Air-Britain

BUSINESS JETS
INTERNATIONAL 2016

Air-Britain supports the fight against terrorism and the efforts of the Police and
other Authorities in protecting airports and airfields from criminal activity.
If you see anything suspicious do not hesitate to call the
Anti-Terrorist Hotline 0800 789321
or alert a Police Officer

BUSINESS JETS INTERNATIONAL 2016

Steven Sowter and Barrie Towey

Thirty-First Edition

Published by:	Air-Britain Publishing
Sales Department:	Unit 1A, Munday Works Industrial Estate, Morley Road, Tonbridge TN9 1RA
Sales e-mail:	sales@air-britain.co.uk
Membership Enquiries:	1 Rose Cottages, 179 Penn Road, Hazelmere, Bucks HP15 7NE, UK (email: membenquiry@air-britain.co.uk)
Web-site:	http://www.air-britain.co.uk

© Air-Britain Publishing

ISBN: 978-0-85130-486-1

Cover photographs:

Front cover:
The Cessna Aircraft Company-operated Cessna 525C CitationJet CJ4 N159CJ seen in a company publicity image. (Cessna/Textron)

Back cover:

Top: Canadair Challenger 605 B-3028 of Wanfeng Aviation on approach at Beijing-Capital on December 5th 2015. (Nick Challoner)

Centre: Aruba-registered Dassault Falcon 7X P4-SCM was a Farnborough visitor on February 12th 2016. (Trevor Warne)

Bottom: The Pilatus PC-24 prototype HB-VXA which first flew on May 11th 2015 is labelled as such on the roofline. (Pilatus Aircraft)

Printed by Bell & Bain Ltd, Glasgow G46 7UQ

CONTENTS

INTRODUCTION

Welcome to the 31st edition of *Business Jets International*, which follows the title's long-established annual format.

The prime purpose of the book continues to be the recording of the registration histories of all purpose-designed business jets, including Experimental and Non-Production types. Supplements also detail airliner variants that have been built or converted for corporate use and our traditional Grumman G159 listing.

Our unique master index shows all registrations in alpha-numeric order, with current registrations in bold print. Generic type designators and construction numbers help locate aircraft in the appropriate production lists, which form the main body of the book. In the case of Citation Is and IIs, the unit number is shown instead of the construction number, as those types are listed by unit number in their respective production lists. Sub-types and military designations can be identified in the main text. Preserved and similar extant aircraft are shown in normal type.

It has always been our policy to include and to distinguish marks that have not yet been fully allocated, for example those only reserved. To identify such marks we use the symbols *, ^ and + and also put unofficial marks within inverted commas. The full description of these symbols can be found within the Explanatory Notes.

The data in this issue of Business Jets International are correct to mid-May 2016. It contains many items from the June 2016 issue of Air-Britain News, our monthly publication that can be used throughout the year to keep the book up to date. Non-subscribers to News will find details of subscriptions and Air-Britain membership at the back of this book or via www.air-britain.co.uk.

In a work of this nature, which can only ever be a snapshot in time, there are bound to be details which have not yet been made known to us, as well as some (hopefully few!) errors; the editorial team at the address below would welcome notification of any such errors or omissions. While we still have problems confirming the identities of aircraft that have been exported to certain countries, particularly Mexico and Venezuela, a growing problem is identifying the fates of early military aircraft which have been retired from service. We would be delighted to hear from anyone who can assist us in this respect.

Much has of course happened in the 12 months since our last book! The General Aviation Manufacturers Association reports that 534 business jets were delivered in the 9 months from June 2015 to March 2016 (the latest date for which figures are available), although at 122 units the January to March 2016 share of that total was nearly 5% down on the previous year's equivalent period. All manufacturers were affected by the downturn in the Chinese economy and the flow of new aircraft to Brazil was more than offset by the number of aircraft being exported from there back to the USA. US and EU sanctions against Russia led to, inter alia, cancelled orders and the dispersal of Finland's Airfix Aviation fleet of Gulfstreams, Globals and Falcons.

Gulfstream Aerospace now has 4 examples of its new wide-bodied GVII-500 carrying out certification flying – the 2nd and 3rd both making their first flight on the same day. The company began deliveries of the ER extended range version of the G650 and also delivered, inter alia, 5 G450s to Flexjet and a G450, G550 and 2 G150s all to the Mexican Air Force. The Royal Australian Air Force placed an order for 2 G550s modified for electronic intelligence use.

Dassault has continued the Falcon 8X certification programme and began ferrying customer aircraft from Bordeaux to the completion centre at Little Rock so that they will be ready for delivery later this year. Development of the Falcon 5X has, however, been delayed by problems with the Snecma Silvercrest engine that will power it – although the prototype was formally rolled out at the beginning of June last year, its first flight had still not taken place at the time of writing.

Deliveries of Bombardier's Challenger 350 continued apace, including significant numbers to NetJets and VistaJet and the first examples for VistaJet USA. Deliveries of the Challenger 650, which has replaced the 605 in production, began – notably to NetJets. The Manx and Maltese registers continued to swell with the addition of new Global 5000s and 6000s. Construction of the first Global 7000 was well under way.

Cessna started delivering Citation Latitudes to customers, including the first NetJets and NetJets Europe examples, two to Turkey and one Manx-registered aircraft to Poland. A non-flying Citation Longitude was exhibited at the NBAA Convention in Las Vegas, where the all-new Citation Hemisphere was also unveiled promising a 4500 nautical mile range and a cabin wider than that of the Gufstream 650. Deliveries of other Citation models were slower than of late.

Embraer Legacy 500 deliveries included examples for the Flexjet fleet, Germany, China, Mexico, Lebanon and the UK. The first Legacy 450s were delivered from Brazil, including one to Belgium, and assembly of the type has begun at the Florida factory. Embraer continued delivering significant numbers of Phenom 300s, with both NetJets and Flexjet continuing to receive new aircraft. NetJets Europe also received its first few examples. Deliveries of the lighter Phenom 100 continued to be slow, however. The decision by Embraer to construct all Phenoms in Florida rather than Brazil affects us as the US test marks used by the company are very difficult to tie up, whereas the Brazilian equivalents appeared on the official register …

On the smaller side, Pilatus flew the second PC-24 'Super Versatile Jet' and Eclipse Aerospace deliveries continued as a mere trickle – but did include two to Germany and one to Austria. Honda finally made its first HondaJet delivery at the tail-end of 2015, since when it has exported examples to Germany and the UK – the latter had just started its delivery journey (under Manx registry) as I was typing these words.

As always, this book should be followed by our *BizQR Quick Reference* annual next January/February.

May 2016

Address for correspondence:
Steven Sowter
78 Laburnum Road
Hayes, Middlesex UB3 4JZ
United Kingdom   email address: stevensowter2@aol.com

ACKNOWLEDGEMENTS

Business Jets International has been produced with the valued past and present assistance of, and from information provided by, the following companies and individuals, sadly some no longer with us:

Aerospatiale/EADS	Canadair Limited	Lockheed Aircraft Co
Ascend Worldwide Ltd	Canadair Challenger Limited	Mitsubishi Aircraft Co
Atlantic Aviation	Cessna Aircraft Co	Raytheon Aircraft Co
Aviation Data Service of Wichita	Gulfstream Aerospace	Rockwell International
British Aerospace plc	Israeli Aircraft Industries	Sabreliner Corp
Beech Aircraft Co	Jetnet LLC Utica NY	

Barry Ambrose	Alan E Clark	Andrew Griffiths	J A Newton	D Sheldon
Joseph Anckner	Colin Clark	Kay Hagby	Ole Nikolajsen	Peter Simmonds
Steve Bailey	Dennis Clement	Philip Hancock	Justin Palmer	Graham Slack
H W Barrett	Paul Compton	Noam Hartoch	Pierre Parvaud	Terry Smith
Colin Berry	Colin Darvill	Richard Hill	Nigel Prevett	Claude Soussi
Bill Blanchard	John Davies	Mike Holdstock	Brian Print	Neville Spalding
Mike Brown	J F Elliott	Gerry Hollands	Glyn Ramsden	David Thompson
David C Buck	Robert D Elliott	Carolos Hopkins	Mark Reavey	Peter Thompson
Peter Budden	David England	Nigel Howarth	Morian Reed	Bob Underwood
B J Burt	Brian Gates	Heinz Kasmanhuber	Doug Robinson	Richard Urbeck
Lyn Buttifant	Wayne Gates	John Kim	Terry Ross	D F Walsh
Jim Cain	Ian Gibson	Bruce Leatherborrow	Ian Sant	Pete Watson
Russell Carter	Jennifer Gradidge	John MacMaster	Don Schofield	
Nick C Challoner	S Graham	Michael Magnusson	Mike Schofield	
Chris Chatfield	Nigel Green	Stephen L Mart	Simon Scott-Kemball	

Plus the many regular contributors to the BIZ-JETS section of *Air-Britain News*. Due acknowledgement is also given to the monograph *Le Morane-Saulnier Paris MS760* by Pierre Parvaud and Pierre Gaillard published by *Le Trait d'Union* (the magazine of the French Branch of Air-Britain) and to the article in the Winter 1989 *Air-Britain Digest* by the same two authors on the HFB320 Hansa. We must also thank the Air-Britain Gulfstream specialist, Alain Jeneve, for his review of the Gulfstream I section. Thanks are also due to Brian Gates for supplying data on the Learjet AvCom fin conversions.

EXPLANATORY NOTES

The following abbreviations have been used in the text:

A/c	Aircraft	cx/canx	cancelled	ntu	not taken up
A/P	Airport	dbr	damaged beyond repair	r/o	rolled out
AFB	Air Force Base	dest	destroyed	TL	total landings
Avn	Aviation	exp	expired	TT	total time
b/u	broken up	ff	first flight	wfs	withdrawn from service
c/s	colour scheme	Inds	Industries	wfu	withdrawn from use
cvtd	converted	Inst	Institute	w/o	written off

+ following a set of marks is to bring the reader's attention to a note which follows, sometimes on the next line, sometimes at the end of the listing

* An asterisk following the last registration indicates that at the time of compilation these marks were only reserved.

^ Indicates marks which the owner/operator of the aircraft has requested. On many occasions such marks may not be taken up.

" " Quotation marks around a registration indicate that the marks were painted on the aircraft, either in error or for publicity purposes, but were not officially allocated.

( ) Brackets around a registration indicate that these marks were not taken up.

NOTE: when an aircraft has been sold to another country and the new marks are not known at the time of compilation, the country prefix only is shown. For Brazil and Mexico PT- and XA- are used even though they may eventually carry other prefixes for these countries.

This year we are undertaking a short survey, which will take you less than five minutes to complete, to gather your views on the physical format of *Business Jets International*.

Please visit www.air-britain.com/bji2016.html for more details.

NOTES

BEECH 390 PREMIER I/1A*

C/n	Srs	Identities						
RB-1		N390RA	[rolled out 19Aug98; ff 23Dec98]		[wfu; cx 18Feb09]			
RB-2		N704T	[wfu; cx 23Feb09]					
RB-3		N390TC	[wfu; cx 18Feb09]					
RB-4		N842PM	N414TE					
RB-5		N155GD	N808V					
RB-6		N390R	N155RM	N391YS				
RB-7		N343PR	(N348PR)	SP-MRD				
RB-8		N460AS						
RB-9		N390EM	N60ME	XA-IAS	XA-ZUL	N21XP		
RB-10		N5010X	[w/o North Las Vegas, NV, 27May04; remains moved to Wichita/Mid-Continent, KS]					
RB-11		N5121P	N50PM	N50PN	(N50PQ)			
RB-12		N390TA	N390P	XA-TSN	N390BW	OE-FRJ	N881AA	
RB-13		N48TC						
RB-14		N969RE						
RB-15		N73WC	N335JB	N929SS				
RB-16		N151KD	N444SS	C-GYPV				
RB-17		N5017T	N88EL	N88ER				
RB-18		N88MM	N711AJ	LX-POO	N23WA	N833PS		
RB-19		N65TB	N16DK	N514AJ				
RB-20		N777MG	N777MQ	(N390BP)	YL-KSC			
RB-21		N390MB	PR-AMA	N390MB				
RB-22		N45NB	N45ND	N223F	N232F	N323CM		
RB-23		N109PM	N488PC	N488RC	VT-RAL	[w/o 19Mar08 Udaipur, India]		
RB-24		N5024J	(ZS-PRF)	ZS-PRM	N124BR	N903MT		
RB-25		N390CL	N808W	N719L	(N713L)	N719D		
RB-26		N390RB	(N390HR)	[w/o 07Jan03 Santo Domingo-Herrera Intl Airport, Dominican Republic]				
RB-27		N3216P	D-IFMC	(HB-...)	N264DL			
RB-28		N128RM	N128JL	N545G				
RB-29		N747BK	N110PR					
RB-30		N390BL	N84ML	N84FM				
RB-31		N3231K	ZS-AVM	N20VA				
RB-32		N5132D	PR-CIM	N1132D	PR-DFG			
RB-33		N50843	N677AS	N92SH				
RB-34		N390DP	N7JT	N390DP				
RB-35		N435K	D-IAGG	M-GDRS	D-ISKO*			
RB-36		N1XT	N36XT					
RB-37		N452A	N567T					
RB-38		N972PF						
RB-39		N39KT	N390JK					
RB-40		N51140	PR-BER	N86RB	N390CE			
RB-41		N142HH	(N111HH)	N43HJ	OE-FMC	N882AA		
RB-42		N390CK	N324AM	[cx 29Oct15; wfu]				
RB-43		N1EG						
RB-44		N5044X	N88MM					
RB-45		N809RM	N100WE					
RB-46		N460L	YL-KSG	N516GW				
RB-47		N5147Y	(N145SD)	N581SF				
RB-48		N51480	D-IATT	HS-KAC				
RB-49		N5049U	N25MC					
RB-50		N344W	N390NS	D-ISXT	N523DR			
RB-51		N4251D	LX-LCG	N530PT				
RB-52		N605TC						
RB-53		N50453	N351CB	N351CW				
RB-54		N61754	ZS-MGK	N354RB				
RB-55		N390PL	N85PL					
RB-56		N390RC	PK-TWL	Indonesia A-9208				
RB-57		N457K	N488PC	VP-CRD	OE-FRC	D-IIMH	T7-OKA	
RB-58		N5158B	N34GN	C-FDAA				
RB-59		N701DF	N622JK					
RB-60		N6160D	LX-PRE	G-PREI	M-PREI			
RB-61		N61161	EC-IOZ	N39JC				
RB-62		N6162Z	N800CS	N808CS				
RB-63		N6163T	ZS-DDM	ZS-SRU				
RB-64		N6164U	LX-PMR	D-IKGT				
RB-65		N4395D	PR-GCA	N67FP				
RB-66		N50586	VP-BAE	N931BR	G-VONJ	ZS-SUW		
RB-67		N6167D	ZS-MGK	N167DP				
RB-68		N447TF	N50648	N133B	ZS-BDG			
RB-69		N205BC						
RB-70		N5070W	N731UG	(N391RB)	ZS-ABG	N70BR	N998PA	
RB-71		N4471P	N71KV					
RB-72		N5072X	N535BC	N535BR	ZS-SGS	ZS-MCO		
RB-73		N371CF	N371CE	N107WR	(N107YR)	F-GVBK		
RB-74		N61474	N902RD	(N9011P)	VP-CWW	N422HS	N144ST	
RB-75		N213PC	N213PQ					
RB-76		N6076Y	N1XH					
RB-77		N6177A	TC-MHS	N32BR	OE-FKW	N889DT		
RB-78		N390JW						
RB-79		N200PR	[w/o 07Apr04 Blackbushe, UK; remains to Air Salvage Int'l, Alton, Hants, UK 07Feb05]					
RB-80		N50280	N50PM	[w/o 17Dec13, Atlanta, GA]				
RB-81		N50468	N390P	N134SW				
RB-82		N61882	D-IBBB					
RB-83		N6183G	N88EL	N88EU	LY-HER	F-HBFA	G-HFAA	F-HLJP	N390AB
RB-84		N61784	PR-JRR					
RB-85		N4485B	N487DT					
RB-86		N390TA	N96NC	N110JD	N407MW			
RB-87		N6187Q	(B-8006)	N952GL	N952GM	N479MM		
RB-88		N4488F	G-OMJC	M-RKAY				
RB-89		N61589	D-IWWW					
RB-90		N32SG						
RB-91		N24YP	N24YD	N45NB				
RB-92		N62LW	N592HC					
RB-93		N322BJ						
RB-94		N6194N	ZS-PFE					

BEECH 390 PREMIER I/1A*

C/n	Srs	Identities					
RB-95		N6195S	N24YP	N888LD	N390LM		
RB-96		N535CD					
RB-97		N6197F	G-FRYL				
RB-98		N61998	N500CZ				
RB-99		N24YP	N24YR	N199RM			
RB-100		N122DS					
RB-101		N6201A	N101PN	N73PJ			
RB-102	*	N6182F	N3901A	N227FH	N200ST		
RB-103		N61930	N701KB	N781KB	N700KB	N730MS	N48KF
RB-104		N5104G	N855JB				
RB-105		N5105A	N777JF				
RB-106		N61706	N20NL	[w/o Lewiston/Sharpe Farms, MO, 23Dec08; parted out by Dodson Int'l, Rantoul, KS]			
RB-107		N61717	N877W	N817W			
RB-108		N61908					
RB-109		N50078	D-IFMG				
RB-110		N701KB	N300SL				
RB-111		N6111F	N713AZ				
RB-112		N60322	N76HL				
RB-113		N11PM	N727KG	N113BR	N390PR	N657NG	
RB-114		N143CM					
RB-115		N6015Y	N72SJ	N193CS			
RB-116		N200LB					
RB-117		N6117G	N1SH				
RB-118		N6118C	B-8018	N390BR	(N30AJ)		
RB-119		N6119C	N1CR	N39DM	N84EA	N14EA	N901MT
RB-120		N6120U	N311SL	UN-P1001	UP-P1001	D-IBBN	OH-ZET
RB-121		N390GM	(N72DV)	N602DV	N520CH	N550CP	
RB-122		N3722Z	G-CJAG	PH-JCI	N810WT		
RB-123		N3723A	N112CM				
RB-124		N6124W	N23SP				
RB-125		N3725F	N312SL	G-PHTO	VQ-BEP		
RB-126		N3726G	G-OEWD				
RB-127		N3727H	N18RF				
RB-128		N6128Y	VT-ANF				
RB-129		N6129U	N390JV				
RB-130		N5030V	N401PP				
RB-131		N36731	G-CJAH	OE-FWW	9H-FWW		
RB-132		N3332C	N9LV	(N48VC)			
RB-133		N3733J	(N545PT)	N575PT	N967F		
RB-134		N3734C	N84VA				
RB-135		N3735V	N390PT				
RB-136	*	N36636	N462CB				
RB-137	*	N6137U	N451MM	VH-TMA	ZS-SHC	(D-ISMV)	(D-IFAP) N428CJ*
RB-138	*	N5118J	VP-BPO	M-VBPO	(N169DT)	N138SJ	
RB-139	*	N3039G	N239RT	N239RF	PR-PRE		
RB-140	*	N3540R	N22VK				
RB-141	*	N3481V	N484AT	N784MA			
RB-142	*	N6142Y	(G-CJAI)	N646S	N767CS	N390ML	
RB-143	*	N61948	N727KG	N729KG	PK-ASB		
RB-144	*	N541RS					
RB-145	*	N37245	N42EL				
RB-146	*	N6146J	N1CR	M-YAIR	G-OOMC	[w/o Blackpool, UK, 12Mar15; cx 19Aug15]	
RB-147	*	N61678	ZS-KBS	N61678	N147FM		
RB-148	*	N6148Z	D-ISAR				
RB-149	*	N36979	F-HAST	OM-TAA			
RB-150	*	N6150Y	(N575PT)	C-FBPL			
RB-151	*	N37071	D-ICJA	N102SK	N103SK	(D-ICJA)	
RB-152	*	N3732Y	HB-VOI	D-IGST			
RB-153	*	N36873	N888MN				
RB-154	*	N36964	(G-CJAJ)	XA-RRG	N176CR		
RB-155	*	N3725L					
RB-156	*	N3726T	N508RN				
RB-157	*	N6178X	N88EL				
RB-158	*	N36758	N727MH	N727ML			
RB-159	*	N37059	N146JF	N145JF			
RB-160	*	N36890	EC-KHH	N43GG			
RB-161	*	N71761	(N606JR)	N6JR	[w/o 27Jul10 Oshkosh, WI; parted out by Atlanta Air Salvage, Griffin, GA]		
RB-162	*	N608CW					
RB-163	*	N7163E	N72GD	(N59RK)	N46CK		
RB-164	*	N36864	D-IDBA				
RB-165	*	N7165X	N800FR	M-FROG			
RB-166	*	N36866					
RB-167	*	N71167	N404JM				
RB-168	*	N7268M	N64PM				
RB-169	*	N7269Z	N837JM	(N237JM)	PR-PRA		
RB-170	*	N7170Y	(N181JT)				
RB-171	*	N17CJ					
RB-172	*	N7102U	G-EVRD	N390GM			
RB-173	*	N73736	N213PC	N213RQ	N329LN		
RB-174	*	N71874	N855RM				
RB-175	*	N71865	VH-VHP				
RB-176	*	N7176J	N906FM	N789DT			
RB-177	*	N37019	(A6-RZA)	A6-RZJ	N37019	N527PM	N527PN
RB-178	*	N3378M	N102CL				
RB-179	*	N7079N	N33PJ				
RB-180	*	N133CM	N133CQ	N835ZT			
RB-181	*	N7081V	VP-BBQ	M-VBBQ	UR-USB		
RB-182	*	N7082V	N246DF	N999ZG	C-GMJJ		
RB-183	*	N994JR	N1J				
RB-184	*	N368CS	N368CC	I-GSAL	N368CC		
RB-185	*	N7085V	N502PM				
RB-186	*	N37086	N2HZ	N36HZ	N685LM		
RB-187	*	N7187J	HB-VOS	T7-NES			
RB-188	*	N7088S	N774KD				
RB-189	*	N7189J	VP-CFW	N255PX			

BEECH 390 PREMIER I/1A*

C/n	Srs	Identities				
RB-190	*	N70890	N537RB			
RB-191	*	N7191K	N992SC			
RB-192	*	N7192M	N91BB	VT-RTR	[dbr by flood water, Chennai, India, 01Dec15]	
RB-193	*	N7193W	N408J	XA-BLE	N390BD	
RB-194	*	N7294E	N276RS	N678AM		
RB-195	*	N74065	A9C-RJA	A6-RZA	G-RIZA	G-ORXI	OM-GLE
RB-196	*	N37346	D-IIMC	OE-FIM	LY-OJB	F-WTAS	F-HTTP
RB-197	*	N7257U	(LX-VAZ)	N115WZ	N116WZ	N213VU
RB-198	*	N7198H	C-FDMM	N7TX		
RB-199	*	N133CM	N716GS			
RB-200	*	N81HR				
RB-201	*	N801BP	I-DMSA	D-ISGE	N390GW	M-ARIE
RB-202	*	N202BP	VP-CAZ	[w/o nr Annemasse, France, 04Mar13]		
RB-203	*	N203BP				
RB-204	*	N204BP	RP-C390			
RB-205	*	N205GY	N801SA	N945LC		
RB-206	*	N306BP	N146JF	N146JE		
RB-207	*	N207AH				
RB-208	*	N208BP	N430GW	N777VG	[w/o Thomson, GA, 20Feb13]	
RB-209	*	N209BP	M-YSKY	G-IOMC		
RB-210	*	N210KP	PT-SBF			
RB-211	*	N701KB	N701KD	(D-IWAJ)	OE-FKK	N851TM
RB-212	*	N42SC				
RB-213	*	N213BP	N952GL			
RB-214	*	N814BP	ZS-CBI			
RB-215	*	N215BR	OE-FAP	LZ-EVB		
RB-216	*	N3216G	YL-MLV	VQ-BDK		
RB-217	*	N3217P	C-GXMB	C-FSDB		
RB-218	*	N3K				
RB-219	*	N34859	VT-VRL			
RB-220	*	N34820	VP-BFU	N390RJ		
RB-221	*	N31921	D-ISAG			
RB-222	*	N32022	PT-CBA			
RB-223	*	N3203L	N427DB			
RB-224	*	N3204P	(PP-LUG)	PR-VPP		
RB-225	*	N3205W	VT-BKG	N3205W	VH-TGQ	N390K
RB-226	*	N97JP	N26DK	(N677DC)	[w/o South Bend, IN, 17Mar13]	
RB-227	*	N166AN				
RB-228	*	N3228M	F-HCJP	OO-JPC	G-RRIA	
RB-229	*	N229RB	N50VM	(N50VH)		
RB-230	*	N3330S	F-HNCY			
RB-231	*	N390GS	PR-PRC			
RB-232	*	N208HP	N208MM			
RB-233	*	N233WC	SP-RDW			
RB-234	*	N367CS	N368CS			
RB-235	*	N33805	D-IIBE	UR-USA		
RB-236	*	N3186C	VT-UPN			
RB-237	*	N33837	PR-RRN	N373MM		
RB-238	*	N3198N	ZS-DDM			
RB-239	*	N3289H	VT-KBN			
RB-240	*	N3400Y	PR-RSN			
RB-241	*	N3241G	I-NGIR	N9930B		
RB-242	*	N390EU	N69SB	N99BC		
RB-243	*	N443BP	N111LP	N111LQ	VT-SSF	
RB-244	*	N3344T	N9CH	N808L		
RB-245	*	N3415A	I-AFOI			
RB-246	*	N3216L	PR-VMD			
RB-247	*	N3187G	N668Z			
RB-248	*	N3188V	N1899	N189K		
RB-249	*	N3194R	D-IAYL	[w/o 19Dec10 nr Samedan, Switzerland]		
RB-250	*	N3200X	N357PT	N390P		
RB-251	*	N3151W	N410SH			
RB-252	*	N3352W	N452AS	N111LP	N950JK	
RB-253	*	N3223G	N78HL			
RB-254	*	N3354S	I-DMSB	N991ML		
RB-255	*	N3355D	C-GYMB	N255AG	N69YM	N853DC
RB-256	*	N3396P	OM-VPB	RA-01809		
RB-257	*	N3197P	N701KB	N701KR	N70NL	
RB-258	*	N3298W	N826TG			
RB-259	*	N3395H	N42LG	C-GLIV	N72JT	
RB-260	*	N3400X	N952SP			
RB-261	*	N3441A	N199BP			
RB-262	*	N42LG	N262RB	SX-FCA		
RB-263	*	N42LG	N42LQ	(D-ISAS)	OE-FDB	UR-FDB	N514GW
RB-264	*	N264HB	N79CB			
RB-265	*	N6465W	ZS-AAM			
RB-266	*	N266AZ	N390MM			
RB-267	*	N64467	C-FJTN			
RB-268	*	N63768	N33EM			
RB-269	*	N60669	F-GDRR	N858Q		
RB-270	*	N6470P	N124EK	N124GV	N323KM	
RB-271	*	N6471N	C-GYMB	C-FCTB		
RB-272	*	N64312	N23HD			
RB-273	*	N64373	N21FM			
RB-274	*	N6174Q	UP-P1002			
RB-275	*	N390P	C-FTIU			
RB-276	*	N76EU	(SP-VVV)	N106PR		
RB-277	*	N6469X	N99MN			
RB-278	*	N6248J	N278AP	OY-FLW		
RB-279	*	N8079R	N775CM			
RB-280	*	N280EU	N722NB			
RB-281	*	N81491	N6JR			
RB-282	*	N282DF				
RB-283	*	N283HB	N707RK	N390HG		
RB-284	*	N8084U	M-MTRM	UR-NST		

BEECH 390 PREMIER I/1A*

C/n	Srs	Identities				
RB-285	*	N85EU	N285EB			
RB-286	*	N81516	TC-ANG	M-SFOZ	N480RE	
RB-287	*	N287AP	UP-P1003	PR-DIA*		
RB-288	*	N8148U	N213PC			
RB-289	*	N289HB	N289BZ	C-FJTA		
RB-290	*	N8110N	N986PB			
RB-291	*	N291EU	N26CS	HB-VTS		
RB-292	*	N8092F	UP-P1004			
RB-293	*	N8113Q	N390MG	[also wore fake serial 12-293]		XA-VWA
RB-294	*	N8144D	N51GM	N440LK*		
RB-295	*	N295HB	N54VM	N84VM	ZS-ETN	

Production complete following the bankruptcy of Hawker Beechcraft Corp in 2012. The following aircraft also had marks assigned but were not completed:

C/n	Srs	Identities	
RB-296	*	(N296AP)	
RB-297	*	(N297EU)	
RB-305	*	(N124EK)	(N305BP)

BEECH 390-2 PREMIER II

The Premier II would have been marketed as the Hawker 200 had it entered production.

C/n	Identities			
RD-1	N392X	[ff 13Mar10] N200HA	[cx Nov15, wfu]
RD-2	N392P	N200HW	[ff 31May11	cx Oct15, wfu]

Type did not enter production due to Hawker Beechcraft Corp's bankruptcy in 2012.

BEECHJET 400

* Denotes aircraft originally manufactured by Mitsubishi as MU300-2s and then converted to Beechjet 400 standard. The c/n shown in brackets in these cases is the old Mitsubishi c/n. C/n RJ-12 is the first pure Beechjet 400.

C/n	Series	Identities									
*RJ-1 (A1001SA)	400	N64VM									
*RJ-2 (A1002SA)	400	N103AD	N402FB	N369EA							
*RJ-3 (A1003SA)	400	N508DM	N203BA	N49JN	N63SN*						
*RJ-4 (A1004SA)	400	N504DM	N92RW	(N401TJ)	N8YM						
*RJ-5 (A1005SA)	400	N77GA	N54TK	N933AC							
*RJ-6 (A1006SA)	400	N106DM	N18JN	YV-737CP	YV-738CP	YV-838CP	N406TS	N111YJ			
*RJ-7 (A1007SA)	400	N507DM	N207BA	N106VC	N25BN	N85BN	N403JP	N644JP			
A1008SA	2	N411BW	[reportedly w/o at unknown location in Mar97; to Dodson Avn, Rantoul, KS, Oct97, for spares use]								
*RJ-9 (A1009SA)	400	N109DM	N209BA	(N248PA)	N42SR	N242SR	N800FT	N65RA			
*RJ-10 (A1010SA)	400	N499DM	N410BA	I-ALSE	N131AP	[parted out Tulsa, OK]					
*RJ-11 (A1011SA)	400	N114DM	N111BA	N72HG							
RJ-12	400	N3112B	N129DB	N3112K	N106CG	[parted out by AvMATS, St Louis, MO]					
RJ-13	400	N3113B	(N400TN)	N428JD	[w/o 18Sep12 Macon/Downtown, GA]	N468JD	[parted out by Atlanta Air Salvage, Griffin, GA]				
RJ-14	400	N3114B	N208R	N208D	N58AU	N672AT	(N770TB)	N599JL	[parted out by White Inds, Bates City, MO]		
RJ-15	400	N3115B	N25W	N25WA	N73BL	N73BE	N902P	N415CT	N222YJ		
RJ-16	400	N165F	N512WP	N803E	(N440MP)	[parted out by Dodson Int'l, Rantoul, KS]					
RJ-17	400	N417BJ	N877S	N400T	N94BJ	N84BJ	N486MJ	N1CG	N455FD	N655CM	
RJ-18	400	N3180T	I-STAP	N940GA	ZS-NOD	N595PT	N824SS	N418RM	LV-COO		
RJ-19	400	N3119W	N800HM	(N700HM)	N880HM	PJ-SOL	N24BA	N101CC	N598JL	[parted out by White Inds, Bates City, MO]	
RJ-20	400	N3120Y	I-ONDO	(N20CV)	N901P	N455DW					
RJ-21	400	N3121B	N721FA	[cx 27Aug12; parted out by MTW Aerospace, Montgomery, AL]							
RJ-22	400	N3122B	9M-ATM	N992GA	(VR-BLG)	I-INCZ	OY-JAT	N724AA	N48CK	N913SF	N913MC	(N315SA)	N567BA
RJ-23	400	N3123T	[rebuilt using parts of RK-11, following accident]	(I-ALSU)	N400GJ	[wfu Lawrenceville, GA]					
RJ-24	400	N3124M	N510WS	N512WS	N800WW	N800WV	[cx 17Feb15; wfu]				
RJ-25	400	N3025T	I-MPIZ	N125RJ	I-OTTY	N425BJ	ZS-OUU	N425BJ			
RJ-26	400	N3026U	N88WG	N90SR	N388DA	N426MD	N91MT	N401GJ			
RJ-27	400	N3127R	N484CC	(N427CW)	N611TG						
RJ-28	400	N31428	I-ACIF	N48GA	N700LP	N51EB					
RJ-29	400	N3129E	N503EB	N193TR	(N597N)	XA-OAC	N129BT	[parted out by Dodson Int'l, Rantoul, KS]			
RJ-30	400	N3130T	(N815BS)	N486MJ	N777FE						
RJ-31	400	N545GM	N5450M	I-ALSI	N5450M	I-ALSI	N114AP	N499P	[parted out by Dodson International, Rantoul, KS]		
RJ-32	400	N31432	XA-RAR								
RJ-33	400	N31733	(N233BJ)	XA-JJA	XA-BNG	XA-JMM					
RJ-34	400	N3134N	I-ALSO	N96WW	(N41TJ)	N80TS	(N800TS)	(N1X)	N1TY	N7EY	N80TS
RJ-35	400	N3035T	N85TT	I-SAMI	N71GA	N737MM	N137MM	N1AG			
RJ-36	400	N3236Q	G-RSRS	N3236Q	G-MARS	I-RDSF	VR-BNV	N52GA	XA-OAC	N555BY	
RJ-37	400	N31437	LV-PAM	LV-RCT	N31437	ZS-ORW					
RJ-38	400	N3238K	N147CC	N447CC	VT-OAM	N438DA	N52AL				
RJ-39	400	N3239K	N48SR	N393BB	N398BB						
RJ-40	400	N3240M	PK-ERA	N3240M	N400DW						
RJ-41	400	N3141G	(N441EE)	(N270BJ)	N241BJ	[wfu Fergus Falls, MN; cx 10Feb12]					
RJ-42	400	N3142E	N31542	N400PL	I-FTAL	N735GA	N444WB	N442JC	N40MA	N418CT	
RJ-43	400	N3143T	N401CG	N500DG	N416CT						
RJ-44	400	N3144A	N3144A	I-GCFA	N22WJ	I-TOPJ	N110GA	N922TR			
RJ-45	400	N3145F	N58AU	N218RG	N241TR						
RJ-46	400	N1546T	N146JB	VT-TEL	[cx 2012; instructional airframe, Hindustan University, Chennai, India]						
RJ-47	400	N1547B	(N900EF)								
RJ-48	400	N1548D	XB-JHE	XC-LJS							
RJ-49	400	N1549J	N88UA								
RJ-50	400	N1550Y	G-OTMC	N56GA	N102MC	N406GJ	N8HQ				
RJ-51	400	N1551B	[converted to RK-1 (qv)]								
RJ-52	400	N196KC	(N196KQ)	(N52EB)	N196JH	N930MG	N324MM	YV3153			
RJ-53	400	N195KC	N195KA	N711EC	N53EB	N520WS					
RJ-54	400	N1554R	XB-FDH	N418MG							
RJ-55	400	N1555P	(VH-...)	N711FG	N711FC	N780GT	N724HB	PP-KIK			
RJ-56	400	N1556W	G-BSZP	OK-UZI	N70DE	OK-RHM	HA-YFK				
RJ-57	400	N1557D	N25BR	[w/o 11Dec91 Lavender Mt, NW of Rome Airport, GA; cx Jun92]							
RJ-58	400	N1558F	XA-RNG	XA-MII	N258BJ	N458HC	(N750KP)				
RJ-59	400	N1559U	ZS-MHN								
RJ-60	400	N1560T	G-BRBZ	N89GA	N400FT	XA-LEG	N250KD	N95RT	N700WH		
RJ-61	400	N1561B	XA-RNE	N701LP	N461EA						
RJ-62	400	N89KM	N89KK	N333RS	N424BT						
RJ-63	400	N848C									
RJ-64	400	N1564B	N195JH	N215TP							
RJ-65	400	N1565B	N16MF								

End of production from Japanese components; production continued with US-built components from c/n RK-1

BEECHJET 400A/ HAWKER 400XP

C/n	Series	Identities									
RK-1	400A	N1551B	[converted from c/n RJ-51]			N294FA	N294AW	(N401CW)	N481CW	[parted out by Alliance Air Parts, Oklahoma City, OK]	
RK-2	400A	N1902W	N272BC	N272BQ	N402CW	N827SB					
RK-3	400A	N400A	XA-CLA	N640AC	N400VG	N400VK	N519RW				
RK-4	400A	N147CC	N147CG	N400BE	N777FL	N771EL	N494CW	N222JE			
RK-5	400A	N501BG	(N405CW)	N495CW	N30XL						
RK-6	400A	N56576	I-IPFC	N3119H	N600CC	(N401FF)	N401EE	N406CW	(N406ML)	N480M	N408M / PR-ALY
RK-7	400A	VR-COG	N416RP	N631RP	(N631RR)	N401AB	N9PW	N848TC			
RK-8	400A	N440DS									
RK-9	400A	N8152H	N315R	(N150TF)							
RK-10	400A	N2842B	(D-CLSG)	D-CEIS	N488DB						
RK-11	400A	N2843B	N5680Z	I-ALSU	[w/o 27Nov91 Parma, Italy; remains to Dodson Av'n, Ottawa, KS – parts used to rebuild RJ-23 (N3123T) qv]						
RK-12	T-1A	[built as Jayhawk c/n TT-1; for USAF]									
RK-13	400A	N56BE	N56BX	N13GB	N610EG	N510TL					
RK-14	400A	N28..B	N81709	(F-GKCJ)	F-GLYO	(N414RK)	N81TJ	N916SB			
RK-15	T-1A	[built as Jayhawk c/n TT-2; for USAF]									
RK-16	400A	N8163G	N71FE	N46FE	N416CW	XA-MGM	N16HD				
RK-17	400A	N505EB	N877S	N877Z	N417CW	(N401LX)	N857C				
RK-18	400A	N5598Q	N717DD	N717DW	N418CW	(N402LX)	TC-ASE	N189GA	ZS-MJD		
RK-19	400A	N1901W	N11GE	(N8ME)	N41ME	N419CW	(N403LX)	N144AW	ZP-BJB	N312JS	
RK-20	400A	N82628	I-UNSA	N82628	N870P	N703LP	PR-MMG				
RK-21	400A	(N401TC)	N1904W	N1881W	N717CW	N717VA	N1920	(N1962)	N2920	HK-4794	N763AJ
RK-22	400A	N56616	N51ML	N85CR	N422CW	(N404LX)	(N522KJ)	N870BB	[cx 15 Mar16; instructional airframe, Skedsmo High School, Norway]		
RK-23	400A	N107BJ	N200BL	(N960AJ)	N250AJ						
RK-24	400A	N8073R	[wfu; parted out by Dodson Intl, Rantoul, KS; cx 01Jul09]								
RK-25	400A	N81918	(VR-CDA)	D-CLBA	N237SP						
RK-26	400A	N8097V	VH-BBJ	VH-IMP	N700GB	N8097V	N80DX	(N80DE)	HK-4446X	HK-4446-W / HK-4446-G	
RK-27	400A	N10FL	N10FQ	N427CW	(N405LX)	N95GK					
RK-28	400XT	N42SK	N411SK	PT-WLM	(N902PC)	N400NS	N401NX	(N401XT)	N75TG		
RK-29	400A	I-IPIZ	N15693	I-IPIZ	OY-JJE						
RK-30	400A	N205R	N430CW	(N406LX)	N494CC						
RK-31	400A	N10J	N10JX	N431CW	(N407LX)	N850C					
RK-32	400A	N999GP	N998GP	N553PF	N432CW	(N408LX)	N932EA				
RK-33	400A	N1878C	N60B	N197PF	N197BE						
RK-34	400A	N400A	N700GM	N74VF	N232BJ	N511JP	N511JF	N721SS	N134FA	N184AR	
RK-35	400A	N81661	VH-BJD	VH-LAW	VH-BJD	VH-BJD	N435CW	(N409LX)	(N936EA)	N492AM	
RK-36	400A	XA-RZG	N56327	N57B	N156DH	N155DH	N568SD				
RK-37	400A	(F-GLPD)	N8014Q	(F-GLOR)	SE-DRS	N998FF					
RK-38	400A	N5685X	N522EE	N522EF	N515MW	YV363T					
RK-39	400A	N400Q	N34VP	N70BJ	(N97XP)	N492P					
RK-40	400A	N8252J	N496EE	N440CW	(N410LX)						
RK-41	400A	N8265Y	I-FSJA	N920SA	N546BZ	N101WR					
RK-42	400A	N8253Y	N442CW	(N411LX)	N443C	N307MT					
RK-43	400A	N56400	N45RK								
RK-44	400XPR	N8249Y	N404VP	N908R	N712GK	N312GK					
RK-45	400A	N56423	N490TN	(N8051H)	N445E	(N600CC)	N445CC	N445CW	(N412LX)	N445PK	
RK-46	400A	N8239E	N515RY								
RK-47	400A	N8053V	N400FT	N408PC	N109CP	[w/o 06Feb10 Washington/Dulles, VA – hangar collapsed]					
RK-48	400A	N8060V	N94HT	N48SE							
RK-49	400A	N8060Y	N54HP	N54HD	(N349HP)						
RK-50	400A	N80KM	N750AB	N450CW	(N413LX)	[cx 24Apr13; parted out by Anglin Aircraft Recovery Services, DE]					
RK-51	400A	N8085T	(N7113Z)								
RK-52	400A	N709JB	(N709EW)	N709EL							
RK-53	400A	N62KM	N200GP	N200GB	N453CW	(N414LX)	N896C	N593M			
RK-54	400A	N80938	PT-WHG								
RK-55	400A	N400Q	N404CC	N42AJ							
RK-56	400A	N89KM	N456CW	(N415LX)	N56FF	XA-JAM	XA-KJM	XA-JPA			
RK-57	400A	N8157H	ZS-NZO	N762BG	N457CW	(N416LX)	N368EA				
RK-58	400A	N56356	PT-WHC								
RK-59	400A	N80544	N50KH	N5PF	N27JJ	N895CP					
RK-60	400A	N8260L	(N794SM)	N61SM	N55SQ						
RK-61	400A	N82378	G-RAHL	N461CW	(N417LX)	N478DR	N479DR				
RK-62	400A	N8083N	N462CW	(N418LX)	N5895K						
RK-63	400A	N2792B	N82412	PT-JQM	N163RK	N304JR					
RK-64	400A	N8164M	N53MS								
RK-65	400A	N39HF	(N97TT)	(N81TT)	PR-AEX	PR-HAW*					
RK-66	400A	N400A	(N400DT)	N400Y	HB-VLM	N6048F	I-AVSS				
RK-67	400A	N8167Y	(N850RG)	N467RG	N429JG	N699PM					
RK-68	400A	N8280J	N295FA	(N419LX)	XA-PYN	N900EF	YV2452				
RK-69	400A	N8169Q	N877S	N877J							
RK-70	400A	C-FOPC	N750T	N73HM	N79HM	N826JH	[w/o Atlanta/DeKalb-Peachtree 18Jun12; parted out by Atlanta Air Salvage, Griffin, GA; remains to Dodson Av'n, Rantoul, KS]				
RK-71	400A	N82497	I-IFPC	N777ND	N73BL	N402GS					
RK-72	400A	N8210W	N709JB	(N72BJ)	N910SH	N428WE	N82QD				
RK-73	400A	N8070Q	PT-WHB								
RK-74	400A	N8146J	N26JP	N93XP							
RK-75	400A	(N275PC)	N82400	N125JG	(PR-TGA)	PR-TGM					
RK-76	400A	N8166A	N261JP								
RK-77	400A	N8277Y	PT-WHD								
RK-78	400A	N8278Z	N611PA	[dbr in hangar collapse at Boca Raton, FL, 24Oct05; to Dodson Av'n, Rantoul, KS, for spares]							
RK-79	400A	N8279G	(N30SF)	OH-RIF	N8279G	[cx 16Oct14; wfu]					
RK-80	400A	N8180Q	AP-BEX	[w/o in hangar collapse at Lahore 06Jun04]							
RK-81	400A	N8167G	PT-WHE								
RK-82	400A	N8282E	PT-WHF								
RK-83	400A	N8283C	XA-SNP	XA-MII	N8283C	N880MG					
RK-84	400A	N8138M	D-CHSW	OE-GFB	VQ-BNJ						
RK-85	400A	N8299Y	N419MS	N419MB	LV-FWF						
RK-86	400A	N1563V	N777GC	(N72PP)	N757CE	N20ZC	(N202RA)				
RK-87	400A	N1567L	N702LP	N87EB	YV3106						
RK-88	400A	N1549W	N654AT	N654AP	N843RH						
RK-89	400A	N1560G	N94HE								
RK-90	400A	N1570L	N165HB	N132WE	N458SF						
RK-91	400A	N1545N	N296FA	N491CW	(N420LX)	N511VB	N400TB				
RK-92	400A	N3240J	N555KK	N124PP							
RK-93	400XT	N3038V	N493CW	(N421LX)	N400XT	N475BC	[cx 21Apr16; wfu]				

BEECHJET 400A/ HAWKER 400XP

C/n	Series	Identities								
RK-94	400A	N3051S	HB-VLN	N585G	N681WD	N661WD				
RK-95	400A	N3114X	HS-UCM	N747RR						
RK-96	400A	N3196N	N924JM	N824JM	N800GF	N800GK	N400XP	[Hawker 400XPR development aircraft]		
RK-97	400A	N3197Q	VH-MGC							
RK-98	400A	N3210X	N400A	N866BB	N999JF	N999YB				
RK-99	400A	N3199Q	N95FA	N575RB						
RK-100	400A	N1570B	N400SH							
RK-101	400A	N3221T	ZS-JRO	N400FT	N490AM					
RK-102	400A	N3232U	N916GR	N111FW						
RK-103	400A	D-CIGM	HB-VLW	N103LP	N403CW	(N422LX)	N12NV	YVO157		
RK-104	400A	N3224X	LV-PLT	LV-WPE	N704SC	PR-DOT	N410ML*			
RK-105	400A	N3235U	(N8252J)	(N423LX)	N127BW	N124BV	N105AX			
RK-106	400A	N3246H	N1HS	N625W						
RK-107	400A	N3227X	N733MK	N907JE						
RK-108	400XT	N3218L N404FL	N498CW	N408CW	(N424LX)	(N408NX)	[Nextant 400XT conversion, ff with Williams FJ44 engines 08Sep10]		(N408XT)	
RK-109	400A	N3269A	N121EZ	N491AM	B-3905					
RK-110	400A	N1090X	(N400A)	XA-FRO						
RK-111	400A	N42SK	N411SK	N412WP	N13SY	N116SS	PK-ELI			
RK-112	400A	N3272L	N94LH	N112BJ						
RK-113	400A	N3263N	N400VG	[w/o 17Apr99 Beckley, WV, cx Dec02]						
RK-114	400A	N1084D	N363K	N698PW	N855RA					
RK-115	400A	N3265A	(N369EA)	N52AW	N512F					
RK-116	400A	N1116R								
RK-117	400A	N1117S	N97FB	N97FF	N12MG	N12MQ	N496AS	N886EP	(N886ER)	
RK-118	400A	N1118Y	LV-PMH	LV-WTP						
RK-119	400A	N1119C	N456JG	(N456NS)	(N7981M)	N450WH				
RK-120	400A	N3261Y	TC-MDJ	N9146Z	N159AK	N702NV	G-ERIE			
RK-121	400A	N1121Z	N419MS	N473JE	PR-IJE					
RK-122	400A	N1102B	PT-WJS							
RK-123	400XT	N1123Z	N110TG	N740TA	N203FL	N410FL				
RK-124	400A	N1124Z	TC-MSA	N124BG	OE-GUK	YU-BVA	4O-BVA			
RK-125	400A	N1105U	N400KP	N400KL	N939GP					
RK-126	400A	N3226B	N197SD	XB-INI						
RK-127	400A	N1127U	N696TR	N686TR	N127UH					
RK-128	400A	N1108Y	N912SH	N621VS						
RK-129	400XT	N1129X	N129MC	N334SR	N129WH	N258AF				
RK-130	400A	N1130B	TC-NEO							
RK-131	400A	N1083Z	N305MD							
RK-132	400XT	N1087Z	N106KC	N954TW	N500PM					
RK-133	400A	N1133T	VP-BMR	N133BP	I-TOPB	OY-JJD				
RK-134	400A	N1094D	N134BJ	N134WF	LV-CBJ					
RK-135	400A	N1135A	N135BJ							
RK-136	400A	N1136Q	N780TP	N397CA	N130WW					
RK-137	400XT	N1117Z	N400AJ	N400XT	N209BK					
RK-138	400A	N40PL	N48PL							
RK-139	400A	N1099S	VH-PNL	VH-MZL	VH-BZL					
RK-140	400A	N1094N	ZS-OCG	A6-ELJ	ZS-OCG	A2-MCG	A2-WIN			
RK-141	400A	N1027S	N974JD	N874JD	N855FC	N824DM	N824D	YV3173		
RK-142	400A	N142BJ	(N223DK)	YV-943CP	N142BJ	N9WW				
RK-143	400A	N191NC	N191NQ	N824HG						
RK-144	400A	N134CM	PR-SKB							
RK-145	400A	N745TA	(N425LX)	N144JS						
RK-146	400XT	N146TA	N746TA	(N426LX)	(N456FL)	ZS-LMF				
RK-147	400A	N147BJ								
RK-148	400A	N1108T	TC-SMB	N663AJ	OE-GHM	C6-SAP				
RK-149	400A	N149TA	(N427LX)	N499LX						
RK-150	400A	N1135U	N100AG	N100AW						
RK-151	400A	N1126V	PT-MAC	N115CD	N586SF	N196CT	N198CT	N548KK		
RK-152	400A	N2252Q	N97FB	YV-754CP	YV213T	N152SV	XB-TNY	XA-TYP		
RK-153	400A	N153BJ	N500HY							
RK-154	400A	N2354B	VH-BJC	VH-EXB	HS-ASC					
RK-155	400A	N2355T	N627RP	N631RP	N631PP	N567DK	PR-JPK			
RK-156	400A	N2056E	N400PU							
RK-157	400A	N397AT	N897AT	ZS-ONP	N897AT	N157WH				
RK-158	400A	N2358X	PT-MPL	N158SN	N475TC					
RK-159	400A	N2159P	N3337J	(N466TS)	N333YJ					
RK-160	400A	N2360F	N54HP							
RK-161	400A	N761TA	N471CW	(N428LX)	N706RM					
RK-162	400A	N2362G	ZS-PDB	N2362G	OY-SIS	N520CH	OE-GMC	OK-PMI		
RK-163	400A	N2363A	N163BJ	I-TOPD						
RK-164	400A	N2164Z	TC-MDB	N2164Z	(N69LS)	N280AJ	(N717CH)	N188HA		
RK-165	400A	N2225Y	N224MC							
RK-166	400A	N2299T	N975CM	N93FT	N93FB					
RK-167	400A	N2267B	N711EC	N501BW						
RK-168	400A	N2168G	N768TA	(N429LX)	N679SJ	XC-LLZ	N679SJ			
RK-169	400A	N2329N	N757WS	PR-SRB						
RK-170	400A	N2289B	TC-MCX	TC-MSB	N70HT	PP-DDR				
RK-171	400A	N2201J	PT-WUF	N287CD	XA-LEG	N888BY	N693GS			
RK-172	400A	N2272K	N615HP	N200GP						
RK-173	400A	N2273Z	HK-4801							
RK-174	400A	N2204J	N174AB	HK-4645						
RK-175	400A	N175BJ								
RK-176	400A	N476BJ								
RK-177	400A	N2277G	N717CF	YV602T						
RK-178	400A	N708TA	(N478CW)	(N430LX)	N406LX					
RK-179	400A	N2279K	N75GF	N75GK	N400CT	OD-DTW				
RK-180	400XT	N709TA	(N480CW)	(N407LX)	OK-EAS					
RK-181	400A	N2235V	N314TL							
RK-182	400A	N2322B	N234DK							
RK-183	400A	N710TA	(N432LX)	N488LX						
RK-184	400A	N2314F	N141DR							
RK-185	400A	N2298L	N140GB	N148GB	(N450AT)	(N185FN)				
RK-186	400A	N712TA	(N433LX)	N12NV	N552CC					
RK-187	400A	N2298S	N400TE	PR-FOL						

BEECHJET 400A/ HAWKER 400XP

C/n	Series	Identities							
RK-188	400A	N2298W	TC-VIN	N2298W	VP-CPH				
RK-189	400A	N715TA	(N434LX)	N440LN					
RK-190	400A	N2290F	TC-YRT	N2290F	N325JG	VT-RPG			
RK-191	400A	N2291T	N960JJ	N960JA	N367EA	N400HD			
RK-192	400A	N492BJ	N272BC	N272BQ	N116AD	N116AP	[Hawker 400XPR development aircraft, first flew with Williams FJ44 engines 03May12]		
RK-193	400A	N13US	N914SH	N366EA	N193BJ				
RK-194	400A	N194BJ	N909ST	PK-ELX					
RK-195	400XT	N718TA	(N485CW)	(N435LX)	(N410LX)	N872MK			
RK-196	400A	N2283T	XA-MEX	N619GA	N619G				
RK-197	400A	N3197A	N214WM	N940VA					
RK-198	400A	N798TA	(N436LX)	N403WC	N168WC				
RK-199	400A	N739TA	N446M	N826JM					
RK-200	400A	N200NA	VP-CKK	N399RA					
RK-201	400A	N741TA	(N437LX)	N402FL					
RK-202	400A	N742TA	N438LX						
RK-203	400A	N2359W	B-3989	N2359W	VP-CHF	N203RK	N262PA	N203DF	
RK-204	400A	N2357K	I-ASER	N204KR	PP-SJJ				
RK-205	400A	N3030D	N143HM	(N17CM)					
RK-206	400A	N3014R	N30046	N982AR					
RK-207	400A	N3015F	N717DD	N257CB					
RK-208	400A	N3101B	N890BH	HI-766SP	HI766	N766AB	N127SJ		
RK-209	400XT	N799TA	(N439LX)	N413LX	ES-CMK				
RK-210	400XT	N111CX	ZK-NXJ						
RK-211	400A	N3028U	TC-NNK	N3028U	N686SC				
RK-212	400A	N3029F	N299AW	N11UB	HK-4756				
RK-213	400A	N3033A	N175PS	N545TC					
RK-214	400A	N79EL							
RK-215	400A	N3038W	N515WA						
RK-216	400A	N3050P	N213BK						
RK-217	400A	N217MB	N385PB						
RK-218	400A	N3068M	N48MF	N426GF					
RK-219	400A	N3059H	N511JP	N80BL	N219SJ	4X-CPY			
RK-220	400A	N220BJ	N799SM	N499AS	N563RJ				
RK-221	400A	N221BJ	N18BR	N400KG	N400SF				
RK-222	400A	N748TA	N482CW	(N440LX)	N482RK	VH-YRC	VH-IPG	HS-EMM	N482RK
RK-223	400A	N3223R	N777FL	N877FL					
RK-224	400A	N3224N	N51NP	N642AC					
RK-225	400XT	N751TA	N415LX	N440LN	N400TC				
RK-226	400A	N3226Q	N59BR	N59BP	N750TA	(N416LX)			
RK-227	400A	N3197K	N362KM	N862KM	N497AS	YV3057			
RK-228	400A	N3228V	N12WF						
RK-229	400A	N3129X	N515TJ						
RK-230	400XT	N753TA	(N441LX)	N417LX	(N431FL)	N722NK	N440XT		
RK-231	400A	N781TP	N615HP						
RK-232	400A	N2355N	N674SF	N674DJ					
RK-233	400A	N2293V	N233MW						
RK-234	400A	N783TA	(N442LX)	N418LX	N1PU				
RK-235	400A	N695BK	N560MT						
RK-236	400A	N2349V	N11WF						
RK-237	400A	N784TA	N437CW	N443LX					
RK-238	400A	N23525	XA-DOS	XA-VRO	N96GA				
RK-239	400XT	N785TA	(N421LX)	N485FL	N868JL	VH-OVS			
RK-240	400A	N3240J	N749SS	N150TF	N393GH				
RK-241	400A	N3241Q	N993H	PR-DDS					
RK-242	400A	N2322B	N32AA	N32AJ	XA-LOA	N400VP			
RK-243	400A	N782TP							
RK-244	400XT	N428HR	N793TA	(N445LX)	N493LX	N188TS			
RK-245	400A	N3199Z	N744TA	(N446LX)	N424LX	HS-CKI	HS-BRM		
RK-246	400A	N500TH							
RK-247	400A	N40252	N20FL	N25XP	XB-MSZ				
RK-248	400XT	N786TA	N447LX	N226WC					
RK-249	400A	N4249K	N611WM	C9-CFM					
RK-250	400A	N2293V	N250HP						
RK-251	400A	N3106Y	N705LP	N495AS	N1853				
RK-252	400XT	N790TA	N490FL						
RK-253	400A	N4053T							
RK-254	400A	N3254P	TC-BYD	N254RK	HA-YFJ				
RK-255	400A	N988JG	N3255B	N960JJ	N400JJ	N960JJ	N402FB		
RK-256	400A	N3079S	N397AT	N387AT	N26PA	N602JC			
RK-257	400A	N739TA	N449LX	N618LT					
RK-258	400A	N40215	(PP-LUA)	PP-WRV					
RK-259	400A	N3259Z	XA-AFS	XA-UKU	N397MG				
RK-260	400XT	N787TA	(N450LX)	N727KG					
RK-261	400A	N3261A	N51B						
RK-262	400A	N300GB							
RK-263	400A	N724MH	N724KW	N724CP					
RK-264	400XT	N792TA	(N451LX)	N428LX	N482MS				
RK-265	400A	N797TA	(N452LX)	N429LX	N498LX				
RK-266	400A	N3166Q	N41283	N10FL	N27XP				
RK-267	400A	N4467X	OY-JJO	N85HP					
RK-268	400XT	N789TA	(N453LX)	(N489FL)	ES-NXT				
RK-269	400A	N400MV	N400MR	N440RC					
RK-270	400A	N3231H	N800SD						
RK-271	400A	N743TA	(N454LX)	(N431LX)	N800GV				
RK-272	400A	N3237H	N701CP						
RK-273	400A	N731TA	(N483CW)	(N455LX)	(N433LX)	N725T	YV2839		
RK-274	400XT	N735TA	(N456LX)	N434LX	N402XT	[first production Nextant 400XT]			
RK-275	400A	N4275K	N426EA						
RK-276	400XT	N775TA	(N457LX)	N435LX	N427DJ	N253AF			
RK-277	400A	N4477X	(N566W)	N101CC					
RK-278	400A	N4378P	N823TT	N750AJ					
RK-279	400XT	N773TA	(N458LX)	N436LX	N436FL				
RK-280	400A	N4480W	N26XP	N75KH	N275KH				
RK-281	400A	N4081L	XA-TDQ	N311JV					
RK-282	400A	N794TA	(N482LX)	(N459LX)	N88CA				

BEECHJET 400A/ HAWKER 400XP

C/n	Series	Identities						
RK-283	400A	N4083N	N600SB	N404MS				
RK-284	400XT	N795TA	(N460LX)	N439LX	N439FL			
RK-285	400A	N3185G	N149SB	N249SB	N249RM			
RK-286	400A	N400MV						
RK-287	400A	N4467E	N361AS	JA78MA				
RK-288	400A	N51VC	N848PF	N41FD				
RK-289	400XT	N796TA	(N461LX)	N440LX	N440FL			
RK-290	400A	N23263	N400QW	N204DH				
RK-291	400A	N3191L	N816DK					
RK-292	400XT	N899TA	N441LX	N444FL				
RK-293	400A	N4293K	EC-HTR	N293RK	XC-LMC	N293RK	OK-BEE	
RK-294	400A	N5094E	HS-TPD	[wfu Bangkok/Don Muang, Thailand; w/o in floods 2011; to Nilai University, Malaysia, as instructional airframe]				
RK-295	400XT	N898TA	(N463LX)	(N406FL)	OK-ESC	(SP-KTB)		
RK-296	400A	N311HS	N68JV	N937RV				
RK-297	400A	N699TA	N497CW	(N464LX)	N497RC			
RK-298	400A	N698TA	N445LX	YV2674	N445LX	XA-MSL		
RK-299	400A	N697TA	N446LX	YV453T	YV2736			
RK-300	400A	N4001M	VP-CVP	N401XR				
RK-301	400A	N696TA	(N465LX)	XA-GOB				
RK-302	400A	N5002G	XA-TTS					
RK-303	400A	N695TA	N400HS	N400HD	SE-RBO	TC-IBO		
RK-304	400XT	N5004Y	N304SE	N527PM				
RK-305	400A	N693TA	N405CW	(N466LX)	N448LX	N705KU		
RK-306	400A	N4056V	YV-968CP	YV198T	YV2698			
RK-307	400A	N692TA	N407CW	(N467LX)	PT-TRA			
RK-308	400A	N51008	N400KP					
RK-309	400A	N3239A	I-VITH					
RK-310	400XT	N695TA	N410CW	(N468LX)	N451LX	N451FL		
RK-311	400A	N755TA	N711GD	N711GL	N311GL	N40SC		
RK-312	400A	N5012U	N75RL	N312GS*				
RK-313	400A	N4483W	(PH-BBC)	PH-DTP	OK-IMO			
RK-314	400A	N5014G	N400HS	N92LP				
RK-315	400A	N3215J	N6MF	N720XP				
RK-316	400A	N3216X	XA-AFA					
RK-317	400A	N691TA	(N469LX)	N452LX	N452SB	N452FL		
RK-318	400A	N3185K	HB-VNE	OK-BII				
RK-319	400A	N689TA	N660CC					
RK-320	400A	N4469E	N717TG	(N290AR)				
RK-321	400A	N688TA	N379DR	XA-TYD				
RK-322	400A	N687TA	N800EL	N800EH	PT-FGV	SP-OHM*		
RK-323	400A	N5003G	N268PA	N369AK				
RK-324	400A	N5024U	N755TA	(N470LX)	(N412FL)	N224FL	N224FD	
RK-325	400A	N272BC	N275BC	N408PC				
RK-326	400A	N749RH	N420DH	N440JR				
RK-327	400XT	N689TA	(N471LX)	N454LX	N454FL			
RK-328	400A	N5028J	N686TA	(N472LX)	N455LX	N423AK	(N70HB)	N424SK
RK-329	400A	N5129U	N580RJ	N580RK				
RK-330	400A	N4330B	(N450CB)	N33NL	N330TS			
RK-331	400A	N5031D	N12MG	N489BH	N744C	XA-ESR		
RK-332	400A	N5032H	XA-TWW					
RK-333	400A	N72FL	N903CG	N160RC				
RK-334	400XT	N5034J	N684TA	N484CW	(N473LX)	N442FL		
RK-335	400A	N5015B	N400GR					
RK-336	400A	N5136T	(N706PL)	N706LP				
RK-337	400A	N5037L	N726PG					
RK-338	400A	N5038V	N116AD					
RK-339	400A	N4309N	N439CW	N400TL	N404LR			
RK-340	400A	N51540	N500LJ					
RK-341	400A	N51241	N61GB					
RK-342	400A	N50552	N400A	N522EE	N522EL			
RK-343	400A	N4357H	N806GG	N106DD	OE-GTM	(SP-GHM)	I-PSCU	
RK-344	400A	N6144S	N99ZB					
RK-345	400A	N4445Y	N425CW	(N474LX)	(N457LX)	N445FL		
RK-346	400A	N446CW	(N475LX)	N422FL				
RK-347	400A	N447CW	N108PJ	N168PJ	N498AS			
RK-348	400A	N448CW	N309AK	(N309BE)	N348BE			
RK-349	400A	N449CW	N975RR					
RK-350	400A	N61850	PR-MVB					
RK-351	400A	N6051C	N371CF					
RK-352	400A	N6052U						
RK-353	400A	N400A	N353AE	XA-GAO				
RK-354	400XP	N5084U	N717EA	EC-KRS	EC-LIO	OY-OYO		
RK-355	400XP	N6055K	N767SB	N400RY				
RK-356	400XP	N6056M	N400XP	N800GR	N800HT	N808HT	N217EC	
RK-357	400XP	N5057Z	N317PC					
RK-358	400XP	N5158D	N865AM					
RK-359	400XP	N61959	XA-UAW	XA-FAF				
RK-360	400XP	N6200D	N823ET					
RK-361	400XP	N61661	N25CU					
RK-362	400XP	N6162V	N362XP	Indonesia P-2034		Indonesia P-8001		
RK-363	400XP	N6193D	(N363XP)	N790SS				
RK-364	400XP	N394BB						
RK-365	400XT	N455CW	N459LX	N456FL				
RK-366	400XP	N466CW	N460LX	N466CW	OD-STW	HZ-ALS1		
RK-367	400XP	N404BL						
RK-368	400XT	N448CW	N461LX	N427FL				
RK-369	400XP	N369XP	N624B	N917EA				
RK-370	400XP	N60270	(N470CW)	N72GH	N432MA			
RK-371	400XP	N371CW	N401CW	N824GB	N72NE			
RK-372	400XP	N6172V	N375DT					
RK-373	400XP	N373XP	N490JC					
RK-374	400XP	N374XP	N109NT	N25SJ*				
RK-375	400XP	N375XP	XA-UCV					
RK-376	400XT	N476CW	N476LX	N426FL	G-SKBD			
RK-377	400XP	N477CW	N477LX	N477FL				

BEECHJET 400XP

C/n	Series	Identities				
RK-378	400XP	N370FC				
RK-379	400XP	N979XP	PP-UQF			
RK-380	400XP	N102QS	N402GJ			
RK-381	400XP	N106QS	N702CS	N381XP		
RK-382	400XP	N108QS	N408GJ			
RK-383	400XP	N115QS	PK-YGK			
RK-384	400XP	N84XP	N302TB			
RK-385	400XT	N116QS	N117XP	OK-PPP		
RK-386	400XP	N524LP	N502N	N300R	N330R	
RK-387	400XP	N478LX	N125DT	N130DT	N959CR*	
RK-388	400XP	N479LX	N45LX	(N45LN)	N997RS	(N202TA)
RK-389	400XP	N50727	N717DD	N28VM		
RK-390	400XP	N480LX	N975RD	PP-AML		
RK-391	400XP	N117QS	N68GS			
RK-392	400XP	N36792	AP-BHQ			
RK-393	400XP	N118QS	N835TB			
RK-394	400XP	N119QS	N281TX	(N125GE)	4L-VIP	N281TX
RK-395	400XP	N7600				
RK-396	400XP	N31496	XA-MEX	[dbr Telluride, CO, 23.12.15]		
RK-397	400XP	N36997	N479LX	N473FL		
RK-398	400XP	N483LX	N480LX	N480FL		
RK-399	400XP	N700FA	N402CB	D2-EAH		
RK-400	400XP	N400XP	ZS-POT	VT-...		
RK-401	400XP	N36701	CS-DMA	N315SL	N140FM	
RK-402	400XP	N485LX	N61CP	OE-GSG	ZS-XPH	
RK-403	400XP	N36803	CS-DMB	N426CB	N732WB	
RK-404	400XP	N37204	CS-DMC	N404XP	N478DR	
RK-405	400XP	N481LX	N40ZH	N94LH		
RK-406	400XP	N140QS	VH-EIG			
RK-407	400XT	N36607	CS-DMD	N363EA	N800WC	N259AF
RK-408	400XP	N37108	CS-DME	N260TX	N411SC	
RK-409	400XP	N120QS	N412TS			
RK-410	400XP	N37310	CS-DMF	N259TX	B-95995	
RK-411	400XP	N611XP	N380JR			
RK-412	400XP	N37312	N412GJ			
RK-413	400XT	N482LX	HB-VPV	OK-RAH		
RK-414	400XP	N136QS	N401NW			
RK-415	400XP	N37115	XA-UFS			
RK-416	400XP	N116XP	N900ST	N900SQ	XA-LMG	N13GG	XA-RFC
RK-417	400XP	N36907	CS-DMG	M-ABFO	N600WM	
RK-418	400XP	N618XP	N418GJ			
RK-419	400XP	N619XP	N279AK			
RK-420	400XP	N620XP	N877S	N400VK		
RK-421	400XP	N145QS	N145WC	N145QS	N152RJ	N345HC
RK-422	400XP	N151QS	N290TX	PR-DIS		
RK-423	400XT	N223XP	N462LX	N429FL		
RK-424	400XP	N24XP	N1JB	N24XP		
RK-425	400XP	N37325	CS-DMH	N261TX	N858EZ	N333EA
RK-426	400XT	N26XP	N463LX	N465FL		
RK-427	400XP	N132QS	N116XP			
RK-428	400XP	N28XP	OE-GYR	EC-JPN	N544LF	PR-BLG
RK-429	400XP	N29XP	N263PA	A2-DBK		
RK-430	400XP	N30XP	N990DF	PR-BED		
RK-431	400XP	N131QS	N311GF			
RK-432	400XP	N142QS	N741RD	N1JP		
RK-433	400XP	N125QS	N113XP	N310GF		
RK-434	400XP	N34XP	(N464LX)	XA-UEV	XC-BJG	
RK-435	400XP	N161QS	PP-SKI			
RK-436	400XP	N147QS	N436RK			
RK-437	400XP	N37337	CS-DMI	N276MM	PR-EKR	
RK-438	400XP	N162QS	N438BC			
RK-439	400XP	N166QS	N159AK	N159AL	PP-DSS	
RK-440	400XP	N152QS	N440WF			
RK-441	400XP	N130QS	N610PR	N43BD		
RK-442	400XP	N124QS	N442GJ			
RK-443	400XP	N36646	CS-DMJ	N258TX		
RK-444	400XP	N465LX	N144XP	N702LP		
RK-445	400XP	N466LX	N45XP	N536V	PR-DIF	
RK-446	400XP	N46XP	N188JF			
RK-447	400XP	N467LX	(N467FL)	XA-AMY		
RK-448	400XP	N146QS	N212FH	OE-GAG	N400RB	PR-LBP	N448SC
RK-449	400XP	N133QS	N127BW			
RK-450	400XP	N650XP	N61VC			
RK-451	400XP	N51XP	N964JD			
RK-452	400XP	N36752	XA-UFR			
RK-453	400XP	N464LX	ZS-AOT	ZS-JPS		
RK-454	400XP	N465LX	N454RJ			
RK-455	400XP	N466LX	N800HT	N915TB	N401XP	N401RL
RK-456	400XP	N61256	LV-BEM			
RK-457	400XP	N6137Y	PR-MMS			
RK-458	400XP	N50858	N339SM			
RK-459	400XP	N459XP	N517MD	XA-TEN		
RK-460	400XP	N460XP	N460KG	(N460JW)		
RK-461	400XP	N61XP	N101AR	N823HM		
RK-462	400XP	N462XP	N689AK	PR-WRR		
RK-463	400XT	N469LX	N469FL			
RK-464	400XP	N36764	CS-DMK	N262TX		
RK-465	400XP	N37165	CS-DML	N500XP	N99VS	
RK-466	400XP	N466XP	N610PR	PR-SCE		
RK-467	400XP	N122QS	N115XP			
RK-468	400XT	N468LX	N467FL			
RK-469	400XP	N37079	(CS-DMM)	N114QS	N114XP	N481MM
RK-470	400XP	N470XP	PR-IND			
RK-471	400XP	N471LX	N471XP			
RK-472	400XP	N36632	CS-DMM	N416TM	N472EM	

BEECHJET 400XP

C/n	Series	Identities					
RK-473	400XP	N149QS	N76GR				
RK-474	400XP	N474XP	N474ME	XA-UQJ			
RK-475	400XP	N61675	CS-DMN	N418TM			
RK-476	400XP	N36846	TC-STA				
RK-477	400XP	N477XP	(N2944M)	N477GJ			
RK-478	400XP	N470LX	N598DR				
RK-479	400XP	N479XP	PP-JCF				
RK-480	400XP	N36880	SU-ZBB	VQ-BIL	M-ABGM		
RK-481	400XP	N472LX	(N481GJ)				
RK-482	400XP	N482XP	N482GS				
RK-483	400XP	N139QS	(N275TX)	N483PA	OD-APA		
RK-484	400XP	N101QS	N29134				
RK-485	400XP	N485XP	[instructional airframe, Wichita Area Technical College National Center for Aviation Training, KS]				
RK-486	400XP	N123QS	N362EA				
RK-487	400XP	N487XP	G-EDCS	N487XP	XA-EGS		
RK-488	400XP	N719EL					
RK-489	400XP	N489XP	N489B				
RK-490	400XP	N153QS	N153Q	(PT-CBT)	PR-CBT		
RK-491	400XP	N491XP	N491HR				
RK-492	400XP	N138QS	(N500XP)	N840JM	N940JM		
RK-493	400XP	N493XP	CC-CRT				
RK-494	400XP	N72594	CS-DMO	XA-ETP			
RK-495	400XP	N495XP	N410CT	N419TM			
RK-496	400XP	N496XP	N410KD	PR-VHB			
RK-497	400XP	N497XP					
RK-498	400XP	N141QS	N276TX	N420BD			
RK-499	400XP	N499XP	I-GFVF	V5-WAW			
RK-500	400XP	N500XP	I-FDED				
RK-501	400XP	N501XP	F-HITM				
RK-502	400XP	N502XP	G-STOB	TC-KJA			
RK-503	400XP	N203XP	XA-FLX	N121GF	XA-FLX		
RK-504	400XP	N204XP	(N45LN)	N202TT			
RK-505	400XP	N505XP					
RK-506	400XP	N471LX	N415FL				
RK-507	400XP	N466LX	N507HB	N507WM			
RK-508	400XP	N70158	CS-DMP	N450TM			
RK-509	400XP	N154QS	N400MX				
RK-510	400XP	N510XP	N225SB				
RK-511	400XP	N511XP	VT-TVR				
RK-512	400XP	N37339	CS-DMQ	N408LH	YV564T		
RK-513	400XP	N513XP					
RK-514	400XP	N514XP	N416RX				
RK-515	400XP	N3735U	I-ALVC				
RK-516	400XP	N74116	CS-DMR	N460TM			
RK-517	400XP	N517XP	N420CT				
RK-518	400XP	N518XP	N473LX	N219DC	PP-MCO	N518TG	(PP-AAW)	N54FB
RK-519	400XP	N72539	CS-DMS	N477TM			
RK-520	400XP	N157QS	N999WW	PP-MFL			
RK-521	400XP	N521XP	EI-ICE	N521XP	PR-MGD		
RK-522	400XP	N522XP	(N385PB)	N522MB			
RK-523	400XP	N523XP	N425CT				
RK-524	400XP	N524XP	PR-OEC				
RK-525	400XP	N502CA					
RK-526	400XP	N7226P	AP-PAL				
RK-527	400XP	N527XP	(N527DF)				
RK-528	400XP	N528XP	HA-YFH				
RK-529	400XP	N167QS	N918TT	N311HS			
RK-530	400XP	N530XP	OY-CJN	AP-KNM			
RK-531	400XP	N435CT					
RK-532	400XP	N532XP	CS-DMT	N481TM			
RK-533	400XP	N533HB	EC-KKD				
RK-534	400XP	N440CT					
RK-535	400XP	N445CT					
RK-536	400XP	N470CT					
RK-537	400XP	N537XP	N537DF				
RK-538	400XP	N538XP	CS-DMU	N482TM			
RK-539	400XP	N539XP	N300RC				
RK-540	400XP	N540RK	N777G				
RK-541	400XP	N32051	N474LX	N420FL			
RK-542	400XP	N542XP	N393BB				
RK-543	400XP	N731PS	N710RA				
RK-544	400XP	N480CT					
RK-545	400XP	N485CT					
RK-546	400XP	N490CT					
RK-547	400XP	N495CT					
RK-548	400XP	N548XP	TC-NEU				
RK-549	400XP	N34249	CS-DMV	N483TM			
RK-550	400XP	N3500R	CS-DMW	N484TM			
RK-551	400XP	N551XP	(N551EU)	YV580T			
RK-552	400XP	N552XP	N552EU	G-KLNR			
RK-553	400XP	N553XP	N975BD				
RK-554	400XP	N475LX	N465TM				
RK-555	400XP	N31975	CS-DMX	N487TM			
RK-556	400XP	N3186B	CS-DMY	N488TM			
RK-557	400XP	N557XP	YV457T	N457CP			
RK-558	400XP	N558XP					
RK-559	400XP	N3289R	CS-DMZ	N489TM			
RK-560	400XP	N560XP	N475TM				
RK-561	400XP	N3501M	CS-DOB	N496TM			
RK-562	400XP	N33062	B-77701				
RK-563	400XP	N63XP	(N475LX)				
RK-564	400XP	N564XP	N491TM				
RK-565	400XP	N565XP	N565EU	HZ-PM3	N565EU	PP-AAO	
RK-566	400XP	N3206K	VT-GRG	N103DD			
RK-567	400XP	N567XP					

BEECHJET 400XP / HAWKER 400XT

C/n	Series	Identities				
RK-568	400XP	N3468D	(N141HB)	PP-JMS		
RK-569	400XP	N180QS	N3438			
RK-570	400XP	N570XP	N979CM			
RK-571	400XP	N979CM	N571TW	HZ-PM2	N571TW	XA-YCC
RK-572	400XP	N3502T	N365KM			
RK-573	400XP	N573XP	N449TM			
RK-574	400XP	N175QS	XA-ABS			
RK-575	400XP	N575XP	N112WC			
RK-576	400XP	N576XP	N451TM			
RK-577	400XP	N577XP	N452TM			
RK-578	400XP	N179QS	N711P			
RK-579	400XP	N579XP	CN-TJD	N579XP	I-TOPX	
RK-580	400XP	N580XP	N492TM			
RK-581	400XP	N481LX	N453TM			
RK-582	400XP	N582XP	N493TM			
RK-583	400XP	N176QS	N583XP	AP-RBA		
RK-584	400XP	N3204Q	VH-NTX	N584SC	LV-CLF	
RK-585	400XP	N585XP	N456TM			
RK-586	400XP	N586XP	N480M			
RK-587	400XP	N587XP	HZ-SPAA			
RK-588	400XP	N588XP	HZ-SPAB			
RK-589	400XP	N589XP	HZ-SPAC			
RK-590	400XP	N3190C	N5031T			
RK-591	400XP	N591XP	HZ-SPAD			
RK-592	400XP	N492TM	N592XP	HZ-SPAE		
RK-593	400XP	N493TM	N593XP	YV471T		
RK-594	400XP	N594XP	HZ-SPAF			
RK-595	400XP	N595XP	N595EU	PR-BCK		
RK-596	400XP	N596XP	N497TM			
RK-597	400XP	N597XP	N410LG			
RK-598	400XP	N598EU	N728EF			
RK-599	400XP	N599XP	N92AJ	PR-BPL		
RK-600	400XP	N60XP	(N600ST)	N31ST		
RK-601	400XP	N601XP	N498TM			
RK-602	400XP	N602XP	N499TM			
RK-603	400XP	N603XP	XA-DVH			
RK-604	400XP	N604XP	N93FT			
RK-605	400XP	N605XP	[aircraft registered but not built]			

Production complete

Nextant Aerospace are refurbishing Beechjet 400As and 400XPs and retro-fitting them with Williams FJ44 engines. The upgraded aircraft are renamed Nextant 400XT. Known conversions are labelled 400XT in the listings above.

T-1A JAYHAWK

C/n	Identities			
TT-1	N2886B	91-0077		
TT-2	N2887B	90-0412	N2887B	90-0412
TT-3	N2892B	90-0400		
TT-4	90-0405			
TT-5	N2876B	89-0284		
TT-6	N2872B	90-0404		
TT-7	N2896B	90-0401		
TT-8	N2868B	90-0402		
TT-9	90-0403			
TT-10	90-0407			
TT-11	90-0406			
TT-12	90-0408			
TT-13	90-0409			
TT-14	90-0410			
TT-15	90-0411			
TT-16	90-0413			
TT-17	91-0076			
TT-18	91-0075			
TT-19	91-0078			
TT-20	91-0079			
TT-21	91-0080			
TT-22	91-0081			
TT-23	91-0082			
TT-24	91-0083			
TT-25	91-0084			
TT-26	91-0085			
TT-27	91-0086			
TT-28	91-0087			
TT-29	91-0088			
TT-30	91-0089			
TT-31	91-0090			
TT-32	91-0091			
TT-33	91-0092			
TT-34	91-0093	[damaged 16Aug03 at Kessler AFB, MS; moved 10Mar05 to Aeronautical Systems Center, Wright Patterson AFB]		
TT-35	91-0094			
TT-36	91-0095			
TT-37	91-0096			
TT-38	91-0097			
TT-39	91-0098			
TT-40	91-0099			
TT-41	91-0100			
TT-42	91-0101			

JAYHAWK

C/n	Identities	
TT-43	91-0102	
TT-44	92-0330	
TT-45	92-0331	
TT-46	92-0332	
TT-47	92-0333	
TT-48	92-0334	
TT-49	92-0335	
TT-50	92-0336	
TT-51	92-0337	
TT-52	92-0338	
TT-53	92-0339	
TT-54	92-0340	
TT-55	92-0341	
TT-56	92-0342	
TT-57	92-0343	
TT-58	92-0344	
TT-59	92-0345	
TT-60	92-0346	
TT-61	92-0347	
TT-62	92-0348	
TT-63	92-0349	
TT-64	92-0350	
TT-65	92-0351	
TT-66	92-0352	
TT-67	92-0353	
TT-68	92-0354	
TT-69	92-0355	
TT-70	92-0356	
TT-71	92-0357	
TT-72	92-0358	
TT-73	92-0359	
TT-74	92-0360	
TT-75	92-0361	
TT-76	92-0362	
TT-77	92-0363	
TT-78	93-0621	
TT-79	93-0622	
TT-80	93-0623	
TT-81	93-0624	
TT-82	N2830B	93-0625
TT-83	93-0626	
TT-84	93-0627	
TT-85	93-0628	
TT-86	93-0629	
TT-87	93-0630	
TT-88	93-0631	
TT-89	93-0632	
TT-90	93-0633	[w/o May08; to National Museum of USAF, Wright-Patterson AFB, OH; loaned to Laughlin AFB Museum, TX]
TT-91	93-0634	
TT-92	93-0635	
TT-93	93-0636	
TT-94	93-0637	
TT-95	93-0638	
TT-96	93-0639	
TT-97	93-0640	
TT-98	93-0641	
TT-99	93-0642	
TT-100	93-0643	
TT-101	93-0644	
TT-102	93-0645	
TT-103	93-0646	
TT-104	93-0647	
TT-105	93-0648	
TT-106	93-0649	
TT-107	93-0650	
TT-108	93-0651	
TT-109	93-0652	
TT-110	93-0653	
TT-111	93-0654	
TT-112	93-0655	
TT-113	93-0656	
TT-114	94-0114	
TT-115	94-0115	
TT-116	94-0116	
TT-117	94-0117	
TT-118	94-0118	
TT-119	94-0119	
TT-120	94-0120	
TT-121	94-0121	
TT-122	94-0122	
TT-123	94-0123	
TT-124	94-0124	
TT-125	94-0125	
TT-126	94-0126	
TT-127	94-0127	
TT-128	94-0128	
TT-129	94-0129	
TT-130	94-0130	
TT-131	94-0131	
TT-132	94-0132	
TT-133	94-0133	
TT-134	94-0134	
TT-135	94-0135	
TT-136	94-0136	
TT-137	94-0137	

JAYHAWK

C/n	Identities
TT-138	94-0138
TT-139	94-0139
TT-140	94-0140
TT-141	94-0141
TT-142	94-0142
TT-143	94-0143
TT-144	94-0144
TT-145	94-0145
TT-146	94-0146
TT-147	94-0147
TT-148	94-0148
TT-149	95-0040
TT-150	95-0041
TT-151	95-0042
TT-152	95-0043
TT-153	95-0044
TT-154	95-0045
TT-155	95-0046
TT-156	95-0047
TT-157	95-0048
TT-158	95-0049
TT-159	95-0050
TT-160	95-0051
TT-161	95-0052
TT-162	95-0053
TT-163	95-0054
TT-164	95-0055
TT-165	95-0056
TT-166	95-0057
TT-167	95-0058
TT-168	95-0059
TT-169	95-0060
TT-170	95-0061
TT-171	95-0062
TT-172	95-0063
TT-173	95-0064
TT-174	95-0065
TT-175	95-0066
TT-176	95-0067
TT-177	95-0068
TT-178	95-0069
TT-179	95-0070
TT-180	95-0071

Production complete

T400 JAYHAWK

C/n	Identities			
TX-1	N82884	Japan 41-5051	[code 051]	
TX-2	N82885	Japan 41-5052	[code 052]	
TX-3	N82886	Japan 41-5053	[code 053]	
TX-4	N3195K	Japan 41-5054	[code 054]	
TX-5	N3195Q	Japan 41-5055	[code 055]	
TX-6	N3195X	Japan 51-5056	[code 056]	
TX-7	N3228M	Japan 51-5057	[code 057]	
TX-8	N3228V	Japan 51-5058	[code 058]	
TX-9	N1069L	Japan 71-5059	[code 059]	
TX-10	"N3221Z"	N32212	Japan 01-5060	[code 060]
TX-11	N50561	Japan 21-5061	[code 061]	
TX-12	N50512	Japan 21-5062	[code 062]	
TX-13	N50543	Japan 41-5063	[code 063]	

Production complete

BRITISH AEROSPACE (RAYTHEON) 125 SERIES

The majority of the series 3, 400 and 700 aircraft which were exported to North America were allocated an additional number in the NA… range, and these numbers are quoted as the c/n. This practice was reintroduced on production 800 and 1000 series aircraft but has since ceased. The production list is in the normal c/n order, and a cross-reference of the two sets of numbers follows the production list.

Early-build aircraft were known as DH125s and then HS125s and subsequently BAe125s. 800 series aircraft above c/n 258208 and 1000 series aircraft above c/n 259024 are known by the nomenclature Corporate Jets BAe125. Following the sale of Corporate Jets by BAe to Raytheon, owner of Beechcraft, yet another nomenclature change took place to Hawker 800 (at c/n 258255) and Hawker 1000 (at c/n 259043).

UK B condition marks from G-5-501 onwards are only shown once against the airframe to which they were allocated, even though they would be re-used whenever that aircraft went to Chester for maintenance.

C/n	Series	Identities									
25001	1	G-ARYA	[ff 13Aug62; CofA exp 01Oct65; wfu Kelsterton College, UK; cockpit section to Mosquito Museum, London Colney UK Feb04]								
25002	1	G-ARYB	[CofA exp 22Jan68; wfu BAe Hatfield, UK; cx 04Mar69; to Midland Air Museum, Coventry, UK]								
25003	1	G-ARYC	[CofA exp 01Aug73; wfu Mosquito Museum, London Colney, UK]								
25004	1/521	G-ASEC	G-FIVE	[wfu by Jun83; cx 14May85, used for spares – wings to c/n 25008]							
25005	1	G-ASNU	(D-CFKG)	D-COMA	G-ASNU	[wfu by Dec82; impounded Lagos, Nigeria; cx 18Nov91]					
25006	1	HB-VAG	I-RACE	[CofA exp Nov87; wfu]							
25007	1	(G-ASSH)	HB-VAH	G-ASTY	HB-VAH	F-BKMF	[w/o 05Jun66 Nice, France]				
25008	1	G-ASSI	5N-AWD	[wfu by Dec83, Luton, UK; to Staggenhoe Farm, Whitewell, Beds UK for use by emergency services in crash exercises 10Sep98]							
25009	1	G-ATPC	XW930	[wfu, scrapped Jordan's scrapyard, Portsmouth, UK by Jun97]							
25010	1/522	G-ASSM	5N-AMK	[wfu by Dec83; to Science Museum, Kensington, London, UK, painted as G-ASSM]							
25011	T1	G-37-65	XS709	[code M]	[wfu 20Jan11; to RAF Museum, Cosford, UK, 11Feb11]						
25012	T1	XS710	[code O]	9259M	[stored RAF Cosford, UK circa 1997]						
25013	1A	G-ASSJ	N125J	N2426	N7125J	N4646S	N88MR	[wfu prior to Jun82; parted out by White Inds, Bates City, MO]			
25014	1A/522	G-ASSK	N125G	N734AK	N621ST	(N125WC)	XA-JUZ	N621ST	[wfu by Dec82; b/u 1985]		
25015	3B	VH-CAO	(9M-AYI)	VH-CAO	(N750D)	[Australian marks cx May91; stripped of re-usable parts by Dodson Av'n during 1998. Fuselage to Australian Air Museum at Sydney-Bankstown, moved to The Oaks, South West of Sydney, NSW by Jun05 to join c/n 25062 reportedly to restore one of the two to flying condition]					
25016	1A	G-ASSL	CF-RWA	CF-OPC	C-FOPC	C6-BPC	N4997E	N222NG	[b/u Fort Lauderdale Executive]		
25017	1A/522	G-ASSH	N3060	N3060F	N306MP	N123JB	N495G	N333M	XA-RSR	[wfu Fort Lauderdale Executive, FL; b/u]	
25018	731	CF-DOM	C-FDOM	N125LM	C-GXPT	N125PT	N118TS	N218TJ	(P4-ZAW)	(XA-…)	N218TJ
25019	1A	G-ASYX	N1125G	N1135K	[w/o 25Feb66 Des Moines, IA]						
25020	731	G-ASZM	N167J	N959KW	N2KW	N2KN	N365DJ	N711WM	(N128TJ)	N55RF	[parted out following landing accident Seattle, WA Dec02; cx Aug 03]
25021	1A/522	G-ASZN	N575DU	N2504	N228G	N228GL	N125BT	N125KC	N711WJ	N300HW	[wfu; parted out by White Inds, Bates City, MO]
25022	1A/522	G-ASZO	CF-SDA	N505PA	N100GB	N50HH	[w/o 02Aug86 Bedford, IN]				
25023	731	G-ASZP	N1125	N338	(N125BW)	N125BM	N58BT	N284DB	N584DB	N62TJ	(N89FF) ZS-PJE ZS-TBN
25024	T1	XS711	[code L]	[wfu]							
25025	1B	D-COME	HB-VAR	F-BOHU	(F-OCGK)	5N-AWB	[wfu by early 87]				
25026	1A	G-5-11	G-ATAY	N225KJ	N225K	N225LL	N4400E	(N40AD)	[wfu by Apr86; used for spares early 86]		
25027	1A	CF-SEN	C-FSEN	N227DH	N125BH	N777RN					
25028	1B	Ghana G.511	(N48172)	C-GLFI	N48172	N50SS	XA-ESQ	N29977	[w/o 14Dec81 as XA-ESQ and parted out; last allocated US marks, N29977, were not worn; cx Apr91; remains to White Inds, Bates City, MO]		
25029	1A/522	G-ATAZ	N10122	N391DA	N10D	[wfu Mar04 Tulsa/Jones Field, OK; parted out by White Inds, Bates City, MO; cx 29Apr09]					
25030	1A	G-ATBA	N413GH	N123VM	(N97VM)	XB-MBM	XA-MBM	XA-RDD	[preserved at Saltillo, Mexico]		
25031	1A	G-ATBB	N1923M	N43WJ	N79AE	N105HS	[wfu circa Oct05 Oklahoma City, OK]				
25032	731	G-ATBC	N65MK	(N657K)	N90WP	N692FC	N98TJ	N942DS	(N16GG)	(9Q-…)	[wfu Lanseria, South Africa]
25033	1A/522	G-ATBD	N125G	N1125G	N111AG	N111AD	(N111AX)	(N700AB)	N63BL	(N32HE)	N125LC N125AL N125LL
		RP-C125	[wfu Lapu-Lapu City, Philippines]								
25034	1A	CF-HLL	C-FHLL	[wfu Quebec City by Jun83, possibly following accident 18Apr83 at Gashe, PQ, Canada; fuselage noted at Montreal-St.Hubert Oct95; wings used on c/n 25027; cx Dec90]							
25035	1A	G-ATCO	N1515P	N1515E	N151SG	(N57TS)	[instructional airframe at Nehru College of Aeronautics & Applied Science, Kuniamuthur, India; cx 03Feb12]				
25036	1A	CF-PQG	C-FPQG	N136DH	[cx Jul95 as destroyed/scrapped]						
25037	1A	G-ATFO	D-CAFI	N787X	N26T	(N26WJ)	(N389DA)	[b/u for spares; cx Jul92]			
25038	731	G-ATCP	N926G	N125G	(N900KC)	N66KC	(N15UB)	N27RC	N301CK	(N417TF)	(N28MM) N28M N42CK
		N806CB	[wfu New Tamiami, FL]								
25039	1A	CF-SIM	C-FSIM	N125TB	N911AS	[wfu to Sanford, FL; b/u & cx Sep03]					
25040	T1	XS712	[code A]	[wfu 20Jan11]	N19CQ	[to RJ Mitchell Aircraft Maintenance Academy, Humberside, UK, 20Feb15 as instructional airframe]					
25041	T1	XS713	[code C]	[wfu 20Jan11; to RAF Shawbury as fire trainer]							
25042	731	CF-ANL	N79TS	(N42FD)	N725WH	[parted out by White Inds, Bates City, MO; cx 25Oct07]					
25043	1A/522	G-ATGA	N125J	N1230V	N3007	N300R	N70HB	N522BW	N522ME	N65TS	(N165AG) [parted out by Dodson Int'l, Rantoul, KS circa Jan01]
25044	T1	XS726	[code T]	9273M	[wfu RAF Cosford, UK circa 1997; to Everett Aero, Sproughton, UK, 2007, then to Newark Air Museum, Newark, UK, Sep14]						
25045	T1	XS727	[code D]	[wfu 20Jan11; preserved RAF Cranwell]							
25046	1A/S-522	G-ATGS	N48UC	N4886	N125P	N666AE	N812TT	N125AD	LV-YGC		
25047	1A/522	G-ATGT	N778SM	N580WS	N75CT	N800DA	(N717GF)				
25048	T1	XS728	[code E]	[wfu 20Jan11]	N19CU	[cx 23Jan15, b/u Kemble, UK]					
25049	T1	XS729	[code G]	9275M	[wfu 1996; to Everett Aero, Sproughton, UK, 2007; to Vilanova i la Geltru, Spain, as instructional airframe]						
25050	T1	XS730	[code H]	[wfu 20Jan11]	N19UG	[cx 23Jan15; to instructional airframe, Lufthansa Resource Technical Training, Kemble, UK]					
25051	731	G-ATGU	N9300	N9300C	N125HD	C6-BEY	N77VK	[wfu 18Dec85; cx Jan87, parted out]			
25052	1A/522	G-ATIK	N816M	N816MC	N812M	N812N	N388WM	N125JR	(N252MA)	XB-JVL	[impounded Jun01 Toluca, Mexico]
25053	1A/522	CF-IPG	CF-IPJ	C-FIPJ	N4465N	N125TB	N254JT	N250JT	N25JT	[cx 30Sep04, wfu at Monterrey/del Norte, Mexico]	
25054	TI	XS714	[code P]	9246M	[wfu; to RAF Manston, UK for fire training use]						
25055	T1	XS731	[code J]	[wfu 20Jan11]	N19XY	[cx 23Jan15, b/u Kemble, UK]					
25056	T1	XS732	[code B]	[wfu Jan91 due to fuselage corrosion; fuselage to Research Establishment, Fort Halstead, Kent, UK 27Mar91; TT 11,955.20, TL 9,067]							
25057	1A/522	G-ATIL	N188K	N125AW	[cx 02Apr86; b/u for spares Pontiac, MI]						
25058	1A	D-COMI	N9308Y	N215G	N470R	N632PB	N632PE	(EC-…)	[used for spares; cx Nov05; b/u]		
25059	T1	XS733	[code Q]	9276M	[wfu 1996; stored RAF Cosford, UK; to Everett Aero, Sproughton, UK, 2007]						
25060	1A/522	G-ATIM	N2601	N26011	N2728	N22DL	N22DE	XB-FIS	XB-EAL	XA-BOJ	XA-HOU XB-CXZ N96SG
		[cx 25Aug09, parted out]									
25061	T1	XS734	[code N]	9260M	[stored RAF Cosford, UK circa 1997; to Everett Aero, Sproughton, UK, 2007]						
25062	3B	VH-ECE	[wfu 21Jul81; to Camden Airport Museum, NSW; TT 13936, TL 53882; derelict at The Oaks, NSW by May97]								
25063	1B	HB-VAN	G-BAXG	G-ONPN	5N-ASZ	[wfu 03Jun86 Southampton, UK; parted out]					
25064	1A/522	G-ATKK	N230H	N125JG	N33BK	N222G	XA-RYW	N222G	XB-GGK	XA-TAL	[w/o 09Jul99 Toluca A/P, Mexico]
25065	1A/522	G-ATKL	N631SC	N631SQ	N1YE	XA-KOF					
25066	731	G-ATKM	N925CT	N369JB	(N374DH)	N373DH	(XA-…)	N372RS	XA-UEX		
25067	1B/522	9J-RAN	ZS-MAN	9J-SAS	9J-EPK	Z-TBX	ZS-MAN				
25068	1A/522	XB-BEA	XA-BEM	XB-VUI	XA-MIR	XB-SBC	[reported Oct89 with dual marks XA-MIR/XB-SBC]	N5274U	[parted out by Dodson Av'n, Rantoul, KS]		
25069	3B	VH-ECF	G-BAXL	G-OBOB	[w/o 31Jan90 Concordia, MO; parted out by White Inds, Bates City, MO]						

BAe 125

C/n		Series	Identities

25070 1A/522 G-ATKN N520M N214JR N2148R N84W N51V N470TS N333GZ [parted out by White Inds, Bates City, MO; cx 29Apr09]

25071 T1 XS735 [code R] [wfu; ground instructional airframe at RAF St Athan, UK May02]

25072 T1 XS736 [code S] [parted out RAF Cranwell, UK; remains to Everett Aero, Sproughton, UK, 2007; then to Winterbourne Gunner, UK]

25073 1A/522 G-ATLI N372CM N372GM N36MK [w/o 28Dec70 Boise, ID]

25074 1A/522 G-ATOV N400NW N400UW N300GB N411FB

25075 731 G-ATLJ N666M CF-MDB C-FMDB N9124N N750GM N731BW N600EG XB-GAM

25076 T1 XS737 [code K] [wfu 20Jan11] N19EK [cx 23Jan15; to instructional airframe, Lufthansa Resource Technical Training, Kemble, UK]

25077 T1 XS738 [code U] 9274M [stored RAF Cosford, UK circa 1997; to RNAS Predannack fire training area by 2007]

25078 1A/522 G-ATLK N40DC N448DC N125NT (N770BC) (N16PJ) XA-DCS

25079 731 G-ATLL N440DC N448DC N40DC N425DC N425FD N79TJ N425FD N942Y N942WN P4-AOC N963YA
[instructional airframe, Tulsa Technical Center, Tulsa/R.L.Jones, OK]

25080 1A/522 VQ-ZIL 3D-AAB G-BDYE EI-BGW C-GLEO N23KL EC-EGT [wfu Jan93; parted out by Dodson Av'n, Rantoul, KS]

25081 T1 XS739 [code F] [wfu 20Jan11] N19UK [to RJ Mitchell Aircraft Maintenance Academy, Humberside, UK, 20Feb15 as instructional airframe]

25082 1A/522 G-ATNM N909B N2125 N125CA N1MY N17SL [wfu; cx Dec92; parted out by White Inds, Bates City, MO]

25083 1A/522 G-ATOW N16777 N435T N437T N533 N538 N50AS [wfu 1988; parted out by OK Aircraft, Gilroy, CA; cx Sep92]

25084 1A/522 G-ATNN N1125G N453CM N154TR N30EF N784AE (N745HG) N71BL N890RC N888CJ [wfu Santo Domingo/ Herrera, Dominican Republic]

25085 1B/522 G-ATPD 5N-AGU G-ATPD [wfu circa Sep00 at Bournemouth A/P, UK, to fire training mid 2002; cx Dec03]

25086 1A/522 CF-DSC N3699T XA-COL [w/o 11Oct73 Acapulco, Mexico]

25087 731/S G-ATOX CF-ALC C-FALC N66AM N330G

25088 1A/522 G-ATNO N1230B 5B-...

25089 1B/522 G-ATPB OO-SKJ 5N-ALH

25090 1B/S522 HB-VAT G-AWYE N102TW N429DA [cx 13May13; wfu]

25091 1A/522 G-ATNP N1230G N20RG N90RG N65FC XA-RSP [wfu Fort Lauderdale Executive, FL; b/u]

25092 1B/522 G-ATPE [CofA exp 01Apr87; to Southampton Airport Fire Svce 1989; canx 14Mar90]

25093 1A/522 G-ATSN N77D N306L N3MF [w/o 26Jan79 Taos NM]

25094 1B/R522 G-ATWH HZ-BO1 G-ATWH G-YUGO [cx 29Mar93 as wfu; remains to Biggin Hill, UK circa 2000 for fire training]

25095 1A/522 G-ATSO N125Y CF-SHZ N1923G N5001G (N5012P) N80CC N61BL N25AW N831LC [w/o 16Mar91 nr San Diego, CA]

25096 1A/522 G-ATNR N235KC [w/o 21Nov66 Grand Bahama, Bahamas]

25097 1A/S522 G-ATSP LN-NPE N125V N12KW N21MF N89HB N67TS [b/u; cx Jan02]

25098 731 G-ATNS N10121 N666SC N57G N11AR N45SL N926LR N29CR YV-815CP (N77LJ) YV2416

25099 1B/522 HB-VAU 5N-AER N2246 N121AC [wfu; located at aircraft trades school Zaira, Nigeria]

25100 1A/522 G-ATNT N125J N952B N7SZ N104 N44TG N44TQ N6SS [cx 06Aug12; wfu]

25101 731/S G-5-11 G-ATXE N142B N124BM XA-RCH XA-RUX N251LA N78AG XA-MBM

25102 1A/522 G-ATUU N756 N756M XB-AKW N3274Q [to spares Houston, TX circa 1995 (cx Feb96) marks N3274Q were never carried]

25103 1A/522 G-ATUV N533 N210M (N700UU) N601UU N60HU N402AC

25104 1A/522 G-ATUW N257H N140AK C-FMTC [derelict Nov97 Vancouver, Canada; hulk removed to Lakeland, FL circa Mar00]

25105 1B/522 (D-CKOW) D-CKCF G-AYRY HZ-FMA [reported wfu]

25106 1B/522 HZ-BIN G-AWUF 5N-ALY G-AWUF G-DJMJ G-OMCA G-BOCB [wfu 1994 Luton, UK; cx 22Feb95; cockpit to Sth.Yorks Aircraft Museum, Doncaster, UK]

25107 1A/522 G-ATUX N7125J N2426 C-GFCL N107BW N694JC XA-GOC XA-HFM XA-UBK

25108 731 N1025C N901TC N901TG N31B C-FTAM N11QD N25LA C-GTTS N46190 [wfu circa Sep04; parted out by White Inds, Bates City, MO, Jly05 still wearing C-GTTS]

25109 1A/S522 G-ATUZ N201H N4CR [wfu Phoenix/Williams Gateway, AZ]

25110 1A/522 G-5-11 G-ATZE N3125B N125E [w/o 30Jun83 Houston Hobby, TX]

25111 3A G-ATYH N1041B N125GC C-GKRL N31AS N177GP N900CD [w/o 30May94 Waukegan Regional A/P, Waukegan, IL; parted out by White Inds, Bates City, MO]

25112 3A G-ATYI N2525 N252V XB-AXP XA-LFU XB-FFV XA-SLR

25113 3B/RA G-5-13 G-AVDX 5N-AVZ [noted semi-derelict Dec96 Lagos, Nigeria]

25114 3A G-ATYJ N425K N44K N44KG N78RZ N25PM XA-SGP N114WD [parted out by Dodson Av'n, Rantoul, KS]

25115 731 G-ATYK N229P N333ME N333MF N317EM N111DT N180ML N21GN N429AC (N750WC) N249BW N249MW N420JC N48DD [w/o 09Mar01 Bridgeport, CT]

25116 3A G-ATZN N93TC N136LK N345DA (N90SR) N345CT N726CC SX-BSS [wfu at Thessalonkia, Greece circa Jul01]

25117 3B 5N-AET 5N-AKT G-BSAA G-DBAL [cx 16Apr93; wfu]

25118 731 G-ATYL N743UT N45PM N731KC N300KC N227HF N14HH N118DA 9Q-CVF

25119 731 G-5-11 G-AVAD N213H N500XY [parted out; still current on USCAR]

25120 3B G-AVGW [w/o 23Dec67 Luton, UK]

25121 731 G-AVAE N795J N307G N807G N200PB N200PF XA-SKZ XB-GHC N125TJ N125LK N685FF [parted out Spirit of St Louis a/p, MO; cx 15Sep07]

25122 3A G-AVAF N12225 N555CB (N123AG) N123AC [parted out 1992, San Jose, CA; remains to OK Aircraft, Gilroy, CA; cx Nov01]

25123 3A G-AVAG N700M N706M N77C N77CD N46TG N44PW N125FD [parted out by Dodson Int'l, Rantoul, KS circa Oct01]

25124 3A G-AVAH N125J N552N N912AS [wfu to Titusville/Cocoa Beach, FL]

25125 F3B G-AVAI LN-NPA G-AVAI F-GFMP 5N-AAN (EL-AMJ) (EL-ELS) [to instructional airframe at Newcastle Aviation Academy, Newcastle UK]

25126 3B G-5-11 G-AVDL N510X N66HA [w/o 13Aug89 Houston, TX – remains to Aviation Warehouse film prop facility, El Mirage, CA]

25127 F3B G-AVPE G-5-623 G-KASS N125GK [w/o 26Jun06 Barcelona, Venezuela; parted out by White Inds, Bates City, MO]

25128 3B G-AVOI F-GECR ZS-SMT [wfu at Lanseria, South Africa]

25129 3A G-5-12 G-AVDM N521M [w/o 12Dec72 Findlay, OH]

25130 3B G-5-14 G-AVRD HB-VAZ F-BSIM TR-LXO F-BSIM TR-LFB [cx; used for fire-fighting demonstrations, Musee de l'Air, Paris/Le Bourget, France]

25131 3B G-5-11 G-AVRE F-BPMC G-FOUR I-RASO F-GFDB 3A-MDB F-GJDE 3A-MDE 7T-VVL

25132 3B OY-DKP G-AZVS G-MRFB G-OCBA EI-WDC G-OCBA EI-WDC G-OCBA S9-PDH

25133 3B G-AVRF G-ILLS VT-EQZ [instructional airframe, Flytech Aviation Academy, Hyderabad, India]

25134 NA700 3A/RA G-5-11 G-AVHA N514V N514VA N338 N366MP N366BR N117TS N725DW N946FS N230TS [to Dodson International Parts May05]

25135 3B G-5-14 HB-VAY G-AXPS [w/o 20Jul70 Edinburgh, UK]

25136 NA701 3A/RA G-5-11 G-AVHB N501W N506N N505W N605W N700RG N700RD N700RG N125HS Brazil VU93-2113

25137 NA702 3A/RA G-5-11 G-AVJD CF-AAG CF-KCI C-FKCI N13MJ N813PR C-GMEA [parted out Arnoni Av'n, Houston, TX circa Sep00; cx Aug99]

25138 3B (G-5-12) G-5-16 G-AVVA HB-VBN I-BOGI 5N-AVV [parted out Coventry, UK, 1997]

25139 NA703 3A/RA G-5-11 G-AVOJ N612G N2G N22GE N140JS XB-JLY XB-KQB [instructional airframe at Patna, India]

25140 3B/RA (G-5-16) G-5-17 G-AVVB G-DJLW C6-MED N140LF [parted out by Dodson Int'l, Rantoul, KS]

25141 NA704 3A/RA G-AVOK N75C N55G N208H N14GD N14GQ (N90WP) N888WK C-GSKV N132RL [parted out by White Inds, Bates City, MO; cx 29Apr09]

25142 NA705 731 G-AVOL N7055 N9040 N688CC N9040 N744CC N7440C N822CC N770DA (N60AM) N25MJ N705EA [parted out by White Inds, Bates City, MO; cx 29Apr09]

25143 3B/RA G-5-18 G-AVXK D-CHTH G-AVXK 5N-AOG [wfu before Jun93; b/u for spares Hurn, UK]

25144 3B/RA G-5-12 G-AVRG G-OHEA [cx Jun94; wfu to Cranfield Inst of Technology, Cranfield, UK, as instructional airframe]

25145 3B G-5-20 G-AVXL LN-NPC G-AVXL I-SNAF [CofA exp 1983; derelict at Milan-Linate 1989; cx 1990]

25146 NA706 3A/RA G-AVRH N77617 N214JR N214TC N711SW N214TC N114PC N21AR N999SA (N899SA) N777GA XA-ADR XB-JKG [wfu Monterrey del Norte, Mexico]

BAe 125

C/n		Series	Identities

25147 3B/RA G-5-14 PK-PJR PK-DJW [CofA expired 20Oct86; wfu; derelict near Jakarta-Halim Airport, Indonesia circa 99]

25148 3A/R G-5-13 G-AVRI N8125J N450JD (N100TT) XB-ERN N814P (N819P) XA-TTH

25149 3A/R G-AVRJ N1125E N99SC N99GC N99KR [wfu 09Sep80; donated to Northrop University nr Los Angeles A/P, CA; cx Apr91; to Malaysian Institute of Aviation Technology, Dengkil nr Kuala Lumpur, 1998, painted as N1125E]

25150 F3A G-5-13 N511BX VR-BKY VP-BKY N42AS [parted out by Alliance Air Parts, Oklahoma City, OK]

25151 3A/RA G-AVTY N125F [wfu at Lima, Peru, circa 1997; fuselage to Collique, Peru, by Feb07]

25152 3A/RA G-AVTZ CF-QNS C-FQNS N45793 N123RZ XA-IIT N28686 N50MJ N23CJ

25153 731 G-5-19 G-AVXM N30F N30FD N731G N336MB N676PC N88DJ N88DU [cx 27Aug13; wfu]

25154 3B/RA G-5-11 EP-AHK G-AZCH [b/u Luton, UK Dec82 due to corrosion; TT 4261hrs, TL 4695, CofA exp 16Aug81; rear fuselage/fin used on c/n 25270; forward fuselage at Cheddington airstrip, Bucks, UK]

25155 3A/RA G-AVXN N32F N466MP (N411MF) N999LF N333CJ N77BT N158AG [still painted as N77BT circa Dec00; wfu Titusville/ Cocoa Beach, FL; b/u; cx Sep03]

25156 3A/RA G-AVZJ N522M N10LN [b/u 1993 Lakeland, FL; fuselage remains only]

25157 3B/RA D-CAMB VR-BGD G-GGAE G-JSAX [wfu Dec82; cx 10Jan86 – at Eastleigh, UK minus outer wings]

25158 3A/RA G-AVZK XB-PUE (N702GA) XA-DAN

25159 731 G-5-19 G-AVZL CF-WOS C-FWOS N4767M N511WM N511WN N67TJ N600SV ZS-CNA

25160 NA707 3A/RA G-5-15 G-AWKH N350NC N873D N873G N627CR SE-DHH N160AG

25161 NA708 3A/RA G-AWKI N9149 N756N N75GN XA-RPT

25162 3B/RC Brazil VC93-2120 Brazil VU93-2120

25163 NA709 731 G-5-16 G-AWMV N208H N55G (N2G) [cx 28Jul14; wfu Fort Lauderdale Executive]

25164 3B/RC Brazil EC93-2125 Brazil EU93-2125

25165 3B/RC Brazil VC93-2121 Brazil EU93-2121 [wfu]

25166 3B/RC Brazil VC93-2122 [w/o 19Jun79 Brasilia, Brazil]

25167 3B/RC Brazil VC93-2123 Brazil VU93-2123

25168 3B/RC Brazil VC93-2124 Brazil VU93-2124 [wfu]

25169 3A/RA G-5-17 G-AWWL VH-BBJ N3AL G-AWWL N84TF (N9300P) N9300C N99SC (N711SC) N122AW N163AG [cx 24Jul08, b/u]

25170 NA710 3A/RA G-AWMW N1259K N226G N228G N223G C-GKCO N500YB C-FMKF N322TP N814ER N314ER (N767LC) [parted out Rantoul, KS]

25171 F3B/RA G-5-19 HB-VBT G-AXPU G-IBIS G-AXPU G-BXPU (N171AV) G-OPOL G-IFTC (N171AV) D2-FEZ

25172 F3B/RA G-AXEG ZS-CAL G-AXEG ZS-CAL

25173 NA711 400A G-AWMX N125J N3711L (N610HC) N711AQ N601JJ ZP-TDF ZP-TKO

25174 NA712 400A G-AWMY N1199M N1199G N511WP N60JC N496G N7777B N712VS N713SS [parted out by White Inds, Bates City, MO circa Oct05]

25175 NA713 731 G-AWPC N217F YV-825CP N272B N773AA XB-MGM [w/o 04Nov13, shot down over Venezuela on suspected drug-running flight]

25176 NA714 731 G-AWPD CF-NER C-FNER N176TS N311JA N811JA N31EP YV299T

25177 400B G-AWXN S Africa 02 [w/o 26May71 Devils Peak, S Africa]

25178 400B G-AWXO 5N-BUA G-OOSP 5N-WMA

25179 NA715 731 G-AWPE N778S N200CC N400CC N800CB N22EH N629P N824TJ N284DB XA-GLS

25180 NA716 731 G-AWPF N196KC N196KQ N888CR N400PH [w/o 05Dec87 Blue Grass Field, Lexington, KY]

25181 400B (G-5-13) G-AXLU S Africa 01 [w/o 26May71 Devils Peak, S Africa]

25182 400B G-AXLV S Africa 03 [w/o 26May71 Devils Peak, S Africa]

25183 NA717 731 G-5-18 G-AWXB N162A N162D N100HF N984HF [w/o 07Nov85 Sparta, TN]

25184 400B G-AXLW S Africa 04 ZS-LPE [wfs – stored at Waterkloof AFB, South Africa]

25185 NA720 400A G-AWXE N140C N4PN N7LG XA-GUB XB-DSQ XA-RMN XB-FRP XA-FRP XB-MSV [wfu Monterrey del Norte, Mexico]

25186 NA721 731 G-AWXF N125G N93BH N933 N40SK N666JT N668JT (N105EJ) N99CK HR-AMD N12YS (N999NM) N186NM N777GD N43TS

25187 NA718 731 G-AWXC N600L N600LP N600JA N900DS (N7WG) N16WG N50SL N141JL XA-SSV N250DH [cx 28Jul14; parted out by Arnoni Av'n, Houston, TX]

25188 NA719 731 G-AWXD N545S XB-IPX

25189 400B G-5-20 (G-AXFY) Malaysia FM1200 FM1801 M24-01 [wfu, to technical school at Alor Setar, Malaysia, wearing fake marks M24-02]

25190 NA722 400A G-AXDO N1393 N75CS N75QS N75TJ N51MN N209NC N38TS (N280CH) XB-ILD [impounded at Portoviejo, Ecuador, Oct03 for drug-running] Ecuador FAE050

25191 NA723 731 G-AXDP N511YP N900KC N100T N723TS N401JR N444HH YV-1145CP YV1687 [dbr Caracas/Simon Bolivar 26Nov15]

25192 NA724 731 CF-SDH C-FSDH N724TS

25193 NA725 400A CF-CFL [w/o 11Nov69 Newfoundland, Canada]

25194 400B G-AXDM [wfu & dismantled at Edinburgh, UK Sep03; to Farnborough, UK; cx as destroyed 13Nov03]

25195 NA726 731 G-AXDR N111MB N949CW N949CV N60B N60BD N731G N31VT YV-141CP N922RR N922GK [parted out by White Inds, Bates City, MO]

25196 NA727 731 G-AXDS N814M N114B N81RR N117RH N100RH XA-TNY

25197 400B G-5-11 PP-EEM PT-LHK N97CS [b/u Fort Lauderdale Executive, FL, Aug12; parted out by Dodson Av'n, Rantoul, KS]

25198 NA728 731 G-AXJD N24CH N400KC N320JJ N410PA N32GM (N232JS) [parted out by Alliance Air Parts, Oklahoma City, OK]

25199 400B G-AXLX HB-VBW G-AXLX (HB-VGU) N3118M (N905Y) [parted out 1994 by Dodson Avn, Ottawa, KS]

25200 NA729 400A G-AXJE N702S N1C N702SS Brazil VU93-2118

25201 NA730 731 G-AXJF N220T N56BL N125MD N800JC N810MC N730TS N101HS N730TS N82CA N800WZ

25202 NA731 400A G-AXJG N65LT N700CC N300LD (N125DC) N31TJ (N700PG) (N600DP) XA-JRF N336AC XB-MAR (XB-ASO)

25203 NA732 400A G-AXOA N500AG N73JH N44CN N21ES N100LR N109LR N2020 N70JC N732TS N400PR [preserved at 1940 Air Terminal Museum, Houston/ Hobby, TX]

25204 NA733 731 G-AXOB N380X N31GT (N125RT) N243JB ZS-PLC [cx; scrapped Sep15]

25205 NA734 731 G-AXOC N125J N111RB N621L N621S N6218 N99ST (N38TS) XA-GTC N20PJ XA-GTC

25206 NA735 400A G-AXPX VP-BDH N125AJ N400AG N11SQ XA-ROJ N165AG N800GE

25207 NA736 400A G-AXOD N30PR N30PP N112M (N400HF) N800AF N736LE [wfu; stored Cambridge, MD]

25208 NA737 400A G-AXOE N2500W N65EC N65DW (N165AG) N643JL N400KD XA-YSM [impounded for drug-running Valencia, Venezuela, Sep07]

25209 400B Malaysia FM1201 FM1802 M24-02 [wfu, to Malaysian Institute of Aviation Technology, Dengkil nr Kuala Lumpur, Malaysia]

25210 NA738 400A G-AXOF N702D Brazil VU93-2117 Brazil XU93-2117 [wfu at Guaratingueta, Brazil, by May05]

25211 NA739 731 G-AXTR N125DH N820MC N820MG [cx Apr10, wfu]

25212 NA740 400A G-AXTS N702P Brazil VU93-2114 [wfu 1998]

25213 NA741 400A CF-CFL C-FCFL [w/o 09Dec77 Newfoundland, Canada]

25214 NA742 731 G-AXTU N40PC N60QA G-AXTU G-5-20 N731HS N12BN N12AE N369CS N569CS (N87DC) N74RT N843B [cx 23Mar15; wfu]

25215 403B HB-VBZ G-BHFT 9M-SSB G-BHFT Z-VEC ZS-NPV D2-EXR [dbr 21Nov03 Luanda, Angola]

25216 NA743 400A G-AXTV N9138 XC-GOB Mexico TP0206 Mexico TP108/XC-UJH N125JW HP-125JW HP-1128P N400D HK-3653X HK-3653 N400LC XA-…

25217 403B G-5-14 G-AXYJ 9Q-CGM 9Q-CHD G-5-651 G-BRXR G-OLFR 5N-EAS

25218 NA744 400A G-AXTW N575DU N575 (N382DA) N711BP N440BC [parted out]

25219 F400A G-5-14 G-AYEP 4W-ACA 9K-AEA G-5-12 N5594U N292GA (N292RC) N128DR N219EC RA-02805 N219EC (ZS-OZU) D2-FFH N114AF [instructional airframe Sinclair University, Dayton, OH]

25220 NA745 731 G-AXYE N41BH N125AR N125AP N427DA N745TS N400XJ N700TR XB-LWC

25221 NA746 731 N42BH CF-BNK C-FBNK N468LM N62CH N74WF N103RR ZS-OIF

25222 NA747 731 G-AXYF N43BH N900EL N400FE N590CH N125NW P4-AOB N401AB [cx 21May13; to instructional airframe, Tulsa Technical Center, Tulsa/R.L.Jones, OK]

25223 403B G-5-15 G-AYIZ PJ-SLB F-BSSL G-AYIZ G-TACE [cx 09Jan90; wfu]

BAe 125

C/n		Series	Identities
25224	NA748	731	G-AXYG N44BH N22DH N222RB N222RG N144PA N189B N199B N143CP N728KA N777SA YV-1111CP N748TS N601KK N748TS N62TW N77WD N748TS (N399JC)
25225	NA749	731	G-AXYH N45BH N81T N119CC N583CM N100HF N100HE N45NC N45NQ (N45ND) SE-DVS N498R N498RS XB-KKS N498RS XB-KNH
25226	NA750	400A	G-AXYI N46BH N300P N304P XA-DIW XB-CCM N3933A N20RG N251AB XA-RWN N131LA [cx 26Jan15; CofR expired]
25227		F403B	G-AYFM G-MKOA 5N-AMY N227MS N355AC XB-MYA
25228	NA751	731	N47BH N640M G-BCLR N640M G-BCLR N120GA N120GB N75RD N75RN N125GH N79B HC-BTT N400FR [cx 20Sep12; wfu]
25229	NA752	731	N48BH N914BD N61MS N61MX N731HS N700PL N700FA N602JR (N998PS)
25230	NA753	731	N49BH N400BH N840H N345GL N145GL
25231		731	D-CBVW G-BEME 5N-AQY G-BEME N125GC N707EZ N707SH (N125TJ) N832MR (N832MB) N831NW N831DF YV113T
25232	NA754	731	CF-TEC C-FTEC C-GVQR N62TF N125VC N125EC N60RE N711HL N227LT N228EA
25233	NA755	400A	N50BH N711SD N755GW (N5MW) XB-AXP XB-LXP XB-AXP N755WJ (N871MA) ZS-MEG [wfu Lanseria, South Africa]
25234	NA756	731	N51BH N701Z N7NP N100MT C-GFCD N40Y N400JK N624PD N624MP
25235		F403B	G-5-18 HB-VCE G-AYNR G-BKAJ G-5-19 N235AV N227LA N297JD N101UD N101UR N330AM
25236	NA757	731	N52BH N125BH N10C N154 (N44BH) N999SC N499SC N50NE (N745WG) N900WG XA-AGL
25237	NA761	400A	N56BH N125BH N1924L N500MA N580MA XA-RIL N814D [cx 01Apr13; wfu]
25238		F403B	G-AYER 9K-ACR G-AYER G-TOPF N125GC N808V VR-BKK VP-BKK G-36-1 VP-BKK [wfu in damaged state at Bournemouth, UK]
25239	NA758	731	G-5-19 N53BH N6709 N731MS N800NP YV586T
25240		400B	G-5-11 G-AYLI I-GJBO VR-BKN VR-BMB [stripped of spares – to fire section at Stansted A/P, UK circa Apr99; b/u there Sep03 and remains removed]
25241	NA759	400A	G-5-20 N54BH N6702 N702M N702MA N810CR N127CM N125CF (N400MR) YV2315
25242		403B	G-5-20 VH-TOM G-BDKF 3D-ABZ ZS-LME [wfu; stored Waterkloof AFB, South Africa]
25243		F400A	G-5-14 (G-AYOI) PT-DTY N243TS VP-CTS N4ES
25244	NA760	400A	G-5-12 N55BH N731X N70LY N456WH YV- ....
25245	NA762	731	N57BH N523M N400GP N125DH [cx 28Aug14; CofR expired]
25246		403B	G-AYOJ 9Q-COH (G-5-16) G-AYOJ G-LORI [derelict Nigeria for many years; cx 21Apr93]
25247		403B	G-AYRR 9Q-CCF G-5-672 G-AYRR 9Q-CSN 9Q-CPR
25248		F403B	D-CFCF G-5-707 G-BTUF G-SHOP (N792A) G-SHOP N792A G-TCDI N189RR YV-1122CP (N119GH) N189RR N505LC
25249		731	G-5-16 G-AZAF N51993 N72HT N72HA N107AW N125KC N200KC N200VT N711VT N54JC N154JC (N303BX) N27UM
25250		731	G-AYOK TR-LQU G-AYOK N20S N24S N300CC N300QC N125G N125HG (N125SJ) N7SJ N888TJ [cx 31Oct12; wfu]
25251		400B	Argentina 5-T-30/0653 LV-AXZ CX-BVD [cx; wfu Monevideo, Uruguay]
25252		400B	G-5-17 XX505 G-BAZB N48US P4-AMB [parted out in 2003]
25253		F400A	G-5-18 OY-APM G-BROD N731HS N3338 N50EB N50FC N610HC XA-SKE N253MT (N253CC) N911RD
25254		F400B	G-AYLG 3D-AVL G-AYLG G-5-624 G-VJAY VT-UBG G-5-624 VT-UBG [wfu; preserved by Kingfisher Airlines, India]
25255		CC1A/F400A	XW788 G-BVTP (N255TS) N4QB
25256		600B	G-AYBH RP-C111 G-5-13 G-AYBH Ireland IAC236 [w/o 27Nov79 Dublin, Ireland]
25257		403B	G-5-19 G-BATA 9M-HLG [wfu Jun93]
25258		F600B	(G-AYRR) G-AZHS G-BFAN VR-CJP VP-CJP G-OJPB TL-ADK 9Q-CBC [wfu Kinshasa/N'Djili, Democratic Republic of Congo]
25259		400B	G-AZEK S Africa 05 ZS-JBA [b/u for spares following accident at Lanseria, South Africa; cx Mar03]
25260		400B	G-AZEL S Africa 06 ZS-JIH D2-EFM
25261	NA763	731	N58BH (N91BH) N246N N46B (N68BW) N246N N55B N125MT N62TC N19H N1QH 6V-AIN
25262	NA764	400A	N59BH XB-CUX N55RZ
25263	NA765	731	N62BH N125PA N700BW N708BW N61MS N68CB N765TS
25264		CC1A/F400A	XW789 N264BH N7171 (N264WD) (N731WB) (N264TS) N93TS N178PC [cx 14Mar12; wfu]
25265	NA766	731	N63BH N711YP N711YR N300LD N200CC N125MD VH-PAB N150SA N854SM
25266		CC1A/F400A	XW790 G-BVTS (N266TS) N135CK N125CK
25267	NA767	400A	N64BH N92BH N28GP N28GE N125CM [parted out Oct94, Spirit of St Louis A/P, MO; cx Jun95; remains to AvMATS, Paynesville, MO]
25268		CC1A/F400A	XW791 G-BVTT (N268TS) N41953 [w/o 07Apr95 Santo Domingo-Herrera Intl Apt, Dominican Republic; parted out by Arnoni Avn, Houston, TX circa Sep00]
25269		400B	G-AZEM S Africa 07 ZS-LPF EX-269 AP-BGI EX-500 [wfu Bishkek, Kyrgystan]
25270		F403B	G-5-13 G-BKBA N270AV N400GP N440RD [parted out by Dodson Int'l, Rantoul, KS]
25271		400A	G-5-14 G-BABL XX506 G-BABL EC-CMU N37516 N103CJ N365DA N400DP N70AP N810HS [parted out by AvMats, St Louis, MO, Jan04; cx]
25272		F400A	G-5-15 G-BAZA N4759D N121VA N121VF N800JT N63EM
25273	NA768	400A	G-5-20 N65BH N125BH N69KA XA-DIN N11FX N7WC XA-SFQ N2155P XA-SFQ
25274		403B	G-5-20 Brazil EU93-2119 [wfu]
25275	NA769	400A	N66BH N872D N972D N125PP N42BL N369JH N900AD [cx 28Aug14; CofR expired]
25276	NA770	731	G-5-11 N67BH N88GA N300CF N74B N7170J N38LB N805WD
25277		403B	G-5-11? Brazil VU93-2126
25278	NA771	731	N68BH CF-AOS C-FAOS N731H VR-BVI N298NM N4WC [wfu; used as fire trainer at Miami a/p, FL]
25279	NA772	400A	G-5-12 N69BH XA-CUZ [w/o 27Dec80 Cancun, Mexico]
25280	NA773	731	N70BH CF-PPN C-FPPN N32KB [parted out Conroe, TX]
25281	NA774	731	N71BH N1BG N18GX N125DB EI-BRG N70338 N774EC RA-02804 G-5-821 RA-02804 N774TS
25282	NA775	731	N72BH N5V N7HV N17HV N333DP XA-EMA N223RR
25283	NA776	403A	N73BH G-BACI XA-LOV XA-SGM XB-GNF XA-LOV [wfu Monterrey del Norte, Mexico]
25284	NA777	731	N74BH N571CH N571GH N228GC N125FM N125MD N101AD (N425JF) [w/o 06May91 Shreveport, LA; cx Sep91 – fuselage at Tulsa, OK, circa Oct99]
25285	NA778	731	N75BH N555CB N733K C-GCEO N2694C N67EC N89SR N88AF N778JA
25286	NA779	731	N76BH N88SJ N33CP N84CP N400WT N408WT N808CC N731JR N781JR (N989AB) [instructional airframe at Fanshawe College, London, Canada]
25287	NA780	731	N78BH N72HC N65DL N265DL N800TG 9Q-CPF
25288		403B	Brazil VU93-2127 [preserved Brasilia International a/p, Brazil]
25289		403B	G-5-16 Brazil VU93-2128 [preserved TAM Museum, Sao Carlos, Brazil]
25290		403B	Brazil VU93-2129 [w/o 08Sep87 Carajas, Brazil]

Production complete

BAe 125 SERIES 600

C/n	Series	Identities									
256001	FA	G-AZUF	N82BH	N711AG	G-BEWW	N711AG	N82RP	N82PP	N444PE	N444PD	N700R	N709R	N561RP
		N61TS	N773JC	N699TS								
256002	A	G-5-15	N79BH	(N925BH)	N631SC	N631SQ	N915JT	N61SB	N602MM	XA-SLP		
256003	A	N80BH	CF-HSS	C-FHSS	N256FC	N42TS	N91KH	N91KP	[cx 29Oct13; wfu Fort Lauderdale Executive, FL]			
256004	A	N81BH	N94BD	N94BB	N19HH	N19HE	VR-BRS	N4TS	(N103RA)	N399GA	N5AH	N600MK	[submerged in
		lake at Athens Scuba Park, Athens, TX, 28May11 for use as diving training aid]										
256005	B	G-BART	(G-BJXV)	(G-BJUT)	EC-EAC	N4253A	[b/u for spares by Western A/C Parts; to White Inds, Bates City, MO; cx Jun95]					
256006	FB	XX507	N606TS	N21SA	[w/o 21Feb05 Bromont, Canada; parted out Montgomery, AL; cx 17Jan08]							
256007	A	N21BH	N125BH	N125KR	N3007	N317TC	[parted out Houston, TX; cx 14Jan08]					
256008	FA	XX508	N256WJ									
256009	A	N22BH	N3PW	N219ST	(N210ST)	N183RD	"N183RM"	N28TS				
256010	A	N23BH	N40PC	[w/o 28Apr77 McLean, VA]								
256011	A	N24BH	N6001H	N555CB	N555GB	VR-BGS	N42622	N81D	EC-EHF	[parted out Oct94, Spirit of St Louis A/P, MO unmarked –		
		remains to Dodson Int'l, Ottawa, KS, circa 1998; fuselage reported at Gary, IN, summer 2012]										
256012	B	G-5-17	G-BAYT	5N-ALX	G-BAYT	G-BNDX	G-BAYT	EC-272	EC-EOQ	N8000Z	[parted out at Houston, TX circa 1995; cx	
		Feb96; allocated marks N8000Z not worn]										
256013	A	N25BH	N25BE	N505W	(N65GB)	N218AC	N627HS	N80TS	VR-CDG	5N-YET		
256014	A	N26BH	N922CR	N922GR	N5SJ	N47HW	N47HV	[parted out by Dodson Int'l, Parts, Rantoul, KS]				
256015	FA	G-5-19	G-BBCL	G-BJCB	G-BBCL	9K-ACZ	G-BBCL	Ireland 239	G-BBCL	G-5-11	(D-CCEX)	G-BBCL	N600AV
		N917K	N777SA	(N74TJ)	(N615TJ)	N777TK	N700XJ	N957MB				
256016	A	N27BH	N99SC	XA-SAI	[parted out by White Inds, Bates City, MO]							
256017	B	G-5-18	G-BBAS	PK-PJD	N600WJ	(N415BA)	N225HR	[parted out by White Inds, Bates City, MO]				
256018	A	N28BH	N500GD	(N780SC)	N880SC	N125E	N600AW	N93TS	N288MW	XA-JRF	N16GA	XA-TNX	XB-ADZ
256019	B	G-BARR	HZ-AA1	G-FANN	[cx 29Mar93, wfu; fuselage on fire dump Dunsfold, UK, still marked as HZ-AA1]							
256020	A	N29BH	(N501H)	N125CU	N334JR	C-GDUP	N334JR	N5NG	XA-NTE	N5NG	[derelict Monterrey, Mexico and scrapped;	
		cx Sep00]										
256021	A	G-5-11	HB-VDL	C-GSTT	N125HS	N125JJ	(N128JJ)	N125JA	XA-SNH	N37SG	C-GKHR	N111UN	N220TS
		3D-BOS	S9-DBG	S9-PDG								
256022	A	N34BH	N701Z	N701A	N1515P	N757M	N757P	XA-XET	N2114E	[parted out by Arnoni Aviation, Houston, TX; marks	
		N2114E not carried]										
256023	A	N35BH	N514V	EC-121	EC-EGL	N523MA	N702HC	[parted out by White Inds, Bates City, MO]				
256024	A	G-BBMD	N50GD	G-BBMD	G-BSHL	G-OMGA	YR-DVA	(N731TC)	N669SC	N411GA	[parted out by Arnoni Av'n, Houston, TX]	
256025	A	N36BH	C-GTPC	N721LH	[parted out by MTW Aerospace, Montgomery, AL]							
256026	FA	N37BH	G-5-16	N124GS	N699SC	N818TP	XA-SWK	N125NA	N450TB	XA-ATC		
256027	FA	D-CJET	G-5-585	D-CJET	OE-GIA	N693TJ	N800NM	N245RS				
256028	A	G-5-12	VP-BDH	C6-BDH	C-GDHW	XA-KUT	[w/o 18Jan88 Houston-Hobby, TX; parted out by Dodson Av'n, Ottawa, KS]					
256029	FB	G-BBRT	PK-PJE	PK-HMG	N629TS	N35WP						
256030	B	G-BBEP	G-BJOY	G-BBEP	5N-ARD	G-BBEP	G-TOMI	N217A	[parted out by Arnoni Av'n, Houston, TX still marked as G-TOMI]			
256031	B	G-5-11	9Q-CFW	"9Q-CFG"	9Q-CGF	9Q-CJF						
256032	A	N38BH	N4BR	(N14BR)	G-DBOW	C-GLBD	N332TA	EC-EAV	N921RD	N801BC	N334PS	[to Alberta Aviation Museum,
		Edmonton, Canada]										
256033	B	F-BUYP	G-DMAN	HZ-YA1	N330G	G-PJWB	G-HALK	N6033	XB-FMF	N303MW	N600HS	N514AJ	N514MH
		N514RD	[wfu California City, CA]									
256034	A	N39BH	N90B	N90BL	N600FL	N600SB	EC-115	EC-EGS	[used for spares Oct94 at Spirit of St Louis A/P, MO; fuselage to		
		Elsberry, MO by Apr96]										
256035	A	F-BKMC	G-SUFC	VP-BCN	"N635PA"	N128YT	[to White Inds, Bates City, MO, 18Jan05 for spares]					
256036	B	(G-BBRT)	[used for paint-spraying trials Chester, UK; aircraft not completed]									
256037	B	(VH-ARJ)	AN-BPR	YN-BPR	VH-NJA	RP-C1600	VP-BBW	(N16VT)	N63810	N228MD	[cx 30Aug12; wfu]	
256038	A	N40BH	N77C	N77CU	SE-DKF	N199SG	XA-ACN	[cx; status?]				
256039	B	G-BCCL	G-BKBM	N61TF	N410AW	G-BKBM	EC-EAO	EC-183	EC-EAO	G-OMGB	[wfu Oct94; TT 6,944 hrs; to spares at	
		Houston, TX]										
256040	A	N41BH	C-GJCM	N4224Y	N125GS	N601BA	N621BA	N16VT	N287DL	(N301JJ)	N287DM	TJ-...	
256041	B	G-5-11	G-BCJU	VR-CBD	N450DA	N888PM	N273K	N42TS	N808RP	N603TS	[wfu Toluca, Mexico]	
256042	B	G-BBRO	G-BKBU	G-5-505	5N-AWS	[w/o 15Dec86 Casablanca, Morocco]						
256043	B	G-BCUX	[w/o 20Nov75 Dunsfold, UK]									
256044	A	N42BH	N600MB	N46B	(N46BE)	C-GKCC	N848W	N992SF	XA-CAH	N9282Y	N116DD	N454DP	N453DP
		[cx 10Sep12; wfu]										
256045	FB	G-5-18	EC-CQT	G-5-11	G-BGYR	N508VM	(N803LL)	[cx 08May15; CofR expired]				
256046	FA	N43BH	N91HR	(N401HR)	N402HR	N117EM	XA-AGL	N299BW	N299GA	N299TJ	(N299DG)	N299GS	
256047	A	G-5-16	"N44BH"	(C-GBNS)	"N4203S"	N4203Y	N400NW	N400NE	N600TT	XA-JEQ	N47EX	N47WU	XA-RYK
		N68GA	9Q-CYA	9Q-CAI								
256048	A	G-5-15	HB-VDS	G-BHIE	YU-BME	N6567G	TC-COS	N852GA	[parted out by Arnoni Av'n, Houston, TX]			
256049	B	G-BCXL	ZS-JHL	G-BCXL	HZ-KA5	P4-VJR	5V-TTP					
256050	B	G-5-12	5N-ANG	G-BLOI	5N-AOL	[wfu, believed scrapped in 1997]						
256051	A	(N45BH)	C-GBNS	N22DL	N5DL	N35DL	N601PS	N601JJ	N616PA	N600AL	N95TS	N601JA	9Q-CFJ
256052	B	G-5-11	G-BDJE	G-BKBH	TR-LAU	G-5-698	G-BKBH	G-5-698	G-BKBH	G-5-698	5N-NBC	5N-DNL	G-5-698
		5N-DNL	G-BKBH	[cx Jly99 wfu Southampton, UK]								
256053	B	D-CFSK	HC-BUR	N125WJ	N5NR	N721RM						
256054	B	G-5-17	G-BCXF	9K-AED	"G-BKFS"	G-BCXF	5N-YFS	5N-RNO	[w/o May01, Lagos, Nigeria]			
256055	A	G-5-19	G-BDOP	N94B	N94BF	N777SA	N100QR	N100QP	N125GS	N20FM	N111UN	(N600GP)	[cx 22Jan13; CofR
		expired]										
256056	B	G-5-13	G-BDOA	G-BKCD	5N-ARN	G-BKCD	G-OMGC	[wfu Sep94; TT 6404 hrs; parted out at Houston, TX circa 1995]				
256057	B	G-5-17	HZ-KA2	G-FFLT	VR-BNW	VP-BNW	N602CF	N11AF	[parted out by Arnoni Av'n, Houston, TX]			
256058	FA	G-5-18	G-BGKN	N9043U	N701Z	N129BA	(N429BA)	(N658TS)	N200XR	N658TS	N658KA	[cx 16Mar16;	
		CofR expired]										
256059	B	G-5-19	HZ-DAC	HZ-SJP	G-BLUW	ZF130	[stored St. Athan, UK, March 2002; wings and tail removed 21Oct02; fuselage to Farnborough,					
		UK, by 24Oct02 for spares, then to Hanningfield Metals scrapyard, Stock, Essex, UK, 07Jan03; to Elektrowerkz nightclub, London EC1, UK, 2006; removed and										
		scrapped 2008]										
256060	B	G-5-12	HZ-MF1	G-BFIC	5N-AYK	N660TC	N422TK	N422TR	N395EJ	[parted out by MTW Aerospace, Montgomery, AL]		
256061	FA	G-5-14	G-BDOB	N125HS	N5253A	N8253A	N707WB	N169B	N189B	N169B	N331DC	N701MS	XA-EXL
		XB-EXC										
256062	B	G-5-15	G-MFEU	G-TMAS	EC-319	EC-ERX	G-TMAS	5N-MAY	5N-DOT	[parted out]		
256063	A	G-5-13	A6-RAK	G-BSPH	N484W	EC-349	EC-ERJ	5N-OPT	N9AZ	YV345T	YV2680	
256064	A	G-5-17	HZ-AMM	N105AS	N666LC	N500MA	N580MA	N600SN	N125HF	XA-MKY	[wfu Monterrey del Norte, Mexico]	
256065	A	G-5-16	G-BJCB	XA-MAH	N73JA	N59JR	VR-CSF	V2-LSF	N125SF	N4SA	N10SA	
256066	FA	G-5-15	G-BDZH	N32RP	N800JP	N600G	(N700SM)	XB-RYP				
256067	A	G-BEIN	N522X	N522C	N270MC	N270MQ	N1884	N67MR	XA-SKH	N822BL	N822BD	(N157RP)	CX-CBS
256068	FA	G-5-20	G-BDZR	N33RP	N90WP	G-5-16	N90WP	N14GD	N54GD	N500R	N501R	N600AE	[disappeared
		11Sep14, believed stolen for drug-running]										
256069	A	G-BEIO	N350MH	N600AG	N369TS	5N-EMA	[wfu Lagos, Nigeria]					
256070	FA	G-5-11	G-BEDT	N322CC	G-5-15	N322CC	N319MF	(N411TC)	N411TP	N83TJ	N365SB	(N76TJ)	N75GA
256071	A	G-5-14	G-BEES	N91884	N571DU	N571E	N121SG	N171TS	[cx May04, parted out in Mexico]			

Production complete

BAe 125 SERIES 700

C/n		Series	Identities											
257001		A	G-BEFZ	VR-HIM	G-BEFZ	N4555E	N700SV	N101SK	N101XS	N80KA	N189GE	N97TS	VH-LYG	N257AJ
			N193TA	N701CW	(N807CW)	N425KG								
257002	NA0201	A	G-5-20	N700HS	N40WB	N40GT	N700NY	N886GB	VR-BNB	G-IECL	N701TS	(N828SA)	N530BL	"N509SM"+
			[+mispainted at Fort Lauderdale Int'l, FL, Jan10]			N529SM	N609AM	[cx 19Feb16; wfu]						
257003	NA0202	A	G-5-19	G-BERP	N64688	N333ME	N727TA	N403BG	XA-ULT					
257004	NA0218	A	G-5-15	G-BGDM	N37975	N222RB	N700RJ	N546BC	N746BC	N648WW	N704CW	N804CW	N804FF
			N903SC	M-JCPO	[cx 23Jul14; b/u]									
257005	NA0203	A	G-BERV	N620M	N104AE	N828PJ								
257006	NA0204	A	G-5-18	G-BERX	N724B									
257007		A	HB-VFA	D-CADA	G-5-721	D-CADA	G-BUNL	RA-02800	G-5-721	RA-02800	(N307TC)	N257TH	N257WJ	N54WJ
			(N545SH)	N49RJ										
257008	NA0205	A	G-5-11	(G-BEWV)	C-GYYZ	N333PC	N807TC	N700FW	N618KR	RP-C8108	[wfu Manila, Philippines]			
257009	NA0206	A	G-5-12	G-BEYC	N813H	(N20GT)	N986H	XA-SNN	N701NW	N818KC	N828KC	N706AM		
257010		A	HZ-MMM	LX-MJM	G-5-631	N700WH	N700ER	N3399P	(N339BW)	(N41CC)	N977CC	N425RJ	N424RJ	N819WG
			N1ES	N819WG	XA-...									
257011	NA0207	A	G-5-13	G-BFAJ	N255CT	(N255QT)	N255TT	N500FC	N33RH	N70X	N7UV	N816JM		
257012	NA0208	A	G-5-14	G-BFBI	N125HS	N700HS	N162A	N700FS	N622AB	N622AD	N37PL	N38PA	N41HF	N449EB
			RA-02810											
257013		A	G-CBBI	N219JA	N75ST	N101HF	N96FT	N36FT	P4-AOH	P4-SKY	N813VC			
257014	NA0209	A	G-5-17	G-BFDW	N46901	N120GA	N60MS	N453EP	N586JR	N74B	N843CP	N209TS		
257015	NA0210	A	G-5-18	G-BFFL	N37P	SE-DPZ	(N725WH)	OY-JPJ	N418RD	P4-AOF	N418RD			
257016	NA0216	A	G-BFFH	N72505	N800CB	N23SB	N23SK	(N23SN)	N999JF	"N197FT"	N98FT	[cx 08Dec14; CofR expired]		
257017	NA0211	A	G-5-19	G-BFFU	N62MS	N454EP	N757M	N757C	(I-DRVM)	I-DVMR	HB-VLH	RA-02806	N211WZ	N411PA
			(N602JJ)											
257018	NA0212	A	G-BFGU	N733H	N662JB	N125CS	(N125MJ)	N425SD	N118CD					
257019	NA0213	A	G-BFGV	N370M	N370RR	N339CA	XA-UPE							
257020		B	(G-BFVN)	G-EFPT	VR-BHE	(N2634B)	N125HM	N818	N311JD	N777EH				
257021	NA0214	A	N34CH	N900KC	N1868M	N1868S	(N526JC)	N926ZT	N926TC	N926MC				
257022		A	(G-5-11)	F-GASL	G-5-17	N34RE	N92RP	N109AF	N700WC	RA-02809				
257023	NA0215	A	G-BFLF	N54555	N125GP	N6JB	N6UB	N35LM	N195XP	N215RS				
257024	NA0217	A	G-BFLG	N94BD	N94BE	N7005	N7006	(N6960)	N700RR					
257025		B	G-5-12	G-BFPI	VR-HIN	G-BFPI	N93TC	N7782	N886S	N205TW				
257026	NA0219	A	G-BFMO	N1230A	N372BC	N372BD	N685FM	N685EM	N788WG	N428AS	N428FS	N219TS	N45BP	
			[w/o 20Sep03 Beaumont, TX]											
257027	NA0220	A	G-BFMP	C-GPPS	N705CC	N725CC	XA-SAU							
257028		A	G-BFSO	G-5-534	N700TL	N603GY	N7728	N899DM	VP-COK	N949EB	[instructional airframe, Tulsa Technical Center,			
			Tulsa/R.L.Jones, OK, then scrapped]											
257029	NA0221	A	N465R	N700PD	(N248JH)	N705JH	C-GTOR							
257030	NA0222	A	G-BFSI	C-GSCL	C-FFAB	HB-VLJ	C-GNAZ	N18CC						
257031		BA	G-BFSP	G-PRMC	G-BFSP	G-5-701	D-CBAE	G-BFSP	G-5-701	N89TJ	HB-VLA	N703TS	N703JN	[wfu Fort
			Lauderdale Int'l, FL]											
257032	NA0223	A	G-5-14	G-BFUE	N700BA	N353WC	N853WC	N154JS	(N158JS)	N154JD	N720PT			
257033	NA0224	A	N50JM	N50TN	N200GX	N200GY	XA-MJI	N336AC	XB-JYS	XB-PAM				
257034		A	G-5-14	G-BFXT	N7007X	N510HS	G-PLGI	N402GJ	N34GG					
257035	NA0225	A	G-5-16	N36NP	SE-DPY	N486MJ	N995SK	(N995SL)	N995SA	N137WR	(N137WK)	9Q-...		
257036	NA0226	A	G-5-17	N60JM	N60TN	N600HC	N902RM	N902PM	N47TJ	N42SR	(N42SE)	N7WC	N1776E	N102BP
			XA-UOW											
257037		B	G-5-18	G-BFVI	G-IFTE									
257038	NA0227	A	G-5-19	N10CZ	N81KA	N216KH	[cx 06Jun14; wfu]							
257039	NA0228	A	G-5-11	N555CB	N555CR	N545GM	[cx to Mexico 03Nov14 but had already been dbr at Roatan, Honduras, 15Dec13]							
257040		B	HZ-RC1	G-OWEB	EC-375	EC-413	EC-ETI	N47TJ	VR-BPE	VP-BPE	HB-VMD	G-BYFO	G-OWDB	P4-LVF
			N67BL	C6-IUE	ZS-SYS									
257041	NA0229	A	G-5-12	N700BB	N400NW	N400NU	(N601UU)	N700LS	N825CT	N820CT	XA-BYP	N820CT		
257042	NA0230	A	G-5-13	N360X	(N360DE)	N881S	N899AB							
257043	NA0232	A	G-BFYV	(N300LD)	N900CC	N500ZB	N22EH	N22KH	N232TN	(N331CG)	[wfu Fort Lauderdale Int'l, FL, after wheels-up			
			landing 1Nov06]											
257044	NA0231	A	G-5-17	G-BFYH	N35D	N5735	N125G	(N125GB)	N225BJ					
257045	NA0240	A	G-BFZJ	N130BA	N700HH	N800E	C6-SVA							
257046		A	4W-ACE	G-BKJV	VH-JCC	VH-LRH	N7465T	XA-LEG	N746TS	N55MT	"N55TS"	N746TS	LV-ZRS	N828AN
			N587VV	N257AM	N770AZ									
257047	NA0233	A	G-BFZI	C-GABX	N79TS	N79EH								
257048	NA0234	A	G-5-16	N711YP	N205BS	N731DL	N323JK	[parted out by Alliance Air Parts, Oklahoma City, OK]						
257049	NA0239	A	G-5-17	G-BGBL	N33BK	C-GKPM	C-GNOW	C-GOHJ						
257050	NA0235	A	G-5-18	N700GB	N10C									
257051	NA0236	A	G-5-11	N700UK	N14JA	N64HA	N236BN	[dbr 20Dec00 Jackson, WY; parted out by Arnoni Av'n, Houston, TX]						
257052	NA0237	A	G-5-19	G-BGBJ	N737X	N697NP	N511GP	N511KA	N700QA					
257053	NA0238	A	G-5-20	N700AR	N33CP	N130MH	N120MH	N200JP	ZS-SDU					
257054		B	C6-BET	G-BVJY	RA-02802	G-BVJY	G-NCFR	G-OURB	OD-HHF	OD-BBF	VP-CFI	[wfu; b/u Bournemouth, UK; fuselage		
			to Birchwood airfield, Yorks, UK]											
257055		A	G-5-16	HZ-RC2	N876JC	G-5-598	G-BOXI	F-WZIG	F-GHHG	N46PL	(N696JH)	(N755TS)	N47PB	N347TC
257056	NA0241	A	G-5-13	N700NT	N492CB	N6VC	N25MK	N300BS	(N388BS)	XA-UCU	N84GA	XA-UCU	N57EJ	
257057	NA0242	A	G-5-14	N700UR	N60HJ	(N60HU)	C-GPCC	N125BW	N701CF	(N988GA)	N418BA	N241RT	[cx 13Aug14; wfu	
			Ontario, CA]											
257058	NA0245	A	G-5-15	N125HS	N700BA	N354WC	N854WC	N750GM	N8PL	N810V	N81QV	VP-CLU	RA-02775	
257059	NA0243	A-II	G-5-17	N130BH	N20S	N20SK	N702BA	XA-JRF	N104JG	N9395Y	N717AF	XA-UQN	N466MM	
257060	NA0244	A	G-5-18	N130BG	N1103	N1183	N230DP	N414RF	[to instructional airframe, North Valley Occupational Center, Los Angeles/Van					
			Nuys, CA]											
257061		A	G-5-19	G-BGGS	G-OJOY	N700SS	N700SF	N810GS	XA-UEA	(N730AA)	N23RT	C9-...		
257062		B	G-5-16	HB-VGF	G-5-708	HB-VGF	G-5-708	N7062B	G-5-708	(G-BWJX)	RA-02809	N62EA	N416RD	EI-WJN
			6V-AIM	[w/o 05Sep15, crashed into Atlantic Ocean]										
257063	NA0246	A	G-5-20	N130BB	N79HC	N700NW								
257064		B/A	HZ-NAD	HZ-OFC	G-BMOS	G-5-519	VH-JFT	N395RD	N48LB	[parted out by AvMATS, St Louis, MO; cx 06Aug14]				
257065	NA0247	A	G-5-11	N130BC	N30PR	N530TL	(N530TE)	N87AG	N120JC	N720JC	(N247PJ)			
257066	NA0248	A	G-5-13	G-BGSR	C-GKCI	C-FBMG	N900CQ	N900CP	XA-...					
257067		B	HZ-DA1	N9113J	(N115RS)	N360N	N144DJ	HB-VKJ	N267TS	N42TS				
257068	NA0249	A	G-5-14	N130BD	N31LG	N799SC	XB-FMK	XA-FMK						
257069	NA0250	A	G-5-15	N130BE	N29GP	N29GD	N308DD	(N900JG)	(N54TJ)	N418DM	XB-SVV			
257070		B	HB-VGG	G-5-604	HB-VGG	G-5-604	G-BWCR	"G-JETG"	G-BWCR	G-DEZC	P4-AMH	[parted out Farnborough, UK, May11;		
			cockpit section to Bombay Night Indian Restaurant, Brentry, Bristol, UK; fuselage to caravan site Birchington, UK]											
257071	NA0251	A	G-5-17	N130BF	N810CR	N571CH	CX-CIB							
257072	NA0252	A	G-5-18	N700HS	N900MR	N401GN	N513GP	N895CC	N237WR	(N237RG)	[w/o 10Nov15 on approach to Akron/Fulton, OH]			
257073		B	G-5-12	G-BGTD	N7788	(N59TJ)	N701TA	N210RK						
257074	NA0253	A	G-5-19	N422X	(N831CJ)									
257075	NA0254	A	G-5-13	(G-BHKF)	N125AM	N125TR	N124AR	N125XX	M-ALUN					

BAe 125 SERIES 700

C/n		Series	Identities										
257076		A	G-5-17	7Q-YJI	MAAW-J1	G-5-524	G-BMWW	G-5-571	XA-LML	N111ZN	N111ZS	N180CH	(N776TS)	N111ZS
257077	NA0255	A	G-5-14	N125AJ	N540B	XA-SEN	N770PJ	[cx 26Nov14; wfu]					
257078	NA0256	A	G-5-15	N125AK	N571CH	N455BK	(N830LR)						
257079	NA0268	A	G-5-16	XA-JIX	N74JA	(N74JE)	N501MM	XA-SON	N111QJ				
257080	NA0257	A	G-5-18	N125HS	N611MC	(N611EL)							
257081	NA0258	A	G-5-19	(N125AM)	N700CU	N711CU	N809M	N812M	N193RC	N227MM			
257082		A	Ireland 238	(N98AF)	XA-TCB	N70HF	N752CM						
257083	NA0259	A	G-5-12	(N150RH)	N125AH	N100Y	N128CS	N941CE					
257084	NA0260	A	G-5-14	N130BK	N202CH	N965JC	N184TB	XB-IRZ	XA-HXM	XB-MWQ	XB-NVE		
257085		B	G-5-15	G-BHIO	RP-C1714	N10TN							
257086	NA0261	A	G-5-17	N125AL	N277CT	N500EF	N983GT	N999CY	N700UJ				
257087	NA0262	A	G-5-16	(N130BL)	C-GKRS	N3234S	N404CB	(N601JR)	N908JE	N988JE	N350DH	N711WM	N3RC	(N313RC)
			N396RC	N561PS									
257088		B	HZ-DA2	G-5-531	N29RP	N222HL	N224EA						
257089	NA0263	A	G-5-18	N130BL	N151AE	(N130AE)	N101FC	(N263TN)	N125RG	N125EK			
257090	NA0264	A	G-5-19	N299CT	N88MX	N264WC	(N160WC)	N161WC	N724EA				
257091		B	G-BHLF	G-OCAA	VP-CLX	C6-IUN							
257092	NA0265	A	G-5-20	N733M	N783M	N91CM	N299WB						
257093	NA0266	A	G-5-11	G-BHMP	C-GBRM	N7UJ	N86MD	N497PT	N804CS	N212XX			
257094		B	G-OBAE	HB-VEK	G-5-16	N49566	N80KM	N713KM	N713K	D-CKIM	(G-....)	9M-STR	N415RD	N483FG
257095	NA0267	A	G-5-12	N125L	N215G	N352WC	N852WC	N427MD	N745TH	N36GS	N267JE	N829SE	[ditched into Loreto Bay,
			Mexico, 05May11; status?]										
257096	NA0276	A	G-5-14	XA-KEW	[w/o 01May81 Monterrey, Mexico]								
257097		B	(G-BHTJ)	G-HHOI	G-BRDI	G-BHTJ	RA-02801	G-5-810	RA-02801				
257098	NA0269	A	G-5-15	N89PP	N70SK	N50HS	XA-NTE	N702NW	N972LM	N438PM	(N61GF)	XA-AMI	
257099	NA0270	A	G-5-16	G-BHSK	C-GDAO	N621JH	N621JA	PK-CTC	N52GA				
257100		A	G-5-19	D-CLVW	G-5-549	G-BNFW	N858JR	N801RA	N925WC				
257101	NA0272	A	G-5-17	(N700E)	N89PP	(N700E)	N109JM	N14SY	N77D	N89GN	N700XF	9V-...		
257102	NA0280	A	G-5-18	XA-KIS	N700CN	N700K	N810M	XA-TCR	N280AJ	N280VC	N500FM		
257103		B	G-5-12	G-BHSU	G-LTEC	VR-BOJ	VP-BOJ	YL-VIP	YL-VIR	G-GIRA	OY-MFL	[cx to Canada, parted out]	
257104	NA0273	A	G-5-20	N10PW	N411SS	N46TJ	N110EJ	(N4477X)	N815TR				
257105	NA0274	A	G-5-11	N125TA	N125TA	N44BB	N700DE	HB-VLL	N560SB	(OY-VIA)	G-CFBP	N700KL	
257106	NA0275	A	G-5-13	N125V	N661JB	N664JB	N404CE	N404CF	N125SJ	(N550JP)	XB-JND	XB-OBS	
257107		A	G-BHSV	G-5-808	N90AR	VR-CVD	N71MA	(N38HH)	N85HH	N900MD	N880RG		
257108	NA0278	A	G-5-14	N45500	N6GG	N6GQ	N86WC	N700FE	N77SA	N130AP	N770CC	N518RR	
257109		B	G-BHSW	VR-BPT	VR-BTZ	VP-BTZ	VP-BOY	OD-BOY					
257110	NA0271	A	G-5-15	XA-KAC	N277JW	N177JW	N154FJ						
257111	NA0277	A	G-5-16	N125AF	N324K	N824K	N500	N509	(N799FL)	N509QC	N972W		
257112		B	D-CMVW	G-5-536	G-BNBO	G-5-553	9M-SSL	(D-CLUB)	G-SVLB	RA-02850			
257113	NA0279	A	G-5-17	N125AD	N204R	N204N	N5511A	N1VQ	N90FF	ZS-ICU			
257114	NA0281	A	G-5-18	N125AN	N533	C-GXYN	N169TA	N403DP	N281BT	N101LT			
257115		A	HZ-DA3	G-5-502	G-BMIH	5N-AMX	G-5-502	G-BMIH	N125YY	N333MS	OD-MAS		
257116	NA0282	A	G-5-19	N125AP	N1982G	N120YB	N150YB	C6-FSI					
257117	NA0283	A	G-5-20	N125AS	N90B	(N90BN)	N220FL	N93CR	N93GR	N26SC			
257118		A	(G-BIHZ)	5N-AVJ	G-BWKL	VP-BBH	VP-CRA	C-GNND	N619TD	N810KB			
257119	NA0284	A	G-5-11	N125AE	N326K	N826K	N125AR	N125AP	N10UC	(N311MG)			
257120	NA0285	A	G-5-13	N125AT	N40CN	(N14WJ)	N130YB	N445UC	C6-JAG				
257121	NA0286	A	G-5-14	N125AU	N20FX	N700SB	N301PH	(N156K)	N150CA	(N501MD)	N83MD		
257122	NA0287	A	G-5-15	N125U	N77LP	N299FB	N3444H	(N731GA)	N564BR				
257123	NA0288	A	G-5-16	N125AH	N700BW	N198GT	XA-EFL						
257124		B	HZ-DA4	OD-FNF	OD-FAF	VP-CFJ							
257125	NA0289	A	G-5-17	N125AJ	N125CG	N62WH	N62WL	N369G	N27KL	N302PC	N802RC	N70QB	
257126	NA0290	A	G-5-18	N700AC	N246VF	N7WG	N17WG	N710AF	XA-NSA	N650TC			
257127		B	G-TJCB	OY-MPA	(F-GNDB)	F-GODB	HB-VLC	N795A	XA-LUN				
257128	NA0291	A	G-5-19	N125BC	N126AR	XA-MSH	N45AF	N947CE					
257129	NA0292	A	G-5-20	N125AK	(N256MA)	N256EN	N805M	N728JW	N748FB	N48FB	N241FB	N966RJ	
257130		A	G-DBBI	G-CCAA	G-BNVU	N700FR	G-5-588	N700FR	G-RJRI	RP-C235	N130TS	N499GA	N405DP	N405TP
			N405DW	[cx 10Dec14; CofR expired]									
257131	NA0293	A	G-5-11	N700BA	N80G	N520M	N52LC	N7CT	N7WG	N700NB	N996RP	N296RG	N406J
257132	NA0294	A	G-BIMY	C-FIPG	N925WC	N925WG	N925DP	N188KA	[cx 07Jan13; wfu]				
257133		B	G-5-14	LV-PMM	LV-ALW	[w/o 11Apr85 Salta, Argentina]							
257134	NA0295	A	G-5-13	N871D	N371D	N888SW	N89MD	N134NW	(N134RT)				
257135	NA0296	A	G-5-15	N490MP	N31AS	N28GP	N28GG	N700DA	N10QJ	N927LL			
257136		B	G-BIRU	G-5-545	OH-JET	N136TN	N318CD	P4-AOE	P4-XZX	[scrapped Kemble, UK, Jun11]			
257137	NA0297	A	G-5-16	N125BD	N78CS	(N78QS)	N589UC	N945CE					
257138	NA0298	A	G-5-17	N125G	N80K	N298TS	N298BP	N917TF	[cx to Mexico but crashed into Caribbean Sea still wearing N917TF while				
			drug-running May15]										
257139		B	(G-GAIL)	G-BKAA	G-MHIH	RA-02803	G-5-875	RA-02803					
257140	NA0299	A	G-5-19	N125BE	VR-BHH	N125BE	N555RB	N703JP	N700NY	N800LM			
257141	NA0300	A	G-5-20	N70PM	N80PM	N80PN	N700SA	N943CE					
257142		B	G-5-12	G-BJDJ	G-RCDI	G-BJDJ	P4-OBE	RA-02802					
257143	NA0325	A	G-5-20	N700HA	N26H	C-GOGM	C-GQGM	C-FCSS					
257144	NA0326	A	G-5-11	N522M	N70AR	N94SA	(N702TJ)	N164WC	N194WC	N819DM	ZS-SOI		
257145	NA0339	A	G-5-18	N70FC	N125BJ	PT-ORJ	N700SA	N83HF	[cx 02Jul14; wfu]				
257146	NA0301	A	G-5-13	N700HB	N711RL	N713RL	N744DC	N421SZ	N107LT	N107ET			
257147	NA0303	A	G-5-14	N125P	N70PM	N70PN	N67PW	N67BW	N900JT				
257148	NA0304	A	G-5-17	N700BB	N707DS	C-GTDN	N99JD	N96PR	N700NH	N237DX			
257149	NA0302	A	G-5-19	N700AA	N700HA	N290PC	N795HE	(N795HL)	C-GEPF	C-GLIG			
257150	NA0305	A	G-5-11	N700HS	N73G	N730H	N305TH	5N-BFC					
257151		B	G-5-12	N161MM	N161G	N613MC	(N613EL)	N825MS	RP-C8101				
257152	NA0306	A	G-5-17	N700DD	N270MH	C-FEXB	N400WP	N800MP	N141AL				
257153	NA0313	A	G-BJOW	XB-CXK	N18G	PK-CTA	N419RD	P4-AOD	[w/o 02Jan06 Karkiv, Ukraine]				
257154	NA0307	A	G-5-18	N700GG	N270MC	N270KA	N888GN						
257155	NA0308	A	G-5-19	N700KK	N1620	C-GYPH	N1843S	N10CN	N9999V	N314RC			
257156	NA0309	A	G-5-17	N15AG	N700MK	N529DM	N526DM	N309WM	N95CM	N57AY			
257157	NA0310	A	G-5-20	N700LL	N64GG	N2640	N18SH	(N168WU)	N128WU	N109BG			
257158		A	G-5-14	G-BJWB	N45KK	XB-DZN	N700VT	XA-NEM	N813NA				
257159	NA0311	A	G-5-15	N91Y	N50JR	(N620CC)	(N502R)	VR-CKP	N311NW	N425WN	N700LP	ZS-WJW	
257160		B	G-5-19	5N-AVK									
257161	NA0323	A	G-5-17	N700RR	C-GZZX	N700RR	N2630	N2830	VT-AAA	[cx 2009, instructional airframe]			
257162	NA0312	A	G-5-18	N700NN	N1896T	N1896F	N176RS	N500GS	N412DP	C-GLBJ	N70HB		
257163		B	G-5-12	7T-VCW									
257164	NA0314	A	G-5-11	N152AE	(N106AE)	N53GH	XA-ERM						
257165	NA0315	A	G-5-14	N869KM	N26ME								
257166		B	G-5-18	F-BYFB	F-GRON	EC-HRQ	RP-C5998						

BAe 125 SERIES 700

C/n		Series	Identities									
257167	NA0316	A	G-5-15	N700PP	N125BA	N2989	N640PM	N63PM	N73PM	N333NR	(N501F)	N18BA
257168	NA0317	A	G-5-20	N700SS	N612MC	(N612EL)	N789BA					
257169		B	G-5-21	(VH-SOA)	VH-HSS	"B-HSS"	VR-HSS	B-HSS	5N-MAZ	[wfu Lanseria, South Africa]		
257170	NA0318	A	G-5-14	N819M	N80CL	EI-RRR	N114BA	N356SR	N431RC			
257171	NA0319	A	G-5-15	N710BP	(N168H)	N120MH	N128MH	N319NW	XB-MLC	N319NW	XA-JAI	XA-TYG
257172		B	5H-SMZ	G-BKFS	5H-SMZ	G-5-568	5H-SMZ	G-5-765	G-BKFS	VT-MPA	N355WJ	ZS-CAG
257173	NA0320	A	G-5-17	N710BN	N500LS	N300LS	N300HB	N100LR	(N100FF)	N320GP	N700HW	N7490A
257174	NA0321	A	G-5-18	N710BL	N469JR	C-GTLG	N165DL	N65DL	N65DU	[parted out Houston, TX; cx 19Sep07]		
257175		B	(C9-TTA)	C9-TAC	N770TJ	VP-CEK	VP-BEK	G-MKSS	RA-02804			
257176	NA0322	A	G-5-20	N109G	C-FCHT	N322BC						
257177	NA0324	A	G-5-11	N710BJ	N711TG	N2000T	N1996F	(N1996E)	N69SB	(N880CR)	N507F	N2KZ	N944TB
257178		A	G-5-14	4W-ACM	G-5-530	G-BMYX	G-5-570	VH-LMP	G-5-747	N700CJ	N621S	EI-COV	N178WB	N803BF
			N175MC	N326TD								
257179	NA0327	A	G-5-15	N810SC	C-GAAA	C-GSQC						
257180	NA0328	A	G-5-16	N710BG	N2HP	N192A	C-FEAE	N910KS				
257181		CC3	G-5-16	ZD620	[wfu Mar15; preserved Bournemouth Aviation Museum, UK]							
257182	NA0329	A	G-5-17	N710BF	(N277CB)	N1824T	N18243	N756N	N512GP	N190WC	5N-DAO	
257183	NA0330	CC3	G-5-20	N710BD	G-5-20	ZD703	[wfu Mar15]					
257184		B	G-5-12	9K-AGA	YI-AKG	9K-AGA	G-OMGD	SU-PIX	G-88-03	SU-PIX	G-36-2	SU-PIX	RA-02808
257185	NA0331	A	G-5-12	N700BA	N900BL	XB-JTN						
257186	NA0332	A	G-5-11	N710BC	N400CH	N400QH	N16GS	XA-STX	N332WE	5N-MAO		
257187		B	G-5-14	9K-AGB	YI-AKH	[dest 1991 during first Gulf War, Muthenna AFB, Iraq]							
257188	NA0333	A	G-5-15	N523M	N125DP	(N301AS)	(N301LX)	N125AS	N511LD	RP-C5808		
257189		B	G-BKHK	(G-OBSM)	G-OSAM	N700BA	N94B	N81HH	N8KG	N45KG		
257190		CC3	ZD621	[wfu Mar15; preserved RAF Northolt, UK]								
257191	NA0336	A	G-5-17	N710BA	N677RW	(N477RW)	N11TS	VT-SRR	N770HS	(N778HS)	XA-UKR	[w/o 19Apr14 Saltillo, Mexico]
257192	NA0337	A	G-5-14	N125MT	N2015M	N201PM	N300TW	N300TK	N818LD			
257193	NA0338	A	G-5-15	N710BZ	N710AG	(N797EM)	N797FA	N350PL				
257194		CC3	ZD704	G-5-870	ZD704	[damaged in hailstorm, possibly w/o, Kandahar, Afghanistan, Apr13; airfreighted back to UK]							
257195	NA0334	A	G-5-18	N710BY	N702M	N93GC	N46WC	N46WQ	TY-SAM	[parted out Farnborough, UK, then scrapped Mar15]		
257196		B	G-5-11	5N-AXO	G-5-693	5N-AXO	G-5-766	5N-AXO	[w/o 17Jan96 Kano, Nigeria]			
257197		A	G-5-12	N790Z	N207PC	N207RC	N3GL	(N2QL)	5N-BEX			
257198	NA0335	A	G-5-18	N710BX	N702E	C-GJBJ	[cx to USA but no N-number allocated; parted out?]					
257199	NA0340	A	G-5-12	N710BW	N702W	VR-BKZ	N921RD	XA-SSY	N23BJ	N23EJ	N804WJ	N242AL	XA-HOM	N391TC
			XC-LNJ	N83CV								
257200		B	G-5-14	G-MSFY	VR-BMD	VP-BMD	RA-02811					
257201	NA0341	A	G-5-19	N710BV	N2KW	I-CIGH	N700KG	I-AZFB	N646AM	D2-...		
257202	NA0342	A	G-5-17	N710BU	N518S	N65LC	N8400E	N93FR	N230R	(ZS-IPI)	ZS-IPE	
257203		B	G-5-14	5N-AXP	[w/o 31Dec85 Kaduna, Nigeria]							
257204	NA0343	A	G-5-15	N524M	N949CE							
257205		CC3	G-5-19	ZE395	[wfu Mar15]							
257206	NA0344	A	G-5-16	N710BT	N1C	N502S	C-FWCE	C-GMBA	N11YR	XA-GIC	N511RG	N27BH	N344BP
257207	NA0345	A	G-5-18	N710BS	N774GF	N686SG	N686FG	N21NY	N21NT	N913V	"N313VR"	N913V	N700NP
257208	NA0346	A	N710BR	G-5-19	(G-BLMJ)	G-BLSM	N501GF	YV575T				
257209		A	G-5-20	VR-BHW	VP-BHW	N127SR	N805CD	RP-C9808				
257210	NA0347	A	N710BQ	G-5-18	(G-BLMK)	G-BLTP	N502GF	ZS-TBT				
257211		CC3	ZE396	[wfu 26Feb15]								
257212		B	G-5-12	G-RACL	N81CH	N81CN	G-IJET	G-5-659	OH-BAP	G-5-659	OH-BAP	LY-ASL	LY-BSK	VP-BMU
			RP-C602									
257213		A	G-5-16	G-BLEK	N213C	N700NP	(N703MJ)	N700CE				
257214		B	G-5-17	HZ-SJP	G-UKCA	G-OMID	VR-BCF	VP-BCF	P4-CMP	VP-CMP	RA-02771	
257215		B	G-5-20	VH-HSP	VT-OBE	[wfu Mumbai, India]						

Production complete

BAe 125 SERIES 800 (HAWKER 800)

(1) * after the c/n indicates US assembled aircraft.

(2) 800SP/800XP2 aircraft are those which have been converted by the addition of Aviation Partners blended winglets and are noted in the series column

C/n	Series	Identities									
258001	B	G-5-11	[ff 26May83]	"N800BA"	G-BKTF	G-5-522	G-UWWB	G-5-557	ZK-TCB	N785CA	OH-JOT	N801CR	N800RM
		(N928KH)	N800JM									
258002	B	(G-5-16)	G-DCCC	(VH-CCC)	VH-III	G-DCCC	VH-NJM	G-DCCC	N800RY	(N1169D)	(N802CW)	N882CW	N15AX
		[parted out Wilmington, DE]										
258003	SP	G-5-20	G-BKUW	N800BA	N800N	N454JB	N803TJ	N803BA	N583VC	N803GE	N803RK	
258004	A	G-5-15	G-BLGZ	N800EE	N94BD	(N98DD)	N94SD	XA-SEH	XA-RET	XA-I VI	N84GA	XA-KTY	XC-LND
		XA-KTY										
258005	A	(G-5-12)	(G-5-19)	G-5-15	G-BLJC	N800GG	(N219JA)	N601UU	N800FL			
258006	A	G-5-17	N800WW	N800S	N70SK	N861CE	N886CW	(N886GW)	N800FH	XA-JUL		
258007	B	G-5-20	G-GAEL	G-5-554	C-GKRL	C-GYPH	C-GWLL	C-GWLE	N258KT	[parted out Roanoke, TX]		
258008	A	G-5-11	N722CC	N850LA	N802WJ							
258009	A	G-5-15	N400AL	N408AL	N45Y	N48Y	N298WB					
258010	A	G-5-19	(G-BLKS)	(G-OVIP)	N84A	N810BG	N810CW	(N800LX)	N810BA	[parted out by AvMATS, St Louis, MO; cx 06Jun14]		
258011	A	G-5-20	N800VV	N1BG	N186G	N811CW	(N144AW)	N820GA	N801RM			
258012	SP	G-5-18	N800TT	N400NW	N80BF	N80BR	N106JL	N644JL	N801CW	(N801LX)	N804MR	
258013	B	G-5-14	G-OCCC	N334	"N500RH"	N300RB	N802RM	XB-VLM	N305AG			
258014	A	G-5-15	N800MM	N294W	N800BS	N94WN	N298AG					
258015	A	G-5-17	G-BLPC	C-FTLA	C-GWFM	C-GWEM	N705BB					
258016	SP	G-5-18	F-GESL	N415PT	N904SB	N906SB	N816CW	N800VR				
258017	A	G-5-16	N800LL	N801G	N801P	(N801R)	N217RM	N888ZZ				
258018	A	G-5-12	N800PP	N818TG	N350WC	N350WG	N601RS	N36TJ	N525CF	N904JR		
258019	A	G-5-12	VH-SGY	VH-LKV	N900MD	G-5-704	N799SC	N799S	(N800NW)	N7996	N880WW	N614AJ
258020	SP	G-5-14	N800ZZ	N270HC	(N251TJ)	5N-QTS						
258021	B	G-5-15	G-GEIL	VR-CEJ	G-RCEJ	(N582CP)	G-IFTF					
258022	B	G-5-16	G-JJCB	G-5-569	HZ-KSA	EC-193	EC-ELK	G-5-874	EC-ELK	N4257R	N822BL	
258023	A	G-5-15	N810AA	(N10AA)	N1910H	N1910J	N47HW					
258024	A	G-5-18	N811AA	N800DP	N802DC	N802D	N337RE					
258025	B	G-5-14	3D-AVL	G-5-742	G-BUIY	N7C	C-GMLR	C-GGYT	PR-LTA			
258026	SP	G-5-18	N800HS	N6TM	N6TU	N826CW	N82SR					
258027	A	G-5-12	N812AA	(N100PM)	N800PM	(N553US)	N553M	N558M	(N80CC)	N880M	XA-MER	
258028	B	G-5-12	G-TSAM	N85KH	N277SS	[cx 23Jan12; wfu]						
258029	A	G-5-16	(N600TH)	N813AA	N600HS	N77LA	N800LR	XA-UUV				
258030	A	G-5-14	N600TH	N6GG	N10WF	N91CH	N616WG					
258031	B	G-5-15	PT-ZAA	PT-LHB								
258032	A	G-5-11	N815AA	N526M	HZ-WBT5							
258033	A	G-5-19	N157H	N57FF	I-CASG	N24RP	N673TM	N833CW	(N802LX)	N408MM	N621WP	
258034	B	G-5-12	G-HYGA	G-5-595	G-HYGA	G-5-595	N85DW	N125HH	[parted out Bangor, ME; cx 16Mar16]			
258035	SP	G-5-20	N816AA	N30F	HB-VKM	PT-ORH	(N.....)	HB-VKM	PT-WIA	N835TS	N835CW	N85MG	(N85VC)
		XA-JMC	XA-RLV									
258036	A	G-5-18	N817AA	N31F	HB-VKN	D-CFRC	N621MT	XA-ISH	[w/o 27Oct03 near Tampico, Mexico]			
258037	B	G-5-15	G-5-501	4W-ACN	7O-ADC	M-HDAM	M-DSML					
258038	SP	G-5-20	N800TR	N206WC	N206PC	N206WC	N550RH	D-CHEF	C-GTNT	C-FDDD		
258039	A	G-5-19	N818AA	N400TB	N200KF	N193TR	N173TR	N731TC				
258040	B	G-5-15	VH-IXL	G-5-697	I-IGNO	N832MJ	N832MR	N713HC	N718HC	(N16CM)		
258041	A	G-5-18	N819AA	N71NP	N626CG							
258042	A	G-5-11	N820AA	N20S	N112K	N804RM	N904BW					
258043	SP	G-5-12	(D-CAZH)	N319AT	N313CC	N313CQ	N937BC	M-ISSY	HA-YFI	N800SN	N829CR	N821MP
258044	A	G-5-12	N821AA	N72NP	N833JP	XA-UEH	N645MS					
258045	SP	G-5-16	N822AA	N800TF	N845CW	(N803LX)	N802SA	(N593WH)	[parted out Wilmington, DE; cx 29Dec15]			
258046	A	G-5-20	N823AA	N800BA	N125SB							
258047	A	G-5-11	N824AA	N84BA	N84FA	N324SA	XA-FGS					
258048	A	G-5-16	G-BMMO	(N125BA)	C-GCIB	N716DB	N716BB*					
258049	A	G-5-19	N800EX	N24SB	N24SP	N93CT	N796CH					
258050	SP	G-5-503	HZ-OFC	G-BUCR	I-OSLO	N9LR	G-ICFR	G-OURA	D-CLBC	N65GD	ZS-PAR	M-SITM	N80BF
		[cx 03Dec15; wfu]										
258051	A	G-5-18	N826AA	N889DH	N888DH	N258SR	N851CW	(N804LX)	XA-ELM			
258052	SP	G-5-20	N360BA	N87EC	N68DA	N233KC	N221HB	C-FKGN	C-GFHJ			
258053	A	G-5-11	N361BA	N5G	N484RA	N489SA	[cx 22Oct14; wfu]					
258054	A	G-5-15	N527M	XB-NYM								
258055	A	G-5-504	N528M	N508MM	XA-UHI	N855BC						
258056	B	G-5-509	G-JETI	M-JETI								
258057	A	G-5-508	N362BA	N300GN	N800GN	N614AF	N614AP					
258058	B	G-5-510	(ZK-EUR)	ZK-EUI	VH-NMR	N125JW	G-5-637	N125JW	G-OMGG	G-JJSI		
258059	SP	G-5-506	N363BA	N400GN	N355RB	N255RB	N355RB	N686CP				
258060	A	G-5-511	N364BA	N686CF	N330X	N330DE	N303SE					
258061	A	G-5-515	N365BA	N161MM	N611MM	(N611CR)	N861CW	(N805LX)	N412DA			
258062	A	G-5-516	N366BA	N961JC	N862CW	(N806LX)	N245TX	(N962DP)	[parted out Wilmington, DE; cx 21Nov14]			
258063	A	G-5-518	N367BA	N684C	N74ND	N391TC	XB-MTG					
258064	B	G-5-514	Malawi MAAW-J1	N803BG	RP-C8082							
258065	A	G-5-520	N368BA	N77CS	N77CU	N65FA	N16GH	[parted out by MTW Aerospace, Montgomery, AL]				
258066	A	G-5-521	N369BA	N75CS	N55RF	N244FL						
258067	B	G-5-525	D-CEVW	G-BUZX	G-5-807	N801MM	N801MB	N801MM	N867CW	N801MM	N867CW	(N807LX)	N469AL
		N469RJ										
258068	B	G-5-539	HZ-SJP	G-5-653	HZ-SJP	G-5-738	G-BUIM	N68GP	N68HR	N167DD	N606	
258069	SP	G-5-526	N519BA	(N743UP)	N746UP	N364WC	N160WC	N517ST				
258070	A	G-5-527	N520BA	N528AC	N255DV	N255DA	N998PA	N798PA				
258071	A	G-5-528	N521BA	N890A	N789LT	N94JT						
258072	SP	G-5-529	N522BA	(N745UP)	N747UP	N164WC						
258073	SP	G-5-532	D-CFVW	G-BVBH	N802MM	VR-BSI	VP-BSI	N2236	N212RG	(N214RG)	N213RG	
258074	A	G-5-541	ZK-MRM	N800MD	G-5-640	N800MD	N800MN	N300BW	N850SM	N103HT	N518S	
258075	A	G-5-533	N188B	N189B	N533P	XA-GFB	N3GU	XA-RYM				
258076	B	G-5-535	D-CGVW	G-BVAS	RA-02807	[w/o near Minsk, Belarus, 26Oct09]						
258077	A	G-5-538	N523BA	N509GP	N877CW	N897CW	(N808LX)					
258078	B	G-5-541	G-BNEH	G-5-713	G-BNEH	ZS-FSI	OE-CHS	YL-VIP	G-88-01	YL-VIP	[scrapped Kemble, UK, Sep11]	
258079	B	G-5-542	G-GJCB	G-BVHW	SE-DRV	9M-DDW	N800LL					
258080	A	G-5-540	N524BA	N800BP	N800WH							
258081	A	G-5-543	N525BA	N650PM	N700PM	N196MC	N196MG					
258082	A	G-5-548	ZK-RJI	N499SC	N90ME	N601BA	(N601BX)	N800S	XA-ASH			
258083	A	G-5-546	N526BA	(N800HS)	N5C	N8UP	N852A	(N805AF)				
258084	A	G-5-547	N527BA	N780A	N877RP	N884CF	N24JG	N124JG	N323SL	PR-WSW		
258085	A	G-5-551	G-WBPR	N285AL	(N910VP)	N457J						

BAe 125 SERIES 800 (HAWKER 800)

C/n		Series	Identities									
258086		A	G-5-550	N528BA	N125BA	N523WC	N523WG	(N523W)				
258087		A	G-5-552	N529BA	N800TR	C-GAWH	C-FIGO	N6200H				
258088		SP	G-5-563	(ZK-RHP)	G-BOOA	G-BTAB	N757BL					
258089		A	G-5-555	N530BA	N125JB	N862CE	N593HR	N598HR				
258090		SP	G-5-556	N531BA	N2SG	N2YG	N410US	N8090	N800FJ	N800FN	N900RL	N901RL	N901RP	N414PE
258091		A	G-5-560	HB-VIK	N165BA	N1776H						
258092		A	G-5-558	N532BA	N2MG	N3007	N3008					
258093		A	G-5-559	N533BA	N331SC	N800S	(A6-HMK)	N358LL	N317CC	N317CQ	N2033	
258094		B	G-5-576	D-CFAN	(LN-BEP)	LN-ESA	HS-EMG					
258095		A	G-5-561	N534BA	N200LS	(N500LL)	C-FPCP	C-GHXY	N40255	ZS-OXY	AP-BJL	ZS-OXY	[parted out Lanseria, South Africa]
258096		SP	G-5-562	N535BA	N800UP	N10TC	N596SW	N311JA	N311JX	N234GF	N233GF	N275RB*
258097		B	G-5-567	HB-VIL	N170BA	N800BV	N384AB					
258098		A	G-5-564	N536BA	N300LS	N181FH						
258099		A	G-5-565	(G-BNUB)	N537BA	C-FAAU	OY-MCL	N10YJ				
258100	NA0401	A	G-5-566	N538BA	N108CF	N815CC	N180NE					
258101	NA0402	A	G-5-572	N539BA	N1125	N757M						
258102	NA0403	A	G-5-573	N540BA	N89K	(N89KT)	N89NC	N316EC	N316CS	N316GS		
258103	NA0404	A	G-5-574	N541BA	N916PT	N494AT	VP-CCH	N801ST	N13SY	N12SY		
258104	NA0405	A	G-5-575	N542BA	N527AC	N211JN						
258105	NA0406	A	G-5-577	(N551BA)	G-BNZW	C-GKLB	C-FSCI	C-FSCY	C-FSCI	C-GCCU	N813AC	
258106		B	G-5-580	PK-WSJ	PK-RGM	(N107CF)	N888SS	G-OLDD	RA-02806			
258107	NA0407	A	G-5-578	N552BA	N70NE							
258108	NA0408	A	G-5-579	N553BA	N61CT	N309G	N703VZ	N118GA				
258109		B	(N554BA)	G-5-581	5N-NPC							
258110		B	(N555BA)	G-5-584	D-CMIR	N710A	(N167SG)	N422CS				
258111	NA0409	SP	(N556BA)	G-5-582	N554BA	N800TR	N375SC	N875SC	XA-TKQ	N870CA	N801LM	
258112		A	G-5-583	Botswana OK-1/Z-1	G-5-664	PT-OBT	N112NW	N331DC	N831DC	N812GJ		
258113	NA0410	A	G-5-587	N555BA	N683E	N683F						
258114	NA0411	SP	G-5-586	N556BA	N600LS	N800EC	(4X-COZ)	N807MC				
258115		B	G-5-599	(G-BPGR)	Saudi Arabia 104	G-5-665	Saudi Arabia 104	G-5-599	G-TCAP	P4-BOB	9H-BOB	P4-JCC
			N666JC									
258116		B	G-5-592	PT-LQP								
258117	NA0412	A	G-5-589	N557BA	N825PS	N826CT	C-GBIS	N955DP				
258118			(G-5-590)	G-5-605	(G-BPGS)	Saudi Arabia 105	HZ-105					
258119	NA0413	SP	G-5-591	N558BA	N203R	N221RE	N239R	N166WC	N413HS			
258120		SP	G-5-606	G-POSN	HB-VLI	VT-EAU	N120AP	G-POSN	N120AP			
258121	NA0414	A	G-5-593	(N559BA)	G-BOTX	C-FRPP	N4361Q	N800WA				
258122	NA0415	A	G-5-594	N560BA	N800VC	N830BA	[parted out by AvMATS, St Louis, MO; cx 06Jun14]					
258123	NA0416	A	G-5-600	N561BA	N353WC	N353WG	C-GCGS					
258124	NA0417	A	G-5-596	N562BA	N800BA	N376SC	N876SC	N801NW	C-GCRP	C-GRGE	N824CW	(N809LX)	N67JF	N620RM
			N668JF									
258125	NA0418	A	G-5-601	N563BA	N802X	(N99DA)	N913SC					
258126	NA0419	SP	G-5-597	N564BA	(N82BL)	HZ-BL2	N196GA	N818WM	RA-02772			
258127	NA0420	A	G-5-602	N565BA	N803X	N3QG						
258128	NA0421	SP	G-5-603	N566BA	N804X	N40GS						
258129		A	G-5-622	N269X	USAF 88-0269		N94	N8029Z	XA-IZA	N956RA		
258130		B	G-5-620	G-FDSL	G-TPHK	G-BVFC	G-ETOM	D-CPAS	G-OSPG	G-DCTA	G-GRGA	G-OGFS	G-GMMR
258131		A	G-5-611	(N271X)	N270X	USAF 88-0270		N95	N8030F	N770SW	N595US	
258132	NA0422	A	G-5-607	N567BA	N125TR	N222MS						
258133		B	G-5-616	G-GSAM	G-5-642	N800FK	G-JETK	N800FK	HP-1262	PT-WAU	N800FK	PR-SOL	PP-ACP	N800FK
			PP-ACP									
258134		A	G-5-634	(N270X)	N271X	USAF 88-0271		N96	N1061	N54ES	N953DP	
258135	NA0423	A	G-5-608	N568BA	N801AB	N801RJ	(N241SM)	N204SM	N423SJ	N952DP		
258136	NA0424	A	G-5-609	N569BA	N452SM	I-SDFG	N80GJ	[cx 05Aug13; parted out by Atlanta Air Salvage, Griffin, GA]				
258137	NA0425	A	G-5-610	N570BA	N733K	(N100MH)	N110MH	N800SE	[parted out by Dodson Int'l, KS]			
258138	NA0428	A	G-5-614	N582BA	N244JM	N384TC	N800FJ					
258139	NA0426	A	G-5-612	N580BA	N125BA	(VR-BPA)	VR-BLP	N47VC	N49VG	(N47TJ)	N795PH	N726EP	N797EP	N218AD
258140	NA0427	A	G-5-613	N581BA	N45Y	N856AF	N858XL	N326N				
258141	NA0429	A	G-5-615	N583BA	N72K	C-FGLF	N106GC	N73WF	N141MR			
258142	NA0430	A	G-5-617	N584BA	N1903P	N850BM	N149VB	N149VP	N50BN	N45GD		
258143		SP	G-5-656	5N-NPF	5N-AGZ	5N-BOO						
258144	NA0431	A	G-5-618	N585BA	N682B	N682D						
258145	NA0432	SP	G-5-619	N586BA	N540M	N805CW	N810LX	N22NF				
258146		B	G-5-629	(G-BPYD)	"HZ-109"	G-5-703	HZ-109					
258147	NA0433	A	G-5-621	N587BA	N919P	N9UP	N9UP					
258148		B	G-5-630	(G-BPYE)	HZ-110	Saudi Arabia 110	HZ-110					
258149		SP	G-5-625	G-FASL	N155T	N577T	YV2477					
258150	NA0434	A	G-5-623	N588BA	N77W	N432AC	N432AQ	XA-RCL	XC-LNG	XA-RCL		
258151		1000	G-EXLR	[prototype BAe125-1000; ff 16Jun90; last flight 10Jly92; wfu Nov93; shipped to Wichita, KS 27Sep95; remains located in scrapyard, Wichita, KS circa Mar96; to Raytheon Svs hangar, Wichita, KS circa Sep99 to train South Korean Hawker 800XP engineers]								
258152		B	G-5-626	HB-VHU	(N42US)	N800WG	XA-UVH					
258153		B	G-5-627	HB-VHV								
258154		A	G-5-655	N272X	USAF 88-0272		N97	N359CF	N950DP			
258155		SP	G-5-628	N800BM	D-CBMW	N159RA	N238AJ	N300BL	(N800LV)	N711PE	N702PE	N723LK
258156		A	G-5-661	N273X	USAF 88-0273		N98	N355FA				
258157	NA0435	A	G-5-632	N589BA	N800BA	C-GMTR						
258158		SP	G-5-667	N274X	USAF 88-0274		N99	N8064Q	N158TN	N800AF		
258159		1000	G-OPFC	[second prototype BAe125-1000; ff 25Nov90]		N10855	[used for ground tests; cx 05Sep03, parted out by APPH Houston Inc, Houston, TX]					
258160	NA0436	A	G-5-633	N590BA	N354WC	N354WG	N369BG	N389BG	N160NW	N803JL	ZS-AOA	
258161	NA0437	A	G-5-636	G-BPXW	C-FFTM	N17DD	XA-QPL					
258162	NA0438	A	G-5-638	N591BA	N753G	N800PA						
258163	NA0443	A	G-5-639	G-BRCZ	C-GMOL	C-FWCE	N360DE	N717MT				
258164		B	G-5-654	Botswana OK1	[code Z2]	Botswana OK2	G-OBLT	(VR-BND)	G-5-654	Saudi Arabia 130	HZ-130	
258165		A	G-5-657	VR-BPG	ZS-BPG	VT-RAY	N324BG					
258166	NA0439	SP	G-5-641	N592BA	N74PC	N74PQ	C-GKPP	C-GFLZ	C-FXGO			
258167		A	G-5-662	N125AS	VR-CAS	VP-CAS	(N802SJ)	N825DA	N48AL	N257PL		
258168	NA0440	A	G-5-643	N593BA	N74NP	N295JR	N816BG					
258169		A	G-5-644	N47CG	N526AC	N255DV	C-FDKJ	N777VW				
258170	NA0441	A	G-5-645	N594BA	N75NP	N79NP	N24JG	XA-EXC				
258171	NA0442	A	G-5-646	N595BA	N754G	N4444J	N707PE	N729HZ	N729EZ	XA-HOM		
258172	NA0444	SP	G-5-647	N596BA	N290EC	N811AM						
258173	NA0447	SP	G-5-648	N599BA	N95AE	N82XP	C-FCRH	C-FCRF	C-GTAU	N41PJ		
258174	NA0445	A	G-5-649	N597BA	N174A	N174NW	N800QC	N119ML				

BAe 125 SERIES 800 (HAWKER 800)

C/n		Series	Identities
258175	NA0446	A	G-5-650 N598BA (VR-BPB) VR-BLQ N204JC HB-VMF N175U N2032 N591CF
258176		B	(N610BA) G-5-652 HB-VJY N176WA XA-TPB N176TL XA-DAS N176TL
258177		A	G-5-668 PT-OJC N411RA N217AL N5119 N52RZ
258178	NA0449	SP	G-5-658 N611BA D-CWIN N800WT N868WC N178AX N430BB N463DD
258179	NA0448	A	G-5-660 N610BA N125BA N60TC N60TG N904GP N904GR
258180		B	G-5-675 G-XRMC G-BZNR VP-BMH
258181	NA0450	SP	G-5-663 N612BA N355WC N355WG C-GAGU C-GAGQ N861CE (N675RW) C-FIQF
258182		B	G-5-676 (VR-B..) G-PBWH G-5-676 N128RS N12F N312LR
258183	NA0451	A	G-5-666 N613BA N50PM N90PM N63PM N599EC CS-DNI N883EJ N731JR XA-GIC N183FM N800DN 4X-CZO
258184		B	G-5-678 (PT-WAW) PT-OSW
258185	NA0452	A	G-5-669 N614BA N207PC (N207RC) XA-SIV N801CF
258186		A	G-5-683 G-BSUL VR-BPM G-BSUL N8186 N818G N818MV [w/o 31Jul08 Owatonna, MN]
258187	NA0453	SP	G-5-670 N615BA N60PM N750RV (N750PB) (N242JG) N4242 XA-LEX
258188	NA0454	A	G-5-671 N616BA N1910A N191BA N180EG (N892BP)
258189	NA0455	A	G-5-673 N617BA N6JB N6UB N195KC N25BB N32PJ
258190		B	G-5-684 G-BTAE PT-OHB PT-JAA
258191	NA0456	A	G-5-674 N618BA N152NS N801P (N730BG)
258192		SP	G-5-691 TR-LDB N192SJ N38CZ N801SA RA-02773
258193	NA0457	A	G-5-677 N619BA N300PM N699EC CS-DNH N893EJ C-GKGD C-GDBC
258194		B	G-5-692 PT-OTC
258195	NA0458	A	G-5-679 N630BA N800BA N800GX N100GX N940HC N941HC N28ZF
258196	NA0459	A	G-5-680 N631BA N125TR N511WM N511WD N929WG N929WQ N189TM
258197		A	G-5-696 G-BTMG G-OMGE N150SB
258198		B	G-5-694 PT-WAL
258199	NA0460	SP	G-5-681 N632BA N4402 N442MS
258200	NA0461	A	G-5-682 N633BA N461W N722A S2-AHS
258201		B	G-5-699 (D-C...) G-OCCI G-BWSY P4-AMF N59DM YV2837
258202	NA0462	A	G-5-685 N634BA N200GX N800DR N800DN A6-MAA N43PJ N462MM
258203	NA0463	A	G-5-686 N635BA YV-735CP N228G N453TM N805JL
258204	NA0464	A	G-5-687 N636BA N341AP N57LN N703SM
258205	NA0465	A	G-5-689 N637BA N805X N939TT
258206	NA0466	A	G-5-688 N638BA (N800BJ) PT-OMC N638BA N466CS N466AE N395HE
258207	NA0467	A	G-5-690 N639BA N600KC (N48DD) N2BG N2QG (N103BG)
258208		SP	"G-5-670" G-5-700 (PT-...) G-BUID TC-ANC N208BG N123HK
258209	NA0468	A	G-5-695 N670BA YV-800CP N168BA N693C N410BT N661JN N9990S TN-AJE
258210		B	G-5-705 G-RAAR HB-VMI VP-CSP
258211		A	G-5-724 PT-OSB N91DV N151TC N855GA
258212		B	G-5-710 G-BUCP D-CSRI RP-C8008 (N323L)
258213		B	G-5-709 D-CWBW G-BURV N10857 [cx 21Jly05; parted out Houston, TX]
258214		B	G-5-706 VR-CCX PT-OOI [wfu Sao Paulo/Congonhas, Brazil]
258215		U-125	G-5-727 G-JFCX Japan 29-3041 [code 041]
258216	NA0469	A	G-5-714 N671BA N500J N50QJ
258217	NA0470	SP	G-5-715 N672BA N600J N60QJ N125GB N800SV
258218	NA0471	SP	G-5-725 N673BA N57PM N118K (N503RJ) N118KL N418CA
258219		A	G-5-740 (9M-WCM) 9M-AZZ N8881J
258220	NA0472	A	G-5-728 N674BA N58PM N125AW N999JF XA-RAA
258221	NA0473	SP	G-5-731 N675BA N25W N25WN VP-BHB N919SS N406VC
258222		B	G-5-745 G-VIPI
258223	NA0474	A	G-5-733 N677BA N800BA N622AB N622AD N44HH N23AN
258224		SP	G-5-763 ZS-NJH N827RH N847RH N618JL N478PM N810V N65DL
258225	NA0475	A	G-5-739 N682BA N800BA N800CJ N935H
258226		A	G-5-755 (9M-...) G-BVCU D-CSRB RP-C1926 N709EA N800MJ PR-HFW
258227		U-125	G-5-769 G-BUUW Japan 39-3042 [code 042]
258228		A	G-5-758 HB-VKV N130LC N889MB
258229		SP	G-5-744 N683BA PT-OTH N229RY TC-TEK N984HM N304HE
258230		A	G-5-748 N678BA N71MT N800RG
258231		A	G-5-750 N685BA N75MT ZS-PSE 5N-BMT
258232		A	G-5-752 N686BA N900KC XA-NGS XA-AEN N723HH C-FBUR
258233		B	G-5-770 D-CAVW F-WQCD (VR-BQH) VR-BTM VP-BTM G-BYHM M-AZAG
258234		B	G-5-757 VR-CDE YV-814CP VR-CDE VP-CDE N65CE (N160H) N68AR
258235		B	G-5-774 D-CBVW G-BWVA OY-RAA N258SA D-CWOL (PH-WOL) OY-RAA
258236		A	G-5-764 N162BA N80PM N800TJ (N39BL) N58BL
258237		A	G-5-775 D-CCVW G-BWRN 9M-DRL VP-BAW N237RA N250JE N250MB
258238		SP	G-5-767 N163BA N70PM N100AG N188AF
258239		A	G-5-768 N164BA VR-BPN N904H N62TC (N262CT) N84CT C-GMLR C-GMFB
258240		B	G-5-772 G-BUWC G-SHEA HB-VLT G-HCFR G-CJAA G-WYNE
258241		SP	G-5-777 N165BA N125CJ N94NB N540BA XA-CHA N855MW
258242		U-125	G-5-793 G-BVFE Japan 49-3043 [code 043] [w/o 06Apr16, crashed nr Roatan, Honduras, 15Dec13]
258243		SP	G-5-778 (G-BUWD) G-SHEB VH-XMO C-GSCL C-FLPH C-FTVC N732AA
258244		SP	G-5-780 N166BA N800CJ N95NB N530BA N252DH N252DT N252DH N252DT N862CE N671RW N671RR
258245		U-125A	G-JHSX Japan 52-3001 [code 001]
258246		A	G-5-782 N387H HB-VKW
258247		U-125A	G-5-813 G-BVRF Japan 52-3002 [code 002]
258248		A	G-5-784 N388H N789LB N260H
258249		A	G-5-786 N933H N326SU (N826SU) N500HF N249SR N117HH
258250		U-125A	G-5-815 G-BVRG Japan 52-3003 [code 003]
258251		A	G-5-787 N937H N194JS N192JS N171MD
258252		A	G-5-788 N938H XB-GCC XA-GCC
258253		A	G-5-790 N942H N801CE N3RC N1310H
258254		A	G-5-791 N943H N2015M N800NY N770JT
258255		SP	G-5-792 [first Hawker 800] N946H N127KC N575MR
258256		SP	G-5-795 N947H N256BC (N256FS) N613CF
258257			G-5-796 N951H N802DC N415BJ N304AT
258258		B	G-5-798 G-BVJI (N953H) G-BVJI N54SB N910JD N910JN N258SP N258MR
258259			G-5-799 N954H (N966L)
258260			G-5-800 N957H
258261			G-5-802 N958H PT-GAF
258262			G-5-803 N959H N521JK
258263			G-5-804 N961H N826GA N826GC
258264			G-5-806 N805H HB-VLF 5N-BMR
258265			G-5-809 N806H HB-VLG 5N-BNE
258266		XP	G-5-811 (N293H) G-BVRW (N293H) N800XP (N800GT) N414XP N800CC
258267			G-5-812 N294H N811CC N980DC N601VC I-SIRF VP-CAF (D-CALI) (D-CKAS) N910CF
258268		U-125A	G-5-829 G-BVYV Japan 62-3004 N809H Japan 62-3004 [code 004]

BAe 125 SERIES 800 (HAWKER 800)

C/n	Series	Identities								
258269		G-5-814	N295H	N380X	N380DE	N302SE	N302EA			
258270	SP	G-5-816	N297H	N802CE	N838JL					
258271		G-5-818	N298H	N803CE	N787CM	N489BM				
258272		G-5-819	N299H	N2426	N4426	N814ST				
258273		G-5-820	N803H	N967L	N258RA	N337WR				
258274		G-5-822	N804H	N2428	N4428	N41HF				
258275		G-5-823	N905H	N77TC	N7775	XA-RBV				
258276	SP	G-5-824	N667H	N126KC						
258277	XP	G-BVYW	N97SH	N333PC	(N339PC)	N339CC				
258278	XP	G-BVZK	N872AT							
258279	XP	G-BVZL	(N817H)	4X-CZM	N817H	N877DM	N880AF			
258280	XP	G-BWDC	N351SP	N351SB	N100LA	(N108LA)	N47HA			
258281	XP	G-BWDD	N914H	VH-ELJ	N281XP	N781TA	N832LX	N801WJ		
258282	XP	G-5-827	G-BWDW	N916H	PT-WHH	N782TA	(N811LX)	(N800LX)	N603MA	
258283	XP	G-5-828	G-BWGB	N918H	(N283XP)	4X-COV	N283BX	N82EA	C-FJHS	
258284	XP	G-5-830	G-BWGC	N919H	(PT-LTA)	PT-WNO	N919H	PR-DBB		
258285	XP2	G-5-831	G-BWGD	N808H	(N800XP)	N285XP				
258286	XP	G-5-832	G-BWGE	N807H	N501F	N304RJ	N504MF			
258287	XP2	G-5-833	N668H	(N287XP)	N801WB	XA-UFK				
258288	U-125A	G-5-848	N816H	Japan 72-3005	[code 005]					
258289	XP2	G-5-834	N669H	N515GP	N863CE	N672RW	(N1957S)	N881AF		
258290	XP	G-5-835	N670H	N348MC	N250GM	4X-CLZ				
258291	XP	"G-5-837"	G-5-836	N672H	N291XP	N291SJ	N791TA	N833LX	N801SS	
258292	XP	G-5-838	N673H	N33BC						
258293	XP	G-5-839	N679H	N404CE	N150NC	N52484				
258294	XP2	G-5-840	N682H	N404BS	N632FW	N35CC				
258295	XP	G-5-841	N683H	VH-LAW	VH-LAT	VH-KEF	VH-EJL	VH-VRC	XA-LAU	
258296	XP2	G-5-842	N685H	N801JT	N707TA	(N812LX)	N934RD			
258297*	XP	[first US-assembled aircraft]		N297XP	N725TA	N725JA	N725TA	N843LX	N553BW	N960TC
258298	XP	G-5-843	N298XP	N880SP	N435JD					
258299	XP	G-5-844	N299XP	(N32BC)	N601DR	N87RB				
258300	XP	G-5-845	N689H	N800VF	N950PC	(N800NE)				
258301*	XP	N1105Z	PT-WMA	(N800XZ)						
258302	XP	G-5-847	N302XP	XA-RUY	XA-GIE	N302MT	XA-GIE	N302PJ		
258303	XP2	G-5-849	N303XP	N876H	N621CH	N4SA	N303DT	N104LR		
258304*	XP	N802JT	N5734							
258305	U-125A	G-5-864	N305XP	Japan 72-3006 [code 006]						
258306*	U-125A	N1103U	Japan 82-3007 [code 007]							
258307	XP2	G-5-850	N307XP	N109TD	N802WM	N307AD	N85CC			
258308	XP	G-5-851	N308XP	(N11WC)	N345BR	N875LP				
258309*	XP	N803JT	N5735	N92UP						
258310	XP2	G-5-852	N310XP	PT-WMG	N33VC	N97XP				
258311*	XP	N804JT	N800RD	N850J	N225RP					
258312	XP2	G-5-853	N312XP	PT-WMD	N251X	B-3998	N251X	N924JM	A6-ZZZ	5N-EXJ
258313*	XP	N2159X	N313XP	N84BA	N908VZ	N411VZ	N313MU	N721KY	(N721KE)	N969JJ
258314	XP	G-5-854	N314XP	OM-SKY	N800NJ	XA-GMM	N316MF			
258315*	XP	N2169X	N9292X							
258316	XP	G-5-855	N316XP	N516GP	C-GDII	N215SP	N75HL			
258317*	XP	N2173X	N9NB	N520BA	N520JF					
258318	XP	G-5-856	N318XP	N1910H	N191GH					
258319*	XP	N2291X	C-FIPE	OD-TSW						
258320*	XP	N2322X	N720TA	(N813LX)	(N801LX)	XB-MCB				
258321	XP	G-5-857	N691H	N32BC	N32BQ*					
258322*	XP2	N722TA	(N814LX)	N307RM						
258323	XP	G-5-858	N323XP	N877S	N877SL	N752CS				
258324	XP	G-5-860	N324XP	N303BC						
258325*	U-125A	N1112N	Japan 82-3008 [code 008]							
258326*	XP2	N326XP	N1897A	N897A						
258327	XP2	G-5-861	N327XP	N111ZN	N801HB	(N219DC)	N22GA	XA-URN	XA-JPF	
258328	XP	G-5-866	N328XP	VH-SGY	VH-SCY	A6-MAH	N91PS			
258329	XP2	G-5-862	N329XP	N901K	N903K	N825CP				
258330	XP2	G-5-869	N330XP	N139M	N86MN					
258331*	XP2	N10NB	N510BA	N160CT	N864CE	N673RW	(N859RP)	(N855ER)		
258332	XP2	G-5-865	N332XP	N36H	N53LB	N214TD				
258333*	U-125A	N3261Y	Japan 82-3009 [code 009]							
258334*	XP2	N334XP	N399JC	N80HD	N60HD	N800YY	N808YY			
258335	XP	G-5-867	N335XP	OY-RAC	OE-GHU	F-HREX				
258336*	XP	N336XP	N2286U	N745UP						
258337	XP	G-5-868	N337XP	[last to be assembled at Chester, UK – rolled out 22Apr97, ff 29Apr97, del to USA 08May97]	(9M-VVV)	N337XP	N733TA			
		(N815LX)	C-FDKL	N606JF						

US Production

C/n	Series	Identities					
258338	XP	N838QS	N838WC	N951DP	PR-GPW*		
258339	XP2	N23395	SE-DVD	N14SA	N294CV		
258340	XP	N840QS	N840WC	N907MC			
258341	U-125A	N3251M	"N2351M"	Japan 92-3010 [code 010]			
258342	XP	N2320J	South Korea 258-342				
258343	XP	N1102U	South Korea 258-343				
258344	XP	N29GP	N29GZ	(N977GR)			
258345	XP	N1135A	D-CBMV	D-CBMW	(G-VONI)	OY-LKG	N100HL
258346	XP	N23204	South Korea 258-346				
258347	XP	N1115G	N40PL	N409AV			
258348	U-125A	N2175W	Japan 92-3011 [code 011]				
258349	XP2	N723TA	VP-BHL	(N74WF)	N349GA	C-FEPC	N377JC	C-FYTZ
258350	XP	N23207	South Korea 258-350				
258351	XP	N23208	South Korea 258-351				
258352	XP	N2321S	South Korea 258-352				
258353	XP	N2321V	South Korea 258-353				
258354	XP	N2G	N262G	N116JG			
258355	XP	N855QS	N291TX	N830TM			
258356	XP	N550H	N55BA				
258357	XP	N2321Z	South Korea 258-357				
258358	XP2	N240B	D-CJET	OY-JBJ			
258359	XP	N25WX	P4-ALE	N359XP	N44UN		
258360	U-125A	N3189H	Japan 92-3012 [code 012]				

BAe 125 SERIES 800 (HAWKER 800)

C/n	Series	Identities							
258361	XP	N861QS	N861WC	N999RZ					
258362	XP	N862QS	N862WC	(N862JA)	N949JA				
258363	XP	N726TA	N816LX						
258364	XP	N728TA	(N817LX)	(N804LX)					
258365	XP2	N865SM	N243BA	N343SC					
258366	XP2	N1133N	(CS-MAI)	N894CA	VH-ZUH	VH-OVE			
258367	XP	N3263E	N367DM	OY-GIP	N704JM				
258368	XP2	N804AC	N804AQ	N248EC					
258369	XP	N800PC	N621WH						
258370	U-125A	N23556	Japan 02-3013 [code 013]	[dbr by tsunami flood waters 11Mar11, Matsushima, Japan]					
258371	XP2	N848N							
258372	XP	N1251K	N372XP	LV-ZHY	N800GN	VH-VLI	N800GN		
258373	XP	N3270X	N168BF	(N808AL)					
258374	XP	N729TA	(N874CW)	(N818LX)	N805LX				
258375	XP	N875QS	N154RR						
258376	XP	N1640	N1645						
258377	XP2	N1251K	N984GC	[1,000th DH/HS/BAe/Raytheon 125 sale]			N993SA	N993SJ	
258378	XP	N494RG	N442MA						
258379	XP	N879QS	[w/o 28Aug06 Carson City, NV]		N879WC	[parted out Atlanta/DeKalb-Peachtree, GA]			
258380	XP2	N8SP	N999JF	N101FC					
258381	U-125A	N23566	Japan 02-3014 [code 014]						
258382	XP	N23451	SE-DYE	EI-WXP					
258383	XP	N730TA	(N819LX)	N806LX	XA-MLP	XA-STK			
258384	XP	N23455	TC-MDC	N23455	N955MC	G-LAOR	M-LAOR	VT-VAP	
258385	XP	N23466	SE-DYV	G-0502	SE-DYV	F-HCSL	M-HASL	S5-AFR	
258386	XP2	N23479	N61DF	N61DN	N715WG	N715WT	XA-FYN	N800CV	
258387	XP	N887QS	N282TX	N835TM					
258388	XP2	N23488	TC-OKN	N809TA	(N809TP)	N809BA	N110WS		
258389	XP	N23493	I-DDVA	YR-VPA	YL-MAR	[b/u Biggin Hill, UK, Mar12; cockpit section to Belgium as flight simulator]			
258390	XP	N23509	(N800SG)	N800FD	N850HS				
258391	XP	N391XP	N771SV	4X-CPS	N543LF				
258392	XP	N23569	"LX-BYG"	LX-GBY	G-0504	LX-GBY	F-HBOM	C-FMIX	
258393	XP	N893QS	N269TX	N840TM					
258394	XP	N394XP	N800DW	N800ER	N800TL				
258395	XP	N23577	PT-WVG	N800UW					
258396	XP	N23585	N21EL						
258397	XP	N752TA	(N887CW)	(N820LX)	(N752LX)	N852LX	XA-WNG		
258398	XP	N168HH	TC-VSC	LY-HCW					
258399	XP2	N899QS	CS-DNJ	N979JB	LY-LTC				
258400	XP	N404JC	N314TC						
258401	XP	N23592	Brazil EU93A-6050						
258402	XP	N729AT							
258403	XP	N23550	ZS-DCK	N25XP	N601RS	N111VG	N333MV		
258404	XP	N30289	VP-BCM	N404DB	N448JM	N930PT			
258405	XP	N405XP	N866RR	N866RB	D-CLBD	M-CLAA	N362AP	N258MS	
258406	XP	N754TA	(N821LX)	N821LX	ZS-EXG				
258407	U-125A	N30562	Japan 02-3015 [code 015]						
258408	XP	N30319	B-3990						
258409	XP	N30337	PT-WPF	N929AK	N929AL	(VP-LV.)	N929AL	VP-BSK	N827NS	XA-TPB
258410	XP2	N755TA	N322LA	N315BK	N885M	OD-EAS			
258411	XP2	N617TM	LV-CJG						
258412	XP	N30682	N990HC						
258413	XP2	N760TA	N813CW	(N822LX)	N807LX	XA-ELX			
258414	XP	N30742	N800XP	N800XM	EI-RNJ	N800XM			
258415	XP	N31016	TC-BHD	TC-STR	N800LR	N444MG	VT-VPA		
258416	XP	N816QS	N274TX	N895TM					
258417	XP	N747NG	N246V	N240V					
258418	XP	N31046	N806XM	(N516TM)	N516TH				
258419	XP	N419XP	N508BP	N559DM					
258420	XP2	N31340	N910JD						
258421	XP	N31820	Brazil EU93A-6051						
258422	XP	N822QS	CS-DNM	VT-SRA					
258423	XP	N925JF	N388BS	N7NY					
258424	XP	N1899K	YL-NST	[parted out Kemble, UK]					
258425	XP2	N825XP	N800VA	N59BR	N89BR	N438PM	N802CF		
258426	XP	N426XP	N27FL						
258427	U-125A	N31833	Japan 02-3016 [code 016]						
258428	XP	N772TA	N828CW	(N823LX)	(N808LX)	N842FL	N885LS		
258429	XP	N88HD	N68HD	ZS-PKY	5N-BNM				
258430	XP	N31590	CS-DNK	N905MT	N905MG	YV572T			
258431	XP	N144HM	XA-TEM						
258432	XP	N432XP	N1650	N165L	N832CW	(N824LX)	N809LX	A6-SKA	A6-GAL
258433	XP	N833QS	N285TX	N822TM					
258434	XP	N40027	Brazil EU93A-6052						
258435	XP	N835QS	CS-DNN	ZS-MNU					
258436	XP	N836QS	N294TX	N845TM					
258437	XP	N780TA	(N825LX)	N812LX	N800WJ				
258438	XP	N40113	VP-BHZ	N827SA	N481SC				
258439	XP	N31596	CS-DNL	N497AG					
258440	XP	N40488	N801MB	N408RT	N8TA				
258441	XP	N800PE	N800PB	N370DE	N715LA				
258442	XP	N40202	PT-XDY	N442XP	N80PK				
258443	XP	N310AS	N489VC	N798KG					
258444	XP	N40489	EC-HJL	LX-ARC	C-GBAP	C-GXPG			
258445	U-125A	N40708	Japan 12-3017 [code 017]						
258446	XP	N529M	(N983EC)	N983CE					
258447	XP	N40310	Brazil EU93A-6053						
258448	XP	N41280	N532PJ	N19DD	N19DU	N15RY			
258449	XP	N41431	N365AT	N717KV					
258450	XP	N41441	D-CTAN	I-DLOH	LY-LTD				
258451	XP	N41534	N475HM						
258452	XPR	N852QS	N270TX	N252XJ	N899TM				
258453	XP	N802TA	N68CB						
258454	XP	N41093	N802TA	(N826LX)	N813LX	N854FL			
258455	XP	N803TA	(N827LX)	N803FL	N500XP				

BAe 125 SERIES 800 (HAWKER 800/850)

C/n	Series	Identities								
258456	XP	N800EM	N41762	G-JMAX	(G-UJET)	M-MIDO				
258457	XP	N41984	CS-DNO	N855TM						
258458	XP	N42685	N228TM	(SE-RIS)	SE-RLX					
258459	XP	N43259	N939LE	N800WW	N800WP					
258460	XP	N81SN	N810N	C-FHRD	N85PK	N460WF	9G-CTH			
258461	XP	N804TA	N881CW	N828LX	N846FL	N32KB				
258462	XP	N43230	LV-PIW	LV-ZTR						
258463	XPR	N863QS	N298TX	N298XJ	N818TM					
258464	XP	N41964	HZ-KSRA	N828NS	N810SC					
258465	XP	N43265	ZS-DDT	VT-RPL						
258466	XP	N805TA	N866CW	N829LX	N866CW	N829LX	LV-FPW			
258467	XP	N5732	N43310	N5732	N42FB	N804JM				
258468	XP	N43436	CS-DNT	N850DP						
258469	U-125A	N43079	Japan 12-3018 [code 018]							
258470	XP	N42830	B-3991							
258471	XP2	N43642	N5736	N513BE						
258472	XPR	N44722	N872QS	N292TX	N272XJ	N820TM				
258473	XP	N73UP								
258474	XPR	N874QS	N283TX	N274XJ	N833TM					
258475	XP	N43675	HZ-KSRB	N829NS	VP-CMB	N220JJ				
258476	XP	N44676	N192NC	N830NS	VT-HCB	N830NS	XA-GGP			
258477	XP	N44767	OE-GEO	VP-BOO	G-CGHY	G-MAXP				
258478	XP2	N44648	N806TA	N800DR	N989ST					
258479	XP	N44779	CS-DNU	N860TM						
258480	XP	N4403	(N73WW)							
258481	XP	N43926	HZ-KSRC							
258482	XPR	N43182	N882QS	N277TX	N285XJ	N808TM				
258483	XP	N44883	N807TA	N830LX	N830FL					
258484	XP	N84UP								
258485	XP	N44515	(HZ-KSRD)	A7-AAL	N485LT	N125XP				
258486	XPR	N886QS	N278TX	N278XJ	N806TM					
258487	XP	N51387	N3007							
258488	XP	N50788	N488HP	N719HG						
258489	XP	N28GP								
258490	XP	N50490	N327LJ	N985CE						
258491	XP	N51191	VP-BKB	N51191	XA-TYH	N544PS				
258492	XP	N51192	N800FJ	N800LF	C-GCIX					
258493	U-125A	N40933	Japan 22-3019 [code 019]							
258494	XP	N808TA	VP-BXP	M-HAWK	N55LB					
258495	XP	N51495	C-GGCH	5B-CKL	SX-FAR	M-OBLA				
258496	XPR	N125TM	N175TM	G-RDMV	EI-ECE	N80AG	[Hawker 800XPR development aircraft; ff 09Jul11]	(OY-JJC)	OY-JJA	
258497	XP	N51197	N825CT	N825QT						
258498	XP	N809TA	N11UL	LY-...						
258499	XP	N51099	CS-DNV	N265TX	ZS-ZIM					
258500	XP	N50600	C-FPCP	C-FPCE	N400CH	N167DF				
258501	XP	N5001S	B-3992							
258502	XP2	N4469B	XA-AET	N502HR	HK-4670					
258503	XP2	N802WM	N801WM	N134CM						
258504	XP	N5004B	TC-AHS	JY-AWG	YI-ASB					
258505	XP	N50005	N805QS	N835QS	N297TX	N865TM				
258506	XP	N50166	I-RONY	(N125JN)						
258507	XP	N507BW	C-GIBU	N5G	(N296G)					
258508	XP2	N5008S	N800PE							
258509	XP	N4109E	N509XP	N313CC	N983CE	N162JB				
258510	XP	N810TA	N890CW	N831LX						
258511	XP	N5011J	CS-DNX	N264TX	N79TS					
258512	XP	N501CT	M-VITO							
258513	U-125A	N50513	Japan 22-3020 [code 020]							
258514	XP	N4021Z	D-CHEF	(M-CHEF)	M-OOUN	5N-IZY				
258515	XP	N321EJ	N321MS							
258516	XP	N811TA	N896CW	(N832LX)	N817LX	N415JA				
258517	XP	N817QS	N293TX	N870TM						
258518	XP	N29B								
258519	XP2	N443M	N72FC							
258520	XP	N4469U	VP-CRS	OE-GEA	VP-CEA	JY-AW4	JY-AWD	JY-WJA	JY-AWD	YI-ASC
258521	XP	N50521	HB-VNJ	N58521	VT-RAN	A6-ICU				
258522	XP	N812TA	N746UP	N18GU	(N284RP)					
258523	XP	N5023J	N824QS	N296TX	N875TM					
258524	XP	N4224H	N7374	(N73741)	(N666BC)	N872BC	N875BC	N875WP*		
258525	XP	N4425R	B-3993							
258526	XP	N50626	B-3995	N526XP	N837RE	N837RF	N595PL	N595PD		
258527	XP2	N813TA	N56BE	XA-RAD						
258528	XP	N828QS	N286TX	N880TM						
258529	XP	N814TA	N259RH							
258530	XP	N890SP	C-FBBF	N76LV	XA-JMR					
258531	850XP	N4469F	N259SP	N622VL	VT-HBC	N259SP	N81SF	N81SJ	N400TJ	N627MZ
258532	XP	N317CC								
258533	U-125A	N50733	JASDF 32-3021 [code 021]							
258534	XP	N815TA	(N833LX)	N818LX						
258535	XP	N51335	N853QS	N255DX						
258536	XP	N51336	B-3996	N102PA	OE-GCE					
258537	XP2	N100NG	N600NG	N650JS	XB-OAE					
258538	XP	N816TA	N25853	4X-CRY	N538LD	P4-SNT	N178BH			
258539	XP	N51239	VP-BKB	JY-AW5	JY-AWE					
258540	XP2	N50440	N700MG	N571CH						
258541	XP2	N50441	N800XP	OY-FCG	N541XP					
258542	XPR	N842QS	N284TX	N286XJ	N877TM					
258543	XP	N806TA	N843CW	(N834LX)	N819LX	(N766CH)	XA-...			
258544	XP	N799JC	D-CXNL							
258545	XP	N50445	N845QS	N279TX	N890TM					
258546	XP2	N50461	N108BP	N488VC	N470EM	N880YY				
258547	XP	N4469N	PR-OPP	N1161G						
258548	XP	N808TA	(N835LX)	N850JL	N860JL	A6-PHS	N116JK	9G-UHI		
258549	XP	N51149	N155NS							
258550	XP	N793RC								

BAe 125 SERIES 800 (HAWKER 800/850)

C/n	Series	Identities							
258551	XP	N44759	N190NC	N777DB	N85594	N800LQ			
258552	XP	N817TA	(N836LX)	N834LX	XA-NIC				
258553	XP	N51453	PR-LUG						
258554	XP	N50034	(5B-CKG)	XA-GTE	N258HH	XA-HHH			
258555	XP	N820TA	N300CQ						
258556	XP2	N51556	N800WY	N512JC					
258557	XP	N51457	N1630	N1638	N987CE				
258558	XP	N51058	N225PB						
258559	XP	N50459	N819AP	N819AB	PR-FAP	N223FA	(PR-CSP)	N977AV	
258560	XP	N50740	N877S	N8778					
258561	XP	N1630	N16300	I-ALHO	N561XP	N901SC			
258562	XP	N5062H	(N877S)	N802DC	N361LA				
258563	XP	N4469M	N981CE						
258564	XP	N864QS	N295TX	N885TM					
258565	XP	N4465M	N240Z						
258566	XP	N4466Z	N664AC						
258567	XP	N50667	N74PC	N24SM					
258568	XP2	N4468K	N96FT						
258569	XP	N4469X	N244LS	N906AS					
258570	XP	N50670	"N873QS"	N880QS	N553BW				
258571	XP	N4471N	RP-C8576						
258572	XP	N5072L	N80FB	N293S	C-GKPP				
258573	XP	N873QS							
258574	850XP	N51274	N915AM	(N915MT)	N915AP				
258575	XP	N3215M	B-3997						
258576	XP	N867QS							
258577	XP	N51027	N800UK						
258578	XP	N50378	N91HK	N81HK	N406TM				
258579	XP	N50309	PK-TVO						
258580	XP	N880QS	N1989D						
258581	XP	N50661	XA-ICF	N581GE	XA-JCT	N687AC	XA-BWB		
258582	850XP	N50182	(N170SK)	XA-JMS	VP-CFS	N48AM	N800EA		
258583	XP	N50983	XA-GLG	N1730M	N55XP				
258584	XP2	N51384	N884VC	N107CE					
258585	XP2	N50285	(N885VC)	N585VC					
258586	XP	N876QS							
258587	XP	N50657	N261PA	N703RK	(N778CC)	(N703RE)	N770CC		
258588	XP	N44888	N799S						
258589	850XP	N51289	N974JD	N874JD	[converted to prototype 850XP]			ZS-PCY	N810AF
258590	XP2	N50910	(N890VC)	(N590VC)	N733H	(N446TW)	N130YB		
258591	XP2	N61791	N380GG	N380GP	PK-EJR				
258592	XP	N892QS	N892VR*						
258593	XP	N898QS	N174WC						
258594	XP2	N61904	N140GB	N323MP	VH-RIO				
258595	XP2	N61495	N76CS	N76CY	N512WC				
258596	XP	N896QS	N596XP	N804BH					
258597	XP	N895QS	N597XP	XA-TYK					
258598	XP2	N61198	(N800JA)	N92FT	(N92FL)	N988RS			
258599	XP	N51169	N59BR						
258600	850XP	N61500	N250SP	N908NR					
258601	XP	N61101	ZS-DDA	N68HB	XA-PBT				
258602	XP2	(N898QS)	N61702	N899SC	N401TM				
258603	XP	N803QS	(N803CW)	N893CW	N893FL	N878MB			
258604	XP	N60664	N8186	N565SK					
258605	XP	N61805	C-GJKI	C-GJKK					
258606	XP	N60506	N895QS						
258607	XP	N60507	N919RT	N500AZ	N118DL				
258608	XP2	N61708	N500BN	I-KREM					
258609	XP	N60159	N80HD	N80HX	M-ABDP				
258610	U-125A	N61320	Japan 42-3022 [code 022]						
258611	XP	N809QS	(N944PP)	N944BB					
258612	XP	(N896QS)	N50522	N711GD	N612XP	OM-OIG			
258613	850XP	N90FB							
258614	XP	N811QS							
258615	XP	N61515	VP-CKN	N615XP	HS-CPH				
258616	XP	N61216	N88HD	N88HX	N900SS	N254SB			
258617	XP	N5117F	N617XP	N551VB	N557VB	P4-SEN			
258618	XP	(N895QS)	N896QS	N618XP	N82GK	G-IWDB	A6-MAB	N527WA	N447SP
258619	XP	N61719	N676JB						
258620	XP	N61920	N620XP	N77CS	N77CX	N77CS	N356SR		
258621	XP2	N61681	(N621XP)	N522EE	N522EF	N123KH			
258622	850XP	N622XP	N800EL	N850RG	N17TV				
258623	XP	N623XP	(N823CW)	N221PB					
258624	XP	N624XP	N866RR	N660HC	N757GS				
258625	XP	N625XP	N305JA	VP-BNK	M-UKHA				
258626	XP	N626XP	N25W	N945SL	XA-LAS				
258627	850XP	N627XP	N929AK						
258628	850XP	N628XP	XA-JET						
258629	U-25A	N61729	Japan 52-3023 [code 023]						
258630	XP	N630XP	N125ZZ	N599AK	N215BB				
258631	XP	N631XP	N74NP	N74NB	OD-MAF				
258632	XP2	N632XP	ZS-PZA	TY-VLT	5V-TTM				
258633	XP	N633XP	N800NS	ZS-PTP	A2-MCB				
258634	XP	N808BL	N851RG						
258635	XP	N635XP	N919SF	N45KN					
258636	XP	N636XP	N800CQ	(N775RB)	N438PM				
258637	XP2	N637XP	PP-ANA	N637XP	OY-JJC				
258638	XP	N638XP	XA-NTE						
258639	XP	N639XP	N95UP						
258640	XP	N640XP	N896QS						
258641	850XP	N641XP	N513ML	N104RF					
258642	XP	N642XP	N12PA	N279CF					
258643	XP	N883CW	(N843TS)	N33NL					
258644	850XP	N644XP	N484JC	HB-VCJ	XA-PYC				
258645	XP	N645XP	N733K	(N645XP)	N733L	N618AR	OY-OAA	HB-VOT	M-HSXP

BAe 125 SERIES 800 (HAWKER 800/850)

C/n	Series	Identities				
258646	850XP	N646XP	N528BP	XA-EBF		
258647	XP	N847CW	(N837LX)	(N847FL)	N864DC	
258648	XP	N848CW	(N823LX)	N848FL	N483AM	N488AM
258649	XP	N649XP	N800EM			
258650	850XP	N650XP	N50AE	N50AN	N821LB	
258651	850XP	N651XP	N470BC	N159FM		
258652	XP	N652XP	N241JS			
258653	XP	N653XP	N203TM	(N203TR)		
258654	XP	N654XP	N149SB			
258655	XP	N655XP	N535BC	N655XP	(N16SM)	N22SM
258656	XP	N656XP	CS-DFX	N850VR	B-3915	
258657	XP	N657XP	(N857CW)	N839LX	N417TM	
258658	850XP	N658XP	(ZS-ARK)	5N-JMA	[wfu Chester, UK]	
258659	850XP	N659XP	5N-JMB			
258660	XP	N660XP	N800RC			
258661	XP	N661XP	N800WW			
258662	XP	N662XP	N305SC	N474CF		
258663	XP	N663XP	CS-DFY	N863GJ		
258664	XP	N664XP	CS-DFW	N808NA	XA-FSA	
258665	XP	N665XP	N689AM			
258666	XP	N876CW	N840LX	N840FL	(N926JR)	N923JR
258667	XP	N667XP	N802DR	N405TM		
258668	XP	N668XP	N156NS			
258669	XP	N669XP	N520SP	N333PC		
258670	850XP	N670XP	N1776N	ZS-PZX	ZS-AOT	
258671	XP	N671XP	N184TB	N184TR		
258672	XP	N672XP	N1CA	N191CA	N120JC	
258673	XP	N673XP	CS-DFZ	N851VR	B-3917	N851VR
258674	XP	N674XP	N841WS	G-OJWB	G-KLOE	N475RS
258675	XP2	N675XP	N351TC	N66ZB		
258676	XP	N676XP	N676GH			
258677	XP2	N677XP	M-CTEM	N840CE		
258678	XP	N678XP	N9867			
258679	XP2	N679XP	N800AH	N800LA	[w/o in hangar collapse at Washington/Dulles, VA, 06Feb10; parted out by AvMATS, St Louis, MO]	
258680	XP	N680XP	N80E	N80EH	N426TM	
258681	XP	N681XP	N80J	N80JE	N119BG	
258682	XP	N682XP	4X-CRU	D-CLBG	N682DK	P4-PRT
258683	XP	N61343	N832QS			
258684	850XP	N684DK				
258685	U-125A	N36685	Japan 62-3024 [code 024]			
258686	XP	N61746	CS-DRA	N851QS		
258687	XP	N61987	N733A	N120YB		
258688	850XP	N688G	C-FMRI	N944KR		
258689	XP	N36689	F-HBFP			
258690	XP	N36690	CS-DRB	XA-RED		
258691	XP	N858QS	XA-...			
258692	XP	N37092	N700R	N90WP		
258693	XP	N693XP	N302PE	N322PE	N277RS	
258694	XP	N36894	N800R	N694FJ	N694ES	
258695	XP	N695XP	N39H	CC-AME	N515JM	
258696	XP2	N36896	N800PL			
258697	XP	N697XP	N530SM	N137LA	N133KS	
258698	XP	N860QS				
258699	850XP	N699XP				
258700	XP2	N108DD				
258701	XP	N501XP	N6NR			
258702	XP2	N841LX	N96SK	N966K	VP-BAS	XA-DAK
258703	XP	N50553	N707JC	N707JQ		
258704	XP2	N614BG	N312KG	N898DD*		
258705	XP	N815QS				
258706	XP	N706XP	N74GW			
258707	XP	N707XP	LV-PJL	LV-BBG		
258708	850XP	N799RM				
258709	XP	N709XP+	[+marks worn but not registered as such]		N821QS	
258710	XP	N37010	G-CDLT	OD-EKF		
258711	XP	N37211	N1910A	N514SK*		
258712	XP	N36672	N18AQ	VH-MBP	VH-MEP	N713SC
258713	850XP	N713XP	N199DF	XA-SJM	N110GD	
258714	XP	N61944	CS-DRC	N852QS		
258715	850XP	N715XP	N715PH	XA-JBT	XA-JBG	
258716	XP	N716XP	VT-RBK	VT-ABG		
258717	850XP	N717XP	ZS-PPH			
258718	XP	N718XP	N718SJ			
258719	XP	N19XP	VP-BCW			
258720	XP	N36820	OM-USS	N720XP	N427TM	
258721	XP	N36621	CS-DRD	N853QS		
258722	XP	N37322	I-PZZR			
258723	850XP	N723XP	N627AK	M-YCEF	VH-RIU	
258724	850XP	N724XP	ZS-AFG	ZS-TNF		
258725	XPi	N30355	CS-DRE	N854QS		
258726	XP2	N726XP	N405LA			
258727	850XP	N787JC	XA-CHK			
258728	XPi	N728XP	N110DD	VP-CXP	N800WF	
258729	850XP	N729XP	N729AG	N232EH		
258730	XPi	N37060	CS-DRF	N855QS		
258731	850XP	N37061	XA-UGO	XA-CHG	XA-LEY	
258732	XPi	N870QS				
258733	XPi	N333XP	HB-VOB	N280CB		
258734	XPi	N884QS				
258735	U-125A	N6135H	Japan 72-3025			
258736	XPi	N136XP	TC-TAV			
258737	850XP	N518M				
258738	XPi	N138XP	TC-ADO			
258739	XPi	N739XP	N499PA			
258740	XP2	N740XP	N824LX	(N824FL)		

BAe 125 SERIES 800 (HAWKER 800/850)

C/n	Series	Identities					
258741	XPi	N36841	CS-DRG	N741VR			
258742	850XP	N742XP	TC-FIN	N742XP	N299JM		
258743	XPi	N885QS					
258744	850XP	N744XP					
258745	850XP	N745XP	VT-FAF				
258746	XPi	N6046J	CS-DRH				
258747	850XP	N519M	N519MN	N100AG			
258748	850XP	N748XP	EC-JNY	TC-ILY	N451RS	OE-GMI	
258749	850XP	N36669	N50UG	XA-GBP			
258750	850XP	N950XP	N1776A	Mozambique FAM-002			
258751	850XP	N751MT					
258752	850XP	N752MT					
258753	850XP	N805M	N546MG	N544MG	XA-DAR		
258754	850XP	N37054	N754AE	N754AF	CC-AEN	N295JM	
258755	850XP	N575JR	VP-CDE				
258756	XPi	N37056	CS-DRI	N75GR			
258757	850XP	N757XP	N345MP	N437JD	N437JR	XA-OLA	
258758	850XP	N37158	N725CS	N858XP			
258759	850XP	N801RR	N426MJ				
258760	XPi	N37160	CS-DRJ	LY-LTA			
258761	850XP	N761XP					
258762	850XP	N762XP	N901SG	N801SG	PR-FAF	N71LG	PR-FNE
258763	XPi	N871QS					
258764	850XP	N764XP	N522EE				
258765	XPi	N61285	CS-DRK	N868QS			
258766	850XP	N542M					
258767	XPi	N767XP	(N143RL)	N825LX	N825FL	N429TM	
258768	850XP	N768XP	N850VP				
258769	850XP	N769XP	CC-CAB	N630GS			
258770	XPi	N36970	CS-DRL				
258771	XPi	N6171U	CS-DRM	N869QS			
258772	XPi	N672XP	CS-DRN				
258773	XPi	N883QS					
258774	850XP	N774XP	N143RL	N820M	N774WF		
258775	XPi	N37105	CS-DRO				
258776	850XP	N36726	N535BC	N776RS	(N2707)		
258777	850XP	N877XP	N900ST	N900SK	N694PD	N694BD	N201LS
258778	850XP	N36578	OE-IPH	N36578	M-IRNE		
258779	XPi	N37179	CS-DRP				
258780	850XP	N37070	VH-SGY				
258781	850XP	N37261	A6-ELC	N146DJ	N73SL		
258782	850XP	N782XP	(N706CW)	(N260G)	N126HY	N830	
258783	XPi	N37146	CS-DRQ				
258784	850XP	N784XP	N76FC	N850RC			
258785	850XP	N785XP	N785VC				
258786	XPi	N36986	CS-DRR				
258787	850XP	N72617	N851CC	(N815RK)			
258788	850XP	N891QS					
258789	850XP	N789XP	N850NS	N850EC			
258790	850XP	N790XP	TC-TKC				
258791	850XP	N70791	N255RB				
258792	850XP	N792XP	A6-TBF	OD-LEA			
258793	850XP	N793XP	TC-STB	M-CSTB	TC-SBL		
258794	850XP	N71794	VT-JHP				
258795	XPi	N37295	CS-DRS				
258796	850XP	N796XP	N850KE	N858KE	C-GTUF		
258797	U-125A	N71907	Japan 82-3026		Japan 92-3026		
258798	850XP	N798XP	N850ZH	N850TM			
258799	850XP	N37009	HB-VOJ	XA-DAD	N452RS	N850EZ*	
258800	850XP	N880XP	N865JT	N465VC	N269AA		
258801	850XP	N7101Z	(N906BL)	TC-DOY	N72LA		
258802	XPi	N7102Z	CS-DRT				
258803	850XP	N853CC					
258804	850XP	N71904	OE-GRS	OD-SKY	[w/o 04Feb11 Sulamaniyah, Iraq]		
258805	850XP	N71025	EI-KJC	A6-AUJ	VT-SSN	RP-C850	
258806	850XP	N36826	N906BL				
258807	850XP	N36878	VH-MQY				
258808	850XP	N70708	TC-CLK	N220PK	N228PK	N850PE	
258809	850XP	N70409	I-TOPH				
258810	850XP	N71010	OE-GJA	G-CERX			
258811	850XP	N71881	LY-DSK	OE-GWP	LY-DSK		
258812	850XP	N812XP	D-CLBH	N359BC			
258813	850XP	N73793	OE-GRF	VQ-BVA			
258814	850XP	N70214	N189TA	VH-TNX	N85NX	C-GMGB	N669CC
258815	850XP	N74155	VT-KNB				
258816	850XP	N74166	(N850ZH)	VP-COD	M-FRZN	M-ABGL	N816TR	PP-CNS
258817	850XP	N37170	N85HH				
258818	850XP	N403CT					
258819	850XP	N405CT	VT-ARR	N277SR			
258820		[Hawker 900XP c/n HA-0001]					
258821	XPi	N73721	CS-DRU				
258822	850XP	N822XP	N103AL	N915TB			
258823	850XP	N823XP	N150GF				
258824	U-125A	N60724	Japan 02-3027				
258825	XPi	N3725Z	CS-DRV				
258826	850XP	N826LX	PT-FPM				
258827	850XP	N7077S	G-HSXP				
258828	850XP	N7128T	C-GCGT				
258829	XPi	N73729	CS-DRW				
258830	850XP	N72520	N111ZN	HS-PEK			
258831	850XP	N676AH					
258832	850XP	N74142	SU-MAN				
258833	850XP	N72233	HS-CPG				
258834	XPi	N71934	CS-DRX				
258835	850XP	N7235R	VP-CMA	VT-AGP			

BAe 125 SERIES 800 (HAWKER 800/850)

C/n	Series	Identities				
258836	850XP	N7236L	N773HR	TC-MAN		
258837	850XP	N662JN				
258838	850XP	N71938	VT-OBR			
258839		[Hawker 900XP c/n HA-0002]				
258840	XPi	N70040	CS-DRY			
258841	850XP	N70431	VP-BMM	N914CE	N159MN	
258842		[Hawker 900XP c/n HA-0003]				
258843	U-125A	N63600	Japan 12-3028			
258844	850XP	N71944	VH-RAM	VH-PNF	N230PA	PP-JFZ
258845	850XP	N72645	TC-STD	M-CSTD	YL-KSD	
258846		[Hawker 900XP c/n HA-0004]				
258847	XPi	N74476	CS-DRZ			
258848	850XP	N827LX	N404TM			

Production continued as a mix of special-order Hawker 850XPs using the old-style 6-digit c/n sequence, Hawker 900XPs with c/ns starting HA- and Hawker 750s with c/ns starting HB-. The latter two models are shown in their own separate production lists.

C/n	Series	Identities				
258849 to 258851		[c/ns not used]				
258852	850XP	N7302P	C-GROG			
258853 to 258854		[c/ns not used]				
258855	850XP	N7255U	LX-OKR	F-GVIA	VP-BNW	
258856	850XP	N7256C	B-3901	N375BC		
258857		[c/n not used]				
258858	850XP	N71958	B-3902	N641RP		
258859	850XP	N859XP	OE-GNY	P4-WIN		
258860		[c/n not used]				
258861	850XP	N861ME	N850ME	N347JR		
258862 to 258871		[c/ns not used]				
258872	850XP	N872XP	TC-SHE			
258873		[c/n not used]				
258874	850XP	N874XP	TC-NUB	N841TC		
258875		[c/n not used]				
258876	850XP	N349AK	N349AS	N850EM	M-ARIA	N97KL
258877 to 258890		[c/ns not used]				
258891	850XP	N31991	(N315ML)	N315JL		
258892		[c/n not used]				
258893	850XP	N1620	N162G	N900WS		
258894		[c/n not used]				
258895	850XP	N3195F	HB-VOY	M-RACE	VH-BMW	
258896 to 258899		[c/ns not used]				
258900	850XP	N850HB	N440CX			
258901	850XP	N3201T	EI-GEM	N658DM	N107LT*	
258902 to 258903		[c/ns not used]				
258904	850XP	N3204T	VT-BTA	N904JC	XA-IJC	
258905 to 258906		[c/ns not used]				
258907	850XP	N3207T	N448H	(N4424)		
258908		[c/n not used]				
258909	850XP	N3289N	VT-BTB	N997BX		
258910 to 258911		[c/ns not used]				
258912	850XP	N32012	VT-BTC	N800CL		
258913 to 258914		[c/ns not used]				
258915	850XP	N3115Y	N383MR	T7-TUN		
258916 to 258920		[c/ns not used]				
258921	850XP	N32061	N888WY			
258922 to 258958		[c/ns not used]				
258959	850XP	N3400S				
258960		[c/n not used]				
258961	850XP	N3201P	N850KE			
258962		[c/n not used]				
258963	850XP	N3193B	N437WR			
258964 to 258976		[c/ns not used]				
258977	850XP	N977LC				
258978 to 258979		[c/ns not used]				
258980	850XP	N3188X	VT-FTL			
258981		[c/n not used]				
258982	850XP	N3482Y	P4-NUR	N982XP	Pakistan 101	
258983	850XP	N62783	N438WR			
258984	850XP	N63984	XA-KBA	N984MS	5N-SPL	

Production complete

HAWKER 900XP

The Hawker 900XP is a re-engined development of the Hawker 850XP.

C/n	Fuselage	Identities					
HA-0001	258820	N90XP	N170DC				
HA-0002	258839	N1776C					
HA-0003	258842	N903XP	A6-PJB	N330GW			
HA-0004	258846	N904XP	N351SP				
HA-0005	258849	N894QS					
HA-0006	258851	N71956	N96SK				
HA-0007	258853	N807HB	N77TC				
HA-0008	258854	N900LD	N855FC				
HA-0009	258857	N809HB	N901K	N907PJ			
HA-0010	258860	N890QS					
HA-0011	258862	N211XP	C-GGMP	N297TX			
HA-0012	258863	N852CC	N526PS	N349JF			
HA-0013	258864	N113XP	N900R				
HA-0014	258865	N897QS					
HA-0015	258866	N915XP	C-GVMP				
HA-0016	258867	N575MA					
HA-0017	258868	N917XP	ZS-KBS	T7-KBS			
HA-0018	258869	N901RD	OK-HWK				
HA-0019	258870	N889QS	N899QS				
HA-0020	258871	N920XP	P4-ALA	N288KR	N900VA		
HA-0021	258873	N899QS	N889QS				
HA-0022	258875	N922XP	N900PF	N900BF			
HA-0023	258877	N923XP	HZ-BIN				
HA-0024	258879	N924XP	N108PJ	N752AR			
HA-0025	258880	N33055	P4-ANG				
HA-0026	258881	N32926	ZS-SAH	M-SAPT	N838LJ	N703CD	
HA-0027	258882	N33527	N799AG				
HA-0028	258883	N31958	B-MBD	N25HA	XA-BNG		
HA-0029	258884	N700WY					
HA-0030	258885	N930XP	N630JS	N638JS*			
HA-0031	258886	N848QS					
HA-0032	258887	N932BC	ZS-SGJ	ZS-BOT	N762JP		
HA-0033	258888	N933XP	EC-KMT	N733DB			
HA-0034	258889	N31624	OK-KAZ	9H-KAZ			
HA-0035	258890	N33235	P4-PET	G-DLTC	N33235	N111MD	
HA-0036	258892	N34956	B-MBE	N130AB	XA-RGO		
HA-0037	258894	N865LS	N918JL				
HA-0038	258896	N34838	HB-VPJ	N900MJ			
HA-0039	258897	N580RJ					
HA-0040	258898	N16SM					
HA-0041	258899	N34441	G-ODUR				
HA-0042	258902	N888QS					
HA-0043	258903	N87PK					
HA-0044	258906	N944XP	VH-EVF				
HA-0045	258908	N3285N	XA-AET				
HA-0046	258910	N31946	TC-KHA				
HA-0047	258911	N22VS					
HA-0048	258914	N34548	A6-RZB	A7-RZB	G-ORYX	(OE-GIS)	TT-ABF
HA-0049	258916	N31959	VH-ACE	N99GM	PP-HVD		
HA-0050	258918	N881QS					
HA-0051	258920	N951XP	CS-DGZ	TC-ACL	TC-ASH	[or TC-NRY, see also c/n HA-0092]	
HA-0052	258922	N104AG	(N952XP)	XA-KBL			
HA-0053	258924	N3193L	B-3903				
HA-0054	258926	N878QS					
HA-0055	258928	N32185	N816SE	N919DW			
HA-0056	258927	N3386A	(D-BGRL)	I-BBGR			
HA-0057	258931	N900PE					
HA-0058	258933	N3088A	M-AJOR				
HA-0059	258935	N3400D	M-INOR				
HA-0060	258937	N3260J	LY-FSK				
HA-0061	258939	N34451	VT-ICA				
HA-0062	258940	N32862	N900XP				
HA-0063	258942	N3363U	N288MB	N190HS			
HA-0064	258943	N31964	VH-NKD	N313ZP			
HA-0065	tbc	N365JR	N819JR				
HA-0066	tbc	N877QS					
HA-0067	tbc	N3217H	ZS-SGV	N309KR			
HA-0068	tbc	N3198C	XA-ESP				
HA-0069	tbc	N3198V	CS-DPA				
HA-0070	258955	N3207Y	N902BE	N131JR	N902BE		
HA-0071	258957	N3371D	(D-CAJA)	(M-ABCE)	PK-JBH		
HA-0072	258959	N33612	M-LCJP	5N-YYY			
HA-0073	258961	N3283V	M-ONAV				
HA-0074	258962	N3204W	I-MFAB				
HA-0075	258966	N869QS	(N975XP)	N979TM	N979TB		
HA-0076	258968	N300R	N330R	N100R			
HA-0077	258970	N710HM	N702CS				
HA-0078	258972	N3378M	PP-ARG				
HA-0079	258975	N190SW					
HA-0080	258980	N31842	A6-HWK				
HA-0081	258978	N3217G	(N902BE)				
HA-0082	258979	N3222W	(N979TM)	N159M	N479M		
HA-0083	258981	N83XP	"M-HARP"+	[+marks worn but ntu]	M-NICO	N901AG	
HA-0084	258984	N984XP	VP-CIS	N991PS			
HA-0085	258986	N985RM	EI-JJJ	VT-AJM			
HA-0086	258988	N986XP	TC-ENK				
HA-0087	258973	N87XP	N865JM	N451CG			
HA-0088	258989	N988AG					
HA-0089	258990	N60089	PR-DBD				
HA-0090	258985	N63890	F-HGBY	VP-CFS			
HA-0091	259101	N61391	CN-RBS				
HA-0092	259103	N64292	CS-DPJ	TC-TSH	TC-NRY	[or TC-ASH, see also c/n HA-0051]	

HAWKER 900XP

C/n	Fuselage	Identities					
HA-0093	259106	N30VP					
HA-0094	258982	N301ML					
HA-0095	259113	N62895	(A6-HBC)	A7-RZD	VP-CBU	G-ORXX	N887PC
HA-0096	259107	N996XP	"LX-KSD"+	[+marks worn at factory but ntu; aircraft not delivered, parted out]			
HA-0097	259111	N62297	D2-EAA	P4-HBS	N375TW		
HA-0098	259112	N6198P	TC-CLG				
HA-0099	259115	N60099	M-LION				
HA-0100	259104	N125ML	VT-UPM				
HA-0101	259116	N15QB	N901MJ				
HA-0102	259109	N6452L	(ZS-HWK)	N955SE			
HA-0103	259120	N6403N	VT-BKL				
HA-0104	259124	N6434R	ZS-SME				
HA-0105	259125	N900FG	N900FU	N105XP	N21FX	N21FZ	N712BS
HA-0106	259118	N803D	N69FR				
HA-0107		N107XP	OE-GYP	N232EA			
HA-0108	259121	N6408F	VQ-BPH				
HA-0109		[not built, order cancelled]					
HA-0110		N804D	N54VM				
HA-0111		[not built, order cancelled]					
HA-0112		N63812	G-OTAZ	N374HM			
HA-0113		N805D					
HA-0114		N62914	TC-MOH				
HA-0115		[not built, order cancelled]					
HA-0116		[not built, order cancelled]					
HA-0117		N117XP	N437JD				
HA-0118		[not built, order cancelled]					
HA-0119		(CS-DPK)	[not built, order cancelled]				
HA-0120		N60820	N239RT				
HA-0121		N6151C	M-JOLY				
HA-0122		N859QS	(N869QS)	N122XP	[registered but not built]		
HA-0123		[not built, order cancelled]					
HA-0124		[not built, order cancelled]					
HA-0125		[not built, order cancelled]					
HA-0126		[not built, order cancelled]					
HA-0127		[not built, order cancelled]					
HA-0128		[not built, order cancelled]					
HA-0129		[not built, order cancelled]					
HA-0130		[not built, order cancelled]					
HA-0131		[not built, order cancelled]					
HA-0132		N857QS	N132XP	[registered but not built]			
HA-0133		[not built, order cancelled]					
HA-0134		[not built, order cancelled]					
HA-0135		[not built, order cancelled]					
HA-0136		[not built, order cancelled]					
HA-0137		[not built, order cancelled]					
HA-0138		[not built, order cancelled]					
HA-0139		[not built, order cancelled]					
HA-0140		N6340T	LX-KAT	G-KTIA	M-CKAY		
HA-0141		[not built, order cancelled]					
HA-0142		[not built, order cancelled]					
HA-0143		N6273X	G-OZAT	9H-ZAT	G-URTH	N900QC	
HA-0144		[not built, order cancelled]					
HA-0145		[not built, order cancelled]					
HA-0146		N146XP	N702A				
HA-0147		N147XP	N703A				
HA-0148		N148XP	OD-MIG				
HA-0149		N149XP	XA-XEL				
HA-0150		N950XP	N916JB				
HA-0151		N6351Y	OM-USS	N154X			
HA-0152		N6452S	G-RGSG	N26XP			
HA-0153		N153XP	HZ-A8				
HA-0154		N154XP	N85PK				
HA-0155		N155XP	N80E	N337CC			
HA-0156		N156XP	N80J				
HA-0157		N157XP	N308GW				
HA-0158		N158XP	CN-TJS				
HA-0159		N6409A	HK-4758				
HA-0160		N160XP	N146JF				
HA-0161		N161XP	OE-GYB	9H-GYB			
HA-0162		N362XP					
HA-0163		N163XP	N459M				
HA-0164		N964XP	N835ZP	N100ZT			
HA-0165		N165XP	VT-LTA				
HA-0166		N166XP	N104AG	VP-CAG	N305KR		
HA-0167		N167XP	B-3909				
HA-0168		N6368D	N50AE				
HA-0169		N81239	N51HH				
HA-0170		N970XP	TC-DMR				
HA-0171		N171XP	N754AE				
HA-0172		N972XP	N627TF				
HA-0173		N173XP	HZ-A9				
HA-0174		N174XP	N844JD				
HA-0175		N975XP	B-3912	N752SC	N234GF		
HA-0176		N176XP	N75CS				
HA-0177		N977XP	9H-BOF	VP-CSD	N144UV		
HA-0178		N178XP	N76CS				
HA-0179		N979XP	N571KG				
HA-0180		N980XP	OE-GOA	N36CD			
HA-0181		N181XP					
HA-0182		N82XP	YR-NAY				
HA-0183		N183XP	N118UF				
HA-0184		N184XP	D-CHGN	N184HA	N977HG		
HA-0185		N985XP	VT-LTC				
HA-0186		N186XP	G-KLNE				
HA-0187		N187XP	VT-UDR				

HAWKER 900XP

C/n	Fuselage	Identities			
HA-0188		N188XP	PK-JBB		
HA-0189		N189XP	N804AC		
HA-0190		N190XP	N1910H		
HA-0191		N191XP	N900ER		
HA-0192		N192XP	N192SA		
HA-0193		N193XP	N193BK		
HA-0194		N194XP	N638MA	5N-...	
HA-0195		N195XP	N979CF		
HA-0196		N396XP	N902MS		
HA-0197		N197XP	UP-HA001		
HA-0198		N198XP	LV-CTE		
HA-0199		N899XP	PP-WAV	N199FJ	
HA-0200		N888XP	PK-CAR		
HA-0201		N901XP	N536BW		
HA-0202		N902XP	N482MG		
HA-0203		N203XP	N251SP		
HA-0204		N204XP	CS-DSE		
HA-0205		N205XP	PR-DPD	N630AB	
HA-0206		N206XP	PT-MIA		
HA-0207		N907XP	PK-LRT		
HA-0208		N908XP	N515JM	XA-CAB	
HA-0209		N909XP	N900PF		
HA-0210		N910XP	M-ALBA	OE-GJL	N963JB
HA-0211		N211XP	N29GP		
HA-0212		N812XP	PK-LRU		
HA-0213		N903XP	N900LD		
HA-0214		(N214XP)	[aircraft built but not delivered; stored unmarked at Wichita/Beech Field, KS]		

Production complete. The following aircraft also had marks assigned in anticipation of being built:

HA-0215		(N915XP)
HA-0216		(N216XP)
HA-0217		(N217XP)
HA-0218		(N218XP)
HA-0219		(N219XP)
HA-0220		(N920XP)
HA-0221		(N221XP)

HAWKER 750

The Hawker 750 is a re-engined development of the Hawker 800XPi.

C/n	Fuselage	Identities				
HB-1	258850	N750HB	(N751NS)	B-MBF	N170FA	XA-MLA
HB-2	258878	N752HB	(N752NS)	(N751NS)	N787FF	N626BS
HB-3	258905	N752NS	N770GS			
HB-4	258913	N804HB	CS-DUA			
HB-5	258917	N31685	CS-DUB			
HB-6	258919	N3206V	(CS-DUA)	CS-DUC		
HB-7	258923	N3207V	(CS-DUB)	(N753NS)	VT-RSR	
HB-8	258925	N3198Z	CS-DUD			
HB-9	258929	N3501Q	B-MBG	N750FA	XA-OAC	
HB-10	258930	N3210N	(N232AV)	XA-DPA		
HB-11	258932	N3211G	CS-DUE			
HB-12	258934	N3212H	N750KH			
HB-13	258936	N3093T	B-MBH	N264TC		
HB-14	258938	N3194Q	(M-OANH)	N555RU	G-NLPA	G-TWIY
HB-15	258941	N3215J	PR-NCJ	N40AG		
HB-16	tbc	N3216R	XA-AFS			
HB-17	tbc	N3217D	HZ-KSRD			
HB-18	tbc	N3418C	N750EL			
HB-19	tbc	N3491F	CS-DUF			
HB-20	258960	N3220K	CS-DUG			
HB-21	258964	N3201K	CS-DUH			
HB-22	258967	N3222S	XA-AEM	N232CS	XA-NXT	
HB-23	258969	N3433D	N751NS			
HB-24	258971	N3417F	(CS-DUI)	EC-KXS	9H-BSA	
HB-25	258974	N3285Q	B-MBI	N90SA	XA-EGE	
HB-26	258977	N3276L	N209HP			
HB-27	258976	N3497J	N666NF	M-INXS	G-ZIPR	F-HOSB
HB-28	258983	N3488P	N752NS			
HB-29	258987	N3197K	N753NS			
HB-30	259110	N730HB	(C-GXMP)	VT-CMO		
HB-31	259102	N731TH	(C-GYMP)	N200RG		
HB-32	259105	N732HB	I-EPAM			
HB-33	259100	N63633	ES-PHR			
HB-34	259119	N760NS	N434HB	YR-MSS	OE-GBG	VP-BSX
HB-35		N735XP	N750HM			
HB-36		[not built, order cancelled]				
HB-37		[not built, order cancelled]				
HB-38		[not built, order cancelled]				
HB-39		[not built, order cancelled]				
HB-40		[not built, order cancelled]				
HB-41		N62991	N219TF			
HB-42		[not built, order cancelled]				
HB-43		N761NS	N743HB	N787CA	N259CA	N787CA	N307ST*
HB-44		[not built, order cancelled]				
HB-45		[not built, order cancelled]				
HB-46		[not built, order cancelled]				
HB-47		[not built, order cancelled]				
HB-48		[not built, order cancelled]				
HB-49		[not built, order cancelled]				
HB-50		[not built, order cancelled]				
HB-51		[not built, order cancelled]				
HB-52		[not built, order cancelled]				
HB-53		[not built, order cancelled]				
HB-54		[not built, order cancelled]				
HB-55		[not built, order cancelled]				
HB-56		[not built, order cancelled]				
HB-57		[not built, order cancelled]				
HB-58		[not built, order cancelled]				
HB-59		[not built, order cancelled]				
HB-60		[not built, order cancelled]				
HB-61		[not built, order cancelled]				
HB-62		N762XP	N93KW			
HB-63		N6173K	N750SG			
HB-64		[not built, order cancelled]				
HB-65		N6405K	M-OLLE			
HB-66		[not built, order cancelled]				
HB-67		N767HB	I-EDLO			
HB-68		N768HB	N605ML			
HB-69		N769HB	N750VM			
HB-70		N770HB	SP-CEO			
HB-71		N771HB	N599LP			
HB-72		N772HB	N327MP			
HB-73		N773HB	XA-JVG			
HB-74		N774HB	D-CFIC	HL7778		

Production complete

SERIES 1000 (BAe 1000) (HAWKER 1000)

C/n	Series	Identities
259001	B	[built as c/n 258151] G-EXLR [ff 16Jun90; reported wfu Nov93; see c/n 258151]
259002	B	[built as c/n 258159] G-OPFC N10855 [see c/n 258159; canx 05Sep03 as b/u]
259003	B	G-5-702 G-ELRA [built between c/ns 258195-6] N503QS (N503LR) N261PA
259004	B	G-LRBJ G-5-779 VR-CPT VP-CPT M-ACPT
259005	NA1000 A	G-BTTX G-5-735 N1AB N81AB N410US N505QS N505LR (N990TB) N982LC
259006	NA1001 A	G-BTTG N1000U N100U (N108U) N850JA
259007	B/A	G-BTSI N84WA N119PW N119U
259008	B/A	G-5-720 HZ-OFC HZ-OFC2 N195L D-CADA N207TT
259009	NA1002 A	G-5-716 G-BTYN N229U N168WU XA-UTB
259010	NA1009 A	G-5-722 (HZ-...) N125CJ N52SM
259011	NA1003 A	G-5-717 G-BTYO N14GD N208R N208L XA-UVY
259012	B/A	G-5-726 HZ-SJP2 N512QS (N512HR) N512LR I-SRAF VP-BMX
259013	NA1004 A	G-5-711 G-BTYP N125BA N513QS (N513RA) N513LR
259014	NA1005 A	G-5-712 G-BTYR N680BA N125CJ N514QS N514LR
259015	NA1006 A	G-5-718 G-BTYS N1000E N515QS N515LR
259016	B/A	(D-BJET) G-5-732 G-BULI (5N-...) G-5-732 N291H N678SB N707HD
259017	B	G-5-719 ZS-NEW ZS-AVL N963H N204R N517QS N517LR A6-ELA N517LR (N868GB)
259018	B	G-5-741 5N-FGR 5N-DGN
259019	NA1007 A	G-5-730 N125CA N792H N2SG N600LS N448CC N730CJ
259020	NA1008 A	G-5-723 N676BA N520QS N520LR (N405FF)
259021	B/A	G-5-736 G-BUKW XA-GRB N5794J VR-CMZ VP-CMZ N137RP N401FF HB-VOQ
259022	B	G-5-734 VH-LMP
259023	NA1010 A	G-5-729 (VH-...) N679BA N523QS N523LR XA-FRC
259024	B	G-5-737 G-BUIX N5ES N263R N524QS N524LR A6-ELB N524LR (G-WWDB) ZS-ABG ZS-CFA N524LR
259025	B	G-5-759 (5N-...) G-BVDL N292H N525QS N501LR N770RG
259026	B	G-5-743 ZS-CCT ZS-ACT N9026 G-GDEZ P4-MAF G-GDEZ F-HMED
259027	B	G-5-746 5H-BLM G-BVLO N333RL N333RU N333RL
259028	B	G-5-749 D-CBWW N46WC N46WE
259029	B	G-5-751 G-BUNW EK-B021+ EZ-B021
259030	B/A	G-5-753 G-BUPL G-DCCI N530QS N430LR LN-SUU HB-VOO N271V [cx 08Oct15; wfu]
259031	B/A	G-5-754 G-BUUY G-HJCB N301PH N301PE N301PB N777VC N511BK
259032	B/A	G-5-760 ZS-NHL F-WQAU G-BWCB VR-CXX VP-CXX N401LS N300LS N850TC N850FC XC-LNC N850FC N70PJ XA-PAG
259033	A	G-5-756 N684BA N850BL N533QS N533LR
259034	B	G-5-761 G-BUWX N290H N81HH G-GMAB
259035	A	G-5-773 N160BA N535QS N525LR N567CL
259036	A	G-5-762 N161BA N1AB N127RP (N402FF) N600MV (N767CJ)
259037	B	G-5-771 G-SCCC G-SHEC XA-TGK XA-RGG G-FINK M-FINK
259038	A	G-5-776 N167BA N125GM N107RP N403FF N67WE
259039	A	G-5-781 N169BA N539QS N539LR
259040	A	G-5-783 N22UP N540QS N540LR N904H*
259041	A	G-5-785 (N937H) N936H N541QS N541LR
259042	A	G-5-789 N941H N542QS N542LR N888GJ
259043		G-5-794 N948H [first Hawker 1000] (N543QS) TC-AKH (N881JT) XA-RYB N698DC (N117CP) N8888H (N626PM)
259044		G-5-797 N956H N544QS N544LR
259045		G-5-801 (N296H) N545QS (N545LR) N207R N207K
259046		G-5-805 N962H N546QS N546LR
259047		G-5-817 N296H N547QS N547LR
259048		G-5-826 N802H N548QS N548LR
259049		G-5-837 N679H N549QS N549LR
259050		G-5-846 N550QS N150LR
259051		G-5-859 N551QS N551LR N880LT
259052		G-5-863 N552QS N552LR N800WD

Production complete

125 NA NUMBER DECODE

NA	C/n	NA	C/n	NA	C/n	NA	C/n	NA	C/n
NA700	25134	NA764	25262	NA0247	257065	NA0311	257159	NA0427	258140
NA701	25136	NA765	25263	NA0248	257066	NA0312	257162	NA0428	258138
NA702	25137	NA766	25265	NA0249	257068	NA0313	257153	NA0429	258141
NA703	25139	NA767	25267	NA0250	257069	NA0314	257164	NA0430	258142
NA704	25141	NA768	25273	NA0251	257071	NA0315	257165	NA0431	258144
NA705	25142	NA769	25275	NA0252	257072	NA0316	257167	NA0432	258145
NA706	25146	NA770	25276	NA0253	257074	NA0317	257168	NA0433	258147
NA707	25160	NA771	25278	NA0254	257075	NA0318	257170	NA0434	258150
NA708	25161	NA772	25279	NA0255	257077	NA0319	257171	NA0435	258157
NA709	25163	NA773	25280	NA0256	257078	NA0320	257173	NA0436	258160
NA710	25170	NA774	25281	NA0257	257080	NA0321	257174	NA0437	258161
NA711	25173	NA775	25282	NA0258	257081	NA0322	257176	NA0438	258162
NA712	25174	NA776	25283	NA0259	257083	NA0323	257161	NA0439	258166
NA713	25175	NA777	25284	NA0260	257084	NA0324	257177	NA0440	258168
NA714	25176	NA778	25285	NA0261	257086	NA0325	257143	NA0441	258170
NA715	25179	NA779	25286	NA0262	257087	NA0326	257144	NA0442	258171
NA716	25180	NA780	25287	NA0263	257089	NA0327	257179	NA0443	258163
NA717	25183			NA0264	257090	NA0328	257180	NA0444	258172
NA718	25187	NA0201	257002	NA0265	257092	NA0329	257182	NA0445	258174
NA719	25188	NA0202	257003	NA0266	257093	NA0330	257183	NA0446	258175
NA720	25185	NA0203	257005	NA0267	257095	NA0331	257185	NA0447	258173
NA721	25186	NA0204	257006	NA0268	257079	NA0332	257186	NA0448	258179
NA722	25190	NA0205	257008	NA0269	257098	NA0333	257188	NA0449	258178
NA723	25191	NA0206	257009	NA0270	257099	NA0334	257195	NA0450	258181
NA724	25192	NA0207	257011	NA0271	257110	NA0335	257198	NA0451	258183
NA725	25193	NA0208	257012	NA0272	257101	NA0336	257191	NA0452	258185
NA726	25195	NA0209	257014	NA0273	257104	NA0337	257192	NA0453	258187
NA727	25196	NA0210	257015	NA0274	257105	NA0338	257193	NA0454	258188
NA728	25198	NA0211	257017	NA0275	257106	NA0339	257145	NA0455	258189
NA729	25200	NA0212	257018	NA0276	257096	NA0340	257199	NA0456	258191
NA730	25201	NA0213	257019	NA0277	257111	NA0341	257201	NA0457	258193
NA731	25202	NA0214	257021	NA0278	257108	NA0342	257202	NA0458	258195
NA732	25203	NA0215	257023	NA0279	257113	NA0343	257204	NA0459	258196
NA733	25204	NA0216	257016	NA0280	257102	NA0344	257206	NA0460	258199
NA734	25205	NA0217	257024	NA0281	257114	NA0345	257207	NA0461	258200
NA735	25206	NA0218	257004	NA0282	257116	NA0346	257208	NA0462	258202
NA736	25207	NA0219	257026	NA0283	257117	NA0347	257210	NA0463	258203
NA737	25208	NA0220	257027	NA0284	257119			NA0464	258204
NA738	25210	NA0221	257029	NA0285	257120	NA0401	258100	NA0465	258205
NA739	25211	NA0222	257030	NA0286	257121	NA0402	258101	NA0466	258206
NA740	25212	NA0223	257032	NA0287	257122	NA0403	258102	NA0467	258207
NA741	25213	NA0224	257033	NA0288	257123	NA0404	258103	NA0468	258209
NA742	25214	NA0225	257035	NA0289	257125	NA0405	258104	NA0469	258216
NA743	25216	NA0226	257036	NA0290	257126	NA0406	258105	NA0470	258217
NA744	25218	NA0227	257038	NA0291	257128	NA0407	258107	NA0471	258218
NA745	25220	NA0228	257039	NA0292	257129	NA0408	258108	NA0472	258220
NA746	25221	NA0229	257041	NA0293	257131	NA0409	258111	NA0473	258221
NA747	25222	NA0230	257042	NA0294	257132	NA0410	258113	NA0474	258223
NA748	25224	NA0231	257044	NA0295	257134	NA0411	258114	NA0475	258225
NA749	25225	NA0232	257043	NA0296	257135	NA0412	258117		
NA750	25226	NA0233	257047	NA0297	257137	NA0413	258119	NA1000	259005
NA751	25228	NA0234	257048	NA0298	257138	NA0414	258121	NA1001	259006
NA752	25229	NA0235	257050	NA0299	257140	NA0415	258122	NA1002	259009
NA753	25230	NA0236	257051	NA0300	257141	NA0416	258123	NA1003	259011
NA754	25232	NA0237	257052	NA0301	257146	NA0417	258124	NA1004	259013
NA755	25233	NA0238	257053	NA0302	257149	NA0418	258125	NA1005	259014
NA756	25234	NA0239	257049	NA0303	257147	NA0419	258126	NA1006	259015
NA757	25236	NA0240	257045	NA0304	257148	NA0420	258127	NA1007	259019
NA758	25239	NA0241	257056	NA0305	257150	NA0421	258128	NA1008	259020
NA759	25241	NA0242	257057	NA0306	257152	NA0422	258132	NA1009	259010
NA760	25244	NA0243	257059	NA0307	257154	NA0423	258135	NA1010	259023
NA761	25237	NA0244	257060	NA0308	257155	NA0424	258136		
NA762	25245	NA0245	257058	NA0309	257156	NA0425	258137		
NA763	25261	NA0246	257063	NA0310	257157	NA0426	258139		

HAWKER 750/900XP FUSELAGE NUMBER DECODE

Airbus UK at Chester, in its capacity as Hawker Beechcraft's fuselage contractor, continues to use the old HS/BAe 6-digit numbering system for the fuselages it builds for the Hawker 750, 900XP and special-order 850XP. These are then given new aircraft c/ns by Hawker Beechcraft after arrival at Wichita/Beech Field. Tie-ups known to us are as follows:

Fuselage	C/n	Fuselage	C/n	Fuselage	C/n	Fuselage	C/n	Fuselage	C/n
258849	HA-0005	258884	HA-0029	258919	HB-6	258954	tba	258989	HA-0088
258850	HB-1	258885	HA-0030	2258920	HA-0051	258955	HA-0070	258990	HA-0089
258851	HA-0006	258886	HA-0031	258921	258921	258956	tba		
258852	258852	258887	HA-0032	258922	HA-0052	258957	HA-0071	259100	HB-33
258853	HA-0007	258888	HA-0033	258923	HB-7	258958	258977	259101	HA-0091
258854	HA-0008	258889	HA-0034	258924	HA-0053	258959	HA-0072	259102	HB-31
258855	258855	258890	HA-0035	258925	HB-8	258960	HB-20	259103	HA-0092
258856	258856	258891	258891	258926	HA-0054	258961	HA-0073	259104	HA-0100
258857	HA-0009	258892	HA-0036	258927	HA-0056	258962	HA-0074	259105	HB-32
258858	258858	258893	258893	258928	HA-0055	258963	258980	259106	HA-0093
258859	258859	258894	HA-0037	258929	HB-9	258964	HB-21	259107	HA-0096
258860	HA-0010	258895	258895	258930	HB-10	258965	258982	259108	
258861	258861	258896	HA-0038	258931	HA-0057	258966	HA-0075	259109	HA-0102
258862	HA-0011	258897	HA-0039	258932	HB-11	258967	HB-22	259110	HB-30
258863	HA-0012	258898	HA-0040	258933	HA-0058	258968	HA-0076	259111	HA-0097
258864	HA-0013	258899	HA-0041	258934	HB-12	258969	HB-23	259112	HA-0098
258865	HA-0014	258900	258900	258935	HA-0059	258970	HA-0077	259113	HA-0095
258866	HA-0015	258901	258901	258936	HB-13	258971	HB-24	259114	
258867	HA-0016	258902	HA-0042	258937	HA-0060	258972	HA-0078	259115	HA-0099
258868	HA-0017	258903	HA-0043	258938	HB-14	258973	HA-0087	259116	HA-0101
258869	HA-0018	258904	258904	258939	HA-0061	258974	HB-25	259117	
258870	HA-0019	258905	HB-3	258940	HA-0062	258975	HA-0079	259118	HA-0106
258871	HA-0020	258906	HA-0044	258941	HB-15	258976	HB-27	259119	HB-34
258872	258872	258907	258907	258942	HA-0063	258977	HB-26	259120	HA-0103
258873	HA-0021	258908	HA-0045	258943	HA-0064	258978	HA-0081	259121	HA-0108
258874	258874	258909	258909	258944	tba	258979	HA-0082	259122	
258875	HA-0022	258910	HA-0046	258945	tba	258980	HA-0080	259123	
258876	258876	258911	HA-0047	258946	tba	258981	HA-0083	259124	HA-0104
258877	HA-0023	258912	258912	258947	tba	258982	HA-0094	259125	HA-0105
258878	HB-2	258913	HB-4	258948	tba	258983	HB-28	259126	
258879	HA-0024	258914	HA-0048	258949	tba	258984	HA-0084	259127	
258880	HA-0025	258915	258915	258950	tba	258985	HA-0090	259128	
258881	HA-0026	258916	HA-0049	258951	tba	258986	HA-0085	259129	
258882	HA-0027	258917	HB-5	258952	tba	258987	HB-29		
258883	HA-0028	258918	HA-0050	258953	tba	258988	HA-0086		

The fuselages numbered 258944 to 258954 inclusive and 258956 were used in the construction of Hawker 900XPs c/n HA-0065 to HA-0069 inclusive, Hawker 750s c/n HB-16 to HB-19 inclusive and Hawker 850XPs c/n 258959, 258961 and 258963 – but their tie-ups remain unknown at present.

Numbers 258991 to 259099 were not used to avoid any clash with the old BAe.125-1000 construction numbers.

HAWKER 4000

The Hawker 4000 was originally known as the Hawker Horizon.

C/n	Identities							
RC-1	N4000R	[ff 11Aug01; wfu Wichita/Beech Field, KS; cx 23Nov15]						
RC-2	N802HH	[ff 10May02]						
RC-3	N803HH	[wfu, cx 29Jun09]						
RC-4	N804HH	[ff 29Apr04]						
RC-5	N805HH	(N974JD)	[wfu Wichita/Beech Field, KS]					
RC-6	(N806HH)	N15QS	N607HB	[cx 31Jan14; wfu]				
RC-7	(N807HH)	N7007Q	N711GD	N700JE*				
RC-8	(N808HH)	N803SA	N715CJ					
RC-9	(N809HH)	N119AK	N508CK					
RC-10	(N810HH)	N126ZZ	N7567T					
RC-11	N974JD	N119AK						
RC-12	N400MR	ZS-DTD	N400MR					
RC-13	N413HB	(ZS-PPR)	N440HB	XA-MMA				
RC-14	N514HB	VP-BCM	LV-CNW					
RC-15	N515HB	ZS-DDT	N115HB	XA-NOI				
RC-16	N455BP	(N988DT)	N699AK					
RC-17	N61407	N408U						
RC-18	N163DK	N163DE	N86LF					
RC-19	N419HB	N163DK						
RC-20	N50QS	N420HB	N899AK					
RC-21	N621HB	(ZK-ABC)	A6-SHH	Pakistan HBC21	N23EA	A6-SHH	AP-SHH	N529AK
RC-22	N10QS	(N422HB)	N339RA	N639RA				
RC-23	N423HB	ZS-ZOT	N230JE					
RC-24	N35004	N995BE	N269LB	N400VR*				
RC-25	N3185G	(VT-VIP)	N143RL					
RC-26	N3186N	VT-HJA						
RC-27	N3187N	(N36QS)	M-KENF					
RC-28	N25QS	N979TM						
RC-29	N14QS	N901SG	N77KV					
RC-30	N830TS	(N921HA)						
RC-31	N12QS	N78KN	N78KX	N31JE				
RC-32	N3502N	N984JC	(N24EA)	Pakistan EYE77	N786ZS	N729JF		
RC-33	N3433T	N440MB	N441MB	N614DJ				
RC-34	N3194F	M-PAUL	G-PROO					
RC-35	N986JC							
RC-36	N616EA	XA-UQZ						
RC-37	N3197H	N33VC						
RC-38	N438HB	5N-NOC						
RC-39	N439HB	N71956						
RC-40	N40VK	XA-ATT	N40RQ					
RC-41	N41HV	(CS-DYA)	VT-VDM					
RC-42	N40QS	N542HB	(CS-DYB)	N349AK				
RC-43	N60143	(CS-DYC)	B-3908	N2KL				
RC-44	N63744	(CS-DYD)	TC-NRN					
RC-45	N6005V	B-3907	N35NP	N51NP				
RC-46	N446HB	N223AF	LX-LOE					
RC-47	N447HB	N402SE						
RC-48	N448HB	XA-CHG	XA-UUG	N480JE				
RC-49	N449HB	B-3910						
RC-50	N950HB	N412TF	(N412TE)	N559AK*				
RC-51	N451HB	M-ABDL	[cx 09May16; broken up]					
RC-52	N452HB	N339RA						
RC-53	N453HB	N453JE						
RC-54	N454HB	N837RE						
RC-55	N6455T	B-3906	N3663T					
RC-56	N984JC	N560RC	ZS-DDT					
RC-57	N457HB	VQ-BRI	OY-JJJ					
RC-58	N158HB	N900ST						
RC-59	N459HB	N117DS	(LV-CWY)	LV-FWC*				
RC-60	N460HB	N860AP						
RC-61	N461HB	N796RM						
RC-62	N8062L	N21FX						
RC-63	N6380H	(OE-HYN)	N46WC					
RC-64	N464HB	N446CC						
RC-65	N465HB	N243PC						
RC-66	N466HB	5N-FGX						
RC-67	N467HB	N826GA						
RC-68	N68HB							
RC-69	N8139T	9H-BOA	(N454RR)	N621TF				
RC-70	N470HB	I-MPGA						
RC-71	N871HB	XA-BUD						
RC-72	N872HB	N713AK						
RC-73	N473HB							
RC-74	N474HB	N411TF						
RC-75	N875HB							
RC-76	N476HB	AP-RRR						

Production complete. The following aircraft also had marks assigned in anticipation of being built.

RC-77	(N477HB)
RC-78	(N478HB)
RC-79	(N179HB)

BOMBARDIER BD-100 CHALLENGER 300/350

The Challenger 300 was originally called the Continental.

C/n	Identities							
20001	C-GJCJ	[ff 14Aug01] [converted to Challenger 350 prototype 2013]						
20002	C-GJCF	[cx 22Aug06, wfu]						
20003	C-GIPX	N303CZ						
20004	C-GJCV	OE-HPK	D-BFJE	N214SG				
20005	C-GIPZ	N850EJ	C-GIPZ					
20006	N5014F	N505FX	N505BX	VT-PIL				
20007	N506FX	XA-JGT						
20008	C-GZDV	N507FX	N507BX	N508XJ				
20009	C-GZDY	N508FX	N306MF					
20010	C-GZEB	N41DP						
20011	C-GZED	N300LJ	(N311DB)	N17UC	N17UE	N228PK		
20012	C-GZEH	N509FX	PR-WSC	N862VP				
20013	C-GZEI	N315LJ	I-SDFC					
20014	C-GZEJ	N27MX	XA-JCP	M-OZZA	(M-DMCD)			
20015	C-GZEM	N115LJ	A6-SMS	N300SM	(N309SM)	A6-SAM	N300SM	PR-BSN	G-LEAZ
20016	C-GZEO	N316LJ	N777VC	C-GFHR				
20017	C-GZEP	N510FX	M-EANS					
20018	C-GZER	N84ZC	N74ZC					
20019	C-GZES	N319RG	N60SB					
20020	C-GZET	N789MB	N828SK	(N630MT)	N905MT			
20021	C-GZDQ	N511FX	N31CA					
20022	C-GZDS	N512FX	HB-JFM	N565RX	N941JR			
20023	C-GZDV	N513FX	N514FX	M-YFLY	G-MRAP	N39ER		
20024	C-GZDY	C-FAUZ	(N515FX)	N184R	XA-CHC			
20025	C-GZEB	N125LJ	EC-JEG	N375WB	N375RF	N497EC	N555GE	
20026	C-GZED	C-FDHV	N26FA	N604RF				
20027	C-GZEH	N448AS	N448CL	N596MC				
20028	C-GZEI	(N328RC)	C-FDIA	N328CC	N121LM			
20029	C-GZEJ	N129LJ	HB-JEC					
20030	C-GZEM	C-FDIH	N300BZ	N30BZ	N430SK			
20031	C-GZEO	N131LJ	N411ST	N411SF	N93NS			
20032	C-GZEP	C-FDIJ	N515FX	N520RP				
20033	C-GZER	C-FCMG	OE-HRR					
20034	C-GZES	C-FCXJ	ZS-ACT					
20035	C-GZET	N900WY						
20036	C-GZDQ	N516FX	N536XJ					
20037	C-GZDS	N885TW						
20038	C-GZDV	(ZS-SCT)	(ZS-ACT)	N517FX				
20039	C-GZDY	N139LJ	HB-JEU	OE-HNL	N847CA	PP-NOC	N724SJ	N727SJ*
20040	C-GZEB	N1967M	N234DP					
20041	C-GZED	N141LJ	VP-CLV	N1870G				
20042	C-GZEH	C-FDSR	A7-AAN	A7-CEC	N550LF	M-BTLT	(D-BHRN)	D-BTLT
20043	C-FCZS	N143LJ	N818KC	XA-GXG				
20044	C-FDSZ	ZS-YES	N74WL	SP-ZSZ				
20045	N145LJ	N618R	N303WS					
20046	N518FX							
20047	C-FEUQ	OE-HPZ	N293KR	N557XJ				
20048	C-FDXU	A6-RJM	N348TS	N70CR				
20049	C-FFZI	N1980Z						
20050	C-FEPU	N350TG	A6-KNH	M-AKVI	M-MTOO			
20051	C-FCZN	C-FFLJ	N424TM	N400CH				
20052	C-FCZV	N606XT						
20053	C-GZDY	C-FGBP	N353PC					
20054	N302EM	N97SH	N1CF					
20055	C-GZEI	C-FFZE	N519FX					
20056	C-GZES	C-FGMR	N520FX					
20057	C-GDZQ	C-FGGF	N521FX					
20058	C-GZDV	C-FGJI	N300DG	(N380DG)				
20059	C-FDAH	C-FGNO	N620JF	N659JF	N304PS			
20060	C-GZEB	C-FGUT	N228N	(N372N)				
20061	C-GZEO	C-FGUD	N422CP	N422CR	N415NG			
20062	C-GZER	N888CN	N300MY					
20063	C-GZET	N363CL						
20064	C-GZDS	C-FGXW	N522FX					
20065	C-FFNT	4X-CPV	OE-HDD	RA-67224				
20066	C-FCZM	C-FGXK	N866TM					
20067	C-FCZS	C-FGZI	N304BC	N300BC				
20068	C-GZEM	C-FGZE	N303EM	N247FS				
20069	C-GZEP	C-FGZD	N987HP					
20070	C-FGYU	N78TC						
20071	C-FGFB	D-BTIM	N371TS	D-BSMI	9H-SMI			
20072	N724SC							
20073	C-FHDN	N731DC	(N731BF)	N1RB				
20074	C-FHDE	N523FX						
20075	C-FHCY	N575WB	N487JA					
20076	C-FGBY	N54HA						
20077	C-FGCD	N304EM						
20078	C-FGCE	"XA-FRO"	[painted in error at completion centre] XA-FRD		M-NYJT	C-GNBN	N285KR	N578XJ
20079	C-FGCJ	D-BETA	OE-HOO					
20080	C-FGCL	N960CR						
20081	C-FGCN	N845UP	N845UR	N801PH				
20082	C-FGCV	N594CA						
20083	C-FGCW	N555DH	N31112	N1DH	N906TC	N903TC	N906TC	N300DH
20084	C-FGCX	XA-GPR						
20085	C-FGCZ	N42GJ						
20086	C-FGVJ	N846UP	N846UR	N806PH				
20087	C-FGVK	N387PC	N924TC					
20088	C-FGVM	N130CH	N723JA	N727FJ				
20089	C-FGVS	N71FA	N605RF					
20090	C-FGWB	N55HA	N300RL					
20091	C-FGWF	N391W						
20092	C-FGWL	N500AL	N300AV					

BOMBARDIER BD-100 CHALLENGER 300

C/n	Identities					
20093	C-FGWR	C-FDOL	C-FDOJ	N618KG		
20094	C-FGWW	I-CCCH	OE-HDU			
20095	C-FGWZ	N524FX				
20096	C-FHMI	C-GPCZ	G-MEGP	M-EVAN		
20097	C-FHMM	LX-PMA				
20098	C-FHMQ	N305EM				
20099	C-FHMS	N991GS	N910CL			
20100	C-FHMZ	(N928MC)	VP-CAO	N456KT		
20101	C-FHNC	N306EM				
20102	C-FHND	N555TF	N926AG	N128TS		
20103	C-FHNF	N926JR				
20104	C-FHNH	N125TM				
20105	C-FHNJ	N56HA	N788MM			
20106	C-FIDX	G-KALS				
20107	C-FIDZ	C-FGIL	C-FGIK	C-FEDG		
20108	C-FIDU	N388WS	N365MC			
20109	C-FIDV	N955H				
20110	C-FIEA	C-GESO	N61TF			
20111	C-FIED	OE-HII				
20112	C-FIEE	N525FX				
20113	C-FIEM	N985FM				
20114	C-FIEP	C-FCSI				
20115	C-FIOB	N57HA	(N197JS)			
20116	C-FIOC	D-BADO				
20117	C-FIOE	N211TB	N202DH			
20118	C-FIOG	N526FX				
20119	C-FIOH	N214RW	N214PW	N307BL	N963EC	
20120	C-FIOJ	N15GT				
20121	C-FIOK	N963RS	N963RB	N104FT	N729JM	
20122	C-FION	N5262				
20123	C-FIOO	N592SP	D-BFLY	M-BFLY	N723MC	
20124	C-FIOP	N527FX				
20125	C-FJQD	N528FX				
20126	C-FJQH	3B-SSD	VQ-BMJ	TC-AFF		
20127	C-FJQP	N297MC				
20128	C-FJQR	N529FX				
20129	C-FJQT	N660AL	N300LV*			
20130	C-FJQX	N300KH				
20131	C-FJQZ	N390DB				
20132	C-FJRE	N518GS				
20133	C-FJRG	3B-NGT	N433DC	M-OIWA	T7-AAB	
20134	C-FLCY	N600LS	N609LS			
20135	C-FLDD	9M-TAN	9M-TST			
20136	C-FLDK	TC-SCR	N37TL	SE-RMA		
20137	C-FLDO	N301TG	HB-JFO	M-ASRY	N318JS	
20138	C-FLDW	N247SS	N12SS	(N812SS)	TC-ISR	N238FJ	N81SF
20139	C-FLDX	N610LS	N848CS			
20140	C-FLEC	VP-CDV				
20141	C-FLEJ	N341TS	LN-AIR	HB-JTB	T7-SIS	
20142	C-FLEK	(N888UD)	N605UK	N228KT	N786FG*	
20143	C-FLEN	N300FS	N593HR			
20144	C-FLQF	N629GB	N302PE			
20145	C-FLQG	D-BUBI				
20146	C-FLQH	N58HA				
20147	C-FLQM	(N600LS)	N480CB			
20148	C-FLQO	N530FX				
20149	C-FLQP	TC-KAR	N377RA	N377MD		
20150	C-FLQR	N531FX				
20151	C-FLQX	M-NEWT	N223TV			
20152	C-FLQY	N487F	N717JJ			
20153	C-FLQZ	N772JS				
20154	C-FMYA	N532FX				
20155	C-FMYB	OH-FLM	N375MH	N197JS		
20156	C-FMXX	N895BB				
20157	C-FMXW	N296SB	N300NB			
20158	C-FMXU	N797CB				
20159	C-FMXQ	LX-TQJ	N70RL	C-GHZD	N70RL	
20160	C-FMXK	N533FX				
20161	C-FMXH	N534FX				
20162	C-FMWX	N888RT	N808RT	N825CT		
20163	C-FMWG	N58LC				
20164	C-FNUH	N782BJ				
20165	C-FOAE	N120GS	N818RC			
20166	C-FOAI	N166CL	N225AR	N697AH		
20167	C-FOAJ	N535FX				
20168	C-FOAQ	(PR-MDB)	PR-IDB	N777MS		
20169	C-FOAT	G-UYGB	A9C-DAR	C-FMHL	C-GMHV	
20170	C-FOMU	C-FOAU	N3975A			
20171	C-FPMQ	N536FX				
20172	C-FPMU	M-TAGB	D-BAVA	RA-67223		
20173	C-FOBJ	RA-67217				
20174	C-FOQR	VT-RAK				
20175	C-FOQW	5A-UAA				
20176	C-FORB	VP-BEK	N287KR	N81CR		
20177	C-FOSB	N896BB				
20178	C-FOSG	PP-BIR	N19DD			
20179	C-FOSM	D-BSKY	M-BSKY	OE-HEO	N716WW	
20180	C-FOSQ	N269MJ				
20181	C-FOSW	TC-ARB				
20182	C-FOSX	C-GRCY				
20183	C-FOTF	N313DS				
20184	C-FPZZ	N384RV				
20185	C-FQCF	N329CH				
20186	C-FQEI	N725CF	N300GM	N330GM	N993MC	N874WD
20187	C-FQOA	N537FX	N155SL			

BOMBARDIER BD-100 CHALLENGER 300

C/n	Identities				
20188	C-FQOF	N414DH	N414DY	N503KJ	
20189	C-FQOI	G-KSFR			
20190	C-FQOK	(TC-THY)	N235AF	N335AF	
20191	C-FQOL	XA-LLA	N585LE		
20192	C-FQOM	C-FJCB	N86DQ		
20193	C-FQOQ	N794RC			
20194	C-FRQA	N194LE	N228Y	N228L	
20195	C-FRQC	N300AH	N632FW		
20196	C-FRQH	VT-JSE			
20197	C-FRQK	N480BA			
20198	C-FRQM	N202XT			
20199	C-FRQN	N703VZ			
20200	C-FRQP	OE-HVJ	N807JD	XA-ARO	
20201	C-FROY	N538FX			
20202	C-FSMO	N539FX	N360PA		
20203	C-FSMW	LN-SOL	XA-DLA		
20204	C-FSNB	N552KF	N302R		
20205	C-FSNP	N540FX			
20206	C-FSNQ	M-NOEL	D-BIVI	M-NOEL	D-BIVI	N763MT
20207	C-FSNU	N746E			
20208	C-FSLL	N729SB	PP-BIC		
20209	C-FSLR	(OH-ZIP)	N184BK		
20210	C-FSLU	N752M			
20211	C-FTKA	N541FX			
20212	C-FTKC	D-BAVB			
20213	C-FTKH	N300LJ	N537XJ		
20214	C-FTKG	OE-HVV	C-GDIK	N214BL	N166WC
20215	C-FTKK	N215BL	RP-C8215		
20216	C-FUBE	N97DK			
20217	C-FUBK	N542FX			
20218	C-FUBM	LX-VPG	TC-VPG		
20219	C-FUBO	LV-BSS			
20220	C-FUBP	N101UD	N205FP		
20221	C-FUBQ	D-BANN			
20222	C-FUBT	OE-HRM	N876DG		
20223	C-FUJA	N229BP			
20224	C-FUJE	N538XJ			
20225	C-FUJM	N7000C			
20226	C-FUJR	OE-HAP	N115LF		
20227	C-FUJT	OE-HAB			
20228	C-FUJX	N30XC	N56BA		
20229	C-FURA	N147AG	N1013		
20230	C-FURB	N539XJ			
20231	C-FURC	N742E			
20232	C-FURD	OE-HAA	(D-BREA)	N320VA	XA-OVA
20233	C-FURF	TC-CMK	C-FURF	M-HSNT	
20234	C-FURH	N825TB			
20235	C-FVNB	RA-67221			
20236	C-FVNC	(I-STEF)	S5-ADE		
20237	C-FVND	HB-JGQ			
20238	C-FVNF	N540XJ	C-FLDD		
20239	C-FVNI	N541XJ	N584D		
20240	C-FVNL	N544FX	N347K		
20241	C-FVNS	N801EL			
20242	C-FVNT	N542XJ	C-FKCI		
20243	C-FVLX	EC-LES	N243RC		
20244	C-FVLZ	N300BY	N301PE		
20245	C-FWUZ	N543XJ	C-FYUQ	C-GJEI	
20246	C-FWUT				
20247	C-FWUO	N402EF			
20248	C-FWUL	N544XJ	N217GH		
20249	C-FWUK	N138CH	(N130CH)		
20250	C-FWUI	N999ND			
20251	C-FWUC	OY-EKS	OE-HPG		
20252	C-FWRE	CS-TFV			
20253	C-FWRG	N545XJ	N300GP		
20254	C-FWRX	N7100C			
20255	C-FWTK	VP-BJT			
20256	C-FWTQ	VP-CPF			
20257	C-FWTY	C-FFBC	N905BA	C-FKXF	N905BA	N694PD
20258	C-FWVH	N672BP	N828SK		
20259	C-FXPB	N83JJ	N57SK		
20260	C-FXPI	(N546XJ)	C-GFCB		
20261	C-FXPL	OE-HDV	YR-TRC		
20262	C-FXPQ	N254DV			
20263	C-FXPR	N526AC			
20264	C-FXPT	N40QG	N44QG	N300TU	
20265	C-FXPW	N265K			
20266	C-FYBG	N411ST	N423JG		
20267	C-FYBJ	N302K			
20268	C-FLDD	C-FYBZ	N1967M	N268CL	N270GP
20269	C-FYBM	N295SG	N508SN		
20270	C-FYBN	N800BD			
20271	C-FYBO	M-CLAB			
20272	C-FYBS	(D-BPWR)	D-BCLA	N551FX	
20273	C-FYBU	VT-JUA	N321GX		
20274	C-FYBV	OE-HCA			
20275	C-FZLX	D-BEKP			
20276	C-FZLY	OE-HMK	N626PS		
20277	C-FZLZ	M-ABCM			
20278	C-GAKE	N545XJ			
20279	C-GAKF	N541XJ			
20280	C-GAKL	N546XJ			
20281	C-GAKN	N547XJ			
20282	C-GAKO	N710DL			

BOMBARDIER BD-100 CHALLENGER 300

C/n	Identities				
20283	C-GAKZ	N307EM			
20284	C-GBZE	(OE-HEP)	M-EDOK	N284JC	TC-RZA
20285	C-GBZI	N808XT			
20286	C-GBZL	N272BC	N286EC		
20287	C-GBZV	N301MB	C-GVFX		
20288	C-GBXZ	F-HAKP	N430WC		
20289	C-GDTF	(OE-HIX)	N711NA	N711NK	
20290	C-GDTQ	N290CL			
20291	C-GDUH	N520CC			
20292	C-GDUJ	N725N			
20293	C-GEVU	N160SB			
20294	C-GEVW	(N845CA)	OE-HLL		
20295	C-GEVX	SP-CON	P4-AMR		
20296	C-GFIA	C-FDOL			
20297	C-GFIG	N612JN			
20298	C-GFIH	N334EC			
20299	C-GFVL	N7670B			
20300	C-GFVN	N830EC			
20301	C-GFVT	N548XJ			
20302	C-GFUF	N545FX			
20303	C-GFUG	B-8106	N88RC		
20304	C-GFUI	N215DA			
20305	C-GFUM	N305CL	N160WC		
20306	C-GIIR	N877RF	N510AF		
20307	C-GIIU	N860SB			
20308	C-GIJP	N219RW	N214RW		
20309	C-GIJZ	N80HD			
20310	C-GJCO	B-8190	OE-HDC		
20311	C-GJCQ	B-8191	N863VP	PP-MQS	
20312	C-GJCX	N300GM	N993JL		
20313	C-GJRG	N670CP			
20314	C-GJSO	M-LIFE	OE-HHH		
20315	C-GJSY	B-8233			
20316	C-GJUZ	N464GR	N463GR		
20317	C-GJVG	OE-HBA			
20318	C-GJVL	N583D			
20319	C-GJVO	N546FX	N1897A		
20320	C-GKIO	B-8192			
20321	C-GKIP	B-8193			
20322	C-GKIU	N549XJ			
20323	C-GKIV	N550XJ			
20324	C-GKIX	N551XJ			
20325	C-GKIY	PR-ADB			
20326	C-GKXH	N595CB			
20327	C-GKXK	N93LA			
20328	C-GKXL	N70FS	(N328CF)		
20329	C-GKXM	N552XJ			
20330	C-GKXN	N293HC			
20331	C-GLKX	N625EL			
20332	C-GLKY	ZS-JDL	N332CG		
20333	C-GLKZ	N108LT			
20334	C-GLLF	OH-STP	OY-SPB		
20335	C-GLLJ	OE-HGL			
20336	C-GLLY	N300KE			
20337	C-GMIC	N3337H	N3337J		
20338	C-GMIV	OE-HZP	N906BP		
20339	C-GMJY	PR-FMW			
20340	C-GMIQ	N300BZ			
20341	C-GMUV	N547FX			
20342	C-GMUW	N300RY	N548FX		
20343	C-GMUX	N311CJ	N406BJ		
20344	C-GMUY	N88HD			
20345	C-GMVD	N19UC	N17UC		
20346	C-GNPT	B-8115			
20347	C-GNPY	N399NC			
20348	C-GNPZ	XA-NTG			
20349	C-GNQA	N607RP			
20350	C-GNQD	B-8116			
20351	C-GNXF	N301JL			
20352	C-GNXH	N21FE			
20353	C-GNXK	N300CY	N200JB		
20354	C-GNXN	N354WG			
20355	C-GNXQ	N24FE			
20356	C-GOIE	VT-RSP			
20357	C-GOIF	OE-HDT	OE-HDI		
20358	C-GOIH	N26FE			
20359	C-GOII	N334AF			
20360	C-GOIJ	N1CA			
20361	C-GOQJ	N28FE			
20362	C-GOQN	N1HP			
20363	C-GOZK	N167RD			
20364	C-GPDU	C-GSUT	C-GSUN		
20365	C-GPEQ	N313V			
20366	C-GPEV	N310VZ			
20367	C-GPEW	XB-NBJ	XA-EZI		
20368	C-GPFI	C-GPDQ			
20369	C-GPFU	N358MY			
20370	C-GPGB	N26DE			
20371	C-GRJQ	N371HA			
20372	C-GRJU	N608RP			
20373	C-GRJV	N300EU			
20374	C-GRKJ	N549FX			
20375	C-GOVY	N91HK			
20376	C-GOWC	N1RH			
20377	C-GOWO	N377DP			

BOMBARDIER BD-100 CHALLENGER 300

C/n	Identities			
20378	C-GOWQ	N707JC		
20379	C-GOWY	N305WM		
20380	C-GOXA	N982JC	N60AD*	
20381	C-GOXB	C-GUOO	C-FGGF	
20382	C-GOXD	N528YT		
20383	C-GOXG	ZS-JPO		
20384	C-GOXM	C-FAJC		
20385	C-GOXN	N300KC		
20386	C-GOXR	N386JC		
20387	C-GOXU	PT-STU		
20388	C-GOXV	VP-CAG		
20389	C-GOXW	N302KC		
20390	C-GOXZ	N304KC		
20391	C-GOYD	N550FX		
20392	C-GOYG	N101UR	N101UD N101UR N947WK	
20393	C-GOYL	N59KG		
20394	C-GOYO	PR-RBZ		
20395	C-GUGS	C-GVDS+	[+ marks assigned in error] C-GUGS C-GVLN VT-APF	
20396	C-GUGV	N567HB		
20397	C-GUGY	N300CF	N939SG N300NZ	
20398	C-GUHA	N300JE	N1901W	
20399	C-GUHE	N370EL		
20400	C-GOVY	C-GVVF	M-ARRH	
20401	C-GOWY	G-VCAN	S5-FUN N401FN	
20402	C-GOWQ	YR-NVY	D-BELO	
20403	C-GOXA	LX-AVT		
20404	C-GOWC	C-GWEP	XA-RUA	
20405	C-GOXB	C-GVZL	CN-CTA	
20406	C-GOWO	N406CL		
20407	C-GOXD	N38BK		
20408	C-GUWH	N35FE		
20409	C-GUWP	[Challenger 350 development a/c] N325PE		
20410	C-GOXM	N738E		
20411	C-GOXN	N37FE		
20412	C-GOXR	N39FE		
20413	C-GOXG	N2425		
20414	C-GOXW	N2428		
20415	C-GOXU	N415BE	N85BE	
20416	C-GOXV	C-FSXR		
20417	C-GOXZ	N585D		
20418	C-GOYD	N723JM		
20419	C-GUGY	D-BIGA	N980JC	
20420	C-GUGV	N420MP		
20421	C-GOYL	N690RB		
20422	C-GUHA	N422MP		
20423	C-GOYG	(D-BIGB)	N300AH N992DC	
20424	C-GUGS	C-GWXH	TC-SPL	
20425	C-GOYO	C-GXVW	N425BD N831FJ	
20426	C-GOVY	N300AN	N813DH	
20427	C-GOWY	C-GYJZ	XA-VFV	
20428	C-GOWQ	N300ER		
20429	C-GUHE	N957DT		
20430	C-GOXB	C-GYFH	N300VC N488VC	
20431	C-GOWC	N431EH	N10EH	
20432	C-GOXA	C-GDIL		
20433	C-GOXD	C-GSJK		
20434	C-GOWO	N235EF		
20435	C-GOXN	N796AC		
20436	C-GOXM	N300AY	N777SJ	
20437	C-GUGS	N914GS		
20438	C-GOXR	N218KF		
20439	C-GOXV	N300DY	XA-BOM	
20440	C-GOXW	N300NC		
20441	C-GOXZ	N441CB	HK-5186*	
20442	C-GOXG	N300BU	N945AC	
20443	C-GOXU	N300LE	PR-YOU [dbr in hangar collapse at Sao Paulo/Congonhas, Brazil, 08Jan15]	
20444	C-GOYD	N339PC	N278PC	
20445	C-GOYG	N300HQ		
20446	C-GOYL	N739E		
20447	C-GUGV	N300HK	N228Y	
20448	C-GUGY	N300CF	N773RC	
20449	C-GUHA	OE-HCZ		
20450	C-GOYO	N44MZ	N44M	
20451	C-GUHE	C-GZKH	C-GWWW	
20452	C-GOXB	D-BEAM		
20453	C-GOXD	N453FD		
20454	C-GOVY	N425XF	N425FX	
20455	C-GOWQ	N325TG		
20456	C-GOWY	N43FE		
20457	C-GOXA	N812KC		

Production complete, replaced by the Challenger 350.

BOMBARDIER BD-100 CHALLENGER 350

C/n	Identities			
20501	C-GYTX	N501BZ		
20502	C-GYTY	N762QS		
20503	C-GOXM	C-FEXI	N801KB	
20504	C-GOXN	OE-HRS		
20505	C-GOXR	N350KM		
20506	C-GOXW	N175DP		
20507	C-GUGC	N824DP		
20508	C-GOXG	SP-KHI		
20509	C-GOXZ	N411SF	N411ST	
20510	C-GOYL	N763QS		
20511	C-GUHE	N50LF		
20512	C-GOXV	N101UD		
20513	C-GOYO	9H-VCA		
20514	C-GOXU	9H-VCB		
20515	C-GOYD	N1987	N467MW	
20516	C-GUGV	N414DH		
20517	C-GUGY	N764QS		
20518	C-GOVY	N358JM		
20519	C-GOXB	C-GJDR		
20520	C-GOYG	N350GS		
20521	C-GUHA	N572FX		
20522	C-GOWQ	N352JM		
20523	C-GOWY	N765QS		
20524	C-GOXA	(PT-PTR)	N10EF	
20525	C-GOXD	C-FJHO	OH-ADM	
20526	C-GOXM	N766QS		
20527	C-GOXR	N570FX		
20528	C-GOXW	C-FIZP	PT-PTR	
20529	C-GUGS	N6PG		
20530	C-GOWC	G-SCAR		
20531	C-GOWO	N350MB		
20532	C-GOXV	N7PG		
20533	C-GOXZ	N767QS		
20534	C-GUHE	N768QS		
20535	C-GOXB	9H-VCC		
20536	C-GOXN	N571FX		
20537	C-GOYL	(P4-AGL)	N718CG	N715CG
20538	C-GOXB	9H-VCD		
20539	C-GOXU	N769QS		
20540	C-GOYD	9H-VCE		
20541	C-GOYO	9H-VCF		
20542	C-GUGV	PR-HNG		
20543	C-GUGY	N770QS		
20544	C-GOVY	CS-CHA		
20545	C-GOYG	9H-VCG		
20546	C-GUGS	9H-VCH		
20547	C-GOXA	OE-HUG		
20548	C-GOWC	N422CP		
20549	C-GOWO	C-FKKI	C-FFBC	
20550	C-GOWQ	9H-VCI		
20551	C-GOWY	N772QS		
20552	C-GOXM	N443DB		
20553	C-GOXR	CS-CHB		
20554	C-GUHA	N774QS		
20555	C-GUHE	N659NR		
20556	C-GOXD	ZS-JDL		
20557	C-GOXN	N775QS		
20558	C-GOXV	N776QS		
20559	C-GOXW	N559SA	N100SA	
20560	C-GOXZ	9H-VCJ		
20561	C-GOYD	N782QS		
20562	C-GOYO	N777QS		
20563	C-GOXU	N778QS		
20564	C-GOYL	N573FX		
20565	C-GUGY	N958CR		
20566	C-GOWO	N779QS		
20567	C-GOXB	N574FX		
20568	C-GOXG	N780QS		
20569	C-GOYG	N350VJ		
20570	C-GOVY	N781QS		
20571	C-GOWQ	C-FLOO	N350PH	
20572	C-GOXA	CS-CHC		
20573	C-GOXM	N351VJ		
20574	C-GUGS	N783QS		
20575	C-GUGV	N784QS		
20576	C-GUHA	N352VJ		
20577	C-GOWY	N575MW		
20578	C-GOXN	N575FX		
20579	C-GOXR	C-FKOC	N721PP	
20580	C-GUHE	N580SB	N509SB	
20581	C-GOXU	(D-BRCR)	M-OCNY	
20582	C-GOXV	N350RX		
20583	C-GOYL	D-BHGN		
20584	C-GUGY	CS-CHD		
20585	C-GOWO	N576FX		
20586	C-GOWQ	N586AL		
20587	C-GOXD	N587FA		
20588	C-GOXZ	M-SGJS		
20589	C-GOYD	N2XT		
20590	C-GOYG	N786QS		
20591	C-FLQZ	VT-JUI		
20592	C-GOVY	9H-VCK		
20593	C-GOWY	N277JH		
20594	C-GOXB	(N577FX)	N350AD	N424MP*

BOMBARDIER BD-100 CHALLENGER 350

C/n	Identities			
20595	C-GOXG	N787QS		
20596	C-GOXR	P4-AGL		
20597	C-GOYO	N356JM		
20598	C-GOXA	C-FOEJ	N350EJ	N247JD*
20599	C-GOXD	N599HA		
20600	C-GOXM	N272BC		
20601	C-GOXN	N578FX^		
20602	C-GOXV	OY-SMS		
20603	C-GOXW	N631RP		
20604	C-GOXZ	N686CB		
20605	C-GOYL	N350AJ	N350RM	
20606	C-GUGS	9H-VCL		
20607	C-GUGV	N788QS		
20608	C-GUHA	N305DL		
20609	C-GUHE	N353VJ		
20610	C-GOWQ	N979KC		
20611	C-GOWO	N350DA		
20612	C-GOWY	N818NX		
20613	C-GOXU	N350EH	N724EH*	
20614	C-GUGY	N354VJ		
20615	C-GOVY	C-FFBE		
20616	C-GOXM	N350FA	N123Q	
20617	C-GOYD	N789QS		
20618	C-GOYG			
20619	C-GOYO	N350CX		
20620	C-GOXA	C-FFIK		
20621	C-GOXB	M-TECH		
20622	C-GOXD	N678HB		
20623	C-GOXG			
20624	C-GOXN			
20625	C-GOXV			
20626	C-GOXW			
20627	C-GOXZ			
20628	C-GOYL			
20629	C-GOWQ			
20630	C-GOXR	C-FALI		
20631	C-GUGS			
20632	C-GUGV			
20633	C-GUHA			
20634				
20635				
20636				
20637				
20638				
20639				
20640				
20641				
20642				
20643				
20644				
20645				
20646				
20647				
20648				
20649				
20650				
20651				
20652				
20653				
20654				
20655				
20656				
20657				
20658				
20659				
20660				

BOMBARDIER BD-700 GLOBAL EXPRESS/GLOBAL 5000

C/n	Series	Identities									
9001		C-FBGX	[rolled out 26Aug96; ff 13Oct96; converted to RAF Airborne Stand-Off Radar test aircraft 2001; later converted to E-11A Battlefield Airborne Communications Node platform for USAF]			N901GX	USAF 11-9001				
9002		C-FHGX	N711MC	N711MN	N881WT						
9003		C-FJGX	C-FBDR	9M-CJG							
9004		C-FKGX	N1TK	C-FKGX	N1TK	(N11TK)	N115HK	HB-JGO	N617JN		
9005		C-GEGX	(VP-CPC)	N700HX	N613WF	(N938WF)	N618WF	(F-GOVV)			
9006		C-GCGY	N1TM	N906GX	N161WC	N420AG	[modified for airborne laser test use]				
9007		C-GCRW	Malaysia M48-01		C-GCRW	Malaysia M48-01		C-GCRW	N907GX	(C-....)	EC-IUQ	N801TK	VH-LEP	VH-LZP
9008		C-GDBG	N9008	(N90005)	N917R						
9009		C-GDGO	N816SR	N816SQ	N813SQ	N998AM	N980GG	N988GG			
9010		C-GDGQ	N701WH	(M-ABAK)	N68005						
9011		C-GDGW	N700KJ	VP-BJJ	HB-IHQ						
9012		C-GDGY	N70PS	N70PX*							
9013		C-GDXU	HB-IUR	C-GZSM	LX-GEX	D-AFAU					
9014		C-GDXV	N700GX	C-FGGX	N700GX	(D-AFLW)	C-FRGX	XA-NGS	N700GX		
9015		C-GDXX	N700KS	N708KS	HB-JEN	N900LF	VH-FMG				
9016		C-GEIM	N700AH	N16GX	N300ES	N309ES	EC-KVU	G-GOYA			
9017		C-GEIR	VP-BDD	HB-JER	N295TX	N90FX					
9018		C-GEVO	VP-BGG	N84SD	N818TS	C-FOXA	PR-VDR				
9019		C-GEVU	N600CC	HL7576	N203JE	N203JZ	N149LP				
9020		C-GEVV	N700GK	VP-BEN	N81ZZ	9H-GBT	(D-AGBT)	F-HGBT	CS-DTW	N344JR	N1JR
9021		C-GEYY	N8VB								
9022		C-GEYZ	N700HG	N622AB	N226HD	N393BZ					
9023		C-GEZD	N324SM	ZS-KDR							
9024		C-GEZF	N700BH	N288Z	N287Z	N9253V					
9025		C-GEZJ	N700AQ	N616DC	N816DC	N322FA	(PR-GEX)	(PR-GBO)	PR-HET*		
9026		C-GEWV	N70EW	N78EW							
9027		C-GEZX	N305CC	N304CC	N850TR						
9028		C-GEZY	N117TF	N717TF	VP-BSE	D-AFAM					
9029		C-GEZZ	HZ-AFA	N929TS	N5UU	N418AB	N829RA				
9030		C-GFAD	VP-BYY	VP-CYY							
9031		C-GFAE	N700VN	N724AF							
9032		C-GFAK	N700HE	(N2T)	G-52-26	G-CBNP	OY-MSI				
9033		C-GFAN	N600AK								
9034		C-GFAP	N700HF	JA005G							
9035		C-GFAQ	(D-AFLW)	N817LS	N711LS	N818LS	N838SC				
9036		C-GFAT	N777GX	HB-ITG	VP-BEM	M-IIII	9H-III				
9037		C-GFJQ	N777SW	N777VU	N400GX	[w/o in hangar collapse at Washington/Dulles, VA, 06Feb10]					
9038		C-GFJR	G-52-24	G-LOBL	N738TS	N20EG	C-GSAP				
9039		C-GFJS	N700GT	N90EW							
9040		C-GFJT	N22BH	N228H	N930EN						
9041		C-GFKT	N195WM	N887WM	N387WM	(N802PF)	N802CB				
9042		C-GFKV	N700WL	N170SW							
9043		C-GFKW	N700BU	N700ML	N416BD	N416BB	(N880NE)	PR-SIR			
9044		C-GFKX	N700BP	I-MOVE	OE-IGS						
9045		C-GFKY	N17GX								
9046		C-GFLS	N700BV	N1TS	N517TT	M-JNJL					
9047		C-GFLU	N410WW	N373SB	(PP-WSC)	PR-HIC					
9048		C-GFLW	N700BY	N4GX	PR-OOF						
9049		C-GFLX	N471DG	N949GP	N471DG	N949GP	M-MDBD				
9050		C-GFLZ	N700FJ	VP-COP	N502JL	M-AFMA					
9051		C-GFWI	N700DZ	N421AL							
9052		C-GFWP	N700DQ	N752DS	N620K	[w/o in hangar collapse at Washington/Dulles, VA, 06Feb10; parted out by Dodson Int'l, Rantoul, KS]					
9053		C-GFWX	N700LJ	N53GX							
9054		C-GFWY	N700LA	HB-IKZ	N550LF	M-RUAT	N356AP	N91FX			
9055		C-GFWZ	N449ML	N540CH							
9056		C-GCGY	N700DU	N421SZ	N928SZ	N670AG					
9057		C-GGIR	(TC-DHG)	N700EX	N18WF	N18WY	VP-BDU				
9058		C-GGJA	N700AD	N79AD	N79AY	(TC-YIL)					
9059		C-GGJF	(VP-BXX)	N700EG	N18WF	N18WZ	N3PC				
9060		C-GGJH	"EC-FPI"	[painted in error at completion centre]	EC-IBD	N542LF	C-GJDU	HL8229	N804TK	C-GJDU	M-ATAR
9061		C-GGJJ	N16FX	ZS-ESA	(VP-C..)	ZS-ESA	N1AR				
9062		C-GGJR	N700CJ	N801PN							
9063		C-GGJS	N700BD	B-HMA	(N733EY)	N933EY					
9064		C-GGJU	N700PL	N264A							
9065		C-GGKA	N700CV	N789TP	N711SW	(N711SQ)	N704MF				
9066		C-GGKC	N898SC	N708SC	N823DF						
9067		C-GGPZ	N700BK	N67RX	N115TR						
9068		C-GGQC	N700BX	(N889JC)							
9069		C-GGQF	N700LD	N1868M	N568M	(N522KM)					
9070		C-GGQG	N700XR	N34U	N14FE	N2FE					
9071		C-GHDQ	D-ADNB	VP-CLY	N888ZJ						
9072		C-GHDV	N700LN	N983J							
9073		C-GHDW	N700XN	N338TP	N801KF						
9074		C-GHEA	N399GS	N2012C							
9075		C-GHEI	N316GS	N1812C	N1812U	N595E					
9076		C-GHER	N700XT	LX-VIP	VP-CGY	9H-GCM					
9077		C-GHET	N700XY	N100A	N200A	N520E	N365CJ				
9078		C-GHEZ	N700AH	N85D							
9079		C-GHFB	N700AP	(N217JC)	VH-VGX						
9080		C-GHFH	N283S	N125CH							
9081		C-GHGC	G-52-25	G-CBNR	G-52-25	C-GZTZ	F-GVML	D-AEGV	OE-IVG		
9082		C-GHYQ	N700AY	JA006G							
9083		C-GHYT	N700AU	C-GKLF	VP-CEB	G-RBEN					
9084		C-GHYX	N700GU	N2T	(N4LZ)	N908BX	N984TS	VP-COU	EC-KKN	LX-NYO	
9085		C-GHZB	N700GQ	N404VL							
9086		C-GHZC	HB-INJ	M-MNAA	M-MMAA	9H-STM					
9087		C-GHZD	N700BQ	N360LA							
9088		C-GHZF	N15FX	C-FDLR	C-GNCB						
9089		C-GHZH	EC-IFS	N65WL							
9090		C-GIOD	N18TM								
9091		C-GIOJ	N700XM	N1FE							
9092		C-GIOK	N15FX	N799WW	N899WW	M-LWSA					
9093		C-GIOW	N17FX	C-GZVZ	VP-CDF						

BOMBARDIER BD-700 GLOBAL EXPRESS/GLOBAL 5000

C/n	Series	Identities						
9094		C-GIOX	(ZS-DAJ)	ZS-DLJ	OY-GLA	A6-EJB	EC-KJH	G-SENT
9095		C-GIPA	HB-IUJ	N97DQ				
9096		C-GIPC	Malaysia M52-01		C-GIPC	Malaysia M48-02	D-ACDF*	
9097		C-GIPD	N903TF	N908TE	N902MM	A6-MHA	M-ALSH	
9098		C-GIPF	N700CE	N149VB	N100VR	N1DS	9H-LLC	P4-MLC	CS-DVE
9099		C-GIPJ	N700CU	C-GZKL	(ZS-DFN)	OE-IEL		
9100		C-GIXI	N700CX	N1SA	XA-PIL	N720CH		
9101		C-GIXJ	VP-BOK	N800TK	VH-VDX			
9102		C-GIXM	N700CY	HB-IGS	VP-CGS	D-AXTM		
9103		C-GIXO	N700CZ	N122BN				
9104		C-GJIU	N190WP	N889CP	N888ZP			
9105		C-GJIW	N700EC	N100A	N500E	N590E		
9106		C-GJIY	N816SG	N816SQ	N10E	OE-IRP		
9107	R-1	C-GJRG	United Kingdom ZJ690					
9108		C-GJRK	N700EK	N100ES	(N150ES)	N625SC	N625SG	N143KB
9109		C-GJRL	N700DU	N700KS				
9110		C-GJTH	N700EL	N14R	N906JW	(SP-WOY)	SP-WOI	
9111		C-GJTK	VT-DHA					
9112		C-GJTP	C-GBLX	OE-IKM	G-FAMT	N703CL	B-7699	
9113		C-GKCG	N920DS	N8762M	N8762W	N2MG		
9114		C-GKCM	N11EA	N1SL	N999YY	N999YA	VT-JSB	N91NG
9115		C-GKCN	(F-GOAK)	LX-PAK	N915AV	C-FNDF	VP-BEB	N915AV	VP-CCK
9116		C-GKGZ	N700EW	N320GX				
9117		C-GKHC	N700EY	N917GL	N724MV			
9118		C-GKHE	N700EZ	N904DS				
9119		C-GKHF	N700FE	C-GZOW	XA-OVR	XA-OVG	XA-AYL	
9120		C-GKHG	N700FG	N887WS	(N910TS)	(D-AGTH)	(OE-IFH)	(N33NN)	G-GLBX
9121		C-GKHH	N700FN	N711MC				
9122		C-GKHI	N700FQ	ZS-GJB	VP-BBK			
9123	R-1	C-FZVM	United Kingdom ZJ691					
9124		C-FZVN	N700GB					
9125		C-FZVS	N700FR	N711SX				
9126		C-FZVV	N60GX	C-GZPT	A7-AAM			
9127	5000	C-GERS	[prototype Global 5000 ff 07Mar03]					
9128		C-FZWB	N700FY	N18WF	(N38WF)	N613WF	N613WE	
9129		C-FZWF	N700FZ	N725LB	N103WG			
9130	5000	C-GLRM	4X-COI	HB-JFB				
9131	R-1	C-FZWW	United Kingdom ZJ692					
9132	R-1	C-FZXC	United Kingdom ZJ693					
9133		C-FZXE	G-XPRS	LX-AAA	N809SD	VH-CCV		
9134		C-FZXZ	A7-GEX	N452CS	N451CS	(N452CS)	N683GA	
9135	R-1	C-FZYL	United Kingdom ZJ694					
9136		C-GZPV	P4-AAA	M-YAAA	M-YFLY			
9137		C-GZPW	C-GCDS					
9138		C-GZRA	N51SE					
9139		C-FYZP	OY-CVS	VQ-BAM	M-GLEX			
9140	5000	C-GAGQ	N140AE	N50DS				
9141		C-GAGS	VP-BOW	N286KR	N804AS	N629KD		
9142		C-GAGT	N700EW	VP-BSC	N442LF	N44GX		
9143		C-FAGU	VH-TGG	VH-TGQ	N777GZ			
9144		C-FAGV	N6VB					
9145		C-FAHN	N914DT	HB-JEX	CS-DVI			
9146		C-FAHQ	EC-JIL					
9147		C-FAHX	P4-VVF	N489JB	N92FX			
9148		C-FAIO	N889JA					
9149	5000	C-FAIY	N356MS	N456MS	VT-BAJ			
9150		C-FAIV	N488CH					
9151		C-FBOC	N81UB	VQ-BHY	N598CH			
9152	5000	C-FBPK	N605VF	N626DJ	N214MD			
9153		C-FBPJ	N454AJ	N120AK	TC-FRK			
9154	5000	C-FBPL	N555EF	N388RF	N3389H			
9155	5000	C-FBPT	N711LS	N717LS	N717MK			
9156	5000	C-FBPZ	N156DG	N1DG				
9157	5000	C-FBQD	VP-BAM	M-AQUA				
9158	5000	C-FCOG	N375G	(N858TS)	C-GPPI			
9159	XRS	C-FCOI	D-ATNR	OH-TNR	(D-AZNF)	OE-ITN		
9160	5000	C-FCOJ	N47					
9161	5000	C-FCOK	N944AM	VP-BWB				
9162		C-FCOZ	N2T					
9163		C-FCPH	OY-ILG	N700FG	VH-FGJ			
9164	5000	C-FCSF	N376G					
9165	XRS	C-FCSH	VP-BOS	M-ASRI				
9166	5000	C-FCSI	N166J	N1990C	M-YSAI			
9167	XRS	C-FCSL	N167GX	(OE-LNX)	HB-JGY	9H-AFP	VH-ZZH	N877AB	N123AB
9168	5000	C-FCSP	OE-INC					
9169	XRS	C-FCSR	G-XXRS					
9170	5000	C-FCSY	D-AAAZ	(VP-CKR)	OE-LAA	D-AAHI*		
9171	XRS	C-FCTE	VP-CGO					
9172	5000	C-FCTK	N729KF	N729KP	M-ANGO			
9173	XRS	C-FCUA	HB-JEY	VH-ZXH	[dbr by hangar fire, Indianapolis, IN, 07Nov10]		N744SD	[parted out by Red Aviation, Georgetown, TX]
9174	5000	C-FCUF	HB-JRS					
9175	XRS	C-FCUG	N771TF	N117TF				
9176	5000	C-FCUK	N720WS					
9177	XRS	C-FCUS	N528J	N528JR	[w/o in hangar collapse at Washington/Dulles, VA, 06Feb10; parted out by Challenger Spares & Support, Georgetown, TX]			
9178	5000	C-FCUX	C-GDPG					
9179	XRS	C-FCVC	HL7748	N905T				
9180	5000	C-FCVD	N818FH	N939AP				
9181	XRS	C-FEAB	N302AK	N382AK	N137BB			
9182	5000	C-FECA	N182GX	OE-IFG	M-AJWA			
9183	XRS	C-FEAD	N821AM					
9184	XRS	C-FEAE	HL7749	N702DR				
9185	XRS	C-FEAG	N1955M	N185GX	N13JS			
9186	5000	C-FECI	P4-HER	OY-FIT				
9187	XRS	C-FEAK	N540WY	N54SL	N11A			
9188	5000	C-FECN	F-HFBY					

BOMBARDIER BD-700 GLOBAL EXPRESS/GLOBAL 5000

C/n	Series	Identities				
9189	XRS	C-FEAQ	LX-GJM	M-GYQM		
9190	5000	C-FECX	N99XN	PR-XDN	M-RIDE	
9191	XRS	C-FEAZ	N91NG	N6D	N28ZD	
9192	5000	C-FECY	N700LK	N267BW		
9193	XRS	C-FEBG	VP-BVG			
9194	XRS	C-FEBH	N313RF			
9195	XRS	C-FEBL	N195GX	N4T		
9196	XRS	C-FEBQ	VP-CRC	G-CEYL		
9197	XRS	C-FEBS	LX-PAK			
9198	5000	C-FECZ	HB-JRR	VQ-BMM		
9199	XRS	C-FEBU	(N799TS)	N379G	PP-SGP*	
9200	XRS	C-FEBX	G-LXRS	N519CP		
9201	5000	C-FHPQ	N95ZZ	N205EL		
9202	XRS	C-FHPB	F-GVMV	N1415N		
9203	XRS	C-FHPG	N203XX	N200A	N210A	N688MC	N121RS
9204	5000	C-FIHP	OE-IAK	LX-ZAK	N709RJ	VP-BSG
9205	XRS	C-FIHL	N205EX	N100A	N102A	N1NE
9206	5000	C-FIIB	N92ZZ	N343DF	N343DE	
9207	5000	C-FIIC	N723AB			
9208	XRS	C-FIHN	EC-KFS	OE-LUB		
9209	5000	C-FIIG	N171JJ	"M-BIJJ"+	[+ fake marks worn at Luton Jul08]	N171JJ	N828CC
9210	XRS	C-FIOT	N190H	M-GBAL	N297SF	
9211	5000	C-FIPH	C-GXPR	[w/o Fox Harbour, Newfoundland, Canada 11Nov07; cx Mar08; parted out]		
9212	5000	C-FIPJ	N13JS	N166MK		
9213	XRS	C-FIOZ	(VP-CAH)	D-AEKT	(VH-ZXH)	VQ-BIS	M-VQBI
9214	5000	C-FIPM	N93ZZ	VT-JSK		
9215	XRS	C-FIPC	N94ZZ	N18WF		
9216	5000	C-FIPN	N900LS	(N530JM)	M-JSMN	
9217	5000	C-FIPP	N700LS	N709LS	N74DH	
9218	XRS	C-FIPF	N96ZZ	N86TW	C-GXBB	
9219	5000	C-FIPQ	N80ZZ	N611VT	SP-ZAK	
9220	XRS	C-FIPG	P4-CBA	C-GHSW	C-GMXP	
9221	5000	C-FIPT	N10SL			
9222	5000	C-FJNJ	N81ZZ	N45JE	N45UE	VP-CAK
9223	XRS	C-FJML	N83ZZ	VP-BAH		
9224	5000	C-FJNQ	N224GX	N989RJ		
9225	XRS	C-FJMP	N36LG	N36EG	VH-CCX	
9226	5000	C-FJNX	A6-DHG	(N381MS)	N900TR	
9227	5000	C-FJNZ	(N200LS)	M-LLGC	M-SKSM	
9228	XRS	C-FJMQ	N87ZZ	N289Z	N288Z	N287Z	VT-SDK
9229	5000	C-FJOA	N84ZZ	YR-TIK		
9230	XRS	C-FJMV	A7-GEY	N57LE	ZS-AMP	VH-IQR
9231	5000	C-FJOK	VP-CAU	G-TSLS	D-AOTL	G-TSLS	CS-TSL
9232	XRS	C-FJMX	D2-ANG			
9233	5000	C-FJOU	(A6-OWC)	N233FJ	C-GGLO	
9234	XRS	C-FLKZ	N234GX	(D-AANA)	OE-LAF	9H-FED	9H-COL	N989SF
9235	XRS	C-FLLA	OE-LXR	N812SD		
9236	XRS	C-FLLF	N624BP	N624BR*		
9237	XRS	C-FLLH	(OE-LNY)	OH-PPS	OE-IRA	
9238	XRS	C-FLLN	HB-JGP			
9239	XRS	C-FLLO	N71ZZ	N421SZ	N928SZ	
9240	XRS	C-FLLV	N999YX	N999YY		
9241	5000	C-FLKY	(G-LLGC)	N941TS	G-OCSA	G-CGFA	B-LRH
9242	XRS	C-FLTB	N942TS	(OH-PPS)	N942TS	N375G
9243	5000	C-FLTH	OE-IMA	VP-CMA		
9244	XRS	C-FLTI	C-FCNN	VP-CZK	N36MM	
9245	5000	C-FLTJ	N200ES	N247WE		
9246	XRS	C-FMFK	VP-BNX	N708RJ		
9247	XRS	C-FMFN	N881TS			
9248	XRS	C-FMFO	N888GX			
9249	5000	C-FMGE	HB-JGN	9H-AFR		
9250	XRS	C-FMGK	D-AKAZ	M-BTAR		
9251	XRS	C-FMKW	N73ZZ	OE-IGG		
9252	XRS	C-FMKZ	LX-FLY			
9253	XRS	C-FMLB	ZS-ZBB	VQ-BZB		
9254	XRS	C-FMLE	N754TS	VQ-BGS		
9255	5000	C-FMLI	N193LA	N199LA	N417CS	
9256	XRS	C-FMLQ	OE-ICN*	[aircraft built in 2007, still not delivered 2014]		
9257	5000	C-FMLT	VP-CVU	5A-UAC		
9258	XRS	C-FMLV	N700ML	PR-MLJ		
9259	XRS	C-FMMH	N89ZZ	Botswana OK1		
9260	XRS	C-FMND	N74ZZ	ZS-XRS	SX-GJN	N651GS	SX-GJN	N218AL
9261	5000	C-FMUI	N878HL			
9262	XRS	C-FMUN	N962TS	VT-STV	N433DC	
9263	5000	C-FMUO	VP-CSB			
9264	XRS	C-FNDN	C-GLUL	SE-RGB		
9265	5000	C-FNDK	N265DE	N501JT	N689WM	
9266	XRS	C-FNDO	N76ZZ	N104DA		
9267	XRS	C-FNDQ	N78ZZ	M-MMAS	OY-LUK	VP-CLP
9268	XRS	C-FNDT	VQ-BJA	N713RJ	M-OGMC	
9269	5000	C-FNRP	OE-IBC			
9270	XRS	C-FNRR	VP-CNY			
9271	5000	C-FNSN	VP-CJC	N898WS		
9272	XRS	C-FNSV	VP-CVV	N15SD		
9273	5000	C-FNZZ	VP-BJN			
9274	XRS	C-FOAB	N974TS	G-EXRS	9H-SRT	
9275	5000	C-FOAD	N87ZZ	VH-KTG	N50XC	N137ZM
9276	XRS	C-FOKD	VP-BJI			
9277	XRS	C-FOKF	N194WM			
9278	XRS	C-FOKH	N709DS			
9279	5000	C-FOKJ	N79ZZ	N468KL		
9280	XRS	C-FOVD	(D-AVIA)	OY-WIN	OE-IDO	
9281	XRS	C-FOVE	N981TS			
9282	5000	C-FOVG	N216PA	A6-FBQ		
9283	XRS	C-FOVH	VQ-BEB	M-YULI	N706RJ	T7-AAA

BOMBARDIER BD-700 GLOBAL EXPRESS/GLOBAL 5000

C/n	Series	Identities				
9284	XRS	C-FOVK	N77UF			
9285	5000	C-FPFF	5A-UAB			
9286	XRS	C-FPGB	C-FHYL	OE-IPA	G-IDRO	LX-AMG
9287	XRS	C-FPGD	N169DT	HB-JGE		
9288	5000	C-FPGI	N375WB			
9289	5000	C-FPQE	N26ZZ	VT-DBA		
9290	XRS	C-FPQF	N774KK	N797KK		
9291	XRS	C-FPQG	OH-PPT	OE-IRN		
9292	XRS	C-FPQH	N837WM	N887WM		
9293	5000	C-FPQI	HZ-SJP	"HZ-BJP"	M-JANP	
9294	XRS	C-FQXW	M-CRVS	A7-CEF		
9295	5000	C-FQXX	B-LIM			
9296	XRS	C-FQXY	N96ZZ	N616DC		
9297	XRS	C-FQYB	VQ-BSC	N703RJ	VH-CCD	
9298	5000	C-FQYD	N900GX			
9299	XRS	C-FQYE	N37ZZ	VH-LAW		
9300	XRS	C-FRJV	N709FG			
9301	5000	C-FRJY	(D-AMOS)	OE-IOO		
9302	5000	C-FRKL	N95ZZ	N352AF		
9303	XRS	C-FRKO	EC-LEB			
9304	XRS	C-FRKQ	N89MX	N3877		
9305	5000	C-FRMW	N815PA			
9306	XRS	C-FRNG	G-SHEF	LX-GXX		
9307	XRS	C-FRNJ	N528MP			
9308	5000	C-FSRX	N103ZZ			
9309	XRS	C-FSRY	G-CJME	G-IRAP		
9310	XRS	C-FSRZ	N38ZZ	VH-ZXH	VP-CKR	
9311	5000	C-FSSE	M-SALE	VH-DNK	VP-CES	
9312	XRS	C-FTIK	PP-VDR			
9313	6000	C-FTIO	[Global Vision Flight Deck test a/c; Global 6000 test a/c]			
9314	XRS	C-FTIQ	N807DC			
9315	5000	C-FTIR	B-LRW			
9316	XRS	C-FTIS	N1328M	N1868M		
9317	XRS	C-FTUX	VT-HMA			
9318	5000	C-FTUY	TC-KRM			
9319	XRS	C-FTVF	OE-IRM	9H-IRA		
9320	XRS	C-FTVK	HB-JGH	N688MC	N283DM	
9321	5000	C-FTVN	VP-CWN			
9322	XRS	C-FTVO	XA-BUA	N717AL	N995ML	
9323	XRS	C-FUCV	OE-LGX	N679JB	F-HXRG	
9324	5000	C-FUCY	G-GRAN	M-GRAN		
9325	5000	C-FUCZ	N723HH	(N291SL)	N73SL	M-BRRB	N636JS
9326	XRS	C-FUDH	VH-OCV			
9327	XRS	C-FUDN	N105ZZ	N118WT		
9328	5000	C-FUOJ	N555HD			
9329	XRS	C-FUOK	9H-XRS	M-SIRI		
9330	5000	C-FUOL	N939ML	N700HM		
9331	XRS	C-FUOM	G-KANL	OY-LNA		
9332	XRS	C-FURP	(LX-GXR)	OH-TNF	(D-ATNF)	LX-TNF
9333	XRS	C-FUSI	G-SANL			
9334	5000	C-FUSR	G-PVEL	9H-PVL		
9335	XRS	C-FUTF	A6-BBD	VP-CTP		
9336	XRS	C-FUTL	(S5-ADE)	CS-DTG	G-OKKI	9H-OKI
9337	5000	C-FUTT	N109ZZ	M-ATAK	N985EL	
9338	XRS	C-FVFW	N18WZ			
9339	XRS	C-FVGP	N112ZZ	C-GFRX	VQ-BNP	D-ABNP*
9340	5000	C-FVGX	N340GF	N501JT	N426CF	N954L
9341	XRS	C-FVHE	VP-CNA			
9342	XRS	C-FVUI	N39ZZ	VQ-BKI		
9343	5000	C-FVUK	OY-SGC	N43GX		
9344	XRS	C-FVUP	VH-VLA	N360HP		
9345	XRS	C-FVUZ	N113ZZ	D-ACBO	A6-CBO	
9346	5000	C-FVVE	VH-LEP	P4-PIF		
9347	XRS	C-FWGB	N115ZZ	HB-JFY		
9348	XRS	C-FWGH	9H-BGL	D-ARKO		
9349	XRS	C-FWGP	(4X-CMB)	M-VANG		
9350	5000	C-FWGV	9M-TAN			
9351	XRS	C-FWHF	G-OXRS	(PP-AHT)		
9352	XRS	C-FWIK	N868SC	C-GILQ	(M-YXRS)	N726AF
9353	5000	C-FWZR	CS-EAM	OH-MAL	9H-FLN	
9354	XRS	C-FWZX	N92ZZ	N113CS	N923SG	N721FF*
9355	E-11A	C-FXAQ	N770AG	USAF 11-9355		
9356	5000	C-FXAY	N404NA			
9357	XRS	C-FXBF	N40ZZ	B-95959		
9358	E-11A	C-FXIY	N760AG	USAF 11-9358		
9359	5000	C-FXJD	HB-JIH	A6-ACE		
9360	XRS	C-FXJM	EC-LJP	N863BA		
9361	XRS	C-FXKE	N65ZZ	N579AT	VP-CYT	
9362	XRS	C-FXKK	B-8101	VP-CCN		
9363	5000	C-FXYK	RP-9363	[dbr Tacloban, Philippines, 17Jan15]		
9364	XRS	C-FXYS	C-GGOL	G-GABY		
9365	XRS	C-FXYY	N75ZZ	TC-YAA	TC-YYA	
9366	5000	C-FYGJ	N59ZZ	N700GR	N560U	
9367	XRS	C-FYGP	HB-JII			
9368	XRS	C-FYGX	VH-TGG			
9369	XRS	C-FYHT	VP-BEB			
9370	5000	C-FYIG	A7-CED			
9371	XRS	C-FYIH	(CS-EAP)	M-UNIS		
9372	5000	C-FYIZ	VP-CGM			
9373	5000	C-FYJC	9H-OVB	HB-JRX		
9374	XRS	C-FYJD	G-FCFC	D-ATOM	VP-CJT	
9375	XRS	C-FYMT	N121ZZ	N416BD		
9376	5000	C-FYMU	RA-67225			
9377	XRS	C-FYNI	(G-HVLD)	G-CGSJ		
9378	XRS	C-FYNQ	N211PB			

BOMBARDIER BD-700 GLOBAL EXPRESS/GLOBAL 5000

C/n	Series	Identities					
9379	5000	C-FYNV	VP-BSK	A7-TAT			
9380	XRS	C-FYOC	M-RSKL				
9381	6000	C-GBTY	N381GX				
9382	5000	C-GBUA	(N119ZZ)	N15PX	N15BX*		
9383	5000	C-GBUI	N188J				
9384	XRS	C-GCKR	HL8230				
9385	XRS	C-GCLI	VQ-BRL	N393BV			
9386	5000	C-GCMJ	N968DS	N117MS			
9387	XRS	C-GCOX	B-8199	N789RR			
9388	XRS	C-GCPI	C-GDPF				
9389	5000	C-GCPV	C-GJCB				
9390	XRS	C-GCWQ	B-8266	N899CH			
9391	XRS	C-GCWU	VP-CHL				
9392	XRS	C-GCWV	N782SF				
9393	XRS	C-GCWX	VQ-BIH	C-GKZW	VH-ICV		
9394	XRS	C-GCXE	VP-CBM				
9395	5000	C-GDCF	Germany 9848		Germany 1401		
9396	XRS	C-GDCZ	VQ-BOK	N290KR	N497EC		
9397	XRS	C-GDEK	N169LL	C-FIPX			
9398	5000	C-GDEV	(B-8198)	N2707	N270F		
9399	XRS	C-GEHF	M-ARRJ				
9400	5000	C-GEHK	N445DB				
9401	5000	C-GEHV	OE-III	M-IBID			
9402	XRS	C-GEIM	N700WR	N1DS			
9403	XRS	C-GEUX	EC-LNM				
9404	5000	C-GEVN	Germany 1402				
9405	5000	C-GEZJ	D-ACDE				
9406	XRS	C-GEZX	N268AA	M-SSSR			
9407	XRS	C-GFAE	C-GWHF				
9408	5000	C-GFAP	TC-MJA				
9409	XRS	C-GFKH	N368HK	S5-GMG	9H-ERO	M-DSUN	
9410	XRS	C-GFKJ	(VT-JSI)	N311NB			
9411	5000	C-GFKL	Germany 1403				
9412	XRS	C-GFKQ	B-8196				
9413	XRS	C-GGFJ	M-GLOB				
9414	5000	[C-GGHN c/n changed to 9998 at customer's request]					
9415	XRS	C-GGHT	(B-LIZ)	B-KTL			
9416	XRS	C-GGIM	VP-CEO				
9417	5000	C-GGSA	Germany 1404				
9418	5000	C-GGSU	M-CCCP				
9419	XRS	C-GGUA	D-ARYR				
9420	XRS	C-GGUG	M-GSKY				
9421	5000	C-GHCE	A7-CEE				
9422	XRS	C-GHCS	HL8238				
9423	XRS	C-GHCZ	G-RAAA				
9424	5000	C-GHVB	4X-COF	India GB8001			
9425	5000	C-GHVN	B-KEZ				
9426	XRS	C-GHVO	P4-GMS				
9427	5000	C-GHVX	(D-APCA)	D-AOHS	OE-INL		
9428	XRS	C-GHWD	N979CB	N976CB			
9429	XRS	C-GHXX	OE-LXX	9H-LXX			
9430	5000	C-GHXY	9H-VSM	P4-MMM	9H-MMM		
9431	5000	C-GHYK	4X-COH	India GB8002			
9432	6000	C-GIOC	VP-CWW				
9433	6000	C-GIOK	OY-LGI				
9434	6000	C-GIOW	M-MNAA	HZ-ATH			
9435	6000	C-GIOX	N797CT				
9436	6000	C-GISY	N302AK				
9437	6000	C-GITG	9H-AMF				
9438	6000	C-GIUD	"C-GUID"+	[+incorrect marks worn at completion centre]		(C-FBDR)	N88AA
9439	6000	C-GIUP	N980GG				
9440	6000	C-GJFD	9H-VJB	9H-OPE			
9441	6000	C-GJFI	9H-VJA				
9442	6000	C-GJFQ	N112MY				
9443	6000	C-GJFW	M-AAAL				
9444	6000	C-GJGE	N1955M	N944GX	N688MC		
9445	5000	C-GJJG	VP-CKM				
9446	5000	C-GJKA	VT-KJB				
9447	6000	C-GJKO	PP-GUL				
9448	6000	C-GJKZ	9H-VJC				
9449	5000	C-GJLH	N346L				
9450	6000	C-GJLY	M-NALE				
9451	6000	C-GKLC	N451GX	(N987JJ)			
9452	6000	C-GKLX	N729KF				
9453	5000	C-GKMO	M-BLUE				
9454	5000	C-GKMU	N678RC				
9455	6000	C-GKNP	OE-IRT				
9456	6000	C-GKOH	F-GVMI				
9457	5000	C-GKOJ	M-IGWT	G-ISAN	N724MF		
9458	5000	C-GKOY	N168JH	C-GKOY	OY-GVI	9H-GVA	
9459	6000	C-GKUZ	N45GX				
9460	6000	C-GKVC	C-GPPX				
9461	5000	C-GKVL	M-SEAS				
9462	5000	C-GKVN	N565RS				
9463	6000	C-GKVO	N115MH				
9464	6000	C-GKYI	EC-LTF				
9465	5000	C-GKYK	N918TA				
9466	6000	C-GKYL	S5-ZFL				
9467	6000	C-GKYN	N320GB	N203JE			
9468	5000	C-GKYO	N755RA				
9469	6000	C-GLEU	N46GX				
9470	6000	C-FHYL	C-GSDU	ZS-SYH	N683JB	OY-GVG	9H-GVG
9471	6000	C-GLFG	M-MYNA				
9472	6000	C-GLFK	(9H-VJC)	9H-VJD			
9473	6000	C-GLFN	N88GZ	B-8197			

BOMBARDIER BD-700 GLOBAL EXPRESS/GLOBAL 5000

C/n	Series	Identities			
9474	5000	C-GLUN	N702LK		
9475	6000	C-GLUP	N160QS		
9476	6000	C-GLUR	N118ZZ	N711LS	
9477	5000	C-GLUS	(N168HH)	B-98888	
9478	6000	C-GLKC	CS-GLA		
9479	6000	C-GLKH	(CS-GLA)	N141QS	
9480	5000	C-GMRX	N100QS		
9481	6000	C-GMSO	CS-GLB		
9482	6000	C-GMSU	M-DADA		
9483	5000	C-GMSY	N101QS		
9484	6000	C-GMTY	N162QS	N914BA	
9485	6000	C-GMWV	N142QS		
9486	5000	C-GMXH	M-SAID		
9487	6000	C-GMXY	(D-ALUK)	D-AGJP	
9488	6000	C-GMYE	B-8195		
9489	5000	C-GMYL	N2707		
9490	6000	C-GNGY	N612FG		
9491	6000	C-GNHB	N8762	N8762M	
9492	5000	C-GNHP	N286JS	(PR-IZB)	
9493	6000	C-GNKK	VT-SNG		
9494	6000	C-GNKW	M-ABFQ		
9495	5000	C-GNZV	OE-LPZ		
9496	6000	C-GOAN	OE-IEO		
9497	6000	C-GOBF	HB-JFE		
9498	5000	C-GOCD	N130QS	N986BA	
9499	6000	C-GODV	N143QS		
9500	6000	C-GOEB	F-GBOL		
9501	5000	C-GOIK	VP-CWQ		
9502	6000	C-GOIM	9H-VJE		
9503	6000	C-GOIP	9H-VJF		
9504	5000	C-GOIR	N933ML		
9505	6000	C-GOIS	VP-BOK		
9506	E-11A	C-GOUR	N9506G	USAF 12-9506	
9507	6000	C-GOUU	OE-IRS		
9508	5000	C-GOUX	N723HH		
9509	6000	C-GPIA	VP-CPT		
9510	6000	C-GPIW	B-8105		
9511	6000	C-GPKI	N806AS		
9512	6000	C-GPKX	N512BH	VP-BVM	
9513	5000	C-GPYF	C-FMPX		
9514	6000	C-GPYW	HB-JRM		
9515	6000	C-GPYX	OH-TRA	N599CH	
9516	5000	C-GPZE	N41SH	M-IUNI	
9517	6000	C-GPZH	M-ABFR		
9518	6000	C-GRRI	(VP-BTD)	M-HAWK	
9519	6000	C-GRSF	N700LS		
9520	5000	C-GRSU	N443PR		
9521	6000	C-GRTU	EI-SSF	M-YSSF	
9522	6000	C-GRUK	N900LS		
9523	6000	C-GSKD	HB-JEH		
9524	6000	C-GSLW	N193LC	N193LA	
9525	6000	C-GSNB	M-AHAH	M-AHAR	M-AHAA
9526	6000	C-GSNF	N526GX	VP-COJ	N526GX
9527	6000	C-GSNG	VT-JSY		
9528	5000	C-GSYX	OE-IXX		
9529	6000	C-GSZB	N1812C		
9530	6000	C-GSZF	N805WB	N805WM	
9531	5000	C-GSZG	N103QS	(N176HT)	N176HS
9532	6000	C-GTUA	VP-CJC		
9533	6000	C-GTUF	CS-GLC		
9534	5000	C-GTUO	A7-CEV		
9535	6000	C-GTUU	9H-CIO		
9536	5000	C-GTUV	N1368M		
9537	6000	C-GTVC	M-YFTA		
9538	6000	C-GTZN	CS-GLD		
9539	5000	C-GTZO	N50VC		
9540	6000	C-GTZS	VP-CZL		
9541	6000	C-GUAK	N41GX	(PR-IZB)	N8998K
9542	5000	C-GUAL	OE-ICA		
9543	6000	C-GUAN	N543GL		
9544	5000	C-GUDZ	OY-VIZ		
9545	6000	C-GUEL	M-RIZA		
9546	6000	C-GUEO	N288DG		
9547	5000	C-GUEP	9H-TOR		
9548	6000	C-GUET	N548GX	N36LG	
9549	6000	C-GUEU	M-BMAL	9H-SMB	
9550	5000	C-GUEV	N627JW		
9551	6000	C-GUIF	N312AF		
9552	5000	C-GUIH	N500VJ		
9553	6000	C-GUIS	OH-MPL	S5-SAD	
9554	6000	C-GUIY	M-ARGO		
9555	5000	C-GUJK	N104QS		
9556	6000	C-GUJM	PP-FCC		
9557	6000	C-GUJP	N9099H		
9558	5000	C-GUOX	N468GH		
9559	6000	C-GUPK	(D-AABE)	(D-AABB)	LX-ABB
9560	5000	C-GUPM	M-TYRA		
9561	6000	C-GUPB	N979CB		
9562	6000	C-GUPL	N562GX	(N14CK)	M-ABCC
9563	5000	C-GUPN	N501VJ		
9564	6000	C-GUPF	XA-OVR		
9565	5000	C-GUSV	9H-VTA	N503VJ	
9566	5000	C-GUTG	9H-VTB		
9567	6000	C-GUTP	F-HFIP		
9568	6000	C-GUSX	VQ-BPG	N68889	

BOMBARDIER BD-700 GLOBAL EXPRESS/GLOBAL 5000

C/n	Series	Identities				
9569	5000	C-GUTN	N3338			
9570	6000	C-GUTE	9H-IGH			
9571	5000	C-GUSU	9H-VTC			
9572	6000	C-GVKL	N181CL			
9573	6000	C-GVGZ	N400BC			
9574	6000	C-GVKO	N533LM			
9575	6000	C-GVKH	N809PT	VP-BMG		
9576	6000	C-GVGY	M-YSKY			
9577	6000	C-GVRO	M-HOME			
9578	5000	C-GVRU	9H-OMK			
9579	6000	C-GVRI	M-SAMA			
9580	6000	C-GVRY	9H-VJG			
9581	5000	C-GVRS	A7-CEI			
9582	6000	C-GVWV	PR-BPT			
9583	6000	C-GVXG	N116SF			
9584	5000	C-GVXD	VP-CBF			
9585	6000	C-GVWR	9H-VJH			
9586	5000	C-GVXF	LX-RAK	N718RJ	M-MICS	
9587	6000	C-GVXB	N99ZM			
9588	6000	C-GWKV	N65XC	N60XC		
9589	5000	C-GWLK	N109QS			
9590	6000	C-GWNY	M-YVVF			
9591	6000	C-GWKY	N7777U			
9592	5000	C-GWLR	N110QS			
9593	6000	C-GWMY	9H-VJI			
9594	5000	C-GWKU	M-FINE			
9595	6000	C-GWKZ	M-IGWT			
9596	6000	C-GXBM	M-YULI			
9597	5000	C-GXAU	M-AGRI	M-BIGG		
9598	6000	C-GXAF	N145QS			
9599	6000	C-GXCE	N626JS			
9600	5000	C-GXBN	A6-RJC			
9601	6000	C-GXAZ	LX-NAD			
9602	5000	C-GXAH	CS-LAM			
9603	6000	C-GXCO	ZS-TDF			
9604	6000	C-GXCA	9H-VJJ			
9605	5000	C-GXBK	N50MG			
9606	6000	C-GXAN	N588LQ			
9607	6000	C-GWZR	N212LE	N212LF		
9608	5000	C-GXCD	N502VJ			
9609	6000	C-GXKK	OE-LII			
9610	5000	C-GXKV	N889ST			
9611	6000	C-GXKO	VP-CJK			
9612	6000	C-GXLG				
9613	5000	C-GXKG	N918TB			
9614	6000	C-GXLC	N878SC			
9615	6000	C-GXRC	N146QS			
9616	5000	C-GXRK	N616GX	N902MY		
9617	6000	C-GXRW	N244DS			
9618	5000	C-GXRD	N618GX	N667BB		
9619	6000	C-GXRA	9H-VJK			
9620	6000	C-GXRU	N620GX	N417LX		
9621	5000	C-GXZL	A6-RJD			
9622	6000	C-GXZD	N810TS			
9623	5000	C-GXZV	M-JGVJ			
9624	6000	C-GXZM	SE-RMT			
9625	6000	C-GXZG	I-PFLY			
9626	6000	C-GXZB	9H-VJL			
9627	5000	C-GXZR	HB-JRI			
9628	6000	C-GYOX	VP-CYA			
9629	5000	C-GYOH	N2QE			
9630	6000	C-GYRF	9H-VJM			
9631	6000	C-GYPW	ZS-OAK			
9632	6000	C-GYOV	N147QS			
9633	5000	C-GYOF	M-DANK			
9634	6000	C-GYPX	N9634	N504R		
9635	6000	C-GZDY	VP-CFO			
9636	5000	C-GZEH	N83FF			
9637	6000	C-GZDS	(M-GABY)+	[+ntu marks worn at factory]	M-YOIL	
9638	6000	C-GZEB	CS-GLE			
9639	5000	C-GZHO	M-KBSD			
9640	6000	C-GZGR	C-GHSW			
9641	6000	C-GZHG	N9641	N12G		
9642	5000	C-GZGP	C-FFIJ			
9643	6000	C-GZHU	N968EX	N88C		
9644	5000	C-GZGS	C-GJET			
9645	6000	C-GZRU	N1955M			
9646	6000	C-GZRE	VQ-BCC			
9647	5000	C-GZRY	N625SC			
9648	6000	C-GZRA	N148QS			
9649	6000	C-GZRP	N70EW			
9650	5000	C-FBUH	N142HC			
9651	6000	C-FBVS	VT-AHI			
9652	6000	C-FBVG	VP-CEW			
9653	6000	C-FBUA	N9653	PR-FIS		
9654	6000	C-FBVL	VH-LEP			
9655	5000	C-FCZV	N5000P			
9656	6000	C-FCYX	N56GX	9H-AMZ		
9657	6000	C-FDIW	N150QS			
9658	5000	C-FCZS	VT-IBG			
9659	6000	C-FCYG	N9TJ			
9660	5000	C-FDHP	N111QS			
9661	6000	C-FCZN	(D-AMPX)	A7-TAA		
9662	6000	C-FDVX	9H-VJN			
9663	5000	C-FDUA	N970DX	N939GS		

BOMBARDIER BD-700 GLOBAL EXPRESS/GLOBAL 5000

C/n	Series	Identities			
9664	6000	C-FDXB	N600JV		
9665	6000	C-FDVO			
9666	5000	C-FDSZ	VP-BCY		
9667	6000	C-FDXA	9H-VJY		
9668	5000	C-FDUV	N968GX	M-SAPT	
9669	6000	C-FEHT	9H-VJO		
9670	6000	C-FEMF	CS-GLF		
9671	5000	C-FEOF	N970NX		
9672	6000	C-FEHU	OE-IGL		
9673	6000	C-FEMN	N403PM		
9674	5000	C-FEHG	N40TE		
9675	6000	C-FELO	N967NX		
9676	5000	C-FFHW	3B-PGT		
9677	6000	C-FFMV	9H-VJP		
9678	6000	C-FFGZ	N968DW	M-MAXX	
9679	6000	C-FFLC	N401PM	N588ZJ	
9680	6000	C-FFMZ	VH-IEJ		
9681	5000	C-FFHA	VP-BGS		
9682	6000	C-FFLZ	N10HD		
9683	5000	C-FFGU	N402PM		
9684	6000	C-FFWP	N588MM		
9685	6000	C-FFVM	N968DZ	N2020Q	
9686	6000	C-FFXS	VP-CAF		
9687	6000	C-FFVX	N968DX	C-FPQJ	M-CVGL
9688	6000	C-FFVE	N688ZJ		
9689	6000	C-FGWV	N410MG	N410M*	
9690	5000	C-FGSU	M-AABG		
9691	6000	C-FGVS	9H-VJQ		
9692	6000	C-FGUD	LX-ZAK		
9693	5000	C-FGWF	9H-CMA		
9694	6000	C-FGSS	N968BX	(N999HY)	
9695	6000	C-FHSX	EC-MKH		
9696	5000	C-FHNN	N898CC		
9697	6000	C-FHMG	N404PM		
9698	6000	C-FHSN	N405PM		
9699	5000	C-FHND	N912MT		
9700	6000	C-FHMF	RA-67241		
9701	6000	C-FHPZ	9H-GFI		
9702	6000	C-FHMZ	N343DF		
9703	6000	C-FIEZ	9H-VJR		
9704	6000	C-FIFP	N161GF		
9705	6000	C-FIIA	VP-CZJ		
9706	6000	C-FIFK	M-NAME		
9707	5000	C-FIHP	N968HX		
9708	6000	C-FIEX			
9709	6000	C-FIFN			
9710	5000	C-FIRT	N112QS		
9711	6000	C-FIPU	9H-VJS		
9712	6000	C-FIRK			
9713	5000	C-FISO	B-7765		
9714	6000	C-FIPT	SE-RMY		
9715	5000	C-FIRG	VP-BLQ		
9716	6000	C-FJDZ	N788ZJ		
9717	5000	C-FJFJ			
9718	6000	C-FJGK			
9719	5000	C-FJDX			
9720	6000	C-FJGI			
9721	6000	C-FJGX	9H-VJT		
9722	5000	C-FJEF			
9723	6000	C-FJXR	D-ANMB*		
9724	6000	C-FJWX	9H-VJU		
9725	6000	C-FJYB	9H-VJV		
9726	6000	C-FJXE			
9727	6000	C-FJXY			
9728	6000	C-FKFY	9H-VJW*		
9729	6000	C-FKEX			
9730	6000	C-FKDN	9H-VJX*		
9731	6000	C-FKFO			
9732	5000	C-FKDK			
9733	6000	C-FKFS			
9734	5000	C-FKRE			
9735	6000	C-FKSN			
9736	6000	C-FKSB			
9737	5000	C-FKPY			
9738	6000	C-FKSF			
9739	6000	C-FKRX			
9740	6000	C-FLGN			
9741	6000	C-FLKU			
9742	6000	C-FLKC			
9743	6000	C-FLGD			
9744	6000	C-FLHA			
9745	6000	C-FLKO			
9746	6000	C-FLFT			
9747	6000	C-FLWV			
9748	6000	C-FLXD			
9749	6000	C-FLVK			
9750	6000	C-FLWX			
9751	6000	C-FMFO			
9752	6000	C-FMCZ			
9753	6000	C-FMHR			
9754	6000	C-FMCH			
9755	5000	C-FMYG			
9756	6000	C-FMZS			
9757	6000	C-FMYD			
9758	6000	C-FMYX			

BOMBARDIER BD-700 GLOBAL EXPRESS/GLOBAL 5000

C/n	Series	Identities		
9759	6000	C-FNIR		
9760	6000	C-FNMC		
9761	6000	C-FNKX		
9762	6000	C-FNIL		
9763	6000	C-FNLH		
9764	6000	C-FNXG		
9765	6000	C-FNVR		
9766	6000	C-FNXK		
9767	6000	C-FODX		
9768	5000	C-FOCF		
9769				
9770				
9771				
9772				
9773				
9774				
9775				
9776				
9777				
9778				
9779				
9780				
9781				
9782				
9783				
9784				
9785				
9786				
9787				
9788				
9789				
9790				
9998	5000	C-GGHN	[c/n changed from 9414 at customer's request]	B-KMF

CANADAIR CL600 CHALLENGER

C/n	Srs	Identities							
1001		C-GCGR-X	[ff 08Nov78; w/o 03Apr80 Mojave, CA, while flight testing]						
1002	S	C-GCGS-X	Canada 144612 code "X"	[displayed Heritage Park, Air Command HQ, Winnipeg, Canada]					
1003/3991	S	C-GCGT-X	C-GCGT	[wfu circa Feb06 to Canadian Aviation Museum, Rockcliffe, Canada for display]					
1004	S	C-GXKQ	N2677S	N227CC	N600BP	N640TS	N50PA	[parted out]	
1005	S	C-GBDH	N600CL	C-GBCC	N444WA	D-BJET	N600CL	N605TS	N180CH	N244AL	[parted out by Dodson Int'l Parts, Rantoul, KS]
1006	S	C-GCSN	N110KS	HZ-AO4	C-GCSN	Canada 144603		N296V	N515BP	(N6972Z)	XB-ODO
1007	S	HZ-TAG	C-GBKC	Canada 144604		N600WJ	(N799HF)	(N607BH)	
1008	S	C-GBEY	(D-BBAD)	Canada 144605		N380V	N604SH		
1009	S	C-GBFY	N606CL	C-GCVQ	Canada 144606		N396V	(N198SD)	
1010	S	C-GCIB	N909MG	N802Q	N7JM	N2105			
1011	S	C-GBHS	N42137	N510PC	N510PS	N601JR	N678ML	N116RA	N3RP	[cx 25Jun15; parted out in South Africa]
1012	S	C-GBKE	N600KC	(N78499)	N750PM	N750BM	N121VA	N8KG	N167SC	N310PE	N604AC	VH-JPQ
1013	S	C-GBHZ	N2428	N601SA	N129BA	N72SR	N16RW			
1014	S	C-GBLL-X	N97941	HZ-TAG	C-GBLL	Canada 144607		N370V	[w/o 02Feb05 Teterboro Airport, NJ]	
1015	S	C-GBLN	N37LB	N604CL	C-GBLN	Canada 144608		N25V		
1016	S	C-GWRT	EI-GPA	VR-BKJ	N757MC	N16TS	N920RV	(N812XL)		
1017	S	C-GBPX	N4247C	N777XX	C-GBPX	Canada 144609		N270V	M-CHLG	N808CH	
1018	S	C-GLWR	N1812C	N198CC	N375PK	N875PK	N771WW	N618AJ	N618RL	C6-SVB
1019	S	C-GLWT	N9071M	N603CL	N600FF	ZS-NER	3B-GFI	N619TS		
1020	S	C-GLWV	N36LB	N602CL	N600MG	N600PD	N808TM	N600BD	N602AJ	
1021	S	C-GLWX	N914X	N914XA	N63HJ	[canx 14Oct04 and parted out]				
1022	S	C-GLWZ	C-GOGO	Canada 144610		N260V	N600JJ			
1023	S	C-GLXB	N630M	N680M	N90UC	(N610TS)	N920DS	(N333TS)	N777GD	N771GD	[parted out by Dodson International Parts, Rantoul, KS]
1024	S	C-GLXD	N637ML	N567ML	N326MM	N810MT	N811MT	[parted out by Dodson Int'l Parts, Rantoul, KS]		
1025	S	C-GLXF	N2636N	N111G	N111J	HB-ILH	N888LW	N620SB	(OY-VIA)	(OY-CKO)	N711GA	N399WB
1026	S	C-GLXH	N507CC	N507HC	(N507WY)	N694JC	N694PG	LV-CGL		
1027	S	C-GLXK	N420L	N420TX	(N456CG)	N678CG	N111FK	N112FK	N93BA	N111JL
1028	S	C-GLXM	HB-VHC	N600ST	5B-CHX	N600BZ	YV-1111CP	N858PJ		
1029	S	C-GLXO	HB-VGA	D-BMTM	(N205A)	OH-WIH	N600TN	N722DJ		
1030	S	C-GLXQ	N1622	N604CL	C-GCZU	Canada 144611		(N196V)	N60S	N630BB	N721ST	ZS-SKC
1031	S	C-GLXS	N620S							
1032	S	C-GLXU	N455SR	N200CN	N11AZ	(N31DC)	N1884	N70X	N70XF	
1033	S	C-GLXW	N2642F	VR-CKK	N600YY	N101SK	N101ST	N357RT	N304TT	(N518FS)
1034		C-GLXY	N2634Y	N153SR	(N151SR)	N209WF	(N209WE)	N481JT	LV-YLB	N134VS
1035	S	C-GLYA	N122TY	N122WF	N64FC	C-FEAQ	(EI-BYD)	VR-BLD	N700CL	N187AP	N163EG	N163ET
1036	S	C-GLYC	C-GBOQ	N80AT	N88AT	N66MF	N900DP	N900LG	N275JP	
1037		C-GLYE	N805C	[w/o 03Jan83 Sun Valley Friedman Memorial, ID]						
1038	S	C-GLYH	N8010X	N1045X	N65HJ	N616DF	N903DD			
1039	S	C-GLYK	N26640	N1868M	N1868S	N722HP	N895CC	N905MP	N420PR*	
1040	S	C-GLYM	Canada 144601	[dbr McDill AFB, FL, 24May12]						
1041	S	C-GLYO	N733K	N733CF	N193DQ	(N95DQ)	N141TS	N141RD		
1042	S	C-GLWV	N770CA	N999SR	N999TF	(N939CG)	N604MH	N604SJ	4X-CZI	
1043	S	C-GLWX	N229GC	C-GJPG	C-FSXG	N43NW	N100QR	(LV-CZU)		
1044	S	C-GLWZ	N541MM	N205MM	N55AR	N800BT				
1045	S	C-GLXB	N55PG	N900FC	C-GBKB	N247CK	G-NREG	[cx 15Feb15; parted out at Kemble, UK; fuselage used as film prop at Leavesden Studios, UK and White Waltham, UK]		
1046	S	C-GLXD	C-GTXV	N46SR	N246JL					
1047	S	C-GLXH	C-GBSZ	N2741Q	N601WW	N818LS	N555WD	N556WD	(N500EX)	N315MK	N249AJ
1048	S	C-GLXK	N29687	N600TT	N500LS	N600LS	N601LS	(EI-BXN)	C-FSIP	C-GDDR
1049	S	C-GLXM	N2720B	HB-VFW	N491DB	N491TS	N39RE	N600CF	N601CT	
1050	S	C-GLXO	N600MK	N82CW	N82CN	N710HL	N650TL			
1051	S	C-GLXQ	N27341	N20CX	(N601CR)	N601SR	N91UC	N27BH	N505PM	
1052	S	C-GLXS	N3330M	N3330L	N110M	N110TD	N409KC	N600LG	N620AC	"N168TS"	N620AC	N152TS	N222LH	N222LM
1053	S	C-GLYA	HB-VHO	N4424P	N32BC	N32BQ	N397BE	N415PT	N54SK	N54SU	LV-BAS
1054	S	C-GLYC	N80TF	N7008	N9008	VR-CLI	N602AS	N660RM	N217RM	N915KH
1055		C-GLYE	N2707T	N1FE	N55SR	N271MB	N643CR	XA-…		
1056	S	C-GLYH	N26895	N600CC	N600TE	N712HL	N1HZ	N2HZ	N777GA	
1057	S	C-GLXU	C-GBTK	(VH-OZZ)	N508CC	N508HC	XA-RAP	XA-TIV	XA-ISR	N78SR	N6MW
1058	S	C-GLXW	N4000X	N60HJ	N658CF	[cx 03Mar16; instructional airframe with Mohawk Valley Community College, Rome/Griffiss, NY]				
1059	S	C-GLXY	N227G	N227GL	(C-FRST)	(C-GFCD)	N3HB	N103HB	N403WY	N396KM
1060	S	C-GLYK	N29984	N22AZ	N74JA					
1061	S	C-GLYO	N600JW	VH-MXX	VH-MCG	N770JC	N661TS	N601KK	(N661TS)	(N604YZ)
1062	S	C-GLWV	C-GBTT	Malaysia M31-01	N4FE	N62BL	N68SD	N95EB	N444ET	
1063	S	C-GLWX	N31240+	N102ML	PT-LXW	N102ML	XA-SOA	N8260D	(N74TJ)	(N711AJ)	(N88TJ)	(N98TW)	N409CC	N457HL
		[+recorded for a while in error on FAA files as N32140]							
1064	S	C-GLWZ	C-GBUB	Malaysia M31-02	N14FE	N64GL	N75B	N100LR		
1065	S	C-GLXB	C-GBVE	Canada 144602		N601WJ	N287DL			
1066	S	C-GLXD	N67B	N721SW	N701QS	N701GA	N51TJ	D-BSNA	ZS-TCW	
1067	S	C-GLXH	"VR-CBP"	C-GLXH	C-GBZE	N50928	N800AB	N205EL	N240AK	M-IFES	G-CIAU
1068	S	C-GLXK	N215RL	N938WH	N160LC	N604EF				
1069	S	C-GLXM	N203G	N816PD	I-LPHZ	N74LM	(N100LR)	N500RH	N788WG	N818TH	(N818E)	N455BE	N817CK	N80CK
1070	S	C-GLXO	N3237S	HZ-MF1	N70DJ	N24JK	N670CL	D-BUSY	N600DP	
1071	S	C-GLXQ	N607CL	N523B	N588UC	N121DF	N127DF	N671SR	N711DB	N220LC	N600HA	ZS-TSN
1072	S	C-GLXW	N82A	(N137FP)	N331FP	N125AC	N10PN	N302PC	N329MP	9Q-CVA	ZS-BGA
1073	S	C-GLXY	N234RG	N234MW	N31WT	(N331WT)	N661JB	N888KS	VH-NKS	N600BP	(VR-BBP)	(N512AC)	N125AN	(N600EC)
		N673TS	N673YS	(N673BH)	N27BH	RP-C5505				
1074		C-GLYK	N317FE	N1FE	N10FE	HZ-SAA	HZ-WT2	HZ-WBT1	HZ-RFM	N800HH	N674CW	N674TB
1075	S	C-GLXO	N600CP	N2FE	N25SR	N751DB	N450AJ	(N458AJ)	N240MC	
1076	S	C-GLXK	N8000	N7SP	I-BLSM	N601WW	N87TR	ZS-YAG		
1077	S	C-GLXM	N994TA	(N778XX)	C-GBZK	N152SM	N71M	N500R	N507R	(N940DH)	N300TK
1078	S	C-GLYO	N600DL	N600CF	I-MRDV	N53SR	N1500	(N1504)	VH-ZSU	
1079	S	C-GLWV	N46ES	N125N	N601Z	N888FW	N600RE	N601SA	N601CM	[cx 14Mar2013, wfu]
1080	S	C-GLWX	N800CC	N3JL	N300TW	N677LM	9Q-CDR	9Q-CRD		
1081	S	C-GLWZ	N19HF	(N54PA)	(N681TS)	N456DK	N19DD	N199D	N19DD	N199D	ZS-ISA
1082	S	C-GLXB	N3854B	N600ST	I-PTCT	N700KK	N777KK	N777KZ	N333KK	N388DD	[wfu Fort Lauderdale Executive, FL]
1083	S	C-GLXD	N47ES	N471SP	N471SB	N399FL				
1084	S	C-GLXH	N730TL	(N10MZ)	N175ST	N550CW				
1085	S	C-GLXQ	N20G	N20GX	N600ST	OE-HET	LZ-YUM	N807CH	[cx 04Jun15; CofR expired]	
1086		C-GLXS	[marks reserved 29Mar83 but aircraft not completed – fuselage to Canadian Forces Fire Fighting Academy, CFB Borden]							
1087		[aircraft not completed – fuselage to Canadian Forces Fire Fighting Academy, CFB Borden]								
1088		[aircraft not completed – fuselage to Canadian Forces Fire Fighting Academy, CFB Borden]								

Production complete–

CANADAIR CL601 CHALLENGER

C/n	Identities									
3001	C-GBUU-X	[ff 17Sep82] N601CL	N601AG	N789DR	N74GR					
3002	C-GBXH	(N509PC)	N4449F	N273G	N601SR	N750GT	N602CW	N227PE	N600NP	[wfu Marco Island, FL, after landing accident 01Mar15]
3003	C-GLXU	N500PC	N500TB	N500TD	C-GESR	N601CL	(N680FA)	VH-MXK		
3004	C-GLXK	N509PC	N967L	N501PC	N45PH	N45WL				
3005	C-FAAL	N601TX	N783DM	N958DP	[cx 01May15; parted out Wilmington, DE]					
3006	C-GLXY	N372G	(N3728)	HB-IKX	N372G	(EI-TAM)	P4-TAM	N606BA	ZS-ONL	N256SD	N601JG
3007	C-GLYE	N711SR	N711SX	N711SZ	N910KB	N275MT				
3008	C-GLYK	N733A	N783A	N61AF	(N999SW)	N38SW	N608CW	N698CW	(N600LX)	N710GA	N214FW	[w/o 29Jan15, shot down by Venezuelan AF near Aruba on suspicion of drug-running]
3009	C-GLYO	N373G	N873G	(N651AC)	[w/o 28Nov04 Montrose, CO]					
3010	C-GLWV	C-GBLX	N80CS	N601UT	N601SQ	N601BD	N411TJ	N957DP		
3011	C-GLWX	C-GBYC	N601AG	N399WW	N899WW	N700MK	N7788	N205EL	N205EE	N202PH	N453GS	[cx 12Dec15; parted out Wilmington, DE]
3012	C-GLXB	N226GL	N226G	C-GMII	VR-BMA	N6165C	XA-SHZ	N603GJ	N23BJ	N23BN	N878RM	C-FKJM
3013	C-GLXD	N601TG	VR-BLA	VP-BLA	N124BC	N633CW	(N602LX)	N213TS	(N32WR)		
3014	C-GLXH	N14PN	N292GA	N698RS	N698RT	C-GDBF	N807MM			
3015	C-GLXM	N374G	XA-KIM	XA-UXK						
3016	C-GLWV	N4562Q	N1107Z	N601CL	VP-BIE	N388DB	N214MD	N813TA		
3017	C-GLWX	N778XX	(HZ-AMA)	HZ-SFS	N778YY	VR-CAR	C-GJPG	C-FBYJ	A6-EJD	JY-RY1	JY-RYA	[wfu Dubai, United Arab Emirates]
3018	C-GLWZ	C-GBXW	N779XX	[w/o 07Feb85 Milan, Italy; cx May91; cockpit section conv to flight simulator and used by Flight Safety Intl at Montreal-Dorval, Canada]							
3019	C-GLXB	N375G	N875G	XA-SMS	N5498G					
3020	C-GLXO	C-GCFI	[parted out Addison, TX]							
3021	C-GLXQ	N5069P	(N711SP)	N711SJ	N967L	N503PC	N966L	N150MH	[cx 20May15; parted out Georgetown, TX]		
3022	C-GLXS	C-GCFG								
3023	C-GLXY	N778YY	N100WC	N967L	N501PC	N524PC	N601KF	N601KE	N601FJ	AP-MIR	
3024	C-GLYA	N711ST	HB-ILM	N98CR	N93CR	N888AZ	VP-COK	N211LM		
3025	C-GLWV	N1620	N529DM	N529D	N363CR	N997GC	T7-GFA			
3026	C-GLWX	N5373U	N927A	N601GL	N300S	N80RP	N716HP	N810MT	(N810MB)	N307SC	N601NP	[parted out Gary, IN]
3027	C-GLWZ	N5402X	N17CN	(N401NK)	N627CW	(N603LX)	C-GPSI	[cx Jul12; instructional airframe, Southern Alberta Institute of Technology, Calgary, Canada]			
3028	C-GLXB	C-FBEL	C-FBEI	[cx May12; instructional airframe, Ecole Nationale d'Aeronautique, Montreal-St Hubert, Canada]							
3029	C-GLXD	N5491V	N1824T	N629TS	N773JC	N629TS	[cx 13Apr15; parted out Wilmington, DE]				
3030	C-GLXH	N611CL	N34CD	N39CD	[parted out Chino, CA; cx 14May11]					
3031	C-GLXK	C-GCTB	N607CL	C-GCTB	Germany 1201	VP-CCF	N303BX	(N631CF)	N54JC	(N181SM)	G-LWDC
3032	C-GLXM	N779YY	HZ-AK1	N7011H	N111G	N111GX	N392FV	N2000C	N177FL		
3033	C-GLXQ	N601TJ	HB-ILK	VP-BBF	M-MTPO	[b/u Kemble, UK, Dec14; cx 20Jan16]				
3034	C-GLXU	N374BC	N372BC	N372BG	N372PG	N120MP	C-GSAP	C-GLOJ	N747LV	[cx 05Jan16; wfu]	
3035	C-GLXW	C-GCUN	Canada 144613	[w/o 24Apr95 Shearwater AFB, Nova Scotia, Canada; to be rebuilt for museum display at CFB Greenwood, Canada]							
3036	C-GLXY	C-GCUP	Canada 144614							
3037	C-GLXB	C-GCUR	Canada 144615							
3038	C-GLYA	C-GCUT	Canada 144616							
3039	C-GLYH	C-GPGD	C-GPCC	N639CL	N500PG	N507PG	N1ES			
3040	C-GLYK	N608CL	Germany 1202	[final German AF flight 31May10]	C-GJNG					
3041	C-GLWV	C-GRBC	N610MS	N600MS	N169TA	N169TD	N418PP			
3042	C-GLWX	N613CL	N900CC	N333GJ	N951RM	N923SL				
3043	C-GLWZ	N609CL	Germany 1203	C5-AFT						
3044	C-GLXD	N921K	N125N	N955DB	N601GB	(N801PA)	LV-BPV	N304CT		
3045	C-GLXH	N914BD	N914BB	N601RP	OE-HCL	N3045	N998JR	N601PR		
3046	C-GLXK	C-GDBX	B-4005	N601HJ	N601TJ	LX-AEN	N46SR	N228PK	N600GA	
3047	C-GLXM	C-GBZQ	B-4006	N602HJ	N602TJ	OE-HLE	N824DH			
3048	C-GLXO	N35FP	N601JM	(N628WC)	[cx 28Apr16; parted out Miami/Opa Locka, FL]					
3049	C-GLXQ	N610CL	C-FQYT	Germany 1204	C-FTDA					
3050	C-GLXS	(N9680N)	N9680Z	N62MS	N62MU	N95SR	N601AE	N802PA	(N626JP)	N528LJ	N1219L
3051	C-GLWR	N445AC	N60MS	N60MU	N4415D	N95SR	N651CW	(N604LX)	N97SG		
3052	C-GLWT	C-GDCQ	B-4007	N603HJ	(N601GF)	N801GC	VP-CRX	N425WN	N515LF		
3053	C-GLWV	N604CL	Germany 1205	C-FDAH						
3054	C-GLWX	N605CL	VH-MZL	N54PR	N601PR	N601TP	N601ZT	N375PK	N315SL	N50TG	N722HP	N57MH	N947KK
3055	C-GLWZ	N100HG	N608RP	N601RC						
3056	C-GLXB	N612CL	Germany 1206	C-FDAU	C-GPAJ					
3057	C-GLXD	N19J	9J-RON	(N602TS)	N747TS	N163WG				
3058	C-GLXU	N125PS								
3059	C-GLXW	N614CL	Germany 1207	C-GDAX						
3060	C-GLXY	(N601SN)	N601S							
3061	C-GLYO	N9708N	N999JR	N597FJ	N601AA	YV3221				
3062	C-GLYK	N601HP	N601GT	N2183N	N628CM					
3063	C-GLYH	C-FURG	[instructional airframe Montreal/St Hubert, Canada]		C-FURB					
3064	C-GLYC	N566N	N356N	N224N	N224F	(N224HF)	N224U	(N424JM)	N664CW	(N606LX)	N425SU
3065	C-GLYA	N602CC	N1623	(N128PE)	N500PE	N601JP	"N603TS"	N601JP	(N54PA)	LX-GDC	G-IMAC	[cx 16Apr15; wfu]
3066	C-GLXQ	N609CL	N144SX	VR-CLE	VP-CLE	N105UP				

MODEL 601-3A

C/n	Identities								
5001	C-GDDP	[ff 28Sep86] N245TT	N245TL	(N59FJ)	N604FJ	N422PR*			
5002	C-GDEQ	N611CL	C-GDEQ	N611CL	N585UC	N43PR	N602TS		
5003	C-GDHP	N778XX	HB-IKT	N601FR					
5004	C-GDKO	N100KT	N180KT	N618DC	N504TS	XA-VDG			
5005	C-GLWR	N613CL	N101PK	HB-IKU	N14GD	N64FE	N902BW		
5006	C-GLWT	C-FLPC	C-GENA	N506TS	N220LC				
5007	C-GLWV	N60GG	N607CL	(N607CZ)	N17TE	N17TZ	N666CT		
5008	C-GLWX	N601CC	N601EG	N1M	N42EE				
5009	C-GLWZ	N399SW	N699CW	(N610LX)	N654CM				
5010	C-GLXB	N57HA	(N57HK)	N1812C	N181AP	N429WG	N601WG		
5011	C-GLXD	N603CC	JA8283	N611MH	N602UK	VR-CIC	VP-CIC		
5012	C-GLXU	N107TB	N1868M	N500LR					
5013	C-GLXW	N711PD	I-CTPT	N604MC	N301MF	N950FB	N116LS		
5014	C-GLXY	N21CX	N31WH	N311G	N311GX	N888DH	(N714TS)	N514TS	
5015	C-GLXH	N601KR	N200DE	N514RB	N204JK				
5016	C-GLXQ	N604CC	N49UR	N622AB	(N622AD)	N868CE	C-GQWI	N325DA	N551SD
5017	C-GLWX	N700KC	N202HG	N7705B	N404HG				

CANADAIR CL601 CHALLENGER

C/n	Identities										
5018	C-GLWV	N606CC	C-FBHX	9Q-CBS	C-FBHX	N601HH	N618DB	(D-AMTM)	N601GS	(N601DR)	(N601GR)	N893AC	N828SK
	N908DG											
5019	C-GLWT	N915BD	N915BB	(N247GA)	N237GA	N602BD	C-GJFQ	N575CF	C-GHGC			
5020	C-GLYA	C-FBKR	I-BEWW	C-GZHZ	N604CF	N39RE	N392JT					
5021	C-GLYC	N64F	N122WF	N48FU	(N305M)	N621CF	N620HF	N989BC				
5022	C-GLYK	N449ML	N449MC	VP-CJP	G-SAJP	VP-CJP	N655TH	N618RR				
5023	C-GLYO	N608CC	EI-LJG	N601CJ	N175ST	N623CW	(OE-...)	D-AAMA	G-JFJC	2-JFJC		
5024	C-GLYH	C-FCDF	B-4010	N604HJ	N601NB	N601DT	N712SD	N142RP				
5025	C-GLWR	C-FCGS	B-4011	N605HJ	N1TK	N11TK	N93DW	N1DW	N931DW	N660AF		
5026	C-GLWT	N601WM	5N-APZ									
5027	C-GLWV	N244BH	N64BH	N421SZ	N420SZ	N420ST	N7PS					
5028	C-GLWX	N601TL	N601RL	(N601EA)	N161JG							
5029	C-GLWZ	C-FDAT	N602CC	VR-BMK	N67MR	N83LC	N594RJ	N375JP	N571NA			
5030	C-GLXB	N312CT	N816SQ	N816SP	N1HZ							
5031	C-GLXD	N900CL	N908CL	N721MC	N721MD	N64LE	(N710TP)					
5032	C-GLXF	N604CC	N667LC	N667CC	4X-COT	N601ER	N950SW	N684SW	LV-BYG			
5033	C-GLXH	VH-ASM	N32GG	N397J	(N397JQ)	N397Q	N144BS	N144BG	N797SA			
5034	C-GLXK	C-GIOH	[to Southern Alberta Institute of Technology, Calgary, as instructional airframe Nov09]									
5035	C-GLXU	N606CC	N333MG	N202W	HB-JRV	N635S						
5036	C-GLXW	N225N	N468KL	N468KE	N400DH							
5037	C-GLXY	N608CC	(JA8360)	N707GG	N353TC	N212LM	N710LM	5N-IGY	[Nigerian marks assumed, not yet confirmed]			
5038	C-GLXQ	C-GBJA	(N602CN)	N1271A	N78RP	(N220LC)	N78PP	N91KH				
5039	C-GLWX	N811BB	N811BP	N811BR	N765WT							
5040	C-GLWV	N652CN	N807Z	N898AK								
5041	C-GLWT	C-FETZ	G-FBMB	C-FTIE	N641CL	N352AF	N352AE	"N541TS"	N953FA	N170FL	N601QA	
5042	C-GLYA	C-FEUV	HB-IKS	N28UA	HB-IKS							
5043	C-GLYC	N779YY	VR-COJ	N601BH	N601VH							
5044	C-GLYK	C-FFBY	I-NNUS	N901BM	VR-CMC	VP-CMC	VP-CBS					
5045	C-GLXS	C-FFSO	N616CC	N500GS	N601AF							
5046	C-GLXW	N6SG	N818TH	N818TY	N426PF	N426PE	N719UW					
5047	C-GLXD	N140CH	N547FP	N900SS	N384MP	N507CZ	N517BB					
5048	C-GLXY	N2004G	N716RD	N907WS	N907WC							
5049	C-GLXF	N721EW	N721SW	N721BW	D-AGKG	N628VK	VR-CVK	VP-CVK	N888JA	B-MAI	N368FJ	
5050	C-GLXK	N826JP	N831CJ	N881CJ	(N25GG)	N710VF	N651JP					
5051	C-GLXM	N1903G	N190GG	N300KC	N190SB	C-GQBQ						
5052	C-GLXO	N4PG	N652CW	N125ST	(N615SA)	XB-CAR						
5053	C-GLXU	N5PG	(N553CW)	N653CW	(N611LX)	N440KM						
5054	C-GLXB	N619FE	N3FE	N954BA								
5055	C-GLXH	N601HC	N46F	N460F	N219YY							
5056	C-GLXQ	N614CC	N153NS	N525SD								
5057	[Was to have been first CL601S with c/n 6001 but built as 601-3A]					C-GLWR	N900NM	N830CB	N830CD	N733CF	(N721KY)	N91KY
5058	C-GLWZ	N404SK	N101SK	N527JA								
5059	C-GLWV	XA-GEO	XA-JFE	XA-TTD	C-GZNC	N627KR	C-FJNS	C-FJNZ	N408JC	N403JC		
5060	C-GLYO	N5060H	N630M	ZS-NKD	N506BA	N573AC	EC-JKT	(D-ADLA)	D-ARTE			
5061	C-GLYH	C-FHHD	9Q-CBS	N661CL	(N575MA)	VP-BEJ						
5062	C-GLWX	N60FC	N540W	N548W	N142B	N727S	N316BG	N601ER				
5063	[Was to have been the second CL601S with c/n 6002 but built as 601-3A, last Cartierville-built airframe]							C-GLXS	N612CC	N79AD	N78AD	N611JW
	N811JW	N801FL	(N315FX)	N304FX	N304BX	N50DS	N563TS	XA-UEW	N9771C			
5064	[First Dorval-built airframe]			C-GLXW	C-FIOB	VH-BRG	N564TS	N601EC	N811NC			
5065	C-GLXD	N601BF	N882C	N103KB								
5066	C-GLXY	N506TN	N100KT	N3PC	N566TS	N221LC	N16KB					
5067	C-GLXF	N603CC	9A-CRO	9A-CRT	N220TW	HB-IUF	VP-CFT	G-OCFT				
5068	C-GLXK	N609CC	N88WG	JA8361	N602WA	D-AOHP	N113WA	C-FNNT	N66NT	C-FNNS	C-FLRP	N360FF	N360
5069	C-GLXM	C-FIGR	I-FIPP	VR-BNF	N655CN	N324B	C-GRTB	N161PB	LV-GDQ			
5070	C-GLXO	N980HC	N780HC	N305FX	(D-AAFX)	OY-CLD	ZS-SGC					
5071	C-GLWT+	N500PC	(N5032H)	TR-AAG	[+shown in Canadian DoT files as C-FLWT in error]							
5072	C-GLYC	N609K	N88HA	[w/o 20Mar94 Bassett, NE; cx Apr95; remains to Executive Aircraft Corp, Wichita, KS; fuselage to Addison, TX, 2008]								
5073	C-GLYK	N60KR	PK-HMK	N5073	(VR-CKC)	(N400KC)	N803RR	N70X				
5074	C-GLXH	N23SB	VH-NSB									
5075	C-GLXU	N65357	N810D	VR-CCV	PT-OSA	N601Z	N409KC	N607AX	N625LR			
5076	C-GLXB	N5TM	XA-GUA									
5077	C-GLXQ	N1622	N64YP	N118MT								
5078	C-GLWR	N601MG	N601MD	N53DF	N553DF	N578FP	N702RV	N227WG				
5079	C-GLWV	C-FJDF	VR-CCR	VP-CCR	N836CM							
5080	C-GLYO	C-FJGR	N601DB	N135BC	N135BD	N903TA	N900H					
5081	C-GLYH	[also reported as C-GLXH]			N619CC	HL7202	N601ST					
5082	C-GLWX	C-GBJA	N611NT	N611GS	N6BB	N82FJ	N794SB					
5083	C-GLYA	N189K	N683UF	N83UF								
5084	C-GLWT	[also reported as C-GLWZ]			N399CF	N622WM	N622WZ	N777GU				
5085	C-GLXD	C-FJPI	N618CC	D-ACTU	D-ACTE	I-DAGS	PH-ABO	M-YONE	G-OWAY	G-XRTV		
5086	C-GLXS	N353K	N343K	N343KA	N601JE	C-GIXI						
5087	C-GLXW	N601CC	C-FLUT	XA-RZD	N587CC	XA-ULQ	XA-OHS	N548CC				
5088	C-GLXH	N601CD	N601HC	C-GPOT	C-GPCS	N613SB	[w/o Chino, CA, 13Jun13; cx 03Aug15]					
5089	C-GLXY	N968L	N516SM	N360SL	N360RL							
5090	C-GLXF	N601CB	N404CB	N818LS	N818TH	N400KC	VP-CAM	HB-ITK	N621CF	N226EC		
5091	C-GLXM	N915BD	(N715BD)	C-FTFC	N366LP							
5092	C-GLXQ	[also reported as C-GLXO]			C-FKIY	HB-IKV	N300CR	N308CR	N4JS			
5093	C-GLYA	N302EC	N601CH	N875H	N375H	N331DC	N331DQ	C-GGMP	C-GMGB	C-GFIG		
5094	C-GLWT	C-FKNN	TC-OVA	TC-DHB	N675CF	VP-BZT	5B-CKK	N774PC	N856JM			
5095	C-GLYC	N95FE	N2FE	N995BA								
5096	C-GLXK	C-FKTD	HB-IKW	C-GSQI	N66NT	N66NS	C-FNNS	C-FJJC				
5097	C-GLXK	C-FKVW	XA-JJS	XA-TLM	N120PA	N227CP						
5098	C-GLXH	N812GS	N808G									
5099	C-GLXU	N509W	N504M	N801P	N801R	N601DW	N203JE	N203JD	(N121GG)	N112GG	YV576T	
5100	C-GLXB	N510	N505M	N225N	N241N							
5101	C-GLXQ	N604CC	N105BN	(N108BN)	N213GS	N243JP						
5102	C-GLWR	C-FLYJ	(HS-TDL)	HS-TVA	VR-CHK	VP-CHK	N604AC	(N983CE)	N494LC	N241FB	N241FR	HZ-OHS
5103	C-GLWV	N76CS	N601BE									
5104	C-GLYO	N777XX	VR-COJ	VR-CEG	N145ST	(N233SG)	9M-SWG	N233SG	(N604TS)	N212CT	N720LM	N111FK
5105	C-GLYH	C-FMVQ	OK-BYA	Czech Republic 5105								
5106	C-GLWX	(N601PR)	N106PR	N523JM								
5107	C-GLWZ	N417CL	N729HZ	N211RG								
5108	C-GLXD	N428CL	N224N	N236N								
5109	C-GLXS	N439CL	N721S	N721G								
5110	C-GLXU	N392PT	N308FX	N308BX	TC-MDG	HZ-FJM						

CANADAIR CL601 CHALLENGER

C/n	Identities											
5111	C-GLXH	C-GBJA	N46SG	N4SG	N502F	N502HE						
5112	C-GLXF	N112NC	N109NC	N404AB	N604ME	N605CK	N800YY					
5113	C-GLXM	N605CC	N163M	N163MR	N733EY	N733EX	N128GB	N770GE	N116HL			
5114	C-GLYA	C-FOSK	VR-BOA	VP-BOA	2-MATO							
5115	C-GLYC	N25SB	(N605AG)	N1800C	N604MB							
5116	C-GLXW	N841PC	N1904P	N436DM								
5117	C-GLXY	N606CC	N80BF	C-FBCR	C-GAOB	N9517	N601WY					
5118	C-GLXK	N824JK	N24JK	N900FN	C-GZUM							
5119	C-GLXO	VR-BNG	VP-BNG	N519DB	C-GJDG	N519DB	N601FS	C-FNEU	N73ML			
5120	C-GLWT	N400TB	(N500TB)	N408TB	PK-JKM							
5121	C-GLYK	N502PC	N702PC	XA-GCD	N328AM	N602NP						
5122	C-GLXS	N908CL	N7046J	N900CL	N65FF	XA-RYK						
5123	C-GLWR	N601UP	N147HH	N613PJ								
5124	C-GLXD	C-FBOM	C-GFCB	C-GFCD	N546LF	N939CC						
5125	C-GLWZ	C-FPIY	HB-IKY	N512BC	N604WB	(N14DP)	P4-EPI	VP-CEI	2-SEXY			
5126	C-GLXU	N21CL	N21NY	N99UG	N650LG	N691CC						
5127	C-GLXB	N718P	N718R	N555LG	N550LG	N993SA						
5128	C-GLWX	C-FPOX	XA-GME	N321GE	N321GL	N307SC						
5129	C-GLXH	N129RH	(N603AF)	N129TF	VP-CRR							
5130	C-GLXQ	N603KS	N601GB	VR-BQA	N601SR	N349JR	N405TC					
5131	C-GLWV	N602JB	N6JB	(N405DP)	XA-HMX							
5132	C-GLYO	N610DB	N289K									
5133	C-GLYH	N53DF	N121DF	N121FF	N486BG							
5134	C-GLXS	N43R	N43RK	N511WM	N511WN	N898EW	C-GPOC	N2369R				

MODEL 601-3R

C/n	Identities											
5135	C-GLWR	N1902J	N1902P	N144MH								
5136	C-GLXW	N51GY	N20G	N20GX	N75EM							
5137	C-GLWZ	N137CL	N90AR	(OY-GSE)	N518JG							
5138	C-GLXF	N138CC	N85									
5139	C-GLXK	N139CD	N34CD	(N348D)	N902TA	(N612LX)	N639TS					
5140	C-GLXM	N1061D	N79AD	N79AN	N630AR	N680AR*						
5141	C-GLXO	N312AT	N601ER	N601TM	N901TA	(N613LX)	N601JP	N358PJ				
5142	C-GLWT	C-FRGV	VR-CJJ	N330TP	(XA-...)	N22AQ	XA-MYN					
5143	C-GLYA	[built as CL604 prototype with c/n 5991 (qv)]										
5144	C-GLYC	N616CC	N347BA	N601CV								
5145	C-GLYK	C-GPGD	C-GDPF	N145LJ	N1DH							
5146	C-GLXW	C-FRQA	LX-MMB	N137MB	C-GWUG	N137MB	N96DS	N88NN				
5147	C-GLWR	C-FRJX	XA-SOR	N514JR	XA-SOR							
5148	C-GLXD	N793CT	N792CT	N601DS								
5149	C-GLXY	N601GR	XA-GRB	N63ST	VP-BFS	VP-BZI	M-YBZI					
5150	C-GLXU	N602CC	N601BW	N710AN								
5151	C-GLXB	C-GBJA	VR-BWB	VP-BWB	N333MX	C-GMMI	N360AP	N405AR				
5152	C-GLWX	N777XX	VR-COJ	VP-COJ	N605BA	N18RF	(N933PG)	N388PG	G-FBFI	N601FB	(HB-JRX)	G-FBFI	G-CHAI
	ZS-ANZ											
5153	C-GLXH	N601EB	VR-CHA	N604BA	OY-APM	N653AC	N115WF	[w/o Aspen, CO, 05Jan14]				
5154	C-GLXQ	N602DP	9M-TAN	N154BA	4X-COY	N601VF	C-FJLA	N601HW				
5155	C-GLWV	N342TC	N401RJ	C-FPDR	N808H	XA-OFM						
5156	C-GLYO	C-FSXH	VR-BAA	N255CC	N601TP							
5157	C-GLYH	N512DG	N471SP	N800KC	N808HG	5N-...						
5158	C-GLXS	C-FSYK	XA-ZTA	XA-MKY	XA-MKI	XA-JZL						
5159	C-GLWR	C-FTNN	EI-SXT	N159TS	C-GICI	N814PS	N659TS	N623BM	N615L			
5160	C-GLXW	N710HM	N94BA	N813VZ	N601MU							
5161	C-GLWZ	N994CT	(N997CT)	N190MP	N805DB	N807DD						
5162	C-GLXF	C-FTNE	VR-BCC	VP-BCC	N850FL	N850FB	N117RY	N949BC				
5163	C-GLXK	N709JM	N980HC	N224F	XA-ABF							
5164	C-GLXM	N715BG	N7008	N164CC	N431CB	XB-PMH	N113SR					
5165	C-GLXO	C-FTOH	VR-CPO	VP-CPO	C-GHCD	N165SC	N723HA	N723HH	XA-PTR	C-GURG		
5166	C-GLWT	N618CC	9M-NSK	N601A	HB-IVS	N410AC	C-GXPZ	N61FF				
5167	C-GLYA	N151CC	N86									
5168	C-GLYC	C-GRPF										
5169	C-GLYK	N773A	N154NS	N620PJ								
5170	C-GL..	N166A	N888WS	N925DD	N441PJ							
5171	C-GLXW	N213MC	N614AF									
5172	C-GLXD	N601FS	C-FUND	N777YG	(N225JF)	N605JF						
5173	C-GLXY	N181JC	D-AKUE	N501KV								
5174	C-GLXU	N605CC	N477DM	N877DM	N47HR	N47HF	C-GHBV	4X-CMH	N28KA	(N386K)	N276GR	
5175	C-GLXB	N601FR	N306FX	N306BX	N601KF	N800YB	N803TK	XA-UTL				
5176	C-GLWX	N142LL	ZS-CCT	N600DR	N600DH	N779AZ	N799AZ	C-GLSW				
5177	C-GLXH	N602MC	N757MC	N601UC	N227RH	N227RE	N895CC					
5178	C-GLXQ	(N602AN)	C-FWGE	CS-MAC	B-MAC	N888FJ						
5179	C-GLWV	(N604CC)	N608CC	N307FX	N307BX	N179TS	N168TS	N168LA	C-GDLI			
5180	C-GLYO	N518CL	5N-PAZ									
5181	C-GLYH	N602D	C-FCIB	C-FCID	N301KR	C-GOHG	N242CK					
5182	C-FVZC	HL7577										
5183	C-GLWR	N601HF	N55HF									
5184	C-GLXW	N605RP	N607RP	N607PH	N843GS							
5185	C-GLWZ	N611CC	N914X	N914Y								
5186	C-GLXF	N612CC	N9700X	N601AD								
5187	C-GLXK	N601KJ	N511DD									
5188	C-GLXM	N614CC	HS-JJA	N575CF	N10FE	N2000C	N221BW					
5189	C-FXCK	PT-WLZ	C-GZWY	N203G	XA-IMY	N54VS						
5190	C-GLWT	N190EK	N87									
5191	C-GLYA	N191BE	N605T									
5192	C-GLYC	N354TC	N750LG									
5193	C-GLYK	N604D	VR-BCI	VP-BCI	(N601HJ)	VP-BIH	N11LK	VP-CLZ				
5194	C-FXIP	EI-MAS	N601R	A9C-BXD	N539CS	N207JB						

CL601 production complete, replaced by CL604

Note: C/ns beginning 6001 were earmarked for the abortive CL601S programme

CANADAIR CL604 CHALLENGER

C/n	Identities									
5991	C-GLYA	[ff 18Sep94] C-FTBZ	"N604CC"+	[+fake marks worn during 1994 NBAA Show at New Orleans/Lakefront, LA]				C-FTBZ	[w/o 10Oct00 Wichita/Mid-	
	Continent A/P, KS; parted out by Dodson Int'l, Rantoul, KS]									
5301	C-FVUC	N604CC	N608CC	N123KH	N604BL					
5302	C-GLXD	C-GBJA	N355CC	N255CC						
5303	C-GLXY	C-FXKE	HL7522	N604BD	(OY-CLE)	N609BD	OY-TNF	OE-INF	(D-ARWE)	(D-AKAT)	N360PL
5304	C-GLXU	C-FXHE	I-MILK	N604VM	C-GITG	N604VM	(N604TS)	N604CA			
5305	C-GLXB	N604B	N747	N747Y	N888DH						
5306	C-GLWX	N309FX	N309BX	N604AB	N604WB						
5307	C-GLXH	C-FXUQ	VR-BHA	VP-BHA	(N604BA)	C-GIDG	LX-FAZ	G-UYAD	N16DA	N34FS	
5308	C-GLYO	N604KS	N604TS	N982J	N713HC	(N713HG)					
5309	C-GLYH	C-FXZS	VR-BAC	VP-BAC	C-GHRK	(N604LM)	N666TR	N666TF	(N509TS)	N814PS	N609TS	N770SW
5310	C-GLXS	C-FCCP	C-GPGD	C-GPFC	C-GWLI						
5311	C-GLWR	N225LY	N604JS	(N989DH)	N604HS						
5312	C-GLXW	N604KC	N312AM	(N905SB)							
5313	C-GLXD	N605KC	N312AT	N906SB	N3HB	N712PR					
5314	C-GLWZ	N604CT	VT-NGS								
5315	C-GLXF	N604LS	N818LS	N818TH							
5316	C-GLXK	N604BB	N411BB	N1848U	N200UL	N203TA	N208R	N484CR			
5317	C-FYXC	D-AMIM	C-GGPK	C-FNNT	C-GYMM	C-GKGN					
5318	C-GLXO	C-FYYH	(TC-DHE)	HB-IKQ	HB-IVR	ZS-LEO	ZS-KEN				
5319	C-GLWT	N604KR	N14R	N14RU	N100SA	N2SA	N5319	N27X	M-LOOK		
5320	C-GLXQ	N605CC	HZ-AFA2	N604MJ	HZ-MEJ1						
5321	C-GLYA	C-FZDY	PT-WXL	C-FZPG	N604CP	N1CP	N604CP	XA-LUF	XA-UWR		
5322	C-GLXY	N604CL	9A-CRO								
5323	C-GLXU	N604DS	N623TS	N604TC	(N604TS)						
5324	C-GLXB	N601CC	N667LC	N667LQ	N55LB	N611AB					
5325	C-GLWX	N60CT	N331TH	N604JW	[w/o 07Nov10 in hangar fire Indianapolis, IN; parted out by Dodson Int'l, Rantoul, KS]						
5326	C-GLYC	N908G	N1903G								
5327	C-GLYK	N609CC	HB-IKJ	D-AJAB	N146BA	N838LJ					
5328	C-GLXH	N712DG	ZS-AVL	(A6-EJB)	N328BX	LN-BWG	N604AZ	XA-JCG			
5329	C-GLWV	N8MC	N1GC	N1QF	N222MC	(N222MZ)					
5330	C-GLYO	N812G									
5331	C-GLYH	N810D									
5332	C-GLXS	C-FZRR	VP-BNF	N606JL	C-FNYU	N606JL					
5333	C-GLWR	N603CC	N811BB	N600MS	N991TW						
5334	C-GLXU	N604RC	N43R								
5335	C-GLXB	C-FZVN	VP-CAN	N8206S	N801P	N604B					
5336	C-GLXW	N310FX	N310BX	N212RR	N2615S	N675BP					
5337	C-GLXD	N270RA	N990AK	N302PC							
5338	C-GLWZ	N604PL	N913JB	N78RP	N426CF	N226CF	N36VV				
5339	C-GLXF	C-GBJA	N604CU	C-GCNR							
5340	C-GLXK	N606CC	N194WM	N134WM							
5341	C-GLXM	C-GBJA	N604SA	N429WG							
5342	C-GLXO	N311FX	N311BX	N371JC	N604AX	VT-DBG					
5343	C-GLWT	C-GAUK	C-GHKY	N307KR	C-GVXX	N323SH					
5344	C-GLXQ	N344BA	N604DH								
5345	C-GLYA	N345BA	N600AM	N2FD							
5346	C-GLXS	N604JP	HZ-SJP3	M-KARN	HZ-HSH						
5347	C-GLXW	C-GBDK	PT-MKO	N747TS	N205EL	N205EE	(N154JC)	N54JC			
5348	C-GLWR	N881TW	N604NC	D-AFAD							
5349	C-GLXY	N312FX	N312BX	N5349	N359V						
5350	C-GLXU	N331TP	VQ-BRZ								
5351	C-GLXB	N374G	N372G	N3726							
5352	C-GLWX	C-GBKE	4X-COE	N5352J	N770BC	N770BQ*					
5353	C-GLXH	C-GRIO	VH-LAM	N758CC							
5354	C-GLYC	N604PM	(N604AG)	N604BM	N11A	N1101A					
5355	C-GLWV	N555WD									
5356	C-GLYO	N605PM	(N605AG)	N880CR	N779WG	5N-BSP					
5357	C-GLYH	N604FS	XA-AST	XA-EVG							
5358	C-GLXS	C-GBRQ	TC-DHE	N127SB	N127SR	C-GJQN	N127SR				
5359	C-GLWR	N497DM	N597DA	SX-KFA							
5360	C-GLXW	N606PM	(N606AG)	N14SR	C-GZEK	C-GHML	M-VICA	C-GHML			
5361	C-GLXD	N346BA	N254AM								
5362	C-GLWZ	N607PM	N995MA	JY-AW3	A6-AAH	VP-CRK					
5363	C-GLXF	N964H	N444CZ								
5364	C-GLXK	C-FBNS	C-GDWF								
5365	C-GLXM	N604DC	N618DC	N280K	N80DX						
5366	C-GLXO	N604DD	Denmark C-066		N604DD	RP-C1937	N604DD	C-GJFC	N906TF	D-AFAI	
5367	C-GCCZ	EI-TAM	VP-COJ	N145DL	C-FZOP	N145DL	N848CC	N898CC	N16YD		
5368	C-GLXQ	N368G	N374G	N3746	9H-MIR						
5369	C-GCQB	(D-AZPP)	HB-IVP	N247WF	N247WE	N248WE	N605JA				
5370	C-GLXS	(N370CL)	N320CL	N755RV	VT-KAV	N370TS	VH-EVJ				
5371	C-GLYK	N371CL	C-GGWH								
5372	C-GLWR	N314FX	(N413LV)	G-LVLV	A6-CPC	N604JC	N976AM				
5373	C-GCVZ	HB-ILL	N604LC								
5374	C-GLXU	N98FJ	N97FJ	N203							
5375	C-GLXB	N604HP	(D-ASTS)	XA-GRB	N352AP	M-ANNA					
5376	C-GLXW	N604CR	N604CC	N604CD	N604ZH	N1102B					
5377	C-GLXH	N315FX	N315BX	N604RB	N604RR	N610TM					
5378	C-GLYC	C-GDBZ	D-ASTS	D-AFAB							
5379	C-GLWV	N604CA	C-GQPA								
5380	C-GLYO	C-GDFA	N604DE	C-GEGM	Denmark C-080						
5381	C-GLYH	N900ES	(N909ES)	PR-TUB	N604MM						
5382	C-GLXS	N604HJ	M-OLOT								
5383	C-GLYK	N383DT	G-EMLI	M-EMLI	C-FGFG						
5384	C-GLXW	C-GDLH	HB-IVV	VP-BNS	N684TS						
5385	C-GLXD	N72NP	C-FCPI	N604SC	LV-FWZ						
5386	C-GLWZ	N315DG	N1DG	N37DG	N119GA	N203R					
5387	C-GLXF	N316FX	N387CL	N999PX							
5388	C-GLXK	C-GDVM	4X-CMY	N488LW	N588AL						
5389	C-GLXM	N604JE	D-AUKE								
5390	C-GLXO	N604KG	ZS-DGB	(N200DE)	N541DE	N200DE					
5391	C-GLWT	N604PA	VP-BCA	N2409W	(N818SL)	N708SC	N788SC	N267BW	N267DW	N267DF	
5392	C-GLXQ	C-GDZE	C-FLPC	C-FCDE	N596CH	N325JJ					

CANADAIR CL604 CHALLENGER

C/n	Identities							
5393	C-GLYA	N355CC	N615TL	(VQ-BUX)	N645TL	VQ-BUX		
5394	C-GLXS	N604CH	HB-IVT	N141DL	N72WY	N350PR		
5395	C-GLYK	N606CC	N82CW	N82CN	N604LV			
5396	C-GLWR	N604SH	N273S	N604SH	N273S	C-GKTO		
5397	C-GLXY	N605PA	VP-BCB	HB-IIV	VP-BJH	A6-PJA	D-AFAA	
5398	C-GLXU	N597DM	N477DM	N577DA	(SX-TFA)			
5399	C-GLXB	N604GM	N901SG					
5400	C-GLWX	N604S	(N237G)	N237GA	N266GA	N60055	(N6550)	N400TJ
5401	C-GLXH	N98FJ	N528GP	(N604GJ)	VT-MGF	M-AWAY	N243BA	
5402	C-GLYC	N603JM	RP-C5610	N15SP	N98AG	VP-BDX	N604CD	
5403	C-GLWV	N604DC	D-ADND	G-JMCW	G-MPJM	G-MPTP	VP-CUP	
5404	C-GLYO	VP-BGO	M-SKZL	M-ADEL	N32UC			
5405	C-GLYH	N311BP	N811BP	N340AK				
5406	C-GLXS	N604MU	N604WW					
5407	C-GLWR	N317FX	N317BX	N604GG	LV-BNO	N548LF	VH-BLM	[wore fake marks N39DJP for film purposes at Archerfield, Australia, 18Jun14]
5408	C-GLXW	N898R	N898AN	N604SA				
5409	C-GLXD	C-GETU	N401NK	N604M				
5410	C-GLWZ	N191BA	N199BA	N805VZ	(N410MU)	C-GFLU	N923KB	
5411	C-GLXF	N604JJ	PP-OSA	N604TS	N3PC	N66ZC	N66ZD	VH-VSZ
5412	C-GLXK	N99FJ	N529GP	TS-IAM				
5413	C-GLXM	C-FSJR	C-FADU	(N802TK)	(N294KR)	N651LS		
5414	C-GLXO	N604AG	N90AG	[w/o 04Jan02 Birmingham A/P, UK]				
5415	C-GLWT	N318FX	VP-CAP	TC-SMZ	N295JL			
5416	C-GLXQ	N604MG	N161MM	N161MN	N161MD	G-FTSL	D-AFAC	
5417	C-GLYA	N605MP	D-AETV	N791BR	C-GNRC			
5418	C-GLXS	N319FX	(N609CR)	N604CR	N529AK	A6-KBB	N309KB	
5419	C-GLYK	N500	N252DH					
5420	C-GLWR	N603CC	VP-BCO	N604TS	C-GBKB	N549LF	(N614MJ)	N39RE	N39RN
5421	C-GLXY	N200JP	N604JP	N604W	N38VS			
5422	C-GLXU	N605DC	D-ADNE	G-JMMD	G-MPCW	G-MPSP	AP-DOD	OE-IHK
5423	C-GLXB	N238SW	N38SW	N38SV	N91MG			
5424	C-GLWX	N604CR	G-DAAC	N604GW				
5425	C-GLXH	N320FX	N604PC	VT-IBR				
5426	C-GLYC	N604JA	JY-ONE	N51VR	G-XONE			
5427	C-GLWV	N321FX	N902CG	USCG 02	[USCG type designation C-143A]	N902CG	N838DB	N828UM
5428	C-GLYO	N640CH	N300TW					
5429	C-GLYH	N604KM	Korea 701					
5430	C-GLXS	(N604MA)	C-GFOE	OY-MMM	D-AONE			
5431	C-GLWR	N276GC						
5432	C-GLXM	C-FDRS	C-GPGD					
5433	C-GLXD	N433FS	N181J	N777J				
5434	C-GLXY	N322FX	N322BX	N604AU				
5435	C-GLWZ	N604PN	OE-IYA	OE-INJ				
5436	C-GLXF	N604LA	(N955CE)	N926SS				
5437	C-GLXK	N437FT	N17TE	N17TZ	N604AV			
5438	C-GLXM	N609CC	AP-GAK					
5439	C-GLXQ	N600ES	N300ES	N350ES	VH-URR			
5440	C-GLXU	N500PE	N208LT	N620TM				
5441	C-GLXB	N641CA	N1CA	N441CL	N33PA	N36HA	N604RM	
5442	C-GLWR	N604PS	G-POAJ	YL-WBD	HB-JRT	B-7696		
5443	C-GLWT	N605JA	JY-TWO	JY-IMK	M-CRCR	G-HOTY		
5444	C-GLWV	N604VF	N604AF					
5445	C-GLWX	N604HD	N877H					
5446	C-GLWZ	N604CE	N156RC					
5447	C-GLYC	N323FX	N323BX	N1NA	N604PS			
5448	C-GLXD	N604CB	TC-DHH	VP-BHH				
5449	C-GLXF	N604GT	N604JR	VP-CCP	LX-SPK	D-AAAX		
5450	C-GLXH	N450DK	4X-CMZ	(N357AP)	M-ABGG			
5451	C-GLXK	N816CC	(N120MT)	N831ET	N604DF			
5452	C-GLXM	N452WU	OH-WIC					
5453	C-GLXO	N453AD	C-FHGC					
5454	C-GLXQ	N324FX	D-ARWE	[w/o Almaty, Kazakstan, 25Dec07]				
5455	C-GLXS	C-GCDS	C-GCDF	N604CW				
5456	C-GLXU	N456MS	VP-BNG	N604LE	VH-MXK	VH-ZZH	VH-VLC	N360SL
5457	C-GLXW	N325FX	D-AKBH	EC-MIT				
5458	C-GLXY	N458MS	C-GZPX					
5459	C-GLYA	N459MT	TC-TAN	Turkey TT4010				
5460	C-GLYH	N460WJ	VP-BMG	N698RS				
5461	C-GLYK	N832SC						
5462	C-GLYO	N462PG	D-AHLE	N604EP				
5463	C-GLXB	N463AG	D-AHEI	N777FF	(N777FN)			
5464	C-GLWR	N326FX	(N326BX)	(OE-IRJ)	I-IRCS	D-AMSC		
5465	C-GLWT	C-GHIH	C-GLBB	N465AV	N604FS			
5466	C-GLWV	N327FX						
5467	C-GLWX	N467RD	G-REYS					
5468	C-GLWZ	C-GHRJ	Denmark C-168					
5469	C-GLYC	N469RC	N78SD	(N32FF)	N770FF			
5470	C-GLXD	N604DW	N604AC	N150BB				
5471	C-GLXF	N471MK	N604WS	N604DE	N604TB			
5472	C-GLXH	C-GHRZ	Denmark C-172					
5473	C-GLXK	N604RP	N303KR	N579RS				
5474	C-GLXM	N328FX	C-FXPB	C-FXCN	C-FBEM	D-ADLD		
5475	C-GLXO	N475AD	D-ASIE	YR-DIP	OE-IAH			
5476	C-GLXQ	N329FX	N343K	A9C-BXH	M-SHLA	N604BA		
5477	C-GLXS	N477AT	A9C-BXB	M-ABEH	N477TX	N529KF		
5478	C-GLXU	N478BA	N604GR	N478U	N604PV			
5479	C-GLXW	N479KA	ZS-CMB	N604ST	N872BC			
5480	C-GLXY	N480LB	N121DF	N500M				
5481	C-GLYA	N481KW	N198DC	JY-AAD	M-AAAD	HZ-TFM	M-AAAD	
5482	C-GLYH	N482BB	N322LA	N581TS				
5483	C-GLYK	N483BA	N483CC	N956PP				
5484	C-GLYO	N484GC	PT-XYW	N684TS	C-GWLL			
5485	C-GLXB	N485CL	"LX-RFBY"	LX-FBY	A9C-BXG	M-ABEI	N485TX	N82RL
5486	C-GLWR	N486EJ	ZS-OSG	9J-ONE				
5487	C-GLWT	N330FX	I-AFMA	G-FABO				

CANADAIR CL604 CHALLENGER

C/n	Identities						
5488	C-GLWV	N604D	N604CC	N870CM	N670CM	(N8570)	N604FM
5489	C-GLWX	N489BA	N604BD	C-GGBL	C-FVSL	N490AJ	N230LC	C-GTJO
5490	C-GLWZ	N604GD	N14GD	N14GU
5491	C-GLYC	N331FX	N331PS	N331FX	N770MS
5492	C-GLXD	N604SX	N711SX	N604SX	N604EM
5493	C-GLXF	N604VK	LV-BHP
5494	C-GLXH	N494JC	D-ANKE	HB-JRN	M-ALII	TC-TRB
5495	C-GLXK	N495BA	N495BC	N495CE
5496	C-GLXM	N496DB	N604UP	N604TH	N604Z
5497	C-GLXO	N604RT	N604LA
5498	C-GLXQ	N598DA	N599DA	N333DS	N226MY
5499	C-GLXS	N499KR	N999VK
5500	C-GLXU	N225AR	N606GG	VP-CAS
5501	C-GLXW	N501AJ	XA-SOL
5502	C-GLXY	N502TF	D-ACTO	D-ACTU	HB-JRY	N598MT	N777DB
5503	C-GLYA	N298DC	N503PC
5504	C-GLYH	N71NP	N71NJ	N604RR
5505	C-GLYK	N505JD	VP-BHS	N655TS	(D-ARTE)	G-OCSC	N664D
5506	C-GLYO	C-GJFI	C-FHYL	C-FLCY	N1821U
5507	C-GLXB	N53DF
5508	C-GLWR	N528DK	P4-FAY	LZ-YUN	9H-MAL	A7-MHA
5509	C-GLWT	N604BG	N112CF
5510	C-GLWV	N511SC	B-7696	N610SA	VP-CHU	HB-JFZ	D-AFAB	N604TX	N100FL
5511	C-GLWX	N815PA	N815RA	N598WC
5512	C-GLWZ	(N626JW)	N512SH	N902AG
5513	C-GLYC	N604NG	N729KF	N729KP	N604RB
5514	C-GLXD	C-GJOE	N880ET
5515	C-GLXF	N515DM	EI-IRE	G-CHVN	Denmark C-215
5516	C-GLXH	N516DG	N1DG	N516DG	N118RH
5517	C-GLXK	C-GJSO	N517RH	LN-SUN
5518	C-GLXM	N8SP	N85PX
5519	C-GLXO	N519MZ	P4-AVJ	N900UC
5520	C-GLXQ	C-GJTR	N520JR	XA-TVG	N116BJ	VP-CBR	A6-MBH	VP-CBR	VP-CST
5521	C-GLXS	N521RF	Australia A37-001
5522	C-GLXU	N522FP	C-GKCB	(N.....)	4X-CMF	M-LRLR
5523	C-GLXW	N552SC	B-7697	N523CL	LX-ZAV	OE-ICL	TC-ICK
5524	C-GLXY	N251VG	N251CP	N601GT
5525	C-GLYA	N525E	XA-JFE
5526	C-GLYH	N804CB	N604CB	I-WISH	G-RCAV
5527	C-GLYK	N554SC	(B-....)	XA-TZF
5528	C-GLYO	N528DT	D-AJAG	G-JMMP	G-MPMP	TC-REA
5529	C-GLXB	C-GJZB	HB-JRA
5530	C-GLWR	C-GJZD	HB-JRB
5531	C-GLWT	N168NQ
5532	C-GLWV	N532DM	N432MC	YL-SKY
5533	C-GLWX	N533DK	C-GKGR	Canada 144617
5534	C-GLWZ	N534RF	Australia A37-002
5535	C-GLYC	C-GKGS	Canada 144618
5536	C-GLXD	N536MP	N25GG	N25ZG
5537	C-GLXF	N537DR	N437MC
5538	C-GLXH	N538RF	Australia A37-003
5539	C-GLXK	N539AB	PP-BIA	VP-BDY	VP-CEO	CS-DTJ	HB-JFC
5540	C-GLXM	C-GKMU	HB-JRC
5541	C-GLXO	N329FX	(D-AMHS)	D-ANGB
5542	C-GLXQ	N876H	B-7766
5543	C-GLXS	N332FX	(N605BA)
5544	C-GLXU	N333FX	N604TS	N50DS	N544TS	N814PS
5545	C-GLXW	N334FX	N6757M	N471RJ
5546	C-GLXY	N335FX	N604BA	N459CS	N100AC
5547	C-GLYA	N350ZE	N426PF
5548	C-GLYH	N548LP	N416BD	N410BD	N604LL	N627AF
5549	C-GLYK	N540JW	N2JW	(N26WK)	N604JE	C-FASD
5550	C-GLYO	N250CC	N1987	N198D	N75KH
5551	C-GLXB+	C-GLXF+	[+shown as C-GLXB in Transport Canada records but reported as C-GLXF while on production line]				N551BT	N604RS	N501PC
5552	C-GLWR	N552CC	ZS-ALT	N552TS	VP-COP
5553	C-GLWT	C-GZTU	HB-JRZ	P4-SAI	N728JP	C-GRLE
5554	C-GLWV	N604KJ
5555	C-GLWX	N555VV	N604HC	N604HM
5556	C-GLWZ	N373G	N3736	C-GBBB
5557	C-GLYC	C-FZSO	C-GAWH
5558	C-GLXD	N604SR	N604KS	N508PC
5559	C-GLXF	N559JA	N902MP
5560	C-GLXH	N604CC	(N560TS)	N604BS
5561	C-GLXK	N561CC	N604WF	VH-MZL	VH-VRE
5562	C-GLXM	N562BA	N562ME	M-EIRE	VP-COD	G-OCOD	N604VG
5563	C-GLXO	N563BA	N300BC	N604BC
5564	C-GLXQ	N564BA	N99KW	N79KW	C-GMIV
5565	C-GLXS	N604KB	D-ABCD
5566	C-GLXU	N604PA
5567	C-GLXW	N567NT	C-FAOL	P4-TAT	RA-67216
5568	C-GLXY	N604JC	N383MB	N456HK
5569	C-GLYA	C-GZVZ	N604SB
5570	C-GLYH	N604CL
5571	C-GLYK	N604BA	N571BA	N907WS
5572	C-GLYO	N572MS	N400	(N472TS)	D-AIND	N790BR	N121RS	N283DM	N512NP
5573	C-GLXB	N573BA	N573BC	N509GE	VH-VLZ
5574	C-GLWR	N574F	N46F	A6-RDJ
5575	C-GLWT	N529DM	N604HF	N950PG
5576	C-GLWV	N1090X	C-GGBL
5577	C-GLWX	N577CJ	C-FEUR	OO-KRC	LX-KRC	VH-LEF
5578	C-GLWZ	N606RP	N604PH	XA-...
5579	C-GLYC	N110BP	C-FBCR
5580	C-GLXD	C-FADG	XA-IGE	P4-CHV	G-OPRM
5581	C-GLXF	N604MC	VP-CMS
5582	C-GLXH	N604BB

CANADAIR CL604 CHALLENGER

C/n	Identities					
5583	C-GLXK	N121ET	A6-ASQ	(D-APJI)	N67ZS	
5584	C-GLXM	C-FAWU	N828KD			
5585	C-GLXO	N585BD	(D-ARTN)	OE-IMB	D-AAOK	SX-KMA
5586	C-GLXQ	N334FX				
5587	C-GLXS	N826JS	(N604UC)	N64UC		
5588	C-GLXU	N88				
5589	C-GLXW	N604SF	N22SF	N228E	OE-IPG	9H-IPG	N585PJ
5590	C-GLXY	N721J	N420SK			
5591	C-GLYA	N604CD	G-OCSD	G-CGFD	CN-IAM	
5592	C-GLYH	N385CT				
5593	C-GLYK	N604SC	VP-BJM			
5594	C-GLYO	N594SF	N43SF	N438E	TC-CEA	
5595	C-GLXB	C-FCOE	(D-AINI)	OE-INI	N351AP	TC-ASL
5596	C-GLWR	C-FCSD	OY-SGM	RA-67222	N605AM	
5597	C-GLWT	N597JA	VP-CKR	VP-CHL	C-GMRL	
5598	C-GLWV	C-FDJN	OE-IGJ	M-MDDE		
5599	C-GLWX	OE-IKP	HB-JFJ			
5600	C-GLWZ	N800BN	N810GT			
5601	C-GLXB	N44SF	N448E			
5602	C-GLXD	C-FDBJ	HB-JRW	LZ-YUP	D-AAAY	
5603	C-GLXF	N76SF	N768E	N349JR*		
5604	C-GLXH	N78RP	(N78RX)	B-LBL	M-AAEL	
5605	C-GLXK	C-FDUY	EC-JNV	N605CL	VP-BJE	
5606	C-GLXM	N606CC	N310TK	N810TK	(N730AS)	
5607	C-GLXO	N607LC	N954L	N610L		
5608	C-GLXQ	C-FDWU	G-DGET	M-TRIX	OE-IPD	M-SIMI
5609	C-GLXS	C-FEFU	N604JC	D-ATTT		
5610	C-GLXU	C-FEFW	G-LGKO	M-ANGO	N801TK	N575AG
5611	C-GLXW	C-FEIH	TC-ARD	(N361AP)		
5612	C-GLXY	C-FEPN	OE-IPK	G-VVPA		
5613	C-GLYA	C-FEPR	HB-JEM	RA-67228		
5614	C-GLYH	N614JA	N614BA	[converted to prototype Boeing Maritime Surveillance Aircraft, ff 28Feb14]		
5615	C-GLYK	N604SG	N904JK			
5616	C-GLYO	C-FEXH	VP-CFD	LX-MDA	D-ANTR	
5617	C-GLXB	C-FEYU	G-PRKR	G-OCOM	M-OCOM	
5618	C-GLXF	C-FEYZ	VP-CMB	D-ASIX	OE-IAA	D-AMIB*
5619	C-GLWT	N335FX	C-FIDT	VH-XNC	[for conversion to Search & Rescue aircraft for Australian government]	
5620	C-GLWV	C-FFGE	OE-IVE	VP-BST	M-YBST	
5621	C-GLWX	C-FFHX	VP-CNK	VP-CBK	(N354AP)	N789SM
5622	C-GLWZ	C-FFLA	B-LLL	VP-CCE	(N688NY)	
5623	C-GLYC	C-FFMQ	VP-CJB	N623HA	G-STCC	G-OCSH	N604AK
5624	C-GLXD	C-FFMS	N604GD	OY-MKS	HB-JGR	9H-JGR
5625	C-GLXF	C-FFQQ	VH-OCV	LZ-YUR	TC-MJB	
5626	C-GLXH	N807RH	VP-BSS	VP-BZM	OH-BZM	G-CGGU	N787LG
5627	C-GLXK	N604DT				
5628	C-GLXM	C-FFZP	P4-ABC	(N30WJ)	TS-IBT	TS-INV	9H-INV
5629	C-GLXO	C-FGBE	(D-AINX)	OE-INX	N356AP	(N317MG)	VT-ZST
5630	C-GLXQ	C-FGBD	XA-SAD	N199GD		
5631	C-GLXS	N724MF	N345XB			
5632	C-GLXU	N604CG	D-AEUK			
5633	C-GLXW	N604CC				
5634	C-GLXY	N336FX	C-FKUL	VH-XND	[for conversion to Search & Rescue aircraft for Australian government]	
5635	C-GLYC	N604SL	N604EG	N604JJ		
5636	C-GLYH	N636HC	(N636TS)	OE-ITH		
5637	C-GLYK	N637TF	N604HT			
5638	C-GLYO	N604MG	N604HT			
5639	C-GLXB	C-FGYI	VP-BJA	M-JSTA		
5640	C-GLXD	N640PN	N910J			
5641	C-GLWT	N641DA	A6-IFA			
5642	C-GLWV	N642JA	OH-WII			
5643	C-GLWX	N643CT	N793CT			
5644	C-GLWZ	C-FHCM	(D-AINY)	OE-INY	(N487LW)	(N297KR)	N395MH
5645	C-GLYC	C-FHCL	4X-CUR			
5646	C-GLXD	N646JC	G-HARK	N438E		
5647	C-GLXF	N337FX	C-FMUS	[for conversion to Search & Rescue aircraft for Australian government]		
5648	C-GLXH	C-FHDV	EC-JYT			
5649	C-GLXK	N649JA	P4-BTA	(D-ATWO)	UP-CL6001	T7-EAA
5650	C-GLXM	C-FIEX	C-FRCI			
5651	C-GLXO	N651JC	HB-JRQ			
5652	C-GLXQ	N604CM	N225N			
5653	C-GLXS	C-FIMF	N720AS	XA-JEP		
5654	C-GLXU	N604MG	OE-IDG			
5655	C-GLXW	N604TF				
5656	C-GLXY	C-FIXN	N338FX	C-FOGX	[for conversion to Search & Rescue aircraft for Australian government]	
5657	C-GLYA	C-FIYA	VP-BNP	N352AP	C-GMBY	
5658	C-GLYH	N658JC	(OH-WIA)	(OH-NEM)	OH-MOL	N1218F
5659	C-GLYK	C-FJCB	G-TAGA	HB-JRG		
5660	C-GLYO	N650KS	N848CC			
5661	C-GLXB	N224NS	N224N			
5662	C-GLWR	N652MC	N868CC			
5663	C-GLWT	N664JC	N604TB	N500PG		
5664	C-GLWV	C-FKDV	OE-IMK			
5665	C-GLWX	N665CT	N657CT			

Production complete

CANADAIR CL605 CHALLENGER

C/n	Identities					
5701	C-FGYM	[ff 23Jan06]	N605KS	N980SK	N2MG	N605KB	N545ZT*
5702	C-FIFK	N605CC	(N225AR)	A6-DNH	N170TY	N138DM
5703	C-FLGN	VP-BML	N605WF
5704	C-FLKC	(D-AIFB)	OE-IFB	M-FBVZ	LX-ZED
5705	C-GLXD	C-FLNZ	N933ML	M-AMRT
5706	C-GLXF	C-FLSF	ZS-SDZ	G-TAGE	VT-AUV
5707	C-GLXH	C-FLSJ	N605BA	OE-INS	(N486LW)	(N298KR)	N864BA	N27AY*
5708	C-GLXK	N605CB	C-GSTG
5709	C-GLXM	C-GCSB	HB-JRP	9H-AFQ	N87878
5710	C-GLXO	C-FMNL	C-GSAP	N710TS	G-OCSE	C-GFTL
5711	C-GLXQ	C-FMNR	N529D	N529DM	N729DM	C-GVVY
5712	C-GLXS	C-FMNW	(OE-IPR)	S5-ADA	N541LF	N605GN
5713	C-GLXU	C-FMVQ	N604D	9H-AFC
5714	C-GLXW	C-FMVN	PP-SCB	N329TL
5715	C-GLXY	C-FNIJ	(OE-IVB)	S5-ADB	CS-DTK	HB-JFA	D-AVPB
5716	C-GLYA	C-FNIN	N605JM	VP-CHH	M-GENT	B-LSB	N688SF
5717	C-GLYH	C-FSCI	N591CH
5718	C-GLYK	C-FNTM	N723HA	N571TS	N555NN	G-NAAL	N592CH	N605KA
5719	C-FOBK	N339FX
5720	C-FNUF	N720HG	N605HC
5721	C-FNTP	N605HG	N4AS	(PR-RSI)	C-GURJ
5722	C-FOGE	M-BIGG	SX-SHC
5723	C-FOGI	N340FX
5724	C-GLWX	C-FOMS	N17TE
5725	C-FOMU	D-ACUA
5726	C-FOXU	N605JP	HB-JRE
5727	C-FOXV	N400ES
5728	C-FOYE	N605GG	A6-MBS
5729	C-FOBF	N540BA
5730	C-FPWI	N605LD	TC-SAB
5731	C-FPQT	M-RLIV
5732	C-FPQV	(OE-III)	OY-GBB	P4-CEO
5733	C-FPQW	N533TS	G-OCSF	G-CGFF	G-MACP	G-MACO	M-ALTI
5734	C-FPQY	G-NCCC	N683UF
5735	C-FPQZ	N605DX	EZ-B022
5736	C-FPSJ	HB-JGT
5737	C-FPSQ	N542BA
5738	C-FPSV	N538TS	N605ZH
5739	C-FQQE	N605AG	VP-CRS	A6-AAG
5740	C-FQQG	N667LC	N667LQ	N605LC
5741	C-FQQH	N741TS	N371G
5742	C-FQQK	N341FX	N950RJ	N3FE
5743	C-FQQO	OE-INN	(N291KR)	N859BA
5744	C-FQQS	N744JC	G-CFSC	M-NHOI
5745	C-FQQW	OE-INP	N593CH	M-BASH
5746	C-FQVE	C-GGBL	N4868
5747	C-FSIP	N605GL	TC-FIB
5748	C-FSIQ	VP-BGM
5749	C-FSIU	N749BA	OE-INU	N594CH	N729HZ
5750	C-FSJH	VT-STV	N605AT	EZ-B023
5751	C-FSJT	N605JA	P4-UNI	M-YUNI
5752	C-FSJV	N342FX	N342F
5753	C-FSJY	HB-JRN	N65HD	N605PA
5754	C-FSKT	S5-ADD
5755	C-FSKX	N605GB	G-NYGB	C-FJNS
5756	C-FTLB	D-ATYA	G-YAGT	9H-LDV
5757	C-FTLH	S5-ADF
5758	C-FTRY	OE-INT	N624EC	C-GVBY	G-KAHR	N307KR	N445BH
5759	C-FTRO	N605CJ	A7-RZC	9H-ALF	C-GRMZ
5760	C-FTRQ	G-SJSS
5761	C-FTRM	N343FX	(N343HM)	N777QX
5762	C-FTRF	9H-AFG	P4-SAT
5763	C-FTQY	N605RJ	VQ-BZB	TC-CLH
5764	C-FTQZ	OE-ISU
5765	C-FUAU	N605FH	C-FYTZ	VQ-BDG	M-ASHI
5766	C-FUAS	N605TX	N605GF
5767	C-FUAK	N605FH	N605H	TC-CMK
5768	C-FUIT	LZ-BVD
5769	C-FUIU	N769CC	N605MM
5770	C-FUIV	VP-BES	(D2-EBR)	N299KR
5771	C-FUVA	N548BA
5772	C-FUVC	C-FKMC	N858CV
5773	C-FUVF	N344FX	N8888G
5774	C-FUVG	(LZ-BVF)	N68888
5775	C-FUVH	N549BA
5776	C-FUUF	(N75NP)	VP-CLJ
5777	C-FUUI	N878CC
5778	C-FUUM	A9C-ACE
5779	C-FUUQ	N520SC
5780	C-FUUW	M-TOPI
5781	C-FVOC	N605BL	M-VSSK	VP-COO
5782	C-FVON	OE-INA	N339MH	N131KJ
5783	C-FVOQ	A7-CEA
5784	C-FVOZ	A7-CEB
5785	C-FWQH	OH-ANS	9H-BOM
5786	C-FWQL	C-FLMK
5787	C-FWQM	VT-APL
5788	C-FWQO	N605S
5789	C-FWQV	N605BT	C-GBKB
5790	C-FWQY	N605TA	N169TA	N189TA
5791	C-FVMI	N899ST
5792	C-FVMW	N605AB	N2JW
5793	C-FXQG	N880HK

CANADAIR CL605 CHALLENGER

C/n	Identities					
5794	C-FXQH	M-ARIE	B-LSC	N446JB	N605L	
5795	C-FXQJ	N605PS				
5796	C-FXQM	C-GHMW				
5797	C-FXQR	OE-IND	N366MH			
5798	C-FXQX	N605RZ	A7-RZA	VP-CBV	D-AJAN	
5799	C-FYAY	P4-KMK	N818AC			
5800	C-FYAW	N605RC				
5801	C-FYAV	N605RP				
5802	C-FYAP	C-FBEL				
5803	C-FYAI	RA-67227				
5804	C-FYAB	N65PX				
5805	C-FXRD	LV-CCW				
5806	C-FYBK	N605FA	C-GJXK	B-3076		
5807	C-FYUD	VP-CIF				
5808	C-FYUH	OE-IPZ	N1220S	XC-LNS	XB-NWD	
5809	C-FYUK	B-3561				
5810	C-FYUP	G-CGJA	M-AAES	N5810B	XA-LPZ	
5811	C-FYUR	N513DL				
5812	C-FYUS	EI-WFI				
5813	C-FYUY	(VT-NKL)	M-ABCU	M-AIZB	T7-AAS	
5814	C-FYTY	M-NOLA	N296KR	VH-LVH		
5815	C-FZLA	N605BX	N89			
5816	C-FZLB	N816CC	N15VC			
5817	C-FZLM	N605JK	N90			
5818	C-FZLR	N880CM				
5819	C-FZLS	N696HS				
5820	C-FZLU	B-3077				
5821	C-FZKY	N605MS	G-URRU	N775RP		
5822	C-GAIP	N605KR	A6-TLH	A9C-TLH	T7-BCH	
5823	C-GAJG	PP-COA				
5824	C-GALP	M-AIRU	N304KR	(N920DS)		
5825	C-GANU	OE-INK				
5826	C-GBYG	B-LOL	M-MARI			
5827	C-GBYH	N605AZ	(HB-JRI)	G-OTAG	N688JH	M-AAAA
5828	C-GBYK	B-3566				
5829	C-GBYM	XA-GRB				
5830	C-GBYS	N1500				
5831	C-GDRJ	N859AG				
5832	C-GDRU	(VQ-BMJ)	N40XC	N926EC		
5833	C-GDRY	C-FGIL				
5834	C-GDSG	N634XJ	N66ZC			
5835	C-GDSO	N635XJ				
5836	C-GDSQ	N636XJ	M-TRBS			
5837	C-GEWI	A6-SAJ				
5838	C-GEWO	OE-IDV	M-KARI	N583TA	XA-KIM	
5839	C-GEWV	N605FR	N807JD	N523AR		
5840	C-GEWX	M-HNOY	M-ACHO			
5841	C-GEXB	M-ERCI	N633AB			
5842	C-GEXD	OE-INE	N290MH	N57MH		
5843	C-GEXY	(VP-CNK)	G-SFRI	M-SFRI	N652BL	LV-FWW
5844	C-GFJB	9M-ATM				
5845	C-GFJE	OE-ING	N692JB	N934TQ		
5846	C-GFJJ	(N878H)	N484JM			
5847	C-GFJO	VP-CSI	9H-ICS	N728JR		
5848	C-GFJQ	VT-MKJ				
5849	C-GFJT	OH-GVI				
5850	C-GFJX	3B-RGT	N989BA	N39RE		
5851	C-GFUQ	N605AK	C-GNYZ	VP-BGO		
5852	C-GFUY	OE-INH	N203MH	N267DW		
5853	C-GHZH	N515KS				
5854	C-GHZQ	C-FSJR				
5855	C-GHZU	N605CR	S5-ADK	D-AZZA*		
5856	C-GIAB	M-AKAS	(D-ACAS)	D-AKAS	VP-BKA	9H-KAS
5857	C-GIAF	A7-CEG				
5858	C-GIVX	N605PW	N261PW			
5859	C-GJOJ	N605PX	N157NS			
5860	C-GJOK	N605JS				
5861	C-GJUR	C-FSEP				
5862	C-GJYV	N890CM				
5863	C-GJXY	D-ABEY				
5864	C-GJYA	N605BB				
5865	C-GJYC	F-HMOB	N312HX			
5866	C-GJYE	A7-MBT	A6-ELD			
5867	C-GJYI	N605AJ	N372G			
5868	C-GJYK	(D-AKAS)	B-7761			
5869	C-GJYN	N825SA				
5870	C-GJYR	N605DJ	N373G			
5871	C-GJYS	B-7796				
5872	C-GKXO	G-LTSK				
5873	C-GKXP	N75NP				
5874	C-GKXQ	N86NP				
5875	C-GKXR	N605RK	N899KK			
5876	C-GKXS	VP-BGT				
5877	C-GLNI	N99KW				
5878	C-GLMU	OE-INM	N423TX	N177FF		
5879	C-GLNF	M-ARKZ				
5880	C-GLNJ	N529DM				
5881	C-GLNP	C-FCIB				
5882	C-GLYV	N508MN	N207R			
5883	C-GLZB	M-SAPL	N955PM			
5884	C-GLZD	A6-MVD				
5885	C-GLZF	N1CP				
5886	C-GNCH	(M-CHAT)	P4-AIM			
5887	C-GNDZ	AP-FFL	M-GINI	AP-FFL		

CANADAIR CL605 CHALLENGER

C/n	Identities			
5888	C-GNEC	B-7768		
5889	C-GNRY	N705AM		
5890	C-GNSG	N605CM	N1CU	
5891	C-GNSI	N605JD	N22SF	
5892	C-GNSJ	M-AYRU		
5893	C-GNSM	N605BR	N43SF	
5894	C-GNVF	N44SF		
5895	C-GNVJ	N605NP		
5896	C-GNVQ	B-LVA		
5897	C-GNVR	N898DL		
5898	C-GNVU	B-LVB		
5899	C-GNVX	N605WV	HZ-ATG	
5900	C-GOVC	N76SF		
5901	C-GOVF	N345FX		
5902	C-GOVG	N726MF		
5903	C-GOVI	B-7769		
5904	C-GOVJ	G-LCDH		
5905	C-GOVR	N97NP		
5906	C-GPUU	B-7763		
5907	C-GPUV	N567YX		
5908	C-GPVD	N530SC		
5909	C-GPVE	N605CL		
5910	C-GPVF	N1967M		
5911	C-GRYI	N200LS		
5912	C-GRYM	N605AB	N156BF	
5913	C-GRYO	N600LS		
5914	C-GRYQ	M-WFAM		
5915	C-GRYR	PR-FTR		
5916	C-GRYT	N732PA		
5917	C-GRYU	N605RT		
5918	C-GRYZ	VP-BOR	D-AMOR*	
5919	C-GRZA	B-7799		
5920	C-GRZF	M-FRZN		
5921	C-GUAZ	C-GIIT		
5922	C-GUBA	A6-TSF	VP-BQN	
5923	C-GUBC	N605LT		
5924	C-GUBD	RA-67238		
5925	C-GUBF	N605BA		
5926	C-GUKT	D-ASHY		
5927	C-GUKS	N882CB		
5928	C-GUKU	VP-BMM	N325MH	N961TC
5929	C-GUKV	M-BAEP		
5930	C-GUKW	N605DA		
5931	C-GUSJ	N817AF		
5932	C-GURO	M-ABGS		
5933	C-GURP	CC-AMX		
5934	C-GURT	N630GA	N171CL	
5935	C-GURZ	N605BF	N605JM	
5936	C-GUSF	(D-ALIK)	M-ABGU	M-MSGG
5937	C-GVEY	(D-AMUC)	PH-HWM	
5938	C-GVFF	N500PB	C-FEUR	C-FCDE
5939	C-GVFH	N605AH	N605GS	
5940	C-GVFI	EI-TAT		
5941	C-GVFJ	M-JMIA		
5942	C-GVFK	N988JC		
5943	C-GVFN	C-FHYL	N227MH	N275GC
5944	C-GVFO	XA-NDY		
5945	C-GVFP	N241EA		
5946	C-GVVQ	B-3365*		
5947	C-GVVU	C-FHRL		
5948	C-GVWE	C-FSCI		
5949	C-GVWF	N880CC		
5950	C-GVWI	(N605BE)	(D-ABIG)	N605BS
5951	C-GWQJ	(N605BK)	N633WM	
5952	C-GWQL	N589MD		
5953	C-GWQM	M-SPBM		
5954	C-GWQQ	N605MX	N232MC	
5955	C-GWQR	Pakistan EYE77		
5956	C-GXNJ	N605BL	C-FGNI	TC-ABN
5957	C-GXNK	N605AM	N905SA	
5958	C-GXNM	9H-JCD		
5959	C-GXNO	N999MY		
5960	C-GXNU	N605MP	N717BN	
5961	C-GXVG	N903AG		
5962	C-GXVJ	M-SEVN		
5963	C-GXVK	HB-JSG		
5964	C-GXVM	TC-KLE		
5965	C-GXVR	N211GS	N213GS	
5966	C-GYLK	(9H-YES)	T7-YES	
5967	C-GYLO	Mexico 3911		
5968	C-GYLP			
5969	C-GYLQ	Mexico AMT-208	Mexico ANX-1208	
5970	C-GYLY	9H-VFA		
5971	C-GYLZ	9H-VFB		
5972	C-GZJK	9H-VFC		
5973	C-GZJQ	9H-VFD		
5974	C-GZJR	9H-VFE		
5975	C-GZJV	N509MM	T7-DMA	
5976	C-GZJW	VP-BKM		
5977	C-FANH	9H-VFF		
5978	C-FAOF	9H-VFG		
5979	C-FAOU	9H-VFH		
5980	C-FAPO	C-FJRG	N605BD	G-RNJP
5981	C-FAPQ	N605M	N46E	

CANADAIR CL605 CHALLENGER

C/n	Identities		
5982	C-FAQB	C-FHYL	
5983	C-FAQD	N605ZK	G-RNFR
5984	C-FAQY	9H-VFI	
5985	C-FAUR	N798RS	
5986	C-FAWU	C-FSJY	
5987	C-FAXN	9H-VFJ	
5988	C-FAYD	B-3028	

Production complete.

CANADAIR CL650 CHALLENGER

C/n	Identities				
6050	C-GZKL				
6051	C-GZSG	N650PP			
6052	C-FAQK	C-FNNI	N200QS`		
6053	C-FAUF	"N201QS"	[fake marks worn at factory]	C-FNOQ	N202QS
6054	C-FAUI	N205QS			
6055	C-FAZC	C-FNQH	N206QS		
6056	C-FAZO	C-FNZS	N208QS		
6057	C-FAZS	N209QS			
6058	C-FAKM	N211QS			
6059	C-FAMN	C-FNSJ	C-FJCB		
6060	C-FAPQ	N541BA			
6061	C-FAWU	N543BA			
6062	C-FAOF				
6063	C-FAOU	XA-GRE			
6064	C-FAPO	N650JF			
6065	C-FANH				
6066	C-FAQB	N212QS			
6067	C-FAQY				
6068	C-FAQD				
6069	C-FAUR				
6070	C-FAXN				
6071	C-FAYD				
6072	C-GZQA				
6073	C-GZQJ				
6074	C-GZQL				
6075	C-GZQO				
6076	C-GZQP				
6077	C-FAQK				
6078	C-FAMN				
6079	C-FAUF				
6080	C-FAZC				
6081	C-FAZO				
6082	C-FAEH				
6083	C-FAKM				
6084	C-FAPQ				
6085	C-FAUI				
6086	C-FAWU				
6087	C-FAZS				
6088					
6089					
6090					
6091					
6092					
6093					
6094					
6095					
6096					
6097					
6098					
6099					
6100					
6101					
6102					
6103					
6104					
6105					
6106					
6107					
6108					
6109					
6110					
6111					
6112					

CESSNA CITATION AND CITATION I

This production list is presented in order of the Unit Number which was used and allocated by Cessna, rather than by the normally used c/n. A c/n-Unit Number cross-reference follows the production list.

Citation Eagle conversions are marked with an asterisk (*) alongside the unit number. Eagle II conversions are aircraft re-engined with Williams FJ44 engines and are shown in the text as such.

Unit No	C/n	Identities									
	669	N500CC	[ff 15Sep69; cx Jan78; scrapped]								
	701	N501CC	[first model 501, converted from model 500 c/n 670; ff 23Jan70; displayed in Smithsonian National Air & Space Museum, Washington, DC, Jun98-Jul00; cx 03Nov09]								
001	500-0001	(N510CC)	N502CC	N20SM	N38SM	N501RM	N501KG	N715JS	N840SP		
002*	500-0002	N8202Q	CF-CPW	C-FCPW	ZS-ONE	[wfu Pretoria/Wonderboom, South Africa]					
003	500-0003	N503CC									
004	500-0004	N504CC	N500GS	N500GE	N5005	N505K	(N22CA)	[w/o 05Nov05 Houston-Hobby, TX]			
005	500-0005	N505CC	N501PC	N981EE	N815HC	PT-OIG					
006	500-0006	OE-FGP	N506CC	N506TF	N500MX	N506MX	N506SR	N500AD	(N500AH)	[cx May91; scrapped for spares]	
007	500-0007	N507CC	N500LF	N555AJ	[w/o 19Nov79 Denver, CO]						
008	500-0008	N508CC	HB-VCX	N502CC	N11TC	N11QC	ZP-TYO	ZP-TYP	PT-WBY		
009	500-0009	N509CC	N500JD	N700JD	N147DA	(N147DA)	N147WS	N55FT			
010	500-0010	N510CC	XC-FIT	XC-SCT	XC-DGA	XB-IKS	N501SE	XB-LVY			
011*	500-0011	N511CC	N227H	N13UR	N18UR	N20FM	C-GJEM	N700VC			
012	500-0012	N6563C	N512CC	XC-FIU	N512CC	[dismantled at Uvalde, TX. Fuselage stored off-airport]					
013	500-0013	N513CC	XC-FIV								
014	500-0014	N514CC	N6563C	N766FT	N900W	N800W	N18FM				
015	500-0015	N515CC	N5867	N58CC	N979EE	(N332GJ)	N14JL	PT-LPZ			
016*	500-0016	N516CC	N3JJ	N15FS	N711CR	N7110K	N9AX	C-GPLN			
017	500-0017	N517CC	(N317AB)	N500PB	N508PB	N49E	N49EA	N565SS	[24Jan05 to Griffin, GA for parting out by Atlanta Air Salvage]		
018	500-0018	N518CC	N5Q	N5QZ	(N58AN)	N978EE	N222MS	C-FDJQ	N70841	C-FSKC	[w/o 25Jly98 at Rawlings, WY, and scrapped]
019*	500-0019	N519CC	USCG 519	N519CC	N11DH	N11DQ	N256WN	N111QP	OB-S-1280	OB-1280	N397SC
020	500-0020	CF-BAX	C-FBAX	N556AT	[scrapped for spares Jun87; canx Feb93]						
021	500-0021	N521CC	JA8421	N5B	N550CC	N208N	(N133N)	XA-JLV	N7GJ	[cx to Mexico but used as instructional airframe at Madrid, Colombia]	
022	500-0022	N522CC	N522JD	N800JD	C-GESZ	[parted out Montreal/Saint Hubert, Canada; cx Mar97]					
023	500-0023	N523CC	N523JD	N900JD	I-ALBS	N523CC	N50FT	N200QC	[parted out 2008 Punta Gorda, FL]		
024	500-0024	N524CC	N524CA	N33TH	VH-ICN	N94AJ					
025	500-0025	N525CC	D-IMAN	N70703	N745US	N976EE	N220W	N57LL			
026	500-0026	N501GP	[w/o 21Jan81 Bluefield, WV]								
027	500-0027	N527CC	N502GP	N51B	N777AN	PT-OVK	[cx; CofA expired]				
028	500-0028	N528CC	N10DG	N103WV	N284AM	N133JM					
029	500-0029	N529CC	N31ST	C-GDWN	N424DA	[cx 16Jan14; parted out]					
030	500-0030	N530CC	N52AN	[cx 11Dec12; parted out]							
031	500-0031	N531CC	YU-BIA	N81883	N666SA	YV-646CP	YV-939CP	YV2245			
032	500-0032	N532CC	N536V	C-GXFZ	(N5364U)	[w/o 26Sep84 Orillia A/P, Ontario, Canada]					
033	500-0033	N533CC	N533BF	N65MA	N58PL	N20RT	N20RF	N990AL	(N130AL)	(N331GC)	
034	500-0034	N534CC	N25HC	N980EE	N500DN	(N111FS)	N11HJ	N716LT			
035	500-0035	N535CC	N10108	YV-2479P	N35SE	XA-JOV	XC-MMM				
036	500-0036	N536CC	OY-DVL	SE-DEU	D-IEXC	N18HJ	OO-LCM	N50812	[parted out at Brussels, Belgium, still marked as OO-LCM]		
037	500-0037	N537CC	N109AL	SE-DPL	N109AL	N407SC	EC-GTS				
038	500-0038	N538CC	HB-VCU	N2EL	N81BA	N777FC	(N207L)	N27L			
039	500-0039	N539CC	N555CC	PT-OOK	N118LA	[to White Inds, Bates City, MO for parts Jly03]					
040	500-0040	N540CC	JA8422	N714US	D-IKAN	OY-ARP	N2170J	N600WM	N98Q		
041	500-0041	N541CC	N541AG	N50AS	N50AM						
042	500-0042	N542CC	CF-BCL	C-FBCL	N	[scrapped circa 1997]					
043	500-0043	N543CC	N104UA	N5072L	N5072E	PT-KXZ	N5072E	N32DD	N502RL	N502RD	(N96EJ) YV1152
		[w/o 02Jul08, Maiquetia, Venezuela]									
044	500-0044	N544CC	N942B	N712US	N892CA	VR-CWW	N501WW	OO-ATS	PH-CTY	N501WW	N501VH ZS-DSA N28AR
045	500-0045	N545CC	N4VF	N6VF	N7KH	N11AQ	N31MW	N666ES	N628BS	(N628FS)	
046	500-0046	N546CC	N50SK	N50SL	N109AP	N109BL	N929CA	N929RW	PT-OTQ		
047	500-0047	N547CC	N180PF	PT-WAB	N7281Z	(N60181)	[cx to Venezuela 08Jan04; wfu Charallave, Venezuela, still wearing marks N7281Z]				
048	500-0048	N548CC	N727LE	N727EE	N11DH	N5500S	N44BW	N67JR	N911GM		
049	500-0049	N549CC	PP-FXB	PT-FXB	PT-LDH	N25UT	[parted out at Montgomery, AL]				
050*	500-0050	N550CC	N471MM	N471MH	N471HH	N333PP	VH-HKX	(N565GW)			
051	500-0051	N551CC	N51BP	(N51BR)	(N61BP)	N61BR	N4646S	VH-ICX	VH-EMM	VH-EGK	[b/u Melbourne/Essendon, Australia, March13
		still wearing marks VH-EMM]									
052	500-0052	N552CC	N52MA	N52FP	YV-2267P	YV-2477P	YV-2628P	YV-881CP	YV1316		
053	500-0053	N553CC	I-CITY	N90WJ	I-KUNA	HB-VGO	I-AEAL				
054	500-0054	N554CC	N54SK	N98MB	(N28U)	(N54FT)	XB-PBT				
055	500-0055	N900KC	N900MP	N999SF	N716CB	[parted out Muskegon, MI, 2007; cx 11Mar13]					
056*	500-0056	N556CC	N777JM	N500DB	C-GCTD	N360DA	N956S	N52FT	N52ET	N777JJ	
057	500-0057	N557CC	PT-ILJ	[w/o 03Jly97 Guanabara Bay/Rio-Santos Dumont A/p, Brazil; parted out by Dodson Av'n, Rantoul, KS]							
058	500-0058	N558CC	N11WC	N11WQ	N46RB	C-GJLQ	N6145Q	YV-901CP	YV1713		
059	500-0059	N559CC	N559BC	N40RD	N40PD	N913RC	N117TW	N501DZ			
060	500-0060	N560CC	N712J	N712G	XA-SEN	XA-PAZ	N712G	PT-OOL			
061	500-0061	N561CC	XC-GAD	XC-ASA	N490EA	N52AJ	N916RC	[US Navy Squadron VT-8 colours, code 01 with legend "T-27A serial 061" where the Bu number would normally appear] ZS-DBS			
062	500-0062	N562CC	N4CH	N4KH	N334RC	XB-ACS	XB-MCN				
063	500-0063	N563CC	SE-DDE	N70451	OO-RST	N70MG	[wfu Chino, CA]				
064	500-0064	N564CC	N27SF								
065	500-0065	N565CC	(N565TW)								
066	500-0066	N566CC	N66CC	C-GQCC	[cx to USA 22Apr05, no N-number allocated – parted out?]					
067	500-0067	N567CC	N3PC	XB-DBA	N5301J	C-FADL	N567EA	(F-GIHT)	(N949SA)	N810RJ	YV2982
068	500-0068	N568CC	N568CM	PT-LAY	N53MJ	N92FA	XB-FDN	XA-RYE	XB-VGT		
069	500-0069	N569CC	PT-IQL	N969SE	N255RD	C-FTMI	N501ZD				
070	500-0070	N570CC	N500TD	N600MT	YV-707CP	VR-CMO	VP-CMO	N227MK			
071	500-0071	N571CC	CF-BCM	C-FBCM	ZS-AMB	D2-EDC	D2-AJL	D2-EDC	V5-LOW	V5-CAL	
072	500-0072	N572CC	N49R	N491	XC-BEZ	N590EA	N103AJ	PT-OYA	N114LA	N72DJ	YV238T
073	500-0073	N573CC	N720C	(N881M)	C-FKMC	[parted out by White Inds, Bates City, MO; cx 22Dec06]					
074	500-0074	N574CC	N574W	N8JG	PT-OOF	N500ML	YV3030				
075	500-0075	N575CC	(N600TT)	N575RD	[parted out by White Inds, Bates City, MO; cx 29Apr10]					
076	500-0076	N576CC	N810SC	N810SG	C-GIAC	N90CC	N500CV	N65WS	ZS-PWT		
077	500-0077	N577CC	N342AP	N869K	ZS-OAM	N147SC	N28WL				
078	500-0078	N578CC	N2HD	ZS-IYY	TL-AAW	N54531	N21TV	N429RC	N110CK	N269RC	
079	500-0079	N579CC	D-INHH	N31088	N40JF	PT-LBN					
080	500-0080	N580CC	N50CC	N419K	C-GJAP	N59019	N222KW	N767PC	N10JP	N10UP	ZS-NGR V5-OGL
081	500-0081	N581CC	N5B	HB-VDA	I-PEGA	D-IEGA*					

CESSNA CITATION AND CITATION I

C/n	Srs	Identities										
082	500-0082	N582CC	EC-CCY	HB-VGD	N4434W	N103JA	N911JD	N500CV	N178HH	N173HH	N482RJ	N428RJ	C-GREK	C-GTRL
083	500-0083	N583CC	N10UC	N10UQ	N800KC	CP-2131	N50602	CP-2131	N50602	[painted as "50602"]	VR-CCP	VR-BMT	N50602
		VR-BMO	VR-CHH	VP-CHH	"VP-CRH"	[painted in error]		VP-CHH	N31LW			
084	500-0084	N584CC	N10	N2	N25	N4	N7	N935GA	XB-FPK	XA-SMH	[w/o 25Mar95 Vera Cruz, Mexico]
085	500-0085	N585CC	N51MW	N515AA	(N64AJ)	5N-BCI	ZS-PTT				
086	500-0086	N586CC	N503GP	C-FMAN	LX-YKH	D-ICIA	(PH-TEU)+	[+ntu marks worn at Rotterdam, Netherlands, Jun09]		PH-TEV
		[cx Nov11, CofA expired; stored Teuge, Netherlands]							
087	500-0087	N587CC	N85AT	(N64792)	N700RY	N500CP	(N911A)	(N911CJ)	N633AT		
088	500-0088	N588CC	PH-CTA	(OO-FAY)	G-HOLL	PH-CTA	N170MD	N251DD	YV....		
089	500-0089	N589CC	EC-EBR	N39LH	[parted out by Int'l Turbine Services, TX; cx May05]				
090	500-0090	N590CC	N590RB	XB-EFR	Mexico ETE-1329		Mexico 3929			
091	500-0091	N591CC	N76RE	(PT-LAW)	N50PR	C-FCHJ	(N1899)	N500AD	PR-FMA		
092	500-0092	N592CC	Venezuela 0222							
093	500-0093	N593CC	PH-CTB	OO-FBY	N611SW	G-OXEC	G-OCPI	N62BR	YV317T	[conv to Citation Long Wing]
094	500-0094	N594CC	N94DE	VR-CEB	N80GB	N96FB				
095	500-0095	N595CC	N2200R	(N578WB)	YV-15CP	N4294A	N500KP	I-AMAW	N950AM	I-ARON	[wfu Rome/Urbe, Italy]
096	500-0096	N596CC	N222SL	N202VS	N202VV	C-GXPT	N202VV	N837MA	(N187AP)	[cx 26Mar15; CofR expired]
097	501-0446	N597CC	N14CF	N63CF	N888MJ	A7-ASA	N308JM	RA-2400G		
098	500-0098	N598CC	PH-CTC	G-BNVY	PH-CTC	N500GR	N500GB	[parted out by White Inds, Bates City, MO]	
099	500-0099	N599CC	N21CC	[to spares circa 1999]						
100	500-0100	N69566	HB-VDC	D-ICPW	OE-FNL	HB-VDC	OE-FNP	D-IFAI	N80AJ	(N58BT)	
101	500-0101	N601CC	N12MB	N101CD	N1HM	N6JL	N6JU	N15CC	N15CQ	C-GKCZ	N666AG	N370LN
102	500-0102	(N602CC)	N800PL	N400K	N491BT	N491PT					
103	500-0103	(N603CC)	N103CC	PT-KIR	C-GJVK						
104	500-0104	(N604CC)	N200KC	N200KQ	C-GPJW	N40HP	N3030C	(N3330)	N353PJ		
105	500-0105	N105CC	N105JJ	N32W	N234UM	[w/o 26Feb01 Sault Ste Marie, MI; scrapped]			
106	500-0106	N606CC	ZS-RCC	[b/u]						
107	500-0107	(N607CC)	N107CC	N107SC	C-GWVC	N230JS	N40RW	N79RS		
108	500-0108	N108CC	EC-CGG	[w/o 22Nov74 Barcelona, Spain]					
109	500-0109	N44SA	G-RAVY	I-AMCU	N221AM	YV1677				
110	500-0110	(N610CC)	N500AB	N154G	(N52WS)	N500Y	N363K	N368K	N172MA	XB-JDG	XB-LSA
111	500-0111	N111CC	N11A	XA-SHO	XA-SLQ	[w/o 16Feb96 Ensenada A/P, Mexico]			
112*	500-0112	N512CC	VH-DRM	N3LG	C-GRJC	N29858	N515DC	N500TM	[wfu Fort Lauderdale Executive, FL]
113	500-0113	(N613CC)	N113CC	N684HA	N684H	N500NJ	[parted out by Alliance Air Parts, Oklahoma City, OK; cx 10Jan14]	
114	500-0114	(N614CC)	N999JB	N899N	(G-BNZP)	I-AMCT	N65SA	N703RT		
115	500-0115	YV-T-AFA	YV-21CP	[w/o 08Mar05 Charallave, Venezuela]					
116	500-0116	N116CC	EC-CJH	D-IATC	EC-HRH	[instructional airframe at Berufskolleg fur Technik & Medien, Monchengladbach, Germany, Oct09]
117	500-0117	N617CC	N90BA	N161WC	N442JB					
118	500-0118	(N618CC)	N220CC	N221CC	N972JD	(N10BF)	N972GW	N50MM	[to spares circa 1999, fuselage to Aviation Fabrications Inc, MO who use it
		to demonstrate their range of Citation modifications]						
119	500-0119	N619CC	N111SU	N11KA	N95Q	N501EJ				
120	500-0120	(N620CC)	N120CC	N10DG	N141DR	N141DP	N999TC	(N500NX)	N127BJ	N712MB
121	500-0121	D-IANE	N9871R	N939SR	OY-SUJ	N3QE	N661AC	YV....		
122*	500-0122	N122CC	CF-ENJ	C-FENJ	N122LM	N122AP	ZS-PFG			
123*	500-0123	N123CC	(PI-C7777)	N523CC	RP-C7777	RP-C102	N123CX	N947CC	VH-LJL	ZK-LJL	VH-ECD	ZS-PMA
124	500-0124	N124CC	N300HC	N300HQ	N303PC	N8FC	N92SM			
125	500-0125	CF-CFP	C-FCFP	XA-SFE	N108RL	YV1475.				
126	500-0126	(N626CC)	HB-VDM	D-IDWH	N404MA	N902DD	[cx 06Apr15; wfu]		
127	500-0127	N701AS	N701AT	N22DN	N500R	N580R	[parted out by Total Aircraft Parts Inc, CT]		
128	500-0128	D-INCC	N53584	N40HL	N501AR	N3490L	[parted out Montgomery, AL, 2007]		
129	500-0129	D-IMLN	N8114G	N500SK						
130*	500-0130	VH-CRM	N4LG	OY-ARW	N4LG	N130G	ZS-MCP	N800AB	N130CE	
131	500-0131	D-IDAU	N1045T	N745DM	(N725DM)	N457CA	PT-OJF	[wfu Mojave, CA]	
132	500-0132	(N632CC)	N35LT	N80CC	(N10GR)	N888JD	N888GA	N881CA	N132BP	N501RB	N713SA	(N992HG)	YV2800
133	500-0133	N133CC	F-BUYL	OO-SEL	N2070K	N1270K	PT-LXH			
134	500-0134	N134CC	PT-JMJ							
135	500-0135	N135CC	N135BC	N900T	N902T	N975EE	N111AM	N220MT	(N500EN)	YV-717CP	[modified with winglets]	HK-3885
		[reportedly crashed into mountains in NW Colombia 07Mar97]						
136	500-0136	(N136CC)	F-BUUL	N136SA	XA-JRV	[instructional airframe at Trident Technical College, North Charleston, SC]	
137	500-0137	N137CC	N12MB	N12ME	ZS-MCU	(N922BA)				
138	500-0138	N3056R	N138SA							
139	500-0139	(N5353J)	OE-FDP	N3771U	N15AW	YV2498	N139FJ			
140	500-0140	N100CC	N300PX	N111AT	(N777SC)	N977EE	XA-EKO	N135JW	N2FA	N4LK	N4ZK	N441TC	N972AB
141	500-0141	N141CC	XA-PIC	XB-EWQ	N727TK					
142	500-0142	N142CC	VH-UCC	N650TF	N200GM	N69XW				
143	500-0143	N143CC	XC-GUQ	XB-CXF	N3W	N14JZ	N14T	N787BA	SE-DUZ	N730RJ	[used as air ambulance exhibit]
144	500-0144	(N644CC)	N332H	OH-CAR	[w/o 19Nov87 Tuusula, Helsinki, Finland]			
145	500-0145	N145CC	N145FC	N145TA	(N415FC)					
146	500-0146	N194AT	N111ME							
147	500-0147	N404G	N494C	N688CF	YV2495					
148	500-0148	(N100JC)	N718VA	N748VA	N410GB	N225DC	LV-PMP	LV-WXJ	N989SC	N500DB
149	500-0149	N4TL	N4TE	(N43TC)	N100RG	(N100FF)	N149PJ	ZS-TMG	[parted out at Lanseria, Sth Africa, then preserved at Muldersdrift, Sth
		Africa]							
150	500-0150	N150CC	N5B	VH-WRM	N5LG	OE-FAU	N501JG	(N78MC)	N9V	N914CD
151	500-0151	N151CC	N6CD	[cx Nov91; parted out by White Inds, Bates City, MO]				
152	500-0152	N152CC	(N194AT)	I-FERN	N53J	N152CC	XB-AMO	N2782D	XB-AMO	
153	500-0153	9J-ADU	N153WB	N153JP	N2RM					
154	500-0154	C-GOCM	N54MC	PT-WFT	C-GRFT					
155	500-0155	(N655CC)	N920W	N5ZZ	N88GJ	(N188DR)	N155MK			
156	500-0156	PT-KBR	[cx, CofA expired; wfu]						
157	500-0157	PH-CTD	N190AB	CS-DCA	EC-HFY	EC-HPQ				
158	500-0158	N999CM	N910Y	N910N	(N158TJ)	OY-TAM	N233DB			
159	500-0159	N36MC	N165BA	N50AC	N831CW	N881JT	N97DD	N159KC		
160	500-0160	N146BF	(N146BE)	N146JC	N1951E	N59TS	C-GNSA	[parted out by White Inds, Bates City, MO; cx 20Jul06]
161	500-0161	(C-GTEL)	C-GHEC	N161CC	ZS-BTC	A2-JDJ	ZS-BTC	[wfu Lanseria, South Africa]	
162	500-0162	PT-JXS	[w/o 16Mar75 Belem, Brazil]						
163	500-0163	N192G	(N94ZG)	N8KH	N54JV					
164	500-0164	N164CC	D-IHSV	N4209K	F-GEPL	N382JP	N334PS	(N164GJ)	N73MP	
165	500-0165	N19M	N19MQ	G-PNNY	VR-CSP	VP-CSP	N501LB	(N501FF)	OD-SAS	[cx Mar08, CofA expired]
166	500-0166	N500WR	N313JL	(N29MW)	N8DE	N511AT	[dbr Beverly, CA, 17Mar07; parted out Punta Gorda, FL; cx 01Nov12]
167	500-0167	PH-CTE	N191AB	N246RR	N801KT	YV-2821P	YV1432			
168	500-0168	N91BA	N918A	N135BK	N135MA	N891CA	(N46JA)			
169	500-0169	N20FL	N19CM	XC-CON	XC-BOC	XA-SJW	N676CW	(N676WE)	N75GM	C-GTNG
170*	500-0170	N60MS	N90237	N818R	N66LE	[parted out by Dodson Av'n, Rantoul, KS]		
171	500-0171	N171CC	YV-370CP	N728US	PT-LIX	(PP-LEM)				

CESSNA CITATION AND CITATION I

C/n	Srs	Identities										
172	500-0172	N172CC	PT-KIU	[w/o 12Nov76 Aracatuba, Brazil]								
173	500-0173	N77CP	N59CL	N500EL	[parted out by White Inds Inc, Bates City, MO]							
174*	500-0174	N26HC	N21NA	N211DB	N14MH	N931CA	N19AJ	N16LG	N15JH			
175	500-0175	N175CC	XA-HOO	XB-CCO	XA-SIG	N175CC	N1DK	[w/o 06Jan98 Pittsburgh-Allegheny County A/P, PA]				
176	500-0176	G-BCII	G-TEFH	N150TT								
177	500-0177	PH-CTF	N192AB	N888XL	N883XL	N431LC						
178	500-0178	D-IKFJ	I-FBCK	(HB-VJP)	HB-VKK	EC-IBA	[w/o 02Aug12 nr Santiago de Compostela, Spain]					
179	500-0179	N444J	N111KR	N427DM	(N997S)	EI-BYM	N179EA	PT-OMT				
180	500-0180	N180CC	I-AMBR	N31079	SE-DDO	HB-VFH	N31079	PT-LAZ	N61MJ	N772C	N500ET	
181	500-0181	N181CC	PT-KPA	[cx by 2000 last permit 1996; reported wfu]								
182	500-0182	D-IABC	N525GA	C-FNOC	N590EA	N13HJ	OO-DCM	N23W	N900TA	[parted out by White Inds, Bates City, MO]		
183	500-0183	N183CC	(VH-FRM)	N1VC	(N721CC)	N1880S	N112CP	N151AS	[parted out Montgomery, AL; cx 24Aug07]			
184	500-0184	N77RC	N71RC	N67SF	N67BE	N67BF	N184NA	N550LT				
185	500-0185	N22EH	N22FH	N500JB	N500WP	N500AZ	C-GIAD	N500AZ	ZP-TZH	N141SA		
186	500-0186	N186MW	N186SC	(N501WL)	N186CP							
187	500-0187	(HB-VDR)	(TI-ACB)	N187MW	N20VP	(N75KC)	N99MC	N345KC	N99BC	(N95TJ)	N5FW	N130DW	YV….
188	500-0188	N5223J	PT-KPB	N505AZ								
189	500-0189	XC-GOV	XA-SJV	N189CC	N500HH	[b/u; cx Jan01]						
190	500-0190	N190CC	(N424RD)	N99BC	N99MC	N500HK	N602BC	N434UM	[parted out; cx 29May09]			
191	500-0191	N5600M	N448EC	N23WK	N155CA	N701BR	LV-YRB					
192	500-0192	N4TK	N508S	N220S	N100JJ	I-AMCY	(N70WA)					
193	500-0193	XC-GOW	XA-SQZ	N293S	OY-PSI							
194	500-0194	D-IMSM	OY-ASR	N310U	PT-LAX	N991SA	(N728RX)	N194TS	N501DG+	[+ flew as N501DG between Oct02 and Apr04 without		
		officially being registered as such]		N225RD	YV2737							
195	500-0195	N14JA	N100AC	N100AQ	N440EZ	N500LJ	N502BE	[parted out by White Inds, Bates City, MO]				
196	500-0196	N74FC	C-GENJ	N499BA	(N969ZS)	(N711FW)	N270PM	[cx 26Aug13; wfu]				
197	500-0197	XC-GOX	XA-SRB	N297S	N95VE	N1TW	N95VE	N316MW				
198	500-0198	G-BCKM	G-JETE	N9UJ	N700MP	N997CA	XB-IJW	XB-IUW	XB-TRN			
199	500-0199	N199SP	C-FGAT	XA-ASR	XB-JVK	N199JK						
200	500-0200	N520CC	N200MW	N250AA	N96G	N96EA	CS-DBM	N102VP	(YV-1071CP)	[wfu Fort Worth/Meacham, TX]		
201	500-0201	XC-GUO	N690EA	(F-GIHU)	N690EA	F-GRCH	C-GLAA	N221DA				
202	500-0202	N202MW	N240AA	N500JK	N500VK	N500WJ	N550RS					
203	500-0203	N95DR	(N724CC)	N101HF	N101HB	CC-PZM	(N51099)	[parted out]				
204	500-0204	C-GBCK	N204Y	TG-OZO	N204Y	N928RD	[parted out]					
205	500-0205	N520N	(N541NC)	N700CW	[w/o 01Apr83 Eagle Pass, TX]							
206	500-0206	N33NH	N946CC	VH-LGL	N771HR	[w/o 30Jun07 Conway, AR]						
207	500-0207	N92BA	N929A	N39J	N107SF	N501TL						
208	500-0208	N82JT	N22JG	(N520SC)	N501AT	(N508CC)	N515WE	N770AF				
209	500-0209	N209MW	(N919AT)	N800AV	EC-HFA	[to parts use circa Feb05 by Atlanta Air Salvage, Griffin, GA]						
210	500-0210	TR-LTI	N9011R	N210MT	N716GA	YV-625CP	[modified with winglets, removed on resale in USA]	N501TK	XB-TRY	XB-NXX		
211	500-0211	N990CB	N999CB	N999CV	[parted out by White Inds, Bates City, MO, 2000]							
212*	500-0212	N1LB	N222LB	N223LB	N223AS	N223MC	N92B	N74LL				
213	500-0213	N62HB	N355H	N741JB	N73WC	N100UF	N100UH	N101HG	(N213CE)	XA-AEI		
214	500-0214	N214CC	N371HH	(N371W)	N214CA	N709TB	N601GN	XB-NKT				
215	500-0215	N215CC	YV-T-000	YV-55CP	YV2030							
216	500-0216	(N216CC)	N314TC	N99CK	N199CK	(N612CA)	YV1686					
217	500-0217	N217CC	N500GA	N560GA	N625GA	XA-ODC	N2201U	XA-SOX	N217S	N55GR	YV2620	
218	500-0218	(N218CC)	N4AC	N271AC	(N271MF)	YV3029						
219	500-0219	N219CC	N25CS	N101KK	(N161KK)	N408CA	PT-LIY	[w/o 01Dec02 Marilia, Brazil]				
220	500-0220	N5220J	N93WD	N932HA	G-BOGA	G-OBEL	N619EA	G-ORHE	[cx 24Jul08, CofA expired]			
221	500-0221	N221CC	XC-GUH	N24AJ								
222	500-0222	N222CC	N636SC	N52PM	[cx 10Jul13; wfu]							
223	500-0223	N223CC	N444LP	N444KV	N400SA	OH-COC	N223P	I-CLAD				
224	500-0224	(N224CC)	N77RE	N3ZD	N5FG	N145CM	N697MB	ZS-ISA	ZS-SGT			
225	500-0225	N5225J	N5B	PH-SAW	OO-GPN	D-IDFD	VH-FSQ	VH-OIL	RP-C1500	[w/o 01Feb97 Mount Balakukan, Mindanao Island,		
		Philippines]										
226	500-0226	N5226J	JA8418	N100AD	PT-LTI							
227	500-0227	(N227CC)	G-BCRM	N423RD	C-GMMO	N227HP	(N776JS)	N227GM	TI-AZX	N916DJ		
228	500-0228	(N228CC)	N6365C	N769K	[parted out by White Inds, Bates City, MO]							
229	500-0229	N22FM	[w/o 26Apr83 Wichita, KS]									
230	500-0230	N5230J	N230CC	HB-VEH	I-PLLL	N92AJ	N24S	(N300TB)	N299TB	N200CG		
231	500-0231	(N5231J)	N99TD	N2TN	C-GMAT	N500SJ	N501GB					
232	500-0232	N5232J	N500PB	N126R	N999AM	(N971AB)						
233	500-0233	N5233J	N233CC	N233VM	N223S	N228S	N233JJ					
234	500-0234	(N5234J)	PH-CTG	N70CA								
235	500-0235	N5235J	N235CC	N12AM	(SE-RKZ)	[to Sweden as instructional airframe; cx 17Dec09]						
236	500-0236	N5236J	N236CC	N24PA	N2801L	N801L	N600SR	N337TV	N236TS	N1X	N742K	N320RG	N70SW
237	500-0237	(N5237J)	N14TT	VH-FSA	[w/o 20Feb84 Proserpine, Queensland, Australia]							
238	500-0238	(N5238J)	N3Q	N3QZ	OO-IBI	N68AG	N53FT	VP-CON	N409S			
239	500-0239	(N5239J)	N239CC	N6034F	PT-LOS	[parted out by Dodson Av'n, Rantoul, KS]						
240	500-0240	N5240J	N240CC	N234AT								
241	500-0241	(N9AT)	N5241J	XA-DAJ	N9060Y	XB-EPN	N288SP	N610ED	[w/o nr Derby, KS, 18Oct13]			
242	500-0242	N5242J	RP-C1964	N888JL	(N884DR)	(N888PA)	[wfu, stored Wichita/Mid-Continent, KS]					
243	500-0243	N5243J	XC-GOY	XC-BEN	XA-SQY	N53AJ	N243SH					
244	500-0244	(N5244J)	(SE-DMM)	SE-DDM	N244WJ	N400BH	N91LS	(N91BS)	N46RD	N516AB	PT-OQD	
245	500-0245	N5245J	(TI-AHE)	TI-AHH	XC-BUR	N2019V	9M-FAZ	(N245MG)	(N245BC)	D-IAJJ	9H-AJJ	
246	500-0246	(N5246J)	N50WM	N227VG	PT-LQR							
247	500-0247	(N5247J)	N4110S	N9065J	XA-JUA	C-GMAJ	[parted out Addison, TX]					
248	500-0248	(N5248J)	N75PX	(N70PB)	N111BB							
249	500-0249	N5249J	N27PA	N411DR	PT-LPF	(N789DD)	N501SE	N1GG	HA-JET			
250	500-0250	(N5250J)	N250CC	N25PA	N25CK	XA-JEL	N444RP	C-GRJQ	N160JS	(N413KA)	(N200BA)	N251P	N251MG	YV3095.
251	500-0251	N5251J	I-COKE	(HB-VGI)	N500LP	XC-QEO	XC-ASB	N790EA	PT-OMS			
252	500-0252	N5252J	N10PS	N200WN	C-GZXA	N244WJ	N501JC	N622AT				
253	500-0253	N5253J	YV-T-MMM	YV-19P	YV-07P	N722US	N8TG	N592WP				
254	500-0254	N5254J	N26PA	C-GJTX	N29991	N79DD	[w/o 24Sep90 San Luis Obispo, CA]					
255	500-0255	N5255J	D-INCI	N37643	N877BP	N885CA	XA-SAM	XB-HND	N907RT	N752CK		
256	500-0256	N256CC	SE-DDN	N83TF	N73TF	N456GB	N73HB	PT-OZT	N131SB	N676DG		
257	500-0257	N5257J	N75MN	N75FN	N75GW	ZS-PXD						
258	500-0258	(N5258J)	TI-AFB	N80639	(N76AM)	N66GE	N886CA	N125DS				
259	500-0259	N5259J	N410ND	JA8247	RP-C1299	N259DH						
260	500-0260	(N5260J)	N260CC	OK-FKA	N50RD	ZS-OGS	N260RD	ZS-OGS	A6-ESJ	N202HM		
261	500-0261	N5261J	N26RD	N55HF	N55LF	N711SE	N711SF	(N124DH)	N58TC	XB-MGS		
262	500-0262	N5262J	N44JF	N111MU	N110AF	N110AB	(N642CT)	ZS-BFS	ZS-LMH			
263	500-0263	N126KR	(N126KP)	N819H	(N90WA)	I-DUMA	N263AL	VH-AQR	VH-AQS	VH-ZMD	[wfu Melbourne/Essendon]	
264*	500-0264	N5264J	N205FM	F-GLJA	G-BWFL	G-OEJA	G-JTNC	G-BWFL				

CESSNA CITATION AND CITATION I

C/n	Srs	Identities									
265	500-0265	N5265J	N504GP	XA-VYF	N38MH	LV-ZPU	N501SC	N595DC			
266	500-0266	N5266J	N5TK	N751CC	N424AD	N7543H	(N40RF)	N11MN			
267	500-0267	N5267J	N28PA	N1UT	N626P	OY-CPK	N70704	N41SH	(N4090P)	N401RD	[parted out by Dodson Av'n, Rantoul, KS, circa 2000]
268	500-0268	N5268J	ZS-JKR	3D-ACR	VH-NEW	A6-RKH	N900G				
269	500-0269	N5269J	(D-IKUC)	D-ICCC	(PH-CTW)	SP-KBM					
270	500-0270	N5270J	N712J	N712N	N72BC	N68CB	N4238X	G-SWET	G-OSCA	N501DR	N915RP	N970RP
271	500-0271	N5271J	N168RL	N4403	N53FB	PT-LQG	[cx Dec97, fate not known]				
272	500-0272	N5272J	N505GP	N30SB	N30JN	N89AJ	[parted out by White Inds, MO; cx 29Apr09]				
273	500-0273	N5273J	N273RC	XA-LEO	XB-OBE	XA-RUR	XB-GBF				
274	500-0274	(N5274J)	N111TH	N140H	XA-IIX	N111TH	XB-ETE	N225BC	N70TF	N5LK	
275	500-0275	(N5275J)	N600SR	N40MM	(N38MM)	N352WC	N352WG	N102HF	N71HB	ZP-TZY	N275GK	(N275MB)	(N275BH)	N411TN
276	500-0276	(N5276J)	N276CC	N100CM	N473LP	N473LR	SE-DEG	(N340TB)	N29EB	SE-DEG	YU-SEG	SE-DEG	[instructional airframe Linkopings, Sweden]
277	500-0277	N277CC	N67MP	N67MA	N652ND	N662CC	N662CG	[wfu Addison, TX; cx 14Jan16]			
278	500-0278	(N5278J)	N278CC	N278SP	(N278SR)	ZS-LYB	N278SP	XB-FQO	XB-UAG	N103PL	VP-BBE	(SE-RDA)	N103PL	OY-PCW EC-JXC
279	500-0279	D-IMEN	OY-AJV	SE-DEX	N70454	VH-NMW	N120S	N501KG	N700LW	N425JS	N138HB
280	500-0280	(N5280J)	N280CC	N100HP	N102AD	N814ER	[w/o 01Feb06 Greensboro, NC; parted out by Dodson Int'l, Rantoul, KS]				
281	500-0281	N5281J	N49R	N72WC	N144JP	(N721TB)	N62TW	N70TS			
282	500-0282	(N5282J)	N282CC	N26WD	N520RB	N501SS	N501CW	N510RC	HB-VNU	N282SA	[stored Zurich, Switzerland, still wearing marks HB-VNU]
283	500-0283	N5283J	N10UC	N18AF	VH-ANQ	[w/o 11May90 Mt Emerald, Cairns, QLD, Australia]					
284	500-0284	(N5284J)	N284CC	YV-43CP	N8508Z	N37DW	PT-LOG				
285	500-0285	(N285CC)	N2U	N86SS	N113SM	[w/o 04Mar08 nr Oklahoma City/Wiley Post, OK]					
286	500-0286	N5286J	N286CC	5N-APN	[wfu Lagos, Nigeria]						
287	500-0287	(N5287J)	N287CC	N73LL	N57MB	OY-CGO	N31LH	PT-WHZ	N287AB	VP-BGE	[crashed on approach to Biggin Hill, England, 30Mar08; w/o]
288	500-0288	(N5288J)	N288CC	D-IDWN	OY-ASD	N9013S	N5TR	(N502BA)	N1DA		
289	500-0289	N5289J	YV-50CP	N5591A	XA-KAH	N939KS	OE-FAN	[w/o 24Feb04 Cagliari, Italy]			
290	500-0290	(N5290J)	N290CC	D-ICFA	N4246Y	N826RD	N88AF	(N390S)	N896MA	N896MB	N400RM
291	500-0291	N5291J	ZS-JOO	N291DS	OE-FGN						
292*	500-0292	N5292J	N10FM	N255LJ	C-FSUN	N18BG	SE-DDX	N501RL	N501HK	N333JH	XB-ESG
293	501-0643	(N5293J)	N8RF	N54CM	N54TS	[Sierra Stallion conversion with Williams FJ44-2A engines, ff 14Jun06]			C-GQPJ		
294	500-0294	N5294J	HL7226	(N501LG)	N924AS	SE-DVB	OY-VIP	OE-FCM	N468PD	[parted out by Dodson Av'n, Rantoul, KS]	
295	500-0295	N5295J	EP-PAO	EP-KIA	N2274B	N44HC	N10FG	XB-NYV			
296	500-0296	(N5296J)	N98DM	N882CA	ZS-NHF	(N245BC)	N296BF	XA-BET			
297	500-0297	N5297J	(N818CD)	YV-62CP	N48DA	N38SA					
298	500-0298	N5298J	N900GC	N570MC	YV....						
299	500-0299	N5299J	HB-VEO	N3JJ	N66TR	N55AK	ZS-MGH	N5133K	YV-940CP	PT-OZX	N80364	(OY-EBD)	OY-TKI	N80364
		[wfu Doncaster/Robin Hood, UK]									
300	500-0300	(N5300J)	OE-FAP	(N500CX)	[parted out by Dodson Av'n, Ottawa, KS, following accident 06Oct84 in Greece; cx Jun90]						
301	500-0301	N5301J	EP-PAP	N81MJ	N747WA	OE-FNG	N305S				
302	500-0302	N5302J	N302CE	N469PW	(N777QE)	N710VL					
303	500-0303	(N5303J)	N19M	N19U	C-GDWS	N8DX					
304	500-0304	N5304J	N304CC	N5253A	N5253E	N70U	N10UH	[cx Jun05, parted out then used for fire training at San Antonio, TX]			
305	500-0305	N5305J	N305BB	N805BB	C-GMLC	N137WC	N100AM				
306	500-0306	N5306J	N36CJ	N36SJ	N606KK	N606KR	(N747BL)				
307	500-0307	N2607	N2613	N777SL							
308	500-0308	(N5308J)	N308CC	N38CJ	N70TG	N6525J	(F-GIRS)	F-GMLH	F-GSMC	F-HDMB	5R-...
309	500-0309	N5309J	(N1GB)	N1JN	N1UG	N1382C	N57LC	SE-DKM	N791MA	N88NW	N83NW
310	500-0310	(N5310J)	N510CC	N1851T	N1851N	N820FJ	N820	XA-STT	N998AA	N222VV	N941JC	N900CC	YV2696
311	500-0311	N5311J	N818CD	OH-COL	N501RL	N39RE	(OY-VIP)	LN-AAF	I-RAGW		
312	F500-0312	N5312J	N33ME	(N233ME)	N33MQ	N82AT	F-GJDG	EC-KGE	F-HBMS	EC-LZP	
313	500-0313	(N5313J)	N76GT	XA-KUJ	XB-DYF	XA-SDS	N313BA	HB-VLE	D-ISKM	N513JK	[cx 06Aug15; derelict at Friedrichshafen, Germany, still wearing D-ISKM]
314	500-0314	N5314J	(N314CC)	N501SC	N100UF	N180UF	N66ES	N668S	N500NT*		
315	500-0315	N5315J	N55SK	N55SH	SE-DRZ	N694PW	[parted out by Alliance Air Parts, Oklahoma City, OK]				
316	500-0316	N5316J	N398RP	N97SK	N711MT	(N127CJ)					
317	500-0317	N53MJ	D-ICCA	N37489	C-GPCO	N317VP	YV-1133CP	YV233T	YV2753		
318	500-0318	N5318J	N518CC	N944B	VR-COM	VP-COM					
319	500-0319	N5319J	HZ-NC1	N5319J	N22LH	D-ICUW	N94MA	"F-GKIL"	F-GKID		
320	500-0320	(N5320J)	N320CC	N341CC	N299WV	N341CC	I-NORT	N74WA	N70WA	I-....	
321	500-0321	N5321J	JA8438	[cx Sep96 as WFU; To Japan Newspaper Museum, Yokohama, Japan]							
322	500-0322	N5322J	N1AP	N108MC							
323	500-0323	N5323J	N300PB	N474L	N523CC	N307EW	(N268GM)	N388GM	N386SC	LV-CDI	
324	500-0324	(N5324J)	N324C	N52TC	N324JC	(N721HW)					
325	500-0325	(N5325J)	N25CJ	N50TR	N60MP	PT-OSD					
326	500-0326	N5326J	N45LC	G-UESS	[w/o 08Dec83 Stornoway, Scotland]						
327	500-0327	N5327J	HL7277	S Korea 5327	S Korea 70327		N399PA	RP-C3958			
328	500-0328	(N5328J)	N328CC	(N571K)	PT-LSF	N168AS	XB-IXE				
329	500-0329	N5329J	ZS-JOK	N5329J	XC-IPP	XC-PPM	N4999H	OY-CEV			
330	500-0330	(N5330J)	N330CC	(N82CF)	I-JESE	N270BH	(N237JP)	N141SG	N800CJ	N812MG	
331	500-0331	N5331J	N331CC	N86RE	N96RE	N40AC	LN-NAT	EC-500	EC-FUM	LN-NAT	G-LOFT	[wfu Caernarfon, UK]
332	500-0332	N5332J	LV-PUY	LV-LZR	N332SE						
333	500-0333	(N5333J)	N275AL	VH-SOU							
334	500-0334	N5334J	N500DD	N44RD	(N527TA)	ZS-MPI	N334JC	[canx Apr98 as scrapped]			
335	500-0335	N5335J	ZP-PNB	ZP-PUP	N2937L	PT-LDI					
336	500-0336	(N5336J)	N336CC	YV-O-MAC-1	[w/o Jun79 Caracas, Venezuela]						
337	500-0337	N5337J	N873D	N22MB	(F-GNAB)	N17KD	N615DS				
338	500-0338	N5338J	(N868D)	HB-VEX	N8499B	N3300M	N92LA	N97LA	N73WC	(N404JW)	N41HL	XB-OIQ
339	500-0339	(N5339J)	G-JEAN	N707US	N300EC	G-JEAN	G-DJAE	[wfu; parted out by Dodson Av'n, Rantoul, KS]			
340	500-0340	(N5340J)	N2630	(N2610)	N505AM	HB-VIV	VR-BTQ	ZS-MBS	N340DN	PT-WOD	(N340RL)	N26NS	N344RJ
		[instructional airframe, Saskatchewan Indian Institute of Technology, Saskatoon, Canada].									
341	500-0341	(N5341J)	N2650	N505JC	C-GVKL	C-FDMB	N383SC	LV-BPW			
342	500-0342	(N5342J)	N530TL	N711TE	N501DR	N501LH					
343	500-0343	(N5343J)	N525AC	C-FRHL	N91D	HB-VJR	N91DZ	C-FOSM	N501JF		
344	500-0344	(N5344J)	N632SC	HB-VHI	VR-BLV	VP-BLV	CX-CCT				
345	500-0345	(N5345J)	N23ND	N410NA	N410N	VR-BUB	N345TL	N747RL	(N747KL)	XA-TOF	XB-CSI
346	500-0346	N5346J	D-IJON	N4234K	(N99WB)	N82SE	N56DV	PT-LUA			
347	500-0347	(N5347J)	N500XY	N876WB	V5-ACE						
348	500-0348	(N5348J)	N300HC	N301HC	C-GCLQ	N712KM					
349	500-0349	(N5349J)	N888AC	(N988AC)	N888GZ	VH-HVM	VH-HVH	N501DA			
350	501-0027	N5350J	N350CC	N10EH	N54DS	JA8380	N783KK				
351	501-0001	N5351J	N51CJ	N506TF	[converted to Sierra Stallion]		(N15FJ)		Mexico 3933		

CESSNA CITATION AND CITATION I

C/n	Srs	Identities										
352	501-0261	N5352J	N52CC	N7NE	N501VP	YV2502						
353	501-0002	N5353J	OE-FPO	N165CB	XA-LUN	N39301	N501WJ	(N501WK)	N88TB	HP-1797		
354	501-0263	N5354J	N948N	N501BE	(N501BF)	[cx 31Aug15; wfu]						
355	501-0003	N5355J	N55CJ	N781L	N81EB							
356	501-0004	N5356J	N88JJ	N86JJ	N142DA							
357	501-0005	N5357J	N661AA	N665JB	N143EP	N284RJ	N455FD					
358	501-0006	(N5358J)	N358CC	N121JW	N121UW	(N1236P)	N5016P	N93TJ	I-ERJA	N501GR		
359	501-0264	(N5359J)	9J-AEJ	N353WB	N27WW							
360	501-0007	N5360J	N222WA									
361	500-0361	N5361J	D-IKPW	N5361J	C-GOIL	N5361J	N90EB	F-GKIR	N501MX			
362	501-0008	N5362J	N362CC	N6HT	(N501DB)	N900PS	N909PS					
363	500-0354	(N5363J)	G-BEIZ	N51GA	G-CCCL	G-TJHI	N354RC	N694LM	HL8037			
364	501-0011	N36842	(N1UB)	N36JG	N770MH	N650AC	N1UM	N130SP	N501			
365	501-0267	N36846	G-DJBB	D-IAEV	N944TG	N565VV	N565V					
366	500-0356	N5366J	N36848	Argentina AE-185		LQ-CLW						
367	501-0009	N36850	N67CC	N715EK	(N715JM)	N505BC	N505RJ					
368	501-0269	N5368J	N36854	YV-120CP	N120RD	N545GA	(N545G)	XB-GVY	N501JJ			
369	501-0012	N36858	N190K	N999RB	N99XY	N99GC	N8P	N8PJ	HI-527	HI-527SP	N4196T	N501GS	N15FJ	N449DT
		[Eagle II conversion]										
370	501-0010	N36859	N7WF	EP-PBC	N7WF	(N500MD)	VH-POZ	EC-EDN				
371	501-0014	N36860	N22TP	N888FL	N645TS							
372	501-0013	N36861	(N622SS)	VR-BJK	N501TJ	[parted out by Dodson Int'l, Rantoul, KS]						
373	501-0015	N36862	N1823B	N18328	XA-MAL	N4446P	N454AC					
374	501-0270	N36863	N300WK	N893CA	N105JM	N501ST						
375	501-0016	N36864	N517A	C-GHOS	N501DL	N38DA	(N58DT)	N58BT	N38DA	(N38DL)	N255TS	N17TJ	N45TL
376	501-0017	N36869	N877C	N100WJ	N501AT							
377	500-0358	N36870	(EP-PAQ)	N82MJ	SE-DEP	I-UUNY						
378	501-0018	N36871	N378CC	N18BG	N550TG	N501GR	N228AK	N228AJ	N228FS	N228ES	XB-JXG	
379	501-0272	N36872	N5072L	N700JR	N44MK							
380	501-0020	N36873	N32JJ	N123EB	(N60GG)	N100GG						
381	501-0041	N36880	N50MC	N173SK	N120ES	[w/o 24Apr95 San Salvador Intl A/P, wreckage parted out by Dodson Av'n, Ottawa, KS; cx 24Apr15]						
382	501-0273	N36881	(I-CCCB)	XA-HEV	N46106	D-IDPD	N333PD	N333PE	N501MD	(N273DA)	N501JF	(N501EM)	N302TS	N302AJ
		N110JA	N301DR									
383	501-0019	N36882	(N301MC)	N501SP	(N5EM)	[dbr Mexicali, Mexico, 03Dec06; cx 04Mar14]						
384	501-0021	N36883	(YV-135CP)	YV-166CP	XA-IEM	N121SJ	N203LH	ZS-MGL	N151SP			
385	501-0022	N36884	N385CC	N11DH	N110H	(N995AU)	N10GE	[w/o 21May85 Harrison Airport, AR]				
386	501-0023	N36885	N56MC	N56MT	(N501FB)	N56MK						
387	501-0024	N36886	(N10CA)	N1CA	N711NR	Z-WSY	N724EA	N70BG				
388	501-0032	N36887	N388CJ	N33AA	N377KC	N690MC	N550T	N550L	N85WP	N642BJ	(N501SK)	N307D
389	501-0025	N36888	N389CC	N21BS	N20RM							
390*	501-0030	N36890	N301MC	N301MG	N100CJ	C-GSLL	N96BA	N911MM	(N911MU)	N655AT		
391	501-0026	N36891	N92C	N92CC	N92BL	N610BD						
392	500-0364	N36892	HB-VFF	N221AC	(N221JB)	N20WP	N40DA	G-OKSP	G-ORJB	N501E	SE-RGN	SX-FDB
393	501-0275	N36893	YV-159CP	N31AJ	ZS-MPN	(N41AJ)	N40AJ	N23AJ				
394	501-0028	N36895	N1234X	N501PV								
395	501-0031	N36896	N395SC	XA-SDI	N510AJ	LV-BFM						
396	500-0370	N36897	SE-DEY	D-IMCE	HA-JEB	OE-FML						
397	501-0262	N36898	YV-O-SID-3	YV-79CP	N9712T	LN-AFC	N50WJ	N794EZ	(N58T)	N20CC	N20CZ	YV593T
398	501-0050	N36901	N20SP	N880CM	N59MA							
399	500-0367	N36906	YV-52CP	YV1541	YV2254							
400	501-0033	N36908	N400GB	N300PB	(N715DG)	N517BA	(N101HC)	N411DS	N411ME	N700LW	C-GQJK	N91PE	[cx 15Jul13]
401	501-0034	N36911	N444MW	N444MV	N501CP							
402	501-0278	N36912	G-BFAR	ZS-LPH	G-BFAR	A6-SMH	G-BFAR	A6-SMH	G-BFAR	G-DANI	N104AB	N53RG	N129AP	N124NB
		N124NS	N322ST									
403	501-0039	N36914	N403CC	N800DC	N800BH	N432DG	N808BC	N507DS	N141M	N212AT	N501SP	
404	501-0035	N36915	(N800M)	N500WN	N112MC	N25MH	(N35K)	N35JF	N501DD			
405	501-0046	N36916	N405CC	N5VP	[parted out by Dodson Int'l, Rantoul, KS]							
406	501-0036	N36918	N406CJ	N36CC	HI-493	N360MC	N2904					
407	501-0279	N36919	SE-DEZ	(N371GP)	(N371GA)	N371GP	N43BG	SE-DEZ	N66HD	SE-DEZ	PH-DEZ	
408	501-0037	N36922	N10J	N19J	N234JW	N501U	LV-CGO					
409	501-0038	N36923	N315S	(N315P)	N501JG	(N510NY)	N501NY					
410	501-0042	N87185	N773FR	I-TOSC	(N120DP)	N420AM	I-AROM	[w/o Rome-Ciampino, Italy, 09Sep05]				
411	501-0029	N87253	(N411CJ)	N411WC	(N411RJ)	N816LL	N31JM	(N45AQ)	XA-TKY	[w/o 06Oct10 Gulf of Mexico nr Coatzacoalcos, Mexico]		
412	501-0040	N87258	N85FS	I-KWYJ	N501E	N21EP	LV-BPZ					
413	501-0047	N87496	HB-VFI	N1021T	N550T	N550U	N9ZB					
414	501-0048	N87510	N414CC	(I-DAEP)	I-OTEL							
415	501-0280	N98449	YU-BKZ	T9-BKA	N212M							
416	501-0045	N98468	N833	N833JL	N22EL							
417	501-0043	N98510	N10NL	N16NL								
418	501-0053	N98528	N59PC	YV-253P	YV-253CP	N14EA	N52TL					
419	501-0054	N98563	N2BT	N501EA								
420	501-0049	N98586	N2ZC	(N36WS)	(N347DA)	OY-SVL	ZS-CWD					
421	501-0062	N98599	D-IBWB	N208W	N900DM	N980DM	N501MR					
422	501-0051	N98601	N422CC	N150TJ	N303CB	N422DA	N501A					
423	501-0281	N36943	LV-PZI	LV-MGB	N501SJ	N501CB						
424	501-0044	N98675	N5TC	N944JD	(N122LG)	N131SY	N50US	N600RM	F-HFRA			
425	501-0055	N98682	N552MD	N400PC	N400PG	N145DF	N145AJ	N223LC	[w/o 18Aug08, crashed into Caribbean Sea]			
426	501-0056	N98688	(N426CC)	(N501SF)	N55WH	CC-CTE	N56WE					
427	501-0052	N98715	N900MC	N677JM	(N13DL)	N5DL						
428	501-0282	(N98718)	N36949	XC-PMX	XA-SQX	N82AJ	[Eagle II conversion]					
429	501-0283	N98749	C-GPTC	N204CA								
430	501-0057	N98751	N500JC	N505BG	N577VM	N577JT						
431	501-0059	N2079A	N431CC	N13RC	ZS-EHL	N16HL	N501AJ					
432	501-0066	N2098A	D-IHEY	N501BG	N501CX	C-GHRX	N945AA	VR-CTB	VP-CTB	N501CD		
433	501-0284	N2131A	N115K	N409AC	VR-BBY	N788SS	N284PC	N729PX	N45AF	[Eagle II conversion]		
434	501-0058	N2627A	N44MC	N444AG	N36GC	N32MJ	N65RA	(N400PG)	N501FT	N211EF	N211X	N501EZ	[w/o 02Dec98
		Grannis, AR]										
435	501-0060	N2741A	N435CC	N500ZC	N5737	N573L	N11TM	N129ZM	N528RM			
436	501-0061	N2757A	N436CC	N34DL	N1401L	N202CF	SE-RBZ	EC-KGX				
437	501-0064	N2768A	(N33KW)	N9TK	N96DS	N12WH						
438	501-0068	N2841A	N438CC	N9GT	N50GT	N68EA	N363TD	N299K				
439	501-0285	N2887A	N100BX	N13ST								
440	501-0065	N2888A	N33WW									
441	501-0069	N2906A	N501EF	N636N								
442	501-0067	N2959A	SE-DEO	D-IGMB	HB-VJB	VR-BLW	HB-VJB					

CESSNA CITATION AND CITATION I

C/n	Srs	Identities											
443	501-0063	N2991A	N305M	N408MM	N408MW	F-GESZ	N501BA	N555KW	(XA-...)				
444	501-0070	N3062A	(N444CW)	N78AB	N21HJ	N96G	N96GT	N70VP	HC-BTQ	(N277RW)	N628ZG	N45MM	YV3025
445	501-0286	N3104M	N445CC	I-ROST	(N789AA)	N381BJ							
446	501-0071	N3105M	N501SR	N501KR	N501KB	N509P	YV-697CP	YV232T	N666TS	(B-M..)	N501SJ		
447	501-0072	N3110M	N1HA	N17HA									
448*	501-0073	N3117M	N100SV	N299RP	(N840MC)	N70FJ	[w/o Hailey, ID 15Mar03; cx Jul03]						
449	501-0074	N3118M	YV-232CP	N888DS	N717RB	N28GC	N552AJ						
450	501-0075	N3120M	N773LP	N773LR	N325BC	(N325PM)	N51ET	N713JD					
451	501-0076	N3122M	N451CJ	N315MR	N315MP	N150RM							
452	501-0077	(N3124M)	N15PR	N42HM	N678JD	(N678JG)	I-FRAI	N501AZ					
453	501-0078	(N3127M)	N13BT	ZS-MZO	N13BT	N501EK	N25MB	(N501VB)	N12VB				
454	500-0369	N3132M	C-GVER	N46253	[parted out circa 06Jly05 Bates City, MO as C-GVER]								
455	500-0374	N3141M	C-GRQA	N501SS	(N501BB)	(N505BB)							
456	501-0079	N3144M	N555EW	N33CX	VP-CFF	D-ICAM	N250GM	N79FT	N791JF				
457	501-0080	N3145M	N51CC	N51CG	N347DA	N37LA	N800BF	N888PN					
458	501-0081	N3146M	N12DE	N12CQ	N12CV								
459	501-0289	N3147M	LV-PAT	LV-MMR	N501NA	N1KC	(N501SK)	N501NZ	N82DT				
460	501-0082	N3150M	N460CC	N84CF	C-GEVF	N6RF	(N386DA)	XB-ERX	N501AB				
461	500-0378	N3156M	C-GBNE	[to instructional airframe Stephenson Technical College, Winnipeg, Canada]									
462	501-0083	N3158M	N462CC	N5YP	N420PC	N420RC	(N83TJ)	N101LD	N910G				
463	501-0084	N3160M	(N463CJ)	(N11JC)	G-CITI	VR-CDM	VP-CDM	G-CITI	EC-ISP				
464	501-0098	N3161M	N44RD	N144AR	(N144AB)	HB-VIC	N92BE						
465	501-0093	N3163M	N88CF	N31RC	N623LB	N501RM	N501AD						
466	501-0090	N3165M	XC-CIR	N41JP	N3GN								
467	501-0099	N3170A	I-FLYA	N216RL	[wfu Sarasota, FL, still wearing I-FLYA]								
468	501-0101	N3170M	C-GDDM	N100TW	N106EA	(N501GS)	(N323JB)	N501KM					
469	501-0095	N3172M	N612DS	XA-AGA									
470	500-0386	N3173M	LV-PAX	LQ-MRM									
471	501-0089	(N3175M)	N471H	N106WV	N588CA	VH-LJG	VH-CCJ	VH-MMC	VH-CSP				
472	501-0292	N3180M	YV-O-MTC-2	YV-2295P	N456R	N339HP							
473	501-0088	(N3181A)	N473CC	N31MT	N22TS	N22TY	N86MT	N23YZ	(N23TZ)	N3WT			
474	501-0087	(N3183M)	N501SE	C-GVVT	(N22508)	N501SJ	N501BB						
475	501-0085	N3189M	N575CC	N475CC	N34AA	N25DD	N707W	N70ZW	XA-...				
476	501-0091	N3194M	(N887DM)	(N55BE)	N33BE	N39BE	(JA8361)	I-OMEP	N2158U	HB-VKY	N2158U		
477	501-0086	N3195M	N8LG	N88CF	(N711AE)	N583MP	N32SX	N501CW	N501JP	N11SQ	(N864TT)	N554T	N11SQ	(N554T)
		EC-INJ	T7-TLM										
478	501-0092	N3197M	(HB-VGD)	N112WC	(N78BT)	LV-PLM	LV-WOI	N501X	N303A				
479	501-0097	N3198M	N479CC	N479JS	N501RS	N251CF	N251CB						
480	501-0096	N3202A	N660AA	(N480CC)	N660KC	N501HS							
481	501-0293	N3202M	Ecuador ANE-201	HC-BVP	N850MA	N597CS	N995JP						
482	501-0107	N3204M	(N333BG)	(N33VV)	N1UL	N107CC	N501LS	N54TB	3A-MTB	(N75471)	EC-GJF		
483	501-0294	N3205M	N2LN	N38TM	N8EH	N80SL							
484	500-0387	N3206M	N484KA	N504D									
485	501-0100	(N3207M)	N485CC	N41ST	(N26MW)	C-GSUN	C-GSUM	N54FT					
486	501-0102	(N2646X)	N486CC	(N223RE)	I-AIRV	N501CG	N45FS	[Eagle II conversion]	VH-FCS				
487	501-0120	N2646Y	N487HR	N487LS	OY-CPW	N71LP							
488	501-0094	(N2646Z)	N488CC	N103PC	N59CC	N159LC	C-FBDS	C-FBDQ					
489	500-0392	N26461	I-FLYB	D-ISSS	3D-IER	4O-OOO	OM-VOV	[cx 2016; status?]					
490	501-0103	(N2647U)	N49WC	N611AT	(N906EA)	ZS-PHP							
491	501-0109	(N2647Y)	N30RL	N30RE	N567WB	LV-BXH							
492	501-0104	(N2647Z)	N312GK	N81CC	N29CA	N33HC	N998EA						
493	501-0105	N2648X	(N231LC)										
494	501-0297	(N2648Y)	VH-SWC	N32DA	N35LD	N41GT	[Stallion conversion, FJ44 engines]						
495	501-0108	(N2648Z)	(N56CJ)	N777AJ	N777GG	N707GG							
496	501-0110	(N26481)	N15NY	[w/o 02Aug79 Akron, OH]									
497	501-0119	(N26486)	N35AA	N35TM	N53RC	N77GJ	N53EZ	N13KD					
498	501-0111	N2649D	N140WC	(N333RB)	N777FE	I-FOMN	N94SL	N59WP	N79BK	N357TX	N501PJ		
499	501-0112	N2649E	(N900LL)	N350M	N14TV	(N84TV)	N74PM	(N74PN)	N112FR	N224GP	LV-FWX		
500	501-0127	N2649H	N500K	N88BM	N96SK	N86SK	N117DJ	N529KT					
501	501-0106	(N2649J)	(N1234F)	OE-FYF	D-IANE	N793AA	(D-ISKY)						
502	501-0113	(N2649S)	(N515CC)	N502CC	N200ES	N502CC							
503	501-0114	N2649Y	N673LP	N673LR	N485RP	N711HL	(N725RH)	N811HL	[to White Inds, MO 17Feb05 for spares]				
504	501-0118	N2649Z	I-DECI	N61572	N311ME	XB-TMG							
505	501-0126	N26492	N505SP	N505JH									
506	501-0117	N26493	LV-PDW	LV-MZG	N91AP								
507	501-0115	N26494	N501GF	(N26540)	N501GK	N95RE	N728MC	N5ZN					
508	501-0122	N26495	N275CC	N275CQ	N400DB	N501HC	(N501MD)	N501MB					
509	501-0116	(N26496)	N500XX	N7CJ	N7QJ	(N90MT)	N7TK						
510	501-0239	N26497	LV-PDZ	LV-MYN	N164CB	OE-FMS	N501TB						
511	501-0298	N26498	(PH-JOB)	I-GERA	OE-FIW	N65M	VR-CMS	N501D	N118RT				
512	501-0129	(N26499)	(N50WP)	N70WP	PT-LQQ	N501JD							
513	501-0123	N2650C	N513CC	N627L	N627E								
514	501-0249	N2650M	RP-C237	N4263X	ZS-LOW	N133DM	G-OHLA	I-DIDY	N249AS	N851BC	XA-OAC	N40MA	(N82MP)	N117MA
515	501-0124	N2650N	N95RE	OE-FFK	[w/o 26Oct88 nr Salzburg, Austria]								
516	501-0134	N2650S	N501LW	N501EM	N841CW	N121EZ	YV3009						
517	501-0130	(N2650V)	N148JB	N148JS	(N726BB)	(N300RN)	N102HS	N505CF					
518	501-0131	N2650X	N490WC	YV-301P	N301PP	YV-2605P	N133SC	(N501NP)					
519	501-0135	N2650Y	N77TW	N711GL	N49MP	N63CG	N501WL						
520	501-0136	(N26502)	N66AT	N66AG	N800TW	N511HC							
521	501-0137	N26503	N46SC	N14VA									
522	501-0128	(N26504)	N522CC	N900MM	N501CF								
523	501-0121	N26506	D-IANO	HB-VID	D-IANO	OE-FHW	[wfu Linz, Austria]						
524	501-0142	N26507	HB-VHA	N310AF	N880M	I-SATV	YV-688CP	N197FS	(N123PL)	N15FJ	N67BE	N142FJ	N174CF
525*	501-0138	(N26509)	8P-BAR	8P-BAB	C-GBTB	N501CE	N74FH	Mexico 3934					
526	501-0139	N2651B	N526CC	N1LQ	(N3UG)	N108JL	N888BH	N501AF					
527	501-0132	N2651G	N50US	N91WZ	N717JL	N39HH							
528	501-0133	N2651J	(N955WP)	N51WP	N700SP	N554T							
529	501-0140	(N2651R)	(N99TD)	N96TD	N96CF	OE-FDM	9A-CHC	[parted out by Atlanta Air Salvage, Griffin, GA]					
530	500-0395	N2651S	XA-JEX	XB-JFV									
531	501-0125	(N2651Y)	(N2DP)	(N501DP)	N45MC	N96TC	N69EP	N125EA					
532	501-0141	N26510	N166CB	VR-BJN	N841MA	N501GG	N501DR	Mexico 3931 [retro-fitted with Williams FJ44 engines]					
533	500-0396	N26514	(XA-JEW)	XC-GTO									
534	501-0156	N26517	N123FG	N44FM	N829MB								
535	501-0143	N26523	D-IGGK	OY-ONE	N501MG	4X-CMG	N520BH	N501WJ					
536	501-0144	N2652U	N270SF	N270NF	OE-FMK								

CESSNA CITATION AND CITATION I

C/n	Srs	Identities												
537	501-0159	N2652Y	D-IGLU	N666JJ	N308AT	N1AT	N8189J	N80CJ	N80HA					
538	501-0145	N2652Z	(ZS-KGF)	VH-LCL	N2652Z	[w/o 22Apr90 Norfolk Island while regd VH-LCL; hulk to Dodson Av'n, Ottawa, KS still marked as VH-LCL for parts use; US marks cx Jly94]								
539	501-0163	N1354G	(I-AGIK)	I-CIGB	D-IGGG*									
540	500-0403	N1710E	G-BPCP	[w/o 01Oct80 Jersey, Channel Is, UK]										
541	501-0147	N1728E	N254TW	CP-2105	N392DA	N27TS	N551MS							
542	501-0148	N1758E	(OO-ECT)	N167CB	N700ER	N500DL	I-GJMA	N148EA	N148ED	XB-KHL				
543	501-0149	(N1772E)	N104CF	N97FD	(N721CG)	N96FP	N72VJ							
544*	501-0302	(N1779E)	(G-BHIW)	XA-JFE	XB-ELU	XA-RLE	XA-JCE	N301EL	N801EL	N7EN				
545*	501-0146	(N1782E)	N545CC	N54MH	N61CD	N1VU	N194RC	N53BB	N804SI	N36KJ*				
546	501-0151	(N1820E)	N269MD	N269CM	N2690M	N797SF	N797SE							
547	501-0152	(N1874E)	N547CC	N501FM	N501ED	N40FJ	N48FJ	N15CV	(N15UJ)	VP-CMA	VP-CCD	N15CY		
548	501-0153	(N1930E)	N105CF	(N118AT)	N99CK	(N484CS)								
549	501-0160	N1951E	(N58BD)	N60PR	C-GAAA	N999PW								
550	501-0161	N1955E	OY-CYD	N5UM	XB-FXO	XB-GRE	N501FP	N96MB	N967B					
551	501-0303	(N1958E)	N6563C	OH-CIT	OY-FFC	SE-DVA	N301JJ	N610GD	N370TP	N303RH	N393PJ*			
552	501-0162	N1959E	N455H	N55H	N44SW	N446V	N501DP							
553	501-0157	N2052A	(N88BR)	N16VG										
554	500-0399	N2069A	YU-BML	T9-SBA	E7-SBA									
555	501-0175	N2072A	EI-BJN	VR-BKP	VP-BKP	VP-BVK	N23VK							
556	501-0158	N2611Y	N1MX	N501WB										
557	501-0165	N2612N	(N20KW)	N557CC	N165NA	N501RC								
558	501-0154	N2613C	N80MF	CC-CWW	N154SC									
559	501-0166	N2614C	N476X	I-CIPA	(N30AF)	OY-INI	N166FA							
560	500-0404	N2614H	G-BHTT	G-ZAPI	N789DD	N789DK	LV-BID							
561	501-0185	N2614K	N653DR	N72787	N111RB	N1CR	N501LL	N505BG	N585BG					
562	501-0150	N2616G	N95MJ	N73FW	N405PC	[w/o 02Apr01 Depere, WI]								
563	501-0167	(N2616L)	N563CC	N323CB	N38RT	N900TW	N723JM	N501FJ						
564	501-0155	N2617B	(N108CT)	N110TV	N110TP	N800DW	VR-CJB	VP-CJB	N299D	N321TS	N347MH	(N38MQ)		
565	500-0401	N2617K	N2651	I-FARN										
566	501-0169	N2617U	D-IBWG	C-GFEE										
567	501-0183	N6777V	ZS-KPA	CS-AYY	(N8NC)									
568	501-0168	(N6777X)	N39LL	PT-LNV	N168EA	N601WT	N328NA							
569	501-0188	N6778C	N1JB	N93JM	N61DT	N251CT	N525PV							
570	501-0164	(N6778L)	N570CC	N223GC	N750LA	N50DS	N170JS	N286PC						
571	501-0193	N6778T	N164CB	XA-LIM	N39300	N45MK	N89MF	N199DJ						
572	501-0173	(N6778V)	OE-FPH	N25GT	N91MS	N91TE								
573	501-0170	(N6778Y)	N501HP	G-GENE	G-MTLE	N170EA	N610TT	N610GG						
574	501-0171	N67780	VH-BNK	N171WJ										
575	501-0184	N67786	N90CF	N433MM	N501VC	N318DN								
576	501-0187	N6779D (N614DD)	N576CC	(N414CB)	N21EH	N23EH	(N576CC)	N137GK	(N600DH)	N900DH	N900DL	N713AL	N7MC	N70CG
577	501-0176	N6779L	N44LC	N49LC	(VR-CIA)	VR-CFG	VP-CFG	N96DA	XB-LYY					
578	501-0177	N6779P	(N999RB)	N22SD	N501DG	N501NC	N501GW	N457CS	N98AV					
579	501-0174	N6779Y	N20GT	N721US	N702NC	N702NY	(N174CF)	N50JG	N454DQ	N1AG	N921BE			
580	501-0186	N67799	LV-PML	N4246A	N83ND	G-FLVU	G-VUEM	[w/o 19Nov10 Birmingham, UK; crash remains to AAIB Farnborough, UK, 22Nov10]						
581	501-0185	(N6780A)	N95EW	N37HW	N999WS									
582	501-0189	N6780C	N80SF	VH-FUM										
583	501-0182	N6780J	N360DJ	I-PALP	N535GA	(N125CA)	D-ISIS	VP-CAP	N220HM					
584	501-0190	(N6780M)	N584CC	N333MS	N393DA	N40AW	N723JR							
585	501-0191	N6780Y	N98ME	N64RT										
586	500-0410	N6780Z	XC-GAW											
587	500-0408	N67805	XA-LUD	XB-DVF										
588	501-0181	N6781C	N250SP	N250SR	N501KK	XB-PMR								
589	501-0179	(N6781D)	N589CJ	N414CB	HB-VLD	N718SA	(N406RH)	LV-CFH						
590	501-0192	(N6781G)	N190K	N650BC										
591	501-0194	N6781L	N28JG	N65WW										
592	501-0222	N6781R	N25HS	N690DM	N690WY									
593	501-0180	(N6781T)	(N593CC)	N695CC	N593DS	N9NE	N180VP	N650MW	N510NJ	LV-BHJ				
594	501-0197	N6781Z	N100SN	N324L										
595	501-0195	N67814	N161CB	N7111H	N109DC	(N123KD)	N109DC	N123KD						
596	500-0409	N67815	XC-FEZ											
597	501-0196	N6782B	(N597JV)	N575SR	N311TP	(N311TT)								
598	500-0412	N6782F	XA-LUV	XB-GDJ										
599	501-0172	(N6782P)	N907KH	HI-581SP	N110JB									
600	501-0311	(N6782T)	SE-DES	OY-JEY	N311VP									
601	501-0199	N6782X	N501MM	N441JT	N62RG	N7SV	N91HG							
602	501-0198	N67822	(N602CC)	N105TW	N500LE	N500LH	N198VP	N800DT	ZK-NBR	ZK-NDT	VH-NOU			
603	500-0406	N67829	SE-DET	OY-FFB										
604	501-0231	N6783C	N55WG	N29HE	N501BP	D-IAWU	N452TS	[w/o Trier, Germany, 12Jan14]						
605	501-0200	N6783L	7Q-YTL	N47TL	LV-CQP									
606	501-0201	N6783U	N801L	N130JS	N123SF	N55BM	N417RC	N417RQ	N78CN	N953SL	N953HC			
607	501-0202	N6783V	N520RP	N607CJ	(XA-PEV)	XA-BOA	N202VP	N477KM	N501G					
608	500-0413	N6783X	(PT-LBZ)	PT-LCC										
609	501-0203	N67830	D-IAEC	[w/o 31May87 Blankensee A/P, Lubeck, Germany]										
610	501-0207	N67839	N968DM	(N207CF)	OE-FYC	VP-BHO	N207JF	D-IABG						
611	501-0204	N6784L	(N123HP)	N345N	(N345HB)	N367HB	N282JG							
612	501-0208	N6784P	N54MJ	I-LAWN	N208EA	N82P	N5942P	[parted out by Alliance Air Parts, Oklahoma City, OK]						
613	501-0205	N6784T	PT-LVB	N6784T	(N501DA)	N528RM	(N501DL)	VH-VPM						
614	501-0209	N6784X	N56MJ	N501CR	N111DT	N36FD	N98RG	N70NB						
615	501-0206	N6784Y	N501HM	N795MA	OE-FBA	N314EB	N943LL	N943RC	N528DS					
616	501-0210	N67848	N32FM	YU-MDV	N1008									
617	501-0211	N6785C	N617CC	[cx Jun96, parted out by Dodson International Parts, Rantoul, KS]										
618	501-0213	N6785D	I-AUNY											
619	501-0212	N6785L	N67GM	N70AA	N2243	N243EE*								
620	501-0314	N6887M	N56MC	N56LW										
621	501-0214	N6887R	I-JUST	(N794WB)	N3312T	N2296S	N2298S	(N340AC)	N241MH	N241BF				
622	501-0215	N1354G	N50MM	ZS-LXT	N215NA									
623	501-0217	N1710E	N623RM	N600SS	N500TW	N7MZ								
624	501-0216	N1758E	N57MJ	(N65T)	N57TW	TG-RIF	TG-RIE							
625	501-0219	N1772E	N25CJ	N678DG	N625CH	N625J	N58BT	N501BW	N12RN	N18RN	N510GA	N56PB		
626	501-0218	N1958E	I-KODE	N218AM	N218JG									
627	501-0223	N1959E	N18HC	(N26HA)										
628	501-0220	N2052A	N628CH	N100CH	N100QH	N100LX								
629	500-0415	N2072A	JA8474	N50KR	N53RD									

CESSNA CITATION AND CITATION I

C/n	Srs	Identities									
630	501-0224	N2611Y	N630CE	N456CE	N825PS						
631	501-0228	N2612N	(N999CB)	N501CM	JA8284	N228EA	XA-SEY	N665MM			
632	501-0260	N2613C	N224RP	N500GA	N7UF	N41LE	N501RG				
633	501-0225	N2614C	N49BL	TG-MIL	TG-KIT	N412SE	N5411				
634	501-0227	(N2614Y)	N2614H	N374GS	N47CF	N83DM					
635	501-0226	(N2615D)	N29AC	N226VP	N501JM						
636	501-0229	(N2615L)	N636CC	N57MC	N57FC						
637	501-0232	(N2616G)	N2616C	N853KB	N35TL	VR-CHF	VR-CAT	VP-CAT	EC-LPP		
638	501-0230	(N2617B)	N2616G	N653F	N5RL	G-ICED	N505CC	HB-VLB	9A-DVR	N999MS	
639	501-0234	N2617B	N61PR	N711RP	PT-LIZ	N643RT	N77PA	N77PX	N123PL	N125PL	N123PL
640	501-0237	(N2617K)	N640BS	N237SC	N831CB	N29UF	N420PC	N712VF	(N712VE)	N420PC	
641	501-0235	N2617U	(N31CF)	(N13BN)							
642	501-0236	N26227	N711VF	C-GQJJ	N109C						
643	501-0221	(N26228)	N643MC	N217RR	N389JP	HB-VKD	N555HR	N221EB	N107GM	N106GM	(N643VP)	N501HG	XB-LVL
644	501-0240	N26232	N13BK	N711BT	OY-JET	N62864	N77UB	N501DY	N238BG		
645	500-0411	N6784Y	G-BIZZ	G-NCMT	SE-DLZ						
646	501-0242	N2623B	N40PL	N500BK	N71L						
647	501-0241	(N2624L)	N174CB	N207G	C-GSTR	N101RR					
648	501-0243	N2624Z	N43SP	N5DL	XB-SHA						
649	501-0238	N2626A	N238JS	I-DVAL	(N501EZ)	N995PA	N737RJ				
650	501-0244	N2626J	N650CJ	(N711VF)	N701VF	N418R	N244SL	N176FB	N501T	(N501HD)	N501MF
651	501-0317	N2626Z	5N-AVL	(N317JQ)	N706DC	N51FT					
652	501-0245	N26263	(N678DG)	ZS-LDO	A2-AGM	ZS-ACE					
653	501-0233	N26264	5N-AVM	N18860	N501Q	[stored dismantled Columbia, MO, awaiting rebuild]					
654	501-0246	N2627N	N85RS	N26LC	OE-FHH	LZ-TBP					
655	501-0247	N2627U	(N24CH)	[w/o 12Nov82 Wichita, KS]							
656	500-0418	N2628B	ZS-LDV								
657	501-0252	N2628Z	N825HL	N574CC	I-TOIO	OY-JJN					
658	501-0254	N2629Z	N84CF	N66BK	(N84GF)						
659	501-0256	N2631N	D-ILLL	I-PAPE	N256P						
660	501-0257	N2631V	(N992NW)	N500NW	OE-FLY	N12NM	N570D	N501WX			
661	501-0255	N661TV	N661TW	N501MR	N707WF	G-SBEC	N400LX	N901NB	N501X		
662	501-0248	N2633N	N7700T	(N711EG)	[w/o Franklin, NC, 15Mar12]						
663	501-0250	N77FD									
664	501-0258	N664CC	N900RB	N900RD	N87FL	VR-BHI	VP-BHI	N16KW	N599BR	N810LG	
665	501-0319	N124KC	N60EW								
666	501-0251	N30BK	N945BC	N400LX	N501RG	N501WD	N581PJ*				
667	501-0320	N2649D	ZS-LHP	3D-ADH	N70467	N401G	C-GPTI	C-GTOL			
668	501-0321	OE-FHP	N321VP	N550MH	N170MK	N510SJ	N986DS	N301MY*			
669	501-0322	N2663J	N374GS	N314GS	(N669DM)	(N769EW)	N527EW				
670	501-0253	N2650Y	N501JE	(N1SH)	C-GKPC	[dbr Stella Maris, Bahamas, 15Feb14; parted out]		N501JE			
671	501-0323	N2651B	N55HL	N501RF	N501LE	(N142AL)	N505BB				
672	501-0324	N2651J	JA8493								
673	501-0325	N1710E	(D-IFGP)	N501LM	N64BH						
674	501-0259	N1758E	(N77111)	(N261WB)	N261WR	N261WD	VR-BJW	N501MS	D-IEIR	(N225WT)	
675	501-0675	N8900M	N501MT	N593BW							
676	501-0676	N1958E	N676CC	(N76JY)							
677	501-0677	(N1958E)	N727MC	(N184SC)	C-GAAA	N54CG	N74HR				
678	501-0678	N2052A	N3FE	N678CF	PT-ODC	(N26AA)					
679	501-0679	N2611Y	N200GF	N679CC	N2611Y	VR-BLF	VP-BLF	N73SK	(N501HH)	4L-MPX	
680	501-0680	N2614C	PT-LFR	PP-EIF							
681	501-0681	N2616G	N82LS	N427SS	N889SH						
682	501-0682	N2617B	N3951	N19GB	N55TK	N682DC	N682HC	N682BF			
683	501-0683	N501BK	N501FR	N170HL	(N49TA)	N96LC	N702RT				
684	501-0684	N3683G	N501TP								
685	501-0685	N5346C	N400SR	N501TB	(N243AB)	N501EG	XB-IXT				
686	501-0686	N6763M	N750PP	N118K							
687	501-0687	N321FM	N154CC	N361DB	N361DE						
688	501-0688	D-IMRX	[w/o 16Feb06 Northern Iraq]								
689	501-0689	N46MT	N689CC	(N88MT)	N88MM	N75TJ	N88MM	N288MM	C-FNHZ		

Production complete

CITATION 500 UNIT NUMBER CROSS-REFERENCE

Note: From c/n 500-0001 to 500-0349 unit numbers match the last three digits of the c/n, then the tie-ups are as follows:

C/n	Unit	C/n	Unit	C/n	Unit	C/n	Unit	C/n	Unit	C/n	Unit	C/n	Unit
500-0354	363	500-0364	392	500-0374	455	500-0392	489	500-0401	565	500-0408	587	500-0412	598
500-0356	366	500-0367	399	500-0378	461	500-0395	530	500-0403	540	500-0409	596	500-0413	608
500-0358	377	500-0369	454	500-0386	470	500-0396	533	500-0404	560	500-0410	586	500-0415	629
500-0361	361	500-0370	396	500-0387	484	500-0399	554	500-0406	603	500-0411	645	500-0418	656

CITATION I CONVERSIONS

The following a/c have been converted from Model 500s to Model 501s (and, in one example, back again):

500-0097 to 501-0446	500-0361 to 501-0265 to 500-0361	500-0376 to 501-0282	500-0398 to 501-0298
500-0293 to 501-0643	500-0362 to 501-0275	500-0377 to 501-0283	500-0400 to 501-0249
500-0350 to 501-0027	500-0363 to 501-0273	500-0379 to 501-0284	500-0402 to 501-0302
500-0351 to 501-0261	500-0365 to 501-0262	500-0381 to 501-0286	500-0405 to 501-0311
500-0352 to 501-0263	500-0366 to 501-0285	500-0383 to 501-0292	500-0414 to 501-0314
500-0353 to 501-0264	500-0368 to 501-0278	500-0389 to 501-0293	500-0416 to 501-0260
500-0355 to 501-0267	500-0371 to 501-0279	500-0391 to 501-0294	500-0417 to 501-0317
500-0357 to 501-0269	500-0372 to 501-0281	500-0393 to 501-0239	500-0476 to 501-0063
500-0359 to 501-0270	500-0373 to 501-0280	500-0394 to 501-0297	500-0667 to 501-0320
500-0360 to 501-0272	500-0375 to 501-0289	500-0397 to 501-0303	

CITATION 501 UNIT NUMBER CROSS-REFERENCE

C/n	Unit	C/n	Unit	C/n	Unit	C/n	Unit	C/n	Unit	C/n	Unit
501-0001	351	501-0054	419	501-0107	482	501-0160	549	501-0213	618	501-0269	368
501-0002	353	501-0055	425	501-0108	495	501-0161	550	501-0214	621	501-0270	374
501-0003	355	501-0056	426	501-0109	491	501-0162	552	501-0215	622	501-0272	379
501-0004	356	501-0057	430	501-0110	496	501-0163	539	501-0216	624	501-0273	382
501-0005	357	501-0058	434	501-0111	498	501-0164	570	501-0217	623	501-0275	393
501-0006	358	501-0059	431	501-0112	499	501-0165	557	501-0218	626	501-0278	402
501-0007	360	501-0060	435	501-0113	502	501-0166	559	501-0219	625	501-0279	407
501-0008	362	501-0061	436	501-0114	503	501-0167	563	501-0220	628	501-0280	415
501-0009	367	501-0062	421	501-0115	507	501-0168	568	501-0221	643	501-0281	423
501-0010	370	501-0063	443	501-0116	509	501-0169	566	501-0222	592	501-0282	428
501-0011	364	501-0064	437	501-0117	506	501-0170	573	501-0223	627	501-0283	429
501-0012	369	501-0065	440	501-0118	504	501-0171	574	501-0224	630	501-0284	433
501-0013	372	501-0066	432	501-0119	497	501-0172	599	501-0225	633	501-0285	439
501-0014	371	501-0067	442	501-0120	487	501-0173	572	501-0226	635	501-0286	445
501 0015	373	501-0068	438	501-0121	523	501-0174	579	501-0227	634	501-0289	459
501-0016	375	501-0069	441	501-0122	508	501-0175	555	501-0228	631	501-0292	472
501-0017	376	501-0070	444	501-0123	513	501-0176	577	501-0229	636	501-0293	481
501-0018	378	501-0071	446	501-0124	515	501-0177	578	501-0230	638	501-0294	483
501-0019	383	501-0072	447	501-0125	531	501-0178	580	501-0231	604	501-0297	494
501-0020	380	501-0073	448	501-0126	505	501-0179	589	501-0232	637	501-0298	511
501-0021	384	501-0074	449	501-0127	500	501-0180	593	501-0233	653	501-0302	544
501-0022	385	501-0075	450	501-0128	522	501-0181	588	501-0234	639	501-0303	551
501-0023	386	501-0076	451	501-0129	512	501-0182	583	501-0235	641	501-0311	600
501-0024	387	501-0077	452	501-0130	517	501-0183	567	501-0236	642	501-0314	620
501-0025	389	501-0078	453	501-0131	518	501-0184	575	501-0237	640	501-0317	651
501-0026	391	501-0079	456	501-0132	527	501-0185	561	501-0238	649	501-0319	665
501-0027	350	501-0080	457	501-0133	528	501-0186	581	501-0239	510	501-0320	667
501-0028	394	501-0081	458	501-0134	516	501-0187	576	501-0240	644	501-0321	668
501-0029	411	501-0082	460	501-0135	519	501-0188	569	501-0241	647	501-0322	669
501-0030	390	501-0083	462	501-0136	520	501-0189	582	501-0242	646	501-0323	671
501-0031	395	501-0084	463	501-0137	521	501-0190	584	501-0243	648	501-0324	672
501-0032	388	501-0085	475	501-0138	525	501-0191	585	501-0244	650	501-0325	673
501-0033	400	501-0086	477	501-0139	526	501-0192	590	501-0245	652	501-0446	097
501-0034	401	501-0087	474	501-0140	529	501-0193	571	501-0246	654	501-0643	293
501-0035	404	501-0088	473	501-0141	532	501-0194	591	501-0247	655	501-0675	675
501-0036	406	501-0089	471	501-0142	524	501-0195	595	501-0248	662	501-0676	676
501-0037	408	501-0090	466	501-0143	535	501-0196	597	501-0249	514	501-0677	677
501-0038	409	501-0091	476	501-0144	536	501-0197	594	501-0250	663	501-0678	678
501-0039	403	501-0092	478	501-0145	538	501-0198	602	501-0251	666	501-0679	679
501-0040	412	501-0093	465	501-0146	545	501-0199	601	501-0252	657	501-0680	680
501-0041	381	501-0094	488	501-0147	541	501-0200	605	501-0253	670	501-0681	681
501-0042	410	501-0095	469	501-0148	542	501-0201	606	501-0254	658	501-0682	682
501-0043	417	501-0096	480	501-0149	543	501-0202	607	501-0255	661	501-0683	683
501-0044	424	501-0097	479	501-0150	562	501-0203	609	501-0256	659	501-0684	684
501-0045	416	501-0098	464	501-0151	546	501-0204	611	501-0257	660	501-0685	685
501-0046	405	501-0099	467	501-0152	547	501-0205	613	501-0258	664	501-0686	686
501-0047	413	501-0100	485	501-0153	548	501-0206	615	501-0259	674	501-0687	687
501-0048	414	501-0101	468	501-0154	558	501-0207	610	501-0260	632	501-0688	688
501-0049	420	501-0102	486	501-0155	564	501-0208	612	501-0261	352	501-0689	689
501-0050	398	501-0103	490	501-0156	534	501-0209	614	501-0262	397		
501-0051	422	501-0104	492	501-0157	553	501-0210	616	501-0263	354		
501-0052	427	501-0105	493	501-0158	556	501-0211	617	501-0264	359		
501-0053	418	501-0106	501	501-0159	537	501-0212	619	501-0267	365		

CESSNA 510 CITATION MUSTANG

C/n	Identities				
712	N27369	[ff 23Apr05; c/n originally quoted as E510-712001]			
0001	N510CE	[ff 29Aug05]	N510ND	N91FP	
0002	N510KS	[ff 27Jan06]	N199ML		
0003	N403CM	[ff 15Jun06]			
0004	N404CM				
0005	N600DE				
0006	N245MU				
0007	N510FF	N4FF			
0008	N396DM	LV-FKG			
0009	N910SY				
0010	N654EA	N24YY	N49MW	LY-VJB	N401DE
0011	N2243W	(VH-SJP)	ZK-LCA		
0012	N443HC	N510DG			
0013	N50HS	(N565VV)	N1VV		
0014	N510VV	(N307TC)			
0015	N406CM				
0016	N416CM				
0017	N17MU	N510WC			
0018	N827DK	N2GS			
0019	N2427N	OK-PPC	OE-FCP		
0020	N24329				
0021	N80HQ	(N12TR)			
0022	N4089Y	OY-LPU	N575TP		
0023	N888TF	N75AP			
0024	N75ES				
0025	N325RR	PH-ORJ	G-LFPT	N510DW	
0026	N1693L	N83EM			
0027	N4092E	N327CM	G-FBLK		
0028	N54PV	N611MW			
0029	N4059H	N45SP	VH-NEQ		
0030	N725JB				
0031	N528DM				
0032	N4107D	N814WS			
0033	N4110T	VH-CCJ	VH-SJP	ZK-PGA	N533VP	C-GNTL
0034	N4155B	XA-JRT			
0035	N4202M	D-ISRM			
0036	N510GH	N999JD			
0037	N33NP	PR-TNP			
0038	N4115W	N821ND	C-GNTZ		
0039	N4159Z	XB-RYE	XA-RYE	N163TC	
0040	N4009F	OE-FID			
0041	N4021E	PP-NNN			
0042	N591ES	C-GMMU			
0043	N4030W	PP-MIS			
0044	XA-BAT	N366FW	OE-FCB		
0045	N761JP	(D-IJKP)	YR-RUS	N510CF	(N1199V)
0046	N946CM	PP-MTG			
0047	N22EM				
0048	D-IEGO	OE-FWF			
0049	N13616	9A-CSG	YU-SPM	OE-FWD	
0050	PH-TXI	G-OAMB	PH-TXI	EC-LZS	
0051	N510JH	N510JM			
0052	G-LEAI				
0053	EC-KNL	OE-FTR	OK-FTR		
0054	N1749L	ZK-MUS	ZK-MOT	N510NZ	
0055	N551WH				
0056	PT-FLO				
0057	PR-MCL				
0058	PR-XSX				
0059	N40770	XA-VMX			
0060	N212C	ZS-CTF	N510J	PP-LDW	
0061	N1EL				
0062	N6183Q	PR-BSA			
0063	PR-DRI				
0064	N13ZM	N60CP			
0065	N61706	OE-FFB			
0066	N902LG				
0067	N967CM	G-FBNK	HB-VWS	G-FBNK	
0068	N968CM	G-FLBK			
0069	N6193S	T7-VIG			
0070	N235SS	VH-YDZ	ZK-YDZ		
0071	N921TX				
0072	G-LEAA				
0073	G-LEAB				
0074	N510LL				
0075	N4084A	G-LEAC			
0076	N4085A	G-NGEL	N301GT		
0077	N774AR				
0078	N724DL	(N884MF)			
0079	ZS-JDM	N816CW			
0080	N4086L	PR-MPM	N305AK		
0081	OE-FHA				
0082	OE-FLR	D-IKOE			
0083	N510GJ				
0084	PR-RDM				
0085	PR-VDL				
0086	N808RD				
0087	N6200C	(PP-PMR)	(PR-FMP)	PR-SBH	
0088	N6197D	(PH-TXA)			
0089	N63223	M-USTG			
0090	N6324L	ZS-LKG	4X-DFZ	T7-DFZ	
0091	N6196M	ZS-KPM			
0092	N6325U	ZS-DIY			

C/n	Identities				
0093	N6332K	ZS-DFI			
0094	N510SA				
0095	N6203C	N102DS			
0096	N40049	N996CM	G-FBKA	N258WC	N963FF
0097	N97HT	N214HT	N544MF		
0098	N510BW				
0099	PP-WGS				
0100	N6202W	HS-IOO			
0101	PP-EVG				
0102	N903JP				
0103	N923JP				
0104	OE-FWH				
0105	N245DR	(N61EP)	N1RS		
0106	N4076J	(OE-FWW)	OE-FMY	G-SCCA	
0107	N710EB	N568VA	N588VA		
0108	N939JC	F-HADT			
0109	N510MW				
0110	N66ES				
0111	(PH-TXB)	PH-TXA			
0112	N801GE	YV2864			
0113	N853JL	C-GDJG	N587AG		
0114	N510PT				
0115	N69AY				
0116	OE-FMZ	OK-AML			
0117	N62076	HS-VIP			
0118	N510MB	N831MF			
0119	PR-NRN				
0120	N4041T	N1RD	N72DA		
0121	N60CP	N510K			
0122	N230BF	CS-DPV			
0123	PT-TOP				
0124	N510AZ				
0125	OO-PRM				
0126	N826CM	G-FBKB			
0127	N627CM	G-FBKC			
0128	N178SF				
0129	PR-FAC				
0130	G-FBLI	N630DB			
0131	(PH-TXC)	N510TX			
0132	LX-FGL	[cx Mar14; parted out Linz, Austria]			
0133	(PH-TXB)	N6206W	N17RP		
0134	ZS-AFD				
0135	N5223F	JA510M	N200KP	N918ST	
0136	C-FDSH	C-GWCL			
0137	ZS-MUS				
0138	N309MT				
0139	N921PP	ZP-...			
0140	N987CM				
0141	N141BG	LZ-AMA	F-GRET		
0142	N609TC	PR-CPT			
0143	N510BA				
0144	N5044V	EI-SFA	OE-FZA		
0145	N6207Z	EI-SFB	OE-FZB		
0146	N4082U	N914GW			
0147	PT-FLC				
0148	N700YY				
0149	F-HDPY				
0150	N220DK				
0151	N738DC	(N33AC)	C-FPCE		
0152	N4085D	EC-LAF	EC-LDK		
0153	N4085S	N442LV			
0154	N510SV	PP-RGL			
0155	N4085Z	N510KB			
0156	G-MICE	ZS-SIO	OE-FDT		
0157	G-KLNW				
0158	N271CS				
0159	N510LF				
0160	I-FITO				
0161	G-ZJET	F-HEND			
0162	(N4RH)	N620WB			
0163	CS-DPN	F-HDPN			
0164	N251MC				
0165	N81WL				
0166	N870HY	XA-UMS			
0167	N638AH				
0168	N510GG				
0169	HB-VWL	F-GLOS			
0170	N426LF	C-GXOP	N68NP		
0171	N510PS	OY-JSW	C-FIPN		
0172	N510K	N510WP	N610PT		
0173	N510CJ				
0174	N40049	XA-ULO			
0175	N42WZ				
0176	N417GR				
0177	N247DR				
0178	N5020J	N662CC			
0179	N520JM				
0180	N884TM				
0181	N59VM				
0182	M-USTG	F-GISH			
0183	N3QE				
0184	N123AD	N128AD			
0185	I-MCAS	OE-FNP			
0186	N4076J	S5-CMT	ES-LCC	OE-FPP	
0187	N453DW	N552M			

CESSNA 510 CITATION MUSTANG

C/n	Identities				
0188	N878SP	N878MM			
0189	SP-KHK				
0190	N4095H	T7-HOT	I-INCH	G-SSLM	N613ML
0191	N509DM	N123TF	N133TF		
0192	N4107D	LX-FGC	M-IFFY		
0193	N530AG	(N533AG)	PP-MTT		
0194	LX-RSQ	F-HERE			
0195	N41227	N52338	PR-HOT		
0196	N41297	EI-SFC	OE-FZC		
0197	PP-PRV				
0198	N995AU				
0199	N4202M	N978PC	N979PC		
0200	N15GJ				
0201	N352AS	N91CH			
0202	N510MD				
0203	N76GP				
0204	N1245				
0205	N4047W	C-GBPL	N34ST		
0206	N620CM				
0207	N101FU				
0208	N510DH				
0209	N209CJ	N888GS			
0210	N54NG				
0211	N369PA	C-FBCI	C-FHFV	N510BE	
0212	N32FM				
0213	N59LW				
0214	VH-EJT				
0215	N603WS				
0216	EI-SFD	OE-FZD			
0217	EI-SFE	OE-FZE			
0218	N949JB				
0219	N625TX				
0220	N510DP				
0221	C-GDLL				
0222	F-GMTJ				
0223	N520KC				
0224	C-GROP	N88CH			
0225	N52733	SU-BQF			
0226	N73AH				
0227	N377RV				
0228	N823M				
0229	N7876C				
0230	N230BF	N7711B			
0231	PR-MDE				
0232	N4082Y	C-GRRD			
0233	N301AJ				
0234	N530AJ				
0235	EC-LCX				
0236	N778JE				
0237	N918WA				
0238	N960PT				
0239	N4085C	N914G			
0240	N510TW				
0241	N270MK	G-GILB			
0242	N530RM				
0243	N520BE	N243MS	N61MR		
0244	N700GD	N510VP	N244CE		
0245	N774ST				
0246	N510EG	RP-C718			
0247	N60GS	N247VP	(N510KA)	XB-JRS	N649JR
0248	N369GC				
0249	N510BD				
0250	N85VR	(D-IGEL)	N510JL		
0251	N510KZ				
0252	N40864	OK-LEO	F-HBIR		
0253	N54CF				
0254	N30NF				
0255	N5274G	SU-BQG			
0256	N991BB				
0257	N257CM				
0258	N5274K	SU-BQH			
0259	N4021E	(D-IMMH)	M-MHDH		
0260	N4030W	OO-ACO			
0261	N52498	PP-DLC			
0262	(D-ICMH)	M-MHBW	D-IEEN	F-HPHD	F-HIBF
0263	N362B				
0264	N4058A	OE-FAJ	N264CJ	N72SR	
0265	LV-CBO				
0266	YR-DAD	N166CJ	YV3148		
0267	N5274M	SU-BQI			
0268	OK-MYS				
0269	VH-PWX				
0270	OM-AES	OK-KUK			
0271	N324DR				
0272	OK-AJA				
0273	N786AF				
0274	N713MD	D-IEMG			
0275	N510EE				
0276	N76BF	N763F	PP-PFD		
0277	N105J				
0278	N278MS	PR-XPI			
0279	N127FJ	C-GWWW	N82824		
0280	PR-ROD	N510BR	N747KS		
0281	YR-DAE	N181CJ	OE-FTS		
0282	N876AM				

CESSNA 510 CITATION MUSTANG

C/n	Identities				
0283	G-XAVB				
0284	N520BE				
0285	M-COOL				
0286	N4059H	N52905	B-8888		
0287	N4073S	XB-JPR			
0288	N4074M	N9002D	PP-MID	N9002D	N323PG
0289	N4074Z	9A-DWD	OK-OBR		
0290	N4075L	N510HW	JA12NT		
0291	N4075Z	N39EG			
0292	N40753	N578CM			
0293	N293MM				
0294	N4077P	N5251F	VH-SQW		
0295	C-FSTX	N246RE			
0296	D-ISIO	N296VP	N495JK		
0297	N4078L	(D-IWHA)	N168TY		
0298	N4078M	C-GTTS	C-FPYP		
0299	N510DT	N61LF	4X-CMA		
0300	N40780	ZK-MUS	VH-MSU		
0301	N4079L	N301DN	N210PM		
0302	N4079S	N9168Y	N479DC		
0303	ZS-YES	PH-JAY	OE-FBD		
0304	N919MB	N510LM			
0305	N1956A				
0306	N146EP	D-IJHO			
0307	N307SH	N215NJ	N872G		
0308	N4082U	N91639	N56PZ		
0309	N9161X	N72AG			
0310	N4083J	N91MB			
0311	N4084A	(EI-...)	N510BK		
0312	N9008U	TC-TAI			
0313	N4085C	N514DD			
0314	N1618L	N223PW			
0315	N4085S	OE-FHK			
0316	N4085Y	N9023F	PJ-DOM		
0317	OO-RAM	N317VR	N850JD	N510WG	
0318	N318CM	N426NS	N426N		
0319	N90082	TC-TAJ			
0320	N9160T	N510HS			
0321	(D-ISIO)	N136MC	JA001Z		
0322	N8MY				
0323	N510KM				
0324	N4087B	N324HS	XA-EGL		
0325	N4087F	N325HS			
0326	N40878	N9048K	RP-C7979	N326CM	HI949
0327	N4088P	N46RC	N951CM		
0328	N4088U	PR-IER	N328CL		
0329	N484VB				
0330	I-STCB	TC-DOU			
0331	N510AT				
0332	N229JR	(EC-...)	N278MW	N820JT	
0333	N262DA	N282DA			
0334	N40339	I-STCA	G-FBKE		
0335	F-GTFB				
0336	N510BT				
0337	(C-....)	N928KG			
0338	C-FMCL	C-FMNL	N935AC		
0339	N428P	N5510	N813CZ		
0340	M-OUSE				
0341	HB-VWZ				
0342	N578CT	5H-LUX			
0343	N90298	VH-SQY			
0344	N771ES				
0345	N1744Z				
0346	N4115W	N9166N	G-FBKD	F-HKIL	
0347	N9043L	VH-SQJ	ZK-JAK		
0348	N678MB				
0349	OE-FRM	OE-FZG			
0350	N350HS				
0351	N262DA	N351V	N771KB		
0352	N929ST				
0353	N544JB				
0354	F-HECG	F-HOUR			
0355	EC-LJC				
0356	N91665	TC-AGR			
0357	N480CM	N795T			
0358	N90573	VH-VSQ			
0359	N510PX				
0360	I-STCC	G-FBKF			
0361	N40770	I-STCD	G-FBKG		
0362	N878PR				
0363	N363MU	VH-MHO			
0364	N35HC				
0365	N91703	N829BC			
0366	D-IFER				
0367	N367CM	N677TW			
0368	N4081M	EC-LNZ	OK-LNZ	CS-DTY	N368TF	N188GS
0369	N369MU	(N373CC)			
0370	N333HS				
0371	N10TR	N371VP			
0372	N295PJ				
0373	N542RK				
0374	N761PA				
0375	N4086L	D-ICCP			
0376	N360KE				
0377	N668JP				

CESSNA 510 CITATION MUSTANG

C/n	Identities			
0378	N378CM			
0379	N40878	N379CZ	N610JL	
0380	N778LC	N778BC		
0381	N264CA	N26WF		
0382	N382MU			
0383	N92958	N111JM		
0384	N72VK			
0385	N87WC			
0386	I-STCE	HB-VPM	N386TA	
0387	VH-KXM			
0388	N4095H	F-HICM		
0389	N885RS			
0390	N61HH	N390CM	N503BB	G-JJET
0391	N248TA	N2Q	N524SM	
0392	N874PW			
0393	N393CM	N61HH		
0394	N394CM			
0395	N789TS			
0396	N62WM			
0397	N397CM			
0398	VH-KJG	ZK-RJZ		
0399	PP-IMP			
0400	N826AG			
0401	N4159Z	PT-AMU		
0402	PP-WEB			
0403	N759SB			
0404	N404CZ			
0405	N93564	ZS-MTG	F-HAHA	
0406	N40512	N862GS		
0407	N511TP	N265GA*		
0408	N662BM			
0409	N4074M	G-RNER		
0410	N575SF	D-IRIZ		
0411	N4075L	N54DT		
0412	N4075X	N171AA		
0413	N678AB	(D-IPRO)	F-HSHA	
0414	N4076Z	N510EM		
0415	N4077P	N117PS		
0416	N416MU	N86WH		
0417	N45VP			
0418	N4078L	N100TP		
0419	N4078M	N486GS		
0420	N4078T	N26DV	N510FD	
0421	N891NY			
0422	PR-FRZ			
0423	N4079S	N427RC		
0424	D-IRUN			
0425	N40805	N910GF		
0426	N4081C	N435HB	N484HB	
0427	N4081M	N747NL	N77TZ	
0428	N4082H	N428SK	JA123F	
0429	N4082U	N422TG		
0430	PP-JCG			
0431	N94731	N802JD		
0432	N194ER			
0433	N9474L	YR-TRQ		
0434	N94749	N171UT		
0435	N94811	N812J		
0436	N94817	N997T		
0437	N94818	N704TP		
0438	N9488B	VT-IAM		
0439	N75RN			
0440	N40854	N94970	N16GS	
0441	N4086H	N570LT		
0442	N4086L	N363BS		
0443	N717ET			
0444	N800FZ			
0445	N445MU			
0446	N422RR	D-ISXT		
0447	N40878	N510MT		
0448	N94979	B-9813		
0449	N254TB			
0450	N234P			
0451	G-FFFC			
0452	N155MM			
0453	N912JD			
0454	B-0408	N454MF		
0455	CC-ANR			
0456	N7QF			
0457	LV-FVY			
0458	N733CF			
0459	N2WG			
0460	N545CM			
0461	C-GCCU			
0462	N40805	N42LJ		
0463	N4081M	N53MU		
0464	N4085S	N464KF		
0465	N40851	N65MU		
0466	N40864			
0467	N4088P	N19CA	N19RP*	
0468	N4009F			
0469	N40339			
0470	N4058A			
0471	N4092E			
0472	N4059H			

CESSNA 510 CITATION MUSTANG

C/n	Identities
0473	N4075X
0474	N4078A
0475	
0476	
0477	
0478	
0479	
0480	
0481	
0482	
0483	
0484	
0485	
0486	
0487	
0488	
0489	
0490	

CESSNA 525 CITATIONJET

C/n	Identities										
702	N525CJ	[prototype; ff 29Apr91 – cx Mar99 re-engineered to serve as the Cessna 525A Citation Jet CJ-2 prototype with c/n 708 q.v.]									
0001	N525CC	[ff 20Nov91; pre-production prototype]				N444RH	"N444RF"	N444RH	N800VT	N800VL	N525VP	N525GV	N133GL
0002	N1326B	N25CJ	N137AL	N46JW	N54BP	(VH-VCJ)	VH-SIY
0003	N1326D	N44FJ	N45FJ	[Citation M2 development aircraft]
0004	N1326G	N4YA	N24CJ	N7CC	N7CQ
0005	N1326H	(N1326D)	N56K	N58KJ	N521PF
0006	N1326P	N106CJ
0007	(N1327E)	N525KN
0008	N1327G	C-GDKI	N525FD	(PP-CMN)	PP-MLA
0009	N1327J	(N529CC)
0010	(N1327K)	N210CJ	ZS-MVX	N525JV	N48GG	N626TM
0011	(N1327N)	N525AL
0012	(N1327Z)	N12PA	N86LA	[retro-fitted with winglets by Tamarack Aerospace Group]
0013	N1328A	N550T	N550TF
0014	N1328D	N70TR	N620TC
0015	(N1328K)	N115CJ	PT-MPE
0016	N1328M	N216CJ	D-IKOP
0017	(N1328Q)	N525AE	N28PT
0018	(N1328X)	N525MC	N525LH
0019	(N1328Y)	N19CJ	N63HB	(N525SP)	N525KA
0020	N1329D	"OO-LFU"	N1329D	OE-FGD	N220JL
0021	(N1329G)	N793CJ
0022	N1329N	G-BVCM	G-THNX	YU-BST
0023	(N1329T)	N525RF	N525RP
0024	N13291	F-GNCJ	N525DJ	F-HAOA	D-IAOA	F-HEQA	N155EC
0025	(N1330D)	N9LR	D-IOBO	D-IBBA	G-CGXM	N33NM
0026	(N1330G)	N525FS	N286CW	(N214LX)	N602CA
0027	N1330N	N825GA	N861PD	N861RD	N700CJ
0028	N1330S	G-OICE	(N25EA)	G-OHAT	G-GRGG	N665DP	N7RL	N525WH	PR-JNW
0029	N13308	D-IWHL	(N525KT)	OK-PBS
0030	N1331X	"PT-MPE"	N177RE	(N93KV)	N53KV
0031	(N13312)	(N131CJ)	N31CJ	N831S	N215RB
0032	(N13313)	N532CJ	N95DJ	N32VP	N900DS
0033	N1354G	ZS-NHE	N526CA	N472SW	N116AP	N501KR
0034	N1772E	N96G	N9GU	N333VS	N525WR
0035	N1779E	N525HS
0036	N1782E	N525MB
0037	N1820E	HB-VKB	EC-IAB	HB-VKB	OO-IDE
0038	N1874E	N135MM	N600HR
0039	N1958E	N39CJ
0040	N1959E	D-ISCH	VP-CCC	N525AJ	OE-FMU
0041	N2098A	N525GG	HB-VJQ	D-IAMM	F-HADA	N565JP	N565JF	N25MB	N86TG
0042	N26105	N96GD	PH-MGT	D-IBWA
0043	N2616L	N525PL
0044	N2617K	XA-SKW	N55DG	D-IDBW	EC-KKE	HB-VPF
0045	N2617P	N525AP	LV-AMB
0046	N26174	N123JN	N127SG
0047	N2621U	N47TH	(N47VP)	N47FH
0048	N2621Z	N500HC	N525NA	N484J
0049	N2633Y	N49CJ	N349SF
0050	N2634E	N70KW	N205BN
0051	N2637R	N800HS	N808HS	N726SC
0052	N26379	N252CJ	N52PK
0053	N2638A	N53CJ	N66ES	N60ES	(N603JC)	N3WB	N654WW
0054	N2638U	N54CJ	N851DB
0055	N2639Y	N923AR	N570DM
0056	N2646X	N56NZ	JA8420	N525KK	PP-BSP
0057	N525DG	N585DG
0058	N2647Y	N525CK	N526CK	N525F	N509SE	N525LX
0059	N2647Z	N71GW	N816FC	N818FC
0060	N2648Y	XA-SOU	XA-TRI	N525WW
0061	N26481	N61CJ	N525PS
0062	N26486	C-FRVE	C-GINT	C-FPWB
0063	N2649J	N55SK
0064	N2649S	D-IHEB
0065	N2649Y	N5259H	EC-704	EC-FZP	N525GC
0066	N26495	N420CH	N545ES	N823ES	N545ES	N824ES
0067	N26499	N594JB	N525TF
0068	N2650V	N68CJ	N303LC	N888KU	N522AJ
0069	N26502	N169CJ	N20FL	N20VL
0070	N26504	(N70HW)	D-ISGW
0071	N26509	N940SW
0072	N2651R	(TG-FIL)	TG-RIF
0073	N2656G	(D-IHEB)	N77794	(N780AJ)	N780AB
0074	N26581	N511TC
0075	N5076K	N719L	N719D	N775TB
0076	N5079V	N80TF	N4TF	N805VC
0077	N50820	N1000E	N1999E	N9410P*
0078	N5085E	N525CH
0079	N5086W	N179CJ	N525WB
0080	N5090A	N80CJ	N33DT
0081	N5090V	N181JT	N525HA
0082	N5090Y	D-IHHS	N525LW
0083	N5091J	N34TC	(N121CP)	(N421CP)	(N50PL)
0084	(N5092D)	D-ITSV	G-CITJ	N306EC	YV549T	YV3184
0085	N5093D	VR-CDN	PT-MJC
0086	(N5093L)	PT-MIL
0087	(N5093Y)	N175PS	(N717DA)	N926CH	N100CH	N100CQ	N606HC
0088	(N50938)	N188CJ	N722SG
0089	N5135K	N189CJ	N920MS	N202BG	EC-KSB	N600HS	T7-MND	D-IMND*
0090	N5136J	N8288R	(N525KF)	LZ-DIN
0091	N5138F	N295DS
0092	N51396	N525AS	N523AS	N534TX	(N534LL)	N801PJ	N800DT

CITATIONJET

C/n	Identities								
0093	N5151S	I-IDAG	N525CM						
0094	(N51522)	N94MZ							
0095	N5153K	N61SH							
0096	N5153X	(EC-...)	D-ICEE						
0097	(N5153Z)	N234WS	N130MR	[w/o 26Mar00 nr Buda, TX; to White Inds, Bates City, MO for spares]					
0098	N5156D	N511AC	N980VP	(HZ-NJ4)					
0099	N5156V	N525SC	N525CP	N526CP					
0100	N51564	N525CC	(N808HS)	N800HS	VH-CIT	VH-KXL			
0101	(N5157E)	F-GPFC	OM-OPR						
0102	N52038	N202CJ	TC-CRO	LX-LOV	HB-VWP				
0103	N5204D	(N203CJ)	D-IVHA	OE-FLG					
0104	N5207A	N606MM	N608MM						
0105	N52081	N305CJ	(D-IAFD)	G-EDCJ	N10R				
0106	N5211A	N21VC	(N444H)						
0107	N5211F	N525WC							
0108	N5211Q	N108CJ							
0109	N52113	N37DG	N393N	C-GDWS	C-GSXX				
0110	N5213S	N195ME							
0111	N52136	N776DF							
0112	N5214J	N1006F	VT-OPJ						
0113	N5214K	N111AM	G-SEAJ	N555BG					
0114	N5214L	N96GM	N294CW	(N215LX)					
0115	N52141	OO-PHI							
0116	N5201M	N41EB	N216CW	(N202LX)	N323JA	N10S			
0117	N5203J	N217CJ	(N349CB)	N26CB	N26QB				
0118	N5203S	N52178	(N61TF)	N118AZ	D-IRWR				
0119	(N5264E)	N47TH	N466F	PT-FBM					
0120	N5264M	PT-WGD	(N665AJ)	N525CZ	PR-VGD				
0121	N5264S	TC-EMA	D-ICSS						
0122	N5264U	N102AF	N41YP	N471MD					
0123	(N52642)	N5223P	D-IRKE						
0124	N5090A	N525JH	VP-CWW	(ZS-BSS)	OE-FRR	N91RB			
0125	N5090V	N525PE	N525PT						
0126	N5090Y	N1264V	N14TV	D-IFUP	VP-CFP	D-IHGW	D-IMPC	D-IAHG	
0127	N5091J	N127CJ	N63LB	N63LF	N6UB				
0128	N5092D	N535LR	N818EE						
0129	N5093D	N52642	N229CJ	C-GPOS					
0130	N5093L	N416KC	N418KC						
0131	N5093Y	(N577SD)	N577SV	N281CW	(N203LX)	N800AJ	N41EA		
0132	N50938	N132AH	(N132RP)						
0133	N52038	EC-261	EC-GIE	N133KT	[parted out Roanoke, TX, still wearing EC-GIE]				
0134	N5204B	N234CJ	N525JM	(N525TL)					
0135	N5207A	N888RA							
0136	N52081	N525KL	[w/o 09Dec99 Branson-Point Lookout, MO]						
0137	N5211A	N810SS	(N525SE)						
0138	N5211F	VH-MOJ	VH-DAA						
0139	N52457	N76AE	N36RG						
0140	N5246Z	N725L	N111BF						
0141	N5250E	N774CA	N237DG	N525TA	N525JJ	N725CF	N545RW		
0142	N5068R	N815MC	N5068R	N815MC					
0143	N51993	D-IOMP	D-IALL	EC-KJV	9A-JSB				
0144	N5200R	D-IDAG							
0145	N52141	N145CJ	N424TV						
0146	N5100J	N1329G	(OE-FGG)						
0147	N52178	N996JR	[w/o 22Jul03 Penn Cove, WA]						
0148	N52144	N148CJ	XB-ATH	N300DL	C-GLBT	N908JP			
0149	N5218R	N67GH	(N57GH)	(N67GU)	N77215	[w/o 12 Jan07 Van Nuys, CA]			
0150	N5090V	ZS-NUW	N8341C						
0151	N5086W	N1015N	9A-CGH	(9A-CAD)	(N151TT)	N7EN	N400RL	N28DM	N242GB	N562PC
0152	N5112K	N152KC	N152KV						
0153	N5090V	N551G	N551Q	(N525EF)	VP-CNF	G-PWNS	N153MR	N36TX	
0154	N51246	N401LG	N401EG	N254CW	(N204LX)	N520DF			
0155	N5132T	N155CJ	I-EDEM						
0156	N156ML								
0157	N51817	N1115V	N57HC	N54HC					
0158	N5093D	N749CP	N800RL	N800RK	N695PA				
0159	N51872	N131RG	N351BC						
0160	N5076J	N66AM							
0161	N5076K	N525BT	(N39GA)						
0162	N5122X	N1XT	N525JW	(N39GA)					
0163	N5138F	N51CD	VH-CDG						
0164	N51444	D-ICGT	N204J						
0165	N5148B	D-IJYP	(OY-FCE)	D-IHCW	N525P				
0166	N5148N	N343PJ	F-GRRM	N252JK					
0167	N5151S	(N4EF)	N1EF	N525RA					
0168	N51522	D-IRON							
0169	N5153K	N68CJ	N230LL	N53KN					
0170	N5153X	N170BG	N170MU						
0171	N5153Z	N97VF							
0172	N5156B	N172CJ	D-IAVB	N350GM	VP-CTA	D-IFUP	OO-CEJ		
0173	N51564	N970SU	N129RP						
0174	N5157E	N817CJ	N417C	(N417Q)	N66BE				
0175	N175CP	N41PG							
0176	N5161J	PT-WLX	[w/o 16Sep05 Rio de Janeiro-Santos Dumont, Brazil]						
0177	N5163C	N1280A	(RP-C717)	G-OCSB	G-OWRC	F-HASC	OE-FWM	D-ITRA	
0178	N525RC								
0179	N5166U	N377GS	N877GS	N608DB					
0180	N5168F	N123AV	(N133AV)	VP-BDS					
0181	N5180K	N181CJ	N88LD	SE-RIO	D-IVPD				
0182	N5183U	(N740JB)	N177JB	N177JF					
0183	N5185J	(N97CJ)	N399G						
0184	N5185V	N525J							
0185	N5187B	N51176	N1241N	(RP-C8288)	N83TR	N13FH	PR-HAP		
0186	N51246	N186CJ	N92ND						
0187	N5130J	N696ST	PR-AEG						

CITATIONJET

C/n	Identities					
0188	N51342	(D-IVID)	D-IVIN	OE-FMA		
0189	N189CM					
0190	N51396	N41NK	N701TF	N708TF	N701TP	N79MX
0191	N5145P	N525BF	(N525BL)	C-FIMA	N15LV	PR-CLB
0192	N51444	N84FG				
0193	N5132T	N193CJ	D-ILCB	HB-VOX	D-IPOD	
0194	N5148B	N81RA	(N194VP)	I-DEAC	N22JM	N600MC
0195	N5138F	N525DC	(N525ST)			
0196	N5135A	D-IURH	N250GM	N525LP		
0197	N5151S	N525KH	EC-HIN			
0198	N51522	N315MR	N198RG	N805KK		
0199	N5153K	N1216K	9A-CAD	N524AF	N525DY	N299CW	(N205LX)
0200	N5153Z	N1276J	N226B	N525LK		
0201	N5156D	N525HV				
0202	N5120U	N202CJ	N747AC			
0203	N5122X	N525GP	N33FW			
0204	N5133E	N1293G	(N323LM)	B-4108	B-7027	
0205	N5156V	N550MC	N275CW	N206LX	(N205NP)	N525DU
0206	N5136J	N17VB	(N45PF)			
0207	N51872	N31SG	N26RL	(N100WQ)		
0208	N5153X	N208JV	N211GM			
0209	N5162W	D-ILAT	N550BD	N580BD		
0210	N5157E	N210CJ	N999EB	XA-CAH	N28CK	
0211	D-IMMD	N525HJ	N1WW	N335MB		
0212	N51176	N67VW	N800NB			
0213	N5168F	N525WM	N486TT	N486CC		
0214	N51743	D-IFAN	N130NM	N130LM		
0215	N5166U	N28GA	N28QA			
0216	N5183V	N18GA	N18QA			
0217	N5202D	(5Y-TCI)	D-IEWS	OE-FMT	N525GJ	
0218	N51881	N64LF	N288CW	(N207LX)	N713SD	
0219	N5197A	N219CJ	N648HE			
0220	N220CJ	C-GHPP	N25MX	PR-HIP	N911Q	
0221	N5203S	D-IWIL				
0222	N52038	N111LR	[w/o 04Apr98 Roswell, GA]			
0223	N5211Q	D-IGAS	OY-INV	OM-HLZ	OE-FKH	N223JF
0224	N52038	N224CJ				
0225	N5211F	N525RM				
0226	N5214J	N1216N	TC-LIM	OE-FSS		
0227	N5214K	N741CC				
0228	N5216A	N668VP	N668VB	N669DB	N525CP	
0229	N5218R	D-IHOL	LX-TRA	LX-FOX	F-GXRK	
0230	N5218T	N323LM	N934AM	(N904AM)	N242BS	
0231	N5223D	N606JR	N606MG	[also wore fake serial 97-0231]		N5255B
0232	N5223Y	N525PF	N525PB	N525GB	C-GABE	
0233	N5235G	N233CJ	N53CG	PR-CAN		
0234	N900P	N950P	(N91GH)			
0235	N5246Z	VP-BZZ	I-ESAI	LX-GCA	F-HIVA	
0236	D-ISWA					
0237	N237CJ	N61YP	[w/o on approach to Elk City, OK, 03Feb14; parted out by Alliance Air Parts, Oklahoma City, OK]			
0238	N5203S	PT-WQI				
0239	N5188N	(PT-WQJ)	PT-XJS	N525VG	N525HY	
0240	N525GM	N524SF				
0241	N52081	N241WS	N207BS	N209BS	N110FD	N307BS
0242	N242LJ	(N27FB)	PP-SDY			
0243	CC-PVJ	CC-CVO	CC-PVJ	CC-CVO	N494BA	PR-OJL
0244	N66ES	N68BS	N525ET	YV533T	YV3182	
0245	N5214J	N33CJ	G-SFCJ	N961RA	N67AZ	
0246	N525EC	N525WF				
0247	N533JF	(N538JF)	N247CW	(N208LX)	N241EP	N609SM
0248	N248CJ	N300FC				
0249	N5214L	N909M	(N909F)			
0250	N250CJ	HB-VMT	F-HMJC	OO-JDK		
0251	N50ET	N1JB	N86JB	N616BM	PR-DCE	
0252	(N5223P)	N740JV	VP-CIS	N252RV		
0253	N5223P	N8940	N894Q	N253CW	(N209LX)	
0254	N5183V	OE-FGI				
0255	N514DS					
0256	(N196DR)	N196HA	C-GPCT			
0257	N9003	N116DK	N26DK	N561BC		
0258	N5203J	N108CR	OY-SML			
0259	N5235G	PT-MSP				
0260	N5197A	D-IGZA	N260AM			
0261	N31HD	(N61CV)				
0262	N52457	N262BK				
0263	N263CT					
0264	(D-IKHV)	VP-CHV	EC-HBC	D-IPCS	N550CM	N531BR*
0265	N198JH					
0266	N52081	N266CJ				
0267	N5201J	PT-XMM				
0268	N850DG	N529NM				
0269	N5219T	N607DB				
0270	N5194J	N525HC				
0271	N860DD	N860DB	HB-VNK	G-OSOH	G-LUBB	
0272	N4GA	N4QP				
0273	(N525HC)	N911NP				
0274	PT-XDB					
0275	N700GW	N42AA	(N174GM)	N69WH		
0276	N800GW	N187MC				
0277	N277CJ	OY-JMC				
0278	N5145V	N1127K	N100SM	N901CJ	N525HX	
0279	D-IGME	SP-DLV				
0280	N5151D	PT-XAC				
0281	N5154J	N1280S	N41NK	N500TL	N508TL	VH-APJ
0282	N625PG					

CITATIONJET/CJ1

C/n	Identities						
0283	N95BS	PP-IZA					
0284	N256JB						
0285	N55PZ	N55PX	PR-SMJ				
0286	N51666	D-ICEY	D-INFS				
0287	N73PM	C-GBPM	N52KX				
0288	N288AG	RP-C525					
0289	D-ISHW	N553EJ	PR-SKW				
0290	N808WA	N97SK					
0291	N51744	F-GPLF	OE-FEM	HB-VPI	(PH-EEJ)	N249CA	
0292	N117W	N171W	N525CU	OE-FCW			
0293	N1127K	[crash-landed in Romania 31Jan01; rebuilt]					
0294	N294AT						
0295	N5209E	N295CM	(PT-MTU)	OE-FJU	YU-MTU		
0296	N296DC						
0297	N316MJ	VP-CAD	N600GK				
0298	G-RSCJ	N55CJ					
0299	N525BE	N711BE	N711BX	[w/o 18Jan16 nr Cedar Fort, UT]			
0300	N300CQ	N881KS	PT-STK				
0301	N27CJ	N270J	N291CW	N915ST			
0302	N302CJ	N326B	C-GSYM				
0303	N51612	D-IMMI	RA-67172				
0304	N1128G	EC-HBX	N154RA	N525TX	(N444L)	N605HP	N525TX	N747AH
0305	N826HS	RA-67428					
0306	(N525BE)	N4RH	N525DY				
0307	N114FW	(N114FG)					
0308	N72SG	N525DR	N373AF				
0309	D-IBMS	EC-LCM					
0310	D-IVBG	D-IIJS	OK-SLA	D-IERF			
0311	N523BT	N270J	N27CJ				
0312	F-GTMD	CN-TLB					
0313	N525MP	N525MR	N525MF				
0314	N5154J	N428PC	N525DM	N525LJ			
0315	(D-IIRR)	D-IAME	S5-BAY	OE-FMI			
0316	N5136J	N187DL	N316EJ	N458MT	PR-BSK		
0317	N51444	N317CJ	N51GS				
0318	N5145P	N525DP					
0319	N5148N	PT-FNP					
0320	N150BV	N30AQ					
0321	D-IAAS	PH-ECI					
0322	N52LT	LX-YSL	F-HCPB	D-IGGW*			
0323	N900GW						
0324	(N428PC)	N5163C	G-IUAN	N525SY			
0325	N464C	N764C	N115BB				
0326	N5183U	N23KG	N226CW	(N211LX)	N188TW		
0327	N398EP	LV-AXN					
0328	N328CJ						
0329	XA-DGP	XB-DGA					
0330	N5153K	N330CJ	N331MS	N38SC			
0331	N888RK	N9UG	PH-KOM	OE-FGK			
0332	N5161J	OO-FNL	(N332VP)	N511BP			
0333	N5185J	N99CJ					
0334	N51872	N44FE	N525M				
0335	N5156D	N335CJ	N335CT	N467F	N620JC	N525XD	
0336	N51564	N105P	PR-EGF				
0337	N5241Z	PT-FJA					
0338	N51575	N525RL	N977DM	N907DK			
0339	N5225K	N339B	N239CW	(N212LX)	N841TC	N810CM	
0340	N5165T	N392RG					
0341	N341AR						
0342	N5216A	N342AC	N9180K	N918CW	N49TH	N56K	N613JG
0343	N5244F	D-IURS					
0344	N77VR	N77VZ	N77VG				
0345	N5185V	G-ZIZI					
0346	N5153J	N5136J	PP-CRS				
0347	N5145P	N1133G	I-DAGF	D-IARI			
0348	N348KH	N248CW	(N213LX)	N8288R			
0349	D-ICWB	RA-67431					
0350	N51444	HP-1410HT	HP-1410	N1348T	N1848T	N720GM	CC-ADB
0351	N5246Z	VP-BRJ	LX-SUP	F-HGOL	OK-DSJ		
0352	N5185V	N99JB	N31JB	N573CM			
0353	N5211Q	D-ICOL	(LN-FDB)	N237CJ			
0354	N5225K	N821P	(D-IMMP)	OE-FCA	I-CABD		
0355	N51396	N205FH	N312SB	N312SE	N525TK	N501CJ*	
0356	N5213S	PP-YOF	N865VP	PP-JJZ			
0357	N5214J	N357JV	N194MG				
0358	N51564	G-HMMV	M-PARK	N358HA			
0359	F-GTRY						

CJ1

C/n	Identities						
0360	N5156D	N31CJ	N525CD				
0361	N5183U	N361RB	N128CS	LV-CKT			
0362	N5214L	N362CJ	N362PE	N362FL	N31WE		
0363	N5161J	N525AS	N523TS				
0364	N5211F	N525DL	N525DE	C-FTKX	VP-CHE	N364WT	PP-WTR
0365	N5130J	N651CJ					
0366	N5223Y	D-IRMA	N850GM	D-IRMA	N173CA	N376RS	
0367	N51872	N525MD	N525FT	(N525CY)	N615AK		
0368	N5185J	N820CE	N525FN				
0369	N5200U	N629DM	N161SM	N525AW			

CJ1

C/n	Identities						
0370	N5145P	N525MW					
0371	N5165T	N175SB	HZ-BL1				
0372	N372CP	N345MG					
0373	N415CS	(N352HC)	N315HC				
0374	N12GS	N12GY					
0375	N5225K	N375KH	HB-VNL	N600XT			
0376	N52352	N802JH	C-GTRG	N814DM			
0377	N5241Z	N15C	N900BT				
0378	N5135K	N525CP	N203BG				
0379	N5188A	I-IMMI					
0380	N5228Z	N381CJ	N525GB	N83DC	B-3669		
0381	N5185J	N856BB	N855BB	(N476JD)			
0382	N5124F	N525LF					
0383	N5231S	N600AL					
0384	N5148B	PP-JET	N684SC				
0385	N5136J	N1326P	N417C	N417Q			
0386	N51993	N45MH	N386RF	N211JH			
0387	N51564	N7715X	N7715Y	N724FS	N33SW	N122HW	
0388	N5162W	N525MH	N525LB	N520GB			
0389	N5156D	N389CJ	D-IDAS	D-IDAZ			
0390	N51396	N100PF					
0391	N5130J	LX-IIH	HB-VWO				
0392	N5165T	N392SM					
0393	D-IBIT	OM-HLY	OE-FFK				
0394	N5132T	N64PM	N64PZ	S5-BAJ	N101PJ		
0395	N5183U	(N525AJ)	N525AR	N507HP			
0396	N51575	D-IMAC	D-IKCS				
0397	N5163C	I-RVRP					
0398	N5183V	N398CJ	C-GMTI				
0399	N5135A	(VP-CTN)	D-ITAN				
0400	N5120U	(C-GPWM)	N525EZ	N526EZ	(N88798)	F-GMDL	N51C
0401	N51246	D-IFFI	N142EA	N44CK			
0402	N525ML						
0403	N51817	PT-PRR	N223CF				
0404	N5145P	N88AD	(N746JB)				
0405	N5125J	N121EB	N7895Q				
0406	N5124F	N72JW					
0407	N51872	N525JL					
0408	N5156D	N408GR	PP-JBS				
0409	N5212M	N657RB	(N334DB)	N530AG	N530AQ	N525BW	
0410	N52144	N4108E					
0411	N51575	N525RF	N535RF	D-ILIF	N411VR		
0412	N5161J	N82AE					
0413	N5185J	N525RK					
0414	N5223P	N726TM	(N26DV)				
0415	N5250E	N26SW	EC-ISS	D-IUWE	HB-VOD	PR-HJH	
0416	N80C	N8UC	N186TW				
0417	N5203B	D-IEAI	PH-SOL	N91BB			
0418	N51444	N300BV					
0419	N7NE	N7XE					
0420	N5183U	N96SK	N86SK	N726CL	CC-AOC		
0421	D-ILME	OE-FET					
0422	N51881	N125DJ	N927CC	N422VP	N525LA		
0423	N5201J	N62SH	N292SG	G-OEBJ	G-ORAN	F-HFMA	N525MX
0424	N5231S	N28SW	N711WG				
0425	N5188A	N335J	C-FWBK	C-GZLM	N85VR		
0426	N5197A	N426ED					
0427	N5202D	N128GW	N525LM				
0428	N5203J	PR-ABV					
0429	N429PK	EC-IVJ					
0430	N52081	N430GR	PR-ARB				
0431	N51993	N431YD	ZS-PWU	N347BC			
0432	N51342	N94AL					
0433	N5223D	N102PT	[w/o 01Feb08 nr Augusta, ME]				
0434	N5226B	N860DD	N860DB				
0435	N5244F	N525AD	G-CJAD	D-IAWU			
0436	N5141F	EC-HVQ					
0437	N5185V	N717NA	G-HEBJ	N489HC	(N489JC)		
0438	N51942	N103CS	N325DM	N525RY			
0439	N5200Z	N395SD	N54CG				
0440	N5233J	C-GPWM	N440CJ	N525NT	(N525JT)		
0441	N5200R	PR-ARA					
0442	N5187Z	D-IFIS	D-ILLY	VH-TFW			
0443	N5136J	N443CJ	N77DB				
0444	N52136	N525BR	(N525WS)				
0445	N445CJ	N207BS					
0446	N5211A	N246GS					
0447	N5120U	N116CS	N952SP	N525LE			
0448	N448JC	EC-JFD	N448EA	F-GMMC	HB-VWW	N88ME	
0449	N5153K	N1259Y	(JA-001T)	JA525A			
0450	N5156D	I-BOAT	OE-FVJ				
0451	N5135A	N165CA					
0452	N52178	N107GM	(N107PK)	N585PK	N585MC		
0453	N5211Q	N103CS	N80VP	N902RD	N929VC	N928VC	N869CB
0454	N5225K	N541CJ	N101U				
0455	N5183V	N75FC	(N15SS)	(N900TW)			
0456	N5185J	PR-LJM					
0457	N118CS	N774GE					
0458	N5188A	LX-MSP	N525NP	PR-BJM			
0459	N459NA						
0460	N5185V	D-IMMM	[rebuilt after accident 12Mar04 Florence, Italy]			N57EC	
0461	N5207A	N200SL					
0462	N5197A	N965LC	N965EC	N86RL			
0463	N5200U	N1284D	Chile 361				
0464	N1284P	Chile 362					

CJ1

C/n	Identities					
0465	N1285P	Chile 363				
0466	N5200Z	N119CS	D-INCS			
0467	N5157E	N620BB				
0468	N468RW					
0469	N52038	N122CS	N520RM			
0470	N901GW					
0471	N768R	N471CJ	B-3668			
0472	N124CS	N525KM				
0473	N5201M	LX-MRC	HB-VOR	F-HJAV		
0474	N31CJ					
0475	N52113	N475CJ	XA-TTG	N88LS		
0476	N476CJ	N50ET	N74PG	D-IRSB		
0477	N5216A	D-INOC	D-IDIG	OE-FOI	OM-OLI	OM-TAB
0478	N5233J	N869GR	(PR-GRN)	N869GS*		
0479	N5200R	N525BP				
0480	N5223Y	N888SF	(N66FH)	OE-FIX	N103SK	OE-FIX
0481	N5204D	N4DF	N795BM	N796BM	N30VR	
0482	N5211Q	PR-EXP				
0483	N5250E	PR-EOB				
0484	N5211F	N484CJ	F-HALO	RA-67433		
0485	N52136	N674JM	N672JM			
0486	N5211A	N334BD	EC-JIU			
0487	N5200U	N243LS	CC-CMS	N191PP	PP-LJR	N487WF	N487CJ
0488	N5218R	N525WH	N488SR			
0489	N5218T	N489ED	N489CB			
0490	N52141	N130CS	(N130MH)	N120CS	N525PJ	N120CS	N907YB
0491	N5244F	N491CJ	N491LT	N926CC	N442CJ*	
0492	N5226B	N492CJ	N888PS	N888PY	N213JT	
0493	N5203J	N65CK	N95CK	(N220JM)	(N315N)	CC-ADN
0494	N71HR	D-ITIP				
0495	N5246Z	OY-RGG	OO-STE			
0496	N5223P	N382EM	PR-TRT			
0497	N5235G	N132CS	N525JJ			
0498	N5223K	N498YY	N5201J	N498YY		
0499	N5200Z	HB-VNP	F-HHSC	D-IBAK		
0500	N525CJ	N111GJ	N44VS			
0501	(N501CJ)	N41LF				
0502	N51881	N133CS	SE-RGX			
0503	N904DP	N909DP	(N818ER)			
0504	N52081	N665CH				
0505	N502TN	(F-HBSC)				
0506	N242ML					
0507	N5263U	Chile 364				
0508	N5225K	N508CJ	EC-JSH	F-HBSC	N918AM	
0509	N993GL					
0510	N5058J	N1DM	N971DM	(N278CA)	G-EDCK	N814SP
0511	N5212M	ZK-TBM	N326JK			
0512	N411MY	(LN-FDC)	PR-GNL			
0513	N52591	N513RV	(N439PW)			
0514	N52136	N514RV	PH-FIS			
0515	N52141	N132CS	N551FP			
0516	N5060K	EC-IRB	N525CF	D-INER	N518RC	
0517	N52626	D-IFDH				
0518	D-ILLL	D-IETZ	F-HAGH			
0519	N926TF	D-IAMF	HB-VPD	T7-SCR		
0520	N135CS	N520CJ	N847JJ	N847JL	N152WR	N525H
0521	N5066U	N521CJ	VH-ANE	VH-YNE		
0522	N138CS	N125CS	(N525BA)	N92AJ	N525RN	
0523	N51246	F-HAJD				
0524	N5202D	N524CJ	N759R	N770BX	N3WB	N525RL	N545JS
0525	N123S					
0526	N5163C	(SP-KCL)	N526LC	SP-KCL	VP-CJI	
0527	N5211Q	N527CJ	N15BV	N358K	N278K	
0528	N50612	N528CJ	G-GEBJ	M-DINO	N716SN	(LV-FUE)	LV-FWT
0529	N50820	N151CS	N151EW			
0530	N5244F	N430JH	N430JF			
0531	N5211A	N333J	N525FC			
0532	N32BG	N323G	PP-INT			
0533	N5180K	(D-IPMM)	D-IPMI	F-GPEB		
0534	N52113	N1269B	JA100C	N534NA	N814LG	
0535	N5090A	N535CJ	JA525Y			
0536	N52369	[re-serialled 525-0600 q.v]				
0537	N5261R	N837AC	N839AC	N678RF	N425WH	
0538	N51564	N525AM				
0539	N152CS	OE-FRF	N90MT			
0540	N5172M	N40CJ				
0541	N458SM	N739LN				
0542	N5125J	N500CW	PR-MFJ			
0543	N5200U	N43NW				
0544	OE-FUJ	HB-VOG	M-OLLY			
0545	N545TG					
0546	N5188N	N981LB	C-GHSB			
0547	N5211Q	N547ST	N547TW			
0548	N5216A	N153CS	N257MV	PP-PIM		
0549	N51995	N549CJ	JA525J			
0550	N5112K	N1288P	SP-KKA	C-GDEK		
0551	N5105F	N1279A	B-3644			
0552	N51564	N1279V	B-3645			
0553	N51612	N902GW				
0554	N5157E	N1290N	B-3647			
0555	N5214L	N1287B	B-3648			
0556	N93LS					
0557	N5250E	N1287F	B-3649			
0558	N51993	N1288N	B-3650			

C/n	Identities							

CJ1+

C/n	Identities							
0600	N525AD	(N55KT)	N919MC	[built from 525-0536; ff 08Oct04; received FAA type certificate 20Jun05]				
0601	N52626	N601CJ	N29ET	N620JW				
0602	N5248V	N602CJ	N46JV	N74UK	D-ISJM			
0603	N51143	N805CJ						
0604	N5183U	N122LM						
0605	N5188A	N800PF						
0606	N51896	N713WH	PR-FSB					
0607	N5218T	N59JN	N58JN					
0608	N52229	N970RP	N4017L	N915RP	N878J			
0609	N5161J	N50VC	M-TEAM					
0610	N51817	N35TK	N43MS					
0611	N52645	D-ICEY						
0612	N5155G	N525RZ						
0613	N5112K	N1309V	PH-CMW					
0614	N51564	(OE-FMU)	D-IMMG	OE-FMD				
0615	N5095N	N65EM	(CS-DPU)	D-IAIB				
0616	N999EB	N525PC						
0617	N18TG	N1TG	N116LJ	D-IWPS	N617VP	B-9641		
0618	N618KA	XA-HPR						
0619	N1317Y	VT-NAB						
0620	N620CJ	N5UD						
0621	N52475	N621AD						
0622	N5270K	N622SL						
0623	N5124F	HB-VOF						
0624	N5141F	D-IOWA						
0625	N5236L	N625CJ	(VH-ODJ)	D-IEPR	N852L	B-....		
0626	N5117U	N626CV						
0627	N5264N	N627MW						
0628	N52433	T7-FRA	G-TFRA					
0629	N56KP							
0630	N50054	N711C						
0631	N5206T	YV2331	N631EC	C-FUTL				
0632	N50715	N1314H	CC-PGK	CC-CSA	JY-AWF	CC-CSA	N1314H	PR-EMX
0633	N5163K	(N28FM)	N43BH					
0634	N5196U	N634CJ	OE-FSR					
0635	N5241R	(N525JN)	N817BT	N817BF				
0636	N5066U	C-GTRG	N636VP	(LN-FDA)	XA-SML	N212RH		
0637	N51993	N637CJ	N779RB	C-GWGZ				
0638	N51342	VH-MYE						
0639	N5201M	(D-ICPO)	D-IMPC					
0640	N5076L	N34DZ						
0641	N5214K	C-GIRL						
0642	N5151D	N466AE	D-ICAO					
0643	N5228Z	N380CR	N380BR	N643RF	N72AC			
0644	N50321	N902DP	EC-LDE					
0645	OE-FPO	N788MP	(D-ILHF)	B-9629				
0646	N5154J	A7-CJI	N646VP					
0647	N1895C	N1865C						
0648	N5152X	G-CJDB						
0649	N51806	N794PF						
0650	N51511	HB-VWF	F-HRCA					
0651	N5267D	N24BC	N886EM					
0652	N5148B	N41159	RA-67705					
0653	N52526	N7715X	XB-MTR					
0654	N52691	N94HL						
0655	N51612	N1367D	B-7777					
0656	N5069E	N388FW						
0657	"N52594"+	[+test marks as quoted, but already in use on a Cessna 182]			N65BK	C-GJOL	N484SE	
0658	N907WL							
0659	N5266F	N659CJ	OE-FNA	LZ-FNA				
0660	N5057F	N197RJ	PR-OUD					
0661	N5244F	N613AL	LN-RYG	(G-STPZ)	F-HKRA			
0662	N5267G	N607TN						
0663	N5244W	N297RJ	PR-GFS					
0664	N664CJ	N88QC	N88QG	D-ILHE				
0665	N5037F	N665CJ	HB-VOV	D-IOBB				
0666	N5076K	N7277	T9-SMS	E7-SMS				
0667	N5061P	N629DR	PP-WBP					
0668	N52613	N557HP						
0669	N5200R	N224BA						
0670	N5161J	VH-LDH	VH-JSO					
0671	N5053R	N525AJ	SE-RIX	D-IZZZ				
0672	N52071	N858SD	N853SD					
0673	N5241Z	N525AJ						
0674	N5061F	N4123S	N324BD					
0675	N5270E	N41196	(D-ILHA)	D-ILHB				
0676	N5120U	N903GW						
0677	N413CQ	(N418CQ)	D-IHKW					
0678	N5250E	N528CB						
0679	N5076K	N525GE						
0680	N5061P	N680KH	(N895CB)					
0681	N5266F	N904GW						
0682	N5245U	N905GW						
0683	N5053R	N397RJ	N70GM					
0684	N5207A	D-IAMS	D-IBTI					
0685	N994JG	[converted to prototype Citation M2; ff as such 09Mar12]			N732M			
0686	N50549	N980MB	HL8201					
0687	"N50904"+	[+test marks as quoted, but already in use on a Cessna 150J]			N687CJ	N535WT		
0688	N5270E	N2259D	HL8283					
0689	N5263D	N101LD						
0690	N52627	HB-VWM						

CJ1+/M2

C/n	Identities			
0691	N52623	N4RH	N691CJ	HL8202
0692	N5266F	N929MM		
0693	N5214K	CN-TJE		
0694	N52609	(D-ILHB)	D-ILHD	
0695	N5201M	D-ILHC		
0696	N51684	(D-ILHD)	D-ILHA	
0697	N5057F	N595DM	N585DM	
0698	N5148N	N619TC		
0699	N5266F	N699CJ		
0700	N51342	N884JG		
0701	N5250P	N805P		

Production complete, replaced by the Citation M2

Note: In 1993-94, Cessna developed a military jet trainer from the Model 525 for the US JPATS contract evaluation. It was given the model number 526 and used many 525 parts, although the complete aircraft bore no actual resemblance to the CitationJet. For the record, two prototypes were built, N526JT c/n 704, ff 20Dec93, and N526JP c/n 705, ff 02Mar94.

CESSNA 525 CITATION M2

C/n	Identities			
0800	N40049	[ff 23Aug13] N800CZ		
0801	N4009F	N123TF		
0802	N46EW			
0803	N186DL			
0804	N600VM			
0805	N958MG			
0806	N778LC	N778EC	N104LW	
0807	N480WB			
0808	N525HL			
0809	N40595	N133TJ		
0810	N260TT			
0811	N1TG	N70LH		
0812	N71FB			
0813	N94972	N1RD		
0814	N371SF			
0815	N525MM			
0816	N30BP			
0817	N318JH			
0818	N4059H	N123AD		
0819	N4073S	N525JD		
0820	N4074M	N525PZ	N625PZ	
0821	N4074Z	N194SF	N77KN	
0822	N4075L	N822CC		
0823	N4075X	N4ST	N888TF	N889TF
0824	N40753	N824MT	JA525M	
0825	N825MT			
0826	N525TG			
0827	N40770	N525HQ		
0828	N828MT	N316CW		
0829	N5L			
0830	N4078M	N63YA		
0831	N71SY			
0832	N40780	N661BP		
0833	N4079L	N265DA	N262DA	
0834	N834FW	ZS-FCW		
0835	N30NS			
0836	N42AL			
0837	N427KP			
0838	N575TM			
0839	N4081C	N575RE		
0840	N304SG	N525LS		
0841	PR-FRC			
0842	(LX-FDJ)	N5KJ		
0843	N4085C	PR-FHI		
0844	N94980	N844MM		
0845	N4085Y	PP-PRB		
0846	N4085Z	PR-RIY		
0847	N248SE			
0848	G-CMTO			
0849	PP-OEG			
0850	N855ED			
0851	T7-FOZ			
0852	N214RT			
0853	N525CG			
0854	N696MM	D-IQXX		
0855	N277JB			
0856	VH-WMY			
0857	OY-MUS			
0858	C-FBCI			
0859	M-CARA			
0860	N408RK			
0861	N1WW			
0862	N862MT	HB-VPH		
0863	N990FV			
0864	N4092E	LX-FDJ		
0865	N865MT			
0866	N866ST			
0867	N4107D	N970MM		
0868	N907LW			
0869	N4059H	N725CG		
0870	N135RU			
0871	N4074M	N819R		

C/n	Identities			
0872	N4075L	N525GL		
0873	N4075X	N842AW		
0874	I-MCAM			
0875	N875MT	N741WY		
0876	N4077P	N876MS		
0877	N40770	N921XT		
0878	N878MT	N487CB		
0879	N188SB			
0880	N4997			
0881	N4079L	N951DH		
0882	N4079S	N52KH		
0883	N4080M	N883MT		
0884	N4081C	N813FM		
0885	N880WC			
0886	N4082U	N886MT	N986PR	
0887	N4082Y	N887SB		
0888	N4083J	N888MQ	N1482B	
0889	N4085A	N95KL		
0890	N890MT			
0891	N4085D	N52ZG		
0892	N4085S	OY-RAW		
0893	N4085Y	N893A	N219GR*	
0894	N4085Z	N689HC		
0895	N40854	N927AA		
0896	N4086H	N96MU		
0897	N4086L	N97MU		
0898	N40863	N898DV	N26DV	
0899	N4087B	C-GTTS		
0900	N4087F	N525AU		
0901	N40878	N901GG		
0902	N4088T	N902MZ		
0903	N4088U	N154RP		
0904	N4088Z	N904MT		
0905	N4089Y	N905MZ	PP-JDF*	
0906	N40049	N906MT		
0907	N4021E	N907MT		
0908	N4030W	N525KH		
0909	N40366	N329CS		
0910	N4042H	N780DC		
0911	N40595	YU-MPC		
0912	N4076A	PR-CYJ*		
0913	N4076J			
0914	N4088H			
0915	N40938			
0916	N4095H			
0917	N4107D	N917AP		
0918	N4110T			
0919	N40512			
0920	N40735	N920MZ		
0921	N4074M	N650VM		
0922	N4074Z			
0923	N4075L			
0924	N40753			
0925	N4076Z			
0926	N4077P			
0927	N40770			
0928	N4078L			
0929				
0930				
0931				
0932				
0933				
0934				
0935				
0936				
0937				
0938				
0939				
0940				
0941				
0942				
0943				
0944				
0945				
0946				
0947				
0948				
0949				
0950				

CESSNA 525A CITATIONJET CJ2

C/n	Identities							
708	N2CJ	[ff 27Apr99 McConnell AFB, Wichita, KS – converted from original C525 prototype c/n 702 qv]				N244CJ	[test-bed for Williams FJ44-4A engine used on the CJ4, ff 02Apr07; cx Nov10, wfu]	
0001	N525AZ	N529PC						
0002	N5252	N765CT	N400WD					
0003	N5148N	N132CJ	N525DT					
0004	N52136	N142CJ	N200KP	N692JM	(N699JM)	N308GT	N7773A	PP-GSM	N713JL
0005	N5235G	N552CJ	N372CT	OY-LLA	I-LALL	9H-ALL		
0006	N5204D	(N411PB)	N411GC	N800WC	N256SP			
0007	N5213S	N7CC	(N8CQ)	N525CC	N257AR	PR-RAQ	N410JL	
0008	N52141	N900EB	N901EB					
0009	N5235G	N525LC	F-HAPP	M-AJDM	N457MD	(N860SC)		
0010	N5194J	N121CP	N25MB					
0011	N51881	N567JP	OE-FLP	[w/o Milan/Linate, Italy, 13Oct14]				
0012	N525MP	N525MA						
0013	N5201M	N4115Q	N8940	N894C	(N177RE)			
0014	N110MG	N110MQ	N18TF					
0015	N125DG	N606XG	N629PA	F-HASF	N610SF			
0016	N5207A	N306CJ	(N547AC)					
0017	N5162W	N172CJ	HB-VOE	LX-VOE	OE-FXE			
0018	N5148N	N96G	N96NJ					
0019	N51942	N57GH	N67GH	S5-BBB	F-GXRL	N5YD		
0020	N52141	N904AM	N323LM	N823L				
0021	N525TG	[cx 16Sep09, corrosion damage]						
0022	N5165T	N217W	(N117W)	N630TF				
0023	N5135K	N525PF						
0024	N5216A	N525TJ	N915MP					
0025	N51396	N550T	N550TB					
0026	N5203S	N126CJ	D-IMYA	D-IHAP	EK-52526	EP-MNZ		
0027	N5194J	N420CH	N420EH					
0028	N5218T	(N592DR)	D-IBBB	N592DR				
0029	N5132T	N92CJ	D-IKJS	OE-FRS				
0030	N5223Y	N302DM	D-ISJP					
0031	N5204D	N312CJ	VP-BFC	M-XONE	G-SONE			
0032	N5250E	D-IOBU	D-IOBO	D-IGIT	N525ME			
0033	N163PB	HB-VNO	(D-IETZ)	EC-JJU	F-HMSG			
0034	N5211F	D-IJOA						
0035	N51564	N288G						
0036	N5246Z	(D-IJOA)	D-IEVX	[w/o 08Oct01 Milan-Linate A/P, Italy]				
0037	N5221Y	N401LG						
0038	N5235G	I-IMMG	N800GF					
0039	N5223P	N842HS	(N525L)	N900HA				
0040	N525HB							
0041	N43ND	D-IHHN	N505RM					
0042	N52352	PR-JET						
0043	N52002	N432CJ	D-IEKU					
0044	N5241Z	PR-JST						
0045	N5214L	N3ST	N525H	N219CM				
0046	N51246	N40RL	N46JW	N46NT	N707LL			
0047	N5148N	N2250G	N225GG	VT-TAX				
0048	N5183U	PT-FTC						
0049	N51575	D-IEFD	OE-FHB	M-CTLX	9A-JSC			
0050	N525DL							
0051	N6M	(N606MM)	N6JR	N415SL	G-OCJZ			
0052	N51881	D-ISCH						
0053	N5194J	PT-FTE						
0054	N5161J	(EI-OPM)	D-IAAS	PH-ECL	OO-SKA	VH-ZGP	N528CJ	N417MH
0055	N5163C	N207BS	N525ZZ					
0056	N5202D	N743JG						
0057	N57EJ	[w/o 07Oct02 Plainville, CT; canx 08Mar05]						
0058	N52035	N811RC	N525KT					
0059	N59CJ	N917SL						
0060	N6877L	N57HC	N525RW					
0061	N5214J	PR-TOP	N272HT					
0062	N5125J	N30HD						
0063	N5135A	N263CJ	N5208F	VH-MOR				
0064	N513SK	EC-IEB	I-OMRA	N746CX	N20JK*			
0065	N5136J	N225EL	N225WW	N55KT				
0066	N51396	N741PC						
0067	N5141F	N525PM						
0068	N51444	N69FH	N69AH	N315MC				
0069	N51564	N757CP						
0070	N5157E	D-ILAM						
0071	N51575	N34RL	N701SF					
0072	N5120U	N65PZ	(N65PX)	N65BZ	N77ND			
0073	N5165T	I-LVNB	N295					
0074	N5125J	N222NF						
0075	N51246	HP-1461	N52AG	PR-REG				
0076	N5156D	N1277E						
0077	N5148N	N377GS	N346US					
0078	N5162W	N113BG						
0079	N51872	N117W	N717HA					
0080	N5135K	N525EZ	N525TK	F-HEKO	N788JB			
0081	N51342	N414FW						
0082	N5183V	N282CJ	OE-FGL	G-CGSB	N58KY	LX-JCL		
0083	N975DM	N975DN	G-EDCL	G-CJTV	N716JS			
0084	N525DG	N523DG	N512TB	N207MM				
0085	N5185J	N85JV						
0086	N5132T	N520JM	N759R	N823DT	N67SB	N970ZG		
0087	N474PC							
0088	N569DM							
0089	OY-JET	[crashed into sea 15May05 off Atlantic City-Bader Field, NJ; repaired]				N525SA	PR-WOB	
0090	N475DH							
0091	N8940	N431MC	(N548ME)	N518ME*				

CJ2

C/n	Identities					
0092	N21RA					
0093	N5216A	N96SK	N93PE	N98PE	N954RM	N327MC
0094	N942CJ	VH-RJB				
0095	N5221Y	I-DEUM				
0096	N5223D	N96CJ	JA525G	N96NA		
0097	N97CJ					
0098	N5223Y	N57HG	N57HC	N57HG		
0099	N5223P	N444RH	N777HN	N747HN	CC-AES	N180YA
0100	N170TM					
0101	N1255J	(N533JF)	N125BJ			
0102	N888KL	D-IWIR				
0103	N5218R	N800VT	N869AC			
0104	N80C					
0105	N13M	N91A	N878JP			
0106	N5148B	D-IUAC	OE-FUX			
0107	N525WD					
0108	N5136J	D-ICMS				
0109	N692JM	N301EL	N22LX	N109VP	C-GVSN	N707EL
0110	N451AJ					
0111	N219FL	N971TB	[w/o in hangar fire 12Sep07 Danbury, CT]			
0112	N51575	N525U	N701TF	N620GB	N112VP	N920NL
0113	N525VV	G-OCJT	M-WMWM			
0114	N726RP					
0115	N115CJ					
0116	N5233J	N711BE	N411BE	N46BE		
0117	N5214K	PT-FTG				
0118	N5163C	N464C	N971TB	N971TE	N718AL	
0119	N525DV	PP-CML	N119CJ			
0120	N5130J	N144EM	N220JD	N35CT		
0121	N121YD	N5YD	YV2152			
0122	N5135A	N224WD	N1901			
0123	N5203S	N37BG	PT-ASX			
0124	N27CJ	N523BT				
0125	N52038	N125CE	N525CC	N525CG	D-IBJJ	
0126	N534CJ	N999WE	VT-MON			
0127	N5211A	N12GS	N112GS			
0128	N5204D	N525CK				
0129	N129SG	N98DH	N715JS			
0130	N51396	N525JD	N550KR	N1962		
0131	N51564	N20GP	N340SP	N109AP		
0132	N5211F	N75PP	D-ITOP	N500SD		
0133	N251KD					
0134	N323SK					
0135	N5211Q	N4RP	(N114RP)	N70KW		
0136	N5141F	N345CJ				
0137	N717VB	N921AP				
0138	N722TS					
0139	N5228Z	N526HV	N365TB			
0140	N140DA					
0141	N51872	PT-FTR	N141JV	N6ZE		
0142	N5207A	OE-FPS	F-HMBG			
0143	D-ISUN					
0144	N144YD					
0145	N7GZ	N192MG*				
0146	N1220W					
0147	N5188W	VP-BJR	D-IVVA	N876UC		
0148	N5132T	N148FB				
0149	N90CJ					
0150	N525GM	OE-FRA	N720SL	N750SL		
0151	N122SM	D-ISCO	SP-KKB*			
0152	N123JW	N128JW	N791JK			
0153	N5233P	N500SV	N153CJ			
0154	N5091J	N708GP				
0155	N5180C	N105PT	EC-KES			
0156	N522KN	N256CJ	JA525B			
0157	N5270E	N88KC	N913DC			
0158	N158CJ	SP-KCK				
0159	N5026	N74GL				
0160	N525KR	N525KP				
0161	N5100J	N28MH	N28NH	N525FF		
0162	N335JJ					
0163	N5151D	ZS-CJT	VT-NJB			
0164	N164CJ	OO-DDA				
0165	N5243K	N30AD				
0166	N5218R	D-IAMO				
0167	N51806	D-ILDL				
0168	N767W	D-IHRA	JY-FMK	D-IHRA	N311HA	(PR-HBO)	PR-HBH
0169	N5262W	F-GPUJ	N2796			
0170	N915RJ	C6-LVU	N170VP	C6-EVU	VT-BJA	N170MR
0171	N271CJ	(F-GPSS)	CC-CHE			
0172	N179DV	N706TF	N525PB			
0173	N525MR					
0174	N5076K	D-IDMH	N613LB			
0175	N525SM					
0176	N100JS	N319R	OE-FYH	VT-TAY	OE-FYP	N525LR	N812PJ
0177	N55KT	N25LZ				
0178	N52655	N7715X	N80AX	N44FJ	N103CL	
0179	N179FZ	OO-FLN	N237MP			
0180	N604LJ					
0181	N5218T	N93AK	N93AQ	N525CE		
0182	N777CJ	N219CQ				
0183	N283CJ	N183TX				
0184	N357J	N1QL	(N357J)	N184CD		
0185	N5257V	N65CK	N65CR	PR-TAP		
0186	N5247U	N350BV				

CJ2/CJ2+

C/n	Identities				
0187	N187MG	N252PC	N956HC		
0188	N5138J	N188JR	N837AC	N505BG	
0189	N5124F	N777DY	N189MS		
0190	N5141F	N680JB	G-OODM	N646TG	SE-RIN
0191	N776LB	G-TBEA			
0192	N688DB	(N688DP)	N193PP		
0193	N5183U	D-IKAL	F-HAMG		
0194	N806MN	N194SJ	[w/o Santa Monica, CA, 29Sep13]		
0195	N51942	D-IMAX			
0196	N5166T	D-INOB			
0197	N197CJ	OO-SKY			
0198	N5162W	N57FL			
0199	N5152X	I-GOSF	LN-AVA	N248RF	
0200	N5203S	F-GZUJ	CS-DGQ	LX-DGQ	N200FT
0201	N888GL				
0202	N202CJ	N719WP	G-EEBJ	G-MROO	SE-RKS	G-ZEUZ
0203	N736LB	OE-FSG	N460RV		
0204	"N5188W"+	[+marks as quoted, already current at the time on a homebuilt] OE-FCY OK-FCY			
0205	N5241Z	N205YY			
0206	N29MR	OO-CIV			
0207	N5117U	N1267B	VT-JSP	N740JS	
0208	N400HT				
0209	N5085E	OY-UCA			
0210	N5214K	N280DM	N28DM	OE-FCU	N721SC
0211	N515EV				
0212	N5226B	N104PC	N702FM		
0213	N5244W	N213CJ	(OE-FJR)	ES-LUX	G-EDCM	N714JS
0214	N51511	N1DM	N7QM	F-HMPR	
0215	N748RE	N748RF	N420CR		
0216	N51246	OY-GGR	EC-JMS	N188JB	N788JS
0217	N5211F	N67GH	N167GH	N771EM	
0218	D-IPVD				
0219	N5247U	F-HEOL	N72JS		
0220	N800RL	N880RL	N75HF	N680SB	
0221	N5153K	N27VQ	YV305T	N27VQ	
0222	N778MA	VT-DOV			
0223	D-IWAN	OK-PBT			
0224	N5264N	N424CJ	N576SC		
0225	N67BC	N67CC			
0226	N5266F	N526DV	PR-CNP	N526DV	
0227	N5174W	N761KG	N450TR		
0228	N5154J	PR-NTX			
0229	N5223P	SX-SMH	OE-FVB	OO-OSD	OE-FAG
0230	N5136J	D-IGRO			
0231	N5211A	D-IWIN	N484CT		
0232	N5245D	[re-serialled 525A0300 q.v. below]			
0233	N5236L	D-IBBE	D-IOHL		
0234	N313CR				
0235	N235KS	C-FTRM	N71EA	VT-BIP	
0236	N5259Y	TC-VYN	VH-IYG		
0237	N5263U	N333BD			
0238	N5117U	N1290Y	N228FS	N227FS	N777AG
0239	N5120U	(OE-FEB)	OE-FIN	OM-OPE	OM-FTS
0240	N5194B	N77VR	(N109TW)		
0241	N52081	N777QP	PR-CFC	N742JS	
0242	N5073G	PH-JNE	N962RA		
0243	N5165T	N551WM			
0244	N52086	N13087	JA525C		

CJ2+

C/n	Identities								
0300	N5245D	[converted from 525A0232 ff 3.4.05, certificated 03Oct05]		N432MA	N486TT	(N486TL)	(N466TT)	N490RM	
0301	N52609	N301PG	N525HD						
0302	N52690	N302CJ	N6M	N302CJ	N832MG*				
0303	N5260M	N85JE	OY-GLO	N525RU	PR-RHG				
0304	N52699	N912GW							
0305	N5213S	N660S							
0306	N5180K	N306JR	N358WC						
0307	N5239J	N674AS	N583SB						
0308	N5188N	N308CJ	N110FD						
0309	N309CJ	M-TSGP	N309CJ						
0310	N5267G	N926JJ							
0311	N5211A	N1317X	JA001T						
0312	N5000R	N786AC	(D-IPAC)						
0313	N5157E	D-IBBS							
0314	N5096S	N1DM	N791DM	N747JJ	(N311DB)				
0315	N5094D	N1414P							
0316	N5165T	PR-NNP	N275ML	N48JM					
0317	N9UD	PR-HAL							
0318	N5268V	N525TA	YV289T	YV2844					
0319	N967TC								
0320	N5188A	F-ONYY							
0321	N13195	OE-FII	OM-BJB						
0322	N51575	(LX-WGR)	F-GMIR	D-IMHA					
0323	N5132T	N65CK							
0324	N5228Z	N586ED	N586FD						
0325	N437JD	N487JD	PP-BBS						
0326	N5223P	OE-FXX	N207BG						
0327	N5226B	N525RF							
0328	N52352	D-IBCT							
0329	N5147B	N525PH							

CJ2+

C/n	Identities				
0330	N5231S	D-IFLY	D-IFEY	N525DR	
0331	N5148B	OY-REN	HB-VPC		
0332	N50282	D-IOBU	D-IOBO	D-IOBC	N725AT
0333	N929BC	N939BC			
0334	N52699	G-HCSA			
0335	N525LD				
0336	N336CJ	N15YD			
0337	N5063P	N525XD	PP-MEO		
0338	N722SM				
0339	N500NB				
0340	N5086W	D-IFIS			
0341	N5064Q	N241CJ	HB-VOL	LX-VOL	OE-FXM
0342	N18TD	N178WG	N615WP		
0343	N5108G	D-IFDN	D-IHTM*		
0344	N5200Z	N45MH			
0345	N5153K	N9180K	PR-NGT		
0346	N525EP	N585EP			
0347	N5262X	M-ICRO	D-IPCH		
0348	N5076J	S5-BAS	D-ISJA		
0349	N52609	N535TV	N535JF		
0350	N5260Y	N117W	N114W		
0351	N909MN				
0352	N51896	N525HG			
0353	N929VC				
0354	N5101J	OE-FOA			
0355	N5079V	D-IWBL	F-HRSC		
0356	N5197A	N617CB	PR-FSA		
0357	N50820	N624PL	D-IVVB	D-IKBO	
0358	N5061F	D-IEFA	N584SB		
0359	N52682	N12742	JA359C		
0360	N52655	N13474	G-HGRC	G-SYGC	G-PEER
0361	N5157E	N361JR			
0362	N51564	OE-FGB	N147WE		
0363	N5197M	D-IETZ	N363VP		
0364	N5090V	D-ITOR			
0365	N50736	OE-FLA	N209AM		
0366	N366CJ	N999QE	N612JD		
0367	N367CJ	D-IAKN			
0368	N5032K	N93AK			
0369	N5181U	OE-FLB	N530DW	N500VA	
0370	N51993	N370JJ	N370RP		
0371	N51160	N574BB			
0372	N5103J	OY-NDP			
0373	N5270E	N41174	VT-BRT		
0374	N5108G	N245RA			
0375	N51055	OE-FOE	HB-VPE		
0376	N51444	PR-JVF			
0377	N5211F	N950DB			
0378	N5214J	N41184	VT-VID		
0379	N5270J	N896P			
0380	N5168Y	N5192U	JA021R		
0381	N52627	EC-KOI	N538CF		
0382	N5241Z	N129CK	D-IPAD*		
0383	N5120U	HB-VWA			
0384	N5218R	N118CJ			
0385	N50820	HB-VOP	N630PA	PR-AIC	
0386	N5270P	N2040E	JA516J		
0387	N5268M	N111JW	N525RG	C-GVCQ	
0388	N5267T	G-CROO	N525NG		
0389	N5153K	M-PSAC	D-ITMA		
0390	N52639	OE-FKO			
0391	"N52391"+	[+test marks as quoted, already current at the time on a Cessna T-50]		N2151Q	JA391C
0392	N52081	PR-ARS			
0393	N51896	N775TF			
0394	N5152X	C-FITC			
0395	N5154J	XA-UJY			
0396	N5162W	N400CV			
0397	N5148B	G-ODAG	G-TWOP		
0398	N5270K	OE-FNB	LZ-FNB		
0399	N5048U	N810PF			
0400	N5235G	D-IMMM			
0401	N5094D	YU-VER	ZS-SOM	N595CH	
0402	N5263U	N2224G	VT-PSB		
0403	N5103J	N250BL	PR-AGC		
0404	N5103J	N85ER	N404CF		
0405	N5180C	N405CJ	N413FC		
0406	N5072X	PR-WAT			
0407	N5225K	N407CJ	N59JN		
0408	N5248V	G-NMRM	OH-SWI		
0409	N5270J	D-IPCC	N409VP		
0410	N5165P	N2297X	VT-BPS		
0411	N5211F	YU-BUU			
0412	N5141F	9A-DWA			
0413	N52086	N19KT			
0414	N5165T	N208BG			
0415	N5225K	OE-FHC			
0416	N108KJ				
0417	N5090A	PR-RJN			
0418	N5265N	N677SL	N642WW		
0419	N52655	N785MT			
0420	N5130J	N10AU	N10GU		
0421	N5265B	N379R			
0422	N757EM	HB-VPB	ZS-PDZ		
0423	N806CJ	S5-BAR	N525JN		
0424	N5136J	N41212	N285JE	N285FW	

C/n	Identities				
0425	N5155G	N2044S	N96SW*		
0426	N426CJ	N476JD			
0427	N5066U	I-CALZ	OE-FCZ		
0428	N51396	SP-DLB	(D-IANP)	D-INDA	N428JF
0429	N5048U	D-ISCV			
0430	N5076L	N2046D	(VT-BJC)	N501KE	
0431	N5163C	OO-ACC			
0432	N5093D	N10WZ			
0433	N5183V	N433CJ	D-IJKP	OE-FPM	
0434	N5200R	9A-CLN	F-HCCP	N434CF	
0435	N52081	VP-BRL	SE-RKM		
0436	N5257V	N2051A	(VT-BJD)	7T-VNF	
0437	N5165T	OE-FPK			
0438	N5026Q	N438TA	EI-ECR		
0439	N52141	N125WT	N923GS		
0440	N52086	PR-KYK			
0441	N50522	N440CJ	N127FJ		
0442	N52655	N2064M	N494TB		
0443	N52645	D-IDAS	OH-SWJ		
0444	N5235G	N20669	D-IWWP		
0445	N50282	N145SF	N503AS		
0446	N5068F	N2067E	N446CJ	LN-BAC	
0447	N5265B	N447CJ	N312SB		
0448	N52446	N360PK	N368PK	N507AS	
0449	N525EG				
0450	N5180K	N926PY			
0451	N5245L	N451FP			
0452	N5090A	N721ES			
0453	N5161J	N484CW	N238RM		
0454	N5057F	N234CJ			
0455	N50054	YR-TOY	N455VP	OK-MAR	
0456	N5136J	C-GTRG			
0457	N5268V	ZS-PAJ	T7-APP		
0458	N52235	N6245J	N674JM		
0459	N5180C	D-IEVB	N459VP		
0460	N525AP				
0461	N5267G	N461CJ	N792CB		
0462	N5197A	OK-ILA	OK-ILC	F-HIJD	
0463	N5207A	(N234CJ)	PP-KYK		
0464	N5185J	N64LW			
0465	N5000R	N380AR	N380CR	N237PT	
0466	N5214L	N466CJ			
0467	N5090V	N525HL	N467CJ	N540AS	
0468	N5090A	N461CQ	N580AS		
0469	N469CJ	N997SS	N469VP	N469LH	
0470	(D-IWWP)	N6033R	VT-TVM		
0471	N5241Z	PP-CIT	N369KL		
0472	N5157E	PP-FRI			
0473	N52369	G-CGUZ	N473CJ	N981WA*	
0474	N50522	N74JE			
0475	N5263D	N858SD			
0476	N5245D	N821PP			
0477	N52114	N477CJ	N22LX		
0478	N5270P	N478CJ	N595DM		
0479	N5130J	M-ICRO			
0480	N52059	N5VU			
0481	N5264A	N518AR	N481VP	N715DL	
0482	N5202D	(XA-TTC)	XA-UPZ		
0483	N5223Y	N188MP			
0484	N5265N	N639TC			
0485	N5062S	G-POWG	OO-KOR		
0486	N5214L	(D-IOBC)	D-IOBU	D-IOBO	
0487	N5264N	D-IPCC			
0488	N5120U	N1895C			
0489	N51743	N53SF	N533F		
0490	N5214K	N82KA	N490VP		
0491	N50756	N535CM	N535VP	XA-TTQ	
0492	N5155G	N278KP	C-FCEU		
0493	N51869	N493CJ			
0494	N5212M	N573BC	N525RL		
0495	N5218T	OO-AMR			
0496	N52446	M-IWPS			
0497	N5245L	N30ST			
0498	N5269X	D-IMGW			
0499	N5269Z	D-IFLY	OE-FLA		
0500	N5235G	N6061U	N5235G	D-ILIB	D-IVVB
0501	N5109W	G-DAGS	D-IENE		
0502	N5030U	D-IMAH			
0503	N5264M	C-FASW			
0504	N50321	N889SW			
0505	N50543	PT-STM			
0506	N5145V	N375DS	(N759R)	G-LFBD	
0507	N5061P	N78RK			
0508	N5247U	C-GZAS			
0509	N5040E	PR-KRT			
0510	N50736	C-GASR			
0511	N5125J	N242AS	C-FIAS		
0512	N5096S	N138GT	N38GT		
0513	N5241R	N759R	N759G		
0514	N5202D	N106CH			
0515	N5223Y	(C-FASP)	PR-MSZ		
0516	N5214K	N575DM	N525DM		
0517	N5270J	N327PD	N517PD*		
0518	N51038	D-IVIV			
0519	N5101J	N242AS	C-FASP		

CJ2+

C/n	Identities		
0520	N5264S	N520SL	VT-RKA
0521	N5188A	N545DL	
0522	N675AB		
0523	PT-FLB		
0524	N5261R	C-FASR	

Production complete

CESSNA 525B CITATIONJET CJ3

C/n	Identities					
711	N3CJ	[ff 17Apr03]				
0001	N753CJ	[ff 08Aug03]	(N929SF)	N53SF	N535F	
0002	N763CJ	N62SH	(N68SH)			
0003	N52059	N103CJ	N432LW	(N627BB)		
0004	N5207A	N1308L	N6525B			
0005	N5270E	N105CJ	N748CX			
0006	N5227G	N1278D	N417C	N525DE		
0007	N5239J	N7CC				
0008	N52627	N51HF	N946RM			
0009	N51806	N777NJ	N5GU			
0010	N5097H	N917RG				
0011	N110MG	N585PK	D-CELE	N551CF	N823LT	
0012	N5093D	N172DH	M-UPCO	N312VP	N525U	
0013	N5228Z	N831V	F-HBPP			
0014	N114CJ	N300ET	(N525JV)	N525BY		
0015	N5163K	N4RH	N747KR	N747KE		
0016	N50820	N200GM	(D-CORA)	S5-BAW	9H-JRF	SE-RLP
0017	N614B					
0018	N51896	N52ET				
0019	N79LB	N11LB	N319VP			
0020	N52038	N899RR	N33UM			
0021	N5073G	N325RC				
0022	N5109W	N528CE	N487TT			
0023	N51055	N77M	N15C			
0024	N5221Y	N525GM	(N525GN)	N525GY		
0025	N5201J	N7NE	(N71NE)	N7NQ	N179WC	
0026	N162EC					
0027	"N5188W"+	[+marks as quoted, already current on a homebuilt] N1287D		ZK-TBM	VH-ARZ	P2-MEH
0028	N5085E	PR-SPO	N50LV			
0029	N726AG					
0030	N5145P	N401CS	N786JS			
0031	N303CJ	N103DS				
0032	N52433	N137BG				
0033	N5243K	N404CS	N783JS			
0034	N52446	N65VM				
0035	N51511	N93JW				
0036	N5244F	N405CS	N779JS			
0037	N52653	C-FXTC	N37VP	N71F		
0038	N51942	N100RC	N100RQ	N159JS		
0039	N526DG	N525DG	N706RT			
0040	N52369	N550T	N540VP	N518GH		
0041	N525PC	N3CT				
0042	N5163K	N69FH	N909EC	N42VP	N721MA	N573BB
0043	N5183V	N406CS	N780JS			
0044	N144AL					
0045	N5221Y	N408CS	N781JS			
0046	N5124F	N860DD	N46VR	N52WK		
0047	N50820	PR-EBD	N347TX			
0048	N853JL	N92MA	N67JR			
0049	N628CB					
0050	N409CS	N784JS				
0051	N5148N	N525L				
0052	N999SM					
0053	N53NW					
0054	N5200U	N535GH				
0055	N5151D	N4GA				
0056	N5093L	N156TW	N748RM	N11TH		
0057	N5239J	N999LB	N999UB	N733CJ		
0058	N5066U	N885BT				
0059	N412CS	N782JS				
0060	N5250P	N125DG				
0061	N361TL					
0062	N5269A	XC-GDC				
0063	N5226B	N123CJ	N128CJ	N611CS		
0064	N5263S	N1CH	N63CJ			
0065	N5269J	N105CQ	LN-HOT	N255RA		
0066	N362JM	N6243M	N602MJ			
0067	N51160	N96MR	OM-LBG	N67CX	N310EG	
0068	N5269Z	N51JJ				
0069	N5231S	N3UD	N535DT			
0070	N51055	N279DV	N279D			
0071	N51511	N531CM				
0072	N5214L	N107CQ	N8106V	N808JN*		
0073	N51995	N899MA	(N550RB)	N575HP		
0074	N5221Y	N742AR				
0075	N528JC	D-CJAK	N390TG	N233FT		
0076	N5207A	N1KA				
0077	N52433	N7877T				
0078	N525DR	VH-MIF				
0079	N52081	N835DM	N25CK	N79VP	C-GTSX	
0080	N52352	N380CJ	N451GP			
0081	N52457	N868EM	N522NJ	N525EE		
0082	N413CS	N785JS				
0083	N5166T	N13001	HS-MCL			
0084	N51744	N841AM				
0085	N51881	D-CLAT	N885LA			
0086	N51993	D-CKJS	(D-CDIG)	D-CVHM	D-CFXJ	N4S
0087	N687DS					
0088	N5264U	N525MP				
0089	N5076J	N525EZ	[w/o in hangar fire 12Sep07 Danbury, CT]			
0090	N5197A	N417CS	N90CZ			
0091	N5214J	N219L	N219F	XA-ACR		
0092	N52653	N852SP				

CJ3

C/n	Identities					
0093	N5259Y	N93PE				
0094	N83TF					
0095	N5214K	N100JS	N100JZ	N423BB		
0096	N5270J	LX-GAP	3A-MRG	N816FC		
0097	N5216A	N888RK	N131MJ			
0098	N5270E	N87VM				
0099	N777NJ					
0100	N50820	N77M	(N563M)	N85GT		
0101	N52113	D-CTEC	PP-AVX	N511VP	CS-DVH	
0102	N5213S	N812JM	N3JM	N812JM		
0103	N5188N	(N103CJ)	N417KM	N221LC	N443PW	
0104	N5192E	N5216A	N560PJ	N590PJ	N525GT	N525GB*
0105	N5135K	N247MV	N651SD			
0106	N5218T	N106JT				
0107	N709PG	D-COBO	D-CEMS			
0108	N5218T	N418CS				
0109	N5145J	N1255J	(N927CC)			
0110	N51246	N28MH				
0111	N5101J	N96PD	N96PB			
0112	N731WH					
0113	N5263U	N55GP				
0114	N52234	N114CJ	N901MV	(D-CELE)	N96G	
0115	N5207A	N420CS	N51EM			
0116	N5244W	ZS-CJT	N80EP			
0117	N5212M	F-GRUJ	N656SM			
0118	N51143	C-GSSC	N532LW			
0119	N5257V	D-CNOB	SE-RMB			
0120	N5211A	D-CEFD				
0121	N52229	N423CS				
0122	N12GS					
0123	N73EM	N73EL	N515TX			
0124	N5203S	PR-ALC				
0125	N5194J	OE-GPO	C-FNCB			
0126	N5030U	N621GA	N525KD*			
0127	N5268A	N107PT				
0128	N17CN	PR-BIR				
0129	N629EE	PR-ALV				
0130	(N910BH)	N329CJ				
0131	N5057E	N331CJ	N30UD	AP-PFL		
0132	N5058J	N425CS				
0133	N5031E	N233MM	N3WS			
0134	N52691	N41ND				
0135	N5059X	OE-GRA				
0136	N5073G	PT-TJS				
0137	N51042	N550MX				
0138	N51942	N356MR	N591MB	N591ME		
0139	N52059	N93CW	(N979TX)	G-RGBY	N139CJ	
0140	N51612	N42AA	N15PG			
0141	N50756	N238SW				
0142	N28DM					
0143	N5185V	N320BP				
0144	N51055	(C-FXFJ)	N847NG			
0145	N332SB	C-FFCM				
0146	CS-DIY	D-CCCG*				
0147	N5168Y	OO-FPC				
0148	N52397	N148CJ	M-ELON	M-ELOW	N523LM	N300MV
0149	N5261R	N123CJ				
0150	N52626	N317BR	OE-GHG	N562PA	(N562PZ)	
0151	N52086	N420CH				
0152	N5262B	N427CS	N825AV			
0153	N5145P	N28FR	G-ODCM	N55FP		
0154	D-CRAH	N53KJ				
0155	N831FC	N222VR				
0156	N5145V	F-GVUJ				
0157	N5096S	N157JL				
0158	N5180K	(OO-FPD)	OO-FPE			
0159	N50275	N565JP				
0160	N5201J	VP-BUG	M-ASRY	M-ABDN	C-GZAM	
0161	N5268M	D-CMHS				
0162	N503LC	M-YEDC	G-YEDC			
0163	N5267K	N80HB	N80HE			
0164	N5125J	N1314V	N500AS			
0165	N5267T	N428CS				
0166	N5061W	N7814				
0167	N450BV					
0168	N970DM					
0169	N5250P	D-CUBA				
0170	N50543	N996PE				
0171	N5172M	N727YB				
0172	N51780	N535DL				
0173	N5228J	OO-LIE				
0174	N174SJ					
0175	N149WW					
0176	N5188N	(F-HAFC)	F-GYFC	N108LA		
0177	N5037F	N429CS				
0178	N5203S	F-GSGL				
0179	N5211A	N179CJ	G-OMBI	HB-VTJ		
0180	N5185J	N360CK				
0181	N5239J	N143JT				
0182	N5243K	N535CM	N533CM			
0183	N5062S	N4115H	A6-SAB	F-HBER	SE-RMJ	
0184	N52639	N914FF	N213F			
0185	N5076K	N430CS	N501DJ			
0186	N186CJ	N111JW	N491JL	N491J		
0187	N5076P	PR-MRG	[w/o Sao Paulo/Congonhas, Brazil, 11Nov12; parted out by Dodson Int'l, Rantoul, KS]		N508EA	

C/n	Identities				
0188	N541WG	N757PC			
0189	N5197A	N525CF			
0190	N5036Q	N81ER	N190VP		
0191	N52626	N379DB			
0192	N5214L	XA-AVX			
0193	N5262B	N1382N	(SX-EDP)	SX-PAP	YU-BTN
0194	N52645	OY-WWW			
0195	N5202D	N400GG	N400TG		
0196	N396CJ	VH-ANE	VH-NNE		
0197	N5262X	D-CUUU	OO-FYS		
0198	N52069	"VP-BJR"+	[+marks worn at factory]	VP-BRJ	OY-TSA
0199	N51817	PR-CVC			
0200	N5073G	OO-EDV			
0201	N5260Y	C-FANJ	N211VR	N525NY	
0202	N51896	N7CH			
0203	N50776	N328RC			
0204	N5066F	N5WN			
0205	N52682	N428BR			
0206	N52086	C-GPMW			
0207	N5262W	N856BB			
0208	N5180K	N414KD	N8880D		
0209	N5228Z	HB-VOW	N80EA		
0210	N52114	N1DM	N771DM		
0211	N51396	ZS-DPP			
0212	N52235	N711BE	N379B		
0213	N5188A	N527HV			
0214	N52433	N92MS			
0215	N5201J	D-CTEC	OE-GBO	D-CMAN	
0216	N5250E	HB-VWB	N216CJ	N688CK	N831HS
0217	N52690	D-CASH	OM-VPT	N651TW	
0218	N5201M	N7725D	PR-PLU		
0219	N5243K	OE-GRZ	OE-GBC		
0220	N52136	(D-CJVC)	D-COWB		
0221	N15ZZ				
0222	N5061W	OE-GRU			
0223	N5117U	N229CN	N7773J*		
0224	N5250P	F-HCIC			
0225	N5296X	N27UB	N10TS		
0226	N50543	N880MR			
0227	N5211A	LX-DCA			
0228	N5000R	N431CS			
0229	N5185J	N826CS			
0230	N5068F	F-GSMG			
0231	N5247U	OE-GJF	G-TSJF	N539KH	
0232	N52682	D-CPAO	G-PAOL		
0233	N5194J	N956GA			
0234	N5214K	EC-KQO			
0235	N5174W	CS-DGW			
0236	N5151D	N308GT			
0237	N50736	N525WL			
0238	N5062S	N525EZ	M-OODY	N525CR	
0239	N5076P	PR-SCF			
0240	N51160	N240CJ	N75JK		
0241	N5226B	N241KA	N241CJ		
0242	N5227G	N899NH	N242KV		
0243	N5101J	C6-LUV	N528BS		
0244	N432CS				
0245	N50776	PR-TBL			
0246	N5266F	N246CZ	N795BM	N800CU	
0247	N5244F	N377GA	J8-JET		
0248	N5109W	N839DM			
0249	N5163C	N608SG			
0250	N5245U	N403CH	N403ND		
0251	N5026Q	N220LC	(N37JK)	N716MB	
0252	N5093L	N941AM	N99RE		
0253	N38M	N38MV	PR-SHC		
0254	N5214J	N307PE			
0255	N5181U	M-BIRD	D-CHAT	OE-GJP	
0256	N52627	N6M	N256CJ	N114CL	N256CJ
0257	N433CS	N32AC			
0258	N5262W	F-HAGA	(D-CFRA)	N99AG	
0259	N5180K	N724CV	UP-CS301		
0260	N5096S	N23BV			
0261	N5223Y	N100DW	N80F	N80FK	
0262	N812HF	C-FNFS			
0263	N5270M	N888PS	N934CT		
0264	N5244W	F-GSCR			
0265	N5262B	N227JP	N265DW	N52MW	
0266	N5218R	N41203	EI-MJC	N330KM	PP-RCA
0267	N5163K	N500WD	N500WJ	N358JJ	
0268	N434CS	N151KD	C-GPLT		
0269	N5194B	OM-OPA	D-CDLC	N411TJ	
0270	N5091J	N58JV	N824DM		
0271	N52144	N39GG			
0272	N52352	HB-VWC	N272CJ	N903MC	
0273	N5228Z	N79JS	N798S	N902SS	
0274	N5201J	N436CS	N436EP		
0275	N52690	OE-GNA			
0276	N5214K	N70NF			
0277	N5213K	N2074H	OE-GET	N369GM	PR-MTQ
0278	N50736	N2111W	PR-ADL		
0279	N51160	N279CJ	N2CP		
0280	N5197A	N150MJ	M-MIKE		
0281	N5174W	LX-JET	D-CIAU*		
0282	N437CS	N578CJ			

CJ3

C/n	Identities					
0283	N283RA					
0284	N5076K	N835CB				
0285	N11UD	PT-OOO				
0286	N5066F	D-CPMI	N286VP			
0287	N5062S	D-CURA	OO-PAR			
0288	N5076P	D-CWIR	N288VP	N721MA	N525MC	
0289	N5226B	N4RP	N204RP	N516TX		
0290	N5101J	N125PL				
0291	N50776	PH-FJK				
0292	N5241Z	N329BH				
0293	N28GA	C-GSLW				
0294	N52229	N108WQ	N106WQ	N294CC		
0295	N5207V	N525EZ	N295VP	N525NE		
0296	N5216A	N296CJ	N296PM	C-GVSN		
0297	N196MR	PP-MPP				
0298	N567HB	N298CJ				
0299	N299CS	N611TK	N299VR	C-FBRP		
0300	N52059	F-GVVB				
0301	N110JC	N256DV	N256DA	N373AG		
0302	N51881	N302CZ	(N88QC)	N18GA		
0303	N5112K	N724BP	N724PB			
0304	N5061F	N20AU				
0305	N5120U	N800FM				
0306	N525H	N949LL	N567RB			
0307	N815LP	XA-ALT				
0308	N5260Y	N27EW	XA-TTC			
0309	N5218R	N41226	TC-GUR	N627V	TC-GUR	N309TX
0310	N5163K	PR-RBO				
0311	N5194B	M-MHMH	N409DJ			
0312	N5091J	N312CJ	OE-GPK			
0313	N123CZ					
0314	N52352	OE-GPD	N369MN			
0315	N315CJ					
0316	N52690	N316BD				
0317	N52613	(CS-EAA)	N880PF	N883PF	(N883PP)	N317VP	N95TX
0318	N5226B	OE-GMZ	N518CJ	N323AD		
0319	N50736	N52WC				
0320	N5124F	UR-PME	(D-CLXG)	N320RH	N321SD	
0321	N52038	N438CS	N5GQ	PR-HMV		
0322	N5108G	UR-DWH	N322PJ			
0323	N5030U	N6132U	UP-CS302			
0324	N5267T	PR-MON				
0325	N5260M	N510RC	N325CJ			
0326	N439CS	N480CC				
0327	N5185V	N527DV	N778BS*			
0328	N51038	N994MP	N421MP			
0329	N5270P	N528DV				
0330	N5066F	D-CAST				
0331	(D-CIOL)	N819CW				
0332	N434CS	N91GT				
0333	N525CJ	C-GMLR				
0334	N5206T	D-CCBH				
0335	N335CJ	N929BC	N928BC	N410PT		
0336	N336CJ	N466F				
0337	N50820	N38M	N38MX	PR-VNA		
0338	N338CZ	N109TW				
0339	(D-CAVB)	D-CBVB	OE-GVB	N70FC		
0340	N111KJ					
0341	N5062S	N808XR	N808SD			
0342	N52639	N885JF				
0343	N5076J	(N91GT)	OM-SYN	N18650		
0344	N47NT					
0345	N5257V	N345NT	N345LT			
0346	N5090Y	N299LS	N346CZ	N710PT		
0347	N5057F	N5MQ				
0348	N5194J	OE-GIE				
0349	N5181U	D-CJET				
0350	N5201J	PR-BHV				
0351	N5197M	N330PK				
0352	N52691	VP-CCX	N906MC			
0353	N5031E	N509SB	N509SD	N971TB		
0354	N5061F	N354CJ	N10TR			
0355	N5268V	N3043F	N480JH	N430JH		
0356	N52457	N820NC				
0357	N777HN	N177HN				
0358	N5059X	N529DV				
0359	N5037F	N777EW	N359CJ	N1LF		
0360	N5072X	N360TD				
0361	N5263S	UR-DWL	N361EV	M-MSVI		
0362	N5045W	PR-RMT	N362TA			
0363	N5103J	N710GD	N700GD			
0364	N5109R	N982BZ				
0365	N52113	N501T	N550T			
0366	N5154J	N861HA				
0367	N5247U	D-CDTZ	D-CJOS			
0368	N5040E	N723SG				
0369	N50736	N777LB				
0370	N5260U	N351AJ				
0371	N5148N	N924TC	N924TD			
0372	N5241Z	N892AB	N356DC			
0373	N5060K	N65LW				
0374	N5156D	N59WG				
0375	N5196U	(PT-MPP)	N863DD	N860DD		
0376	N5066F	(PP-CMP)	N386SF			
0377	N5061F	N88GA				

CJ3/CJ3+

C/n	Identities			
0378	N5117U	D-CHIO		
0379	N51342	N379SM		
0380	N5157E	N181EA	N568CM	
0381	N5201M	N6062M	N77NT	
0382	N52229	N6061Z	N73EM	
0383	N52235	N383CJ	N383JR*	
0384	N5223D	N6060S	N919SV	
0385	N5262B	N370MR		
0386	N5270K	PR-DRP		
0387	N5270M	N216TM		
0388	N51666	N81110	N81ER	
0389	N5214J	N56WN	PT-GMU	
0390	N52626	PT-GBF		
0391	N50715	N1MG	[also wears fake serial 12-391]	
0392	N5093L	N392RS	N392MG	
0393	N5037F	N513PN	N393VP	N500WD
0394	N5260U	PR-JRV		
0395	N5151D	N196JH		
0396	N5203J	N730GA		
0397	N5245D	N787EV		
0398	N5162W	N895CB		
0399	N5063P	N128WT		
0400	N51780	N54FL		
0401	N51806	N988MM		
0402	N52114	N73AD		
0403	N5270P	N578WZ		
0404	N5236L	N525GK		
0405	N5214J	N405CZ	PR-EDB	
0406	N52613	N559HF		
0407	N5265B	N38HD		
0408	(D-COBC)	N906GW		
0409	N52655	N32PM	N363AL	
0410	N525TH			
0411	N435CM	N535CM		
0412	N412AR	N518AR		
0413	N5265N	N278KP		
0414	D-COBC	D-COBO		
0415	N523DV			

CJ3+

C/n	Identities			
0451	N30CJ	[r/o 29May14, ff 28Jul14] N531AJ*		
0452	N51GZ			
0453	N1MF			
0454	N52653	N160BR		
0455	N80VM			
0456	N5174W	N95LL		
0457	N426NS			
0458	N5241R	N543PD		
0459	N989RS			
0460	N5196U	N778LC		
0461	N766LF			
0462	N50715	N84WC		
0463	N865MK			
0464	N550BW			
0465	N525CW			
0466	N5181U	N504PS		
0467	N5194B	N816BL		
0468	N468CJ	N468EC		
0469	N528HV			
0470	N5206T	(D-CUGF)	N309TW	
0471	N285ER	N85ER		
0472	N5180C	N225TJ		
0473	N5267D	N491AM		
0474	N5076P	N474CC	N525GM	
0475	N5124F	N122WY		
0476	N5093D	N223GB		
0477	N5145U	N872J		
0478	N212GB	N304TC		
0479	N5165P	D-CUGF		
0480	N5208J	PP-MRX		
0481	N5270J	N888TF		
0482	N52114	N327RD		
0483	N5058J	N327JA		
0484	N52690	N494CJ+	[+ marks allocated in error for one day only]	N484CJ
0485	N5214L	N485CZ		
0486	N5100J	N19537	N486JR	
0487	N5265S	N93MW		
0488	N5097H	N725TM		
0489	N5157E	C-FASY		
0490	N5166U	N858CB		
0491	N52699	N85VM		
0492	N52639			
0493	N5200Z	N302JK		
0494	N5268V	N248PM		
0495	N5076J			
0496	N5244F			
0497	N5101J			
0498	N5233J			
0499	N5156D			
0500				

CJ3+

C/n	Identities
0501	
0502	
0503	
0504	
0505	
0506	
0507	
0508	
0509	
0510	
0511	
0512	
0513	
0514	
0515	
0516	
0517	
0518	
0519	
0520	
0521	
0522	
0523	
0524	

CESSNA 525C CITATIONJET CJ4

C/n	Identities				
714001	N4CJ	[ff 05May08]			
0001	N525NG	[ff 19Aug08]	N14CJ		
0002	N525KS	[ff 02Dec08]	N747HS	N747KR	(N747HR)	XA-MKA
0003	N52141	N525NB	N990H	N233VP	XA-GZZ
0004	N5269Z	N525CZ	N88QC		
0005	N5211Q	N941KN			
0006	N615PL				
0007	N5061W	N1DM	N6QM	N407CJ	N525EM
0008	N5130J	N868HC			
0009	N5245L	N100JS	(N100JZ)	M-AZIA	
0010	N52229	N96PD	N787JJ		
0011	N52653	N429MR			
0012	N4M				
0013	N52609	N105AD			
0014	N5201M	N627RP	N627RR		
0015	N5155G	N1CH			
0016	N5101J	N518TT			
0017	N51995	N80HB			
0018	N5228Z	N926TF			
0019	N52655	N80F			
0020	N5270K	N2250G			
0021	N51564	N817CJ	N417C		
0022	N5216A	N450CM			
0023	N50231	N219L			
0024	N51780	N424CJ	N87FL		
0025	N52645	XA-LPK			
0026	N5200R	N588MM	(N426VP)	XA-UTG	
0027	N5267G	N545JF			
0028	N51396	N428CJ	N909EC	N907SF	
0029	N5218T	N481AM			
0030	N5105F	N460PK	N360PK		
0031	N50275	N631TJ			
0032	N5263U	N740AK			
0033	N50715	N94JW			
0034	N5136J	N577TH			
0035	N52352	N163M			
0036	N5221Y	N436RV	PR-VON	N80CH	N548AJ	PR-MRE*
0037	N52178	N80LD	N82LD		
0038	N5253S	XA-HOF			
0039	N5093D	N38M	N38MJ	N3RC	
0040	N5093Y	N181CN			
0041	N51872	N718MV			
0042	N5228J	N442RR	PR-RAR	N42VP	
0043	N50282	D-CEVB	OE-GWB	N543TX	
0044	N5153K	D-CEFA	N544TX		
0045	N5200Z	N8GQ			
0046	N5260Y	N446CJ			
0047	N5076L	N220BA			
0048	N51744	N126PG			
0049	N5154J	N816DV	N716DV		
0050	N5244W	PR-NJR			
0051	N51055	N999WC			
0052	N5135K	N279DV			
0053	N5207V	N322SB			
0054	N5269A	XA-UQG			
0055	N51038	D-CMOM	OE-GXB	N455TX	
0056	N5079V	(PP-CFO)	PR-GML		
0057	N5267T	PT-MPP			
0058	N5185V	D-CHRA	(D-CEFE)		
0059	N5069E	PP-CMP			
0060	N51143	N4B	N357BV		
0061	N5181U	N44GL			
0062	N5197M	N503TF			
0063	N5076K	N5254C			
0064	N5263D	ZS-AML	N43LJ		
0065	N5048U	N329CF			
0066	N5112K	N67GH			
0067	N51160	N545GH			
0068	N5162X	N7NE			
0069	N5163K	N569CJ	C-GDSH		
0070	N5180K	N929BC			
0071	N5200U	N181HB	N44FJ*		
0072	N52144	N65CD	PR-VZN		
0073	N5026Q	M-NSJS	N473SC	HK-5120	
0074	N5061W	N74CJ	N869KA		
0075	N5073F	N765DF			
0076	N5101J	N277C	N300KK		
0077	N5135A	N400ET			
0078	N51564	N59JM	C-FXTC		
0079	N51612	N79HM			
0080	N5188N	N271MP			
0081	N52086	N851AC	N511AC		
0082	N5211Q	N482CJ	N82KA		
0083	N5236L	C-FANJ			
0084	N52397	N719L			
0085	N5239J	N1BL	N585VP	N485CJ	OK-ILA
0086	N5243K	N525KR			
0087	N52609	N87ED	N586ED		
0088	N5260M	N95FP			
0089	N5268M	C-FIMP	C-FMCI	N989CJ	
0090	N50275	PP-WMA			
0091	N52623	N271CQ	N752KP*		
0092	N51511	N2004D	5N-DIA		

CJ4

C/n	Identities			
0093	N5188A	D-CBCT		
0094	N5244F	N800RL		
0095	N52613	N770LE		
0096	N5000R	N5253Z	N525EZ	
0097	N5268A	N98CH		
0098	N5174W	N511TK	N611TK	
0099	N5201J	N1440W		
0100	N5095N	OE-GTI		
0101	N5094D	N1DM	N1WX	
0102	N51396	N1BL		
0103	N52178	PR-MJM		
0104	N5168Y	N34LA		
0105	N5250P	N460RG		
0106	N5228J	(D-COJS)	D-CCJS	M-FLYI
0107	N50282	N573AB	N721MA	
0108	N5153K	D-CKNA		
0109	N5148N	N827BT	N817BT	
0110	N5241Z	N9542G	N747LA	
0111	N5156D	N38M	N826BM	
0112	N52699	ZK-PGA	ZK-OCB	
0113	N5267D	N95CT		
0114	N52591	F-HGLO		
0115	N5076L	F-HATG		
0116	N51744	N525KB	HB-VPA	
0117	N5188N	N713WD	N218MB	
0118	N51942	D-CWIR		
0119	N51881	N45FS	N500SV	
0120	N5068R	N513NN	RP-C7513	
0121	N5245U	N606MC		
0122	N5254Y	N339KC		
0123	N5244W	N43KA		
0124	N51055	D-CVHA	D-CWIT	
0125	N5269A	N888KG		
0126	N5048U	N255MV		
0127	N5112K	N636DS		
0128	N51160	N47PB		
0129	N5152X	N129CJ		
0130	N5163K	N622GB	N620GB	
0131	N5000R	N892AB	N431TX*	
0132	N50275	M-OBIL		
0133	N50549	N133CJ	N577RT	
0134	N5067U	N94FP	G-SDRY	
0135	N5068F	N55MZ		
0136	N5072X	N55BW		
0137	N5076K	N137JQ		
0138	N51072	N79JS		
0139	N5203S	N6064A	N810GW	
0140	N5166U	C-FLBS		
0141	N5161J	N953FF		
0142	N52136	N589GB		
0143	N5045W	M-SSYS		
0144	N5262W	D-CHRB		
0145	N5058J	N899NB	N899NH	
0146	N5091J	N146CJ	N950RG	
0147	N133RC	N100RC		
0148	N601FM			
0149	N5204D	N627RP		
0150	N5086W	N938LN		
0151	N5097H	N65DD		
0152	N152CZ	N111LP		
0153	N5197M	D-CHRC		
0154	N154GV	JA008G		
0155	N5153K	N525KJ		
0156	N51744	N485HB	N435HB	
0157	N50282	(D-CCTS)	N4751	
0158	C-GLUV			
0159	N51612	N159CJ		
0160	N189MM	N18MM		
0161	D-CJUG			
0162	N51444	N1886X		
0163	N5130J	N448CJ		
0164	N5157E	F-ONCP		
0165	N300BB			
0166	N1492J			
0167	N5109W	N167H	N886CA	N843CA	N888LB
0168	N522EP	N525EP		
0169	N5244W	N701AL		
0170	N329SH	N525SJ		
0171	N194SS			
0172	N52235	N292ST		
0173	N52626	N173NL	N754RL	
0174	N5270P	LX-GJM		
0175	N414KU			
0176	N38M			
0177	N51072	D-CEFE		
0178	N41KN			
0179	N179GV	JA009G		
0180	N910SS			
0181	N986ST			
0182	N5141T	N22UB		
0183	N888RK			
0184	N389AL	N53SF		
0185	N185GV	JA010G		
0186	N709CB			
0187	N5148N	N187CJ	N309CQ	

CJ4

C/n	Identities		
0188	N51511	N225CJ	M-SIXT
0189	N52059	N679TC	
0190	N52699	N32PM	
0191	N5192E	CC-AOR	
0192	N51342	N492CA	
0193	N193CF	N437MR	
0194	N51564	N329SH	
0195	N5211F	N159H	
0196	N326PZ	N525PZ	
0197	N5244F	M-NTOS	
0198	N5061P	N449BZ	
0199	N51869	C-FSTX	
0200	N5135A	ZJ-THC	
0201	N5227G	N604DR	
0202	N5136J	N207RT	
0203	N51038	N759R	
0204	N51780	N100Y	
0205	N5076K	N415KA	
0206	N5207V	N939AM	
0207	N5246Z	N207CJ	
0208	N5265N	N601JL	
0209	N51942	N888KJ	
0210	N52645	N10AU	
0211	N5117U	N57HC	
0212	N51143	N254AB	
0213	N5130J	N213CJ	
0214	N5000R	N2286B	
0215	N5194B	N215CJ	
0216	N5180C	N159WG	
0217	N5270E	N217CJ	
0218	N5148N	D-CBRO*	
0219	N5147B		
0220	N5152X	N220GV	
0221	N52609		
0222	N5168Y		
0223	N51995		
0224	N5270M		
0225	N5201M		
0226	N5214J		
0227	N52653		
0228	N5221Y		
0229	N5211Q		
0230			
0231			
0232			
0233			
0234			
0235			
0236			
0237			
0238			
0239			
0240			
0241			
0242			
0243			
0244			
0245			
0246			
0247			
0248			
0249			
0250			

CESSNA CITATION II/BRAVO

This production list is presented in order of the Unit Number which was used and allocated by Cessna, rather than by the normally-used c/n. A c/n-Unit Number cross-reference follows the production list.

Unit No	C/n	Identities
	686	N550CC [ff 31Jan77; cvtd to S550 standards;cx Apr91 presumed wfu]
001	550-0001	(N98751) (N551CC) N5050J N560CC [converted to Model 560; canx 11Apr05; wfu]
002	551-0027	N98753 N552CC N44GT N552CC N522CC N46PJ
003	550-0003	N98784 N553CJ YV-19CP N19CP N199Q N19CP
004	F550-0004	N98786 C-GPAW N312GA F-GNCP [cx 09Dec13; b/u]
005	550-0005	N98817 OE-GKP N77ND [w/o 30Sep05 70 miles North of Fairbanks, AK; wreck parted out by White Inds, Bates City, MO]
006	550-0006	N98820 N2 N6 N152GA N725RH N550LA
007	550-0007	N98830 N300PB (N447FM) N650WC N650WG (N550TY) N127JJ N127CL
008	550-0008	N98840 N575W OE-GIW (N108AJ) N550JF N70X N70XA G-VUEZ "M-VUEZ"+ N70XA [+fake marks worn at Doncaster/Robin Hood Oct12]
009	550-0009	N98853 N744SW N744DC N656PS
010	550-0010	N98858 OE-GEP N550PL N806C PT-LPK
011	550-0021	N98871 N296AB (N171CB) N900LJ N52RF (N252RF) N529F N15H
012	550-0011	(N99876) Venezuela 0002
013	550-0012	N3208M N513CC C-GHOL N11FH N586CP N586GR
014	550-0002	N3210M YV-140CP N20FM N700AS XA-SLD N39ML N502CL LV-CEN
015	550-0014	N3212M N702R N780GT (N94FS) N780CF
016	550-0013	N3216M YV-151CP N3952B N21SW N21SV PT-LML [w/o 15Aug87 Criciuma, Brazil: wreck parted out by Dodson Av'n, Rantoul, KS; cx Aug97]
017	550-0016	N3221M N276AL (N216VP) HC-BTJ N204MC N116LA
018	551-0007	N3223M YV-169CP (N169CP) YV-169CP YV-05CP N60FJ N42MJ [parted out by Marklyn Jet Parts, TX]
019	550-0018	(N3225M) N752CC [wfu]
020	551-0006	N3227A YV-06CP YV-O-CVG-2 Venezuela 1967
021	550-0017	N3230M VH-MAY P2-RDZ N771ST N744AT
022	550-0019	N3232M N1851T N1851D (HI-530) HI-534 HI-534CA N1851D (N200GP) N900AF N7RC [w/o 26Apr95 Walkers Cay, Bahamas; cx Oct95 – remains to Dodson Avn, KS]
023	551-0071	N3236M PH-HES OO-RJT PH-HES N4578F N79CD N790D N551DS N551HH
024	551-0003	N3237M YV-205CP N4445N N72RC I-MESK [wfu Nairobi. Kenya]
025	550-0025	N3239M (EP-KID) EP-KIC N9014S N664JB N664J N78PH N78PR 9H-ACR OY-GMC N551DA
026	550-0026	N3240M N256W (N2231B) N30AV
027	550-0027	N3245M N527CC G-BFRM N222DE N222D N127PM
028	550-0028	(N3246M) (G-BFLY) OE-GAU N501BL N888MW N100CX (F-GHUA) 5Y-HAB N310AV N551CZ (N370CD) [retro-fitted with Williams FJ44 engines]
029	550-0029	(N3247M) G-JEEN N502AL N718VA N202PB N7CC N550TJ N524MA
030	550-0030	(N3249M) G-DJBI G-FERY G-MSLY N64CA VR-CSS N507AB N501KC (N200G) N601KK N4TS N16TS
031	550-0031	N3250M RP-C550 RP-C296 N22GA N9DC C6-MAS
032	550-0032	N3251M N810SC N810SG N55BP N66ES N50US N905EM N112JS N232CW
033	550-0033	(N3252M) TR-LYE N59MJ N755CM N46DA F-GPLT F-WPLT LX-GDL LX-JET LX-GDL G-CEUO N300GH
034	550-0034	N3258M N771A N697A N60CC N922SL
035	550-0219	(N3261M) N108WG HB-VGK N4457A N108WG VH-ORE N12AC YV-606CP N550RP N550PM N10JA N321KR [parted out by Alliance Air Parts, Oklahoma City, OK]
036	550-0036	(N3262M) N58AN N5Q (N54DA) N36CE N711BP (N789RR) N789BR N336MA
037	550-0037	(N3268M) N37HG N361DJ XA-SDV (N551NA) N535MA N829NL N237CW (N37GA) N622PG
038	550-0038	(N3271M) N526AC N526AG C-FLDO N642CC (N842CC) N550JC
039	550-0039	(N3273M) G-BJHH EI-BJL N78FA ZP-TYO N848D N33PB
040	550-0040	(N3274M) N220CC N277CJ N900LC HK-3607X N554BA N550SC (N551GA) N545GA N554MB
041	550-0024	N3276M N533M N85MG N313CK XA-SJZ N313CK N413CK N404RP
042	550-0035	N3278M N8417B N50XX N333X N74G (N50GG) N15JA [parted out by MTW Aerospace, AL]
043	550-0041	N3279M N8418B N341AG N985BA N177HH OE-GCI D-CHSA
044	550-0042	N3283M N666RC N57MB N66AT C-FPEL C-FLBC N41GA
045	550-0045	N3284M N4CH N4CR 5N-AMR [w/o 21May91 private airstrip Bauchi, Nigeria]
046	550-0043	N3285M N6Q VR-CCI N801JP N112SH N551RM
047	550-0044	N3286M N3526 N550HM N300TW N308TW (N452AJ)
048	550-0048	N3288M N534M N161BH N384DA N10BF N19ER
049	551-0010	N3291M YV-137CP N55AL D-ICAC
050	550-0046	(N3292M) C-GRHC
051	551-0095	N3296M N1AP N66LB G-HOTL N999WA N49TJ N314CK N200TJ (N127TA) C-GAMW N627TA N400PC N402TJ N48DK
052	F550-0050	(N3298M) N102FC N362DJ D-CJJJ N250CF F-ODUT F-GMCI N342AJ
053	550-0053	(N3300M) N4VF N53VP N53KB TC-NKB N550EC N519AA
054	550-0054	(N3301M) N501AA VH-WGJ VH-OYW VH-FOJ [cx; wfu]
055	550-0055	(N3308M) N55CC N2JZ (N1466K) N10EG
056	550-0047	N3313M (N66VM) OB-M-1171 N66VM N44AS
057	550-0075	N3314M N55BH N58BH C-GSFA N710MT N910MT PR-LIG
058	550-0068	N3319M N558CC N558CB N402ST N1WB N91VB (N406CJ)
059	550-0242	N1955E N551BC
060	550-0051	N1958E C-GJAP C-GBCB N678CA ZS-RKV
061	550-0263	N1959E D-IMTM (N458N) N13VP [w/o 20May02 Oklahoma-Wiley Post,OK: b/u for spares by Dodson Int'l Parts circa Oct02; but cx to Italy 20Dec04]
062	551-0017	N2052A N1UH (N33FW) N53WF N811VC N811VG
063	550-0069	N2069A F-GBPL 3A-MWA HZ-AAA HZ-ALJ N550CE OE-GIN (N269AJ) N551JF N550AB C-FFCL N712PD N550MN
064	550-0070	N2072A N564CC N108DB N777FL N550KA N892PB YV....
065	550-0065	N4191G N55SX ZS-RCS N144GA
066	550-0064	N4308G C-GDPD N404BF (N404BV) CS-DCI (OY-GMB) OY-GMK (D-CIRR) OE-GAD SE-RIM
067	550-0052	N4620G (OO-LFX) OY-ASV N90MJ N534MW N67TM PH-CTZ N550DR N302SJ
068	F550-0073	N4621G F-GBTL VP-CTJ G-JBIZ
069	550-0074	N4754G N48ND (N86JM) LN-AAI N386MA (N551GN) (N10GN) D-CIFA LX-THS N174DR
070	550-0056	N5342J N752RT N444FJ N89D
071	550-0058	N5348J N71CJ N100HB
072	550-0072	(N2661H) N360N N36QN (N700EA) N969MT N551SR N770JM N778JM N905CW [parted out by White Inds, Bates City, MO]
073	550-0057	(N2661N) VH-WNZ VH-FOJ
074	550-0338	(N2661P) (D-ICWB) (N71RL) N22RJ HB-VGE N28968 N550DW N500GM N500QM N900SE N900MF N992AS
075	550-0060	N26610 (N550KR) N75KR N98BE N315CK OE-GIL ZA-AMA
076	551-0015	N26613 YV-213CP YV-2671P YV2073 YV2662
077	550-0061	(N26614) N456N N458N
078	550-0062	(N26615) (N77SF) C-GDLR [cx 07Feb13; wfu]
079	551-0117	(N26616) C-GHYD N11AB OO-SKS N551AD 4X-CZD
080	550-0064	N26617 YV-36CP N64TF (N550TJ)
081	550-0066	N26619 (N3031) N3032 N733H N783H N10JP (N410JP) N19HU N360RP N425GT
082	550-0077	(N2662A) N582CC N578W XA-PIJ XA-AGN XA-GAA
083	550-0078	(N2662B) N31KW N71FM N78GA C-GPTR (N277A) N533MA N432NM

CITATION II

Unit No	C/n	Identities									
084	551-0122	(N2662F)	N10LR	N922EH							
085	550-0090	N2662Z	N4110S	N4110C	N410NA	N290VP	N818RJ*				
086	550-0371	(N26621)	N551MC	C-GCJN	N585DM	N550LS					
087	550-0079	(N26622)	N930BS	(N26DA)	N789SS	N33RH	N232DM	YV3124			
088	550-0089	(N26623)	N88MJ	(N44JX)	(N444WJ)	N43RW	N81CC	N800RR	(N111DT)	N61SS	
089	550-0080	(N26624)	G-BFLY	HB-VGR	N22511	N45ME	ZP-BMG				
090	550-0081	N26626	I-FBCT	N254AM	I-AROO	N394AM	I-GGLC				
091	550-0082	N26627	G-BMCL	N21DA	N49U						
092	551-0024	N26628	N2CA	[w/o 18Dec82 Mountain View, MO]							
093	550-0084	N26229	N222LB	N808DM	N156N	N226N	N226L	N521WM	(N467MW)	N391AN	N84NP	N550SS
094	550-0067	N26263B	N81TC	N74TC	N867CW	N267CW	N267BB				
095	551-0018	N2663F	N455DM	N666AJ	N556CC	LN-AAD	N387MA	D-IEAR			
096	550-0086	N2663G	N414GC	(N93CW)	N43SA	XC-JCY+	[+marks worn when flying Mexican Customs missions]			N43SA	[wfu]
097	551-0132	N2663J	(C-FCFP)	C-GTBR	N78GA	SE-DYR	N170AR	N551MW			
098	551-0133	N2663N	G-JRCT	N222TG	I-JESA	HB-VDO					
099	550-0076	(N2663X)	LN-HOT	VH-LSW	VH-TFY	VH-XDD	P2-MBD	VH-QQZ			
100	550-0085	(N2663Y)	OY-GKC	N57AJ	OE-GBA	EI-MED	G-IMED	N143TW			
101	550-0094	(N26630)	G-JETA	G-RDBS	G-JETA	[wfu Doncaster/Robin Hood, UK]					
102	550-0095	N26631	N400DT	N100UF	N550CG	LV-CTT					
103	550-0096	N26632	N550EW	N30UC	N87SF	N96NF	[parted out by Dodson Int'l, KS]				
104	550-0097	N26634	N404G	N404E	N202CE	N999GR	C-GRQC	N207AP	N550ME		
105	550-0098	(N26635)	N17S	N212H	N211JS	N211MT					
106	550-0374	N26638	YV-147CP	YV-1478P	(N772AC)	YV-678CP	N477A	(N999LL)	N695TA		
107	551-0021	N26639	N107BB	N307AJ	N551CF	N55LS	N1HA				
108	551-0141	N2664F	(N108CT)	N95CC	N210MJ	N888RF	N888HW	N100SC	N388MA	CC-CWZ	N451DA	(N636MA)	N311TT
		N451DA									
109	550-0099	N2664L	N109JC								
110	550-0100	N2664T	(N801L)	N801G	N2S	C-FKHD	N140DA	C-GLMK			
111	550-0101	(N2664U)	N91MJ	(N42BM)	[w/o 31Dec95 Marco Island Airport, FL]						
112	550-0102	N2664Y	VH-WNP	VH-JCG	VH-JPG	VH-OYC	VH-INT				
113	550-0376	N26640	N313BT	N30FJ	N30EJ	N73ST					
114	F550-0092	(N26643)	N89B	N89Q	F-GFPO	N89Q	F-GNLF	N567CA	N550GZ		
115	551-0026	(N26648)	N551R	N12TV	N25NH	N32PB	N612VR				
116	550-0105	N26649	N116CC	D-CNCP	I-MTNT	N105BA	N550LH				
117	550-0106	N2665A	Argentina AE-129	LQ-TFM	AE-129	(N83MA)	N37CR	N308CK	N820MC	(N820MQ)	
118	551-0149	N2665D	N550CB	N225AD	N225FM	N550JS	(N715PS)	N5WT	N255WT	N451MP	
119	550-0108	(N2665F)	N4TL	N4EK	(N65SA)	VP-CBE	N36NA	N690EW			
120	550-0109	N2665N	N753CC	[w/o Oklahoma City, OK, 21Dec12]							
121	550-0091	(N2665S)	N527AC	N527AG	N601BC						
122	550-0110	(N2665Y)	N222SG	N122G	N550SF						
123	550-0111	N26652	N3R	N34WP	(N3184Z)	N123VP	HP-7JH				
124	550-0112	(N26656)	(C-GDPE)	C-GDPF	N550PS	N3FA	N213CF	YV2317			
125	550-0113	N2666A	N227PC	C-GDMF	C-FIMP	N90DA	N550KD				
126	550-0114	N2745G	(N89B)	N55HF	N88HF	N83HF	(N900BM)	N991BM	N819KR		
127	550-0115	N2745L	N127SC	SE-DDY	OY-CCU	SE-DDY					
128	550-0116	N2745M	HZ-AAA	HZ-AA1	PT-LGM	N413CA	N669MA	N575BW	N94PL		
129	550-0117	N2745R	N575FM	N150HR	N150HE	N550RB	N490DC				
130	550-0162	N2745T	VH-UOH	N550KP	N1UA	N85HD	N85HE				
131	550-0118	N2745X	LV-PHH	N131ET	N999BL	N162DW	EC-743	EC-FIL	N118EA	N138J	N650BP	N143BL
132	551-0163	N27457	N80BS	D-IGRC	ZS-ARG						
133	550-0378	N2746B	YV-299CP	N3999H	OH-CAT	D-CIFA	SE-RIK	PH-SVZ			
134	550-0121	N2746C	N655PC	OB-M-1195	OB-1195	N850BA	N51FT	N896MA	N899MA	N121HL	
135	550-0122	N2746E	N135CC	N70GM	C-FCEL	G-OSMC	HB-VKH	N221GA	C-GCUL	N89GA	
136	550-0123	N2746F	(CC-CGX)	N36CJ	N81TF	SE-DEV	LN-NEA	SE-DEV	LN-NLA	N748DC	N948DC	N550NT
137	550-0124	N2746U	LN-VIP	N4557W	N57MK	N57MF	N124CR	N109GA	(N789DD)		
138	550-0125	N2746Z	N5500F	N320S	N125RR	5N-NPF					
139	551-0169	(N2747R)	OE-GHP	N26863	N82RP	N82RZ	N50HW	N700YM	N14RM		
140	550-0103	N2747U	XA-JEZ	N90MA							
141	551-0171	N26178	(9V-PUW)	ZS-PMC	5R-MHF	N26178					
142	550-0184	N2619M	N80DR	N813DH	N200NC	(N20TV)					
143	550-0127	N2631N	N29TC	(N29TG)	N550TJ	G-GAUL	G-ESTA				
144	550-0128	N2631V	N536M	N220LA	YU-BPU	RC-BPU	9A-BPU	F-WLEF	EI-CIR	N60AR	EI-CIR	F-GJOB
145	550-0129	N2632Y	N537M	N129TC	N122MM	(N550RD)	N237WC				
146	550-0104	N2633N	CC-ECN	Chile E-301	CC-CLC						
147	550-0132	N2633Y	G-CJHH	N13627	N500VB	(N330MG)	PT-LLU				
148	550-0133	N2634Y	G-BHBH	C-GRIO	N228CC	N198NS	YV....				
149	551-0179	N2635D	HZ-AAI	HZ-ZTC	N203BE	N127BU					
150	551-0029	N26369	(G-BHGH)	N168CB	N551PL	N500ER	D-ICUR	N450GM	N35403	[w/o 01Jan05 Ainsworth, TX; parted out]	
151	551-0180	N8520J	(D-CACS)	N852WR	D-ICAB	N166MA	(N729MJ)	N222VV	D-IHAG		
152	551-0181	N2638A	N56GT	N137CF	N29B	N565VV	(N61442)	N551GE			
153	550-0138	N2646X	XC-SCT								
154	550-0139	N2646Y	ZS-KOO	N222MJ	PT-LJA	N39FA	PT-ORD	(PT-WQG)	OY-ELY	9H-LEO	
155	550-0140	N2646Z	N55WL	(N45WL)							
156	550-0141	N2646I	VH-ING	VH-INX	VH-EJY						
157	550-0142	N2648Z	PT-LCR	N387SC	N550TJ	YV....					
158	550-0143	N2649D	N100VV	N550TT	PT-LQW	(N660AC)	N150RD	N50JP	N507EC	[wfu Fort Lauderdale Executive, FL]	
159	550-0144	N2649E	RP-C689	N418MA	[w/o 18Nov03 Mineral Wells, TX]		N97315				
160	550-0145	N2653R	N444JJ	VH-TFQ	P2-MBN	P2-TAA	[w/o 30Aug10 Misima Island, Papua New Guinea]				
161	550-0146	N26610	N580AV	(N611RR)	N501LC						
162	551-0036	N2661P	N162CC	N160D	N317SM	N3170B	N889FA	VH-JMM			
163	551-0191	N222AG	N550CP	(N771R)	N107SB	D-IVOB	N127KR	N386AM	YV470T		
164	550-0149	N116K	N116KC								
165	550-0150	N2668A	N1SV								
166	550-0279	(N88838)	N566CC	N886AT	N566CC	N550KA					
167	550-0152	N88840	(N107)	RP-C581	N88840	N550CA	VH-FYP				
168	550-0153	(N88842)	N27BA	N278A	N50HS	N50HE	N27MH	N37MH			
169	550-0130	(N88845)	N77RC	N778C	N630CC						
170	550-0381	(N88848)	N170CC	N155PT	N155BT	(N49VP)	N391BC	N391KC	N381VP		
171	550-0154	(N8777N)	G-DJBE	G-EJET	G-JETJ	N80AX	YV600T				
172	550-0382	(N98715)	YV-300CP	N551TT	N852SP	N852SB	N852HA				
173	550-0383	(N98718)	N551AB	N561AS	[cx 22Apr13; CofR expired]						
174	551-0031	(N98749)	N6565C	YV-301CP	N75TG	N5T	N5TQ	EC-JTH	(N25AQ)	T7-XXV	(PR-EVC)	N25AQ
175	550-0155	N6566C	(YV-209CP)	YV-298CP	N65TF	N31RC	N155TJ	N168AM	N215CW	(N155FF)	C-FNCT
176	550-0156	N98784	N6567C	(N31F)	N205SG	N205SC	EC-IAX				
177	551-0201	N177CJ	C-GGSP	N550JB	N550GB	D-ISEC	EC-MCF				

CITATION II

Unit No	C/n	Identities									
178	550-0175	N10JK	C-FWWW	C-GHWW	N550CU	N1FM	N75WL				
179	550-0165	N98871	3D-ACQ	ZS-LHU	N976GA						
180	550-0166	N88731	PH-MBX	N166CF	N166VP	N367JC	N867JC				
181	551-0205	N88732	N999AU	XA-KIQ	N3951Z	N342DA	HB-VIO	N828SS	(N175TN)	N69AH	
182	550-0167	N88737	N100CJ	N717DT	YV182T						
183	550-0158	N88738	(N662AA)	N423D	N550AJ	N2JW	N49HS	N258CW	N769H	[parted out by White Inds, Bates City, MO]	
184	550-0168	N88740	(VH-ICT)	VH-TNP	VH-LJK	N785CA	VH-LJK	N68GA	ZS-NII		
185	550-0169	(N88743)	N185CC	N6001L	XC-JDA+	[+marks worn when flying Mexican Customs missions]			N6001L	[wfu]	
186	550-0170	N88791	N550TP	N550TR	N37BM	N500CV	N508CV	N550DA	YV3111		
187	550-0172	N88795	(N28MM)	N72MM	N88JJ	N78CS	N412P	N800TV	SE-RCZ	M-LEFB	
188	550-0171	(N88797)	(C-GDPE)	N43D	N934H	(N984H)	N333CG	EI-BYN	(N171VP)	N19AJ	N1TY
189	550-0234	N88798	N511WC	C-FLPD	N65DA	N173AA	(N353HA)				
190	551-0214	N8881N	N107T	N163DA	N178HH	N9SS	N800CU	N71KG			
191	551-0215	N88822	(N36NW)	N286G	N169JM	(N169DA)	N550HP	(N151PR)	N500PX	N551CL	
192	550-0179	N88824	N60MM	N673LP	N673LR						
193	550-0180	N88825	N320V	N77WD	N77WU	N3030C	(N303GC)	(N89TA)	N3030T	N219MS	(N619MS)
194	550-0181	N88826	RP-C653	N550GP	N50US	N50VS					
195	550-0182	N88830	(F-BKFB)	F-GCSZ	N78TF	F-GEFB	N30XX	N165MC	(F-....)	N107CF	F-HACA	[cx to Denmark 09Apr09 but no
		Danish marks allocated]									
196	551-0050	N98403	N1823B	N196HA	N196HR	N228AK	N228MH				
197	550-0186	N98418	N80AW	YV-187CP	N80AW	N676CM					
198	550-0187	N98432	N303X	N143DA	N6WU	N57CE	N57CK	C-GHOM	N598CA	N111GJ	
199	550-0218	N98436	N45EP	PT-LPP	(N250DR)						
200	551-0223	N98468	(N200MR)	N550LP	LN-AFG	5B-CIS	LN-AAC	N754AA	YV-2567P	(N28GZ)	YV1776
201	550-0174	(N98510)	N201CC	N666WW	N87PT						
202	550-0151	(N98528)	N35HC	N495CM							
203	550-0176	N98563	N552TF	N900TF	(N900TE)	N900TJ	N83SF	N83SE	(N24TR)	N61MA	
204	551-0023	N98599	N155TA	N34DL	PT-LME	[w/o 23Jly03 Sorocaba, Brazil]					
205	550-0189	N98601	D-CAAT	HB-VGP	D-CCCF						
206	550-0183	N98630	(XC-DUF)	HB-VGS	G-JMDW	G-CGOA					
207	550-0188	N98675	VH-SWL	HB-VIZ	N38NA	N280PM					
208	550-0147	N98682	N155JK	N80GM							
209	550-0190	N98715	F-BTEL	F-GZLC	F-BTEL	F-GZLC	EC-JON				
210	550-0083	N98718	N54CC	N200VT	YV....						
211	550-0164	N164CC	N7YP	(N24PT)	N916RC	N721DR	[cx 12Sep13; wfu]				
212	551-0033	N88692	D-IJHM	[w/o 19May82 Kassel, Germany]							
213	550-0191	N88707	C-GWCR	C-GWCJ	N550PA	YV2968					
214	550-0192	N88716	N44ZP	YV-900CP	N192DW	N941BB					
215	550-0249	N88718	N829JM	(N401U)	N201U	PT-LZO	(N48NA)	N39GA	N456AB	N456TX	
216	550-0159	(N88721)	N45ZP	N188SF	C-GAPT	N444GB	N550PW				
217	550-0194	N88723	N91B	C6-PCA	N519RJ						
218	550-0205	(N88727)	N30JD	XB-SGT							
219	550-0196	N6798Y	N68DS	N1212H	N800EC	N88ML	N400DK	HB-VLS	N196JS	N104WV	
220	550-0197	N6798Z	(N30F)	N44FC	HB-VIT	N510JC					
221	550-0198	(N67980)	XC-DOK	XA-SQV							
222	550-0199	N67983	N586RE								
223	550-0260	N67986	N32JJ	N82JJ	N8CF	N6HF					
224	551-0245	N67988	N224CC	LN-AAE	[w/o 15Nov89 Mt Langfjelltind, nr Bardufoss, Norway]						
225	550-0200	N67989	(G-BHVA)	N34SS	N287	N28S	N284	N810MC	(N810MG)	N797SF	N606KK
226	550-0206	N6799C	XC-DUF	XA-SQW	N280TA						
227	550-0201	N6799E	N334AM	N566TX	N1GH						
228	550-0185	N6799L	N815GK	N600EZ	N370AC	N511DR	N511DL	N317HC	N550RT		
229	550-0157	N6799T	N550K	N101BX	N257CW	N535PC	N61HT				
230	550-0202	N6799Y	N590RB	N10CF	(N5GA)	N175VB	N550NE	N704DA			
231	550-0203	N67990	N12JA	N62HA	N766AE	(N766AF)	(N857BT)	YV252T			
232	550-0209	N67997	N121C	N101KK	(N877GB)	N444G					
233	550-0238	N67999	N97S	N204CF							
234	550-0207	N6800C	(N95CC)	N163CB	N60BB	N1823C	HB-VJH	N207BA	N196RJ		
235	550-0135	N6800J	VH-KDI	N39142	ZS-LLO	N555BC	TF-JET	N555BC	N550BP	YV-888CP	YV2103
236	550-0214	N6800S	N13BJ	N44WF	N75Z	N75ZA	YV205T	YV2443			
237	550-0222	N6800Z	N17RG	PT-LNC							
238	550-0215	N68003	N500WP	(N400MT)	N40MT	N550MJ					
239	550-0204	(N6801H)	N820	N200JR	(N300PR)	N815CE	YV474T				
240	550-0216	N6801L	N240AR	(N911NJ)	N550PG	(N304TH)	XA-...				
241	550-0208	N6801P	N54RC	N222WL	[parted out, cx Mar91]						
242	550-0223	N6801Q	N900BA	N901RM	N701RM	N400PC	N81TJ	N239CD	N550WL		
243	550-0284	N6801R	I-ARIB	OY-JEV							
244	550-0211	N6801T	XA-LOT	N611CF	N77PH	N77PR					
245	550-0212	(N6801V)	N245CC								
246	551-0038	N6801Z	D-IBPF	N550DA	N103M	N551BB	YU-BTT				
247	550-0210	N68018	N762PF	(N177CM)	N3PC	N37WP	(N3184V)	N19VP	XA-SDN	XA-KMX	N850PM	XA-...
248	550-0220	N6802S	N95CC	N275CC	N288CC	HI-500	HI-500SP	HI-500CT	N80513	(N962HA)	N4CS	N4ZS	N123RF
		N614SJ	YV....									
249	550-0193	N6802T	(N47RP)	XC-FOO	XC-ROO	N2160N	N492ST	N72FL	N260J	N485AK	PP-CST
250	550-0213	N6802X	N420P	N421TX	N550HB	N213CC					
251	550-0224	N6802Y	YV-O-MTC	YV-O-MTC-20	Venezuela 2222						
252	550-0228	N6802Z	(N702BC)	5N-AWJ	N96CS	VH-EXM	N334ED	N334RJ			
253	550-0221	N68026	N253W	N95AX	N31GA						
254	550-0227	N68027	N254CC	(N71CG)	PT-LND	N227DR	XA-GMP				
255	550-0229	N6803E	N550JM	OY-GRC	N50FC	C-FGAT	N229MC				
256	550-0239	N6803L	8P-BAR	N4720T	N66MC						
257	550-0235	(N6803T)	N67SG	I-PNCA	D-CNCA*						
258	550-0225	(N6803Y)	(N34SS)	N258CC	PT-LTJ						
259	550-0195	N68032	N60JD	(N41CK)	N61CK	N343CM					
260	550-0236	N68033	N611ER	N611CR	N711VR	LN-AAD	N823NA	N550G	[cx 26Aug15; wfu]		
261	550-0248	N6804C	N550SA	N233ST	N125RG						
262	550-0226	N6804F	N29WS	N300JK	N550RG	N772HP	N872RT	N872RD	YV2596		
263	550-0217	N6804L	N88DD	N66DD	N66DN	N340DA	I-CIGA	N217SA			
264	550-0237	N6804M	3D-ACT	ZS-NHO	N41WJ	XA-LFJ					
265	550-0230	(N6804N)	(G-OTKI)	N3254G	N270RA	N141DA	N550EK	N550WB	N558WB	PR-NFT	
266	551-0285	N6804S	(N550RL)	N551SR	ZS-MLN	Venda VDF-030		ZS-MLN			
267	551-0046	N6804Y	C-GDDC	N34YL	N81GD	N518MV					
268	550-0241	N6804Z	N10FN	N268J	(N32TJ)	XC-BCS	N241FT	XA-TQL	N241FT	VH-EUV	P2-EUV
269	550-0390	N6805T	N58GG	(N500EE)	N500AE	N135BC	N136BC	VT-VPS	N14RZ	N717LC	
270	550-0250	N68599	N9LR	N33GK	N250VP						

CITATION II

Unit No	C/n	Identities									
271	550-0231	N6860A	N28RF	(N221BW)	N671B	N88TB	N140DR	N148DR	N41SM	N922RV	
272	551-0289	N6860C	N98GC	N666JT	N551BW	PT-LJF					
273	550-0243	N6860L	TI-APZ	VR-BHG	N1333Z	XA-POR	XA-REN	N214MD	N67SF		
274	550-0307	N6860R	N37BM	N550VW							
275	550-0254	N6860S	N171CB	XA-TEL	(N828SH)	N112SA	N888RT	N888RL			
276	550-0247	N6860T	(N18DD)	N928DS	PT-LJJ	(N85NA)	[dbr Manhuacu, Brazil, 07Oct11; wreck dumped at Belo Horizonte/Pampulha, Brazil]				
277	551-0035	N6860U	N277HM	N277JM							
278	551-0039	N6860Y	ECT-023	EC-DOH	N71LP	N550TA	N551GF				
279	550-0245	N68607	N505GP	N388SB							
280	550-0257	N68609	XC-HEQ	XA-SQQ	N187TA	N53RG	F-HCRT				
281	550-0303	N6861D	(N281AM)	N160VE	N40FJ	N4JS	N450CC	XB-GLZ			
282	550-0246	N6861E	N72TC	N78TC	N69ME	(N396DA)	N68ME	N35BP	N551TK	N550BP	[w/o 04Jun07 Lake Michigan nr Milwaukee, MI]
283	550-0255	N6861L	I-DEAF	N28GA	I-JESO	D-CIAO					
284	550-0232	N6861P	N929DS	N797CW							
285	550-0258	N6861S	N172CB	(N550DD)	N550CM	N463C	N550FB	N258JS	N550PR	N424TG	N752GS [cx 12Aug14; parted out by Atlanta Air Salvage, Griffin, GA]
286	550-0256	N6861X	N3300L	N550SM	N550BM	N75HS	N75TP	N55TP	N111AF		
287	550-0251	N68615	PK-WSO	PK-TRV	N550HF	N20FB	XA-GYA	XB-NCR			
288	550-0261	N68616	N40GS	C-FLDM	N41JP	C-FLDM	(N261VP)	N261SS	N50AZ	N551WL	
289	550-0259	N68617	VH-KDP	N810JT	OY-BZT						
290	551-0304	N6862C	G-DJHH	G-TIFF	N7028U	N702KH	N304KT	N999MK	N551NH		
291	550-0393	N6862D	N12GK	I-FLYD	N228AM	I-GGLB					
292	550-0264	N6862L	N550KC	N777WY	N771WY	N610JC					
293	550-0265	N6862Q	(N314MC)	(N265QS)	CN-TKK	N16PL					
294	550-0252	N6862R	N507GP	N6JL	N6JU	N525JA					
295	550-0253	N68621	N23ND	N18ND	N31DA	N75EC	N202TS	N953FT	N157DW	N127JM	
296	550-0266	N68622	N296CC	N296PH	N296CF	OE-GEC	N15NA	N825JW	N825JV	N550TT	N550TP	N330DK
297	550-0267	N68624	N932LM	N15Y	(N194JM)	N502BG	XA-OAC	N910RB			
298	550-0268	N68625	N298CJ	N500EX	N500FX	N38TT					
299	550-0289	N68629	D-CBAT	OE-GST	N550MD	N820FJ	N820SA	N22HP	C-FTIL	C-FTMS	VH-JMK	P2-JMK	VH-JMK
300	551-0313	N6863B	OE-GLS	N270CF	YV-2426P	YV1820					
301	551-0051	N6863C	(D-IHAT)	D-ICTA							
302	550-0269	N6863G	N74MG	N760	N28RC	N1MM	N28RC	N1MM	N550HJ	N550TR	
303	550-0271	N6863J	(N303EC)	N555EW	N655EW	N550CA	N303J	PT-ORO	N167MA	N729MJ	N1NL	N320JT
304	550-0290	N6863L	VH-JBH	OE-GCH	N290BA	N217LG	N312NC				
305	550-0285	N6863T	N20CN	N20CF	(N17PL)	N40PL	N989TW	N989TV	C-GQCC		
306	550-0286	N68631	N306SC	SE-DLY	N78BA	N2GG	N2GQ				
307	550-0272	N68633 N247JM	9M-WAN	VH-JPK	HB-VKX	VR-BVV	VP-BVV	SE-DVV	Sweden 103001	SE-DVV	YU-BVV	N550SM
308	550-0273	N68637	N217FS	N121KM							
309	550-0277	N6864B	N44LF	(N550MT)	N550WJ	N550BJ	YV2332	Venezuela 1113			
310	550-0274	N6864C	ZS-LDK	N14GA	HB-VKT	VP-CCM	EC-HJD	N75GA	XB-JLJ	N2057H	
311	551-0323	N6864L	(N990Y)	N819Y	N555RT						
312	551-0056	N6864X	(N312CC)	I-GAMB	N214AM	I-NIAR	N36WJ	N826RT			
313	550-0280	N6864Y	N280MH	N864D	N300TC	N7SN	C-GKAU				
314	550-0281	N6864Z	N31RK	N33EK							
315	550-0282	N68644	G-JETC	G-JCFR	G-JETC	[b/u Southend, Essex, UK, Jan13; fuselage to Bedworth, Warks, UK, 2013, then to Hangar Number 4 Restaurant, Warrington, UK, as customer attraction 2014]					
316	550-0283	(N68646)	N316CC	N316CF	N316CC	TC-BAY	N124GA	N225J	N257DW		
317	550-0287	N68648	N444MM	N65LC	N67LC	N920E	YV-909CP	N550RL	N771AA	(N221JS)	N527DS	YV2788
318	550-0276	N68649	C-GGFW	N53FT	[parted out by White Inds, Bates City, MO]						
319	550-0288	N6865C	G-JETB	N4564P	G-JETB	G-MAMA	G-JETB	(G-OXEH)	[w/o 26May93 Eastleigh, Southampton, UK]		
320	550-0291	N6887T	ZP-PNB	ZP-TNB	N550CD	N41C	N1AF	N40MA	N262Y	[w/o 01Oct10 Manteo, NC; parted out by Atlanta Air Salvage, Griffin, GA]	
321	550-0292	N6887X	N114EL	(N63FS)	C-FTOM	C-FTOC	C-GTDK	C-GREK	N554GR		
322	550-0293	N6887Y	[w/o 19Dec92 Billings, MT; cx May93]								
323	550-0294	N68872	PH-HET	N323CJ	PT-LPN						
324	550-0298	N68873	N74KV	N431DS	D-ILCC	N888FG					
325	550-0295	N68876	N483G	N800LA	N345JR	(N295EA)	N339MC	N48KH			
326	550-0296	N6888C	G-BJIR	G-DWJM	[b/u Staverton, UK, Apr12; fuselage to Southend, UK, then to Milton Hall Primary School, Westcliff-on-Sea, UK, Mar16]						
327	550-0304	N6888D	N208TC	N369DA	(N70PH)	N42PH					
328	550-0299	N6888L	N538M	HB-VIR	N511AB						
329	550-0302	N6888T	N329CC	N441T	N133BC	N33BC	N792MA	(SE-RCX)	SE-RCY	[to instructional airframe, Stockholm/Skavsta, Sweden]	
330	550-0306	N6888X	N303EC	N550MT	N341CW	N296CW	N206AG	VH-NSB	N539CC	[cx 04Dec15; wfu]	
331	550-0396	N6888Z	N8AD	N99DE	N99CN	N289CP	(N289CR)				
332	550-0300	N68881	YV-162CP	YV2246							
333	550-0310	N68887	N130TC	(N779DD)	(N730TC)	N779DD	N7798D	N530P	LV-CFS		
334	551-0059	N68888	N114DS	N59FA	N59FY	N59DY	CC-ARV				
335	550-0312	N6889E	N58H	N61HA	N61CF	YV-1055CP	YV255T				
336	550-0313	N6889K	(N393HC)	N393RC	N246NW	N960CP	N32TM	N32TK	N941JP		
337	550-0311	N6889L	N43TC	N43TE	N44TC	N121CP	N2RC	N211SP	N300GC		
338	550-0398	N6889T	VH-BRX	N101DD	I-KESO	(N550SC)	N398S	PH-CTX	N610ED	N707LM	
339	550-0318	N6889Y	N642BB	PT-LJT	PT-WJZ						
340	550-0315	N6889Z	N90JD	N618DB	N59GU	SE-RBK	(LN-AWF)	N833JP			
341	550-0308	N68891	3D-AVH	N30SA	(F-GIRS)	N15XM					
342	550-0399	(N6890C)	N66MS	N165RD							
343	550-0320	(N6890D)	N343CC	N300GM	N800SB	N800EL	N800VJ	N3MB	N57MB	N204PM	
344	551-0351	(N6890E)	N7FD	N612CC	N27U	N322CS	N5TR				
345	550-0319	N6890G	N8BX	N26SC	N26CT	N76CK	N78CK				
346	550-0316	N5428G	N143RW	N42KC	N129TS	N741JC	N26HH				
347	550-0321	N5430G	N321SE	TC-COY	N321GN	VP-CCO	YU-FCS	PH-MKL	D-COMK	6V-AIQ	F-HAJX
348	551-0355	N5451G	N551AS	I-ALPG	F-HHHH	T7-JET					
349	550-0327	N5474G	N74JA	N74JN	PT-LLT						
350	550-0400	N5492G	N350CC	N888EB	N53CC	[w/o 02Oct89 Roxboro, NC; cx Jul90]					
351	550-0323	(N5703C)	OE-GCP	TC-FAL	TC-FMB	TC-YZB	(N323AM)	VP-CLD	N550LD		
352	550-0324	N5873C	N171LE	I-JESJ	N23W	HB-VLQ	F-HBMB	OM-PTT			
353	551-0359	N67983	(N551SE)	N142TJ	N740JB	5Y-WEC	[not delivered; still wearing N740JB at Wichita/Mid-Continent, KS, May11]				
354	551-0360	N67988	G-BJIL	N550MD	C-GSCR	N24CJ	N551EA				
355	551-0361	N6799C	LV-PNB	LV-APL	LQ-APL						
356	550-0275	N6799L	N550JR	N550CP	N555DS						
357	550-0301	N6799T	China 091	B-4103	B-7024						
358	550-0333	N67990	PT-LCW	N313CE	N123GM	N365WA					
359	550-0305	N67999	China 090	B-4105	B-7026	[w/o 28Mar11 Xinjiang Uygur Region, China]					
360	550-0329	N6800C	(N49N)	N491N	N949SA	N939SA					
361	550-0334	N6800S	N92LT	N404KS	N755BP	N44FR					

CITATION II

Unit No	C/n	Identities									
362	550-0297	N68003	China 092	B-4104	B-7025						
363	551-0369	N696A	N999GP	N998GP	N68BK	N778JC					
364	550-0401	N6825X	N242WT	(N551GC)	N550KT						
365	550-0335	N6829Y	N1847B	N1847P	N51PS	N667CG	N204AB	N235TS	N187JN	YV3188	
366	550-0402	N6830X	N700LB	N717PC	N57SF	N624RL					
367	550-0336	N6830Z	N90Z								
368	550-0337	N6802S	N727C	N75F	(N78BA)	N54HJ	(N54HC)	N406SS	N3FW	N93AJ	
369	550-0326	N6802T	N12FC	PT-OAF	(N983AJ)	N390AJ	(N390JP)	YV589T			
370	550-0339	N6802Y	VH-KTK	VH-SCD	VH-EEE						
371	550-0403	N68027	N101RL	N637EH	N362CP	N404BS	Venezuela 0403				
372	550-0332	N6803L	N372CC	N1880F	N12CQ	N120Q	C-FFCC				
373	550-0341	N68032	C-GJAP	N182U	C-FDYL	N141JC	(N367EA)				
374	550-0340	N6804F	N374FC	N219SC	N219CS	N219SC	N235DB	ZP-TWN	N38DD		
375	551-0378	N6804L	G-BJVP	N4581Y	(N43D)	N115VH	N6EL	(F-OGUO)	(F-OGVA)	N322MA	
376	550-0345	N6804Y	N312DC	N3GT	N30CZ	N267TG	N267TC	(N782NA)	(N50NA)	N982NA	(N982LC)
377	551-0060	N6805T	N465D	N46SD	N458HW	(N458H)	(N60HW)	N59GB			
378	550-0344	(N6806Y)	N6806X	N532M	PT-LKR	N550GM	C-GVGM	N550GM			
379	550-0357	N6808C	N632SC	N29G	HB-VJA	N29FA	PT-OAG				
380	550-0347	N6826U	ZS-LEE	VH-ZLE							
381	550-0348	N381CC	I-VIKI	N550CA	C-GSCX	XA-RIV					
382	550-0346	N550CF	N106SP	N106SR							
383	550-0349	N6801L	N8FD	N870PT	(N221LC)	N600ST	N600SZ	N525LC	N61CS		
384	550-0350	N86SG									
385	550-0405	YV-276CP	YV-604P	YV-778CP	YV1813						
386	550-0351	N99KW	I-ALKA	(N167WE)	N351CJ						
387	551-0388	N68321	N711WM [w/o 06Nov86; no details known; cx Nov87]								
388	550-0354	N121CG	N121C	VR-CJR	VP-CJR	SE-RBD	S5-BBG				
389	550-0358	N6801Q	Myanmar 4400								
390	550-0356	N6801Z	PT-OER	N133WA	N21UA						
391	550-0343	(N1214D)	G-MINE	N721US	N20GT	N56FB	A6-SMS	G-ORCE	N789TT		
392	551-0393	N1214H	(N18CC)	N122SP							
393	550-0352	(N1214J)	(N140DV)	N140V	(N72B)	I-ALKB	N352AM	VT-EUN	N352DA	N550WJ	
394	550-0363	N1214S	(N777NJ)	N444CC	HK-3400X	N363SP	N741T	(N46NR)			
395	551-0396	(N1214Z)	N395CC	N39K	N39KY	N45GA	LV-WXD				
396	550-0362	N12142	N396M	(N440PJ)							
397	550-0353	(N12149)	G-GAIL	N3251H	N922RA	N922RT	LN-AAB	N922RT	N477KM	N353FT	YV2959
398	550-0406	(N1215A)	N398CC	C-GHKY	N551CE	C-FTAM	N781SC	LV-ZPD	N815MA	[w/o 04Jan09 Wilmington, NC]	
399	550-0366	N1215G	N200E	N2008	N773LP	N55FM	(N614GA)	N110LD			
400	551-0400	(N67983)	N550WR	N95CT	N280JS	D-IMME					
401	550-0407	(N1215S)	N600CR	(N767TR)	N758S	(N950FC)	N55MV	YV2619			
402	550-0368	(N12155)	N94ME	N94MF	N718CK						
403	550-0364	N12157	N100AC	N550AV	C-GLTG	N180FW	N10VT	N420KH			
404	550-0365	(N12159)	N712J	N100AG	N100AY	N129DV	N122WW				
405	550-0367	(N1216A)	N95CC	N17LK	N17LV	N3MB	N45ML	LV-FWA*			
406	550-0408	N1216H	N400TX	N110WA	N82ML						
407	550-0409	N1216J	N22T	HI-496	(N22TZ)	HI-496SP	N7153X	VR-CIT	N102HB		
408	550-0410	N1216K	(N258P)	N46MK	N46MF	C-GNWM					
409	550-0411	N1216N	N200YM	C-FMPP	N550KW	[cx 29Aug12; wfu]					
410	550-0412	N1216Q	N410CC	N830VL	N223J	N450KD	[cx 23Nov15; wfu]				
411	550-0355	(N1216Z)	N122CG	N125CJ	N440TX	N500BR	N355DF	N52LT			
412	551-0412	N12160	G-OMCL	N413VP	OY-PDN	EC-KJR					
413	550-0414	N12162	N342CC	(N414VP)	N814AM	N503BG	N983AG*				
414	550-0415	N12164	D-CNCI	OH-CUT	N1949B	N1949M	F-GJYD	EC-KJJ	9H-TRT	EC-MAM	
415	550-0416	N12167	N416CC								
416	550-0417	N1217D	ZS-LHW	N17DM	N303SD						
417	550-0418	N1217H	N550J	N418CG	N214JT						
418	550-0419	N1217N	G-JETD	VH-JVS	G-WYLX	G-DCFR	G-FJET				
419	550-0420	N1217P	N200RT	N200RN	(N10PX)	I-AGSM	N555KT	N585KT			
420	550-0421	N1217S	N67HW	N510GP							
421	551-0421	N1217V	N421CJ	OO-RJE	SE-DEF	OE-GES	N550RD	D-IAWA	3A-MRB	G-LUXY	
422	550-0423	N12171	N45MC	C-GUUU	C-FCCC	N248HA	N15WT				
423	550-0424	(N12173)	N18CC	N46A	(N469)	N24AJ	N555DH	N271CG	N551BP	N435UM	C-FHLG
424	550-0425	N1218A	(LN-FOX)	Spain U.20-1/01-405							
425	550-0426	N1218F	N404SB	N434SB	(N426SP)						
426	550-0427	N1218K	N923RL	PT-LHY	N527EA	N840MC	N840MQ	N711CC	YV2855		
427	550-0428	(N1218P)	N7004	N7864J	N107WV	N97BG	N550PF				
428	551-0428	N1218S	(N70HC)	(N147RP)	[w/o 22Dec99 Crisp County-Cordele, GA; cx Jun00]						
429	550-0430	N1218T	N264A	N1278	HB-VLY	N567S	N56FT	XB-AGV			
430	551-0431	N1218W	N21EH	N218H	N900TN	N59CC	(N431JC)	N4MM	N4NM	N551GS	
431	550-0369	N1218Y	(N342CC)	N324CC	N431CB	N55MT	N725BA	N725BF	N725FL	N181EB	
432	550-0433	N1219D	I-KIWI	N131GA	N7ZU	C-GMJN					
433	550-0434	(N1219G)	N1109	N1178	(N515M)	N152JC	(N152JQ)	(D-CVAU)	N53FP		
434	550-0435	(N1219N)	N434CC	N20CL	N390DA	N674G					
435	550-0436	N1219P	N711Z	N717DM	N717TR						
436	551-0436	N1219Z	N235KK	N437CF	N11SS	N102DR					
437	550-0438	N12190	(N555TD)	N437CC	N643TD	N100CH	N686RC				
438	550-0432	(N12191)	N432CC	I-ASAZ	N76AS	(N258TT)					
439	550-0439	N1220A	ZS-LHT	N550RS	HK-3191X	N550RS	N511WS	N1250V			
440	550-0440	(N1220D)	N31F	N31FT	N120TC	OY-CYV					
441	550-0441	N1220J	N50LM	N56PC	VR-CCE	HB-VKS	N221GA	G-RVHT	N80LA	G-JETO	(CN-...)	N476RS
442	550-0442	(N1220N)	N32F	N53M	N943LL	N442MR	N442ME	N668AJ			
443	550-0443	N1220S	N777FE	N777FB	OY-CYT	D-CGAS	EC-IMF				
444	550-0444	(N1248G)	N67MP	(N67ME)	N47SW	N71GA	C-FMJM	C6-...			
445	550-0445	N1248K	(N666WW)	N453S							
446	550-0446	N1248N	Spain U.20-2/01-406								
447	550-0447	"N1248K"	N12482	(N447CJ)	HB-VIS	G-JBIS					
448	550-0448	N1249B	N964J	N309AT	N82GA	N93DW	(N39HD)	N938W	N994CF	N994CE	
449	550-0449	N1249H	(YV-1107)	YV-2338P	Venezuela 1107	YV-2338P					
450	550-0450	N1249K	N15EA	N505RP	N899RJ						
451	550-0451	N1249P									
452	550-0452	(N1249T)	N452CJ	N150DM	N707WF	N707PE	N707PF				
453	550-0453	N1249V	N962JC	N962J							
454	550-0454	N1216K	(N258P)	N12490	N93BD	N938D	(N250KD)	N905MH			
455	550-0455	N1250B	(YV-04CP)	N90SF	PT-MMO						
456	550-0456	N1250C	(N456CM)	N549CC	N24RF	N20RF	C-GMPQ	N283DF			

Unit No	C/n	Identities										
457	550-0457	N1250L	N220CC	N457CF	N63TM	OY-TMA						
458	550-0458	N1250P	N458CC	(N458DS)	XA-SET	N25MK	N664SS	LV-BCO				
459	550-0459	N12500	N15TW	N15TV	N315ES	N604PJ						
460	550-0460	N12505	N818TP	N818TB	(PT-...)	N6523A	PT-OKP					
461	550-0461	N12507	N22FM									
462	550-0462	N12508	N509TC	N67JW	XA-LTH	XB-LTH	N501DK	N550AL	N62TL	(N550DK)		
463	551-0463	N1251B	N121JW	(N131EL)	YV-05C	YV-713CP	YV1563					
464	550-0464	N1251D	XC-HEP	XA-SQR	N117TA	N822HA						
465	550-0465	N1251H	N206TC	N68JW	HB-VIU	N784A	N387HA	N551WJ	N90PT			
466	550-0466	N1251K	HI-420	(N1251K)	HI-420	N1251K	I-TNTR	N412MA	N10LY			
467	550-0467	N1251N	N1883	N64PM	N64CM	YV-810CP	YV2166					
468	550-0468	(N1251P)	N468CJ	D-CBEL	N123FH	N120JP						
469	550-0469	N1251V	G-BKSR	VR-BIZ	HB-VIP	N123SR	N50N	[crashed 18Oct01 Bolzano A/P Italy; cx Nov01]		(OY-ERY)	N50N	(I-....)
		(OY-...)	N420SS	N550GT								
470	550-0470	N1251Z	N10RU	F-GFJL	N10RU	N202SW	N60FT					
471	550-0471	N12510	N797WC	N787WC	N92B	(N623KC)	N271AG	N770TB	N1HE			
472	550-0472	N12511	HZ-AFP	N12511	N492MA	N492AT	[w/o 24Jan07 Butler, PA; parted out]					
473	550-0473	N12513	HZ-AFQ	N12513	N484MA	XB-HZF	N70224	XB-IZK	XC-LLL			
474	550-0474	N12514	ZS-LIG									
475	550-0475	N1252B	N870MH	N475WA	N475HC							
476	551-0476	N1252D										
477	550-0477	N1252J	N1515P	N151JC	N648WW	N649WW	N47TW	(N477JR)	N269JR	N269JD	N344KK	(N846L)	YV210T
		YV2932										
478	550-0478	N1252N	N4FE	N57BC	N214RW	N17WC	N32SM					
479	550-0479	N1252P	N999RC	PT-OOM	N45NS	N68TS	N600HW					
480	550-0480	(N12522)	N72K	N72U	YU-BPL	SL-BAC	S5-BAC	N335CC	N380MS	ZS-OIE		
481	550-0481	N1253D	N550MW	D-IADD	N531A	CC-LLM	N481VP	N97EM	N97FM			
482	550-0482	N1253K	N62GC	N62WG	N594G	N99DY	N550WR					
483	550-0483	(N1253K)	N141AB	N483AS	N83AG	N147PS	N483SC	N412PE	N17FS	N17VP	N729TA	N917BB
484	550-0484	N1253N	N84EA	N501GG								
485	550-0485	N1253P	N474SP	N74SP	N485A	PT-WBV	N727C	PR-LJJ				
486	550-0486	N1253Y	A4O-SC	N410CS	(N35PN)	XA-AAK	XA-ATA	CC-AHQ				
487	550-0487	N12532	(N487CC)	N444BL	N550DW							
488	550-0488	N12536	N84EB	C-FCSS	N990MM	N990MR						
489	550-0489	N12539	N63CC	N15RL	(N801TA)	N489SS	N121MJ					
490	550-0490	N1254C	N490CC	(N490CD)	J8-JTS							
491	550-0491	(N1254D)	I-AVRM	D-CVRM	[stored Rome/Ciampino, Italy]							
492	550-0492	(N1254G)	I-AVGM	D-CVGM	[stored Rome/Ciampino, Italy]							
493	550-0493	N1254P	(N258P)	N84AW	N84GC							
494	550-0494	N1254X	XC-JBR+	[+marks worn when flying Mexican Customs missions]								
495	550-0495	(N1254Y)	N495CC	JA8495	N505GL	PT-LLQ	(N400MC)	N10TC				
496	551-0496	(N12543)	N232CC	N8008F	N999GH	LX-PRS	LN-ACX	OE-FAD	9A-DOF			
497	550-0497	(N12549)	N1257B	XC-JBQ+	[+marks worn when flying Mexican Customs missions]			N1257B				
498	550-0498	(N1255D)	N550CJ	N1823B	N78FK	N772SB						
499	550-0499	(N1255G)	N550PT	PT-LIV								
500	551-0500	N1255J	N90RC	N501MC	N9CR	N568PC						
501	550-0501	N12549										
502	550-0502	N1255D	Turkey 12-001		Turkey 84-007		Turkey 007					
503	550-0503	N1255G	Turkey 12-002		Turkey 84-008		Turkey 008					
504	550-0504	(N1255J)	N979C	N979G	N72SL	XA-TQA						
505	550-0505	N1255K	XC-JAY+	[+marks worn when flying Mexican Customs missions]			N1255K					

Unit numbers 506 to 549 not used (506 to 531 built as S550s c/n 0001 to 0026 – qv)

550	550-0550	N1299N	PT-LOC	N550FM	HK-4128W	N550FM	N177RJ			
551	550-0551	N487LD	N600AT							
552	551-0552	OE-FPA	D-IADV							
553	550-0553	N553CC	N46MT	XA-ODC	(N555SL)	N5XR	N553MJ			
554	550-0554	N1297Y	ZS-NAT	N2140L	N40FC	(N40WE)	N40YC	N700JR	(N705JT)	N750SL	N758SL
555	550-0555	N1297Z	(EI-BUN)	EI-BUY	D-IRKE	N93BA	N560CB	N104HW	[parted out by Dodson Int'l, Rantoul, KS]		
556	551-0556	(N12979)	N200GF	N513WT							
557	550-0557	N1298C	N711NV								
558	550-0558	(N1298G)	N209G	N558VP	N558AG	LV-WJN					
559	550-0559	(N1298H)	G-BNSC	VR-CHB	D-ICHE	OO-MMP	N409ST				
560	550-0560	N1298J	ZS-LNP	N560AJ	D-IMMF	N550GX	(YV....)				
561	550-0561	N1298K	I-SALV	N916WJ	PT-OYP	(N234RA)	C-GYCJ	[canx 14Oct03 as sold in USA; to Dodsons Intl Parts following accident 12Nov02			
		Sandspit, BC, Canada]									
562	550-0562	(N1298N)	D-CBAT	N562CD	PT-OJT	N813A	N54RM	N45FS			
563	550-0563	N1298P	G-THCL	N518N							
564	550-0564	N1298X	PH-MCX	(N87683)	N564VP	C-GBCF	N674CA	D-CASH	[w/o 19Feb96 nr Freilassing, Salzburg, Austria]		
565	550-0565	N1298Y	N565CJ	N88BM	N565JS	N565NC	N568ST				
566	550-0566	(N1299G)	N15SP	N15SN	N900PB						
567	550-0567	(N1299H)	N321F	N41BH	N926RM	N191TF					
568	550-0568	N1299K	N988RS	N83KE	N47SM						
569	550-0569	N1299P	G-JFRS	G-OSNB	5Y-TWE	ZS-SCX	C-GQYL				
570	550-0570	(N1299T)	N2KH	N570VP	N570WD	N270CW	(N189WW)	(N550AZ)			
571	550-0571	N12990	N90JJ	(N278S)							
572	551-0572	N12992	N193SS	N719EH	D-IRUP						
573	550-0573	(N12993)	C-FJOE	N944AF	PT-OKM	N155AC	YV2831				
574	551-0574	N12998	N60GL	N60GF	OE-FBS	N22AA	N1RV*				
575	550-0575	N12999	N910G	N46BA	N337RE	N387RE					
576	550-0576	(N1300G)	N576CC	N438SP	N675SS	(N183JN)	PR-MGT				
577	550-0577	(N1300J)	N557CC	N100CX	N120HC	N827JB	N8344M				
578	550-0578	N1300N	PT-LQJ	N54NS	N203PM	N15DF					
579	550-0579	(N13001)	N579L	N750TB							
580	550-0580	(N13006)	N912BD	N18NA							
581	550-0581	(N13007)	N905LC	N805LC							
582	550-0582	(N1301A)	Colombia FAC1211								
583	550-0583	N1301B	N62WA	(N583VP)	N12L	N12LW	N22PC	(N22PQ)	(N228G)		
584	550-0584	N1301D	N550WW	N550WV	N25QT	N25QF	N979WC				
585	550-0585	N1301K	C-GTCI	N94AF	N79SE	N89SE	N65AR	N585PS	VP-CRA	N585RA	
586	550-0586	N1301N	F-GGGA								
587	550-0587	N1301S	ZS-MBX	N550SM	N1301S	N18HJ					
588	550-0588	N1301V	N255CC	N92BD	(N747RT)	N633RT					
589	550-0589	N1301Z	N679BC	N787JD	N589SJ	N12LD					

CITATION II

Unit No	C/n	Identities									
590	550-0590	C-GBCA	N673CA	N88NM	XA-UGG	XB-OFK	N941SC				
591	551-0591	C-GBCE	N672CA	N1AT	N608JR						
592	550-0592	N1302N	Spain U.20-3/01-407								
593	550-0593	N1302V	N26621	XC-JBT+	[+marks worn when flying Mexican Customs missions]				N26621		
594	550-0594	N1302X	N2531K								
595	550-0595	N2734K	XC-JCV+	[+marks worn when flying Mexican Customs missions]							
596	550-0596	N96TD	D-CAWA	EC-HGI							
597	550-0597	N13027	G-SSOZ	G-MRTC	N24EP	N400LX	N400EX	N213JS			
598	550-0598	N13028	(PT-...)	XC-ROO	N7WY	N888XL					
599	550-0599	G-SYKS	N599FW	VR-BPF	VR-BYE	N571BC					
600	550-0600	N1303H	PT-LSR	N415AJ							
601	550-0601	(N1303M)	G-ELOT	G-OCDB	G-CBTU	N42NA	N501RL				
602	550-0602	N2663Y	XC-JAZ+	[+marks worn when flying Mexican Customs missions]				N2663Y			
603	550-0603	N603CJ	C-GMSM	N560AB	N550TW						
604	550-0604	N821G	N30WE	LV-WIT	N64VP	N827JB	N887SA	N904SJ			
605	550-0605	N26494									
606	550-0606	N770BB	N602AT								
607	550-0607	N26496	XC-JCW+	[+marks worn when flying Mexican Customs missions]				N26496			
608	550-0608	N12419	PT-LTL	(N675DM)	N608VP	N608AM	N990M				
609	550-0609	(N1242A)	N609TC	D-CHOP	N344A	F-GLTK					
610	550-0610	N1242B	"M-JMF"	9M-JMF	(9M-UEM)	9M-NSA	N610BL	N610JB	YV2875		
611	550-0611	(N1242K)	F-GGGT								
612	550-0612	N1244V	N300AK	N380AK	(N534M)	N578M					
613	550-0613	N1250P	PT-OAC	N664AJ							
614	551-0614	(N1251P or N1251V)	D-ILAN	N26HG							
615	550-0615	N12522	N88HF	N87CF	CS-AYS	N615EA	N577VM	N577VN	N803SC		
616	550-0616	(N1253K)	N55LS	(D-IAFA)	PT-OVV	N611NM	(PP-ONA)	PR-OLB			
617	551-0617	(N1253Y)	N617CM	D-ILTC	N450GM	N747JB	N881SA	N40EP	(N551GK)		
618	550-0618	N1254C	PT-LXG	PP-ESC							
619	550-0619	(N1254D)	N170TC	(N619BA)	N550BD	XA-LRL	N15FJ	N522FJ	N552FJ	N67BE	
620	550-0620	N1254G	PT-LYA	N250GM	N508DW	(N508AJ)	N477JE	(N391DH)	N391DT		
621	550-0621	N12543	ZS-MLS	N502SU	OY-RDD	N102PA	N99TK				
622	550-0622	(N1255J)	N326EW	N826EW	HB-VKP	LX-VAZ	F-HAJV				
623	550-0623	(N1255L)	N89LS	PR-VIR	PR-VLJ*						
624	550-0624	N1255Y	PT-LYS	N662AJ	N65DV						
625	550-0625	(N12554)	PT-LYN	N625EA	N6846T	(F-HCCN)	F-HBFK				
626	550-0626	(N1256G)	N117GS	N626VP	LV-PLR	LV-WOZ	N466SS				
627	550-0627	(N1256N)	N17FL	N650WC	N804BC	N494GP					
628	550-0628	(N1256P)	N183AJ	N183AB	Ecuador IGM-628						
629	550-0629	N1256T	D-CHVB	[w/o 25Jan95 Allendorf, Germany; cx Mar95]							
630	550-0630	N1257K	PH-CSA	N220AB	N198DF	N198ND	PP-CMG	N18GY			
631	550-0631	(N1257M)	N631CC	XA-RUD	XA-ICP	N631EA	N631TS				
632	550-0632	N12570	5N-AYA	Nigeria NAF050		Nigeria NAF960					
633	550-0633	N12576	PT-OSK	N388FA	N7AB	N550AB					
634	550-0634	(N1258B)	PH-MDX	N550SB	SE-DVT	F-HDGT	EC-LBO				
635	550-0635	N1258H	PT-OAA	N550NS	(N622EX)	N622VH	(N214CP)	N277JE	N550HW	N760M	
636	550-0636	N1258M	N4EW	N50NF	YV565T						
637	550-0637	(N1258U)	YV-376CP	YV2286							
638	550-0638	(N12582)	N500RR	N1717L	N255TC						
639	550-0639	(N1259B)	N22RG	N62RG	N100DS						
640	550-0640	(N1259K)	N1308V	PT-ODL							
641	550-0641	(N1259N)	N1309A	PT-OOA	N1309A	PT-WON	N395HE	(N391DT)	N895HE	N996AC	
642	550-0642	(N1259R)	N1309K	XA-JRF	XA-SEX	XB-TTT					
643	550-0643	(N1259S)	N13091	PT-ODW	N643MC	N747CR	G-EJEL				
644	550-0644	(N1259Y)	(N13092 or N1310B)	XC-PGM							
645	550-0645	(N1259Z)	N1310C	PT-ODZ							
646	550-0646	(N12593)	(N1310G)	N9VF	N562RM						
647	550-0647	(N12596)	N647CC	N205BE	N140MD	N800MT	N604DS	YV603T			
648	550-0648	N1260G	(N1310Q)	XC-PGP	[instructional airframe, Instituto Politecnico Nacional Centro de Estudios Cientifico y Tecnologicos, Mexico City, Mexico]						
649	550-0649	(N1310Z)	I-ATSE	N4320P	N44LC	N44LQ	HB-VMH	N649DA	G-SOVA	VH-VDF	
650	550-0650	(N1311A)	PK-WSG+	[+ marks worn but not officially reg'd]	N28RC	N824CT	N823CT	C-GBBX	N38MR	N50CZ	N569GB
		XB-BRT	XB-ODN								
651	550-0651	(N1131K)	N24E								
652	550-0652	(N1311P)	N3262M	XC-HJF+	[+marks worn when flying Mexican Customs missions]						
653	550-0653	N36854	N30RL								
654	550-0654	N36886	XA-RZB	XB-BON	XB-LWN						
655	550-0655	N37201	XC-LHH+	[+marks worn when flying Mexican Customs missions]							
656	550-0656	N30GR									
657	550-0657	N3986G	CC-DGA								
658	550-0658	N550MZ	RP-C1180	N137PA	RP-C5538						
659	550-0659	N4614N	XC-HGZ+	[+marks worn when flying Mexican Customs missions]							
660	550-0660	N5233J	D-CMJS	5B-CIQ	N550JF	D-CILL	N160SP	N827DP	[w/o 03Aug08 Reading, PA; parted out by AvMATS, St Louis, MO]		
		N825LH	[cx 27Jun11]								
661	550-0661	N5252C	N550RA	N847HS	N3444B	N3444P	XA-AFU	N550AR	VT-CLB		
662	550-0662	N5294C	N911CB	N911QB	N623DS	N623JL	XA-UME				
663	550-0663	N5314J	XC-JCX+	[+marks worn when flying Mexican Customs missions]							
664	550-0664	N5315J	N67LH	XA-RYR	N70PC	N45BE					
665	550-0665	N5348J	N665MC	N998BC							
666	550-0666	(N5703C)	N5408G	XC-JBS+	[+marks worn when flying Mexican Customs missions]						
667	550-0667	EC-621	EC-FDL	N668EA	VR-CWM	VP-CWM	N167EA	N107EE			
668	550-0668	N668CM	N1879M	(N866VP)	XA-TVH	N48PJ					
669	550-0669	N6170C	N98TJ	N6170C	N846HS	N677GS	VH-CFO	P2-SOS	VH-VBK	N881JG	N425WY*
670	550-0670	N6637G	XC-JCZ+	[+marks worn when flying Mexican Customs missions]							
671	550-0671	(N6761L)	9M-TAA	N671EA	G-BWOM	G-VUEA	[cx 15Sep14; wfu Cambridge, UK]				
672	550-0672	N6763C	PT-OMB	N550PF	G-OTIS	(N394MA)	OY-VIS	SE-RHP	G-IBZA		
673	550-0673	N6763L	XC-HHA+	[+marks worn when flying Mexican Customs missions]			[w/o Greenwood, SC, 17Nov12]				
674	550-0674	(N6770S)	(N550FB)	N1883M	N1888M	N45TP	N65TP	N910HM	N918HM	N690AN	XB-ACS
675	550-0675	N6773P	XC-OJK	N275BD	PT-WKQ						
676	550-0676	N67741	PT-OJG								
677	550-0677	N6775C	XC-HJC+	[+marks worn when flying Mexican Customs missions]							
678	550-0678	N6775U	EC-777	EC-FES	SE-RCI	EC-KBZ					
679	550-0679	(N6776P)	I-FJTO	N250GM	N622EX	N782ST	(N64JY)				
680	550-0680	N6776T	XC-HJE+	[+marks worn when flying Mexican Customs missions]							
681	550-0681	(N6776Y)	N1200N	XC-LHA+	[+marks worn when flying Mexican Customs missions]						
682	550-0682	N682CM	YV-662CP	N682CJ	N90BL	N90BY	N73HH				

Unit No	C/n	Identities							
683	550-0683	YV-701CP	YV1192						
684	550-0684	N6778L	C-FJXN						
685	550-0685	C-FJWZ							
686	550-0686	C-FKCE							
687	550-0687	N6778Y	C-FKDX						
688	550-0688	C-FKEB							
689	550-0689	N12001	XA-JPA	XA-JYO	N689VP				
690	550-0690	N6780C	OE-GLZ	VH-VLZ	M-AGGY	D-CAAB*			
691	550-0691	N910H	C-GAPD	C-GAPV	N600JB				
692	550-0692	N692TT	N75RJ	N814LC					
693	550-0693	VR-BTR	VP-BTR	N594WP					
694	550-0694	N694CM	N550KE	N807MB					
695	550-0695	N6782T	N695VP	N870WC	N7851M	N77DD	N153TH	N466SG	
696	550-0696	N29PF	N67PC	N67NC	N696VP	(N74EH)			
697	550-0697	N6851C	ZS-NFL	N697EA	HB-VMP	D-CHEP	N697BA	LV-BRE	
698	550-0698	N12003	YV-911CP	N550RM	VT-CLC				
699	550-0699	C-FKLB							
700	550-0700	C-FJCZ							
701	550-0701	C-FLZA							
702	550-0702	C-FMFM							
703	550-0703	N308A							
704	550-0704	N704CD	(N197GH)	N197HF	(N187HF)	N197PR			
705	550-0705	N521TM							
706	550-0706	7Q-YLF	N706NA	N168ES					
707	550-0707	N1202T	RP-C4654	(SE-DYY)	N707EA	OE-GDM	HS-RBL	OE-GRD	SX-FDA
708	550-0708	N12022	N720WC	N923JH					
709	550-0709	N1203D	N709CC	N12RN	N18RN	N85KC	N709VP	N709RS	VT-SGT	N425ST
710	550-0710	N1203N	ZP-TCA	N510VP	N90BJ	N678GS			
711	550-0711	N1203S	N711CN	N58LC	XB-ZZZ	N711ZC	N53DD		
712	550-0712	(N12030)	PH-LAB						
713	550-0713	N12033	N293PC	N95HE	N283CW	N400EC			
714	550-0714	N12035	N593EM	G-SPUR					
715	550-0715	N1204A	PT-OTN	N715AB	LV-PNL	LV-YHC			
716	550-0716	N1205A	N4VR	(N800KC)	VR-CTE	VP-CTE	VP-CTF	N550TL	XA-...
717	550-0717	(N1205M)	XA-TCM	N600GH	TC-SES	Sweden 103002	SE-RBM	OE-GBC	F-HBMR
718	550-0718	N12060	XA-FIR	N142GA	N129ED	N550HM			
719	550-0719	N12068	(N550BG)	YV1504	YV2766				
720	550-0720	(N1207A)	N720CC	XA-SMV	N72WE	N848HS	N260TB	N550MW	
721	550-0721	N1207B	N721CC	YV3023					
722	550-0722	N1207C	XA-SMT	N1886G	N220LE	PP-JAS			
723	550-0723	N1207D	N5NE	(N888NA)	N777JE	PR-SNV			
724	550-0724	N1207F	LV-PGU	LV-WEJ					
725	550-0725	N1207Z	N222FA	N725CC					
726	550-0726	N1209T	XT-AOK	N918GA	VP-CMD	N726BM	N726AM	XA-CSM	
727	550-0727	(N1209X)	N727CM	N521BH	LV-ZNR	N232JS	N550DG	N550KR	VT-CLD
728	550-0728	(N1210N)	N728CC	LV-PHN	LV-WJO				
729	550-0729	N1210V	VR-CBM	VP-CBM	N38NA				
730	550-0730	N1211M	N730BR	(N730VP)	N2NT	N773VP	(N650JP)	N501JP	XA-WWG	XA-UPX
731	550-0731	N12117	N550BP	XC-SST					
732	550-0732	N1213S	N101AF	N902DK	N36WL	N232KS			
733	550-0733	N1213Z	C-GFCI	N4347F	N550VR	N550TR	N44SW	N37HF	YV....
734	550-0734	[first Bravo model]	(N1214J)	N550BB					

Production continued as Citation Bravo

CITATION BRAVO

C/n	Identities							
550-0801	N5135K	N801BB						
550-0802	N5135R	N802CB	N550HH					
550-0803	N52113	N550FB	N141HL	N251CF	N251CM			
550-0804	N5214J	N804CB	N550BC	(N41VY)				
550-0805	N5214K	N108RF	N4AT					
550-0806	N52141	N300PY	C-GKUT	N100RJ				
550-0807	N52144	C-FANS	C-GPGA	C-FJDS				
550-0808	N5216A	N1299B	SE-DVZ	YU-BSM	M-SGCR			
550-0809	N800AK	N300AK	N380AK	(N35KT)				
550-0810	N5218T	VH-MGC	VH-XCJ	VH-XBP				
550-0811	N5221Y	PT-MMV						
550-0812	N5223P	C-FJBO	N808MV	N238EJ				
550-0813	N5096S	N813CB	N100KU	YV611T				
550-0814	N5093L	PT-WNH	N303CS	C-GOKO				
550-0815	N51038	N126TF						
550-0816	N5225K	C-FMCI	N550HK					
550-0817	N5076J	N817CB	(YV....)	N123GF	N550RZ			
550-0818	N5097H	LV-PMV	LV-WYH	N818AJ	N300CS	YV521T		
550-0819	N5092D	N1259B	N15CV	N15CN	N324JT			
550-0820	N5117U	N820CB	N302CS	N774KD	N779KD			
550-0821	N5093Y	N77797	N225WT	N129LT				
550-0822	N5214L	N550TG	N822CB	N52MW	N2029E	N725DS		
550-0823	N50715	(N823CB)	N25FS					
550-0824	N5121N	N824CB	N26AP					
550-0825	N5060P	N25HV	(N45HV)	N305CS	N717TF	N717RA	N717CH	
550-0826	N51072	N595PC						
550-0827	N51042	D-CCAB						
550-0828	N5058J	N6FR						
550-0829	N5096S	N829CB						
550-0830	N5076J	(N550KE)	N830KE	N717CB				
550-0831	N5145P	N331PR						
550-0832	N5148B	PT-WSO	N832UJ	N77VZ	N109DC			
550-0833	N5145P	PT-WVC	N833PA	PR-FEP				
550-0834	N834CB	D-CALL						
550-0835	N835CB	N198SL	(N835VP)	(N10PZ)	N226PC			
550-0836	N51872	N122NC						
550-0837	N5185J	OE-GPS						
550-0838	N49FW	N49KW	N813JD					
550-0839	N839DW	N101FG	N101ND	N80PT				
550-0840	N5086W	N442SW	N773CA	N256PH				
550-0841	N5086W	N841WS	N841W	N999CX				
550-0842	N86AJ	N842CB	N621KR	N621KM				
550-0843	N5079V	N627L	AP-BHE					
550-0844	N550KL							
550-0845	N51817	N550WS						
550-0846	N5101J	N517AF						
550-0847	N5076K	N133AV	N304CS	N544PS	N584PS	(N550JN)		
550-0848	N997HT	N550J						
550-0849	(N849CB)	N51143	N541JG	N246CB	N315N	N623N	N71LU	N560JA
550-0850	N5073G	N551G	N551V					
550-0851	N7NN	N711KT						
550-0852	N5076J	VH-FGK	[w/o Lismore, Australia, 05Sep15]		N674ND	[parted out by Dodson Int'l, KS]		
550-0853	N5086W	N398LS						
550-0854	N5188A	N550KH	N550KJ	XB-FIR				
550-0855	N132LF	N232JR	XB-LVV	XA-LVV				
550-0856	N820JM	N300GF	N300GP	N426JK	N103CX			
550-0857	N51246	VP-CNM	VP-CCP	N984BK				
550-0858	N1273Q	N100WT						
550-0859	N551KH	(N550KH)	I-BENN					
550-0860	N860JH	(N860J)	N844DR	N220DH				
550-0861	N861BB	N26CB	N26CV	N577MC				
550-0862	N442SW	N1962J	N888HS	N1967J	N467HS			
550-0863	N704JW	N709JW	N577VM					
550-0864	N864CB	OE-GTZ	D-CCWD	HB-VOH	TJ-ROA			
550-0865	N505X	D-CPPP	OE-GRM	OM-ATS				
550-0866	N866CB	D-CHZF						
550-0867	N161TM							
550-0868	N5117U	N627BC						
550-0869	N98RX	N499WM						
550-0870	N50612	VP-CED	M-ISKY					
550-0871	N5108G	N871CB	I-GIWW	D-CIWW	N1Q	N76RB		
550-0872	N5093L	OE-GKK	5N-IZZ	G-SPRE				
550-0873	N5109R	PT-XSX						
550-0874	N5194B	D-CHAN	LX-EJH	D-CHMC	N237MB			
550-0875	N51055	TG-BAC	N800AB	N877SD	N7CP			
550-0876	N5135A	N876CB	5Y-MNG					
550-0877	N5085J	N21SL						
550-0878	N5135K	VH-ZLT						
550-0879	N5000R	N4M	N35ET					
550-0880	N5112K	N7YA						
550-0881	N5105F	N546MT	(N312RD)	N306CS	N546MT	N306CS	N108MV	
550-0882	N5068R	N488A	N12MA	N438SP	VH-VFP	N882WF		
550-0883	N469DE							
550-0884	N5090Y	N602BW	N1318Y	N361DB	VP-CGL	D-CSWM	N50W	
550-0885	N5109W	N820JM	N88AJ					
550-0886	N550KH	N500TS	N139RN					
550-0887	N887BB	XA-ABE						
550-0888	N550BF	N162TJ	(N218G)					
550-0889	N619JM	N360HS	N368HS					
550-0890	N1961S							
550-0891	N5093L	N82MA	N86PC					
550-0892	N22GR	(N84CF)						
550-0893	N5073G	N333EB						
550-0894	N51160	N550TE	N107EG	N413ST				

C/n	Identities							
550-0895	N199BB	N87GS	N17FS					
550-0896	N121L	N58WV	N157WW					
550-0897	N5079V	EI-GHP	G-GHPG	N897SC	LV-CVC			
550-0898	N550GH	N149HC						
550-0899	N5076K	N899DC	N535SW	N235BS				
550-0900	N327LJ	N327LN	N214TJ	N138CA				
550-0901	N5058J	N857AA						
550-0902	N5095N	N770JM	N770UM	N688JD	N898BA			
550-0903	N51055	N14HB	N903VP	PR-ERP				
550-0904	N5093Y	N904BB						
550-0905	N5101J	N505AG						
550-0906	N5166T	C-GLCE	N850GM	D-CSSS	HB-VNZ	N906MS		
550-0907	N5155G	N316MA	HB-VMM	SX-BMK				
550-0908	N5264M	N242SW	(N208FC)					
550-0909	N5076J	N706CP	(N909CA)	C-GDSH	N40KW	N44KW	N391BC	
550-0910	N5207V	N574M						
550-0911	N52655	N575M	[parted out by Alliance Air Parts, Oklahoma City, OK]					
550-0912	N5117U	N588AC						
550-0913	N5096S	N232BC	N66MT					
550-0914	N5105F	N897MC	N499GS	N399GS	N858RM			
550-0915	N51143	N915BB	N346CM	N348CM				
550-0916	N5265N	N555BK						
550-0917	N5100J	EI-DAB	(SE-RBY)	G-IDAB	G-MHIS	N127RG		
550-0918	N5109R	N45VM						
550-0919	N52601	N100Y	(N919TX)	N565AR				
550-0920	N5109W	N63LB	N854JA					
550-0921	N5073G	N40MF						
550-0922	N51896	I-FJTB	OE-GAH	N508UJ	N365EG			
550-0923	N51160	N676BB	N676PB	N23YC				
550-0924	N5090Y	XT-COK	N550VC	YU-BZZ				
550-0925	N5090V	N1305C	5N-DUK	N550PF	N10UH			
550-0926	N5154J	N72PB	N100Z	N144Z				
550-0927	N5061P	PH-DYE	G-OPEM	G-IPLY				
550-0928	N5000R	PH-DYN	(N928DA)	N928CB				
550-0929	N5086W	N552SM						
550-0930	N5066U	PP-ORM						
550-0931	N233DW	C-FAMJ						
550-0932	N5103J	G-MIRO	I-MTVB	5Y-BYD	9H-PAL			
550-0933	N5262X	N417KW	N325WP					
550-0934	N5260Y	N200AS						
550-0935	N5264A	EI-PAL	G-IPAL	G-IPAC	G-YPRS	HS-...		
550-0936	N5101J	N550TM						
550-0937	N51666	N440CE						
550-0938	N51038	N5VN	EC-HRO	LX-VVR	N938AM			
550-0939	N5076K	(N939BB)	VP-BNS	N48NS				
550-0940	N5263S	G-FIRM	N125JJ					
550-0941	N5093Y	N900SS	N878AG	4X-CPW	N796MA			
550-0942	N5095N	N72SG	N265TS	ZS-BVO				
550-0943	N5117U	N706CP	YV-2711P	YV266T	YV3086			
550-0944	N5267J	N723RE	(TG-PIB)	N813AK				
550-0945	N5109R	N585KS						
550-0946	N52229	HB-VMX						
550-0947	N947CB	N514BC	XA-UQO					
550-0948	N5264E	N49FW	N48FW					
550-0949	N550KG	N45NS	N49NS	N550WB				
550-0950	N555HM							
550-0951	N5076J	TC-TPE	N51KR	LN-SUV	G-CGEI			
550-0952	N5268V	N952CH	N749FF	N749FB	N811JA			
550-0953	N50612	N953GM	C-GZEK	N550WG	VH-CCJ			
550-0954	N5079V	PP-OAA						
550-0955	N50715	HB-VMW	EC-KHP					
550-0956	N51666	N572PB	N800VA					
550-0957	N51780	N957PH	G-IKOS					
550-0958	N5168Y	N333BD	N833BD	N404RK	D2-EPI			
550-0959	N5172M	N418KW	N511JP	N418KW				
550-0960	N52229	N960CB	TC-MKA					
550-0961	N5181U	N961BB	HK-4250X	HK-4250	N641L	HK-4597X	HK-4597	N960SC	N82P
550-0962	N5212M	N797TE						
550-0963	N52114	N24QT	N24QF	N990TC				
550-0964	N52234	HB-VMY	N550TA					
550-0965	N52086	N741PP	N965BB	N741PP	N256CC	XA-USS		
550-0966	N51806	N36PT						
550-0967	N52397	N967CB	N432RJ					
550-0968	N51612	N551G						
550-0969	N5228J	N401KC	N119LC					
550-0970	N5243K	N367BP	N78MD					
550-0971	N5239J	N717KQ	N717GK					
550-0972	N52462	PH-HMA	S5-BBL					
550-0973	N5245U	N129PB						
550-0974	N307CS	N307MS	OE-GAL					
550-0975	N975HM	5Y-MSR						
550-0976	N5168Y	N308CS	N308MS	OE-GML	N8892D	HS-MED		
550-0977	N5172M	N309CS	(OE-GLM)	OE-GLG				
550-0978	N52475	N696CM	N95AN					
550-0979	N5147B	N311CS						
550-0980	N51666	N312CS	N146CT	N67JB				
550-0981	N5093L	N313CS	N800MT					
550-0982	N5260U	C-GDSH	C-GVIJ	C-FMOS	C-FMOI	N156GW		
550-0983	N51055	XA-SDI						
550-0984	N5227G	VH-HVM	(N984VP)					
550-0985	N5269J	G-FCDB	G-EHGW	N410TG				
550-0986	N52690	N986PA	N45NF	N458F	XB-DBT			
550-0987	N51780	N987GR	N471WR	N500VA	N500VT	N998TS		
550-0988	N5174W	N32FJ	I-FJTC	(D-CFTC)	OE-GVR	E7-FRA	N524XA	(N275TA)
550-0989	N5270E	XA-LOF						

BRAVO

C/n	Identities					
550-0990	N5154J	N990JM	N448RL			
550-0991	N5270J	N4190A	N628CB	N628GB		
550-0992	N52086	N777NG	G-EKWS	D-COFY	EC-KKO	
550-0993	N5244W	N721T				
550-0994	N580SH	C-GLGB	C-GGQF			
550-0995	N550PD	5Y-SIR				
550-0996	N5270P	CC-LLM	Chile C-53			
550-0997	N5192E	N67BK				
550-0998	N5165P	OE-GHP	(D-CGHP)	D-CELI		
550-0999	N5270E	XA-UVA	XB-UVA	XA-GEN		
550-1000	N5194B	N121CN				
550-1001	N26CB					
550-1002	N52397	N101JL				
550-1003	N51743	N777UU	Pakistan 1003			
550-1004	N314CS	N114VP	N355DF	LV-CZD		
550-1005	N5247U	CS-DHA	N366EA	N847JJ	(N847JA)	N589HH
550-1006	N5212M	N106BB	N992HE			
550-1007	N51995	N717CB	N67PC	N67PV	N117VP	N664DF
550-1008	N5181U	N40435	D2-ECE			
550-1009	N5155G	CS-DHB	(LV-CZH)	N363CA		
550-1010	N5228J	N316CS	N116VP	N544PS	N116VP	
550-1011	N51780	C-FRST	N1000E			
550-1012	N20AU	N20RU	XA-GPO			
550-1013	N5166U	CS-DHC	N371EA	N886YS		
550-1014	N52475	N610CB				
550-1015	N5253S	N81ER	N81LR	N140TF	PR-PAB	
550-1016	N926ED	N926EC	N958GC			
550-1017	N51666	CS-DHD	N406CA	D-CYKP		
550-1018	N5259Y	SU-HEC	(D-CEFM)	OO-IIG	G-JBLZ	
550-1019	N5231S	N317CS	N117VP	N799JL	N519VP	N14CG*
550-1020	N5166T	N212BH	N219LC	N495MH	N447SF	
550-1021	N5174W	N49KW				
550-1022	N5168Y	CS-DHE	SE-DJH	LN-IDD		
550-1023	N4405	C-FEVC				
550-1024	N5254Y	N550FP	A2-BCL			
550-1025	N5172M	CS-DHF	N712BG	N712BD		
550-1026	N5180K	N552CB	N438SP			
550-1027	N52691	OO-FYG	N328SB	N299RK		
550-1028	N442LW	N442LV	C-FYUL	C-GWUL	N831HS	N851HS
550-1029	N5270J	N318CS	N118VP	N550AR		
550-1030	N52397	N322GT				
550-1031	N525PE					
550-1032	N5223X	N880CM	N910N	N31AD		
550-1033	N52114	N933BB	N701VV			
550-1034	N52086	CS-DHG	N802CA			
550-1035	N585TH	YV....				
550-1036	N319CS	N119VP	LV-CTF			
550-1037	N5180C	N1258B	YU-BTB	D-CKLS*		
550-1038	N551VB	(N551VP)	SE-RBY			
550-1039	N320CS	N711HA	N511HA	OE-GRB	N139JA	D-CESA
550-1040	N52446	N12378	OK-VSZ	OM-ATN		
550-1041	N5206T	N412ET	N7725D	N7765D	N31JB	XA-UTI
550-1042	N51869	G-ORDB	G-OJMW	M-WOOD		
550-1043	N52235	CS-DHH	N490CA			
550-1044	N52369	N141AB	PR-HCA			
550-1045	N52690	PP-BMG				
550-1046	N300GF	N900GF				
550-1047	N5231S	N889B				
550-1048	N5253S	CS-DHI	N484CA			
550-1049	N5267G	N249CB	N299HS	YU-BSG	[w/o 15Jul10 Brac, Croatia]	
550-1050	N5268E	N105BX	A9C-BXC	D-CMIX	OY-EVO	
550-1051	N5155G	N251CB	N745CC	VH-EYJ		
550-1052	N322CS	N152VP	CP-2790			
550-1053	N57MC	N57ME				
550-1054	N5239J	N254CB	N600ST	5R-MGX		
550-1055	N896CG					
550-1056	N52601	N45678	N5852K			
550-1057	N5245U	N714RM				
550-1058	N52691	VH-SCC				
550-1059	N324CS	N159VP	N693SV	ZS-SUA		
550-1060	N669B	N927MM				
550-1061	N5267K	N325CS	N161VP	PP-LCE		
550-1062	N662CB					
550-1063	N5268V	N96TM	N151TM	N6TM	(N166TM)	N335RJ
550-1064	N823PM					
550-1065	N326CS	N175CW	N896MA			
550-1066	N573M					
550-1067	N5085E	N6TM	N114TM	N44SW		
550-1068	N668CB					
550-1069	N5093Y	OE-GLL				
550-1070	N5296X	N327CS	XA-CAP			
550-1071	N5090A	N104FL	XB-MNV			
550-1072	N5148B	N143BP	YV2877			
550-1073	N899B					
550-1074	N328CS	N404LS				
550-1075	N5162W	N275BB	N8701L	N87011	N26T	
550-1076	N51872	N359GW	N550TT	VT-IBS		
550-1077	N329CS	N107VP	N336SC			
550-1078	N442NR	N807CT				
550-1079	N5268E	C-FRNG	N1271B	N444EA		
550-1080	N132MT	YV3183				
550-1081	N332CS	N181VP	N193PC			
550-1082	N5180C	CS-DHJ	N510CA	N550MK	N550ML	
550-1083	N5201M	I-PABL	G-PABL	G-PJDS		
550-1084	N52141	N338CS	N184VP	HI915		

C/n	Identities					
550-1085	N5068R	N339CS	N633PC			
550-1086	N52446	N58HK	G-OMRH	N623AR	N5171M	Argentina AE-186
550-1087	N5265B	[test marks not confirmed]		N151FD	N876BB	
550-1088	N153SG	N158SG	N188VP	5Y-CCB		
550-1089	N334CS	(N186VP)	N189VP			
550-1090	N51038	CS-DHK	N514CA	N942EB		
550-1091	N335CS					
550-1092	N52645	CS-DHL	N92VR			
550-1093	N5263D	CS-DHM	N93VR			
550-1094	N5109W	N308DT				
550-1095	N336CS	(N195VP)	LV-CQV			
550-1096	N52626	N877B	N707HP	VT-BNF		
550-1097	N5148B	N337CS	[stored Phoenix/Williams Gateway, AZ]			
550-1098	N5132T	CS-DHN	N363WC			
550-1099	N5180C	CS-DHO	N595VR	XA-MXN		
550-1100	N5203S	N110BR	G-WAIN	N110VR		
550-1101	N5264U	N342CS	C-FMCG			
550-1102	N5214L	N1276A	AP-BHD			
550-1103	N50612	LZ-ABV	N1276Z	LZ-ABV	HS-PSL	
550-1104	N52144	CS-DHP	N504VR			
550-1105	N5117U	N332MT				
550-1106	N341CS	N106VP	HI925			
550-1107	N51744	TC-AHE				
550-1108	N5181U	N717VL	N717VF	PR-BVO		
550-1109	N5212M	N1281A	CS-DHQ	N109VR		
550-1110	N877B	LV-CED				
550-1111	N5165P	OK-ACH	[w/o 14Feb10 nr Dresden, Germany]			
550-1112	N5202D	N47NM				
550-1113	N5218R	N724EH	N724EB	N569CC		
550-1114	N5223Y	N1298Y	CS-DHR	N114VR		
550-1115	N5223X	N4002Y	HZ-133			
550-1116	N52457	N4060Y	HZ-134			
550-1117	N52591	OO-FPB				
550-1118	N550CY	PR-SCP				
550-1119	N51072	N630JS	N230JS	N63NW	N1SU	N830TA	C-GBZF
550-1120	N5109W	N112BR	LV-BEU			
550-1121	N5061W	N1309B	9M-ZAB*			
550-1122	N5211Q	N984GB	OE-GEN	LZ-GEN	N396PB	PR-GPE
550-1123	N5212M	N106FT	N675SS			
550-1124	N5076K	N417JD	N417JP	N410PS		
550-1125	N5262X	VH-YXY	N28SP			
550-1126	N5233J	N12993	HZ-135			
550-1127	N52623	N1298P	HZ-136			
550-1128	N5296X	N23AJ	PR-MGB			
550-1129	N52059	N60LW	M-BRVO			
550-1130	N5125J	D-CSMB				
550-1131	N5227G	N110TP				
550-1132	N5165P	N338B				
550-1133	N5201M	N579M				
550-1134	N5068R	N412ET	N412BT			
550-1135	N5180C	D2-GES				
550-1136	N51743	N998SR	OE-GMV	LZ-GMV		

Production complete

CITATION 550 UNIT NUMBER CROSS-REFERENCE

C/n	Unit	C/n	Unit	C/n	Unit	C/n	Unit	C/n	Unit	C/n	Unit
550-0001	001	550-0082	091	550-0170	186	550-0249	215	550-0332	372	550-0430	429
550-0003	003	550-0083	210	550-0171	188	550-0250	270	550-0333	358	550-0432	438
550-0004	004	550-0084	093	550-0172	187	550-0251	287	550-0334	361	550-0433	432
550-0005	005	550-0085	100	550-0174	201	550-0252	294	550-0335	365	550-0434	433
550-0006	006	550-0086	096	550-0175	178	550-0253	295	550-0336	367	550-0435	434
550-0007	007	550-0089	088	550-0176	203	550-0254	275	550-0337	368	550-0436	435
550-0008	008	550-0090	085	550-0179	192	550-0255	283	550-0338	074	550-0438	437
550-0009	009	550-0091	121	550-0180	193	550-0256	286	550-0339	370	550-0439	439
550-0010	010	550-0092	114	550-0181	194	550-0257	280	550-0340	374	550-0440	440
550-0011	012	550-0094	101	550-0182	195	550-0258	285	550-0341	373	550-0441	441
550-0012	013	550-0095	102	550-0183	206	550-0259	289	550-0343	391	550-0442	442
550-0013	016	550-0096	103	550-0184	142	550-0260	223	550-0344	378	550-0443	443
550-0014	015	550-0097	104	550-0185	228	550-0261	288	550-0345	376	550-0444	444
550-0016	017	550-0098	105	550-0186	197	550-0262	282	550-0346	382	550-0445	445
550-0017	021	550-0099	109	550-0187	198	550-0263	061	550-0347	380	550-0446	446
550-0018	019	550-0100	110	550-0188	207	550-0264	292	550-0348	381	550-0447	447
550-0019	022	550-0101	111	550-0189	205	550-0265	293	550-0349	383	550-0448	448
550-0021	011	550-0102	112	550-0190	209	550-0266	296	550-0350	384	550-0449	449
550-0024	041	550-0103	140	550-0191	213	550-0267	297	550-0351	386	550-0450	450
550-0025	025	550-0104	146	550-0192	214	550-0268	298	550-0352	393	550-0451	451
550-0026	026	550-0105	116	550-0193	249	550-0269	302	550-0353	397	550-0452	452
550-0027	027	550-0106	117	550-0194	217	550-0271	303	550-0354	388	550-0453	453
550-0028	028	550-0108	119	550-0195	259	550-0272	307	550-0355	411	550-0454	454
550-0029	029	550-0109	120	550-0196	219	550-0273	308	550-0356	390	550-0455	455
550-0030	030	550-0110	122	550-0197	220	550-0274	310	550-0357	379	550-0456	456
550-0031	031	550-0111	123	550-0198	221	550-0275	356	550-0358	389	550-0457	457
550-0032	032	550-0112	124	550-0199	222	550-0276	318	550-0362	396	550-0458	458
550-0033	033	550-0113	125	550-0200	225	550-0277	309	550-0363	394	550-0459	459
550-0034	034	550-0114	126	550-0201	227	550-0279	166	550-0364	403	550-0460	460
550-0035	042	550-0115	127	550-0202	230	550-0280	313	550-0365	404	550-0461	461
550-0036	036	550-0116	128	550-0203	231	550-0281	314	550-0366	399	550-0462	462
550-0037	037	550-0117	129	550-0204	239	550-0282	315	550-0367	405	550-0464	464
550-0038	038	550-0118	131	550-0205	218	550-0283	316	550-0368	402	550-0465	465
550-0039	039	550-0121	134	550-0206	226	550-0284	243	550-0369	431	550-0466	466
550-0040	040	550-0122	135	550-0207	234	550-0285	305	550-0370	076	550-0467	467
550-0041	043	550-0123	136	550-0208	241	550-0286	306	550-0371	086	550-0468	468
550-0042	044	550-0124	137	550-0209	232	550-0287	317	550-0374	106	550-0469	469
550-0043	046	550-0125	138	550-0210	247	550-0288	319	550-0376	113	550-0470	470
550-0044	047	550-0127	143	550-0211	244	550-0289	299	550-0378	133	550-0471	471
550-0045	045	550-0128	144	550-0212	245	550-0290	304	550-0381	170	550-0472	472
550-0046	050	550-0129	145	550-0213	250	550-0291	320	550-0382	172	550-0473	473
550-0047	056	550-0130	169	550-0214	236	550-0292	321	550-0383	173	550-0474	474
550-0048	048	550-0132	147	550-0215	238	550-0293	322	550-0390	269	550-0475	475
550-0050	052	550-0133	148	550-0216	240	550-0294	323	550-0393	291	550-0476	476
550-0051	060	550-0135	235	550-0217	263	550-0295	325	550-0396	331	550-0477	477
550-0052	067	550-0138	153	550-0218	199	550-0296	326	550-0398	338	550-0478	478
550-0053	053	550-0139	154	550-0219	035	550-0297	362	550-0399	342	550-0479	479
550-0054	054	550-0140	155	550-0220	248	550-0298	324	550-0400	350	550-0480	480
550-0055	055	550-0141	156	550-0221	253	550-0299	328	550-0401	364	550-0482	482
550-0056	070	550-0142	157	550-0222	237	550-0300	332	550-0402	366	550-0483	483
550-0057	073	550-0143	158	550-0223	242	550-0301	357	550-0403	371	550-0484	484
550-0058	071	550-0144	159	550-0224	251	550-0302	329	550-0405	385	550-0485	485
550-0060	075	550-0145	160	550-0225	258	550-0303	281	550-0406	398	550-0486	486
550-0061	077	550-0146	161	550-0226	262	550-0304	327	550-0407	401	550-0487	487
550-0062	078	550-0147	208	550-0227	254	550-0305	359	550-0408	406	550-0488	488
550-0064	080	550-0149	164	550-0228	252	550-0306	330	550-0409	407	550-0489	489
550-0065	065	550-0150	165	550-0229	255	550-0307	274	550-0410	408	550-0490	490
550-0066	081	550-0151	202	550-0230	265	550-0308	341	550-0411	409	550-0491	491
550-0067	094	550-0152	167	550-0231	271	550-0310	333	550-0412	410	550-0492	492
550-0068	058	550-0153	168	550-0232	284	550-0311	337	550-0414	413	550-0493	493
550-0069	063	550-0154	171	550-0234	189	550-0312	335	550-0415	414	550-0494	494
550-0070	064	550-0155	175	550-0235	257	550-0313	336	550-0416	415	550-0495	495
550-0071	066	550-0156	176	550-0236	260	550-0315	340	550-0417	416	550-0497	497
550-0072	072	550-0157	229	550-0237	264	550-0316	346	550-0418	417	550-0498	498
550-0073	068	550-0158	183	550-0238	233	550-0318	339	550-0419	418	550-0499	499
550-0074	069	550-0159	216	550-0239	256	550-0319	345	550-0420	419	550-0501	501
550-0075	057	550-0162	130	550-0241	268	550-0320	343	550-0421	420	550-0502	502
550-0076	099	550-0164	211	550-0242	059	550-0321	347	550-0423	422	550-0503	503
550-0077	082	550-0165	179	550-0243	273	550-0323	351	550-0424	423	550-0504	504
550-0078	083	550-0166	180	550-0245	279	550-0324	352	550-0425	424	550-0505	505
550-0079	087	550-0167	182	550-0246	282	550-0326	369	550-0426	425		
550-0080	089	550-0168	184	550-0247	276	550-0327	349	550-0427	426		
550-0081	090	550-0169	185	550-0248	261	550-0329	360	550-0428	427		

Note: From c/n 550-0550 onwards, unit number and c/n are the same.

CITATION 551 UNIT NUMBER CROSS-REFERENCE

C/n	Unit	C/n	Unit	C/n	Unit	C/n	Unit	C/n	Unit	C/n	Unit
551-0001	–	551-0027	002	551-0059	334	551-0171	141	551-0289	272	551-0496	495
551-0002	014	551-0029	150	551-0060	377	551-0179	149	551-0304	290	551-0400	400
551-0003	024	551-0031	174	551-0071	023	551-0180	151	551-0313	300	551-0412	412
551-0006	020	551-0033	212	551-0095	051	551-0181	152	551-0323	311	551-0421	421
551-0007	018	551-0035	277	551-0117	079	551-0191	163	551-0355	348	551-0428	428
551-0010	049	551-0036	162	551-0122	084	551-0201	177	551-0359	353	551-0431	430
551-0017	062	551-0038	246	551-0132	097	551-0205	181	551-0360	354	551-0436	436
551-0018	095	551-0039	278	551-0133	098	551-0214	190	551-0361	355	551-0463	463
551-0021	107	551-0046	267	551-0141	108	551-0215	191	551-0369	363	551-0481	481
551-0023	204	551-0050	196	551-0149	118	551-0223	200	551-0378	375	551-0351	344
551-0024	092	551-0051	301	551-0163	132	551-0245	224	551-0388	387	551-0496	496
551-0026	115	551-0056	312	551-0169	139	551-0285	266	551-0393	392		

Note: From c/n 551-0550 onwards, unit number and c/n are the same.

CITATION CONVERSIONS

The following Citations have been converted from 550 to 551 or 551 to 550:

550-0002 to 551-0027
550-0020 to 551-0071
550-0030 to 551-0077
550-0040 to 551-0085 to 550-0040
550-0044 to 551-0092 to 550-0044
550-0049 to 551-0095
550-0059 to 551-0122
550-0063 to 551-0117
550-0074 to 551-0109 to 550-0074
550-0084 to 551-0129 to 550-0084
550-0087 to 551-0132
550-0088 to 551-0133
550-0092 to 551-0146
550-0093 to 551-0141
550-0098 to 551-0140 to 550-0098
550-0100 to 551-0143 to 550-0100
550-0107 to 551-0149
550-0118 to 551-0162 to 550-0118
550-0126 to 551-0169
550-0128 to 551-0174 to 550-0128
550-0131 to 551-0201
550-0134 to 551-0179
550-0136 to 551-0180
550-0137 to 551-0181
550-0139 to 551-0184
550-0148 to 551-0191
550-0160 to 551-0171
550-0161 to 551-0205
550-0163 to 551-0214
550-0177 to 551-0223 to 550-0177 to 551-0223
550-0178 to 551-0245
550-0240 to 551-0285
550-0244 to 551-0289
550-0246 to 551-0296
550-0249 to 551-0236 to 550-0249
550-0253 to 551-0308 to 550-0253
550-0262 to 551-0304
550-0266 to 551-0309 to 550-0266
550-0268 to 551-0311
550-0270 to 551-0313
550-0278 to 551-0323
550-0298 to 551-0335
550-0299 to 551-0339 to 550-0299

550-0306 to 551-0341
550-0313 to 551-0345 to 550-0313
550-0314 to 551-0396
550-0317 to 551-0355
550-0322 to 551-0351
550-0328 to 551-0360
550-0331 to 551-0369
550-0342 to 551-0378
550-0353 to 551-0398 to 550-0353
550-0359 to 551-0400
550-0373 to 551-0018
550-0397 to 551-0059
550-0413 to 551-0413
550-0420 to 551-0419
550-0422 to 551-0422
550-0429 to 551-0428
550-0435 to 551-0434
550-0437 to 551-0436
550-0450 to 551-0450
550-0452 to 551-0452
550-0476 to 551-0476
550-0459 to 551-0459
550-0460 to 551-0460 to 550-0460
550-0463 to 551-0463
550-0475 to 551-0475 to 550-0475
550-0476 to 551-0476 to 550-0476
550-0481 to 551-0481 to 550-0481
550-0485 to 551-0485 to 550-0485
550-0487 to 551-0487 to 550-0487
550-0490 to 551-0491 to 550-0490
550-0496 to 551-0496
550-0559 to 551-0559
550-0572 to 551-0572
550-0574 to 551-0575
550-0584 to 551-0584
550-0591 to 551-0591
550-0604 to 551-0604 to 550-0604
550-0617 to 551-0617
551-0004 to 550-00031
551-0005 to 550-0013
551-0008 to 550-0219
551-0009 to 550-0263 to 551-0009 to 550-0263
551-0012 to 550-0242

551-0014 to 550-0068
551-0016 to 550-0338 to 551-0016 to 550-0338
551-0018 to 550-0373
551-0019 to 550-0371
551-0020 to 550-0374
551-0022 to 550-0376
551-0025 to 550-0378
551-0026 to 550-0377 to 551-0026
551-0029 to 550-0379 to 551-0029
551-0030 to 550-0383
551-0032 to 550-0382
551-0047 to 550-0390
551-0048 to 550-0307
551-0049 to 550-0381
551-0050 to 550-0385 to 551-0050
551-0052 to 550-0228
551-0053 to 550-0399
551-0055 to 550-0400
551-0057 to 550-0402
551-0058 to 550-0403
551-0059 to 550-0397 to 551-0059
551-0062 to 550-0406
551-0065 to 550-0396
551-0066 to 550-0401
551-0077 to 550-0030
551-0084 to 550-0039
551-0109 to 550-0074
551-0296 to 550-0246
551-0311 to 550-0268
551-0335 to 550-0298
551-0341 to 550-0306
551-0345 to 550-0313
551-0351 to 550-0322
551-0419 to 550-0420
551-0445 to 550-0445
551-0496 to 550-0496 to 551-0496
551-0551 to 550-0551
551-0555 to 550-0555
551-0557 to 550-0557
551-0559 to 550-0559
551-0560 to 550-0560
551-0567 to 550-0567
551-0584 to 550-0584

CESSNA S550 CITATION II

C/n	Unit No	Identities									
0001	(0506)	(N1255L)	N95CC	(N969MC)	(N36H)	N969MC	N969MQ	N151DD	N86BA	(N550VS)	
0002	(0507)	(N1255Y)	(N507CC)	N507CJ	N111VP	N211VP	CC-CWW				
0003	(0508)	(N12554)	(N21AG)	N847G	N847C	N847G					
0004	(0509)	N1256B	N830CB	N554CA	N72AM	N178DA					
0005	(0510)	(N1256G)	N666LN	N123FF							
0006	(0511)	(N1256N)	N101EC	N71FM	N71EM	N27MH	(N66EA)	N29EA	N65DT	N181G	
0007	(0512)	(N1256P)	N51JH	N573CC	TC-SAM	N30CX	CS-DCE	OO-MMJ	CS-DCE	OO-SKP	EC-LQF
0008	(0513)	(N1256T)	N40PL	SE-DKI	N204A	(N40KM)	N600KM	[dbr Nov11; cx 24Sep12; parted out by Air Care Inc, Warsaw, IN]			
0009	(0514)	N1256Z	N550A	N165JB	N819EK						
0010	(0515)	(N1257K)	N651CC	N49MJ	N47MJ	XA-INF	XA-INK	N747RL	N747KL	N422MJ	N550F	N829TG
0011	(0516)	(N1257M)	N68SK	N211QS	N25GZ						
0012	(0517)	(N12570)	N550TB	N550RV	N777GG	YV....					
0013	(0518)	(N12576)	(N518AS)	N277AL	N389L	N561PS	N551PS	N84LG			
0014	(0519)	(N12583)	N32JJ	N32TJ	N214QS	N777AM	N84EC				
0015	(0520)	(N1258U)	C-GMTV	N600EA							
0016	(0521)	(N1259B)	(N99VC)	N85MP	N557CS						
0017	(0522)	(N1259G)	(N47LP)	N1259G	N88G	(N1259G)	(N188G)	N88GD	N86PC	N413CT	
0018	(0523)	(N1259K)	N501NB	N814CC	N1AF	N145DF	N627X	N614JK			
0019	(0524)	(N1259M)	N15TT	N519CJ	N29AU	N119EA	(N600VE)	N550TB	N670JD	N670DD	
0020	(0525)	(N1259R)	N550AS	N550JT							
0021	(0526)	(N1259S)	N593M	N693M	N320DG	N945ER					
0022	(0527)	(N1259Y)	N258P	N360M	N460M						
0023	(0528)	(N1259Z)	N420CC	N94RT	N293RT	N500ZB					
0024	(0529)	(N12593)	PT-LGI	N34NS	N790AL						
0025	(0530)	(N12596)	PT-LGJ	[w/o 06Sep88 Rio-Santos Dumont, Brazil]							
0026	(0531)	(N1260G)	N19AF	(N126LP)	N24PH	N24PF	N32TX				
0027		N1260K	D-CBUS	N27EA	N27FP	N5WC	C-GSSK	N4HK	N112BR		
0028		(N1260L)	HB-VHH	S5-BAX	9H-MCM						
0029		(N1260N)	N185SF	N608LB	HB-VMJ	N257JC	C-FBDS				
0030		(N1260V)	N7007V	N7007Q	(N999GL)	N999HC	N509RP				
0031		(N12605)	N531CC	N50DS	N54WJ	N50BK	[w/o 13Aug02 Big Bear, CA]				
0032		(N1261A)	N532CC	N532CF	N232QS	CS-DNA	N232WC	N48BV			
0033		(N1261K)	(G-BLSG)	G-BLXN	N550ST	N531CM	N581CM	N256CP			
0034		(N1261M)	OE-GAP	N34CJ	N59EC	N610GD	N220BP				
0035		(N1261P)	N712S	N711JG	N711JN	XA-THO	N834DC				
0036		(N12615)	N95CC	N36H	N36HR	N27B	N63JG	N63JU	N63CR	C-FRGY	C-FOBQ	N308GL
0037		(N12616)	C-GERC	N72WC	N573BB	N578BB	N12S				
0038		N3D	N1982U	N100KP	(N801CC)	N214PN	N406CT				
0039		N22UL	YV....								
0040		(N1269D)	C-FEMA	[instructional airframe, Stevenson Aviation & Aerospace Training Centre, Portage La Prairie, Canada]							
0041		(N1269E)	N772M	N592M	N692M	N74BJ	N74LM	[retro-fitted with Williams FJ44 engines]		ZS-BEN	
0042		(N1269J)	N250AL	N250AF	N241DS						
0043		(N1269N)	N101EG	(N727NA)	(N727AL)	N727NA	N727EF				
0044		(N1269P)	N92ME								
0045		N1269Y	YU-BOE	BH-BIH	T9-BIH	N97CC	N750JM				
0046		(N12690)	N553CC	N760NB	N103VF	N198ST	N63RS				
0047		N12695	I-CEFI	N16RP							
0048		N1270D	N797TJ	N999TJ	N705SP						
0049		N1270K	B-4101								
0050		N1270S	B-4102								
0051		N1270Y	N251QS	CS-DNB	N132WC	N77PA	N311AF				
0052		N12703	N4TL	N4TU	(N552CF)	N27SD	N27GD	N57BJ			
0053		N12705	N75BL	N253QS	N1223N	N393E					
0054		N12709	N717LS	N57MB	N999CB	N599CB	N812HA				
0055		N1271A	N374GS	N374GC	N87FL	N417RC	N408CT				
0056		(N1271B)	C-GERL	N550F	N52FT						
0057		N1271D	N1UL	N1UH	N1UL	N57CJ	N800HW				
0058		N1271E	N633EE	N936BR							
0059		(N1271N)	PT-LHD	N36NS	N829JC	N329JC	(N904VA)	N531PM	N329JC	N71WH	
0060		(N1271T)	N85AB	N588CT	N314G	N260QS	N442KM				
0061		(N12712)	N540JB	N46A	(N464)	N53JM	N200LX	N811RG	N45NC		
0062		N12715	I-AVVM	D-CVVM							
0063		(N12717)	VH-EMO								
0064		(N1272G)	N2000X	N200CX	(N990HP)	N45H	N200CX	N200CV	N575SG	(N557MG)	
0065		(N1272N)	N7118A	N612ST	(N900RG)	(N909RG)	N995DC	N90FJ	XB-PAX		
0066		N1272P	N711MD								
0067		(N1272V)	N550FS	C-GMAV	N70AF	N789MA	(N67VP)	"EW94228"	HC-BTY	N550HA	N900DM	N828AF	N917GP
0068		N1272Z	N404G	N4049	N7070A						
0069		(N12720)	N43VS								
0070		(N12722)	N570CC	N570RC	XB-EEP	N550SG					
0071		(N12727)	N571CC	N1865M	YV....						
0072		(N1273A)	(N572CC)	N1273A	N186MT	N686MC	TC-NMC	N62NS	N627HS		
0073		(N1273E)	N1958N	[parted out by White Industries, Bates City, MO]							
0074		N1273J	N550LC	N22EH	N274QS	N274PG	N74JE	N74GZ			
0075		(N1273N)	N554CC	N882KB	N882RB	(N275VP)					
0076		(N1273Q)	N95CC	C-GQMH	N89TD	N52CK	N25DY	VH-JLU			
0077		(N1273R)	N747CP	(N747GP)	N277QS	CS-DNC	N202WC	N999EA	N999QH		
0078		N1273X	ZS-CAR								
0079		(N1273Z)	N1000W	N100QW	N97AJ	N97LB	(N27TB)	5N-BEL	N578GG		
0080		N12730	C-GTDO	N581EA	(N269MT)	XA-TMI	N260BS	XA-VGF	N712MG		
0081		(N1274B)	N168HC	N550KM	PR-MCN	N404KK	YV2692				
0082		N1274D	N97TJ	N9KH	N282QS	N27TB					
0083		N1274K	N511BB	N511BR	OE-GNS	N511BR	N883PF	N683PF	N688AT		
0084		N1274N	PT-LJL								
0085		N1274P	N683MB	N683CF	N54AM	(N285CF)	N220CA	N8BG	N143BP	N550BT	YV3125	
0086		(N1274X)	N586CC	N900RB	N86QS	4X-COO	OB-1792-T	OB-1792	N11SU	D-CJJJ	VH-SQM	
0087		N1274Z	N21EG	ZS-DES							
0088		(N12744)	N825HL	N288QS	N127RC	(N557TC)	N67FT				
0089		N12745	(N289CC)	N134GB	VT-RHM	VT-ETG					
0090		N12746	N777GF	N320S	N76FC	(N4BP)	N97BP	(N50BM)	N113VP	XA-AEZ	N113VP	N499RC
0091		(N12747)	N595CC	N595CM	N241LA	N477LC+	[+ marks reserved in error]		N476LC		
0092		(N1275A)	N92QS	N923S	N489GM						
0093		N1275B	N593CC	N33DS	N93QS	N400RE	N629RA	YV3019			
0094		(N1275D)	N594CC	(N347CP)	F-OHAH	N560AJ	N6LL	N1H	N19ZA		

CESSNA S550 CITATION II

C/n	Unit No	Identities								
0095	N1275H	N200NK	N200NV	N345CC	N409CT	XB-MYO				
0096	(N1275N)	N95CC	N29X	N29XA	[w/o 05Mar89 Poughkeepsie, NY]					
0097	N1290B	N97QS	N828WB	N551BE	N551RF	N302MB				
0098	N1290E	N98QS	CS-DDA	N598WC	N598KW					
0099	N1290G	N44GT	N299QS	N777FD	YV2469					
0100	(N1290N)	N3000W	(N616GB)	N300QW	N550SJ					
0101	(N1290Y)	N101QS	C-FABF							
0102	N1290Z	N287MC	N285MC							
0103	N12900	N103QS	N22HP	[w/o 03May07 Dillon, MT]						
0104	N12903	N224KC	[retro-fitted with Williams FJ44 engines]							
0105	(N12907)	N105BG	(N1058G)	N623BG						
0106	(N12909)	N106QS	N666TR	N9072U						
0107	N1291E	N474L	N713DH	N550HT	C-GBGC	N553SD	YV2988			
0108	(N1291K)	N108QS	N316MH	N192RS	N132GS					
0109	N1291P	N509CC	N1GC	N7QC	N38EC	N61TL	N75MC	(N50SL)	N501VE	YV....
0110	N1291V	N45GP	(N116LD)	N550WD						
0111	(N1291Y)	N111QS	(N777HN)	N57KF	HP-18BLM					
0112	(N12910)	N112QS	A2-MCB	ZS-PSG						
0113	(N12911)	N553CC	PT-LJQ							
0114	N1292A	PT-LKS								
0115	(N1292B)	N505CC	N520RP	C-FDDD	C-GWBF	N92JT	N92JC	N724JK		
0116	N1292K	N125CG	N550HC							
0117	N1292N	PT-LKT	[w/o 01Dec92 Sao Paulo-Congonhas, Brazil]							
0118	N12920	N600TF	N820FJ	N820F	VH-IWU	N118AJ	N110LH	N721LR	4X-COZ	
0119	(N12922)	N261WR	N261WD	N700SW	N700SV	(N500LH)	N11TS	N11TR	N11TS	N63HA	N616TG*
0120	N12924	N1283M	N716DB	N716DD	(N716QW)					
0121	(N12925)	D-CLOU	N23NM	(N20NM)	N711XR	N550JE				
0122	N12929	I-TALG	N122WS	N163C						
0123	N1293A	N121CG								
0124	(N1293E)	N1867W	N52CK	N550JC	N554T	N555WV	N123TL			
0125	N1293G	N122CG	N97CT	(N552SM)	N125QA	YV3152				
0126	N1293K	N126QS	(N127RC)	ZS-EDA						
0127	N1293N	N14UM	(N127CF)	PT-OSL	N14UM	N674JM	N874JM	N97SK	N431MS	
0128	N1293V	N911BB	N370M	N550CZ						
0129	N1293X	N87TH	N480CC	N488CC	N323JR					
0130	(N1293Z)	N130CC	N302PC	N550PL	N552SD	N552SE	YV....			
0131	N12934	D-CHJH	N87BA							
0132	(N1294D)	N533CC	N91ME	N91ML	N394HA					
0133	(N1294K)	G-VKRS	N7047K	I-ZAMP	N133VP	N431WM	N133VP	YV2853		
0134	N1294M	N134QS	D-CFAI	SE-DYO	OY-GMJ	N66HD	SE-DYO	N51DA		
0135	(N1294N)	OE-GPD	D-CIAO	N2235	VT-KMB					
0136	(N1294P)	[converted on line to prototype Citation V c/n 560-0001]								
0137	(N12945)	D-CNCA	HB-VKA	N100TB	PT-WIB					
0138	(N1295A)	N538CC	N305PC	N138QS	N713HH	(N501BE)	N552BE	N20CS	ZS-CWG	
0139	(N1295B)	N906SB	N706SB	N39TF	N881A					
0140	(N1295G)	C-GLCR	N575EW							
0141	(N1295J)	N907SB	N707SB	N26JJ	N550AJ					
0142	(N1295M)	N542CC	C-FALI	C-GCRG	N701BG					
0143	(N1295N)	N143QS	N1VA	N458PE	CC-CWZ					
0144	(N1295P)	D-CNCB	N6516V	N543SC	VQ-BFT	N543SC				
0145	(N1295Y)	(PH-HMC)	(PH-HMA)	PH-RMA	N145VP	4X-CPT	N900LM			
0146	(N1296B)	(G-JBCA)	N1296B	N81SH	N815H	YV327T	YV2671			
0147	N1296N	OO-OSA	CS-DDV							
0148	N1296Z	ZS-IDC	N170RD	D-CSFD	N550BG	(SE-RCY)	(SE-RCX)	M-BULL		
0149	N149QS	C-GMGB	N816V	N810V	N43RC	N777AX				
0150	(N1297B)	N150CJ	N107RC							
0151	(N2634E)	N151QS	N151Q	N550SP	N88NW					
0152	N26369	N848G	N843G	N987CJ						
0153	(N2637R)	N153QS	N242LA	N476LC+	[+ marks reserved in error]		N477LC			
0154	N26379	PT-LQI	N910DS	N660AJ	N550DS					
0155	(N2638A)	N155QS	N155GB	N550DL	[retro-fitted with winglets and Williams FJ44 engines]					
0156	(N2638U)	N156QS	N766NB	(N400AJ)	N901PV	N63JT				
0157	N2639N	N157QS	N157BM	N802Q						
0158	(N2639Y)	N158QS	N301QS	N158QS	N66EH	N886RP	N889RP	N550EZ		
0159	(N2646X)	N50GT	N289CC	N9GT	N9GY	YV3040				
0160	N2642Z	N550GT	PT-OSM	N121WF	YV3098					

Production complete

CESSNA 552 CITATION (T-47A)

C/n	Identities			
0001	N552CC	N12855	162755	[w/o 20Jly93 in hangar fire Forbes Field, Topeka, KS]
0002	N12756	162756	[w/o 20Jly93 in hangar fire Forbes Field, Topeka, KS]	
0003	N12557	162757	[w/o 20Jly93 in hangar fire Forbes Field, Topeka, KS]	
0004	N12058	162758	[w/o 20Jly93 in hangar fire Forbes Field, Topeka, KS; cx Sep93]	
0005	N12859	162759	[w/o 20Jly93 in hangar fire Forbes Field, Topeka, KS; cx Sep93]	
0006	N12660	162760	[w/o 20Jly93 in hangar fire Forbes Field, Topeka, KS; cx Sep93]	
0007	N12761	162761	[w/o 20Jly93 in hangar fire Forbes Field, Topeka, KS; cx Sep93]	
0008	N12762	162762	[w/o 20Jly93 in hangar fire Forbes Field, Topeka, KS; cx Sep93]	
0009	N12763	162763	[w/o 20Jly93 in hangar fire Forbes Field, Topeka, KS; cx Sep93]	
0010	N12564	162764	[w/o 20Jly93 in hangar fire Forbes Field, Topeka, KS; cx Sep93]	
0011	N12065	162765	[w/o 20Jly93 in hangar fire Forbes Field, Topeka, KS; cx Sep93]	
0012	N12566	162766	[in compound outside Columbus State Community College hangar at Columbus Bolton Field, OH as N12566]	
0013	N12967	162767	[w/o 20Jly93 in hangar fire Forbes Field, Topeka, KS; cx Sep93]	
0014	N12568	162768	[cx 03Nov09, scrapped]	
0015	N12269	162769	[w/o 20Jly93 in hangar fire Forbes Field, Topeka, KS; cx Sep93]	

Production complete

CESSNA 560 CITATION V/ULTRA/ENCORE

C/n	Identities									
707	N5079V	N560VU	[Citation Ultra Encore prototype, c/n 0424 reworked qv; cx Nov10, wfu]							
550-0001	N560CC	[Model 550 aircraft cvtd to 560 standard]								
560-0001	(N1294P)	N560CV	N1217V	N561VP	[cvtd on production line from c/n S550-0136]					
0002	N1209T	N562CV	N90PG	N101HB	N560VP	N560CZ				
0003	(N1209X or N1216A)	N563CV	SY-AAP	Seychelles SY-001		S7-AAP	Seychelles SY-001	N560BA	N560ER	N413LC	N561CF
0004	(N1210N or N1216J)	N189H								
0005	(N1210V or N1216K)	N953F								
0006	(N1211M or N1216N)	N962JC	N566VP	N570MH	N269TA	N569TA				
0007	(N12117 or N1216Q)	N964JC	(N57VP)	N717MB	N763D	N933SP	(N560C)			
0008	(N1213S or N1216Z)	N561B								
0009	(N1213Z or N12160)	N456FB	VH-HEY	N77HN	N77HU	N77NR	N37NR	N91CV		
0010	(N1214J or N12162)	N205PC	N205BC	N643RT	N560JM					
0011	(N1214Z or N1217H)	N700TF	N913BJ							
0012	N1217N	N560ME	N560RR							
0013	(N1217P)	N560WH								
0014	N1217S	N1MC	N88TJ	N12ST	(N650ST)	N900SM				
0015	N12171	N800DL	N560MR	N580MR	N480DG					
0016	N12173	N68HC	N68HQ	N462B						
0017	(N1218P or N1223A)	N89BM	N560H	C-FPJT	N560JZ					
0018	(N1218Y or N12249)	N164DW	N114CP	N500FZ						
0019	(N1219D or N1226X)	N99WR	OE-GRW	N61TW	N643RT					
0020	(N1219G or N1228N)	N520CV	N560HC	N560HG	N7867T					
0021	N1228V	N682D	C-FDLT	N560DC	N669AJ	N410DW	N83EP			
0022	(N1228Y)	N211MA	N574BB	N574BP						
0023	(N12283)	OE-GDP	VR-CTL	N560JM	N31RC	N345MB	N3FA			
0024	(N12284)	N501QS	N4CS	N560FN	N140U					
0025	(N12285)	CNA-NV								
0026	(N12286)	N560LC	N49MJ	N350RD	N380RD					
0027	(N12289)	N560JR	N20CC	(N20YC)	N560JR	N531MB	N531MF	N625WA	N540PA*	
0028	(N1229A)	N6FE	N6FZ	N757CK	N753MB					
0029	(N1229C)	N590A								
0030	(N1229D)	N560W	XB-MTS	N570BJ	N40HT					
0031	N1229F	D-CHDE	N198MM	N520BP						
0032	N1229M	G-DBII	N96MT	N96MY	N560BC					
0033	N1229N	I-ATSB	N4333W	C-GAPC						
0034	(N1229Q)	N895LD	N401MC	N560PY	ZP-BTP					
0035	N1229Z	N36H	N561EJ							
0036	(N12295 or N2663B)	(N107CF)	(N107CR)	HZ-ZTC	N532MA	(N560EJ)	N200MM	N50EL		
0037	(N12297 or N2663X)	N17LK	N416HF	N560GG						
0038	(N12298 or N2663Y)	N301QS	N2296S	N212BW	N560CV					
0039	(N1230A or N26630)	CNA-NW								
0040	(N1230G or N2664U)	N12403	N71NK	N91NK	N91NL	N560CF				
0041	N26643	VH-NTH	N400KS							
0042	(N26648)	N42CV	D-CAWU	N142GA	N500SX					
0043	(N2665F)	N991PC	[w/o 30Dec95 Eagle River Airport, WI; cx May96; to White Inds, Bates City, MO, for spares]							
0044	N2665S	N111VP	N331CC	N560JL						
0045	N2665Y	PT-LZQ	N560WF	N560WJ						
0046	(N26656)	G-CZAR	G-CJAE	N846MA	JA118N					
0047	N2666A	N500FK	N560WW							
0048	N2667X	N4TL	N74TL	N57CE	N57CN	N870AJ	N220CM	N240CM	N561PF	
0049	(N2672X)	N560EL								
0050	(N26771)	(N208BC)	N208PC	N208BC	N501CW	YV2655				
0051	N2680A	N599SC	N599SG	N314RW	N318RW					
0052	N2680D	N500LE	N500UB	N777RB						
0053	(N2680X)	N53CV	I-NYCE	N111CF	C-GCUW	C-FACO	C-FACC	C-GNGV	N560LW	
0054	(N26804)	N531F	N100SC	N100SY	(N748DC)					
0055	N2681F	HB-VJZ	N282RH	(N21JJ)	(N560CP)	N200CP	(N201CP)	N209CP	N715PS	N55EA
0056	N2682F	N78AM	(N56EP)	N560AE	N406VJ					
0057	(N2683L)	N560BL	N561BC	N561TS	N553SC	LV-CRL				
0058	(N2686Y)	F-GKGL	N62GA	N710LC						
0059	(N2687L)	F-GKHL	G-PPLC	A7-AKA						
0060	(N2689B)	N2697Y	N90MF	PT-FTB						
0061	(N2697X)	N2701J	D-CNCI	N46GA	N603HC					
0062	N2716G	ZS-MVV	N560EA	EC-411	EC-GLM	N500UJ	(N405RH)	(N328SB)		
0063	(N2701J)	N7FE	(N7FZ)	N68CK	N63FF					
0064	N2717X	(ZS-MYN)	ZS-MVZ	N45GA	OE-GPC	OY-NUD	N560AG	N560CC		
0065	N2721F	N77711	N560JV	N608CT						
0066	(N27216)	N60S	N501JS	N810BE	N382AG*					
0067	N2722F	N45BA	JA119N							
0068	N2722H	(N40PL)	N711GF	N712GF	N246NW	N560LM	N569LM			
0069	(N2724R)	D-CNCP	N65229	N70TG	N357WC	N857WC	N367JC			
0070	(N2725A)	F-GJXX	N570VP	5H-ETG						
0071	(N2725X)	N271CA								
0071A	N2728N	N45RC								
0072	N2726J	(N72FE)	(N91FA)	N572CV	N72CT	(N772KC)	JA120N			
0073	(N2726X)	N100WP								
0074	N2727F	N27WW	N174JS	N593MD	C-GBNX					
0075	(N2745L)	N75CV	N617PD	(N619PD)	N817PD					
0076	(N2745M)	N777FE	N777FH	N777FN	N94NB	N623KC	N217GL			
0077	N2745R	G-BSVL	C-GNND	N42NA	HB-VLV	[w/o 20Dec01 Zurich A/P, Switzerland]				
0078	N2748B	SE-DLI	OY-CKT	D-CSUN	PH-ILA	OY-CKT	N797MM			
0079	(N2746C)	N560GL	N224GP							
0080	N2746E	JA8576	(N803EA)	N5JU	N300CH					
0081	(N2746F)	OE-GID	N560HP	N318CT						
0082	(N2746U)	N950WA	C-FETJ	N247DG						
0083	(N2747R)	N22LP	N568WC	N577XW						
0084	(N2747U)	N16NM	C-GHEC	N51C	XB-IML					
0085	(N2748F)	N591M	N891M	N85VP	N599LP	N599LR	LV-COV			
0086	(N2748V)	SE-DPG	N560CX	N560CJ	N218SE	N560CJ				
0087	N2749B	5N-IMR	N167WE	N600BW	N60QB					
0088	(N6783X)	OE-GSW	D-CMCM	OK-SLS						
0089	N67830	ZS-MPT	N54DD							

CITATION V

C/n	Identities							
0090	(N67839)	N30PC	N30PQ	LV-AHX				
0091	N6784P	(N18SK)	N56GT	N3GT	(N8GY)	N32PB	N103BG	N604NB	YV3178
0092	N6784X	XA-RTT	XB-RTT	N719RM				
0092A	N6784Y	N906SB	N592VP	(N713HH)				
0093	(N6785C)	F-GKJL	N93EA	YV2686				
0094	N6785D	N1823S	(N594VP)	N340DR	N1827S	N94VP		
0095	N6788P	N707CV	N404G					
0096	N67890	(N96JJ)	N10TD					
0097	(N6790L)	N898CB	YV....					
0098	(N6790P)	(N18SK)	N59DF					
0099	(N67905)	OE-GPA	D-CDUW	N560GM	N565EJ			
0100	(N6792A)	PH-PBM	N560WE	N560AF				
0101	(N67980)	N101CV	N560EC	N560DM	N560EP	N560PW		
0102	(N67988)	VR-BUL	VP-BUL	N560BA	N555PG			
0103	(N67989)	N98E	YV616T					
0104	(N6799L)	(N560CT)	N400CT	(N416H)	N815CM	(N907EA)		
0105	(N6800C)	N105CV	LN-AAA	N147VC	N149VG	N560MH	(N800WT)	
0106	N6801H	(HB-V..)	(N560PT)	N60SH	N525RD			
0107	(N6801L)	N78NP	N560RJ	N365EA				
0108	(N6801P)	N8HJ	VH-NHJ	N777KY	N73ME	N73MN	N573BB	(N573BP)	N579BB
0109	(N6801Q)	N6801V	N2	N27	N109VP	N480RL		
0109A	(N68018)	N907SB	N560RS	(N22YP)	N4MM	N387MM		
0110	(N6802S)	N560LC	N832CB	N832QB	N26DY	N95TD		
0111	(N6802T)	(N91AN)	OE-GAA	[cx Oct14; status?]				
0112	(N68027)	N4110S	N145MK	N560G				
0113	N6803L	N26	N4	N113VP	N555FD			
0114	(N6803T)	OE-GPS	D-CZAR	PH-ILI	OY-CKJ	N401MM	N506RL	
0115	N6803Y	I-NEWY	N91YC	N87JK				
0116	N68032	N901RM	N49NS	N561PA				
0117	(N6804F)	D-CMEI						
0118	N6804L	XA-RXO	XA-SKX	N118DF	N626SL	N900PS		
0119	(N6804N)	F-GLIM	N119CV	N450MM				
0120	(N6804Y or N6806X)	N120CV	N1824S	N560PS	(N994CF)	N129MC		
0121	N6808C	PT-MTG	N898GF	N821VP	N960CD	N560WR		
0122	(N6808Z)	N261WR	N510MT	N561MT				
0123	(N6809G)	N611ST	(N321VP)	N583CW	N92TE			
0124	(N6809T)	D-CBIG	N124VP	OB-1626	N7513D	N823WB	N560VS	
0125	N6809V	OE-GCC	C-GMAE					
0126	N68097	LV-PFN	LV-RED					
0127	(N6810L)	N64HA	N127VP	(C-....)	N127VP	XB-JHD	N150GP	
0128	(N6810N)	N19MK	N19ME	N85KC	N504BW	N154JK		
0129	(N6811F)	N22AF						
0130	(N6811T)	N130CV	N14VF	(N19VF)	PR-CCV			
0131	(N6811X)	N131CV	PT-ORE	N223JV				
0132	N6811Z	HZ-SFA	N226JV	N521LF				
0133	(N68118)	N77HF	N88HF	N93DW	N560PK			
0134	N6812D	YV-811CP	YV1022					
0135	(N6812L or N6871L)	N560BB	N560RL	N19HU				
0136	(N6812Z or N6872T)	(N136CV)	N501T	N772AA	N999AD	N560PA		
0137	(N560RB)	N6874Z	N7338	N733H	N193G	N137JC		
0138	(N68746)	(OY-JET)	OY-FFV	N511WV	N561SR			
0139	(N68753)	N561A	N75F	(N75FV)	N59NH	N77JD		
0140	(N6876Q)	N562E	N75G	(N75GV)	N24JD	N329PV		
0141	N6876S	N141AQ						
0142	N6876Z	PT-OLV	N7220L	PT-WPC	N560FA	N560GT	N64FT	
0143	N6877C	N65HA	(N543VP)	N744WW	N10TB	N734DB		
0144	N6877G	N2000X	N500VC					
0145	(N6877L)	N57MK	N57ML	D-CFLY	PH-ILZ	N308MM	N50US	
0146	(N6877Q)	N2000M	N500AT	[w/o 16Feb05 Pueblo, CO; cx]				
0147	(N6877R)	N27SD	XA-RKX	N125RH	N410J	N147RJ	(N880EF)	N508KD
0148	N68770	N92HW	N560FB	N115K				
0149	(N68786)	N565JW	N61GK					
0150	(N6879L)	D-CTAN	(N560ED)	N191VF	N191VE			
0151	N6881Q	ZS-NDU	V5-CDM	N6881Q				
0152	N6882R	ZS-NDX						
0153	N6804Y	N502T	N502F	(N153VP)	N1SN	SE-DYZ	OO-SKV	EC-LEP
0154	N6805T	N503T	(N503F)	(N154SV)	N154VP	N96MB	N432TX	
0155	N6872T	N40WP	N155VP	N630TK				
0156	(F-GLIM)	N6885L	XA-RKH	N560L	N75B			
0157	N6885V	N5734	N5704	N502TS	N88WC	N157TF		
0158	(N6885Y)	N601AB	N801AB	N560RP				
0159	(N68854)	N68MA	D-CLEO	G-JOPT	N18CV			
0160	N6886X	ZS-NDT	N458CK					
0161	N68860	Spain TR.20-01/403-11						
0162	N68864	[painted as N6864 for a short while end 1991]			XA-SDT	N388RD	XB-PEM	
0163	N68869	N529X	N953C	(N163L)	N97JL	N104LR	N904LR	(N904SR)
0164	(N6887T)	N164CV	N392BS	N570EJ	N830JB			
0165	(N6887X)	N910V	C-GAPD	N24HX				
0166	N68872	ZS-NDW	N166JV	HB-VMV	N203M	N17TX		
0167	(N68873)	N20CN	(N167WE)	N211DG	N311DG	N560JT	N580JT	N922KG
0168	(N68876)	N168CV	N168EA					
0169	N6888C	N80AB						
0170	N6888L	N170CV	N814CM	(N417H)	LV-CAK			
0171	(N6888T)	N5735	N573F	N567F				
0172	(N6888X)	N172CV	N560BP	(N560BD)				
0173	N68881	N918BD	N247CN					
0174	N6889E	N563C	N164TC	N560JD				
0175	(N564D)	N1279Z	N49LD	N43LD	YV463T			
0176	N12798	PT-OOR	N176VP	PT-WOM	N661AJ	N83ZA		
0177	N12799	VR-CNS	D-CHHS	N242AC	N650CM			
0178	N1280A	N531CC	N500PX	N997EA				
0179	(N179CJ)	N1280D	N865M	N885M	N65RL			
0180	N1280K	N550WW	N558WW					
0181	N1280R	N181SG						
0182	(N1280S)	N560RA	N920PM	C-FCRH	C-FEPG	N561WF		

C/n	Identities									
0183	N12807	N83RR	N83RE	Spain TR.20-03						
0184	N1281A	N873DB	N410DM							
0185	N1281K	N29WE	N29WF	N989TW	N939TW					
0186	N1281N	N583M	(N586CC)	N583N	N586CC	N47PW				
0187	N12812	N60GL	N80GE	N922AC						
0188	N12813	(N188CJ)	N64PM	N395R	N62CR	N180HL				
0189	N12815	N189CV	N62HA	N63JG						
0190	N12816	LV-PGC	LV-VFY	N555WF	N303CB	(N214LS)	N404LN	N650JS	N200NG	N655JS
0191	N12817	PT-ORT	N2JW	N45KB	C-FBCW	[retro-fitted with cargo door by Sierra Industries, Uvalde, TX]			[cx to USA 07Feb13 but no US marks assigned – status?]	
0192	(N1282D)	D-CEWR	N713HH	N238JC	N3444B	N621CD	[parted out by Alliance Air Parts, Oklahoma City, OK]			
0193	N1282K	Spain TR.20-02/403-12								
0194	(N1282M)	N194CV	N352WC	(N352WQ)	N852WC	N413CK	N413GK	N628CK	N700LP	
0195	N1282N	PT-ORC								
0196	N12824	N196CV	XA-SEJ	N560JS	N4JS	(N560JS)	N357AZ	N560RW		
0197	N12826	N197CV	(EI-DUN)	XA-SJC	N21LG					
0198	N1283F	N135BC	N560RG	N560BG	(N198VP)	N598CW	N198CV	N550DC		
0199	(N1283K)	N63HA	N7895Q	N4895Q	N500DW	N560PH				
0200	N1283M	OE-GDA	YR-TIC	YR-SMD						
0201	N1283N	ZS-NGM	N98GA	SU-EWA	N255RM					
0202	N1283V	(N202CV)	ZS-NGL	N1283V	N815LT					
0203	N1283X	(N203CV)	ZS-NHC	N7700L	N9700T					
0204	N1283Y	N1000W	YV483T							
0205	N12838	F-GLYC	N205VP	N1AK	N11AK					
0206	N1284A	N560TX	N900E							
0207	(N1284B)	N207CV	N52SN	N780BF	N560CK	N320CB				
0208	(N1284D)	N208CV	N892SB	N88G	N208VP	(N758PM)				
0209	(N1284F)	N209CV								
0210	N1284N	N20MK	N420DM	N277RC						
0211	(N1284P)	N250SP	N250SR							
0212	N1284X	TC-LAA	TC-ARI	TC-LAA						
0213	N12845	PT-OTS								
0214	(N1285D)	OE-GCP	N938GR	N618VH						
0215	(N1285G)	PT-OTT	N23NS	N315EJ						
0216	N1285N	TC-LAB	TC-BOR	TC-LAB						
0217	N1285P	N602AB	N802AB							
0218	N1285V	XA-SIT	N218BR	N218DF	N5T	N5GE	N561AC	N901LB		
0219	N12850	N318MM	N318MN	N229VP	N515RW	LV-CNJ				
0220	N12852	N23UD	N23UB	N73KH						
0221	(N1286A)	N24UD	N24UB	N701DK	N626RB					
0222	N1286C	N456SW	N767LD							
0223	N1286N	N575PC	N93AG	N500MG	N223VP	N593CW	N223CV	N560MG		
0224	N1287B	N224CV	N523KW	N528KW	(N47TW)					
0225	N1287C	(N1865S)	N1823S	N525CW	N225CV	N545PL	N969GB			
0226	N1287D	N893CM	N226CV							
0227	N1287F	(N227CV)	LV-PGR	LV-WDR						
0228	N1287G	N228CV	XA-SLA	N87GA	N560MM					
0229	N1287K	XA-SNX	N98GA	N193SB	N193SE					
0230	N1287N	YV-169CP	N169CP	N394AJ	N384AJ					
0231	N1287Y	N501E	N12CQ							
0232	(N12879)	N502E	C-GJYL							
0233	N1288A	Pakistan 0233								
0234	N1288B	N234AQ								
0235	N1288D	N22RG	N52RG	N129PJ	N560MM	N335EJ	N92BF	N633SA	N608BC	
0236	N1288N	N506E	N840CT	M-EMCT	N840CT					
0237	N1288P	N593M	N893M	N237VP						
0238	N238CV	N1288T	N46WB	(N95HW)	N194SA					
0239	N1288Y	N239CV	N1GC	N93CV	(N560RB)					
0240	N1289G	N91ME	N966JM	N55CH	N387A					
0241	N1289N	N241CV	ZS-NGS							
0242	N1289Y	N242CV	N605AT	N826AC						
0243	N12890	N39N	D-CAMS	N243VP	[wfu; fuselage stored Wichita/Mid-Continent]					
0244	(N12895)	(N244CV)	N60RD	N701NB	C-GBNE					
0245	N12896	N615AT	(N508DW)	N508KD	N43RC	N824CK				
0246	N1290N	N5060P	LV-PHD	LV-WGY						
0247	N12907	N94TX	N750ML							
0248	N12909	N248CV	N226N	(N229N)	(N123NW)	(N226U)	N50DR	N749TT		
0249	N1291K	N10CN	N733M	N2000X						
0250	(N1291K)	(N250CV)	N1291Y	N205CM						
0251	N12910	LV-PGZ	LV-WGO	N625AC	(N621AC)					
0252	N12911	N252CV	N44GT	N252CV	N8996					
0253	N1292B	N253CV	N46MT	N20LT	N553CW	N858ME				
0254	N12921	N560GB	(N561GB)	N568GB	N710MT	N710ML				
0255	N12922	N255CV	ZS-NHD	N255WA	N355EJ	N61KM				
0256	N12929	N22KW	N52KW	N356EJ	N356SA					
0257	N1293E	N155PT								
0258	N1293Y	PT-OZB	N60NS	PP-ISJ						
0259	N1293Z	N37WP	N56GA	N559BM						

CITATION ULTRA

C/n	Identities								
0260	N1294B	N260CV	C-GPAW	N888RE	N888RT	N883RT	N180FW	N69VT	N863JB
0261	N1294K	N261CV	XB-PYC	N261UH	N305QS	N135WC			
0262	N1294N	N262CV	N444GG						
0263	N12945	N979C	N560GS						
0264	N1295A	N5250K	N264CV	N264U	N294RT				
0265	N1295P	N5270K	LV-PHJ	LV-WIJ	N86CE	[w/o 24Jan06 Carlsbad, CA]			
0266	N1295G	N456JW	N458JW	N269JR	N288JR	N306QS	N350WC		
0267	N1295J	N96NB	N197JH	N267VP	N267WG				
0268	N1295M	"N5270M"	(XA-...)	N12012	N269CM	N750FL			
0269	N1295N	N331EC	N357EC	C-GRCC	C-GRQQ				

CITATION ULTRA

C/n	Identities									
0270	N1295Y	N68HC	N68HQ	N159JH	(N259JH)	N4FC	N394CK	N404MU	N888PA	C6-AIP
0271	N1296N	PH-VLG	N49TT	HB-VNB	CS-DTA	N560TP				
0272	N5094B	N220JT	N372EJ	N672SA	N790PS	N15SL				
0273	N5095N	N910PC	N61JB	N861CE	(N861CF)	N521LL	N77MA*			
0274	N5096S	N751CF	N511DR	(N511DP)	N137LA	(N137LX)	N560HD			
0275	(N5097H)+	N1297V	D-CVHA	(N560LW)	N560LT	N717D				
0276	N5100J	N183AJ	N376QS	N376WC	N145KK					
0277	(N5101J)+	D-CFOX	N804WA	N308QS	N130WC	N560BG	N525JZ			
0278	N5103J	N2HJ	VH-FHJ	N560EM	N180B					
0279	(N51038)+	(N331EC)	N361EC	N594M	N190K					
0280	(N51042)+	PH-MDC	HB-VNA							
0281	(N5105F)+	N511ST	N281VP	N716SX	N560HW					
0282	N51055	D-CBEN	N282VR	YV3225						
0283	(N51072)+	N560JC	N1CH	N560JC	N568JC					
0284	N5108G	N966SW	(N369TC)							
0285	(N5109R)+	N285CV	N147VC	N285CC						
0286	(N5109W)+	N286CV	N57MB	N31NS						
0287	(N5112K)+	N287CV	N117CC	N117MR	N863RD					
0288	N5141F	N522JA								
0289	N51444	LV-PHY	LV-WLS							
0290	N5145P	N97BH								
0291	N5148B	N744R	N470DP							
0292	N5148N	N1295N	HL7501							
0293	N51575	N293QS	N131WC	N50CV	N136JD					
0294	N5161J	N1295Y	HL7502							
0295	(N5162W)+	N295CV	N61HA	N80LP	N80EP	N295BM	N903BH	N510JN		
0296	(N5163C)+	N560LC								
0297	N5165T	N1296N	HL7503							
0298	N5166U	N200CK	N25CV	N112CW	N656JG					
0299	N5168F	(N550TM)	VT-EUX							
0300	N51743	N1297V	HL7504							
0301	N5180K	(HB-V..)	VR-BQB	N560AG	HB-VOC					
0302	(N5223Y)	N560CE	I-NYSE	N560CE	N580CE	N302EJ	(N602SA)	N901AB		
0303	N5225K	(N560BD)	(D-CAFB)	N560BJ	N190JH	N190JK				
0304	N5226B	N47VC	N401KH	C-GWWU						
0305	N5228Z	LV-PLE	LV-WMT	N284HS						
0306	N5231S	N49MJ	N306TR	N753BD	(N753BB)	(N753GL)	N753GJ			
0307	N5233J	N307QS	N139WC	N51FK						
0308	N5235G	PT-WFD								
0309	N52352	N212BD	N560RN	N615HR						
0310	N5241Z	N410CV	N868JT	N228PC	N228PG					
0311	(N5244F)	N311QS	(N211WC)	N531VP	N421LT	N469ES				
0312	(N52457)	N312QS	N521VP	(N127JW)						
0313	N5246Z	N313CV								
0314	N5250E	N314CV	C-FYMM	C-FYMT	N561DA					
0315	(N5250K)	N315QS	(N215WC)	N515VP	N220LC	N105BG				
0316	(N5251Y)	N12RN	N120QM							
0317	(N52526)	N317QS	N217WC	N818BL	N818BF					
0318	N5261R	N1273R	N877RF	N877RB	N910HM					
0319	N52613	N1319D	N52613	LV-WOE	N2RC					
0320	N5262B	N46WB	(N28ET)	VR-CCV	VP-CCV	N320VP	VH-SMF	VH-MXJ	VH-OHE	
0321	N5262W	N320QS	N220WC	N560AV						
0322	N5262X	"ZS-NNV"	ZS-NVV	N850BA	N300QS	N300WC	N607HM	N560JS		
0323	(N5097H)	N323QS	N808AC							
0324	N5100J	N55LC	N55LQ	N342QS	N152WC	N853CR				
0325	(N5101J)	N96AT	N313QS	N140WC	N566KB					
0326	N5103J	N583M	(N711Z)	N200SC	N220SC	(N902AV)				
0327	(N51038)	N327QS	(N101EC)	C-GKZJ	N80JH					
0328	(N5104Z)	N554R	N554EJ	(N554UJ)	N984GA	N926NC				
0329	N5105F	N330QS	N302WC							
0330	(N51055)	N351WC	N851WC	N330VP						
0331	N51072	N331QS	N231WC	[parted out by Dodson Int'l, Rantoul, KS]						
0332	(N5108G)	N332LC	N332AR	VH-SJP	VH-MMC					
0333	(N5109R)	N333QS	(N397WC)	YV2798						
0334	N5109W	N4TL	N905LC							
0335	N335QS	N301WC	VH-WFE							
0336	N5265B	N336QS	(N128WC)	N690ES						
0337	N5265N	N108LJ								
0338	N52645	N592M	N338R							
0339	N339QS	N539VP	YV516T							
0340	N5267T	N21CV								
0341	N341QS	N541VP	N560HL							
0342	N5267T	(N14VF)	XA-RDM	N86CW	(N82CW)	N86CV				
0343	N5268A	N343CV	N60AE	N303QS	N325WC	N327VP				
0344	N5268M	N344QS	N126WC	N501JG						
0345	N5268E	N345CV	N75Z	(N560NS)	N64LV					
0346	N5269A	N346CC	C-GFCL	C-FNTM	N399AF					
0347	N5268V	N72FC	N72FE	N106SP	N50LD	N50LQ				
0348	N52682	N348QS	(N399WC)	N980AG						
0349	N5151S	N1127P	JA001A							
0350	N51522	N645M	N250JH	N991L	N2500N	Colombia FAC5760				
0351	N5153K	N699CC	N560DM	C-GAWR	C-GAWU	N151VP	N31CV			
0352	N5153X	N352QS	(N133WC)	(N106EC)	C-GKZD	N215H				
0353	N51564	N353CV	N1873	N187S	N353Z	N20SM	N53SM			
0354	N5157E	N4200K								
0355	N51575	N355CV	N67GW	N67GU	HK-4304	N560MV	HK-4304			
0356	N5153Z	N354QS	(N130WC)	PR-BEE						
0357	N5148N	N81SH	N347QS	N110WC	ZP-BZH					
0358	N5163C	N358CV	N12TV	(N12TU)	N30TV	N284CP				
0359	N5166U	ZS-SMB	N416BA							
0360	N5168F	N6780A	N62WA	N62WD						
0361	N5156B	N361QS	N560VP	N217MW						
0362	N5183U	OE-GMI	PH-ILO	N831MM	N998TW					
0363	N5180K	N59KG	N59KC	C-GUWT						
0364	N5260Y	N991PC	N560A	N51ND						

CITATION ULTRA

C/n	Identities							
0365	N5235G	N7547P	N375CM	N712L	N2500D	Peru 721	N2500D	Colombia FAC5763
0366	N52352	SX-DCI	(N361CA)	N131RR				
0367	N5161J	N367QS	N395WC	N747GV				
0368	N5194J	N343CC	N348CC	N555KT				
0369	N52113	N5200	N520G	N5200	N680GW	N210CM		
0370	N5262B	N607RJ	N749DC	N560MF				
0371	N5262X	N371CV	N315CS					
0372	N52601	N372CV	N76CK	N372QS	N372WC	N592MA		
0373	N373QS	(N113EC)	C-GKZC					
0374	N5214L	N7728T	N166KB	N163L	Colombia FAC5761	N1066W	Colombia FAC5761	
0375	N375QS	N575VP	XA-SEB	N478SB				
0376	N5097H	VR-BCY	N1217H	N713DH	N600LF	N600EF	N554T	N554TS
0377	N5264A	N377RA	N450RA	N377QS	N377WC	N537VP	N100SN	N560HS
0378	N5090A	N350WC	N850WC	(N378VP)	N808TH	HP-3010	HP-3010HTB	
0379	N5101J	C-GWCR	N560RF	N560PE				
0380	N5103J	N380CV	N190KL	N147SB	N827DP			
0381	N2762J	N857BL	N214L	N5373D	Columbia FAC5764			
0382	N382QS	N582VP	N560TX					
0383	N51038	N57ST	N63TM	N631M	N579BJ	(N241KP)		
0384	N5231S	N196SA	(N86DD)	N950TC	N331MW			
0385	N5109R	N333WM	(N833WM)	N444DN				
0386	N7274A	N720SJ	N615L	N2500B	Columbia FAC5762			
0387	N5108G	US Army 95-0123	[UC-35A]					
0388	N5269A	N92SS						
0389	N5092B	PT-WRR	N389JV	N118RK	(N118RY)	N118RW		
0390	N5093L	N390CV	C-GMGB	N390VP	N560SE	C-GNLQ	N217TH	
0391	N5092D	N391CV	N92DE	YV2940				
0392	N5124F	US Army 95-0124	[UC-35A]					
0393	N5156V	N393QS	(N116WC)	(N126EC)	C-FCBQ			
0394	N5093Y	N394QS	(N127EC)	C-GKZK	[stored Scottsdale, AZ]			
0395	N5093Y	(N395QS)	N19MK	(N19MU)	N15SK			
0396	N50938	N396QS	N596VP	ZK-AWK	N3937E	ZK-AWK	N396VP	LV-CTX
0397	N50715	PT-WKS	N397AF	N560RC	N44LV			
0398	N5061W	ZS-NUZ	ZS-TSB					
0399	N51881	N97NB	N560WD	(N560DW)	N969DW	N322VA		
0400	N51942	N916CS	N916CG	N42ND	N443EA			
0401	N5197A	N401CV	VP-CSN	OY-KLG				
0402	N5200U	N302QS	(N122WC)	N691ES				
0403	N5201J	N1202D	JA01TM	N403SC	N5150K	N14RP		
0404	N5201M	US Army 96-0107	[UC-35A]					
0405	N5202D	PT-WMQ	N137FA	N45TP	N45TE	N616TD		
0406	N5203S	PT-WMZ						
0407	N5204D	N1218Y	F-OHRU	N560RK				
0408	N5207A	PT-WOA	N560NS	N304QS	N408JT	YV1018		
0409	N52081	PT-WVH	(N409VP)	N390BA	C-FKBC			
0410	N5211A	US Army 96-0108	[UC-35A]					
0411	N5226B	PT-WNE	N38NS	N731TR				
0412	N5228Z	PT-WNF	(N412EA)	N412CW	N513EF	N17PL	N38MR	
0413	N5233J	N413CV	VP-CKM	N8041R	N561JS			
0414	N5235G	ZS-CDS	SE-RGY	PJ-TOM				
0415	N52457	US Army 96-0109	[UC-35A]					
0416	N5109R	N19PV	N713DH	N713DA	N416VP	N561CC		
0417	N5090A	N1248B	RP-C8818	N560TJ	VH-XTT	N525BA	N560RV	
0418	N5112K	N318QS	(N128EC)	C-GCFL				
0419	N5233J	EC-GOV						
0420	N51942	US Army 96-0110	[UC-35A]					
0421	N322QS	(N138EC)	C-GKZG	N555LG				
0422	N20SB	N5XP	N58RG	N59TF	N297CP			
0423	N5073G	N324QS	N523VP	N528VM	C-GKHD			
0424	(N324QS)	N424CV	[cx Sep97 cvtd to prototype Citation Ultra Encore with c/n 707 in the Cessna prototype series]					
0425	N325QS	(N139EC)	C-GKZH					
0426	N5101J	US Army 96-0111	[UC-35A]					
0427	N5105F	N11LC	N11LQ	N573AB	N891FV			
0428	N328QS	N140EC	C-GKZQ	N117JL				
0429	N392QS	(N146EC)	C-FLBQ	N650NV	N560NV*			
0430	N433CV	C-GLIM	N560TA					
0431	N5076K	PT-WZW	N431JV	N560JP	N76TF			
0432	N51143	N356WC	N856CW	N564TJ				
0433	N5231S	N33LX	N88EX	XA-CDF	N660SB	N840AA		
0434	N334QS	(N148EC)	C-GKZO					
0435	N52352	N410NA	N5263					
0436	N5086W	N36LX	N86EX	N96FC	N560BJ	N97TE	N605PR	
0437	N337QS	(N149EC)	C-GKZR					
0438	N5207A	(PT-WQE)	N438MC	N228FS	N459MB			
0439	N50612	(N39LX)	VP-CSC	N6NY				
0440	N5076K	PT-WSN	N400MC	N560HB	N910TF			
0441	N314QS	(N151EC)	C-GMXD					
0442	N5226B	N23UD	N152JH	N752JH	N888SV	N778FW	N323NE	
0443	N5228Z	N24UD	N568RL	N561CM	N317JM	N818RU		
0444	N343QS	(N153EC)	C-GKZT					
0445	N5000R	N345QS	(N156EC)	C-GKZP				
0446	N51038	HB-VLZ	9H-VLZ	[wfu Dusseldorf, Germany]				
0447	N5108G	N51246	N261WR					
0448	N5100J	C-GSUN	C-GSUM	N4ZL				
0449	N5120U	N560BP	N555WF	N555WK	N75WP			
0450	N51246	PT-XCF						
0451	N5124F	N351QS	(N160EC)	C-GKZA	CP-2823			
0452	N5130J	US Army 97-0101	[UC-35A]					
0453	N5132T	N453CV	N400LX	N60KM				
0454	N5135K	TC-ROT	N1216Z	TC-ROT	N454RT	N63GB	C-GOOB	
0455	N51396	N358QS	(N161EC)	C-FUBQ				
0456	N51444	US Army 97-0102	[UC-35A]					
0457	N51564	N59HA	VP-CMS	G-GRGS	HB-VNW	N5UU		
0458	N5161J	LV-PNR	LV-YMA	N458DA				
0459	N5162W	N79PM	N76WR	N776WR				

C/n	Identities						
0460	N5157E	N360QS	(N163EC)	C-GKZS	N303HC		
0461	N5185V	XA-ICO	N461VP	N61TL	N765WG		
0462	N5183U	US Army 97-0103	[UC-35A]				
0463	N50612	N56K	N58KJ	N48LC	N48LQ	D-CEMG	N463EA	N114KN
0464	N420DM	N53PE					
0465	N5086W	N465CV	N848G				
0466	N366QS	(N224WC)	N981AG				
0467	N5096S	ZS-OFM	N98NA	N20CC			
0468	N51042	US Army 97-0104	[UC-35A]				
0469	N5183V	N701CR	N7010R	N469DN			
0470	N44FG	N290BB					
0471	N5188A	N371QS	(N164EC)	C-GKZB			
0472	N5097H	US Army 97-0105	[UC-35A]				
0473	N5093D	N9LR	N473SB	N1CF	N716S		
0474	N51160	N474CV	XA-TKZ	N474VP	N321GG	N474PE	
0475	N374QS	N374WC	YV504T				
0476	N150S	N941RM					
0477	N5085E	N50GP	N560FF				
0478	N5095N	N70BR	N111JW	N458NC			
0479	N5125J	N379QS	N743DB	N811MB	YV3170		
0480	N51246	N71JJ	N560VR	N566VR			
0481	N5153K	C-GXCO	C-GXCG				
0482	N5156D	N44LC	N44LQ				
0483	N383QS	(N166EC)	C-GKZE	N212LP			
0484	N5125J	C-GYMM	C-FWHH	[wfu; to instructional airframe, South Alberta Institute of Technology, Calgary, Canada]			
0485	N998SA						
0486	N386QS	(N168EC)	C-FIBQ				
0487	N50820	N46MW	N43KW	N51EF			
0488	N12688	N555WF	N555WL				
0489	N66U						
0490	N390QS	N390WC	N565NC	N629EP			
0491	N51564	N404MM	N484MM				
0492	N5152X	N492CV	C-GDSH	N41VP	N41VR	N85EB	
0493	N391QS	(N173EC)	C-GKZF	N93HA			
0494	N5166T	N80GR	N86GR	N452AJ	N977DM		
0495	US Army 98-0006	[UC-35A]					
0496	N395QS	(N175EC)	C-GKZL				
0497	N5161J	TC-MET	N497EA	OE-GCD	G-OBCC	N560EM	
0498	(N24QT)	N26QT	N26QL				
0499	N556BG						
0500	N500CU	N35TF	N960CR	N860CR			
0501	N51896	US Army 98-0007	[UC-35A]				
0502	N1298X	D2-EBA					
0503	N52059	(ZS-FCB)	VP-BDB	N204BG			
0504	N504CC						
0505	N52229	US Army 98-0008	[UC-35A]				
0506	N50820	G-RIBV	G-OGRG	EC-JFT			
0507	N5095N	N1129L	N994HP				
0508	N5085E	US Army 98-0009	[UC-35A]				
0509	N309QS	N509VE	YV....				
0510	N399QS	(N176EC)	C-GKZM				
0511	N200NK	YV2110					
0512	N29WE	N10AU	N10RU				
0513	N5061W	US Army 98-0010	[UC-35A]				
0514	N340QS	N850MA					
0515	N51042	VH-PSU					
0516	N316QS	N316WH	YV3103				
0517	N5145V	G-OTGT	N424HH	OE-GCB	N767KC		
0518	N51817	N1295B	JA02AA	N581SC	N93FS		
0519	N319QS	(N177EC)	C-GKZN	N100GY	N909LB		
0520	N51072	N620AT	N101KP				
0521	N5086W	N521CV	N22LC	N22LQ	N560AT		
0522	N398QS	N795AJ	YV3190				
0523	N332QS	N166MC					
0524	N5091J	US Marines 165740	[UC-35C]				
0525	N5093Y	N593M	N777WY				
0526	N326QS	YV534T	YV3128				
0527	N51396	N627AT	N102KP				
0528	N52WF						
0529	N5097H	US Marines 165741	[UC-35C]				
0530	N353QS	(N560PM)	N331BR				
0531	N397QS	[w/o 02May02 Leaky, TX; by Jan05 remains at Lancaster TX]					
0532	N5268V	N5209E	US Army 99-0100	[UC-35A]			
0533	N591M	XA-GSS					
0534	N5112K	US Army 99-0101	[UC-35A]	N403ET			
0535	N5267D	N1247V	N57MK	(N57ML)	N403ET		
0536	N363QS	N701GP	ZS-FLJ				
0537	N5181U	G-TTFN	OO-CLX	SE-RLU			
0538	N51143	US Army 99-0102	[UC-35A]				

CITATION ENCORE

C/n	Identities						
0539	N5108G	N539CE	N303CP				
0540	N540CV	N154JS	N158JS				
0541	N51780	N541CV	(N486BG)	N812DC	C-FXSS		
0542	N5093L	N542CE	(N120SB)	N12MW	N12MY	I-CMCC	N430AM
0543	N51995	N543LE	N1UM				
0544	N901DK	N701DK	D-CASA	N544VP	C-FTJC		
0545	N5091J	US Army 99-0103	[UC-35B]				
0546	N5151D	N368BE					
0547	N51995	N68MA	N906AS	N908AS	N610GD		

CITATION ENCORE

C/n	Identities							
0548	N5097H	US Army 99-0104	[UC-35B]					
0549	N5090A	N713DH	N486BG	N11TS	N33TS	N560CS		
0550	N51072	N865M	N3865M	N563M				
0551	N52670	N560RG	N86SK	N927PK				
0552	N5154J	N55HV	N552HV					
0553	N5145V	G-KDMA	VH-YUL					
0554	N5154J	N747RL	N749RL	N8486	N554VP			
0555	N5155G	N154JH						
0556	N5165P	N539WA	N556VP	N707W				
0557	N221CE	N557PG						
0558	N5174W	N560RV	N558V	N558CG	(D-CEBM)	N558GG	N558AK	N558NC	N80SN
0559	N5192E	N359EJ	(N659SA)	N359EC	N444RF			
0560	N5180C	N560JW						
0561	N5197M	N120SB	N511TH	(N60AE)				
0562	N5180K	N60NF	N911UM					
0563	N51995	N59KG	N56KG					
0564	N5241R	N7895Q	N660LT	N5601T				
0565	N5211A	US Army 00-1051	[UC-35A]					
0566	N5000R	N560BL	C-FAMI	N560FP				
0567	N5268A	US Marines 165938	[UC-35C]	[w/o 10Mar04 NAS Miramar, CA]				
0568	N52639	N155JH	N582WP					
0569	N52433	(N600LF)	N1315C	N600LF	D-CEBM	N569P	N564M	
0570	N5262W	US Marines 165939	[UC-35C]					
0571	N5244W	N3616						
0572	N174JS							
0573	N162TF	C-FALI	C-FRKI	C-FRKL	N804BG	N804BC*		
0574	N52526	US Army 00-1052	[UC-35A]					
0575	N5257C	N156JH	N912DP					
0576	N51072	N200JR	N280JR	C-GTGO	N560H			
0577	N5207V	US Army 00-1053	[UC-35A]					
0578	N5264N	D-CAUW						
0579	N5259Y	N579CE	N977DT					
0580	N5267G	N580CE	N1871R	N486SB	[w/o Upland, CA, 24Jun06]			
0581	N5269Z	N157JH	N560JE					
0582	N52229	N843HS	N560CX					
0583	N52591	N583CE						
0584	N5296X	N7HB	N90HB	N428SJ	N232JS			
0585	N5254Y	N221VP	(N585VP)	N832R				
0586	N52691	N201SU						
0587	N5270K	N120SB	(N587K)	N4TL				
0588	N5243K	C-GJEI	C-FQYB	N560GT				
0589	N5151D	US Army 01-0301	[UC-35A]					
0590	N5166T	OE-GPH	N403SR	N21H				
0591	N591DK							
0592	N5180C	US Marines 166374	[UC-35D]					
0593	N5260M	N121LS	N300AK	N308AK	N554SD	N243SL		
0594	N52446	N560MR						
0595	N560TE	N595KW						
0596	N52235	N844HS	N507PD					
0597	N51869	N597KC	JA002A					
0598	N5250P	N800QS	N806WC	N757TR				
0599	N52690	N288HL						
0600	N52369	PR-LAM	N915DK					
0601	N5239J	N801QS	N108VR					
0602	N5206T	N9CN						
0603	(N66W)	N5236L	N603CV	N313HC	N89PR			
0604	N911CB	N998JL						
0605	N5257C	N605CE	N250AL					
0606	N5245U	N802QS	N606CE	N91AG	N166ST			
0607	N5270K	ZS-UCH	SE-RGZ	N254DR				
0608	N52059	N608CE						
0609	N5269Z	N847HS	N242AC	N203NM				
0610	N52699	N804QS						
0611	N98AC	N98AQ	N560CH	N568CH	N611MR	N611MP		
0612	N5260U	N89MD						
0613	N44SH	N448H	N25QT	N25QA	N189WT			
0614	N5296X	N806QS						
0615	N510BG	N152JH						
0616	N52114	N616CE	N80GR					
0617	N5207A	N807QS						
0618	N51995	N933PB						
0619	N52135	N808QS						
0620	N101WY							
0621	N102WY							
0622	N5197A	N560KL	N743DB					
0623	N51993	N977MR						
0624	N5257V	N1242K	N500MG	N93CL	N2U	N53ST*		
0625	N810QS							
0626	N41VP							
0627	N5260M	N191VB	N191VF					
0628	N812QS							
0629	N844QS							
0630	N5180K	US Marines 166474 [UC-35C]						
0631	N813QS	N8130S	N560HC					
0632	N5228J	N6521F	N109WS	N105TD				
0633	N866QS	(N860Q)	N427CD	C-FTOM	N560BL			
0634	(N911CB)	N5254Y	N90NB					
0635	N5257C	N535CE	N5WT					
0636	N83TF	N83TK	N636SE	[w/o Cresco, IA, 19Jul06]				
0637	N5073G	CS-DIG	(PR-ALL)	LN-IDB				
0638	N5263S	(N814QS)	N1269P	N23YZ	N560ET			
0639	N5214L	N639CV	N24GF	(N2QE)				
0640	N640CE	N800BW						
0641	N5270J	N67GW	N1967G					
0642	N642LF	N379BC						

CITATION ENCORE/ENCORE+

C/n	Identities					
0643	N5264N	N960JH	(N990JH)	(N960BM)	C-FTJF	
0644	N5270K	N814QS	N95NB	N93NB	N644VP	N988PG
0645	N5269A	N299DH				
0646	N5260U	N846QS	N535BP			
0647	N647CE	C-GDSH	C-FYUL	N230JK		
0648	N5248V	N820QS	C-GTOG	C-FVEJ	N648VP	C-FAMI	C-GIJP
0649	N5267T	US Army 03-0016	[UC-35B]			
0650	N5260Y	N820QS				
0651	US Marines 166500		N5156D	US Marines 166500	[UC-35D]	
0652	N652NR	YR-ELV	LN-IDC			
0653	N5265N	PR-SCR				
0654	N52653	N654CE				
0655	N825QS					
0656	N656Z					
0657	N5214L	N778BC	N450MQ			
0658	N52234	N560RM				
0659	N191KL	N721NB				
0660	N5264M	N844TM				
0661	N5162W	N591CF	N682CE			
0662	N5212M	N560CR	N338MC	N560LF		
0663	N5266F	N357BE				
0664	N5151D	N664CE				
0665	N5200R	OE-GEJ	YR-RPG	M-FRED	OM-ATM	N504U
0666	N51160	N700JR	N708JR			
0667	N52462	US Army 03-0726	[UC-35B]			
0668	N5214L	N560TG	(N560TP)	N45TP		
0669	N5216A	N834QS				
0670	N5243K	N670CE	N611CS	N560JT	N962KC	
0671	N52457	N600BW				
0672	N5253G	US Navy 166712	[UC-35D]			
0673	N5245U	N96NB	N98NB	N673VP	N682DG	
0674	N52601	N552TC	N552CN			
0675	N29QC					
0676	N227WS	C-FSNC				
0677	N5079V	US Navy 166713	[UC-35D]			
0678	N5203J	N399HS	N177JE			
0679	US Marines 166714	[UC-35D]				
0680	N5245L	N595MA	N595JJ	N958GB		
0681	N5265B	N681CE				
0682	N5204D	US Navy 166715*	[UC-35D]			
0683	N51042	F-HLIM				
0684	N5161J	N684CE	N684BM	(N827TV)	N370TC	N774SB
0685	N5086W	N837QS				
0686	N5188A	[c.f. c/n 0751 below]				
0687	N5207V	XA-UEF	XC-LNN			
0688	N5248B	N254AD				
0689	N52059	XC-GDT				
0690	N5218T	N839QS				
0691	N5241Z	N300PX	N500PX	N560PX	N960M	
0692	N5166T	N40166	N999CB	N852AC*		
0693	N5076K	US Navy 166766	[UC-35D]			
0694	N5079V	N4018S	JA560Y			
0695	N5172M	N695V	N345NF			
0696	N50715	US Navy 166767	[UC-35D]			
0697	N5093D	N697CE	LV-CBB			
0698	N5216A	N809QS				
0699	N52462	N560HM				
0700	N5268E	N700NK				
0701	N113US					
0702	N702AM	C-GRYC	C-GRFC			
0703	N52144	VH-VPL	VH-VRL			
0704	N5248V	PR-GQG	N866VP			
0705	N52639	C-FYMM				
0706	N802QS					
0707	N13092	(HL7778)				

CITATION ENCORE+

C/n	Identities					
0751	N560CC	[Encore+ prototype, believed to originally be c/n 560-0686, ff 22Mar06 Cedar Rapids, IA]				N560KW
0752	N5112K	N752CE				
0753	N5095N	N753CE	N120SB	C-FACC	C-FACO	
0754	N5100J	(N960JH)	N990JH			
0755	N5218R	N56TE				
0756	N52645	N545BP				
0757	N52141	YV2389	N657RH			
0758	N62WA	N83WA				
0759	N387SV	N229N				
0760	N5245L	PR-CTB	N760WF			
0761	N5036Q	N560DL				
0762	N68HC	N68NC	N24QT	N24QA		
0763	N50612	N926CE				
0764	N5174W	N764CE	LN-AKA	N64SV		
0765	N5245U	N713WD	(N719WD)	N587MV	(N589MV)	N946TS
0766	N766CE	N15CV				
0767	N5247U	I-ZACK				
0768	N5085E	N179RP	EC-KKB	EC-KOV	N562CL	
0769	N5241Z	N769CS				
0770	N5093Y	EC-KKK	N770VR	C-GRYC		
0771	N237BG	N765F				
0772	N5244F	N772CS				
0773	N5207A	M-ANSL	SE-RIT	N560RH		

CITATION ENCORE+

C/n	Identities					
0774	N774CC	N422JT	N404SP	N853AC		
0775	N5211Q	N803QS				
0776	N5223D	N814QS				
0777	N5216A	N777EN	N475JC			
0778	N5223X	N818QS				
0779	N5185V	N787CW	N779RK			
0780	N780CE	N560CL				
0781	N781CE	C-GDSH	C-GPLS	N380LV	YV546T	N555JA
0782	N826QS					
0783	N5091J	N560CH				
0784	N830QS					
0785	N5257C	N203WS				
0786	N819QS					
0787	N887CS					
0788	N5259Y	N788CE	N468CE	N468CF	N717VL	
0789	N822QS					
0790	N843QS					
0791	N5079V	N507CR	N44GT			
0792	N831QS					
0793	N793CS	N416BS				
0794	N823QS					
0795	N51942	N114EB				
0796	N829QS					
0797	N846QS					
0798	N5214L	N808PL				
0799	N841QS					
0800	N800CV	N101CP	LQ-CVO			
0801	N827QS					
0802	N52136	N866TC				
0803	N5247U	N865M	N803CJ	(N69LD)	N49LD	
0804	N804CV					
0805	N5188A	N571AP				
0806	N5196U	D-CAPB				
0807	N5064M	N807CE	VH-MXD			
0808	N5152X	N360HS				
0809	N5097H	N610BK	N196JP			
0810	N5204D	N810CV	N337CC	N657DM		
0811	N50736	N811WE				
0812	N5268A	N812CV	C-GAWU	N812VP	N917TL	
0813	N51942	N100U	N813CJ	N505RH		
0814	N5200Z	D-CIFM	N814TX	OE-GDM		
0815	N488JD	N815CJ	N2426	N272P	C-FNDF	
0816	N5135K	[aircraft scrapped before completion]				
0817	[aircraft scrapped before completion]					
0818	[aircraft not built]					
0819	[aircraft not built]					
0820	(D-CNSC)	[aircraft not built]				
0821	[aircraft not built]					
0822	[aircraft not built]					
0823	N823CE	[aircraft registered but not built]				

Production complete

+ after a registration indicates test marks not fully confirmed

CESSNA 560XL CITATION EXCEL/XLS/XLS+

C/n	Identities							
706	N560XL	[ff 29Feb96]						
5001	N561XL	[cx Jan11; b/u]						
5002	N5060K	N562XL	N12L					
5003	N5165T	N563XL	(PT-WZO)	PT-FPP	N814BR			
5004	N5148N	OE-GAP	N504VP	N504BM	Pakistan J-754			
5005	N51575	N208PC	SE-RBB	N166MB	N77UW			
5006	N5141F	N8005	N569MK					
5007	N5200R	N83RR	N97VN	OE-GTK	I-CDBS	N70TH		
5008	N5204D	N207PC	SE-RBC	N944AH				
5009	N52113	N398RS						
5010	N52178	N27XL	VT-CLA					
5011	N52141	N560L						
5012	N52144	N561DA	I-JETS	N560CE				
5013	N5216A	N1243C	N1PB	N191PB	N977SD			
5014	N5221Y	N60GL	(N58KJ)	N56K	N1SN	N10SN	(N16SN)	N989TW	N531MB
5015	N5223D	N523KW	N560HN					
5016	N615RG							
5017	N517XL	N157AE	N600BJ	N500PX	(N300PX)	N865CE	N580AW	
5018	N5250E	ZS-FCB	N223AM	N410MT				
5019	N980DK	N990DK	N380PK					
5020	N5246Z	PT-XCL	(N61850)	N18JE				
5021	N5244F	D-CMIC	N560GM	N862CE	N862CF	N909LA		
5022	N522XL	HZ-FYZ	D-CSFD					
5023	N51933	N822MJ	N236LD	N236LB	N3444B			
5024	N654EL	N622PC	N622PL					
5025	N534CC	N584CC	LV-BMH	LQ-BMH				
5026	N5201M	N17UC	(N17UG)	C-GJRB	N697FF			
5027	N5202D	N560GB	N560GP	N560ML				
5028	N5203J	N528XL	CS-DDB	OO-MLG				
5029	N5203S	(PT-...)	SE-DYX	OE-GYX	N96TE			
5030	N52038	N1228N	N899BC	N17AN				
5031	N531BJ	N560BT						
5032	N165JB	N108EK						
5033	N5211Q	N456JW	XA-UVA	N50LD				
5034	N52113	PP-RAA						
5035	N5213S	N35XL	N4JS	N4KS				
5036	N52136	N884BB	N36XL	N884BB	N910CS	N317ML	N526SM	N528SM	N705WL
5037	N5214J	D-CIII	OE-GTI	(D-CGTI)	D-CADY	N900WL		
5038	N5214K	N404BT	N590AK					
5039	N39JV	N88WU	N87WU					
5040	N5214L	N54HA	N840CC					
5041	N52141	N1XL	N39RC					
5042	N52178	N42XL	SU-EWC	N418CK	N413CK	N418CK	N842A	
5043	N5218R	PT-XIB						
5044	N5218T	N544XL						
5045	N5221Y	PP-JFM						
5046	N5223D	N966MT	A9C-BXA	N83GG	[cx Dec10; b/u]			
5047	N5223P	C-FCEL	N838RT	N888RT	N838RT	N847A		
5048	N868JB	N548XL	VP-CAI					
5049	N5223Y	N24PH	N24PY	N680VR	N560VR	N305LX		
5050	N5225K	N184G	N88HP					
5051	N5226B	N1324B	SX-DCM	TC-TMO				
5052	N5228Z	N990MF						
5053	N5231S	I-BENT	N620GS	N991RW				
5054	N5233J	N1306V	N80X					
5055	N488CP	(N560KN)						
5056	N51993	D-CVHB	EC-IRU	N688AG	SE-RBX	OH-RBX		
5057	N52457	N350RD	N240B	N53WF				
5058	N5235G	N555WF	N555WE	HB-VNC	S5-BBD	OE-GGK		
5059	N55HA	N55HX	N580BC					
5060	N5201J	PT-WYU						
5061	N5200R	HB-VMO	OE-GUN					
5062	N5197A	N22KW	N23LM	N97EM				
5063	N5200U	N56HA	N56HX	N71LU				
5064	N5194J	N2JW	N555WF	N586SF	N386SF	N227MC		
5065	N5204D	N100SC	N112CW					
5066	N134SW	HB-VMU	N192RW					
5067	N42PA	HB-VMZ	OE-GPZ	N864CC	N309BT	N202CW		
5068	N52081	N57HA	N57HX	N56LP				
5069	N5201M	N404SB	N189WW					
5070	N5207A	VP-CNM	N507VP	N789CN	HB-VOU			
5071	N51881	N671QS	N579MH					
5072	N52178	N565AB	N565BA	N180FW	N51VT			
5073	N5214K	D-CDBW	N79EA	N121TL	N121TE	N560DR		
5074	N636GS	N466LM	4X-CPU	N574AV	N66LM	N958AP		
5075	N558R	N568R						
5076	N521RA	N55VW						
5077	N51575	N221LC	N46VE	N76VE	XA-PLA	N960HD		
5078	N5203J	C-FPWC	N560HJ	SE-RHJ				
5079	N5218T	ZS-OHZ						
5080	N52141	N90CF	N475PD					
5081	N4000K							
5082	N145SM	N469RS						
5083	N52144	N520G	N520Q	XA-SID				
5084	N5211A	N684QS	N384WC	N12ND				
5085	N52113	N85XL	N883PF	N803PF	5Y-WHB			
5086	N51817	N62GB	N269JR	N394WJ	N957BJ			
5087	N5165T	PT-MSK						
5088	N52081	VP-BSD	G-WCIN	EC-KOL				
5089	N51942	N868JB	N868J	N21MA	N560GC			
5090	N51246	N690QS	N590VP					
5091	N5183V	N560CH	N83SD	N170SD				
5092	N5125J	N692QS	C-GYMC					

CITATION EXCEL

C/n	Identities						
5093	N5203S	N19MK	N19MZ	N903DK	N210VS		
5094	N1094L						
5095	N5135A	N95XL	PR-LPG				
5096	N5202D	C-GCXL					
5097	N5226B	C-GLMI	N597TX	N900TV			
5098	N5244F	N200PF	N502BC				
5099	N58XL	N58HA	N58HX				
5100	N51444	N510XL	N49MJ	N49MU	N100CJ		
5101	N5216A	N88845	N81SH				
5102	N5153K	N997CB					
5103	N5218R	N68HC	N68HG				
5104	N5223D	(F-HACD)	LX-JCD	(F-GXXX)	N104XL	N717CD	
5105	N5185V	PR-RAA	PP-JGV				
5106	N5221Y	N506AM	HB-VND	G-ELOA	N316GK	N712GK	
5107	N51342	N560DA	I-NYNY	N300SJ			
5108	N562DB	N562DD					
5109	N324LX	(N324LE)	N561GR	N58LC	N458LC	N58LQ	
5110	N5200Z	PH-RSA					
5111	N5141F	N532CC	(N530CC)	N522CC	N380M		
5112	N52457	N1129E	ZS-CCW				
5113	N52178	OE-GME	N810JB				
5114	N5223P	N20SB	N717MB	N38HG	N877RW		
5115	N5157E	N20WE	VT-ARA				
5116	N5246Z	N498AB					
5117	N5233J	N202RL					
5118	N5214L	N1241K	B-7019				
5119	N5197A	N357WC	N75HU				
5120	N5211Q	PR-AAA					
5121	N5223Y	N560CG					
5122	N5211F	N67TW	N673W	(N373MJ)	N317JM*		
5123	N5201J	N699BC	N59EC				
5124	N5207A	N24NG	N883SC				
5125	N5214K	N4JB					
5126	N626QS	N39FW					
5127	N560KT	N560FH					
5128	N5228Z	PH-CJI					
5129	N5214J	N359WC	N94LA	N680AT			
5130	N52113	N630QS	N29ZR				
5131	N52136	N631QS	N131VP	5R-AHF			
5132	N5225K	N632QS	N513VP	LV-CBK			
5133	N23NG	N359CC	N510FS				
5134	(N5250E)	N52352	N561BP	LV-BRX			
5135	N5200U	N135ET	LV-ZXW	N885BB			
5136	N52639	N4005G	VP-CWM	N560JP	N522RA	N100YB	
5137	N637QS	N300WC	LV-CCG	N785DW			
5138	N5265N	N704JW	N924JE	N138HW			
5139	N639QS	N239WC	N560HX				
5140	N52655	N884B					
5141	N52235	N17AN	N701CR	N901CR			
5142	N5093D	N705SG					
5143	N5096S	N1836S	N966JM	N150BL			
5144	N5108G	C-GOEL	N713DF	N713DH	N52MW	N560TS	N552SC
5145	N52645	N645QS	N645Q	N507D			
5146	N291DV						
5147	N52059	N24UD					
5148	N52234	N777FH	N200SC	XA-UTD			
5149	N627XL						
5150	N5100J	N650QS	N150WC	LV-CCF	N817LF		
5151	N5147B	N79PF	C-GHCB	N560KS			
5152	N5101J	N652QS	(N650RJ)	N888RP			
5153	N5105F	N916CS	N816CS				
5154	N51160	N154XL	HB-VNI	OE-GXL			
5155	N5095N	N1837S					
5156	N5155G	N2ZC					
5157	N5163G	N40577	OH-ONE	OE-GCA			
5158	N5151D	N917EE	N615EC				
5159	N5163K	C-GMNC	N336MA	N326MA			
5160	N51869	N595A	N903FH	N901FH	N902FH		
5161	N404MM	N405MM	G-VECT	N561HH			
5162	N51511	N168BG	N600BS				
5163	N5166T	N63LX	N68LX	N591MA			
5164	N5166U	N64LX	N84LX				
5165	N5109W	N665QS	N190PR				
5166	N52059	N5068R	N580RC	N580EE			
5167	N5188N	N250SM	G-REDS	B-9429			
5168	N565DR	N780CS	VT-SWC	M-TIME	N562SC	N155FS	N919WG*
5169	N923PC	OE-GPN	C-GKXS				
5170	N670QS	N261GC					
5171	N5236L	SU-EWB	N632BL	N1219M			
5172	N5086W	HB-VNH	N105RJ	I-BEDT			
5173	N51743	N5173F	N560JF				
5174	N5223X	N624AT	N624WP				
5175	N52114	N625AT					
5176	N676QS						
5177	N5061P	N841DW					
5178	N562TS	(N258TT)					
5179	N51984	N512DR	N86TW	N188WS	(N186WS)		
5180	N52235	N868JB	N868J	N845JS			
5181	N681QS	N696M	N604SN*				
5182	N5058J	N98RX	N563CH	N712GC	N712CG		
5183	N5090V	G-CFRA	G-IAMS	OK-CAA			
5184	N5061W	N184XL	N531RC	N531RQ			
5185	N51042	G-SIRS					
5186	N186XL						
5187	N687QS	C-FKHJ					

C/n	Identities						
5188	N688QS	N647MK					
5189	N5073G	OY-GKC	OO-SAV	N560ZF	B-9465		
5190	N51038	N560S	G-XLSB	N104LV			
5191	N5090A	N767BS					
5192	N50820	N119LP	N192XL	N164AS	N176DL		
5193	N811ST	N968BS					
5194	N694QS	N708M*					
5195	N51143	D-CVHI	D-CINI	(D-CJOY)	N237NA	N800AM	
5196	N51038	XA-ICO	N905AC				
5197	N697QS	N697SD					
5198	N552MA	N560NY	N86WU				
5199	N699QS	N950MA*					
5200	N5109R	C-GXCO	N950BA				
5201	N5096S	N533CC	N523CC	N828CK	(N760RE)	N760ED	
5202	N5095N	N50XL	N82KW	N600CF			
5203	N603QS	N137BW					
5204	N604QS						
5205	N5100J	N503CS	N525VP	N503CS	(N502VP)	N503QF	
5206	N5101J	N821DG	N921DG	N206CX	N561CE		
5207	N5076J	N62GB	N62GR	N592CF			
5208	N5109W	XA-TKZ					
5209	N5093Y	N501XL	(PH-DYX)	HB-VNS	S5-BDC	5R-HMR	
5210	N610QS						
5211	N5076K	PR-VRD	N399PV				
5212	N5090Y	N560DP					
5213	N5108G	N1130G	(D-CASH)	N24EP			
5214	N57KW	N75EB					
5215	N50612	N560TH	N5091J	VP-CPC	N560TH	M-CEXL	S5-BDG	N560SJ
5216	N5103J	CS-DNY	N926HL				
5217	N5079V	(OY-LEG)	OY-EKC	SE-RCL	HB-VWJ	N550DU	ZP-...
5218	N218AM	P4-ALM	VP-CFM	T7-FAY			
5219	N5079H	N877RF	N871RF				
5220	N5112K	N318MM					
5221	N5094D	CS-DNW	N551QS				
5222	N2HB	N560JP	N426CH				
5223	N5068R	PR-EMS					
5224	N5093L	N146EP	N595G				
5225	N5117U	N351WC	N351CG				
5226	N5196U	N350WC	N562WD	N411KQ			
5227	N5197M	N627QS					
5228	N5000R	EI-PAX	G-IPAX				
5229	N5105F	N504CS	N529VP	YV508T	N560CR		
5230	N5085E	G-NETA	OO-PGG				
5231	N231XL	N417JD	N511DN	N153SG	N876RA		
5232	N451W	N34WP	N9U				
5233	N233XL						
5234	N5076J	C-FCXL					
5235	N5086W	CS-DNZ	N300AK				
5236	N51072	N236LD	S5-BAZ	S5-ICR	D-CICR*		
5237	N5061W	N751PL					
5238	N5061P	N238SM					
5239	N239XL	N626AT	N192W				
5240	N51055	N640QS					
5241	N5090V	N100AR					
5242	N51042	TC-LMA	G-LDFM	N560FS			
5243	N5093D	N567CH	N243CH	(D-CSLX)	OK-SLX		
5244	N51743	N5090A	N244XL	N898MC	N898PP		
5245	N50820	N245J	N1MM				
5246	N646QS						
5247	N51038	N7RL	N57RL	G-CIEL			
5248	N5109R	HB-VNR	OO-FPA	(N414XL)	N28XL	XA-HTL	
5249	N5096S	N80LP	N429JS				
5250	N5095N	N25NG	N56FE	N90HH	N115TL		
5251	N651QS						
5252	N5145V	N505CS	(N552VP)	N501UP			
5253	N5154J	N72SG	(N62SG)	N73SG	C-FTIL	N600PY	
5254	N631RP	N681RP	N626TN				
5255	N52081	N60AG	N15TF	N716LD			
5256	N5194B	N4107V	PR-GAM				
5257	N5196U	CS-DFM	N770CK				
5258	N52334	C-GWII	PH-DRK	LX-VMF			
5259	N52526	G-XLMB	G-XLGB	N26SJ	VT-AVV		
5260	N527SC	N711HA	N711VH	N712BG	N450AJ		
5261	N5091J	N75TP	N57TP	C-FLFE			
5262	N662QS						
5263	N663QS						
5264	N5066U	N664QS					
5265	N5100J	OE-GPA	N5535	G-PEPE	N248SF		
5266	N5245D	G-CBRG	N562SC	N21GD			
5267	N5246Z	N506CS	V5-NDB				
5268	N668QS						
5269	N51160	HB-VAA	Switzerland T-784				
5270	N5058J	N356WC	N300DA				
5271	N5103J	LN-SUX	G-CGMF				
5272	N5079V	N1326A					
5273	N5073G	N1268D	N617PD				
5274	N5060K	PR-ACC	N753JL				
5275	N675QS						
5276	N276A	N556LS					
5277	N5076K	N560CM	N695QE				
5278	N16GS	N176GS	N95CC	N278XL			
5279	N679QS						
5280	N621QS	N561LS					
5281	N68AA	N142AA					
5282	N5094D	N507CS	N528VP	YV540T			

CITATION EXCEL

C/n	Identities					
5283	N5097H	CS-DFN	N1122K			
5284	N5109W	N560DE	(OO-VIZ)	N560JP	C-GUPC	N284VP	C-FMOS
5285	N5112K	N285XL	N422AB	N58FE	N45NS	
5286	N51143	N622QS				
5287	N118ST	YV2975				
5288	N5117U	SX-DCE	N560RS			
5289	N5105F	PR-NBR	N44EJ	N1980M*		
5290	N691QS					
5291	N5086W	N829JC	N829JQ	N397BC		
5292	N5101J	N666MX	N848JS			
5293	N695QS					
5294	N5068R	N508CS	(N294VP)	N500UP		
5295	N50820	N641QS				
5296	N696QS					
5297	N51612	N821DG	(N721DG)	N1871R	C-GRCC	
5298	N5061P	C-GSEC	C-FBXL			
5299	N623QS					
5300	N5085E	N613GY	N613KS	(N618KS)	N829LC	
5301	N601QS					
5302	(N118ST)	N624QS				
5303	N1867M					
5304	N636QS	N636EJ				
5305	N628QS					
5306	N629QS					
5307	N51072	XA-DRM	N894MA			
5308	N608QS					
5309	N5093D	N309XL	C-GMKZ			
5310	N509CS	N502UP				
5311	N5090A	N712KC	N560JP	N560PD		
5312	N612QS					
5313	N562XL	[first Citation XLS; re-serialled 560-5501 q.v.]				
5314	N5000R	CS-DFO	N91GY			
5315	N5095N	CS-DFP	OE-GRI			
5316	N5096S	D-CWWW	OE-GCG			
5317	N5269J	N57WP				
5318	N51743	N102FS	OO-FTS			
5319	N625QS					
5320	N5194J	N66W	N151KV	N847JS		
5321	N605QS					
5322	N5196U	N1838S	N183JS	N183YS		
5323	N606QS	N606Q	N560RS	N561RW	N440ML	
5324	N511CS	(N324VP)	N504UP			
5325	N52397	N568DM	N48NA	N560FM		
5326	N512CS	(N326VP)	N503UP			
5327	N175WS	N178WS	YV3147			
5328	N514CS	N818BL				
5329	N848DM					
5330	N638QS	(N638Q)	N395WJ			
5331	N643QS	N6430S	N946TC	N510HF		
5332	N727YB	N710MT				
5333	N533XL	N2				
5334	N5093L	CS-DFQ	N552QS			
5335	N515CS	N335XL				
5336	N5165P	N336XL	(N404PK)	(N336BC)		
5337	N51942	N198DF	N560JP	N79BC	YR-RPR	N17ED
5338	N5094D	N606QS				
5339	N51143	OE-GNW	HA-JED			
5340	N50820	N607QS				
5341	N5061W	N3				
5342	N5223P	N7337F	N777JV	N228Y	N228L	N342BL
5343	N5145V	G-WINA	N969XX	N843JS*		
5344	N51055	I-CMAL	N1NA			
5345	N616QS					
5346	N517CS	N346XL				
5347	N47HF					
5348	N470SK					
5349	N676BB	N670BB	N447MJ			
5350	N5270M	N325FN	LV-AIW	N325FN	N562HC	
5351	N5101J	N53XL	N1HS	N71HS	N560AW	
5352	N5245D	ZS-IDC	ZS-FOS	N846JS		
5353	N678QS	N5250E	EC-ISQ			
5354	N518CS	(N71RL)	N178BR			
5355	N659QS	N5200Z	CS-DFR	N168MC		
5356	N5101J	N519CS	XA-UAF			
5357	N5161J	N567MC				
5358	N5235G	N635QS				
5359	N659QS					
5360	N5079V	N615QS				
5361	N52397	N361XL	VP-CGG	G-CFGL	N112AB	N561JL
5362	N521CS	N506UP				
5363	N638QS					
5364	N522CS	(N364VP)	N880P			
5365	N667QS					
5366	N5216A	N585PC	N555WF	N555WZ	(N560WF)	
5367	N677QS					
5368	N5094D	N12686	VT-CSP			
5369	N5197A	N678QS	N504PK	N504LV		
5370	N5270P	N770JM	N421LT			
5371	N371P	PR-OUR				
5372	N5091J	CS-DFS	N553QS			

C/n	Identities

CITATION XLS

C/n	Identities						
5501	N562XL	[converted from c/n 560-5313]			N633RP	N683RP	N883RP
5502	N52144	N502XL	N502EG				
5503	N503XS	N732JR	N553VP	XA-AEA			
5504	N5223Y	N111GU					
5505	N901DK						
5506	N618QS						
5507	N523CS	N270PR					
5508	N72SG						
5509	N617QS						
5510	N52352	N41118	N357EC	N941KA			
5511	N52609	N670MW					
5512	N52433	CS-DFT	N898MP	N669CC	N283MM		
5513	N196SB						
5514	N5086W	N143DH	N611MR				
5515	N5157E	N4118K	N361EC	N110PG			
5516	N540CS	N719TT					
5517	N52639	PR-RAV	N778BC	N475JC	N478JC	N106SP	N106SJ	N456HC*
5518	N52699	N602QS					
5519	N52655	N43HF					
5520	N5269A	CS-DFU	N554QS				
5521	N541CS	HI955					
5522	N51872	N609QS					
5523	N542CS	N900KD					
5524	N5267G	N546CS					
5525	N5264A	N370BA	N624GF				
5526	N5194B	N633QS					
5527	N5254Y	N713DH	(N712DH)	N321CL			
5528	N5296X	N579BJ	N456SL	HB-VON	N715MM	N613BB	
5529	N5262X	OE-GEG	SE-RIZ				
5530	N5270J	N4107W	N491N	N2Q			
5531	N52229	N560JG	N748W				
5532	N5270E	N562DB	N562LD				
5533	N711NK	N711NR	N917EE	N104PC	N913KZ		
5534	N5165P	N424HH					
5535	N5141F	PT-ORM	N535TF				
5536	N25XL	D-CHSP	G-XLTV				
5537	N5152X	I-TAKA					
5538	N5163C	N538XL	OE-GCM	D-CMMI	N789KG		
5539	N52178	N4007J	B-3642				
5540	N5090Y	N4008S	B-3643				
5541	N5201J	N560JC	LV-BCS	N63FT			
5542	N5267K	N547CS	N507UP				
5543	N5165T	CS-DFV	N555QS				
5544	N5268M	PP-BRS	N754V	PP-SBR	N137TN	N900XL	
5545	N5269J	N45XL	N560TV				
5546	N51881	N549CS	N508UP				
5547	N5156D	N647QS					
5548	N5168Y	N611QS					
5549	N51780	CS-DXA	N39GA	N727MH	N527EE		
5550	N200JR	N632BL	N682BL	N21FR			
5551	N550CS	N509UP					
5552	N5231S	PP-MDB					
5553	N5103J	N12778	CS-DXB	N556QS			
5554	N5166U	JY-AW1	EC-JZK	G-CIFJ	N255RC		
5555	N51869	(D-CLDI)	D-CAAA	M-CESA	LV-FQD		
5556	N385MG	C-GSLC					
5557	N5197M	N551CS	N5NR				
5558	N52609	N634QS					
5559	N5093L	N1281N	CS-DXC	N557QS			
5560	N51984	N553CS	N264SC	N560CR	(N1PB)	N97TE	
5561	N5296X	N642QS					
5562	N5109R	N619QS					
5563	N5226B	N45NF	(N457F)	N563CS			
5564	N560TM	EC-JVF	OE-GAC	LX-NAT			
5565	N5196U	N370M	N560MU				
5566	N52113	N70XL					
5567	N5213S	(D-CKLI)	D-CBBB	M-CESB	N567KS	N870SB	
5568	N5197A	N6779D	CS-DXD	N558QS			
5569	D-CTLX	OE-GHB					
5570	N10VQ	N155RW					
5571	N5211F	N24PH					
5572	N5194B	N554CS	N510UP				
5573	N51881	(OE-GAL)	D-CTTT				
5574	N5090A	N648QS					
5575	N5267J	N75XL	N851AC				
5576	N5245U	HB-VNY	CS-DPZ	N707MT	N394AG		
5577	N5267K	N556CS	N758CP				
5578	N5261R	N1299H	CS-DXE	N578VR			
5579	N5253S	N2HB	PP-RST				
5580	N614QS						
5581	N5153K	N577PS					
5582	N644QS						
5583	N5076J	PR-CON					
5584	N51342	G-CDOL	I-CDOL				
5585	N51396	(D-CTLX)	N558CS	N560BA	N560TW		
5586	N5145V	N1299K	CS-DXF				
5587	N5135A	N806MN	N808MN				
5588	N643QS						
5589	N5262W	N842DW	N500PX				
5590	N5197M	N590XL	N103PG	N101PG	N559VP		
5591	N771DE						

C/n	Identities				
5592	N52639	N586SF			
5593	N5152X	N559CS	N593XL	EC-JXI	D-CCEA	D-CGMR
5594	N5180C	N4017R	(VT-XLS)	VT-JSS	
5595	N5135K	CS-DXG			
5596	N5181U	N82GM	N1HS	N96XL	N906AC
5597	N5228J	N562CS	N780CC	N711LV	
5598	N5264A	N12990	PK-ILA	PK-RJT	
5599	N613QS				
5600	N51780	N560PL	N228PC		
5601	N5268M	N563CS	N563XL	N867W	
5602	N52235	N499HS			
5603	N5244W	N868XL			
5604	N562DB	N562DL	N134FM		
5605	N5101J	OB-1824			
5606	N566F				
5607	N52038	N7HB	(N560HB)	N301HB	PR-XLS
5608	N5103J	LN-XLS	SX-ADK	G-GXLS	
5609	N5162W	N442LW	N442LU	N90BL	
5610	N52613	LX-GDX	G-OMEA		
5611	N654QS				
5612	N5141F	N564CS	N926DR	N441BP	
5613	N5265B	N613XL	G-PKRG	G-CXLS	
5614	N5206T	N45PK	N614XL	N484SF	
5615	N5266F	CS-DXH			
5616	N5267T	N678QS			
5617	N5201J	N563XP	[XLS+ prototype]		
5618	N52136	N618XL	C-GRPB	PH-JND	XA-LAP
5619	N5246Z	PR-LFT			
5620	N5264E	D-CAIR			
5621	N52682	N1300J	CS-DXI		
5622	N52691	N561MK			
5623	N5244F	D-CDDD	N562VP		
5624	N5267K	N1312K	SE-RCM		
5625	N5245D	N916CS	N913CS		
5626	N5197M	N68GW	N515CP		
5627	N51396	CS-DXJ			
5628	N51038	N890LE			
5629	N5261R	N560VH	N1897A	N1397A	5N-BOQ	N560PM
5630	N51612	D-CEEE			
5631	N51042	SX-SMR	G-ECAI	N631JD	
5632	N5262W	N632XL			
5633	N5185J	N13218	CS-DXK		
5634	N51612	D-CFFF	N634VP	N823DT	
5635	N51806	N1312T	N573AB	N493RP	N486TT
5636	N657QS				
5637	N5225K	N568CS	N511UP		
5638	N4086L	N64LX	N737D		
5639	N5152X	XA-MMX	N639VP	N212CE	
5640	"N5188W"+	[+Marks current on a homebuilt]		N1319X	CS-DXL
5641	N51342	PH-JNX	D-CCSG	YU-SMK	
5642	N5181U	N642XL	D-CRUW	HB-VOM	OE-GKE
5643	N683QS				
5644	N52626	PR-TRJ			
5645	N5223X	N88SF	D-COBI		
5646	N5223P	N921MW			
5647	N660QS				
5648	N5109W	N1320P	N711HA		
5649	N5155G	SP-KCS			
5650	N685QS				
5651	N5228J	N673QS			
5652	N5183V	N226JT			
5653	N5257C	N698QS			
5654	N5264S	N682QS			
5655	N5161J	N655QS			
5656	N52369	N35SE	N40HC		
5657	N693QS				
5658	N5135A	A9C-BXI	HZ-BSA	HZ-KME1	
5659	N689QS				
5660	N5247U	N602MA	S5-BAV	N560LS	
5661	N686QS				
5662	N5211Q	SX-DCD	N362CA	N894KS	
5663	N5268E	N672QS			
5664	N5241R	N600QS			
5665	N52601	N658QS			
5666	N51780	LN-EXL	EI-XLS	N68MY	
5667	N5192E	XA-UGQ	N128AW	D-CKHG	
5668	N5183U	(I-LAST)	(I-AGLS)	OE-GZK	
5669	N5202D	N633RP	N637RP	N357TW	
5670	N52655	N670XL	(D-CCWD)	D-CAJK	N936EA
5671	N5269Z	N55NG			
5672	(N656QS)	N5207V	C-FTXL		
5673	N5269J	VH-XCJ	VH-XCU		
5674	N51160	D-CHHH	9H-VMK		
5675	N5266F	G-OXLS			
5676	N5265N	A9C-BXJ	N560RB	N612AC	
5677	N5180K	N661QS			
5678	N52613	N702AC	N513SK	(N513XX)	N513CC
5679	N5263S	N1230F	A6-GJB	N679CF	(N560PS)	Peru EP-861
5680	N52690	N571CS	N512UP		
5681	N5221Y	C-GPAW			
5682	N50549	F-GVYC			
5683	N5256Z	N1130X	CS-DXM		
5684	N5061P	N669TT			
5685	N5259Y	N11963	CS-DXN		
5686	N5061W	N86XL	C-FNXL	N892SB	

CITATION XLS

C/n	Identities						
5687	N5068F	N533CC	N588CC				
5688	N50639	D-CVHB	N469ED				
5689	N50275	N669QS					
5690	N5130J	(VP-BWC)	N560FC	M-BWFC	N690XL		
5691	N5264E	C-FWXL	C-FYUL				
5692	N5026Q	N1198V	CS-DXO				
5693	N5069E	TC-LNS	N693EA	N631HH			
5694	N5072X	N717NB					
5695	N5166T	OE-GSR	N859AE	N528AC			
5696	N5105F	LV-BIB	N569VP	PR-HOF			
5697	N5136J	N594QS					
5698	N5091J	G-XBEL	N698VP	N75HF			
5699	N5148N	G-RSXL	N699XL	N177E			
5700	N52235	ES-SKY	N813DH	N713DH	N916DK		
5701	N5264U	N414AA	A6-GJC	N570CF	OE-GGP		
5702	N1275T	CS-DXP					
5703	N5250E	N560MF	5N-BJS				
5704	N1281R	CS-DXQ					
5705	N50736	N574CS	N705TX	N514UP			
5706	N592QS						
5707	N5253S	N534CC	N580HC				
5708	N576QS						
5709	N5227G	XA-UHQ					
5710	N5254Y	N1312T	5A-DRK				
5711	N51744	N1315D	(VT-...)	N560TD			
5712	N595QS	G-LEAX					
5713	N51881	N614EP	N854AN				
5714	N599QS						
5715	N32KM						
5716	N38KW						
5717	N52369	C-GAWR	N886BH				
5718	N399SF	N913CL					
5719	N5236L	N12UD	D-CMMP	N75PS			
5720	N52397	N121KL					
5721	N588QS						
5722	N5165T	D-CLLL	(TC-OHY)	TC-LLL			
5723	N5260M	D-CVVV	OK-IRI	9H-IRI			
5724	N5263U	G-OROO	VT-AON				
5725	N5260U	N725XL					
5726	N50054	N577CS	(N726XL)	N515UP			
5727	N5192E	VH-NGH	LX-INS	SE-RMR			
5728	N5264A	N946PC	N811MB				
5729	N5264N	C-GKEG	C-GTOG	N560DW			
5730	N575QS						
5731	N51995	I-CMAB					
5732	N656QS						
5733	N51143	OO-AIE	N735XL				
5734	N411EC						
5735	N577QS						
5736	N52229	N777LX					
5737	N404MM	N454MM					
5738	N590QS						
5739	N52623	"PR-FJU"+	[+marks worn at factory]	PR-FJA			
5740	N166RD						
5741	N580QS						
5742	N5221Y	N911EK	N597BJ				
5743	N52613	N806AD					
5744	N5063P	N2003J	PR-MMV	N560QG			
5745	N5067U	PH-ANO					
5746	N50715	N8000U					
5747	N5040E	N47XL	C-FSXL				
5748	N5246Z	N585QS	CS-DXR				
5749	N5076L	N169SM	OE-GBR	D-CEBM*			
5750	N5095N	PR-ANP					
5751	N8701L						
5752	N412AB						
5753	N52653	EC-KPB					
5754	N51042	N578QS	CS-DXS				
5755	N51038	OE-GEH	LX-SEH				
5756	N5265B	OE-GSP	G-ZENT				
5757	N51246	OY-CKK	N57VP	N401AS			
5758	N5241R	N758XL	N178JC				
5759	N575NR	N959CC					
5760	N50756	YU-SPA	OE-GHA	G-LXWD			
5761	N5156D	N2060V	B-3666				
5762	N51780	D-CRON					
5763	N51869	OE-GSZ	N258PC	N855SC			
5764	N51666	EC-KPE					
5765	N5233J	CS-DXT					
5766	N5155G	N2065X	B-3667				
5767	N5059X	CC-CDE					
5768	N5064Q	N75TP	N768TX				
5769	N5066U	N1387E	TC-DAG				
5770	N5030U	"G-SOVM"+	[+marks worn at factory]	G-OSVM	M-SNAP	M-XJOB	N311MB
5771	N5068R	XA-UJP	PP-CTU				
5772	N5076J	OE-GVL	YU-SVL				
5773	N5109R	N579QS					
5774	N5263S	N357MP	N828DR				
5775	N50522	CS-DXU					
5776	N51342	XA-VGR	N776VP	N499MD*			
5777	N5069E	SE-RIL					
5778	N52141	PR-TEN					
5779	N5085E	N579CL	TC-LAC				
5780	N5204D	C-GFCL	N400LV				
5781	N51984	PH-MHM	OO-SLM				

CITATION XLS/XLS+

C/n	Identities					
5782	N5145P	CS-DXV				
5783	N52113	N783XL	VT-VDD			
5784	N5264M	D-CCVD				
5785	N5260U	G-KPEI	N721RN			
5786	N5267D	D-CNNN	M-CESC	N786TX	N786TT	
5787	N5145V	CS-DXW				
5788	N5259Y	D-CWWW	D-CLIC	(D-CFLO)	G-XSTV	
5789	N5211Q	CS-DXX				
5790	N5223D	D-CZZZ	M-CESD	N790TX		
5791	N5268A	CS-DXY				
5792	N5200Z	PH-DRS	N777AT	PP-IVA		
5793	N5264A	G-FCAP	YR-DPH	N413SK		
5794	N576CS	N513UP				
5795	N52229	N595CL	TC-LAD			
5796	N5268E	CS-DXZ				
5797	N52061	D-CAWU				
5798	N5157E	CS-DQA				
5799	N50321	N771PM				
5800	N578CS	N560ES				
5801	N5267J	I-CMAD	OE-GDA			
5802	N5263D	N731BP				
5803	N50715	CS-DQB				
5804	N52626	N41233	PK-BKS			
5805	N587QS					
5806	N51612	N67PK	N67PC			
5807	N579CS	SE-RGS	YU-SPB			
5808	N5060K	N2067V	5A-DRL			
5809	N5203J	N145PK				
5810	N589QS					
5811	N5086W	(D-CSYB)	OE-GKM			
5812	N583QS					
5813	N52591	XA-UKQ				
5814	N5161J	(D-CMIC)	D-CNOC			
5815	N580CS	N728EC	N629EC			
5816	N5108G	N41237	VT-BSL			
5817	N581CS					
5818	N565QS					
5819	N5267G	XA-DST				
5820	N574QS					
5821	N51038	N2116N	N673MG			
5822	N5228J	(G-XMAR)	(OE-GEM)	PP-ADD		
5823	N5264N	PP-PRR	N533ES	N806DE		
5824	N5090V	N2087K	TC-DLZ			
5825	N566QS					
5826	N5000R	OE-GWV				
5827	N573QS					
5828	N52235	N21076	B-9330			
5829	N568QS					
5830	N51995	N2112X	5N-BMM	[dbr Port Harcourt, Nigeria, 14Jul11; parted out by Dodson Av'n, Rantoul, KS]		

CITATION XLS+

C/n	Identities					
6001						
6002	N51806	N502XL	(D-CRUW)	D-CAWM		
6003	N5040E	N563XL	OO-CEH			
6004	N5253S	N343CC				
6005	N52609	N575JC	N562DB	N285FA		
6006	N5200U	N508MV	N412CC	N808W	N952RB	
6007	N892Z					
6008	N5130J	N748RE	N748RB	N717FH	N717EH	
6009	N560DG					
6010	N33LX					
6011	N68HC	N68HQ	N458FS			
6012	N595S	PP-VYV				
6013	N5061W	N2011Z	OE-GGG			
6014	N868JB	D-CFLY				
6015	N5211A	N488JD				
6016	N51666	N906DK				
6017	N52653	N7877D	OE-GNP			
6018	N51780	N881VP				
6019	N5233J	N193SB	N299DB			
6020	N5103J	N310BN	N620VP	OE-GWS		
6021	N5223X	(HB-VWE)	HB-VWD	(N941AA)	D-CEHM	
6022	N52691	(HB-VWG)	HB-VWE	N622XL	N423LM	N990DW
6023	N5085E	N623CL	7T-VCX			
6024	N50321	SP-ARK	M-AKAL			
6025	N5153K	OO-EBE	LX-EBE			
6026	N52639	LX-FGB	N560AR			
6027	N5076J	(D-CHAM)	D-CXLS			
6028	N5059X	N712DH	N7TM			
6029	N826AG	OE-GWH				
6030	N5241R	N560GB				
6031	N51342	N853JA	N95NB			
6032	N5250P	N932XL	N743JA	(N713AG)		
6033	N5223Y	YR-GCI	N888RT			
6034	N5218T	PR-RMC	N634BE			
6035	N949LL	N635CJ	PK-DPD			
6036	N5105F	OE-GES				
6037	N50275	YU-BZM				
6038	N5202D	N563WD				
6039	N50756	D-CCWD				

C/n	Identities				
6040	N5100J	TC-TSY			
6041	N5147B	(D-CDCC)	N100U	N417JD	
6042	N5261R	N2370S	CN-AMJ		
6043	N51806	PT-FPG			
6044	N221AM	I-GGLA	G-GGLA		
6045	N5072X	I-CNDG			
6046	N5248V	PR-RTS	N646RH		
6047	N5096S	N2384K	CN-AMK		
6048	N5192E	N61442	TC-DAK		
6049	N5270M	(D-CDCD)	N900FS	N90FD	
6050	N50612	N565AP	N565AB	N595AB	N713DH	RP-C8568
6051	N5157E	N912EL	PR-JSR	N651TK	D-CKHK
6052	N52626	N332BN			
6053	N52433	N2401X	N53XL	N883PF	
6054	N50715	N54XL	N98MD	N25CK	
6055	N5264U	N2009A	TC-SSH	VP-CSS	
6056	N51896	N156XL			
6057	N5037F	N868RB			
6058	N5262W	N58XL	N155SM		
6059	N5262Z	N268CM			
6060	N51160	OK-XLS			
6061	N5269A	N61XL	PP-JSR	N316TF	
6062	N5254Y	(D-CDCE)	N916CS		
6063	N51042	(D-CDCF)	N533CC		
6064	N5231S	(N583CS)	N664AF		
6065	N5068R	XA-LOS			
6066	N5162W	PR-AFA	[w/o on approach to Santos, Brazil, 13Aug14]		
6067	N5212M	N30423	5N-HAR		
6068	N5067U	PR-AJP			
6069	N51869	N814PE			
6070	N5085E	N534CC			
6071	N5223X	N907CR	N507CR	N607VP	N6TM
6072	N52136	N43TJ	N72XL		
6073	N5268M	VP-BJR			
6074	N5227G	N96NB			
6075	N5223J	YR-TYA			
6076	N5218R	N487JA	N487AV		
6077	N52230	(OO-OIL)	PH-PKD	N566VP	N824HH
6078	N50639	B-LCT	RP-C1290		
6079	N5165T	N716JN	N79XL	Turkey EM-805	
6080	N50944	XA-URQ			
6081	N5211A	N789HU			
6082	N51817	(N282XL)	D-CEFO		
6083	N51612	N599CS			
6084	N5226B	PP-SFY			
6085	N5194B	N1SU			
6086	N5248V	N26XL			
6087	N5096S	N52FE			
6088	N5241R	N270BC			
6089	N52690	D-CBEN			
6090	N5086W	N690XS	N54FE		
6091	N5063P	N865M			
6092	N5145V	N564CH			
6093	N5151D	D-CSEB			
6094	N5203J	N82KW			
6095	N5061P	N475JC	N476JC		
6096	N50820	N27XL			
6097	N5064Q	(PH-EER)	(PH-HRA)	PH-HRM	
6098	N5076J	N98XL	N681WA*		
6099	N5245D	N5901D	N732JR		
6100	N5036Q	N167JN			
6101	N5132T	N301L			
6102	N51942	D-CSUN			
6103	N51881	N807AD			
6104	N5068R	N800KV			
6105	N5076P	N299RR	PR-TAQ		
6106	N5248V	G-EPGI	VT-BIR		
6107	N5192E	N965LC			
6108	N5064M	CS-DTX	LX-MMB		
6109	N52141	OY-GKC	D-CPOS		
6110	N5200R	N768LP	N768LR	N110XL	N60S
6111	N5213S	N790ZK			
6112	N5067U	N676BB			
6113	N51817	N1401L			
6114	N5211F	LV-CYL			
6115	N52081	N613JT	N613WM		
6116	N5268E	G-EYUP			
6117	N51984	PR-OFF			
6118	N50522	N532MT			
6119	N52475	G-DEIA			
6120	N5257V	N224JV	N224JW		
6121	N5227G	D-CPMI			
6122	N5228Z	N764JA			
6123	N5226B	D-CAAA			
6124	N5194B	N768LP			
6125	N5066U	D-CBBB			
6126	N5065S	D-CCLA	N626SG		
6127	N5100J	D-CNNN			
6128	N50820	D-CZZZ			
6129	N5064Q	N600CB			
6130	N5076J	N918RZ			
6131	N52601	N242JT			
6132	N5225K	N278HN			
6133	N5212M	N920CG	N133XL		
6134	N52645	D-CQQQ			

CITATION XLS+

C/n	Identities				
6135	N5265N	N539CC	N539WA		
6136	N5062S	YU-SPC			
6137	N5214L	D-CUUU			
6138	N5264N	N188ST	(PK-RGE)	N15TF	
6139	N5120U	G-CHUI			
6140	N51743	UR-UQA	(D-CZEC)	D-CECH	
6141	N5132T	N100SC			
6142	N5245D	N42XL	N512AB		
6143	N5180K	N7671G	TC-KIP		
6144	N5200U	N144XL	N985BC	N1BC	N144XL
6145	N52144	PR-RCN			
6146	N5026Q	N54SB	N838CT		
6147	N5207A	RP-C6038			
6148	N5031E	G-OJER			
6149	N5154J	N237EE			
6150	N660AS				
6151	N5207V	N151XL			
6152	N5105F	PP-BBL			
6153	N5263U	EC-LYL			
6154	N52623	N897SS	N997SS		
6155	N5226B	PR-TUC			
6156	N5194B	N1088R			
6157	N52601	N157XL			
6158	PP-WEE				
6159	N106ST				
6160	N303ST				
6161	N5141F	B-9823			
6162	N5090A	OO-XLS			
6163	N63XL	PR-VTO			
6164	N5263D	N838CC			
6165	D-CAHO				
6166	D-CDDD				
6167	N5260Y	XA-TVG			
6168	D-CVHB				
6169	N52645	XA-VGR			
6170	N52691	D-CFFF			
6171	N5218T	N617SA	7T-VNC		
6172	N52446	N1865K			
6173	N5245L	D-CGAA			
6174	N921CG				
6175	N165DS				
6176	N51245	N3104R	B-3266		
6177	N5124F	N3103L	B-3299		
6178	D-CIFM				
6179	N101ER				
6180	N420PL				
6181	N491JL				
6182	N31031				
6183	N175TP	N75TP			
6184	N3101N				
6185	N5200U	SE-RHD			
6186	N52136	N560JV	N560GJ		
6187	N5245D	D-CLHS			
6188	N3103D	RP-C6188			
6189	N561JV	N5267T	N168GW	N68GW	
6190	N5213S	N212HF			
6191	N5147B	N701KB	N701KR*		
6192	N5221Y	N746PC			
6193	N562JV	N5163C	M-YXLS		
6194	N5248V	N255SM			
6195	N563JV	N5268V	N679LG		
6196	N51995	N130WE			
6197	N5085E	(D-CSCT)	N197XL	N510RC*	
6198	N52457	G-RSXP			
6199	N5214K	N199XL	YU-RDA		
6200	N5125J	N404MM			
6201	N5223P	N1907M			
6202	N5270K	G-XLSR			
6203	N51160	N623SA			
6204	N50549	N777HN			
6205	N5261R	N62WA			
6206	N5257V	N19539	N7148J		
6207	N5264M	N7146T			
6208	N5265B	N7146D			
6209	N51612				
6210	N5267T				
6211	N5213S	N564HV			
6212	N5262W	N560N			
6213	N5090A				
6214	N5266F				
6215	N5045W				
6216	N5211A				
6217	N5105F				
6218	N5135K				
6219	N5072X				
6220	N50776				
6221	N5262Z				
6222					
6223					
6224					
6225					
6226					
6227					
6228					
6229					

CITATION XLS+

C/n	Identities
6230	
6231	
6232	
6233	
6234	
6235	
6236	
6237	
6238	
6239	
6240	
6241	
6242	
6243	
6244	
6245	

CESSNA 650 CITATION III

C/n	Identities									

696	N650CC	[ff 30May79 cx Nov89; wfu]								
697	N650	[converted to Citation VII standards 1991; used as GMA3007 turbofan testbed for Citation X programme 1992; b/u circa 2001; front section used for training purposes, rear to scrapyard at Wichita Mid-Continent, KS]								
0001	N651CC	N1AP	(N651AP)	N654CC	N651CC	N651CG	N345SK	N945SK		
0002	N652CC	N5000C	(N650BG)	N650AS						
0003	N653CC	HZ-AAA	N187CP	N92LA	OY-CCG	N166MC	N411SL	CC-AGR		
0004	(N654AR)	N654GC	N650GT	N650LA	LV-FVT					
0005	N137S	N439H	N693BA	N700RY	[wfu Oberpfaffenhofen, Germany, Aug08; cx 14May15]					
0006	N656CC	N44HS	(N306QS)	N58RW	N1TS	N650TS	N39RE	N27TS	N128GB	N129GB
0007	(N13047)	(N3Q)	N657CC	N929DS	C-FLTL	(N20EA)	N52SY	N719HG	N650MG	XA-UND	N117BG
0008	(N13049)	N618CC	N10TC	N84TJ	N84WU	N926CB	N926CR	N777XS		
0009	(N1305C)	N933DB	N933SH	[parted out by Alliance Air Parts, OK]						
0010	(N1305N)	N2UP	N2EP	(N610VP)	OK-NKN	N650LW	[parted out Roanoke, TX]			
0011	N1305U	(C-GWPA)	(N90LA)	N91LA	N17TE	N17TN	N311CW	N362TW		
0012	N1305V	N15VF	OE-GCO	HA-JEN						
0013	(N13052)	N119EL	(N13QS)	N313QS	N377JE	N770GF	N25TG			
0014	(N1306B)	(N664RB)	N650CJ	C-GHOO	OE-GCN	(N855DH)	OY-EDP			
0015	(N1306F)	N83CT	N369G	N15QS	N766MH					
0016	N1306V	N720ML	N720ME	N555DH	(N45US)	N32MG	N316CW	N21LL	[wfu]	
0017	N1307A	C-GHLM	N900CM	N900QM	(N650BP)	N651BP				
0018	(N1307C)	N715BC	N275WN	N650SB	N650KK					
0019	(N1307D)	(N44BH)	N30CJ	N333RL	N833RL	XA-TBA	N650JL	N650MS	N707MS	N71LU	N970GW
0020	N1307G	XA-VIT	N488JT	N10PN	N650WB	N420GT	(N341MB)	YV....		
0021	N2624M	N2604	N650SS	N460CP	N94GH					
0022	N650J	PR-DIO								
0023	N889G	C-GHKY	N658MA	VR-CCC	N38DD	N650CG				
0024	N1UP	N1UH	N624VP	N643CR	N95SR	N650SL	N422BC			
0025	N10PX	N200RT	(N376HW)	(N277HG)	N700RR	N650VP	N625VP	N16FE	(N522GS)	N16SU
0026	(N656CC)	[damaged on production line early 1984 and not completed; fuselage used as test frame]								
0027	N375SC	N875SC	N650NY	N433LF	N993LC					
0028	N148C	N328QS	LN-NLC	N38ED	N650BW	PP-USA				
0029	(N30CJ)	N600GH	N70TT	(N81TT)	N89AC	N409SF	N67FS			
0030	N650SC	SE-DHL	N650SC	N380CW	N51EM	N651EM				
0031	N631CC	N1ZC	N7ZG							
0032	N54WC	N38WP	N3184Z	N332FW	XA-HVP	(N632VP)	XA-PRO			
0033	(N1309A)	CC-ECE	Chile E-302	[w/o 09Jly92 4km from runway 20 Concepcion, Chile]						
0034	N80CC	N34QS	N777LF	(N45US)	N650GH	N650SF				
0035	N650MD	N400JD	N408JD	XA-GJC						
0036	N700CS	(N700RD)	N20RD	N36CD	N43TC	(N143RC)	XA-TGA	N650BS	N651CV	
0037	N411BB	N37CD	VH-OZI	N37VP	I-GASD	(D-CLDF)	D-CVAI	C-GTKI		
0038	N366G	N366GE	N373DJ	XB-PGC						
0039	N81TC	N39WP	N171L	XA-KMX	N71NT	PP-NPC				
0040	N82TC	VR-BJY	HB-VIY	N650WE						
0041	N55BH									
0042	N142AB	N342QS	N342AS	C-GPOP						
0043	(N1310B)	OY-GKL	N643CC	N953JF						
0044	(N234HM)	N650M	(D-CRRR)	N129PJ	N126MT					
0045	N84G	N67SF	N67SE	N669W	N689W					
0046	N658CC	N57TT	N650TT	C-FBNA						
0047	N1102	(N1109)	N650CN	N33BC	N33BQ	N711VH	N711VZ	N706HB		
0048	N98BD	N98DD	N986M	N650MM	(A6-GAN)	VP-CGK	A6-CGK	A7-CGK	N122TA	
0049	(N1311A)	C-FJOE	PJ-MAR	PT-LSN	N30AF	(N650AN)				
0050	(N1311K)	N44M	N44MU	N51JV						
0051	(N1311P)	N910F	N651BH	N777MX						
0052	N20MW	XA-SDU								
0053	N367G	N306PA								
0054	(N1312D)	N1103	N1183	(N26RG)	N17AN	N47AN	N224PG*			
0055	N173LP	N173LR	N515VC	N16AS	N652CV	N125RH	N105RH			
0056	N273LP	(N273LB)	N760EW	N397CS	N56JV	N78AP	N641MS			
0057	N368G	N101YC	(N101PC)	N400PC	N31TJ	N400PC	N955HG			
0058	N88DD	N70DJ	(N282PC)	(N292PC)	(N650JS)	N143PL	N72EP	[dbr in hangar collapse at Atlanta/Paulding County, GA, 02Mar12; parted out by Team Aero LLC, Olathe, KS]		
0059	N1313G	PT-LHA	N660AA	N370TP						
0060	(N1313J)	HB-VHW	N848US	TC-CAO	N660TJ	N220TW	N220TV	OY-JPJ		
0061	(N1313T)	N137X	(N129TC)	N137X	N650TP	N650TC	N450RS	N440PC	N400PC	N939RT
0062	N626CC	C-GHGK	N388DA	N19FR	N342HM	N650CN	N475M	N84PH		
0063	N13138	N41ST	N72LE	N650AT	N651AT					
0064	(N1314H)	N801CC	N650TC	N444CW						
0065	(N1314T)	N500E	C-FIMO							
0066	(N1314V)	N138M	N138V	N650CD	N496RA	(N156DT)				
0067	(N1314X)	N210F	N9AX	N232CF	N232CE					
0068	(N1314X)	N273W	N985M	N9KL	N650AJ	XA-TMZ				
0069	(N13142)	N910M	XB-GRN	N455JD						
0070	(N1315A)	N149C	N370QS	N370TG	LN-NLD	OY-NLA	N38ED	OY-NLA		
0071	(N1315B)	N334H	N297DD	N97DD	XA-VYM					
0072	(N1315C)	N277W	N651CN	N72ST	N139MY					
0073	(N1315D)	N650JA	N673JS	N85DA	XA-LEY	N849AC				
0074	(N1315G)	(N555EW)	N234YP	N194DC	N93CL	N81SF	N949SA			
0075	N1315T	N16AJ	N85MS							
0076	N1315V	N376SC	N876SC	HB-VJT	N731GA	XA-SEP	N424LB	XA-PVR	N760LB	
0077	(N1315Y)	N677CC	N701AG	VR-BGB	(N42NA)	TC-EES	TC-SIS	(N701AG)	N800GM	
0078	(N13150)	N652CC	PK-TRJ	PK-WSE	N650WJ	N50DS	(XA-...)	N650WL	N650KB	
0079	(N1316A)	N66ME	N290SC	N288CC	N59CD	N217RR	N211RR	N69VC	N217RJ	N650RB	(N96SS)	N96SN
0080	N1316E	N69LD	C-FDJC	N802DB						
0081	(N1316H)	PT-LGT	(N881BA)	N910DP	N910DF					
0082	(N13162)	N651AP	N1AP	N81AP	N82VP	N4VF	N4VY	N825JW	N825UW	
0083	N13166	N944H	N944CA	TC-TOP	N2NR	N5NR	N677LM	N650HG		
0084	(N13168)	N85AW	N431CB	(N431CQ)	N650CB					
0085	N1317G	JA8249	N650DA	I-CIST	[w/o 04Nov00 Rome-Ciampino A/P, Italy; parted out by White Inds, Bates City MO circa Oct01]					
0086	(N1317X)	PT-LHC								
0087	(N1317Y)	N988H	N988HL	N687VP	C-FQCY	N680BC	N37VP	PP-AIO	PR-MPF	
0088	(N13170)	PT-LGZ	N290AS	N590AS	N650TA					
0089	(N13175)	N653CC	N650JC	N86WP	N86VP	(N229J)	N15ZT			
0090	(N1318A)	N694CC	N1823S	N651TC	N850MC	N1DH	N555DH	N651PW	N650JA	

CITATION III

C/n	Identities
0091	N1318E N68HC N58HC PT-LUE
0092	(N1318L) N692CC N692BE
0093	(N1318M) (N693CC) N773M N93VP N222GT CS-DND N196SG N196SD LV-CQK
0094	(N1318P) N5114 N6114 N94VP N94TJ 5B-CSM N650SP N651RS N650SP N926HC N699MG N438AD*
0095	(N1318Q) N5115 N6115 (N95VP) N882KB N883KB N941KA N650PF N650KP
0096	(N1318X) N5116 N96VP N700SW N702SW N629RM N629MD
0097	(N1318Y) N697MC N725WH N697MC [w/o 27Oct07 Atlantic City, NJ; parted out by White Inds, Bates City, MO]
0098	(N13189) N399W N389W N54HC N398CW N398DL (TI-BFY) TI-BFT
0099	N1319B (N555EW) N26SD N403CB XA-PYN N994U XA-AEB
0100	(N1319D) N200LH N200LL N202JK
0101	N1319M N847G C-GPEA N330TJ N650HR XB-GXV XA-LTH N9NL VH-SPJ
0102	(N1319X) (N406M) N406MM N406LM N24237 PP-FMA
0103	(N13194) (N407M) N407MM N407LM N2411A (N907RM)
0104	N13195 I-BETV N650CF C-FLMJ C-GOXB C-FORJ N82FD
0105	(N1320B) N655CC N15TT N48TT N67BG I-FEEV [w/o nr Rome/Ciampino, Italy, 07Feb09]
0106	(N1320K) N106CC N650CE N725RH (N404LN)
0107	(N1320P) N8000U N650MP N650JG N397CW N397DR
0108	(N1320U) N650Z C5-MAC
0109	(N1320V) (N650AT) N20AT N134M (N134MJ) (N649AF) N109ST N106ST VH-SBU N353HA
0110	(N1320X) N76D N303PC N304PC
0111	(N13204) N500CM N381CW (N381EM) (N650RJ)
0112	N1321A N60BE N93DK N598C N598AW N500JS
0113	N1321C N10ST N872EC (N650AF) N652JM N393CW N393JC
0114	(N1321J) N7000G N651AF N650DA N650DD
0115	N1321K PT-LJC N1419J N541S
0116	(N1321L) N78D (N78DL) N788BA C-FJJC C-FJJG N928PS
0117	N1321N F-GGAL
0118	(N13210) N6000J N118CD N770MP N770MR N79KF N727TX
0119	(N13217) VR-BJS HB-VIN N100WH EC-EQX N96AF 8P-KAM N770AF N147PS N147TA N650HM N888KG N181MG
0120	N13218 N143AB (N818TP) (N650AF) I-SALG N650AF N1223N N30NM N907DF
0121	(N1322D) D-CATP N1322D N121AG N24VB N818DE
0122	(N1322K) EC-EAS N650TT (N650MT) N65WL N122EJ N515MB
0123	(N1322X) N624CC N434H N59FT (N491SS) (N14NB)
0124	(N1322Y) N95CC N7HV N650HC N776GM
0125	(N13222) EC-EAP N650AF N170HL N178HL
0126	(N1323A) N55HF N65HF XA-RZQ N65HF N311MA N101PG N131PG (N127CA)
0127	N1323D N723BH N92TX (N18PV) N95TJ N95UJ+ [+ marks worn at 2002 NBAA but not officially registered] N700MH
0128	(N1323K) N628CC N125Q LV-CAE
0129	(N1323N) N61BE (N309TA) PT-LUO N125N N330MB N989PT
0130	(N1323Q) N227LA N227BA N543SC N159M N159MR N130TS (N130RK) N603HC N603HP N918BH N901RH
0131	(N1323R) CC-ECL Chile E-303 Chile 303 CC-ANT
0132	N1323V N24KT N49SM N727AW
0133	N1323X N633CC N133LE N133LH ZK-NLJ N133LE N250CM N213HP
0134	(N1323Y) N75RD N75RN N27SD N123SL N1239L D-CARE (PH-EVY) PH-MSX N6707L [parted out]
0135	(N1324B) N5109 N135AF VP-CAR N702SS
0136	(N1324D) N841G N60AF N779AZ N779AF N650DF N3170B
0137	(N1324G) N874G N4Y
0138	(N1324R) N828G N650JV N35PN N717JM
0139	(N13242) N4EG N96CP N650AH
0140	(N1325D) N95CC N290SC N220CC N90CN (N650SS) N4FC N1400M
0141	N1325E N110TM TC-CMY N21WJ N140TS
0142	(N1325L) N142CC N20RD D-CRHR (N492BA) HA-JEO
0143	N1325X N143WR N11NZ N28S N312CF N40FC
0144	N1325Y N644CC VH-KTI N644CC N650KM N2605 PK-TSM N2605 N384CW N384EM
0145	N1325Z C-GCFP N650AF N29AU N385CW N385EM [w/o in Venezuela 18Feb08]
0146	N13256 N646CC XA-PIP N650FC
0147	N13259 OE-GNK N148N N141M N456AF N94BJ N151DR
0148	N1326A N55SC N55SQ N50PH N50EJ N7HF N92RP N413MH*
0149	N1326B N649CC N139M N139N (CS-DNE) D-CBPL HA-AXA OE-GAE D-CSAO HA-JEP
0150	N1326D N150F N61CK XA-RIB
0151	N1326G G-MLEE N91D PK-KIG N660AF N321AR N797VS
0152	(N1326H) (N4EG) N650AE (N152VP) N627R N327R N260VP N255VP (N260VP) N605SA N404BY
0153	N1326K N95CC N653CC N47CM N777ZC N1DH N2DH N845FW N308MR
0154	(N1326P) N154CC N696HC N650CH
0155	N13264 N788NB N97AL
0156	N13267 N68SK N38SK XA-ARS N209A N74VF N650CC [cx 02Jul15; parted out by Dodson Int'l, Rantoul, KS]
0157	N1327A N657CC N516SM N10JP N650RP
0158	N1327B N658CJ N121AT N135HC N735HC (N745EA) N721ST VH-SSZ
0159	N13113 N683MB N267TG N359CW YV3213
0160	N1312D N95CC N24UM N831CB N830CB (N830GB) N33UL N650PT N220CM
0161	(N1312K) N161CC I-ATSA N500AE N510SD
0162	N1312Q N202RB N275GC N660Q N85WT
0163	N1312T N137M (N137MR) N163AF N749CP N163JM
0164	N1312V N138M N138MR N164AF N364CW N162DS
0165	N1312X XA-FCP XC-PGN (N650GJ)
0166	N1313J PT-LTB
0167	N667CC N532CC (N532C) N832CC N88DJ N25EG
0168	N1314H N175J
0169	N169CC N88JJ N749DC N73HM N650PT
0170	N1314V N95CC N170CC N32JJ XA-RIE N476AC (YV....) N476AC
0171	N1354G PT-LVF PR-ITN
0172	(N1772E) N672CC N934H [cx Oct10; b/u]
0173	(N1779E) N843G N173VP
0174	(N1782E) N674CC D-CLUE
0175	(N175J) N1820E N235KK N835KK N175SR
0176	N176L N1874E N1526L N2TF N48TF N176AF N504RP
0177	N1930E JA8367 N707HJ N834H XB-OBM XA-UVV
0178	N1958E N95CC N178CC JA8378 N178CC N603AT TC-RAM N650BA N57CE N605DS N896RJ N427RR
0179	N1959E N679CC XA-RMY N35FC N63GC N287CD
0180	N2098A N768NB N498CS
0181	N2131A (N181CC) PT-OBX N743CC N650DR N857DN
0182	N26105 N682CC N491JB YV527T
0183	N2614Y EI-SNN N820FJ (N820F) (N376CW)
0184	N2615D N95CC N1128B N11288 (N650DW)
0185	N2615L N708CT N708CF N185VP VR-BMG N650HS N533CC N538CC (N650MG) 4X-CMR N521BH N468ES

C/n	Identities											
0186	N2616L	PT-OAK	N186VP	N386CW	XA-UIS							
0187	N2617K	N187CM	N500RP	(N55PC)	N70PT	(N78PT)	D-CAYK	N39VP	LN-AAA	D-CRRR	N226EM	4X-CZA
0188	N2617P	N587S	N650FP	XA-PMH								
0189	N26174	XA-RGS										
0190	(N2621U)	N142B	N190JJ	N350CD	N260VP	D-CCEU	HA-JEC					
0191	(N2621Z)	N191CM	N59B	TC-KLS	N650TJ	N650SG						
0192	N2622C	N15TT	N15TZ	LN-AAU	N78EM	D-CREY	SX-FDK					
0193	N2622Z	N95CC	N95CM	N55HF	N55HD	N650CC	N2DH	N91KK				
0194	N26228	N111VW	N2606	N831GA	N831VP							
0195	N26233	N411BB	N411BP	C-GAPT	N800MC	N140WH						
0196	(N2625C)	N196CM	N896EC	N534H								
0197	N2625Y	N95CC	N197CC	(N197VP)	N797T	N800R	N840R	N100R	N50QN	N111F		
0198	N2624L	(N650GA)	N198CM	N553AC	(N650BW)	XA-INF	N650BC	XA-XGX				
0199	(N2626X)	(N900JD)	N65KB	N890MC	N527CP	N400RE						
0200	[Built as Citation VI (qv)]											
0201	[Built as Citation VI (qv)]											
0202	[Built as Citation VI (qv)]											
0203	N26271	N95CC	(N203CD)	N4612	(N4612S)	N4612Z	N350M	N350MQ	VT-IPA			
0204	N2630B	XA-RZK	(N691DE)	N811JT	N108WV							
0205	N2630N	PT-OMU										
0206	N2630U	PT-OKV	N39H	N826RP	N610RP	N119ES						

Production complete

CESSNA 650 CITATION VI

Note: The Citation VI was to have used model number 660 but in the end used 650 in common with the Citation III and VII.

C/n	Identities								
0200	(N2626Z)	N650CM	PT-OMV	[w/o 23Mar94 25 miles NW Bogota, Colombia]					
0201	(N26264)	N40PH	N347BG	N1419J	XA-GMG	N777AL			
0202	N2627A	(N202CV)	PT-OJO	N202TJ	N65BP	UP-CS401			
0203	[Built as Citation III qv]								
0204	[Built as Citation III qv]								
0205	[Built as Citation III qv]								
0206	[Built as Citation III qv]								
0207	(N2632Y or N6812D)	N207CC	N334WC	N107CG	N818SE				
0208	N6812L	N91TG	I-TALW	N500FR					
0209	(N6812Z)	N650L	N198DF	N198D	N902VP	N930MG	N830MG		
0210	(N6868P)	N610CM	VR-CVP	N7059U	N733H	N783H	N891SH		
0211	N6820T	N335WC	N333WC	(N59CC)	N211CC	N211CQ	N650CE	XB-ELJ	
0212	(N6820Y)	N805GT	N972VZ	N651AR	D-CCSD				
0213	(N6823L)	N900JD	N900UD	PR-KKA					
0214	N68231	N95CC	N95CM	TC-CEY	N771JB	N7777B	N7717B		
0215	(N900JD)	(N6824G)	N215CM	N650KC	N650GC				
0216	N68269	I-BLUB	(D-CCUB)	HA-JES	CN-TKS				
0217	(N6828S)	N217CM	PH-MEX	5Y-YAH					
0218	N6829X	XA-GAN	N218CC	XA-MTZ	XA-ACH	XC-CFE			
0219	N6829Z	N219CC	G-HNRY	(N211MA)	N650TS	XB-GTT			
0220	N6830T	B-4106	B-7022						
0221	N1301A	B-4107	B-7023	[w/o 02Sep02 Xichang, China]					
0222	N222CD	N733K	N738K	N780GT	N333AH				
0223	N1301D	N111Y	N111YW						
0224	N224CD	N1UP	(N7UL)						
0225	N1301Z	(N225CV)	N606AT	XB-MXK					
0226	N1302A	N400JH	XA-GPS						
0227	N1302C	(N227CV)	N2UP	(N2UX)					
0228	N1302V	N228CM	XA-SLB						
0229	N1302X	TC-ANT	Turkey TT2020						
0230	N1305N	N616AT	N660PA						
0231	N13052	LV-WHY	N67SF	N400WK	(N650FA)				
0232	N1303A	F-GKJS	N517MT	(N512MT)	N711LV	N711LT			
0233	N1303H	CC-DAC							
0234	N1306V+	N334CM	TC-SBH	N733AU	N733A	(N735A)	XA-GBM		
0235	(N1307A)	N1303V	N235CM	N235SV					
0236	(N1307C)	N1303M	N600JD	N600UD	N184GP				
0237	(N1307D)	N1306B	N650MC	(N656LE)	N650W				
0238	N1304B	(N9UC)	N19UC	N19QC	(N13QG)	(N650QF)			
0239	N1304G	N17UC	N17QC	N68ED	XA-...				
0240	N51143	PH-MFX	D-CAKE	PH-MFX					
0241	N5202D	(N651JM)	N666JM	N651JM	N651EJ				

Production complete

CESSNA 650 CITATION VII

Note: The Citation VII was to have used model number 670 but in the end used 650 in common with the Citation III and VI.

C/n	Identities							
7001	N1259B	N701CD	N111RF	N404JF	N701HA			
7002	N1259K	N702CM	N95CC	N19SV				
7003	N1259N	N1AP	N17AP	N888TX	(N650RJ)			
7004	N1259R	N708CT	N913SQ	N174VP	N144CA			
7005	N1259S	N200LH						
7006	(N1259Y)	N966H	N966K	(N706VP)	TC-KOC	OE-GCH	N650MK	PR-VII
7007	N1259Z	N944H	N944L	N28TX				
7008	N12593	(N708CM)	N95CC	N901SB	N902SB	N909SB	N16KB	N678EQ	PR-RVW
7009	N12596	(N709CM)	N93TX	N709VP	N711NB			
7010	N1260G	N1S	(N1902)	N317MZ	N150JP	(N403BL)	N406CJ	
7011	N1260N	N5111	(N6111)	N700VP	SE-DVY	VH-DHN		
7012	N1260V	N712CM	N5112	N5144	N317MB	N817MB		
7013	N12605	N5113	N5118	(N713VP)	N2NT	N15LN		
7014	N1261A	N864EC	(N865EC)	(N714VP)	N375E	XA-EMY		
7015	N1261K	N5115	N5119	(N715VP)	(N317MX)	N317MQ	N817MQ	N750CK
7016	N1261M	N18SK	N68SK	N650RP	N650CP	N710BB		
7017	(N1261M)	N775M						
7018	(N1261P)	N5114	N5174	N718VP	N119RM	N623PM	(N51LN)	
7019	N12616	XA-TCZ	XA-TRE	N105GV	XA-GAV			
7020	N1262A	N95CC	N700RR	N832CB				
7021	N1262B	PT-MGS						
7022	N1262E	N722CM	N902RM	N902F	[2000th Citation]			
7023	N1262G	N6110						
7024	N1262Z	Turkey 93-7024		[code ETI-024]		Turkey 93-004		
7025	N1263B	N442WT	N442WJ	N68BC	XA-RTS	XA-UHO	XA-RRQ	XA-GIT	N125TN
7026	N1263G	Turkey 93-7026		[code ETI-026]		Turkey 93-005		
7027	N1263P	N500	N657ER	N900MN	N622PM			
7028	(N1263V)	N728CM	XA-SPQ	N569RS	XB-RSC			
7029	(N1263Y)	N95CM	XA-SOK	N650RL	N444KE	JY-RYN	[wfu, stored Zurich, Switzerland]	
7030	N12632	N1263Z	N8JC	(N703VP)	N95CC	N782CC		
7031	N12636	N40N	N4QN					
7032	N12637	XA-XIS	N32FJ					
7033	N1264B	PT-OVU						
7034	N1264E	XA-SWM	N4360S	VP-CDW	N650K	N583SD		
7035	N1264M	VR-CIM	N3273H	PT-WLC	N95RX	N757MB	N650AT	
7036	N1264P	N95CC	N95HF	N77HF				
7037	(N1264V)	N737CC	N95TX	N787CV				
7038	N12642	N399W	N398W	PR-PTL	N156BA	N398W	PR-JAP	
7039	N12643	D-CACM	OY-GGG	D-CBIZ	N521RF			
7040	N1265B	N504T						
7041	N1265C	N430SA	(N449SA)					
7042	N1265K	N657T						
7043	N1265P	N78D	N78DL	TC-ATC	N650DH	N44M	N44MQ	
7044	N1265U	N7005	N650CJ					
7045	N12652	N95CM	CC-PGL	CC-CPS	N745VP	CS-DGR		
7046	N51160	N746CM	N746BR	N747TX	N703RB	(N328BT)	N270AB	
7047	N5117U+	N647CM	N1828S	N198TX	N650DD	N650KD	N650RA	
7048	N51176	N18GB						
7049	N5120U	N749CM	N900FL	N750FB	N182PA	N73UC	N937TC	N458RM
7050	N5121N	N6150B	N33GK	N83GK	N650CZ			
7051	N51817	(N95CC)	N965JC	N77LX				
7052	N5183U	N752CM	N24NB	N24KT				
7053	(N5183V)	N344AS	N650AS	N650AB	N123SL	N128SL	N650AT	XB-JCM
7054	N5185J	(N754CM)	PT-WFC	N7243U	LV-WTN	LQ-WTN		
7055	N5185V	N755CM	N317M	N317MZ	N817MZ	D-CMPI	N611NS	
7056	N52144	N6781C	N60PL	N444EX	N325RD			
7057	N5216A	N157CM	N653EJ	N361EE	N808VA	N597AF		
7058	N52178	N625CC	N98XS					
7059	N5218R	(N95CC)	N4EG	N76PR	N144MH	N14DG	N625G	N963U	N650PJ
7060	N5218T	N55SC						
7061	N5221Y	N903SB	N908SB	N202CW	N102CE	N132CE		
7062	N5262Z	N876G	(N337GM)					
7063	N52623	N95CC	N877G	[dbr Fort Lauderdale Executive 28Dec11; parted out by AvMATS, St Louis, MO]				
7064	N52626	HB-VLP	N5117	N5112	N82GM	N901LK		
7065	N52627	(N765W)	N650W	N96MT	N650UA			
7066	N5263D	N766CG	N669W	N161SD				
7067	(N5263S)	N51143	N502T	C-FTOR				
7068	N51160	N111HZ	N111BZ	N7AB				
7069	N5117U	(N769CM)	XA-TMX	N191JT	XA-CTK	N478PA		
7070	N51176	N95CM	N22RG	N322RG	(N770VP)	N654EJ	OY-CKE	N556RA	CS-DVN
7071	N5120U	HS-DCG	N1130N	HS-DCG	HS-LNG			
7072	N5141F	(N8494C)	N35HS	N77SF				
7073	N51444	N1867M	N1887M	XA-UAM	PK-YRL	PK-RJB	PK-RSO	
7074	N5183V	PT-WLY	N32AJ	YV552T				
7075	N52613	N12295	N711GF					
7076	N5213S	N286MC						
7077	N5203J	N877CM	N532JF	(N582JF)	VP-CGE	N603HD	N603HC	N650HW
7078	N5079V	N78BR	N84NG					
7079	N779QS	(N132WC)	N779VP	Spain U.21-01		[code 01-408]		
7080	N780QS	CS-DNF	S5-BBA	YU-BTM				
7081	N781QS	CS-DNG	N8VX	XA-FRI	N650RF			
7082	N5086W	N782QS	(N133WC)	N782VP	N2RF	N91KC	N773HA	N181BR*
7083	N50820	PT-WQH	[w/o 10Nov15 between Brasilia and Sao Paulo, Brazil]					
7084	N5094D	TC-KON	N1127G	TC-KON				
7085	N5112K	N785QS	(N136WC)	N785CC	D-CLDF			
7086	N51342	N860W						
7087	N5163C	N787QS	(N139WC)	N149WC	N43FC			
7088	N5073G	N449SA	N440SA	XA-UGX	XA-PYN	N650PD	[parted out by Dodson Int'l, Rantoul, KS]	
7089	N5117U	N789QS	N789VP	VH-VRC	N789VP	N87SF		
7090	N790QS	N790VP	(D-CVII)	T7-VII	D-CWII	9H-WII		
7091	N791QS	N791VP	TC-STO					
7092	N792QS	(N792VP)	N792CC	C-GCIX	C-FSBC			

CITATION VII

C/n	Identities						
7093	N793QS	CS-DNE	OY-CLP				
7094	N794QS	N794VP	D-CVII	N650WT			
7095	N795QS	N795VP	VH-LYM				
7096	N5162W	N796QS	N287MC	N513TS			
7097	N797QS	N797CC					
7098	N5212M	N798QS	N601AB	(N612AB)	N621AB	N1254C	(N777MS)	N303PC
7099	N5141F	PT-XFG	N17NN				
7100	N710QS	N710VP					
7101	N5157E	N602AB	(N621AB)	N612AB	N650JL	N602DS*	
7102	N5223X	D-CNCJ	OE-GMG				
7103	N713QS	N713VP	LV-FQW				
7104	N5148B	VH-ING					
7105	N715QS	N118MM	(N56BP)				
7106	N5188A	N716QS	N71NK	N33RL	N7WF*		
7107	N559AM	N652CC					
7108	N202AV						
7109	N5269A	N709QS	[w/o Dec99 in ground accident Wichita A/P, KS; cx Feb11]				
7110	N52235	(N12909)	RP-C650	N657JW	OE-GLS		
7111	N5172M	N256W	N226W	PR-AJG	N815TK	PT-RMB	
7112	N5174W	N257W	(N267W)	N269TA			
7113	N5192E	PP-JRA	N650JB	N737MM			
7114	N5194B	N68BR	N926CB				
7115	N5267K	N314SL	(N848FP)	N845FP			
7116	N5268M	N175DP	N653CC				
7117	N5263D	N33D	N135HC	PH-MYX	D-CEAC*		
7118	N5264U	N33L					
7119	N5152X	N651CC					

Production complete

+ indicates test marks not fully confirmed

CESSNA 680 CITATION SOVEREIGN

C/n	Identities				
709	N680CS	[ff 27Feb02]			
0001	N681CS	N605CS	[ff 27Jun02; fitted with experimental winglets 2013] HI985		
0002	N682CS	N747RL	N747RC	N682SV	N168PX
0003	N52114	N103SV	N602CS	N683SV	
0004	N5233J	XA-GMO	XA-CIA		
0005	N52229	N105SV	OE-GMM		
0006	N5264U	N409GB	N499GB		
0007	N52081	N604CS	(N687VP)	PP-SGM	
0008	N900EB				
0009	N682DB				
0010	N5135A	N301QS			
0011	N5135K	N338QS			
0012	N970RC	N61DF	N680VP	VH-ZEK	
0013	N5136J	N346QS			
0014	N5270K	XA-HIT			
0015	N272MH	CC-ALZ			
0016	N616CS	(D-CNIC)	(N21FR)	XA-RTS	
0017	N5248V	N757EG	(N121LS)	N446RT	N448RT	C-GJAE
0018	N79PG	N889DF			
0019	N5188N	N63TM			
0020	N5245U	N914SP	N7777B	N77773	
0021	N5200Z	N1276L	N621SV	N174TM	N988TM
0022	N1901	N110LE			
0023	N52235	N44SH			
0024	N5241R	N565A	N304AC		
0025	N52475	N680AR	N121GG		
0026	N5260Y	SU-EWD			
0027	N5264S	N532CC	N522CC	VH-EXA	N827DC	N966JM
0028	N5264E	N865EC			
0029	N5183V	N349QS			
0030	N680PH	N86LF	N808WC	N200Y	
0031	N5223P	N156PH			
0032	N51575	N52433	N132SV	C-FDHD	
0033	N52114	ZS-JDL	D-CAFE	OE-GEM	
0034	N5260U	N2426	N211CC		
0035	N5155G	N157PH			
0036	N5108G	N350QS			
0037	N5130J	N631RP	N681RP	N126AA	N637SV
0038	N456SM				
0039	N39SV	N680SB	VP-CFP	N184G	N755LL
0040	N5241R	N785RC			
0041	N5200U	N789H			
0042	N5090V	N29WE			
0043	N5233J	N718MN	XA-GAN		
0044	N52623	N680SW	N680CG		
0045	N5203S	N145BL	Chile 304		
0046	N5260M	N2428	N2478		
0047	N5267G	N737KB	N544KB	ZS-SUM	
0048	N52601	N777UT			
0049	N5058J	N158PH			
0050	N5257V	D-CVHA	N685VP	XA-CAR	
0051	N362QS				
0052	N5203J	N12925	N19MK	N19MQ	LV-CIQ
0053	N5076K	N53HS	XA-FUD		
0054	N5168Y	N2425	N2475		
0055	N5147B	OE-GNB	N333MG		
0056	N747CC	(N5YH)	N680SV	VT-VED	N915FG
0057	N51872	N365QS			
0058	N5060K	N121TL	ZK-JTH	N121TL	N339B
0059	N5214J	N4017X	SE-RFH		
0060	N5207A	N51246	PR-SUN	(N68GA)	
0061	N51575	N606CS	XA-CRS		
0062	N364QS				
0063	N5148B	N608CS	N655MM		
0064	N5214L	C-GNEQ	N413CK		
0065	N901G	N901S			
0066	N5223D	OE-GUP	D-CUPI	OE-GBY	N307LS
0067	N5203S	(OY-JET)	OY-WET		
0068	N68HC	(N68HQ)	C-GSUN	N422ML	
0069	N5166U	N1315Y	PR-SOV	(N209CR)	N720HW
0070	N51869	N927LT	N978BE		
0071	N5061P	C-GJKI	C-FRKI		
0072	N5254Y	VH-EXG			
0073	N5264S	N368QS			
0074	N5105F	N391KK			
0075	N5163C	N1312V	A6-GJA	D-CLIF	N680GT	N250AT*
0076	N5270M	N121LS			
0077	N961TC	N933SC			
0078	N51872	N678SV	(OO-SIN)	N680SE	
0079	N5172M	N680HC	D-CHEC		
0080	N5090V	OE-GLP	N345PF	N106SP	
0081	N369QS				
0082	N7402				
0083	N50612	N44M	N44MV	N672PP	
0084	N5250E	N4087B	N63LX	N137WH	N717MB
0085	N5202D	N1ZC			
0086	N5090Y	N227DH	N86LQ	N73UC	
0087	N5093Y	(N666BK)	EC-JYG	N680EV	
0088	N305QS				
0089	N380QS				
0090	N868GM	(N84LF)	PR-RCB		
0091	N5200R	N595SY	PP-ACV		
0092	N51444	N610CS	(N692VP)	N95CC	

CITATION SOVEREIGN

C/n	Identities					
0093	N5245U	N204RP	(N4RP)	N497KK	N131GM	
0094	N5263D	G-SVSB	N94SV	N201RC	N694TX	5Y-PAA
0095	N5136J	N711NK	(N711NL)	N363AP		
0096	N5200Z	N16GS	N214LV			
0097	N381QS					
0098	N52178	N202DF	N475BC*			
0099	N370QS					
0100	N5120U	C-GAGU				
0101	N51072	N696HC	N686HC	N153SG		
0102	N617CS	N680WC				
0103	N378QS					
0104	N51872	N680GG	(G-GALI)	N928JK		
0105	N389QS	N305EJ	N105HC			
0106	N51869	N83SD				
0107	N5235G	N531RC	N531FC			
0108	N680VR	N680PG				
0109	N900JD	N394CK				
0110	N384QS					
0111	N282DR					
0112	N52446	N829JC	N329JC			
0113	N388QS					
0114	N5223D	N11084	SE-RFI	D-CCFF	N614TX	
0115	N5250P	N385QS				
0116	N5225K	N308QS				
0117	N5094D	N681SV	EC-KKC	N680CF		
0118	N52653	(N2UJJ)	SU-SMA	N261NA		
0119	N5260M	N387QS				
0120	N52038	N621CS				
0121	N5188N	N822DS	C-GTOG			
0122	N52526	N122SV	N468SA	N63CR	N899JF	
0123	N52582	N396BB				
0124	N5233J	N622CS	D-CHRE*			
0125	N5053R	N666FH	D-CBAY			
0126	N5270M	N359QS				
0127	N51038	N111Y				
0128	N5062S	N228RH				
0129	N50522	VH-EXQ	N1314T	VH-EXQ		
0130	N52178	N307QS				
0131	N5000R	N624CS	(N131SV)	N247TA		
0132	N5090A	PR-SPR	N132SV	C-FDNA		
0133	N5060K	(LN-TIH)	LN-SSS			
0134	N5076K	N323QS				
0135	N5172M	N229LC	N138BG			
0136	N5093D	N320TM				
0137	N5093L	N192CN	N37VP	XA-FLM		
0138	N51984	M-AGIC	N477RT			
0139	N52081	OK-UNI				
0140	N313QS					
0141	N230LC	N905WS				
0142	N51817	N685CS	D-CHRD			
0143	N5257C	N1318X	G-XBLU	N483TW		
0144	N397QS					
0145	N5117U	OE-GVO	G-GEVO	N145WF	PT-TNE	N680PB
0146	N599GB					
0147	N52462	N1TG	N11GU			
0148	N51072	N515TB	N112MV			
0149	N5030U	N389QS				
0150	D-CHDC					
0151	N5204D	N681LF	N175WS	N271PH		
0152	N52113	N152SV	N930MG			
0153	N5223P	OE-GTT	D-CGTT	D-CATE	D-COST	N680UT
0154	N52234	N888SF				
0155	N5040E	N357QS				
0156	N5235G	D-CHIP	D-CHIL	D-CYOU	N611NJ	
0157	N5226B	C-FCPR				
0158	N158SV	C-GKEG	C-FMFN			
0159	N51872	TC-IST	N159TF	N793KK		
0160	N51869	N317QS				
0161	N5268V	G-NSJS	N161SV	N14DG	N650JC	
0162	N5218T	D-CMES	N710MS			
0163	N5267J	N1RF				
0164	N52627	N300QS	N334QS			
0165	N5268A	N629CS	XA-XDC			
0166	N5086W	N1FJ	N75SJ			
0167	N5180C	SU-SMB	N262NA			
0168	N5094D	N442LW	N442EW			
0169	N5263D	N320QS				
0170	N5268E	N630CS	N250CM			
0171	N5093D	(D-CLLS)	VP-CMH	N680BD	PR-BCO	
0172	N5045W	N633RP				
0173	N52475	N1315G	JA680C			
0174	N5212M	TC-TKN				
0175	N52144	D-CCJS	N175VP	PR-SVG	N680TG	
0176	N5072X	N701CR				
0177	N52446	N338TM				
0178	N5163K	EC-KMK	D-CLEO	N178RH		
0179	N5200Z	N2UJJ	(A6-DPD)	HB-JIL	M-ARIA	
0180	N5124F	N376QS				
0181	N5174W	N751BG				
0182	N5194B	PR-HLW				
0183	N5130J	LN-SOV				
0184	N5231S	PP-BST				
0185	N50275	PH-CIJ	D-CEIS			
0186	N5135K	"OE-GAC"+	[+marks worn at factory]	OE-GAK	XA-UJP	
0187	N5135A	N377QS				

CITATION SOVEREIGN

C/n	Identities				
0188	N51881	N626CS			
0189	N5245D	G-CJCC	N884RS	N333KG	
0190	N52352	ZS-SAP			
0191	N5136J	N339QS			
0192	N680RC				
0193	N5257V	ZS-JDL	N289KR		
0194	N52526	N680CM			
0195	N5207V	N973AC	C-GSOC		
0196	N5203S	N311QS			
0197	N5061F	N631CS	N7HB	N67HB	N716GC	N151YD
0198	N51072	G-SVGN	M-SVGN		
0199	N50655	N806MN	N12LE		
0200	N51564	N100KZ	OE-GKZ	N830GS	
0201	N5223P	N372QS			
0202	N5197M	VP-CAV	PR-JJA*		
0203	N50282	N203DN			
0204	N51511	SX-BMI	N6EQ	PR-SVR	
0205	N5112K	N1406S	SE-RFJ	N799MJ	
0206	N5269Z	N606SV	N120SB	XA-CDF	
0207	N50612	N306QS			
0208	N50549	N68EU			
0209	N5090Y	N1388J	ZS-DRS	N1388J	N310LV
0210	N52059	N680GR			
0211	N5058J	N2208L	N402SF		
0212	N52369	PH-RID			
0213	N52397	G-TLFK	SP-EAR		
0214	N5188W	N342QS			
0215	N5093Y	OH-WIA			
0216	N5100J	G-SIRJ	N997C		
0217	N52446	PR-BNP			
0218	N51881	N444A	N218SV		
0219	N5061F	N843DW	N683SL		
0220	N5109R	N315QS			
0221	N5096S	N401PG			
0222	N632CS	N7403			
0223	N223SV	C-GSOE			
0224	N5166T	ZS-IDC			
0225	N5135K	N341QS			
0226	N5135A	VP-CRH	D-CAHH	N226VP	N680NY
0227	N5105F	N631CB			
0228	N5264U	N41199	SE-RFK	N221LC	
0229	N5147B	N61KT	JA04AA		
0230	N375QS				
0231	N5264S	N570RZ	XA-GIM		
0232	N51444	TC-ATP			
0233	N5036Q	N208MF			
0234	N5057F	G-CFGB			
0235	N50054	N361QS			
0236	N633CS	N680LN	N12F		
0237	N51042	N21NR	PR-EGS	N405JD	PP-UTC
0238	N28WE	C-FLFI	N80FW		
0239	N680RP	N636BC			
0240	N52623	N396QS			
0241	N5246Z	N2157D	PR-BRS	(N745BD)	N745DB	PR-BBP
0242	N52178	N324QS			
0243	N51896	N520G			
0244	N634CS	N955KC	N680BF		
0245	N5221Y	N382QS			
0246	N5162W	SU-SMC			
0247	N5185J	N9661S	N777DY		
0248	N5269Z	N312QS	N95SJ		
0249	N456CJ	N219LC			
0250	N5231S	N680JG	VH-VPL		
0251	N5201M	C-GDCP			
0252	N5296X	PR-SMK			
0253	N51869	LX-DEC			
0254	N5194J	ZS-AKG			
0255	N5206T	(N681MR)	N680PA	N860SM	
0256	N5068R	N631RP	N201RC		
0257	N188TL				
0258	N51744	N21654	N702AB		
0259	N5212M	N310QS	PR-AGP		
0260	N5031E	PP-AAD			
0261	N5227G	N261SV	N261AH		
0262	N5257C	N262SV	N84EE	VH-PYN	
0263	N51072	N263SV	N41225	TC-TVA	N263TA
0264	N5065S	N68SL			
0265	N5203S	M-ISLE	N265SV	OK-JUR	
0266	N5154J	N696HC	N686HC		
0267	N51564	PR-RTJ	N753MS		
0268	N5197M	N6GU			
0269	N51511	SU-BRF			
0270	N52699	N41221	SU-SMD		
0271	N5132T	OO-ALX			
0272	N5063P	N2465N	TC-RED		
0273	N5145P	N6242R	CN-TLA		
0274	N5267D	N41222	SU-SME		
0275	N635CS	N72UK			
0276	N5223D	G-CPRR			
0277	N5094D	N88JJ			
0278	N5201J	N278SV	N259CK		
0279	N5264A	OK-EMA			
0280	N5064Q	HB-JIG	N680G		
0281	N5145V	N149JS			
0282	N5203J	OE-GJM	N582CJ	N868EM	

CITATION SOVEREIGN/SOVEREIGN+

C/n	Identities				
0283	N52369	(SU-SMF)	N680AK		
0284	N5109R	N284RP	Mexico 3930		
0285	N5264S	N61855	JY-AWH	N680AJ	
0286	N5036Q	N715WE			
0287	N5262W	N681HS			
0288	N5267J	N288JA	JA68CE		
0289	N5247U	N680FD			
0290	N5270J	N9022D	TC-ICT		
0291	N5268E	N682HS			
0292	N292CS	N8608			
0293	PT-FIS	N578AN	D2-EPL		
0294	N51444	N122PH			
0295	N5135A	SU-BRG			
0296	N52178	N446RT			
0297	N5125J	N6026T	B-9300		
0298	N5026Q	N60286	B-9301		
0299	N5172M	N60280	B-9329		
0300	N5188N	PR-FOR			
0301	N5103J	N688JG			
0302	N5183V	LX-GSP			
0303	N5117U	LV-CFQ			
0304	N5076P	N19MK			
0305	N5245U	D-CWIN	N81NT		
0306	N5093L	N3099			
0307	N5032K	(PP-JSR)	N9021H	N115WZ	N370M
0308	N5145P	N21NG			
0309	N5192E	I-TAOS			
0310	N5244F	N680MB	N622PC		
0311	N5264E	N16GS	N59TF		
0312	N52627	PR-WDM	N77778	N7777B	
0313	N5270E	N288HK			
0314	N5183U	N724RM			
0315	N50054	N468CE			
0316	N5235G	N316MJ	B-KTS	N680BA	N215WS
0317	N5066U	N18WE			
0318	N5065S	XA-ICO			
0319	N5100J	N680AB	D-CAWB		
0320	N5147B	N67TW			
0321	N50612	N103HB	PP-SVG		
0322	N50776	M-DMMH	D-CMDH		
0323	N5180C	N102CE			
0324	N52699	OK-UGJ			
0325	N5125J	N708BG			
0326	N51042	UR-LDB	N326TF		
0327	N52639	N327SV			
0328	N5185J	N682AB	D-CAWS		
0329	N52234	N610F	N61DF		
0330	N5085E	C-GREQ	N630TX	N521BU	
0331	N5145P	N568VA			
0332	N51995	N227SE			
0333	N5218R	N542CC			
0334	N5231S	N777GD	B-9630		
0335	N5261R	C-GUPC			
0336	N5267G	N201PG	N101PG		
0337	N5267J	N555MB	C-GAWU	C-GAWR	
0338	N5073G	N680HB	N20H		
0339	N52433	N339ES			
0340	N5057F	N680LK	N24PR		
0341	N5259Y	N341ES			
0342	N5204D	N342CC	5N-EMS		
0343	N5086W	N680SG	TC-NTA		
0344	N5136J	N344GL	TC-OYD		
0345	N52352	C-FJRX			
0346	N51478	M-IMOR	N346EC	N3ZC	
0347	N50612	N971MD	N831GA		
0348	N5165T	N81EA			
0349	N5172M	N680RB			

CITATION SOVEREIGN+

C/n	Identities		
0501	N681GF		
0502	N682SS	N354JR	
0503	N52627	N503SV	
0504	N5270E	N504SV	N680HA
0505	N5183U	N505SV	N259CA
0506	N50054	N989H	N990H
0507	N52639	N507SV	N507SF
0508	N5165P	N508SV	N885M
0509	N50360	N16YF	
0510	N5032K	N510WD	N294GM
0511	N5124F	N511SV	N742AW
0512	N5185J	N38WE	
0513	N52234	N513SV	N680SC
0514	N5085E	N683AB	D-CARO
0515	N5145P	N680MC	
0516	N51995	N311BN	N310BN
0517	N5103J	N517SV	N425PQ
0518	N518SV	N68VC	N68HC
0519	N5216A	N179PG	
0520	N680SV		
0521	N5066U	N680KJ	

CITATION SOVEREIGN+/LATITUDE

C/n	Identities			
0522	N5065S	XA-GME		
0523	N5225K	N523SV	N105CD	
0524	N671MD			
0525	N5218R	PH-CTR		
0526	N680NA			
0527	N23NG			
0528	N17EE			
0529	N314TM			
0530	N5206T	PH-HGT		
0531	PH-RLG			
0532	N52113	N101EF		
0533	N5135A	N533SV	C-GSOV	C-GLMI
0534	N52086	(D-CORA)	PP-JMT	
0535	N684AB	D-CAWX		
0536	N30884	RP-C2910		
0537	N3088R	PP-LBM		
0538	N956MB			
0539	N442LW			
0540	N5236M	N578AB		
0541	N541SV			
0542	N5093L	C-GREQ		
0543	N5152K	C-GLVE		
0544	N52035	N544SV	N715GB	
0545	N5152X	N680RH		
0546	N5262W	N47SB		
0547	N50054	N4RP		
0548	N5065S	N711FS		
0549	N516CM			
0550	N52352	N15KJ		
0551	N5228J	N551DN		
0552	N52691	N5264N	C-FMCI	
0553	N5296X	N660HC		
0554	N5269Z	N606KG		
0555	N5076L	N999CA		
0556	N51896	N45NF		
0557	N557SV			
0558	N5263S	OK-JRT		
0559	N5064Q			
0560	N50736	N680TR		
0561	N52038			
0562	N50054			
0563	N52475			
0564	N5183U			
0565	N5057F			
0566	N5060K			
0567	N5202D			
0568	N5069E			
0569	N50275			
0570	N5154J			
0571	N52136			
0572				
0573				
0574				
0575				
0576				
0577				
0578				
0579				
0580				
0581				
0582				
0583				
0584				
0585				
0586				
0587				
0588				
0589				
0590				
0591				
0592				
0593				
0594				
0595				

CESSNA 680A CITATION LATITUDE

C/n	Identities			
E68A-719001	N3765L	[ff 18Feb14]		
680A0001	N681CL			
680A0002	N682A			
680A0003	N683CL	N444A*		
680A0004	N684CL	[r/o 29.1.15, first production model]	N717FH	
680A0005	N685CL			
680A0006	N5194J	N632BL		
680A0007	N52234	N275BS		
680A0008	N5103J	N328N		
680A0009	N52691	N985BC		
680A0010	N5218T	N388JR	N8JR	
680A0011	N52446	N80LD		
680A0012	N50776	N680CT		
680A0013	N5268A	N613CL		
680A0014	N5239J	N11TR		
680A0015	N5211Q	N550QS		
680A0016	N5268E	N684DB		
680A0017	N5262Z	M-MJLD		
680A0018	N5243K	N968AG	TC-TVH	
680A0019	N5073G	N61JD		
680A0020	N5040E	N920CL		
680A0021	N52627	N621LA	TC-GRS	
680A0022	N52086	N868MJ		
680A0023	N5228Z	N996UA		
680A0024	N5148B	N868MJ	N763JA	
680A0025	N5188A			
680A0026	N51806	N626LA		
680A0027	N52038	CS-LAT		
680A0028	N5059X	N992AB		
680A0029	N5073F	N778SC		
680A0030	N5093Y	N680DJ		
680A0031	N5196U	N399DH		
680A0032	N5068F			
680A0033	N5174W	N558R		
680A0034	N5241R			
680A0035	N5268M			
680A0036	N5093L			
680A0037	N5181U	N501QS		
680A0038	N51072			
680A0039	N5235G			
680A0040	N5161J	N503QS		
680A0041	N5086W	N504QS		
680A0042	N5064M	N505QS		
680A0043	N5192E	N506QS		
680A0044	N5248V			
680A0045	N5061P			
680A0046	N5267G			
680A0047	N51869			
680A0048	N5223Y			
680A0049	N52144			
680A0050	N5026Q			
680A0051	N5223D			
680A0052	N50175			
680A0053				
680A0054				
680A0055				
680A0056				
680A0057				
680A0058				
680A0059				
680A0060				
680A0061				
680A0062				
680A0063				
680A0064				
680A0065				
680A0066				
680A0067				
680A0068				
680A0069				
680A0070				
680A0071				
680A0072				
680A0073				
680A0074				
680A0075				
680A0076				
680A0077				
680A0078				
680A0079				
680A0081				
680A0082				
680A0083				
680A0084				
680A0085				
680A0086				
680A0087				
680A0088				
680A0089				
680A0090				

CESSNA 750 CITATION X

WL alongside the c/n indicates the aircraft has been fitted with winglets.

C/n		Identities						
703	WL	N750CX	[ff 21Dec93; ff with winglets 25Sep07]					
0001		N751CX	[ff 27Sep94]	TC-ATV	N754SE	HB-JGU	XA-USA	XA-GMG
0002		N752CX	N902QS	(N752VP)	C-FPUI	N902VP		
0003		N5223D	N1AP	N200AP	(N300AT)	(N300VP)	PT-MMN	
0004	WL	N5223P	N754CX	(N96UD)	N597U	N62VE	PR-LUZ	HB-JLL
0005		N5263S	N99BB	N1JM				
0006		N5263U	N76D	N484T	N484H	N706VP	N706XJ	
0007	WL	N52655	N750EC					
0008		N5266F	N1014X	N353WC	N853WC	N708VP	N750CW	
0009	WL	N5223Y	N96TX	N909QS	(N109VP)	N978DB		
0010		N5225K	N5112	N5112S	N808CZ	PR-CTA	N417NZ	PP-LAR
0011		N5122X	N944H	N944D	N960KC	N845TX		
0012		N52136	N966H	N912QS	N712VP	VH-RCA	N712TX	[wfu Wichita/Mid-Continent, KS, still wearing marks VH-RCA]
0013		N5241Z	N5113	N5113S	LV-BRJ	N405LS		
0014		N5244F	N757T	(N14VP)	N478PM			
0015		N5085E	N715CX	N326SU	N915QS	N715VP	VH-XCJ	
0016		N5263U	N206PC	N521FP				
0017	WL	N51072	N5114	N5144	N619AT			
0018		N5091J	N95CC	N5115	N199WT	N287TG		
0019		N5109W	N5116	N199XP				
0020		N5125J	N95CM	N8JC	N8JQ	C-FJIC		
0021		N5131M	(N164M)	N138A	N630M	N61KB	N49FW	VP-CFP
0022		N51313	(N5116)	N52639	(N722CX)	N10JM	OH-CXO	(N750AG) N750VP
0023	WL	N5000R	N923QS	N923VP	N725DT			
0024		N52682	N164M	N5125J	N924EJ	N504SU	N942QS	N942QB N201HR
0025		N50612	N750RL	[2500th Citation built]	N760BP	N444BC		
0026	WL	N5066U	N926QS	N926VP	N926VR			
0027	WL	N5068R	N354WC	N854WC	N27VP	N733FL		
0028		N5058J	N728CX	N100FF	PR-FNP	N228CF	[cx 29Sep14; wfu]	
0029		N5090V	N500RP	N500FP	(N992QS)	N929EJ	N945QS	N729VP
0030		N5095N	N355WC	N369B	[w/o 29May08 Kearney, NE; parted out by Dodson Av'n, Rantoul, KS]			
0031	WL	N5061W	N22RG					
0032		N932QS	(N214BM)	N214WT				
0033		N5093D	N710AW	N808GG				
0034		N934QS	N34VP	N34VR				
0035		N5071M	N97DK	N96DK	N60ES			
0036		N5085E	N936QS	N541CX				
0037		N51160	N75HS					
0038		N51176	(N938QS)	N739CX	N938EJ	N938CC	(N788CW)	N700LX N710FL
0039	WL	N51055	N98TX	N750LM	N22NG	N32NG	N736FL	
0040		N52136	N68LP	N68LF	N740VP	N40KW	N110PK	
0041		N5066U	(N95CC)	(N22NG)	N98TX	C-GIWD	C-GIWZ	
0042		N5090A	N95CM	N915RB				
0043		N5090Y	N943QS	N943EL				
0044		N5103J	N96RX					
0045		N5109R	N45BR	N621FP				
0046		N5109W	N746CX	N946EJ	N749DX	N749P		
0047		N5091J	N947QS	(N752EL)	N947EL			
0048		N5135A	N84PJ	P4-MAA				
0049		N5153K	N949QS	N517CF				
0050		N5156D	N950QS	N750VR	N720CC			
0051		N5058J	N750J	(N1419J)	N119RM	(N119PM)		
0052		N5000R	N712JC	N681WD	PR-LAT			
0053		N5061P	N795HG	(N795HC)	N53VP	N753XJ		
0054	WL	N45ST	N450T	N610HC				
0055		N5068R	N955QS					
0056	WL	N5105F	PP-JQM	N156VP				
0057	WL	N505MA	N74VF					
0058		N5120U	N758CX	(N87N)	(N750XB)			
0059	WL	N5108G	N751BH	N750RB				
0060		N5090Y	N95CM	N98CX	PR-JAQ			
0061		N5109R	N961QS	N751EL	N104PC			
0062		N724CC	N301HR					
0063	WL	N51038	N750JB	N999GY				
0064		N964QS	N964EJ	N931QS	N964EL			
0065		N5163C	(N965QS)	N750JJ	N514X			
0066		N750GM						
0067		N967QS	N767XJ					
0068		N5100J	N377SF	N750PT				
0069		N51055	N100FR	N96TX				
0070		N970QS	N790XJ					
0071		N971QS	N771XJ	(N710TX)	N864MM			
0072		XA-VER	N72FD	N777CX				
0073		(N532JF)	N999CX	N269JR	N706LX	N716FL		
0074		N774CZ	N2418Y	N2418N	N2418F	N7418F	N703LX	N713FL
0075		N5196U	G-HERS	(SE-DZX)	N21HE	N21HQ	P4-AND	
0076		N5197M	N400RB	N702LX	N702FL			
0077		N977QS	N797XJ	(N977TX)	N110CX			
0078		N51160	N199NP	(N711HE)	N121HE	N711HE	N711HQ	N707LX N730FL
0079		N979QS	N979EL	N125DT				
0080		N5165T	ZS-SAB	(N178AT)	PT-PTL	N703DM		
0081		N810X	N1BS					
0082	WL	N82BG	(N242LT)	N705LX	N712FL			
0083		N983QS	(N256TX)	N783XJ				
0084		N984QS	(N253TX)	N784XJ				
0085		(N985QS)	N5103J	D-BTEN				
0086		N5124F	N888CN	N986QS				
0087		N987QS	N87VR	N100MA*				
0088		N5130J	N88EJ	N712WB				
0089	WL	N989QS	(N251TX)	N989VR	N900KM			
0090		N5132T	N1932P	N193ZP	C-GCUL	C-FSDS		

CITATION X

C/n		Identities									
0091		N5061P	N991EJ	N991CX	(N791CW)	N704LX	N721FL				
0092		N5066U	PT-WUM								
0093		N993QS	N71RP	N114VW	N793XJ						
0094		N51038	N750XX	N84EA							
0095		N415FW	N19DD	N95CX	N104RP						
0096		N585M									
0097		N5060K	(N81SN)	VP-CYK	C-FTEL	C-GIGT	C-GMNC	N92TH			
0098		N5090V	N998EJ	N998CX	(N798CW)						
0099		N5090A	N442WT	N442WJ	N93TX	HI1001					
0100		N5100J	N104CT	(N104UT)	N170HL	N612EM					
0101		N901QS	N881G	N711VT	N711VJ						
0102		N51995	N901QS								
0103		N5260Y	N96TX	N750HS	N737FL						
0104		N5147B	N5T	N750NA							
0105		N905QS									
0106		N52642	N106CX	N955GH							
0107		N5086W	N107CX	(N332CM)	N520CM	N307RX	N107CX	D-BEEP			
0108	WL	N51744	N908QS	(N249TX)	N908VR	C-GAUH	C-GTCI				
0109		N900EJ	N750PT	N708LX	N708FL						
0110	WL	N910QS	(N255TX)	N910VP							
0111		N5264A	N750BP								
0112		N51072	N1107Z	N173WF	(N910RL)	PR-GRD	N194SR				
0113		N913QS									
0114		N50820	N114CX	N701LX	N732FL						
0115		N5085E	OH-PPI	ES-ELI							
0116		N916QS									
0117		N50612	N426CM								
0118	WL	N5266F	N753BD	PR-XDY	C-FTLH						
0119		N5223X	XA-FMX	XA-SAR	N187CR						
0120		N920QS									
0121		N51042	N358WC	N93LA	N910E						
0122		N800W	N577JC								
0123		N51038	N900QS								
0124		N924QS	(N248TX)	XA-MIL							
0125		N5061W	N444CX	N977AE	N977AF						
0126		N5076K	N962QS								
0127		N52639	N15TT	N15TZ							
0128		N5145V	N67CX	N1873							
0129		N929QS									
0130		N930QS									
0131		N5155G	N131CX	C-GAPT							
0132		N51055	N627R	N75TX							
0133		N933QS									
0134		N51780	CS-DCT	[impounded at Caracas-La Carlotta, Venezuela, 24Oct04]			(YV1969)	Venezuela 1060	YV2470	Venezuela 1060		
		(YV2818)	[wfu Caracas/Miranda]								
0135		N935QS									
0136		N5058J	N799TG	N1DH	N8TU	XA-BAE					
0137		N937QS									
0138		N5241Z	N138SP								
0139		N5196U	N26MJ								
0140		N5112K	D-BLUE	CS-DGO	PT-TBR	CS-DVB	N750RT	N601DL			
0141		N5068R	N941QS								
0142		N5172M	N700SW								
0143	WL	N51744	N825GA	N751AJ	(N884JL)	N13SY					
0144		N944QS									
0145	WL	N5174W	N145CX	(N745CW)	N709LX	N709FL					
0146		N5152X	N750DM	N751MM							
0147	WL	N5085E	N147CX	(N787CW)	N2AZ						
0148		N700LH									
0149		N52601	N948QS								
0150		N51896	TC-VZR	N750MD	N750TX						
0151		N951QS									
0152		N51744	OH-PPJ	N934BD	N750GS						
0153		N953QS									
0154		N5206T	N8JC								
0155		N551AM	N73ME								
0156		N956QS									
0157		N52081	B-7021								
0158		N958QS									
0159		N5245D	N1128V	N7600G							
0160		N960QS									
0161		N5245L	I-KETO	N280DM	N232CF						
0162		N903QS									
0163		N5253S	N610GR	N618GR	N675CS						
0164		N964QS									
0165		N5257V	N15RL								
0166		N966QS									
0167		N5117U	N802W	N4165Y	N721VT	N610RT	N610RW				
0168		N52653	N1288B	N123SL							
0169		N5248V	N68LP	N563BA							
0170	WL	N5060K	N90NF								
0171		N51160	(B-....)	N399W							
0172	WL	N5066U	N750NS	N750WR							
0173		N5093D	N173CX	N749DX	D2-EZR						
0174		N5270M	N174CX	N87SL	N174CH						
0175		N975QS									
0176		N51806	N1AP								
0177		N177EL	N3B	N125TH							
0178		N5152X	N275NM	N750BL							
0179		N5147B	OE-HFE	HB-JEZ	N719XJ						
0180		N51511	N353WC								
0181		N181BR	N600AW								
0182		N982QS									
0183		N938QS									
0184		N51896	I-JETX	HS-CDY							

C/n		Identities							
0185		N5223X	N7SB	N185CX	N45ST	N185CX	N370EK	N750DD	
0186		N5188N	N970SK						
0187		N978QS							
0188		N5163K	C-FTEN	N750EA					
0189		N51984	N93S						
0190		N990QS							
0191		N5267G	N354WC						
0192		N51817	N5FF	N750XX					
0193		N939QS							
0194		N5192E	N194CX	G-CDCX	N194VP	ZS-MRH	N194B	N19DD	N199D	N125RH
0195		N5241R	N946QS						
0196		N996QS							
0197	WL	N585T							
0198		N998QS							
0199	WL	N5245L	N484T						
0200		N952QS							
0201		N907QS							
0202		N300JD	N202KC						
0203		N999QS							
0204		N5197M	N22NG	XA-KYE					
0205		N5181U	N4005T	C-GSUX	N700RH				
0206		N906QS							
0207		N5152X	N751GM	N49PW*					
0208		N997QS							
0209		N52229	N7SB						
0210		N51666	N904QS						
0211	WL	N5247U	N954QS	N954Q	N65ST	N686T			
0212		N51744	N4101Z	N69SB	OY-LKS	LN-HST	SE-RIC	C-FWRX	
0213		N50715	N9NG						
0214		N5154J	OE-HGG	N44PR					
0215		N215CX	VH-TEN	N546MD					
0216		N51817	N1268F	N882KB					
0217		N5166T	N217CX	(N221AL)	N217AL	N717XJ			
0218		N5223X	D-BLDI						
0219		N5192E	D-BKLI	N288CX	[w/o on approach to Egelsbach, Germany, 01Mar12]				
0220		N52613	N48HF						
0221		N51042	N256W	XA-FJM					
0222		N5166U	N222CX	(N850PT)	N750PT	N722XJ			
0223		N52526	N918QS						
0224		N919QS							
0225		N52526	N5223D	N921QS	N5223D	N215RX	N827SL		
0226		N5262X	N226CX	N257AL	N726XJ				
0227		N5267J	P4-LJG	M-DKDI	OH-DDI	EI-TEN	(D-BTAG)	D-BAVG	
0228		N5269Z	N228BD	N228DB					
0229		N5268A	N229CE						
0230		N750WM	N10XT						
0231		N5109R	N432AC	N527NP					
0232		N5120U	N232CX	OE-HAC	EI-LEO				
0233		N51612	N442WT	N442WP	(N233VP)	N228WH			
0234		N52526	PP-AAA	N750WS					
0235		N400JD	N480JD						
0236	WL	N5246Z	N53HF	N349RR	N5FF				
0237		N5228J	N5197M	PR-MJC	LV-CEP				
0238		N5183U	N238CX	N78SL					
0239		N5268V	N500N	N50QN	N910DP				
0240		N51666	N40CX	N1962J					
0241		N5197M	N921QS						
0242		N5194J	N1289G	9M-ATM	9M-VAM	M-MOON			
0243	WL	N5214J	N373AB						
0244		N52655	N750GF						
0245		N5269A	N200CQ	N200CV					
0246	WL	N5214K	C-GSEC	C-GSEO	N812KD	N15SD	N409CC	C-GAXX	
0247		N5257C	N751PT	N747XJ					
0248	WL	N5268A	N1298G	N48VE	(N750CR)	N750ME			
0249		N5109R	N49VE	N265RX					
0250		N52526	N752PT	N750XJ					
0251	WL	N5096S	N251CX	VP-CFZ	M-ABGR	N17XR			
0252		N5000R	N252CX	G-CEDK					
0253		N5268V	N253CX						
0254	WL	N52627	N254CX	M-ARCH	N999TJ	N751EM			
0255		N51666	N712KC						
0256		N5268A	N753PT	N756XJ					
0257		N5090A	N754PT	N757XJ					
0258		N5264N	N755PT	N758XJ					
0259		N52114	OE-HAL	D-BOOC					
0260		N5260Y	N260CX	N760PI	N760XJ				
0261	WL	N5079V	OE-HJA	HB-JFD	T7-TAN				
0262		N5093D	N262CX	SX-ECI					
0263		N52609	N750DX						
0264		N52462	N764PT	N764XJ					
0265		N5262Z	N765PT	N765XJ					
0266		N5201M	N355WC	N355PX					
0267	WL	N5267G	N17CX	N92MK					
0268		N5262W	CC-CPS						
0269		N5066F	N769PT	N769XJ					
0270		N5165P	N270CX	N570PT	N770XJ				
0271		N271CX	(M-KAZZ)	P4-BUS	N250BC	N896RJ			
0272		N5200R	N772PT	N772XJ					
0273	WL	N5132T	OE-HUB						
0274		N5109W	N874PT	N774XJ					
0275	WL	N5141F	N4119S	N104CT	N1HS	N115HS			
0276		N51743	N776PT	N776XJ	N752GM	N347RL			
0277	WL	N52178	(OE-HEC)	[ntu marks worn at completion centre] UP-CS501		VP-CEG	M-BEST		
0278		N5203J	N778PT	N778XJ					
0279		N5031E	N879PT	N779XJ					

CITATION X/X+

C/n		Identities				
0280		N5163C	N780PT	N780XJ		
0281	WL	N50639	G-CTEN	N281VP	N9192W	
0282		N5064M	N282CX	N782PT	N782XJ	
0283		N5221Y	N711VT	N711VP	N610RT*	
0284		N52178	N784PT	N784XJ	N750HH	
0285		N5060K	N940QS			
0286	WL	N5245L	N786XJ			
0287	WL	N5183V	N787XJ	XA-FGL		
0288		N928QS				
0289		N52457	N789XJ			
0290		N5032K	N927QS			
0291		N5125J	N2068G	M-PRVT		
0292		N51743	N792XJ			
0293		N5090A	N922QS			
0294		N5168Y	N794XJ			
0295		N5264E	N795XJ			
0296		N914QS				
0297	WL	N5268M	N797XJ	N797CX		
0298		N52114	N20768	HS-KCS		
0299		N925QS	N299CX			
0300		N50639	(N800XJ)	OE-HAK	[cx; impounded at Minsk-1, Belarus, 20Oct11]	
0301	WL	N5156D	N92CX	N92RX		
0302		N750JT				
0303	WL	N5244F	N442WT	N442WE		
0304	WL	N5109W	PP-JMJ			
0305	WL	N305CX	C-FNRG			
0306	WL	N5032K	N110NB			
0307	WL	N52601	N98FG			
0308	WL	N51666	N308CX	N795HG		
0309	WL	N5225K	N411NB			
0310	WL	N5165P	N359TJ	N953TJ		
0311	WL	N51246	G-OTEN	N950M		
0312	WL	N5246Z	N858TH			
0313	WL	N5053R	PH-PKX	(LX-ITS)	OO-PKX	

Replaced in production by the Citation X+, a stretched (by 15") variant with upgraded engines and avionics and winglets fitted as standard.

CITATION X+

C/n	Identities				
E750-716001	N750CT	[ff 17Jan12]			
0501	N751CT				
0502	N5233J	N502NX	[r/o 15Apr13]	N68ES	
0503	N52141	N900JD	N503CX		
0504	N5200R	N750GB			
0505	N5064M	N15TT	N15TN		
0506	N5192E	N586M			
0507	N5248V	N900JD			
0508	N5163C	N747RX			
0509	N51817	N509CX			
0510	N5201J	N555QB	N510CX		
0511	N5136J	N511CX	N752TX		
0512	N5148B	N512CX			
0513	N52609	(PP-OAS)	N680KG		
0514	N5201M	N442WT			
0515	N300JD				
0516	N516CX	N555QB			
0517	N745RP				
0518	N5201M	C-FTLS			
0519	N5263D	N500CG			
0520	N5026Q	N520CX			
0521	N5207A	N71273	N3B		
0522	N5172M	N7145D	N504WV^		
0523					
0524	N50612				
0525					
0526					
0527					
0528	N5108G				
0529	N51246				
0530					
0531					
0532					
0533					
0534					

DASSAULT FALCON 10/100

C/n	Series	Identities
01	10	F-WFAL [ff 01Dec70] [w/o 31Oct72 Romorantin, France]
02	10	F-WTAL [ff 15Oct71] F-ZJTA France 02/F-ZACB [wfu; preserved at Aeroscopia museum, Toulouse-Blagnac, France]
03	10	F-WSQN [ff 14Oct72] F-BSQN [CofA expired Apr81, wfu, cx 1988]
1	10	F-WSQU [ff 30Apr73] F-BSQU PH-ILT F-WJLH F-BJLH N333FJ [parted out by Alliance Air Parts, Oklahoma City, OK]
2	10	F-WJMM N10FJ N103JM C-GRIS [cx 29Sep11, wfu]
3	10	F-WJMJ N100FJ N731FJ N661GL (N10PN) N52TJ (N149DG) [wfu, cx 06Aug08]
4	10	F-WJMK N101FJ XB-SII EC-353 EC-FTV XA-SYY N888FJ [parted out by White Inds, Bates City, MO]
5	100	F-WLCT F-BVPR F-V10F F-WVPR F-BVPR [cx 19Oct15; scrapped]
6	10	F-WJML N102FJ N600BT (N110FJ) N10AG N139DD C-GRDT N54H N999MH N32BL N32VC N59CC N77JW [parted out by Dodson Int'l Parts,, Rantoul, KS]
7	10	F-WJMN VR-BFF F-BXAG HB-VDE I-LUBE HB-VKE D-CASH HB-VKE N769SC [parted out by White Inds, Bates City, MO]
8	10	F-WJMN N104FJ N21ES N21ET N21EK N88ME N108KC
9	10	F-WJMM N103FJ N10TX N149TJ N510CL N189JW [cx 15Sep14; wfu]
10	10	F-WJMJ N105FJ N253K [w/o 30Jan80 Chicago, IL; remains to White Inds, Bates City, MO, for spares]
11	10	F-WJMK N106FJ N23ES N23ET (N23ED) N942C N452DP (N190DB) N211TJ (N11WC) N419WC N858SP
12	10	F-WJML N107FJ N3100X N10F (N76TJ)
13	10	F-WLCS N108FJ N734S N210FJ N72EU N10JZ N777SN N15TX [b/u for spares 1992; cx Feb93]
14	10	F-WJMK SE-DEL N59TJ (N50B) N333KE
15	10	F-WJMM N109FJ N60MB [w/o 03Apr77 Denver, CO]
16	10	F-WLCT N110FJ N48TT F-GELA N416AS N416HC N127WL [wfu Scottsdale, AZ]
17	10	F-WLCS OH-FFB VH-FFB N29966 N27DA N33HL F-GHDZ EC-949 F-GNDZ
18	10	F-WJMJ N111FJ N78MD N48MS (N74TJ) N1TJ N80CC N1TJ N241RS [parted out by Dodson Int'l Parts, Rantoul, KS; canx Feb06]
19	10	F-WLCU N112FJ N30JM (N30JH) (N36KA) N36JM N937J F-GJFZ 3A-MGT [while regd and painted as 3A-MGT used call sign C-GORI at 1995 NBAA] LX-TRG N600HL [parted out by Alliance Air Parts, Oklahoma City, OK]
20	10	F-WLCV N113FJ N42G
21	10	F-WJMK (HB-VDT) 3D-ACB N40WJ N60ND N40ND [parted out by Alliance Air Parts, Oklahoma City, OK]
22	10	F-WLCX N114FJ N44JC N48JC F-GJLL VP-BWA M-GACB
23	10	F-WLCY N115FJ N73B N310FJ N91MH N20WP N90LC XA-GPA C-GRBP
24	10	F-WJML N116FJ N1924V F-GBTI N301JJ N991RV N230RS N69GB [cx; parted out by Dodson Int'l Parts, Rantoul, KS]
25	10	F-WJMJ N117FJ N40N N83RG N22EH N83RG N60FC N600GM N719AL N177BC C-GJET N725CJ
26	10	F-WJMK N118FJ N592DC N707AM N720DF
27	10	F-WLCX SE-DDF OK-EEH N38DA XA-AAY
28	10	F-WJML N119FJ N130B N813AV N500DS N42EH (N655DB)
29	10	F-WJMM N120FJ N234U N66MF N332J N999F N404JW [parted out by Alliance Air Parts, Oklahoma City, OK]
30	10	F-WLCT N121FJ N294W N30FJ N156X N3WZ N191MC N171MC [w/o 24Jan96 Romulus, MI, as N191MC; to White Inds, Bates City, MO, for spares]
31	10	F-WLCU N122FJ N2MP N27C N50TC N81P (N952TC) (N29AA) N27AJ
32	MER	France 32
33	10	F-WJMJ N123FJ N881P (N246N) N900UC F-GHFO N54WJ (N18BG) TC-ORM N20373 C-FBVF N33BV (N933TS) [parted out by Alliance Air Parts, Oklahoma City, OK]
34	10	F-WLCS N124FJ N110M N220M N18SK
35	10	F-WLCV N125FJ N54V N777JJ N83TJ N726MR N17WG N73LR
36	10	F-WJMJ HB-VDD N10UN N224CC N894CA N676PC N76AF XA-MMM
37	10	F-WJML C-GFCS N39515 N123VV N123TG N347K N48JC N72GW N945MC [b/u for spares by Air Salvage, Griffin, GA cx Feb04]
38	10	F-WJMM N127FJ N20ES N20ET N20EE F-GBRF [wfu]
39	MER	F-WPUX France 39 [w/o 30Jan80 Toul-Rosieres, France]
40	10	F-WJMN N128FJ N10XX N15SJ XA-LIO N11697 [parted out by Dodson Int'l Parts, Rantoul, KS]
41	10	F-WLCS N129FJ N1HM N50DM N53DB F-GKLV N61TJ N116DD N34TJ
42	10	F-WLCU N126FJ N18X (N9147F) N100UB N282T
43	10	F-WJMN N135FJ N1515P N510CP (F-GHFI) F-GIQP N17TJ [wfu Alton, IL, 2005; used for paint trials]
44	10	F-WJMJ N130FJ N205X N62TJ N277SF N244TJ (N90AB) C-FZOP
45	10	F-WJML N131FJ N120HC N110CG C-FTEN N444CR PR-EGB
46	10	F-WLCT N134FJ N911RF N815LC (N908SB) N908RF N401JW
47	10	F-WLCY N132FJ N07-07CP PJ-AYA YV-221CP YV-101CP N3914L N101GZ N91LA N90LA N79PB (N190MD) F-GJGB [w/o 30Sep93 Besancon, France]
48	10	F-WJMM N133FJ N720ML N720ME N333SR F-WGTF F-GHRV LX-EPA N20LW
49	10	F-WLCV N136FJ (N490A) N49AS N449A N26EN N700TT PT-LMO N67LC [parted out by Dodson International, Rantoul, KS]
50	10	F-WLCS VH-MEI (ZK-WNL) N133FJ PT-OHM N411SC N299DB N299DP
51	10	F-WJML N137FJ N51BP N909TF N683WS*
52	10	F-WLCX N138FJ N342G N52TJ N8100E N860E N711TF (N117RR) N828KW [cx 05Aug11, scrapped]
53	10	F-WLCS N139FJ N8100E N810US N125EM (N890E) N891CQ I-LCJG N53WA HI-836SP N824LA [parted out by Alliance Air Parts, Oklahoma City, OK]
54	10	F-WPUU N140FJ (XA-SAR) N464AC N4875 N53SN N54FJ VR-BFW VP-BFW N561D N110LA N791CP
55	10	F-WPUV N141FJ N55FJ N702NC N702NG N700AL (N700PD)
56	10	F-WPUY HB-VDX OY-FRM N56WJ N16DD N56WJ N297PF (XA-...) N297FF [parted out by Alliance Air Parts, Oklahoma City, OK]
57	10	F-WJMJ N142FJ N142V N50TB (N50YJ) N10YJ (N6366W) [w/o 30Jun97 White Plains, NY; parted out by White Inds, Bates City, MO]
58	10	F-WJMM N143FJ N76FJ N58AS N458A N500FF (F-GHJL) N170CS [cx 29Oct07 after cracks found in fuselage]
59	10	F-WJMN N144FJ N300GN N300A N302A N633WW N52JA
60	10	F-WJML N145FJ N77GT N810E SE-DKD N69WJ N769BH [parted out by White Inds, Bates City, MO]
61	10	F-WPUV D-CBMB F-WZGD (F-BIPF) F-BFDG 3D-ART [w/o 03Oct86 Magoebaskloof, Transvaal, S Africa]
62	10	F-WJMM N146FJ N12LB N6VG [parted out by Alliance Air Parts, Oklahoma City, OK]
63	10	F-WLCX N147FJ PT-KTO N70TS N876MA N976M [parted out by Alliance Air Parts, Oklahoma City, OK]
64	10	F-WLCT N148FJ N100BG N721DP N500DE N718CA N444WJ [parted out by White Inds, Bates City, MO]
65	10	F-WJMJ N149FJ XB-BAK N21DB (F-GJMA) N66CF [cx 11Jun13; CofR expired]
66	10	F-WJMN N150FJ N50RL YV-70CP N63TS [parted out by AvMATS, St Louis, MO; cx 27Jun11]
67	10	F-WLCU N151FJ D-COME N427CJ YV2474
68	10	F-WLCV N152FJ N7NP (N7NL) N11DH N91DH N80MP F-GFPF [wfu]
69	10	F-WJML N153FJ N43CC N3RC F-GELE N7TJ N711JC N530TC [cx 15Jun15; CofR expired]
70	10	F-WJMM HB-VEG F-WQCO VR-BCH VP-BCH N349JC
71	10	F-WJMM D-CMAN N229JB (N728SA) (N203PV) N190H (N202PV) N341DB N220KS
72	10	F-WLCX N154FJ N10TB N31SJ N50TY ZS-FOX
73	10	F-WNGL N155FJ N88AT C-GDCO N130FJ YV-601CP N130FJ VR-BNT N378C N362PT (N810MK)
74	10	F-WJMJ N156FJ N30TH N34TH N518S N108MR N5JY N55FJ [displayed at Aerospace Museum of California, Sacramento/McClellan, CA]
75	10	F-WNGM N157FJ N12U N937D (N75MH) N97TJ N796SF N97DD N97DX N71TS [cx Mar06, b/u]
76	10	F-WPUU F-BYCC N727TS N528JD N528JL
77	10	F-WNGN N158FJ N82MD N301HC N53TS N107TB N607TC N915FB
78	10	F-WLCT N159FJ N83MD (N83MF) N784CE N178TJ N199SA C-FEXD
79	10	F-WPXB F-BPXB N160FJ N73B N692US
80	10	F-WPXD N161FJ N48R F-GMJS N1080Q N39RE (N320GP) N577RT N4RT (N803RA) N567RA

FALCON 10/100

C/n	Series	Identities											
81	10	F-WPXF	N162FJ	N700BD	N81TX								
82	10	F-WPXE	N168FJ	N97MC	N602NC	N101HS	[parted out by Alliance Air Parts, Oklahoma City, OK]						
83	10	F-WPXG	N163FJ	N5GD	XA-FIU	N83EA	N67TJ	N76MB	N724AS	[cx 12Oct11, parted out Oshawa, Canada]			
84	10	F-WPXH	N164FJ	N8447A	JA8447	N8447A	N526D	N6PA	N192MC	(N100TW)	N106TW		
85	10	F-WPXI	N165FJ	N85JM	(N95DW)	(OE-...)	[w/o 17Feb93 Aurillac, France; to White Inds, Bates City, MO, for spares 1993]						
86	10	F-WPXJ	N166FJ	N410WW	N411WW	N50TE	[w/o at McCall, ID, 18Dec1992; to White Inds, Bates City, MO, for spares]						
87	10	F-WPXK	N167FJ	(N200AF)	N662D	N682D	C-FBSS	N80TS	N99BL	N549AS	C-FNND	N156BF	N156BE	N515LP
		[parted out by Alliance Air Parts, Oklahoma City, OK]											
88	10	F-WPXL	N169FJ	N3600X	(F-GKCD)	F-GHER	N71M						
89	10	F-WPXM	D-CADB	F-WZGF	I-CAIC	3X-GCI	HB-VIG	I-EJIC	HB-VKF	D-CENT	TC-AND	(N888WJ)	N23TJ
90	10	F-WNGD	N170FJ	N14U	N12TX	[parted out by White Inds, Bates City, MO, Jun06]							
91	10	F-WJMJ	D-CBAG	N790US	N23VP	[parted out by Alliance Air Parts, Oklahoma City, OK]							
92	10	F-WNGM	N172FJ	(N61BP)	N1PB	(N58B)	F-GHLT	N95TJ	N724DS	N824DS			
93	10	F-WNGN	F-BYCV	N40180	(N98TW)	[parted out by White Inds, Bates City, MO; cx 01Feb13]							
94	10	F-WNGO	N171FJ	N54RS	N13BK	N54DR							
95	10	F-WPXD	N173FJ	PT-ASJ	[w/o 17Feb89 nr Rio-Santos Dumont, Brazil]								
96	10	F-WNGD	N174FJ	XA-SAR	OE-GLG	I-LCJT	N174FJ	N96TJ	N115TD				
97	10	F-WPXF	N175FJ	N6FJ									
98	10	F-WPXG	D-CBUR	[w/o 08Aug96 near Offenburg, Germany]									
99	10	F-WPXH	N176FJ	N10TJ	(N65HS)	N656PC	N500GM	N67JW	F-GKBC	N63BA	N923HB	(N923HE)	N715JC
100	10	F-WPXI	N177FJ	N10FJ	YV-17CP	(N217CP)	N100FJ	XA-MGM	XA-UKD	XA-UML	C-GSXJ		
101	MER	F-WPXJ	France 101										
102	10	F-WPXK	N178FJ	N61BP	N908TF								
103	10	F-WPXL	F-GBMH	N103TJ	N339TG	N103TJ	N9TE	N26TJ	N63XG	N68XG	N316GB		
104	10	F-WPUU	N179FJ	N90DM	VR-BHJ	N4557P	N913V	N913VL	N800SB	N100CU			
105	10	F-WPUV	N180FJ	N942B	N71TJ	N711MT	N16DD	N16WJ	N804JJ				
106	10	F-WPUX	N181FJ	N1JN	N10FJ	N730PV	(N918PC)	N902PC	N913VS	N103MM	N20CF		
107	10	F-WPUY	N182FJ	XB-ZRB	XB-CAM	XB-FWX	XC-ZRB	N160TJ	N100T	N91BP	N907TF		
108	10	F-WPUZ	(HZ-KAI)	HZ-AKI	F-WZGF	F-BIPC	N246FJ	N11DH	N91DH	N88LD	(F-GFJK)	F-GJHK	[w/o 26Mar92
		Brest, France; scrapped Mar93]											
109	10	F-WNGD	N183FJ	N77NR	C6-BEN	N69EC	N89EC	N840GL	YV2806				
110	10	F-WNGO	N184FJ	N90MH	N901MH	I-SHIP	N712US	N104DD	N43US	N653FJ			
111	10	F-WNGO	N185FJ	N8200E	N820CE	N10HE	N289CA						
112	10	F-WPXD	N186FJ	N12XX	N12MB	N598JC	[parted out by White Inds, Bates City, MO; cx 29Apr09]						
113	10	(I-SHOP)	I-CHOC	HB-VIW	(F-GFHG)	F-GFHH	LX-DPA	VP-BGD	N220PA	(N716JC)	(N168DN)	(N210MJ)	
		[cx 1Jul14; parted out at Pompano Air Park, FL]											
114	10	F-WPXF	N187FJ	N200YM	N100YM	N807F	N15TM	N555DH	N108TG	N982MC	[cx 03Feb10, scrapped]		
115	10	F-WPXH	N188FJ	N511S	N211SR	N420JD	F-GGAR	I-ITPR	N115WA	N636SC	N169LS		
116	10	F-WNGL	N189FJ	N4DS	(N927DS)	N925DS	N525RC	F-GJMA	[w/o 27Sep96 Madrid-Barajas, Spain, but still current with no C of A]				
117	10	F-WPXG	N190FJ	N23DS	N923DS	N18MX							
118	10	F-WPXI	HZ-AMA	HZ-NOT	HZ-AO2	N848MP	I-DNOR	F-GJJL	HB-VJN	F-GIJG	N41TJ	(N97RJ)	N118AD N100FJ
119	10	F-WPXK	N191FJ	N257W	N257V	N119SJ	C-GNDJ	[parted out Oshawa, Canada]					
120	10	F-WPXM	N192FJ	N20ES	N359V	N369V	N100WG	N402JW	N710JC	N631KA	CN-TLD		
121	10	F-WPUU	(HB-VFS)	HB-VFT	F-GDLR	N381MF	[parted out by Dodson Int'l, Rantoul, KS]						
122	10	F-WPUV	N193FJ	N22ES	N312A	N312AT	OE-GSC	N911UN	(N104KW)	[parted out by White Inds, Bates City, MO]			
123	10	F-WPUX	N194FJ	N23ES	N312AT	N312AM	N312AN	N50TK	N25FF	SE-DKC	N23WJ	N110TP	N689WC N54JE
124	10	F-WPUY	F-GBTC	[w/o 15Jan86 nr Chalon-Vatry, France]									
125	10	F-WNGD	N195FJ	N400SP	N100CK	XA-SAR	N269SW	[cx 13May15; CofR expired]					
126	10	F-WNGM	(N196FJ)	I-CHIC	F-WZGS	I-CHIC	HB-VIX	(F-GFHH)	F-GFHG	N26WJ	N36WJ	PR-CDF	
127	10	F-WZGG	F-GCTT	I-CALC	N8GA	(N7RZ)	ZS-SEB						
128	10	F-WNGO	N197FJ	N1871R	N79HA	N79PB	N99MC	N99BC	N175BC	N228SJ	P4-AVN	CN-TKN	
129	MER	F-WZGA	France 129										
130	10	F-WZGB	I-SFRA	(N777ND)	N921GS	N432EZ	N454DP						
131	10	F-WZGC	I-196FJ	N654PC	(D-CAJC)	HB-VME	N133EP	C-FSXX					
132	10	F-WZGD	N198FJ	N500GS	N580GS	SE-DKB	N250MA	TC-ATI	[dbr Nov94 Le Bourget A/P, Paris, France; cx Mar95]	N9258U			
		[fuselage with White Inds, Bates City, MO by Apr96; cx 29Oct07]											
133	MER	F-WZGE	F-ZGTI	France 133									
134	10	F-WZGF	N202FJ	N900T	N509TC	VH-MCX	VH-WJW	[wfu; cx Sep11]					
135	10	F-WZGG	N199FJ	N835F	N969F	N707CX	N245SP	N707CX	N272DN				
136	10	F-WZGH	I-MUDE	F-WZGS	F-GFMD	[wfu]							
137	10	F-WZGI	N200FJ	N837F	C-GTVO	[cx to USA 24May05, no N-number allocated – parted out?]							
138	10	F-WZGJ	N203FJ	N30TH	N100BG	(N942M)	F-GGVR	N236DJ	C-GNVT	[w/o 14Jan01 Kuujuaq, Quebec]			
139	10	F-WZGK	N204FJ	N10AH	(N810J)	(N110J)	(N803SR)	N110J	(N518RJ)	[wfu Fort Lauderdale Executive, FL]			
140	10	F-WZGL	N205FJ	N70WC	N88WL	F-GHDX	5Y-CAX						
141	10	F-WZGM	N206FJ	(N10AH)	N900D	N77SF	N7781	[parted out by Alliance Air Parts, Oklahoma City, OK]					
142	10	F-WZGN	N207FJ	N10HK	N11DH	N5LP	N174B						
143	MER	F-WZGO	France 143										
144	10	F-WZGP	N208FJ	N1TC	(N79FJ)	N101TF	(N144HE)	N502BG	N502PG				
145	10	F-WZGQ	N209FJ	N244A									
146	10	F-WZGR	N211FJ	F-GHVK	(N17ZU)	N461AS	XA-CEG	N110GF	XA-CEG	XA-UJG	N957EC		
147	10	F-WZGS	N212FJ	N12TX	F-GHPL	N125GA	N212FJ	[parted out by Dodson Int'l Parts, Rantoul, KS]					
148	10	F-WZGT	N213FJ	N103PJ	N79TJ	ZS-BDC							
149	10	F-WZGU	N214FJ	N711FJ	(N830SR)	N711EJ	C6-LPV	N149BL					
150	10	F-WZGV	N215FJ	N212N	N212NC	(HB-V..)	N99WA	9Q-CCA	ZS-FGS				
151	10	F-WZGX	N217FJ	N26CP	OE-GAG	N4581R	N27AC	N256W	N256V	RP-C9999	N256V		
152	10	F-WZGY	N216FJ	N8463	JA8463	N8463	F-GDRN	SE-DPK	N152WJ	N999LL	(N999AH)	N9TE	
153	10	F-WZGZ	N218FJ	N344A	N81P	N81PX	N600TW						
154	10	F-WZGA	N219FJ	PT-LCO	N777FJ	N149HP	[parted out by White Inds, Bates City, MO]						
155	10	F-WZGC	(N220FJ)	D-CIEL	N725PA	F-GTOD							
156	10	F-WZGE	N221FJ	N618S	SE-DEK	ZS-SEA							
157	10	F-WZGF	N222FJ	(N900AR)	N101EF	N80GP	F-GFBG	N157EA	N64AM	N703JS	(N157JA)	(N814AA)	(N450CT)
		N76AM	9V-...										
158	10	F-WZGI	N223FJ	N81LB	N220SC	N790FH	N700FH						
159	10	F-WZGJ	N224FJ	N224RP	N224BP	(N88TB)	N10WE	N707DC	N707AM				
160	10	F-WZGK	N225FJ	N223HS	N31TM	F-GFFP	LX-JCG	(ZS-SEB)	N160FJ	PR-FDE			
161	10	F-WZGM	N230FJ	N30CN	N50SL	I-CREM	F-WWZK	I-CREM	G-ECJI	(F-GOJI)	M-ECJI		
162	10	F-WZGN	N226FJ	N664JB	N796MA	N47RK	(N162TJ)	(N713G)	N170MK	N602DM	N425JR		
163	10	F-WZGP	N227FJ	N151WC	N163F	F-GJRN	(N2CH)	N163CH	N163AV	(N73TJ)	N983CC	N83JJ	N50HT
		N163MJ											
164	10	F-WZGQ	N228FJ	N222MU									
165	10	F-WZGR	N229FJ	N111WW	N56LP	N707CG	[cx Oct05; parted out by Dodson Int'l Parts, Rantoul, KS]						
166	10	F-WZGS	N232FJ	N94MC	(F-GIPH)	F-GJFB	N94MG	N747AC	N21CL	(N166SS)	N211EC		
167	10	F-WZGT	N233FJ	N39K	5V-TAE	5V-MBG	5V-TAE	N167AC	N516SM	N82CG	N111WW	N111WH	
168	10	F-WZGU	N234FJ	N175BL	N43EC								
169	10	F-WZGV	N235FJ	VH-DJT	N725P	F-GHFB	(N107AF)	PT-WSF					

FALCON 10/100

C/n	Series	Identities								
170	10	F-WZGX	N236FJ	N821LG	[w/o 22Feb86 Westchester, PA]					
171	10	F-WZGY	N237FJ	N30TB	N26ES	PT-OIC	N42US			
172	10	F-WZGZ	N238FJ	YV-99CP	N172CP	N10NC				
173	10	F-WZGA	N239FJ	N72BB	N441DM	N211CN	N555SR	N554SR	9A-CRL	N8LT
174	10	F-WZGE	N240FJ	N5ES	N402ES	RP-C1911				
175	10	F-WZGF	N241FJ	XA-LOK	N12EP	C6-NPV	N175CJ			
176	10	F-WZGI	N242FJ	HK-2968X	HK-2968	N179AG	N66HH	N231JH		
177	10	F-WZGJ	N243FJ	N533CS	F-GFGB	N101VJ	N100ND			
178	10	F-WZGK	N244FJ	N10QD	N79BP	N87TH	(N210MJ)			
179	10	F-WZGL	I-DJMA	(F-GGRA)	F-GERO	N100RR	N3PW	N777RF		
180	10	F-WZGM	N245FJ	N593DC	N398DC	N25MC	N211JL			
181	10	F-WZGC	N247FJ	N87GT	N151GS	(N151DC)	F-GJHG	N138DM	N204WS	
182	10	F-WZGN	N248FJ	N111MU	N809F	C-GOJC				
183	100	F-WZGO	N249FJ	N82CR	N183SR	SE-DLB	N100HV			
184	10	F-WZGP	N250FJ	N346P	N4AC	(C-....)	N725DM			
185	MER	F-WZGQ	France 185	F-WQBJ	France 185					
186	10	F-WZGB	N251FJ	N2426	N2426G	N63TJ	N420PC	N186TJ	N555DH	N555DZ
187	10	F-WZGR	N252FJ	N2427F	"N2427N"	N81TJ	N303PL	N555DH	N1DH	(N600AP) N5CA
188	10	F-WZGS	N253FJ	N188DH	N64F	D-CLLL	HB-VJM	I-TFLY	N84TJ	
189	10	F-WZGT	N254FJ	N605T	N60SL	N600PB	N812KC	N189JM	N155PX	
190	10	F-WZGU	N255FJ	N1887S	N36BG	N190L	C-FBNW			
191	10	F-WZGV	N256FJ	N700DK	[w/o 23Sep85 Palwaukee, IL]					
192	100	F-WZGX	N258FJ	N100FJ	N121FJ	[w/o 15Oct87 Sacramento, CA]				
193	100	F-WZGY	N259FJ	N3BY	OH-AMB	(N30TN)	EC-HVV			
194	100	F-WZGZ	N260FJ	N100FJ	N61FC	F-GIPH				
195	100	F-WZGA	N261FJ	N561NC	N5736	N10NL	(N10NV)	N95WJ	TS-IAM	F-WWZL TS-IAM N1993
196	100	F-WZGB	N262FJ	N581NC	N5734	N573J	N125CA	C-FICA		
197	100	F-WZGC	F-GEDB	F-WEDB	F-GEDB	N888G	N52N	N197MJ		
198	100	F-WZGF	N263FJ	N551NC	N5738	N100RB	N1PB	N91PB	N25ST	
199	100	F-WZGG	N264FJ	N330MC	(N1CN)	N39TH	PT-OXB	N886MJ	N486MJ	N96VR N60HM N655PE
200	100	F-WZGG	N265FJ	N662D	(N682D)	N80BL	N808L	N1JW		
201	100	F-WZGH	N266FJ	N8494	JA8494	N30TH	(F-GKPZ)	F-GKCC	N100NW	N844F
202	100	F-WZGD	F-GDSA	3D-ADR	N80WJ	N202DN	[w/o 09Dec01 Lawrence A/P, KS. To White Inds, Bates City, MO, for spares]			
203	100	F-WZGJ	N267FJ	VR-CLA	N100CT	XA-TBL	N45JB	N54FH	F-WQBM	I-FJDC F-GPGL
204	100	F-WZGK	N268FJ	N101EU	F-WGTG	XA-TAB	XA-UDP	C-FFEV		
205	100	F-WZGL	N269FJ	N700DW	N606AM					
206	100	F-WZGM	N270FJ	N100FJ	N367F	N46MK				
207	100	F-WZGN	N271FJ	N711MT	F-GKPB	(N107US)	N207US	N456CM	N55DG	N456CM N55DG ZS-JLK
208	100	F-WZGO	F-GELS	I-OANN	N71M	F-WQBJ	F-GSLZ			
209	100	F-WZGP	N272FJ	N312AT	(N312AR)	HB-VKR	OY-PHN	EC-KPP		
210	100	F-WZGR	N273FJ	N312AM	N812AM	N85WN	N35WN	N110PP	N210EM	VP-BAF [w/o Samedan, Switzerland, 12Feb09]
211	100	F-WZGT	F-GELT	(N446BM)						
212	100	F-WZGU	CN-TNA	F-WWZM	CN-TNA	CN-ANZ	CN-MNZ			
213	100	F-WZGV	N274FJ	ZK-MAZ	F-GKAE	F-WKAE	N711HF			
214	100	F-WZGX	N275FJ	N147G	N147GX					
215	100	F-WZGY	F-GHPB	N550FJ						
216	100	F-WZGZ	N276FJ	N100H	VH-JDW	9M-ATM	N999WJ	SE-DYB	N707CX	
217	100	F-WZGA	N277FJ	N100FJ	N100WG	F-GIFL	N68GT	N214RV		
218	100	F-WZGB	F-GHSK	TC-ARK	N218BA	N130DS	N303FZ	[dbr Jeffersonville, IN, 23Mar11; parted out by Alliance Air Parts, Oklahoma City, OK]		
219	100	F-WZGC	N123FJ	N2649	PT-ORS	N219JW	N485AS			
220	100	F-WZGD	N124FJ	N368F	N326EW	N326LW	N702NC	N569DW	N220CV	
221	100	F-WZGH	OE-GHA	F-GPFD	TR-...					
222	100	F-WZGF	N125FJ	N100CK	N98VR	N100YP				
223	100	F-WZGG	N126FJ	PT-LVD						
224	100	F-WZGH	N128FJ	(PT-...)	C-FREE	N135FJ	SE-DVP	F-WWZN	SE-DVP	N100TM N35CD
225	100	F-WZGI	N127FJ	PT-LXJ	N225CC	(N814PJ)				
226	100	F-WZGJ	N130FJ	XA-RLX	N121AT					

Production complete

DASSAULT FALCON 20/200

Notes: European Line Numbers" are quoted alongside the c/n where appropriate. These were numbers allocated by Dassault for administrative purposes but do from time to time get quoted as the c/n on its own, or jointly with the actual c/n.

Aircraft converted as part of the TFE-731 re-engining programme are known as 20-5s; known conversions are shown in the series column. Aircraft with TFE-731-5A engines (the earlier conversion) retain the series number in the designation, eg 20C-5 (c/n 24), while later conversions which use the TFE-731-5B engines (as also used in the Falcon 900B) do not retain the series letter; we have however retained this so that readers can be aware of the original model type.

Was known as the CC117 while in Canadian military service

C/n	Series	Identities
01	20	F-WLKB [ff 04May63] F-BLKB F-WLKB [last flt 06Feb76; used as mock-up for Guardian trials: donated to Musee de L'Air, Le Bourget, Paris, France]
1/401	20C	F-WMSH [ff 01Jan65] F-BMSH F-WMSH France 1/F-ZACV [wfu 31Dec81; TT 6,248 hrs, with 13,329 landings; to Bordeaux-Merignac Museum as F-WMSH]
2/402	20C	F-WMSS F-BMSS [canx Jan04 as wfu; to Musee de l'Air et de l'Espace site at Le Bourget, France on 02Mar05]
3/403	20C	F-WMKG F-BMSX VR-BCG HB-VAV N92MH N301R [wfu Oscoda, MI]
4	20C	F-WMKF N801F N116JD N121GW [w/o 18May78 Memphis, TN]
5	20C	F-WMKI N804F N747W F-GJPR N295TW [cx 03May16; wfu Addison, TX]
6	20C	F-WMKH F-BMKH N805F N20JM N21JM (N21DT) C-GOQG N65311 N497 N750SS EC-EDC
7	20C	F-WMKK N807F N607S N740L CF-GWI N777FA N20GH N12GH N110CE N93CP N600JC XA-ACI N666BT [canx 28Jly05; b/u]
8	20C	F-WMKJ N806F N1500 N150CG N1500 N190BD N612GA N277RA
9	20C	F-WMKI N809F N366G N3668 C-GSKA LV-PLC LV-WMF N611GA [wfu; cx 24Dec08]
10	20C	F-WMKK N810F N111M [cx Aug87; parted out by AvMATS, Paynesville, MO]
11	20C	F-WMKH N808F CF-SRZ N2200M N220CM N30CC N30CQ N4351M N4351N N409PC OO-DDD N983AJ N216CA [wfu at Addison, TX]
12	20C	F-WMKI N803F N221B N51SF LN-AAB [cx Mar89; to USA, no marks allocated; b/u for spares Jul89 Memphis, TN]
13	20C	F-WMKH F-BOEF TR-LOL F-BOEF D-CILL F-BTCY N977TW [wfu Addison, TX]
14	20C	F-WMKJ N804F CF-DML N22DL N22HC N91JF N41MH
15	20C	F-WMKK N806F N622R N1502 N151CG N1501 [wfu at Detroit-Willow Run by Nov03; cx 15Aug13]
16	20DC	F-WNGL N807F N354H N10FE N122CA N120AF N216TW N216SA [parted out by Dodson Av'n, Rantoul, KS]
17	20C	F-WMKF N802F N545C N5450 N5C N5CE N55TH N234CA [wfu at Addison, TX]
18	20C	F-WNGM N840F N803LC D-COLO N777JF N9DM N210RS [wfu 1996 for spares]
19	20C	F-WNGN N841F N500PC N500PX N41PC (N41PD) C-GKHA [b/u for spares Mar04 at Ottawa-Rockcliffe, Canada]
20	20DC	F-WMKJ N842F N367G N367GA N5FE (N146FE) (N25FR) N903FR G-FRAJ
21	20C	F-WMKI N843F N3444G N370 (N500NU) N500EW N91TS XA-SWC N20LT C-FTUT N50446 [wfu Addison, TX]
22/404	20C	F-WMKK F-BMKK France 22/F-ZACS [wfu Bonneuil-en-France, nr Le Bourget, France]
23	20C	F-WNGL F-BNKX N844F N424JX N15CC N256EN N256MA (N582G) Venezuela 5761 [stored El Libertador, Venezuela]
24	20C-5	F-WNGM N845F N297AR N30JM (N13FE) N2255Q N738RH N60SM N60SN N703SC N20YA N25TX N204JP N1M N240TJ (N794SB) N240CK
25/405	20C	F-WNGN F-BOON HB-VCO F-BSYF N813AA TG-GGA N813AA [wfu Detroit-Willow Run, MI; parted out]
26	20C	F-WNGO N846F N802F N11827 N819AA [wfu Detroit-Willow Run, MI; cx 28Aug14]
27	20C-5	F-WMKJ N847F N677SW N33TP N174GA N326VW N481FL
28	20C	F-WMKG N848F N367EJ N10WA N573EJ YV-78CP N50CA (N280RC) (N126JM) N50CA C-GEAQ N333AV [at Montreal – Saint Hubert Aeronautical College]
29	20C	F-WMKI N849F N368G N368L C-GSKC LV-PLD? LV-WMM [parted out Buenos Aires/San Fernando]
30	20CF	F-WMKF N804F N368EJ YV-126CP N368EJ N407PC CS-ATD F-GPIM N514SA N123RA
31	20C	F-WNGM N806F N34C N814AA N828AA N131MV
32	20C	F-WNGL N805F N418S N218S 5B-CGB TL-AJK F-GIVT N232TW
33	20C	F-WNGO N807F N369EJ N888AR [w/o 07Aug76 Acapulco, Mexico]
34	20C	F-WMKJ N808F N369G N3690 C-GSKS LV-PHV LV-WLH [w/o 07Feb97 in mountains near Salta, Argentina]
35	20C	F-WMKG N809F (N1777R) N809P 9M-BCR [wfu by 2005; for sale in stripped down state for static use]
36	20C	F-WMKI N810F N900P N711BC N644X N85N OE-GUS N818AA [wfu Detroit-Willow Run, MI]
37/406	20C	F-WMKF (HB-VWW) HB-VAP (N7922) (N11WA) [w/o 01Oct77 Goose Bay, Canada; parts used in rebuild of c/n 28]
38	20C	F-WMKF N842F N1107M N957TH [wfu 1987; cx Jan93; remains to Elberry, MO]
39	20C	F-WNGM N843F N5555U N6565A N50MM N910U XA-LOB XB-EDU XA-RMA [wfu Toluca, Mexico]
40	20C	F-WNGL N870F CF-BFM N19BC N354H N354WC N854WC N65LC N65LE C-GSKQ N240TW
41/407	20F-5B	F-WNGL (S Africa 431)F-BOED LN-FOI Norway 041 [ECM Aircraft]
42	20C	F-WNGO N871F N1503 N7824M [w/o 16Jan74 Fort Worth, TX]
43	20C	F-WMKJ N872F N990L [w/o 03Mar75 Dallas, TX]
44	20C	F-WNGN N873F N355WB N355WC N355WG N692G N76TS N377BT (N773HS) N800PP (N120EN) [parted out Chino, CA; cx 08Dec14]
45	20C	F-WMKI N876F N147X N159FC N90JF N202KH N175GA N589DC
46	20DC	F-WMKG CF-ESO N23555 N7FE (N144FE) N46VG EC-EHC [wfu; instructional airframe Fuenlabrada, Spain]
47	20C	F-WNGM N875F N1846 [w/o 13Mar68 Parkersburg, WV]
48	20C-5	F-WMKG N878F N910Y N91CV (N23NQ) N23ND N541FL
49/408	20C	F-WNGN France 49/F-RAFJ F-TEOA France 49/F-RHFA [code 120-FA; preserved Villacoublay, France]
50	20DC	F-WMGO N879F N804F N565A N6FE (N145FE) N56VG EC-EDO N699TW
51	20C	F-WMKJ N880F N880P N218US N425JF N425JA [scrapped for spares Aug91; cx Oct94]
52	20C	F-WNGN N881F N72ET N85DB N825TC D-CLBR UR-CLG [wfu Paderborn, Germany]
53/417	20C	F-WNGO F-BNRE LN-FOD Norway 053 [ECM Aircraft]
54	20C-5	F-WMKI N886F N200P N2005 N10726 N54SN N100HG (N205TS) (N103RA) N380RA N405JW D2-JMM
55/410	20C	F-WNGO VR-BCJ HB-VBS EC-EHD N550AL CCCP-01100 UR-EFA N520FD N830AA [wfu at Detroit-Willow Run, MI; cx 25Nov14]
56	20C	F-WNGM N882F N671SR N100SR N185S N932S (OO-PPP) OO-OOO N388AJ N560RA [b/u for parts at Detroit-Willow Run, MI circa May05]
57	20C	F-WNGO N883F N499MJ N678BM N677BM N3JJ N76RY N711KG N812AA [cx 24Apr09; to Saudi Arabia as instructional airframe]
58	20C	F-WNGL N884F N600KC F-BTQZ HB-VDG N2954T [scrapped for spares 1987 Van Nuys, CA]
59	20DC	F-WNGO N971F N263MW N710MW N710MR N710MT N227GC N227CC N202TA N72BB N771LD N159MV N900RA
60	20C	F-WMKJ N885F N805F [w/o 05Jly71 Boca Raton, FL]
61	20C	F-WMKI N887F N299NW N20NY
62/409	20C	F-WMKJ F-BOLX LN-FOE (N17401) [w/o 12Dec73 Norwich, UK; used by Federal Express for spares, marks N17401 were reserved after the w/o]
63/411	20C	F-WMKI PH-LPS D-CBNA [w/o 04Aug01 Narssarssuaq, Greenland]
64	20C	F-WMKG N889F N806F N200JW N916AN N513AN N513AG N425JF
65	20C	F-WNGN N890F N383RF (N393RF) N393F N777WJ N777WL N1U N5052U C-GSKN N165TW [w/o Jamestown, NY, 21Dec08]
66	20C	F-WNGL N891F N401AB N581SS N109RK N181RB N766NW N830RA N814ER
67/414	20C	F-WJMN F-BOOA F-BTML N821AA N826AA
68	20C-5	F-WMKJ N892F N577S N458SW N521FL
69	20C	F-WMKF N893F N176NP N176BN N31LT [Parted out by March Aviation, Naples, FL, 2006]
70	20C	F-WMKH N966F N647JP (N647SA) N78JR (N400NL) [wfu 20Mar89; b/u for spares Mojave, CA (TT 4,326 hrs); remains to Aviation Warehouse film prop yard, El Mirage, CA]
71	20C	F-WNGM N967F N807F N807PA N33SC N818SH N818CP (N293GT) N195AS N209CA [wfu at Addison, TX]
72/413	20C	F-WNGO HB-VAW N1270F N99KT VH-DWA N725P F-GJCC (N172MV) [wfu by Sep04 Middletown, OH]

FALCON 20/200

C/n	Series	Identities
73/419	20C	F-WJML VH-BIZ (F-BRHB) F-WMKG 9Q-CKZ (OO-RJX) (OO-ADA) LX-AAA LN-AAA [cx Dec89; scrapped for spares May89 Memphis, TN]
74 ʻ	20C-5	F-WMKG N968F N1851T N1MB N57HH N800MC N800PA N800DC N702DM N702DD N522DD N8TP N221BR [cx 06May15; wfu]
75	20C	F-WNGL N969F N100V N256MA N2568 N800DC N77QM UR-EFB N217CA N962AA
76	20C	F-WMKF N970F N937GC N776DS F-GGFO F-GJDB
77/429	20C	F-WNGO I-RIED (F-GJBR) F-GHDN F-WGTF F-GHSG N613GA N844SL [wfu by Sep04 Toledo, OH still wearing N613GA; fuselage to Pontiac, MI by Oct05 for parts; cx 03Oct07]
78/412	20C	F-WNGM Australia A11-078 VH-JSX N6555C [canx 10Nov04 for parts; b/u]
79/415	20C	F-WMKH F-BNRH France 79/F-ZACT
80	20C	F-WMKI N972F N115K N356WB N356WC N356JB N76MB N24TW N925BE [fuselage noted 28Aug05 on trailer Pontiac, MI]
81	20C	F-WNGN N973F N799G N661JB N661J N747T N93RS N810RA [wfu Oscoda, MI; cx 18Nov14]
82/418	20C	F-WJMM Canada 20501 Canada 117501 G-FRAS
83	20C	F-WJMJ N974F N805CC N80506 N22JW N12WP N1TC N55ME N68JK N20PL (N82SR) N283SA
84	20C	F-WJMK N975F N530L N1FE (N150FE) N9FE [exhibited in Federal Express HQ, Memphis, TN]
85/425	20C	F-WMKH Australia A11-085 VH-JSY N6555L [cx 30Apr15; wfu Spirit of St Louis, MO]
86	20C	F-WMKI N976F N808F N622R (G-BBEK) F-BUYI G-BBEK (HB-VDW) F-WRGQ France 86/F-ZACG [wfu; to Musee Europeen de l'Aviation de Chasse, Montelimar, France]
87/424	20C	F-WJMJ Canada 20502 Canada 117502 G-FRAT
88	20C	F-WNGN N977F N130B N665P N665B N41CD N617GA [parted out by White Inds, Bates City, MO]
89	20C	F-WMKG N978F N345BM N71CP N505AJ [cx 30Jul12; b/u]
90/426	20C	F-WNGL Australia A11-090 VH-JSZ VH-CIR PK-CIR [wfu by Dec04 Jakarta-Soekarno, Indonesia]
91	20C-5	F-WMKJ N979F N115TW N25DB N8WN (N91MH) N777DC N20UA (N200SS)
92/421	20C	F-WJMM Canada 20503 Canada 117503 C-GWPB [in use as instructional airframe at BC Institute of Technology, Vancouver, Canada; wore marks "N9747I" in 2000 for film 'Josie & The Pussycats']
93/435	20C	F-WMKF F-RAFN F-RBQA France 93/F-RAFN France 93/F-RAEC France 93/F-RAED [code 65-ED] [wfu Chateaudun, France]
94/428	20C	F-WNGO I-ATMO F-ODSK CS-ATE F-GLNL N614GA N566YT N461FL
95	20C	F-WNGO N980F N802F N664P (OO-EEF) N664B N950RA N995CK
96	20C	F-WNGM N981F N511S N5RT N89SC F-GERT France 96/F-ZACB
97/422	20C	F-WJMJ Canada 20504 Canada 117504 G-FRAU
98/434	20C	F-WNGN TU-VAD OY-AZT N408PC OO-RRR N781AJ N980R N998CK
99	20C	F-WJMK N982F N921ML
100	20C	F-WJMN N983F N605RP N200FT I-VEPA N179GA [w/o 08Apr03 Mississippi River landing at St Louis-Lambert, MO; parted out by Dodson Int'l Parts, Rantoul, KS]
101	20C	F-WMKJ N984F N342K N342F N97WJ
102	20C	F-WMKI N985F N223B N53SF N710EC (N710EG) N710WB N403JW N204AN
103/423	20C	F-WMKH Canada 20505 Canada 117505 [ECM Aircraft] G-FRAV F-GPAA
104/454	20C	F-WJMK (OT-JFA) F-BOXV France 104/F-ZACW
105	20C	F-WNGL N986F N243K N77GR N97FJ N460MC [b/u for spares Jly87 Memphis, TN; cx Mar89; remains to Spirit of St.Louis A/P, MO circa Jan02]
106	20C	F-WJMM N987F F-GBPG N9300M N31V EC-EKK
107	20C	F-WMKJ N988F N965BC N155NK N330PC N213LS N107J
108/430	20DC	F-WNGO (D-CDAS) D-CBAT N5CA N4FE (N147FE) N26VG N101ZE N108R [wfu Oscoda, MI] N808CK*
109/427	20C	F-WNGM Canada 20506 Canada 117506 [ECM Aircraft] C-FIGD [biofuel test aircraft]
110	20C	F-WMKG N989F CF-WRA C-FWRA VH-FWO [b/u for spares Oct88 Memphis, TN; cx Feb89]
111	20C	F-WMKI N990F N111AC N990F N111AM N111BP (XC-HIX) [cx 17Oct14; CofR expired]
112	20C	F-WJMJ N991F N2989 N830MF N200CX (HB-V..) CS-ATF UR-CCD UR-NIK [parted out by Atlanta Air Salvage, Griffin, GA]
113	20C-5	F-WNGL N993F PP-FOH PT-FOH (N713PE) N100WK N333WF N315PA N500HK (N731RG) F-WTFF N731F N129JE N129JF N400PC N400PG N22WJ N531FL
114/420	20C	F-WJMM Canada 20507 Canada 117507 [ECM Aircraft] G-FRAW
115/432	20SNA	F-WJML France 115/F-UGWL France F-UKJG [code 339-JG; stored Chateaudun, France by Jun02]
116	20C-5	F-WMKJ N994F HB-VJD OO-JBB F-WGTH (F-GPNG) F-GLMM F-WLMM F-GLMM N770FG
117	20C-5	F-WMKH N995F N171PF N421ZC TS-IRS HB-VKC EC-855 EC-FJP F-GLMD N207JS
118	20C	F-WMKG N996F N512T F-GGKE N820AA [wfu at Detroit-Willow Run, MI]
119/431	20C	F-WJMK I-SNAV F-GHFP N20FJ
120	20C-5	F-WMKI N4340F N410US N205FJ (F-GKAF) F-GICF N20AF N647JP N820CK
121	20C	F-WJMJ N4341F N242LB N813PA N1199M N25CP N500BG N121DJ [parted out by Dodson Av'n, Rantoul, KS]
122	20C-5	F-WNGL N4342F N779P N335WR N335WJ N32PB N900LC N33QS N302TT N511FL
123	20C	F-WNGM N4343F N513T N45MR N223TW
124/433	20C	F-WJMJ France 124/F-ZACC [instructional airframe Toussus-le-Noble, France]
125	20C-5B	F-WJMN N4344F N6810J N812PA LN-FOE Norway 0125 [ECM Aircraft]
126/438	20C	F-WMKH HB-VBL PH-BAG N1047T N10VG N102ZE N126R [wfu Detroit-Willow Run, MI circa Oct01]
127	20C	F-WNGN N4345F N50AD XB-EPB XA-REY XB-GCR XB-HRA
128/436	20C	F-WMKJ 5A-DAF YN-BZH C-GNAA EC-FAM N228CK N70CK
129	20C	F-WJMM N4346F N1823F N1823A N666DA N68TS PT-WUV N119LA PR-SUL
130	20C	F-WMKJ N4347F N514T XA-SCL (N130MV) (N130TJ) N722KS [canx 21Apr04; b/u; by Oct04 fuselage dumped at Ontario CA]
131/437	20C	F-WJMK France 131/F-ZACD [wfu Chateaudun, France]
132	20DC	F-WMKG N4348F N560L N2FE (N149FE) (N23FR) N902FR G-FFRA
133	20C	F-WNGO N4349F N894F VR-BKR F-GJLA N133FJ N200JE [dbr 21Jan04 Pueblo, CO; to Dodson Intl Parts for parts]
134	20C	F-WMKH N4350F N895F N897DM N897D I-NLAE [w/o 25Sep91 Kiel-Holtenau, Germany]
135	20C-5	F-WMKI N4351F N6820J N40XY N9999E N194MC N800DW N4MB [parted out by Dodson Int'l, Rantoul, KS]
136/439	20C	F-WJMJ HB-VBM 9K-ACQ F-GCGU HB-VBM SP-FCP LX-IAL N20MY RA-09007 [w/o 20May05 Moscow-Sheremetyevo, Russia]
137	20C	F-WLLK F-BLLK F-WLLK N4352F N8999A N777PV N200GT [parted out by AvMATS, St Louis, MO; cx 27Jun11]]
138/440	20C	F-WLCS D-CALL D-CGJH (G-BAOA) F-BUIC France 138/F-ZACR
139	20C	F-WNGM N4353F N334JR N926LR N1868M N1868N N23PL N900WB N235CA [wfu Addison, TX]
140	20C	F-WNGN N4354F N4350M N3350M N160WC N314AE N165WC [Volpar PW305 conversion; ff 05Feb91] [wfu 1994 Detroit-Willow Run, MI; b/u for spares by Active Aero cx Aug03]
141/441	20C-5	F-WMKF F-BPIO F-BIHY (UR-BCA) UR-CCB UR-SBS [cx; wfu Rotterdam, Netherlands]
142	20C-5	F-WJMM N4355F N100S N1BF N298W N777WJ N511T N511TA N43SM N220RT (N205FJ) XA-RNB N300BA
143/442	20C	F-WMKH 5A-DAG
144	20C	F-WJMJ N4356F N888L N888JR N800LS (N200WF) N800KR N911RG N385AC N960AA
145/443	20C	F-WNGN F-BPJB OO-PJB F-GCGY France 145/F-ZACU
146	20CF	F-WJMN N964M N777EG N11TC C-FCDS N182GA N345FH N299RA [cx Oct10; wfu]
147/444	20CF	F-WLCH PH-ILF (D-CORT) (D-CCNA) N41154 N183GA [w/o 08Apr03 Toledo, OH]
148	20C	F-WMKG N4358F N120HC N126HC N657MC N888WS N148WC N148TW
149	20C	F-WNGO N4359F N1818S (N4359F) N568Q EC-263 EC-EQP
150/445	20C	F-WMKH HB-VBO (N95591) N8227V N777XX N679RE N123RE (VR-C..) TG-RBW HC-BSS
151	20DC	F-WMKI N4360F N810F N810PA N3FE (N148FE) (N24FR) N904FR G-FRAL
152/446	20DC	F-WJMJ CN-MBG CN-ANN
153	20C	F-WLCT N4361F N70MD N207CA
154/447	20C	F-WLCV France 154/F-RAFK [w/o 22Jan76 nr Villacoublay, France]

FALCON 20/200

C/n	Series	Identities										
155	20C	F-WJMK	N4362F	N500Y	N205SC	N212C	(N205SE)	N404R	N68BC	N68BP		
156/448	20C	F-WMKI	7T-VRE	[w/o 30May81 Bamako, Mali]								
157	20C	F-WJMM	N4363F	N166RS	Canada 117508		C-GRSD-X	C-GRSD	N5096F	[wfu]		
158/449	20C	F-WMKJ	D-CMAX	N158TW								
159	20C	F-WMKJ	N4364F	N5RC	N411CC	N96WC	N96RT	XA-ICG	XA-PCC	N67AX	XA-PCC	
160/450	20C	F-WMKG	I-DKET	F-GHBT	N48BT	N100UF	N301TT	[cx 27Jun11; parted out]				
161	20C	F-WMKF	N4365F	N93CD	N19BD	N93FH	N21NC	N10PP	N10RZ	N503RV	N620RB	[parted out by Alliance Air Parts, Oklahoma City, OK]
162/451	20C	F-WNGO	OO-WTB	D-CBBT	HB-VED	F-ODOK	OO-DOK	(F-GFLL)	F-GFUN	N162CT	N911DG	(N389AC) [cx 25Nov13; wfu]
163	20D	F-WNGM	N4366F	(N500HD)	N500FE	N500LD	N178GA	N258PE	N471FL			
164	20C	F-WJMN	N4367F	N654E	N164NW	[cx 23Apr13; CofR expired]						
165/452	20C	F-WJMJ	CN-MBH	CNA-NM	[ECM Aircraft]							
166	20C-5	F-WLCS	N4368F	N33D	N33DY	N71TJ	N201BR					
167/453	20C	F-WMKG	France 167/F-RAFL		France 167/F-RAEB		[code 65-EB; wore full "reg'n"; wfu; preserved Espaces Aero Lyon Corbas museum, Lyon, France]					
168	20C-5	F-WLCX	N4369F	N100KW	N108NC	N300FJ	N731RG	N112CT	N514JJ	N168DJ		
169	20C	F-WNGN	N4370F	XC-SEY	XC-MIC							
170/455	20C	F-WPUV	I-EKET	F-GHPA	RA-09004	[cx; to scrapyard, Geneva, Switzerland, 14Mar06]						
171	20D-5	F-WMKG	N4371F	N570L	N900JL	(F-GHRE)	F-GICB	N217AJ	LV-BRZ			
172/456	20C	F-WNGM	F-BRHB	I-LIAB	[cx, C of A expired]							
173	20D	F-WLCU	F-BLCU	N70PA	N729S	PK-TRI						
174/457	20C	F-WNGL	TL-AAY	TL-KAZ	(HB-VER)	F-WSHT	HZ-KA3	HZ-NES	(D-CFAI)	N174BD	[wfu parted out at Fayetteville, AR circa Oct05]	
175	20D-5	F-WMKF	N4373F	N866MM	F-BUFG	D-COFG	F-ODHA	F-GBMS	I-CAIB	N4246R	N688MC	N116BK	HB-VJW
		SU-OAE	5A-DKQ	[parted out by Atlanta Air Salvage, Griffin, GA Sep08]								
176/458	20C-5	F-WMKG	I-SNAM	F-WGTM	F-GHDT	F-WQBM	EC-JJH	N179CJ				
177	20D	F-WMKI	N4374F	N6701	N14FG	N41BP	N82PJ	[cx 14Oct11; wfu]				
178/459	20C	F-WPXF	OH-FFA	G-FRBA	[cx 06Dec11; CofA expired]							
179	20D	F-WNGO	N4375F	N10LB	N12LB	N12MF	M17JT	XA-ACA	N341PF	XA-PVM	XB-NOR	
180/460	20C-5	F-WMKF	OY-BDS	I-GOBJ	F-GVJR	F-OVJR	[w/o 15Mar06 Kiel, Germany]					
181	20D	F-WNGL	N4376F	N836UC	N966L	N200GH	N200GL	N817JS	N5225G	[cx 06May13; wfu]		
182/461	20C	F-WNGN	HB-VCB	F-WTDJ	I-ROBM	F-WVFV	F-BVFV	France 182/F-ZJTA	France 182/F-UKJA	[preserved Canopee museum, Chateaudun, France]		
183	20D	F-WLCY	N4377F	N2979	EC-EFR	RA-09003	[wfu at Moscow/Domodedovo by Aug07]					
184/462	20D	F-WRQQ	F-BTMF	D-COMF	F-GAPC	OE-GCJ	EC-HCX					
185/467	20D-5	F-WMKF	I-IRIF	N3WN	N147X	N813LS	N818LS	N653MF	[parted out by Alliance Air Parts, Oklahoma City, OK]			
186/463	20SNA	F-WPXL	France 463/F-UGWM	[code 339-WM]		France 463/F-UKJE		[code 339-JE; stored Chateaudun, France by Jun02]				
187	20D	F-WLCV	N4379F	N40AC	N750R	N811AA						
188/464	20C	F-WJMK	F-BRPK	France 188/F-ZACX								
189	20D	F-WPUU	N4380F	N950L	N47JF	N47JE	N444BF	EC-EFI	[w/o 11Oct87 off Keflavik, Iceland]			
190/465	20SNA	F-WNGN	Libya 002	5A-DCO								
191	20D-5	F-WPUX	N4381F	N910L	N200DE	N200CG	N800CF	OE-GCR	N20HF	[parted out by Alliance Air Parts, Oklahoma City, OK]		
192	20DF	F-WPUY	N4382F	N920L	N57JF	N910W	N192R	N192CK				
193	20D	F-WMKG	N4383F	N930L	N37JF	N400DB	9Q-CTT	N219CA	[wfu Addison, TX]			
194	20DF	F-WPUZ	N4384F	N100M	N555RA	N297W	N287W	[w/o 11Feb88 Akron, OH; b/u Jun89; cx Jun92; parted out by AvMATS, Paynesville, MO]				
195	20D	F-WPXD	N4385F	N200SR	N186S	N191C	N500GM	N43JK	N195MP	N822AA		
196	20D	F-WPXE	N4386F	N811PA	N701MG	N369WR	N216BG	N79AE	N255RK	N196TS	(N141JF)	(N142JF) [cx Oct10; wfu]
197	20D	F-WPXF	N4387F	N399SW	C-GTAK	N5098F	[cx 21May13; CofR expired]					
198/466	20D	F-WNGO	VR-BDK	(N14FE)	N74196	(XC-GAM)	XC-BIN	XA-SQS	N520TJ	N339TG	N724DS	
199	20DC	F-WMKH	N4388F	N8FE	[wfu Aug83; displayed National Air & Space (Smithsonian) Museum, Steven F. Udvar-Hazy Center, Washington-Dulles, VA]							
200	20D	F-WMKJ	N4389F	N550MC	N44MC	N44CC	N48CC	N38CC	YV-200C	HC-BUP	YV-876C	N12AR [b/u Ontario, CA, May03 still marked as YV-876C cx Jun03; fuselage still present 2009]
201/469	20D	F-WLCY	D-CELL	"D-CEUU"	D-CELL	I-DRIB	[wfu by 2004 Rome-Ciampino, Italy]					
202	20D-5	F-WNGM	N4391F	N814PA	N33L	N33LV	N48TJ	N9TE	N29TE	N9TE	N365CD	N100FT	N604PT
203	20D	F-WPXH	N4378F	N1857B	N20BE	N911WT	OE-GDR	N36P	N821AA	[parted out by Dodson Av'n, Rantoul, KS]		
204	20DC	F-WMKI	N4392F	N26FE	N120FS	EC-113	EC-EGM	N204TW				
205	20D	F-WPXF	N4393F	N21W	N82A	N4LH	(N426CC)	N815AA	N915SA	N585AC	N961AA	
206	20D	F-WLCS	N4394F	N815AC	N632PB	N801SC	N28RK	(N410FJ)	[crashed into sea off Bahamas 17Dec09, w/o; cx 13Jun11]]			
207	20DC	F-WMKF	N4395F	N27FE	N908FR	G-FRAP						
208/468	20D	F-WPXD	HB-VCA	VH-BRR	N300JJ	N125CA	[w/o 29Jun89 Cartersville, GA]					
209	20DC	F-WLCX	N4396F	N28FE	N909FR	G-FRAR						
210	20DC	F-WNGL	N4397F	N29FE	N66VG	EC-ECB	[w/o 30Sep87 Las Palmas, Canary Islands, Spain]					
211	20DC	F-WJMK	N4398F	N30FE	Portugal 8101		Portugal 17101	N618GA	N764LA	N120RA		
212	20DC	F-WPXG	N4399F	N31FE	N212R	[wfu Oscoda, MI]						
213	20DC	F-WJMM	N4390F	N32FE	N905FR	G-FRAK	(N213FC)					
214	20DC	F-WNGO	N4400F	N33FE	N906FR	G-FRAO						
215	20DC	F-WLCS	N4401F	N34FE	Portugal 8102		Portugal 17102		N619GA	N510BM	[wfu for parts use; fuselage at Pontiac, MI by Oct05; canx Jan06 as b/u]	
216	20DC	F-WLCT	N4402F	N9FE	Venezuela 5840		[stored El Libertador, Venezuela]					
217	20DC	F-WLCY	N4403F	N35FE	Portugal 8103		Portugal 17103	[wfu; preserved Museo do Ar, Sintra, Portugal]				
218	20DC	F-WMKJ	N4372F	N36FE	N86VG	OO-STE	N86VG	EC-EEU	N218CA			
219/470	20D	F-WPXH	EC-BVV	Spain TM.11-3/401-04		Spain TM.11-3/45-04		Spain TM.11-3/408-11		Spain TM.11-3/47-23		
220	20DC	F-WPUU	N4404F	N24FE	N36VG	OO-STF	EC-EDL	"EC-EDC"+	[+ reported painted as EC-EDC for at least one flight (to Luton, UK) during 1987]			
		N220CA	[wfu Addison, TX]									
221	20DC	F-WPUV	N4406F	N25FE	N300NL	EC-165	EC-EIV	N221TW				
222/471	20D	F-WNGL	EC-BXV	Spain TM.11-2/401-03		Spain TM.11-2/45-03		Spain TM.11-2/47-22				
223	20DC	F-WPUX	N4407F	N22FE	(N904FR)	N900FR	G-60-01	G-FRAH				
224	20DC	F-WPUY	N4408F	N23FE	N907FR	G-FRAM	9M-FRA					
225/472	20D	F-WPXD	TR-KHA	TR-LRU	F-BOFH	OH-FFJ	N125MJ	N37WT	N332FE	N338DB	(N30AD)	N102AD	C-FONX
		N5098H	[parted out Milwaukee, WI]									
226	20DC	F-WPXI	F-WSQK	N4409F	N21FE	N226R	N226CK					
227	20DC	F-WMKG	N4410F	N14FE	N24EV	N227R	N227CK					
228/473	20D	F-WNGL	ZS-LAL	ZS-LLG	3D-LLG	C-GWSA	HB-VEZ	5N-AYM	OE-GRU	N823AA	[cx 06May15; CofR expired]	
229	20DC	F-WJMJ	N4411F	N15FE	N25EV	N229R	N229CK					
230	20DC	F-WJML	N4412F	N16FE	N26EV	N230RA	[wfu Oscoda, MI]					
231/474	20D	F-WPXE	HB-VCG	[w/o 20Feb72 nr St Moritz, Switzerland]								
232	20DC	F-WJMN	N4413F	N17FE	N27EV	N232RA	[w/o 15Feb89 Bingham, NY; cx Mar91]					
233	20DC	F-WLCV	N4414F	N18FE	N76VG	I-TIAG	N817AA	[parted out by Dodson Av'n, Rantoul, KS]				
234/475	20D	F-WLCU	(D-CIBM)	D-COLL	I-LIAC	[cx, C of A expired]						
235	20DC	F-WPXJ	N4415F	N20FE	Venezuela 0442		[stored El Libertador, Venezuela]					
236	20D	F-WPXK	(N4416F)	CF-JES	C-FJES	N375PK	N375BK	YR-DSA	N128AP	N618GH	N936NW	N236TW
237/476	20D-5	F-WPXF	(D-CHCH)	(D-CALM)	D-CITY	N4227Y	VR-CBT	VR-BKH	HB-VJV	EC-JDVUR-MOA	N119TA	
238/477	20C	F-WRQP	France 238/F-RAFM		France 238/F-RAED		France 238/F-RAEE		France 238/F-RAFM		France 238/F-RAEE	[code 65-EE; wfu; instructional airframe Toussus-le-Noble, France]

FALCON 20/200

C/n	Series	Identities										
239	20F	F-WPXM	N4417F	N10MT	C-GBFL	N134CJ	I-AGEC	PH-OMC	N39WJ	N697BH	N239CD	N239BD	N300BP
		[cx 08Jul13; wfu; parted out Denton, TX]
240/478	20E-5	F-WLCX	I-SNAG	N240AT	HB-VMN	F-GYCA	T7-ALM
241/479	20E	F-WRQP	SE-DCO	N48AD	HZ-PL7	I-FLYK	N241JC	[cx 25Jun07, wfu]
242	20F	F-WPUZ	N4418F	N800CF	(N320FJ)	N2622M	N911TR	N66WB	YR-DSB	N129AP	(N711RT)	"N4RT"	(N242RJ)
		N513AC	(N242MA)
243/480	20F	F-WMKH	OH-FFW	[w/o 01Mar72 nr Montreal, Canada; remains to Sunstream Avn, Chicago-DuPage A/P, MI, gone by Jun95]
244	20F	F-WMKI	N4420F	N20FJ	N11LB	N226G	N61LL	VR-BJB	[w/o 15Jan88 Lugano, Switzerland; remains to Dodson Avn, Ottawa, KS]
245/481	20E	F-WLCS	SX-ABA	F-BUIX	HB-VDP	HB-VDY	EL-VDY	[parted out by Dodson Int'l Parts, Rantoul, KS circa Oct98]
246/482	20F	F-WJMK	F-BSTR	(F-GLMT)	N970GA	[b/u for spares at White Inds. Bates City, MO]
247	20E	F-WPXE	N4419F	N730K	VH-FAX	N730S	N67JR	N95JR	N70PL	N247PL
248/483	20F	F-WRQV	OH-FFV	N37JJ	XB-AQU	XB-OEM	XB-VRM	XC-HIX	XB-NET
249	20F	F-WJMM	N4421F	N11AK	N777JF	N451DP	N431FL
250	20F	F-WMKF	N4422F	N111AM	XA-HEW	N223BG
251/484	20E	F-WRQR	EP-VAP	EP-FIE	EP-IPA	Iran 0110
252/485	20E	F-WRQP	I-GIAZ	France 252/F-ZACA
253/486	20E	F-WRQS	EC-BZV	Spain T.11-1/401-02		Spain T.11-1/45-02		Spain T.11-1/47-21
254	20F	F-WNGO	N4423F	CF-YPB	C-FYPB	G-FRAC	F-GPAB	[cx 19Oct15; scrapped]
255/487	20E	F-WRQP	Jordan 122	HB-VDZ	N2724K	VH-HIF	VH-MIQ	N721J	F-GHLN	[w/o 20Jan95 Paris-Le Bourget A/P, France]
256	20F	F-WNGL	N4416F	N3RC	C-GNTZ	F-GKME	UR-CCA	N368DS	N868DS	N15SL	N651SD	N733JB
257	20F-5	F-WMKH	N4425F	N781W	N300CC	C-GNTL	(F-GJPI)	F-GKDD	HB-VKO	N18HN	[wfu; cx 05Dec15]
258	20F	F-WNGM	N4426F	N20JM	N544X	N20AE	N300SF	N380SF	N68UP
259	20F	F-WLCT	N4418F	N212H	N45WH	N45WN	SE-DHK	F-GIFP	N569BW	N569DW	N569D	[cx Mar11; to Finland as instructional airframe]
260/488	20E	F-WMKJ	France 260/F-RAEA		[code 65-EA; wfu Chateaudun, France]
261	20F-5	F-WLCU	N4368F	N200WK
262	20F-5	F-WJMK	N4427F	N720ML	N750ME	VH-WLH	N501AS	C-GTLU	F-GHVR	(N.....)	D2-ESV	(OO-MDN)	(OO-RYB)
		N795AB	N189RB
263/489	20E	F-WMKJ	HB-VCR	(PH-LEN)	F-BSBU	France 263/F-ZACY
264	20F	F-WJMN	N4428F	N373KC	N777V	N773V	(N86BL)	F-GJJS	CS-ATG	N264TN	XA-III	XA-NCC
265	20F	F-WLCX	N4429F	N606RP	N265MP
266/490	20EF	F-WRQR	PH-ILX	N4115B	N184GA	[w/o 13Jun00 Peterborough, Canada; to White Inds. Bates City, MO for parts use circa Jan01]
267/491	20E	F-WRQZ	I-REAL	N731G	N627JG	N267H	N129JE	[parted out by Alliance Air Parts, Oklahoma City, OK]
268/492	20E	F-WNGN	France 268/F-RAEB		France 268/F-RAFK		France 268/F-RAEF	[code 65-EF; wfu Chateaudun, France]
269	20F	F-WPUX	N4430F	N1902W	N501F	XA-NAY	XA-DUC
270	20DC	F-WPUZ	N4435F	N37FE	(N907FR)	N901FR	G-FRAI
271/493	20E	F-WNGN	7T-VRP	(F-GHPO)	F-GKDB	[cx to Switzerland 08Mar05 but no Swiss marks allocated; b/u; fuselage used as cabin trainer]
272	20F	F-WMKF	N4431F	N20FJ	N732S	N888RF	N913MK	N813MK	(N803MM)	XA-TAN	(N272FA)	N272JP	N885BH N20FE
		N770RR	N224WE
273	20F-5	F-WPUU	N4432F	N212T	N212TC	N212TG	5N-EPN	F-WQBK	N596DA	N720JC	N632KA	CN-TNM
274	20F-5	F-WJMM	N4433F	N370WT	N121WT	N256M	N26LA	(D-CHEF)	N260MB	N100AS
275	20E	F-WMKH	N4434F	N661JB	N9FB	VR-BRJ	SX-DKI	N999EQ	(N999BG)	N200CP
276/494	20E	F-WNGL	Belgium CM-01
277/501	20E	F-WPXD	Pakistan J-753
278/495	20E-5	F-WNGM	Belgium CM-02		F-WQBN	Belgium CM-02
279/502	20E	F-WMKJ	I-FKET	F-GHFQ	N279AL	F-GROC	N854GA	D-CLBE	UR-CLE
280/503	20E	F-WPXK	I-EDIS	N910FR	G-FRAE	F-GPAD
281/496	20E	F-WRQR	D-CORF	LN-AAC	N70830	N347K	N281JJ	N341K	N341KA	N116GB	[wfu Easton MD; cx 18May12]
282	20E	F-WRMKG	N4436F	N131JA	N282JJ	N282C	XC-DIP	XB-IYK	XC-HID	[code PF-203]
283/497	20E	F-WRQX	EP-AGX	[w/o 21Nov74 Kermanshah, Iran]
284	20E	F-WPXM	N4437F	N132JA	N284JJ	N98RH	N444FJ	N441FA	XA-BCC	N441FA	N284CE	N501MD	(N801MD)
		N201GF
285/504	20EF	F-WRQT	A4O-AA	A4O-GA	PH-WMS	VR-CCF	PH-WMS	N285AP	N285TW
286/498	20E	F-WRQU	EP-AGY	Iran 15-2234
287	20E	F-WMKF	N4438F	YV-T-AVA	YV-38CP	XB-ALO	XA-SAG	XC-PFJ/PF-239		XC-QER
288/499	20E	F-WRQZ	F-BUYE	France 288/F-ZACV
289	20F	F-WMKG	N4439F	N20FJ	N54J	N54JJ	N1HF	N40994	N211HF	N105TW	N75TJ	N450CP
290	20E	F-WMKH	N4440F	N133JA	I-TIAL	N816AA	[instructional airframe, Doha, Qatar]
291/505	20E	F-WRQT	France 291/F-RAEC		France 291/F-RCAP		France 291/F-RAEG	[code 65-EG; wfu Mar07, stored Chateaudun, France]
292	20F-5B	F-WMKI	N4441F	N733S	N510WS	9M-LLJ
293	20E-5	F-WMKJ	N4442F	N2615	N2613	HZ-PL1	HB-VJX	OY-CKY	F-WQBN	F-GOBZ	I-GOBZ	F-WQVA	RA-09005
		UR-CLF	N570ZD
294/506	20E-5B	F-WRQT	F-BVPM	SU-AXN
295/500	20E	F-WRQQ	I-EDIM	N911FR	G-FRAF
296/507	20F-5	F-WRQP	HB-VDB	D2-EBB	J5-GAS	N4960S	N214JP	N297CK	N19TX	N20TX	N220LA
297	20E	F-WMKF	N4443F	(N370EU)	N121EU	PK-TIR	"N297AG"	CS-DCK
298	20E	F-WMKG	N4444F	N86W	N98LB	OE-GNN	N827AA
299	20F	F-WMKI	(N734S)	N21FJ	N456SR	N90CN	N585UC	F-GJSF	TC-EZE	(N669AC)	N299JC
300/508	20E	F-WRQP	I-EDIF	(F-GIBT)	(F-GEJX)	F-GGMM	N300FJ	(N953DC)	N600WD
301/509	20E	F-WNGL	EP-AKC
302/510	20E	F-WRQP	D-COMM	OE-GDP	N84V	F-WQBM	F-GOPM
303	20F	F-WMKH	N4445F	N27R	[w/o 12Nov76 Naples, FL]
304/511	20E	F-WRQP	G-BCYF	G-FRAD	9M-BDK	G-FRAD
305	20F-5	F-WMKJ	N4446F	N16R	N56SL	VR-CDB	N282U	N34CW	N715WS
306/512	20E	F-WRQS	(HB-VDY)	(HB-VDO)	D-CGSO	VH-HFJ	(N725P)	N76662	N205WM	N205WP
307/513	20E-5	F-WRQT	HB-VDV	I-GCAL	OE-GLL	F-GKIS	F-GYPB	F-GYMC	CS-DPW	F-HJYL
308	20F	F-WMKF	N4447F	N668P	N668S	N37RM	SE-DKA	N81AJ	N453SB	N458SB
309/514	20SNA	F-WRQT	TR-LUW	France 309/F-RAFU		France 309/F-UGWP		[code 339-WP; named L'Etoile du Berger]		[w/o 02Dec91 Villacoublay, France]
310	20F	F-WMKH	N4450F	(N370ME)	N121AM	N831HG	N31FJ	N724JC	N20WK
311/515	20F-5	F-WRQS	F-BVPN	N......
312	20F	F-WMKH	N4448F	N2605	N619MW	N1971R	N132AP	N741MR	[cx 30May14; wfu]
313	20F-5B	F-WMKF	N4449F	N744CC	N56CC	N560R	I-PERF	F-GHCR	N212PB	N183TS	N184TS	N339RK	[parted out by Alliance Air Parts, Oklahoma City, OK]
314/516	20E	F-WNGL	D-COTT	F-GDLU	N314TW
315/517	20E-5	F-WRQP	F-BVPQ	OO-VPQ	F-GDLO	F-SEBI	F-GSXF	D-CLBB	UR-CLD	N204ED	(N208MD)
316	20F-5	F-WMKF	N4451F	N734S	N242CT	N424XT
317	20F	F-WMKG	N4452F	N31CM	N99E	N92K	N88FE	HB-VEV	N939CK
318/518	20E	F-WRQT	(EP-VAS)	EP-VSP	EP-FIG	Iran 15-2235
319	20F-5	F-WMKF	N4453F	N730V	N44NT	C-GNTM	N70LG	N77LA	N205K	N724CP	N520TC
320/519	20E	F-WRQS	EP-AHV	EP-FIF
321	20F-5	F-WJMJ	N4454F	N2525	N702SC	N244CA	N20FM	(PH-BPS)	N104SB	PH-BPS	[cx Jun10; CofA expired]
322	20F	F-WMKH	N4455F	N1971R	N999DC	N94GW	N464M	N300CV	YV2723
323/520	20E	F-WRQS	HB-VEB	I-FCIM	OE-GLF	XU-008	[instructional airframe, Singapore/Seletar]

FALCON 20/200

C/n	Series	Identities
324	20F	F-WMKF N4456F N444SC N324TC N312K N373DN
325	20F	F-WMKG N4457F N100GN N400GN (N400GX) (N700GN) VH-RRC N7WG N599RR N555TF (N325MC) N877JG
326/521	20E	F-WRQQ PH-ILY TC-CEN TC-GGG
327	20F	F-WMKI N4458F N3H N2H N96L VH-NMN N900DB N25WG XA-HHF XA-ABF N327BC XA-MSA XA-UPO
328/522	20F	F-WMKJ (N4459F) YK-ASA [crashed Damascus, Syria, 19Oct08; rebuilt at Le Bourget, France, 2010]
329/523	20E	F-WRQV D-CMET
330	20E	F-WNGM N4460F N300AL C-GNTY N770MC (N227LA) N30FT
331/524	20F	F-WRQS YK-ASB
332/525	20E	F-WRQP EC-CTV Spain TM.11-4/401-05 Spain TM.11-4/45-01 Spain TM.11-4/408-12 Spain TM.11-4/47-24
333/526	20E	F-WNGL Iran 5-2801 Iran 15-2233 [w/o 09Jan06 Aidinlou, NW Iran]
334/527	20E	F-WRQU EP-FIC [w/o 03Mar14 nr Kish Island, Iran]
335	20F	F-WMKF N4459F N901TC N903SB D-CFAI N335AJ N707JC (N707JZ) (N301FC) N335TW
336/528	20E	F-WRQP Iran 5-2802 [wfu Tehran, Iran]
337/529	20F	F-WRQR YI-AHH Iran 5-9014
338/530	20E	F-WMKG EP-FID
339	20F-5	F-WMKH N4461F N200GN N100GN N200GN (N200GX) N131DB (N402NC) N22FS N19MX SE-DSA N38TJ N239CD
340/531	20E	F-WRQX Iran 5-2803 Iran 803
341	20F-5B	F-WMKF N4462F N20FJ N66GA N511WP N511WR N78BC N311JS VR-CDT F-OHCJ F-GYSL [cx 11Dec13, b/u]
342/532	20F	F-WRQP YI-AHI J2-KAC France 342/F-RAEC France 342/F-RAEG France 342/F-RAEC [code 65-EC]
343/533	20F	F-WRQR YI-AHJ Iran 5-9015
344/534	20F-5	F-WRQP A6-HEM A6-EXA N344FJ (N731F) N731AS (N731AE) N227WE N227WL [parted out by Alliance Air Parts, Oklahoma City, OK]
345	20F	F-WMKI N4463F N678BM F-GHMD N133AP OH-FPC UR-NOA N345FJ UR-NOA
346/535	20E	F-WRQP Iran 5-2804 [wfu Tehran, Iran]
347	20F	F-WMKF N4464F N744CC N298CK N347HS N20VF N711FJ N211FJ N730RA
348/536	20E	F-WRQR Iran 5-4039 Iran 5-3020 [w/o 03Mar97 Ardabil, Iran]
349	20E	F-WMKG N4465F N273K N66NT N767AC N767AG N287SA N220WE (N159RA)
350/537	20E	F-WRQS Iran 5-4040 Iran 5-3021
351/538	20F	F-WMKJ Iran 5-9001 [reportedly destroyed Feb91, no other details known]
352	20F-5	F-WMKF N4466F N920G N184WW
353/539	20F	F-WRQP Iran 5-9002 [reportedly destroyed Jan91, no other details known]
354/540	20F	F-WRQR Iran 5-9003 Iran 5-9016
355	20F-5	F-WMKF N4467F N20FJ N27AC N344G N550M N63PM N61PM N200MK N712ME N803WC N335MC N632PB
356	20F	F-WMKG N4468F N27R N27RX G-FRAB F-GPAE N111F N11UF N69SW N621JS [cx 16Sep13; wfu; parted out Denton, TX]
357	20F-5	F-WMKI N4469F N435T N435TP N342K N342KF N357PS M-ABCD N370AG VH-PNY
358/541	20F-5B	F-WRQS SU-AZJ F-WRQY SU-AZJ
359/542	20F	F-WRQR (N64769) HZ-TAG HZ-AO1 N64769 N647JP N35RZ N50SL (N508L) N369CA N369CE OH-WIP N829TS N359BR
360	20F	F-WMKJ N1010F N901YP N905SB N911SB F-GJEA N165PA N865VP N390AG N349MR N766RA
361/543	20F-5	F-WMKF SU-AYD
362	20G	(F-WZAS) F-WATF F-WDFJ F-GDFJ F-WDFJ [wfu Istres, France circa Sep00; preserved as 'gate guardian' Martignas-sur-Jalle, France]
363/544	20F-5	F-WRQV HZ-DC2 N363FJ N3VF N9TE N78MB (N68BC)
364	20F	F-WMKI N1013F N235U N285U OE-GCS N285U XA-FLM N134PA XB-KBW XA-FLG
365	20F	F-WMKJ N1018F N777TX N50BH N50BV [cx 11Mar13; wfu]
366	20F	F-WMKG N1020F N83V N300CT N100AC N100AQ N404DH
367/545	20F	F-WRQR EP-SEA
368	20F-5	F-WMKI N1036F N800CF N200DE N800CF VH-NCF N83D I-FIPE N110TJ F-GHTK N110TJ N65TS N107LW N23A N15H N987AB N913SH
369	20F	F-WRQP N1037F N20SR (N414JC) N415JW N509WP N420J N138FJ N138FN N887DR
370	20F	F-WMKG N1038F HL7234 N370HF N269SR N20WN
371	HU25C	F-WMKJ N1039F USCG 2141
372/546	20F	F-WRQV ST-PRS
373	20F-5	F-WMKI N1041F N53DS N922DS N91Y (N620CC) N610CC N620CC N399FG C-FSJI
374	HU25A	F-WRQP N1045F USCG 2101
375/547	20F	F-WRQR F-GBMD France 375/F-ZACZ
376	20F-5B	F-WRQS N103F N2624M N2614 N2616H N1892S N1897S N367BL
377/548	20F-5	F-WRQP D-CCMB N30FT N5VJ N377RP N600CD
378	20F-5	F-WRQT N107F (N662PP) N662P (N6621) N305AR N500JD N97SJ N378DB
379	20F-5	F-WMKF N130F (N37AH) (N33AJ) N33AH F-GGBL N62570 N892SB N892S (N724JS) XA-RHA N205ZZ
380	20F-5	F-WMKI N136F N8BX N1BX N9654N N922ML (N288MM) N289MM N3848U I-ULJA N380CJ VH-FAI
381/549	20F-5	F-WRQS (I-LAFA) D-CCDB N20TZ N20T N85TZ N602LP N840DP
382	20F	F-WMKG N138F HP-1A N138F N138E N382E N10AZ N453SB N459SB
383/550	20F-5	F-WRQR D-CONU 5N-AYO HB-VJS N900CH N908CH N706SB
384/551	20F-5	F-WRQU OO-PSD N384JK N120CG N120TF N120DE N82TN N384PS
385	20F-5	F-WJMJ N139F N118R G-FRAA N120WH N87TN N385FJ ZS-KGS
386	HU25A	F-WJMK N149F USCG 2102
387	20F	F-WJML N162F N56CC N676DW N387CE N676DW N384K N650MG
388	20F-5	F-WJMM N169F N90GS N920CF F-WTFE N731RG N756 N502BG N579DN
389/552	20F	I-CMUT UR-KKA [b/u Geneva, Switzerland, Sep12; fuselage to GVA airport fire training area]
390	HU25C	F-WJMN N173F USCG 2104 [preserved USCGAS Astoria, OR]
391	20F	F-WLCS N175F N376SC N876SC VH-HPF N503F N995PT N990PT N550PT N420DP N420CL N420GL TR-LGZ
392/553	20F	F-WRQT D-CALL N328EW N326EW N326LW (N392FJ) N713MC
393	20F	F-WLCT N176F N21NL N76TA N809F XA-REY XA-PUE XB-FVH XC-FVH XC-SON
394	HU25A	F-WMKF N178F USCG 2103
395/554	20F	F-WRQX (HZ-AKI) OD-PAL (N395BB) [parted out by White Inds, Bates City, MO, circa Oct98]
396	20F-5	F-WMKG N179F N881J N711GL N711WV N811WV N711KU
397/555	20F	F-WRQP F-GBTM F-WBTM F-GBTM
398	HU25A	F-WMKF N183F USCG 2105 [wfu; preserved as 'gate guardian' Corpus Christi, TX]
399	20F-5	F-WMKI N184F N881G N70NE N70NF N70U N21FE N728JC N633KA
400/556	20F	F-WRQR RP-C1980 [w/o 24Apr96 at Davao City, Philippines; parted out by White Inds, Bates City, MO]
401	200	F-WZAH F-GATF (F-WDHA) N200FJ N207FJ F-GATF VR-BJJ F-GATF VR-BJJ F-GEXF Chile 301 code VP-1 N699GA N501KC [cx 13May15, CofR expired]
402	HU25A	F-WJMJ N187F USCG 2106 [wfu AMARC Davis-Monthan, AZ 04Jul95; park code AC410007]
403	20F	F-WJMK N189F N15AT N108BG N960TX (N175BC) [preserved in flying condition, Spirit of Flight Center museum, Erie, CO]
404	20F	F-WJMK N404F N28C N313K
405	HU25A	F-WMKI N405F USCG 2108 [wfu AMARC Davis-Monthan, AZ 10Aug01; park code AC410016]
406/557	20F	F-WMKF G-BGOP N800FF
407	HU25A	F-WJMJ N406F USCG 2109
408	20F-5	F-WRQS (PK-CAJ) PK-CAG (N508TC) N408PA N757CX N200FJ
409	HU25A	F-WMKJ N407F USCG 2107 [wfu AMARC Davis-Monthan, AZ 04Sep01; park code AC410018]
410	20F-5B	F-WRQT N200CP N200J N410SB N410AZ

FALCON 20/200

C/n	Series	Identities									
411	HU25A	F-WMKG	N408F	USCG 2110	N524NA						
412	20F-5	F-WMKI	N409F	N85V	N85VE	N2FU	N12FU	N620A	N97TD		
413	HU25A	F-WJMK	N410F	USCG 2111	[wfu; placed into Atlantic Ocean 6 miles off N.Carolina coast to create new reef 04May05]						
414	20F-5B	F-WJML	N412F	N1881Q							
415	HU25A	F-WLCV	N413F	USCG 2112	[wfu]						
416	20F	F-WLCT	N415F	N416F	N88NT	N9VG	N416F	N725JG	N19TD		
417	HU25A	F-WJMM	N416F	N416FJ	USCG 2113	N417MD					
418	HU25A	F-WJMN	N417F	USCG 2114	[wfu; to instructional airframe, North Valley Occupational Center, Los Angeles/Van Nuys, CA]						
419	HU25A	F-WMKJ	N419F	USCG 2115	[wfu AMARC Davis-Monthan, AZ 04Sep01; park code AC410017]						
420	HU25A	F-WMKG	N420F	USCG 2116	[wfu AMARC Davis-Monthan, AZ 25Apr94; park code AC410005]						
421	HU25A	F-WMKI	N422F	USCG 2117	(N107AV)	[wfu]					
422	20F	F-WRQU	(N422F)	F-ZJTJ	France 422/F-RCAL		France 422/F-RAEH	[code 65-EH]			
423	HU25B	F-WJMJ	N423F	USCG 2118							
424	HU25A	F-WMKF	N424F	USCG 2119	[damaged in storms Nov93 Mobile, AL; wfu AMARC Davis-Monthan, AZ, circa Jan94; park code AC410002]						
425	HU25A	F-WMKG	N425F	USCG 2120							
426	20F-5B	F-WJMK	N427F	N123WH	N555PT	N416RM	I-BAEL	HB-VNM	N426ST		
427	20F	F-WRQV	5N-AYN	I-ACTL	N42WJ						
428	20F-5B	F-WMKI	N426F	N98R	I-FLYF	N98R	N148MC	N93MC	N98AS	N373MG	
429	20F-5B	F-WMKF	VR-BHL	HB-VHY	N4286A	N149MC	N702CA	N331DM			
430	20F-5	F-WMKG	N428F	N660P	N243FJ						
431	HU25A	F-WMKJ	N429F	USCG 2121	[wfu; preserved New England Air Museum, Windsor Locks/Bradley, CT]						
432	20F-5B	F-WJMK	N430F	N667P	N237PT	N855DG	N355DG	N4TB	N760RA		
433	HU25B	F-WJML	N432F	USCG 2122	[wfu AMARC Davis-Monthan, AZ 07Sep01; park code AC410020]						
434	20F	F-WRQP	Peru 300/OB-1433	[w/o 18Jun10 Chiclayo, Peru]							
435	HU25A	F-WJMM	N433F	USCG 2123	[damaged in storms Nov93 Mobile, AL; wfu AMARC Davis-Monthan, AZ, circa Jan94; park code AC410003]						
436	20F-5	F-WJMN	N434F	N181CB	N436MP	N8000U	N436RB	N70PL			
437	HU25A	F-WMKG	N435F	USCG 2124	[wfu AMARC Davis-Monthan, AZ; park code AC410022]						
438	20F-5	F-WMKI	N442F	N263K	N256A	N258A	N438SJ				
439	HU25B	F-WMKJ	N443F	USCG 2125	[AMARC Davis-Monthan, AZ; park code AC410023]	N523NA	N448TB	N523NA	N448TB		
440	20F	F-WRQQ	N452F	N5152	N768J	(N768V)	VR-CAR	N32TC	N32TE	N7000G	N205JC	N581FL
441	HU25A	F-WJMK	N445F	USCG 2126	[wfu AMARC, Davis-Monthan, AZ; park code AC410021]						
442	20F-5	F-WJML	N446F	VH-FJZ	N203TA	I-SREG	N747CX				
443	HU25A	F-WMKG	N447F	USCG 2127	[wfu AMARC Davis-Monthan, AZ, circa Jul91; park code AC410001]		USCG 2127	[returned to USCG service by Jan08]			
444	20F-5B	F-WJMJ	N453F	N665P	N244FJ	LV-BIY					
445	HU25A	F-WJMM	N449F	USCG 2128	N513YF	[parted out by Dodson Int'l, Rantoul, KS]					
446	20F	F-WJMN	N454F	N31WT	N901SB	N904SB	N270RA	N446D	N81P		
447	HU25A	F-WLCS	N455F	USCG 2129	N525NA						
448	20G	F-WJMK	France 48/F-ZWVF								
449	20F	F-WLCT	N457F	N39TT	N73MR	N166RA					
450	HU25A	F-WMKG	N458F	USCG 2130	[wfu AMARC Davis-Monthan, AZ, 25Apr94; park code AC410004]	N513XF	[parted out by Dodson Int'l, Rantoul, KS]				
451	20F	F-WRQR	F-ZJTS	France 339/F-UGWN	[code 339-WN]		France 339/F-UKJC	[code 339-JC]		[wfu Chateaudun, France]	
452	HU25A	F-WMKI	N459F	USCG 2131							
453	20F	F-WJMK	N460F	N25S	N189MM	N520AW					
454	HU25A	F-WJML	N461F	USCG 2132	[wfu AMARC Davis-Monthan, AZ 06Sep01; park code AC410019]						
455	20F-5	F-WRQS	F-GKAL	N555SR	N404HR						
456	HU25A	F-WJMJ	N462F	USCG 2133	[preserved Cape Cod Air Station, MA]						
457	20F-5	F-WJMM	N463F	N4351M	N4362M	N47LP					
458	HU25B	F-WJMN	N465F	USCG 2134							
459	HU25A	F-WMKJ	N466F	USCG 2135							
460	HU25B	F-WJML	N467F	USCG 2136	[preserved Elizabeth City USCGAS, NC]						
461	20F	F-WMKG	N469F	N747V	N353CP	OH-WIF	N221H				
462	HU25A	F-WMKI	N470F	USCG 2137	[wfu AMARC Davis-Monthan, AZ 10Apr95; park code AC410008]	N513VF	[parted out by Dodson Int'l, Rantoul, KS]				
463	20F	F-WJMJ	N471F	N134JA	N132EP	C-GZOX					
464	HU25A	F-WJMK	N472F	USCG 2138	[wfu AMARC Davis-Monthan, AZ 13Apr95; park code AC410009]	N513UT	[parted out by Dodson Int'l, Rantoul, KS]				
465	20G	F-ZJTS	France 65/F-ZJTS								
466	HU25C	F-WJML	N473F	USCG 2139	[wfu AMARG Davis-Monthan, AZ 20Oct10]		N513ZF	[parted out by Dodson Int'l, Rantoul, KS]			
467	HU25A	F-WJMM	N474F	USCG 2140	[wfu]						
468	20F	F-WMKG	Pakistan J-468								
469	20F	F-WMKI	Pakistan J-469								
470	20F-5	F-WJMJ	N477F	N607RP	N470G	N500NH	N470FJ				
471	20F-5	F-WJMK	N478F	N44JC	N44JQ	N911DT	(N611DT)	N2BW	XC-HIX		
472	20G	France 72									
473	20F	F-WRQT	F-GEJR	3A-MGR	3A-MJV	N473SH	3A-MJV	N473SH	N393S	N404FZ	
474	20F-5	F-WMKF	F-GFFS	I-ACCG	F-WGTG	N211HF	N1HF	N998BM			
475	20F	F-WJML	Spain T.11-5/45-05	N475EZ	XA-YUR						
476	20F	F-WJMM	France 76/F-ZJTD		Venezuela 1650		YV2919				
477	20G	France 77									
478	20F-5	F-WJMN	N161WT	N181WT	N300RT	N39RP	C-GBCI				
479	200	F-WPUU	N200FJ	(N200FX)	N200WD	(N200FJ)	N200LS	N400WT	(N60DD)	(N200SA)	N349MG	N240RS	N7KC
		N767AG	HB-...								
480	20G	France 80/F-ZJSA									
481	20F-5B	F-WLCS	N502F	N250RA	OH-WIN	N599ZM	[parted out by Alliance Air Parts, Oklahoma City, OK]				
482	200	F-WPUZ	F-WDSB	F-GDSB	SE-DDZ	F-WGDZ	VR-CCL	VP-CCL	(N94TJ)		
483	20F	F-WRQQ	France 483/F-UKJI	[code 339-JI]							
484	200	F-WPUV	N202FJ	N28U	N357CL	N422MU	N24JG	N425RJ	N690EC		
485	20F-5	F-WLCT	N161EU	N997TT	(N23SJ)	N22FW	N485FW				
486	20F-5	F-WLCV	N6VF	N852E							
487	200	F-WZZB	(N206FJ)	F-GDSD	"I-WDSD"	I-SOBE	N137TA	(N387FJ)	XB-NCM	XB-NVT	
488	200	F-WZZF	HB-VHS	N682JB	N123CC	N2HW	C-GTNT	N146CF	N200NP	N488KF	
489	200	F-WPUX	N203FJ	(N109FC)	N109NC	N109NQ	N200RT	(TC-...)	N7654F	TC-DEM	N489TK	N489BB	N613BS
		N613PB	XA-...								
490	200	F-WPUY	N204FJ	N14EN	N806F	N2TF	N95JT	N200RT	(N208RT)	HC-BVH	N917JC	N917JG	PH-APV	N490SJ
		M-JETT									
491	200	F-WZZA	N205FJ	N200FJ	N120FJ	VH-PDJ	VH-HPJ	N491MB	N343MG	N843MG	N500RR	N25HU
492	200	F-WPUV	VR-BHZ	N805C	N803F	N412AB	N492CC	YV....			
493	200	F-WZZC	N208FJ	N901SB	N1847B	VH-ECG	ZS-SOS	ZS-JVS	[wfu Lanseria, South Africa]		
494	200	F-WZZD	N209FJ	N85LB	LV-PFM	LV-BAI	N49US	N204DD	EC-HEG	N200FJ	RA-2058G	
495	200	F-WZZE	N210FJ	(N290BC)	VH-BGL	N522C	N48FU	N48HU	N800HM	C-GSCL	C-GSCR	N800EG	N1D
		N109TT	[parted out by Alliance Air Parts, Oklahoma City, OK]								
496	200	F-WZZC	VR-BHY	F-GFAY	I-LXOT	(F-GGAR)	F-OGSR	F-WGSR	Chile 302	CC-PES	N496RT	N227TA	N256JC
		N202AR									
497	200	F-WZZA	N212FJ	N720HC	N20CL						
498	200	F-WPUV	N215FJ	N200ET	N422D	N422L	N69EC				
499	200	F-WZZJ	N213FJ	N565A	N14CJ	N200CU					

FALCON 20/200

C/n	Series	Identities											
500	200	F-WPUU	N214FJ	N595DC	C-GMPO	C-GRPM	N734DB	N777TE	[cx 22Apr13; CofR expired]				
501	200	F-WZZD	I-MAFU	F-WWGP	F-GOJT	N200TJ	N57TT	N214AS					
502	200	F-WPUU	N216FJ	N5732	N573E	N232F	N64YP	N64YR	HB-VNG	VP-CCP	C6-MIV	(N64YR)	N502SV
503	200	F-WPUY	N218FJ	N300HA	N50MW	(N50MX)							
504	200	F-WPUX	N217FJ	N902SB	N702SB	VH-CPE	(N504CL)	N504FJ	XB-OAP				
505	200	F-WZZA	N221FJ	ZK-MAY	VH-NGF	XA-SKO	N221FJ	N45JB	M-DEJB				
506	200	F-WPUZ	I-CNEF	N147TA	XA-MAM								
507	200	F-WPUU	N220FJ	N200FJ	(N122FJ)	C-FCEH	N79MB	N50MG	N50LG	N22HS	XB-SJA		
508	200	F-WPUU	N219FJ	N1851T	XA-RKE	N777FC							
509	200	F-WPUX	N222FJ	(N8495B)	JA8270	N70TH	N200WY	(N277AT)	PR-SMT	N202AT	N270MF	(N721JJ)	
510	200	F-WPUY	N223FJ	N79PM	N515DB	N510LF	N36DA	N84MJ					
511	200	F-WWGR	F-OGSI	F-WGTF	F-OLET	(F-GNMF)	VT-TTA	F-WQBK	EC-JBH	M-ENTA			
512	200	F-WPUU	N224FJ	N45WH	N999TH	N767PJ							
513	200	F-WPUV Rantoul, KS]	N225FJ	XB-ECR	XA-ECR	N881JT	(N200UP)	(N10UU)	N5UU	N5UQ	N618GH	[parted out by Dodson Av'n,	
514	200	F-WWGP	(F-GJIS)	F-OHES	PT-OQG	N531WB	(N81AG)	N87AG	N322RR				
515	200	F-WWGO	VR-CCQ	VR-CHC	F-GOBE	XA-PFM	N181RK						

Production complete

DASSAULT FALCON 50

* Denotes Falcon 50EX

C/n	Identities
1	F-WAMD [ff 07Nov76] "F-BAMD"+ [+ marks worn at 1977 Paris Air Show] F-WNDB F-BNDB F-WNDB F-BNDB F-WNDB [wfu fuselage to Conservatoire de l'Air et de l'Espace d'Aquitaine, Merignac, France, circa Oct99
2	F-WINR F-BINR France 2/F-RAFJ F-BINR F-GSER N50BL
3	F-WFJC F-GBIZ N50FJ N50EJ N880F N8805 N728LW
4	F-WZHA N110FJ N50FJ YV-452CP YV-O-SATA-12 YV-462CP YV2165
5	(F-WZHB) (F-GBRF) France 5/F-RAFI France 5/F-ZWVA
6	F-WZHB N50FB N1871R N815CA 9XR-NN [w/o 06Apr94 Kigali, Rwanda]
7	F-WZHA HZ-AKI HZ-AO3 N8516Z N26LB N5DL N50HE F-WQBN France 7
8	F-WZHC N50FE N50PG N409ER (N408ER) (N119HB) (N119HT) N119PH N508EJ N550CL N550CE [parted out by AvMATS, St Louis, MO]
9	F-WZHD I-SAFP XA-LOH (HB-IED) VR-CBR "N100WJ" F-GGCP TR-LGY
10	F-WZHD N50FG N65B N420CL
11	F-WZHE N50FH N501NC N5739 F-GGVB F-HADH
12	F-WZHC CN-ANO
13	F-WZHF N50FK N150BG (N150NW) N150TX
14	F-WZHG N50FL N233U N283U N9X N955E N917SB N880TD
15	F-WZHM PH-ILR N350JS (N595CW)
16	F-WZHH (N50FM) D-BIRD D-BFAR F-WQBL (F-GYBM) F-HBBM F-WQBL F-HBBM N516CJ
17	F-WZHI 5A-DGI TY-BBM HB-IEB N4679T N3456F N349K N349KS N727S N517CW (N550LX) N9TE N114TD
18	F-WZHJ N50FN N187S N720M N1102A N82RP N82LP N518EJ (N525MA) (N10UG) N963JF
19	F-WZHB N50FM N63A N253L N519CW (N551LX) N519EM
20	F-WZHK N50FR C6-BER N63537 N590CW (N552LX) N590RA
21	F-WZHN (9K-ACQ) 9K-AEE N299W (F-GJKT) F-GHGT N70AF N77CE N770E N56LT
22	F-WZHF N50FS N203BT N866FP XA-SFP XA-AVE XA-TUH N220JP N50FL Venezuela 0018 YV1083
23	F-WZHG (D-BBAD) D-BBWK PH-ILD N725PA N821BS N523CW (N553LX) N523PB [parted out Wilmington, DE]
24	F-WZHL N51FJ N817M N200RT N280RT N929T
25	F-WZHI Yugoslavia 72101/YU-BPZ [carried both marks] YU-BPZ "N34S"+ [+marks worn but ntu] N502EZ N753JC N877DF N977KG
26	F-WZHA N52FJ N190MC N190MQ
27	F-WZHN HB-IEU F-WGTG France 27/F-RAFK France 27/F-ZWMM
28	F-WZHE N53FJ N131WT PH-LEM N47UF N800FM N752JC
29	F-WZHB I-SAFR F-WGTH CS-TMF N534MA N290TJ N529CW N529MM C-GRGE N309SF
30	F-WZHD I-SNAC (YV-553CP) I-SNAC F-WQFZ France 30
31	F-WZHC (N54FJ) I-KIDO N211CN N145W N145WF N105EJ XA-AAS N931CC (N931EJ) N890FH N292FH N987RC N250RJ N468AM N921EW
32	F-WZHJ VR-BTT N80TR N717LA N717LF XA-UWJ N717LF
33	F-WZHA N56FJ N8100E N8300E
34	F-WZHH HB-IEV F-WEFS France 34/F-RAFL France 34/F-ZWMT
35	F-WZHF N57FJ N800BD N907M N350AF XA-FVK N35YP
36	F-WZHJ N54FJ N345PA N450AF N59GS F-WWHZ F-ZWTA F-ZJTL France 36
37	F-WZHM (I-CAIK) I-SAME F-GMCU F-HAIR [w/o Paris-Le Bourget, France, 13Aug10; b/u Sep12]
38	F-WZHK N58FJ N993 N505CL N500FJ N951DJ
39	F-WZHL N59FJ N754S N326FB N850EP
40	F-WZHG 9K-AEF N90005 N50GF N1PR N695ST N150JT N156DB N47NS
41	F-WZHI N60FJ N546EX (N760DL) N76FD (N76FB) N352JS (N541FJ) (N841FJ) N888MF N888ME N956DP
42	F-WZHE N61FJ N82MP D-BDWO OE-HCS OO-LFT (N250UC) N442AM ZS-LBB N185BA N405DC N167BD N167BR
43	F-WZHO Yugoslavia 72102 YU-BNA
44	F-WZHA N62FJ N150JP N50LT N44MK N285CP YV2346 (N485VL) N144PA [parted out Roanoke, TX]
45	F-WZHF N63FJ N731F N9BX N569BW
46	F-WZHK N64FJ N908EF N911RF N725LB N728LB N347K N547K N777ZL
47	F-WZHP N65FJ N150WC N23AC N23AQ N1BX (N81CH) (N601CH) N37ER
48	F-WZHK HB-IET I-ERDN N134AP N247EM (N2478) N247BC C-FBVF
49	F-WZHL N66FJ N43ES N43BE N978W N650AL N800DW N805DW
50	F-WZHQ N67FJ N747 N747Y XA-GCH N406SA
51	F-WZHR N70FJ N52DC N52DQ F-GMGA N113WA N551CW (N554LX) (N551S) N524S
52	F-WZHV F-BMER F-WZHV JY-HAH N18G N86AK N163WW N900KE
53	F-WZHS N150JT (N77SW) N45SJ (N50SJ) N22T N22TZ N90AM N53FJ N22YP N53FJ YV1128
54	F-WZHT N71FJ N450X (N50EF) N204DD N202DD N392U N130A (OY-GDA) LX-GED N589KM N100DV N51MJ N400KE N954DP N954SG
55	F-WZHU N73FJ N839F (N30N) N1CN N332MC N332MQ N625CR N300CR N96UH N200UP N504WE N12QP
56	F-WZHR F-WDFE F-GDFE N112FJ N84HP (N844J) C-FCRH C-FFGI
57	F-WZHC HB-IER N57B N138F N138E N505TC
58	F-WZHA N72FJ N744X N50KR N451CF [cx 13Sep12]
59	F-WZHB N75FJ N31DM N31V N900JB N910CN
60	F-WZHD JY-HZH N900W (N50RG) N560EJ CS-DFJ N105WC
61	F-WZHI HB-IES VP-CRF [wfu Basle, Switzerland]
62	F-WZHE N77FJ N292BC N50FH N562EJ (CS-DFK) N230BT [parted out Roanoke, TX]
63	F-WZHF N78FJ N841F HB-IAL VR-CGP N48GP C-FKCI N63FJ YV1129
64	F-WZHH N79FJ N418S N300A N731DD N496PT
65	F-WZHT N50FJ N90FJ N65HS D-BFFB N50LV N1EV F-GPPF
66	F-WZHP (PH-SDL) F-WZHP N500BL N50BL N4413N (VR-B..) 9U-BTB N789JC [trialled with spiroid wingtip devices then fitted with winglets] N711HT
67	F-WZHG N76FJ HB-IEP Switzerland T-783 N260ER
68	F-WZHQ 5A-DGM
69	F-WZHJ N80FJ N650X (N69VJ) N909VJ
70	F-WZHL N81FJ N230S N130K (N651SB) N699SC N300ES N306ES N700MP
71	F-WZHF YI-ALB J2-KBA N352WB
72	F-WZHM N82FJ N1181G [w/o 12May85 Lake Geneva, WI; remains to Clarkesville, MO]
73	F-WPXE HZ-SAB F-WGTG VR-CCQ N48TW N15TW (N15TA) N573CW (N556LX) N67JF
74	F-WZHA N83FJ
75	F-WZHH N95FJ N45ES N45BE N850CA N78LT
76	F-WZHB N84FJ N85MD N410WW N411WW N450CL
77	F-WZHC N85FJ N366F N992 N77NT N78LF N680KT
78	F-WPXF F-ODEO TR-LAI F-GEOY France 78/F-RAFJ France 78/F-ZWMO
79	F-WZHE N86FJ N60CN (N881K) (N79FJ) N56LN
80	F-WZHN N87FJ XB-OEM XA-FTC N4154G XA-GFC N80WE N50SJ N50BZ N50XJ N711RA
81	F-WZHA N89FJ N718DW N504CX [converted to Falcon 50-4]
82	F-WZHG N88FJ N293BC RP-C754 (N767W) (N40F) N511GG N450KP N150BP N582EJ N613PD
83	F-WZHJ N88U N881M N50HD N50XY
84	F-WZHK N2711B F-WZHK Spain T.16-1/401-09 Spain T.16-1/45-20 N503EZ N500JD N700JD
85	F-WZHO N90FJ N50FJ N40TH N254DV N82ST N107CV
86	F-WPXD N94FJ N238U F-GKDR HB-IAT N150UC N86JC N960S
87	F-WZHS N91FJ N283K N55NT C-GLRP C-GOIL C-GOIH N87FJ PR-FJL

FALCON 50

C/n	Identities											
88	F-WZHU	N92FJ	XA-OVR	N188FJ	F-WQCP	VR-CRT	VP-CRT	N588FJ	F-WQBK	F-GYOL	LZ-OIO	F-GYOL	(D-CHIC)
	N943RL	N510GT										
89	F-WZHV	N93FJ	N212K	N212KM	N890GA	N400PC	(N400LC)	N120TJ	N97BZ	N589EJ	CS-DFI	N156WC	TR-LGV
90	F-WZHX	N290W	N298W	N600AS	(N650AS)	N4351M	N925GS	N963JN					
91	F-WZHY	(ZS-BFB)	ZS-BMB	ZS-CAS									
92	F-WZHZ	N97FJ	N85A	N40CN	(N881J)	N929ML	T7-FGD	N92CJ					
93	F-WZHB	N98FJ	N844X	N868BT									
94	F-WZHC	N99FJ	N82NC	N212JP	XA-MVR	(XA-AFG)	XA-TVQ	N504PA	[converted to Falcon 50-4]			N946TC	
95	F-WPXD	VR-CBL	N3950N	N331MC	C-GSSS	TC-KAM	F-WQBJ	N29YY	N70FL	N95FJ	N101ET	N903JS	
96	F-WPXE	N4AC	C-FMFL										
97	F-WZHL	(N101FJ)	C-FSCL	N33GG	N33GQ	LZ-OII	N597FJ	C-FPDO	N850MC	N412PG			
98	F-WPXF	VR-CBO	N39461	N50MK	(N50ML)	N600WG							
99	F-WZHM	(N96FJ)	C-FMYB	N816M	N292PC								
100	F-WZHN	N102FJ	N14CG	N450AK									
101	F-WPXH	YI-ALC	Iran 5-9012	EP-TFA									
102	F-WZHO	N103FJ	N50BX	(N50WB)	N350WB								
103	F-WZHQ	N104FJ	N83MP	N370KP	N303PM								
104	F-WZHR	N105FJ	N90AE	F-GFGQ	F-WWHK	N50VG	SE-DVG	N351JS	LX-UAE	F-GUAE	HB-IGR	N725PA	N49KR
	N452CF												
105	F-WZHS	N106FJ	N80CN	(N881L)	N100EG	(N214GA)	N990MM						
106	F-WZHT	N96FJ	N50BF	N9300C	N74TS								
107	F-WPXK	(ZS-LJM)	LX-RVR	VR-BUC	VP-BUC	F-WQBM	F-GIQZ	VP-BCZ	F-GTCD	F-WQBM	N253SJ	F-GLSJ	N108BK
108	F-WZHM	N101FJ	N350X	N150K	N399GG								
109	F-WZHV	N109FJ	N280BC	N280BG	N5107								
110	F-WPXG	5N-ARE	VR-BJA	N77TE	N84TN								
111	F-WZHZ	N297W	F-GKTV	VR-CDF	N50AH	F-GMOT	[b/u Geneva, Switzerland, Aug12]						
112	F-WZHA	N107FJ	N144AD	N193TR	N652AL	N216WD							
113	F-WZHB	N108FJ	N186S	N394U	N35RZ	N75RZ	N450DR	N900JB	N654CP				
114	F-WPXM	ST-PSR											
115	F-WZHC	N111FJ	N777MJ	N50TC	N522GS	(N369CA)	N569CA	N569CC	N502JB	N950S	N850BA	N70BR	
116	F-WZHD	N112FJ	N781B	N69R	F-GIDC	N70AF	XA-SOL	XB-SOL	N678MA				
117	F-WPXI	HB-ITH	N50TG	N124HM	N50J	N896DA	(N896TW)						
118	F-WZHF	N113FJ	N784B	(N183B)	N784B	[w/o 10Nov85 on approach to Teterboro A/P, NJ]							
119	F-WZHN	N114FJ	N83FC	N57DC	XA-SSS	N168JC	TS-JBT	N929WT					
120	F-WPXJ	YI-ALD	Iran 5-9011	EP-TFI									
121	F-WZHO	N115FJ	N9311	N824R	N121FJ	N51FE	N150MJ						
122	F-WZHG	YI-ALE	Iran 5-9013										
123	F-WZHH	(F-GDSC)	VH-SFJ	N211EF	F-GPSA	N5123							
124	F-WZHA	N116FJ	N711TU	N6666R	N500RE	N600JM	N25JM	VP-BFM	N50MV	N987F			
125	F-WZHB	N118FJ	N711KT	I-DENR	HB-IBQ	TS-JAM	N102TF	N250MJ					
126	F-WZHI	N119FJ	(YV-269CP)	N9312	N931G	N52DC	N52DQ	N200RT	(N986PA)	N650TC	N838BB		
127	F-WZHD	N121FJ	N1896T	N1896F	N129JE	N48KR	N453CF	N154LA					
128	F-WZHF	N122FJ	N9313	N733E	N223DD	N42NA							
129	F-WZHQ	N123FJ	N1903W	N4903W	N99JD	N751JC	N634KA						
130	F-WZHR	N124FJ	N9314	N630L	N988T	C-GSRS	P4-BAK	N315SC					
131	F-WPXD	HZ-BB2	I-ADAG	(F-GPLH)	F-WGTF	F-GOAL	N750BR						
132	F-WPXF	I-EDIK	France 132										
133	F-WPXH	HB-IEA	HZ-AKI	HB-IEA	ZS-CAQ								
134	F-WPXK	HB-IEC	VR-CLD	VP-CLD	F-GOGL	VP-BCD	F-GUDP	F-WQBN	N134FJ	F-GOCT	(OY-CKH)	F-HALM	
135	F-WZHA	N125FJ	N293BC										
136	F-WZHB	N126FJ	N204HC	(N500HC)	N50HC	VR-BLL	N6550W	YV-455CP	YV1495	N136FJ	XB-YJA		
137	F-WZHC	N127FJ	N50FJ	(N119FJ)	C-GTPL	N119FJ	N117SF	C-FJUH	N137FA				
138	F-WPXD	N75G	N941CC	I-CAFB	N138NW	VR-CEZ	VP-CEZ	N380TJ	N138AV	N903CS			
139	F-WZHD	N128FJ	N96CE	N1S	N7GX								
140	F-WPXH	VR-BHX	(F-GJTR)	F-WGTF	I-MMEA	N303JW	N750DF	N914JH	N510MP				
141	F-WZHE	N129FJ	N16R	(N222MC)	N86MC	N96NX	N924WJ						
142	F-WZHK	N132FJ	N4350M	N860BA									
143	F-WZHI	N130FJ	N77CP	N444PE									
144	F-WZHL	N133FJ	N70FL	VR-BZE	VP-BZE	N544RA	(LX-FTJ)	N7011	N950BD				
145	F-WPXE	F-GEXE	A6-ZKM	I-CAFC	N50KD								
146	F-WZHA	N131FJ	N747	N7228K	XA-DUQ	N430AC							
147	F-WPXG	HB-IED	F-WPXG	VR-BKG	VP-BKG	N526CC	N844NX	N1CG	N50SQ*				
148	F-WZHB	N134FJ	N81R	N81U	YR-FNA	N28KB	N254NA	N50LQ	N770JD				
149	F-WZHJ	N135FJ	N1904W	F-GHAQ	N149MD	N1971R	N198M	N198MR	N950CL				
150	F-WZHC	N136FJ	HB-IAE	N8200E	N8400E								
151	F-WPXD	Italy (MM151)		Italy MM62020		F-WQBM	I-DARK	F-GPGS	TR-...				
152	F-WZHD	N137FJ	N1841F	N75W	N75WE	N152FJ							
153	F-WZHE	N138FJ	N50FJ	N16CP	N50HM	N50HN							
154	F-WZHA	N139FJ	N320K	N920K	N404R	N404E	N154PA	N117AJ					
155	F-WPXH	Italy MM62021		F-WQBM	I-RODJ	F-GTHS	F-GKGO	TR-CHB					
156	F-WZHF	N140FJ	N5733	N4MB	N4MR	N377HW	N500RE	N156RE					
157	F-WPXG	N141FJ	N312A	N341M	N911HB	N901RK	N15FX	N19FX	N345SK	N89TD			
158	F-WZHH	N142FJ	N54YR	N54YP	N15VX								
159	F-WZHC	LX-NUR	I-LXAG	VR-CWI	VP-CWI	HB-ISD	N839RM	N343PM	VH-FOL				
160	F-WZHI	N143FJ	N48R	N487F	N4VF	N82CA							
161	F-WZHA	N144FJ	N863BD	N800BD	TC-EYE	N301JJ	N770MP	N766HK					
162	F-WZHB	N145FJ	N90R	C-GYPJ	N244AD	N750JC	N750LQ	N954AM					
163	F-WZHA	N146FJ	N50FJ	(N165FJ)	N185FJ	N5VF	N5VH	N85HP	(N854W)	N521DC			
164	F-WZHD	N164FJ	HB-IAM	N164MA	N164GB	(N132MS)							
165	F-WZHF	HZ-SM3	LX-FMR	HB-JSR	F-GXTM								
166	F-WZHE	N165FJ	N500AF	(N3115U)	N500AE	N316PA	N5VF						
167	F-WZHG	N166FJ	N186HG	N2T	N2FQ								
168	F-WZHH	N167FJ	N711SC	N48GL	XA-RXZ	N48GL	VR-CQZ	N48GL	(N420JP)	N514MB			
169	F-WPXD	I-SNAB	F-GUAJ	F-HISI									
170	F-WZHI	N169FJ	N293K	N500AF	N508AF	N504YP	[converted to Falcon 50-4]						
171	F-WZHJ	N170FJ	N171FJ	N40AS	(N650AS)	N750H							
172	F-WZHK	N170FJ	N98R	N9000F	N256A								
173	F-WZHL	N172FJ	(JA....)	PT-LJI	N544CM	N37KJ							
174	F-WPXE	HB-IAG	N79PF	N565A	N8KG	N988SB	N50FX						
175	F-WZHM	N177FJ	N50FJ	N334MC	N330MC	N200RT	(VR-B..)	N530AR	N50FX	M-AGER	N200V	N20GP	
176	F-WZHN	N178FJ	VH-PDJ	N157SP	N95GC	I-DEGF	VR-CFI	C-FNNC	N568VA	N711T	N777XY	N777UV	
177	F-WPXF	9Q-CGK	9Q-CPK	(N68BA)	ZS-PFB	N14NE	XA-UCN	XA-TAB	N177MJ				
178	F-WZHO	N179FJ	N239R	N59PM	N634H	T7-AWO							
179	F-WZHP	N180FJ	HL7386	N222MC	N212Q	N232PR	N500TS	N508TS*					
180	F-WWHC	I-POLE	N45FG	N2254S	N50SF	N626HJ							

FALCON 50

C/n	Identities											
181	F-WWHA	N181FJ	N345AP	N367TP	N93AX	N600CH	N26WJ					
182	F-WWHB	N182FJ	N250AS	N713SN	N116GB	N227GJ						
183	F-WWHF	I-CAFD										
184	F-WWHD	N183FJ	N50FJ	N89FC	N25MB	N25ME	N633W	VP-CDG				
185	F-WWHE	N184FJ	C-GDCO	N23SY	N238Y	F-GKBZ	LX-THS	F-HFMB	T7-DFX			
186	F-WWHH	N278FJ	N450K	N25SJ	N107A	N16NK*						
187	F-WWHG	N279FJ	N4CP	N4QP	VH-PPF	N187PN	N133NM*					
188	F-WWHA	N280FJ	N50FJ	PT-WAN	LV-WXV	N160AF	XA-ALA	N188FJ				
189	F-WWHB	N281FJ	N50WG	N55SN	N51V	N51VT	N51V					
190	F-WWHG	I-CAFE	CS-TMJ	F-GXMC								
191	F-WWHD	N282FJ	N950F									
192	F-WWHE	N283FJ	N212T	N96LT	N96UT	N96UJ						
193	F-WWHH	Italy MM62026		Italy CSX62026		Italy MM62026						
194	F-WWHM	N284FJ	N10AT	N10LT	N95PH	N194K	N28PH					
195	F-WWHK	Portugal 7401		Portugal 17401								
196	F-WWHD	N285FJ	N8575J	JA8575	N71TH	D-BNTH	VP-BSA	N388TC	N196FJ	N56CL	N566L	
197	F-WWHA	N286FJ	N50FJ	N500KJ	N404JF	N57MK						
198	F-WWHC	Portugal 7402		Portugal 17402								
199	F-WWHB	N287FJ	N291BC	N290MX								
200	F-WWHE	N288FJ	N664P	N664B	N595JS	N749CP	N769CP	N62DT				
201	F-WWHA	N289FJ	N41TH	N54DA	N553M	N504ST	N526SM					
202	F-WWHB	N290FJ	N212N	N97LT	N97UT	N202CP	N750MC	N512JB				
203	F-WWHA	I-CSGA	C-GNCA	N203NC								
204	F-WWHD	F-GKAR	VR-CGP	VP-CGP	EC-GPN	EC-HHS	(F-HDCB)	N725PA	F-HDCB	N147GB		
205	F-WWHD	N291FJ	N57EL	N59EL	N52JJ	N348K	(N848K)	N504MK	N314AM			
206	F-WWHB	VR-BMF	VP-BMF	N801DL	N607BF	N607RJ						
207	F-WWHC	N292FJ	N55BP	N50CS	N396EG	N275HH	N192RS					
208	F-WWHP	I-CSGB	VR-CCQ	C-GWEI	N50AE	N50HC	N90HC					
209	F-WWHE	N293FJ	N59CF	N59CH	EC-168	EC-FPG	N1902W	N96DS	VP-BSL	N358MH		
210	F-WWHL	F-GICN	XA-TXB	N411GC	N803AC							
211	F-WWHR	Italy MM62029										
212	F-WWHH	N294FJ	N50FJ	N30TH	N40TH	N85WN	LX-APG	UR-CCF				
213	F-WWHW	N295FJ	XA-RVV	N991LB								
214	F-WWHX	N296FJ	N55AS	(N214FJ)	N265G							
215	F-WWHT	N297FJ	XA-SIM	D-BOOK	(D-BOOI)	HB-JSV	F-GOLV	9H-MSL				
216	F-WWHZ	N298FJ	N180AR	N56SN	N84NW	N722FS	(N270FX)	N650JS				
217	F-WWHV	N122FJ	N5732	N573AC	N573TR							
218	F-WWHA	N50NK	N218WA	D-BERT	N750FJ	N703TM	N979JC*					
219	F-WWHS	N129FJ	YV-450CP	YV1496	N256JC	(N509MD)	N98DH					
220	F-WWHG	N131FJ	N75RD	N100RR	N528JR	N50FF	N557LZ	N800TA				
221	F-WWHL	Portugal 7403		Portugal 17403								
222	F-WWHM	D-BELL	OE-HIT	N722MK								
223	F-WWHN	N132FJ	N633L	N840FJ	N451CL							
224	F-WWHO	N133FJ	VR-CNV	XA-SDK	XA-BEG	N800BD	N87TN	N258FV				
225	F-WWHP	N134FJ	N50FJ	N32TC	N428CC							
226	F-WWHC	N119AM	F-WQBN	VP-BBD	CS-DPO	SX-CRC	TN-AJN					
227	F-WWHE	N226FJ	N50FJ	(N227FJ)	N1848U	N630SR	N37LC	(N37LQ)	C-GGFP	N365DF		
228	F-WWHR	(F-GNFS)	F-GNFF	VR-BJJ	F-GJEK	F-WWHR	N313GH	VR-CAE	C-GAZU	N228FJ		
229	F-WWHH	N114FJ	C-GMII	C-GMID	N550WM							
230	F-WWHD	F-GNGL	HB-IAV	3B-NSY	OY-LIN	F-OMON	N506BA	N930JG				
231	F-WWHA	N228FJ	(VR-B..)	XA-SIF	N10PQ	N10PP	N199FG					
232	F-WWHT	F-WNLR	F-GNLR	N244FJ	N45NC	N45NQ	N100KP	N108KP	ZS-MGS			
233	F-WWHB	(N233FJ)	N232FJ	N48HB	N318GA	(N919GA)						
234	F-WWHC	N233FJ	PT-AAF	PR-WYW								
235	F-WWHM	F-GKRU	(UR-ACA)	UR-CCC	[destroyed by shellfire, Donetsk, Ukraine, 2014]							
236	F-WWHD	N234FJ	N50FJ	N70FJ	XA-HGF	N195SV	N196SV	XA-HHF	N725PA	N347K	N50FJ	N394AJ	N497SB
237	F-WWHE	N237FJ	N2425	(N5425)	N94BJ	N74BJ	N89BM	N85TN				
238	F-WWHF	N238FJ	N50FJ	XA-LRA	N796A	N238DL	SE-DVL	N970S				
239	F-WWHG	N239FJ	N200SG									
240	F-WWHH	F-GNMO	(N40SK)	N780F	N33TY	N34TY	(N200BN)	N398AC	(N798AC)	N550JP		
241	F-WWHF	F-OKSI	N233BC	N86TN								
242	F-WWHA	N241FJ	XA-SPM	N599SC	N9000F	N733M	N733N	N733K	N28US			
243	F-WWHM	N243FJ	N742R	N62HM								
244	F-WWHK	N243FJ	N50FJ	N95HC	N954ME*							
245	F-WWHL	N240FJ	N720ML	N720ME	N530DG	N827CT						
246	F-WWHF	N246FJ	TC-YSR	F-GTJF	3C-LGE							
247	F-WWHP	N247FJ	N740R	N520AF								
248	F-WWHB	N249FJ	N25UD	N25UB	N67PW							
249	F-WWHN	N248FJ	(XA-DMS)	N663MN	SE-DVK	N247CJ	N980S					
250	F-WWHR	N250FJ	N696HC	N696HQ	N277JW	N917JC	N917JG	N111WW				
251*	F-WOND	[ff 10Apr96]	(F-GOND)	VR-CLN	VP-CLN	(F-GIVD)	N870	N565	N171TG			
252	F-WWHE	(N313GH)	N93GH	N50FJ	XA-TDD	N52FJ	XA-RUY	N959DM				
253*	F-WWHA	N253EX	PT-WSC	N85F	N3VF							
254*	F-WWHB	N50FJ	N50AE	N345AP	N94PC	N67MT						
255*	F-WWHC	N255CM	N50MG	N60ME								
256*	F-WWHD	VP-CBT	N600N									
257*	F-WWHE	F-OKSY	N925BC	ZS-LAC								
258*	F-WWHF	F-WQHU	VP-BST	N48G	N726JG	PR-GJS						
259*	F-WWHG	VP-CHG	N373RS	N373RR								
260*	F-WWHK	N586CS	N777									
261*	F-WWHL	N140RT	(N97FJ)	N73GH								
262*	F-WWHM	N262EX	N1896T	C-GOFJ								
263*	F-WWHN	N8550A	N503PC	N503PQ								
264*	F-WWHO	F-GVDN	C6-BHD	N900CH	C-GWFM	C-GWFK						
265*	F-WWHP	N9550A	N501PC	N838DB	N868DB							
266*	F-WWHQ	VP-BPA	N50NM	(N266EC)								
267*	F-WWHR	(D-BETI)	F-OHFO	D-BETI								
268*	F-WWHS	EC-GTR	CS-TMS	PH-JNL	F-WQBL	N268FJ	F-WQBL	G-ITIH	G-DASO	M-DASO	G-DASA	N133JA
269*	F-WWHT	F-GPBG	F-GJBZ	N52RF								
270*	F-WWHU	N270EX	N148M	C-GJLB								
271*	F-WWHV	TC-BHO	N30FE	N30FT	N865PC							
272*	F-WWHW	N272EX	N50FJ	C-GMII	N272F	C-GKCI	C-FZYB	N695JB				
273*	F-WWHX	N158M	N198M									
274*	F-WWHY	N138M	N80GP	N299DB	N205JA							
275*	F-WWHA	F-GODP	N56LC	N44LC	N44EQ	N75FJ	N52YP					

FALCON 50

C/n	Identities								
276*	F-WWHB	N159M	N128M	N789ME	N96UT				
277*	F-WWHC	N368M	N198M	N192F	N818KF				
278*	F-WWHD	VP-CFI	N623QW	C-GXBB	M-SNSS	N421AE	N732AM		
279*	F-WWHE	N181MC	N928WK	N411SK	N58HL				
280*	F-WWHF	N50FJ	N1829S	N3BM					
281*	F-WWHG	N17AN	C-GNET	N463JD					
282*	F-WWHH	N191MC							
283*	F-WWHK	VP-CEF	VP-BEF	N283FJ	N223HD	(N868NB)	N248BT		
284*	F-WWHL	N904SB	N703AW	N900SS					
285*	F-WWHM	N901TF							
286*	F-WWHN	(F-GKIN)	VP-BMI	N286ZT	VP-BEA	N286ZT	[retro-fitted with winglets]		
287*	F-WWHO	ZS-ONG							
288*	F-WWHP	N288EX	N33TY	N83TY	(N89TY)				
289*	F-WWHQ	N214DV	N315DV	(N589FJ)	M-GPIK	F-HUNT	Bolivia FAB-002		
290*	F-WWHR	N44SK	N42SK	(N660AH)	(N302WY)	N50HM	N68YB		
291*	F-WWHS	N294EX	XA-GMD	XA-UDW	N291FJ				
292*	F-WWHT	N292EX	N38WP	XA-KMX					
293*	F-WWHU	N293EX	N195SV						
294*	F-WWHV	N39WP							
295*	F-WWHW	I-FJDN	P4-JET	9H-AVE					
296*	F-WWHX	N296EX	N50FJ	N23FM					
297*	F-WWHY	N119AG	F-WQBJ	OE-HHH	F-HCDD				
298*	F-WWHZ	N615SR							
299*	F-WWHA	N299EX	PP-PMV	N299MV	N299PR				
300*	F-WWHB	N344CM	N749CP	N549CP	N214FT				
301*	F-WWHC	N301EX	N476MK	N504MS	N353H	N715CB			
302*	F-WWHD	N302FJ	N45NC	N115RL	N115RN				
303*	F-WWHE	N902TF							
304*	F-WWHF	N918JM	N909JM						
305*	F-WWHG	TC-BNT	F-WQBK	N302BG	N102BG	N102BQ	N710BG	N710BQ	N114HC
306*	F-WWHH	LX-AKI	F-HCEF						
307*	F-WWHK	N950H							
308*	F-WWHL	N902SB	N719DW	N50PC					
309*	F-WWHM	N903SB	N37WX						
310*	F-WWHN	N310EX	N50FJ	N310EX	N50FQ	N50SN			
311*	F-WWHO	N507AS	VP-CBF	N136MV					
312*	F-WWHP	N26WP							
313*	F-WWHR	G-JPSI	F-WQBM	N921EC	N225HD	N50CZ			
314*	F-WWHT	N314EX	N55LC	N55LQ	N311BP				
315*	F-WWHU	N668P	PH-LSV	LX-LXL					
316*	F-WWHV	N316EX	N696HC	N696HQ	N1838S	N4911			
317*	F-WWHW	N1839S	N607SG	N500RE					
318*	F-WWHX	N416KC	N410KC	N771HM					
319*	F-WWHY	N319EX	N50FJ	(N319EX)	N85CL	N85DN	XA-PRR	XA-UVS	
320*	F-WWHZ	N662P	N500AF	M-VGIN	M-CFLY				
321*	F-WWHA	N321EX	N900CM	N556HD					
322*	F-WWHB	N5322							
323*	F-WWHC	N323EX	N500N	N50QN	N500R	N500GR	N500LY		
324*	F-WWHD	N324EX	F-WWHD	LX-IRE	N150RJ				
325*	F-WWHE	N325EX	N146AS						
326*	F-WWHF	N37LC	N33LC	N33EQ	N850EN				
327*	F-WWHG	N327EX	N188DM	N1978G					
328*	F-WWHH	N328EX	N308DM	N223F	N918RD				
329*	F-WWHK	N329EX	(N50FJ)	N98AC					
330*	F-WWHL	N330EX	N115SK	N115MF					
331*	F-WWHM	N331EX	(N331SE)	N1839S	N963U				
332*	F-WWHN	N332EX	N280BC	N280BD					
333*	F-WWHO	N334EX	N701WC	N701WQ	N54YR				
334*	F-WWHP	N335EX	OE-HPS	F-HDPB					
335*	F-WWHQ	N535EX	C-GMII	C-GMIU	N505BL	PP-NOB	[retro-fitted with winglets]		
336*	F-WWHR	N224HD	N50FJ						
337*	F-WWHS	N50FJ	N89NC	N988GC					
338*	F-WWHT	N338FJ	N883RA	N883RW	(PP-AAH)	(N137LR)	N513SK	PP-LVY*	
339*	F-WWHU	5B-CKN	I-PBRA						
340*	F-WWHV	N340EX	N109CQ	N733G					
341*	F-WWHW	I-ZUGR	G-KPTN						
342*	F-WWHX	N342EX	N649TT						
343*	F-WWHY	N343EX	N733M						
344*	F-WWHZ	N344EX	N50YP						
345*	F-WWHA	VP-BMP	M-NICK	M-CICO					
346*	F-WWHB	N346EX	F-HAPM	HB-IGV					
347*	F-WWHC	F-HAPN							
348*	F-WWHD	N905SB	P4-SNS	F-GLSA	[w/o Moscow/Vnukovo 20Oct14]				
349*	F-WWHE	N906SB	N30JC	N575JC					
350*	F-WWHF	N350DV	N214DV						
351*	F-WWHH	N158M	N191CP						
352*	F-WWHK	N1836S	N180NL						

Production complete

DASSAULT FALCON 900

C/n	Series	Identities									
1	B	F-WIDE	[ff 21Sep84] F-GIDE	[converted to prototype 900B]		F-HOCI	G-HMEI	(F-GOEI)			
2		F-WFJC	F-GFJC	France 2/F-RAFP							
3		F-WWFA	N403FJ	N327K	N991RF	N728GH	N345KM				
4		F-WWFC	(HB-...)	VR-BJX	F-WWFA	France 4/F-RAFQ					
5	B	F-WWFB	N404FJ	VH-BGF	F-GGRH	N905TS	PT-WQM	N905FJ	(D-ACDC)	G-HMEV	(F-GOEV)	N905FJ
6	B	F-WWFD	N405FJ	N80F	N885						
7	B	F-WWFG	TR-LCJ	3B-XLA	F-GMOH						
8	B	F-WWFE	N406FJ	N5731	N316SS						
9		F-WWFJ	(PH-ILC)	HB-IAB	C6-BHN	N900TR	N193TR	N232CL			
10	B	F-WWFF	N407FJ	N900FJ	(N910FJ)	N26LB	N96LB	N5MC	N349K	N349H	N403HR	N91MS
11		F-WWFK	LX-AER	F-WEFX	UN-09002	F-GLGY	N251SJ	F-GKHJ			
12	B	F-WWFH	N408FJ	N991AS	N77CE	N8VF					
13	B	F-WWFI	N409FJ	N328K	(N75V)	(N75W)	N75V	N61TS	N297AP		
14		F-WWFL	N410FJ	N900SB	N906SB	N324SR	VP-BLP	N44EG	(N47EG)	N900CZ	(PR-IMP)	PP-IPR
15		F-WWFM	HB-IAK	XA-RGB	(N115FJ)	N999EH					
16	B	F-WWFN	N412FJ	(N187HG)	N187H	VR-CTA	N619BD	VP-CBD	N64BD	N900SF	
17	B	F-WWFO	N411FJ	N944AD	N790JC	N884BB					
18		F-WWFA	N413FJ	N72PS	N72PX	N900YB*					
19		F-WWFB	N414FJ	N900SJ	N45SJ	N1L					
20		F-WWFC	N415FJ	(N711T)	N999PM	N70FJ	N911RF	N256DV	N920DB	N900LP	
21	B	F-WWFJ	(HZ-R4A)	HZ-AFT							
22	B	F-WWFD	N416FJ	N54DC	OE-ICF	N988AK					
23		F-WWFK	I-BEAU								
24		F-WWFE	N417FJ	N901B	N67WB	N93GR	N93CR	N93GR	N202WR		
25	B	F-WWFF	N418FJ	N70EW	N75EW	N660BD	N615MS	N615ME	N922LJ		
26	B	F-WWFM	HB-IAC	SX-ECH	N900RN	VP-CJF	YR-CJF	N926CJ			
27	B	F-WWFH	N419FJ	N90EW	N91EW	N5VJ	N15VJ	N777XY			
28		F-WWFK	N420FJ	N85D	N86MC	N1S	N696JM				
29		F-WWFA	N421FJ	C-GTCP	N19VF						
30		F-WWFL	HB-IAF	F-WGTH	(F-GIRZ)	I-DIES	(PH-ERB)	PH-ERB	M-EBRB		
31	B	F-WWFB	N422FJ	N900FJ	N910JW						
32	B	F-WWFG	N423FJ	VH-BGV	F-GJBT	N800BL	N500BL	N10MZ	N18MZ		
33	B	F-WWFC	N424FJ	N298W	F-GHEA	N9138Y	N901SB	N931SB	N203CW	TY-AOM	5V-TTS	
34	B	F-WWFD	N425FJ	N8100E	N8200E						
35		F-WWFC	HB-IAD	F-GLMU	PP-PPA	F-GNDK	PH-OLI	N139AL	F-HJJB	N82MF	
36	B	F-WWFE	N426FJ	N96PM	N91MK	N922JW					
37	B	F-WWFN	N427FJ	N45SJ	N41SJ	VH-FCP	VH-ACE	N394WJ	N377HW		
38		F-WWFE	Spain T.18-1/45-40								
39	B	F-WWFF	N428FJ	(N900BF)	N1818S	N181BS	N5733	N573J	N239AX		
40	B	F-WWFH	N429FJ	N904M	N145W	N369BG	(N389BG)	(N940SJ)	N924S	N839RM	N900MK	
41		F-WWFJ	N430FJ	N404F	N404FF	N76FD					
42	B	F-WWFJ	N431FJ	N900FJ	N42FJ	N117TF	N901BB	N990BB			
43	B	F-WWFC	I-MTDE	N288Z	N388Z	(N692SH)	N693SH	N410KA	[retro-fitted with winglets]		N504PA
44	B	F-WWFA	N432FJ	N914J	N914JL	HB-IBY	N100UP				
45	B	F-WWFB	N433FJ	N64BE	N298W	(N798W)	N670JD				
46		F-WWFD	N434FJ	N329K	N779SG	N46FJ	TR-AFJ				
47		F-WWFA	A6-ZKM	F-WQBJ	(F-GOFC)	F-GNMF	F-WQBK	N678CH	LV-CRI	N687HS	
48	B	F-WWFM	N435FJ	N900MJ	N233KC						
49		F-WWFD	VR-BLB	VP-BLB	N920SA						
50	B	F-WWFH	N436FJ	N330K	N900TA	(N711WK)	N950SF				
51	B	F-WWFG	N437FJ	N59LB	N26LB	(N50RG)	N9RG	N528JR	N328JR	VP-BMB	N51FJ	(N888TD)	N74TD
52		F-WWFC	5N-FGO	5N-BOH	(N367TA)						
53		F-WWFN	N438FJ	JA8570							
54		F-WWFC	(LX-IMN)	I-FICV	F-GKAY	N954FJ	F-GZME	9H-SVA			
55	B	F-WWFO	N439FJ	C-FJES	N495GA	N404R	N704R	(N955FJ)	C-GSMR	N117SF	
56		F-WWFB	N440FJ	JA8571							
57	B	F-WWFK	N441FJ	N900WK	C-FCRH						
58	B	F-WWFE	OE-ILS	HB-IGL	N116RW						
59	B	F-WWFD	N442FJ	N32B	TR-AFR						
60		F-WWFG	N443FJ	N900FJ	N91TH	N900VL	N860ST	N990LT			
61	B	F-WWFB	VR-CSA	HZ-AB2	HZ-AFZ						
62	B	F-WWFJ	F-GIVR	N62FJ	F-WQBL	F-GSCN	F-WQBJ	LX-LFB	OO-LFQ	LX-LFB	VP-CAX	9H-WLD	CS-DTV	TT-DIT
63		F-WWFF	N445FJ	N90TH	N127EM	N75W	N311JA	N211JA	N583JF			
64		F-WWFH	N446FJ	Malaysia M37-01							
65		F-WWFM	N447FJ	N216FP	N216FB	N990MC	(N990MQ)	N988T			
66		F-WWFE	F-GJPM	CS-TMK	CS-TFN						
67	B	F-WWFD	N448FJ	N900MA	N900MG	T7-OSB					
68	B	F-WWFL	N449FJ	N900HC	N900HE	N900HW	N610RL				
69		F-WWFD	I-SNAX	F-WQBM	HB-JSP	F-GPGK					
70		F-WWFN	N450FJ	Australia A26-070	VH-VIW	N105BK					
71	B	F-WWFB	N451FJ	(N900BF)	PK-TRP	N280BC	N280BQ	N642JC	N1PR	N711FJ	
72		F-WWFF	VR-BLM	VP-BLM							
73		F-WWFA	N452FJ	Australia A26-073	VH-WII	N109BK	Spain T.18-5/45-44				
74		F-WWFF	N453FJ	Australia A26-074	VH-WIZ	N108BK	Spain T.18-4/45-43				
75		F-WWFC	N458FJ	C-FWSC	HB-IAI	N60RE	N60TL	C-GOIL			
76		F-WWFE	N454FJ	Australia A26-076	VH-WIZ	N106BK	N54SK	HZ-DME			
77		F-WWFG	N455FJ	Australia A26-077	VH-WIM	N107BK	Spain T.18-3/45-42				
78	B	F-WWFH	N456FJ	N332MC	C-GSSS	N522KM	LX-GES	F-GVMO	G-FLCN		
79	B	F-WWFM	N457FJ	N900FJ	N901FJ	N6BX	N6PX	N952GD	N800DW		
80	B	F-WWFA	N459FJ	N914BD	N914DD	N882SS					
81		F-WWFL	7T-VPA	N81GN	I-TLCM	N33GG	N484FM				
82		F-WWFM	7T-VPB	N82GP	(N561CM)	N649TT	N699BG				
83	B	F-WWFG	N460FJ	N900WG	N900NE	N361K					
84		F-WWFD	A6-AUH	F-WQBM	ST-PSA						
85		F-WWFC	N461FJ	N74FS							
86		F-WWFE	A6-UAE	F-GVAE	HB-JEI	OE-IOD	N904RS	C-FXOO			
87	B	F-WWFA	N462FJ	N33GG	N402FG	VQ-BZZ	C-FDOW				
88	B	F-WWFH	VR-BLT	F-GNDA	N987QK	N987GK	N122A				
89		F-WWFB	I-NUMI	F-HKMO							
90		F-WWFG	Spain T.18-2/45-41								
91		F-WWFH	A7-AAD	N91WF	CS-DFA	N991EJ	CS-DFH				
92		F-WWFL	N463FJ	PT-OEX							
93	B	F-WWFM	EC-617	EC-FEN	N900Q	N780SP	[retro-fitted with winglets]				
94		F-WWFC	A7-AAE	N94WA	CS-DFB	N889TD	N889TR	N960CL*			

FALCON 900

C/n	Series	Identities											
95	B	F-WWFO	N464FJ	N478A	N343MG	N898TS							
96		F-WWFF	F-GHTD	F-WWFF	5N-OIL	5N-FGE	Nigeria NAF961						
97	B	F-WWFA	EC-765	EC-FFO	XA-SJX	(N900DU)	N902NC	N595PL					
98	B	F-WWFM	N465FJ	N900FJ	(N903FJ)	N59CF	N590F						
99		F-WWFE	ZS-NAN										
100		F-WWFN	YK-ASC										
101	B	F-WWFO	N466FJ	D-ALME	VP-CAB	N101FJ	N56CL	N568L					
102		F-WWFK	N467FJ	N906WK	N906CM								
103	B	F-WWFL	F-GHYB	F-WWFJ	V5-NAM								
104	B	F-WWFA	N468FJ	N104FJ	N881G	N900CS	N945TM	N610CX					
105	B	F-WWFD	N469FJ	N8572	JA8572	N71TH	F-GTGJ	F-WQBJ	F-GTGJ	CN-TFU	N767CF	N405EJ	N225KS
		N974BK	N979BK*										
106	B	F-WWFL	F-GKDI	9M-BAN	F-GJRH	N332EC	N333EC	EC-JVR					
107	B	F-WWFJ	N470FJ	XA-GTR	N823BJ	N23BJ	N71GK						
108	B	F-WWFN	N471FJ	N334MC	N511WM	N229HD	(N108FJ)	YV2039	N108FJ				
109	B	F-WWFB	G-BTIB	Belgium CD-01									
110	B	F-WWFH	OY-CKK	F-GHGO	N110FJ	C-GJPG	C-GJPT	N900EJ					
111	B	F-WWFH	N472FJ	N8BX	TS-JSM								
112	B	F-WWFM	N473FJ	N246AG	N248AG	N908JB							
113	B	F-WWFB	HZ-SAB2	N612NL	N525MH								
114	B	F-WWFC	N474FJ	XA-SIM	N114GS	XA-FSB							
115	B	F-WWFL	EC-235	EC-FPI	LX-TAG	HB-IBG	LX-MEL	I-FLYS	F-GSNK	N115FJ	N900JS		
116	B	F-WWFO	N475FJ	N900FJ	N5VF	N5VN	N82RP	N782RP					
117	B	F-WWFA	N476FJ	N70TH	N900WF	(N995P)	N2111P	N111P					
118	B	F-WWFB	F-GNFI	RA-09000									
119	B	F-WWFD	N477FJ	N22T	N22FW								
120	B	F-WWFN	VR-BNJ	VP-BNJ	F-GRAX	F-WQBM	CS-DLA	F-GXDZ	C-FWKX				
121	B	F-WWFE	N478FJ	9M-BAB	HB-IFQ	RP-C9121							
122	B	F-WWFF	N479FJ	XA-SGW	N612BH	N247CJ							
123	B	F-WWFL	RA-09001										
124	B	F-WWFG	N480FJ	VR-BWS	VP-BWS	N14NA							
125	B	F-WWFL	F-GPAX	F-WWFL	VR-BSK	VP-BSK	RP-C7808	N978PW	N976PW	N85KB			
126	B	F-WWFM	N481FJ	N900FJ	N733A	N733HL	N910CS	N94NA	N3HB				
127	B	F-WWFC	N482FJ	N654CN	N390F	N909AS	N963RS	N964RS	XA-VAL				
128	B	F-WWFM	N128FJ	N999PM	(N999PN)	N11LK	N98NX	N404BC					
129	B	F-WWFD	N483FJ	XA-VTO	N909VT	XA-VTO							
130	B	F-WWFC	F-GOAB	F-WWFB	VR-CID	VP-CID	F-WQBN	F-GKBQ	G-HAAM	A6-SAC	HZ-SPAL	F-WHLV	F-GKOM
131	B	F-WWFH	N131FJ	N900FJ	N158JA	XA-TJG	N900VT	N900KD	N900D				
132	B	F-WWFI	N132FJ	N707WB	N767WB								
133	B	F-WWFH	F-GODE	HZ-OFC3	N395L	N5UU	N813TS	YV2040					
134	B	F-WWFA	N134FJ	N88YF	N322CP								
135	B	F-WWFJ	VR-BPW	VP-BPW	F-GYCP	CS-DTP							
136	B	F-WWFE	N137FJ	N1818S	N187S	(N1836S)	N609SG	YV2726					
137	B	F-WWFF	N139FJ	XA-GAE	N99DQ	(N98DQ)	N35RZ						
138	B	F-WWF.	VR-BHJ	VP-BHJ	VH-FHR	C-FGFI	N346SK	N345SK					
139	B	F-WWFG	N140FJ	N523AC	(N523AG)	N900SX							
140	B	F-WWFL	VR-CES	N70HS	N900UT	M-RURU	N140FJ						
141	B	F-WWFK	N141FJ	XA-OVR	XA-OVA	C-GHML	M-SAIR						
142	B	F-WWFN	N142FJ	N10AT	F-WSMF	F-GSMF	TC-CAG	F-HAAP	N103DT	VP-BPC	N100FF	F-GXRM	N211WG
143	B	F-WWFH	F-GNMR	ZS-ZBB	VP-BZB	CS-DDI	PH-LCG	N24FJ					
144	B	F-WWFO	N144FJ	N453JS	N512JY	N111	N111MU						
145	B	F-WWFK	VR-CGB	VP-CGB	F-GOFX								
146	B	F-WWFF	N146FJ	N216FP	N881P	N4MB	N81SV	N900KR					
147	B	F-WWFG	N147FJ	N900FJ	(N901FJ)	OE-IMI	N147FJ	XA-ISR	N195CR				
148	B	F-WWFD	N148FJ	N522AC	N900DV	N900VG	(N900VH)	N148FJ					
149	B	F-WWFH	VR-BPI	VP-BPI	ZS-DAV	N88879	N924S						
150	B	F-WWFC	N150FJ	N335MC	HB-IUW								
151	B	F-WWFK	G-OPWH	EC-HHK	N908CA	N906KW*							
152	B	F-WWFJ	N337MC	N660EG	N902M	N902MK	N18FX	N544CM					
153	B	F-WWFK	N153FJ	N57EL	N67EL								
154	B	F-WWFL	VR-BJA	VP-BJA	F-WQBJ	VP-BGF	F-WQBK	F-GVBF	LX-LFA	I-TCGR			
155	B	F-WWFM	N2056	N730SA	N814M	N155FJ	N900TG	N939SS					
156	B	F-WWFA	N202FJ	HL7301	N910Q	N918MV							
157	B	F-WWFB	N157FJ	N1868M	N1868S	N626EK	N62NW						
158	B	F-WWFC	N158FJ	N900FJ	N404VL	N404VC	N721HM						
159	B	F-WWFD	P4-NAN	N263PW	LX-NAN	F-WQBL	LX-NAN	LX-COS	CS-DPE	M-JMMM	D2-ANT		
160	B	F-WWFE	N176CF	N506BA									
161	B	F-WWFF	F-GSAB	VP-CTT	G-GSEB	PH-ILC	N161PE	N874VT					
162	B	F-WWFJ	N162FJ	N611JW	N1726M	[retro-fitted with winglets]							
163	B	F-WWFM	N163FJ	F-WWFM	(PH-EFA)	(F-GSAD)	VP-BEH	VP-CGP	N25MB	N82SV	N600ME		
164	B	F-WWFC	G-MLTI	F-WQBM	VP-CFL	VP-CDA	N454AJ						
165	B	F-WWFD	G-EVES	VP-BEC	N183WW								
166	B	F-WWFG	N166FJ	N900FJ	F-GLHI	N995SK	N711WV						
167	B	F-WWFO	F-GUEQ	3C-ONM									
168	B	F-WWFA	N167FJ	XA-TEL									
169	C	F-WWFP	F-GRDP	VP-BGC	EC-KFA	N727GW							
170	B	F-WWFR	VP-BKA	N900DA	N900TR	N901TX	XA-...						
171	B	F-WWFW	TC-AKK	VP-CAB									
172	B	F-WWFD	N177FJ	N352AF	N352AE	N910SD							
173	B	F-WWFI	PH-LBA	VP-BFH	M-FASH								
174	B	F-WWFK	N138FA	N138F	XA-FXL	N167BS	N167BD						
175	B	F-WWFN	CS-TMQ	PH-NDK									
176	B	F-WWFW	N900SM	N909PM									
177	B	F-WWFY	N886DC										
178	B	F-WWFF	N179FJ	XA-APE									
179	C	F-WWFQ	N900FJ	N900DW	N902DW								
180	C	F-WWFX	N90TH										
181	C	F-WWFZ	HB-IUY	N833AV	EC-JNZ	F-WHLV	F-GXMF	ZS-JCC					
182	C	F-WWFB	N168HT	EC-JBB									
183	C	F-WWFK	N900CC	(N900WP)	N900RX								
184	C	F-WWFP	N129KJ	N184FJ	N247FR								
185	C	F-WWFF	HB-IGT	VH-PPD									
186	C	F-WWFJ	N900LC										
187	C	F-WWFO	N181FJ	N901SS	N900BK								
188	C	F-WWFZ	PH-EDM	F-HDSD									

FALCON 900

C/n	Series	Identities							
189	C	F-WWFD	N189FJ	C-GMND	N144FH				
190	C	F-WWFI	N900NB	N906NB	N468GH	N500JD			
191	C	F-WWFM	N31D	N48KZ					
192	C	F-WWFQ	N192FJ	PR-SEA	N192LW	VH-LAW	VH-LAL	VH-LUL	N820M
193	C	F-WWFV	N193FJ	(VP-CGR)	F-WQBL	VP-BCX	N917BC		
194	C	F-WWFZ	OO-ACT	PH-STB					
195	C	F-WWFB	N195FJ	N100ED	(N100EQ)	N666TR	N666DJ	N655TC	
196	C	F-WWFH	N196FJ	N501DB					
197	C	F-WWFQ	N197FJ	F-WWFQ	(LX-MAM)	LX-GJL			
198	C	F-WWFR	N198FJ	C-GAZU					
199	C	F-WWFA	N199FJ	N900KJ					
200	C	F-WWFG	N207FJ	N404ST	N404TR	N144BS			
201	C	F-WWFA	N210FJ	LX-FTA	N888LG				
202	C	F-WWFF	VP-BMV	UR-CRD	M-TSKW				

Production complete

DASSAULT FALCON 900DX

C/n	Identities					
601	F-WWFA	[ff 13May05]	HB-JSW	A6-RTS		
602	F-WWFB	N950JB				
603	F-WWFC	OO-VMI				
604	F-WWFD	OE-IDX	G-TAGF	C-GFLU		
605	F-WWFE	N605FJ	N453JS	M-OEPL		
606	F-WWFF	D-AUCR				
607	F-WWFI	(N607DX)	N907DX	C-GPOT		
608	F-WWFN	N50LB				
609	F-WWFO	VP-BNS	F-GRCV	M-WING	F-HTMS	N900VL
610	F-WWFI	VP-CIT	OD-MIK			
611	F-WWFP	N886BB	N890BB			
612	F-WWFJ	HB-JSU	M-MNDD			
613	F-WWFQ	B-8021				
614	F-WWFS	VP-CHA	G-TAGK	M-GSIR		
615	F-WWFX	LX-AFD	N232SF			
616	F-WWFM	A6-SMS	F-HATB	SX-ZHT	VP-CBT	
617	F-WWFH	OE-ISM	TC-SHU			
618	F-WWFO	N416KC				
619	F-WWVB	LX-SVW	LX-SAB			
620	F-WWFI	N620DX				
621	F-WWFA	N16FX	N790T			
622	F-WWFO	M-DADI	D-ADDI*			
623	F-WWFA	D-AMIG	G-ECHB			
624	F-WWFY	N14FX	N906D			
625	F-WWFS	[status?]				

Production complete

DASSAULT FALCON 900EX/900LX

* after the c/n indicates 900EX EASy cockpit-configured aircraft
+ after the c/n indicates a 900LX model

C/n	Identities									
1	F-WREX	[ff 01Jun95]	F-GREX	PH-ERP	N900HG	[retro-fitted with winglets]				
2	F-WWFA	N200L	N209FJ	N970CC						
3	F-WWFG	N903FJ	JA50TH	N760						
4	F-WWJC	N204FJ	N8100E							
5	F-WWFJ	N205FJ	9M-JJS	N905EX	N500VM	N600JM				
6	F-WWFK	F-OIBL	EC-GMO	N143DL	N900FH	N711T				
7	F-WWFN	N907FJ	N45SJ	N374MV	N900SJ					
8	F-WWFB	N30LB	N500BL							
9	F-WWFE	N909FJ	N70LF							
10	F-WWFG	N910FJ	N22CS	N900Q	N910EX					
11	F-WWFI	F-GOYA	CS-DTB	N111SW	[retro-fitted with winglets]					
12	F-WWFJ	N913FJ	N900EX	(N900SB)	N912EX	F-WQBL	F-HAXA			
13	F-WWFK	VP-BRO	N127SF							
14	F-WWFN	N72WS	N7KC	[retro-fitted with winglets]						
15	F-WWFO	N915EX	N914J	N914JL	C-GOAG					
16	F-WWFA	N916EX	N67WB	N950RD						
17	F-WWFB	N600AS	N990H	VP-BEG	N170PF	TJ-TRI	N170PF	RP-C9018		
18	F-WWFE	N918EX	N18RF	N166FB	T7-ZOR					
19	F-WWFJ	N919EX	N7301	N96DS	N900CX	N88ND	[retro-fitted with winglets]			
20	F-WWFN	N920EX	N158JA	(F-OIBE)	D-AWKG					
21	F-WWFH	N330MC	N901MM							
22	F-WWFQ	N331MC	(N332MC)	(N21HJ)						
23	F-WWFS	SE-DVE	OH-FFC	N291MJ						
24	F-WWFU	TR-LEX								
25	F-WWFV	N925EX	N55TY	N607CV	N602CV					
26	F-WWFX	N900SB								
27	F-WWFY	N927EX	N900EX	N626CC	I-FLYW	N99FG				
28	F-WWFZ	HB-IAH	G-CGPT	N328PT	VQ-BYT	T7-MJB	VQ-BYT	[retro-fitted with winglets]		
29	F-WWFA	N25UD	N900MK	N17FX	N490S					
30	F-WWFB	N662P	N860FJ	N100NG	N900CQ					
31	F-WWFC	F-GSAI	HZ-OFC4	M-FALC	N940CL					
32	F-WWFE	N2425	N4425	N97NX	N794SE					
33	F-WWFF	N933EX	(N810M)	XA-TMH	XA-BEG	N903EX	N900WG			
34	F-WWFI	VP-CLB								
35	F-WWFJ	N2BD	HB-IAQ	N96NX	N913SN	N717LA				
36	F-WWFM	N326K	N826K							
37	F-WWFV	N327K	N900BZ	N900FJ						
38	F-WWFX	N328K	N68CG	N901MD	7Q-ONE	ZS-FCI				
39	F-WWFA	N939EX	VP-BID	N39NP						
40	F-WWFB	N940EX	N900EX	N606DR	N990WM					
41	F-WWFC	N5737	N81SN							
42	F-WWFD	N942EX	VP-BMS	N942CK	N909CK					
43	F-WWFE	F-GSDP	F-WQBK	EC-HOB						
44	F-WWFG	G-JCBG	N900PL	N947LF	PR-WRI	N128JL				
45	F-WWFJ	Italy MM62171								
46	F-WWFM	N946EX	XA-FEX	N40ML	N107CC	C-FGCT				
47	F-WWFO	N58CG								
48	F-WWFP	G-GPWH	G-CBHT	N627CR						
49	F-WWFR	N949EX	N404F							
50	F-WWFS	F-GPNJ								
51	F-WWFU	F-GVDP	OE-IDM							
52	F-WWFV	Italy MM62172								
53	F-WWFW	N953EX	PT-WQS	VP-BDZ	N53FJ					
54	F-WWFY	HB-IUX	PH-LAU							
55	F-WWFA	N498A	(N399CG)	N388GS	XA-BNM	N555ZT				
56	F-WWFC	N956EX	N404A	N909SB						
57	F-WWFD	N900MT	N900MJ	N10HZ	N10HQ	C-GXPZ				
58	F-WWFF	N958EX	N11WM							
59	F-WWFH	N959EX	N694JP	(N6940P)	N900EF					
60	F-WWFI	N960EX	PT-XSC	N60EX	YV2053					
61	F-WWFL	N961EX	N240LG							
62	F-WWFM	EC-HNU	N960SF							
63	F-WWFO	N963EX	N900EX	N435T						
64	F-WWFR	N900VM	D-AJAD	C-GBBX	N745TM	N945TM				
65	F-WWFW	N965EX	N965M	VP-CGD						
66	F-WWFA	N377SC	(N677SC)	N66FJ						
67	F-WWFB	N967EX	N312P	N312PV						
68	F-WWFC	N390DE	N271DV	N271DU						
69	F-WWFD	N969EX	C-FJOI							
70	F-WWFE	N970EX	N999PM							
71	F-WWFG	N111NG	(N971EX)	N110EX						
72	F-WWFH	N2BD	N72FJ*							
73	F-WWFI	N973M	VP-CGE							
74	F-WWFK	N315KP	N811AV	N600LF	G-HNJC	VP-CNZ	N740LM			
75	F-WWFL	(F-GYDP)	VP-BEH	F-WQBK	F-GXBV					
76	F-WWFN	F-GLJV	F-WLJV	N80F	C-GMLH					
77	F-WWFQ	N977LP	N83SV							
78	F-WWFR	G-DAEX	D-AGSI	F-GXHG	D-AHER					
79	F-WWFS	N788CG								
80	F-WWFV	N881Q	N900CM							
81	F-WWFW	N404N	N404R	N908SB						
82	F-WWFX	N982EX	PR-GPA							
83	F-WWFY	HB-IGI								
84	F-WWFA	N984EX	N900EX	N984EX	N326K	(N82KK)	N420KK	N420PD		
85	F-WWFB	N985EX	(N410MW)	N910MW	N76PW					
86	F-WWFC	N986EX	HB-IGX	VP-BEZ	M-ODKZ					
87	F-WWFE	OE-IMA	N487MA	C-GGMI	OE-IMI					
88	F-WWFF	N909MM	C-GLBB	(D-AHRO)	N900ZM	C-GWFM				
89	F-WWFH	N990EX	N871MM	(N802CB)	N802CJ	VT-SBK				
90	F-WWFG	VP-CLO								
91	F-WWFJ	N989EX	F-WWFJ	(F-OINA)	F-WQBJ	I-CAEX	N91EX	ZS-FCN	[retro-fitted with winglets]	N436RB

FALCON 900EX/900LX

C/n	Identities									
92	F-WWFK	HB-IFJ	N921WC	N992FJ	N902YP					
93	F-WWFL	N993EX	N993GT	C-FPFS						
94	F-WWFN	N994EX	N663MK	N731SR						
95	F-WWFO	HB-IGY								
96	F-WWFP	N93CR	N900ZA	HB-JSY	D-AHRN					
97+	F-WNCO	(F-GNCO)+	(F-GOEA)+	[+ both sets of ntu marks reserved simultaneously]		CS-DFL	N970RJ	N963RS		
98	F-WWFR	N998EX	N900KX	N209CQ						
99	F-WWFS	N996EX	N890FH	XA-GMD	N5VJ					
100	F-WWFU	N997EX	JA55TH	N550TH						
101	F-WWFW	N966H	(N875F)	N730LM						
102	F-WWFX	N6666P	N6666R	N70TT						
103	F-WWFY	N103EX	N900EX	N327K	F-GYCM	N103FJ	N900HD			
104	F-WWFA	N588GS	N805WM	N440DM						
105	F-WWFC	G-LCYA	(D-AHRN)	N552SD	[retro-fitted with winglets]		N94UT			
106	F-WWFD	F-GSDA	LX-ZAK	SE-DJM	N106EX					
107	F-WWFE	F-HBOL	HB-JIN							
108	F-WWFF	G-JCBX	N9WV	N501MK						
109	F-WWFG	VP-BEE	F-HDOM	I-SLNI						
110	F-WWFI	N176CL	N137SF							
111	F-WWFJ	N101EX	N57EL	N508PC	VP-BFV	OE-IEX	N900VE			
112	F-WWFK	G-JJMX	N900MF	N587DZ						
113	F-WWFL	G-RBSG	F-GYRB	N121DF						
114	F-WWFM	N114EX	N900EX	(N114EX)	N900YP					
115	F-WWFN	N720ML	N720ME	N44VP						
116	F-WWFO	Italy MM62210								
117	F-WWFP	N117EX	(N900EX)	N900SN						
118	F-WWFS	OH-PPR	OE-IRL	F-HFOX	CN-RAK					
119	F-WWFU	N119EX	N958DM	N719SH						
120*	F-WWFV	(N120EZ)	N900EX	F-WWFV	N900EX	N106RW	[w/o in hangar collapse at Washington/Dulles, VA, 06Feb10; parted out by Dodson International, Rantoul, KS]			
121*	F-WWFW	F-GSEF	F-WWFW	F-GSEF	OO-FOI	N793CG				
122*	F-WWFX	N901SB								
123*	F-WWFY	N990ML	N990MC	N80Q						
124*	F-WWFZ	N919SA								
125*	F-WWFB	N988H								
126*	F-WWFC	N966H	N966E	N889H						
127*	F-WWFD	N900HC	N984BX							
128*	F-WWFE	OY-OKK	(N900LK)	M-ABEB	N1SA					
129*	F-WWFF	N129EX	XA-RGB	XA-PGB	C-GLBU	C-GJPG				
130*	F-WWFH	VP-BEF								
131+	F-WWFI	VP-BFM	N900MV	N297GB						
132*	F-WWFJ	G-JPSX	N590CL							
133*	F-WWFK	F-WQBJ	D-AZEM							
134*	F-WWFL	VP-CEZ	VP-CFR	EI-ZMA						
135*	F-WWFM	N246AG								
136*	F-WWFN	N22LC	(N22LQ)	N822WW						
137*	F-WWFO	N88LC	N50NL	N50NU						
138*	F-WWFP	OE-IVK	(OY-VIK)	OY-IVK	F-GNVK					
139*	F-WWFQ	N139EX	N265H							
140*	F-WWFR	N940EX	(N900EX)	N54HG						
141*	F-WWFS	N141EX	HB-JSX	OE-IWG	F-HMCH	D-ASBG				
142*	F-WWFU	N142EX	RA-09008							
143*	F-WWFV	HA-LKN								
144*	F-WWFW	N144EX	VP-BSO							
145*	F-WWFX	F-GSNA	(LN-SEH)							
146*	F-WWFZ	N146EX								
147*	F-WWFE	N193F	N622WM							
148*	F-WWFG	5A-DCN								
149*	F-WWFH	Italy MM62244								
150*	F-WWFI	N900NS	G-SABI	F-HUBB						
151+	F-WWFJ	VP-BSP	G-EGVO							
152*	F-WWFK	P4-SCM	UR-WIG	F-WHLV	N592CL					
153*	F-WWFL	N7818S	N1818S							
154+	F-WWFM	N47EG								
155*	F-WWFN	(F-GSMT)	N955EX	F-WQBN	F-GSMT	(LN-SEH)	LN-AOC	N852CA	G-FFFG	N91GL	N978PW
156*	F-WWFO	MM62245								
157*	F-WWFP	N227HD	N82HD							
158*	F-WWFQ	N15FF	N18DF							
159+	F-WWFR	N959EX	N900EX	N900SG	G-FNES	VH-MQK	VH-MQR	N6VF		
160+	F-WWFS	I-DAKO	LX-DSP	N731FJ	N615MS					
161*	F-WWFU	TC-MMG	TC-FTG							
162*	F-WWFW	N962EX	PR-CCC	N876C						
163*	F-WWFX	G-GALX	I-FLYN	N731FJ	N575JJ					
164*	F-WWFY	RA-09006								
165*	F-WWFZ	N165FJ	(N777SA)	(F-GUDA)	OE-IMC	F-HDLJ				
166*	F-WWFM	VT-ISH								
167*	F-WWFP	N167EX	N85CL	N902SB						
168*	F-WWFQ	N900JG	(N900JF)	N900JQ	N446TD					
169+	F-WWFH	N900NF	N900NB	(N906NB)	N169FJ	N885B				
170*	F-WWFJ	N585BP	N700FL							
171*	F-WWFK	SE-DJA	N889TA	N889TD						
172*	F-WWFL	G-SIRO								
173*	F-WWFE	N7600S								
174*	F-WWFR	F-HCBM	F-WQBN	VP-BOZ	N789ZZ					
175*	F-WWFV	N513HS								
176*	F-WWFW	N176EX	(LX-GDX)	D-AMBI	OE-IBN					
177*	F-WWFZ	N900KM	F-WQBM	VT-AKU						
178*	F-WWFA	N178EX	N900EX	N178EX	N900VG	N900VQ	N1836S			
179*	F-WWFC	SE-DJB	N718MM							
180+	F-WWFD	HZ-OFC5	M-ROWL	C-FJOA	N278RF					
181+	F-WWFH	N181EX	PR-FRU	N920JS	N13JS	N539CA				
182*	F-WWFU	N93KD	N1828S							
183*	F-WWFG	A6-MAF	A6-MMF	F-GVFL	I-SEAR					
184*	F-WWFN	G-JMMX	N512TF	F-....						
185*	F-WWFV	LN-AKR								

FALCON 900EX/900LX

C/n	Identities					
186*	F-WWFY	N186EX	(XA-SCO)	XA-TEI		
187*	F-WWFA	N904JY				
188*	F-WWFW	N460D				
189*	F-WWFZ	OE-INB	G-RMMA			
190*	F-WWFF	N190FJ	C-GLXC	C-GLXG	N990FL	
191*	F-WWFP	N191AE				
192*	F-WWFR	I-SEAS				
193+	F-WWFU	G-REYG	N843MG	N343MG	N843MG	
194*	F-WWFK	N987AL	(PR-OLD)	N970SF		
195*	F-WWFL	C6-SZN	3A-MGA	3A-MGC	HB-JIO	Switzerland T-785
196*	F-WWVA	N196EX	YV2485			
197*	F-WWFC	N197EX	YV2486			
198*	F-WWFF	CS-DPF				
199*	F-WWFJ	N199FJ	N918JM			
200*	F-WWFW	F-HBDA	M-AFAJ			
201*	F-WWFY	N900EX	C-GIPX	N718AK		
202*	F-WWVC	N606SG				
203*	F-WWVD	N203FJ	XA-RET	N203FJ		
204*	F-WWVE	I-FLYI	[w/o 28Nov08 Brindisi, Italy; parted out Tarbes, France; b/u]			
205*	F-WWFB	(M-TECH)	VT-CAP	M-VGAL		
206*	F-WWFD	N206EX	N33LC			
207*	F-WWFE	N907EX	PR-PMV			
208*	F-WWFG	N286MJ				
209*	F-WWFK	N209EX	(N900RF)+	[+ntu marks worn at completion centre]		Bolivia FAB-001
210*	F-WWFM	N210FJ	(N600US)	(N984H)		
211*	F-WWFN	G-WTOR	LX-GLD			
212*	F-WWFC	N212EX	N48CG			
213*	F-WWFI	N213EX	N28VL			
214*	F-WWFH	OE-IOE				
215*	F-WWFJ	N375SC				
216*	F-WWFQ	N44LC				
217+	F-WWFS	LX-GET	M-ROWL			
218*	(F-WWFV)	F-WWFL	N606US	P2-ANW		
219*	(F-WWFX)	F-WWFR	(TC-...)	G-ENXA		
220*	(F-WWFZ)	F-WWFD	OH-FFE	OO-FFE		
221*	(F-WWVA)	F-WWFE	N221EX	N5MV		
222*	(F-WWVF)	F-WWFF	N399EX	N63XF		
223*	(F-WWVG)	F-WWFG	N223EX	(B-MBL)	RA-09003	
224*	(F-WWVH)	F-WWFC	G-JPSZ	N980SF		
225*	(F-WWVI)	F-WWFK	VP-BPW			
226*	F-WWVJ	N7600P				
227*	F-WWFI	(D-ASIE)	D-ALMS	N368FK		
228*	F-WWFJ	N228EX	N18CG			
229*	F-WWFP	N229DK				
230*	F-WWFL	F-GMDS	LN-BRG	M-MIDY		
231*	F-WWFQ	N231FJ	N720ML			
232*	F-WWFU	G-WABB	N685DC			
233*	F-WWFE	N900FJ	N707WB			
234*	F-WWFV	N432FJ	N672WM			
235*	F-WWFF	N235FJ	(PR-RJZ)	PR-ROZ	N580CB	
236*	F-WWFW	TC-AZR	F-HEBO			
237*	F-WWFX	F-GZVA	M-EAGL			
238*	F-WWFG	LX-EMO				
239*	F-WWFZ	P4-GEM				
240+	F-WWFH	RA-09600				
241*	F-WWFM	9G-EXE				
242+	F-WWFN	XA-BEG				
243+	F-WWVA	N90LX	N175BC			
244+	F-WWFJ	M-ATOS	N91FE			
245+	F-WWFQ	N777QG	B-8030	M-LANG		
246+	F-WWFA	N900YG				
247+	F-WWFD	9H-GMT	D-AETD*			
248+	F-WWFE	N248LX				
249+	F-WWFB	(F-HBFL)	N63JP			
250+	F-WWFC	N250FJ	VQ-BJW	M-ATEX		
251+	F-WWFF	N311JA				
252+	F-WWFI	OH-GPE	OO-GPE			
253+	F-WWFY	I-DIEM				
254+	F-WWVB	N264C	(N264G)			
255+	F-WWVC	I-NEMO				
256+	F-WWVD	G-YCKF				
257+	F-WWVE	TC-MKR				
258+	F-WWFP	N258LX	VQ-BNH			
259+	F-WWVF	N529SG				
260+	F-WWVG	C-GTLA				
261+	F-WWVH	N261CH				
262+	F-WWVI	N577QT				
263+	F-WWVJ	F-GLYD	TC-AKE			
264+	F-WWFK	OY-SLS	ES-SLS			
265+	F-WWFV	N265LX	N993AM			
266+	F-WWFW	VP-CHG				
267+	F-WWFL	B-8208				
268+	F-WWFU	N234SA				
269+	F-WWVA	M-JPLC	N115PL			
270+	F-WWFX	M-WING				
271+	F-WWFM	(TC-IRR)	M-ISRK	M-ABGZ	F-HIBR	
272+	F-WWFC	N40LB				
273+	F-WWFR	OY-MHM				
274+	F-WWFA	M-AGIK				
275+	F-WWFY	N248DV				
276+	F-WWFF	B-8212				
277+	F-WWFD	F-HNLX	M-TINK	F-HDDP		
278+	F-WWVB	N278FJ				
279+	F-WWFB	HB-JTA				
280+	F-WWVC	N215EF				

FALCON 900EX/900LX

C/n	Identities				
281+	F-WWFQ	F-HNDO	N1130B		
282+	F-WWFH	VP-BFM			
283+	F-WWFG	TC-AOM	F-HVRO	M-PATH	F-HJMD
284+	F-WWFE	N46R			
285+	F-WWVE	OO-LMS			
286+	F-WWFN	N900VG			
287+	F-WWFI	N95BD			
288+	F-WWFP	F-HRAY			
289+	F-WWFZ	N73PS			
290+	F-WWFJ	N72PS			
291+	F-WWFY	N373RS			
292+	F-WWFX				
293+	F-WWFW				
294+	F-WWFV	N18UD			
295+	F-WWFU				
296+	F-WWFS				
297+	F-WWFR				
298+	F-WWFA				
299+	F-WWFC				
300+					
301+					
302+					
303+	D-ABBA*				
304+					
305+					
306+					
307+					
308+					
309+					
310+					

DASSAULT FALCON 2000

C/n	Identities											
1	(F-WNEW)	F-WNAV	[r/o 10Feb93; ff 04Mar93]	(F-GMIR)	F-GMOE	VP-CAS	F-GXJC	G-YUMN	M-YUMN			
2	F-WNEW	[rolled out Dec93; ff 11Jly94]		ZS-NNF	F-GJHJ	N201CR						
3	F-WWFA	N2000A	N15AS	N203AF								
4	F-WWMA	N925AJ										
5	F-WWMB	N27R	[parted out by Pollard Spares, Roanoke, TX]									
6	F-WWMD	F-GPAM	F-WQBL	N93GH	N93GT	PR-WSM	N55EY	N954SC	M-....			
7	F-WWME	N28R										
8	F-WWMF	N610AS	F-WQBK	VT-VLM								
9	F-WWMG	N435T	N435TM	N209FJ	N783FS							
10	F-WWMH	N652PC	N131EP									
11	F-WWMK	N101NS	(N787RA)	N721BS	N248JF	N48FB						
12	F-WWMM	I-SNAW	(F-GLHJ)	N105AF								
13	F-WWML	N2004	N722JB									
14	F-WWMN	N2034	N70KS	N51MN								
15	F-WWMO	N790L	N502BG									
16	F-WWMB	HB-IAW										
17	F-WWMA	N2035	N77A	N88TY	N89TY	N659FM	N658FM	N62MF				
18	F-WWMG	F-GMPR	EI-LJR	VP-CJA	[retro-fitted with winglets]							
19	F-WWMC	N790M										
20	F-WWME	N389GS	N822TP	N405ST	N427GW							
21	F-WWMA	N390GS	N11BV									
22	F-WWMF	N200NE	N609CH	N202CE	N644RV							
23	F-WWMH	N2036	N375SC	N575SC	N23FJ	N10JP						
24	F-WWMK	N2039	N376SC	N876SC	N18MV							
25	F-WWML	N2042	N96FG	N122SC	(N406ST)	N25FJ	M-NIKO	T7-NIK	G-TNIK			
26	F-WWMN	N2046	N2000A	F-WQFL	TC-CIN	VP-BHC	TC-CIN	F-WQBN	N112CD	HB-ISF	OY-ICE	(F-GSAE)	LX-SAM
	N358PR											
27	F-WWMM	G-JCBI	F-GJSK	D-BSIK	F-WQBL	LX-SIK	F-WQBK	F-GSYC	B-8020	N27FJ	VH-FJO	
28	F-WWMO	N596A	N160WS	N8888	[retro-fitted with winglets]							
29	F-WWMA	N2028	XA-TDU	N700FL	N889MC	[retro-fitted with winglets]						
30	F-WWMB	HB-IAZ	N480CF									
31	F-WWMC	N2032	N790Z									
32	F-WWMD	N65SD	N324CL	N175BC	N132FJ	N37MD	[retro-fitted with winglets]					
33	F-WWME	HB-IAX	N974HR									
34	F-WWMF	HB-IAY	N234FJ									
35	F-WWMG	N27WP	N1927G	N623HD								
36	F-WWMA	F-GSAA	(PH-WOL)	PH-INJ	F-GNBL	VT-COT	N480LP	N602LP				
37	F-WWMH	EC-GNK										
38	F-WWMI	N3BM	N8QM	(N800BG)	N710ET							
39	F-WWMJ	N2061	N151AE	N42ST								
40	F-WWMK	N1C	N212US	N200CD								
41	F-WWMD	N2073	N48CG	N148CG	N214LD							
42	F-WWMG	HB-IBH	F-WHLX	CS-DTZ	[retro-fitted with winglets]							
43	F-WWMK	(N2077)	PT-MML	N101BE	N43FJ	N86TW	(N86TY)	N775ST				
44	F-WWML	N2074	N2000A	N49MW	N37TH	N623QW	N303CL					
45	F-WWMM	N45SC	N190MC									
46	F-WWMN	N2080	(N220JM)	F-WWMN	F-GMCK	CS-DCM	N505RR					
47	F-WWMB	N220JM	N800BL	N435JF								
48	F-WWMC	N2089	N701WC	N701WG	N48WK	N888FC						
49	F-WWMD	(PH-EFB)	VP-BEF	G-GEDI	F-GHGO	F-WQBK	VT-TBT					
50	F-WWME	D-BEST										
51	F-WWMF	N82AT	N2AT	N797CM								
52	F-WWMI	N212T	N749GP	N955SL								
53	F-WWMJ	N981	N149VB	N149V	N149VB							
54	F-WWML	D-BIRD	D-BOND	I-JAMY	N254FJ							
55	F-WWMM	HB-IVM	F-WQBK	F-GJTG	EC-JXR							
56	F-WWMO	TC-CYL	N784BX									
57	F-WWMA	N2132	N18CG	N918CG	N122PR							
58	F-WWMB	N2133	N326EW	N826EW								
59	F-WWMC	N2146	PT-WYC									
60	F-WWMD	N2147	XA-GNI	(N260FJ)	XA-TYT	N524SA	N898CT					
61	F-WWME	HB-IVN	F-WQBJ	F-GJTH	EC-JVI	N61RN						
62	F-WWMF	HB-IVO	CX-MBS									
63	F-WWMG	N2155	N2000A	N804JH	N800JH	N806JH	N302JC	(N863TS)	N68GL			
64	F-WWMH	N996AG	N553GR									
65	F-WWMI	F-GODO	(F-OIBA)	VT-TAT								
66	F-WWMJ	N30TH	N429SJ	N793WF								
67	F-WWMK	N150BC	N406NL									
68	F-WWMN	N200GN	N629TG									
69	F-WWMA	N220JN	(N220JM)	N220EJ	(N220MR)	N220DF	(N346SR)	N910LA*				
70	F-WWMB	N2168	N207QS	P4-IKR	D-BAMA	F-WQBK	VT-HDL					
71	F-WWMC	N92LT	N811AV	N811AG	N811TY	N811AG	C-FWTF	N630TS				
72	F-WWMD	N2169	N96LT	N769JW	N768JW	N61JE						
73	F-WWMG	N2176	(N97LT)	N273JC	N273JE	N73FJ						
74	F-WWMH	HB-IUZ	F-GJSC	OO-VMB	N988DV	N986DV	(N829AM)	N468AM				
75	F-WWMK	N275QS	N229DA	[retro-fitted with winglets]								
76	F-WWML	OY-CKN	F-WQBN	OY-CKN								
77	F-WWMM	N278QS	N273TX	N888NA								
78	F-WWMJ	G-PYCO	N262PC	N78FJ	[retro-fitted with winglets]							
79	F-WWMN	N929HG	N772MC	N774MC	N79FJ	(JY-RYG)						
80	F-WWMO	N2CW	N60TC	N60TQ	N323EG							
81	F-WWVA	N281QS										
82	F-WWVB	N752S										
83	F-WWVC	N1128B										
84	F-WWVD	N1929Y										
85	F-WWVE	N220JM	N221EJ	N344GC	XA-HHF							
86	F-WWVF	N111HZ	N101HZ									
87	F-WWVG	N287QS	N4200	N910CS								
88	F-WWVH	N753S	C-FJPV	C-GSCL	C-GSMR							
89	F-WWVI	N2189	N2000A	N800GH								
90	F-WWVJ	F-GKIP	F-WQBM	N930SD	N5200							
91	F-WWVK	N46HA										
92	F-WWVL	N2191	N2000L	N850TC								
93	F-WWVM	N292QS										

FALCON 2000

C/n	Identities								
94	F-WWVN	N48HA	N517PJ	N286MG	(N94FJ)	M-IIII	N923JE		
95	F-WWVO	N628CC	[retro-fitted with winglets]						
96	F-WWVP	N88DD	N50TG	N53TG	N755FL				
97	F-WWVQ	N620AS	N922H	N922J	N12MW	N12MQ	[retro-fitted with winglets]		
98	F-WWVR	N298QS	N289TX	M-ABCD					
99	F-WWVS	(N2099)	N111VU	N111VW	N770MP				
100	F-WWVT	VP-CGA	N518SS						
101	F-WWVU	N2093	N399FA	OO-GFD	F-WHLX	VT-RVL			
102	F-WWVV	N515TK	N440AS	N410AS	N286CX				
103	F-WWVX	I-FLYP	F-WHLX	VT-AVH					
104	F-WWVY	N204QS							
105	F-WWVZ	N220EJ	N105LF	N711PE					
106	F-WWVA	N635E							
107	F-WWVB	VP-CGC	N107VP	XA-RHA					
108	F-WWVC	I-FLYV							
109	F-WWVD	CS-DNP	N2218	F-WWVD	CS-DNP	N2000L			
110	F-WWVE	N2194	PP-CFF	[retro-fitted with winglets]					
111	F-WWVF	VP-BDL	F-WHLY	N132DA	G-FBJL	N925AK	[retro-fitted with winglets]		
112	F-WWVG	N2197	N2000A	N2112L	N410GS	N112FJ			
113	F-WWVH	N213QS							
114	F-WWVI	ZS-PKR							
115	F-WWVK	CS-DNQ	N30AJ	N48MF					
116	F-WWVL	N2216	N52DC	N382KU*					
117	F-WWVM	N2217	N54DC						
118	F-WWVN	N218QS							
119	F-WWVO	F-GXDP	F-WQBN	D-BDNL	F-GESP	CS-DTR			
120	F-WWVP	CS-DNR							
121	F-WWVQ	HZ-KSDA	F-ORAX	(F-GVDA)	VP-BNT	N78NT	M-TANA	OD-ONE	F-HFLX	M-SFOZ
122	F-WWVR	N222QS							
123	F-WWVS	LZ-OOI							
124	F-WWVU	N224QS							
125	F-WWVV	N313GH	N813GH	N911SH	N118AD				
126	F-WWVW	N226QS							
127	F-WWVY	N227QS							
128	F-WWVZ	N228EJ	N628SA	N350M	N200JW				
129	F-WWVD	N229QS							
130	F-WWVE	N99TY	N202TH	N902MC					
131	F-WWVG	N707MM	N707MN	N317ML					
132	F-WWVH	N97NX	N905B						
133	F-WWVI	HZ-KSDB	F-WQBK	LX-SVW	F-WQBJ	B-MBK	F-WHLX	F-HKLB	TC-DGS	TC-GNC
134	F-WWVF	SX-DCF	N493S	(N493SV)	N622QW	N462ST			
135	F-WWVJ	N222BN	N196RG	N797HD					
136	F-WWVL	N236QS							
137	F-WWVM	N61KW	N510RR						
138	F-WWVN	N799BC	N856F	(N138MM)	N250DL				
139	F-WWVR	CS-DNS	N26NJ						
140	F-WWVT	N797SM	N797WC						
141	F-WWVU	N2227	N2000A	N54J					
142	F-WWVV	HZ-KSDC							
143	F-WWVW	N2230	N872EC	VT-ARF					
144	F-WWVX	F-GUJP	N317ML	N317MR	N203WB	N233EM	N233EH		
145	F-WWVZ	N245QS							
146	F-WWVA	N844AV	N866AV	N317MN	N455DX				
147	F-WWVB	N999BE	N777MN	N700CH					
148	F-WWVC	CS-DFC	N248VR	N921SA					
149	F-WWVG	N2235	XA-MAV	XA-URK	N555GS				
150	F-WWVH	EC-HYI							
151	F-WWVI	G-IBSF	N151GR	N151CM	N10JM*				
152	F-WWVJ	N98NX	N70XC	N317MQ	N246V	N243V			
153	F-WWVK	N253QS							
154	F-WWVL	OY-CKI	LN-RTG						
155	F-WWVM	N255QS							
156	F-WWVN	N844UP	N844UR	N187AA					
157	F-WWVO	TC-RMK	[retro-fitted with winglets]		TC-CTN				
158	F-WWVP	N258QS							
159	F-WWVQ	N259QS							
160	F-WWVZ	VP-CGM	TC-PLM	F-WQBL	VP-BBP	N889MU			
161	F-WWVA	I-DDVF	N411YF						
162	F-WWVU	N262QS							
163	F-WWVW	N163J	OY-CKF	G-CGHI	N755BB	N991CE			
164	F-WWVY	N44JC							
165	F-WWVE	N265QS							
166	F-WWVD	(N2259)	TC-DGC	OY-CKW	F-WQBL	F-GVTC	(A6-SAF)	OY-TJF	TC-RSN	T7-RSN
167	F-WWVG	3A-MGR	3A-MGA	3A-MMA	VP-BHD	B-MAU	PR-SFB		
168	F-WWVV	N268QS							
169	F-WWVJ	N269QS							
170	F-WWVC	N220AB							
171	F-WWVK	(HZ-KSDD)	F-ORAV	N797HT	HB-JSB				
172	F-WWVN	N272EJ	N36EP						
173	F-WWVR	N673BA	OY-SIR	N988S					
174	F-WWMA	CS-DFD	N53NJ						
175	F-WWMB	N2258	XA-AVE						
176	F-WWMC	N676BA	N313AV						
177	F-WWMD	N277QS							
178	F-WWME	N279QS	N884WY	N100WY	N101NY				
179	F-WWMF	OH-FIX	N22TS						
180	F-WWMG	N2260	(N203DD)	N680DF					
181	F-WWMH	N280QS							
182	F-WWMI	N2264	N2000A	N329K	N826KR				
183	F-WWMJ	N2265	N88MX	N903GS					
184	F-WWMK	N2261	XA-RET	N71AX	G-MDBA	N228MN	N557PK		
185	F-WWML	N284QS							
186	F-WWMM	N2270	N551SS	N98RP					
187	F-WWMN	(F-GZAK)	LX-ZAK	F-GNDO	N87FJ	VP-BCV	N343AT	PT-SRU	N72BC
188	F-WWMD	N2288	N317MZ	N317M					

FALCON 2000/2000DX

C/n	Identities						
189	F-WWMB	N2267	N2000A	N330K			
190	F-WWVA	N290QS					
191	F-WWVB	F-GUYM	TC-PRK	F-WQBJ	I-BNTN	(F-GULK)	F-GZJR	I-GEFD
192	F-WWVC	N2289	N2000A	N515PV	N458SW	N718PM	
193	F-WWVE	N239QS	N278GS	N279GS			
194	F-WWVF	N671WM					
195	F-WWVH	N297QS	N196KC				
196	F-WWVI	N296QS					
197	F-WWVJ	N2290	N215KH	I-KERE			
198	F-WWVL	N203QS					
199	F-WWVM	N2295	N899U	N15BY			
200	F-WWVN	I-SEAE					
201	F-WWVO	N201WR					
202	F-WWVP	N251QS					
203	F-WWVQ	I-ARIF					
204	F-WWVR	N240QS	N2317	N88DD			
205	F-WWVS	CS-DFE	N205VR				
206	F-WWVT	N208QS	N2319	N414CC	N331DC	N831DC	N900NH
207	F-WWVU	N207EM	OE-HEM	OM-OPF	OE-HBG		
208	F-WWVV	G-GEDY	LX-MBE				
209	F-WWVW	N209FS	N209TM	OE-HPH			
210	F-WWVX	N270QS	N2325	N850K	C-GEPG		
211	F-WWVY	N210QS					
212	F-WWVZ	N2322	N523W	N523WC			
213	F-WWVA	N212QS	N684KF				
214	F-WWVB	N214FJ	N215QS				
215	F-WWVC	N215RE	N203CK	N215RE			
216	F-WWVD	N718KS	OE-HFA	9H-MAT	S5-CWA		
217	F-WWVE	N863TM	OE-HVA	N771AT	PP-LFS		
218	F-WWVF	N218PH					
219	F-WWVG	N219FJ	N1999	(N219FJ)	C-GOCX		
220	F-WWVH	N620BA	N306BH				
221	F-WWVI	N102MG	N1MG	N950RL			
222	F-WWVJ	N297RG	N296RG	N138FJ			
223	F-WWVK	OE-HAF	M-WING	M-WIND	OY-SNK		
224	F-WWVL	N33FJ	N33D	N40N			
225	F-WWVM	VT-AAT					
226	F-WWVN	OE-HKY	D-BSKY				
227	F-WWVO	P4-IKF					
228	F-WWVP	N900MC					
229	F-WWVQ	F-GXDA	TC-SNK				
230	F-WWVR	(F-HDFS)	N230FJ	N532CC	N522CC	N97FG	
231	F-WWVS	VT-HGL					

Production complete, replaced by the Falcon 2000DX

DASSAULT FALCON 2000DX

C/n	Identities		
601	F-WWGY	[ff 19Jun07]	N331DC
602	F-WWMC	N30LF	[retrofitted with winglets]
603	F-WWGD	LX-ATD	N473K
604	F-WWGV	VT-VKR	

Production complete

DASSAULT FALCON 2000EX/2000EX EASy/2000LX

* alongside the c/n indicates a 2000EX EASy cockpit-configured aircraft
+ alongside the c/n indicates a 2000LX aircraft

C/n		Identities							
1		F-WMEX	[r/o 19Jly01; ff 25Oct01]	(F-GMEX)	VP-BMJ	N900CH			
2		F-WWGA	N202EX						
3		F-WWGC	HB-IAJ						
4		F-WWGD	N200CH	N909CF					
5		F-WWGE	LX-DKC	F-GUDN	PH-VBG				
6	+	F-WXEY	[retrofitted with 2000LX winglets 2008]						
7		F-WWGF	D-BIRD	N40TH					
8		F-WWGG	G-JOLI	F-GUTD	OO-IAR	OE-HRA	LX-AAM	OE-HNM	S5-ADG	N1978X
9		F-WWGH	(N209EX)	HB-IGQ	OM-IGQ	EP-FSC			
10		F-WWGI	(SE-RBV)	VP-BER	OE-HKK				
11		F-WWGJ	I-NATS	OE-HGM	D-BGGM*				
12		F-WWGK	N313CC						
13		F-WWGL	N500R	N500FE	N71FE	(D-BJGM)	N263XF		
14		F-WWGM	HB-IAU						
15		F-WWGN	N215EX	N97GM	S5-ABR	Slovenia L1-01			
16	+	F-WWGO	PP-AAF	N16XY					
17		F-WWGP	N217EX	F-WWGP	N977CP				
18		F-WWGQ	F-GUHB	N943JB	N104MT				
19		F-WWGR	N528BD	N855TJ					
20	+	F-WWGS	N219EX	XA-GNI	XA-CDT				
21		F-WWGT	N221EX	N521CD	N801WW	N801WC			
22		F-WWGU	N218EX	PR-WQT	N218EX	VP-BDV	N122FJ	N118T	
23		F-WWGV	N223EX	N101PV					
24		F-WWGW	N224EX	N341AP					
25		F-WWGX	N225EX	N699MC	N83LT				
26		F-WWGY	N226EX	N6453	N6458	N880RJ			
27		F-WWGZ	OH-FEX	ER-KVI	N23LT				
28	*	F-WWGC	F-GUFM	N2CC	N4QG	(N28EX)	M-RONE		
29	*	F-WWGD	SX-DCA	N382CA	N12MW				
30	*	F-WWGG	D-BERT	M-PDCS					
31	*	F-WWGJ	N31EX	N620MS					
32	*	F-WWGK	N666BE	N999BE	N377GM	N377AG			
33	*	F-WWGL	D-BILL	D-BOSS	N924BC	N790DC			
34	+	F-WWGM	HB-JEG	C-FJAJ	C-GJKI				
35	+	F-WWGQ	OY-CLN	N626NT					
36	*	F-WWGR	N185G	N163EB					
37	*	F-WWGS	N308U						
38	*	F-WWGT	N3BM	N8QM	N909MM				
39	*	F-WWGU	CS-TLP	9H-SFA					
40	*	F-WWGV	N240EX	PR-PPN	N888NX	PH-CHT	N131A		
41	*	F-WWGW	CS-DFF						
42	*	F-WWGX	F-GUTC	D-BMVV					
43	*	F-WWGY	N9871R						
44	*	F-WWGA	CS-DFG						
45	+	F-WWGE	VP-BVP	N205CW	N659FM				
46	*	F-WWGF	N21HE	N10EU					
47	+	F-WWGH	N711HE	N404UK	N365FJ	G-LSMB			
48	*	F-WWGI	N48NC	N1NC					
49	+	F-WWGN	F-GUDC	N50TG	N249FJ				
50	*	F-WWGO	N57MN	N133RL	N250LX	N726DC			
51	*	F-WWGP	ZS-MGD	N581GM					
52	*	F-WWMA	G-KWIN	M-ABFF	EP-TTI				
53	*	F-WWMB	N36TH	N98TH	N510CT				
54	*	F-WWMC	N221QS						
55	*	F-WWMD	N226EW	N326EW	N326LW	N57AL			
56	*	F-WWME	N56EX	N954SP	N600BL	C-FNCG			
57	*	F-WWMF	N376SC	N818BH	N707MT				
58	*	F-WWMG	N158EX	VH-CRQ	VH-CRW	VH-KRW	N37EA		
59	*	F-WWMH	N230QS						
60	*	F-WWMI	N100MB						
61	*	F-WWMJ	LX-NLK	VP-CBC	OO-FDG				
62	+	F-WWMK	N346PC						
63	+	F-WWML	OY-EJD	F-HPAD	9H-BEC				
64	*	F-WWMM	N493SF	N493S					
65	*	F-WWMN	CS-DFK						
66	+	F-WWMO	N822ST	N303QW	N318CL				
67	*	F-WWGA	OH-FOX	G-YFOX					
68	*	F-WWGC	N934ST	N360M					
69	*	F-WWGD	N56EL	N57EL	N47EL	N888WL			
70	*	F-WWGE	D-BOOK	N237BB					
71	*	F-WWGG	N71EL	N56EL	(N46EL)	N56EG	N904TF		
72	*	F-WWGH	N613GH	(N431GH)	N995GH	N172FJ			
73	*	F-WWGJ	N85MQ	N85M	N85MQ	N273SW			
74	*	F-WWGK	D-BAMM	N925BC					
75	*	F-WWGL	F-GUPH	OO-GML	F-GZLX	D-BTIG*			
76	*	F-WWGM	A6-SMS	F-WQBL	(D-BBED)	D-BIKA			
77	*	F-WWGN	N377EX	XA-LFA					
78	*	F-WWGO	(F-GOTF)	I-JETF	G-JETF	OE-HCB			
79	*	F-WWGP	N88HE	N886CE					
80	*	F-WWGQ	CS-DLB						
81	*	F-WWGR	N81EX	N89CE					
82	*	F-WWGS	VP-CMD	C-GSEC					
83	+	F-WWGT	N83EX	F-WWGT	N83EX	N283SL	N669HP		
84	*	F-WWGU	N522BD						
85	*	F-WWGV	N993GH						
86	*	F-WWGW	N223QS						
87	+	F-WWGX	N287F	C-GTPL					
88	*	F-WWGY	OE-HOT	M-ILES	G-LATE				
89	+	F-WWGZ	VP-CAM	M-XJOB	M-SNAP	N642TA	N542AP		
90	*	F-WWGC	N190EX	C-GOHB	C-GOAB				
91	*	F-WWGD	N91EX	[trialled with temporary winglets Jun06-Aug06]		N233QS			

FALCON 2000EX EASy/2000LX

C/n		Identities						
92	+	F-WWGG	N176CG					
93	*	F-WWGH	D-BFFB					
94	*	F-WWGI	N912MT	N912VV				
95	+	F-WWGJ	N168CE	N887CE	M-ROWL	M-SNER		
96	*	F-WWGN	5B-CKO	F-WWMA	5B-CKO			
97	*	F-WWGA	N12AR	N855DG				
98	*	F-WWGP	CS-DLC					
99	*	F-WWMA	PP-MJC					
100	*	F-WWMB	N310U					
101	+	F-WWMC	N204CW	M-ORAD				
102	*	F-WWMD	G-ITIG	CS-DTF	OE-IEN			
103	*	F-WWME	(OY-FPN)	OY-PNO	F-HIKJ	B-3211		
104	*	F-WWGE	TC-DGN					
105	*	F-WWGR	N994GP	M-JETZ				
106	+	F-WWGU	N771DV					
107	*	F-WWGV	N367BW	N267BW	N367BW	N612HT		
108	*	F-WWGW	I-JAMJ					
109	*	F-WWGX	CS-DLD					
110	*	F-WWMG	VP-BAK	M-STCO	N157AL			
111	*	F-WWMH	D-BASE	HB-IGU				
112	*	F-WWMI	N619SM					
113	*	F-WWMJ	VP-CMI	M-CIMO				
114	*	F-WWMK	F-GVNG	[fitted with mock Falcon 2000LX winglets 2007, later removed]		M-AMND	N671PB	N671PP
115	*	F-WWML	N232QS					
116	*	F-WWMM	N116EX	N72PS	N72PU	N80RP*		
117	*	F-WWMO	VT-VLN					
118	*	F-WWGC	D-BONN					
119	*	F-WWGD	N2000A	N62YC	[w/o in hangar collapse at Washington/Dulles, VA, 06Feb10; parted out by Alliance Air Parts, Oklahoma City, OK]			
120	*	F-WWGG	N333MX					
121	+	F-WWGI	N121EX	XA-CMM				
122	*	F-WWGF	N147G					
123	+	F-WWGJ	OO-PAP	N925AK	N1933G			
124	+	F-WWGK	N124EX	N888CE				
125	*	F-WWGM	(D-BONN)	VP-BVV	N125FJ	XA-JBT		
126	+	F-WWGO	N669PG	VP-BGI	C-FJOA	N810U		
127	*	F-WWGQ	CS-DLE					
128	+	F-WWGS	(VP-BOE)	M-CHEM				
129	+	F-WWGU	N129EX	C-GENW				
130	*	F-WWGA	N1JK					
131	+	F-WWGH	N131AG	N117AL	PT-FCS			
132	*	F-WWGN	G-OJAJ	OO-OFP	N899BC			
133	*	F-WWGP	"VP-BAH"+	[+ painted in error at completion centre]			VP-BRA	
134	*	F-WWGV	CS-DLF					
135	+	F-WWGE	N414TR	N820EC				
136	+	F-WWGF	TC-ATC	F-HLDB				
137	*	F-WWGG	N137EM	N119EM				
138	+	F-WWGI	N168AM	N880PC				
139	*	F-WWGZ	N470D	VP-CTT				
140	*	F-WWMA	OO-DFG	D-BHER*				
141	+	F-WWGK	G-WLVS	N267WB				
142	+	F-WWGO	N100KP	N500N	N623CT			
143	+	F-WWGR	(P4-LGM)	M-LJGI	N806DB	N805DB		
144	*	F-WWGW	CS-DLG					
145	+	F-WWMB	N345EX	N47WS	C-FDBJ	N345GA		
146	+	F-WWGH	N268DM	N785AD				
147	+	F-WWGU	N278DM	N786AD	N147CJ			
148	+	F-WWGE	M-YJET	N888MX				
149	*	F-WWGJ	CS-DLH					
150	+	F-WWGL	N150FJ	N772MC				
151	+	F-WWMD	N151EX	N2000A	N151EX	M-GOLX	N257AL	
152	+	F-WWGA	OE-HMR					
153	+	F-WWGC	VT-AYV					
154	+	F-WWGG	HB-JET	N94AM	N716GC			
155	+	F-WWGZ	(CS-DLH)	N155EX	CS-DLI	N606TJ	N609TJ	N274SW
156	+	F-WWME	OY-MHA	N156FJ	N500RR			
157	+	F-WWGQ	N157EX	(PT-FLX)	PR-NXG	N107RG		
158	+	F-WWGS	N234QS	N60FK				
159	+	F-WWGT	VT-TDT					
160	+	F-WWGH	(G-CNGM)	OY-CKH	N552GR			
161	+	F-WWGX	(G-LSMB)	OY-MGO	F-....			
162	+	F-WWMB	N162NS	VH-RAM	OO-PSE			
163	+	F-WWMC	N480D	N209SU	N500R			
164	+	F-WWMF	N64EX	PP-PPN				
165	+	F-WWGL	N204CE					
166	+	F-WWGN	(M-PNRE)	HS-RBR				
167	+	F-WWGP	N167EX	C-GSLU				
168	+	F-WWGU	(N168NS)	N460SJ				
169	+	F-WWGY	VT-BRK					
170	+	F-WWMG	N404UK	(N170LX)	N2000A	N515CF		
171	*	F-WWMH	N449SA					
172	+	F-WWMI	N75EK					
173	+	(F-WWMJ)	F-WWGI	M-ALRV				
174	+	(F-WWMK)	F-WWGK	N250QS	N174LX	N716CG	N716CQ	
175	+	(F-WWML)	F-WWGO	N175EX	N747RL	N747KL		
176	+	(F-WWMM)	F-WWGF	N609LS	N376SF			
177	+	(F-WWMN)	F-WWGQ	(N177NS)	M-DARA	N900FS		
178	+	(F-WWMO)	F-WWGS	N429SA	PP-AUL			
179	+	F-WWMA	N179EX	PR-OBE				
180	+	F-WWMJ	TC-SGO					
181	+	F-WWMK	(N928GC)+	[+ntu marks worn at completion centre]			LX-EVM	
182	+	F-WWML	G-EDHY	ZA-EVA	N197KA	N197JK	N300FS	
183	+	F-WWGW	N183FJ	VH-WIO	N183FJ	N928WK		
184	+	F-WWMC	N9895					
185	+	F-WWMM	HB-JGF	F-HEFG	N49HT			
186	+	F-WWMN	B-MAZ					

FALCON 2000EX EASy/2000LX

C/n		Identities					
187	+	F-WWMO	N781EX	PR-ETY			
188	+	F-WWGE	HB-JGG				
189	+	F-WWGL	N720WY				
190	+	F-WWGP	EI-TDV	N810ET			
191	+	F-WWMD	N257QS	F-GVEL	I-PBRB		
192	+	F-WWGA	(N192LX)	(OY-GLO)	(D-BSKY)	B-8025	N497DC
193	+	F-WWGD	TC-MRK				
194	+	F-WWGG	PH-CTH				
195	+	F-WWGK	F-GVFX	OY-GKJ			
196	+	F-WWGO	OY-ZWO	OO-VRO			
197	+	F-WWMF	N325B				
198	+	F-WWGR	EC-LGV				
199	+	F-WWGS	OE-HTO	M-FTHD			
200	+	F-WWME	M-ABAK	SX-MLA	F-HPKR	N501RR	
201	+	F-WWMG	D-BEKY				
202	+	F-WWMA	PP-MMF				
203	+	F-WWMH	N203LX	N801DE	N901FH		
204	+	F-WWJN	I-FEDN				
205	+	F-WWJO	N205LX	N769JW			
206	+	F-WWJP	N696SB				
207	+	F-WWJQ	(M-TANG)	N741SP			
208	+	F-WWJR	N1903W				
209	+	F-WWJS	(N209LX)	I-UCBT	PR-RNY		
210	+	F-WWJT	(D-BEKY)	N410SG			
211	+	F-WWJU	N988DV				
212	+	F-WWJV	ZS-SAB				
213	+	F-WWJX	I-MOFI				
214	+	F-WWJY	F-GZBJ	VQ-BIJ			
215	+	F-WWJZ	N215FJ	RP-C9215			
216	+	F-WWGB	N70FA	M-IKEL	N201PG		
217	+	F-WWGJ	N262MW	N58MW			
218	+	F-WWGL	N218LX	PR-JJR			
219	+	F-WWGM	N733H				
220	+	F-WWGT	M-IKAT				
221	+	F-WWGD	TC-LIA				
222	+	F-WWGE	N12LX				
223	+	F-WWGH	N223LX	PR-OLD	N885FJ	PR-DLX	
224	+	F-WWGI	N917JC				
225	+	F-WWGS	OY-SKL	N225FJ	N790R		
226	+	F-WWGV	N801WW				
227	+	F-WWGY	N377SC				
228	+	F-WWGZ	(OY-ZWO)	F-HBIP	N228BL		
229	+	F-WWJN	N1C				
230	+	F-WWJO	TC-MAA	F-HSAM			
231	+	F-WWGF	F-GTDA	F-WTDA	France 231/F-RAFC		
232	+	F-WWGX	C-GOHB				
233	+	F-WWJP	N448AS	N560US			
234	+	F-WWJR	VP-CAM	D-BLTA			
235	+	F-WWJT	(D-BOBI)	N2000A	(N235EX)	N733A	
236	+	F-WWJU	N36TH	PR-ALS			
237	+	F-WWMG	F-GTDK	F-WTDK	France 237/F-RAFD		
238	+	F-WWMC	N532CC				
239	+	F-WWMD	I-PBRP	N919BA	N1897S		
240	+	F-WWMH	M-STCO				
241	+	F-WWMJ	N688CP				
242	+	F-WWMK	N242FJ	VP-CJS	N242FJ	XA-FLC	
243	+	F-WWML	OO-GHE				
244	+	F-WWMO	HB-JKL				
245	+	F-WWMM	OE-HAM	9H-HAM			
246	+	F-WWMF	D-BOBI				
247	+	F-WWGK	PP-NPP				
248	+	F-WWJS	N326EW				
249	+	F-WWJZ	N620V				
250	+	F-WWME	N86HD				
251	+	F-WWGC	N251FJ	XA-BLZ			
252	+	F-WWGR	PP-AMK				
253	+	F-WWGO	F-HOME	M-TINK	M-FIVE	F-HLDS	B-1999
254	+	F-WWGJ	F-WWGT	PR-MDB	N80BL		
255	+	F-WWGL	N255FJ	N2000A	N544S		
256	+	F-WWJX	HB-JFI				
257	+	F-WWGB	G-WWFC				
258	+	F-WWMI	N258FJ	C-FVMW			
259	+	F-WWGW	N259EX	VH-WIO			
260	+	F-WWJY	OE-HEY				
261	+	F-WWGD	G-VPCM				
262	+	F-WWGY	N383MH	N905TF			
263	+	F-WWMN	D-BVHA				
264	+	F-WWGE	P4-DBB				
265	+	F-WWJN	N885A				
266	+	F-WWJO	N409GB				
267	+	F-WWMK	N325AP				
268	+	F-WWMG	N268LX	N65NY			
269	+	F-WWGZ	F-HLXS	G-PULA			
270	+	F-WWMF	N918MJ				
271	+	F-WWJS	D-BERT				
272	+	F-WWGH	N70TF				
273	+	F-WWJP	N231TJ				
274	+	F-WWMH	N327RX				
275	+	F-WWGR	G-FLXS				
276	+	F-WWGK	OE-HTR				
277	+	F-WWGJ	D-BOOK				
278	+	F-WWGX	N881Q				
279	+	F-WWJT	N666TR				
280	+	F-WWMJ	PT-FKY				
281	+	F-WWMA	OY-CKK				

FALCON 2000EX EASy/2000LX

C/n		Identities			
282	+	F-WWMI	F-HLPM		
283	+	F-WWGB	N225FD	N225DF	
284	+	F-WWGQ	(PT-FKY)	N482JC	N515AN
285	+	F-WWJY	N58GG		
286	+	F-WWJV	C-GOFS		
287	+	F-WWMC	N844UP		
288	+	F-WWJQ	F-HJCD		
289	+	F-WWMB	XA-DFN		
290	+	F-WWGD	F-HALG		
291	+	F-WWGY	N84SV		
292	+	F-WWGV	N78KN		
293	+	F-WWGT	N1HS		
294	+	F-WWMG	TC-SMC		
295	+	F-WWGG	N812RX		
296	+	F-WWGS	F-HLPN		
297	+	F-WWMN	M-AERO		
298	+	F-WWGN	PH-PKF		
299	+	F-WWJU	N133RL		
300	+	F-WWJS	N307PS		
301	+	F-WWJX	G-FLLY		
302	+	F-WWJP	LN-RTN		
303	+	F-WWGA	N84PJ		
304	+	F-WWGE	N14GD		
305	+	F-WWGF	N488GB		
306	+	F-WWGI	(N2000A)		
307	+	F-WWGJ	N87HD		
308	+	F-WWGK	XA-CHD		
309	+	F-WWGL	PR-VEN		
310	+	F-WWGR	N81SV		
311	+	F-WWGW	OY-MGA		
312	+	F-WWGB	N541Z		
313	+	F-WWGC			
314	+	F-WWGQ			
315	+	F-WWGX	N376SC		
316	+	F-WWGZ			
317	+	F-WWMA			
318	+	F-WWMB			
319	+	F-WWMC			
320	+	F-WWME			
321					
322	+	F-WWMH			
323					
324					
325					
326					
327					
328					
329					
330					
331					
332					
333					
334					
335					
336					
337					
338					
339					
340					

DASSAULT FALCON 2000S

C/n	Identities			
701	F-WWGP	[ff 17Feb11]		
702	F-WWJV	N702FJ	N515PV	
703	F-WWJQ	F-HMCG	N957CP	
704	F-WWMA	TC-TOS		
705	F-WWGQ	G-TTJF		
706	F-WWGT	LY-GVS		
707	F-WWGG	ES-TEP	F-HCRK	M-LCFC	HS-KPA
708	F-WWGV	N748RE		
709	F-WWGS	N1824S		
710	F-WWJR	XA-KAR		
711	F-WWGN	M-ABGP	N775TM	N491N
712	F-WWGA	PT-TRJ		
713	F-WWJU	C-GMII		
714	F-WWMC	N714RK	[for Republic of Korea Air Force]	
715	F-WWMD	OY-GWK		
716	F-WWGF	N716FJ	HB-JGD	
717	F-WWMO	N427MJ		
718	F-WWGL	SP-ARG	SP-ARK	
719	F-WWGI	XA-GMO		
720	F-WWMM	N720NP	HK-5068X	HK-5068
721	F-WWJX	B-8210		
722	F-WWJZ	N498DC		
723	F-WWME	TC-VGP		
724	F-WWGU	N657DB		
725	F-WWGM	OY-SWO		
726	F-WWGC	N726RK	[cx 22Dec14 to Republic of Korea Air Force]	
727	F-WWML	N845UP		
728	F-WWGO	N728FJ		
729	F-WWJR	N846UP		
730	F-WWJO	N184G		
731	F-WWJN	N410GS		
732	F-WWGH	N278GS		
733	F-WWGM	N639M		
734	F-WWMD	N995G		
735	F-WW..	EC-MLA*		
736				
737				
738				
739				
740				
741				
742				
743				
744				
745				
746				
747				
748				
749				
750				

DASSAULT FALCON 7X

The Falcon 7X was originally known as the Falcon FNX.

C/n	Identities				
1	F-WFBW	[rolled out 15Feb05; ff 05May05]			
2	F-WTDA	[ff 05Jly05]	(F-HNFG)	HB-JSS	
3	F-WSKY	[ff 20Sep05]	VP-BIL	N56CL	
4	F-WWUA	[ff 08Jun06]	HB-JSZ	F-HDPO	N570RF
5	F-WWUB	VP-BGG	F-GZLP	N705FJ	F-HFDA
6	F-WWUC	(N200L)	N607X	PR-WRM	N191ST
7	F-WWUD	N70FL	N2016A		
8	F-WWUE	N999BE			
9	F-WWUF	(N9707X)+	[+ ntu marks worn at completion centre]	VP-BVY	TC-YHK
10	F-WWUG	XA-MAR			
11	F-WWUH	VP-BAR	M-ALMA		
12	F-WWUI	HB-JSO	N250LG		
13	F-WWUJ	N907SB	N713L		
14	F-WWUK	VP-BZE			
15	F-WWUL	CS-TLY			
16	F-WWUM	(HB-JSS)+	[+ ntu marks worn at completion centre]	N7707X	
17	F-WWUN	HB-JST			
18	F-WWUO	N273JC			
19	F-WWUP	F-GYDA	F-WWUP	F-HAKA	CS-DTS	N221HJ
20	F-WWUQ	M-SVNX	OH-FFD	RA-09007	
21	F-WWUR	VP-BEH			
22	F-WWUS	PR-DNZ			
23	F-WWZK	N188SW			
24	F-WWZL	N171EX			
25	F-WWZM	N8000E			
26	F-WWZN	N7MR			
27	F-WWZO	VQ-BFN			
28	F-WWZP	TC-GMM	F-HCRM		
29	F-WWZQ	N671WB			
30	F-WWZR	CS-DSA	LX-DSA	M-OPDE	
31	F-WWZS	N786CS			
32	F-WWZT	XA-CXW			
33	F-WWZU	N7X			
34	F-WWZV	(F-GVRB)	I-AFIT		
35	F-WWZW	(N100HC)+	[+ ntu marks worn at completion centre]	N207TR	N82RP
36	F-WWZX	G-SRDG			
37	F-WWZY	HB-JSI			
38	F-WWZZ	N55LC			
39	F-WWVK	N900DW			
40	F-WWVL	M-ROLL	SE-DJL		
41	F-WWVM	N741FJ	OO-NAD		
42	F-WWVN	F-HCCX	F-WHLV	OE-IVA	M-YORK
43	F-WWVO	CS-DSB			
44	F-WWVP	HB-JLK			
45	F-WWVQ	B-8029			
46	F-WWVR	VQ-BAA			
47	F-WWVS	(CS-DSC)	RA-09009	F-HVIB	
48	F-WWVT	N748FJ	N138BT	VQ-BVS	
49	F-WWUA	VT-RGX			
50	F-WWUB	C-GMGX			
51	F-WWUC	N817X	N9997X		
52	F-WWUD	G-CNUK	N740AC		
53	F-WWVU	N12U			
54	F-WWVV	OY-JDE	F-HLIV	M-SCOT	
55	F-WWVX	OE-LLL	N54TN	PR-CSE	
56	F-WWVY	LX-ZXP			
57	F-WWVZ	OO-AAA	N157BR	C-GCUL	
58	F-WWHA	VQ-BSN			
59	F-WWHB	G-PVHT	SE-DJK		
60	F-WWHC	CS-DTD			
61	F-WWHD	B-8026			
62	F-WWHE	N62FJ	N11HD	N4VF	
63	F-WWHF	N763FJ	B-8027		
64	F-WWHH	VQ-BSO			
65	F-WWHK	C-FAWZ			
66	F-WWHL	(D-AJAB)	OH-FFF	CS-DVX	
67	F-WWUE	HB-JGI			
68	F-WWUG	F-GJLQ	France 68/F-RAFA		
69	F-WWUH	G-CGGN	OH-FFI	OY-FFI	
70	F-WWUJ	C-GRGM			
71	F-WWHM	F-HCLS	RA-09010		
72	F-WWHN	N312P	N312PY	M-HKND	
73	F-WWHO	N787AD	N144AD*		
74	F-WWHP	N906NB	N900NB		
75	F-WWHQ	N906SB			
76	F-WWHR	HB-JSN			
77	F-WWHS	D-ACGN	D-APLC		
78	F-WWHT	SE-DJC			
79	F-WWHU	HZ-SPAG			
80	F-WWUF	HB-JOB			
81	F-WWUI	I-JAMI			
82	F-WWUK	M-YNNS	M-YNNG	N317SK	
83	F-WWUL	VQ-BSP			
84	F-WWUM	VQ-BHA			
85	F-WWUN	OY-VIK			
86	F-WWUS	F-GUJC	France 86/F-RAFB		
87	F-WWUO	HZ-SPAH			
88	F-WWUP	N333KG	LX-TQJ	N887XF	
89	F-WWUQ	N966H			
90	F-WWUR	5N-FGU			
91	F-WWZL	M-MNBB			
92	F-WWZM	HZ-OFC6	CS-DSD		
93	F-WWZN	VQ-BGG			

FALCON 7X

C/n	Identities					
94	F-WWZQ	I-FFRR				
95	F-WWZT	OY-SNZ				
96	F-WWZU	M-SCMG				
97	F-WWZX	LX-MES	M-ZJBT			
98	F-WWNA	(PP-AKT)	N407KT	OY-TSS		
99	F-WWNB	N199FJ	N722AZ			
100	F-WWNC	N15FX	N714K			
101	F-WWND	N940EX	B-8028			
102	F-WWNE	PH-AJX				
103	F-WWNF	N150BC				
104	F-WWVO	A6-SMS	VP-CTG			
105	F-WWVR	G-VITA	G-DYXH	B-8213		
106	F-WWZK	PR-BTG	N106FJ	VP-CSG	M-ABGO	VP-CSG	F-HMOD
107	F-WWZR	A6-MAF				
108	F-WWZS	VP-CMX	M-ABFM	XT-EBO	F-HLTI	
109	F-WWVL	SX-GRC				
110	F-WWVM	M-CELT				
111	F-WWVN	SX-DCV	G-IONX			
112	F-WWVK	HZ-SPAI				
113	F-WWVP	VP-CSJ	F-WHLU	F-HVON	VQ-BSF	
114	F-WWZO	G-UMKA	9H-MAK			
115	F-WWZW	N900JG				
116	F-WWZY	HB-JFN				
117	F-WWZV	EC-LLV				
118	F-WWZZ	LX-AMB				
119	F-WWHA	F-HSAS				
120	F-WWHB	OO-IDY				
121	F-WWHC	OY-EKC				
122	F-WWHE	VP-CIG				
123	F-WWHF	G-SVNX				
124	F-WWHH	OO-EJA				
125	F-WWHL	OE-ILM	D-AFSX	OE-IMF		
126	F-WWHS	5N-FGV				
127	F-WWHT	V5-GON				
128	F-WWHU	G-ITIM	M-INER			
129	F-WWUA	SE-DJD				
130	F-WWUB	N85DN				
131	F-WWUC	N950X				
132	F-WWUD	VQ-BLP				
133	F-WWUG	N733LX	B-8023			
134	F-WWUH	F-HECD				
135	F-WWUL	VQ-BNT				
136	F-WWUM	HZ-SPAJ				
137	F-WWUN	N111HZ				
138	F-WWUS	M-OMAN				
139	F-WWVQ	P4-GIS				
140	F-WWVS	M-AKOL				
141	F-WWVU	VP-CDY				
142	F-WWVV	N142FJ	B-8207	N577JF		
143	F-WWVX	VP-CSW				
144	F-WWVY	F-GYBJ	B-8206			
145	F-WWVZ	N577CF				
146	F-WWHO	PR-PCT	N906TF			
147	F-WWHK	N147FJ	VP-CSX			
148	F-WWHN	G-STMT				
149	F-WWHP	B-8201	N996MS			
150	F-WWHM	N887X				
151	F-WWHQ	N151NS	C-FLKX	C-FBNS		
152	F-WWZN	OO-LMG				
153	F-WWUO	(CS-DTT)	N66DD			
154	F-WWUF	CS-DTT				
155	F-WWHD	OY-CLS				
156	F-WWUE	M-MNCC				
157	F-WWUK	B-8215				
158	F-WWZM	N747RL				
159	F-WWNC	N159FJ	B-8202			
160	F-WWUQ	D-AFPR				
161	F-WWZQ	HB-JSA				
162	F-WWUI	N771RS	PP-RFA	N17XX		
163	F-WWNB	N163FJ				
164	F-WWZX	CS-DSC				
165	F-WWZP	(VP-CYL)	PR-YVL			
166	F-WWVR	F-HSTF	OO-ABC			
167	F-WWVO	LX-USM				
168	F-WWZL	N268FJ	M-DTBP			
169	F-WWUP	N783SL				
170	F-WWUR	N889AB				
171	F-WWVT	PP-CFJ				
172	F-WWZR	N1216K	C-FMHL			
173	F-WWNE	N173CN				
174	F-WWZS	N988NW				
175	F-WWNA	(M-ALAA)	(M-LMAA)	VQ-BTV		
176	F-WWVL	N76FJ	C-GLXC			
177	F-WWZT	B-8209	N166CK			
178	F-WWNF	M-LJGI				
179	F-WWVM	D-ALIL				
180	F-WWVN	N191MD				
181	F-WWVK	HB-JSM				
182	F-WWZY	LX-FDA				
183	F-WWZV	N183MK	VH-MQK	M-GMKM		
184	F-WWHC	SX-JET				
185	F-WWZZ	Ecuador FAE-052				
186	F-WWHE	M-EDIA	M-YJET			
187	F-WWHH	PP-OSM				
188	F-WWHT	F-HVBL				

FALCON 7X

C/n	Identities			
189	F-WWZO	B-8218		
190	F-WWVP	TC-OIL		
191	F-WWUB	RA-09616		
192	F-WWHS	N192FJ	XA-JHS	
193	F-WW..	[test marks either F-WWHL or F-WWUD]		B-8203
194	F-WWUC	HB-JSL		
195	F-WWHU	A6-SMS		
196	F-WW..	[test marks either F-WWHL or F-WWUD]		OE-IRR
197	F-WWHB	LX-TQJ		
198	F-WWUS	OY-FWO		
199	F-WWUA	B-8216		
200	F-WWHA	M-ABFX	3A-MGA	
201	F-WWUH	(PT-YVL)	VP-CUH	
202	F-WWVX	N977GS		
203	F-WWHF	N24TH		
204	F-WWUL	VP-CBY		
205	F-WWUM	PP-VEL		
206	F-WWZU	N559AM		
207	F-WWHR	F-HGHF	(OO-AAM)	M-RTFS
208	F-WWZK	N817X		
209	F-WWVQ	B-8205		
210	F-WWND	VP-CGS		
211	F-WWUG	N496AC		
212	F-WWVV	B-8211		
213	F-WWVZ	OO-TOI	M-MNAA	
214	F-WWHO	PR-NAK		
215	F-WWZN	N715FJ		
216	F-WWZW	M-ARVY		
217	F-WWHD	VH-CRW		
218	F-WWUE	HB-JSE		
219	F-WWZQ	VP-CBG	T7-CBG	
220	F-WWVS	N120FJ	VP-CJS	
221	F-WWZX	N487C		
222	F-WWUF	N37TY		
223	F-WWVY	F-HEXR		
224	F-WWHN	M-FALZ		
225	F-WWZP	TC-SZA		
226	F-WWUP	VP-CLS		
227	F-WWHK	TC-MMM		
228	F-WWUN	9H-ZSN		
229	F-WWHM	M-ISRK	LX-ISR	
230	F-WWHQ	M-IAMI		
231	F-WWUO	OH-WIX		
232	F-WWZM	TN-ELS		
233	F-WWUI			
234	F-WWVO	(F-HLBG)	N814TP	
235	F-WWNE	N606TJ		
236	F-WWZR	OY-EJD		
237	F-WWVT	PP-DBS		
238	F-WWNC	OE-IPW		
239	F-WWHP			
240	F-WWVM	N269BK		
241	F-WWVK	N2237X		
242	F-WWUJ	LX-LMF		
243	F-WWUR			
244	F-WWVL	N1227W		
245	F-WWHA	P4-SCM		
246	F-WWUQ			
247	F-WWVN			
248	F-WWVP	N347BD		
249	F-WWHC	N343MG		
250	F-WWUC	N998SS		
251	F-WWNF	B-8217		
252	F-WWZS	XA-GNI		
253	F-WWHE	RA-09601		
254	F-WWUB	TC-KMR		
255	F-WWVR	N716CG		
256	F-WWHT	RA-09602		
257	F-WWHH	(PP-CSC)	VP-CZS	
258	F-WWHU	F-HIPK		
259	F-WWVU	PH-TLP		
260	F-WWZL			
261	F-WWZT	XA-GOR		
262	F-WWZV	N770LM		
263	F-WWUD			
264	F-WWHB			
265	F-WWUS	N343AP		
266	F-WWUL	M-TINK		
267	F-WWUA	VP-CMW		
268	F-WWUE	VP-CRS		
269	F-WWUF			
270	F-WWUG			
271	F-WWUH			
272	F-WWUJ			
273	F-WWUK			
274				
275				
276				
277	F-WWUP			
278				
279				
280				
281				
282				
283				

C/n	Identities
284	
285	
286	
287	
288	
289	
290	

DASSAULT FALCON 8X

C/n	Identities	
401	F-WWQA	[rolled out 17Dec14; ff 6Feb15]
402	F-WWQB	[ff 30Mar15]
403	F-WWQC	[ff 11May15]
404	F-WWQD	
405	F-WWQE	
406	F-WWQF	
407	F-WWQG	
408		
409		
410		
411		
412		
413		
414		
415		
416		
417		
418		
419		
420		
421		
422		
423		
424		
425		
426		
427		
428		
429		
430		

ECLIPSE AVIATION ECLIPSE 500

C/n	Identities			
EX500-100	N500EA	[rolled out Albuquerque-Double Eagle II 13Jly02; ff 26Aug02; retired Oct03, tt 55hrs]		
EX500-101	(N502EA)	"N500EA"	[Not completed following decision to change from Williams EJ22 to P&W PWF610F engines; used as display exhibit]	
EX500-102	[Not built following decision to change from Williams EJ22 to P&W PWF610F engines]			
EX500-103	N502EA	[ff 14Apr05]		
EX500-104	[static test airframe completed 11May05]			
EX500-105	[fatigue test airframe completed 20Dec05]			
EX500-106	N505EA	[Beta test aircraft 1; ff 09Jly05]		
EX500-107	N506EA	[Beta test aircraft 2; ff 24Aug05]		
EX500-108	N503EA	[ff 31Dec04]		
EX500-109	N504EA	[ff 21Apr05]		
000001	N508JA			
000002	N126DJ	N102TE	N147KN	N11PC
000003	N816KD			
000004	N229BW	N403LB	N440NE	
000005	N504RS			
000006	N109DJ	N106TE	N375KD	
000007	N110DJ	(N107TE)	TC-KEA	
000008	N941NC			
000009	N513EA			
000010	N500VK	XB-ODY		
000011	N777VE	N80NE		
000012	N651FC	N61HF		
000013	N317BH	N770TE	N878BW	
000014	N705PT			
000015	N515MP			
000016	N15ND	N320LA	N58KY	
000017	N17AE			
000018	N875NA	N140NE		
000019	N519EJ			
000020	N115DJ	N220TE	N312BL	
000021	N116DJ	N521TE	N800TE	
000022	N119DJ	N522TE	N22NJ	
000023	N130DJ	N223TE	2-LIFE	
000024	N561EA			
000025	N546BW			
000026	N612KB			
000027	N502LT	N563MJ		
000028	N963JG			
000029	N55BX			
000030	N768JF			
000031	N531EA			
000032	N80TF			
000033	N131DJ	N133TE	N51GJ	
000034	N132DJ	N134TE	N760NE	N124KK*
000035	N134DJ	N135TE	N889CM	
000036	N135DJ	N136TE		
000037	N136DJ	N37TE	PR-CCA	
000038	N112EA			
000039	N858GS			
000040	N444RL			
000041	N541LB			
000042	N168TT	[w/o Nome, AK, 01Jun11; parted out Henderson, NV]		
000043	N62RC			
000044	N489JC	N53WA		
000045	N500CD			
000046	N6100			
000047	N218JT			
000048	N570RG			
000049	N549AF			
000050	N456MF			
000051	N500UK			
000052	N502ET			
000053	N514EA	[cx 08Mar13, wfu]		
000054	N139DJ	N54TE		
000055	N141DJ	N255TE	N99XG	
000056	N142DJ	N156TE	(N868SB)	N838SB
000057	N145DJ	(N57TE)	N411VP	(AP-...)
000058	N146DJ	N158TE		
000059	N147DJ	N159TE	N322PL	
000060	N429CC			
000061	N148DJ	(N61TE)	N434MT	
000062	N150DJ	N62TE		
000063	N778VW			
000064	N717LK			
000065	N23PJ	N65TE	N384TC	
000066	N370P			
000067	N568PB			
000068	(N370P)	N615RH		
000069	N71MT			
000070	N570EA			
000071	N152DJ	N508JP		
000072	N153DJ	N94GA	N843TE	
000073	N156DJ	N173TE	N505XX	N73EJ
000074	N158DJ	(N74TE)	N179TD	
000075	N575CC			
000076	N576EA			
000077	N160DJ	N77TE		
000078	N161DJ	N78TE	N45DJ	
000079	N162DJ	(N168TE)		
000080	N580WC			
000081	N163DJ	N565FP		
000082	N382EA			
000083	N38DA			
000084	N509JA			

ECLIPSE 500

C/n	Identities			
000085	N778TC			
000086	N990NA			
000087	N50EJ			
000088	N457TB			
000089	N44EJ	N316CP		
000090	N2486B			
000091	N54KJ			
000092	N355BM			
000093	(N457TB)	N233MT	N7601B*	
000094	N417CG			
000095	N317DJ	N995TE	N581VC	
000096	N464PG			
000097	N502TS			
000098	N598EA			
000099	N911MX			
000100	N9922F			
000101	N539RM			
000102	N277G			
000103	N333MY	[w/o 30Jul08 West Chester/Brandywine, PA; parted out by White Inds, Bates City, MO]		
000104	N117EA			
000105	N522DK			
000106	N516EA			
000107	N706PT			
000108	N812MJ	XA-...		
000109	N777ZY			
000110	N501DX			
000111	N175JE			
000112	N112EJ			
000113	N717HD			
000114	N197AR			
000115	N727HD			
000116	N75EA			
000117	N117UH			
000118	N105LB			
000119	N815WT			
000120	N27052			
000121	N855MS			
000122	N164MW			
000123	N696NA	N352BB		
000124	N227G			
000125	N370EA			
000126	N953JB			
000127	N261DC			
000128	N528EA			
000129	N500DG			
000130	N322JG	N411TE	N58VL	
000131	N67NV	ZS-YTC		
000132	N964S			
000133	N21EK			
000134	N800EJ			
000135	N3MT			
000136	N136EA	(N326LA)		
000137	N36FD			
000138	N100VA			
000139	N500MM			
000140	N100MZ	N561MJ		
000141	N504TC			
000142	N2711H	ZS-DKS	[w/o nr Swellendam, South Africa, 07Dec15]	
000143	N533DK			
000144	N545MA			
000145	N145EA			
000146	N146EA			
000147	N414TW			
000148	N148LG			
000149	N149EA			
000150	N920GB			
000151	N85SM			
000152	N113EA	EC-LHC	N113EA	
000153	N800AZ			
000154	N66BX			
000155	N114EA	EC-LET	N114EA	
000156	N234EA	N562MJ		
000157	N500CE			
000158	N500ZH			
000159	N727CW			
000160	N2YU			
000161	N448HC			
000162	N224ZQ			
000163	N63AD			
000164	N884AM			
000165	N669CM	N450RB		
000166	N23FK			
000167	N800JR			
000168	N568EA	(N335LA)		
000169	N166EA			
000170	N170EA			
000171	N58EH			
000172	N964JG			
000173	N173PD			
000174	N21YP	N21YR		
000175	N512MB			
000176	N9900R			
000177	N177EA	D-ILAC		
000178	N721MA	N721NA	N48KY	
000179	N220BW	N207TB		

ECLIPSE 500

C/n	Identities			
000180	N712WG			
000181	N99KP			
000182	N177CK			
000183	N555EJ			
000184	N118EA	EC-LII	N118EA	
000185	N500FB	(N808KD)		
000186	N204ZQ			
000187	N187EA			
000188	N652FC			
000189	N435NF			
000190	N190CK	TC-ATS		
000191	N678PS			
000192	N61DT			
000193	N193EA	N125DB		
000194	N70EJ			
000195	N227LS			
000196	N508CP			
000197	N218G			
000198	N888DZ	T7-AEB		
000199	N165DJ	N120EA	(N477JN)	
000200	N166DJ	N119EA		
000201	N167DJ	N201EA		
000202	N169DJ	N202EA		
000203	N883LC			
000204	N607LM			
000205	N653FC	N740DM		
000206	N977VH			
000207	N207EA			
000208	N55TJ			
000209	N209EA			
000210	N140EA	N160FF		
000211	N500VH			
000212	N212EA			
000213	N888ZY			
000214	N301MK			
000215	N762DL	(N792DL)		
000216	N375ET			
000217	N7FY			
000218	N142EA	N165DL		
000219	N219EA			
000220	N724ML	N18BM		
000221	N666TM			
000222	N161BB			
000223	N141EA			
000224	N722TD			
000225	N5005	N646WT		
000226	N226BR	T7-AEA		
000227	N654FC	(N227UH)		
000228	N478F			
000229	N229EA			
000230	N256DP			
000231	N619RJ			
000232	N707ES	PR-SDD*		
000233	N869AW			
000234	N461N			
000235	N747LG			
000236	N67LP			
000237	N828PA			
000238	N989RF			
000239	N867K			
000240	N929KD			
000241	N279E			
000242	N23VA			
000243	N121G			
000244	N20KS			
000245	N853TC			
000246	N144EA	D-INDY		
000247	N207WM	N287WM		
000248	N889BW			
000249	N29MR			
000250	N163BB			
000251	N147EA			
000252	N214MS			
000253	N427X			
000254	N618SR	N290JP		
000255	N49PL			
000256	N375SH			
000257	N257K			
000258	N257AK			
000259	N84UR			
000260	N877PM			
000261	N159EA	N985AS	N261TD	
000262	N511ED	N262DJ		
000263	(N522EA)	[aircraft not completed; components used in Eclipse 550 c/n 550-0263]		
000264	(N29SS)	[aircraft not completed; components used in Eclipse 550 c/n 550-0264]		
000265	(N767PW)	[aircraft not completed; components used in Eclipse 550 c/n 550-0265]		
000266	N143EA	N263CA		
000267	N533GT			

Production complete following the liquidation of Eclipse Aviation in February 2009. Work had begun on the following aircraft, most with N-numbers assigned, but they were not completed:

000268	(N106WH)	[components used in Eclipse 550 c/n 550-0268]
000269	(N500YD)	[components used in Eclipse 550 c/n 550-0269]
000270	(N202JG)	[components used in Eclipse 550 c/n 550-0270]
000271		[components used in Eclipse 550 c/n 550-0271]

C/n	Identities		
000272	(N444EJ)	[components used in Eclipse 550 c/n 550-0272]	
000273	[components used in Eclipse 550 c/n 550-0273]		
000274	(N610PW)	[components used in Eclipse 550 c/n 550-0274]	
000275	(N89RF)	[components used in Eclipse 550 c/n 550-0275]	
000276	[components used in Eclipse 550 c/n 550-0276]		
000277	(N510JA)	[components used in Eclipse 550 c/n 550-0277]	
000278	(N278JC)	[components used in Eclipse 550 c/n 550-0278]	
000279	(N10HH)	[components used in Eclipse 550 c/n 550-0279]	
000280	(N502BH)	[components used in Eclipse 550 c/n 550-0280]	
000281	[components intended for Eclipse 550 c/n 550-0281 but not completed]		
000282	[components used in Eclipse 550 c/n 550-0282]		
000283	[components used in Eclipse 550 c/n 550-0283]		
000284	[components used in Eclipse 550 c/n 550-0284]		
000297	(N79EA)	[aircraft not built]	

ECLIPSE AEROSPACE ECLIPSE 550

New company Eclipse Aerospace resumed Eclipse production with the model 550 in June 2012, being the Eclipse 500 airframe with uprated avionics.

C/n	Identities		
550-0263	(N263EJ)	N550LJ	N550AD
550-0264	N279EJ	N264EJ	N229BW
550-0265	N265EA	N656FP	
550-0268	N268EJ	N268EM	
550-0269	N285EA	N269EJ	D-ILAT
550-0270	(N270EJ)	N550UZ	
550-0271	N271EJ	N80WP	
550-0272	N272EJ		
550-0273	(N273EJ)	N771MT	
550-0274	N274EJ	N288JR	
550-0275	N275EJ	N113HX	
550-0276	N276EJ	N322BH	
550-0277	N277EJ	N317SA	
550-0278	N278EJ	N146HA	
550-0279	N279EJ		
550-0280	N280EJ	N450NE	
550-0281	(N281EJ)	[fuselage noted on production line Sep13 but not completed]	
550-0282	N282EJ	N826ES	
550-0283	N283EJ	N777VE	
550-0284	N284EJ	N284BG	
550-1001	N550F	[first Eclipse 550 built from 'scratch']	
550-1002	N150NE		
550-1003	N160NE	OE-FMO	
550-1004	N170NE	D-ILAV	
550-1005	N190NE		
550-1006	N200NE		
550-1007			
550-1008			
550-1009			
550-1010			
550-1011			
550-1012			

EMBRAER EMB-500 PHENOM 100

C/n	Identities			
50099801	PP-XPH	[rolled out 16Jun07; ff 26Jul07; wfu, preserved Rio de Janeiro/Jacarepagua, Brazil]		
50000001	PP-XOM	[ff 26Sep07]		
50000002	PP-XOJ	[ff 21Dec07]		
50000003	PP-XOH	[ff 26Mar08]		
50000004	PP-XOG			
50000005	PP-XON	PP-SGF		
50000006	PP-XOO	N131ML	N175EW	N580JH
50000007	PP-XOQ	PR-DDO		
50000008	PP-XOR	N82DU		
50000009	PP-XPD	N26SH	C-FLOX	
50000010	PP-XPE	N673DC		
50000011	PP-XPF	N68ER		
50000012	PP-XPG	N168FG	N6DQ	N168FG	N933MA
50000013	PT-ZYA	N76EM		
50000014	PT-ZYB	(N777SG)	Pakistan V-4102	
50000015	PT-ZYC	N100PZ	N247SK	
50000016	PT-ZYD	N484JH		
50000017	PT-ZYE	Pakistan V-4101		
50000018	PT-ZYF	N600AS	N665AS	
50000019	PT-ZYG	N458LM		
50000020	PT-ZYH	N73DB		
50000021	PT-ZYI	N300LJ		
50000022	PT-ZYT	N389MW		
50000023	PT-ZYX	N108JA		
50000024	PT-ZYL	M-INXY	G-NUDD	N390TP
50000025	PT-TFA	N605AS		
50000026	PT-TFB	PT-MAH		
50000027	PT-TFC	PR-DCJ		
50000028	PT-TFD	N190BW		
50000029	PT-TFE	N200XT	VH-YYT	N899JC	N700AJ
50000030	PT-TFF	N102PA		
50000031	PT-TFG	PP-LGT		
50000032	PT-TFH	PR-IVI		
50000033	PT-TFI	PP-CTC		
50000034	PT-TFJ	PR-DHC		
50000035	PT-TFK	SX-NSS	C-FLIX	
50000036	PT-TFL	N600HT		
50000037	PT-TFM	N100WX		
50000038	PT-TFN	N353SB		
50000039	PT-TFO	N514AF		
50000040	PT-TFP	D-IPHE	M-KELY	
50000041	PT-TFQ	N777BF	N630EE	N328MY	N685AS
50000042	PT-TFR	PR-FBS		
50000043	PT-TFS	(EI-JBA)	PR-NPP	
50000044	PT-TFT	N610AS	N639AS	
50000045	PT-TFU	N620AS		
50000046	PT-TFV	N574JS		
50000047	PT-TFW	Pakistan V-4103		
50000048	PT-TFX	PR-CSW		
50000049	PT-TFY	PP-AFM	[w/o 12Oct09 Angra dos Reis, Brazil; fuselage stored Sorocaba, Brazil]	
50000050	PT-TFZ	HB-VWQ	N981WA	N316BG
50000051	PT-TGA	N575JS		
50000052	PT-TGB	N430TB		
50000053	PT-TGC	N999RN		
50000054	PT-TGD	PR-DRC		
50000055	PT-TGE	G-DRBN	SP-AVP	
50000056	PT-TGF	G-SRBN	N80EJ	N936SM*
50000057	PT-TGG	N576JS	N224MD	[w/o Sedona, AZ, 25May11; to scrapyard near Phoenix Sky Harbor airport, AZ]
50000058	PT-TGH	N27WP		
50000059	PT-TGI	N206AH		
50000060	PT-TGJ	(EI-EHN)	PP-ELE	
50000061	PT-TGK	N644RM	(N644RP)	
50000062	PT-TGL	(EI-EHO)	HB-JFK	D-IHER*
50000063	PT-TGM	N32KC		
50000064	PT-TGN	N579JS		
50000065	PT-TGO	PR-DAY		
50000066	PT-TGP	(PR-SKD)	PP-SKD	N237JA	N321VA*
50000067	PT-TGQ	N629AS	N557TC	N647AS
50000068	PT-TGR	PR-VEL		
50000069	PT-TGS	ZS-STS		
50000070	PT-TGT	N241DE		
50000071	PT-TGU	N226CP	N226KV	
50000072	PT-TGV	N777JQ		
50000073	PT-TGW	(EI-EHS)	PP-IME	
50000074	PT-TGX	N784JP		
50000075	PT-TGY	N639AS	N876JC	
50000076	PT-TGZ	(EI-EHT)	PR-SPJ	
50000077	PT-THA	PR-PTA	N770EC	N770BR
50000078	(PT-THB)	[not built, cancelled order]		
50000079	PT-THC	N580JS		
50000080	PT-THD	YV2609		
50000081	PT-THE	N59PW		
50000082	PT-THF	N100EQ	[w/o Gaithersburg/Montgomery County apt, MD, 8Dec14]	
50000083	PT-THG	PR-JAJ		
50000084	PT-THH	N725MW	N600CS	
50000085	PT-THI	PR-IEI		
50000086	PT-THJ	(EI-EHU)	PP-MRV	
50000087	PT-THK	N149GK		
50000088	PT-THL	N210FF		
50000089	PT-THM	N354RX		
50000090	PT-THN	N91TQ	N56SB	
50000091	PT-THO	N6745		
50000092	PT-THP	M-PHNM	OE-FOM	9H-FOM
50000093	PT-THQ	PR-UUT		

EMBRAER EMB-500 PHENOM 100

C/n	Identities						
50000094	PT-THR	PR-LMP					
50000095	PT-THS	OO-NOA	PT-THS	PR-NTO			
50000096	PT-THT	PR-MJD					
50000097	PT-THU	N208DX					
50000098	PT-THV	PR-DLM					
50000099	PT-THW	PT-FCC					
50000100	PT-THX	OE-FAM	9H-FAM				
50000101	PT-THY	PR-ADQ					
50000102	PT-THZ	N102EP					
50000103	PT-TIH	N511WK					
50000104	PT-TII	PP-KPL					
50000105	PT-TIJ	N67WG	N932MA				
50000106	PT-TIK	N175EM	HP-500E	N175EM			
50000107	PT-TIL	N926JK					
50000108	PT-TIM	PR-OFP					
50000109	PT-TIN	PP-VDP					
50000110	PT-TIO	N581JS					
50000111	PT-TIP	N723GB					
50000112	PT-TIQ	M-YTOY					
50000113	PT-TIR	Pakistan V-4104					
50000114	PT-TIS	N645AS					
50000115	PT-TIT	CS-DTC					
50000116	PT-TIU	N917LJ	N100NV				
50000117	PT-TIV	N777ZA	N636SD	N1PB*			
50000118	PT-TIW	N663LS	N627DB				
50000119	(PT-TIX)	[not built, cancelled order]					
50000120	PT-TIY	(F-HDMG)	PR-DFC				
50000121	PT-TIZ	N130EC					
50000122	PT-TYA	(HB-VWS)	OE-FGR	N991CA			
50000123	PT-TYB	N661EP					
50000124	PT-TYC	N190HL	N188TM				
50000125	PR-CPC						
50000126	PP-KKA						
50000127	(PT-FQA)	PT-TYD	PR-OVD				
50000128	PT-FQB	N43AG					
50000129	PT-FQC	N43EP					
50000130	PT-FQD	N600PB	CS-DVS				
50000131	PT-FQE	N583JS					
50000132	PT-FQF	PH-PST					
50000133	PT-FQG	N80EJ	N637AS				
50000134	PT-FQH	PP-VIP	OK-VAN				
50000135	PT-FQI	N582JS					
50000136	PT-FQJ	N937DM	(N536EC)	C-GVJV			
50000137	PT-FQK	N100FZ	(N69HT)				
50000138	PT-FQL	N585JS					
50000139	PT-FQM	N988BC					
50000140	PT-FQN	N584JS					
50000141	PT-FQO	N100FF					
50000142	PT-FQP	N893MW	N917MM				
50000143	PT-FQQ	N888PT					
50000144	PT-FQR	PR-PNM					
50000145	PT-FQS	M-KICK	G-VKGO	N63007			
50000146	PT-FQT	G-CGNP	N724RN				
50000147	PT-FQU	OO-GJP	D-ISTP				
50000148	PT-FQV	N623DT					
50000149	PT-FQW	N646AS					
50000150	PT-FQX	N86DC	N427RR	N89JJ			
50000151	PT-FQY	G-RAAL	N196EC	N299PP			
50000152	PT-FQZ	PR-PCM					
50000153	PT-FUA	N121PZ					
50000154	PT-FUB	N21SB					
50000155	PT-FUC	PR-TPA					
50000156	PT-FUD	PR-JJD					
50000157	PT-FUE	N665AS	N629JJ				
50000158	PT-FUF	PR-VPJ					
50000159	PT-FUG	N525EC	N367ER				
50000160	PT-FUH	PR-PHD					
50000161	PT-FUI	PT-GCP					
50000162	PT-FUJ	M-MACH	D-IAAT				
50000163	PT-FUK	PR-BET					
50000164	PT-FUL	PP-MOR					
50000165	PT-FUM	G-PHNM					
50000166	PT-FUN	(G-COQI)	N288DX				
50000167	PT-FUO	PR-JIP					
50000168	PT-FUP	N668AS	N500TB				
50000169	PT-FUQ	(JY-AWG)	N161PA				
50000170	PT-FUR	N170AP					
50000171	PT-FUS	N625EL	C-GXMP				
50000172	PT-FUT	XA-UOB	N218RG				
50000173	PT-FUU	N173GH					
50000174	PT-FUV	PT-FLX					
50000175	PT-FUW	PR-PHE					
50000176	PT-FUX	N648DX					
50000177	PT-FUY	OO-MCV	N142TL				
50000178	PT-FUZ	N88DW	N784KS				
50000179	PT-FYA	G-ROOB	OE-FHT	N646TG	N199BA	N179PH	
50000180	PT-FYB	OE-FTF	N720MV				
50000181	PT-FYC	N400PZ					
50000182	PT-FYD	N669AS					
50000183	PT-FYE	N586JS					
50000184	PT-FYF	N450JF					
50000185	PT-FYG	(PP-WAJ)	G-RUBO	OE-FHO	G-ITSU		
50000186	PT-FYH	PP-WAJ	N9990M				
50000187	PT-FYI	OO-HPG	G-LGMG				
50000188	PT-FYJ	N670AS	N830NF				

EMBRAER EMB-500 PHENOM 100

C/n	Identities			
50000189	(PT-FYK)	[not built, cancelled order]		
50000190	PT-FYL	OH-EPA		
50000191	(PT-FYM)	[not built, cancelled order]		
50000192	PT-FYN	VT-IAJ	N264AG	
50000193	PT-FYO	OE-FGV	9H-FGV	
50000194	PT-FYP	N649DX		
50000195	(PT-FYQ)	[not built, cancelled order]		
50000196	PT-FYR	OO-MAS	[w/o Berlin/Schoenefeld, Germany, 15Feb13] N508ML [parted out Denton, TX]	
50000197	PT-FYS	PR-FIL		
50000198	(PT-FYT)	[not built, cancelled order]		
50000199	PR-REX			
50000200	(PT-FYU)	[not built, cancelled order]		
50000201	PT-FYV	(PR-TED)	OH-EPB	
50000202	PR-TED			
50000203	PT-FYW	VT-IAG		
50000204	PT-FYX	VT-AVS		
50000205	PT-FYY	N4200	VT-AJI	
50000206	PT-FYZ	VH-PNM		
50000207	(PT-PYA)	[not built, cancelled order]		
50000208	(PT-PYB)	[not built, cancelled order]		
50000209	(PT-PYC)	[not built, cancelled order]		
50000210	PT-PYD	VT-SFM		
50000211	(PT-PYE)	[not built, cancelled order]		
50000212	(PT-PYF)	[not built, cancelled order]		
50000213	PT-PYG	N996LP	N996LF	
50000214	PT-PYH	C-GYMP		
50000215	PT-PYI	D-IAAD		
50000216	PT-PYJ	N899DX		
50000217	(PT-PYK)	[not built, cancelled order]		
50000218	PT-PYL	N222GP	N387MB	
50000219	PT-PYM	PR-RHB		
50000220	PT-PYN	N100PU		
50000221	PT-PYO	PP-UBS		
50000222	PT-PYP	N101FG		
50000223	PT-PYQ	N615SM	N456RF*	
50000224	(PR-ENY)	C-FSTP	N39K	
50000225	PR-ARR			
50000226	PT-LBM	N108MG	N109LE	
50000227	PT-LBR	PP-BIO		
50000228	PT-LBS	N630AS		
50000229	PT-LBV	N85JG		
50000230	PT-LBL			
50000231	PT-LBZ	(PP-MAS)	PR-VFC	
50000232	PP-LBQ	N244MD		
50000233	PP-LBW	PP-BGG		
50000234	PP-LBX	PP-COR		
50000235	PT-TDJ	N525MN		
50000236	(PR-VBS)	PR-TLS		
50000237	PT-TDL	VH-FJP		
50000238	PT-TDM	N238KJ	VT-TSK	
50000239	PT-TDN	N225AS		
50000240	(PT-TDO)	[not built, cancelled order]		
50000241	PT-TDP	N19SG		
50000242	PT-TDQ	PR-PER		
50000243	PT-TDR	OO-OTU	D-IAAY	
50000244	PT-TDS	PR-TDV		
50000245	PT-TES	D-IAAW		
50000246	N602EE	N600AS		
50000247	PT-TGO	C-FCEX	N121PC	
50000248	PT-TGP	N917NS	(D-IAAT)	
50000249	[instructional airframe]			
50000250	PT-TJK	UR-ALB	4L-ALF	
50000251	[instructional airframe]			
50000252	PT-TJL	N74GH	C-FMPU	
50000253	PT-TJM	UR-ALA		
50000254	(PT-TJN)	[not built, cancelled order]		
50000255	N255EE	C-GYMD		
50000256	PP-NIV			
50000257	PT-TJO	PR-IMR		
50000258	PT-TJP	N787PJ		
50000259	PT-TJQ	N161PL		
50000260	PT-TNO	(N260AL)	N888WS	N851RV
50000261	PT-TNP	PP-JJB		
50000262	(PT-TNQ)	[not built, cancelled order]		
50000263	PT-TNR	F-HCJE		
50000264	(PT-TNS)	PT-MMP		
50000265	(PT-TNT)	C-GTLP	C-GTLG	N611EC
50000266	(PT-TNU)	PR-REV		
50000267	(PT-TNV)	N670AS		
50000268	PT-TNW	N131BV		
50000269	PT-TNJ	N452AR		
50000270	(PT-TOA)	N60312	N999TN	
50000271	PT-TPX	XB-MRQ	XB-MUL	XA-ASS
50000272	N60318	XA-TPA		
50000273	PT-TPY	PT-HRI		
50000274	N161CE			
50000275	PT-TPZ	PT-TAT		
50000276	PT-TRD	PT-FSF		
50000277	HP-1776	HP-1776AJQ	N88FW	
50000278	PT-TRG	PP-LMH		
50000279	PT-TSX	PT-STR		
50000280	N316N			
50000281	PT-TUA	D-IMOR		
50000282	PT-TOJ	PR-LIQ		
50000283	N6004N	N1008U	HP-1778	

EMBRAER EMB-500 PHENOM 100

C/n	Identities			
50000284	(PT-TAN)	PP-OLY		
50000285	N285GC			
50000286	N60126	N10153	HP-1779	HP-1779AJQ
50000287	PP-JLS	PR-EBK		
50000288	PT-TAR	D-ILAP		
50000289	N289EE	N289RZ		
50000290	N6014A	N1015G	N520RB	
50000291	N60231	N48VC		
50000292	PT-TAS	HB-VRV		
50000293	N6051D	N1015J	N221AA	YR-DDM
50000294	N60298	N900WS	N435SC	
50000295	N60237	N10160	N100RY	D-IBSL
50000296	N60231	C-GSAM		
50000297	PR-EAT*			
50000298	N60318	N214PC		
50000299	N6032F	N1016M	C-FGGH	N677MS
50000300	PT-TBO	N911YA		
50000301				
50000302	N1018S	N6005Y	N123RX	
50000303				
50000304	N1019L	N8KD		
50000305	N1019Q	N305PL		
50000306	N10200	VH-LWZ		
50000307	PR-VOG*			
50000308				
50000309	PP-EMB			
50000310	N60126	N390EE	N575JT	
50000311	N1020G	N60312	N374N	
50000312				
50000313	N984EP	XA-...		
50000314	N6051D	N5237R		
50000315	N60318	N122CR		
50000316	N823CR			
50000317	N330XX	N44WS		
50000318	(PR-PAA)	PR-FBU		
50000319	N305PG	T7-VYT		
50000320	PR-PAO	PR-CMQ		
50000321	N6004N	N321KM		
50000322	PR-PAP	PP-JEL		
50000323	PR-PBH	N914TQ		
50000324	(PT-TJG)	PR-FYB		
50000325	PR-PBT	PP-JSZ		
50000326	PP-VRL			
50000327	(PP-AHW)	PR-HNZ		
50000328	PP-AHW			
50000329	4X-CMN			
50000330	PT-RMI			
50000331	N531EE	C-GDCC		
50000332	PR-TDM			
50000333	PR-PBM	N7913M		
50000334	N500RB			
50000335	N356N			
50000336	PR-RLM	[300th Phenom 100 delivered]		
50000337	PR-PHX			
50000338	PR-PCG	N826E	VT-ZAP	
50000339	(PR-PHX)	PP-IVN		
50000340	(PP-IVN)	PR-PCH	PR-PLO	
50000341	PR-PCN	PR-PLR		
50000342	PR-PCI	XA-ATT		
50000343	PR-PCP	N658MB		
50000344	PR-PCQ	N589WT		
50000345	PR-PCR	PR-PMK		
50000346	PP-MKB			
50000347	PR-PCY	XA-MSO		
50000348	N548EE			
50000349	PR-LFL	N250YB		
50000350	PR-PEI	PR-JIE		
50000351	PR-PEJ	PP-WPM		
50000352	PR-PEW	N348N		
50000353	PR-PFF	F-HSBL		
50000354	PR-PFI	F-HLRY		
50000355	PR-PFH			
50000356	PR-PFL	B-3113		
50000357	PR-PFS	N188MR		
50000358	PR-PFT	N615DM		
50000359	N234FP			
50000360	PR-PFW	N598LG		
50000361	PR-PGE			
50000362	PR-PGI	N100MZ		
50000363	PR-PGJ			
50000364	(PR-PGK)			
50000365	PR-PAE	D-IDAS*		
50000366	PR-PGK			
50000367	PR-PGP			
50000368	SP-IAF			
50000369	PR-PGV	A6-...*		
50000370				
50000371	PR-PGY	A6-...*		
50000372	D-IUCR*			
50000373	PR-PGZ	A6-...*		
50000374	PR-PHF			
50000375	PR-PHK			
50000376				
50000377				
50000378				

EMBRAER EMB-500 PHENOM 100

C/n	Identities
50000379	
50000380	
50000381	
50000382	
50000383	
50000384	
50000385	
50000386	
50000387	
50000388	
50000389	
50000390	
50000391	
50000392	
50000393	
50000394	
50000395	
50000396	
50000397	
50000398	
50000399	
50000400	

EMBRAER EMB-505 PHENOM 300

C/n	Identities				
50599801	PP-XVI	[rolled out 12Apr08; ff 29Apr08]			
50500001	PP-XVJ				
50500002	PP-XVK				
50500003	PP-XVL				
50500004	PP-XVM	[ff 08Aug09] PT-PVY	N914LJ	N917LJ	
50500005	PT-ZXS	N454DR	(N973ME)		
50500006	PT-ZXT	N585TV			
50500007	PT-ZXW	PT-PVA	PR-DHP		
50500008	PT-ZXX	N308MJ	N999GC		
50500009	PT-ZXY	N392AS			
50500010	PT-ZXZ	PT-MLJ			
50500011	PP-ZZC	N525PC	N6DQ		
50500012	PP-ZZD	PP-OAC			
50500013	(PP-ZZE)	[not built, order cancelled]			
50500014	PP-PVB				
50500015	(PT-PVC)	[not built, order cancelled]			
50500016	PT-PVD	F-HIPE			
50500017	PT-PVE	G-MGNE	N135BC		
50500018	PT-PVF	N492BB			
50500019	PT-PVG	N117DD	N717DD		
50500020	PT-PVH				
50500021	PT-PVI	ZS-MPD	(G-....)	ZS-SYU	N521EC ZS-SYU
50500022	PT-PVJ	PP-MCL			
50500023	PT-PVL	G-GEIR	HB-VYM		
50500024	PT-PVN	(PP-MCL)	PR-ALU		
50500025	(PT-PVN)	(PT-PVZ)	CN-MBR	[w/o 06Aug12 Altenrhein, Switzerland] N538WS	[parted out by Dodson Int'l Parts, Rantoul KS]
50500026	PT-PVO	N69GY	PK-JCO		
50500027	PT-PVP	N300FL			
50500028	PT-PVQ	N304FL			
50500029	PT-PVK	N305FL	N833CL		
50500030	PT-PVR	N306FL			
50500031	PT-PVS	N300R	N88DW	N284PD	N428P
50500032	PT-PVT	N307FL			
50500033	PT-PVU	N960ES	N247JK		
50500034	PT-PVV	N311FL			
50500035	PT-PVW	N394AS			
50500036	PT-PVX	N301TG	N523DM		
50500037	PT-PVZ	(PR-PAY)	N312FL		
50500038	PT-PYR	PP-ITU	N38VC		
50500039	PT-PYW	A4O-CY	N539TA	PR-EMD	N505EC N500AD
50500040	PT-PYS	N715MS	HZ-IBN	[w/o Blackbushe, UK, 31Jul15]	
50500041	PT-PYT	(PT-TIC)	PR-WRT	N341EC	PT-SBC N282GS
50500042	PT-PYU	N448TM			
50500043	PT-PYV	N300VR			
50500044	PT-PUB	N20T			
50500045	PT-PUC	PP-ABV			
50500046	PT-PUE	N300FJ			
50500047	PT-PUF	N318FL			
50500048	PT-TDI	N898MW			
50500049	PP-OGX				
50500050	PP-TDT	N314FL			
50500051	PT-TDU	PR-STA			
50500052	(PP-PFA)	PP-LGD			
50500053	PT-TDV	N525LS	N67WG		
50500054	PT-TDW	N315FL	N918DG	N82161	
50500055	PP-OVD				
50500056	PT-THT	N697AS			
50500057	PT-TJJ	N316FL			
50500058	PT-TJR	D-CFMI			
50500059	PT-TJT	N317FL	N562TM		
50500060	(PT-TJU)	PR-ERE			
50500061	PT-TJV	N900HT			
50500062	PT-TJW	OK-PHE	OE-GDP		
50500063	PT-TKL	N505TM			
50500064	PT-TLW	XA-LOB	(N505EC)	N364PF	XA-CAN
50500065	PT-TNA	N14AH	N14AQ		
50500066	PT-TNB	D-CHLR			
50500067	PT-TNC	(PT-TIC)	N319FL	N116DK	
50500068	PT-TND	HB-VPG			
50500069	PT-TNF	D-CRCR			
50500070	PT-TNH	N732AC			
50500071	PT-TNI	N896LS			
50500072	(PT-TNJ)	PP-UTI			
50500073	PT-TNK	N583KD			
50500074	PT-TNL	N322FL	N345PY*		
50500075	PT-TNM	N324FL			
50500076	PT-TRH	N3300			
50500077	PT-TNS	PR-GCR			
50500078	PT-TRK	N330AG	PK-BSW		
50500079	PT-TNU	N335AS			
50500080	(PT-RAB)	PK-RJD			
50500081	(PT-TVN)	N729JF	N729JE	N11TE	
50500082	PT-TRN	M-VAKE	UP-EM009		
50500083	PT-TNV	CS-DTQ			
50500084	PT-TRP	N100FG			
50500085	PT-TPM	A4O-CY			
50500086	PP-MDA				
50500087	PT-TRQ	M-APLE			
50500088	PT-TRT	N614TH	N618TH		
50500089	PT-TRR	C-GJOL			
50500090	PT-TRV	N325FL			
50500091	PT-TRS	N300QS	CS-PHZ	N391VR	N85BZ
50500092	PT-TRW	PP-WLP			
50500093	PT-TSS	N326FL			

EMBRAER EMB-505 PHENOM 300

C/n	Identities			
50500094	PT-TST	N327FL	N347FX	
50500095	PT-TSU	N195MC		
50500096	PT-TSV	D-CHIC		
50500097	PT-TRE	N328FL		
50500098	PT-TSW	N175MC		
50500099	PT-TRF	TC-KEH	F-HJFG	
50500100	(PT-GPX)	N329FL		
50500101	PT-TRJ	D-CSAG		
50500102	PT-TRO	OY-PWO	(D-CNJK)	N323EP
50500103	PT-TRP	N65KZ		
50500104	PT-TOA	N657GF	N300GV	
50500105	PT-TRU	N330FL		
50500106	PT-TOB	N585BC	N585PF	N443BB
50500107	PT-TOC	PR-WIN		
50500108	PT-TOD	D-CLAM		
50500109	PT-TOG	N332FL		
50500110	PT-TOH	PP-EMO		
50500111	PT-TOI	C-FMPN		
50500112	PT-TAU	N1505P	N347PP	
50500113	PT-TAY	PP-CGG		
50500114	PT-TAZ	PP-CMJ		
50500115	PT-TBI	N335FL		
50500116	PT-TBM	M-MDMH		
50500117	PT-TBU	(PT-PTT)	G-CHKE	UR-ALD	N322LV
50500118	N1039V	[ff 05Dec12 Melbourne, FL – first US-built Phenom 300]	N505EE	N43RC
50500119	PT-TBW	N301AS		
50500120	PT-TBP	N535BC		
50500121	PP-URA			
50500122	N85JE			
50500123	PT-TBX	N302QS		
50500124	PT-TCJ	N977JK		
50500125	PT-TDM	N316TA		
50500126	PP-PRP	N192DM		
50500127	PT-TDL	ZS-MPD		
50500128	(PT-TAS)	PT-TDN	N528TM	
50500129	(PT-TBT)	PT-TDO	PP-NMM	
50500130	(PT-TCU)	PT-TDQ		
50500131	(PT-TBY)	PT-TDP	N344PL	
50500132	PR-EFT			
50500133	PT-TDJ	ZS-CSB		
50500134	PR-PAE	G-JAGA		
50500135	PR-PAH	N337FL	N354FX	
50500136	PP-MPB			
50500137	(PT-TJH)	PP-SCN		
50500138	N894JH			
50500139	PR-PAL	N338FL	N355FX	
50500140	PR-HJM			
50500141	PR-PAU	N303QS		
50500142	N932DM			
50500143	PR-PBD	N304QS		
50500144	N801WZ			
50500145	PR-PAY	PP-EPH		
50500146	PR-PBG	B-9060		
50500147	PR-PBI	N310QS		
50500148	N340AS			
50500149	C-FAJV			
50500150	PR-PBJ	(D-CAXO)	D-CHGS	
50500151	N628DS			
50500152	PR-PBK	N309QS		
50500153	PR-PBL	N312QS		
50500154	N899EE			
50500155	N6032F	N342FL	N356FX	
50500156	N343FL	N357FX		
50500157	PR-PBM	PP-HUC		
50500158	PR-PBN	N314QS		
50500159	N9300	VT-AJJ		
50500160	PP-BPS			
50500161	PR-PBO	N316QS		
50500162	PR-PBP	N318QS		
50500163	N862LG			
50500164	(PP-MMP)	N319QS		
50500165	PR-PBQ	N322QS	N505PJ	
50500166	N440XX			
50500167	N713WD	(N589MV)		
50500168	PR-PBU	N325QS		
50500169	N800CS			
50500170	PR-PBV	N327QS		
50500171	N344FL	N358FX		
50500172	N7JW			
50500173	PR-PBX	D-CLBM		
50500174	N895JH			
50500175	PR-PBW	N328QS		
50500176	N6013X	N361CE		
50500177	PP-LMR			
50500178	PR-BJA			
50500179	N598TB	N598TP		
50500180	PR-PBD	N330QS		
50500181	HB-VYS			
50500182	PP-NRN			
50500183	PR-PBI	N331QS		
50500184	PR-PBJ	N332QS		
50500185	N585EE	C-GDJG		
50500186	PR-PBK	N333QS		
50500187	M-BEAR	N157AF		
50500188	N588EE	N505GP		

EMBRAER EMB-505 PHENOM 300

C/n	Identities			
50500189	N340QS			
50500190	PR-NGM			
50500191	N715DE			
50500192	PR-AJN			
50500193	PP-NEF			
50500194	N343QS			
50500195	PR-PBL	HB-VPR		
50500196	PP-MCG			
50500197	M-ELON			
50500198	PR-PBN	D-CDTZ		
50500199	N377N			
50500200	(PR-HUC)	N335QS		
50500201	(PP-JBE)	N336QS		
50500202	PR-PBZ	N337QS		
50500203	CS-PHA			
50500204	PR-PCB	N300HJ		
50500205	N613R			
50500206	PR-PCD	M-KGTS		
50500207	D-COLT			
50500208	PR-PCE	N345FL	N359FX	
50500209	CS-PHB			
50500210	N1887B			
50500211	PP-LJA			
50500212	N110AP			
50500213	PP-IBR			
50500214	CS-PHC			
50500215	N896JH			
50500216	PR-PCF	LX-MAR	F-HBDX	
50500217	N865BB			
50500218	PR-PCJ	PR-DRJ		
50500219	N344QS			
50500220	PR-SAD			
50500221	N724MH			
50500222	N585PC			
50500223	PR-PCK	N969GC		
50500224	PT-PVC			
50500225	CS-PHD			
50500226	N505FF			
50500227	(PT-PVC)	PR-DLN		
50500228	N300RZ			
50500229	PT-PCH			
50500230	N345QS			
50500231	N40ML			
50500232	PR-PCS	D-CCWM		
50500233	N360FX			
50500234	N361FX			
50500235	N235EE			
50500236	PR-PCO	PP-CTS		
50500237	N351QS			
50500238	PR-PCU	N645B		
50500239	N362FX			
50500240	PR-PCV	N29GS		
50500241	PR-PCW	N851AB		
50500242	N363FX			
50500243	PR-PCX	N168J		
50500244	N352QS			
50500245	PP-NBB			
50500246	N364FX	N68TJ		
50500247	PR-BEB	F-HMML		
50500248	N1505P			
50500249	PP-JDB			
50500250	N358QS			
50500251	PR-PEE	N500EC		
50500252	CS-PHE			
50500253	PR-PEF	CC-AND		
50500254	N360QS			
50500255	(PP-JDB)	PR-PEH	N73FE	
50500256	N363QS			
50500257	PR-LFH	N347QS		
50500258	N119EP			
50500259	PR-LFJ	N348QS		
50500260	CS-PHF			
50500261	PR-LFK	M-ANAP	T7-ANA	
50500262	PR-PEN	G-CRBN	N262PF	
50500263	PR-PEO	N353QS		
50500264	CS-PHG			
50500265	PR-PEQ	N354QS		
50500266	N566EE			
50500267	PR-PEU	N337AS		
50500268	N366QS			
50500269	PR-PEV	N365FX		
50500270	CS-PHH			
50500271	N571EE			
50500272	PR-PFA	N272NR		
50500273	PR-PEK	N367QS		
50500274	PR-PEY	F-HPJL		
50500275	N373QS			
50500276	PR-PEZ	M-HPIN		
50500277	N300FP			
50500278	PR-PFB	F-HJBR		
50500279	N371QS			
50500280	N317N			
50500281	PR-PFJ	N419PJ		
50500282	N974SC			
50500283	N200BF			

EMBRAER EMB-505 PHENOM 300

C/n	Identities		
50500284	PR-PFK	C-GMSO	N569EE
50500285	N843M		
50500286	PR-PFM	LX-TAC	
50500287	N805PG		
50500288	N947AS		
50500289	N374QS		
50500290	PR-PFO	N750LC	N199BA
50500291	PR-PFU	PP-VFV	
50500292	N48VM		
50500293	N909BK		
50500294	N379QS		
50500295	PR-PFV	N603WM	
50500296	N795W		
50500297	N588CB		
50500298	N975SC		
50500299	PR-PFY	N750SC	
50500300	(D-CHMS)	N66LD	
50500301	PR-PFZ	N577JM	
50500302	N383QS		
50500303	PR-PGA	XA-LOB	
50500304	F-HJLM		
50500305	PR-PGB	(PP-KCB)	N217CB
50500306	N300PH		
50500307	C-FWTF		
50500308	PR-PGD	HB-VRW	
50500309	N386QS		
50500310	N302TG		
50500311	N9688R		
50500312	N318PT		
50500313	PR-PGG	N361AS	
50500314	N30MN		
50500315	PR-PGH	T7-ANB	
50500316	N848AM		
50500317	D-CDAS		
50500318	N897JH		
50500319	N124EK		
50500320	N10193	PR-HRO	
50500321	N995LP		
50500322	N302GV		
50500323	N7DR		
50500324	N60298	D-CHMS	
50500325	PR-PGN	OE-GDF	
50500326	N6013X	N366FX	
50500327	N597TB		
50500328	N390QS		
50500329	PR-PGO	T7-AAK	
50500330	N978PC		
50500331	N391QS		
50500332	CS-PHI		
50500333	N10139	D-CWWP	
50500334	PR-PGQ	N168JC	
50500335	N10204	XA-CSS	
50500336			
50500337			
50500338	N505EE		
50500339			
50500340			
50500341	PR-PGR	N368AS	
50500342			
50500343	PR-PGT	D-CBBS	
50500344	N383CH		
50500345	N545EE		
50500346	PR-PGU	N804SW	
50500347	N10163	N4B	
50500348			
50500349	N392QS		
50500350	PR-PGW		
50500351			
50500352	PR-PGX	N858EE	
50500353			
50500354	N359AS		
50500355			
50500356	N393QS		
50500357	N557EE		
50500358	PR-PHC	G-KRBN	
50500359			
50500360			
50500361			
50500362	N394QS		
50500363			
50500364			
50500365	N395QS		
50500366	PR-PHG	(T7-ANC)	G-JMBO
50500367			
50500368			
50500369			
50500370			
50500371	N398QS		
50500372			
50500373	PR-PHH	D-CMOR*	
50500374	PR-PHJ		
50500375			
50500376	PR-PHN		
50500377			
50500378			

EMBRAER EMB-505 PHENOM 300

C/n	Identities
50500379	N300QS
50500380	
50500381	
50500382	
50500383	
50500384	
50500385	
50500386	
50500387	
50500388	
50500389	
50500390	
50500391	
50500392	
50500393	
50500394	
50500395	
50500396	
50500397	
50500398	
50500399	
50500400	
50500401	
50500402	
50500403	
50500404	
50500405	
50500406	
50500407	
50500408	
50500409	
50500410	

EMBRAER EMB-550 LEGACY 500

C/n	Identities		
55000001	PT-ZEX	[rolled out 23Dec11; ff 27Nov12]	
55000002	PT-ZEY	[ff 15Feb13]?	
55000003	PT-ZFV	[ff 22Mar13] PR-LJN	D-BJKP
55000004	PT-ZHY	PP-JJA	
55000005	PT-ZJF	PR-EUF	
55000006	PR-LFO	N762CC	
55000007	PR-LFW	N598DB	N498EE	N424ML
55000008	PR-LFQ	N878EE	PR-LFQ	N142GZ
55000009	PT-ZIJ	[prototype Legacy 450; ff 28Dec13]	
55000010	PR-LGL	HZ-A7	
55000011	PR-LGO	N657GF	
55000012	PR-LGQ	N576EE	N614TH
55000013	[believed not built due superstition over unlucky number 13]		
55000014	PR-LGW	N895EE	
55000015	PR-LHE	Brazil 3601	[military designation IU-50]
55000016	PR-LGY	TC-MLA	
55000017	PR-LGZ	N878EE	N886CA*
55000018	PR-LHJ	XA-TUB	
55000019	PR-LHG	PR-HIL	
55000020	PR-LGV	[second Legacy 450]	N456LG
55000021	PR-LHK	N725EE	
55000022	PR-LHL	B-3385	
55000023	PR-LHM	Brazil 3602	[military designation IU-50]
55000024	PR-LHO	N401EE	N550HD
55000025	PR-LHS	N400FX	
55000026	PR-LHT	N298EE	N718RA
55000027	PR-LHX	N401FX	
55000028	PR-LHY	N402FX	
55000029	PR-LIC	N403FX*	
55000030	PR-LIE	XA-EMB	
55000031	PR-LIJ	N729MM	
55000032	PR-LIK	N368EE	
55000033	PR-LIR	N585BC	
55000034	PR-LIU	N661HS	
55000035	PR-LIW	N275EE	
55000036	PR-LIX	N404FX	
55000037	PR-LIY	OD-CXJ	
55000038	PR-LJB	N159M	
55000039	PR-LJD	G-HARG	
55000040	PR-LJO		
55000041	PR-LJU	N250LC	
55000042	PR-LJW		
55000043	PR-LJY		
55000044	PR-LKB		
55000045	PR-LKE		
55000046	PR-LKF	N721EE	
55000047	PR-LKO		
55000048	PR-LKL		
55000049	PR-LKM		
55000050	PR-LKQ		
55000051	PR-LKP		
55000052	PR-LKT		
55000053			
55000054			
55000055			
55000056			
55000057			
55000058			
55000059			
55000060			
55000061			
55000062			
55000063			
55000064			
55000065			
55000066			
55000067			
55000068			
55000069			
55000070			
55000071			
55000072			
55000073			
55000074			
55000075			

EMBRAER EMB-545 LEGACY 450

C/n	Identities	
55010001	[c/n not used, built as 55000009]	
55010002	[c/n not used, built as 55000020]	
55010003	PR-LJH	OO-NEY
55010004	PR-LJK	N450CH
55010005	PR-LJZ	N801EE
55010006	PR-LKG	
55010007	PR-LKI	N214EE
55010008	PR-LKN	
55010009	PR-LKU	
55010010	PR-LKV	
55010011		
55010012		
55010013		
55010014		
55010015		
55010016		
55010017		
55010018		
55010019		
55010020		
55010021		
55010022		

G1159 GULFSTREAM II

Notes: G1159B Gulfstream 2B conversion programme numbers have been included alongside the c/n (see also at the end of the production list)
TT indicates aircraft with tip tanks (some 2Bs were built as "TT" models and converted later)
SP indicates a specialist conversion by Aviation Partners with winglets, known as Gulfstream 2SPs; these are not 2B aircraft. The prototype was c/n 12
* in the series column indicates that engine hush kits have been fitted

C/n	Series	Identities									
1	SP	N801GA	[ff 02Oct66]	N55RG	[to Carolinas Aviation Museum, Charlotte,NC, Sep12]						
2	SP	N802GA	N801GA	N369CS	N869CS	N721SW	N434JW	N902GT	[cx Jly03; to Air Classics Museum, IL, then to Aviation Warehouse, El Mirage, CA]		
3		N831GA	N214GP	N311JJ	N555RS	N300GP	(N417RD)	N300RD	[parted out Hagerstown, MD]		
4/8	2B	N832GA	N680RW	N680RZ	9K-ACY	VR-CAS	HZ-MPM	N8490P	N36RR	[parted out California City, CA; cx 27Jan14]	
5		N100PJ	N100PJ	N65ST	N655TJ	N34S	N3LH	[parted out California City, CA]			
6		N834GA	N430R	N122DJ	N122DU	[broken up Geneva, Switzerland, 2006; remains to Air Salvage Int'l, Alton, Hants, UK, for parts; removed from site by Aug08]					
7	SP	CF-HOG	N9300	N93QQ	N118NP	N701JA	[parted out by Int'l Turbine Service circa Nov 03; cx Nov03]				
8	SP	N833GA	N18N	N400SJ	N400SA	HB-IMV	N400SA	N777GG	PJ-ARI	N504TF	N5UD	N225CC	N11UF	N22CX
		S9-CRH	S9-GOT	ZS-TGG	N267PS	N225MS	[parted out by Dodson International, Rantoul, KS]				
9/33	2B	CF-SBR	N320FE	(N115RS)	N209GA	N343K	N48EC	N129WA	[cx 20Jan16, wfu Dallas/Redbird, TX]		
10	SP	N343K	N343N	N888CF	XA-ROI	N555LG	N51TJ	N667CX	XB-JPL	HR-AUJ	N900CE	[wfu; cx 15Sep08]
11		N835GA	N902	N902GA	N611TJ	N463HK	[wfu 2006; broken up; cockpit & forward fuselage preserved in Banyan Pilot Shop at Fort Lauderdale Executive]				
12	SP	N500R	N11UM	N154X	N115MR	N121EA	N160WC	[temporarily fitted with spiroid winglets for 50hrs of test flights in 1993]		N212TJ	
		N794SB	N622RR	[cx 13Aug13; wfu]							
13		N678RW	N678RZ	N98AM	5N-AMN	N2GP	N373LP	N373LB	VR-BOS	N269MH	N269HM	N169HM
14	SP	N663P	N663B	N217JD	N369AP	N500JW	XA-RBS	XA-RBP			
15		N375PK	N77SW	N416SH	N125JJ	N571BJ	[parted out at Islip, NY, 2004 onwards]				
16/13	2B	N890A	N697A	N711MT	N38GL	N24YS					
17	SP	N119K	N819GA	N456AS	N91AE	N305AF	N917R	N217GA	N1PR	(N121PR)	N422DV	N143G	N143V
		N202PX	(N217DA)	[cx 27Aug12; wfu]							
18		N838GA	N205M	N43R	(N48RA)	XA-SDE	XA-LZZ	XC-AA70			
19	SP	N839GA	N1929Y	N19NW	N590CH	(N213DC)	ZS-LOG	[b/u Lanseria, South Africa]			
20		N2PG	N755S	N4SP	N331P	N747NB	N88LN				
21		N4PG	N7ZX	N8PG	N8PQ	[cx Jan93; to CIS but unable to obtain CofA]			N8PQ	N244DM	[cx to Panama 25Jun07]	"PP-EMS"	[fake marks noted crudley applied to fin at Campo Grande, Brazil, Mar11]
22	SP	N862GA	N5152	N145ST	N22FS	N683FM	N206MD	(N800TE)	(N655JH)	N217RR	N216RR	[instructional airframe Wilson Technological Center, Farmingdale, NY]
23		N863GA	USCG 01 [VC-11A]	N7TJ	N890TJ	[cx 05Jun13; wfu]					
24		N536CS	N4S	(N98G)	N26WP	(N224TS)	N800XL	(N800XC)	XB-KFU		
25		N327K	N527K	N711RL	N711RZ	YV1681	N137GJ				
26	SP	N328K	N202GA	PK-PJZ	N975GA	(N711RT)	N4RT	ZS-PYY			
27	SP	N1807Z	N121JJ	N430BC	N227TS	(N227TJ)	N227BA	XB-MZK	N227BA	XB-NRX	
28		N695ST	N700ST	N7004T	C-GCFB	N120EA	N85EQ	N68DM	N17KW		
29	SP	N869GA	N930BS	N919G	N41RC	N71TJ	N941CW	N188JS	[cx 20Jan16, wfu Dallas/Redbird, TX]		
30/4	2B	N870GA	N788S	N2601	N2607	N333AX	N338AX	N47HR	XA-FHR	XA-TRG	N30438	XA-EHR	XA-STT	XB-KBO
		XB-KCX	XC-LKN								
31		N1621	N685TA	N789FF	N200CC	N105TB	[test a/c with nose probe and underwing pods]				
32/2	2B	N7602	(N7601)	N976B	N971EC	N971EQ	N200AQ	[cx 18May15, CofR expired]			
33	SP	N1624	N1324	N217TL	(N217TE)	N327TL	N327TC	N926NY	N747NB	N747JX	
34		N230E	N130A	N11SX	VR-CBM	N500JR	N204RC	[w/o 17Jun91 Caracas-Oscar Machada, Venezuela; cx Oct91]			
35		N1004T	N830TL	N30PR							
36/3	2B	N26L	N26LA	N5400G	(N211GA)	N901K	N901KB	N74A			
37		N179AR	N179AP	N994JD	N397RD	[cx Nov02; b/u, remains to Aviation Warehouse film prop facility at El Mirage, CA]					
38		N80A	N880A	[Quiet Spey development a/c with BAC1-11 thrust reverser on starboard engine]			[cx Jun95; wfu for spares]				
39	SP	N80Q	N8000	N401NW	(N124BN)	N425A	(N12BN)	N1TJ	N87HB	N87TD	[wfu at Chino, CA, 2006]
40		N1040	(N5040)	N1039	VR-BLJ	[w/o 20Jun96 Jos, 465m NE of Lagos, Nigeria]					
41	SP	N38N	(N417GA)	N401GA	N416K	N365TC	N311MG	[parted out Mojave, CA]			
42/12	2B	N8000J	N937M	N880GM	VR-BMQ	N1164A	N36PN				
43		N17583	F-BRUY	N84X	N33ME	N691RC	(N243TS)	N270TS	N899GA	(N247LG)	[impounded Toluca, Mexico, for drug-running Aug07; moved to Mexico City, Mexico, and stored]
44		N814GA	N830G	N585A	N830G	[b/u Fort Lauderdale Executive, FL circa Jan02; cx Feb02]					
45	SP	N815GA	N711R	PK-PJG	N152RG	N215RL	VR-BHA	N115GA	N40CE	US Army 89-0266	N51741	US Army 89-0266
		N245GA	N250MS	[cx 24Mar15, CofR expired]							
46	TT	N806CC	N40CC	N111RF	C-GSLK	N9272K	N721CP	N9BF	N505JT	N565KC	[canx 19Jly05 aircraft b/u at, then removed from, Islip, NY]
47	SP	N803GA	N35JM	N553MD	N809GA	N809LS	N800FL	N800RT	[cx 18Sep12; parted out California City, CA]		
48/29	2B	N109G	N4411	N711MC	N61WH	N61WE	N865AA				
49		N871GA	N747G	N74JK	N830TL	N830TE	N830TL	(N830TE)	N830BH	N511PA	N511BA	(N33EN)	[cx 09Dec14, CofR expired]
50		N39N	N39NX	N767FL	N800FL	N220FL	N220JR	N650KA	HI…		
51	SP*	N2013M	VR-BNE	N7C	N20H	N20HE	N20H	N20HE	N30HE		
52		CF-FNM	C-FFNM	N69SF	N38KM	N5SJ	(N52NE)	"N52TJ"	N711MT	N211MT	N52NW	[canx 28Oct05 parted out]
53	SP	N107A	N167A	N102AB	N104CD	N104VV					
54/36	2B	N123H	CF-NOR	C-FNOR	N955CC	N148V					
55		N875GA	N225SF	N225SE	N125DC						
56	SP	N10XY	N20XY	N105Y	N805GA	N610CC	N690PC	N2000			
57	SP	N876GA	N770AC	N300DK	N300DL	(N333ST)	N33PJ	N466JB	N605RA	[cx 25Mar13; parted out California City, CA]	
58		N878GA	N720Q	[w/o 24Jun74 Kline, SC]							
59	SP	N879GA	N1823D	[b/u; cx 19Nov08]							
60		N892GA	N500J	[w/o 26Sep76 Hot Springs, VA]							
61	SP	N18N	N711MM	N497TJ	N800MC	N57BG	N61LH	N41AV	[instructional airframe, South Georgia Technical College, Americus, GA]		
62		N834GA	N372CM	N372GM	N1PG	N3ZQ	N7PG	N7PQ	Russia 62 [Black or Dark Blue]	(N777TX)	N20LW
		N262PA	N128KG								
63		N835GA	N238U	N239P	N149JW	N17ND	(N20GP)	N12GP			
64/27	2B	N836GA	N940BS	N950BS	N341NS	N95SV	N620K	N82CK	N43RJ	N95SJ	N351SE	[impounded Bissau, Guinea-Bissau, 12Jul08]
65		N837GA	N720E	N1JG	N500PC	N58JF	(N300FN)				
66		N838GA	N720F	N165W	N165U	N718JS	N718JA	[parted out by Dodson Int'l, Rantoul, KS]			
67	SP	N839GA	N711S	EL-WRT	N10HR	N400JD	N67PR	N568TN	ZS-WHG	[b/u Lanseria, South Africa, 09Jul15]	
68		N308EL	N308EE	[cx to Panama 22Jun06, shot down over Colombia 12Aug06]							
69	SP	N69NG	N25JM	N33CR	N45JM	N45Y	N45YP	VH-HKR	N21066	N123CC	N440DR	N701S	XA-MEM	XC-LKA
70/1	2B	N711SC	N711SB	VR-BML	N165A	N451CS	N451GS	N908EJ	N908CE	N510SR	N510SE	N660AF	[wfu at Mojave, CA; cx 25Feb2010]
71		N4CP	N4CQ	N711SW	N907SW	N48JK	N47A	N200AB	N200EL	[cx 20Jan16, wfu Dallas/Redbird, TX]	
72		N397F	[w/o 22Feb76 Burlington, VT]								

G1159 GULFSTREAM II

C/n	Series	Identities									
73/9	2B	N116K	N555CS	N920DS	N436JW	3D-TCB	7P-TCB	N436JW	N1B	9Q-…	
74	SP	N845GA	N111AC	N311AC	(3X-GBD)	N204GA	N92SV	N74TJ	N74HH	[parted out by Dodson Int'l, Rantoul, KS]	
75/7	2B	N823GA	N1000	N100AC	N100CC	N600CS	N760U	N94TJ	N211SJ	Venezuela 0010	[wfu Caracas/La Carlota, Venezuela]
76	SP	N711LS	N227G	N227GL	N227GX	N227G	N227GA	[canx 25May04; wfu]			
77		N824GA	N100WK	N40CH	N140CH	N34MZ	N84MZ	N777JS	N385M	N7TJ	N707SH	N7TJ	N700JP
		N125WM	N994GC	N994GG	N277GS						
78	SP*	N17585	PH-FJP	CF-IOT	C-FIOT	N90HH	HP-1A	HP-1691	[wfu Jan10]		
79	SP	N826GA	N719GA	N204A	XA-SFB	XA-STO	XA-ARA	[b/u Houston/Hobby, TX, 2008]			
80	SP	N827GA	N85V	N85VT	N500RH	N510RH	N82CR	[structurally modified for US Navy BAMS system development]			
81	SP	N828GA?	N777SW	N44MD	N281GA	N283MM	N688MC	N681AR	XC-PGR+	N681AR	(N281NW)	N151SD	N419MS
		[parted out by MTW Aerospace Inc, Montgomery, AL]									
82	SP	N711DP	N10LB	N9040	N600B	N600BT	N728T	N492JT	[preserved Georgia Aviation Hall of Fame, Warner Robins, GA]		
83		N404M	N409M	N409MA	(N48MS)	[w/o 03May95 Quito, Ecuador]					
84		N5101	N5101T	N27SL							
85	SP	N5102	Denmark F-085	N5102	N510G	N86SK	N931CW	N93AT	N524MM	N598GS	ZS-MMG
86/16	2B	N880GA	N179T	(N179DE)	[parted out Mojave, CA]						
87/775/6	2B	N804GA	N13GW	N723J	N6PC	N692EB	N165PA				
88/21	2B	N881GA	N2600	N2637M	HB-IMZ	N901AS	N80WD	N779LC			
89	SP*	N882GA	N100A	N203A	N36MW	[conv to prototype "Paragon" before SP]		N98WJ	[cx 03May16, CofR expired]		
90		N883GA	N7789	N20GP	N671LW						
91	SP	N17586	G-AYMI	VH-ASM	N219GA	G-OVIP	VR-BRM	N291GA	N99ST	N183SC	N81FC	N914MH	XB-KIV	XC-LKS
92	SP	N884GA	N300L	N300U	N114HC	N994JD	N430SA	N722TP	N589HM	N691HM	(N584DM)	N629TD	N374PS
		(N883KF)	N888YZ								
93	SP	N885GA	N8785R	TJ-AAK	N215GA	N62K	N484TL	N396BC	N922MR	(N159DA)		
94	SP	N886GA	N200A	N202A	N623MW	N420JM	N420JT	N18AQ	N685SF	N665SF		
95/39	2B	N887GA	VH-ASG	N427AC	N836MF	N836ME	N113CS	N118GS	N889DF	N2DF	N608CM	[wfu Mojave, CA, Feb11]
96	SP	N888GA	N100KS	N100WC	N75WC	N75SR	XC-MEX	XB-EBI	N3005P	XA-EYA	N396CF	[wfu Kingman, AZ]
97	SP	N889GA	I-SMEG	N66TF	N11AL	N930SD	N397J	(N397L)	N55HY	N25GJ	XB-RRC	[wfu 2013, stored Chino, CA]
98/38	2B	N850GA	N93M	N955H	N988H	N988DS	N925DS	N17MX	XA-CHR	XA-PSD	N198AV	N812RS	N888CS	N888ES
		N883ES	N982B	N44YS							
99	SP	N851GA	N99GA	N822CA	N900VL	N900MP	N1218C	(N1273G)			
100	SP	N852GA	N4000X	N400CX	N234DB	N911DB	XB-FVL	N400D			
101	SP	N853GA	N1159K	(N237LM)	N240CX	N623CX	N512JT	N412JT	[wfu Pachuca, Mexico; cx 11Dec14]		
102/32	2B	N854GA	N88AE	N210GA	N119CC	N400CC	N102CX	N511PK			
103	SP	N855GA	G-BDMF	N833GA	P2-PNF	P2-PNG	N833GA	HZ-MS4	(N103WJ)	N89TJ	[parted out circa Feb05 by Dodson Intl Parts, Rantoul, KS]
104/10	2B/2	N856GA	N856W	N858W	[cvtd back to G2 standards 1989; wings to G3 c/n 303]			C-FHPM	N712MQ	[b/u Houston/Hobby, TX]	
105	SP	N807GA	N23M	N5997K	N405GA	N6060	N711TE	N754JB	[b/u Fort Lauderdale Executive, FL, Nov10]		
106		N808GA	N33M	(N519TW)	N397LE	N226GA	(N106TJ)	N141JF	(N473JF)	[wfu Chino, CA]	
107	*	N809GA	N5113H	N10123	[modified for aerial survey use]						
108	SP	N810GA	N11UC	N60GG	N600MB	N700FS	N801GA	N200GH	(N200GL)	N900AK	N183PA	N189PA
109	SP	N811GA	N679RW	N882W	N86CE	N862CE	N73AW	N581MB	[parted out]		
110	SP	N814GA	N5000G	N200GN	N200PB	N21AM	N21AX	N92AG	N417EK	[cx 13May15; wfu Houston/Hobby, TX]	
111		N815GA	N10LB	N13LB	N765A	N900BR	N900DH	[flying testbed for Snecma Silvercrest turbofan 2014]			
112	SP	N816GA	N102ML	N102HS	VR-BJG	N36JK	N909L	N108DB	N87AG	N168VA	N168DA	XB-NXC	XB-OCC
113	SP	N817GA	N30RP	N34RP	N60CT	N203GA	N2S	N32HC	N2S	N216HE	(N216MF)	N1BL	N211BL	N217JS
		N74RT	N74RQ	[dbr 19Jan05 Logan, UT; to White Inds, Bates City, MO for spares; cx 22Jan09]								
114		N818GA	N100PM	N25BF	XA-TDK	(N114WJ)	XB-KBE	XB-KCW	XC-LKL	XB-NKS	[destroyed by fire at clandestine airstrip nr Calabozo, Venezuela, Oct15, presumed used for drug-running]
115	SP	N819GA	N677S	N457SW	N47JK	N200BP	N700BH	N40AG	N42PP	N424GC	[b/u Mojave, CA; cx 02Jul09]
116		N821GA	9M-ARR	N20XY	N23W	(N410LR)	N716TE	N218SE	[cx 12Apr12; wfu]		
117	SP	N822GA	N580RA	N888SW	N75CC	N7500	N750RA				
118		N823GA	N399CB	(N301FP)	N399FP	N650PF/NASA650 [for Prop Fan Experiments]		(N651NA)	N945NA	[to be preserved at US Space & Rocket Center, Huntsville, AL]	
119/22	2B	N824GA	TU-VAF	N825GA	C-FHBX	N2991Q	N60HJ	(N875E)	N720G	N73LP	N928GF	(N103EL)	N305SJ
		N500MA	XB-KKU	[w/o in Venezuela 07Oct07]							
120	SP	N825GA	N901BM	N777V	N677V	N20FX	N393BD	N392BD	C-GTEW	N711VL	
121	SP	N200P	N90EA	N507JC	N721RL	N721PL	N892TM	[parted out by White Inds, Bates City, MO]			
122		N832GA	N429JX	N4290X	N61SM	N84A	N500RL	N500RQ	[parted out Mojave, CA, Aug10, then to El Mirage, CA, for film prop use]		
123/25	2B	N805CC	N345CP	N345AA	N344AA	N344AB	N368DS	N868DS	[cx 11Dec14, CofR expired]		
124		N834GA	HB-IEW	VR-BGL	VR-BGO	N203GA	Venezuela 0004	(N980EF)	N124TV	[wfu Mojave, CA circa Sep03; cx 15Jun05 as b/u; fuselage to Long Beach, CA, Nov07 for training use; tail unit still at Mojave Oct11]
125/26	2B	N870GA	N367G	N364G	N3643	N92LA	N92NA	N178B			
126		N43M	N581WD	(HB-I..)	N578DF	N416K	N901WG	[cx 13Jan10; b/u Savannah, GA, Oct10, remains to Atlanta Air Salvage, Griffin, GA]			
127	TT	N17581	TR-KHB	[w/o 06Feb80 Ngaoundere, Cameroun]							
128		N73M	N367EG	N128TS	N829NL	[cx 25Nov14, CofR expired]					
129	SP	N871GA	N1H	N711DS	N83TE	N626TC	N711EV	[b/u cx Nov03]			
130	SP	N872GA	N127V	N518GS	N512SD	A6-PHY	N666SA				
131/23	2B	N17582	9M-ATT	N759A	N2JR						
132	SP	N873GA	N400M	[wfu London, Canada]							
133	TT	N88906	N17583	5X-UPF	N44UP	N444QG	N442QG	N930LS	[wfu Mojave, CA; cx 31Mar09]		
134		N806CC	C-FROC	N555KH	N628HC	(N810MY)	[impounded Guatemala City/La Aurora 26Jun13]				
135	SP*	N83M	N113EV	(N518FE)	N518JT	N515JT	N552JT	N525XL	[cx 12Dec11; b/u]		
136	SP	N874GA	N65M	ZS-JIS	3D-AAC	N207GA	6V-AFL	6V-AGQ	N26WB	XA-ABA	XA-AFP	XA-FCP	N95RT
		N190RP	[parted out California City, CA; cx 26Nov14]								
137	SP	N875GA	N1875P	N2711M	VR-BJT	N23AH	N115MC	N485GM	N435GM	[dbr by Hurricane Rita at Beaumont, TX, Sep05; parted out by Dodson Av'n, Rantoul, KS; cx 12Nov14]
138		N6JW	YV….								
139/11	2B	N880GA	N18N	HZ-PET	HB-ITV	N2UJ	(N763PD)	N663PD	N339GA	N139CF	N113AR	N139CF	[wfu Conakry, Guinea]
140/40	2B*	N881GA	C-GTWO	N2667M	(N101AR)	N104AR	N212GA	VR-BJQ	N189TC	N730TK	N159NB	
141		N17584	JA8431	[Mitsubishi special test aircraft]							
142		N882GA	N60CC	N5RD	N742TS	N588SS	[cx 04Jun13; wfu]				
143		N883GA	N334	N204C	[w/o 04Sep91 Kota Kinabalu, Borneo; cx Nov93]						
144		N17585	HB-ITR	N944NA	[preserved Dryden Flight Research Center, Edwards, CA]						
145	SP	N894GA	N871D	N871E	N339H	N226RM	[wfu Okeechobee, FL]				
146		N897GA	N946NA	[preserved Texas Air & Space Museum, Amarillo, TX]							
147		N898GA	N947NA	[preserved Evergreen Aviation & Space Museum, McMinnville, OR]							
148/5	2B	N710MR	N710MP	N2615	N180AR						
149		N896GA	N17586	5V-TAA	[w/o 26Dec74 Lome, Togo]						
150	SP	N803GA	N966H	N988H	N636MF	N638MF	(N631CK)	N613CK	N319GP	N60GU	ZS-TPG	[parted out Lanseria, South Africa]
151/24	2B	N804GA	N979RA	N979GA	N908JE	(N988JE)	N909JE	YV569T			

G1159 GULFSTREAM II

C/n	Series	Identities									
152		N17587	XA-FOU	N202GA	N62WB	N559LC	N559L				
153	SP	N881GA	N23A	(N602CM)	N111VW	N110VW	N132FP				
154/28	2B	N1625	N1JN	N18JN	N836MF	N110GD	N719SA	N719SQ	HI871		
155/14	2B	N308A	XA-GAC	N477GG							
156/31	2B	N806GA	N400SJ	N7000G	N16NK	N18NK	N525JT	N83TE	N864YD	(N159DJ)	ZS-DJA	[parted out Lanseria, South Africa]
157		N805GA	N914BS	N940BS	N74JK	N658PC	N683EC	N468HW	(N488HW)	[parted out by Dodson Int'l, Rantoul, KS]		
158	SP	N76CS	N76QS	N401M	N2S	N889JC	[cx 29Sep14; wfu]				
159	SP	N345UP	N800DM	N800DJ	N880RJ	N510AG	[has extensive fuselage modifications]				
160		N80J	N801	N214GA	N900TP	N919TG	N1123G	N241MH	E3-AAT		
161	*	N17589	XA-ABC	XC-FEZ	XC-CFE	Mexico TP-04/XC-UJK	XB-GSN	XA-RUS	XA-AHM	XA-AHC	
162		(C-GANE)	N530SW	N74RV	C-GTCB	N74RV	N666JT	N668JT	[cx 13Jun12; wfu]		
163	SP	N17581	(YV-60CP)	PJ-ABA	N117JJ	N117JA	N117JJ	[wfu Fort Pierce/St Lucie, FL]		
164	SP	N17582	9K-ACX	A6-HHZ	N93LA	N80AG	XA-ESC	XA-BBO	XB-BBO		
165/37	2B*	N810GA	N7000C	N788C	VR-BHR	N26L	N965CC	N183V	N696MJ	N945PK	
166/15	2B	N811GA	N515KA	N66AL	(N84AL)	N826GA	N826AG	XA-SWP	N776MA	ZS-DGW	
167	SP*	N17583	5V-TAC	VR-CBC	N204GA	N900SF	N430DP	N681FM	N82204	N682FM	N683FM	N120GS	N368AG
		N868AG	XA-UEC	XA-CVS							
168	SP	N812GA	N10LB	N26LB	N193CK	N635AV	N168JW	N317AF	(N370SP)	N318SP	N501JV
169	SP	N17584	HB-IEX	N39JK	N31SY	N710JL	N7155P	N169P	N169EA	N467AM	N467AN	XA-...
170		N991GA	N14PC	N502PC	(N318GD)	N111GD	N202XT	N111GD	[cx Nov10; parted out Mojave, CA]		
171		N17585	HZ-AFH	SX-BTX	[b/u Geneva, Switzerland, Nov09; fuselage to Lanseria, South Africa]						
172	SP	N804GA	N903G	N903GA	N903AG	N987SA	[shot down while drug-running in Mexico 24Sep07, w/o]				
173	TT	N801GA	XC-PET	XA-SQU	N98FT	N173EL	(N444ML)	[parted out Van Nuys, CA]		
174	SP	N805GA	N401M	N144ST	N7766Z	N900ES	N540EA				
175	SP	N17586	HZ-AFG	5T-UPR	N770PA	XA-FNY	XC-PFT	[code PF-210]		
176	SP	N806GA	N176P	N176SB	N15UC	N15UG	N794SB	N794SC	N550WP	N959QP	
177		N17587	5N-AGV	"5N-BLV"	5N-BGV	(N1513)	[wfu Atlanta/Falcon-Peachtree, GA]			
178	SP	N819GA	N390F	N104ME	(N128AD)	N42LC	N720JW	N502RG	[cx 23Jul11; parted out]		
179		N17588	HZ-CAD	HZ-PCA	[wfu Jeddah, Saudi Arabia]						
180	SP	N859GA	N329K	N359K	N37WH	(N47WH)	N702JA	N416CG	XB-MUX		
181		N860GA	N24DS	N924DS	N48CC	N48CQ	[wfu Tulsa, OK circa Nov02; cx 02Dec05, believed b/u]			
182	TT*	N17589	CN-ANL								
183	SP	N17581	A4O-AA	N23AZ	(N10NW)	N801WC	N806WC	N400PJ	N821PA	[cx 05Jan12; wfu]	
184		N861GA	N80E	N220GA	N254CR	N777RW					
185	SP	N862GA	N372CM	N372GM	N3E	N3EU	N511WP	XA-BRE	N297GB	N950NA	[modified for use as USAF YAL-1A (Airborne Laser) target aircraft]
186	SP	N17582	(D-ACVG)	D-AFKG	5N-AML	(D-AAMD)	VR-BJV	VP-BJV	VP-BFF	[parted out California City, CA]	
187		N17583	N804GA	HZ-ADC	N202GA	N802CC					
188		N823GA	N862G	N662G	N555MW	N555MU	N188DC	[wfu Fort Pierce/St Lucie, FL; cx 29Oct14]		
189/42	2B*	N333AR	N512VB	(N515JT)	N555XL	N404AC	N711MQ	[wfu Miami/Opa Locka, FL]		
190	SP	N130K	N159B	N169B	N900WJ	N1WP	N7WQ	N59CD	N59JR	N914DZ	N914CF	N190CS
191	SP	N810GA	N680RW	N679RW	N677RW	N675RW	N951RK	[abandoned Roatan, Honduras, 22Mar13 – presumed drug-running]		
192	SP	N811GA	N678RW	N677RW	HB-ITW	N273LP	N192FG	N192WF	[wfu Toluca, Mexico; cx 10Dec14]		
193	SP	N808GA	N26L	N26LT	N54J	N54JJ	N227LA	N117LB			
194		N17584	HB-IMW	C6-BEJ	C6-BFE	VR-BRM	N194MA	N57HJ	N57HE	[parted out Cartersville, GA; cx 25Nov14]	
195		N212K	N71TP	XA-ILV	N195AR	[parted out San Antonio, TX, 2006]					
196		N400J	N200BE	N610MC	N619MC	N829GL					
197		N800GA	N5117H	(N217AH)	N608MD	[wfu Okeechobee, FL]					
198/35	2B	N825GA	N365G	N3652	N91LA	N91NA					
199/19	2B*	N829GA	N75WC	N75RP	N74RP	N71RP	VR-BND	VP-BND	N900TJ	N338CL	N511TL	[b/u Chino, CA]
200	SP	N826GA	N1806P	N135CP	N99VA	XA-AVR	N17GG	N281RB	N17KJ	(N200UJ)	[cx 21Jun12; parted out California City, CA]
201	TT	N17585	HZ-AFI	N105AJ	[cx 26Jul12; wfu]						
202	TT	N17586	A9C-BG								
203	TT	N17587	HZ-AFJ	[wfu circa Dec05 Geneva, Switzerland; b/u Oct07]							
204	SP	N17588	G-CXMF	N806CC	N937US	N659PC	N659WL	VR-CPA	VP-CPA	N659WL	
205	SP*	N25UG	N1000	N205BL	N623BM	N345GL	(N345GV)				
206	SP	N2PK	N900BF	N721CN	(N609PA)						
207/34	2B	N700PM	(N780PM)	N111UB	VR-CUB	VP-CUB	N4UB	[cx 14Oct14; parted out California City, CA]		
208	SP	N808GA	N62CB	C-FNCG	N818DA	N247AD	N247AB	[cx 26Jun13; wfu]		
209	SP*	N806GA	N277T	N720DR							
210	SP	HB-IEY	G-IIRR	(HK-....)	8P-LAD	N30FW	N826GW	[cx 12Aug14; instructional airframe Rome/Griffiss, NY]		
211	SP	N17581	VR-BGT	VP-BGT	N7079N	XA-FNY	XA-UTP				
212	SP	N807GA	N551MD	N807CC	N706TJ	[parted out California City, CA]					
213	SP	N1707Z	N96JA	(N96BK)	N213X						
214	SP	N17585	G-BSAL	A4O-HA	Oman 601	N11NZ	N214NW	N914KA	N914KB	N707KD	[abandoned Roatan, Honduras, 01Apr14 still – presumed drug-running]
215	SP	N816GA	N748MN								
216	TT	HB-IEZ	N63SD	N200RG	HZ-ND1	HZ-HA1					
217		N88GA	N81728	N880WD	N880WE	[cx 25Jan12; parted out California City, CA]					
218		TU-VAC	N218GA	N187PH	(N187PA)	N188MR	ZS-CTL	[parted out California City, CA]		
219/20	2B	N84V	VR-BJD	N307AF	N923ML	N505RX	N575E	N74RT			
220		N805GA	N404M	N405MM	M405MM	N315TS	N117GL	[parted out Los Angeles/Van Nuys, CA; fuselage to Long Beach, CA, as cabin trainer]		
221	SP	N575SF	N575SE	N2HF	N600CD	N827K	N949NA	N805NA			
222		N817GA	N5253A	N948NA	[to Pima Air & Space Museum, Tucson, AZ, for display Jul07; cx 30Apr15]						
223	SP	N510US	N257H	N510US	[wfu Mojave, CA, 23Jun09]						
224	TT	N17584	N810GA	N631SC	N90CP	N800PM	N860PM	[cx 02Mar15; wfu]		
225	SP	N17585	G-BGLT	N55922	N289K	N225TR	N450MH	N169MM			
226	SP	N1902P	N1902L	N5DL	N448PC	N355KM					
227	SP	N818GA	N1841D	N1841L	N1BX	N18XX	N200LS	N264CL	[instructional airframe, North Valley Occupational Center, Los Angeles/Van Nuys, CA]		
228	SP	N819GA	(N700CQ)	(N30B)	N157LH	N189WS	[cx 03May16, CofR expired]			
229		N821GA	N702H	N117FJ	[parted out Islip, NY]						
230		N17586	7T-VHB	[w/o 03May82 over NW Iranian border]							
231		N808GA	N1102	VR-CAG	VR-BHD	N18RN	N205K	N47EC	N416KD	[parted out California City, CA; cx 04Jun13]	
232		N806GA	C-GDPB	N71WS	N508T	N10RQ					
233	TT	N807GA	N320TR	N233RS	N720LH						
234	TT	N808GA	N910S	N910R	N480GA	N222PV	(N220GA)	N500JW	(N956MJ)	[parted out California City, CA]	
235	TT	N17581	G-HADI	N5519C	N16FG	N256M	N430RG	N840RG	[cx 07Aug14; wfu]		
236	TT	N812GA	N2998	N630PM	N50PM	N54BM	N211DH	N311DH	N311BD		
237/43	2B	N816GA	N25BH	XA-MIX	XA-BAL	XA-SDM	EC-363	EC-FRV	N237RF	N302DP	[parted out California City, CA]
238	TT	N831GA	N335H	N72BP							
239	TT	N17582	HZ-AFK	(N239WJ)	[wfu Jeddah, Saudi Arabia]						
240		5A-DDR	TT-AAI	(N240EA)							
241	SP	N830GA	(N60TA)	(N801GA)	N90MD	N902MP	(N902MK)	N909MK	N909FK	N380AC	

G1159 GULFSTREAM II

C/n	Series	Identities								
242		5A-DDS								
243		N119R	N119RC	N46TE	[w/o 19Jan90 Little Rock, AR]					
244	SP	N17584	9K-AEB	N500T	N509T	N509TT	N811DF	N811DE		
245/30	2B	N829GA	N141GS	N871D	N99WJ	N222NB	N222NP	(YV....)		
246	TT*	N17587	HB-IEZ	N14LT	N81RR	[used by NASA as High Ice Water Content research aircraft but wfu due US Gov't budget cuts; stored Chino, CA; cx 05Dec14]				
247	SP*	N828GA	N888MC	C-GTEP	N73MG	N75MG	N530GA			
248	SP	N17589	9K-AEC	N501T	N510T	N510TL	N248TH	N7WG	(N70WG)	N71WJ	N457BE	[cx 03Mar15; wfu Rome/ Griffiss, NY]
249		[Gulfstream 3 airframe]								
250	TT	N821GA	N309EL	(N94SF)	N985BB	[cx 16Nov12; wfu]				
251		N944H	N9PG	N9PY	N567A	N36GS	N251JS	N933RD	[cx 20May15; CofR expired]	
252		[Gulfstream 3 airframe]								
253	SP	N15TG	N154C	N915C	XB-LHW	XA-GEG	N16YY	N522HS	[impounded Puerto Plata, Honduras, Nov14]	
254/41	2B	N254AR	N706TS	N868SM						
255/18	2B	N442A	N4NR							
256		N17581	HZ-MSD	(N135WJ)	N61TJ	[parted out Nov04 by Dodson Av'n, Rantoul, KS]				
257/17	2B	N822GA	N872E	N411WW	N911WW	N56D	N1CC	N1159B		
258	SP	N823GA	N301EC	N929GV	N437H	N87GS	N689JE			
775		see c/n 87								

GULFSTREAM G1159B CONVERSION PROGRAMME

No	C/n	Completion date	No	C/n	Completion date	No	C/n	Completion date	No	C/n	Completion date
1	70	17Sep81	10	104	09Feb83	19	199	04Jan84	28	154	15Oct84
2	32	02Apr82	11	139	15Mar83	20	219	17Feb84	29	48	02Nov84
3	36	13Aug82	12	42	05May83	21	88	18Feb84	30	245	10Jan85
4	30	06Aug82	13	16	09May83	22	119	27Mar84	31	156	19Feb85
5	148	18Aug82	14	155	22Jun83	23	131	25Apr84	32	102	07Mar85
6	775	19Sep82	15	166	14Jly83	24	151	04Jun84	33	9	30Apr85
7	75	16Nov82	16	86	09Aug83	25	123	11Jun84	34	207	02May85
8	4	29Nov82	17	257	17Oct83	26	125	11Jly84	35	198	07May85
9	73	15Dec82	18	255	09Nov83	27	64	28Sep84	36	54	05Jly85

PLUS

37	165	Dec85
38	98	Jan86
39	95	Mar86
40	140	Jun86
41	254	Sep86 (rolled out as G1159B 06Oct86)
42	189	Jly87
43	237	Oct87

G1159A GULFSTREAM III

* alongside the c/n indicates fitted with engine hush kits

C/n	Identities									
249	N300GA	[ff 02Dec79]	N901GA	Denmark F-249		N163PA				
252	(N777SL)	N17582	(N301GA)	XA-MEY	N247RG	N516TR				
300*	N300GA	N700VA	N71TJ	N918BG	N234LR					
301	N100P	N21NY	(N100P)	N110BR	N444GA	N973MW	(N973MV)	N480RW	[cx 26Feb15; parted out Mojave, CA]	
302	N302GA	N62GG	N2610	N56L	N56LA	(XA-TOT)	(N561ST)	VP-BCT	N49US	N109ST	N302ST	N818VB
	[wfu Okeechobee, FL]									
303	N300GA	N303GA	TU-VAF	[rebuilt with wings from G2B c/n 104/10]			N1761W	N303GA	[w/o 29Mar01 Aspen, CO]	
304	N17583	HZ-NR2	N600YY	N768J	N763J	(N18SL)	VR-BSL	N304TS	[cx 26Dec13; parted out Mojave, CA]	
305*	N305GA	N235U	N305MD	N682FM	PK-OCN	N552JT	N553JT	N106KM	(9M-...)	
306	N306GA	N777SW	N72RK	N72PK	N862CE	N863CE	(N868CE)	N104BK	N360MB	
307	N17584	C-GSBR	C-GGPM	N111FA						
308	N717A	N606PT	VR-BNO	N308GA	N308HG	N921MG				
309	N18LB	N1NA	N2NA	N803NA	N992NA					
310	N719A	C-FYAG	N6513X	(N373LP)	(N173LP)	N982RK	[cx 7Jul14; wfu]			
311	N17585	HZ-AFL	N311GA	N721RB	N711SW	(N311BK)	N127BK	N127GK	[instructional airframe, Embry-Riddle Aeronautical University, Daytona Beach, FL]	
312*	N304GA	N100GN	N200GN	N200JJ	N800JH	N312NW	XA-RCM	N116AR	ZS-JGC	
313	Denmark F-313		N173PA							
314	N1040	N1540	N1640	N93CX	N99PD	(N99YD)	[wfu Dallas/Redbird, TX; cx 20Jan16]			
315	N315GA	N2600	N2600Z	N315GS	N710EC	N718EC	N21PJ	(N901JF)	N90ML	
316	N316GA	N2601	N26018	PK-CAP	PK-BND	N316FA	N691AC	(N69EH)	N300UJ	
317*	C-GKRL	N344GA	A6-CKZ	N83D	HZ-DG2	N90EP	N186PA			
318	N308GA	N300L	(N300LF)	(XA-...)	N70050	N150GX	N150QX	N150RK	N500WW	N17NC	N184PA
319	N319Z	N200SK								
320*	N873E	N69FF	VR-BNX	N320WE	N624BP	N624PP	N410UJ	N190PA		
321	N30RP	N94GC	N321GA	N100GX	N100QX	N313RG	N310RG	N9KL	(N91KL)	N830SU
322	N130A	N110LE	(N110EE)	N322GA	N555NT	N600ES	N606ES	N706JA	[cx 09Jan13, wfu]	
323	XA-MIC	N323G	XA-ERH	XA-LNP						
324	N17587	HZ-AFM	N44200	N67JR	N96MR	N450CB	N324JW			
325	N890A	N89QA	N393U	N155MM	N55ME	N59ME				
326	N17582	TR-KHC	N333GA	(N326DD)	N420JC					
327	N70PS	(N72PS)	N57BJ	N777RY	N711LT	N829MG	N259SK	ZS-LUX		
328	N309GA	N75RP	N78RP	N98RP	N97AG	N36WL	ZS-LAH			
329	N301GA	N862G	N1JN	(N329N)	N327JJ	N1LW	A6-ZAB	N15ZA	N197PA	
330	Denmark F-330		[w/o 03Aug96 nr Vagar, Faroe Islands]							
331	N307GA	N17LB	HZ-RC3	(N231WJ)						
332	N310GA	N77TG	N300BE	N65BE	N121JM	(N121JN)	N921AS	N909RR	N939RR	
333	N600PM	N50PM	N901FH	N901EH						
334	N1PG	(N1PU)	N41PG	N700SB	N3DP					
335	HB-IMX	N117MS	N717MS	N456BE						
336	N3PG	N3PY	(N523TX)	(N523PT)	(N102PT)	N147X	N378MB			
337	N456SW	N330WR								
338	N862GA	N372CM	N372GM	N87HP	(N338RJ)	N750SW				
339	N302GA	N522SB	N339A	N684AT	N774AK	N774MB	[wfu Okeechobee, FL]			
340	F-WDHK	F-GDHK	N99WJ	N90WJ	N340GA	N4PC	N2LY	N57NP	N557JK	
341	N263C	N1PR	V5-PJM							
342	N441A	N91LJ	N82A	N82AE	N1AQ	N1JK	N818SS	N555XS	[parted out California City, CA]	
343	N305GA	N664P	N664S	N400AL	N221CM					
344	N306GA	N7000C	5N-IMR	N344DD	N344GW	N804NA	[NASA testbed for new wing-flap assemblies]			
345*	N17585	G-BSAN	VR-CCN	G-GIII	5X-UOI	N76TJ	N454JB	N550PP		
346*	N17581	HZ-RH2	HZ-HR2	(N126AH)	VP-BHR	N103VV				
347	N17583	VR-BJE	N545JT	N888LV	N39LF					
348	N756S	N357PR								
349*	N89AE	N89AB	N1KE	N6453	N6458	N711EG	N111ES	N911HJ	[parted out California City, CA]	
350	N317GA	N1454H	N1454	[cx May10, parted out Mojave, CA]						
351	N888MC	N308AF	N836MF	N18TM	N623MS					
352	N17586	HB-ITM	Mexico TP-06/XC-UJN		[wfu]					
353	N26619	HZ-BSA	HZ-108	N212BA						
354*	3D-AAC	3D-AAI	N16NK	N420RC	N429DD	N913PD	[wfu Okeechobee, FL]			
355	N318GA	N676RW	(N103HS)	N876RW	8P-GAC	(N105HS)	N355TS	ZS-TEX	(N355TR)	
356*	N17608	A6-HEH	N356TJ	N356BR						
357	N303GA	N340	N802GA	N891MG	N723MM	N623NP	[wfu Bournemouth, UK; last flew 30Mar12]			
358*	N1761B	HZ-DA1	N9711N	N200DE	(N1149E)	N475DJ	(N475CY)	N358CY		
359	N800J	N305TC	N25MT	N50BH						
360	N341GA	N90LC	(N405LM)	N705JA	N425SV					
361	(N875E)	N874RA	(N361RA)	(N863A)	(N874RR)	[wfu Okeechobee, FL]				
362	N408M	N800AR	N400AA							
363*	N83AL	N77FK	N77EK	N855SA						
364	N1761D	HZ-AFN								
365*	N1761J	HZ-AFO	CN-ANU							
366	N2SP	N90SF	N222KC	N333KC	(N333KD)	N555KC	N333LX	N366JA	[cx 9Dec14; CofR expired]	
367	(N910A)	N17588	HB-ITN	(N6164Z)	N367GA	N700FS	N300FS	N933PA	N888SM	
368	N17509	7T-VRB	N368GA	(N368TJ)	C-GBBB	(N112GS)	[cx 04Dec12; parted out California City, CA]			
369*	N910A	N740SS	N17ND	N15HE	(4X-CMM)					
370	N319GA	N100A	N200A	N400K	N697BJ	N463LM	N105VS	N323MK		
371	HZ-NR3	N680FM	N8220F	N681FM	N353VA	[cx 03Jan13; parted out Mojave, CA]				
372	N320GA	N200A	N500E	N500EX	N724DB	N724DD	N523AM			
373	N340GA	N232HC	VR-BAB	VP-BAB	N162JC	N373GS	N373RR	N550RM		
374	N339GA	N122DJ	VR-CMF	N24GA	N270MC					
375	N955CP	VR-BOB	N375GA	N375NM	N375NW	(N75GJ)	N375LT			
376	N17582	A6-HHS	N70AG	(N5HG)	N60AG	N376EJ	N376PJ	N380AG		
377*	N342GA	N40CH	N707RX	N760AC	N377RX	N748JX	N377LR*			
378	N343GA	N955H	N378HC	N803CC	N960DC	N141MH	N444KM	N378SE	[cx 20Feb13; parted out California City, CA]	
379	N17586	HZ-MAL	N379RH	N282Q	N28QQ	N900LA	N96757			
380	N345GA	N159B	N30WR							
381	N304GA	N277NS	(N46ES)	N747G	N1871R	N621S	N221WR			
382	N305GA	83-0500	US Navy 830500	[C20A]	[wfu; to Southern Illinois University, Carbondale, IL, as instructional airframe]					
383	N308GA	83-0501	[C20A]	N65CE	N30501					
384	N1982C	N399WW	N399BH	N369CS	N112GS	N818TJ	N461AR			
385	N1761K	HZ-MS3	N883PA	N183PA						
386	N316GA	N902K	N902KB	Mexico TP-07/XC-UJO	[wfu]					
387	N26L	N621JH	N621JA	N620JH	N620JA	N485GM	N484GM	[cx 25Jun13; wfu]		

G1159A GULFSTREAM III

C/n	Identities											
388	N309GA	N902C	N1C	N748T	N561ST	N8JL	N797BD	N388LR				
389	N310GA	83-0502	[C20A – transferred to NASA]									
390*	N200SF	VR-BKS	VR-BLO	VR-BOK	VP-BOK	N67TJ	N1M	N102AK	N102AQ	N124DT		
391	N349GA	N29S	N1S	N194	(N222AP)	N94BN	N14SY	N288KA	[cx 1May14; parted out]			
392	N30AH	N6BX	N6BZ	N60GN	N1GN	N9WN	N800WC	N805WC	N801WC	N391SH	N734TJ	
393	N17587	A9C-BB	HZ-MWD	N33GZ	XA-ABD	N33GZ	N519AF	N200EL	N300EL	N200AB		
394	N1761P	N311GA	N379XX	N99WJ	N888WE							
395	N1761Q	PK-PJA	N5NW	N395EJ	N422TK							
396	N1761S	7T-VRC	N437GA	N800MK	N175BG							
397	N351GA	N59HA	N978FL	N692TV	N767CB	(N888WZ)	XA-PCH	N767CB				
398	N315GA	N88AE	N827GA	N827G	N777RZ	N610AB	(N628JG)					
399*	N17581	7T-VRD	N188TJ	N528AP	N399AP	N818EC						
400	N17585	Venezuela 0005		N990ML	N500EF	(N964MP)						
401	N352GA	N717	N400LH	(N80AG)	Denmark F-400		N97AG	N370JL	(N370J)			
402	N301GA	N303HB	N3338	VR-BLN	VP-BLN	[w/o 06Feb98 Lac du Bourget, Chambery, France]						
403	N347GA	N39NA	N39N	XA-TCO	(N333KC)	N403NW	XB-HIZ	N403WJ	N555GL	[wfu Dubai/World Central, UAE]		
404	N355GA	N404M	N404MM	N403LM	(N402LM)	N8115N	N560SH					
405	N348GA	N40NB	N40N	N91CH	N91CR	N990WC	N991WC	(N9718P)	N789TP	N789TR	N456AL	
406	N356GA	N80L	N406FA	XA-STT	N12EN	[cx 26Sep14; parted out California City, CA]						
407	N17603	G-XMAF	N407GA	N913MK	N813MK	[parted out California City, CA]						
408	N17608	9K-AEG	YI-AKI	[w/o 1991 Baghdad Airport, Iraq during Operation Desert Storm]								
409*	(N353GA)	N300BK	N320GA	N1526M	N1526R	N457ST	N457SF	N828MG	N555RE	N224KL		
410	N350GA	HZ-AFR										
411	N314GA	N966H	N461GT	N461GB								
412	N354GA	N20XY	N50XY	N610CC	N105Y	N527CC	N450BD					
413	N357GA	N77SW	N778W	N1	N8226M	Ireland 249	N166WC	N766WC	N59AJ	N762GS	N16AJ	[wfu Okeechobee, FL]
414	N358GA	N165ST	N165G									
415	N17582	(HZ-SOG)	HZ-HR4	HZ-NR2	N21NR	N109DD						
416*	N312GA	N500AL	N883A	N4500X	(N500XB)	N19H						
417	N317GA	N111AC	N1119C	N300M	N431JT	N431JG	[cx 4Sep14; parted out Miami/Opa Locka, FL]					
418*	N17583	JY-ABL	JY-AMN	N717TR	PT-ALK	N103CD	[w/o Biggin Hill, UK, 24Nov14; parted out Bruntingthorpe, UK]					
419	9K-AEH	YI-AKJ	[w/o 1991 Baghdad Airport, Iraq during Operation Desert Storm]									
420	N333GA	"40420"	N47449	India K-2960/VT-ENR		[but marks K-2960 not actually worn]						
421	N318GA	N99GA	N421GM	N721FF	N921FF	N711UF	[parted out by Dodson Int'l, Rantoul, KS]					
422	N319GA	N750AC	(N128AG)	N407CA	N903G	(N903GL)	N820BA	N171TV	N222G	YV....		
423*	N1761D	HZ-MIC	(VR-CMC)	N7134E	N225SF	N399RV	N712AS					
424	N320GA	N60AC	N228G	N94FL								
425	N344GA	N425SP	N492A									
426	N321GA	N151MZ	N751MZ	VR-CNJ	VP-CNJ	N703JA	XA-ABA					
427*	N327GA	N44MD	N42MD	N87AC	N300WY	N308WY	XA-MDC					
428	N322GA	N760A	N760G	N702DM								
429	N323GA	N429SA	N423SA	N100HG	N100HZ	N77BT	N77HG					
430	N324GA	N760C	N23A	N600BG	N608BG							
431*	N25SB	(N259B)	PK-CTP	N99WJ	P4-AEA	N17LK						
432	N333GA	N713KM	N995BC	N997CM	(N997HM)	N704JA	N469BT					
433	N325GA	N399CB	N579TG	N45KR								
434	N326GA	N811JK	N311JK	N226G	N226GC	XA-SNG	XB-FXD	N23ET	(N23SK)	(N73ET)	N323JH	N18ZL
435	N17581	HB-ITS	N435U	N888PM	N32KA	N357KM						
436	N346GA	V8-HB3	V8-A11	V8-007	V8-009	N436GA	N10EH	N243MW				
437*	N380TT	N100AK	N171AM									
438	N302GA	N1841D	N911KT	N473KT	N30LX	[modified as Airborne Multi-INT Laboratory]						
439	N17586	SU-BGU										
440*	N304GA	N5103	(N3PY)	N222BW	N265A	N71RP	N458BE	N124EP				
441	N306GA	N80J	N214WY	N467AM								
442	N17587	SU-BGV										
443	N315GA	N5104	N21AM	N813LS								
444	N328GA	N110MT	N555HD	N554HD	ZS-VIP							
445*	N316GA	(N5103)	N5105	N599DA	N590DA	N606DH	N850PG					
446	N309GA	N446U	N58AJ									
447	N186DS	N186DC	N144PK	N707JA	N776MA	[parted out Miami/Opa Locka, FL]						
448	N339GA	N117JJ	N255SB	I-MADU	N123AP	N178HH	N710CF	[testbed for Next Generation Jammer electronic warfare system]				
449	N310GA	XA-FOU	N7C	N85V	N85VT	[w/o 22Nov04 Houston-Hobby Airport, TX]						
450	N329GA	HZ-AFS	N329GA	PT-AAC	VR-CTG	N888VS	N801MJ	N36DA				
451	(N370GA)	N330GA	Italy MM62022		N351FJ	N500RH	N5159Y	N600RH	N693PB	N951XF	[cx 31Oct12; wfu]	
452	N331GA	N27R	N633P	VR-BNZ	VP-BNZ	N123TL	N800TD					
453	N332GA	HZ-109	Saudi Arabia 103		HZ-103	N213BA						
454*	N334GA	N60CT	N1GT	N273G	N111G	N111GX	N903TC	N740VC				
455	N335GA	N1SF	(N103GA)	N103GC	N123CC	N123MR	N147MR	N28YC	N818DD	N935DH	XA-DHM	
456	N336GA	US Army 85-0049	[C20C]	[wfu; to AMARG Davis-Monthan, AZ, 02Dec13]								
457	N337GA	N457H	N972G	N457JC								
458	N338GA	US Army 85-0050	[C20C]	[wfu; to AMARG Davis-Monthan, AZ, 02Dec13]								
459	N321GA	N600B	N586C	N566C	N54HF	N555DW						
460*	N322GA	N500LS	N500VS	N500MM	N500MN	I-FCHI	N2TQ	N2TF	N317ML	N460PG	N32MJ	
461	N323GA	N104AR	N108AR									
462	N324GA	N303GA	TU-VAF									
463	N327GA	N80AT	N808T	VR-BMY	VP-BMY	N463GE	N886DT	N196CC				
464	N340GA	N535CS	N83AG	N83PP	N513MA							
465*	N17586	86-0200	[C20B]	N465GA	Chile 911	N35GZ	(N33GZ)	N33NT	N35GZ	N53GL	N35GZ	N36JE
466*	N17583	N325GA	N37HE	N102AK	N817MF							
467*	N341GA	JY-HAH	N551AC	N400WY	N218MD							
468	N342GA	86-0202	[C20B]	[wfu; to AMARG Davis-Monthan, AZ, 03Sep15]								
469*	N343GA	JY-HZH	N1956M	N469TB	N598GS	N698GS	YV2896					
470	N344GA	86-0201	[C20B]	N770GA	86-0201							
471	N347GA	N888WL	N583D	N57TT	N975RG							
472*	N348GA	N800CC	N806CC	N800CC	N806CC	N357H	N780RH	N780RA	(N454BE)	N353MA	LV-CEG	
473	N326GA	US Army 86-0403	[C20C]	[wfu; to AMARG Davis-Monthan, AZ, 02Dec13]								
474	N311GA	D2-ECB										
475	N312GA	86-0203	[C20B]									
476	N314GA	86-0204	[C20B]									
477	N317GA	86-0205	USCG 01	[VC20B]	N477SJ	N477WG	[parted out California City, CA; cx 15Apr15]					
478	N318GA	86-0206	[C20B]									
479	N319GA	Italy MM62025		N50RL	N556AF	[parted out Miami/Opa Locka, FL; cx 25Aug15]						
480	N302GA	USN 163691 [C20D]										
481	N304GA	USN 163692 [C20D]										
482	N306GA	N333HK	N600BL	N164RJ	N268RJ	N111HC						

G1159A GULFSTREAM III

C/n	Identities									
483*	N309GA	N66DD	N766DD	N19H	(N483H)	N343DF	N343DP	N794ME		
484	N310GA	N4UP	N856W	N506T	VP-BOR	N62MW	N62MV			
485	N315GA	N721CW	N777MW	N80SR	N5G	N95NM				
486	N316GA	TJ-AAW								
487*	N324GA	(TJ-...)	TC-GAP	N377GA	N90005	N488SB	N618KM	N416WM		
488	N325GA	N700CN	(N100BG)	N800BG	N446GA	N401RJ	N401PJ	N399SC	(N45PG)	N500GF
489*	N328GA	N272JS	N888CW	N388CW	XA-LCA	N218EE				
490	N332GA	N28R	N388MM							
491	N337GA	N73RP	N998JB	N531JF	(N531JC)	N101PT	N51MF	N51FF	A6-INF	HZ-HHT	[parted out California City, CA]
492	N339GA	N212AT	N212AD	PT-WRC	N492DD	N188TC	N848RJ	N939KM		
493	N322GA	N400J	N40QJ	Ghana G540	N7513H					
494	N370GA	India K-2961								
495	N371GA	India K-2962								
496	N372GA	N310SL	N21NY	N89AE	N89AB	N99SC	(N99SU)	N843HS	VP-CNP	N384BB
497	N373GA	US Army 87-0139		N7096G	US Army 87-0139	[C20E]	[wfu; to AMARG Davis-Monthan, AZ, 30Jan15]			
498	N374GA	US Army 87-0140		N7096E	US Army 87-0140	[C20E]	[wfu; to AMARG Davis-Monthan, AZ, 28Jul14]			
875	N333GA	N333GU	N210GK	N290GA	N728CP	N845FW	N298TB	N416NP	N300JZ	

Production complete

GULFSTREAM IV/GULFSTREAM 300/350/400/450

We have been advised by Gulfstream Aerospace that the Gulfstream IV does not have the model number G1159C as has been quoted elsewhere.

C/n	Series	Identities							
1000		N404GA	[ff 19Sep85] N234DB	N404DB	N971EC	N552WF			
1001		N17581	N441GA	N400GA	VR-BSS	VP-BSS	N31001	N981SW	N181CW	N181CR
1002		N440GA	N168WC	N168WM						
1003		N403GA	N986AH	N685TA	N885TA	N864YC	N250RG			
1004		N424GA	N184CW	(N199LX)	N124TF					
1005		N17582	VR-BJZ	N823GA	[w/o 13Jul12 Le Castellet, France]					
1006		N99GM	N3338	N614RD						
1007		N420GA	N100GN	N100GJ	N59JR	N575E	N710WJ			
1008		N26LB	N10LQ	N10LB	VR-BLH	N412GA	N119R	N85WD		
1009		N423GA	N500LS	N500VS	N700LS	N780LS	VR-BOY	Netherlands V-11		
1010		N426GA	N444TJ	N824CA	N950DM	XA-AVZ				
1011		N17581	A6-HHH	[cx; status?]						
1012		N445GA	N636MF	N838MF	N713VT	(N713VL)	N636GD	N836MF	N458BE	
1013		N446GA	N130B	N321PT	N321RT	N1625	(N16251)	N97FT	N64AL	XA-BVG	N3150C	(N771JG)
1014		N447GA	N777SW	N779SW	Sweden 102001 [code 021]					
1015		N17583	VR-BRF	VP-BRF	N450BF	N772AV				
1016		N427GA	N95AE	N29GY	N880GC	N21FJ				
1017		N405GA	N678RW	(C-FNCG)	VR-BHG	VP-BHG	N402KC	N818BA		
1018		N407GA	N300L	N43KS	N418QA	N113AR	N25VG	[parted out Dallas/Redbird, TX; fuselage to Roanoke, TX]		
1019		N17584	TU-VAD							
1020		N408GA	N600CS	N9300	N93AT					
1021		N412GA	N3M	N3NU	EC-HGH	N310EL	(N310EN)	N21DH		
1022		"N63M"	[painted on a/c but not officially reg'd] N23M	N23MU	N663PD					
1023		N415GA	N77SW	N778W	N85M	N85MG	N830EF	N300JA		
1024		(N130B)	N412GA	N96AE	"N16JM"	N116HM	N820HB	N1BB		
1025		N419GA	N5BK	N420SZ	N420SL	N421SZ	N928SZ	N928ST	N900GB	N595E	N250KC
1026		N17584	N151A	N277RP	(N277AG)	N100HG	N400HG			
1027		N416GA	TC-GAP	Turkey 001	[wore dual marks TC-GAP/001]		TC-GVB			
1028		N428GA	N712CW	N712CC	N605RA					
1029		N429GA	VR-BKI	VP-BKI	VP-BKH	N44ZF				
1030		N430GA	N811JK	N1WP	N24JR					
1031		N434GA	HZ-AFU							
1032		N17585	C-FSBR	N315MA	N315MC	N888UE	N432QS	N254GA	N2DF	
1033		(HB-IMY)	N69GP	N173LP	N1KE	N6453	N6458	N711SW	N711FW	N76EJ	(N400EE)
1034		N413GA	N800BG	N800BQ	N841PA	N388CA				
1035		N435GA	HZ-AFV							
1036		N152A	N45AC	N701DB						
1037		N17588	VR-BKE	HZ-ADC	HZ-103					
1038		N17603	N438GA	HZ-AFW						
1039		(N431GA)	N1901M	N726RW						
1040		N432GA	N74RP	N620DS	N908DH	N163EG				
1041		N433GA	N366F	N888FR						
1042		N17608	N400GA	N22	N220GA	N71TJ	N68SL	N217RR	N889TC	[parted out by Dodson Int'l Parts, Rantoul, KS]
1043		N1761B	TC-ANA	TC-ATA	TC-GVA					
1044		N423GA	N1040	N1540	N154G					
1045		N420GA	N227G	N227GH	N247EM	N217EM	[cx 18Nov13; wfu]			
1046		N1761D	(HB-ITT)	VR-BKU	(HB-ITE)	HB-ITP	N119K	N400CC	3B-PGF	
1047		N1761J	N461GA	N23AC	[w/o 30Oct96 Palwaukee, IL; cx Apr97]					
1048		N1761K	N448GA	(VR-BKL)	SU-BGM					
1049		N402GA	N372CM	N372GM	N113CS	N829CS	N136ZC	N385GP	N840ER	
1050		N153RA	N195WS	N1AM	N214BM	N517ML				
1051		N403GA	N399CC	N919CT	(N903JF)	(N903KP)	N515UJ	N515JA		
1052		N419GA	N800CC	N940DC	N152TS	N722MM	N48GL			
1053		N47SL	N26SL	N91AE	N165ST	N17ND	N168PK			
1054		N426GA	N400UP	N480UP	N745UP	N745UR	N789DK	(N1DC)	N860JB	N220LH	N254CA
1055		N1761P	VR-BKV	XB-EXJ	XB-OEM	N255GA	N450MS			
1056		N436GA	N33M	N33MX	N770SC	N685SF	N685MF			
1057		N437GA	N43M	N43MU	N222AD	N226AL	N842PA			
1058		N458GA	N70PS	VP-BSF	VP-BME	[w/o 01Dec04 Teterboro, NJ; cx 17Aug05; parted out by 818 Aviation, Mojave, CA]				
1059		N17581	V8-RB1	V8-ALI	V8-SR1	V8-007	N415GA	N701QS	N799WW	N199WW	N612AC	N271PS
1060		N427GA	N1SF	VT-AMA	[cx 17Jun10; parted out Mojave, CA]					
1061		N17582	N457GA	F-GPAK	N161AK	N429AL	HB-IWZ	N999GP		
1062		N17583	N462GA	N688H	VR-CMF	VP-CMF	N104JG	N619KK	N619ML	
1063		N17584	N54SB	N333AX	N720LH	N745RS	9Q-CGC			
1064		N439GA	HB-ITT	N7RP	N797CM	XA-AEX				
1065		N442GA	N584D	N511C	N599CN	C-FCNR	N835AA			
1066		N443GA	N118R	N466TS	N773JC	N1JR	N5JR	N63NM*		
1067		N446GA	N145ST	N200LC						
1068		N17585	N95AE	N90AE	N82A	N189J	(N189WJ)			
1069		N459GA	N765A	N450AR	N1AR	N813PD				
1070		N407GA	N107A	N40KJ						
1071		N410GA	N1							
1072		N17586	N100A	N500E	N260CH	N472MM				
1073		N75RP	N75PP	N177BB						
1074		N17587	(HB-I..)	VR-BKT	VP-BKT	N740JA	N995GG			
1075		N412GA	N901K	N121JJ	N121JV	N61WH				
1076		N17586	HZ-MNC	N338MM						
1077		N445GA	N119R	N119RC	PK-NSP	N477TS	N457DS			
1078		N17589	(G-BPJM)	G-DNVT	N211DK					
1079		N17603	XA-PUV	(N100WJ)	(N15WJ)	N479TS	N691RC	N794MH		
1080		N447GA	N20XY	N205X	M-YGIV	N108GS				
1081		N955H	(N955HC)	N777SA	N797SA	XA-RCM				
1082		N1082A	(N82BR)	M-GULF	N384MS	N555KE				
1083		N1761Q	HB-ITZ	VH-CCC	VH-CGF					
1084		(N448GA)	N1761S	HB-IMY						
1085		N449GA	N88GA	N864CE	N677RP	N423TT	N212JE			
1086		N460GA	N888MC	N23SY	N1086					
1087		N463GA	(N94SL)	N310SL	N1TM	N110TM	N368AG			
1088		N464GA	N4UP	N2600	N2600J	N1JN	N71JN	N93MK	N385PD	N305PB*
1089		N465GA	N53M	N53MU	Chile 911					
1090		N466GA	VR-CYM	VP-CYM	N9999M	VP-CYM	N9999M	N8989N		
1091		N467GA	N364G	N984JW						
1092		N468GA	N937US	N3H	N3HX	N661R	N18RF	N515PL	N515PE	N786JB	N13SA

GULFSTREAM IV/IVSP

C/n	Series	Identities									
1093		VR-BLC	HB-ITX	N399PA	N624BP	N100JF	N770KS				
1094		N2610	N740K	(N628NP)	N818BK						
1095		N469GA	N311EL								
1096		N17582	(G-....)	VR-CBW	VP-CBW	N167AA					
1097		N402GA	N900AL	N900AP							
1098		N403GA	N404CC	XA-AIS	N282CD	N7800	VP-BSF	N198GS			
1099		N489H	N299FB	(N499QS)	N199QS	N999LX	N36RR				
1100		N100AR	N100GX	B-8080	N483DJ						
1101		N404GA	N365G	N900EG							
1102		N405GA	N910B	XA-RBS	N522VR						
1103		N433GA	N90005	N103BC	VP-BIV	N3KN	C-FHPM				
1104		N600ML	N700GD	N2SA	[w/o Bakavu, Democratic Republic of Congo, 12Feb12]						
1105		N408GA	N312EL								
1106		N17608	9M-ISJ								
1107		N17581	(JA8366)	N101MU	N11FX	VH-CCO	N74TJ	N844GS	N844GF	N848GF	N606MH
1108		N17584	N410GA	N114AN	(N11AN)	N522AC	VH-NCP	N778MT	N463MA		
1109		N1761D	V8-ALI	V8-SR1	V8-007	N101GA	EC-IKP	G-MATF	N310EJ	N310	
1110		N415GA	N404M	N404MY	N88MX	N526EE	N888MX	N721MC	N883LS		
1111		N416GA	N111JL	N111ZT	N511PA						
1112		N417GA	N12UT	N12U	N12UM	N112WJ					
1113		N423GA	N902K	N168TR	N169TT	XA-JJS					
1114		N428GA	N444LT	N555WL	XA-BAL	XA-TOO	N314GA	N44LX	N763DB		
1115		N430GA	N410M	N410MY	N440TC	VH-TXS					
1116		N431GA	N971L	N305TC							
1117		N1761J	G-HARF	N105BH	VP-CMR	N117JF	N2121	N2129			
1118		N439GA	N1526M	N2WL	N440CP	N418TT	N720CH	N269HM			
1119		N407GA	N614HF	N768J	N524AN	N716AS					
1120		N410GA	VR-BOB	N400SA	N70AG	N20H	N888ES				
1121		N412GA	N7776	N411WW	N811WW	N214TS	N962SS	N178MH	N962SS		
1122		N40N	N226G	N317M	N317MJ	N600LY*					
1123		N457GA	I-LUBI	N529AL	N619A						
1124		N420GA	N1900W	N277GM							
1125		N432GA	N415SH	N700WB	N888LK	N888LG	N56AG	N49PP	N44CE		
1126		N426GA	5N-FGP	5N-BOD							
1127		N427GA	VR-BLR	VR-BUS	VP-BUS	N127DK	[w/o Tahiti 30Jan11]				
1128		N429GA	HZ-MFL								
1129		N17585	EI-CAH	ZS-NMO	N1129X	N8MC					
1130		N436GA	N401MM	N404LM	N711GL						
1131		N437GA	N679RW	N55TD							
1132		N442GA	A6-ALI	N60NY	N604M	N80BR	N4T	N71NR	N7JM		
1133		N443GA	N700CN	N375TC	N385GP						
1134		N445GA	VR-BJD	VP-BJD	N334JC	N8796J	N990PT	(N990PJ)	N990PM	(N34S)	N3H
1135		N435GA	N500MM	N100ES	N190ES	N456BE	N85KV	N930LS			
1136		N401GA	N27CD	N75VB							
1137		N402GA	N299DB	N21CZ	N7RX	N37RX	N777TC	N605CM			
1138		N403GA	N200A	(N501E)	N520E	N520EP	N777SA	N501RB			
1139		N404GA	N99WJ	N21KR	N21KP	N325RC	N331P	N134BR	N572EC		
1140		N405GA	N811JK	(N827JK)	N827JM	N77WL					
1141		N407GA	N767FL	N767EL	N115FL	N729TY					
1142		N408GA	I-LADA	N142NW	N222	N222GY					
1143		N410GA	HZ-AFX								
1144		N415GA	N100PM	N250J	B-HWA	N114GA	B-3999	N233GA	B-8091		
1145		N416GA	N102MU	N797CD	N569CW	LV-BYC	N569CW	N973MW			
1146		N417GA	N77SW	(N778W)	N777UE	N776US	N970SJ	N970SY			
1147		N419GA	N200PM	N820MS							
1148		N427GA	(JA8380)	N427GA	HB-IEJ	N306TT					
1149		N430GA	N777SW	N149GU	N152KB	N108DB	N108DU				
1150		N433GA	V8-ALI	V8-009	V8-SR1	N151G	VP-BIS	N386AG	N900RL		
1151		N375GA	N80AT	N109ST	N151ST	9U-BKB					
1152		N446GA	N63M	N63MU	[cx 10May13; parted out California City, CA]						
1153		N448GA	N110LE	N589HM	N590HM	N589HM	N546MG				
1154		N1761D	N150PG	N150GX	N151GX	N186DS					
1155		N1761B	N910S	N719SA							
1156		N1761K	N987AC	N987AR	VH-TGG	VH-XGG	N156TS	N5RD	N57LQ		
1157		N17581	9K-AJA	N457GA	OE-IJA	N157FQ	B-8082	N960DP			
1158		N17582	N917W								
1159		N17583	9K-AJB	N458FA	HB-IKR	(D-AAGF)	[cx; status?]				
1160		N17584	Ireland 251	N297PJ							
1161		N17585	9K-AJC	N459FA	N20EG	N461TS	N495RS				
1162	C20F	N457GA	US Army 91-0108	N7096B	US Army 91-0108						
1163		N458GA	Turkey 12-003		Turkey 91-003						
1164		N459GA	N300GX	N420CC	N218KD	(N103HF)					
1165		N460GA	N780E	N780N	N877LC						
1166		N461GA	HZ-SAR	HZ-AFY							
1167		N17586	N1SL	N49SL	N1SL	N275DJ					
1168		N462GA	A4O-AB	Oman 557							
1169		N463GA	N500DG	N600DW	N600CK						
1170		N464GA	N711SW	(N811SW)	N997BC	N880WD	N765RM				
1171		N465GA	N72RK	N686CG	N3SA	N1WE					
1172		N466GA	XA-SEC	N472TS	N85V	N85VM	N227SV				
1173		N17587	Botswana OK1		Botswana OK2		N731AE	N113WJ			
1174		N467GA	N174LM	HB-IEQ	N174SJ	N4PC	N6VB	N41VB	N10ZK	N914EG	N71NE
1175		N17588	HB-ITJ	(N1175B)	VH-CCA	N18WF	G-EVLN	5N-PZE			
1176		N468GA	V8-008	N176G	VP-CRY	N9253V	HB-IWY	N786CM			
1177		N469GA	N677RW	N236MJ							
1178		N470GA	N900LS	N909LS	N611JM						
1179		N471GA	N41CP	N41QR	N265ST	N527JC					
1180		N472GA	N700LS	N709LS	N827K	XA-ASI					
1181	C20H	N473GA	USAF 90-0300		N473GA	N906GA	USAF 90-0300				
1182		N475GA	N200LS	N202LS	N75CC	Chile 912					
1183	SP	N476GA	[ff as Gulfstream IV 23Dec91; cvtd to SP prototype and ff as such 24Jun92]			VR-BDC	HB-IBX	N510ST	N510SR	N510SP	
1184		N477GA	N111NL	(N508JM)	(N805JM)	N583AJ					
1185	SP	N478GA	N485GA	N635AV	N570DC						
1186		N479GA	8P-MAK	N345AA	N344AA	N915G*					
1187	C20G	N481GA	US Navy 165093								

GULFSTREAM IV/IVSP

C/n	Series	Identities								
1188		N482GA	HL7222	N102AK						
1189	C20G	N402GA	US Navy 165094							
1190		N403GA	JA001G							
1191	SP	N404GA	N979RA	N317M	N317MR	N317MB	N403TB			
1192	SP	N407GA	N212K	N180CH						
1193	SP	N412GA	(N980ML)	N163M	N620K	N620KA	N608CL			
1194	SP	N415GA	N77CP	N77QR	N473CW					
1195	SP	N419GA	XA-CHR	N47HR	N867CE	N888PM				
1196		N420GA	A4O-AC	Oman 558						
1197		N423GA	N150GX	XA-CAG	N969SG	N4753	N771AV			
1198		N425GA	N99GA	N68AL						
1199	C20G	N428GA	US Navy 165151 [code RG]							
1200	C20G	N430GA	US Marines 165153							
1201	C20G	N431GA	US Navy 165152							
1202		N432GA	V8-MSB	V8-009	JY-RAY	N369XL	HB-ITF	G-CFOH	M-PZPZ	N236CA
1203	SP	N434GA	N410WW	N411WW	N412WW	(N199PZ)	N417NK*			
1204		N435GA	N212AT	N252CH	N178PT					
1205	SP	N439GA	VH-ASQ	N8203K	N393BD	N671AF				
1206		N437GA	N1040	N1620	N162G	N315MK				
1207		N441GA	C-FDCS	C-FJES	N77SW	(N77VU)	N344AA	(N344AB)	N30LH	
1208	SP	N443GA	VR-BNY	VP-BNY	N297GB	N110SN				
1209		N445GA	N157H	N724DB	N724DD	N1D				
1210		N448GA	(N909SP)	N9PC	N410QS	N144PK				
1211		N447GA	N2107Z							
1212	SP	N413GA	VR-BOT	VP-BOT	N88HP	N884L	(N38NZ)	(N777NZ)	N502JT	N939PG
1213		N416GA	N56L							
1214		N405GA	N414BM	N2615	N2615B	N477JB				
1215	SP	N426GA	Sweden 102002							
1216	SP	N440GA	Sweden 102003							
1217	SP	N417GA	N981HC	N711MC	N711HE	(N711PE)	N979CB	N977CB		
1218	SP	N418SP	N5MC							
1219	SP	N446GA	PK-NZK	N50HE	N87HP	N874C				
1220	SP	N449GA	N79RP	N688TT	N688TF	N268VT				
1221	SP	N451GA								
1222	SP	N452GA	N71RP	N171JC						
1223	SP	N453GA	N935SH	N257H						
1224	SP	N454GA	N18TM	N18TD	N124TS	C-GEIV	M-IVSP	2-TRAV		
1225	SP	N459GA	N316GS	N816GS	N773MJ	N773AJ	N450KK	N450KD*		
1226	SP	N460GA	N41PR	N41PL	N50MG	N415WW	N96JA			
1227	SP	N463GA	(XA-VAD)	XA-DPS	N626TG	N626TC	N600VC	N958BX		
1228	SP	N464GA	N18AN	(VP-C..)	N30GD					
1229	SP	N465GA	N830EC	N270SC						
1230	SP	N467GA	9M-TRI	N101CV						
1231	SP	N470GA	N250VC	N250VZ	N255TS	VT-DLF	VT-ONE			
1232	SP	N471GA	N232K							
1233	SP	N472GA	N575SF	VP-BFW	A6-OME	N450JE	N700MV			
1234	SP	N475GA	N924ML	I-LXGR	VP-BNB	N999NB				
1235	SP	N477GA	N100A	N500E	N500EP	N17JK	N1AZ			
1236	SP	N478GA	N100GN	N99SC	N99EJ					
1237	SP	N480GA	N1904W	N277GR*						
1238	SP	N483GA	N499SC	(N71LA)	N92LA	(N92LU)	N415PG	C-GCPM		
1239	SP	N484GA	N1JN	N909RX	(N105TR)	N699HH	N950DM			
1240	SP	N486GA	N333PV	N212AW	N705PC	N789TN				
1241	SP	N487GA	N169CA	N343DF	N843DF	N117MS	N917MS			
1242	SP	N490GA	N982HC	N407GC						
1243	SP	N491GA	N404SP	VR-CBL	N39WH	N37WH	(N39WH)			
1244	SP	N404GA	JA002G							
1245	SP	N405GA	N101HC	(N7602)	N7601	N459BE	N588LS			
1246	SP	N407GA	N49RF							
1247	SP	N408GA	(N990UH)	N14UH	N477RP	N211MA	N94PC	N6PC		
1248	SP	N422GA	N62MS	N6VN	N244DS	N72RK	N700PP			
1249	SP	N423GA	N63HS	N634S	N151SD					
1250	SP	N425GA	VR-CBB	VP-CBB	N47HR	XA-CHR	N169JC	XA-JPS	XA-RUI	N169JC	XA-KTX
1251	SP	N429GA	(N321PT)	N60PT	N60PE	N165JF				
1252	SP	N433GA	N252C	N394TR	N707CW					
1253	SP	N435GA	N676RW	N225DC						
1254	SP	N436GA	N801CC	N930DC	N920DS	N920TB	VT-PLL	HZ-MKG	VT-PLP	N445BJ
1255	SP	N437GA	N600PM	VP-BNN	N934DF	VP-BKI	M-PBKI	N504ST		
1256	C20H	N438GA	USAF 92-0375							
1257	SP	N448GA	N4CP	N4QP	(N99PD)	N603CS	N1JN	(D-AGIV)	N603CS	N776MA
1258	SP	N416GA	N400UP	N585D	N598GS					
1259	SP	N495GA	N1PG	N4PG	N4UG	N559LC				
1260	SP	N461GA	N3PG	N810LP	(N415P)					
1261	SP	N469GA	N399CB	N57HJ						
1262	SP	N496GA	N462QS	N326AZ	N432HC					
1263	SP	N497GA	N830CB	N263S	N128TS	N147X				
1264	SP	N499GA	N464QS	N120JJ						
1265	SP	N465GA	N540W	VP-CFF	N165GD	N141CP	N450TL	VH-WXK	N370RS	
1266	SP	N412GA	N300K	N61LA	N91LA	(N91LU)	N77DY	N77D	VP-BOL	N267LG
1267	SP	N417GA	N301K	N624GJ						
1268	SP	N427GA	N990WC	N600BG	N888MF					
1269	SP	N434GA	N677SW	N677VU	N250LB	N925JS				
1270	U4	N442GA	Japan 75-3251							
1271	U4	N452GA	Japan 75-3252							
1272	SP	N454GA	N621JH	N621JA	N620JH					
1273	SP	N457GA	N372BC	N372BG	N102BG	N102BQ				
1274	SP	N458GA	"LV-WOW"	[painted in error at completion centre]		LV-WOM	Sweden 102004			
1275	SP	N459GA	N475QS	N505GF						
1276	SP	N460GA	N1955M	N1990C	N515XL	N856AF	N557WY			
1277	SP	N462GA	N5GF							
1278	SP	N464GA	VR-CTA	N98LT						
1279	SP	N466GA	N2002P	(N451C)	N925DC					
1280	SP	N468GA	N531MD	N688LS						
1281	SP	N470GA	N481QS	N129NS						
1282	SP	N471GA	(N96FL)	VR-CFL	VP-CFL	N9KN	N1925M			

GULFSTREAM IVSP

C/n	Series	Identities										
1283	SP	N472GA	N401JL	N402JP	N898AW							
1284	SP	N475GA	N1GN	N21GN	N150CM	(N577SW)	N90AM	N575CT	N707EA			
1285	SP	N477GA	N874A	N972MS								
1286	SP	N480GA	(N486GA)	N286GA	N464SP	N4SP	N464SP	N880G	N192NC	N192N	N7LA	N999AA	(N620HF)
1287	SP	N484GA	N487QS	N99GY								
1288	SP	N403GA	7T-VPR									
1289	SP	N405GA	N844HS	N802WC	N804WC	N800WC	N334MC	N202VZ	N289MU	N677FR	N607MH	N624MH*
1290	SP	N408GA	N6NB	N730BA	N71VR	N988LS						
1291	SP	N412GA	7T-VPS									
1292	SP	N413GA	N1GT	N917VZ	N292MU	N492JR	N1JN					
1293	SP	N415GA	N493QS	N429DD								
1294	SP	N416GA	HZ-MAL	N416GA	HZ-KAA	N718GM	N131SW	N294G				
1295	SP	N417GA	N495QS	N450MB								
1296	SP	N419GA	N725LB	N728LB								
1297	SP	N420GA	LV-WSS	N728JP	N710LX							
1298	SP	N422GA	N501PC	N961V								
1299	SP	N423GA	N499QS	N555LK								
1300	SP	N432GA	N1BN	N321BN	(N500BL)	N226MP						
1301	SP	N433GA	N92AE	N974JD								
1302	SP	N434GA	(N98AE)	N93AE	N818SS	N819SS						
1303	U4	N435GA	Japan 85-3253									
1304	SP	N436GA	N404QS	N287TX	N526EE							
1305	SP	N439GA	(N913SC)	N888SQ	N305GA	M-FMHG	N44GV					
1306	SP	N441GA	N540CH	N811DF	N89888							
1307	SP	N443GA	N94AE	N94AN	(N130WB)	N137WS						
1308	SP	N446GA	N408QS	N288TX	XA-STS							
1309	SP	N447GA	N309GA	N824CA	N56D	N992MS						
1310	SP	N448GA	(N2425)	N902	N902H	N850LG						
1311	SP	N449GA	N411QS	N271TX	N485GM							
1312	SP	N453GA	9M-ABC	N4FL	N619FL	N910AF*						
1313	SP	N455GA	N94LT	N100DF								
1314	SP	N461GA	N429SA	N427SA								
1315	SP	N413GA	N315GA	N950CM	N525KF	N580KF						
1316	SP	N427GA	N416QS	N168RT								
1317	SP	N417GA	N929WT	N333PY								
1318	SP	N418GA	N1624	N15Y								
1319	SP	N429GA	N878SM									
1320	SP	N437GA	N420QS	N116WJ								
1321	SP	N444GA	(N600CC)	N500CD	N905LP							
1322	SP	N445GA	N422QS	N272TX								
1323	SP	N454GA	N503PC	N565RV								
1324	SP	N457GA	N424QS	N817RA								
1325	SP	N459GA	N102FM	(N24EE)	Pakistan J-755							
1326	U4	N325GA	Japan 95-3254									
1327	SP	N327GA	TR-KHD	TR-KSP								
1328	SP	N328GA	N428QS	N450WG								
1329	SP	N329GA	SU-BNC									
1330	SP	N324GA	N400J	N40QJ	N168BB							
1331	SP	N331GA	N878G	EC-KEY	N74GG	(N322MG)	(N755CS)					
1332	SP	N332GA	SU-BND									
1333	SP	N333GA	N800J	N80QJ								
1334	SP	N334QS	N434QS	N626JS	N626LJ	N800CR						
1335	SP	N335GA	N720BA	N918CC	N978CC							
1336	SP	N636GA	N41CP	N235LP	C-FORB							
1337	SP	N637GA	N52MK	T7-DRM								
1338	SP	N638GA	N401WT	N100HF	XA-HNY							
1339	SP	N339GA	N327TL									
1340	SP	N340GA	N1TF	N800AL	N77D	N550GN						
1341	SP	N341GA	N441QS	N886LS								
1342	SP	N342GA	N555KC	N808T								
1343	SP	N343GA	N99SC	N2CC								
1344	SP	N344GA	N18AC	N411LL								
1345	SP	N345GA	(JY-ONE)	N457ST	N857ST	(N121PP)						
1346	SP	N346GA	N104AR	N104PR	RP-C8346							
1347	SP	N347GA	N988H	N933JJ	N155RJ	N156WJ						
1348	SP	N348GA	N80A	PP-WJB								
1349	SP	N349GA	HZ-KS1	N349GA	N616DC	N616DG	N510MG					
1350	SP	N330GA	N396U	N1JN	N396U							
1351	SP	N351GA	N451QS	N265SJ								
1352	SP	N352GA	N452QS	N572MS								
1353	SP	N353GA	A9C-BAH	A9C-BRF								
1354	SP	N354GA	N397J	N397JJ								
1355	SP	N355GA	N66DD	N66ED	N107TD							
1356	SP	N319GA	(JY-TWO)	N600DR	N970KG							
1357	SP	N357GA	N77FK									
1358	SP	N358GA	N1625									
1359	SP	N359GA	Japan 05-3255									
1360	SP	N360GA	N460QS	N428KS*								
1361	SP	N361GA	N545CS									
1362	SP	N362GA	N888LK	(N888LF)	ZK-KFB	N662GA	VQ-BMT					
1363	SP	N363GA	N463QS	N463G	N48CC	VH-DBT	N1363G	N869MD				
1364	SP	N364GA	N143KS	N711SK								
1365	SP	N365GA	HZ-MS04	HZ-MS4								
1366	SP	N320GA	N404M	N404XT	N445MD							
1367	SP	N367GA	HZ-KS2	N367GA	N422ML	N1EB	N618SA	N335LL	N335L	N415LT		
1368	SP	N322GA	N1967M	N610MC	N411AL	N125SJ						
1369	SP	N323GA	N469QS	N469G	N400MP							
1370	SP	N370GA	N240CX	N340CX								
1371	SP	N371GA	VP-CIP	N371FP	(N279AP)							
1372	SP	N372GA	N472QS	N926TT*								
1373	SP	N373GA	N373KM	N106KA	N595PE							
1374	SP	N374GA	N7PG	N1PG	N896AC							
1375	SP	N375GA	N247KB	B-8088	N484DJ	N222RA						
1376	SP	N376GA	N12NZ	N400CK								
1377	SP	N377GA	N477QS									

C/n	Series	Identities							
1378	SP	N378GA	N2PG	N269WR					
1379	SP	N379GA	N60PT	VT-MST	VP-CTR	N450EF			
1380	SP	N380QS	N480VR						
1381	SP	N381GA	VP-BZA	VP-BIV	VP-BYS	A6-NMA	PK-TWY		
1382	SP	N382GA	N1TF	(N222MC)	N1GC	N428M	C-GMRX		
1383	SP	N383GA	N955H	N955E	(N507TE)	N707TE			
1384	SP	N384GA	(HZ-KS3)	N404AC	N945GS				
1385	SP	N485GA	N577SW	N577VU	N1818C	N4818C			
1386	SP	N486GA	N486QS	N889CG*					
1387	SP	N487GA	N254SD	N854SD	N4387	N108RT			
1388	SP	N477GA	N38BG	N4SP	XA-EYA	N990EA			
1389	SP	N389GA	N489QS						
1390	SP	N490GA	N1874M	VP-CSF	N30JE				
1391	SP	N391GA	N827GA						
1392	SP	N392GA	N492QS						
1393	SP	N393GA	N297MC	N352BH					
1394	SP	N394GA	N721RL						
1395	SP	N395GA	N961SV	N396NS					
1396	SP	N396GA	N890A	N664JN					
1397	SP	N397GA	N669BJ						
1398	SP	N398GA	N498QS						
1399	SP	N499GA	N121JM	[w/o Bedford/Hanscom Field, MA, 31May14]					
1400	SP	N478GA	N215TM	N700FS					
1401	SP	N401GA	N900LS	N300CR					
1402	SP	N479GA	N602PM	(N602AG)	(N602KF)	N602PL	VP-CLA	M-ABCT	N80AE	N799CP
1403	SP	N403GA	N403QS						
1404	SP	N404GA	N404HS	XA-FCP					
1405	SP	N310GA	N45ET						
1406	SP	N311GA	VP-BNZ	N404GA	N526EE	N104AD			
1407	SP	N312GA	N407QS	N40HB	N407NS				
1408	SP	N316GA	(N448QS)	N401QS					
1409	SP	N317GA	N67TM						
1410	SP	N318GA	N80AT						
1411	SP	N411GA	N56MD	N56D	N303TP	N404TC	(N808TC)	N444QC	
1412	SP	N412GA	N700LS	N709LS	A6-DWD	N65CC			
1413	SP	N413GA	5X-UEF	N92SA	PP-CSW	N197SW	(N413VS)		
1414	SP	N323GA	"N819JF"	N5VS	N505VS	N333EC	(N787AF)		
1415	SP	N415GA	N71BD						
1416	SP	N416GA	N900WR						
1417	SP	N417GA	(N417QS)	N122RS	XA-RYR				
1418	SP	N418GA	7T-VPC						
1419	SP	N419GA	EI-CVT	VP-BVT	(N419GA)	N600AR	N617WM		
1420	SP	N420GA	N72BD	N106CE	N724DB				
1421	SP	N324GA	7T-VPM						
1422	SP	N422GA	N999GP	N7UF					
1423	SP	N423GA	N621JH						
1424	SP	N328GA	SU-BNO						
1425	SP	N425GA	XA-ABA	P4-TAK	P4-DDA	P4-NMD			
1426	SP	N426GA	N426QS						
1427	SP	N427GA	SU-BNP						
1428	SP	N330GA	N512C	N990NB	N991NB				
1429	SP	N429GA	N777KK						
1430	SP	N331GA	N530JD	N14456	N913SQ	N71TV			
1431	SP	N334GA	N818ME						
1432	SP	N335GA	N211DH						
1433	SP	N433GA	N1SN						
1434	SP	N434GA	N663P	N9106					
1435	SP	N435GA	N144KK	N435GA	N994GC	N502PC			
1436	SP	N436GA	N436QS						
1437	SP	N437GA							
1438	SP	N388GA	N228RE						
1439	SP	N439GA	N586D	N505UP					
1440	SP	N391GA	N997AG	N76RP	N84HD	N40AA			
1441	SP	N341GA	N1289M	N123LC	VH-OSW	N950LG			
1442	SP	N442GA	N481FB	N345LC	N718DW	N106TD			
1443	SP	N443GA	N305LM						
1444	SP	N344GA	(N444GV)	N400HF	N904TC	N944TC	HZ-SK1		
1445	SP	N445GA	N445QS	N474D	N474X				
1446	SP	N446GA	N317M	N317ML	N817ME				
1447	SP	N447GA	N667P	N822A					
1448	SP	N448GA	N1LB	N300LB	N808MF				
1449	SP	N449GA	N200LS	N209LS	(N4SP)	N309SG	N551CB		
1450	SP	N370GA	N809C	N435HC					
1451	SP	N351GA	N372CM	N522BP	N522BR	N244J			
1452	SP	N452GA	N603PM	(N603AG)	N603KF	N603KE	N816SP		
1453	SP	N453GA	N444QG						
1454	SP	N454GA	N454QS						
1455	SP	N455GA	N616CC						
1456	SP	N396GA	N507SA	N207AA					
1457	SP	N357GA	N234DB	N234DN	N305CF				
1458	SP	N358GA	N235KK						
1459	SP	N399GA	(D-AJJJ)	D-AJGK	N1459A				
1460	SP	N460GA	(N825LM)	HB-ILV	N331LV	(N326LM)	N326JD	N386JD	
1461	SP	N461GA	N877A						
1462	SP	N462GA	N462CS	N462CK	N457H	N1SG			
1463	SP	N463GA	N465QS						
1464	SP	N464GA	N950AV	N950HB	N119FM				
1465	SP	N465GA	RA-10201						
1466	SP	N266GA	VP-BSH	N888ZF					
1467	SP	N467GA	(N225BK)	N225CX	N226CX	XA-BLZ	XA-PTR		
1468	SP	N468GA	N700NY	N814RR					
1469	SP	N269GA	N5956B						
1470	SP	N470GA	N34UH	N394AK					
1471	SP	N471GA	N471CR	N923CL					
1472	SP	N372GA	N4DA	N475LC					

GULFSTREAM IVSP/300/400/350/450

C/n	Series	Identities						
1473	SP	N373GA	XA-EOF	N620M	N711EG			
1474	SP	N374GA	(N948AV)	N248AB	N7799T			
1475	SP	N475GA	N24TH	N67TH	N324FP			
1476	SP	N476GA	N59AP	N52AP	N221EA			
1477	SP	N477GA	(N949AV)	N244DS	N284DS	N468AB	N100EW	N100ZW	N606PS
1478	SP	N378GA	N478GS					
1479	SP	N479GA	N1479G	N226RS				
1480	SP	N480GA	N482QS	CS-DKA	N36MW			
1481	SP	N281GA	N621SC	N691SC	4X-CPX			
1482	SP	N482GA	N13J	N121JJ				
1483	SP	N483GA	N810TM					
1484	SP	N484GA	N721FF	N717AL				
1485	SP	N485GA	N5NG					
1486	SP	N486GA	N608PM	(N608AG)	(N608KF)	M-YWAY		
1487	SP	N487GA	N428AS	N428AZ	XA-SKY	M-GFOR	VH-TSL	
1488	SP	N488GA	N490QS					
1489	SP	N389GA	N142HC	N142HQ	N212WZ	N119AF		
1490	SP	N490GA	(N490QS)	N1TM				
1491	SP	N491GA	N491EC					
1492	SP	N392GA	N123MR	N500PC				
1493	SP	N493GA	N235DX	N717DX	N104DX	N154C		
1494	SP	N494GA	N400FJ					
1495	SP	N495GA	N250VC	N251MM	N33LR	N899AL*		
1496	SP	N496GA	N308AB	N800AR				
1497	SP	N397GA	(N497QS)	N702GH				
1498	SP	N398GA	N780RH	N757MC				
1499	SP	N499GA	N941AM	N918TB	N918TD	N55ME*	[last a/c to bear the Gulfstream IV name]	
1500	400	N520GA	N400GA	(N55GJ)	N50EE			
1501	400	N401GA	(N402QS)	N128AB	N176MG			
1502	400	N202GA	N710EC					
1503	300	N403GA	A6-RJA	(D-AONE)	HZ-FM2			
1504	400	N374GA	(N402QS)	N902L	N570BY			
1505	300	N405GA	A6-RJB					
1506	400	N306GA	SU-BPE					
1507	300	N307GA	N91KL	N826RP				
1508	300	N508GA	N820TM	(B-MJZ)	B-LSZ	N388AJ		
1509	300	N509GA	N607PM	N607KF	N789RR	XA-RIN		
1510	300	N510GA	N609PM	(N609KF)	(N609RM)	N349K		
1511	400	N201GA	N161MM					
1512	300	N512GA	N606PM	(N606KF)	N958TB			
1513	400	N113GA	N4UC	N928GC	N500RL			
1514	400	N314GA	N1932P	(N1931P)	LV-CAZ			
1515	400	N415GA	N851EL	N342AP				
1516	400	N516GA	N400GA	N721BS				
1517	300	N517GA	N129MH	N130MH	N900CC			
1518	400	N218GA	SU-BPF					
1519	400	N519GA	N527JG					
1520	300	N520GA	HZ-MF3					
1521	400	N221GA	N413QS					
1522	400	N522GA	N251DV	N254SD	N854SD			
1523	400	N423GA	N401FT					
1524	400	N524GA	N522AC	N522AG	XA-CHG			
1525	300	N425GA	HZ-MF4					
1526	300	N526GA	N160TM					
1527	400	N327GA	N402FT					
1528	400	N528GA	N523AC	N706VA	N702JF*			
1529	400	N529GA	N477SA	(N171RH)	N702RH*			
1530	400	N330GA	N650PW					
1531	400	N531GA	N212VZ	N531MU	A6-HHH			
1532	300	N532GA	HZ-MF5					
1533	400	N533GA	N467QS	N167TV				
1534	400	N434GA	(N650PW)	(N616KF)	N616KG	N721KJ		
1535	300	N435GA	N825T					

GULFSTREAM 350/450

The Gulfstream 450 was originally dubbed the GIV-X and was awarded its FAA Type certificate 13Aug04
The Gulfstream 350 is essentially a shorter-range Gulfstream 450

C/n	Series	Identities						
4001	450	N401SR						
4002	450	N442SR	N820AV	N4FC	N820AV			
4003	450	N403SR	N821AV	N704JW				
4004	450	N404SR	N450GA	N428TT	(N8875)	D-ARKK	N156WC	N4500X	N4570X
4005	450	N165GA	N512JT	N512LT	(N980CM)			
4006	450	N166GA	N111CQ					
4007	450	N185GA	N142HC	N142HQ	HZ-A13	HZ-SK5		
4008	450	N608GA	N97FT	N97FL	XA-XTR			
4009	450	N909GA	N885AR	(N885RR)	(N299AJ)			
4010	450	N910GA	N425QS					
4011	350	N121GA	N502GM					
4012	450	N812GA	N80Q	N80QL	N450Z			
4013	350	N913GA	N5113	N211FZ	N931DC			
4014	450	N314GA	N415QS					
4015	350	N915GA	N117WR					
4016	350	N816GA	N5114	N551GR	XC-PFM			
4017	450	N917GA	N7RX					
4018	450	N618GA	B-KHK					
4019	350	N989GA	"N350GA"+	[+ fake marks worn in NBAA Static park Nov05 Orlando Executive, FL]		N5115	N82CW	

GULFSTREAM 350/450

C/n	Series	Identities					
4020	450	N990GA	(N450GA)+	[+ ntu marks worn in NBAA Static park Nov05 Orlando Executive, FL]		N588AT	N326AZ
4021	450	N621GA	N430QS				
4022	450	N622GA	N464ST	N461GT*			
4023	350	N623GA	N5116				
4024	450	N624GA	N451CM	(N927EM)			
4025	450	N998GA	N440QS				
4026	350	N626GA	N5117	XA-LAA	N906JC		
4027	450	N627GA	HB-JEQ	S5-ADC	G-SADC	D-AFLY	N251HR
4028	450	N628GA	N915BD	N881E	PK-TMI		
4029	450	N629GA	N888HH				
4030	450	N630GA	N235CG	N285CG	C-GXDN	N348RS	
4031	450	N631GA	(N450JK)	N1JK	VP-CAE	N450FK	(PT-FKK)
4032	450	N632GA	N24XC	N82A	N823A		
4033	450	N633GA	N989WS	N404PX			
4034	450	N634GA	N122GV	N442HM			
4035	450	N635GA	N409CC	N119AD			
4036	450	N936GA	N922H	N922N	N1MC		
4037	450	N537GA	N445QS				
4038	350	N538GA	N450RG				
4039	450	N439GA	N450GA	N760G	N539VE	N937BG	
4040	350	N440GA	N350FK				
4041	450	N401GA	N451DC				
4042	450	N442GA	N776JB				
4043	450	N443GA	N450AB				
4044	450	N644GA	N663CP	N450KR			
4045	450	N445GA	4K-AZ888				
4046	450	N446GA	N450QS				
4047	450	N447GA	N664CP	C-GFCP			
4048	450	N448GA	N900AL	N950AV			
4049	450	N449GA	N665CP	N665P	N918E		
4050	450	N850GA	N244DS	N865R			
4051	450	N351GA	N908VZ	N405MU	N868BB*		
4052	450	N452GA	N500J	N50UJ	N918CC		
4053	450	N453GA	N845G				
4054	450	N454GA	N405QS				
4055	450	N455GA	N237GA	N240JA*			
4056	450	N556GA	(N450PG)	N500N	N778CR		
4057	450	N457GA	N500RP	N457GA	N2LA		
4058	450	N458GA	N218WW	N18NY			
4059	450	N459GA	N222NB	N221NB	N18S		
4060	450	N460GA	G-TAYC				
4061	450	N461GA	N450LV				
4062	450	N462GA	N450XX				
4063	450	N463GA	N930DC				
4064	450	N464GA	N768JJ	N763JJ	N338TZ		
4065	450	N465GA	N450GD	(N555LR)	N767DX	N767DT	PR-ETE	N450EA
4066	450	N466GA	OY-GVG	P4-BFL			
4067	450	N467GA	N475M	HZ-...			
4068	450	N468GA	N435QS				
4069	450	N469GA	N612AF				
4070	450	N470GA	N818G	N100EW			
4071	450	N471GA	N24TH	N76TH			
4072	450	N372GA	N450PG				
4073	450	N373GA	N474M	HZ-...			
4074	450	N374GA	N455QS				
4075	450	N375GA	N440AS	N913MK			
4076	450	N376GA	N779CS	N796MA	B-8098	N407GA	
4077	350	N377GA	N723MM				
4078	450	N378GA	N310GJ	N865JM			
4079	450	N379GA	N450NS	HZ-KSGA			
4080	450	N380GA	N555TF				
4081	450	N381GA	N926RR				
4082	450	N382GA	N451NS				
4083	450	N383GA	N251VP				
4084	450	N384GA	N470QS				
4085	450	N385GA	N711SW	(N711SZ)	N711FW	N88WR	
4086	350	N486GA	N722MM	N722MN	VH-NKD		
4087	450	N387GA	N800AL				
4088	450	N388GA	N450EJ	VP-CKD	B-LIS		
4089	450	N389GA	N606CH	N779AZ			
4090	450	N490GA	Pakistan J-756				
4091	450	N391GA	N450GA	(N450GQ)	D-AABB	N274TX	PR-VCO
4092	450	N392GA	VP-BIV	VQ-BGA			
4093	450	N393GA	VP-CMG				
4094	450	N494GA	N452NS	M-ABRJ			
4095	450	N495GA	N450PU				
4096	450	N496GA	VP-BMY	B-LWX			
4097	450	N397GA	N59CF				
4098	450	N398GA	N608CH	N600AR			
4099	450	N199GA	N841WS				
4100	450	N120GA	N448QS				
4101	450	N401GA	N424PX				
4102	450	N702GA	XA-GMX				
4103	450	N603GA	VP-BTB				
4104	450	N704GA	OE-ICH	M-AAMM			
4105	450	N405GA	N450T				
4106	450	N606GA	A6-FLG	4L-GAF			
4107	450	N607GA	N717DX				
4108	450	N608GA	N227RH				
4109	450	N609GA	N950SW				
4110	450	N610GA	N450WB				
4111	450	N131GA	N178SD				
4112	450	N612GA	N703LH	N3918Y			
4113	450	N913GA	D-AGVS				
4114	450	N614GA	N421QS				

GULFSTREAM 350/450

C/n	Series	Identities				
4115	450	N815GA	SX-SEE	VP-BSA		
4116	450	N216GA	N990PT	N516VE	N483CM	
4117	450	N417GA	N450GD	N770XB		
4118	450	N418GA	N7GU	N667LC		
4119	450	N819GA	VP-BAE	M-ARAE	OE-LAR	
4120	450	N420GA	N851GG			
4121	450	N821GA	OE-IMZ			
4122	450	N422GA	HB-JGJ	OK-ILE		
4123	450	N423GA	A6-DJL	HB-JUS	N450PJ	VQ-BZM
4124	450	N424GA	N944AL	N512RJ		
4125	450	N425GA	N461QS			
4126	450	N426GA	N192NC			
4127	450	N427GA	N450LC	N59AP		
4128	450	N528GA	N988AL	Mexico AMT-205	XC-LMF	
4129	450	N429GA	N596DC			
4130	450	N130GA	OE-IAG	HB-JGB		
4131	450	N531GA	N667HS			
4132	450	N532GA	N851CB			
4133	450	N433GA	N478QS	(N478WC)	A6-ORX	
4134	450	N434GA	N9939T			
4135	450	N535GA	N499SC			
4136	450	N436GA	N65QT	A6-AZH		
4137	450	N337GA	VP-CFB	M-YGLK		
4138	450	N138GA	N458X			
4139	450	N439GA	N212LF	N212LE	N922WC	
4140	450	N740GA	N1BX			
4141	450	N541GA	N451QS	N18CJ		
4142	450	N742GA	N432AS	N1TT		
4143	450	N843GA	N884WT	N884WE		
4144	450	N444GA	N450GA	N72LN		
4145	450	N545GA	N9BX			
4146	450	N146GA	N468QS			
4147	450	N447GA	N10SN	N728MM	N728MN	
4148	450	N448GA	VQ-BCE			
4149	450	N449GA	N246V			
4150	450	N950GA	VP-BMV			
4151	450	N651GA	(N459X)	N1818C		
4152	450	N152GA	N451JC	N608D		
4153	450	N453GA	N27YA			
4154	450	N454GA	N92HL	N975GR	B-8155	
4155	450	N455GA	A6-FLH			
4156	450	N656GA	A9C-BHR			
4157	450	N657GA	N451BH			
4158	450	N458GA	N202VZ			
4159	450	N459GA	N451C			
4160	450	N360GA	N844GF			
4161	450	N461GA	VP-BSR			
4162	450	N462GA	N37JL			
4163	450	N463GA	N450GD	N450EE		
4164	450	N464GA	N718JS			
4165	450	N565GA	B-8093			
4166	450	N126GA	VP-CET			
4167	450	N467GA	N597DC			
4168	450	N468GA	B-8099			
4169	450	N569GA	N922CB			
4170	450	N570GA	B-8128			
4171	450	N571GA	N225CX			
4172	450	N572GA	SX-GAB			
4173	450	N175GA	N936MP			
4174	450	N574GA	N9SC			
4175	450	N475GA	TC-KHB			
4176	450	N178GA	N1DW			
4177	450	N577GA	N918LL			
4178	450	N478GA	B-8096			
4179	450	N479GA	N915AM	N919AM		
4180	450	N418GA	SX-MAW	N427MG	B-8158	
4181	450	N181GA	N123LV	M-SWAN		
4182	450	N482GA	B-LCK			
4183	450	N483GA	N903G			
4184	450	N984GA	N333SZ	B-8252		
4185	450	N985GA	VH-MBP			
4186	450	N986GA	N510AK	N511AK		
4187	450	N187GA	B-LWW			
4188	450	N188GA	N188DX			
4189	450	N989GA	N450GA	N555LR		
4190	450	N790GA	B-8127			
4191	450	N491GA	(N235WL)	N235PZ	N4CP	N814CP
4192	450	N492GA	N1902P			
4193	450	N693GA	N77XM	B-8253		
4194	450	N494GA	N803AG			
4195	450	N495GA	N451LC	N65HD		
4196	450	N996GA	B-8133			
4197	450	N397GA	N167AD			
4198	450	N398GA	N917VZ			
4199	450	N499GA	N804AG			
4200	450	N820GA	OE-IZK			
4201	450	N401GA	XA-CHE			
4202	450	N202GA	VP-CSH	B-LAS		
4203	450	N403GA	HB-JKF	VP-CMY		
4204	450	N904GA	N818KE			
4205	450	N452GA	(N229LS)	B-8150	N333GW	
4206	450	N906GA	N236LP			
4207	450	N907GA	N807BC			
4208	450	N608GA	N888KJ	N818TS		
4209	450	N909GA	N300ES			

GULFSTREAM 350/450

C/n	Series	Identities				
4210	450	N120GA	N60TC			
4211	450	N711GA	B-8322			
4212	450	N922GA	TC-DYO	N451SC	OB-2017-P	N451SC	N20G
4213	450	N413GA	N450L			
4214	450	N214GA	N450BE			
4215	450	N425GA	N847RC			
4216	450	N216GA	B-8166			
4217	450	N427GA	(N289HC)	D-ADSE	N450HE	
4218	450	N218GA	N450JR	(N450MK)	XA-ELK	
4219	450	N429GA	N213TG			
4220	450	N920GA	M-DKVL			
4221	450	N712GA	N57EL			
4222	450	N422GA	N280BC			
4223	450	N423GA	N104AR			
4224	450	N924GA	N701WC			
4225	450	N622GA	N450GD	N81GK		
4226	450	N426GA	N494EC			
4227	450	N627GA	N268ND	B-8262		
4228	450	N822GA	N85M			
4229	450	N229GA	N222NB			
4230	450	N730GA	N56EL			
4231	450	N931GA	N502P			
4232	450	N432GA	N129MH			
4233	450	N433GA	N175BL			
4234	450	N434GA	B-8250			
4235	450	N735GA	PR-LHW			
4236	450	N436GA	(N428TT)	N426TT	N236FS	
4237	450	N374GA	OE-LAI			
4238	450	N938GA	B-8161			
4239	450	N439GA	TC-IPK			
4240	450	N940GA	I-DLGH	TC-GAP		
4241	450	N641GA	M-VICI	N224BH		
4242	450	N942GA	B-8251			
4243	450	N943GA	OH-GIV	D-AGVI		
4244	450	N444GA	(N1100A)	N125TF		
4245	450	N445GA	N7777N			
4246	450	N446GA	VP-BSQ	TC-REC		
4247	450	N647GA	P4-MVP			
4248	450	N348GA	VP-CTH			
4249	450	N249GA	TC-MZA			
4250	450	N345GA	N450CE			
4251	450	N151GA	B-8257			
4252	450	N252GA	(N383XX)	N383KK		
4253	450	N453GA	N533SR			
4254	450	N354GA	XA-ATI			
4255	450	N455GA	VP-CLI			
4256	450	N456GA	(N888JE)	N888DC		
4257	450	N457GA	N818SS			
4258	450	N258GA	B-8265			
4259	450	N459GA	N702TR			
4260	450	N460GA	OE-IOK	M-YANG		
4261	450	N261GA	N250AF			
4262	450	N462GA	M-KBBG			
4263	450	N463GA	N7GF	N721MJ		
4264	450	N964GA	B-8290			
4265	450	N465GA	OH-JVA	S5-JVA		
4266	450	N466GA	M-MNDG	N426GA		
4267	450	N467GA	B-8267			
4268	450	N468GA	N1963N			
4269	450	N469GA	HB-JKJ	VP-CMC		
4270	450	N470GA	VP-CHH	Pakistan 4270		
4271	450	N471GA	B-8271			
4272	450	N272GA	B-8291			
4273	450	N372GA	M-AVOS			
4274	450	N274GA	B-8295			
4275	450	N275GA	N450GA	N90AE		
4276	450	N176GA	B-8263			
4277	450	N477GA	B-8299			
4278	450	N178GA	N278NA			
4279	450	N279GA	I-XPRA			
4280	450	N980GA	N400J			
4281	450	N281GA	N268RB			
4282	450	N282GA	VP-CQQ			
4283	450	N483GA	M-MNVN			
4284	450	N284GA	M-NELS	M-PING		
4285	450	N885GA	B-8279			
4286	450	N286GA	B-8316			
4287	450	N287GA	B-8278			
4288	450	N488GA	N142HC	N142HQ	N142HC	N142HQ
4289	450	N289GA	N299SC			
4290	450	N890GA	N1Z			
4291	450	N491GA	OE-IRE			
4292	450	N292GA	N440MB			
4293	450	N493GA	B-8293			
4294	450	N294GA	PT-MTP			
4295	450	N495GA	N617XT			
4296	450	N296GA	N500N			
4297	450	N297GA	B-8301			
4298	450	N998GA	N900PY			
4299	450	N299GA	N668EM			
4300	450	N400GA	B-8300			
4301	450	N901GA				
4302	450	N902GA	N71GE			
4303	450	N303GA	M-SOBR			
4304	450	N934GA	N456SW			

GULFSTREAM 350/450

C/n	Series	Identities			
4305	450	N805GA	OY-APM		
4306	450	N306GA	M-KKCO		
4307	450	N307GA	OE-IIE		
4308	450	N308GA	N450GD	C-FDBJ*	
4309	450	N309GA	B-8308		
4310	450	N110GA	VP-BAK		
4311	450	N931GA	N666ZW		
4312	450	N312GA	N451PW		
4313	450	N413GA	HZ-MS4A		
4314	450	N314GA	VP-CAX		
4315	450	N315GA	B-3029		
4316	450	N316GA	N238MH		
4317	450	N317GA	N229AR		
4318	450	N718GA	N154FV		
4319	450	N319GA	M-WONE		
4320	450	N820GA	N903TC		
4321	450	N432GA	N321LV	A6-VPS	
4322	450	N422GA	M-MAEE		
4323	450	N323GA	5N-AZK		
4324	450	N324GA	HZ-MS4B		
4325	450	N425GA	N212VZ		
4326	450	N426GA	I-BMPG		
4327	450	N427GA	N904TC		
4328	450	N328GA	HZ-MS4C		
4329	450	N429GA	N908VZ		
4330	450	N330GA	N450FX		
4331	450	N833GA	N450GA		
4332	450	N832GA	N451FX		
4333	450	N433GA	Mexico 3915/XC-LOJ	Mexico TP-06/XC-LOJ	
4334	450	N434GA	N452FX		
4335	450	N835GA			
4336	450	N436GA	N453FX		
4337	450	N337GA	N169TA		
4338	450	N838GA	N899FS		
4339	450	N439GA	N454FX		
4340	450	N440GA	N455FX		
4341	450	N841GA	N584A		
4342	450	N942GA	PR-CBK		
4343	450	N443GA	N888ND		
4344	450	N444GA	N450JS		
4345	450	N445GA	N587DV		
4346	450	N446GA			
4347	450	N447GA	N904TS*		
4348	450	N448GA			
4349	450	N449GA			
4350	450	N850GA	N844CB*		
4351	450	N351GA			
4352	450	N352GA			
4353	450	N453GA			
4354	450	N354GA			
4355	450	N355GA			
4356	450	N356GA			
4357	450	N957GA			
4358	450	N458GA			
4359	450	N459GA			
4360	450	N360GA			
4361	450	N361GA			
4362	450	N362GA			
4363	450	N363GA			
4364	450	N964GA			
4365	450	N465GA			
4366	450	N466GA			
4367	450	N467GA			
4368	450	N468GA			
4369	450	N369GA			
4370	450	N370GA			
4358	450	N458GA			
4359	450	N459GA			
4360	450	N360GA			
4361	450	N361GA			
4362	450	N362GA			
4363	450	N363GA			
4364	450	N964GA			
4365	450	N465GA			
4366	450	N466GA			
4367	450	N467GA			
4368	450	N468GA			
4369	450	N369GA			
4370	450	N370GA			

GULFSTREAM V/GULFSTREAM 500/550

We have been advised by Gulfstream Aerospace that the Gulfstream V does not have the model number G1159D as has been quoted elsewhere.

C/n	Series	Identities										
501		N501GV	[rolled out 22Sep95; ff 28Nov95]		N22	N99NG						
502		N502GV	N502KA	N5GV	N502KA							
503		N503GV	N767FL									
504		N504GV	N313RG									
F5		[Static test airframe]										
505		N505GV	EI-WGV	N505AX	N371JC							
506		N506GV	N158AF	N500GV	N33XE	(N506GV)	M-FISH					
507		N507GA	N300L	N507DW								
508		N508GA	N777GV	N899GM	N777TY	[w/o Palm Beach Int'l, FL, 14Feb02]		N777PY	[cx 10Aug04; b/u Palm Beach Int'l, FL; remains to Savannah, GA, by Oct04]			
509		N509GA	V8-009	V8-001	V8-009	N509GA	"N61GV"	N5GA	VP-BNZ	N509GV	N855RB	N888XY
510		N598GA	N513MW	B-8092	N194MF							
511		N511GA	VP-CBX	N779WA								
512		N512GV	N636MF	N838MF	N863MF							
513		N513GA	HB-IVL	N85NV								
514		N514GA	N777SW	N304K	N320K	N256LK	B-KDP					
515		N599GA	V8-007	V8-001	N55GV							
516		N516GA	N555CS	N740BA	N882WT							
517		N517GA	HB-IMJ									
518		N518GA	HZ-MIC	N555GN	(N36GA)	N1GN	N555GN	N555GV	N5GV	(N55GV)	N885G	(N917ND) N17ND
519		N597GA	VP-CMG	N526EE	N452AC	N549CP						
520		N596GA	N17GV	N450AR	N818DA	(N786CW)	N767CW					
521	C-37A	N521GA	USAF 97-0400									
522		N595GA	(N158RA)	N39PY	N20H	N20HN	N70AG					
523		N523GA	N711SW	N790MC	N54TG							
524		N524GA	N400JD	N674RW	N1892	N474MJ						
525		N594GA	N252JS	N40SR	VT-SMI							
526		N526GA	N675RW	N125GH								
527		N527GA	N5SA	N25CP								
528		N528GA	N80RP	N75RP	N9UX							
529		N529GA	N73RP	N529TA	T7-TIL	N677FP						
530		N530GA	N780F	N780W								
531		N531GA	(N8CA)	N531AF	N1GT	N279PH						
532		N532GA	N282Q	(N282QT)	N282QA	N740SS						
533		N533GA	XA-CPQ									
534		N534GA	(N158JJ)	N920DC	N127GG							
535		N593GA	N775US	(N535GV)	N535V							
536		N536GA	N5UH	N688TY	N318AG							
537		N537GA	8P-MAK	N132SD								
538		N538GA	N601MD	N1JN	N223GA							
539		N539GA	N1GC	N162JC								
540		N640GA	XA-OEM									
541		N641GA	N405LM	N405DR	N53LT	N459BE						
542	C-37A	N642GA	USAF 97-0401									
543		N643GA	N91CW									
544		N644GA	N910DC	N383LS								
545		N645GA	N1HC	N55GV	N5GV	N888CW	N545CC	N209MG				
546		N646GA	XA-BAL	XA-DAB								
547		N647GA	N73M	N625TF								
548		N648GA	N245TT	N245TJ	N32BD	XA-AHM						
549		N649GA	N317JD	N718MC	N718MD	N123FT						
550		N650GA	N5101	N105CX								
551		N651GA	N5102	N9102								
552		N652GA	N9SC	N189SC	B-8130	N552WS						
553		N653GA	N516GH									
554		N654GA	N589HM	N450BE	HB-JKA	N38NZ	XA-AZT					
555		N655GA	VP-BSM	VP-BSJ	N813WP	N102DZ						
556		N656GA	N556AR	HB-JES								
557		N657GA	N83M	N557E	N833E							
558		N658GA	N750BA	N600RH	N500RH							
559		N659GA	N559GV	N144KK	N59JE							
560		N660GA	9K-AJD									
561		N661GA	N108CE									
562		N662GA	N95AE	N970SJ								
563		N463GA	N8CA	N169CA	(N169PG)	(N180CH)	N225EE					
564		N664GA	(JY-...)	"N18VS"	N664GA	N54PR	A6-DEJ	N238FJ	N1GN			
565		N460GA	N77CP	N940AJ								
566	C-37A	N466GA	US Army 97-0049		N8VQ	US Army 05-1944						
567		N467GA	N93M	N50JE								
568		N461GA	N845HS	N568JC	HB-INQ	N5HN	N89HE	N168CE				
569		N469GA	9K-AJE									
570		N470GA	N451CS	N521HN	N820HB							
571	C-37A	N671GA	USAF 99-0402									
572		N472GA	(N223SS)	P4-FAZ	HB-IIS	OE-IIS						
573		N673GA	9K-AJF									
574		N674GA	N1KE	N6453	N6458							
575		N475GA	N410M	N625GN								
576		N476GA	N991LF	N80PS	N80PN							
577		N577GA	HB-IVZ	VP-CAR								
578		N578GA	N1GN	N21GN	N410LM	N801AR						
579		N579GA	N23M	N866AB								
580		N580GA	N1540									
581		N581GA	N379P	N8068V	N44982	N126CH	VH-CCC	N280PH				
582		N582GA	N271JG	EC-IRZ	N582GV	(N312GV)	N598KZ					
583		N583GA	HZ-MS05	HZ-MS5	HZ-MS5B							
584		N584GA	N84GV									
585		N585GA	N18NK	N16NK	N776RB							
586		N586GA	N2N	N586GV								
587		N587GA	N300K	N416RJ								
588		N588GA	VP-BAC	N588GV	HS-WEH							
589		N589GA	N15UC	(N15UQ)								
590	C-37A	N590GA	USAF 99-0404									
591		N591GA	N301K	N25GV								

GULFSTREAM V

C/n	Series	Identities					
592		N592GA	N90AM	N950CM			
593		N593GA	(I-MPUT)	I-DEAS	N977SA		
594		N594GA	N33M	N363JG			
595		N595GA	N85V	(N595GV)			
596		N596GA	(USAF 99-0405)		N383JA	N977GA	N996GA
597		N495GA	N302K	N540M	N595E	N595B	
598		N598GA	N1SF	N598F	N808JG		
599		N496GA	N401WJ	N428WT	N800PM		
600		N650GA	N100GV				
601		N536GA	N502QS				
602		N538GA	N602GV	VP-BKZ	N783MB		
603		N539GA	N35CD	VH-CRQ	N881HS		
604		N551GA	LV-ZXI	N551GA	XA-EAJ	(D-AHER)	XA-JEF	XA-KUO
605		N554GA	N62MS	N62ML	N691RC	N37AL	
606		N558GA	N63HS	N53HS	N551GA	N1222P	
607		N559GA	N303K	VP-BNL	P4-SBR	N17FJ	
608		N561GA	N111LX	N608WB	N505SS		
609		N566GA	N5733	N418SG	N418SM	N101MH	
610		N567GA	(N610CM)	N253CM			
611		N568GA	N5000X				
612		N569GA	N350C	N88D	N88DZ		
613		N570GA	N504QS	N721MM	B-8097	N727PR	
614		N571GA	N614CM				
615		N572GA	N914J	N318XX	N324CX		
616		N574GA	(N457ST)	N1HC	N141HC	N5616	
617		N575GA	7T-VPG				
618		N585GA	N585JC	(N123H)			
619		N608GA	N1454H	N4377			
620	C-37A	N535GA	USAF 01-0028				
621		N621GA	(N605M)	N605CH	N702TY		
622		N622GA	N304K	N806AC	VP-BBX	HB-JTT	
623		N623GA	N506QS	N285TX	N1AM		
624	C-37A	N624GA	USAF 01-0029				
625		N625GA	N507QS	N269TX	N100HG		
626		N626GA	N5JR	N846QM			
627		N627GA	N54KB	N54BS			
628		N628GA	N18RF	N42GX	N628BD		
629		N629GA	N711RL	N711RQ	N707GW	N188ES	
630		N630GA	N130GV				
631		N631GA	N508QS				
632	V-SP	N632GA	N5SP	N532SP	[first GV-SP; ff 31Aug01]		
633		N633GA	N222LX				
634		N534GA	ZS-AOL	ZS-AJZ	N731AE	N700HA	
635		N522GA	N83CP	N709AA			
636		N556GA	N910V	VP-BEP	N886DT	N328MM	
637		N637GA	N509QS				
638		N638GA	HB-IIY	N888HE	(N888HK)	US Coast Guard 02	
639		N639GA	N501CV				
640		N580GA	N752BA	N600JD	N278PH		
641		N641GA	HB-IIZ	OE-IIA	N506RD	C-GUGU	
642		N562GA	N510QS	CS-DKB	N626JS	N626JE	
643		N523GA	5N-FGS				
644		N644GA	HZ-MS5A				
645	C-37A	N645GA	USAF 01-0076				
646		N524GA	N51FL	(N617JS)	N17JS	N856TD	N749CP
647		N647GA	N511QS	[w/o, hit by truck while parked at San Francisco, CA, 22Sep12; parted out by AvMATS, St Louis, MO]			
648		N648GA	N85M	N85ML	VP-BSN	N626UT	
649		N649GA	N83CW	N183CW	N87WD		
650		N520GA	N1040				
651		N581GA	N651GV	N1DC			
652	C-37A	N582GA	USAF 01-0065				
653	VC-37A	N527GA	US Coast Guard 01				
654		N584GA	(N654GV)	N960AV	VP-BLA	N404M	XA-MPS
655		N529GA	N825LM				
656		N256GA	(N218CP)	N218EC	N724AG		
657	C-37B	N587GA	USN 166375				
658		N532GA	N516QS				
659		N589GA	N50KC				
660		N533GA	N130TM	N21NE			
661		N561GA	N405HG				
662		N662GA	N697A	N427HG			
663	C-37A	N663GA	USAF 01-0030				
664		N664GA	N564QS+	[+marks were applied but ntu]		N664GA	XA-MKI
665		N565GA	N845HS	N223MD	N128GV	N128GB	N765SG	N999LX
666		N566GA	(N958AV)	N699GA	[c/n changed to 699 on rereg'n to N699GA qv]		
667		N567GA	N1BN	N121BN	N123M	N168NJ	N168NB	N136ZC
668		N568GA	N721S				
669		N569GA	N144KK	N544KK	N1UB	VP-CES	3C-LLX
670	C-37A	N670GA	USAF 02-1863				
671		N571GA	N671LE	N671LB	N703RK		
672		N672GA	VP-BJD	N225GV	N3546		
673		N873GA	N282QT	N673P	N169LL*		
674		N674GA	N25GV	(N26GV)	N36GV		
675		N675GA	N505RX	N1956M			
676		N676GA	Israel 676	["Nachshon Shavit" ELINT platform]			
677		N677GA	N677F				
678		N678GA	Greece 678				
679		N679GA	Israel 679	["Nachshon Shavit" ELINT platform]			
680		N680GA	(OK-ONE)	M-USBA			
681		N981GA	(N519QS)	N624N			
682		N682GA	(VP-BFD)	G-JCBV	N551M	N38BA	N919YC
683		N683GA	JA500A	[code LAJ500]			
684		N684GA	Israel 684	["Nachshon Shavit" ELINT platform]			
685		N585GA	N685TA	N108NY			
686		N686GA	N524AC	N524AG			

GULFSTREAM V/GULFSTREAM 500/550

C/n	Series	Identities						
687		N687GA	OE-IVY					
688		N688GA	(N254W)	N543H				
689		N689GA	JA501A	[code LAJ501]				
690		N690GA	N914BD	N915BD				
691		N691GA	N250DV	N525AC	N523AG	N721MC		
692		N692GA	N100TM	C-GLFV				
693		N693GA	N508P	N617EA				
694		c/n not used						
695		c/n not used						
696		c/n not used						
697		c/n not used						
698		c/n not used						
699		N566GA	(N958AV)	N699GA	N885KT	[orginally built as c/n 666]		

GULFSTREAM 500/550

C/n	Series	Identities						
5001	500	N901GA	[rolled out 19Jun02 ff 18Jly02]		N5SP	N621KD	N501ZK	N501HM
5002	550	N702GA	N550GA	N92LA				
5003	550	N703GA	N245TT					
5004	550	N904GA	HB-IGM	N145MG				
5005	550	N805GA	N4CP	N499CP	B-8152			
5006	550	N906GA	N550GW	(N345AA)	(N550AA)			
5007	550	N907GA	N754BA	N383T				
5008	550	N908GA	XA-EOF	N378L	N551GT			
5009	550	N909GA	N1HC					
5010	550	N910GA	N711RL	N711RZ	N701RH*			
5011	550	N991GA	(N522QS)	VP-BGN	N811GA	(N827DC)		
5012	550	N812GA	N888LK	N918SM				
5013	550	N913GA	N63HS					
5014	550	N914GA	Israel 514	Singapore 010	[AEW platform]			
5015	550	N915GA	N565ST					
5016	550	N916GA	N944H	N599H				
5017	550	N917GA	N62MS					
5018	550	N518GA	N818RF	N111AM				
5019	550	N919GA	SE-RDX	G-GSSO	N15019	B-8270		
5020	550	N920GA	N221DG	N243DG	N550AA			
5021	550	N921GA	N5DA	N510SR				
5022	550	N922GA	N550GV	OE-ISS	N550GV	(PR-CPD)	M-GLFV	N122TN	(PR-GFV)	PR-GMV
5023	550	N923GA	N1GN	N125N	B-8135			
5024	550	N924GA	VP-BLA	N424GA	B-8100			
5025	550	N925GA	HB-JEE	N356WW				
5026	550	N926GA	N550MT	N550TA	N921WC			
5027	550	N927GA	N91LA					
5028	550	N928GA	N55UH	HL7799	N311TK	N310TK		
5029	550	N929GA	(N550RN)	N155AN	N155AD	TU-VAR	N155AD	
5030	550	N830GA	5H-ONE					
5031	550	N931GA	N795BA					
5032	550	N932GA	G-HRDS	N550JD				
5033	550	N933GA	VP-BNR					
5034	550	N934GA	US Army 04-1778	[C37A]				
5035	550	N935GA	N1TF	N607CV				
5036	550	N936GA	N1BN					
5037	550	N637GA	Israel 537	["Nachshon Eitam" AEW platform]				
5038	550	N938GA	N372BG	N102BG	N192BG	N192BH	HZ-A6	HZ-SK6
5039	550	N939GA	N401HF	N94LF				
5040	550	N940GA	N418SG	(N13J)	HB-JEV	N74VW		
5041	550	N841GA	US Navy 166376	[C37A]				
5042	550	N942GA	N528QS					
5043	550	N943GA	N550GA	N83TE	VP-BGL	N107VS		
5044	550	N944GA	Israel 544	Singapore 016	[AEW platform]			
5045	550	N945GA	N789RR	N560DM				
5046	550	N946GA	N5PG					
5047	550	N947GA	(N550YM)	(PR-NYM)	N848JA			
5048	550	N948GA	VP-CIF	VP-CIP				
5049	550	N949GA	N109ST	N89NC				
5050	550	N950GA	VP-BNO	M-SAWO				
5051	550	N851GA	VP-BNE					
5052	550	N952GA	XA-ATL					
5053	550	N953GA	N2929					
5054	550	N954GA	OE-IVV	XA-ZTK				
5055	550	N955GA	N144KK	N755VE				
5056	550	N956GA	N45ST	N556TT				
5057	550	N957GA	CS-DKC	N8228N				
5058	550	N958GA	N74RP					
5059	550	N959GA	VP-BLR	N659GA	B-8095			
5060	550	N960GA	G-JCBC	N143G	N254SD			
5061	550	N961GA	N718MC					
5062	550	N962GA	N159JA					
5063	550	N963GA	N759WR	N411WW	N897AW	N897AT*		
5064	550	N964GA	VP-BJD					
5065	550	N965GA	N747AE	N75CC				
5066	550	N966GA	N250DV					
5067	500	N967GA	N50HA					
5068	550	N968GA	EI-GDL	N407GK				
5069	550	N969GA	Israel 569	["Nachshon Eitam" AEW platform]				
5070	550	N870GA	HB-JEP	M-BJEP				
5071	550	N571GA	(N550GA)+	[+ ntu marks worn in NBAA Static display, Orlando Executive, FL, Nov05]		I-LUXO		
5072	550	N572GA	(N25GV)	N572EC	N528M	N378L		
5073	550	N673GA	N800JH					

GULFSTREAM 500/550

C/n	Series	Identities				
5074	550	N574GA	HZ-ARK			
5075	550	N575GA	N518QS	D-AGAZ*		
5076	550	N576GA	N870CM			
5077	550	N577GA	N933H			
5078	550	N578GA	EC-JPK			
5079	550	N579GA	N860AA			
5080	550	N580GA	SE-RDY			
5081	550	N581GA	CS-DKD			
5082	550	N582GA	N550FG	N709DW	B-8136	
5083	550	N583GA	N985JC	N474D		
5084	550	N584GA	VP-BSI			
5085	550	N585GA	N235DX	N5585		
5086	550	N586GA	N609PM	N620JF		
5087	550	N587GA	US Navy 166377			
5088	550	N588GA	N5VS			
5089	550	N589GA	N771JT			
5090	550	N590GA	N282Q			
5091	550	N591GA	N3PG			
5092	550	N592GA	VP-CVI	VP-CVK		
5093	550	N593GA	D-ADLR	[High Altitude Long-Range research aircraft]		
5094	550	N594GA	CS-DKE			
5095	550	N595GA	N550KF	N550MZ		
5096	550	N696GA	N3050			
5097	550	N597GA	N550GA	N806AC	N801AS	
5098	550	N598GA	US Navy 166378			
5099	550	N699GA	CS-DKF			
5100	500	N820GA	N51MF	N760CC	N760CG	N789LR
5101	550	N821GA	N550M	N904G		
5102	550	N822GA	VP-CVT	(B-HVT)		
5103	550	N923GA	N534QS			
5104	550	N824GA	N661CP	N314TP		
5105	500	N935GA	N500RD	PR-WQY		
5106	550	N986GA	N234DB			
5107	550	N937GA	N662CP	N335LL		
5108	550	N828GA	N311CG	N611CG	N1LA	
5109	550	N829GA	VP-BIP	N818HK		
5110	550	N940GA	N585A			
5111	550	N981GA	B-KGV	VP-CKC		
5112	550	N832GA	N636MF	N363MF		
5113	550	N833GA	VP-CNR	N919PE		
5114	550	N834GA	D-ADCA	N720JS		
5115	550	N835GA	B-KID	N42FD	N838LM	
5116	550	N836GA	EC-JYR	XA-ALC		
5117	550	N967GA	N595A			
5118	550	N838GA	N855G			
5119	550	N519GA	RA-10202			
5120	550	N920GA	N254SD	N284SD	B-8108	
5121	550	N921GA	N550PR	N1972N		
5122	550	N522GA	N837BA			
5123	550	N523GA	VP-BBO			
5124	550	N524GA	EC-KBR			
5125	550	N295GA	N550GD	N388AC		
5126	550	N526GA	N676RW	N665JN		
5127	550	N527GA	CS-DKG			
5128	550	N928GA	N940DC	(N1759)	N1759C	
5129	550	N529GA	VP-BLW			
5130	550	N130GA	N671LE			
5131	550	N531GA	N671RW	M-GVSP		
5132	550	N432GA	Israel 532	Singapore 017	[AEW platform]	
5133	550	N533GA	N531QS			
5134	550	N534GA	N712KT	N712DA	N5GV	
5135	550	N535GA	N522BP			
5136	500	N536GA	N110ED			
5137	550	N287GA	8P-MSD			
5138	550	N638GA	N600J	N60QJ	N551RC	
5139	550	N539GA	OE-IRG	N673MM		
5140	550	N740GA	N838BA			
5141	550	N541GA	N10MZ			
5142	550	N42GA	D-ADCB	T7-ARG		
5143	550	N643GA	Singapore 018	[AEW platform]		
5144	500	N644GA	N515PL	N515PE	PR-NOC	
5145	550	N545GA	N345LC			
5146	550	N646GA	N607PM	N1852B		
5147	550	N647GA	B-LUE	VP-CEM		
5148	500	N648GA	N551KF	N650PL	VP-BCC	
5149	550	N649GA	VP-CGN	VP-CGI	N970SG	
5150	550	N43GA	CS-DKH			
5151	550	N921GA	EC-KJS	M-HOTB		
5152	550	N652GA	06-0500			
5153	550	N923GA	SE-RDZ	M-ARDI		
5154	550	N654GA	N557GA	N113CS	N113GS	N808TC
5155	550	N935GA	N550GA	EC-KUM		
5156	550	N936GA	N529QS			
5157	550	N657GA	N785QS			
5158	500	N998GA	N56UH			
5159	550	N659GA	N607CH			
5160	550	N660GA	N813QS			
5161	550	N261GA	N725MM	N725MN		
5162	550	N662GA	EC-KLS	VT-BRS		
5163	550	N663GA	N57UH			
5164	550	N764GA	N372BG			
5165	550	N965GA	N245BD			
5166	550	N966GA	CS-DKI			
5167	550	N967GA	G-EGNS	(D-AMAN)	M-ANIE	N878DB
5168	550	N668GA	N528AP			

GULFSTREAM 500/550

C/n	Series	Identities				
5169	550	N569GA	N203A	N5569		
5170	550	N770GA	N105ST			
5171	550	N971GA	N550BM	D-AUTO		
5172	550	N972GA	HB-JGX	G-LGKD	N688CB	
5173	550	N673GA	N401HB			
5174	550	N974GA	CS-DKJ			
5175	550	N975GA	HB-JGC	N887AG	N883A	
5176	550	N476GA	VP-BTC	G-CGUL	N7325	
5177	550	N977GA	VP-BCO	OE-IZM		
5178	550	N978GA	HB-JKB	N188WR		
5179	550	N979GA	VP-BZC	M-SQAR		
5180	550	N980GA	N108DB	N108DN	N1FS	
5181	550	N181GA	N550AN	VP-CEA	VP-CJM	
5182	550	N782GA	XA-CHR			
5183	550	N983GA	N88D	N868D	N88D	(N135RG) N35RG
5184	550	N284GA	N550GD	N550RP		
5185	550	N185GA				
5186	550	N286GA	G-JCBB	N10XG		
5187	550	N187GA	N816MG			
5188	550	N188GA	N554CE			
5189	550	N189GA	D-AAAM	G-YAAZ	D-AVAR	OK-VPI
5190	550	N290GA	N546QS			
5191	550	N291GA	D-AJJK			
5192	550	N492GA	N323BD	N990NB		
5193	550	N293GA	P4-TPS	P4-PPP	N117AL	
5194	550	N394GA	N1EB			
5195	550	N295GA	N1LB	N550SN		
5196	550	N196GA	N45ST	N385WL	N554DG	
5197	550	N597GA	SX-MFA	N888HZ		
5198	550	N298GA	LZ-FIA			
5199	550	N399GA	N443M			
5200	550	N990GA	VP-BJK	Sweden 102005		
5201	550	N991GA	CS-DKK			
5202	550	N992GA	N1SF			
5203	550	N203GA	EC-KXF	N575PK		
5204	550	N104GA	4K-MEK8			
5205	500	N405GA	(VT-ADA)	(D-ADSE)	(N51FL)	
5206	550	N806GA	N211HS	(N721V)	N169SD	N469SD
5207	550	N607GA	N101CP	N418SG	N550A	
5208	550	N908GA	5X-UGF			
5209	550	N609GA	N517QS			
5210	550	N610GA	M-ONEM			
5211	550	N711GA	N550GA	(N550JE)	N653MK	
5212	550	N512GA	TC-DAP			
5213	550	N413GA	N888HK			
5214	550	N314GA	N4PG	N550WW		
5215	550	N615GA	VQ-BLA			
5216	550	N516GA	VP-CJL	B-HVP		
5217	550	N517GA	N768JJ			
5218	550	N518GA	VQ-BGN			
5219	550	N419GA	(N885AR)	B-KVC		
5220	550	N520GA	G-TFKR	M-TFKR	HB-JOE	
5221	550	N221GA	VQ-BLV	VQ-BLY		
5222	550	N622GA	N801TM			
5223	550	N623GA	N550SG	N557H	N727TE	
5224	550	N624GA	N678SC	(N88WR)	N700MK	
5225	550	N325GA	M-VRNY			
5226	550	N526GA	N803TM			
5227	550	N217GA	M-FPIA	M-FUAD		
5228	550	N828GA	B-KCK			
5229	550	N509GA	N535QS	N55AL	N668P	
5230	550	N330GA	C-GNDN	C-GXDN	N898CE	
5231	550	N131GA	N899SR	N398TA	B-8138	N8889 N8810
5232	550	N932GA	N773MJ	N773AJ	N231CE	
5233	550	N733GA	HL8200			
5234	550	N934GA	N674RW	N897NC		
5235	550	N435GA	N589K			
5236	550	N563GA	PR-WRO			
5237	550	N937GA	N885WT			
5238	550	N838GA	B-KGP			
5239	550	N339GA	N928GC			
5240	550	N840GA	HB-JKC			
5241	550	N841GA	Turkey 09-001	TC-KOP	Turkey 09-001	
5242	550	N842GA	A9C-BRN			
5243	550	N924GA	(N803TG)	B-99888		
5244	550	N744GA	N800DL			
5245	550	N845GA	N802AG			
5246	550	N846GA	M-IPHS			
5247	550	N847GA	USAF 09-0501	09-0525		
5248	550	N748GA	9K-GFA			
5249	550	N849GA	N757PL			
5250	550	N952GA	"N592GA"+	[+incorrect marks worn for test-flight at Long Beach 18Nov09]	N952GA	B-LSM
5251	550	N351GA	HZ-ALFA	N251GV		
5252	550	N552GA	N550PM			
5253	550	N523GA	PR-OGX	N1005	N446VG	
5254	550	N554GA	Turkey 10-002	TC-CBK		
5255	550	N955GA	N94924	N94124*		
5256	550	N856GA	N1932P			
5257	550	N957GA	N253DV			
5258	550	N558GA	N780E			
5259	550	N959GA	VH-LAL			
5260	550	N960GA	ZK-KFB	SE-RKL		
5261	550	N561GA	N780F			
5262	550	N562GA	(D-ASAF)	N315RG		
5263	550	N263GA	N605CH			

GULFSTREAM 500/550

C/n	Series	Identities				
5264	550	N564GA	N551CS	N551TG		
5265	550	N965GA	N247EM			
5266	550	N926GA	VQ-BMC	N131LK		
5267	550	N867GA	XA-EAJ			
5268	550	N568GA	VQ-BHP			
5269	550	N369GA	B-8122			
5270	550	N370GA	VP-CRO			
5271	550	N971GA	CN-AMS			
5272	550	N772GA	N235PE	N77CP		
5273	550	N927GA	N273A			
5274	550	N174GA	B-8123			
5275	550	N575GA	VP-CTA			
5276	550	N276GA	B-8125			
5277	550	N527GA	4K-AI06			
5278	550	N528GA	N512JT			
5279	550	N579GA	EC-LIY			
5280	550	N508GA	(PR-EVS)	PR-FGA		
5281	550	N581GA	XA-FEM			
5282	550	N282GA	XA-RGB	N335MC	XA-RET	
5283	550	N283GA	N332MM			
5284	550	N584GA	TC-TTC			
5285	550	N285GA	N5GV	N555GV		
5286	550	N526GA	N235PV	N83CP		
5287	550	N587GA	VH-PFL			
5288	550	N588GA	N552GA			
5289	550	N589GA	B-8131			
5290	550	N290GA	N3M			
5291	550	N591GA	B-8132			
5292	550	N592GA	M-MOMO			
5293	550	N829GA	XA-SKY			
5294	550	N594GA	VT-TMS	N117AL	N887TM	
5295	550	N295GA	HL8288			
5296	550	N896GA	B-KEQ	N296GC	Mexico 3910	
5297	550	N792GA	USAF 11-0550			
5298	550	N598GA	B-8168			
5299	550	N529GA	N550MT	N17JS		
5300	550	N300GA	B-90609			
5301	550	N901GA	N550SA	M-SAJJ	M-SAAJ	
5302	550	N532GA	D-ASAF	OE-IZI		
5303	550	N303GA	B-KHJ			
5304	550	N604GA	N550GA	VP-CTE		
5305	550	N535GA	(N725AF)	N550GD	Mexico ANX-207	Mexico ANX-1207
5306	550	N836GA	C-GBGC	C-GGPM		
5307	550	N507GA	N288A			
5308	550	N638GA	PR-PSE			
5309	550	N509GA	N300A			
5310	550	N510GA	5N-FGW			
5311	550	N531GA	N818LK	N818LF		
5312	550	N112GA	N415P			
5313	550	N633GA	N888VS			
5314	550	N834GA	I-ADVD			
5315	550	N835GA	G-GRZD			
5316	550	N916GA	M-YBJK	N316GD	N418SG	
5317	550	N917GA				
5318	550	N718GA	N989JC			
5319	550	N519GA	B-8137			
5320	550	N732GA	A4O-AD			
5321	550	N921GA	N891E			
5322	550	N632GA	N900ES			
5323	550	N923GA	N505D			
5324	550	N524GA	VP-CJL	VP-CPY		
5325	550	N352GA	A4O-AE			
5326	550	N126GA	N510QS			
5327	550	N772GA	VP-CKG	N881WR		
5328	550	N778GA	N1911W			
5329	550	N129GA	B-8288			
5330	550	N830GA	N725AF	N550PR		
5331	550	N131GA	N53M			
5332	550	N992GA	PR-CIP			
5333	550	N833GA	N119LE			
5334	550	N934GA	N76RP			
5335	550	N853GA	B-LDL			
5336	550	N936GA	D-ABMW			
5337	550	N537GA	B-8156	N88AY		
5338	550	N988GA	N550AU			
5339	550	N339GA	N989AR	PP-JFH*		
5340	550	N740GA	M-ATPS			
5341	550	N541GA	N200A			
5342	550	N854GA	B-8157			
5343	550	N843GA	ZS-AOL	N343AR		
5344	550	N944GA	N888XS			
5345	550	N954GA	N235DX			
5346	550	N946GA	M-JIGG	TC-ATA		
5347	550	N987GA	N79RP			
5348	550	N948GA	B-8256			
5349	550	N949GA	B-8126			
5350	550	N750GA	SX-GJJ			
5351	550	N751GA	N636MF			
5352	550	N152GA	B-8255			
5353	550	N953GA	N581D			
5354	550	N454GA	D-ATIM			
5355	550	N155GA	N625JK	HB-JKI		
5356	550	N356GA	B-KVE			
5357	550	N757GA	B-8259			
5358	550	N758GA	B-8160			

GULFSTREAM 500/550

C/n	Series	Identities			
5359	550	N559GA	N168NJ		
5360	550	N360GA	B-8258		
5361	550	N361GA	N616KG	N616RK	
5362	550	N562GA	N462MK		
5363	550	N763GA	N128GV		
5364	550	N764GA	B-8261		
5365	550	N565GA	N550VE		
5366	550	N566GA	N312P		
5367	550	N767GA	N96UA		
5368	550	N368GA	N550GS	XA-WOW	
5369	550	N569GA	N85JM		
5370	550	N570GA	N721MM		
5371	550	N371GA	N890A		
5372	550	N753GA	N999FH		
5373	550	N703GA	B-8260		
5374	550	N574GA	N551PM		
5375	550	N375GA	N407TR		
5376	550	N376GA	N63M		
5377	550	N577GA	B-HHI		
5378	550	N578GA	RA-10203		
5379	550	N579GA	(D-AMKA)	OE-ISN	
5380	550	N380GA	N506SA		
5381	550	N381GA	N551VL		
5382	550	N582GA	N552PM		
5383	550	N583GA	N999HZ		
5384	550	N384GA	N558GA		
5385	550	N585GA	N977HS		
5386	550	N536GA	N5092		
5387	550	N387GA	B-8268		
5388	550	N588GA	B-LMF		
5389	550	N389GA	N3788B		
5390	550	N590GA	N552X		
5391	550	N591GA	M-ALAY		
5392	550	N492GA	N504AC		
5393	550	N593GA	XA-MAV	N586MS	XA-MAV
5394	550	N494GA	M-USIC		
5395	550	N195GA	OE-LPN		
5396	550	N596GA	N550DV	G-MRLX	
5397	550	N397GA	N582D		
5398	550	N398GA	N838KE		
5399	550	N399GA	B-8273		
5400	550	N500GA	N34U	N506HG	
5401	550	N340GA	N899NC		
5402	550	N342GA			
5403	550	N983GA	N662P		
5404	550	N904GA	B-8269		
5405	550	N545GA	B-8272		
5406	550	N346GA	M-UGIC		
5407	550	N407GA	N676AS		
5408	550	N908GA	OH-GVA	D-AGVA	
5409	550	N349GA	D-AKAR	VP-CUA	
5410	550	N910GA	N284CC		
5411	550	N311GA	N523AC		
5412	550	N412GA	N721V		
5413	550	N213GA	N550DR		
5414	550	N814GA	B-8275		
5415	550	N415GA	VP-CHI		
5416	550	N516GA	N540W	N640W	
5417	550	N517GA	N517DW		
5418	550	N418GA	N550GA	P4-BFY	
5419	550	N219GA	N800J		
5420	550	N120GA	(G-GENT)	G-NOYA	OE-IPE
5421	550	N142GA	N155AN	N421GD	
5422	550	N842GA	B-8292		
5423	550	N423GA	B-8297		
5424	550	N324GA	N524VE		
5425	550	N425GA	G-ZNSF		
5426	550	N526GA	OK-KKF		
5427	550	N927GA	VT-CPA		
5428	550	N928GA	N73M		
5429	550	N849GA	Israel 429	[being fitted out at Tel Aviv for Italian Air Force]	
5430	550	N850GA	(D-ADCL)	EC-LYO	
5431	550	N531GA	I-SEAM		
5432	550	N732GA	N1905W		
5433	550	N233GA	N524AC		
5434	550	N834GA	OE-IGO		
5435	550	N435GA	D-ADCL		
5436	550	N936GA	N568SP	N126HR	
5437	550	N537GA	B-8302		
5438	550	N938GA	N447TR		
5439	550	N539GA	N728EC		
5440	550	N940GA	N550MC		
5441	550	N541GA	N441GC		
5442	550	N424GA	N550JU		
5443	550	N443GA	N550AL		
5444	550	N344GA	N344RS		
5445	550	N445GA	B-8306		
5446	550	N146GA	N45JE		
5447	550	N147GA	B-8298		
5448	550	N148GA	N586RW		
5449	550	N944GA	B-8296	N730EA	
5450	550	N745GA	N998FA		
5451	550	N351GA	N451GV		
5452	550	N352GA	N8JK	M-TRAV	
5453	550	N353GA	G-OGSE		

GULFSTREAM 500/550

C/n	Series	Identities			
5454	550	N554GA			
5455	550	N355GA	N169SD		
5456	550	N356GA	N456GA		
5457	550	N957GA	PR-CGI		
5458	550	N458GA	N1RP		
5459	550	N559GA	TC-KHG		
5460	550	N760GA	N75RP		
5461	550	N461GA	VP-CNP		
5462	550	N762GA	OE-LOK		
5463	550	N563GA	N514VA		
5464	550	N464GA	XA-BUA		
5465	550	N265GA	N5465M		
5466	550	N566GA	N866BB		
5467	550	N867GA	N588PX		
5468	550	N568GA	N550XY		
5469	550	N969GA	B-3196		
5470	550	N870GA	N83M		
5471	550	N571GA	G-LSCW		
5472	550	N572GA	B-3226		
5473	550	N473GA	N793CP		
5474	550	N974GA	N795CP		
5475	550	N475GA	B-8309		
5476	550	N476GA	N138GL		
5477	550	N267GA	N550GD	N550GH	
5478	550	N478GA	B-3003		
5479	550	N479GA	N797CP		
5480	550	N580GA	(N550KP)	HS-KPI	
5481	550	N581GA	N999LR		
5482	550	N482GA	N464GR		
5483	550	N583GA	B-8373		
5484	550	N584GA	N486RW		
5485	550	N585GA	N585DW		
5486	550	N586GA	N586G		
5487	550	N587GA	N942JT		
5488	550	N588GA	N588G		
5489	550	N489GA	N559X		
5490	550	N590GA	N550AV		
5491	550	N591GA	N276A		
5492	550	N492GA	(D-ADES)	D-ADSE	
5493	550	N593GA	9M-TMJ		
5494	550	N594GA	N6HJ		
5495	550	N595GA	N550RH		
5496	550	N596GA	N500J		
5497	550	N597GA	N552AV		
5498	550	N598GA	N97FT		
5499	550	N499GA	N600J		
5500	550	N500GA	N100GA	N900AL	
5501	550	N751GA	N83CW		
5502	550	N702GA	N667P		
5503	550	N703GA	N914X		
5504	550	N904GA	N525KF		
5505	550	N305GA	PR-NZV		
5506	550	N856GA	N111		
5507	550	N807GA	N322K		
5508	550	N908GA	Mexico 3916/XC-LOK	Mexico TP-07/XC-LOK	
5509	550	N909GA	N68989		
5510	550	N510GA	N70EL		
5511	550	N851GA	VP-CLK		
5512	550	N512GA	N550TY		
5513	550	N853GA	N319PP		
5514	550	N854GA	N34HS		
5515	550	N955GA	N931FL		
5516	550	N516GA	N324K		
5517	550	N517GA	N550DX		
5518	550	N518GA	I-DELO		
5519	550	N519GA	M-MNDG		
5520	550	N952GA	N587G		
5521	550	N921GA	N906FS		
5522	550	N822GA	N260Z		
5523	550	N523GA	(N237GA)		
5524	550	N524GA	OE-LCY		
5525	550	N325GA	N336EB		
5526	550	N526GA	N550GA		
5527	550	N527GA	N38NG		
5528	550	N528GA	N73RP		
5529	550	N529GA	N561SK		
5530	550	N830GA	N316VA		
5531	550	N531GA			
5532	550	N532GA	B-3988		
5533	550	N533GA	TU-...		
5534	550	N534GA	N360WF		
5535	550	N535GA	N613WF		
5536	550	N536GA			
5537	550	N537GA			
5538	550	N538GA	N565JM*		
5539	550	N539GA	N80AD*		
5540	550	N540GA			
5541	550	N541GA			
5542	550	N542GD			
5543	550	N543GD			
5544	550	N544GD			
5545	550	N545GA			
5546	550	N546GD			
5547	550	N547GA			
5548	550	N548GD			

GULFSTREAM 500/550

C/n	Series	Identities
5549	550	N549GA
5550	550	N750GA
5551	550	N551GD
5552	550	N552GD
5553	550	N553GD
5554	550	N554GD
5555	550	N255GA
5556	550	N556GD
5557	550	N557GD
5558	550	N558GD
5559	550	N559GA
5560	550	N560GD
5561		
5562		
5563		
5564		
5565		
5566		
5567		
5568		
5569		
5570		
5571		
5572		
5573		
5574		
5575		
5576		
5577		
5578		
5579		
5580		

GULFSTREAM VI/650

Gulfstream's new wide-bodied aircraft, officially the Gulfstream VI but marketed as the Gulfstream 650. The G650ER, an extended-range version, was made available in 2014 – including as a retro-upgrade option for existing G650s. Those known to us are indicated below.

C/n		Identities				
6001		N601GD	N650GA	[r/o 29Sep09, ff 25Nov09] N650GX		
6002		N602GD	N652GD	[ff 25Feb10; w/o 02Apr11 Roswell, NM]		
6003		N603GD	N653GD	N211HS		
6004	ER	N604GD	N650GD	[ff 06Jun10] N104GA	N650RG	
6005	ER	N605GD	N655GA	[ff 24Jan11] N914BD		
6006		N606GD	M-YGVI	OH-GVV	9H-GVI	
6007	ER	N607GD	N711SW	N288WR		
6008	ER	N608GD	N762MS			
6009	ER	N609GD	VQ-BNZ	N923WC		
6010	ER	N110GA	N100A			
6011		N611GD	N102BG			
6012	ER	N612GD	N524EA			
6013		N613GD	N650PH	(D-AJKI)	N871FR	
6014	ER	N614GD	N100ES			
6015		N615GD	N1AL	N515PL	N516PL*	
6016		N616GA	VP-CZA			
6017		N617GA	N886WT			
6018		N618GA	N673HA			
6019		N609GA	N650RR			
6020		N520GA	N922H			
6021		N221GA	N305CC			
6022		N722GA	N650HC	(N650HE)	N658HC	
6023		N623GA	G-OMRE	HS-VSK		
6024		N624GA	N1KE			
6025		N325GA	VP-CZZ			
6026		N626GA	N919SB			
6027		N607GA	N521HN			
6028		N328GA	G-ULFS			
6029		N629GA	EC-LYK			
6030		N330GA	N650MT			
6031	ER	N331GA	N606GA			
6032		N932GA	M-GSIX	N4FL		
6033		N633GA	XA-BAL			
6034		N603GA	VP-CNR			
6035		N635GA	N880MD	N712KT		
6036		N636GD	N650SS	N666KQ	N13MS	
6037		N637GA	M-USIK			
6038		N638GD	N278L			
6039	ER	N639GA	N650DX	(N650CP)	N4CP	
6040		N640GA	OY-GLF	N999NN	VP-COR	
6041	ER	N641GD	N650CK	N657AT		
6042		N604GD	N28LL	N838MF		
6043		N643GA	ZK-KFB			
6044		N604GA	N22T	N829JV		
6045	ER	N645GA	N67WB			
6046		N646GA	N788AC	N650JK		
6047		N647GD	M-KSSN	M-KSOI		
6048		N648GA	N773MJ			
6049		N649GA	M-JCBB			
6050		N605GD	N650PR	N650PE		
6051		N601GA	N650TP			
6052		N602GA	N927MC			
6053		N653GA	N2N			
6054		N654GA	N650GL			
6055	ER	N655GA	N44KJ			
6056		N656GA	N374FS			
6057		N657GA	N650DA			
6058		N658GA	N511DB			
6059		N659GA	N8833			
6060	ER	N660GA	N651CH			
6061		N661GA	N221DG			
6062		N662GA	(OY-IZM)	HB-IVJ		
6063		N663GA	N451CS			
6064		N664GA	N311CG			
6065		N965GA	N1TF			
6066		N606GA	EC-LZU			
6067		N667GA	N650GU			
6068		N668GA	(N650KG)	VP-CKB		
6069	ER	N669GD	N650EW			
6070		N670GA	EI-JSK			
6071		N671GA	N650XY			
6072		N672GA	N711RL			
6073		N673GA	OE-LZM			
6074	ER	N674GA	N652CH			
6075		N675GA	G-REFO			
6076		N676GA	N650JH	N1F		
6077		N677GD	M-NNNN	M-NGNG		
6078		N678GA	N5GV	N6453		
6079		N679GA	(N168D)	N88D	N83DZ	N650NY
6080		N608GA	N7780	M-WIND		
6081		N681GD	A9C-BAH			
6082		N682GD	VP-CTS			
6083		N683GD	M-BADU			
6084	ER	N684GA	N650ER	N585GS		
6085		N985GA	N691LC	VP-CRZ		
6086		N686GD	VH-LUY	VP-BLF		
6087		N687GA	N650GA	N711SW		
6088		N688GA	N380SE			
6089		N689GA	N747SC	N650AF		
6090	ER	N690GA	N212LF	N113CS		
6091		N691GA	N1AL			

GULFSTREAM VI/650

C/n		Identities			
6092		N692GA	SX-GSB		
6093		N693GA	N288Z		
6094		N694GA	N1777M		
6095		N695GA	LX-GVI		
6096		N696GA	M-INSK		
6097		N697GA	N650HC		
6098		N698GA	B-KEY		
6099		N699GA	M-VITA		
6100	ER	N601GD	N650AB		
6101		N611GA	N47TR		
6102		N612GA	VQ-BMZ		
6103		N603GD	9K-GGA		
6104	ER	N641GA	N998PB		
6105		N615GA	N1454H		
6106	ER	N616GD	N388RF	N3CP	
6107		N617GD	4K-AI88		
6108		N618GD	N761LE		
6109		N619GA	N326JD		
6110		N610GA	VP-BBF		
6111		N611GD	N817GS		
6112		N612GD	VP-CGN		
6113		N613GD	M-PLUS		
6114		N614GD	RA-10205		
6115		N615GD	VT-NKR*		
6116		N616GA	9H-ZMB	N251TD	
6117		N617GA	N650ZK	N650HF	
6118		N618GA	HB-JUF		
6119	ER	N619GD	N40D		
6120		N620GD	9H-IKO	M-YNNS	
6121		N621GD	VP-CVI		
6122	ER	N622GA	VP-CYL	VP-CCW	
6123	ER	N623GA	VP-CJJ		
6124		N624GA	N887WT		
6125	ER	N625GD	N898NC		
6126	ER	N626GA	N6D		
6127		N627GA	N650HH	N899YF	
6128		N628GD	N108DB		
6129		N629GA	VP-CZB		
6130	ER	N630GD	N652BA		
6131		N631GA	N240CX		
6132		N632GA	M-BHBH		
6133	ER	N633GA	N651AV	N271DV	
6134		N634GA	OE-IIH		
6135		N635GA	EC-MHZ		
6136		N636GA	VP-BMP		
6137	ER	N637GA	TR-KGM		
6138	ER	N638GA	N650PA		
6139		N639GA	PP-WSR		
6140		N640GD	P4-LSM	LX-DLF	
6141	ER	N641GD	N651WE		
6142		N142GA	N305KN		
6143		N643GA	D-ADSK		
6144	ER	N644GA	N650GY		
6145	ER	N645GA	N616KG		
6146		N646GD	D-AYSM		
6147		N647GA	(M-ABIU)	P4-AZG	T7-AZG
6148	ER	N648GA	B-LHK		
6149	ER	N649GA	N650GD		
6150		N601GA	M-ABIU	N968FA	
6151		N651GA	N22T		
6152		N652GD	(N341MM)	VP-CMM	
6153	ER	N653GA	A7-CGA		
6154		N654GA	N108R		
6155		N655GA	9K-GGB		
6156	ER	N656GD	M-YSIX		
6157		N657GD	N946JB		
6158	ER	N658GD	VQ-BNZ		
6159		N659GD	VP-BCO		
6160		N660GA	G-GSVI		
6161		N661GA	N650GA		
6162		N662GA	C-GNDN		
6163		N663GA	N900KS		
6164		N664GA	N270LE		
6165	ER	N605GD	B-99988		
6166		N766GA	N94924^		
6167	ER	N667GD	A7-CGB		
6168		N668GA			
6169		N669GD	VP-BCT		
6170		N670GA	RA-10204		
6171	ER	N671GA	N2437		
6172		N672GA			
6173	ER	N673GD	N688JR		
6174	ER	N674GA	N827DC		
6175	ER	N175GA	N650FJ		
6176		N676GA	VP-B..		
6177	ER	N677GD	N628TS		
6178		N678GA			
6179		N679GA			
6180	ER	N680GD	N566NS		
6181		N681GD			
6182		N682GD	XA-EAJ*		
6183		N183GA	9K-GGC*		
6184		N684GA			
6185		N685GD			
6186		N686GD			

GULFSTREAM VI/650

C/n		Identities		
6187		N687GD	N155AN*	
6188		N688GA		
6189		N689GA		
6190		N690GA	PP-ADZ*	
6191		N691GD		
6192		N692GA	(D-ADSK)	N891WW*
6193		N693GD	N912GG*	
6194		N694GA		
6195		N695GA		
6196		N696GA		
6197		N697GA	N720LF*	
6198		N698GD		
6199		N699GA		
6200		N620GD		
6201		N621GD	N650XA*	
6202		N622GD		
6203		N623GD		
6204		N624GD		
6205		N602GA		
6206		N626GD		
6207		N627GD		
6208		N628GD		
6209		N629GD		
6210	ER	N650ER*		
6211		N611GD		
6212		N612GD		
6213		N613GD		
6214		N614GD		
6215		N615GA		
6216		N616GA		
6217		N617GA		
6218		N618GA		
6219		N619GA		
6220		N620GS		
6221		N621GS		
6222		N602GD		
6223		N623GA		
6224		N624GS		
6225		N625GD		
6226		N626GA		
6227		N627GA		
6228		N628GA		
6229		N629GA		
6230		N630GD		
6231		N631GD		
6232		N632GA		
6233		N633GA		
6234		N634GA		
6235		N635GA		
6236		N636GA		
6237		N637GA		
6238		N638GA		
6239		N639GA		
6240		N640GA		
6241		N641GA		
6242		N642GS		
6243		N643GA		
6244		N644GA		
6245		N645GA		
6246				
6247				
6248				
6249				
6250				
6251				
6252				
6253				
6254				
6255				
6256				
6257				
6258				
6259				
6260				

GULFSTREAM VII/500

A new wide-bodied aircraft, officially the Gulfstream VII-G500 but marketed as the Gulfstream 500.

C/n	Identities	
72001	N500GA	[ff 18May15, Savannah, GA]
72002	N502GS	[ff 20Nov15, Savannah, GA]
72003	N503G	[ff 20Nov15, Savannah, GA]
72004	N504GS	[ff 20Feb16, Savannah, GA]
72005	N505GD	
72006	N506GD	
72007	N507GD	
72008	N508GD	
72009		
72010		
72011		
72012		
72013		
72014		
72015		
72016		
72017		
72018		
72019		
72020		
72021		
72022		
72023		
72024		

HONDA HA-420 HONDAJET

C/n	Identities			
P001	N420HA	[ff 03Dec03]		
42000001	N420HJ	[ff 20Dec10]		
42000002	N420HM	[ff 18Nov11]		
42000003	N420AH	[ff 04May12]		
42000004	N420NC	[ff 16May13]		
42000005	[c/n not used]			
42000006	[c/n not used]			
42000007	[c/n not used]			
42000008	[c/n not used]			
42000009	[c/n not used]			
42000010	[c/n not used]			
42000011	N420EX	[first production aircraft, ff 27Jun14]		
42000012	N959EN			
42000013	N420KA			
42000014	N21HJ			
42000015	N420AZ			
42000016	N420HE	N420ET	N420EA	
42000017	N420TG	N420EA	N420DE	N420HE
42000018	N420EU	M-HNDA		
42000019	N420MX	XA-MHU		
42000020	N774RC			
42000021	N141HJ	N557MW	N527MW	
42000022	N420BT			
42000023	N682TM			
42000024	N25HJ			
42000025	N527MW	N41JJ		
42000026	N21671			
42000027	N20ZA			
42000028	N420JB			
42000029	N816LS			
42000030	N421EK			
42000031	N575DM			
42000032	N71TS			
42000033				
42000034				
42000035				
42000036				
42000037				
42000038				
42000039				
42000040				
42000041				
42000042				
42000043				
42000044				
42000045				
42000046				
42000047				
42000048				
42000049				
42000050				
42000051				
42000052				
42000053				
42000054				
42000055				
42000056				
42000057				
42000058				
42000059				
42000060				

IAI 1125 ASTRA/GULFSTREAM 100

Note: The SPX has model number 1125A

C/n	Series	Identities									
001		4X-WIN	[ff 19Mar84; wfu Aug86]								
002		4X-WIA									
003		[non-flying test airframe]									
004		4X-CUA	N96PC	"N425TS"	N96PC	N425TS	OB-1703	OB-2108-P			
005		)									
006		)									
007		) [Aircraft not built as the owner of the first aircraft to be delivered specified that he did									
008		) not want one of the first ten aircraft being built!]									
009		)									
010		)									
011		4X-CUK	N450PM	N450BM	N705MA	N991RV	N500FA	N765A			
012		4X-CUL	N1125A	N25AG	N312W	N27BH	N610HC	N618HC	N939MC	(YV....)	
013		4X-CUM	(N413SC)	N713SC	N112PR	N25N					
014		4X-CUN	N400J	N400JF	N8484P	N116JC					
015		4X-CUP	N887PC	N46UF	N46UP	N14SR	N755PA	N157GA			
016		4X-CUK	N716W	N36FD	N221DT	N221PA	YV3046				
017		4X-CUD	N717WW	VR-BES	N996JP	N711JG	N711JQ	N455SH	(N800JS)	N555KE	N565KE
018		4X-CUR	N1188A	N500M	N500MQ	N72FL	N72EL	N1700A	YV3049		
019		4X-CUE	N30AJ	N49MW	(N499MW)	N49MN					
020		4X-CUS	N279DP	N212LD	N917SC	N15BA					
021		4X-CUR	N1125A	N1125S	N1125	N200CK	N7AG	N307FT			
022		4X-CUT	PT-MBZ								
023		4X-CUG	N125GB	N23TJ	N345GC	N112EM					
024		4X-CUT	N300JJ	N999BL	N763RR	YV501T					
025		4X-CUH	N387PA	N887PA	N902AU						
026		4X-CUI	N120BJ	N120WH	N120WS	N9VL	N24PR	N1900A			
027		4X-CUJ	N199GH	N199HF	N199HE						
028		N10MZ	N11MZ	N816HB	N800ZZ	[cx 7Jul14; wfu Wilmington, DE]					
029		N79AD	N15TW	N94TW	N154DD	N131DA	N956PP	N959PP			
030		4X-CUI	N50AJ	N90U	N90UG	N902G	N900DL	N13AD			
031		N40AJ	N125AJ	N987GK	N987G	N962A					
032		4X-CUN	N1125A	N232S	N125MG	N116PB	(N716PT)	N113PT	N514BB		
033		4X-CUP	N980ML	N922RA	N52KS	N441BC	[cx 18Jun15; wfu]				
034		4X-CUJ	N53SF	VR-CMG	N511WA	N541RL					
035		N1125K									
036		I-FLYL	N82RT	N195FC	N230AJ	N757BD	N727HE	YV2872			
037		N3PC	N589TB	N100SR	(N100SQ)	N400XS					
038		N803JW	N930SC	N930UC	N777AM						
039		N359V	N359VP	N359VS	N402TS	N885CA	XA-JRM	N636BC	N686BC*		
040		N279DS	N666K	N666KL	(N530CM)						
041	SP	N96AR	VR-BME	N45MS	N41AU	(N29UC)					
042	SP	N60AJ	N575ET	N575EW	EC-339	EC-GIA	N588R	N528RR			
043	SP	N56AG	(N34CE)	N90CE	N1M	N43MH	[cx 12Mar13]				
044	SP	N50AJ	N676TC	N844GA	N1UA	N334MM					
045	SP	N91FD	VH-FIS	D-CFIS	VH-FIS	N880CH	N916BG	N916CG			
046	SP	N140DR	N630S								
047	SP	N30AJ	(N134RV)	N166RM							
048	SP	N1125V	N88MF	N43RP							
049	SP	N1125Y	JA8379	N4420E	N145AS	N323P	(N1M)	N293P			
050	SP	N4EM	XA-TJF	N501JT	N45H	YV2682					
051	SP	N1125A									
052	SP	N90AJ									
053	SP	N227N	N227NL	(N315S)	N853SP	N121SG	N717CP	N419WC			
054	SP	N70AJ	N198HF	N187HF	N770FF	N770SC					
055	SP	4X-CUI	N1125Z	N1MC	N828C	N880CA	VP-CDR	N120GA	ZS-MDA	N111EL	N111EQ	N63XG
056	SP	4X-CUG	N3175T	N790FH							
057	SP	4X-CUH	N3175S	YV-2199P	YV-785CP	YV-2564P	YV-785CP	N157SP	YV484T		
058	SP	N1125E	C-FDAX								
059	SP/100	N4341S	D-CCAT	HB-VNF	LX-GOL	D-CABB	[rebranded as Gulfstream 100 – but has no winglets!]			N666HA
060	SP	N227AN	YV-757CP	VR-BON	VP-BON	N577AN					
061	SP	4X-CUG	N60AJ	N550M	N200ST	YV2679					
062	SP	4X-CUJ	N999GP	N9990P	N100AK	N262SP	N866G	N866Q	N874WD	N944RS	
063	SP	4X-CUI	Eritrea 901	N74TJ	N331SK	(N60RV)					
064	SP	4X-CUG	N650GE	N650GF	N858WW						
065	SP	4X-CUJ	N75TT	N50TG	N50TQ	N30GC					
066	SP	N101NS	N419MK	C-FMHL	C-FMHB	N419MK					
067	SP	N20FE	N28NP	(N28NR)	N28NF	N267SP	N467MW	N46386	N730DF		
068	SP	N1125Z	N401WT								
069	SP	N804JW	N247PS	[cx 21Feb13; to Savannah Technical College, GA, as instructional airframe]								
070	SP/100	N300AJ	N805JW	N100GA	(N100GQ)	N448GR	(N149LP)	[rebranded as Gulfstream 100 – but has no winglets!]			
071	SP	4X-CUW	N60AJ	N71FS							
072	SP	N1125L	N314AD	N32TM	N365GA	[wfu; cx 06Jun13]					
073	SPX	4X-WIX	[first model SPX]	N173W	N918MJ	N24ZD					
074	SP	N500AJ	N789CA								
075	SP	4X-CUW	ZS-BCT	N75GZ	(N175SP)	N225AL	N928JA				
076	SP	4X-CUV	N1125	4X-CUV	N1125G	N699MC	N699MQ	N20YL			
077	SP	N220AJ	N771CP	YV-771CP	YV1771						
078	SP	N1125J									
079	SPX	4X-CUX	C-FCFP	N800PW	N928WG						
080	SPX	4X-CUY	(D-CCBT)	N333AJ	N333CZ	VP-CUT	C-GSSS	N411MM	C-FPSB		
081	SPX	N800AJ	N801G	N415BS							
082	SPX	N121GV	N882GA								
083	SPX	N383SF									
084	SPX	N795HP	N795HB	N801RS							
085	SPX	N796HP	N796HR								
086	SPX	N793A	PT-WBC	N880GP							
087	SPX	4X-CUU	C-FRJZ								
088	C-38A	N398AG	USAF 94-1569								
089	SPX	N918MK	N89HS								
090	C-38A	N399AG	USAF 94-1570								
091	SPX	N297GA	N500MZ	N500M	N91GX	N818WF					
092	SPX	N789A	VP-BMA	N92UJ	N8MC	N8MN	N100G	[crash-landed 14Sep07 Atlanta/DeKalb-Peachtree, GA; parted out]			
093	SPX	N65TD	N149TD	N707BC	N207BC						

IAI 1125 ASTRA/GULFSTREAM 100

C/n	Series	Identities						
094	SPX	N294S	N500MA					
095	SPX	N98AD	C6-JET	N98AD	N608DC			
096	SPX	N66KG	VP-CKG	N96AL	N323P			
097	SPX	N273RA	N363NH					
098	SPX	N275RA	N98FJ	N919CH	N819CH*			
099	SPX	N987A	5B-CJG	N830DB	N838DB	N115BR	N34FS	N917SM
100	SPX	N807JW	N907DP					
101	SPX	N202GA	N297GA	N711WK	(N291WK)	N610SM		
102	SPX	N525M	N359V	N359D	N877D	N858WZ	[parted out by Alliance Air Parts, OK]	
103	SPX	N755A						
104	SPX	N957P	(N104GA)	N957F	N6EL			
105	SPX	N217PT	HB-VMG	N105FN				
106	SPX	N122GV	N876GA	N800MK	N800WS	N550HB		
107	SPX	N997GA	D-CRIS	OE-GBE				
108	SPX	N998GA	N999GP	N998GP	N302TS	N108CG		
109	SPX	N96FL	N377AC					
110	SPX	N97FL	N212T					
111	SPX	N848GA	N297GA	OE-GAM	HB-VOA	OY-YAM	N760JR	
112	SPX	N633GA	N1MC	N61JE	N81JE			
113	SPX	N113GA	HB-VMK	N35GX	(N297GA)	N82BE	N242BG	N617RA
114	SPX	N114GA	N114SN					
115	SPX	N526GA	HB-VMR	C-GRGE	OE-GPG	N514MM	(PH-DEQ)	(D-CENT) B-58813
116	SPX	N527GA	N456PR	N12ND	N125GR			
117	SPX	N528GA	C-FTDB	C-GGHZ	C-FACG			
118	SPX	N529GA	N28NP					
119	SPX	4X-CUZ	B-20001					
120	SPX	N635GA	N770UP	C-GPDA	N100GY	N989SE		
121	SPX	N843GA	N100AK	N188AK				
122	SPX	N69GX	(N297GA)	N419TK	N110MG	N2HZ		
123	SPX	4X-CVJ	N36GX	"C-GWST"	VH-WSM	N36GX	N307JW	
124	SPX	4X-CVE	N42GX	N777FL	N777FZ			
125	SPX	4X-CVG	N44GX	N248SL	N2488L	N625MM	N625BE	
126	SPX	4X-CVJ	India L3458					
127	SPX	4X-CVG	N621KD	N327GA	N247PS	N919DS		
128	SPX	4X-CVF	N45GX	N179DC	N676TC	N314AD		
129	SPX	4X-CVG	N52GX	N424MP	N180TA	N546LS		
130	SPX	4X-CVI	N55GX	N297GA	N100GA	C-GBSW		
131	SPX	4X-CVG	N57GX	N400CP				
132	SPX	4X-CVI	N1125V	N775DF	N722AZ	N728AZ	N632BE	
133	SPX	4X-CVG	N65GX	VP-CAR	D-CGMA	OE-GBD		
134	SPX	4X-CVG	N64GX	N1125S	N666K			
135	SPX	4X-CVI	N58GX	N809JW				
136	SPX	4X-CVG	N68GX	N43RJ	(N32UC)			
137	SPX	4X-CVI	N75GX	N620KE				
138	SPX	4X-CVG	N80GX	N810JW	N10FH	N776JS		
139	100	4X-CVI	N99GX	N100GA	N420CE	N948LM	N250EX	
140	SPX	4X-CVK	N104GX	N811JW	N50MS			
141	SPX	4X-CVI	N106GX	CC-CWK	N223GA	M-YEDT	N505PL	
142	100	4X-CVK	N109GX					
143	SPX	4X-CVH	N261GA	VT-BAV	N143FS	(YV....)	N174JF	
144	SPX	4X-CVK	N262GA	VP-BMT	N144GX	N82HH		
145	SPX	4X-CVK	N264GA	N387PA	N3FD	(N37DE)	YV3194	
146	100	4X-CVI	N646GA	VP-BMW	N853M	C-GTLG	N590TA	
147	100	4X-CVF	N647GA	N147SW				
148	100	4X-CVI	N648GA	4X-CVI	India L3467			
149	100	N749GA						
150	100	4X-CVK	N750GA	C-FHRL	C-FIPP	OE-GKW		
151	100	4X-CVG	N751GA	C-GTDO	N907TP			
152	100	4X-CVE	N352GA	N150CT	N160CT	N900DP	N525PG	N1UA*
153	100	4X-CVJ	N353GA	OE-GBE	N133SN	N100AK		
154	100	N354GA	N221AL	XA-MEG				
155	100	4X-CVJ	N445AK					
156	100	N996GA	C-FHNS					
157	100	4X-CVK	N327GA					
158	100	4X-CVJ	N995GA	EC-JXE	ZS-SFY	EC-JXE	EC-LDS	N662EP N158LC*

Production complete

Note: Most, if not all, aircraft were first test flown with 4X- marks, some of which remain unknown to us.

The Astra was replaced by the Gulfstream 150.

IAI GULFSTREAM 150

C/n	Identities						
201	4X-TRA	[rolled out at Tel Aviv 18Jan05; ff 05May05]			N150RT	N150GV	
202	4X-WID	[ff 2.9.05]	N150GA	N703HA	(N901VB)		
203	4X-CVK	N528GA	N530GP				
204	4X-WID	N373ML					
205	4X-CVK	N405GA	N715WG	N301SG	N552CB		
206	4X-WID	N806GA	N830DB	N150KM			
207	4X-CVK	N807GA	N531GP				
208	4X-WID	N208GA	N150CT				
209	4X-CVK	N409GA	N501RP	N290GA	N92AJ		
210	4X-WID	N510GA	N650GE	N428JD			
211	4X-CVK	N757GA	N248SL				
212	4X-WID	N412GA	N502RP				
213	4X-CVK	N613GA	N5950C				
214	4X-WID	N314GA	N777FL				
215	4X-CVK	N615GA	N503RP	N215GA	N247PS		
216	4X-WID	N216GA	N192SW				
217	4X-CVK	N217GA	N150GD	N217MS			
218	4X-WID	N218GA	N969WR				
219	4X-CVL	N219GA	CC-CWK				
220	4X-CVM	N220GA	N197HF				
221	4X-WID	N532GP					
222	4X-CVL	N422GA	N717EP	C-FTXX			
223	4X-CVK	N350BN	N611NC				
224	4X-CVM	N424GA	N590FA				
225	4X-WID	N399GA	N150PU	N365GA			
226	4X-CVL	N8821C					
227	4X-CVK	N451R	OB-1951-P	N275SC	N100SR		
228	4X-CVM	N628GA	VP-BMA	N100GX			
229	4X-WID	N8841C					
230	4X-CVK	N630GA	N722SW				
231	4X-CVL	N9611Z	N787BN				
232	4X-CVM	N928ST					
233	4X-WID	N633GA	EC-KMF	N100VP	VH-PFV		
234	4X-CVK	N511CT					
235	4X-CVL	N635GA	D-CKDM	M-CKDM	N371GA	PR-FSN	N250EA
236	4X-TRA	N77709					
237	4X-CVM	N537GA	EC-KMS	CC-AOA			
238	4X-WID	N150GA	N222LR				
239	4X-CVK	N639GA	AP-MMM				
240	4X-TRA	N360AV					
241	4X-CVL	N631GA	N480JJ	[w/o Key West, FL, 31Oct11]			
242	4X-CVM	N442GA	UR-KAS	OE-GAS			
243	4X-WID	N443GA	EC-KPJ				
244	4X-CVK	N744GA	N950N	N302SG	N553CB		
245	4X-TRA	N745GA	OE-GSK	M-STEP	N162RU		
246	4X-CVL	N96AD					
247	4X-CVM	N110FS					
248	4X-WID	N637SF					
249	4X-CVK	N191CP	N67KP				
250	4X-TRA	N850GA	N918MJ	N434JM			
251	4X-CVL	N351GA	N22ST				
252	4X-CVK	N352GA	N769MS	N789MS	N247PS	N150GA	
253	4X-WID	N353GA	EC-KTV	N253DE	N591MB		
254	4X-CVM	N354GA	EC-KTK	N254GS	N901SS		
255	4X-TRA	N556GA	XA-PAZ	XA-UUX			
256	4X-CVL	N262GA	N150GD	N546MM			
257	4X-WID	N457GA	XA-ADR				
258	4X-CVK	N458GA	N10RZ				
259	4X-CVM	N746GA	RP-C5168				
260	4X-TRA	N260GA	N802RR	N150GV	N150HM		
261	4X-CVL	N261GA	OE-GLF				
262	4X-WID	N272CB	N101RX				
263	4X-CVK	N263GA	(N150GV)	N802RR			
264	4X-CVM	N264GA	C-GXNW				
265	4X-CVL	N465GA	N993AC	XA-CHY			
266	4X-WID	N888YC					
267	4X-TRA	N367GA	N119KW				
268	4X-CVK	N268GA	(D-CKDN)	N365SC			
269	4X-CVM	N469GA	(D-CKDO)	N520CH	(N520SH)	XA-CPL	
270	4X-CVL	N470GA	(D-CKDP)	N110JJ	N480JJ		
271	4X-WID	N471GA	C-FTRP				
272	4X-TRA	N372GA	N399SC	N819AM			
273	4X-CVK	N373GA	C-GZCZ				
274	4X-CVM	N374GA	N1FC	N3FS			
275	4X-WID	N375GA	N116HW	C-GNYH	C-GWWW	C-FTIX	
276	4X-CVL	N46WY	N15PV*				
277	4X-CVK	N7FF	N1FS	N636SF			
278	4X-TRA	N700FA					
279	4X-CVM	N489GA	N935SS	N200LR			
280	4X-WID	N980GA	VP-CEP	VT-GKB			
281	4X-CVK	N631GA	N372AS	N57RG			
282	4X-TRA	N382GA	C-GPDQ	C-GZDO	N2282	N22G	
283	4X-CVL	N683GA	C-GXVK	N283GA	9H-JET	SP-TBF	
284	4X-WID	N484GA	TC-AEH				
285	4X-CVM	N485GA	C-FZCC	C-FZCG	N285GA		
286	4X-CVK	N486GA	N150GA	N1924D			
287	4X-TRA	N487GA	(D-CGPE)	D-CGEP			
288	4X-WID	N208GA	C-GWPK				
289	4X-CVL	N489GA	N650MP	N2289	N24G		
290	4X-CVM	N490GA	(XA-ATP)	XB-OMG	XA-ATZ		
291	4X-CVK	N391GA	N1920				
292	4X-TRA	N392GA	N557GA				
293	4X-WID	N393GA	PR-NTR	N935GB			
294	4X-CVL	N994GA	N565AB				

IAI GULFSTREAM 150

C/n	Identities				
295	4X-CVM	N595GA	N194SW		
296	4X-CVK	N996GA	C-FREE		
297	4X-CVL	N217GA	N639SF		
298	4X-CVM	N298GA	N150GD	N685JF	
299	4X-TRA	N199GA	M-GASG		
300	4X-...	N300GA	OE-GKA		
301	4X-CVK	N101GA	PP-ESV		
302	4X-CVL	N702GA	N589MD	N888YV	
303	4X-CVM	N203GA	N13WF		
304	4X-CVK	N104GA	PR-CBA		
305	4X-CVL	N305GA	N150PG		
306	4X-CVM	N806GA	N500RP		
307	4X-CVK	N907GA	N503RP		
308	4X-TRA	N208GA	N501RP		
309	4X-WID	N209GA	N116NC		
310	4X-CVL	N310GA	N151PW		
311	4X-CVK	N311GA	(N150GA)	N72AM	N150GD
312	4X-TRA	N112GA	YV3119		
313	4X-CVK	N913GA	Mexico 3913/XC-LOH	Mexico TP-08/XC-LOH	
314	4X-TRA	N914GA	Mexico 3914/XC-LOI	Mexico TP-09/XC-LOI	
315	4X-WID	N915GA	RP-C8150		
316	4X-CVL	N916GA	N963CH		
317	4X-CVM	N817GA	N622SF		
318	4X-CVK	N918GA			
319	4X-CVL	N819GA	N651DH*		
320	4X-CVM	N120GA			
321	4X-CVK	N221GA			
322					
323					
324					
325					
326					

IAI 1126 GALAXY/GULFSTREAM 200

Note: Some Galaxys have been re-branded as Gulfstream 200s, as shown

C/n	Series	Identities								
001		[reportedly non-flying test airframe]								
002		[reportedly non-flying test airframe]								
003		4X-IGA	[rolled out 04Sep97; ff 25Dec97; wfu Tel Aviv, Israel]							
004	200	4X-IGO	4X-CVF [not confirmed]	(N7AU)	N844GA	N711JG	(N711JU)	(N711JQ)	VP-CHW	N789AT	PR-WTR
005	200	4X-IGB	N505GA							
006		N7AU	N81TT	N8MF						
007		N847GA	(C-GRJZ)	HB-IUT	N844RC					
008		N998G	(N288GA)	VP-CRS	N479PR					
009	200	N849GA	N83EJ	N200AX	PR-FKK	N9889	(N173BF)			
010		N808JW	N121LS	N672PS						
011		N634GA	HB-IUU	N634GA	"HB-IGA"	HB-IUU	N56AG	(N223AM)	LZ-FIB	
012		4X-CVE	"N1TA"	N845GA	(HB-IGK)	YR-TIG	[w/o 16Jan09 Oradea, Romania]			
013	200	4X-CVG	N13GX	N200GA	"XA-MAK"	N200GA	(N13GX)	XA-MAK	N160HA	HB-IGP	N200BH
014	200	N37GX	N121GV	N121GX	N467MW	N469MW	(N140GH)	N20BD		
015		4X-CVI	N38GX	N622SV						
016		4X-CVK	N40GX	N35BP	N135BP	N35BP				
017		4X-CVF	N48GX	(N406LM)+	[+marks worn but ntu]	N415PR				
018	200	4X-CVH	N47GX	N18GZ	4X-COG	HB-JKH	N917DP			
019		4X-CVI	N39GX	N407LM	N219GA	N219AX	N612MH	N812FT*		
020		4X-CVI	N46GX	N516CC	N816CC	C-FLPB				
021		4X-CVF	N321SF	(N41GX)	N321SF					
022	200	4X-CVE	N43GX	N414KD	N414KB	N200AX	N322AD	N330WJ		
023	200	4X-CVH	N50GX	N414DH	N414DK	N32TM	(N32JN)			
024		4X-CVI	N101L	N101LD	N188ML	N818CR	N251LB			
025		4X-CVK	N54GX	N2HL	N263GA	N302MC	N866G			
026		4X-CVE	N56GX	N800PJ						
027		4X-CVF	N878CS	PR-OFT						
028		4X-CVH	N60GX	N199HF	N139HF	N225JD				
029		4X-CVK	N61GX	VP-BLH	VP-CAS	D-BAIR	N929GA			
030	200	4X-CVF	N303MC	B-HWB	N133BA	B-8086				
031		4X-CVH	N62GX	N671PP	N671BP					
032	200	4X-CVE	N66GX	N406LM	HB-JEB	N320LV				
033		4X-CVK	N31SJ	N212MP	YV3130					
034	200	4X-CVF	N34GX	(N200GA)	N134AX	N274JC	(N216YM)	PH-YMA	N108SC	OB-2023
035	200	4X-CVE	N59GX	N110HA						
036		4X-CVK	N67GX	N144KK	N408LM	N408LN	B-KSJ			
037	200	4X-CVH	N337JD	N204AB	B-8083					
038		4X-CVE	N168EC	N602VC	N858DN					
039		4X-CVE	N72RK	N132JC	(N302HM)	YV....				
040		4X-CVH	N90GX	4X-CLL						
041		4X-CVE	N101GX	YV-772CP	YV1401					
042		4X-CVF	N102GX	N701HB	N755PA					
043		4X-CVH	N103GX	N122GV	N123GV	C-FHYB				
044		4X-CVE	N105GX	N621KD	N621KB	N882LT	N882ET			
045		4X-CVF	N107GX	N70TT	N440TT	N1221G				
046	200	4X-CVH	N108GX	PR-MEN	N889G	N878DN	C-GJFG			
047	200	4X-CVE	N110GX	N601AB	N721CJ					
048	200	4X-CVF	N112GX	N602AB	N200GA	N921TH				
049	200	4X-CVH	N290GA	N751BC	N753BC	B-8090	B-LUX	N188AJ		
050	200	4X-CVE	N291GA	N789RR	N789PR	OE-HFC	HB-JKD	N505JC	HK-4907	
051		4X-CVF	N293GA	OY-RAK	LN-SUS	N140KR	B-8089	N283DJ		
052		4X-CVG	N294GA	N402TX						
053	200	4X-CVE	N295GA	(N601AV)	N815JW					
054	200	4X-CVI	N296GA	N200GA	N54AX	N272JC	(N254SC)	C-FLMS		
055		4X-CVF	N255JT	N885AR	N885RR	N212SL	(HS-AAH)	HS-JAA		
056		4X-CVE	N298GA	N929WG	N929WD	XA-PCO				
057	200	4X-CVG	N299GA	N886G						
058	200	4X-CVI	N360GA	(N702QS)+	[+marks worn but ntu]	N272MW	N726DC	N726DR		
059	200	4X-CVE	N361GA	(N602AV)	N409BM					
060	200	4X-CVF	N270GA	N703QS	N409TX	N513RB*				
061	200	4X-CVG	N271GA	N705QS	N413TX	N35RF*				
062	200	4X-CVH	N362GA	N957P	XA-DRE					
063	200	4X-CVE	N363GA	N20PL	N363GA	N20PL	N363GA	SX-IFB	N810AA	HK-5154
064	200	4X-CVF	N364GA	(N706QS)	N2BG					
065	200	4X-CVG	N275GA	(N628RC)	N118KA	(SX-MAD)	SX-ONE	OE-HSG	OO-OSG	OE-HAG
066	200	4X-CVH	N276GA	N707QS	N419TX	N70HQ				
067	200	4X-CVK	N367GA	N916GR	N916GB					
068	200	4X-CVE	N368GA	N179AE	N360SJ					
069	200	4X-CVF	N279GA	N708QS	N403TX	N334JK				
070	200	4X-CVG	N268GA	N702QS	N415TX					
071	200	4X-CVH	N371GA	(N706QS)	N459BN	N458BN				
072	200	4X-CVK	N272GA	N65R	N679RW	N892SB	N110WA			
073	200	4X-CVF	N673GA	N712QS	HB-IUV					
074	200	4X-CVJ	N274GA	N80R	N889MR					
075	200	4X-CVG	N875GA	N200YB	N365CX					
076	200	4X-CVK	N376GA	N200BA						
077	200	4X-CVH	N277GA	VT-PLA						
078	200	4X-CVJ	N278GA	(HB-IUS)						
079	200	4X-CVE	N379GA	N382G	N379GA					
080	200	4X-CVK	N380GA	XA-MDK						
081	200	4X-CVG	N881GA	N414DH	N86CW	N186CW				
082	200	4X-CVJ	N282GA	N402LM						
083	200	4X-CVE	N283GA	N403LM	N830DT					
084	200	4X-CVK	N284GA	N414KD	N1Z	N111ZD	N882SG			
085	200	4X-CVJ	N285GA	N720QS	N406TX	N585DD				
086	200	4X-CVH	N286GA	XA-JHE						
087	200	4X-CVE	N287GA	(N747SG)	N707SG					
088	200	4X-CVJ	N388GA	(N721QS)	N200GA	N704JW	N179JA			
089	200	4X-CVH	N289GA	OE-HTI	YR-TII					
090	200	4X-CVK	N790GA	B-KMJ	HS-LEE					
091	200	4X-CVJ	N391GA	N2HL	(N19HL)	(N918JT)	N990JT			
092	200	4X-CVH	N492GA	N721QS	N417TX	N329PK				
093	200	4X-CVK	N393GA	N722QS	N422TX	N318JF				

IAI GULFSTREAM 200

C/n	Series	Identities							
094	200	4X-CVI	N394GA	N121GV					
095	200	4X-CVF	N595GA	N331BN	N311MK				
096	200	4X-CVG	N196GA	N600YB	N454TH				
097	200	4X-CVI	N397GA	N816JW					
098	200	4X-CVK	N398GA	ZS-PKD	VT-ARV				
099	200	4X-CVF	N499GA	N723QS	XA-MYM				
100	200	4X-CVI	N500GA	N724QS	N408TX	N483AM			
101	200	4X-CVJ	N201GA	N415SE					
102	200	4X-CVK	N702GA	N601DV	OE-HAZ	N412AP			
103	200	4X-CVH	N203GA	EC-JGN	LX-GRS	XA-POS			
104	200	4X-CVI	N104GA	N271RA					
105	200	4X-CVJ	N305GA	N725QS	N932BA	N645PM			
106	200	4X-CVG	N606GA	"N200GA"+	[+ marks worn in NBAA static display at Orlando Executive, FL, Nov05]		N851LE	N2G	
107	200	4X-CVF	N107GA	N707BC	N311WK^				
108	200	4X-CVI	N508GA	N726QS	N324WK*				
109	200	4X-CVE	N409GA	N819AP	N819VE				
110	200	4X-CVG	N510GA	N721BS	N221BS	N967PC	N489VC*		
111	200	4X-CVH	N995GA	N88WU	N818ER				
112	200	4X-CVI	N112GA	C-GTRL	N856T				
113	200	4X-CVK	N413GA	N727QS	N144JE				
114	200	4X-CVE	N214GA	B-LSJ	N833BA	B-8085	VP-CEK	N888NS	
115	200	4X-CVF	N615GA	N200LV	N765WM				
116	200	4X-CVF	N216GA	N728QS	N921BA				
117	200	4X-CVG	N217GA	N62GB	N162GB				
118	200	4X-CVJ	N118GA	N729QS	N620JE				
119	200	4X-CVI	N419GA	C-GWPB					
120	200	4X-CVE	N220GA	N730QS	N970BA	N200GN*			
121	200	4X-CVH	N818JW						
122	200	4X-CVG	N422GA	N200GA	N173JM	(N607AW)			
123	200	4X-CVJ	N223GA	N731QS	N468JJ				
124	200	4X-CVF	N765M						
125	200	4X-CVI	N221GA	EC-JQE					
126	200	4X-CVG	N126GA	N916GR					
127	200	4X-CVH	N424GA	N737QS	N977BA	N573PT*			
128	200	4X-CVE	N102FD						
129	200	4X-CVF	N229GA	N711QS	N980BA	N100EK			
130	200	4X-CVG	N330GA	N565GB	PR-MMP				
131	200	4X-CVH	N771GA	N706QS	N946BA				
132	200	4X-CVI	N732GA	N751BC					
133	200	4X-CVE	N433GA	N200GX	(N202GJ)	N200VR			
134	200	4X-CVJ	N434GA	N88AY	B-8129				
135	200	4X-CVG	N435GA	B-8081					
136	200	4X-CVF	N436GA	N718QS	N299PS*				
137	200	4X-CVH	N137WB						
138	200	4X-CVI	N787PR	N32BG					
139	200	4X-CVJ	N139GA	N204DD					
140	200	4X-CVE	N640GA	PR-AUR					
141	200	4X-CVG	N641GA	N701QS	N929BA				
142	200	4X-CVF	N842GA	N235LC	SX-IRP	G-OIRP	HS-VNT		
143	200	4X-CVH	N143GA	(N81TT)	C-GSQE	C-FJOJ			
144	200	4X-CVI	N217BA						
145	200	4X-CVJ	N645GA	EC-KBC					
146	200	4X-CVE	N138GA	N602RF	N333LX	N789SB			
147	200	4X-CVF	N603RF						
148	200	4X-CVG	N844GA	N716QS	N951BA	N991RL			
149	200	4X-CVH	N404GA	(SX-IFB)	SX-IDA	N899AU	VT-EHT	[dbr by flood water Chennai, India, 01Dec15]	
150	200	4X-CVI	N698GA	EC-KCA					
151	200	4X-CVJ	N651GA	N200GA	N619KS				
152	200	4X-CVE	N152GA	N752QS					
153	200	4X-CVF	N653GA	B-LMJ	HS-HAN				
154	200	4X-CVG	N236LC						
155	200	4X-CVH	N136FT	N135FT					
156	200	4X-CVI	N656GA	N101L					
157	200	4X-CVJ	N557GA	N748QS					
158	200	4X-CVE	N658GA	ZK-RGB	N818TS	N500AG			
159	200	4X-CVF	N559GA	(VP-CSG)	SX-SMG	M-MSGG	N259JP	N159JH*	
160	200	4X-CVG	N670RW	N452AC					
161	200	4X-CVH	(N361GA)	N49VC	N80GK	N765WS			
162	200	4X-CVI	N562GA	N719QS					
163	200	4X-CVJ	N360GA	N35BP	SX-SEA	N680RW	G-ZZOO	M-ZZOO	G-ZZOO
164	200	4X-CVF	N164GA	N200JB	N900GA	N212U			
165	200	4X-CVE	N565GA	N749QS					
166	200	4X-CVG	N566GA	N631DV					
167	200	4X-CVH	N367GA	N200GV	N178TM	N888GQ	M-GULF	OK-GLF	
168	200	4X-CVI	N368GA	N755QS					
169	200	4X-CVF	N10XQ						
170	200	4X-CVJ	N370GA	N745QS					
171	200	4X-CVE	N671GA	EC-KLL	N636CN				
172	200	4X-CVG	N672GA	N172EX					
173	200	4X-CVI	N403GA	N200GA	N125JF				
174	200	4X-CVH	N674GA	B-8087	N148KB	N851SC	M-SBUR		
175	200	4X-CVF	N675GA	N62GB	N148MC				
176	200	4X-CVJ	N276GA	N761QS					
177	200	4X-CVE	N677GA	EC-KOR	N200KN				
178	200	4X-CVG	N678GA	N758QS					
179	200	4X-CVM	N479GA	N797M					
180	200	4X-CVF	N480GA	EC-KPF	LZ-EVL	N991EA	5N-...		
181	200	4X-CVJ	N461GA	N929WC					
182	200	4X-CVE	N482GA	N282CM					
183	200	4X-CVG	N636GA	EC-KPL	N636GA	PR-EST			
184	200	4X-CVF	N384GA	HB-JKG	N581JB	N322SW			
185	200	4X-CVH	N285GA	N750QS					
186	200	4X-CVJ	N486GA	N715WG					
187	200	N387GA	VP-BPH						
188	200	4X-CVG	N388GA	EC-KRN					

IAI GULFSTREAM 200

C/n	Series	Identities				
189	200	4X-CVF	N289GA	4K-AZ88		
190	200	4X-CVH	N590GA	N369JK	N769MS	
191	200	4X-CVJ	N391GA	N819AP		
192	200	4X-CVE	N692GA	N501DV	N929AW	
193	200	4X-CVG	N493GA	HB-JGL		
194	200	4X-CVI	N494GA	N740QS		
195	200	4X-CVF	N595GA	N459BN	N480BN	N441JW
196	200	4X-CVH	N696GA	N988KD	N196X	
197	200	4X-CVJ	N116FE			
198	200	4X-CVE	N398GA	N739QS		
199	200	4X-CVG	N139GA	LX-LAI	N401JK	N621AB
200	200	4X-CVI	N910GA	P4-ADD		
201	200	4X-CVF	N901GA	N332TM		
202	200	4X-CVH	N682GA			
203	200	4X-CVE	N683GA	N98SP	N365GC	
204	200	4X-CVG	N804GA	N738QS		
205	200	4X-CVJ	N805GA	M-OSPB	N205GP	B-23068
206	200	4X-CVI	N306GA	OE-HAS		
207	200	4X-CVE	N307GA	SX-MAJ	M-ILTD	
208	200	4X-CVF	N94FT	N94FY		
209	200	4X-CVH	N809GA	N90FT	N878G	
210	200	4X-CVG	N510GA	N333SZ	B-LSS	N881ST
211	200	4X-CVI	N378GA	N184TB		
212	200	4X-CVJ	N612GA	N741QS	N612GA	N104SG
213	200	4X-CVE	N379GA	VT-JUM	N543WW	
214	200	4X-CVF	N614GA			
215	200	4X-CVH	N715GA	SX-TAJ	UR-PRM	T7-PRM
216	200	4X-CVG	N616GA	N743QS		
217	200	4X-CVI	N417GA	N168RR		
218	200	4X-CVJ	N618GA	PR-BBD		
219	200	4X-CVE	N619GA	EC-LAE		
220	200	4X-CVF	N420GA	VQ-BDS		
221	200	4X-CVH	N381GA	N200BN	N408H	
222	200	4X-CVG	N722GA	EC-LBB		
223	200	4X-CVJ	N383GA	OE-HSB	VP-CIM	M-ALIK
224	200	4X-CVI	N824GA	M-GZOO	G-GZOO	
225	200	4X-CVE	N385GA	OE-HSN		
226	200	4X-CVF	(N525GF)	N525AG	N831BG	
227	200	4X-CVG	N627GA	N742QS	N367GA	B-8121
228	200	4X-CVH	N928GA	N488RC		
229	200	4X-CVI	N629GA	B-8120		
230	200	4X-CVJ	N630GA	N331BN	N331BD	
231	200	4X-CVG	N631GA	HB-JKE	N203GA	OE-HNG
232	200	4X-CVE	N632GA	N262GA	B-8139	
233	200	4X-CVF	N533GA	(ZK-VGL)	M-SWAN	M-SASS
234	200	4X-CVH	N534GA	PR-JPP		
235	200	4X-CVG	N935GA	N244S		
236	200	4X-CVE	N536GA	N200MP		
237	200	4X-CVF	N417GA	N415VF	M-ROIL	
238	200	4X-CVG	N538GA	OE-HGO	OK-GLX	
239	200	4X-CVH	N379GA	N929WG		
240	200	4X-CVE	N440GA	OE-HGE	AP-NST	
241	200	4X-CVF	N341GA	N121DX		
242	200	4X-CVE	N842GA	N688AJ		
243	200	4X-CVG	N373GA	B-8159		
244	200	4X-CVE	N264GA	VT-SNP		
245	200	4X-CVF	N945GA	B-8151	OE-HMA	
246	200	4X-CVH	N146GA	M-NICE		
247	200	4X-CVE	N472GA	B-8277		
248	200	4X-CVF	N848GA	N383AZ		
249	200	4X-CVG	N449GA	VP-CSA		
250	200	4X-CVH	N250GD	N221AE	PR-DEA	

Production complete

IAI GULFSTREAM 280

The Gulfstream 280 was originally named the Gulfstream 250 but was rebranded to improve its sales potential in China.

C/n	Identities						
1998	[static test airframe]						
1999	[fatigue test airframe]						
2001	"N250GA"+	[+ fake marks N250GA worn for roll-out ceremony at Tel Aviv, Israel, 06Oct09]	4X-WSJ	[ff 11Dec09] N101GA	N280GD		
2002	4X-WSM	[ff 24Mar10] N202GA	4X-CVG	N202GA	4X-WSM	N202GA	
2003	4X-WBJ	[ff 28Jun10] "N250GA"+	[+ fake marks N250GA worn in NBAA static display, Atlanta/DeKalb-Peachtree, GA, 18-21Oct10]		N280GT	N280GC	
2004	4X-CVP	N280GD	N38GL				
2005	4X-CVI	N280CC					
2006	4X-CVJ	N260GA	N281CC				
2007	4X-CVE	N280FR	N280GC	XA-BAY			
2008	4X-CVF	N208GA	4K-AZ280				
2009	4X-CVG	N209GA	C-FZCC				
2010	4X-CVH	N310GA	M-AYBE				
2011	4X-CVI	N711GA	N280DX				
2012	4X-CVJ	N112GA	N300R				
2013	4X-CVE	N913GA	M-ASIK				
2014	4X-CVF	N214GA	N282CC				
2015	4X-CVG	N215GA	N259FG				
2016	4X-CVH	N216GA	4K-AZ208				
2017	4X-CVI	N817GA	N280PU				
2018	4X-CVJ	N918GA	N209FS				
2019	4X-CVE	N919GA	N1640				
2020	4X-CVF	N202GA	N516CC				
2021	4X-CVG	N921GA	N7HB				
2022	4X-CVH	N922GA	N28357				
2023	4X-CVI	N923GA	N158FM	N518MB			
2024	4X-CVJ	N924GA	N459BN				
2025	4X-CVE	N225GD	B-8303				
2026	4X-CVF	N226GA	N285DX				
2027	4X-CVG	N427GA	N1FC				
2028	4X-CVH	N828GA	N1620				
2029	4X-CVI	N229GA	N1630				
2030	4X-CVJ	N830GA	B-8280				
2031	4X-CVE	N131GA	N206FS				
2032	4X-CVF	N832GA	B-8305				
2033	4X-CVG	N833GA	N711VT				
2034	4X-CVH	N534GA	N603D				
2035	4X-CVI	N835GA	N331BN				
2036	4X-CVJ	N836GA	N710BG				
2037	4X-CVE	N137GA	TC-KHD				
2038	4X-CVF	N138GA	N92FT				
2039	4X-CVG	N139GA	N280EX				
2040	4X-CVH	N840GA	N280KR				
2041	4X-CVI	N214GA	N280GU	N62AE			
2042	4X-CVJ	N742GA	P4-NAV				
2043	4X-CVC	N943GA	(N604D)	N927LT			
2044	4X-CVD	N744GA	N855A				
2045	4X-CVE	N845GA					
2046	4X-CVF	N246GA	N604D				
2047	4X-CVG	N947GA	N280PF				
2048	4X-CVI	N248GA	XA-PAZ				
2049	4X-CVJ	N249GA	M-ELAS				
2050	4X-CVC	N250GA	N286RW				
2051	4X-CVD	N151GA	"N280HF"+	[+ fake marks N280HF worn at completion centre]	N199HF		
2052	4X-CVE	N252GA	N386RW				
2053	4X-CVF	N253GA	XA-FMX	XA-FAX			
2054	4X-CVG	N254GA	N186RW				
2055	4X-CVH	N255GA	N702BV				
2056	4X-CVI	N256GA	PR-FRT				
2057	4X-CVJ	N257GA	N977AE				
2058	4X-CVC	N258GA	N697CC				
2059	4X-CVD	N259GA	PP-MAO				
2060	4X-CVE	N260GA	N650MP				
2061	4X-CVF	N261GA	N280TD				
2062	4X-CVG	N262GA	CN-TRS				
2063	4X-CVH	N163GA	N164GD	(D-BOSA)	[ntu German marks worn at Dallas/Love Field, TX, completion centre]	N164GD	
2064	4X-CVI	N164GA	N456JA				
2065	4X-CVJ	N965GA	N531RC				
2066	4X-CVC	N266GA	PR-CRC				
2067	4X-CVD	N367GA	N905G				
2068	4X-CVE	N368GA	N308KB				
2069	4X-CVF	N269GA	N806JK				
2070	4X-CVG	N270GA	D-BKAT				
2071	4X-CVI I	N271GA	N029JC				
2072	4X-CVI	N272GA	VP-CVH				
2073	4X-CVJ	N373GA	B-66666				
2074	4X-CVC	N274GA	N28SJ				
2075	4X-CVD	N275GA	N882LT				
2076	4X-CVE	N276GA	N280FW				
2077	4X-CVF	N277GA	N280C				
2078	4X-CVG	N978GA	N696HC				
2079	4X-CVH	N279GA	N3FB				
2080	4X-CVI	N980GA	N280SD				
2081	4X-CVJ	N281GA	N98AD				
2082	4X-CVC	N282GA	N370Z				
2083	4X-CVD	N203GA	N86CW				
2084	4X-CVE	N284GA	HS-KPG				
2085	4X-CVF	N208GA	M-ISTY				
2086	4X-CVG	N286GA	M-INTY				
2087	4X-CVH	N287GA	N199SC				
2088	4X-CVI	N288GA	SP-NVM				
2089	4X-CVJ	N289GA	N283EM				
2090	4X-CVC	N209GA	N283BA				
2091	4X-CVD	N291GA	N94FT*				

IAI GULFSTREAM 280

C/n	Identities		
2092	4X-CVE	N292GA	N15TT*
2093	4X-CVF	N293GA	
2094	4X-CVH	N294GA	N284EM*
2095	4X-CVI	N295GA	N285BA
2096	4X-CVJ	N296GA	N960DT*
2097	4X-CVC	N297GA	
2098	4X-CVD	N998GA	
2099	4X-CVE	N299GA	
2100	4X-CVF	N100GA	
2101	4X-CVG	N101GA*	
2102	4X-...	N902GA*	
2103	4X-...	N703GA*	
2104			
2105			
2106			
2107			
2108			
2109			
2110			
2111			
2112			
2113			
2114			

JET COMMANDER/WESTWIND

C/n	Series	Identities
1	1121	N610J [ff 27Jan63; dismantled 1975]
2	1121	N611JC [test aircraft for static fatigue]
3	1121	N612J N316 N316E N400WT N409WT
4	1121	N77F N77TC N72TC N72TQ [cx 08Aug13; wfu]
5	1121	N364G N334RK N18CA C-GKFT N18CA [cx Oct86; b/u Miami, FL mid 1986; remains to Dodson Avn, Ottawa, KS]
6	1121	N5418 CF-ULG N420P N42QB [wfu; cx Dec91; b/u 1982 by White Inds, Bates City, MO]
7	1121	N112JC N1173Z N22CH N30RJ (N711VK) N77KT N77NT [b/u for spares 1989; cx Nov91]
8	1121	N157JF N31CF N749MC N749MP N101LB [wfu 1998 Tucson, AZ; b/u circa Nov00 at Tucson, AZ]
9	1121	N450JD N459JD CF-WUL N9BY N66EW N89MR (N98KK) [wfu cx Jan94; to Aviation Warehouse film prop facility at El Mirage, CA]
10	1121	N31S N31SB N600CD N5BP N9023W [wfu Jly87 to Bardufoss Videregarude Skole, Norway; TT 5322 hrs as technical airframe – circa 2002 reported b/u]
11	1121	N1172Z N1172L N111TD [parted out St. Simons Island, GA circa late 03; cx 24Jul12]
12	1121	N8300 N613J N777V N37BB N711GW N302AT N344DA LV-RDD [w/o (details unknown); wreckage noted 14May92 Moron, Argentina]
13	1121	N450RA N50VF N12CJ N1JU (N404PC) XA-SFS [wfu; b/u 1983 by White Inds, Bates City, MO]
14	1121	N350M N121BN N87DC N87DG [b/u remains with White Inds, Bates City, MO; cx Jly94]
15	1121	N365G HB-VAX N125K N320W [wfu; b/u 1983 by White Inds, Bates City, MO; cx Apr91]
16	1121	N96B N217PM N177A YV-123CP [wfu Mar93 Caracas, Venezuela; derelict Feb97]
17	1121	(HB-VAL) CF-SUA C-FSUA N91669 [wfu; to Aviation Warehouse film prop facility, El Mirage CA; cx Nov14]
18	1121	N1166Z N121HM [wfu Dec79, to Skolen for Luftfahrtsuddannel, Copenhagen-Kastrup, Denmark; scrapped 2008]
19	1121	N95B [sold May88 in Norway as technical airframe – circa 2002 reported b/u]
20	1121	N334LP N1121E [cx 11Apr13; parted out]
21	1121	N252R CF-WOA N2579E [wfu; parted out by White Inds, Bates City, MO; last allocated US marks not worn; cx Mar91]
22	1121	N148E [w/o 13Sep68 Burbank, CA]
23	1121	N2100X N349M [b/u 1983 by White Inds, Bates City, MO]
24	1121	N94B N360M N360MC N7GW N360MC N560MC [wfu 1993; cx 04Jun13]
25	1121	N555DM [to spares 1992 with Dodson Avn, Ottawa, KS; cx Aug92]
26	1121	N614J N614JC N10MC N77FV [cx Oct88; to spares Aug88 Wiley Post, OK]
27	1121	N93B N93BE [b/u for spares 1989 by White Inds, Bates City, MO; cx Apr91]
28	1121	N1190Z N77NR N234G
29	1121	N615J 4X-COJ [w/o 21Jan70 Tel Aviv, Israel]
30	1121	N401V N400CP [w/o 21Jan71 Burlington, VT]
31	1121	N399D N99GS [wfu 1994]
32	1121B	N92B N92BT N32JC N101BU N98SC [wfu Washington County A/P, PA circa 2001; canx 09Dec05 presumed b/u]
33	1121	N1180Z N151CR N104CJ VT-ERO [wfu and b/u in India, rear fuselage and some other parts to Hollister, CA]
34	1121	N1210 N1210G N102SV N102SY N329HN N777MH N130RC N111XL N500MF TG-OMF N500MF [wfu; parted out by White Inds, Bates City, MO]
35	1121	N6504V N22AC N100TH N101GS N189G N7HL N710JW [cx Nov92 as "destroyed/scrapped"]
36	1121	N1121M N730PV N780PV [sold May88 to Norway as technical airframe; scrap late 1990]
37	1121	N967L N123JB N723JB N445 [noted derelict 11May88 Wiley Post, OK; cx 08Mar11]
38	1121	N901JL N217PM N217AL N1776F (N200WN) N106CJ N37SJ [parted out by White Inds, Bates City, MO]
39	1121	N6505V N550NM N666JD N66TS N80TF N1BC N16FP N10EA [wfu May82 to Skolen for Luftfahrtsuddannel, Copenhagen-Kastrup, Denmark; cx Apr91; to Teknisk Erhvervsskole Centre, Hvidovre, Copenhagen, 2008]
40	1121	N913HB N40JC N40AJ N40UA [wfu; remains with White Inds, Bates City, MO]
41	1121	N6510V N187G N41FL ZP- N40593 N499TR [canx 02Mar06; parted out by Dodson Av'n, Rantoul, KS]
42	1121	N6511V N599KC N3DL N6361C N111Y (N359C) N111YL [noted derelict 12Mar86 Wiley Post, OK; cx Jly94, wfu]
43	1121	N6518V N271E N186G N121CS (N385G) N386G [wfu; b/u for parts 1989; cx Oct90]
44	1121	N200M N700C N700CB N273LP N273LF N69GT N60CD [b/u for parts Rantoul, KS circa Jan01]
45	1121	N920R N340DR N340ER N121PG N910MH [wfu; to instructional airframe at Vaughn College nr.La Guardia A/P, NY, then scrapped]
46	1121	N1500C N200BP N200RM N200GT N220ST N99W [wfu for spares at Tamiami, FL; cx 03Dec14]
47	1121	N6513V HB-VBX N33GL N222GL N222HM N200LF [cx Sep87; b/u for parts by White Inds, Bates City, MO]
48	1121	N541SG N541M N400LR N444WL N8LC N486G N85MA N929GV N502U N301AJ [w/o 13Aug90 Cozumel, Mexico; cx Oct92]
49	1121	N430C N5JR [wfu; remains with White Inds, Bates City, MO]
50	1121	N612JC N133ME [in scrapyard Oct88 Wiley Post, OK; cx 27Nov12]
51	1121	N618JC SE-DCK N303LA N69WW N21BC N93JR N18JL N1EC [b/u Dodson Avn, Ottawa, KS; cx Sep94]
52	1121	N701AP N1121G N696GW N159YC N159MP N159DP [wfu; displayed Darwin Aviation Museum, Australia; some parts to Dodson Avn, Ottawa, KS]
53	1121	N1230 N1230D N10MF N103F N925HB N27BD [wfu; parted out White Inds, Bates City, MO]
54	1121	N6534V N848C [cx Aug88; b/u for spares 1989]
55	1121B	(D-CHAS) D-CEAS 4X-CON N11MC N747LB [b/u; cx Jan04]
56	1121	N6550V (N53AA) N382AA XA-... N382AA Panama SAN-301 [wfu Panama City/Gelabert, Panama]
57	1121	N6544V N770WL N121AJ [wfu May82; b/u for spares]
58	1121	N90B N721AS N120GH N660W N957RC CP-2263 N580NJ [to spares; cx Dec00]
59	1121	N6538V N59JC N21AK [cx 23Aug12; parted out]
60	1121	N6545V N100RC [w/o 14Nov70 Lexington, KY]
61	1121	N1196Z N666DC N51CH N100NR N999FB N29LP N29LB [w/o 19Dec80 Many Airport, LA]
62	1121	N5415 N1777T C-GKFS N1777T [wfu circa 1995 at Tucson, AZ & b/u 9-10Dec00]
63	1121	N6546V N7784 N15G N9DM N8GA N8GE [wfu to spares White Inds, Bates City, MO]
64	1121	N6512V N500GJ N124JB N124VS [wfu Manila, Philippines circa 1999]
65	1121	N500JR [w/o 26Sep66 North Platte, SD]
66	1121	N1966J [wfu; parted out by White Inds, Bates City, MO; hulk to Salina, KS, for training use 2011]
67	1121	N650M N1121G [wfu; used for spares by Dodson Avn, Ottawa, KS]
68	1121	N196KC [w/o 01Jly68 Fayetteville, AR]
69	1121	N6527V N89B N10SN N50JP [wfu; remains with Dodson Avn, Ottawa, KS]
70	1121	N1194Z N129K [parted out by White Inds, Bates City, MO; cx 12Jun12]
71	1121	N1500M N150CM N150CT N150HR N721GB 4X-COA [preserved Israeli Air Force Museum, Hatzerim, with Mig-21 nose]
72	1121	N757AL N777WJ N7KR I-LECO N2WU VR-CAU N2WU [w/o 02Dec90 Laguna del Saule, Uruguay]
73	1121	N98SA N98S N100W N100WM [parted out at Sarasota, FL]
74	1121	N6610V N535D N47DM N300DH N93RM N74GM N274MA (N149SF)
75	1121	N6611V N1121R N212CW [parted out by White Inds, Bates City, MO]
76	1121	N6612V N1121C CF-VVX N100DG N100DR N100TR [wfu with OK Aircraft, Gilroy, CA; fuselage reported at Hollister, CA, Sep95; cx 08Sep14]
77	1121	N1121X N523AC N442WT N11BK N21JW N121JC N177JC [cx 22Dec14; CofR expired]
78	1121	N6613V N1121E N866DH N102CJ [used as spares at Opa-Locka, FL, circa Dec95]
79	1121	N454SR N100LL N36PT [reportedly scrapped; cx Jan97]
80	1121	N87B N900JL N173A N173AR N925R [wfu 1994; cx 18Mar11]
81	1121	N6617V CF-KBI C-FEYG [w/o 26May78 Winnipeg, Canada]
82	1121	N9932 N4NK N82JC N927S C-GPDH N103BW N240AA [parted out & b/u Sep03]
83	1121A	N4550E N23FF N83AL C-GHPR N503U [w/o 19Dec95 Guatemala City, Guatemala]
84	1121	N312S N600TD N600TP N600ER N16MK [wfu Dallas-Redbird, TX circa Dec05]
85	1121	N4554E N201S XC-HAD [b/u 1990 Mexico City, Mexico]
86	1121	N1100M N2JW N13TV N116MC XA-RIW XA-SHA [wfu Houston-Hobby, TX, parted out by Dodson Int'l Parts, Rantoul, KS]

JET COMMANDER/WESTWIND

C/n	Series	Identities
87	1121	N920G N920GP N400PC N430PC N430DC N116KX [wfu; parted out at Hollister, CA]
88	1121	N963WM N70CS N751CR [b/u May87; remains to Aviation Warehouse film prop facility, El Mirage, CA; cx 08May13]
89	1121	N6B N1195N N10BK N163DC [wfu New Orleans-Lakefront A/P, LA]
90	1121	N188WP N1121E N93SC [with Dodson Int'l Parts, Rantoul, KS circa May00]
91	1121	N365RJ N1972W N73535 N711JT [w/o 13Mar75 Tullahoma, TN]
92	1121	N5420 N524X N33PS N401DE [b/u; remains at Wiley Post, OK 12May88; cx Mar89]
93	1121	N619JC N221CF N50LB (N999RA) N1PT [wfu; cx Oct94 "destroyed/scrapped" – parted out]
94	1121	N1424 N1424Z (N144JC) N1424 N94WA N64AH [wfu San Juan, PR]
95	1121B	N5412 N6412 N7090 N709Q N210FE N100CA N200MP (N3031) N200MZ N95JK N614MH CP-2259 N85JW N55HL
96	1121	N56S N56WH N59CT N7EC N1QL N1QH N10JP N10JV (N2ES) YV-2454P [wfu by Jun05 at Caracas-Charallave, Venezuela]
97	1121	N4644E N96B N3032 N3082B N34SW [parted out at Hollister, CA; cx 28Apr06]
98	1121	N1121N C-FWRN N6DB N101DE N482G N301L N333BG [parted out & b/u]
99	1121B	N4661E N922CR N922CP N22RT N22RD N63357 [cx 27Jun13; wfu]
100	1121	N4663E N605V N16GR N11WP N305AJ [wfu; still regd; remains to Aviation Warehouse film prop facility at El Mirage, CA]
101	1121	N899S N100KY N45JF N5JC N16A N16MA N16SK [sold May88 in Norway as technical airframe; later to Bodo Aviation Museum, Bodo, Norway]
102	1121	N27MD [wfu 1986; parted out by White Inds, Bates City, MO; cx 11Jun13]
103	1121	N1121S N136K N487G N10HV N13AD N77HH N998RD [parted out by Dodson Int'l Parts, Rantoul, KS]
104	1121	N4674E N87B N8RA [cx 23Aug13; wfu]
105	1121	N618JC F-BPIB N230RC C-GWPV N5094B [wfu with White Inds, Bates City, MO & b/u; cx Dec03]
106	1121B	N4690E N3711H N40AB N88AD N114HH (N114HE) N180TJ N814K N814T
107	1123	N4691E 4X-COL (4X-COK) Israel 4X-JYG/064 N2120Q Ciskei CA-01 N2120Q [b/u at Oklahoma City, OK; cx Dec90]
108	1121B	N1121Z N1WP N12JA N12JX N77ST LV-WHZ
109	1121	N350X N9DC N379TH N1MW TG-VWA XA-THF [wfu Guatemala City, Guatemala]
110	1121B	N4716E 4X-CPA N101SV N181SV N16GH N1121N [parted out at Hollister, CA]
111	1121	N344PS N999CA C-GDJW N1121M [cx Aug92; wfu for spares by OK Aircraft, Gilroy, CA; remains to scrapyard Long Beach, CA]
112	1121B	N4730E N91B N91WG N4WG N44WG N773WB N372Q N710DC (C-....) N710DC [instructional airframe at British Columbia Institute of Technology, Vancouver, Canada]
113	1121	N4732E 4X-CPB N8534 [b/u circa early 2003, remains at Deland, FL]
114	1121	N4734E 4X-CPC N442WT N448WT N111ST N10GR N85MR N333SV [to spares at Hollister, CA, circa 1995; fuselage used as static testbed for overhauled engines]
115	1121	CF-WEC C-FWEC N3252J N500VF XB-FJI [b/u Monterrey, Mexico]
116	1121	N4743E N236JP [w/o 31Oct69 Marion, VA]
117	1121	N237JF N200BP N400HC N220KP N54WC N34NW [parted out by White Inds, Bates City, MO, 1997; cx 15Nov12]
118	1121	N312S N438 N117GM (N712GM) N716BB N381DA N696RV [cx 22Dec14; wfu Cairo, Egypt]
119	1121	C-FFBC N119AC (LV-...) [reported parted out in Argentina as N119AC, after cancellation]
120	1121	N200M N203M [scrapped during 1984; cx Jan85]
121	1121A	N1121X N840AR N250JP N1121R N250UA (N121JC) [w/o 27Apr78 Flatwood, LA]
122	1121B	N4940E N801NM N122JC N666BP N122HL N122ST (XA-SCV)
123	1121A	N5410 N155VW N1121A N580WE [parted out by Dodson Int'l Parts at Rantoul, KS]
124	1121B	N1300M N300M XA-REO XA-RQT N8070U [for spares; cx Jan99]
125	1121A	N1121N N30LS N1121R
126	1121B	4X-COM N4983E N315SA N113MR N87DC N87DL LV-WEN [w/o 28Sep94 Cordoba, Argentina]
127	1121A	N6B N27X N34HD N209RR N20GB N100SR N550K N277MG [to Dodson Int'l Parts 01Apr05 for parting out]
128	1121A	N660RW N74XL N74XE N1121U N386MC (N386JM) N404WC [to Virginia Museum of Transportation, Roanoke, VA]
129	1121A	N5032E N525AW N110ST (N1121B) N102CE N121PA [to Dodson Int'l Parts Oct05 for parts use]
130	1121A	N5038E 4X-CPD N84 N44 [w/o 02Nov88 en route Westmoreland County A/P, Latrobe, PA]
131	1121A	N5039E 4X-CPE N83 N43 N7028F [at Fairmont State College, WV; canx as "possibly scrapped" Aug96]
132	1121	N200M N403M [w/o 16Dec79 Salt Lake City, UT]
133	1121B	N5041E N1172Z N56AG N56AZ N133JC N666JM N22976 N161X N122JB XA-LYM XB-GBZ N132LA
134	1121B	N111E 4X-FVN UAF1 5X-AAB 4X-COP N7638S N134N [wfu Chino, CA; cx 18May15]
135	1121B	N5043E N700HB N2DB N1KT N721GB N1121N XC-COL N900PJ P4-...
136	1121	N5044E SE-DCY [w/o 04Dec69 Stockholm, Sweden]
137	1121B	N5045E SE-DCZ N50VF N3VF N873 N500LS N300LS N5BP N700BF (N700GA) N707TE XB-FKV N47CE
138	1121B	N5046E 4X-COB N5BA N972TF [cx 22Aug13; wfu]
139	1121B	N5047E 4X-CPF N8535 I-ARNT N188G N481DH [parted out by White Inds, Bates City, MO. cx 09May13]
140	1121	N9040N 4X-CPG N200RC [w/o 25Sep73 Tampa, FL]
141	1121B	N9041N 4X-CPH N100CJ N160WC N177PC N177HB N163WC N163WS 5N-EZE N163WS [wfu Columbia Metropolitan, SC; cx Dec03]
142	1121C	N9042N 4X-CPI N82 N42 N50138 N51038 N1944P [instructional airframe at Pittsburgh Inst of Aeronautics]
143	1121C	N9043N 4X-CPJ N81 N41 N30AD [scrapped at Boeing Field, WA circa May98]
144	1121C	N9044N 4X-CPK N80 N45 N20K (N920KP) [wfu with White Industries, KS]
145	1121B	N9045N HB-VCC (N17DW) F-BTDA N349DA N145BW N145AJ (N805SA) N805SM [cx 28Oct13; wfu Deland, FL]
146	1121B	N9046N N99CV N99CK N923JA N926JM N444TJ [b/u for spares at Atlanta Air Salvage, Griffin, GA circa 1999]
147	1121B	N9047N N720ML N728MC N147JK N912DA (N888MP)
148	1121B	N9048N 4X-CPL N8536 N200DE N200DF N101NK N600K (N22LL) [cx Jun99; parted out at Hollister, CA mid 99]
149	1121B	N9049N 4X-CPM N100MC N100PC N45SL N489G N78MN N700R N1121E (N9LP) (N149BP) N606JM N666JM (N129ME) N343DA N303AJ (N308AU) N149SF [wfu Kingston, Jamaica; cx Nov03]
150	1121B	N9050N 4X-CPN N1884Z N173MC N121FM N1121F [w/o 20May97 San Louis Potosi, Mexico]
151	1123	4X-CJD N1123E N88WP ZP-AGD [b/u Fort Lauderdale Executive, FL]
152	1124N	4X-CJC Israel 4X-JYF/029 4X-CJC Israel 4X-JYR/035 Israel 4X-JYR/929
153	1123	4X-CJB N773EJ N200WC N223WW XA-PUF
154	1124	4X-CJA (D-CBBE) N919JH D-CBBE N722AW N176AK N176DT
155	1123	4X-CJE N23Y N707TE N707TF
156	1123	4X-CJF N1123H N40AS N40BG (N666MP) N566MP N35D [b/u 2006]
157	1123	4X-CJG N1123Q N10MB (N820RT) [wfu; b/u c 1989-90; cx Aug92; remains with OK Aircraft, Gilroy, CA]
158	1123	4X-CJH N1123G N123DR [wfu Buenos Aires/Aeroparque, Argentina]
159	1123	4X-CJI N1123E (N12FH) N123Z N344CK N96TS [wfu to spares at Hollister, CA; cx 25Mar05]
160	1123	4X-CJJ USCG 160 4X-CJJ N1123W N221MJ N221RJ XA-AVE XA-MUI XA-RIZ
161	1123	4X-CJK D-CGLS (N653J) N185G N33WD XA-POJ [wfu after accident (no details known); remains to Dodson Av'n, Ottawa, KS, for spares]
162	1123	4X-CJL N1123S N78LB N234RC N9VC N9VQ XA-SDW (N163W) N13GW HK-.... [cx from USCAR Mar95 but still marked N13GW Feb97 at Bogota-El Dorado, Columbia]
163	1123	4X-CJM N1123T N4444U N47DC N163DL [canx Oct97, status?]
164	1123	4X-CJN D-CAAS N9114S N32WE [parted out by White Inds, Bates City, MO; cx 04Jun13]
165	1123	4X-CJO N1123R C-GWSH N102BW N22RD N30156 [wfu Deland, FL; cx 20May15]
166	1123	4X-CJP C-GDOC N360HK [b/u 1989]
167	1123	4X-CJQ N873EJ N1123H [being parted out by White Industries 1998]
168	1123	4X-CJR N973EJ N66SM N111NF [b/u Dallas-Love Field, TX circa 1998]
169	1123	4X-CJS N1123U N1500C N1100D N44PR [wfu; cx 18Feb09]
170	1123	4X-CJT N1123W N112RC N150HR N90HM [wfu; cx May94]
171	1123	4X-CJU C-GJLL N223PA N89XL (ZS-ODP) [stored at Lanseria, South Africa]
172	1123	4X-CJV N1123H XB-AER N19EE YV-58CP YV-2482P [wfu]

C/n	Series	Identities										
173	1123	4X-CJW	N1123Q	N680K	N30JM	N30AN	[film prop at Aviation Warehouse, El Mirage CA]					
174	1124	4X-CJX	N1123X	N112MR	N124VF	N74TS	N760C	XA-PVR	XA-UHJ	N92RB	[cx 18Dec12; parted out by Dodson Int'l,	
		Rantoul, KS]										
175	1123	4X-CJY	N1123R	N500M	N500ML	N51TV	N523RB	(N571MC)	N384AT	[parted out by Dodson Int'l Parts, Rantoul, KS]		
176	1123	4X-CJZ	N1123T	C-GJCD	N661MP	C-FNRW	N661MP	N27AT	N35CR			
177	1123	4X-CKA	N1123U	N11WC	N777CJ	N118AF	(N114ED)	[cx 1991 wfu]				
178	1123	4X-CKB	N1123Z	N999U	U123CV	[wfu Columbia Metropolitan, SC; cx 01Oct04]						
179	1123	4X-CKC	N1123Y	LV-WJU	N114RA	[cx Apr10; parted out]						
180	1123	4X-CKD	HP-1A	N1019K	(N180JS)	N72LT	N72ET	(N190LH)	N192LH	N3VL	[cx May01, b/u]	
181	1124	4X-CKE	HK-2150X	HK-2150	N107CF	N325AJ	N325LJ	N345BS	N821CN	PP-...		
182	1123	4X-CKF	N1123Q	N200HR	N700EC	N13KH	N18BL	N78BL	N10122	LV-WYL	[wfu Buenos Aires/San Fernando,	
		Argentina]										
183	1123	4X-CKG	Honduras 318		HR-001	XB-DNY	N51990	LV-WLR				
184	1123	4X-CKH	N1123T	N666JM	N866JM	YV-119P	CC-CRK	N481MC	[instructional airframe Midland College, Midland, TX]			
185	1124N	4X-CKI	N1123U	Israel 4X-JYJ/027		Israel 4X-JYJ/927						
186	1123N	4X-CKJ	N1123R	Israel 4X-JYO/031		Israel 4X-JYO/931						
187	1124	4X-CKK	N1124N	N18GW	(N943CL)	(N715GW)	(N416NL)	N516AC	(N789DD)	N1M	N280DB	(N1TS)	(N187TS)
		N241RH	N187TJ									
188	1124	4X-CKL	N1124G	C-GRDP	N118RJ	[parted out by Dodson Int'l Parts, Rantoul, KS]						
189	1124	4X-CKM	N26DS	N926DS	N200DL	N42CM						
190	1124	4X-CKN	N50AL	N890WW	N190WW	N313TW	N510GT	N518GT				
191	1124	4X-CKO	N3VF	N13VF	N711MR	YV-777CP	(N771AC)	N326AJ	N900FS	N900JF	[wfu Tamiami, FL; cx 22May16]	
192	1124	4X-CKP	N71M	(N736US)	N319BG	N819RC						
193	1124	4X-CKQ	N60AL	(YV-37CP)	N101HS	N420J	N420JM	N428JM	N515LG	N98BM		
194	1124	4X-CKR	N222SR	N343AP	N124FM	N40TA	N807BF					
195	1124	4X-CKS	N887PL	N880WW	(N24TE)	TC-ASF	(N195ML)	N951DB	(N920AD)	[parted out]		
196	1124	4X-CKT	N1124E	N250JP	N505U	N500WK	(N615DM)	N863AB	N606MA			
197	1124	4X-CKU	N214CC	N29GH	N29CL	SE-DLK	[w/o 21Sep92 Umea, Sweden; cx Jan93]					
198	1124	4X-CKV	N800Y	N744JR	N600TJ	N98TS	N51MN	N71PT	N750SP	(N750SB)	PR-NJT	
199	1124	4X-CKW	N1124P	N111AG	N999MS	D-CHDL	N199WW	C-FTWO				
200	1124	4X-CKX	N1124X	N4WG								
201	1124	4X-CKY	N1124Q	N1124N	N56AG	N58WW	N85EQ	(N85EA)	N95CP	N300TE	(N29UF)	C-FOIL	N124WW
		[instructional airframe, Western Michigan University, Kalamazoo, MI]										
202	1124	4X-CKZ	D-CBAY	N49968	N54MC	(N254MC)	N202DD	(N37WC)	N141LB	N168DB	YV-297CP	N274HM	N59PT
		N469WC	PP-JJK*									
203	1124	4X-CLA	N1124G	N124WW	N880Z	N22RD						
204	1124	4X-CLB	N221MJ	N156CW	N26TJ	N10UJ	(N100XJ)	[b/u; cx Jly03]				
205	1124	4X-CLC	N96BA	N967A	N124NY	N125AC	SE-DLL	N205AJ	(N775JC)	N331AP	YV2032	
206	1124	4X-CLD	N215G	N215C	N215M	N943LL	N943JL	N100ME	N148H			
207	1124	4X-CLE	N1124P	N6053C	N330PC	N519ME	N666K	D-CHAL	N207WW	C-FTWR	[wfu; cx 24Mar16]	
208	1124	4X-CLF	N961JC	(N961JD)	N961JE	N208MD	N208ST	N324AJ	N311DB	N57PT		
209	1124	4X-CLG	N661JB	N663JB	N662JB	N938WH	N988WH	N222LH	N705AC			
210	1124	4X-CLH	N662JB	N69HM	N661CP	N662JB	N23AC	N38WW	N444MM	N59KC	N337RE	N425JF	N428JF
		N2150H										
211	1124	4X-CLI	YV-160CP	[w/o 19Feb97 near Guatemala City/La Aurora, Guatemala]								
212	1124	4X-CLJ	N212WW	N900CS	N700MD							
213	1124	4X-CLK	N213WW	N555J	N530GV	N580GV	N30YM	(4X-NOY)	4X-CLK	N27TZ		
214	1124	4X-CLL	N1124N	N214WW	N24RH	(N248H)	N46BK	N21SF				
215	1124	4X-CLM	N215DH	N500WH	N946GM	N238DB						
216	1124	4X-CLN	N216SC	N1124G	(N65BK)	N290CA	C-FAPK					
217	1124	4X-CLO	N8QP	N8QR	N217SC	N217SQ	N217WC	N163WC				
218	1124	4X-CLP	N218WW	N100AK	C-GFAN	N218DJ	N74GR	N218PM	N425RJ	N426RJ		
219	1124	4X-CLQ	YV-190CP	N290CP								
220	1124	4X-CLR	N1124G	C-GHBQ	N9134Q	N106BC	N9RD					
221	1124	4X-CLS	N108GM	N969PW	N969KC	(N969EG)	VH-AJS	[w/o 27Apr95 Alice Springs, Australia]				
222	1124	4X-CLT	N294W	N294B	N36EF	N86EF	N700R	N3RC	N598JM			
223	1124	4X-CLU	N1124P	N124TY	N303PC	N20KH	N518WA					
224	1124	4X-CLV	N898SR	XA-KUG	N2756T	N349MC						
225	1124	4X-CLW	N1124U	N30MR								
226	1124	4X-CLX	N500LS	N300LS	N100BC	(N10BY)	N124MB	N120S	D-CHBL	N226WW	C-FTWV	[wfu; cx 11Mar16]
227	1124	4X-CLY	N250PM	N64FG	N624KM							
228	1124	4X-CLZ	N305BB	N795FM								
229	1124	4X-CMA	N1212G	N1625	N162E	N40GG	[parted out by Alliance Air Parts, Oklahoma City, OK]					
230	1124	4X-CMB	N4995N	XC-HCP	XC-HDA	N102U	N1KT					
231	1124	4X-CMC	HB-VFP	N8514Y	N777CF	N70CA	(N27TA)	N331CW	N331GW	N600NY		
232	1124	4X-CMD	N1124Q	N19UC	N190M	N773AW	N4MH					
233	1124	4X-CME	N1124X	N650GE	N650G	N67DF	N36SF	[parted out by Dodson Int'l Parts, KS]				
234	1124	4X-CMF	(N1124Z)	HC-BGL	N1124Z	N161X	[cx Apr13; parted out Denton, TX]					
235	1124	4X-CMG	N1124E	(N24PP)	N65A	N30AB	N903MM	YV....				
236	1124	4X-CMH	N35LH	N236W	N22LZ	N618WA	YV....					
237	1124	4X-CMI	N39GW	N723M	N28TJ	N24KL						
238	1124	4X-CMJ	VH-AJP	[wfu 2015 Nowra, Australia]								
239	1124A	4X-CMK	[conv to 1124A prototype]		HK-2485	HK-2485W	HK-2485G					
240	1124	4X-CML	N240WW	(N400Q)	N400SJ	N400NE	N72787	N298HM				
241	1124	4X-CMM	N789TE	N300TC								
242	1124	4X-CMN	N340DR	N140DR	N500BJ							
243	1124	4X-CMO	N1124G	N59WK	N215SC	4X-AIP	[w/o 23Jly96 Rosh-Pina/Mahanaim-I-Ben-Yaakov, Israel]					
244	1124	4X-CMP	N124PA	N911SP	N124PA	N911SP						
245	1124	4X-CMQ	N1124P	N404CB	N270LC							
246	1124	4X-CMR	N101SV	N911CU								
247	1124	4X-CMS	N1125G	N280LM	N280AZ	N280AT	[w/o 02Jly04 Panama City-Tocumen; dbf]					
248	1124	4X-CMT	N25RE	VH-AJJ	[wfu 2015 Wagga Wagga, Australia]							
249	1124	4X-CMU	N1JS	[reported stolen/crashed 1985 in Mexico; cx Jul10]								
250	1124	4X-CMV	N250WW	C-GFAO	N29995	N60RV	(N250KD)	N914MM	N418WA	N912PM*		
251	1124	4X-CMW	N6MJ	CX-CMJ	PT-LDY							
252	1124	4X-CMX	N1WS	(N9WW)	N553MC	N121JD						
253	1124	4X-CMY	N511CC	N511CQ	N800WW	N800WS	N253MD	VH-LLW	[b/u Perth-Jandakot, Australia by 06Apr98]			
254	1124	4X-CMZ	N600TD	N888R	N112AB	N72HB	N60AV	RP-C59	RP-C5988			
255	1124	4X-CNA	N222MW	N202MW	N424CS	LV-CLS*						
256	1124	4X-CNB	VH-AJK	[wfu; to fire dump at Nowra, NSW, Australia]								
257	1124	4X-CNC	N573P	N317M	N317MB	N755CM	N942FA	N124UF	N79LC	N576LC	[cx 30Dec15; technical airframe Delaware	
		Technical Community College, Georgetown, DE]										
258	1124	4X-CND	N10MR	N1857W	N29AP	N24DS	YV-770CP	N258AV	(N258CF)	N572M	N58FB	N771B	[parted out by
		White Inds, Bates City, MO]										
259	1124	4X-CNE	N1124N	C-GSWS	N19AP	N315JM	VH-LLX	[b/u Perth-Jandakot, Australia by 06Apr98]				

JET COMMANDER/WESTWIND

C/n	Series	Identities							
260	1124	4X-CNF	N401BP	N525ML	C-GAGP	N49TA	(N503RH)	N80FD	N525AK
261	1124	4X-CNG	N167C	N249E	N87GS	N39JN	N11LN		
262	1124	4X-CNH	N262WW	N40DG	YV-393CP	N262WC	N79KP	N150EX	
263	1124	4X-CNI	N29PC	N918SS					
264	1124	4X-CNJ	N351C	XA-MAR	N351C	(N125NY)	N88PV	N351C	N809VC	N810CC
265	1124	4X-CNK	N167J	N7DJ	[parted out by Alliance Air Parts, Oklahoma City, OK]				
266	1124	4X-CNL	N24KT	N24KE	N50DR	N7HM	N5HQ		
267	1124	4X-CNM	N297W	N297A	N100SR	N241CT	N55FG		
268	1124	4X-CNN	(N13HH)	N821H	N606AB	N21CX	N200HR	N41WH	N56BP	N56BN	[parted out by Alliance Air Parts, Oklahoma City, OK]
269	1124	4X-CNO	N3031	N50SL	N21DX	[parted out by Alliance Air Parts, Oklahoma City, OK]				
270	1124	4X-CNP	(N270WW)	N270A	(N27SJ)	(N270DT)	N501DT	N475AT	[w/o May06 Exuma Island, Bahamas]
271	1124	4X-CNQ	N368S	N102KJ	N218SC	C-GWKF	C-FREE	C-FJOJ	C-GSQE
272	1124	4X-CNR	N26GW	N723R	VH-LLY	[b/u Perth-Jandakot, Australia by 06Apr98]			
273	1124	4X-CNS	N104RS	(N566PG)					
274	1124	4X-CNT	N701Z	N701W	N274K	[parted out by Alliance Air Parts, Oklahoma City, OK]			
275	1124	4X-CNU	N1141G	N1621	N36PT	N6TM	N96TM		
276	1124	4X-CNV	VR-CAD	XA-BQA	N269AJ	N800XL	N300XL		
277	1124	4X-CNW	N288WW	(N2AJ)	N504JC	D-CHCL	N277WW	C-GAWJ	N277WW	C-FTWX
278	1124	4X-CNX	N505BC	C-GJLK	N10S	C-GHYD			
279	1124	4X-CNY	N1126G	N885RD	N230TL	N230JK	N952HF	N400TF	XC-COL	[w/o 24Feb05 Sapotita, Mexico]
280	1124	4X-CNZ	N290W	(N5BP)	(N5S)	N29LP	N250RA	N500R	N508R	N949CC
281	1124	4X-CQA	VH-AJQ	N4251H	N1124F	(N200XJ)	VH-AJG	[wfu 2015 Wagga Wagga, Australia]	
282	1124	4X-CQB	N711MB	N186G	VH-AJV	[wfu 2015 Wagga Wagga, Australia]			
283	1124	4X-CQC	N483A	N666JM	(N70WW)	N17UC	N95JK		
284	1124	4X-CQD	N99WH	N296NW	N217BL	N727AT			
285	1124	4X-CQE	VR-CAC	XA-LIJ	VR-CBK	XA-LIJ	N85PT		
286	1124	4X-CQF	N1124U	C-GMBH	N4447T	N92FE	N111LP	N110LP	N113GH	N743PB
287	1124	4X-CQG	N146BF	N530DL					
288	1124	4X-CQH	N1124Q	C-GMTT	N116AT	N94AT	N48AH	N711KE		
289	1124	4X-CQI	N711CJ	N45SJ	N23SJ	VR-CIL	N900VP	[cx 15May15; CofR expired]	
290	1124	4X-CQJ	N800JJ	N719CC					
291	1124	4X-CQK	N124WK	N917BE	N917BF	N816LC			
292	1124	4X-CQL	N292JC	N741C	N741AK				
293	1124	4X-CQM	N26TV	N26T	N26TZ				
294	1124	4X-CQN	D-CBBA	N24DB	(N73GB)	HK-3884X	N147A		
295	1124A	4X-CQO	N295WW	N100AK	N100AQ	N555CW	N730CA		
296	1124	4X-CQP	D-CBBB	N64KT	N770JJ	N92WW	N89TJ	N710SA	
297	1124	4X-CQQ	D-CBBC	N76TG	N51PD	N801SM	N335VB		
298	1124	4X-CQR	N610JA	C-GESO	C-GRGE	N298CM	N809JC	[parted out]	
299	1124A	4X-CQS	N922CR	N922CK	N74JM	N600TC	(N288SJ)	N67TJ	
300	1124A	4X-CQT	N500M	N500MD	(N20NW)	N10MV	PR-STJ		
301	1124A	4X-CQU	N500GK	N815RC	N815BC	XB-GRN	N230JS	N301KF	N890BA
302	1124A	4X-CQV	N600J	N60QJ	N100AK	N422BC	[w/o 26Dec99 Milwaukee, WI]		
303	1124A	4X-CQW	N500J	N50QJ	N211ST				
304	1124A	4X-CQX	N304WW	N369BG	N389BG	N10NL	N13NL	N78PT	
305	1124A	4X-CQY	N464EC	N717LA	N717EA	N629WH	N804CC		
306	1124A	4X-CQZ	YV-387CP	N555BY	(N9WW)	(N722W)	HK-3971X	HK-4204X	HK-4204	N306PT	N123EG
307	1124A	4X-CRA	YV-388CP	N1124K	(N301HC)	N300HC	N825JL	N925Z	N97SM	N494BP	N4SQ	YV2908
308	1124A	4X-CRB	YV-210CP	YV-O-CVG-1	N308JS	N308TS	N628KM	N639AT	[parted out by Worthington Av'n Parts, MN]
309	1124A	4X-CRC	(N200LH)	N240S	N50SK	[w/o 04Apr86 nr Rosewater, TX]			
310	1124	4X-CRD	D-CBBD	N78GJ					
311	1124	4X-CRE	N700MM	N50XX	N700MM	N788MA	N53LM	N696RG	
312	1124	4X-CRF	N200LH	N300LH	N97HW	N24FJ	N316TD		
313	1124	4X-CRG	N146J	C-FAWW	N711WU	N711WV	N611WV	C-GDSR	
314	1124	4X-CRH	VH-IWW	N2454M	N84PH	N2HZ	N49CT		
315	1124A	4X-CRI	N371H	N400YM	VH-BCL	VH-NJW	N315TR	(N89TJ)	N124GR	YV374T
316	1124	4X-CRJ	VH-ASR	N93KE	N33TW				
317	1124	4X-CRK	VH-AYI	P2-BCM	VH-JPW	(VH-NIJ)	VH-UUZ	VH-KNU	[wfu 2015 Wagga Wagga, Australia]
318	1124	4X-CRL	N298W	N298A	N10FG	N38AE	N599DP	[cx 25Nov14; CofR expired]	
319	1124A	4X-CRM	XA-LOR	N560SH	N700WM	(N50XX)	N200KC	N225N	N783FS	N788FS
320	1124	4X-CRN	N60JP	N204TM	YV....				
321	1124	4X-CRO	N900WW	N1124N	N83CT	N93WW	N666K	N666KL	N217F	N810VC	[wfu Fort Worth/Meacham, TX; cx 08Aug13]
322	1124A	4X-CRP	N2AV	N990S					
323	1124	4X-CRQ	N816H	VH-KNS	[wfu 2015 Wagga Wagga, Australia]				
324	1124A	4X-CRR	N3VF	N90CL	C-FCEJ	N91MK	N404HR	N323MR	N406HR
325	1124	4X-CRS	VH-WWY	N504U	N124HL	SE-DPT	N467MW	N68PT	
326	1124	4X-CRT	(N88JE)	N66JE	[w/o 21Feb95 Denver-Stapleton Airport, CO]				
327	1124	4X-CRU	N50M						
328	1124A	4X-CRV	N816JA	N819JA	C-GPFC	N328PC			
329	1124	4X-CRW	N30NS	N711SE	N7HM	N124HS	[impounded Caracas/Simon Bolivar, Venezuela]		
330	1124A	4X-CRX	N52GW	N723K	YV-332CP	YV1685			
331	1124	4X-CRY	N556N	N228N	N228L	LV-WOV	N228L	N811VC	[wfu Fort Worth/Meacham, TX; cx 08Aug13]
332	1124A	4X-CRZ	N24SR	N332DF	N43RP	N43RU	N913CW		
333	1124	4X-CTA	HR-002	HR-CEF	HR-PHO				
334	1124A	4X-CTB	(N45MP)	N40MP	N325LW	N42NF			
335	1124A	4X-CTC	N300HR	N359JS	N501BW	EC-254	EC-GIB	N21HR	
336	1124	4X-CTD	N245S	C-FOIL	N336SV	N255RB	N525XX	N112EM	[w/o Cincinnati/Lunken, OH, 18Jun13; parted out by Alliance Air Parts, Oklahoma City, OK]
			N497HA						
337	1124A	4X-CTE	N14BN	N639J	N900NW	4X-CTE	N2518M	VP-BLT	N127PT
338	1124A	4X-CTF	N338W	N350PM	N850WW	N114WL	N50PL	[w/o 12Dec99, Gouldsboro, PA; cx Sep03]	
339	1124A	4X-CTG	(XC-HDA)	N333CG	N782PC	N74AG	N90KC	ZK-RML	ZK-PJA
340	1124A	4X-CTH	4X-CUA	(XC-BDA)	N1124L	N212CP	PT-OLN	N340PM	N118MP	N3RC	N118MP	VH-KNR
341	1124A	4X-CTI	4X-CUB	N1124P	N23AC	N23AQ	N80RE	N555HD	N556HD	N728LW	N728LM	N868CP	N52KS	N818JH
342	1124A	4X-CTJ	XA-MAK	N342AJ	N39RE	N342TS	N204AB	N274HM	N1VT
343	1124A	4X-CTK	YV-451CP	YV-O-CVG-3		YV-O-FMO-6		N343RD	N999AZ	N911GU
344	1124A	4X-CTL	N334	N311BR	N849HS	N379AV	N769MS	N769M	
345	1124A	4X-CTM	N1424	(N533)	N534	N534R	N345TR		
346	1124A	4X-CTN	N100AG	N1124N	N610HC	N610SE			
347	1124	4X-CTO	N347WW	N30PD	N21GG	YV-666CP	N666CP	N178HH	N347GA
348	1124A	4X-CTP	N348WW	N348SJ	N960FA	N16SF			
349	1124A	4X-CTQ	N78WW	N65GW	N723L	N728L	N123RC		
350	1124A	4X-CTR	VR-CBB	XA-MAK	N3838J	N777LU	N309CK	[w/o 15Dec93 Orange County A/P, CA; cx Oct95]	
351	1124A	4X-CTS	N106WT	N351TC	N722AZ	N728AZ	N111EL	N124BC	
352	1124A	4X-CTT	N15BN	N117JW	N117AH	[cx 04Mar13; parted out by Dodson Av'n, Rantoul, KS]			

JET COMMANDER/WESTWIND

C/n	Series	Identities										
353	1124A	4X-CTU	N379JR	N90CH	N86UR	N89UH	C-GRGE	EC-GSL	RP-C5880			
354	1124	4X-CTV	N443A	N512CC	N506U	N124LS	N894TW					
355	1124A	4X-CUI	N355WW	N355JK	N241CT							
356	1124A	4X-CUJ	N356WW	N8GA	N533	N530GV	N929GV	N43ZZ	N861GS	N767AC	N38TJ	N993DS YV....
357	1124	4X-CUK	(N357W)	C-GDUC	N357EA	N66FG	N357BC	N914DM				
358	1124A	4X-CUL	N358CT	N13UR	N800MA	N830MA	N787RP	N720MC	N404PG	N900DM		
359	1124A	4X-CUM	N8JL	N86RR	N500RR	N500AX	C-GRGE	N14CN	VH-IER			
360	1124	4X-CUN	N816S	N816ST	N816S	N500KE						
361	1124A	4X-CUO	N6053C	N610HC	N3AV							
362	1124	4X-CUP	N445A	YV251T								
363	1124	4X-CUQ	N3320G	N1629	N54PT	(N723JM)	N420JM	(PR-AWB)	PR-OMX			
364	1124A	4X-CUR	N60DG	N199GH	N198GH	N198HF	N198HE	RP-C2480	N944M	N67DT	[cx 27Mar13; wfu]	
365	1124A	4X-CUS	N793JR	(N185BR)	N185MB	N2BG	N73CL					
366	1124	4X-CUT	VH-SQH	VH-LOF	N388GA	N707BC	N65TD	N320MD				
367	1124	4X-CUD	N446A	N511CC	N455S	N367WW						
368	1124A	4X-CUE	N28WW	N368MD	N83SG							
369	1124A	4X-CUF	N24SB	(N54BC)	N300JK	N85WC	N76ER	[parted out by Alliance Air Parts, Oklahoma City, OK]				
370	1124	4X-CUG	N641FG	N471TM	N875HS	N875P						
371	1124	4X-CUH	VH-IWJ	[w/o 10Oct85 nr Sydney, Australia]								
372	1124	4X-CUB	N372WW	N988NA	N810MT	(N800MT)	N810ME	(N5TH)	N921DT	N502BG	N444MW	N404MW N406CH
		N224GP	N942EB	N922EB								
373	1124A	4X-CUK	N373CM	N900LM	N555DH	N794TK						
374	1124A	4X-CUL	N18SF	N56AG	N248H	N33MK	N43W	N30TK				
375	1124	4X-CUF	N79AD	N79AP	N66LX	N66VA						
376	1124A	4X-CUH	4X-CJP	N1124P	N110SF	N376WA	N376BE	VH-ZYH				
377	1124A	4X-CUJ	N301PC									
378	1124	4X-CUI	N84LA	N481NS	C-GXKF	N481NS						
379	1124	4X-CUJ	N52FC	N62ND	N302SG	N851E	YV588T					
380	1124A	4X-CUM	N50DW	N380DA	C-FMWW	[w/o 27Jan94 Meadow Lake, Saskatchewan, Canada; cx Jly94]						
381	1124A	4X-CUO	VH-KNJ	N501U	N929GV	N928GV	N928G	N92EB	N381W	N50FD		
382	1124A	4X-CUP	N900BF	N410NA	(N445BL)	N999BL	N445BL	[w/o 01May92 Waterbury, Oxford, CT; cx Mar93]				
383	1124	4X-CUQ	(N301PC)	N82HH	N20DH	N84WU	N84VV	N942WC				
384	1124A	4X-CUB	N48WW	N61RS	(N50MF)	[w/o 08Nov02, Taos, NM; cx Mar03]						
385	1124A	4X-CUC	N96AL	YV-962CP	N962MV	N317JS						
386	1124	4X-CUE	N68WW	(VH-JPL)	N348DH	N386RL						
387	1124A	4X-CUJ	N97AL	VH-NGA	[w/o 18Nov09 off Norfolk Island, Australia]							
388	1124	4X-CUH	N1124K	N900H	N388WW							
389	1124A	4X-CUF	N49WW	N812M	(N612M)	N812G	N100WP	N812G	N89AM	YV3219		
390	1124A	4X-CUB	N57WW	N3RL	(N303E)	N290RA	ZS-MZM	(HB-...)	N59SM	N122MP		
391	1124	4X-CUG	N24WW	N24VH	C-GMPF	N155ME	N303SG	N59PT	(N205B)			
392	1124A	4X-CUA	N92WW	N95WC	N793BG	[w/o 18Jun14, Huntsville, AL; parted out by Atlanta Air Salvage, Griffin, GA]						
393	1124	4X-CUK	N53WW	N491AN								
394	1124A	4X-CUM	N94WW	N314AD	N352TC	N516CC	N21RA	N63PP	N98HG			
395	1124A	4X-CUC	N95WW	VH-SGY	VH-APU	N395SR	N395TJ					
396	1124	4X-CUR	8P-BAR	N1124N	N37BE	[parted out by White Inds, Bates City, MO; cx 02Apr14]						
397	1124A	4X-CUN	N52SM	N11CS	N777HD							
398	1124	4X-CUO	N98WW	N59AP	N41C							
399	1124A	4X-CUF	N78WW	N48SD								
400	1124A	4X-CUP	N200LS	N300LS	N900PA	N900TN	N917LH	N917LE				
401	1124	4X-CUQ	N84WW	N980S	N30GF	N936AA	YV....					
402	1124A	4X-CUS	N87WW	N999LC	N51TV	N325LB	N63WD					
403	1124	4X-CUH	N403W	(N825EC)	YV2981							
404	1124A	4X-CUG	4X-CJR	N404W	N29CL							
405	1124A	4X-CUJ	N1124L	N211DB	N420TJ	N420CE	N424JR					
406	1124	4X-CUA	N406W	N651E	(N651ES)	N100CH	N830	N8QX	N57KE			
407	1124A	4X-CUK	N407W									
408	1124	4X-CUB	N408W	N408MJ	N125HF	[parted out by Alliance Air Parts, Oklahoma City, OK]						
409	1124A	4X-CUM	VH-JJA	4X-CUM?	4X-CUO	Chile 130	N7051J	N409WW	XA-RET	N4426Z	N217RM	N217BM N26KL
		N629WH										
410	1124A	4X-CUO	N1124Z	(N410EL)	N22BG	N26VF	N26VB	N777DC				
411	1124	4X-CUC	N96WW	N47LP	N47LR	HC-BVX	N224PA					
412	1124A	4X-CUP	N412W	N412SC	N50XX	N50HS	N999MC	N870BA				
413	1124	4X-CJS	4X-CUD	N413WW	N35LH	[parted out by Alberth Air Parts, Tomball, TX; cx 21Nov13]						
414	1124A	4X-CPO	4X-CUC	N86MF	(N66MF)	N980AW	N24MN	N524RH	N550HB	N110JD		
415	1124A	4X-CUS	N415EL	N105BE	N415EL	N415TH	N417PC	N928HR				
416	1124	4X-CUD	N416W	N303TS	N815RK	N600KE						
417	1124A	4X-CUE	N417EL	(N417GW)	N700WE	N115BP	(N99WF)	N34FS	N64FS			
418	1124	4X-CUB	PT-LIP	N124PA	N662K	N317MX	(N317MV)	N420MP	N26T	N26TN		
419	1124A	4X-CUF	N419W	N551TP	N51MN	N411HB	N728MB					
420	1124A	4X-CUH	N420W	N91SA	N728TG							
421	1124	4X-CUJ	N111HN	N801MS	N317MQ	N520MP						
422	1124A	4X-COC	4X-CUI	N422AW	N251SP	N87GS	N87GJ	C6-IRM				
423	1124	4X-CUC	N223WA	N680ME								
424	1124A	4X-CUJ	N424W	N790JR								
425	1124A	4X-CUK	N425WA	N600LE	N365CX	(N365QX)	N328SA	N167JB				
426	1124	4X-CUF	N426WW	N75BC								
427	1124A	4X-CUN	N427WW	N256N	N229N	N229D						
428	1124A	4X-CUO	N428W	(N92BE)	N327SA	N57BE						
429	1124	4X-CUK	(N429W)	C-FROY	N42FL	YV3140						
430	1124	4X-CUM	N430W	N821LG	N430A	N430BJ	N430PT					
431	1124	4X-CUN	N431AM	C-FGGH	N431WA							
432	1124	4X-CUH	N87NS	N317M	N62276	N317MB	(N317MT)	N320MP	N432HS	N282SM	N60BT	
433	1124A	4X-CUH	N433WW	N433WR	N433GM	CP-2784						
434	1124A	4X-CUC	N330MG	(N346CP)	N222KC	N601DR	N187EC	N919BT	(N102AK)	N564RM	YV606T	
435	1124	4X-CUG	(N435W)	N501CB	(N501CP)	(N669SB)	N297JS	N140VJ	N500MA	N435WW	N99PS	
436	1124A	4X-CUE	N436WW	N50XX	N436WW	N110AF	N1904G	N100AK	N444EP			
437	1124A	4X-CUF	N437WW	N437SJ								
438	1124	4X-CUJ	(N438W)	N438AM	N100BC	(N438FS)						
439	1124A	4X-CUG	N439WW									
440	1124A	4X-CUJ	N440WW	N127SA	N220DH	PP-SDW						
441	1124	4X-CUP	PT-LPV	HK-3893X	C-FZEI	C-FPEP	N822QL					
442	1124A	4X-CUO	N406W	N830	N71WF	N830C						

Production complete

LEARJET MODELS 23 & 24

C/n	Model	Identities
001	23	N801L [ff 07Oct63; w/o 04Jun64 Wichita, KS]
002	23	N802L [ff 05May64; last flight 17Jun66; displayed at Smithsonian National Air & Space Museum Steven F Udvar-Hazy Center, Washington-Dulles, VA]
003	23	N803L N200Y N2008 N10MC N3BL
004	23	N804LJ [became c/n 23-015A]
005	23	N232R N570FT N994SA N721HW N721GB N15BE N500JW [b/u for spares around Mar87; cx Aug87 – remains to Bounty Av'n Scrapyard, Detroit-Willow Run, MI]
006	23	N505PF N578LJ N23CH N111JD N505PF [donated Oct93 to Kansas Aviation Museum]
007	23	N826L D-IHAQ [w/o 12Dec65 Zurich]
008	23	N825LJ N1203 N20S N20BD N20EP [wfu circa Mar93; exhibited outside White Inds, Bates City, MO]
009	23	N425EJ N5BL N13SN N49CK N23BY [to Arkansas Air Museum, Fayetteville, AR 2008]
010	23	N805LJ N292BC N2920C N333BF N29BF N400BF N500BF [b/u for spares Oct88 Detroit-Willow Run, MI – remains to Bounty Av'n Scrapyard, Detroit-Willow Run, MI]
011	24A	N806LJ N233VW N1966K N150WL N50JF N711PJ N711TJ N225LJ N24LG (N40TV)
012	24	N1965L N1967L N1966L
013	23	N613W N201BA N888DS N37BL N28ST [w/o 31Jul87 10km east of Guatemala City/La Aurora A/P, Guatemala; cx Dec89]
014	23	N814L N426EJ JY-AEG (HB-VEL) F-BXPT [wfu by Jun05 Limoges, France]
015	24	N88B [donated 28Feb92 to Pima County Air Museum, AZ; cx Mar92]
015A	23	N804LJ [w/o 21Oct65 nr Jackson, MI]
016	23	N500K N7CF N7GF N96CK [fuselage and detached wingset at compound near Davis-Monthan, AZ by Feb02; remains to Aviation Warehouse, El Mirage, CA by Oct04]
017	23	N233R N658L N32SD N30BP F-GBTA F-GDAV [w/o 30Jan89 Lisbon, Portugal; wreckage to Troyes, France, by Jun90; cx Nov92]
018	23	N807LJ N661FS D-IKAA N652J N866DB N866JS [w/o 06May80 Richmond, VA; remains with White Inds, Bates City, MO]
019	24	N4641J HB-VAI N889JF N654DN N100EA N747SC (N954SC) [cx May10; to Thakur Institute of Aviation Technology, Mumbai, India as instructional airframe]
020	23	N388R N338KK N2GP N210GP N310KR (N144WC) N388R N820L
021	23	N427EJ N427NJ N133W [w/o Burbank, CA; cx Jul81, parted out]
022	23	N428EJ N400CS N103TC N88TC N456SC [b/u; cx Feb93; remains to White Inds, Bates City, MO]
023	23	N429EJ JY-AEH HB-VEL F-GAMA [w/o after on-board fire 05Jun81 Le Bourget, France; cx 10Feb92 – to technical college at Perigueux, France]
024	23	N202Y N21U N488J N803JA (N702RK) N3ZA [b/u for spares 1982; cx Apr91; remains to White Inds, Bates City, MO]
025	23	N600G N60QG N5DM N3JL N37DM N50DM N508M N24SA [b/u for spares after accident 21Jun85; cx May89]
026	23	N706L HB-VBA F-BSTP N26008 N404AJ N222GH N404DB N540CL [parted out at Hollister, CA circa early 2000; cx 28Apr06 as b/u]
027	23	N430EJ JY-AEI HB-VES F-GAPY (N108TW) [b/u for spares 1983 Kansas City, KS; remains to White Inds, Bates City, MO; rear fuselage & tail unit used as engineering testbed for Avcom Intl ventral fin retrofit programme]
028	23	N818LJ N5DM (N56PR) N500YY) N5QY N37CP [b/u for spares 1994 Kansas City, KS; remains to White Inds, Bates City, MO]
028A	23	N803LJ N432EJ [w/o 25Oct67 Muskegon, MI]
029	23	N7000K N715BC N1BU N66AS N61TS [wfu Sep88; b/u for spares Detroit-Willow Run, MI; cx Jan96]
030	23	N431EJ N431CA ZS-JWC N431CA ZS-JWC [sold in USA circa May02, to be used for spares for c/n 23-081; remains to Aviation Warehouse, El Mirage, CA]
031	24A	N175FS N477BL N777TF N777TE N202BA N175FS [stored dismantled at Paso Robles, CA, awaiting possible restoration – was owned by Frank Sinatra Jun65-Jun67]
032	23	N235R [w/o 23Apr66 Clarendon, TX]
033	23	N158MJ N453LJ N453JT XA-LGM XA-GAM N60DH N23TJ [wfu Sep87; cx Feb93 remains to scrapyard at Hastings-Earls Air Park, FL by Mar01]
034	23	N242WT N241BN N24FF N154AG [to Museum of Flight, Seattle WA. Displayed at Everett/Paine Field, WA] "N407V"
035	23	N100X (N10QX) N992TD [wfu; cx23Jul08]
036	23	N477K N210PC N111WM N38DM YV-278CP N123MJ
037	23	N266JP N988SA N51AJ N65LJ N41AJ N13LJ N10LJ N50AJ XA-ESS XC-UJP XC-AA28 XC-LGD [w/o 07Dec08 Lake Atlangatepec, Mexico]
038	23	N812LJ VR-BCF LN-NPE N1002B 9Q-CGM 9Q-CHB N433J N433JB N100TA N100JZ N300TA N175BA PT-LKQ [wfu Detroit-Willow Run, MI; to Detroit technical school as instructional airframe – then reportedly b/u circa 2000]
039	23	N43B N800JA N15SC N30SC N9JJ (N43CT) N121CK XA-... N121CK [b/u Niagara Falls A/P, NY, May13]
040	23	N433EJ N673WM YV-01CP N98386 (N12HJ) [b/u for spares 1989]
041	23	N205RJ N666MP C-GDDB N77VJ [b/u for spares circa 2001]
042	23	N293BC N2932C N1ZA N701RZ N69KB [b/u for spares 1982 by White Inds, Bates City, MO; cx Dec91; remains still present Nov94]
043	24	N368MJ N39T N24MW N50BA (N43AC) [sold for spares during 1987; cx Sep89]
044	23	N22B HB-VAM [w/o 28Aug72 Innsbruck, Austria]
045	23	N242F N711MR N100TA [w/o 06May82 Savannah, GA]
045A	23	N803LJ HB-VBB F-BSUX N959SC [w/o 23Jly91 Detroit City, MI]
046	23	N434EJ [w/o 09May70 Pellston, MI]
047	23	N2503L N347J YV-E-GPA YV-15CP N9260A N444WC N2503L [parted out at Rantoul, KS, circa early 2000]
048	23	N805LJ N1GW N48MW N140RC [wfu at Montgomery, AL by Jul04]
049	23	NASA701 N701NA N933NA (N933N) N605NA
050	24	N828MW N828M N823M N650CA N24ET N24NJ [instructional airframe at Bombay Flying Club College of Aviation, Mumbai/Juhu, India]
050A	23	N808LJ N808JA [w/o 23May(?) 1982 in ground fire; probably at Sarasota-Bradenton, FL, where burnt fuselage was noted 25Jun82; remains to Taylorville, IL]
051	24	N1500B N1500G N100MJ (N69LL) N990TM N70JC N24VM [parted out by White Inds, Bates City, MO, 1987]
052	23	N360EJ HB-VBD N360EJ N856JB
053	23	N361EJ HB-VBC F-BTQK N23AJ [parted out by Dodson Av'n, Rantoul, KS, 1988; cx Sep92; hulk to Aviation Film Prop Warehouse, El Mirage, CA, wearing fake marks N464CL]
054	23	CF-TEL N351WB N351WC N351NR N351N [parted out by Dodson Av'n, Rantoul, KS]
055	24	N809LJ N2366Y N511WH N711CW [preserved at Tillamook Air Museum, OR]
056	23	N362EJ N332PC [w/o 06Jan77 Flint, MI; parted out by White Inds, Bates City, MO]
057	23	N448GC N448GG [parted out by Dodson Av'n, Ottawa, KS]
058	23	N363EJ N66MP N7FJ N153AG [cx 13Nov14, CofR expired]
059	23	N364EJ N31DP N331DP [b/u for spares Jun87 Detroit-Willow Run, MI – remains to Bounty Av'n Scrapyard]
060	24	N889WF N90J XA-ADJ
061	23	N316M [w/o 19Mar66 Lake Michigan, MI]
062	23	N670MF N20TA [cx 06Sep12, wfu]
063	23	N243F [w/o 14Nov65 Palm Springs, CA]
064	23	N365EJ N200G N400RB N401RB N73JT N66AM ZS-MBR 3D-AFJ ZS-MBR [wfu Oct93 Lanseria, S Africa] N259DB [parted out by Atlanta Air Salvage, Griffin, GA; cx 16May13]
065	24	N2000M N200DM N7500K (N750QK) N750WJ N957SC N707SC (XA-...) N707SC [wfu Rio Negro, Columbia]
065A	23	N388Q N28BP (N28BR) N1GZ N122M (N156AG) [fuselage and detached wingset in compound nr Davis-Monthan, AZ, by Feb02; remains to Aviation Warehouse, El Mirage, CA, by Oct04; tail unit used in 'Telle Mere Tel Fils' sculpture by Adel Abdessemed 2008]
066	23	N216RG N72MK N66MW XA-RVE XA-SDP N211TS XB-MYE
067	23	N815LJ N2ZA N703DC N720UA N331DP [w/o 18Jan90 nr Dayton, OH; cx Oct90]
068	23	N460F N902AR N902AB N575HW N9RA N400PG N152AG XA-ARG XB-GRR N73CE [to Yanks Air Museum, Chino, CA]
069	23	N814LJ N9AJ N6GJ N37BL (N34TR) [converted at some time to Model 24 standards; w/o 04Mar98 Oakland, CA, remains to White Ind's, Bates City, MO circa Oct98]
070	23	CF-ARE N1976L N197GL N111CT N101DB XA-RZM XA-TII XC-AA104 XC-JDX XB-KMY
071	23	N1001A N71LJ XA-RZC N6262T [with Dodson Avn, Rantoul, KS, for parts Jly95, still marked as XA-RZC]

LEARJET 23/24

C/n	Model	Identities
072	23	N331WR N331JR N4VS N31S N2SN RP-C848
073	23	N806LJ
074	23	5A-DAC D-IATD N23TC N74MW N23AN N68WM N150AG XA-LAR XB-GRQ N83CE [sold to Maricopa County Community College, AZ]
075	23	5A-DAD [w/o 05Jun67 Damascus, Syria]
076	23	N1966W N801JA N12GP N50PJ N83LJ [cx Aug10, wfu]
077	23	N812LJ N740J N868J N500P N90658 N88EA (N611CA) N745F [w/o 30Jul88 March AFB, Riverside, CA; cx Mar90]
078	23	N690LJ [w/o 30Nov67 Orlando, FL]
079	23	N240AG N240AQ N31CK [fuselage and detached wingset in compound nr Davis-Monthan, AZ by Feb02; remains to Aviation Warehouse, El Mirage, CA by Oct04; tail unit used in 'Telle Mere Tel Fils' sculpture by Adel Abdessemed 2008]
080	23	N822LJ [w/o 09Dec67 Detroit, MI]
081	23	N369EJ N437LJ XC-JOA N418LJ (N81LJ) ZS-MDN N265DC [cx 18Apr07, wfu]
082	23	N280C N805JA N7GP (N700NP) (N216SA) [wfu Hampton – Tara Field, Atlanta GA]
082A	23	N823LJ N255ES N744CF N100TA N613BR N618BR (N118LS) [instructional airframe Blackhawk Technical College, Janesville, WI]
083	23	N824LJ [donated to the Kalamazoo Air Zoo, MI for public static display]
084	23	N788DR N101JR N119BA
085	23	N825LJ N385J N101PP [w/o 04Jun84 Windsor Locks, CT]
086	23	N1021B [w/o 06Nov69 Racine, WI]
087	24	N407V CF-UYT N7VS D-IKAB C-GEEN N998RL N24YA N24YE [parted out by Dodson Int'l Parts, Rantoul, KS cx Feb03]
088	23	N816LJ N616PS N11JK N804JA N48AS N500FM (N500LH) [w/o 02Jul91 Columbia, TN; noted dumped Oct91 Bounty Avn Scrapyard, Detroit-Willow Run, MI; cx Jun99]
089	23	N869B N969B N1968W [cx Apr01; b/u for spares by Dodson Int'l Parts, Rantoul, KS, circa 2002]
090	23	PP-FMX [w/o 30Aug69 Rio de Janeiro, Brazil]
091	23	N430JA N430J N110M N11QM [cx Dec89; b/u for spares 1989]
092	23	N415LJ N422JR N105BJ N344WC N415LJ [cx Aug10, wfu Smyrna, TN]
093	23	N416LJ N3350 N416LJ N12TA N38JD N486G N101AR N101AD N97MJ XA-SHN N80775 N7GF XA-... [still wearing N7GF at Toluca, Mexico, May11]
094	23	N417LJ N20M [w/o 15Dec72 Detroit, MI]
095	23	N366EJ N974D N5D N9RA N46452 [cx 27Oct09; to India as instructional airframe]
096	24A	N1967W N421L N527ER N33BK N1972L N1973L N1972L N464CL
097	23	N425SC N79LS N1968A N1963A [to spares 1995 remains at Hampton – Tara Field, Atlanta, GA]
098	23	N112T N11111 N2DD N711 N711AE N99TC [b/u May87, Cincinnati/Lunken Field, OH; parted out by Brandis Avn, Taylorville, IL]
099	23	N7200K [cx 06May13; wfu]
100	24A	N427LJ CF-BCJ N144X N989SA N424NJ N361AA N24BA N616SC N427LJ N224SC [w/o 26Sep99 Gainsville, GA; remains to Atlanta Air Salvage, Griffin, GA]
101	24	N316M N316MF N15PL N473EJ N473 N68DM (N68FN) N24GJ XA-SGU N24WX [noted wfu at Corona Municipal apt, CA 1997; moved to Mesa/Falcon Field, AZ, by Feb08 for rebuild]
102	24A	N436LJ N365EJ N705NA N805NA [w/o 07Jun01 Victorville, CA; cx Sep01]
103	24	N430LJ N714X N72442 ZS-LTK N90532 ZS-LTK N90532 ZS-LTK N90532 ZS-LTK N105EC XB-ADR
104	24	N433LJ N924ED N45ED
105	24	N425NJ N111EK N111EJ TR-LYB F-GDAE [cx Aug96 as wfu; reported w/o in 1989, no details]
106	24	N888NS N969J N100GP N70RL N103RB N888MC C-FNMC N888MC [cx Mar11; to India as instructional airframe]
107	24A	N48L [cx 05May15; CofR expired]
108	24	N1966L N745W N661CP N661BS N661SS C-GSIV N45811 N29LA N900JA N315AJ [b/u circa Apr04 for spares by White Industries, Bates City, MO]
109	24	HB-VAS OY-RYA SE-DCW (F-GBBV(2)) N900DL XA-NLK [wfu Toluca, Mexico]
110	24A	N388R N1969H N362AA N35JF N88JF [b/u Oct86 possibly following accident at Detroit, MI in Oct86; cx Jul89; remains with Brandis Avn, Taylorville, IL]
111	24A	N900Y N500FM N44WD N900NA
112	24	N447LJ CF-ECB N2200T N10CP (OB-....) N112DJ N104GA XA-TRQ
113	24	N438LJ (N402Y) N204Y N100SQ [to spares 1989 by Brandis Avn, Taylorville, IL]
114	24	N443LJ N999M N99DM PT-LNE [wfu at Belo Horizonte, Brazil by 2005]
115	24	N449LJ N458LJ N591D N591DL N86CC [b/u for spares during 1989 Denver, CO; remains with Brandis Avn, Taylorville, IL]
116	24A	N461F N52EN N77GH N8FM N400EP N40BP N51B N105GA (N12MB) (N1420)
117	24XR	N288VW F-BRAL N16MJ HZ-SMB N90DH N92DF N140EX N24SA
118	24	N452LJ N100GS N1008S N1919W N31SK [w/o 27Mar87 Eagle County A/P, Vail, CO]
119	24	N453LJ N453SA N605GA N994SA N110W N500PP N500P (N500PJ) N61CK N63CK [b/u for spares by Dodson Int'l Parts, Rantoul, KS circa Oct02]
120	24	N457LJ N633J N633NJ N44AJ N44NJ PT-LMF N244RD [b/u for spares by Dodson Int'l Parts, Rantoul, KS, circa Oct02]
121	24	N454LJ N454GL N454RN [w/o 26Feb73 Atlanta, GA]
122	24	N461LJ PT-CXK [w/o 04May73 Rio Galeon, Brazil]
123	24	N262HA N700C (N700ET) XA-JSC XA-JSO N35EC N25LJ N3137
124	24	N462LJ OY-EGE SE-DCU (N252DL) XA-RTV N991TD [cx 20Jul12; to Malaysia as instructional airframe]
125	24A	N651LJ [crashed 03Jan76 Anchorage, AK]
126	24	N653LJ N352WR N332FP (N345SF) N16HC [instructional airframe Craven Community College Institute of Aeronautical Technology, Havelock, NC]
127	24	N654LJ N654JC N654LD N111LJ N127LJ N37CB (N6462) N124JL [cx 19May15; CofR expired]
128	24	N655LJ HB-VBK N914BA N333X N383X N4CR HB-VBK N37594 N802W (D-CJAD) N128BJ N911KB XA-TDP (N128WD) [to spares by Dodson Int'l Parts, Rantoul, KS, circa 1999]
129	24	N656LJ D-IFUM N44GA C-GSAX N44GA [w/o 30Jan84 Santa Catalina, CA; cx Nov86]
130	24	N657LJ N420WR N1871R N1871P N130J N33CJ N330J N234MR [b/u for spares Dec87]
131	24	N659LJ N232R N282R N11FH N241JA [to Wings Over the Rockies Museum, Denver, CO]
132	24	N658LJ N233R N238R N32CA [cx Sep01; aircraft was b/u]
133	24	N660LJ N40JF N40JE N555PV N46WB N16WJ N133DF N133BL [b/u; cx Feb04]
134	24	N231R N281R N282R N215J N200GP (N202GP) N200TC N270TC N7GN N911TR N26BA [parted out at Rantoul, KS circa early 2000]
135	24	N85W N77LB LV-WMR [w/o 28Aug95 Pasadas, Argentina; fuselage at Buenos Aires-Aeroparque, for spares]
136	24	N664LJ N222RB N954S N24LW XA-JLV [wfu following flood damage; to spares Oct94 Spirit of St Louis A/P, MO]
137	24	N907CS N73HG N77RY N72FP N151AG [parted out by White Inds, Bates City, MO]
138	24	N37P N808DP N808D N575G N106CA N45JF (N106CA) N400RS N94JJ N130RS [was being converted to a 4-seat 'suborbital spaceplane' fitted with a Rocketdyne RS-88 rocket, new wings and new tail assembly. First flight was planned for Jul06, current project status unknown]
139	24	N590GA N52JH N42AJ N481EZ N96AA [b/u for spares by Dodson Int'l, Rantoul, KS circa Oct02]
140	24	N663LJ N663L N663LJ N593KR N252M N100VC N100VQ [to instructional airframe, National Aviation Academy, St Petersburg-Clearwater, FL by Oct02]
141	24	N348VL N348BJ N43AJ N141PJ XB-FJW XB-GHO [w/o 18Feb11 Pachuca, Mexico]
142	24	N591GA N200NR N777MR N723JW [instructional airframe Delaware Technical Community College, Georgetown, DE]
143	24	N592GA N145JN N778GA N49AJ N900BD N2YY (N727LG) N724LG N24WF [wfu still painted as N724LG; in compound nr Davis-Monthan, AZ, by Nov02; cx 19Jul04; hulk to Aviation Warehouse, El Mirage, CA by Oct04]
144	24	N593GA N397L N397BC N9KC N700C N303AF [parted out by White Inds, Bates City, MO, 1986; cx 11Mar05]
145	24	N690J N57ND (N57NB) N282AC (ZS-PBI) [cx 30Mar09; wfu in South Africa]
146	24	N672LJ N235Z N44CJ [w/o 02Oct81 Felt, OK]
147	24	N673LJ N595GA N16CP N444KW N33NJ N825AA (N67CK) N147KH N147CK [instructional airframe JRN Institute of Aviation Technology, India; cx 21Jan09]

LEARJET 23/24

C/n	Model	Identities									
148	24	N406L	N80CB	N133TW	HB-VDH	N8482B	N426PS	(N47NR)	N41MP	N24ET	[cx 13Aug13; impounded at Charallave, Venezuela]
149	24	N294BC	N2945C	N300HH	N300LB	N64HB	N995TD	[cx 09Mar06; aircraft used as instructional airframe]			
150	24XR	N3807G	N596GA	N596HF	N211HJ	N211BL	N24XR	XA-RQB	[parted out by Dodson Av'n, Rantoul, KS Oct04]		
151	24	N153H	N111HJ	N664CL	N664GL	N50JF	N24AJ	N53GH	N6177Y	[cx 12Dec14, CofR expired]	
152	24	N3807G	N597GA	N21U	N98DK	N9LM	N48BA	[wfu 1993 Kissimmee, FL; cx Aug93; parted out by Dodson Av'n, Rantoul, KS]			
153	24	N524SC	N1TK	N159J	(N53DE)	N878DE	(N555DH)	N153BR	N120RA	[wfu; cx 13Jan09]	
154	24	N123VW	N12315	N424RD	N7HA	N11AK	N123RE	[w/o 17Oct78 Lancaster, CA]			
155	24	N598GA	N422U	N462B	N462BA	N833GA	N210FP	N660A	[parted out 1987; hulk to Aviation Film Prop Warehouse, El Mirage, CA]		
156	24	N599GA	N468DM	N111RF	N111RP	N712R	LZ-VTS	[wfu; fire training aid at Nurnberg a/p]			
157	24	N640GA	N1919W	N1919W	N191DA	N94HC	N124WL	N43ZP	N659AT	(N157BP)	XA-SNZ	(N650AT)	N659AT
		N157TW	[cx 15May15; CofR expired]								
158	24	N642GA	N392T	N855GA	N500MH	PT-LPX	N500MH	N220PM	PT-WEW		
159	24	N647GA	N855W	N661JB	N66MR	N710TV	(N269AL)				
160	24	N645G	N111WJ	C-GTJT	N4791C	N989TL					
161	24	N649G	N224KT	N24KT	N24KF	N222TW					
162	24	N841GA	N338DS	N91MK	N919K	N835AC	N835AG	N55NJ	[w/o 07May86, Hollywood, FL; remains to Dodson Av'n, Ottawa, KS; rear fuselage & tail to Guthrie, OK]		
163	24	N701AP	N1AP	N65339	N77AE	(N777JA)	N65WM	N68LU	[wfu, donated to mechanics school, Lewis University, IL Jul86]		
164	24	N711L	N464J	N924BW	N831RA	XA-RYN	N831RA	XA-TKC+	N831RA	[+ remained current on USCAR, while also on the Mexican register]	
165	24	N844GA	N469J	ZS-KJY	V5-KJY	ZS-KJY	V5-KJY	ZS-KJY			
166	24	N993KL	N500SB	N124PJ	N124HF	N993TD	[to India as instructional airframe]				
167	24	N847GA	N841LC	N888B	N664CL	[instructional airframe, North Valley Occupational Center, Van Nuys, CA]					
168	24	N109JR	N109JB	N51CH	C-GBWB	N155BT	N333TW				
169	24	D-ICAR	N9033X	(N127DN)	N127DM	N927AA	N93BP	[parted out by Dodson Int'l Parts, Rantoul, KS circa Oct02]			
170	24	N200DH	N151WW	[wfu Addison, TX]							
171	24	N737FN	N417WW	[cx Jan11; to India as instructional airframe]							
172	24	N675L	N234WR	N48AJ	[parted out by White Inds, Bates City, MO]						
173	24	N852GA	N872JR	N110SQ	N33ST	N102GP	N3GL	N623RC	YV-824CP	YV1079	
174	24	N854GA	N661CP	N661JG	N999JR	N321GL	N77WD	N77GJ	XA-LNK		
175	24	N859GM	N859L	N288K	N28BK	N881FC	[w/o 02Feb92 New Tamiami, FL; cx Mar93]				
176	24	PT-CXJ	N3034B	[cx 31Jan05; b/u]							
177	24	N321Q	N104MB	N555LB	N555LA	N555LB	(N524DW)	[fuselage and detached wing set in compound near Davis-Monthan, AZ by Feb02; remains to Aviation Warehouse, El Mirage, CA by Oct04]			
178	24	N674LJ	N55KS	N55KX	N56LB	N56LS	N24AJ	N41BJ	N723JW	N11AQ	[parted out at Addison, TX, circa 2005]
179	24	N920FF	N300CC	N111RA	N111RE	N410PD	N410PB	N412PD	N717DB	XC-GII	XA-RQP	N994TD	[cx 11Jul13; wfu]
180	24	N566RB	N802JA	N100RA	XA-SBR	XA-NLA					
181	24B	N234Q	N1QC	N651J	N44PA	(N144PA)	N87CF	N254JT	N426TA		
182	24B	N945GA	N171L	N500ZA	N500ZH	N155J	RP-C2324	[wfu, stored at private address Quezon City, Philippines]			
183	24B	N676LJ	OY-AGZ	F-BRNL	[w/o 18Dec85 Toulouse, France]						
184	24B	N950GA	D-IMWZ	N84J	N36RS	N78BH	N28DL	N58DM	N58FN	[Instructional airframe, Hampton University, Newport News, VA, then scrapped]	
185	24B	N754M	N44CP	N144CP	[parted out at Rantoul, KS circa early 2000]						
186	24B	N266P	N100AJ	N1SS	N18G	(N7300G)	N7300K	N73PS	N196CF	[b/u for parts; cx Feb06]	
187	24B	ZS-SGH	F-GAJD	N5WJ	N129DM	[b/u for spares Feb90]					
188	24B	N230R	N280R	[cx 14Jan08, wfu Guthrie, OK]							
189	24B	D-CJET	D-IKAF	D-CONA	N14MJ	N711DS	N711DX	N915US	[cx 21Feb06, parted out]		
190	24B	N4291G	N9HM	N50TC	HZ-GP4	F-GBLA	N190SC	(N190DB)	N190BP	N600XJ	[w/o 23Dec03 Helendale, CA]
191	24B	N855W	N44LJ	(N44TL)	N80DH	[b/u 1984 after accident; cx Mar89; remains to Dodson Av'n, Ottawa, KS]					
192	24B	N1919W	N12MK	[w/o 06Jan77 Palm Springs, CA]							
193	24B	D-IOGI	N31TC	N500RP	N500RE	N33RE	N140CA	N83H	N83HC	(N488BL)	N193JF	N193DB
194	24B	N952GA	N77LS	N851BA	N62DM	(N62FN)	N2093A	[wfu Newton, KS]			
195	24B	N202BT	N272GL	F-BUUV	N803L	N555LJ	(N721MD)	(N46LM)			
196	24B	N99SC	N1125E	N99ES	N99E	N173LP	N573LP	N573LR	N88RD	N196AF	N196TB
197	24B	N953GA	CF-CSS	C-FCSS	S52GH	N87AC	C-FCSS	N711CN	N711	N711UR	N710TJ	XB-SUD	XA-RXA	N84CT
		XA-	N24FU	N89ES							
198	24B	N66RP	N111GW	N21XL	N21XB	N39KM	[to India as instructional airframe; cx 12Nov08]				
199	24B	N333CR	N855W	N444HC	N70TJ	XA-TTT					
200	24B	(N24NP)	N721J	N721JA	N246CM	N119MA	[being parted out at Bates City, MO circa early 2000]				
201	24B	N3871J	N273GL	D-IDDD	D-CDDD	C-GTFA	N100DL	[w/o 23May98, Orlando Executive, FL; parted out at Bates City, MO, circa early 2000]			
202	24B	N3816G	N77JN	F-BUFN	N26MJ	N999MF	N123SV	N814HH	N814JR	N333RY	[parted out San Antonio, TX; cx 14Aug13]
203	24B	N515WC	N3GW	(N43TL)	N55LJ	N55MJ	N203CK	N203JL	[to Evergreen Aviation & Space Museum, McMinnville, OR]		
204	24B	N957GA	N957E	N176CP	N510ND	N510MS	[fuselage with OK Turbines, Hollister, CA by Feb05]				
205	24B	N974JD	N64CF	N64CE	(N721J)	[wfu; cx 16Sep08]					
206	24B	HB-VBY	F-BTYV	N116RM	N24YA	[parted out by White Inds, Bates City, MO; cx 18Apr13]					
207	24XR	N851JH	N878W	N457JA	ZS-MGJ						
208	24B	D-ILDE	N72335	N42HC	N444AG	N32MJ	N444AG	N444AQ	N14PT	XA-AAA	[wfu Monterrey del Norte, Mexico]
209	24B	N970GA	N16MT	N14BC	ZS-LWU						
210	24B	ZS-LLG	F-BSRL	[w/o 10Jun85 over Provins nr Paris, France]							
211	24B	N388P	N30EH	N222AP	N31LB	N413WF	N680CJ	[cx 27Aug13; wfu]			
212	24B	N291BC	N328TL	N328JK	[cx 17Apr14, wfu Charallave, Venezuela]						
213	24B	N555MH	N986WC	N886WC	N999RA	N43KC	N103TC	N95AB	N895J	N24JZ	XA-...	N24JZ
214	24B	N192MH	N192MB	N666CC	N668MC	N214MJ	N42NF	N234CM	[w/o 16Dec88 nr Monclova, Mexico; cx Apr91]		
215	24B	N971GA	N201WL	N10EC	N29CA	(N57JR)	N29CA	(N57JR)	N400EP	[cx 9Oct14, CofR expired]	
216	24B	N212LF	N723LL	N711DB	N411SP	(N821LL)	N777LB	N900GG	XA-...		
217	24B	N777MC	N777MQ	C-GPDB	N8536Y	C-GDKS	N45824	N217AT	C-FZHT	N876MC	
218	24B	N682LJ	N101VS								
219	24B	N658AT	N711CE	N100KK	F-GECI	N977GA	ZS-TOY				
220	24B	N292BC	N248J	N17FN	[wfu for spares by Dodson Avn, Ottawa, KS]						
221	24B	N977GA	N570P	(N570JG)	N59JG	N233TW					
222	24B	N692LJ	N740E	N740F	N740EJ	[cx 19Jly05 as b/u]					
223	24B	D-IOGA	D-COGA	D-IFVG	D-CFVG	N7074A	[wfu for spares by Feb94]				
224	24B	D-IOGE	N99606	N30DH	C-GPCL	N102PA	(N722DM)	N61DM	(N61FN)	(N51GJ)	XA-TCA	[wfu Toluca, Mexico]
225	24B	N618R	D-IHLZ	[w/o 18Jun73 Marlensel, W Germany]							
226	24B	N454LJ	N335JW	(N335JR)	N335RY	RP-C2424					
227	24B	N244GL	XA-TIP	N90797	N1DD	N10CB	N43W	N4576T	N28AT	N27BJ	
228	24B	N245GL	N4292G	N7DL	(D-IIDD)	D-IIPD	N777SA	N150AB	PT-OBD	[wfu at Belo Horizonte, Brazil by 2005]	
229	24B	N293BC	N298H	N551AS	N864CL	[w/o 08Oct84 San Francisco, CA]					
230	24D	N252GL	N329HN	N93C	N93CB	N433J	N433JA	N18SD	N477JB	N482CP	N819GF	N67JR	N7121K
		XA-VVI	N32287	XA-SSU							
231	24D	HB-VBU	I-CART	N693LJ	N37DH	N93BR	[wfu; remains with Brandis Avn, Taylorville, IL; still regd]				
232	24D	N123CB	[w/o 17Apr71 Butte, MT]								
233	24R	N253GL	D-IGSO	N78AF	N23SG	N23SQ	N500RW	N124TS	(N56GH)	N143GB	N19LJ	[wfu Newton, KS]
234	24D	LV-PRA	LV-JTZ	[wfu Buenos Aires/Ezeiza, Argentina]							

LEARJET 23/24

C/n	Model	Identities										
235	24XR	N51VL	N701SC									
236	24D	N26VM	N48JW	N25ZW	N55DD	N3TJ	N25LJ	N236TS	N236WJ	N93DD	N990PT	N890PT	N47TK N59AL
237	24D	N902AR	N111TT	N25TA	N112J	N32AA	N353J	N889WF	XA-...	N25RJ	N825DM	N237TW	
238	24D	N262GL	N472EJ	N49DM	N48FN	[to Hampton University, Newport News, VA, as instructional airframe then scrapped]							
239	24D	D-ILVW	D-ILHM	F-GBLZ	N83MJ	PT-LAU	[w/o 10Sep94 Brasilia A/P, Brazil]						
240	24D	LV-PRB	LV-JXA	[possibly to spares with Dodson Int'l Parts, Olathe/New Century Air Center, KS circa Oct00]									
241	24D	HB-VCT	N120J	N363BC	(N61TJ)	N63GA							
242	24D	N1972G	N45CP	N1972G	N999WA	[to India as instructional airframe; cx 28Aug09]							
243	24XR	HB-VCI	N2909W	(N85DH)	N83RG	N56WS	N57FL	N37HT	N929HF	N929MC			
244	24D	PT-DZU	[w/o 23Aug71 Sao Paulo, Brazil]										
245	24D	N275LE	N275E	JA8446	N275E	(N44KB)							
246	24D	N215Z	N21NA	N5SJ	N35SJ	N50SJ	(N69SF)	N61BA	N184AL	N600JC	N444SC	(N444HE)	N24TE N99JB
		N6JM	N500MS	N400MS									
247	24D	HB-VCN	D-ICAP	N23AM	N42PG	N247DB	N997TD	[w/o 10Dec01 on approach to El Paso, TX]					
248	24D	OO-LFA	9Q-CBC	[w/o 18Jan94 Kinshasa, Zaire]									
249	24D	9J-ADF	N27MJ	N999M	N998M	XA-POS	XC-AA63	N249RA	N440KT	[cx 19Mar13, CofR expired]			
250	24D	N112C	D-IMAR	N122CG	N2U	N1U	N85CA	N85CD	Venezuela 0006	[wfu; preserved Caracas/La Carlota,			
		Venezuela]											
251	24D	N333X	N338X	N251TJ	N95DD	XA-SBZ	XA-RIC	N46JA	N69XW	N39EL	[wfu Carlsbad, CA; cx 19May15]		
252	24D	N711L	N711LD	N972	N157AG	(N252TJ)	(C6-BGF)	XA-...	N157AG				
253	24D	N123VW	N999U	N30FL	N711DB	(N30FL)	N97DM	N417JD	N97DM	[w/o 05Mar86; collided with Learjet N39DM c/n 35-040			
		over Pacific Ocean nr San Clemente Islands]											
254	24D	D-ICAY	D-CCAT	N13606	PT-LCV								
255	24D	XC-SAG	XA-BBE	XA-SMU	N255AR	[cx Jun10; to Finland as instructional airframe]							
256	24D	HB-VCW	N703J	C-GWFG	C-GWEG	N256MJ	N256WM	[b/u Jan06 Mankato, MN; cx 04Apr06; fuselage to Guthrie, OK, by 01Oct06]					
257	24D	N427JX	C-GHDP	N888FA	[instructional airframe Southern Illinois University, Carbondale, IL]								
258	24D	N75KV	N25VZ	N25GW	N19TJ	N24CK	(N24DZ)	(N77RS)	N424RS				
259	24D	N200JR	N22MH	(N24EA)	(N22ML)	I-EJIA	N22MH	XA-RRC	[parted out by White Inds, Bates City, MO]				
260	24D	N60GL	C-GFJB	XA-ROX	XA-GBA	XC-PFP	XC-AGU						
261	24D	D-IDAT	D-COOL	C-GBWA	[b/u for spares 1993 by Global Inds; cx Jun94; remains to Bounty Av'n Scrapyard, Detroit-Willow Run, MI]								
262	24D	N2GR	OH-GLB	N38788	N110PS	OH-GLB	[wfu; cx Apr03 – to RAOL Technical Vocational School, Rovaniemi, Finland, as instructional						
		airframe]											
263	24D	N3812G	XB-JOY	[w/o 29Jun76 Mexico City, Mexico]									
264	24XR	PI-C1747	RP-C1747	[wfu Manila, Philippines]									
265	24D	N2WL	N32WL	N456JA	[w/o 24Oct85 Juneau, AK]								
266	24D	N266BS	VH-BSJ	N266BS	N266TW								
267	24XR	HB-VCY	N46032	N78AE	N124GA	VR-BHC	HB-VCY	N95DA	VR-BMN	N267MP	ZS-OEA		
268	24D	N53GL	N111WW	N123CC	N92TC	(N66FN)	N58BL	N98WJ	N24TK				
269	24D	XA-DIJ	XA-MOV	XA-DIJ	XB-MZX								
270	24D	XB-NAG	XA-BUY	N3979P	PT-LEM	[w/o 07Apr99 Ribeirao Preto, Brazil]							
271	24D	N3818G	HB-VDK	F-BVEC	N4305U	XA-SCE							
272	24D	N51GL	N117K	[cx 22Jul13; wfu]									
273	24D	OH-GLA	N118J	5Y-GEO	N51AJ	XC-DOP	XB-DZR						
274	24D	N3871J	N1U	N48CT									
275	24D	XB-NUR	N24TC	N216HB	PT-LPH								
276	24D	PT-JGU	N25CV	N56PT	(N814HP)								
277	24D	N131CA	N181CA	(N163ME)	(N181RW)	N106MC	N57BC	N277TW					
278	24D	PT-JKR	N5695H	N202JS									
279	24D	VH-SBC	N849GL	N3DU	N3DZ	I-FREU	N75CJ	N101AR	N955EA				
280	24XR	D-ICHS	N79RS	ZS-NGG	[b/u for spares at Nelspruit, South Africa]								
281	24D	SE-DFB	OY-BIZ	N23MJ	N281FP	[to Frontiers of Flight Museum, Dallas-Love Field, TX]							
282	24D	D-INKA	N300JA	[w/o 02Dec79 Dutch Harbor, AK]									
283	24D	SE-DFA	D-IEGO	N51JT	N20GT	N31WT	N47WT	(N711SC)	N24XR	XA-UHT			
284	24D	PT-JKQ											
285	24D	XC-AZU	XA-REK	XB-GBC	N995DR	(N995RD)	N430JW	N300TJ	[cx 9Dec14, CofR expired]				
286	24XR	N59GL	N86GC	N56RD	N57DB	N77JL	[w/o 12Nov03 St. Louis Downtown apt, IL]						
287	24D	HB-VDN	EC-CJA	HB-VDN	I-MABU	N92565	PT-LCN	[w/o 04Apr84 Florianapolis, Brazil]					
288	24D	N288DF	N7701L										
289	24D	(HB-VDO)	F-BRGF	N131MA	XA-RUJ	N131MA	N289SA	N289G	N98CG	[wfu Carlsbad, CA; cx 21May15]			
290	24D	N462B	N23JC	N934H	N87AP	N24EA	N24TK	XA-RMF	N24TK	N88LJ	N308SM	XB-AFA	
291	24D	ZS-GLD	N45862	N148J	N24PJ	PT-LYL	N114WC	(N919MA)	N488DM	N483DM	[cx 25Apr11; instructional airframe, South		
		Georgia Technical College; Americus, GA]											
292	24D	N426NA	N600PC	N426NA	N800PC	N888TW							
293	24D	XA-TIP	N917BF	N293MC									
294	24D	N4F	PT-LNK	PP-EIW	PT-WKL								
295	24D	N717HB	N717HE	N49TJ	(N160GC)	N590CH	N295NW						
296	24D	XA-FIW	N222BN	N500RK	N500DJ	PT-LMS							
297	24D	N297EJ	XA-ACC	N716US	(N317MR)	HK-3265	N8094U	N24S					
298	24D	N298EJ	XA-ADD	N98AC	N151AG	N470TR	N169US						
299	24D	N299EJ	XA-ABB	XC-JCN	XB-GJS	N299TW	[cx 22Sep14, wfu]						
300	24D	N300EJ	N455JA	[w/o 20Aug85 Gulkana, AK]									
301	24D	N137JL	N111TT	(N87MJ)	N31BG	N249HP							
302	24D	N302EJ	N39DM	N302EJ	[w/o 14Apr83 Puerta Vallarta, Mexico]								
303	24D	N303EJ	PT-LOJ	N303EJ	[to White Inds, Bates City, MO 21Jun04 for spares; cx 26Oct07]								
304	24D	N304FJ	N304LP	N500CG	N588CG	[wfu at Detroit-Willow Run, MI]							
305	24D	N305EJ	N98DK	N305EJ	(N725DM)	N43DM	(N43FN)	N510PA	N666MW	N930PJ	[cx 3Dec14, CofR expired]		
306	24D	N306EJ	N55CD	N98AA	N132MA	XA-SAV	XA-SAA	N306JA	(N243RK)				
307	24D	N307EJ	N307BJ	XA-RRK	[w/o 02Jan98 Tampico, Mexico; to spares by Dodson Int'l Parts, Rantoul, KS]								
308	24D	N308EJ	N99AA	N39TT	(N308LJ)	N89AA	XB-IRH						
309	24D	N310LJ	N45FC	N45AJ	(N4445J)	N789AA	N80CK	N309TC	[wfu Detroit/Willow Run, MI, still marked N80CK]				
310	24D	HB-VDU	I-AMME	[w/o 06Feb76 Bari, Italy]									
311	24D	N66LW	N5TR	N5TD	N19HM	N19FM	N50DR	N56DR	N748GM	N10WJ	(N76PW)	N311LJ	[to Finland as
		instructional airframe May11]											
312	24D	Ecuador IGM-401		N312NA	N80AP	[cx 25Aug15; wfu]							
313	24D	Mexico MTX-01		Mexico MTX-02		[w/o 20Nov98 Mexico City, Mexico; parted out by White Inds, Bates City, MO]							
314	24D	N501MH	N13MJ	[w/o 06Nov82 Elizabeth City, NC; cx Sep92]									
315	24D	PT-KPE	[wfu Sao Paulo/Congonhas, Brazil circa Sep99; fuselage to Jundiai, Brazil]										
316	24D	LV-LRC	Argentina T-03		LV-LRC								
317	24D	N133GL	ZS-JJO	N45AJ	XA-JIQ								
318	24D	N114JT	N611DB										
319	24XR	XC-SUP	XA-SUP	XC-SUP	N174RD	[cx Aug10; wfu in Australia]		N174RD					
320	24D	N3802G	YU-BIH	SL-BAB	S5-BAB	N996TD	[cx Feb10; to Singapore as instructional airframe]						
321	24D	N10WF	N122RW	N224JB	C-FRNR	N33TP	N351MH						
322	24D	XA-DAT	N105GL	N972H	N7RL	(N322TJ)	N322RS	[cx 01Aug12, wfu]					

LEARJET 23/24

C/n	Model	Identities							
323	24D	N61AW	N744JC	N104MC	N453	N27AX	[wfu 2005]	'N1TL'+	[+displayed in Tulsa Air & Space Museum, Tulsa, OK, wearing fake marks N1TL 2005-2011; scrapped by Oct11]
324	24D	N107GL	(possibly XA-SUY)		XA-SCY	N324TW			
325	24D	N76RV	N416G	N500SW	N500SQ	N721SF	[instructional airframe, Redstone College, Denver, CO]		
326	24D	N326EJ	(N400XB)	N326KE	N322AU	XA-MMD			
327	24D	N327EJ	F-GGPG	N327GJ	N711PC	[instructional airframe VARIA-Vantaa Vocational School, Helsinki, Finland Dec08; cx 10Mar09]			
328	24D	D-IMMM	D-CMMM	[w/o Bornholm, Denmark, 15Sep12]					
329	24E	N102GL	N21AG	N22MJ	XA-PFA	N329TJ	N24FW		
330	24E	N511AT	N330TW	[cx 05Mar16; wfu]					
331	24E	N12MJ	XA-REA	N32DD	[instructional airframe, Lake Area Technical Institute, Watertown, SD]				
332	24F	N13KL	N56MM						
333	24E	N76TR	N32WT	N75GP	N75GR	PT-LQK			
334	24E	N6KM	N66MJ	N944KM	[cx Dec10; to India as instructional airframe]				
335	24E	N721GL	N87JL	N2DD	N8AE	N2DD	N894CJ		
336	24F	N3818G	I-DDAE	N162J	N9LD	N49GS			
337	24F	XA-GEO	XA-DET						
338	24E	N729GL	N30LM	N30EM	[b/u for spares 1989; cx Dec89; remains with Brandis Av'n, Taylorville, IL]				
339	24E	N15MJ	N851CC	N690	N60FN	N1TJ	N52DD	N207RG	T7-SAM
340	24E	N10FU	C-FHFP	N54JC	(N95CP)	N106TJ	N457GM	N825AM	N627JJ [cx 29Apr14, believed wfu in Venezuela]
341	24E	N22BM	N22NM	N3PW	(N103JW)	N14DM			
342	24F	N40144	YV-178CP	N824GA	N123DG				
343	24E	N102B	N102C	N1DK	N7EJ	(N602JF)	[cx 11May15; CofR expired]		
344	24F	N81MC	[w/o 10Nov84 St Thomas, Virgin Islands]						
345	24E	N500RP	N500RR	D-CFPD	N435AS	N217JS	(N99UP)	N217AJ	
346	24E	N61SF	N41TC	N117AJ	N117AE	N69AX	(HP-....)	XC-LJE	XB-JXZ
347	24E	N724GL	N124EZ	N500LL	N500TS	N500SR	N508SR		
348	24F	N725GL	N4RT	N4RU	(N106M)	N8BG	N444TW	[w/o Guadalajara, Mexico, 09Jan07]	
349	24F	VH-FLJ	N349BS	XA-CAP	XB-DZD	XB-KJW			
350	24F	N741GL	N500ZA	N504JV*					
351	24E	N19MJ	N31WT	N81WT	N77MR	(N94BD)	N75NE	[cx 9Dec14, CofR expired]	
352	24F	N101US	(N449JS)	N352MD					
353	24F	N740GL	N711PD	N411MM	N63BW	PT-LMA	[w/o 24Feb88 Macre, Brazil]		
354	24F	N678SP	PT-LYE	ZS-FUN	[possibly w/o 14Jan06 Kinshasa, Republic of Congo]				
355	24E	N7AB	N7ZB	N500NH	N165CM				
356	24F	N3283M	N677SW	N113JS	PT-LKD				
357	24F	N288J	N129ME	HZ-S3					

Production complete

LEARJET MODEL 25

C/n	Series	Identities									
001		N463LJ	[used in construction of 25-002]
002		N661LJ	[wfu Jly72 and used for AiResearch engine tests]
003		N594GA	N11JC	N4PN	N97DM	N97FN	[Instructional airframe, Hampton University, Norfolk News, NC, then scrapped]
004		N641GA	N1121	N1121C	N7GJ	N47MJ	N251AF	N225KA
005		N646GA	N1969W	N777RA	N707TR	(N707TP)	(N24FN)	N28FN	N711SQ	XA-SDQ	N39CK
006		N6804L	N256P	N90MH	N88CJ	(N88GJ)	N522SC	N852SC	N188FC	(N25JX)	(N857SC)	N252SC	N44CP	XB-KQN
007		N644GA	N551MD	N551MB	N7TJ	N25NM	N500JA	N52JA	(N58JA)	N726WR
008		N648GA	N744W	VP-BDM	N744W	N1976S	N645L	N88NJ	N800GG	XA-MUU
009		N843GA	N670LJ	9Q-CHC	N40LB	[w/o 25Sep73 Omaha, NB]
010		N846GA	N846HC	N671WM	N102PS	(N10BF)	(N82UH)	(N121GL)	N121EL	[cx May03 to Kingston University, UK as instructional airframe]
011		N167J	N49BA	C-GHMH	N108GA	N525TW
012		N853GA	N853DS	N191DA	N846YT	N846YC	N102AR	[parted out by White Inds, Bates City, MO; cx 29Apr09]
013		N856G	N515VW	[w/o 17Apr69 Delemont, Switzerland]
014		N857GA	N914SB	N204A	N316M	N127AJ	N8CL	N14LJ	N754DB	[cx 07Jun04; b/u by Clay Lacy Av'n for parts]
015		N858GM	CF-HMV	N713US	N708TR	N25FN	N25GJ	N125U	XA-LLL
016		N145JN	CF-KAX	N424RD	N711EV	N83TH	N8FF	N976BS	(N35WE)	[canx 12Sep05; b/u for parts by Jet Components Aircraft Parts, TX; hulk to Alliance Air Parts, Oklahoma City, OK]
017		N720AS	N101WR	N16JP	N666WL	N55WJ	N128DM	N123JS	N53FL	[wfu; cx 27Aug12]
018		N861GA	N323WA	N77SA	N32PC	N99ES	N117CH	N15MJ	(N23FN)	N29FN	[parted out by Brandis Avn, Taylorville, IL; cx 07Jun13]
019		N591KR	N88EP	N88FP	N100MK	[w/o 21Oct78 Sandusky, OH]
020		N941GA	N215Z	N30TT	(N90TC)	N113AK	N900JD	N900CJ	N500JS	N76CK	[wfu; cx 09Oct15]
021		N942GA	N111LL	N1JR	N1LL	N40SW	N40SN	N6NF	[wfu; cx Apr95; displayed Ozark Municipal A/P, AL]
022	XR	N943GA	N925WP	N1ZC	N99CQ	(N93JH)	N131MS	N24BS	N111WB	N111WR	ZS-SSM
023		N577LJ	N72CD	N13CR	(N861L)	N47AJ	(N820RT)	(N12RA)	N850SC	N767SC	N147TW
024		N425RD	N125ST	N137BC	N20HJ	N20RZ
025		N920S	N928S	N920S	N92V	N49BB	N242AG	N225DS	(N111LM)	N110RA	[cx Apr13; wfu Pontiac, MI]
026		N4005S	N7ZA	C-GMAP	N283R	N281R	N25EC
027		N7000G	N423RD	N35WB	N835WB	(N835GM)	EC-EBM	N500DL	N900AJ	[b/u]
028		N592KR	N263GL	N277LE	N33PF	N727LJ	[instructional airframe, Augusta Technical College, Thomson, GA]
029	XR	N280LC	N28LA	N107HF	[parted out by White Inds, Bates City, MO; cx 29Apr09]
030		N951GA	N999M	N999MK	N745W	N30PS	N48HM	N380LC	N45DM	N51CA	[w/o 30Mar83 Newark, NJ]
031		N294NW	(N294M)
032		N373W	N711DB	N712DC	N357HC	XA-ZYZ	XA-RQI	[was on display in terminal at Mexico City A/P, Mexico, in 1994 but has since been removed]
033		HB-VBP	N143J	N786MS	YV-88CP	N77NJ	[cx Aug03; parted out]
034		N954GA	N954FA	N242WT	N6GC	N3UC	N17AR	N19FN	N309AJ	N309LJ	[cx Oct03; instructional airframe at Staverton UK then Kemble UK then City of Bristol College, UK]
035		N683LJ	N33GF	N33TR	N616NA
036	TF	N956GA	N956J	N741E	N741ED	N15CC	N15M	[also carried "N25TF"]	N45BK
037		N737EF	N18JF	N28AA	N155AG	[parted out circa Nov00; fuselage used as a cabin interior display exhibit by Best AeroNet Ltd TX; canx 18Sep03]
038		HB-VBR	EC-CKD	HB-VBR	N738GL	N36MW	N444WS	N83GG	N400AJ	N813JW	N130CK	[cx 2Dec14, CofR expired]
039		N959GA	N959RE	N17JF	N66NJ	N308AJ	(N25VJ)	N273CA	[to India as instructional airframe; cx 12Nov09]
040		N687LJ	HB-VBI	F-BSUR	(N2273G)	C-GOSL	N41AJ	N9CZ	(N98RH)	N23FN	N238CA	[to India as instructional airframe 2009]
041		N960GA	N205SC	N205SA	N31AA	(N25RE)	[parted out by White Inds, Bates City, MO]
042		N958GA	N958DM	(N429TJ)	N50DT	N800JA	N797SC	(N25LG)	(N125WD)	[derelict at Deland, FL since 2002]
043		N30LJ	N808DP	N234ND	N473TC
044		N962GA	N658TC	[w/o 18Jan72 Victoria, TX]
045		N963GA	CF-DWW	N815J	N33CJ	N123EL	N24FN	N28CK	[fuselage noted at MTW Aerospace's facility near Montgomery, AL in Apr02; canx 07Apr05]
046		N964GA	N55KC	N55KQ	N33PT	N345MC	[w/o 09Dec12, crashed in mountains near Monterrey, Mexico]
047		N222B	(N68CK)	[cx 16Sep14, CofR expired]
048		N965GA	N200G	XA-TCY	N48GR
049		N966GA	N900P	N900Q	HP-1141P	N900Q	N70HJ	N70SK	[w/o 21Jul07 St Augustine, FL]
050		N44EL	N44EE	D-CONE	N27MJ	N55FN	N999MF
051		N973GA	N70MP	PT-LPT	N12WW	N76UM	(N760A)
052		N232MD	N8280	N828QA	N250CC	(N132MA)	N133MA	N692FC	N692FG	(N69LJ)	[cx 29Oct13; wfu]
053		N974GA	N974M	N37MB	N37GB	N153TW	[w/o 24Aug01 Lansing, NY; cx Jan02]
054		OY-AKL	N12373	N500JW	N509G	N25MD
055		N1500B	N65RC	N511AJ	[parted out by White Inds, Bates City, MO]
056	XR	N780A	PT-LBW
057		CF-TXT	C-FTXT	N920EA	(N225EA)	N507HF	[parted out by White Inds, Bates City, MO; cx 29Apr09]
058		N2366Y	N273LP	N273LR	[parted out by Alliance Air Parts, Oklahoma City, OK]
059		N425JX	N211MB	[w/o 03Mar80 Port au Prince, Haiti]
060		N695LJ	N564CL
061	C	N251GL	PT-DUO	N9CN	YV-203CP	(YV2365)	[wfu Fort Lauderdale Executive, FL]
062		OY-AKZ	N4981	N105BJ	N303JJ	HZ-GP4	N86MJ	N27FN	N25ME	N21FN	[Instructional airframe, Hampton University, Norfolk News, NC, then scrapped]
063		N919S	C-GPDZ	N184J	N680J	N68PJ	N5DM	N24LT	N25FM
064		N266GL	[rebuilt to Model 28 standard to act as prototype; reverted to Model 25 standards]				N566NA	[wfu 1998; cx 07Apr03; preserved at John C.Stennis Space Center, MS; moved to Keystone Airpark, FL, by Feb16]
065		[airframe not built]
066		[airframe not built]
067		[airframe not built]
068		[airframe not built]
069		[airframe not built]
070	C	N255GL	CF-ROX	C-FROX	N32SM	C-FZHU	N911LM	[parted out Griffin, GA]
071	C	N257GL	YV-T-DTT	YV-130P	YV-132CP	N97AM	LV-ZTH
072	C	N256GL	PT-IBR	[w/o 26Sep76 Sao Paulo, Brazil]
073	XR	HB-VCM	I-TAKY	N3JL	N3JX	HZ-SMB	N63SB	N85FJ	N888DB	N45CP	[w/o 30Aug02 Lexington, KY – remains with Atlanta Air Salvage, Griffin, GA]
074	B	N251GL	SX-ASO	[w/o 18Feb72 Antibes, France]
075	B	N241AG	N241AQ	N417PJ	N138JB	VR-CGD	VR-CHT	VP-CHT	VP-CJF	N82025	N307HF	[parted out by White Inds Bates City, MO; cx 29Apr09]
076	B	HB-VCL	D-CCWK	N160J	N711CA	N831WM	N222MC	N222MQ	N77KW	XA-SJS	XB-LTD	[abandoned at Roatan, Honduras, 16Jul15]
077	B	PT-DVL	[w/o 12Nov76 Sao Paulo, Brazil]
078	B	N258GL	N64MP	N64MR	N276LE	N188BC	N778JC	N778GM	N229GS
079	B	D-CCAT	OE-GLA	N50DH	N36CC	(N85HR)	XA-SVG	XA-AVV
080	B	N1976L	N1978L	(N90DH)	N30AP	XA-POG	[wfu Toluca, Mexico]
081	B	N111GL	N110GL	HZ-MOA	HZ-AZP	HZ-BB1	N66TJ	N524DW
082	B	HB-VCK	N30P	N427RD	N15AK	N11AK	N654	N700FC	N62DM	N67SY
083	C	N31CS	N200Y	N200MH	N54FN
084	C	N2000M	(C-GWUZ)	N200QM	N200SF	F-BYAL	N777TX
085	B	N8MA	N8MQ	[b/u for spares – fuselage in compound near Lake City, FL]

LEARJET MODEL 25

C/n	Series	Identities
086	B	N123DM N28BP N23DB N65WH [wfu Perris, CA, by Sep09 then moved to Quartzsite, AZ]
087	C	N723LF N777LF N99XZ N25TE [dbr 09Feb03 Bethel, AK; parted out by White Inds, Bates City, MO; cx 29Apr09]
088	B	N88GC N88GQ N123SF N176G N42FE N125JL N5UJ [w/o 22Nov01 Pittsburgh, PA]
089	C	PT-IIQ (N890K)
090	B	N265GL N112CT N112CH N112ME C-GBOT N754CA C-FPUB [to India as instructional airframe]
091	B	N500CA N500CD N500MJ D-CBPD N96MJ C-FDAC N2138T (N816JA) VR-CCH N91PN
092	B	N1ED N9671A N258G N18AK N113ES N60DK N80EL N92SH N84SH YV....
093	B	N33HM N33NM PT-LEN
094	C	SX-CBM VR-BFV N97J N77RS [w/o 14Dec78 Anchorage, AK; remains to White Inds, Bates City, MO, for spares]
095	B	N200BC N303SC N303SQ C-GRCO N2094L
096	B	N742E N742Z N48FN N405RS C-GCJD N235JW N20NW XB-KPR
097	C	HB-VCS (OY-ASK) I-SFER N22NJ (N220AR) N79EV N252LJ YV3198
098	C	N7JN VR-BEM N139J VR-BGF YV-26CP N96MJ N502MH ZS-NYG
099	C	PT-IKR PT-FAF PT-LHU [w/o 28Jly92 Icuape, Brazil]
100	B	N262JE N741E N741F "N59AC"+ [+marks worn at 1988 NBAA Convention, Dallas/Love Field, TX] N25TK N829AA [cx 04Apr13, to instructional airframe, Dublin Institute of Technology, Dublin, Ireland]
101	B	N268GL N575GD N269AS N30AP N156CB N600HT N600HD N74JL N821AW N47MR [to India as instructional airframe; cx 08Jul09]
102	B	N267GL N999M N999ML N311CC N52AJ N962 N52AJ N64WH N254SC N325SJ XA-...
103	B	N428JX [dbr Richmond, VA, 03Jul75; parted out by Brandis Av'n, Taylorville, IL]
104	B	N1JR N101JR N392T XA-JAX XA-RIN N128TJ N35WJ N104WJ
105	B	N1BR N1RA N711WE N713Q N234RB N905WJ N7AT N55PD XA-SXD N55PD LY-AJB N25WJ
106	XR	N10NP N10FL N974JD N458JA N458J [w/o 01Jly91 Columbus, OH; cx Aug91]
107	B	N225CC N57DM N25NP N25NB N252BK [parted out Houston/Hobby, TX]
108	C	PT-CMY [w/o 06Apr90 Juiz de Fora, Brazil]
109	B	N888DH N333HP C-GSAS N860MX [parted out by Dodson Av'n, Rantoul, KS]
110	B	N50GL N63ET N75CA N110HA N52SD N343RK LV-... N198MA N343RK
111	B	N30TP N55ES PT-LXS N825A N45BS N25PJ
112	B	OY-BFC N173J N279LE N157G
113	C	PT-ISN [w/o 04Nov89 Belo Horizonte-Pampulha, Brazil]
114	B	N47HC (C-GLRE) N45HB N77PK N25JD N114HC XA-VMC
115	C	PT-ISO
116	C	CF-CXY N600PC N819GY (N818GY) N666TW [w/o 19Sep03 Del Rio TX, cx Nov03]
117	B	N40AS N170GT N170RL N4402 N4405 C-FMGM N731CW N7810W [parted out by White Inds, Bates City, MO]
118	B	OO-LFZ (D-CITO) N601J N118SE (N800JA) N124MA (N79AX) VP-CMB N118MB N818CK
119	B	N3810G PT-JBQ [w/o 04Sep82 Rio Branco, Brazil]
120	B	N111AF N744MC N278LE N10BD N10BU VH-OVS (N100FU) N101FU N120SL XA-AJL
121	B	N7GA HZ-MRP N39JJ N500PP N1036N [may have been XA-SAL] XA-SIO N8005Y (N821MS) [to India as instructional airframe; cx 12Nov09]
122	B	N23TA N332LS N122BS N122WC N751CA C-FSYO N751CA XB-KVX XB-LCI XB-LXL XB-MEH XB-MKO
123	B	N360AA N973JD (N914RA) N906SU N688GS
124	B	N44MJ N39JE N59BP N15CC N15CU N54H N54HU (N400DB) (N95TW) N33TW XA-ALV [to museum at Cajititlan, Mexico, Sep08]
125	B	N4MR N9AT (N85AT) N89AT N94AT N97AC (N11MC) N10VG N1VG N10VG
126	C	N12WK N114CC (N162AC) N14FN YV2465
127	B	N93C N93CE N83JM N450 N450SC N222AK N425JL N225LC [cx 19May15; CofR expired]
128	B	N67PC N1MX N40BC [w/o 06Jly79 Pueblo, CO; parted out by White Inds, Bates City, MO]
129	C	N551WC N71DM (N193DR) N25MR N25MT
130	B	N111BL N25PL N26AT [instructional airframe Del Mar College, TX]
131	C	N3803G PT-JDX [w/o 26Dec78 Sao Paulo-Congonhas, Brazil; front of fuselage in use at Belo Horizonte-Pampulha, Brazil as a link trainer]
132	B	N202BT N132GL N54MC N54MQ N715JF N715MH [w/o 26Oct01 Ciudad Victoria, Mexico; cx Oct02; parted out by Dodson Av'n, Rantoul, KS]
133	B	N10RE N10RZ N51MJ N58CP XA-RZY N233CA [cx Dec10; to India as instructional airframe]
134	B	N52GL N15BH N712JA N26FN N65A [wfu; cx 06Jun11]
135	B	G-BBEE N3803G N1103R G-BBEE N7600K (N1RW) N50RW [cx 19Dec15; CofR expired]
136	B	N920CC N920US N180YA N221TC N71CE (N48WA) N753CA N48WA
137	B	N400 N37BJ N500WW N752CA N752EA
138	B	N11BU N100EP N36204 N777PD N711PD N811PD (N2HE) N73LJ N911RF [parted out by Atlanta Air Salvage, Griffin, GA]
139	XR	N618R N225AC N12MH (N14PT) N605NE N111MP [cx 10Dec14, CofR expired]
140	B	N42G N42GX N68TJ N401AC N403AC N140CA [cx Jun10; to India as instructional airframe]
141	XR	N52L N424JR N424JP N94RS N25HA ZS-BXR
142	B	N515WH N42HC (N142HC) N70CE (N70WA) N49WA
143	B	N96VF (N33VF) N111RF N113RF N143CK
144	B	N10NT N44PA [w/o 23Dec91 Carlsbad, CA; b/u Jun92]
145	B	N131GL C-GRDR N2127E N145SH LV-CFW
146	C	N146LJ N9HM N9HN C-GRQX N9HN N6KJ I-BMFE
147	B	N55KC N25KC N150WW N911JG N147BP XA-GGG
148	XR	N58GL N336WR N98RS (N98JA) YV2786
149	C	HB-VDI EC-CIM N149J N239CA [cx Jun09; instructional airframe Singapore/Seletar]
150	B	N714K N714KP N888RB (N25LP) N251JA N150CK
151	B	N366AA [w/o 31Aug74 Briggsdale, CO]
152	XR	N50L N515SC N452ET XA-POI XA-JSC N105BA N165AA
153	B	N501PS [w/o 26May77 Detroit, MI; parted out by Dodson Av'n, Ottawa, KS]
154	B	N100K N30DK N47DK N82TS N210NC N82TS [wfu Pontiac, MI]
155	B	N24TA PT-LEA
156	C	PT-KAP N613SZ N75BL N725JS
157	B	N2427F N157CA N57CK N50CK
158	B	N158GL HZ-GP3 N85MJ N334LS N71RB N924BW
159	B	Peru FAP 522/OB-1429 N24RZ [w/o 20Feb04 Fort Lauderdale Executive, FL; cx 03Feb05; parted out by Dodson Intl Parts, Rantoul, KS]
160	B	ZS-MTD VP-WKY Z-WKY ZS-MTD 3D-AEZ ZS-MTD
161	B	N4VC N61EW N236CA [cx Dec10; to India as instructional airframe]
162	XR	N62ZS N661MP N663JB N97RS N97JJ N150RS YV525T
163	B	SE-DFC N70606 N173LP N173LR C-FBEA N333AW N59SG N25RE (N65RC) N911AJ
164	B	Peru FAP 523/OB-1430 N23RZ
165	C	PT-KBC [w/o 04Jun96 Ribeirao Preto, Brazil; cx Aug97]
166	B	PT-KBD N918TD N166PC
167	B	C-GBFP
168	B	N72TP N88BT N88BY [wfu Pontiac, MI]
169	B	N471MM N743E N743F N893WA N59FL XA-KKK
170	B	N131G N711DS N170EV (N170EP) N98796 N627WS [w/o 13Jan98 Houston Intercontinental, TX; cx Oct98]
171	B	I-ELEN N1DD OY-ASP N1DD N55MF N55PT N42DG N888LR N401AJ N171WW [cx 22Mar13; to instructional airframe, Estonian Aviation Academy, Tartu, Estonia]
172	C	PT-KKV [w/o 11Jan91 nr Belo Horizonte, Brazil]
173	XR	N780AC N780AQ N777NJ N104BW XA-JSC
174	B	N74G N410SP N412SP N16KK
175	XR	N462B N462BA N96RS (N96JJ) N307AJ N75SJ N127GB

LEARJET MODEL 25

C/n	Series	Identities										
176	C	N55VL	N50PE	N25KV	N28KV	PT-LLN						
177	B	N11PH	N745W	D-CDPD	[w/o 18May83 in Atlantic approx 320 km S of Reykjavik, Iceland]							
178	B	N75B	N999M	N999MV	N999HG	[w/o 08Sep77 Sanford, NC]						
179	B	N659HX	C-GBQC	C-GSKL	[parted out by White Inds, Bates City, MO; cx 02Jun08]							
180	B	VH-BLJ	N95BS	C-FEWB	N95BS	VH-LJB	N266BS	N102VS				
181	C	VH-TNN	N94PK	N73TW	N73TA	N100NB	[wfu Newton, KS]					
182	B	C-GLBT	N4300L	F-GFMZ	N225JL	N99MC						
183	B	N66JD	N5LL	N83CK	[cx 29Oct14, CofR expired]							
184	B	EC-CKR	[w/o 13Aug96 RAF Northolt, UK; to spares by White Inds, Bates City, MO 1998]									
185	B	N666LP	N55V	N988DB	N988AA	N988AC	N606SM					
186	B	YU-BJH	[w/o 18Jan77 Sarajevo, Yugoslavia]									
187	B	YU-BJG	N187CA									
188	B	G-BCSE	A4O-AJ	N1JR	[w/o 28Jly84 Waterville, ME and used for spares; remains to White Inds, Bates City, MO]							
189	B	N111SF	N111SZ	N352SC	N888DF	N67HB	[to Museum of Aeronautical Sciences, Tokyo/Narita, Japan 2008]					
190	B	XA-DAK	N190AR	XA-...								
191	B	N1DD	N78BT	N38DJ	[w/o 12Jun92 Sheboygan, WI; cx Dec94; remains to Hampton/Tara Field, Atlanta, GA]							
192	B	Bolivia FAB-008		Bolivia FAB-010								
193	B	HB-VEF	I-KISS	HB-VIE	I-SIMD	N80GR	N350DH	N125RM	N125TN	XA-WWW		
194	B	XA-COC	XB-EGP	XA-SXG	XC-NSP	XB-KYK	XB-MSW					
195	B	OB-M-1004	N108PA	[b/u for spares 1984; cx 05May06]								
196	B	N711WD	N25TA	[w/o 11Apr80 New Mexico]								
197	B	N104GL	N240AG	N197WC	N197CF	(N96DM)						
198	B	N20DK	N29TS	N198JA								
199	XR	HB-VEI	HZ-RI1	HZ-GP5	[w/o 11Jan82 Narssarssuaq, Greenland]							
200	B	N2022R	N680BC	N350JH	[parted out by White Inds, Bates City, MO]							
201	B	N227RW	N777SA	N111AD	N11TK	N713B	N43TS	N59BL	N251TS			
202	B	N3807G	Yugoslavia 10401		Yugoslavia 70401		YU-BRA	N343CA	[wfu; to Aviation Warehouse, El Mirage, CA]			
203	B	N3811G	Yugoslavia 10402		Yugoslavia 70402		YU-BRB	N344CA	N927FW	(N212GW)		
204	B	N376SC	N373SC	N472J	PT-KZY	[w/o 16May82 Uberaba, Brazil]						
205	B	N1468B	YU-BKJ	Z3-BAA								
206	D	N206EC	N206EQ	ZS-LXH								
207	D	N3513F	(I-GIAN)	I-LEAR	(N3513F)	N207JC	[parted out by White Industries, Bates City, MO circa 99]					
208	D	N54YR	N54YP	C-GZIM	"N500PP"	N54YP	N500PP	N500MP	N300SC	N188CA		
209	D	N36SC	N770AC	(N770PA)	N770AQ	N18NM	N30LJ	[wfu Curacao]				
210	D	N133MR	XA-JIN	XA-RPV	N97FT	N75TJ	N764RH	XA-ULS				
211	D	N3514F	Bolivia FAB-010									
212	D	N1450B	N911MG	N212NE	[b/u for spares during 1989]							
213	D	N551DP	HZ-SS2	VR-CDH	N803PF	N925DW	N910JB	XA-CST				
214	D	N30W	N3UW	N90BR	I-AVJD	N61826	N214ME	N214LJ	N245BS	N70TF	N56MD	N555VH
215	D	N44FE	N325JL	N25UJ	[cx 9Dec14, CofR expired]							
216	D	N3556F	N2426	(N345FJ)	N80RE	N80RP	(N87MW)	XA-PRO	N216SA	N767SA	N68AX	N724TN	XA-...	N724TN
		N77FN	XA-...									
217	D	N41H	N217WM	YV436T								
218	D	N18MJ	N155AU	XA-RAX	N14NA	N251DS	[parted out by Dodson Av'n, Rantoul, KS]					
219	XR	N55SL	XA-CCC	XA-MCC								
220	XR	N220HS	(N419BL)	(N25WL)	N220NJ	N99NJ	N969AR					
221	D	N3819G	YU-BKR	N147CA	XA-UKH							
222	XR	N1476B	N726GL	N4MR	XA-KEY	XA-MHA	N4MR	N225TJ	N134WE	XA-UNC	[w/o 01Apr10 Huatulco, Mexico]	
223	D	N23AM	XC-DAD	XA-BBA	[w/o 18Jun94 Washington-Dulles A/P, VA]							
224	D	N50B	(N32TJ)	N711NM	N80AX	XB-MGM	XB-OZA	XB-AZD	XB-DDG			
225	D	9J-AED	N222AP	N808DS	N140GC	[parted out by Dodson Av'n, Rantoul, KS]						
226	D	N333SG	N234SV	N90LJ								
227	D	N44BB	N444PB	N882SB	XA-ROO	(N25RE)	N227EW	N25RE	[cx 23Jun15; CofR expired]			
228	D	N228SW	[parted out by Dodson International Parts Inc, Rantoul, KS]									
229	D	N39415	LV-MBP	CX-ECO	N229WJ	N890BJ						
230	D	N16GT	N16LJ	N161AC	N7RL	N207HF	[parted out by White Inds, Bates City, MO; cx 29Apr09]					
231	D	(OO-LFW)	(OO-HFW)	N999M	N999ME	N60DK	N31MJ	N225HW	N531CW	[cx 30Sep14; to Centro Ensenanza Tecnica Aeronautica de		
		Canaria, Tenerife, as instructional airframe]										
232	D	N744LC	N500EW	N500LW	N264TW							
233	D	N55LJ	N75LM	N947TC								
234	D	N3815G	(N27GW)	N234KK	(N234EJ)	(N28CC)	XA-ESQ	N234KK	(N11SQ)	N300JE	N39BL	N88DJ	(N432AS)	N18BL
		N764KF	YV2681									
235	XR	N400PC	N400JS	N400VC	(N25XR)	N221LV	YV2675					
236	D	N1466B	XC-RPP									
237	D	(N28BP)	N137GL	(N55MF)	[w/o 19Jan79 Detroit, MI]							
238	D	N39416	N40SW	N45ZP	N238MP	N500TL	N300TL	N41NK				
239	D	N192MH	N45H	N499EH	N499BS							
240	D	N78GL	N83EA	N33PT	(N339BA)							
241	D	N432SL	N25TA	N25TB	N711WD	N712BW	N713RR	N713LJ	N213CA	[cx Nov10; to India as instructional airframe]		
242	D	N749GL	N363HA	N102RA	N242GM	(N242AF)	N242GS					
243	D	N711JT	PT-LSD	[w/o 02Mar96 Serra de Cantareira, near Sao Paulo, Brazil]								
244	D	N7LA	XA-LET	N24EP	N831LH	N125PT	[w/o 12Aug07 Farmingdale, NY; parted out by MTW Aerospace, Montgomery, AL]					
245	XR	N39398	LV-PAF	LV-MST	N245DK	N60DK	N606GB	(N531GC)				
246	XR	N40162	N51DN	[w/o 21Oct86 nr Jeddah, Saudi Arabia]								
247	D	N300PI	[cx 05Sep12; parted out]									
248	D	N80BT	N80BE	N500PP	N900WA	N95CK	(N248LJ)	N248CK				
249	D	N20PY	N249SC	N211JB	(N500EF)	N249LJ	XA-FMU	N800L	XA-FMU	N34TN		
250	D	N30LM	N438DM	(N60DK)	N112JM	N19JM	N127BH	[cx 27Aug12; wfu]				
251	D	N752GL	N78SD	N290	N25FA	TG-VOC	N85TW					
252	D	N1468B	N44FH	N444MK	[wfu Addison, TX; cx 10May11]							
253	D	N253EJ	N97DK	(N202DR)	N253J	N253M	N253SC	N8MF	N321AU	YV-1049CP	YV129T	N69PL	YV1346
254	D	N973	I-AVJE	N76AX								
255	D	N1433B	N1ED	N91ED	N91MT	N25GJ	N717EP	N219RB	N219RR			
256	D	N6LL	N75CK									
257	D	N700BJ	N377C	N377Q	N988AS	[cx 30Apr15; CofR expired]						
258	D	N144FC	(N54888)	N54TA	N888GC	N333CD	N258MD	PT-LLL	[w/o 18Mar91 Brasilia, Brazil]			
259	D	LV-PAW	LV-MMV	[w/o 23Sep89 in Marana River, nr Posadas, Argentina – fuselage and detached wingset noted at Moron AFB Apr04, still present Apr07]									
260	D	N39413	(D-CHBM)	D-CHEF	N43783	N74RD	N80PJ	N314AJ				
261	D	N3802G	N180MC	N24JK	N261WC							
262	D	N23HM	N440F	N333CG	[w/o 12Jun01 Salina A/P, KS; parted out]							
263	D	N40162	N14VC	N20DL	N825D	XA-YYY						
264	D	N716NC	N133JF	N502JC	N547JG	XA-...						
265	D	N1462B	N265EJ	N279TG	N265LJ	N31WT	(N61WT)	N69GF	N265TW	[w/o nr Nuevo Michoacan, Mexico, 19Dec14]		
266	D	N3807G	PT-KYR	[reported w/o circa Aug89; no further details; cx during 1990]								
267	D	N15ER	(N400VC)									

LEARJET MODEL 25

C/n	Series	Identities								
268	D	N268WC	XA-SPL	N268WC	XA-...	N268WC	[wfu Pachuca, Mexico; cx 10Dec14]			
269	D	N109SJ	N269MD	N51BL	LV-PLL	LV-WOC				
270	D	N842GL	(N123CG)	N842GL	N123CG	(N45KB)	N75AX	XB-LPD	N842GL	N25XA
271	D	N183AP	N125NE	[w/o 21May80 Gulf of Mexico; cx Nov82]						
272	D	N272EJ	N272JM	N747AN	N717AN	N520SR	N25CY			
273	D	N321AS	N73DJ	XA-...						
274	D	N600CD	D-CEPD	N3131G	N602NC	N602N	N110FP	N274LJ	XA-MAL	XA-RZE	XA-FMR
275	D	N211CD	N254CL							
276	D	N188TC	N188TQ	N188TA	XA-UUU	[wfu Monterrey del Norte, Mexico]				
277	D	N20MJ	N34CW	N283U	N321GL	N81MW	N9RA	(XA-...)	N277RG	XA-...
278	D	N70JF	[parted out by White Inds, Bates City, MO; cx 29Apr09]							
279	D	N41ZP	N81AX	[wfu; cx 29Sep15]						
280	D	N280LA	N18TA	N18RA	N225AC	N95EC	(N510L)	N280C	N901PM	N405SD	XA-...	N405FM
281	D	(N245KK)	N45KK	N45KB	N555PG	N800RF				
282	D	N711WD	XA-SKA	XA-CAO						
283	D	N40144	XC-DAA	N45826	N312GK	N444WW				
284	D	XC-CFM	N284TJ							
285	D	N6666R	(N28RW)	N6666K	N666KK	N422G	I-COTO	[w/o Feb86 Paris-Le Bourget, France]		
286	D	N28MJ	XA-ROZ	N6596R	XA-RVI	XC-AA83+	XA-TAQ	N850MX	N9QM	[cx 01Mar07, wfu][+ marks not confirmed]
287	D	N39416	RP-C4121	N63KH	N287MF	XA-ZYZ	N20AD	XA-ZZZ	[parted out by White Inds, Bates City, MO, circa 2001]	
288	D	N31WT	N61WT	N40BC	N100WN	(N40BC)	[instructional airframe Columbus/Bolton, OH]			
289	D	N1087T	RP-C6610	RP-C400	N389GA	N321GL	N321GE	XA-TWH		
290	D	N221AP	XA-ELR	N221EL	N321RB	N600GM				
291	D	N1088D	N666RB	N952	N600JT	N530DC	(N477MM)	N453MA	XB-MCW	
292	D	N1088C	N92MJ	N92CS	N711VT	N711VK	N604AS			
293	D	N999TH	N97JP	XA-PIU						
294	D	N27K	N419GL	N125TJ	N161RB	N88NJ	N881J	[parted out by Dodson Av'n, Rantoul, KS; cx 20Apr06]		
295	D	N229AP	N137K	ZS-LUD	OE-GHL	N295DJ	(N298GS)	N45ES	XC-AGR	N25HF	XB-MYG
296	D	N712RW	N712SJ	N55DD	N55MJ	PT-OHD	[destroyed by Venezuelan armed forces 10Apr14 on suspicion of drug-running]?			
297	D	N297EJ	N36NW	N297EJ	N24KW	N389AT				
298	D	N923GL	N711TG	N711TQ	(N712CB)	XA-ABH	N298DR	N242PF	YV448T	
299	D	N222LW	I-KIOV	(N8217W)	N299MW	(N5B)	N117SH	[wfu; cx 07Jul15]		
300	D	(N46BA)	N659HX	N108FL						
301	D	N416RM	N610LM	(N888JA)	N25CZ	N82AX	N301MT	HI...		
302	D	N521JP	N28BP	N740K	N700DA	N702DA	N25CY	N881P	YV592T	YV3116
303	D	XA-JOC								
304	D	N25NY								
305	D	N88JA	N53TC	N188R	XA-AAS	XA-TAK	XA-TAQ	XA-MET		
306	D	XA-DUB	XC-GUB							
307	D	LV-PEU	LV-OEL							
308	D	N23AM	XA-RMF	N2721U	XB-GDR	XA-SXY	N102RR	N727LM		
309	D	XA-GRB	XB-DKS	XA-DAZ	XA-PAZ	XB-KWN				
310	D	N1088C	N211PD	N211JC	(N211JE)	YV2611	YV2699			
311	D	N39391	N199BT	ZS-NJF	N199BT	N502JV				
312	D	N94MJ	XC-HIS							
313	D	N31MJ	N31GS	N37RR	N727AW	N727CS	N631CW	N727CS	N251AL	
314	D	N1466B	I-DEAN	HB-VHM	N38328	N30AD	N40AD	XA-LUZ	XA-REE	N42825	N95BP	N305AR
315	D	N10873	N3798A	N83TC	N273KH	N273M	XA-TSL	N315FW	XA-ASP	
316	D	N3793X	N1AH	(N782JR)	N17AH	[fitted with Williams-Rolls FJ44 engines ff 09Jan03 at Guthrie, OK]				
317	D	N821LM	N660TC	N969SS	(N96DC)	N317TS	N317FN	N25CY	N35DL	XB-OAC
318	D	N522JP	N522TA	N999BH	[w/o 05Sep93 Rowe Mera, 30m from Santa Fe Municipal A/P, NM; cx May94]					
319	D	N319EJ	N911EM	N680JC	N712DP	[instructional airframe at Savo Vocational College, Finland; cx 23Nov09]				
320	D	N320EJ	OO-LFR	N690JC						
321	D	N25AM								
322	D	5N-AOC	N19GE							
323	D	N323EJ	N70SE	N6YY	PT-LMM					
324	D	N711BF	XA-POP	N970WJ						
325	D	N123NC	N523SA	N1411S	XA-RXB	N1411S	N2U	XA-TBV	N325JB	XB-HGE	XB-GCP
326	D	N771CB	N25NB							
327	D	N54GP	N52DA	(N54JC)	(N327BC)	N444TG				
328	D	N7LC	(N12FS)	OB-R-1313	OB-1313	N58DJ	N200NR	N725DM	N328JW	N518JG	XB-JLU	XB-MBW
329	D	N3799B	XC-GNL	XA-GNL	N613GL	N83TE	N401DP			
330	D	(N523JP)	N521JP	XA-RZT	XA-RCG	XC-AA84	N330LJ	N330L		
331	D	N462B	N422B	N462CP	N657BM					
332	D	XC-FIF	XB-DZQ	XA-AFH						
333	D	N34MJ	N555SD	[cx 8Jul14, CofR expired]						
334	D	N20RD	N57DL	N334MD	XA-RYH	N23W	XB-JKK	XA-ULG		
335	D	N27KG	PT-LUZ							
336	D	XA-LAP	N6354N	XA-VYA	XA-JYL					
337	G	N3810G	N937GL	N337GL	LV-P...	LV-WBP	N14CK	XA-UKK		
338	D	XA-LOF	N4447P	[wfu Fort Pierce/St Lucie, FL]						
339	D	N3798D	HK-2624X	HK-2624P	N21HR	Mexico MTX-03		Mexico AMT-202		
340	D	N980A	N625AU	N891P						
341	D	N341FW	N101DL	XA-TAM	(N.....)	XA-SAE	N58HC			
342	D	N820M	N984JD	(N187DY)	I-RJVA	N707CA	XA-RXQ	N342AA	N342GG	N25PW
343	D	N3797L	N456CG	(N458CG)						
344	D	N3798L	N37943	5N-ASQ	[w/o 22Jly83 Lagos, Nigeria]					
345	D	N345EJ	N345KB	N711SC	LV-PHU	LV-WLG				
346	D	N39412	N3798V	N300WG	N41TC	N72AX	XA-ZZZ	N181PA	YV....	
347	D	N39415	N347EJ	D-CHIC	N25NM	N347MD	N347AC	N202JW	N347AC	(N347JW)	N347JV	N203VS
348	D	N37949	N440DM	N522GS	N522JS	N988AA				
349	D	N40146	N349EJ	N20GT	XA-NOG	[w/o 02Sep93 Tijuana, Mexico]				
350	D	N350AG	(N428CH)	N648JW	LV-BZC					
351	D	N878ME	XA-POQ	N837CS	N302PC	N402DP	N425RH	N425RA	N21NW	
352	D	N3794P	RP-C1261	N7035C	XA-MMO	(N352XR)	N25FN	N125JW		
353	D	N353EJ	N800DR	(N50MT)	XA-RKP	XA-RLI	N510TP	N71AX	N43DR	
354	D	N3795U	N515TC	N304VS						
355	D	(N830WM)	N202WM	N7801L	N713DJ	XA-SNO	XA-EAS	N355AM	LV-WRE	
356	D	N78DT	N100NR	N108NR	N25PT	N251MD	N62DK	YV544T		
357	D	N40149	N3797U	N148JW	N812MM	XA-ROC	N250LB	N27KG	LV-WXY	
358	D	N1461B	N37971							
359	D	N6307H	N37973	N359SK	N666RE	N666PE	N116JR	XA-LRJ	XB-MXZ	
360	D	N6340T	N8563B	N618R	N618P	N360JG	XA-...			
361	D	N4291K	N218NB	N218NR	N804PH	N804RH	XA-TYW			
362	D	N39398	N25GL	N52CT	N717CW	(N107MS)	N107RM			

LEARJET MODEL 25

C/n	Series	Identities										
363	D	N39416	N85654	N91MT	N2PW	XA-RSU	N197LS	YV1738				
364	D	N10873	N8565Y	N25TZ	XA-TIE	XB-LYG						
365	D	N1473B	N7260C	N218R	N365CM	XA-SJN	XB-KDQ					
366	D	N1088D	N7261B	(ZS-LRI)	XA-SWX	N366LJ	ZS-CAT	N366LJ	XB-IFW	XA-SOH		
367	D	N7262A	N51DT	VT-SWP	N4488W	N25HF						
368	D	N1088A	N8567J	XA-PIM	N8567J	N368D	YV3191					
369	D	N10872	N8566Z	N369MJ	N2213T	N369D	XB-JJS					
370	D	N39399	N72600	N610JR	N610JB	N220TG	N223TG	C-GSWS	XA-SJO	N370LJ	N252HS	N972H	N888DV	[parted out
		by Dodson Av'n, Rantoul, KS]										
371	D	N1468B	N72603	N125DB	N44SK	N1WT	N1U	(N102U)	N4ZB	N72WC	N188PR	LV-FDB*
372	D	N40149	N72606	N5NC	N722EM	N418KS	YV2873					
373	D	N3819G	N29EW	EC-EGY	XA-ACX	XA-RCH						

Production complete

LEARJET MODEL 28

C/n	Identities							
28-001	N9RS	N9KH	N128MA	N3AS	N128LR			
28-002	N39404	N511DB	XC-VSA					
28-003	N157CB	N42ZP	N555JK	N44QG	N14QG	N28LR	N25GW	N800GA
28-004	N39394	N125NE	HB-VGB	XA-KAJ	N225MS	XA-KAJ	N28AY	N43PJ	N769CA
28-005	(N31WT)	N8LL	N500LG					

Production complete

LEARJET MODEL 29

C/n	Identities				
29-001	N929GL	HB-VFY	N929GL	XC-IST	
29-002	N723LL	N920GL	XC-DFS	XC-HIE/PF-201	XB-JHV
29-003	N289CA	VT-EHS	India K-2995 [wfu]		
29-004	N39412	N294CA	VT-EIH	India K-2996 [wfu]	

Production complete

LEARJET MODEL 31

C/n	Series	Identities								
001		N311DF	N984JD	[w/o 23Feb90 Taiyuan, China; cx Mar90; to spares by Dodson Avn, Ottawa, KS]						
002		N7262Y	PT-LVO	N102NW	N350DS	N322TS	N386MM			
003		N10873	N31CG	N331CC	N888CP					
004		N1088D	XA-ZTH	N314SC	LV-CNQ					
005		N39415	XA-GMD	XA-RFS	N942BY	(N963Y)	N431BC	PR-AVM		
006		N6331V	N26LC	C-GKMS	N103TD					
007		N3819G	PT-LXX							
008		N71JC	[w/o 02Sep97 Aberdeen, MS; to Atlanta Air Salvage, GA Nov97 for spares]							
009		OO-JBA	N173PS	N727CP	N38MG					
010		N31LJ	N446	PT-LLK	N311TS	N89HB	PP-LFV			
011		N3803G	HB-VJI	D-CTWO	M-LEAR	D-CFST				
012		N917MC	XA-RUU	XA-TUL	XA-LMS	(N510TL)				
013		PT-LVR	N213PA	PT-XTA						
014		N1468B	N5VG	PT-OFJ	N5VG					
015		N111TT	N260LF							
016		N4291K	N666RE	N92LJ	N1DE					
017		N4289U	N17VG	PT-OFK	[crashed 26Feb93 Rio de Janeiro-Santos Dumont, Brazil; rebuilt with new wingset]			N17VG	N600AW	N801CT
		PR-LRR								
018		N40144	HB-VIM	N19TJ	(N20LL)	N90BA				
019		(N19LT)	PT-OFL	N19LT	N818LJ	(N631LA)				
020		N42905	N31LJ	N337FP	XA-UJQ					
021		N3802G	XA-RNK	XA-CYA						
022		N331N								
023		N111VV	PR-SFA							
024		N30LJ	LV-PFK	LV-RBV	N90PB	N92EC	N912TB	XA-MRS	N731GA	
025		N39399	I-AIRW	N50AN	[stored Milan/Linate still wearing I-AIRW]					
026		N91164	XA-HRM	XA-HGF	XA-DIN	N39TJ	N45HG	N706SA	(N184RM)	N103JL
027		N91201	N30LJ	N2FU						
028		N90WA								
029		N9173L	(XB-ZRB)	XB-FKT						
030		N525AC	N255DV	N255DY	XA-JYC	[impounded at Houston/Hobby, TX, Apr11]				
031		N5000E	N9132Z	N31HA	ZS-OFW	N878MA	ZS-OFW	N878MA	N93SK	N111YA
032		N5010U	XA-AAP	XA-BRG	XB-KDK					
033		N5012H	9V-ATA	N603LJ	N632PB	(N638PB)	N407BS			
033A		N2603S	9V-ATC	N311GC	N156JS	N990GC				
033B		N2600S	9V-ATD	[w/o 21Jly97 30m S of Ranong, Thailand]						
033C		N5013L	9V-ATE	N310LJ	N158JS	N555VR	N55VR	VH-OVX		
033D		N5023D	9V-ATF	N312LJ	N157JS	N539BA	(N777YL)			
034		N5015U	9V-ATB	N604LJ	N45PK	N394SA	CS-DDZ			
035	A	N50111	N618R	N618RF	N3VJ					
036	A	N31LJ	N88MM	D-CVGP	N316LJ	N127V	N127VL	(N127V)		
037	A	N31TF	PT-OVZ							
038	A	N5016V	N4	N131NA	N500WR	N2RW	N338CW			
039	A	N90LJ	N10ST	N16ST	N22AX	N23AX	N71AL			
040	A	VR-CHJ	N9HJ	VR-CHJ	VR-CGS	N340LJ	N314MK	N55VY	N613SZ	N2SM
041	A	N131TA	N9CH	N319CH	RP-C8822					
042	A	D-CGGG	D-CURT							
043	A	N5009V	C-GLRJ	N43LJ	N531SK					
044	A	N50163	XA-MJG	XA-HRM	XA-OLE					
045	A	N50159	N67SB	YU-BRZ						
046	A	D-CCKV	N131PT	N352EF						
047	A	N31UK	N39TW	LV-CNF						
048	A	N43SF	N43SE	N314XS	N864KB					
049	A	D-CDEN	D-CADC	N107GM	N131TT	N61VW				
050	A	N92UG	N38SK	(N166AA)	N548LM					
051	A	N9152R	N1905H	N351AC						
052	A	N50LJ	N301AS	N75MC	N899CS	XA-TGM				
053	A	N9173Q	N44QG	(N44ZG)	N31FF	(N555JS)	N163AL			
054	A	N2603G	N92FD	N82KK	N82KL	N54TN	LV-BFG			
055	A	N9143F	N666RE	N425M						
056	A	N25685	N303WB	N56LF	XA-UUQ					
057	A	N9147Q	D-CSAP	D-CJPD						
058	A	N5017J	N26018	N770CC	"ZS-OJO"	(N258SC)	N590MH	N298CH	N825AC	LV-BRC
059	A	N25999	(N31LJ)	N31TK	(N67MP)					
060	A	N2600Z	N156SC	N156EC	N696PA	N699CP	N52SY			
061	A	N51057	(N740E)	N9152X	N740E	N740F	N261SC	XA-RCF		
062	A	N25997	AP-BEK							
063	A	(N27)	N2	N995AW	N707NV	(N31AX)	N131LJ	N510AB		
064	A	N142GT	N444HC							
065	A	N50153	N26005	N44SF	N44SU	N64NB				
066	A	N5009V	N26006	PK-CAH						
067	A	N9173M	TG-AIR	TG-MYS						
068	A	N2603X	N743E	N743F	N500CG	(N500CQ)	N500EW	C-GWXK	N680AF	N131GR
069	A	N9173V	N744E	N744N	(N169SC)					
070	A	N2602Y	N741E	N741F	(N270SC)	N370SC	XA-CTL			
071	A	N9173N	N742E	N742F	N271SC	XA-MCA				
072	A	N31LJ	N45UF	(N14WT)	N211RN					
073	A	N46UF	XA-ZYZ							
074	A	N999AU	(VP-B..)	N999AU	N128GB	N174TS	N131BR			
075	A	N418R	N418RT	N631SF	N636SF	N636SE				
076	A	N40339	XA-SPR	XA-PIC	N518SA	N215TT	N456JN			
077	A	N26002	PK-CAJ							
078	A	N40280	N31LJ	XA-SNM	N112CM	N539LB	XA-RDL	XC-LNF	XA-RDL	
079	A	N40349	N41DP	N91DP						
080	A	N2601K	N80LJ	N986MA						
081	A	N31LJ	N81LJ	N83WM	N83WN	LV-YMB				
082	A	N5014F	N4022X	PT-MVI	N727BT	XA-CCC				
083	A	N5012Z	N40363	N789SR						
084	A	N4034H	N196HA	N840SW						
085	A	N5013Y	N4005G	XA-PEN	N531AT	N321GL	N480ME			
086	A	N2603Q	N867JS	N105FX	OY-LJB	N166BA	N969	N1BR	N11BR	
087	A	N9173T	N868JS	N106FX	OY-LJC	N167BA	N535PS			
088	A	N50088	N31LJ	N500JE	N508J	N500JE				
089	A	N5009L	N77PH	N77PY						

LEARJET 31

C/n	Series	Identities							
090	A	N9173X	N78PH	N78PR	N557PK	N557BK			
091	A	N5019Y	V5-NAG						
092	A	N50302	N711FG						
093	A	N4031K	(N917BD)	N916BD	N716BD				
094	A	N4027K	N31AX	(N916BD)	N917BD	N817BD	N36BL		
095	A	N50459	N163JD	OK-AJD	N395LJ				
096	A	N5009V	N4006G	N30LX	N30TK	(N31TK)	N37BM		
097	A	N50207	N31LJ						
098	A	N5012H	N50378	N148C	N721MJ	(N521MJ)	N797KB	N200KB	
099	A	N5049J	N1932P	N1932K					
100	A	N5001X	N31LR	PT-MCB	N31LK	PR-SCB	N342JP		
101	A	N5010J	N293SA	N900R	N79BJ	XA-MGM	ZS-LJC	V5-TUC	
102	A	N5002D	N107FX	N731RA	C-GWXP	N681AF	C-GHJJ	N102WG	N25BB
103	A	N5003F	(N31AZ)	PT-TOF	N766AJ	N407RA	PT-BBB	N213BR	LV-FKB
104	A	N4010N	N108FX	OY-LJI	N104BX	N631CC			
105	A	N51054	N5005K	N109FX	N109HV	N109FX	N109HV	PR-PLM	
106	A	N29RE	N531RA	N581RA	N531TS	N784AM			
107	A	N5012H	N31HY	C-GHCY	N107TS	N107LP	N213AR	N942RC	
108	A	N110FX	(N110BX)	(N288BF)	N288FF				
109	A	N5029F	N261PC	N261PQ	N722JS	N882JD	N728CL		
110	A	N40130	PT-WIV						
111	A	N50114	C-GRVJ	N113AF	N111AF	N420LJ	LV-BTF		
112	A	N5082S	LX-PCT	N359RA	(PT-PPP)	(N190MM)			
113	A	N31LJ	N331SJ	(N642GG)	N131GG				
114	A	N524HC							
115	A	(N5005M)	N112FX	N31NR	ZS-NYV	(PP-NYV)	PR-NYV		
116	A	N113FX	N112FX	N112HV	N31UJ	LV-CLK			
117	A	N317LJ	N517CC						
118	A	N318LJ	N815A	N815E	PP-JNY				
119	A	N114FX	N114HY	N996JS					
120	A	N5020Y	I-TYKE	N200TJ	C-GHJU				
121	A	N121LJ							
122	A	(N112FX)	N122LJ	PT-WLO					
123	A	N323LJ	N48AM	N23NP	N23VG	N85KH	HK-4891		
124	A	N124LJ	N931FD	N931ED					
125	A	N125LJ	N527JG	N125FS					
126	A	N8066P	N22SF	N22UF	N18BL	N100BL	N239CA		
127	A	N80727	HB-VLR	N54HT					
128	A	N8082J	N400	(N469)	N365GL				
129	A	N8079Q	N115FX	N115BX	N645HA				
130	A	N5013N	N31PV	TG-SHV					
131	A	N80631	N31LR	N319SC	PR-WMA				
132	A	N116FX	N116BX	N929JH					
133	A	N8073Y	N117FX	OY-LJL	N331ZX	N314SG	(N820AT)		
134	A	N5014E	N118FX	N118BX	N977AR	N134LJ	N164AL		
135	A	N80645	PT-WSB						
136	A	N119FX	N119BX	N119FX	N131DA	N47TR	N509AB		
137	A	N120FX	N120RV	N459A	N165AL				
138	A	N138LJ	V5-NPC						
139	A	N139LJ	N131AR	N229KD	N29KD				
140	A	N140LJ	N96LF	VP-BML	N314AC	N45HG	N95HG	N977JP	
141	A	N121FX	(N121HV)	N121PX	XA-ARQ				
142	A	N142LJ	ZS-EAG	N698MM	N382AL	N372JL			
143	A	N122FX	N122BX	XA-EGU					
144	A	N144LJ	JA01CP						
145	A	N124FX	N145LJ	N29RE	N89RF	(N696RB)	LV-BDM		
146	A	N30046	N218NB	(ZS-DCT)	ZS-AGT	N218NB			
147	A	N198KF	N202LC	N157EC	N45KK	N31GQ			
148	A	N148LJ	(PT-XIT)	PT-XPP					
149	A	N1904S	N685RC	PR-JJV					
150	A	N31NR	N6666R	N6666A	N316RS	N316AS	N595PA	N381AL	
151	A	N3019S	N583PS	N583LJ	N31NF	PR-ENE			
152	A	N517GP							
153	A	N6666R	N30111	RP-C6153	(N37RA)	N153NP	N349HP	N153RB	
154	A	N337RB	N154RT						
155	A	N525GP	D-CPRO						
156	A	N124FX	(N29RE)	N181PA	N5007	N484BA			
157	A	N125FX	N800CK	LV-CXE	N800CK				
158	A	N126FX	N126BX	PR-LRJ					
159	A	N127FX	N127BX	XA-AFX					
160	A	N31LR	VP-BMX	LX-EAR	(D-CPRO)	N160CF			
161	A	N3016X	N177JB						
162	A	N525GP	N162LJ	N125GP	ES-PVH				
163	A	N128FX	N431DA						
164	A	N131GM	N164SB	XA-USF					
165	A	N31TD	N885TW	N808W	N608W				
166	A	N166DT	N811PS	N366TS	PR-GBN	N296SF	XB-GYB	[w/o Apaseo del Alto, Mexico, 22Oct15]	
167	A	N167LJ	I-ERJB	N613SA	D-CGOM	LX-OMC	I-CFLY		
168	A	N168LJ	N811CP	N31CV	YV-952CP	N952VS	PP-CTA		
169	A	N197PH	N659BX						
170	A	N31NR	(ZS-DHL)	ZS-OML	(OY-LJN)				
171	A	N50157	N129FX	N31MW	N820MT	N31NV	N171AR		
172	A	N197PH	N130FX	N312CC	N312TL				
173	A	N173LC	N31KH						
174	A	N9VL	Mexico MTX-02		Mexico AMT-201				
175	A	N131FX	N175FF	N27AL	N31WU	N240B			
176	A	N176WS	XA-LRD						
177	A	N132FX	N569SC						
178	A	N50145	RP-C6178	N178NP	PR-MKB				
179	A	N133FX	N133BG	XA-RAN					
180	A	N1926S							
181	A	N134FX	N526GP	N418DL					
182	A	N136FX	N527GP	N399RW	N699GG				
183	A	N183DT	N183ML	LV-BFE					
184	A	N931RS							

LEARJET 31

C/n	Series	Identities							
185	A	N31LR	N110SC	N31MJ	N515CS				
186	A	N137FX	N45PK	N45PD	RP-C1432				
187	A	N932FD	N932ED	C-FVNC					
188	A	N70AE	N70AY						
189	A	N138FX	N316RS	N158R	N239AY				
190	A	N316AC	N8TG						
191	A	N631AT	OE-GTA	Mexico AMT-206		Mexico ANX-1206			
192	A	N50088	N531RA	N382AL					
193	A	N44SF	N44SZ	N129JD					
194	A	N29SM	N29SN						
195	A	N134FX	N134CG	XA-NTR					
196	A	N136FX	N136BX	N1JM	N54CH	N331US			
197	A	N20XP							
198	A	N500MP							
199	A	N900P	N901P	N895DM					
200	A	N31NR	N797WB	N599CT	N900EL				
201	A	N4003K	N137FX	N776PH	N32HH				
202	A	N4003L	ZS-PNP	ZS-AJD	OO-ENZ	D-CAAY	N99AT		
203	A	N63SE	VP-BAW	OD-PWC	N595SA	PR-GJC	N221EJ		
204	A	N204RT							
205	A	N50153	VP-CFB	N71FB	YR-TYC	D-CGFK			
206	A	N5000E	N79SE						
207	A	N50126	D-CSIE	D-CGFM					
208	A	N138FX	N138FY	N751BP	N518JG	N518JC	N227KT	N131AR	XB-NZS
209	A	N139FX	N139FY	N209HR	N428BB	XA-ARD			
210	A	N927DJ	(N928DJ)	N631SF					
211	A	N5013Y	N574DA	N574BA	N5NC	N276PS			
212	A	N31KJ	N480JJ	N481JJ	N128BG				
213	A	N5009V	D-CMRM	N213MF	PR-MVF	N213NU	PK-...		
214	A	N5000E	N124DF	PT-FZA	N125DF	PR-PJD			
215	A	N40075	N30051	N786YA	(N784LB)	N31MC			
216	A	N40077	N999GH	N321GL	N311JS				
217	A	N40078	N10SE	N110SE					
218	A	N30050	N1ED						
219	A	N214RW	N214PW	N518JG	N638SF				
220	A	N5009T	N220LJ	N521CH	N521WH	N54AP			
221	A	N68ES	N278JM	XB-MBP					
222	A	N5013U	N200CH	N770CH	N14T	LV-BSO			
223	A	N40012	N8064K	N800CH	N501RS				
224	A	N3001H	(XA-VMX)	N224LJ	N411DJ				
225	A	N3003S	N334AF	N834AF					
226	A	N138FX	N226LJ	N7SN	N32PF				
227	A	N30054	N40073	D-CGGG					
228	A	N3018P	N955JS						
229	A	N50005	(N11TK)	N229LJ					
230	A	N5004Z	N295PS	N556HD	N558HD	XA-GCM	N558HD	XA-JMB	
231	A	N5005Q	XA-VTR	N712EJ	(N759FS)	N724FS			
232	A	N5008S	N668VP	N68VP					
233	A	N5005X	LX-PAT	N233BX	EI-MAX	N726MP	PR-MUR		
234	A	N5028E	N376MB	XA-EFX	XA-UMV				
235	A	N31NR	N317K	XA-UBI					
236	A	N314DT	N57TS						
237	A	N23UP	N19UP	N84MJ	N44LG	N37LG	N962FM		
238	A	N36UP							
239	A	N686AB							
240	A	N998AL	N990AE	N440SC	N48VP				
241	A	N335AF	N633SF						
242	A	N40043	(PR-BOI)+	[+ ntu marks worn at Tucson completion centre Apr03]			N40031	N903LJ	N600AW N600AN N680SW N132PH

Production complete

LEARJET MODEL 35

* after the series letter or in the series column indicates the aircraft has been fitted with Avcom delta fins.

C/n	Series	Identities								
001		N731GA	[ff 22Aug73] N351GL	[on display at entrance to Learjet factory, Wichita, KS]						
002		N352GL	N35SC	C-GVVA	N11382	[parted out by Alliance Air Parts, Oklahoma City, OK]				
003		N731GA	N931BA	N263GL	N370EC	N4RT	N960AA	N700WL	N703MA	N111WB
004		N74MP	N74MB	N74MJ	C-GIRE	[cx Feb15; to Algonquin College, Rockcliffe, Canada, as instructional airframe]				
005		EC-CLS	TR-LXP	EC-CLS	N175J	N178CP				
006		N356P	N39DM	N39FN						
007		D-CONI	N75DH	N47JR	(N65FN)	N35UJ	N357RM	N110UN	[cx 25Jun12; to Singapore as instructional airframe]	
008		N673M	PT-LFS	PP-ERR						
009		N44EL	N14EL	N275J	N263GL	PT-LGR	N335AT			
010		N888DH	N888DE	N35AJ						
011		N3816G	N400RB	N408RB	N531AJ	XA-RJT	XB-WID			
012		N711	N71LA	C-GVCB	N2242P	N95SC	N975AA	N975AD	N97TJ	XA-SVX
013	*	N1DA	N7TJ	N304AF	N35JN	N35BN	N535TA	N913CK		
014		N71TP	N73TP	(N72TB)	N98VA	N69PS	N77LJ	N190GC	N844L	[wfu El Paso, TX]
015		N291BC	N57FF	N58FF	N58CW	N335JL	(N335SS)	N354PM	[parted out by Alliance Air Parts, Oklahoma City, OK]	
016		N136GL	N5867	N9CN	N1SC	N18CV	VP-CLT	N31HK		
017		N119GS	N456MS	N551CC	N600DT					
018		D-CORA	F-GBMB	N696SC	N435JL	N696SC	N435JL	(N435EC)	[Parted out by White Inds, Bates City, MO; cx 29Apr09]	
019	*	N959AT	PT-LGF	N19NW	N71LG	N1AK	N157AK	N750RM	YV1828	
020		XA-BUX	N95TC	[w/o 20Dec84 Waco Airport, TX; remains to White Inds, Bates City, MO]						
021	A	N101GP	N91CH	N33TS	N442JT	N4415S	N53FN	N220NJ	N535LC	
022		OY-BLG	N90WR	[cx 05May15; CofR expired]						
023		N986WC	N886WC	N886CS	N443RK	[cx 08Aug13; wfu]				
024		N316	N24GA	N528JD	N528EA	N241RT	N411BA	N159RA		
025		9K-ACT	N40TF	N135TX	N510LJ	N185BA	(N188JA)	N435UJ	[parted out by Dodson Int'l, Rantoul, KS]	
026		D-CDHS	D-CBRK	N54754	N89TC					
027		N31WS								
028		N135GL	N20BG	XC-IPP	[carried dual marks XC-IPP/TP104]		Mexico TP104			
029		N711AF	[w/o Katab, Egypt 11Aug79 en route Athens-Jeddah]							
030	*	N816M	N16FN	N542PA [code "TX"]	(N30TK)	C-GKPE	N542PA			
031		N77FC	N77U	N77TE	N160AT	N233CC	N19WG			
032		N711CH	(N711QH)	N711MA	N235JW	N711MA	N710GS			
033		N7KA	HZ-KA1	N2297B	N31FN	N524PA				
034		N37TA								
035		N711R	(N711RQ)	N7125	N350TS	N92TS	YV....			
036		N134GL	N76GL	N76GP	N90AH	N351AJ	N135AJ			
037	*	N1462B	N100GL	N58M	N35GQ	N600WT	N520PA	N45TK	N333KC	N24NW
038		(VH-UDC)	VH-ELJ	C-FBFP	N10972	[parted out by Alliance Air Parts, Oklahoma City,OK]				
039		N1HP	N382TC							
040		C-GGYV	N39DM	[w/o 05Mar86 over Pacific Ocean nr San Clemente Island; collided with Learjet 24D-253 N97DM qv]						
041		N202BT	N202BD	N711BH	N41PJ	(N433JW)	N41NW	(N694PG)	[parted out by Alliance Air Parts, Oklahoma City, OK]	
042		N221UE	N73TJ	N270CS	XA-FFF	XB-RYT				
043		C-GVCA	N575WW	[parted out at Scottsdale, AZ]						
044		N38TA	N44MW	N44VW	N130F	[parted out by Alliance Air Parts, Oklahoma City,OK]				
045	*	N1461B	HB-VEN	N35HB	N99786	N999M	XA-HOS	N45MJ	N117CH	N304TZ	N304AT	N1140A	(N40AN)
		[parted out by Alliance Air Parts, Oklahoma City, OK]								
046		VH-SLJ	VH-FSX	VH-LJL	N58EM					
047	A	XA-ALE	N13MJ	N701AS	[parted out by Alliance Air Parts, Oklahoma City, OK]					
048	*	N233R	N64MH	F-GHMP	N8040A	[parted out by Alliance Air Parts, Oklahoma City,OK]				
049		JY-AEV	N3759C	C-GBWL	N235JL	N899WA	LV-ZZF			
050		CC-ECO	Chile 351							
051		SE-DEA	N2BA	(N123MJ)						
052		JY-AEW	[w/o 28Apr77 Riyadh, Saudi Arabia]							
053		N1976L	N53FN	N541PA						
054		VR-BFX	N53650	N54PR	N109MC	N435MS				
055		D-CONO	N70WW	I-NIKJ	N255RG	N255JH	C-GCJD	N354LQ		
056		(JY-AEX)	N106GL	N645G						
057		N551MD	N57FL	C-GHOO	N57GL	N35MR	C-GTDE			
058		C-GPUN	[w/o 11Jan95 Massett, Queen Charlotte Islands, BC, Canada]							
059		N221Z	N51FN	[w/o 02Apr90 Carlsbad, CA; remains to White Inds, Bates City, MO]						
060		N64MP	N64MR	N47BA	(N590CH)	[w/o 25Oct99 near Mina, SD]				
061		N424DN	N4246N	N238RC	N235EA					
062		N217CS	ZS-LII	TL-ABD	N701US	N310BA	N31DP			
063		N828M	N663CA	N80PG						
064		N290BC	N291BC	N100GP	(N257DP)	N257SD	N622RB	N921TM		
065		N425DN	N4358N	[parted out by Alliance Air Parts, Oklahoma City, OK]						
066		CC-ECP	Chile 352							
067	A	N118K	N888DJ	(N66FN)	N32FN	(N52FL)	N135FA			
068	A	HB-VEM	Switzerland T-781	N168TR						
069	A	N103GL	N591D	N1CA	N10AQ	N35NW	N48GP	N51FN		
070	A	D-CITA	N3GL	N503RP	N50FN	N543PA	N50FN			
071	A	JY-AFD	F-WDCP	F-GDCP	N82GA	N199CJ	N99FN	VH-ESW		
072	A	N2015M	N4415M	PR-MLA						
073	A	N108GL	N163A	(N64FN)	N352TX	N610GA	N536KN			
074	A	N5000B	N530J	N666JR	N100T	N198T	N351PJ			
075	A	N3503F	HB-VEV	JY-AFE	N3503F	(N117DA)	N48RW	N30FN	SE-DHP	
076	A	N959SA	N76CK							
077	A	N814M	N819JE	(N707BJ)	N46TJ	(XA-...)	ZS-NRZ	N98LC	[parted out by Alliance Air Parts, Oklahoma City, OK]	
078	A	N95BA	N95BH	N711SW	N711SD	N440JB	N112EL	N45AW	N145AM	
079	A	N6000J	N660CJ	N560KC	N7777B	N500DS	N68QB			
080	A	N109GL	N23HB	N10AZ	N17AZ					
081	A	N3523F	JY-AFF	N3523F	N118DA	N81FR	N353CK			
082	A	N235HR	N285HR	N700GB	N700SJ	[parted out by Alliance Air Parts, Oklahoma City,OK]				
083	A	(N600CC)	N400CC	(N400MJ)	(N45SL)	N500CD	N121CL	YV-100CP	N400LV	N581CC	N581PH
084	A	N111GL	N56HF	N135WB	N184TS	(N696JH)	N903AL	D-CFAY	[parted out Nurnberg, Germany]	
085	A	N15WH	(N353CK)							
086	A	N435M	N26DA	N98MD	N86CS	N860S	[parted out by Alliance Air Parts, Oklahoma City, OK]			
087	A	N720GL	N835GA	N862PD	(N862BD)	N18AX	N48ES			
088	A	N3545F	HB-VEW	N35GE	OE-GBR	N72JF	[parted out by Alliance Air Parts, Oklahoma City, OK]			
089	A	N3547F	D-CCHB							
090	A	HB-VEY	I-FIMI	N88BG	N290CK					
091	A	VH-TLJ	C-GBLF	N8GA	D-CIRS	N37FA	(N900JV)	XB-LWW		
092	A	N722GL	N424JR	C-GPFC	N46931	N92NE	N92EJ	N39WA	N73CK	

LEARJET 35

C/n	Series	Identities								
093	A	N804CC	C-GFRK	N5474G	N44PT	PT-LOT				
094	A	N506C	N935BD	N200EC	N92EC	N94GP	(N65PF)	(N35PF)	N94AF	
095	A*	N971H	N971F	N68UW	N66KK	N500LL				
096	A	N214LS	(N11JV)	N87AT	(D-CHRC)	N96FA	N94RL			
097	A	N135J	N108RB							
098	A*	N20CR	N21GL	N44UC	(N998DJ)	(N998M)	N72DA	[b/u; cx 23Jan12]		
099	A	N40146	HB-VFC	I-MCSA	[w/o 22Feb78 Palermo, Sicily]					
100	A	N550E	N558E	C-GRFO	[cx 29Nov12, wfu]					
101	A	N40149	N109JR	N109JU	N721AS	N751AC				
102	A	N1451B	N232R	PT-OEF	[w/o 02May92 Morelia, Mexico; remains to Dodson Int'l for spares]					
103	A	N96RE	N50MJ	PT-LCD						
104	A	N87W	N873LP	[w/o 22Sep85 Auburn, AL]						
105	A	(N720GH)	N102GH	N102GP	N612KC	N18FN	N444WB			
106	A	N101BG	N15TW	[w/o 08Dec85 Minneapolis, MN; remains to Brandis Avn, Taylorville, IL]						
107	A	N723GL	[w/o 12Dec85 Esterwood, TX]							
108	A*	D-COCO	F-GCLE	N86PC	(N86PQ)	D-CJPG				
109	A	N506GP	N911AE	[parted out by White Inds, Bates City, MO]						
110	A	(N12EP)	N4J	[parted out by Alliance Air Parts, Oklahoma City, OK]						
111	A	N3815G	(HB-VFE)	(I-SIDU)	OE-GMA	I-LIAD	D-CONE			
112	A	N3810G	D-CCAY	N247TA	N299LR	N999ND	N20HJ	(N120WH)	N354JC	(N354DT)	N354SS
113	A	N763GL	N35CL	N35RN	N14M	N684LA	N684HA	(N113AN)	[cx 19May15; CofR expired]	
114	A	N3807G	D-CONA	N18G	N851L	[w/o 14Dec94 Moscow-Sheremetyevo A/P, Russia; to Dodson Int'l, Rantoul, KS, for parts use]		N851L		
115	A	Argentina T-21	[w/o 09Mar06 La Paz, Bolivia]							
116	A	I-MMAE	N116AM	N58CW						
117	A	N3155B	N78MC	YV499T	YV3027					
118	A	N39391	HB-VFK	N115MA	N50MT	N88JA	N118FN			
119	A	HB-VFG	D-CHER	N93MJ	OY-ASO	N93MJ	N36FN	(N64DH)	N549PA [code "GA"]	
120	A*	N400JE	(N400RV)	N220CK*						
121	A	N43EL	(D-CFVG)	N43TJ	N752AC	VH-LJG				
122	A	D-CCHS	OE-GMP	N27TT	[parted out by Alliance Air Parts, Oklahoma City, OK]					
123	A	N3802G	N900JE	N900BJ						
124	A	N1500E	N35WG	N8LA	C-GTJL					
125	A	N3803G	N777MC	N777NQ	N111MZ	N125GA	N351EF			
126	A	N744GL	N15EH							
127	A	N727GL	N351TX	(N800VL)	[parted out by White Inds, Bates City, MO]					
128	A	N231R	N257AL	N39PJ						
129	A	N22BX	N229X	XA-ZAP						
130	A	N230R	(N44KW)	N757AL	(N116PR)	[cx Apr11; wfu]				
131	A	N3812G	N26GB	N26GD	N155AM					
132	A	N431M	N420PC	N37TJ	N135AG					
133	A	N728GL	N35NB	N58RW	I-ALPM	N133GJ	N133EJ			
134	A	N1473B	N88EP	N235DH	N238JA	[parted out by White Inds, Bates City, MO; cx 29Apr10]				
135	A*	(OO-LFX)	N22MJ	D-CDAX	N719US	N11AK	I-ZOOM	N135GJ	D-CFAX	[w/o 26Oct14, Tamanrasset, Algeria]
136	A	Argentina T-22								
137	A	N3819G	HB-VFL	EC-DEB	N41FN	N35TJ	[wfu; cx 10May11]			
138	A	N7735A	N31FB	N3RA	N83TJ	N35WH	N100MS	N138NA	N124ZT	[parted out by Alliance Air Parts, Oklahoma City, OK]
139	A*	N15SC	D-CGFD							
140	A	N742GL	N888BL	N72TP	N40BD	N76RA				
141	A	N743GL	N66WM	N553M	N553V					
142	A	N815A	N815L	N241CA						
143	A*	N3811G	N301SC	OE-GER	N20DK	LV-BPA				
144	A	N39398	D-CCAP	N705US	N35KC	OY-CCT	N118MA	N135JW	(N118MA)	N56HF	N56EM	[parted out by White Inds, Bates City, MO]
145	A	N39394	HB-VFB	Switzerland T-782	N145GJ	(N166AG)	VH-SLD	[wfu 2015 Wagga Wagga, Australia]		
146	A	N55AS	N351AS							
147	A	N717W	HZ-KTC	N499G	N717W	N55F	[parted out by Alliance Air Parts, Oklahoma City, OK]			
148	A	N103GH	N103GP	N333RP	N500RW	[w/o 24May88 Teterboro, NJ]				
149	A	OO-KJG	HB-VGN	N85351	N273MC	N273MG	N600LE	N600AE	N600AW	N800AW	(N40AN)	[w/o 19Mar04 Utica-Oneida County, NY; parted out by Dodson Int'l, KS, circa Dec05]
150	A	N100EP	[w/o 12May87 West Mifflin, PA; cx 01May90]							
151	A	N39399	N711L	N813M	[aircaft stolen 13Apr85; fate unknown]					
152	A*	N101HB	N964CL	[confiscated in Bolivia and donated post 12Jun90 to AF]			Bolivia FAB-009	N964CL	XA-RIN	XA-WIN
153	A	C-GZVV	N573LP	N573LR						
154	A	N650NL	N117RB	N244RG						
155	A	N760LP	N760DL	N110KG	"N1001L"	N110AE	N70AX	(N892AC)	N703DJ	
156	A	N170L	N190EB	N190DA	N35WE	N720RA	[crashed on approach to PalWaukee, IL, 05Jan10, w/o]			
157	A	N746GL	YV-01CP	N57FF	N57FP	N157DJ	ZS-MWW	N26GP	N389AW*	
158	A	N835AC	N158MJ	N158NE	N800GP	[w/o Springfield, IL, 06Jan11; cx 05Dec11]				
159	A	N93C	N93CK	(N135CK)	D-CAPO					
160	A*	D-CCCA								
161	A	N39415	YV-65CP	N433DD						
162	A	N751GL	(HB-VFO)	N711HH	N1978L	N222SL	XA-CZG			
163	A	YV-173CP	N27BL	N163CK						
164	A	N1473B	N248HM	N50MJ	[cx Apr11; wfu]					
165	A	N40144	A4O-CA	VH-HOF	N16BJ	N72CK				
166	A	N831CJ	N831I	N719IR	N10UF					
167	A*	N725P	N813AS	[parted out by Alliance Air Parts, Oklahoma City, OK]						
168	A	N22SF	N22SY	N36TJ	N75RJ	N68TJ	C-GPDO	C-FZQP	[cx 29Nov12, wfu]	
169	A	N135ST	N48CN	N500JS	N707RG					
170	A	N100K	N354RZ	C-GPDQ	C-GFEH	N335NA	N335AS	N88NJ	N870CK	
171	A*	N747GL	C-GNSA	N823J	N1968A	N1968T	N196DT	(N48DK)	N40DK	N171WH	XA-ICU
172	A	N748GL	SE-DDG	N72TJ	N32JA	SX-BFJ	(N32JA)	N50AK	(ZS-ZZZ)	
173	A	N750GL	HZ-MIB	N750GL	(HZ-NCI)	N100GU	N116EL	(N83DM)	YU-BPY	N326DD
174	A	TR-LYC	N65DH	D-CAVI	(F-GGRG)	N130TA	D-CAMB	N82283	N38AM	N773DL	N474KA
175	A	D-CDWN	SE-RCA							
176	A	N317MR	XA-ACC	N176JE	(N67GA)	XA-BUX				
177	A	N1461B	N77CP	N77CQ	N174CP	D-CITY				
178	A	N40146	N22CP	N22CQ	N35GG	N900JC	(N104AA)	[parted out by Alliance Air Parts, Oklahoma City, OK]		
179	A*	N39412	D-CCAR	D-CAPD	N718SW	(N696SC)	C-FHLO	N801PF	D-CGFA	
180	A	N3819G	N222BE	N222BK	N35CX	N44HG	N701DA			
181	A	N35LJ	N35PR	N35PD	N5114G	PT-LSJ				
182	A	N1450B	N33HB	N3HB	N3HA	N221SG	[cx 30Jan14; wfu]			
183	A	N3802G	N720M	N72JM	N106XX	N51TJ	N137RS	(N137TS)	N183FD	N717AJ
184	A	N1462B	HB-VFO	[damaged 06Dec82 Paris-Le Bourget, France; believed repaired]		N7092C	[cx 04Nov13; parted out]			
185	A	N99ME	N99VA	N10BF	N99VA	N900EM	TC-GEM	OE-GAV	ZS-SES	RP-C5354

LEARJET 35

C/n	Series	Identities										
186	A	N753GL	N590	N96DM	(N317JD)	N96FN	[cx 10Oct14; wfu]					
187	A	N755GL	N32HM	(N888DT)	N799TD							
188	A	VH-AJS	N39293	N20RT	(N38FN)	N3MJ	N343MG	N135AC	N35TK	N88TJ	N999JF	N924AM CX-JYE N352RJ
189	A	N3811G	VH-AJV	N39292	(N189TC)	N32TC	N32FN	N35KC	N18NM	N727JP	I-AVJG	[w/o 24Oct99 on approach to
		Genoa A/P, Italy]										
190	A	N32BA	N202VS	N202WR	(N208WR)	N181EF						
191	A	N3810G	(YV-15CP)	HB-VFX	N75TF	N35NP	N35SE	N535AF				
192	A	N4995A	N225CC	N225QC	N49PE	N49BE	VH-LRX					
193	A	N1465B	(YV-131CP)	VH-SBJ	N620J	VH-SBJ	N2743T	N9EE	N359EF			
194	A	N91W	N86BL	N86BE	[w/o 5Apr00 Marianna Municipal apt, FL]							
195	A	N1471B	D-CONY	N555JE	SE-DHO							
196	A	HB-VFU	EC-DFA	[w/o 13Aug80 Palma, Spain]								
197	A	N754GL	N754WS	HK-4982								
198	A	N25FS	I-ALPT	N198GJ								
199	A	N40144	N9HM	(N9HV)	N30DH	N34TC	N444HC	N235JS				
200	A	N3818G	D-CCAR	OO-LFY	N200LJ	N606	N80UT	N200LJ	P4-TID			
201	A	N39415	N79MJ	N35RT	N35RF	XA-PIN	N35AZ	N136WE	N135AV	N234MR		
202	A	VH-MIQ	N499G	D-CGPD	N55FN							
203	A	N744E	N744P	VR-CUC	N203RW	N97CE						
204	A	N1466B	D-COSY	N87MJ	N99ME	N7PE	(N277AM)	D-CFTG				
205	A	N39418	N80SM	N59DM	N59FN	N568PA						
206	A	N760GL	(N66HM)	HB-VGH	N189TC	N123CC	N38PS	(N46KB)				
207	A	N40146	N711	N3PW	N620JM	[w/o 15Jul05 Vail/Eagle County, CO]						
208	A	N40149	N40TA	(N691NS)	N39DK	(N39DJ)	N67PA					
209	A	N399W	N339W	N711DS	N22MS	[w/o McMinnville, OR, 13May13]						
210	A	N840GL	(N35HM)	N42HM	N721CM	XB-FNF	N210WL	N770JP				
211	A	N1461B	D-CATY	N15MJ	N600LC	N500KK	N500GM	N998JP	N44TT	N621RB	N920TM	
212	A	N3803G	N180MC	N291A	N989AL							
213	A	N800RD	(N935NA)	XC-CUZ								
214	A	N279DM	[parted out by White Inds, Bates City, MO]									
215	A	VH-UPB	N2951P	N80CD	N80GD	N35ED	N41RA					
216	A	N3819G	D-CATE	N24MJ	N39MB	N142LG	N335RD	N991AL				
217	A*	N39412	N111RF	N122JW	N217CK							
218	A	N256TW	N481FM	(N601WT)	(N83TE)	N781RS	[w/o 28Dec05 Truckee-Tahoe, CA]					
219	A	N39416	VH-BJQ	N502G	N350JF	[shot down 29Aug99 Ethiopia/Eritrea Border]						
220	A	N79BH	N333RB	N220GH	N873LP	N873LR	(N373LP)	N220GS				
221	A	N1462B	N845GL	VH-WFE	VH-FSY	N221TR	XA-...					
222	A*	N1468B	HB-VFZ	I-EJID	N90AL	HB-VFZ	N789KW	D-CGFG				
223	A	N215JW	D-CGRC									
224	A*	N96AC	N56PB	N40RW	N28MJ	N269JR						
225	A	N225MC	TG-JAY	N34TJ	N225CF	[wfu Houston Intercontinental Sep06]						
226	A	N1127M	N30HJ	[parted out by White Industries Inc, Bates City, MO; cx 29Apr09]								
227	A	N211BY	N25RF	N88NE	N85GW	(N227MJ)	N902JC	N366TT	[parted out by Alliance Air Parts, Oklahoma City, OK]			
228	A	N101PG	N4GB	SX-BNT	N100NW	N72LG	N921CH					
229	A	N1476B	N8MA	N717JB	N718EA	N41WT	N31WT	(N214LS)	N415LS	N4415W	[parted out by Dodson Int'l, Rantoul, KS]	
230	A	N39418	N714K	PT-WAR	N81458	N356AC	N37HJ	N595BA				
231	A*	(N10AB)	(N712DM)	N911DB	N62DK	VH-JCR						
232	A	N8281	N4415S	N503LB								
233	A	N35SL	N35AW	(N442HC)	N23A							
234	A	N35WR										
235	A	N841GL	N600CN	N256MA	(N256MB)	N166HL	N166HE	LV-ZSZ	[w/o Buenos Aires/San Fernando, Argentina, 19Oct15]			
236	A	G-ZOOM	N8537B	N90LP	N4XL	N900EC	N600GP	(N415RD)	EC-HLB	N65RZ		
237	A	N843GL	N78MN	I-KUSS	N35RJ	(N37DJ)	N72LE	N237TJ	(N36BP)	N300TW	N300TE	N11UF N237CK
238	A	N844GL	N80HK	ZS-INS	3D-ACZ	ZS-INS	N248DA	N500CG	N500HG	N500HZ	N32RZ	[dismantled at Boca Raton, FL while
		still painted as N500HZ circa Jan04; to White Inds, Bates City, MO for spares use]										
239	A	N1473B	N847GL	(HB-VGC)	VH-KTI	VH-LEQ	N239GJ	N521PA	[w/o 14Dec94 Fresno, CA; cx Jun95]			
240	A	N240B	N249B	N135WE	N35LJ							
241	A	N42FE	N500GP	N500FD	N240JS	N500EX	N500ED					
242	A	N846GL	VH-WFJ	VH-FSZ	N242DR							
243	A	N3812G	HZ-ABM	N81863	I-AGEB	N2217Q	XA-HYS	N152TJ	XA-THD	N747RY		
244	A	N1451B	RP-57	RP-C57	N244TS	N244LJ	(N116KV)					
245	A	N2WL	N1526L	N30PA								
246	A	N50PH	N50PL	N555GB	N1DC	N628DB	YV543T					
247	A	YV-265CP	N110JD	N38FN	N523PA	N544PA						
248	A	N3811G	C-GBFA	N128CA								
249	A	N107JM	I-KALI	N249DJ	N300DA	C-FICU	[parted out in USA; cx 16Feb09]		(N374LJ)			
250	A	N3250	(N87RS)	N63LE	N63LF	N947GS						
251	A	N27NB	N27HF	N251CT	N387HA							
252	A	N28CR	PT-KZR									
253	A	N40144	N211DH	N611CM	N611SH	N129TS	N129TK					
254	A	N666CC	N34FN	N522PA	(N54TK)	N254US	N720WW					
255	A	N44EL	N44ET	N610HC	N616HC	XB-LHS	XB-FNW	XB-USD	XA-USD	[w/o 19Nov13, crashed into sea on departure from Fort
		Lauderdale International, FL; wreckage parted out by Atlanta Air Salvage, Griffin, GA]										
256	A	N712L	N6GG	N50DD	N911ML	(N402FW)	(N811ML)	(N66PJ)	N335RC			
257	A	F-GCMS	N257DJ	N417BA								
258	A	(N1700)	N28BG	N35MH	N583PS	N583BS	(N218CR)	N17UF	[w/o 10Nov14 Grand Bahama, Bahamas]			
259	A	N39413	HB-VGC	N9113F	N259HA	(N259JC)	HK-3983X	N25AN	[parted out by Alliance Air Parts, Oklahoma City, OK]			
260	A	N40PK										
261	A	N900RD	XA-ELU	N35SJ	N35FN	N63DH	N58MM					
262	A	N237GA	N237AF									
263	A	D-CCAD	N4577Q	N37FN	EC-GXX	N8228P	EC-GXX	(N2422J)	(ZS-PBA)	[dbr Olbia, Italy, as EC-GXX 25Aug02; ntu reservations made
		later, for parts use]										
264	A*	XA-ATA	N35GX	N40DK	N3056R	VR-CDI	N64CP	N264CK				
265	A	N1462B	(G-ZEST)	G-LEAR	United Arab Emirates 801 A6-RJI		G-LEAR	SX-SEM				
266	A	N3904	SE-DDI	N922GL	N35GC							
267	A	N39418	XA-LAN	[w/o 08Jan93 nr Hermosillo, Mexico]								
268	A*	N10870	YV-286CP	N3857N	(N286CP)	N510SG	N2U	D-CGFB				
269	A	N881W	N225F	N211WH	N886R							
270	A	N10871	(YV-15CP)	YV-O-MRI-1		Venezuela FAV0013	N31MC	[w/o 17Oct07, Goodland, KS; parted out by Alliance Air Parts, Oklahoma
		City, OK]										
271	A*	N1088A	LV-PET	LV-OAS	N40AN	[w/o 10Jan07 Columbus, OH; parted out by Alliance Air Parts, Oklahoma City, OK]						
272	A	N39398	N272HS	N500EF	N321AN	N89TB						
273	A	N1465B	N35FH	N103C	N103CL	N273LJ						
274	A	N1087Y	N274JS	N274JH	N83CP	N711BE	(N35WG)	N274FD	N274JS	N53G		
275	A	N10872	G-ZEAL	(N43PE)	N43FE	(N65WH)	N235SC	N72LL	ZS-SFV			

LEARJET 35

C/n	Series	Identities										
276	A	N44LJ	N613RR	N69BH	[cx 04Nov14; wfu]							
277	A	N925GL	N723LL	N70CN	N127HC	XA-PUI	N350MD	(N9876S)	N27TJ	N42B	(N6362D)	(N489)	N2WQ	N999JS
278	A	N1476B	HB-VGL	ECT-028	EC-DJC	N300ES	N17GL	N12RP					
279	A	N19LH	[w/o 15Jly97 Avon Park, FL]										
280	A(C21A)	N80MJ	HP-912	YN-BVO	US Army 87-0026		N35AX	N142LM	N542LM				
281	A	N80WG	N425M	N425AS									
282	A	N504Y	N80CD	N80GD	N9CH	N444CM	N62MB						
283	A	N920C	N205EL	N205FL	N386CM								
284	A	(D-CEFL)	D-CCAX	OO-GBL	N43MF								
285	A	N777RA	N75KV	N34TB	VH-MZL	N818WS	N42PJ	(N528VP)	N725ST	CX-PYB			
286	A	N333X	(N333XX)	N200SX	PT-LSW	N286WL	N286SD						
287	A	N17EM	N71HS	N929SR	N929SL	N156BA	N170LD	N177LD					
288	A	N1476B	HB-VGM	N43DD	N288NE	N288JE	N288JP	N1441M					
289	A	N3JL	N802CC	N289MJ	N289NE	N289LJ	N36TJ	N217TA					
290	A	N2022L	XA-RAV	XA-ORO									
291	A	N7US	N535PC	[w/o 14Feb91 2 miles N of Aspen Airport, CO; cx Jly91]									
292	A	N634H	N292ME										
293	A	N182K	[w/o Groton, CT, 02Jun06]										
294	A	N745E	N745F	N35VP	N440HM	[w/o 27Feb97 Greenville, SC; remains to White Inds, Bates City, MO]							
295	A	PT-LAA	N94AA	N474AN	N295CK								
296	A	N296BS	XA-LML	N51JA	N66NJ	[cx 14Oct15; parted out by DK Turbines, CA]							
297	A	N746E	N746F	N38US	N777DM	N3313C							
298	A	I-FLYC	N298NW	N298CK									
299	A	N244FC	PT-LGS	N148X	(PT-PMV)	PT-XLI	[cx, CofA suspended]						
300	A	N365N	N104PH										
301	A	N301TP	N999RB	N102ST	N102BT	N190VE	N98AC	N945W					
302	A	N717DS	N780A	N78QA	N41ST	N631CW	N51LC	[parted out by Alliance Air Parts, Oklahoma City, OK]					
303	A	N771A	PT-LLS										
304	A	N464HA	N112PG	N534H	N534A	N53GH	N53GL	(N97QA)	N995CR	ZS-BLE			
305	A	N3VG	N33NJ	N519GE	[parted out by Alliance Air Parts, Oklahoma City, OK]								
306	A	N926GL	N66LM	N601MC	N77LN	N111US	N1110S	N71E	(N63602)	(N485)	N9ZD		
307	A	N120MB	(N119HB)	N677CT	N623KM								
308	A	N99MJ	N747GM	(N7LA)	(N747RL)	XA-UPR							
309	A	(YV-328CP)	HB-VGT	OE-GAR	N8216Z	N100MN	D-CHPD	C-GUAC					
310	A	N97JL	N13HB	(N13HQ)	N8280	N310ME	N310PJ						
311	A	D-CDHS	N723US	N35BG	OE-GPN	N311BP	HC-BSZ	N121JT	N581AS	N711EC			
312	A	LV-PHX	LV-OFV	N369BA	N62RA								
313	A	N39413	(F-GCLT)	TR-LZI	N31WR	N352CK							
314	A	N35AK	(N118GM)	N777LD									
315	A	N927GL	N662AA	D-CCAA	(N121JT)								
316	A	N39398	N1503	N1507	N35AH	N18ST	N99GK	N89GK	N384JW	N884JW	XA-UKF		
317	A	N10871	SE-DEM	N98TE	N317TT								
318	A	N444WB	N103CF	N318NW	(N35WU)								
319	A	Argentina T-23											
320	A	N905LC	N905LD	N35FS	N320M	N30GJ	N393JP	N32PJ	N727MG	N35RT			
321	A	N14TX	(N19LM)	N77LP	XA-RVB	XC-AA60	(N321WJ)	Mexico TP-106		Mexico 3909/XC-UJG			
322	A	N305SC	PT-WGF										
323	A*	N735A	N357EF										
324	A	G-JJSG	G-JETN	G-JETG	N8064A	VH-LJJ							
325	A	D-CARO	I-FFLY	N325NW									
326	A	PT-LAS	N155WL	N255JC	N612DG	N35SA	XA-...						
327	A	N3797N	N135UT	N327F	N32PF	N32PE	YV....						
328	A	N3807G	N1502	N35NY	N35NX	N392JP	N408MG	N731RA					
329	A	N39412	N53DM	N261PC	N261PG	XA-...							
330	A	N930GL	[partially destroyed Dec89 during US invasion of Panama; b/u for spares; cx Jly91]										
331	A*	N10870	HB-VGU	I-EJIB	N700NW	N435JW	D-CGFC						
332	A	N600LN	N332FG	(N598WW)	N543WW	N827CR	XA-LBS						
333	A	Argentina T-24	[w/o 07Jun82 S Atlantic]										
334	A	N2815	N350RB	N334SP	(N334AB)	N235MC							
335	A	N25MJ	N8YY	N15Y	N335DJ	N335NE	N335EE	N800CD	N800CH	N880CH	N3MB	N135SH	
336	A	HB-VGW	N590J	N166RM	N782JR	XA-PYC	(N336EA)	XA-BNO	XC-DGO				
337	A	N80ED	N337WC	N710AT	N39HJ								
338	A	N1473B	RP-C7272	N610GE	RP-C610	[cx, wfu Manilla, Philippines]							
339	A	N24JK	N24CK	N15CC	N1500	PT-LZP							
340	A*	N11AM	N11YM	N504F	XA-DAZ	XC-LNE	XA-DAZ						
341	A	N3802G	D-CARE	XA-HOS	N259WJ	ZS-CEW	P4-KIS	OE-GMS	OE-GPI	M-EASY			
342	A	N1088D	N37931	VH-SDN	VH-LGH	N678S	YV-15CP	N56JA	[parted out by Alliance Air Parts, Oklahoma City, OK]				
343	A	N135MB	N80BT	N21NA	N21NG	N998GC	LV-BPO						
344	A	N40149	YV-327CP	N344MC	N630SJ	(N111BJ)	N45MF						
345	A	N3818G	N10RE	VH-EMP	N345LJ	N30DK	[w/o 24Oct04 San Diego-Brown Field, CA]						
346	A	N3803G	C-GMGA	N35AJ	I-DLON	(N34LZ)	EC-IIC	D-CTRI					
347	A	OE-GNP	N85SV										
348	A	(N17ND)	N3798B	N600BE	N500MJ	N35TL	N35DL	(N8JA)	N7ZH				
349	A	N272T	XA-TCI	N252WJ	(N349TS)	ZS-ARA							
350	A	N88NE	N35WB										
351	A	N500RP	N500DD	N500ND	[w/o 11Aug07 Melville Hall, Dominica; parted out by Alliance Air Parts, Oklahoma City, OK; cx 12Jan10]								
352	A	YV-326CP	N30GD	N600G	N71A	(N999JA)	N35CZ	N800GJ	N47RA				
353	A	N3819G	C-GDJH										
354	A	N1450B	D-CART	N212GA	N405GJ								
355	A	N1468B	LV-PJZ	LV-ONN	N64RV	N345	N351WB	N721EC					
356	A	N54YR	N54YP	N800WJ	(VR-C..)	PT-LUG							
357	A	N3797S	N1001L	(N289GA)	ZS-MGK	(N100L)	N104SB	N357LJ					
358	A	N524HC	N358PG	N108JN									
359	A	(N127RM)	HB-VHB	N136JP									
360	A	N185FP	N1129M	(N360GL)	N360LJ	(N901MS)	(N987DK)	YV2661					
361	A	N924GL	PT-LBS	PT-FAT	PT-OCZ								
362	A	N3794M	N888MV	N399KL	N773LP	N633DS	N362FW						
363	A	N52MJ	N183JC	N19RP	PP-CRT								
364	A	N3794Z	(N65TA)	N981TH	N950CS	N490BC	N353EF	HK-4826					
365	A	G-ZONE	(N4564S)	G-ZIPS	G-SEBE	G-CJET	G-GJET	D-CFAI	[w/o 12Jun08 Kinsangani, DR Congo]				
366	A	N411LC	N49AT	(N94AA)	N119CP	N350DA	HS-CFS	VH-YPT					
367	A	N714S	(N67TJ)	N97RJ	N232CC	N360AX							
368	A	N35FM	SE-DHE	N368BG	N99KW	N450MC	N351TV						
369	A	Argentina VR-17		Argentina T-24		Argentina T-26							
370	A	HB-VGY	N11MY	N1MY	(N56PR)	VR-BKB	N8216Q	XA-RKY	XA-OFA	XA-CVD	N87GA	XA-CVD	XB-JOA

LEARJET 35

C/n	Series	Identities
371	A	LV-PLY LV-ALF N399BA
372	A	HB-VGX N372AS PT-LJK
373	A	SE-DER XA-BRE XA-RUY N97AN N971K LV-BNR
374	A	HZ-106 HZ-MS1A [parted out by Atlanta Air Salvage, Griffin, GA, 2009]
375	A	(YV-270CP) HZ-107 HZ-MS1B [parted out by Atlanta Air Salvage, Griffin, GA, 2009]
376	A	N458JA N77FK N33WB XA-SBF N979RF
377	A	(N711EV) N933GL N10WF N18WE N46MF
378	A	CX-BOI/FAU 500 (N900DG) N354ME N354EF
379	A	N23VG N18LH N217RT XB-IWL XB-KPB [damaged at Guadalajara 02Aug08]
380	A	N82JL N291BX N291BC N281BC XA-SBA N11SQ XA-SGK XA-MSH N903WJ C-GAJS
381	A	D-CORA N65DH (N40TM) N300CM N335K N35NA N131AJ
382	A	N382BL N382BP OE-GAF N60WL
383	A	N66FE N364CL
384	A	N37984 N811DF N811DD N384CF
385	A	N535MC N350EF D-CFIV
386	A	N13VG N999FA LV-BAW
387	A*	D-CARL
388	A	N1929S N388PD N388LS [w/o 24Dec96 Smarts Mountain on approach to Lebanon-Municipal, NH; cx May98]
389	A	N59MJ N377C N31WT N31WE VR-BLU N436DM N79AX N389KA
390	A	N500PP N508P N831CW C-FJEF C-FPRP [parted out by Alliance Air Parts Inc, Oklahoma City, OK] N831CW
391	A	N3793D N444BF N813RR N89AT I-RYVA N888PT XA-SWF [w/o 23Jun95 Tepico, Mexico]
392	A	N931GL N1ED N18DY N1XL [parted out by Precision Jet Service, Stuart, FL; cx 10Apr14]
393	A	N932GL N666RB N700WJ PT-LOE
394	A	N1466K N816JA N94MJ N60DK N626JS N232PR N238PR C-GLNL
395	A	HB-VHD N3261L N30GL N246CM N395MY C-GVGH Argentina VR-24
396	A	N2000M N938GL N5139W VR-CBU N5FF N74JL PT-OPJ
397	A	N33PT D-CLAN N200TW (N335JD)
398	A	N3797A N1AH [w/o 16May97 Great Falls, MT; cx Nov97; to spares by White Inds, Bates City, MO, 1998]
399	A	N37965 N540HP (N399DJ) N399AZ PT-OVC (N399AZ) [w/o 04Nov07 Sao Paulo, Brazil]
400	A	VH-CPH (VH-CPQ) VH-TPR VH-JIG VH-RHQ VH-OVB
401	A	N66LJ (N177SB) N771SB N535JM XC-LNH XA-USI
402	A	N3402 N610JR N7AB N35BG
403	A	N37966 N312CT N312CF N312CE N100NR N101HW N100HW N403FW [parted out by Alliance Air Parts, Oklahoma City, OK]
404	A	N500JS N404BB N404KA N404DP N804TF
405	A	N41MJ (N181GL) N35AS N35FS N442DM N135DA D-CVFL*
406	A	N764G N35Q I-KELM ER-LGA HS-EMS [cx, wfu Bangkok/Don Mueang, Thailand]
407	A	N3793P N234DT N221MC N407MR C-GIWD C-GIWO
408	A	(N33VG) N3798P LV-POG LV-AIT
409	A	N50PD N858TM N123LC N888BS N35FE N351AM
410	A	N12109 N1210M C-FHDM N441CW (N21WS) N820RP N89RP N352TV
411	A	PT-LBY N94GP
412	A	N37980 N6666R N412GL (N31LM) N314C XA-RGH
413	A	HB-VHE N2637Z F-GHAE N413MA N27KG D-CFCF
414	A	(N135AB) N39MW PT-SMO N414TJ N196SD N196SP N815DD
415	A	N125AX N19GL N415DJ D-COSY SE-DZZ
416	A	N306M N35MV N40GG N841TT N841TF
417	A	N934GL N117FJ (N117RJ) D-CONO N97D N90RK HC-BTN (N37HR) N281CD LX-ONE C-GXCB
418	A	XA-KCM XA-SCA N366AC LV-BPL
419	A	N935GL N25EL N53JM N35SM N72AX
420	A	N35RT N35PT N100KK N100KZ N181CA
421	A	N44MJ N85CA N85QA (N88AH) N3AH N413JP I-VULC D-CDSF D-CQAJ
422	A	YV-434CP N86BL N45AE
423	A	N369XL N200TC (N335GA) D-CAVE [cx, wfu Karlsruhe]
424	A	N2844 N508GP N52FN
425	A	N111KK N111KZ N425SA
426	A*	D-CARD N43W N43H ZS-NID N1128J RP-C1426 N143LG N543LM
427	A	N1087Z VH-FOX N42LL N358AC N36HJ [parted out by MTW Aerospace, AL]
428	A	N1465B VH-ELC N17LH VH-SLE [wfu 2015 Wagga Wagga, Australia]
429	A	G-ZING G-GAYL G-ZENO United Arab Emirates 800 A6-RJH G-ZING (D-CSOS) (SX-SEN) 9H-MRQ
430	A	N10870 Finland LJ-1
431	A	N1088A YV-433CP N34FD N431CW N431AS N355PC N431CK
432	A	F-GDCN N4445Y N330BC VR-CAD G-HUGG VH-VLJ
433	A	N39416 D-CARG HB-VCZ N26583 N95AC (N93RC) PT-LIH [w/o 15Mar91 Uberlandia, Brazil]
434	A	N4401 N469BB (N434CJ)
435	A	N435N XC-HHJ
436	A	N37988 PT-LDN N436BL N100AT LV-CMO
437	A	N3803G YV-432CP YV2044
438	A	N17ND N600LL N12GJ N300R N308R N308BW N35WL
439	A	N439ME HK-3121X HK-3121 N55RZ N35LW (N35FT) N402DP N911WX N611TA
440	A	N101HK N101CK N903HC (N354EM) N917SC N300SC
441	A	N1471B N551WC TC-MEK N441PC N441PG N74SP N404JS RP-C1404 N699ST [wfu Fort Lauderdale Executive]
442	A	N40149 N3799C N35BK N442NE [w/o 26Jul88 Morristown, NJ; parted out by White Inds, Bates City, MO]
443	A	N135RJ N258G N335MR (N335SJ)
444	A	N3818G D-CARH N44695 N444MJ N144WB N1U N44SK N615HP N615HB
445	A	N3802G HB-VHG I-MOCO [w/o 08Feb01 Nurnberg, Germany]
446	A	N37962 N80AS N96CP N96CR N794GC N403DP
447	A	N127K N300FN D-COKE
448	A	N48MJ N222BG N595PL N577AC
449	A	N37947 N777LF N449QS XA-GDO XB-GDO
450	A	N450KK N950SP
451	A	N1462B Finland LJ-2
452	A	N25MJ N279SP N452DA
453	A	N124MC N802JW (N802EC) N453AM
454	A	N3794W (N379BW) N80AR (N80KR) N661MS
455	A	N3794U N455NE N988QC
456	A	N711CD N456CL
457	A	N1451B N900P N974JD (N113LB) N874JD N113LB N49WL
458	A	N276JS YV-997CP N86RX N4EA
459	A	VH-MIE N306SP N80BL N969MT N829CA [w/o 13Jul04 Charlestown, St. Kitts & Nevis; to Dodson Av'n, Rantoul, KS for spares]
460	A	XC-PGR XA-MPS XA-JJJ N994EA
461	A	N64CF
462	A	N3811G N8562W N147K N801K N7117 N135TP N394PA LV-BXU
463	A	N1088D VH-ULT VH-FSW VH-FSU N68LL N32HJ N699BA C-GTWX
464	A	(N75PK) N1DC PT-LHX N464WL VP-BJS N111KR
465	A	N465NW

LEARJET 35

C/n	Series	Identities										
466	A	VH-WFP	N39SA	(N700WJ)	N600WJ	D-COCO	[w/o 08Jun93 Cologne-Bonn, Germany; remains to Dodson Av'n, Rantoul, KS for spares]					
467	A	N3796Q	HZ-MS1	HZ-MS1C	[parted out by Atlanta Air Salvage, Griffin, GA, 2009]							
468	A*	VH-ANI	N468LM	OY-CCJ								
469	A	N39416	N3202A	N660SA	N444TG	N71MH	N35JN	N35EG				
470	A	N3810G	Finland LJ-3									
471	A	VH-BQR	N95AP	N110FT	N529BC							
472	A	N1468B	N448GC	N448WC	N448WG	PT-ONK	(N472AS)	N54HF	N35TN	N335MW	N138WE	N612SQ	N81RA
473	A	N3796P	PT-LFT	N3UJ	N44AB	N35TH	N777LB	N35CY				
474	A	N39413	N37975	PT-LEB	[wfu Jundiai, Brazil]							
475	A	N10873	N3797K	3D-ADC	ZS-TOW	(N42AJ)						
476	A	N3818G	N476VC	N777LB	N1TW							
477	A	N40162	N3797B	N82GL	N80CD	N95EC	N477WB	(N477MS)	N24JG	N235UJ	N155RD	N608GF	N376HA	N480YA
		[parted out by Alliance Air Parts, Oklahoma City,OK]										
478	A	N3815G	LV-TDF	[w/o 15May84 Ushuaia, Argentina]								
479	A	N3816G	N8565J	N31WT	N30SA	PT-LHT						
480	A*	N3819G	(VH-ALH)	N8563A	N35CK	(N484)	(N35FH)	N39DK	[parted out by Alliance Air Parts, Oklahoma City, OK]			
481	A	N1466B	N6666K	N666KK	N728MP	N729HS	HK-3122X	HK-3122	N729HS	N27NR	OO-LFV	N99NJ	[cx 30Jun14; wfu]
482	A	N482U	[w/o 13Feb83 en route Kuala Lumpur-Colombo]		N2286D	[reason for new N-number not yet known; cx 07Nov13; CofR expired]						
483	A	N40144	N8562Y	N202BT	(N203AL)	N327CB	N990LC					
484	A	N4289U	Argentina VR-18		Argentina T-25							
485	A	N4290C	N485S	XA-RZZ	N710WL	N485AC	N90J					
486	A	N4291G	N821PC	N117EL	N810CC	N925DM	N817EM					
487	A*	N4289Y	N206FC	N206EC	N400MC	N391JP	N391JR	N487FW	N890LR	N890LJ		
488	A	N8563G	N848GL	N30W	N30WY	N900R	N907R	XA-UGK	N61SJ	XC-OAH	XB-NKR	XA-SKI
489	A	N1473B	N222BE	N312LG								
490	A	N1087Z	N64MP	N502JF	C-GTWL							
491	A	N1087Y	N8563N	N491HS	N241AG	N485	I-AGEN	N135PG	N394JP	N35NK		
492	A	N39399	N8566B	N35NP	N37SV	N335UJ	N492RM	N994CR	N492RM	N490JP		
493	A	N3811G	N8564M	N482SG	I-FFRI	N493NW	N493CH	N354CL				
494	A	N1476B	PT-LDM									
495	A	N1088D	N440MC	N383AL	N47MF							
496	A	N3803G	N8564K	N856RR	N496SW	N39TH	N496SW	(N496LJ)	N825LJ			
497	A	N1450B	N8565N	N50PH	N21DA	N15RH	N518PR	N758JA				
498	A	N3815G	N8564P	I-FLYH	N498JR	N400FF	C-GTDM					
499	A	N3818G	N85645	N84AD	PT-LII	HK-3921	N38AL	N499WJ	N1TS	N911DX	N32HM	
500	A*	N1465B	N8566X	N66LN	N101US	N81CH	N81QH	N144LG	N544LM			
501	A*	N3816G	HB-VHR	N711PR	N35HW	N326HG	N565GG					
502	A	N1476B	N8565X	N747CP								
503	A	N1087Z	N8567A	HB-VII	HK-3646X	N8567A	N77NR	N542SA				
504	A*	N10871	N8568B	G-RAFF	N505DH	OE-GMJ	D-CTWO					
505	A	N1471B	N7259J	N505EE	N494PA	N60DK	N90PN	C-GJDA	N505GJ			
506	A	N3819G	N317BG	N10BD	[on display in the terminal at Denver Int'l by May03 having been the first aircraft to land at the new airport in 1993]							
507	A	N3802G	N35GJ	N35HP	N42HP	N42HN						
508	A	N40144	N741E	N741F	N7777B	N881CA	N508TF	N452AC	LV-BOX			
509	C21A	N6317V	N7263C	84-0063	N35AL	N826RD	N135PT	[w/o 04Aug03 Poquonock River, Groton, CT]				
510	C21A	N6331V	N7263D	84-0064	[preserved Wright-Patterson AFB USAF museum, OH]							
511	C21A	N4289X	N7263E	84-0065								
512	C21A	N4290J	N7263F	84-0066	[w/o Decatur, IL, 02Oct06]							
513	C21A	N4291G	N7263H	84-0067	N35AQ	N117PK	HK-4662					
514	C21A	N4289Z	N7263K	84-0068	[wfu AMARC 26Jan07, park code AACJ0020]							
515	C21A	N4290K	N7263L	84-0069	[to Embry-Riddle Aeronautical University, Daytona Beach, FL]							
516	C21A	N4291K	N7263N	84-0070								
517	C21A	N6340T	N7263R	84-0071								
518	C21A	N4289Y	N7263X	84-0072								
519	C21A	N6307H	N400AD	84-0073	[wfu AMARC 16Jan07, park code AACJ0011]							
520	C21A	N42905	N400AK	84-0074	[wfu AMARC 08Jan07, park code AACJ0005]							
521	C21A	N4291N	N400AN	84-0075	[wfu]							
522	C21A	N4290Y	N400AP	84-0076	N506HL							
523	C21A	N4289U	N400AQ	84-0077								
524	C21A	N6317V	N400AS	84-0078	[wfu AMARC 08Jan07, park code AACJ0006]							
525	C21A	N6331V	N400AT	84-0079								
526	C21A	N4289X	N400AU	84-0080	[wfu AMARC 10Jan07, park code AACJ0007]							
527	C21A	N4290J	N400AX	84-0081	N527Z	[wfu]						
528	C21A	N4289Z	N400AY	84-0082	N528L	[wfu; stored Springfield, OH]						
529	C21A	N4291G	N400AZ	84-0083								
530	C21A	N4290K	N400BA	84-0084	N352PJ							
531	C21A	N4291K	N400FY	84-0085								
532	C21A	N6340T	N400BN	84-0086	[wfu AMARC 18Jan07, park code AACJ0013]							
533	C21A	N4289Y	N400BQ	84-0087								
534	C21A	N6307H	N400BU	84-0088	[wfu AMARC 22Jan07, park code AACJ0015]							
535	C21A	N4290C	N400BY	84-0089	(N61905)	[wfu AMARC 10Jan07 park code AACJ0008]						
536	C21A	N42905	N400BZ	84-0090	[wfu]							
537	C21A	N4290Y	N400CD	84-0091	N506LG							
538	C21A		N400CG	84-0092	[wfu AMARC 27Sep11]							
539	C21A		N400CJ	84-0093	[wfu]							
540	C21A		N400CK	84-0094								
541	C21A		N400CQ	84-0095								
542	C21A		N400CR	84-0096								
543	C21A		N400CU	84-0097	[w/o 02Feb02 Ellsworth AFB, SD]							
544	C21A		N400CV	84-0098	N865SP							
545	C21A		N400CX	84-0099								
546	C21A		N400CY	84-0100	N400CY	[wfu; instructional airframe Eastern Florida State College, Cocoa, FL]						
547	C21A		N400CZ	84-0101	N400CZ	[parted out by Dodson Int'l, Rantoul, KS]						
548	C21A		N400DD	84-0102	N400FQ	[parted out by Dodson Int'l, Rantoul, KS]						
549	C21A		N400DJ	84-0103								
550	C21A		N400DL	84-0104	[wfu AMARC 16Jan07, park code AACJ0012]							
551	C21A		N400DN	84-0105	[wfu AMARC 08Jan07, park code AACJ0004]							
552	C21A		N400DQ	84-0106								
553	C21A		N400DR	84-0107	[wfu AMARC 28Sep11]							
554	C21A		N400DU	84-0108	[wfu AMARC 12Jan07, park code AACJ0010]							
555	C21A		N400DV	84-0109								
556	C21A		N400DX	84-0110								
557	C21A		N400DY	84-0111	N38VM							
558	C21A		N400DZ	84-0112	[wfu AMARC 27Sep11]							
559	C21A		N400EC	84-0113	[wfu AMARC 24Jan07, park code AACJ0018]							

LEARJET 35

C/n	Series	Identities								
560	C21A	N400EE	84-0114	N21VN						
561	C21A	N400EF	84-0115	[wfu AMARC 12Jan07, park code AACJ0009]						
562	C21A	N400EG	84-0116	[wfu AMARC 24Jan07, park code AACJ0017]						
563	C21A	N400EJ	84-0117	[wfu AMARC 22Jan07, park code AACJ0016]						
564	C21A	N400EK	84-0118	[wfu; stored Springfield, OH]						
565	C21A	N400EL	84-0119	N400EL	[parted out by Dodson Int'l, Rantoul, KS]					
566	C21A	N400EM	84-0120							
567	C21A	N400EN	84-0121	[w/o 15Jan87 Alabama, LA]						
568	C21A	N400EQ	84-0122	[wfu AMARC 18Jan07, park code AACJ0014]						
569	C21A	N400ER	84-0123	N118MD						
570	C21A	N400ES	84-0124							
571	C21A	N400ET	84-0125							
572	C21A	N400EU	84-0126							
573	C21A	N400EV	84-0127	N508YV	[parted out by Dodson Int'l, Rantoul, KS]					
574	C21A	N400EX	84-0138	[wfu AMARC, park code AACJ0001]						
575	C21A	N400EY	84-0128	N499UM	[instructional airframe Seattle, WA]					
576	C21A	N400EZ	84-0129							
577	C21A	N400FE	84-0130	(N499YK)	N36SP					
578	C21A	N400FG	84-0131	[wfu; stored Springfield, OH]						
579	C21A	N400FH	84-0132	[wfu AMARC 26Jan07, park code AACJ0019]						
580	C21A	N400FK	84-0133	[wfu AMARC 08Jan07, park code AACJ0002]						
581	C21A	N400FM	84-0134	N72GH	[instructional airframe, Pittsburgh Institute of Aeronautics, PA]					
582	C21A	N400FN	84-0135							
583	C21A	N400FP	84-0136	[w/o 17Apr95 Alexandra City, AL]						
584	C21A	N400FQ	84-0141	[wfu AMARC 03Jan07, park code AACJ0003]		N400FQ	[reg'd 21Feb14, believed in error; cx 12Mar14]			
585	C21A	N400FR	84-0137							
586	C21A	N400FT	84-0142							
587	C21A	N400FU	84-0139							
588	C21A	N400FV	84-0140	N335KB						
589	A	N1087T	N8567K	PT-GAP	(N3215K)	[cx, CofA expired]				
590	A	N1451B	N35GA	N35KT	N969MC	N827CA	(N822SF)	N882SC		
591	A	N3803G	N8567Z	N72626	N500EX	N822CA	N822CP	N9ZM	N9ZB	N880Z
592	A	N3810G	N952GL	N45KK	N93LE					
593	A*	N40146	N32B	I-FLYG	N593LR	N593PN	VH-PPF	VH-LPJ		
594	A	N1088C	N72596	N7007V	(ZS-PTL)	(ZS-EFD)	OY-LJA	N410BD	N747BW	
595	A	N3815G	N85PM	N414KL	N95JN					
596	A	N1473B	N72612	N62WM	YV-850CP	N850MM	N826CA	N826CP	N352HS	
597	A	N39394	N8567R	N54GL	N597BL	N597JT	N355CA	N604S		
598	A	N39415	N8567T	PT-LGW						
599	A	N40144	N58GL	N367DA						
600	A	N823CA	N823CP	N995DP						
601	A	N3818G	China HY986							
602	A	N10873	China HY987 B-4187							
603	A	N1471B	China HY988 B-4188							
604	A	N1462B	N59GL	N604BL	N73LP	N604GS				
605	A	N1088D	N185HA	N35AS	N825CA	N925CA	YV526T			
606	A	N3803G	N1735J	N35PD	N3WP	N96GS				
607	A	N39399	N72614	PT-LIJ	N68MJ	D-CGFH				
608	A	N40162	N8567Z	N111SF	N14T	N96AX	ZS-IGP			
609	A	N4290J	N36NW	N788QC	XA-JRH	N609TF	N986SA			
610	A	N1473B	N101AR	N161MA	N610LJ	(N354GG)	(N354GE)			
611	A*	N39413	N622WG	N611TW	VH-ESM					
612	A	N3812G	N8568D	N2FU	N501TW	N551TW	N551HM	N36BP	D-CGFI	[w/o near Olsberg, Germany, 23Jun14 after mid-air collision
		with Luftwaffe Eurofighter]								
613	R-35A	N4289X	Brazil 6000							
614	A	N3815G	G-PJET	HB-VJC	G-SOVN	G-VIPS	G-OCFR	N335EA	N683EL	N683EF	D-CFOR	D-CGFO
615	R-35A	N1466B	N7260E	Brazil 6001						
616	A	N3807G	N8568Q	PT-LQF	N616LJ	N876CS	N876C	D-CEXP		
617	R-35A	N4289Z	Brazil 6002							
618	A	N10871	YU-BOL	SL-BAA	S5-BAA	N618DM	N618CF	N9099		
619	A	N4290K	N8568V	PT-POK						
620	A*	N1451B	I-KODM	VR-BNI	N232FX	XA-COI	N620EM	N500CG	N500CQ	XA-...
621	A	N1468B	N999TH	N999TN	PT-OFW	N242MT	PR-ABP			
622	A	N4290C	N7260H	N610R	N81MR					
623	A	N40149	N7260Q	Thailand B.TL12-1/30 60504		Thailand B.TL12-1/30 40207				
624	C21A	N39404	86-0374							
625	C21A	N4289Y	86-0375	N625BL	(N522AG)	N625CY				
626	A	N39398	N7261R	N35AJ	N711NF	C-GNPT	N335MG	(N385MG)	N21BK	
627	A	N4289U	N7260T	PT-LMY						
628	C21A	N3810G	86-0376	N628BL	N628WJ	CX-VRH	N628DC	N628GZ	LX-TWO	
629	C21A	N40144	86-0377							
630	A	N42905	N72630	N742E	N742P	N388PD				
631	VU-35A	N3818G	Brazil 2710	[converted to R-35AM aerial reconnaissance platform 2010/2011]						
632	VU-35A	N1461B	Brazil 2711	[converted to R-35AM aerial reconnaissance platform 2010/2011]						
633	VU-35A	N39416	Brazil 2712	[converted to R-35AM aerial reconnaissance platform 2010/2011]						
634	ZR	N1462B	I-EAMM	N626BM	[has Raisbeck modified wing set]					
635	A	N1471B	Thailand B.TL12-2/31 60505		Thailand B.TL12-2/31 40208		[w/o 08Non06 Nakhon Sawan, Thailand]			
636	VU-35A	N1476B	Brazil 2713							
637		[airframe not built]								
638	A/VU35A	N39412	Brazil 2714							
639	A/VU35A	N6317V	Brazil 2715							
640	A/VU35A	N3816G	N8568Y	Brazil 2716						
641	A/VU35A	N1087Y	N7261H	Brazil 2717						
642	A/VU35A	N1465B	N7262X	Brazil 2718						
643	A	N39418	G-LJET	(N35NK)	N643MJ	D-CGFJ				
644	A	N1088C	N1043B	PT-LLF	(N54SB)	C-GMMY	N893AC	C-GYFB		
645	A*	N43TR	N645AM							
646	A	N3812G	XA-UMA	N646EA	N717JB	N712JB	G-MURI	[w/o 2May00 Lyon-Satolas A/P, France; crash remains to Fort Lauderdale Executive, FL]		
647	A	N410RD	N915RB	N815RB	(N647TJ)	ZS-DJB	N335PR			
648	A	N1045J	N974JD	XB-LHS	N648JW	RP-C648	N648J	N97LE		
649	A*	N10870	HB-VJJ	N35QB	ZK-XVL	VH-LJA				
650	A*	N1022G	PT-LYF	N135MW	N650LR	N393SC				
651	A	HB-VJK	N405PC	N9RA*						
652	A	N6307H	N99FN	D-CURE	N652SA	N49AZ	N2KZ	N652KZ		
653	A	HB-VJL	LX-LAR							

LEARJET 35

C/n	Series	Identities									
654	A	N4290K	N633WW	N600LF	(N95EC)	(B-98183)	ZS-NSB	B-98183	N8189	N770BM	D-CGFN*
655	A	N1088A	N16FG	PT-MFR	N785JM	C-GMMA	N355GA	N655JH	YV523T	N655JH	
656	A*	N3810G	G-JETL	N335SB	N356JW	G-ZMED	D-CFOR				
657	A	N1473B	N1CA	N10AH							
658	A*	N39404	N573LP	N162EM	N77NJ	N592UA	[parted out by Alliance Air Parts, Oklahoma City, OK]				
659	A	N4290Y	N873LP	(N878LP)	N413LC	N776BG					
660	A	N1087Z	C-GLJQ	N660L	C-GLJQ	N421SV					
661	A	(N8888D)	N1268G	VH-PFA	[operated by Singapore AF as a target towing aircraft]						
662	A	G-NEVL	G-BUSX	N35UK	N27AX	N663TW					
663	A	N91480	D-CCCB								
664	A	N9130F	N117RJ	C-GRMJ	N640BA						
665	A	N5009T	N291K	N35UA	LV-BRT						
666		[airframe not built as this number is considered unlucky in the USA]									
667	A	N5018G	N91566	N135DE							
668	A	N5011L	N9168Q	N441PC							
669	A*	N5014F	N91452	OO-JBS	N7XJ	(N487LP)	A6-FAJ	N669LJ	N393CF	N893CF	C-GWFG
670	A	N5012K	N35UK	N599SC	OY-CCO	(HP-....)	HK-3949X	(N670WJ)	OY-CCO	N787LP	N987LP	N460SB
671	A*	N9141N	(ZS-NEX)	(ZS-NFS)	ZS-NFK	N671BA	LV-PLV	LV-WPZ	N671BX	N671TS	G-JMED	D-CTIL
672	A	N9140Y	N672DK	N45KK	XA-FMT	XB-GSM					
673	A	N5014F	N9173G	C-FBDH	C-GPDO	N835MC	9M-NOR	Malaysia M102-01			
674	A	N2601G	N22SF	N22SN	N900JE	N674LJ	LV-BIE				
675	A	N2602M	B-98181	[w/o 17Sep94, shot down in error while target-towing off coast of Taiwan]							
676	A	N5012Z	N35LJ	N235AC	N620MJ						

Production complete

LEARJET MODEL 36

* after the series letter or in the series column indicates the aircraft has been fitted with Avcom delta fins.

C/n	Series	Identities
001		N26GL [ff 09Jan73 as a model 26 c/n 26-001; used as development airframe for both the model 35 and 36] C-GBRW-X C-GBRW [has winglets in place of tip tanks; cx Apr97 to Montreal/St Hubert Aeronautical College painted as C-XPWC to celebrate its active life as a flying test bed with Pratt & Whitney Canada]
002		N362GL D-CMAR YV-T-ASG YV-161P YV-89CP (N2297G) N18AT D-CELA N3239A N84DM N84FN
003	*	N363GL N36TA N55CJ N361PJ
004	*	N1918W (D-CCAC) D-CCPD N50DT N180GC N54PA
005	*	LV-LOG N9108Z N905CK
006		(I-CRYS) HB-VEA D-CAFO D-CDFA [w/o 25Mar80 Libya]
007	*	N138GL N173JA N226CC SX-AHF VR-BHB N83DM N83FN
008	*	N20JA VR-BJD VR-BJO N84MJ N101AR (N701AR) N101AJ (N43A)
009		N2000M N704J N44GL N25CL N15CC N505RA N505HG
010	*	N50SF N45FG
011		PT-KQT N26MJ N26FN
012		N139GL VR-BFR N2267Z C-GBWD N666TB N36CW N222AW N55GH N712JE N547PA [code "AK"]
013	*	N352WC (N852WC) SE-DDH N3280E N3PC N13JE D-CBRD N71PG
014		N900Y N200Y VH-SLJ [wfu2015, Wagga Wagga, Australia]
015	*	N14CF N10FN
016	*	HB-VEE JY-AET F-GBGD N616DJ N12FN
017	*	N1010A N17LJ (N32JA) (N361PJ) N362PJ
018	A*	PT-KTU N418CA PT-ACC (N7379M) N418CA N779CM
019	A	N300CC N89MJ C-GLMK N718US N300DK N300DL C-GLAL N719JE N540PA N527PA
020	A	JY-AFC [w/o 21Sep77 Amman, Jordan]
021	A	N3524F I-AIFA [w/o 10Dec79 Forli, Italy]
022	A*	N761A N38WC N36PD N44EV N31GJ
023	A	N1871R N1871P N187MZ (N64FN) N767RA N6YY N56PA
024	A	N38D N978E C-FEMT
025	A	N774AB N730GL OE-GLP C-GVVB N500MJ (N98A) N800BL N32PA
026	A	(N762L) N762GL N23G C-GGPF N6617B N8U (N888TN) (N8UB) N1U N8UA N86BL
027	A*	N836GA N484HB N27MJ N16FN
028	A	N731GA N75TD N545PA [code "HI"]
029	A	(N79JS) HB-VFD N116MA
030	A	N71TP N74TP N360LS N36PJ (N36AX) N160GC
031	A	N20UC N20UG D-CFOX N20UG N62PG
032	A*	N40146 N745GL N22BM N36BP HB-VLK N950G (N16AJ) VH-CMS N132LJ
033	A	N762L [w/o 06Dec96 Stephenville, Newfoundland, Canada. Parted out by White Industries Inc, Bates City, MO]
034	A	N763R China HY985 B-4599
035	A	N3807G VH-BIB N266BS VH-BIB N71CK
036	A*	N1462B N610GE N36MJ N136DH
037	A	RP-C5128 N555WH C-GRJL C-FCLJ
038	A	N304E N15FN N548PA N700GG N363PJ
039	A	N217CS C-GSRN N4998Z N25PK N99RS
040	A	HB-VFV N902WJ N110PA N70UT N70UP (N444SC) (N442SC) N500SV N72AV N82GG
041	A	N79SF [w/o 08Jan88 Monroe, LA]
042	A	N39391 HB-VFS [w/o 23Sep95 Zarzaitine, Algeria]
043	A	N1010G N43LJ N53JA (N143JW) N432JW (N521JW) XB-JPX
044	A	N1010H N44LJ N54JA (N77JW) N286AB N70LJ
045	A	(N700MD) N900MD N13FN N546PA [w/o 03Dec02, Astoria, WA; parted out; cx Jun03]
046	A*	F-BKFB N4448Y N146MJ N17A
047	A	G-ZEIZ N2972Q N14CN N36SK OE-GMD N36PJ
048	A*	HB-VHF N3999B (N14FU) N2FU N24PT N3NP PT-WGM N32AJ D-CFGG
049	A	N661AA N136ST VH-SLF [wfu 2015, Wagga Wagga, Australia]
050	A	N3456L XA-RIA Mexico TP-105/XC-AA24 Mexico TP-105/XC-UJP
051	A	N4290J Peru 524/OB-1431
052	A	N1087T Peru 525/OB-1432
053	A	N39418 China HY984 B-4184
054	A/U36A	(N54GL) N1087Z Japan 9201
055	A	N10871 OE-GNL N365AS PP-JAA S9-CRH ZS-CRH N41GJ
056	A/U36A	N3802G Japan 9202 [w/o 21May03 Iwakuni AFB, Japan]
057	A	N39394 HB-VIF VH-JCX
058	A/U36A	N4290J Japan 9203 [w/o 28Feb91 Shikoku Island, Japan]
059	A/U36A	N1087Z Japan 9204
060	A/U36A	N1088A Japan 9205
061	A/U36A	N50154 N2601B Japan 9206
062	A*	N4291N D-CGFE
063	A*	N6340T N1048X D-CGFF

Production complete

LEARJET MODEL 40

C/n	Identities						
45-001	N45XL	N40LX	[converted from model 45 circa 2002 and ff as such on 31Aug02]				
2001	N40LJ	[ff 05Sep02] N401LJ					
2002	N40KJ	N789AH	N482ES	PR-JOF			
2003	N404MK	LQ-BFS					
2004	N40082	N605FX	N605BX				
2005	N40083	N606FX	M-LRJT	N657MP			
2006	N50111	D-CNIK	PR-WSB				
2007	N50126	N40PX	G-MOOO	N990JT	N64HT		
2008	N5013U	N2408	N99GK				
2009	N40LJ	CC-CMS					
2010	N50163	N46E	N46FE				
2011	N4001G	N51001	N411AJ				
2012	N607FX	N479JS					
2013	N5018G	XA-GRR					
2014	N608FX	N499GS					
2015	N40077	I-ERJG	OE-GGC				
2016	N40078	I-ELYS					
2017	N5009T	N502JM	N700KG				
2018	N5018G	OE-GGB	D-CGGB	N118AV	PP-ASV		
2019	N50111	G-FORN	I-FORR				
2020	N50153	PR-ONE					
2021	N5013U	N401EG					
2022	N5013Y	N609FX	N510GW				
2023	N50163	N521CH					
2024	N424LF	N40ML	I-YLFC	9H-CFL			
2025	N225LJ	N240RP					
2026	N5014E	OE-GVI	EC-JYY	N77CJ	XA-…		
2027	N50154	N40LJ	N610FX	N684JB	N116DJ		
2028	N40XR						
2029	N40073	N996AL	N998AL	[w/o 18Jun09 Fort Worth/Meacham, TX; parted out by Alliance Air Parts, Oklahoma City, OK]			N998AQ
2030	N40076	XA-SNI					
2031	N40085	RP-C3110					
2032	N5015U	N10SE					
2033	N404EL						
2034	N5018G	I-PARS	N151VA	PT-FRD			
2035	N40050	N1848T	N1348T	PR-PPG			
2036	N100HW						
2037	N237LJ	N611FX	N689JB	N119DJ			
2038	N22GM	N290GS					
2039	N612FX	N256MH	N120DJ				
2040	N5009V	(XA-GPE)	XA-CGF	N112DJ	PR-WNA		
2041	N614FX	[wfu Jan16; stored Addison, TX]					
2042	N256AH	N258AH	XA-PAR				
2043	N4001G	C-FMHA					
2044	N5016V	N140LJ	N232PH				
2045	N176CA	N88LJ					
2046	N4004Q	N40LJ	N773RS	XC-TJN			
2047	N616FX	N473BD	XA-RAB				
2048	N40077	N80169	PR-JBS	N586CC			
2049	N5012K	N140WW	N422KS	N239SR			
2050	N5015U	VP-BHT					
2051	N615FX						
2052	N784CC						
2053	N5018G	I-ERJJ	N253EC	N253RM*			
2054	N50111	G-MEET	XA-USP				
2055	N5010U	N55XR	N506KS				
2056	N411HC						
2057	N616FX	N200KJ					
2058	N71NF	N71NX	N219RB				
2059	N619FX	N695BD	I-GURU				
2060	N999EK						
2061	N5016Z	D-CLUX	N108JE				
2062	N4005Q	PT-XDN					
2063	N240WG	N740KG					
2064	N5000E	(OY-KVP)	"OY-KPV"	"N34AG"	N540LH	OY-KVP	
2065	N617FX	N356RR					
2066	N50154	N2758W					
2067	N618FX	XA-NJM					
2068	N5012G	PP-FMW	N286KR	N137BR			
2069	N24VP	N29RN	N29RE				
2070	N77HN						
2071	N40077	OY-ZAN	D-CLUZ	(D-CFAF)	D-CLOZ	N550VT	
2072	N4003K	N83JJ	N15UB	N25UB			
2073	N40083	N975DM					
2074	N40012	G-STUF	N268KR	N41UA			
2075	N75XR	N484CH	PR-MFX				
2076	N618FX						
2077	N5015U	XA-VFV	N951FM				
2078	N40079	I-GOCO					
2079	N40082	D-CVJP	OE-GVA	N427DC	PP-LRJ		
2080	N40076	D-CPDR	F-HPEB				
2081	N24VP	PR-DIB	(N288KR)				
2082	N619FX						
2083	N51054	N419ET	N412ET	N740KD			
2084	N40LJ	N65TP					
2085	N620FX						
2086	N4003W	PR-PTR					
2087	N40NB	N779CF					
2088	N288AS						
2089	N621FX						
2090	N4003K	N90XR					
2091	N5009T	D-CVJN	N431DC	OE-GHF			
2092	N426JK	N173DS					

LEARJET 40

C/n	Identities					
2093	N5016Z	D-CAHB	N880MS	PR-BCC		
2094	N40079	CS-TFO				
2095	N622FX	[wfu Jan16; stored Addison, TX]				
2096	N40083	OY-RED	LV-CJY			
2097	N40078	(D-CVJT)	OE-GVX	N480ES		
2098	N40043	N346CN	N346CM	N810JK		
2099	N623FX	[wfu Jan16; stored Addison, TX]				
2100	N959RP	(N959RB)				
2101	N152UT	VT-VSA	N152UT	N725BH		
2102	N4003K	G-HPPY	C-GLRP	PR-LJG*		
2103	N140HM					
2104	N624FX					
2105	N40085	N295SG	N296SG	(N998AL)	N4003L	PR-JEC
2106	N700MB					
2107	N50145	D-CGGC	N204PG	PP-CRV		
2108	N5009T	(G-RMPI)	N718EJ	N945EJ		
2109	N625FX	N77NR	N905ST			
2110	N50157	N556HD	N554HD			
2111	N40PD					
2112	N40050	OE-GXX				
2113	N40075	N477XR	N123AC			
2114	N40083	N663LB	PR-PVI			
2115	N5012Z	N115LJ				
2116	N625FX					
2117	N4004Q	(XA-LOA)	PP-CRC			
2118	N4008G	N289JP	N57MC			
2119	N40082	N119NJ	N300GF			
2120	(D-COIN)	N626FX	[wfu Jan16; stored Addison, TX]			
2121	N40081	(D-COIN)	N140EP	N24QT		
2122	N40162	N990WA				
2123	N4003W	N255AH	N256AH			
2124	N50126	(N627FX)	N403LS			
2125	N5016Z	N44LG				
2126	N5017J	N46MW				
2127	N5016V	N209MD				
2128	N5012H	N802AK				
2129	N785BC	[prototype Learjet 70]				
2130	N50185	N998AL	(N998AB)	N998NJ		
2131	N40075	N25TQ	N25QT			
2132	N51053	N641K	N341K			
2133	N40079	N49HM	PR-RNF	M-DMBP		

LEARJET 70

Although officially registered as Learjet 40s with c/ns following that model's sequence, Learjet 70s have also been allocated secondary c/ns by Learjet Inc as listed below. This second c/n has been painted on many (if not all) of the Learjet 70s built so far.

C/n	Identities			
2134	70-001	N40085	N9CH	
2135	70-002	N4001G	N356K	
2136	70-003	N50185	N959RC	
2137	70-004	N40162	N137LJ	N444KM
2138	70-005	N4002P	(N359K)	N352K
2139	70-006	N70NJ		
2140	70-007	N10870	N359H	N359K
2141	70-008	N5012H	N15UB	
2142	70-009	N4004Q	C-GTLP	
2143	70-010	N40050	N342K	
2144	70-011	N4001G	N998AB	N998AL
2145	70-012	N50153	C-GFFT	
2146	70-013	N98QC		
2147	70-014			
2148	70-015			
2149	70-016			
2150	70-017			
2151	70-018			
2152	70-019			
2153	70-020			
2154	70-021			
2155	70-022			
2156	70-023			
2157	70-024			
2158	70-025			
2159	70-026			
2160	70-027			

LEARJET MODEL 45

C/n	Identities							
001	N45XL	[ff 07Oct95]	N40LX	[converted to Model 40 circa 2002 qv]				
002	N45LJ	N452LJ	[instructional airframe, Wichita Area Technical College National Center for Aviation Training, KS]					
003	N453LJ	(N789H)	[to ground instruction airframe, Pima Community College, Tucson, AZ]					
004	N454LJ	[w/o 27Oct98 Wallops Island, VA]						
005	N455LJ	G-ZXZX						
006	N456LJ	ZS-OIZ	N456LM	N721CP	YV351T	N445BH	N45YF	
007	N457LJ	(ZS-JBR)	(ZS-BAR)	ZS-OPD	VH-EJK	(ZS-ITT)	TC-CMB	
008	N745E	N80RP	N458DP					
009	N984GC	N459LJ	N500CG	N395WB				
010	(D-CWER)	N41DP	N903HC	N311BP	N811BP	N556JP		
011	N741E	N741F	N89RP	N459DP				
012	N5009V	N412LJ	(OE-...)	D-COMM	D-CMLP	N450TJ		
013	N5010U	N413LJ	D-CEWR	D-CFWR	N45LR			
014	N708SP	(N202JR)						
015	N31V	N30AB	N781RX					
016	N743E	N743F	N74SG	XA-WNG	N797CH	XA-UVA	N716SC	N607BF
017	(D-CWER)	N417LJ	D-CESH	D-CSMS	M-CSMS			
018	N418LJ	OO-LFS	D-CDOC					
019	N56WD	N45LJ	C-GCMP	(N.....)	C-GLRJ	N442LF	VT-CRA	
020	N5000E	HB-VMA	N45NP	C-GVVZ				
021	N5009T	HB-VMB	CS-TFI	N440JJ				
022	N5012G	PT-TJB	N453BL	N345RL	N845RL	C-GSWQ		
023	N740E	(N740SG)	N353AP	N45HM				
024	N145ST	C-FBCL	C-FVSL	D-CNMB				
025	N742E	N742F	(N354AP)	(N909DD)	N200KP			
026	N405FX	N405BX	XC-HIE					
027	N156PH	N156PB	N445SB	N838TH	N1250			
028	N5014E	HB-VMC	XC-VMC	[w/o 04Nov08 Mexico City, Mexico]				
029	N5013Y	9V-ATG	N290LJ	N170LS				
030	N5012H	N157PH	N157PB					
031	N5016V	9V-ATH	N310LJ					
032	N4FE	N932JC	N774MC					
033	N50162	9V-ATI	VH-SQD	T7-SCI				
034	N45FE	N454LP	XA-VYC					
035	N5013U	9V-ATJ	VH-SQM	A4O-..				
036	N345WB	I-FORU						
037	N50145	OE-GDI	G-CPRI	ZS-CJB				
038	N454AS	(N454RR)	N14FE	N14BX	XA-RIU			
039	N456AS	N15FE	(N390AB)	N45FE	N238LM			
040	(N145MC)	N68PC	N68PQ	N501CG	N930TC			
041	N541LJ	C-GPDQ	C-GPDB					
042	N10R	N917LH	XA-JAO					
043	D-CRAN	N45VB						
044	D-CLUB	N888CX	4O-MNE					
045	N4545	PR-SZA						
046	ZS-PTL	ZS-OLJ	ZS-BAR	ZS-OXB	N136MA	N336UB	XB-RMT	XA-RMT
047	N158PH	N158PD	N206CK	[2000th Learjet built]				
048	PT-XLR							
049	N711R							
050	N16PC	N16PQ	LV-BOU					
051	N145KC	N927SK						
052	N5011L	ZS-DCT	N745SA	N233MK				
053	N685RC	N3211Q	N1904S					
054	N345MA							
055	N63MJ	N45LR	G-JRJR	G-OLDF	G-GOMO	G-PFCT		
056	N196PH	VH-LJX						
057	N75TE	N83TN	N83TZ	XA-SUK	XA-UVW			
058	N50111	RP-C1944	N660HC	N237DM	N55DG			
059	N50153	VP-CVL	N590JC	ZS-PNP				
060	N1MG	N459LC						
061	N111KK	N443SL						
062	N512RB	N543CM						
063	N10J	N10JY						
064	N800MA	N800UA	EC-ILK	I-AVND				
065	N100KK	N100KZ						
066	N94CK	D2-FFX						
067	N5087B	XA-LRX	XA-QUE	N220AR	XA-PRA			
068	I-ERJD	OE-GJC	N145RG					
069	N50157	SU-MSG	D2-EBN					
070	N50163	LX-IMS	N450JC					
071	N145K	N145KL	N989PA	N103EZ				
072	N5016Z	I-ERJC	N720CC	N720GB				
073	N65U	N66SG						
074	N815A	N740TF						
075	N450BC							
076	N245K	N2451Y	N988PA	N881MJ				
077	N5018G	PT-XVA	N770DS	XA-AIM	N273LM	N476CA		
078	N5016Z	N116AS						
079	N5FE	N100GY						
080	N42HP	N45UJ	N451DJ	(N451DZ)	N45EJ			
081	N76TE	N145GM	N30TL	PT-FLE				
082	N40082	N1HP	N473YH	N184R	N95VS			
083	N5013Y	OY-LJG	ZS-TJS					
084	N5009V	HB-VML	OE-GVM	HB-VML	N845SC	[dbr in refuelling incident at Bangor, ME, 23Dec14; parted out by Alliance Air Parts, Oklahoma City, OK]		
085	N454CG	C-FPBX						
086	N4001G	N386K	C-GMRO					
087	N645HJ	N64HH						
088	N454MK	C-FMGL	C-FLLH	N484VL	N910LJ			
089	N406FX	N406BX	XA-EFM					
090	N407FX	N452CJ						
091	N408FX	(N408BX)	N451WM	[parted out by Deer Valley Aviation Parts, Wilmington, DE]				
092	N5016V	ZS-LOW	(ZS-PPR)	ZS-PDG	D2-SRR			
093	N5014F	N450TR	(PT-XLF)	I-ERJC	[w/o 01Jun03 Milan-Linate, Italy]			

LEARJET 45

C/n	Identities						
094	N300JE	N800WC	N49CJ	LQ-CPS			
095	N409FX	N409F	N786CC				
096	N5009T	C-GDMI	N450JG	C-FNJT			
097	N5017J	D-CMSC					
098	N6FE	N450HA					
099	(N545RS)	N7FE	N745TT				
100	N50145	N45LJ	RP-C1958	N345BH			
101	N410FX	N410BX	N22AX				
102	N411FX	N411BX	N810YS	XA-EEA	XA-UUB		
103	N412FX	(N412F)	N720MC	N45XT			
104	N40012	OH-IPJ	N450BK	3D-BIS	4O-SEV		
105	N105LJ	N397AT	(N17LJ)	N89ZZ	N99NJ		
106	N145XL						
107	N145CG	(N145CM)	N762EL				
108	N50154	N313BW	N313BH				
109	N60PC	N451CF	N945HC				
110	N4002P	N222MW					
111	N414FX	N414BX	XA-BFX	XC-HIF			
112	N415FX	CN-TJB					
113	N416FX	N124BP	N869DL				
114	N417FX	N318SA					
115	N90UG	(N405MW)	N45MW				
116	N50111	OY-LJJ	A6-MED	OY-LJJ	N116WE	PP-CPN	
117	N40081	ZS-DCA					
118	N50163	N5XP	N75XP				
119	N5016V	N316SR	N1RB	N145LR			
120	N418FX	N418FA	N45TU				
121	N316SR	(N666BG)	N45HF				
122	N945FD						
123	N454LC	N484LC	N21AX	N750CR			
124	N4003Q	G-OLDL	N124AV	G-JANV	N526CF		
125	N419FX	N145MW	N145MN	PP-JAW			
126	N420FX	C-FXHN	C-GMCP				
127	N421FX	N421FY	XA-ALF				
128	N10NL						
129	N4003W	N9CH	N455DG				
130	N583FH	N4001G	(ZS-OSP)	N418MN			
131	N444MW	N218JL					
132	N132LJ	N889CA					
133	N645KM	N183CM					
134	N4004Q	N423FX	N423FA	N751JC			
135	N4004Y	N422FX	N423DC	XA-UJR			
136	N45BA	(N136LJ)	N583PS	N883BS	N654AT	N659AT	
137	N45AJ	N800AB					
138	N5018G	G-OLDJ	N138AX	G-SOVB			
139	N45VL	XA-UAG	XA-EMM				
140	N40050	XA-AED	N345SV				
141	N142HC	N142HQ	N858MK				
142	N145SB	(N450DS)	CC-ADC	N129FS	N188SG		
143	N4005Q	N145GS	N334AF	N384AF	N917BE		
144	N5011L	D-CEMM	CS-TLW				
145	N50145	N421FX	N942FK				
146	N424FX	N460DC	PR-OPF				
147	N425FX	N425LW	N44NJ				
148	N40075	N8084R	D-CDEN	OE-GAR	M-ROMA	N148LJ	N33NJ
149	N451CL	N451GL	N904HD				
150	N245KC	N348K	(N848K)	N546DH			
151	N345K	N345FM					
152	N3013Q	N5014E	VH-CXJ				
153	N30137	C-GCMP	N302KR	N345FF			
154	N3008P	N886CA	N918EG				
155	N145MC	N882CA					
156	N3017F	G-OLDC	N156AV	C-FLRJ	N495EC		
157	N545RA	N341K	N371K	PR-LEB			
158	N3019T	LX-DSL	I-DFSL	D-CPSG	N523BM	N979DR	
159	N5001J	N828CA					
160	N455PM	N455DE	N863CA	N863LB			
161	N3000S	G-OLDR	N161AV	G-SOVC	SE-RKY	D-CSOS	
162	N426FX	N426LW	PR-BFM	N455EA			
163	N427FX	N427BX	5N-BGR	C-FZAU	N45NY		
164	N428FX	PR-OSF					
165	N429FX	XA-SEG					
166	N430FX	(N430BX)	(PR-MIS)	C-GEJD			
167	N5012V	G-GMAA					
168	N50088	VH-PFS					
169	N5013D	N77HN	N332K	N424TG			
170	N5013E	(XA-SKY)	N50154	N45UP	N45VS		
171	N171DP	N342K	(N322K)	XA-PBX			
172	N70PC	N1893N					
173	N900P	N906P					
174	N45HC	N887SG					
175	N328RR	N30SF	N41TF				
176	N5016S	N45TK	N176TK	XA-IKE			
177	N431FX	N695GL	PP-MPJ				
178	N50207	XA-JMF					
179	N5023U	N863CA	N541AL	N45MR	N179MR		
180	N880LJ	N345RL					
181	N5024E	ZS-PTL	(ZS-FUL)	(ZS-AJN)	V5-TTO		
182	N50248	N345AW					
183	N5025K	N511WP	C-GHMP				
184	N45VP	N866CA					
185	N273LP						
186	N158EC						
187	N5030J	N146XL					
188	N5018G	N21BD	XA-UJZ				

LEARJET 45

C/n	Identities						
189	N5030N	N800MA	D-CSUL	XA-CMA			
190	N41PC	N41PQ	N787EJ	N988RC			
191	N158EC	N191LJ	XA-LVS				
192	N433FX	PP-MMX					
193	N434FX	N865CA					
194	N5040W	ZS-YES	ZS-ULT				
195	N5040Y	VH-SQR	N113RX	N713RX*			
196	N50353	N473LP	N531AC				
197	N432FX	PP-JLY	N197EC				
198	N5048K	N45UG	N229BK				
199	N545EC	N1925P	N1925B				
200	N451ST	HK-5107					
201	N473LP	N452ST	(N451SC)	N617RX			
202	N5048Q	N445N					
203	N145AR						
204	N5010U	N204MK	VH-ZZH	N45NP			
205	N5011L	N5052K	N88AF				
206	N45UG	N5042A	N45AX	N445AX	N445RM		
207	N5000E	VH-SQV	N131RX	N431RX*			
208	N5009V	N5050G	N715CG	N719CG	N615CG		
209	N435FX	(N435FA)	N300JC	N209KM	XA-CFX		
210	N5009V	N866RA	N29RE	N29ZE	XA-ALA	N233TM	N1TK
211	N50145	N50490	N300AA	N300AQ	(N299BB)	M-MRBB	
212	N50111	N434FX	N599TA				
213	N50126	D-CEWR	G-MUTD	G-RWGW	M-RWGW	C-FHCW	
214	N214LF	N29SM	N555CK				
215	N5018G	N822CA	N352K	N852K			
216	N5016V	C-GHCY	N359K	(N559K)	N777QL	(N977AR)	
217	N5016Z	N1RL	N400	N401Q	N217MJ	(N977AR)	
218	N50163	N310ZM	N451JC	ZS-OPY			
219	N4003K	ZS-BAR	ZS-OPR				
220	N40077	N825CA					
221	N823CA						
222	N673LP	N673LB	N826CA				
223	N40081	(D-CTAN)	C-FNRG	C-GPKS	N338K	ZS-LRJ	
224	N822CA	N822GA	N77702	C-GQPM			
225	N436FX	N518GS	N558GS	N90GS			
226	N40085	I-ERJE	N126EC				
227	N437FX	N721BS	N821BS	N903RL	N70AE	N645FD	
228	N5012Z	ZS-LOW	V5-LRJ				
229	N40079	N159EC					
230	N4008G	N451N					
231	N40073	N30PC	N30PF	N145HC	N145GP	XA-ALN	
232	N40076	N45XR	LV-ARD				
233	N5000E	N45KX					
234	N5009T	Ireland 258					
235	N50145	N30PC	N30PQ	XA-JPG			
236	N5018G	N125GW	N66DN	G-LLOD	XA-SAA		
237	N5017J	N45QG	N44QG	N43QG	PP-HSI	N556CG	
238	N570AM	(N577CC)					
239	N45LJ	C-GJCY					
240	N5016Z	(D-CTAN)	N50579	N9FE	N45ZR		
241	N241LJ						
242	N4003W	N45SY	PR-OTA				
243	N4004Q	G-IOOX	OE-GFF	XA-ZZZ			
244	N5009V	N545K					
245	N5010U	N745K					
246	N5012G	XA-HFM	N1019K	XA-SAP			
247	N50154	N3AS	N401SF				
248	N4004Y	N48TF	(N83TR)	N48TE	LV-CAR		
249	N40075	C-GLRS	M-GLRS	N435DC			
250	N40050	OO-LFN	ZS-CVU				
251	N40073	N145XR	XA-MVG	N45VG	N918DG		
252	N40076	N272BC	N876BC	N272BC	N876BC	XA-...	
253	N4008G	N45NM					
254	N729SB	N728SB	LV-BXD				
255	N40081	C-FSDL	C-GUSM				
256	N5011L	B-3988	N97XR	XA-GTP			
257	N5012H	N555VR					
258	N5015U	N45LJ	N395BC				
259	N40PC	N451LJ	(N778T)				
260	N745TC						
261	N5010U	N451BW					
262	N50126	VH-VVI	N45AU	VH-VVI			
263	N50157	N263RA	N263MR				
264	N5016V	N910BD	N916BD	N816BD	N1899	N189PP	
265	N5017J	G-OLDT	N630BB	P4-BFS			
266	N40012	"LX-IMS" [wrongly painted at completion centre]			LX-IMZ	(D-CLHM)	D-CHLM	N787CH
267	N4002P	N451HC	N219JL				
268	N5009V	N145K					
269	N4003W	N245K					
270	N4004Q	(ZS-FUL)	C-FBLJ	C-FXYN	N820AT		
271	N4004Y	N45XR	N435FX	XB-NHM	XA-EXE	XA-QLO	
272	N40043	N288CB					
273	N4005Q	N183TS					
274	N40075	N274CZ	N728VG				
275	N40082	C-FRYS					
276	N40084	N88WV					
277	N40086	N912BD	N918BD	N818BD			
278	N63WR	(N63WL)	N63WJ				
279	N4008G	N45LJ	N279AJ	[w/o 03Jan09 Telluride, CO; parted out by Alliance Air Parts Oklahoma City, OK]			
280	N40079	G-CDNK	CS-DTL	N145JP	M-RBIG		
281	N5012H	N617BD	N917BD	N817BD	XA-JRS		
282	N456Q	N45QQ					
283	N4DA						

LEARJET 45

C/n	Identities					
284	N40078	XA-ARB				
285	N5012Z	N300AA				
286	N50126	G-CDSR	CS-DTM	VH-LJQ		
287	N5013Y	CS-TLT	F-HACP	(D-CBCP)	9H-BCP	
288	N5014F	C-FBCL	C-GKDT	N547LF	N651AY	
289	N5013U	N68PC	N68PQ	N840JM		
290	N45BZ	VT-TRI				
291	N4002P	OO-EPU	N291LJ			
292	N4003W	JA01GW	N98XR	N273TA	N852BA	N95AX*
293	N45XR	(N694SC)	TG-ABY	N45HD		
294	N5014E	G-OLDW	G-IZIP	N595LA		
295	N4004Y	XA-UFB				
296	N4003K	N454LC	N484LC	N118RK		
297	N50154	(N145CG)	N145CM			
298	N5000E	N191TD				
299	N453ST	N445WF				
300	N145AP					
301	N45KJ	N996BP	N45VA			
302	N4008G	JA02GW	N99XR	CS-TFQ		
303	N40043	C-FANS	N303LJ			
304	N40086	N400	N4009	N90RZ	(N473AC)	N117WH
305	N40073	N45XR	N808KS	ZS-KAA	T7-KAA	
306	N5009T	OY-OCV	M-EOCV	N306AV	(N245LH)	
307	N425G					
308	N436FX	N415CL	ZS-OPM	LX-LAA		
309	N436FX	LV-BXV				
310	N5014F	N345K				
311	N40078	G-OLDK	G-IZAP	G-XJET		
312	N575AG	N808AK	PR-PAK	N808AK		
313	N45KH					
314	N74PT					
315	N437FX					
316	N50145	AP-BHY				
317	N438FX	N605SE	N87SK			
318	N45LJ	(N45XR)	N196CT	N797ES	N793ES	
319	N16PC	N451XR	YV3193			
320	N452A	PR-CAO				
321	N4002P	ZS-OPN	LX-EAA			
322	N5011L	N313BW				
323	N50157	N125BW				
324	N50126	N12VU				
325	N40085	N390GG	Mexico 3912			
326	N50126	N507FG	XB-GTH			
327	N50153	N726EL	N816LP	N526EL	5N-LDM	
328	N40081	F-HCGD	G-HCGD	N87AX		
329	N5012K	N454JF	PR-CSM			
330	N5009V	N45XT	N2HP	N36GL		
331	N40084	N583PS				
332	N45XR	N445TG				
333	N438FX					
334	N4003Q	N445SE				
335	N435HH					
336	N40073	N45YH	4X-CYH	M-EANS	N55EP	
337	N10J					
338	N45TK	N46TK	N45TQ	N45KV	XA-ABD	
339	N454N					
340	N5014F	N300JQ	N300JC	N922KM	N657PP	
341	N439FX					
342	N5011L	ZS-OPO	D-CDRF	LX-ONE		
343	N45HG					
344	N607FG	N196AT				
345	N5017J	N45MR	(N45MX)	Peru 526		
346	N440FX					
347	N40050	D-CINS				
348	N4005Q	N744E				
349	N45HK					
350	N50153	5N-BLW				
351	N60PC	N351XR	N392DL			
352	N988MC					
353	N903BT	PP-SCE	N903BT			
354	N40077	N135CG				
355	N4008G	N45XP				
356	N745E					
357	N441FX					
358	N40081	5N-DAL				
359	N710R					
360	N5012H	C-FMGL	N249TX	N80AE		
361	N45LJ	N44QG	N547LF	N505BC		
362	N40075	C-GLYS	N251TX	N119GM		
363	N453A					
364	N442FX	N442FP*				
365	N5XP	ZS-SGU				
366	N20FE	N301KR	N366LV			
367	N741E					
368	N4003W	EI-WFO	N350AP	[prototype Learjet 75]		
369	N40082	ZS-AJD				
370	N4005Q	N743E				
371	N443FX	N21AX	N31AX	N654AT		
372	N5009V	4O-BBB	D-CRBE	SE-RMO		
373	N5013U	N984XR				
374	N5014F	VP-BSF	M-ABEU			
375	N4003L	G-SNZY	N24AX	N256TT		
376	N4002P	N145GR	N145GM	N15CF		
377	N50163	N54AX	N45AX			
378	N444FX					

C/n	Identities					
379	N50154	N379LJ				
380	N45XR	N774CC	N729JM	N729JV	N818AF	
381	N5010U	N45XR	RP-C8338	N296JA		
382	N40073	CS-TFR				
383	N5016V	N176MG	PR-VPO	N91FG	N145PJ	
384	N5012H	N694LP	N745KD			
385	N5015U	XA-HUR				
386	N545CG					
387	N41PC	N325PT				
388	N40078	LV-BTO				
389	N389CG	YV2565				
390	N390CG	YV2567				
391	N40086	G-OSRL				
392	N40144	N45LJ	N81FJ			
393	N40146	N93XR	N504WV	N245FH*		
394	N40043	(N45LJ)	N818CH	N918DG	N145VG	
395	N40149	D-CLMS				
396	N396GC	YV1118				
397	N40079	(N445FX)	N458A	N192TD		
398	N398CG	N818CH	N694SH	N5014E	LX-JAG	
399	N50145	(N545K)	N545KS	N32AA		
400	N40085	N145MW				
401	N50111	N848CA	N848AG			
402	N10873	(N745K)	N26QT	N945K		
403	N40012	N245CM				
404	N4001G	OO-KJD	G-DDDJ	N961AS		
405	N5015U	(N451K)	N474TC			
406	N40149	(N452K)	N624EC	N821LC		
407	N5011L	N359JR	YV2670	YV2734		
408	N4005Q	C-FVSL	N286KR	N960AS		
409	N40077	(N453K)	N667MC			
410	N940K	N94CK				
411	N40082	N411VE	N45TK	N451SD		
412	N5010U	N309KC	PT-SAF			
413	N40012	"N45XR"+	[+ fake marks N45XR worn in NBAA static display Atlanta/DeKalb-Peachtree, GA, 19-21Oct10]		N451A	
414	N4001G	N414VE	N414VF	N45RR		
415	N40162	N415VE	YV2716			
416	N5012G	C-FBCL	N590CH	N450FC		
417	N5014E	N30PC				
418	N4002P	N411FG				
419	N4003K	N454LC				
420	N50157	N511FG				
421	N5009V	C-FSDL	N589CH	N5015U	M-ABGV	
422	N40073	PR-HVN				
423	N40144	N70GM	N45XR	N545AR	N808W	
424	N5018L	N424VE	YV2738			
425	N10872	N425VE	YV2739			
426	N5012H	N681P				
427	N5016V	N98AS	N3AS			
428	N4003L	N46TQ	N46TK	N452SD*		
429	N4004Q	N999LB	N399LB	N121GZ		
430	N5012K	N618CW				
431	N5015U	N28QT				
432	N50154	N70PC				
433	N5010U	LV-CVQ				
434	N50157	N34XR	C-GCMP			
435	N5016Z	N45LD	N916BD	N845BA	N501KT	
436	N5017J	N45MX	N528JJ			
437	N4002P	N437LJ	N422AJ			
438	N4003K	HB-VDW				
439	N50111	N826EP				
440	N40050	LV-CYQ				
441	N40076	N2476	N2426			
442	N40078	N104DN	N925ST			
443	N40082	N443LJ	N21AX			
444	N40144	AP-BKP				
445	N40149	N445FD	N483SC			
446	N10871	[Learjet 75 development a/c]		N446LJ		
447	N50185	N45GH				
448	N40084	N365LP				
449	N5009V	N986BL				
450	N5011L	N917BD	N846BA	N131JX		
451	N5012H	N925MW				
452	N50126	N247MX				
453	N5016V	N68PC				
454	N5009T	N918BD	N849BA	N5015U	M-ABJA	
455	N5012Z	N445FD				

LEARJET 75

Although officially registered as Learjet 45s with c/ns following that model's sequence, Learjet 75s have also been allocated secondary c/ns by Learjet Inc as listed below. This second c/n has been painted on many (if not all) of the Learjet 75s built so far.

C/n	Identities					
456	75-001	N50145	N157MW			
457	75-002	N5013Y	N457LJ	XA-MBU		
458	75-003	N575AR				
459	75-004	N5015U	N353K			
460	75-005	N40043	N999LB			
461	75-006	N40081	N461LJ	N75FP		
462	75-007	N5014F	N354K			
463	75-008	N5017J	C-FMGL			
464	75-009	N5013U	N1845T	N1848T		
465	75-010	N40012	C-GLYS			
466	75-011	N40073	C-FVSL			
467	75-012	N5012G	C-FBCL			
468	75-013	N10872	C-FSDL			
469	75-014	N40079	N984BH			
470	75-015	N5016Z	N19GR			
471	75-016	N5000E	N366CM	N346CM		
472	75-017	N5009T	N228H	N2HP		
473	75-018	N5009V	N475JT			
474	75-019	N50111	N455SC			
475	75-020	N5012Z	N275DE			
476	75-021	N50126	V5-RON			
477	75-022	N5014E	N60PL	N60PC		
478	75-023	N5010U	N977RJ			
479	75-024	N5016V	(N445FX)	N470FX		
480	75-025	N10873	N495RJ			
481	75-026	N5011L	N26QT			
482	75-027	N50157	N482LJ	XA-MBD		
483	75-028	N4003K	N101KK			
484	75-029	N4003W	N342SP			
485	75-030	N4005Q	N752R			
486	75-031	N40076	N63WG	N63WR		
487	75-032	N40082	N178TM			
488	75-033	N40077	F-HINC			
489	75-034	N40078	N100SA	N991GS	N800CH	
490	75-035	N4008G	SP-AAW			
491	75-036	N50163	OE-GEC			
492	75-037	N5016Z	N492LJ	XA-MBT		
493	75-038	N5009V	XA-SKA			
494	75-039	N5009T	9H-DDJ			
495	75-040	N5000E	N16PC			
496	75-041	N5018G	N877W			
497	75-042	N5012K	N175MX			
498	75-043	N50145	N333KK	N111KK		
499	75-044	N50111	N504CR			
500	75-045	N5012Z	N471FX			
501	75-046	N5013U	N472FX			
502	75-047	N4002P	N473FX			
503	75-048	N5013Y	N751LJ			
504	75-049	N5014E	N75LY			
505	75-050	N5014F	N812BR			
506	75-051	N50154	N474FX			
507	75-052	N40083	N45HC	N46F		
508	75-053	N5011L	N475FX			
509	75-054	N5010U	(XA-RAN)+	[+ ntu marks worn at the factory]	XA-VRM	
510	75-055	N40079	N300JC			
511	75-056	N4003K	N476FX			
512	75-057	N4003Q	N234TG	N176TG		
513	75-058	N4003L	RP-C629			
514	75-059	N50126	N477FX			
515	75-060	N5017J	N40PC			
516	75-061	N5012H	N478FX			
517	75-062	N50157	N912BD	N917BD		
518	75-063	N4003W	N918DD	N918BD		
519	75-064	N5016V	N1878C			
520	75-065	N4004Q	N916DD			
521	75-066	N4004Y	XA-MBC			
522	75-067	N40043	XA-MBS			
523	75-068	N4005Q	N72NF	N71NF		
524	75-069	N40075	XA-MBO			
525	75-070	N5021G	N282TA	N273TA		
526	75-071	N40076	XA-UXC			
527	75-072	N40050	XA-UXD			
528	75-073	N40073	N753A			
529	75-074					
530	75-075	N40078	C-GAJG			
531	75-076	N4008G				
532	75-077	N40081				
533	75-078	N40082	N173DX			
534	75-079	N40084				
535	75-080	N40085				
536	75-081	N40086	N75LJ			
537	75-082	N10870				
538	75-083	N10871				
539	75-084	N40077				
540	75-085	N10872				
541	75-086	N10873				
542	75-087	N40144				
543	75-088	N40146				
544	75-089	N40149				
545	75-090	N40162				

LEARJET 75

C/n	Identities	
546	75-091	
547	75-092	N50185
548	75-093	N5000E
549	75-094	
550	75-095	
551	75-096	
552	75-097	
553	75-098	
554	75-099	
555	75-100	

LEARJET MODEL 55

C/n	Series	Identities											
001	60	N551GL	[model 55 prototype converted to 55C prototype]		N551DF		[converted to Model 60 prototype]		N60XL		[cx Sep96; wfu]		
002		N552GL	[given new c/n 55-139A on conversion to 55C standards (qv); cx Apr91]										
003		N553GP	N162GA	N553DJ	(N553GJ)	N612EQ	YV487T	YV2904					
004		N90E	N50L	N24JK	N24CK	D-CLIP	(N500FA)	N155DD	N155PJ	N728MG	YV2868		
005		N40ES	N128VM	N550CS	(N94TJ)	N440DM	N440BM	N999CM					
006		N113EL	N212JP	N126EL	N355DB	N228PK	N427TL	N655TR					
007		N41ES	I-KILO	[w/o 04Apr94 San Pablo Airport, Seville, Spain; remains to Atlanta Air Salvage, Griffin, GA]									
008		N551SC	N322GC										
009		N42ES	N55SJ	HB-VIB	N955FD	N955MD	N955LS	N559BC	N800LJ				
010		N57TA	[w/o 13Nov81 Waterkloof AFB, S Africa]										
011		N37951	(N57TA)	N411GL	N574W	D-CREW	N200BA	ES-PVV	LY-LRJ	SE-RCK	D-CMAX	[wfu Nurnberg, Germany]	
012		N55GH	N23G	N104BS	N48HC	N85XL	N666TV	N135GL					
013		N10872	(D-CCHS)	OE-GNK	N3238K	PT-LEL	N82679	(N519AC)	(N155AJ)	(D-CEWR)	D-CUTE	N82679	D-CUTE	N155SB
		N550JB	YV598T										
014		N40144	N90BS	N55KC	XA-PIL	N550RH	N155MP	(N554EM)	N455EM	N551CG	N1CG	N441CG	N303PM	N308PM
		N52LJ	YV....										
015		(YV-41CP)	N39413	HB-VGV	N515DJ	N550LJ	D-CION	N27DD	N551MF				
016		N646G	N717EP	N717EB	(N116GL)								
017		N760AC	N760AQ	D-CCGN									
018		N39E	N599EC	N797CS	N822MC	N805PC							
019		YV-41CP	N141SM	C-GSWP									
020		N720M	N20DL	N57B	N8GT	N123LC	N35PF	N55NY					
021		N3794B	N700TG	EI-BSA	I-LOOK	N619MJ	(N721GS)	N211GS					
022		N64WM	VR-BOL	VP-BOL	N155GM	N712MC	N414TB						
023		N3796B	N7784	N110ET	(N236PJ)	[parted out by Alliance Air Parts, OK]							
024		HB-VGZ	N224DJ	HB-VGZ	N900FA	(N54NW)	N824CC						
025		N236R	N57PM	N57FM	N92MG	N979RD	YV....						
026		N8565H	N55HD	N21VB	D-CILY	(N96AF)	N421QL	(N321GL)	N318JH	N1324B	N285DH		
027		N3796X	OE-GKN	N3796X	N123LC	B-3980	N227A	B-3980	N59HJ	[parted out by Florida Jet Parts, Fort Lauderdale, FL]			
028		N3794C	PT-LDR	N3794C	PT-LOF	N7244W	(N53HJ)	N556GA	N556HJ	N515CY			
029		N4CP	D-CLIP	N29DJ	N10CP	PT-OHU	N10CP	N82JA	N100VA	N29NW	(N55PJ)	N915RT	
030		N986WC	N959WC	N117WC	N55LJ	(N155CD)	N122LX						
031		YV-12CP	YV1794										
032		N75TP	(N72TP)	N71TP	N81CH	N11TS	N83SD	N183SD	N255UJ	N125LR	XA-UCI		
033		N96CE	N960E	N917S	N414RF	N155CS	(VR-CJA)	VR-CML	PT-OOW	N38JA	(N377JW)	(N77JW)	N971EC	N398AC
		N355UJ	N355RM										
034		N3795Y	D-CARX	N84DJ	D-CLUB	N77JW	N37JA	(N234LC)	(N334JW)	N123LC	N550TC		
035		N115EL	(N100GU)	N1968A	N127EL	D-CVIP	N97AF	C-GPCS	VP-CUC	N816MC	VP-CTY	N60GD	
036		N3803G	N555GL	N81CH	N76AW	N81CH	N236JW	N155HM	N723CC				
037		N41CP	N86AJ	PT-OBR	N53HJ								
038		N551HB	N50AF	N666TK									
039		N39418	N770JM	N97J	VR-BQF	N339BC	N539JM	N399RL					
040		N3802G	HZ-AM11	HZ-AM2	N426EM	N55HK	N554CL						
041		N401JE	N155PJ	N41EA	N550RH	(HP-....)	HK-4016X	N141FM	N550LJ	N802GJ	N17LJ	N923AL	N928AL
042		N1462B	N3796U	N160TL	D-CMTM	N575GH							
043		N5543G	N785B	(N500JC)	N500JW	N30AF	N430HM	(N455EC)	N83WM	YV....			
044		N3797C	PT-LHR										
045		N1451B	HB-VHK	EC-DSI	VR-BHV	EC-DSI	(N90583)	N49PE	(N49PD)	I-AGER	N550AK	(N123LC)	[cx 15Nov14, CofR
		expired]											
046		N23HB	(N13HB)	N3HB	N55HL	N855PT							
047		N600C											
048		(N734)	N3796Z	VH-LGH	N73TP	N67RW	PT-OBS	N558AC	N558HJ	N831JP			
049		N6317V	N3796C	D-CCHS	N150MS								
050		N4289X	D-CARP	(HB-...)	(N122JD)	OY-FLK	N220JC	(N552BA)	(N55UJ)	[w/o 23Jun00 Boca Raton, FL]			
051		N734	N22G	N22GH	N55KS	N55KD	D-CATL	[United Nations code UN-453]		N832JP	HI929		
052		N4289Z	YV-292CP	N55GF	N551DB	D-COOL							
053		N4290Z	N85653	YV-374CP	(N1450B)	N500RP	N501RP	N205EL	(N205EF)	N253S	N531K		
054		N42905	N54GL	HB-VHL	N54NW	(N54LZ)	(N54JZ)						
055		(N155JC)	N155LP	N970H	N970F	N825MG	N852PA	N1JG	N5QG	YV3164			
056		N8563E	(N854GA)	N946FP	N59GS	N272TB	N270AS	OH-IPP	N156JC	N607BF	N607BR	N62LJ	
057		N4290Y	N10CR	N733EY	N733E								
058		(N55BE)	N500BE	N200PC	N129SP	N58SR	YV2961						
059		(N211BY)	D-CAEP	N50AF	N59LJ	OE-GRR	M-KRRR	D-CMED					
060		N6331V	N60MJ	N53JL	N86AJ	N8YY	N60LT	PT-OUG	N6364U	N255TS	N996CR	N24NV	
061		N117EL	N222MC	N132EL	D-CFUX	ES-PVT	D-CFAI	N655NC					
062		N62GL	N24G	N316	N292RC	N855DB	(N107MC)	N69VH					
063		N40146	N8563P	N1744P	N74RY	N63AX	N5XR						
064		N255ST	N121LT	N900PJ	N912MM	(N17LZ)	N400AT						
065		N1088C	N8565K	N555GL	N1125M	(N565B)	N75LJ	N477YP					
066		N237R	(N550DD)	N50DD	N717HB								
067		N39412	N120EL	N127GT	N505EH								
068		N1088A	N38D	N135LR									
069		N551UT	N102ST	N817AM									
070		N1471B	F-GDHR	[w/o 05Feb87 over Cameroons nr Nigerian border]									
071		N3807G	(N155UT)	N155JC	N113YS								
072		N58AS	N55AS	N55AQ	PT-MSM	N72ET	SX-BNS	N5572					
073		N1087Z	HB-VHN	I-VIKY	D-CARE	N355DH	N73WE	N357PR	N857PR	N155V	N667MB		
074		N5574	N74GL	N151PJ	N701DB	N155LR	N905RL	N755CL					
075		N39415	N8563Z	N675M	N55GM	N55GH	N90NE	N117LR					
076		N155JC	N2855	N30GL	C-GKTM	N551RA							
077		N3812G	N8563M	N58M	N85NC	N245MS	(N99YB)						
078		N39391	(N55GJ)	N55GV	N56TG	(N120GR)	I-ALPR	N55VK	N345RJ	N270JP			
079		N39404	(N2855)	N1983Y	N700SR								
080		N1465B	N85632	PT-LET									
081		N1468B	N85631	N777MC	N777MQ	N903JC	N61SJ						
082		N39394	N1075X	N33GL	N68LP	N817AM	N139SK	N599TC					
083		N40149	N55GZ	N6789	(N6780)	N551AS	(N500HG)	N550HG	(N550CK)				
084		N39413	N85643	N740AC	I-FLYJ	D-CWDL	ZS-ELI	[parted out Lanseria, South Africa]					
085		N238R	N58PM	N58FM	N55NM	(N551MD)	(N146PA)	N225MD					
086		N40162	D-CACP	N8227P	PT-LUK	N558RA							
087	ER	N1451B	N8564Z	N103C	N520SC	N520SQ	N554PF	N902RL	SE-RGU	N1852	M-TNTJ	N955NC	D-C...
088		N1461B	N55GJ	N155GS	N900JB	N901JC	N522WK	N60ND					
089		N4289U	N8564X	N170VE	N555CJ	N789PF	N628PT	N312AL	C-GLRJ	C-GCIL			
090		N40146	N723H	D-CGIN	N181EF	N55UJ	XA-BZA						

LEARJET 55

C/n	Series	Identities										
091		N3810G	N8566F	N91CH	N991CH	N91PR	(N69B)	N700JE	(N567SC)	N591SC	N30TK	N911FC	N429FC
092		N1462B	N724J	N400JT	D-CLUB	N500FA	N40DK	N890AC					
093		N725K	N32KJ	N531P									
094		N1088C	N235HR	(N236HR)									
095		N39398	N8565Z	N55RT	D-CAAE								
096		N1087T	N1045X	N8010X	N126KD	N126KL							
097		N4290C	N8566Q	N40CR	N20CR								
098	ER	N726L	D-CCON	N550SC	(N455UJ)	N1324P	(N132TP)	N155ER					
099		(N5599)	N2992	N17GL	N95WK								
100		N3807G	N552UT	N552SQ	N500NH	(N500NB)	N717AM						
101	ER	N39415	N101HK	N101PK	N101HK	N211EF	N501TW	N251VG	(C-FNRG)	N251NG	C-FNRG	N1129M	N112WQ	N307JA
		YV....											
102	ER	N1087Y	N55DG	I-OSUA	N44GA	PT-WSS	N112FK	N604FK	N155TS	N155SJ			
103	ER	N10870	N921FP	[w/o 06Aug86 Rutland, VT]									
104		N39404	N18CG	N18CQ	(N95TJ)	N277AL							
105		N39391	N55GK	N22G	N274	C-GQBR	N55AR						
106		N3812G	N60E	N90AM	N318JH	N824MG	(N850PA)						
107	ER	N1466B	N760G	N155JT	N304AT	D-CWAY	PH-ABU	D-CWAY					
108		(N888FK)	N77FK	N78FK	N222MC	N220VE	(N551AM)	N517AM	(D-CMAX)	D-CUNO	N855NC		
109		N348HM	D-CVIP	ZS-ELJ									
110		N39412	N55GY	(N24RH)	N455RH								
111		N1461B	N7260G	PT-LIG	[w/o 09Nov94 Guanabara Bay, Rio de Janeiro, Brazil; parted out by Dodson Avn, Ottawa, KS]								
112		N3802G	(YV-325CP)	N325CP	LN-VIP	N7AU	EC-HAI	N55LF	[w/o 19Jul04 Fort Lauderdale Executive, FL; canx 17Mar05]				
113		N1450B	N7262M	N713M	N236HR	N57MH	N57MV						
114		N39398	N72608	N34GB	N355UA								
115		N1476B	N6666R	N6666K	N633AC	N155BC	N803GJ						
116		N1087Y	N85GL	N116DA	N51V	N51VL	N801GJ						
117		N3807G	N8567X	N255MB	N155RB	N385RC							
118		N39416	C-FCLJ	N257SJ									
119		N3816G	N72613	N273MC	N273MG	N237PJ							
120		N39418	N72629	N55LK	(N486)	N1127M	N120LJ	N777YC	N329TJ				
121		N3811G	N8568J	N65Y	N155SC	N747AN	N1VG						
122		N10870	N8568P	N18ZD	N99KW	N99KV	C-FHJB	OE-GRO	D-CGBR				
123		N6331V	N44EL	N121US	N150NE	N417AM	N420BG						
124		N39391	N58CG	N58CQ	SX-BTV	D-CONU							
125	ER	N6307H	N610JR										
126		N4291G	N7260J	YV-125CP	N7260J	N16LJ	(N162JG)						
127	B	N6340T	HZ-AM2	N73GP									
128	B	N1087T	N255BL	N7US	N7UA	N10BF	N717JB	N8MF	N655GP	N787GT			
129	B	N4290Y	N75GP	N655AL	N60WA	N72LJ							
130	B	N4291N	N55VC										
131	B	N1088A	N7260K	N52CT	YV2770								
132	B	N4291K	N67WM	N133WB	(N333GJ)	(N133SU)	N122SU	N242RB	N795HA	[parted out by MTW Aerospace, Montgomery, AL]			
133	B	N155PL	N155LJ	N55LF	N700R	N810V	EC-INS						
134	B	N39399	N7261D	PT-LDR									
135	C	N1055C	PT-LXO	[w/o Rio de Janeiro/Santos Dumont, Brazil, 12Aug10]									
136	C	N3811G	N767AZ	N767NY	N155PS	OE-GCF	PH-MED	OE-GCF	D-CFAZ	N990CH			
137	C	N39413	N95SC	N155SP	PR-ERR								
138	C	N4291G	TC-MEK	TC-FBS	VR-CDK	N9LR	N338FP	N270WS	N234ES	YV3102			
139	C	N39391	N1039L	PT-LZS	PT-GMN	N139ST	N552TL						
139A	C	[converted from 55-002 (qv)]			N4289X	N994JD	N984JD	N55GM	(N55ZT)	N518SA	N518SB		
140	C	N72616	PT-OCA	Brazil FAB6100									
141	C	N155DB											
142	C	N555MX	N755VT										
143	C	N10871	D-CMAD	ES-PVD	N143LJ								
144	C	N144LT	PT-OJH	N40CR	N178AM								
145	C	N66WM	N10CR	N211BC	N721AH								
146	C	N9125M	PT-ORA	N559RA									
147	C	N55UK	N499SC	N111US	N160NE	N177AM	YV3179						

Production complete

LEARJET MODEL 60

C/n	Identities											
55-001	N551GL	N551DF	N60XL	[prototype Model 55 converted to Model 60 standards]								
001	N601LJ	[rolled out 05May92; ff 15Jun92]										
002	N602LJ	C-GLRS	C-GLRL	N602LJ	N190AS	N1940	(N602DM)	N170MK	N32SW			
003	N60LJ	N961MR	N808ML	N60FE	N48KZ	N117KB						
004	N60UK	N194AL	N600PJ	N863PA	N44RM							
005	N5011L	N610TM	N869JS	N205FX	OY-LJD	N104SD	N60KJ	VP-BGB	N60KJ	N160AJ	[parted out by Bizav Support LLC, FL]	
006	N60VE	N60VL	N606TS	N606BR	N8783							
007	N448HM	(N212FX)	N219FX	N204FX	(N204BX)	N60UJ	N760CF	N733SW				
008	N608LJ	PT-OVI	N608LJ	N222FX	N222HV	N260UJ	(N359RM)	N808SK				
009	N26029	N54										
010	N5012H	N477DM	N477BM	HB-VLU	N525CF	N928CD	N928GD	C-FBDR	N610TS	N561TC	N610TS	N692PC	N212JA
011	N5013U	N60T	OY-LJE	N61YC	N611TS	N843CP						
012	N5014H	N123CC	N147CC	N626KM	N80DX	N25MX						
013	(N960H)	N26011	N55									
014	N7US	N862PA										
015	N960H	(N960HL)	N826SS	N861PA	N711SE	N711SZ*						
016	N50153	TC-MEK	N788MM	UR-CHH	UR-NAC							
017	N50157	N9173R	N760AC	N660AH	(N860AH)	N60GG	N864PA	N498SW	N500SW	[w/o Aspen A/P, CO, 07Jun12}		N794AA
	[parted out by Alliance Air Parts, Oklahoma City, OK, still wearing marks N500SW]											
018	N5009T	N4016G	N24G	N24GU								
019	N50153	N40366	HB-VKI	D-CRAN	D-CFAN							
020	N600L	N606L										
021	N600LC	N600LG	N600GA	N732LH	N260AJ							
022	N2602Z	N22G	N22GU									
023	N40323	N60SB	N60SR	N588BA								
024	N2601V	LV-PGX	LV-WFM	N415NP								
025	N9155Z	N299SC	N299SG	N919RS	N479PF							
026	N4026Z	N60LJ	N700GS	N60LJ	N347GS	N14T	N14TU					
027	N4027S	XA-ICA	N4230S	N12FU	N69LJ	M-AUTO	N271SC	N878RG				
028	N50298	N870JS	N206FX	N206HY								
029	N4029P	N55KS	C-FBLU	C-GFAX	N296TS	N64SL	N119FD	[w/o Valencia, Venezuela 05May13]				
030	N4030W	N164PA	TC-ELL	YR-RPB	9H-AFJ							
031	N4031L	N228N	N841TT									
032	N5013D	OE-GNL	D-CPMU	D-CIFA*								
033	N4031A	N56										
034	N5034Z	9M-CAL										
035	N50353	VR-BST	N116AS	N1DC	[w/o 14Jan01 Troy, AL]	N1498G						
036	N5014E	N60LR	N44EL									
037	N5017J	N4037A	N637LJ	N101HW	N101ND							
038	N4007J	N638LJ	C-FJGG									
039	N50154	N5003X	N57	N8071J	N57							
040	N399SC	N899SC	N660AS	N600AS	N600CN							
041	N5004Y	N699SC	N166HL									
042	N4010K	N90AG	N90AQ	N60MG	N821DF							
043	N5043D	C-GHKY	N43NR									
044	N5044N	N618R	(N618P)	(N1618R)	N613R	N668RC	LV-CPL					
045	N5045S	N60WM	N711VT	N711VJ	N903AG	N454AN						
046	N50157	N5006G	(PT-WGB)	N214FX	N214BX	N239RC	N710TP	(N710TF)	N137RH			
047	N5007P	N418R	N50DS	N850DS	N647TS	N647EF	N600LJ					
048	N5008Z	N648LJ	N730M	N551ST								
049	N50298	N227N	N247N	N126CX	N459SF							
050	N50450	N207FX	N207BX	N923SK	N924PS							
051	N5051X	N63BL	OY-LJH	D-CHER	ES-PVC							
052	N5022C	ZS-NTV	(N42AJ)	N120HV	N247CP	N900KK	N769DS	XA-MGM	N60LJ			
053	N5012Z	N5053Y	B-3981	N91772	N360UJ	N744DB	N744RD					
054	N65BL	VP-BMM	N301RJ	N777YY								
055	N5014E	N5055F	N1CA	(N143CA)	N660CB	N574DA	(N574BA)	B-3925				
056	N5013Y	N60LR	N117RJ	N700CH	(N556SA)	N92FG						
057	(N5010U)	N50050	N58									
058	N5016V	N92BL	XA-BRE	XA-IRE								
059	N5059J	N208FX	N208BX	N60KF	N159SC	LV-BFR						
060	N50602	N209FX	OY-LJM	N209FX	OY-LJM	N175BA	N909SK	N604SL				
061	N50162	N98BL	N219DC	C-FRGY								
062	N5012H	N5006T	(N510SG)	N707SG	N707SQ	C-GLRS	N62BX	N551BD	LV-CPC			
063	N5015U	N5003U	N8270	N660BC	N496WH							
064	N210FX	N210HV	N529KF	N529KE	N405DC							
065	N5006V	N30W	N718AN	N654AN								
066	N5006K	N8271	N176KS	Colombia FAC1214								
067	N799SC	N118HC	N60HM	N504AB								
068	(N96ZC)	N95ZC	N823TR	N64LE	N160JD	LV-CKK						
069	N50324	N60CE	D-CITA									
070	N5035R	N21AC										
071	N60LJ	N940P	N658KS									
072	N5072L	9M-FCL										
073	N50761	N256M	N860PD									
074	N8074W	N620JF	N674BP	N600PH								
075	N675LJ	N9CU	(N609LC)	N233VR								
076	N211FX	N211BX	N494PA	LV-CCO								
077	N212FX	N677LJ	C-GLRS	N227FX	N227BX	N60GF						
078	N5068F	N188TC	N188TG	N168ZZ								
079	N319LJ	N95AG	LV-FDQ									
080	N8080W	N59										
081	N681LJ	N60LJ	N180CP									
082	N682LJ	N600LN	N534TP	[parted out by Alliance Air Parts, Oklahoma City, OK}								
083	N683LJ	N383MB	N255RK	N725SC	N512TB	LV-GCK						
084	N684LJ	N59FD	N100R	N306R	N8JR	N600TD						
085	N685LJ	N99KW	N89KW	N814GF								
086	(N213FX)	N686LJ	(N777CB)	N797CB	N797CP	N607SB						
087	N687LJ	N411ST	N410ST	N787LP	N601CN							
088	N688LJ	XA-TZF	XA-TZI									
089	N8089Y	XA-MDM										
090	N8090P	PT-WMO	N460BG	N85NC	N255SP	N143LP						
091	N8071L	N896R	N91LE	N156DH								

LEARJET 60

C/n	Identities					
092	N5092R	C-FBLJ	C-FBLO	N907SK	N226SF	N92NS
093	N80683	RP-C648	N109JE	N109JR	N129JR	N717JB	N160EE
094	N60LR	A6-SMS	(N511CL)	N93BA	TC-ARC	N789MS
095	N5005X	N602SC	N82KK	(N82KD)		
096	N8086L	N603SC				
097	N8067Y	N897R	N60TX	N688DB		
098	N50758	N218FX	N218BX	N797PA	N16CS	
099	N212FX	N212BX	N60AN	N173KR		
100	N6100	N60MN	N876SF			
101	N215FX	N215BX	N179LF			
102	N8082B	LV-WXN	N102LJ			
103	N216FX	N216BX	N298EF	N399JR*		
104	N104LJ	N83WM	N903AM	N614TS	N160BL	N60VV
105	N217FX	N217BX	N60BC			
106	N106LJ	N140JC	N945GS	N945G		
107	N107LJ	D-CFFB	D-CFAF			
108	N220FX	(N220PX)	N60RY	N38CP		
109	N109LJ	N707SG	N747SG	N177KS	N215KM	N78FR
110	N60LJ	N928CD	N600CL			
111	N221FX	N898PA	(N898PR)			
112	N299SC	N808WG	N160BS			
113	N599SC	N60LH	N700R	N702R	N160GG	
114	N3014R	N199SC	N114PJ	N154AK		
115	N3015F	N500	N500ZH	N600GG		
116	N116LJ	XA-VIG				
117	N889DW					
118	N3018C	N11AM				
119	N119LJ	N626LJ	N8811A			
120	N120LJ	D-CSIX	(N141MB)			
121	N621LJ	PT-XFS				
122	N622LJ	N61DP	A6-IAS			
123	N356WA					
124	N223FX	(N223BX)	N260AN	XA-IBC		
125	N60LR	VP-CRB	N917SC			
126	N224FX	N160AN	N660CJ			
127	N225FX	(N225BX)	N460AN	XA-ONE		
128	N226FX	(N660AN)	N61ZZ	N8888	N8889	N975LV
129	N629LJ	D-CBAD	N45US	N160GH	N717BK	
130	N630LJ	N90MC	N384JW			
131	N631LJ	XA-JJS	XB-JCG	XA-MHP		
132	N228FX	N9200M	XA-UUP			
133	N133LJ	C-FIDO	C-FBCD	C-FCMG	N500CW	
134	N134LJ	XA-ZTA				
135	N135LJ	N98JV				
136	N136LJ	N60RL	N60RU			
137	N229FX	N360AN	N240JK			
138	N230FX	(N230BX)	N560AN	N160BP		
139	N233FX	N139XX	EI-IAT	N370AT	N7734T	(N77511)
140	N98JV	N140LJ	Argentina T-10			
141	N234FX	N141LJ	OY-JKH	N163BA	N655TH	N888KL
142	(N642LJ)	N426JN	(N940RL)	N116LM		
143	N235FX	N6666R	N6666A	N393TA	N143FA	N143AA	N759SH
144	N60144	D-CKKK	N94BA	N929SR		
145	N145LJ	LX-PRA	I-PRAD	N960TT	N826LJ	
146	N50776	N261PC	N800R	N809R	N790SU	
147	N138SP	N133SR	N160RM	(N158JP)	N420JP	(N42JP)	N727SJ	N69ZJ
148	N80701	D-CETV	N648TS	HB-VOZ	D-CHER	
149	N149LJ	(ZS-JRM)	SU-BNL	SU-EZI	VP-BEZ	N260CA	EI-REX	N160EM
150	N80667	A6-SMS	N150BX	N200MT		
151	N234FX	N9ZM	N11TS	(N11TR)		
152	N50126	Mexico MTX-01		Mexico AMT-200		Mexico ANX-1200	
153	N235FX	(N235BX)	N424KW			
154	N233FX	N969JD	N523MV	N313AR		
155	N88V					
156	N76SF	N76QF	N605SB			
157	N236FX	N114LJ	YV3146			
158	N237FX	N50EL	N460JD	HB-VWN	N838MA	VH-NPP
159	N43SF	N43QF	N721MJ	PP-WIN		
160	D-CDNY	D-CGEO	T7-SOV			
161	D-CDNZ	EC-JVM				
162	N99ZC					
163	N238FX	N238BX	N326HG			
164	N60LJ	PT-XGS				
165	N929GW	N929GV	LV-FUF			
166	N239FX	N60ZD	N114BD			
167	N240FX	N240BX	OE-GVB	N167XX	LZ-AXA	(D-CHRN)	M-WISO	LV-CZX
168	N706CJ	N706CR	N724JS	N721SE		
169	N5014F	OE-GII	D-COMO			
170	N50154	D-COWS	9H-AEE	F-HAVB	D-CNUE	
171	N422CP	N422CR	N424MW	N422CR	N424MW	
172	N241FX	N241BX	XA-DGO	XA-RIN	XA-URG	N121TN
173	OY-LJF	D-CEJA	ZS-TEJ			
174	N242FX	N242ZX	XA-COI	N174BL		
175	N243FX	N243F	XB-KYZ	XB-LBO	XB-LEJ	XB-LLT	N175PC	XA-JKM
176	N176MB	N10MB				
177	N60LR	N991DB				
178	N244FX	N178MM				
179	N9012H	C-FCNR	HB-VNV	D-CIII	N17XL	LV-FUT
180	N777MC					
181	N273MC					
182	N245FX	N600NM	N600EF			
183	N246FX	N810Y	XB-SLL	XA-GSL		
184	TC-DHF	N184LJ	N752BP	N606SB		
185	N464TF	N604GJ				
186	N186ST	N58ST	N294DD			

LEARJET 60

C/n	Identities								
187	N247FX	N27ZH	N470MD						
188	N248FX	N255SL							
189	N189LJ	PR-XJS							
190	N5012K	N190LJ	EI-IAU	ES-PVS					
191	N40073	N30154	N660AS	N710SG					
192	N601GG								
193	N249FX	N627AF	N193AF	N876MA					
194	N250FX	N250SG	(N96FF)	LV-CIO					
195	N251FX	N251SD							
196	N252FX	(N252RD)	(XA-XOX)	N358AP	(D-CHRO)	LV-CUE			
197	N5010U	N23PZ	P4-AVM	OE-GYG	N420KM	N420KV*			
198	N198HB								
199	N253FX	N502RP	N502RB	N600AJ					
200	N254FX	N254FY	(OY-TCG)	(OY-LJK)	A6-EJA	D-CSLT			
201	N411ST	N411SK	N614JH	N269JH					
202	N1RB	N202LJ	XA-TSA	N202LJ	XA-UQP				
203	N770BC	N770BG	LZ-BVV	(D-CFAG)					
204	N4008G	I-NATZ	N30GJ	(N90GJ)	N50GJ				
205	N40043	N205ST	N12ST	N64HA	(N64HX)	N358P	(N358PP)		
206	N40076	(N254FX)	N500RP	N916BG	N909JS	N448GL			
207	N777VC	(N207VC)	N777VQ	N706CJ	N207LJ				
208	N40084	(N235HR)	N821CC	(N112MT)	N208BH				
209	N40085	N1221J							
210	N40086	ZS-NVP+	[+marks worn for at least 16 months at the Tucson, AZ, completion centre but ntu]				N700JE	C-FGJC	C-FCTK	N427PM
211	N5012Z	D-CHLE	I-MRGC	N849WC					
212	N5012H	LX-RPL	I-RPLY	N295KR	N708CF				
213	N40079	N65T	N14T	N717FF					
214	N5016Z	D-CIMM	OE-GFA	C6-ZIP					
215	N40083	N44SF	N44QF	VP-BCY	N275HZ				
216	N131TR	N888LJ							
217	N5012G	N60LJ	N600ML	XA-VLA					
218	N50157	N8084J	EI-IAW	C-GRBZ	N727BG				
219	N660KS	N552SK							
220	N80857	N254FX	N254FZ	N255FX	(N447FA)	(XA-ONE)	N359AP	VP-BOD	N260GD
221	N255BD	XA-JWM	XA-FGP						
222	N8088U	N60VE	N1128M						
223	N3006J	N109JR	N109JZ	N309MG	N375BW				
224	N61VE	N64MG							
225	N30170	N22SF	N22QF	N60HS	N60TG	(N770JB)	N312AL		
226	N3011F	N128V	N596MC	N596MG	N229TS				
227	N253FX	N503RP	N503RE	N582MM					
228	N255FX	N10ST	N65HA	N65HU					
229	N23SR	N38SV							
230	N50031	N826SR	N235CG	N356CG	N600LG				
231	N3015M	N40012	D-CDNX	SX-BNR					
232	N5004J	LV-ZYF	N232LJ	N95BD	N95BQ				
233	N5008F	N33DC	N520SC	N520S	N405TK				
234	N5013J	N24SR	LV-CAY						
235	N5013N	N252RP							
236	N5015T	I-IINL	OE-GNI	N716BG	N916BG	N555EH			
237	N699DA	PR-WBW							
238	N5018U	N753BP	(N140CT)	N260BS					
239	N5019R	(ZS-SCT)	N503BC						
240	N5019V	N29LJ							
241	N5026Q	N253FX	N603GP	N603GR					
242	N5027Q	PR-LDF	N5027Q	[w/o 07Oct02 Santa Cruz do Sul, Brazil]					
243	N50287	OY-LGI	EC-JVB	N65LJ					
244	N5031R	N884TW	N335AF	N835AF	N160MG				
245	N50330	XA-ORA	N290KR	N474PT					
246	N5035F	D-CWHS	N64JP						
247	N254FX	N645MD	LV-FVZ						
248	N5038N	OE-GMR	N248L	N787LP	N787LD	N248LA			
249	N50422	N4004Q	D-CLUB	EC-JYQ	(D-CFAK)	D-CFAX			
250	N50433	XA-FLY	N50433	XA-FLY					
251	N50458	N747DP							
252	N5012H	N5051X	N749SS						
253	N5012K	C-GIIT	C-FBLU	N1127M					
254	N5015U	RP-C6003	N773SW						
255	N5013U	OO-TME	ER-LGB	N166MS					
256	N5013Y	OY-LJK	D-CCGG	N401SY					
257	N50157	N256FX	N977SS	N671CB					
258	N202N								
259	N40075	N600L							
260	N40050	N257FX	N973HR						
261	N4003Q	D-CROB	N397JK						
262	N4003W	N5051A	N126KD	N440DM	N440DN	N604BK			
263	N258FX	N876CS							
264	N40084	N214RW	N214PW	N811RA					
265	N40086	N600LC	[parted out by Alliance Air Parts, Oklahoma City, OK]						
266	N259FX	N266LJ	N156BF	(N156BE)	N506AB				
267	N5009V	N50558	N60YC	N60SN	PP-LRR	N166MS	N618L		
268	N5011L	N268WS	N21NV						
269	N5012H	N100NR	N903AM						
270	N5012K	VH-MZL	LV-BDX	N247SC	A6-MAJ	OE-GMA			
271	N271L	N954WS							
272	N50157	N60KH	P4-BAZ	N272DJ	LV-CBI				
273	N4002P	VH-OCV	RP-C2956	VH-EXJ	N60SE				
274	N4003K	D-CSIM							
275	N101UD	ES-PVI							
276	N5000E	N838RC	OE-GDF	D-CDSM	M-AIRS	N276BG			
277	N40079	LX-LOU	N404CD						
278	N5012K	N60RL							
279	N50145	Z3-MKD							
280	"N50127"+	[+marks as reported but not a recognized Learjet test reg'n]					OE-GKP	G-SXTY		
281	N5013U	"OE-GTS"+	[+marks painted in error at Wichita, KS in Feb05]			OE-GTF	D-CGTF	OH-GVE	ES-LVC	D-CFAG

LEARJET 60/60XR

C/n	Identities							
282	N5013Y	TC-RKS	N207AW					
283	N5009T	N60LJ	PR-GCL	N160JA	N415SG			
284	N5000E	EC-JIE	N284L	N461MC				
285	N5009T	N72CE	N183BX					
286	N4003K	(D-CSIS)	N262DB	G-LGAR	N875CA			
287	N4003L	OE-GGL	M-ALEX	ES-PVJ				
288	N40077	N103LS	N719JB					
289	N40083	N785DR	VP-BGS	M-ABGI	N770BM			
290	N5012K	N260DB	D-CFLG	(D-CHRN)	N60FZ	PP-BIN	N548WC	VH-XPN
291	N4003Q	XA-KCM						
292	N5011L	N380BA	N580BA					
293	N60SE	N772PP						
294	N50163	[first LJ60XR, ff 3.4.06]	N60XR	N160BG	D2-EPC			
295	N259FX	N314CM						
296	N5016Z	EC-JPV	N296L					
297	N5012G	XA-KLZ						
298	N40012	N729LJ	N812GR					
299	N50153	N75CT						
300	N40081	OH-AEM	G-CJMC	EI-DXW	YL-ABA	OE-GSV	(D-CFAX)	D-CFAK*
301	N50157	ZS-GSG	N301LJ	N440MC				
302	N5012H	(OE-GJA)	ES-PVP					
303	N40075	(OE-GJA)	(OH-GVI)	OE-GTO	OH-III	ES-III		
304	N40076	(D-CGNF)	OE-GNF	N355AP	VH-SBU	N604ED		
305	N40050	OH-VIV	EI-VIV	M-IGOR	OE-GMD			
306	N5013Y	N80177	N500	N5009	N869AV			
307	N260FX							
308	N115AN							
309	N460MC							
310	N222BR	PP-BED						
311	N710SG	N202SJ	VP-BLC	N327AR	XA-JGC			
312	N5013U	OH-VMF	VP-CCD	HZ-OSR	VP-CCD			
313	N4003L	N613H	G-HOIL	M-HOIL	N61WF			
314	N999LJ	[w/o 19Sep08 Columbia Metropolitan, SC; parted out by Atlanta Air Salvage, Griffin, GA]						
315	N604KT							
316	N5017J	N50LK	N923AL					
317	N5012Z	(OH-GVI)	OE-GSU	N292KR	Colombia FAC1216			
318	N777VC	N770PC						
319	N261FX	(D-CVIP)	N814TS					
320	N60LJ	N229BP	N229RP	(C-....)				
321	N5010U	N675BP	N574DA	(PP-BRP)	XA-MES			
322	N710SG	N724CJ	N5014F	OY-MIR	OE-GSC	N924KW		
323	N50157	N262FX	N98UF					
324	N50126	N707CS	N797CS					
325	N5013Y	P4-SSV	M-SSSV	N608JA	PP-JAE			
326	N5018G	N80172	OD-MHA	M-APWC	M-MHAC			
327	N5016Z	9H-AFB	N545LF	LV-CKA				
328	N5000E	VP-BBZ	G-XXZZ	M-URAL				
329	N50111	LZ-BVE						
330	N5102G	OK-JDM						
331	N4001G	(D-CDEF)	N331PL	HK-4565				
332	N5013U	OE-GLX	N804JD	LV-FPM				
333	N4003L	OE-GLY	N805JD	N943RM	YV3065	YV3167		
334	N263FX	(N334BG)	XA-ORI					
335	N5014E	TC-MEN						
336	N4004Y	A6-NGN	HZ-NGN	N781SC	N770X			
337	N60LJ	N337BG	XA-FMT					
338	N5016V	N338PR	A6-SBF	CS-EAE	A9C-BXK	A6-SBF	N398AA	N121EL
339	N5010U	N160TG	N610CR					
340	N264FX	N714TS						
341	N5012K	A6-CYS	M-YCYS					
342	N40073	SP-CEZ						
343	N5015U	C-FEDG	C-FEDU	N60XA	PP-CTP	N343EC		
344	N40076	OO-ADH	LV-BZJ					
345	N265FX							
346	N724EH	N724EB	AP-BKB					
347	N5012Z	P4-EXG	UP-LJ001	N786SC	XA-...			
348	N266FX	N550DG						
349	N40012	C-GJLN						
350	N5011L	D-COMO	VP-COO	VP-CBO	VP-CIO			
351	N5013Y	D-CJAF						
352	N4003Q	(G-DOKK)	VH-THG	N352XR				
353	N5017J	N999YC	LV-BTA					
354	N5000E	(PP-ONE)	N60LE	PP-ONE				
355	N40077	OH-IVS	N483VL					
356	N267FX	N356JH						
357	N50111	PR-MLR						
358	N60XR	N358JA						
359	N5018G	OE-GVJ	N806JD	LV-FPN				
360	N5012G	OE-GVT	N809SD	LV-CRC				
361	N5014E	N361TS	N487LP					
362	N10870	N62XR	CS-DTH	N306KR	9H-LJE			
363	N50145	N1JB						
364	N40076	OE-GVV	N810SD	N604WC				
365	N4004Y	N65LR	(C-....)	(N53LV)				
366	(N268FX)	N988P	N900P	N60AX*				
367	N5012K (N437JL)	"N60XR"+	[+fake marks N60XR worn in NBAA static displays at Orlando Executive, FL, Oct09 and Atlanta/DeKalb-Peachtree Oct10]					N5012K N367LJ
368	N10872	(N420JP)	N42JP	N468JM	N368XR*			
369	N10873	OY-KYS	M-MARI	UR-ISH	T7-ISH			
370	N326SM	HZ-MS1A						
371	N4003K	HZ-MS1B						
372	N50153	(N269FX)	ES-LVA					
373	N5018L	(D-CGVD)	OE-GVD	N811SD	M-ELHI			
374	N5000E	N60LJ	N83TR					
375	N3099	N106FF						

LEARJET 60XR

C/n	Identities								
376	N50157	(OK-YXY)	N76XR	N40149	XA-TCO	N561CT			
377	N4002P	C-FLTB	N357AP	TG-AIR					
378	N50163	(D-CBOB)	N984BD	N60HJ					
379	N50154	(CS-DJA)	N79XR	N51054	I-SDAG	(D-CFAS)	D-CURE		
380	N4003L	N380L	XB-RGB						
381	N4003Q	B-3926							
382	N5013U	M-IGHT							
383	N5009V	N383LJ	A6-RJE						
384	N5013Y	VT-DBC							
385	N694HC	N10871	5A-UAE						
386	N40076	N60SJ	OE-GVE	N812SD	D-CFAD	D-CLUZ			
387	N40078	N201UD	C-FJOL						
388	N60LJ	N724EH	N724EF						
389	N50153	N883RA							
390	N5018G	N649SP							
391	N50111	B-3935							
392	N5016Z	N90CE							
393	N5017J	N393AC	N668JH	VP-CHU	N60AJ				
394	N40084	VT-MAM							
395	N5000E	N168KS							
396	N50126	N396LJ	LV-CRB						
397	N50145	N810YS							
398	N40086	N787LC	N787LP						
399	N5013U	LZ-TRH							
400	N40043	N80170	XA-RAV						
401	N40146	OE-GVF	N60AJ	TC-AEK					
402	N40083	N93EW							
403	N40085	OE-GVG	N716RJ	XA-AIG					
404	N5009T	N901PM							
405	N5011L	OE-GVH	N718RJ	XA-MGM					
406	N5012Z	OE-GVN	N731RJ	"XA-UOC"	[incorrect marks worn at Tucson service centre Oct15]				XB-UOC
407	N50163	OE-GVP	N732RJ	N956RS*					
408	N4003Q	N95CE							
409	N5014F	(D-CAEX)	OE-GVQ	N738RJ					
410	N10870	N717EL	N717EP						
411	N5014E	N88MZ							
412	N5018G	VT-UNO							
413	N4001G	N27LJ							
414	N40012	I-GSIN							
415	N4005Q	N81GD							
416	N5012G	N603GP							
417	N4003W	N249S	N844S						
418	N40077	N220AZ							
419	N4008G	N20GJ	N30GJ						
420	N10873	N723HC							
421	N40162	N268FX	N421XR	M-GLFZ	M-YETD	D-CETD	N588BF		
422	N40086	N269FX	N422XR	N104RJ					
423	N5018L	N270FX	(N423XR)	N760AA	N1972H				
424	N50163	N271FX	(N424XR)	N424LJ	N600LN				
425	N5012K	N425GS							
426	N4003Q	C-GJDR	N377PT	N357PT					
427	N4004Y	N929GX	N929GW						
428	N50154	N60FP							
429	N50153	XA-USZ							
430	N40146	XA-JWM							
431	(N40075)	[test marks allocated but aircraft not built]							
432	(N40083)	[test marks allocated but aircraft not built]							

Production complete

LOCKHEED JETSTAR

Aircraft which were converted to -731s by Garrett AiResearch were given a sequential conversion number by that company; these numbers appear alongside the c/n in the production list.

C/n	Series	Identities
1001		N329J [ff 04Sep57; last flight 16Aug82; donated to Pacific Vocational Inst, Vancouver, Canada; to Seattle Museum of Flight, WA, circa Aug04]
1002		N329K N711Z [displayed Andrews AFB, MD, in USAF colours, code 89001]
5001/53	731	N9201R [ff 21Oct60] N1 N21 N1 N11 N7145V [wfu; to Pratt Community College, KS; to White Ind's, Bates City, MO, for spares 1998]
5002	6	N9202R EP-VRP N106GM N69TP N81JJ N148PE [b/u for spares Mar85, Minneapolis/St Paul, MN. Fuselage still in nearby scrapyard Feb07]
5003	6	N9203R NASA14 N814NA [cx Dec89; for disp Plant 42 Heritage Airpark, Palmdale, CA]
5004	6	N9204R N13304 N524AC N777EP N69HM N777EP [displayed Graceland Estate, Memphis, TN]
5005	6	N161LM N176LG N12121 N716RD N712RD N70TP XA-SIN XB-DLV (N22265) [wfu as XB-DLV Van Nuys, CA and scrapped]
5006/40	731	N9280R N12R N227K N731JS N222Y N6NE (VR-CCC) [wfu Southampton, UK, after landing accident; was on fire dump; remains to Florida]
5007/45	731	N9205R N110G N72CT N971AS [impounded 1992 Atlanta-Peachtree, GA; b/u for spares 1993; fuselage dumped in field adjacent to Atlanta-Peachtree]
5008	6	N500Z N400M [w/o 27Dec72 Saranac Lake, NY]
5009	6	N9206R N540G N767Z N717X N717 (HB-VET) N717JM [cx Sep84; b/u for spares]
5010	6/C140A	59-5958 [preserved Travis AFB, CA, originally in museum then elsewhere on base]
5011/1	731	N9282R Indonesia T17845 PK-PJS 9V-BEE PK-PJH N731A C-GKRS N10461 N159B N88JM [b/u for spares late 1985; fuselage at Lincoln, NE 1988]
5012	6	N9283R D-BABE N10123 N1012B N500SJ N501AL [wfu Opa-Locka, FL; cx Jan94; derelict Mar94]
5013	8	N9284R N322K N523AC N11JC HZ-MAC N11JC N8AD N158DP (N5AX) [b/u for spares Mar88 by White Inds, Bates City, MO]
5014	6	N58CG N158CG N9MD N54BW N95GS [b/u for spares 1989 Miami, FL; cx 17Mar03]
5015	6	NASA4 N172L N103KC N505T N9046F N66MP [wfu; to South Seattle Community College, WA, as instructional airframe; cx Oct00]
5016	6	N9210R N2222R (N222R) N20TF HZ-AFS HZ-SH2 N4258P N712GW N440RM [open storage Roswell, NM circa Oct97]
5017	6/VC140B	N9286R 61-2488 [AMARC park code CL001] [preserved Warner-Robins AFB, GA]
5018	6	N9287R (CF-DTX) C-FDTX [preserved National Aviation Museum, Rockcliffe, Canada]
5019	6	N9288R N105GM N105GN (N70TP) N5UD N50UD [b/u 1986; tail section at North Perry, FL 1989; fuselage converted into mobile home, derelict at Big Guy's Auto facility nr Gainesville, GA]
5020	6	N9207R N371H N300CR N308WC [cx Sep88; b/u for spares]
5021	6	CF-ETN C-FETN N564MG [b/u for spares Memphis, TN]
5022	6/VC140B	61-2489 [AMARC park code CL006] [preserved Pima County Museum, Tucson, AZ]
5023	6	N9221R I-SNAL N711Z N1107Z N767Z N979RA N879RA N723ST N20PY N2ES (N6ES) [b/u for spares Mar88 by White Inds, Bates City, MO]
5024	6/VC140B	61-2490 [stored AMARC Davis-Monthan AFB, AZ with park code CL004 then preserved Lyndon B Johnson National Historical Park, TX, Aug10]
5025	6	(62-12166) W Germany CA101 W Germany 1101 SU-DAF ST-JRM [not confirmed if marks have been taken up]
5026	6/C140A	59-5959 [noted preserved 29Sep92 Scott AFB]
5027	6/VC140B	61-2491 [displayed Rhein-Main AFB, Germany]
5028	6/C140A	59-5960 [wfu; stored Greenville, TX, auctioned for scrap 2010]
5029/38	731	N3E N3EK N340 N39BL N1BL N166AC N112TJ (N25TX) (N1406) [to Aviation Warehouse, El Mirage, CA by Oct04]
5030	6/C140A	59-5961 [w/o 07Nov62 Warner-Robins AFB, GA]
5031	6/VC140B	61-2492 [preserved USAF Museum, Wright Patterson AFB, OH]
5032	6/C140A	59-5962 [at Edwards AFB, CA, for Museum]
5033/56	731	N1620 N16200 N33EA N100CC N100AC N200CC N200CG XB-FIS N25WA N50EC (N890MC) N500MA [cx Oct02, b/u; fuselage at Conroe, TX, in 2005 but removed by Feb08]
5034	6/VC140B	61-2493 [stored AMARC Davis-Monthan AFB, AZ with park code CL003; to Western Air Parts]
5035	6	(62-12167) W Germany CA102 [w/o 16Jan68 Bremen, W Germany; reported stored Bremen]
5036/42	731	N1622 N1622D N41TC N776JM N444JH N90KR N900CR [b/u circa 2001; cx Oct01]
5037/24	731	N9211R N2600 [damaged in pressurisation tests; rebuilt as c/n 5128, but still known as c/n 5037] N519L N3060 N60CN N60CH N11UF (N71UF) N90TC N10DR N6JL N552JH N770JR [cx Jun08, wfu Palm Beach International, FL]
5038	6	N9212R N341NS N341N N22CH N11UF N11UE (N44KF) [b/u; cx Dec92; remains to Aviation Warehouse film prop yard at El Mirage, CA]
5039	6	N600J N60QJ N81MR N86HM N200CK [cx Sep90; was stored Spirit of St Louis A/P, MO; presumed since scrapped]
5040	6	N505C N518L N7SZ N888RW [cx May88; spares May88; remains blown up Fort Lauderdale, FL for film]
5041	6/C140B	62-4197 [stored AMARC Davis-Monthan AFB, AZ with park code CL007; parted out; used in artwork at Pima Air & Space Museum, Tucson, AZ]
5042	6/C140B	62-4198 [to Battle Damage Repair Unit, Mildenhall AFB, UK; b/u by 22Jan92 Mildenhall]
5043	6/C140B	62-4199 [stored AMARC Davis-Monthan AFB, AZ, park code CL002, then to Western Air Parts]
5044	6/C140B	62-4200 [stored AMARC Davis-Monthan AFB, AZ, park code CL005, then to Western Air Parts; used in artwork at Pima Air & Space Museum, Tucson, AZ]
5045	6/C140B	62-4201 [stored AMARC Davis-Monthan AFB, AZ, park code CL008, then to Hill AFB Museum, UT]
5046	6	N9282R PK-IJS Indonesia T-9446 Indonesia A-9446 [wfu Jakarta-Halim AFB, Indonesia; later put on display at Garuda's training centre at Kushadasi, Indonesia]
5047	6	N9214R N409M N409MA N555PB [cx Oct90; scrapped]
5048	6	N9215R N40N N40NC N98KR N98MD N500WN N500WZ N428DA (N130LW) [preserved Marietta Aviation Museum, GA; cx 15Aug13]
5049	6	N9216R N1230R N96B N96BB [wfu at South Seattle Community College, WA]
5050/34	731	N207L N208L N141TC HZ-THZ N434AN [b/u Apr94 by Atlanta Air Salvage, Griffin, GA]
5051	6	N9217R N400KC N44MF N31S N310AD N555BS N488JS N488GR [part of 'Disaster' attraction at Universal Studios, Orlando, FL, since Jan08]
5052	6	N9218R N300P N66CR CF-DTM C-FDTM N9739B [b/u for spares early 1989 Bi-States Park, St Louis, MO; cx Jun92]
5053/2	731	N9219R N12R N121CN N69CN N14WJ XA-POU XC-JCC XA-BCE XC-JCC [wfu Topeka/Forbes Field, KS by 2007]
5054/59	731	N9220R N7600J N7600 N20AP N354CA N721PA [parted out by White Inds, Bates City, MO]
5055/21	731	N9222R N296AR N303H N90ZP N85BP (N43JK) (N86BP) (N79MB) N304CK N707EZ N99FT [wfu at Chino, CA, circa Sep95; cx Mar96; parted out remains to scrapyard at Long Beach, CA]
5056	6	N9223R N105G N105GH N300AG HZ-FNA [b/u Spirit of St Louis A/P, MO]
5057	6	N1007 N90U N90ME [cx Mar87; b/u Memphis, TN during 1988]
5058/4	731	N100A N100AL N1500M N50AS N600TT (N600DT) N600TP N381AA N131EL N200DW XA-TTE XB-JIZ [wfu circa 2006 Toluca. Mexico]
5059	6	Indonesia T-1645 Indonesia A-1645 [preserved in museum Yogyakarta-Adisutjipto, Indonesia painted as A-9446]
5060	6	N9225R N31F N55NC [cx May88; b/u Jun88 Fort Lauderdale International, FL]
5061/48	731	N9226R N506T N506D N47BA N67GT N152GS N161GS N123GA (N888WW) N488MR N488EC N333EC N338EC [b/u Palm Beach Int'l, FL, 2006]
5062/12	731	N679RW N2200M RP-57 N111G VR-BHF EC-697 EC-FGX [reported parted out in US circa 2005]
5063	6	N9228R N420L N420A N420G N499PB XC-LIT
5064/51	731	N184GP N3QS N3QL [parted out Rantoul, KS circa early 2000]
5065	6	N9229R N1966G S9-NAD [wfu 1989; used as spares for c/n 5085]
5066/46	731	N9230R N228Y N7782 XA-HRM XA-JHR XA-SAE XA-MIK [reported w/o 16Nov95, no other details]
5067	6	N871D N711Z N207L (N267AD) N267L [w/o 29Mar81 Luton, UK]
5068/27	731	N9231R N96GS [w/o 06Jan90 Miami A/P, FL; used as spares; cx Jan91]
5069/20	731	N910M N918MM XA-PGO N197JS [reported for spares; cx Feb99]
5070/52	731	N992 N9921 C-GAZU N9921 N177NC N731AG N114CL N888CF N888WT N712TE N731WL [cx 26Jan05; parted out]
5071	6	(62-12845) W Germany CA103 1103 SU-DAH ST-PRE [wfu Khartoum, Sudan]

LOCKHEED JETSTAR

C/n	Series	Identities											
5072/23	731	N9233R	N500Z	N74AG	[b/u; cx Dec99]								
5073	6	N7775	[fuselage used as interior mock-up by KC Avn, Dallas, TX]										
5074/22	731	N9234R	N67B	N267P	N267GF	N168DB	N777SG	N171JL	[parted out circa 2001; cx Oct01 fuselage at City Museum, St.Louis, MO]				
5075/19	731	N397B	N540G	N2345M	N1DB	N500ES	[b/u Rockford, IL, Apr06]						
5076/17	731	N9235R	N100C	N3E	N3EK	N69ME	N76HG	[b/u Rockford, IL, May06]					
5077	6	N9236R	N1924V	N1EM	[w/o 25Mar76 Chicago, IL]								
5078/3	731	N711Z	N7105	N472SP	N52TJ	N916RC	(N916RG)	N515AJ	N124RM	[cx 19Apr04; preserved at Aviation Institute of Maintenance, Houston/Hobby, TX]			
5079/33	731	N9238R	XA-RGB	XA-MAZ	N58TS	[parted out by Alliance Air Parts, Oklahoma City, OK]							
5080	6	N914X	N914P	N77HW	[wfu & scrapped – details not known]								
5081	8	N200A	N200AL	N4SP	N4SX	[cx Sep87; b/u for spares during 1987]							
5082/36	731	N320S	N917J	N82SR	TC-OMR	P4-CBJ	3C-QQU						
5083/49	731	N208L	N141LM	N161LM	N257H	N257HA	C-GAZU	N27FW	N817BD	N198DL	[cx 09Nov15; wfu Wilmington, DE]		
5084/8	731	N9240R	N83M	N732M	N910E	N520S	[w/o 11Feb81 Westchester, NY]						
5085	6	N9241R	N586	N5861	S9-NAE	VR-CCY	[to Abu Dhabi Higher College of Technology, marked as "HCT"]						
5086/44	731	N9242R	N27R	N27RL	N600J	N60UJ	HZ-FBT	N711AG	N27RC	(N65JW)	N313JS		
5087/55	731	N9243R	N41N	N800J	N31LJ	N31WG	N75MG	N33SJ	[cx 25Apr13; CofR expired. Fuselage to Planes of Fame museum, Chino, CA]				
5088	6	N9244R	CF-DTF	C-FDTF	[cx late 1986; preserved in Atlantic Canada Aviation Museum, Halifax, Canada]								
5089	8	N9245R	N324K	N120AR	(N85DL)	(XA-…)	N120AR	[used for spares Jan94 by TAESA Mexico City, Mexico]					
5090	8	N9246R	N106G	N10MJ	N55CJ	N555SG	[wfu 1989 Fort Lauderdale Executive, FL (cf c/n 5094)]						
5091	6	N9247R	N107G	N107GH	N118B	N118BA	[wfu; remains to White Inds, Bates City, MO; cx May93]						
5092/58	731	N9248R	N372H	N901H	N110AN	N110DD	VR-CSM	VP-CSM					
5093	6	N9249R	N711Z	N5000C	N5000B	N76EB	N22RB	[cx Oct90; b/u for spares circa Sep90]					
5094	6	N9250R	N3030	N3080	[rebuilt with tail section from c/n 5090; wfu Opa-Locka, FL; derelict there Feb94; cx 09Dec14]								
5095/30	731	N9251R	N78MP	N780RH	N731L	[b/u; cx Jan04]							
5096/10	731	N9252R	N530G	[cx 17Jun04; b/u; fuselage at Conroe, TX in 2005 but removed by Feb08]									
5097/60	731	N9253R	N300L	N306L	N77D	N81366	N1BL	N922MS	[parted out by Dodson Int'l Parts, Rantoul, KS; fuselage to Sir Sandford Fleming College, Peterboro, Canada, by Sep08, instructional airframe painted as 'C-FCCC']				
5098/28	731	N9254R	N1967G	N5098G	(N98MD)	N417PJ	N199LA	N792AA	N942Y	(N963Y)	XA-TVK		
5099/5	731	N9255R	N533EJ	N594KR	N277NS	N323P	N62K	N62KK	N18BH	(N117J)	[wfu Fort Pierce/St Lucie, FL; cx 24Jun11]		
5100/41	731	N9256R	N207L	XA-FIU	N35JJ	XA-GZA	N510TS	N800GD	[wfu Conroe, TX]				
5101/15	731	N9208R	N7008	N7008J	N760DL	N760DE	XA-JJS	N26MJ	N800AF	N511TS	[wfu Aug05 Guthrie, OK; cx to Australia, but only engines went – fuselage remained in USA]		
5102	8	N9235K	N326K	N500ZB	N75CC	N7500	N85CC	N601JJ	[wfu Oct94 Spirit of St Louis A/P, MO & scrapped cx Feb00]				
5103	8	N23M	N672M	N176BN	N176AN	N101AW	XA-TAZ	(N101AW)	XA-TAV	[used for fire training at Aruba wearing its previous US marks N101AW]			
5104/6	731	N902K	N902KB	N155AV	N155TJ	[parted out; cx 22May13]							
5105	8	N277T	N2277T	N7005	N17005	HZ-MA1	[to Lycee Saint-Exupery Blagnac, Toulouse, France, for training use]						
5106/9	731	N238U	N288U	CF-GWI	N8SC	N1329K	YV-03CP	[wfu Maracaibo, Venezuela]					
5107	8	N118K	N337US	N7788	YV-187CP	N7788	N69MT	[parted out Jun93 Hollister, CA]					
5108	8	N7953S	N1207Z	N24UG	N68CT	N680TT	XA-SWD	N104CE					
5109/13	731	N7954S	N968GN	N968BN	N678BC	[b/u for spares 1992 Chandler Municipal A/P, AZ; fuselage noted Apr94 on fire dump Phoenix-Skyharbor A/P, AZ; gone by Oct98]							
5110/47	731	N7955S	N2600	N2601	N788S	N49UC	[b/u for spares during 1990; cx Dec93]						
5111	8	N7956S	N5111H	N11SX	N115MR	N115DX	[b/u circa Aug91 Addison, TX; wings to Spirit of St Louis A/P, MO]						
5112/7	731	N7957S	N910G	N99MR	N499PC	N728PX	N475MD	[parted out by White Inds, Bates City, MO]					
5113/25	731	N7958S	N505C	N124RP	N303LE	(N1967J)	(N65JW)	N1962J	N77BT	N542TW	[parted out by White Inds, Bates City, MO, Nov05; cx 29Apr09]		
5114/18	731	N7959S	N930MT	N930M	N94K	N111GU	N26GL	5B-CHE	5A-DBZ				
5115/39	731	N933LC	N933CY	N26TR	N40XY	N8300E	N1151K	[b/u Willard A/P, Champaign, IL Aug95]					
5116	8	N7961S	N222QA	N3HB	N60BC	[wfu 29Sep92 Spirit of St Louis A/P, MO; fuselage still present circa Apr96]							
5117/35	731	N7962S	N210EK	N310CK	VR-BSH	VP-BSH	(N858SH)	VP-BLD	[wfu Toulouse, France]				
5118	8	N7963S	N333QA	N333KN	N222KN	[b/u 1987 Memphis, TN]							
5119/29	731	N7964S	N11HM	N508T	N508TA	N500AU	N1DB	N9GU	[parted out by White Inds, Bates City, MO]				
5120/26	731	N7965S	N40DC	HZ-TNA	[wfu Geneva, Switzerland by mid 2004; b/u 22-25Mar11]								
5121	8	N7966S	W Germany 1102	SU-DAG	ST-PRM	[still at Cairo, Egypt as SU-DAG Oct02]							
5122	8	N7967S	N1107Z	N1107M	N213AP	[cx Mar89; b/u during 1989]							
5123/14	731	N7968S	N1844S	N559GP	N441A	N47UC	N123GN	N57NP	N57NR	(N425MK)	N725MK		
5124	8	N7969S	N46F	N7SZ	XA-SBQ	XA-SKI	XC-SKI						
5125/31	731	N7970S	N47UC	N48UC	N31BP	[parted out by Aerovision International, OK]							
5126	8	N7971S	N955H	N955HL	N20S	N39E	N39Q	[b/u for spares Aug83]					
5127	8	N7972S	N42G	N42GB	N3GR	N636C	(N636MC)	N636	N171CC	[derelict 1991 Van Nuys, CA; cx Jun92 to Aviation Warehouse film prop yard, El Mirage, CA, wearing marks "N171SG"; cockpit section used in 'Telle Mere Tel Fils' sculpture by Adel Abdessemed 2008]			
5128/16	731	N7973S	N26S	5B-CGP	N128BP	N777PZ	[parted out Houston-Hobby, TX]						
5128S		[see c/n 5037/24]											
5129	8	N7974S	Saudi Arabia 101		XA-TJW	XA-TZW	[parted out Toluca, Mexico]						
5130	8	N7975S	Saudi Arabia 103		Saudi Arabia 102		XA-TJV	XA-TZV	XA-PES	[wfu Toluca, Mexico]			
5131	8/Fanstar	N7976S	N30RP	N31RP	N64C	N212JW	N380AA	[derelict 1991 Van Nuys, CA; cx Mar92]					
5132/57	731	N7977S	N1620	N1620N	N100GL	N801	N1JN	N989JN	XA-PSD	XA-BEB			
5133	8	N7978S	N329K	N322K	C-GPGD	VR-CAW	HZ-WBT	HZ-WT1	HZ-FK1	XA-ROF	XA-ROK	[wfu Jan95 Mexico City A/P, Mexico, used as ticket office in car park of Wal-Mart store in eastern Mexico City]	
5134/50	731	N7979S	N295AR	N500S	N50PS	N72HT	N136MA	XA-JMN	XA-TPD	[wfu Addison, TX, by Sep03; removed from airport by road March14]			
5135	8	N7980S	N636	N900H	N500WN	N500FG	[parted out Spirit of St.Louis, MO, still marked N500WN; cx 28Aug09]						
5136	8	N5500L	Libya 001	5A-DAJ	[wfu]								
5137	8	N5501L	EP-VRP	Iran 1004	Iran 5-9001								
5138	8	N5502L	N1301P	N333RW	N31DK	N801	(N700MJ)	[wfu at Greenville Technical College, SC; used as an instructional airframe]					
5139/54	731	N5503L	N991	N991F	N10DR	XA-RVG	N1189A	[to Atlanta Air Salvage, Griffin, GA, Apr97 still marked as XA-RVG; US marks cx Apr97]					
5140	8	N5504L	XB-VIW	XA-JCG	XA-EMO	[wfu Jan06 Toluca, Mexico]							
5141	8	N5505L	N711Z	N7967S	N12241	N244	N4436S	HZ-SH1	N4493S	XB-CXO	N3982A	N747GB	[derelict at Lagos, Nigeria, circa Jan98]
5142	8	N5506L	N5113H	N1UP	N20SH	HZ-SH3	N90658	N86TP	N91LJ	N91UJ	N86TP	N39LG	N23FE	XA-SOY [wfu by 2006 Toluca, Mexico]
5143	8	N5507L	N100UA	N31UT	N5070L	N5878D	C-GATU	N620JB	N326CB	[b/u; cx Jan00]			
5144	8	N5508L	Mexico JS10201		Mexico DN-01		Mexico JS10201		Mexico 3908	[wfu 2013; preserved in Mexican Air Force museum, Santa Lucia, Mexico]			
5145	8	N5509L	N46K	XB-DBJ	XB-JFE	XA-JFE	N511TD	[to Greater St Louis Air & Space Museum, IL; cx 27Aug12]					
5146	8	N5510L	N80GM	C-GWSA	N4990D	N499AS	N545BF	[b/u for spares Jan87]					
5147	8	N5511L	N744UT	N718R	N212AP	[wfu for spares Jan93 Greenwood, LA]							
5148	8	N5512L	N964M	N21SH	HZ-SH4	N900SA	XA-ROK	XA-ROF	XA-OLI	[cx]			
5149/11	731	N5513L	N711Z	N157JF	N157QP	N524AC	N110MN	N110MT	N100MZ	VR-BJI	[b/u for spares Feb91]		
5150/37	731	N5514L	N516WC	N200CC	N200CG	N42C	N312CK	N100TM	(N345CK)	(N710JA)	N721CR	N911CR	[parted out by White Inds, Bates City, MO]

LOCKHEED JETSTAR

C/n	Series	Identities										
5151	8	N5515L	N711Z	N46KJ	N45K	XA-PUL	[wfu Jan94 for spares by TAESA Mexico City, Mexico, used as ticket office in car park of Wal-Mart store in southern Mexico City]					
5152	8	N5516L	N500JD	N113KH	XA-SOC	[b/u for spares Toluca, Mexico circa Jan03]						
5153/61	731	N5517L	N711JS	N500PG	N430MB	N416KD	N416SJ					
5154	8	N5518L	N3031	N756	N766	XC-SRH	N43AR	[parted out Fort Lauderdale Executive, FL circa Jly00]				
5155/32	731	N5519L	N711Z	XA-FES	N4248Z	N55NE	N10PN	N79AE	N59CD	N1DB	(VR-BQG)	(N120RL)	VR-BRL	VP-BRL
		N84GA	N116DD	[w/o Dallas/Love Field, TX, 10Mar06, cx]								
5156	8	N5520L	9K-ACO	N70TP	XB-DBT	N16AZ	[wfu]	N1B				
5157	8	N5521L	N9WP	N29WP	XB-DUH	[displayed at entrance to Dodson Av'n at Rantoul, KS painted as "N001DT"]						
5158	8	N5522L	N516DM	C-GTCP	N1DT	XA-POO	XA-FHR	XA-TDG				
5159	8	N5523L	N520M	XB-DBS	[wfu]							
5160	8	N5524L	C-FRBC	(N60EE)	[b/u late 1988 Memphis, TN]							
5161/43	731	N5525L	N22ES	N60SM	N119SE	N1329L	N200PB	N99VR	LY-AMB	N5161R	XB-KCV	XB-KFR	[impounded at
		Valencia, Venezuela, 07Sep07 for drug-running]										
5162	8	N5526L	N10CX	N10JJ	XA-HNY	XB-KLV						

One of 5A-DAJ c/n 5136 or 5A-DBZ c/n 5114 was dbr by munitions fire at Tripoli in July 2014.

C/n	Series	Identities										
5201	2	N5527L	N711Z	N711DZ	(N93JD)	N93JM	N745DM	N777AY	[cx 14May14, wfu Miami/Opa Locka, FL]			
5202	2	N5528L	N717	N717X	N333KN	N20GB	EC-232	EC-FQX	VP-CBH	P4-CBG	3C-QRK	N25AG	[b/u Kemble, UK,
		2006; remains to Air Salvage Int'l, Alton, Hants, UK]										
5203	2	N5529L	EP-VLP	Iran 1003	[reported w/o 05Jan95 Isfahan, Iran]							
5204	2	N5530L	N19ES	N59AC	N500PR	N167R	N25WZ	(N220ES)	N202ES	N814K	[parted out 2008; to Cavanaugh Flight	
		Museum, Addison, TX]										
5205	2	N5531L	N5000C	N500QC	N718R	N713R	YV-826CP	N16BL	N454JB	N72GW		
5206	2	N5532L	N107GM	XA-STG	XA-JML	N329JS	[to White Inds, Bates City, MO Dec04 for parts]					
5207	2	N5533L	N176BN	N34WR								
5208	2	N5534L	N322CS	N123CC	(N29TC)	N38BG	N95BD	N95BK	[cx 13Aug12, wfu]			
5209	2	N5535L	N500S	N297AP	N529TS	N375MD	[damaged 24Oct05 by Hurricane Wilma at Fort Lauderdale Executive, FL; parted out by Dodson					
		Int'l Parts, KS]										
5210	2	N5536L	N400KC	N707WB	N787WB	[parted out; fuselage at Aircraft Support Group facility at Conroe, TX in 2005 but removed by Feb08]						
5211	2	N5537L	N500T	(N500YY)	N56PR	N821MD	N118B	XA-PWR	N261US	[wfu Fort Pierce/St Lucie, FL, still wearing XA-PWR]		
5212	2	N5538L	N3030	N5030	N167G	XA-ACC	N167G	(N95SR)	[b/u; cx Aug03; fuselage at Aircraft Support Group facility at Conroe, TX		
		in 2005 but removed by Feb08]										
5213	2	N5539L	N501T	N501J	N60JM	(N600JT)	N65JT	N710RM				
5214	2	N5540L	N530M	N601CM	N760DL	N760DE	(N9366Q)	N106JL	N848AB	N221CR	N3RC	N50KP	XA-CVE
		N50127	XA-RCR	[parted out by Alliance Air Parts, Oklahoma City, OK, still wearing marks N50127]								
5215	2	N5541L	(N215HZ)	VR-BJH	N329MD	N777WJ	XA-FHS	N215DL	N215TS	(N1X)	N1TS	N1X	N800TS	N80TS
		N808RP	N175MD	[cx 27Jan12, wfu; engines sold, airframe to private museum]								
5216	2	N5542L	N95BA	N99E	N797WC	N797WQ						
5217	2	N5543L	N106G	N814CE	N500EX	N504EX	N1MJ	N486MJ	N1MJ	9G-ABF		
5218	2	N5544L	N716RD	N816RD	N901C	[cx 20Dec05; presumed wfu]						
5219	2	N5545L	N107G	N21VB	C-GBDX	N219MF	N104BK	N770DR	5H-APH	LY-EWC	N522AG	N500DB	(N5VN)
		N800GD										
5220	2	N5546L	N32KR	A6-KAH	TC-NOA	VP-CGH						
5221	2	N5547L	5A-DAR	[w/o 16Jan83 en route Libya-Algeria]								
5222	2	N5548L	N509T	(N509TF)	N509J	C-GAZU	VP-BCP	A6-CPC	N813P	N311RS		
5223	2	N5549L	N105G	N341K	N1DB	N644JW	N1MJ	N886DT	N887DT	ZS-ICC	[parted out Lanseria, South Africa]	
5224	2	N4016M	N1924G	N285LM	N3QS	N6QZ	N116DD	N700RM				
5225	2	N4021M	N746UT	N990CH	N42KR	TC-IHS	N900DB	(N9KE)				
5226	2	N4026M	N2MK	N815RC	N308SG	TC-SSS						
5227	2	N4033M	N211PA	N23SB	N30Y	(N811)	N110AN	N171SG	N117AJ	N375MD	[cx 14May14, wfu Miami/Opa Locka, FL]	
5228	2	N4034M	N372H	XA-RMD	N400MP	N400MR	XA-CON					
5229	2	N4038M	N7NP	N351WC	N851WC	(N50NM)	N500NM	VR-CNM	N222MF	XA-TCN	N224MF	N377SA	
5230	2	N4042M	N257H	N901FH	N901EH	N701JH	N275MD	[cx 14May14, wfu Miami/Opa Locka, FL]				
5231	2	N4043M	N196KC	(N788JS)	N988MW	N112MC	XA-FHR	XA-TPJ	XA-AAL	[wfu Toluca, Mexico]		
5232	2	N4046M	N90CP	N90QP	N77C							
5233	2	N4048M	YI-AKA	7T-VHP	OD-KMI	HB-JGK						
5234	2	N4049M	N357H	N920DY	N920DG	"N234TS"	XA-EKT	XB-NZJ				
5235	2	N4055M	YI-AKB	[destroyed at Quadisiya Air Base, Iraq, during Gulf War Jan91]								
5236	2	N4056M	N531M	N2JR	N34TR	N741AM	(A6-...)	ST-FSA				
5237	2	N4058M	YI-AKC	Iran 5-9003								
5238	2	N4062M	YI-AKD	[destroyed at Quadisiya Air Base, Iraq, during Gulf War Jan91]								
5239	2	N4063M	YI-AKE	[destroyed at Quadisiya Air Base, Iraq, during Gulf War Jan91]								
5240	2	N4065M	YI-AKF	[destroyed at Al Muthana Air Base, Iraq, during Gulf War Jan91]								

Production complete

MBB HFB 320 HANSA JET

C/n	Series	Identities							
V1/1001		D-CHFB	[ff 21Apr64; w/o 12May65 Torrejon, Spain]						
V2/1002		D-CLOU	(D-CASE)	[wfu 24Sep70; preserved Deutsches Museum, Munich, Germany, but removed to Flugwerft Schleissheim museum at Oberschleissheim until 2019 to allow Deutches Museum refurbishment]					
1021		D-CARA	[wfu Braunschweig 25May84; on static display at Finkenwerder, Germany]						
1022		D-CARE	[CofA exp 28Apr72; under restoration Berlin/Gatow, Germany]						
1023		D-CARI	N320J	N1320U	N320AF	N103F	[b/u for spares]		
1024		D-CARO	W Germany (YA111)	W Germany (CA111)	W Germany D9536	W Germany 1607	F-WZIH	[preserved Musee de l'Air, Paris, France]	
1025		D-CARU	W Germany (YA112)	W Germany (CA112)	W Germany D9537	W Germany 1608	[in open storage at Manching, Germany by 2001; to Finkenwerder, Germany, by road Aug07 for restoration to flying condition]		
1026		D-CARY "D-CARY"	N890HJ	N71CW	(N1026)	N71DL	TC-FNS	[cx 1991; wfu Hannover, Germany circa Sep88; to Museum Hannover Laatzen marked	
1027		D-CASO	I-TALC	(D-CASO)	D-CITO	N905MW	N127MW	[w/o 05Oct84 Aberdeen, SD]	
1028		D-CASU	5N-AMF	[w/o 25Jly77 Abidjan, Ivory Coast]					
1029		D-CASY	[w/o 29Jun72 Blackpool, UK]						
1030		D-CATE	N247GW	N111DC	[wfu; noted dismantled at Monroe, MI Aug95; cx 28Aug14]				
1031		D-CERA	N300SB	N750SB	[cx Dec90; wfu Fort Lauderdale Executive, FL; hulk stored Opa-Locka, FL for spares]				
1032		D-CERE	PH-HFA	N130MW	N132MW	[wfu; b/u]			
1033		D-CERI	PH-HFB	N132MW	N130MW	[b/u 1989]			
1034		D-CERO	N320J	N320MC	[w/o 09Mar73 Phoenix, AZ and b/u; cx Oct90]				
1035		D-CERU	PH-HFC	N128SD	[wfu for spares use Monroe, MI circa Aug97]				
1036		D-CESA	N891HJ	N380EX	N2MK	N136MW	(N92047)	[cx 22Aug13; wfu]	
1037		D-CESE	N892HJ	N5ZA	N6MK	N6ML	N555JM	YV-999P	N604GA	[w/o 30Nov04 Spirit of St. Louis Airport, MO]
1038		D-CESI	N110WS	N5627	(N18RA)	N192AT	N301AT	N605GA	[instructional airframe at Jefferson County Technical College/Bowman Field, KY]
1039		D-CESO	N118RA	N893HJ	CF-WDU	N666LC	N666LQ	N205MM	N208MM	N171GA	[submerged into Portage Quarry nr Bowling Green, OH, 2006 for diver training]
1040		D-CESU	I-ITAL	N7158Q	[b/u for spares Mojave, CA; remains to Aviation Warehouse film prop facility at El Mirage, CA; canx 27Jan06 as wfu]				
1041		D-CIRA	W Germany 1601	(D-CIRA)	N92045	(N62452)	N602GA	[wfu Toledo, OH noted Mar00 devoid of marks]	
1042		D-CIRE	W Germany 1602	TC-LEY	TC-SEN	TC-GSB	(N7684X)	N106TF	(N603GA)	[b/u circa 2000 – remains being used by Fire Department at Louisville, KY]
1043		D-CIRI	W Germany 1603	TC-KHE	TC-LEY	(D-CHFB)	[to M.Rahmi Koc Museum, Istanbul, Turkey, 14Dec12 for public display]		
1044		D-CIRO	[w/o 18Dec70 Texel Is, Netherlands]						
1045		D-CIRU	N5602	N894HJ	N4ZA	N7ES	[wfu Fort Lauderdale Executive, FL, for spares; remains to Opa-Locka, FL; scrapped]		
1046		D-CISA	W Germany 1604	TC-NSU	[cx 1991; wfu]				
1047		D-CISE	W Germany 1605	TC-OMR	[cx 1991; wfu]				
1048		D-CISI	W Germany 1606	[preserved GAF Museum, Gatow, Berlin]					
1049		D-CISO	XC-DGA	XC-TIJ	[b/u 1991, possibly following accident at San Diego, CA 11Jun84; remains to Mojave, CA]				
1050		D-CISU	LV-POP	LQ-JRH	(N1184L)	N2675W	N777PV	N777PS	N777PZ	N777PQ	[wfu for spares use Monroe, MI circa Aug97]
1051		D-CORE	N895HJ	N6ZA	N888DL	[b/u Jly 90 for spares – remains to Aviation Warehouse film prop yard at El Mirage, CA]			
1052		D-CORI	PT-IDW	N173GA	[instructional airframe at Jefferson County Technical College/Bowman Field, KY]				
1053		D-CORO	PT-IOB	N176GA	[wfu, cx Feb07]				
1054		D-CORU	N896HJ	N480LR	[cx Feb87; to spares use Monroe, MI circa Aug97]				
1055		D-CORY	N897HJ	N11NT	N87950	N30AV	(N21SU)	TC-GSA	(N7685T)	N105TF	[cx 27Feb13, b/u]
1056		D-COSA	[to instructional airframe at Manching, Germany; later to museum at Niederaltaich, Germany (minus engines & wings)]						
1057		D-CLMA	D-COSE	(N107TW)	VR-CYR	YV-388CP	[impounded for drug-smuggling Venezuela Aug2004]		
1058	ECM	D-COSI	Germany 1621	N322AF	[b/u at Hollister, CA circa Jly98]				
1059	ECM	D-COSO	W Germany 9825	W Germany 1622	[w/o 27Nov76 Schwabmuenchen, W Germany]				
1060	ECM	D-COSU	W Germany 9826	Germany 1623	(D-CCCH)	N321AF	[b/u at Hollister, CA, circa Jly98]		
1061	ECM	(D-CUNA)	D-CANI	Germany 1624	(D-CEDL)	N320AF	[cx 05Sep12, b/u]		
1062	ECM	(D-CURE)	D-CANO	Germany 1625	N323AF	[b/u at Hollister, CA circa Jly98]		
1063	ECM	(D-CURI)	D-CANU	Germany 1626	[preserved GAF Museum, Gatow, Berlin]				
1064	ECM	(D-CURO)	D-CAMA	Germany 1627	N324AF	[b/u at Hollister, CA circa Jly98]		
1065	ECM	(D-CURU)	D-CAME	Germany 1628	N325AF	[b/u at Hollister, CA circa Jly98]		
1066		(D-CURY)	(D-CAMO)						
1067		(D-CUSA)	(D-CAMU)						
1068		(D-CUSE)	(D-CALA)						
1069		(D-CUSI)	(D-CALE)						
1070		(D-CUSO)	(D-CALI)						
1071		(D-CUSU)	(D-CALO)						
1072		(D-CUSY)	(D-CALU)						
1073		(D-CADA)							
1074		(D-CADE)							
1075		(D-CADI)							
1076		(D-CADO)							
1077		(D-CADU)							
1078		(D-CATI)							
1079		(D-CANA)							
1080		(D-CANE)	(D-CINA)	(D-CCVW)	(D-CDVW)				

Notes: 1021 to 1065 above also have a secondary c/n (S1 to S45)
1066 to 1080 not completed; used for spares

MU300 DIAMOND

C/n	Series	Identities
001SA	2	JQ8001 N181MA [to Beech Field, Wichita, KS fire department for training; cx 18Feb09]
002	1	JQ8002 N81DM JQ8003 JA8248 [cx, wfu]
A003SA	1A	N300DM N300TS (N300TJ) N303JH*
A004SA	1A	JQ8004 N302DM (N40BK) N59TJ N102WR (N88TJ) N541CW (N484CW) (N541TM) [parted out by White Industries, Bates City, MO; cx 04Feb09]
A005SA	1A	JQ8005 N304DM N450TJ N15AR N40GC N700LP N30HD N110DS [parted out by White Industries, Bates City, MO]
A006SA	1	N325DM C-FPAW N400TJ N777JJ N750TJ N200LP
A007SA	1A	N301DM N707CW N507CW N485CW N507CW N24HD N567JK [parted out by Alliance Air Parts, Oklahoma City, OK]
A008SA	1A	N303DM (N56SK) N399DM (N442JC)
A009SA	1A	N305DM N909GA N306P N318RS N360CA [parted out by White Inds, Bates City, MO]
A010SA	1A	N306DM N69PC (N9FC) N300DH N703JH N931MA
A011SA	1A	N307DM (N77GA) N114DM N211GA
A012SA	1A	N308DM N82CT N7RC N107T I-GIRL N112GA N316LP [cx 2Oct14, CofR expired]
A013SA	1	N81HH I-VIGI [w/o 15Oct99 Parma, Italy]
A014SA	1	N15TW N339DM OH-KNE OY-FYN (N517KR)
A015SA	1A	N315DM N415RC N271MB N870P N789DD N789DJ
A016SA	1A	N133RC N100DE N208F N530RD N10NM N706JH N411RE
A017SA	1A	N14DM N75BL (N33MM) N399MM
A018SA	1A	N900LH C-GRDS N138DM N118GA N83BG (N831TJ)
A019SA	1	N311DM N9LP N6PA N319DM N400GK (N438AM)
A020SA	1A	N399RP (N911JJ) [parted out by White Inds, Bates City MO; cx 29Apr09]
A021SA	1	N222Q N4LK N678PC N405MG
A022SA	1A	N313DM N18KE (N816S) N322MD N322BE N800TJ N811DJ (N397SL) N400UF
A023SA	1A	N314DM OY-BPC SE-DDW OY-BPC N79GA N17TJ N22BN N150CA [parted out by White Inds, Bates City, MO]
A024SA	1A	N316DM N320CH N95TJ N450PC N674AC XB-CTC
A025SA	1	N317DM N63GH N1843S N1843A N400HH
A026SA	1	N5UE N55JM N900DW N140AK N526CW N326CW N486CW (N426TM) (N26FA) N28FM [cx11Jun13; wfu]
A027SA	1	N319DM N237CC N800RD N27TJ N7PW [cx13May13; wfu]
A028SA	1A	N320DM N331DC N900WJ [to Dodson Int'l Parts, Rantoul, KS; parted out]
A029SA	1A	N321DM N1UT N10TE N89TJ N100RS (N22CX) [cx 14Mar13, wfu]
A030SA	1A	N322DM N191GS N41UT N58TJ N301P N83SA (N800GC)
A031SA	1A	N174B N2220G N956PP N958PP [parted out by White Inds, Bates City, MO]
A032SA	1A	N323DM N132GA N320T N929WG N83CG (N996DR)
A033SA	1A	N312DM N520TT N223S N5EJ N717CF N717DF N148J [parted out by White Inds, Bates City, MO]
A034SA	1A	N318DM N303P N334KC PR-WTZ
A035SA	1A	N300HH HB-VHX N135GA N702JH N37CB
A036SA	1	N326DM N18BA N997MX
A037SA	1A	N327DM OY-CCB LN-SJA N109TW N134RG [parted out by White Inds, Bates City MO;cx 29Apr09]
A038SA	1	N338DM N147DA N147WC N42SR (N212PA) [Parted out by White Inds, Bates City, MO]
A039SA	1A	N328DM C-GRDX N139DM N399MJ PT-OXT
A040SA	1A	(N329DM) N82CS N188ST N40GA [cx 18Jul13; wfu]
A041SA	1A	N330DM (N444SL) N45GL N83AE N300AA N300AR N104GB
A042SA	1A	N331DM N420TJ N8LE (N420FA)
A043SA	1A	N332DM N19R
A044SA	1A	N334DM N110DK N146GA N606JM N600GW
A045SA	1A	N335DM N334DM N99FF N154GA N60B N61GA N777DC N545TP N395WB N393WB
A046SA	1A	N346DM (YV-274CP) (N146GA) N151SP N272BC N272BG N900BT N109PW HA-YFE
A047SA	1	N347DM N138RC N76LE N47TJ N45NP N47PB N333TS N2WC
A048SA	1A	N335DM (OO-EBA) VH-JEP N335DM PT-LNN [w/o 23Mar03 Santos Air Base, Brazil]
A049SA	1A	N336DM N300LA YV-309P YV-29CP N40MF XA-SOD N411SP PP-JCP
A050SA	1A	N350DM N257CB N826JH N528LG
A051SA	1A	(N357DM) N351DM N550HS (N35P) D-CGFV TC-YIB [w/o in ground accident; to Dodson Avn, Rantoul, KS, for spares] (N550HS)
A052SA	1	N352DM HB-VHT I-FRAB N70XX [Oct05 to White Industries, Bates City MO for parts]
A053SA	1	N353DM D-CDRB JA30DA
A054SA	1A	N354DM N850TJ N141H N491BT
A055SA	1A	N877S N877T N89EM N600MS N600CG XA-UIC [wfu Monterrey del Norte, Mexico]
A056SA	1A	N341DM N101AD N156GA I-FRTT N255DG
A057SA	1A	N342DM N119MH N334WM N510BC
A058SA	1A	N343DM N384DM VR-BKA N7050V N442EA
A059SA	1A	N345DM N344DM I-DOCA N126GA N1JC (N259JM)
A060SA	1A	N345DM (N300SJ) N585TC [parted out by White Inds, Bates City, MO; cx 29Apr09]
A061SA	1A	N348DM N18T N500PP
A062SA	1A	N349DM G-JMSO N362MD 3D-AFH N426DA TG-LAR N64EZ N616MM N817GR
A063SA	1A	N363DM N54BE N51B N51BE N984SA [parted out by Atlanta Air Salvage, Griffin, GA]
A064SA	1A	N364DM N246GA I-SELM N800LE HI-646SP N2225J N400ML YV195T YV2347
A065SA	1A	N361DM N65JN N165GA OY-CDK I-GENC N54RM N16MF N925MJ
A066SA	1A	N366DM N1TX (N185GA) "N66FG" N88MF N88ME PR-JTS
A067SA	1A	N367DM N123VJ I-ALGU N184SC N65SA N63DR N617BG [parted out by White Industries, Bates City, MO; cx 04Feb09]
A068SA	1A	N368DM N368PU N103HC
A069SA	1A	N355DM N56MC N250GP (N197SL) (N501EZ)
A070SA	1A	N370DM D-CNEX OY-BPI N84GA N60EF
A071SA	1A	N371DM (N106GA) N70GA N71GH
A072SA	1A	N372DM PT-LGD N174SA N777DC N779DC
A073SA	1A	N356DM N717VL N1715G N94LH N94LD
A074SA	1A	N374DM N22WJ JA8298 N19GA N32HP [parted out by Dodson Int'l, Rantoul, KS]
A075SA	1A	N375DM N11WF N824DW [wfu; cx 14May11]
A076SA	1A	N376DM N76LE C-GLIG [w/o 01Mar95 Jasper-Hinton A/P, Alberta, Canada] N8221M [parted out by White Inds, Bates City, MO; regn cx Aug01 a/c b/u]
A077SA	1A	N377DM N68PL N66PL N975GR N851C
A078SA	1A	N378DM N710MB [w/o 15Dec93 nr Goodland, KS. Parted out by White Industries, Bates City, MO]
A079SA	1A	N379DM (N574U) N574CF N213LG N765KC
A080SA	1A	N380DM N380CM N770PC N925WC N275HS N44MM
A081SA	1A	N381DM N381MG N81TJ N317CC N317GC N750TJ N50EF XA-...
A082SA	1A	N382DM N105HS N555FA N62CH N214PG [wfu Chino, CA]
A083SA	1A	N383DM N12WF N83TK N417KT [Parted out by White Inds, Bates City, MO]
A084SA	1A	N484DM (N484VS) (N84DT) N840TJ N160S N160H EC-JKL
A085SA	1A	N485DM I-TORA N485DM N777MJ (N911JJ) N70VT N87DY [cx 21May12, wfu]
A086SA	1A	N486DM N515KK N428NG*
A087SA	1A	N487DM HB-VIA (PH-JSL) N870AM I-AVEB
A088SA	1A	N482DM
A089SA	1A	N483DM N100EA N89SC N88CR N20PA PP-ELT
A090SA	1A	N312DM G-TOMY N300LG (N64EZ) C-GLIG N464AM
A091SA	1A	N357DM (N357MD) PT-OVM (N485DM) N611AG N400HG N400NF N301AE
A092SA	1A	JA8246 [w/o 23Jly86 Sado Island, Japan]

Production complete

Note: Diamond 2s are included under Beechjet 400s.

MS760 PARIS

C/n	Series	Identities
01		F-WGVO [ff 29Jly54] F-BGVO EP-GVO+ [+ temporary marks used for demonstration flight from 1957 Paris Air Show] F-BGVO [w/o 01May58 Lisbon, Portugal]
02		[used as static test airframe and b/u]
03		F-BHOK France 03 F-SDIA (F-Z…) F-SDIA [w/o 24Dec64 Mont de Marsan, France]
001		F-WIET France 1 F-ZADS F-SDIB F-ZADS F-SDIB 330-DB/F-SDDB [to Musee de l'Air et de l'Espace, Le Bourget, France, Oct09]
002		EP-HIM F-BOJO N760MM N1EP N207MJ
003		Argentina A-01/E-201 [wfu 1994; to IV Brigada Museum, Mendoza, Argentina]
004	2	Argentina A-02/E-202 [wfu 2007; stored Mendoza, Argentina]
005	1A	F-WJAA N760H N2NC N2TE XB-FJO N2TE (N760LB) [w/o 30Nov96 Santa Ana/Orange County, CA; cx Mar97]
006		F-WJAB N84J N760J [b/u 05Apr81; cx May81]
007		Argentina A-03/E-203 [w/o 27Jan61 Mendoza, Argentina]
008		F-WJAC G-36-2 G-APRU N60GT
009		F-WJAD N300ND N722Q
010		Argentina A-04/E-204 [wfu 1998; stored Mendoza, Argentina]
011		Argentina A-05/E-205 [wfu 2006; stored Mendoza, Argentina]
012		France 12/F-YDJ? [w/o 13Apr59 Hyeres, France]
013		Argentina A-06/E-206 [w/o 11Mar88 Mendoza, Argentina; rebuilt with tail unit and fuselage parts from c/n 016 for display at Ezeiza, Argentina]
014		France 14 France 312-DF/F-RHDF [dismantled at Long Beach, CA circa Dec97; fuselage at San Luis Obispo, CA circa May01; to Estrella Warbirds Museum, Paso Robles, CA]
015		Argentina A-07/E-207 [wfu 2007; to Museo Aeronautico, Moron, Argentina]
016		Argentina A-08/E-208 [wfu 2001; parts used in rebuild of c/n 013 for display purposes]
017		Argentina A-09/E-209 [wfu 1995; preserved Rio Gallegas, Argentina]
018		Argentina A-10/E-210 [w/o 09Nov59 Cordoba, Argentina]
019		France 19 France 41-AR/F-SCAR [stored Chateaudun, France Apr97]
020		France 20 F-SDIC 20-Q/F-RABQ [w/o 26Oct62 Bernay en Brie, France]
021		Argentina A-11/E-211 [w/o 06Oct89 Mendoza, Argentina]
022		Argentina A-12/E-212 [wfu 2007]
023		France 23 330-DO/F-SDDO [stored Chateaudun, France Apr97]
024		France 24 65-KW/F-FBLW [to Ailes Anciennes Toulouse for restoration Nov03; preserved wearing code 330-DB in Aeroscopia museum, Toulouse/Blagnac, France]
025		France 25 42-AP/F-SCAP 116-CB [stored Chateaudun, France circa Mar01]
026		F-WJAA France 26 -LN/F-RBLN [stored Chateaudun, France circa Sep99]
027		France 27 -DE/F-RHDE N760PJ
028		F-WJAE I-SNAI N760X
029		France 29 65-LC/F-RBLC [stored Chateaudun, France Apr97]
030		France 30 65-LI/F-RBLW N370AS N761X
031		France 31/F-YCB. [wfu 23Jly72; instructional airframe Rochefort, France]
032		32 Aeronavale/Marine F-AZLT
033		33 Aeronavale/Marine [preserved Musee de Tradition de l'Aeronautique Navale, Rochefort, France]
034		France 34 43-BB/F-SCBB 113-CG N371AS
035		France 35 43-BL/F-SCBC
036		France 36 44-CC/F-SCCC 316-DH N373AS [cx 16Sep13; CofR expired]
037		France 37 34-Z/F-RABZ [w/o 07Dec67 Les Loges, France]
038		France 38 41-A/F-SCAS 115-ME N374AS
039	1A	F-WJAA F-BJET [stored Reims-Prunay, France circa Jly99; to USA for spares 2007]
040		40 Aeronavale/Marine [instructional airframe at Lycee Professionel Robert & Nelly de Rothschild, St Maxim, France]
041		41 Aeronavale/Marine N41NY [parted out]
042		42 Aeronavale/Marine [instructional airframe at Morlaix-Ploujean May03]
043		(N888JK) (N776JK) N776K N760C N760S
044		France 44 4D-L/F-RBLD N375AS
045		France 45 43-B./F-SCB. 316-DI N378AS
046		46 Aeronavale/Marine [in Ailes Anciennes Pays Beaunois collection at Chateau de Savigny les Beaunois]
047		47 Aeronavale/Marine [wfu]
048		France 48 Aeronavale/Marine [w/o 04Jan68]
049		N760M [w/o 03May69 Evadale, TX]
050	2	CN-MAJ CF-MAJ N6068 N111ER N42BL N23ST [w/o 11Sep90 Albuquerque, NM; cx Jun91]
051		Brazil C41-2912 France 51 330-DC/F-SDDC N751PJ [to Den Helder, Netherlands 16Apr04 for restoration towards flying condition]
052		Brazil C41-2911 [wfu]
053		Brazil C41-2910 France 53 OD/F-RHDD N53PJ [to China Jan16 for refurbishment and resale]
054		Brazil C41-2913 France 54 41-A./F-SCA. N354AS [cx 24Sep13; CofR expired]
055		Brazil C41-2914 [wfu]
056		Brazil C41-2915 France 56 65-LG/F-RBLG 133-CM N956P [cx 24Sep13; CofR expired]
057		Brazil C41-2918 France 57 41-AC/F-SCAC N657P [cx 24Sep13; CofR expired]
058		Brazil C41-2920 France 58 65-LB/F-RBLB 312-DG N760F
059		Brazil C41-2916 France 59 41-A./F-SCA. 133-CF N959P [cx 18Mar13, CofR expired]
060		Brazil C41-2917 France 60 41-AT/F-SCAT N7601R [to China Jan16 for refurbishment and resale]
061		Brazil C41-2919 France 61 -LY/F-RBLY N961P [cx 18Mar13, CofR expired]
062		Brazil C41-2921 France 62 65-LV/F-RBLV 314-DO [stored Chateaudun, France circa Mar01]
063		Brazil C41-2923 [wfu]
064		Brazil C41-2922 [stored Santa Cruz, Brazil]
065		Brazil C41-2924 France 65 65-LF/F-RBLF 330-DP
066		Brazil C41-2925 [wfu]
067		Brazil C41-2926 [w/o 29Oct62 Nova Lima, Brazil]
068		Brazil C41-2927 France 68 NB/F-ZJNB
069		HB-PAA Switzerland J-4117 HB-PAA [cx Jun84; to Musee Europeen de l'Aviation de Chasse Montelimar-Ancone, France] N760FB
070		Brazil C41-2928 France 70 65-LF/F-RBLF [displayed at Tarbes-Lourdes, France marked as "F-MSAD"]
071		Brazil C41-2929 France 71 65-LE/F-RBLE N571P [cx 19Mar13, CofR expired]
072	1A	F-BJLV N760FR [parted out Mojave, CA]
073		France 73
074		Brazil C41-2930 France 74 [w/o 02Dec80 Natal, Brazil]
075		Brazil C41-2931 France 75 65-LZ/F-RBLZ N975P
076		Brazil C41-2932 [preserved Brazilian AF Museum, Camp de Abonsas, nr Rio de Janeiro, Brazil]
077		Brazil C41-2933 France 77 65-LP/F-RBLP [to Estrella Warbirds Museum, Paso Robles, CA, by Feb10]
078		Brazil C41-2934 France 78 65-LY/F-RBLY115-ME [stored Chateaudun, France Apr97]
079		Brazil C41-2935 France 79 [wfu 15Apr79; to SOPEMEA Villacoublay, France 31Jan89 for stress tests]
080		Brazil C41-2936 France 80 314-D/F-RHD. GE-316 80/DE [wfu Chateaudun, France – on dump by 20Jun98]
081		Brazil C41-2937 France 81 41-A./F-RBLL ELA61 N81PJ
082		Brazil C41-2938 France 82 65-L./F-RBL. N761JS [cx 21Oct10, wfu]
083		Brazil C41-2939 France 83 NC/F-ZJNC [code 316-DB] [stored Chateudun, France circa Jly00]
084		84 Aeronavale/Marine [w/o 23Dec70 Le Bourget, Paris, France]
085		85 Aeronavale/Marine F-AZTL*
086	1A	F-BJLX N9035Y [b/u Mojave, CA]
087		87 Aeronavale/Marine N87NY
088		88 Aeronavale/Marine N88NY N626TC N760JS
089	2	F-BJLY N999PJ

MS760 PARIS

C/n	Series	Identities					
090		D-INGE	N334RK	N454HC	N69X		
091		France 91	65-LU/F-RBLU	[to Musee d'Aeronautique, Orange, France, by Apr07]			
092		France 92	118-DA/F-RHDA	316-DL	N763JS		
093		France 93	65-LD/F-RBLD	N764JS	[cx 30Nov10, wfu]		
094		France 94	65-L./F-RBL. N765JS	[cx 17Dec10, wfu]			
095		France 95	/F-RBL.	[w/o 03Aug67 Melun, France]			
096		France 96	65-LU/F-RBLU	[w/o 29May82 Villacoublay, France]			
097		France 97	65-LH/F-RBLH	[reported as G1-330 "330 DC"]	N97PJ	PP-XUM	
098	2	D-INGA	F-BOHN	HB-VEP	3A-MPP	F-GKPP	[w/o Oct91 Calvi, Corsica; [used for spares for c/n 111]
099		I-SNAP	[w/o 27Oct62 Milan, Italy]				
100		F-ZJNJ	France 100				
101	2	France 101	F-BNRG	(N7038Z)	N760PJ	N444ET	(N760PJ) N520DB
102	2B	F-BJZQ	PH-MSR	N760E	HB-VEU	N99HB	N20DA
103	2B	F-BJZR	PH-MSS	N760N	YV-163CP	N760N	N760T [wfu Oct94 Mojave, CA]
104	2B	F-BJZS	PH-MST	N760P	N760R	[stored Santa Maria, CA]	
105	2B	F-BJZT	PH-MSU	N760Q	F-BXQL	[stored Reims-Prunay, France circa Jly99; to USA for spares 2007]	
106	2B	F-BJZU	PH-MSV	N5878	[used as a source of spare parts for c/n 008 N60GT]		
107	2B	F-BJZV	PH-MSW	N5879			
108	2B	F-BJZX	PH-MSX	N760AR			
109		(F-BJZY)	[airframe not built; RLS, Netherlands, option cx]				
110		(F-BJZZ)	[airframe not built; RLS, Netherlands, option cx]				
111	2	I-FINR	C6-BEV	N760FM	[cx 31Jan13, CofR expired]		
112		F-EXAA	HB-PAC	F-BOJY	N65218	N7277X	N710K [b/u Mojave, CA; cx10May13]
113		France 113	F-ZJNI				
114		France 114	F-ZJNJ	[preserved Villacoublay, France]			
115		France 115	F-ZJOV	[instructional airframe Toussus-le-Noble, France]			
116		France 116	F-ZJON				
117		France 117	F-ZJAZ				
118		France 118	F-ZJNQ				
119		France 119	F-ZLNL	[wfu by 05Jun05 Istres, France; to museum at Saint Victoret, Marseille, France, 27Feb06]			
01	3	F-WLKL	F-BLKL	[being refurbished at Le Bourget, France, 2011, after over 10 years stored at Reims-Prunay, France]			

Production complete

Production by FMA in Argentina

C/n	Series	Identities	
A-1		Argentina E-213	[w/o 29Mar73; collided with E-217 c/n A-5 Santa Luis, Argentina]
A-2		Argentina E-214	[w/o 30Dec74 Cordoba, Argentina]
A-3		Argentina E-215	[wfu 1998; preserved Ameghino, Argentina]
A-4		Argentina E-216	[w/o 26Apr62 Moron, Argentina]
A-5		Argentina E-217	[w/o 29Mar73; collided with E-213 c/n A-1 Santa Luis, Argentina]
A-6		Argentina E-218	[w/o 11Feb81 Mendoza, Argentina – but see A-35]
A-7		Argentina E-219	[wfu 1998 and by 2005 displayed on a roundabout near Mendoza apt, Argentina]
A-8		Argentina E-220	[wfu 2005; stored Mendoza, Argentina]
A-9		Argentina E-221	[wfu 1994; preserved Mendoza, Argentina]
A-10		Argentina E-222	[wfu 1994 and stored by Lockheed Martin Aircraft Argentina SA]
A-11		Argentina E-223 [code 23]	[wfu 1994 and std by Escuela de Suboficiales de la Fuerza Aerea (ESFA)]
A-12		Argentina E-224	[wfu 1998; to museum at Santa Romana, Argentina]
A-13		Argentina E-225	[wfu 1994; stored with Area Material Quilmes (AMQ), Argentina]
A-14		Argentina E-226	[wfu 1994; preserved Cordoba, Argentina]
A-15		Argentina E-227	[wfu 2006; dismantled at Mendoza, Argentina]
A-16		Argentina E-228 [code 28]	[w/o 16Aug65 Formosa, Argentina]
A-17		Argentina E-229 [code 29]	[wfu 1994 and stored by Lockheed Martin Aircraft Argentina SA]
A-18		Argentina E-230	[wfu 1994; to Escuela Nacional Education Tecnica, Mendoza, Argentina as instructional airframe]
A-19		Argentina E-231	[w/o 09Dec64 "EAM"?]
A-20		Argentina E-232	[wfu 2002; to instructional airframe, Mendoza, Argentina]
A-21		Argentina E-233	[wfu 1995; preserved Mendoza, Argentina]
A-22		Argentina E-234	[w/o 1990 Mendoza, Argentina]
A-23		Argentina E-235	[wfu 1998; stored Mendoza, Argentina; an FMA Paris painted as E-235 is displayed at Museo de Aera de Material, Rio Cuarto but is believd not to be c/n A-23]
A-24		Argentina E-236	[wfu 2005; stored Mendoza, Argentina]
A-25		Argentina E-237	[w/o 04Nov83 San Luis, Argentina]
A-26		Argentina E-238	[w/o 30Dec78 Mendoza, Argentina]
A-27		Argentina E-239	[w/o Jun78 Mendoza, Argentina]
A-28		Argentina E-240	[w/o 20Mar85 San Juan, Argentina]
A-29		Argentina E-241	[wfu 2006]
A-30		Argentina E-242	[wfu 2007]
A-31		Argentina E-243	[wfu 1998; by 2005 displayed by San Justo Aero Club, San Justo, Argentina]
A-32		Argentina E-244	[wfu 1998; preserved San Juan, Argentina, wearing marks E-245]
A-33		Argentina E-245	[wfu 1998; stored Bahia Blanca, Argentina]
A-34		Argentina E-246	[w/o 09Feb77 Cordoba, Argentina]
A-35		Argentina E-247	[wfu 1993 to Museo Nacional de Aeronautica, by Apr04 displayed on a pole at Moron, Argentina painted as E-218]
A-36		Argentina E-248	[w/o 08Nov77 Cordoba, Argentina]

Production complete

PIAGGIO PD808

C/n	Series	Identities	
501	TA	MM577	[wfu by 1996, on dump at Pratica di Mare by Mar98]
502	TA	MM578	[on dump at Pratica di Mare by Mar98; b/u]
503	VIP	I-PIAI	[w/o 18Jun68 San Sebastian, Spain]
504	VIP	I-PIAL	[wfu 1998]
505	GE1	MM61958	[wfu at Pratica di Mare by Nov97]
506	VIP	MM61948	[wfu; preserved at Cadimare former seaplane base, La Spezia,Italy]
507	VIP	MM61949	[wfu mid-1990s; to Ditellandia Air Park, Castel Volturno by Jul99]
508	VIP	MM61950	[wfu Rome/Ciampino 2006]
509	VIP	MM61951	[wfu at Pratica di Mare by Mar98]
510	TP	MM61952	[converted to PD808 GE2; wfu at Pratica di Mare by Aug04; preserved at ITISM, Faraday college, Ostia, Rome, Italy by May09]
511	TP	MM61953	[w/o 15Sep93 Venice, Italy]
512	TP	MM61954	[wfu at Pratica di Mare by Aug98]
513	TP	MM61955	[converted to PD808 GE2; wfu by May05; preserved as gate guardian at Parma, Italy]
514	TP	MM61956	[wfu to dump at Pratica di Mare by Mar98; b/u]
515	TP	MM61957	[wfu at Pratica di Mare by Mar98]
516	GE1	MM61959	[wfu by Mar98; preserved near Ciampino airport, Rome, Italy]
517	GE1	MM61960	[wfu at Pratica di Mare by Aug04; b/u]
518	GE1	MM61961	[wfu; preserved at Italian Air Force Museum, Vigna di Valle, Italy]
519	GE1	MM61962	[wfu by Aug04; stored at Naples airport, Italy]
520	GE1	MM61963	[wfu before Jun93 Pisa, Italy; dismantled at Pratica di Mare by Nov97; remains to Ditellandia Air Park, Castel Volturno by Nov99]
521	RM	MM62014	[wfu; preserved Vialo Europa, Lucca, Italy]
522	RM	I-PIAY	MM62015 [wfu at Pratica di Mare by Mar98; b/u]
523	RM	MM62016	[wfu at Pratica di Mare by Nov97]
524	RM	MM62017	[wfu at Pratica di Mare by Feb98; b/u]

Production complete

NORTH AMERICAN/ROCKWELL SABRE MODELS

T-39 SERIES

C/n	Series	Identities				
265-1	CT-39A	59-2868	N2259V	[displayed Kirtland AFB, NM as 59-2868]		
265-2	CT-39A	59-2869	N4999G	59-2869	[AMARC park code TG033; std wfu Sep93 Memphis Airport, TN]	
265-3	NT-39A	59-2870	[to AMARC 21Aug03, park code AATG0105]			
265-4	T-39A	59-2871	[w/o 13Nov69 Eglin AFB, FL]			
265-5	CT-39A	59-2872	N2296C	59-2872	[AMARC park code TG015]	
265-6	T-39A	60-3478	[to AMARC 22Aug03, park code AATG0106]			
265-7	CT-39A	60-3479	[AMARC park code TG082]			
265-8	CT-39A	60-3480	[AMARC park code TG013]			
265-9	CT-39A	60-3481	[AMARC park code TG085]		[to Lane Community College, Eugene, OR; to Evergreen Aviation & Space Museum,Mcminnville, OR; to Classic Aircraft Aviation Museum, Hillsboro, OR]	
265-10	CT-39A	60-3482	[AMARC park code TG016]	N510TA	XA-TFD	[w/o 4Feb00 Merida, Mexico]
265-11	T-39A	60-3483	[preserved Travis AFB, CA]			
265-12	CT-39A	60-3484	[AMARC park code TG024]	N7043U	XB-GDU	XA-TFC [w/o 16May97 20km S of Monterrey-Del Norte, Mexico]
265-13	CT-39A	60-3485	[AMARC park code TG003]	[West Intl Aviation, Tucson, AZ]		
265-14	CT-39A	60-3486	[AMARC park code TG008]	XA-TIY	[wfu; stored Laredo, TX]	
265-15	CT-39A	60-3487	[AMARC park code TG021]	N510TD	[cx Sep98 still in AMARC as 60-3486]	
265-16	CT-39A	60-3488	N431NA	[instructional airframe at Des Moines Educational Resource Center, IA; cx 21May13]		
265-17	CT-39A	60-3489	[AMARC park code TG058]	[to Houston Community College, TX]		
265-18	CT-39A	60-3490	[AMARC park code TG062]	N8052V	[South Seattle Community College, WA]	
265-19	CT-39A	60-3491	[AMARC park code TG009]			
265-20	CT-39A	60-3492	[AMARC park code TG007]	[to Thief River Falls Tech College, MN]		
265-21	CT-39A	60-3493	[AMARC park code TG057]	[to Moses Lake, WA for instructional use]		
265-22	CT-39A	60-3494	[AMARC park code TG094]			
265-23	CT-39A	60-3495	[displayed Scott AFB, IL]			
265-24	CT-39A	60-3496	[AMARC park code TG072]	[to Cochise College, Douglas, AZ]		
265-25	CT-39A	60-3497	[AMARC park code TG066]			
265-26	CT-39A	60-3498	[AMARC park code TG077]	[at Chandler Williams Gateway, AZ, Apr94]		
265-27	CT-39A	60-3499	[AMARC park code TG037]			
265-28	CT-39A	60-3500	[AMARC park code TG030]	[to Letourneau College, Longview, TX]		
265-29	CT-39A	60-3501	[AMARC park code TG093]			
265-30	CT-39A	60-3502	[AMARC park code TG095]	[to Dr Robert Smirnow, E Northport, NY]		
265-31	GCT-39A	60-3503	[preserved Air Classics Museum, Aurora, IL]			
265-32	CT-39A	60-3504	[to Bi-States College, St Louis, MO, then to Wyoming Technical College, Oakland, CA; to Oakland Aviation Museum, Oakland, CA]		(N3504)	
265-33	T-39A	60-3505	[displayed Edwards Flight Test Museum, CA]			
265-34	T-39A	60-3506	[w/o 09Feb74 Colorado, CO]			
265-35	CT-39A	60-3507	[AMARC park code TG061]	[West LA College, Los Angeles, CA marked as "0350" – painted as N3507W (these marks used on a PA-32)]		
265-36	CT-39A	60-3508	[AMARC park code TG042]	[believed b/u]		
265-37	CT-39A	61-0634	[displayed Dyess AFB, TX]			
265-38	CT-39A	61-0635	[AMARC park code TG054]	[to Lafayette Regional A/P, LA]		
265-39	CT-39A	61-0636	[AMARC park code TG089]			
265-40	CT-39A	61-0637	[AMARC park code TG035]			
265-41	CT-39A	61-0638	[AMARC park code TG096]	[to Jett Paqueteria S.A. for parts use circa 2006 noted 14Apr06 Laredo TX]		
265-42	CT-39A	61-0639	[AMARC park code TG086]	N21092	[instructional airframe at Blackhawk Technical College, Janesville, WI, then disposed of]	
265-43	T-39A	61-0640	[w/o 16Apr70 Halifax County A/P, NC (midair collision with a TA-4F)]			
265-44	CT-39A	61-0641	[AMARC park code TG036]	[to Rock Valley College, Rockford, IL]		
265-45	CT-39A	61-0642	[AMARC park code TG045]			
265-46	CT-39A	61-0643	[AMARC park code TG022]			
265-47	T-39A	61-0644	[w/o 07May63 Andrews AFB, VA]			
265-48	CT-39A	61-0645	[AMARC park code TG091]	N6CF	XA-TFL	[w/o Culiacan, Mexico 05Jul07]
265-49	T-39A	61-0646	[w/o 14May75 10 miles north of Richmond, VA]			
265-50	CT-39A	61-0647	[AMARC park code TG078]	[to Coast Community College, Costa Mesa, CA]		
265-51	CT-39A	61-0648	[AMARC park code TG017]	[to scrapyard of West Intl Aviation,in 1993]		
265-52	T-39A	61-0649	N1064	[AMARC park code TG047; to Portland A/P fire service, OR, still wearing 61-0649; no longer present Oct10]		
265-53	CT-39A	61-0650	[AMARC park code TG043]	[instructional airframe, Everett Community College, WA]		
265-54	CT-39A	61-0651	[AMARC park code TG040]	[instructional airframe, Trident Technical College, Moncks Corner, SC]		
265-55	CT-39A	61-0652	N4999H	61-0652	[AMARC park code TG087]	
265-56	CT-39A	61-0653	[AMARC park code TG071]	[to Community College of San Francisco, CA]		
265-57	CT-39A	61-0654	[AMARC park code TG044]	"N1ERAU"	[to Jett Paqueteria S.A. for parts use circa 2006 noted 14Apr06 Laredo TX]	
265-58	CT-39A	61-0655	[AMARC park code TG005]	[sold 1992 to Av-mats, St Louis, MO; ex storage]		
265-59	CT-39A	61-0656	[AMARC park code TG010]			
265-60	CT-39A	61-0657	[AMARC park code TG023]	[to Rice Aviation, Houston-Hobby, TX]		
265-61	CT-39A	61-0658	[AMARC park code TG034]	[to Frederick Community College, Frederick, MD; removed by road 15Aug00, reportedly to Texas]		
265-62	CT-39A	61-0659	[AMARC park code TG026]	XA-TNP	[w/o Culiacan, Mexico, 30Dec06]	
265-63	T-39A	61-0660	[displayed McClellan AFB, CA]			
265-64	T-39A	61-0661	[w/o 29Jul62 Paine Field-Seattle, WA]			
265-65	CT-39A	61-0662	[AMARC park code TG032]	[b/u Spirit of St Louis, MO; remains to Clarkesville, MO, by 1993]		
265-66	CT-39A	61-0663	[AMARC park code TG067]	[b/u nose/forward fuselage by firestation at New Orleans/Lakefront A/P, LA; removed by road late Apr01]		
265-67	T-39A	61-0664	[AMARC park code TG063]	[to Deuel Vo-Tech Inst, Tracy, CA, 08Jun90; to Castle Air Museum, Atwater, CA, 05Dec07]		
265-68	CT-39A	61-0665	[AMARC park code TG028]			
265-69	CT-39A	61-0666	[AMARC park code TG014]			
265-70	CT-39A	61-0667	[AMARC park code TG088]	N7143N	[w/o Khartoum A/P, Sudan in either 1993 or 1994; to Fujairah, UAE minus wings & engines; noted Jan04]	
265-71	CT-39A	61-0668	[AMARC park code TG051]	[believed b/u]		
265-72	CT-39A	61-0669	[AMARC park code TG075]	[to Metro Tech Aviation Career Center, Oklahoma City, OK]		
265-73	CT-39A	61-0670	[operational Maxwell AFB, AL]			
265-74	CT-39A	61-0671	[AMARC park code TG090]	[to ground trainer Keesler AFB, MS]		
265-75	T-39A	61-0672	[w/o 13Mar79 S Korea]			
265-76	CT-39A	61-0673	[AMARC park code TG038]	N4313V	XA-TJZ	[wfu; stored Laredo, TX]
265-77	CT-39A	61-0674	[displayed Hill AFB, UT]			
265-78	CT-39A	61-0675	[displayed Yokota AFB, Japan; reported b/u circa 1998]			
265-79	CT-39A	61-0676	[AMARC park code TG049]			
265-80	T-39A	61-0677	N9166Y	[at Helena Vocational Technical Center, Helena ND]		
265-81	CT-39A	61-0678	[AMARC park code TG012]			
265-82	T-39A	61-0679	[AMARC park code TG069]	N6581E	[at Spokane Community College, WA]	
265-83	CT-39A	61-0680	[AMARC park code TG039]	N32010	[Central Missouri State University, MO; at Warrensburg, MO marked "1068"]	
265-84	CT-39A	61-0681	[instructional airframe at Michigan Institute of Aeronautics, Canton, MI]			
265-85	CT-39A	61-0682	[AMARC park code TG031]	[to Southwest Michigan College, Dowagiac, MI]		
265-86	CT-39A	61-0683	[AMARC park code TG025]	N510TB	XB-GDW	XA-GDW [wfu; stored Laredo, TX]
265-87	T-39A	61-0684	[scrapyard Davis-Monthan, AZ/"Bob's Air Park"; believed b/u]			
265-88	T-39A	61-0685	[preserved US Army Aviation Museum, Fort Rucker, AL]			
270-1	T-39B	59-2873	[preserved Wright-Patterson AFB, OH, until 1986 then stored at China Lake NWC, CA]			

SABRE T-39

C/n	Series	Identities
270-2	T-39B	59-2874 [AMARC park code TG103]
270-3	T-39B	60-3474 [operational Edwards AFB, CA]
270-4	T-39B	60-3475 [AMARC park code TG098]
270-5	T-39B	60-3476 [AMARC park code TG102]
270-6	T-39B	60-3477 [AMARC park code TG101]
276-1	T-39A	62-4448 [w/o 28Jan64, Erfurt, East Germany – shot down by Soviet Air Force]
276-2	CT-39A	62-4449 [AMARC park code TG092] [preserved Pima County Museum, Tucson, AZ]
276-3	CT-39A	62-4450 [AMARC park code TG006] [to Jett Paqueteria S.A. for parts use circa 2006 noted 14Apr06 Laredo TX]
276-4	CT-39A	62-4451 [AMARC park code TG060] N31403 XA-TQR [wfu; stored Laredo, TX]
276-5	T-39A	62-4452 [preserved Travis AFB, CA]
276-6	T-39A	62-4453 N6552R XA-TGO [wfu; stored Laredo, TX]
276-7	CT-39A	62-4454 [AMARC park code TG018]
276-8	CT-39A	62-4455 [AMARC park code TG065] N4314B XA-TJU [w/o Monterrey, Mexico, 19Dec06]
276-9	CT-39A	62-4456 [AMARC park code TG056] [at Westwood College of Aviation Technology, Los Angeles, CA painted as N1965W]
276-10	CT-39A	62-4457 [AMARC park code TG002]
276-11	T-39A	62-4458 [w/o 25Mar65 Clark AFB, Philippines]
276-12	CT-39A	62-4459 [AMARC park code TG041] [to Clover Park Vo-Tech, Tacoma, WA]
276-13	T-39A	62-4460 [w/o 28Feb70 Torrejon AFB, Spain]
276-14	T-39A	62-4461 [displayed Warner-Robins AFB, GA, until 2013, then disposed of]
276-15	CT-39A	62-4462 [AMARC park code TG046] [instructional airframe at Trident Technical College, Moncks Corner, SC, wearing fake marks N24462]
276-16	CT-39A	62-4463 [AMARC park code TG043]
276-17	CT-39A	62-4464 [AMARC park code TG004] [to Utah State University, Salt Lake City, UT]
276-18	T-39A	62-4465 [preserved March AFB, CA]
276-19	CT-39A	62-4466 [AMARC park code TG019] [to technical school at Detroit City airport, MI]
276-20	CT-39A	62-4467 [AMARC park code TG083] [at GTCC Aviation Center, Greensboro, NC; wears fake marks 66866]
276-21	CT-39A	62-4468 [AMARC park code TG020] N63611 XA-TIX [wfu; stored Laredo, TX]
276-22	CT-39A	62-4469 [AMARC park code TG064] [to Wyotech, Bedford, MA. Scrapped 2007]
276-23	CT-39A	62-4470 [displayed Maxwell AFB, AL]
276-24	CT-39A	62-4471 [displayed Ramstein AFB, W Germany]
276-25	CT-39A	62-4472 [AMARC park code TG011] N39RG XA-...
276-26	CT-39A	62-4473 [AMARC park code TG029] [forward fuselage at Greater St Louis Aviation Museum, St Louis, MO]
276-27	CT-39A	62-4474 [AMARC park code TG027] XB-GDV N510TC XA-TDX [wfu; stored Laredo, TX]
276-28	CT-39A	62-4475 [AMARC] [noted flying during 1991 ex storage at AMARC; to Milwaukee Area Technical College, WI, by Sep92]
276-29	T-39A	62-4476 [AMARC park code TG099]
276-30	CT-39A	62-4477 [AMARC park code TG048; to Milwaukee Area Technical College, WI] "N269Y" [fake marks]
276-31	T-39A	62-4478 [preserved USAF Museum Wright-Patterson AFB, OH]
276-32	CT-39A	62-4479 [AMARC park code TG052] N988MT [to Metro-Tech Aviation Center, Oklahoma, OK]
276-33	CT-39A	62-4480 [AMARC park code TG068] N24480 N39FS
276-34	CT-39A	62-4481 N33UT [to University of Tennessee, Tullahoma, TN] N741MT [to Middle Tennessee State University, Murfreesboro, TN, 2006]
276-35	CT-39A	62-4482 [displayed Kelly AFB, TX, then to AMARC 30Jan04, park code AATG0107]
276-36	CT-39A	62-4483 [AMARC park code TG055] [to Indian Hills Community College, IA]
276-37	T-39A	62-4484 [displayed Kadena AFB, Japan]
276-38	CT-39A	62-4485 [displayed Yokota AFB, Japan]
276-39	CT-39A	62-4486 [AMARC park code TG050] N265WB XA-TJY [wfu; stored Laredo, TX]
276-40	CT-39A	62-4487 [displayed SAC Museum, Ashland, NE]
276-41	CT-39A	62-4488 [operational Andrews AFB, MD]
276-42	CT-39A	62-4489 [AMARC park code TG074] N65618 [to Colorado Northwestern Community College, Rangely, CO; cx Sep95; status?]
276-43	CT-39A	62-4490 [AMARC park code TG079] [to Jett Paqueteria S.A. for parts use circa 2006, noted 14Apr06 Laredo TX]
276-44	CT-39A	62-4491 [AMARC park code TG081] N63811 XA-TIW [wfu; stored Laredo, TX]
276-45	CT-39A	62-4492 [painted as N1SJ with San Jose University's Avn Dept, San Jose Airport, CA (the real N1SJ used by Cessna 310 (U-3) s/n 57-5856)]
276-46	CT-39A	62-4493 [AMARC park code TG076] [to instructional airframe, Penn College, Williamsport, PA, wearing fake marks N1PC]
276-47	CT-39A	62-4494 [displayed Chanute Air Museum, Rantoul, IL]
276-48	CT-39A	62-4495 [AMARC park code TG059] N6612S N1929P [to college in Yunlin, Taiwan, as instructional airframe]
276-49	CT-39A	62-4496 [w/o 20Apr85 Scranton/Wilkes Barre, PA]
276-50	CT-39A	62-4497 [AMARC park code TG053] [to Wyotech, Bedford, MA] "N15EC"
276-51	CT-39A	62-4498 [AMARC park code TG080] [to Salt Lake City Community College, UT]
276-52	CT-39A	62-4499 [w/o 24Jun69 McCook, NB]
276-53	CT-39A	62-4500 [AMARC park code TG070] [to Milwaukee Area Technical College, WI]
276-54	CT-39A	62-4501 [AMARC park code TG073] [to O'Fallon Technical College, St Louis, MO]
276-55	T-39A	62-4502 [w/o 31Dec68 Langley AFB, VA]
277-1	T-39D	150542 [stored China Lake NWC, CA]
277-2	T-39D	150543 [AMARC park code 7T-027] (N960M) (XA-AAG)
277-3	T-39D	150544 [code F18] [AMARC park code 7T-006]
277-4	T-39D	150545 [wfu and b/u]
277-5	T-39D	150546 [code F201] [AMARC park code 7T-014]
277-6	T-39D	150547 [code F211] [AMARC park code 7T-021] (N959M) (XA-AAI)
277-7	T-39D	150548 [code F10] [AMARC park code 7T-008] (N956M) (XA-AAF)
277-8	T-39D	150549 [code F11] [AMARC park code 7T-011]
277-9	T-39D	150550 [at Pensacola NAS, FL]
277-10	T-39D	150551 [AMARC park code 7T-002] [believed b/u]
285-1	T-39D	150969 [AMARC park code 7T-026] (N957M) (XA-AAJ)
285-2	T-39D	150970 N431NA [cx Dec91; wfu and b/u]
285-3	T-39D	150971 [AMARC park code 7T-001] [believed b/u]
285-4	T-39D	150972 [at Pensacola NAS, FL]
285-5	T-39D	150973 [code F203] [AMARC park code 7T-013]
285-6	T-39D	150974 [code F204] [AMARC park code 7T-015]
285-7	T-39D	150975 [code F12] [AMARC park code 7T-007]
285-8	T-39D	150976 [code F205] [AMARC park code 7T-016]
285-9	T-39D	150977 [at Pensacola NAS, FL]
285-10	T-39D	150978 [code F218] [AMARC park code 7T-009]
285-11	T-39D	150979 [code F206] [AMARC park code 7T-017]
285-12	T-39D	150980 [code F14] [AMARC park code 7T-004]
285-13	T-39D	150981 [AMARC park code 7T-012] [believed b/u]
285-14	T-39D	150982 [code F219] [AMARC park code 7T-022]
285-15	T-39D	150983 [code F212] [AMARC park code 7T-023]
285-16	T-39D	150984 [code F208] [AMARC park code 7T-010]
285-17	T-39D	150985 N32508 [preserved Pensacola, FL]
285-18	T-39D	150986 [displayed Warner-Robins AFB, GA]
285-19	T-39D	150987 [preserved NAS Patuxent River, MD]
285-20	T-39D	150988 [code F209] [AMARC park code 7T-005]
285-21	T-39D	150989 [stored China Lake NWC, CA]
285-22	T-39D	150990 [code F213] [AMARC park code 7T-024]

SABRE T-39/SABRE 40

C/n	Series	Identities										
285-23	T-39D	150991	[code F17]	[AMARC park code 7T-003]								
285-24	T-39D	150992	[active at China Lake NWC, CA circa May97]									
285-25	T-39D	151336	[code F214]	[AMARC park code 7T-025]		(N961M)	(XA-AAH)					
285-26	T-39D	151337	[at Pensacola NAS, FL]									
285-27	T-39D	151338	[preserved Southern Museum of Flight, Birmingham, AL]									
285-28	T-39D	151339	[preserved US Naval Aviation Museum, NAS Pensacola, FL]									
285-29	T-39D	151340	[code F216]	[AMARC park code 7T-018]		[wfu to DMI scrapyard at AMARC]						
285-30	T-39D	151341	[code F217]	[AMARC park code 7T-019]								
285-31	T-39D	151342	[AMARC park code TG-097]		[to Milwaukee Area Technical College, WI]							
285-32	T-39D	151343	[dumped NAS Pensacola, FL; believed b/u]									

Production complete

AMARC or AMARG indicates aircraft at Aerospace Maintenance and Regeneration Center, Davis-Monthan, AZ

SABRE 40

C/n	Series	Identities											
282-1	R	N7820C	N177A	N766R	XC-OAH	XC-JCK	(N351JM)	N116SC	[cx Jul10; wfu]				
282-2	T-39N	N577R	N577PM	N100WF	N108W	N108U	N57GS	N67WW	N16TA	N304NT	US Navy 165512	[wfu; to AMARG	
		Davis Monthan, AZ, 23May14]											
282-3		N570R	(N57QR)	N467H	[wfu Van Nuys A/P, CA, circa 2002; parted out; cx Jun11]								
282-4		N6358C	N14M	N75JD	N111MS	N408TR	[cx Sep03; in use as instructional airframe by Toledo Public Schools, OH]						
282-5		N30W	[w/o 21Dec67 Perryville, MO]										
282-6		N6360C	N600R	XB-HHF	XA-SBS	XA-GYR	XA-UCS	[w/o Mexico City 05Jul06]					
282-7		N6361C	N360J	N576R	N1102D	N43NR	N101US	N43NR	N122RP	XA-SEN	XB-EZV	XA-STU	N706A	[wfu;
		b/u Opa-Locka, FL]											
282-8		N6362C	N520S	N366N	N369N	N140MM	[wfu Sep93 and parted out; cx Nov96]						
282-9	T-39N	N6363C	N620M	N620K	N327JB	(N327RH)	N329SS	N301NT	US Navy 165509	[wfu; to instructional airframe,			
		NAS Pensacola, FL]											
282-10		N6364C	N525N	N9503Z	[w/o 07Mar73 Blaine, MN]								
282-11		N6365C	N167H	N167G	N73PC	N10SL	[wfu for spares & b/u Fort Lauderdale Executive, FL; cx Jun03]						
282-12		N6366C	N905M	N888PM	N368DA	N107CJ	[wfu Opa-Locka, FL; cx Mar97]						
282-13		N6367C	N899TG	N408S	N408CS	N408CC	XA-SMP	N502RR	XA-TKW				
282-14		N6368C	N2009	N31BC	N31BQ	N30BE	(N30PN)	[b/u during 1986; remains at Clarkesville, MO]					
282-15		N6369C	N106G	N1062	N32BC	N32BQ	(N19MS)	N40SE	N21PF	N43W	N43WL	[cx 02Dec14; wfu]	
282-16		N6370C	N227SW	N227S	N40GP	N41GS	[b/u for spares Miami A/P, FL during		1989]				
282-17		N6371C	N911Q	N382RF	N392F	N900CS	XA-HOK	[wfu; remains at Clarkesville, MO]					
282-18		N6372C	N107G	N1072	N113SC	N15TS	N131BH	[cx 02May07; b/u]					
282-19	R/T-39N	N6373C	N881MC	N881MD	N100CE	N100E	(N40R)	N311NT	US Navy 165519				
282-20	T-39N	N6374C	N265R	N3298D	N40YA	(N282AM)	N315NT/US Navy 165523 [wore dual marks]		[wfu; to AMARG Davis Monthan, AZ, 22May14]				
282-21		N6375C	N168H	N168D	N87CM	[wfu Clarkesville, MO; parted out; cx 30Apr15]							
282-22		N6376C	N747	N747E	[w/o 21Dec94 Buenos Aires-Aeroparque, Argentina; parted out Buenos Aires-Don Torcuato]								
282-23		N6377C	N282NA	N8400B	N800M	N80QM	N301HA	N50TX	(N265AC)	N123CD	(N55ME)		
282-24		N6378C	N720J	N360Q	N40DW	N8AF	XA-JDN						
282-25		N6379C	HB-VAK	I-SNAK	N40SJ	I-NICK	[wfu; to White Inds, Bates City, MO, for spares Oct98]						
282-26		N6380C	N60Y	N6087	N737E	N153G	N300CH	XA-RED	XA-DAN	XA-RED	[cx; fate?]		
282-27		N6381C	N720R	N129GP	N129GB	N111EA	N61RH	[wfu Oct93 to Spartan College of Aeronautics & Technology, Tulsa Int'l A/P, OK]					
282-28	T-39N	N6382C	N6565A	N6565K	N524AC	N524AG	N27DA	N197DA	N40CD	N482HC	N314NT	US Navy 165522	[w/o
		Gulf of Mexico 08May02 in mid-air collision with 165525 c/n 282-100]											
282-29	T-39N	N6383C	N910E	N170JL	N170AL	N170DD	N303NT	US Navy 165511	[wfu; to AMARG, Davis-Monthan, AZ, 22May13]				
282-30	T-39N	N6384C	N526N	N7090	N709Q	N801MS	N306NT	US Navy 165514	[wfu; to AMARG Davis Monthan, AZ, 03Sep14]				
282-31		N23G	N236Y	N800Y	N700R	N577VM	N34AM	[wfu; to spares 1993 Spirit of St Louis, MO; remains with Fire Service at Springfield					
		Airport, IL]											
282-32	T-39N	N100Y	N100HC	N711UC	N40SL	N40WP	N8GA	N456JP	N312NT	US Navy 165520	[wfu; to George Stone Technical		
		Center, Pensacola, FL, as instructional airframe 20Oct14]											
282-33		N737R	N903K	N903KB	N168W								
282-34		N6389C	N575R	N5PC	N5PQ	N400CS	N940CC	[cx 15Nov12, wfu]					
282-35		N6390C	N341AP	N341AR	N567DW	[b/u circa 1985; remains to Clarkesville, MO]							
282-36		N6391C	N1903W	N1908W	N22BN	N59PK	N59K	N59KQ	N63A	N88JM	N200MP	N40LB	[cx 30Aug12, wfu
		Fort Lauderdale Executive A/P, FL]											
282-37		N6392C	N265W	N77AP	[w/o 07Nov77 New Orleans, LA]								
282-38		N6393C	N2997	N299LR	N100FS	(N68AA)	N999VT	N921JG	N339PM	[parted out by AvMATS, St Louis, MO; cx Jun11]			
282-39	R	N6394C	N442A	N947R	N333B	XA-BAF	(N4492V)	XA-RGC	XA-RTM	XA-PIC	[wfu Toluca, Mexico]		
282-40		N6395C	N738R	N715MR	N40BP	[wfu Oct93; parted out Clarkesville, MO; remains form part of MonstroCity exhibit at City Museum, St Louis, MO]							
282-41		N6396C	N661P	N300RC	N300RG	N707JM	N57RM	(N300TK)	(N116AC)	N240AC	XB-AYJ	[impounded Panama City	
		Balboa/Paitilla, Panama, Dec01]											
282-42		N6397C	N727R	N904K	(N61FC)	N40EL	N500RK	N50CD	[w/o 03Feb90 Detroit, MI; cx Oct91; remains to Spirit of St				
		Louis A/P, MO 1995]											
282-43	R	N6398C	N730R	XA-JUD	N4469F	Ecuador 043							
282-44		N6399C	N4567	N1DC	N1QC	N44NP	N600JS	N64MA	[instructional airframe, Middle Georgia College Aviation Campus,				
		Eastman, GA]											
282-45		N6552C	N747UP	N344UP	N255GM	N333GM	N333NM						
282-46	CT-39E	N6553C	N339NA	157352	[w/o 21Dec75 Alameda AFB, CA]								
282-47		N740R	N34W	[w/o 04Jan74 Midland, TX]									
282-48	R	N6555C	N747UP	N90GM	(N153G)	XA-JUE	N4469M	XA-CPQ	N4469M	XA-RGC	N47VL	[parted out Perryville, MO]	
282-49		N6556C	N757R	N905K	N905KB	Sweden 86001							
282-50		N6557C	N757E	N956	N956CC	XA-SMQ	N282CA	[wfu Spirit of St Louis, MO, still wearing previous identity XA-SMQ; b/u; cx 24Jul08]					
282-51		N733R	N108G	N108X	N227LS	N225LS	(N51MN)	[noted 31Aug91 wfu Spirit of St Louis A/P, MO; remains to Elsberry, MO]					
282-52	R	N7502V	N200A	N2000	N2004	N40R	N77MR	(N77MK)	N303A	N282MC	N64DH		
282-53		N7503V	N999BS	N123MS	N101T	N62K	N62Q	(ZS-GSB)	ZS-PTJ	N67201	N600BP	N555PT	[cx Jan91; parted
		out Spirit of St.Louis, MO]											
282-54		N7504V	N255CT	N256CT	XA-EEU	[w/o 1980 ground accident in Mexico]							
282-55		N7505V	N2007	N353WB	N353WC	N68HC	N68HQ	N221PH	(N221PX)	[b/u during 1986; cx Feb91; fuselage to Spirit of St.Louis			
		A/P, MO circa Aug00]											
282-56		N7506V	N322CS	N10CC	N722ST	N722FD	(N722ED)	N204TM	N85DA	XA-RPS	[reported wfu]		
282-57		N7507V	N27C	N545C	N1909R	N1909D	[to spares at Spirit of St Louis A/P, MO circa May97]						
282-58		N7508V	N1101G	N110FS	[wfu; remains at Spirit of St.Louis A/P, MO circa Oct00; cx Sep01]								
282-59		N7509V	N48WS	N48WP	(N2SN)	N17LT	XA-ESR	N465S	N40SE	N43CF	[parted out Perryville, MO; cx Aug95]		
282-60	T-39N	N7510V	N903G	N66TP	N22TP	N256MA	N256EN	N256EA	N555AE	N555AB	N141H	N316NT	US Navy 165524
		[w/o northwest Georgia, USA, 10Jan06]											

SABRE 40

C/n	Series	Identities
282-61	T-39N	N550L N550LL N231A XA-RGC XA-EGC N2568S (N60WL) N33TW N309NT US Navy 165517 [wfu; to AMARG Davis Monthan, AZ,03Sep14]
282-62		N1863T [cx Sep87, wfu]
282-63		N325K XA-AFW XB-IHB
282-64		N7514V N9000V N9000S N800CS [b/u 1986; cx Feb90]
282-65		N2232B N145G XA-GGR XA-MJE
282-66	T-39N	N2233B N355MJ N4943A N737R N40NR N40HC N48TC N54CF N98CF N305NT US Navy 165513 [w/o 12Apr10 nr Morgantown, GA]
282-67	A	N2234B N711T N140RF [cx Aug10; parted out by AvMATS, St Louis, MO]
282-68	R	N2235B N788R N801NC N22MY N22MV N60RB XA-LEL N4469N Ecuador 068 [w/o 03Jun88 Quito A/P, Ecuador]
282-69		N2236B N125N N256MA N125NL N1MN N43NR N777V N777VZ N49RJ [canx 09Dec04; b/u]
282-70		N2236C N377P N874AJ N111AB N654E N22CH N70SL N17LT N34LP N3280G [impounded Mexico City, Mexico; cx 06Jul13, CofR expired; current status not known]
282-71		N2239B N957 N957CC XA-SMR [dbr Saltillo, Mexico, 30Jun07]
282-72	T-39N	N744R (N880HL) (N69CG) N78GP N986JB N307NT US Navy 165515 [wfu; to AMARG Davis Monthan, AZ, 28Aug14]
282-73		N630M N630N [cx Jun85; b/u for spares; remains at Spirit of St.Louis A/P, MO, circa Oct00]
282-74		N2241B N572R N707TG N707FH [b/u and cx Nov02]
282-75		N2241C N48CG (N48CE) [b/u 1983; remains to Clarkesville, MO]
282-76		N2242B N474VW D-CAVW N787R N124H N415CS N415GS N350E N58025 N8345K N265CM N257TM [b/u circa May02, cx Jun02]
282-77	T-39N	N2244B N608S N608AR N189AR N96CM N27KG N310NT US Navy 165518 [wfu; to AMARG Davis Monthan, AZ, 20Feb14]
282-78		N739R [w/o 16May67 Ventura, CA]
282-79		N2248C N797R N701NC N35CC N111AC XA-CYS
282-80		N2249B N36050 N360E N40JF N40WH XA-FTN XB-JGI [parted out Perryville, MO]
282-81	T-39N	N2250B N36065 N360N N99CR N416CS N1GY N302NT US Marines 165510 [wfu; to AMARG Davis Monthan, AZ, 23Jul14]
282-82		N574R N736R N713MR (N777ST) N19MS N366DA XB-EQR N39RG [to Tulsa Technology Center, Tulsa, OK, as instructional airframe 2006]
282-83		N726R N642LR N232T N160TC N82ML [wfu for spares c Oct94 Clarkesville, MO; cx Mar95]
282-84	CT-39E	N2254B 157353 [code 353RW] [AMARC park code 7T-028]
282-85	CT-39E	N2255B 157354 N958M XA-AAW [substantial damage 02Jun03 in hanger collapse at Laredo, TX still wearing 157354]
282-86		N86 [cx Sep92; wfu; stored in bare metal Oklahoma City, OK, no marks visible]
282-87		N87 N36P N399P [at Pittsburgh Inst of Aeronautics, PA]
282-88		N88 [cx Dec93; instructional airframe Hampton University/Hughes Training Inc Aero Science Center, Newport News, VA, then scrapped]
282-89		N89 [cx Oct91; b/u for spares]
282-90	T-39N	N2569M N928R CF-NCG C-FNCG N3831C N155GM N362DA N308NT US Navy 165516 [wfu; to AMARG Davis Monthan, AZ, 28Aug14]
282-91		N9500B N5511A N5511Z N66ES N40NR Sweden 86002
282-92	CT-39E	N2676B 158382 N825SB [to Tulsa Technology Center, Tulsa, OK, as instructional airframe 2005]
282-93	CT-39E	N4701N 158381 [w/o during 1991 nr Spratley Islands, S China Sea]
282-94	T-39N	N4703N N16R N216R N6TE N147CF N40TA N313NT US Navy 165521
282-95	CT-39E	N4704N 158380 N425NA 158380
282-96	CT-39E	N4705N 158383 [wfu; to Dodson International Parts, KS circa 2004]
282-97		N4706N N85 [w/o 14Jan76 Recife, Brazil]
282-98	A	N4707N N40SC N516WP N516LW N767JH YV416T YV2871
282-99	A	N7594N N78TC N22CH N400GM N100FG N12BW N211BR
282-100	A/T-39N	N19HF N82CF XA-LEG N71325 (N302NT) N317NT US Navy 165525 [w/o Gulf of Mexico 08May02 in mid-air collision with 165522 c/n 282-28]
282-101	A	N7596N N1BX N111XB N101RR N160W
282-102	A	N7597N N2WR N800DC N74MG N74MJ (N157AT) XA-PIH XB-JKV XA-UGB
282-103	A	N7598N N44P N9MS N217A N217TE N217E N730CA N730CP [cx 21Oct13; wfu]
282-104	A	N40CH N78BC N99XR N100KS N26SC N26SE N925BL XA-SEU N104SL [b/u; cx 24Jul08]
282-105	A	N2HW N2QW N22BJ N312K N921JG XA-SCN XC-AA73 [noted derelict at Mexico City, Mexico in Jan03]
282-106	A	N7595N XB-DUS XA-RKG (N22NB) N333GM N854RB YV-1144CP YV120T [wfu Caracas/Simon Bolivar, Venezuela]
282-107	A	N7584N N40NR CF-BRL [w/o 27Feb74 Frobisher Bay, Canada]
282-108	A	N7596N N442WT N442WP N306CW N85CC N8500
282-109	A	N4NP N700CF N93AC N77AT Ecuador 047
282-110	A	N7597N N477X N477A N250EC [wfu Entebbe, Uganda after suffering gunfire damage in Democratic Republic of Congo circa May03; cx 04Jun04, w/o]
282-111	A	N7662N N9NR XA-SAG N32654 N213BM (N200CK) (N431DA) (N246GS) N7KG [to Tulsa Technology Center, Tulsa, OK, as instructional airframe 2006]
282-112	A	N7667N N6789 N6789D N301PC N306PC N55MT N164DA N74MB N164DA N164DN N40ZA XA-UBG XA-UEY
282-113	A	N8311N N40SC N40BT N30AF N430MB N430MP
282-114	A	N64MC N64MG XA-ATC XC-SUB XA-ATC (N7SL) XB-RGS XB-RGO XB-MDG XA-UNV
282-115	A	N8333N N376D N376DD N376RP XA-MNA XA-GCH XA-LML
282-116	A	N4PH XB-BBL [wfu Toluca, Mexico]
282-117	A	N8338N (HB-VCZ) I-MORA N1WZ Mexico TP108/XC-UJH N3159U N265SC (N298AS)
282-118	A	N8339N PT-JNJ N19BG [wfu Aug93 still as PT-JNJ; to spares cOct94 Clarkesville,MO; cx Aug95]
282-119	A	N8341N N5565 [w/o 15Jan74 Oklahoma City, OK]
282-120	A	N73HP N73DR YV225T
282-121	A	N8349N PP-SED [fuselage to Spirit of St.Louis A/p, MO circa Sep97]
282-122	A	N40JW N188PS "N409GL" N188PS N409GL [parted out by AvMATS, St Louis, MO]
282-123	A	N8350N XA-APD XB-ESS
282-124	A	N193AT N200E N2006 N40JE N20ES N70ES XA-TYZ XB-EGO
282-125	A	N8356N XB-NIB XA-SQA
282-126	A	N40NS XA-SNI N40GT
282-127	A	N110PM N183AR N63SL OB-T-1319 OB-1319 [w/o 03Sep93 Buenos Aires, Argentina; remains to Opa-Locka, FL]
282-128	A	N99AP XA-LIX N99114 XB-JPS
282-129	A	N75W N75WA N75MD (N99FF) XA-RLH [b/u Monterrey del Norte, Mexico]
282-130	A	N33LB N44NR XC-SRA Mexico TP107 Mexico TP105/XC-UJG XC-HEY Mexico TP105/XC-UJI XC-PGE XA-REG XC-AA51
282-131	A	N9251N N3BM N3QM N82R LV-WND
282-132	A	N9252N N28TP N70BC N240CF N240JR [cx 15Apr13; CofR expired]
282-133	A	N65740 N41NR I-RELT
282-134	A	N40NR N60RC (YV-64CP) N66CD XA-MVG XB-MVG N134JJ N40NJ
282-135	A	N4GV N777SL N7778L N55PP N820JR N200E N2006 (N67BK) [cx 06Jun13; wfu]
282-136	A	N44PH N211SF N112ML CP-2317 (N68ML)
282-137	A	N65763 N5511A N5512A N53WC N9NR N87CR N870R N881DM XA-LMA [wfu Mexico City, Mexico]

Production complete

SABRE 60

C/n	Series	Identities									

Note: The following T-39N aircraft "converted" by Sabreliner Corp for use in US Navy training contract had the serials applied as shown above, while still current on the USCAR 282-2, 282-9, 282-19, 282-20, 282-28, 282-29, 282-30, 282-32, 282-60, 282-61, 282-66, 282-72, 282-77, 282-81, 282-90, 282-94 and 282-100

C/n	Series	Identities									
306-1		N306NA	N978R	N521N	N571NC	XA-REC	N359WJ				
306-2		N307NA	N968R	N22MA	N277CT	N2710T	N666BR	XA-PUR	N36RZ	[cx 08Aug13; wfu]	
306-3		N177A	N1001G	N925Z	N61MD	N424R	N160CF	LV-WPO	[w/o 16Jly98 Cordoba, Argentina]		
306-4		N4709N	N178W	N1210	N121JE						
306-5	A	N365N	N302H	N7090	OO-IBS	N7090	(N477JM)	N161CM	[parted out by White Inds, Bates City, MO; cx 29Apr09]		
306-6	A	N4712N	N662P	N662F	N311RM	XA-HHR	XA-ADC	XA-SMF	XB-IYS		
306-7		N4715N	N523N	N63NC	N531NC	N30PY	N60GH	N60EX	N60CR	N64AM	XA-SND	XB-HDL	XB-KPC
		XA-UOO									
306-8		N4716N	N73G	N73GR	N361DA	N84LP	N613BR	N813BR	[instructional airframe, Middle Georgia College Aviation Campus, Eastman, GA]		
306-9		N4717N	N47MN	N998R	N958R	N1298	N32UT	N5071L	N4LG	[to Greenville Technical College, SC, as instructional airframe]	
306-10		N4720N	N30W	N9000V	N9001V	N19CM	N125MC	N946JR	[parted out at Paynesville, MO circa early 2000]		
306-11		N4721N	N723R	N743R	[w/o 13Apr73 Montrose, CO]						
306-12		N4722R	N90N	N9QN	N18N	N900P	XA-ACE	XA-CCB	XC-HHL	XC-AA26	[parted out following flood damage reportedly in 1994; fuselage at Festus, MO, circa Apr96]
306-13		N4723N	N60Y	N555SL	N33BC	N33BQ	(N256MT)	N60EL	N306CF	RA-3077K	RF-14423
306-14		N4724N	N24G	N24GB	(N60AG)	N24GB	N1JN	N43GB	N60JN	[wfu; fuselage at Festus, MO, circa Apr96]	
306-15		N4725N	N101L	N60BK	N360CH	N221PH	N221PF	XA-RUQ	N604MK	N600SJ	[rebuilt with parts from c/n 306-16; canx 06Apr06 as b/u]
306-16	A	N4726N	N787R	N5415	(N542S)	N7090	N967R	N100PW	N160RW	N105UA	N33UT	N38UT	N5075L
		[parted out Sep92 Spirit of St Louis, MO; remains to Clarkesville, MO; cx May95]									
306-17		N4727N	(D-COUP)	N988R	N2UP	N2UR	N135L	N401MS	[has been parted out]		
306-18		N4728N	N908R	N339GW	N18HH	N36HH	(N60RL)	N11AQ	N12PB	N29PB	XB-LOA
306-19		N4729N	N918R	N8000U	N50DG	[to spares Perryville, MO; cx Jan99]					
306-20		N4730N	N938R	N330U	N22JW	N44SB	N78JP	N55BP	N155EC	XA-PEI	N155EC	XA-REI	XA-TLL
		XC-AAJ	XA-UJW								
306-21		N4731N	N948R	N442A	N60HC	XB-LRD	XB-QND	XC-AAC			
306-22		N4732N	N746UP	N743UP	(N450CE)	XA-CHP	[wfu Toluca, Mexico]				
306-23		N4733N	N908R	CF-BLT	C-FBLT	N15RF	N77AT	N68MA	N85HS	N616TR	
306-24	A	N4734N	N958R	N5419	N300TB	N58JM	N990AC	(N995RD)	N600GL	(N600GE)	[cx 08Jul13; wfu]
306-25		N4735N	N210F	N212F	N47MM	(N613E)	N60DL	N60DE	OB-1550	N60DE	LV-WOF	[derelict at San Fernando, Argentina by Nov01]
306-26		N4736N	N644X	N323R	N71CD	N31CJ	(N377EM)	XA-CEN	[wfu Toluca, Mexico]		
306-27		N4737N	N978R	I-SNAD	N11AL	N888WL	N105DM	(N777CR)	(N55ME)	(N105SS)	N103TA	[wfu Banjul, Gambia, after taxying accident 22Apr09]
306-28		N741R	N741RL	N353CA	[wfu]						
306-29		N4741N	N3000	N3008	N995	N3008	N771WW	[cx Jan95 as destroyed reportedly on 10Jan95 – cabin fire at Lexington-Blue Grass Airport, KY; to White Inds, Bates City, MO]			
						N771WB	[cx Aug98; parted out]				
306-30		N4742N	N905R	N905BG	N2440G	N2440C	N1116A	N104SS	[wfu Fort Lauderdale, FL; parted out by White Inds, Bates City, MO]		
306-31		N307D	N274CA	[cx Jun11; parted out]							
306-32		N4743N	N3278	[parted out at Spirit of St Louis, MO circa early 2000; cx Sep01]							
306-33		N4745N	N600B	XB-APD	XA-APD	N3FC	N30TC	N711TW	N60JF	(N660BW)	N78RR	N500RR	N399SR
		HC-BQT	CC-CGT	N633SL							
306-34		N4746N	N3533	N747RC	XA-VIO	Mexico MTX-02		Mexico MTX-01		Mexico MTX-04		Mexico AMT-203
		XB-RGO									
306-35		N4748N	N3456B	XB-JMR							
306-36		N4749N	N918R	N18N	N90R	N436CC	XA-RIR	[wfu by 2006 Toluca, Mexico]			
306-37		N4750N	N4S	N4SE	(N60EX)	N562R	[canx 23May05 as b/u]				
306-38		N4751N	N253MZ	N251MA	N229LS	N230A	XA-PEK	XA-DCO	XC-HGY	[preserved Plaza Estado de Mexico, Ciudad de Toluca, Mexico]	
306-39		N4752N	N10PF	N888MC	N507TF	N747UP	N745UP	XA-RTH	XA-SLH	N82197	(N39SL)	[to spares Sep97 at Spirit of St.Louis, MO still as XA-SLH; marks N82197 cx Jun00 as b/u]
306-40		N4753N	N907R	N711WK	N1UP	N1UT	N997ME	XA-SBX	N306SA	[wfu]	
306-41		N4754N	N925R	N173A	N1909R	(N8909R)	N614MM	LV-WLX	(N62DW)	N856MA	[reported destroyed in unknown circumstances in early 2003 in Democratic Republic of Congo; cx Aug03]
306-42		N4755N	N915R	N80L	N58CG	N60EL	N120JC	N128JC	XA-VEL	XB-IZR	
306-43		N4757N	N5420	N6NR	N6NP	N6NE	N60AH	N10UM	N115CR		
306-44		N4760N	D-CEVW	N111VW	N45RS	N86Y	N60RS	(N83RH)	N129KH	HC-BQU	N562MS	[parted out by AvMATS, St Louis, MO; cx Jun11]
306-45		N4763N	N742R	N742K	N169RF	[w/o 07Nov92 Phoenix-Sky Harbor A/P, AZ; cx Jan95]					
306-46		N4764N	N3600X	N100FL	N100FN	N642RP	[cx Jun11; parted out]				
306-47	A	N4765N	N927R	XB-ZUM	XA-ZUM	XA-ZOM	XB-ESX	XB-CVS			
306-48		N7519N	N938R	N234U	N284U	N60AG	N75HP	N86HP	N4228A	N4NT	[cx 04Aug14; wfu]
306-49		N7522N	N29S	N29SX	XA-POR	XA-RNR	[reported wfu 1991]				
306-50		N7529N	N948R	N100Y	XA-VIT	XA-MUL	XA-FSZ	N601GL	[cx 19Nov14, CofR expired]		
306-51		N7531N	N928R	C-GDCC	N141JA	N60JC					
306-52	CT-39G	N7571N	N955R	158843	[AMARC park code 7T031]						
306-53		N7573N	N957R	N99AA	N963WL	N963WA	N624FA	N48MG	N68TA	N999KG	(N999LG)	N699RD
		[canx 26Jly05 as b/u]									
306-54		N7574N	N370VS	N1020P	N38JM	N100EU	N38JM	N33TR	N97SC	N610RA	[cx 27Aug13; wfu Toluca, Mexico]
306-55	CT-39G	N7575N	N908R	N5419	158844	[AMARC park code 7T034]	[returned to service]	158844	[wfu; to AMARG, Davis-Monthan, AZ, 22May13]		
306-56		N7576N	N935R	N14M	N19M	N19U	XA-CMN	XA-RXP	XA-DSC	[wfu Toluca, Mexico]	
306-57		N7577N	N937R	N7NR	N53G	N22EH	N122EH	N701FW	N465JH	XA-RLS	[noted wfu at Toluca, Mexico, Jan02]
306-58		N7578N	N80E	N80ER	N1MN	N1PN	N529SC	N529SQ	N529CF	XA-AGT	[wfu Toluca, Mexico]
306-59		N945R	N20G	N20GX	N10LX	[cx 26Feb16; b/u Goodyear, AZ]					
306-60		N947R	N115L	N31BC	N555RR	N15H	N15HF	[modified to act as flying testbed for Williams EJ22 engine, 2002; to instructional airframe, Michigan Institute of Aviation & Technology, Canton, MI]			
306-61		N965R	N961R	(N1VC)	N76GT	N1JN	N1JX	[instructional airframe at Battle Creek, MI, since Nov04]			
306-62		N967R	N66NR	N7090	N905R	N905P	N32BC	N62CF	N162JB	[b/u circa 2001]	
306-63		N978R	XB-BIP	XA-CIS	XA-ABC	XA-LRA	XB-FST	XB-FUZ	XA-FNP	XB-ZNP	XA-TSS	XB-MBV
306-64		N8357N	N21BM	N370L	N1024G	(N500RK)	N96CP	N74BS	[a/c dismantled, fuselage noted at Spirit of St Louis, MO 08Dec02]		
306-65	CT-39G	N8364N	159361	[reported wfu Sigonella, Italy 1992]							
306-66	CT-39G	N8365N	159362	[AMARC park code 7T032]							
306-67	CT-39G	159363	[wfu; dumped Jan97 Edwards AFB, CA circa 1996]								
306-68		N8000	N2HW	N2HX	N265DP	Ecuador 049					
306-69	CT-39G	159364	[AMARC park code 7T-030]		[returned to service circa 2000]		159364	[wfu; to AMARG, Davis-Monthan, AZ, 31Jan14]			
306-70	CT-39G	159365	[wfu; to AMARG, Davis-Monthan, AZ, 21Nov13]								
306-71	A	N31BM	N370M	N1028Y	N71CC						
306-72		N231CA	N231A	N550SL	N6TM	N60TM	XA-RYD	N97SC	XA-GIH	XA-PRO	XB-MMN
306-73		N65745	N7NR	N601MG	N90EC	XC-OAH	XA-TNW	N442RM	[w/o in mid-air collison on approach to San Diego/Brown Field, CA, 16Aug15; cx 05Nov15]		

SABRE 60/65

C/n	Series	Identities											
306-74		N920G	[w/o 27Dec74 Lancaster, PA]										
306-75		N110G	N666WL	N709AB	N509AB	N11LX							
306-76		N65750	N67NR	N333PC	N333NC	N82MW	N86CP	(N760SA)	[cx 23Mar15, wfu]				
306-77		N65751	N180AR	N787R	[wfu; to spares 1994 Spirit of St Louis A/P, MO; cx Apr95]								
306-78		N65752	C-GRRS	N140JA	N477X	[b/u; cx 24Jul08]							
306-79		N4NR	N4NE	N768DV	(N7682V)	N43JG	N539PG	[parted out by White Inds, Bates City, MO; cx 08Nov12]					
306-80		N65756	PT-KOT	N61FB									
306-81	A	N6NR	N6ND	N30CC	[wfu; to spares circa Oct94; remains to Av-Mats Clarkville, MO; cx Jan96]								
306-82		N65759	N60SL	N59K									
306-83		N14CG	N14CQ	N411MD	N300YM	N99FF	XA-RLL	XB-KQY					
306-84		N65762	PT-KOU	N8025X	N383TS	N55ZM	N265GM	[wfu; cx 19Jun09]					
306-85		N65764	N217A	N500RK	N355CD	N855CD	N211BR	[dbr by fire-suppressant foam Mojave, CA, 2007; parted out by AvMATS, St Louis, MO; cx Jul10]					
306-86		N65765	N60SL	N60TG	XA-ICK	XB-KSL	XB-MRU						
306-87		N65767	N100CE	N60RS	N100MA	N400CE	N200CE	XA-RFB	XB-PCJ				
306-88		N65769	N992	N22CG	XA-RAP								
306-89		N65770	N23DS	N86RM	XA-ECM	N86RM	XA-STI	[wfu by 2006 Toluca, Mexico]					
306-90		N65772	N181AR	N13SL	N148JP	N123FG	N265MK	XB-FMB					
306-91		N65774	N204R	N204G	N60BP	N660RM	(N45MM)	LV-WXX					
306-92		N65775	N711S	N328JS	N74AB	N33JW							
306-93		N65777	N366N	N182AR	N200CX	N507U	XA-JCE	XB-IXJ	XB-MXG				
306-94		N65778	HZ-MA1	HZ-NCB	N75JT	N217RM	N217RN	N348W	[cx 14Aug12, parted out by AvMATS, St Louis, MO]				
306-95		N65783	N999DC	N124DC	N124VC								
306-96		N65784?	N54784	N68HC	N48HC	(N1318E)	N315JM	XB-ETV					
306-97		N65785	I-FBCA	N3WQ	N344K	N85DB	N707DB	N98LB	XA-RWY	XA-SVH	N90TT	N97NL	N15DJ	XA-SVG
306-98		N65786	N6MK	N169AC	N531AB	XA-GUR	XB-MXU						
306-99		N65789	N905R	N16PN	N66GE	N66GZ	[parted out]						
306-100		N65790	N881MC	N81HP	N5379W	N60SE	XA-RLR	XB-LAW	XA-TMF				
306-101	A	N65791	N68NR	N376D	N60FS	N376D	N378D						
306-102		N65792	N108G	N555AE	N444MA	N265TJ	N70HL						
306-103		N65794	N11UL	N40TL	N234DC	[cx 11May15; wfu Fort Myers/Page Field, FL]							
306-104	CT-39G	N65795	160053	[wfu; to AMARG, Davis-Monthan, AZ, 24Sep13]									
306-105	CT-39G	N65796	160054	[wfu; preserved NAS Pensacola]									
306-106	CT-39G	N65797	160055	[wfu; to AMARG, Davis Monthan, AZ, 06Mar13]									
306-107	CT-39G	N65798	160056	[AMARC park code 7T-029]		[to museum at Pensacola NAS, FL, by Feb09]							
306-108	CT-39G	N65799	160057	[w/o 03Mar91 approx 1.5 miles from Glenview NAS, IL]									
306-109	A	N2101J	N522N	N64NC	N521NC	N602KB	XA-SBV	N60SQ	XA-…				
306-110		N2103J	N60RS	HZ-MA1	N13SL	XA-RTP	N75GM	XB-HJS					
306-111		N2106J	N300RC	XA-SKB	XC-PFN	[code PF-213]		[w/o 28Jly04 Mexicali, Mexico]					
306-112		N2107J	N740R	N740RC	CC-CTC	N700AU							
306-113		N2108J	N712MR	N2626M	N113T	XA-TVZ	XC-LMP						
306-114	65	N2109J	N65R	N60TF	N65R	N65RN	N990PT	N990PA					
306-115		N2118J	(XA-LEI)	Bolivia FAB-001		Bolivia FAB-002	[cx; wfu 2013]						
306-116	A	N2119J	N605RG	N44WD	N39CB								
306-117		N2120J	N22MY	Ecuador FAE-001A	[reported wfu]								
306-118		N2122J	N65NR	N711MR	N2635M	N607SR	N607CF						
306-119	A	N2123J	N167H	N110MH	XA-JMD	N109MC	N41RG						
306-120		N2124J	N265C	N265SR	N1GM	[cx 20May13; parted out Perryville, MO]							
306-121		N2130J	N880KC	(N15CK)	N880CK	XA-SYS	N789SG	XA-…					
306-122	A	N2131J	N168H	N56RN	XA-GUR	N110JG	[cx Jun11; parted out]						
306-123		N2132J	N710MR	N2627M	N128VM	(N213BE)	N28VM	XA-PAX	N97SC	XA-ATE			
306-124	A	N2133J	N65NR	N60RS	N48WS	XB-MDO							
306-125		N2134J	XA-RGC	N265RW	N261T	XA-SLJ	N28HH	XA-AEV	XA-JML				
306-126		N2141J	N60SL	N7NR	N7NF	N1CH	N85HP	N4227N	HC-BUN	N111F	XA-TGA	XB-MQN	
306-127		N2142J	N5NE	N60DD	XA-CUR	XB-JTG							
306-128		N2143J	N80CR	N100CE	N117JL	"N24TK"	N117JL	XA-SJM	XB-SOL	XA-CUN	XB-NOA		
306-129		N2144J	N711ST	N749UP	N95RC	N60ML	XB-ULF						
306-130		N2145J	XA-OVR	XA-JIK	XB-JMM	XA-AFG	XA-UFQ	[dbf Calaya, Mexico, 18Dec08, w/o]					
306-131		N2149J	N5DL	N35DL	N61DF	N131JR	(N131SE)	XA-GUR	[w/o Nov04 Toluca, Mexico]				
306-132		N2150J	N60RS	N108W	(N994W)	N60AG	N265U	XB-MMW	XB-KLQ	[w/o 09Dec14; shot down over Venezuela on drug-running flight]			
306-133		N2151J	N6NE	N9NP	N700WS	I-PATY	N360CF	N400JH	N468RB				
306-134		N2152J	N323EC	N282WW	[cx 08May15; wfu Guatemala City/La Aurora, Guatemala]								
306-135		N2535E	N9NR	N9NT	N64CM	N59JM	N60AM	N921MB	HC-…				
306-136	65	N2501E	N465S	N65RS	[redesignated c/n 465-1 1981 as first Sabre 65 (qv)]								
306-137		N2506E	N60SL	N650C	N18X	XA-SAH							
306-138		N2508E	N22BX	N800RM	N700JR	N702JR	XA-RVT						
306-139		Mexico TP105		Mexico TP103/XC-UJE	XC-UJS								
306-140		N636	N636MC	N60AF	N26SC	N26SQ	XA-SSV						
306-141		N8NR	(N89N)	(N8NF)	N141SL	(N707GP)							
306-142		N60RS	N80CR	N742R	N742RC	N190MD	N40KJ	(N70LW)	N700MH	(N700DA)	N143DZ		
306-143		N800M	N80QM	N741R	N741RC	XA-SIM	XA-SUN	XA-TPU	XA-URI				
306-144		N2519E	Mexico TP106		Mexico TP104/XC-UJF	Mexico AMT-204							
306-145		N60SL	N730CA	XA-LOQ	XC-JDC	XC-CAM							
306-146		N301MC	N301MG	N360CH	XA-ARE	(N146BJ)	N31CR	N44DD					

Production complete

SABRE 65

C/n	Identities								
465-1	N2501E	N465S	N65RS	N77A	N65KJ	N117MB	(N117MN)	N65HH	[originally Sabre 60 c/n 306-136]
465-2	N465T	N251JE	N45H	N624DS	N124SD				
465-3	N65RS	N6K	N170JL	N170CC	N1CF	N65BT			
465-4	N1058X	N14M	N141PB	N800TW	N804PA				
465-5	N24G	N55KS	N52GG	N60CE	N241H	[w/o 11May00 Molokai, HI]			
465-6	N65NC	N511NC	N65SR	N1CC	N41CQ	(N652CC)	N2CC	N432CC	
465-7	N10580	N2000	N2800	N2000	N2700				
465-8	N10581	XA-GAP	XB-UNA						
465-9	N6NP	N769KC	(N769EG)	N6GV					
465-10	N65SL	N77TC	N336RJ						
465-11	N3000	N3030	N25UG	N5739	N57MQ				

SABRE 65/75

C/n	Identities									
465-12	XA-OVR	XA-PVR	XB-GMD	N112PR	N112PV	N529SC	N73TJ	N77GU		
465-13	N7HF	N13MF	N945CC	N95TL						
465-14	N651S	N301MC	N67SC	N71RB	N740R	N25SR	XA-SPM			
465-15	N2513E	XA-ZUM	N465TS	N25VC						
465-16	N31BC	N7000G	N700QG	N65SR	N112CF	N920CC	N603MA	N75HL	N75HE	XA-APC	XC-LNI	XA-APC
465-17	N2537E	N905K	N4MB	N32290	(N322TW)	N74VC				
465-18	N4M	N696US	XA-XPA							
465-19	N65RC	N91BZ	[parted out by AvMATS, St Louis, MO]							
465-20	N2544E	N173A								
465-21	N2586E	(N65HM)	N465LC	(N265CA)	N701FW					
465-22	N996W	N678AM	9H-ABO	VR-CEE	N927AA	N883RA	N889RA	XB-RSH	XA-UUS	
465-23	N904K	(N904KB)	N223LB	XA-...	N65JR					
465-24	N65NR	N2545E	N8000U	N800CU	N65JR	N265PC	N741R	N777SK	N271MB	N22CS	XA-INM
465-25	N9000F	N25MF	N125BP	N324ZR	N812WN	N42DC				
465-26	N465SL	N2548E	N65DD	N31SJ	N488DM	N770MD				
465-27	XA-ARE	XA-AVR	XA-FVK	N351AF	N111AD	N39TR	N4CS	N247CS		
465-28	N2549E	N333PC	N742R	N24RF	(N129BA)	N66GE				
465-29	N6NR	N976SR	N779CS							
465-30	N25ZC	(N25ZG)	N89MM	N65TC	N465SC					
465-31	N2550E	N65FC	N265M	N670AC						
465-32	N97RE	N303A	HB-VCN	N329Z						
465-33	N994	N869KC	(N869EG)	(N271MB)	N465SR	N265C	VP-CBG	N265VP	N70SK	
465-34	(N50DG)	N112KM	N80FH	N65TS	N47SE					
465-35	N2590E	N65AK								
465-36	N651GL	N652MK	N424JM	N65MC						
465-37	N750CS	N750CC	YV415T	N465NH	N465PD					
465-38	N850CS	N850CC	(N4LQ)							
465-39	N2551E	N5511A	N551FA	N203JK	N41LV	N901CD	[b/u Fort Lauderdale Executive, FL, Aug13]			
465-40	N341AP	N465RM	N465PM	N801SS	N861SS	[parted out by White Inds, Bates City, MO]				
465-41	N2556E	N800M								
465-42	N2561E	N415CS	N41TC	N15CC	N150HN	N15CC	N64SL	N45NP	N875CA	N799MW
465-43	N950CS	N228LS	N83TF	N955PR	N65T					
465-44	N7NR	N74BJ								
465-45	N442WT	N448WT	N65TJ	(N265DR)	N65DR	N265DS				
465-46	N20UC	N79CD	N65FF	N65CC	N307ST	N265FT				
465-47	N265A	N33TR								
465-48	N2539E	XA-MLG	N500WD	N265SP	N265CP	[canx 15Jun15; CofR expired]				
465-49	N455SF	N455LB	N500RR	N82CR	N697US					
465-50	N2570E	N129GP	N959C	N920DY	(N920DG)	XB-MYP				
465-51	N3BM	N3QM	N114LG	N69WU						
465-52	N500E	N96RE								
465-53	N76NX	N80R	N80RN	N465BC						
465-54	N2579E	N6000J	N600QJ	N1909R	N65SR	[cx 28Mar15, wfu]				
465-55	N2574E	XA-LUC	XA-RYO	XB-RYO	XA-TOM	XB-RSC	[w/o Las Vegas/McCarran, NV, 05Jul13; to scrapyard nr Phoenix Sky Harbor, AZ]			
465-56	N544PH	N265JS	N65TL	N499NH						
465-57	N903K	N355CD								
465-58	N65AM	N670AS	N670H							
465-59	N65AN	HB-VJF	N59SR	N61DF	N8500	N35CC	N35CQ			
465-60	N2580E	N88BF	(N688WS)	N654YS						
465-61	N23BX	N117JW								
465-62	N56NW	N65AF	N265WS							
465-63	N2N	N605Y	N2N	N2NL						
465-64	N99S	[w/o 11Jan83 Toronto, Canada; cx Aug91]								
465-65	N29S	N29SZ	N65AD	(N925WL)	N963WL	XA-SCR	N600TG	N395GA		
465-66	N964C									
465-67	N65AR	N921CC								
465-68	N65AH	OO-IBC	N68LX	N165NA	N930RA	N6NR	N888UP			
465-69	N33BC	(N31BC)	N400KV	N25KL	N65ML					
465-70	N15AK	N15EN	N58CM	N58HT						
465-71	N728C	N75G	N75GL	N75VC						
465-72	N857W	(OO-RSA)	(OO-RSB)	OO-RSE	N465SP	XB-PTC				
465-73	N64MC	N64MQ	N651MK							
465-74	N700JC									
465-75	N2581E	N570R								
465-76	N65L	N376D								

Production complete

SABRE 75

C/n	Series	Identities									
370-1		N7572N	[used as parts for other test aircraft]								
370-2		N7585N	N75NR	N8NR	N80K	N10M	[wfu; cx 08Sep06]				
370-3		N7586N	N70NR	N125N	N125NX	[wfu; cx 19May09]					
370-4		N7587N	N75U	N75UA	N37GF	N370BH	N400DB	(N404DB)	N726JR	[dbr San Jose, Costa Rica, 03Sep07]	
370-5		N7588N	N75NR	N23G	N55KS	N55KZ	N58KS	N250BC	N265SR	XA-RYJ	
370-6		N7589N	N2TE	XA-SGR	N29019	(N30EV)	[wfu; cx Sep91; remains to Clarkesville, MO]				
370-7	A	N7590N	N75NR	N60PM	N60PT	N75DE	XB-ERU	N670C	(N26TJ)	(N272HS)	[cx 03Dec14; CofR expired]
370-8		N7591N	N3TE	N70HC	[b/u for spares Sep90 Little Rock, AR; canx Jun96; remains to Paynesville, MO]						
370-9		N7592N	N8NR	N8NB	N55CR	XA-RZW	XB-GJO	N370SL	[parted out at Spirit of St Louis, MO circa early 2000 still wearing its previous identity XB-GJO; cx Jan01, scrapped]		

SABRE 75A

C/n	Series	Identities									

Production complete

380-1   N7593N   N6K   N87Y   N30GB   N100EJ   (N200UN)

380-2   N8445N   N2440G   N2440C   N19PC   N380SR   N9GN   N642TS   N406PW   YV265T

380-3   N8467N   Argentina T-10   Argentina T-11   [wfu Cordoba/Rio Cuarto, Argentina]

380-4   80A   N65733   N5105   N510AA   N75SE   XA-RLP   N11887   (LV-…)   N11887

380-5   N51   N125MS   N223LP   N71460   XA-TUD   [wfu Toluca, Mexico]

380-6   80A   N65741   N5106   N50GG   N75TJ   N711GL   N711GD   N184PC   [preserved on barge at Fort Lauderdale, FL]

380-7   N65744   N67KM   [w/o 14Jun75 Watertown, SD]

380-8   N65749   N5107   N500NL   [wfu; parted out Feb93 – possibly following an accident on 23Feb75 at Oakland-Pontiac, MI]

380-9   80A   N5108   N510BB   N6SP   N383CF   N995RD

380-10   N52   [cx Sep95 wfu; in use as an instructional airframe at Burlington, VT]

380-11   80A   N5109   N5109T   N265SR   N151TB   [cx 11Jan05; parted out by White Industries, Bates City, MO]

380-12   N65758   (N335K)   HB-VEC   D-CLAN   N75SL   D-CLAN   N120YB   (N4WJ)   N75BS   [b/u; cx 24Jul08]

380-13   N65761   Argentina AE-175

380-14   N53   N72028   [being parted out at Rantoul, KS circa early 2000]

380-15   N65766   (N338K)   N80NR   N1841D   N1841F   N15PN   N18TF   N18TZ   XA-LEG   N22JW   N424R

380-16   N54   N126MS   N12659   N801FT

380-17   80A   N65768   (N339K)   N80RS   5N-AMM   N70TF   N15RF   N111Y   N1115   N380BC   [parted out]

380-18   N55   N127MS   [wfu; parted out Perryville, MO; cx Jly95]

380-19   N65771   D-CLUB   N500TF   N100RS   XB-EPM   XA-EPM   N54HH   N80HG   N80TN   [b/u and cx Jun02]

380-20   N56   N773W   N109SB

380-21   80A   N65773   N711A   N75A   N22NT   N25AT   N577SW   N111AG   N840MA   N647JP   N82AF   N380MS   XA-…

380-22   N57   N132MS   N131MS   [wfu; parted out Perryville, MO; cx Jly95]

380-23   N65776   N68KM   N102RD   N800CD

380-24   80   N58   N219TT   [parted out by AvMATS, St Louis, MO]

380-25   N50PM   N90AM   N16LF   N13NH   N400RS

380-26   N59   N128MS   N2200A   [parted out circa Jan02 Spirit of St Louis A/P, MO; cx Jun11]

380-27   N65787   N8NR   N8NB   N10CN   N6NR   N6NG   N90GM   N90GW   N85DW   [w/o 14Aug00 near Ironwood, MI]

380-28   N60   [cx Jun96; wfu]

380-29   N61   N131MS   N58966   N132MS   N71543   [used for fire training by University of Illinois, Champaign, IL and destroyed as a result]

380-30   N65793   N69KM   N265CH   N265DP   N818DW   N818LD   N42799   [cx Jun11; parted out]

380-31   N62   N75CN   [parted out at Rantoul, KS circa early 2000]

380-32   80A   N2100J   N75RS   N64MP   N64MQ   N66ES   N66ED   (N86SH)   N380DJ   N198GB   XA-JRF

380-33   N63   N129MS   N7148J   N802FT

380-34   N2104J   N6LG   (N112KH)   N382MC   Ecuador FAE-034   Ecuador AEE-403   N97SC   XC-DDA

380-35   N64   [w/o 29Sep86 Liberal, KS; cx Aug88]

380-36   N2105J   N75A   JY-AFM   N75HL   (N835MA)   XA-MCB   N377HS   [canx 22Feb05 as b/u]

380-37   N65   N774W   [cx 06May15; CofR expired]

380-38   N2102J   D-CAVW   N85031   N3RN   HZ-AMN   N95TJ   N75AK   N316EC   N316EQ   [cx 11Dec14; CofR expired]

380-39   N2110J   N7NR   N102MJ   N88JM   N38JM   (N60WP)   N40WP   XA-PON   N2093P   XA-SXK   XC-ONA   N354SH
     (N805HD)   (N55HD)   N105HD

380-40   N2112J   N4NR   N4NB   N75NL   N920DY   N820DY   N14TN   XA-UBH   XA-UEK   [wfu Toluca, Mexico]

380-41   N2113J   N33NT   N400N   N400NR   [parted out by White Inds, Bates City, MO]

380-42   N2114J   N75RS   D-CHIC   N75AG   XA-MVT   N6YL   N3RP   N80KR   [parted out by MTW Aerospace, Montgomery, AL]

380-43   N2115J   N6NR   N2265Z   [wfu prior Sep90 Clarkesville, MO]

380-44   80A   N2116J   N2440G   N380GK   YV338T

380-45   N2117J   D-CCVW   N218US   (N218UB)   N753TW   Ecuador FAE-045   Ecuador AEE-402   [not confirmed]   [AEE-402 was w/o
     10Dec92 nr Quito A/P, Ecuador]

380-46   N2125J   (N50K)   N90C   XA-RIH   XC-HFY   XC-AA89

380-47   N2126J   N25BH   N25BX   N33RZ   XA-…

380-48   80A   N2127J   N8NR   N8NG   N805RG   N6PG   N27TS   N132DB   N100BP   XB-JYZ

380-49   80A   N2128J   N4PG   (N41B)   N4PQ   N673SH   N673FH   N221PH   N265KC

380-50   80A   N2129J   N5PG   N5EQ   N5PG   N179S   XA-ROD   XA-RLR   XA-TDQ   XA-ACD   XB-ACD

380-51   N2135J   N43R   N4343   N711BY   (N12GP)   N808EB   N80LX   N180NA   N382LS   N380CF   [cx to Mexico 28Jul10 but w/o
     Queretaro, Mexico, 30Jan16 still as N380CF]

380-52   N2136J   N75A   N177NC   N177NQ   N70KM   N84NG   N34NG   N929GC   N929CG

380-53   N2137J   N75NR   JY-AFN   HZ-THZ   N8526A   N75HZ   XC-FIA   XB-DVP   N380SR   N827SL   XB-CYA

380-54   N2138J   N6NR   N62NR   N10CN   N350MT   N81GD   N999M   N176DC   N380CF   N910BH   N380FP   XA-…
     [although cx to Mexico 28Oct13, still flying as N380CF]

380-55   N2139J   N33KA   HZ-CA1   N120KC   XA-OAF   XB-RDB   XB-GSP

380-56   N2146J   JY-AFL   N14JD   (N914JC)   N22NB   [cx 10Jul14, wfu]

380-57   N2147J   N80RS   N75A   HZ-RBH   JY-AFH   [wfu]

380-58   N2148J   N75RS   N380T   XA-CHA   XA-SEB   XA-GHR   N8267D   XA-UEQ   XC-LKB

380-59   N80AB   (N935PC)   N83AB   N911CR   N27LT   N1LT   [parted out Tulsa, OK; cx 31Jul08]

380-60   N2521E   D-CBVW   N4260K   N100TM   XB-RSG   XB-SHA   XA-RDY   N60SL   XA-AOV

380-61   N2522E   JY-AFO   9L-LAW   N727US   [parted out at Spirit of St.Louis, MO circa 1996 cx Jan00]

380-62   JY-AFP   [wfu]

380-63   N75RS   N448W

380-64   N75NR   N75Y   N942CC   JY-JAS   [w/o Alexandria, Egypt, May06]

380-65   YU-BLY   RC-BLY   9A-BLY   N88JJ   N69JN   N972NR

380-66   N2536E   N6PG   N6VL   N6PG   N75L   N943CC   N819GY   [parted out by AvMATS, St Louis, MO]

380-67   N2528E   Mexico TP 103   Mexico TP 101/XC-UJC   [w/o 26Oct89 Saltillo, Mexico; fuselage to Spirit of St.Louis A/P, MO]

380-68   N2538E   Mexico TP 104   Mexico TP 102/XC-UJD   XC-UJU   [preserved at military base near Mexico City]

380-69   N2542E   N111VW   (N111VS)   N111VX   N547JL   [w/o 18Jly98 near Marion, KS]

380-70   (N13ME)   (N15ME)   N101ME   N1NR   (N380RS)   N110AJ   [wfu Fort Lauderdale Executive, FL]

380-71   HZ-NR1   N80HK   XA-TSZ

380-72   HZ-SOG   N380N   N90N   N555JR   N933JC   [cx 21May15; wfu Pontiac, MI]

Production complete

SN601 CORVETTE

C/n	Identities							
01	F-WRSN	[ff 16Jly70; w/o 23Mar71 Marseille, France (model SN600)]						
1	F-WUAS	[ff 20Dec72] F-BUAS	F-WUAS	F-BUAS	France (CEV) 1/F-ZVMV coded MV	[wfu by Jun05 at Istres, France]		
2	F-WRNZ	F-BRNZ	France (CEV) 2/F-ZVMW coded MW	[to Vitrolles Engineering College nr Marseille, France]				
3	F-WUQN	F-BUQN	F-WUQN	F-BUQN	[w/o 16Oct00 Toulouse-Blagnac, France; repaired to non-flying condition and painted as "F-WUQN" on display at entrance to Airbus facility St. Nazaire, France]			
4	F-WUQP	F-BUQP	[wfu Toulouse, France; instructional airframe at Vitrolles, France]					
5	F-BVPA	F-ODJX	F-BVPA	CN-TDE				
6	F-WUQR	F-BVPB	F-OGJL	F-BVPB	[regn cx circa 2000; CofA expired; instructional airframe at St.Yan, France; moved to Le Bourget by 10Apr03]			
7	F-OBZR	N611AC	F-BVPK					
8	F-WPTT	6V-AEA	F-GJAS					
9	F-WRQK	F-BRQK	N612AC	F-BTTR	F-OCRN	TN-ADI	[reported wfu South of France]	
10	F-BVPO	N600AN	F-GFEJ	France (CEV) 10/F-ZVMX coded MX	[instructional airframe at Lycee Stella, Reunion]			
11	(F-WIFU)	N613AC	F-BTTS	TR-LWY	F-ODKS	F-BTTV	EI-BNY	F-WFPD	(F-GFPD) F-GKGA [wfu; cx 08Dec09; preserved in Aeroscopia museum, Toulouse/Blagnac, France]
12	F-BVPC	TR-LYM	TJ-AHR	F-GMOF	[parted out; broken up at Le Bourget, France, by Mar12]			
13	F-BVPD	N601AN	F-GFDH	[wfu; cx 08Dec09]				
14	F-BVPS	SP-FOA	(F-GIRH)	[last noted 29Mar06 dismantled on a low-loader at Le Bourget, France]				
15	F-WIFA	SE-DEN	OO-MRA	OO-MRE	F-GDUB	SE-DEN	N17AJ	F-GEQF	D6-ECB F-GNAF EC-HHZ [wfu]
16	F-BVPT	5R-MVN	5R-MBR	[wfu Antananarivo, Madagascar]				
17	F-WNGQ	N614AC	F-BTTM	F-ODTM	YV-572CP	[w/o 21Jun91 Las Delicias A/P, Santa Barbara del Zulia, Venezuela]		
18	F-WNGR	N615AC	F-BTTO	N604AN	[cx Dec90; sold to Drenair, Spain, for spares use]			
19	F-BVPL	F-OCJL	F-BVPL	TZ-PBF	(F-GDRC)	F-SEBH	F-GEPQ	EC-HIA	[wfu; cx 2006]
20	F-WNGS	N616AC	F-BTTN	TR-LZT	F-GKJB	[wfu 31Mar93 for spares at Toulouse, France; wings used in rebuild of c/n 28; forward fuselage to cabin trainer use]		
21	F-BVPE	OY-SBS	[w/o 03Sep79 Nice, France]					
22	F-WNGT	N617AC	F-BTTU	F-ODFE	TN-ADB	[w/o 30Mar79 Nkayi, Congo Republic]		
23	F-BVPF	OY-SBR	[wfu Aalborg, Denmark circa Feb05; last flight 26Dec04; to Danmarks Flymuseum, Stauning, Denmark]					
24	F-BVPI	EC-DQC	[sold in USA for scrap/spares and b/u Mar92 Toulouse, France]					
25	F-WNGU	F-BVPG	F-OBZV	F-BVPG	[cx Oct06, C of A expired]			
26	F-WNGV	N618AC	F-ODFQ	PH-JSB	F-GDAY	EC-DQE	[noted dismantled 2000 at Dieupentule, France; intended as a museum exhibit but cut up by local gypsies]	
27	F-BVPH	N26674+	[+ marks not confirmed] EC-DQG	[w/o 25Nov00 Cordoba, Spain]				
28	F-WNGX	F-BTTL	(OO-TTL)	F-GPLA				
29	F-WNGY	F-BVPJ	F-OBZP	F-BVPJ	F-OBZP	TY-BBK	[w/o 16Nov81 Lagos, Nigeria]	
30	F-WNGQ	F-BTTP	OO-MRC	TR-LAH	OO-MRC	EC-DUE	(F-GKGB)	F-GLEC	[wfu; cx 27Oct09]
31	F-WNGZ	F-BTTK	N602AN	F-WZSB	EC-DYE	F-GJAP	[to Musee de l'Air et de l'Espace, Le Bourget, France 17Oct09; cx 08Dec09]	
32	F-WNGR	F-BTTQ	OY-ARA	SE-DED	OY-ARA	EC-DUF	F-GILM	[wfu 08Dec09; preserved at entrance to Airbus factory, Meaulte, France]
33	F-BTTT	OY-SBT	[wfu]					
34	F-WNGS	F-BYCR	OY-ARB	SE-DEE	OY-ARB	SE-DEE	F-GKGD	CN-TCS	5R-MHK
35	PH-JSC	F-GDAZ	YV-589CP	YV-01CP	F-ODSR	5R-MVD	F-ODSR	[wfu]
36	F-BTTS	PH-JSD	F-OCDE	XB-CYA	XB-EWF	XA-BCC	N601RC	N600RA	[parted out by Atlanta Air Salvage, Griffin, GA]
37	F-BTTU	[w/o 31Jul90 St Yan, France; cx 12Feb91 as "reformed" 04Dec90]						
38	F-ODIF	5A-DCK						
39	F-WNGY	F-OBYG	TL-SMI	TL-RCA	F-GJLB	CN-THL		
40	F-WNGZ	F-ODJS	XB-CYI	N601CV	N200MT	N220MT	[parted out by Atlanta Air Salvage, Griffin, GA circa Feb05]	

Production complete

SYBERJET SJ30

Originally called the Swearingen SA-30 Gulfjet, then the Swearingen SJ-30 and SJ30-1, then the Sino Swearingen SJ30-2, then the Emivest SJ30.

C/n	Identities		
001	N30SJ	[ff 13Feb91 Stinson Field, TX. Stretched to become SJ30-2 prototype and ff 8Nov96; cx Oct99, wfu. To Lone Star Flight Museum, Galveston, TX, Dec06. Scrapped following storm damage sustained in Sep08]	
002	N138BF	[rolled out 17Jly00; ff 30Nov00; crashed near Del Rio, TX, 26Apr03 during high-speed test-flight, killing Sino-Swearingen's chief test pilot; w/o]	
003	N30SJ	N110SJ	
004	N709JB	N404SJ	
005	N50SJ	[ff Jan05]	
006	N60SJ	N901HB	N30SJ
007	N70SJ	N7SJ	
008	(N80SJ)	N200DV	
009	[in production, not yet completed]		
010	N30GZ		
011			
012			
TF-2	[static test frame]		
TF-3	[static test frame]		

EXPERIMENTAL & NON-PRODUCTION TYPES

ADAM AIRCRAFT A700

A 6-8 seat very light jet powered by 2 Williams FJ-33 engines

C/n	Identities		
0001	N700JJ	N700AJ	[ff 27Jly03; cx 08Jun07, wfu]
0002	N700LJ	[ff 06Feb06; cx 02Oct12, wfu]	
0003	N703AJ	[cx 29May09, wfu]	
0004	N700AJ	[cx 06May09, wfu]	

Company filed for bankruptcy February 2008, production ceased.

CHICHESTER-MILES LEOPARD

C/n	Identities	
001	G-BKRL	[first flight late 1988; cx 25Jan99, wfu; to Bournemouth Aviation Museum, UK, in dismantled state circa Feb05]
002	G-BRNM	[preserved Bournemouth Aviation Museum, UK 2003-2008 then Midland Air Museum, Coventry, UK]

CIRRUS VISION SF50

A 6-passenger "personal" jet powered by a single Williams FJ-33 engine. Was previously known as the SJ50.

C/n	Identities	
0001	N280CJ	[ff 03Jul08 Duluth, MN]
0002	N250CV	[ff 24Mar14 Duluth, MN]
0003	N251CV	
0004	N252CV	
0005	N253CV	

DASSAULT FALCON 30

C/n	Identities	
01	F-WAMD	[wfu Bordeaux, France; never entered production; fuselage at Vitrolles Engineering University, nr Marseille, France, 1990]

DASSAULT FALCON 5X

A new long-range super-midsize twin-jet under development but subject to a 2-year delay due to problems with the new Snecma Silvercrest engines selected to power it. First flight is currently scheduled for 2017 with customer deliveries following in 2020.

C/n	Identities	
1	F-WIDE	[r/o 02Jun15, Bordeaux, France]

DIAMOND D-JET

A 4-passenger, single pilot "personal" jet powered by a single Williams FJ-33 engine giving a range of 1350NM at an operating altitude of 25,000 ft.

C/n	Identities	
10-0001	C-GVLJ	[ff 18Apr06 London, ONT, Canada; cx 31Oct08, wfu]
DJ1-0002	C-FPTM	[ff 14Sep07]
DJ1-0003	C-GUPJ	[ff 14Apr08]

ECLIPSE 400 CONCEPT JET

A 4-seat, single-engined "personal jet" built to test the single-engined jet market. Officially registered as a Swift Engineering Inc Mark 400.

C/n	Identities	
SE-400-001	N5184U	[ff 02Jul07]

EPIC ELITE

A 6-seat very light jet powered by two Williams FJ-33-4A engines.

C/n	Identities	
001J	C-GROL	[ff 07Jun07]

EPIC VICTORY

A 4-seat "personal jet" powered by a single Williams FJ-33-4A engine.

C/n	Identities		
001	N370EJ	[ff 06Jul07]	
002	N975AR	N952R	

GROB G180 SPn Utility Jet

Grob Aerospace unveiled its ten-seat (including crew), carbon-fibre SPn Utility jet at the 2005 Paris Air Show. Development of the type drove the company into insolvency. H3 Aerospace purchased the company in January 2009 but decided not to continue the SPn programme.

C/n	Identities		
90001	D-ISPN	[ff 20Jly05] D-CSPN	[to Deutsches Museum Flugwerft Schleissheim, Munich, Germany, 2012]
90002	D-CGSP	[ff 29Sep06, w/o Tussenhausen-Mattsies 29Nov06]	
90003	D-CSPJ	[ff 29Oct07] F-WINT	
90004	D-CSPG	[ff 07Aug08]	
90005	[assembly commenced but not completed]		

GULFSTREAM 550 PEREGRINE

C/n	Identities			
551	N9881S	N550GA	N84GP	[wfu Mar92; to Oklahoma Air & Space Museum, Oklahoma City, OK]

HONDA MH02

C/n	Identities	
001	N3097N	[ff 05Mar93 – undertook 170 hours of test flying which ended in Aug96, displayed in the Honda Hall, Motegi, Japan]

LEARJET MODEL 85

Official Bombardier designation was LJ-200-1A10. Development was ceased in 2014 due to weak demand and Bombardier management's desire to focus resources on the new Global 7000 and 8000.

C/n	Identities	
3001	N851LJ	[r/o 07Sep13; ff 09Apr14; stored Wichita/Mid-Continent, KS]
3002	(N852LJ)	[marks requested but aircraft not completed; stored Wichita/Mid-Continent, unmarked]
3003	(N853LJ)	[marks requested but aircraft not built]
3004	(N854LJ)	[marks requested but aircraft not built]
3005	(N855LJ)	[marks requested but aircraft not built]
3006	(N856LJ)	[marks requested but aircraft not built]

McDONNELL MD220

C/n	Identities			
1	N119M	N220N	N4AZ	[never entered production; ferried Albuquerque, NM, to El Paso, TX 21Dec85 – where it is wfu]

NORTH AMERICAN UTX

C/n	Identities	
C/n	Identities	
246-1	N4060K	[b/u circa 1967]

PILATUS PC-24

C/n	Identities	
P01	HB-VXA	[rolled out 1Aug14, Stans, Switzerland; ff 11May15]
P02	HB-VXB	[rolled out Feb15, Stans, Switzerland; ff 16Nov15]

PIPER PA-47 PIPERJET/ALTAIRE

A 6-seat "personal" jet powered by a single Williams FJ44 engine, development work on which was suspended in 2011.

C/n	Identities	
4798E001	N360PJ	[ff 30Jul08 Vero Beach, FL; to Florida Air Museum, Lakeland, FL, Dec11; cx 15Feb12]

EXPERIMENTAL & NON-PRODUCTION TYPES

SABRE 50

C/n	Identities		
287-1	N287NA	N50CR	[did not enter production; preserved Evergreen Aviation & Space Museum, McMinnville, OR]

SCALED COMPOSITES 143 TRIUMPH

C/n	Identities	
001	N143SC	[ff 12Jly88; further development abandoned; wfu Sep92 Mojave, CA; placed on display outside Scaled Composites premises at Mojave, CA]

SPECTRUM 33

C/n	Identities	
0001	N322LA	[ff 07Jan06, w/o 25Jly06 Spanish Fork, UT. Powered by 2 rear-mounted Williams FJ33 engines giving a range of 2000nm, the aircraft had a cabin slightly larger than that of the CitationJet CJ2. Current project status uncertain]

VISIONAIRE VANTAGE/EVIATION EV-20

C/n	Identities	
001	N247VA	[ferried to Brazil Nov04 for conversion to EV-20 powered by 2 Williams FJ44 turbofans; project abandoned, returned to Ames, IA, 18Feb06 and wfu; subsequently moved to Hickory, NC]

WILLIAMS V-JET II

C/n	Identities	
001	N222FJ	[wfu and presented to the EAA AirVenture Museum, Oshkosh, WI on 27Jly00]

Officially registered as a Scale Composites 271. The V-Jet II is a small, all-composite 6-seat jet powered by a single Williams FJX-2 engine. It was built primarily as a test-bed for the FJX-2 engine rather than for series production.

MASTER INDEX

Civil-registered bizjets are arranged in order of country registration prefix, registrations relating to each country being listed in alphabetical or numerical order as appropriate. For each registration, a four-letter character abbreviation for the type of aircraft is given (see decode below), followed by the c/n (except for Citation I and II models, where the unit number is quoted where this is known). This code is to help locate the aircraft in the main text, not to indicate any subtypes etc.

All civil registered aircraft which are in current use are indicated by bold typeface; reserved marks are given in the normal typeface.

Bizjets in military use are arranged in alphabetical order of country name.

MASTER INDEX DE-CODE

Code	Type	Code	Type
A700	Adam Aircraft A700	G280	IAI Gulfstream 280
ASTR	IAI1125 Astra/Gulfstream 100	GALX	IAI1126 Galaxy/Gulfstream 200
BE40	Beechjet 400/400A/Hawker 400XP/T-1A Jayhawk	GLEX	BD700 Global Express/Global 5000
C500	Cessna 500/501 Citation I/ISP	GLF2	G1159 Gulfstream II
C510	Cessna 510 Citation Mustang	GLF3	G1159A Gulfstream III
C525	Cessna 525 CitationJet/CJ1+/M2	GLF4	Gulfstream IV/300/350/400/450
C52A	Cessna 525A CitationJet CJ2/CJ2+	GLF5	Gulfstream V/500/550
C52B	Cessna 525B CitationJet CJ3	GLF6	Gulfstream VI/650
C52C	Cessna 525C CitationJet CJ4	GLF7	Gulfstream VII/500
C550	Cessna 550/551 Citation II/IISP/Bravo	GPER	Gulfstream Peregrine
C552	Cessna 552 Citation (T-47A)	HDJT	Honda HA-420 Hondajet
C560	Cessna 560 Citation V/Ultra/Encore	HFB3	MBB HFB320 Hansa
C56X	Cessna 560XL Citation Excel/XLS	HMH2	Honda MH02
C650	Cessna 650 Citation III/VI/VII	HA4T	Hawker 4000 (formerly Horizon)
C680	Cessna 680 Citation Sovereign	HS25	HS/BAe/Raytheon 125 (all models)
C750	Cessna 750 Citation X	JSTR	Lockheed Jetstar
CL30	BD100 Challenger 300	LEG5	Embraer EMB-550 Legacy 500
CL60	CL600 Challenger	LEOP	Chichester-Miles Leopard
CL61	CL601 Challenger	LJ24	Learjet 23/24
CL64	CL604 Challenger	LJ25	Learjet 25
CL65	CL605 Challenger	LJ28	Learjet 28/29
CRVT	SN601 Corvette	LJ31	Learjet 31
CS55	Cessna S550 Citation SII	LJ35	Learjet 35
DDJT	Diamond D-Jet	LJ36	Learjet 36
EA40	Eclipse 400	LJ40	Learjet 40/70
EA50	Eclipse 500	LJ45	Learjet 45/75
EPC1	Epic Victory	LJ55	Learjet 55
EPC2	Epic Elite	LJ60	Learjet 60
E50P	Embraer EMB-500 Phenom 100	LJ85	Learjet 85
E55P	Embraer EMB-505 Phenom 300	M220	McDonnell MD220
FA10	Dassault Falcon 10	MS76	MS760 Paris
FA20	Dassault Falcon 20	MU30	MU300 Diamond
FA30	Dassault Falcon 30	NUTX	North American UTX
FA50	Dassault Falcon 50	P808	Piaggio PD808
FA5X	Dassault Falcon 5X	PC24	Pilatus PC-24
FA7X	Dassault Falcon 7X	PJET	Piper PA-47 Piperjet
FA8X	Dassault Falcon 8X	PRM1	Beech 390 Premier I
F900	Dassault Falcon 900	SBRL	Sabreliner (all models)
F9DX	Dassault Falcon 900DX	SJ30	Syberjet SJ30
F9EX	Dassault Falcon 900EX/900LX	SJ50	Cirrus Vision SJ50
F2TH	Dassault Falcon 2000/2000DX	SPEC	Spectrum 33
F2TS	Dassault Falcon 2000S	T143	Scaled Composites 143 Triumph
F2EX	Dassault Falcon 2000EX/2003210LX	VVAN	Visionaire Vantage
G150	IAI Gulfstream 150	WVII	Williams V-Jet II
G180	Grob G180 SPn Utility Jet	WW24	Jet Commander/Westwind

CIVIL INDEX

Current marks (as at publication date) are in **bold** typeface.

Preserved aircraft and others not in service are shown in normal typeface.

Nicaragua

AN-BPR	HS25	256037

Pakistan

(AP-...)	EA50	000057
AP-BEK	**LJ31**	**062**
AP-BEX	BE40	RK-80
AP-BGI	HS25	25269
AP-BHD	**C550**	**550-1102**
AP-BHE	**C550**	**550-0843**
AP-BHQ	**BE40**	**RK-392**
AP-BHY	**LJ45**	**316**
AP-BJL	HS25	258095
AP-BKB	**LJ60**	**346**
AP-BKP	**LJ45**	**444**
AP-DOD	CL64	5422
AP-FFL	**CL65**	**5887**
AP-GAK	**CL64**	**5438**
AP-KNM	**BE40**	**RK-530**
AP-MIR	**CL61**	**3023**
AP-MMM	**G150**	**239**
AP-NST	**GALX**	**240**
AP-PAL	**BE40**	**RK-526**
AP-PFL	**C52B**	**0131**
AP-RBA	**BE40**	**RK-583**
AP-RRR	**HA4T**	**RC-76**
AP-SHH	HA4T	RC-21

Botswana

A2-AGM	C500	652
A2-BCL	**C550**	**550-1024**
A2-DBK	**BE40**	**RK-429**
A2-JDJ	C500	161
A2-MCB	C555	0112
A2-MCB	**HS25**	**258633**
A2-MCG	BE40	RK-140
A2-WIN	**BE40**	**RK-140**

Oman

A4O-..	**LJ45**	**035**
A4O-AA	FA20	285/504
A4O-AA	GLF2	183
A4O-AB	GLF4	1168
A4O-AC	GLF4	1196
A4O-AD	**GLF5**	**5320**
A4O-AE	**GLF5**	**5325**
A4O-AJ	LJ25	188
A4O-CA	LJ35	165
A4O-CY	E55P	50500039
A4O-CY	**E55P**	**50500085**
A4O-GA	FA20	285/504
A4O-HA	GLF2	214
A4O-SC	C550	486

United Arab Emirates

(A6-...)	JSTR	5236
A6-...	E50P	50000369
A6-...	E50P	50000371
A6-...	E50P	50000373
A6-AAG	**CL65**	**5739**
A6-AAH	CL64	5362
A6-ACE	GLEX	9359
A6-ALI	GLF4	1132
A6-ASQ	CL64	5583
A6-AUH	F900	84
A6-AUJ	HS25	258805
A6-AZH	**GLF4**	**4136**
A6-BBD	GLEX	9335
A6-CBO	**GLEX**	**9345**
A6-CGK	C650	0048
A6-CKZ	GLF3	317
A6-CPC	CL64	5372
A6-CPC	JSTR	5222
A6-CYS	LJ60	341
A6-DEJ	GLF5	564
A6-DHG	GLEX	9226
A6-DJL	GLF4	4123
A6-DNH	CL65	5702
(A6-DPD)	C680	0179
A6-DWD	GLF4	1412
A6-EJA	LJ60	200
A6-EJB	GLEX	9094
(A6-EJB)	CL64	5328
A6-EJD	CL61	3017
A6-ELA	HS25	259017
A6-ELB	HS25	259024
A6-ELC	HS25	258781
A6-ELD	**CL65**	**5866**
A6-ELJ	BE40	RK-140
A6-ESJ	C500	260
A6-EXA	FA20	344/534
A6-FAJ	LJ35	669
A6-FBQ	**GLEX**	**9282**
A6-FLG	GLF4	4106
A6-FLH	**GLF4**	**4155**
A6-GAL	**HS25**	**258432**
(A6-GAN)	C650	0048
A6-GJA	C680	0075
A6-GJB	C56X	5679
A6-GJC	C56X	5701
(A6-HBC)	HS25	HA-0095
A6-HEH	GLF3	356
A6-HEM	FA20	344/534
A6-HHH	GLF4	1011
A6-HHH	**GLF4**	**1531**
A6-HHS	GLF3	376
A6-HHZ	GLF2	164
(A6-HMK)	HS25	258093
A6-HWK	**HS25**	**HA-0080**
A6-IAS	**LJ60**	**122**
A6-ICU	**HS25**	**258521**
A6-IFA	**CL64**	**5641**
A6-INF	GLF3	491
A6-KAH	JSTR	5220
A6-KBB	CL64	5418
A6-KNH	CL30	20050
A6-MAA	HS25	258202
A6-MAB	HS25	258618
A6-MAF	F9EX	183
A6-MAF	**FA7X**	**107**
A6-MAH	HS25	258328
A6-MAJ	LJ60	270
A6-MBH	CL64	5520
A6-MBS	**CL65**	**5728**
A6-MED	LJ45	116
A6-MHA	GLEX	9097
A6-MMF	F9EX	183
A6-MVD	**CL65**	**5884**
A6-NGN	LJ60	336
A6-NMA	GLF4	1381
A6-OME	GLF4	1233
A6-ORX	**GLF4**	**4133**
(A6-OWC)	GLEX	9233
A6-PHS	HS25	258548
A6-PHY	GLF2	130
A6-PJA	CL64	5397
A6-PJB	HS25	HA-0003
A6-RAK	HS25	256063
A6-RDJ	**CL64**	**5574**
A6-RJA	GLF4	1503
A6-RJB	**GLF4**	**1505**
A6-RJC	**GLEX**	**9600**
A6-RJD	**GLEX**	**9621**
A6-RJE	**LJ60**	**383**
A6-RJH	LJ35	429
A6-RJI	LJ35	265
A6-RJM	CL30	20048
A6-RKH	C500	268
A6-RTS	**F9DX**	**601**
A6-RZA	PRM1	RB-195
(A6-RZA)	PRM1	RB-177
A6-RZB	HS25	HA-0048
A6-RZJ	PRM1	RB-177
A6-SAB	C52B	0183
A6-SAC	F900	130
(A6-SAF)	F2TH	166
A6-SAJ	**CL65**	**5837**
A6-SAM	CL30	20015
A6-SBF	LJ60	338
A6-SHH	HA4T	RC-21
A6-SKA	HS25	258432
A6-SMH	C500	402
A6-SMS	C550	391
A6-SMS	CL30	20015
A6-SMS	F2EX	76
A6-SMS	F9DX	616
A6-SMS	FA7X	104
A6-SMS	**FA7X**	**195**
A6-SMS	LJ60	094
A6-SMS	LJ60	150
A6-TBF	HS25	258792
A6-TLH	CL65	5822
A6-TSF	CL65	5922
A6-UAE	F900	86
A6-VPS	**GLF4**	**4321**
A6-ZAB	GLF3	329
A6-ZKM	F900	47
A6-ZKM	FA50	145
A6-ZZZ	HS25	258312

Qatar

A7-AAD	F900	91
A7-AAE	F900	94
A7-AAL	HS25	258485
A7-AAM	**GLEX**	**9126**
A7-AAN	CL30	20042
A7-AKA	**C560**	**0059**
A7-ASA	C500	097
A7-CEA	**CL65**	**5783**
A7-CEB	**CL65**	**5784**
A7-CEC	CL30	20042
A7-CED	**GLEX**	**9370**
A7-CEE	**GLEX**	**9421**
A7-CEF	**GLEX**	**9294**
A7-CEG	**CL65**	**5857**
A7-CEI	**GLEX**	**9581**
A7-CEV	**GLEX**	**9534**
A7-CGA	**GLF6**	**6153**
A7-CGB	**GLF6**	**6167**
A7-CGK	C650	0048
A7-CJI	C525	0646
A7-GEX	GLEX	9134
A7-GEY	GLEX	9230
A7-MBT	CL65	5866
A7-MHA	**CL64**	**5508**
A7-RZA	CL65	5798
A7-RZB	HS25	HA-0048
A7-RZC	CL65	5759
A7-RZD	HS25	HA-0095
A7-TAA	**GLEX**	**9661**
A7-TAT	**GLEX**	**9379**

Bahrain

A9C-ACE	**CL65**	**5778**
A9C-BAH	GLF4	1353
A9C-BAH	**GLF6**	**6081**
A9C-BB	GLF3	393
A9C-BG	**GLF2**	**202**
A9C-BHR	**GLF4**	**4156**
A9C-BRF	**GLF4**	**1353**
A9C-BRN	**GLF5**	**5242**
A9C-BXA	C56X	5046
A9C-BXB	CL64	5477
A9C-BXC	C550	550-1050
A9C-BXD	CL61	5194
A9C-BXG	CL64	5485
A9C-BXH	CL64	5476
A9C-BXI	C56X	5658
A9C-BXJ	C56X	5676
A9C-BXK	LJ60	338
A9C-DAR	CL30	20169
A9C-RJA	PRM1	RB-195
A9C-TLH	CL65	5822

China

B-....	**C525**	**0625**
(B-....)	C750	0171
(B-....)	CL64	5527
B-0408	C510	0454
B-1999	**F2EX**	**253**
B-3003	**GLF5**	**5478**
B-3028	**CL65**	**5988**
B-3029	**GLF4**	**4315**
B-3076	**CL65**	**5806**
B-3077	**CL65**	**5820**
B-3113	**E50P**	**50000356**
B-3196	**GLF5**	**5469**
B-3211	**F2EX**	**103**
B-3226	**GLF5**	**5472**
B-3266	**C56X**	**6176**
B-3299	**C56X**	**6177**
B-3365	CL65	5946
B-3385	**LEG5**	**55000022**
B-3561	**CL65**	**5809**
B-3566	**CL65**	**5828**
B-3642	**C56X**	**5539**
B-3643	**C56X**	**5540**
B-3644	**C525**	**0551**
B-3645	**C525**	**0552**
B-3647	**C525**	**0554**
B-3648	**C525**	**0555**
B-3649	**C525**	**0557**
B-3650	**C525**	**0558**
B-3666	**C56X**	**5761**
B-3667	**C56X**	**5766**
B-3668	**C525**	**0471**
B-3669	**C525**	**0380**
B-3901	HS25	258856
B-3902	HS25	258858
B-3903	**HS25**	**HA-0053**
B-3905	**BE40**	**RK-109**
B-3906	HA4T	RC-55
B-3907	HA4T	RC-45
B-3908	HA4T	RC-43
B-3909	**HS25**	**HA-0167**
B-3910	**HA4T**	**RC-49**
B-3912	HS25	HA-0175
B-3915	**HS25**	**258656**
B-3917	HS25	258673
B-3925	**LJ60**	**055**
B-3926	**LJ60**	**381**
B-3935	**LJ60**	**391**
B-3980	LJ55	027
B-3981	LJ60	053
B-3988	**GLF5**	**5532**
B-3988	LJ45	256
B-3989	BE40	RK-203
B-3990	**HS25**	**258408**
B-3991	**HS25**	**258470**
B-3992	**HS25**	**258501**
B-3993	**HS25**	**258525**
B-3995	HS25	258526
B-3996	HS25	258536
B-3997	**HS25**	**258575**
B-3998	HS25	258312
B-3999	GLF4	1144
B-4005	CL61	3046
B-4006	CL61	3047
B-4007	CL61	3052
B-4010	CL61	5024
B-4011	CL61	5025
B-4101	**C555**	**0049**
B-4102	**C555**	**0050**
B-4103	C550	357
B-4104	C550	362
B-4105	C550	359
B-4106	C650	0220
B-4107	C650	0221
B-4108	C525	0204
B-4184	**LJ36**	**053**
B-4187	**LJ35**	**602**
B-4188	**LJ35**	**603**
B-4599	**LJ36**	**034**
B-7019	**C56X**	**5118**
B-7021	**C750**	**0157**
B-7022	**C650**	**0220**
B-7023	C650	0221
B-7024	**C550**	**357**
B-7025	**C550**	**362**
B-7026	C550	359
B-7027	**C525**	**0204**
B-7696	**CL64**	**5442**
B-7696	CL64	5510
B-7697	CL64	5523
B-7699	**GLEX**	**9112**
B-7761	**CL65**	**5868**
B-7763	**CL65**	**5906**
B-7765	**GLEX**	**9713**
B-7766	**CL64**	**5542**
B-7768	**CL65**	**5888**
B-7769	**CL65**	**5903**
B-7777	**C525**	**0655**
B-7796	**CL65**	**5871**
B-7799	**CL65**	**5919**
(B-8006)	PRM1	RB-87
B-8018	PRM1	RB-118
B-8020	F2TH	27
B-8021	**F9DX**	**613**
B-8023	**FA7X**	**133**
B-8025	F2EX	192
B-8026	**FA7X**	**61**
B-8027	**FA7X**	**63**
B-8028	**FA7X**	**101**
B-8029	**FA7X**	**45**
B-8030	F9EX	245
B-8080	GLF4	1100
B-8081	**GALX**	**135**
B-8082	GLF4	1157
B-8083	**GALX**	**037**
B-8085	GALX	114
B-8086	**GALX**	**030**
B-8087	GALX	174
B-8088	GLF4	1375
B-8089	GALX	051
B-8090	GALX	049
B-8091	**GLF4**	**1144**
B-8092	GLF5	510
B-8093	**GLF4**	**4165**
B-8095	**GLF5**	**5059**
B-8096	**GLF4**	**4178**
B-8097	GLF5	613
B-8098	GLF4	4076
B-8099	**GLF4**	**4168**
B-8100	**GLF5**	**5024**
B-8101	GLEX	9362
B-8105	**GLEX**	**9510**
B-8106	CL30	20303
B-8108	**GLF5**	**5120**
B-8115	**CL30**	**20346**
B-8116	**CL30**	**20350**
B-8120	**GALX**	**229**
B-8121	**GALX**	**227**
B-8122	**GLF5**	**5269**
B-8123	**GLF5**	**5274**
B-8125	**GLF5**	**5276**
B-8126	**GLF5**	**5349**
B-8127	**GLF4**	**4190**
B-8128	**GLF4**	**4170**
B-8129	**GALX**	**134**
B-8130	GLF5	552
B-8131	**GLF5**	**5289**
B-8132	**GLF5**	**5291**
B-8133	**GLF4**	**4196**
B-8135	**GLF5**	**5023**
B-8136	**GLF5**	**5082**
B-8137	**GLF5**	**5319**
B-8138	GLF5	5231
B-8139	**GALX**	**232**
B-8150	GLF4	4205
B-8151	GALX	245
B-8152	**GLF5**	**5005**
B-8155	**GLF4**	**4154**
B-8156	GLF5	5337
B-8157	**GLF5**	**5342**
B-8158	**GLF4**	**4180**
B-8159	**GALX**	**243**
B-8160	**GLF5**	**5358**
B-8161	**GLF4**	**4238**
B-8166	**GLF4**	**4216**
B-8168	**GLF5**	**5298**
B-8190	CL30	20310
B-8191	CL30	20311
B-8192	**CL30**	**20320**
B-8193	**CL30**	**20321**
B-8195	**GLEX**	**9488**
B-8196	**GLEX**	**9412**
B-8197	**GLEX**	**9473**
(B-8198)	GLEX	9398
B-8199	GLEX	9387
B-8201	FA7X	149
B-8202	**FA7X**	**159**
B-8203	**FA7X**	**193**
B-8205	**FA7X**	**209**
B-8206	**FA7X**	**144**
B-8207	FA7X	142
B-8208	**F9EX**	**267**
B-8209	FA7X	177
B-8210	**F2TS**	**721**
B-8211	**FA7X**	**212**
B-8212	**F9EX**	**276**
B-8213	**FA7X**	**105**
B-8215	**FA7X**	**157**
B-8216	**FA7X**	**199**
B-8217	**FA7X**	**251**
B-8218	**FA7X**	**189**
B-8233	**CL30**	**20315**
B-8250	**GLF4**	**4234**
B-8251	**GLF4**	**4242**
B-8252	**GLF4**	**4184**
B-8253	**GLF4**	**4193**
B-8255	**GLF5**	**5352**
B-8256	**GLF5**	**5348**
B-8257	**GLF4**	**4251**
B-8258	**GLF5**	**5360**
B-8259	**GLF5**	**5357**
B-8260	**GLF5**	**5373**
B-8261	**GLF5**	**5364**
B-8262	**GLF4**	**4227**
B-8263	**GLF4**	**4276**
B-8265	**GLF4**	**4258**
B-8266	GLEX	9390
B-8267	**GLF4**	**4267**
B-8268	**GLF5**	**5387**
B-8269	**GLF5**	**5404**
B-8270	**GLF5**	**5019**
B-8271	**GLF4**	**4271**
B-8272	**GLF5**	**5405**
B-8273	**GLF5**	**5399**
B-8275	**GLF5**	**5414**
B-8277	**GALX**	**247**
B-8278	**GLF4**	**4287**
B-8279	**GLF4**	**4285**
B-8280	**G280**	**2030**
B-8288	**GLF5**	**5329**
B-8290	**GLF4**	**4264**
B-8291	**GLF4**	**4272**
B-8292	**GLF5**	**5422**
B-8293	**GLF4**	**4293**
B-8295	**GLF4**	**4274**
B-8296	GLF5	5449
B-8297	**GLF5**	**5423**
B-8298	**GLF5**	**5447**
B-8299	**GLF4**	**4277**
B-8300	**GLF4**	**4300**
B-8301	**GLF4**	**4297**
B-8302	**GLF5**	**5437**
B-8303	**G280**	**2025**
B-8305	**G280**	**2032**
B-8306	**GLF5**	**5445**
B-8308	**GLF4**	**4309**
B-8309	**GLF5**	**5475**
B-8316	**GLF4**	**4286**
B-8322	**GLF4**	**4211**
B-8373	**GLF5**	**5483**
B-8888	**C510**	**0286**
B-9060	**E55P**	**50500146**
B-9300	**C680**	**0297**
B-9301	**C680**	**0298**
B-9329	**C680**	**0299**
B-9330	**C56X**	**5828**

B-9429 C56X 5167
B-9465 C56X 5189
B-9629 C525 0645
B-9630 C680 0334
B-9641 C525 0617
B-9813 C510 0448
B-9823 C56X 6161

Taiwan

B-20001 ASTR 119
B-23068 GALX 205
B-58813 ASTR 115
B-66666 G280 2073
B-77701 BE40 RK-562
B-90609 GLF5 5300
B-95959 GLEX 9357
B-95995 BE40 RK-410
B-98181 LJ35 675
B-98183 LJ35 654
B-98888 GLEX 9477
B-99888 GLF5 5243
B-99988 GLF6 6165

China – Hong Kong

B-HHI GLF5 5377
B-HMA GLEX 9063
B-HSS HS25 257169
"B-HSS" HS25 257169
B-HVP GLF5 5216
(B-HVT) GLF5 5102
B-HWA GLF4 1144
B-HWB GALX 030

B-KCK GLF5 5228
B-KDP GLF5 514
B-KEQ GLF5 5296
B-KEY GLF6 6098
B-KEZ GLEX 9425
B-KGP GLF5 5238
B-KGV GLF5 5111
B-KHJ GLF5 5303
B-KHK GLF4 4018
B-KID GLF5 5115
B-KMF GLEX 9998
B-KMJ GALX 090
B-KSJ GALX 036
B-KTL GLEX 9415
B-KTS C680 0316
B-KVC GLF5 5219
B-KVE GLF5 5356
B-LAS GLF4 4202

B-LBL CL64 5604
B-LCK GLF4 4182
B-LCT C56X 6078
B-LDL GLF5 5335
B-LHK GLF6 6148
B-LIM GLEX 9295
B-LIS GLF4 4088
(B-LIZ) GLEX 9415
B-LLL CL64 5622
B-LMF GLF5 5388
B-LMJ GALX 153
B-LOL CL65 5826
B-LRH GLEX 9241
B-LRW GLEX 9315
B-LSB CL65 5716
B-LSC CL65 5794
B-LSJ GALX 114
B-LSM GLF5 5250
B-LSS GALX 210
B-LSZ GLF4 1508
B-LUE GLF5 5147
B-LUX GALX 049
B-LVA CL65 5896
B-LVB CL65 5898
B-LWW GLF4 4187
B-LWX GLF4 4096

China – Macau

(B-M..) C500 446
B-MAC CL61 5178
B-MAI CL61 5049
B-MAU F2TH 167
B-MAZ F2EX 186
B-MBD HS25 HA-0028
B-MBE HS25 HA-0036
B-MBF HS25 HB-1
B-MBG HS25 HB-9
B-MBH HS25 HB-13
B-MBI HS25 HB-25
B-MBK F2TH 133
(B-MBL) F9EX 223
(B-MJZ) GLF4 1508

Bosnia

BH-BIH CS55 0045

Canada

(C-....) C510 0337
(C-....) C560 0127
(C-....) FA10 184
(C-....) GLEX 9007
(C-....) LJ60 320
(C-....) LJ60 365
(C-....) WW24 112
C-FAAL CL61 3005
C-FAAU HS25 258099
C-FABF CS55 0101
C-FACC C560 0053
C-FACC C560 0753
C-FACG ASTR 117
C-FACO C560 0053
C-FACO C560 0753
C-FADG CL64 5580
C-FADL C500 067
C-FADU CL64 5413
C-FAEH CL65 6082
C-FAGU GLEX 9143
C-FAGV GLEX 9144
C-FAHN GLEX 9145
C-FAHQ GLEX 9146
C-FAHX GLEX 9147
C-FAIO GLEX 9148
C-FAIV GLEX 9150
C-FAIY GLEX 9149
C-FAJC CL30 20384
C-FAJV E55P 50500149
C-FAKM CL65 6058
C-FAKM CL65 6083
C-FALC HS25 25087
C-FALI C560 0573
C-FALI CL30 20630
C-FALI CS55 0142
C-FAMI C560 0566
C-FAMI C560 0648
C-FAMJ C550 550-0931
C-FAMN CL65 6059
C-FAMN CL65 6078
C-FANH CL65 5977
C-FANH CL65 6065
C-FANJ C52B 0201
C-FANJ C52C 0083
C-FANL HS25 25042
C-FANS C550 550-0807
C-FANS LJ45 303
C-FAOF CL65 5978
C-FAOF CL65 6062
C-FAOL CL64 5567
C-FAOS HS25 25278
C-FAOU CL65 5979
C-FAOU CL65 6063
C-FAPK WW24 216
C-FAPO CL65 5980
C-FAPO CL65 6064
C-FAPQ CL65 5981
C-FAPQ CL65 6060
C-FAPQ CL65 6084
C-FAQB CL65 5982
C-FAQB CL65 6066
C-FAQD CL65 5983
C-FAQD CL65 6068
C-FAQK CL65 6052
C-FAQK CL65 6077
C-FAQY CL65 5984
C-FAQY CL65 6067
C-FASD CL64 5549
C-FASP C52A 0519
(C-FASP) C52A 0515
C-FASR C52A 0524
C-FASW C52A 0503
C-FASY C52B 0489
C-FAUF CL65 6053
C-FAUF CL65 6079
C-FAUI CL65 6054
C-FAUI CL65 6085
C-FAUR CL65 5985
C-FAUR CL65 6069
C-FAUZ CL30 20024
C-FAWU CL64 5584
C-FAWU CL65 5986
C-FAWU CL65 6061
C-FAWU CL65 6086
C-FAWW WW24 313
C-FAWZ FA7X 65
C-FAXN CL65 5987
C-FAXN CL65 6070
C-FAYD CL65 5988
C-FAYD CL65 6071
C-FAZC CL65 6055
C-FAZC CL65 6080
C-FAZO CL65 6056
C-FAZO CL65 6081
C-FAZS CL65 6057
C-FAZS CL65 6087
C-FBAX C500 020
C-FBBF HS25 258530
C-FBCD LJ60 133
C-FBCI C510 0211
C-FBCI C525 0858
C-FBCL C500 042
C-FBCL LJ45 024
C-FBCL LJ45 288
C-FBCL LJ45 416
C-FBCL LJ45 467
C-FBCM C500 071
C-FBCR CL61 5117
C-FBCR CL64 5579
C-FBCW C560 0191
C-FBDH LJ35 673
C-FBDQ C500 488
C-FBDR GLEX 9003
C-FBDR LJ60 010
(C-FBDR) GLEX 9438
C-FBDS C500 488
C-FBDS CS55 0029
C-FBEA LJ25 163
C-FBEI CL61 3028
C-FBEL CL61 3028
C-FBEL CL65 5802
C-FBEM CL64 5474
C-FBFP LJ35 038
C-FBGX GLEX 9001
C-FBHX CL61 5018
C-FBKR CL61 5020
C-FBLJ LJ45 270
C-FBLJ LJ60 092
C-FBLO LJ60 092
C-FBLT SBRL 306-23
C-FBLU LJ60 029
C-FBLU LJ60 253
C-FBMG HS25 257066
C-FBNA C650 0046
C-FBNK HS25 25221
C-FBNS CL64 5364
C-FBNS FA7X 151
C-FBNW FA10 190
C-FBOC GLEX 9151
C-FBOM CL61 5124
C-FBPJ GLEX 9153
C-FBPK GLEX 9152
C-FBPL GLEX 9154
C-FBPL PRM1 RB-150
C-FBPT GLEX 9155
C-FBPZ GLEX 9156
C-FBQD GLEX 9157
C-FBRP C52B 0299
C-FBSS FA10 87
C-FBUA GLEX 9653
C-FBUH GLEX 9650
C-FBUR HS25 258232
C-FBVF FA10 33
C-FBVF FA50 48
C-FBVG GLEX 9652
C-FBVL GLEX 9654
C-FBVS GLEX 9651
C-FBXL C56X 5298
C-FBYJ CL61 3017
C-FCBQ C560 0393
C-FCCC C550 422
C-FCCP CL64 5310
C-FCDE CL64 5392
C-FCDE CL65 5938
C-FCDF CL61 5024
C-FCDS FA20 146
C-FCEH FA20 507
C-FCEJ WW24 324
C-FCEL C550 135
C-FCEL C56X 5047
C-FCEU C52A 0492
C-FCEX E50P 50000247
C-FCFL HS25 25213
C-FCFP ASTR 079
C-FCFP C500 125
(C-FCFP) C550 097
C-FCGS CL61 5025
C-FCHJ C500 091
C-FCHT HS25 257176
C-FCIB CL61 5181
C-FCIB CL65 5881
C-FCID CL61 5181
C-FCLJ LJ36 037
C-FCLJ LJ55 118
C-FCMG CL30 20033
C-FCMG LJ60 133
C-FCNN GLEX 9244
C-FCNR GLF4 1065
C-FCNR LJ60 179
C-FCOE CL64 5595
C-FCOG GLEX 9158
C-FCOI GLEX 9159
C-FCOJ GLEX 9160
C-FCOK GLEX 9161
C-FCOZ GLEX 9162
C-FCPH GLEX 9163
C-FCPI CL64 5385
C-FCPR C680 0157
C-FCPW C500 002
C-FCRF HS25 258173
C-FCRH C560 0182
C-FCRH F900 57
C-FCRH FA50 56
C-FCRH HS25 258173
C-FCSD CL64 5596
C-FCSF GLEX 9164
C-FCSH GLEX 9165
C-FCSI CL30 20114
C-FCSI GLEX 9166
C-FCSL GLEX 9167
C-FCSP GLEX 9168
C-FCSR GLEX 9169
C-FCSS C550 488
C-FCSS HS25 257143
C-FCSS LJ24 197
C-FCSY GLEX 9170
C-FCTB PRM1 RB-271
C-FCTE GLEX 9171
C-FCTK GLEX 9172
C-FCTK LJ60 210
C-FCUA GLEX 9173
C-FCUF GLEX 9174
C-FCUG GLEX 9175
C-FCUK GLEX 9176
C-FCUS GLEX 9177
C-FCUX GLEX 9178
C-FCVC GLEX 9179
C-FCVD GLEX 9180
C-FCXJ CL30 20034
C-FCXL C56X 5234
C-FCYG GLEX 9659
C-FCYX GLEX 9656
C-FCZM CL30 20066
C-FCZN CL30 20051
C-FCZN GLEX 9661
C-FCZS CL30 20043
C-FCZS CL30 20067
C-FCZS GLEX 9658
C-FCZV CL30 20052
C-FCZV GLEX 9655
C-FDAA PRM1 RB-58
C-FDAC LJ25 091
C-FDAH CL30 20059
C-FDAH CL61 3053
C-FDAT CL61 5029
C-FDAU CL61 3056
C-FDAX ASTR 058
C-FDBJ CL64 5602
C-FDBJ F2EX 145
C-FDBJ GLF4 4308
C-FDCS GLF4 1207
C-FDDD CS55 0115
C-FDDD HS25 258038
C-FDHD C680 0032
C-FDHP GLEX 9660
C-FDHV CL30 20026
C-FDIA CL30 20028
C-FDIH CL30 20030
C-FDIJ CL30 20032
C-FDIW GLEX 9657
C-FDJC C650 0080
C-FDJN CL64 5598
C-FDJQ C500 018
C-FDKJ HS25 258169
C-FDKL HS25 258337
C-FDLR GLEX 9088
C-FDLT C560 0021
C-FDMB C500 341
C-FDMM PRM1 RB-198
C-FDNA C680 0132
C-FDOJ CL30 20093
C-FDOL CL30 20093
C-FDOL CL30 20296
C-FDOM HS25 25018
C-FDOW F900 87
C-FDRS CL64 5432
C-FDSH C510 0136
C-FDSR CL30 20042
C-FDSZ CL30 20044
C-FDSZ GLEX 9666
C-FDTF JSTR 5088
C-FDTM JSTR 5052
C-FDTX JSTR 5018
C-FDUA GLEX 9663
C-FDUV GLEX 9668
C-FDUY CL64 5605
C-FDVO GLEX 9665
C-FDVX GLEX 9662
C-FDWU CL64 5608
C-FDXA GLEX 9667
C-FDXB GLEX 9664
C-FDXU CL30 20048
C-FDYL C550 373
C-FEAB GLEX 9181
C-FEAD GLEX 9183
C-FEAE GLEX 9184
C-FEAE HS25 257180
C-FEAG GLEX 9185
C-FEAK GLEX 9187
C-FEAQ CL60 1035
C-FEAQ GLEX 9189
C-FEAZ GLEX 9191
C-FEBG GLEX 9193
C-FEBH GLEX 9194
C-FEBL GLEX 9195
C-FEBQ GLEX 9196
C-FEBS GLEX 9197
C-FEBU GLEX 9199
C-FEBX GLEX 9200
C-FECA GLEX 9182
C-FECI GLEX 9186
C-FECN GLEX 9188
C-FECX GLEX 9190
C-FECY GLEX 9192
C-FECZ GLEX 9198
C-FEDG CL30 20107
C-FEDG LJ60 343
C-FEDU LJ60 343
C-FEFU CL64 5609
C-FEFW CL64 5610
C-FEHG GLEX 9674
C-FEHT GLEX 9669
C-FEHU GLEX 9672
C-FEIH CL64 5611
C-FELO GLEX 9675
C-FEMA CS55 0040
C-FEMF GLEX 9670
C-FEMN GLEX 9673
C-FEMT LJ36 024
C-FENJ C500 122
C-FEOF GLEX 9671
C-FEPC HS25 258349
C-FEPG C560 0182
C-FEPN CL64 5612
C-FEPR CL64 5613
C-FEPU CL30 20050
C-FETJ C560 0082
C-FETN JSTR 5021
C-FETZ CL61 5041
C-FEUQ CL30 20047
C-FEUR CL64 5577
C-FEUR CL65 5938
C-FEUV CL61 5042
C-FEVC C550 550-1023
C-FEWB LJ25 180
C-FEXB HS25 257152
C-FEXD FA10 78
C-FEXH CL64 5616
C-FEXI CL30 20503
C-FEYG WW24 81
C-FEYU CL64 5617
C-FEYZ CL64 5618
C-FFAB HS25 257030
C-FFBC CL30 20257
C-FFBC CL30 20549
C-FFBC WW24 119
C-FFBE CL30 20615
C-FFBY CL61 5044
C-FFCC C550 372
C-FFCL C550 063
C-FFCM C52B 0145
C-FFEV FA10 204
C-FFGE CL64 5620
C-FFGI FA50 56
C-FFGU GLEX 9683
C-FFGZ GLEX 9678
C-FFHA GLEX 9681
C-FFHW GLEX 9676
C-FFHX CL64 5621
C-FFIJ GLEX 9642
C-FFIK CL30 20620
C-FFLA CL64 5622
C-FFLC GLEX 9679
C-FFLJ CL30 20051
C-FFLZ GLEX 9682
C-FFMQ CL64 5623
C-FFMS CL64 5624
C-FFMV GLEX 9677
C-FFMZ GLEX 9680
C-FFNM GLF2 52
C-FFNT CL30 20065
C-FFQQ CL64 5625
C-FFSO CL61 5045
C-FFTM HS25 258161
C-FFVE GLEX 9688
C-FFVM GLEX 9685
C-FFVX GLEX 9687
C-FFWP GLEX 9684
C-FFXS GLEX 9686
C-FFZE CL30 20055
C-FFZI CL30 20049
C-FFZP CL64 5628
C-FGAT C500 199
C-FGAT C550 255
C-FGBD CL64 5630
C-FGBE CL64 5629
C-FGBP CL30 20053
C-FGBY CL30 20076
C-FGCD CL30 20077
C-FGCE CL30 20078
C-FGCJ CL30 20079
C-FGCL CL30 20080
C-FGCN CL30 20081
C-FGCT F9EX 46
C-FGCV CL30 20082
C-FGCW CL30 20083
C-FGCX CL30 20084
C-FGCZ CL30 20085
C-FGFB CL30 20071
C-FGFG CL64 5383
C-FGFI F900 138
C-FGGF CL30 20057
C-FGGF CL30 20381
C-FGGH E50P 50000299
C-FGGH WW24 431
C-FGGX GLEX 9014
C-FGIK CL30 20107
C-FGIL CL30 20107
C-FGIL CL65 5833
C-FGJC LJ60 210
C-FGJI CL30 20058
C-FGLF HS25 258141
C-FGMR CL30 20056
C-FGNI CL65 5956
C-FGNO CL30 20059
C-FGSS GLEX 9694
C-FGSU GLEX 9690
C-FGUD CL30 20061
C-FGUD GLEX 9692
C-FGUT CL30 20060
C-FGVJ CL30 20086
C-FGVK CL30 20087
C-FGVM CL30 20088
C-FGVS CL30 20089
C-FGVS GLEX 9691
C-FGWB CL30 20090

C-FGWF	CL30	20091
C-FGWF	GLEX	9693
C-FGWL	CL30	20092
C-FGWR	CL30	20093
C-FGWV	GLEX	9689
C-FGWW	CL30	20094
C-FGWZ	CL30	20095
C-FGXK	CL30	20066
C-FGXW	CL30	20064
C-FGYI	CL64	5639
C-FGYM	CL65	5701
C-FGYU	CL30	20070
C-FGZD	CL30	20069
C-FGZE	CL30	20068
C-FGZI	CL30	20067
C-FHBX	GLF2	119/22
C-FHCL	CL64	5645
C-FHCM	CL64	5644
C-FHCW	**LJ45**	**213**
C-FHCY	CL30	20075
C-FHDE	CL30	20074
C-FHDM	LJ35	410
C-FHDN	CL30	20073
C-FHDV	CL64	5648
C-FHFP	LJ24	340
C-FHFV	C510	0211
C-FHGC	**CL64**	**5453**
C-FHGX	GLEX	9002
C-FHHD	CL61	5061
C-FHJB	LJ55	122
C-FHLG	**C550**	**423**
C-FHLL	HS25	25034
C-FHLO	LJ35	179
C-FHMF	GLEX	9700
C-FHMG	GLEX	9697
C-FHMI	CL30	20096
C-FHMM	CL30	20097
C-FHMQ	CL30	20098
C-FHMS	CL30	20099
C-FHMZ	CL30	20100
C-FHMZ	GLEX	9702
C-FHNC	CL30	20101
C-FHND	CL30	20102
C-FHND	GLEX	9699
C-FHNF	CL30	20103
C-FHNH	CL30	20104
C-FHNJ	CL30	20105
C-FHNN	GLEX	9696
C-FHNS	**ASTR**	**156**
C-FHPB	GLEX	9202
C-FHPG	GLEX	9203
C-FHPM	GLF2	104/10
C-FHPM	**GLF4**	**1103**
C-FHPQ	GLEX	9201
C-FHPZ	GLEX	9701
C-FHRD	HS25	258460
C-FHRL	ASTR	150
C-FHRL	**CL65**	**5947**
C-FHSN	GLEX	9698
C-FHSS	HS25	256003
C-FHSX	GLEX	9695
C-FHYB	**GALX**	**043**
C-FHYL	CL64	5506
C-FHYL	CL65	5943
C-FHYL	**CL65**	**5982**
C-FHYL	GLEX	9286
C-FHYL	GLEX	9470
C-FIAS	**C52A**	**0511**
C-FIBQ	**C560**	**0486**
C-FICA	**FA10**	**196**
C-FICU	**LJ35**	**249**
C-FIDO	LJ60	133
C-FIDT	CL64	5619
C-FIDU	CL30	20108
C-FIDV	CL30	20109
C-FIDX	CL30	20106
C-FIDZ	CL30	20107
C-FIEA	CL30	20110
C-FIED	CL30	20111
C-FIEE	CL30	20112
C-FIEM	CL30	20113
C-FIEP	CL30	20114
C-FIEX	CL64	5650
C-FIEX	**GLEX**	**9708**
C-FIEZ	GLEX	9703
C-FIFK	CL65	5702
C-FIFK	GLEX	9706
C-FIFN	**GLEX**	**9709**
C-FIFP	GLEX	9704
C-FIGD	**FA20**	**109/427**
C-FIGO	HS25	258087
C-FIGR	CL61	5069
C-FIHL	GLEX	9205
C-FIHN	GLEX	9208
C-FIHP	GLEX	9204
C-FIHP	GLEX	9707
C-FIIA	GLEX	9705
C-FIIB	GLEX	9206
C-FIIC	GLEX	9207
C-FIIG	GLEX	9209
C-FIMA	C525	0191
C-FIMF	CL64	5653
C-FIMO	**C650**	**0065**
C-FIMP	C52C	0089
C-FIMP	C550	125
C-FIOB	CL30	20115
C-FIOB	CL61	5064
C-FIOC	CL30	20116
C-FIOE	CL30	20117
C-FIOG	CL30	20118
C-FIOH	CL30	20119
C-FIOJ	CL30	20120
C-FIOK	CL30	20121
C-FION	CL30	20122
C-FIOO	CL30	20123
C-FIOP	CL30	20124
C-FIOT	GLEX	9210
C-FIOT	GLF2	78
C-FIOZ	GLEX	9213
C-FIPC	GLEX	9215
C-FIPE	HS25	258319
C-FIPF	GLEX	9218
C-FIPG	GLEX	9220
C-FIPG	HS25	257132
C-FIPH	GLEX	9211
C-FIPJ	GLEX	9212
C-FIPJ	HS25	25053
C-FIPM	GLEX	9214
C-FIPN	**C510**	**0171**
C-FIPN	GLEX	9216
C-FIPP	ASTR	150
C-FIPP	GLEX	9217
C-FIPQ	GLEX	9219
C-FIPT	GLEX	9221
C-FIPT	GLEX	9714
C-FIPU	GLEX	9711
C-FIPX	**GLEX**	**9397**
C-FIQF	**HS25**	**258181**
C-FIRG	GLEX	9715
C-FIRK	**GLEX**	**9712**
C-FIRT	GLEX	9710
C-FISO	GLEX	9713
C-FITC	**C52A**	**0394**
C-FIXN	CL64	5656
C-FIYA	CL64	5657
C-FIZP	CL30	20528
C-FJAJ	F2EX	34
C-FJBO	C550	550-0812
C-FJCB	CL30	20192
C-FJCB	CL64	5659
C-FJCB	**CL65**	**6059**
C-FJCZ	**C550**	**700**
C-FJDF	CL61	5079
C-FJDS	**C550**	**550-0807**
C-FJDX	**GLEX**	**9719**
C-FJDZ	GLEX	9716
C-FJEF	**GLEX**	**9722**
C-FJEF	LJ35	390
C-FJES	F900	55
C-FJES	FA20	236
C-FJES	GLF4	1207
C-FJFJ	**GLEX**	**9717**
C-FJGG	**LJ60**	**038**
C-FJGI	**GLEX**	**9720**
C-FJGK	**GLEX**	**9718**
C-FJGR	CL61	5080
C-FJGX	GLEX	9003
C-FJGX	GLEX	9721
C-FJHO	CL30	20525
C-FJHS	**HS25**	**258283**
C-FJIC	**C750**	**0020**
C-FJJC	C650	0116
C-FJJC	**CL61**	**5096**
C-FJJG	C650	0116
C-FJLA	CL61	5154
C-FJML	GLEX	9223
C-FJMP	GLEX	9225
C-FJMQ	GLEX	9228
C-FJMV	GLEX	9230
C-FJMX	GLEX	9232
C-FJNJ	GLEX	9222
C-FJNQ	GLEX	9224
C-FJNS	CL61	5059
C-FJNS	**CL65**	**5755**
C-FJNX	GLEX	9226
C-FJNZ	CL61	5059
C-FJNZ	GLEX	9227
C-FJOA	F2EX	126
C-FJOA	F9EX	180
C-FJOA	GLEX	9229
C-FJOE	C550	573
C-FJOE	C650	0049
C-FJOI	**F9EX**	**69**
C-FJOJ	**GALX**	**143**
C-FJOJ	WW24	271
C-FJOK	GLEX	9231
C-FJOL	**LJ60**	**387**
C-FJOU	GLEX	9233
C-FJPI	CL61	5085
C-FJPV	F2TH	88
C-FJQD	CL30	20125
C-FJQH	CL30	20126
C-FJQP	CL30	20127
C-FJQR	CL30	20128
C-FJQT	CL30	20129
C-FJQX	CL30	20130
C-FJQZ	CL30	20131
C-FJRE	CL30	20132
C-FJRG	CL30	20133
C-FJRG	CL65	5980
C-FJRX	**C680**	**0345**
C-FJTA	**PRM1**	**RB-289**
C-FJTN	**PRM1**	**RB-267**
C-FJUH	FA50	137
C-FJWX	GLEX	9724
C-FJWZ	**C550**	**685**
C-FJXE	**GLEX**	**9726**
C-FJXN	**C550**	**684**
C-FJXR	**GLEX**	**9723**
C-FJXY	**GLEX**	**9727**
C-FJYB	GLEX	9725
C-FKBC	**C560**	**0409**
C-FKCE	**C550**	**686**
C-FKCI	**CL30**	**20242**
C-FKCI	FA50	63
C-FKCI	HS25	25137
C-FKDK	**GLEX**	**9732**
C-FKDN	**GLEX**	**9730**
C-FKDV	CL64	5664
C-FKDX	**C550**	**687**
C-FKEB	**C550**	**688**
C-FKEX	**GLEX**	**9729**
C-FKFO	**GLEX**	**9731**
C-FKFS	**GLEX**	**9733**
C-FKFY	**GLEX**	**9728**
C-FKGN	HS25	258052
C-FKGX	GLEX	9004
C-FKHD	C550	110
C-FKHJ	**C56X**	**5187**
C-FKIY	CL61	5092
C-FKJM	**CL61**	**3012**
C-FKKI	CL30	20549
C-FKLB	**C550**	**699**
C-FKMC	C500	073
C-FKMC	CL65	5772
C-FKNN	CL61	5094
C-FKOC	CL30	20579
C-FKPY	**GLEX**	**9737**
C-FKRE	**GLEX**	**9734**
C-FKRX	**GLEX**	**9739**
C-FKSB	**GLEX**	**9736**
C-FKSF	**GLEX**	**9738**
C-FKSN	**GLEX**	**9735**
C-FKTD	CL61	5096
C-FKUL	CL64	5634
C-FKVW	CL61	5097
C-FKXF	CL30	20257
C-FLBC	C550	044
C-FLBQ	C560	0429
C-FLBS	**C52C**	**0140**
C-FLCY	CL30	20134
C-FLCY	CL64	5506
C-FLDD	CL30	20135
C-FLDD	**CL30**	**20238**
C-FLDD	CL30	20268
C-FLDK	CL30	20136
C-FLDM	C550	288
C-FLDO	C550	038
C-FLDO	CL30	20137
C-FLDW	CL30	20138
C-FLDX	CL30	20139
C-FLEC	CL30	20140
C-FLEJ	CL30	20141
C-FLEK	CL30	20142
C-FLEN	CL30	20143
C-FLFE	**C56X**	**5261**
C-FLFI	C680	0238
C-FLFT	**GLEX**	**9746**
C-FLGD	**GLEX**	**9743**
C-FLGN	CL65	5703
C-FLGN	**GLEX**	**9740**
C-FLHA	**GLEX**	**9744**
C-FLIX	**E50P**	**50000035**
C-FLKC	CL65	5704
C-FLKC	**GLEX**	**9742**
C-FLKO	**GLEX**	**9745**
C-FLKU	**GLEX**	**9741**
C-FLKX	FA7X	151
C-FLKY	GLEX	9241
C-FLKZ	GLEX	9234
C-FLLA	GLEX	9235
C-FLLF	GLEX	9236
C-FLLH	GLEX	9237
C-FLLH	LJ45	088
C-FLLN	GLEX	9238
C-FLLO	GLEX	9239
C-FLLV	GLEX	9240
C-FLMJ	C650	0104
C-FLMK	**CL65**	**5786**
C-FLMS	**GALX**	**054**
C-FLNZ	CL65	5705
C-FLOO	CL30	20571
C-FLOX	**E50P**	**50000009**
C-FLPB	**GALX**	**020**
C-FLPC	CL61	5006
C-FLPC	CL64	5392
C-FLPD	C550	189
C-FLPH	HS25	258243
C-FLQF	CL30	20144
C-FLQG	CL30	20145
C-FLQH	CL30	20146
C-FLQM	CL30	20147
C-FLQO	CL30	20148
C-FLQP	CL30	20149
C-FLQR	CL30	20150
C-FLQX	CL30	20151
C-FLQY	CL30	20152
C-FLQZ	CL30	20153
C-FLQZ	CL30	20591
C-FLRJ	LJ45	156
C-FLRP	CL61	5068
C-FLSF	CL65	5706
C-FLSJ	CL65	5707
C-FLTB	GLEX	9242
C-FLTB	LJ60	377
C-FLTH	GLEX	9243
C-FLTI	GLEX	9244
C-FLTJ	GLEX	9245
C-FLTL	C650	0007
C-FLUT	CL61	5087
C-FLVK	**GLEX**	**9749**
C-FLWV	**GLEX**	**9747**
C-FLWX	**GLEX**	**9750**
C-FLXD	**GLEX**	**9748**
C-FLYJ	CL61	5102
C-FLZA	**C550**	**701**
C-FMAN	C500	086
C-FMCG	**C550**	**550-1101**
C-FMCH	**GLEX**	**9754**
C-FMCI	C52C	0089
C-FMCI	C550	550-0816
C-FMCI	**C680**	**0552**
C-FMCL	C510	0338
C-FMCZ	**GLEX**	**9752**
C-FMDB	HS25	25075
C-FMFK	GLEX	9246
C-FMFL	**FA50**	**96**
C-FMFM	**C550**	**702**
C-FMFN	**C680**	**0158**
C-FMFN	GLEX	9247
C-FMFO	GLEX	9248
C-FMFO	**GLEX**	**9751**
C-FMGE	GLEX	9249
C-FMGK	GLEX	9250
C-FMGL	LJ45	088
C-FMGL	LJ45	360
C-FMGL	**LJ45**	**463**
C-FMGM	LJ25	117
C-FMHA	**LJ40**	**2043**
C-FMHB	ASTR	066
C-FMHL	ASTR	066
C-FMHL	CL30	20169
C-FMHL	**FA7X**	**172**
C-FMHR	**GLEX**	**9753**
C-FMIX	**HS25**	**258392**
C-FMJM	C550	444
C-FMKF	HS25	25170
C-FMKW	GLEX	9251
C-FMKZ	GLEX	9252
C-FMLB	GLEX	9253
C-FMLE	GLEX	9254
C-FMLI	GLEX	9255
C-FMLQ	**GLEX**	**9256**
C-FMLT	GLEX	9257
C-FMLV	GLEX	9258
C-FMMH	GLEX	9259
C-FMND	GLEX	9260
C-FMNL	C510	0338
C-FMNL	CL65	5710
C-FMNR	CL65	5711
C-FMNW	CL65	5712
C-FMOI	C550	550-0982
C-FMOS	C550	550-0982
C-FMOS	**C56X**	**5284**
C-FMPN	**E55P**	**50500111**
C-FMPP	C550	409
C-FMPU	**E50P**	**50000252**
C-FMPX	**GLEX**	**9513**
C-FMRI	HS25	258688
C-FMTC	HS25	25104
C-FMUI	GLEX	9261
C-FMUN	GLEX	9262
C-FMUO	GLEX	9263
C-FMUS	**CL64**	**5647**
C-FMVN	CL65	5714
C-FMVQ	CL61	5105
C-FMVQ	CL65	5713
C-FMWG	CL30	20163
C-FMWW	WW24	380
C-FMWX	CL30	20162
C-FMXH	CL30	20161
C-FMXK	CL30	20160
C-FMXQ	CL30	20159
C-FMXU	CL30	20158
C-FMXW	CL30	20157
C-FMXX	CL30	20156
C-FMYA	CL30	20154
C-FMYB	CL30	20155
C-FMYB	FA50	99
C-FMYD	**GLEX**	**9757**
C-FMYG	**GLEX**	**9755**
C-FMYX	**GLEX**	**9758**
C-FMZS	**GLEX**	**9756**
C-FNCB	**C52B**	**0125**
C-FNCG	**F2EX**	**56**
C-FNCG	GLF2	208
C-FNCG	SBRL	282-90
(C-FNCG)	GLF4	1017
C-FNCT	**C550**	**175**
C-FNDF	**C560**	**0815**
C-FNDF	GLEX	9115
C-FNDK	GLEX	9265
C-FNDN	GLEX	9264
C-FNDO	GLEX	9266
C-FNDQ	GLEX	9267
C-FNDT	GLEX	9268
C-FNER	HS25	25176
C-FNEU	CL61	5119
C-FNFS	**C52B**	**0262**
C-FNHZ	**C500**	**689**
C-FNIJ	CL65	5715
C-FNIL	**GLEX**	**9762**
C-FNIN	CL65	5716
C-FNIR	**GLEX**	**9759**
C-FNJT	**LJ45**	**096**
C-FNKX	**GLEX**	**9761**
C-FNLH	**GLEX**	**9763**
C-FNMC	**GLEX**	**9760**
C-FNMC	LJ24	106
C-FNNC	FA50	176
C-FNND	FA10	87
C-FNNI	CL65	6052
C-FNNS	CL61	5068
C-FNNS	CL61	5096
C-FNNT	CL61	5068
C-FNNT	CL64	5317
C-FNOC	C500	182
C-FNOQ	CL65	6053
C-FNOR	GLF2	54/36
C-FNQH	CL65	6055
C-FNRG	**C750**	**0305**
C-FNRG	LJ45	223
C-FNRG	LJ55	101
C-FNRP	GLEX	9269
C-FNRR	GLEX	9270
C-FNRW	WW24	176
C-FNSJ	CL65	6059
C-FNSN	GLEX	9271
C-FNSV	GLEX	9272
C-FNTM	C560	0346
C-FNTM	CL65	5718
C-FNTP	CL65	5721
C-FNUF	CL65	5720
C-FNUH	CL30	20164
C-FNVR	**GLEX**	**9765**
C-FNXG	**GLEX**	**9764**
C-FNXK	**GLEX**	**9766**
C-FNXL	C56X	5686
C-FNYU	CL64	5332
C-FNZS	CL65	6056
C-FNZZ	GLEX	9273
C-FOAB	GLEX	9274
C-FOAD	GLEX	9275
C-FOAE	CL30	20165
C-FOAI	CL30	20166
C-FOAJ	CL30	20167
C-FOAQ	CL30	20168
C-FOAT	CL30	20169
C-FOAU	CL30	20170
C-FOBF	CL65	5729
C-FOBJ	CL30	20173
C-FOBK	CL65	5719
C-FOBQ	CS55	0036
C-FOCF	**GLEX**	**9768**
C-FODX	**GLEX**	**9767**
C-FOEJ	CL30	20598
C-FOGE	CL65	5722
C-FOGI	CL65	5723
C-FOGX	**CL64**	**5656**
C-FOIL	WW24	201
C-FOIL	WW24	336
C-FOKD	GLEX	9276
C-FOKF	GLEX	9277
C-FOKH	GLEX	9278
C-FOKJ	GLEX	9279
C-FOMS	CL65	5724
C-FOMU	CL30	20170
C-FOMU	CL65	5725
C-FONX	FA20	225/472
C-FOPC	HS25	25016
C-FOPC	BE40	RK-70
C-FOQR	CL30	20174
C-FOQW	CL30	20175
C-FORB	CL30	20176
C-FORB	**GLF4**	**1336**
C-FORJ	C650	0104
C-FOSB	CL30	20177
C-FOSG	CL30	20178
C-FOSK	CL61	5114
C-FOSM	C500	343
C-FOSM	CL30	20179
C-FOSQ	CL30	20180
C-FOSW	CL30	20181
C-FOSX	CL30	20182
C-FOTF	CL30	20183
C-FOVD	GLEX	9280
C-FOVE	GLEX	9281
C-FOVG	GLEX	9282
C-FOVH	GLEX	9283
C-FOVK	GLEX	9284
C-FOXA	GLEX	9018
C-FOXU	CL65	5726
C-FOXV	CL65	5727
C-FOYE	CL65	5728
C-FPAW	MU30	A006SA
C-FPBX	**LJ45**	**085**
C-FPCE	**C510**	**0151**
C-FPCE	HS25	258500
C-FPCP	HS25	258095
C-FPCP	HS25	258500
C-FPDO	FA50	97
C-FPDR	CL61	5155
C-FPEL	C550	044
C-FPEP	WW24	441
C-FPFF	GLEX	9285

C-FPFS	**F9EX**	**93**
C-FPGB	GLEX	9286
C-FPGD	GLEX	9287
C-FPGI	GLEX	9288
C-FPIY	CL61	5125
C-FPJT	C560	0017
C-FPMQ	CL30	20171
C-FPMU	CL30	20172
C-FPOX	CL61	5128
C-FPPN	HS25	25280
C-FPQE	GLEX	9289
C-FPQF	GLEX	9290
C-FPQG	GLEX	9291
C-FPQG	HS25	25036
C-FPQH	GLEX	9292
C-FPQI	GLEX	9293
C-FPQJ	GLEX	9687
C-FPQT	CL65	5731
C-FPQV	CL65	5732
C-FPQW	CL65	5733
C-FPQY	CL65	5734
C-FPQZ	CL65	5735
C-FPRP	LJ35	390
C-FPSB	**ASTR**	**080**
C-FPSJ	CL65	5736
C-FPSQ	CL65	5737
C-FPSV	CL65	5738
C-FPTM	**DDJET**	**DJ1-0002**
C-FPUB	LJ25	090
C-FPUI	C750	0002
C-FPWB	**C525**	**0062**
C-FPWC	C56X	5078
C-FPWI	CL65	5730
C-FPYP	**C510**	**0298**
C-FPZZ	CL30	20184
C-FQCF	CL30	20185
C-FQCY	C650	0087
C-FQEI	CL30	20186
C-FQNS	HS25	25152
C-FQOA	CL30	20187
C-FQOF	CL30	20188
C-FQOI	CL30	20189
C-FQOK	CL30	20190
C-FQOL	CL30	20191
C-FQOM	CL30	20192
C-FQOQ	CL30	20193
C-FQQE	CL65	5739
C-FQQG	CL65	5740
C-FQQH	CL65	5741
C-FQQK	CL65	5742
C-FQQO	CL65	5743
C-FQQS	CL65	5744
C-FQQW	CL65	5745
C-FQVE	CL65	5746
C-FQXW	GLEX	9294
C-FQXX	GLEX	9295
C-FQXY	GLEX	9296
C-FQYB	C560	0588
C-FQYB	GLEX	9297
C-FQYD	GLEX	9298
C-FQYE	GLEX	9299
C-FQYT	CL61	3049
C-FRBC	JSTR	5160
C-FRCI	**CL64**	**5650**
C-FREE	FA10	224
C-FREE	**G150**	**296**
C-FREE	WW24	271
C-FRGV	CL61	5142
C-FRGX	GLEX	9014
C-FRGY	C555	0036
C-FRGY	**LJ60**	**061**
C-FRHL	C500	343
C-FRJV	GLEX	9300
C-FRJX	CL61	5147
C-FRJY	GLEX	9301
C-FRJZ	**ASTR**	**087**
C-FRKI	C560	0573
C-FRKI	**C680**	**0071**
C-FRKL	C560	0573
C-FRKL	GLEX	9302
C-FRKO	GLEX	9303
C-FRKQ	GLEX	9304
C-FRMW	GLEX	9305
C-FRNG	C550	550-1079
C-FRNG	GLEX	9306
C-FRNJ	GLEX	9307
C-FRNR	LJ24	321
C-FROC	GLF2	134
C-FROX	LJ25	070
C-FROY	CL30	20201
C-FROY	WW24	429
C-FRPP	HS25	258121
C-FRQA	CL30	20194
C-FRQA	CL61	5146
C-FRQC	CL30	20195
C-FRQH	CL30	20196
C-FRQK	CL30	20197
C-FRQM	CL30	20198
C-FRQN	CL30	20199
C-FRQP	CL30	20200
C-FRST	C550	550-1011
(C-FRST)	CL60	1059
C-FRVE	C525	0062
C-FRYS	**LJ45**	**275**
C-FSBC	**C650**	**7092**
C-FSBR	GLF4	1032
C-FSCI	CL65	5717

C-FSCI	**CL65**	**5948**
C-FSCI	HS25	258105
C-FSCL	FA50	97
C-FSCY	HS25	258105
C-FSDB	**PRM1**	**RB-217**
C-FSDH	HS25	25192
C-FSDL	LJ45	255
C-FSDL	LJ45	421
C-FSDL	**LJ45**	**468**
C-FSDS	**C750**	**0090**
C-FSEN	HS25	25027
C-FSEP	**CL65**	**5861**
C-FSIM	HS25	25039
C-FSIP	CL60	1048
C-FSIP	CL65	5747
C-FSIQ	CL65	5748
C-FSIU	CL65	5749
C-FSJH	CL65	5750
C-FSJI	**FA20**	**373**
C-FSJR	CL64	5413
C-FSJR	**CL65**	**5854**
C-FSJT	CL65	5751
C-FSJV	CL65	5752
C-FSJY	CL65	5753
C-FSJY	**CL65**	**5986**
C-FSKC	C500	018
C-FSKT	CL65	5754
C-FSKX	CL65	5755
C-FSLL	CL30	20208
C-FSLR	CL30	20209
C-FSLU	CL30	20210
C-FSMO	CL30	20202
C-FSMW	CL30	20203
C-FSNB	CL30	20204
C-FSNC	**C560**	**0676**
C-FSNP	CL30	20205
C-FSNQ	CL30	20206
C-FSNU	CL30	20207
C-FSRX	GLEX	9308
C-FSRY	GLEX	9309
C-FSRZ	GLEX	9310
C-FSSE	GLEX	9311
C-FSTP	E50P	50000224
C-FSTX	C510	0295
C-FSTX	**C52C**	**0199**
C-FSUA	WW24	17
C-FSUN	C500	292
C-FSXG	CL60	1043
C-FSXH	CL61	5156
C-FSXL	**C56X**	**5747**
C-FSXR	**CL30**	**20416**
C-FSXX	**FA10**	**131**
C-FSYK	CL61	5158
C-FSYO	LJ25	122
C-FTAM	C550	398
C-FTAM	HS25	25108
C-FTBZ	CL64	5991
C-FTDA	**CL61**	**3049**
C-FTDB	ASTR	117
C-FTEC	HS25	25232
C-FTEL	C750	0097
C-FTEN	C750	0188
C-FTEN	FA10	45
C-FTFC	CL61	5091
C-FTIE	CL61	5041
C-FTIK	GLEX	9312
C-FTIL	C550	299
C-FTIL	C56X	5253
C-FTIO	**GLEX**	**9313**
C-FTIQ	GLEX	9314
C-FTIR	GLEX	9315
C-FTIS	GLEX	9316
C-FTIU	**PRM1**	**RB-275**
C-FTIX	**G150**	**275**
C-FTJC	**C560**	**0544**
C-FTJF	**C560**	**0643**
C-FTKA	CL30	20211
C-FTKC	CL30	20212
C-FTKG	CL30	20214
C-FTKH	CL30	20213
C-FTKK	CL30	20215
C-FTKX	C525	0364
C-FTLA	HS25	258015
C-FTLB	CL65	5756
C-FTLH	**C750**	**0118**
C-FTLH	CL65	5757
C-FTLS	**C750**	**0518**
C-FTMI	C500	069
C-FTMS	C550	299
C-FTNE	CL61	5162
C-FTNN	CL61	5159
C-FTOC	C550	321
C-FTOH	CL61	5165
C-FTOM	C550	321
C-FTOM	C560	0633
C-FTOR	**C650**	**7067**
C-FTQY	CL65	5763
C-FTQZ	CL65	5764
C-FTRF	CL65	5762
C-FTRM	C52A	0235
C-FTRM	CL65	5761
C-FTRO	CL65	5759
C-FTRP	**G150**	**271**
C-FTRQ	CL65	5760
C-FTRY	CL65	5758
C-FTUT	FA20	21
C-FTUX	GLEX	9317

C-FTUY	GLEX	9318
C-FTVC	HS25	258243
C-FTVF	GLEX	9319
C-FTVK	GLEX	9320
C-FTVN	GLEX	9321
C-FTVO	GLEX	9322
C-FTWO	**WW24**	**199**
C-FTWR	WW24	207
C-FTWV	WW24	226
C-FTWX	**WW24**	**277**
C-FTXL	**C56X**	**5672**
C-FTXT	LJ25	057
C-FTXX	**G150**	**222**
C-FUAK	CL65	5767
C-FUAS	CL65	5766
C-FUAU	CL65	5765
C-FUBE	CL30	20216
C-FUBK	CL30	20217
C-FUBM	CL30	20218
C-FUBO	CL30	20219
C-FUBP	CL30	20220
C-FUBQ	**C560**	**0455**
C-FUBQ	CL30	20221
C-FUBT	CL30	20222
C-FUCV	GLEX	9323
C-FUCY	GLEX	9324
C-FUCZ	GLEX	9325
C-FUDH	GLEX	9326
C-FUDN	GLEX	9327
C-FUIT	CL65	5768
C-FUIU	CL65	5769
C-FUIV	CL65	5770
C-FUJA	CL30	20223
C-FUJE	CL30	20224
C-FUJM	CL30	20225
C-FUJR	CL30	20226
C-FUJT	CL30	20227
C-FUJX	CL30	20228
C-FUND	CL61	5172
C-FUOJ	GLEX	9328
C-FUOK	GLEX	9329
C-FUOL	GLEX	9330
C-FUOM	GLEX	9331
C-FURA	CL30	20229
C-FURB	CL30	20230
C-FURB	**CL61**	**3063**
C-FURC	CL30	20231
C-FURD	CL30	20232
C-FURF	CL30	20233
C-FURG	CL61	3063
C-FURH	CL30	20234
C-FURP	GLEX	9332
C-FUSI	GLEX	9333
C-FUSR	GLEX	9334
C-FUTF	GLEX	9335
C-FUTL	**C525**	**0631**
C-FUTL	GLEX	9336
C-FUTT	GLEX	9337
C-FUUF	CL65	5776
C-FUUI	CL65	5777
C-FUUM	CL65	5778
C-FUUQ	CL65	5779
C-FUUW	CL65	5780
C-FUVA	CL65	5771
C-FUVC	CL65	5772
C-FUVF	CL65	5773
C-FUVG	CL65	5774
C-FUVH	CL65	5775
C-FVEJ	C560	0648
C-FVFW	GLEX	9338
C-FVGP	GLEX	9339
C-FVGX	GLEX	9340
C-FVHE	GLEX	9341
C-FVLX	CL30	20243
C-FVLZ	CL30	20244
C-FVMI	CL65	5791
C-FVMW	CL65	5792
C-FVMW	**F2EX**	**258**
C-FVNB	CL30	20235
C-FVNC	CL30	20236
C-FVNC	**LJ31**	**187**
C-FVND	CL30	20237
C-FVNF	CL30	20238
C-FVNI	CL30	20239
C-FVNL	CL30	20240
C-FVNS	CL30	20241
C-FVNT	CL30	20242
C-FVOC	CL65	5781
C-FVON	CL65	5782
C-FVOQ	CL65	5783
C-FVOZ	CL65	5784
C-FVSL	CL64	5489
C-FVSL	LJ45	024
C-FVSL	LJ45	408
C-FVSL	**LJ45**	**466**
C-FVUC	CL64	5301
C-FVUI	GLEX	9342
C-FVUK	GLEX	9343
C-FVUP	GLEX	9344
C-FVUZ	GLEX	9345
C-FVVE	GLEX	9346
C-FVZC	CL61	5182
C-FWBK	C525	0425
C-FWCE	HS25	257206
C-FWCE	HS25	258163
C-FWEC	WW24	115
C-FWGB	GLEX	9347

C-FWGE	CL61	5178
C-FWGH	GLEX	9348
C-FWGP	GLEX	9349
C-FWGV	GLEX	9350
C-FWHF	GLEX	9351
C-FWHH	C560	0484
C-FWIK	GLEX	9352
C-FWKX	**F900**	**120**
C-FWOS	HS25	25159
C-FWQH	CL65	5785
C-FWQL	CL65	5786
C-FWQM	CL65	5787
C-FWQO	CL65	5788
C-FWQV	CL65	5789
C-FWQY	CL65	5790
C-FWRA	FA20	110
C-FWRE	CL30	20252
C-FWRG	CL30	20253
C-FWRN	WW24	98
C-FWRX	**C750**	**0212**
C-FWRX	CL30	20254
C-FWSC	F900	75
C-FWTF	**E55P**	**50500307**
C-FWTF	F2TH	71
C-FWTK	CL30	20255
C-FWTQ	CL30	20256
C-FWTY	CL30	20257
C-FWUC	CL30	20251
C-FWUI	CL30	20250
C-FWUK	CL30	20249
C-FWUL	CL30	20248
C-FWUO	CL30	20247
C-FWUT	**CL30**	**20246**
C-FWUZ	CL30	20245
C-FWVH	CL30	20258
C-FWWW	C550	178
C-FWXL	C56X	5691
C-FWZR	GLEX	9353
C-FWZX	GLEX	9354
C-FXAQ	GLEX	9355
C-FXAY	GLEX	9356
C-FXBF	GLEX	9357
C-FXCK	CL61	5189
C-FXCN	CL64	5474
(C-FXFJ)	C52B	0144
C-FXGO	**HS25**	**258166**
C-FXHE	CL64	5304
C-FXHN	LJ45	126
C-FXIP	CL61	5194
C-FXIY	GLEX	9358
C-FXJD	GLEX	9359
C-FXJM	GLEX	9360
C-FXKE	CL64	5303
C-FXKE	GLEX	9361
C-FXKK	GLEX	9362
C-FXOO	**F900**	**86**
C-FXPB	CL30	20259
C-FXPB	CL64	5474
C-FXPI	CL30	20260
C-FXPL	CL30	20261
C-FXPQ	CL30	20262
C-FXPR	CL30	20263
C-FXPT	CL30	20264
C-FXPW	CL30	20265
C-FXQG	CL65	5793
C-FXQH	CL65	5794
C-FXQJ	CL65	5795
C-FXQM	CL65	5796
C-FXQR	CL65	5797
C-FXQX	CL65	5798
C-FXRD	CL65	5805
C-FXSS	**C560**	**0541**
C-FXTC	C52B	0037
C-FXTC	**C52C**	**0078**
C-FXUQ	CL64	5307
C-FXYK	GLEX	9363
C-FXYN	LJ45	270
C-FXYS	GLEX	9364
C-FXYY	GLEX	9365
C-FXZS	CL64	5309
C-FYAB	CL65	5804
C-FYAG	GLF3	310
C-FYAI	CL65	5803
C-FYAP	CL65	5802
C-FYAV	CL65	5801
C-FYAW	CL65	5800
C-FYAY	CL65	5799
C-FYBG	CL30	20266
C-FYBJ	CL30	20267
C-FYBK	CL65	5806
C-FYBM	CL30	20269
C-FYBN	CL30	20270
C-FYBO	CL30	20271
C-FYBS	CL30	20272
C-FYBU	CL30	20273
C-FYBV	CL30	20274
C-FYBZ	CL30	20268
C-FYGJ	GLEX	9366
C-FYGP	GLEX	9367
C-FYGX	GLEX	9368
C-FYHT	GLEX	9369
C-FYIG	GLEX	9370
C-FYIH	GLEX	9371
C-FYIZ	GLEX	9372
C-FYJC	GLEX	9373
C-FYJD	GLEX	9374
C-FYMM	C560	0314

C-FYMM	**C560**	**0705**
C-FYMT	C560	0314
C-FYMT	GLEX	9375
C-FYMU	GLEX	9376
C-FYNI	GLEX	9377
C-FYNQ	GLEX	9378
C-FYNV	GLEX	9379
C-FYOC	GLEX	9380
C-FYPB	FA20	254
C-FYTY	CL65	5814
C-FYTZ	CL65	5765
C-FYTZ	**HS25**	**258349**
C-FYUD	CL65	5807
C-FYUH	CL65	5808
C-FYUK	CL65	5809
C-FYUL	C550	550-1028
C-FYUL	C560	0647
C-FYUL	**C56X**	**5691**
C-FYUP	CL65	5810
C-FYUQ	CL30	20245
C-FYUR	CL65	5811
C-FYUS	CL65	5812
C-FYUY	CL65	5813
C-FYXC	CL64	5317
C-FYYH	CL64	5318
C-FYZP	GLEX	9139
C-FZAU	LJ45	163
C-FZCC	G150	285
C-FZCC	**G280**	**2009**
C-FZCG	G150	285
C-FZDY	CL64	5321
C-FZEI	WW24	441
C-FZHT	LJ24	217
C-FZHU	LJ25	070
C-FZKY	CL65	5821
C-FZLA	CL65	5815
C-FZLB	CL65	5816
C-FZLM	CL65	5817
C-FZLR	CL65	5818
C-FZLS	CL65	5819
C-FZLU	CL65	5820
C-FZLX	CL30	20275
C-FZLY	CL30	20276
C-FZLZ	CL30	20277
C-FZOP	CL64	5367
C-FZOP	**FA10**	**44**
C-FZPG	CL64	5321
C-FZQP	LJ35	168
C-FZRR	CL64	5332
C-FZSO	CL64	5557
C-FZVM	GLEX	9123
C-FZVN	CL64	5335
C-FZVN	GLEX	9124
C-FZVS	GLEX	9125
C-FZVV	GLEX	9126
C-FZWB	GLEX	9128
C-FZWF	GLEX	9129
C-FZWW	GLEX	9131
C-FZXC	GLEX	9132
C-FZXE	GLEX	9133
C-FZXZ	GLEX	9134
C-FZYB	FA50	272
C-FZYL	GLEX	9135
C-GAAA	C500	549
C-GAAA	C500	677
C-GAAA	HS25	257179
C-GABE	**C525**	**0232**
C-GABX	HS25	257047
C-GAGP	WW24	260
C-GAGQ	GLEX	9140
C-GAGQ	HS25	258181
C-GAGS	GLEX	9141
C-GAGT	GLEX	9142
C-GAGU	**C680**	**0100**
C-GAGU	HS25	258181
C-GAIP	CL65	5822
C-GAJG	CL65	5823
C-GAJG	**LJ45**	**530**
C-GAJS	**LJ35**	**380**
C-GAKE	CL30	20278
C-GAKF	CL30	20279
C-GAKL	CL30	20280
C-GAKN	CL30	20281
C-GAKO	CL30	20282
C-GAKZ	CL30	20283
C-GALP	CL65	5824
C-GAMW	C550	051
(C-GANE)	GLF2	162
C-GANU	CL65	5825
C-GAOB	CL61	5117
C-GAPC	**C560**	**0033**
C-GAPD	C550	691
C-GAPD	C560	0165
C-GAPT	C550	216
C-GAPT	C650	0195
C-GAPT	**C750**	**0131**
C-GAPV	C550	691
C-GASR	**C52A**	**0510**
C-GATU	JSTR	5143
C-GAUH	C750	0108
C-GAUK	CL64	5343
C-GAWH	**CL64**	**5557**
C-GAWH	HS25	258087
C-GAWJ	WW24	277
C-GAWR	C560	0351
C-GAWR	C56X	5717
C-GAWR	**C680**	**0337**

C-GAWU	C560	0351
C-GAWU	C560	0812
C-GAWU	C680	0337
C-GAXX	**C750**	**0246**
C-GAZU	**F900**	**198**
C-GAZU	FA50	228
C-GAZU	JSTR	5070/52
C-GAZU	JSTR	5083/49
C-GAZU	JSTR	5222
C-GBAP	HS25	258444
C-GBBB	**CL64**	**5556**
C-GBBB	GLF3	368
C-GBBX	C550	650
C-GBBX	F9EX	64
C-GBCA	C550	590
C-GBCB	C550	060
C-GBCC	CL60	1005
C-GBCE	C550	591
C-GBCF	C550	564
C-GBCI	**FA20**	**478**
C-GBCK	C500	204
C-GBDH	CL60	1005
C-GBDK	CL64	5347
C-GBDX	JSTR	5219
C-GBEY	CL60	1008
C-GBFA	LJ35	248
C-GBFL	FA20	239
C-GBFP	**LJ25**	**167**
C-GBFY	CL60	1009
C-GBGC	C555	0107
C-GBGC	GLF5	5306
C-GBHS	CL60	1011
C-GBHZ	CL60	1013
C-GBIS	HS25	258117
C-GBJA	CL61	5038
C-GBJA	CL61	5082
C-GBJA	CL61	5111
C-GBJA	CL61	5151
C-GBJA	CL64	5302
C-GBJA	CL64	5339
C-GBJA	CL64	5341
C-GBKB	CL60	1045
C-GBKB	CL64	5420
C-GBKB	**CL65**	**5789**
C-GBKC	CL60	1007
C-GBKE	CL60	1012
C-GBKE	CL64	5352
C-GBLF	LJ35	091
C-GBLL	CL60	1014
C-GBLL-X	CL60	1014
C-GBLN	CL60	1015
C-GBLX	CL61	3010
C-GBLX	GLEX	9112
C-GBNE	C500	461
C-GBNE	**C560**	**0244**
C-GBNS	HS25	256051
(C-GBNS)	HS25	256047
C-GBNX	**C560**	**0074**
C-GBOQ	CL60	1036
C-GBOT	LJ25	090
C-GBPL	C510	0205
C-GBPM	C525	0287
C-GBPX	CL60	1017
C-GBQC	LJ25	179
C-GBRM	HS25	257093
C-GBRQ	CL64	5358
C-GBRW	LJ36	001
C-GBRW-X	LJ36	001
C-GBSW	**ASTR**	**130**
C-GBSZ	CL60	1047
C-GBTB	C500	525
C-GBTK	CL60	1057
C-GBTT	CL60	1062
C-GBTY	GLEX	9381
C-GBUA	GLEX	9382
C-GBUB	CL60	1064
C-GBUI	GLEX	9383
C-GBUU-X	CL61	3001
C-GBVE	CL60	1065
C-GBWA	LJ24	261
C-GBWB	LJ24	168
C-GBWD	LJ36	012
C-GBWL	LJ35	049
C GBXH	CL61	3002
C-GBXW	CL61	3018
C-GBXZ	CL30	20288
C-GBYC	CL61	3011
C-GBYG	CL65	5826
C-GBYH	CL65	5827
C-GBYK	CL65	5828
C-GBYM	CL65	5829
C-GBYS	CL65	5830
C-GBZE	CL30	20284
C-GBZE	CL60	1067
C-GBZF	**C550**	**550-1119**
C-GBZI	CL30	20285
C-GBZK	CL60	1077
C-GBZL	CL30	20286
C-GBZQ	CL61	3047
C-GBZV	CL30	20287
C-GCCU	**C510**	**0461**
C-GCCU	HS25	258105
C-GCCZ	CL64	5367
C-GCDF	CL64	5455
C-GCDS	CL64	5455
C-GCDS	**GLEX**	**9137**
C-GCEO	HS25	25285
C-GCFB	GLF2	28
C-GCFG	**CL61**	**3022**
C-GCFI	CL61	3020
C-GCFL	**C560**	**0418**
C-GCFP	C650	0145
C-GCGR-X	CL60	1001
C-GCGS	**HS25**	**258123**
C-GCGS-X	CL60	1002
C-GCGT	CL60	1003/3991
C-GCGT	**HS25**	**258828**
C-GCGT-X	CL60	1003/3991
C-GCGY	GLEX	9006
C-GCGY	GLEX	9056
C-GCIB	CL60	1010
C-GCIB	HS25	258048
C-GCIL	**LJ55**	**089**
C-GCIX	C650	7092
C-GCIX	**HS25**	**258492**
C-GCJD	LJ25	096
C-GCJD	LJ35	055
C-GCJN	C550	086
C-GCKR	GLEX	9384
C-GCLI	GLEX	9385
C-GCLQ	C500	348
C-GCMJ	GLEX	9386
C-GCMP	LJ45	019
C-GCMP	LJ45	153
C-GCMP	**LJ45**	**434**
C-GCNR	**CL64**	**5339**
C-GCOX	GLEX	9387
C-GCPI	GLEX	9388
C-GCPM	**GLF4**	**1238**
C-GCPV	GLEX	9389
C-GCQB	CL64	5369
C-GCRG	C555	0142
C-GCRP	HS25	258124
C-GCRW	GLEX	9007
C-GCSB	CL65	5709
C-GCSN	CL60	1006
C-GCTB	CL61	3031
C-GCTD	C500	056
C-GCUL	C550	135
C-GCUL	C750	0090
C-GCUL	**FA7X**	**57**
C-GCUN	CL61	3035
C-GCUP	CL61	3036
C-GCUR	CL61	3037
C-GCUT	CL61	3038
C-GCUW	C560	0053
C-GCVQ	CL60	1009
C-GCVZ	CL64	5373
C-GCWQ	GLEX	9390
C-GCWU	GLEX	9391
C-GCWV	GLEX	9392
C-GCWX	GLEX	9393
C-GCXE	GLEX	9394
C-GCXL	**C56X**	**5096**
C-GCZU	CL60	1030
C-GDAO	HS25	257099
C-GDAX	**CL61**	**3059**
C-GDBC	**HS25**	**258193**
C-GDBF	CL61	3014
C-GDBG	GLEX	9008
C-GDBX	CL61	3046
C-GDBZ	CL64	5378
C-GDCC	**E50P**	**50000331**
C-GDCC	SBRL	306-51
C-GDCF	GLEX	9395
C-GDCO	FA10	73
C-GDCO	FA50	185
C-GDCP	**C680**	**0251**
C-GDCQ	CL61	3052
C-GDCZ	GLEX	9396
C-GDDB	LJ24	041
C-GDDC	C550	267
C-GDDM	C500	468
C-GDDP	CL61	5001
C-GDDR	**CL60**	**1048**
C-GDEK	**C525**	**0550**
C-GDEK	GLEX	9397
C-GDEQ	CL61	5002
C-GDEV	GLEX	9398
C-GDFA	CL64	5380
C GDGO	GLEX	9009
C-GDGQ	GLEX	9010
C-GDGW	GLEX	9011
C-GDGY	GLEX	9012
C-GDHP	CL61	5003
C-GDHW	HS25	256028
C-GDII	HS25	258316
C-GDIK	CL30	20214
C-GDIL	**CL30**	**20432**
C-GDJG	C510	0113
C-GDJG	**E55P**	**50500185**
C-GDJH	**LJ35**	**353**
C-GDJW	WW24	111
C-GDKI	C525	0008
C-GDKO	CL61	5004
C-GDKS	LJ24	217
C-GDLH	CL64	5384
C-GDLI	**CL61**	**5179**
C-GDLL	**C510**	**0221**
C-GDLR	C550	078
C-GDMF	C550	125
C-GDMI	LJ45	096
C-GDOC	WW24	166
C-GDPB	GLF2	232
C-GDPD	C550	066
(C-GDPE)	C550	124
(C-GDPE)	C550	188
C-GDPF	C550	124
C-GDPF	CL61	5145
C-GDPF	**GLEX**	**9388**
C-GDPG	**GLEX**	**9178**
C-GDRJ	CL65	5831
C-GDRU	CL65	5832
C-GDRY	CL65	5833
C-GDSG	CL65	5834
C-GDSH	**C52C**	**0069**
C-GDSH	C550	550-0909
C-GDSH	C550	550-0982
C-GDSH	C560	0492
C-GDSH	C560	0647
C-GDSH	C560	0781
C-GDSO	CL65	5835
C-GDSQ	CL65	5836
C-GDSR	**WW24**	**313**
C-GDTF	CL30	20289
C-GDTQ	CL30	20290
C-GDUC	WW24	357
C-GDUH	CL30	20291
C-GDUJ	CL30	20292
C-GDUP	HS25	256020
C-GDVM	CL64	5388
C-GDWF	**CL64**	**5364**
C-GDWN	C500	029
C-GDWS	C500	303
C-GDWS	C525	0109
C-GDXU	GLEX	9013
C-GDXV	GLEX	9014
C-GDXX	GLEX	9015
C-GDZE	CL64	5392
C-GDZQ	CL30	20057
C-GEAQ	FA20	28
C-GEEN	LJ24	087
C-GEGM	CL64	5380
C-GEGX	GLEX	9005
C-GEHF	GLEX	9399
C-GEHK	GLEX	9400
C-GEHV	GLEX	9401
C-GEIM	GLEX	9016
C-GEIM	GLEX	9402
C-GEIR	GLEX	9017
C-GEIV	GLF4	1224
C-GEJD	**LJ45**	**166**
C-GENA	CL61	5006
C-GENJ	C500	196
C-GENW	**F2EX**	**129**
C-GEPF	HS25	257149
C-GEPG	**F2TH**	**210**
C-GERC	C555	0037
C-GERL	C555	0056
C-GERS	**GLEX**	**9127**
C-GESO	CL30	20110
C-GESO	WW24	298
C-GESR	CL61	3003
C-GESZ	C500	022
C-GETU	CL64	5409
C-GEUX	GLEX	9403
C-GEVF	C500	460
C-GEVN	GLEX	9404
C-GEVO	GLEX	9018
C-GEVU	CL30	20293
C-GEVU	GLEX	9019
C-GEVV	GLEX	9020
C-GEVW	CL30	20294
C-GEVX	CL30	20295
C-GEWI	CL65	5837
C-GEWO	CL65	5838
C-GEWV	CL65	5839
C-GEWV	GLEX	9026
C-GEWX	CL65	5840
C-GEXB	CL65	5841
C-GEXD	CL65	5842
C-GEXY	CL65	5843
C-GEYY	GLEX	9021
C-GEYZ	GLEX	9022
C-GEZD	GLEX	9023
C-GEZF	GLEX	9024
C-GEZJ	GLEX	9025
C-GEZJ	GLEX	9405
C-GEZX	GLEX	9027
C-GEZX	GLEX	9406
C-GEZY	GLEX	9028
C-GEZZ	GLEX	9029
C-GFAD	GLEX	9030
C-GFAE	GLEX	9031
C-GFAE	GLEX	9407
C-GFAK	GLEX	9032
C-GFAN	GLEX	9033
C-GFAN	WW24	218
C-GFAO	WW24	250
C-GFAP	GLEX	9034
C-GFAP	GLEX	9408
C-GFAQ	GLEX	9035
C-GFAT	GLEX	9036
C-GFAX	LJ60	029
C-GFCB	**CL30**	**20260**
C-GFCB	CL61	5124
C-GFCD	CL61	5124
C-GFCD	HS25	25234
(C-GFCD)	CL60	1059
C-GFCI	C550	733
C-GFCL	C560	0346
C-GFCL	C56X	5780
C-GFCL	HS25	25107
C-GFCP	**GLF4**	**4047**
C-GFCS	FA10	37
C-GFEE	**C500**	**566**
C-GFEH	LJ35	170
C-GFFT	**LJ40**	**2145**
C-GFHJ	**HS25**	**258052**
C-GFHR	**CL30**	**20016**
C-GFIA	CL30	20296
C-GFIG	CL30	20297
C-GFIG	**CL61**	**5093**
C-GFIH	CL30	20298
C-GFJB	CL65	5844
C-GFJB	LJ24	260
C-GFJE	CL65	5845
C-GFJJ	CL65	5846
C-GFJO	CL65	5847
C-GFJQ	CL65	5848
C-GFJQ	GLEX	9037
C-GFJR	GLEX	9038
C-GFJS	GLEX	9039
C-GFJT	CL65	5849
C-GFJT	GLEX	9040
C-GFJX	CL65	5850
C-GFKH	GLEX	9409
C-GFKJ	GLEX	9410
C-GFKL	GLEX	9411
C-GFKQ	GLEX	9412
C-GFKT	GLEX	9041
C-GFKV	GLEX	9042
C-GFKW	GLEX	9043
C-GFKX	GLEX	9044
C-GFKY	GLEX	9045
C-GFLS	GLEX	9046
C-GFLU	CL64	5410
C-GFLU	**F9DX**	**604**
C-GFLU	GLEX	9047
C-GFLW	GLEX	9048
C-GFLX	GLEX	9049
C-GFLZ	GLEX	9050
C-GFLZ	HS25	258166
C-GFOE	CL64	5430
C-GFRK	LJ35	093
C-GFRX	GLEX	9339
C-GFTL	**CL65**	**5710**
C-GFUF	CL30	20302
C-GFUG	CL30	20303
C-GFUI	CL30	20304
C-GFUM	CL30	20305
C-GFUQ	CL65	5851
C-GFUY	CL65	5852
C-GFVL	CL30	20299
C-GFVN	CL30	20300
C-GFVT	CL30	20301
C-GFWI	GLEX	9051
C-GFWP	GLEX	9052
C-GFWX	GLEX	9053
C-GFWY	GLEX	9054
C-GFWZ	GLEX	9055
C-GGBL	CL64	5489
C-GGBL	**CL64**	**5576**
C-GGBL	CL65	5746
C-GGCH	HS25	258495
C-GGFJ	GLEX	9413
C-GGFP	FA50	227
C-GGFW	C550	318
C-GGHN	GLEX	9998
C-GGHT	GLEX	9415
C-GGHZ	ASTR	117
C-GGIM	GLEX	9416
C-GGIR	GLEX	9057
C-GGJA	GLEX	9058
C-GGJF	GLEX	9059
C-GGJH	GLEX	9060
C-GGJJ	GLEX	9061
C-GGJR	GLEX	9062
C-GGJS	GLEX	9063
C-GGJU	GLEX	9064
C-GGKA	GLEX	9065
C-GGKC	GLEX	9066
C-GGLO	**GLEX**	**9233**
C-GGMI	F9EX	87
C-GGMP	CL61	5093
C-GGMP	HS25	HA-0011
C-GGOL	GLEX	9364
C-GGPF	LJ36	026
C-GGPK	CL64	5317
C-GGPM	GLF3	307
C-GGPM	**GLF5**	**5306**
C-GGPZ	GLEX	9067
C-GGQC	GLEX	9068
C-GGQF	**C550**	**550-0994**
C-GGQF	GLEX	9069
C-GGQG	GLEX	9070
C-GGSA	GLEX	9417
C-GGSP	C550	177
C-GGSU	GLEX	9418
C-GGUA	GLEX	9419
C-GGUG	GLEX	9420
C-GGWH	**CL64**	**5371**
C-GGYT	HS25	258025
C-GGYV	LJ35	040
C-GHBQ	WW24	220
C-GHBV	CL61	5174
C-GHCB	C56X	5151
C-GHCD	CL61	5165
C-GHCE	GLEX	9421
C-GHCS	GLEX	9422
C-GHCY	LJ31	107
C-GHCY	LJ45	216
C-GHCZ	GLEX	9423
C-GHDP	LJ24	257
C-GHDQ	GLEX	9071
C-GHDV	GLEX	9072
C-GHDW	GLEX	9073
C-GHEA	GLEX	9074
C-GHEC	C500	161
C-GHEC	C560	0084
C-GHEI	GLEX	9075
C-GHER	GLEX	9076
C-GHET	GLEX	9077
C-GHEZ	GLEX	9078
C-GHFB	GLEX	9079
C-GHFH	GLEX	9080
C-GHGC	**CL61**	**5019**
C-GHGC	GLEX	9081
C-GHGK	C650	0062
C-GHIH	CL64	5465
C-GHJJ	LJ31	102
C-GHJU	**LJ31**	**120**
C-GHKY	C550	398
C-GHKY	C650	0023
C-GHKY	CL64	5343
C-GHKY	LJ60	043
C-GHLM	C650	0017
C-GHMH	LJ25	011
C-GHML	**CL64**	**5360**
C-GHML	F900	141
C-GHMP	**LJ45**	**183**
C-GHMW	**CL65**	**5796**
C-GHOL	C550	013
C-GHOM	C550	198
C-GHOO	C650	0014
C-GHOO	LJ35	057
C-GHOS	C500	375
C-GHPP	C525	0220
C-GHPR	WW24	83
C-GHRJ	CL64	5468
C-GHRK	CL64	5309
C-GHRX	C500	432
C-GHRZ	CL64	5472
C-GHSB	**C525**	**0546**
C-GHSW	GLEX	9220
C-GHSW	**GLEX**	**9640**
C-GHVB	GLEX	9424
C-GHVN	GLEX	9425
C-GHVO	GLEX	9426
C-GHVX	GLEX	9427
C-GHWD	GLEX	9428
C-GHWW	C550	178
C-GHXX	GLEX	9429
C-GHXY	GLEX	9430
C-GHXY	HS25	258095
C-GHYD	C550	079
C-GHYD	**WW24**	**278**
C-GHYK	GLEX	9431
C-GHYQ	GLEX	9082
C-GHYT	GLEX	9083
C-GHYX	GLEX	9084
C-GHZB	GLEX	9085
C-GHZC	GLEX	9086
C-GHZD	CL30	20159
C-GHZD	GLEX	9087
C-GHZF	GLEX	9088
C-GHZH	CL65	5853
C-GHZH	GLEX	9089
C-GHZQ	CL65	5854
C-GHZU	CL65	5855
C-GIAB	CL65	5856
C-GIAC	C500	076
C-GIAD	C500	185
C-GIAF	CL65	5857
C-GIBU	HS25	258507
C-GICI	CL61	5159
C-GIDG	CL64	5307
C-GIGT	C750	0097
C-GIIR	CL30	20306
C-GIIT	**CL65**	**5921**
C-GIIT	LJ60	253
C-GIIU	CL30	20307
C-GIJP	**C560**	**0648**
C-GIJP	CL30	20308
C-GIJZ	CL30	20309
C-GILQ	GLEX	9352
C-GINT	C525	0062
C-GIOC	GLEX	9432
C-GIOD	GLEX	9090
C-GIOH	**CL61**	**5034**
C-GIOJ	GLEX	9091
C-GIOK	GLEX	9092
C-GIOK	GLEX	9433
C-GIOW	GLEX	9093
C-GIOW	GLEX	9434
C-GIOX	GLEX	9094
C-GIOX	GLEX	9435
C-GIPA	GLEX	9095
C-GIPC	GLEX	9096
C-GIPD	GLEX	9097
C-GIPF	GLEX	9098
C-GIPJ	GLEX	9099
C-GIPX	CL30	20003
C-GIPX	F9EX	201
C-GIPZ	**CL30**	**20005**

C-GIRE	LJ35	004
C-GIRL	**C525**	**0641**
C-GISY	GLEX	9436
C-GITG	CL64	5304
C-GITG	GLEX	9437
C-GIUD	GLEX	9438
C-GIUP	GLEX	9439
C-GIVX	CL65	5858
C-GIWD	C750	0041
C-GIWD	LJ35	407
C-GIWO	**LJ35**	**407**
C-GIWZ	**C750**	**0041**
C-GIXI	**CL61**	**5086**
C-GIXI	GLEX	9100
C-GIXJ	GLEX	9101
C-GIXM	GLEX	9102
C-GIXO	GLEX	9103
C-GJAE	**C680**	**0017**
C-GJAP	C500	080
C-GJAP	C550	060
C-GJAP	C550	373
C-GJBJ	HS25	257198
C-GJCB	**GLEX**	**9389**
C-GJCD	WW24	176
C-GJCF	CL30	20002
C-GJCJ	**CL30**	**20001**
C-GJCM	HS25	256040
C-GJCO	CL30	20310
C-GJCQ	CL30	20311
C-GJCV	CL30	20004
C-GJCX	CL30	20312
C-GJCY	**LJ45**	**239**
C-GJDA	LJ35	505
C-GJDG	CL61	5119
C-GJDR	**CL30**	**20519**
C-GJDR	LJ60	426
C-GJDU	GLEX	9060
C-GJEI	C560	0588
C-GJEI	**CL30**	**20245**
C-GJEM	C500	011
C-GJET	FA10	25
C-GJET	**GLEX**	**9644**
C-GJFC	CL64	5366
C-GJFD	GLEX	9440
C-GJFG	**GALX**	**046**
C-GJFI	CL64	5506
C-GJFI	GLEX	9441
C-GJFQ	CL61	5019
C-GJFQ	GLEX	9442
C-GJFW	GLEX	9443
C-GJGE	GLEX	9444
C-GJIU	GLEX	9104
C-GJIW	GLEX	9105
C-GJIY	GLEX	9106
C-GJJG	GLEX	9445
C-GJKA	GLEX	9446
C-GJKI	C680	0071
C-GJKI	**F2EX**	**34**
C-GJKI	HS25	258605
C-GJKK	**HS25**	**258605**
C-GJKO	GLEX	9447
C-GJKZ	GLEX	9448
C-GJLB	**FA50**	**270**
C-GJLH	GLEX	9449
C-GJLK	WW24	278
C-GJLL	WW24	171
C-GJLN	**LJ60**	**349**
C-GJLQ	C500	058
C-GJLY	GLEX	9450
C-GJNG	**CL61**	**3040**
C-GJOE	CL64	5514
C-GJOJ	CL65	5859
C-GJOK	CL65	5860
C-GJOL	C525	0657
C-GJOL	**E55P**	**50500089**
C-GJPG	CL60	1043
C-GJPG	CL61	3017
C-GJPG	F900	110
C-GJPG	**F9EX**	**129**
C-GJPT	F900	110
C-GJQN	CL64	5358
C-GJRB	C56X	5026
C-GJRG	CL30	20313
C-GJRG	GLEX	9107
C-GJRK	GLEX	9108
C-GJRL	GLEX	9109
C-GJSO	CL30	20314
C-GJSO	CL64	5517
C-GJSY	CL30	20315
C-GJTH	GLEX	9110
C-GJTK	GLEX	9111
C-GJTP	GLEX	9112
C-GJTR	CL64	5520
C-GJTX	C500	254
C-GJUR	CL65	5861
C-GJUZ	CL30	20316
C-GJVG	CL30	20317
C-GJVK	**C500**	**103**
C-GJVL	CL30	20318
C-GJVO	CL30	20319
C-GJXK	CL65	5806
C-GJXY	CL65	5863
C-GJYA	CL65	5864
C-GJYC	CL65	5865
C-GJYE	CL65	5866
C-GJYI	CL65	5867
C-GJYK	CL65	5868
C-GJYL	**C560**	**0232**
C-GJYN	CL65	5869
C-GJYR	CL65	5870
C-GJYS	CL65	5871
C-GJYV	CL65	5862
C-GJZB	CL64	5529
C-GJZD	CL64	5530
C-GKAU	**C550**	**313**
C-GKCB	CL64	5522
C-GKCC	HS25	256044
C-GKCG	GLEX	9113
C-GKCI	FA50	272
C-GKCI	HS25	257066
C-GKCM	GLEX	9114
C-GKCN	GLEX	9115
C-GKCO	HS25	25170
C-GKCZ	C500	101
C-GKDT	LJ45	288
C-GKEG	C56X	5729
C-GKEG	C680	0158
C-GKFS	WW24	62
C-GKFT	WW24	5
C-GKGD	HS25	258193
C-GKGN	**CL64**	**5317**
C-GKGR	CL64	5533
C-GKGS	CL64	5535
C-GKGZ	GLEX	9116
C-GKHA	FA20	19
C-GKHC	GLEX	9117
C-GKHD	**C560**	**0423**
C-GKHE	GLEX	9118
C-GKHF	GLEX	9119
C-GKHG	GLEX	9120
C-GKHH	GLEX	9121
C-GKHI	GLEX	9122
C-GKHR	HS25	256021
C-GKIO	CL30	20320
C-GKIP	CL30	20321
C-GKIU	CL30	20322
C-GKIV	CL30	20323
C-GKIX	CL30	20324
C-GKIY	CL30	20325
C-GKLB	HS25	258105
C-GKLC	GLEX	9451
C-GKLF	GLEX	9083
C-GKLX	GLEX	9452
C-GKMO	GLEX	9453
C-GKMS	LJ31	006
C-GKMU	CL64	5540
C-GKMU	GLEX	9454
C-GKNP	GLEX	9455
C-GKOH	GLEX	9456
C-GKOJ	GLEX	9457
C-GKOY	GLEX	9458
C-GKPC	C500	670
C-GKPE	LJ35	030
C-GKPM	HS25	257049
C-GKPP	HS25	258166
C-GKPP	**HS25**	**258572**
C-GKRL	GLF3	317
C-GKRL	HS25	25111
C-GKRL	HS25	258007
C-GKRS	HS25	257087
C-GKRS	JSTR	5011/1
C-GKTM	LJ55	076
C-GKTO	**CL64**	**5396**
C-GKUT	C550	550-0806
C-GKUZ	GLEX	9459
C-GKVC	GLEX	9460
C-GKVL	GLEX	9461
C-GKVN	GLEX	9462
C-GKVO	GLEX	9463
C-GKXH	CL30	20326
C-GKXK	CL30	20327
C-GKXL	CL30	20328
C-GKXM	CL30	20329
C-GKXN	CL30	20330
C-GKXO	CL65	5872
C-GKXP	CL65	5873
C-GKXQ	CL65	5874
C-GKXR	CL65	5875
C-GKXS	**C56X**	**5169**
C-GKXS	CL65	5876
C-GKYI	GLEX	9464
C-GKYK	GLEX	9465
C-GKYL	GLEX	9466
C-GKYN	GLEX	9467
C-GKYO	GLEX	9468
C-GKZA	C560	0451
C-GKZB	**C560**	**0471**
C-GKZC	**C560**	**0373**
C-GKZD	C560	0352
C-GKZE	C560	0483
C-GKZF	C560	0493
C-GKZG	C560	0421
C-GKZH	**C560**	**0425**
C-GKZJ	C560	0327
C-GKZK	C560	0394
C-GKZL	**C560**	**0496**
C-GKZM	**C560**	**0510**
C-GKZN	C560	0519
C-GKZO	**C560**	**0434**
C-GKZP	**C560**	**0445**
C-GKZQ	C560	0428
C-GKZR	**C560**	**0437**
C-GKZS	C560	0460
C-GKZT	**C560**	**0444**
C-GKZW	GLEX	9393
C-GL..	CL61	5170
C-GLAA	C500	201
C-GLAL	LJ36	019
C-GLBB	CL64	5465
C-GLBB	F9EX	88
C-GLBD	HS25	256032
C-GLBJ	HS25	257162
C-GLBT	C525	0148
C-GLBT	LJ25	182
C-GLBU	F9EX	129
C-GLCE	C550	550-0906
C-GLCR	C555	0140
C-GLEO	HS25	25080
C-GLEU	GLEX	9469
C-GLFG	GLEX	9471
C-GLFI	HS25	25028
C-GLFK	GLEX	9472
C-GLFN	GLEX	9473
C-GLFV	**GLF5**	**692**
C-GLGB	C550	550-0994
C-GLIG	**HS25**	**257149**
C-GLIG	MU30	A076SA
C-GLIG	MU30	A090SA
C-GLIM	C560	0430
C-GLIV	PRM1	RB-259
C-GLJQ	LJ35	660
C-GLKC	GLEX	9478
C-GLKH	GLEX	9479
C-GLKX	CL30	20331
C-GLKY	CL30	20332
C-GLKZ	CL30	20333
C-GLLF	CL30	20334
C-GLLJ	CL30	20335
C-GLLY	CL30	20336
C-GLMI	C56X	5097
C-GLMI	**C680**	**0533**
C-GLMK	**C550**	**110**
C-GLMK	LJ36	019
C-GLMU	CL65	5878
C-GLNF	CL65	5879
C-GLNI	CL65	5877
C-GLNJ	CL65	5880
C-GLNL	**LJ35**	**394**
C-GLNP	CL65	5881
C-GLOJ	CL61	3034
(C-GLRE)	LJ25	114
C-GLRJ	LJ31	043
C-GLRJ	LJ45	019
C-GLRJ	LJ55	089
C-GLRL	LJ60	002
C-GLRM	GLEX	9130
C-GLRP	FA50	87
C-GLRP	**LJ40**	**2102**
C-GLRS	LJ45	249
C-GLRS	LJ60	002
C-GLRS	LJ60	062
C-GLRS	LJ60	077
C-GLSW	**CL61**	**5176**
C-GLTG	C550	403
C-GLUL	GLEX	9264
C-GLUN	GLEX	9474
C-GLUP	GLEX	9475
C-GLUR	GLEX	9476
C-GLUS	GLEX	9477
C-GLUV	**C52C**	**0158**
C-GLVE	**C680**	**0543**
C-GLWR	CL60	1018
C-GLWR	CL61	3051
C-GLWR	CL61	5005
C-GLWR	CL61	5025
C-GLWR	CL61	5057
C-GLWR	CL61	5078
C-GLWR	CL61	5102
C-GLWR	CL61	5123
C-GLWR	CL61	5135
C-GLWR	CL61	5147
C-GLWR	CL61	5159
C-GLWR	CL61	5183
C-GLWR	CL64	5311
C-GLWR	CL64	5333
C-GLWR	CL64	5348
C-GLWR	CL64	5359
C-GLWR	CL64	5372
C-GLWR	CL64	5396
C-GLWR	CL64	5407
C-GLWR	CL64	5420
C-GLWR	CL64	5431
C-GLWR	CL64	5442
C-GLWR	CL64	5464
C-GLWR	CL64	5486
C-GLWR	CL64	5508
C-GLWR	CL64	5530
C-GLWR	CL64	5552
C-GLWR	CL64	5574
C-GLWR	CL64	5596
C-GLWR	CL64	5662
C-GLWT	CL60	1019
C-GLWT	CL61	3052
C-GLWT	CL61	5006
C-GLWT	CL61	5019
C-GLWT	CL61	5026
C-GLWT	CL61	5041
C-GLWT	CL61	5071
C-GLWT	CL61	5084
C-GLWT	CL61	5094
C-GLWT	CL61	5120
C-GLWT	CL61	5142
C-GLWT	CL61	5166
C-GLWT	CL61	5190
C-GLWT	CL64	5319
C-GLWT	CL64	5343
C-GLWT	CL64	5391
C-GLWT	CL64	5415
C-GLWT	CL64	5443
C-GLWT	CL64	5465
C-GLWT	CL64	5487
C-GLWT	CL64	5509
C-GLWT	CL64	5531
C-GLWT	CL64	5553
C-GLWT	CL64	5575
C-GLWT	CL64	5597
C-GLWT	CL64	5619
C-GLWT	CL64	5641
C-GLWT	CL64	5663
C-GLWV	CL60	1020
C-GLWV	CL60	1042
C-GLWV	CL60	1062
C-GLWV	CL60	1079
C-GLWV	CL61	3010
C-GLWV	CL61	3016
C-GLWV	CL61	3025
C-GLWV	CL61	3041
C-GLWV	CL61	3053
C-GLWV	CL61	5007
C-GLWV	CL61	5018
C-GLWV	CL61	5027
C-GLWV	CL61	5040
C-GLWV	CL61	5059
C-GLWV	CL61	5079
C-GLWV	CL61	5103
C-GLWV	CL61	5131
C-GLWV	CL61	5155
C-GLWV	CL61	5179
C-GLWV	CL64	5329
C-GLWV	CL64	5355
C-GLWV	CL64	5379
C-GLWV	CL64	5403
C-GLWV	CL64	5427
C-GLWV	CL64	5444
C-GLWV	CL64	5466
C-GLWV	CL64	5488
C-GLWV	CL64	5510
C-GLWV	CL64	5532
C-GLWV	CL64	5554
C-GLWV	CL64	5576
C-GLWV	CL64	5598
C-GLWV	CL64	5620
C-GLWV	CL64	5642
C-GLWV	CL64	5664
C-GLWX	CL60	1021
C-GLWX	CL60	1043
C-GLWX	CL60	1063
C-GLWX	CL60	1080
C-GLWX	CL61	3011
C-GLWX	CL61	3017
C-GLWX	CL61	3026
C-GLWX	CL61	3042
C-GLWX	CL61	3054
C-GLWX	CL61	5008
C-GLWX	CL61	5017
C-GLWX	CL61	5028
C-GLWX	CL61	5039
C-GLWX	CL61	5062
C-GLWX	CL61	5082
C-GLWX	CL61	5106
C-GLWX	CL61	5128
C-GLWX	CL61	5152
C-GLWX	CL61	5176
C-GLWX	CL64	5306
C-GLWX	CL64	5325
C-GLWX	CL64	5352
C-GLWX	CL64	5400
C-GLWX	CL64	5424
C-GLWX	CL64	5445
C-GLWX	CL64	5467
C-GLWX	CL64	5489
C-GLWX	CL64	5511
C-GLWX	CL64	5533
C-GLWX	CL64	5555
C-GLWX	CL64	5577
C-GLWX	CL64	5599
C-GLWX	CL64	5621
C-GLWX	CL64	5643
C-GLWX	CL64	5665
C-GLWX	CL65	5724
C-GLWZ	CL60	1022
C-GLWZ	CL60	1044
C-GLWZ	CL60	1064
C-GLWZ	CL60	1081
C-GLWZ	CL61	3018
C-GLWZ	CL61	3027
C-GLWZ	CL61	3043
C-GLWZ	CL61	3055
C-GLWZ	CL61	5009
C-GLWZ	CL61	5029
C-GLWZ	CL61	5058
C-GLWZ	CL61	5107
C-GLWZ	CL61	5125
C-GLWZ	CL61	5137
C-GLWZ	CL61	5161
C-GLWZ	CL61	5185
C-GLWZ	CL64	5314
C-GLWZ	CL64	5338
C-GLWZ	CL64	5362
C-GLWZ	CL64	5386
C-GLWZ	CL64	5410
C-GLWZ	CL64	5435
C-GLWZ	CL64	5446
C-GLWZ	CL64	5468
C-GLWZ	CL64	5490
C-GLWZ	CL64	5512
C-GLWZ	CL64	5534
C-GLWZ	CL64	5556
C-GLWZ	CL64	5578
C-GLWZ	CL64	5600
C-GLWZ	CL64	5622
C-GLWZ	CL64	5644
C-GLXB	CL60	1023
C-GLXB	CL60	1045
C-GLXB	CL60	1065
C-GLXB	CL60	1082
C-GLXB	CL61	3012
C-GLXB	CL61	3019
C-GLXB	CL61	3028
C-GLXB	CL61	3037
C-GLXB	CL61	3056
C-GLXB	CL61	5010
C-GLXB	CL61	5030
C-GLXB	CL61	5054
C-GLXB	CL61	5076
C-GLXB	CL61	5100
C-GLXB	CL61	5127
C-GLXB	CL61	5151
C-GLXB	CL61	5175
C-GLXB	CL64	5305
C-GLXB	CL64	5324
C-GLXB	CL64	5335
C-GLXB	CL64	5351
C-GLXB	CL64	5375
C-GLXB	CL64	5399
C-GLXB	CL64	5423
C-GLXB	CL64	5441
C-GLXB	CL64	5463
C-GLXB	CL64	5485
C-GLXB	CL64	5507
C-GLXB	CL64	5529
C-GLXB	CL64	5551
C-GLXB	CL64	5573
C-GLXB	CL64	5595
C-GLXB	CL64	5601
C-GLXB	CL64	5617
C-GLXB	CL64	5639
C-GLXB	CL64	5661
C-GLXC	F9EX	190
C-GLXC	**FA7X**	**176**
C-GLXD	CL60	1024
C-GLXD	CL60	1046
C-GLXD	CL60	1066
C-GLXD	CL60	1083
C-GLXD	CL61	3013
C-GLXD	CL61	3029
C-GLXD	CL61	3044
C-GLXD	CL61	3057
C-GLXD	CL61	5011
C-GLXD	CL61	5031
C-GLXD	CL61	5047
C-GLXD	CL61	5065
C-GLXD	CL61	5085
C-GLXD	CL61	5108
C-GLXD	CL61	5124
C-GLXD	CL61	5148
C-GLXD	CL61	5172
C-GLXD	CL64	5302
C-GLXD	CL64	5313
C-GLXD	CL64	5337
C-GLXD	CL64	5361
C-GLXD	CL64	5385
C-GLXD	CL64	5409
C-GLXD	CL64	5433
C-GLXD	CL64	5448
C-GLXD	CL64	5470
C-GLXD	CL64	5492
C-GLXD	CL64	5514
C-GLXD	CL64	5536
C-GLXD	CL64	5558
C-GLXD	CL64	5580
C-GLXD	CL64	5602
C-GLXD	CL64	5624
C-GLXD	CL64	5640
C-GLXD	CL64	5646
C-GLXD	CL65	5705
C-GLXF	CL60	1025
C-GLXF	CL61	5032
C-GLXF	CL61	5049
C-GLXF	CL61	5067
C-GLXF	CL61	5090
C-GLXF	CL61	5112
C-GLXF	CL61	5138
C-GLXF	CL61	5162
C-GLXF	CL61	5186
C-GLXF	CL64	5315
C-GLXF	CL64	5339
C-GLXF	CL64	5363
C-GLXF	CL64	5387
C-GLXF	CL64	5411
C-GLXF	CL64	5436
C-GLXF	CL64	5449
C-GLXF	CL64	5471
C-GLXF	CL64	5493
C-GLXF	CL64	5515

C-GLXF	CL64	5537
C-GLXF	CL64	5551
C-GLXF	CL64	5559
C-GLXF	CL64	5581
C-GLXF	CL64	5603
C-GLXF	CL64	5618
C-GLXF	CL64	5625
C-GLXF	CL64	5647
C-GLXF	CL65	5706
C-GLXG	F9EX	190
C-GLXH	CL60	1026
C-GLXH	CL60	1047
C-GLXH	CL60	1067
C-GLXH	CL60	1084
C-GLXH	CL61	3014
C-GLXH	CL61	3030
C-GLXH	CL61	3045
C-GLXH	CL61	5015
C-GLXH	CL61	5033
C-GLXH	CL61	5055
C-GLXH	CL61	5074
C-GLXH	CL61	5088
C-GLXH	CL61	5098
C-GLXH	CL61	5111
C-GLXH	CL61	5129
C-GLXH	CL61	5153
C-GLXH	CL61	5177
C-GLXH	CL64	5307
C-GLXH	CL64	5328
C-GLXH	CL64	5353
C-GLXH	CL64	5377
C-GLXH	CL64	5401
C-GLXH	CL64	5425
C-GLXH	CL64	5450
C-GLXH	CL64	5472
C-GLXH	CL64	5494
C-GLXH	CL64	5516
C-GLXH	CL64	5538
C-GLXH	CL64	5560
C-GLXH	CL64	5582
C-GLXH	CL64	5604
C-GLXH	CL64	5626
C-GLXH	CL64	5648
C-GLXH	CL65	5707
C-GLXK	CL60	1027
C-GLXK	CL60	1048
C-GLXK	CL60	1068
C-GLXK	CL60	1076
C-GLXK	CL61	3004
C-GLXK	CL61	3031
C-GLXK	CL61	3046
C-GLXK	CL61	5034
C-GLXK	CL61	5050
C-GLXK	CL61	5068
C-GLXK	CL61	5097
C-GLXK	CL61	5118
C-GLXK	CL61	5139
C-GLXK	CL61	5163
C-GLXK	CL61	5187
C-GLXK	CL64	5316
C-GLXK	CL64	5340
C-GLXK	CL64	5364
C-GLXK	CL64	5388
C-GLXK	CL64	5412
C-GLXK	CL64	5437
C-GLXK	CL64	5451
C-GLXK	CL64	5473
C-GLXK	CL64	5495
C-GLXK	CL64	5517
C-GLXK	CL64	5539
C-GLXK	CL64	5561
C-GLXK	CL64	5583
C-GLXK	CL64	5605
C-GLXK	CL64	5627
C-GLXK	CL64	5649
C-GLXK	CL65	5708
C-GLXM	CL60	1028
C-GLXM	CL60	1049
C-GLXM	CL60	1069
C-GLXM	CL60	1077
C-GLXM	CL61	3015
C-GLXM	CL61	3032
C-GLXM	CL61	3047
C-GLXM	CL61	5051
C-GLXM	CL61	5069
C-GLXM	CL61	5091
C-GLXM	CL61	5113
C-GLXM	CL61	5140
C-GLXM	CL61	5164
C-GLXM	CL61	5188
C-GLXM	CL64	5341
C-GLXM	CL64	5365
C-GLXM	CL64	5389
C-GLXM	CL64	5413
C-GLXM	CL64	5432
C-GLXM	CL64	5438
C-GLXM	CL64	5452
C-GLXM	CL64	5474
C-GLXM	CL64	5496
C-GLXM	CL64	5518
C-GLXM	CL64	5540
C-GLXM	CL64	5562
C-GLXM	CL64	5584
C-GLXM	CL64	5606
C-GLXM	CL64	5628
C-GLXM	CL64	5650
C-GLXM	CL65	5709
C-GLXO	CL60	1029
C-GLXO	CL60	1050
C-GLXO	CL60	1070
C-GLXO	CL60	1075
C-GLXO	CL61	3020
C-GLXO	CL61	3048
C-GLXO	CL61	5052
C-GLXO	CL61	5070
C-GLXO	CL61	5119
C-GLXO	CL61	5141
C-GLXO	CL61	5165
C-GLXO	CL64	5318
C-GLXO	CL64	5342
C-GLXO	CL64	5366
C-GLXO	CL64	5390
C-GLXO	CL64	5414
C-GLXO	CL64	5453
C-GLXO	CL64	5475
C-GLXO	CL64	5497
C-GLXO	CL64	5519
C-GLXO	CL64	5541
C-GLXO	CL64	5563
C-GLXO	CL64	5585
C-GLXO	CL64	5607
C-GLXO	CL64	5629
C-GLXO	CL64	5651
C-GLXO	CL65	5710
C-GLXQ	CL60	1030
C-GLXQ	CL60	1051
C-GLXQ	CL60	1071
C-GLXQ	CL60	1085
C-GLXQ	CL61	3021
C-GLXQ	CL61	3033
C-GLXQ	CL61	3049
C-GLXQ	CL61	3066
C-GLXQ	CL61	5016
C-GLXQ	CL61	5038
C-GLXQ	CL61	5056
C-GLXQ	CL61	5077
C-GLXQ	CL61	5092
C-GLXQ	CL61	5101
C-GLXQ	CL61	5130
C-GLXQ	CL61	5154
C-GLXQ	CL61	5178
C-GLXQ	CL64	5320
C-GLXQ	CL64	5344
C-GLXQ	CL64	5368
C-GLXQ	CL64	5392
C-GLXQ	CL64	5416
C-GLXQ	CL64	5439
C-GLXQ	CL64	5454
C-GLXQ	CL64	5476
C-GLXQ	CL64	5498
C-GLXQ	CL64	5520
C-GLXQ	CL64	5542
C-GLXQ	CL64	5564
C-GLXQ	CL64	5586
C-GLXQ	CL64	5608
C-GLXQ	CL64	5630
C-GLXQ	CL64	5652
C-GLXQ	CL65	5711
C-GLXS	CL60	1031
C-GLXS	CL60	1052
C-GLXS	CL60	1086
C-GLXS	CL61	3022
C-GLXS	CL61	3050
C-GLXS	CL61	5045
C-GLXS	CL61	5063
C-GLXS	CL61	5086
C-GLXS	CL61	5109
C-GLXS	CL61	5122
C-GLXS	CL61	5134
C-GLXS	CL61	5158
C-GLXS	CL64	5310
C-GLXS	CL64	5332
C-GLXS	CL64	5346
C-GLXS	CL64	5358
C-GLXS	CL64	5370
C-GLXS	CL64	5382
C-GLXS	CL64	5394
C-GLXS	CL64	5406
C-GLXS	CL64	5418
C-GLXS	CL64	5430
C-GLXS	CL64	5455
C-GLXS	CL64	5477
C-GLXS	CL64	5499
C-GLXS	CL64	5521
C-GLXS	CL64	5543
C-GLXS	CL64	5565
C-GLXS	CL64	5587
C-GLXS	CL64	5609
C-GLXS	CL64	5631
C-GLXS	CL64	5653
C-GLXS	CL65	5712
C-GLXU	CL60	1032
C-GLXU	CL60	1057
C-GLXU	CL61	3003
C-GLXU	CL61	3034
C-GLXU	CL61	3058
C-GLXU	CL61	5012
C-GLXU	CL61	5035
C-GLXU	CL61	5053
C-GLXU	CL61	5075
C-GLXU	CL61	5099
C-GLXU	CL61	5110
C-GLXU	CL61	5126
C-GLXU	CL61	5150
C-GLXU	CL61	5174
C-GLXU	CL64	5304
C-GLXU	CL64	5323
C-GLXU	CL64	5334
C-GLXU	CL64	5350
C-GLXU	CL64	5374
C-GLXU	CL64	5398
C-GLXU	CL64	5422
C-GLXU	CL64	5440
C-GLXU	CL64	5456
C-GLXU	CL64	5478
C-GLXU	CL64	5500
C-GLXU	CL64	5522
C-GLXU	CL64	5544
C-GLXU	CL64	5566
C-GLXU	CL64	5588
C-GLXU	CL64	5610
C-GLXU	CL64	5632
C-GLXU	CL64	5654
C-GLXU	CL65	5713
C-GLXW	CL60	1033
C-GLXW	CL60	1058
C-GLXW	CL60	1072
C-GLXW	CL61	3035
C-GLXW	CL61	3059
C-GLXW	CL61	5013
C-GLXW	CL61	5036
C-GLXW	CL61	5046
C-GLXW	CL61	5064
C-GLXW	CL61	5087
C-GLXW	CL61	5116
C-GLXW	CL61	5136
C-GLXW	CL61	5146
C-GLXW	CL61	5160
C-GLXW	CL61	5171
C-GLXW	CL61	5184
C-GLXW	CL64	5312
C-GLXW	CL64	5336
C-GLXW	CL64	5347
C-GLXW	CL64	5360
C-GLXW	CL64	5376
C-GLXW	CL64	5384
C-GLXW	CL64	5408
C-GLXW	CL64	5457
C-GLXW	CL64	5479
C-GLXW	CL64	5501
C-GLXW	CL64	5523
C-GLXW	CL64	5545
C-GLXW	CL64	5567
C-GLXW	CL64	5589
C-GLXW	CL64	5611
C-GLXW	CL64	5633
C-GLXW	CL64	5655
C-GLXW	CL65	5714
C-GLXY	CL60	1034
C-GLXY	CL60	1059
C-GLXY	CL60	1073
C-GLXY	CL61	3006
C-GLXY	CL61	3023
C-GLXY	CL61	3036
C-GLXY	CL61	3060
C-GLXY	CL61	5014
C-GLXY	CL61	5037
C-GLXY	CL61	5048
C-GLXY	CL61	5066
C-GLXY	CL61	5089
C-GLXY	CL61	5117
C-GLXY	CL61	5149
C-GLXY	CL61	5173
C-GLXY	CL64	5303
C-GLXY	CL64	5322
C-GLXY	CL64	5349
C-GLXY	CL64	5397
C-GLXY	CL64	5421
C-GLXY	CL64	5434
C-GLXY	CL64	5458
C-GLXY	CL64	5480
C-GLXY	CL64	5502
C-GLXY	CL64	5524
C-GLXY	CL64	5546
C-GLXY	CL64	5568
C-GLXY	CL64	5590
C-GLXY	CL64	5612
C-GLXY	CL64	5634
C-GLXY	CL64	5656
C-GLXY	CL65	5715
C-GLYA	CL60	1035
C-GLYA	CL60	1053
C-GLYA	CL61	3024
C-GLYA	CL61	3038
C-GLYA	CL61	3065
C-GLYA	CL61	5020
C-GLYA	CL61	5042
C-GLYA	CL61	5083
C-GLYA	CL61	5093
C-GLYA	CL61	5114
C-GLYA	CL61	5143
C-GLYA	CL61	5167
C-GLYA	CL61	5191
C-GLYA	CL64	5321
C-GLYA	CL64	5345
C-GLYA	CL64	5393
C-GLYA	CL64	5417
C-GLYA	CL64	5459
C-GLYA	CL64	5481
C-GLYA	CL64	5503
C-GLYA	CL64	5525
C-GLYA	CL64	5547
C-GLYA	CL64	5569
C-GLYA	CL64	5591
C-GLYA	CL64	5613
C-GLYA	CL64	5657
C-GLYA	CL64	5991
C-GLYA	CL65	5716
C-GLYC	CL60	1036
C-GLYC	CL60	1054
C-GLYC	CL61	3064
C-GLYC	CL61	5021
C-GLYC	CL61	5043
C-GLYC	CL61	5072
C-GLYC	CL61	5095
C-GLYC	CL61	5115
C-GLYC	CL61	5144
C-GLYC	CL61	5168
C-GLYC	CL61	5192
C-GLYC	CL64	5326
C-GLYC	CL64	5354
C-GLYC	CL64	5378
C-GLYC	CL64	5402
C-GLYC	CL64	5426
C-GLYC	CL64	5447
C-GLYC	CL64	5469
C-GLYC	CL64	5491
C-GLYC	CL64	5513
C-GLYC	CL64	5535
C-GLYC	CL64	5557
C-GLYC	CL64	5579
C-GLYC	CL64	5623
C-GLYC	CL64	5635
C-GLYC	CL64	5645
C-GLYE	CL60	1037
C-GLYE	CL60	1055
C-GLYE	CL61	3007
C-GLYH	CL60	1038
C-GLYH	CL60	1056
C-GLYH	CL61	3039
C-GLYH	CL61	3063
C-GLYH	CL61	5024
C-GLYH	CL61	5061
C-GLYH	CL61	5081
C-GLYH	CL61	5105
C-GLYH	CL61	5133
C-GLYH	CL61	5157
C-GLYH	CL61	5181
C-GLYH	CL64	5309
C-GLYH	CL64	5331
C-GLYH	CL64	5357
C-GLYH	CL64	5381
C-GLYH	CL64	5405
C-GLYH	CL64	5429
C-GLYH	CL64	5460
C-GLYH	CL64	5482
C-GLYH	CL64	5504
C-GLYH	CL64	5526
C-GLYH	CL64	5548
C-GLYH	CL64	5570
C-GLYH	CL64	5592
C-GLYH	CL64	5614
C-GLYH	CL64	5636
C-GLYH	CL64	5658
C-GLYH	CL65	5717
C-GLYK	CL60	1039
C-GLYK	CL60	1060
C-GLYK	CL60	1074
C-GLYK	CL61	3008
C-GLYK	CL61	3040
C-GLYK	CL61	3062
C-GLYK	CL61	5022
C-GLYK	CL61	5044
C-GLYK	CL61	5073
C-GLYK	CL61	5096
C-GLYK	CL61	5121
C-GLYK	CL61	5145
C-GLYK	CL61	5169
C-GLYK	CL61	5193
C-GLYK	CL64	5327
C-GLYK	CL64	5371
C-GLYK	CL64	5383
C-GLYK	CL64	5395
C-GLYK	CL64	5419
C-GLYK	CL64	5461
C-GLYK	CL64	5483
C-GLYK	CL64	5505
C-GLYK	CL64	5527
C-GLYK	CL64	5549
C-GLYK	CL64	5571
C-GLYK	CL64	5593
C-GLYK	CL64	5615
C-GLYK	CL64	5637
C-GLYK	CL64	5659
C-GLYK	CL65	5718
C-GLYM	CL60	1040
C-GLYO	CL60	1041
C-GLYO	CL60	1061
C-GLYO	CL60	1078
C-GLYO	CL61	3009
C-GLYO	CL61	3061
C-GLYO	CL61	5023
C-GLYO	CL61	5060
C-GLYO	CL61	5080
C-GLYO	CL61	5104
C-GLYO	CL61	5132
C-GLYO	CL61	5156
C-GLYO	CL61	5180
C-GLYO	CL64	5308
C-GLYO	CL64	5330
C-GLYO	CL64	5356
C-GLYO	CL64	5380
C-GLYO	CL64	5404
C-GLYO	CL64	5428
C-GLYO	CL64	5462
C-GLYO	CL64	5484
C-GLYO	CL64	5506
C-GLYO	CL64	5528
C-GLYO	CL64	5550
C-GLYO	CL64	5572
C-GLYO	CL64	5594
C-GLYO	CL64	5616
C-GLYO	CL64	5638
C-GLYO	CL64	5660
C-GLYS	LJ45	362
C-GLYS	**LJ45**	**465**
C-GLYV	CL65	5882
C-GLZB	CL65	5883
C-GLZD	CL65	5884
C-GLZF	CL65	5885
C-GMAE	**C560**	**0125**
C-GMAJ	C500	247
C-GMAP	LJ25	026
C-GMAT	C500	231
C-GMAV	CS55	0067
C-GMBA	HS25	257206
C-GMBH	WW24	286
C-GMBY	**CL64**	**5657**
C-GMCP	**LJ45**	**126**
C-GMEA	HS25	25137
C-GMFB	**HS25**	**258239**
C-GMGA	LJ35	346
C-GMGB	C560	0390
C-GMGB	CL61	5093
C-GMGB	CS55	0149
C-GMGB	HS25	258814
C-GMGX	**FA7X**	**50**
C-GMHV	**CL30**	**20169**
C-GMIC	CL30	20337
C-GMID	FA50	229
C-GMII	CL61	3012
C-GMII	**F2TS**	**713**
C-GMII	FA50	229
C-GMII	FA50	272
C-GMII	FA50	335
C-GMIQ	CL30	20340
C-GMIU	FA50	335
C-GMIV	CL30	20338
C-GMIV	**CL64**	**5564**
C-GMJJ	**PRM1**	**RB-182**
C-GMJN	**C550**	**432**
C-GMJY	CL30	20339
C-GMKZ	**C56X**	**5309**
C-GMLC	C500	305
C-GMLH	**F9EX**	**76**
C-GMLR	**C52B**	**0333**
C-GMLR	HS25	258025
C-GMLR	HS25	258239
C-GMMA	LJ35	655
C-GMMI	CL61	5151
C-GMMO	C500	227
C-GMMU	**C510**	**0042**
C-GMMY	LJ35	644
C-GMNC	C56X	5159
C-GMNC	C750	0097
C-GMND	F900	189
C-GMOL	HS25	258163
C-GMPF	WW24	391
C-GMPO	FA20	500
C-GMPQ	C550	456
C-GMRL	**CL64**	**5597**
C-GMRO	**LJ45**	**086**
C-GMRX	GLEX	9480
C-GMRX	**GLF4**	**1382**
C-GMSM	C550	603
C-GMSO	E55P	50500284
C-GMSO	GLEX	9481
C-GMSU	GLEX	9482
C-GMSY	GLEX	9483
C-GMTI	**C525**	**0398**
C-GMTR	**HS25**	**258157**
C-GMTT	WW24	288
C-GMTV	CS55	0015
C-GMTY	GLEX	9484
C-GMUV	CL30	20341
C-GMUW	CL30	20342
C-GMUX	CL30	20343
C-GMUY	CL30	20344
C-GMVD	CL30	20345
C-GMWV	GLEX	9485
C-GMXD	**C560**	**0441**
C-GMXH	GLEX	9486
C-GMXP	**GLEX**	**9220**
C-GMXY	GLEX	9487
C-GMYE	GLEX	9488
C-GMYL	GLEX	9489
C-GNAA	FA20	128/436
C-GNAZ	HS25	257030
C-GNBN	CL30	20078
C-GNCA	FA50	203
C-GNCB	**GLEX**	**9088**
C-GNCH	CL65	5886
C-GNDJ	FA10	119
C-GNDN	GLF5	5230
C-GNDN	**GLF6**	**6162**

C-GNDZ	CL65	5887
C-GNEC	CL65	5888
C-GNEQ	C680	0064
C-GNET	FA50	281
C-GNGV	C560	0053
C-GNGY	GLEX	9490
C-GNHB	GLEX	9491
C-GNHP	GLEX	9492
C-GNKK	GLEX	9493
C-GNKW	GLEX	9494
C-GNLQ	C560	0390
C-GNND	C560	0077
C-GNND	HS25	257118
C-GNOW	HS25	257049
C-GNPT	CL30	20346
C-GNPT	LJ35	626
C-GNPY	CL30	20347
C-GNPZ	CL30	20348
C-GNQA	CL30	20349
C-GNQD	CL30	20350
C-GNRC	**CL64**	**5417**
C-GNRY	CL65	5889
C-GNSA	C500	160
C-GNSA	LJ35	171
C-GNSG	CL65	5890
C-GNSI	CL65	5891
C-GNSJ	CL65	5892
C-GNSM	CL65	5893
C-GNTL	**C510**	**0033**
C-GNTL	FA20	257
C-GNTM	FA20	319
C-GNTY	FA20	330
C-GNTZ	**C510**	**0038**
C-GNTZ	FA20	256
C-GNVF	CL65	5894
C-GNVJ	CL65	5895
C-GNVQ	CL65	5896
C-GNVR	CL65	5897
C-GNVT	FA10	138
C-GNVU	CL65	5898
C-GNVX	CL65	5899
C-GNWM	**C550**	**408**
C-GNXF	CL30	20351
C-GNXH	CL30	20352
C-GNXK	CL30	20353
C-GNXN	CL30	20354
C-GNXQ	CL30	20355
C-GNYH	G150	275
C-GNYZ	CL65	5851
C-GNZV	GLEX	9495
C-GOAB	**F2EX**	**90**
C-GOAG	**F9EX**	**15**
C-GOAN	GLEX	9496
C-GOBF	GLEX	9497
C-GOCD	GLEX	9498
C-GOCM	C500	154
C-GOCX	**F2TH**	**219**
C-GODV	GLEX	9499
C-GOEB	GLEX	9500
C-GOEL	C56X	5144
C-GOFJ	**FA50**	**262**
C-GOFS	**F2EX**	**286**
C-GOGM	HS25	257143
C-GOGO	CL60	1022
C-GOHB	**F2EX**	**232**
C-GOHB	F2EX	90
C-GOHG	CL61	5181
C-GOHJ	**HS25**	**257049**
C-GOIE	CL30	20356
C-GOIF	CL30	20357
C-GOIH	CL30	20358
C-GOIH	FA50	87
C-GOII	CL30	20359
C-GOIJ	CL30	20360
C-GOIK	GLEX	9501
C-GOIL	C500	361
C-GOIL	**F900**	**75**
C-GOIL	FA50	87
C-GOIM	GLEX	9502
C-GOIP	GLEX	9503
C-GOIR	GLEX	9504
C-GOIS	GLEX	9505
C-GOJC	**FA10**	**182**
C-GOKO	**C550**	**550-0814**
C-GOOB	**C560**	**0454**
C-GOQG	FA20	6
C-GOQJ	CL30	20361
C-GOQN	CL30	20362
C-GOSL	LJ25	040
C-GOUR	GLEX	9506
C-GOUU	GLEX	9507
C-GOUX	GLEX	9508
C-GOVC	CL65	5900
C-GOVF	CL65	5901
C-GOVG	CL65	5902
C-GOVI	CL65	5903
C-GOVJ	CL65	5904
C-GOVR	CL65	5905
C-GOVY	CL30	20375
C-GOVY	CL30	20400
C-GOVY	CL30	20426
C-GOVY	CL30	20454
C-GOVY	CL30	20518
C-GOVY	CL30	20544
C-GOVY	CL30	20570
C-GOVY	CL30	20592
C-GOVY	CL30	20615
C-GOWC	CL30	20376
C-GOWC	CL30	20404
C-GOWC	CL30	20431
C-GOWC	CL30	20530
C-GOWC	CL30	20548
C-GOWO	CL30	20377
C-GOWO	CL30	20406
C-GOWO	CL30	20434
C-GOWO	CL30	20531
C-GOWO	CL30	20549
C-GOWO	CL30	20566
C-GOWO	CL30	20585
C-GOWO	CL30	20611
C-GOWQ	CL30	20378
C-GOWQ	CL30	20402
C-GOWQ	CL30	20428
C-GOWQ	CL30	20455
C-GOWQ	CL30	20522
C-GOWQ	CL30	20550
C-GOWQ	CL30	20571
C-GOWQ	CL30	20586
C-GOWQ	CL30	20610
C-GOWQ	**CL30**	**20629**
C-GOWY	CL30	20379
C-GOWY	CL30	20401
C-GOWY	CL30	20427
C-GOWY	CL30	20456
C-GOWY	CL30	20523
C-GOWY	CL30	20551
C-GOWY	CL30	20577
C-GOWY	CL30	20593
C-GOWY	CL30	20612
C-GOXA	CL30	20380
C-GOXA	CL30	20403
C-GOXA	CL30	20432
C-GOXA	CL30	20457
C-GOXA	CL30	20524
C-GOXA	CL30	20547
C-GOXA	CL30	20572
C-GOXA	CL30	20598
C-GOXA	CL30	20620
C-GOXB	C650	0104
C-GOXB	CL30	20381
C-GOXB	CL30	20405
C-GOXB	CL30	20430
C-GOXB	CL30	20452
C-GOXB	CL30	20519
C-GOXB	CL30	20535
C-GOXB	CL30	20538
C-GOXB	CL30	20567
C-GOXB	CL30	20594
C-GOXB	CL30	20621
C-GOXD	CL30	20382
C-GOXD	CL30	20407
C-GOXD	CL30	20433
C-GOXD	CL30	20453
C-GOXD	CL30	20525
C-GOXD	CL30	20556
C-GOXD	CL30	20587
C-GOXD	CL30	20599
C-GOXD	CL30	20622
C-GOXG	CL30	20383
C-GOXG	CL30	20413
C-GOXG	CL30	20442
C-GOXG	CL30	20508
C-GOXG	CL30	20568
C-GOXG	CL30	20595
C-GOXG	**CL30**	**20623**
C-GOXM	CL30	20384
C-GOXM	CL30	20410
C-GOXM	CL30	20436
C-GOXM	CL30	20503
C-GOXM	CL30	20526
C-GOXM	CL30	20552
C-GOXM	CL30	20573
C-GOXM	CL30	20600
C-GOXM	CL30	20616
C-GOXN	CL30	20385
C-GOXN	CL30	20411
C-GOXN	CL30	20435
C-GOXN	CL30	20504
C-GOXN	CL30	20536
C-GOXN	CL30	20557
C-GOXN	CL30	20578
C-GOXN	**CL30**	**20601**
C-GOXN	**CL30**	**20624**
C-GOXR	CL30	20386
C-GOXR	CL30	20412
C-GOXR	CL30	20438
C-GOXR	CL30	20505
C-GOXR	CL30	20527
C-GOXR	CL30	20553
C-GOXR	CL30	20579
C-GOXR	CL30	20596
C-GOXR	CL30	20630
C-GOXU	CL30	20387
C-GOXU	CL30	20415
C-GOXU	CL30	20443
C-GOXU	CL30	20514
C-GOXU	CL30	20539
C-GOXU	CL30	20563
C-GOXU	CL30	20581
C-GOXU	CL30	20613
C-GOXV	CL30	20388
C-GOXV	CL30	20416
C-GOXV	CL30	20439
C-GOXV	CL30	20512
C-GOXV	CL30	20532
C-GOXV	CL30	20558
C-GOXV	CL30	20582
C-GOXV	CL30	20602
C-GOXV	**CL30**	**20625**
C-GOXW	CL30	20389
C-GOXW	CL30	20414
C-GOXW	CL30	20440
C-GOXW	CL30	20506
C-GOXW	CL30	20528
C-GOXW	CL30	20559
C-GOXW	CL30	20603
C-GOXW	**CL30**	**20626**
C-GOXZ	CL30	20390
C-GOXZ	CL30	20417
C-GOXZ	CL30	20441
C-GOXZ	CL30	20509
C-GOXZ	CL30	20533
C-GOXZ	CL30	20560
C-GOXZ	CL30	20588
C-GOXZ	CL30	20604
C-GOXZ	**CL30**	**20627**
C-GOYD	CL30	20391
C-GOYD	CL30	20418
C-GOYD	CL30	20444
C-GOYD	CL30	20515
C-GOYD	CL30	20540
C-GOYD	CL30	20561
C-GOYD	CL30	20589
C-GOYD	CL30	20617
C-GOYG	CL30	20392
C-GOYG	CL30	20423
C-GOYG	CL30	20445
C-GOYG	CL30	20520
C-GOYG	CL30	20545
C-GOYG	CL30	20569
C-GOYG	CL30	20590
C-GOYG	**CL30**	**20618**
C-GOYL	CL30	20393
C-GOYL	CL30	20421
C-GOYL	CL30	20446
C-GOYL	CL30	20510
C-GOYL	CL30	20537
C-GOYL	CL30	20564
C-GOYL	CL30	20583
C-GOYL	CL30	20605
C-GOYL	**CL30**	**20628**
C-GOYO	CL30	20394
C-GOYO	CL30	20425
C-GOYO	CL30	20450
C-GOYO	CL30	20513
C-GOYO	CL30	20541
C-GOYO	CL30	20562
C-GOYO	CL30	20597
C-GOYO	CL30	20619
C-GOZK	CL30	20363
C-GPAJ	**CL61**	**3056**
C-GPAW	C550	004
C-GPAW	C560	0260
C-GPAW	**C56X**	**5681**
C-GPCC	CL61	3039
C-GPCC	HS25	257057
C-GPCL	LJ24	224
C-GPCO	C500	317
C-GPCS	CL61	5088
C-GPCS	LJ55	035
C-GPCT	**C525**	**0256**
C-GPCZ	CL30	20096
C-GPDA	ASTR	120
C-GPDB	LJ24	217
C-GPDB	**LJ45**	**041**
C-GPDH	WW24	82
C-GPDO	LJ35	168
C-GPDO	LJ35	673
C-GPDQ	**CL30**	**20368**
C-GPDQ	G150	282
C-GPDQ	LJ35	170
C-GPDQ	LJ45	041
C-GPDU	CL30	20364
C-GPDZ	LJ25	063
C-GPEA	C650	0101
C-GPEQ	CL30	20365
C-GPEV	CL30	20366
C-GPEW	CL30	20367
C-GPFC	CL64	5310
C-GPFC	LJ35	092
C-GPFC	WW24	328
C-GPFI	CL30	20368
C-GPFU	CL30	20369
C-GPGA	C550	550-0807
C-GPGB	CL30	20370
C-GPGD	CL61	3039
C-GPGD	CL61	5145
C-GPGD	CL64	5310
C-GPGD	**CL64**	**5432**
C-GPGD	JSTR	5133
C-GPIA	GLEX	9509
C-GPIW	GLEX	9510
C-GPJW	C500	104
C-GPKI	GLEX	9511
C-GPKS	LJ45	223
C-GPKX	GLEX	9512
C-GPLN	**C500**	**016**
C-GPLS	C560	0781
C-GPLT	**C52B**	**0268**
C-GPMW	**C52B**	**0206**
C-GPOC	CL61	5134
C-GPOP	**C650**	**0042**
C-GPOS	**C525**	**0129**
C-GPOT	CL61	5088
C-GPOT	**F9DX**	**607**
C-GPPI	**GLEX**	**9158**
C-GPPS	HS25	257027
C-GPPX	**GLEX**	**9460**
C-GPSI	CL61	3027
C-GPTC	C500	429
C-GPTI	C500	667
C-GPTR	C550	083
C-GPUN	LJ35	058
C-GPUU	CL65	5906
C-GPUV	CL65	5907
C-GPVD	CL65	5908
C-GPVE	CL65	5909
C-GPVF	CL65	5910
C-GPWM	C525	0440
(C-GPWM)	C525	0400
C-GPYF	GLEX	9513
C-GPYW	GLEX	9514
C-GPYX	GLEX	9515
C-GPZE	GLEX	9516
C-GPZH	GLEX	9517
C-GQBQ	**CL61**	**5051**
C-GQBR	LJ55	105
C-GQCC	C500	066
C-GQCC	**C550**	**305**
C-GQGM	HS25	257143
C-GQJJ	C500	642
C-GQJK	C500	400
C-GQMH	CS55	0076
C-GQPA	**CL64**	**5379**
C-GQPJ	**C500**	**293**
C-GQPM	**LJ45**	**224**
C-GQWI	CL61	5016
C-GQYL	**C550**	**569**
C-GRBC	CL61	3041
C-GRBP	**FA10**	**23**
C-GRBZ	LJ60	218
C-GRCC	C560	0269
C-GRCC	**C56X**	**5297**
C-GRCO	LJ25	095
C-GRCY	**CL30**	**20182**
C-GRDP	WW24	188
C-GRDR	LJ25	145
C-GRDS	MU30	A018SA
C-GRDT	FA10	6
C-GRDX	MU30	A039SA
C-GREK	C500	082
C-GREK	C550	321
C-GREQ	C680	0330
C-GREQ	**C680**	**0542**
C-GRFC	**C560**	**0702**
C-GRFO	LJ35	100
C-GRFT	**C500**	**154**
C-GRGE	ASTR	115
C-GRGE	FA50	29
C-GRGE	HS25	258124
C-GRGE	WW24	298
C-GRGE	WW24	353
C-GRGE	WW24	359
C-GRGM	**FA7X**	**70**
C-GRHC	**C550**	**050**
C-GRIO	C550	148
C-GRIO	CL64	5353
C-GRIS	FA10	2
C-GRJC	C500	112
C-GRJL	LJ36	037
C-GRJQ	C500	250
C-GRJQ	CL30	20371
C-GRJU	CL30	20372
C-GRJV	CL30	20373
(C-GRJZ)	GALX	007
C-GRKJ	CL30	20374
C-GRLE	**CL64**	**5553**
C-GRMJ	LJ35	664
C-GRMZ	**CL65**	**5759**
C-GROG	**HS25**	**258852**
C-GROL	**EPC2**	**001J**
C-GROP	C510	0224
C-GRPB	C56X	5618
C-GRPF	**CL61**	**5168**
C-GRPM	FA20	500
C-GRQA	C500	455
C-GRQC	C550	104
C-GRQQ	**C560**	**0269**
C-GRQX	LJ25	146
C-GRRD	**C510**	**0232**
C-GRRI	GLEX	9518
C-GRRS	SBRL	306-78
C-GRSD	FA20	157
C-GRSD-X	FA20	157
C-GRSF	GLEX	9519
C-GRSU	GLEX	9520
C-GRTB	CL61	5069
C-GRTU	GLEX	9521
C-GRUK	GLEX	9522
C-GRVJ	LJ31	111
C-GRYC	C560	0702
C-GRYC	**C560**	**0770**
C-GRYI	CL65	5911
C-GRYM	CL65	5912
C-GRYO	CL65	5913
C-GRYQ	CL65	5914
C-GRYR	CL65	5915
C-GRYT	CL65	5916
C-GRYU	CL65	5917
C-GRYZ	CL65	5918
C-GRZA	CL65	5919
C-GRZF	CL65	5920
C-GSAM	**E50P**	**50000296**
C-GSAP	CL61	3034
C-GSAP	CL65	5710
C-GSAP	**GLEX**	**9038**
C-GSAS	LJ25	109
C-GSAX	LJ24	129
C-GSBR	GLF3	307
C-GSCL	F2TH	88
C-GSCL	FA20	495
C-GSCL	HS25	257030
C-GSCL	HS25	258243
C-GSCR	C550	354
C-GSCR	FA20	495
C-GSCX	C550	381
C-GSDU	GLEX	9470
C-GSEC	C56X	5298
C-GSEC	C750	0246
C-GSEC	**F2EX**	**82**
C-GSEO	C750	0246
C-GSFA	C550	057
C-GSIV	LJ24	108
C-GSJK	**CL30**	**20433**
C-GSKA	FA20	9
C-GSKC	FA20	29
C-GSKD	GLEX	9523
C-GSKL	LJ25	179
C-GSKN	FA20	65
C-GSKQ	FA20	40
C-GSKS	FA20	34
C-GSKV	HS25	25141
C-GSLC	**C56X**	**5556**
C-GSLK	GLF2	46
C-GSLL	C500	390
C-GSLU	**F2EX**	**167**
C-GSLW	**C52B**	**0293**
C-GSLW	GLEX	9524
C-GSMR	**F2TH**	**88**
C-GSMR	F900	55
C-GSNB	GLEX	9525
C-GSNF	GLEX	9526
C-GSNG	GLEX	9527
C-GSOC	**C680**	**0195**
C-GSOE	**C680**	**0223**
C-GSOV	C680	0533
C-GSQC	**HS25**	**257179**
C-GSQE	GALX	143
C-GSQE	**WW24**	**271**
C-GSQI	CL61	5096
C-GSRN	LJ36	039
C-GSRS	FA50	130
C-GSSC	C52B	0118
C-GSSK	CS55	0027
C-GSSS	ASTR	080
C-GSSS	F900	78
C-GSSS	FA50	95
C-GSTG	**CL65**	**5708**
C-GSTR	C500	647
C-GSTT	HS25	256021
C-GSUM	C500	485
C-GSUM	C560	0448
C-GSUN	C500	485
C-GSUN	C560	0448
C-GSUN	C680	0068
C-GSUN	**CL30**	**20364**
C-GSUT	CL30	20364
C-GSUX	C750	0205
C-GSWP	**LJ55**	**019**
C-GSWQ	**LJ45**	**022**
C-GSWS	LJ25	370
C-GSWS	WW24	259
C-GSXJ	**FA10**	**100**
C-GSXX	**C525**	**0109**
C-GSYM	**C525**	**0302**
C-GSYX	GLEX	9528
C-GSZB	GLEX	9529
C-GSZF	GLEX	9530
C-GSZG	GLEX	9531
C-GTAK	FA20	197
C-GTAU	HS25	258173
C-GTBR	C550	097
C-GTCB	GLF2	162
C-GTCI	C550	585
C-GTCI	**C750**	**0108**
C-GTCP	F900	29
C-GTCP	JSTR	5158
C-GTDE	**LJ35**	**057**
C-GTDK	C550	321
C-GTDM	**LJ35**	**498**
C-GTDN	HS25	257148
C-GTDO	ASTR	151
C-GTDO	CS55	0080
(C-GTEL)	C500	161
C-GTEP	GLF2	247
C-GTEW	GLF2	120
C-GTFA	LJ24	201
C-GTGO	C560	0576
C-GTJL	**LJ35**	**124**
C-GTJO	**CL64**	**5489**
C-GTJT	LJ24	160
C-GTKI	**C650**	**0037**
C-GTLA	**F9EX**	**260**
C-GTLG	ASTR	146
C-GTLG	E50P	50000265

C-GTLG	HS25	257174
C-GTLP	E50P	50000265
C-GTLP	**LJ40**	**2142**
C-GTLU	FA20	262
C-GTNG	**C500**	**169**
C-GTNT	FA20	488
C-GTNT	HS25	258038
C-GTOG	C560	0648
C-GTOG	C56X	5729
C-GTOG	**C680**	**0121**
C-GTOL	**C500**	**667**
C-GTOR	**HS25**	**257029**
C-GTPC	HS25	256025
C-GTPL	**F2EX**	**87**
C-GTPL	FA50	137
C-GTRG	C525	0376
C-GTRG	C525	0636
C-GTRG	**C52A**	**0456**
C-GTRL	**C500**	**082**
C-GTRL	GALX	112
C-GTSX	**C52B**	**0079**
C-GTTS	C510	0298
C-GTTS	**C525**	**0899**
C-GTTS	HS25	25108
C-GTUA	GLEX	9532
C-GTUF	GLEX	9533
C-GTUF	**HS25**	**258796**
C-GTUO	GLEX	9534
C-GTUU	GLEX	9535
C-GTUV	GLEX	9536
C-GTVC	GLEX	9537
C-GTVO	FA10	137
C-GTWL	**LJ35**	**490**
C-GTWO	GLF2	140/40
C-GTWX	**LJ35**	**463**
C-GTXV	CL60	1046
C-GTZN	GLEX	9538
C-GTZO	GLEX	9539
C-GTZS	GLEX	9540
C-GUAC	**LJ35**	**309**
C-GUAK	GLEX	9541
C-GUAL	GLEX	9542
C-GUAN	GLEX	9543
C-GUAZ	CL65	5921
C-GUBA	CL65	5922
C-GUBC	CL65	5923
C-GUBD	CL65	5924
C-GUBF	CL65	5925
C-GUDZ	GLEX	9544
C-GUEL	GLEX	9545
C-GUEO	GLEX	9546
C-GUEP	GLEX	9547
C-GUET	GLEX	9548
C-GUEU	GLEX	9549
C-GUEV	GLEX	9550
C-GUGC	CL30	20507
C-GUGS	CL30	20395
C-GUGS	CL30	20424
C-GUGS	CL30	20437
C-GUGS	CL30	20529
C-GUGS	CL30	20546
C-GUGS	CL30	20574
C-GUGS	CL30	20606
C-GUGS	**CL30**	**20631**
C-GUGU	**GLF5**	**641**
C-GUGV	CL30	20396
C-GUGV	CL30	20420
C-GUGV	CL30	20447
C-GUGV	CL30	20516
C-GUGV	CL30	20542
C-GUGV	CL30	20575
C-GUGV	CL30	20607
C-GUGV	**CL30**	**20632**
C-GUGY	CL30	20397
C-GUGY	CL30	20419
C-GUGY	CL30	20448
C-GUGY	CL30	20517
C-GUGY	CL30	20543
C-GUGY	CL30	20565
C-GUGY	CL30	20584
C-GUGY	CL30	20614
C-GUHA	CL30	20398
C-GUHA	CL30	20422
C-GUHA	CL30	20449
C-GUHA	CL30	20521
C-GUHA	CL30	20554
C-GUHA	CL30	20576
C-GUHA	CL30	20608
C-GUHA	**CL30**	**20633**
C-GUHE	CL30	20399
C-GUHE	CL30	20429
C-GUHE	CL30	20451
C-GUHE	CL30	20511
C-GUHE	CL30	20534
C-GUHE	CL30	20555
C-GUHE	CL30	20580
C-GUHE	CL30	20609
"C-GUID"	GLEX	9438
C-GUIF	GLEX	9551
C-GUIH	GLEX	9552
C-GUIS	GLEX	9553
C-GUIY	GLEX	9554
C-GUJK	GLEX	9555
C-GUJM	GLEX	9556
C-GUJP	GLEX	9557
C-GUKS	CL65	5927
C-GUKT	CL65	5926

C-GUKU	CL65	5928
C-GUKV	CL65	5929
C-GUKW	CL65	5930
C-GUOO	CL30	20381
C-GUOX	GLEX	9558
C-GUPB	GLEX	9561
C-GUPC	C56X	5284
C-GUPC	**C680**	**0335**
C-GUPF	GLEX	9564
C-GUPJ	**DDJET**	**DJ1-0003**
C-GUPK	GLEX	9559
C-GUPL	GLEX	9562
C-GUPM	GLEX	9560
C-GUPN	GLEX	9563
C-GURG	**CL61**	**5165**
C-GURJ	**CL65**	**5721**
C-GURO	CL65	5932
C-GURP	CL65	5933
C-GURT	CL65	5934
C-GURZ	CL65	5935
C-GUSF	CL65	5936
C-GUSJ	CL65	5931
C-GUSM	**LJ45**	**255**
C-GUSU	GLEX	9571
C-GUSV	GLEX	9565
C-GUSX	GLEX	9568
C-GUTE	GLEX	9570
C-GUTG	GLEX	9566
C-GUTN	GLEX	9569
C-GUTP	GLEX	9567
C-GUUU	C550	422
C-GUWH	CL30	20408
C-GUWP	CL30	20409
C-GUWT	**C560**	**0363**
C-GVBY	CL65	5758
C-GVCA	LJ35	043
C-GVCB	LJ35	012
C-GVCQ	**C52A**	**0387**
C-GVDS	CL30	20395
C-GVER	C500	454
C-GVEY	CL65	5937
C-GVFF	CL65	5938
C-GVFH	CL65	5939
C-GVFI	CL65	5940
C-GVFJ	CL65	5941
C-GVFK	CL65	5942
C-GVFN	CL65	5943
C-GVFO	CL65	5944
C-GVFP	CL65	5945
C-GVFX	**CL30**	**20287**
C-GVGH	LJ35	395
C-GVGM	C550	378
C-GVGY	GLEX	9576
C-GVGZ	GLEX	9573
C-GVIJ	C550	550-0982
C-GVJV	**E50P**	**50000136**
C-GVKH	GLEX	9575
C-GVKL	C500	341
C-GVKL	GLEX	9572
C-GVKO	GLEX	9574
C-GVLJ	DDJET	10-0001
C-GVLN	CL30	20395
C-GVMP	**HS25**	**HA-0015**
C-GVQR	HS25	25232
C-GVRI	GLEX	9579
C-GVRO	GLEX	9577
C-GVRS	GLEX	9581
C-GVRU	GLEX	9578
C-GVRY	GLEX	9580
C-GVSN	C52A	0109
C-GVSN	**C52B**	**0296**
C-GVVA	LJ35	002
C-GVVB	LJ36	025
C-GVVF	CL30	20400
C-GVVQ	**CL65**	**5946**
C-GVVT	C500	474
C-GVVU	CL65	5947
C-GVVY	**CL65**	**5711**
C-GVVZ	**LJ45**	**020**
C-GVWE	CL65	5948
C-GVWF	CL65	5949
C-GVWI	CL65	5950
C-GVWR	GLEX	9585
C-GVWV	GLEX	9582
C-GVXB	GLEX	9587
C-GVXD	GLEX	9584
C-GVXF	GLEX	9586
C-GVXG	GLEX	9583
C-GVXX	CL64	5343
C-GVZL	CL30	20405
C-GWBF	C555	0115
C-GWCJ	C550	213
C-GWCL	**C510**	**0136**
C-GWCR	C550	213
C-GWCR	C560	0379
C-GWEG	LJ24	256
C-GWEI	FA50	208
C-GWEM	HS25	258015
C-GWEP	CL30	20404
C-GWFG	LJ24	256
C-GWFG	**LJ35**	**669**
C-GWFK	**FA50**	**264**
C-GWFM	**F9EX**	**88**
C-GWFM	FA50	264
C-GWFM	HS25	258015
C-GWGZ	**C525**	**0637**
C-GWHF	**GLEX**	**9407**

C-GWII	C56X	5258
C-GWKF	WW24	271
C-GWKU	GLEX	9594
C-GWKV	GLEX	9588
C-GWKY	GLEX	9591
C-GWKZ	GLEX	9595
C-GWLE	HS25	258007
C-GWLI	**CL64**	**5310**
C-GWLK	GLEX	9589
C-GWLL	**CL64**	**5484**
C-GWLL	HS25	258007
C-GWLR	GLEX	9592
C-GWMY	GLEX	9593
C-GWNY	GLEX	9590
(C-GWPA)	C650	0011
C-GWPB	FA20	92/421
C-GWPB	**GALX**	**119**
C-GWPK	**G150**	**288**
C-GWPV	WW24	105
C-GWQJ	CL65	5951
C-GWQL	CL65	5952
C-GWQM	CL65	5953
C-GWQQ	CL65	5954
C-GWQR	CL65	5955
C-GWRT	CL60	1016
C-GWSA	FA20	228/473
C-GWSA	JSTR	5146
C-GWSH	WW24	165
"C-GWST"	ASTR	123
C-GWUG	CL61	5146
C-GWUL	C550	550-1028
(C-GWUZ)	LJ25	084
C-GWVC	C500	107
C-GWWU	**C560**	**0304**
C-GWWW	C510	0279
C-GWWW	**CL30**	**20451**
C-GWWW	G150	275
C-GWXH	CL30	20424
C-GWXK	LJ31	068
C-GWXP	LJ31	102
C-GWZR	GLEX	9607
C-GXAF	GLEX	9598
C-GXAH	GLEX	9602
C-GXAN	GLEX	9606
C-GXAU	GLEX	9597
C-GXAZ	GLEX	9601
C-GXBB	FA50	278
C-GXBB	**GLEX**	**9218**
C-GXBK	GLEX	9605
C-GXBM	GLEX	9596
C-GXBN	GLEX	9600
C-GXCA	GLEX	9604
C-GXCB	**LJ35**	**417**
C-GXCD	GLEX	9608
C-GXCE	GLEX	9599
C-GXCG	**C560**	**0481**
C-GXCO	C560	0481
C-GXCO	C56X	5200
C-GXCO	GLEX	9603
C-GXDN	GLF4	4030
C-GXDN	GLF5	5230
C-GXFZ	C500	032
C-GXKF	WW24	378
C-GXKG	GLEX	9613
C-GXKK	GLEX	9609
C-GXKO	GLEX	9611
C-GXKQ	CL60	1004
C-GXKV	GLEX	9610
C-GXLC	GLEX	9614
C-GXLG	**GLEX**	**9612**
C-GXMB	PRM1	RB-217
C-GXMP	**E50P**	**50000171**
(C-GXMP)	HS25	HB-30
C-GXNJ	CL65	5956
C-GXNK	CL65	5957
C-GXNM	CL65	5958
C-GXNO	CL65	5959
C-GXNU	CL65	5960
C-GXNW	**G150**	**264**
C-GXOP	C510	0170
C-GXPG	**HS25**	**258444**
C-GXPR	GLEX	9211
C-GXPT	C500	096
C-GXPT	HS25	25018
C-GXPZ	CL61	5166
C-GXPZ	**F9EX**	**57**
C-GXRA	GLEX	9619
C-GXRC	GLEX	9615
C-GXRD	GLEX	9618
C-GXRK	GLEX	9616
C-GXRU	GLEX	9620
C-GXRW	GLEX	9617
C-GXVG	CL65	5961
C-GXVJ	CL65	5962
C-GXVK	CL65	5963
C-GXVK	G150	283
C-GXVM	CL65	5964
C-GXVR	CL65	5965
C-GXVW	CL30	20425
C-GXYN	HS25	257114
C-GXZB	GLEX	9626
C-GXZD	GLEX	9622
C-GXZG	GLEX	9625
C-GXZL	GLEX	9621
C-GXZM	GLEX	9624
C-GXZR	GLEX	9627
C-GXZV	GLEX	9623

C-GYCJ	C550	561
C-GYFB	**LJ35**	**644**
C-GYFH	CL30	20430
C-GYJZ	CL30	20427
C-GYLK	CL65	5966
C-GYLO	CL65	5967
C-GYLP	**CL65**	**5968**
C-GYLQ	CL65	5969
C-GYLY	CL65	5970
C-GYLZ	CL65	5971
C-GYMB	PRM1	RB-255
C-GYMB	PRM1	RB-271
C-GYMC	**C56X**	**5092**
C-GYMD	**E50P**	**50000255**
C-GYMM	C560	0484
C-GYMM	CL64	5317
C-GYMP	**E50P**	**50000214**
(C-GYMP)	HS25	HB-31
C-GYOF	GLEX	9633
C-GYOH	GLEX	9629
C-GYOV	GLEX	9632
C-GYOX	GLEX	9628
C-GYPH	HS25	257155
C-GYPH	HS25	258007
C-GYPJ	FA50	162
C-GYPV	**PRM1**	**RB-16**
C-GYPW	GLEX	9631
C-GYPX	GLEX	9634
C-GYRF	GLEX	9630
C-GYTX	CL30	20501
C-GYTY	CL30	20502
C-GYYZ	HS25	257008
C-GZAM	**C52B**	**0160**
C-GZAS	**C52A**	**0508**
C-GZCZ	**G150**	**273**
C-GZDO	G150	282
C-GZDQ	CL30	20021
C-GZDQ	CL30	20036
C-GZDS	CL30	20022
C-GZDS	CL30	20037
C-GZDS	CL30	20064
C-GZDS	GLEX	9637
C-GZDV	CL30	20008
C-GZDV	CL30	20023
C-GZDV	CL30	20038
C-GZDV	CL30	20058
C-GZDY	CL30	20009
C-GZDY	CL30	20024
C-GZDY	CL30	20039
C-GZDY	CL30	20053
C-GZDY	GLEX	9635
C-GZEB	CL30	20010
C-GZEB	CL30	20025
C-GZEB	CL30	20040
C-GZEB	CL30	20060
C-GZEB	GLEX	9638
C-GZED	CL30	20011
C-GZED	CL30	20026
C-GZED	CL30	20041
C-GZEH	CL30	20012
C-GZEH	CL30	20027
C-GZEH	CL30	20042
C-GZEH	GLEX	9636
C-GZEI	CL30	20013
C-GZEI	CL30	20028
C-GZEI	CL30	20055
C-GZEJ	CL30	20014
C-GZEJ	CL30	20029
C-GZEK	C550	550-0953
C-GZEK	CL64	5360
C-GZEM	CL30	20015
C-GZEM	CL30	20030
C-GZEM	CL30	20068
C-GZEO	CL30	20016
C-GZEO	CL30	20031
C-GZEO	CL30	20061
C-GZEP	CL30	20017
C-GZEP	CL30	20032
C-GZEP	CL30	20069
C-GZER	CL30	20018
C-GZER	CL30	20033
C-GZER	CL30	20062
C-GZES	CL30	20019
C-GZES	CL30	20034
C-GZES	CL30	20056
C-GZET	CL30	20020
C-GZET	CL30	20035
C-GZET	CL30	20063
C-GZGP	GLEX	9642
C-GZGR	GLEX	9640
C-GZGS	GLEX	9644
C-GZHG	GLEX	9641
C-GZHO	GLEX	9639
C-GZHU	GLEX	9643
C-GZHZ	CL61	5020
C-GZIM	LJ25	208
C-GZJK	CL65	5972
C-GZJQ	CL65	5973
C-GZJR	CL65	5974
C-GZJV	CL65	5975
C-GZJW	CL65	5976
C-GZKH	CL30	20451
C-GZKL	**CL65**	**6050**
C-GZKL	GLEX	9099
C-GZLM	C525	0425
C-GZNC	CL61	5059
C-GZOW	GLEX	9119

C-GZOX	**FA20**	**463**
C-GZPT	GLEX	9126
C-GZPV	GLEX	9136
C-GZPW	GLEX	9137
C-GZPX	**CL64**	**5458**
C-GZQA	**CL65**	**6072**
C-GZQJ	**CL65**	**6073**
C-GZQL	CL65	6074
C-GZQO	**CL65**	**6075**
C-GZQP	**CL65**	**6076**
C-GZRA	GLEX	9138
C-GZRA	GLEX	9648
C-GZRE	GLEX	9646
C-GZRP	GLEX	9649
C-GZRU	GLEX	9645
C-GZRY	GLEX	9647
C-GZSG	CL65	6051
C-GZSM	GLEX	9013
C-GZTU	CL64	5553
C-GZTZ	GLEX	9081
C-GZUM	**CL61**	**5118**
C-GZVV	LJ35	153
C-GZVZ	CL64	5569
C-GZVZ	GLEX	9093
C-GZWY	CL61	5189
C-GZXA	C500	252
C-GZZX	HS25	257161

Chile

CC-ADB	**C525**	**0350**
CC-ADC	LJ45	142
CC-ADN	**C525**	**0493**
CC-AEN	HS25	258754
CC-AES	C52A	0099
CC-AGR	**C650**	**0003**
CC-AHQ	**C550**	**486**
CC-ALZ	**C680**	**0015**
CC-AME	HS25	258695
CC-AMX	**CL65**	**5933**
CC-AND	**E55P**	**50500253**
CC-ANR	**C510**	**0455**
CC-ANT	**C650**	**0131**
CC-AOA	**G150**	**237**
CC-AOC	**C525**	**0420**
CC-AOR	**C52C**	**0191**
CC-ARV	**C550**	**334**
CC-CAB	HS25	258769
CC-CDE	**C56X**	**5767**
CC-CGT	SBRL	306-33
(CC-CGX)	C550	136
CC-CHE	**C52A**	**0171**
CC-CLC	**C550**	**146**
CC-CMS	C525	0487
CC-CMS	**LJ40**	**2009**
CC-CPS	C650	7045
CC-CPS	**C750**	**0268**
CC-CRK	WW24	184
CC-CRT	**BE40**	**RK-493**
CC-CSA	C525	0632
CC-CTC	SBRL	306-112
CC-CTE	C500	426
CC-CVO	C525	0243
CC-CWK	ASTR	141
CC-CWK	**G150**	**219**
CC-CWW	C500	558
CC-CWW	**C555**	**0002**
CC-CWZ	C550	108
CC-CWZ	**C555**	**0143**
CC-DAC	**C650**	**0233**
CC-DGA	**C550**	**657**
CC-ECE	C650	0033
CC-ECL	C650	0131
CC-ECN	C550	146
CC-ECO	LJ35	050
CC-ECP	LJ35	066
CC-LLM	C550	481
CC-LLM	C550	550-0996
CC-PES	FA20	496
CC-PGK	C525	0632
CC-PGL	C650	7045
CC-PVJ	C525	0243
CC-PZM	C500	203

Russia

CCCP-01100	FA20	55/410

Canada

CF-AAG	HS25	25137
CF-ALC	HS25	25087
CF-ANL	HS25	25042
CF-AOS	HS25	25278
CF-ARE	LJ24	070
CF-BAX	C500	020
CF-BCJ	LJ24	100
CF-BCL	C500	042
CF-BCM	C500	071
CF-BFM	FA20	40
CF-BLT	SBRL	306-23
CF-BNK	HS25	25221
CF-BRL	SBRL	282-107
CF-CFL	HS25	25193
CF-CFL	HS25	25213
CF-CFP	C500	125
CF-CPW	C500	002
CF-CSS	LJ24	197
CF-CXY	LJ25	116
CF-DML	FA20	14

CF-DOM	HS25	25018
CF-DSC	HS25	25086
CF-DTF	JSTR	5088
CF-DTM	JSTR	5052
(CF-DTX)	JSTR	5018
CF-DWW	LJ25	045
CF-ECB	LJ24	112
CF-ENJ	C500	122
CF-ESO	FA20	46
CF-ETN	JSTR	5021
CF-FNM	GLF2	52
CF-GWI	FA20	7
CF-GWI	JSTR	5106/9
CF-HLL	HS25	25034
CF-HMV	LJ25	015
CF-HOG	GLF2	7
CF-HSS	HS25	256003
CF-IOT	GLF2	78
CF-IPG	HS25	25053
CF-IPJ	HS25	25053
CF-JES	FA20	236
CF-KAX	LJ25	016
CF-KBI	WW24	81
CF-KCI	HS25	25137
CF-MAJ	MS76	050
CF-MDB	HS25	25075
CF-NCG	SBRL	282-90
CF-NER	HS25	25176
CF-NOR	GLF2	54/36
CF-OPC	HS25	25016
CF-PPN	HS25	25280
CF-PQG	HS25	25036
CF-QNS	HS25	25152
CF-ROX	LJ25	070
CF-RWA	HS25	25016
CF-SBR	GLF2	9/33
CF-SDA	HS25	25022
CF-SDH	HS25	25192
CF-SEN	HS25	25027
CF-SHZ	HS25	25095
CF-SIM	HS25	25039
CF-SRZ	FA20	11
CF-SUA	WW24	17
CF-TEC	HS25	25232
CF-TEL	LJ24	054
CF-TXT	LJ25	057
CF-ULG	WW24	6
CF-UYT	LJ24	087
CF-VVX	WW24	76
CF-WDU	HFB3	1039
CF-WEC	WW24	115
CF-WOA	WW24	21
CF-WOS	HS25	25159
CF-WRA	FA20	110
CF-WUL	WW24	9
CF-YPB	FA20	254

Morocco

(CN-...)	C550	441
CN-AMJ	**C56X**	**6042**
CN-AMK	**C56X**	**6047**
CN-AMS	**GLF5**	**5271**
CN-ANL	**GLF2**	**182**
CNA-NM	**FA20**	**165/452**
CN-ANN	**FA20**	**152/446**
CN-ANO	**FA50**	**12**
CN-ANU	**GLF3**	**365**
CNA-NV	**C560**	**0025**
CNA-NW	**C560**	**0039**
CN-ANZ	FA10	212
CN-CTA	**CL30**	**20405**
CN-IAM	**CL64**	**5591**
CN-MAJ	MS76	050
CN-MBG	FA20	152/446
CN-MBH	FA20	165/452
CN-MBR	E55P	50500025
CN-MNZ	**FA10**	**212**
CN-RAK	**F9EX**	**118**
CN-RBS	**HS25**	**HA-0091**
CN-TCS	CRVT	34
CN-TDE	**CRVT**	
CN-TFU	**F900**	**105**
CN-THL	**CRVT**	**39**
CN-TJB	**LJ45**	**112**
CN-TJD	BE40	RK-579
CN-TJE	**C525**	**0693**
CN-TJS	**HS25**	**HA-0158**
CN-TKK	C550	293
CN-TKN	**FA10**	**128**
CN-TKS	**C650**	**0216**
CN-TLA	**C680**	**0273**
CN-TLB	**C525**	**0312**
CN-TLD	**FA10**	**120**
CN-TNA	FA10	212
CN-TNM	**FA20**	**273**
CN-TRS	**G280**	**2062**

Bolivia

CP-2105	C500	541
CP-2131	C500	083
CP-2259	WW24	95
CP-2263	WW24	58
CP-2317	**SBRL**	**282-136**
CP-2784	**WW24**	**433**
CP-2790	**C550**	**550-1052**
CP-2823	**C560**	**0451**

Portugal

CS-ATD	FA20	30
CS-ATE	FA20	94/428
CS-ATF	FA20	112
CS-ATG	FA20	264
CS-AYS	C550	615
CS-AYY	**C500**	**567**
CS-CHA	**CL30**	**20544**
CS-CHB	**CL30**	**20553**
CS-CHC	**CL30**	**20572**
CS-CHD	**CL30**	**20584**
CS-DBM	C500	200
CS-DCA	C500	157
CS-DCE	C555	0007
CS-DCI	C550	066
CS-DCK	**FA20**	**297**
CS-DCM	F2TH	46
CS-DCT	C750	0134
CS-DDA	C555	0098
CS-DDB	C56X	5028
CS-DDI	F900	143
CS-DDV	**C555**	**0147**
CS-DDZ	**LJ31**	**034**
CS-DFA	F900	91
CS-DFB	F900	94
CS-DFC	F2TH	148
CS-DFD	F2TH	174
CS-DFE	F2TH	205
CS-DFF	**F2EX**	**41**
CS-DFG	**F2EX**	**44**
CS-DFH	**F900**	**91**
CS-DFI	FA50	89
CS-DFJ	FA50	60
CS-DFK	**F2EX**	**65**
(CS-DFK)	FA50	62
CS-DFL	F9EX	97
CS-DFM	C56X	5257
CS-DFN	C56X	5283
CS-DFO	C56X	5314
CS-DFP	C56X	5315
CS-DFQ	C56X	5334
CS-DFR	C56X	5355
CS-DFS	C56X	5372
CS-DFT	C56X	5512
CS-DFU	C56X	5520
CS-DFV	C56X	5543
CS-DFW	HS25	258664
CS-DFX	HS25	258656
CS-DFY	HS25	258663
CS-DFZ	HS25	258673
CS-DGO	C750	0140
CS-DGQ	C52A	0200
CS-DGR	**C650**	**7045**
CS-DGW	**C52B**	**0235**
CS-DGZ	HS25	HA-0051
CS-DHA	C550	550-1005
CS-DHB	C550	550-1009
CS-DHC	C550	550-1013
CS-DHD	C550	550-1017
CS-DHE	C550	550-1022
CS-DHF	C550	550-1025
CS-DHG	C550	550-1034
CS-DHH	C550	550-1043
CS-DHI	C550	550-1048
CS-DHJ	C550	550-1082
CS-DHK	C550	550-1090
CS-DHL	C550	550-1092
CS-DHM	C550	550-1093
CS-DHN	C550	550-1098
CS-DHO	C550	550-1099
CS-DHP	C550	550-1104
CS-DHQ	C550	550-1109
CS-DHR	C550	550-1114
CS-DIG	C560	0637
CS-DIY	**C52B**	**0146**
(CS-DJA)	LJ60	379
CS-DKA	GLF4	1480
CS-DKB	GLF5	642
CS-DKC	GLF5	5057
CS-DKD	**GLF5**	**5081**
CS-DKE	**GLF5**	**5094**
CS-DKF	**GLF5**	**5099**
CS-DKG	**GLF5**	**5127**
CS-DKH	**GLF5**	**5150**
CS-DKI	**GLF5**	**5166**
CS-DKJ	**GLF5**	**5174**
CS-DKK	**GLF5**	**5201**
CS-DLA	F900	120
CS-DLB	**F2EX**	**80**
CS-DLC	**F2EX**	**98**
CS-DLD	**F2EX**	**109**
CS-DLE	**F2EX**	**127**
CS-DLF	**F2EX**	**134**
CS-DLG	**F2EX**	**144**
CS-DLH	**F2EX**	**149**
(CS-DLH)	F2EX	155
CS-DLI	F2EX	155
CS-DMA	BE40	RK-401
CS-DMB	BE40	RK-403
CS-DMC	BE40	RK-404
CS-DMD	BE40	RK-407
CS-DME	BE40	RK-408
CS-DMF	BE40	RK-410
CS-DMG	BE40	RK-417
CS-DMH	BE40	RK-425
CS-DMI	BE40	RK-437
CS-DMJ	BE40	RK-443
CS-DMK	BE40	RK-464
CS-DML	BE40	RK-465
CS-DMM	BE40	RK-472
(CS-DMM)	BE40	RK-469
CS-DMN	BE40	RK-475
CS-DMO	BE40	RK-494
CS-DMP	BE40	RK-508
CS-DMQ	BE40	RK-512
CS-DMR	BE40	RK-516
CS-DMS	BE40	RK-519
CS-DMT	BE40	RK-532
CS-DMU	BE40	RK-538
CS-DMV	BE40	RK-549
CS-DMW	BE40	RK-550
CS-DMX	BE40	RK-555
CS-DMY	BE40	RK-556
CS-DMZ	BE40	RK-559
CS-DNA	C555	0032
CS-DNB	C555	0051
CS-DNC	C555	0077
CS-DND	C650	0093
CS-DNE	C650	7093
(CS-DNE)	C650	0149
CS-DNF	C650	7080
CS-DNG	C650	7081
CS-DNH	HS25	258193
CS-DNI	HS25	258183
CS-DNJ	HS25	258399
CS-DNK	HS25	258430
CS-DNL	HS25	258439
CS-DNM	HS25	258422
CS-DNN	HS25	258435
CS-DNO	HS25	258457
CS-DNP	F2TH	109
CS-DNQ	F2TH	115
CS-DNR	**F2TH**	**120**
CS-DNS	F2TH	139
CS-DNT	HS25	258468
CS-DNU	HS25	258479
CS-DNV	HS25	258499
CS-DNW	C56X	5221
CS-DNX	HS25	258511
CS-DNY	C56X	5216
CS-DNZ	C56X	5235
CS-DOB	BE40	RK-561
CS-DPA	**HS25**	**HA-0069**
CS-DPE	F900	159
CS-DPF	**F9EX**	**198**
CS-DPJ	HS25	HA-0092
(CS-DPK)	HS25	HA-0119
CS-DPN	C510	0163
CS-DPO	FA50	226
(CS-DPU)	C525	0615
CS-DPV	**C510**	**0122**
CS-DPW	FA20	307/513
CS-DPZ	C56X	5576
CS-DQA	**C56X**	**5798**
CS-DQB	**C56X**	**5803**
CS-DRA	HS25	258686
CS-DRB	HS25	258690
CS-DRC	HS25	258714
CS-DRD	HS25	258721
CS-DRE	HS25	258725
CS-DRF	HS25	258730
CS-DRG	HS25	258741
CS-DRH	**HS25**	**258746**
CS-DRI	HS25	258756
CS-DRJ	HS25	258760
CS-DRK	HS25	258765
CS-DRL	**HS25**	**258770**
CS-DRM	HS25	258771
CS-DRN	**HS25**	**258772**
CS-DRO	**HS25**	**258775**
CS-DRP	**HS25**	**258779**
CS-DRQ	**HS25**	**258783**
CS-DRR	**HS25**	**258786**
CS-DRS	**HS25**	**258795**
CS-DRT	**HS25**	**258802**
CS-DRU	**HS25**	**258821**
CS-DRV	**HS25**	**258825**
CS-DRW	**HS25**	**258829**
CS-DRX	**HS25**	**258834**
CS-DRY	**HS25**	**258840**
CS-DRZ	**HS25**	**258847**
CS-DSA	FA7X	30
CS-DSB	**FA7X**	**43**
CS-DSC	**FA7X**	**164**
(CS-DSC)	FA7X	47
CS-DSD	**FA7X**	**92**
CS-DSE	**HS25**	**HA-0204**
CS-DTA	C560	0271
CS-DTB	F9EX	11
CS-DTC	**E50P**	**50000115**
CS-DTD	**FA7X**	**60**
CS-DTF	F2EX	102
CS-DTG	GLEX	9336
CS-DTH	LJ60	362
CS-DTJ	CL64	5539
CS-DTK	CL65	5715
CS-DTL	LJ45	280
CS-DTM	LJ45	286
CS-DTP	**F900**	**135**
CS-DTQ	**E55P**	**50500083**
CS-DTR	**F2TH**	**119**
CS-DTS	FA7X	19
CS-DTT	**FA7X**	**154**
(CS-DTT)	FA7X	153
CS-DTV	F900	62
CS-DTW	GLEX	9020
CS-DTX	C56X	6108
CS-DTY	C510	0368
CS-DTZ	**F2TH**	**42**
CS-DUA	**HS25**	**HB-4**
(CS-DUA)	HS25	HB-6
CS-DUB	**HS25**	**HB-5**
(CS-DUB)	HS25	HB-7
CS-DUC	**HS25**	**HB-6**
CS-DUD	**HS25**	**HB-8**
CS-DUE	**HS25**	**HB-11**
CS-DUF	**HS25**	**HB-19**
CS-DUG	**HS25**	**HB-20**
CS-DUH	**HS25**	**HB-21**
(CS-DUI)	HS25	HB-24
CS-DVB	C750	0140
CS-DVE	**GLEX**	**9098**
CS-DVH	**C52B**	**0101**
CS-DVI	**GLEX**	**9145**
CS-DVN	**C650**	**7070**
CS-DVS	**E50P**	**50000130**
CS-DVX	**FA7X**	**66**
CS-DXA	C56X	5549
CS-DXB	C56X	5553
CS-DXC	C56X	5559
CS-DXD	C56X	5568
CS-DXE	C56X	5578
CS-DXF	**C56X**	**5586**
CS-DXG	**C56X**	**5595**
CS-DXH	**C56X**	**5615**
CS-DXI	**C56X**	**5621**
CS-DXJ	**C56X**	**5627**
CS-DXK	**C56X**	**5633**
CS-DXL	**C56X**	**5640**
CS-DXM	**C56X**	**5683**
CS-DXN	**C56X**	**5685**
CS-DXO	**C56X**	**5692**
CS-DXP	**C56X**	**5702**
CS-DXQ	**C56X**	**5704**
CS-DXR	**C56X**	**5748**
CS-DXS	**C56X**	**5754**
CS-DXT	**C56X**	**5765**
CS-DXU	**C56X**	**5775**
CS-DXV	**C56X**	**5782**
CS-DXW	**C56X**	**5787**
CS-DXX	**C56X**	**5789**
CS-DXY	**C56X**	**5791**
CS-DXZ	**C56X**	**5796**
(CS-DYA)	HA4T	RC-41
(CS-DYB)	HA4T	RC-42
(CS-DYC)	HA4T	RC-43
(CS-DYD)	HA4T	RC-44
(CS-EAA)	C52B	0317
CS-EAE	LJ60	338
CS-EAM	GLEX	9353
(CS-EAP)	GLEX	9371
CS-GLA	**GLEX**	**9478**
(CS-GLA)	GLEX	9479
CS-GLB	**GLEX**	**9481**
CS-GLC	**GLEX**	**9533**
CS-GLD	**GLEX**	**9538**
CS-GLE	**GLEX**	**9638**
CS-GLF	**GLEX**	**9670**
CS-LAM	**GLEX**	**9602**
CS-LAT	**C680**	**680A0027**
CS-PHA	**E55P**	**50500203**
CS-PHB	**E55P**	**50500209**
CS-PHC	**E55P**	**50500214**
CS-PHD	**E55P**	**50500225**
CS-PHE	**E55P**	**50500252**
CS-PHF	**E55P**	**50500260**
CS-PHG	**E55P**	**50500264**
CS-PHH	**E55P**	**50500270**
CS-PHI	**E55P**	**50500332**
CS-PHZ	E55P	50500091
CS-TFI	LJ45	021
CS-TFN	**F900**	**66**
CS-TFO	**LJ40**	**2094**
CS-TFQ	**LJ45**	**302**
CS-TFR	**LJ45**	**382**
CS-TFV	**CL30**	**20252**
CS-TLP	F2EX	39
CS-TLT	LJ45	287
CS-TLW	**LJ45**	**144**
CS-TLY	**FA7X**	**15**
CS-TMF	FA50	29
CS-TMJ	FA50	190
CS-TMK	F900	66
CS-TMQ	F900	175
CS-TMS	FA50	268
CS-TSL	**GLEX**	**9231**

Macau

CS-MAC	CL61	5178
(CS-MAI)	HS25	258366

Uruguay

CX-BOI	LJ35	378
CX-BVD	HS25	25251
CX-CBS	**HS25**	**256067**
CX-CCT	**C500**	**344**
CX-CIB	**HS25**	**257071**
CX-CMJ	WW24	251
CX-ECO	LJ25	229
CX-JYE	LJ35	188
CX-MBS	**F2TH**	**62**
CX-PYB	**LJ35**	**285**
CX-VRH	LJ35	628

Gambia

C5-AFT	**CL61**	**3043**
C5-MAC	**C650**	**0108**

Bahamas

C6-...	**C550**	**444**
C6-AIP	**C560**	**0270**
C6-BDH	HS25	256028
C6-BEJ	GLF2	194
C6-BEN	FA10	109
C6-BER	FA50	20
C6-BET	HS25	257054
C6-BEV	MS76	111
C6-BEY	HS25	25051
C6-BFE	GLF2	194
(C6-BGF)	LJ24	252
C6-BHD	FA50	264
C6-BHN	F900	9
C6-BPC	HS25	25016
C6-EVU	C52A	0170
C6-FSI	**HS25**	**257116**
C6-IRM	**WW24**	**422**
C6-IUE	HS25	257040
C6-IUN	**HS25**	**257091**
C6-JAG	**HS25**	**257120**
C6-JET	ASTR	095
C6-LPV	FA10	149
C6-LUV	C52B	0243
C6-LVU	C52A	0170
C6-MAS	**C550**	**031**
C6-MED	HS25	25140
C6-MIV	FA20	502
C6-NPV	FA10	175
C6-PCA	C550	217
C6-SAP	**BE40**	**RK-148**
C6-SVA	**HS25**	**257045**
C6-SVB	**CL60**	**1018**
C6-SZN	F9EX	195
C6-ZIP	**LJ60**	**214**

Mozambique

C9-...	**HS25**	**257061**
C9-CFM	**BE40**	**RK-249**
C9-TAC	HS25	257175
(C9-TTA)	HS25	257175

Germany

D-AAAM	GLF5	5189
D-AAAX	**CL64**	**5449**
D-AAAY	**CL64**	**5602**
D-AAAZ	GLEX	9170
D-AABB	GLF4	4091
(D-AABB)	GLEX	9559
(D-AABE)	GLEX	9559
(D-AAFX)	CL61	5070
(D-AAGF)	GLF4	1159
D-AAHI	GLEX	9170
D-AAMA	CL61	5023
(D-AAMD)	GLF2	186
(D-AANA)	GLEX	9234
D-AAOK	CL64	5585
D-ABBA	F9EX	303
D-ABCD	**CL64**	**5565**
D-ABEY	**CL65**	**5863**
(D-ABIG)	CL65	5950
D-ABMW	**GLF5**	**5336**
D-ABNP	GLEX	9339
(D-ACAS)	CL65	5856
D-ACBO	GLEX	9345
(D-ACDC)	F900	5
D-ACDE	**GLEX**	**9405**
D-ACDF	GLEX	9096
D-ACGN	FA7X	77
D-ACTE	CL61	5085
D-ACTO	CL64	5502
D-ACTU	CL61	5085
D-ACTU	CL64	5502
D-ACUA	**CL65**	**5725**
(D-ACVG)	GLF2	186
D-ADCA	GLF5	5114
D-ADCB	GLF5	5142
D-ADCL	**GLF5**	**5435**
(D-ADCL)	GLF5	5430
D-ADDI	F9DX	622
(D-ADES)	GLF5	5492
(D-ADLA)	CL61	5060
D-ADLD	**CL64**	**5474**
D-ADLR	**GLF5**	**5093**
D-ADNB	GLEX	9071
D-ADND	CL64	5403
D-ADNE	CL64	5422
D-ADSE	GLF4	4217
D-ADSE	**GLF5**	**5492**
(D-ADSE)	GLF5	5205
D-ADSK	**GLF6**	**6143**
(D-ADSK)	GLF6	6192
D-AEGV	GLEX	9081
D-AEKT	GLEX	9213
D-AETD	F9EX	247
D-AETV	CL64	5417
D-AEUK	**CL64**	**5632**
D-AFAA	**CL64**	**5397**
D-AFAB	**CL64**	**5378**
D-AFAB	CL64	5510

D-AFAC	**CL64**	**5416**
D-AFAD	**CL64**	**5348**
D-AFAI	**CL64**	**5366**
D-AFAM	**GLEX**	**9028**
D-AFAU	**GLEX**	**9013**
D-AFKG	GLF2	186
(D-AFLW)	GLEX	9014
(D-AFLW)	GLEX	9035
D-AFLY	GLF4	4027
D-AFPR	**FA7X**	**160**
D-AFSX	FA7X	125
D-AGAZ	GLF5	5075
(D-AGBT)	GLEX	9020
(D-AGIV)	GLF4	1257
D-AGJP	**GLEX**	**9487**
D-AGKG	CL61	5049
D-AGSI	F9EX	78
(D-AGTH)	GLEX	9120
D-AGVA	**GLF5**	**5408**
D-AGVI	**GLF4**	**4243**
D-AGVS	**GLF4**	**4113**
D-AHEI	CL64	5463
D-AHER	**F9EX**	**78**
(D-AHER)	GLF5	604
D-AHLE	CL64	5462
D-AHRN	**F9EX**	**96**
(D-AHRN)	F9EX	105
(D-AHRO)	F9EX	88
(D-AIFB)	CL65	5704
D-AIND	CL64	5572
(D-AINI)	CL64	5595
(D-AINX)	CL64	5629
(D-AINY)	CL64	5644
D-AJAB	CL64	5327
(D-AJAB)	FA7X	66
D-AJAD	F9EX	64
D-AJAG	CL64	5528
D-AJAN	**CL65**	**5798**
D-AJGK	GLF4	1459
(D-AJJJ)	GLF4	1459
D-AJJK	**GLF5**	**5191**
(D-AJKI)	GLF6	6013
D-AKAR	GLF5	5409
D-AKAS	CL65	5856
(D-AKAS)	CL65	5868
(D-AKAT)	CL64	5303
D-AKAZ	GLEX	9250
D-AKBH	CL64	5457
D-AKUE	CL61	5173
(D-ALIK)	CL65	5936
D-ALIL	**FA7X**	**179**
D-ALME	F900	101
D-ALMS	F9EX	227
(D-ALUK)	GLEX	9487
(D-AMAN)	GLF5	5167
D-AMBI	F9EX	176
(D-AMHS)	CL64	5541
D-AMIB	CL64	5618
D-AMIG	F9DX	623
D-AMIM	CL64	5317
(D-AMKA)	GLF5	5379
D-AMOR	CL65	5918
(D-AMOS)	GLEX	9301
(D-AMPX)	GLEX	9661
D-AMSC	**CL64**	**5464**
(D-AMTM)	CL61	5018
(D-AMUC)	CL65	5937
D-ANGB	**CL64**	**5541**
D-ANKE	CL64	5494
D-ANMB	GLEX	9723
D-ANTR	**CL64**	**5616**
D-AOHP	CL61	5068
D-AOHS	GLEX	9427
D-AONE	**CL64**	**5430**
(D-AONE)	GLF4	1503
D-AOTL	GLEX	9231
(D-APCA)	GLEX	9427
(D-APJI)	CL64	5583
D-APLC	**FA7X**	**77**
D-ARKK	GLF4	4004
D-ARKO	**GLEX**	**9348**
D-ARTE	**CL61**	**5060**
(D-ARTE)	CL64	5505
(D-ARTN)	CL64	5585
D-ARWE	CL64	5454
(D-ARWE)	CL64	5303
D-ARYR	**GLEX**	**9419**
D-ASAF	GLF5	5302
(D-ASAF)	GLF5	5262
D-ASBG	**F9EX**	**141**
D-ASHY	**CL65**	**5926**
D-ASIE	CL64	5475
(D-ASIE)	F9EX	227
D-ASIX	CL64	5618
D-ASTS	CL64	5378
(D-ASTS)	CL64	5375
D-ATIM	**GLF5**	**5354**
(D-ATNF)	GLEX	9332
D-ATNR	GLEX	9159
D-ATOM	GLEX	9374
D-ATTT	**CL64**	**5609**
(D-ATWO)	CL64	5649
D-ATYA	CL65	5756
D-AUCR	**F9DX**	**606**
D-AUKE	**CL64**	**5389**
D-AUTO	**GLF5**	**5171**
D-AVAR	GLF5	5189
(D-AVIA)	GLEX	9280
D-AVPB	**CL65**	**5715**
D-AWKG	**F9EX**	**20**
D-AXTM	**GLEX**	**9102**
D-AYSM	**GLF6**	**6146**
D-AZEM	**F9EX**	**133**
(D-AZNF)	GLEX	9159
(D-AZPP)	CL64	5369
D-AZZA	CL65	5855
D-BABE	JSTR	5012
D-BADO	**CL30**	**20116**
D-BAIR	GALX	029
D-BAMA	F2TH	70
D-BAMM	F2EX	74
D-BANN	**CL30**	**20221**
D-BASE	F2EX	111
D-BAVA	CL30	20172
D-BAVB	**CL30**	**20212**
D-BAVG	**C750**	**0227**
(D-BBAD)	CL60	1008
(D-BBAD)	FA50	23
(D-BBED)	F2EX	76
D-BBWK	FA50	23
D-BCLA	CL30	20272
D-BDNL	F2TH	119
D-BDWO	FA50	42
D-BEAM	**CL30**	**20452**
D-BEEP	**C750**	**0107**
D-BEKP	**CL30**	**20275**
D-BEKY	**F2EX**	**201**
(D-BEKY)	F2EX	210
D-BELL	FA50	222
D-BELO	**CL30**	**20402**
D-BERT	**F2EX**	**271**
D-BERT	F2EX	30
D-BERT	FA50	218
D-BEST	**F2TH**	**50**
D-BETA	CL30	20079
D-BETI	**FA50**	**267**
D-BFAR	FA50	16
D-BFFB	**F2EX**	**93**
D-BFFB	FA50	65
D-BFJE	CL30	20004
D-BFLY	CL30	20123
D-BGGM	F2EX	11
(D-BGRL)	HS25	HA-0056
D-BHER	F2EX	140
D-BHGN	**CL30**	**20583**
(D-BHRN)	CL30	20042
D-BIGA	CL30	20419
(D-BIGB)	CL30	20423
D-BIKA	**F2EX**	**76**
D-BILL	F2EX	33
D-BIRD	F2EX	7
D-BIRD	F2TH	54
D-BIRD	FA50	16
D-BIVI	CL30	20206
D-BJET	CL60	1005
(D-BJET)	HS25	259016
(D-BJGM)	F2EX	13
D-BJKP	**LEG5**	**55000003**
D-BKAT	**G280**	**2070**
D-BKLI	C750	0219
D-BLDI	**C750**	**0218**
D-BLTA	**F2EX**	**234**
D-BLUE	C750	0140
D-BMTM	CL60	1029
D-BMVV	**F2EX**	**42**
D-BNTH	FA50	196
D-BOBI	**F2EX**	**246**
(D-BOBI)	F2EX	235
D-BOND	F2TH	54
D-BONN	**F2EX**	**118**
(D-BONN)	F2EX	125
D-BOOC	**C750**	**0259**
(D-BOOI)	FA50	215
D-BOOK	**F2EX**	**277**
D-BOOK	F2EX	70
D-BOOK	FA50	215
(D-BOSA)	G280	2063
D-BOSS	F2EX	33
(D-BPWR)	CL30	20272
(D-BRCR)	CL30	20581
(D-BREA)	CL30	20232
D-BSIK	F2TH	27
D-BSKY	CL30	20179
D-BSKY	**F2TH**	**226**
(D-BSKY)	F2EX	192
D-BSMI	CL30	20071
D-BSNA	CL60	1066
(D-BTAG)	C750	0227
D-BTEN	**C750**	**0085**
D-BTIG	F2EX	75
D-BTIM	CL30	20071
D-BTLT	**CL30**	**20042**
D-BUBI	**CL30**	**20145**
D-BUSY	CL60	1070
D-BVHA	**F2EX**	**263**
D-C...	**LJ55**	**087**
(D-C...)	HS25	258201
D-CAAA	C56X	5555
D-CAAA	**C56X**	**6123**
D-CAAB	C550	690
D-CAAE	**LJ55**	**095**
D-CAAS	WW24	164
D-CAAT	C550	205
D-CAAY	LJ31	202
D-CABB	ASTR	059
D-CACM	C650	7039
D-CACP	LJ55	086
(D-CACS)	C550	151
D-CADA	HS25	257007
D-CADA	HS25	259008
(D-CADA)	HFB3	1073
D-CADB	FA10	89
D-CADC	LJ31	049
(D-CADE)	HFB3	1074
(D-CADI)	HFB3	1075
(D-CADO)	HFB3	1076
(D-CADU)	HFB3	1077
D-CADY	C56X	5037
D-CAEP	LJ55	059
(D-CAEX)	LJ60	409
(D-CAFB)	C560	0303
D-CAFE	C680	0033
D-CAFI	HS25	25037
D-CAFO	LJ36	006
D-CAHB	LJ40	2093
D-CAHH	C680	0226
D-CAHO	**C56X**	**6165**
D-CAIR	**C56X**	**5620**
(D-CAJA)	HS25	HA-0071
(D-CAJC)	FA10	131
D-CAJK	C56X	5670
D-CAKE	C650	0240
(D-CALA)	HFB3	1068
(D-CALE)	HFB3	1069
(D-CALI)	HFB3	1070
(D-CALI)	HS25	258267
D-CALL	**C550**	**550-0834**
D-CALL	FA20	138/440
D-CALL	FA20	392/553
(D-CALM)	FA20	237/476
(D-CALO)	HFB3	1071
(D-CALU)	HFB3	1072
D-CAMA	HFB3	1064
D-CAMB	HS25	25157
D-CAMB	LJ35	174
D-CAME	HFB3	1065
(D-CAMO)	HFB3	1066
D-CAMS	C560	0243
(D-CAMU)	HFB3	1067
(D-CANA)	HFB3	1079
(D-CANE)	HFB3	1080
D-CANI	HFB3	1061
D-CANO	HFB3	1062
D-CANU	HFB3	1063
D-CAPB	**C560**	**0806**
D-CAPD	LJ35	179
D-CAPO	**LJ35**	**159**
D-CARA	HFB3	1021
D-CARD	LJ35	426
D-CARE	C650	0134
D-CARE	HFB3	1022
D-CARE	LJ35	341
D-CARE	LJ55	073
D-CARG	LJ35	433
D-CARH	LJ35	444
D-CARI	HFB3	1023
D-CARL	**LJ35**	**387**
D-CARO	**C680**	**0514**
D-CARO	HFB3	1024
D-CARO	LJ35	325
D-CARP	LJ55	050
D-CART	LJ35	354
D-CARU	HFB3	1025
D-CARX	LJ55	034
D-CARY	HFB3	1026
D-CASA	C560	0544
(D-CASE)	HFB3	V2/1002
D-CASH	C52B	0217
D-CASH	C550	564
D-CASH	FA10	7
(D-CASH)	C56X	5213
D-CASO	HFB3	1027
D-CAST	**C52B**	**0330**
D-CASU	HFB3	1028
D-CASY	HFB3	1029
D-CATE	C680	0153
D-CATE	HFB3	1030
D-CATE	LJ35	216
(D-CATI)	HFB3	1078
D-CATL	LJ55	051
D-CATP	C650	0121
D-CATY	LJ35	114
D-CATY	LJ35	211
D-CAUW	**C560**	**0578**
(D-CAVB)	C52B	0339
D-CAVE	LJ35	423
D-CAVI	LJ35	174
D-CAVW	HS25	258233
D-CAVW	SBRL	282-76
D-CAVW	SBRL	380-38
D-CAWA	C550	596
D-CAWB	**C680**	**0319**
D-CAWM	**C56X**	**6002**
D-CAWS	**C680**	**0328**
D-CAWU	C560	0042
D-CAWU	**C56X**	**5797**
D-CAWX	**C680**	**0535**
(D-CAXO)	E55P	50500150
D-CAYK	C650	0187
(D-CAZH)	HS25	258043
D-CBAD	LJ60	129
D-CBAE	HS25	257031
D-CBAG	FA10	91
D-CBAT	C550	299
D-CBAT	C550	562
D-CBAT	FA20	108/430
D-CBAY	**C680**	**0125**
D-CBAY	WW24	202
D-CBBA	WW24	294
D-CBBB	C56X	5567
D-CBBB	**C56X**	**6125**
D-CBBB	WW24	296
D-CBBC	WW24	297
D-CBBD	WW24	310
D-CBBE	WW24	154
D-CBBS	**E55P**	**50500343**
D-CBBT	FA20	162/451
(D-CBCP)	LJ45	287
D-CBCT	**C52C**	**0093**
D-CBEL	C550	468
D-CBEN	C560	0282
D-CBEN	**C56X**	**6089**
D-CBIG	C560	0124
D-CBIZ	C650	7039
D-CBMB	FA10	61
D-CBMV	HS25	258345
D-CBMW	HS25	258155
D-CBMW	HS25	258345
D-CBNA	FA20	63/411
(D-CBOB)	LJ60	378
D-CBPD	LJ25	091
D-CBPL	C650	0149
D-CBRD	LJ36	013
D-CBRK	LJ35	026
D-CBRO	C52C	0218
D-CBUR	FA10	98
D-CBUS	CS55	0027
D-CBVB	C52B	0339
D-CBVW	HS25	25231
D-CBVW	HS25	258235
D-CBVW	SBRL	380-60
D-CBWW	HS25	259028
D-CCAA	**LJ35**	**315**
D-CCAB	**C550**	**550-0827**
(D-CCAC)	LJ36	004
D-CCAD	LJ35	263
D-CCAP	LJ35	144
D-CCAR	LJ35	179
D-CCAR	LJ35	200
D-CCAT	ASTR	059
D-CCAT	LJ24	254
D-CCAT	LJ25	079
D-CCAX	LJ35	284
D-CCAY	LJ35	112
D-CCBH	**C52B**	**0334**
(D-CCBT)	ASTR	080
D-CCCA	**LJ35**	**160**
D-CCCB	**LJ35**	**663**
D-CCCF	**C550**	**205**
D-CCCG	C52B	0146
(D-CCCH)	HFB3	1060
D-CCDB	FA20	381/549
D-CCEA	C56X	5593
D-CCEU	C650	0190
(D-CCEX)	HS25	256015
D-CCFF	C680	0114
D-CCGG	LJ60	256
D-CCGN	**LJ55**	**017**
D-CCHB	**LJ35**	**089**
D-CCHS	LJ35	122
D-CCHS	LJ55	049
(D-CCHS)	LJ55	013
D-CCJS	C52C	0106
D-CCJS	C680	0175
D-CCKV	LJ31	046
D-CCLA	C56X	6126
D-CCMB	FA20	377/548
(D-CCNA)	FA20	147/444
D-CCON	LJ55	098
D-CCPD	LJ36	004
D-CCSD	**C650**	**0212**
D-CCSG	C56X	5641
(D-CCTS)	C52C	0157
(D-CCUB)	C650	0216
D-CCVD	**C56X**	**5784**
D-CCVW	HS25	258237
D-CCVW	SBRL	380-45
(D-CCVW)	HFB3	1080
D-CCWD	C550	550-0864
D-CCWD	**C56X**	**6039**
(D-CCWD)	C56X	5670
D-CCWK	LJ25	076
D-CCWM	**E55P**	**50500232**
D-CDAS	**E55P**	**50500317**
(D-CDAS)	FA20	108/430
D-CDAX	LJ35	135
D-CDBW	C56X	5073
(D-CDCC)	C56X	6041
(D-CDCD)	C56X	6049
(D-CDCE)	C56X	6062
(D-CDCF)	C56X	6063
D-CDDD	C56X	5623
D-CDDD	**C56X**	**6166**
D-CDDD	LJ24	201
(D-CDEF)	LJ60	331
D-CDEN	LJ31	049
D-CDEN	LJ45	148
D-CDFA	LJ36	006
D-CDHS	LJ35	026
D-CDHS	LJ35	311
(D-CDIG)	C52B	0086
D-CDLC	C52B	0269
D-CDNX	LJ60	231
D-CDNY	LJ60	160
D-CDNZ	LJ60	161
D-CDOC	**LJ45**	**018**
D-CDPD	LJ25	177
D-CDRB	MU30	A053SA
D-CDRF	LJ45	342
D-CDSF	LJ35	421
D-CDSM	LJ60	276
D-CDTZ	C52B	0367
D-CDTZ	**E55P**	**50500198**
D-CDUW	C560	0099
(D-CDVW)	HFB3	1080
D-CDWN	LJ35	175
D-CEAC	C650	7117
D-CEAS	WW24	55
D-CEBM	C560	0569
D-CEBM	C56X	5749
(D-CEBM)	C560	0558
D-CECH	**C56X**	**6140**
(D-CEDL)	HFB3	1061
D-CEEE	**C56X**	**5630**
D-CEFA	C52C	0044
D-CEFD	**C52B**	**0120**
D-CEFE	**C52C**	**0177**
(D-CEFE)	C52C	0058
(D-CEFL)	LJ35	284
(D-CEFM)	C550	550-1018
D-CEFO	**C56X**	**6082**
D-CEHM	**C56X**	**6021**
D-CEIS	**C680**	**0185**
D-CEIS	BE40	RK-10
D-CEJA	LJ60	173
D-CELA	LJ36	002
D-CELE	C52B	0011
(D-CELE)	C52B	0114
D-CELI	**C550**	**550-0998**
D-CELL	FA20	201/469
D-CEMG	C560	0463
D-CEMM	LJ45	144
D-CEMS	**C52B**	**0107**
D-CENT	FA10	89
(D-CENT)	ASTR	115
D-CEPD	LJ25	274
D-CERA	HFB3	1031
D-CERE	HFB3	1032
D-CERI	HFB3	1033
D-CERO	HFB3	1034
D-CERU	HFB3	1035
D-CESA	**C550**	**550-1039**
D-CESA	HFB3	1036
D-CESE	HFB3	1037
D-CESH	LJ45	017
D-CESI	HFB3	1038
D-CESO	HFB3	1039
D-CESU	HFB3	1040
D-CETD	LJ60	421
D-CETV	LJ60	148
"D-CEUU"	FA20	201/469
D-CEVB	C52C	0043
D-CEVW	HS25	258067
D-CEVW	SBRL	306-44
D-CEWR	C560	0192
D-CEWR	LJ45	013
D-CEWR	LJ45	213
(D-CEWR)	LJ55	013
D-CEXP	**LJ35**	**616**
D-CFAD	LJ60	386
D-CFAF	**LJ60**	**107**
(D-CFAF)	LJ40	2071
D-CFAG	**LJ60**	**281**
(D-CFAG)	LJ60	203
D-CFAI	CS55	0134
D-CFAI	FA20	335
D-CFAI	LJ35	365
D-CFAI	LJ55	061
(D-CFAI)	FA20	174/457
D-CFAK	LJ60	300
(D-CFAK)	LJ60	249
D-CFAN	HS25	258094
D-CFAN	**LJ60**	**019**
(D-CFAS)	LJ60	379
D-CFAX	LJ35	135
D-CFAX	**LJ60**	**249**
(D-CFAX)	LJ60	300
D-CFAY	LJ35	084
D-CFAZ	LJ55	136
D-CFCF	HS25	25248
D-CFCF	**LJ35**	**413**
D-CFFB	LJ60	107
D-CFFF	C56X	5634
D-CFFF	**C56X**	**6170**
D-CFGG	**LJ36**	**048**
D-CFIC	HS25	HB-74
D-CFIS	ASTR	045
D-CFIV	**LJ35**	**385**
(D-CFKG)	HS25	25005
D-CFLG	LJ60	290
(D-CFLO)	C56X	5788
D-CFLY	C560	0145
D-CFLY	**C56X**	**6014**
D-CFMI	**E55P**	**50500058**
D-CFOR	LJ35	614

D-CFOR	**LJ35**	**656**
D-CFOX	C560	0277
D-CFOX	LJ36	031
D-CFPD	LJ24	345
(D-CFRA)	C52B	0258
D-CFRC	HS25	258036
D-CFSK	HS25	256053
D-CFST	**LJ31**	**011**
(D-CFTC)	C550	550-0988
D-CFTG	**LJ35**	**204**
D-CFUX	LJ55	061
D-CFVG	LJ24	223
(D-CFVG)	LJ35	121
D-CFVW	HS25	258073
D-CFWR	LJ45	013
D-CFXJ	C52B	0086
D-CGAA	**C56X**	**6173**
D-CGAS	C550	443
D-CGBR	**LJ55**	**122**
D-CGEO	LJ60	160
D-CGEP	**G150**	**287**
D-CGFA	**LJ35**	**179**
D-CGFB	**LJ35**	**268**
D-CGFC	**LJ35**	**331**
D-CGFD	**LJ35**	**139**
D-CGFE	**LJ36**	**062**
D-CGFF	**LJ36**	**063**
D-CGFG	**LJ35**	**222**
D-CGFH	**LJ35**	**607**
D-CGFI	LJ35	612
D-CGFJ	**LJ35**	**643**
D-CGFK	**LJ31**	**205**
D-CGFM	**LJ31**	**207**
D-CGFN	LJ35	654
D-CGFO	**LJ35**	**614**
D-CGFV	MU30	A051SA
D-CGGB	LJ40	2018
D-CGGC	LJ40	2107
D-CGGG	LJ31	042
D-CGGG	**LJ31**	**227**
(D-CGHP)	C550	550-0998
D-CGIN	LJ55	090
D-CGJH	FA20	138/440
D-CGLS	WW24	161
D-CGMA	ASTR	133
D-CGMR	**C56X**	**5593**
(D-CGNF)	LJ60	304
D-CGOM	LJ31	167
D-CGPD	LJ35	202
(D-CGPE)	G150	287
D-CGRC	**LJ35**	**223**
D-CGSO	FA20	306/512
D-CGSP	G180	90002
D-CGTF	LJ60	281
(D-CGTI)	C56X	5037
D-CGTT	C680	0153
(D-CGVD)	LJ60	373
D-CGVW	HS25	258076
D-CHAL	WW24	207
(D-CHAM)	C56X	6027
D-CHAN	C550	550-0874
(D-CHAS)	WW24	55
D-CHAT	C52B	0255
D-CHBL	WW24	226
(D-CHBM)	LJ25	260
(D-CHCH)	FA20	237/476
D-CHCL	WW24	277
D-CHDC	**C680**	**0150**
D-CHDE	C560	0031
D-CHDL	WW24	199
D-CHEC	**C680**	**0079**
D-CHEF	HS25	258038
D-CHEF	HS25	258514
D-CHEF	LJ25	260
(D-CHEF)	FA20	274
D-CHEP	C550	697
D-CHER	LJ35	119
D-CHER	LJ60	051
D-CHER	**LJ60**	**148**
D-CHFB	HFB3	V1/1001
(D-CHFB)	HFB3	1043
D-CHGN	HS25	HA-0184
D-CHGS	**E55P**	**50500150**
D-CHHH	C56X	5674
D-CHHS	C560	0177
D-CHIC	**E55P**	**50500096**
D-CHIC	LJ25	347
D-CHIC	SBRL	380-42
(D-CHIC)	FA50	88
D-CHIL	C680	0156
D-CHIO	**C52B**	**0378**
D-CHIP	C680	0156
D-CHJH	C555	0131
D-CHLE	LJ60	211
D-CHLM	LJ45	266
D-CHLR	**E55P**	**50500066**
D-CHMC	C550	550-0874
D-CHMS	**E55P**	**50500324**
(D-CHMS)	E55P	50500300
D-CHOP	C550	609
D-CHPD	LJ35	309
D-CHRA	**C52C**	**0058**
D-CHRB	**C52C**	**0144**
D-CHRC	**C52C**	**0153**
(D-CHRC)	LJ35	096
D-CHRD	**C680**	**0142**
D-CHRE	C680	0124
(D-CHRN)	LJ60	167
(D-CHRN)	LJ60	290
(D-CHRO)	LJ60	196
D-CHSA	**C550**	**043**
D-CHSP	C56X	5536
D-CHSW	BE40	RK-84
D-CHTH	HS25	25143
D-CHVB	C550	629
D-CHZF	**C550**	**550-0866**
D-CIAO	**C550**	**283**
D-CIAO	C555	0135
D-CIAU	C52B	0281
(D-CIBM)	FA20	234/475
D-CICR	C56X	5236
D-CIEL	FA10	155
D-CIFA	C550	069
D-CIFA	C550	133
D-CIFA	LJ60	032
D-CIFM	C560	0814
D-CIFM	**C56X**	**6178**
D-CIGM	BE40	RK-103
D-CIII	C56X	5037
D-CIII	LJ60	179
D-CILL	C550	660
D-CILL	FA20	13
D-CILY	LJ55	026
D-CIMM	LJ60	214
(D-CINA)	HFB3	1080
D-CINI	C56X	5195
D-CINS	**LJ45**	**347**
(D-CIOL)	C52B	0331
D-CION	LJ55	015
D-CIRA	HFB3	1041
D-CIRE	HFB3	1042
D-CIRI	HFB3	1043
D-CIRO	HFB3	1044
(D-CIRR)	C550	066
D-CIRS	LJ35	091
D-CIRU	HFB3	1045
D-CISA	HFB3	1046
D-CISE	HFB3	1047
D-CISI	HFB3	1048
D-CISO	HFB3	1049
D-CISU	HFB3	1050
D-CITA	LJ35	070
D-CITA	**LJ60**	**069**
D-CITO	HFB3	1027
(D-CITO)	LJ25	118
D-CITY	FA20	237/476
D-CITY	**LJ35**	**177**
D-CIWW	C550	550-0871
(D-CJAD)	LJ24	128
D-CJAF	**LJ60**	**351**
D-CJAK	C52B	0075
D-CJET	**C52B**	**0349**
D-CJET	HS25	256027
D-CJET	HS25	258358
D-CJET	LJ24	189
D-CJJJ	C550	052
D-CJJJ	C555	0086
D-CJOS	**C52B**	**0367**
(D-CJOY)	C56X	5195
D-CJPD	**LJ31**	**057**
D-CJPG	**LJ35**	**108**
D-CJUG	**C52C**	**0161**
(D-CJVC)	C52B	0220
(D-CKAS)	HS25	258267
D-CKCF	HS25	25105
D-CKDM	G150	235
(D-CKDN)	G150	268
(D-CKDO)	G150	269
(D-CKDP)	G150	270
D-CKHG	**C56X**	**5667**
D-CKHK	**C56X**	**6051**
D-CKIM	HS25	257094
D-CKJS	C52B	0086
D-CKKK	LJ60	144
(D-CKLI)	C56X	5567
D-CKLS	C550	550-1037
D-CKNA	**C52C**	**0108**
(D-CKOW)	HS25	25105
D-CLAM	**E55P**	**50500108**
D-CLAN	LJ35	397
D-CLAN	SBRL	380-12
D-CLAT	C52B	0085
D-CLBA	BE40	RK-25
D-CLBB	FA20	315/517
D-CLBC	HS25	258050
D-CLBD	HS25	258405
D-CLBE	FA20	279/502
D-CLBG	HS25	258682
D-CLBH	HS25	258812
D-CLBM	**E55P**	**50500173**
D-CLBR	FA20	52
D-CLDF	**C650**	**7085**
(D-CLDF)	C650	0037
(D-CLDI)	C56X	5555
D-CLEO	C560	0159
D-CLEO	C680	0178
(D-CLHM)	LJ45	266
D-CLHS	**C56X**	**6187**
D-CLIC	C56X	5788
D-CLIF	C680	0075
D-CLIP	LJ55	004
D-CLIP	LJ55	029
D-CLLL	C56X	5722
D-CLLL	FA10	188
(D-CLLS)	C680	0171
D-CLMA	HFB3	1057
D-CLMS	**LJ45**	**395**
D-CLOU	C555	0121
D-CLOU	HFB3	V2/1002
D-CLOZ	LJ40	2071
(D-CLSG)	BE40	RK-10
D-CLUB	LJ45	044
D-CLUB	LJ55	034
D-CLUB	LJ55	092
D-CLUB	LJ60	249
D-CLUB	SBRL	380-19
(D-CLUB)	HS25	257112
D-CLUE	**C650**	**0174**
D-CLUX	LJ40	2061
D-CLUZ	LJ40	2071
D-CLUZ	**LJ60**	**386**
D-CLVW	HS25	257100
(D-CLXG)	C52B	0320
D-CMAD	LJ55	143
D-CMAN	**C52B**	**0215**
D-CMAN	FA10	71
D-CMAR	LJ36	002
D-CMAX	FA20	158/449
D-CMAX	LJ55	011
(D-CMAX)	LJ55	108
D-CMCM	C560	0088
D-CMDH	**C680**	**0322**
D-CMED	**LJ55**	**059**
D-CMEI	**C560**	**0117**
D-CMES	C680	0162
D-CMET	**FA20**	**329/523**
D-CMHS	**C52B**	**0161**
D-CMIC	C56X	5021
(D-CMIC)	C56X	5814
D-CMIR	HS25	258110
D-CMIX	C550	550-1050
D-CMJS	C550	660
D-CMLP	LJ45	012
D-CMMI	C56X	5538
D-CMMM	LJ24	328
D-CMMP	C56X	5719
D-CMOM	C52C	0055
D-CMOR	E55P	50500373
D-CMPI	C650	7055
D-CMRM	LJ31	213
D-CMSC	**LJ45**	**097**
D-CMTM	LJ55	042
D-CMVW	HS25	257112
D-CNCA	C550	257
D-CNCA	C555	0137
D-CNCB	C555	0144
D-CNCI	C550	414
D-CNCI	C560	0061
D-CNCJ	C650	7102
D-CNCP	C550	116
D-CNCP	C560	0069
D-CNEX	MU30	A070SA
(D-CNIC)	C680	0016
D-CNIK	LJ40	2006
(D-CNJK)	E55P	50500102
D-CNMB	**LJ45**	**024**
D-CNNN	C56X	5786
D-CNNN	**C56X**	**6127**
D-CNOB	C52B	0119
D-CNOC	**C56X**	**5814**
(D-CNSC)	C560	0820
D-CNUE	**LJ60**	**170**
D-COBC	C52B	0414
(D-COBC)	C52B	0408
D-COBI	**C56X**	**5645**
D-COBO	C52B	0107
D-COBO	**C52B**	**0414**
D-COCO	LJ35	108
D-COCO	LJ35	466
D-COFG	FA20	175
D-COFY	C550	550-0992
D-COGA	LJ24	223
(D-COIN)	LJ40	2120
(D-COIN)	LJ40	2121
(D-COJS)	C52C	0106
D-COKE	**LJ35**	**447**
D-COLL	FA20	234/475
D-COLO	FA20	18
D-COLT	**E55P**	**50500207**
D-COMA	HS25	25005
D-COME	FA10	67
D-COME	HS25	25025
D-COMF	FA20	184/462
D-COMI	HS25	25058
D-COMK	C550	347
D-COMM	FA20	302/510
D-COMM	LJ45	012
D-COMO	**LJ60**	**169**
D-COMO	LJ60	350
D-CONA	LJ24	189
D-CONA	LJ35	114
D-CONE	LJ25	050
D-CONE	**LJ35**	**111**
D-CONI	LJ35	007
D-CONO	LJ35	055
D-CONO	LJ35	417
D-CONU	FA20	383/550
D-CONU	**LJ55**	**124**
D-CONY	LJ35	195
D-COOL	LJ24	261
D-COOL	**LJ55**	**052**
D-CORA	LJ35	018
D-CORA	LJ35	381
(D-CORA)	C52B	0016
(D-CORA)	C680	0534
D-CORE	HFB3	1051
D-CORF	FA20	281/496
D-CORI	HFB3	1052
D-CORO	HFB3	1053
(D-CORT)	FA20	147/444
D-CORU	HFB3	1054
D-CORY	HFB3	1055
D-COSA	HFB3	1056
D-COSE	HFB3	1057
D-COSI	HFB3	1058
D-COSO	HFB3	1059
D-COST	C680	0153
D-COSU	HFB3	1060
D-COSY	LJ35	204
D-COSY	LJ35	415
D-COTT	FA20	314/516
(D-COUP)	SBRL	306-17
D-COWB	**C52B**	**0220**
D-COWS	LJ60	170
D-CPAO	C52B	0232
D-CPAS	HS25	258130
D-CPDR	LJ40	2080
D-CPMI	C52B	0286
D-CPMI	**C56X**	**6121**
D-CPMU	**LJ60**	**032**
D-CPOS	**C56X**	**6109**
D-CPPP	C550	550-0865
D-CPRO	**LJ31**	**155**
(D-CPRO)	LJ31	160
D-CPSG	LJ45	158
D-CQAJ	**LJ35**	**421**
D-CQQQ	**C56X**	**6134**
D-CRAH	C52B	0154
D-CRAN	LJ45	043
D-CRAN	LJ60	019
D-CRBE	LJ35	372
D-CRCR	**E55P**	**50500069**
D-CREW	LJ55	011
D-CREY	C650	0192
D-CRHR	C650	0142
D-CRIS	ASTR	107
D-CROB	LJ60	261
D-CRON	**C56X**	**5762**
D-CRRR	C650	0187
(D-CRRR)	C650	0044
D-CRUW	C56X	5642
(D-CRUW)	C56X	6002
D-CSAG	**E55P**	**50500101**
D-CSAO	C650	0149
D-CSAP	LJ31	057
(D-CSCT)	C56X	6197
D-CSEB	**C56X**	**6093**
D-CSFD	**C56X**	**5022**
D-CSFD	C555	0148
D-CSIE	LJ31	207
D-CSIM	**LJ60**	**274**
(D-CSIS)	LJ60	286
D-CSIX	**LJ60**	**120**
D-CSLT	**LJ60**	**200**
(D-CSLX)	C56X	5243
D-CSMB	**C550**	**550-1130**
D-CSMS	LJ45	017
D-CSOS	**LJ45**	**161**
(D-CSOS)	LJ35	429
D-CSPG	**G180**	**90004**
D-CSPJ	G180	90003
D-CSPN	G180	90001
D-CSRB	HS25	258226
D-CSRI	HS25	258212
D-CSSS	C550	550-0906
D-CSUL	LJ45	189
D-CSUN	C560	0078
D-CSUN	**C56X**	**6102**
D-CSWM	C550	550-0884
(D-CSYB)	C56X	5811
D-CTAN	C560	0150
D-CTAN	HS25	258450
(D-CTAN)	LJ45	223
(D-CTAN)	LJ45	240
D-CTEC	C52B	0101
D-CTEC	C52B	0215
D-CTIL	**LJ35**	**671**
D-CTLX	C56X	5569
(D-CTLX)	C56X	5585
D-CTRI	**LJ35**	**346**
D-CTTT	**C56X**	**5573**
D-CTWO	LJ31	011
D-CTWO	**LJ35**	**504**
D-CUBA	**C52B**	**0169**
D-CUGF	**C52B**	**0479**
(D-CUGF)	C52B	0470
(D-CUNA)	HFB3	1061
D-CUNO	LJ55	108
D-CUPI	C680	0066
D-CURA	C52B	0287
D-CURE	LJ35	652
D-CURE	**LJ60**	**379**
(D-CURE)	HFB3	1062
(D-CURI)	HFB3	1063
(D-CURO)	HFB3	1064
D-CURT	**LJ31**	**042**
(D-CURU)	HFB3	1065
(D-CURY)	HFB3	1066
(D-CUSA)	HFB3	1067
(D-CUSE)	HFB3	1068
(D-CUSI)	HFB3	1069
(D-CUSO)	HFB3	1070
(D-CUSU)	HFB3	1071
(D-CUSY)	HFB3	1072
D-CUTE	LJ55	013
D-CUUU	C52B	0197
D-CUUU	**C56X**	**6137**
D-CVAI	C650	0037
(D-CVAU)	C550	433
D-CVFL	LJ35	405
D-CVGM	C550	492
D-CVGP	LJ31	036
D-CVHA	C52C	0124
D-CVHA	C560	0275
D-CVHA	C680	0050
D-CVHB	C56X	5056
D-CVHB	C56X	5688
D-CVHB	**C56X**	**6168**
D-CVHI	C56X	5195
D-CVHM	C52B	0086
D-CVII	C650	7094
(D-CVII)	C650	7090
D-CVIP	LJ55	035
D-CVIP	LJ55	109
(D-CVIP)	LJ60	319
D-CVJN	LJ40	2091
D-CVJP	LJ40	2079
(D-CVJT)	LJ40	2097
D-CVRM	C550	491
D-CVVM	**C555**	**0062**
D-CVVV	C56X	5723
D-CWAY	**LJ55**	**107**
D-CWBW	HS25	258213
D-CWDL	LJ55	084
(D-CWER)	LJ45	010
(D-CWER)	LJ45	017
D-CWHS	LJ60	246
D-CWII	C650	7090
D-CWIN	C680	0305
D-CWIN	HS25	258178
D-CWIR	C52B	0288
D-CWIR	**C52C**	**0118**
D-CWIT	**C52C**	**0124**
D-CWOL	HS25	258235
D-CWWP	**E55P**	**50500333**
D-CWWW	C56X	5316
D-CWWW	C56X	5788
D-CXLS	**C56X**	**6027**
D-CXNL	**HS25**	**258544**
D-CYKP	**C550**	**550-1017**
D-CYOU	C680	0156
D-CZAR	C560	0114
(D-CZEC)	C56X	6140
D-CZZZ	C56X	5790
D-CZZZ	**C56X**	**6128**
D-IAAD	**E50P**	**50000215**
D-IAAS	C525	0321
D-IAAS	C52A	0054
D-IAAT	**E50P**	**50000162**
(D-IAAT)	E50P	50000248
D-IAAW	**E50P**	**50000245**
D-IAAY	**E50P**	**50000243**
D-IABC	C500	182
D-IABG	**C500**	**610**
D-IADD	C550	481
D-IADV	**C550**	**552**
D-IAEC	C500	609
D-IAEV	C500	365
(D-IAFA)	C550	616
(D-IAFD)	C525	0105
D-IAGG	PRM1	RB-35
D-IAHG	**C525**	**0126**
D-IAIB	**C525**	**0615**
D-IAJJ	C500	245
D-IAKN	**C52A**	**0367**
D-IALL	C525	0143
D-IAME	C525	0315
D-IAMF	C525	0519
D-IAMM	C525	0041
D-IAMO	**C52A**	**0166**
D-IAMS	C525	0684
D-IANE	C500	121
D-IANE	C500	501
D-IANO	C500	523
(D-IANP)	C52A	0428
D-IAOA	C525	0024
D-IARI	**C525**	**0347**
D-IATC	C500	116
D-IATD	LJ24	074
D-IATT	PRM1	RB-48
D-IAVB	C525	0172
D-IAWA	C550	421
D-IAWU	C500	604
D-IAWU	**C525**	**0435**
D-IAYL	PRM1	RB-249
D-IBAK	**C525**	**0499**
D-IBBA	C525	0025
D-IBBB	C52A	0028
D-IBBB	**PRM1**	**RB-82**
D-IBBE	C52A	0233
D-IBBN	PRM1	RB-120
D-IBBS	**C52A**	**0313**
D-IBCT	**C52A**	**0328**
D-IBIT	C525	0393
D-IBJJ	**C52A**	**0125**

D-IBMS	C525	0309
D-IBPF	C550	246
D-IBSL	**E50P**	**50000295**
D-IBTI	**C525**	**0684**
D-IBWA	**C525**	**0042**
D-IBWB	C500	421
D-IBWG	C500	566
D-ICAB	C500	151
D-ICAC	**C550**	**049**
D-ICAM	C500	456
D-ICAO	**C525**	**0642**
D-ICAP	LJ24	247
D-ICAR	LJ24	169
D-ICAY	LJ24	254
D-ICCA	C500	317
D-ICCC	C500	269
D-ICCP	**C510**	**0375**
D-ICEE	**C525**	**0096**
D-ICEY	C525	0286
D-ICEY	**C525**	**0611**
D-ICFA	C500	290
D-ICGT	C525	0164
D-ICHE	C550	559
D-ICHS	LJ24	280
D-ICIA	C500	086
D-ICJA	PRM1	RB-151
(D-ICMH)	C510	0262
D-ICMS	**C52A**	**0108**
D-ICOL	C525	0353
(D-ICPO)	C525	0639
D-ICPW	C500	100
D-ICSS	**C525**	**0121**
D-ICTA	**C550**	**301**
D-ICUR	C550	150
D-ICUW	C500	319
D-ICWB	C525	0349
(D-ICWB)	C550	074
D-IDAG	**C525**	**0144**
D-IDAS	C525	0389
D-IDAS	C52A	0443
D-IDAS	E50P	50000365
D-IDAT	LJ24	261
D-IDAU	C500	131
D-IDAZ	**C525**	**0389**
D-IDBA	**PRM1**	**RB-164**
D-IDBW	C525	0044
D-IDDD	LJ24	201
D-IDFD	C500	225
D-IDIG	C525	0477
D-IDMH	C52A	0174
D-IDPD	C500	382
D-IDWH	C500	126
D-IDWN	C500	288
D-IEAI	C525	0417
D-IEAR	**C550**	**095**
D-IEEN	C510	0262
D-IEFA	C52A	0358
D-IEFD	C52A	0049
D-IEGA	C500	081
D-IEGO	C510	0048
D-IEGO	LJ24	283
D-IEIR	**C500**	**674**
D-IEKU	**C52A**	**0043**
D-IEMG	**C510**	**0274**
D-IENE	**C52A**	**0501**
D-IEPR	C525	0625
D-IERF	**C525**	**0310**
D-IETZ	C525	0518
D-IETZ	C52A	0363
(D-IETZ)	C52A	0033
D-IEVB	C52A	0459
D-IEVX	C52A	0036
D-IEWS	C525	0217
D-IEXC	C500	036
D-IFAI	C500	100
D-IFAN	C525	0214
(D-IFAP)	PRM1	RB-137
D-IFDH	**C525**	**0517**
D-IFDN	**C52A**	**0343**
D-IFER	**C510**	**0366**
D-IFEY	C52A	0330
D-IFFI	C525	0401
(D-IFGP)	C500	673
D-IFIS	C525	0442
D-IFIS	**C52A**	**0340**
D-IFLY	C52A	0330
D-IFLY	C52A	0499
D-IFMC	PRM1	RB-27
D-IFMG	**PRM1**	**RB-109**
D-IFUM	LJ24	129
D-IFUP	C525	0126
D-IFUP	C525	0172
D-IFVG	LJ24	223
D-IGAS	C525	0223
(D-IGEL)	C510	0250
D-IGGG	C500	539
D-IGGK	C500	535
D-IGGW	C525	0322
D-IGIT	C52A	0032
D-IGLU	C500	537
D-IGMB	C500	442
D-IGME	C525	0279
D-IGRC	C550	132
D-IGRO	**C52A**	**0230**
D-IGSO	LJ24	233
D-IGST	**PRM1**	**RB-152**
D-IGZA	C525	0260

D-IHAG	**C550**	**151**
D-IHAP	C52A	0026
D-IHAQ	LJ24	007
(D-IHAT)	C550	301
D-IHCW	C525	0165
D-IHEB	**C525**	**0064**
(D-IHEB)	C525	0073
D-IHER	E50P	50000062
D-IHEY	C500	432
D-IHGW	C525	0126
D-IHHN	C52A	0041
D-IHHS	C525	0082
D-IHKW	**C525**	**0677**
D-IHLZ	LJ24	225
D-IHOL	C525	0229
D-IHRA	C52A	0168
D-IHSV	C500	164
D-IHTM	C52A	0343
D-IIBE	PRM1	RB-235
(D-IIDD)	LJ24	228
D-IIJS	C525	0310
D-IIMC	PRM1	RB-196
D-IIMH	PRM1	RB-57
D-IIPD	LJ24	228
(D-IIRR)	C525	0315
D-IJHM	C550	212
D-IJHO	**C510**	**0306**
D-IJKP	C52A	0433
(D-IJKP)	C510	0045
D-IJOA	**C52A**	**0034**
(D-IJOA)	C52A	0036
D-IJON	C500	346
D-IJYP	C525	0165
D-IKAA	LJ24	018
D-IKAB	LJ24	087
D-IKAF	LJ24	189
D-IKAL	C52A	0193
D-IKAN	C500	040
D-IKBO	**C52A**	**0357**
D-IKCS	**C525**	**0396**
D-IKFJ	C500	178
D-IKGT	**PRM1**	**RB-64**
(D-IKHV)	C525	0264
D-IKJS	C52A	0029
D-IKOE	**C510**	**0082**
D-IKOP	**C525**	**0016**
D-IKPW	C500	361
(D-IKUC)	C500	269
D-ILAC	**EA50**	**000177**
D-ILAM	**C52A**	**0070**
D-ILAN	C550	614
D-ILAP	**E50P**	**50000288**
D-ILAT	C525	0209
D-ILAT	**EA50**	**550-0269**
D-ILAV	**EA50**	**550-1004**
D-ILCB	C525	0193
D-ILCC	C550	324
D-ILDE	LJ24	208
D-ILDL	**C52A**	**0167**
D-ILHA	**C525**	**0696**
(D-ILHA)	C525	0675
D-ILHB	**C525**	**0675**
(D-ILHB)	C525	0694
D-ILHC	**C525**	**0695**
D-ILHD	**C525**	**0694**
(D-ILHD)	C525	0696
D-ILHE	**C525**	**0664**
(D-ILHF)	C525	0645
D-ILHM	LJ24	239
D-ILIB	C52A	0500
D-ILIF	C525	0411
D-ILLL	C500	659
D-ILLL	C525	0518
D-ILLY	C525	0442
D-ILME	C525	0421
D-ILTC	C550	617
D-ILVW	LJ24	239
D-IMAC	C525	0396
D-IMAH	**C52A**	**0502**
D-IMAN	C500	025
D-IMAR	LJ24	250
D-IMAX	**C52A**	**0195**
D-IMCE	C500	396
D-IMEN	C500	279
D-IMGW	**C52A**	**0498**
D-IMHA	**C52A**	**0322**
D-IMLN	C500	129
D-IMMD	C525	0211
D-IMME	**C550**	**400**
D-IMMF	C550	560
D-IMMG	C525	0614
(D-IMMH)	C510	0259
D-IMMI	C525	0303
D-IMMM	C525	0460
D-IMMM	**C52A**	**0400**
D-IMMM	LJ24	328
(D-IMMP)	C525	0354
D-IMND	C525	0089
D-IMOR	**E50P**	**50000281**
D-IMPC	C525	0126
D-IMPC	**C525**	**0639**
D-IMRX	C500	688
D-IMSM	C500	194
D-IMTM	C550	061
D-IMWZ	LJ24	184
D-IMYA	C52A	0026
D-INCC	C500	128

D-INCI	C500	255
D-INCS	**C525**	**0466**
D-INDA	C52A	0428
D-INDY	**EA50**	**000246**
D-INER	C525	0516
D-INFS	**C525**	**0286**
D-INGA	MS76	098
D-INGE	MS76	090
D-INHH	C500	079
D-INKA	LJ24	282
D-INOB	**C52A**	**0196**
D-INOC	C525	0477
D-IOBB	**C525**	**0665**
D-IOBC	C52A	0332
(D-IOBC)	C52A	0486
D-IOBO	C525	0025
D-IOBO	C52A	0032
D-IOBO	C52A	0332
D-IOBO	**C52A**	**0486**
D-IOBU	C52A	0032
D-IOBU	C52A	0332
D-IOBU	C52A	0486
D-IOGA	LJ24	223
D-IOGE	LJ24	224
D-IOGI	LJ24	193
D-IOHL	**C52A**	**0233**
D-IOMP	C525	0143
D-IOWA	**C525**	**0624**
(D-IPAC)	C52A	0312
D-IPAD	C52A	0382
D-IPCC	C52A	0409
D-IPCC	**C52A**	**0487**
D-IPCH	**C52A**	**0347**
D-IPCS	C525	0264
D-IPHE	E50P	50000040
D-IPMI	C525	0533
(D-IPMM)	C525	0533
D-IPOD	**C525**	**0193**
(D-IPRO)	C510	0413
D-IPVD	**C52A**	**0218**
D-IQXX	**C525**	**0854**
D-IRIZ	**C510**	**0410**
D-IRKE	**C525**	**0123**
D-IRKE	C550	555
D-IRMA	C525	0366
D-IRON	**C525**	**0168**
D-IRSB	**C525**	**0476**
D-IRUN	**C510**	**0424**
D-IRUP	**C550**	**572**
D-IRWR	**C525**	**0118**
D-ISAG	**PRM1**	**RB-221**
D-ISAR	**PRM1**	**RB-148**
(D-ISAS)	PRM1	RB-263
D-ISCH	C525	0040
D-ISCH	**C52A**	**0052**
D-ISCO	**C52A**	**0151**
D-ISCV	**C52A**	**0429**
D-ISEC	C550	177
D-ISGE	PRM1	RB-201
D-ISGW	**C525**	**0070**
D-ISHW	C525	0289
D-ISIO	C510	0296
(D-ISIO)	C510	0321
D-ISIS	C500	583
D-ISJA	**C52A**	**0348**
D-ISJM	**C525**	**0602**
D-ISJP	**C52A**	**0030**
D-ISKM	C500	313
D-ISKO	PRM1	RB-35
(D-ISKY)	C500	501
(D-ISMV)	PRM1	RB-137
D-ISPN	G180	90001
D-ISRM	**C510**	**0035**
D-ISSS	C500	489
D-ISTP	**E50P**	**50000147**
D-ISUN	**C52A**	**0143**
D-ISWA	**C525**	**0236**
D-ISXT	**C510**	**0446**
D-ISXT	PRM1	RB-50
D-ITAN	**C525**	**0399**
D-ITIP	**C525**	**0494**
D-ITMA	**C525**	**0389**
D-ITOP	C52A	0132
D-ITOR	**C52A**	**0364**
D-ITRA	**C525**	**0177**
D-ITSV	C525	0084
D-IUAC	C52A	0106
D-IUCR	E50P	50000372
D-IURH	C525	0196
D-IURS	**C525**	**0343**
D-IUWE	C525	0415
D-IVBG	C525	0310
D-IVHA	C525	0103
(D-IVID)	C525	0188
D-IVIN	C525	0188
D-IVIV	**C52A**	**0518**
D-IVOB	C550	163
D-IVPD	**C525**	**0181**
D-IVVA	C52A	0147
D-IVVB	C52A	0357
D-IVVB	**C52A**	**0500**
(D-IWAJ)	PRM1	RB-211
D-IWAN	C52A	0223
D-IWBL	C52A	0355
(D-IWHA)	C510	0297
D-IWHL	C525	0029
D-IWIL	**C525**	**0221**

D-IWIN	C52A	0231
D-IWIR	**C52A**	**0102**
D-IWPS	C525	0617
D-IWWP	**C52A**	**0444**
(D-IWWP)	C52A	0470
D-IWWW	**PRM1**	**RB-89**
D-IZZZ	**C525**	**0671**

Angola

D2-...	**HS25**	**257201**
D2-AJL	C500	071
D2-ANG	**GLEX**	**9232**
D2-ANT	**F900**	**159**
D2-EAA	HS25	HA-0097
D2-EAH	**BE40**	**RK-399**
D2-EBA	**C560**	**0502**
D2-EBB	FA20	296/507
D2-EBN	**LJ45**	**069**
(D2-EBR)	CL65	5770
D2-ECB	**GLF3**	**474**
D2-ECE	**C550**	**550-1008**
D2-EDC	C500	071
D2-EFM	**HS25**	**25260**
D2-EPC	**LJ60**	**294**
D2-EPI	**C550**	**550-0958**
D2-EPL	**C680**	**0293**
D2-ESV	FA20	262
D2-EXR	HS25	25215
D2-EZR	**C750**	**0173**
D2-FEZ	**HS25**	**25171**
D2-FFH	HS25	25219
D2-FFX	**LJ45**	**066**
D2-GES	**C550**	**550-1135**
D2-JMM	**FA20**	**54**
D2-SRR	**LJ45**	**092**

Comores

D6-ECB	CRVT	15

Spain

(EC-...)	C510	0332
(EC-...)	C525	0096
(EC-...)	HS25	25058
EC-113	FA20	204
EC-115	HS25	256034
EC-121	HS25	256023
EC-165	FA20	221
EC-168	FA50	209
EC-183	HS25	256039
EC-193	HS25	258022
EC-232	JSTR	5202
EC-235	F900	115
EC-254	WW24	335
EC-261	C525	0133
EC-263	FA20	149
EC-272	HS25	256012
EC-319	HS25	256062
EC-339	ASTR	042
EC-349	HS25	256063
EC-353	FA10	4
EC-363	GLF2	237/43
EC-375	HS25	257040
EC-411	C560	0062
EC-413	HS25	257040
EC-500	C500	331
EC-551	FA20	128/436
EC-617	F900	93
EC-621	C550	667
EC-697	JSTR	5062/12
EC-704	C525	0065
EC-743	C550	131
EC-765	F900	97
EC-777	C550	678
EC-855	FA20	117
EC-949	FA10	17
EC-BVV	FA20	219/470
EC-BXV	FA20	222/471
EC-BZV	FA20	253/486
EC-CCY	C500	082
EC-CGG	C500	108
EC-CIM	LJ25	149
EC-CJA	LJ24	287
EC-CJH	C500	116
EC-CKD	LJ25	038
EC-CKR	LJ25	184
EC-CLS	LJ35	005
EC-CMU	HS25	25271
EC-CQT	HS25	256045
EC-CTV	FA20	332/525
EC-DEB	LJ35	137
EC-DFA	LJ35	196
EC-DJC	LJ35	278
EC-DOH	C550	278
EC-DQC	CRVT	24
EC-DQE	CRVT	26
EC-DQG	CRVT	27
EC-DSI	LJ55	045
EC-DUE	CRVT	30
EC-DUF	CRVT	32
EC-DYE	CRVT	31
EC-EAC	HS25	256005
EC-EAO	HS25	256039
EC-EAP	C650	0125
EC-EAS	C650	0122
EC-EAV	HS25	256032
EC-EBM	LJ25	027
EC-EBR	C500	089
EC-ECB	FA20	210
EC-EDC	**FA20**	**6**
"EC-EDC"	FA20	220
EC-EDL	FA20	220
EC-EDN	**C500**	**370**
EC-EDO	FA20	50
EC-EEU	FA20	218
EC-EFI	FA20	189
EC-EFR	FA20	183
EC-EGL	HS25	256023
EC-EGM	FA20	204
EC-EGS	HS25	256034
EC-EGT	HS25	25080
EC-EGY	LJ25	373
EC-EHC	FA20	46
EC-EHD	FA20	55/410
EC-EHF	HS25	256011
EC-EIV	FA20	221
EC-EKK	**FA20**	**106**
EC-ELK	HS25	258022
EC-EOQ	HS25	256012
EC-EQP	**FA20**	**149**
EC-EQX	C650	0119
EC-ERJ	HS25	256063
EC-ERX	HS25	256062
EC-ETI	HS25	257040
EC-FAM	FA20	128/436
EC-FDL	C550	667
EC-FEN	F900	93
EC-FES	C550	678
EC-FFO	F900	97
EC-FGX	JSTR	5062/12
EC-FIL	C550	131
EC-FJP	FA20	117
EC-FPG	FA50	209
EC-FPI	F900	115
"EC-FPI"	GLEX	9060
EC-FQX	JSTR	5202
EC-FRV	GLF2	237/43
EC-FTV	FA10	4
EC-FUM	C500	331
EC-FZP	C525	0065
EC-GIA	ASTR	042
EC-GIB	WW24	335
EC-GIE	C525	0133
EC-GJF	**C500**	**482**
EC-GLM	C560	0062
EC-GMO	F9EX	6
EC-GNK	**F2TH**	**37**
EC-GOV	**C560**	**0419**
EC-GPN	FA50	204
EC-GSL	WW24	353
EC-GTR	FA50	268
EC-GTS	**C500**	**037**
EC-GXX	LJ35	263
EC-HAI	LJ55	112
EC-HBC	C525	0264
EC-HBX	C525	0304
EC-HCX	**FA20**	**184/462**
EC-HEG	FA20	494
EC-HFA	C500	209
EC-HFY	C500	157
EC-HGH	GLF4	1021
EC-HGI	**C550**	**596**
EC-HHK	F900	151
EC-HHS	FA50	204
EC-HHZ	CRVT	15
EC-HIA	CRVT	19
EC-HIN	**C525**	**0197**
EC-HJD	C550	310
EC-HJL	HS25	258444
EC-HLB	LJ35	236
EC-HNU	F9EX	62
EC-HOB	**F9EX**	**43**
EC-HPQ	**C500**	**157**
EC-HRH	C500	116
EC-HRO	C550	550-0938
EC-HRQ	HS25	257166
EC-HTR	BE40	RK-293
EC-HVQ	**C525**	**0436**
EC-HVV	**FA10**	**193**
EC-HYI	**F2TH**	**150**
EC-IAB	C525	0037
EC-IAX	**C550**	**176**
EC-IBA	C500	178
EC-IBD	GLEX	9060
EC-IEB	C52A	0064
EC-IFS	GLEX	9089
EC-IIC	LJ35	346
EC-IKP	GLF4	1109
EC-ILK	LJ45	064
EC-IMF	**C550**	**443**
EC-INJ	C500	477
EC-INS	**LJ55**	**133**
EC-IOZ	PRM1	RB-61
EC-IRB	C525	0516
EC-IRU	C56X	5056
EC-IRZ	GLF5	582
EC-ISP	**C500**	**463**
EC-ISQ	**C56X**	**5353**
EC-ISS	C525	0415
EC-IUQ	GLEX	9007
EC-IVJ	**C525**	**0429**
EC-JBB	**F900**	**182**
EC-JBH	FA20	511
EC-JDV	FA20	237/476
EC-JEG	CL30	20025

EC-JFD	C525	0448
EC-JFT	**C560**	**0506**
EC-JGN	GALX	103
EC-JIE	LJ60	284
EC-JIL	**GLEX**	**9146**
EC-JIU	**C525**	**0486**
EC-JJH	FA20	176/458
EC-JJU	C52A	0033
EC-JKL	**MU30**	**A084SA**
EC-JKT	CL61	5060
EC-JMS	C52A	0216
EC-JNV	CL64	5605
EC-JNY	HS25	258748
EC-JNZ	F900	181
EC-JON	**C550**	**209**
EC-JPK	**GLF5**	**5078**
EC-JPN	BE40	RK-428
EC-JPV	LJ60	296
EC-JQE	**GALX**	**125**
EC-JSH	C525	0508
EC-JTH	C550	174
EC-JVB	LJ60	243
EC-JVF	C56X	5564
EC-JVI	F2TH	61
EC-JVM	**LJ60**	**161**
EC-JVR	**F900**	**106**
EC-JXC	**C500**	**278**
EC-JXE	ASTR	158
EC-JXI	C56X	5593
EC-JXR	**F2TH**	**55**
EC-JYG	C680	0087
EC-JYQ	LJ60	249
EC-JYR	GLF5	5116
EC-JYT	**CL64**	**5648**
EC-JYY	LJ40	2026
EC-JZK	C56X	5554
EC-KBC	**GALX**	**145**
EC-KBR	**GLF5**	**5124**
EC-KBZ	**C550**	**678**
EC-KCA	**GALX**	**150**
EC-KES	**C52A**	**0155**
EC-KEY	GLF4	1331
EC-KFA	F900	169
EC-KFS	GLEX	9208
EC-KGE	C500	312
EC-KGX	**C500**	**436**
EC-KHH	PRM1	RB-160
EC-KHP	**C550**	**550-0955**
EC-KJH	GLEX	9094
EC-KJJ	C550	414
EC-KJR	**C550**	**412**
EC-KJS	GLF5	5151
EC-KJV	C525	0143
EC-KKB	C560	0768
EC-KKC	C680	0117
EC-KKD	**BE40**	**RK-533**
EC-KKE	C525	0044
EC-KKK	C560	0770
EC-KKN	GLEX	9084
EC-KKO	**C550**	**550-0992**
EC-KLL	GALX	171
EC-KLS	GLF5	5162
EC-KMF	G150	233
EC-KMK	C680	0178
EC-KMS	G150	237
EC-KMT	HS25	HA-0033
EC-KNL	C510	0053
EC-KOI	C52A	0381
EC-KOL	**C56X**	**5088**
EC-KOR	GALX	177
EC-KOV	C560	0768
EC-KPB	**C56X**	**5753**
EC-KPE	**C56X**	**5764**
EC-KPF	GALX	180
EC-KPJ	**G150**	**243**
EC-KPL	GALX	183
EC-KPP	**FA10**	**209**
EC-KQO	**C52B**	**0234**
EC-KRN	**GALX**	**188**
EC-KRS	BE40	RK-354
EC-KSB	C525	0089
EC-KTK	G150	254
EC-KTV	G150	253
EC-KUM	**GLF5**	**5155**
EC-KVU	GLEX	9016
EC-KXF	GLF5	5203
EC-KXS	HS25	HB-24
EC-LAE	**GALX**	**219**
EC-LAF	C510	0152
EC-LBB	**GALX**	**222**
EC-LBO	**C550**	**634**
EC-LCM	**C525**	**0309**
EC-LCX	**C510**	**0235**
EC-LDE	**C525**	**0644**
EC-LDK	**C510**	**0152**
EC-LDS	ASTR	158
EC-LEB	**GLEX**	**9303**
EC-LEP	**C560**	**0153**
EC-LES	CL30	20243
EC-LET	EA50	000155
EC-LGV	**F2EX**	**198**
EC-LHC	EA50	000152
EC-LII	EA50	000184
EC-LIO	BE40	RK-354
EC-LIY	**GLF5**	**5279**
EC-LJC	**C510**	**0355**
EC-LJP	GLEX	9360
EC-LLV	**FA7X**	**117**
EC-LNM	**GLEX**	**9403**
EC-LNZ	C510	0368
EC-LPP	**C500**	**637**
EC-LQF	**CS55**	**0007**
EC-LTF	**GLEX**	**9464**
EC-LYK	**GLF6**	**6029**
EC-LYL	**C56X**	**6153**
EC-LYO	**GLF5**	**5430**
EC-LZP	**C500**	**312**
EC-LZS	**C510**	**0050**
EC-LZU	**GLF6**	**6066**
EC-MAM	**C550**	**414**
EC-MCF	**C550**	**177**
EC-MHZ	**GLF6**	**6135**
EC-MIT	**CL64**	**5457**
EC-MKH	**GLEX**	**9695**
EC-MLA	F2TS	735
ECT-023	C550	278
ECT-028	LJ35	278

Ireland

(EI-...)	C510	0311
EI-BGW	HS25	25080
EI-BJL	C550	039
EI-BJN	C500	555
EI-BNY	CRVT	11
EI-BRG	HS25	25281
EI-BSA	LJ55	021
(EI-BUN)	C550	555
EI-BUY	C550	555
(EI-BXN)	CL60	1048
(EI-BYD)	CL60	1035
EI-BYM	C500	179
EI-BYN	C550	188
EI-CAH	GLF4	1129
EI-CIR	C550	144
EI-COV	HS25	257178
EI-CVT	GLF4	1419
EI-DAB	C550	550-0917
(EI-DUN)	C560	0197
EI-DXW	LJ60	300
EI-ECE	HS25	258496
EI-ECR	**C52A**	**0438**
(EI-EHN)	E50P	50000060
(EI-EHO)	E50P	50000062
(EI-EHS)	E50P	50000073
(EI-EHT)	E50P	50000076
(EI-EHU)	E50P	50000086
EI-GDL	GLF5	5068
EI-GEM	HS25	258901
EI-GHP	C550	550-0897
EI-GPA	CL60	1016
EI-IAT	LJ60	139
EI-IAU	LJ60	190
EI-IAW	LJ60	218
EI-ICE	BE40	RK-521
EI-IRE	CL64	5515
(EI-JBA)	E50P	50000043
EI-JJJ	HS25	HA-0085
EI-JSK	**GLF6**	**6070**
EI-KJC	HS25	258805
EI-LEO	**C750**	**0232**
EI-LJG	CL61	5023
EI-LJR	F2TH	18
EI-MAS	CL61	5194
EI-MAX	LJ31	233
EI-MED	C550	100
EI-MJC	C52B	0266
(EI-OPM)	C52A	0054
EI-PAL	C550	550-0935
EI-PAX	C56X	5228
EI-REX	LJ60	149
EI-RNJ	HS25	258414
EI-RRR	HS25	257170
EI-SFA	C510	0144
EI-SFB	C510	0145
EI-SFC	C510	0196
EI-SFD	C510	0216
EI-SFE	C510	0217
EI-SNN	C650	0183
EI-SSF	GLEX	9521
EI-SXT	CL61	5159
EI-TAM	CL64	5367
(EI-TAM)	CL61	3006
EI-TAT	**CL65**	**5940**
EI-TDV	F2EX	190
EI-TEN	C750	0227
EI-VIV	LJ60	305
EI-WDC	HS25	25132
EI-WFI	**CL65**	**5812**
EI-WFO	LJ45	368
EI-WGV	GLF5	505
EI-WJN	HS25	257062
EI-WXP	**HS25**	**258382**
EI-XLS	C56X	5666
EI-ZMA	**F9EX**	**134**

Armenia

EK-52526	C52A	0026
EK-B021	HS25	259029

Liberia

(EL-AMJ)	HS25	25125
(EL-ELS)	HS25	25125
EL-VDY1	FA20	245/481
EL-WRT	GLF2	67

Iran

EP-AGX	FA20	283/497
EP-AGY	FA20	286/498
EP-AHK	HS25	25154
EP-AHV	FA20	320/519
EP-AKC	**FA20**	**301/509**
EP-FIC	FA20	334/527
EP-FID	**FA20**	**338/530**
EP-FIE	FA20	251/484
EP-FIF	**FA20**	**320/519**
EP-FIG	FA20	318/518
EP-FSC	**F2EX**	**9**
EP-GVO	MS76	01
EP-HIM	MS76	002
EP-IPA	FA20	251/484
EP-KIA	C500	295
EP-KIC	C550	025
(EP-KID)	C550	025
EP-MNZ	**C52A**	**0026**
EP-PAO	C500	295
EP-PAP	C500	301
(EP-PAQ)	C500	377
EP-PBC	C500	370
EP-SEA	**FA20**	**367/545**
EP-TFA	**FA50**	**101**
EP-TFI	**FA50**	**120**
EP-TTI	**F2EX**	**52**
EP-VAP	FA20	251/484
(EP-VAS)	FA20	318/518
EP-VLP	JSTR	5203
EP-VRP	JSTR	5002
EP-VRP	JSTR	5137
EP-VSP	FA20	318/518

Moldova

ER-KVI	F2EX	27
ER-LGA	LJ35	406
ER-LGB	LJ60	255

Estonia

ES-CMK	**BE40**	**RK-209**
ES-ELI	**C750**	**0115**
ES-III	**LJ60**	**303**
ES-LCC	C510	0186
ES-LUX	C52A	0213
ES-LVA	**LJ60**	**372**
ES-LVC	LJ60	281
ES-NXT	**BE40**	**RK-268**
ES-PHR	**HS25**	**HB-33**
ES-PVC	**LJ60**	**051**
ES-PVD	LJ55	143
ES-PVH	**LJ31**	**162**
ES-PVI	**LJ60**	**275**
ES-PVJ	**LJ60**	**287**
ES-PVP	**LJ60**	**302**
ES-PVS	**LJ60**	**190**
ES-PVT	LJ55	061
ES-PVV	LJ55	011
ES-SKY	C56X	5700
ES-SLS	**F9EX**	**264**
ES-TEP	F2TS	707

Belarus

"EW94228"	CS55	0067

Kyrgyzstan

EX-269	HS25	25269
EX-500	HS25	25269

Turkmenistan

EZ-B021	**HS25**	**259029**
EZ-B022	**CL65**	**5735**
EZ-B023	**CL65**	**5750**

Eritrea

E3-AAT	**GLF2**	**160**

Boznia-Herzegovina

E7-FRA	C550	550-0988
E7-SBA	**C500**	**554**
E7-SMS	**C525**	**0666**

France

F-....	**F2EX**	**161**
F-....	**F9EX**	**184**
(F-....)	C550	195
F-AZLT	**MS76**	**032**
F-AZTL	MS76	085
"F-BAMD"	FA50	1
F-BFDG	FA10	61
F-BGVO	MS76	01
F-BHOK	MS76	03
F-BIHY	FA20	141/441
F-BINR	FA50	2
F-BIPC	FA10	108
(F-BIPF)	FA10	61
F-BJET	MS76	039
F-BJLH	FA10	1
F-BJLV	MS76	072
F-BJLX	MS76	086
F-BJLY	MS76	089
F-BJZQ	MS76	102
F-BJZR	MS76	103
F-BJZS	MS76	104
F-BJZT	MS76	105
F-BJZU	MS76	106
F-BJZV	MS76	107
F-BJZX	MS76	108
(F-BJZY)	MS76	109
(F-BJZZ)	MS76	110
F-BKFB	LJ36	046
(F-BKFB)	C550	195
F-BKMC	HS25	256035
F-BKMF	HS25	25007
F-BLCU	FA20	173
F-BLKB	FA20	01
F-BLKL	MS76	01
F-BLLK	FA20	137
F-BMER	FA50	52
F-BMKH	FA20	6
F-BMKK	FA20	22/404
F-BMSH	FA20	1/401
F-BMSS	FA20	2/402
F-BMSX	FA20	3/403
F-BNDB	FA50	1
F-BNKX	FA20	23
F-BNRE	FA20	53/417
F-BNRG	MS76	101
F-BNRH	FA20	79/415
F-BOED	FA20	41/407
F-BOEF	FA20	13
F-BOFH	FA20	225/472
F-BOHN	MS76	098
F-BOHU	HS25	25025
F-BOJO	MS76	002
F-BOJY	MS76	112
F-BOLX	FA20	62/409
F-BOOA	FA20	67/414
F-BOON	FA20	25/405
F-BOXV	FA20	104/454
F-BPIB	WW24	105
F-BPIO	FA20	141/441
F-BPJB	FA20	145/443
F-BPMC	HS25	25131
F-BPXB	FA10	79
F-BRAL	LJ24	117
F-BRGF	LJ24	289
F-BRHB	FA20	172/456
(F-BRHB)	FA20	73/419
F-BRNL	LJ24	183
F-BRNZ	CRVT	2
F-BRPK	FA20	188/464
F-BRQK	CRVT	9
F-BRUY	GLF2	43
F-BSBU	FA20	263/489
F-BSIM	HS25	25130
F-BSQN	FA10	03
F-BSQU	FA10	1
F-BSRL	LJ24	210
F-BSSL	HS25	25223
F-BSTP	LJ24	026
F-BSTR	FA20	246/482
F-BSUR	LJ25	040
F-BSUX	LJ24	045A
F-BSYF	FA20	25/405
F-BTCY	FA20	13
F-BTDA	WW24	145
F-BTEL	C550	209
F-BTMF	FA20	184/462
F-BTML	FA20	67/414
F-BTQK	LJ24	053
F-BTQZ	FA20	58
F-BTTK	CRVT	31
F-BTTL	CRVT	28
F-BTTM	CRVT	17
F-BTTN	CRVT	20
F-BTTO	CRVT	18
F-BTTP	CRVT	30
F-BTTQ	CRVT	32
F-BTTR	CRVT	9
F-BTTS	CRVT	11
F-BTTS	CRVT	36
F-BTTT	CRVT	33
F-BTTU	CRVT	22
F-BTTU	CRVT	37
F-BTTV	CRVT	11
F-BTYV	LJ24	206
F-BUAS	CRVT	1
F-BUFG	FA20	175
F-BUFN	LJ24	202
F-BUIC	FA20	138/440
F-BUIX	FA20	245/481
F-BUQN	CRVT	3
F-BUQP	CRVT	4
F-BUUL	C500	136
F-BUUV	LJ24	195
F-BUYE	FA20	288/499
F-BUYI	FA20	86
F-BUYL	C500	133
F-BUYP	HS25	256033
F-BVEC	LJ24	271
F-BVFV	FA20	182/461
F-BVPA	CRVT	5
F-BVPB	CRVT	6
F-BVPC	CRVT	12
F-BVPD	CRVT	13
F-BVPE	CRVT	21
F-BVPF	CRVT	23
F-BVPG	CRVT	25
F-BVPH	CRVT	27
F-BVPI	CRVT	24
F-BVPJ	CRVT	29
F-BVPK	**CRVT**	**7**
F-BVPL	CRVT	19
F-BVPM	FA20	294/506
F-BVPN	FA20	311/515
F-BVPO	CRVT	10
F-BVPQ	FA20	315/517
F-BVPR	FA10	5
F-BVPS	CRVT	14
F-BVPT	CRVT	16
F-BXAG	FA10	7
F-BXPT	LJ24	014
F-BXQL	MS76	105
F-BYAL	LJ25	084
F-BYCC	FA10	76
F-BYCR	CRVT	34
F-BYCV	FA10	93
F-BYFB	HS25	257166
F-GAJD	LJ24	187
F-GAMA	LJ24	023
F-GAPC	FA20	184/462
F-GAPY	LJ24	027
F-GASL	HS25	257022
F-GATF	FA20	401
(F-GBBV)	LJ24	109
F-GBGD	LJ36	016
F-GBIZ	FA50	3
F-GBLA	LJ24	190
F-GBLZ	LJ24	239
F-GBMB	LJ35	018
F-GBMD	FA20	375/547
F-GBMH	FA10	103
F-GBMS	FA20	175
F-GBOL	**GLEX**	**9500**
F-GBPG	FA20	106
F-GBPL	C550	063
F-GBRF	FA10	38
(F-GBRF)	FA50	5
F-GBTA	LJ24	017
F-GBTC	FA10	124
F-GBTI	FA10	24
F-GBTL	C550	068
F-GBTM	**FA20**	**397/555**
F-GCGU	FA20	136/439
F-GCGY	FA20	145/443
F-GCLE	LJ35	108
(F-GCLT)	LJ35	313
F-GCMS	LJ35	257
F-GCSZ	C550	195
F-GCTT	FA10	127
F-GDAE	LJ24	105
F-GDAV	LJ24	017
F-GDAY	CRVT	26
F-GDAZ	CRVT	35
F-GDCN	LJ35	432
F-GDCP	LJ35	071
F-GDFE	FA50	56
F-GDFJ	FA20	362
F-GDHK	GLF3	340
F-GDHR	LJ55	070
F-GDLO	FA20	315/517
F-GDLR	FA10	121
F-GDLU	FA20	314/516
(F-GDRC)	CRVT	19
F-GDRN	FA10	152
F-GDRR	PRM1	RB-269
F-GDSA	FA10	202
F-GDSB	FA20	482
(F-GDSC)	FA50	123
F-GDSD	FA20	487
F-GDUB	CRVT	15
F-GECI	LJ24	219
F-GECR	HS25	25128
F-GEDB	FA10	197
F-GEFB	C550	195
F-GEFS	FA20	486
F-GEJR	FA20	473
(F-GEJX)	FA20	300/508
F-GELA	FA10	16
F-GELE	FA10	69
F-GELS	FA10	208
F-GELT	**FA10**	**211**
F-GEOY	FA50	78
F-GEPL	C500	164
F-GEPQ	CRVT	19
F-GEQF	CRVT	15
F-GERO	FA10	179
F-GERT	FA20	96
F-GESL	HS25	258016
F-GESP	F2TH	119
F-GESZ	C500	443
F-GEXE	FA50	145
F-GEXF	FA20	401
F-GFAY	FA20	496
F-GFBG	FA10	157
F-GFDB	HS25	25131
F-GFDH	CRVT	13
F-GFEJ	CRVT	10
F-GFFP	FA10	160
F-GFFS	FA20	474
F-GFGB	FA10	177
F-GFGQ	FA50	104
F-GFHG	FA10	126
(F-GFHG)	FA10	113
F-GFHH	FA10	113
(F-GFHH)	FA10	126
F-GFJC	F900	2
(F-GFJK)	FA10	108
F-GFJL	C550	470

(F-GFLL)	FA20	162/451
F-GFMD	FA10	136
F GFMP	HS25	25125
F-GFMZ	LJ25	182
(F-GFPD)	CRVT	11
F-GFPF	FA10	68
F-GFPO	C550	114
F-GFUN	FA20	162/451
F-GGAL	**C650**	**0117**
F-GGAR	FA10	115
(F-GGAR)	FA20	496
F-GGBL	FA20	379
F-GGCP	FA50	9
F-GGFO	FA20	76
F-GGGA	**C550**	**586**
F-GGGT	**C550**	**611**
F-GGKE	FA20	118
F-GGMM	FA20	300/508
F-GGPG	LJ24	327
(F-GGRA)	FA10	179
(F-GGRG)	LJ35	174
F-GGRH	F900	5
F-GGVB	FA50	11
F-GGVR	FA10	138
F-GHAE	LJ35	413
F-GHAQ	FA50	149
F-GHBT	FA20	160/450
F-GHCR	FA20	313
F-GHDN	FA20	77/429
F-GHDT	FA20	176/458
F-GHDX	FA10	140
F-GHDZ	FA10	17
F-GHEA	F900	33
F-GHER	FA10	88
F-GHFB	FA10	169
(F-GHFI)	FA10	43
F-GHFO	FA10	33
F-GHFP	FA20	119/431
F-GHFQ	FA20	279/502
F-GHGO	F2TH	49
F-GHGO	F900	110
F-GHGT	FA50	21
F-GHHG	HS25	257055
(F-GHJL)	FA10	58
F-GHLN	FA20	255/487
F-GHLT	FA10	92
F-GHMD	FA20	345
F-GHMP	LJ35	048
F-GHPA	FA20	170/455
F-GHPB	FA10	215
F-GHPL	FA10	147
(F-GHPO)	FA20	271/493
(F-GHRE)	FA20	171
F-GHRV	FA10	48
F-GHSG	FA20	77/429
F-GHSK	FA10	218
F-GHTD	F900	96
F-GHTK	FA20	368
(F-GHUA)	C550	028
F-GHVK	FA10	146
F-GHVR	FA20	262
F-GHYB	F900	103
(F-GIBT)	FA20	300/508
F-GICB	FA20	171
F-GICF	FA20	120
F-GICN	FA50	210
F-GIDC	FA50	116
F-GIDE	F900	1
F-GIFL	FA10	217
F-GIFP	FA20	259
(F-GIHT)	C500	067
(F-GIHU)	C500	201
F-GIJG	FA10	118
F-GILM	CRVT	32
F-GIPH	**FA10**	**194**
(F-GIPH)	FA10	166
F-GIQP	FA10	43
F-GIQZ	FA50	107
(F-GIRH)	CRVT	14
(F-GIRS)	C500	308
(F-GIRS)	C550	341
(F-GIRZ)	F900	30
F-GISH	**C510**	**0182**
(F-GIVD)	FA50	251
F-GIVR	F900	62
F-GIVT	FA20	32
F-GJAP	CRVT	31
F-GJAS	**CRVT**	**8**
(F-GJBR)	FA20	77/429
F-GJBT	F900	32
F-GJBZ	FA50	269
F-GJCC	FA20	72/413
F-GJDB	**FA20**	**76**
F-GJDE	HS25	25131
F-GJDG	C500	312
F-GJEA	FA20	360
F-GJEK	FA50	228
F-GJFB	FA10	166
F-GJFZ	FA10	19
F-GJGB	FA10	47
F-GJHG	FA10	181
F-GJHJ	F2TH	2
F-GJHK	FA10	108
(F-GJIS)	FA20	514
F-GJJL	FA10	118
F-GJJS	FA20	264
(F-GJKT)	FA50	21
F-GJLA	FA20	133
F-GJLB	CRVT	39
F-GJLL	FA10	22
F-GJLQ	FA7X	68
F-GJMA	FA10	116
(F-GJMA)	FA10	65
F-GJOB	**C550**	**144**
(F-GJPI)	FA20	257
F-GJPM	F900	66
F-GJPR	FA20	5
F-GJRH	F900	106
F-GJRN	FA10	163
F-GJSC	F2TH	74
F-GJSF	FA20	299
F-GJSK	F2TH	27
F-GJTG	F2TH	55
F-GJTH	F2TH	61
(F-GJTR)	FA50	140
F-GJXX	C560	0070
F-GJYD	C550	414
F-GKAE	FA10	213
(F-GKAF)	FA20	120
F-GKAL	FA20	455
F-GKAR	FA50	204
F-GKAY	F900	54
F-GKBC	FA10	99
F-GKBQ	F900	130
F-GKBZ	FA50	185
F-GKCC	FA10	201
(F-GKCD)	FA10	88
(F-GKCJ)	BE40	RK-14
F-GKDB	FA20	271/493
F-GKDD	FA20	257
F-GKDI	F900	106
F-GKDR	FA50	86
F-GKGA	CRVT	11
(F-GKGB)	CRVT	30
F-GKGD	CRVT	34
F-GKGL	C560	0058
F-GKGO	FA50	155
F-GKHJ	**F900**	**11**
F-GKHL	C560	0059
F-GKID	**C500**	**319**
"F-GKIL"	C500	319
(F-GKIN)	FA50	286
F-GKIP	F2TH	90
F-GKIR	C500	361
F-GKIS	FA20	307/513
F-GKJB	CRVT	20
F-GKJL	C560	0093
F-GKJS	C650	0232
F-GKLV	FA10	41
F-GKME	FA20	256
F-GKOM	**F900**	**130**
F-GKPB	FA10	207
F-GKPP	MS76	098
(F-GKPZ)	FA10	201
F-GKRU	FA50	235
F-GKTV	FA50	111
F-GLEC	CRVT	30
F-GLGY	F900	11
F-GLHI	F900	166
(F-GLHJ)	F2TH	12
F-GLIM	C560	0119
(F-GLIM)	C560	0156
F-GLJA	C500	264
F-GLJV	F9EX	76
F-GLMD	FA20	117
F-GLMM	FA20	116
(F-GLMT)	FA20	246/482
F-GLMU	F900	35
F-GLNL	FA20	94/428
(F-GLOR)	BE40	RK-37
F-GLOS	**C510**	**0169**
(F-GLPD)	BE40	RK-37
F-GLSA	FA50	348
F-GLSJ	FA50	107
F-GLTK	**C550**	**609**
F-GLYC	C560	0205
F-GLYD	F9EX	263
F-GLYO	BE40	RK-14
F-GMCI	C550	052
F-GMCK	F2TH	46
F-GMCU	FA50	37
F-GMDL	C525	0400
F-GMDS	F9EX	230
(F-GMEX)	F2EX	1
F-GMGA	FA50	51
F-GMIR	C52A	0322
(F-GMIR)	F2TH	
F-GMJS	FA10	80
F-GMLH	C500	308
F-GMMC	C525	0448
F-GMOE	F2TH	1
F-GMOF	CRVT	12
F-GMOH	**F900**	**7**
F-GMOT	**FA50**	**111**
F-GMPR	F2TH	18
F-GMTJ	**C510**	**0222**
(F-GNAB)	C500	337
F-GNAF	CRVT	15
F-GNBL	F2TH	36
F-GNCJ	C525	0024
(F-GNCO)	F9EX	97
F-GNCP	C550	004
F-GNDA	F900	88
(F-GNDB)	HS25	257127
F-GNDK	F900	35
F-GNDO	F2TH	187
F-GNDZ	**FA10**	**17**
F-GNFF	FA50	228
F-GNFI	F900	118
(F-GNFS)	FA50	228
F-GNGL	FA50	230
F-GNLF	C550	114
F-GNLR	FA50	232
F-GNMF	F900	47
(F-GNMF)	FA20	511
F-GNMO	FA50	240
F-GNMR	F900	143
F-GNVK	**F9EX**	**138**
F-GOAB	F900	130
(F-GOAK)	GLEX	9115
F-GOAL	FA50	131
F-GOBE	FA20	515
F-GOBZ	FA20	293
F-GOCT	FA50	134
F-GODB	HS25	257127
F-GODE	F900	133
F-GODO	F2TH	65
F-GODP	FA50	275
(F-GOEA)	F9EX	97
(F-GOEI)	F900	1
(F-GOEV)	F900	5
(F-GOFC)	F900	47
F-GOFX	**F900**	**145**
F-GOGL	FA50	134
(F-GOJI)	FA10	161
F-GOJT	FA20	501
F-GOLV	FA50	215
(F-GOND)	FA50	251
F-GOPM	**FA20**	**302/510**
(F-GOTF)	F2EX	78
(F-GOVV)	GLEX	9005
F-GOYA	F9EX	11
F-GPAA	**FA20**	**103/423**
F-GPAB	FA20	254
F-GPAD	**FA20**	**280/503**
F-GPAE	FA20	356
F-GPAK	GLF4	1061
F-GPAM	F2TH	6
F-GPAX	F900	125
F-GPBG	FA50	269
F-GPEB	**C525**	**0533**
F-GPFC	C525	0101
F-GPFD	FA10	221
F-GPGK	**F900**	**69**
F-GPGL	**FA10**	**203**
F-GPGS	FA50	151
F-GPIM	FA20	30
F-GPLA	**CRVT**	**28**
F-GPLF	C525	0291
(F-GPLH)	FA50	131
F-GPLT	C550	033
(F-GPNG)	FA20	116
F-GPNJ	**F9EX**	**50**
F-GPPF	**FA50**	**65**
F-GPSA	FA50	123
(F-GPSS)	C52A	0171
F-GPUJ	C52A	0169
F-GRAX	F900	120
F-GRCH	C500	201
F-GRCV	F9DX	609
F-GRDP	F900	169
F-GRET	**C510**	**0141**
F-GREX	F9EX	1
F-GROC	FA20	279/502
F-GRON	HS25	257166
F-GRRM	C525	0166
F-GRUJ	C52B	0117
F-GSAA	F2TH	36
F-GSAB	F900	161
(F-GSAD)	F900	163
(F-GSAE)	F2TH	26
F-GSAI	F9EX	31
F-GSCN	F900	62
F-GSCR	**C52B**	**0264**
F-GSDA	F9EX	106
F-GSDP	F9EX	43
F-GSEF	F9EX	121
F-GSER	FA50	2
F-GSGL	**C52B**	**0178**
F-GSLZ	**FA10**	**208**
F-GSMC	C500	308
F-GSMF	F900	142
F-GSMG	**C52B**	**0230**
F-GSMT	F9EX	155
F-GSNA	**F9EX**	**145**
F-GSNK	F900	115
F-GSXF	FA20	315/517
F-GSYC	F2TH	27
F-GTCD	FA50	107
F-GTDA	F2EX	231
F-GTDK	F2EX	237
F-GTFB	**C510**	**0335**
F-GTGJ	F900	105
F-GTHS	FA50	155
F-GTJF	FA50	246
F-GTMD	C525	0312
F-GTOD	**FA10**	**155**
F-GTRY	**C525**	**0359**
F-GUAE	FA50	104
F-GUAJ	FA50	169
(F-GUDA)	F9EX	165
F-GUDC	F2EX	49
F-GUDN	F2EX	5
F-GUDP	FA50	134
F-GUEQ	F900	167
F-GUFM	F2EX	28
F-GUHB	F2EX	18
F-GUJC	FA7X	86
F-GUJP	F2TH	144
(F-GULK)	F2TH	191
F-GUPH	F2EX	75
F-GUTC	F2EX	42
F-GUTD	F2EX	8
F-GUYM	F2TH	191
F-GVAE	F900	86
F-GVBF	F900	154
F-GVBK	**PRM1**	**RB-73**
(F-GVDA)	F2TH	121
F-GVDN	FA50	264
F-GVDP	F9EX	51
F-GVEL	F2EX	191
F-GVFL	F9EX	183
F-GVFX	F2EX	195
F-GVIA	HS25	258855
F-GVJR	FA20	180/460
F-GVMI	**GLEX**	**9456**
F-GVML	GLEX	9081
F-GVMO	F900	78
F-GVMV	GLEX	9202
F-GVNG	F2EX	114
(F-GVRB)	FA7X	34
F-GVTC	F2TH	166
F-GVUJ	**C52B**	**0156**
F-GVVB	**C52B**	**0300**
F-GVYC	**C56X**	**5682**
F-GXBV	**F9EX**	**75**
F-GXDA	F2TH	229
F-GXDP	F2TH	119
F-GXDZ	F900	120
F-GXHG	F9EX	78
F-GXJC	F2TH	1
F-GXMC	**FA50**	**190**
F-GXMF	F900	181
F-GXRK	**C525**	**0229**
F-GXRL	C52A	0019
F-GXRM	F900	142
F-GXTM	**FA50**	**165**
(F-GXXX)	C56X	5104
F-GYBJ	FA7X	144
(F-GYBM)	FA50	16
F-GYCA	FA20	240/478
F-GYCM	F9EX	103
F-GYCP	F900	135
F-GYDA	FA7X	19
(F-GYDP)	F9EX	75
F-GYFC	C52B	0176
F-GYMC	FA20	307/513
F-GYOL	FA50	88
F-GYPB	FA20	307/513
F-GYRB	F9EX	113
F-GYSL	FA20	341
(F-GZAK)	F2TH	187
F-GZBJ	F2EX	214
F-GZJR	F2TH	191
F-GZLC	C550	209
F-GZLP	FA7X	5
F-GZLX	**F2EX**	**75**
F-GZME	F900	54
F-GZUJ	C52A	0200
F-GZVA	F9EX	237
F-HAAP	F900	142
F-HACA	C550	195
(F-HACD)	C56X	5104
F-HACP	LJ45	287
F-HADA	C525	0041
F-HADH	**FA50**	**11**
F-HADT	**C510**	**0108**
(F-HAFC)	C52B	0176
F-HAGA	C52B	0258
F-HAGH	**C525**	**0518**
F-HAHA	**C510**	**0405**
F-HAIR	FA50	37
F-HAJD	**C525**	**0523**
F-HAJV	**C550**	**622**
F-HAJX	**C550**	**347**
F-HAKA	FA7X	19
F-HAKP	CL30	20288
F-HALG	**F2EX**	**290**
F-HALM	**FA50**	**134**
F-HALO	C525	0484
F-HAMG	**C52A**	**0193**
F-HAOA	C525	0024
F-HAPM	FA50	346
F-HAPN	**FA50**	**347**
F-HAPP	C52A	0009
F-HASC	C525	0177
F-HASF	C52A	0015
F-HAST	PRM1	RB-149
F-HATB	F9DX	616
F-HATG	**C52C**	**0115**
F-HAVB	LJ60	170
F-HAXA	**F9EX**	**12**
F-HBBM	FA50	16
F-HBDA	F9EX	200
F-HBDX	**E55P**	**50500216**
F-HBER	C52B	0183
F-HBFA	PRM1	RB-83
F-HBFK	**C550**	**625**
(F-HBFL)	F9EX	249
F-HBFP	**HS25**	**258689**
F-HBIP	F2EX	228
F-HBIR	**C510**	**0252**
F-HBMB	C550	352
F-HBMR	**C550**	**717**
F-HBMS	C500	312
F-HBOL	F9EX	107
F-HBOM	HS25	258392
F-HBPP	**C52B**	**0013**
F-HBSC	C525	0508
(F-HBSC)	C525	0505
F-HCBM	F9EX	174
(F-HCCN)	C550	625
F-HCCP	C52A	0434
F-HCCX	FA7X	42
F-HCDD	**FA50**	**297**
F-HCEF	**FA50**	**306**
F-HCGD	LJ45	328
F-HCIC	**C52B**	**0224**
F-HCJE	**E50P**	**50000263**
F-HCJP	PRM1	RB-228
F-HCLS	FA7X	71
F-HCPB	**C525**	**0322**
F-HCRK	F2TS	707
F-HCRM	**FA7X**	**28**
F-HCRT	**C550**	**280**
F-HCSL	HS25	258385
F-HDCB	FA50	204
F-HDDP	**F9EX**	**277**
(F-HDFS)	F2TH	230
F-HDGT	C550	634
F-HDLJ	**F9EX**	**165**
F-HDMB	C500	308
(F-HDMG)	E50P	50000120
F-HDOM	F9EX	109
F-HDPB	**FA50**	**334**
F-HDPN	**C510**	**0163**
F-HDPO	FA7X	4
F-HDPY	**C510**	**0149**
F-HDSD	**F900**	**188**
F-HEBO	**F9EX**	**236**
F-HECD	**FA7X**	**134**
F-HECG	C510	0354
F-HEFG	F2EX	185
F-HEKO	C52A	0080
F-HEND	**C510**	**0161**
F-HEOL	C52A	0219
F-HEQA	C525	0024
F-HERE	**C510**	**0194**
F-HEXR	**FA7X**	**223**
F-HFBY	**GLEX**	**9188**
F-HFDA	**FA7X**	**5**
F-HFIP	**GLEX**	**9567**
F-HFLX	F2TH	121
F-HFMA	C525	0423
F-HFMB	FA50	185
F-HFOX	F9EX	118
F-HFRA	**C500**	**424**
F-HGBT	GLEX	9020
F-HGBY	HS25	HA-0090
F-HGHF	FA7X	207
F-HGLO	**C52C**	**0114**
F-HGOL	C525	0351
F-HHHH	C550	348
F-HHSC	C525	0499
F-HIBF	**C510**	**0262**
F-HIBR	**F9EX**	**271**
F-HICM	**C510**	**0388**
F-HIJD	**C52A**	**0462**
F-HIKJ	F2EX	103
F-HINC	**LJ45**	**488**
F-HIPE	**E55P**	**50500016**
F-HIPK	**FA7X**	**258**
F-HISI	**FA50**	**169**
F-HITM	**BE40**	**RK-501**
F-HIVA	**C525**	**0235**
F-HJAV	**C525**	**0473**
F-HJBR	**E55P**	**50500278**
F-HJCD	**F2EX**	**288**
F-HJFG	**E55P**	**50500099**
F-HJJB	F900	35
F-HJLM	**E55P**	**50500304**
F-HJMD	**F9EX**	**283**
F-HJYL	**FA20**	**307/513**
F-HKIL	**C510**	**0346**
F-HKLB	F2TH	133
F-HKMO	**F900**	**89**
F-HKRA	**C525**	**0661**
(F-HLBG)	FA7X	234
F-HLDB	**F2EX**	**136**
F-HLDS	F2EX	253
F-HLIM	**C560**	**0683**
F-HLIV	FA7X	54
F-HLJP	PRM1	RB-83
F-HLPM	**F2EX**	**282**
F-HLPN	**F2EX**	**296**
F-HLRY	**E50P**	**50000354**
F-HLTI	**FA7X**	**108**
F-HLXS	F2EX	269
F-HMBG	**C52A**	**0142**
F-HMCG	F2TS	703
F-HMCH	F9EX	141
F-HMED	**HS25**	**259026**
F-HMJC	C525	0250
F-HMML	**E55P**	**50500247**
F-HMOB	CL65	5865

F-HMOD	**FA7X**	**106**
F-HMPR	**C52A**	**0214**
F-HMSG	**C52A**	**0033**
F-HNCY	**PRM1**	**RB-230**
F-HNDO	F9EX	281
(F-HNFG)	FA7X	2
F-HNLX	F9EX	277
F-HOCI	F900	1
F-HOME	F2EX	253
F-HOSB	**HS25**	**HB-27**
F-HOUR	**C510**	**0354**
F-HPAD	F2EX	63
F-HPEB	**LJ40**	**2080**
F-HPHD	C510	0262
F-HPJL	**E55P**	**50500274**
F-HPKR	F2EX	200
F-HRAY	**F9EX**	**288**
F-HRCA	**C525**	**0650**
F-HREX	**HS25**	**258335**
F-HRSC	**C52A**	**0355**
F-HSAM	**F2EX**	**230**
F-HSAS	**FA7X**	**119**
F-HSBL	**E50P**	**50000353**
F-HSHA	**C510**	**0413**
F-HSTF	FA7X	166
F-HTMS	F9DX	609
F-HTTP	**PRM1**	**RB-196**
F-HUBB	**F9EX**	**150**
F-HUNT	FA50	289
F-HVBL	**FA7X**	**188**
F-HVIB	**FA7X**	**47**
F-HVON	FA7X	113
F-HVRO	F9EX	283
F-HXRG	**GLEX**	**9323**

France D'Outremer

F-OBYG	CRVT	39
F-OBZP	CRVT	29
F-OBZR	CRVT	7
F-OBZV	CRVT	25
F-OCDE	CRVT	36
(F-OCGK)	HS25	25025
F-OCJL	CRVT	19
F-OCRN	CRVT	9
F-ODEO	FA50	78
F-ODFE	CRVT	22
F-ODFQ	CRVT	26
F-ODHA	FA20	175
F-ODIF	CRVT	38
F-ODJS	CRVT	40
F-ODJX	CRVT	5
F-ODKS	CRVT	11
F-ODOK	FA20	162/451
F-ODSK	FA20	94/428
F-ODSR	CRVT	35
F-ODTM	CRVT	17
F-ODUT	C550	052
F-OGJL	CRVT	6
F-OGSI	FA20	511
F-OGSR	FA20	496
(F-OGUO)	C550	375
(F-OGVA)	C550	375
F-OHAH	C555	0094
F-OHCJ	FA20	341
F-OHES	FA20	514
F-OHFO	FA50	267
F-OHRU	C560	0407
(F-OIBA)	F2TH	65
(F-OIBE)	F9EX	20
F-OIBL	F9EX	6
(F-OINA)	F9EX	91
F-OKSI	FA50	241
F-OKSY	FA50	257
F-OLET	FA20	511
F-OMON	FA50	230
F-ONCP	**C52C**	**0164**
F-ONYY	**C52A**	**0320**
F-ORAV	F2TH	171
F-ORAX	F2TH	121
F-OVJR	FA20	180/460

France – Military Callsigns

F-EXAA	MS76	112
F-FBLW	MS76	024
F-RAEA	FA20	260/488
F-RAEB	FA20	167/453
F-RAEB	FA20	268/492
F-RAEC	FA20	291/505
F-RAEC	**FA20**	**342/532**
F-RAEC	FA20	93/435
F-RAED	FA20	238/477
F-RAED	FA20	93/435
F-RAEE	FA20	238/477
F-RAEF	FA20	268/492
F-RAEG	FA20	291/505
F-RAEG	FA20	342/532
F-RAEH	**FA20**	**422**
F-RAFA	**FA7X**	**68**
F-RAFB	**FA7X**	**86**
F-RAFC	**F2EX**	**231**
F-RAFD	**F2EX**	**237**
F-RAFI	FA50	5
F-RAFJ	FA20	49/408
F-RAFJ	FA50	2
F-RAFJ	FA50	78
F-RAFK	FA20	154/447
F-RAFK	FA20	268/492
F-RAFK	FA50	27
F-RAFL	FA20	167/453
F-RAFL	FA50	34
F-RAFM	FA20	238/477
F-RAFN	FA20	93/435
F-RAFP	**F900**	**2**
F-RAFQ	**F900**	**4**
F-RAFU	**FA20**	**309/514**
F-RABQ	MS76	020
F-RABZ	MS76	037
F-RAFN	FA20	93/435
F-RBL.	MS76	082
F-RBL.	MS76	094
F-RBL.	MS76	095
F-RBLB	MS76	058
F-RBLC	MS76	029
F-RBLD	MS76	044
F-RBLD	MS76	093
F-RBLE	MS76	071
F-RBLF	MS76	065
F-RBLF	MS76	070
F-RBLG	MS76	056
F-RBLH	MS76	097
F-RBLL	MS76	081
F-RBLN	MS76	026
F-RBLP	MS76	077
F-RBLU	MS76	091
F-RBLU	MS76	096
F-RBLV	MS76	062
F-RBLW	MS76	030
F-RBLY	MS76	061
F-RBLY	MS76	078
F-RBLZ	MS76	075
F-RBQA	FA20	93/435
F-RCAL	FA20	422
F-RCAP	FA20	291/505
F-RHD.	MS76	080
F-RHDA	MS76	092
F-RHDD	MS76	053
F-RHDE	MS76	027
F-RHDF	MS76	014
F-RHFA	FA20	49/408
F-SCA.	MS76	054
F-SCA.	MS76	059
F-SCAC	MS76	057
F-SCAP	MS76	025
F-SCAR	MS76	019
F-SCAS	MS76	038
F-SCAT	MS76	060
F-SCB.	MS76	045
F-SCBB	MS76	034
F-SCBC	**MS76**	**035**
F-SCCC	MS76	036
F-SDDB	MS76	001
F-SDDC	MS76	051
F-SDDO	MS76	023
F-SDIA	MS76	03
F-SDIB	MS76	001
F-SDIC	MS76	020
F-SEBH	CRVT	19
F-SEBI	FA20	315/517
F-TEOA	FA20	49/408
F-UGWL	FA20	115/432
F-UGWM	FA20	186/463
F-UGWN	FA20	451
F-UGWP	FA20	309/514
F-UKJA	FA20	182/461
F-UKJC	FA20	451
F-UKJE	FA20	186/463
F-UKJG	FA20	115/432
F-UKJI	**FA20**	**483**
F-V10F	FA10	5
F-YCB.	MS76	031
F-YDJ?	MS76	012

France – Temporary

F-WAMD	FA30	01
F-WAMD	FA50	1
F-WATF	FA20	362
F-WBTM	FA20	397/555
F-WDCP	LJ35	071
F-WDFE	FA50	56
F-WDFJ	FA20	362
(F-WDHA)	FA20	401
F-WDHK	GLF3	340
F-WDSB	FA20	482
F-WEDB	FA10	197
F-WEFS	FA50	34
F-WEFX	F900	11
F-WFAL	FA10	01
F-WFBW	**FA7X**	**1**
F-WFJC	F900	2
F-WFJC	FA50	3
F-WFPD	CRVT	11
F-WGDZ	FA20	482
F-WGSR	FA20	496
F-WGTF	FA10	48
F-WGTF	FA20	511
F-WGTF	FA20	77/429
F-WGTF	FA50	131
F-WGTF	FA50	140
F-WGTG	FA10	204
F-WGTG	FA20	474
F-WGTG	FA50	27
F-WGTG	FA50	73
F-WGTH	F900	30
F-WGTH	FA20	116
F-WGTH	FA50	29
F-WGTM	FA20	176/458
F-WGVO	MS76	01
F-WHLU	FA7X	113
F-WHLV	F900	130
F-WHLV	F900	181
F-WHLV	F9EX	152
F-WHLV	FA7X	42
F-WHLX	F2TH	101
F-WHLX	F2TH	103
F-WHLX	F2TH	133
F-WHLX	F2TH	42
F-WHLY	F2TH	111
F-WIDE	F900	1
F-WIDE	**FA5X**	**1**
F-WIET	MS76	001
F-WIFA	CRVT	15
(F-WIFU)	CRVT	11
F-WINR	FA50	2
F-WINT	**G180**	**90003**
F-WJAA	MS76	005
F-WJAA	MS76	026
F-WJAA	MS76	039
F-WJAB	MS76	006
F-WJAC	MS76	008
F-WJAD	MS76	009
F-WJAE	MS76	028
F-WJLH	FA10	1
F-WJMJ	FA10	10
F-WJMJ	FA10	18
F-WJMJ	FA10	25
F-WJMJ	FA10	3
F-WJMJ	FA10	33
F-WJMJ	FA10	36
F-WJMJ	FA10	44
F-WJMJ	FA10	57
F-WJMJ	FA10	65
F-WJMJ	FA10	74
F-WJMJ	FA10	91
F-WJMJ	FA20	112
F-WJMJ	FA20	121
F-WJMJ	FA20	124/433
F-WJMJ	FA20	136/439
F-WJMJ	FA20	144
F-WJMJ	FA20	152/446
F-WJMJ	FA20	165/452
F-WJMJ	FA20	229
F-WJMJ	FA20	321
F-WJMJ	FA20	385
F-WJMJ	FA20	402
F-WJMJ	FA20	407
F-WJMJ	FA20	423
F-WJMJ	FA20	444
F-WJMJ	FA20	456
F-WJMJ	FA20	463
F-WJMJ	FA20	470
F-WJMJ	FA20	83
F-WJMJ	FA20	87/424
F-WJMJ	FA20	97/422
F-WJMK	FA10	11
F-WJMK	FA10	14
F-WJMK	FA10	21
F-WJMK	FA10	26
F-WJMK	FA10	4
F-WJMK	FA20	104/454
F-WJMK	FA20	119/431
F-WJMK	FA20	131/437
F-WJMK	FA20	155
F-WJMK	FA20	188/464
F-WJMK	FA20	211
F-WJMK	FA20	246/482
F-WJMK	FA20	262
F-WJMK	FA20	386
F-WJMK	FA20	403
F-WJMK	FA20	404
F-WJMK	FA20	413
F-WJMK	FA20	426
F-WJMK	FA20	432
F-WJMK	FA20	441
F-WJMK	FA20	448
F-WJMK	FA20	453
F-WJMK	FA20	464
F-WJMK	FA20	471
F-WJMK	FA20	84
F-WJMK	FA20	99
F-WJML	FA10	12
F-WJML	FA10	24
F-WJML	FA10	28
F-WJML	FA10	37
F-WJML	FA10	45
F-WJML	FA10	51
F-WJML	FA10	6
F-WJML	FA10	60
F-WJML	FA10	69
F-WJML	FA20	115/432
F-WJML	FA20	230
F-WJML	FA20	387
F-WJML	FA20	414
F-WJML	FA20	433
F-WJML	FA20	442
F-WJML	FA20	454
F-WJML	FA20	460
F-WJML	FA20	466
F-WJML	FA20	475
F-WJML	FA20	73/419
F-WJMM	FA10	15
F-WJMM	FA10	2
F-WJMM	FA10	29
F-WJMM	FA10	38
F-WJMM	FA10	48
F-WJMM	FA10	58
F-WJMM	FA10	62
F-WJMM	FA10	70
F-WJMM	FA10	71
F-WJMM	FA10	9
F-WJMM	FA20	106
F-WJMM	FA20	114/420
F-WJMM	FA20	129
F-WJMM	FA20	142
F-WJMM	FA20	157
F-WJMM	FA20	213
F-WJMM	FA20	249
F-WJMM	FA20	274
F-WJMM	FA20	388
F-WJMM	FA20	417
F-WJMM	FA20	435
F-WJMM	FA20	445
F-WJMM	FA20	457
F-WJMM	FA20	467
F-WJMM	FA20	476
F-WJMM	FA20	82/418
F-WJMM	FA20	92/421
F-WJMN	FA10	40
F-WJMN	FA10	43
F-WJMN	FA10	59
F-WJMN	FA10	66
F-WJMN	FA10	7
F-WJMN	FA10	8
F-WJMN	FA20	100
F-WJMN	FA20	125
F-WJMN	FA20	146
F-WJMN	FA20	164
F-WJMN	FA20	232
F-WJMN	FA20	264
F-WJMN	FA20	390
F-WJMN	FA20	418
F-WJMN	FA20	436
F-WJMN	FA20	446
F-WJMN	FA20	458
F-WJMN	FA20	478
F-WJMN	FA20	67/414
F-WKAE	FA10	213
F-WLCH	FA20	147/444
F-WLCS	FA10	13
F-WLCS	FA10	17
F-WLCS	FA10	34
F-WLCS	FA10	41
F-WLCS	FA10	50
F-WLCS	FA10	53
F-WLCS	FA20	138/440
F-WLCS	FA20	166
F-WLCS	FA20	206
F-WLCS	FA20	215
F-WLCS	FA20	245/481
F-WLCS	FA20	391
F-WLCS	FA20	447
F-WLCS	FA20	481
F-WLCT	FA10	16
F-WLCT	FA10	30
F-WLCT	FA10	46
F-WLCT	FA10	5
F-WLCT	FA10	64
F-WLCT	FA10	78
F-WLCT	FA20	153
F-WLCT	FA20	216
F-WLCT	FA20	259
F-WLCT	FA20	393
F-WLCT	FA20	416
F-WLCT	FA20	449
F-WLCT	FA20	485
F-WLCU	FA10	19
F-WLCU	FA10	31
F-WLCU	FA10	42
F-WLCU	FA10	67
F-WLCU	FA20	173
F-WLCU	FA20	234/475
F-WLCU	FA20	261
F-WLCV	FA10	20
F-WLCV	FA10	35
F-WLCV	FA10	49
F-WLCV	FA10	68
F-WLCV	FA20	154/447
F-WLCV	FA20	187
F-WLCV	FA20	233
F-WLCV	FA20	415
F-WLCV	FA20	486
F-WLCX	FA10	22
F-WLCX	FA10	27
F-WLCX	FA10	52
F-WLCX	FA10	63
F-WLCX	FA10	72
F-WLCX	FA20	168
F-WLCX	FA20	209
F-WLCX	FA20	240/478
F-WLCX	FA20	265
F-WLCY	FA10	23
F-WLCY	FA10	47
F-WLCY	FA20	183
F-WLCY	FA20	201/469
F-WLCY	FA20	217
F-WLEF	C550	144
F-WLJV	F9EX	76
F-WLKB	FA20	01
F-WLKL	MS76	01
F-WLLK	FA20	137
F-WLMM	FA20	116
F-WMEX	F2EX	1
F-WMGO	FA20	50
F-WMKF	FA20	141/441
F-WMKF	FA20	161
F-WMKF	FA20	17
F-WMKF	FA20	175
F-WMKF	FA20	180/460
F-WMKF	FA20	185/467
F-WMKF	FA20	207
F-WMKF	FA20	250
F-WMKF	FA20	272
F-WMKF	FA20	287
F-WMKF	FA20	297
F-WMKF	FA20	30
F-WMKF	FA20	308
F-WMKF	FA20	316
F-WMKF	FA20	319
F-WMKF	FA20	324
F-WMKF	FA20	335
F-WMKF	FA20	341
F-WMKF	FA20	347
F-WMKF	FA20	352
F-WMKF	FA20	355
F-WMKF	FA20	361/543
F-WMKF	FA20	37/406
F-WMKF	FA20	379
F-WMKF	FA20	38
F-WMKF	FA20	394
F-WMKF	FA20	398
F-WMKF	FA20	4
F-WMKF	FA20	406/557
F-WMKF	FA20	424
F-WMKF	FA20	429
F-WMKF	FA20	474
F-WMKF	FA20	69
F-WMKF	FA20	76
F-WMKF	FA20	93/435
F-WMKG	FA20	110
F-WMKG	FA20	118
F-WMKG	FA20	132
F-WMKG	FA20	148
F-WMKG	FA20	160/450
F-WMKG	FA20	167/453
F-WMKG	FA20	171
F-WMKG	FA20	176/458
F-WMKG	FA20	193
F-WMKG	FA20	227
F-WMKG	FA20	28
F-WMKG	FA20	282
F-WMKG	FA20	289
F-WMKG	FA20	298
F-WMKG	FA20	3/403
F-WMKG	FA20	317
F-WMKG	FA20	325
F-WMKG	FA20	338/530
F-WMKG	FA20	349
F-WMKG	FA20	35
F-WMKG	FA20	356
F-WMKG	FA20	366
F-WMKG	FA20	370
F-WMKG	FA20	382
F-WMKG	FA20	396
F-WMKG	FA20	411
F-WMKG	FA20	420
F-WMKG	FA20	425
F-WMKG	FA20	430
F-WMKG	FA20	437
F-WMKG	FA20	443
F-WMKG	FA20	450
F-WMKG	FA20	46
F-WMKG	FA20	461
F-WMKG	FA20	468
F-WMKG	FA20	48
F-WMKG	FA20	64
F-WMKG	FA20	73/419
F-WMKG	FA20	74
F-WMKG	FA20	89
F-WMKH	FA20	103/423
F-WMKH	FA20	11
F-WMKH	FA20	117
F-WMKH	FA20	126/438
F-WMKH	FA20	13
F-WMKH	FA20	134
F-WMKH	FA20	143/442
F-WMKH	FA20	150/445
F-WMKH	FA20	199
F-WMKH	FA20	243/480
F-WMKH	FA20	257
F-WMKH	FA20	275
F-WMKH	FA20	290
F-WMKH	FA20	303
F-WMKH	FA20	310
F-WMKH	FA20	312
F-WMKH	FA20	322
F-WMKH	FA20	339
F-WMKH	FA20	6
F-WMKH	FA20	70
F-WMKH	FA20	79/415
F-WMKH	FA20	85/425
F-WMKI	FA20	102
F-WMKI	FA20	111
F-WMKI	FA20	12
F-WMKI	FA20	120
F-WMKI	FA20	135
F-WMKI	FA20	151

F-WMKI	FA20	156/448
F-WMKI	FA20	177
F-WMKI	FA20	204
F-WMKI	FA20	21
F-WMKI	FA20	244
F-WMKI	FA20	29
F-WMKI	FA20	292
F-WMKI	FA20	299
F-WMKI	FA20	327
F-WMKI	FA20	345
F-WMKI	FA20	357
F-WMKI	FA20	36
F-WMKI	FA20	364
F-WMKI	FA20	368
F-WMKI	FA20	373
F-WMKI	FA20	380
F-WMKI	FA20	399
F-WMKI	FA20	405
F-WMKI	FA20	412
F-WMKI	FA20	421
F-WMKI	FA20	428
F-WMKI	FA20	438
F-WMKI	FA20	45
F-WMKI	FA20	452
F-WMKI	FA20	462
F-WMKI	FA20	469
F-WMKI	FA20	5
F-WMKI	FA20	54
F-WMKI	FA20	61
F-WMKI	FA20	63/411
F-WMKI	FA20	80
F-WMKI	FA20	86
F-WMKI	FA20	9
F-WMKJ	FA20	101
F-WMKJ	FA20	107
F-WMKJ	FA20	116
F-WMKJ	FA20	128/436
F-WMKJ	FA20	130
F-WMKJ	FA20	14
F-WMKJ	FA20	158/449
F-WMKJ	FA20	159
F-WMKJ	FA20	20
F-WMKJ	FA20	200
F-WMKJ	FA20	218
F-WMKJ	FA20	260/488
F-WMKJ	FA20	263/489
F-WMKJ	FA20	27
F-WMKJ	FA20	279/502
F-WMKJ	FA20	293
F-WMKJ	FA20	305
F-WMKJ	FA20	313
F-WMKJ	FA20	328/522
F-WMKJ	FA20	34
F-WMKJ	FA20	351/538
F-WMKJ	FA20	360
F-WMKJ	FA20	365
F-WMKJ	FA20	371
F-WMKJ	FA20	409
F-WMKJ	FA20	419
F-WMKJ	FA20	43
F-WMKJ	FA20	431
F-WMKJ	FA20	439
F-WMKJ	FA20	459
F-WMKJ	FA20	51
F-WMKJ	FA20	60
F-WMKJ	FA20	62/409
F-WMKJ	FA20	68
F-WMKJ	FA20	8
F-WMKJ	FA20	91
F-WMKK	FA20	10
F-WMKK	FA20	15
F-WMKK	FA20	22/404
F-WMKK	FA20	7
F-WMSH	FA20	1/401
F-WMSS	FA20	2/402
F-WNAV	F2TH	1
F-WNCO	F9EX	97
F-WNDB	FA50	1
F-WNEW	F2TH	2
(F-WNEW)	F2TH	1
F-WNGD	FA10	109
F-WNGD	FA10	125
F-WNGD	FA10	90
F-WNGD	FA10	96
F-WNGL	FA10	116
F-WNGL	FA10	73
F-WNGL	FA20	105
F-WNGL	FA20	113
F-WNGL	FA20	122
F-WNGL	FA20	16
F-WNGL	FA20	174/457
F-WNGL	FA20	181
F-WNGL	FA20	210
F-WNGL	FA20	222/471
F-WNGL	FA20	228/473
F-WNGL	FA20	23
F-WNGL	FA20	256
F-WNGL	FA20	276/494
F-WNGL	FA20	301/509
F-WNGL	FA20	314/516
F-WNGL	FA20	32
F-WNGL	FA20	333/526
F-WNGL	FA20	40
F-WNGL	FA20	41/407
F-WNGL	FA20	58
F-WNGL	FA20	66
F-WNGL	FA20	75
F-WNGL	FA20	90/426
F-WNGM	FA10	126
F-WNGM	FA10	75
F-WNGM	FA10	92
F-WNGM	FA20	109/427
F-WNGM	FA20	123
F-WNGM	FA20	139
F-WNGM	FA20	163
F-WNGM	FA20	172/456
F-WNGM	FA20	18
F-WNGM	FA20	202
F-WNGM	FA20	24
F-WNGM	FA20	258
F-WNGM	FA20	278/495
F-WNGM	FA20	31
F-WNGM	FA20	330
F-WNGM	FA20	39
F-WNGM	FA20	47
F-WNGM	FA20	56
F-WNGM	FA20	71
F-WNGM	FA20	78/412
F-WNGM	FA20	96
F-WNGN	FA10	77
F-WNGN	FA10	93
F-WNGN	FA20	127
F-WNGN	FA20	140
F-WNGN	FA20	145/443
F-WNGN	FA20	169
F-WNGN	FA20	182/461
F-WNGN	FA20	19
F-WNGN	FA20	190/465
F-WNGN	FA20	25/405
F-WNGN	FA20	268/492
F-WNGN	FA20	271/493
F-WNGN	FA20	44
F-WNGN	FA20	49/408
F-WNGN	FA20	52
F-WNGN	FA20	65
F-WNGN	FA20	81
F-WNGN	FA20	88
F-WNGN	FA20	98/434
F-WNGO	FA10	110
F-WNGO	FA10	111
F-WNGO	FA10	128
F-WNGO	FA10	94
F-WNGO	FA20	108/430
F-WNGO	FA20	133
F-WNGO	FA20	149
F-WNGO	FA20	162/451
F-WNGO	FA20	179
F-WNGO	FA20	198/466
F-WNGO	FA20	214
F-WNGO	FA20	254
F-WNGO	FA20	26
F-WNGO	FA20	33
F-WNGO	FA20	42
F-WNGO	FA20	53/417
F-WNGO	FA20	55/410
F-WNGO	FA20	57
F-WNGO	FA20	59
F-WNGO	FA20	72/413
F-WNGO	FA20	77/429
F-WNGO	FA20	94/428
F-WNGO	FA20	95
F-WNGQ	CRVT	17
F-WNGQ	CRVT	30
F-WNGR	CRVT	18
F-WNGR	CRVT	32
F-WNGS	CRVT	20
F-WNGS	CRVT	34
F-WNGT	CRVT	22
F-WNGU	CRVT	25
F-WNGV	CRVT	26
F-WNGX	CRVT	28
F-WNGY	CRVT	29
F-WNGY	CRVT	39
F-WNGZ	CRVT	31
F-WNGZ	CRVT	40
F-WNLR	FA50	232
F-WOND	FA50	251
F-WPLT	C550	033
F-WPTT	CRVT	8
F-WPUU	FA10	104
F-WPUU	FA10	121
F-WPUU	FA10	54
F-WPUU	FA10	76
F-WPUU	FA20	189
F-WPUU	FA20	220
F-WPUU	FA20	273
F-WPUU	FA20	479
F-WPUU	FA20	500
F-WPUU	FA20	502
F-WPUU	FA20	508
F-WPUU	FA20	512
F-WPUV	FA10	105
F-WPUV	FA10	122
F-WPUV	FA10	55
F-WPUV	FA10	61
F-WPUV	FA20	170/455
F-WPUV	FA20	221
F-WPUV	FA20	484
F-WPUV	FA20	492
F-WPUV	FA20	498
F-WPUV	FA20	507
F-WPUV	FA20	513
F-WPUX	FA10	106
F-WPUX	FA10	123
F-WPUX	FA10	39
F-WPUX	FA20	191
F-WPUX	FA20	223
F-WPUX	FA20	269
F-WPUX	FA20	489
F-WPUX	FA20	504
F-WPUX	FA20	509
F-WPUY	FA10	107
F-WPUY	FA10	124
F-WPUY	FA10	56
F-WPUY	FA20	192
F-WPUY	FA20	224
F-WPUY	FA20	490
F-WPUY	FA20	503
F-WPUY	FA20	510
F-WPUZ	FA10	108
F-WPUZ	FA20	194
F-WPUZ	FA20	242
F-WPUZ	FA20	270
F-WPUZ	FA20	482
F-WPUZ	FA20	506
F-WPXB	FA10	79
F-WPXD	FA10	112
F-WPXD	FA10	80
F-WPXD	FA10	95
F-WPXD	FA20	195
F-WPXD	FA20	208/468
F-WPXD	FA20	225/472
F-WPXD	FA20	277/501
F-WPXD	FA50	131
F-WPXD	FA50	138
F-WPXD	FA50	151
F-WPXD	FA50	169
F-WPXD	FA50	86
F-WPXD	FA50	95
F-WPXE	FA10	113
F-WPXE	FA10	82
F-WPXE	FA20	196
F-WPXE	FA20	231/474
F-WPXE	FA20	247
F-WPXE	FA50	145
F-WPXE	FA50	174
F-WPXE	FA50	73
F-WPXE	FA50	96
F-WPXF	FA10	114
F-WPXF	FA10	81
F-WPXF	FA10	97
F-WPXF	FA20	178/459
F-WPXF	FA20	197
F-WPXF	FA20	205
F-WPXF	FA20	237/476
F-WPXF	FA50	132
F-WPXF	FA50	177
F-WPXF	FA50	78
F-WPXF	FA50	98
F-WPXG	FA10	117
F-WPXG	FA10	83
F-WPXG	FA10	98
F-WPXG	FA20	212
F-WPXG	FA50	110
F-WPXG	FA50	147
F-WPXG	FA50	157
F-WPXH	FA10	115
F-WPXH	FA10	84
F-WPXH	FA10	99
F-WPXH	FA20	203
F-WPXH	FA20	219/470
F-WPXH	FA50	101
F-WPXH	FA50	133
F-WPXH	FA50	140
F-WPXH	FA50	155
F-WPXI	FA10	100
F-WPXI	FA10	118
F-WPXI	FA10	85
F-WPXI	FA20	226
F-WPXI	FA50	117
F-WPXJ	FA10	101
F-WPXJ	FA10	86
F-WPXJ	FA20	235
F-WPXJ	FA50	120
F-WPXK	FA10	102
F-WPXK	FA10	119
F-WPXK	FA10	87
F-WPXK	FA20	236
F-WPXK	FA20	280/503
F-WPXK	FA50	107
F-WPXK	FA50	134
F-WPXL	FA10	103
F-WPXL	FA10	88
F-WPXL	FA20	186/463
F-WPXM	FA10	120
F-WPXM	FA10	89
F-WPXM	FA20	239
F-WPXM	FA20	284
F-WPXM	FA50	114
F-WQAU	HS25	259032
F-WQBJ	F2TH	133
F-WQBJ	F2TH	191
F-WQBJ	F2TH	61
F-WQBJ	F900	105
F-WQBJ	F900	154
F-WQBJ	F900	47
F-WQBJ	F900	62
F-WQBJ	F9EX	133
F-WQBJ	F9EX	91
F-WQBJ	FA10	185
F-WQBJ	FA10	208
F-WQBJ	FA50	297
F-WQBJ	FA50	95
F-WQBK	F2TH	133
F-WQBK	F2TH	27
F-WQBK	F2TH	49
F-WQBK	F2TH	55
F-WQBK	F2TH	70
F-WQBK	F2TH	8
F-WQBK	F900	154
F-WQBK	F900	47
F-WQBK	F9EX	43
F-WQBK	F9EX	75
F-WQBK	FA20	273
F-WQBK	FA20	511
F-WQBK	FA50	305
F-WQBK	FA50	88
F-WQBL	F2EX	76
F-WQBL	F2TH	160
F-WQBL	F2TH	166
F-WQBL	F2TH	27
F-WQBL	F2TH	6
F-WQBL	F900	159
F-WQBL	F900	193
F-WQBL	F900	62
F-WQBL	F9EX	12
F-WQBL	FA50	16
F-WQBL	FA50	268
F-WQBM	F2TH	90
F-WQBM	F900	120
F-WQBM	F900	164
F-WQBM	F900	69
F-WQBM	F900	84
F-WQBM	F9EX	177
F-WQBM	FA10	203
F-WQBM	FA20	176/458
F-WQBM	FA20	302/510
F-WQBM	FA50	107
F-WQBM	FA50	151
F-WQBM	FA50	155
F-WQBM	FA50	313
F-WQBN	F2TH	119
F-WQBN	F2TH	26
F-WQBN	F2TH	76
F-WQBN	F900	130
F-WQBN	F9EX	155
F-WQBN	F9EX	174
F-WQBN	FA20	278/495
F-WQBN	FA20	293
F-WQBN	FA50	134
F-WQBN	FA50	226
F-WQBN	FA50	7
F-WQCD	HS25	258233
F-WQCO	FA10	70
F-WQCP	FA50	88
F-WQFL	F2TH	26
F-WQFZ	FA50	30
F-WQHU	FA50	258
F-WQVA	FA20	293
F-WREX	F9EX	1
F-WRGQ	FA20	86
F-WRNZ	CRVT	2
F-WRQK	CRVT	9
F-WRQP	FA20	238/477
F-WRQP	FA20	241/479
F-WRQP	FA20	252/485
F-WRQP	FA20	255/487
F-WRQP	FA20	296/507
F-WRQP	FA20	300/508
F-WRQP	FA20	302/510
F-WRQP	FA20	304/511
F-WRQP	FA20	315/517
F-WRQP	FA20	332/525
F-WRQP	FA20	336/528
F-WRQP	FA20	342/532
F-WRQP	FA20	344/534
F-WRQP	FA20	346/535
F-WRQP	FA20	353/539
F-WRQP	FA20	369
F-WRQP	FA20	374
F-WRQP	FA20	377/548
F-WRQP	FA20	397/555
F-WRQP	FA20	434
F-WRQQ	FA20	184/462
F-WRQQ	FA20	295/500
F-WRQQ	FA20	326/521
F-WRQQ	FA20	440
F-WRQQ	FA20	483
F-WRQR	FA20	251/484
F-WRQR	FA20	266/490
F-WRQR	FA20	281/496
F-WRQR	FA20	337/529
F-WRQR	FA20	343/533
F-WRQR	FA20	348/536
F-WRQR	FA20	354/540
F-WRQR	FA20	359/542
F-WRQR	FA20	367/545
F-WRQR	FA20	375/547
F-WRQR	FA20	383/550
F-WRQR	FA20	400/556
F-WRQR	FA20	451
F-WRQS	FA20	253/486
F-WRQS	FA20	306/512
F-WRQS	FA20	311/515
F-WRQS	FA20	320/519
F-WRQS	FA20	323/520
F-WRQS	FA20	331/524
F-WRQS	FA20	350/537
F-WRQS	FA20	358/541
F-WRQS	FA20	376
F-WRQS	FA20	381/549
F-WRQS	FA20	408
F-WRQS	FA20	455
F-WRQT	FA20	285/504
F-WRQT	FA20	291/505
F-WRQT	FA20	294/506
F-WRQT	FA20	307/513
F-WRQT	FA20	309/514
F-WRQT	FA20	318/518
F-WRQT	FA20	378
F-WRQT	FA20	392/553
F-WRQT	FA20	410
F-WRQT	FA20	473
F-WRQU	FA20	286/498
F-WRQU	FA20	334/527
F-WRQU	FA20	384/551
F-WRQU	FA20	422
F-WRQV	FA20	248/483
F-WRQV	FA20	329/523
F-WRQV	FA20	363/544
F-WRQV	FA20	372/546
F-WRQV	FA20	389/552
F-WRQV	FA20	427
F-WRQX	FA20	283/497
F-WRQX	FA20	340/531
F-WRQX	FA20	395/554
F-WRQY	FA20	358/541
F-WRQZ	FA20	267/491
F-WRQZ	FA20	288/499
F-WRSN	CRVT	01
F-WSHT	FA20	174/457
F-WSK	FA7X	3
F-WSMF	F900	142
F-WSQK	FA20	226
F-WSQN	FA10	03
F-WSQU	FA10	1
F-WTAL	FA10	02
F-WTAS	PRM1	RB-196
F-WTDA	F2EX	231
F-WTDA	FA7X	2
F-WTDJ	FA20	182/461
F-WTDK	F2EX	237
F-WTFE	FA20	388
F-WTFF	FA20	113
F-WUAS	CRVT	1
F-WUQN	CRVT	3
F-WUQP	CRVT	4
F-WUQR	CRVT	6
F-WVFV	FA20	182/461
F-WVPR	FA10	5
F-WW..	**F2TS**	**735**
F-WW..	FA7X	193
F-WW..	FA7X	196
F-WWF.	F900	138
F-WWFA	F2TH	3
F-WWFA	F900	104
F-WWFA	F900	117
F-WWFA	F900	134
F-WWFA	F900	156
F-WWFA	F900	168
F-WWFA	F900	18
F-WWFA	F900	199
F-WWFA	F900	201
F-WWFA	F900	29
F-WWFA	F900	3
F-WWFA	F900	4
F-WWFA	F900	44
F-WWFA	F900	47
F-WWFA	F900	73
F-WWFA	F900	80
F-WWFA	F900	87
F-WWFA	F900	97
F-WWFA	F9DX	601
F-WWFA	F9DX	621
F-WWFA	F9DX	623
F-WWFA	F9EX	104
F-WWFA	F9EX	16
F-WWFA	F9EX	178
F-WWFA	F9EX	187
F-WWFA	F9EX	2
F-WWFA	F9EX	246
F-WWFA	F9EX	274
F-WWFA	F9EX	29
F-WWFA	**F9EX**	**298**
F-WWFA	F9EX	39
F-WWFA	F9EX	55
F-WWFA	F9EX	66
F-WWFA	F9EX	84
F-WWFB	F900	109
F-WWFB	F900	113
F-WWFB	F900	118
F-WWFB	F900	130
F-WWFB	F900	157
F-WWFB	F900	182
F-WWFB	F900	19
F-WWFB	F900	195
F-WWFB	F900	31
F-WWFB	F900	45
F-WWFB	F900	5
F-WWFB	F900	56
F-WWFB	F900	61
F-WWFB	F900	71
F-WWFB	F900	89
F-WWFB	F9DX	602
F-WWFB	F9EX	125

F-WWFB	F9EX	17
F-WWFB	F9EX	205
F-WWFB	F9EX	249
F-WWFB	F9EX	279
F-WWFB	F9EX	30
F-WWFB	F9EX	40
F-WWFB	F9EX	67
F-WWFB	F9EX	8
F-WWFB	F9EX	85
F-WWFC	F900	114
F-WWFC	F900	127
F-WWFC	F900	130
F-WWFC	F900	150
F-WWFC	F900	158
F-WWFC	F900	164
F-WWFC	F900	20
F-WWFC	F900	33
F-WWFC	F900	35
F-WWFC	F900	4
F-WWFC	F900	43
F-WWFC	F900	52
F-WWFC	F900	54
F-WWFC	F900	75
F-WWFC	F900	85
F-WWFC	F900	94
F-WWFC	F9DX	603
F-WWFC	F9EX	105
F-WWFC	F9EX	126
F-WWFC	F9EX	179
F-WWFC	F9EX	197
F-WWFC	F9EX	212
F-WWFC	F9EX	224
F-WWFC	F9EX	250
F-WWFC	F9EX	272
F-WWFC	**F9EX**	**299**
F-WWFC	F9EX	31
F-WWFC	F9EX	41
F-WWFC	F9EX	56
F-WWFC	F9EX	68
F-WWFC	F9EX	86
F-WWFD	F900	105
F-WWFD	F900	119
F-WWFD	F900	129
F-WWFD	F900	148
F-WWFD	F900	159
F-WWFD	F900	165
F-WWFD	F900	172
F-WWFD	F900	189
F-WWFD	F900	22
F-WWFD	F900	34
F-WWFD	F900	46
F-WWFD	F900	49
F-WWFD	F900	59
F-WWFD	F900	6
F-WWFD	F900	67
F-WWFD	F900	69
F-WWFD	F900	84
F-WWFD	F9DX	604
F-WWFD	F9EX	106
F-WWFD	F9EX	127
F-WWFD	F9EX	180
F-WWFD	F9EX	206
F-WWFD	F9EX	220
F-WWFD	F9EX	247
F-WWFD	F9EX	277
F-WWFD	F9EX	42
F-WWFD	F9EX	57
F-WWFD	F9EX	69
F-WWFE	F900	121
F-WWFE	F900	136
F-WWFE	F900	160
F-WWFE	F900	24
F-WWFE	F900	36
F-WWFE	F900	38
F-WWFE	F900	58
F-WWFE	F900	66
F-WWFE	F900	76
F-WWFE	F900	8
F-WWFE	F900	86
F-WWFE	F900	99
F-WWFE	F9DX	605
F-WWFE	F9EX	107
F-WWFE	F9EX	128
F-WWFE	F9EX	147
F-WWFE	F9EX	173
F-WWFE	F9EX	18
F-WWFE	F9EX	207
F-WWFE	F9EX	221
F-WWFE	F9EX	233
F-WWFE	F9EX	248
F-WWFE	F9EX	284
F-WWFE	F9EX	32
F-WWFE	F9EX	43
F-WWFE	F9EX	70
F-WWFE	F9EX	87
F-WWFE	F9EX	9
F-WWFF	F900	10
F-WWFF	F900	122
F-WWFF	F900	137
F-WWFF	F900	146
F-WWFF	F900	161
F-WWFF	F900	178
F-WWFF	F900	185
F-WWFF	F900	202
F-WWFF	F900	25
F-WWFF	F900	39
F-WWFF	F900	63
F-WWFF	F900	72
F-WWFF	F900	74
F-WWFF	F900	96
F-WWFF	F9DX	606
F-WWFF	F9EX	108
F-WWFF	F9EX	129
F-WWFF	F9EX	190
F-WWFF	F9EX	198
F-WWFF	F9EX	222
F-WWFF	F9EX	235
F-WWFF	F9EX	251
F-WWFF	F9EX	276
F-WWFF	F9EX	33
F-WWFF	F9EX	58
F-WWFF	F9EX	88
F-WWFG	F900	124
F-WWFG	F900	139
F-WWFG	F900	147
F-WWFG	F900	166
F-WWFG	F900	200
F-WWFG	F900	32
F-WWFG	F900	51
F-WWFG	F900	60
F-WWFG	F900	7
F-WWFG	F900	77
F-WWFG	F900	83
F-WWFG	F900	90
F-WWFG	F9EX	10
F-WWFG	F9EX	109
F-WWFG	F9EX	148
F-WWFG	F9EX	183
F-WWFG	F9EX	208
F-WWFG	F9EX	223
F-WWFG	F9EX	238
F-WWFG	F9EX	283
F-WWFG	F9EX	3
F-WWFG	F9EX	44
F-WWFG	F9EX	71
F-WWFG	F9EX	90
F-WWFH	F900	110
F-WWFH	F900	111
F-WWFH	F900	12
F-WWFH	F900	131
F-WWFH	F900	133
F-WWFH	F900	143
F-WWFH	F900	149
F-WWFH	F900	196
F-WWFH	F900	27
F-WWFH	F900	40
F-WWFH	F900	50
F-WWFH	F900	64
F-WWFH	F900	78
F-WWFH	F900	88
F-WWFH	F900	91
F-WWFH	F9DX	617
F-WWFH	F9EX	130
F-WWFH	F9EX	149
F-WWFH	F9EX	169
F-WWFH	F9EX	181
F-WWFH	F9EX	21
F-WWFH	F9EX	214
F-WWFH	F9EX	240
F-WWFH	F9EX	282
F-WWFH	F9EX	59
F-WWFH	F9EX	72
F-WWFH	F9EX	89
F-WWFI	F900	13
F-WWFI	F900	132
F-WWFI	F900	173
F-WWFI	F900	190
F-WWFI	F900	41
F-WWFI	F9DX	607
F-WWFI	F9DX	610
F-WWFI	F9DX	620
F-WWFI	F9EX	11
F-WWFI	F9EX	110
F-WWFI	F9EX	131
F-WWFI	F9EX	150
F-WWFI	F9EX	213
F-WWFI	F9EX	227
F-WWFI	F9EX	252
F-WWFI	F9EX	287
F-WWFI	F9EX	34
F-WWFI	F9EX	60
F-WWFI	F9EX	73
F-WWFJ	F900	103
F-WWFJ	F900	107
F-WWFJ	F900	135
F-WWFJ	F900	152
F-WWFJ	F900	162
F-WWFJ	F900	186
F-WWFJ	F900	21
F-WWFJ	F900	42
F-WWFJ	F900	62
F-WWFJ	F900	9
F-WWFJ	F9DX	612
F-WWFJ	F9EX	111
F-WWFJ	F9EX	12
F-WWFJ	F9EX	132
F-WWFJ	F9EX	151
F-WWFJ	F9EX	170
F-WWFJ	F9EX	19
F-WWFJ	F9EX	199
F-WWFJ	F9EX	215
F-WWFJ	F9EX	228
F-WWFJ	F9EX	244
F-WWFJ	F9EX	290
F-WWFJ	F9EX	35
F-WWFJ	F9EX	45
F-WWFJ	F9EX	5
F-WWFJ	F9EX	91
F-WWFK	F900	102
F-WWFK	F900	11
F-WWFK	F900	141
F-WWFK	F900	145
F-WWFK	F900	151
F-WWFK	F900	153
F-WWFK	F900	174
F-WWFK	F900	183
F-WWFK	F900	23
F-WWFK	F900	28
F-WWFK	F900	57
F-WWFK	F9EX	112
F-WWFK	F9EX	13
F-WWFK	F9EX	133
F-WWFK	F9EX	152
F-WWFK	F9EX	171
F-WWFK	F9EX	194
F-WWFK	F9EX	209
F-WWFK	F9EX	225
F-WWFK	F9EX	264
F-WWFK	F9EX	6
F-WWFK	F9EX	74
F-WWFK	F9EX	92
F-WWFL	F900	103
F-WWFL	F900	106
F-WWFL	F900	115
F-WWFL	F900	123
F-WWFL	F900	125
F-WWFL	F900	14
F-WWFL	F900	140
F-WWFL	F900	154
F-WWFL	F900	30
F-WWFL	F900	68
F-WWFL	F900	81
F-WWFL	F900	92
F-WWFL	F9EX	113
F-WWFL	F9EX	134
F-WWFL	F9EX	153
F-WWFL	F9EX	172
F-WWFL	F9EX	195
F-WWFL	F9EX	218
F-WWFL	F9EX	230
F-WWFL	F9EX	267
F-WWFL	F9EX	61
F-WWFL	F9EX	75
F-WWFL	F9EX	93
F-WWFM	F900	112
F-WWFM	F900	126
F-WWFM	F900	128
F-WWFM	F900	15
F-WWFM	F900	155
F-WWFM	F900	163
F-WWFM	F900	191
F-WWFM	F900	26
F-WWFM	F900	48
F-WWFM	F900	65
F-WWFM	F900	79
F-WWFM	F900	82
F-WWFM	F900	93
F-WWFM	F900	98
F-WWFM	F9DX	616
F-WWFM	F9EX	114
F-WWFM	F9EX	135
F-WWFM	F9EX	154
F-WWFM	F9EX	166
F-WWFM	F9EX	210
F-WWFM	F9EX	241
F-WWFM	F9EX	271
F-WWFM	F9EX	36
F-WWFM	F9EX	46
F-WWFM	F9EX	62
F-WWFN	F900	100
F-WWFN	F900	108
F-WWFN	F900	120
F-WWFN	F900	142
F-WWFN	F900	16
F-WWFN	F900	175
F-WWFN	F900	37
F-WWFN	F900	53
F-WWFN	F900	70
F-WWFN	F9DX	608
F-WWFN	F9EX	115
F-WWFN	F9EX	136
F-WWFN	F9EX	14
F-WWFN	F9EX	155
F-WWFN	F9EX	184
F-WWFN	F9EX	20
F-WWFN	F9EX	211
F-WWFN	F9EX	242
F-WWFN	F9EX	286
F-WWFN	F9EX	7
F-WWFN	F9EX	76
F-WWFN	F9EX	94
F-WWFO	F900	101
F-WWFO	F900	116
F-WWFO	F900	144
F-WWFO	F900	167
F-WWFO	F900	17
F-WWFO	F900	187
F-WWFO	F900	55
F-WWFO	F900	95
F-WWFO	F9DX	609
F-WWFO	F9DX	618
F-WWFO	F9DX	622
F-WWFO	F9EX	116
F-WWFO	F9EX	137
F-WWFO	F9EX	15
F-WWFO	F9EX	156
F-WWFO	F9EX	47
F-WWFO	F9EX	63
F-WWFO	F9EX	95
F-WWFP	F900	169
F-WWFP	F900	184
F-WWFP	F9DX	611
F-WWFP	F9EX	117
F-WWFP	F9EX	138
F-WWFP	F9EX	157
F-WWFP	F9EX	167
F-WWFP	F9EX	191
F-WWFP	F9EX	229
F-WWFP	F9EX	258
F-WWFP	F9EX	288
F-WWFP	F9EX	48
F-WWFP	F9EX	96
F-WWFQ	F900	179
F-WWFQ	F900	192
F-WWFQ	F900	197
F-WWFQ	F9DX	613
F-WWFQ	F9EX	139
F-WWFQ	F9EX	158
F-WWFQ	F9EX	168
F-WWFQ	F9EX	216
F-WWFQ	F9EX	22
F-WWFQ	F9EX	231
F-WWFQ	F9EX	245
F-WWFQ	F9EX	281
F-WWFQ	F9EX	77
F-WWFR	F900	170
F-WWFR	F900	198
F-WWFR	F9EX	140
F-WWFR	F9EX	159
F-WWFR	F9EX	174
F-WWFR	F9EX	192
F-WWFR	F9EX	219
F-WWFR	F9EX	273
F-WWFR	**F9EX**	**297**
F-WWFR	F9EX	49
F-WWFR	F9EX	64
F-WWFR	F9EX	78
F-WWFR	F9EX	98
F-WWFS	F9DX	614
F-WWFS	**F9DX**	**625**
F-WWFS	F9EX	118
F-WWFS	F9EX	141
F-WWFS	F9EX	160
F-WWFS	F9EX	217
F-WWFS	F9EX	23
F-WWFS	**F9EX**	**296**
F-WWFS	F9EX	50
F-WWFS	F9EX	79
F-WWFS	F9EX	99
F-WWFU	F9EX	100
F-WWFU	F9EX	119
F-WWFU	F9EX	142
F-WWFU	F9EX	161
F-WWFU	F9EX	182
F-WWFU	F9EX	193
F-WWFU	F9EX	232
F-WWFU	F9EX	24
F-WWFU	F9EX	268
F-WWFU	**F9EX**	**295**
F-WWFU	F9EX	51
F-WWFV	F900	193
F-WWFV	F9EX	120
F-WWFV	F9EX	143
F-WWFV	F9EX	175
F-WWFV	F9EX	185
F-WWFV	F9EX	234
F-WWFV	F9EX	25
F-WWFV	F9EX	265
F-WWFV	F9EX	294
F-WWFV	F9EX	37
F-WWFV	F9EX	52
F-WWFV	F9EX	80
(F-WWFV)	F9EX	218
F-WWFW	F900	171
F-WWFW	F900	176
F-WWFW	F9EX	101
F-WWFW	F9EX	121
F-WWFW	F9EX	144
F-WWFW	F9EX	162
F-WWFW	F9EX	176
F-WWFW	F9EX	188
F-WWFW	F9EX	200
F-WWFW	F9EX	236
F-WWFW	F9EX	266
F-WWFW	**F9EX**	**293**
F-WWFW	F9EX	53
F-WWFW	F9EX	65
F-WWFW	F9EX	81
F-WWFX	F900	180
F-WWFX	F9DX	615
F-WWFX	F9EX	102
F-WWFX	F9EX	122
F-WWFX	F9EX	145
F-WWFX	F9EX	163
F-WWFX	F9EX	237
F-WWFX	F9EX	26
F-WWFX	F9EX	270
F-WWFX	**F9EX**	**292**
F-WWFX	F9EX	38
F-WWFX	F9EX	82
(F-WWFX)	F9EX	219
F-WWFY	F900	177
F-WWFY	F9DX	624
F-WWFY	F9EX	103
F-WWFY	F9EX	123
F-WWFY	F9EX	164
F-WWFY	F9EX	186
F-WWFY	F9EX	201
F-WWFY	F9EX	253
F-WWFY	F9EX	27
F-WWFY	F9EX	275
F-WWFY	F9EX	291
F-WWFY	F9EX	54
F-WWFY	F9EX	83
F-WWFZ	F900	181
F-WWFZ	F900	188
F-WWFZ	F900	194
F-WWFZ	F9EX	124
F-WWFZ	F9EX	146
F-WWFZ	F9EX	165
F-WWFZ	F9EX	177
F-WWFZ	F9EX	189
F-WWFZ	F9EX	239
F-WWFZ	F9EX	28
F-WWFZ	F9EX	289
(F-WWFZ)	F9EX	220
F-WWGA	F2EX	130
F-WWGA	F2EX	152
F-WWGA	F2EX	192
F-WWGA	F2EX	2
F-WWGA	F2EX	303
F-WWGA	F2EX	44
F-WWGA	F2EX	67
F-WWGA	F2EX	97
F-WWGA	F2TS	712
F-WWGB	F2EX	216
F-WWGB	F2EX	257
F-WWGB	F2EX	283
F-WWGB	F2EX	312
F-WWGC	F2EX	118
F-WWGC	F2EX	153
F-WWGC	F2EX	251
F-WWGC	F2EX	28
F-WWGC	F2EX	3
F-WWGC	**F2EX**	**313**
F-WWGC	F2EX	68
F-WWGC	F2EX	90
F-WWGC	F2TS	726
F-WWGD	F2EX	119
F-WWGD	F2EX	193
F-WWGD	F2EX	221
F-WWGD	F2EX	261
F-WWGD	F2EX	29
F-WWGD	F2EX	290
F-WWGD	F2EX	4
F-WWGD	F2EX	69
F-WWGD	F2EX	91
F-WWGD	F2TH	603
F-WWGE	F2EX	104
F-WWGE	F2EX	135
F-WWGE	F2EX	148
F-WWGE	F2EX	188
F-WWGE	F2EX	222
F-WWGE	F2EX	264
F-WWGE	F2EX	304
F-WWGE	F2EX	45
F-WWGE	F2EX	5
F-WWGE	F2EX	70
F-WWGF	F2EX	122
F-WWGF	F2EX	136
F-WWGF	F2EX	176
F-WWGF	F2EX	231
F-WWGF	F2EX	305
F-WWGF	F2EX	46
F-WWGF	F2EX	7
F-WWGF	F2TS	716
F-WWGG	F2EX	120
F-WWGG	F2EX	137
F-WWGG	F2EX	154
F-WWGG	F2EX	194
F-WWGG	F2EX	295
F-WWGG	F2EX	30
F-WWGG	F2EX	71
F-WWGG	F2EX	8
F-WWGG	F2EX	92
F-WWGG	F2TS	707
F-WWGH	F2EX	131
F-WWGH	F2EX	146
F-WWGH	F2EX	160
F-WWGH	F2EX	223
F-WWGH	F2EX	272
F-WWGH	F2EX	47
F-WWGH	F2EX	72
F-WWGH	F2EX	9
F-WWGH	F2EX	93
F-WWGH	F2TS	732
F-WWGI	F2EX	10
F-WWGI	F2EX	121
F-WWGI	F2EX	138
F-WWGI	F2EX	173
F-WWGI	F2EX	224
F-WWGI	**F2EX**	**306**
F-WWGI	F2EX	48
F-WWGI	F2EX	94
F-WWGI	F2TS	719

F-WWGJ	F2EX	11
F-WWGJ	F2EX	123
F-WWGJ	F2EX	149
F-WWGJ	F2EX	217
F-WWGJ	F2EX	254
F-WWGJ	F2EX	277
F-WWGJ	F2EX	307
F-WWGJ	F2EX	31
F-WWGJ	F2EX	73
F-WWGJ	F2EX	95
F-WWGK	F2EX	12
F-WWGK	F2EX	124
F-WWGK	F2EX	141
F-WWGK	F2EX	174
F-WWGK	F2EX	195
F-WWGK	F2EX	247
F-WWGK	F2EX	276
F-WWGK	F2EX	308
F-WWGK	F2EX	32
F-WWGK	F2EX	74
F-WWGL	F2EX	13
F-WWGL	F2EX	150
F-WWGL	F2EX	165
F-WWGL	F2EX	189
F-WWGL	F2EX	218
F-WWGL	F2EX	255
F-WWGL	F2EX	309
F-WWGL	F2EX	33
F-WWGL	F2EX	75
F-WWGL	F2TS	718
F-WWGM	F2EX	125
F-WWGM	F2EX	14
F-WWGM	F2EX	219
F-WWGM	F2EX	34
F-WWGM	F2EX	76
F-WWGM	F2TS	725
F-WWGM	F2TS	733
F-WWGN	F2EX	132
F-WWGN	F2EX	15
F-WWGN	F2EX	166
F-WWGN	F2EX	298
F-WWGN	F2EX	49
F-WWGN	F2EX	77
F-WWGN	F2EX	96
F-WWGN	F2TS	711
F-WWGO	F2EX	126
F-WWGO	F2EX	142
F-WWGO	F2EX	16
F-WWGO	F2EX	175
F-WWGO	F2EX	196
F-WWGO	F2EX	253
F-WWGO	F2EX	50
F-WWGO	F2EX	78
F-WWGO	F2TS	728
F-WWGO	FA20	515
F-WWGP	F2EX	133
F-WWGP	F2EX	167
F-WWGP	F2EX	17
F-WWGP	F2EX	190
F-WWGP	F2EX	51
F-WWGP	F2EX	79
F-WWGP	F2EX	98
F-WWGP	**F2TS**	**701**
F-WWGP	FA20	501
F-WWGP	FA20	514
F-WWGQ	F2EX	127
F-WWGQ	F2EX	157
F-WWGQ	F2EX	177
F-WWGQ	F2EX	18
F-WWGQ	F2EX	284
F-WWGQ	**F2EX**	**314**
F-WWGQ	F2EX	35
F-WWGQ	F2EX	80
F-WWGQ	F2TS	705
F-WWGR	F2EX	105
F-WWGR	F2EX	143
F-WWGR	F2EX	19
F-WWGR	F2EX	198
F-WWGR	F2EX	252
F-WWGR	F2EX	275
F-WWGR	F2EX	310
F-WWGR	F2EX	36
F-WWGR	F2EX	81
F-WWGR	FA20	511
F-WWGS	F2EX	128
F-WWGS	F2EX	158
F-WWGS	F2EX	178
F-WWGS	F2EX	199
F-WWGS	F2EX	20
F-WWGS	F2EX	225
F-WWGS	F2EX	296
F-WWGS	F2EX	37
F-WWGS	F2EX	82
F-WWGS	F2TS	709
F-WWGT	F2EX	159
F-WWGT	F2EX	21
F-WWGT	F2EX	220
F-WWGT	F2EX	254
F-WWGT	F2EX	293
F-WWGT	F2EX	38
F-WWGT	F2EX	83
F-WWGT	F2TS	706
F-WWGU	F2EX	106
F-WWGU	F2EX	129
F-WWGU	F2EX	147
F-WWGU	F2EX	168
F-WWGU	F2EX	22
F-WWGU	F2EX	39
F-WWGU	F2EX	84
F-WWGU	F2TS	724
F-WWGV	F2EX	107
F-WWGV	F2EX	134
F-WWGV	F2EX	226
F-WWGV	F2EX	23
F-WWGV	F2EX	292
F-WWGV	F2EX	40
F-WWGV	F2EX	85
F-WWGV	F2TH	604
F-WWGV	F2TS	708
F-WWGW	F2EX	108
F-WWGW	F2EX	144
F-WWGW	F2EX	183
F-WWGW	F2EX	24
F-WWGW	F2EX	259
F-WWGW	F2EX	311
F-WWGW	F2EX	41
F-WWGW	F2EX	86
F-WWGX	F2EX	109
F-WWGX	F2EX	161
F-WWGX	F2EX	232
F-WWGX	F2EX	25
F-WWGX	F2EX	278
F-WWGX	F2EX	315
F-WWGX	F2EX	42
F-WWGX	F2EX	87
F-WWGY	F2EX	169
F-WWGY	F2EX	227
F-WWGY	F2EX	26
F-WWGY	F2EX	262
F-WWGY	F2EX	291
F-WWGY	F2EX	43
F-WWGY	F2EX	88
F-WWGY	F2TH	601
F-WWGZ	F2EX	139
F-WWGZ	F2EX	155
F-WWGZ	F2EX	228
F-WWGZ	F2EX	269
F-WWGZ	F2EX	27
F-WWGZ	**F2EX**	**316**
F-WWGZ	F2EX	89
F-WWHA	FA50	181
F-WWHA	FA50	188
F-WWHA	FA50	197
F-WWHA	FA50	201
F-WWHA	FA50	203
F-WWHA	FA50	218
F-WWHA	FA50	231
F-WWHA	FA50	242
F-WWHA	FA50	253
F-WWHA	FA50	275
F-WWHA	FA50	299
F-WWHA	FA50	321
F-WWHA	FA50	345
F-WWHA	FA7X	119
F-WWHA	FA7X	200
F-WWHA	FA7X	245
F-WWHA	FA7X	58
F-WWHB	FA50	182
F-WWHB	FA50	189
F-WWHB	FA50	199
F-WWHB	FA50	202
F-WWHB	FA50	206
F-WWHB	FA50	233
F-WWHB	FA50	248
F-WWHB	FA50	254
F-WWHB	FA50	276
F-WWHB	FA50	300
F-WWHB	FA50	322
F-WWHB	FA50	346
F-WWHB	FA7X	120
F-WWHB	FA7X	197
F-WWHB	**FA7X**	**264**
F-WWHB	FA7X	59
F-WWHC	FA50	180
F-WWHC	FA50	198
F-WWHC	FA50	207
F-WWHC	FA50	226
F-WWHC	FA50	234
F-WWHC	FA50	255
F-WWHC	FA50	277
F-WWHC	FA50	301
F-WWHC	FA50	323
F-WWHC	FA50	347
F-WWHC	FA7X	121
F-WWHC	FA7X	184
F-WWHC	FA7X	249
F-WWHC	FA7X	60
F-WWHD	FA50	184
F-WWHD	FA50	191
F-WWHD	FA50	196
F-WWHD	FA50	204
F-WWHD	FA50	205
F-WWHD	FA50	230
F-WWHD	FA50	236
F-WWHD	FA50	256
F-WWHD	FA50	278
F-WWHD	FA50	302
F-WWHD	FA50	324
F-WWHD	FA50	348
F-WWHD	FA7X	155
F-WWHD	FA7X	217
F-WWHD	FA7X	61
F-WWHE	FA50	185
F-WWHE	FA50	192
F-WWHE	FA50	200
F-WWHE	FA50	209
F-WWHE	FA50	227
F-WWHE	FA50	237
F-WWHE	FA50	252
F-WWHE	FA50	257
F-WWHE	FA50	279
F-WWHE	FA50	303
F-WWHE	FA50	325
F-WWHE	FA50	349
F-WWHE	FA7X	122
F-WWHE	FA7X	186
F-WWHE	FA7X	253
F-WWHE	FA7X	62
F-WWHF	FA50	183
F-WWHF	FA50	238
F-WWHF	FA50	241
F-WWHF	FA50	246
F-WWHF	FA50	258
F-WWHF	FA50	280
F-WWHF	FA50	304
F-WWHF	FA50	326
F-WWHF	FA50	350
F-WWHF	FA7X	123
F-WWHF	FA7X	203
F-WWHF	FA7X	63
F-WWHG	FA50	187
F-WWHG	FA50	190
F-WWHG	FA50	220
F-WWHG	FA50	239
F-WWHG	FA50	259
F-WWHG	FA50	281
F-WWHG	FA50	305
F-WWHG	FA50	327
F-WWHH	FA50	186
F-WWHH	FA50	193
F-WWHH	FA50	212
F-WWHH	FA50	229
F-WWHH	FA50	240
F-WWHH	FA50	282
F-WWHH	FA50	306
F-WWHH	FA50	328
F-WWHH	FA50	351
F-WWHH	FA7X	124
F-WWHH	FA7X	187
F-WWHH	FA7X	257
F-WWHH	FA7X	64
F-WWHK	FA50	104
F-WWHK	FA50	195
F-WWHK	FA50	244
F-WWHK	FA50	260
F-WWHK	FA50	283
F-WWHK	FA50	307
F-WWHK	FA50	329
F-WWHK	FA50	352
F-WWHK	FA7X	147
F-WWHK	FA7X	227
F-WWHK	FA7X	65
F-WWHL	FA50	210
F-WWHL	FA50	221
F-WWHL	FA50	245
F-WWHL	FA50	261
F-WWHL	FA50	284
F-WWHL	FA50	308
F-WWHL	FA50	330
F-WWHL	FA7X	125
F-WWHL	FA7X	66
F-WWHM	FA50	194
F-WWHM	FA50	222
F-WWHM	FA50	235
F-WWHM	FA50	243
F-WWHM	FA50	262
F-WWHM	FA50	285
F-WWHM	FA50	309
F-WWHM	FA50	331
F-WWHM	FA7X	150
F-WWHM	FA7X	229
F-WWHM	FA7X	71
F-WWHN	FA50	223
F-WWHN	FA50	249
F-WWHN	FA50	263
F-WWHN	FA50	286
F-WWHN	FA50	310
F-WWHN	FA50	332
F-WWHN	FA7X	148
F-WWHN	FA7X	224
F-WWHN	FA7X	72
F-WWHO	FA50	224
F-WWHO	FA50	264
F-WWHO	FA50	287
F-WWHO	FA50	311
F-WWHO	FA50	333
F-WWHO	FA7X	146
F-WWHO	FA7X	214
F-WWHO	FA7X	73
F-WWHP	FA50	208
F-WWHP	FA50	225
F-WWHP	FA50	247
F-WWHP	FA50	265
F-WWHP	FA50	288
F-WWHP	FA50	312
F-WWHP	FA50	334
F-WWHP	FA7X	149
F-WWHP	**FA7X**	**239**
F-WWHP	FA7X	74
F-WWHQ	FA50	266
F-WWHQ	FA50	289
F-WWHQ	FA50	335
F-WWHQ	FA7X	151
F-WWHQ	FA7X	230
F-WWHQ	FA7X	75
F-WWHR	FA50	211
F-WWHR	FA50	228
F-WWHR	FA50	250
F-WWHR	FA50	267
F-WWHR	FA50	290
F-WWHR	FA50	313
F-WWHR	FA50	336
F-WWHR	FA7X	207
F-WWHR	FA7X	76
F-WWHS	FA50	219
F-WWHS	FA50	268
F-WWHS	FA50	291
F-WWHS	FA50	337
F-WWHS	FA7X	126
F-WWHS	FA7X	192
F-WWHS	FA7X	77
F-WWHT	FA50	215
F-WWHT	FA50	232
F-WWHT	FA50	269
F-WWHT	FA50	292
F-WWHT	FA50	314
F-WWHT	FA50	338
F-WWHT	FA7X	127
F-WWHT	FA7X	188
F-WWHT	FA7X	256
F-WWHT	FA7X	78
F-WWHU	FA50	270
F-WWHU	FA50	293
F-WWHU	FA50	315
F-WWHU	FA50	339
F-WWHU	FA7X	128
F-WWHU	FA7X	195
F-WWHU	FA7X	258
F-WWHU	FA7X	79
F-WWHV	FA50	217
F-WWHV	FA50	271
F-WWHV	FA50	294
F-WWHV	FA50	316
F-WWHV	FA50	340
F-WWHW	FA50	213
F-WWHW	FA50	272
F-WWHW	FA50	295
F-WWHW	FA50	317
F-WWHW	FA50	341
F-WWHX	FA50	214
F-WWHX	FA50	273
F-WWHX	FA50	296
F-WWHX	FA50	318
F-WWHX	FA50	342
F-WWHY	FA50	274
F-WWHY	FA50	297
F-WWHY	FA50	319
F-WWHY	FA50	343
F-WWHZ	FA50	216
F-WWHZ	FA50	298
F-WWHZ	FA50	320
F-WWHZ	FA50	344
F-WWHZ	FA50	36
F-WWJC	F9EX	4
F-WWJN	F2EX	204
F-WWJN	F2EX	229
F-WWJN	F2EX	265
F-WWJN	F2TS	731
F-WWJO	F2EX	205
F-WWJO	F2EX	230
F-WWJO	F2EX	266
F-WWJO	F2TS	730
F-WWJP	F2EX	206
F-WWJP	F2EX	233
F-WWJP	F2EX	273
F-WWJP	F2EX	302
F-WWJQ	F2EX	207
F-WWJQ	F2EX	288
F-WWJQ	F2TS	703
F-WWJR	F2EX	208
F-WWJR	F2EX	234
F-WWJR	F2TS	710
F-WWJR	F2TS	729
F-WWJS	F2EX	209
F-WWJS	F2EX	218
F-WWJS	F2EX	271
F-WWJS	F2EX	300
F-WWJT	F2EX	210
F-WWJT	F2EX	235
F-WWJT	F2EX	279
F-WWJU	F2EX	211
F-WWJU	F2EX	236
F-WWJU	F2EX	299
F-WWJU	F2TS	713
F-WWJV	F2EX	212
F-WWJV	F2EX	286
F-WWJV	F2TS	702
F-WWJX	F2EX	213
F-WWJX	F2EX	256
F-WWJX	F2EX	301
F-WWJX	F2TS	721
F-WWJY	F2EX	214
F-WWJY	F2EX	260
F-WWJY	F2EX	285
F-WWJZ	F2EX	215
F-WWJZ	F2EX	249
F-WWJZ	F2TS	722
F-WWMA	F2EX	140
F-WWMA	F2EX	179
F-WWMA	F2EX	202
F-WWMA	F2EX	281
F-WWMA	**F2EX**	**317**
F-WWMA	F2EX	52
F-WWMA	F2EX	96
F-WWMA	F2EX	99
F-WWMA	F2TH	17
F-WWMA	F2TH	174
F-WWMA	F2TH	21
F-WWMA	F2TH	29
F-WWMA	F2TH	36
F-WWMA	F2TH	4
F-WWMA	F2TH	57
F-WWMA	F2TH	69
F-WWMA	F2TS	704
F-WWMB	F2EX	100
F-WWMB	F2EX	145
F-WWMB	F2EX	162
F-WWMB	F2EX	289
F-WWMB	**F2EX**	**318**
F-WWMB	F2EX	53
F-WWMB	F2TH	16
F-WWMB	F2TH	175
F-WWMB	F2TH	189
F-WWMB	F2TH	30
F-WWMB	F2TH	47
F-WWMB	F2TH	5
F-WWMB	F2TH	58
F-WWMB	F2TH	70
F-WWMC	F2EX	101
F-WWMC	F2EX	163
F-WWMC	F2EX	184
F-WWMC	F2EX	238
F-WWMC	F2EX	287
F-WWMC	**F2EX**	**319**
F-WWMC	F2EX	54
F-WWMC	F2TH	176
F-WWMC	F2TH	19
F-WWMC	F2TH	31
F-WWMC	F2TH	48
F-WWMC	F2TH	59
F-WWMC	F2TH	602
F-WWMC	F2TH	71
F-WWMC	F2TS	714
F-WWMD	F2EX	102
F-WWMD	F2EX	151
F-WWMD	F2EX	191
F-WWMD	F2EX	239
F-WWMD	F2EX	55
F-WWMD	F2TH	177
F-WWMD	F2TH	188
F-WWMD	F2TH	32
F-WWMD	F2TH	41
F-WWMD	F2TH	49
F-WWMD	F2TH	6
F-WWMD	F2TH	60
F-WWMD	F2TH	72
F-WWMD	F2TS	715
F-WWMD	F2TS	734
F-WWME	F2EX	103
F-WWME	F2EX	156
F-WWME	F2EX	200
F-WWME	F2EX	250
F-WWME	**F2EX**	**320**
F-WWME	F2EX	56
F-WWME	F2TH	178
F-WWME	F2TH	20
F-WWME	F2TH	33
F-WWME	F2TH	50
F-WWME	F2TH	61
F-WWME	F2TH	7
F-WWME	F2TS	723
F-WWMF	F2EX	164
F-WWMF	F2EX	197
F-WWMF	F2EX	246
F-WWMF	F2EX	270
F-WWMF	F2EX	57
F-WWMF	F2TH	179
F-WWMF	F2TH	22
F-WWMF	F2TH	34
F-WWMF	F2TH	51
F-WWMF	F2TH	62
F-WWMF	F2TH	8
F-WWMG	F2EX	110
F-WWMG	F2EX	170
F-WWMG	F2EX	201
F-WWMG	F2EX	237
F-WWMG	F2EX	268
F-WWMG	F2EX	294
F-WWMG	F2EX	58
F-WWMG	F2TH	18
F-WWMG	F2TH	180
F-WWMG	F2TH	35
F-WWMG	F2TH	42
F-WWMG	F2TH	63
F-WWMG	F2TH	73
F-WWMG	F2TH	9
F-WWMH	F2EX	111
F-WWMH	F2EX	171
F-WWMH	F2EX	203
F-WWMH	F2EX	240
F-WWMH	F2EX	274
F-WWMH	**F2EX**	**322**
F-WWMH	F2EX	59
F-WWMH	F2TH	10
F-WWMH	F2TH	181

F-WWMH	F2TH	23
F-WWMH	F2TH	37
F-WWMH	F2TH	64
F-WWMH	F2TH	74
F-WWMI	F2EX	112
F-WWMI	F2EX	172
F-WWMI	F2EX	258
F-WWMI	F2EX	282
F-WWMI	F2EX	60
F-WWMI	F2TH	182
F-WWMI	F2TH	38
F-WWMI	F2TH	52
F-WWMI	F2TH	65
F-WWMJ	F2EX	113
F-WWMJ	F2EX	180
F-WWMJ	F2EX	241
F-WWMJ	F2EX	280
F-WWMJ	F2EX	61
F-WWMJ	F2TH	183
F-WWMJ	F2TH	39
F-WWMJ	F2TH	53
F-WWMJ	F2TH	66
F-WWMJ	F2TH	78
(F-WWMJ)	F2EX	173
F-WWMK	F2EX	114
F-WWMK	F2EX	181
F-WWMK	F2EX	242
F-WWMK	F2EX	267
F-WWMK	F2EX	62
F-WWMK	F2TH	11
F-WWMK	F2TH	184
F-WWMK	F2TH	24
F-WWMK	F2TH	40
F-WWMK	F2TH	43
F-WWMK	F2TH	67
F-WWMK	F2TH	75
(F-WWMK)	F2EX	174
F-WWML	F2EX	115
F-WWML	F2EX	182
F-WWML	F2EX	243
F-WWML	F2EX	63
F-WWML	F2TH	13
F-WWML	F2TH	185
F-WWML	F2TH	25
F-WWML	F2TH	44
F-WWML	F2TH	54
F-WWML	F2TH	76
F-WWML	F2TS	727
(F-WWML)	F2EX	175
F-WWMM	F2EX	116
F-WWMM	F2EX	185
F-WWMM	F2EX	245
F-WWMM	F2EX	64
F-WWMM	F2TH	12
F-WWMM	F2TH	186
F-WWMM	F2TH	27
F-WWMM	F2TH	45
F-WWMM	F2TH	55
F-WWMM	F2TH	77
F-WWMM	F2TS	720
(F-WWMM)	F2EX	176
F-WWMN	F2EX	186
F-WWMN	F2EX	263
F-WWMN	F2EX	297
F-WWMN	F2EX	65
F-WWMN	F2TH	14
F-WWMN	F2TH	187
F-WWMN	F2TH	26
F-WWMN	F2TH	46
F-WWMN	F2TH	68
F-WWMN	F2TH	79
(F-WWMN)	F2EX	177
F-WWMO	F2EX	117
F-WWMO	F2EX	187
F-WWMO	F2EX	244
F-WWMO	F2EX	66
F-WWMO	F2TH	15
F-WWMO	F2TH	28
F-WWMO	F2TH	56
F-WWMO	F2TH	80
F-WWMO	F2TS	717
(F-WWMO)	F2EX	178
F-WWNA	FA7X	175
F-WWNA	FA7X	98
F-WWNB	FA7X	163
F-WWNB	FA7X	99
F-WWNC	FA7X	100
F-WWNC	FA7X	159
F-WWNC	FA7X	238
F-WWND	FA7X	101
F-WWND	FA7X	210
F-WWNE	FA7X	102
F-WWNE	FA7X	173
F-WWNE	FA7X	235
F-WWNF	FA7X	103
F-WWNF	FA7X	178
F-WWNF	FA7X	251
F-WWQA	**FA8X**	**401**
F-WWQB	**FA8X**	**402**
F-WWQC	**FA8X**	**403**
F-WWQD	**FA8X**	**404**
F-WWQE	**FA8X**	**405**
F-WWQF	**FA8X**	**406**
F-WWQG	**FA8X**	**407**
F-WWUA	FA7X	129
F-WWUA	FA7X	199
F-WWUA	FA7X	267
F-WWUA	FA7X	4
F-WWUA	FA7X	49
F-WWUB	FA7X	130
F-WWUB	FA7X	191
F-WWUB	FA7X	254
F-WWUB	FA7X	5
F-WWUB	FA7X	50
F-WWUC	FA7X	131
F-WWUC	FA7X	194
F-WWUC	FA7X	250
F-WWUC	FA7X	51
F-WWUC	FA7X	6
F-WWUD	FA7X	132
F-WWUD	**FA7X**	**263**
F-WWUD	FA7X	52
F-WWUD	FA7X	7
F-WWUE	FA7X	156
F-WWUE	FA7X	218
F-WWUE	FA7X	268
F-WWUE	FA7X	67
F-WWUE	FA7X	8
F-WWUF	FA7X	154
F-WWUF	FA7X	222
F-WWUF	**FA7X**	**269**
F-WWUF	FA7X	80
F-WWUF	FA7X	9
F-WWUG	FA7X	10
F-WWUG	FA7X	133
F-WWUG	FA7X	211
F-WWUG	**FA7X**	**270**
F-WWUG	FA7X	68
F-WWUH	FA7X	11
F-WWUH	FA7X	134
F-WWUH	FA7X	201
F-WWUH	**FA7X**	**271**
F-WWUH	FA7X	69
F-WWUI	FA7X	12
F-WWUI	FA7X	162
F-WWUI	**FA7X**	**233**
F-WWUI	FA7X	81
F-WWUJ	FA7X	13
F-WWUJ	FA7X	242
F-WWUJ	**FA7X**	**272**
F-WWUJ	FA7X	70
F-WWUK	FA7X	14
F-WWUK	FA7X	157
F-WWUK	**FA7X**	**273**
F-WWUK	FA7X	82
F-WWUL	FA7X	135
F-WWUL	FA7X	15
F-WWUL	FA7X	204
F-WWUL	FA7X	266
F-WWUL	FA7X	83
F-WWUM	FA7X	136
F-WWUM	FA7X	16
F-WWUM	FA7X	205
F-WWUM	FA7X	84
F-WWUN	FA7X	137
F-WWUN	FA7X	17
F-WWUN	FA7X	228
F-WWUN	FA7X	85
F-WWUO	FA7X	153
F-WWUO	FA7X	18
F-WWUO	FA7X	231
F-WWUO	FA7X	87
F-WWUP	FA7X	169
F-WWUP	FA7X	19
F-WWUP	FA7X	226
F-WWUP	**FA7X**	**277**
F-WWUP	FA7X	88
F-WWUQ	FA7X	160
F-WWUQ	FA7X	20
F-WWUQ	**FA7X**	**246**
F-WWUQ	FA7X	89
F-WWUR	FA7X	170
F-WWUR	FA7X	21
F-WWUR	**FA7X**	**243**
F-WWUR	FA7X	90
F-WWUS	FA7X	138
F-WWUS	FA7X	198
F-WWUS	FA7X	22
F-WWUS	FA7X	265
F-WWUS	FA7X	86
F-WWVA	F2TH	106
F-WWVA	F2TH	146
F-WWVA	F2TH	161
F-WWVA	F2TH	190
F-WWVA	F2TH	213
F-WWVA	F2TH	81
F-WWVA	F9EX	196
F-WWVA	F9EX	243
F-WWVA	F9EX	269
(F-WWVA)	F9EX	221
F-WWVB	F2TH	107
F-WWVB	F2TH	147
F-WWVB	F2TH	191
F-WWVB	F2TH	214
F-WWVB	F2TH	82
F-WWVB	F9DX	619
F-WWVB	F9EX	254
F-WWVB	F9EX	278
F-WWVC	F2TH	108
F-WWVC	F2TH	148
F-WWVC	F2TH	170
F-WWVC	F2TH	192
F-WWVC	F2TH	215
F-WWVC	F2TH	83
F-WWVC	F9EX	202
F-WWVC	F9EX	255
F-WWVC	F9EX	280
F-WWVD	F2TH	109
F-WWVD	F2TH	129
F-WWVD	F2TH	166
F-WWVD	F2TH	216
F-WWVD	F2TH	84
F-WWVD	F9EX	203
F-WWVD	F9EX	256
F-WWVE	F2TH	110
F-WWVE	F2TH	130
F-WWVE	F2TH	165
F-WWVE	F2TH	193
F-WWVE	F2TH	217
F-WWVE	F2TH	85
F-WWVE	F9EX	204
F-WWVE	F9EX	257
F-WWVE	F9EX	285
F-WWVF	F2TH	111
F-WWVF	F2TH	134
F-WWVF	F2TH	194
F-WWVF	F2TH	218
F-WWVF	F2TH	86
F-WWVF	F9EX	259
(F-WWVF)	F9EX	222
F-WWVG	F2TH	112
F-WWVG	F2TH	131
F-WWVG	F2TH	149
F-WWVG	F2TH	167
F-WWVG	F2TH	219
F-WWVG	F2TH	87
F-WWVG	F9EX	260
(F-WWVG)	F9EX	223
F-WWVH	F2TH	113
F-WWVH	F2TH	132
F-WWVH	F2TH	150
F-WWVH	F2TH	195
F-WWVH	F2TH	220
F-WWVH	F2TH	88
F-WWVH	F9EX	261
(F-WWVH)	F9EX	224
F-WWVI	F2TH	114
F-WWVI	F2TH	133
F-WWVI	F2TH	151
F-WWVI	F2TH	196
F-WWVI	F2TH	221
F-WWVI	F2TH	89
F-WWVI	F9EX	262
(F-WWVI)	F9EX	225
F-WWVJ	F2TH	135
F-WWVJ	F2TH	152
F-WWVJ	F2TH	169
F-WWVJ	F2TH	197
F-WWVJ	F2TH	222
F-WWVJ	F2TH	90
F-WWVJ	F9EX	226
F-WWVJ	F9EX	263
F-WWVK	F2TH	115
F-WWVK	F2TH	153
F-WWVK	F2TH	171
F-WWVK	F2TH	223
F-WWVK	F2TH	91
F-WWVK	FA7X	112
F-WWVK	FA7X	181
F-WWVK	FA7X	241
F-WWVK	FA7X	39
F-WWVL	F2TH	116
F-WWVL	F2TH	136
F-WWVL	F2TH	154
F-WWVL	F2TH	198
F-WWVL	F2TH	224
F-WWVL	F2TH	92
F-WWVL	FA7X	109
F-WWVL	FA7X	176
F-WWVL	FA7X	244
F-WWVL	FA7X	40
F-WWVM	F2TH	117
F-WWVM	F2TH	137
F-WWVM	F2TH	155
F-WWVM	F2TH	199
F-WWVM	F2TH	225
F-WWVM	F2TH	93
F-WWVM	FA7X	110
F-WWVM	FA7X	179
F-WWVM	FA7X	240
F-WWVM	FA7X	41
F-WWVN	F2TH	118
F-WWVN	F2TH	138
F-WWVN	F2TH	156
F-WWVN	F2TH	172
F-WWVN	F2TH	200
F-WWVN	F2TH	226
F-WWVN	F2TH	94
F-WWVN	FA7X	111
F-WWVN	FA7X	180
F-WWVN	**FA7X**	**247**
F-WWVN	FA7X	42
F-WWVO	F2TH	119
F-WWVO	F2TH	157
F-WWVO	F2TH	201
F-WWVO	F2TH	227
F-WWVO	F2TH	95
F-WWVO	FA7X	104
F-WWVO	FA7X	167
F-WWVO	FA7X	234
F-WWVO	FA7X	43
F-WWVP	F2TH	120
F-WWVP	F2TH	158
F-WWVP	F2TH	202
F-WWVP	F2TH	228
F-WWVP	F2TH	96
F-WWVP	FA7X	113
F-WWVP	FA7X	190
F-WWVP	FA7X	248
F-WWVP	FA7X	44
F-WWVQ	F2TH	121
F-WWVQ	F2TH	159
F-WWVQ	F2TH	203
F-WWVQ	F2TH	229
F-WWVQ	F2TH	97
F-WWVQ	FA7X	139
F-WWVQ	FA7X	209
F-WWVQ	FA7X	45
F-WWVR	F2TH	122
F-WWVR	F2TH	139
F-WWVR	F2TH	173
F-WWVR	F2TH	204
F-WWVR	F2TH	230
F-WWVR	F2TH	98
F-WWVR	FA7X	105
F-WWVR	FA7X	166
F-WWVR	FA7X	255
F-WWVR	FA7X	46
F-WWVS	F2TH	123
F-WWVS	F2TH	205
F-WWVS	F2TH	231
F-WWVS	F2TH	99
F-WWVS	FA7X	140
F-WWVS	FA7X	220
F-WWVS	FA7X	47
F-WWVT	F2TH	100
F-WWVT	F2TH	140
F-WWVT	F2TH	206
F-WWVT	FA7X	171
F-WWVT	FA7X	237
F-WWVT	FA7X	48
F-WWVU	F2TH	101
F-WWVU	F2TH	124
F-WWVU	F2TH	141
F-WWVU	F2TH	162
F-WWVU	F2TH	207
F-WWVU	FA7X	141
F-WWVU	FA7X	259
F-WWVU	FA7X	53
F-WWVV	F2TH	102
F-WWVV	F2TH	125
F-WWVV	F2TH	142
F-WWVV	F2TH	168
F-WWVV	F2TH	208
F-WWVV	FA7X	142
F-WWVV	FA7X	212
F-WWVV	FA7X	54
F-WWVW	F2TH	126
F-WWVW	F2TH	143
F-WWVW	F2TH	163
F-WWVW	F2TH	209
F-WWVX	F2TH	103
F-WWVX	F2TH	144
F-WWVX	F2TH	210
F-WWVX	FA7X	143
F-WWVX	FA7X	202
F-WWVX	FA7X	55
F-WWVY	F2TH	104
F-WWVY	F2TH	127
F-WWVY	F2TH	164
F-WWVY	F2TH	211
F-WWVY	FA7X	144
F-WWVY	FA7X	223
F-WWVY	FA7X	56
F-WWVZ	F2TH	105
F-WWVZ	F2TH	128
F-WWVZ	F2TH	145
F-WWVZ	F2TH	160
F-WWVZ	F2TH	212
F-WWVZ	FA7X	145
F-WWVZ	FA7X	213
F-WWVZ	FA7X	57
F-WWZK	FA10	161
F-WWZK	FA7X	106
F-WWZK	FA7X	208
F-WWZK	FA7X	23
F-WWZL	FA10	195
F-WWZL	FA7X	168
F-WWZL	FA7X	24
F-WWZL	**FA7X**	**260**
F-WWZL	FA7X	91
F-WWZM	FA10	212
F-WWZM	FA7X	158
F-WWZM	FA7X	232
F-WWZM	FA7X	25
F-WWZM	FA7X	92
F-WWZN	FA10	224
F-WWZN	FA7X	152
F-WWZN	FA7X	215
F-WWZN	FA7X	26
F-WWZN	FA7X	93
F-WWZO	FA7X	114
F-WWZO	FA7X	189
F-WWZO	FA7X	27
F-WWZP	FA7X	165
F-WWZP	FA7X	225
F-WWZP	FA7X	28
F-WWZQ	FA7X	161
F-WWZQ	FA7X	219
F-WWZQ	FA7X	29
F-WWZQ	FA7X	94
F-WWZR	FA7X	107
F-WWZR	FA7X	172
F-WWZR	FA7X	236
F-WWZR	FA7X	30
F-WWZS	FA7X	108
F-WWZS	FA7X	174
F-WWZS	FA7X	252
F-WWZS	FA7X	31
F-WWZT	FA7X	177
F-WWZT	FA7X	261
F-WWZT	FA7X	32
F-WWZT	FA7X	95
F-WWZU	FA7X	206
F-WWZU	FA7X	33
F-WWZU	FA7X	96
F-WWZV	FA7X	117
F-WWZV	FA7X	183
F-WWZV	FA7X	262
F-WWZV	FA7X	34
F-WWZW	FA7X	115
F-WWZW	FA7X	216
F-WWZW	FA7X	35
F-WWZX	FA7X	164
F-WWZX	FA7X	221
F-WWZX	FA7X	36
F-WWZX	FA7X	97
F-WWZY	FA7X	116
F-WWZY	FA7X	182
F-WWZY	FA7X	37
F-WWZZ	FA7X	118
F-WWZZ	FA7X	185
F-WWZZ	FA7X	38
F-WXEY	**F2EX**	**6**
F-WZAH	FA20	401
(F-WZAS)	FA20	362
F-WZGA	FA10	129
F-WZGA	FA10	154
F-WZGA	FA10	173
F-WZGA	FA10	195
F-WZGA	FA10	217
F-WZGB	FA10	130
F-WZGB	FA10	186
F-WZGB	FA10	196
F-WZGB	FA10	218
F-WZGC	FA10	131
F-WZGC	FA10	155
F-WZGC	FA10	181
F-WZGC	FA10	197
F-WZGC	FA10	219
F-WZGD	FA10	132
F-WZGD	FA10	202
F-WZGD	FA10	220
F-WZGD	FA10	61
F-WZGE	FA10	133
F-WZGE	FA10	156
F-WZGE	FA10	174
F-WZGF	FA10	108
F-WZGF	FA10	134
F-WZGF	FA10	157
F-WZGF	FA10	175
F-WZGF	FA10	198
F-WZGF	FA10	222
F-WZGF	FA10	89
F-WZGG	FA10	127
F-WZGG	FA10	135
F-WZGG	FA10	199
F-WZGG	FA10	200
F-WZGG	FA10	223
F-WZGH	FA10	136
F-WZGH	FA10	201
F-WZGH	FA10	221
F-WZGH	FA10	224
F-WZGI	FA10	137
F-WZGI	FA10	158
F-WZGI	FA10	176
F-WZGI	FA10	225
F-WZGJ	FA10	138
F-WZGJ	FA10	159
F-WZGJ	FA10	177
F-WZGJ	FA10	203
F-WZGJ	FA10	226
F-WZGK	FA10	139
F-WZGK	FA10	160
F-WZGK	FA10	178
F-WZGK	FA10	204
F-WZGL	FA10	140
F-WZGL	FA10	179
F-WZGL	FA10	205
F-WZGM	FA10	141
F-WZGM	FA10	161
F-WZGM	FA10	180
F-WZGM	FA10	206
F-WZGN	FA10	142
F-WZGN	FA10	162
F-WZGN	FA10	182
F-WZGN	FA10	207
F-WZGO	FA10	143
F-WZGO	FA10	183
F-WZGO	FA10	208
F-WZGP	FA10	144
F-WZGP	FA10	163
F-WZGP	FA10	184
F-WZGP	FA10	209
F-WZGQ	FA10	145

F-WZGQ	FA10	164
F-WZGQ	FA10	185
F-WZGR	FA10	146
F-WZGR	FA10	165
F-WZGR	FA10	187
F-WZGR	FA10	210
F-WZGS	FA10	126
F-WZGS	FA10	136
F-WZGS	FA10	147
F-WZGS	FA10	166
F-WZGS	FA10	188
F-WZGT	FA10	148
F-WZGT	FA10	167
F-WZGT	FA10	189
F-WZGT	FA10	211
F-WZGU	FA10	149
F-WZGU	FA10	168
F-WZGU	FA10	190
F-WZGU	FA10	212
F-WZGV	FA10	150
F-WZGV	FA10	169
F-WZGV	FA10	191
F-WZGV	FA10	213
F-WZGX	FA10	151
F-WZGX	FA10	170
F-WZGX	FA10	192
F-WZGX	FA10	214
F-WZGY	FA10	152
F-WZGY	FA10	171
F-WZGY	FA10	193
F-WZGY	FA10	215
F-WZGZ	FA10	153
F-WZGZ	FA10	172
F-WZGZ	FA10	194
F-WZGZ	FA10	216
F-WZHA	FA50	112
F-WZHA	FA50	124
F-WZHA	FA50	135
F-WZHA	FA50	146
F-WZHA	FA50	154
F-WZHA	FA50	161
F-WZHA	FA50	163
F-WZHA	FA50	26
F-WZHA	FA50	33
F-WZHA	FA50	4
F-WZHA	FA50	44
F-WZHA	FA50	58
F-WZHA	FA50	7
F-WZHA	FA50	74
F-WZHA	FA50	81
F-WZHB	FA50	113
F-WZHB	FA50	125
F-WZHB	FA50	136
F-WZHB	FA50	148
F-WZHB	FA50	162
F-WZHB	FA50	19
F-WZHB	FA50	29
F-WZHB	FA50	59
F-WZHB	FA50	6
F-WZHB	FA50	76
F-WZHB	FA50	93
(F-WZHB)	FA50	5
F-WZHC	FA50	115
F-WZHC	FA50	12
F-WZHC	FA50	137
F-WZHC	FA50	150
F-WZHC	FA50	159
F-WZHC	FA50	31
F-WZHC	FA50	57
F-WZHC	FA50	77
F-WZHC	FA50	8
F-WZHC	FA50	94
F-WZHD	FA50	10
F-WZHD	FA50	116
F-WZHD	FA50	127
F-WZHD	FA50	139
F-WZHD	FA50	152
F-WZHD	FA50	164
F-WZHD	FA50	30
F-WZHD	FA50	60
F-WZHD	FA50	9
F-WZHE	FA50	11
F-WZHE	FA50	141
F-WZHE	FA50	153
F-WZHE	FA50	166
F-WZHE	FA50	28
F-WZHE	FA50	42
F-WZHE	FA50	62
F-WZHE	FA50	79
F-WZHF	FA50	118
F-WZHF	FA50	128
F-WZHF	FA50	13
F-WZHF	FA50	156
F-WZHF	FA50	165
F-WZHF	FA50	22
F-WZHF	FA50	35
F-WZHF	FA50	45
F-WZHF	FA50	63
F-WZHF	FA50	71
F-WZHG	FA50	122
F-WZHG	FA50	14
F-WZHG	FA50	167
F-WZHG	FA50	23
F-WZHG	FA50	40
F-WZHG	FA50	67
F-WZHG	FA50	82
F-WZHH	FA50	123
F-WZHH	FA50	158
F-WZHH	FA50	16
F-WZHH	FA50	168
F-WZHH	FA50	34
F-WZHH	FA50	64
F-WZHH	FA50	75
F-WZHI	FA50	126
F-WZHI	FA50	143
F-WZHI	FA50	160
F-WZHI	FA50	17
F-WZHI	FA50	170
F-WZHI	FA50	25
F-WZHI	FA50	41
F-WZHI	FA50	61
F-WZHJ	FA50	149
F-WZHJ	FA50	171
F-WZHJ	FA50	18
F-WZHJ	FA50	32
F-WZHJ	FA50	36
F-WZHJ	FA50	69
F-WZHJ	FA50	83
F-WZHK	FA50	142
F-WZHK	FA50	172
F-WZHK	FA50	20
F-WZHK	FA50	38
F-WZHK	FA50	46
F-WZHK	FA50	48
F-WZHK	FA50	84
F-WZHL	FA50	144
F-WZHL	FA50	173
F-WZHL	FA50	24
F-WZHL	FA50	39
F-WZHL	FA50	49
F-WZHL	FA50	70
F-WZHL	FA50	97
F-WZHM	FA50	108
F-WZHM	FA50	15
F-WZHM	FA50	175
F-WZHM	FA50	37
F-WZHM	FA50	72
F-WZHM	FA50	99
F-WZHN	FA50	100
F-WZHN	FA50	119
F-WZHN	FA50	176
F-WZHN	FA50	21
F-WZHN	FA50	27
F-WZHN	FA50	80
F-WZHO	FA50	102
F-WZHO	FA50	121
F-WZHO	FA50	178
F-WZHO	FA50	43
F-WZHO	FA50	85
F-WZHP	FA50	179
F-WZHP	FA50	47
F-WZHP	FA50	66
F-WZHQ	FA50	103
F-WZHQ	FA50	129
F-WZHQ	FA50	50
F-WZHQ	FA50	68
F-WZHR	FA50	104
F-WZHR	FA50	130
F-WZHR	FA50	51
F-WZHR	FA50	56
F-WZHS	FA50	105
F-WZHS	FA50	53
F-WZHS	FA50	87
F-WZHT	FA50	106
F-WZHT	FA50	54
F-WZHT	FA50	65
F-WZHU	FA50	55
F-WZHU	FA50	88
F-WZHV	FA50	109
F-WZHV	FA50	52
F-WZHV	FA50	89
F-WZHX	FA50	90
F-WZHY	FA50	91
F-WZHZ	FA50	111
F-WZHZ	FA50	92
F-WZIG	HS25	257055
F-WZIH	HFB3	1024
F-WZSB	CRVT	31
F-WZZA	FA20	491
F-WZZA	FA20	497
F-WZZA	FA20	505
F-WZZB	FA20	487
F-WZZC	FA20	493
F-WZZC	FA20	496
F-WZZD	FA20	494
F-WZZD	FA20	501
F-WZZE	FA20	495
F-WZZF	FA20	488
F-WZZJ	FA20	499

France – Govt Operated

(F-Z…)	MS76	03
F-ZACA	**FA20**	**252/485**
F-ZACB	FA10	02
F-ZACB	**FA20**	**96**
F-ZACC	FA20	124/433
F-ZACD	FA20	131/437
F-ZACG	FA20	86
F-ZACR	**FA20**	**138/440**
F-ZACS	FA20	22/404
F-ZACT	**FA20**	**79/415**
F-ZACU	**FA20**	**145/443**
F-ZACV	FA20	1/401
F-ZACV	**FA20**	**288/499**
F-ZACW	**FA20**	**104/454**
F-ZACX	**FA20**	**188/464**
F-ZACY	**FA20**	**263/489**
F-ZACZ	**FA20**	**375/547**
F-ZADS	MS76	001
F-ZGTI	FA10	133
F-ZJAZ	**MS76**	**117**
F-ZJNB	**MS76**	**068**
F-ZJNC	MS76	083
F-ZJNI	**MS76**	**113**
F-ZJNJ	MS76	100
F-ZJNJ	MS76	114
F-ZJNQ	**MS76**	**118**
F-ZJON	**MS76**	**116**
F-ZJOV	MS76	115
F-ZJSA	**FA20**	**480**
F-ZJTA	FA10	02
F-ZJTA	FA20	182/461
F-ZJTD	FA20	476
F-ZJTJ	FA20	422
F-ZJTL	FA50	36
F-ZJTS	**FA20**	**465**
F-ZJTS	FA20	451
F-ZLNL	MS76	119
F-ZVMV	CRVT	1
F-ZVMW	CRVT	2
F-ZVMX	CRVT	10
F-ZWMM	**FA50**	**27**
F-ZWMO	**FA50**	**78**
F-ZWMT	**FA50**	**34**
F-ZWTA	FA50	36
F-ZWVA	**FA50**	**5**
F-ZWVF	**FA20**	**448**

United Kingdom Class B

G-0502	HS25	258385
G-0504	HS25	258392
G-5-11	HS25	25026
G-5-11	HS25	25101
G-5-11	HS25	25110
G-5-11	HS25	25119
G-5-11	HS25	25126
G-5-11	HS25	25131
G-5-11	HS25	25134
G-5-11	HS25	25137
G-5-11	HS25	25139
G-5-11	HS25	25154
G-5-11	HS25	25197
G-5-11	HS25	25240
G-5-11	HS25	25276
G-5-11	HS25	256015
G-5-11	HS25	256021
G-5-11	HS25	256045
G-5-11	HS25	256052
G-5-11	HS25	256070
G-5-11	HS25	257008
G-5-11	HS25	257039
G-5-11	HS25	257051
G-5-11	HS25	257065
G-5-11	HS25	257093
G-5-11	HS25	257105
G-5-11	HS25	257119
G-5-11	HS25	257131
G-5-11	HS25	257144
G-5-11	HS25	257150
G-5-11	HS25	257164
G-5-11	HS25	257177
G-5-11	HS25	257186
G-5-11	HS25	257196
G-5-11	HS25	258001
G-5-11	HS25	258008
G-5-11	HS25	258032
G-5-11	HS25	258042
G-5-11	HS25	258047
G-5-11	HS25	258053
(G-5-11)	HS25	257022
G-5-11?	HS25	25277
G-5-12	HS25	25129
G-5-12	HS25	25141
G-5-12	HS25	25144
G-5-12	HS25	25219
G-5-12	HS25	25244
G-5-12	HS25	25279
G-5-12	HS25	256028
G-5-12	HS25	256050
G-5-12	HS25	256060
G-5-12	HS25	257009
G-5-12	HS25	257025
G-5-12	HS25	257041
G-5-12	HS25	257073
G-5-12	HS25	257083
G-5-12	HS25	257095
G-5-12	HS25	257103
G-5-12	HS25	257142
G-5-12	HS25	257151
G-5-12	HS25	257163
G-5-12	HS25	257184
G-5-12	HS25	257185
G-5-12	HS25	257197
G-5-12	HS25	257199
G-5-12	HS25	257212
G-5-12	HS25	258018
G-5-12	HS25	258019
G-5-12	HS25	258027
G-5-12	HS25	258028
G-5-12	HS25	258034
G-5-12	HS25	258043
G-5-12	HS25	258044
(G-5-12)	HS25	25138
(G-5-12)	HS25	258005
G-5-13	HS25	25113
G-5-13	HS25	25148
G-5-13	HS25	25150
G-5-13	HS25	25256
G-5-13	HS25	25270
G-5-13	HS25	256041
G-5-13	HS25	256056
G-5-13	HS25	256063
G-5-13	HS25	257011
G-5-13	HS25	257042
G-5-13	HS25	257056
G-5-13	HS25	257066
G-5-13	HS25	257075
G-5-13	HS25	257106
G-5-13	HS25	257120
G-5-13	HS25	257134
G-5-13	HS25	257146
(G-5-13)	HS25	25181
G-5-14	HS25	25130
G-5-14	HS25	25135
G-5-14	HS25	25147
G-5-14	HS25	25217
G-5-14	HS25	25219
G-5-14	HS25	25243
G-5-14	HS25	25271
G-5-14	HS25	256031
G-5-14	HS25	256061
G-5-14	HS25	256071
G-5-14	HS25	257012
G-5-14	HS25	257032
G-5-14	HS25	257034
G-5-14	HS25	257057
G-5-14	HS25	257068
G-5-14	HS25	257077
G-5-14	HS25	257084
G-5-14	HS25	257096
G-5-14	HS25	257108
G-5-14	HS25	257121
G-5-14	HS25	257133
G-5-14	HS25	257147
G-5-14	HS25	257158
G-5-14	HS25	257165
G-5-14	HS25	257170
G-5-14	HS25	257178
G-5-14	HS25	257187
G-5-14	HS25	257192
G-5-14	HS25	257200
G-5-14	HS25	257203
G-5-14	HS25	258013
G-5-14	HS25	258020
G-5-14	HS25	258025
G-5-14	HS25	258030
G-5-15	HS25	25160
G-5-15	HS25	25223
G-5-15	HS25	25272
G-5-15	HS25	256002
G-5-15	HS25	256048
G-5-15	HS25	256062
G-5-15	HS25	256066
G-5-15	HS25	256070
G-5-15	HS25	257004
G-5-15	HS25	257058
G-5-15	HS25	257069
G-5-15	HS25	257078
G-5-15	HS25	257085
G-5-15	HS25	257098
G-5-15	HS25	257110
G-5-15	HS25	257122
G-5-15	HS25	257135
G-5-15	HS25	257159
G-5-15	HS25	257167
G-5-15	HS25	257171
G-5-15	HS25	257179
G-5-15	HS25	257188
G-5-15	HS25	257193
G-5-15	HS25	257204
G-5-15	HS25	258004
G-5-15	HS25	258005
G-5-15	HS25	258009
G-5-15	HS25	258014
G-5-15	HS25	258021
G-5-15	HS25	258023
G-5-15	HS25	258031
G-5-15	HS25	258037
G-5-15	HS25	258040
G-5-15	HS25	258054
G-5-16	HS25	25138
G-5-16	HS25	25163
G-5-16	HS25	25249
G-5-16	HS25	25289
G-5-16	HS25	256026
G-5-16	HS25	256047
G-5-16	HS25	256065
G-5-16	HS25	256068
G-5-16	HS25	257035
G-5-16	HS25	257048
G-5-16	HS25	257055
G-5-16	HS25	257062
G-5-16	HS25	257079
G-5-16	HS25	257087
G-5-16	HS25	257094
G-5-16	HS25	257099
G-5-16	HS25	257111
G-5-16	HS25	257123
G-5-16	HS25	257137
G-5-16	HS25	257180
G-5-16	HS25	257181
G-5-16	HS25	257206
G-5-16	HS25	257213
G-5-16	HS25	258017
G-5-16	HS25	258022
G-5-16	HS25	258029
G-5-16	HS25	258045
G-5-16	HS25	258048
(G-5-16)	HS25	25140
(G-5-16)	HS25	25246
(G-5-16)	HS25	258002
G-5-17	HS25	25140
G-5-17	HS25	25169
G-5-17	HS25	25252
G-5-17	HS25	256012
G-5-17	HS25	256054
G-5-17	HS25	256057
G-5-17	HS25	256064
G-5-17	HS25	257014
G-5-17	HS25	257022
G-5-17	HS25	257036
G-5-17	HS25	257044
G-5-17	HS25	257049
G-5-17	HS25	257059
G-5-17	HS25	257071
G-5-17	HS25	257076
G-5-17	HS25	257086
G-5-17	HS25	257101
G-5-17	HS25	257113
G-5-17	HS25	257125
G-5-17	HS25	257138
G-5-17	HS25	257148
G-5-17	HS25	257152
G-5-17	HS25	257156
G-5-17	HS25	257161
G-5-17	HS25	257173
G-5-17	HS25	257182
G-5-17	HS25	257191
G-5-17	HS25	257202
G-5-17	HS25	257214
G-5-17	HS25	258006
G-5-17	HS25	258015
G-5-18	HS25	25143
G-5-18	HS25	25183
G-5-18	HS25	25235
G-5-18	HS25	25253
G-5-18	HS25	256017
G-5-18	HS25	256045
G-5-18	HS25	256058
G-5-18	HS25	257006
G-5-18	HS25	257015
G-5-18	HS25	257037
G-5-18	HS25	257050
G-5-18	HS25	257060
G-5-18	HS25	257072
G-5-18	HS25	257080
G-5-18	HS25	257089
G-5-18	HS25	257102
G-5-18	HS25	257114
G-5-18	HS25	257126
G-5-18	HS25	257139
G-5-18	HS25	257145
G-5-18	HS25	257154
G-5-18	HS25	257162
G-5-18	HS25	257166
G-5-18	HS25	257174
G-5-18	HS25	257195
G-5-18	HS25	257198
G-5-18	HS25	257207
G-5-18	HS25	257210
G-5-18	HS25	258012
G-5-18	HS25	258016
G-5-18	HS25	258024
G-5-18	HS25	258026
G-5-18	HS25	258036
G-5-18	HS25	258041
G-5-18	HS25	258051
G-5-19	HS25	25153
G-5-19	HS25	25159
G-5-19	HS25	25171
G-5-19	HS25	25235
G-5-19	HS25	25239
G-5-19	HS25	25257
G-5-19	HS25	256015
G-5-19	HS25	256055
G-5-19	HS25	256059
G-5-19	HS25	257003
G-5-19	HS25	257017
G-5-19	HS25	257038
G-5-19	HS25	257052
G-5-19	HS25	257061
G-5-19	HS25	257074
G-5-19	HS25	257081
G-5-19	HS25	257090
G-5-19	HS25	257100
G-5-19	HS25	257116
G-5-19	HS25	257128
G-5-19	HS25	257140
G-5-19	HS25	257149
G-5-19	HS25	257155
G-5-19	HS25	257160
G-5-19	HS25	257201
G-5-19	HS25	257205
G-5-19	HS25	257208
G-5-19	HS25	258010

G-5-19	HS25	258033
G-5-19	HS25	258039
G-5-19	HS25	258049
(G-5-19)	HS25	258005
G-5-20	HS25	25145
G-5-20	HS25	25189
G-5-20	HS25	25214
G-5-20	HS25	25241
G-5-20	HS25	25242
G-5-20	HS25	25273
G-5-20	HS25	25274
G-5-20	HS25	256068
G-5-20	HS25	257002
G-5-20	HS25	257053
G-5-20	HS25	257063
G-5-20	HS25	257092
G-5-20	HS25	257104
G-5-20	HS25	257117
G-5-20	HS25	257129
G-5-20	HS25	257141
G-5-20	HS25	257143
G-5-20	HS25	257157
G-5-20	HS25	257168
G-5-20	HS25	257176
G-5-20	HS25	257183
G-5-20	HS25	257209
G-5-20	HS25	257215
G-5-20	HS25	258003
G-5-20	HS25	258007
G-5-20	HS25	258011
G-5-20	HS25	258035
G-5-20	HS25	258038
G-5-20	HS25	258046
G-5-20	HS25	258052
G-5-21	HS25	257169
G-5-501	HS25	258037
G-5-502	HS25	257115
G-5-503	HS25	258050
G-5-504	HS25	258055
G-5-505	HS25	256042
G-5-506	HS25	258059
G-5-508	HS25	258057
G-5-509	HS25	258056
G-5-510	HS25	258058
G-5-511	HS25	258060
G-5-514	HS25	258064
G-5-515	HS25	258061
G-5-516	HS25	258062
G-5-518	HS25	258063
G-5-519	HS25	257064
G-5-520	HS25	258065
G-5-521	HS25	258066
G-5-522	HS25	258001
G-5-524	HS25	257076
G-5-525	HS25	258067
G-5-526	HS25	258069
G-5-527	HS25	258070
G-5-528	HS25	258071
G-5-529	HS25	258072
G-5-530	HS25	257178
G-5-531	HS25	257088
G-5-532	HS25	258073
G-5-533	HS25	258075
G-5-534	HS25	257028
G-5-535	HS25	258076
G-5-536	HS25	257112
G-5-538	HS25	258077
G-5-539	HS25	258068
G-5-540	HS25	258080
G-5-541	HS25	258074
G-5-542	HS25	258079
G-5-543	HS25	258081
G-5-544	HS25	258078
G-5-545	HS25	257136
G-5-546	HS25	258083
G-5-547	HS25	258084
G-5-548	HS25	258082
G-5-549	HS25	257100
G-5-550	HS25	258086
G-5-551	HS25	258085
G-5-552	HS25	258087
G-5-553	HS25	257112
G-5-554	HS25	258007
G-5-555	HS25	258089
G-5-556	HS25	258090
G-5-557	HS25	258001
G-5-558	HS25	258092
G-5-559	HS25	258093
G-5-560	HS25	258091
G-5-561	HS25	258095
G-5-562	HS25	258096
G-5-563	HS25	258088
G-5-564	HS25	258098
G-5-565	HS25	258099
G-5-566	HS25	258100
G-5-567	HS25	258097
G-5-568	HS25	257172
G-5-569	HS25	258022
G-5-570	HS25	257178
G-5-571	HS25	257076
G-5-572	HS25	258101
G-5-573	HS25	258102
G-5-574	HS25	258103
G-5-575	HS25	258104
G-5-576	HS25	258094
G-5-577	HS25	258105
G-5-578	HS25	258107
G-5-579	HS25	258108
G-5-580	HS25	258106
G-5-581	HS25	258109
G-5-582	HS25	258111
G-5-583	HS25	258112
G-5-584	HS25	258110
G-5-585	HS25	256027
G-5-586	HS25	258114
G-5-587	HS25	258113
G-5-588	HS25	257130
G-5-589	HS25	258117
(G-5-590)	HS25	258118
G-5-591	HS25	258119
G-5-592	HS25	258116
G-5-593	HS25	258121
G-5-594	HS25	258122
G-5-595	HS25	258034
G-5-596	HS25	258124
G-5-597	HS25	258126
G-5-598	HS25	257055
G-5-599	HS25	258115
G-5-600	HS25	258123
G-5-601	HS25	258125
G-5-602	HS25	258127
G-5-603	HS25	258128
G-5-604	HS25	257070
G-5-605	HS25	258118
G-5-606	HS25	258120
G-5-607	HS25	258132
G-5-608	HS25	258135
G-5-609	HS25	258136
G-5-610	HS25	258137
G-5-611	HS25	258131
G-5-612	HS25	258139
G-5-613	HS25	258140
G-5-614	HS25	258138
G-5-615	HS25	258141
G-5-616	HS25	258133
G-5-617	HS25	258142
G-5-618	HS25	258144
G-5-619	HS25	258145
G-5-620	HS25	258130
G-5-621	HS25	258147
G-5-622	HS25	258129
G-5-623	HS25	25127
G-5-624	HS25	25254
G-5-625	HS25	258150
G-5-626	HS25	258152
G-5-627	HS25	258153
G-5-628	HS25	258155
G-5-629	HS25	258146
G-5-630	HS25	258148
G-5-631	HS25	257010
G-5-632	HS25	258157
G-5-633	HS25	258160
G-5-634	HS25	258134
G-5-635	HS25	258149
G-5-636	HS25	258161
G-5-637	HS25	258058
G-5-638	HS25	258162
G-5-639	HS25	258163
G-5-640	HS25	258074
G-5-641	HS25	258166
G-5-642	HS25	258133
G-5-643	HS25	258168
G-5-644	HS25	258169
G-5-645	HS25	258170
G-5-646	HS25	258171
G-5-647	HS25	258172
G-5-648	HS25	258173
G-5-649	HS25	258174
G-5-650	HS25	258175
G-5-651	HS25	25217
G-5-652	HS25	258176
G-5-653	HS25	258068
G-5-654	HS25	258164
G-5-655	HS25	258154
G-5-656	HS25	258143
G-5-657	HS25	258165
G-5-658	HS25	258178
G-5-659	HS25	257212
G-5-660	HS25	258179
G-5-661	HS25	258156
G-5-662	HS25	258167
G-5-663	HS25	258181
G-5-664	HS25	258112
G-5-665	HS25	258115
G-5-666	HS25	258183
G-5-667	HS25	258158
G-5-668	HS25	258177
G-5-669	HS25	258185
G-5-670	HS25	258187
"G-5-670"	HS25	258208
G-5-671	HS25	258188
G-5-672	HS25	25247
G-5-673	HS25	258189
G-5-674	HS25	258191
G-5-675	HS25	258180
G-5-676	HS25	258182
G-5-677	HS25	258193
G-5-678	HS25	258184
G-5-679	HS25	258195
G-5-680	HS25	258196
G-5-681	HS25	258199
G-5-682	HS25	258200
G-5-683	HS25	258186
G-5-684	HS25	258190
G-5-685	HS25	258202
G-5-686	HS25	258203
G-5-687	HS25	258204
G-5-688	HS25	258206
G-5-689	HS25	258205
G-5-690	HS25	258207
G-5-691	HS25	258192
G-5-692	HS25	258194
G-5-693	HS25	257196
G-5-694	HS25	258198
G-5-695	HS25	258209
G-5-696	HS25	258197
G-5-697	HS25	258040
G-5-698	HS25	256052
G-5-699	HS25	258201
G-5-700	HS25	258208
G-5-701	HS25	257031
G-5-702	HS25	259003
G-5-703	HS25	258146
G-5-704	HS25	258019
G-5-705	HS25	258210
G-5-706	HS25	258214
G-5-707	HS25	25248
G-5-708	HS25	257062
G-5-709	HS25	258213
G-5-710	HS25	258212
G-5-711	HS25	259013
G-5-712	HS25	259014
G-5-713	HS25	258078
G-5-714	HS25	258216
G-5-715	HS25	258217
G-5-716	HS25	259009
G-5-717	HS25	259011
G-5-718	HS25	259015
G-5-719	HS25	259017
G-5-720	HS25	259008
G-5-721	HS25	257007
G-5-722	HS25	259010
G-5-723	HS25	259020
G-5-724	HS25	258211
G-5-725	HS25	258218
G-5-726	HS25	259012
G-5-727	HS25	258215
G-5-728	HS25	258220
G-5-729	HS25	259023
G-5-730	HS25	259019
G-5-731	HS25	258221
G-5-732	HS25	259016
G-5-733	HS25	258223
G-5-734	HS25	259022
G-5-735	HS25	259005
G-5-736	HS25	259021
G-5-737	HS25	259024
G-5-738	HS25	258068
G-5-739	HS25	258225
G-5-740	HS25	258219
G-5-741	HS25	259018
G-5-742	HS25	258025
G-5-743	HS25	259026
G-5-744	HS25	258229
G-5-745	HS25	258222
G-5-746	HS25	259027
G-5-747	HS25	257178
G-5-748	HS25	258230
G-5-749	HS25	259028
G-5-750	HS25	258231
G-5-751	HS25	259029
G-5-752	HS25	258232
G-5-753	HS25	259030
G-5-754	HS25	259031
G-5-755	HS25	258226
G-5-756	HS25	259033
G-5-757	HS25	258234
G-5-758	HS25	258228
G-5-759	HS25	259025
G-5-760	HS25	259032
G-5-761	HS25	259034
G-5-762	HS25	259036
G-5-763	HS25	258224
G-5-764	HS25	258236
G-5-765	HS25	257172
G-5-766	HS25	257196
G-5-767	HS25	258238
G-5-768	HS25	258239
G-5-769	HS25	258227
G-5-770	HS25	258233
G-5-771	HS25	259037
G-5-772	HS25	258240
G-5-773	HS25	259035
G-5-774	HS25	258235
G-5-775	HS25	258237
G-5-776	HS25	259038
G-5-777	HS25	258241
G-5-778	HS25	258243
G-5-779	HS25	259004
G-5-780	HS25	258244
G-5-781	HS25	259039
G-5-782	HS25	258246
G-5-783	HS25	259040
G-5-784	HS25	258248
G-5-785	HS25	259041
G-5-786	HS25	258249
G-5-787	HS25	258251
G-5-788	HS25	258252
G-5-789	HS25	259042
G-5-790	HS25	258253
G-5-791	HS25	258254
G-5-792	HS25	258255
G-5-793	HS25	258242
G-5-794	HS25	259043
G-5-795	HS25	258256
G-5-796	HS25	258257
G-5-797	HS25	259044
G-5-798	HS25	258258
G-5-799	HS25	258259
G-5-800	HS25	258260
G-5-801	HS25	259045
G-5-802	HS25	258261
G-5-803	HS25	258262
G-5-804	HS25	258263
G-5-805	HS25	259046
G-5-806	HS25	258264
G-5-807	HS25	258067
G-5-808	HS25	257107
G-5-809	HS25	258265
G-5-810	HS25	257097
G-5-811	HS25	258266
G-5-812	HS25	258267
G-5-813	HS25	258247
G-5-814	HS25	258269
G-5-815	HS25	258250
G-5-816	HS25	258270
G-5-817	HS25	259047
G-5-818	HS25	258271
G-5-819	HS25	258272
G-5-820	HS25	258273
G-5-821	HS25	25281
G-5-822	HS25	258274
G-5-823	HS25	258275
G-5-824	HS25	258276
G-5-826	HS25	259048
G-5-827	HS25	258282
G-5-828	HS25	258283
G-5-829	HS25	258268
G-5-830	HS25	258284
G-5-831	HS25	258285
G-5-832	HS25	258286
G-5-833	HS25	258287
G-5-834	HS25	258289
G-5-835	HS25	258290
G-5-836	HS25	258291
G-5-837	HS25	259049
"G-5-837"	HS25	258291
G-5-838	HS25	258292
G-5-839	HS25	258293
G-5-840	HS25	258294
G-5-841	HS25	258295
G-5-842	HS25	258296
G-5-843	HS25	258298
G-5-844	HS25	258299
G-5-845	HS25	258300
G-5-846	HS25	259050
G-5-847	HS25	258302
G-5-848	HS25	258288
G-5-849	HS25	258303
G-5-850	HS25	258307
G-5-851	HS25	258308
G-5-852	HS25	258310
G-5-853	HS25	258312
G-5-854	HS25	258314
G-5-855	HS25	258316
G-5-856	HS25	258318
G-5-857	HS25	258321
G-5-858	HS25	258323
G-5-859	HS25	259051
G-5-860	HS25	258324
G-5-861	HS25	258327
G-5-862	HS25	258329
G-5-863	HS25	259052
G-5-864	HS25	258305
G-5-865	HS25	258332
G-5-866	HS25	258328
G-5-867	HS25	258335
G-5-868	HS25	258337
G-5-869	HS25	258330
G-5-870	HS25	257194
G-5-874	HS25	258022
G-5-875	HS25	257139
G-36-1	HS25	25238
G-36-2	HS25	257184
G-36-2	MS76	008
G-37-65	HS25	25011
G-52-24	GLEX	9038
G-52-25	GLEX	9081
G-52-26	GLEX	9032
G-60-01	FA20	223
G-88-01	HS25	258078
G-88-03	HS25	257184

United Kingdom

(G-….)	E55P	50500021
(G-….)	GLF4	1096
(G-….)	HS25	257094
G-APRU	MS76	008
G-ARYA	HS25	25001
G-ARYB	HS25	25002
G-ARYC	HS25	25003
G-ASEC	HS25	25004
G-ASNU	HS25	25005
G-ASSH	HS25	25017
(G-ASSH)	HS25	25007
G-ASSI	HS25	25008
G-ASSJ	HS25	25013
G-ASSK	HS25	25014
G-ASSL	HS25	25016
G-ASSM	HS25	25010
G-ASTY	HS25	25007
G-ASYX	HS25	25019
G-ASZM	HS25	25020
G-ASZN	HS25	25021
G-ASZO	HS25	25022
G-ASZP	HS25	25023
G-ATAY	HS25	25026
G-ATAZ	HS25	25029
G-ATBA	HS25	25030
G-ATBB	HS25	25031
G-ATBC	HS25	25032
G-ATBD	HS25	25033
G-ATCO	HS25	25035
G-ATCP	HS25	25038
G-ATFO	HS25	25037
G-ATGA	HS25	25043
G-ATGS	HS25	25046
G-ATGT	HS25	25047
G-ATGU	HS25	25051
G-ATIK	HS25	25052
G-ATIL	HS25	25057
G-ATIM	HS25	25060
G-ATKK	HS25	25064
G-ATKL	HS25	25065
G-ATKM	HS25	25066
G-ATKN	HS25	25070
G-ATLI	HS25	25073
G-ATLJ	HS25	25075
G-ATLK	HS25	25078
G-ATLL	HS25	25079
G-ATNM	HS25	25082
G-ATNN	HS25	25084
G-ATNO	HS25	25088
G-ATNP	HS25	25091
G-ATNR	HS25	25096
G-ATNS	HS25	25098
G-ATNT	HS25	25100
G-ATOV	HS25	25074
G-ATOW	HS25	25083
G-ATOX	HS25	25087
G-ATPB	HS25	25089
G-ATPC	HS25	25009
G-ATPD	HS25	25085
G-ATPE	HS25	25092
G-ATSN	HS25	25093
G-ATSO	HS25	25095
G-ATSP	HS25	25097
G-ATUU	HS25	25102
G-ATUV	HS25	25103
G-ATUW	HS25	25104
G-ATUX	HS25	25107
G-ATUY	HS25	25108
G-ATUZ	HS25	25109
G-ATWH	HS25	25094
G-ATXE	HS25	25101
G-ATYH	HS25	25111
G-ATYI	HS25	25112
G-ATYJ	HS25	25114
G-ATYK	HS25	25115
G-ATYL	HS25	25118
G-ATZE	HS25	25110
G-ATZN	HS25	25116
G-AVAD	HS25	25119
G-AVAE	HS25	25121
G-AVAF	HS25	25122
G-AVAG	HS25	25123
G-AVAH	HS25	25124
G-AVAI	HS25	25125
G-AVDL	HS25	25126
G-AVDM	HS25	25129
G-AVDX	HS25	25113
G-AVGW	HS25	25120
G-AVHA	HS25	25134
G-AVHB	HS25	25136
G-AVJD	HS25	25137
G-AVOI	HS25	25128
G-AVOJ	HS25	25139
G-AVOK	HS25	25141
G-AVOL	HS25	25142
G-AVPE	HS25	25127
G-AVRD	HS25	25130
G-AVRE	HS25	25131
G-AVRF	HS25	25133
G-AVRG	HS25	25144
G-AVRH	HS25	25146
G-AVRI	HS25	25148
G-AVRJ	HS25	25149
G-AVTY	HS25	25151
G-AVTZ	HS25	25152
G-AVVA	HS25	25138
G-AVVB	HS25	25140
G-AVXK	HS25	25143
G-AVXL	HS25	25145
G-AVXM	HS25	25153
G-AVXN	HS25	25155
G-AVZJ	HS25	25156
G-AVZK	HS25	25158
G-AVZL	HS25	25159
G-AWKH	HS25	25160
G-AWKI	HS25	25161
G-AWMS	HS25	25150
G-AWMV	HS25	25163
G-AWMW	HS25	25170
G-AWMX	HS25	25173
G-AWMY	HS25	25174

G-AWPC	HS25	25175
G-AWPD	HS25	25176
G-AWPE	HS25	25179
G-AWPF	HS25	25180
G-AWUF	HS25	25106
G-AWWL	HS25	25169
G-AWXB	HS25	25183
G-AWXC	HS25	25187
G-AWXD	HS25	25188
G-AWXE	HS25	25185
G-AWXF	HS25	25186
G-AWXN	HS25	25177
G-AWXO	HS25	25178
G-AWYE	HS25	25090
G-AXDM	HS25	25194
G-AXDO	HS25	25190
G-AXDP	HS25	25191
G-AXDR	HS25	25195
G-AXDS	HS25	25196
G-AXEG	HS25	25172
(G-AXFY)	HS25	25189
G-AXJD	HS25	25198
G-AXJE	HS25	25200
G-AXJF	HS25	25201
G-AXJG	HS25	25202
G-AXLU	HS25	25181
G-AXLV	HS25	25182
G-AXLW	HS25	25184
G-AXLX	HS25	25199
G-AXOA	HS25	25203
G-AXOB	HS25	25204
G-AXOC	HS25	25205
G-AXOD	HS25	25207
G-AXOE	HS25	25208
G-AXOF	HS25	25210
G-AXPS	HS25	25135
G-AXPU	HS25	25171
G-AXPX	HS25	25206
G-AXTR	HS25	25211
G-AXTS	HS25	25212
G-AXTT	HS25	25213
G-AXTU	HS25	25214
G-AXTV	HS25	25216
G-AXTW	HS25	25218
G-AXYE	HS25	25220
G-AXYF	HS25	25222
G-AXYG	HS25	25224
G-AXYH	HS25	25225
G-AXYI	HS25	25226
G-AXYJ	HS25	25217
G-AYBH	HS25	25256
G-AYEP	HS25	25219
G-AYER	HS25	25238
G-AYFM	HS25	25227
G-AYIZ	HS25	25223
G-AYLG	HS25	25254
G-AYLI	HS25	25240
G-AYMI	GLF2	91
G-AYNR	HS25	25235
(G-AYOI)	HS25	25243
G-AYOJ	HS25	25246
G-AYOK	HS25	25250
G-AYRR	HS25	25247
(G-AYRR)	HS25	25258
G-AYRY	HS25	25105
G-AZAF	HS25	25249
G-AZCH	HS25	25154
G-AZEK	HS25	25259
G-AZEL	HS25	25260
G-AZEM	HS25	25269
G-AZHS	HS25	25258
G-AZUF	HS25	256001
G-AZVS	HS25	25132
G-BABL	HS25	25271
G-BACI	HS25	25283
(G-BAOA)	FA20	138/440
G-BARR	HS25	256019
G-BART	HS25	256005
G-BATA	HS25	25257
G-BAXG	HS25	25063
G-BAXL	HS25	25069
G-BAYT	HS25	256012
G-BAZA	HS25	25272
G-BAZB	HS25	25252
G-BBAS	HS25	256017
G-BBCL	HS25	256015
G-BBEE	LJ25	135
G-BBEK	FA20	86
G-BBEP	HS25	256030
G-BBGU	HS25	25270
G-BBMD	HS25	256024
G-BBRO	HS25	256042
G-BBRT	HS25	256029
(G-BBRT)	HS25	256036
G-BCCL	HS25	256039
G-BCII	C500	176
G-BCJU	HS25	256041
G-BCKM	C500	198
G-BCLR	HS25	25228
G-BCRM	C500	227
G-BCSE	LJ25	188
G-BCUX	HS25	256043
G-BCXF	HS25	256054
G-BCXL	HS25	256049
G-BCYF	FA20	304/511
G-BDJE	HS25	256052
G-BDKF	HS25	25242
G-BDMF	GLF2	103
G-BDOA	HS25	256056
G-BDOB	HS25	256061
G-BDOP	HS25	256055
G-BDYE	HS25	25080
G-BDZH	HS25	256066
G-BDZR	HS25	256068
G-BEDT	HS25	256070
G-BEES	HS25	256071
G-BEFZ	HS25	257001
G-BEIN	HS25	256067
G-BEIO	HS25	256069
G-BEIZ	C500	363
G-BEME	HS25	25231
G-BERP	HS25	257003
G-BERV	HS25	257005
G-BERX	HS25	257006
G-BETV	HS25	256035
(G-BEWV)	HS25	257008
G-BEWW	HS25	256001
G-BEYC	HS25	257009
G-BFAJ	HS25	257011
G-BFAN	HS25	25258
G-BFAR	C500	402
G-BFBI	HS25	257012
G-BFDW	HS25	257014
G-BFFH	HS25	257016
G-BFFL	HS25	257015
G-BFFU	HS25	257017
G-BFGU	HS25	257018
G-BFGV	HS25	257019
G-BFIC	HS25	256060
G-BFLF	HS25	257023
G-BFLG	HS25	257024
G-BFLY	C550	089
(G-BFLY)	C550	028
G-BFMO	HS25	257026
G-BFMP	HS25	257027
G-BFPI	HS25	257025
G-BFRM	C550	027
G-BFSI	HS25	257030
G-BFSO	HS25	257028
G-BFSP	HS25	257031
(G-BFTP)	HS25	257020
G-BFUE	HS25	257032
G-BFVI	HS25	257037
(G-BFVN)	HS25	257020
G-BFXT	HS25	257034
G-BFYH	HS25	257044
G-BFYV	HS25	257043
G-BFZI	HS25	257047
G-BFZJ	HS25	257045
G-BGBJ	HS25	257052
G-BGBL	HS25	257049
G-BGDM	HS25	257004
G-BGGS	HS25	257061
G-BGKN	HS25	256058
G-BGLT	GLF2	225
G-BGOP	FA20	406/557
G-BGSR	HS25	257066
G-BGTD	HS25	257073
G-BGYR	HS25	256045
G-BHBH	C550	148
G-BHFT	HS25	25215
(G-BHGH)	C550	150
G-BHIE	HS25	256048
G-BHIO	HS25	257085
(G-BHIW)	C500	544
(G-BHKF)	HS25	257075
G-BHLF	HS25	257091
G-BHMP	HS25	257093
G-BHSK	HS25	257099
G-BHSU	HS25	257103
G-BHSV	HS25	257107
G-BHSW	HS25	257109
G-BHTJ	HS25	257097
G-BHTT	C500	560
(G-BHVA)	C550	225
(G-BIHZ)	HS25	257118
G-BIMY	HS25	257132
G-BIRU	HS25	257136
G-BIZZ	C500	645
G-BJCB	HS25	256015
G-BJCB	HS25	256065
G-BJDJ	HS25	257142
G-BJHH	C550	039
G-BJIL	C550	354
G-BJIR	C550	326
G-BJOW	HS25	257153
G-BJOY	HS25	256030
(G-BJUT)	HS25	256005
G-BJVP	C550	375
G-BJWB	HS25	257158
(G-BJXV)	HS25	256005
G-BKAA	HS25	257139
G-BKAJ	HS25	25235
G-BKBA	HS25	25270
G-BKBH	HS25	256052
G-BKBM	HS25	256039
G-BKBU	HS25	256042
G-BKCD	HS25	256056
G-BKFS	HS25	257172
"G-BKFS"	HS25	256054
G-BKHK	HS25	257189
G-BKJV	HS25	257046
G-BKRL	LEOP	001
G-BKSR	C550	469
G-BKTF	HS25	258001
G-BKUW	HS25	258003
G-BLEK	HS25	257213
G-BLGZ	HS25	258004
G-BLJC	HS25	258005
(G-BLKS)	HS25	258010
(G-BLMJ)	HS25	257208
(G-BLMK)	HS25	257210
G-BLOI	HS25	256050
G-BLPC	HS25	258015
(G-BLSG)	C555	0033
G-BLSM	HS25	257208
G-BLTP	HS25	257210
G-BLUW	HS25	256059
G-BLXN	C555	0033
G-BMCL	C550	091
G-BMIH	HS25	257115
G-BMMO	HS25	258048
G-BMOS	HS25	257064
G-BMWW	HS25	257076
G-BMYX	HS25	257178
G-BNBO	HS25	257112
G-BNDX	HS25	256012
G-BNEH	HS25	258078
G-BNFW	HS25	257100
G-BNSC	C550	559
(G-BNUB)	HS25	258099
G-BNVU	HS25	257130
G-BNVY	C500	098
(G-BNZP)	C500	114
G-BNZW	HS25	258105
G-BOCB	HS25	25106
G-BOGA	C500	220
G-BOOA	HS25	258088
G-BOTX	HS25	258121
G-BOXI	HS25	257055
G-BPCP	C500	540
(G-BPGR)	HS25	258115
(G-BPGS)	HS25	258118
(G-BPJM)	GLF4	1078
G-BPXW	HS25	258161
(G-BPYD)	HS25	258146
(G-BPYE)	HS25	258148
G-BRBZ	BE40	RJ-60
G-BRCZ	HS25	258163
G-BRDI	HS25	257097
G-BRNM	LEOP	002
G-BROD	HS25	25253
G-BRXR	HS25	25217
G-BSAA	HS25	25117
G-BSAL	GLF2	214
G-BSAN	GLF3	345
G-BSHL	HS25	256024
G-BSPH	HS25	256063
G-BSUL	HS25	258186
G-BSVL	C560	0077
G-BSZP	BE40	RJ-56
G-BTAB	HS25	258088
G-BTAE	HS25	258190
G-BTIB	F900	109
G-BTMG	HS25	258197
G-BTSI	HS25	259007
G-BTTG	HS25	259006
G-BTTX	HS25	259005
G-BTUF	HS25	25248
G-BTYN	HS25	259009
G-BTYO	HS25	259011
G-BTYP	HS25	259013
G-BTYR	HS25	259014
G-BTYS	HS25	259015
G-BUCP	HS25	258212
G-BUCR	HS25	258050
G-BUID	HS25	258208
G-BUIM	HS25	258068
G-BUIX	HS25	259024
G-BUIY	HS25	258025
G-BUKW	HS25	259021
G-BULI	HS25	259016
G-BUNL	HS25	257007
G-BUNW	HS25	259029
G-BUPL	HS25	259030
G-BURV	HS25	258213
G-BUSX	LJ35	662
G-BUUW	HS25	258227
G-BUUY	HS25	259031
G-BUWC	HS25	258240
(G-BUWD)	HS25	258243
G-BUWX	HS25	259034
G-BUZX	HS25	258067
G-BVAS	HS25	258076
G-BVBH	HS25	258073
G-BVCM	C525	0022
G-BVCU	HS25	258226
G-BVDL	HS25	259025
G-BVFC	HS25	258130
G-BVFE	HS25	258242
G-BVHW	HS25	258079
G-BVJI	HS25	258258
G-BVJY	HS25	257054
G-BVLO	HS25	259027
G-BVRF	HS25	258247
G-BVRG	HS25	258250
G-BVRW	HS25	258266
G-BVTP	HS25	25255
G-BVTR	HS25	25264
G-BVTS	HS25	25266
G-BVTT	HS25	25268
G-BVYV	HS25	258268
G-BVYW	HS25	258277
G-BVZK	HS25	258278
G-BVZL	HS25	258279
G-BWCB	HS25	259032
G-BWCR	HS25	257070
G-BWDC	HS25	258280
G-BWDD	HS25	258281
G-BWDW	HS25	258282
G-BWFL	**C500**	**264**
G-BWGB	HS25	258283
G-BWGC	HS25	258284
G-BWGD	HS25	258285
G-BWGE	HS25	258286
(G-BWJX)	HS25	257062
G-BWKL	HS25	257118
G-BWOM	C550	671
G-BWRN	HS25	258237
G-BWSY	HS25	258201
G-BWVA	HS25	258235
G-BXPU	HS25	25171
G-BYFO	HS25	257040
G-BYHM	HS25	258233
G-BZNR	HS25	258180
G-CBBI	HS25	257013
G-CBHT	F9EX	48
G-CBNP	GLEX	9032
G-CBNR	GLEX	9081
G-CBRG	C56X	5266
G-CBTU	C550	601
G-CCAA	HS25	257130
G-CCCL	C500	363
G-CDCX	C750	0194
G-CDLT	HS25	258710
G-CDNK	LJ45	280
G-CDOL	C56X	5584
G-CDSR	LJ45	286
G-CEDK	**C750**	**0252**
G-CERX	**HS25**	**258810**
G-CEUO	C550	033
G-CEYL	**GLEX**	**9196**
G-CFBP	HS25	257105
G-CFGB	**C680**	**0234**
G-CFGL	C56X	5361
G-CFOH	GLF4	1202
G-CFRA	C56X	5183
G-CFSC	CL65	5744
G-CGEI	**C550**	**550-0951**
G-CGFA	GLEX	9241
G-CGFD	CL64	5591
G-CGFF	CL65	5733
G-CGGN	FA7X	69
G-CGGU	CL64	5626
G-CGHI	F2TH	163
G-CGHY	HS25	258477
G-CGJA	CL65	5810
G-CGMF	**C56X**	**5271**
G-CGNP	E50P	50000146
G-CGOA	**C550**	**206**
G-CGPT	F9EX	28
G-CGSB	C52A	0082
G-CGSJ	**GLEX**	**9377**
G-CGUL	GLF5	5176
G-CGUZ	C52A	0473
G-CGXM	C525	0025
G-CHAI	CL61	5152
G-CHKE	E55P	50500117
G-CHUI	**C56X**	**6139**
G-CHVN	CL64	5515
G-CIAU	**CL60**	**1067**
G-CIEL	**C56X**	**5247**
G-CIFJ	C56X	5554
G-CITI	C500	463
G-CITJ	C525	0084
G-CJAA	HS25	258240
G-CJAD	C525	0435
G-CJAE	C560	0046
G-CJAG	PRM1	RB-122
G-CJAH	PRM1	RB-131
(G-CJAI)	PRM1	RB-142
(G-CJAJ)	PRM1	RB-154
G-CJCC	C680	0189
G-CJDB	**C525**	**0648**
G-CJET	LJ35	365
G-CJHH	C550	147
G-CJMC	LJ60	300
G-CJME	GLEX	9309
G-CJTV	C52A	0083
G-CMTO	**C525**	**0848**
(G-CNGM)	F2EX	160
G-CNUK	FA7X	52
(G-COQI)	E50P	50000166
G-CPRI	LJ45	037
G-CPRR	**C680**	**0276**
G-CRBN	E55P	50500262
G-CROO	C52A	0388
G-CTEN	C750	0281
G-CXLS	**C56X**	**5613**
G-CXMF	GLF2	204
G-CYII	HS25	256005
G-CZAR	C560	0046
G-DAAC	CL64	5424
G-DAEX	F9EX	78
G-DAGS	C52A	0501
G-DANI	C500	402
G-DASA	FA50	268
G-DASO	FA50	268
G-DBAL	HS25	25117
G-DBBI	HS25	257130
G-DBII	C560	0032
G-DBOW	HS25	256032
G-DCCC	HS25	258002
G-DCCI	HS25	259030
G-DCFR	C550	418
G-DCTA	HS25	258130
G-DDDJ	LJ45	404
G-DEIA	**C56X**	**6119**
G-DEZC	HS25	257070
G-DGET	CL64	5608
G-DJAE	C500	339
G-DJBB	C500	365
G-DJBE	C550	171
G-DJBI	C550	030
G-DJHH	C550	290
G-DJLW	HS25	25140
G-DJMJ	HS25	25106
G-DLTC	HS25	HA-0035
G-DMAN	HS25	256033
G-DNVT	GLF4	1078
(G-DOKK)	LJ60	352
G-DRBN	E50P	50000055
G-DWJM	C550	326
G-DYXH	FA7X	105
G-ECAI	C56X	5631
G-ECHB	**F9DX**	**623**
G-ECJI	FA10	161
G-EDCJ	C525	0105
G-EDCK	C525	0510
G-EDCL	C52A	0083
G-EDCM	C52A	0213
G-EDCS	BE40	RK-487
G-EDHY	F2EX	182
G-EEBJ	C52A	0202
G-EFPT	HS25	257020
G-EGNS	GLF5	5167
G-EGVO	**F9EX**	**151**
G-EHGW	C550	550-0985
G-EJEL	**C550**	**643**
G-EJET	C550	171
G-EKWS	C550	550-0992
G-ELOA	C56X	5106
G-ELOT	C550	601
G-ELRA	HS25	259003
G-EMLI	CL64	5383
G-ENXA	**F9EX**	**219**
G-EPGI	C56X	6106
G-ERIE	**BE40**	**RK-120**
G-ESTA	**C550**	**143**
G-ETOM	HS25	258130
G-EVES	F900	165
G-EVLN	GLF4	1175
G-EVRD	PRM1	RB-172
G-EXLR	HS25	258151
G-EXLR	HS25	259001
G-EXRS	GLEX	9274
G-EYUP	**C56X**	**6116**
G-FABO	**CL64**	**5487**
G-FAMT	GLEX	9112
G-FANN	HS25	256019
G-FASL	HS25	258149
G-FBFI	CL61	5152
G-FBJL	F2TH	111
G-FBKA	C510	0096
G-FBKB	**C510**	**0126**
G-FBKC	**C510**	**0127**
G-FBKD	C510	0346
G-FBKE	**C510**	**0334**
G-FBKF	**C510**	**0360**
G-FBKG	**C510**	**0361**
G-FBLI	C510	0130
G-FBLK	**C510**	**0027**
G-FBMB	CL61	5041
G-FBNK	**C510**	**0067**
G-FCAP	C56X	5793
G-FCDB	C550	550-0985
G-FCFC	GLEX	9374
G-FDSL	HS25	258130
G-FERY	C550	030
G-FFFC	**C510**	**0451**
G-FFFG	F9EX	155
G-FFLT	HS25	256057
G-FFRA	**FA20**	**132**
G-FINK	HS25	259037
G-FIRM	C550	550-0940
G-FIVE	HS25	25004
G-FJET	**C550**	**418**
G-FLBK	**C510**	**0068**
G-FLCN	**F900**	**78**
G-FLLY	**F2EX**	**301**
G-FLVU	C500	580
G-FLXS	**F2EX**	**275**
G-FNES	F9EX	159
G-FORN	LJ40	2019
G-FOUR	HS25	25131
G-FRAA	FA20	385
G-FRAB	FA20	356
G-FRAC	FA20	254
G-FRAD	**FA20**	**304/511**
G-FRAE	FA20	280/503
G-FRAF	**FA20**	**295/500**
G-FRAH	**FA20**	**223**
G-FRAI	**FA20**	**270**
G-FRAJ	**FA20**	**20**
G-FRAK	**FA20**	**213**

G-FRAL	**FA20**	**151**
G-FRAM	FA20	224
G-FRAO	**FA20**	**214**
G-FRAP	**FA20**	**207**
G-FRAR	**FA20**	**209**
G-FRAS	**FA20**	**82/418**
G-FRAT	**FA20**	**87/424**
G-FRAU	**FA20**	**97/422**
G-FRAV	FA20	103/423
G-FRAW	**FA20**	**114/420**
G-FRBA	FA20	178/459
G-FRYL	**PRM1**	**RB-97**
G-FTSL	CL64	5416
G-GABY	**GLEX**	**9364**
G-GAEL	HS25	258007
G-GAIL	C550	397
(G-GAIL)	HS25	257139
(G-GALI)	C680	0104
G-GALX	F9EX	163
G-GAUL	C550	143
G-GAYL	LJ35	429
G-GDEZ	HS25	259026
G-GEBJ	C525	0528
G-GEDI	F2TH	49
G-GEDY	F2TH	208
G-GEIL	HS25	258021
G-GEIR	E55P	50500023
G-GENE	C500	573
(G-GENT)	GLF5	5420
G-GEVO	C680	0145
G-GGAE	HS25	25157
G-GGLA	**C56X**	**6044**
G-GHPG	C550	550-0897
G-GIII	GLF3	345
G-GILB	**C510**	**0241**
G-GIRA	HS25	257103
G-GJCB	HS25	258079
G-GJET	LJ35	365
G-GLBX	**GLEX**	**9120**
G-GMAA	**LJ45**	**167**
G-GMAB	**HS25**	**259034**
G-GMAC	GLF4	1058
G-GMMR	**HS25**	**258130**
G-GOMO	LJ45	055
G-GOYA	**GLEX**	**9016**
G-GPWH	F9EX	48
G-GRAN	GLEX	9324
G-GRGA	HS25	258130
G-GRGG	C525	0028
G-GRGS	C560	0457
G-GRZD	**GLF5**	**5315**
G-GSAM	HS25	258133
G-GSEB	F900	161
G-GSSO	GLF5	5019
G-GSVI	**GLF6**	**6160**
G-GXLS	**C56X**	**5608**
G-GZOO	**GALX**	**224**
G-HAAM	F900	130
G-HADI	GLF2	235
G-HALK	HS25	256033
G-HARF	GLF4	1117
G-HARG	**LEG5**	**55000039**
G-HARK	CL64	5646
G-HCFR	HS25	258240
G-HCGD	LJ45	328
G-HCSA	**C52A**	**0334**
G-HEBJ	C525	0437
G-HERS	C750	0075
G-HFAA	PRM1	RB-83
G-HGRC	C52A	0360
G-HHOI	HS25	257097
G-HJCB	HS25	259031
G-HMEI	**F900**	**1**
G-HMEV	**F900**	**5**
G-HMMV	C525	0358
G-HNJC	F9EX	74
G-HNRY	C650	0219
G-HOIL	LJ60	313
G-HOLL	C500	088
G-HOTL	C550	051
G-HOTY	**CL64**	**5443**
G-HPPY	LJ40	2102
G-HRDS	GLF5	5032
G-HSXP	**HS25**	**258827**
G-HUGG	LJ35	432
(G-HVLD)	GLEX	9377
G-HYGA	HS25	258034
G-IAMS	C56X	5183
G-IBIS	HS25	25171
G-IBSF	F2TH	151
G-IBZA	**C550**	**672**
G-ICED	C500	638
G-ICFR	HS25	258050
G-IDAB	C550	550-0917
G-IDRO	GLEX	9286
G-IECL	HS25	257002
G-IFTC	HS25	25171
G-IFTE	**HS25**	**257037**
G-IFTF	**HS25**	**258021**
G-IIRR	GLF2	210
G-IJET	HS25	257212
G-IKOS	**C550**	**550-0957**
G-ILLS	HS25	25133
G-IMAC	CL61	3065
G-IMED	C550	100
G-IOMC	**PRM1**	**RB-209**
G-IONX	**FA7X**	**111**
G-IOOX	LJ45	243
G-IPAC	C550	550-0935
G-IPAL	C550	550-0935
G-IPAX	**C56X**	**5228**
G-IPLY	**C550**	**550-0927**
G-IRAP	**GLEX**	**9309**
G-ISAN	GLEX	9457
G-ITIG	F2EX	102
G-ITIH	FA50	268
G-ITIM	FA7X	128
G-ITSU	**E50P**	**50000185**
G-IUAN	C525	0324
G-IWDB	HS25	258618
G-IZAP	LJ45	311
G-IZIP	LJ45	294
G-JAGA	**E55P**	**50500134**
G-JANV	LJ45	124
(G-JBCA)	C555	0146
G-JBIS	**C550**	**447**
G-JBIZ	**C550**	**068**
G-JBLZ	**C550**	**550-1018**
G-JCBB	GLF5	5186
G-JCBC	GLF5	5060
G-JCBG	F9EX	44
G-JCBI	F2TH	27
G-JCBV	GLF5	682
G-JCBX	F9EX	108
G-JCFR	C550	315
G-JEAN	C500	339
G-JEEN	C550	029
G-JETA	C550	101
G-JETB	C550	319
G-JETC	C550	315
G-JETD	C550	418
G-JETE	C500	198
G-JETF	F2EX	78
G-JETG	LJ35	324
"G-JETG"	HS25	257070
G-JETI	HS25	258056
G-JETJ	C550	171
G-JETK	HS25	258133
G-JETL	LJ35	656
G-JETN	LJ35	324
G-JETO	C550	441
G-JFCX	HS25	258215
G-JFJC	CL61	5023
G-JFRS	C550	569
G-JHSX	HS25	258245
G-JJCB	HS25	258022
G-JJET	**C510**	**0390**
G-JJMX	F9EX	112
G-JJSG	LJ35	324
G-JJSI	**HS25**	**258058**
G-JMAX	HS25	258456
G-JMBO	**E55P**	**50500216**
G-JMCW	CL64	5403
G-JMDW	C550	206
G-JMED	LJ35	671
G-JMMD	CL64	5422
G-JMMP	CL64	5528
G-JMMX	F9EX	184
G-JMSO	MU30	A062SA
G-JOLI	F2EX	8
G-JOPT	C560	0159
G-JPSI	FA50	313
G-JPSX	F9EX	132
G-JPSZ	F9EX	224
G-JRCT	C550	098
G-JRJR	LJ45	055
G-JSAX	HS25	25157
G-JTNC	C500	264
G-KAHR	CL65	5758
G-KALS	**CL30**	**20106**
G-KANL	GLEX	9331
G-KASS	HS25	25127
G-KDMA	C560	0553
G-KLNE	**HS25**	**HA-0186**
G-KLNR	**BE40**	**RK-552**
G-KLNW	**C510**	**0157**
G-KLOE	HS25	258674
G-KPEI	C56X	5785
G-KPTN	**FA50**	**341**
G-KRBN	**E55P**	**50500358**
G-KSFR	**CL30**	**20189**
G-KTIA	HS25	HA-0140
G-KWIN	F2EX	52
G-LAOR	HS25	258384
G-LATE	**F2EX**	**88**
G-LCDH	**CL65**	**5904**
G-LCYA	F9EX	105
G-LDFM	C56X	5242
G-LEAA	**C510**	**0072**
G-LEAB	**C510**	**0073**
G-LEAC	**C510**	**0075**
G-LEAI	**C510**	**0052**
G-LEAR	LJ35	265
G-LEAX	**C56X**	**5712**
G-LEAZ	**CL30**	**20015**
G-LFBD	**C52A**	**0506**
G-LFPT	C510	0025
G-LGAR	LJ60	286
G-LGKD	GLF5	5172
G-LGKO	CL64	5610
G-LGMG	**E50P**	**50000187**
G-LJET	LJ35	643
(G-LLGC)	GLEX	9241
G-LLOD	LJ45	236
G-LOBL	GLEX	9038
G-LOFT	C500	331
G-LORI	HS25	25246
G-LRBJ	HS25	259004
G-LSCW	**GLF5**	**5471**
G-LSMB	**F2EX**	**47**
(G-LSMB)	F2EX	161
G-LTEC	HS25	257103
G-LTSK	**CL65**	**5872**
G-LUBB	**C525**	**0271**
G-LUXY	**C550**	**421**
G-LVLV	CL64	5372
G-LWDC	**CL61**	**3031**
G-LXRS	GLEX	9200
G-LXWD	**C56X**	**5760**
G-MACO	CL65	5733
G-MACP	CL65	5733
G-MAMA	C550	319
G-MARS	BE40	RJ-36
G-MATF	GLF4	1109
G-MAXP	**HS25**	**258477**
G-MDBA	F2TH	184
G-MEET	LJ40	2054
G-MEGP	CL30	20096
G-MFEU	HS25	256062
G-MGNE	E55P	50500017
G-MHIH	HS25	257139
G-MHIS	C550	550-0917
G-MICE	C510	0156
G-MINE	C550	391
G-MIRO	C550	550-0932
G-MKOA	HS25	25227
G-MKSS	HS25	257175
G-MLEE	C650	0151
G-MLTI	F900	164
G-MOOO	LJ40	2007
G-MPCW	CL64	5422
G-MPJM	CL64	5403
G-MPMP	CL64	5528
G-MPSP	CL64	5422
G-MPTP	CL64	5403
G-MRAP	CL30	20023
G-MRFB	HS25	25132
G-MRLX	**GLF5**	**5396**
G-MROO	C52A	0202
G-MRTC	C550	597
G-MSFY	HS25	257200
G-MSLY	C550	030
G-MTLE	C500	573
G-MURI	LJ35	646
G-MUTD	LJ45	213
G-NAAL	CL65	5718
G-NCCC	CL65	5734
G-NCFR	HS25	257054
G-NCMT	C500	645
G-NETA	C56X	5230
G-NEVL	LJ35	662
G-NGEL	C510	0076
G-NLPA	HS25	HB-14
G-NMRM	C52A	0408
G-NOYA	GLF5	5420
G-NREG	CL60	1045
G-NSJS	C680	0161
G-NUDD	E50P	50000024
G-NYGB	CL65	5755
G-OAMB	C510	0050
G-OBAE	HS25	257094
G-OBCC	C560	0497
G-OBEL	C500	220
G-OBLT	HS25	258164
G-OBOB	HS25	25069
(G-OBSM)	HS25	257189
G-OCAA	HS25	257091
G-OCBA	HS25	25132
G-OCCC	HS25	258013
G-OCCI	HS25	258201
G-OCDB	C550	601
G-OCFR	LJ35	614
G-OCFT	**CL61**	**5067**
G-OCJT	C52A	0113
G-OCJZ	**C52A**	**0051**
G-OCOD	CL64	5562
G-OCOM	CL64	5617
G-OCPI	C500	093
G-OCSA	GLEX	9241
G-OCSB	C525	0177
G-OCSC	CL64	5505
G-OCSD	CL64	5591
G-OCSE	CL65	5710
G-OCSF	CL65	5733
G-OCSH	CL64	5623
G-ODAG	C52A	0397
G-ODCM	C52B	0153
G-ODUR	**HS25**	**HA-0041**
G-OEBJ	C525	0423
G-OEJA	C500	264
G-OEWD	**PRM1**	**RB-126**
G-OGFS	HS25	258130
G-OGRG	C560	0506
G-OGSE	**GLF5**	**5453**
G-OHAT	C525	0028
G-OHEA	HS25	25144
G-OHLA	C500	514
G-OICE	C525	0028
G-OIRP	GALX	142
G-OJAJ	F2EX	132
G-OJER	**C56X**	**6148**
G-OJMW	C550	550-1042
G-OJOY	HS25	257061
G-OJPB	HS25	25258
G-OJWB	HS25	258674
G-OKKI	GLEX	9336
G-OKSP	C500	392
G-OLDC	LJ45	156
G-OLDD	HS25	258106
G-OLDF	LJ45	055
G-OLDJ	LJ45	138
G-OLDK	LJ45	311
G-OLDL	LJ45	124
G-OLDR	LJ45	161
G-OLDT	LJ45	265
G-OLDW	LJ45	294
G-OLFR	HS25	25217
G-OMBI	C52B	0179
G-OMCA	HS25	25106
G-OMCL	C550	412
G-OMEA	**C56X**	**5610**
G-OMGA	HS25	256024
G-OMGB	HS25	256039
G-OMGC	HS25	256056
G-OMGD	HS25	257184
G-OMGE	HS25	258197
G-OMGG	HS25	258058
G-OMID	HS25	257214
G-OMJC	PRM1	RB-88
G-OMRE	GLF6	6023
G-OMRH	C550	550-1086
G-ONPN	HS25	25063
G-OODM	C52A	0190
G-OOMC	PRM1	RB-146
G-OOSP	HS25	25178
G-OPEM	C550	550-0927
G-OPFC	HS25	258159
G-OPFC	HS25	259002
G-OPOL	HS25	25171
G-OPRM	**CL64**	**5580**
G-OPWH	F900	151
G-ORAN	C525	0423
G-ORCE	C550	391
G-ORDB	C550	550-1042
G-ORHE	C500	220
G-ORJB	C500	392
G-OROO	C56X	5724
G-ORXI	PRM1	RB-195
G-ORXX	HS25	HA-0095
G-ORYX	HS25	HA-0048
G-OSAM	HS25	257189
G-OSCA	C500	270
G-OSMC	C550	135
G-OSNB	C550	569
G-OSOH	C525	0271
G-OSPG	HS25	258130
G-OSRL	**LJ45**	**391**
G-OSVM	C56X	5770
G-OTAG	CL65	5827
G-OTAZ	HS25	HA-0112
G-OTEN	C750	0311
G-OTGT	C560	0517
G-OTIS	C550	672
(G-OTKI)	C550	265
G-OTMC	BE40	RJ-50
G-OURA	HS25	258050
G-OURB	HS25	257054
G-OVIP	GLF2	91
(G-OVIP)	HS25	258010
G-OWAY	CL61	5085
G-OWDB	HS25	257040
G-OWEB	HS25	257040
G-OWRC	C525	0177
G-OXEC	C500	093
(G-OXEH)	C550	319
G-OXLS	**C56X**	**5675**
G-OXRS	**GLEX**	**9351**
G-OZAT	HS25	HA-0143
G-PABL	C550	550-1083
G-PAOL	**C52B**	**0232**
G-PBWH	HS25	258182
G-PEER	**C52A**	**0360**
G-PEPE	C56X	5265
G-PFCT	**LJ45**	**055**
G-PHNM	**E50P**	**50000165**
G-PHTO	PRM1	RB-125
G-PJDS	**C550**	**550-1083**
G-PJET	LJ35	614
G-PJWB	HS25	256033
G-PKRG	C56X	5613
G-PLGI	HS25	257034
G-PNNY	C500	165
G-POAJ	CL64	5442
G-POSN	HS25	258120
G-POWG	C52A	0485
G-PPLC	C560	0059
G-PREI	PRM1	RB-60
G-PRKR	CL64	5617
G-PRMC	HS25	257031
G-PROO	**HA4T**	**RC-34**
G-PULA	**F2EX**	**269**
G-PVEL	GLEX	9334
G-PVHT	FA7X	59
G-PWNS	C525	0153
G-PYCO	F2TH	78
G-RAAA	**GLEX**	**9423**
G-RAAL	E50P	50000151
G-RAAR	HS25	258210
G-RACL	HS25	257212
G-RAFF	LJ35	504
G-RAHL	BE40	RK-61
G-RAVY	C500	109
G-RBEN	**GLEX**	**9083**
G-RBSG	F9EX	113
G-RCAV	**CL64**	**5526**
G-RCDI	HS25	257142
G-RCEJ	HS25	258021
G-RDBS	C550	101
G-RDMV	HS25	258496
G-REDS	C56X	5167
G-REFO	**GLF6**	**6075**
G-REYG	F9EX	193
G-REYS	**CL64**	**5467**
G-RGBY	C52B	0139
G-RGSG	HS25	HA-0152
G-RIBV	C560	0506
G-RIZA	PRM1	RB-195
G-RJRI	HS25	257130
G-RMMA	**F9EX**	**189**
(G-RMPI)	LJ40	2108
G-RNER	**C510**	**0409**
G-RNFR	**CL65**	**5983**
G-RNJP	**CL65**	**5980**
G-ROOB	E50P	50000179
G-RRIA	**PRM1**	**RB-228**
G-RSCJ	C525	0298
G-RSRS	BE40	RJ-36
G-RSXL	C56X	5699
G-RSXP	**C56X**	**6198**
G-RUBO	E50P	50000185
G-RVHT	C550	441
G-RWGW	LJ45	213
G-SABI	F9EX	150
G-SADC	GLF4	4027
G-SAJP	CL61	5022
G-SANL	**GLEX**	**9333**
G-SBEC	C500	661
G-SCAR	**CL30**	**20530**
G-SCCA	**C510**	**0106**
G-SCCC	HS25	259037
G-SDRY	**C52C**	**0134**
G-SEAJ	C525	0113
G-SEBE	LJ35	365
G-SENT	**GLEX**	**9094**
G-SFCJ	C525	0245
G-SFRI	CL65	5843
G-SHEA	HS25	258240
G-SHEB	HS25	258243
G-SHEC	HS25	259037
G-SHEF	GLEX	9306
G-SHOP	HS25	25248
G-SIRJ	C680	0216
G-SIRO	**F9EX**	**172**
G-SIRS	**C56X**	**5185**
G-SJSS	**CL65**	**5760**
G-SKBD	**BE40**	**RK-376**
G-SNZY	LJ45	375
G-SONE	**C52A**	**0031**
G-SOVA	C550	649
G-SOVB	**LJ45**	**138**
G-SOVC	LJ45	161
"G-SOVM"	C56X	5770
G-SOVN	LJ35	614
G-SPRE	**C550**	**550-0872**
G-SPUR	**C550**	**714**
G-SRBN	E50P	50000056
G-SRDG	**FA7X**	**36**
G-SSLM	C510	0190
G-SSOZ	C550	597
G-STCC	CL64	5623
G-STMT	**FA7X**	**148**
G-STOB	BE40	RK-502
(G-STPZ)	C525	0661
G-STUF	LJ40	2074
G-SUFC	HS25	256035
G-SVGN	C680	0198
G-SVLB	HS25	257112
G-SVNX	**FA7X**	**123**
G-SVSB	C680	0094
G-SWET	C500	270
G-SXTY	**LJ60**	**280**
G-SYGC	C52A	0360
G-SYKS	C550	599
G-TACE	HS25	25223
G-TAGA	CL64	5659
G-TAGE	CL65	5706
G-TAGF	F9DX	604
G-TAGK	F9DX	614
G-TAYC	**GLF4**	**4060**
G-TBEA	**C52A**	**0191**
G-TCAP	HS25	258115
G-TCDI	HS25	25248
G-TEFH	C500	176
G-TFKR	GLF5	5220
G-TFRA	**C525**	**0628**
G-THCL	C550	563
G-THNX	C525	0022
G-TIFF	C550	290
G-TJCB	HS25	257127
G-TJHI	C500	363
G-TLFK	C680	0213
G-TMAS	HS25	256062
G-TNIK	**F2TH**	**25**
G-TOMI	HS25	256030
G-TOMY	MU30	A090SA

G-TOPF	HS25	25238
G-TPHK	HS25	258130
G-TSAM	HS25	258028
G-TSJF	C52B	0231
G-TSLS	GLEX	9231
G-TTFN	C560	0537
G-TTJF	**F2TS**	**705**
G-TWIY	**HS25**	**HB-14**
G-TWOP	**C52A**	**0397**
G-UESS	C500	326
(G-UJET)	HS25	258456
G-UKCA	HS25	257214
G-ULFS	**GLF6**	**6028**
G-UMKA	FA7X	114
G-URRU	CL65	5821
G-URTH	HS25	HA-0143
G-UWWB	HS25	258001
G-UYAD	CL64	5307
G-UYGB	CL30	20169
G-VCAN	CL30	20401
G-VECT	C56X	5161
G-VIPI	**HS25**	**258222**
G-VIPS	LJ35	614
G-VITA	FA7X	105
G-VJAY	HS25	25254
G-VKGO	E50P	50000145
G-VKRS	C555	0133
(G-VONI)	HS25	258345
G-VONJ	PRM1	RB-66
G-VPCM	**F2EX**	**261**
G-VUEA	C550	671
G-VUEM	C500	580
G-VUEZ	C550	008
G-VVPA	**CL64**	**5612**
G-WABB	F9EX	232
G-WAIN	C550	550-1100
G-WBPR	HS25	258085
G-WCIN	C56X	5088
G-WINA	C56X	5343
G-WLVS	F2EX	141
G-WTOR	F9EX	211
(G-WWDB)	HS25	259024
G-WWFC	**F2EX**	**257**
G-WYLX	C550	418
G-WYNE	**HS25**	**258240**
G-XAVB	**C510**	**0283**
G-XBEL	C56X	5698
G-XBLU	C680	0143
G-XJET	**LJ45**	**311**
G-XLGB	C56X	5259
G-XLMB	C56X	5259
G-XLSB	C56X	5190
G-XLSR	**C56X**	**6202**
G-XLTV	**C56X**	**5536**
G-XMAF	GLF3	407
(G-XMAR)	C56X	5822
G-XONE	**CL64**	**5426**
G-XPRS	GLEX	9133
G-XRMC	HS25	258180
G-XRTV	**CL61**	**5085**
G-XSTV	**C56X**	**5788**
G-XXRS	**GLEX**	**9169**
G-XXZZ	LJ60	328
G-YAAZ	GLF5	5189
G-YAGT	CL65	5756
G-YCKF	**F9EX**	**256**
G-YEDC	**C52B**	**0162**
G-YFOX	**F2EX**	**67**
G-YPRS	C550	550-0935
G-YUGO	HS25	25094
G-YUMN	F2TH	1
G-ZAPI	C500	560
G-ZEAL	LJ35	275
G-ZEIZ	LJ36	047
G-ZENO	LJ35	429
G-ZENT	**C56X**	**5756**
(G-ZEST)	LJ35	265
G-ZEUZ	**C52A**	**0202**
G-ZING	LJ35	429
G-ZIPR	HS25	HB-27
G-ZIPS	LJ35	365
G-ZIZI	**C525**	**0345**
G-ZJET	C510	0161
G-ZMED	LJ35	656
G-ZNSF	**GLF5**	**5425**
G-ZONE	LJ35	365
G-ZOOM	LJ35	236
G-ZXZX	**LJ45**	**005**
G-ZZOO	**GALX**	**163**

Hungary

HA-AXA	C650	0149
HA-JEB	C500	396
HA-JEC	**C650**	**0190**
HA-JED	**C56X**	**5339**
HA-JEN	**C650**	**0012**
HA-JEO	**C650**	**0142**
HA-JEP	**C650**	**0149**
HA-JES	C650	0216
HA-JET	**C500**	**249**
HA-LKN	**F9EX**	**143**
HA-YFE	**MU30**	**A046SA**
HA-YFH	**BE40**	**RK-528**
HA-YFI	HS25	258043
HA-YFJ	**BE40**	**RK-254**
HA-YFK	**BE40**	**RJ-56**

Switzerland

HB-...	**FA20**	**479**
(HB-...)	F900	4
(HB-...)	LJ55	050
(HB-...)	PRM1	RB-27
(HB-...)	WW24	390
(HB-I..)	GLF2	126
(HB-I..)	GLF4	1074
HB-IAB	F900	9
HB-IAC	F900	26
HB-IAD	F900	35
HB-IAE	FA50	150
HB-IAF	F900	30
HB-IAG	FA50	174
HB-IAH	F9EX	28
HB-IAI	F900	75
HB-IAJ	**F2EX**	
HB-IAK	**F900**	**15**
HB-IAL	FA50	63
HB-IAM	FA50	164
HB-IAQ	F9EX	35
HB-IAT	FA50	86
HB-IAU	**F2EX**	**14**
HB-IAV	FA50	230
HB-IAW	**F2TH**	**16**
HB-IAX	F2TH	33
HB-IAY	F2TH	34
HB-IAZ	F2TH	30
HB-IBG	F900	115
HB-IBH	F2TH	42
HB-IBQ	FA50	125
HB-IBX	GLF4	1183
HB-IBY	F900	44
HB-IEA	FA50	133
HB-IEB	FA50	17
HB-IEC	FA50	134
HB-IED	FA50	147
(HB-IED)	FA50	
HB-IEJ	GLF4	1148
HB-IEP	FA50	67
HB-IEQ	GLF4	1174
HB-IER	FA50	57
HB-IES	FA50	61
HB-IET	FA50	48
HB-IEU	FA50	27
HB-IEV	FA50	34
HB-IEW	GLF2	124
HB-IEX	GLF2	169
HB-IEY	GLF2	210
HB-IEZ	GLF2	216
HB-IEZ	GLF2	246
HB-IFJ	F9EX	92
HB-IFQ	F900	121
"HB-IGA"	GALX	011
HB-IGI	**F9EX**	**83**
(HB-IGK)	GALX	012
HB-IGL	F900	58
HB-IGM	GLF5	5004
HB-IGP	GALX	013
HB-IGQ	F2EX	9
HB-IGR	FA50	104
HB-IGS	GLEX	9102
HB-IGT	F900	185
HB-IGU	**F2EX**	**111**
HB-IGV	**FA50**	**346**
HB-IGX	F9EX	86
HB-IGY	**F9EX**	**95**
HB-IHQ	**GLEX**	**9011**
HB-IIS	GLF5	572
HB-IIV	CL64	5397
HB-IIY	GLF5	638
HB-IIZ	GLF5	641
HB-IKJ	CL64	5327
HB-IKQ	CL64	5318
HB-IKR	GLF4	1159
HB-IKS	**CL61**	**5042**
HB-IKT	CL61	5003
HB-IKU	CL61	5005
HB-IKV	CL61	5092
HB-IKW	CL61	5096
HB-IKX	CL61	3006
HB-IKY	CL61	5125
HB-IKZ	GLEX	9054
HB-ILH	CL60	1025
HB-ILK	CL61	3033
HB-ILL	CL64	5373
HB-ILM	CL61	3024
HB-ILV	GLF4	1460
HB-IMJ	**GLF5**	**517**
HB-IMV	GLF2	8
HB-IMW	GLF2	194
HB-IMX	GLF3	335
HB-IMY	**GLF4**	**1084**
(HB-IMY)	GLF4	1033
HB-IMZ	GLF2	88/21
HB-INJ	GLEX	9086
HB-INQ	GLF5	568
HB-ISD	FA50	159
HB-ISF	F2TH	26
(HB-ITE)	GLF4	1046
HB-ITF	GLF4	1202
HB-ITG	GLEX	9036
HB-ITH	FA50	117
HB-ITJ	GLF4	1175
HB-ITK	CL61	5090
HB-ITM	GLF3	352
HB-ITN	GLF3	367
HB-ITP	GLF4	1046
HB-ITR	GLF2	144
HB-ITS	GLF3	435
HB-ITT	GLF4	1064
(HB-ITT)	GLF4	1046
HB-ITV	GLF2	139/11
HB-ITW	GLF2	192
HB-ITX	GLF4	1093
HB-ITZ	GLF4	1083
HB-IUF	CL61	5067
HB-IUJ	GLEX	9095
HB-IUR	GLEX	9013
(HB-IUS)	GALX	078
HB-IUT	GALX	007
HB-IUU	GALX	011
HB-IUV	**GALX**	**073**
HB-IUW	**F900**	**150**
HB-IUX	F9EX	54
HB-IUY	F900	181
HB-IUZ	F2TH	74
HB-IVJ	**GLF6**	**6062**
HB-IVL	GLF5	513
HB-IVM	F2TH	55
HB-IVN	F2TH	61
HB-IVO	F2TH	62
HB-IVP	CL64	5369
HB-IVR	CL64	5318
HB-IVS	CL61	5166
HB-IVT	CL64	5394
HB-IVV	CL64	5384
HB-IVZ	GLF5	577
HB-IWY	GLF4	1176
HB-IWZ	GLF4	1061
HB-JEB	GALX	032
HB-JEC	**CL30**	**20029**
HB-JEE	GLF5	5025
HB-JEG	F2EX	34
HB-JEH	**GLEX**	**9523**
HB-JEI	F900	86
HB-JEM	CL64	5613
HB-JEN	GLEX	9015
HB-JEP	GLF5	5070
HB-JEQ	GLF4	4027
HB-JER	GLEX	9017
HB-JES	**GLF5**	**556**
HB-JET	F2EX	154
HB-JEU	CL30	20039
HB-JEV	GLF5	5040
HB-JEX	GLEX	9145
HB-JEY	GLEX	9173
HB-JEZ	C750	0179
HB-JFA	CL65	5715
HB-JFB	**GLEX**	**9130**
HB-JFC	**CL64**	**5539**
HB-JFD	C750	0261
HB-JFE	**GLEX**	**9497**
HB-JFI	**F2EX**	**256**
HB-JFJ	**CL64**	**5599**
HB-JFK	**E50P**	**50000062**
HB-JFM	CL30	20022
HB-JFN	**FA7X**	**116**
HB-JFO	CL30	20137
HB-JFY	**GLEX**	**9347**
HB-JFZ	CL64	5510
HB-JGB	**GLF4**	**4130**
HB-JGC	GLF5	5175
HB-JGD	**F2TS**	**716**
HB-JGE	**GLEX**	**9287**
HB-JGF	F2EX	185
HB-JGG	**F2EX**	**188**
HB-JGH	GLEX	9320
HB-JGI	**FA7X**	**67**
HB-JGJ	GLF4	4122
HB-JGK	**JSTR**	**5233**
HB-JGL	**GALX**	**193**
HB-JGN	GLEX	9249
HB-JGO	GLEX	9004
HB-JGP	**GLEX**	**9238**
HB-JGQ	**CL30**	**20237**
HB-JGR	CL64	5624
HB-JGT	**CL65**	**5736**
HB-JGU	C750	0001
HB-JGX	GLF5	5172
HB-JGY	GLEX	9167
HB-JIG	C680	0280
HB-JIH	GLEX	9359
HB-JII	**GLEX**	**9367**
HB-JIL	C680	0179
HB-JIN	**F9EX**	**107**
HB-JIO	**F9EX**	**195**
HB-JKA	GLF5	554
HB-JKB	GLF5	5178
HB-JKC	**GLF5**	**5240**
HB-JKD	GALX	050
HB-JKE	GALX	231
HB-JKF	GLF4	4203
HB-JKG	GALX	184
HB-JKH	GALX	018
HB-JKI	**GLF5**	**5355**
HB-JKJ	GLF4	4269
HB-JKL	**F2EX**	**244**
HB-JLK	**FA7X**	**44**
HB-JLL	**C750**	**0004**
HB-JOB	**FA7X**	**80**
HB-JOE	**GLF5**	**5220**
HB-JRA	**CL64**	**5529**
HB-JRB	**CL64**	**5530**
HB-JRC	**CL64**	**5540**
HB-JRE	**CL65**	**5726**
HB-JRG	**CL64**	**5659**
HB-JRI	**GLEX**	**9627**
(HB-JRI)	CL65	5827
HB-JRM	**GLEX**	**9514**
HB-JRN	CL64	5494
HB-JRN	CL65	5753
HB-JRP	CL65	5709
HB-JRQ	**CL64**	**5651**
HB-JRR	GLEX	9198
HB-JRS	**GLEX**	**9174**
HB-JRT	CL64	5442
HB-JRV	CL61	5035
HB-JRW	CL64	5602
HB-JRX	**GLEX**	**9373**
(HB-JRX)	CL61	5152
HB-JRY	CL64	5502
HB-JRZ	CL64	5553
HB-JSA	**FA7X**	**161**
HB-JSB	**F2TH**	**171**
HB-JSE	**FA7X**	**218**
HB-JSG	**CL65**	**5963**
HB-JSI	**FA7X**	**37**
HB-JSL	**FA7X**	**194**
HB-JSM	**FA7X**	**181**
HB-JSN	**FA7X**	**76**
HB-JSO	FA7X	12
HB-JSP	F900	69
HB-JSR	FA50	165
HB-JSS	**FA7X**	**2**
(HB-JSS)	FA7X	16
HB-JST	**FA7X**	**17**
HB-JSU	F9DX	612
HB-JSV	FA50	215
HB-JSW	F9DX	601
HB-JSX	F9EX	141
HB-JSY	F9EX	96
HB-JSZ	FA7X	4
HB-JTA	**F9EX**	**279**
HB-JTB	CL30	20141
HB-JTT	**GLF5**	**622**
HB-JUF	**GLF6**	**6118**
HB-JUS	GLF4	4123
HB-PAA	MS76	069
HB-PAC	MS76	112
(HB-V..)	C560	0106
(HB-V..)	C560	0301
(HB-V..)	FA10	150
(HB-V..)	FA20	112
HB-VAA	C56X	5269
HB-VAG	HS25	25006
HB-VAH	HS25	25007
HB-VAI	LJ24	019
HB-VAK	SBRL	282-25
(HB-VAL)	WW24	17
HB-VAM	LJ24	044
HB-VAN	HS25	25063
HB-VAP	FA20	37/406
HB-VAR	HS25	25025
HB-VAS	LJ24	109
HB-VAT	HS25	25090
HB-VAU	HS25	25099
HB-VAV	FA20	3/403
HB-VAW	FA20	72/413
HB-VAX	WW24	15
HB-VAY	HS25	25135
HB-VAZ	HS25	25130
HB-VBA	LJ24	026
HB-VBB	LJ24	045A
HB-VBC	LJ24	053
HB-VBD	LJ24	052
HB-VBI	LJ25	040
HB-VBK	LJ24	128
HB-VBL	FA20	126/438
HB-VBM	FA20	136/439
HB-VBN	HS25	25138
HB-VBO	FA20	150/445
HB-VBP	LJ25	033
HB-VBR	LJ25	038
HB-VBS	FA20	55/410
HB-VBT	HS25	25171
HB-VBU	LJ24	231
HB-VBW	HS25	25199
HB-VBX	WW24	47
HB-VBY	LJ24	206
HB-VBZ	HS25	25215
HB-VCA	FA20	208/468
HB-VCB	FA20	182/461
HB-VCC	WW24	145
HB-VCE	HS25	25235
HB-VCG	FA20	231/474
HB-VCI	LJ24	243
HB-VCJ	HS25	258644
HB-VCK	LJ25	082
HB-VCL	LJ25	076
HB-VCM	LJ25	073
HB-VCN	LJ24	247
HB-VCN	SBRL	465-32
HB-VCO	FA20	25/405
HB-VCR	FA20	263/489
HB-VCS	LJ25	097
HB-VCT	LJ24	241
HB-VCU	C500	038
HB-VCW	LJ24	256
HB-VCX	C500	008
HB-VCY	LJ24	267
HB-VCZ	LJ35	433
(HB-VCZ)	SBRL	282-117
HB-VDA	C500	081
HB-VDB	FA20	296/507
HB-VDC	C500	100
HB-VDD	FA10	36
HB-VDE	FA10	7
HB-VDG	FA20	58
HB-VDH	LJ24	148
HB-VDI	LJ25	149
HB-VDK	LJ24	271
HB-VDL	HS25	256021
HB-VDM	C500	126
HB-VDN	LJ24	287
HB-VDO	**C550**	**098**
(HB-VDO)	FA20	306/512
(HB-VDO)	LJ24	289
HB-VDP	FA20	245/481
(HB-VDR)	C500	187
HB-VDS	HS25	256048
(HB-VDT)	FA10	21
HB-VDU	LJ24	310
HB-VDV	FA20	307/513
HB-VDW	**LJ45**	**438**
(HB-VDW)	FA20	86
HB-VDX	FA10	56
HB-VDY	FA20	245/481
(HB-VDY)	FA20	306/512
HB-VDZ	FA20	255/487
HB-VEA	LJ36	006
HB-VEB	FA20	323/520
HB-VEC	SBRL	380-12
HB-VED	FA20	162/451
HB-VEE	LJ36	016
HB-VEF	LJ25	193
HB-VEG	FA10	70
HB-VEH	C500	230
HB-VEI	LJ25	199
HB-VEK	HS25	257094
HB-VEL	LJ24	023
(HB-VEL)	LJ24	014
HB-VEM	LJ35	068
HB-VEN	LJ35	045
HB-VEO	C500	299
HB-VEP	MS76	098
(HB-VER)	FA20	174/457
HB-VES	LJ24	027
(HB-VET)	JSTR	5009
HB-VEU	MS76	102
HB-VEV	FA20	317
HB-VEV	LJ35	075
HB-VEW	LJ35	088
HB-VEX	C500	338
HB-VEY	LJ35	090
HB-VEZ	FA20	228/473
HB-VFA	HS25	257007
HB-VFB	LJ35	145
HB-VFC	LJ35	099
HB-VFD	LJ36	029
(HB-VFE)	LJ35	111
HB-VFF	C500	392
HB-VFG	LJ35	119
HB-VFH	C500	180
HB-VFI	C500	413
HB-VFK	LJ35	118
HB-VFL	LJ35	137
HB-VFO	LJ35	184
(HB-VFO)	LJ35	162
HB-VFP	WW24	231
HB-VFS	LJ36	042
(HB-VFS)	FA10	121
HB-VFT	FA10	121
HB-VFU	LJ35	196
HB-VFV	LJ36	040
HB-VFW	CL60	1049
HB-VFX	LJ35	191
HB-VFY	LJ28	29-001
HB-VFZ	LJ35	222
HB-VGA	CL60	1029
HB-VGB	LJ28	28-004
HB-VGC	LJ35	259
(HB-VGC)	LJ35	239
HB-VGD	C500	082
(HB-VGD)	C500	478
HB-VGE	C550	074
HB-VGF	HS25	257062
HB-VGG	HS25	257070
HB-VGH	LJ35	206
(HB-VGI)	C500	251
HB-VGK	C550	035
HB-VGL	LJ35	278
HB-VGM	LJ35	288
HB-VGN	LJ35	149
HB-VGO	C500	053
HB-VGP	C550	205
HB-VGR	C550	089
HB-VGS	C550	206
HB-VGT	LJ35	309
HB-VGU	LJ35	331
(HB-VGU)	HS25	25199
HB-VGV	LJ55	015
HB-VGW	LJ35	336
HB-VGX	LJ35	372
HB-VGY	LJ35	370
HB-VGZ	LJ55	024
HB-VHA	C500	524
HB-VHB	LJ35	359

HB-VHC	CL60	1028
HB-VHD	LJ35	395
HB-VHE	LJ35	413
HB-VHF	LJ36	048
HB-VHG	LJ35	445
HB-VHH	C555	0028
HB-VHI	C500	344
HB-VHK	LJ55	045
HB-VHL	LJ55	054
HB-VHM	LJ25	314
HB-VHN	LJ55	073
HB-VHO	CL60	1053
HB-VHR	LJ35	501
HB-VHS	FA20	488
HB-VHT	MU30	A052SA
HB-VHU	HS25	258152
HB-VHV	**HS25**	**258153**
HB-VHW	C650	0060
HB-VHX	MU30	A035SA
HB-VHY	FA20	429
HB-VIA	MU30	A087SA
HB-VIB	LJ55	009
HB-VIC	C500	464
HB-VID	C500	523
HB-VIE	LJ25	193
HB-VIF	LJ36	057
HB-VIG	FA10	89
HB-VII	LJ35	503
HB-VIK	HS25	258091
HB-VIL	HS25	258097
HB-VIM	LJ31	018
HB-VIN	C650	0119
HB-VIO	C550	181
HB-VIP	C550	469
HB-VIR	C550	328
HB-VIS	C550	447
HB-VIT	C550	220
HB-VIU	C550	465
HB-VIV	C500	340
HB-VIW	FA10	113
HB-VIX	FA10	126
HB-VIY	C650	0040
HB-VIZ	C550	207
HB-VJA	C550	379
HB-VJB	**C500**	**442**
HB-VJC	LJ35	614
HB-VJD	FA20	116
HB-VJE	BE40	RJ-44
HB-VJF	SBRL	465-59
HB-VJH	C550	234
HB-VJI	LJ31	011
HB-VJJ	LJ35	649
HB-VJK	LJ35	651
HB-VJL	LJ35	653
HB-VJM	FA10	188
HB-VJN	FA10	118
(HB-VJP)	C500	178
HB-VJQ	C525	0041
HB-VJR	C500	343
HB-VJS	FA20	383/550
HB-VJT	C650	0076
HB-VJV	FA20	237/476
HB-VJW	FA20	175
HB-VJX	FA20	293
HB-VJY	HS25	258176
HB-VJZ	C560	0055
HB-VKA	C555	0137
HB-VKB	C525	0037
HB-VKC	FA20	117
HB-VKD	C500	643
HB-VKE	FA10	7
HB-VKF	FA10	89
HB-VKH	C550	135
HB-VKI	LJ60	019
HB-VKJ	HS25	257067
HB-VKK	C500	178
HB-VKM	HS25	258035
HB-VKN	HS25	258036
HB-VKO	FA20	257
HB-VKP	C550	622
HB-VKR	FA10	209
HB-VKS	C550	441
HB-VKT	C550	310
HB-VKV	HS25	258228
HB-VKW	**HS25**	**258246**
HB-VKX	C550	307
HB-VKY	C500	476
HB-VLA	HS25	257031
HB-VLB	C500	638
HB-VLC	HS25	257127
HB-VLD	C500	589
HB-VLE	C500	313
HB-VLF	HS25	258264
HB-VLG	HS25	258265
HB-VLH	HS25	257017
HB-VLI	HS25	258120
HB-VLJ	HS25	257030
HB-VLK	LJ36	032
HB-VLL	HS25	257105
HB-VLM	BE40	RK-66
HB-VLN	BE40	RK-94
HB-VLP	C650	7064
HB-VLQ	C550	352
HB-VLR	LJ31	127
HB-VLS	C550	219
HB-VLT	HS25	258240
HB-VLU	LJ60	010

HB-VLV	C560	0077
HB-VLW	BE40	RK-103
HB-VLY	C550	429
HB-VLZ	C560	0446
HB-VMA	LJ45	020
HB-VMB	LJ45	021
HB-VMC	LJ45	028
HB-VMD	HS25	257040
HB-VME	FA10	131
HB-VMF	HS25	258175
HB-VMG	ASTR	105
HB-VMH	C550	649
HB-VMI	HS25	258210
HB-VMJ	C555	0029
HB-VMK	ASTR	113
HB-VML	LJ45	084
HB-VMM	C550	550-0907
HB-VMN	FA20	240/478
HB-VMO	C56X	5061
HB-VMP	C550	697
HB-VMR	ASTR	115
HB-VMT	C525	0250
HB-VMU	C56X	5066
HB-VMV	C560	0166
HB-VMW	C550	550-0955
HB-VMX	**C550**	**550-0946**
HB-VMY	C550	550-0964
HB-VMZ	C56X	5067
HB-VNA	**C560**	**0280**
HB-VNB	C560	0271
HB-VNC	C56X	5058
HB-VND	C56X	5106
HB-VNE	BE40	RK-318
HB-VNF	ASTR	059
HB-VNG	FA20	502
HB-VNH	C56X	5172
HB-VNI	C56X	5154
HB-VNJ	HS25	258521
HB-VNK	C525	0271
HB-VNL	C525	0375
HB-VNM	FA20	426
HB-VNO	C52A	0033
HB-VNP	C525	0499
HB-VNR	C56X	5248
HB-VNS	C56X	5209
HB-VNU	C500	282
HB-VNV	LJ60	179
HB-VNW	C560	0457
HB-VNY	C56X	5576
HB-VNZ	C550	550-0906
HB-VOA	ASTR	111
HB-VOB	HS25	258733
HB-VOC	**C560**	**0301**
HB-VOD	C525	0415
HB-VOE	C52A	0017
HB-VOF	**C525**	**0623**
HB-VOG	C525	0544
HB-VOH	C550	550-0864
HB-VOI	PRM1	RB-152
HB-VOJ	HS25	258799
HB-VOL	C52A	0341
HB-VOM	C56X	5642
HB-VON	C56X	5528
HB-VOO	HS25	259030
HB-VOP	C52A	0385
HB-VOQ	**HS25**	**259021**
HB-VOR	C525	0473
HB-VOS	PRM1	RB-187
HB-VOT	HS25	258645
HB-VOU	**C56X**	**5070**
HB-VOV	C525	0665
HB-VOW	C52B	0209
HB-VOX	C525	0193
HB-VOY	HS25	258895
HB-VOZ	LJ60	148
HB-VPA	**C52C**	**0116**
HB-VPB	C52A	0422
HB-VPC	**C52A**	**0331**
HB-VPD	C525	0519
HB-VPE	**C52A**	**0375**
HB-VPF	**C525**	**0044**
HB-VPG	**E55P**	**50500068**
HB-VPH	**C525**	**0862**
HB-VPI	C525	0291
HB-VPJ	HS25	HA-0038
HB-VPM	C510	0386
HB-VPR	**E55P**	**50500195**
HB-VRV	**E50P**	**50000292**
HB-VRW	**E55P**	**50500308**
HB-VTJ	**C52B**	**0179**
HB-VTS	**PRM1**	**RB-291**
HB-VWA	**C52A**	**0383**
HB-VWB	C52B	0216
HB-VWC	C52B	0272
HB-VWD	C56X	6021
HB-VWE	C56X	6022
(HB-VWE)	C56X	6021
HB-VWF	C525	0650
(HB-VWG)	C56X	6022
HB-VWJ	C56X	5217
HB-VWL	C510	0169
HB-VWM	**C525**	**0690**
HB-VWN	LJ60	158
HB-VWO	**C525**	**0391**
HB-VWP	**C525**	**0102**
HB-VWQ	E50P	50000050
HB-VWS	C510	0067

(HB-VWS)	E50P	50000122
HB-VWW	C525	0448
(HB-VWW)	FA20	37/406
HB-VWZ	**C510**	**0341**
HB-VXA	**PC24**	**P01**
HB-VXB	**PC24**	**P02**
HB-VYM	**E55P**	**50500023**
HB-VYS	**E55P**	**50500181**

Ecuador

HC-...	**SBRL**	**306-135**
HC-BGL	WW24	234
HC-BQT	SBRL	306-33
HC-BQU	SBRL	306-44
HC-BSS	**FA20**	**150/445**
HC-BSZ	LJ35	311
HC-BTJ	C550	017
HC-BTN	LJ35	417
HC-BTQ	C500	444
HC-BTT	HS25	25228
HC-BTY	C555	0067
HC-BUN	SBRL	306-126
HC-BUP	FA20	200
HC-BUR	HS25	256053
HC-BVH	FA20	490
HC-BVP	C500	481
HC-BVX	WW24	411

Dominican Republic

HI-420	C550	466
HI-493	C500	406
HI-496	C550	407
HI-496SP	C550	407
HI-500	C550	248
HI-500CT	C550	248
HI-500SP	C550	248
HI-527	C500	369
HI-527SP	C500	369
(HI-530)	C550	022
HI-534	C550	022
HI-534CA	C550	022
HI-581SP	C500	599
HI-646SP	MU30	A064SA
HI-766SP	BE40	RK-208
HI-836SP	FA10	53
HI...	**GLF2**	**50**
HI...	**LJ25**	**301**
HI766	BE40	RK-208
HI871	**GLF2**	**154/28**
HI915	**C550**	**550-1084**
HI925	**C550**	**550-1106**
HI929	**LJ55**	**051**
HI949	**C510**	**0326**
HI955	**C56X**	**5521**
HI985	**C680**	**0001**
HI1001	**C750**	**0099**

Colombia

HK-....	WW24	162
(HK-....)	GLF2	210
HK-2150	WW24	181
HK-2150X	WW24	181
HK-2485	WW24	239
HK-2485G	**WW24**	**239**
HK-2485W	WW24	239
HK-2624P	LJ25	339
HK-2624X	LJ25	339
HK-2968	FA10	176
HK-2968X	FA10	176
HK-3121	LJ35	439
HK-3121X	LJ35	439
HK-3122	LJ35	481
HK-3122X	LJ35	481
HK-3191X	C550	439
HK-3265	LJ24	297
HK-3400X	C550	394
HK-3607X	C550	040
HK-3646X	LJ35	503
HK-3653	HS25	25216
HK-3653X	HS25	25216
HK-3884X	WW24	294
HK-3885	C500	135
HK-3893X	WW24	441
HK-3921	LJ35	499
HK-3949X	LJ35	670
HK-3971X	WW24	306
HK-3983X	LJ35	259
HK-4016X	LJ55	041
HK-4128W	C550	550
HK-4204	WW24	306
HK-4204X	WW24	306
HK-4250	C550	550-0961
HK-4250X	C550	550-0961
HK-4304	**C560**	**0355**
HK-4446-G	**BE40**	**RK-26**
HK-4446-W	BE40	RK-26
HK-4446X	BE40	RK-26
HK-4565	**LJ60**	**331**
HK-4597	C550	550-0961
HK-4597X	C550	550-0961
HK-4645	**BE40**	**RK-174**
HK-4662	**LJ35**	**513**
HK-4670	**HS25**	**258502**
HK-4756	**BE40**	**RK-212**
HK-4758	**HS25**	**HA-0159**
HK-4794	BE40	RK-21
HK-4801	**BE40**	**RK-173**
HK-4826	**LJ35**	**364**
HK-4891	**LJ31**	**123**
HK-4907	**GALX**	**050**
HK-4982	**LJ35**	**197**
HK-5068	**F2TS**	**720**
HK-5068X	F2TS	720
HK-5107	**LJ45**	**200**
HK-5120	**C52C**	**0073**
HK-5154	**GALX**	**063**
HK-5186	CL30	20441

South Korea

HL7202	CL61	5081
HL7222	GLF4	1188
HL7226	C500	294
HL7234	FA20	370
HL7277	C500	327
HL7301	F900	156
HL7386	FA50	179
HL7501	**C560**	**0292**
HL7502	**C560**	**0294**
HL7503	**C560**	**0297**
HL7504	**C560**	**0300**
HL7522	CL64	5303
HL7576	GLEX	9019
HL7577	**CL61**	**5182**
HL7748	GLEX	9179
HL7749	GLEX	9184
HL7778	**HS25**	**HB-74**
(HL7778)	C560	0707
HL7799	GLF5	5028
HL8037	**C500**	**363**
HL8200	**GLF5**	**5233**
HL8201	**C525**	**0686**
HL8202	**C525**	**0691**
HL8229	GLEX	9060
HL8230	**GLEX**	**9384**
HL8238	**GLEX**	**9422**
HL8283	**C525**	**0688**
HL8288	**GLF5**	**5295**

Panama

(HP-....)	LJ24	346
(HP-....)	LJ35	670
(HP-....)	LJ55	041
HP-1A	FA20	382
HP-1A	GLF2	78
HP-1A	WW24	180
HP-7JH	**C550**	**123**
HP-18BLM	**C555**	**0111**
HP-125JW	HS25	25216
HP-500E	E50P	50000106
HP-912	LJ35	280
HP-1128P	HS25	25216
HP-1141P	LJ25	049
HP-1262	HS25	258133
HP-1410	C525	0350
HP-1410HT	C525	0350
HP-1461	C52A	0075
HP-1691	GLF2	78
HP-1776	E50P	50000277
HP-1776AJQ	E50P	50000277
HP-1778	**E50P**	**50000283**
HP-1779	E50P	50000286
HP-1779AJQ	**E50P**	**50000286**
HP-1797	**C500**	**353**
HP-3010	C560	0378
HP-3010HTB	**C560**	**0378**

Honduras

HR-001	WW24	183
HR-002	WW24	333
HR-AMD	HS25	25186
HR-AUJ	GLF2	10
HR-CEF	WW24	333
HR-PHO	**WW24**	**333**

Thailand

HS-...	**C550**	**550-0935**
(HS-AAH)	GALX	055
HS-ASC	**BE40**	**RK-154**
HS-BRM	**BE40**	**RK-245**
HS-CDY	**C750**	**0184**
HS-CFS	LJ35	366
HS-CKI	BE40	RK-245
HS-CPG	**HS25**	**258833**
HS-CPH	**HS25**	**258615**
HS-DCG	C650	7071
HS-EMG	**HS25**	**258094**
HS-EMM	BE40	RK-222
HS-EMS	LJ35	406
HS-HAN	**GALX**	**153**
HS-IOO	**C510**	**0100**
HS-JAA	**GALX**	**055**
HS-JJA	CL61	5188
HS-KAC	**PRM1**	**RB-48**
HS-KCS	**C750**	**0298**
HS-KPA	**F2TS**	**707**
HS-KPG	**G280**	**2084**
HS-KPI	**GLF5**	**5480**
HS-LEE	**GALX**	**090**
HS-LNG	**C650**	**7071**
HS-MCL	**C52B**	**0083**
HS-MED	**C550**	**550-0976**
HS-PEK	**HS25**	**258830**
HS-PSL	**C550**	**550-1103**
HS-RBL	C550	707
HS-RBR	**F2EX**	**166**
(HS-TDL)	CL61	5102
HS-TPD	BE40	RK-294
HS-TVA	CL61	5102
HS-UCM	BE40	RK-95
HS-VIP	**C510**	**0117**
HS-VNT	**GALX**	**142**
HS-VSK	**GLF6**	**6023**
HS-WEH	**GLF5**	**588**

Saudi Arabia

(HZ-...)	HS25	259010
HZ-...	**GLF4**	**4067**
HZ-...	**GLF4**	**4073**
HZ-103	GLF3	453
HZ-103	**GLF4**	**1037**
HZ-105	**HS25**	**258118**
HZ-106	LJ35	374
HZ-107	LJ35	375
HZ-108	GLF3	353
HZ-109	GLF3	453
HZ-109	**HS25**	**258146**
"HZ-109"	HS25	258146
HZ-110	**HS25**	**258148**
HZ-130	**HS25**	**258164**
HZ-133	**C550**	**550-1115**
HZ-134	**C550**	**550-1116**
HZ-135	**C550**	**550-1126**
HZ-136	**C550**	**550-1127**
HZ-A6	GLF5	5038
HZ-A7	**LEG5**	**55000010**
HZ-A8	**HS25**	**HA-0153**
HZ-A9	**HS25**	**HA-0173**
HZ-A13	GLF4	4007
HZ-AA1	C550	128
HZ-AA1	HS25	256019
HZ-AAA	C550	063
HZ-AAA	C550	128
HZ-AAA	C650	0003
HZ-AAI	C550	149
HZ-AB2	F900	61
HZ-ABM	LJ35	243
HZ-ADC	GLF2	187
HZ-ADC	GLF4	1037
HZ-AFA	GLEX	9029
HZ-AFA2	CL64	5320
HZ-AFG	GLF2	175
HZ-AFH	GLF2	171
HZ-AFI	GLF2	201
HZ-AFJ	GLF2	203
HZ-AFK	GLF2	239
HZ-AFL	GLF3	311
HZ-AFM	GLF3	324
HZ-AFN	**GLF3**	**364**
HZ-AFO	GLF3	365
HZ-AFP	C550	472
HZ-AFQ	C550	473
HZ-AFR	**GLF3**	**410**
HZ-AFS	GLF3	450
HZ-AFS	JSTR	5016
HZ-AFT	**F900**	**21**
HZ-AFU	**GLF4**	**1031**
HZ-AFV	**GLF4**	**1035**
HZ-AFW	**GLF4**	**1038**
HZ-AFX	**GLF4**	**1143**
HZ-AFY	**GLF4**	**1166**
HZ-AFZ	**F900**	**61**
HZ-AK1	CL61	3032
HZ-AKI	FA10	108
HZ-AKI	FA50	133
HZ-AKI	FA50	7
(HZ-AKI)	FA20	395/554
HZ-ALFA	GLF5	5251
HZ-ALJ	C550	063
HZ-ALS1	**BE40**	**RK-366**
HZ-AM11	LJ55	040
HZ-AM2	LJ55	040
HZ-AM2	LJ55	127
HZ-AMA	FA10	118
(HZ-AMA)	CL61	3017
HZ-AMM	HS25	256064
HZ-AMN	SBRL	380-38
HZ-AO1	FA20	359/542
HZ-AO2	FA10	118
HZ-AO3	FA50	7
HZ-AO4	CL60	1006
HZ-ARK	**GLF5**	**5074**
HZ-ATG	**CL65**	**5899**
HZ-ATH	**GLEX**	**9434**
HZ-AZP	LJ25	081
HZ-BB1	LJ25	081
HZ-BB2	FA50	131
HZ-BIN	HS25	25106
HZ-BIN	**HS25**	**HA-0023**
"HZ-BJP"	GLEX	9293
HZ-BL1	**C525**	**0371**
HZ-BL2	HS25	258126
HZ-BO1	HS25	25094
HZ-BSA	C56X	5658
HZ-BSA	GLF3	353
HZ-CA1	SBRL	380-55
HZ-CAD	GLF2	179
HZ-DA1	GLF3	358
HZ-DA1	HS25	257067
HZ-DA2	HS25	257088
HZ-DA3	HS25	257115
HZ-DA4	HS25	257124

HZ-DAC	HS25	256059
HZ-DC2	FA20	363/544
HZ-DG2	GLF3	317
HZ-DME	**F900**	**76**
HZ-FBT	JSTR	5086/44
HZ-FJM	**CL61**	**5110**
HZ-FK1	JSTR	5133
HZ-FM2	**GLF4**	**1503**
HZ-FMA	HS25	25105
HZ-FNA	JSTR	5056
HZ-FYZ	C56X	5022
HZ-GP3	LJ25	158
HZ-GP4	LJ24	190
HZ-GP4	LJ25	062
HZ-GP5	LJ25	199
HZ-HA1	**GLF2**	**216**
HZ-HE4	FA20	241/479
HZ-HHT	GLF3	491
HZ-HR2	GLF3	346
HZ-HR4	GLF3	415
HZ-HSH	**CL64**	**5346**
HZ-IBN	E55P	50500040
HZ-KA1	LJ35	033
HZ-KA2	HS25	256057
HZ-KA3	FA20	174/457
HZ-KA5	HS25	256049
HZ-KAA	GLF4	1294
(HZ-KAI)	FA10	108
HZ-KME1	**C56X**	**5658**
HZ-KS1	GLF4	1349
HZ-KS2	GLF4	1367
(HZ-KS3)	GLF4	1384
HZ-KSA	HS25	258022
HZ-KSDA	F2TH	121
HZ-KSDB	F2TH	133
HZ-KSDC	**F2TH**	**142**
(HZ-KSDD)	F2TH	171
HZ-KSGA	**GLF4**	**4079**
HZ-KSRA	HS25	258464
HZ-KSRB	HS25	258475
HZ-KSRC	**HS25**	**258481**
HZ-KSRD	**HS25**	**HB-17**
(HZ-KSRD)	HS25	258485
HZ-KTC	LJ35	147
HZ-MA1	JSTR	5105
HZ-MA1	SBRL	306-110
HZ-MA1	SBRL	306-94
HZ-MAC	JSTR	5013
HZ-MAL	GLF3	379
HZ-MAL	GLF4	1294
HZ-MEJ1	**CL64**	**5320**
HZ-MF1	CL60	1070
HZ-MF1	HS25	256060
HZ-MF3	**GLF4**	**1520**
HZ-MF4	**GLF4**	**1525**
HZ-MF5	**GLF4**	**1532**
HZ-MFL	**GLF4**	**1128**
HZ-MIB	LJ35	173
HZ-MIC	GLF3	423
HZ-MIC	GLF5	518
HZ-MKG	GLF4	1254
HZ-MMM	HS25	257010
HZ-MNC	GLF4	1076
HZ-MOA	LJ25	081
HZ-MPM	GLF2	4/8
HZ-MRP	LJ25	121
HZ-MS04	GLF4	1365
HZ-MS05	GLF5	583
HZ-MS1	LJ35	467
HZ-MS1A	LJ35	374
HZ-MS1A	**LJ60**	**370**
HZ-MS1B	LJ35	375
HZ-MS1B	**LJ60**	**371**
HZ-MS1C	LJ35	467
HZ-MS3	GLF3	385
HZ-MS4	GLF2	103
HZ-MS4	**GLF4**	**1365**
HZ-MS4A	**GLF4**	**4313**
HZ-MS4B	**GLF4**	**4324**
HZ-MS4C	**GLF4**	**4328**
HZ-MS5	GLF5	583
HZ-MS5A	**GLF5**	**644**
HZ-MS5B	**GLF5**	**583**
HZ-MSD	GLF2	256
HZ-MWD	GLF3	393
HZ-NAD	HS25	257064
HZ-NC1	C500	319
HZ-NCB	SBRL	306-94
(HZ-NCI)	LJ35	173
HZ-ND1	GLF2	216
HZ-NES	FA20	174/457
HZ-NGN	LJ60	336
(HZ-NJ4)	C525	0098
HZ-NOT	FA10	118
HZ-NR1	SBRL	380-71
HZ-NR2	GLF3	304
HZ-NR2	GLF3	415
HZ-NR3	GLF3	371
HZ-OFC	HS25	257064
HZ-OFC	HS25	258050
HZ-OFC	HS25	259008
HZ-OFC2	HS25	259008
HZ-OFC3	F900	133
HZ-OFC4	F9EX	31
HZ-OFC5	F9EX	180
HZ-OFC6	FA7X	92
HZ-OHS	**CL61**	**5102**

HZ-OSR	LJ60	312
HZ-PCA	GLF2	179
HZ-PET	GLF2	139/11
HZ-PL1	FA20	293
HZ-PL7	FA20	241/479
HZ-PM2	BE40	RK-571
HZ-PM3	BE40	RK-565
(HZ-R4A)	F900	21
HZ-RBH	SBRL	380-57
HZ-RC1	HS25	257040
HZ-RC2	HS25	257055
HZ-RC3	**GLF3**	**331**
HZ-RFM	CL60	1074
HZ-RH2	GLF3	346
HZ-RI1	LJ25	199
HZ-S3	**LJ24**	**357**
HZ-SAA	CL60	1074
HZ-SAB	FA50	73
HZ-SAB2	F900	113
HZ-SAR	GLF4	1166
HZ-SFA	C560	0132
HZ-SFS	CL61	3017
HZ-SH1	JSTR	5141
HZ-SH2	JSTR	5016
HZ-SH3	JSTR	5142
HZ-SH4	JSTR	5148
HZ-SJP	GLEX	9293
HZ-SJP	HS25	256059
HZ-SJP	HS25	257214
HZ-SJP	HS25	258068
HZ-SJP2	HS25	259012
HZ-SJP3	CL64	5346
HZ-SK1	**GLF4**	**1444**
HZ-SK5	**GLF4**	**4007**
HZ-SK6	**GLF5**	**5038**
HZ-SM3	FA50	165
HZ-SMB	LJ24	117
HZ-SMB	LJ25	073
HZ-SOG	SBRL	380-72
(HZ-SOG)	GLF3	415
HZ-SPAA	**BE40**	**RK-587**
HZ-SPAB	**BE40**	**RK-588**
HZ-SPAC	**BE40**	**RK-589**
HZ-SPAD	**BE40**	**RK-591**
HZ-SPAE	**BE40**	**RK-592**
HZ-SPAF	**BE40**	**RK-594**
HZ-SPAG	**FA7X**	**79**
HZ-SPAH	**FA7X**	**87**
HZ-SPAI	**FA7X**	**112**
HZ-SPAJ	**FA7X**	**136**
HZ-SPAL	F900	130
HZ-SS2	LJ25	213
HZ-TAG	CL60	1007
HZ-TAG	CL60	1014
HZ-TAG	FA20	359/542
HZ-TFM	CL64	5481
HZ-THZ	JSTR	5050/34
HZ-THZ	SBRL	380-53
HZ-TNA	JSTR	5120/26
HZ-WBT	JSTR	5133
HZ-WBT1	CL60	1074
HZ-WBT5	**HS25**	**258032**
HZ-WT1	JSTR	5133
HZ-WT2	CL60	1074
HZ-YA1	HS25	256033
HZ-ZTC	C550	149
HZ-ZTC	C560	0036

Italy

I-....	**C500**	**320**
(I-....)	C550	469
I-ACCG	FA20	474
I-ACIF	BE40	RJ-28
I-ACTL	FA20	427
I-ADAG	FA50	131
I-ADVD	**GLF5**	**5314**
I-AEAL	**C500**	**053**
I-AFIT	**FA7X**	**34**
I-AFMA	CL64	5487
I-AFOI	**PRM1**	**RB-245**
I-AGEB	LJ35	243
I-AGEC	FA20	239
I-AGEN	LJ35	491
I-AGER	LJ55	045
(I-AGIK)	C500	539
(I-AGLS)	C56X	5668
I-AGSM	C550	419
I-AIFA	LJ36	021
I-AIRV	C500	486
I-AIRW	LJ31	025
I-ALBS	C500	023
I-ALGU	MU30	A067SA
I-ALHO	HS25	258561
I-ALKA	C550	386
I-ALKB	C550	393
I-ALPG	C550	348
I-ALPM	LJ35	133
I-ALPR	LJ55	078
I-ALPT	LJ35	198
I-ALSE	BE40	RJ-10
I-ALSI	BE40	RJ-31
I-ALSO	BE40	RJ-34
I-ALSU	BE40	RK-11
(I-ALSU)	BE40	RJ-23
I-ALVC	**BE40**	**RK-515**
I-AMAW	C500	095
I-AMBR	C500	180

I-AMCT	C500	114
I-AMCU	C500	109
I-AMCY	**C500**	**192**
I-AMME	LJ24	310
I-ARIB	C550	243
I-ARIF	**F2TH**	**203**
I-ARNT	WW24	139
I-AROM	C500	410
I-ARON	C500	095
I-AROO	C550	090
I-ASAZ	C550	438
I-ASER	BE40	RK-204
I-ATMO	FA20	94/428
I-ATSA	C650	0161
I-ATSB	C560	0033
I-ATSE	C550	649
I-AUNY	**C500**	**618**
I-AVEB	**MU30**	**A087SA**
I-AVGM	C550	492
I-AVJD	LJ25	214
I-AVJE	LJ25	254
I-AVJG	LJ35	189
I-AVND	**LJ45**	**064**
I-AVRM	C550	491
I-AVSS	**BE40**	**RK-66**
I-AVVM	C555	0062
I-AZFB	HS25	257201
I-BAEL	FA20	426
I-BBGR	**HS25**	**HA-0056**
I-BEAU	**F900**	**23**
I-BEDT	**C56X**	**5172**
I-BENN	**C550**	**550-0859**
I-BENT	C56X	5053
I-BETV	C650	0104
I-BEWW	CL61	5020
I-BLSM	CL60	1076
I-BLUB	C650	0216
I-BMFE	**LJ25**	**146**
I-BMPG	**GLF4**	**4326**
I-BNTN	F2TH	191
I-BOAT	C525	0450
I-BOGI	HS25	25138
I-CABD	**C525**	**0354**
I-CAEX	F9EX	91
I-CAFB	FA50	138
I-CAFC	FA50	145
I-CAFD	**FA50**	**183**
I-CAFE	FA50	190
I-CAIB	FA20	175
I-CAIC	FA10	89
(I-CAIK)	FA50	37
I-CALC	FA10	127
I-CALZ	C52A	0427
I-CART	LJ24	231
I-CASG	HS25	258033
(I-CCCB)	C500	382
I-CCCH	CL30	20094
I-CDBS	C56X	5007
I-CDOL	**C56X**	**5584**
I-CEFI	C555	0047
I-CFLY	**LJ31**	**167**
I-CHIC	FA10	126
I-CHOC	FA10	113
I-CIGA	C550	263
I-CIGB	**C500**	**539**
I-CIGH	HS25	257201
I-CIPA	C500	559
I-CIST	C650	0085
I-CITY	C500	053
I-CLAD	**C500**	**223**
I-CMAB	**C56X**	**5731**
I-CMAD	C56X	5801
I-CMAL	C56X	5344
I-CMCC	C560	0542
I-CMUT	FA20	389/552
I-CNDG	**C56X**	**6045**
I-CNEF	FA20	506
I-COKE	C500	251
I-COTO	LJ25	285
I-CREM	FA10	161
(I-CRYS)	LJ36	006
I-CSGA	FA50	203
I-CSGB	FA50	208
I-CTPT	CL61	5013
(I-DAEP)	C500	414
I-DAGF	C525	0347
I-DAGS	CL61	5085
I-DAKO	F9EX	160
I-DARK	FA50	151
I-DDAE	LJ24	336
I-DDVA	HS25	258389
I-DDVF	F2TH	161
I-DEAC	C525	0194
I-DEAF	C550	283
I-DEAN	LJ25	314
I-DEAS	GLF5	593
I-DECI	C500	504
I-DEGF	FA50	176
I-DELO	**GLF5**	**5518**
I-DENR	FA50	125
I-DEUM	**C52A**	**0095**
I-DFSL	LJ45	158
I-DIDY	C500	514
I-DIEM	**F9EX**	**253**
I-DIES	F900	30
I-DJMA	FA10	179
I-DKET	FA20	160/450

I-DLGH	GLF4	4240
I-DLOH	HS25	258450
I-DLON	LJ35	346
I-DMSA	PRM1	RB-201
I-DMSB	PRM1	RB-254
I-DNOR	FA10	118
I-DOCA	MU30	A059SA
I-DRIB	FA20	201/469
(I-DRVM)	HS25	257017
I-DUMA	C500	263
I-DVAL	C500	649
I-DVMR	HS25	257017
I-EAMM	LJ35	634
I-EDEM	**C525**	**0155**
I-EDIF	FA20	300/508
I-EDIK	FA50	132
I-EDIM	FA20	295/500
I-EDIS	FA20	280/503
I-EDLO	**HS25**	**HB-67**
I-EJIA	LJ24	259
I-EJIB	LJ35	331
I-EJIC	FA10	89
I-EJID	LJ35	222
I-EKET	FA20	170/455
I-ELEN	LJ25	171
I-ELYS	**LJ40**	**2016**
I-EPAM	**HS25**	**HB-32**
I-ERDN	FA50	48
I-ERJA	C500	358
I-ERJB	LJ31	167
I-ERJC	LJ45	072
I-ERJC	LJ45	093
I-ERJD	LJ45	068
I-ERJE	LJ45	226
I-ERJG	LJ40	2015
I-ERJJ	LJ40	2053
I-ESAI	C525	0235
I-FARN	**C500**	**565**
I-FBCA	SBRL	306-97
I-FBCK	C500	178
I-FBCT	C550	090
I-FCHI	GLF3	460
I-FCIM	FA20	323/520
I-FDED	**BE40**	**RK-500**
I-FEDN	**F2EX**	**204**
I-FEEV	C650	0105
I-FERN	C500	152
I-FFLY	LJ35	325
I-FFRI	LJ35	493
I-FFRR	**FA7X**	**94**
I-FICV	F900	54
I-FIMI	LJ35	090
I-FINR	MS76	111
I-FIPE	FA20	368
I-FIPP	CL61	5069
I-FITO	**C510**	**0160**
I-FJDC	FA10	203
I-FJDN	FA50	295
I-FJTB	C550	550-0922
I-FJTC	C550	550-0988
I-FJTO	C550	679
I-FKET	FA20	279/502
I-FLYA	C500	467
I-FLYB	C500	489
I-FLYC	LJ35	298
I-FLYD	C550	291
I-FLYF	FA20	428
I-FLYG	LJ35	593
I-FLYH	LJ35	498
I-FLYI	F9EX	204
I-FLYJ	LJ55	084
I-FLYK	FA20	241/479
I-FLYL	ASTR	036
I-FLYN	F9EX	163
I-FLYP	F2TH	103
I-FLYS	F900	115
I-FLYV	**F2TH**	**108**
I-FLYW	F9EX	27
I-FOMN	C500	498
I-FORR	**LJ40**	**2019**
I-FORU	**LJ45**	**036**
I-FRAB	MU30	A052SA
I-FRAI	C500	452
I-FREU	LJ24	279
I-FRTI	MU30	A056SA
I-FSJA	BE40	RK-41
I-FTAL	BE40	RJ-42
I-GAMB	C550	312
I-GASD	C650	0037
I-GCAL	FA20	307/513
I-GCFA	BE40	RJ-44
I-GEFD	**F2TH**	**191**
I-GENC	MU30	A065SA
I-GERA	C500	511
I-GFVF	BE40	RK-499
I-GGLA	C56X	6044
I-GGLB	**C550**	**291**
I-GGLC	**C550**	**090**
(I-GIAN)	LJ25	207
I-GIAZ	FA20	252/485
I-GIRL	MU30	A012SA
I-GIWW	C550	550-0871
I-GJBO	HS25	25240
I-GJMA	C500	542
I-GOBJ	FA20	180/460
I-GOBZ	FA20	293
I-GOCO	**LJ40**	**2078**

I-GOSF	C52A	0199
I-GSAL	PRM1	RB-184
I-GSIN	**LJ60**	**414**
I-GURU	**LJ40**	**2059**
I-IDAG	C525	0093
I-IFPC	BE40	RK-71
I-IGNO	HS25	258040
I-IINL	LJ60	236
I-IMMG	C52A	0038
I-IMMI	**C525**	**0379**
I-INCH	C510	0190
I-INCZ	BE40	RJ-22
I-IPFC	BE40	RK-6
I-IPIZ	BE40	RK-29
I-IRCS	CL64	5464
I-IRIF	FA20	185/467
I-ITAL	HFB3	1040
I-ITPR	FA10	115
I-JAMI	**FA7X**	**81**
I-JAMJ	**F2EX**	**108**
I-JAMY	F2TH	54
I-JESA	C550	098
I-JESE	C500	330
I-JESJ	C550	352
I-JESO	C550	283
I-JETF	F2EX	78
I-JETS	C56X	5012
I-JETX	C750	0184
I-JUST	C500	621
I-KALI	LJ35	249
I-KELM	LJ35	406
I-KERE	**F2TH**	**197**
I-KESO	C550	338
I-KETO	C750	0161
I-KIDO	FA50	31
I-KILO	LJ55	007
I-KIOV	LJ25	299
I-KISS	LJ25	193
I-KIWI	C550	432
I-KODE	C500	626
I-KODM	LJ35	620
I-KREM	**HS25**	**258608**
I-KUNA	C500	053
I-KUSS	LJ35	237
I-KWYJ	C500	412
I-LADA	GLF4	1142
(I-LAFA)	FA20	381/549
I-LALL	C52A	0005
(I-LAST)	C56X	5668
I-LAWN	C500	612
I-LCJG	FA10	53
I-LCJT	FA10	96
I-LEAR	LJ25	207
I-LECO	WW24	72
I-LIAB	FA20	172/456
I-LIAC	FA20	234/475
I-LIAD	LJ35	111
I-LOOK	LJ55	021
I-LPHZ	CL60	1069
I-LUBE	FA10	7
I-LUBI	GLF4	1123
I-LUXO	**GLF5**	**5071**
I-LVNB	C52A	0073
I-LXAG	FA50	159
I-LXGR	GLF4	1234
I-LXOT	FA20	496
I-MABU	LJ24	287
I-MADU	GLF3	448
I-MAFU	FA20	501
I-MCAM	**C525**	**0874**
I-MCAS	C510	0185
I-MCSA	LJ35	099
I-MESK	C550	024
I-MFAB	**HS25**	**HA-0074**
I-MILK	CL64	5304
I-MMAE	LJ35	116
I-MMEA	FA50	140
I-MOCO	LJ35	445
I-MOFI	**F2EX**	**213**
I-MORA	SBRL	282-117
I-MOVE	GLEX	9044
I-MPGA	**HA4T**	**RC-70**
I-MPIZ	BE40	RJ-25
(I-MPUT)	GLF5	593
I-MRDV	CL60	1070
I-MRGC	LJ60	211
I-MTDE	F900	43
I-MTNT	C550	116
I-MTVB	C550	550-0932
I-MUDE	FA10	136
I-NATS	F2EX	11
I-NATZ	LJ60	204
I-NEMO	**F9EX**	**255**
I-NEWY	C560	0115
I-NGIR	PRM1	RB-241
I-NIAR	C550	312
I-NICK	SBRL	282-25
I-NIKJ	LJ35	055
I-NLAE	FA20	134
I-NNUS	CL61	5044
I-NORT	C500	320
I-NUMI	F900	89
I-NYCE	C560	0053
I-NYNY	C56X	5107
I-NYSE	C560	0302
I-OANN	FA10	208
I-OMEP	C500	476

I-OMRA	C52A	0064
I-ONDO	BE40	RJ-20
I-OSLO	HS25	258050
I-OSUA	LJ55	102
I-OTEL	**C500**	**414**
I-OTTY	BE40	RJ-25
I-PABL	C550	550-1083
I-PALP	C500	583
I-PAPE	C500	659
I-PARS	LJ40	2034
I-PATY	SBRL	306-133
I-PBRA	**FA50**	**339**
I-PBRB	**F2EX**	**191**
I-PBRP	F2EX	239
I-PEGA	**C500**	**081**
I-PERF	FA20	313
I-PFLY	**GLEX**	**9625**
I-PIAI	P808	503
I-PIAL	P808	504
I-PIAY	P808	522
I-PLLL	C500	230
I-PNCA	**C550**	**257**
I-POLE	FA50	180
I-PRAD	LJ60	145
I-PSCU	**BE40**	**RK-343**
I-PTCT	CL60	1082
I-PZZR	**HS25**	**258722**
I-RACE	HS25	25006
I-RAGW	**C500**	**311**
I-RASO	HS25	25131
I-RDSF	BE40	RJ-36
I-REAL	FA20	267/491
I-RELT	**SBRL**	**282-133**
I-RIED	FA20	77/429
I-RJVA	LJ25	342
I-ROBM	FA20	182/461
I-RODJ	FA50	155
I-RONY	**HS25**	**258506**
I-ROST	C500	445
I-RPLY	LJ60	212
I-RVRP	**C525**	**0397**
I-RYVA	LJ35	391
I-SAFP	FA50	9
I-SAFR	FA50	29
I-SALG	C650	0120
I-SALV	C550	561
I-SAME	FA50	37
I-SAMI	BE40	RJ-35
I-SATV	C500	524
I-SDAG	LJ60	379
I-SDFC	**CL30**	**20013**
I-SDFG	HS25	258136
I-SEAE	**F2TH**	**200**
I-SEAM	**GLF5**	**5431**
I-SEAR	**F9EX**	**183**
I-SEAS	**F9EX**	**192**
I-SELM	MU30	A064SA
I-SFER	LJ25	097
I-SFRA	FA10	130
I-SHIP	FA10	110
(I-SHOP)	FA10	113
(I-SIDU)	LJ35	111
I-SIMD	LJ25	193
I-SIRF	HS25	258267
I-SLNI	**F9EX**	**109**
I-SMEG	GLF2	97
I-SNAB	FA50	169
I-SNAC	FA50	30
I-SNAD	SBRL	306-27
I-SNAF	HS25	25145
I-SNAG	FA20	240/478
I-SNAI	MS76	028
I-SNAK	SBRL	282-25
I-SNAL	JSTR	5023
I-SNAM	FA20	176/458
I-SNAP	MS76	099
I-SNAV	FA20	119/431
I-SNAW	F2TH	12
I-SNAX	F900	69
I-SOBE	FA20	487
I-SRAF	HS25	259012
I-SREG	FA20	442
I-STAP	BE40	RJ-18
I-STCA	C510	0334
I-STCB	C510	0330
I-STCC	C510	0360
I-STCD	C510	0361
I-STCE	C510	0386
(I-STEF)	CL30	20236
I-TAKA	**C56X**	**5537**
I-TAKY	LJ25	073
I-TALC	HFB3	1027
I-TALG	CS55	0122
I-TALW	C650	0208
I-TAOS	**C680**	**0309**
I-TCGR	**F900**	**154**
I-TFLY	FA10	188
I-TIAG	FA20	233
I-TIAL	FA20	290
I-TLCM	F900	81
I-TNTR	C550	466
I-TOIO	C500	657
I-TOPB	BE40	RK-133
I-TOPD	**BE40**	**RK-163**
I-TOPH	**HS25**	**258809**
I-TOPJ	BE40	RJ-44
I-TOPX	**BE40**	**RK-579**
I-TORA	MU30	A085SA
I-TOSC	C500	410
I-TYKE	LJ31	120
I-UCBT	F2EX	209
I-ULJA	FA20	380
I-UNSA	BE40	RK-20
I-UUNY	**C500**	**377**
I-VEPA	FA20	100
I-VIGI	MU30	A013SA
I-VIKI	C550	381
I-VIKY	LJ55	073
I-VITH	**BE40**	**RK-309**
I-VULC	LJ35	421
"I-WDSD"	FA20	487
I-WISH	CL64	5526
I-XPRA	**GLF4**	**4279**
I-YLFC	LJ40	2024
I-ZACK	**C560**	**0767**
I-ZAMP	CS55	0133
I-ZOOM	LJ35	135
I-ZUGR	FA50	341

Japan

(JA....)	FA50	173
(JA-001T)	C525	0449
JA001A	**C560**	**0349**
JA001G	**GLF4**	**1190**
JA001T	**C52A**	**0311**
JA001Z	**C510**	**0321**
JA002A	**C560**	**0597**
JA002G	**GLF4**	**1244**
JA005G	**GLEX**	**9034**
JA006G	**GLEX**	**9082**
JA008G	**C52C**	**0154**
JA009G	**C52C**	**0179**
JA010G	**C52C**	**0185**
JA01CP	**LJ31**	**144**
JA01GW	LJ45	292
JA01TM	C560	0403
JA021R	**C52A**	**0380**
JA02AA	C560	0518
JA02GW	LJ45	302
JA04AA	**C680**	**0229**
JA12NT	**C510**	**0290**
JA30DA	**MU30**	**A053SA**
JA50TH	F9EX	3
JA55TH	F9EX	100
JA68CE	**C680**	**0288**
JA78MA	**BE40**	**RK-287**
JA100C	C525	0534
JA118N	**C560**	**0046**
JA119N	**C560**	**0067**
JA120N	**C560**	**0072**
JA123F	**C510**	**0428**
JA359C	**C52A**	**0359**
JA391C	**C52A**	**0391**
JA500A	**GLF5**	**683**
JA501A	**GLF5**	**689**
JA510M	C510	0135
JA516J	**C52A**	**0386**
JA525A	**C525**	**0449**
JA525B	**C52A**	**0156**
JA525C	**C52A**	**0244**
JA525G	C52A	0096
JA525J	**C525**	**0549**
JA525M	**C525**	**0824**
JA525Y	**C525**	**0535**
JA560Y	**C560**	**0694**
JA680C	**C680**	**0173**
JA8246	MU30	A092SA
JA8247	C500	259
JA8248	MU30	002
JA8249	C650	0085
JA8270	FA20	509
JA8283	CL61	5011
JA8284	C500	631
JA8298	MU30	A074SA
(JA8360)	CL61	5037
JA8361	CL61	5068
(JA8361)	C500	476
(JA8366)	GLF4	1107
JA8367	C650	0177
JA8378	C650	0178
JA8379	ASTR	049
JA8380	C500	350
(JA8380)	GLF4	1148
JA8418	C500	226
JA8420	C525	0056
JA8421	C500	021
JA8422	C500	040
JA8431	**GLF2**	**141**
JA8438	C500	321
JA8446	LJ24	245
JA8447	FA10	84
JA8463	FA10	152
JA8474	C500	629
JA8493	**C500**	**672**
JA8494	FA10	201
JA8495	C550	495
JA8570	**F900**	**53**
JA8571	**F900**	**56**
JA8572	F900	105
JA8575	FA50	196
JA8576	C560	0080
JQ8001	MU30	001SA
JQ8002	MU30	002
JQ8003	MU30	002
JQ8004	MU30	A004SA
JQ8005	MU30	A005SA

Jordan

(JY-...)	GLF5	564
JY-AAD	CL64	5481
JY-ABL	GLF3	418
JY-AEG	LJ24	014
JY-AEH	LJ24	023
JY-AEI	LJ24	027
JY-AET	LJ36	016
JY-AEV	LJ35	049
JY-AEW	LJ35	052
(JY-AEX)	LJ35	056
JY-AFC	LJ36	020
JY-AFD	LJ35	071
JY-AFE	LJ35	075
JY-AFF	LJ35	081
JY-AFH	SBRL	380-57
JY-AFL	SBRL	380-56
JY-AFM	SBRL	380-36
JY-AFN	SBRL	380-53
JY-AFO	SBRL	380-61
JY-AFP	SBRL	380-62
JY-AMN	GLF3	418
JY-AW1	C56X	5554
JY-AW3	CL64	5362
JY-AW4	HS25	258520
JY-AW5	HS25	258539
JY-AWD	HS25	258520
JY-AWE	**HS25**	**258539**
JY-AWF	C525	0632
JY-AWG	HS25	258504
(JY-AWG)	E50P	50000169
JY-AWH	C680	0285
JY-FMK	C52A	0168
JY-HAH	FA50	52
JY-HAH	GLF3	467
JY-HZH	FA50	60
JY-HZH	GLF3	469
JY-IMK	CL64	5443
JY-JAS	SBRL	380-64
JY-ONE	CL64	5426
(JY-ONE)	GLF4	1345
JY-RAY	GLF4	1202
JY-RY1	CL61	3017
JY-RYA	CL61	3017
(JY-RYG)	F2TH	79
JY-RYN	C650	7029
JY-TWO	CL64	5443
(JY-TWO)	GLF4	1356
JY-WJA	HS25	258520

Djibouti

J2-KAC	FA20	342/532
J2-KBA	FA50	71

Guinea-Bissau

J5-GAS	FA20	296/507

St Vincent & Grenadines

J8-JET	**C52B**	**0247**
J8-JTS	**C550**	**490**

Norway

LN-AAA	C560	0105
LN-AAA	C650	0187
LN-AAA	FA20	73/419
LN-AAB	C550	397
LN-AAB	FA20	12
LN-AAC	C550	200
LN-AAC	FA20	281/496
LN-AAD	C550	095
LN-AAD	C550	260
LN-AAE	C550	224
LN-AAF	C500	311
LN-AAI	C550	069
LN-AAU	C650	0192
LN-ACX	C550	496
LN-AFC	C500	397
LN-AFG	C550	200
LN-AIR	CL30	20141
LN-AKA	C560	0764
LN-AKR	**F9EX**	**185**
LN-AOC	F9EX	155
LN-AVA	C52A	0199
(LN-AWF)	C550	340
LN-BAC	**C52A**	**0446**
(LN-BEP)	HS25	258094
LN-BRG	F9EX	230
LN-BWG	CL64	5328
LN-ESA	HS25	258094
LN-EXL	C56X	5666
(LN-FDA)	C525	0636
(LN-FDB)	C525	0353
(LN-FDC)	C525	0512
LN-FOD	FA20	53/417
LN-FOE	FA20	125
LN-FOE	FA20	62/409
LN-FOI	FA20	41/407
(LN-FOX)	C550	424
LN-HOT	C52B	0065
LN-HOT	C550	099
LN-HST	C750	0212
LN-IDB	**C560**	**0637**
LN-IDC	**C560**	**0652**
LN-IDD	**C550**	**550-1022**
LN-NAT	C500	331
LN-NEA	C550	136
LN-NLA	C550	136
LN-NLC	C650	0028
LN-NLD	C650	0070
LN-NPA	HS25	25125
LN-NPC	HS25	25145
LN-NPE	HS25	25097
LN-NPE	LJ24	038
LN-RTG	**F2TH**	**154**
LN-RTN	**F2EX**	**302**
LN-RYG	C525	0661
(LN-SEH)	F9EX	145
(LN-SEH)	F9EX	155
LN-SJA	MU30	A037SA
LN-SOL	CL30	20203
LN-SOV	**C680**	**0183**
LN-SSS	**C680**	**0133**
LN-SUN	**CL64**	**5517**
LN-SUS	GALX	051
LN-SUU	HS25	259030
LN-SUV	C550	550-0951
LN-SUX	C56X	5271
(LN-TIH)	C680	0133
LN-VIP	C550	137
LN-VIP	LJ55	112
LN-XLS	C56X	5608

Argentina

LQ-APL	**C550**	**355**
LQ-BFS	**LJ40**	**2003**
LQ-BMH	**C56X**	**5025**
LQ-CLW	**C500**	**366**
LQ-CPS	**LJ45**	**094**
LQ-CVO	**C560**	**0800**
LQ-JRH	HFB3	1050
LQ-MRM	**C500**	**470**
LQ-TFM	C550	117
LQ-WTN	**C650**	**7054**
LV-...	LJ25	110
(LV-...)	SBRL	380-4
(LV-...)	WW24	119
LV-AHX	C560	0090
LV-AIT	**LJ35**	**408**
LV-AIW	C56X	5350
LV-ALF	LJ35	371
LV-ALW	HS25	257133
LV-AMB	**C525**	**0045**
LV-APL	C550	355
LV-ARD	**LJ45**	**232**
LV-AXN	**C525**	**0327**
LV-AXZ	HS25	25251
LV-BAI	FA20	494
LV-BAS	**CL60**	**1053**
LV-BAW	**LJ35**	**386**
LV-BBG	**HS25**	**258707**
LV-BCO	**C550**	**458**
LV-BCS	C56X	5541
LV-BDM	**LJ31**	**145**
LV-BDX	LJ60	270
LV-BEM	**BE40**	**RK-456**
LV-BEU	**C550**	**550-1120**
LV-BFE	**LJ31**	**183**
LV-BFG	**LJ31**	**054**
LV-BFM	**C500**	**395**
LV-BFR	**LJ60**	**059**
LV-BHJ	**C500**	**593**
LV-BHP	**CL64**	**5493**
LV-BIB	C56X	5696
LV-BID	**C500**	**560**
LV-BIE	**LJ35**	**674**
LV-BIY	**FA20**	**444**
LV-BMH	C56X	5025
LV-BNO	CL64	5407
LV-BNR	**LJ35**	**373**
LV-BOU	**LJ45**	**050**
LV-BOX	**LJ35**	**508**
LV-BPA	**LJ35**	**143**
LV-BPL	**LJ35**	**418**
LV-BPO	**LJ35**	**343**
LV-BPV	CL61	3044
LV-BPW	**C500**	**341**
LV-BPZ	**C500**	**412**
LV-BRC	**LJ31**	**058**
LV-BRE	**C550**	**697**
LV-BRJ	C750	0013
LV-BRT	**LJ35**	**665**
LV-BRX	**C56X**	**5134**
LV-BRZ	**FA20**	**171**
LV-BSO	**LJ31**	**222**
LV-BSS	**CL30**	**20219**
LV-BTA	**LJ60**	**353**
LV-BTF	**LJ31**	**111**
LV-BTO	**LJ45**	**388**
LV-BXD	**LJ45**	**254**
LV-BXH	**C500**	**491**
LV-BXU	**LJ35**	**462**
LV-BXV	**LJ45**	**309**
LV-BYC	GLF4	1145
LV-BYG	**CL61**	**5032**
LV-BZC	**LJ25**	**350**
LV-BZJ	**LJ60**	**344**
LV-CAE	**C650**	**0128**
LV-CAK	**C560**	**0170**
LV-CAR	**LJ45**	**248**
LV-CAY	**LJ60**	**234**
LV-CAZ	**GLF4**	**1514**
LV-CBB	**C560**	**0697**
LV-CBI	**LJ60**	**272**
LV-CBJ	**BE40**	**RK-134**
LV-CBK	**C56X**	**5132**
LV-CBO	**C510**	**0265**
LV-CCF	C56X	5150
LV-CCG	C56X	5137
LV-CCO	**LJ60**	**076**
LV-CCW	**CL65**	**5805**
LV-CDI	**C500**	**323**
LV-CED	**C550**	**550-1110**
LV-CEG	**GLF3**	**472**
LV-CEN	**C550**	**014**
LV-CEP	**C750**	**0237**
LV-CFH	**C500**	**589**
LV-CFQ	**C680**	**0303**
LV-CFS	**C550**	**333**
LV-CFW	**LJ25**	**145**
LV-CGL	**CL60**	**1026**
LV-CGO	**C500**	**408**
LV-CIO	**LJ60**	**194**
LV-CIQ	**C680**	**0052**
LV-CJG	**HS25**	**258411**
LV-CJY	**LJ40**	**2096**
LV-CKA	**LJ60**	**327**
LV-CKK	**LJ60**	**068**
LV-CKT	**C525**	**0361**
LV-CLF	**BE40**	**RK-584**
LV-CLK	**LJ31**	**116**
LV-CLS	WW24	255
LV-CMO	**LJ35**	**436**
LV-CNF	**LJ31**	**047**
LV-CNJ	**C560**	**0219**
LV-CNQ	**LJ31**	**004**
LV-CNW	**HA4T**	**RC-14**
LV-COO	**BE40**	**RJ-18**
LV-COV	**C560**	**0085**
LV-CPC	**LJ60**	**062**
LV-CPL	**LJ60**	**044**
LV-CQK	**C650**	**0093**
LV-CQP	**C500**	**605**
LV-CQV	**C550**	**550-1095**
LV-CRB	**LJ60**	**396**
LV-CRC	**LJ60**	**360**
LV-CRI	F900	47
LV-CRL	**C560**	**0057**
LV-CTE	**HS25**	**HA-0198**
LV-CTF	**C550**	**550-1036**
LV-CTT	**C550**	**102**
LV-CTX	**C560**	**0396**
LV-CUE	**LJ60**	**196**
LV-CVC	**C550**	**550-0897**
LV-CVQ	**LJ45**	**433**
(LV-CWY)	HA4T	RC-59
LV-CXE	LJ31	157
LV-CYL	**C56X**	**6114**
LV-CYQ	**LJ45**	**440**
LV-CZD	**C550**	**550-1004**
(LV-CZH)	C550	550-1009
(LV-CZU)	CL60	1043
LV-CZX	**LJ60**	**167**
LV-FDB	LJ25	371
LV-FDQ	**LJ60**	**079**
LV-FKB	**LJ31**	**103**
LV-FKG	**C510**	**0008**
LV-FPM	**LJ60**	**332**
LV-FPN	**LJ60**	**359**
LV-FPW	**HS25**	**258466**
LV-FQD	**C56X**	**5555**
LV-FQW	**C650**	**7103**
(LV-FUE)	C525	0528
LV-FUF	**LJ60**	**165**
LV-FUT	**LJ60**	**179**
LV-FVT	**C650**	**0004**
LV-FVY	**C510**	**0457**
LV-FVZ	**LJ60**	**247**
LV-FWA	C550	405
LV-FWC	HA4T	RC-59
LV-FWF	**BE40**	**RK-85**
LV-FWT	**C525**	**0528**
LV-FWW	**CL65**	**5843**
LV-FWX	**C500**	**499**
LV-FWZ	**CL64**	**5385**
LV-GCK	**LJ60**	**083**
LV-GDQ	**CL61**	**5069**
LV-JTZ	LJ24	234
LV-JXA	LJ24	240
LV-LOG	LJ36	005
LV-LRC	**LJ24**	**316**
LV-LZR	C500	332
LV-MBP	LJ25	229
LV-MGB	C500	423
LV-MMR	C500	459
LV-MMV	LJ25	259
LV-MST	LJ25	245
LV-MYN	C500	510
LV-MZG	C500	506
LV-OAS	LJ35	271
LV-OEL	**LJ25**	**307**
LV-OFV	LJ35	312
LV-ONN	LJ35	355
LV-P...	LJ25	337
LV-PAF	LJ25	245
LV-PAM	BE40	RJ-37
LV-PAT	C500	459
LV-PAW	LJ25	259
LV-PAX	C500	470

LV-PDW	C500	506
LV-PDZ	C500	510
LV-PET	LJ35	271
LV-PEU	LJ25	307
LV-PFK	LJ31	024
LV-PFM	FA20	494
LV-PFN	C560	0126
LV-PGC	C560	0190
LV-PGR	C560	0227
LV-PGU	C550	724
LV-PGX	LJ60	024
LV-PGZ	C560	0251
LV-PHD	C560	0246
LV-PHH	C550	131
LV-PHJ	C560	0265
LV-PHN	C550	728
LV-PHU	LJ25	345
LV-PHV	FA20	34
LV-PHX	LJ35	312
LV-PHY	C560	0289
LV-PIW	HS25	258462
LV-PJL	HS25	258707
LV-PJZ	LJ35	355
LV-PLC	FA20	9
LV-PLD?	FA20	29
LV-PLE	C560	0305
LV-PLL	LJ25	269
LV-PLM	C500	478
LV-PLR	C550	626
LV-PLT	BE40	RK-104
LV-PLV	LJ35	671
LV-PLY	LJ35	371
LV-PMH	BE40	RK-118
LV-PML	C500	580
LV-PMM	HS25	257133
LV-PMP	C500	148
LV-PMV	C550	550-0818
LV-PNB	C550	355
LV-PNL	C550	715
LV-PNR	C560	0458
LV-POG	LJ35	408
LV-POP	HFB3	1050
LV-PRA	LJ24	234
LV-PRB	LJ24	240
LV-PUY	C500	332
LV-PZI	C500	423
LV-RBV	LJ31	024
LV-RCT	BE40	RJ-37
LV-RDD	WW24	12
LV-RED	**C560**	**0126**
LV-TDF	LJ35	478
LV-VFY	C560	0190
LV-WBP	LJ25	337
LV-WDR	**C560**	**0227**
LV-WEJ	**C550**	**724**
LV-WEN	WW24	126
LV-WFM	LJ60	024
LV-WGO	C560	0251
LV-WGY	**C560**	**0246**
LV-WHY	C650	0231
LV-WHZ	**WW24**	**108**
LV-WIJ	C560	0265
LV-WIT	C550	604
LV-WJN	**C550**	**558**
LV-WJO	**C550**	**728**
LV-WJU	WW24	179
LV-WLG	**LJ25**	**345**
LV-WLH	FA20	34
LV-WLR	**WW24**	**183**
LV-WLS	**C560**	**0289**
LV-WLX	SBRL	306-41
LV-WMF	FA20	9
LV-WMM	FA20	29
LV-WMR	LJ24	135
LV-WMT	C560	0305
LV-WND	**SBRL**	**282-131**
LV-WOC	**LJ25**	**269**
LV-WOE	C560	0319
LV-WOF	SBRL	306-25
LV-WOI	C500	478
LV-WOM	GLF4	1274
LV-WOV	WW24	331
"LV-WOW"	GLF4	1274
LV-WOZ	C550	626
LV-WPE	BE40	RK-104
LV-WPO	SBRL	306-3
LV-WPZ	LJ35	671
LV-WRE	**LJ25**	**355**
LV-WSS	GLF4	1297
LV-WTN	C650	7054
LV-WTP	**BE40**	**RK-118**
LV-WXD	**C550**	**395**
LV-WXJ	C500	148
LV-WXN	LJ60	102
LV-WXV	FA50	188
LV-WXX	**SBRL**	**306-91**
LV-WXY	**LJ25**	**357**
LV-WYH	C550	550-0818
LV-WYL	WW24	182
LV-YGC	**HS25**	**25046**
LV-YHC	**C550**	**715**
LV-YLB	CL60	1034
LV-YMA	C560	0458
LV-YMB	**LJ31**	**081**
LV-YRB	**C500**	**191**
LV-ZHY	HS25	258372
LV-ZNR	C550	727
LV-ZPD	C550	398
LV-ZPU	C500	265
LV-ZRS	HS25	257046
LV-ZSZ	LJ35	235
LV-ZTH	**LJ25**	**071**
LV-ZTR	**HS25**	**258462**
LV-ZXI	GLF5	604
LV-ZXW	C56X	5135
LV-ZYF	LJ60	232
LV-ZZF	**LJ35**	**049**

Luxembourg

LX-AAA	FA20	73/419
LX-AAA	GLEX	9133
LX-AAM	F2EX	8
LX-ABB	**GLEX**	**9559**
LX-AEN	CL61	3046
LX-AER	F900	11
LX-AFD	F9DX	615
LX-AKI	FA50	306
LX-AMB	**FA7X**	**118**
LX-AMG	**GLEX**	**9286**
LX-APG	FA50	212
LX-ARC	HS25	258444
LX-ATD	F2TH	603
LX-AVT	**CL30**	**20403**
"LX-BYG"	HS25	258392
LX-COS	F900	159
LX-DCA	**C52B**	**0227**
LX-DEC	**C680**	**0253**
LX-DGQ	C52A	0200
LX-DKC	F2EX	5
LX-DLF	**GLF6**	**6140**
LX-DPA	FA10	113
LX-DSA	FA7X	30
LX-DSL	LJ45	158
LX-DSP	F9EX	160
LX-EAA	**LJ45**	**321**
LX-EAR	LJ31	160
LX-EBE	**C56X**	**6025**
LX-EJH	C550	550-0874
LX-EMO	**F9EX**	**238**
LX-EPA	FA10	48
LX-EVM	**F2EX**	**181**
LX-FAZ	CL64	5307
LX-FBY	CL64	5485
LX-FDA	**FA7X**	**182**
LX-FDJ	**C525**	**0864**
(LX-FDJ)	C525	0842
LX-FGB	C56X	6026
LX-FGC	C510	0192
LX-FGL	C510	0132
LX-FLY	**GLEX**	**9252**
LX-FMR	FA50	165
LX-FOX	C525	0229
LX-FTA	F900	201
(LX-FTJ)	FA50	144
LX-GAP	C52B	0096
LX-GBY	HS25	258392
LX-GCA	C525	0235
LX-GDC	CL61	3065
LX-GDL	C550	033
LX-GDX	C56X	5610
(LX-GDX)	F9EX	176
LX-GED	FA50	54
LX-GES	F900	78
LX-GET	F9EX	217
LX-GEX	GLEX	9013
LX-GJL	**F900**	**197**
LX-GJM	**C52C**	**0174**
LX-GJM	GLEX	9189
LX-GLD	**F9EX**	**211**
LX-GOL	ASTR	059
LX-GRS	GALX	103
LX-GSP	**C680**	**0302**
LX-GVI	**GLF6**	**6095**
(LX-GXR)	GLEX	9332
LX-GXX	**GLEX**	**9306**
LX-IAL	FA20	136/439
LX-IIH	C525	0391
(LX-IMN)	F900	54
LX-IMS	LJ45	070
"LX-IMS"	LJ45	266
LX-IMZ	LJ45	266
LX-INS	C56X	5727
LX-IRE	FA50	324
LX-ISR	**FA7X**	**229**
(LX-ITS)	C750	0313
LX-JAG	**LJ45**	**398**
LX-JCD	C56X	5104
LX-JCG	FA10	160
LX-JCL	**C52A**	**0082**
LX-JET	**C52B**	**0281**
LX-JET	C550	033
LX-KAT	HS25	HA-0140
LX-KRC	CL64	5577
"LX-KSD"	HS25	HA-0096
LX-LAA	**LJ45**	**308**
LX-LAI	GALX	199
LX-LAR	**LJ35**	**653**
LX-LCG	PRM1	RB-51
LX-LFA	F900	154
LX-LFB	F900	62
LX-LMF	**FA7X**	**242**
LX-LOE	**HA4T**	**RC-46**
LX-LOU	LJ60	277
LX-LOV	C525	0102
LX-LXL	**FA50**	**315**
(LX-MAM)	F900	197
LX-MAR	E55P	50500216
LX-MBE	**F2TH**	**208**
LX-MDA	CL64	5616
LX-MEL	F900	115
LX-MES	FA7X	97
LX-MJM	HS25	257010
LX-MMB	**C56X**	**6108**
LX-MMB	CL61	5146
LX-MRC	C525	0473
LX-MSP	C525	0458
LX-NAD	**GLEX**	**9601**
LX-NAN	F900	159
LX-NAT	**C56X**	**5564**
LX-NLK	F2EX	61
LX-NUR	FA50	159
LX-NYO	**GLEX**	**9084**
LX-OKR	HS25	258855
LX-OMC	LJ31	167
LX-ONE	LJ35	417
LX-ONE	**LJ45**	**342**
LX-PAK	GLEX	9115
LX-PAK	**GLEX**	**9197**
LX-PAT	LJ31	233
LX-PCT	LJ31	112
LX-PMA	**CL30**	**20097**
LX-PMR	PRM1	RB-64
LX-POO	PRM1	RB-18
LX-PRA	LJ60	145
LX-PRE	PRM1	RB-60
LX-PRS	C550	496
LX-RAK	GLEX	9586
"LX-RFBY"	CL64	5485
LX-RPL	LJ60	212
LX-RSQ	C510	0194
LX-RVR	FA50	107
LX-SAB	**F9DX**	**619**
LX-SAM	F2TH	26
LX-SEH	**C56X**	**5755**
LX-SIK	F2TH	27
LX-SPK	CL64	5449
LX-SUP	C525	0351
LX-SVW	F2TH	133
LX-SVW	F9DX	619
LX-TAC	**E55P**	**50500286**
LX-TAG	F900	115
LX-THS	C550	069
LX-THS	FA50	185
LX-TNF	**GLEX**	**9332**
LX-TQJ	CL30	20159
LX-TQJ	**FA7X**	**197**
LX-TQJ	FA7X	88
LX-TRA	C525	0229
LX-TRG	FA10	19
LX-TWO	**LJ35**	**628**
LX-UAE	FA50	104
LX-USM	**FA7X**	**167**
LX-VAZ	C550	622
(LX-VAZ)	PRM1	RB-197
LX-VIP	GLEX	9076
LX-VMF	**C56X**	**5258**
LX-VOE	C52A	0017
LX-VOL	C52A	0341
LX-VPG	CL30	20218
LX-VVR	C550	550-0938
(LX-WGR)	C52A	0322
LX-YKH	C500	086
LX-YSL	C525	0322
LX-ZAK	F2TH	187
LX-ZAK	F9EX	106
LX-ZAK	GLEX	9204
LX-ZAK	**GLEX**	**9692**
LX-ZAV	CL64	5523
LX-ZED	**CL65**	**5704**
LX-ZXP	**FA7X**	**56**

Lithuania

LY-...	**HS25**	**258498**
LY-AJB	LJ25	105
LY-AMB	JSTR	5161/43
LY-ASL	HS25	257212
LY-BSK	HS25	257212
LY-DSK	**HS25**	**258811**
LY-EWC	JSTR	5219
LY-FSK	**HS25**	**HA-0060**
LY-GVS	**F2TS**	**706**
LY-HCW	**HS25**	**258398**
LY-HER	PRM1	RB-83
LY-LRJ	LJ55	011
LY-LTA	**HS25**	**258760**
LY-LTC	**HS25**	**258399**
LY-LTD	**HS25**	**258450**
LY-OJB	PRM1	RB-196
LY-VJB	C510	0010

Bulgaria

LZ-ABV	C550	550-1103
LZ-AMA	C510	0141
LZ-AXA	LJ60	167
LZ-BVD	**CL65**	**5768**
LZ-BVE	**LJ60**	**329**
(LZ-BVF)	CL65	5774
LZ-BVV	**LJ60**	**203**
LZ-DIN	**C525**	**0090**
LZ-EVB	**PRM1**	**RB-215**
LZ-EVL	GALX	180
LZ-FIA	**GLF5**	**5198**
LZ-FIB	**GALX**	**011**
LZ-FNA	**C525**	**0659**
LZ-FNB	**C52A**	**0398**
LZ-GEN	C550	550-1122
LZ-GMV	**C550**	**550-1136**
LZ-OII	FA50	97
LZ-OIO	FA50	88
LZ-OOI	**F2TH**	**123**
LZ-TBP	**C500**	**654**
LZ-TRH	**LJ60**	**399**
LZ-VTS	LJ24	156
LZ-YUM	CL60	1085
LZ-YUN	CL64	5508
LZ-YUP	CL64	5602
LZ-YUR	CL64	5625

Isle of Man

M-....	**F2TH**	**6**
M-AAAA	**CL65**	**5827**
M-AAAD	**CL64**	**5481**
M-AAAL	**GLEX**	**9443**
M-AABG	**GLEX**	**9690**
M-AAEL	**CL64**	**5604**
M-AAES	CL65	5810
M-AAMM	**GLF4**	**4104**
M-ABAK	F2EX	200
(M-ABAK)	GLEX	9010
M-ABCC	**GLEX**	**9562**
M-ABCD	**F2TH**	**98**
M-ABCD	FA20	357
(M-ABCE)	HS25	HA-0071
M-ABCM	**CL30**	**20277**
M-ABCT	GLF4	1402
M-ABCU	CL65	5813
M-ABDL	HA4T	RC-51
M-ABDN	C52B	0160
M-ABDP	**HS25**	**258609**
M-ABEB	F9EX	128
M-ABEH	CL64	5477
M-ABEI	CL64	5485
M-ABEU	**LJ45**	**374**
M-ABFF	F2EX	52
M-ABFM	FA7X	108
M-ABFO	BE40	RK-417
M-ABFQ	**GLEX**	**9494**
M-ABFR	**GLEX**	**9517**
M-ABFX	FA7X	200
M-ABGG	**CL64**	**5450**
M-ABGI	LJ60	289
M-ABGL	HS25	258816
M-ABGM	**BE40**	**RK-480**
M-ABGO	FA7X	106
M-ABGP	F2TS	711
M-ABGR	C750	0251
M-ABGS	**CL65**	**5932**
M-ABGU	CL65	5936
M-ABGV	**LJ45**	**421**
M-ABGZ	F9EX	271
M-ABIU	GLF6	6150
(M-ABIU)	GLF6	6147
M-ABJA	**LJ45**	**454**
M-ABRJ	**GLF4**	**4094**
M-ACHO	**CL65**	**5840**
M-ACPT	**HS25**	**259004**
M-ADEL	CL64	5404
M-AERO	**F2EX**	**297**
M-AFAJ	**F9EX**	**200**
M-AFMA	**GLEX**	**9050**
M-AGER	FA50	175
M-AGGY	**C550**	**690**
M-AGIC	C680	0138
M-AGIK	**F9EX**	**274**
M-AGRI	GLEX	9597
M-AHAA	**GLEX**	**9525**
M-AHAH	GLEX	9525
M-AHAR	GLEX	9525
M-AIRS	LJ60	276
M-AIRU	CL65	5824
M-AIZB	CL65	5813
M-AJDM	C52A	0009
M-AJOR	**HS25**	**HA-0058**
M-AJWA	**GLEX**	**9182**
M-AKAL	**C56X**	**6024**
M-AKAS	CL65	5056
M-AKOL	**FA7X**	**140**
M-AKVI	CL30	20050
(M-ALAA)	FA7X	175
M-ALAY	**GLF5**	**5391**
M-ALBA	HS25	HA-0210
M-ALEX	LJ60	287
M-ALII	CL64	5494
M-ALIK	**GALX**	**223**
M-ALMA	**FA7X**	**11**
M-ALRV	**F2EX**	**173**
M-ALSH	**GLEX**	**9097**
M-ALTI	**CL65**	**5733**
M-ALUN	**HS25**	**257075**
M-AMND	F2EX	114
M-AMRT	**CL65**	**5705**
M-ANAP	E55P	50500261
M-ANGO	CL64	5610
M-ANGO	**GLEX**	**9172**
M-ANIE	GLF5	5167
M-ANNA	**CL64**	**5375**
M-ANSL	C560	0773
M-APLE	**E55P**	**50500087**
M-APWC	LJ60	326
M-AQUA	**GLEX**	**9157**
M-ARAE	GLF4	4119
M-ARCH	C750	0254
M-ARDI	**GLF5**	**5153**
M-ARGO	**GLEX**	**9554**
M-ARIA	**C680**	**0179**
M-ARIA	HS25	258876
M-ARIE	CL65	5794
M-ARIE	**PRM1**	**RB-201**
M-ARKZ	**CL65**	**5879**
M-ARRH	**CL30**	**20400**
M-ARRJ	**GLEX**	**9399**
M-ARVY	**FA7X**	**216**
M-ASHI	**CL65**	**5765**
M-ASIK	**G280**	**2013**
M-ASRI	**GLEX**	**9165**
M-ASRY	C52B	0160
M-ASRY	CL30	20137
M-ATAK	GLEX	9337
M-ATAR	**GLEX**	**9060**
M-ATEX	**F9EX**	**250**
M-ATOS	F9EX	244
M-ATPS	**GLF5**	**5340**
M-AUTO	LJ60	027
M-AVOS	**GLF4**	**4273**
M-AWAY	CL64	5401
M-AYBE	**G280**	**2010**
M-AYRU	**CL65**	**5892**
M-AZAG	**HS25**	**258233**
M-AZIA	**C52C**	**0009**
M-BADU	**GLF6**	**6083**
M-BAEP	**CL65**	**5929**
M-BASH	**CL65**	**5745**
M-BEAR	E55P	50500187
M-BEST	**C750**	**0277**
M-BFLY	CL30	20123
M-BHBH	**GLF6**	**6132**
M-BIGG	CL65	5722
M-BIGG	**GLEX**	**9597**
"M-BIJJ"	GLEX	9209
M-BIRD	C52B	0255
M-BJEP	**GLF5**	**5070**
M-BLUE	**GLEX**	**9453**
M-BMAL	GLEX	9549
M-BRRB	GLEX	9325
M-BRVO	**C550**	**550-1129**
M-BSKY	CL30	20179
M-BTAR	**GLEX**	**9250**
M-BTLT	CL30	20042
M-BULL	**CS55**	**0148**
M-BWFC	C56X	5690
M-CARA	**C525**	**0859**
M-CCCP	**GLEX**	**9418**
M-CELT	**FA7X**	**110**
M-CESA	C56X	5555
M-CESB	C56X	5567
M-CESC	C56X	5786
M-CESD	C56X	5790
M-CEXL	C56X	5215
M-CFLY	**FA50**	**320**
(M-CHAT)	CL65	5886
(M-CHEF)	HS25	258514
M-CHEM	**F2EX**	**128**
M-CHLG	CL60	1017
M-CICO	**FA50**	**345**
M-CIMO	**F2EX**	**113**
M-CKAY	**HS25**	**HA-0140**
M-CKDM	G150	235
M-CLAA	HS25	258405
M-CLAB	**CL30**	**20271**
M-COOL	**C510**	**0285**
M-CRCR	CL64	5443
M-CRVS	GLEX	9294
M-CSMS	**LJ45**	**017**
M-CSTB	HS25	258793
M-CSTD	HS25	258845
M-CTEM	HS25	258677
M-CTLX	C52A	0049
M-CVGL	**GLEX**	**9687**
M-DADA	**GLEX**	**9482**
M-DADI	**F9DX**	**622**
M-DANK	**GLEX**	**9633**
M-DARA	F2EX	177
M-DASO	FA50	268
M-DEJB	**FA20**	**505**
M-DINO	C525	0528
M-DKDI	C750	0227
M-DKVL	**GLF4**	**4220**
M-DMBP	**LJ40**	**2133**
(M-DMCD)	CL30	20014
M-DMMH	C680	0322
M-DSML	**HS25**	**258037**
M-DSUN	**GLEX**	**9409**
M-DTBP	**FA7X**	**168**
M-EAGL	**F9EX**	**237**
M-EANS	**CL30**	**20017**
M-EANS	LJ45	336
M-EASY	**LJ35**	**341**
M-EBRB	**F900**	**30**
M-ECJI	**FA10**	**161**
M-EDIA	FA7X	186
M-EDOK	CL30	20284
M-EIRE	CL64	5562
M-ELAS	**G280**	**2049**
M-ELHI	**LJ60**	**373**
M-ELON	C52B	0148

M-ELON	**E55P**	**50500197**
M-ELOW	C52B	0148
M-EMCT	C560	0236
M-EMLI	CL64	5383
M-ENTA	**FA20**	**511**
M-EOCV	LJ45	306
M-ERCI	CL65	5841
M-EVAN	**CL30**	**20096**
M-FALC	F9EX	31
M-FALZ	**FA7X**	**224**
M-FASH	**F900**	**173**
M-FBVZ	CL65	5704
M-FINE	**GLEX**	**9594**
M-FINK	**HS25**	**259037**
M-FISH	**GLF5**	**506**
M-FIVE	F2EX	253
M-FLYI	**C52C**	**0106**
M-FMHG	GLF4	1305
M-FPIA	GLF5	5227
M-FRED	C560	0665
M-FROG	**PRM1**	**RB-165**
M-FRZN	**CL65**	**5920**
M-FRZN	HS25	258816
M-FTHD	**F2EX**	**199**
M-FUAD	**GLF5**	**5227**
(M-GABY)	GLEX	9637
M-GACB	**FA10**	**22**
M-GASG	**G150**	**299**
M-GBAL	GLEX	9210
M-GDRS	**PRM1**	**RB-35**
M-GENT	CL65	5716
M-GFOR	GLF4	1487
M-GINI	CL65	5887
M-GLEX	**GLEX**	**9139**
M-GLFV	GLF5	5022
M-GLFZ	LJ60	421
M-GLOB	**GLEX**	**9413**
M-GLRS	LJ45	249
M-GMKM	**FA7X**	**183**
M-GOLX	F2EX	151
M-GPIK	FA50	289
M-GRAN	**GLEX**	**9324**
M-GSIR	**F9DX**	**614**
M-GSIX	GLF6	6032
M-GSKY	**GLEX**	**9420**
M-GULF	GALX	167
M-GULF	GLF4	1082
M-GVSP	**GLF5**	**5131**
M-GYQM	**GLEX**	**9189**
M-GZOO	GALX	224
"M-HARP"	HS25	HA-0083
M-HASL	HS25	258385
M-HAWK	**GLEX**	**9518**
M-HAWK	HS25	258494
M-HDAM	HS25	258037
M-HKND	**FA7X**	**72**
M-HNDA	**HDJT**	**42000018**
M-HNOY	CL65	5840
M-HOIL	LJ60	313
M-HOME	**GLEX**	**9577**
M-HOTB	**GLF5**	**5151**
M-HPIN	**E55P**	**50500276**
M-HSNT	**CL30**	**20233**
M-HSXP	**HS25**	**258645**
M-IAMI	**FA7X**	**230**
M-IBID	**GLEX**	**9401**
M-ICRO	C52A	0347
M-ICRO	**C52A**	**0479**
M-IFES	CL60	1067
M-IFFY	**C510**	**0192**
M-IGHT	**LJ60**	**382**
M-IGOR	LJ60	305
M-IGWT	GLEX	9457
M-IGWT	**GLEX**	**9595**
M-IIII	F2TH	94
M-IIII	GLEX	9036
M-IKAT	**F2EX**	**220**
M-IKEL	F2EX	216
M-ILES	F2EX	88
M-ILTD	**GALX**	**207**
M-IMOR	C680	0346
M-INER	**FA7X**	**128**
M-INOR	**HS25**	**HA-0059**
M-INSK	**GLF6**	**6096**
M-INTY	**G280**	**2086**
M-INXS	HS25	HB-27
M-INXY	E50P	50000024
M-IPHS	**GLF5**	**5246**
M-IRNE	**HS25**	**258778**
M-ISKY	**C550**	**550-0870**
M-ISLE	C680	0265
M-ISRK	F9EX	271
M-ISRK	FA7X	229
M-ISSY	HS25	258043
M-ISTY	**G280**	**2085**
M-IUNI	**GLEX**	**9516**
M-IVSP	GLF4	1224
M-IWPS	**C52A**	**0496**
M-JANP	**GLEX**	**9293**
M-JCBB	**GLF6**	**6049**
M-JCPO	HS25	257004
M-JETI	**HS25**	**258056**
M-JETT	**FA20**	**490**
M-JETZ	**F2EX**	**105**
M-JGVJ	**GLEX**	**9623**
M-JIGG	GLF5	5346
"M-JMF"	C550	610

M-JMIA	**CL65**	**5941**
M-JMMM	F900	159
M-JNJL	**GLEX**	**9046**
M-JOLY	**HS25**	**HA-0121**
M-JPLC	F9EX	269
M-JSMN	**GLEX**	**9216**
M-JSTA	**CL64**	**5639**
M-KARI	CL65	5838
M-KARN	CL64	5346
(M-KAZZ)	C750	0271
M-KBBG	**GLF4**	**4262**
M-KBSD	**GLEX**	**9639**
M-KELY	**E50P**	**50000040**
M-KENF	**HA4T**	**RC-27**
M-KGTS	**E55P**	**50500206**
M-KICK	E50P	50000145
M-KKCO	**GLF4**	**4306**
M-KRRR	LJ55	059
M-KSOI	**GLF6**	**6047**
M-KSSN	GLF6	6047
M-LANG	**F9EX**	**245**
M-LAOR	HS25	258384
M-LCFC	F2TS	707
M-LCJP	HS25	HA-0072
M-LEAR	LJ31	011
M-LEFB	**C550**	**187**
M-LIFE	CL30	20314
M-LION	**HS25**	**HA-0099**
M-LJGI	F2EX	143
M-LJGI	**FA7X**	**178**
M-LLGC	GLEX	9227
(M-LMAA)	FA7X	175
M-LOOK	**CL64**	**5319**
M-LRJT	LJ40	2005
M-LRLR	**CL64**	**5522**
M-LWSA	**GLEX**	**9092**
M-MACH	E50P	50000162
M-MAEE	**GLF4**	**4322**
M-MARI	**CL65**	**5826**
M-MARI	LJ60	369
M-MAXX	**GLEX**	**9678**
M-MDBD	**GLEX**	**9049**
M-MDDE	**CL64**	**5598**
M-MDMH	**E55P**	**50500116**
M-MHAC	**LJ60**	**326**
M-MHBW	C510	0262
M-MHDH	**C510**	**0259**
M-MHMH	C52B	0311
M-MICS	**GLEX**	**9586**
M-MIDO	**HS25**	**258456**
M-MIDY	**F9EX**	**230**
M-MIKE	**C52B**	**0280**
M-MJLD	**C680**	**680A0017**
M-MMAA	GLEX	9086
M-MMAS	GLEX	9267
M-MNAA	**FA7X**	**213**
M-MNAA	GLEX	9086
M-MNAA	GLEX	9434
M-MNBB	**FA7X**	**91**
M-MNCC	**FA7X**	**156**
M-MNDD	**F9DX**	**612**
M-MNDG	GLF4	4266
M-MNDG	**GLF5**	**5519**
M-MNVN	**GLF4**	**4283**
M-MOMO	**GLF5**	**5292**
M-MOON	**C750**	**0242**
M-MRBB	**LJ45**	**211**
M-MSGG	**CL65**	**5936**
M-MSGG	GALX	159
M-MSVI	**C52B**	**0361**
M-MTOO	**CL30**	**20050**
M-MTPO	CL61	3033
M-MTRM	PRM1	RB-284
M-MYNA	**GLEX**	**9471**
M-NALE	**GLEX**	**9450**
M-NAME	**GLEX**	**9706**
M-NELS	GLF4	4284
M-NEWT	CL30	20151
M-NGNG	**GLF6**	**6077**
M-NHOI	**CL65**	**5744**
M-NICE	**GALX**	**246**
M-NICK	FA50	345
M-NICO	HS25	HA-0083
M-NIKO	F2TH	25
M-NNNN	GLF6	6077
M-NOEL	CL30	20206
M-NOLA	CL65	5814
M-NSJS	C52C	0073
M-NTOS	**C52C**	**0197**
M-NYJT	CL30	20078
(M-OANH)	HS25	HB-14
M-OBIL	**C52C**	**0132**
M-OBLA	**HS25**	**258495**
M-OCNY	**CL30**	**20581**
M-OCOM	**CL64**	**5617**
M-ODKZ	**F9EX**	**86**
M-OEPL	**F9DX**	**605**
M-OGMC	**GLEX**	**9268**
M-OIWA	CL30	20133
M-OLLE	**HS25**	**HB-65**
M-OLLY	**C525**	**0544**
M-OLOT	**CL64**	**5382**
M-OMAN	**FA7X**	**138**
M-ONAV	**HS25**	**HA-0073**
M-ONEM	**GLF5**	**5210**
M-OODY	C52B	0238
M-OOUN	HS25	258514

M-OPDE	**FA7X**	**30**
M-ORAD	**F2EX**	**101**
M-OSPB	GALX	205
M-OUSE	**C510**	**0340**
M-OZZA	**CL30**	**20014**
M-PARK	C525	0358
M-PATH	F9EX	283
M-PAUL	HA4T	RC-34
M-PBKI	GLF4	1255
M-PDCS	**F2EX**	**30**
M-PHNM	E50P	50000092
M-PING	**GLF4**	**4284**
M-PLUS	**GLF6**	**6113**
(M-PNRE)	F2EX	166
M-PREI	**PRM1**	**RB-60**
M-PRVT	**C750**	**0291**
M-PSAC	C52A	0389
M-PZPZ	GLF4	1202
M-RACE	HS25	258895
M-RBIG	**LJ45**	**280**
M-RIDE	**GLEX**	**9190**
M-RIZA	**GLEX**	**9545**
M-RKAY	**PRM1**	**RB-88**
M-RLIV	**CL65**	**5731**
M-ROIL	**GALX**	**237**
M-ROLL	FA7X	40
M-ROMA	LJ45	148
M-RONE	**F2EX**	**28**
M-ROWL	F2EX	95
M-ROWL	F9EX	180
M-ROWL	**F9EX**	**217**
M-RSKL	**GLEX**	**9380**
M-RTFS	**FA7X**	**207**
M-RUAT	GLEX	9054
M-RURU	F900	140
M-RWGW	LJ45	213
M-SAAJ	**GLF5**	**5301**
M-SAID	**GLEX**	**9486**
M-SAIR	**F900**	**141**
M-SAJJ	GLF5	5301
M-SALE	GLEX	9311
M-SAMA	**GLEX**	**9579**
M-SAPL	CL65	5883
M-SAPT	**GLEX**	**9668**
M-SAPT	HS25	HA-0026
M-SASS	**GALX**	**233**
M-SAWO	**GLF5**	**5050**
M-SBUR	**GALX**	**174**
M-SCMG	**FA7X**	**96**
M-SCOT	**FA7X**	**54**
M-SEAS	**GLEX**	**9461**
M-SEVN	**CL65**	**5962**
M-SFOZ	**F2TH**	**121**
M-SFOZ	PRM1	RB-286
M-SFRI	CL65	5843
M-SGCR	**C550**	**550-0808**
M-SGJS	**CL30**	**20588**
M-SHLA	CL64	5476
M-SIMI	**CL64**	**5608**
M-SIRI	**GLEX**	**9329**
M-SITM	HS25	258050
M-SIXT	**C52C**	**0188**
M-SKSM	**GLEX**	**9227**
M-SKZL	CL64	5404
M-SNAP	C56X	5770
M-SNAP	F2EX	89
M-SNER	**F2EX**	**95**
M-SNSS	FA50	278
M-SOBR	**GLF4**	**4303**
M-SPBM	**CL65**	**5953**
M-SQAR	**GLF5**	**5179**
M-SSSR	**GLEX**	**9406**
M-SSSV	LJ60	325
M-SSYS	**C52C**	**0143**
M-STCO	F2EX	110
M-STCO	**F2EX**	**240**
M-STEP	G150	245
M-SVGN	**C680**	**0198**
M-SVNX	FA7X	20
M-SWAN	GALX	233
M-SWAN	**GLF4**	**4181**
M-TAGB	CL30	20172
M-TANA	F2TH	121
(M-TANG)	F2EX	207
M-TEAM	**C525**	**0609**
M-TECH	**CL30**	**20621**
(M-TECH)	F9EX	205
M-TFKR	GLF5	5220
M-TIME	C56X	5168
M-TINK	F2EX	253
M-TINK	F9EX	277
M-TINK	**FA7X**	**266**
M-TNTJ	LJ55	087
M-TOPI	**CL65**	**5780**
M-TRAV	**GLF5**	**5452**
M-TRBS	**CL65**	**5836**
M-TRIX	CL64	5608
M-TSGP	C52A	0309
M-TSKW	**F900**	**202**
M-TYRA	**GLEX**	**9560**
M-UGIC	**GLF5**	**5406**
M-UKHA	**HS25**	**258625**
M-UNIS	**GLEX**	**9371**
M-UPCO	C52B	0012
M-URAL	**LJ60**	**328**
M-USBA	**GLF5**	**680**
M-USIC	**GLF5**	**5394**

M-USIK	**GLF6**	**6037**
M-USTG	**C510**	**0089**
M-USTG	C510	0182
M-VAKE	E55P	50500082
M-VANG	**GLEX**	**9349**
M-VBBQ	PRM1	RB-181
M-VBPO	PRM1	RB-138
M-VGAL	**F9EX**	**205**
M-VGIN	FA50	320
M-VICA	CL64	5360
M-VICI	GLF4	4241
M-VITA	**GLF6**	**6099**
M-VITO	**HS25**	**258512**
M-VQBI	**GLEX**	**9213**
M-VRNY	**GLF5**	**5225**
M-VSSK	CL65	5781
"M-VUEZ"	C550	008
M-WFAM	**CL65**	**5914**
M-WIND	F2TH	223
M-WIND	**GLF6**	**6080**
M-WING	F2TH	223
M-WING	F9DX	609
M-WING	**F9EX**	**270**
M-WISO	LJ60	167
M-WMWM	**C52A**	**0113**
M-WONE	**GLF4**	**4319**
M-WOOD	**C550**	**550-1042**
M-XJOB	C56X	5770
M-XJOB	F2EX	89
M-XONE	C52A	0031
M-YAAA	GLEX	9136
M-YAIR	PRM1	RB-146
M-YANG	**GLF4**	**4260**
M-YBJK	GLF5	5316
M-YBST	**CL64**	**5620**
M-YBZI	**CL61**	**5149**
M-YCEF	HS25	258723
M-YCYS	**LJ60**	**341**
M-YEDC	C52B	0162
M-YEDT	ASTR	141
M-YETD	LJ60	421
M-YFLY	CL30	20023
M-YFLY	**GLEX**	**9136**
M-YFTA	**GLEX**	**9537**
M-YGIV	GLF4	1080
M-YGLK	**GLF4**	**4137**
M-YGVI	GLF6	6006
M-YJET	F2EX	148
M-YJET	**FA7X**	**186**
M-YNNG	FA7X	82
M-YNNS	FA7X	82
M-YNNS	**GLF6**	**6120**
M-YOIL	**GLEX**	**9637**
M-YONE	CL61	5085
M-YORK	**FA7X**	**42**
M-YSAI	**GLEX**	**9166**
M-YSIX	**GLF6**	**6156**
M-YSKY	**GLEX**	**9576**
M-YSKY	PRM1	RB-209
M-YSSF	**GLEX**	**9521**
M-YTOY	**E50P**	**50000112**
M-YULI	GLEX	9283
M-YULI	**GLEX**	**9596**
M-YUMN	**F2TH**	**1**
M-YUNI	**CL65**	**5751**
M-YVVF	**GLEX**	**9590**
M-YWAY	**GLF4**	**1486**
M-YXLS	**C56X**	**6193**
(M-YXRS)	GLEX	9352
M-ZJBT	**FA7X**	**97**
M-ZZOO	GALX	163

United States of America

N.....	C500	042
N.....	**FA20**	**311/515**
(N.....)	CL64	5522
(N.....)	FA20	262
(N.....)	HS25	258035
(N.....)	LJ25	341
(N.....)	LJ45	019
N1	GLF3	413
N1	**GLF4**	**1071**
N1	JSTR	5001/53
N1AB	HS25	259005
N1AB	HS25	259036
N1AF	C550	320
N1AF	C555	0018
N1AG	C500	579
N1AG	**BE40**	**RJ-35**
N1AH	LJ25	316
N1AH	LJ35	398
N1AK	C560	0205
N1AK	LJ35	019
N1AL	GLF6	6015
N1AL	**GLF6**	**6091**
N1AM	GLF4	1050
N1AM	**GLF5**	**623**
N1AP	C500	322
N1AP	C550	051
N1AP	C650	0001
N1AP	C650	0082
N1AP	C650	7003
N1AP	C750	0003
N1AP	**C750**	**0176**
N1AP	LJ24	163
N1AQ	GLF3	342
N1AR	**GLEX**	**9061**

N1AR	GLF4	1069
N1AT	C500	537
N1AT	C550	591
N1AZ	**GLF4**	**1235**
N1B	GLF2	73/9
N1B	**JSTR**	**5156**
N1BB	**GLF4**	**1024**
N1BC	C56X	6144
N1BC	WW24	39
N1BF	FA20	142
N1BG	HS25	25281
N1BG	HS25	258011
N1BL	C52C	0085
N1BL	**C52C**	**0102**
N1BL	GLF2	113
N1BL	JSTR	5029/38
N1BL	JSTR	5097/60
N1BN	GLF4	1300
N1BN	**GLF5**	**5036**
N1BN	GLF5	667
N1BR	LJ25	105
N1BR	LJ31	086
N1BS	**C750**	**0081**
N1BU	LJ24	029
N1BX	FA20	380
N1BX	FA50	47
N1BX	GLF2	227
N1BX	**GLF4**	**4140**
N1BX	SBRL	282-101
N1C	**F2EX**	**229**
N1C	F2TH	40
N1C	GLF3	388
N1C	HS25	25200
N1C	HS25	257206
N1CA	C500	387
N1CA	**CL30**	**20360**
N1CA	CL64	5441
N1CA	HS25	258672
N1CA	LJ35	069
N1CA	LJ35	657
N1CA	LJ60	055
N1CC	GLF2	257/17
N1CC	SBRL	465-6
N1CF	C560	0473
N1CF	**CL30**	**20054**
N1CF	SBRL	465-3
N1CG	**FA50**	**147**
N1CG	LJ55	014
N1CG	BE40	RJ-17
N1CH	C52B	0064
N1CH	**C52C**	**0015**
N1CH	C560	0283
N1CH	SBRL	306-126
N1CN	FA50	55
(N1CN)	FA10	199
N1CP	CL64	5321
N1CP	**CL65**	**5885**
N1CR	C500	561
N1CR	PRM1	RB-119
N1CR	PRM1	RB-146
N1CU	**CL65**	**5890**
N1D	FA20	495
N1D	**GLF4**	**1209**
N1DA	**C500**	**288**
N1DA	LJ35	013
N1DB	JSTR	5075/19
N1DB	JSTR	5119/29
N1DB	JSTR	5155/32
N1DB	JSTR	5223
N1DC	**GLF5**	**651**
N1DC	LJ35	246
N1DC	LJ35	464
N1DC	LJ60	035
N1DC	SBRL	282-44
(N1DC)	GLF4	1054
N1DD	LJ24	227
N1DD	LJ25	171
N1DD	LJ25	191
N1DE	**LJ31**	**016**
N1DG	CL64	5386
N1DG	CL64	5516
N1DG	**GLEX**	**9156**
N1DH	C650	0090
N1DH	C650	0153
N1DH	C750	0136
N1DH	CL30	20083
N1DH	**CL61**	**5145**
N1DH	FA10	187
N1DK	C500	175
N1DK	LJ24	343
N1DM	C525	0510
N1DM	C52A	0214
N1DM	C52A	0314
N1DM	C52B	0210
N1DM	C52C	0007
N1DM	C52C	0101
N1DS	GLEX	9098
N1DS	**GLEX**	**9402**
N1DT	JSTR	5158
N1DW	CL61	5025
N1DW	**GLF4**	**4176**
N1EB	GLF4	1367
N1EB	**GLF5**	**5194**
N1EC	WW24	51
N1ED	LJ25	092
N1ED	LJ25	255
N1ED	**LJ31**	**218**

N1ED	LJ35	392
N1EF	C525	0167
N1EG	**PRM1**	**RB-43**
N1EL	**C510**	**0061**
N1EM	JSTR	5077
N1EP	MS76	002
"N1ERAU"	SBRL	265-57
N1ES	**CL61**	**3039**
N1ES	HS25	257010
N1EV	FA50	65
N1F	**GLF6**	**6076**
N1FC	G150	274
N1FC	**G280**	**2027**
N1FE	CL60	1055
N1FE	CL60	1074
N1FE	FA20	84
N1FE	**GLEX**	**9091**
N1FJ	C680	0166
N1FM	C550	178
N1FS	G150	277
N1FS	**GLF5**	**5180**
(N1GB)	C500	309
N1GC	C560	0239
N1GC	CL64	5329
N1GC	CS55	0109
N1GC	GLF4	1382
N1GC	GLF5	539
N1GG	C500	249
N1GH	**C550**	**227**
N1GM	SBRL	306-120
N1GN	GLF3	392
N1GN	GLF4	1284
N1GN	GLF5	5023
N1GN	GLF5	518
N1GN	**GLF5**	**564**
N1GN	GLF5	578
N1GT	GLF3	454
N1GT	GLF4	1292
N1GT	GLF5	531
N1GW	LJ24	048
N1GY	SBRL	282-81
N1GZ	LJ24	065A
N1H	CS55	0094
N1H	GLF2	129
N1HA	C500	447
N1HA	**C550**	**107**
N1HC	**GLF5**	**5009**
N1HC	GLF5	545
N1HC	GLF5	616
N1HE	**C550**	**471**
N1HF	FA20	289
N1HF	FA20	474
N1HM	C500	101
N1HM	FA10	41
N1HP	**CL30**	**20362**
N1HP	LJ35	039
N1HP	LJ45	082
N1HS	C56X	5351
N1HS	C56X	5596
N1HS	C750	0275
N1HS	**F2EX**	**293**
N1HS	BE40	RK-106
N1HZ	CL60	1056
N1HZ	**CL61**	**5030**
N1J	**PRM1**	**RB-183**
N1JB	C500	569
N1JB	C525	0251
N1JB	**LJ60**	**363**
N1JB	BE40	RK-424
N1JC	**MU30**	**A059SA**
N1JG	GLF2	65
N1JG	LJ55	055
N1JK	**F2EX**	**130**
N1JK	GLF3	342
N1JK	GLF4	4031
N1JM	**C750**	**0005**
N1JM	LJ31	196
N1JN	C500	309
N1JN	FA10	106
N1JN	GLF2	154/28
N1JN	GLF3	329
N1JN	GLF4	1088
N1JN	GLF4	1239
N1JN	GLF4	1257
N1JN	**GLF4**	**1292**
N1JN	GLF4	1350
N1JN	GLF5	538
N1JN	JSTR	5132/57
N1JN	SBRL	306-14
N1JN	SBRL	306-61
N1JP	**BE40**	**RK-432**
N1JR	**GLEX**	**9020**
N1JR	GLF4	1066
N1JR	LJ25	021
N1JR	LJ25	104
N1JR	LJ25	188
N1JS	WW24	249
N1JU	WW24	13
N1JW	**FA10**	**200**
N1JX	SBRL	306-61
N1KA	**C52B**	**0076**
N1KC	C500	459
N1KE	GLF3	349
N1KE	GLF4	1033
N1KE	GLF5	574
N1KE	**GLF6**	**6024**
N1KT	WW24	135

N1KT	**WW24**	**230**
N1L	**F900**	**19**
N1LA	**GLF5**	**5108**
N1LB	C500	212
N1LB	GLF4	1448
N1LB	GLF5	5195
N1LF	**C52B**	**0359**
N1LL	LJ25	021
N1LQ	C500	526
N1LT	SBRL	380-59
N1LW	GLF3	329
N1M	ASTR	043
N1M	CL61	5008
N1M	FA20	24
N1M	GLF3	390
N1M	WW24	187
(N1M)	ASTR	049
N1MB	FA20	74
N1MC	ASTR	055
N1MC	ASTR	112
N1MC	C560	0014
N1MC	**GLF4**	**4036**
N1MF	**C52B**	**0453**
N1MG	**C52B**	**0391**
N1MG	F2TH	221
N1MG	LJ45	060
N1MJ	JSTR	5217
N1MJ	JSTR	5223
N1MM	C550	302
N1MM	**C56X**	**5245**
N1MN	SBRL	282-69
N1MN	SBRL	306-58
N1MW	WW24	109
N1MX	C500	556
N1MX	LJ25	128
N1MY	HS25	25082
N1MY	LJ35	370
N1NA	**C56X**	**5344**
N1NA	CL64	5447
N1NA	GLF3	309
N1NC	**F2EX**	**48**
N1NE	**GLEX**	**9205**
N1NL	C550	303
N1NR	SBRL	380-70
N1PB	C56X	5013
N1PB	E50P	50000117
N1PB	FA10	198
N1PB	FA10	92
(N1PB)	C56X	5560
N1PG	GLF2	62
N1PG	GLF3	334
N1PG	GLF4	1259
N1PG	GLF4	1374
N1PN	SBRL	306-58
N1PR	F900	71
N1PR	FA50	40
N1PR	GLF2	17
N1PR	GLF3	341
N1PT	WW24	93
N1PU	**BE40**	**RK-234**
(N1PU)	GLF3	334
N1Q	C550	550-0871
N1QC	LJ24	181
N1QC	SBRL	282-44
N1QF	CL64	5329
N1QH	HS25	25261
N1QH	WW24	96
N1QL	C52A	0184
N1QL	WW24	96
N1RA	LJ25	105
N1RB	**CL30**	**20073**
N1RB	LJ45	119
N1RB	LJ60	202
N1RD	C510	0120
N1RD	**C525**	**0813**
N1RF	**C680**	**0163**
N1RH	**CL30**	**20376**
N1RL	LJ45	217
N1RP	**GLF5**	**5458**
N1RS	**C510**	**0105**
N1RV	C550	574
(N1RW)	LJ25	135
N1S	C650	7010
N1S	F900	28
N1S	FA50	139
N1S	GLF3	391
N1SA	**F9EX**	**128**
N1SA	GLEX	9100
N1SC	LJ35	016
N1SF	GLF3	455
N1SF	GLF4	1060
N1SF	**GLF5**	**5202**
N1SF	GLF5	598
N1SG	**GLF4**	**1462**
N1SH	**PRM1**	**RB-117**
(N1SH)	C500	670
N1SL	GLEX	9114
N1SL	GLF4	1167
N1SN	C560	0153
N1SN	C56X	5014
N1SN	**GLF4**	**1433**
N1SS	LJ24	186
N1SU	C550	550-1119
N1SU	**C56X**	**6085**
N1SV	**C550**	**165**
"N1TA"	GALX	012
N1TC	FA10	144

N1TC	FA20	83
N1TF	GLF4	1340
N1TF	GLF4	1382
N1TF	GLF5	5035
N1TF	**GLF6**	**6065**
N1TG	C525	0617
N1TG	C525	0811
N1TG	C680	0147
N1TJ	FA10	18
N1TJ	GLF2	39
N1TJ	LJ24	339
N1TK	CL61	5025
N1TK	GLEX	9004
N1TK	LJ24	153
N1TK	**LJ45**	**210**
"N1TL"	LJ24	323
N1TM	GLEX	9006
N1TM	GLF4	1087
N1TM	**GLF4**	**1490**
N1TS	C650	0006
N1TS	GLEX	9046
N1TS	JSTR	5215
N1TS	LJ35	499
(N1TS)	WW24	187
N1TT	**GLF4**	**4142**
N1TW	C500	197
N1TW	**LJ35**	**476**
N1TX	MU30	A066SA
N1TY	**C550**	**188**
N1TY	BE40	RJ-34
N1U	FA20	65
N1U	LJ24	250
N1U	LJ24	274
N1U	LJ25	371
N1U	LJ35	444
N1U	LJ36	026
N1UA	ASTR	044
N1UA	ASTR	152
N1UA	C550	130
N1UB	GLF5	669
(N1UB)	C500	364
N1UG	C500	309
N1UH	C550	062
N1UH	C650	0024
N1UH	CS55	0057
N1UL	C500	482
N1UL	CS55	0057
N1UM	C500	364
N1UM	**C560**	**0543**
N1UP	C650	0024
N1UP	**C650**	**0224**
N1UP	JSTR	5142
N1UP	SBRL	306-40
N1UT	C500	267
N1UT	MU30	A029SA
N1UT	SBRL	306-40
N1VA	CS55	0143
N1VC	C500	183
(N1VC)	SBRL	306-61
N1VG	LJ25	125
N1VG	**LJ55**	**121**
N1VQ	HS25	257113
N1VT	**WW24**	**342**
N1VU	C500	545
N1VV	**C510**	**0013**
N1WB	C550	058
N1WE	**GLF4**	**1171**
N1WP	GLF2	190
N1WP	GLF4	1030
N1WP	WW24	108
N1WS	WW24	252
N1WT	LJ25	371
N1WW	C525	0211
N1WW	**C525**	**0861**
N1WX	**C52C**	**0101**
N1WZ	SBRL	282-117
N1X	C500	236
N1X	JSTR	5215
(N1X)	BE40	RJ-34
N1XH	**PRM1**	**RB-76**
N1XL	C56X	5041
N1XL	LJ35	392
N1XT	C525	0162
N1XT	PRM1	RB-36
N1YE	HS25	25065
N1Z	GALX	084
N1Z	**GLF4**	**4290**
N1ZA	LJ24	042
N1ZC	C650	0031
N1ZC	**C680**	**0085**
N1ZC	LJ25	022
N2	C500	084
N2	C550	006
N2	C560	0109
N2	**C56X**	**5333**
N2	LJ31	063
(N2AJ)	WW24	277
N2AT	F2TH	51
N2AV	WW24	322
N2AZ	**C750**	**0147**
N2BA	**LJ35**	**051**
N2BD	F9EX	35
N2BD	**F9EX**	**72**
N2BG	**GALX**	**064**
N2BG	HS25	258207
N2BG	WW24	365
N2BT	C500	419

N2BW	FA20	471
N2CA	C550	092
N2CC	F2EX	28
N2CC	**GLF4**	**1343**
N2CC	SBRL	465-6
(N2CH)	FA10	163
N2CJ	C52A	708
N2CP	**C52B**	**0279**
N2CW	F2TH	80
N2DB	WW24	135
N2DD	LJ24	098
N2DD	LJ24	335
N2DF	GLF2	95/39
N2DF	**GLF4**	**1032**
N2DH	C650	0153
N2DH	C650	0193
(N2DP)	C500	531
N2EL	C500	038
N2EP	C650	0010
N2ES	JSTR	5023
(N2ES)	WW24	96
N2FA	C500	140
N2FD	**CL64**	**5345**
N2FE	CL60	1075
N2FE	CL61	5095
N2FE	FA20	132
N2FE	**GLEX**	**9070**
N2FQ	**FA50**	**167**
N2FU	FA20	412
N2FU	**LJ31**	**027**
N2FU	LJ35	612
N2FU	LJ36	048
N2G	**GALX**	**106**
N2G	HS25	25139
N2G	HS25	258354
(N2G)	HS25	25163
N2GG	C550	306
N2GP	GLF2	13
N2GP	LJ24	020
N2GQ	**C550**	**306**
N2GR	LJ24	262
N2GS	**C510**	**0018**
N2H	FA20	327
N2HB	C56X	5222
N2HB	C56X	5579
N2HD	C500	078
(N2HE)	LJ25	138
N2HF	GLF2	221
N2HJ	C560	0278
N2HL	GALX	025
N2HL	GALX	091
N2HP	HS25	257180
N2HP	LJ45	330
N2HP	**LJ45**	**472**
N2HW	FA20	488
N2HW	SBRL	282-105
N2HW	SBRL	306-68
N2HX	SBRL	306-68
N2HZ	**ASTR**	**122**
N2HZ	CL60	1056
N2HZ	PRM1	RB-186
N2HZ	WW24	314
N2JR	**GLF2**	**131/23**
N2JR	JSTR	5236
N2JW	C550	183
N2JW	C560	0191
N2JW	C56X	5064
N2JW	CL64	5549
N2JW	**CL65**	**5792**
N2JW	WW24	86
N2JZ	C550	055
N2KH	C550	570
N2KL	**HA4T**	**RC-43**
N2KN	HS25	25020
N2KW	HS25	25020
N2KW	HS25	257201
N2KZ	HS25	257177
N2KZ	LJ35	652
N2LA	**GLF4**	**4057**
N2LN	C500	483
N2LY	GLF3	340
N2MG	CL65	5701
N2MG	**GLEX**	**9113**
N2MG	HS25	258092
N2MK	HFB3	1036
N2MK	JSTR	5226
N2MP	FA10	31
N2N	GLF5	586
N2N	**GLF6**	**6053**
N2N	SBRL	465-63
N2NA	GLF3	309
N2NC	MS76	005
N2NL	**SBRL**	**465-63**
N2NR	C650	0083
N2NT	C550	730
N2NT	C650	7013
N2PG	GLF2	20
N2PG	GLF4	1378
N2PK	GLF2	206
N2PW	LJ25	363
N2Q	C510	0391
N2Q	**C56X**	**5530**
N2QE	**GLEX**	**9629**
(N2QE)	C560	0639
N2QG	**HS25**	**258207**
(N2QL)	HS25	257197
N2QW	SBRL	282-105

N2RC	C550	337
N2RC	**C560**	**0319**
N2RF	C650	7082
N2RM	**C500**	**153**
N2RW	LJ31	038
N2S	C550	110
N2S	GLF2	113
N2S	GLF2	158
N2SA	CL64	5319
N2SA	GLF4	1104
N2SG	HS25	258090
N2SG	HS25	259019
N2SM	**LJ31**	**040**
N2SN	LJ24	072
(N2SN)	SBRL	282-59
N2SP	GLF3	366
N2T	FA50	167
N2T	GLEX	9084
N2T	**GLEX**	**9162**
(N2T)	GLEX	9032
N2TE	MS76	005
N2TE	SBRL	370-6
N2TF	C650	0176
N2TF	FA20	490
N2TF	GLF3	460
N2TN	C500	231
N2TQ	GLF3	460
N2U	C500	285
N2U	**C560**	**0624**
N2U	LJ24	250
N2U	LJ25	325
N2U	LJ35	268
N2UJ	C680	0179
N2UJ	GLF2	139/11
(N2UJ)	C680	0118
N2UP	C650	0010
N2UP	**C650**	**0227**
N2UP	SBRL	306-17
N2UR	SBRL	306-17
(N2UX)	C650	0227
N2WC	**MU30**	**A047SA**
N2WG	**C510**	**0459**
N2WL	GLF4	1118
N2WL	LJ24	265
N2WL	LJ35	245
N2WQ	LJ35	277
N2WR	SBRL	282-102
N2WU	WW24	72
N2XT	**CL30**	**20589**
N2YG	HS25	258090
N2YU	**EA50**	**000160**
N2YY	LJ24	143
N2ZA	LJ24	067
N2ZC	C500	420
N2ZC	**C56X**	**5156**
N3	**C56X**	**5341**
N3AH	LJ35	421
N3AL	HS25	25169
N3AS	LJ28	28-001
N3AS	LJ45	247
N3AS	**LJ45**	**427**
N3AV	**WW24**	**361**
N3B	C750	0177
N3B	**C750**	**0521**
N3BL	**LJ24**	**003**
N3BM	F2EX	38
N3BM	F2TH	38
N3BM	**FA50**	**280**
N3BM	SBRL	282-131
N3BM	SBRL	465-51
N3BY	FA10	193
N3CJ	**C52B**	**711**
N3CP	**GLF6**	**6106**
N3CT	**C52B**	**0041**
N3D	CS55	0038
N3DL	WW24	42
N3DP	**GLF3**	**334**
N3DU	LJ24	279
N3DZ	LJ24	279
N3E	GLF2	185
N3E	JSTR	5029/38
N3E	JSTR	5076/17
N3EK	JSTR	5029/38
N3EK	JSTR	5076/17
N3EU	GLF2	185
N3FA	C550	124
N3FA	**C560**	**0023**
N3FB	**G280**	**2079**
N3FC	SBRL	306-33
N3FD	ASTR	145
N3FE	C500	678
N3FE	CL61	5054
N3FE	**CL65**	**5742**
N3FE	FA20	151
N3FS	**G150**	**274**
N3FW	C550	368
N3GL	HS25	257197
N3GL	LJ24	173
N3GL	LJ35	070
N3GN	**C500**	**466**
N3GR	JSTR	5127
N3GT	C550	376
N3GT	C560	0091
N3GU	HS25	258075
N3GW	LJ24	203
N3H	FA20	327
N3H	GLF4	1092

N3H	**GLF4**	**1134**
N3HA	LJ35	182
N3HB	CL60	1059
N3HB	CL64	5313
N3HB	**F900**	**126**
N3HB	JSTR	5116
N3HB	LJ35	182
N3HB	LJ55	046
N3HX	GLF4	1092
N3JJ	C500	016
N3JJ	C500	299
N3JJ	FA20	57
N3JL	CL60	1080
N3JL	LJ24	025
N3JL	LJ25	073
N3JL	LJ35	289
N3JM	C52B	0102
N3JX	LJ25	073
N3K	**PRM1**	**RB-218**
N3KN	GLF4	1103
N3LG	C500	112
N3LH	GLF2	5
N3M	GLF4	1021
N3M	**GLF5**	**5290**
N3MB	C550	343
N3MB	C550	405
N3MB	LJ35	335
N3MF	HS25	25093
N3MJ	LJ35	188
N3MT	**EA50**	**000135**
N3NP	LJ36	048
N3NU	GLF4	1021
N3PC	ASTR	037
N3PC	C500	067
N3PC	C550	247
N3PC	CL61	5066
N3PC	CL64	5411
N3PC	**GLEX**	**9059**
N3PC	LJ36	013
N3PG	GLF2	21
N3PG	GLF3	336
N3PG	GLF4	1260
N3PG	**GLF5**	**5091**
N3PW	FA10	179
N3PW	HS25	256009
N3PW	LJ24	341
N3PW	LJ35	207
N3PY	GLF3	336
(N3PY)	GLF3	440
N3Q	C500	238
(N3Q)	C650	0007
N3QE	C500	121
N3QE	**C510**	**0183**
N3QG	**HS25**	**258127**
N3QL	JSTR	5064/51
N3QM	SBRL	282-131
N3QM	SBRL	465-51
N3QS	JSTR	5064/51
N3QS	JSTR	5224
N3QZ	C500	238
N3R	C550	123
N3RA	LJ35	138
N3RC	**C52C**	**0039**
N3RC	FA10	69
N3RC	FA20	256
N3RC	HS25	257087
N3RC	HS25	258253
N3RC	JSTR	5214
N3RC	WW24	222
N3RC	WW24	340
N3RL	WW24	390
N3RN	SBRL	380-38
N3RP	CL60	1011
N3RP	SBRL	380-42
N3SA	GLF4	1171
N3ST	C52A	0045
N3TE	SBRL	370-8
N3TJ	LJ24	236
N3UC	LJ25	034
N3UD	C52B	0069
(N3UG)	C500	526
N3UJ	LJ35	473
N3UW	LJ25	214
N3VF	FA20	363/544
N3VF	**FA50**	**253**
N3VF	WW24	137
N3VF	WW24	191
N3VF	WW24	324
N3VG	LJ35	305
N3VJ	**LJ31**	**035**
N3VL	WW24	180
N3W	C500	143
N3WB	C525	0053
N3WB	C525	0524
N3WN	FA20	185/467
N3WP	LJ35	606
N3WQ	SBRL	306-97
N3WS	**C52B**	**0133**
N3WT	**C500**	**473**
N3WZ	FA10	30
N3ZA	LJ24	024
N3ZC	**C680**	**0346**
N3ZD	C500	224
N3ZQ	GLF2	62
N4	C500	084
N4	C560	0113
N4	LJ31	038
N4AC	C500	218
N4AC	FA10	184
N4AC	FA50	96
N4AS	CL65	5721
N4AT	**C550**	**550-0805**
N4AZ	M220	1
N4B	C52C	0060
N4B	**E55P**	**50500347**
(N4BP)	C555	0090
N4BR	HS25	256032
N4CH	C500	062
N4CH	C550	045
N4CJ	**C52C**	**714001**
N4CP	FA50	187
N4CP	GLF2	71
N4CP	GLF4	1257
N4CP	GLF4	4191
N4CP	GLF5	5005
N4CP	**GLF6**	**6039**
N4CP	LJ55	029
N4CQ	GLF2	71
N4CR	C550	045
N4CR	HS25	25109
N4CR	LJ24	128
N4CS	C550	248
N4CS	C560	0024
N4CS	SBRL	465-27
N4DA	GLF4	1472
N4DA	**LJ45**	**283**
N4DF	C525	0481
N4DS	FA10	116
N4EA	**LJ35**	**458**
(N4EF)	C525	0167
N4EG	C650	0139
N4EG	C650	7059
(N4EG)	C650	0152
N4EK	C550	119
N4EM	ASTR	050
N4ES	**HS25**	**25243**
N4EW	C550	636
N4F	LJ24	294
N4FC	C560	0270
N4FC	C650	0140
N4FC	GLF4	4002
N4FE	C550	478
N4FE	CL60	1062
N4FE	FA20	108/430
N4FE	LJ45	032
N4FF	**C510**	**0007**
N4FL	GLF4	1312
N4FL	**GLF6**	**6032**
N4GA	C525	0272
N4GA	**C52B**	**0055**
N4GB	LJ35	228
N4GV	SBRL	282-135
N4GX	GLEX	9048
N4HK	C555	0027
N4J	LJ35	110
N4JB	**C56X**	**5125**
N4JS	C550	281
N4JS	C560	0196
N4JS	C56X	5035
N4JS	**CL61**	**5092**
N4KH	C500	062
N4KS	**C56X**	**5035**
N4LG	C500	130
N4LG	SBRL	306-9
N4LH	FA20	205
N4LK	C500	140
N4LK	MU30	A021SA
(N4LQ)	SBRL	465-38
(N4LZ)	GLEX	9084
N4M	**C52C**	**0012**
N4M	C550	550-0879
N4M	SBRL	465-18
N4MB	F900	146
N4MB	FA20	135
N4MB	FA50	156
N4MB	SBRL	465-17
N4MH	**WW24**	**232**
N4MM	C550	430
N4MM	C560	0109A
N4MR	FA50	156
N4MR	LJ25	125
N4MR	LJ25	222
N4NB	SBRL	380-40
N4NE	SBRL	306-79
N4NK	WW24	82
N4NM	C550	430
N4NP	SBRL	282-109
N4NR	**GLF2**	**255/18**
N4NR	SBRL	306-79
N4NR	SBRL	380-40
N4NT	SBRL	306-48
N4PC	GLF3	340
N4PC	GLF4	1174
N4PG	CL61	5052
N4PG	GLF2	21
N4PG	GLF4	1259
N4PG	GLF5	5214
N4PG	SBRL	380-49
N4PH	SBRL	282-116
N4PN	HS25	25185
N4PQ	SBRL	380-49
N4QB	**HS25**	**25255**
N4QG	F2EX	28
N4QN	**C650**	**7031**
N4QP	**C525**	**0272**
N4QP	FA50	187
N4QP	GLF4	1257
N4RH	C525	0306
N4RH	C525	0691
N4RH	C52B	0015
(N4RH)	C510	0162
N4RP	C52A	0135
N4RP	C52B	0289
N4RP	**C680**	**0547**
(N4RP)	C680	0093
N4RT	FA10	80
N4RT	GLF2	26
N4RT	LJ24	348
N4RT	LJ35	003
"N4RT"	FA20	242
N4RU	LJ24	348
N4S	**C52B**	**0086**
N4S	GLF2	24
N4S	SBRL	306-37
N4SA	HS25	256065
N4SA	HS25	258303
N4SE	SBRL	306-37
N4SG	CL61	5111
N4SP	GLF2	20
N4SP	GLF4	1286
N4SP	GLF4	1388
N4SP	JSTR	5081
(N4SP)	GLF4	1449
N4SQ	WW24	307
N4ST	C525	0823
N4SX	JSTR	5081
N4T	**GLEX**	**9195**
N4T	GLF4	1132
N4TB	FA20	432
N4TE	C500	149
N4TF	C525	0076
N4TK	C500	192
N4TL	C500	149
N4TL	C550	119
N4TL	C560	0048
N4TL	C560	0334
N4TL	**C560**	**0587**
N4TL	C555	0052
N4TS	C550	030
N4TS	HS25	256004
N4TU	C555	0052
N4UB	GLF2	207/34
N4UC	GLF4	1513
N4UG	GLF4	1259
N4UP	GLF3	484
N4UP	GLF4	1088
N4VC	LJ25	161
N4VF	C500	045
N4VF	C550	053
N4VF	C650	0082
N4VF	FA50	160
N4VF	**FA7X**	**62**
N4VR	C550	716
N4VS	LJ24	072
N4VY	C650	0082
N4WC	HS25	25278
N4WG	WW24	112
N4WG	**WW24**	**200**
(N4WJ)	SBRL	380-12
N4XL	LJ35	236
N4Y	**C650**	**0137**
N4YA	C525	0004
N4ZA	HFB3	1045
N4ZB	LJ25	371
N4ZK	C500	140
N4ZL	**C560**	**0448**
N4ZS	C550	248
N5AH	HS25	256004
(N5AX)	JSTR	5013
N5B	C500	021
N5B	C500	081
N5B	C500	150
N5B	C500	225
(N5B)	LJ25	299
N5BA	WW24	138
N5BK	GLF4	1025
N5BL	LJ24	009
N5BP	WW24	10
N5BP	WW24	137
(N5BP)	WW24	280
N5C	FA20	17
N5C	HS25	258083
N5CA	**FA10**	**187**
N5CA	FA20	108/430
N5CE	FA20	17
N5D	LJ24	095
N5DA	GLF5	5021
N5DL	**C500**	**427**
N5DL	C500	648
N5DL	FA50	7
N5DL	GLF2	226
N5DL	HS25	256051
N5DL	SBRL	306-131
N5DM	LJ24	025
N5DM	LJ24	028
N5DM	LJ25	063
N5EJ	MU30	A033SA
(N5EM)	C500	383
N5EQ	SBRL	380-50
N5ES	FA10	174
N5ES	HS25	259024
N5FE	FA20	20
N5FE	LJ45	079
N5FF	C750	0192
N5FF	**C750**	**0236**
N5FF	LJ35	396
N5FG	C500	224
N5FW	C500	187
N5G	GLF3	485
N5G	HS25	258053
N5G	**HS25**	**258507**
N5GA	GLF5	509
(N5GA)	C550	230
N5GD	FA10	83
N5GE	C560	0218
N5GF	**GLF4**	**1277**
N5GQ	C52B	0321
N5GU	**C52B**	**0009**
N5GV	GLF5	502
N5GV	**GLF5**	**5134**
N5GV	GLF5	518
N5GV	GLF5	5285
N5GV	GLF5	545
N5GV	GLF6	6078
(N5HG)	GLF3	376
N5HN	GLF5	568
N5HQ	**WW24**	**266**
N5JC	WW24	101
N5JR	**GLF4**	**1066**
N5JR	GLF5	626
N5JR	WW24	49
N5JU	C560	0080
N5JY	FA10	74
N5KJ	**C525**	**0842**
N5L	**C525**	**0829**
N5LG	C500	150
N5LK	**C500**	**274**
N5LL	LJ25	183
N5LP	FA10	142
N5MC	F900	10
N5MC	**GLF4**	**1218**
N5MQ	**C52B**	**0347**
N5MV	**F9EX**	**221**
(N5MW)	HS25	25233
N5NC	LJ25	372
N5NC	LJ31	211
N5NE	C550	723
N5NE	SBRL	306-127
N5NG	**GLF4**	**1485**
N5NG	HS25	256020
N5NR	**C56X**	**5557**
N5NR	C650	0083
N5NR	HS25	256053
N5NW	GLF3	395
N5PC	SBRL	282-34
N5PF	BE40	RK-59
N5PG	CL61	5053
N5PG	**GLF5**	**5046**
N5PG	SBRL	380-50
N5PQ	SBRL	282-34
N5Q	C500	018
N5Q	C550	036
N5QG	LJ55	055
N5QY	LJ24	028
N5QZ	C500	018
N5RC	FA20	159
N5RD	GLF2	142
N5RD	GLF4	1156
N5RL	C500	638
N5RT	FA20	96
(N5S)	WW24	280
N5SA	GLF5	527
N5SJ	GLF2	52
N5SJ	HS25	256014
N5SJ	LJ24	246
N5SP	GLF5	5001
N5SP	GLF5	632
N5T	C550	174
N5T	C560	0218
N5T	C750	0104
N5TC	C500	424
N5TD	LJ24	311
(N5TH)	WW24	372
N5TK	C500	266
N5TM	CL61	5076
N5TQ	C550	174
N5TR	C500	288
N5TR	**C550**	**344**
N5TR	LJ24	311
N5UD	**C525**	**0620**
N5UD	GLF2	8
N5UD	JSTR	5019
N5UE	MU30	A026SA
N5UH	GLF5	536
N5UJ	LJ25	088
N5UM	C500	550
N5UQ	FA20	513
N5UU	**C560**	**0457**
N5UU	F900	133
N5UU	FA20	513
N5UU	GLEX	9029
N5V	HS25	25282
N5VF	F900	116
N5VF	FA50	163
N5VF	**FA50**	**166**
N5VG	**LJ31**	**014**
N5VH	FA50	163
N5VJ	F900	27
N5VJ	**F9EX**	**99**
N5VJ	FA20	377/548
N5VN	C550	550-0938
N5VN	F900	116
(N5VN)	JSTR	5219
N5VP	C500	405
N5VS	GLF4	1414
N5VS	**GLF5**	**5088**
N5VU	**C52A**	**0480**
N5WC	C555	0027
N5WF	C500	460
N5WJ	LJ24	187
N5WN	**C52B**	**0204**
N5WT	C550	118
N5WT	**C560**	**0635**
N5XP	C560	0422
N5XP	LJ45	118
N5XP	LJ45	365
N5XR	C550	553
N5XR	LJ55	063
N5YD	**C52A**	**0019**
N5YD	C52A	0121
(N5YH)	C680	0056
N5YP	C500	462
N5ZA	HFB3	1037
N5ZN	**C500**	**507**
N5ZZ	C500	155
N6	C550	006
N6B	WW24	127
N6B	WW24	89
N6BB	CL61	5082
N6BX	F900	79
N6BX	GLF3	392
N6BZ	GLF3	392
N6CD	C500	151
N6CF	SBRL	265-48
N6D	GLEX	9191
N6D	**GLF6**	**6126**
N6DB	WW24	98
N6DQ	E50P	50000012
N6DQ	**E55P**	**50500011**
N6EL	**ASTR**	**104**
N6EL	C550	375
N6EQ	C680	0204
(N6ES)	JSTR	5023
N6FE	C560	0028
N6FE	FA20	50
N6FE	LJ45	098
N6FJ	**FA10**	**97**
N6FR	**C550**	**550-0828**
N6FZ	C560	0028
N6GC	LJ25	034
N6GG	HS25	257108
N6GG	HS25	258030
N6GG	LJ35	256
N6GJ	LJ24	069
N6GQ	HS25	257108
N6GU	**C680**	**0268**
N6GV	**SBRL**	**465-9**
N6HF	**C550**	**223**
N6HJ	**GLF5**	**5494**
N6HT	C500	362
N6JB	CL61	5131
N6JB	HS25	257023
N6JB	HS25	258189
N6JL	C500	101
N6JL	C550	294
N6JL	JSTR	5037/24
N6JM	LJ24	246
N6JR	C52A	0051
N6JR	PRM1	RB-161
N6JR	**PRM1**	**RB-281**
N6JU	C500	101
N6JU	C550	294
N6JW	GLF2	138
N6K	SBRL	380-1
N6K	SBRL	465-3
N6KJ	LJ25	146
N6KM	LJ24	334
N6LG	SBRL	380-34
N6LL	C555	0094
N6LL	LJ25	256
N6M	C52A	0051
N6M	C52A	0302
N6M	C52B	0256
N6MF	BE40	RK-315
N6MJ	WW24	251
N6MK	HFB3	1037
N6MK	SBRL	306-98
N6ML	HFB3	1037
N6MW	**CL60**	**1057**
N6NB	GLF4	1290
N6ND	SBRL	306-81
N6NE	JSTR	5006/40
N6NE	SBRL	306-133
N6NE	SBRL	306-43
N6NF	LJ25	021
N6NG	SBRL	380-27
N6NP	SBRL	306-43
N6NP	SBRL	465-9
N6NR	**HS25**	**258701**
N6NR	SBRL	306-43
N6NR	SBRL	306-81
N6NR	SBRL	380-27
N6NR	SBRL	380-43
N6NR	SBRL	380-54
N6NR	SBRL	465-29

N6NR	SBRL	465-68
N6NY	**C560**	**0439**
N6PA	FA10	84
N6PA	MU30	A019SA
N6PC	GLF2	87/775/6
N6PC	**GLF4**	**1247**
N6PG	**CL30**	**20529**
N6PG	SBRL	380-48
N6PG	SBRL	380-66
N6PX	F900	79
N6Q	C550	046
N6QM	C52C	0007
N6QZ	JSTR	5224
N6RF	C500	460
N6SG	CL61	5046
N6SP	SBRL	380-9
N6SS	HS25	25100
N6TE	SBRL	282-94
N6TM	C550	550-1063
N6TM	C550	550-1067
N6TM	**C56X**	**6071**
N6TM	HS25	258026
N6TM	SBRL	306-72
N6TM	WW24	275
N6TU	HS25	258026
N6UB	**C525**	**0127**
N6UB	HS25	257023
N6UB	HS25	258189
N6VB	**GLEX**	**9144**
N6VB	GLF4	1174
N6VC	HS25	257056
N6VF	C500	045
N6VF	**F9EX**	**159**
N6VF	FA20	486
N6VG	FA10	62
N6VL	SBRL	380-66
N6VN	GLF4	1248
N6WU	C550	198
N6YL	SBRL	380-42
N6YY	LJ25	323
N6YY	LJ36	023
N6ZA	HFB3	1051
N6ZE	**C52A**	**0141**
N7	C500	084
N7AB	C550	633
N7AB	**C650**	**7068**
N7AB	LJ24	355
N7AB	LJ35	402
N7AG	ASTR	021
N7AT	LJ25	105
N7AU	GALX	006
N7AU	LJ55	112
(N7AU)	GALX	004
N7C	GLF2	51
N7C	GLF3	449
N7C	HS25	258025
N7CC	C525	0004
N7CC	C52A	0007
N7CC	**C52B**	**0007**
N7CC	C550	029
N7CF	LJ24	016
N7CH	**C52B**	**0202**
N7CJ	C500	509
N7CP	**C550**	**550-0875**
N7CQ	**C525**	**0004**
N7CT	HS25	257131
N7DJ	WW24	265
N7DL	LJ24	228
N7DR	**E55P**	**50500323**
N7EC	WW24	96
N7EJ	LJ24	343
N7EN	**C500**	**544**
N7EN	C525	0151
N7ES	HFB3	1045
N7EY	BE40	RJ-34
N7FD	C550	344
N7FE	C560	0063
N7FE	FA20	46
N7FE	LJ45	099
N7FF	G150	277
N7FJ	LJ24	058
N7FY	**EA50**	**000217**
(N7FZ)	C560	0063
N7GA	LJ25	121
N7GF	GLF4	4263
N7GF	LJ24	016
N7GF	LJ24	093
N7GJ	C500	021
N7GJ	LJ25	004
N7GN	LJ24	134
N7GP	LJ24	082
N7GU	GLF4	4118
N7GW	WW24	24
N7GX	**FA50**	**139**
N7GZ	**C52A**	**0145**
N7HA	LJ24	154
N7HB	C560	0584
N7HB	C56X	5607
N7HB	C680	0197
N7HB	**G280**	**2021**
N7HF	C650	0148
N7HF	SBRL	465-13
N7HL	WW24	35
N7HM	WW24	266
N7HM	WW24	329
N7HV	C650	0124
N7HV	HS25	25282
N7JM	CL60	1010
N7JM	**GLF4**	**1132**
N7JN	LJ25	098
N7JT	PRM1	RB-34
N7JW	**E55P**	**50500172**
N7KA	LJ35	033
N7KC	**F9EX**	**14**
N7KC	FA20	479
N7KG	SBRL	282-111
N7KH	C500	045
N7KR	WW24	72
N7LA	GLF4	1286
N7LA	LJ25	244
(N7LA)	LJ35	308
N7LC	LJ25	328
N7LG	HS25	25185
N7MC	C500	576
N7MR	**FA7X**	**26**
N7MZ	**C500**	**623**
N7NE	C500	352
N7NE	C525	0419
N7NE	C52B	0025
N7NE	**C52C**	**0068**
N7NF	SBRL	306-126
(N7NL)	FA10	68
N7NN	C550	550-0851
N7NP	FA10	68
N7NP	HS25	25234
N7NP	JSTR	5229
N7NQ	C52B	0025
N7NR	SBRL	306-126
N7NR	SBRL	306-57
N7NR	SBRL	306-73
N7NR	SBRL	380-39
N7NR	SBRL	465-44
N7NY	**HS25**	**258423**
N7PE	LJ35	204
N7PG	**CL30**	**20532**
N7PG	GLF2	62
N7PG	GLF4	1374
N7PQ	GLF2	62
N7PS	**CL61**	**5027**
N7PW	MU30	A027SA
N7QC	CS55	0109
N7QF	**C510**	**0456**
N7QJ	C500	509
N7QM	C52A	0214
N7RC	C550	022
N7RC	MU30	A012SA
N7RL	C525	0028
N7RL	C56X	5247
N7RL	LJ24	322
N7RL	LJ25	230
N7RP	GLF4	1064
N7RX	GLF4	1137
N7RX	**GLF4**	**4017**
(N7RZ)	FA10	127
N7SB	C750	0185
N7SB	**C750**	**0209**
N7SJ	HS25	25250
N7SJ	**SJ30**	**007**
(N7SL)	SBRL	282-114
N7SN	C550	313
N7SN	LJ31	226
N7SP	CL60	1076
N7SV	C500	601
N7SZ	HS25	25100
N7SZ	JSTR	5040
N7SZ	JSTR	5124
N7TJ	FA10	69
N7TJ	GLF2	23
N7TJ	GLF2	77
N7TJ	LJ25	007
N7TJ	LJ35	013
N7TK	**C500**	**509**
N7TM	**C56X**	**6028**
N7TX	**PRM1**	**RB-198**
N7UA	LJ55	128
N7UF	C500	632
N7UF	**GLF4**	**1422**
N7UJ	HS25	257093
(N7UL)	C650	0224
N7US	LJ35	291
N7US	LJ55	128
N7US	LJ60	014
N7UV	HS25	257011
N7VS	LJ24	087
N7WC	HS25	25273
N7WC	HS25	257036
N7WF	C500	370
N7WF	C650	7106
N7WG	FA20	325
N7WG	GLF2	248
N7WG	HS25	257126
N7WG	HS25	257131
(N7WG)	HS25	25187
N7WQ	GLF2	190
N7WY	C550	598
N7X	**FA7X**	**33**
N7XE	**C525**	**0419**
N7XJ	LJ35	669
N7YA	**C550**	**550-0880**
N7YP	C550	211
N7ZA	LJ25	026
N7ZB	LJ24	355
N7ZG	**C650**	**0031**
N7ZH	**LJ35**	**348**
N7ZU	C550	432
N7ZX	GLF2	21
N8AD	C550	331
N8AD	JSTR	5013
N8AE	LJ24	335
N8AF	SBRL	282-24
N8BG	CS55	0085
N8BG	LJ24	348
N8BX	C550	345
N8BX	F900	111
N8BX	FA20	380
N8CA	GLF5	563
(N8CA)	GLF5	531
N8CF	C550	223
N8CL	LJ25	014
(N8CQ)	C52A	0007
N8DE	C500	166
N8DX	**C500**	**303**
N8EH	C500	483
N8FC	C500	124
N8FD	C550	383
N8FE	FA20	199
N8FF	LJ25	016
N8FM	LJ24	116
N8GA	FA10	127
N8GA	LJ35	091
N8GA	SBRL	282-32
N8GA	WW24	356
N8GA	WW24	63
N8GE	WW24	63
N8GQ	**C52C**	**0045**
N8GT	LJ55	020
(N8GY)	C560	0091
N8HJ	C560	0108
N8HQ	**BE40**	**RJ-50**
(N8JA)	LJ35	348
N8JC	C650	7030
N8JC	C750	0020
N8JC	**C750**	**0154**
N8JG	C500	074
N8JK	GLF5	5452
N8JL	GLF3	388
N8JL	WW24	359
N8JQ	C750	0020
N8JR	**C680**	**680A0010**
N8JR	LJ60	084
N8KD	**E50P**	**50000304**
N8KG	CL60	1012
N8KG	FA50	174
N8KG	HS25	257189
N8KH	C500	163
N8LA	LJ35	124
N8LC	WW24	413
N8LE	**MU30**	**A042SA**
N8LG	C500	477
N8LL	LJ28	28-005
N8LT	**FA10**	**173**
N8MA	LJ25	085
N8MA	LJ35	229
N8MC	ASTR	092
N8MC	CL64	5329
N8MC	**GLF4**	**1129**
(N8ME)	BE40	RK-19
N8MF	**GALX**	**006**
N8MF	LJ25	253
N8MF	LJ55	128
N8MN	ASTR	092
N8MQ	LJ25	085
N8MY	**C510**	**0322**
N8NB	SBRL	370-9
N8NB	SBRL	380-27
(N8NC)	C500	567
(N8NF)	SBRL	306-141
N8NG	SBRL	380-48
N8NR	SBRL	306-141
N8NR	SBRL	370-2
N8NR	SBRL	370-9
N8NR	SBRL	380-27
N8NR	SBRL	380-48
N8P	C500	369
N8PG	GLF2	21
N8PJ	C500	369
N8PL	HS25	257058
N8PQ	GLF2	21
N8QM	F2EX	38
N8QM	F2TH	38
N8QP	WW24	217
N8QR	WW24	217
N8QX	WW24	406
N8RA	WW24	104
N8RF	C500	293
N8SC	JSTR	5106/9
N8SP	CL64	5518
N8SP	HS25	258380
N8TA	**HS25**	**258440**
N8TG	C500	253
N8TG	**LJ31**	**190**
N8TP	FA20	74
N8TU	C750	0136
N8U	LJ36	026
N8UA	LJ36	026
(N8UB)	LJ36	026
N8UC	C525	0416
N8UP	HS25	258083
N8VB	**GLEX**	**9021**
N8VF	**F900**	**12**
N8VQ	GLF5	566
N8VX	C650	7081
N8WN	FA20	91
N8YM	**BE40**	**RJ-4**
N8YY	LJ35	335
N8YY	LJ55	060
N9AJ	LJ24	069
N9AT	LJ25	125
(N9AT)	C500	241
N9AX	C500	016
N9AX	C650	0067
N9AZ	HS25	256063
N9BF	GLF2	46
N9BX	FA50	45
N9BX	**GLF4**	**4145**
N9BY	WW24	9
N9CH	LJ31	041
N9CH	LJ35	282
N9CH	**LJ40**	**2134**
N9CH	LJ45	129
N9CH	PRM1	RB-244
N9CN	**C560**	**0602**
N9CN	LJ25	061
N9CN	LJ35	016
N9CR	C550	500
N9CU	LJ60	075
N9CZ	LJ25	040
N9DC	C550	031
N9DC	WW24	109
N9DM	FA20	18
N9DM	WW24	63
N9EE	LJ35	193
N9FB	FA20	275
(N9FC)	MU30	A010SA
N9FE	FA20	216
N9FE	FA20	84
N9FE	LJ45	240
N9GN	SBRL	380-2
N9GT	C500	438
N9GT	CS55	0159
N9GU	C525	0034
N9GU	JSTR	5119/29
N9GY	CS55	0159
N9HJ	LJ31	040
N9HM	LJ24	190
N9HM	LJ25	146
N9HM	LJ35	199
N9HN	LJ25	146
(N9HV)	LJ35	199
N9JJ	LJ24	039
N9KC	LJ24	144
(N9KE)	JSTR	5225
N9KH	CS55	0082
N9KH	LJ28	28-001
N9KL	C650	0068
N9KL	GLF3	321
N9KN	GLF4	1282
N9LD	LJ24	336
N9LM	LJ24	152
N9LP	MU30	A019SA
(N9LP)	WW24	149
N9LR	C525	0025
N9LR	C550	270
N9LR	C560	0473
N9LR	HS25	258050
N9LR	LJ55	138
N9LV	**PRM1**	**RB-132**
N9MD	JSTR	5014
N9MS	SBRL	282-103
N9NB	HS25	258317
N9NE	C500	593
N9NG	**C750**	**0213**
N9NL	C650	0101
N9NP	SBRL	306-133
N9NR	SBRL	282-111
N9NR	SBRL	282-137
N9NR	SBRL	306-135
N9NT	SBRL	306-135
N9PC	GLF4	1210
N9PG	GLF2	251
N9PW	BE40	RK-7
N9PY	GLF2	251
N9QM	LJ25	286
N9QN	SBRL	306-12
N9RA	LJ24	068
N9RA	LJ24	095
N9RA	LJ25	277
N9RA	LJ35	651
N9RD	**WW24**	**220**
N9RG	F900	51
N9RS	LJ28	28-001
N9SC	**GLF4**	**4174**
N9SC	GLF5	552
N9SS	C550	190
N9TE	FA10	103
N9TE	**FA10**	**152**
N9TE	FA20	202
N9TE	FA20	363/544
N9TE	FA50	17
N9TJ	**GLEX**	**9659**
N9TK	C500	437
N9U	**C56X**	**5232**
(N9UC)	C650	0238
N9UD	C52A	0317
N9UG	C525	0331
N9UJ	C500	198
N9UP	HS25	258147
N9UX	**GLF5**	**528**
N9V	C500	150
N9VC	WW24	162
N9VF	C550	646
N9VG	FA20	416
N9VL	ASTR	026
N9VL	LJ31	174
N9VQ	WW24	162
N9WN	GLF3	392
N9WP	JSTR	5157
N9WV	F9EX	108
N9WW	**BE40**	**RK-142**
(N9WW)	WW24	252
(N9WW)	WW24	306
N9X	FA50	14
N9ZB	**C500**	**413**
N9ZB	LJ35	591
N9ZD	**LJ35**	**306**
N9ZM	LJ35	591
N9ZM	LJ60	151
N10	C500	084
(N10AA)	HS25	258023
(N10AB)	LJ35	231
N10AG	FA10	6
N10AH	FA10	139
N10AH	**LJ35**	**657**
(N10AH)	FA10	141
N10AQ	LJ35	069
N10AT	F900	142
N10AT	FA50	194
N10AU	C52A	0420
N10AU	**C52C**	**0210**
N10AU	C560	0512
N10AZ	FA20	382
N10AZ	LJ35	080
N10BD	LJ25	120
N10BD	LJ35	506
N10BF	C550	048
N10BF	LJ35	185
N10BF	LJ55	128
(N10BF)	C500	118
(N10BF)	LJ25	010
N10BK	WW24	89
N10BU	LJ25	120
(N10BY)	WW24	226
N10C	HS25	25236
N10C	**HS25**	**257050**
(N10CA)	C500	387
N10CB	LJ24	227
N10CC	SBRL	282-56
N10CF	C550	230
N10CN	C560	0249
N10CN	HS25	257155
N10CN	SBRL	380-27
N10CN	SBRL	380-54
N10CP	LJ24	112
N10CP	LJ55	029
N10CR	LJ55	057
N10CR	LJ55	145
N10CX	JSTR	5162
N10CZ	HS25	257038
N10D	HS25	25029
N10DG	C500	028
N10DG	C500	120
N10DR	JSTR	5037/24
N10DR	JSTR	5139/54
N10E	GLEX	9106
N10EA	WW24	39
N10EC	LJ24	215
N10EF	**CL30**	**20524**
N10EG	**C550**	**055**
N10EH	C500	350
N10EH	**CL30**	**20431**
N10EH	GLF3	436
N10EU	**F2EX**	**46**
N10F	**FA10**	**12**
N10FE	CL60	1074
N10FE	CL61	5188
N10FE	FA20	16
N10FG	C500	295
N10FG	WW24	318
N10FH	ASTR	138
N10FJ	FA10	100
N10FJ	FA10	106
N10FJ	FA10	2
N10FL	LJ25	106
N10FL	BE40	RK-266
N10FL	BE40	RK-27
N10FM	C500	292
N10FN	C550	268
N10FN	**LJ36**	**015**
N10FQ	BE40	RK-27
N10FU	LJ24	340
N10GE	C500	385
(N10GN)	C550	069
N10GR	WW24	114
(N10GR)	C500	132
N10GU	**C52A**	**0420**
N10HD	**GLEX**	**9682**
N10HE	FA10	111
(N10HH)	EA50	000279
N10HK	FA10	142
N10HQ	F9EX	57
N10HR	GLF2	67
N10HV	WW24	103
N10HZ	F9EX	57
N10J	C500	408
N10J	LJ45	063

N10J	**LJ45**	**337**
N10J	BE40	RK-31
N10JA	C550	035
N10JJ	JSTR	5162
N10JK	C550	178
N10JM	C750	0022
N10JM	F2TH	151
N10JP	C500	080
N10JP	C550	081
N10JP	C650	0157
N10JP	**F2TH**	**23**
N10JP	WW24	96
N10JV	WW24	96
N10JX	BE40	RK-31
N10JY	**LJ45**	**063**
N10JZ	FA10	13
N10LB	FA20	179
N10LB	GLF2	111
N10LB	GLF2	168
N10LB	GLF2	82
N10LB	GLF4	1008
N10LJ	LJ24	037
N10LN	HS25	25156
N10LQ	GLF4	1008
N10LR	C550	084
N10LT	FA50	194
N10LX	SBRL	306-59
N10LY	**C550**	**466**
N10M	SBRL	370-2
N10MB	**LJ60**	**176**
N10MB	WW24	157
N10MC	LJ24	003
N10MC	WW24	26
N10MF	WW24	53
N10MJ	JSTR	5090
N10MR	WW24	258
N10MT	FA20	239
N10MV	WW24	300
N10MZ	ASTR	028
N10MZ	F900	32
N10MZ	**GLF5**	**5141**
(N10MZ)	CL60	1084
N10NB	HS25	258331
N10NC	**FA10**	**172**
N10NL	C500	417
N10NL	FA10	195
N10NL	**LJ45**	**128**
N10NL	WW24	304
N10NM	MU30	A016SA
N10NP	LJ25	106
N10NT	LJ25	144
(N10NV)	FA10	195
(N10NW)	GLF2	183
N10PF	SBRL	306-39
N10PN	C650	0020
N10PN	CL60	1072
N10PN	JSTR	5155/32
(N10PN)	FA10	3
N10PP	FA20	161
N10PP	FA50	231
N10PQ	FA50	231
N10PS	C500	252
N10PW	HS25	257104
N10PX	C650	0025
(N10PX)	C550	419
(N10PZ)	C550	550-0835
N10QD	FA10	178
N10QJ	HS25	257135
N10QS	HA4T	RC-22
(N10QX)	LJ24	035
N10R	**C525**	**0105**
N10R	LJ45	042
N10RE	LJ25	133
N10RE	LJ35	345
N10RQ	**GLF2**	**232**
N10RU	C550	470
N10RU	**C560**	**0512**
N10RZ	FA20	161
N10RZ	**G150**	**258**
N10RZ	LJ25	133
N10S	**C525**	**0116**
N10S	WW24	278
N10SA	**HS25**	**256065**
N10SE	LJ31	217
N10SE	**LJ40**	**2032**
N10SL	**GLEX**	**9221**
N10SL	SBRL	282-11
N10SN	C56X	5014
N10SN	GLF4	4147
N10SN	WW24	69
N10ST	C650	0113
N10ST	LJ31	039
N10ST	LJ60	228
N10TB	C560	0143
N10TB	FA10	72
N10TC	**C550**	**495**
N10TC	C650	0008
N10TC	HS25	258096
N10TD	**C560**	**0096**
N10TE	MU30	A029SA
N10TJ	FA10	99
N10TN	**HS25**	**257085**
N10TR	C510	0371
N10TR	**C52B**	**0354**
N10TS	**C52B**	**0225**
N10TX	FA10	9
N10UC	C500	083

N10UC	C500	283
N10UC	**HS25**	**257119**
N10UF	**LJ35**	**166**
(N10UG)	FA50	18
N10UH	C500	304
N10UH	**C550**	**550-0925**
N10UJ	WW24	204
N10UM	SBRL	306-43
N10UN	FA10	36
N10UP	C500	080
N10UQ	C500	083
(N10UU)	FA20	513
N10VG	FA20	126/438
N10VG	**LJ25**	**125**
N10VQ	C56X	5570
N10VT	C550	403
N10WA	FA20	28
N10WE	FA10	159
N10WF	HS25	258030
N10WF	LJ24	321
N10WF	LJ35	377
N10WJ	LJ24	311
N10WZ	**C52A**	**0432**
N10XG	**GLF5**	**5186**
N10XQ	**GALX**	**169**
N10XT	**C750**	**0230**
N10XX	FA10	40
N10XY	GLF2	56
N10YJ	FA10	57
N10YJ	**HS25**	**258099**
N10ZK	GLF4	1174
N11	JSTR	5001/53
N11A	C500	111
N11A	CL64	5354
N11A	**GLEX**	**9187**
N11AB	C550	079
N11AF	HS25	256057
N11AK	**C560**	**0205**
N11AK	FA20	249
N11AK	LJ24	154
N11AK	LJ25	082
N11AK	LJ35	135
N11AL	GLF2	97
N11AL	SBRL	306-27
N11AM	LJ35	340
N11AM	**LJ60**	**118**
(N11AN)	GLF4	1108
N11AQ	C500	045
N11AQ	LJ24	178
N11AQ	SBRL	306-18
N11AR	HS25	25098
N11AZ	CL60	1032
N11BK	WW24	77
N11BR	**LJ31**	**086**
N11BU	LJ25	138
N11BV	**F2TH**	**21**
N11CS	WW24	397
N11DH	C500	019
N11DH	C500	048
N11DH	C500	385
N11DH	FA10	108
N11DH	FA10	142
N11DH	FA10	68
N11DQ	C500	019
N11EA	GLEX	9114
N11FH	C550	013
N11FH	LJ24	131
N11FX	GLF4	1107
N11FX	HS25	25273
N11GE	BE40	RK-19
N11GU	**C680**	**0147**
N11HD	FA7X	62
N11HJ	C500	034
N11HM	JSTR	5119/29
N11JC	JSTR	5013
(N11JC)	C500	463
N11JK	LJ24	088
(N11JV)	LJ35	096
N11KA	C500	119
N11LB	C52B	0019
N11LB	FA20	244
N11LC	C560	0427
N11LK	CL61	5193
N11LK	F900	128
N11LN	**WW24**	**261**
N11LQ	C560	0427
N11LX	**SBRL**	**306-75**
N11MC	WW24	55
(N11MC)	LJ25	125
N11MN	**C500**	**266**
N11MY	LJ35	370
N11MZ	ASTR	028
N11NT	HFB3	1055
N11NZ	C650	0143
N11NZ	GLF2	214
N11PC	**EA50**	**000002**
N11PH	LJ25	177
N11PM	PRM1	RB-113
N11QC	C500	008
N11QD	HS25	25108
N11QM	LJ24	091
N11SQ	C500	477
N11SQ	HS25	25206
N11SQ	LJ35	380
(N11SQ)	LJ25	234
N11SS	C550	436
N11SU	C555	0086

N11SX	GLF2	34
N11SX	JSTR	5111
N11TC	C500	008
N11TC	FA20	146
N11TE	**E55P**	**50500081**
N11TH	**C52B**	**0056**
N11TK	CL61	5025
N11TK	LJ25	201
(N11TK)	GLEX	9004
(N11TK)	LJ31	229
N11TM	C500	435
N11TR	**C680**	**680A0014**
N11TR	C555	0119
(N11TR)	LJ60	151
N11TS	C560	0549
N11TS	C555	0119
N11TS	HS25	257191
N11TS	LJ55	032
N11TS	**LJ60**	**151**
N11UB	BE40	RK-212
N11UC	GLF2	108
N11UD	C52B	0285
N11UE	JSTR	5038
N11UF	FA20	356
N11UF	GLF2	8
N11UF	JSTR	5037/24
N11UF	JSTR	5038
N11UF	LJ35	237
N11UL	HS25	258498
N11UL	SBRL	306-103
N11UM	GLF2	12
(N11WA)	FA20	37/406
N11WC	C500	058
N11WC	WW24	177
(N11WC)	FA10	11
(N11WC)	HS25	258308
N11WF	MU30	A075SA
N11WF	**BE40**	**RK-236**
N11WM	**F9EX**	**58**
N11WP	WW24	100
N11WQ	C500	058
N11YM	LJ35	340
N11YR	HS25	257206
N12AC	C550	035
N12AE	HS25	25214
N12AM	C500	235
N12AR	F2EX	97
N12AR	FA20	200
N12BN	HS25	25214
(N12BN)	GLF2	39
N12BW	SBRL	282-99
N12CJ	WW24	13
N12CQ	C500	458
N12CQ	C550	372
N12CQ	**C560**	**0231**
N12CV	**C500**	**458**
N12DE	C500	458
N12EN	GLF3	406
N12EP	FA10	175
(N12EP)	LJ35	110
N12F	**C680**	**0236**
N12F	HS25	258182
N12FC	C550	369
(N12FH)	WW24	159
N12FN	**LJ36**	**016**
(N12FS)	LJ25	328
N12FU	FA20	412
N12FU	LJ60	027
N12G	**GLEX**	**9641**
N12GH	FA20	7
N12GJ	LJ35	438
N12GK	C550	291
N12GP	**GLF2**	**63**
N12GP	LJ24	076
(N12GP)	SBRL	380-51
N12GS	C525	0374
N12GS	C52A	0127
N12GS	**C52B**	**0122**
N12GY	**C525**	**0374**
(N12HJ)	LJ24	040
N12JA	C550	231
N12JA	WW24	108
N12JX	WW24	108
N12KW	HS25	25097
N12L	C550	583
N12L	**C56X**	**5002**
N12LB	FA10	62
N12LB	FA20	179
N12LD	**C550**	**589**
N12LE	**C680**	**0199**
N12LW	C550	583
N12LX	**F2EX**	**222**
N12MA	C550	550-0882
N12MB	C500	101
N12MB	C500	137
N12MB	FA10	112
(N12MB)	LJ24	116
N12ME	C500	137
N12MF	FA20	179
N12MG	BE40	RK-117
N12MG	BE40	RK-331
N12MH	LJ25	139
N12MJ	LJ24	331
N12MK	LJ24	192
N12MQ	**F2TH**	**97**
N12MQ	BE40	RK-117
N12MW	C560	0542

N12MW	**F2EX**	**29**
N12MW	F2TH	97
N12MY	C560	0542
N12ND	ASTR	116
N12ND	**C56X**	**5084**
N12NM	C500	660
N12NV	BE40	RK-103
N12NV	BE40	RK-186
N12NZ	GLF4	1376
N12PA	C525	0012
N12PA	HS25	258642
N12PB	SBRL	306-18
N12QP	**FA50**	**55**
N12QS	HA4T	RC-31
N12R	JSTR	5006/40
N12R	JSTR	5053/2
(N12RA)	LJ25	023
N12RN	C500	625
N12RN	C550	709
N12RN	C560	0316
N12RP	**LJ35**	**278**
N12S	**C555**	**0037**
N12SS	CL30	20138
N12ST	C560	0014
N12ST	LJ60	205
N12SY	**HS25**	**258103**
N12TA	LJ24	093
(N12TR)	C510	0021
(N12TU)	C560	0358
N12TV	C550	115
N12TV	C560	0358
N12TX	FA10	147
N12TX	FA10	90
N12U	FA10	75
N12U	**FA7X**	**53**
N12U	GLF4	1112
N12UD	C56X	5719
N12UM	GLF4	1112
N12UT	GLF4	1112
N12VB	**C500**	**453**
N12VU	**LJ45**	**324**
N12WF	MU30	A083SA
N12WF	**BE40**	**RK-228**
N12WH	**C500**	**437**
N12WK	LJ25	126
N12WP	FA20	83
N12WW	LJ25	051
N12XX	FA10	112
N12YS	HS25	25186
N13AD	**ASTR**	**030**
N13AD	WW24	103
N13BJ	C550	236
N13BK	C500	644
N13BK	FA10	94
(N13BN)	C500	641
N13BT	C500	453
N13CR	LJ25	023
(N13DL)	C500	427
(N13FE)	FA20	24
N13FH	C525	0185
N13FN	LJ36	045
N13GB	BE40	RK-13
N13GG	BE40	RK-416
N13GW	GLF2	87/775/6
N13GW	WW24	162
N13GX	GALX	013
N13HB	LJ35	310
(N13HB)	LJ55	046
(N13HH)	WW24	268
N13HJ	C500	182
(N13HQ)	LJ35	310
N13J	GLF4	1482
(N13J)	GLF5	5040
N13JE	LJ36	013
N13JS	F9EX	181
N13JS	**GLEX**	**9185**
N13JS	GLEX	9212
N13KD	**C500**	**497**
N13KH	WW24	182
N13KL	LJ24	332
N13LB	GLF2	111
N13LJ	LJ24	037
N13M	C52A	0105
(N13ME)	SBRL	380-70
N13MF	SBRL	465-13
N13MJ	HS25	25137
N13MJ	LJ24	314
N13MJ	LJ35	047
N13MS	**GLF6**	**6036**
N13NH	SBRL	380-25
N13NL	WW24	304
(N13QG)	C650	0238
(N13QS)	C650	0013
N13RC	C500	431
N13SA	**GLF4**	**1092**
N13SL	SBRL	306-110
N13SL	SBRL	306-17
N13SL	SBRL	306-90
N13SN	LJ24	009
N13ST	**C500**	**439**
N13SY	**C750**	**0143**
N13SY	HS25	258103
N13SY	BE40	RK-111
N13TV	WW24	86
N13UR	C500	011
N13UR	WW24	358
N13US	BE40	RK-193

N13VF	WW24	191
N13VG	LJ35	386
N13VP	C550	061
N13WF	**G150**	**303**
N13ZM	C510	0064
N14AH	E55P	50500065
N14AQ	**E55P**	**50500065**
N14BC	LJ24	209
N14BN	WW24	337
(N14BR)	HS25	256032
N14BX	LJ45	038
N14CF	C500	097
N14CF	LJ36	015
N14CG	C550	550-1019
N14CG	FA50	100
N14CG	SBRL	306-83
N14CJ	**C52C**	**0001**
N14CJ	FA20	499
N14CK	LJ25	337
(N14CK)	GLEX	9562
N14CN	LJ36	047
N14CN	WW24	359
N14CQ	SBRL	306-83
N14DG	C650	7059
N14DG	C680	0161
N14DM	**LJ24**	**341**
N14DM	MU30	A017SA
(N14DP)	CL61	5125
N14EA	C500	418
N14EA	PRM1	RB-119
N14EL	LJ35	009
N14EN	FA20	490
N14FE	CL60	1064
N14FE	FA20	227
N14FE	GLEX	9070
N14FE	LJ45	038
(N14FE)	FA20	198/466
N14FG	FA20	177
N14FN	LJ25	126
(N14FU)	LJ36	048
N14FX	F9DX	624
N14GA	C550	310
N14GD	CL61	5005
N14GD	CL64	5490
N14GD	**F2EX**	**304**
N14GD	HS25	25141
N14GD	HS25	256068
N14GD	HS25	259011
N14GQ	HS25	25141
N14GU	CL64	5490
N14HB	C550	550-0903
N14HH	HS25	25118
N14JA	C500	195
N14JA	HS25	257051
N14JD	SBRL	380-56
N14JL	C500	015
N14JZ	C500	143
N14LJ	LJ25	014
N14LT	GLF2	246
N14M	LJ35	113
N14M	SBRL	282-4
N14M	SBRL	306-56
N14M	SBRL	465-4
N14MH	C500	174
N14MJ	LJ24	189
N14NA	**F900**	**124**
N14NA	LJ25	218
(N14NB)	C650	0123
N14NE	FA50	177
N14PC	GLF2	170
N14PN	CL61	3014
N14PT	LJ24	208
(N14PT)	LJ25	139
N14QG	LJ28	28-003
N14QS	HA4T	RC-29
N14R	CL64	5319
N14R	GLEX	9110
N14RM	**C550**	**139**
N14RP	**C560**	**0403**
N14RU	CL64	5319
N14RZ	C550	269
N14SA	HS25	258339
N14SR	ASTR	015
N14SR	CL64	5360
N14SY	GLF3	391
N14SY	HS25	257101
N14T	C500	143
N14T	LJ31	222
N14T	LJ35	608
N14T	LJ60	026
N14T	LJ60	213
N14TN	SBRL	380-40
N14TT	C500	237
N14TU	**LJ60**	**026**
N14TV	C500	499
N14TV	C525	0126
N14TX	LJ35	321
N14TX	LJ36	033
N14U	FA10	90
N14UH	GLF4	1247
N14UM	C555	0127
N14VA	**C500**	**521**
N14VC	LJ25	263
N14VF	C560	0130
(N14VF)	C560	0342
(N14VP)	C750	0014
N14WJ	JSTR	5053/2

(N14WJ)	HS25	257120
(N14WT)	LJ31	072
N15AG	HS25	257156
N15AK	LJ25	082
N15AK	SBRL	465-70
N15AR	MU30	A005SA
N15AS	F2TH	3
N15AT	FA20	403
N15AW	C500	139
N15AX	HS25	258002
N15BA	**ASTR**	**020**
N15BE	LJ24	005
N15BH	LJ25	134
N15BN	WW24	352
N15BV	C525	0527
N15BX	GLEX	9382
N15BY	**F2TH**	**199**
N15C	C525	0377
N15C	**C52B**	**0023**
N15CC	C500	101
N15CC	FA20	23
N15CC	LJ25	036
N15CC	LJ25	124
N15CC	LJ35	339
N15CC	LJ36	009
N15CC	SBRL	465-42
N15CF	**LJ45**	**376**
(N15CK)	SBRL	306-121
N15CN	C550	550-0819
N15CQ	C500	101
N15CU	LJ25	124
N15CV	C500	547
N15CV	C550	550-0819
N15CV	**C560**	**0766**
N15CY	**C500**	**547**
N15DF	**C550**	**578**
N15DJ	SBRL	306-97
N15EA	C550	450
"N15EC"	SBRL	276-50
N15EH	**LJ35**	**126**
N15EN	SBRL	465-70
N15ER	**LJ25**	**267**
N15FE	FA20	229
N15FE	LJ45	039
N15FF	F9EX	158
N15FJ	C500	369
N15FJ	C500	524
N15FJ	C550	619
(N15FJ)	C500	351
N15FN	LJ36	038
N15FS	C500	016
N15FX	FA50	157
N15FX	FA7X	100
N15FX	GLEX	9088
N15FX	GLEX	9092
N15G	WW24	63
N15GJ	**C510**	**0200**
N15GT	**CL30**	**20120**
N15H	**C550**	**011**
N15H	FA20	368
N15H	SBRL	306-60
N15HE	**GLF3**	**369**
N15HF	SBRL	306-60
N15JA	C550	042
N15JH	**C500**	**174**
N15KJ	**C680**	**0550**
N15LN	**C650**	**7013**
N15LV	C525	0191
N15M	LJ25	036
(N15ME)	SBRL	380-70
N15MJ	LJ24	339
N15MJ	LJ25	018
N15MJ	LJ35	211
N15NA	C550	296
N15ND	EA50	000016
N15NY	C500	496
N15PG	**C52B**	**0140**
N15PL	LJ24	101
N15PN	SBRL	380-15
N15PR	C500	452
N15PV	G150	276
N15PX	**GLEX**	**9382**
N15QB	HS25	HA-0101
N15QS	C650	0015
N15QS	HA4T	RC-6
N15RF	SBRL	306-23
N15RF	SBRL	380-17
N15RH	LJ35	497
N15RL	C550	489
N15RL	**C750**	**0165**
N15RY	**HS25**	**258448**
N15SC	LJ24	039
N15SC	LJ35	139
N15SD	C750	0246
N15SD	**GLEX**	**9272**
N15SJ	FA10	40
N15SK	**C560**	**0395**
N15SL	**C560**	**0272**
N15SL	FA20	256
N15SN	C550	566
N15SP	C550	566
N15SP	CL64	5402
(N15SS)	C525	0455
(N15TA)	FA50	73
N15TF	C56X	5255
N15TF	**C56X**	**6138**
N15TG	GLF2	253
N15TM	FA10	114
N15TN	**C750**	**0505**
N15TS	SBRL	282-18
N15TT	C650	0105
N15TT	C650	0192
N15TT	C750	0127
N15TT	C750	0505
N15TT	CS55	0019
N15TT	G280	2092
N15TV	C550	459
N15TW	ASTR	029
N15TW	C550	459
N15TW	FA50	73
N15TW	LJ35	106
N15TW	MU30	A014SA
N15TX	FA10	13
N15TZ	C650	0192
N15TZ	**C750**	**0127**
N15UB	LJ40	2072
N15UB	**LJ40**	**2141**
(N15UB)	HS25	25038
N15UC	GLF2	176
N15UC	**GLF5**	**589**
N15UG	GLF2	176
(N15UJ)	C500	547
(N15UQ)	GLF5	589
N15VC	**CL65**	**5816**
N15VF	C650	0012
N15VJ	F900	27
N15VX	**FA50**	**158**
N15WH	**LJ35**	**085**
(N15WJ)	GLF4	1079
N15WT	**C550**	**422**
N15XM	**C550**	**341**
N15Y	C550	297
N15Y	**GLF4**	**1318**
N15Y	LJ35	335
N15YD	**C52A**	**0336**
N15ZA	GLF3	329
N15ZT	**C650**	**0089**
N15ZZ	**C52B**	**0221**
N16A	WW24	101
N16AJ	C650	0075
N16AJ	GLF3	413
(N16AJ)	LJ36	032
N16AS	C650	0055
N16AZ	JSTR	5156
N16BJ	LJ35	165
N16BL	JSTR	5205
(N16CM)	HS25	258040
N16CP	FA50	153
N16CP	LJ24	147
N16CS	**LJ60**	**098**
N16DA	CL64	5307
N16DD	FA10	105
N16DD	FA10	56
N16DK	PRM1	RB-19
N16FE	C650	0025
N16FE	FA20	230
N16FG	GLF2	235
N16FG	LJ35	655
N16FN	LJ35	030
N16FN	**LJ36**	**027**
N16FP	WW24	39
N16FX	F9DX	621
N16FX	GLEX	9061
N16GA	HS25	256018
(N16GG)	HS25	25032
N16GH	HS25	258065
N16GH	WW24	110
N16GR	WW24	100
N16GS	**C510**	**0440**
N16GS	C56X	5278
N16GS	C680	0096
N16GS	C680	0311
N16GS	HS25	257186
N16GT	LJ25	230
N16GX	GLEX	9016
N16HC	LJ24	126
N16HD	**BE40**	**RK-16**
N16HL	C500	431
"N16JM"	GLF4	1024
N16JP	LJ25	017
N16KB	C650	7008
N16KB	**CL61**	**5066**
N16KK	**LJ25**	**174**
N16KW	C500	664
N16LF	SBRL	380-25
N16LG	C500	174
N16LJ	LJ25	230
N16LJ	**LJ55**	**126**
N16MA	WW24	101
N16MF	MU30	A065SA
N16MF	**BE40**	**RJ-65**
N16MJ	LJ24	117
N16MK	WW24	84
N16MT	LJ24	209
N16NK	FA50	186
N16NK	GLF2	156/31
N16NK	GLF3	354
N16NK	GLF5	585
N16NL	**C500**	**417**
N16NM	C560	0084
N16PC	LJ45	050
N16PC	LJ45	319
N16PC	**LJ45**	**495**
(N16PJ)	HS25	25078
N16PL	**C550**	**293**
N16PN	SBRL	306-99
N16PQ	LJ45	050
N16R	FA20	305
N16R	FA50	141
N16R	SBRL	282-94
N16RP	**CS55**	**0047**
N16RW	**CL60**	**1013**
N16SF	**WW24**	**348**
N16SK	WW24	101
N16SM	**HS25**	**HA-0040**
(N16SM)	HS25	258655
(N16SN)	C56X	5014
N16ST	LJ31	039
N16SU	**C650**	**0025**
N16TA	SBRL	282-2
N16TS	**C550**	**030**
N16TS	CL60	1016
N16VG	**C500**	**553**
N16VT	HS25	256040
(N16VT)	HS25	256037
N16WG	HS25	25187
N16WJ	FA10	105
N16WJ	LJ24	133
N16XY	**F2EX**	**16**
N16YD	**CL64**	**5367**
N16YF	**C680**	**0509**
N16YY	GLF2	253
N17A	**LJ36**	**046**
N17AE	**EA50**	**000017**
N17AH	LJ25	316
N17AJ	CRVT	15
N17AN	**C56X**	**5030**
N17AN	C56X	5141
N17AN	C650	0054
N17AN	FA50	281
N17AP	C650	7003
N17AR	LJ25	034
N17AZ	**LJ35**	**080**
N17CJ	**PRM1**	**RB-171**
(N17CM)	BE40	RK-205
N17CN	C52B	0128
N17CN	CL61	3027
N17CX	C750	0267
N17DD	HS25	258161
N17DM	C550	416
(N17DW)	WW24	145
N17ED	**C56X**	**5337**
N17EE	**C680**	**0528**
N17EM	LJ35	287
N17FE	FA20	232
N17FJ	**GLF5**	**607**
N17FL	C550	627
N17FN	LJ24	220
N17FS	C550	483
N17FS	**C550**	**550-0895**
N17FX	F9EX	29
N17FX	GLEX	9093
N17GG	GLF2	200
N17GL	LJ35	278
N17GL	LJ55	099
N17GV	GLF5	520
N17GX	**GLEX**	**9045**
N17HA	**C500**	**447**
N17HV	HS25	25282
N17JF	LJ25	039
N17JK	GLF4	1235
N17JS	**GLF5**	**5299**
N17JS	GLF5	646
N17JT	FA20	179
N17KD	C500	337
N17KJ	GLF2	200
N17KW	**GLF2**	**28**
N17LB	GLF3	331
N17LH	LJ35	428
N17LJ	LJ36	017
N17LJ	LJ55	041
(N17LJ)	LJ45	105
N17LK	C550	405
N17LK	C560	0037
N17LK	**GLF3**	**431**
N17LT	SBRL	282-59
N17LT	SBRL	282-70
N17LV	C550	405
(N17LZ)	LJ55	064
N17MU	C510	0017
N17MX	GLF2	98/38
N17NC	GLF3	318
N17ND	GLF2	63
N17ND	GLF3	369
N17ND	GLF4	1053
N17ND	**GLF5**	**518**
N17ND	LJ35	438
(N17ND)	LJ35	348
N17NN	**C650**	**7099**
N17PL	C560	0412
(N17PL)	C550	305
N17QC	C650	0239
N17RG	C550	237
N17RP	**C510**	**0133**
N17S	C550	105
N17SL	HS25	25082
N17TE	C650	0011
N17TE	CL61	5007
N17TE	CL64	5437
N17TE	**CL65**	**5724**
N17TJ	C500	375
N17TJ	FA10	43
N17TJ	MU30	A023SA
N17TN	C650	0011
N17TV	**HS25**	**258622**
N17TX	**C560**	**0166**
N17TZ	CL61	5007
N17TZ	CL64	5437
N17UC	C56X	5026
N17UC	C650	0239
N17UC	CL30	20011
N17UC	**CL30**	**20345**
N17UC	WW24	283
N17UE	CL30	20011
N17UF	LJ35	258
(N17UG)	C56X	5026
N17VB	**C525**	**0206**
N17VG	LJ31	017
N17VP	C550	483
N17WC	C550	478
N17WG	FA10	35
N17WG	HS25	257126
N17XL	LJ60	179
N17XR	**C750**	**0251**
N17XX	**FA7X**	**162**
(N17ZU)	FA10	146
N18AC	GLF4	1344
N18AF	C500	283
N18AK	LJ25	092
N18AN	GLF4	1228
N18AQ	GLF2	94
N18AQ	HS25	258712
N18AT	LJ36	002
N18AX	LJ35	087
N18BA	**HS25**	**257167**
N18BA	MU30	A036SA
N18BG	C500	292
N18BG	C500	378
(N18BG)	FA10	33
N18BH	JSTR	5099/5
N18BL	LJ25	234
N18BL	LJ31	126
N18BL	WW24	182
N18BM	**EA50**	**000220**
N18BR	BE40	RK-221
N18CA	WW24	5
N18CC	C550	423
N18CC	**HS25**	**257030**
(N18CC)	C550	392
N18CG	F2TH	57
N18CG	**F9EX**	**228**
N18CG	LJ55	104
N18CJ	**GLF4**	**4141**
N18CQ	LJ55	104
N18CV	**C560**	**0159**
N18CV	LJ35	016
(N18DD)	C550	276
N18DF	**F9EX**	**158**
N18DY	LJ35	392
N18FE	FA20	233
N18FM	**C500**	**014**
N18FN	LJ35	105
N18FX	F900	152
N18G	FA50	52
N18G	HS25	257153
N18G	LJ24	186
N18G	LJ35	114
N18GA	C525	0216
N18GA	**C52B**	**0302**
N18GB	**C650**	**7048**
N18GU	**HS25**	**258522**
N18GW	WW24	187
N18GX	HS25	25281
N18GY	**C550**	**630**
N18GZ	GALX	018
N18HC	**C500**	**627**
N18HH	SBRL	306-18
N18HJ	C500	036
N18HJ	**C550**	**587**
N18HN	FA20	257
N18JE	**C56X**	**5020**
N18JF	LJ25	037
N18JL	WW24	51
N18JN	GLF2	154/28
N18JN	BE40	RJ-6
N18KE	MU30	A022SA
N18LB	GLF3	309
N18LH	LJ35	379
N18MJ	LJ25	218
N18MM	**C52C**	**0160**
N18MV	**F2TH**	**24**
N18MX	**FA10**	**117**
N18MZ	**F900**	**32**
N18N	GLF2	139/11
N18N	GLF2	61
N18N	GLF2	8
N18N	SBRL	306-12
N18N	SBRL	306-36
N18NA	**C550**	**580**
N18ND	C550	295
N18NK	GLF2	156/31
N18NK	GLF5	585
N18NM	LJ25	209
N18NM	LJ35	189
N18NY	**GLF4**	**4058**
(N18PV)	C650	0127
N18QA	**C525**	**0216**
N18RA	LJ25	280
(N18RA)	HFB3	1038
N18RF	CL61	5152
N18RF	F9EX	18
N18RF	GLF4	1092
N18RF	GLF5	628
N18RF	**PRM1**	**RB-127**
N18RN	C500	625
N18RN	C550	709
N18RN	GLF2	231
N18S	**GLF4**	**4059**
N18SD	LJ24	230
N18SF	WW24	374
N18SH	HS25	257157
N18SK	C650	7016
N18SK	**FA10**	**34**
(N18SK)	C560	0091
(N18SK)	C560	0098
(N18SL)	GLF3	304
N18ST	LJ35	316
N18T	MU30	A061SA
N18TA	LJ25	280
N18TD	C52A	0342
N18TD	GLF4	1224
N18TF	**C52A**	**0014**
N18TF	SBRL	380-15
N18TG	C525	0617
N18TM	**GLEX**	**9090**
N18TM	GLF3	351
N18TM	GLF4	1224
N18TZ	SBRL	380-15
N18UD	**F9EX**	**294**
N18UR	C500	011
"N18VS"	GLF5	564
N18WE	**C680**	**0317**
N18WE	LJ35	377
N18WF	GLEX	9057
N18WF	GLEX	9059
N18WF	GLEX	9128
N18WF	**GLEX**	**9215**
N18WF	GLF4	1175
N18WY	GLEX	9057
N18WZ	GLEX	9059
N18WZ	**GLEX**	**9338**
N18X	FA10	42
N18X	SBRL	306-137
N18XX	GLF2	227
N18ZD	LJ55	122
N18ZL	**GLF3**	**434**
N19AF	CS55	0026
N19AJ	C500	174
N19AJ	C550	188
N19AP	WW24	259
N19BC	FA20	40
N19BD	FA20	161
N19BG	SBRL	282-118
N19CA	**C510**	**0467**
N19CJ	C525	0019
N19CM	C500	169
N19CM	SBRL	306-10
N19CP	**C550**	**003**
N19CQ	HS25	25040
N19CU	HS25	25048
N19DD	C750	0095
N19DD	C750	0194
N19DD	CL30	20178
N19DD	CL60	1081
N19DD	HS25	258448
N19DU	HS25	258448
N19EE	WW24	172
N19ER	**C550**	**048**
N19ES	JSTR	5204
N19FM	LJ24	311
N19FN	LJ25	034
N19FR	C650	0062
N19FX	FA50	157
N19GA	MU30	A074SA
N19GB	C500	682
N19GE	**LJ25**	**322**
N19GL	LJ35	415
N19GR	**LJ45**	**470**
N19H	**GLF3**	**416**
N19H	GLF3	483
N19H	HS25	25261
N19HE	HS25	256004
N19HF	CL60	1001
N19HF	SBRL	282-100
N19HH	HS25	256004
(N19HL)	GALX	091
N19HM	LJ24	311
N19HU	C550	081
N19HU	**C560**	**0135**
N19J	C500	408
N19J	CL61	3057
N19JM	LJ25	250
N19KT	**C52A**	**0413**
N19LH	LJ35	279
N19LJ	LJ24	233
(N19LM)	LJ35	321
N19LT	LJ31	019
N19M	C500	165
N19M	C500	303
N19M	SBRL	306-56
N19ME	C560	0128
N19MJ	LJ24	351
N19MK	C560	0128
N19MK	C560	0395
N19MK	C56X	5093

N19MK	C680	0052
N19MK	**C680**	**0304**
N19MQ	C500	165
N19MQ	C680	0052
N19MS	SBRL	282-82
(N19MS)	SBRL	282-15
(N19MU)	C560	0395
N19MX	FA20	339
N19MZ	C56X	5093
N19NW	GLF2	19
N19NW	LJ35	019
N19PC	SBRL	380-2
N19PV	C560	0416
N19QC	**C650**	**0238**
N19R	**MU30**	**A043SA**
N19RP	C510	0467
N19RP	LJ35	363
N19SG	**E50P**	**50000241**
N19SV	**C650**	**7002**
N19TD	**FA20**	**416**
N19TJ	LJ24	258
N19TJ	LJ31	018
N19TX	FA20	296/507
N19U	C500	303
N19U	SBRL	306-56
N19UC	C650	0238
N19UC	CL30	20345
N19UC	WW24	232
N19UK	HS25	25081
N19UP	LJ31	237
N19VF	**F900**	**29**
(N19VF)	C560	0130
N19VP	C550	247
N19WG	**LJ35**	**031**
N19XP	HS25	258719
N19ZA	**CS55**	**0094**
N20AD	LJ25	287
N20AE	FA20	258
N20AF	FA20	120
N20AP	JSTR	5054/59
N20AT	C650	0109
N20AU	**C52B**	**0304**
N20AU	C550	550-1012
N20BD	**GALX**	**014**
N20BD	LJ24	008
N20BE	FA20	203
N20BG	LJ35	028
N20CC	C500	397
N20CC	C560	0027
N20CC	**C560**	**0467**
N20CF	C550	305
N20CF	**FA10**	**106**
N20CG	FA20	281/496
N20CL	C550	434
N20CL	**FA20**	**497**
N20CN	C550	305
N20CN	C560	0167
N20CR	LJ35	098
N20CR	**LJ55**	**097**
N20CS	CS55	0138
(N20CV)	BE40	RJ-20
N20CX	CL60	1051
N20CZ	C500	397
N20DA	**MS76**	**102**
N20DH	WW24	383
N20DK	LJ25	198
N20DK	LJ35	143
N20DL	LJ25	263
N20DL	LJ55	020
(N20EA)	C650	0007
N20EE	FA10	38
N20EG	GLEX	9038
N20EG	GLF4	1161
N20EP	LJ24	008
N20ES	FA10	120
N20ES	FA10	38
N20ES	SBRL	282-124
N20ET	FA10	38
N20FB	C550	287
N20FE	ASTR	067
N20FE	FA20	235
N20FE	FA20	272
N20FE	LJ45	366
N20FJ	**FA20**	**119/431**
N20FJ	FA20	244
N20FJ	FA20	272
N20FJ	FA20	289
N20FJ	FA20	341
N20FJ	FA20	355
N20FL	C500	169
N20FL	C525	0069
N20FL	BE40	RK-247
N20FM	C500	011
N20FM	C550	014
N20FM	FA20	321
N20FM	HS25	256055
N20FM	HS25	256058
N20FX	GLF2	120
N20FX	HS25	257121
N20G	CL60	1085
N20G	CL61	5136
N20G	**GLF4**	**4212**
N20G	SBRL	306-59
N20GB	JSTR	5202
N20GB	WW24	127
N20GH	FA20	7
N20GJ	LJ60	419
N20GP	C52A	0131
N20GP	**FA50**	**175**
N20GP	GLF2	90
(N20GP)	GLF2	63
N20GT	C500	579
N20GT	C550	391
N20GT	LJ24	283
N20GT	LJ25	349
(N20GT)	HS25	257009
N20GX	CL60	1085
N20GX	CL61	5136
N20GX	SBRL	306-59
N20H	**C680**	**0338**
N20H	GLF2	51
N20H	GLF4	1120
N20H	GLF5	522
N20HE	GLF2	51
N20HF	FA20	191
N20HJ	LJ25	024
N20HJ	LJ35	112
N20HN	GLF5	522
N20JA	LJ36	008
N20JK	C52A	0064
N20JM	FA20	258
N20JM	FA20	6
N20K	WW24	144
N20KH	WW24	223
N20KS	**EA50**	**000244**
(N20KW)	C500	557
(N20LL)	LJ31	018
N20LT	C560	0253
N20LT	FA20	21
N20LW	**FA10**	**48**
N20LW	GLF2	62
N20M	LJ24	094
N20MJ	LJ25	277
N20MK	C560	0210
N20MW	C650	0052
N20MY	FA20	136/439
N20NL	PRM1	RB-106
(N20NM)	CS55	0121
N20NW	LJ25	096
(N20NW)	WW24	300
N20NY	**FA20**	**61**
N20PA	MU30	A089SA
N20PJ	HS25	25205
N20PL	FA20	83
N20PL	GALX	063
N20PY	JSTR	5023
N20PY	LJ25	249
N20RD	C650	0036
N20RD	C650	0142
N20RD	LJ25	334
N20RF	C500	033
N20RF	C550	456
N20RG	HS25	25091
N20RG	HS25	25226
N20RM	**C500**	**389**
N20RT	C500	033
N20RT	LJ35	188
N20RU	C550	550-1012
N20RZ	**LJ25**	**024**
N20S	HS25	25250
N20S	HS25	257059
N20S	HS25	258042
N20S	JSTR	5126
N20S	LJ24	008
N20SB	C560	0422
N20SB	C56X	5114
N20SH	JSTR	5142
N20SK	HS25	257059
N20SM	C500	001
N20SM	C560	0353
N20SP	C500	398
N20SR	FA20	369
N20T	**E55P**	**50500044**
N20T	FA20	381/549
N20TA	LJ24	062
N20TF	JSTR	5016
(N20TV)	C550	142
N20TX	FA20	296/507
N20TZ	FA20	381/549
N20UA	**FA20**	**91**
N20UC	LJ36	031
N20UC	SBRL	465-46
N20UG	LJ36	031
N20VA	**PRM1**	**RB-31**
N20VF	FA20	347
N20VL	**C525**	**0069**
N20VP	C500	187
N20WE	C56X	5115
N20WK	**FA20**	**310**
N20WN	**FA20**	**370**
N20WP	C500	392
N20WP	FA10	23
N20XP	**LJ31**	**197**
N20XY	GLF2	116
N20XY	GLF2	56
N20XY	GLF3	412
N20XY	GLF4	1080
N20YA	FA20	24
(N20YC)	C560	0027
N20YL	**ASTR**	**076**
N20ZA	**HDJT**	**42000027**
N20ZC	**BE40**	**RK-86**
N21	JSTR	5001/53
N21AC	**LJ60**	**070**
N21AG	LJ24	329
(N21AG)	CS55	0003
N21AK	WW24	59
N21AM	GLF2	110
N21AM	GLF3	443
N21AR	HS25	25146
N21AX	GLF2	110
N21AX	LJ45	123
N21AX	LJ45	371
N21AX	**LJ45**	**443**
N21BC	WW24	51
N21BD	LJ45	188
N21BH	HS25	256007
N21BK	**LJ35**	**626**
N21BM	SBRL	306-64
N21BS	C500	389
N21CC	C500	099
N21CL	CL61	5126
N21CL	FA10	166
N21CV	**C560**	**0340**
N21CX	CL61	5014
N21CX	WW24	268
N21CZ	GLF4	1137
N21DA	C550	091
N21DA	LJ35	497
N21DB	FA10	65
N21DH	**GLF4**	**1021**
(N21DT)	FA20	6
N21DX	WW24	269
N21EG	CS55	0087
N21EH	C500	576
N21EH	C550	430
N21EK	**EA50**	**000133**
N21EK	FA10	8
N21EL	**HS25**	**258396**
N21EP	C500	412
N21ES	FA10	8
N21ES	HS25	25203
N21ET	FA10	8
N21FE	**CL30**	**20352**
N21FE	FA20	226
N21FE	FA20	399
N21FJ	FA20	299
N21FJ	**GLF4**	**1016**
N21FM	**PRM1**	**RB-273**
N21FN	LJ25	062
N21FR	**C56X**	**5550**
(N21FR)	C680	0016
N21FX	**HA4T**	**RC-62**
N21FX	HS25	HA-0105
N21FZ	HS25	HA-0105
N21GD	**C56X**	**5266**
N21GG	WW24	347
N21GL	LJ35	098
N21GN	GLF4	1284
N21GN	GLF5	578
N21GN	HS25	25115
N21H	**C560**	**0590**
N21HE	C750	0075
N21HE	F2EX	46
N21HJ	C500	444
N21HJ	**HDJT**	**42000014**
(N21HJ)	F9EX	22
N21HQ	C750	0075
N21HR	LJ25	339
N21HR	**WW24**	**335**
(N21JJ)	C560	0055
N21JM	FA20	6
N21JW	WW24	77
N21KP	GLF4	1139
N21KR	GLF4	1139
N21LG	**C560**	**0197**
N21LL	C650	0016
N21MA	C56X	5089
N21MF	HS25	25097
N21NA	C500	174
N21NA	LJ24	246
N21NA	LJ35	343
N21NC	FA20	161
N21NE	**GLF5**	**660**
N21NG	**C680**	**0308**
N21NG	LJ35	343
N21NL	FA20	393
N21NR	C680	0237
N21NR	GLF3	415
N21NT	HS25	257207
N21NV	**LJ60**	**268**
N21NW	**LJ25**	**351**
N21NY	CL61	5126
N21NY	GLF3	301
N21NY	GLF3	496
N21NY	HS25	257207
N21PF	SBRL	282-15
N21PJ	GLF3	315
N21RA	**C52A**	**0092**
N21RA	WW24	394
N21SA	HS25	256006
N21SB	**E50P**	**50000154**
N21SF	**WW24**	**214**
N21SH	JSTR	5148
N21SL	**C550**	**550-0877**
(N21SU)	HFB3	1055
N21SV	C550	016
N21SW	C550	016
N21TV	C500	078
N21U	LJ24	024
N21U	LJ24	152
N21UA	**C550**	**390**
N21VB	JSTR	5219
N21VB	LJ55	026
N21VC	**C525**	**0106**
N21VN	**LJ35**	**560**
N21W	FA20	205
N21WJ	C650	0141
(N21WS)	LJ35	410
N21XB	LJ24	198
N21XL	LJ24	198
N21XP	**PRM1**	**RB-9**
N21YP	EA50	000174
N21YR	**EA50**	**000174**
N22	GLF4	1042
N22	GLF5	501
N22AA	**C550**	**574**
N22AC	WW24	35
N22AF	**C560**	**0129**
N22AQ	CL61	5142
N22AX	LJ31	039
N22AX	**LJ45**	**101**
N22AZ	CL60	1060
N22B	LJ24	044
N22BG	WW24	410
N22BH	GLEX	9040
N22BH	HS25	256009
N22BJ	SBRL	282-105
N22BM	LJ24	341
N22BM	LJ36	032
N22BN	MU30	A023SA
N22BN	SBRL	282-36
N22BX	LJ35	129
N22BX	SBRL	306-138
(N22CA)	C500	004
N22CG	SBRL	306-88
N22CH	JSTR	5038
N22CH	SBRL	282-70
N22CH	SBRL	282-99
N22CH	WW24	7
N22CP	LJ35	178
N22CQ	LJ35	178
N22CS	F9EX	10
N22CS	SBRL	465-24
N22CX	GLF2	8
(N22CX)	MU30	A029SA
N22DE	HS25	25060
N22DH	HS25	25224
N22DL	FA20	14
N22DL	HS25	25060
N22DL	HS25	256051
N22DN	C500	127
N22EH	C500	185
N22EH	CS55	0074
N22EH	FA10	25
N22EH	HS25	25179
N22EH	HS25	257043
N22EH	SBRL	306-57
N22EL	**C500**	**416**
N22EM	**C510**	**0047**
N22ES	FA10	122
N22ES	JSTR	5161/43
N22FE	FA20	223
N22FH	C500	185
N22FM	C500	229
N22FM	**C550**	**461**
N22FS	FA20	339
N22FS	GLF2	22
N22FW	**F900**	**119**
N22FW	FA20	485
N22G	**G150**	**282**
N22G	LJ55	051
N22G	LJ55	105
N22G	LJ60	022
N22GA	C550	031
N22GA	HS25	258327
N22GE	HS25	25139
N22GH	LJ55	051
N22GM	LJ40	2038
N22GR	**C550**	**550-0892**
N22GU	**LJ60**	**022**
N22HC	FA20	14
N22HP	C550	299
N22HP	CS55	0103
N22HS	FA20	507
N22JG	C500	208
N22JM	C525	0194
N22JW	FA20	83
N22JW	SBRL	306-20
N22JW	SBRL	380-15
N22KH	HS25	257043
N22KW	C560	0256
N22KW	C56X	5062
N22LC	C560	0521
N22LC	F9EX	136
N22LH	C500	319
(N22LL)	WW24	148
N22LP	C560	0083
N22LQ	C560	0521
(N22LQ)	F9EX	136
N22LX	C52A	0109
N22LX	**C52A**	**0477**
N22LZ	WW24	236
N22MA	SBRL	306-2
N22MB	C500	337
N22MH	LJ24	259
N22MJ	LJ24	329
N22MJ	LJ35	135
(N22ML)	LJ24	259
N22MS	LJ35	209
N22MV	SBRL	282-68
N22MY	SBRL	282-68
N22MY	SBRL	306-117
N22NB	SBRL	380-56
(N22NB)	SBRL	282-106
N22NF	**HS25**	**258145**
N22NG	C750	0039
N22NG	C750	0204
(N22NG)	C750	0041
N22NJ	**EA50**	**000022**
N22NJ	LJ25	097
N22NM	LJ24	341
N22NT	SBRL	380-21
N22PC	**C550**	**583**
(N22PQ)	C550	583
N22QF	LJ60	225
N22RB	JSTR	5093
N22RD	WW24	165
N22RD	**WW24**	**203**
N22RD	WW24	99
N22RG	C550	639
N22RG	C560	0235
N22RG	C650	7070
N22RG	**C750**	**0031**
N22RJ	C550	074
N22RT	WW24	99
N22SD	C500	578
N22SF	CL64	5589
N22SF	**CL65**	**5891**
N22SF	LJ31	126
N22SF	LJ35	168
N22SF	LJ35	674
N22SF	LJ60	225
N22SM	**HS25**	**258655**
N22SN	LJ35	674
N22ST	**G150**	**251**
N22SY	LJ35	168
N22T	C550	407
N22T	F900	119
N22T	FA50	53
N22T	GLF6	6044
N22T	**GLF6**	**6151**
N22TP	C500	371
N22TP	SBRL	282-60
N22TS	C500	473
N22TS	**F2TH**	**179**
N22TY	C500	473
N22TZ	FA50	53
(N22TZ)	C550	407
N22UB	**C52C**	**0182**
N22UF	LJ31	126
N22UL	CS55	0039
N22UP	HS25	259040
N22VK	**PRM1**	**RB-140**
N22VS	**HS25**	**HA-0047**
N22WJ	FA20	113
N22WJ	MU30	A074SA
N22WJ	BE40	RJ-44
N22YP	FA50	53
(N22YP)	C560	0109A
N23A	FA20	368
N23A	GLF2	153
N23A	GLF3	430
N23A	**LJ35**	**233**
N23AC	FA50	47
N23AC	GLF4	1047
N23AC	WW24	210
N23AC	WW24	341
N23AH	GLF2	137
N23AJ	**C500**	**393**
N23AJ	C550	550-1128
N23AJ	LJ24	053
N23AM	LJ24	247
N23AM	LJ25	223
N23AM	LJ25	308
N23AN	**HS25**	**258223**
N23AN	LJ24	074
N23AQ	FA50	47
N23AQ	WW24	341
N23AX	LJ31	039
N23AZ	GLF2	183
N23BH	HS25	256010
N23BJ	CL61	3012
N23BJ	F900	107
N23BJ	HS25	257199
N23BN	CL61	3012
N23BV	**C52B**	**0260**
N23BX	SBRL	465-61
N23BY	LJ24	009
N23CH	LJ24	006
N23CJ	**HS25**	**25152**
N23DB	LJ25	086
N23DS	FA10	117
N23DS	SBRL	306-89
N23EA	HA4T	RC-21
(N23ED)	FA10	11
N23EH	C500	576
N23EJ	HS25	257199
N23ES	FA10	11
N23ES	FA10	123
N23ET	FA10	11
N23ET	GLF3	434
N23FE	FA20	224
N23FE	JSTR	5142
N23FF	WW24	83

N23FJ	F2TH	23
N23FK	**EA50**	**000166**
N23FM	**FA50**	**296**
N23FN	LJ25	040
(N23FN)	LJ25	018
(N23FR)	FA20	132
N23G	LJ36	026
N23G	LJ55	012
N23G	SBRL	282-31
N23G	SBRL	370-5
N23HB	LJ35	080
N23HB	LJ55	046
N23HD	**PRM1**	**RB-272**
N23HM	LJ25	262
N23JC	LJ24	290
N23KG	C525	0326
N23KL	HS25	25080
N23LM	C56X	5062
N23LT	**F2EX**	**27**
N23M	GLF2	105
N23M	GLF4	1022
N23M	GLF5	579
N23M	JSTR	5103
N23MJ	LJ24	281
N23MU	GLF4	1022
N23ND	C500	345
N23ND	C550	295
N23ND	FA20	48
N23NG	C56X	5133
N23NG	**C680**	**0527**
N23NM	CS55	0121
N23NP	LJ31	123
(N23NQ)	FA20	48
N23NS	C560	0215
N23PJ	EA50	000065
N23PL	FA20	139
N23PZ	LJ60	197
N23RT	HS25	257061
N23RZ	**LJ25**	**164**
N23SB	CL61	5074
N23SB	HS25	257016
N23SB	JSTR	5227
N23SG	LJ24	233
N23SJ	WW24	289
(N23SJ)	FA20	485
N23SK	HS25	257016
(N23SK)	GLF3	434
(N23SN)	HS25	257016
N23SP	**PRM1**	**RB-124**
N23SQ	LJ24	233
N23SR	LJ60	229
N23ST	MS76	050
N23SY	FA50	185
N23SY	GLF4	1086
N23TA	LJ25	122
N23TC	LJ24	074
N23TJ	ASTR	023
N23TJ	**FA10**	**89**
N23TJ	LJ24	033
(N23TZ)	C500	473
N23UB	C560	0220
N23UD	C560	0220
N23UD	C560	0442
N23UP	LJ31	237
N23VA	**EA50**	**000242**
N23VG	LJ31	123
N23VG	LJ35	379
N23VK	**C500**	**555**
N23VP	FA10	91
N23W	C500	182
N23W	C550	352
N23W	GLF2	116
N23W	LJ25	334
N23WA	PRM1	RB-18
N23WJ	FA10	123
N23WK	C500	191
N23Y	WW24	155
N23YC	**C550**	**550-0923**
N23YZ	C500	473
N23YZ	C560	0638
N24AJ	**C500**	**221**
N24AJ	C550	423
N24AJ	LJ24	151
N24AJ	LJ24	178
N24AX	LJ45	375
N24BA	LJ24	100
N24BA	BE40	RJ-19
N24BC	C525	0651
N24BH	HS25	256011
N24BS	LJ25	022
N24CH	HS25	25198
(N24CH)	C500	655
N24CJ	C525	0004
N24CJ	C550	354
N24CK	LJ24	258
N24CK	LJ35	339
N24CK	LJ55	004
N24DB	WW24	294
N24DS	GLF2	181
N24DS	WW24	258
(N24DZ)	LJ24	258
N24E	**C550**	**651**
(N24EA)	HA4T	RC-32
(N24EA)	LJ24	259
(N24EE)	GLF4	1325
N24EP	C550	597
N24EP	**C56X**	**5213**
N24EP	LJ25	244
N24ET	LJ24	050
N24ET	LJ24	148
N24EV	FA20	227
N24FE	**CL30**	**20355**
N24FE	FA20	220
N24FF	LJ24	034
N24FJ	**F900**	**143**
N24FJ	WW24	312
N24FN	LJ25	045
(N24FN)	LJ35	005
(N24FR)	FA20	151
N24FU	LJ24	197
N24FW	**LJ24**	**329**
N24G	**G150**	**289**
N24G	LJ55	062
N24G	LJ60	018
N24G	SBRL	306-14
N24G	SBRL	465-5
N24GA	GLF3	374
N24GA	LJ35	024
N24GB	SBRL	306-14
N24GF	**C560**	**0639**
N24GJ	LJ24	101
N24GU	**LJ60**	**018**
N24HD	MU30	A007SA
N24HX	**C560**	**0165**
N24JD	C560	0140
N24JG	FA20	484
N24JG	HS25	258084
N24JG	HS25	258170
N24JG	LJ35	477
N24JK	CL60	1070
N24JK	CL61	5118
N24JK	LJ25	261
N24JK	LJ35	339
N24JK	LJ55	004
N24JR	**GLF4**	**1030**
N24JZ	**LJ24**	**213**
N24KE	WW24	266
N24KF	LJ24	161
N24KL	**WW24**	**237**
N24KT	C650	0132
N24KT	**C650**	**7052**
N24KT	LJ24	161
N24KT	WW24	266
N24KW	LJ25	297
N24LG	**LJ24**	**011**
N24LT	LJ25	063
N24LW	LJ24	136
N24MJ	LJ35	216
N24MN	WW24	414
N24MW	LJ24	043
N24NB	C650	7052
N24NG	C56X	5124
N24NJ	LJ24	050
(N24NP)	LJ24	200
N24NV	**LJ55**	**060**
N24NW	**LJ35**	**037**
N24PA	C500	236
N24PF	CS55	0026
N24PH	C56X	5049
N24PH	**C56X**	**5571**
N24PH	CS55	0026
N24PJ	LJ24	291
(N24PP)	WW24	235
N24PR	ASTR	026
N24PR	**C680**	**0340**
N24PT	LJ36	048
(N24PT)	C550	211
N24PY	C56X	5049
N24QA	**C560**	**0762**
N24QF	C550	550-0963
N24QT	C550	550-0963
N24QT	C560	0762
N24QT	**LJ40**	**2121**
(N24QT)	C560	0498
N24RF	C550	456
N24RF	SBRL	465-28
N24RH	WW24	214
(N24RH)	LJ55	110
N24RP	HS25	258033
N24RZ	LJ25	159
N24S	C500	230
N24S	HS25	25250
N24S	**LJ24**	**297**
N24SA	LJ24	025
N24SA	**LJ24**	**117**
N24SB	HS25	258049
N24SB	WW24	369
N24SM	**HS25**	**258567**
N24SP	HS25	258049
N24SR	LJ60	234
N24SR	WW24	332
N24TA	LJ25	155
N24TC	LJ24	275
N24TE	LJ24	246
(N24TE)	WW24	195
N24TH	**FA7X**	**203**
N24TH	GLF4	1475
N24TH	GLF4	4071
(N24TJ)	GLF3	404
N24TK	**LJ24**	**268**
N24TK	LJ24	290
"N24TK"	SBRL	306-128
(N24TR)	C550	203
N24TW	FA20	80
N24UB	C560	0221
N24UD	C560	0221
N24UD	C560	0443
N24UD	**C56X**	**5147**
N24UG	JSTR	5108
N24UM	C650	0160
N24VB	C650	0121
N24VH	WW24	391
N24VM	LJ24	051
N24VP	LJ40	2069
N24VP	LJ40	2081
N24WF	LJ24	143
N24WW	WW24	391
N24WX	LJ24	101
N24XC	GLF4	4032
N24XP	**BE40**	**RK-424**
N24XR	LJ24	150
N24XR	LJ24	283
N24YA	LJ24	087
N24YA	LJ24	206
N24YD	PRM1	RB-91
N24YE	LJ24	087
N24YP	PRM1	RB-91
N24YP	PRM1	RB-95
N24YP	PRM1	RB-99
N24YR	PRM1	RB-99
N24YS	**GLF2**	**16/13**
N24YY	C510	0010
N24ZD	**ASTR**	**073**
N25	C500	084
N25AG	ASTR	012
N25AG	JSTR	5202
N25AM	**LJ25**	**321**
N25AN	LJ35	259
N25AQ	**C550**	**174**
N25AT	SBRL	380-21
N25AW	HS25	25095
N25BB	HS25	258189
N25BB	**LJ31**	**102**
N25BE	HS25	256013
N25BF	GLF2	114
N25BH	GLF2	237/43
N25BH	HS25	256013
N25BH	SBRL	380-47
N25BN	BE40	RJ-7
N25BR	BE40	RJ-57
N25BX	SBRL	380-47
N25CJ	C500	325
N25CJ	C500	625
N25CJ	C525	0002
N25CK	C500	250
N25CK	C52B	0079
N25CK	**C56X**	**6054**
N25CL	LJ36	009
N25CP	FA20	121
N25CP	**GLF5**	**527**
N25CS	C500	219
N25CU	**BE40**	**RK-361**
N25CV	C560	0298
N25CV	LJ24	276
N25CY	**LJ25**	**272**
N25CY	LJ25	302
N25CY	LJ25	317
N25CZ	LJ25	301
N25DB	FA20	91
N25DD	C500	475
N25DY	CS55	0076
(N25EA)	C525	0028
N25EC	**LJ25**	**026**
N25EG	**C650**	**0167**
N25EL	LJ35	419
N25EV	FA20	229
N25FA	LJ25	251
N25FE	FA20	221
N25FF	FA10	123
N25FJ	F2TH	25
N25FM	**LJ25**	**063**
N25FN	LJ25	015
N25FN	LJ25	352
(N25FR)	FA20	20
N25FS	**C550**	**550-0823**
N25FS	LJ35	198
N25GG	CL64	5536
(N25GG)	CL61	5050
N25GJ	GLF2	97
N25GJ	LJ25	015
N25GJ	LJ25	255
N25GL	LJ25	362
N25GT	C500	572
N25GV	**GLF5**	**591**
N25GV	GLF5	674
(N25GV)	GLF5	5072
N25GW	LJ24	258
N25GW	LJ28	28-003
N25GZ	**CS55**	**0011**
N25HA	HS25	HA-0028
N25HA	LJ25	141
N25HC	C500	034
N25HF	LJ25	295
N25HF	**LJ25**	**367**
N25HJ	**HDJT**	**42000024**
N25HS	C500	592
N25HU	**FA20**	**491**
N25HV	C550	550-0825
N25JD	LJ25	114
N25JM	FA50	124
N25JM	GLF2	69
N25JT	HS25	25053
(N25JX)	LJ25	006
N25KC	LJ25	147
N25KL	SBRL	465-69
N25KV	LJ25	176
N25LA	HS25	25108
(N25LG)	LJ25	042
N25LJ	LJ24	123
N25LJ	LJ24	236
(N25LP)	LJ25	150
N25LZ	**C52A**	**0177**
N25MB	C500	453
N25MB	C525	0041
N25MB	**C52A**	**0010**
N25MB	F900	163
N25MB	FA50	184
N25MC	FA10	180
N25MC	**PRM1**	**RB-49**
N25MD	**LJ25**	**054**
N25ME	FA50	184
N25ME	LJ25	062
N25MF	SBRL	465-25
N25MH	C500	404
N25MJ	HS25	25142
N25MJ	LJ35	335
N25MJ	LJ35	452
N25MK	C550	458
N25MK	HS25	257056
N25MR	LJ25	129
N25MT	GLF3	359
N25MT	**LJ25**	**129**
N25MX	C525	0220
N25MX	**LJ60**	**012**
N25N	**ASTR**	**013**
N25NB	LJ25	107
N25NB	**LJ25**	**326**
N25NG	C56X	5250
N25NH	C550	115
N25NM	LJ25	007
N25NM	LJ25	347
N25NP	LJ25	107
N25NY	**LJ25**	**304**
N25PA	C500	250
N25PJ	**LJ25**	**111**
N25PK	LJ36	039
N25PL	LJ25	130
N25PM	HS25	25114
N25PT	LJ25	356
N25PW	**LJ25**	**342**
N25QA	C560	0613
N25QF	C550	584
N25QS	HA4T	RC-28
N25QT	C550	584
N25QT	C560	0613
N25QT	**LJ40**	**2131**
N25RE	LJ25	163
N25RE	LJ25	227
N25RE	WW24	248
(N25RE)	LJ25	041
N25RF	LJ35	227
N25RJ	LJ24	237
N25S	FA20	453
N25SB	CL61	5115
N25SB	GLF3	431
N25SJ	FA50	186
N25SJ	BE40	RK-374
N25SR	CL60	1075
N25SR	SBRL	465-14
N25ST	**FA10**	**198**
N25TA	LJ24	237
N25TA	LJ25	196
N25TA	LJ25	241
N25TB	LJ25	241
N25TE	LJ25	087
N25TG	**C650**	**0013**
N25TK	LJ25	100
N25TQ	LJ40	2131
N25TX	FA20	24
(N25TX)	JSTR	5029/38
N25TZ	LJ25	364
N25UB	FA50	248
N25UB	**LJ40**	**2072**
N25UD	F9EX	29
N25UD	FA50	248
N25UG	GLF2	205
N25UG	SBRL	465-11
N25UJ	LJ25	215
N25UT	C500	049
N25V	**CL60**	**1015**
N25VC	**SBRL**	**465-15**
N25VG	GLF4	1018
(N25VJ)	LJ25	039
N25VZ	LJ24	258
N25W	HS25	258221
N25W	HS25	258626
N25W	BE40	RJ-15
N25WA	JSTR	5033/56
N25WA	BE40	RJ-15
N25WG	FA20	327
N25WJ	**LJ25**	**105**
(N25WL)	LJ25	220
N25WN	HS25	258221
N25WX	HS25	258359
N25WZ	JSTR	5204
N25XA	**LJ25**	**270**
N25XL	C56X	5536
N25XP	HS25	258403
N25XP	BE40	RK-247
(N25XR)	LJ25	235
N25ZC	SBRL	465-30
N25ZG	**CL64**	**5536**
(N25ZG)	SBRL	465-30
N25ZW	LJ24	236
N26	C560	0113
(N26AA)	C500	678
N26AP	**C550**	**550-0824**
N26AT	LJ25	130
N26BA	LJ24	134
N26BH	HS25	256014
N26CB	C525	0117
N26CB	C550	550-0861
N26CB	**C550**	**550-1001**
N26CP	FA10	151
N26CS	PRM1	RB-291
N26CT	C550	345
N26CV	C550	550-0861
N26DA	LJ35	086
(N26DA)	C550	087
N26DE	**CL30**	**20370**
N26DK	C525	0257
N26DK	PRM1	RB-226
N26DS	WW24	189
N26DV	C510	0420
N26DV	**C525**	**0898**
(N26DV)	C525	0414
N26DY	C560	0110
N26EN	FA10	49
N26ES	FA10	171
N26EV	FA20	230
N26FA	CL30	20026
(N26FA)	MU30	A026SA
N26FE	**CL30**	**20358**
N26FE	FA20	204
N26FN	LJ25	134
N26FN	**LJ36**	**011**
N26GB	LJ35	131
N26GD	LJ35	131
N26GL	JSTR	5114/18
N26GL	LJ36	001
N26GP	**LJ35**	**157**
(N26GV)	GLF5	674
N26GW	WW24	272
N26H	HS25	257143
(N26HA)	C500	627
N26HC	C500	174
N26HG	**C550**	**614**
N26HH	**C550**	**346**
N26JJ	CS55	0141
N26JP	BE40	RK-74
N26KL	WW24	409
N26L	GLF2	165/37
N26L	GLF2	193
N26L	GLF2	36/3
N26L	GLF3	387
N26LA	FA20	274
N26LA	GLF2	36/3
N26LB	F900	10
N26LB	F900	51
N26LB	FA50	7
N26LB	GLF2	168
N26LB	GLF4	1008
N26LC	C500	654
N26LC	LJ31	006
N26LT	GLF2	193
N26ME	**HS25**	**257165**
N26MJ	**C750**	**0139**
N26MJ	JSTR	5101/15
N26MJ	LJ24	202
N26MJ	LJ36	011
(N26MW)	C500	485
N26NJ	**F2TH**	**139**
N26NS	C500	340
N26PA	C500	254
N26PA	BE40	RK-256
N26QB	**C525**	**0117**
N26QL	**C560**	**0498**
N26QT	C560	0498
N26QT	LJ45	402
N26QT	**LJ45**	**481**
(N26RG)	C650	0054
N26RL	**C525**	**0207**
N26S	JSTR	5128/16
N26SC	C550	345
N26SC	**HS25**	**257117**
N26SC	SBRL	282-104
N26SC	SBRL	306-140
N26SD	C650	0099
N26SE	SBRL	282-104
N26SH	E50P	50000009
N26SJ	C56X	5259
N26SL	GLF4	1053
N26SQ	SBRL	306-140
N26SW	C525	0415
N26T	**C550**	**550-1075**
N26T	HS25	25037
N26T	WW24	293
N26T	WW24	418
N26TJ	FA10	103
N26TJ	WW24	204
(N26TJ)	SBRL	370-7
N26TL	HS25	25037
N26TN	**WW24**	**418**
N26TR	JSTR	5115/39
N26TV	WW24	293

N26TZ	**WW24**	**293**
N26VB	WW24	410
N26VF	WW24	410
N26VG	FA20	108/430
N26VM	LJ24	236
N26WB	GLF2	136
N26WD	C500	282
N26WF	**C510**	**0381**
N26WJ	FA10	126
N26WJ	**FA50**	**181**
(N26WJ)	HS25	25037
(N26WK)	CL64	5549
N26WP	**FA50**	**312**
N26WP	GLF2	24
N26XL	**C56X**	**6086**
N26XP	**HS25**	**HA-0152**
N26XP	BE40	RK-280
N26XP	BE40	RK-426
N26ZZ	GLEX	9289
N27	C560	0109
(N27)	LJ31	063
N27AC	FA10	151
N27AC	FA20	355
N27AJ	**FA10**	**31**
N27AL	LJ31	175
N27AT	WW24	176
N27AX	LJ24	323
N27AX	LJ35	662
N27AY	CL65	5707
N27B	CS55	0036
N27BA	C550	168
N27BD	WW24	53
N27BH	ASTR	012
N27BH	CL60	1051
N27BH	CL60	1073
N27BH	HS25	256016
N27BH	HS25	257206
N27BJ	**LJ24**	**227**
N27BL	LJ35	163
N27C	FA10	31
N27C	SBRL	282-57
N27CD	GLF4	1136
N27CJ	C525	0301
N27CJ	**C525**	**0311**
N27CJ	C52A	0124
N27DA	FA10	17
N27DA	SBRL	282-28
N27DD	LJ55	015
N27EA	CS55	0027
N27EV	FA20	232
N27EW	C52B	0308
(N27FB)	C525	0242
N27FE	FA20	207
N27FJ	F2TH	27
N27FL	**HS25**	**258426**
N27FN	LJ25	062
N27FP	CS55	0027
N27FW	JSTR	5083/49
N27GD	CS55	0052
(N27GW)	LJ25	234
N27HF	LJ35	251
N27JJ	BE40	RK-59
N27K	LJ25	294
N27KG	LJ25	335
N27KG	LJ25	357
N27KG	LJ35	413
N27KG	SBRL	282-77
N27KL	HS25	257125
N27L	**C500**	**038**
N27LJ	**LJ60**	**413**
N27LT	SBRL	380-59
N27MD	WW24	102
N27MH	C550	168
N27MH	CS55	0006
N27MJ	LJ24	249
N27MJ	LJ25	050
N27MJ	LJ36	027
N27MX	CL30	20014
N27NB	LJ35	251
N27NR	LJ35	481
N27PA	C500	249
N27R	F2TH	5
N27R	FA20	303
N27R	FA20	356
N27R	GLF3	452
N27R	JSTR	5086/44
N27RC	HS25	25038
N27RC	JSTR	5086/44
N27RL	JSTR	5086/44
N27RX	FA20	356
N27SD	C560	0147
N27SD	C650	0134
N27SD	CS55	0052
N27SF	**C500**	**064**
(N27SJ)	WW24	270
N27SL	**GLF2**	**84**
(N27TA)	WW24	231
N27TB	**CS55**	**0082**
(N27TB)	CS55	0079
N27TJ	LJ35	277
N27TJ	MU30	A027SA
N27TS	C500	541
N27TS	C650	0006
N27TS	SBRL	380-48
N27TT	LJ35	122
N27TZ	**WW24**	**213**
N27U	C550	344
N27UB	C52B	0225
N27UM	**HS25**	**25249**
N27VP	C750	0027
N27VQ	**C52A**	**0221**
N27WP	**E50P**	**50000058**
N27WP	F2TH	35
N27WW	**C500**	**359**
N27WW	C560	0074
N27X	CL64	5319
N27X	WW24	127
N27XL	C56X	5010
N27XL	**C56X**	**6096**
N27XP	**BE40**	**RK-266**
N27YA	**GLF4**	**4153**
N27ZH	LJ60	187
N28..B	BE40	RK-14
N28AA	LJ25	037
N28AR	**C500**	**044**
N28AT	LJ24	227
N28AY	LJ28	28-004
N28BG	LJ35	258
N28BH	HS25	256018
N28BK	LJ24	175
N28BP	LJ24	065A
N28BP	LJ25	086
N28BP	LJ25	302
(N28BP)	LJ25	237
(N28BR)	LJ24	065A
N28C	FA20	404
(N28CC)	LJ25	234
N28CK	**C525**	**0210**
N28CK	LJ25	045
N28CR	LJ35	252
N28DL	LJ24	184
N28DM	C525	0151
N28DM	C52A	0210
N28DM	**C52B**	**0142**
(N28ET)	C560	0320
(N28EX)	F2EX	28
N28FE	**CL30**	**20361**
N28FE	FA20	209
N28FM	MU30	A026SA
(N28FM)	C525	0633
N28FN	LJ25	005
N28FR	C52B	0153
N28GA	C525	0215
N28GA	C52B	0293
N28GA	C550	283
N28GC	C500	449
N28GE	HS25	25267
N28GG	HS25	257135
N28GP	HS25	25267
N28GP	HS25	257135
N28GP	**HS25**	**258489**
(N28GZ)	C550	200
N28HH	SBRL	306-125
N28JG	C500	591
N28KA	CL61	5174
N28KB	FA50	148
N28KV	LJ25	176
N28LA	LJ25	029
N28LL	GLF6	6042
N28LR	LJ28	28-003
N28M	HS25	25038
N28MH	C52A	0161
N28MH	**C52B**	**0110**
N28MJ	LJ25	286
N28MJ	LJ35	224
(N28MM)	C550	187
(N28MM)	HS25	25038
N28NF	ASTR	067
N28NH	C52A	0161
N28NP	ASTR	067
N28NP	**ASTR**	**118**
(N28NR)	ASTR	067
N28PA	C500	267
N28PH	**FA50**	**194**
N28PT	**C525**	**0017**
N28QA	**C525**	**0215**
N28QQ	GLF3	379
N28QT	**LJ45**	**431**
N28R	**F2TH**	
N28R	**GLF3**	**490**
N28RC	C550	302
N28RC	C550	650
N28RF	C550	271
N28RK	FA20	206
(N28RW)	LJ25	285
N28S	C550	225
N28S	C650	0143
N28SJ	**G280**	**2074**
N28SP	**C550**	**550-1125**
N28ST	LJ24	013
N28SW	C525	0424
N28TJ	WW24	237
N28TP	SBRL	282-132
N28TS	**HS25**	**256009**
N28TX	**C650**	**7007**
N28U	FA20	484
(N28U)	C500	054
N28UA	CL61	5042
N28US	**FA50**	**242**
N28VL	**F9EX**	**213**
N28VM	SBRL	306-123
N28VM	**BE40**	**RK-389**
N28WE	C680	0238
N28WL	**C500**	**077**
N28WW	WW24	368
N28XL	C56X	5248
N28XP	BE40	RK-428
N28YC	GLF3	455
N28ZD	**GLEX**	**9191**
N28ZF	**HS25**	**258195**
(N29AA)	FA10	31
N29AC	C500	635
N29AP	WW24	258
N29AU	C650	0145
N29AU	CS55	0019
N29B	C550	152
N29B	**HS25**	**258518**
N29BF	LJ24	010
N29BH	HS25	256020
N29CA	C500	492
N29CA	LJ24	215
N29CL	WW24	197
N29CL	**WW24**	**404**
N29CR	HS25	25098
N29DJ	LJ55	029
N29EA	CS55	0006
N29EB	C500	276
N29ET	C525	0601
N29EW	LJ25	373
N29FA	C550	379
N29FE	FA20	210
N29FN	LJ25	018
N29G	C550	379
N29GD	HS25	257069
N29GH	WW24	197
N29GP	HS25	257069
N29GP	HS25	258344
N29GP	**HS25**	**HA-0211**
N29GS	**E55P**	**50500240**
N29GY	GLF4	1016
N29GZ	**HS25**	**258344**
N29HE	C500	604
N29KD	**LJ31**	**139**
N29LA	LJ24	108
N29LB	WW24	61
N29LJ	**LJ60**	**240**
N29LP	WW24	280
N29LP	WW24	61
N29MR	C52A	0206
N29MR	**EA50**	**000249**
(N29MW)	C500	166
N29NW	LJ55	029
N29PB	SBRL	306-18
N29PC	WW24	263
N29PF	C550	696
N29QC	**C560**	**0675**
N29RE	LJ31	106
N29RE	LJ31	145
N29RE	**LJ40**	**2069**
N29RE	LJ45	210
(N29RE)	LJ31	156
N29RN	LJ40	2069
N29RP	HS25	257088
N29S	GLF3	391
N29S	SBRL	306-49
N29S	SBRL	465-65
N29SM	LJ31	194
N29SM	LJ45	214
N29SN	**LJ31**	**194**
(N29SS)	EA50	000264
N29SX	SBRL	306-49
N29SZ	SBRL	465-65
N29TC	C550	143
(N29TC)	JSTR	5208
N29TE	FA20	202
(N29TG)	C550	143
N29TS	LJ25	198
(N29UC)	ASTR	041
N29UF	C500	640
(N29UF)	WW24	201
N29WE	C560	0185
N29WE	C560	0512
N29WE	**C680**	**0042**
N29WF	C560	0185
N29WP	JSTR	5157
N29WS	C550	262
N29X	CS55	0096
N29XA	CS55	0096
N29XP	BE40	RK-429
N29YY	FA50	95
N29ZE	LJ45	210
N29ZR	**C56X**	**5130**
N30AB	LJ45	015
N30AB	WW24	235
N30AD	**C52A**	**0165**
N30AD	LJ25	314
N30AD	WW24	143
(N30AD)	FA20	225/472
N30AF	**C650**	**0049**
N30AF	LJ55	043
N30AF	SBRL	282-113
(N30AF)	C500	559
N30AH	GLF3	392
N30AJ	ASTR	019
N30AJ	ASTR	047
N30AJ	F2TH	115
(N30AJ)	PRM1	RB-118
N30AN	WW24	173
N30AP	LJ25	080
N30AP	LJ25	101
N30AQ	**C525**	**0320**
N30AV	**C550**	**026**
N30AV	HFB3	1055
(N30B)	GLF2	228
N30BE	SBRL	282-14
N30BK	C500	666
N30BP	**C525**	**0816**
N30BP	LJ24	017
N30BZ	CL30	20030
N30CC	FA20	11
N30CC	SBRL	306-81
N30CJ	**C52B**	**0451**
N30CJ	C650	0019
(N30CJ)	C650	0029
N30CN	FA10	161
N30CQ	FA20	11
N30CX	CS55	0007
N30CZ	C550	376
N30DH	LJ24	224
N30DH	LJ35	199
N30DK	LJ25	154
N30DK	LJ35	345
N30EF	HS25	25084
N30EH	LJ24	211
N30EJ	C550	113
N30EM	LJ24	338
(N30EV)	SBRL	370-6
N30F	HS25	25153
N30F	HS25	258035
(N30F)	C550	220
N30FD	HS25	25153
N30FE	FA20	211
N30FE	FA50	271
N30FJ	C550	113
N30FJ	FA10	30
N30FL	LJ24	253
N30FN	LJ35	075
N30FT	**FA20**	**330**
N30FT	FA20	377/548
N30FT	FA50	271
N30FW	GLF2	210
N30GB	SBRL	380-1
N30GC	**ASTR**	**065**
N30GD	**GLF4**	**1228**
N30GD	LJ35	352
N30GF	WW24	401
N30GJ	LJ35	320
N30GJ	LJ60	204
N30GJ	**LJ60**	**419**
N30GL	LJ35	395
N30GL	LJ55	076
N30GR	**C550**	**656**
N30GZ	**SJ30**	**010**
N30HD	**C52A**	**0062**
N30HD	MU30	A005SA
N30HE	**GLF2**	**51**
N30HJ	LJ35	226
N30JC	FA50	349
N30JD	C550	218
N30JE	**GLF4**	**1390**
(N30JH)	FA10	19
N30JM	FA10	19
N30JM	FA20	24
N30JM	WW24	173
N30JN	C500	272
N30LB	F9EX	8
N30LF	**F2TH**	**602**
N30LH	**GLF4**	**1207**
N30LJ	LJ25	043
N30LJ	LJ25	209
N30LJ	LJ31	024
N30LJ	LJ31	027
N30LM	LJ24	338
N30LM	LJ25	250
N30LS	WW24	125
N30LX	**GLF3**	**438**
N30LX	LJ31	096
N30MN	**E55P**	**50500314**
N30MR	**WW24**	**225**
(N30N)	FA50	55
N30NF	**C510**	**0254**
N30NM	C650	0120
N30NS	**C525**	**0835**
N30NS	WW24	329
N30P	LJ25	082
N30PA	**LJ35**	**245**
N30PC	C560	0090
N30PC	LJ45	231
N30PC	LJ45	235
N30PC	**LJ45**	**417**
N30PD	WW24	347
N30PF	LJ45	231
(N30PN)	SBRL	282-14
N30PP	HS25	25207
N30PQ	C560	0090
N30PQ	LJ45	235
N30PR	**GLF2**	**35**
N30PR	HS25	25207
N30PR	HS25	257065
N30PS	LJ25	030
N30PY	SBRL	306-7
N30RE	C500	491
N30RJ	WW24	7
N30RL	C500	491
N30RL	**C550**	**653**
N30RP	GLF2	113
N30RP	GLF3	321
N30RP	JSTR	5131
N30SA	C550	341
N30SA	LJ35	479
N30SB	C500	272
N30SC	LJ24	039
N30SF	LJ45	175
(N30SF)	BE40	RK-79
N30SJ	SJ30	001
N30SJ	SJ30	003
N30SJ	**SJ30**	**006**
N30ST	**C52A**	**0497**
N30TB	FA10	171
N30TC	SBRL	306-33
N30TH	F2TH	66
N30TH	FA10	138
N30TH	FA10	201
N30TH	FA10	74
N30TH	FA50	212
N30TK	LJ31	096
N30TK	LJ55	091
N30TK	**WW24**	**374**
(N30TK)	LJ35	030
N30TL	LJ45	081
(N30TN)	FA10	193
N30TP	LJ25	111
N30TT	LJ25	020
N30TV	C560	0358
N30UC	C550	103
N30UD	C52B	0131
N30VP	**HS25**	**HA-0093**
N30VR	**C525**	**0481**
N30W	LJ25	214
N30W	LJ35	488
N30W	LJ60	065
N30W	SBRL	282-5
N30W	SBRL	306-10
N30WE	C550	604
(N30WJ)	CL64	5628
N30WR	**GLF3**	**380**
N30WY	LJ35	488
N30XC	CL30	20228
N30XL	**BE40**	**RK-5**
N30XP	BE40	RK-430
N30XX	C550	195
N30Y	JSTR	5227
N30YM	WW24	213
N31AA	LJ25	041
N31AD	**C550**	**550-1032**
N31AJ	C500	393
N31AS	HS25	25111
N31AS	HS25	257135
N31AX	LJ31	094
N31AX	LJ45	371
(N31AX)	LJ31	063
(N31AZ)	LJ31	103
N31B	HS25	25108
N31BC	SBRL	282-14
N31BC	SBRL	306-60
N31BC	SBRL	465-16
(N31BC)	SBRL	465-69
N31BG	LJ24	301
N31BM	SBRL	306-71
N31BP	JSTR	5125/31
N31BQ	SBRL	282-14
N31CA	**CL30**	**20021**
N31CF	WW24	8
(N31CF)	C500	641
N31CG	LJ31	003
N31CJ	C525	0031
N31CJ	C525	0360
N31CJ	**C525**	**0474**
N31CJ	SBRL	306-26
N31CK	LJ24	079
N31CM	FA20	317
N31CR	SBRL	306-146
N31CS	LJ25	083
N31CV	**C560**	**0351**
N31CV	LJ31	168
N31D	F900	191
N31DA	C550	295
(N31DC)	CL60	1032
N31DK	JSTR	5138
N31DM	FA50	59
N31DP	LJ24	059
N31DP	**LJ35**	**062**
N31EP	HS25	25176
N31EX	F2EX	31
N31F	C550	440
N31F	HS25	258036
N31F	JSTR	5060
(N31F)	C550	176
N31FB	LJ35	138
N31FE	FA20	212
N31FF	LJ31	053
N31FJ	FA20	310
N31FN	LJ35	033
N31FT	C550	440
N31GA	**C550**	**253**
N31GJ	**LJ36**	**022**
N31GQ	**LJ31**	**147**
N31GS	LJ25	313
N31GT	HS25	25204
N31HA	LJ31	031
N31HD	**C525**	**0261**
N31HK	**LJ35**	**016**
N31HY	LJ31	107
N31JB	C525	0352
N31JB	C550	550-1041

N31JE	**HA4T**	**RC-31**
N31JM	C500	411
N31KH	**LJ31**	**173**
N31KJ	LJ31	212
N31KW	C550	083
N31LB	LJ24	211
N31LG	HS25	257068
N31LH	C500	287
N31LJ	JSTR	5087/55
N31LJ	LJ31	010
N31LJ	LJ31	020
N31LJ	LJ31	036
N31LJ	LJ31	072
N31LJ	LJ31	078
N31LJ	LJ31	081
N31LJ	LJ31	088
N31LJ	**LJ31**	**097**
N31LJ	LJ31	113
(N31LJ)	LJ31	059
N31LK	LJ31	100
(N31LM)	LJ35	412
N31LR	LJ31	100
N31LR	LJ31	131
N31LR	LJ31	160
N31LR	LJ31	185
N31LT	FA20	69
N31LW	**C500**	**083**
N31MC	**LJ31**	**215**
N31MC	LJ35	270
N31MJ	LJ25	231
N31MJ	LJ25	313
N31MJ	LJ31	185
N31MT	C500	473
N31MW	C500	045
N31MW	LJ31	171
N31NF	LJ31	151
N31NR	LJ31	115
N31NR	LJ31	150
N31NR	LJ31	170
N31NR	LJ31	200
N31NR	LJ31	235
N31NS	**C560**	**0286**
N31NV	LJ31	171
N31PV	LJ31	130
N31RC	C500	465
N31RC	C550	175
N31RC	C560	0023
N31RK	C550	314
N31RP	JSTR	5131
N31S	JSTR	5051
N31S	LJ24	072
N31S	WW24	10
N31SB	WW24	10
N31SG	C525	0207
N31SJ	FA10	72
N31SJ	GALX	033
N31SJ	SBRL	465-26
N31SK	LJ24	118
N31ST	C500	029
N31ST	**BE40**	**RK-600**
N31SY	GLF2	169
N31TC	LJ24	193
N31TD	LJ31	165
N31TF	LJ31	037
N31TJ	C650	0057
N31TJ	HS25	25202
N31TK	**LJ31**	**059**
(N31TK)	LJ31	096
N31TM	FA10	160
N31UJ	LJ31	116
N31UK	LJ31	047
N31UT	JSTR	5143
N31V	FA20	106
N31V	FA50	59
N31V	LJ45	015
N31VT	HS25	25195
N31WE	**C525**	**0362**
N31WE	LJ35	389
N31WG	JSTR	5087/55
N31WH	CL61	5014
N31WR	LJ35	313
N31WS	**LJ35**	**027**
N31WT	CL60	1073
N31WT	FA20	446
N31WT	LJ24	283
N31WT	LJ24	351
N31WT	LJ25	265
N31WT	LJ25	288
N31WT	LJ35	229
N31WT	LJ35	389
N31WT	LJ35	479
(N31WT)	LJ28	28-005
N31WU	LJ31	175
N32AA	LJ24	237
N32AA	**LJ45**	**399**
N32AA	BE40	RK-242
N32AC	**C52B**	**0257**
N32AJ	C650	7074
N32AJ	LJ36	048
N32AJ	BE40	RK-242
N32B	F900	59
N32B	LJ35	593
N32BA	LJ35	190
N32BC	CL60	1053
N32BC	**HS25**	**258321**
N32BC	SBRL	282-15
N32BC	SBRL	306-62
(N32BC)	HS25	258299
N32BD	GLF5	548
N32BG	C525	0532
N32BG	**GALX**	**138**
N32BL	FA10	6
N32BQ	CL60	1053
N32BQ	HS25	258321
N32BQ	SBRL	282-15
N32BR	PRM1	RB-77
N32CA	LJ24	132
N32DA	C500	494
N32DD	C500	043
N32DD	LJ24	331
N32F	C550	442
N32F	HS25	25155
N32FE	FA20	213
(N32FF)	CL64	5469
N32FJ	C550	550-0988
N32FJ	**C650**	**7032**
N32FM	C500	616
N32FM	**C510**	**0212**
N32FN	LJ35	067
N32FN	LJ35	189
N32GG	CL61	5033
N32GM	HS25	25198
N32HC	GLF2	113
(N32HE)	HS25	25033
N32HH	**LJ31**	**201**
N32HJ	LJ35	463
N32HM	LJ35	187
N32HM	**LJ35**	**499**
N32HP	MU30	A074SA
N32JA	LJ35	172
(N32JA)	LJ36	017
N32JC	WW24	32
N32JJ	C500	380
N32JJ	C550	223
N32JJ	C650	0170
N32JJ	CS55	0014
(N32JN)	GALX	023
N32KA	GLF3	435
N32KB	HS25	25280
N32KB	**HS25**	**258461**
N32KC	**E50P**	**50000063**
N32KJ	LJ55	093
N32KM	**C56X**	**5715**
N32KR	JSTR	5220
N32MG	C650	0016
N32MJ	C500	434
N32MJ	**GLF3**	**460**
N32MJ	LJ24	208
N32NG	C750	0039
N32PA	**LJ36**	**025**
N32PB	C550	115
N32PB	C560	0091
N32PB	FA20	122
N32PC	LJ25	018
N32PC	SBRL	306-125
N32PE	LJ35	327
N32PF	**LJ31**	**226**
N32PF	LJ35	327
N32PJ	**HS25**	**258189**
N32PJ	LJ35	320
N32PM	C52B	0409
N32PM	**C52C**	**0190**
N32RP	HS25	256066
N32RZ	LJ35	238
N32SD	LJ24	017
N32SG	**PRM1**	**RB-90**
N32SM	**C550**	**478**
N32SM	LJ25	070
N32SW	**LJ60**	**002**
N32SX	C500	477
N32TC	FA20	440
N32TC	FA50	225
N32TC	LJ35	189
N32TE	FA20	440
N32TJ	CS55	0014
(N32TJ)	C550	268
(N32TJ)	LJ25	224
N32TK	C550	336
N32TM	ASTR	072
N32TM	C550	336
N32TM	**GALX**	**023**
N32TX	**CS55**	**0026**
N32UC	**CL64**	**5404**
(N32UC)	ASTR	136
N32UT	SBRL	306-9
N32VC	FA10	6
N32VP	C525	0032
N32W	C500	105
N32WE	WW24	164
N32WL	LJ24	265
(N32WR)	CL61	3013
N32WT	LJ24	333
N33AA	C500	388
(N33AC)	C510	0151
N33AH	FA20	379
(N33AJ)	FA20	379
N33BC	C550	329
N33BC	C650	0047
N33BC	**HS25**	**258292**
N33BC	SBRL	306-13
N33BC	SBRL	465-69
N33BE	C500	476
N33BK	HS25	25064
N33BK	HS25	257049
N33BK	LJ24	096
N33BQ	C650	0047
N33BQ	SBRL	306-13
N33BV	FA10	33
N33CJ	C525	0245
N33CJ	LJ24	130
N33CJ	LJ25	045
N33CP	HS25	25286
N33CP	HS25	257053
N33CR	GLF2	69
N33CX	C500	456
N33D	C650	7117
N33D	F2TH	224
N33D	FA20	166
N33DC	LJ60	233
N33DS	CS55	0093
N33DT	**C525**	**0080**
N33DY	FA20	166
N33EA	JSTR	5033/56
N33EK	**C550**	**314**
N33EM	**PRM1**	**RB-268**
(N33EN)	GLF2	49
N33EQ	FA50	326
N33FE	FA20	214
N33FJ	F2TH	224
N33FW	**C525**	**0203**
(N33FW)	C550	062
N33GF	LJ25	035
N33GG	F900	81
N33GG	F900	87
N33GG	FA50	97
N33GK	C550	270
N33GK	C650	7050
N33GL	LJ55	082
N33GL	WW24	47
N33GQ	FA50	97
N33GZ	GLF3	393
(N33GZ)	GLF3	465
N33HB	LJ35	182
N33HC	C500	492
N33HL	FA10	17
N33HM	LJ25	093
N33JW	**SBRL**	**306-92**
N33KA	SBRL	380-55
(N33KW)	C500	437
N33L	**C650**	**7118**
N33L	FA20	202
N33LB	SBRL	282-130
N33LC	**F9EX**	**206**
N33LC	FA50	326
N33LR	**GLF4**	**1495**
N33LV	FA20	202
N33LX	C560	0433
N33LX	**C56X**	**6010**
N33M	GLF2	106
N33M	GLF4	1056
N33M	GLF5	594
N33ME	C500	312
N33ME	GLF2	43
N33MK	WW24	374
(N33MM)	MU30	A017SA
N33MQ	C500	312
N33MX	GLF4	1056
N33NH	C500	206
N33NJ	LJ24	147
N33NJ	LJ35	305
N33NJ	**LJ45**	**148**
N33NL	**HS25**	**258643**
N33NL	BE40	RK-330
N33NM	**C525**	**0025**
N33NM	LJ25	093
(N33NN)	GLEX	9120
N33NP	C510	0037
N33NT	GLF3	465
N33NT	SBRL	380-41
N33PA	CL64	5441
N33PB	**C550**	**039**
N33PF	LJ25	028
N33PJ	GLF2	57
N33PJ	**PRM1**	**RB-179**
N33PS	WW24	92
N33PT	LJ25	046
N33PT	**LJ25**	**240**
N33PT	LJ35	397
N33QS	FA20	122
N33RE	LJ24	193
N33RH	C550	087
N33RH	HS25	257011
N33RL	**C650**	**7106**
N33RP	HS25	256068
N33RZ	SBRL	380-47
N33SC	FA20	71
N33SJ	JSTR	5087/55
N33ST	LJ24	173
N33SW	C525	0387
N33TH	C500	024
N33TP	FA20	27
N33TP	LJ24	321
N33TR	LJ25	035
N33TR	SBRL	306-54
N33TR	**SBRL**	**465-47**
N33TS	C560	0549
N33TS	LJ35	021
N33TW	LJ25	124
N33TW	SBRL	282-61
N33TW	**WW24**	**316**
N33TY	FA50	240
N33TY	FA50	288
N33UL	C650	0160
N33UM	**C52B**	**0020**
N33UT	SBRL	276-34
N33UT	SBRL	306-16
N33VC	**HA4T**	**RC-37**
N33VC	HS25	258310
(N33VF)	LJ25	143
(N33VG)	LJ35	408
(N33VV)	C500	482
N33WB	LJ35	376
N33WD	WW24	161
N33WW	**C500**	**440**
N33XE	GLF5	506
N34AA	C500	475
"N34AG"	LJ40	2064
N34AM	SBRL	282-31
N34BH	HS25	256022
N34C	FA20	31
N34CD	CL61	3030
N34CD	CL61	5139
(N34CE)	ASTR	043
N34CH	HS25	257021
N34CJ	CS55	0034
N34CW	FA20	305
N34CW	LJ25	277
N34DL	C500	436
N34DL	C550	204
N34DZ	**C525**	**0640**
N34FD	LJ35	431
N34FE	FA20	215
N34FN	LJ35	254
N34FS	ASTR	099
N34FS	**CL64**	**5307**
N34FS	WW24	417
N34GB	LJ55	114
N34GG	**HS25**	**257034**
N34GN	PRM1	RB-58
N34GX	GALX	034
N34HD	WW24	127
N34HS	**GLF5**	**5514**
N34LA	**C52C**	**0104**
N34LP	SBRL	282-70
(N34LZ)	LJ35	346
N34MJ	LJ25	333
N34MZ	GLF2	77
N34NG	SBRL	380-52
N34NS	CS55	0024
N34NW	WW24	117
N34QS	C650	0034
N34RE	HS25	257022
N34RL	C52A	0071
N34RP	GLF2	113
N34S	GLF2	5
"N34S"	FA50	25
(N34S)	GLF4	1134
N34SS	C550	225
(N34SS)	C550	258
N34ST	**C510**	**0205**
N34SW	WW24	97
N34TB	LJ35	285
N34TC	**C525**	**0083**
N34TC	LJ35	199
N34TH	FA10	74
N34TJ	**FA10**	**41**
N34TJ	LJ35	225
N34TN	**LJ25**	**249**
N34TR	JSTR	5236
(N34TR)	LJ24	069
N34TY	FA50	240
N34U	GLEX	9070
N34U	GLF5	5400
N34UH	GLF4	1470
N34UT	C500	043
N34VP	C750	0034
N34VP	BE40	RK-39
N34VR	**C750**	**0034**
N34W	SBRL	282-47
N34WP	C550	123
N34WP	C56X	5232
N34WR	**JSTR**	**5207**
N34XP	BE40	RK-434
N34XR	LJ45	434
N34YL	C550	267
N35AA	C500	497
N35AH	LJ35	316
N35AJ	**LJ35**	**010**
N35AJ	LJ35	346
N35AJ	LJ35	626
N35AK	LJ35	314
N35AL	LJ35	509
N35AQ	LJ35	513
N35AS	LJ35	405
N35AS	LJ35	605
N35AW	LJ35	233
N35AX	LJ35	280
N35AZ	LJ35	201
N35BG	LJ35	311
N35BG	**LJ35**	**402**
N35BH	HS25	256023
N35BK	LJ35	442
N35BN	LJ35	013
N35BP	C550	282
N35BP	**GALX**	**016**
N35BP	GALX	163
N35CC	**HS25**	**258294**
N35CC	SBRL	282-79
N35CC	SBRL	465-59
N35CD	**FA10**	**224**
N35CD	GLF5	603
N35CK	LJ35	480
N35CL	LJ35	113
N35CQ	**SBRL**	**465-59**
N35CR	**WW24**	**176**
N35CT	**C52A**	**0120**
N35CX	LJ35	180
N35CY	**LJ35**	**473**
N35CZ	LJ35	352
N35D	HS25	257044
N35D	WW24	156
N35DL	HS25	256051
N35DL	LJ25	317
N35DL	LJ35	348
N35DL	SBRL	306-131
N35EC	LJ24	123
N35ED	LJ35	215
N35EG	**LJ35**	**469**
N35ET	**C550**	**550-0879**
N35FC	C650	0179
N35FE	**CL30**	**20408**
N35FE	FA20	217
N35FE	LJ35	409
N35FH	LJ35	273
(N35FH)	LJ35	480
N35FM	LJ35	368
N35FN	LJ35	261
N35FP	CL61	3048
N35FS	LJ35	320
N35FS	LJ35	405
(N35FT)	LJ35	439
N35GA	LJ35	590
N35GC	**LJ35**	**266**
N35GE	LJ35	088
N35GG	LJ35	178
N35GJ	LJ35	507
N35GQ	LJ35	037
N35GX	ASTR	113
N35GX	LJ35	264
N35GZ	GLF3	465
N35HB	LJ35	045
N35HC	**C510**	**0364**
N35HC	C550	202
(N35HM)	LJ35	210
N35HP	LJ35	507
N35HS	C650	7072
N35HW	LJ35	501
N35JF	C500	404
N35JF	LJ24	110
N35JJ	JSTR	5100/41
N35JM	GLF2	47
N35JN	LJ35	013
N35JN	LJ35	469
(N35K)	C500	404
N35KC	LJ35	144
N35KC	LJ35	189
N35KT	LJ35	590
(N35KT)	C550	550-0809
N35LD	C500	494
N35LH	WW24	236
N35LH	WW24	413
N35LJ	LJ35	181
N35LJ	**LJ35**	**240**
N35LJ	LJ35	676
N35LM	HS25	257023
N35LT	C500	132
N35LW	LJ35	439
N35MH	LJ35	258
N35MR	LJ35	057
N35MV	LJ35	416
N35NA	LJ35	381
N35NB	LJ35	133
N35NK	**LJ35**	**491**
(N35NK)	LJ35	643
N35NP	HA4T	RC-45
N35NP	LJ35	191
N35NP	LJ35	492
N35NW	LJ35	069
N35NX	LJ35	328
N35NY	LJ35	328
(N35P)	MU30	A051SA
N35PD	LJ35	181
N35PD	LJ35	606
N35PF	LJ55	020
(N35PF)	LJ35	094
N35PN	C650	0138
(N35PN)	C550	486
N35PR	LJ35	181
N35PT	LJ35	420
N35Q	LJ35	406

N35QB	LJ35	649
N35RF	GALX	061
N35RF	LJ35	201
N35RG	**GLF5**	**5183**
N35RN	LJ35	113
N35RT	LJ35	201
N35RT	**LJ35**	**320**
N35RT	LJ35	420
N35RZ	**F900**	**137**
N35RZ	FA20	359/542
N35RZ	FA50	113
N35SA	LJ35	326
N35SC	LJ35	002
N35SE	C500	035
N35SE	C56X	5656
N35SE	LJ35	191
N35SJ	LJ24	246
N35SJ	LJ35	261
N35SL	LJ35	233
N35SM	LJ35	419
N35TF	C560	0500
N35TH	LJ35	473
N35TJ	LJ35	137
N35TK	C525	0610
N35TK	LJ35	188
N35TL	C500	637
N35TL	LJ35	348
N35TM	C500	497
N35TN	LJ35	472
N35UA	LJ35	665
N35UJ	LJ35	007
N35UK	LJ35	662
N35UK	LJ35	670
N35VP	LJ35	294
N35WB	LJ25	027
N35WB	**LJ35**	**350**
N35WE	LJ35	156
(N35WE)	LJ25	016
N35WG	LJ35	124
(N35WG)	LJ35	274
N35WH	LJ35	138
N35WJ	LJ25	104
N35WL	**LJ35**	**438**
N35WN	FA10	210
N35WP	**HS25**	**256029**
N35WR	**LJ35**	**234**
(N35WU)	LJ35	318
N35XL	C56X	5035
N35YP	**FA50**	**35**
(N36AX)	LJ36	030
N36BG	FA10	190
N36BH	HS25	256025
N36BL	**LJ31**	**094**
N36BP	LJ35	612
N36BP	LJ36	032
(N36BP)	LJ35	237
N36CC	C500	406
N36CC	LJ25	079
N36CD	C650	0036
N36CD	**HS25**	**HA-0180**
N36CE	C550	036
N36CJ	C500	306
N36CJ	C550	136
N36CW	LJ36	012
N36DA	FA20	510
N36DA	**GLF3**	**450**
N36EF	WW24	222
N36EG	GLEX	9225
N36EP	**F2TH**	**172**
N36FD	ASTR	016
N36FD	C500	614
N36FD	**EA50**	**000137**
N36FE	FA20	218
N36FN	LJ35	119
N36FT	HS25	257013
(N36GA)	GLF5	518
N36GC	C500	434
N36GL	**LJ45**	**330**
N36GS	GLF2	251
N36GS	HS25	257095
N36GV	**GLF5**	**674**
N36GX	ASTR	123
N36H	C560	0035
N36H	CS55	0036
N36H	HS25	258332
(N36H)	CS55	0001
N36HA	CL64	5441
N36HH	SBRL	306-18
N36HJ	LJ35	427
N36HR	CS55	0036
N36HZ	PRM1	RB-186
N36JE	**GLF3**	**465**
N36JG	C500	364
N36JK	GLF2	112
N36JM	FA10	19
(N36KA)	FA10	19
N36KJ	C500	545
N36LB	CL60	1020
N36LG	GLEX	9225
N36LG	**GLEX**	**9548**
N36LX	C560	0436
N36MC	C500	159
N36MJ	LJ36	036
N36MK	HS25	25073
N36MM	**GLEX**	**9244**
N36MW	GLF2	89
N36MW	**GLF4**	**1480**
N36MW	LJ25	038
N36NA	C550	119
N36NP	HS25	257035
N36NS	CS55	0059
N36NW	LJ25	297
N36NW	LJ35	609
(N36NW)	C550	191
N36P	FA20	203
N36P	SBRL	282-87
N36PD	LJ36	022
N36PJ	LJ36	030
N36PJ	**LJ36**	**047**
N36PN	**GLF2**	**42/12**
N36PT	**C550**	**550-0966**
N36PT	WW24	275
N36PT	WW24	79
N36QN	C550	072
(N36QS)	HA4T	RC-27
N36RG	**C525**	**0139**
N36RR	GLF2	4/8
N36RR	**GLF4**	**1099**
N36RS	LJ24	184
N36RZ	SBRL	306-2
N36SC	LJ25	209
N36SF	WW24	233
N36SJ	C500	306
N36SK	LJ36	047
N36SP	**LJ35**	**577**
N36TA	LJ36	003
N36TH	F2EX	236
N36TH	F2EX	53
N36TJ	HS25	258018
N36TJ	LJ35	168
N36TJ	LJ35	289
N36TX	**C525**	**0153**
N36UP	**LJ31**	**238**
N36VG	FA20	220
N36VV	**CL64**	**5338**
N36WJ	C550	312
N36WJ	FA10	126
N36WL	C550	732
N36WL	GLF3	328
(N36WS)	C500	420
N36XL	C56X	5036
N36XT	**PRM1**	**RB-36**
(N37AH)	FA20	379
N37AL	**GLF5**	**605**
N37BB	WW24	12
N37BE	WW24	396
N37BG	C52A	0123
N37BH	HS25	256026
N37BJ	LJ25	137
N37BL	LJ24	013
N37BL	LJ24	069
N37BM	C550	186
N37BM	C550	274
N37BM	**LJ31**	**096**
N37CB	LJ24	127
N37CB	**MU30**	**A035SA**
N37CD	C650	0037
N37CP	LJ24	028
N37CR	C550	117
(N37DE)	ASTR	145
N37DG	C525	0109
N37DG	CL64	5386
N37DH	LJ24	231
(N37DJ)	LJ35	237
N37DM	LJ24	025
N37DW	C500	284
N37EA	**F2EX**	**58**
N37ER	**FA50**	**47**
N37FA	LJ35	091
N37FE	**CL30**	**20411**
N37FE	FA20	270
N37FN	LJ35	263
(N37GA)	C550	037
N37GB	LJ25	053
N37GF	SBRL	370-4
N37GX	GALX	014
N37HE	GLF3	466
N37HF	C550	733
N37HG	C550	037
N37HJ	LJ35	230
(N37HR)	LJ35	417
N37HT	LJ24	243
N37HW	C500	581
N37JA	LJ55	034
N37JF	FA20	193
N37JJ	FA20	248/483
(N37JK)	C52B	0251
N37JL	**GLF4**	**4162**
N37KJ	**FA50**	**173**
N37LA	C500	457
N37LB	CL60	1015
N37LC	FA50	227
N37LC	FA50	326
N37LG	LJ31	237
(N37LQ)	FA50	227
N37MB	LJ25	053
N37MD	**F2TH**	**32**
N37MH	**C550**	**168**
N37NR	C560	0009
N37P	HS25	257015
N37P	LJ24	138
N37PL	HS25	257012
(N37RA)	LJ31	153
N37RM	FA20	308
N37RR	LJ25	313
N37RX	GLF4	1137
N37SG	HS25	256021
N37SJ	WW24	38
N37SV	LJ35	492
N37TA	**LJ35**	**034**
N37TE	EA50	000037
N37TH	F2TH	44
N37TJ	LJ35	132
N37TL	CL30	20136
N37TY	**FA7X**	**222**
N37VP	C52B	0037
N37VP	C650	0037
N37VP	C650	0087
N37VP	C680	0137
(N37WC)	WW24	202
N37WH	GLF2	180
N37WH	**GLF4**	**1243**
N37WP	C550	247
N37WP	C560	0259
N37WT	FA20	225/472
N37WX	**FA50**	**309**
N37ZZ	GLEX	9299
N38AE	WW24	318
N38AL	LJ35	499
N38AM	LJ35	174
N38BA	GLF5	682
N38BG	GLF4	1388
N38BG	JSTR	5208
N38BH	HS25	256032
N38BK	**CL30**	**20407**
N38CC	FA20	200
N38CJ	C500	308
N38CP	**LJ60**	**108**
N38CZ	HS25	258192
N38D	LJ36	024
N38D	LJ55	068
N38DA	C500	375
N38DA	**EA50**	**000083**
N38DA	FA10	27
N38DD	**C550**	**374**
N38DD	C650	0023
N38DJ	LJ25	191
(N38DL)	C500	375
N38DM	LJ24	036
N38EC	CS55	0109
N38ED	C650	0028
N38ED	C650	0070
N38FN	LJ35	247
(N38FN)	LJ35	188
N38GL	**G280**	**2004**
N38GL	GLF2	16/13
N38GT	**C52A**	**0512**
N38GX	GALX	015
N38HD	**C52B**	**0407**
N38HG	C56X	5114
(N38HH)	HS25	257107
N38JA	LJ55	033
N38JD	LJ24	093
N38JM	SBRL	306-54
N38JM	SBRL	380-39
N38KM	GLF2	52
N38KW	**C56X**	**5716**
N38LB	HS25	25276
N38M	C52B	0253
N38M	C52B	0337
N38M	C52C	0039
N38M	C52C	0111
N38M	**C52C**	**0176**
N38MG	**LJ31**	**009**
N38MH	C500	265
N38MJ	C52C	0039
(N38MM)	C500	275
(N38MQ)	C500	564
N38MR	C550	650
N38MR	**C560**	**0412**
N38MV	C52B	0253
N38MX	C52B	0337
N38N	GLF2	41
N38NA	C550	207
N38NA	**C550**	**729**
N38NG	**GLF5**	**5527**
N38NS	C560	0411
N38NZ	GLF5	554
(N38NZ)	GLF4	1212
N38PA	HS25	257012
N38PS	**LJ35**	**206**
N38RT	C500	563
N38SA	**C500**	**297**
N38SC	**C525**	**0330**
N38SK	C650	0156
N38SK	LJ31	050
N38SM	C500	001
N38SV	CL64	5423
N38SV	**LJ60**	**229**
N38SW	CL61	3008
N38SW	CL64	5423
N38TA	LJ35	044
N38TJ	FA20	339
N38TJ	WW24	356
N38TM	C500	483
N38TS	HS25	25190
(N38TS)	HS25	25205
N38TT	**C550**	**298**
N38US	LJ35	297
N38UT	SBRL	306-16
N38VC	**E55P**	**50500038**
N38VM	**LJ35**	**557**
N38VS	**CL64**	**5421**
N38WC	LJ36	022
N38WE	**C680**	**0512**
(N38WF)	GLEX	9128
N38WP	C650	0032
N38WP	FA50	292
N38WW	WW24	210
N38ZZ	GLEX	9310
N39BE	C500	476
N39BH	HS25	256034
N39BL	JSTR	5029/38
N39BL	LJ25	234
(N39BL)	HS25	258236
N39CB	**SBRL**	**306-116**
N39CD	CL61	3030
N39CJ	**C525**	**0039**
N39CK	**LJ25**	**005**
(N39DJ)	LJ35	208
N39DK	LJ35	208
N39DK	LJ35	480
N39DM	LJ24	302
N39DM	LJ35	006
N39DM	LJ35	040
N39DM	PRM1	RB-119
N39E	JSTR	5126
N39E	LJ55	018
N39EG	**C510**	**0291**
N39EL	LJ24	251
N39ER	**CL30**	**20023**
N39FA	C550	154
N39FE	**CL30**	**20412**
N39FN	**LJ35**	**006**
N39FS	**SBRL**	**276-33**
N39FW	**C56X**	**5126**
N39GA	C550	215
N39GA	C56X	5549
(N39GA)	C525	0161
(N39GA)	C525	0162
N39GG	**C52B**	**0271**
N39GW	WW24	237
N39GX	GALX	019
N39H	C650	0206
N39H	HS25	258695
(N39HD)	C550	448
N39HF	BE40	RK-65
N39HH	**C500**	**527**
N39HJ	**LJ35**	**337**
N39J	C500	207
N39JC	**PRM1**	**RB-61**
N39JE	LJ25	124
N39JJ	LJ25	121
N39JK	GLF2	169
N39JN	WW24	261
N39JV	C56X	5039
N39K	C550	395
N39K	**E50P**	**50000224**
N39K	FA10	167
N39KM	LJ24	198
N39KT	PRM1	RB-39
N39KY	C550	395
N39LF	**GLF3**	**347**
N39LG	JSTR	5142
N39LH	C500	089
N39LL	C500	568
(N39LX)	C560	0439
N39MB	LJ35	216
N39ML	C550	014
N39MW	LJ35	414
N39N	C560	0243
N39N	GLF2	50
N39N	GLF3	403
N39NA	GLF3	403
N39NP	**F9EX**	**39**
N39NX	GLF2	50
N39PJ	LJ35	128
N39PY	GLF5	522
N39Q	JSTR	5126
N39RC	**C56X**	**5041**
N39RE	C500	311
N39RE	C650	0006
N39RE	CL60	1049
N39RE	CL61	5020
N39RE	CL64	5420
N39RE	**CL65**	**5850**
N39RE	FA10	80
N39RE	WW24	342
N39RG	SBRL	276-25
N39RG	SBRL	282-82
N39RN	**CL64**	**5420**
N39RP	FA20	478
N39SA	LJ35	466
(N39SL)	SBRL	306-39
N39SV	C680	0039
N39T	LJ24	043
N39TF	CS55	0139
N39TH	FA10	199
N39TH	LJ35	496
N39TJ	LJ31	026
N39TR	SBRL	465-27
N39TT	FA20	449
N39TT	LJ24	308
N39TW	LJ31	047
N39VP	C650	0187
N39WA	LJ35	092
N39WH	GLF4	1243
N39WJ	FA20	239
N39WP	C650	0039
N39WP	**FA50**	**294**
N39ZZ	GLEX	9342
N40AA	**GLF4**	**1440**
N40AB	WW24	106
N40AC	C500	331
N40AC	FA20	187
N40AD	LJ25	314
(N40AD)	HS25	25026
N40AG	GLF2	115
N40AG	**HS25**	**HB-15**
N40AJ	ASTR	031
N40AJ	C500	393
N40AJ	WW24	40
N40AN	LJ35	271
(N40AN)	LJ35	045
(N40AN)	LJ35	149
N40AS	FA50	171
N40AS	LJ25	117
N40AS	WW24	156
N40AW	C500	584
N40BC	LJ25	128
N40BC	LJ25	288
(N40BC)	LJ25	288
N40BD	LJ35	140
N40BG	WW24	156
N40BH	HS25	256038
(N40BK)	MU30	A004SA
N40BP	LJ24	116
N40BP	SBRL	282-40
N40BT	SBRL	282-113
N40CC	GLF2	46
N40CD	SBRL	282-28
N40CE	GLF2	45
N40CH	GLF2	77
N40CH	GLF3	377
N40CH	SBRL	282-104
N40CJ	**C525**	**0540**
N40CN	FA50	92
N40CN	HS25	257120
N40CR	LJ55	097
N40CR	LJ55	144
N40CX	C750	0240
N40D	**GLF6**	**6119**
N40DA	C500	392
N40DC	HS25	25078
N40DC	HS25	25079
N40DC	JSTR	5120/26
N40DG	WW24	262
N40DK	LJ35	171
N40DK	LJ35	264
N40DK	LJ55	092
N40DW	SBRL	282-24
N40EL	SBRL	282-42
N40EP	**C550**	**617**
N40ES	LJ55	005
(N40F)	FA50	82
N40FC	C550	554
N40FC	**C650**	**0143**
N40FJ	C500	547
N40FJ	C550	281
N40GA	MU30	A040SA
N40GC	MU30	A005SA
N40GG	LJ35	416
N40GG	WW24	229
N40GP	SBRL	282-16
N40GS	C550	288
N40GS	**HS25**	**258128**
N40GT	HS25	257002
N40GT	**SBRL**	**282-126**
N40GX	GALX	016
N40HB	GLF4	1407
N40HC	**C56X**	**5656**
N40HC	SBRL	282-66
N40HL	C500	128
N40HP	C500	104
N40HT	**C560**	**0030**
N40JC	WW24	40
N40JE	LJ24	133
N40JE	SBRL	282-124
N40JF	C500	079
N40JF	LJ24	133
N40JF	SBRL	282-80
N40JW	SBRL	282-122
N40KJ	**GLF4**	**1070**
N40KJ	LJ40	2002
N40KJ	SBRL	306-142
(N40KM)	CS55	0008
N40KW	C550	550-0909
N40KW	C750	0040
N40LB	**F9EX**	**272**
N40LB	LJ25	009
N40LB	SBRL	282-36
N40LJ	LJ40	2001
N40LJ	LJ40	2009
N40LJ	LJ40	2027
N40LJ	LJ40	2046
N40LJ	LJ40	2084
N40LX	**LJ40**	**45-001**
N40LX	LJ45	001
N40MA	C500	514
N40MA	C550	320
N40MA	BE40	RJ-42
N40MF	**C550**	**550-0921**
N40MF	MU30	A049SA
N40ML	**E55P**	**50500231**
N40ML	F9EX	46

N40ML	LJ40	2024
N40MM	C500	275
N40MP	WW24	334
N40MT	C550	238
N40N	C650	7031
N40N	**F2TH**	**224**
N40N	FA10	25
N40N	GLF3	405
N40N	GLF4	1122
N40N	JSTR	5048
N40NB	GLF3	405
N40NB	LJ40	2087
N40NC	JSTR	5048
N40ND	FA10	21
N40NJ	**SBRL**	**282-134**
N40NR	SBRL	282-107
N40NR	SBRL	282-134
N40NR	SBRL	282-66
N40NR	SBRL	282-91
N40NS	SBRL	282-126
N40PC	HS25	25214
N40PC	HS25	256010
N40PC	LJ45	259
N40PC	**LJ45**	**515**
N40PD	C500	059
N40PD	**LJ40**	**2111**
N40PH	C650	0201
N40PK	**LJ35**	**260**
N40PL	C500	646
N40PL	C550	305
N40PL	CS55	0008
N40PL	HS25	258347
N40PL	BE40	RK-138
(N40PL)	C560	0068
N40PX	LJ40	2007
N40QG	CL30	20264
N40QJ	GLF3	493
N40QJ	GLF4	1330
N40QS	HA4T	RC-42
N40R	SBRL	282-52
(N40R)	SBRL	282-19
N40RD	C500	059
(N40RF)	C500	266
N40RL	C52A	0046
N40RQ	**HA4T**	**RC-40**
N40RW	C500	107
N40RW	LJ35	224
N40SC	SBRL	282-113
N40SC	SBRL	282-98
N40SC	**BE40**	**RK-311**
N40SE	SBRL	282-15
N40SE	SBRL	282-59
N40SJ	SBRL	282-25
N40SK	HS25	25186
(N40SK)	FA50	240
N40SL	SBRL	282-32
N40SN	LJ25	021
N40SR	GLF5	525
N40SW	LJ25	021
N40SW	LJ25	238
N40TA	LJ35	208
N40TA	SBRL	282-94
N40TA	WW24	194
N40TE	**GLEX**	**9674**
N40TF	LJ35	025
N40TH	**F2EX**	**7**
N40TH	FA50	212
N40TH	FA50	85
N40TL	SBRL	306-103
(N40TM)	LJ35	381
(N40TV)	LJ24	011
N40UA	WW24	40
N40VK	HA4T	RC-40
N40WB	HS25	257002
(N40WE)	C550	554
N40WH	SBRL	282-80
N40WJ	FA10	21
N40WP	C560	0155
N40WP	SBRL	282-32
N40WP	SBRL	380-39
N40XC	CL65	5832
N40XR	**LJ40**	**2028**
N40XY	FA20	135
N40XY	JSTR	5115/39
N40Y	HS25	25234
N40YA	SBRL	282-20
N40YC	C550	554
N40ZA	SBRL	282-112
N40ZH	BE40	RK-405
N40ZZ	GLEX	9357
N41	WW24	143
N41AJ	LJ24	037
N41AJ	LJ25	040
(N41AJ)	C500	393
N41AU	**ASTR**	**041**
N41AV	GLF2	61
(N41B)	SBRL	380-49
N41BH	C550	567
N41BH	HS25	25220
N41BH	HS25	256040
N41BJ	LJ24	178
N41BP	FA20	177
N41C	C550	320
N41C	**WW24**	**398**
(N41CC)	HS25	257010
N41CD	FA20	88
(N41CK)	C550	259
N41CP	GLF4	1179
N41CP	GLF4	1336
N41CP	LJ55	037
N41CQ	SBRL	465-6
N41DP	**CL30**	**20010**
N41DP	LJ31	079
N41DP	LJ45	010
N41EA	**C525**	**0131**
N41EA	LJ55	041
N41EB	C525	0116
N41ES	LJ55	007
N41FD	**BE40**	**RK-288**
N41FL	WW24	41
N41FN	LJ35	137
N41GA	**C550**	**044**
N41GJ	**LJ36**	**055**
N41GS	SBRL	282-16
N41GT	C500	494
N41GX	GLEX	9541
(N41GX)	GALX	021
N41H	LJ25	217
N41HF	HS25	257012
N41HF	**HS25**	**258274**
N41HL	C500	338
N41HV	HA4T	RC-41
N41JJ	**HDJT**	**42000025**
N41JP	C500	466
N41JP	C550	288
N41KN	**C52C**	**0178**
N41LE	C500	632
N41LF	**C525**	**0501**
N41LV	SBRL	465-39
N41ME	BE40	RK-19
N41MH	**FA20**	**14**
N41MJ	LJ35	405
N41MP	LJ24	148
N41N	JSTR	5087/55
N41ND	**C52B**	**0134**
N41NK	C525	0190
N41NK	C525	0281
N41NK	**LJ25**	**238**
N41NR	SBRL	282-133
N41NW	LJ35	041
N41NY	MS76	041
N41PC	FA20	19
N41PC	LJ45	190
N41PC	LJ45	387
(N41PD)	FA20	19
N41PG	**C525**	**0175**
N41PG	GLF3	334
N41PJ	**HS25**	**258173**
N41PJ	LJ35	041
N41PL	GLF4	1226
N41PQ	LJ45	190
N41PR	GLF4	1226
N41QR	GLF4	1179
N41RA	**LJ35**	**215**
N41RC	GLF2	29
N41RG	**SBRL**	**306-119**
N41SH	C500	267
N41SH	GLEX	9516
N41SJ	F900	37
N41SM	C550	271
N41ST	C500	485
N41ST	C650	0063
N41ST	LJ35	302
N41TC	JSTR	5036/42
N41TC	LJ24	346
N41TC	LJ25	346
N41TC	SBRL	465-42
N41TF	**LJ45**	**175**
N41TH	FA50	201
N41TJ	FA10	118
(N41TJ)	BE40	RJ-34
N41UA	**LJ40**	**2074**
N41UT	MU30	A030SA
N41VB	GLF4	1174
N41VP	C560	0492
N41VP	**C560**	**0626**
N41VR	C560	0492
(N41VY)	C550	550-0804
N41WH	WW24	268
N41WJ	C550	264
N41WT	LJ35	229
N41YP	C525	0122
N41ZP	LJ25	279
N42	WW24	142
N42AA	C525	0275
N42AA	C52B	0140
N42AJ	LJ24	139
N42AJ	**BE40**	**RK-55**
(N42AJ)	LJ35	475
(N42AJ)	LJ60	052
N42AL	**C525**	**0836**
N42AS	HS25	25150
N42B	LJ35	277
N42BH	HS25	25221
N42BH	HS25	256044
(N42BJ)	LJ25	127
N42BL	HS25	25275
N42BL	MS76	050
(N42BM)	C550	111
N42C	JSTR	5150/37
N42CK	HS25	25038
N42CM	**WW24**	**189**
N42CV	C560	0042
N42DC	**SBRL**	**465-25**
N42DG	LJ25	171
N42EE	**CL61**	**5008**
N42EH	**FA10**	**28**
N42EL	**PRM1**	**RB-145**
N42ES	LJ55	009
N42FB	HS25	258467
N42FD	GLF5	5115
(N42FD)	HS25	25042
N42FE	LJ25	088
N42FE	LJ35	241
N42FJ	F900	42
N42FL	WW24	429
N42G	**FA10**	**20**
N42G	JSTR	5127
N42G	LJ25	140
N42GA	GLF5	5142
N42GB	JSTR	5127
N42GJ	**CL30**	**20085**
N42GX	ASTR	124
N42GX	GLF5	628
N42GX	LJ25	140
N42HC	LJ24	208
N42HC	LJ25	142
N42HM	C500	452
N42HM	LJ35	210
N42HN	**LJ35**	**507**
N42HP	LJ35	507
N42HP	LJ45	080
N42JP	LJ60	368
(N42JP)	LJ60	147
N42KC	C550	346
N42KR	JSTR	5225
N42LC	GLF2	178
N42LG	PRM1	RB-259
N42LG	PRM1	RB-262
N42LG	PRM1	RB-263
N42LJ	**C510**	**0462**
N42LL	LJ35	427
N42LQ	PRM1	RB-263
N42MD	GLF3	427
N42MJ	C550	018
N42NA	C550	601
N42NA	C560	0077
N42NA	**FA50**	**128**
(N42NA)	C650	0077
N42ND	C560	0400
N42NF	LJ24	214
N42NF	**WW24**	**334**
N42PA	C56X	5067
N42PG	LJ24	247
N42PH	**C550**	**327**
N42PJ	LJ35	285
N42PP	GLF2	115
N42QB	WW24	6
N42SC	**PRM1**	**RB-212**
(N42SE)	HS25	257036
N42SK	FA50	290
N42SK	BE40	RK-111
N42SK	BE40	RK-28
N42SR	HS25	257036
N42SR	MU30	A038SA
N42SR	BE40	RJ-9
N42ST	**F2TH**	**39**
N42TS	HS25	256003
N42TS	HS25	256041
N42TS	**HS25**	**257067**
N42US	**FA10**	**171**
(N42US)	HS25	258152
N42VP	C52B	0042
N42VP	**C52C**	**0042**
N42WJ	**FA20**	**427**
N42WZ	**C510**	**0175**
N42XL	C56X	5042
N42XL	C56X	6142
N42ZP	LJ28	28-003
N43	WW24	131
(N43A)	LJ36	008
(N43AC)	LJ24	043
N43AG	**E50P**	**50000128**
N43AJ	LJ24	141
N43AR	JSTR	5154
N43B	LJ24	039
N43BD	**BE40**	**RK-441**
N43BE	FA50	49
N43BG	C500	407
N43BH	**C525**	**0633**
N43BH	HS25	25222
N43BH	HS25	256046
N43CC	FA10	69
N43CF	SBRL	282-59
(N43CT)	LJ24	039
N43D	C550	188
(N43D)	C550	375
N43DD	LJ35	288
N43DM	LJ24	305
N43DR	**LJ25**	**353**
N43EC	**FA10**	**168**
N43EL	LJ35	121
N43EP	**E50P**	**50000129**
N43ES	FA50	49
N43FC	**C650**	**7087**
N43FE	**CL30**	**20456**
N43FE	LJ35	275
N43FJ	F2TH	43
(N43FN)	LJ24	305
N43GA	GLF5	5150
N43GB	SBRL	306-14
N43GG	**PRM1**	**RB-160**
N43GX	GALX	022
N43GX	**GLEX**	**9343**
N43H	LJ35	426
N43HF	**C56X**	**5519**
N43HJ	PRM1	RB-41
N43JG	SBRL	306-79
N43JK	FA20	195
(N43JK)	JSTR	5055/21
N43KA	**C52C**	**0123**
N43KC	LJ24	213
N43KS	GLF4	1018
N43KW	C560	0487
N43LD	C560	0175
N43LJ	**C52C**	**0064**
N43LJ	LJ31	043
N43LJ	LJ36	043
N43M	GLF2	126
N43M	GLF4	1057
N43MF	**LJ35**	**284**
N43MH	ASTR	043
N43MS	**C525**	**0610**
N43MU	GLF4	1057
N43ND	C52A	0041
N43NR	**LJ60**	**043**
N43NR	SBRL	282-69
N43NR	SBRL	282-7
N43NW	**C525**	**0543**
N43NW	CL60	1043
(N43PE)	LJ35	275
N43PJ	HS25	258202
N43PJ	LJ28	28-004
N43PR	CL61	5002
N43QF	LJ60	159
N43QG	LJ45	237
N43R	CL61	5134
N43R	**CL64**	**5334**
N43R	GLF2	18
N43R	SBRL	380-51
N43RC	C560	0245
N43RC	CS55	0149
N43RC	**E55P**	**50500118**
N43RJ	**ASTR**	**136**
N43RJ	GLF2	64/27
N43RK	CL61	5134
N43RP	**ASTR**	**048**
N43RP	WW24	332
N43RU	WW24	332
N43RW	C550	088
N43SA	C550	096
N43SE	LJ31	048
N43SF	CL64	5594
N43SF	**CL65**	**5893**
N43SF	LJ31	048
N43SF	LJ60	159
N43SM	FA20	142
N43SP	C500	648
N43TC	C550	337
N43TC	C650	0036
(N43TC)	C500	149
N43TE	C550	337
N43TJ	C56X	6072
N43TJ	LJ35	121
(N43TL)	LJ24	203
N43TR	LJ35	645
N43TS	**HS25**	**25186**
N43TS	LJ25	201
N43US	FA10	110
N43VS	**CS55**	**0069**
N43W	LJ24	227
N43W	LJ35	426
N43W	SBRL	282-15
N43W	WW24	374
N43WJ	HS25	25031
N43WL	SBRL	282-15
N43ZP	LJ24	157
N43ZZ	WW24	356
N44	WW24	130
N44AB	LJ35	473
N44AJ	LJ24	120
N44AS	**C550**	**056**
N44BB	HS25	257105
N44BB	LJ25	227
N44BH	HS25	25224
"N44BH"	HS25	256047
(N44BH)	C650	0019
(N44BH)	HS25	25236
N44BW	C500	048
N44CC	FA20	200
N44CE	**GLF4**	**1125**
N44CJ	LJ24	146
N44CK	**C525**	**0401**
N44CN	HS25	25203
N44CP	LJ24	185
N44CP	LJ25	006
N44DD	**SBRL**	**306-146**
N44EE	LJ25	050
N44EG	F900	14
N44EJ	**C56X**	**5289**
N44EJ	EA50	000089
N44EL	LJ25	050
N44EL	LJ35	009
N44EL	LJ35	255
N44EL	LJ55	123
N44EL	**LJ60**	**036**
N44EQ	FA50	275
N44ET	LJ35	255
N44EV	LJ36	022
N44FC	C550	220
N44FE	C525	0334
N44FE	LJ25	215
N44FG	C560	0470
N44FH	LJ25	252
N44FJ	C525	0003
N44FJ	C52A	0178
N44FJ	C52C	0071
N44FM	C500	534
N44FR	**C550**	**361**
N44GA	LJ24	129
N44GA	LJ55	102
N44GL	**C52C**	**0061**
N44GL	LJ36	009
N44GT	C550	002
N44GT	C560	0252
N44GT	**C560**	**0791**
N44GT	CS55	0099
N44GV	**GLF4**	**1305**
N44GX	ASTR	125
N44GX	**GLEX**	**9142**
N44HC	C500	295
N44HG	LJ35	180
N44HH	HS25	258223
N44HS	C650	0006
N44JC	**F2TH**	**164**
N44JC	FA10	22
N44JC	FA20	471
N44JF	C500	262
N44JQ	FA20	471
(N44JX)	C550	088
N44K	HS25	25114
(N44KB)	LJ24	245
(N44KF)	JSTR	5038
N44KG	HS25	25114
N44KJ	**GLF6**	**6055**
N44KW	C550	550-0909
(N44KW)	LJ35	130
N44LC	C500	577
N44LC	C550	649
N44LC	C560	0482
N44LC	**F9EX**	**216**
N44LC	FA50	275
N44LF	C550	309
N44LG	LJ31	237
N44LG	**LJ40**	**2125**
N44LJ	LJ24	191
N44LJ	LJ35	276
N44LJ	LJ36	044
N44LQ	C550	649
N44LQ	**C560**	**0482**
N44LV	**C560**	**0397**
N44LX	GLF4	1114
N44M	C650	0050
N44M	C650	7043
N44M	C680	0083
N44M	**CL30**	**20450**
N44MC	C500	434
N44MC	FA20	200
N44MD	GLF2	81
N44MD	GLF3	427
N44MF	JSTR	5051
N44MJ	LJ25	124
N44MJ	LJ35	421
N44MK	**C500**	**379**
N44MK	FA50	44
N44MM	**MU30**	**A080SA**
N44MQ	**C650**	**7043**
N44MU	C650	0050
N44MV	C680	0083
N44MW	LJ35	044
N44MZ	CL30	20450
N44NJ	LJ24	120
N44NJ	**LJ45**	**147**
N44NP	SBRL	282-44
N44NR	SBRL	282-130
N44NT	FA20	319
N44P	SBRL	282-103
N44PA	LJ24	181
N44PA	LJ25	144
N44PH	SBRL	282-136
N44PR	**C750**	**0214**
N44PR	WW24	169
N44PT	LJ35	093
N44PW	HS25	25123
N44QF	LJ60	215
N44QG	CL30	20264
N44QG	LJ28	28-003
N44QG	LJ31	053
N44QG	LJ45	237
N44QG	LJ45	361
N44RD	C500	334
N44RD	C500	464
N44RM	**LJ60**	**004**
N44SA	C500	109
N44SB	SBRL	306-20
N44SF	CL64	5601
N44SF	**CL65**	**5894**
N44SF	LJ31	065
N44SF	LJ31	193
N44SF	LJ60	215
N44SH	C560	0613
N44SH	**C680**	**0023**
N44SK	FA50	290
N44SK	LJ25	371
N44SK	LJ35	444

N44SU	LJ31	065
N44SW	C500	552
N44SW	**C550**	**550-1067**
N44SW	C550	733
N44SZ	LJ31	193
N44TC	C550	337
N44TG	HS25	25100
(N44TL)	LJ24	191
N44TQ	HS25	25100
N44TT	LJ35	211
N44UC	LJ35	098
N44UN	**HS25**	**258359**
N44UP	GLF2	133
N44VP	**F9EX**	**115**
N44VS	**C525**	**0500**
N44VW	LJ35	044
N44WD	LJ24	111
N44WD	SBRL	306-116
N44WF	C550	236
N44WG	WW24	112
N44WS	**E50P**	**50000317**
N44YS	**GLF2**	**98/38**
N44ZF	**GLF4**	**1029**
(N44ZG)	LJ31	053
N44ZP	C550	214
N45	WW24	144
N45AC	GLF4	1036
N45AE	**LJ35**	**422**
N45AF	C500	433
N45AF	HS25	257128
N45AJ	LJ24	309
N45AJ	LJ24	317
N45AJ	LJ45	137
(N45AQ)	C500	411
N45AU	LJ45	262
N45AW	LJ35	078
N45AX	LJ45	206
N45AX	**LJ45**	**377**
N45BA	C560	0067
N45BA	LJ45	136
N45BE	**C550**	**664**
N45BE	FA50	75
N45BH	HS25	25225
(N45BH)	HS25	256051
N45BK	**LJ25**	**036**
N45BP	HS25	257026
N45BR	C750	0045
N45BS	LJ25	111
N45BZ	LJ45	290
N45CP	LJ24	242
N45CP	LJ25	073
N45DJ	**EA50**	**000078**
N45DM	LJ25	030
N45ED	**LJ24**	**104**
N45EJ	**LJ45**	**080**
N45EP	C550	199
N45ES	FA50	75
N45ES	LJ25	295
N45ET	**GLF4**	**1405**
N45FC	LJ24	309
N45FE	LJ45	034
N45FE	LJ45	039
N45FG	FA50	180
N45FG	**LJ36**	**010**
N45FJ	**C525**	**0003**
N45FS	C500	486
N45FS	C52C	0119
N45FS	**C550**	**562**
N45GA	C550	395
N45GA	C560	0064
N45GD	**HS25**	**258142**
N45GH	**LJ45**	**447**
N45GL	MU30	A041SA
N45GP	CS55	0110
N45GX	ASTR	128
N45GX	**GLEX**	**9459**
N45H	ASTR	050
N45H	CS55	0064
N45H	LJ25	239
N45H	SBRL	465-2
N45HB	LJ25	114
N45HC	LJ45	174
N45HC	LJ45	507
N45HD	**LJ45**	**293**
N45HF	**LJ45**	**121**
N45HG	LJ31	026
N45HG	LJ31	140
N45HG	**LJ45**	**343**
N45HK	**LJ45**	**349**
N45HM	**LJ45**	**023**
(N45HV)	C550	550-0825
N45JB	FA10	203
N45JB	FA20	505
N45JE	GLEX	9222
N45JE	**GLF5**	**5446**
N45JF	LJ24	138
N45JF	WW24	101
N45JM	GLF2	69
N45K	JSTR	5151
N45KB	C560	0191
N45KB	LJ25	281
(N45KB)	LJ25	270
N45KG	**HS25**	**257189**
N45KH	**LJ45**	**313**
N45KJ	LJ45	301
N45KK	HS25	257158
N45KK	LJ25	281
N45KK	LJ31	147
N45KK	LJ35	592
N45KK	LJ35	672
N45KN	**HS25**	**258635**
N45KR	**GLF3**	**433**
N45KV	LJ45	338
N45KX	**LJ45**	**233**
N45LC	C500	326
N45LD	LJ45	435
N45LJ	LJ45	002
N45LJ	LJ45	019
N45LJ	LJ45	100
N45LJ	LJ45	239
N45LJ	LJ45	258
N45LJ	LJ45	279
N45LJ	LJ45	318
N45LJ	LJ45	361
N45LJ	LJ45	392
(N45LJ)	LJ45	394
(N45LN)	BE40	RK-388
(N45LN)	BE40	RK-504
N45LR	**LJ45**	**013**
N45LR	LJ45	055
N45LX	BE40	RK-388
N45MC	C500	531
N45MC	C550	422
N45ME	C550	089
N45MF	**LJ35**	**344**
N45MH	C525	0386
N45MH	**C52A**	**0344**
N45MJ	LJ35	045
N45MK	C500	571
N45ML	**C550**	**405**
N45MM	C500	444
(N45MM)	SBRL	306-91
(N45MP)	WW24	334
N45MR	FA20	123
N45MR	LJ45	179
N45MR	LJ45	345
N45MS	ASTR	041
N45MW	**LJ45**	**115**
N45MX	LJ45	436
(N45MX)	LJ45	345
N45NB	PRM1	RB-22
N45NB	**PRM1**	**RB-91**
N45NC	**CS55**	**0061**
N45NC	FA50	232
N45NC	FA50	302
N45NC	HS25	25225
N45ND	PRM1	RB-22
(N45ND)	HS25	25225
N45NF	C550	550-0986
N45NF	C56X	5563
N45NF	**C680**	**0556**
N45NM	**LJ45**	**253**
N45NP	LJ45	020
N45NP	**LJ45**	**204**
N45NP	MU30	A047SA
N45NP	SBRL	465-42
N45NQ	FA50	232
N45NQ	HS25	25225
N45NS	C550	479
N45NS	C550	550-0949
N45NS	**C56X**	**5285**
N45NY	**LJ45**	**163**
N45PD	LJ31	186
(N45PF)	C525	0206
(N45PG)	GLF3	488
N45PH	CL61	3004
N45PK	C56X	5614
N45PK	LJ31	034
N45PK	LJ31	186
N45PM	HS25	25118
N45QG	LJ45	237
N45QQ	**LJ45**	**282**
N45RC	**C560**	**0071A**
N45RK	**BE40**	**RK-43**
N45RR	**LJ45**	**414**
N45RS	SBRL	306-44
N45SC	F2TH	45
N45SJ	F900	19
N45SJ	F900	37
N45SJ	F9EX	7
N45SJ	FA50	53
N45SJ	WW24	289
N45SL	HS25	25098
N45SL	WW24	149
(N45SL)	LJ35	083
N45SP	C510	0029
N45ST	C750	0054
N45ST	C750	0185
N45ST	GLF5	5056
N45ST	GLF5	5196
N45SY	LJ45	242
N45TE	C560	0405
N45TK	LJ35	037
N45TK	LJ45	176
N45TK	LJ45	338
N45TK	LJ45	411
N45TL	**C500**	**375**
N45TP	C550	674
N45TP	C560	0405
N45TP	**C560**	**0668**
N45TQ	LJ45	338
N45TU	**LJ45**	**120**
N45UE	GLEX	9222
N45UF	LJ31	072
N45UG	LJ45	198
N45UG	LJ45	206
N45UJ	LJ45	080
N45UP	LJ45	170
N45US	LJ60	129
(N45US)	C650	0016
(N45US)	C650	0034
N45VA	**LJ45**	**301**
N45VB	**LJ45**	**043**
N45VG	LJ45	251
N45VL	LJ45	139
N45VM	**C550**	**550-0918**
N45VP	**C510**	**0417**
N45VP	LJ45	184
N45VS	**LJ45**	**170**
N45WH	FA20	259
N45WH	FA20	512
N45WL	**CL61**	**3004**
(N45WL)	C550	155
N45WN	FA20	259
N45XL	C56X	5545
N45XL	LJ40	45-001
N45XL	LJ45	001
N45XP	**LJ45**	**355**
N45XP	BE40	RK-445
N45XR	LJ45	232
N45XR	LJ45	271
N45XR	LJ45	293
N45XR	LJ45	305
N45XR	LJ45	332
N45XR	LJ45	380
N45XR	LJ45	381
N45XR	LJ45	423
"N45XR"	LJ45	413
(N45XR)	LJ45	318
N45XT	**LJ45**	**103**
N45XT	LJ45	330
N45Y	GLF2	69
N45Y	HS25	258009
N45Y	HS25	258140
N45YF	**LJ45**	**006**
N45YH	LJ45	336
N45YP	GLF2	69
N45ZP	C550	216
N45ZP	LJ25	238
N45ZR	**LJ45**	**240**
N46A	C550	423
N46A	CS55	0061
N46B	HS25	25261
N46B	HS25	256044
N46BA	C550	575
(N46BA)	LJ25	300
N46BE	**C52A**	**0116**
(N46BE)	HS25	256044
N46BH	HS25	25226
N46BK	WW24	214
N46CK	**PRM1**	**RB-163**
N46DA	C550	033
N46E	**CL65**	**5981**
N46E	LJ40	2010
(N46EL)	F2EX	71
N46ES	CL60	1079
(N46ES)	GLF3	381
N46EW	**C525**	**0802**
N46F	CL61	5055
N46F	CL64	5574
N46F	JSTR	5124
N46F	**LJ45**	**507**
N46FE	**LJ40**	**2010**
N46FE	BE40	RK-16
N46FJ	F900	46
N46GA	C560	0061
N46GX	GALX	020
N46GX	**GLEX**	**9469**
N46HA	**F2TH**	**91**
N46JA	LJ24	251
(N46JA)	C500	168
N46JV	C525	0602
N46JW	C525	0002
N46JW	C52A	0046
N46K	JSTR	5145
(N46KB)	LJ35	206
N46KJ	JSTR	5151
(N46LM)	LJ24	195
N46MF	C550	408
N46MF	**LJ35**	**377**
N46MK	C550	408
N46MK	**FA10**	**206**
N46MT	C500	689
N46MT	C550	553
N46MT	C560	0253
N46MW	C560	0487
N46MW	**LJ40**	**2126**
(N46NR)	C550	394
N46NT	C52A	0046
N46PJ	**C550**	**002**
N46PL	HS25	257055
N46R	**F9EX**	**284**
N46RB	C500	058
N46RC	C510	0327
N46RD	C500	244
N46SC	C500	521
N46SD	C550	377
N46SG	CL61	5111
N46SR	CL60	1046
N46SR	CL61	3046
N46TE	GLF2	243
N46TG	HS25	25123
N46TJ	HS25	257104
N46TJ	LJ35	077
N46TK	LJ45	338
N46TK	**LJ45**	**428**
N46TQ	LJ45	428
N46UF	ASTR	015
N46UF	LJ31	073
N46UP	ASTR	015
N46VE	C56X	5077
N46VG	FA20	46
N46VR	C52B	0046
N46WB	C560	0238
N46WB	C560	0320
N46WB	LJ24	133
N46WC	**HA4T**	**RC-63**
N46WC	HS25	257195
N46WC	HS25	259028
N46WE	**HS25**	**259028**
N46WQ	HS25	257195
N46WY	**G150**	**276**
N46XP	BE40	RK-446
N47	**GLEX**	**9160**
N47A	GLF2	71
N47AJ	LJ25	023
N47AN	**C650**	**0054**
N47BA	JSTR	5061/48
N47BA	LJ35	060
N47BH	HS25	25228
N47CE	**WW24**	**137**
N47CF	C500	634
N47CG	HS25	258169
N47CM	C650	0153
N47DC	WW24	163
N47DK	LJ25	154
N47DM	WW24	74
N47EC	GLF2	231
N47EG	**F9EX**	**154**
(N47EG)	F900	14
N47EL	F2EX	69
N47ES	CL60	1083
N47EX	HS25	256047
N47FH	**C525**	**0047**
N47GX	GALX	018
N47HA	**HS25**	**258280**
N47HC	LJ25	114
N47HF	**C56X**	**5347**
N47HF	CL61	5174
N47HR	CL61	5174
N47HR	GLF2	30/4
N47HR	GLF4	1195
N47HR	GLF4	1250
N47HV	HS25	256014
N47HW	HS25	256014
N47HW	**HS25**	**258023**
N47JE	FA20	189
N47JF	FA20	189
N47JK	GLF2	115
N47JR	LJ35	007
N47LP	**FA20**	**457**
N47LP	WW24	411
(N47LP)	CS55	0017
N47LR	WW24	411
N47MF	**LJ35**	**495**
N47MJ	CS55	0010
N47MJ	LJ25	004
N47MM	SBRL	306-25
N47MN	SBRL	306-9
N47MR	LJ25	101
N47NM	**C550**	**550-1112**
(N47NR)	LJ24	148
N47NS	**FA50**	**40**
N47NT	**C52B**	**0344**
N47PB	**C52C**	**0128**
N47PB	HS25	257055
N47PB	MU30	A047SA
N47PW	**C560**	**0186**
N47RA	**LJ35**	**352**
N47RK	FA10	162
(N47RP)	C550	249
N47SB	**C680**	**0546**
N47SE	**SBRL**	**465-34**
N47SL	GLF4	1053
N47SM	**C550**	**568**
N47SW	C550	444
N47TH	C525	0047
N47TH	C525	0119
N47TJ	HS25	257036
N47TJ	HS25	257040
N47TJ	MU30	A047SA
(N47TJ)	HS25	258139
N47TK	LJ24	236
N47TL	C500	605
N47TR	**GLF6**	**6101**
N47TR	LJ31	136
N47TW	C550	477
(N47TW)	C560	0224
N47UC	JSTR	5123/14
N47UC	JSTR	5125/31
N47UF	FA50	28
N47VC	C560	0304
N47VC	HS25	258139
N47VL	SBRL	282-48
(N47VP)	C525	0047
(N47WH)	GLF2	180
N47WS	F2EX	145
N47WT	LJ24	283
N47WU	HS25	256047
N47XL	C56X	5747
N48AD	FA20	241/479
N48AH	WW24	288
N48AJ	LJ24	172
N48AL	HS25	258167
N48AM	HS25	258582
N48AM	LJ31	123
N48AS	LJ24	088
N48BA	LJ24	152
N48BH	HS25	25229
N48BT	FA20	160/450
N48BV	**CS55**	**0032**
N48CC	FA20	200
N48CC	GLF2	181
N48CC	GLF4	1363
(N48CE)	SBRL	282-75
N48CG	F2TH	41
N48CG	**F9EX**	**212**
N48CG	SBRL	282-75
N48CK	BE40	RJ-22
N48CN	LJ35	169
N48CQ	GLF2	181
N48CT	**LJ24**	**274**
N48DA	C500	297
N48DD	HS25	25115
(N48DD)	HS25	258207
N48DK	**C550**	**051**
(N48DK)	LJ35	171
N48EC	GLF2	9/33
N48ES	**LJ35**	**087**
N48FB	**F2TH**	**11**
N48FB	HS25	257129
N48FJ	C500	547
N48FN	LJ24	238
N48FN	LJ25	096
N48FU	CL61	5021
N48FU	FA20	495
N48FW	**C550**	**550-0948**
N48G	FA50	258
N48GA	BE40	RJ-28
N48GG	C525	0010
N48GL	FA50	168
N48GL	**GLF4**	**1052**
N48GP	FA50	63
N48GP	LJ35	069
N48GR	**LJ25**	**048**
N48GX	GALX	017
N48HA	F2TH	94
N48HB	FA50	233
N48HC	LJ55	012
N48HC	SBRL	306-96
N48HF	**C750**	**0220**
N48HM	LJ25	030
N48HU	FA20	495
N48JC	FA10	22
N48JC	FA10	37
N48JK	GLF2	71
N48JM	**C52A**	**0316**
N48JW	LJ24	236
N48KF	**PRM1**	**RB-103**
N48KH	**C550**	**325**
N48KR	FA50	127
N48KY	**EA50**	**000178**
N48KZ	**F900**	**191**
N48KZ	LJ60	003
N48L	LJ24	107
N48LB	HS25	257064
N48LC	C560	0463
N48LQ	C560	0463
N48MF	**F2TH**	**115**
N48MF	BE40	RK-218
N48MG	SBRL	306-53
N48MJ	LJ35	448
N48MS	FA10	18
(N48MS)	GLF2	83
N48MW	LJ24	048
N48NA	C56X	5325
(N48NA)	C550	215
N48NC	F2EX	48
N48ND	C550	069
N48NS	**C550**	**550-0939**
N48PJ	**C550**	**668**
N48PL	**BE40**	**RK-138**
N48R	FA10	80
N48R	FA50	160
(N48RA)	GLF2	18
N48RW	LJ35	075
N48SD	**WW24**	**399**
N48SE	**BE40**	**RK-48**
N48SR	BE40	RJ-39
N48TC	**PRM1**	**RB-13**
N48TC	SBRL	282-66
N48TE	LJ45	248
N48TF	C650	0176
N48TF	LJ45	248
N48TJ	FA20	202
N48TT	C650	0105
N48TT	FA10	16
N48TW	FA50	73
N48UC	HS25	25046
N48UC	JSTR	5125/31
N48US	HS25	25252
N48VC	**E50P**	**50000291**
(N48VC)	PRM1	RB-132
N48VE	C750	0248
N48VM	**E55P**	**50500292**

Reg	Type	Serial	Reg	Type	Serial	Reg	Type	Serial	Reg	Type	Serial	Reg	Type	Serial
N48VP	LJ31	240	N50BF	FA50	106	N50GP	C560	0477	N50QN	C650	0197	N51FE	FA50	121
N48WA	LJ25	136	N50BH	FA20	365	N50GT	C500	438	N50QN	C750	0239	N51FF	GLF3	491
N48WK	F2TH	48	N50BH	GLF3	359	N50GT	CS55	0159	N50QN	HA4T	RC-20	N51FJ	F900	51
N48WP	SBRL	282-59	N50BH	HS25	25233	N50GX	GALX	023	N50QS	HA4T	RC-20	N51FJ	FA50	24
N48WS	SBRL	282-59	N50BK	CS55	0031	N50HA	GLF5	5067	N50RD	C500	260	N51FK	C560	0307
N48WS	SBRL	306-124	N50BL	FA50	66	N50HC	FA50	136	(N50RG)	F900	51	N51FL	GLF5	646
N48WW	WW24	384	(N50BM)	CS55	0090	N50HC	FA50	208	(N50RG)	FA50	60	(N51FL)	GLF5	5205
N48Y	HS25	258009	N50BN	HS25	258142	N50HD	FA50	83	N50RL	FA10	66	N51FN	LJ35	059
N49AJ	LJ24	143	N50BV	FA20	365	N50HE	C550	168	N50RL	GLF3	479	N51FN	LJ35	069
N49AS	FA10	49	N50BX	FA50	102	N50HE	FA50	7	N50RW	LJ25	135	N51FT	C500	651
N49AT	LJ35	366	N50BZ	FA50	80	N50HE	GLF4	1219	N50SF	FA50	180	N51FT	C550	134
N49AZ	LJ35	652	N50CA	FA20	28	N50HH	HS25	25022	N50SF	LJ36	010	N51GA	C500	363
N49BA	LJ25	011	N50CC	C500	080	N50HM	FA50	153	N50SJ	FA50	80	N51GJ	EA50	000033
N49BB	LJ25	025	N50CD	SBRL	282-42	N50HM	FA50	290	N50SJ	LJ24	246	(N51GJ)	LJ24	224
N49BE	LJ35	192	N50CK	LJ25	157	N50HN	FA50	153	N50SJ	SJ30	005	N51GL	LJ24	272
N49BH	HS25	25230	N50CR	SBRL	287-1	N50HS	C510	0013	(N50SJ)	FA50	53	N51GM	PRM1	RB-294
N49BL	C500	633	N50CS	FA50	207	N50HS	C550	168	N50SK	C500	046	N51GS	C525	0317
N49CJ	C525	0049	N50CV	C560	0293	N50HS	HS25	257098	N50SK	WW24	309	N51GY	CL61	5316
N49CJ	LJ45	094	N50CZ	C550	650	N50HS	WW24	412	N50SL	C500	046	N51GZ	C52B	0452
N49CK	LJ24	009	N50CZ	FA50	313	N50HT	FA10	163	N50SL	FA10	161	N51HF	C52B	0008
N49CT	WW24	314	N50DD	LJ35	256	N50HW	C550	139	N50SL	FA20	359/542	N51HH	HS25	HA-0169
N49DM	LJ24	238	N50DD	LJ55	066	N50J	FA50	117	N50SL	HS25	25187	N51JA	LJ35	296
N49E	C500	017	N50DG	SBRL	306-19	N50JE	GLF5	567	N50SL	WW24	269	N51JH	CS55	0007
N49EA	C500	017	(N50DG)	SBRL	465-34	N50JF	LJ24	011	(N50SL)	CS55	0109	N51JJ	C52B	0068
N49FW	C550	550-0838	N50DH	LJ25	079	N50JF	LJ24	151	N50SN	FA50	310	N51JT	LJ24	283
N49FW	C550	550-0948	N50DM	FA10	41	N50JG	C500	579	N50SQ	FA50	147	N51JV	C650	0050
N49FW	C750	0021	N50DM	LJ24	025	N50JM	HS25	257033	N50SS	HS25	25028	N51KR	HS25	550-0951
N49GS	LJ24	336	N50DR	C560	0248	N50JP	C550	158	N50TB	FA10	57	N51LC	LJ35	302
N49HM	LJ40	2133	N50DR	LJ24	311	N50JP	WW24	69	N50TC	FA10	31	(N51LN)	C650	7018
N49HS	C550	183	N50DR	WW24	266	N50JR	HS25	257159	N50TC	FA50	115	N51MF	GLF3	491
N49HT	F2EX	185	N50DS	C500	570	(N50K)	SBRL	380-46	N50TC	LJ24	190	N51MF	GLF5	5100
N49JN	BE40	RJ-3	N50DS	C650	0078	N50KC	GLF5	659	N50TE	FA10	86	N51MJ	FA50	54
N49KR	FA50	104	N50DS	CL61	5063	N50KD	FA50	145	N50TG	ASTR	065	N51MJ	LJ25	133
N49KW	C550	550-0838	N50DS	CL64	5544	N50KH	BE40	RK-59	N50TG	CL61	3054	N51ML	BE40	RK-22
N49KW	C550	550-1021	N50DS	CS55	0031	N50KP	JSTR	5214	N50TG	F2EX	49	N51MN	F2TH	14
N49LC	C500	577	N50DS	GLEX	9140	N50KR	C500	629	N50TG	F2TH	96	N51MN	HS25	25190
N49LD	C560	0175	N50DS	LJ60	047	N50KR	FA50	58	N50TG	FA50	117	N51MN	WW24	198
N49LD	C560	0803	N50DT	LJ25	042	N50L	LJ25	152	N50TK	FA10	123	N51MN	WW24	419
N49MJ	C560	0026	N50DT	LJ36	004	N50L	LJ55	004	N50TN	HS25	257033	(N51MN)	SBRL	282-51
N49MJ	C560	0306	N50DW	WW24	380	N50LB	F9DX	608	N50TQ	ASTR	065	N51MW	C500	085
N49MJ	C56X	5100	N50EB	HS25	25253	N50LB	WW24	93	N50TR	C500	325	N51ND	C560	0364
N49MJ	C55	0010	N50EC	JSTR	5033/56	N50LD	C550	0347	N50TX	SBRL	282-23	N51NP	HA4T	RC-45
N49MN	ASTR	019	N50EE	GLF4	1500	N50LD	C56X	5033	N50TY	FA10	72	N51NP	BE40	RK-224
N49MP	C500	519	N50EF	MU30	A081SA	N50LF	CL30	20511	N50UD	JSTR	5019	N51PD	WW24	297
N49MU	C56X	5100	(N50EF)	FA50	54	N50LG	FA20	507	N50UG	HS25	258749	N51PS	C550	365
N49MW	ASTR	019	N50EJ	C650	0148	N50LJ	LJ31	052	N50UJ	GLF4	4052	N51SE	GLEX	9138
N49MW	C510	0010	N50EJ	EA50	000087	N50LK	LJ60	316	N50US	C500	424	N51SF	FA20	12
N49MW	F2TH	44	N50EJ	FA50	3	N50LM	C550	441	N50US	C500	527	N51TJ	CL60	1066
(N49N)	C550	360	N50EL	C560	0036	N50LQ	C560	0347	N50US	C550	032	N51TJ	GLF2	10
N49NS	C550	550-0949	N50EL	LJ60	158	N50LQ	FA50	148	N50US	C550	194	N51TJ	LJ35	183
N49NS	C550	0116	N50ET	C525	0251	N50LT	FA50	44	N50US	C560	0145	N51TV	WW24	175
(N49PD)	LJ55	045	N50ET	C525	0476	N50LV	C52B	0028	N50VC	C525	0609	N51TV	WW24	402
N49PE	LJ35	192	N50FB	FA50	6	N50LV	FA50	65	N50VC	GLEX	9539	N51V	FA50	189
N49PE	LJ55	045	N50FC	C550	255	N50M	WW24	327	N50VF	WW24	13	N51V	HS25	25070
N49PL	EA50	000255	N50FC	HS25	25253	N50MC	C500	381	N50VF	WW24	137	N51V	LJ55	116
N49PP	GLF4	1125	N50FD	WW24	381	(N50MF)	WW24	384	N50VG	FA50	104	N51VC	BE40	RK-288
N49PW	C750	0207	N50FE	FA50	8	N50MG	FA20	507	(N50VH)	PRM1	RB-229	N51VL	LJ24	235
N49R	C500	072	N50FF	FA50	220	N50MG	FA50	255	N50VM	PRM1	RB-229	N51VL	LJ55	116
N49R	C500	281	N50FG	FA50	10	N50MG	GLEX	9605	N50VS	C550	194	N51VR	CL64	5426
N49RF	GLF4	1246	N50FH	FA50	11	N50MG	GLF4	1226	N50W	C550	550-0884	N51VT	C56X	5072
N49RJ	HS25	257007	N50FH	FA50	62	N50MJ	HS25	25152	(N50WB)	C500	102	N51VT	FA50	189
N49RJ	SBRL	282-69	N50FJ	FA50	137	N50MJ	LJ35	103	N50WG	FA50	189	N51WP	C500	528
N49SL	GLF4	1167	N50FJ	FA50	153	N50MJ	LJ35	164	N50WJ	C500	397	N51XP	BE40	RK-451
N49SM	C650	0132	N50FJ	FA50	163	N50MK	FA50	98	N50WM	C500	246	N52	SBRL	380-10
N49TA	WW24	260	N50FJ	FA50	175	(N50ML)	FA50	98	(N50WP)	C500	512	N52AG	C52A	0075
(N49TA)	C500	683	N50FJ	FA50	184	N50MM	C500	118	N50XC	GLEX	9275	N52AJ	C500	061
N49TH	C525	0342	N50FJ	FA50	188	N50MM	C500	622	N50XJ	FA50	80	N52AJ	LJ25	102
N49TJ	C550	051	N50FJ	FA50	197	N50MM	FA20	39	N50XL	C56X	5202	N52AL	BE40	RJ-38
N49TJ	LJ24	295	N50FJ	FA50	212	N50MS	ASTR	140	N50XX	C550	042	N52AN	C500	030
N49TT	C560	0271	N50FJ	FA50	225	N50MT	LJ35	118	N50XX	WW24	311	N52AP	GLF4	1476
N49U	C550	091	N50FJ	FA50	227	(N50MT)	LJ25	353	N50XX	WW24	412	N52AW	BE40	RK-115
N49UC	JSTR	5110/47	N50FJ	FA50	236	N50MV	C550	124	N50XX	WW24	436	N52BH	HS25	25236
N49UR	CL61	5016	N50FJ	FA50	238	N50MW	FA20	503	(N50XX)	WW24	319	N52CC	C500	352
N49US	FA20	494	N50FJ	FA50	244	(N50MX)	FA20	503	N50XY	FA50	83	N52CK	CS55	0076
N49US	GLF3	302	N50FJ	FA50	252	N50N	C550	469	N50XY	GLF3	412	N52CK	CS55	0124
N49VC	GALX	161	N50FJ	FA50	254	(N50NA)	C550	376	(N50YJ)	FA10	57	N52CT	LJ25	362
N49VE	C750	0249	N50FJ	FA50	272	N50NE	HS25	25236	N50YP	FA50	344	N52CT	LJ55	131
N49VG	HS25	258139	N50FJ	FA50	280	N50NF	C550	636	N51	SBRL	380-5	N52DA	LJ25	327
(N49VP)	C550	170	N50FJ	FA50	296	N50NK	FA50	218	N51AJ	LJ24	037	N52DC	F2TH	116
N49WA	LJ25	142	N50FJ	FA50	3	N50NL	F9EX	137	N51AJ	LJ24	273	N52DC	FA50	126
N49WC	C500	490	N50FJ	FA50	310	N50NM	C550	266	N51B	LJ25	027	N52DC	FA50	51
N49WL	LJ35	457	N50FJ	FA50	319	(N50NM)	JSTR	5229	N51B	LJ24	116	N52DD	LJ24	339
N49WW	WW24	389	N50FJ	FA50	336	N50NU	F9EX	137	N51B	MU30	A063SA	N52DQ	FA50	126
N50AC	C500	159	N50FJ	FA50	337	N50PA	CL60	1004	N51B	BE40	RK-261	N52DQ	FA50	51
N50AD	FA20	127	N50FJ	FA50	4	N50PC	FA50	308	N51BE	MU30	A063SA	(N52EB)	BE40	RJ-32
N50AE	FA50	208	N50FJ	FA50	65	N50PD	LJ35	409	N51BH	HS25	25234	N52EN	LJ24	116
N50AE	FA50	254	N50FJ	FA50	85	N50PE	LJ25	176	N51BL	LJ25	269	N52ET	C500	056
N50AE	HS25	258650	(N50FJJ)	FA50	329	N50PG	FA50	8	N51BP	C500	051	N52ET	C52B	0018
N50AE	HS25	HA-0168	N50FK	FA50	13	N50PH	C650	0148	N51BP	FA10	51	N52FC	WW24	379
N50AF	LJ55	038	N50FL	FA50	14	N50PH	LJ35	246	(N51BR)	C500	051	N52FE	C56X	6087
N50AF	LJ55	059	N50FL	FA50	22	N50PH	LJ35	497	N51C	C525	0400	N52FJ	FA50	252
N50AH	FA50	111	N50FM	FA50	19	N50PJ	LJ24	076	N51C	C560	0084	N52FJ	FA50	26
N50AJ	ASTR	030	(N50FM)	FA50	16	N50PL	LJ35	246	N51CA	LJ25	030	(N52FL)	LJ35	067
N50AJ	ASTR	044	N50FN	FA50	18	N50PL	WW24	338	N51CC	C500	457	N52FN	LJ35	424
N50AJ	LJ24	037	N50FN	LJ35	070	(N50PL)	C525	0083	N51CD	C525	0163	N52FP	C500	052
N50AK	LJ35	172	N50FQ	FA50	310	N50PM	GLF2	236	N51CG	C500	457	N52FT	C500	056
N50AL	WW24	190	N50FR	FA50	20	N50PM	GLF3	333	N51CH	LJ24	168	N52FT	CS55	0056
N50AM	C500	041	N50FS	FA50	22	N50PM	HS25	258183	N51CH	WW24	61	N52GA	HS25	257099
N50AN	HS25	258650	N50FT	FA50	023	N50PM	PRM1	RB-11	N51CJ	C500	351	N52GA	BE40	RJ-36
N50AN	LJ31	025	N50FX	FA50	174	N50PM	PRM1	RB-80	N51DA	CS55	0134	N52GG	SBRL	465-5
N50AS	C500	041	N50FX	FA50	175	N50PM	SBRL	380-25	N51DB	LJ25	246	N52GH	LJ24	197
N50AS	HS25	025083	N50GD	HS25	256024	N50PN	PRM1	RB-11	N51DT	LJ25	367	N52GL	LJ25	134
N50AS	JSTR	5058/4	N50GF	FA50	40	(N50PQ)	PRM1	RB-11	N51EB	BE40	RJ-28	N52GW	WW24	330
N50AZ	C550	288	N50GG	SBRL	380-6	N50PR	C500	091	N51EF	C560	0487	N52GX	ASTR	129
N50B	LJ25	224	(N50GG)	C550	042	N50PS	C56X	5134/50	N51EM	C52B	0115	N52JA	FA10	59
(N50B)	FA10	14	N50GJ	LJ60	204	N50QJ	HS25	258216	N51EM	C650	0030	N52JA	LJ25	007
N50BA	LJ24	043	N50GL	LJ25	110	N50QJ	WW24	303	N51ET	C500	450	N52JH	LJ24	139

N52JJ	FA50	205
N52KH	**C525**	**0882**
N52KS	ASTR	033
N52KS	WW24	341
N52KW	C560	0256
N52KX	**C525**	**0287**
N52L	LJ25	141
N52LC	HS25	257131
N52LJ	LJ55	014
N52LT	C525	0322
N52LT	**C550**	**411**
N52MA	C500	052
N52MJ	LJ35	363
N52MK	GLF4	1337
N52MW	**C52B**	**0265**
N52MW	C550	550-0822
N52MW	C56X	5144
N52N	FA10	197
(N52NE)	GLF2	52
N52NW	GLF2	52
N52PK	**C525**	**0052**
N52PM	C500	222
N52RF	C550	011
N52RF	**FA50**	**269**
N52RG	C560	0235
N52RZ	**HS25**	**258177**
N52SD	LJ25	110
N52SM	**HS25**	**259010**
N52SM	WW24	397
N52SN	C560	0207
N52SY	C650	0007
N52SY	**LJ31**	**060**
N52TC	C500	324
N52TJ	FA10	3
N52TJ	FA10	52
N52TJ	JSTR	5078/3
"N52TJ"	GLF2	52
N52TL	**C500**	**418**
N52WC	**C52B**	**0319**
N52WF	**C560**	**0528**
N52WK	**C52B**	**0046**
(N52WS)	C500	110
N52YP	**FA50**	**275**
N52ZG	**C525**	**0891**
N53	SBRL	380-14
(N53AA)	WW24	56
N53AJ	C500	243
N53BB	C500	545
N53BH	HS25	25239
N53CC	C550	350
N53CG	C525	0233
N53CJ	C525	0053
N53CV	C560	0053
N53DB	FA10	41
N53DD	**C550**	**711**
(N53DE)	LJ24	153
N53DF	CL61	5078
N53DF	CL61	5133
N53DF	**CL64**	**5507**
N53DM	LJ35	329
N53DS	FA20	373
N53EB	BE40	RJ-53
N53EZ	C500	497
N53FB	C500	271
N53FJ	**F9EX**	**53**
N53FJ	FA50	28
N53FJ	FA50	53
N53FL	LJ25	017
N53FN	LJ35	021
N53FN	LJ35	053
N53FP	**C550**	**433**
N53FT	C500	238
N53FT	C550	318
N53G	**LJ35**	**274**
N53G	SBRL	306-57
N53GH	HS25	257164
N53GH	LJ24	151
N53GH	LJ35	304
N53GL	GLF3	465
N53GL	LJ24	268
N53GL	LJ35	304
N53GX	**GLEX**	**9053**
N53HF	C750	0236
N53HJ	**LJ55**	**037**
(N53HJ)	LJ55	028
N53HS	C680	0053
N53HS	GLF5	606
N53J	C500	152
N53JA	LJ36	043
N53JL	LJ55	060
N53JM	CS55	0061
N53JM	LJ35	419
N53KB	C550	053
N53KJ	**C52B**	**0154**
N53KN	**C525**	**0169**
N53KV	**C525**	**0030**
N53LB	HS25	258332
N53LM	WW24	311
N53LT	GLF5	541
(N53LV)	LJ60	365
N53M	C550	442
N53M	GLF4	1089
N53M	**GLF5**	**5331**
N53MJ	C500	068
N53MJ	C500	317
N53MS	**BE40**	**RK-64**
N53MU	**C510**	**0463**
N53MU	GLF4	1089
N53NJ	**F2TH**	**174**
N53NW	**C52B**	**0053**
N53PE	**C560**	**0464**
N53PJ	MS76	053
N53RC	C500	497
N53RD	**C500**	**629**
N53RG	C500	402
N53RG	C550	280
N53SF	ASTR	034
N53SF	C52A	0489
N53SF	C52B	0001
N53SF	**C52C**	**0184**
N53SF	FA20	102
N53SM	**C560**	**0353**
N53SN	FA10	54
N53SR	CL60	1078
N53ST	C560	0624
N53TC	LJ25	305
N53TG	F2TH	96
N53TS	FA10	77
N53VP	C550	053
N53VP	C750	0053
N53WA	**EA50**	**000044**
N53WA	FA10	53
N53WC	SBRL	282-137
N53WF	C550	062
N53WF	**C56X**	**5057**
N53WW	WW24	393
N53XL	C56X	5351
N53XL	C56X	6053
N54	**LJ60**	**009**
N54	SBRL	380-16
N54AM	CS55	0085
N54AP	**LJ31**	**220**
N54AX	GALX	054
N54AX	LJ45	377
(N54BC)	WW24	369
N54BE	MU30	A063SA
N54BH	HS25	25241
N54BM	GLF2	236
N54BP	C525	0002
N54BS	**GLF5**	**627**
N54BW	JSTR	5014
N54CC	C550	210
N54CF	**C510**	**0253**
N54CF	SBRL	282-66
N54CG	C500	677
N54CG	**C525**	**0439**
N54CH	LJ31	196
N54CJ	C525	0054
N54CM	C500	293
N54DA	FA50	201
(N54DA)	C550	036
N54DC	**F2TH**	**117**
N54DC	F900	22
N54DD	**C560**	**0089**
N54DR	**FA10**	**94**
N54DS	C500	350
N54DT	**C510**	**0411**
N54ES	HS25	258134
N54FB	**BE40**	**RK-518**
N54FE	**C56X**	**6090**
N54FH	FA10	203
N54FJ	FA10	54
N54FJ	FA50	36
(N54FJ)	FA50	31
N54FL	**C52B**	**0400**
N54FN	**LJ25**	**083**
N54FT	**C500**	**485**
(N54FT)	C500	054
N54GD	HS25	256068
N54GL	LJ35	597
N54GL	LJ55	054
(N54GL)	LJ36	054
N54GP	LJ25	327
N54GX	GALX	025
N54H	FA10	6
N54H	LJ25	124
N54HA	C56X	5040
N54HA	**CL30**	**20076**
N54HC	**C525**	**0157**
N54HC	C650	0098
(N54HC)	C550	368
N54HD	**BE40**	**RK-49**
N54HF	GLF3	459
N54HF	LJ35	472
N54HG	**F9EX**	**140**
N54HH	SBRL	380-19
N54HJ	C550	368
N54HP	**BE40**	**RK-160**
N54HP	BE40	RK-49
N54HT	**LJ31**	**127**
N54HU	LJ25	124
N54J	**F2TH**	**141**
N54J	FA20	289
N54J	GLF2	193
N54JA	LJ36	044
N54JC	CL61	3031
N54JC	**CL64**	**5347**
N54JC	HS25	25249
N54JC	LJ24	340
(N54JC)	LJ25	327
N54JE	**FA10**	**123**
N54JJ	FA20	289
N54JJ	GLF2	193
N54JV	**C500**	**163**
(N54JZ)	LJ55	054
N54KB	GLF5	627
N54KJ	**EA50**	**000091**
(N54LZ)	LJ55	054
N54MC	C500	154
N54MC	LJ25	132
N54MC	WW24	202
N54MH	C500	545
N54MJ	C500	612
N54MQ	LJ25	132
N54NG	**C510**	**0210**
N54NS	C550	578
N54NW	**LJ55**	**054**
(N54NW)	LJ55	024
N54PA	**LJ36**	**004**
(N54PA)	CL60	1081
(N54PA)	CL61	3065
N54PR	CL61	3054
N54PR	GLF5	564
N54PR	LJ35	054
N54PT	WW24	363
N54PV	C510	0028
N54RC	C550	241
N54RM	C550	562
N54RM	MU30	A065SA
N54RS	FA10	94
N54SB	C56X	6146
N54SB	GLF4	1063
N54SB	HS25	258258
(N54SB)	LJ35	644
N54SK	C500	054
N54SK	CL60	1053
N54SK	F900	76
N54SL	GLEX	9187
N54SN	FA20	54
N54SU	CL60	1053
N54TA	LJ25	258
N54TB	C500	482
N54TE	**EA50**	**000054**
N54TG	**GLF5**	**523**
(N54TJ)	HS25	257069
N54TK	BE40	RJ-5
(N54TK)	LJ35	254
N54TN	FA7X	55
N54TN	LJ31	054
N54TS	C500	293
N54V	FA10	35
N54VM	**HS25**	**HA-0110**
N54VM	PRM1	RB-295
N54VS	**CL61**	**5189**
N54WC	C650	0032
N54WC	WW24	117
N54WJ	CS55	0031
N54WJ	FA10	33
N54WJ	HS25	257007
N54XL	C56X	6054
N54YP	FA50	158
N54YP	LJ25	208
N54YP	LJ35	356
N54YR	FA50	158
N54YR	**FA50**	**333**
N54YR	LJ25	208
N54YR	LJ35	356
N55	**LJ60**	**013**
N55	SBRL	380-18
N55AK	C500	299
N55AL	C550	049
N55AL	GLF5	5229
N55AQ	LJ55	072
N55AR	CL60	1044
N55AR	**LJ55**	**105**
N55AS	FA50	214
N55AS	LJ35	146
N55AS	LJ55	072
N55B	HS25	25261
N55BA	**HS25**	**258356**
(N55BE)	C500	476
(N55BE)	LJ55	058
N55BH	C550	057
N55BH	**C650**	**0041**
N55BH	HS25	25244
N55BM	C500	606
N55BP	C550	032
N55BP	FA50	207
N55BP	SBRL	306-20
N55BW	**C52C**	**0136**
N55BX	**EA50**	**000029**
N55CC	C550	055
N55CD	LJ24	306
N55CH	C560	0240
N55CJ	C500	355
N55CJ	**C525**	**0298**
N55CJ	JSTR	5090
N55CJ	LJ36	003
N55CR	SBRL	370-9
N55DD	LJ24	236
N55DD	LJ25	296
N55DG	C525	0044
N55DG	FA10	207
N55DG	**LJ45**	**058**
N55DG	LJ55	102
N55EA	**C560**	**0055**
N55EP	**LJ45**	**336**
N55ES	LJ25	111
N55EY	F2TH	6
N55F	LJ35	147
N55FG	**WW24**	**267**
N55FJ	FA10	55
N55FJ	FA10	74
N55FM	C550	399
N55FN	LJ25	050
N55FN	**LJ35**	**202**
N55FP	**C52B**	**0153**
N55FT	**C500**	**009**
N55G	HS25	25141
N55G	HS25	25163
N55GF	LJ55	052
N55GH	LJ36	012
N55GH	LJ55	012
N55GH	LJ55	075
N55GJ	LJ55	088
(N55GJ)	GLF4	1500
(N55GJ)	LJ55	078
N55GK	LJ55	105
N55GM	LJ55	075
N55GM	LJ55	139A
N55GP	**C52B**	**0113**
N55GR	C500	217
N55GV	**GLF5**	**515**
N55GV	GLF5	545
N55GV	LJ55	078
(N55GV)	GLF5	518
N55GX	ASTR	130
N55GY	LJ55	110
N55GZ	LJ55	083
N55H	C500	552
N55HA	C56X	5059
N55HA	CL30	20090
N55HD	C650	0193
N55HD	LJ55	026
(N55HD)	SBRL	380-39
N55HF	C500	261
N55HF	C550	126
N55HF	C650	0126
N55HF	C650	0193
N55HF	**CL61**	**5183**
N55HK	LJ55	040
N55HL	C500	671
N55HL	LJ55	046
N55HL	**WW24**	**95**
N55HV	C560	0552
N55HX	C56X	5059
N55HY	GLF2	97
N55JM	MU30	A026SA
N55KC	LJ25	046
N55KC	LJ25	147
N55KC	LJ55	014
N55KD	LJ55	051
N55KQ	LJ25	046
N55KS	LJ24	178
N55KS	LJ55	051
N55KS	LJ60	029
N55KS	SBRL	370-5
N55KS	SBRL	465-5
N55KT	**C52A**	**0065**
N55KT	C52A	0177
(N55KT)	C525	0600
N55KX	LJ24	178
N55KZ	SBRL	370-5
N55LB	CL64	5324
N55LB	**HS25**	**258494**
N55LC	C560	0324
N55LC	FA50	314
N55LC	**FA7X**	**38**
N55LF	C500	261
N55LF	LJ55	112
N55LF	LJ55	133
N55LJ	LJ24	203
N55LJ	LJ25	233
N55LJ	LJ55	030
N55LK	LJ55	120
N55LQ	C560	0324
N55LQ	FA50	314
N55LS	C550	107
N55LS	C550	616
N55ME	FA20	83
N55ME	GLF3	325
N55ME	GLF4	1499
(N55ME)	SBRL	282-23
(N55ME)	SBRL	306-27
N55MF	LJ25	171
(N55MF)	LJ25	237
N55MJ	LJ24	203
N55MJ	LJ25	296
N55MT	C550	431
N55MT	HS25	257046
N55MT	SBRL	282-112
N55MV	C550	401
N55MZ	**C52C**	**0135**
N55NC	JSTR	5060
N55NE	JSTR	5155/32
N55NG	**C56X**	**5671**
N55NJ	LJ24	162
N55NM	LJ55	085
N55NT	FA50	87
N55NY	**LJ55**	**020**
(N55PC)	C650	0187
N55PD	LJ25	105
N55PG	CL60	1045
(N55PJ)	LJ55	029
N55PP	SBRL	282-135
N55PT	LJ25	171
N55PX	C525	0285
N55PZ	C525	0285
N55RF	HS25	25020
N55RF	HS25	258066
N55RG	GLF2	1
N55RT	LJ55	095
N55RZ	**HS25**	**25262**
N55RZ	LJ35	439
N55SC	C650	0148
N55SC	**C650**	**7060**
N55SH	C500	315
N55SJ	LJ55	009
N55SK	C500	315
N55SK	**C525**	**0063**
N55SL	LJ25	219
N55SN	FA50	189
N55SQ	C650	0148
N55SQ	**BE40**	**RK-60**
N55SR	CL60	1055
N55SX	C550	065
N55TD	**GLF4**	**1131**
N55TH	FA20	17
N55TJ	**EA50**	**000208**
N55TK	C500	682
N55TP	C550	286
"N55TS"	HS25	257046
N55TY	F9EX	25
N55UH	GLF5	5028
N55UJ	LJ55	090
(N55UJ)	LJ55	050
N55UK	LJ55	147
N55V	LJ25	185
N55VC	**LJ55**	**130**
N55VK	LJ55	078
N55VL	LJ25	176
N55VR	LJ31	033C
N55VW	**C56X**	**5076**
N55VY	LJ31	040
N55WG	C500	604
N55WH	C500	426
N55WJ	LJ25	017
N55WL	**C550**	**155**
N55XP	**HS25**	**258583**
N55XR	LJ40	2055
N55ZM	SBRL	306-84
(N55ZT)	LJ55	139A
N56	**LJ60**	**033**
N56	SBRL	380-20
N56AG	ASTR	043
N56AG	GALX	011
N56AG	GLF4	1125
N56AG	WW24	133
N56AG	WW24	201
N56AG	WW24	374
N56AZ	WW24	133
N56BA	**CL30**	**20228**
N56BE	HS25	258527
N56BE	BE40	RK-13
N56BH	HS25	25237
N56BL	HS25	25201
N56BN	WW24	268
N56BP	WW24	268
(N56BP)	C650	7105
N56BX	BE40	RK-13
N56CC	FA20	313
N56CC	FA20	387
(N56CJ)	C500	495
N56CL	F900	101
N56CL	FA50	196
N56CL	**FA7X**	
N56D	**GLF2**	**257/17**
N56D	GLF4	1309
N56D	GLF4	1411
N56DR	LJ24	311
N56DV	C500	346
N56EG	F2EX	71
N56EL	F2EX	69
N56EL	F2EX	71
N56EL	**GLF4**	**4230**
N56EM	LJ35	144
(N56EP)	C560	0056
N56EX	F2EX	56
N56FB	C550	391
N56FE	C56X	5250
N56FF	BE40	RK-56
N56FJ	FA50	33
N56FT	C550	429
N56GA	C560	0259
N56GA	BE40	RJ-50
(N56GH)	LJ24	233
N56GT	C550	152
N56GT	C560	0091
N56GX	GALX	026
N56GX	GLEX	9656
N56HA	C56X	5063
N56HA	CL30	20105
N56HF	LJ35	084
N56HF	LJ35	144
N56HX	C56X	5063
N56JA	LJ35	342
N56JV	C650	0056
N56K	C525	0005
N56K	C525	0342
N56K	C560	0463
N56K	C56X	5014
N56KG	**C560**	**0563**
N56KP	**C525**	**0629**
N56L	GLF3	302
N56L	**GLF4**	**1213**

N56LA	GLF3	302
N56LB	LJ24	178
N56LC	FA50	275
N56LF	LJ31	056
N56LN	**FA50**	**79**
N56LP	**C56X**	**5068**
N56LP	FA10	165
N56LS	LJ24	178
N56LT	**FA50**	**21**
N56LW	**C500**	**620**
N56MC	C500	386
N56MC	C500	620
N56MC	MU30	A069SA
N56MD	GLF4	1411
N56MD	LJ25	214
N56MJ	C500	614
N56MK	**C500**	**386**
N56MM	**LJ24**	**332**
N56MT	C500	386
N56NW	SBRL	465-62
N56NZ	C525	0056
N56PA	**LJ36**	**023**
N56PB	**C500**	**625**
N56PB	LJ35	224
N56PC	C550	441
N56PR	JSTR	5211
(N56PR)	LJ24	028
(N56PR)	LJ35	370
N56PT	**LJ24**	**276**
N56PZ	**C510**	**0308**
N56RD	LJ24	286
N56RN	SBRL	306-122
N56S	WW24	96
N56SB	**E50P**	**50000090**
(N56SK)	MU30	A008SA
N56SL	FA20	305
N56SN	FA50	216
N56TE	**C560**	**0755**
N56TG	LJ55	078
N56UH	**GLF5**	**5158**
N56VG	FA20	50
N56WD	LJ45	019
N56WE	**C500**	**426**
N56WH	WW24	96
N56WJ	FA10	56
N56WN	C52B	0389
N56WS	LJ24	243
N57	**LJ60**	**039**
N57	SBRL	380-22
N57AJ	C550	100
N57AL	**F2EX**	**55**
N57AY	**HS25**	**257156**
N57B	FA50	57
N57B	LJ55	020
N57B	BE40	RK-36
N57BC	C550	478
N57BC	LJ24	277
N57BE	**WW24**	**428**
N57BG	GLF2	61
N57BH	HS25	25245
N57BJ	**C555**	**0052**
N57BJ	GLF3	327
N57CE	C550	198
N57CE	C560	0048
N57CE	C650	0178
N57CJ	C555	0057
N57CK	C550	198
N57CK	LJ25	157
N57CN	C560	0048
N57DB	LJ24	286
N57DC	FA50	119
N57DL	LJ25	334
N57DM	LJ25	107
N57EC	**C525**	**0460**
N57EJ	C52A	0057
N57EJ	**HS25**	**257056**
N57EL	F2EX	69
N57EL	F900	153
N57EL	F9EX	111
N57EL	FA50	205
N57EL	**GLF4**	**4221**
N57FC	**C500**	**636**
N57FF	HS25	258033
N57FF	LJ35	015
N57FF	LJ35	157
N57FJ	FA50	35
N57FL	**C52A**	**0198**
N57FL	LJ24	243
N57FM	LJ55	025
N57FP	LJ35	157
N57G	HS25	25098
N57GH	C52A	0019
(N57GH)	C525	0149
N57GL	LJ35	057
N57GS	SBRL	282-2
N57GX	ASTR	131
N57HA	C56X	5068
N57HA	**CL30**	**20115**
N57HA	CL61	5010
N57HC	C525	0157
N57HC	C52A	0060
N57HC	C52A	0098
N57HC	**C52C**	**0211**
N57HE	GLF2	194
N57HG	**C52A**	**0098**
N57HH	FA20	74
N57HJ	GLF2	194

N57HJ	**GLF4**	**1261**
(N57HK)	CL61	5010
N57HX	C56X	5068
N57JF	FA20	192
(N57JR)	LJ24	215
N57KE	**WW24**	**406**
N57KF	C555	0111
N57KW	C56X	5214
N57LC	C500	309
N57LE	GLEX	9230
N57LL	**C500**	**025**
N57LN	HS25	258204
N57LQ	**GLF4**	**1156**
N57MB	C500	287
N57MB	C550	044
N57MB	C550	343
N57MB	C560	0286
N57MB	C555	0054
N57MC	C500	636
N57MC	C550	550-1053
N57MC	**LJ40**	**2118**
N57ME	**C550**	**550-1053**
N57MF	C550	137
N57MH	CL61	3054
N57MH	**CL65**	**5842**
N57MH	LJ55	113
N57MJ	C500	624
N57MK	C550	137
N57MK	C560	0145
N57MK	C560	0535
N57MK	**FA50**	**197**
N57ML	C560	0145
(N57ML)	C560	0535
N57MN	F2EX	50
N57MQ	**SBRL**	**465-11**
N57MV	**LJ55**	**113**
(N57NB)	LJ24	145
N57ND	LJ24	145
N57NP	GLF3	340
N57NP	JSTR	5123/14
N57NR	JSTR	5123/14
N57PM	HS25	258218
N57PM	LJ55	025
N57PT	**WW24**	**208**
(N57QR)	SBRL	282-3
N57RG	**G150**	**281**
N57RL	C56X	5247
N57RM	SBRL	282-41
N57SF	C550	366
N57SK	**CL30**	**20259**
N57ST	C560	0383
N57TA	LJ55	010
(N57TA)	LJ55	011
(N57TE)	EA50	000057
N57TP	C56X	5261
N57TS	**LJ31**	**236**
(N57TS)	HS25	25035
N57TT	C650	0046
N57TT	FA20	501
N57TT	GLF3	471
N57TW	C500	624
N57UH	**GLF5**	**5163**
N57VP	C56X	5757
(N57VP)	C560	0007
N57WP	**C56X**	**5317**
N57WW	WW24	390
N58	**LJ60**	**057**
N58	SBRL	380-24
N58AJ	**GLF3**	**446**
N58AN	C550	036
(N58AN)	C500	018
N58AS	FA10	58
N58AS	LJ55	072
N58AU	BE40	RJ-14
N58AU	BE40	RJ-45
(N58B)	FA10	92
(N58BD)	C500	549
N58BH	C550	057
N58BH	HS25	25261
N58BL	**HS25**	**258236**
N58BL	LJ24	268
N58BT	C500	375
N58BT	C500	625
N58BT	HS25	25023
(N58BT)	C500	100
N58CC	C500	015
N58CG	**F9EX**	**47**
N58CG	JSTR	5014
N58CG	LJ55	124
N58CG	SBRL	306-42
N58CM	SBRL	465-70
N58CP	LJ25	133
N58CQ	LJ55	124
N58CW	LJ35	015
N58CW	**LJ35**	**116**
N58DJ	LJ25	328
N58DM	LJ24	184
(N58DT)	C500	375
N58EH	**EA50**	**000171**
N58EM	**LJ35**	**046**
N58FB	WW24	258
N58FE	C56X	5285
N58FF	LJ35	015
N58FJ	FA50	38
N58FM	LJ55	085
N58FN	LJ24	184
N58GG	C550	269

N58GG	**F2EX**	**285**
N58GL	LJ25	148
N58GL	LJ35	599
N58GX	ASTR	135
N58H	C550	335
N58HA	C56X	5099
N58HA	**CL30**	**20146**
N58HC	C650	0091
N58HC	**LJ25**	**341**
N58HK	C550	550-1086
N58HL	**FA50**	**279**
N58HT	**SBRL**	**465-70**
N58HX	**C56X**	**5099**
(N58JA)	LJ25	007
N58JF	**GLF2**	**65**
N58JM	SBRL	306-24
N58JN	**C525**	**0607**
N58JV	C52B	0270
N58KJ	C525	0005
N58KJ	C560	0463
(N58KJ)	C56X	5014
N58KS	SBRL	370-5
N58KY	C52A	0082
N58KY	**EA50**	**000016**
N58LC	C550	711
N58LC	C56X	5109
N58LC	**CL30**	**20163**
N58LQ	**C56X**	**5109**
N58M	LJ35	037
N58M	LJ55	077
N58MM	**LJ35**	**261**
N58MW	**F2EX**	**217**
N58PL	C500	033
N58PM	HS25	258220
N58PM	LJ55	085
N58RG	C560	0422
N58RW	C650	0006
N58RW	LJ35	133
N58SR	LJ55	058
N58ST	LJ60	186
(N58T)	C500	397
N58TC	C500	261
N58TJ	MU30	A030SA
N58TS	JSTR	5079/33
N58VL	**EA50**	**000130**
N58WV	C550	550-0896
N58WW	WW24	201
N58XL	C56X	5099
N58XL	C56X	6058
N59	**LJ60**	**080**
N59	SBRL	380-26
N59AC	JSTR	5204
"N59AC"	LJ25	100
N59AJ	GLF3	413
N59AL	**LJ24**	**236**
N59AP	GLF4	1476
N59AP	**GLF4**	**4127**
N59AP	WW24	398
N59B	C650	0191
N59BH	HS25	25262
N59BL	LJ25	201
N59BP	LJ25	124
N59BP	BE40	RK-226
N59BR	HS25	258425
N59BR	**HS25**	**258599**
N59BR	BE40	RK-226
N59CC	C500	488
N59CC	C550	430
N59CC	FA10	6
(N59CC)	C650	0211
N59CD	C650	0079
N59CD	GLF2	190
N59CD	JSTR	5155/32
N59CF	F900	98
N59CF	FA50	209
N59CF	**GLF4**	**4097**
N59CH	FA50	209
N59CJ	C52A	0059
N59CL	C500	173
N59CT	WW24	96
N59DF	**C560**	**0098**
N59DM	HS25	258201
N59DM	LJ35	205
N59DY	C550	334
N59EC	**C56X**	**5123**
N59EC	C555	0034
N59EL	FA50	205
N59FA	C550	334
N59FD	LJ60	084
N59FJ	FA50	39
(N59FJ)	CL61	5001
N59FL	LJ25	169
N59FN	LJ35	205
N59FT	**C650**	**0123**
N59FY	C550	334
N59GB	**C550**	**377**
N59GL	LJ24	286
N59GL	LJ35	604
N59GS	FA50	36
N59GS	LJ55	056
N59GU	C550	340
N59GX	GALX	035
N59HA	C560	0457
N59HA	GLF3	397
N59HJ	LJ55	027
N59JC	WW24	59
N59JE	**GLF5**	**559**

N59JG	LJ24	221
N59JM	C52C	0078
N59JM	SBRL	306-135
N59JN	C525	0607
N59JN	**C52A**	**0407**
N59JR	GLF2	190
N59JR	GLF4	1007
N59JR	HS25	256065
N59K	SBRL	282-36
N59K	**SBRL**	**306-82**
N59KC	C560	0363
N59KC	WW24	210
N59KG	C560	0363
N59KG	C560	0563
N59KG	**CL30**	**20393**
N59KQ	SBRL	282-36
N59LB	F900	51
N59LJ	LJ55	059
N59LW	**C510**	**0213**
N59MA	**C500**	**398**
N59ME	**GLF3**	**325**
N59MJ	C550	033
N59MJ	LJ35	389
N59NH	C560	0139
N59PC	C500	418
N59PK	SBRL	282-36
N59PM	FA50	178
N59PT	WW24	202
N59PT	**WW24**	**391**
N59PW	**E50P**	**50000081**
(N59RK)	PRM1	RB-163
N59SG	LJ25	163
N59SM	WW24	390
N59SR	SBRL	465-59
N59TF	C560	0422
N59TF	**C680**	**0311**
N59TJ	FA10	14
N59TJ	MU30	A004SA
(N59TJ)	HS25	257073
N59TS	C500	160
N59VM	**C510**	**0181**
N59WG	**C52B**	**0374**
N59WK	WW24	243
N59WP	C500	498
N59ZZ	GLEX	9366
N60	SBRL	380-28
N60AC	GLF3	424
N60AD	CL30	20380
N60AE	C560	0343
(N60AE)	C560	0561
N60AF	C650	0136
N60AF	SBRL	306-140
N60AG	C56X	5255
N60AG	GLF3	376
N60AG	SBRL	306-132
N60AG	SBRL	306-48
(N60AG)	SBRL	306-14
N60AH	SBRL	306-43
N60AJ	ASTR	042
N60AJ	ASTR	061
N60AJ	ASTR	071
N60AJ	**LJ60**	**393**
N60AJ	LJ60	401
N60AL	WW24	193
N60AM	SBRL	306-135
(N60AM)	HS25	25142
N60AN	LJ60	099
N60AR	C550	144
N60AV	WW24	254
N60AX	LJ60	366
N60B	HS25	25195
N60B	MU30	A045SA
N60B	BE40	RK-33
N60BB	C550	234
N60BC	JSTR	5116
N60BC	**LJ60**	**105**
N60BD	HS25	25195
N60BE	C650	0112
N60BK	SBRL	306-15
N60BP	SBRL	306-91
N60BT	**WW24**	**432**
N60CC	C550	034
N60CC	GLF2	142
N60CD	WW24	44
N60CE	LJ60	069
N60CE	SBRL	465-5
N60CH	JSTR	5037/24
N60CN	FA50	79
N60CN	JSTR	5037/24
N60CP	**C510**	**0064**
N60CP	C510	0121
N60CR	SBRL	306-7
N60CT	CL64	5325
N60CT	GLF2	113
N60CT	GLF3	454
N60DD	SBRL	306-127
(N60DD)	FA20	479
N60DE	SBRL	306-25
N60DG	WW24	364
N60DH	LJ24	033
N60DK	LJ25	092
N60DK	LJ25	231
N60DK	LJ25	245
N60DK	LJ35	394
N60DK	LJ35	505
(N60DK)	LJ25	250
N60DL	SBRL	306-25

N60E	LJ55	106
(N60EE)	JSTR	5160
N60EF	**MU30**	**A070SA**
N60EL	SBRL	306-13
N60EL	SBRL	306-42
N60ES	C525	0053
N60ES	**C750**	**0035**
N60EW	**C500**	**665**
N60EX	F9EX	60
N60EX	SBRL	306-7
(N60EX)	SBRL	306-37
N60FC	CL61	5062
N60FC	FA10	25
N60FE	LJ60	003
N60FJ	C550	018
N60FJ	FA50	41
N60FK	**F2EX**	**158**
N60FN	LJ24	339
N60FP	**LJ60**	**428**
N60FS	SBRL	306-101
N60FT	**C550**	**470**
N60FZ	LJ60	290
N60GD	**LJ55**	**035**
N60GF	C550	574
N60GF	**LJ60**	**077**
N60GG	CL61	5007
N60GG	GLF2	108
N60GG	LJ60	017
(N60GG)	C500	380
N60GH	SBRL	306-7
N60GL	C550	574
N60GL	C560	0187
N60GL	C56X	5014
N60GL	LJ24	260
N60GN	GLF3	392
N60GS	C510	0247
N60GT	**MS76**	**008**
N60GU	GLF2	150
N60GX	GALX	028
N60GX	GLEX	9126
N60HC	SBRL	306-21
N60HD	HS25	258334
N60HJ	CL60	1058
N60HJ	GLF2	119/22
N60HJ	HS25	257057
N60HJ	**LJ60**	**378**
N60HM	FA10	199
N60HM	LJ60	067
N60HS	LJ60	225
N60HU	HS25	25103
(N60HU)	HS25	257057
(N60HW)	C550	377
N60JC	HS25	25174
N60JC	**SBRL**	**306-51**
N60JD	C550	259
N60JF	SBRL	306-33
N60JM	HS25	257036
N60JM	JSTR	5213
N60JN	SBRL	306-14
N60JP	WW24	320
N60KF	LJ60	059
N60KH	LJ60	272
N60KJ	LJ60	005
N60KM	**C560**	**0453**
N60KR	CL61	5073
N60LE	LJ60	354
N60LH	LJ60	113
N60LJ	LJ60	003
N60LJ	LJ60	026
N60LJ	**LJ60**	**052**
N60LJ	LJ60	071
N60LJ	LJ60	081
N60LJ	LJ60	110
N60LJ	LJ60	164
N60LJ	LJ60	217
N60LJ	LJ60	283
N60LJ	LJ60	320
N60LJ	LJ60	337
N60LJ	LJ60	374
N60LJ	LJ60	388
N60LR	LJ60	036
N60LR	LJ60	056
N60LR	LJ60	094
N60LR	LJ60	125
N60LR	LJ60	177
N60LT	LJ55	060
N60LW	C550	550-1129
N60MB	FA10	15
N60ME	**FA50**	**255**
N60ME	PRM1	RB-9
N60MG	LJ60	042
N60MJ	LJ55	060
N60ML	SBRL	306-129
N60MM	C550	192
N60MN	LJ60	100
N60MP	C500	325
N60MS	C500	170
N60MS	CL61	3051
N60MS	HS25	257014
N60MU	CL61	3051
N60ND	FA10	21
N60ND	**LJ55**	**088**
N60NF	C560	0562
N60NS	C560	0258
N60NY	GLF4	1132
N60PC	HS25	25214
N60PC	LJ45	109

N60PC	LJ45	351
N60PC	**LJ45**	**477**
N60PE	GLF4	1251
N60PL	C650	7056
N60PL	LJ45	477
N60PM	HS25	258187
N60PM	SBRL	370-7
N60PR	C500	549
N60PT	GLF4	1251
N60PT	GLF4	1379
N60PT	SBRL	370-7
N60QA	HS25	25214
N60QB	**C560**	**0087**
N60QG	LJ24	025
N60QJ	GLF5	5138
N60QJ	HS25	258217
N60QJ	JSTR	5039
N60QJ	WW24	302
N60RB	SBRL	282-68
N60RC	SBRL	282-134
N60RD	C560	0244
N60RE	F900	75
N60RE	HS25	25232
N60RL	LJ60	136
N60RL	**LJ60**	**278**
(N60RL)	SBRL	306-18
N60RS	SBRL	306-110
N60RS	SBRL	306-124
N60RS	SBRL	306-132
N60RS	SBRL	306-142
N60RS	SBRL	306-44
N60RS	SBRL	306-87
N60RU	**LJ60**	**136**
N60RV	WW24	250
(N60RV)	ASTR	063
N60RY	LJ60	108
N60S	C560	0066
N60S	**C56X**	**6110**
N60S	CL60	1030
N60SB	**CL30**	**20019**
N60SB	LJ60	023
N60SE	**LJ60**	**273**
N60SE	LJ60	293
N60SE	SBRL	306-100
N60SH	C560	0106
N60SJ	LJ60	386
N60SJ	SJ30	006
N60SL	FA10	189
N60SL	SBRL	306-126
N60SL	SBRL	306-137
N60SL	SBRL	306-145
N60SL	SBRL	306-82
N60SL	SBRL	306-86
N60SL	SBRL	380-60
N60SM	FA20	24
N60SM	JSTR	5161/43
N60SN	FA20	24
N60SN	LJ60	267
N60SQ	SBRL	306-109
N60SR	LJ60	023
N60T	LJ60	011
(N60TA)	GLF2	241
N60TC	F2TH	80
N60TC	**GLF4**	**4210**
N60TC	HS25	258179
N60TF	SBRL	306-114
N60TG	HS25	258179
N60TG	LJ60	225
N60TG	SBRL	306-86
N60TL	F900	75
N60TM	SBRL	306-72
N60TN	HS25	257036
N60TQ	F2TH	80
N60TX	LJ60	097
N60UJ	JSTR	5086/44
N60UJ	LJ60	007
N60UK	LJ60	004
N60VE	LJ60	006
N60VE	LJ60	222
N60VL	LJ60	006
N60VV	**LJ60**	**104**
N60WA	LJ55	129
N60WL	**LJ35**	**382**
(N60WL)	SBRL	282-61
N60WM	LJ60	045
(N60WP)	SBRL	380-39
N60XA	LJ60	343
N60XC	**GLEX**	**9588**
N60XL	LJ55	001
N60XL	LJ60	55-001
N60XP	BE40	RK-600
N60XR	LJ60	294
N60XR	LJ60	358
"N60XR"	LJ60	367
N60Y	SBRL	282-26
N60Y	SBRL	306-13
N60YC	LJ60	267
N60ZD	LJ60	166
N61	SBRL	380-29
N61AF	CL61	3008
N61AW	LJ24	323
N61BA	LJ24	246
N61BE	C650	0129
N61BL	HS25	25095
N61BP	FA10	102
(N61BP)	C500	051
(N61BP)	FA10	92
N61BR	C500	051
N61CD	C500	545
N61CF	C550	335
N61CJ	C525	0061
N61CK	C550	259
N61CK	C650	0150
N61CK	LJ24	119
N61CP	BE40	RK-402
N61CS	**C550**	**383**
N61CT	HS25	258108
(N61CV)	C525	0261
N61DF	C680	0012
N61DF	**C680**	**0329**
N61DF	HS25	258386
N61DF	SBRL	306-131
N61DF	SBRL	465-59
N61DM	LJ24	224
N61DN	HS25	258386
N61DP	LJ60	122
N61DT	C500	569
N61DT	**EA50**	**000192**
(N61EP)	C510	0105
N61EW	LJ25	161
N61FB	**SBRL**	**306-80**
N61FC	FA10	194
(N61FC)	SBRL	282-42
N61FF	**CL61**	**5166**
N61FJ	FA50	42
(N61FN)	LJ24	224
N61GA	MU30	A045SA
N61GB	**BE40**	**RK-341**
(N61GF)	HS25	257098
N61GK	**C560**	**0149**
"N61GV"	GLF5	509
N61GX	GALX	029
N61HA	C550	335
N61HA	C560	0295
N61HF	**EA50**	**000012**
N61HH	C510	0390
N61HH	**C510**	**0393**
N61HT	**C550**	**229**
N61JB	C560	0273
N61JD	**C680**	**680A0019**
N61JE	ASTR	112
N61JE	**F2TH**	**72**
N61KB	C750	0021
N61KM	**C560**	**0255**
N61KT	C680	0229
N61KW	F2TH	137
N61LA	GLF4	1266
N61LF	C510	0299
N61LH	GLF2	61
N61LL	FA20	244
N61MA	**C550**	**203**
N61MD	SBRL	306-3
N61MJ	C500	180
N61MR	**C510**	**0243**
N61MS	HS25	25229
N61MS	HS25	25263
N61MX	HS25	25229
N61PM	FA20	355
N61PR	C500	639
N61RH	SBRL	282-27
N61RN	**F2TH**	**61**
N61RS	WW24	384
N61SB	HS25	256002
N61SF	LJ24	346
N61SH	**C525**	**0095**
N61SJ	LJ35	488
N61SJ	**LJ55**	**081**
N61SM	GLF2	122
N61SM	BE40	RK-60
N61SS	**C550**	**088**
(N61TE)	EA50	000061
N61TF	**CL30**	**20110**
N61TF	HS25	256039
(N61TF)	C525	0118
N61TJ	FA10	41
N61TJ	GLF2	256
(N61TJ)	LJ24	241
N61TL	C560	0461
N61TL	CS55	0109
N61TS	F900	13
N61TS	HS25	256001
N61TS	LJ24	029
N61TW	C560	0019
N61VC	**BE40**	**RK-450**
N61VE	LJ60	224
N61VW	**LJ31**	**049**
N61WE	GLF2	48/29
N61WF	**LJ60**	**313**
N61WH	GLF2	48/29
N61WH	**GLF4**	**1075**
N61WT	LJ25	288
(N61WT)	LJ25	265
N61XL	C56X	6061
N61XP	BE40	RK-461
N61YC	LJ60	011
N61YP	C525	0237
N61ZZ	LJ60	128
N62	SBRL	380-31
N62AE	**G280**	**2041**
N62BH	HS25	25263
N62BL	CL60	1062
N62BR	C500	093
N62BX	LJ60	062
N62CB	GLF2	208
N62CF	SBRL	306-62
N62CH	HS25	25221
N62CH	MU30	A082SA
N62CR	C560	0188
N62DK	LJ25	356
N62DK	LJ35	231
N62DM	LJ24	194
N62DM	LJ25	082
N62DT	**FA50**	**200**
(N62DW)	SBRL	306-41
N62EA	HS25	257062
N62FJ	F900	62
N62FJ	FA50	44
N62FJ	FA7X	62
(N62FN)	LJ24	194
N62GA	C560	0058
N62GB	C56X	5086
N62GB	C56X	5207
N62GB	GALX	117
N62GB	GALX	175
N62GC	C550	482
N62GG	GLF3	302
N62GL	LJ55	062
N62GR	C56X	5207
N62GX	GALX	031
N62HA	C550	231
N62HA	C560	0189
N62HB	C500	213
N62HM	**FA50**	**243**
N62K	GLF2	93
N62K	JSTR	5099/5
N62K	SBRL	282-53
N62KK	JSTR	5099/5
N62KM	BE40	RK-53
N62LJ	**LJ55**	**056**
N62LW	PRM1	RB-92
N62MB	**LJ35**	**282**
N62MF	**F2TH**	**17**
N62ML	GLF5	605
N62MS	CL61	3050
N62MS	GLF4	1248
N62MS	**GLF5**	**5017**
N62MS	GLF5	605
N62MS	HS25	257017
N62MU	CL61	3050
N62MV	**GLF3**	**484**
N62MW	GLF3	484
N62ND	WW24	379
N62NR	SBRL	380-54
N62NS	CS55	0072
N62NW	**F900**	**157**
N62PG	**LJ36**	**031**
N62Q	SBRL	282-53
N62RA	**LJ35**	**312**
N62RC	**EA50**	**000043**
N62RG	C500	601
N62RG	C550	639
(N62SG)	C56X	5253
N62SH	C525	0423
N62SH	**C52B**	**0002**
N62TC	HS25	25261
N62TC	HS25	258239
N62TE	**EA50**	**000062**
N62TF	HS25	25232
N62TJ	FA10	44
N62TJ	HS25	25023
N62TL	**C550**	**462**
N62TW	C500	281
N62TW	HS25	25224
N62VE	C750	0004
N62WA	C550	583
N62WA	C560	0360
N62WA	C560	0758
N62WA	**C56X**	**6205**
N62WB	GLF2	152
N62WD	**C560**	**0360**
N62WG	C550	482
N62WH	HS25	257125
N62WL	HS25	257125
N62WM	**C510**	**0396**
N62WM	LJ35	596
N62XR	LJ60	362
N62YC	F2EX	119
N62ZS	LJ25	162
N63	SBRL	380-33
N63A	FA50	19
N63A	SBRL	282-36
N63AD	**EA50**	**000163**
N63AX	LJ55	063
N63BA	FA10	99
N63BH	HS25	25265
N63BL	HS25	25033
N63BL	LJ60	051
N63BW	LJ24	353
N63CC	C550	489
N63CF	C500	097
N63CG	C500	519
N63CJ	**C52B**	**0064**
N63CK	LJ24	119
N63CR	C680	0122
N63CR	CS55	0036
N63DH	LJ35	261
N63DR	MU30	A067SA
N63EM	**HS25**	**25272**
N63ET	LJ25	110
N63FF	**C560**	**0063**
N63FJ	FA50	45
N63FJ	FA50	63
(N63FS)	C550	321
N63FT	**C56X**	**5541**
N63GA	**LJ24**	**241**
N63GB	C560	0454
N63GC	C650	0179
N63GH	MU30	A025SA
N63HA	C560	0199
N63HA	**CS55**	**0119**
N63HB	C525	0019
N63HJ	CL60	1021
N63HS	GLF4	1249
N63HS	**GLF5**	**5013**
N63HS	GLF5	606
N63JG	**C560**	**0189**
N63JG	CS55	0036
N63JP	**F9EX**	**249**
N63JT	**CS55**	**0156**
N63JU	CS55	0036
N63KH	LJ25	287
N63LB	C525	0127
N63LB	C550	550-0920
N63LE	LJ35	250
N63LF	C525	0127
N63LF	LJ35	250
N63LX	C56X	5163
N63LX	C680	0084
N63M	GLF4	1152
N63M	**GLF5**	**5376**
"N63M"	GLF4	1022
N63MJ	LJ45	055
N63MU	GLF4	1152
N63NC	SBRL	306-7
N63NM	GLF4	1066
N63NW	C550	550-1119
N63PM	FA20	355
N63PM	HS25	257167
N63PM	HS25	258183
N63PP	WW24	394
N63RS	**CS55**	**0046**
N63SB	LJ25	073
N63SD	GLF2	216
N63SE	LJ31	203
N63SL	SBRL	282-127
N63SN	BE40	RJ-3
N63ST	CL61	5149
N63TJ	FA10	186
N63TM	C550	457
N63TM	C560	0383
N63TM	**C680**	**0019**
N63TS	FA10	66
N63WD	**WW24**	**402**
N63WG	LJ45	486
N63WJ	**LJ45**	**278**
(N63WL)	LJ45	278
N63WR	LJ45	278
N63WR	**LJ45**	**486**
N63XF	**F9EX**	**222**
N63XG	**ASTR**	**055**
N63XG	FA10	103
N63XL	C56X	6163
N63XP	**BE40**	**RK-563**
N63YA	**C525**	**0830**
N64	SBRL	380-35
N64AH	WW24	94
(N64AJ)	C500	085
N64AL	GLF4	1013
N64AM	FA10	157
N64AM	SBRL	306-7
N64BD	F900	16
N64BE	F900	45
N64BH	**C500**	**673**
N64BH	CL61	5027
N64BH	HS25	25267
N64C	JSTR	5131
N64CA	C550	030
N64CE	LJ24	205
N64CF	LJ24	205
N64CF	**LJ35**	**461**
N64CM	C550	467
N64CM	SBRL	306-135
N64CP	LJ35	264
N64DH	**SBRL**	**282-52**
(N64DH)	LJ35	119
N64EX	F2EX	164
N64EZ	MU30	A062SA
(N64EZ)	MU30	A090SA
N64F	CL61	5021
N64F	FA10	188
N64FC	CL60	1035
N64FE	CL61	5005
N64FG	WW24	227
N64FJ	FA50	46
(N64FN)	LJ35	073
(N64FN)	LJ36	023
N64FS	**WW24**	**417**
N64FT	**C560**	**0142**
N64GG	HS25	257157
N64GL	CL60	1064
N64GX	ASTR	134
N64HA	C560	0127
N64HA	HS25	257051
N64HA	LJ60	205
N64HB	LJ24	149
N64HH	**LJ45**	**087**
N64HT	**LJ40**	**2007**
(N64HX)	LJ60	205
N64JP	**LJ60**	**246**
(N64JY)	C550	679
N64KT	WW24	296
N64LE	**CL61**	**5031**
N64LE	LJ60	068
N64LF	C525	0218
N64LV	**C560**	**0345**
N64LW	**C52A**	**0464**
N64LX	C56X	5164
N64LX	C56X	5638
N64MA	SBRL	282-44
N64MC	SBRL	282-114
N64MC	SBRL	465-73
N64MG	**LJ60**	**224**
N64MG	SBRL	282-114
N64MH	LJ35	048
N64MP	LJ25	078
N64MP	LJ35	060
N64MP	LJ35	490
N64MP	SBRL	380-32
N64MQ	SBRL	380-32
N64MQ	SBRL	465-73
N64MR	LJ25	078
N64MR	LJ35	060
N64NB	**LJ31**	**065**
N64NC	SBRL	306-109
N64PM	C525	0394
N64PM	C550	467
N64PM	C560	0188
N64PM	**PRM1**	**RB-168**
N64PZ	C525	0394
N64RT	**C500**	**585**
N64RV	LJ35	355
N64SL	LJ60	029
N64SL	SBRL	465-42
N64SV	**C560**	**0764**
N64TF	**C550**	**080**
N64UC	**CL64**	**5587**
N64VM	**BE40**	**RJ-1**
N64VP	C550	604
N64WH	LJ25	102
N64WM	LJ55	022
N64YP	CL61	5077
N64YP	FA20	502
N64YR	FA20	502
N65	SBRL	380-37
N65A	LJ25	134
N65A	WW24	235
N65AD	SBRL	465-65
N65AF	SBRL	465-62
N65AH	SBRL	465-68
N65AK	**SBRL**	**465-35**
N65AM	SBRL	465-58
N65AN	SBRL	465-59
N65AR	C550	585
N65AR	SBRL	465-67
N65B	FA50	10
N65BE	GLF3	332
N65BH	HS25	25273
N65BK	C525	0657
(N65BK)	WW24	216
N65BL	LJ60	054
N65BP	C650	0202
N65BT	**SBRL**	**465-3**
N65BZ	C52A	0072
N65CC	**GLF4**	**1412**
N65CC	SBRL	465-46
N65CD	C52C	0072
N65CE	GLF3	383
N65CE	HS25	258234
N65CK	C525	0493
N65CK	C52A	0185
N65CK	**C52A**	**0323**
N65CR	C52A	0185
N65DA	C550	189
N65DD	**C52C**	**0151**
N65DD	SBRL	465-26
N65DH	LJ35	174
N65DH	LJ35	381
N65DL	HS25	25287
N65DL	HS25	257174
N65DL	**HS25**	**258224**
N65DR	SBRL	465-45
N65DT	CS55	0006
N65DU	HS25	257174
N65DV	**C550**	**624**
N65DW	HS25	25208
N65EC	HS25	25208
N65EM	C525	0615
N65FA	HS25	258065
N65FC	HS25	25091
N65FC	SBRL	465-31
N65FF	CL61	5122
N65FF	SBRL	465-46
N65FJ	FA50	47
(N65FN)	LJ35	00
(N65GB)	HS25	256013
N65GD	HS25	258050
N65GW	WW24	349
N65GX	ASTR	133
N65HA	C560	0143
N65HA	LJ60	228
N65HD	CL65	5753
N65HD	**GLF4**	**4195**
N65HF	C650	0126
N65HH	SBRL	465-1
N65HJ	CL60	1038

(N65HM)	SBRL	465-21
N65HS	FA50	65
(N65HS)	FA10	99
N65HU	**LJ60**	**228**
N65JN	MU30	A065SA
N65JR	**SBRL**	**465-23**
N65JR	SBRL	465-24
N65JT	JSTR	5213
(N65JW)	JSTR	5086/44
(N65JW)	JSTR	5113/25
N65KB	C650	0199
N65KJ	SBRL	465-1
N65KZ	**E55P**	**50500103**
N65L	SBRL	465-76
N65LC	C550	317
N65LC	FA20	40
N65LC	HS25	257202
N65LE	FA20	40
N65LJ	LJ24	037
N65LJ	**LJ60**	**243**
N65LR	**LJ60**	**365**
N65LT	HS25	25202
N65LW	**C52B**	**0373**
N65M	C500	511
N65M	GLF2	136
N65MA	C500	033
N65MC	**SBRL**	**465-36**
N65MK	HS25	25032
N65ML	**SBRL**	**465-69**
N65MU	**C510**	**0465**
N65NC	SBRL	465-6
N65NR	SBRL	306-118
N65NR	SBRL	306-124
N65NR	SBRL	465-24
N65NY	**F2EX**	**268**
(N65PF)	LJ35	094
N65PX	**CL65**	**5804**
(N65PX)	C52A	0072
N65PZ	C52A	0072
N65QT	GLF4	4136
N65R	GALX	072
N65R	SBRL	306-114
N65RA	C500	434
N65RA	**BE40**	**RJ-9**
N65RC	LJ25	055
N65RC	SBRL	465-19
(N65RC)	LJ25	163
N65RL	**C560**	**0179**
N65RN	SBRL	306-114
N65RS	SBRL	306-136
N65RS	SBRL	465-1
N65RS	SBRL	465-3
N65RZ	**LJ35**	**236**
N65SA	C500	114
N65SA	MU30	A067SA
(N65SA)	C550	119
N65SD	F2TH	32
N65SL	SBRL	465-10
N65SR	SBRL	465-16
N65SR	SBRL	465-54
N65SR	SBRL	465-6
N65ST	C750	0211
N65ST	GLF2	5
N65T	LJ60	213
N65T	**SBRL**	**465-43**
(N65T)	C500	624
(N65TA)	LJ35	364
N65TB	PRM1	RB-19
N65TC	SBRL	465-30
N65TD	ASTR	093
N65TD	WW24	366
N65TE	EA50	000065
N65TF	C550	175
N65TJ	SBRL	465-45
N65TL	SBRL	465-56
N65TP	C550	674
N65TP	**LJ40**	**2084**
N65TS	FA20	368
N65TS	HS25	25043
N65TS	SBRL	465-34
N65U	LJ45	073
N65VM	**C52B**	**0034**
N65WH	LJ25	086
(N65WH)	LJ35	275
N65WL	C650	0122
N65WL	**GLEX**	**9089**
N65WM	LJ24	163
N65WS	C500	076
N65WW	**C500**	**591**
N65XC	GLEX	9588
N65Y	LJ55	121
N65ZZ	GLEX	9361
N66AG	C500	520
N66AL	GLF2	166/15
N66AM	**C525**	**0160**
N66AM	HS25	25087
N66AM	LJ24	064
N66AS	LJ24	029
N66AT	C500	520
N66AT	C550	184
N66BE	**C525**	**0174**
N66BH	HS25	25275
N66BK	**C500**	**658**
N66BX	**EA50**	**000154**
N66CC	C500	066
N66CD	SBRL	282-134
N66CF	FA10	65
N66CR	JSTR	5052
N66DD	C550	263
N66DD	**FA7X**	**153**
N66DD	GLF3	483
N66DD	GLF4	1355
N66DN	C550	263
N66DN	LJ45	236
(N66EA)	CS55	0006
N66ED	GLF4	1355
N66ED	SBRL	380-32
N66EH	CS55	0158
N66ES	C500	314
N66ES	**C510**	**0110**
N66ES	C525	0053
N66ES	C525	0244
N66ES	C550	032
N66ES	SBRL	282-91
N66ES	SBRL	380-32
N66EW	WW24	9
N66FE	LJ35	383
N66FG	WW24	357
"N66FG"	MU30	A066SA
(N66FH)	C525	0480
N66FJ	**F9EX**	**66**
N66FJ	FA50	49
(N66FN)	LJ24	268
(N66FN)	LJ35	067
N66GA	FA20	341
N66GE	C500	258
N66GE	SBRL	306-99
N66GE	**SBRL**	**465-28**
N66GX	GALX	032
N66GZ	SBRL	306-99
N66HA	HS25	25126
N66HD	C500	407
N66HD	CS55	0134
N66HH	FA10	176
(N66HM)	LJ35	206
N66JD	LJ25	183
N66JE	WW24	326
N66KC	HS25	25038
N66KG	ASTR	096
N66KK	LJ35	095
N66LB	C550	051
N66LD	**E55P**	**50500300**
N66LE	C500	170
N66LJ	LJ35	401
N66LM	C56X	5074
N66LM	LJ35	306
N66LN	LJ35	500
N66LW	LJ24	311
N66LX	WW24	375
N66MC	**C550**	**256**
N66ME	C650	0079
N66MF	CL60	1036
N66MF	FA10	29
(N66MF)	WW24	414
N66MJ	LJ24	334
N66MP	JSTR	5015
N66MP	LJ24	058
N66MR	LJ24	159
N66MS	C550	342
N66MT	**C550**	**550-0913**
N66MW	LJ24	066
N66NJ	LJ25	039
N66NJ	LJ35	296
N66NR	SBRL	306-62
N66NS	CL61	5096
N66NT	CL61	5068
N66NT	CL61	5096
N66NT	FA20	349
(N66PJ)	LJ35	256
N66PL	MU30	A077SA
N66RP	LJ24	198
N66SG	**LJ45**	**073**
N66SM	WW24	168
N66TF	GLF2	97
N66TJ	LJ25	081
N66TP	SBRL	282-60
N66TR	C500	299
N66TS	WW24	39
N66U	**C560**	**0489**
N66VA	**WW24**	**375**
N66VG	FA20	210
N66VM	C550	056
N66W	C56X	5320
(N66W)	C560	0603
N66WB	FA20	242
N66WM	LJ35	141
N66WM	LJ55	145
N66ZB	**HS25**	**258675**
N66ZC	CL64	5411
N66ZC	**CL65**	**5834**
N66ZD	CL64	5411
N67AX	FA20	159
N67AZ	**C525**	**0245**
N67B	CL60	1066
N67B	JSTR	5074/22
N67BC	C52A	0225
N67BE	C500	184
N67BE	C500	524
N67BE	**C550**	**619**
N67BF	C500	184
N67BG	C650	0105
N67BH	HS25	25276
N67BK	**C550**	**550-0997**
(N67BK)	SBRL	282-135
N67BL	HS25	257040
N67CC	C500	367
N67CC	**C52A**	**0225**
(N67CK)	LJ24	147
N67CX	C52B	0067
N67CX	C750	0128
N67DF	WW24	233
N67DT	WW24	364
N67EC	HS25	25285
N67EL	**F900**	**153**
N67FJ	FA50	50
N67FP	**PRM1**	**RB-65**
N67FS	**C650**	**0029**
N67FT	**CS55**	**0088**
(N67GA)	LJ35	176
N67GH	C525	0149
N67GH	C52A	0019
N67GH	C52A	0217
N67GH	**C52C**	**0066**
N67GM	C500	619
N67GT	JSTR	5061/48
N67GU	C560	0355
(N67GU)	C525	0149
N67GW	C560	0355
N67GW	C560	0641
N67GX	GALX	036
N67HB	C680	0197
N67HB	LJ25	189
N67HW	C550	420
N67JB	**C550**	**550-0980**
N67JF	**FA50**	**73**
N67JF	HS25	258124
N67JR	C500	048
N67JR	**C52B**	**0048**
N67JR	FA20	247
N67JR	GLF3	324
N67JR	LJ24	230
N67JW	C550	462
N67JW	FA10	99
N67KM	SBRL	380-7
N67KP	**G150**	**249**
N67LC	C550	317
N67LC	FA10	49
N67LH	C550	664
N67LP	**EA50**	**000236**
N67MA	C500	277
(N67ME)	C550	444
N67MP	C500	277
N67MP	C550	444
(N67MP)	LJ31	059
N67MR	CL61	5029
N67MR	HS25	256067
N67MT	**FA50**	**254**
N67NC	C550	696
N67NR	SBRL	306-76
N67NV	EA50	000131
N67PA	**LJ35**	**208**
N67PC	C550	550-1007
N67PC	C550	696
N67PC	**C56X**	**5806**
N67PC	LJ25	128
N67PK	C56X	5806
N67PR	GLF2	67
N67PV	C550	550-1007
N67PW	**FA50**	**248**
N67PW	HS25	257147
N67RW	LJ55	048
N67RX	GLEX	9067
N67SB	C52A	0086
N67SB	LJ31	045
N67SC	SBRL	465-14
N67SE	C650	0045
N67SF	C500	184
N67SF	**C550**	**273**
N67SF	C650	0045
N67SF	C650	0231
N67SG	C550	257
N67SY	**LJ25**	**082**
N67TH	GLF4	1475
N67TJ	FA10	83
N67TJ	GLF3	390
N67TJ	HS25	25159
N67TJ	**WW24**	**299**
(N67TJ)	LJ35	367
N67TM	C550	067
N67TM	**GLF4**	**1409**
N67TS	HS25	25097
N67TW	C56X	5122
N67TW	**C680**	**0320**
(N67VP)	CS55	0067
N67VW	C525	0212
N67WB	F900	24
N67WB	F9EX	16
N67WB	**GLF6**	**6045**
N67WE	**HS25**	**259038**
N67WG	E50P	50000105
N67WG	**E55P**	**50500053**
N67WM	LJ55	132
N67WW	SBRL	282-2
N67ZS	**CL64**	**5583**
N68AA	C56X	5281
(N68AA)	SBRL	282-38
N68AG	C500	238
N68AL	**GLF4**	**1198**
N68AR	**HS25**	**258234**
N68AX	LJ25	216
(N68BA)	FA50	177
N68BC	C650	7025
N68BC	FA20	155
(N68BC)	FA20	363/544
N68BH	HS25	25278
N68BK	C550	363
N68BP	**FA20**	**155**
N68BR	C650	7114
N68BS	C525	0244
(N68BW)	HS25	25261
N68CB	C500	270
N68CB	HS25	25263
N68CB	**HS25**	**258453**
N68CG	F9EX	38
N68CJ	C525	0068
N68CJ	C525	0169
N68CK	C560	0063
(N68CK)	LJ25	047
N68CT	JSTR	5108
N68DA	HS25	258052
N68DM	GLF2	28
N68DM	LJ24	101
N68DS	C550	219
N68EA	C500	438
N68ED	C650	0239
N68ER	**E50P**	**50000011**
N68ES	**C750**	**0502**
N68ES	LJ31	221
N68EU	**C680**	**0208**
(N68FN)	LJ24	101
N68GA	C550	184
N68GA	HS25	256047
(N68GA)	C680	0060
N68GL	**F2TH**	**63**
N68GP	HS25	258068
N68GS	**BE40**	**RK-391**
N68GT	FA10	217
N68GW	C56X	5626
N68GW	**C56X**	**6189**
N68GX	ASTR	136
N68HB	**HA4T**	**RC-68**
N68HB	HS25	258601
N68HC	C560	0016
N68HC	C560	0270
N68HC	C560	0762
N68HC	C56X	5103
N68HC	C56X	6011
N68HC	C650	0091
N68HC	C680	0068
N68HC	**C680**	**0518**
N68HC	SBRL	282-55
N68HC	SBRL	306-96
N68HD	HS25	258429
N68HG	**C56X**	**5103**
N68HQ	C560	0016
N68HQ	C560	0270
N68HQ	C56X	6011
N68HQ	SBRL	282-55
(N68HQ)	C680	0068
N68HR	HS25	258068
N68JK	FA20	83
N68JV	BE40	RK-296
N68JW	C550	465
N68KM	SBRL	380-23
N68LF	C750	0040
N68LL	LJ35	463
N68LP	C750	0040
N68LP	C750	0169
N68LP	LJ55	082
N68LU	LJ24	163
N68LX	C56X	5163
N68LX	SBRL	465-68
N68MA	C560	0159
N68MA	C560	0547
N68MA	SBRL	306-23
N68ME	C550	282
N68MJ	LJ35	607
(N68ML)	SBRL	282-136
N68MY	**C56X**	**5666**
N68NC	C560	0762
N68NP	**C510**	**0170**
N68NR	SBRL	306-101
N68PC	LJ45	040
N68PC	LJ45	289
N68PC	**LJ45**	**453**
N68PJ	LJ25	063
N68PL	MU30	A077SA
N68PQ	LJ45	040
N68PQ	LJ45	289
N68PT	**WW24**	**325**
N68QB	**LJ35**	**079**
N68SD	CL60	1062
(N68SH)	C52B	0002
N68SK	C650	0156
N68SK	C650	7016
N68SK	CS55	0011
N68SL	**C680**	**0264**
N68SL	GLF4	1042
N68TA	SBRL	306-53
N68TJ	**E55P**	**50500246**
N68TJ	LJ25	140
N68TJ	LJ35	168
N68TS	C550	479
N68TS	FA20	129
N68UP	**FA20**	**258**
N68UW	LJ35	095
N68VC	C680	0518
N68VP	**LJ31**	**232**
N68WM	LJ24	074
N68WW	WW24	386
N68XG	FA10	103
N68YB	**FA50**	**290**
N69AH	C52A	0068
N69AH	**C550**	**181**
N69AX	LJ24	346
N69AY	**C510**	**0115**
(N69B)	LJ55	091
N69BH	HS25	25279
N69BH	LJ35	276
(N69CG)	SBRL	282-72
N69CN	JSTR	5053/2
N69EC	FA10	109
N69EC	**FA20**	**498**
(N69EH)	GLF3	316
N69EP	C500	531
N69FF	GLF3	320
N69FH	C52A	0068
N69FH	C52B	0042
N69FR	**HS25**	**HA-0106**
N69GB	FA10	24
N69GF	LJ25	265
N69GP	GLF4	1033
N69GT	WW24	44
N69GX	ASTR	122
N69GY	E55P	50500026
N69HM	JSTR	5004
N69HM	WW24	210
(N69HT)	E50P	50000137
N69JN	SBRL	380-65
N69KA	HS25	25273
N69KB	LJ24	042
N69KM	SBRL	380-30
N69LD	C650	0080
(N69LD)	C560	0803
N69LJ	LJ60	027
(N69LJ)	LJ25	052
(N69LL)	LJ24	051
(N69LS)	BE40	RK-164
N69ME	C550	282
N69ME	JSTR	5076/17
N69MT	JSTR	5107
N69NG	GLF2	69
N69PC	MU30	A010SA
N69PL	LJ25	253
N69PS	LJ35	014
N69R	FA50	116
N69SB	C750	0212
N69SB	HS25	257177
N69SB	PRM1	RB-242
N69SF	GLF2	52
(N69SF)	LJ24	246
N69SW	FA20	356
N69TP	JSTR	5002
N69VC	C650	0079
N69VH	**LJ55**	**062**
(N69VJ)	FA50	69
N69VT	C560	0260
N69WH	**C525**	**0275**
N69WJ	FA10	60
N69WU	**SBRL**	**465-51**
N69WW	WW24	51
N69X	**MS76**	**090**
N69XW	**C500**	**142**
N69XW	LJ24	251
N69YM	PRM1	RB-255
N69ZJ	**LJ60**	**147**
N70AA	C500	619
N70AE	LJ31	188
N70AE	LJ45	227
N70AF	CS55	0067
N70AF	FA50	116
N70AF	FA50	21
N70AG	GLF3	376
N70AG	GLF4	1120
N70AG	**GLF5**	**522**
N70AJ	ASTR	054
N70AP	HS25	25271
N70AR	HS25	257144
N70AX	LJ35	155
N70AY	**LJ31**	**188**
N70BC	SBRL	282-132
N70BG	**C500**	**387**
N70BH	HS25	25280
N70BJ	BE40	RK-39
N70BR	C560	0478
N70BR	**FA50**	**115**
N70BR	PRM1	RB-70
N70CA	**C500**	**234**
N70CA	WW24	231
N70CE	LJ25	142
N70CG	**C500**	**576**
N70CK	**FA20**	**128/436**
N70CN	LJ35	277
N70CR	**CL30**	**20048**
N70CS	WW24	88
N70DE	BE40	RJ-56
N70DJ	C650	0058
N70DJ	CL60	1070
N70EJ	**EA50**	**000194**
N70EL	**GLF5**	**5510**
N70ES	SBRL	282-124
N70EW	F900	25
N70EW	GLEX	9026
N70EW	**GLEX**	**9649**
N70FA	F2EX	216

N70FC	**C52B**	**0339**
N70FC	HS25	257145
N70FJ	C500	448
N70FJ	F900	20
N70FJ	FA50	236
N70FJ	FA50	51
N70FL	FA50	144
N70FL	FA50	95
N70FL	FA7X	7
N70FS	**CL30**	**20328**
N70GA	MU30	A071SA
N70GM	**C525**	**0683**
N70GM	C550	135
N70GM	LJ45	423
N70HB	HS25	25043
N70HB	**HS25**	**257162**
(N70HB)	BE40	RK-328
N70HC	SBRL	370-8
(N70HC)	C550	428
N70HF	HS25	257082
N70HJ	LJ25	049
N70HL	**SBRL**	**306-102**
N70HQ	**GALX**	**066**
N70HS	F900	140
N70HT	BE40	RK-170
(N70HW)	C525	0070
N70JC	HS25	25203
N70JC	LJ24	051
N70JF	LJ25	278
N70KM	SBRL	380-52
N70KS	F2TH	14
N70KW	C525	0050
N70KW	**C52A**	**0135**
N70LF	**F9EX**	**9**
N70LG	**FA20**	**319**
N70LH	**C525**	**0811**
N70LJ	**LJ36**	**044**
(N70LW)	SBRL	306-142
N70LY	HS25	25244
N70MD	FA20	153
N70MG	C500	063
N70MP	LJ25	051
N70NB	**C500**	**614**
N70NE	FA20	399
N70NE	**HS25**	**258107**
N70NF	**C52B**	**0276**
N70NF	FA20	399
N70NJ	**LJ40**	**2139**
N70NL	**PRM1**	**RB-257**
N70NR	SBRL	370-3
N70PA	FA20	173
(N70PB)	C500	248
N70PC	C550	664
N70PC	LJ45	172
N70PC	**LJ45**	**432**
(N70PH)	C550	327
N70PJ	HS25	259032
N70PL	FA20	247
N70PL	**FA20**	**436**
N70PM	HS25	257141
N70PM	HS25	257147
N70PM	HS25	258238
N70PN	HS25	257147
N70PS	**GLEX**	**9012**
N70PS	GLF3	327
N70PS	GLF4	1058
N70PT	C650	0187
N70PX	GLEX	9012
N70QB	**HS25**	**257125**
N70RL	**CL30**	**20159**
N70RL	LJ24	106
N70SE	LJ25	323
N70SJ	SJ30	007
N70SK	HS25	257098
N70SK	HS25	258006
N70SK	LJ25	049
N70SK	**SBRL**	**465-33**
N70SL	SBRL	282-70
N70SW	**C500**	**236**
N70TF	C500	274
N70TF	**F2EX**	**272**
N70TF	LJ25	214
N70TF	SBRL	380-17
N70TG	C500	308
N70TG	C560	0069
N70TH	**C56X**	**5007**
N70TH	F900	117
N70TH	FA20	509
N70TJ	LJ24	199
N70TP	JSTR	5005
N70TP	JSTR	5156
(N70TP)	JSTR	5019
N70TR	C525	0014
N70TS	**C500**	**281**
N70TS	FA10	63
N70TT	C650	0029
N70TT	**F9EX**	**102**
N70TT	GALX	045
N70U	C500	304
N70U	FA20	399
N70UP	LJ36	040
N70UT	LJ36	040
N70VP	C500	444
N70VT	MU30	A085SA
N70WA	C500	320
(N70WA)	C500	192
(N70WA)	LJ25	142

N70WC	FA10	140
(N70WG)	GLF2	248
N70WP	C500	512
N70WW	LJ35	055
(N70WW)	WW24	283
N70X	C550	008
N70X	CL60	1032
N70X	**CL61**	**5073**
N70X	HS25	257011
N70XA	**C550**	**008**
N70XC	F2TH	152
N70XF	**CL60**	**1032**
N70XL	**C56X**	**5566**
N70XX	MU30	A052SA
N70ZW	C500	475
N71A	LJ35	352
N71AL	**LJ31**	**039**
N71AX	F2TH	184
N71AX	LJ25	353
N71BD	**GLF4**	**1415**
N71BH	HS25	25281
N71BL	HS25	25084
N71CC	**SBRL**	**306-71**
N71CD	SBRL	306-26
N71CE	LJ25	136
(N71CG)	C550	254
N71CJ	C550	071
N71CK	**LJ36**	**035**
N71CP	FA20	89
N71CW	HFB3	1026
N71DL	HFB3	1026
N71DM	LJ25	129
N71E	LJ35	306
N71EA	C52A	0235
N71EL	F2EX	71
N71EM	CS55	0006
N71F	**C52B**	**0037**
N71FA	CL30	20089
N71FB	**C525**	**0812**
N71FB	LJ31	205
N71FE	F2EX	13
N71FE	BE40	RK-16
N71FJ	FA50	54
N71FM	C550	083
N71FM	CS55	0006
N71FS	**ASTR**	**071**
N71GA	C550	444
N71GA	BE40	RJ-35
N71GE	**GLF4**	**4302**
N71GH	**MU30**	**A071SA**
N71GK	**F900**	**107**
N71GW	C525	0059
N71HB	C500	275
N71HR	C525	0494
N71HS	C56X	5351
N71HS	LJ35	287
N71JC	LJ31	008
N71JJ	C560	0480
N71JN	GLF4	1088
N71KG	**C550**	**190**
N71KV	**PRM1**	**RB-71**
N71L	**C500**	**646**
N71LA	LJ35	012
(N71LA)	GLF4	1238
N71LG	HS25	258762
N71LG	LJ35	019
N71LJ	LJ24	071
N71LP	**C500**	**487**
N71LP	C550	278
N71LU	C550	550-0849
N71LU	**C56X**	**5063**
N71LU	C650	0019
N71M	CL60	1077
N71M	FA10	208
N71M	**FA10**	**88**
N71M	WW24	192
N71MA	HS25	257107
N71MH	LJ35	469
N71MT	**EA50**	**000069**
N71MT	HS25	258230
N71NE	**GLF4**	**1174**
(N71NE)	C52B	0025
N71NF	LJ40	2058
N71NF	**LJ45**	**523**
N71NJ	CL64	5504
N71NK	C560	0040
N71NK	C650	7106
N71NP	CL64	5504
N71NP	HS25	258041
N71NR	GLF4	1132
N71NT	C650	0039
N71NX	LJ40	2058
N71PG	**LJ36**	**013**
N71PT	WW24	198
N71RB	LJ25	158
N71RB	SBRL	465-14
N71RC	C500	184
(N71RL)	C550	074
(N71RL)	C56X	5354
N71RP	C750	0093
N71RP	GLF2	199/19
N71RP	GLF3	440
N71RP	GLF4	1222
N71SY	**C525**	**0831**
N71TH	F900	105
N71TH	FA50	196
N71TJ	FA10	105

N71TJ	FA20	166
N71TJ	GLF2	29
N71TJ	GLF3	300
N71TJ	GLF4	1042
N71TP	GLF2	195
N71TP	LJ35	014
N71TP	LJ36	030
N71TP	LJ55	032
N71TS	FA10	75
N71TS	**HDJT**	**42000032**
N71TV	**GLF4**	**1430**
(N71UF)	JSTR	5037/24
N71VR	GLF4	1290
N71WF	WW24	442
N71WH	**CS55**	**0059**
N71WJ	GLF2	248
N71WS	GLF2	232
N71ZZ	GLEX	9239
N72AC	**C525**	**0643**
N72AG	**C510**	**0309**
N72AM	CS55	0004
N72AM	G150	311
N72AV	LJ36	040
N72AX	LJ25	346
N72AX	**LJ35**	**419**
(N72B)	C550	393
N72BB	FA10	173
N72BB	FA20	59
N72BC	C500	270
N72BC	**F2TH**	**187**
N72BD	GLF4	1420
N72BH	HS25	25282
(N72BJ)	BE40	RK-72
N72BP	**GLF2**	**238**
N72CD	LJ25	023
N72CE	LJ60	285
N72CK	**LJ35**	**165**
N72CT	C560	0072
N72CT	JSTR	5007/45
N72DA	**C510**	**0120**
N72DA	LJ35	098
N72DJ	C500	072
(N72DV)	PRM1	RB-121
N72EL	ASTR	018
N72EP	C650	0058
N72ET	FA20	52
N72ET	LJ55	072
N72ET	WW24	180
N72EU	FA10	13
N72FC	C560	0347
N72FC	**HS25**	**258519**
N72FD	C750	0072
N72FE	C560	0347
(N72FE)	C560	0072
N72FJ	F9EX	72
N72FJ	FA50	58
N72FL	ASTR	018
N72FL	C550	249
N72FL	BE40	RK-333
N72FP	LJ24	137
N72GD	PRM1	RB-163
N72GH	LJ35	581
N72GH	BE40	RK-370
N72GW	FA10	37
N72GW	**JSTR**	**5205**
N72HA	HS25	25249
N72HB	WW24	254
N72HC	HS25	25287
N72HG	**BE40**	**RJ-11**
N72HT	HS25	25249
N72HT	JSTR	5134/50
N72JF	LJ35	088
N72JM	LJ35	183
N72JS	**C52A**	**0219**
N72JT	**PRM1**	**RB-259**
N72JW	**C525**	**0406**
N72K	C550	480
N72K	HS25	258141
N72LA	**HS25**	**258801**
N72LE	C650	0063
N72LE	LJ35	237
N72LG	LJ35	228
N72LJ	**LJ55**	**129**
N72LL	LJ35	275
N72LN	**GLF4**	**4144**
N72LT	WW24	180
N72MK	LJ24	066
N72MM	C550	187
N72NE	**BE40**	**RK-371**
N72NF	LJ45	523
N72NP	CL64	5385
N72NP	HS25	258044
N72PB	C550	550-0926
N72PK	GLF3	306
(N72PP)	BE40	RK-86
N72PS	F2EX	116
N72PS	F900	18
N72PS	**F9EX**	**290**
(N72PS)	GLF3	327
N72PU	**F2EX**	**116**
N72PX	**F900**	**18**
N72RC	C550	024
N72RK	GALX	039
N72RK	GLF3	306
N72RK	GLF4	1171
N72RK	GLF4	1248
N72SG	C525	0308

N72SG	C550	550-0942
N72SG	C56X	5253
N72SG	**C56X**	**5508**
N72SJ	PRM1	RB-115
N72SL	C550	504
N72SR	**C510**	**0264**
N72SR	CL60	1013
N72ST	C650	0072
(N72TB)	LJ35	014
N72TC	C550	282
N72TC	WW24	4
N72TJ	LJ35	172
N72TP	LJ25	168
N72TP	LJ35	140
(N72TP)	LJ55	032
N72TQ	WW24	4
N72U	C550	480
N72UK	**C680**	**0275**
N72VJ	**C500**	**543**
N72VK	**C510**	**0384**
N72WC	C500	281
N72WC	CS55	0037
N72WC	LJ25	371
N72WE	C550	720
N72WS	F9EX	14
N72WY	CL64	5394
N72XL	**C56X**	**6072**
N73AD	**C52B**	**0402**
N73AH	**C510**	**0226**
N73AW	GLF2	109
N73B	FA10	23
N73B	FA10	79
N73BE	BE40	RJ-15
N73BH	HS25	25283
N73BL	BE40	RJ-15
N73BL	BE40	RK-71
N73CE	LJ24	068
N73CK	**LJ35**	**092**
N73CL	**WW24**	**365**
N73DB	**E50P**	**50000020**
N73DJ	LJ25	273
N73DR	SBRL	282-120
N73EJ	**EA50**	**000073**
N73EL	C52B	0123
N73EM	C52B	0123
N73EM	**C52B**	**0382**
(N73ET)	GLF3	434
N73FE	**E55P**	**50500255**
N73FJ	**F2TH**	**73**
N73FJ	FA50	55
N73FW	C500	562
N73G	HS25	257150
N73G	SBRL	306-8
(N73GB)	WW24	294
N73GH	**FA50**	**261**
N73GP	**LJ55**	**127**
N73GR	SBRL	306-8
N73HB	C500	256
N73HG	LJ24	137
N73HH	**C550**	**682**
N73HM	C650	0169
N73HM	BE40	RK-70
N73HP	SBRL	282-120
N73JA	HS25	256065
N73JH	HS25	25203
N73JT	LJ24	064
N73KH	**C560**	**0220**
N73LJ	LJ25	138
N73LL	C500	287
N73LP	GLF2	119/22
N73LP	LJ35	604
N73LR	**FA10**	**35**
N73M	GLF2	128
N73M	**GLF5**	**5428**
N73M	GLF5	547
N73ME	C560	0108
N73ME	**C750**	**0155**
N73MG	GLF2	247
N73ML	**CL61**	**5119**
N73MN	C560	0108
N73MP	**C500**	**164**
N73MR	FA20	449
N73PC	SBRL	282-11
N73PJ	**PRM1**	**RB-101**
N73PM	C525	0287
N73PM	HS25	257167
N73PS	**F9EX**	**289**
N73PS	LJ24	186
N73RP	GLF3	491
N73RP	GLF5	529
N73RP	**GLF5**	**5528**
N73SG	C56X	5253
N73SK	C500	679
N73SL	GLEX	9325
N73SL	**HS25**	**258781**
N73ST	**C550**	**113**
N73TA	LJ25	181
N73TF	C500	256
N73TJ	LJ35	042
N73TJ	SBRL	465-12
(N73TJ)	FA10	163
N73TP	LJ35	014
N73TP	LJ55	048
N73TW	LJ25	181
N73UC	C650	7049
N73UC	**C680**	**0086**
N73UP	**HS25**	**258473**

N73WC	C500	213
N73WC	C500	338
N73WC	PRM1	RB-15
N73WE	LJ55	073
N73WF	HS25	258141
(N73WW)	HS25	258480
N73ZZ	GLEX	9251
N74A	**GLF2**	**36/3**
N74AB	SBRL	306-92
N74AG	JSTR	5072/23
N74AG	WW24	339
N74B	HS25	25276
N74B	HS25	257014
N74BH	HS25	25284
N74BJ	CS55	0041
N74BJ	FA50	237
N74BJ	**SBRL**	**465-44**
N74BS	SBRL	306-64
N74CJ	C52C	0074
N74DH	**GLEX**	**9217**
(N74EH)	C550	696
N74FC	C500	196
N74FH	C500	525
N74FS	**F900**	**85**
N74G	C550	042
N74G	LJ25	174
N74GG	**GLF4**	**1331**
N74GH	E50P	50000252
N74GL	**C52A**	**0159**
N74GL	LJ55	074
N74GM	WW24	74
N74GR	**CL61**	**3001**
N74GR	WW24	218
N74GW	**HS25**	**258706**
N74GZ	**CS55**	**0074**
N74HH	GLF2	74
N74HR	**C500**	**677**
N74JA	C550	349
N74JA	**CL60**	**1060**
N74JA	HS25	257079
N74JE	**C52A**	**0474**
N74JE	CS55	0074
(N74JE)	HS25	257079
N74JK	GLF2	157
N74JK	GLF2	49
N74JL	LJ25	101
N74JL	LJ35	396
N74JM	WW24	299
N74JN	C550	349
N74KV	C550	324
N74LL	**C500**	**212**
N74LM	CL60	1069
N74LM	CS55	0041
N74MB	LJ35	004
N74MB	SBRL	282-112
N74MG	C550	302
N74MG	SBRL	282-102
N74MJ	LJ35	004
N74MJ	SBRL	282-102
N74MP	LJ35	004
N74MW	LJ24	074
N74NB	HS25	258631
N74ND	HS25	258063
N74NP	HS25	258168
N74NP	HS25	258631
N74PC	HS25	258166
N74PC	HS25	258567
N74PG	C525	0476
N74PM	C500	499
(N74PN)	C500	499
N74PQ	HS25	258166
N74PT	**LJ45**	**314**
N74RD	LJ25	260
N74RP	GLF2	199/19
N74RP	GLF4	1040
N74RP	**GLF5**	**5058**
N74RQ	GLF2	113
N74RT	GLF2	113
N74RT	**GLF2**	**219/20**
N74RT	HS25	25214
N74RV	GLF2	162
N74RY	LJ55	063
N74SG	LJ45	016
N74SP	C550	485
N74SP	LJ35	441
N74TC	C550	094
N74TD	**F900**	**51**
(N74TE)	EA50	000074
N74TJ	ASTR	063
N74TJ	GLF2	74
N74TJ	GLF4	1107
(N74TJ)	CL60	1063
(N74TJ)	FA10	18
(N74TJ)	HS25	256015
N74TL	C560	0048
N74TP	LJ36	030
N74TS	**FA50**	**106**
N74TS	WW24	174
N74UK	C525	0602
N74VC	**SBRL**	**465-17**
N74VF	C650	0156
N74VF	**C750**	**0057**
N74VF	BE40	RK-34
N74VW	**GLF5**	**5040**
N74WA	C500	320
N74WF	HS25	25221
(N74WF)	HS25	258349

N74WL	CL30	20044
N74XE	WW24	128
N74XL	WW24	128
N74ZC	**CL30**	**20018**
N74ZZ	GLEX	9260
N75A	SBRL	380-21
N75A	SBRL	380-36
N75A	SBRL	380-52
N75A	SBRL	380-57
N75AG	SBRL	380-42
N75AK	SBRL	380-38
N75AP	**C510**	**0023**
N75AX	LJ25	270
N75B	**C560**	**0156**
N75B	CL60	1064
N75B	LJ25	178
N75BC	**WW24**	**426**
N75BH	HS25	25285
N75BL	CS55	0053
N75BL	LJ25	156
N75BL	MU30	A017SA
N75BS	SBRL	380-12
N75C	HS25	25141
N75CA	LJ25	110
N75CC	GLF2	117
N75CC	GLF4	1182
N75CC	**GLF5**	**5065**
N75CC	JSTR	5102
N75CJ	LJ24	279
N75CK	**LJ25**	**256**
N75CN	SBRL	380-31
N75CS	HS25	25190
N75CS	HS25	258066
N75CS	**HS25**	**HA-0176**
N75CT	HS25	25047
N75CT	**LJ60**	**299**
N75CV	C560	0075
N75DE	SBRL	370-7
N75DH	LJ35	007
N75EA	**EA50**	**000116**
N75EB	**C56X**	**5214**
N75EC	C550	295
N75EK	**F2EX**	**172**
N75EM	**CL61**	**5136**
N75ES	**C510**	**0024**
N75EW	F900	25
N75F	C550	368
N75F	C560	0139
N75FC	**C525**	**0455**
N75FJ	FA50	275
N75FJ	FA50	59
N75FN	C500	257
N75FP	**LJ45**	**461**
(N75FV)	C560	0139
N75G	C560	0140
N75G	FA50	138
N75G	SBRL	465-71
N75GA	C550	310
N75GA	**HS25**	**256070**
N75GF	BE40	RK-179
(N75GJ)	GLF3	375
N75GK	BE40	RK-179
N75GL	SBRL	465-71
N75GM	C500	169
N75GM	SBRL	306-110
N75GN	HS25	25161
N75GP	LJ24	333
N75GP	LJ55	129
N75GR	**HS25**	**258756**
N75GR	LJ24	333
(N75GV)	C560	0140
N75GW	C500	257
N75GX	ASTR	137
N75GZ	ASTR	075
N75HE	SBRL	465-16
N75HF	C52A	0220
N75HF	**C56X**	**5698**
N75HL	**HS25**	**258316**
N75HL	SBRL	380-36
N75HL	SBRL	465-16
N75HP	SBRL	306-48
N75HS	C550	286
N75HS	**C750**	**0037**
N75HU	**C56X**	**5110**
N75HZ	SBRL	380-53
N75JD	SBRL	282-4
N75JK	**C52B**	**0240**
N75JT	SBRL	306-94
(N75KC)	C500	187
N75KH	**CL64**	**5550**
N75KH	BE40	RK-280
N75KR	C550	075
N75KV	LJ24	258
N75KV	LJ35	285
N75L	SBRL	380-66
N75LJ	**LJ45**	**536**
N75LJ	LJ55	065
N75LM	LJ25	233
N75LY	**LJ45**	**504**
N75MC	CS55	0109
N75MC	LJ31	052
N75MD	SBRL	282-129
N75MG	GLF2	247
N75MG	JSTR	5087/55
(N75MH)	FA10	75
N75MN	C500	257
N75MT	HS25	258231

N75NE	LJ24	351
N75NL	SBRL	380-40
N75NP	**CL65**	**5873**
N75NP	HS25	258170
(N75NP)	CL65	5776
N75NR	SBRL	370-2
N75NR	SBRL	370-5
N75NR	SBRL	370-7
N75NR	SBRL	380-53
N75NR	SBRL	380-64
(N75PK)	LJ35	464
N75PP	C52A	0132
N75PP	GLF4	1073
N75PS	**C56X**	**5719**
N75PX	C500	248
N75QS	HS25	25190
N75RD	C650	0134
N75RD	FA50	220
N75RD	HS25	25228
N75RJ	C550	692
N75RJ	LJ35	168
N75RL	**BE40**	**RK-312**
N75RN	**C510**	**0439**
N75RN	C650	0134
N75RN	HS25	25228
N75RP	GLF2	199/19
N75RP	GLF3	328
N75RP	GLF4	1073
N75RP	GLF5	528
N75RP	**GLF5**	**5460**
N75RS	SBRL	380-32
N75RS	SBRL	380-42
N75RS	SBRL	380-58
N75RS	SBRL	380-63
N75RZ	FA50	113
N75SE	SBRL	380-4
N75SJ	**C680**	**0166**
N75SJ	LJ25	175
N75SL	SBRL	380-12
N75SR	GLF2	96
N75ST	HS25	257013
N75TD	LJ36	028
N75TE	LJ45	057
N75TF	LJ35	191
N75TG	C550	174
N75TG	**BE40**	**RK-28**
N75TJ	C500	689
N75TJ	FA20	289
N75TJ	HS25	25190
N75TJ	LJ25	210
N75TJ	SBRL	380-6
N75TP	C550	286
N75TP	C56X	5261
N75TP	C56X	5768
N75TP	**C56X**	**6183**
N75TP	LJ55	032
N75TT	ASTR	065
N75TX	**C750**	**0132**
N75U	SBRL	370-4
N75UA	SBRL	370-4
N75V	F900	13
N75VB	**GLF4**	**1136**
N75VC	**SBRL**	**465-71**
N75W	F900	63
N75W	FA50	152
N75W	SBRL	282-129
(N75W)	F900	13
N75WA	SBRL	282-129
N75WC	GLF2	199/19
N75WC	GLF2	96
N75WE	FA50	152
N75WL	**C550**	**178**
N75WP	**C560**	**0449**
N75XL	C56X	5575
N75XP	**LJ45**	**118**
N75XR	LJ40	2075
N75Y	SBRL	380-64
N75Z	C550	236
N75Z	C560	0345
N75ZA	C550	236
N75ZZ	GLEX	9365
N76AE	C525	0139
N76AF	FA10	36
N76AM	FA10	157
(N76AM)	C500	258
N76AS	**C550**	**438**
N76AW	LJ55	036
N76AX	**LJ25**	**254**
N76BF	C510	0276
N76BH	HS25	25286
N76CK	C550	345
N76CK	C560	0372
N76CK	LJ25	020
N76CK	**LJ35**	**076**
N76CS	CL61	5103
N76CS	GLF2	158
N76CS	HS25	258595
N76CS	**HS25**	**HA-0178**
N76CY	HS25	258595
N76D	C650	0110
N76D	C750	0006
N76EB	JSTR	5093
N76EJ	**GLF4**	**1033**
N76EM	**E50P**	**50000013**
N76ER	WW24	369
N76EU	PRM1	RB-276
(N76FB)	FA50	41

N76FC	CS55	0090
N76FC	HS25	258784
N76FD	**F900**	**41**
N76FD	FA50	41
N76FJ	FA10	58
N76FJ	FA50	67
N76FJ	FA7X	176
N76GL	LJ35	036
N76GP	**C510**	**0203**
N76GP	LJ35	036
N76GR	**BE40**	**RK-473**
N76GT	C500	313
N76GT	SBRL	306-61
N76HG	JSTR	5076/17
N76HL	**PRM1**	**RB-112**
(N76JY)	C500	676
N76LE	MU30	A047SA
N76LE	MU30	A076SA
N76LV	HS25	258530
N76MB	FA10	83
N76MB	FA20	80
N76NX	SBRL	465-53
N76PR	C650	7059
N76PW	**F9EX**	**85**
(N76PW)	LJ24	311
N76QF	LJ60	156
N76QS	GLF2	158
N76RA	**LJ35**	**140**
N76RB	**C550**	**550-0871**
N76RE	C500	091
N76RP	GLF4	1440
N76RP	**GLF5**	**5334**
N76RV	LJ24	325
N76RY	FA20	57
N76SF	CL64	5603
N76SF	**CL65**	**5900**
N76SF	LJ60	156
N76TA	FA20	393
N76TE	LJ45	081
N76TF	**C560**	**0431**
N76TG	WW24	297
N76TH	**GLF4**	**4071**
N76TJ	GLF3	345
(N76TJ)	FA10	12
(N76TJ)	HS25	256070
N76TR	LJ24	333
N76TS	FA20	44
N76UM	**LJ25**	**051**
N76VE	C56X	5077
N76VG	FA20	233
N76WR	C560	0459
N76XR	LJ60	376
N76ZZ	GLEX	9266
N77A	F2TH	17
N77A	SBRL	465-1
N77AE	LJ24	163
N77AP	SBRL	282-37
N77AT	SBRL	282-109
N77AT	SBRL	306-23
N77BT	GLF3	429
N77BT	HS25	25155
N77BT	JSTR	5113/25
N77C	HS25	25123
N77C	HS25	256038
N77C	**JSTR**	**5232**
N77CD	HS25	25123
N77CE	F900	12
N77CE	FA50	21
N77CJ	LJ40	2026
N77CP	C500	173
N77CP	FA50	143
N77CP	GLF4	1194
N77CP	**GLF5**	**5272**
N77CP	GLF5	565
N77CP	LJ35	177
N77CQ	LJ35	177
N77CS	HS25	258065
N77CS	HS25	258620
N77CU	HS25	256038
N77CU	HS25	258065
N77CX	HS25	258620
N77D	GLF4	1266
N77D	GLF4	1340
N77D	HS25	25093
N77D	HS25	257101
N77D	JSTR	5097/60
N77DB	**C525**	**0443**
N77DD	C550	695
N77DY	GLF4	1266
N77EK	GLF3	363
N77F	WW24	4
N77FC	LJ35	031
N77FD	**C500**	**663**
N77FJ	FA50	62
N77FK	GLF3	363
N77FK	**GLF4**	**1357**
N77FK	LJ35	376
N77FK	LJ55	108
N77FN	LJ25	216
N77FV	WW24	26
N77GA	BE40	RJ-5
(N77GA)	MU30	A011SA
N77GH	LJ24	116
N77GJ	C500	497
N77GJ	LJ24	174
N77GR	FA20	105
N77GT	FA10	60

N77GU	**SBRL**	**465-12**
N77HF	C560	0133
N77HF	**C650**	**7036**
N77HG	**GLF3**	**429**
N77HH	WW24	103
N77HN	C560	0009
N77HN	**LJ40**	**2070**
N77HN	LJ45	169
N77HU	C560	0009
N77HW	JSTR	5080
N77JD	**C560**	**0139**
N77JL	LJ24	286
N77JN	LJ24	202
N77JW	FA10	6
N77JW	LJ55	034
(N77JW)	LJ36	044
(N77JW)	LJ55	033
N77KN	**C525**	**0821**
N77KT	WW24	7
N77KV	**HA4T**	**RC-29**
N77KW	LJ25	076
N77LA	FA20	319
N77LA	HS25	258029
N77LB	LJ24	135
N77LJ	LJ35	014
(N77LJ)	HS25	25098
N77LN	LJ35	306
N77LP	HS25	257122
N77LP	LJ35	321
N77LS	LJ24	194
N77LX	**C650**	**7051**
N77M	C52B	0023
N77M	C52B	0100
N77MA	C560	0273
(N77MK)	SBRL	282-52
N77MR	LJ24	351
N77MR	SBRL	282-52
N77ND	**C52A**	**0072**
N77ND	C550	005
N77NJ	LJ25	033
N77NJ	LJ35	658
N77NR	C560	0009
N77NR	FA10	109
N77NR	LJ35	503
N77NR	LJ40	2109
N77NR	WW24	28
N77NT	**C52B**	**0381**
N77NT	FA50	77
N77NT	WW24	7
N77PA	C500	639
N77PA	CS55	0051
N77PH	C550	244
N77PH	LJ31	089
N77PK	LJ25	114
N77PR	**C550**	**244**
N77PX	C500	639
N77PY	**LJ31**	**089**
N77QM	FA20	75
N77QR	GLF4	1194
N77RC	C500	184
N77RC	C550	169
N77RE	C500	224
N77RS	LJ25	094
(N77RS)	LJ24	258
N77RY	LJ24	137
N77SA	HS25	257108
N77SA	LJ25	018
N77SF	**C650**	**7072**
N77SF	FA10	141
(N77SF)	C550	078
N77ST	WW24	108
N77SW	GLF2	15
N77SW	GLF3	413
N77SW	GLF4	1023
N77SW	GLF4	1146
N77SW	GLF4	1207
(N77SW)	FA50	53
N77TC	HS25	258275
N77TC	**HS25**	**HA-0007**
N77TC	SBRL	465-10
N77TC	WW24	4
N77TE	**EA50**	**000077**
N77TE	FA50	110
N77TE	LJ35	031
N77TG	GLF3	332
N77TW	C500	519
N77TZ	**C510**	**0427**
N77U	LJ35	031
N77UB	C500	644
N77UF	**GLEX**	**9284**
N77UW	**C56X**	**5005**
N77VG	**C525**	**0344**
N77VJ	LJ24	041
N77VK	HS25	25051
N77VR	C525	0344
N77VR	**C52A**	**0240**
(N77VU)	GLF4	1207
N77VZ	C525	0344
N77VZ	C550	550-0832
N77W	HS25	258150
N77WD	C550	193
N77WD	HS25	25224
N77WD	LJ24	174
N77WL	**GLF4**	**1140**
N77WU	C550	193
N77XM	GLF4	4193
N78AB	C500	444

N78AD	CL61	5063
N78AE	LJ24	267
N78AF	LJ24	233
N78AG	HS25	25101
N78AM	C560	0056
N78AP	C650	0056
N78BA	C550	306
(N78BA)	C550	368
N78BC	FA20	341
N78BC	SBRL	282-104
N78BH	HS25	25287
N78BH	LJ24	184
N78BL	WW24	182
N78BR	C650	7078
N78BT	LJ25	191
(N78BT)	C500	478
N78CK	**C550**	**345**
N78CN	C500	606
N78CS	C550	187
N78CS	HS25	257137
N78D	C650	0116
N78D	C650	7043
N78DL	C650	7043
(N78DL)	C650	0116
N78DT	LJ25	356
N78EM	C650	0192
N78EW	**GLEX**	**9026**
N78FA	C550	039
N78FJ	**F2TH**	**78**
N78FJ	FA50	63
N78FK	C550	498
N78FK	LJ55	108
N78FR	**LJ60**	**109**
N78GA	C550	083
N78GA	C550	097
N78GJ	**WW24**	**310**
N78GL	LJ25	240
N78GP	SBRL	282-72
N78HL	**PRM1**	**RB-253**
N78JP	SBRL	306-20
N78JR	FA20	70
N78KN	**F2EX**	**292**
N78KN	HA4T	RC-31
N78KX	HA4T	RC-31
N78LB	WW24	162
N78LF	FA50	77
N78LT	**FA50**	**75**
N78MB	**FA20**	**363/544**
N78MC	LJ35	117
(N78MC)	C500	150
N78MD	**C550**	**550-0970**
N78MD	FA10	18
N78MN	LJ35	237
N78MN	WW24	149
N78MP	JSTR	5095/30
N78NP	C560	0107
N78NT	F2TH	121
N78PH	C550	025
N78PH	LJ31	090
N78PP	CL61	5038
N78PR	C550	025
N78PR	LJ31	090
N78PT	**WW24**	**304**
(N78PT)	C650	0187
N78QA	LJ35	302
(N78QS)	HS25	257137
N78RK	**C52A**	**0507**
N78RP	CL61	5038
N78RP	CL64	5338
N78RP	CL64	5604
N78RP	GLF3	328
N78RR	SBRL	306-33
(N78RX)	CL64	5604
N78RZ	HS25	25114
N78SD	CL64	5469
N78SD	LJ25	251
N78SL	**C750**	**0238**
N78SR	CL60	1057
N78TC	C550	282
N78TC	**CL30**	**20070**
N78TC	SBRL	282-99
N78TE	EA50	000078
N78TF	C550	195
N78WW	WW24	349
N78WW	WW24	399
N78ZZ	GLEX	9267
N79AD	ASTR	029
N79AD	CL61	5063
N79AD	CL61	5140
N79AD	GLEX	9058
N79AD	WW24	375
N79AE	FA20	196
N79AE	HS25	25031
N79AE	JSTR	5155/32
N79AN	CL61	5140
N79AP	WW24	375
N79AX	LJ35	389
(N79AX)	LJ25	118
N79AY	**GLEX**	**9058**
N79B	HS25	25228
N79BC	C56X	5337
N79BH	HS25	256002
N79BH	LJ35	220
N79BJ	LJ31	101
N79BK	C500	498
N79BP	FA10	178
N79CB	**PRM1**	**RB-264**

N79CD	C550	023
N79CD	SBRL	465-46
N79DD	C500	254
N79EA	C56X	5073
(N79EA)	EA50	000297
N79EH	**HS25**	**257047**
N79EL	**BE40**	**RK-214**
N79EV	LJ25	097
N79FJ	**F2TH**	**79**
N79FJ	FA50	64
(N79FJ)	FA10	144
(N79FJ)	FA50	79
N79FT	C500	456
N79GA	MU30	A023SA
N79HA	FA10	128
N79HC	HS25	257063
N79HM	**C52C**	**0079**
N79HM	BE40	RK-70
N79JS	C52B	0273
N79JS	**C52C**	**0138**
(N79JS)	LJ36	029
N79KF	C650	0118
N79KP	WW24	262
N79KW	CL64	5564
N79LB	C52B	0019
N79LC	WW24	257
N79LS	LJ24	097
N79MB	FA20	507
(N79MB)	JSTR	5055/21
N79MJ	LJ35	201
N79MX	**C525**	**0190**
N79NP	HS25	258170
N79PB	FA10	128
N79PB	FA10	47
N79PF	C56X	5151
N79PF	FA50	174
N79PG	C680	0018
N79PM	C560	0459
N79PM	FA20	510
N79RP	GLF4	1220
N79RP	**GLF5**	**5347**
N79RS	**C500**	**107**
N79RS	LJ24	280
N79SE	C550	585
N79SE	**LJ31**	**206**
N79SF	LJ36	041
N79TJ	FA10	148
N79TJ	HS25	25079
N79TS	HS25	25042
N79TS	HS25	257047
N79TS	**HS25**	**258511**
N79VP	C52B	0079
N79XL	C56X	6079
N79XR	LJ60	379
N79ZZ	GLEX	9279
N80	WW24	144
N80A	GLF2	38
N80A	GLF4	1348
N80AB	**C560**	**0169**
N80AB	SBRL	380-59
N80AD	GLF5	5539
N80AE	GLF4	1402
N80AE	**LJ45**	**360**
N80AG	GLF2	164
N80AG	HS25	258496
(N80AG)	GLF3	401
N80AJ	**C500**	**100**
N80AP	LJ24	312
N80AR	LJ35	454
N80AS	LJ35	446
N80AT	CL60	1036
N80AT	GLF3	463
N80AT	GLF4	1151
N80AT	**GLF4**	**1410**
N80AW	C550	197
N80AX	C52A	0178
N80AX	C550	171
N80AX	LJ25	224
N80BE	LJ25	248
N80BF	CL61	5117
N80BF	HS25	258012
N80BF	HS25	258050
N80BH	HS25	256003
N80BL	**F2EX**	**254**
N80BL	FA10	200
N80BL	LJ35	459
N80BL	BE40	RK-219
N80BR	GLF4	1132
N80BR	HS25	258012
N80BS	C550	132
N80BT	LJ25	248
N80BT	LJ35	343
N80C	C525	0416
N80C	**C52A**	**0104**
N80CB	LJ24	148
N80CC	C500	132
N80CC	C650	0034
N80CC	FA10	18
N80CC	HS25	25095
(N80CC)	HS25	258027
N80CD	LJ35	215
N80CD	LJ35	282
N80CD	LJ35	477
N80CH	C52C	0036
N80CJ	C500	537
N80CJ	C525	0080
N80CK	**CL60**	**1069**
N80CK	LJ24	309
N80CL	HS25	257170
N80CN	FA50	105
N80CR	SBRL	306-128
N80CR	SBRL	306-142
N80CS	CL61	3010
(N80DE)	BE40	RK-26
N80DH	LJ24	191
N80DR	C550	142
N80DX	**CL64**	**5365**
N80DX	LJ60	012
N80DX	BE40	RK-26
N80E	GLF2	184
N80E	HS25	258680
N80E	HS25	HA-0155
N80E	SBRL	306-58
N80EA	**C52B**	**0209**
N80ED	LJ35	337
N80EH	HS25	258680
N80EJ	**E50P**	**50000056**
N80EJ	E50P	50000133
N80EL	LJ25	092
N80EP	**C52B**	**0116**
N80EP	C560	0295
N80ER	SBRL	306-58
N80F	C52B	0261
N80F	**C52C**	**0019**
N80F	F900	6
N80F	F9EX	76
N80FB	HS25	258572
N80FD	WW24	260
N80FH	SBRL	465-34
N80FJ	FA50	69
N80FK	**C52B**	**0261**
N80FW	**C680**	**0238**
N80G	HS25	257131
N80GB	C500	094
N80GD	LJ35	215
N80GD	LJ35	282
N80GE	C560	0187
N80GJ	HS25	258136
N80GK	GALX	161
N80GM	**C550**	**208**
N80GM	JSTR	5146
N80GP	FA10	157
N80GP	FA50	274
N80GR	C560	0494
N80GR	**C560**	**0616**
N80GR	LJ25	193
N80GX	ASTR	138
N80HA	**C500**	**537**
N80HB	C52B	0163
N80HB	**C52C**	**0017**
N80HD	**CL30**	**20309**
N80HD	HS25	258334
N80HD	HS25	258609
N80HE	**C52B**	**0163**
N80HG	SBRL	380-19
N80HK	LJ35	238
N80HK	SBRL	380-71
N80HQ	**C510**	**0021**
N80HX	HS25	258609
N80J	GLF2	160
N80J	GLF3	441
N80J	HS25	258681
N80J	**HS25**	**HA-0156**
N80JE	HS25	258681
N80JH	**C560**	**0327**
N80K	HS25	257138
N80K	SBRL	370-2
N80KA	HS25	257001
N80KM	HS25	257094
N80KM	BE40	RK-50
N80KR	SBRL	380-42
(N80KR)	LJ35	454
N80L	GLF3	406
N80L	SBRL	306-42
N80LA	C550	441
N80LD	C52C	0037
N80LD	**C680**	**680A0011**
N80LJ	LJ31	080
N80LP	C560	0295
N80LP	C56X	5249
N80LX	SBRL	380-51
N80MF	C500	558
N80MJ	LJ35	280
N80MP	FA10	68
N80NE	**EA50**	**000011**
N80NR	SBRL	380-15
N80PG	**LJ35**	**063**
N80PJ	LJ25	260
N80PK	**HS25**	**258442**
N80PM	HS25	257141
N80PM	HS25	258236
N80PN	**GLF5**	**576**
N80PN	HS25	257141
N80PS	GLF5	576
N80PT	**C550**	**550-0839**
N80Q	**F9EX**	**123**
N80Q	GLF2	39
N80Q	GLF4	4012
N80QJ	**GLF4**	**1333**
N80QL	GLF4	4012
N80QM	SBRL	282-23
N80QM	SBRL	306-143
N80R	GALX	074
N80R	SBRL	465-53
N80RE	LJ25	216
N80RE	WW24	341
N80RN	SBRL	465-53
N80RP	CL61	3026
N80RP	F2EX	116
N80RP	GLF5	528
N80RP	LJ25	216
N80RP	LJ45	008
N80RS	SBRL	380-17
N80RS	SBRL	380-57
N80SF	C500	582
(N80SJ)	SJ30	008
N80SL	**C500**	**483**
N80SM	LJ35	205
N80SN	**C560**	**0558**
N80SR	GLF3	485
N80TF	C525	0076
N80TF	CL60	1054
N80TF	**EA50**	**000032**
N80TF	WW24	39
N80TN	SBRL	380-19
N80TR	FA50	32
N80TS	FA10	87
N80TS	HS25	256013
N80TS	JSTR	5215
N80TS	**BE40**	**RJ-34**
N80UT	LJ35	200
N80VM	**C52B**	**0455**
N80VP	C525	0453
N80WD	GLF2	88/21
N80WE	FA50	80
N80WG	LJ35	281
N80WJ	FA10	202
N80WP	**EA50**	**550-0271**
N80X	**C56X**	**5054**
N80ZZ	GLEX	9219
N81	WW24	143
N81AB	HS25	259005
(N81AG)	FA20	514
N81AJ	FA20	308
N81AP	C650	0082
N81AX	LJ25	279
N81BA	C500	038
N81BH	HS25	256004
N81CC	C500	492
N81CC	C550	088
N81CH	HS25	257212
N81CH	LJ35	500
N81CH	LJ55	032
N81CH	LJ55	036
(N81CH)	FA50	47
N81CN	HS25	257212
N81CR	**CL30**	**20176**
N81D	HS25	256011
N81DM	MU30	002
N81EA	**C680**	**0348**
N81EB	**C500**	**355**
N81ER	C52B	0190
N81ER	**C52B**	**0388**
N81ER	C550	550-1015
N81EX	F2EX	81
N81FC	GLF2	91
N81FJ	FA50	70
N81FJ	**LJ45**	**392**
N81FR	LJ35	081
N81GD	C550	267
N81GD	**LJ60**	**415**
N81GD	SBRL	380-54
N81GK	**GLF4**	**4225**
N81GN	F900	81
N81HH	HS25	257189
N81HH	HS25	259034
N81HH	MU30	A013SA
N81HK	HS25	258578
N81HP	SBRL	306-100
N81HR	**PRM1**	**RB-200**
N81JE	**ASTR**	**112**
N81JJ	JSTR	5002
N81KA	HS25	257038
N81LB	FA10	158
N81LJ	LJ31	081
(N81LJ)	LJ24	081
N81LR	C550	550-1015
N81MC	LJ24	344
N81MJ	C500	301
N81MR	JSTR	5039
N81MR	**LJ35**	**622**
N81MW	LJ25	277
N81NT	**C680**	**0305**
N81P	FA10	153
N81P	FA10	31
N81P	**FA20**	**446**
N81PJ	**MS76**	**081**
N81PX	FA10	153
N81QH	LJ35	500
N81QV	HS25	257058
N81R	FA50	148
N81RA	C525	0194
N81RA	**LJ35**	**472**
N81RR	GLF2	246
N81RR	HS25	25196
N81SF	C650	0074
N81SF	**CL30**	**20138**
N81SF	HS25	258531
N81SH	C560	0357
N81SH	**C56X**	**5101**
N81SH	C555	0146
N81SJ	HS25	258531
N81SN	**F9EX**	**41**
N81SN	HS25	258460
(N81SN)	C750	0097
N81SV	**F2EX**	**310**
N81SV	F900	146
N81T	HS25	25225
N81TC	C550	094
N81TC	C650	0039
N81TF	C550	136
N81TJ	C550	242
N81TJ	FA10	187
N81TJ	MU30	A081SA
N81TJ	BE40	RK-14
N81TT	GALX	006
(N81TT)	C650	0029
(N81TT)	GALX	143
(N81TT)	BE40	RK-65
N81TX	**FA10**	**81**
N81U	FA50	148
N81UB	GLEX	9151
N81WL	**C510**	**0165**
N81WT	LJ24	351
N81ZZ	GLEX	9020
N81ZZ	GLEX	9222
N82	WW24	142
N82A	CL60	1072
N82A	FA20	205
N82A	GLF3	342
N82A	GLF4	1068
N82A	GLF4	4032
N82AE	**C525**	**0412**
N82AE	GLF3	342
N82AF	SBRL	380-21
N82AJ	C500	428
N82AT	C500	312
N82AT	F2TH	51
N82AX	LJ25	301
N82BE	ASTR	113
N82BG	C750	0082
N82BH	HS25	256001
(N82BL)	HS25	258126
(N82BR)	GLF4	1082
N82CA	**FA50**	**160**
N82CA	HS25	25201
N82CF	SBRL	282-100
(N82CF)	C500	330
N82CG	FA10	167
N82CK	GLF2	64/27
N82CN	CL60	1050
N82CN	CL64	5395
N82CR	FA10	183
N82CR	**GLF2**	**80**
N82CR	SBRL	465-49
N82CS	MU30	A040SA
N82CT	MU30	A012SA
N82CW	CL60	1050
N82CW	CL64	5395
N82CW	**GLF4**	**4019**
(N82CW)	C560	0342
N82DT	**C500**	**459**
N82DU	**E50P**	**50000008**
N82EA	HS25	258283
N82FD	**C650**	**0104**
N82FJ	CL61	5082
N82FJ	FA50	72
N82GA	C550	448
N82GA	LJ35	071
N82GG	**LJ36**	**040**
N82GK	HS25	258618
N82GL	LJ35	477
N82GM	C56X	5596
N82GM	C650	7064
N82GP	F900	82
N82HD	**F9EX**	**157**
N82HH	**ASTR**	**144**
N82HH	WW24	383
N82JA	LJ55	029
N82JC	WW24	82
N82JJ	C550	223
N82JL	LJ35	380
N82JT	C500	208
N82KA	C52A	0490
N82KA	**C52C**	**0082**
(N82KD)	LJ60	095
N82KK	LJ31	054
N82KK	**LJ60**	**095**
(N82KK)	F9EX	84
N82KL	LJ31	054
N82KW	C56X	5202
N82KW	**C56X**	**6094**
N82LD	**C52C**	**0037**
N82LP	FA50	18
N82LS	C500	681
N82MA	C550	550-0891
N82MD	FA10	77
N82MF	**F900**	**35**
N82MJ	C500	377
N82ML	**C550**	**406**
N82ML	SBRL	282-83
N82MP	FA50	42
(N82MP)	C500	514
N82MW	SBRL	306-76
N82NC	FA50	94
N82P	C500	612
N82P	**C550**	**550-0961**
N82PJ	FA20	177
N82PP	HS25	256001
N82QD	**BE40**	**RK-72**
N82R	SBRL	282-131
N82RL	**CL64**	**5485**
N82RP	C550	139
N82RP	F900	116
N82RP	FA50	18
N82RP	**FA7X**	**35**
N82RP	HS25	256001
N82RT	ASTR	036
N82RZ	C550	139
N82SE	C500	346
N82SR	**HS25**	**258026**
N82SR	JSTR	5082/36
(N82SR)	FA20	83
N82ST	FA50	85
N82SV	F900	163
N82TC	C650	0040
N82TN	FA20	384/551
N82TS	LJ25	154
(N82UH)	LJ25	010
N82VP	C650	0082
N82XP	HS25	258173
N82XP	HS25	HA-0182
N83	WW24	131
N83AB	SBRL	380-59
N83AE	MU30	A041SA
N83AG	C550	483
N83AG	GLF3	464
N83AL	GLF3	363
N83AL	WW24	83
N83BG	**MU30**	**A018SA**
N83CE	LJ24	074
N83CG	**MU30**	**A032SA**
N83CK	LJ25	183
N83CP	**GLF5**	**5286**
N83CP	GLF5	635
N83CP	LJ35	274
N83CT	C650	0015
N83CT	WW24	321
N83CV	**HS25**	**257199**
N83CW	**GLF5**	**5501**
N83CW	GLF5	649
N83D	FA20	368
N83D	GLF3	317
N83DC	C525	0380
N83DM	**C500**	**634**
N83DM	LJ36	007
(N83DM)	LJ35	173
N83DZ	GLF6	6079
N83EA	FA10	83
N83EA	LJ25	240
N83EJ	GALX	009
N83EM	**C510**	**0026**
N83EP	**C560**	**0021**
N83EX	F2EX	83
N83FC	FA50	119
N83FF	**GLEX**	**9636**
N83FJ	**FA50**	**74**
N83FN	**LJ36**	**007**
N83GG	C56X	5046
N83GG	LJ25	038
N83GK	C650	7050
N83H	LJ24	193
N83HC	LJ24	193
N83HF	C550	126
N83HF	HS25	257145
N83JJ	CL30	20259
N83JJ	FA10	163
N83JJ	LJ40	2072
N83JM	LJ25	127
N83KE	C550	568
N83LC	CL61	5029
N83LJ	LJ24	076
N83LT	**F2EX**	**25**
N83M	GLF2	135
N83M	**GLF5**	**5470**
N83M	GLF5	557
N83M	JSTR	5084/8
(N83MA)	C550	117
N83MD	FA10	78
N83MD	**HS25**	**257121**
(N83MF)	FA10	78
N83MJ	LJ24	239
N83MP	FA50	103
N83ND	C500	580
N83NW	**C500**	**309**
N83PP	GLF3	464
N83RE	C560	0183
N83RG	FA10	25
N83RG	LJ24	243
(N83RH)	SBRL	306-44
N83RR	C560	0183
N83RR	C56X	5007
N83SA	**MU30**	**A030SA**
N83SD	C56X	5091
N83SD	**C680**	**0106**
N83SD	LJ55	032
N83SE	C550	203
N83SF	C550	203
N83SG	**WW24**	**368**
N83SV	**F9EX**	**77**
N83TC	LJ25	315
N83TE	GLF2	129
N83TE	GLF2	156/31
N83TE	GLF5	5043
N83TE	LJ25	329

(N83TE)	LJ35	218
N83TF	C500	256
N83TF	**C52B**	**0094**
N83TF	C560	0636
N83TF	SBRL	465-43
N83TH	LJ25	016
N83TJ	FA10	35
N83TJ	HS25	256070
N83TJ	LJ35	138
(N83TJ)	C500	462
N83TK	C560	0636
N83TK	MU30	A083SA
N83TN	LJ45	057
N83TR	C525	0185
N83TR	**LJ60**	**374**
(N83TR)	LJ45	248
N83TY	**FA50**	**288**
N83TZ	LJ45	057
N83UF	**CL61**	**5083**
N83V	FA20	366
N83WA	**C560**	**0758**
N83WM	LJ31	081
N83WM	LJ55	043
N83WM	LJ60	104
N83WN	LJ31	081
N83XP	HS25	HA-0083
N83ZA	**C560**	**0176**
N83ZZ	GLEX	9223
N84	WW24	130
N84A	GLF2	122
N84A	HS25	258010
N84AD	LJ35	499
(N84AL)	GLF2	166/15
N84AW	C550	493
N84BA	HS25	258047
N84BA	HS25	258313
N84BJ	BE40	RJ-17
N84CF	C500	460
N84CF	C500	658
(N84CF)	C550	550-0892
N84CP	HS25	25286
N84CT	HS25	258239
N84CT	LJ24	197
N84DJ	LJ55	034
N84DM	LJ36	002
(N84DT)	MU30	A084SA
N84EA	C550	484
N84EA	**C750**	**0094**
N84EA	PRM1	RB-119
N84EB	C550	488
N84EC	**CS55**	**0014**
N84EE	C680	0262
N84FA	HS25	258047
N84FG	**C525**	**0192**
N84FJ	FA50	76
N84FM	**PRM1**	**RB-30**
N84FN	**LJ36**	**002**
N84G	C650	0045
N84GA	HS25	257056
N84GA	HS25	258004
N84GA	JSTR	5155/32
N84GA	MU30	A070SA
N84GC	**C550**	**493**
(N84GF)	C500	658
N84GP	GPER	551
N84GV	**GLF5**	**584**
N84HD	GLF4	1440
N84HP	FA50	56
N84J	LJ24	184
N84J	MS76	006
N84LA	WW24	378
(N84LF)	C680	0090
N84LG	**CS55**	**0013**
N84LP	SBRL	306-8
N84LX	**C56X**	**5164**
N84MJ	**FA20**	**510**
N84MJ	LJ31	237
N84MJ	LJ36	008
N84ML	PRM1	RB-30
N84MZ	GLF2	77
N84NG	**C650**	**7078**
N84NG	SBRL	380-52
N84NP	C550	093
N84NW	FA50	216
N84PH	**C650**	**0062**
N84PH	WW24	314
N84PJ	C750	0048
N84PJ	**F2EX**	**303**
N84SD	GLEX	9018
N84SH	LJ25	092
N84SV	**F2EX**	**291**
N84TF	HS25	25169
N84TJ	C650	0008
N84TJ	**FA10**	**188**
N84TN	**FA50**	**110**
(N84TV)	C500	499
N84UP	**HS25**	**258484**
N84UR	**EA50**	**000259**
N84V	FA20	302/510
N84V	GLF2	219/20
N84VA	**PRM1**	**RB-134**
N84VM	PRM1	RB-295
N84VV	WW24	383
N84W	HS25	25070
N84WA	HS25	259007
N84WC	**C52B**	**0462**
N84WU	C650	0008

N84WU	WW24	383
N84WW	WW24	401
N84X	GLF2	43
N84XP	BE40	RK-384
N84ZC	CL30	20018
N84ZZ	GLEX	9229
N85	**CL61**	**5138**
N85	SBRL	282-97
N85A	FA50	92
N85AB	CS55	0060
N85AT	C500	087
(N85AT)	LJ25	125
N85AW	C650	0084
N85BE	**CL30**	**20415**
N85BN	BE40	RJ-7
N85BP	JSTR	5055/21
N85BZ	**E55P**	**50500091**
N85CA	LJ24	250
N85CA	LJ35	421
N85CC	**HS25**	**258307**
N85CC	JSTR	5102
N85CC	SBRL	282-108
N85CD	LJ24	250
N85CL	F9EX	167
N85CL	FA50	319
N85CR	BE40	RK-22
N85D	F900	28
N85D	**GLEX**	**9078**
N85DA	C650	0073
N85DA	SBRL	282-56
N85DB	FA20	52
N85DB	SBRL	306-97
(N85DH)	LJ24	243
(N85DL)	JSTR	5089
N85DN	FA50	319
N85DN	**FA7X**	**130**
N85DW	HS25	258034
N85DW	SBRL	380-27
(N85EA)	WW24	201
N85EB	**C560**	**0492**
N85EQ	GLF2	28
N85EQ	WW24	201
N85ER	C52A	0404
N85ER	**C52B**	**0471**
N85EU	PRM1	RB-285
N85F	FA50	253
N85FJ	FA50	77
N85FJ	LJ25	073
N85FS	C500	412
N85GL	LJ55	116
N85GT	**C52B**	**0100**
N85GW	LJ35	227
N85HD	C550	130
N85HE	**C550**	**130**
N85HH	HS25	257107
N85HH	**HS25**	**258817**
N85HP	FA50	163
N85HP	SBRL	306-126
N85HP	**BE40**	**RK-267**
(N85HR)	LJ25	079
N85HS	SBRL	306-23
N85JE	C52A	0303
N85JE	**E55P**	**50500122**
N85JG	**E50P**	**50000229**
N85JM	FA10	85
N85JM	**GLF5**	**5369**
N85JV	**C52A**	**0085**
N85JW	WW24	95
N85KB	**F900**	**125**
N85KC	C550	709
N85KC	C560	0128
N85KH	HS25	258028
N85KH	LJ31	123
N85KV	GLF4	1135
N85LB	FA20	494
N85M	F2EX	73
N85M	GLF4	1023
N85M	**GLF4**	**4228**
N85M	GLF5	648
N85MA	WW24	48
N85MD	FA50	76
N85MG	C550	041
N85MG	GLF4	1023
N85MG	HS25	258035
N85MJ	LJ25	158
N85ML	GLF5	648
N85MP	CS55	0016
N85MQ	F2EX	73
N85MR	WW24	114
N85MS	**C650**	**0075**
N85N	FA20	36
(N85NA)	C550	276
N85NC	LJ55	077
N85NC	LJ60	090
N85NV	**GLF5**	**513**
N85NX	HS25	258814
N85PK	HS25	258460
N85PK	**HS25**	**HA-0154**
N85PL	**PRM1**	**RB-55**
N85PM	LJ35	595
N85PT	**WW24**	**285**
N85PX	**CL64**	**5518**
N85QA	LJ35	421
N85RS	C500	654
N85SM	**EA50**	**000151**
N85SV	**LJ35**	**347**
N85TN	**FA50**	**237**

N85TT	BE40	RJ-35
N85TW	**LJ25**	**251**
N85TZ	FA20	381/549
N85V	FA20	412
N85V	GLF2	80
N85V	GLF3	449
N85V	GLF4	1172
N85V	**GLF5**	**595**
(N85VC)	HS25	258035
N85VE	FA20	412
N85VM	**C52B**	**0491**
N85VM	GLF4	1172
N85VP	C560	0085
N85VR	C510	0250
N85VR	**C525**	**0425**
N85VT	GLF2	80
N85VT	GLF3	449
N85W	LJ24	135
N85WC	WW24	369
N85WD	**GLF4**	**1008**
N85WN	FA10	210
N85WN	FA50	212
N85WP	C500	388
N85WT	**C650**	**0162**
N85XL	C56X	5085
N85XL	LJ55	012
N86	**CL61**	**5167**
N86	SBRL	282-86
N86AJ	C550	550-0842
N86AJ	LJ55	037
N86AJ	LJ55	060
N86AK	FA50	52
N86BA	**CS55**	**0001**
N86BE	LJ35	194
N86BL	LJ35	194
N86BL	LJ35	422
N86BL	**LJ36**	**026**
(N86BL)	FA20	264
(N86BP)	JSTR	5055/21
N86CC	LJ24	115
N86CE	C560	0265
N86CE	GLF2	109
N86CP	SBRL	306-76
N86CS	LJ35	086
N86CV	**C560**	**0342**
N86CW	C560	0342
N86CW	**G280**	**2083**
N86CW	GALX	081
N86DC	E50P	50000150
(N86DD)	C560	0384
N86DQ	**CL30**	**20192**
N86EF	WW24	222
N86EX	C560	0436
N86FJ	FA50	79
N86GC	LJ24	286
N86GR	C560	0494
N86HD	**F2EX**	**250**
N86HM	JSTR	5039
N86HP	SBRL	306-48
N86JB	C525	0251
N86JC	FA50	86
N86JJ	C500	356
(N86JM)	C550	069
N86LA	**C525**	**0012**
N86LF	C680	0030
N86LF	**HA4T**	**RC-18**
N86LQ	C680	0086
N86MC	F900	28
N86MC	FA50	141
N86MD	HS25	257093
N86MF	WW24	414
N86MJ	LJ25	062
N86MN	**HS25**	**258330**
N86MT	C500	473
N86NP	**CL65**	**5874**
N86PC	**C550**	**550-0891**
N86PC	CS55	0017
N86PC	LJ35	108
(N86PQ)	LJ35	108
N86QS	CS55	0086
N86RB	PRM1	RB-40
N86RE	C500	331
N86RL	**C525**	**0462**
N86RM	SBRL	306-89
N86RR	WW24	359
N86RX	LJ35	458
N86SG	**C550**	**384**
(N86SH)	SBRL	380-32
N86SK	C500	500
N86SK	C525	0420
N86SK	C560	0551
N86SK	GLF2	85
N86SS	C500	285
N86TG	**C525**	**0041**
N86TN	**FA50**	**241**
N86TP	JSTR	5142
N86TW	C56X	5179
N86TW	F2TH	43
N86TW	GLEX	9218
(N86TY)	F2TH	43
N86UR	WW24	353
N86VG	FA20	218
N86VP	C650	0089
N86W	FA20	298
N86WC	HS25	257108
N86WH	**C510**	**0416**
N86WP	C650	0089

N86WU	**C56X**	**5198**
N86XL	C56X	5686
N86Y	SBRL	306-44
N87	**CL61**	**5190**
N87	SBRL	282-87
N87AC	GLF3	427
N87AC	LJ24	197
N87AG	FA20	514
N87AG	GLF2	112
N87AG	HS25	257065
N87AP	LJ24	290
N87AT	LJ35	096
N87AX	**LJ45**	**328**
N87B	WW24	104
N87B	WW24	80
N87BA	**CS55**	**0131**
N87CF	C550	615
N87CF	LJ24	181
N87CM	SBRL	282-21
N87CR	SBRL	282-137
N87DC	WW24	126
N87DC	WW24	14
(N87DC)	HS25	25214
N87DG	WW24	14
N87DL	WW24	126
N87DY	MU30	A085SA
N87EB	BE40	RK-87
N87EC	HS25	258052
N87ED	C52C	0087
N87FJ	F2TH	187
N87FJ	FA50	80
N87FJ	FA50	87
N87FL	C500	664
N87FL	**C52C**	**0024**
N87FL	CS55	0055
N87GA	C560	0228
N87GA	LJ35	370
N87GJ	WW24	422
N87GS	C550	550-0895
N87GS	GLF2	258
N87GS	WW24	261
N87GS	WW24	422
N87GT	FA10	181
N87HB	GLF2	39
N87HD	**F2EX**	**307**
N87HP	GLF3	338
N87HP	GLF4	1219
N87JK	**C560**	**0115**
N87JL	LJ24	335
N87MJ	LJ35	204
(N87MJ)	LJ24	301
(N87MW)	LJ25	216
(N87N)	C750	0058
N87NS	WW24	432
N87NY	**MS76**	**087**
N87PK	**HS25**	**HA-0043**
N87PT	**C550**	**201**
N87RB	**HS25**	**258299**
(N87RS)	LJ35	250
N87SF	C550	103
N87SF	**C650**	**7089**
N87SK	**LJ45**	**317**
N87SL	C750	0174
N87TD	GLF2	39
N87TH	CS55	0129
N87TH	**FA10**	**178**
N87TN	FA20	385
N87TN	FA50	224
N87TR	CL60	1076
N87VM	**C52B**	**0098**
N87VR	**C750**	**0087**
N87W	LJ35	104
N87WC	**C510**	**0385**
N87WD	**GLF5**	**649**
N87WU	**C56X**	**5039**
N87WW	WW24	402
N87XP	HS25	HA-0087
N87Y	SBRL	380-1
N87ZZ	GLEX	9228
N87ZZ	GLEX	9275
N88	**CL64**	**5588**
N88	SBRL	282-88
N88AA	**GLEX**	**9438**
N88AD	**C525**	**0404**
N88AD	WW24	106
N88AE	GLF2	102/32
N88AE	GLF3	398
N88AF	C500	290
N88AF	HS25	25285
N88AF	**LJ45**	**205**
(N88AH)	LJ35	421
N88AJ	**C550**	**550-0885**
N88AT	CL60	1036
N88AT	FA10	73
N88AY	GALX	134
N88AY	**GLF5**	**5337**
N88B	LJ24	015
N88BF	SBRL	465-60
N88BG	LJ35	090
N88BM	C500	500
N88BM	C550	565
(N88BR)	C500	553
N88BT	LJ25	168
N88BY	LJ25	168
N88C	**GLEX**	**9643**
N88CA	**BE40**	**RK-282**
N88CF	C500	465

N88CF	C500	477
N88CH	**C510**	**0224**
N88CJ	LJ25	006
N88CR	MU30	A089SA
N88D	GLF5	5183
N88D	GLF5	612
N88D	GLF6	6079
N88DD	C550	263
N88DD	C650	0058
N88DD	**F2TH**	**204**
N88DD	F2TH	96
N88DJ	C650	0167
N88DJ	HS25	25153
N88DJ	LJ25	234
N88DU	HS25	25153
N88DW	E50P	50000178
N88DW	E55P	50500031
N88DZ	**GLF5**	**612**
N88EA	LJ24	077
N88EJ	C750	0088
N88EL	**PRM1**	**RB-157**
N88EL	PRM1	RB-17
N88EL	PRM1	RB-83
N88EP	LJ25	019
N88EP	LJ35	134
N88ER	**PRM1**	**RB-17**
N88EU	PRM1	RB-83
N88EX	C560	0433
N88FE	FA20	317
N88FJ	FA50	82
N88FP	LJ25	019
N88FW	**E50P**	**50000277**
N88G	C560	0208
N88G	CS55	0017
N88GA	**C52B**	**0377**
N88GA	GLF2	217
N88GA	GLF4	1085
N88GA	HS25	25276
N88GC	LJ25	088
N88GD	CS55	0017
N88GJ	C500	155
(N88GJ)	LJ25	006
N88GQ	LJ25	088
N88GZ	GLEX	9473
N88HA	CL61	5072
N88HD	**CL30**	**20344**
N88HD	HS25	258429
N88HD	HS25	258616
N88HE	F2EX	79
N88HF	C550	126
N88HF	C550	615
N88HF	C560	0133
N88HP	**C56X**	**5050**
N88HP	GLF4	1212
N88HX	HS25	258616
N88JA	LJ25	305
N88JA	LJ35	118
(N88JE)	WW24	326
N88JF	LJ24	110
N88JJ	C500	356
N88JJ	C550	187
N88JJ	C650	0169
N88JJ	**C680**	**0277**
N88JJ	SBRL	380-65
N88JM	JSTR	5011/1
N88JM	SBRL	282-36
N88JM	SBRL	380-39
N88KC	C52A	0157
N88LC	F9EX	137
N88LD	C525	0181
N88LD	FA10	108
N88LJ	LJ24	290
N88LJ	**LJ40**	**2045**
N88LN	**GLF2**	**20**
N88LS	**C525**	**0475**
N88ME	**C525**	**0448**
N88ME	FA10	8
N88ME	MU30	A066SA
N88MF	ASTR	048
N88MF	MU30	A066SA
N88MJ	C550	088
N88ML	C550	219
N88MM	C500	689
N88MM	LJ31	036
N88MM	PRM1	RB-18
N88MM	**PRM1**	**RB-44**
N88MR	HS25	25013
(N88MT)	C500	689
N88MX	F2TH	183
N88MX	GLF4	1110
N88MX	HS25	257090
N88MZ	**LJ60**	**411**
N88ND	**F9EX**	**19**
N88NE	LJ35	227
N88NE	LJ35	350
N88NJ	LJ25	008
N88NJ	LJ25	294
N88NJ	LJ35	170
N88NM	C550	590
N88NN	**CL61**	**5146**
N88NT	FA20	416
N88NW	C500	309
N88NW	**CS55**	**0151**
N88NY	MS76	088
N88PV	WW24	264
N88QC	C525	0664
N88QC	**C52C**	**0004**

(N88QC)	C52B	0302
N88QG	C525	0664
N88RC	**CL30**	**20303**
N88RD	LJ24	196
N88SF	C56X	5645
N88SJ	HS25	25286
N88TB	C500	353
N88TB	C550	271
(N88TB)	FA10	159
N88TC	LJ24	022
N88TJ	C560	0014
N88TJ	LJ35	188
(N88TJ)	CL60	1063
(N88TJ)	MU30	A004SA
N88TY	F2TH	17
N88U	FA50	83
N88UA	**BE40**	**RJ-49**
N88V	**LJ60**	**155**
N88WC	C560	0157
N88WG	CL61	5068
N88WG	BE40	RJ-26
N88WL	FA10	140
N88WP	WW24	151
N88WR	**GLF4**	**4085**
(N88WR)	GLF5	5224
N88WU	C56X	5039
N88WU	GALX	111
N88WV	**LJ45**	**276**
N88YF	F900	134
N89	**CL65**	**5815**
N89	SBRL	282-89
N89AA	LJ24	308
N89AB	GLF3	349
N89AB	GLF3	496
N89AC	C650	0029
N89AE	GLF3	349
N89AE	GLF3	496
N89AJ	C500	272
N89AM	WW24	389
N89AT	LJ25	125
N89AT	LJ35	391
N89B	C550	114
N89B	WW24	69
(N89B)	C550	126
N89BM	C560	0017
N89BM	FA50	237
N89BR	HS25	258425
N89CE	**F2EX**	**81**
N89D	**C550**	**070**
N89EC	FA10	109
N89EM	MU30	A055SA
N89ES	**LJ24**	**197**
N89FC	FA50	184
(N89FF)	HS25	25023
N89FJ	FA50	81
N89GA	**C550**	**135**
N89GA	BE40	RJ-60
N89GK	LJ35	316
N89GN	HS25	257101
N89HB	HS25	25097
N89HB	LJ31	010
N89HE	GLF5	568
N89HS	**ASTR**	**089**
N89JJ	**E50P**	**50000150**
N89K	HS25	258102
N89KK	BE40	RJ-62
N89KM	BE40	RJ-62
N89KM	BE40	RK-56
(N89KT)	HS25	258102
N89KW	LJ60	085
N89LS	C550	623
N89MD	**C560**	**0612**
N89MD	HS25	257134
N89MF	C500	571
N89MJ	LJ36	019
N89MM	SBRL	465-30
N89MR	WW24	9
N89MX	GLEX	9304
(N89N)	SBRL	306-141
N89NC	FA50	337
N89NC	**GLF5**	**5049**
N89NC	HS25	258102
N89PP	HS25	257098
N89PP	HS25	257101
N89PR	**C560**	**0603**
N89Q	C550	114
N89QA	GLF3	325
N89RF	LJ31	145
(N89RF)	EA50	000275
N89RP	LJ35	410
N89RP	LJ45	011
N89SC	FA20	96
N89SC	MU30	A089SA
N89SE	C550	585
N89SR	HS25	25285
(N89TA)	C550	193
N89TB	**LJ35**	**272**
N89TC	**LJ35**	**026**
N89TD	C555	0076
N89TD	**FA50**	**157**
N89TJ	GLF2	103
N89TJ	HS25	257031
N89TJ	MU30	A029SA
N89TJ	WW24	296
(N89TJ)	WW24	315
N89TY	F2TH	17
(N89TY)	FA50	288
N89UH	WW24	353
N89XL	WW24	171
N89ZZ	GLEX	9259
N89ZZ	LJ45	105
N90	**CL65**	**5817**
(N90AB)	FA10	44
N90AE	FA50	104
N90AE	GLF4	1068
N90AE	**GLF4**	**4275**
N90AG	CL64	5414
N90AG	LJ60	042
N90AH	LJ35	036
N90AJ	**ASTR**	**052**
N90AL	LJ35	222
N90AM	FA50	53
N90AM	GLF4	1284
N90AM	GLF5	592
N90AM	LJ55	106
N90AM	SBRL	380-25
N90AQ	LJ60	042
N90AR	CL61	5137
N90AR	HS25	257107
N90B	HS25	256034
N90B	HS25	257117
N90B	WW24	58
N90BA	C500	117
N90BA	**LJ31**	**018**
N90BJ	C550	710
N90BL	C550	682
N90BL	**C56X**	**5609**
N90BL	HS25	256034
(N90BN)	HS25	257117
N90BR	LJ25	214
N90BS	LJ55	014
N90BY	C550	682
N90C	SBRL	380-46
N90CC	C500	076
N90CE	ASTR	043
N90CE	**LJ60**	**392**
N90CF	C500	575
N90CF	C56X	5080
N90CH	WW24	353
N90CJ	**C52A**	**0149**
N90CL	WW24	324
N90CN	C650	0140
N90CN	FA20	299
N90CP	GLF2	224
N90CP	JSTR	5232
N90CZ	**C52B**	**0090**
N90DA	C550	125
N90DH	LJ24	117
(N90DH)	LJ25	080
N90DM	FA10	104
N90E	LJ55	004
N90EA	GLF2	121
N90EB	C500	361
N90EC	SBRL	306-73
N90EP	GLF3	317
N90EW	F900	27
N90EW	**GLEX**	**9039**
N90FB	**HS25**	**258613**
N90FD	**C56X**	**6049**
N90FF	HS25	257113
N90FJ	C555	0065
N90FJ	FA50	65
N90FJ	FA50	85
N90FT	GALX	209
N90FX	**GLEX**	**9017**
(N90GJ)	LJ60	204
N90GM	SBRL	282-48
N90GM	SBRL	380-27
N90GS	FA20	388
N90GS	**LJ45**	**225**
N90GW	SBRL	380-27
N90GX	GALX	040
N90HB	C560	0584
N90HC	**FA50**	**208**
N90HH	C56X	5250
N90HH	GLF2	78
N90HM	WW24	170
N90J	LJ24	060
N90J	**LJ35**	**485**
N90JD	C550	340
N90JF	FA20	45
N90JJ	**C550**	**571**
N90KC	WW24	339
N90KR	JSTR	5036/42
N90LA	FA10	47
(N90LA)	C650	0011
N90LC	FA10	23
N90LC	GLF3	360
N90LJ	**LJ25**	**226**
N90LJ	LJ31	039
N90LP	LJ35	236
N90LX	F9EX	243
N90MA	**C550**	**140**
N90MC	LJ60	130
N90MD	GLF2	241
N90ME	HS25	258082
N90ME	JSTR	5057
N90MF	C560	0060
N90MH	FA10	110
N90MH	LJ25	006
N90MJ	C550	067
N90ML	**GLF3**	**315**
N90MT	**C525**	**0539**
(N90MT)	C500	509
N90N	SBRL	306-12
N90N	SBRL	380-72
N90NB	**C560**	**0634**
N90NE	LJ55	075
N90NF	**C750**	**0170**
N90PB	LJ31	024
N90PG	C560	0002
N90PM	HS25	258183
N90PN	LJ35	505
N90PT	**C550**	**465**
N90QP	JSTR	5232
N90R	FA50	162
N90R	SBRL	306-36
N90RC	C550	500
N90RG	HS25	25091
N90RK	LJ35	417
N90RZ	LJ45	304
N90SA	HS25	HB-25
N90SF	C550	455
N90SF	GLF3	366
N90SR	BE40	RJ-26
(N90SR)	HS25	25116
N90TC	JSTR	5037/24
(N90TC)	LJ25	020
N90TH	**F900**	**180**
N90TH	F900	63
N90TT	SBRL	306-97
N90U	ASTR	030
N90U	JSTR	5057
N90UC	CL60	1023
N90UG	ASTR	030
N90UG	LJ45	115
N90WA	**LJ31**	**028**
(N90WA)	C500	263
N90WJ	C500	053
N90WJ	GLF3	340
N90WP	HS25	25032
N90WP	HS25	256068
N90WP	**HS25**	**258692**
(N90WP)	HS25	25141
N90WR	LJ35	022
N90XP	HS25	HA-0001
N90XR	**LJ40**	**2090**
N90Z	**C550**	**367**
N90ZP	JSTR	5055/21
N91A	C52A	0105
N91AE	GLF2	17
N91AE	GLF4	1053
N91AG	C560	0606
(N91AN)	C560	0111
N91AP	**C500**	**506**
N91B	C550	217
N91B	WW24	112
N91BA	C500	168
N91BB	**C525**	**0417**
N91BB	PRM1	RB-192
(N91BH)	HS25	25261
N91BP	FA10	107
(N91BS)	C500	244
N91BZ	SBRL	465-19
N91CH	**C510**	**0201**
N91CH	GLF3	405
N91CH	HS25	258030
N91CH	LJ35	021
N91CH	LJ55	091
N91CM	HS25	257092
N91CR	GLF3	405
N91CV	**C560**	**0009**
N91CV	FA20	48
N91CW	**GLF5**	**543**
N91D	C500	343
N91D	C650	0151
N91DH	FA10	108
N91DH	FA10	68
N91DP	**LJ31**	**079**
N91DV	HS25	258211
N91DZ	C500	343
N91ED	LJ25	255
N91EW	F900	27
N91EX	F2EX	91
N91EX	F9EX	91
(N91FA)	C560	0072
N91FD	ASTR	045
N91FE	**F9EX**	**244**
N91FG	LJ45	383
N91FJ	FA50	87
N91FP	**C510**	**0001**
N91FX	**GLEX**	**9054**
(N91GH)	C525	0234
N91GL	F9EX	155
N91GT	**C52B**	**0332**
(N91GT)	C52B	0343
N91GX	ASTR	091
N91GY	**C56X**	**5314**
N91HG	**C500**	**601**
N91HK	**CL30**	**20375**
N91HK	HS25	258578
N91HR	HS25	256046
N91JF	FA20	14
N91KC	C650	7082
N91KH	**CL61**	**5038**
N91KH	HS25	256003
N91KK	**C650**	**0193**
N91KL	GLF4	1507
(N91KL)	GLF3	321
N91KP	HS25	256003
N91KY	**CL61**	**5057**
N91LA	C650	0011
N91LA	FA10	47
N91LA	GLF2	198/35
N91LA	GLF4	1266
N91LA	**GLF5**	**5027**
N91LE	LJ60	091
N91LJ	GLF3	342
N91LJ	JSTR	5142
N91LS	C500	244
(N91LU)	GLF4	1266
N91MB	**C510**	**0310**
N91ME	C560	0240
N91ME	C555	0132
N91MG	**CL64**	**5423**
N91MH	FA10	23
(N91MH)	FA20	91
N91MJ	C550	111
N91MK	F900	36
N91MK	LJ24	162
N91MK	WW24	324
N91ML	C555	0132
N91MS	C500	572
N91MS	**F900**	**10**
N91MT	LJ25	255
N91MT	LJ25	363
N91MT	BE40	RJ-26
N91NA	**GLF2**	**198/35**
N91NG	**GLEX**	**9114**
N91NG	GLEX	9191
N91NK	C560	0040
N91NL	C560	0040
N91PB	FA10	198
N91PE	C500	400
N91PN	**LJ25**	**091**
N91PR	LJ55	091
N91PS	**HS25**	**258328**
N91RB	**C525**	**0124**
N91SA	WW24	420
N91TE	**C500**	**572**
N91TG	C650	0208
N91TH	F900	60
N91TQ	E50P	50000090
N91TS	FA20	21
N91UC	CL60	1051
N91UJ	JSTR	5142
N91VB	**C550**	**058**
N91W	LJ35	194
N91WF	F900	91
N91WG	WW24	112
N91WZ	C500	527
N91Y	FA20	373
N91Y	HS25	257159
N91YC	C560	0115
N92AE	GLF4	1301
N92AG	GLF2	110
N92AJ	C500	230
N92AJ	C525	0522
N92AJ	**G150**	**209**
N92AJ	BE40	RK-599
N92B	C500	212
N92B	C550	471
N92B	WW24	32
N92BA	C500	207
N92BD	C550	588
N92BE	**C500**	**464**
(N92BE)	WW24	428
N92BF	C560	0235
N92BH	HS25	25267
N92BL	C500	391
N92BL	LJ60	058
N92BT	WW24	32
N92C	C500	391
N92CC	C500	391
N92CJ	C52A	0029
N92CJ	**FA50**	**92**
N92CS	LJ25	292
N92CX	C750	0301
N92DE	C560	0391
N92DF	LJ24	117
N92EB	WW24	381
N92EC	LJ31	024
N92EC	LJ35	094
N92EJ	LJ35	092
N92FA	C500	068
N92FD	LJ31	054
N92FE	WW24	286
N92FG	**LJ60**	**056**
N92FJ	FA50	88
(N92FL)	HS25	258598
N92FT	**G280**	**2038**
N92FT	HS25	258598
N92FX	**GLEX**	**9147**
N92HL	GLF4	4154
N92HW	C560	0148
N92JC	C555	0115
N92JT	C555	0115
N92K	FA20	317
N92LA	C500	338
N92LA	C650	0003
N92LA	GLF2	125/26
N92LA	GLF4	1238
N92LA	**GLF5**	**5002**
N92LJ	LJ31	016
N92LP	**BE40**	**RK-314**
N92LT	C550	361
N92LT	F2TH	71
(N92LU)	GLF4	1238
N92MA	C52B	0048
N92ME	**C555**	**0044**
N92MG	LJ55	025
N92MH	FA20	3/403
N92MJ	LJ25	292
N92MK	**C750**	**0267**
N92MS	**C52B**	**0214**
N92NA	GLF2	125/26
N92ND	**C525**	**0186**
N92NE	LJ35	092
N92NS	**LJ60**	**092**
N92QS	C555	0092
N92RB	WW24	174
N92RP	**C650**	**0148**
N92RP	HS25	257022
N92RW	BE40	RJ-4
N92RX	**C750**	**0301**
N92SA	GLF4	1413
N92SH	LJ25	092
N92SH	**PRM1**	**RB-33**
N92SM	**C500**	**124**
N92SS	**C560**	**0388**
N92SV	GLF2	74
N92TC	LJ24	268
N92TE	**C560**	**0123**
N92TH	**C750**	**0097**
N92TS	LJ35	035
N92TX	C650	0127
N92UG	LJ31	050
N92UJ	ASTR	092
N92UP	**HS25**	**258309**
N92V	LJ25	025
N92VR	**C550**	**550-1092**
N92WW	WW24	296
N92WW	WW24	392
N92ZZ	GLEX	9206
N92ZZ	GLEX	9354
N93AC	SBRL	282-109
N93AE	GLF4	1302
N93AG	C560	0223
N93AJ	**C550**	**368**
N93AK	C52A	0181
N93AK	**C52A**	**0368**
N93AQ	C52A	0181
N93AT	GLF2	85
N93AT	**GLF4**	**1020**
N93AX	FA50	181
N93B	WW24	27
N93BA	C550	555
N93BA	CL60	1027
N93BA	LJ60	094
N93BD	C550	454
N93BE	WW24	27
N93BH	HS25	25186
N93BP	LJ24	169
N93BR	LJ24	231
N93C	LJ24	230
N93C	LJ25	127
N93C	LJ35	159
N93CB	LJ24	230
N93CD	FA20	161
N93CE	LJ25	127
N93CK	LJ35	159
N93CL	C560	0624
N93CL	C650	0074
N93CP	FA20	7
N93CR	CL61	3024
N93CR	F900	24
N93CR	F9EX	96
N93CR	HS25	257117
N93CT	HS25	258049
N93CV	**C560**	**0239**
N93CW	C52B	0139
(N93CW)	C550	096
N93CX	GLF3	314
N93DD	LJ24	236
N93DK	C650	0112
N93DW	C550	448
N93DW	C560	0133
N93DW	CL61	5025
N93EA	C560	0093
N93EW	**LJ60**	**402**
N93FB	**BE40**	**RK-166**
N93FH	FA20	161
N93FJ	FA50	89
N93FR	HS25	257202
N93FS	**C560**	**0518**
N93FT	BE40	RK-166
N93FT	**BE40**	**RK-604**
N93GC	HS25	257195
N93GH	F2TH	6
N93GH	FA50	252
N93GR	F900	24
N93GR	HS25	257117
N93GT	F2TH	6
N93HA	**C560**	**0493**
(N93JD)	JSTR	5201
(N93JH)	LJ25	022
N93JM	C500	569
N93JM	JSTR	5201
N93JR	WW24	51
N93JW	**C52B**	**0035**
N93KD	F9EX	182
N93KE	WW24	316
(N93KV)	C525	0030
N93KW	**HS25**	**HB-62**
N93LA	C750	0121

N93LA	**CL30**	**20327**
N93LA	GLF2	164
N93LE	**LJ35**	**592**
N93LS	**C525**	**0556**
N93M	GLF2	98/38
N93M	GLF5	567
N93MC	FA20	428
N93MJ	LJ35	119
N93MK	GLF4	1088
N93MW	**C52B**	**0487**
N93NB	C560	0644
N93NS	**CL30**	**20031**
N93PE	C52A	0093
N93PE	**C52B**	**0093**
N93QQ	GLF2	7
N93QS	CS55	0093
(N93RC)	LJ35	433
N93RM	WW24	74
N93RS	FA20	81
N93S	**C750**	**0189**
N93SC	WW24	90
N93SK	LJ31	031
N93TC	HS25	25116
N93TC	HS25	257025
N93TJ	C500	358
N93TS	HS25	25264
N93TS	HS25	256018
N93TX	C650	7009
N93TX	C750	0099
N93VP	C650	0093
N93VR	**C550**	**550-1093**
N93WD	C500	220
N93WW	WW24	321
N93XP	**BE40**	**RK-74**
N93XR	LJ45	393
N93ZZ	GLEX	9214
N94	HS25	258129
N94AA	LJ35	295
(N94AA)	LJ35	366
N94AE	GLF4	1307
N94AF	C550	585
N94AF	**LJ35**	**094**
N94AJ	**C500**	**024**
N94AL	**C525**	**0432**
N94AM	F2EX	154
N94AN	GLF4	1307
N94AT	LJ25	125
N94AT	WW24	288
N94B	HS25	256055
N94B	HS25	257189
N94B	WW24	24
N94BA	CL61	5160
N94BA	LJ60	144
N94BB	HS25	256004
N94BD	HS25	256004
N94BD	HS25	257024
N94BD	HS25	258004
(N94BD)	LJ24	351
N94BE	HS25	257024
N94BF	HS25	256055
N94BJ	C650	0147
N94BJ	FA50	237
N94BJ	BE40	RJ-17
N94BN	GLF3	391
N94CK	LJ45	066
N94CK	**LJ45**	**410**
N94DE	C500	094
N94FJ	FA50	86
(N94FJ)	F2TH	94
N94FL	**GLF3**	**424**
N94FP	C52C	0134
(N94FS)	C550	015
N94FT	G280	2091
N94FT	GALX	208
N94FY	**GALX**	**208**
N94GA	EA50	000072
N94GC	GLF3	321
N94GH	**C650**	**0021**
N94GP	LJ35	094
N94GP	**LJ35**	**411**
N94GW	FA20	322
N94HC	LJ24	157
N94HE	**BE40**	**RK-89**
N94HL	**C525**	**0654**
N94HT	BE40	RK-48
N94JJ	LJ24	138
N94JT	**HS25**	**258071**
N94JW	**C52C**	**0033**
N94K	JSTR	5114/18
N94LA	C56X	5129
N94LD	**MU30**	**A073SA**
N94LF	**GLF5**	**5039**
N94LH	MU30	A073SA
N94LH	BE40	RK-112
N94LH	**BE40**	**RK-405**
N94LT	GLF4	1313
N94MA	C500	319
N94MC	FA10	166
N94ME	C550	402
N94MF	C550	402
N94MG	FA10	166
N94MJ	LJ25	312
N94MJ	LJ35	394
N94MZ	**C525**	**0094**
N94NA	F900	126
N94NB	C560	0076
N94NB	HS25	258241
N94PC	FA50	254
N94PC	GLF4	1247
N94PK	LJ25	181
N94PL	**C550**	**128**
N94RL	**LJ35**	**096**
N94RS	LJ25	141
N94RT	CS55	0023
N94SA	HS25	257144
N94SD	HS25	258004
(N94SF)	GLF2	250
N94SL	C500	498
(N94SL)	GLF4	1087
N94SV	C680	0094
N94TJ	C650	0094
N94TJ	GLF2	75/7
(N94TJ)	FA20	482
(N94TJ)	LJ55	005
N94TW	ASTR	029
N94TX	C560	0247
N94UT	**F9EX**	**105**
N94VP	**C560**	**0094**
N94VP	C650	0094
N94WA	F900	94
N94WA	WW24	94
N94WN	HS25	258014
N94WW	WW24	394
(N94ZG)	C500	163
N94ZZ	GLEX	9215
N95	HS25	258131
N95AB	LJ24	213
N95AC	LJ35	433
N95AE	GLF4	1016
N95AE	GLF4	1068
N95AE	GLF5	562
N95AE	HS25	258173
N95AG	LJ60	079
N95AN	**C550**	**550-0978**
N95AP	LJ35	471
N95AX	C550	253
N95AX	LJ45	292
N95B	WW24	19
N95BA	JSTR	5216
N95BA	LJ35	078
N95BD	**F9EX**	**287**
N95BD	JSTR	5208
N95BD	LJ60	232
N95BH	LJ35	078
N95BK	JSTR	5208
N95BP	LJ25	314
N95BQ	**LJ60**	**232**
N95BS	C525	0283
N95BS	LJ25	180
N95CC	C550	108
N95CC	C550	248
N95CC	C550	405
N95CC	C56X	5278
N95CC	C650	0124
N95CC	C650	0140
N95CC	C650	0153
N95CC	C650	0160
N95CC	C650	0170
N95CC	C650	0178
N95CC	C650	0184
N95CC	C650	0193
N95CC	C650	0197
N95CC	C650	0203
N95CC	C650	0214
N95CC	C650	7002
N95CC	C650	7008
N95CC	C650	7020
N95CC	C650	7030
N95CC	C650	7036
N95CC	C650	7063
N95CC	**C680**	**0092**
N95CC	C750	0018
N95CC	CS55	0001
N95CC	CS55	0036
N95CC	CS55	0076
N95CC	CS55	0096
(N95CC)	C550	234
(N95CC)	C650	7051
(N95CC)	C650	7059
(N95CC)	C750	0041
N95CE	**LJ60**	**408**
N95CK	C525	0493
N95CK	LJ25	248
N95CM	C650	0193
N95CM	C650	0214
N95CM	C650	7029
N95CM	C650	7045
N95CM	C650	7070
N95CM	C750	0020
N95CM	C750	0042
N95CM	C750	0060
N95CM	HS25	257156
N95CP	WW24	201
(N95CP)	LJ24	340
N95CT	**C52C**	**0113**
N95CT	C550	400
N95CX	C750	0095
N95DA	LJ24	267
N95DD	LJ24	251
N95DJ	C525	0032
(N95DQ)	CL60	1041
N95DR	C500	203
(N95DW)	FA10	85
N95EB	CL60	1062
N95EC	LJ25	280
N95EC	LJ35	477
(N95EC)	LJ35	654
N95EW	C500	581
N95FA	BE40	RK-99
N95FE	CL61	5095
N95FJ	FA50	75
N95FJ	FA50	95
N95FP	**C52C**	**0088**
N95GC	FA50	176
N95GK	**BE40**	**RK-27**
N95GS	JSTR	5014
N95HC	**FA50**	**244**
N95HE	C550	713
N95HF	C650	7036
N95HG	LJ31	140
(N95HW)	C560	0238
N95JK	**WW24**	**283**
N95JK	WW24	95
N95JN	**LJ35**	**595**
N95JR	FA20	247
N95JT	FA20	490
N95KL	**C525**	**0889**
N95LL	**C52B**	**0456**
N95MJ	C500	562
N95NB	C560	0644
N95NB	**C56X**	**6031**
N95NB	HS25	258244
N95NM	**GLF3**	**485**
N95PH	FA50	194
N95Q	C500	119
N95RC	SBRL	306-129
N95RE	C500	507
N95RE	C500	515
N95RT	GLF2	136
N95RT	BE40	RJ-60
N95RX	C650	7035
N95SC	LJ35	012
N95SC	LJ55	137
N95SJ	**C680**	**0248**
N95SJ	GLF2	64/27
N95SR	C650	0024
N95SR	CL61	3050
N95SR	CL61	3051
(N95SR)	JSTR	5212
N95SV	GLF2	64/27
N95TC	LJ35	020
N95TD	**C560**	**0110**
N95TJ	C650	0127
N95TJ	FA10	92
N95TJ	MU30	A024SA
N95TJ	SBRL	380-38
(N95TJ)	C500	187
(N95TJ)	LJ55	104
N95TL	**SBRL**	**465-13**
N95TS	HS25	256051
(N95TW)	LJ25	124
N95TX	**C52B**	**0317**
N95TX	C650	7037
N95UJ	C650	0127
N95UP	**HS25**	**258639**
N95VE	C500	197
(N95VP)	C650	0095
N95VS	**LJ45**	**082**
N95WC	WW24	392
N95WJ	FA10	195
N95WK	**LJ55**	**099**
N95WW	WW24	395
N95XL	C56X	5095
N95ZC	LJ60	068
N95ZZ	GLEX	9201
N95ZZ	GLEX	9302
N96	HS25	258134
N96AA	LJ24	139
N96AC	LJ35	224
N96AD	**G150**	**246**
N96AE	GLF4	1024
N96AF	C650	0119
(N96AF)	LJ55	026
N96AL	ASTR	096
N96AL	WW24	385
N96AR	ASTR	041
N96AT	C560	0325
N96AX	LJ35	608
N96B	JSTR	5049
N96B	WW24	16
N96B	WW24	97
N96BA	C500	390
N96BA	WW24	205
N96BB	JSTR	5049
(N96BK)	GLF2	213
N96CE	FA50	139
N96CE	LJ55	033
N96CF	C500	529
N96CJ	C52A	0096
N96CK	LJ24	016
N96CM	SBRL	282-77
N96CP	C650	0139
N96CP	LJ35	446
N96CP	SBRL	306-64
N96CR	LJ35	446
N96CS	C550	252
N96DA	C500	577
(N96DC)	LJ25	317
N96DK	C750	0035
N96DM	LJ35	186
(N96DM)	LJ25	197
N96DS	C500	437
N96DS	CL61	5146
N96DS	F9EX	19
N96DS	FA50	209
N96EA	C500	200
(N96EJ)	C500	043
N96FA	LJ35	096
N96FB	**C500**	**094**
N96FC	C560	0436
(N96FF)	LJ60	194
N96FG	F2TH	25
N96FJ	FA50	106
(N96FJ)	FA50	99
N96FL	ASTR	109
(N96FL)	GLF4	1282
N96FN	LJ35	186
N96FP	C500	543
N96FT	HS25	257013
N96FT	**HS25**	**258568**
N96G	C500	200
N96G	C500	444
N96G	C525	0034
N96G	C52A	0018
N96G	**C52B**	**0114**
N96GA	**BE40**	**RK-238**
N96GD	C525	0042
N96GM	C525	0114
N96GS	JSTR	5068/27
N96GS	**LJ35**	**606**
N96GT	C500	444
N96JA	GLF2	213
N96JA	**GLF4**	**1226**
(N96JJ)	C560	0096
(N96JJ)	LJ25	175
N96L	FA20	327
N96LB	F900	10
N96LC	C500	683
N96LF	LJ31	140
N96LT	F2TH	72
N96LT	FA50	192
N96MB	C500	550
N96MB	C560	0154
N96MJ	LJ25	091
N96MJ	LJ25	098
N96MR	C52B	0067
N96MR	GLF3	324
N96MT	C560	0032
N96MT	C650	7065
N96MU	**C525**	**0896**
N96MY	C560	0032
N96NA	**C52A**	**0096**
N96NB	C560	0267
N96NB	C560	0673
N96NB	**C56X**	**6074**
N96NC	PRM1	RB-86
N96NF	C550	103
N96NJ	**C52A**	**0018**
N96NX	F9EX	35
N96NX	FA50	141
N96PB	**C52B**	**0111**
N96PC	ASTR	004
N96PD	C52B	0111
N96PD	C52C	0010
N96PM	F900	36
N96PR	HS25	257148
N96RE	C500	331
N96RE	LJ35	103
N96RE	**SBRL**	**465-52**
N96RS	LJ25	175
N96RT	FA20	159
N96RX	**C750**	**0044**
N96SG	HS25	25060
N96SK	C500	500
N96SK	C525	0420
N96SK	C52A	0093
N96SK	HS25	258702
N96SK	**HS25**	**HA-0006**
N96SN	**C650**	**0079**
(N96SS)	C650	0079
N96SW	**C52A**	**0425**
N96TC	C500	531
N96TD	C500	529
N96TD	C550	596
N96TE	**C56X**	**5029**
N96TJ	FA10	96
N96TM	C550	550-1063
N96TM	**WW24**	**275**
N96TS	WW24	159
N96TX	C750	0009
N96TX	**C750**	**0069**
N96TX	C750	0103
N96UA	**GLF5**	**5367**
(N96UD)	C750	0004
N96UH	FA50	55
N96UJ	**FA50**	**192**
N96UT	FA50	192
N96UT	**FA50**	**276**
N96VF	LJ25	143
N96VP	C650	0096
N96VR	FA10	199
N96WC	FA20	159
N96WW	WW24	411
N96WW	BE40	RJ-34
N96XL	C56X	5596
(N96ZC)	LJ60	068
N96ZZ	GLEX	9218
N96ZZ	GLEX	9296
N97	HS25	258154
N97AC	LJ25	125
N97AF	LJ55	035
N97AG	GLF3	328
N97AG	GLF3	401
N97AJ	CS55	0079
N97AL	**C650**	**0155**
N97AL	WW24	387
N97AM	LJ25	071
N97AN	LJ35	373
N97BG	C550	427
N97BH	**C560**	**0290**
N97BP	CS55	0090
N97BZ	FA50	89
N97CC	CS55	0045
N97CE	**LJ35**	**203**
N97CJ	**C52A**	**0097**
(N97CJ)	C525	0183
N97CS	HS25	25197
N97CT	CS55	0125
N97D	LJ35	417
N97DD	C500	159
N97DD	C650	0071
N97DD	FA10	75
N97DK	C750	0035
N97DK	**CL30**	**20216**
N97DK	LJ25	253
N97DM	LJ24	253
N97DQ	**GLEX**	**9095**
N97DX	FA10	75
N97EM	C550	481
N97EM	**C56X**	**5062**
N97FB	BE40	RK-117
N97FB	BE40	RK-152
N97FD	C500	543
N97FF	BE40	RK-117
N97FG	**F2TH**	**230**
N97FJ	CL64	5374
N97FJ	FA20	105
N97FJ	FA50	92
(N97FJ)	FA50	261
N97FL	ASTR	110
N97FL	GLF4	4008
N97FM	**C550**	**481**
N97FT	GLF4	1013
N97FT	GLF4	4008
N97FT	**GLF5**	**5498**
N97FT	LJ25	210
N97GM	F2EX	15
N97HT	C510	0097
N97HW	WW24	312
N97J	LJ25	094
N97J	LJ55	039
N97JJ	LJ25	162
N97JL	C560	0163
N97JL	LJ35	310
N97JP	LJ25	293
N97JP	PRM1	RB-226
N97KL	**HS25**	**258876**
N97LA	C500	338
N97LB	CS55	0079
N97LE	**LJ35**	**648**
N97LT	FA50	202
(N97LT)	F2TH	73
N97MC	FA10	82
N97MJ	LJ24	093
N97MU	**C525**	**0897**
N97NB	C560	0399
N97NL	SBRL	306-97
N97NP	**CL65**	**5905**
N97NX	F2TH	132
N97NX	F9EX	32
N97PJ	MS76	097
(N97QA)	LJ35	304
N97QS	CS55	0097
N97RE	SBRL	465-32
N97RJ	LJ35	367
(N97RJ)	FA10	118
N97RS	LJ25	162
N97S	C550	233
N97SC	SBRL	306-123
N97SC	SBRL	306-54
N97SC	SBRL	306-72
N97SC	SBRL	380-34
N97SG	**CL61**	**3051**
N97SH	CL30	20054
N97SH	HS25	258277
N97SJ	FA20	378
N97SK	C500	316
N97SK	**C525**	**0290**
N97SK	CS55	0127
N97SM	WW24	307
N97TD	**FA20**	**412**
N97TE	C560	0436
N97TE	**C56X**	**5560**
N97TJ	CS55	0082
N97TJ	FA10	75
N97TJ	LJ35	012
N97TS	HS25	257001
(N97TT)	BE40	RK-65
N97UT	FA50	202
N97VF	**C525**	**0171**
(N97VM)	HS25	25030
N97VN	C56X	5007
N97WJ	**FA20**	**101**
N97XP	**HS25**	**258310**

(N97XP)	BE40	RK-39
N97XR	LJ45	256
N98	HS25	258156
(N98A)	LJ36	025
N98AA	LJ24	306
N98AC	C560	0611
N98AC	**FA50**	**329**
N98AC	LJ24	298
N98AC	LJ35	301
N98AD	ASTR	095
N98AD	**G280**	**2081**
(N98AE)	GLF4	1302
(N98AF)	HS25	257082
N98AG	CL64	5402
N98AM	GLF2	13
N98AQ	C560	0611
N98AS	FA20	428
N98AS	LJ45	427
N98AV	**C500**	**578**
N98BD	C650	0048
N98BE	C550	075
N98BL	LJ60	061
N98BM	**WW24**	**193**
N98CF	SBRL	282-66
N98CG	LJ24	289
N98CH	**C52C**	**0097**
N98CR	CL61	3024
N98CX	C750	0060
N98DD	C650	0048
(N98DD)	HS25	258004
N98DH	C52A	0129
N98DH	**FA50**	**219**
N98DK	LJ24	152
N98DK	LJ24	305
N98DM	C500	296
(N98DQ)	F900	137
N98E	C560	0103
N98FG	**C750**	**0307**
N98FJ	ASTR	098
N98FJ	CL64	5374
N98FJ	CL64	5401
N98FJ	FA50	93
N98FT	GLF2	173
N98FT	HS25	257016
(N98G)	GLF2	24
N98GA	C560	0201
N98GA	C560	0229
N98GC	C550	272
N98HG	**WW24**	**394**
(N98JA)	LJ25	148
N98JV	**LJ60**	**135**
N98JV	LJ60	140
(N98KK)	WW24	9
N98KR	JSTR	5048
N98LB	FA20	298
N98LB	SBRL	306-97
N98LC	LJ35	077
N98LT	**GLF4**	**1278**
N98MB	C500	054
N98MD	C56X	6054
N98MD	JSTR	5048
N98MD	LJ35	086
(N98MD)	JSTR	5098/28
N98ME	C500	585
N98NA	C560	0467
N98NB	C560	0673
N98NX	F2TH	152
N98NX	F900	128
N98PE	C52A	0093
N98Q	**C500**	**040**
N98QC	**LJ40**	**2146**
N98QS	CS55	0098
N98R	FA20	428
N98R	FA50	172
N98RG	C500	614
N98RH	FA20	284
(N98RH)	LJ25	040
N98RP	**F2TH**	**186**
N98RP	GLF3	328
N98RS	LJ25	148
N98RX	C550	550-0869
N98RX	C56X	5182
N98S	WW24	73
N98SA	WW24	73
N98SC	WW24	32
N98SP	GALX	203
N98TE	LJ35	317
N98TH	F2EX	53
N98TJ	C550	669
N98TJ	HS25	25032
N98TS	WW24	198
(N98TW)	CL60	1063
(N98TW)	FA10	93
N98TX	C750	0039
N98TX	C750	0041
N98UF	**LJ60**	**323**
N98VA	LJ35	014
N98VR	FA10	222
N98WJ	GLF2	89
N98WJ	LJ24	268
N98WW	WW24	398
N98XL	**C56X**	**6098**
N98XR	LJ45	292
N98XS	**C650**	**7058**
N99	HS25	258158
N99AA	LJ24	308
N99AA	SBRL	306-53
N99AG	**C52B**	**0258**
N99AP	SBRL	282-128
N99AT	**LJ31**	**202**
N99BB	C750	0005
N99BC	C500	187
N99BC	C500	190
N99BC	FA10	128
N99BC	**PRM1**	**RB-242**
N99BL	FA10	87
N99CJ	**C525**	**0333**
N99CK	C500	216
N99CK	**C500**	**548**
N99CK	HS25	25186
N99CK	WW24	146
N99CN	C550	331
N99CQ	LJ25	022
N99CR	SBRL	282-81
N99CV	WW24	146
(N99DA)	HS25	258125
N99DE	C550	331
N99DM	LJ24	114
N99DQ	F900	137
N99DY	C550	482
N99E	FA20	317
N99E	JSTR	5216
N99E	LJ24	196
N99EJ	**GLF4**	**1236**
N99ES	LJ24	196
N99ES	LJ25	018
N99FF	MU30	A045SA
N99FF	SBRL	306-83
(N99FF)	SBRL	282-129
N99FG	**F9EX**	**27**
N99FJ	CL64	5412
N99FJ	FA50	94
N99FN	LJ35	071
N99FN	LJ35	652
N99FT	JSTR	5055/21
N99GA	GLF2	99
N99GA	GLF3	421
N99GA	GLF4	1198
N99GC	C500	369
N99GC	HS25	25149
N99GK	LJ35	316
N99GK	**LJ40**	**2008**
N99GM	GLF4	1006
N99GM	HS25	HA-0049
N99GS	WW24	31
N99GX	ASTR	139
N99GY	**GLF4**	**1287**
N99HB	MS76	102
N99JB	C525	0352
N99JB	LJ24	246
N99JD	FA50	129
N99JD	HS25	257148
N99KP	**EA50**	**000181**
N99KR	HS25	25149
N99KT	FA20	72/413
N99KV	LJ55	122
N99KW	C550	386
N99KW	CL64	5564
N99KW	**CL65**	**5877**
N99KW	LJ35	368
N99KW	LJ55	122
N99KW	LJ60	085
N99MC	C500	187
N99MC	C500	190
N99MC	FA10	128
N99MC	**LJ25**	**182**
N99ME	LJ35	185
N99ME	LJ35	204
N99MJ	LJ35	308
N99MN	**PRM1**	**RB-277**
N99MR	JSTR	5112/7
N99NG	**GLF5**	**501**
N99NJ	LJ25	220
N99NJ	LJ35	481
N99NJ	**LJ45**	**105**
N99PD	GLF3	314
(N99PD)	GLF4	1257
N99PS	**WW24**	**435**
N99RE	**C52B**	**0252**
N99RS	**LJ36**	**039**
N99S	SBRL	465-64
N99SC	GLF3	496
N99SC	GLF4	1236
N99SC	GLF4	1343
N99SC	HS25	25149
N99SC	HS25	25169
N99SC	HS25	256016
N99SC	LJ24	196
N99ST	GLF2	91
N99ST	HS25	25205
(N99SU)	GLF3	496
N99TC	LJ24	098
N99TD	C500	231
(N99TD)	C500	529
N99TK	**C550**	**621**
N99TY	F2TH	130
N99UG	CL61	5126
(N99UP)	LJ24	345
N99VA	GLF2	200
N99VA	LJ35	185
(N99VC)	CS55	0016
N99VR	JSTR	5161/43
N99VS	**BE40**	**RK-465**
N99W	WW24	46
N99WA	FA10	150
(N99WB)	C500	346
(N99WF)	WW24	417
N99WH	WW24	284
N99WJ	GLF2	245/30
N99WJ	GLF3	340
N99WJ	GLF3	394
N99WJ	GLF3	431
N99WJ	GLF4	1139
N99WR	C560	0019
N99XG	**EA50**	**000055**
N99XN	GLEX	9190
N99XR	LJ45	302
N99XR	SBRL	282-104
N99XY	C500	369
N99XZ	LJ25	087
(N99YB)	LJ55	077
(N99YD)	GLF3	314
N99ZB	**BE40**	**RK-344**
N99ZC	**LJ60**	**162**
N99ZM	**GLEX**	**9587**
N100A	GLEX	9077
N100A	GLEX	9105
N100A	GLEX	9205
N100A	GLF2	89
N100A	GLF3	370
N100A	GLF4	1072
N100A	GLF4	1235
N100A	**GLF6**	**6010**
N100A	JSTR	5058/4
N100AC	C500	195
N100AC	C550	403
N100AC	**CL64**	**5546**
N100AC	FA20	366
N100AC	GLF2	75/7
N100AC	JSTR	5033/56
N100AD	C500	226
N100AG	C550	404
N100AG	HS25	258238
N100AG	**HS25**	**258747**
N100AG	WW24	346
N100AG	BE40	RK-150
N100AJ	LJ24	186
N100AK	ASTR	062
N100AK	ASTR	121
N100AK	**ASTR**	**153**
N100AK	GLF3	437
N100AK	WW24	218
N100AK	WW24	295
N100AK	WW24	302
N100AK	WW24	436
N100AL	JSTR	5058/4
N100AM	**C500**	**305**
N100AQ	C500	195
N100AQ	FA20	366
N100AQ	WW24	295
N100AR	**C56X**	**5241**
N100AR	GLF4	1100
N100AS	**FA20**	**274**
N100AT	LJ35	436
N100AW	**BE40**	**RK-150**
N100AY	C550	404
N100BC	WW24	226
N100BC	**WW24**	**438**
N100BG	FA10	138
N100BG	FA10	64
(N100BG)	GLF3	488
N100BL	LJ31	126
N100BP	SBRL	380-48
N100BX	C500	439
N100C	JSTR	5076/17
N100CA	WW24	95
N100CC	GLF2	75/7
N100CC	JSTR	5033/56
N100CE	SBRL	282-19
N100CE	SBRL	306-128
N100CE	SBRL	306-87
N100CH	C500	628
N100CH	C525	0087
N100CH	C550	437
N100CH	WW24	406
N100CJ	C500	390
N100CJ	C550	182
N100CJ	**C56X**	**5100**
N100CJ	WW24	141
N100CK	FA10	125
N100CK	FA10	222
N100CM	C500	276
N100CQ	C525	0087
N100CT	FA10	203
N100CU	**FA10**	**104**
N100CX	C550	028
N100CX	C550	577
N100DE	MU30	A016SA
N100DF	**GLF4**	**1313**
N100DG	WW24	76
N100DL	LJ24	201
N100DR	WW24	76
N100DS	**C550**	**639**
N100DV	FA50	54
N100DW	C52B	0261
N100EA	LJ24	019
N100EA	MU30	A089SA
N100ED	F900	195
N100EG	FA50	105
N100EJ	**SBRL**	**380-1**
N100EK	**GALX**	**129**
N100EP	LJ25	138
N100EP	LJ35	150
N100EQ	E50P	50000082
(N100EQ)	F900	195
N100ES	GLEX	9108
N100ES	GLF4	1135
N100ES	**GLF6**	**6014**
N100EU	SBRL	306-54
N100EW	GLF4	1477
N100EW	**GLF4**	**4070**
N100FF	C750	0028
N100FF	**E50P**	**50000141**
N100FF	F900	142
(N100FF)	C500	149
(N100FF)	HS25	257173
N100FG	**E55P**	**50500084**
N100FG	SBRL	282-99
N100FJ	FA10	100
N100FJ	**FA10**	**118**
N100FJ	FA10	192
N100FJ	FA10	194
N100FJ	FA10	206
N100FJ	FA10	217
N100FJ	FA10	3
N100FL	**CL64**	**5510**
N100FL	SBRL	306-46
N100FN	SBRL	306-46
N100FR	C750	0069
N100FS	SBRL	282-38
N100FT	FA20	202
(N100FU)	LJ25	120
N100FZ	**E50P**	**50000137**
N100G	ASTR	092
N100GA	ASTR	070
N100GA	ASTR	130
N100GA	ASTR	154
N100GA	**G280**	**2100**
N100GA	GLF5	5500
N100GB	HS25	25022
N100GG	**C500**	**380**
N100GJ	GLF4	1007
N100GL	JSTR	5132/57
N100GL	LJ35	037
N100GN	FA20	325
N100GN	FA20	339
N100GN	GLF3	312
N100GN	GLF4	1007
N100GN	GLF4	1236
N100GP	LJ24	106
N100GP	LJ35	064
(N100GQ)	ASTR	070
N100GS	LJ24	118
N100GU	LJ35	173
(N100GU)	LJ55	035
N100GV	**GLF5**	**600**
N100GX	**G150**	**228**
N100GX	GLF3	321
N100GX	GLF4	1100
N100GX	HS25	258195
N100GY	ASTR	120
N100GY	C560	0519
N100GY	**LJ45**	**079**
N100H	FA10	216
N100HB	**C550**	**071**
N100HC	SBRL	282-32
(N100HC)	FA7X	35
N100HE	HS25	25225
N100HF	GLF4	1338
N100HF	HS25	25183
N100HF	HS25	25225
N100HG	CL61	3055
N100HG	FA20	54
N100HG	GLF3	429
N100HG	GLF4	1026
N100HG	**GLF5**	**625**
N100HL	**HS25**	**258345**
N100HP	C500	280
N100HV	**FA10**	**183**
N100HW	LJ35	403
N100HW	**LJ40**	**2036**
N100HZ	GLF3	429
(N100JC)	C500	148
N100JF	GLF4	1093
N100JF	HS25	257135
N100JJ	C500	192
N100JS	C52A	0176
N100JS	C52B	0095
N100JS	C52C	0009
N100JZ	C52B	0095
N100JZ	LJ24	038
(N100JZ)	C52C	0009
N100K	LJ25	154
N100K	LJ35	170
N100KK	LJ24	219
N100KK	LJ35	420
N100KK	LJ45	065
N100KP	CS55	0038
N100KP	F2EX	142
N100KP	FA50	232
N100KS	GLF2	96
N100KS	SBRL	282-104
N100KT	CL61	5004
N100KT	CL61	5066
N100KU	C550	550-0813
N100KW	FA20	168
N100KY	WW24	101
N100KZ	C680	0200
N100KZ	LJ35	420
N100KZ	**LJ45**	**065**
(N100L)	LJ35	357
N100LA	HS25	258280
N100LL	WW24	79
N100LR	**CL60**	**1064**
N100LR	HS25	25203
N100LR	HS25	257173
(N100LR)	CL60	1069
N100LX	**C500**	**628**
N100M	FA20	194
N100MA	C750	0087
N100MA	SBRL	306-87
N100MB	**F2EX**	**60**
N100MC	WW24	149
N100ME	WW24	206
(N100MH)	HS25	258137
N100MJ	LJ24	051
N100MK	LJ25	019
N100MN	LJ35	309
N100MS	LJ35	138
N100MT	HS25	25234
N100MZ	**E50P**	**50000362**
N100MZ	EA50	000140
N100MZ	JSTR	5149/11
N100NB	LJ25	181
N100ND	**FA10**	**177**
N100NG	F9EX	30
N100NG	HS25	258537
N100NR	LJ25	356
N100NR	LJ35	403
N100NR	LJ60	269
N100NR	WW24	61
N100NV	**E50P**	**50000116**
N100NW	FA10	201
N100NW	LJ35	228
N100P	GLF2	5
N100P	GLF3	301
N100PC	WW24	149
N100PF	**C525**	**0390**
N100PJ	GLF2	5
N100PM	GLF2	114
N100PM	GLF4	1144
(N100PM)	HS25	258027
N100PU	**E50P**	**50000220**
N100PW	SBRL	306-16
N100PZ	E50P	50000015
N100QH	C500	628
N100QP	HS25	256055
N100QR	**CL60**	**1043**
N100QR	HS25	256055
N100QS	**GLEX**	**9480**
N100QW	CS55	0079
N100QX	GLF3	321
N100R	C650	0197
N100R	**HS25**	**HA-0076**
N100R	LJ60	084
N100RA	LJ24	180
N100RB	FA10	198
N100RC	C52B	0038
N100RC	**C52C**	**0147**
N100RC	WW24	60
N100RG	C500	149
N100RH	HS25	25196
N100RJ	**C550**	**550-0806**
N100RQ	C52B	0038
N100RR	FA10	179
N100RR	FA50	220
N100RS	MU30	A029SA
N100RS	SBRL	380-19
N100RY	E50P	50000295
N100S	FA20	142
N100SA	**CL30**	**20559**
N100SA	CL64	5319
N100SA	LJ45	489
N100SC	C550	108
N100SC	C560	0054
N100SC	C56X	5065
N100SC	**C56X**	**6141**
N100SM	C525	0278
N100SN	C500	594
N100SN	C560	0377
N100SQ	LJ24	113
(N100SQ)	ASTR	037
N100SR	ASTR	037
N100SR	FA20	56
N100SR	**G150**	**227**
N100SR	WW24	127
N100SR	WW24	267
N100SV	C500	448
N100SY	**C560**	**0054**
N100T	FA10	107
N100T	HS25	25191
N100T	LJ35	074
N100TA	LJ24	038
N100TA	LJ24	045
N100TA	LJ24	082A
N100TB	CS55	0137
N100TH	WW24	35
N100TM	FA10	224
N100TM	GLF5	692
N100TM	JSTR	5150/37
N100TM	SBRL	380-60
N100TP	**C510**	**0418**
N100TR	WW24	76
(N100TT)	HS25	25148
N100TW	C500	468

(N100TW)	FA10	84
N100U	C560	0813
N100U	C56X	6041
N100U	HS25	259006
N100UA	JSTR	5143
N100UB	FA10	42
N100UF	C500	213
N100UF	C500	314
N100UF	C550	102
N100UF	FA20	160/450
N100UH	C500	213
N100UP	**F900**	**44**
N100V	FA20	75
N100VA	**EA50**	**000138**
N100VA	LJ55	029
N100VC	LJ24	140
N100VP	G150	233
N100VQ	LJ24	140
N100VR	GLEX	9098
N100VV	C550	158
N100W	WW24	73
N100WC	CL61	3023
N100WC	GLF2	96
N100WE	**PRM1**	**RB-45**
N100WF	SBRL	282-2
N100WG	FA10	120
N100WG	FA10	217
N100WH	C650	0119
N100WJ	C500	376
"N100WJ"	FA50	9
(N100WJ)	GLF4	1079
N100WK	FA20	113
N100WK	GLF2	77
N100WM	WW24	73
N100WN	LJ25	288
N100WP	**C560**	**0073**
N100WP	WW24	389
(N100WQ)	C525	0207
N100WT	**C550**	**550-0858**
N100WX	**E50P**	**50000037**
N100WY	F2TH	178
N100X	LJ24	035
(N100XJ)	WW24	204
N100Y	**C52C**	**0204**
N100Y	C550	550-0919
N100Y	HS25	257083
N100Y	SBRL	282-32
N100Y	SBRL	306-50
N100YB	**C56X**	**5136**
N100YM	FA10	114
N100YP	**FA10**	**222**
N100Z	C550	550-0926
N100ZT	**HS25**	**HA-0164**
N100ZW	GLF4	1477
N101AD	HS25	25284
N101AD	LJ24	093
N101AD	MU30	A056SA
N101AF	C550	732
N101AJ	**LJ36**	**008**
N101AR	LJ24	093
N101AR	LJ24	279
N101AR	LJ35	610
N101AR	LJ36	008
N101AR	BE40	RK-461
(N101AR)	GLF2	140/40
N101AW	JSTR	5103
N101BE	F2TH	43
N101BG	LJ35	106
N101BU	WW24	32
N101BX	C550	229
N101CC	BE40	RJ-19
N101CC	**BE40**	**RK-277**
N101CD	C500	101
N101CP	C560	0800
N101CP	GLF5	5207
N101CV	C560	0101
N101CV	**GLF4**	**1230**
N101DB	LJ24	070
N101DD	C550	338
N101DE	WW24	98
N101DL	LJ25	341
N101EC	C555	0006
(N101EC)	C560	0327
N101EF	**C680**	**0532**
N101EF	FA10	157
N101EG	C555	0043
N101ER	**C56X**	**6179**
N101ET	FA50	95
N101EU	FA10	204
N101EX	F9EX	111
N101FC	HS25	257089
N101FC	**HS25**	**258380**
N101FG	C550	550-0839
N101FG	**E50P**	**50000222**
N101FJ	F900	101
N101FJ	FA10	4
N101FJ	FA50	108
(N101FJ)	FA50	97
N101FU	**C510**	**0207**
N101FU	LJ25	120
N101GA	G150	301
N101GA	G280	2001
N101GA	G280	2101
N101GA	GLF4	1109
N101GP	LJ35	021
N101GS	WW24	35
N101GX	GALX	041
N101GZ	FA10	47
N101HB	C500	203
N101HB	C560	0002
N101HB	LJ35	152
N101HC	GLF4	1245
(N101HC)	C500	400
N101HF	C500	203
N101HF	HS25	257013
N101HG	C500	213
N101HK	LJ35	440
N101HK	LJ55	101
N101HS	FA10	82
N101HS	HS25	25201
N101HS	WW24	193
N101HW	LJ35	403
N101HW	LJ60	037
N101HZ	**F2TH**	**86**
N101JL	**C550**	**550-1002**
N101JR	LJ24	084
N101JR	LJ25	104
N101KK	C500	219
N101KK	C550	232
N101KK	**LJ45**	**483**
N101KP	**C560**	**0520**
N101L	GALX	024
N101L	**GALX**	**156**
N101L	SBRL	306-15
N101LB	WW24	8
N101LD	C500	462
N101LD	**C525**	**0689**
N101LD	GALX	024
N101LT	**HS25**	**257114**
N101ME	SBRL	380-70
N101MH	**GLF5**	**609**
N101MU	GLF4	1107
N101ND	C550	550-0839
N101ND	**LJ60**	**037**
N101NK	WW24	148
N101NS	ASTR	066
N101NS	F2TH	11
N101NY	**F2TH**	**178**
(N101PC)	C650	0057
N101PG	C56X	5590
N101PG	C650	0126
N101PG	**C680**	**0336**
N101PG	LJ35	228
N101PJ	**C525**	**0394**
N101PK	CL61	5005
N101PK	LJ35	440
N101PK	LJ55	101
N101PN	PRM1	RB-101
N101PP	LJ24	085
N101PT	GLF3	491
N101PV	**F2EX**	**23**
N101QS	C555	0101
N101QS	**GLEX**	**9483**
N101QS	BE40	RK-484
N101RL	C550	371
N101RR	**C500**	**647**
N101RR	SBRL	282-101
N101RX	**G150**	**262**
N101SK	CL60	1033
N101SK	CL61	5058
N101SK	HS25	257001
N101ST	CL60	1033
N101SV	WW24	110
N101SV	WW24	246
N101T	SBRL	282-53
N101TF	FA10	144
N101U	**C525**	**0454**
N101UD	CL30	20220
N101UD	CL30	20392
N101UD	**CL30**	**20512**
N101UD	HS25	25235
N101UD	LJ60	275
N101UR	CL30	20392
N101UR	HS25	25235
N101US	LJ24	352
N101US	LJ35	500
N101US	SBRL	282-7
N101VJ	FA10	177
N101VS	**LJ24**	**218**
N101WR	LJ25	017
N101WR	**BE40**	**RK-41**
N101WY	**C560**	**0620**
N101XS	HS25	257001
N101YC	C650	0057
N101ZE	FA20	108/430
N102A	GLEX	9205
N102AB	GLF2	53
N102AD	C500	280
N102AD	FA20	225/472
N102AF	C525	0122
N102AK	GLF3	390
N102AK	GLF3	466
N102AK	**GLF4**	**1188**
(N102AK)	WW24	434
N102AQ	GLF3	390
N102AR	LJ25	012
N102B	LJ24	343
N102BG	FA50	305
N102BG	GLF4	1273
N102BG	GLF5	5038
N102BG	**GLF6**	**6011**
N102BP	HS25	257036
N102BQ	FA50	305
N102BQ	**GLF4**	**1273**
N102BT	LJ35	301
N102BW	WW24	165
N102C	LJ24	343
N102CE	C650	7061
N102CE	**C680**	**0323**
N102CE	WW24	129
N102CJ	WW24	78
N102CL	**PRM1**	**RB-178**
N102CX	GLF2	102/32
N102DR	**C550**	**436**
N102DS	**C510**	**0095**
N102DZ	**GLF5**	**555**
N102EP	**E50P**	**50000102**
N102FC	C550	052
N102FD	**GALX**	**128**
N102FJ	FA10	6
N102FJ	FA50	100
N102FM	GLF4	1325
N102FS	C56X	5318
N102GH	LJ35	105
N102GL	LJ24	329
N102GP	LJ24	173
N102GP	LJ35	105
N102GX	GALX	042
N102HB	**C550**	**407**
N102HF	C500	275
N102HS	C500	517
N102HS	GLF2	112
N102KJ	WW24	271
N102KP	**C560**	**0527**
N102LJ	**LJ60**	**102**
N102MC	BE40	RJ-50
N102MG	F2TH	221
N102MJ	SBRL	380-39
N102ML	CL60	1063
N102ML	GLF2	112
N102MU	GLF4	1145
N102NW	LJ31	002
N102PA	C550	621
N102PA	**E50P**	**50000030**
N102PA	HS25	258536
N102PA	LJ24	224
N102PS	LJ25	010
N102PT	C525	0433
(N102PT)	GLF3	336
N102QS	BE40	RK-380
N102RA	LJ25	242
N102RD	SBRL	380-23
N102RR	LJ25	308
N102SK	PRM1	RB-151
N102ST	LJ35	301
N102ST	LJ55	069
N102SV	WW24	34
N102SY	WW24	34
N102TE	EA50	000002
N102TF	FA50	125
N102TW	HS25	25090
N102U	WW24	230
(N102U)	LJ25	371
N102VP	C500	200
N102VS	**LJ25**	**180**
N102WG	LJ31	102
N102WR	MU30	A004SA
N102WY	**C560**	**0621**
N102ZE	FA20	126/438
N103AD	BE40	RJ-2
N103AJ	C500	072
N103AL	HS25	258822
N103BC	GLF4	1103
N103BG	C560	0091
(N103BG)	HS25	258207
N103BW	WW24	82
N103C	LJ35	273
N103C	LJ55	087
N103CC	C500	103
N103CD	GLF3	418
N103CF	LJ35	318
N103CJ	C52B	0003
N103CJ	HS25	25271
(N103CJ)	C52B	0103
N103CL	**C52A**	**0178**
N103CL	LJ35	273
N103CS	C525	0438
N103CS	C525	0453
N103CX	**C550**	**550-0856**
N103DD	**BE40**	**RK-566**
N103DS	**C52B**	**0031**
N103DT	F900	142
(N103EL)	GLF2	119/22
N103EX	F9EX	103
N103EZ	**LJ45**	**071**
N103F	FA20	376
N103F	HFB3	1023
N103F	WW24	53
N103FJ	F9EX	103
N103FJ	FA10	9
N103FJ	FA50	102
(N103GA)	GLF3	455
N103GC	GLF3	455
N103GH	LJ35	148
N103GL	LJ35	069
N103GP	LJ35	148
N103GX	GALX	043
N103HB	C680	0321
N103HB	CL60	1059
N103HC	**MU30**	**A068SA**
(N103HF)	GLF4	1164
(N103HS)	GLF3	355
N103HT	HS25	258074
N103JA	C500	082
N103JL	**LJ31**	**026**
N103JM	FA10	2
(N103JW)	LJ24	341
N103KB	**CL61**	**5065**
N103KC	JSTR	5015
N103LP	BE40	RK-103
N103LS	LJ60	288
N103M	C550	246
N103MM	FA10	106
N103PC	C500	488
N103PG	C56X	5590
N103PJ	FA10	148
N103PL	C500	278
N103QS	C555	0103
N103QS	GLEX	9531
(N103RA)	FA20	54
(N103RA)	HS25	256004
N103RB	LJ24	106
N103RR	HS25	25221
N103SK	C525	0480
N103SK	**PRM1**	**RB-151**
N103SV	C680	0003
N103TA	SBRL	306-27
N103TC	LJ24	022
N103TC	LJ24	213
N103TD	**LJ31**	**006**
N103TJ	FA10	103
N103VF	C555	0046
N103VV	**GLF3**	**346**
N103WG	**GLEX**	**9129**
(N103WJ)	GLF2	103
N103WV	C500	028
N103ZZ	**GLEX**	**9308**
N104	HS25	25100
(N104AA)	LJ35	178
N104AB	C500	402
N104AD	**GLF4**	**1406**
N104AE	HS25	257005
N104AG	HS25	HA-0052
N104AG	HS25	HA-0166
N104AR	GLF2	140/40
N104AR	GLF3	461
N104AR	GLF4	1346
N104AR	**GLF4**	**4223**
N104BK	GLF3	306
N104BK	JSTR	5219
N104BS	LJ55	012
N104BW	LJ25	173
N104BX	LJ31	104
N104CD	GLF2	53
N104CE	**JSTR**	**5108**
N104CF	C500	543
N104CJ	WW24	33
N104CT	C750	0100
N104CT	C750	0275
N104DA	**GLEX**	**9266**
N104DD	FA10	110
N104DN	LJ45	442
N104DX	GLF4	1493
N104FJ	F900	104
N104FJ	FA10	8
N104FJ	FA50	103
N104FL	C550	550-1071
N104FT	CL30	20121
N104GA	G150	304
N104GA	GALX	104
N104GA	GLF5	5204
N104GA	GLF6	6004
N104GA	LJ24	112
(N104GA)	ASTR	104
N104GB	**MU30**	**A041SA**
N104GL	LJ25	197
N104GX	ASTR	140
N104HW	C550	555
N104JG	GLF4	1062
N104JG	HS25	257059
(N104KW)	FA10	122
N104LJ	LJ60	104
N104LR	C560	0163
N104LR	**HS25**	**258303**
N104LV	**C56X**	**5190**
N104LW	**C525**	**0806**
N104MB	LJ24	177
N104MC	LJ24	323
N104ME	GLF2	178
N104MT	**F2EX**	**18**
N104PC	C52A	0212
N104PC	C56X	5533
N104PC	**C750**	**0061**
N104PH	**LJ35**	**300**
N104PR	GLF4	1346
N104QS	**GLEX**	**9555**
N104RF	**HS25**	**258641**
N104RJ	**LJ60**	**422**
N104RP	**C750**	**0095**
N104RS	**WW24**	**273**
N104SB	FA20	321
N104SB	LJ35	357
N104SD	LJ60	005
N104SG	**GALX**	**212**
N104SL	SBRL	282-104
N104SS	SBRL	306-30
N104UA	C500	043
(N104UT)	C750	0100
N104VV	**GLF2**	**53**
N104WJ	**LJ25**	**104**
N104WV	**C550**	**219**
N104XL	C56X	5104
N105AD	**C52C**	**0013**
N105AF	**F2TH**	**12**
N105AJ	GLF2	201
N105AS	HS25	256064
N105AX	**BE40**	**RK-105**
N105BA	C550	116
N105BA	LJ25	152
N105BE	WW24	415
N105BG	**C560**	**0315**
N105BG	C555	0105
N105BH	GLF4	1117
N105BJ	LJ24	092
N105BJ	LJ25	062
N105BK	**F900**	**70**
N105BN	CL61	5101
N105BX	C550	550-1050
N105CC	C500	105
N105CD	**C680**	**0523**
N105CF	C500	548
N105CJ	C52B	0005
N105CQ	C52B	0065
N105CV	C560	0105
N105CX	**GLF5**	**550**
N105DM	SBRL	306-27
N105EC	LJ24	103
N105EJ	FA50	31
(N105EJ)	HS25	25186
N105FJ	FA10	10
N105FJ	FA50	104
N105FN	**ASTR**	**105**
N105FX	LJ31	086
N105G	JSTR	5056
N105G	JSTR	5223
N105GA	**LJ24**	**116**
N105GH	JSTR	5056
N105GL	LJ24	322
N105GM	JSTR	5019
N105GN	JSTR	5019
N105GV	C650	7019
N105GX	GALX	044
N105HC	**C680**	**0105**
N105HD	**SBRL**	**380-39**
N105HS	HS25	25031
N105HS	MU30	A082SA
(N105HS)	GLF3	355
N105J	**C510**	**0277**
N105JJ	C500	105
N105JM	C500	374
N105LB	**EA50**	**000118**
N105LF	F2TH	105
N105LJ	LJ45	105
N105P	C525	0336
N105PT	C52A	0155
N105RH	**C650**	**0055**
N105RJ	C56X	5172
(N105SS)	SBRL	306-27
N105ST	**GLF5**	**5170**
N105SV	C680	0005
N105TB	**GLF2**	**31**
N105TD	**C560**	**0632**
N105TF	HFB3	1055
(N105TR)	GLF4	1239
N105TW	C500	602
N105TW	FA20	289
N105UA	SBRL	306-16
N105UP	**CL61**	**3066**
N105VS	GLF3	370
N105WC	**FA50**	**60**
N105XP	HS25	HA-0105
N105Y	GLF2	56
N105Y	GLF3	412
N105ZZ	GLEX	9327
(N106AE)	HS25	257164
N106BB	C550	550-1006
N106BC	WW24	220
N106BK	F900	76
N106CA	LJ24	138
N106CC	C650	0106
N106CE	GLF4	1420
N106CG	BE40	RJ-12
N106CH	**C52A**	**0514**
N106CJ	**C525**	**0006**
N106CJ	WW24	38
N106CX	C750	0106
N106DD	BE40	RK-343
N106DM	BE40	RJ-6
N106EA	C500	468
(N106EC)	C560	0352
N106EX	**F9EX**	**106**
N106FF	**LJ60**	**375**
N106FJ	FA10	11
N106FJ	FA50	105
N106FJ	FA7X	106
N106FT	C550	550-1123
N106FX	LJ31	087
N106G	JSTR	5090
N106G	JSTR	5217
N106G	SBRL	282-15
(N106GA)	MU30	A071SA
N106GC	HS25	258141
N106GL	LJ35	056
N106GM	C500	643
N106GM	JSTR	5002

N106GX	ASTR	141
N106JL	HS25	258012
N106JL	JSTR	5214
N106JT	**C52B**	**0106**
N106KA	GLF4	1373
N106KC	BE40	RK-132
N106KM	**GLF3**	**305**
N106LJ	LJ60	106
(N106M)	LJ24	348
N106MC	LJ24	277
N106PR	CL61	5106
N106PR	**PRM1**	**RB-276**
N106QS	CS55	0106
N106QS	BE40	RK-381
N106RW	F9EX	120
N106SJ	**C56X**	**5517**
N106SP	C550	382
N106SP	C560	0347
N106SP	C56X	5517
N106SP	**C680**	**0080**
N106SR	**C550**	**382**
N106ST	**C56X**	**6159**
N106ST	C650	0109
N106TD	**GLF4**	**1442**
N106TE	EA50	000006
N106TF	HFB3	1042
N106TJ	LJ24	340
(N106TJ)	GLF2	106
N106TW	**FA10**	**84**
N106VC	BE40	RJ-7
N106VP	C550	550-1106
(N106WH)	EA50	000268
N106WQ	C52B	0294
N106WT	WW24	351
N106WV	C500	471
N106XX	LJ35	183
(N107)	C550	167
N107A	**FA50**	**186**
N107A	GLF2	53
N107A	GLF4	1070
(N107AF)	FA10	169
(N107AV)	FA20	421
N107AW	HS25	25249
N107BB	C550	107
N107BJ	BE40	RK-23
N107BK	F900	77
N107BW	HS25	25107
N107CC	C500	107
N107CC	C500	482
N107CC	F9EX	46
N107CE	**HS25**	**258584**
N107CF	C550	195
N107CF	WW24	181
(N107CF)	C560	0036
(N107CF)	HS25	258106
N107CG	C650	0207
N107CJ	SBRL	282-12
N107CQ	C52B	0072
(N107CR)	C560	0036
N107CV	**FA50**	**85**
N107CX	C750	0107
N107EE	**C550**	**667**
N107EG	C550	550-0894
N107ET	**HS25**	**257146**
N107F	FA20	378
N107FJ	FA10	12
N107FJ	FA50	112
N107FX	LJ31	102
N107G	JSTR	5091
N107G	JSTR	5219
N107G	SBRL	282-18
N107GA	GALX	107
N107GH	JSTR	5091
N107GL	LJ24	324
N107GM	C500	643
N107GM	C525	0452
N107GM	JSTR	5206
N107GM	LJ31	049
N107GX	GALX	045
N107HF	LJ25	029
N107J	**FA20**	**107**
N107JM	LJ35	249
N107LJ	LJ60	107
N107LP	LJ31	107
N107LT	HS25	257146
N107LT	HS25	258901
N107LW	FA20	368
(N107MC)	LJ55	062
(N107MS)	LJ25	362
(N107PK)	C525	0452
N107PT	**C52B**	**0127**
N107RC	**CS55**	**0150**
N107RG	**F2EX**	**157**
N107RM	**LJ25**	**362**
N107RP	HS25	259038
N107SB	C550	163
N107SC	C500	107
N107SF	C500	207
N107T	C550	190
N107T	MU30	A012SA
N107TB	CL61	5012
N107TB	FA10	77
N107TD	**GLF4**	**1355**
(N107TE)	EA50	000007
N107TS	LJ31	107
(N107TW)	HFB3	1057
(N107US)	FA10	207

N107VP	C550	550-1077
N107VP	F2TH	107
N107VS	**GLF5**	**5043**
N107WR	PRM1	RB-73
N107WV	C550	427
N107XP	HS25	HA-0107
(N107YR)	PRM1	RB-73
(N108AJ)	C550	008
N108AR	**GLF3**	**461**
N108BG	FA20	403
N108BK	F900	74
N108BK	**FA50**	**107**
(N108BN)	CL61	5101
N108BP	HS25	258546
N108CC	C500	108
N108CE	**GLF5**	**561**
N108CF	HS25	258100
N108CG	**ASTR**	**108**
N108CJ	**C525**	**0108**
N108CR	C525	0258
(N108CT)	C500	564
(N108CT)	C550	108
N108DB	C550	064
N108DB	GLF2	112
N108DB	GLF4	1149
N108DB	GLF5	5180
N108DB	**GLF6**	**6128**
N108DD	**HS25**	**258700**
N108DN	GLF5	5180
N108DU	**GLF4**	**1149**
N108EK	**C56X**	**5032**
N108FJ	**F900**	**108**
N108FJ	FA10	13
N108FJ	FA50	113
N108FL	**LJ25**	**300**
N108FX	LJ31	104
N108G	SBRL	282-51
N108G	SBRL	306-102
N108GA	LJ25	011
N108GL	LJ35	073
N108GM	WW24	221
N108GS	**GLF4**	**1080**
N108GX	GALX	046
N108JA	**E50P**	**50000023**
N108JE	**LJ40**	**2061**
N108JL	C500	526
N108JN	**LJ35**	**358**
N108KC	**FA10**	**8**
N108KJ	**C52A**	**0416**
N108KP	FA50	232
N108LA	**C52B**	**0176**
(N108LA)	HS25	258280
N108LJ	**C560**	**0337**
N108LT	**CL30**	**20333**
N108MC	**C500**	**322**
N108MG	E50P	50000226
N108MR	FA10	74
N108MV	**C550**	**550-0881**
N108NC	FA20	168
N108NR	LJ25	356
N108NY	**GLF5**	**685**
N108PA	LJ25	195
N108PJ	HS25	HA-0024
N108PJ	BE40	RK-347
N108QS	CS55	0108
N108QS	BE40	RK-382
N108R	FA20	108/430
N108R	**GLF6**	**6154**
N108RB	**LJ35**	**097**
N108RF	C550	550-0805
N108RL	C500	125
N108RT	**GLF4**	**1387**
N108SC	GALX	034
N108TG	FA10	114
(N108TW)	LJ24	027
N108U	SBRL	282-2
(N108U)	HS25	259006
N108VR	**C560**	**0601**
N108W	SBRL	282-2
N108W	SBRL	306-132
N108WG	C550	035
N108WQ	C52B	0294
N108WV	**C650**	**0204**
N108X	SBRL	282-51
N109AF	HS25	257022
N109AL	C500	037
N109AP	C500	046
N109AP	**C52A**	**0131**
N109BG	**HS25**	**257157**
N109BK	F900	73
N109BL	C500	046
N109C	**C500**	**642**
N109CP	BE40	RK-47
N109CQ	FA50	340
N109DC	C500	595
N109DC	**C550**	**550-0832**
N109DD	**GLF3**	**415**
N109DJ	EA50	000006
N109DM	BE40	RJ-9
(N109FC)	FA20	489
N109FJ	FA10	15
N109FJ	FA50	109
N109FX	LJ31	105
N109G	GLF2	48/29
N109G	HS25	257176
N109GA	**C550**	**137**
N109GL	LJ35	080

N109GX	**ASTR**	**142**
N109HV	LJ31	105
N109JB	LJ24	168
N109JC	**C550**	**109**
N109JE	LJ60	093
N109JM	HS25	257101
N109JR	LJ24	168
N109JR	LJ35	101
N109JR	LJ60	093
N109JR	LJ60	223
N109JU	LJ35	101
N109JZ	LJ60	223
N109LE	**E50P**	**50000226**
N109LJ	LJ60	109
N109LR	HS25	25203
N109MC	LJ35	054
N109MC	SBRL	306-119
N109NC	CL61	5112
N109NC	FA20	489
N109NQ	FA20	489
N109NT	**BE40**	**RK-374**
N109PM	PRM1	RB-23
N109PW	MU30	A046SA
N109QS	**GLEX**	**9589**
N109RK	FA20	66
N109SB	**SBRL**	**380-20**
N109SJ	LJ25	269
N109ST	C650	0109
N109ST	GLF3	302
N109ST	GLF4	1151
N109ST	GLF5	5049
N109TD	HS25	258307
N109TT	FA20	495
N109TW	**C52B**	**0338**
N109TW	MU30	A037SA
(N109TW)	C52A	0240
N109VP	C52A	0109
N109VP	C560	0109
(N109VP)	C750	0009
N109VR	**C550**	**550-1109**
N109WS	C560	0632
N109ZZ	GLEX	9337
N110AB	C500	262
N110AE	LJ35	155
N110AF	C500	262
N110AF	WW24	436
N110AJ	SBRL	380-70
N110AN	JSTR	5092/58
N110AN	JSTR	5227
N110AP	**E55P**	**50500212**
N110BP	CL64	5579
N110BR	C550	550-1100
N110BR	GLF3	
301		
(N110BX)	LJ31	108
N110CE	FA20	7
N110CG	FA10	45
N110CK	C500	078
N110CX	**C750**	**0077**
N110DD	HS25	258728
N110DD	JSTR	5092/58
N110DJ	EA50	000007
N110DK	MU30	A044SA
N110DS	MU30	A005SA
N110ED	**GLF5**	**5136**
(N110EE)	GLF3	322
N110EJ	HS25	257104
N110ET	LJ55	023
N110EX	**F9EX**	**71**
N110FD	C525	0241
N110FD	**C52A**	**0308**
N110FJ	F900	110
N110FJ	FA10	16
N110FJ	FA50	4
(N110FJ)	FA10	6
N110FP	LJ25	274
N110FS	**G150**	**247**
N110FS	SBRL	282-58
N110FT	LJ35	471
N110FX	LJ31	108
N110G	JSTR	5007/45
N110G	SBRL	306-75
N110GA	GLF4	4310
N110GA	GLF6	6010
N110GA	BE40	RJ-44
N110GD	GLF2	154/28
N110GD	**HS25**	**258713**
N110GF	FA10	146
N110GL	LJ25	081
N110GX	GALX	047
N110H	C500	385
N110HA	**GALX**	**035**
N110HA	LJ25	110
N110J	FA10	139
N110JA	C500	382
N110JB	**C500**	**599**
N110JC	C52B	0301
N110JD	LJ35	247
N110JD	PRM1	RB-86
N110JD	**WW24**	**414**
N110JG	SBRL	306-122
N110JJ	G150	270
N110KG	LJ35	155
N110KS	CL60	1006
N110LA	FA10	54
N110LD	**C550**	**399**
N110LE	**C680**	**0022**

N110LE	GLF3	322
N110LE	GLF4	1153
N110LH	CS55	0118
N110LP	WW24	286
N110M	CL60	1052
N110M	FA10	34
N110M	LJ24	091
N110MG	ASTR	122
N110MG	C52A	0014
N110MG	C52B	0011
N110MH	HS25	258137
N110MH	SBRL	306-119
N110MN	JSTR	5149/11
N110MQ	C52A	0014
N110MT	GLF3	444
N110MT	JSTR	5149/11
N110NB	**C750**	**0306**
N110PA	LJ36	040
N110PG	**C56X**	**5515**
N110PK	**C750**	**0040**
N110PM	SBRL	282-127
N110PP	FA10	210
N110PR	**PRM1**	**RB-29**
N110PS	LJ24	262
N110QS	**GLEX**	**9592**
N110RA	LJ25	025
N110SC	LJ31	185
N110SE	**LJ31**	**217**
N110SF	WW24	376
N110SJ	**SJ30**	**003**
N110SN	**GLF4**	**1208**
N110SQ	LJ24	173
N110ST	WW24	129
N110TD	CL60	1052
N110TG	BE40	RK-123
N110TJ	FA20	368
N110TM	C650	0141
N110TM	GLF4	1087
N110TP	C500	564
N110TP	**C550**	**550-1131**
N110TP	FA10	123
N110TV	C500	564
N110UN	LJ35	007
N110VR	**C550**	**550-1100**
N110VW	GLF2	153
N110W	LJ24	119
N110WA	C550	406
N110WA	**GALX**	**072**
N110WC	C560	0357
N110WS	HFB3	1038
N110WS	**HS25**	**258388**
N110XL	C56X	6110
N111	F900	144
N111	**GLF5**	**5506**
N111AB	SBRL	282-70
N111AC	FA20	111
N111AC	GLF2	74
N111AC	GLF3	417
N111AC	SBRL	282-79
N111AD	HS25	25033
N111AD	LJ25	201
N111AD	SBRL	465-27
N111AF	**C550**	**286**
N111AF	LJ25	120
N111AF	LJ31	111
N111AG	HS25	25033
N111AG	SBRL	380-21
N111AG	WW24	199
N111AM	C500	135
N111AM	C525	0113
N111AM	FA20	111
N111AM	FA20	250
N111AM	**GLF5**	**5018**
N111AT	C500	140
(N111AX)	HS25	25033
N111BA	BE40	RJ-11
N111BB	**C500**	**248**
N111BF	**C525**	**0140**
(N111BJ)	LJ35	344
N111BL	LJ25	130
N111BP	FA20	111
N111BZ	C650	7068
N111CC	C500	111
N111CF	C560	0053
N111CQ	**GLF4**	**4006**
N111CT	LJ24	070
N111CX	BE40	RK-210
N111DC	HFB3	1030
N111DT	C500	614
N111DT	HS25	25115
(N111DT)	C550	088
N111E	WW24	134
N111EA	SBRL	282-27
N111EJ	LJ24	105
N111EK	LJ24	105
N111EL	ASTR	055
N111EL	WW24	351
N111EQ	ASTR	055
N111ER	MS76	050
N111ES	GLF3	349
N111F	**C650**	**0197**
N111F	FA20	356
N111F	SBRL	306-126
N111FA	**GLF3**	**307**
N111FJ	FA10	18
N111FJ	FA50	115
N111FK	CL60	1027

N111FK	**CL61**	**5104**
(N111FS)	C500	034
N111FW	**BE40**	**RK-102**
N111G	CL60	1025
N111G	CL61	3032
N111G	GLF3	454
N111G	JSTR	5062/12
N111GD	GLF2	170
N111GJ	C525	0500
N111GJ	**C550**	**198**
N111GL	LJ25	081
N111GL	LJ35	084
N111GU	**C56X**	**5504**
N111GU	JSTR	5114/18
N111GW	LJ24	198
N111GX	CL61	3032
N111GX	GLF3	454
N111HC	**GLF3**	**482**
(N111HH)	PRM1	RB-41
N111HJ	LJ24	151
N111HN	WW24	421
N111HZ	C650	7068
N111HZ	F2TH	86
N111HZ	**FA7X**	**137**
N111J	CL60	1025
N111JD	LJ24	006
N111JL	**CL60**	**1027**
N111JL	GLF4	1111
N111JM	**C510**	**0383**
N111JW	C52A	0387
N111JW	C52B	0186
N111JW	C560	0478
N111KJ	**C52B**	**0340**
N111KK	LJ35	425
N111KK	LJ45	061
N111KK	**LJ45**	**498**
N111KR	C500	179
N111KR	**LJ35**	**464**
N111KZ	LJ35	425
N111LJ	LJ24	127
N111LL	LJ25	021
(N111LM)	LJ25	025
N111LP	**C52C**	**0152**
N111LP	PRM1	RB-243
N111LP	PRM1	RB-252
N111LP	WW24	286
N111LQ	PRM1	RB-243
N111LR	C525	0222
N111LX	GLF5	608
N111M	FA20	10
N111MB	HS25	25195
N111MD	**HS25**	**HA-0035**
N111ME	**C500**	**146**
N111MP	LJ25	139
N111MS	SBRL	282-4
N111MU	C500	262
N111MU	**F900**	**144**
N111MU	FA10	182
N111MZ	LJ35	125
N111NF	WW24	168
N111NG	F9EX	71
N111NL	GLF4	1184
N111P	**F900**	**117**
N111QJ	**HS25**	**257079**
N111QP	C500	019
N111QS	CS55	0111
N111QS	**GLEX**	**9660**
N111RA	LJ24	179
N111RB	C500	561
N111RB	HS25	25205
N111RE	LJ24	179
N111RF	C650	7001
N111RF	GLF2	46
N111RF	LJ24	156
N111RF	LJ25	143
N111RF	LJ35	217
N111RP	LJ24	156
N111SF	LJ25	189
N111SF	LJ35	608
N111ST	WW24	114
N111SU	C500	119
N111SW	**F9EX**	**11**
N111SZ	LJ25	189
N111TD	WW24	11
N111TH	C500	274
N111TT	LJ24	237
N111TT	LJ24	301
N111TT	LJ31	015
N111UB	GLF2	207/34
N111UN	HS25	256021
N111UN	HS25	256055
N111US	LJ35	306
N111US	LJ55	147
N111VG	HS25	258403
N111VP	C560	0044
N111VP	CS55	0002
(N111VS)	SBRL	380-69
N111VU	F2TH	99
N111VV	LJ31	023
N111VW	C650	0194
N111VW	F2TH	99
N111VW	GLF2	153
N111VW	SBRL	306-44
N111VW	SBRL	380-69
N111VX	SBRL	380-69
N111WB	LJ25	022
N111WB	**LJ35**	**003**

N111WH	**FA10**	**167**
N111WJ	LJ24	160
N111WM	LJ24	036
N111WR	LJ25	022
N111WW	FA10	165
N111WW	FA10	167
N111WW	**FA50**	**250**
N111WW	LJ24	268
N111XB	SBRL	282-101
N111XL	WW24	34
N111Y	C650	0223
N111Y	**C680**	**0127**
N111Y	SBRL	380-17
N111Y	WW24	42
N111YA	**LJ31**	**031**
N111YJ	**BE40**	**RJ-6**
N111YL	WW24	42
N111YW	**C650**	**0223**
N111ZD	GALX	084
N111ZN	HS25	257076
N111ZN	HS25	258327
N111ZN	HS25	258830
N111ZS	**HS25**	**257076**
N111ZT	GLF4	1111
N112AB	C56X	5361
N112AB	WW24	254
N112BJ	**BE40**	**RK-112**
N112BR	C550	550-1120
N112BR	**CS55**	**0027**
N112C	LJ24	250
N112CD	F2TH	26
N112CF	**CL64**	**5509**
N112CF	SBRL	465-16
N112CH	LJ25	090
N112CM	LJ31	078
N112CM	**PRM1**	**RB-123**
N112CP	C500	183
N112CT	FA20	168
N112CT	LJ25	090
N112CW	C560	0298
N112CW	**C56X**	**5065**
N112DJ	LJ24	112
N112DJ	LJ40	2040
N112EA	**EA50**	**000038**
N112EB	C500	499
N112EJ	**EA50**	**000112**
N112EL	LJ35	078
N112EM	**ASTR**	**023**
N112EM	WW24	336
N112FJ	**F2TH**	**112**
N112FJ	FA10	19
N112FJ	FA50	116
N112FJ	FA50	56
N112FK	CL60	1027
N112FK	LJ55	102
N112FX	LJ31	115
N112FX	LJ31	116
(N112FX)	LJ31	122
N112GA	G150	312
N112GA	G280	2012
N112GA	GALX	112
N112GA	GLF5	5312
N112GA	MU30	A012SA
N112GG	CL61	5099
N112GS	**C52A**	**0127**
N112GS	GLF3	384
(N112GS)	GLF3	368
N112GX	GALX	048
N112HV	LJ31	116
N112J	LJ24	237
N112JC	WW24	7
N112JM	LJ25	250
N112JS	C550	032
N112K	HS25	258042
(N112KH)	SBRL	380-34
N112KM	SBRL	465-34
N112M	HS25	25207
N112MC	C500	404
N112MC	JSTR	5231
N112ME	LJ25	090
N112ML	SBRL	282-136
N112MR	WW24	174
(N112MT)	LJ60	208
N112MV	**C680**	**0148**
N112MY	**GLEX**	**9442**
N112NC	CL61	5112
N112NW	HS25	258112
N112PG	LJ35	304
N112PR	ASTR	013
N112PR	SBRL	465-12
N112PV	SBRL	465-12
N112QS	CS55	0112
N112QS	**GLEX**	**9710**
N112RC	WW24	170
N112SA	C550	275
N112SH	C550	046
N112T	LJ24	098
N112TJ	JSTR	5029/38
N112VP	C52A	0112
N112WC	C500	478
N112WC	**BE40**	**RK-575**
N112WJ	**GLF4**	**1112**
N112WQ	LJ55	101
N112ZZ	GLEX	9339
N113AF	LJ31	111
N113AK	LJ25	020
(N113AN)	LJ35	113
N113AR	GLF2	139/11
N113AR	GLF4	1018
N113BG	**C52A**	**0078**
N113BR	PRM1	RB-113
N113CC	C500	113
N113CS	GLEX	9354
N113CS	GLF2	95/39
N113CS	GLF4	1049
N113CS	GLF5	5154
N113CS	**GLF6**	**6090**
N113EA	**EA50**	**000152**
(N113EC)	C560	0373
N113EL	LJ55	006
N113ES	LJ25	092
N113EV	GLF2	135
N113FJ	FA10	20
N113FJ	FA50	118
N113FX	LJ31	116
N113GA	ASTR	113
N113GA	GLF4	1513
N113GH	WW24	286
N113GS	GLF5	5154
N113HX	**EA50**	**550-0275**
N113JS	LJ24	356
N113KH	JSTR	5152
N113LB	LJ35	457
N113MR	WW24	126
N113PT	ASTR	032
N113RF	LJ25	143
N113RX	**LJ45**	**195**
N113SC	SBRL	282-18
N113SH	C500	285
N113SR	**CL61**	**5164**
N113T	SBRL	306-113
N113US	**C560**	**0701**
N113VP	C560	0113
N113VP	CS55	0090
N113WA	CL61	5068
N113WA	FA50	51
N113WJ	**GLF4**	**1173**
N113XP	HS25	HA-0013
N113XP	BE40	RK-433
N113YS	**LJ55**	**071**
N113ZZ	GLEX	9345
N114AF	HS25	25219
N114AN	GLF4	1108
N114AP	BE40	RJ-31
N114B	HS25	25196
N114BA	HS25	257170
N114BD	**LJ60**	**166**
N114CC	LJ25	126
N114CJ	C52B	0014
N114CJ	C52B	0114
N114CL	C52B	0256
N114CL	JSTR	5070/52
N114CP	C560	0018
N114CX	C750	0114
N114DM	MU30	A011SA
N114DM	BE40	RJ-11
N114DS	C550	334
N114EA	**EA50**	**000155**
N114EB	**C560**	**0795**
(N114ED)	WW24	177
N114EL	C550	321
N114EX	F9EX	114
(N114FG)	C525	0307
N114FJ	FA10	22
N114FJ	FA50	119
N114FJ	FA50	229
N114FW	**C525**	**0307**
N114FX	LJ31	119
N114GA	ASTR	114
N114GA	GLF4	1144
N114GB	LJ24	022
N114GS	F900	114
N114HC	**FA50**	**305**
N114HC	GLF2	92
N114HC	LJ25	114
(N114HE)	WW24	106
N114HH	WW24	106
N114HY	LJ31	119
N114JT	LJ24	318
N114KN	**C560**	**0463**
N114LA	C500	072
N114LG	SBRL	465-51
N114LJ	LJ60	157
N114PC	HS25	25146
N114PJ	LJ60	114
N114QS	BE40	RK-469
N114RA	WW24	179
(N114RP)	C52A	0135
N114SN	**ASTR**	**114**
N114TD	**FA50**	**17**
N114TM	C550	550-1067
N114VP	C550	550-1004
N114VR	**C550**	**550-1114**
N114VW	C750	0093
N114W	**C52A**	**0350**
N114WC	LJ24	291
N114WD	HS25	25114
(N114WJ)	GLF2	114
N114WL	WW24	338
N114XP	BE40	RK-469
N115AN	**LJ60**	**308**
N115BB	**C525**	**0325**
N115BP	WW24	417
N115BR	ASTR	099
N115BX	LJ31	129
N115CD	BE40	RK-151
N115CJ	C525	0015
N115CJ	**C52A**	**0115**
N115CR	**SBRL**	**306-43**
N115DJ	EA50	000020
N115DX	JSTR	5111
N115EL	LJ55	035
N115FJ	F900	115
N115FJ	FA10	23
N115FJ	FA50	121
(N115FJ)	F900	15
N115FL	GLF4	1141
N115FX	LJ31	129
N115GA	GLF2	45
N115HB	HA4T	RC-15
N115HK	GLEX	9004
N115HS	**C750**	**0275**
N115K	C500	433
N115K	**C560**	**0148**
N115K	FA20	80
N115L	SBRL	306-60
N115LF	**CL30**	**20226**
N115LJ	CL30	20015
N115LJ	**LJ40**	**2115**
N115MA	LJ35	118
N115MC	GLF2	137
N115MF	**FA50**	**330**
N115MH	**GLEX**	**9463**
N115MR	GLF2	12
N115MR	JSTR	5111
N115PL	**F9EX**	**269**
N115QS	BE40	RK-383
N115RL	FA50	302
N115RN	**FA50**	**302**
(N115RS)	GLF2	9/33
(N115RS)	HS25	257067
N115SK	FA50	330
N115TD	**FA10**	**96**
N115TL	**C56X**	**5250**
N115TR	**GLEX**	**9067**
N115TW	FA20	91
N115VH	C550	375
N115WA	FA10	115
N115WF	CL61	5153
N115WZ	C680	0307
N115WZ	PRM1	RB-197
N115XP	**BE40**	**RK-467**
N115ZZ	GLEX	9347
(N116AC)	SBRL	282-41
N116AD	BE40	RK-192
N116AD	**BE40**	**RK-338**
N116AM	LJ35	116
N116AP	C525	0033
N116AP	BE40	RK-192
N116AR	GLF3	312
N116AS	**LJ45**	**078**
N116AS	LJ60	035
N116AT	WW24	288
N116BJ	CL64	5520
N116BK	FA20	175
N116BX	LJ31	132
N116CC	C500	116
N116CC	C550	116
N116CS	C525	0447
N116DA	LJ55	116
N116DD	FA10	41
N116DD	HS25	256044
N116DD	JSTR	5155/32
N116DD	JSTR	5224
N116DJ	EA50	000021
N116DJ	**LJ40**	**2027**
N116DK	C525	0257
N116DK	**E55P**	**50500067**
N116EL	LJ35	173
N116EX	F2EX	116
N116FE	**GALX**	**197**
N116FJ	FA10	24
N116FJ	FA50	124
N116FX	LJ31	132
N116GB	FA20	281/496
N116GB	FA50	182
(N116GL)	LJ55	016
N116HL	**CL61**	**5113**
N116HM	GLF4	1024
N116HW	G150	275
N116JC	**ASTR**	**014**
N116JD	FA20	4
N116JG	**HS25**	**258354**
N116JK	HS25	258548
N116JR	LJ25	359
N116K	C550	164
N116K	GLF2	73/9
N116KC	**C550**	**164**
(N116KV)	LJ35	244
N116KX	WW24	87
N116LA	**C550**	**017**
(N116LD)	CS55	0110
N116LJ	C525	0617
N116LJ	LJ60	116
N116LM	**LJ60**	**142**
N116LS	**CL61**	**5013**
N116MA	**LJ36**	**029**
N116MC	WW24	86
N116NC	**G150**	**309**
N116PB	ASTR	032
(N116PR)	LJ35	130
N116QS	BE40	RK-385
N116RA	CL60	1011
N116RM	LJ24	206
N116RW	**F900**	**58**
N116SC	SBRL	282-1
N116SF	**GLEX**	**9583**
N116SS	BE40	RK-111
N116VP	**C550**	**550-1010**
(N116WC)	C560	0393
N116WE	LJ45	116
N116WJ	**GLF4**	**1320**
N116WZ	PRM1	RB-197
N116XP	BE40	RK-416
N116XP	**BE40**	**RK-427**
N117AE	LJ24	346
N117AH	WW24	352
N117AJ	**FA50**	**154**
N117AJ	JSTR	5227
N117AJ	LJ24	346
N117AL	F2EX	131
N117AL	**GLF5**	**5193**
N117AL	GLF5	5294
N117BG	**C650**	**0007**
N117CC	C560	0287
N117CH	LJ25	018
N117CH	LJ35	045
(N117CP)	HS25	259043
(N117DA)	LJ35	075
N117DD	E55P	50500019
N117DJ	C500	500
N117DS	**HA4T**	**RC-59**
N117EA	**EA50**	**000104**
N117EL	LJ35	486
N117EL	LJ55	061
N117EM	HS25	256046
N117EX	F9EX	117
N117FJ	FA10	25
N117FJ	GLF2	229
N117FJ	LJ35	417
N117FX	LJ31	133
N117GL	GLF2	220
N117GM	WW24	118
N117GS	C550	626
N117HH	**HS25**	**258249**
(N117J)	JSTR	5099/5
N117JA	GLF2	163
N117JF	GLF4	1117
N117JJ	GLF2	163
N117JJ	GLF3	448
N117JL	**C560**	**0428**
N117JL	SBRL	306-128
N117JW	**SBRL**	**465-61**
N117JW	WW24	352
N117K	LJ24	272
N117KB	**LJ60**	**003**
N117LB	**GLF2**	**193**
N117LR	**LJ55**	**075**
N117MA	**C500**	**514**
N117MB	SBRL	465-1
(N117MN)	SBRL	465-1
N117MR	C560	0287
N117MS	**GLEX**	**9386**
N117MS	GLF3	335
N117MS	GLF4	1241
N117PK	LJ35	513
N117PS	**C510**	**0415**
N117QS	BE40	RK-391
N117RB	LJ35	154
N117RH	HS25	25196
N117RJ	LJ35	664
N117RJ	LJ60	056
(N117RJ)	LJ35	417
(N117RR)	FA10	52
N117RY	CL61	5162
N117SF	**F900**	**55**
N117SF	FA50	137
N117SH	LJ25	299
N117TA	C550	464
N117TF	F900	42
N117TF	GLEX	9028
N117TF	**GLEX**	**9175**
N117TS	HS25	25134
N117TW	C500	059
N117UH	**EA50**	**000117**
N117VP	C550	550-1007
N117VP	C550	550-1019
N117W	C525	0292
N117W	C52A	0079
N117W	C52A	0350
(N117W)	C52A	0022
N117WC	LJ55	030
N117WH	**LJ45**	**304**
N117WR	**GLF4**	**4015**
N117XP	HS25	HA-0117
N117XP	BE40	RK-385
N118AD	**F2TH**	**125**
N118AD	FA10	118
N118AF	WW24	177
N118AJ	CS55	0118
(N118AT)	C500	548
N118AV	LJ40	2018
N118AZ	C525	0118
N118B	JSTR	5091
N118B	JSTR	5211
N118BA	JSTR	5091
N118BX	LJ31	134
N118CD	C650	0118
N118CD	**HS25**	**257018**
N118CJ	**C52A**	**0384**
N118CS	C525	0457
N118DA	HS25	25118
N118DA	LJ35	081
N118DF	C560	0118
N118DL	**HS25**	**258607**
N118EA	C550	131
N118EA	**EA50**	**000184**
N118FJ	FA10	26
N118FJ	FA50	125
N118FN	**LJ35**	**118**
N118FX	LJ31	134
N118GA	GALX	118
N118GA	**HS25**	**258108**
N118GA	MU30	A018SA
(N118GM)	LJ35	314
N118GS	GLF2	95/39
N118HC	LJ60	067
N118J	LJ24	273
N118K	**C500**	**686**
N118K	HS25	258218
N118K	JSTR	5107
N118K	LJ35	067
N118KA	GALX	065
N118KL	HS25	258218
N118LA	C500	039
(N118LS)	LJ24	082A
N118MA	LJ35	144
N118MB	LJ25	118
N118MD	**LJ35**	**569**
N118MM	**C650**	**7105**
N118MP	WW24	340
N118MT	**CL61**	**5077**
N118NP	GLF2	7
N118QS	BE40	RK-393
N118R	FA20	385
N118R	GLF4	1066
N118RA	HFB3	1039
N118RH	**CL64**	**5516**
N118RJ	WW24	188
N118RK	C560	0389
N118RK	**LJ45**	**296**
N118RT	**C500**	**511**
N118RW	**C560**	**0389**
(N118RY)	C560	0389
N118SE	LJ25	118
N118ST	C56X	5287
(N118ST)	C56X	5302
N118T	**F2EX**	**22**
N118TS	HS25	25018
N118UF	**HS25**	**HA-0183**
N118VP	C550	550-1029
N118WT	**GLEX**	**9327**
N118ZZ	GLEX	9476
N119AC	WW24	119
N119AD	**GLF4**	**4035**
N119AF	**GLF4**	**1489**
N119AG	FA50	297
N119AK	**HA4T**	**RC-11**
N119AK	HA4T	RC-9
N119AM	FA50	226
N119BA	**LJ24**	**084**
N119BG	**HS25**	**258681**
N119BX	LJ31	136
N119CC	GLF2	102/32
N119CC	HS25	25225
N119CJ	**C52A**	**0119**
N119CP	LJ35	366
N119CS	C525	0466
N119CV	C560	0119
N119DJ	EA50	000022
N119DJ	**LJ40**	**2037**
N119EA	CS55	0019
N119EA	**EA50**	**000200**
N119EL	C650	0013
N119EM	**F2EX**	**137**
N119EP	**E55P**	**50500258**
N119ES	**C650**	**0206**
N119EX	F9EX	119
N119FD	LJ60	029
N119FJ	FA10	28
N119FJ	FA50	126
N119FJ	FA50	137
N119FM	**GLF4**	**1464**
N119FX	LJ31	136
N119GA	CL64	5386
(N119GH)	HS25	25248
N119GM	**LJ45**	**362**
N119GS	LJ35	017
(N119HB)	FA50	8
(N119HB)	LJ35	307
(N119HT)	FA50	8
N119K	GLF2	17
N119K	GLF4	1046
N119KW	**G150**	**267**
N119LA	FA20	129
N119LC	**C550**	**550-0969**
N119LE	**GLF5**	**5333**
N119LJ	LJ60	119
N119LP	C56X	5192
N119M	M220	1
N119MA	LJ24	200
N119MH	MU30	A057SA
N119ML	**HS25**	**258174**
N119NJ	LJ40	2119
N119PH	FA50	8

(N119PM)	C750	0051
N119PW	HS25	259007
N119QS	BE40	RK-394
N119R	GLF2	243
N119R	GLF4	1008
N119R	GLF4	1077
N119RC	GLF2	243
N119RC	GLF4	1077
N119RM	C650	7018
N119RM	**C750**	**0051**
N119SE	JSTR	5161/43
N119SJ	FA10	119
N119TA	**FA20**	**237/476**
N119U	**HS25**	**259007**
N119VP	C550	550-1036
(N119ZZ)	GLEX	9382
N120AF	FA20	16
N120AK	GLEX	9153
N120AP	**HS25**	**258120**
N120AR	JSTR	5089
N120BJ	ASTR	026
N120CC	C500	120
N120CG	FA20	384/551
N120CS	C525	0490
N120CV	C560	0120
N120DE	FA20	384/551
N120DJ	**LJ40**	**2039**
(N120DP)	C500	410
N120EA	**EA50**	**000199**
N120EA	GLF2	28
N120EL	LJ55	067
(N120EN)	FA20	44
N120ES	C500	381
(N120EZ)	F9EX	120
N120FJ	FA10	29
N120FJ	FA20	491
N120FJ	FA7X	220
N120FS	FA20	204
N120FX	LJ31	137
N120GA	ASTR	055
N120GA	**G150**	**320**
N120GA	GLF4	4100
N120GA	GLF4	4210
N120GA	GLF5	5420
N120GA	HS25	25228
N120GA	HS25	257014
N120GB	HS25	25228
N120GH	WW24	58
(N120GR)	LJ55	078
N120GS	CL30	20165
N120GS	GLF2	167
N120HC	C550	577
N120HC	FA10	45
N120HC	FA20	148
N120HV	LJ60	052
N120J	LJ24	241
N120JC	HS25	257065
N120JC	**HS25**	**258672**
N120JC	SBRL	306-42
N120JJ	**GLF4**	**1264**
N120JP	**C550**	**468**
N120KC	SBRL	380-55
N120LJ	LJ55	120
N120LJ	LJ60	120
N120MB	LJ35	307
N120MH	HS25	257053
N120MH	HS25	257171
N120MP	CL61	3034
(N120MT)	CL64	5451
N120PA	CL61	5097
N120Q	C550	372
N120QM	**C560**	**0316**
N120QS	BE40	RK-409
N120RA	**FA20**	**211**
N120RA	LJ24	153
N120RD	C500	368
(N120RL)	JSTR	5155/32
N120RV	LJ31	137
N120S	C500	279
N120S	WW24	226
N120SB	C560	0561
N120SB	C560	0587
N120SB	C560	0753
N120SB	C680	0206
(N120SB)	C560	0542
N120SL	LJ25	120
N120TC	C550	440
N120TF	FA20	384/551
N120TJ	FA50	89
N120WH	ASTR	026
N120WH	FA20	385
(N120WH)	LJ35	112
N120WS	ASTR	026
N120YB	HS25	257116
N120YB	**HS25**	**258687**
N120YB	SBRL	380-12
N121AC	HS25	25099
N121AG	C650	0121
N121AJ	WW24	57
N121AM	FA20	310
N121AT	C650	0158
N121AT	**FA10**	**226**
N121BN	GLF5	667
N121BN	WW24	14
N121C	C550	232
N121C	C550	388
N121CG	C550	388
N121CG	**CS55**	**0123**
N121CK	LJ24	039
N121CL	LJ35	083
N121CN	**C550**	**550-1000**
N121CN	JSTR	5053/2
N121CP	C52A	0010
N121CP	C550	337
(N121CP)	C525	0083
N121CS	WW24	43
N121DF	CL60	1071
N121DF	CL61	5133
N121DF	CL64	5480
N121DF	**F9EX**	**113**
N121DJ	FA20	121
N121DX	**GALX**	**241**
N121EA	GLF2	12
N121EB	C525	0405
N121EL	LJ25	010
N121EL	**LJ60**	**338**
N121ET	CL64	5583
N121EU	FA20	297
N121EX	F2EX	121
N121EZ	C500	516
N121EZ	BE40	RK-109
N121FF	CL61	5133
N121FJ	FA10	192
N121FJ	FA10	30
N121FJ	FA50	121
N121FJ	FA50	127
N121FM	WW24	150
N121FX	LJ31	141
N121G	**EA50**	**000243**
N121GA	GLF4	4011
N121GF	BE40	RK-503
N121GG	**C680**	**0025**
(N121GG)	CL61	5099
(N121GL)	LJ25	010
N121GV	ASTR	082
N121GV	GALX	014
N121GV	**GALX**	**094**
N121GW	FA20	4
N121GX	GALX	014
N121GZ	**LJ45**	**429**
N121HE	C750	0078
N121HL	**C550**	**134**
N121HM	WW24	18
(N121HV)	LJ31	141
N121JC	WW24	77
(N121JC)	WW24	121
N121JD	**WW24**	**252**
N121JE	**SBRL**	**306-4**
N121JJ	GLF2	27
N121JJ	GLF4	1075
N121JJ	**GLF4**	**1482**
N121JM	GLF3	332
N121JM	GLF4	1399
(N121JN)	GLF3	332
N121JT	LJ35	311
(N121JT)	LJ35	315
N121JV	GLF4	1075
N121JW	C500	358
N121JW	C550	463
N121KL	**C56X**	**5720**
N121KM	**C550**	**308**
N121L	C550	550-0896
N121LJ	**LJ31**	**121**
N121LM	**CL30**	**20028**
N121LS	C560	0593
N121LS	**C680**	**0076**
N121LS	GALX	010
(N121LS)	C680	0017
N121LT	LJ55	064
N121MJ	**C550**	**489**
N121PA	WW24	129
N121PC	**E50P**	**50000247**
N121PG	WW24	45
(N121PP)	GLF4	1345
(N121PR)	GLF2	17
N121PX	LJ31	141
N121PZ	**E50P**	**50000153**
N121RS	CL64	5572
N121RS	**GLEX**	**9203**
N121SG	ASTR	053
N121SG	HS25	256071
N121SJ	C500	384
N121TE	C56X	5073
N121TL	C56X	5073
N121TL	C680	0058
N121TN	**LJ60**	**172**
N121US	LJ55	123
N121UW	C500	358
N121VA	CL60	1012
N121VA	HS25	25272
N121VF	HS25	25272
N121WF	CS55	0160
N121WT	FA20	274
N121YD	C52A	0121
N121ZZ	GLEX	9375
N122A	**F900**	**88**
N122AP	C500	122
N122AW	HS25	25169
N122BN	**GLEX**	**9103**
N122BS	LJ25	122
N122BX	LJ31	143
N122CA	FA20	16
N122CC	C500	122
N122CG	C550	411
N122CG	CS55	0125
N122CG	LJ24	250
N122CR	**E50P**	**50000315**
N122CS	C525	0469
N122DJ	GLF2	6
N122DJ	GLF3	374
N122DS	**PRM1**	**RB-100**
N122DU	GLF2	6
N122EH	SBRL	306-57
N122EJ	C650	0122
N122FJ	F2EX	22
N122FJ	FA10	31
N122FJ	FA50	128
N122FJ	FA50	217
(N122FJ)	FA20	507
N122FX	LJ31	143
N122G	C550	122
N122GV	ASTR	106
N122GV	GALX	043
N122GV	GLF4	4034
N122HL	WW24	122
N122HM	C550	145
N122HW	**C525**	**0387**
N122JB	WW24	133
N122JC	WW24	122
(N122JD)	LJ55	050
N122JW	LJ35	217
(N122LG)	C500	424
N122LJ	LJ31	122
N122LM	C500	122
N122LM	**C525**	**0604**
N122LX	**LJ55**	**030**
N122M	LJ24	065A
N122MM	C550	145
N122MP	**WW24**	**390**
N122NC	**C550**	**550-0836**
N122PH	**C680**	**0294**
N122PR	**F2TH**	**57**
N122QS	BE40	RK-467
N122RP	SBRL	282-7
N122RS	GLF4	1417
N122RW	LJ24	321
N122SC	F2TH	25
N122SM	C52A	0151
N122SP	**C550**	**392**
N122ST	**WW24**	**122**
N122SU	LJ55	132
N122SV	C680	0122
N122TA	**C650**	**0048**
N122TN	GLF5	5022
N122TY	CL60	1035
N122WC	LJ25	122
(N122WC)	C560	0402
N122WF	CL60	1035
N122WF	CL61	5021
N122WS	CS55	0122
N122WW	**C550**	**404**
N122WY	**C52B**	**0475**
N122XP	HS25	HA-0122
N123AB	**GLEX**	**9167**
N123AC	HS25	25122
N123AC	**LJ40**	**2113**
N123AD	C510	0184
N123AD	**C525**	**0818**
(N123AG)	HS25	25122
N123AP	GLF3	448
N123AV	C525	0180
N123CB	LJ24	232
N123CC	C500	123
N123CC	FA20	488
N123CC	GLF2	69
N123CC	GLF3	455
N123CC	JSTR	5208
N123CC	LJ24	268
N123CC	LJ35	206
N123CC	LJ60	012
N123CD	**SBRL**	**282-23**
N123CG	LJ25	270
N123CJ	C52B	0063
N123CJ	**C52B**	**0149**
N123CV	WW24	178
N123CX	C500	123
N123CZ	**C52B**	**0313**
N123DG	**LJ24**	**342**
N123DM	LJ25	086
N123DR	WW24	158
N123EB	C500	380
N123EG	**WW24**	**306**
N123EL	LJ25	045
N123FF	**CS55**	**0005**
N123FG	C500	534
N123FG	SBRL	306-90
N123FH	C550	468
N123FJ	FA10	219
N123FJ	FA10	33
N123FJ	FA50	129
N123FT	**GLF5**	**549**
N123GA	JSTR	5061/48
N123GF	C550	550-0817
N123GM	C550	358
N123GN	JSTR	5123/14
N123GV	GALX	043
N123H	GLF2	54/36
(N123H)	GLF5	618
N123HK	**HS25**	**258208**
(N123HP)	C500	611
N123JB	HS25	25017
N123JB	WW24	37
N123JN	C525	0046
N123JS	LJ25	017
N123JW	C52A	0152
N123KD	**C500**	**595**
N123KH	CL64	5301
N123KH	**HS25**	**258621**
N123LC	GLF4	1441
N123LC	LJ35	409
N123LC	LJ55	020
N123LC	LJ55	027
N123LC	LJ55	034
(N123LC)	LJ55	045
N123LV	GLF4	4181
N123M	GLF5	667
N123MJ	**LJ24**	**036**
(N123MJ)	LJ35	051
N123MR	GLF3	455
N123MR	GLF4	1492
N123MS	SBRL	282-53
N123NC	LJ25	325
(N123NW)	C560	0248
N123PL	**C500**	**639**
(N123PL)	C500	524
N123Q	**CL30**	**20616**
N123QS	BE40	RK-486
N123RA	**FA20**	**30**
N123RC	**WW24**	**349**
N123RE	FA20	150/445
N123RE	LJ24	154
N123RF	C550	248
N123RX	**E50P**	**50000302**
N123RZ	HS25	25152
N123S	**C525**	**0525**
N123SF	C500	606
N123SF	LJ25	088
N123SL	C650	0134
N123SL	C650	7053
N123SL	**C750**	**0168**
N123SR	C550	469
N123SV	LJ24	202
N123TF	C510	0191
N123TF	**C525**	**0801**
N123TG	FA10	37
N123TL	**CS55**	**0124**
N123TL	GLF3	452
N123VJ	MU30	A067SA
N123VM	HS25	25030
N123VP	C550	123
N123VV	FA10	37
N123VW	LJ24	154
N123VW	LJ24	253
N123WH	FA20	426
N124AR	HS25	257075
N124AV	LJ45	124
N124BC	CL61	3013
N124BC	**WW24**	**351**
N124BG	BE40	RK-124
N124BM	HS25	25101
(N124BN)	GLF2	39
N124BP	LJ45	113
N124BR	PRM1	RB-24
N124BV	BE40	RK-105
N124CC	C500	124
N124CR	C550	137
N124CS	C525	0472
N124DC	SBRL	306-95
N124DF	LJ31	214
(N124DH)	C500	261
N124DT	**GLF3**	**390**
N124EK	**E55P**	**50500319**
N124EK	PRM1	RB-270
(N124EK)	PRM1	RB-305
N124EP	**GLF3**	**440**
N124EX	F2EX	124
N124EZ	LJ24	347
N124FJ	FA10	220
N124FJ	FA10	34
N124FJ	FA50	130
N124FM	WW24	194
N124FX	LJ31	145
N124FX	LJ31	156
N124GA	C550	316
N124GA	LJ24	267
N124GR	WW24	315
N124GS	HS25	256026
N124GV	PRM1	RB-270
N124H	SBRL	282-76
N124HF	LJ24	166
N124HL	WW24	325
N124HM	FA50	117
N124HS	WW24	329
N124JB	WW24	64
N124JG	HS25	258084
N124JL	LJ24	127
N124KC	C500	665
N124KK	EA50	000034
N124LJ	LJ31	124
N124LS	WW24	354
N124MA	LJ25	118
N124MB	WW24	226
N124MC	LJ35	453
N124NB	C500	402
N124NS	C500	402
N124NY	WW24	205
N124PA	WW24	244
N124PA	WW24	418
N124PJ	LJ24	166
N124PP	**BE40**	**RK-92**
N124QS	BE40	RK-442
N124RM	JSTR	5078/3
N124RP	JSTR	5113/25
N124SD	**SBRL**	**465-2**
N124TF	**GLF4**	**1004**
N124TS	GLF4	1224
N124TS	LJ24	233
N124TV	GLF2	124
N124TY	WW24	223
N124UF	WW24	257
N124VC	**SBRL**	**306-95**
N124VF	WW24	174
N124VP	C560	0124
N124VS	WW24	64
N124WK	WW24	291
N124WL	LJ24	157
N124WW	WW24	201
N124WW	WW24	203
N124ZT	LJ35	138
N125AC	CL60	1072
N125AC	WW24	205
N125AD	HS25	25046
N125AD	HS25	257113
N125AE	HS25	257119
N125AF	HS25	257111
N125AH	HS25	257083
N125AH	HS25	257123
N125AJ	ASTR	031
N125AJ	HS25	25206
N125AJ	HS25	257077
N125AJ	HS25	257125
N125AK	HS25	257078
N125AK	HS25	257129
N125AL	HS25	25033
N125AL	HS25	257086
N125AM	HS25	257075
(N125AM)	HS25	257081
N125AN	CL60	1073
N125AN	HS25	257114
N125AP	HS25	25220
N125AP	HS25	257116
N125AP	HS25	257119
N125AR	HS25	25220
N125AR	HS25	257119
N125AS	HS25	257117
N125AS	HS25	257188
N125AS	HS25	258167
N125AT	HS25	257120
N125AU	HS25	257121
N125AW	HS25	25057
N125AW	HS25	258220
N125AX	LJ35	415
N125BA	HS25	257105
N125BA	HS25	257167
N125BA	HS25	258086
N125BA	HS25	258139
N125BA	HS25	258179
N125BA	HS25	259013
(N125BA)	HS25	258048
N125BC	HS25	257128
N125BD	HS25	257137
N125BE	HS25	257140
N125BH	HS25	25027
N125BH	HS25	25236
N125BH	HS25	25237
N125BH	HS25	25273
N125BH	HS25	256007
N125BJ	**C52A**	**0101**
N125BJ	HS25	257145
N125BM	HS25	25023
N125BP	SBRL	465-25
N125BT	HS25	25021
N125BW	HS25	257057
N125BW	**LJ45**	**323**
(N125BW)	HS25	25023
N125CA	FA10	196
N125CA	FA20	208/468
N125CA	HS25	25082
N125CA	HS25	259019
(N125CA)	C500	583
N125CE	C52A	0125
N125CF	HS25	25241
N125CG	CS55	0116
N125CG	HS25	257125
N125CH	**GLEX**	**9080**
N125CJ	C550	411
N125CJ	HS25	258241
N125CJ	HS25	259010
N125CJ	HS25	259014
N125CK	**HS25**	**25266**
N125CM	HS25	25267
N125CS	C525	0522
N125CS	HS25	257018
N125CU	HS25	256020
N125DB	**EA50**	**000193**
N125DB	HS25	25281
N125DB	LJ25	371
N125DC	**GLF2**	**55**
(N125DC)	HS25	25202
N125DF	LJ31	214
N125DG	C52A	0015
N125DG	**C52B**	**0060**
N125DH	HS25	25211
N125DH	HS25	25245
N125DJ	C525	0422

N125DP	HS25	257188
N125DS	**C500**	**258**
N125DT	**C750**	**0079**
N125DT	BE40	RK-387
N125E	HS25	25110
N125E	HS25	256018
N125EA	**C500**	**531**
N125EC	HS25	25232
N125EH	HS25	25222
N125EK	**HS25**	**257089**
N125EM	FA10	53
N125F	HS25	25151
N125FD	HS25	25123
N125FJ	F2EX	125
N125FJ	FA10	222
N125FJ	FA10	35
N125FJ	FA50	135
N125FM	HS25	25284
N125FS	LJ31	125
N125FX	LJ31	157
N125G	HS25	25014
N125G	HS25	25033
N125G	HS25	25038
N125G	HS25	25186
N125G	HS25	25250
N125G	HS25	257044
N125G	HS25	257138
N125GA	FA10	147
N125GA	LJ35	125
N125GB	ASTR	023
N125GB	HS25	258217
(N125GB)	HS25	257044
N125GC	HS25	25111
N125GC	HS25	25231
N125GC	HS25	25238
(N125GE)	BE40	RK-394
N125GH	**GLF5**	**526**
N125GH	HS25	25228
N125GK	HS25	25127
N125GM	HS25	259038
N125GP	HS25	257023
N125GP	LJ31	162
N125GR	**ASTR**	**116**
N125GS	HS25	256040
N125GS	HS25	256055
N125GW	LJ45	236
N125HD	HS25	25051
N125HF	HS25	256064
N125HF	WW24	408
N125HG	HS25	25250
N125HH	HS25	258034
N125HM	HS25	257020
N125HS	HS25	25136
N125HS	HS25	256021
N125HS	HS25	256061
N125HS	HS25	257012
N125HS	HS25	257058
N125HS	HS25	257080
N125J	HS25	25013
N125J	HS25	25043
N125J	HS25	25100
N125J	HS25	25124
N125J	HS25	25173
N125J	HS25	25205
N125JA	HS25	256021
N125JB	HS25	258089
N125JF	**GALX**	**173**
N125JG	HS25	25064
N125JG	BE40	RK-75
N125JJ	**C550**	**550-0940**
N125JJ	GLF2	15
N125JJ	HS25	256021
N125JL	LJ25	088
(N125JN)	HS25	258506
N125JR	HS25	25052
N125JW	HS25	25216
N125JW	HS25	258058
N125JW	**LJ25**	**352**
N125K	WW24	15
N125KC	HS25	25021
N125KC	HS25	25249
N125KR	HS25	256007
N125L	HS25	257095
N125LC	HS25	25033
N125LJ	CL30	20025
N125LJ	LJ31	125
N125LK	HS25	25121
N125LL	HS25	25033
N125LM	HS25	25018
N125LR	LJ55	032
N125MC	SBRL	306-10
N125MD	HS25	25201
N125MD	HS25	25265
N125MD	HS25	25284
N125MG	ASTR	032
N125MJ	FA20	225/472
(N125MJ)	HS25	257018
N125ML	HS25	HA-0100
N125MS	SBRL	380-5
N125MT	HS25	25261
N125MT	HS25	257192
N125N	C650	0129
N125N	CL60	1079
N125N	CL61	3044
N125N	GLF5	5023
N125N	SBRL	282-69
N125N	SBRL	370-3
N125NA	HS25	256026
N125NE	LJ25	271
N125NE	LJ28	28-004
N125NL	SBRL	282-69
N125NT	HS25	25078
N125NW	HS25	25222
N125NX	SBRL	370-3
(N125NY)	WW24	264
N125P	HS25	25046
N125P	HS25	257147
N125PA	HS25	25263
N125PL	C500	639
N125PL	**C52B**	**0290**
N125PP	HS25	25275
N125PS	**CL61**	**3058**
N125PT	HS25	25018
N125PT	LJ25	244
N125Q	C650	0128
N125QA	C555	0125
N125QS	BE40	RK-433
N125RG	**C550**	**261**
N125RG	HS25	257089
N125RH	C560	0147
N125RH	C650	0055
N125RH	**C750**	**0194**
N125RJ	BE40	RJ-25
N125RM	LJ25	193
N125RR	C550	138
(N125RT)	HS25	25204
N125SB	**HS25**	**258046**
N125SF	HS25	256065
N125SJ	**GLF4**	**1368**
N125SJ	HS25	257106
(N125SJ)	HS25	25250
N125ST	CL61	5052
N125ST	LJ25	024
N125TA	HS25	257105
N125TB	HS25	25039
N125TB	HS25	25053
N125TF	**GLF4**	**4244**
N125TH	**C750**	**0177**
N125TJ	HS25	25121
N125TJ	LJ25	294
(N125TJ)	HS25	25231
N125TM	**CL30**	**20104**
N125TM	HS25	258496
N125TN	**C650**	**7025**
N125TN	LJ25	193
N125TR	HS25	257075
N125TR	HS25	258132
N125TR	HS25	258196
N125U	HS25	257122
N125U	LJ25	015
N125V	HS25	25097
N125V	HS25	257106
N125VC	HS25	25232
(N125WC)	HS25	25014
(N125WD)	LJ25	042
N125WJ	HS25	256053
N125WM	GLF2	77
N125WT	C52A	0439
N125XP	**HS25**	**258485**
N125XX	HS25	257075
N125Y	HS25	25095
N125Y	HS25	257098
N125YY	HS25	257115
N125ZZ	HS25	258630
N126AA	C680	0037
(N126AH)	GLF3	346
N126AR	HS25	257128
N126BX	LJ31	158
N126CH	GLF5	581
N126CJ	C52A	0026
N126CX	LJ60	049
N126DJ	EA50	000002
N126EC	**LJ45**	**226**
(N126EC)	C560	0393
N126EL	LJ55	006
N126FJ	FA10	223
N126FJ	FA10	42
N126FJ	FA50	136
N126FX	LJ31	158
N126GA	GALX	126
N126GA	GLF4	4166
N126GA	GLF5	5326
N126GA	MU30	A059SA
N126HC	FA20	148
N126HR	**GLF5**	**5436**
N126HY	HS25	258782
(N126JM)	FA20	28
N126KC	**HS25**	**258276**
N126KD	LJ55	096
N126KD	LJ60	262
N126KL	**LJ55**	**096**
(N126KP)	C500	263
N126KR	C500	263
(N126LP)	C555	0026
N126MS	SBRL	380-16
N126MT	**C650**	**0044**
N126PG	**C52C**	**0048**
N126QS	C555	0126
N126R	C500	232
N126R	FA20	126/438
N126TF	**C550**	**550-0815**
N126WC	C560	0344
N126ZZ	HA4T	RC-10
N127AJ	LJ25	014
N127BH	LJ25	250
N127BJ	C500	120
N127BK	GLF3	311
N127BU	**C550**	**149**
N127BW	BE40	RK-105
N127BW	**BE40**	**RK-449**
N127BX	LJ31	159
(N127CA)	C650	0126
(N127CF)	C555	0127
N127CJ	C525	0127
(N127CJ)	C500	316
N127CL	**C550**	**007**
N127CM	HS25	25241
N127DF	CL60	1071
N127DK	GLF4	1127
N127DM	LJ24	169
(N127DN)	LJ24	169
(N127EC)	C560	0394
N127EL	LJ55	035
N127EM	F900	63
N127FJ	C510	0279
N127FJ	**C52A**	**0441**
N127FJ	FA10	225
N127FJ	FA10	38
N127FJ	FA50	137
N127FX	LJ31	159
N127GB	**LJ25**	**175**
N127GG	**GLF5**	**534**
N127GK	GLF3	311
N127GT	LJ55	067
N127HC	LJ35	277
N127JJ	C550	007
N127JM	**C550**	**295**
(N127JW)	C560	0312
N127K	LJ35	447
N127KC	HS25	258255
N127KR	C550	163
N127LJ	LJ24	127
N127MS	SBRL	380-18
N127MW	HFB3	1027
N127PM	**C550**	**027**
N127PT	**WW24**	**337**
N127RC	C555	0088
(N127RC)	C555	0126
N127RG	**C550**	**550-0917**
(N127RM)	LJ35	359
N127RP	HS25	259036
N127SA	WW24	440
N127SB	CL64	5358
N127SC	C550	127
N127SF	**F9EX**	**13**
N127SG	**C525**	**0046**
N127SJ	**BE40**	**RK-208**
N127SR	**CL64**	**5358**
N127SR	HS25	257209
(N127TA)	C550	051
N127UH	**BE40**	**RK-127**
N127V	GLF2	130
N127V	LJ31	036
N127VL	**LJ31**	**036**
N127VP	C560	0127
N127WL	FA10	16
N128AB	GLF4	1501
N128AD	**C510**	**0184**
(N128AD)	GLF2	178
(N128AG)	GLF3	422
N128AP	FA20	236
N128AW	C56X	5667
N128BG	**LJ31**	**212**
N128BJ	LJ24	128
N128BP	JSTR	5128/16
N128CA	**LJ35**	**248**
N128CJ	C52B	0063
N128CS	C525	0361
N128CS	HS25	257083
N128DM	LJ25	017
N128DR	HS25	25219
(N128EC)	C560	0418
N128FJ	F900	128
N128FJ	FA10	224
N128FJ	FA10	40
N128FJ	FA50	139
N128FX	LJ31	163
N128GB	C650	0006
N128GB	CL61	5113
N128GB	GLF5	665
N128GB	LJ31	074
N128GV	**GLF5**	**5363**
N128GV	GLF5	665
N128GW	C525	0427
N128JC	SBRL	306-42
(N128JJ)	HS25	256021
N128JL	**F9EX**	**44**
N128JL	PRM1	RB-28
N128JW	C52A	0152
N128KG	**GLF2**	**62**
N128LR	**LJ28**	**28-001**
N128M	FA50	276
N128MA	LJ28	28-001
N128MH	HS25	257171
N128MS	SBRL	380-26
(N128PE)	CL61	3065
N128RM	PRM1	RB-28
N128RS	HS25	258182
N128SD	HFB3	1035
N128SL	C650	7053
N128TJ	LJ25	104
(N128TJ)	HS25	25020
N128TS	**CL30**	**20102**
N128TS	GLF2	128
N128TS	GLF4	1263
N128V	LJ60	226
N128VM	LJ55	005
N128VM	SBRL	306-123
(N128WC)	C560	0336
(N128WD)	LJ24	128
N128WT	**C52B**	**0399**
N128WU	HS25	257157
N128YT	HS25	256035
N129AP	C500	402
N129AP	FA20	242
N129BA	CL60	1013
N129BA	HS25	256058
(N129BA)	SBRL	465-28
N129BT	BE40	RJ-29
N129CJ	**C52C**	**0129**
N129CK	**C52A**	**0382**
N129DB	BE40	RJ-12
N129DM	LJ24	187
N129DV	C550	404
N129ED	C550	718
N129EX	F2EX	129
N129EX	F9EX	129
N129FJ	FA10	41
N129FJ	FA50	141
N129FJ	FA50	219
N129FS	LJ45	142
N129FX	LJ31	171
N129GA	GLF5	5329
N129GB	**C650**	**0006**
N129GB	SBRL	282-27
N129GP	SBRL	282-27
N129GP	SBRL	465-50
N129JD	**LJ31**	**193**
N129JE	FA20	113
N129JE	FA20	267/491
N129JE	FA50	127
N129JF	FA20	113
N129JR	LJ60	093
N129K	WW24	70
N129KH	SBRL	306-44
N129KJ	F900	184
N129LJ	CL30	20029
N129LT	**C550**	**550-0821**
N129MC	**C560**	**0120**
N129MC	BE40	RK-129
N129ME	LJ24	357
(N129ME)	WW24	149
N129MH	GLF4	1517
N129MH	**GLF4**	**4232**
N129MS	SBRL	380-33
N129NS	**GLF4**	**1281**
N129PB	**C550**	**550-0973**
N129PJ	C560	0235
N129PJ	C650	0044
N129RH	CL61	5129
N129RP	**C525**	**0173**
N129SG	C52A	0129
N129SP	LJ55	058
N129TC	C550	145
(N129TC)	C650	0061
N129TF	CL61	5129
N129TK	**LJ35**	**253**
N129TS	C550	346
N129TS	LJ35	253
N129WA	GLF2	9/33
N129WH	BE40	RK-129
N129ZM	C500	435
N130A	FA50	54
N130A	GLF2	34
N130A	GLF3	322
N130AB	HS25	HA-0036
(N130AE)	HS25	257089
(N130AL)	C500	033
N130AP	HS25	257108
N130B	FA10	28
N130B	FA20	88
N130B	GLF4	1013
(N130B)	GLF4	1024
N130BA	HS25	257045
N130BB	HS25	257063
N130BC	HS25	257065
N130BD	HS25	257068
N130BE	HS25	257069
N130BF	HS25	257071
N130BG	HS25	257060
N130BH	HS25	257059
N130BK	HS25	257084
N130BL	HS25	257089
(N130BL)	HS25	257087
N130CC	C555	0130
N130CE	**C500**	**130**
N130CH	CL30	20088
(N130CH)	CL30	20249
N130CK	LJ25	038
N130CS	C525	0490
N130CV	C560	0130
N130DJ	EA50	000023
N130DS	FA10	218
N130DT	**BE40**	**RK-387**
N130DW	C500	187
N130EC	**E50P**	**50000121**
N130F	FA20	379
N130F	LJ35	044
N130FJ	FA10	226
N130FJ	FA10	44
N130FJ	FA10	73
N130FJ	FA50	143
N130FX	LJ31	172
N130G	C500	130
N130GA	GLF4	4130
N130GA	GLF5	5130
N130GV	**GLF5**	**630**
N130J	LJ24	130
N130JS	C500	606
N130K	FA50	70
N130K	GLF2	190
N130LC	HS25	258228
N130LM	**C525**	**0214**
(N130LW)	JSTR	5048
N130MH	GLF4	1517
N130MH	HS25	257053
(N130MH)	C525	0490
N130MR	C525	0097
(N130MV)	FA20	130
N130MW	HFB3	1032
N130MW	HFB3	1033
N130NM	C525	0214
N130QS	GLEX	9498
N130QS	BE40	RK-441
N130RC	WW24	34
(N130RK)	C650	0130
N130RS	LJ24	138
N130SP	C500	364
N130TA	LJ35	174
N130TC	C550	333
(N130TJ)	FA20	130
N130TM	GLF5	660
N130TS	C650	0130
N130TS	HS25	257130
(N130WB)	GLF4	1307
N130WC	C560	0277
(N130WC)	C560	0356
N130WE	**C56X**	**6196**
N130WW	**BE40**	**RK-136**
N130YB	HS25	257120
N130YB	**HS25**	**258590**
N131A	**F2EX**	**40**
N131AG	F2EX	131
N131AJ	**LJ35**	**381**
N131AP	BE40	RJ-10
N131AR	LJ31	139
N131AR	LJ31	208
N131BH	SBRL	282-18
N131BR	**LJ31**	**074**
N131BV	**E50P**	**50000268**
N131CA	LJ24	277
(N131CJ)	C525	0031
N131CV	C560	0131
N131CX	C750	0131
N131DA	ASTR	029
N131DA	LJ31	136
N131DB	FA20	339
N131DJ	EA50	000033
N131EL	JSTR	5058/4
(N131EL)	C550	463
N131EP	**F2TH**	**10**
N131ET	C550	131
N131FJ	F900	131
N131FJ	FA10	45
N131FJ	FA50	146
N131FJ	FA50	220
N131FX	LJ31	175
N131G	LJ25	170
N131GA	C550	432
N131GA	G280	2031
N131GA	GLF4	4111
N131GA	GLF5	5231
N131GA	GLF5	5331
N131GG	**LJ31**	**113**
N131GL	LJ25	145
N131GM	**C680**	**0093**
N131GM	LJ31	164
N131GR	**LJ31**	**068**
N131JA	FA20	282
N131JR	HS25	HA-0070
N131JR	SBRL	306-131
N131JX	**LJ45**	**450**
N131KJ	**CL65**	**5782**
N131LA	HS25	25226
N131LJ	CL30	20031
N131LJ	LJ31	063
N131LK	**GLF5**	**5266**
N131MA	LJ24	289
N131MJ	**C52B**	**0097**
N131ML	E50P	50000006
N131MS	LJ25	022
N131MS	SBRL	380-22
N131MS	SBRL	380-29
N131MV	**FA20**	**31**
N131NA	LJ31	038
N131PG	**C650**	**0126**
N131PT	LJ31	046
N131QS	BE40	RK-431
N131RG	C525	0159
N131RR	**C560**	**0366**
N131RX	**LJ45**	**207**
N131SB	C500	256
(N131SE)	SBRL	306-131
(N131SV)	C680	0131
N131SW	GLF4	1294

N131SY	C500	424
N131TA	LJ31	041
N131TR	LJ60	216
N131TT	LJ31	049
N131VP	C56X	5131
N131WC	C560	0293
N131WT	FA50	28
N132AH	**C525**	**0132**
N132AP	FA20	312
N132BP	C500	132
N132CE	**C650**	**7061**
N132CJ	C52A	0003
N132CS	C525	0497
N132CS	C525	0515
N132DA	F2TH	111
N132DB	SBRL	380-48
N132DJ	EA50	000034
N132EL	LJ55	061
N132EP	FA20	463
N132FJ	F2TH	32
N132FJ	F900	132
N132FJ	FA10	47
N132FJ	FA50	142
N132FJ	FA50	223
N132FP	**GLF2**	**153**
N132FX	LJ31	177
N132GA	MU30	A032SA
N132GL	LJ25	132
N132GS	**CS55**	**0108**
N132JA	FA20	284
N132JC	GALX	039
N132LA	**WW24**	**133**
N132LF	C550	550-0855
N132LJ	**LJ36**	**032**
N132LJ	LJ45	132
N132MA	LJ24	306
(N132MA)	LJ25	052
N132MS	SBRL	380-22
N132MS	SBRL	380-29
(N132MS)	FA50	164
N132MT	C550	550-1080
N132MW	HFB3	1032
N132MW	HFB3	1033
N132PH	**LJ31**	**242**
N132QS	BE40	RK-427
N132RL	HS25	25141
(N132RP)	C525	0132
N132SD	**GLF5**	**537**
N132SV	C680	0032
N132SV	C680	0132
(N132TP)	LJ55	098
N132WC	CS55	0051
(N132WC)	C650	7079
N132WE	BE40	RK-90
N132XP	HS25	HA-0132
N133AP	FA20	345
N133AV	C550	550-0847
(N133AV)	C525	0180
N133B	PRM1	RB-68
N133BA	GALX	030
N133BC	C550	329
N133BG	LJ31	179
N133BL	LJ24	133
N133BP	BE40	RK-133
N133CC	C500	133
N133CJ	C52C	0133
N133CM	PRM1	RB-180
N133CM	PRM1	RB-199
N133CQ	PRM1	RB-180
N133CS	C525	0502
N133DF	LJ24	133
N133DM	C500	514
N133EJ	**LJ35**	**133**
N133EP	FA10	131
N133FJ	FA10	48
N133FJ	FA10	50
N133FJ	FA20	133
N133FJ	FA50	144
N133FJ	FA50	224
N133FX	LJ31	179
N133GJ	LJ35	133
N133GL	**C525**	**0001**
N133GL	LJ24	317
N133JA	FA20	290
N133JA	**FA50**	**268**
N133JC	WW24	133
N133JF	LJ25	264
N133JM	**C500**	**028**
N133KS	**HS25**	**258697**
N133KT	C525	0133
N133LE	C650	0133
N133LH	C650	0133
N133LJ	LJ60	133
N133MA	LJ25	052
N133ME	WW24	50
N133MR	LJ25	210
(N133N)	C500	021
N133NM	FA50	187
N133QS	BE40	RK-449
N133RC	C52C	0147
N133RC	MU30	A016SA
N133RL	**F2EX**	**299**
N133RL	F2EX	50
N133SC	**C500**	**518**
N133SN	ASTR	153
N133SR	LJ60	147
(N133SU)	LJ55	132
N133TE	EA50	000033
N133TF	**C510**	**0191**
N133TJ	**C525**	**0809**
N133TW	LJ24	148
N133VP	CS55	0133
N133W	LJ24	021
N133WA	C550	390
N133WB	LJ55	132
(N133WC)	C560	0352
(N133WC)	C650	7082
N133XL	**C56X**	**6133**
N134AP	FA50	48
N134AX	GALX	034
N134BJ	BE40	RK-134
N134BR	GLF4	1139
N134CC	C500	134
N134CG	LJ31	195
N134CJ	FA20	239
N134CM	**HS25**	**258503**
N134CM	BE40	RK-144
N134DJ	EA50	000035
N134FA	BE40	RK-34
N134FJ	F900	134
N134FJ	FA10	46
N134FJ	FA50	134
N134FJ	FA50	148
N134FJ	FA50	225
N134FM	**C56X**	**5604**
N134FX	LJ31	181
N134FX	LJ31	195
N134GB	CS55	0089
N134GL	LJ35	036
N134JA	FA20	463
N134JJ	SBRL	282-134
N134LJ	LJ31	134
N134LJ	LJ60	134
N134M	C650	0109
(N134MJ)	C650	0109
N134N	WW24	134
N134NW	**HS25**	**257134**
N134PA	FA20	364
N134QS	CS55	0134
N134RG	MU30	A037SA
(N134RT)	HS25	257134
(N134RV)	ASTR	047
N134SW	C56X	5066
N134SW	**PRM1**	**RB-81**
N134TE	EA50	000034
N134VS	**CL60**	**1034**
N134WE	LJ25	222
N134WF	BE40	RK-134
N134WM	**CL64**	**5340**
(N135AB)	LJ35	414
N135AC	LJ35	188
N135AF	C650	0135
N135AG	**LJ35**	**132**
N135AJ	**LJ35**	**036**
N135AV	LJ35	201
N135BC	C500	135
N135BC	C550	269
N135BC	C560	0198
N135BC	CL61	5080
N135BC	**E55P**	**50500017**
N135BD	CL61	5080
N135BJ	**BE40**	**RK-135**
N135BK	C500	168
N135BP	GALX	016
N135CC	C500	135
N135CC	C550	135
N135CG	**LJ45**	**354**
N135CK	HS25	25266
(N135CK)	LJ35	159
N135CP	GLF2	200
N135CS	C525	0520
N135DA	**LJ35**	**405**
N135DE	**LJ35**	**667**
N135DJ	EA50	000036
N135ET	C56X	5135
N135FA	**LJ35**	**067**
N135FJ	FA10	224
N135FJ	FA10	43
N135FJ	FA50	149
N135FT	**GALX**	**155**
N135GA	MU30	A035SA
N135GJ	LJ35	135
N135GL	LJ35	028
N135GL	**LJ55**	**012**
N135HC	C650	0158
N135HC	C650	7117
N135J	LJ35	097
N135JW	C500	140
N135JW	LJ35	144
N135LJ	LJ60	135
N135LR	**LJ55**	**068**
N135MA	C500	168
N135MB	LJ35	343
N135MM	C525	0038
N135MW	LJ35	650
N135PG	LJ35	491
N135PT	LJ35	509
(N135RG)	GLF5	5183
N135RJ	LJ35	443
N135RU	**C525**	**0870**
N135SH	**LJ35**	**335**
N135ST	LJ35	169
N135TE	EA50	000035
N135TP	LJ35	462
N135TX	LJ35	025
N135UT	LJ35	327
N135WB	LJ35	084
N135WC	**C560**	**0261**
N135WE	LJ35	240
(N135WJ)	GLF2	256
N136BC	C550	269
N136BX	LJ31	196
(N136CC)	C500	136
(N136CV)	C560	0136
N136DH	HS25	25036
N136DH	**LJ36**	**036**
N136DJ	EA50	000037
N136EA	**EA50**	**000136**
N136F	FA20	380
N136FJ	FA10	49
N136FJ	FA50	136
N136FJ	FA50	150
N136FT	GALX	155
N136FX	LJ31	182
N136FX	LJ31	196
N136GL	LJ35	016
N136JD	**C560**	**0293**
N136JP	**LJ35**	**359**
N136K	WW24	103
N136LJ	LJ60	136
(N136LJ)	LJ45	136
N136LK	HS25	25116
N136MA	JSTR	5134/50
N136MA	LJ45	046
N136MC	C510	0321
N136MV	**FA50**	**311**
N136MW	HFB3	1036
N136QS	BE40	RK-414
N136SA	C500	136
N136ST	LJ36	049
N136TE	**EA50**	**000036**
N136TN	HS25	257136
(N136WC)	C650	7085
N136WE	LJ35	201
N136XP	HS25	258736
N136ZC	GLF4	1049
N136ZC	**GLF5**	**667**
N137AL	C525	0002
N137BB	**GLEX**	**9181**
N137BC	LJ25	024
N137BG	**C52B**	**0032**
N137BR	**LJ40**	**2068**
N137BW	**C56X**	**5203**
N137CC	C500	137
N137CF	C550	152
N137CL	CL61	5137
N137EM	F2EX	137
N137FA	C560	0405
N137FA	**FA50**	**137**
N137FJ	F900	136
N137FJ	FA10	51
N137FJ	FA50	152
(N137FP)	CL60	1072
N137FX	LJ31	186
N137FX	LJ31	201
N137GA	G280	2037
N137GJ	**GLF2**	**25**
N137GK	C500	576
N137GL	LJ25	237
N137JC	**C560**	**0137**
N137JL	LJ24	301
N137JQ	**C52C**	**0137**
N137K	LJ25	295
N137LA	C560	0274
N137LA	HS25	258697
N137LJ	LJ40	2137
(N137LR)	FA50	338
(N137LX)	C560	0274
N137M	C650	0061
N137M	C650	0163
N137MB	CL61	5146
N137MM	BE40	RJ-35
(N137MR)	C650	0163
N137PA	C550	658
N137RH	**LJ60**	**046**
N137RP	HS25	259021
N137RS	LJ35	183
N137S	C650	0005
N137SF	**F9EX**	**110**
N137TA	FA20	487
N137TN	C56X	5544
(N137TS)	LJ35	183
N137WB	**GALX**	**137**
N137WC	C500	305
N137WH	C680	0084
(N137WK)	HS25	257035
N137WR	HS25	257035
N137WS	**GLF4**	**1307**
N137X	C650	0061
N137ZM	**GLEX**	**9275**
N138A	C750	0021
N138AV	FA50	138
N138AX	LJ45	138
N138BF	SJ30	002
N138BG	**C680**	**0135**
N138BT	FA7X	48
N138CA	**C550**	**550-0900**
N138CC	CL61	5138
N138CH	**CL30**	**20249**
N138CS	C525	0522
N138DM	**CL65**	**5702**
N138DM	FA10	181
N138DM	MU30	A018SA
N138E	FA20	382
N138E	FA50	57
(N138EC)	C560	0421
N138F	F900	174
N138F	FA20	382
N138F	FA50	57
N138FA	F900	174
N138FJ	**F2TH**	**222**
N138FJ	FA10	52
N138FJ	FA20	369
N138FJ	FA50	153
N138FN	FA20	369
N138FX	LJ31	189
N138FX	LJ31	208
N138FX	LJ31	226
N138FY	LJ31	208
N138GA	G280	2038
N138GA	GALX	146
N138GA	GLF4	4138
N138GL	**GLF5**	**5476**
N138GL	LJ36	007
N138GT	C52A	0512
N138HB	**C500**	**279**
N138HW	**C56X**	**5138**
N138J	C550	131
N138JB	LJ25	075
N138LJ	LJ31	138
N138M	C650	0066
N138M	C650	0164
N138M	FA50	274
(N138MM)	F2TH	138
N138MR	C650	0164
N138NA	LJ35	138
N138NW	FA50	138
N138QS	CS55	0138
N138QS	BE40	RK-492
N138RC	MU30	A047SA
N138SA	**C500**	**138**
N138SJ	**PRM1**	**RB-138**
N138SP	**C750**	**0138**
N138SP	LJ60	147
N138V	C650	0066
N138WE	LJ35	472
N138XP	HS25	258738
N139AL	F900	35
N139CD	CL61	5139
N139CF	GLF2	139/11
N139CJ	**C52B**	**0139**
N139DD	FA10	6
N139DJ	EA50	000054
N139DM	MU30	A039SA
(N139EC)	C560	0425
N139EX	F9EX	139
N139F	FA20	385
N139FJ	**C500**	**139**
N139FJ	F900	137
N139FJ	FA10	53
N139FJ	FA50	154
N139FX	LJ31	209
N139FY	LJ31	209
N139GA	G280	2039
N139GA	GALX	139
N139GA	GALX	199
N139GL	LJ36	012
N139HF	GALX	028
N139J	LJ25	098
N139JA	C550	550-1039
N139LJ	CL30	20039
N139LJ	LJ31	139
N139M	C650	0149
N139M	HS25	258330
N139MY	**C650**	**0072**
N139N	C650	0149
N139QS	BE40	RK-483
N139RN	**C550**	**550-0886**
N139SK	LJ55	082
N139ST	LJ55	139
N139WC	C560	0307
(N139WC)	C650	7087
N139XX	LJ60	139
N140AE	GLEX	9140
N140AK	HS25	25104
N140AK	MU30	A026SA
N140C	HS25	25185
N140CA	LJ24	193
N140CA	LJ25	140
N140CC	C500	140
N140CH	CL61	5047
N140CH	GLF2	77
(N140CJ)	LJ60	238
N140DA	**C52A**	**0140**
N140DA	C550	110
N140DR	ASTR	046
N140DR	C550	271
N140DR	WW24	242
(N140DV)	C550	393
N140EA	EA50	000210
N140EC	C560	0428
N140EP	LJ40	2121
N140EX	LJ24	117
N140FJ	F900	139
N140FJ	**F900**	**140**
N140FJ	FA10	54
N140FJ	FA50	156
N140FM	**BE40**	**RK-401**
N140GB	HS25	258594
N140GB	BE40	RK-185
N140GC	LJ25	225
(N140GH)	GALX	014
N140H	C500	274
N140HM	**LJ40**	**2103**
N140JA	SBRL	306-78
N140JC	LJ60	106
N140JS	HS25	25139
N140KR	GALX	051
N140LF	HS25	25140
N140LJ	LJ31	140
N140LJ	LJ40	2044
N140LJ	LJ60	140
N140MD	C550	647
N140MM	SBRL	282-8
N140NE	**EA50**	**000018**
N140QS	BE40	RK-406
N140RC	LJ24	048
N140RF	SBRL	282-67
N140RT	FA50	261
N140TF	C550	550-1015
N140TS	**C650**	**0141**
N140U	**C560**	**0024**
N140V	C550	393
N140VJ	WW24	435
N140WC	C500	498
N140WC	C560	0325
N140WH	**C650**	**0195**
N140WW	LJ40	2049
N141AB	C550	483
N141AB	C550	550-1044
N141AL	**HS25**	**257152**
N141AQ	**C560**	**0141**
N141BG	C510	0141
N141CC	C500	141
N141CP	GLF4	1265
N141DA	C550	265
N141DJ	EA50	000055
N141DL	CL64	5394
N141DP	C500	120
N141DR	C500	120
N141DR	**BE40**	**RK-184**
N141EA	**EA50**	**000223**
N141EX	F9EX	141
N141FJ	F900	141
N141FJ	FA10	55
N141FJ	FA50	157
N141FM	LJ55	041
N141GS	GLF2	245/30
N141H	MU30	A054SA
N141H	SBRL	282-60
(N141HB)	BE40	RK-568
N141HC	GLF5	616
N141HJ	HDJT	42000021
N141HL	C550	550-0803
N141JA	SBRL	306-51
N141JC	**C550**	**373**
N141JF	GLF2	106
(N141JF)	FA20	196
N141JL	HS25	25187
N141JV	C52A	0141
N141LB	WW24	202
N141LJ	CL30	20041
N141LJ	LJ60	141
N141LM	JSTR	5083/49
N141M	C500	403
N141M	C650	0147
(N141MB)	LJ60	120
N141MH	GLF3	378
N141MR	**HS25**	**258141**
N141PB	SBRL	465-4
N141PJ	LJ24	141
N141QS	**GLEX**	**9479**
N141QS	BE40	RK-498
N141RD	**CL60**	**1041**
N141SA	**C500**	**185**
N141SG	C500	330
N141SL	**SBRL**	**306-141**
N141SM	LJ55	019
N141TC	JSTR	5050/34
N141TS	CL60	1041
N142AA	**C56X**	**5281**
N142AB	C650	0042
(N142AL)	C500	671
N142B	C650	0190
N142B	CL61	5062
N142B	HS25	25101
N142BJ	BE40	RK-142
N142CC	C500	142
N142CC	C650	0142
N142CJ	C52A	0004
N142DA	**C500**	**356**
N142DJ	EA50	000056
N142EA	C525	0401
N142EA	EA50	000218
N142EX	F9EX	142
N142FJ	C500	524
N142FJ	F900	142
N142FJ	FA10	57
N142FJ	FA50	158
N142FJ	FA7X	142
N142GA	C550	718
N142GA	C560	0042
N142GA	GLF5	5421
N142GA	GLF6	6142
N142GT	LJ31	064

N142GZ	**LEG5**	**55000008**
N142HC	**GLEX**	**9650**
N142HC	GLF4	1489
N142HC	GLF4	4007
N142HC	GLF4	4288
N142HC	LJ45	141
(N142HC)	LJ25	142
N142HH	PRM1	RB-41
N142HQ	GLF4	1489
N142HQ	GLF4	4007
N142HQ	**GLF4**	**4288**
N142HQ	LJ45	141
(N142JF)	FA20	196
N142LG	LJ35	216
N142LJ	LJ31	142
N142LL	CL61	5176
N142LM	LJ35	280
N142NW	GLF4	1142
N142QS	**GLEX**	**9485**
N142QS	BE40	RK-432
N142RP	**CL61**	**5024**
N142TJ	C550	353
N142TL	**E50P**	**50000177**
N142V	FA10	57
N143AA	LJ60	143
N143AB	C650	0120
N143BL	**C550**	**131**
N143BP	C550	550-1072
N143BP	C555	0085
(N143CA)	LJ60	055
N143CC	C500	143
N143CK	**LJ25**	**143**
N143CM	**PRM1**	**RB-114**
N143CP	HS25	25224
N143DA	C550	198
N143DH	C56X	5514
N143DL	F9EX	6
N143DZ	**SBRL**	**306-142**
N143EA	EA50	000266
N143EP	C500	357
N143FA	LJ60	143
N143FJ	FA10	58
N143FJ	FA50	160
N143FS	ASTR	143
N143G	GLF2	17
N143G	GLF5	5060
N143GA	GALX	143
N143GB	LJ24	233
N143HM	**BE40**	**RK-205**
N143J	LJ25	033
N143JT	**C52B**	**0181**
(N143JW)	LJ36	043
N143KB	**GLEX**	**9108**
N143KS	GLF4	1364
N143LG	LJ35	426
N143LJ	CL30	20043
N143LJ	**LJ55**	**143**
N143LP	**LJ60**	**090**
N143PL	C650	0058
N143QS	C555	0143
N143QS	**GLEX**	**9499**
(N143RC)	C650	0036
N143RL	**HA4T**	**RC-25**
N143RL	HS25	258774
(N143RL)	HS25	258767
N143RW	C550	346
N143SC	T143	001
N143TW	**C550**	**100**
N143V	GLF2	17
N143WR	C650	0143
(N144AB)	C500	464
N144AD	FA50	112
N144AD	FA7X	73
N144AL	**C52B**	**0044**
N144AR	C500	464
N144AW	BE40	RK-19
(N144AW)	HS25	258011
N144BG	CL61	5033
N144BS	CL61	5033
N144BS	**F900**	**200**
N144CA	**C650**	**7004**
N144CP	LJ24	185
N144DJ	HS25	257067
N144EA	EA50	000246
N144EM	C52A	0120
N144EX	F9EX	144
N144FC	LJ25	258
(N144FE)	FA20	46
N144FH	**F900**	**189**
N144FJ	F900	144
N144FJ	FA10	59
N144FJ	FA50	161
N144GA	**C550**	**065**
N144GX	ASTR	144
(N144HE)	FA10	144
N144HM	HS25	258431
(N144JC)	WW24	94
N144JE	**GALX**	**113**
N144JP	C500	281
N144JS	**BE40**	**RK-145**
N144KK	GALX	036
N144KK	GLF4	1435
N144KK	GLF5	5055
N144KK	GLF5	559
N144KK	GLF5	669
N144LG	LJ35	500
N144LJ	LJ31	144
N144LT	LJ55	144
N144MH	C650	7059
N144MH	**CL61**	**5135**
N144PA	FA50	44
N144PA	HS25	25224
(N144PA)	LJ24	181
N144PK	GLF3	447
N144PK	**GLF4**	**1210**
N144ST	GLF2	174
N144ST	**PRM1**	**RB-74**
N144SX	CL61	3066
N144UV	**HS25**	**HA-0177**
N144WB	LJ35	444
(N144WC)	LJ24	020
N144X	LJ24	100
N144XL	**C56X**	**6144**
N144XP	BE40	RK-444
N144YD	**C52A**	**0144**
N144Z	**C550**	**550-0926**
N145AJ	C500	425
N145AJ	WW24	145
N145AM	**LJ35**	**078**
N145AP	**LJ45**	**300**
N145AR	**LJ45**	**203**
N145AS	ASTR	049
N145BL	C680	0045
N145BW	WW24	145
N145CC	C500	145
N145CG	LJ45	107
(N145CG)	LJ45	297
N145CJ	C525	0145
N145CM	C500	224
N145CM	**LJ45**	**297**
(N145CM)	LJ45	107
N145CX	C750	0145
N145DF	C500	425
N145DF	C555	0018
N145DJ	EA50	000057
N145DL	CL64	5367
N145EA	**EA50**	**000145**
N145FC	C500	145
(N145FE)	FA20	50
N145FJ	FA10	60
N145FJ	FA50	162
N145G	SBRL	282-65
N145GJ	LJ35	145
N145GL	**HS25**	**25230**
N145GM	LJ45	081
N145GM	LJ45	376
N145GP	LJ45	231
N145GR	LJ45	376
N145GS	LJ45	143
N145HC	LJ45	231
N145JF	**PRM1**	**RB-159**
N145JN	LJ24	143
N145JN	LJ25	016
N145JP	LJ45	280
N145K	LJ45	071
N145K	**LJ45**	**268**
N145KC	LJ45	051
N145KK	**C560**	**0276**
N145KL	LJ45	071
N145LJ	CL30	20045
N145LJ	CL61	5145
N145LJ	LJ31	145
N145LJ	LJ60	145
N145LR	**LJ45**	**119**
N145MC	LJ45	155
(N145MC)	LJ45	040
N145MG	**GLF5**	**5004**
N145MK	C560	0112
N145MN	LJ45	125
N145MW	LJ45	125
N145MW	**LJ45**	**400**
N145PJ	**LJ45**	**383**
N145PK	**C56X**	**5809**
N145QS	**GLEX**	**9598**
N145QS	BE40	RK-421
N145RG	**LJ45**	**068**
N145SB	LJ45	142
(N145SD)	PRM1	RB-47
N145SF	C52A	0445
N145SH	LJ25	145
N145SM	C56X	5082
N145ST	CL61	5104
N145ST	GLF2	22
N145ST	GLF4	1067
N145ST	LJ45	024
N145TA	**C500**	**145**
N145VG	**LJ45**	**394**
N145VP	C555	0145
N145W	F900	40
N145W	FA50	31
N145WC	BE40	RK-421
N145WF	C680	0145
N145WF	FA50	31
N145XL	**LJ45**	**106**
N145XR	LJ45	251
N146AS	**FA50**	**325**
N146BA	CL64	5327
(N146BE)	C500	160
N146BF	C500	160
N146BF	WW24	287
(N146BJ)	SBRL	306-146
N146CF	FA20	488
N146CJ	C52C	0146
N146CT	C550	550-0980
N146DJ	EA50	000058
N146DJ	HS25	258781
N146EX	**EA50**	**000146**
(N146EC)	C560	0429
N146EP	C510	0306
N146EP	C56X	5224
N146EX	**F9EX**	**146**
(N146FE)	FA20	20
N146FJ	F900	146
N146FJ	FA10	62
N146FJ	FA50	163
N146GA	GALX	246
N146GA	GLF4	4146
N146GA	GLF5	5446
N146GA	MU30	A044SA
(N146GA)	MU30	A046SA
N146HA	**EA50**	**550-0278**
N146J	WW24	313
N146JB	BE40	RJ-46
N146JC	C500	160
N146JE	**PRM1**	**RB-206**
N146JF	**HS25**	**HA-0160**
N146JF	PRM1	RB-159
N146JF	PRM1	RB-206
N146LJ	LJ25	146
N146MJ	LJ36	046
(N146PA)	LJ55	085
N146QS	**GLEX**	**9615**
N146QS	BE40	RK-448
N146TA	BE40	RK-146
N146XL	**LJ45**	**187**
N146XP	HS25	HA-0146
N147A	**WW24**	**294**
N147AG	CL30	20229
N147BJ	**BE40**	**RK-147**
N147BP	LJ25	147
N147CA	LJ25	221
N147CC	LJ60	012
N147CC	BE40	RJ-38
N147CC	BE40	RK-4
N147CF	SBRL	282-94
N147CG	BE40	RK-4
N147CJ	**F2EX**	**147**
N147CK	LJ24	147
N147CX	C750	0147
N147DA	C500	009
N147DA	MU30	A038SA
N147DB	C500	009
N147DJ	EA50	000059
N147EA	**EA50**	**000251**
(N147FE)	FA20	108/430
N147FJ	F900	147
N147FJ	FA10	63
N147FJ	FA7X	147
N147FM	**PRM1**	**RB-147**
N147G	**F2EX**	**122**
N147G	FA10	214
N147GA	GLF5	5447
N147GB	**FA50**	**204**
N147GX	**FA10**	**214**
N147HH	CL61	5123
N147JK	WW24	147
N147K	LJ35	462
N147KH	LJ24	147
N147KN	EA50	000002
N147MR	GLF3	455
N147PS	C550	483
N147PS	C650	0119
N147QS	**GLEX**	**9632**
N147QS	BE40	RK-436
N147RJ	C560	0147
(N147RP)	C550	428
N147SB	C560	0380
N147SC	C500	077
N147SW	**ASTR**	**147**
N147TA	C650	0119
N147TA	FA20	506
N147TW	**LJ25**	**023**
N147VC	C560	0105
N147VC	C560	0285
N147WC	MU30	A038SA
N147WE	**C52A**	**0362**
N147WS	C500	009
N147X	FA20	185/467
N147X	FA20	45
N147X	GLF3	336
N147X	**GLF4**	**1263**
N147XP	HS25	HA-0147
N148C	C650	0028
N148C	LJ31	098
N148CG	F2TH	41
N148CJ	C525	0148
N148CJ	C52B	0148
N148DJ	EA50	000061
N148DR	C550	271
N148E	WW24	22
N148EA	C500	542
(N148EC)	C560	0434
N148ED	C500	542
N148FB	**C52A**	**0148**
(N148FE)	FA20	151
N148FJ	**F900**	**148**
N148FJ	FA10	64
N148GA	GLF5	5448
N148GB	**BE40**	**RK-185**
N148H	**WW24**	**206**
N148J	LJ24	291
N148J	MU30	A033SA
N148JB	C500	517
N148JP	SBRL	306-90
N148JS	C500	517
N148JW	LJ25	357
N148KB	GALX	174
N148LG	**EA50**	**000148**
N148LJ	LJ31	148
N148LJ	LJ45	148
N148M	FA50	270
N148MC	FA20	428
N148MC	**GALX**	**175**
N148N	C650	0147
N148PE	JSTR	5002
N148QS	**GLEX**	**9648**
N148TW	**FA20**	**148**
N148V	**GLF2**	**54/36**
N148WC	FA20	148
N148X	LJ35	299
N148XP	HS25	HA-0148
N149BL	**FA10**	**149**
(N149BP)	WW24	149
N149C	C650	0070
(N149DG)	FA10	3
N149EA	**EA50**	**000149**
(N149EC)	C560	0437
N149F	FA20	386
(N149FE)	FA20	132
N149FJ	FA10	65
N149GK	**E50P**	**50000087**
N149GU	GLF4	1149
N149HC	**C550**	**550-0898**
N149HP	FA10	154
N149J	LJ25	149
N149JS	**C680**	**0281**
N149JW	GLF2	63
N149LJ	LJ60	149
N149LP	**GLEX**	**9019**
(N149LP)	ASTR	070
N149MC	FA20	429
N149MD	FA50	149
N149PJ	C500	149
N149QS	C555	0149
N149QS	BE40	RK-473
N149SB	**HS25**	**258654**
N149SB	BE40	RK-285
N149SF	WW24	149
(N149SF)	WW24	74
N149TA	BE40	RK-149
N149TD	ASTR	093
N149TJ	FA10	9
N149V	F2TH	53
N149VB	**F2TH**	**53**
N149VB	GLEX	9098
N149VB	HS25	258142
N149VG	C560	0105
N149VP	HS25	258142
N149WC	C650	7087
N149WW	**C52B**	**0175**
N149XP	HS25	HA-0149
N150AB	LJ24	228
N150AG	LJ24	074
N150BB	**CL64**	**5470**
N150BC	F2TH	67
N150BC	**FA7X**	**103**
N150BG	FA50	13
N150BL	**C56X**	**5143**
N150BP	FA50	82
N150BV	C525	0320
N150BX	LJ60	150
N150CA	HS25	257121
N150CA	MU30	A023SA
N150CC	C500	150
N150CG	FA20	8
N150CJ	C555	0150
N150CK	**LJ25**	**150**
N150CM	GLF4	1284
N150CM	WW24	71
N150CT	ASTR	152
N150CT	**G150**	**208**
N150CT	WW24	71
N150DJ	EA50	000062
N150DM	C550	452
(N150ES)	GLEX	9108
N150EX	**WW24**	**262**
N150F	C650	0150
(N150FE)	FA20	84
N150FJ	F2EX	150
N150FJ	F900	150
N150FJ	FA10	66
N150GA	G150	202
N150GA	G150	238
N150GA	**G150**	**252**
N150GA	G150	286
(N150GA)	G150	311
N150GD	G150	217
N150GD	G150	256
N150GD	G150	298
N150GD	**G150**	**311**
N150GF	**HS25**	**258823**
N150GP	**C560**	**0127**
N150GV	**G150**	**201**
N150GV	G150	260
(N150GV)	G150	263
N150GX	GLF3	318
N150GX	GLF4	1154
N150GX	GLF4	1197
N150HE	C550	129
N150HM	**G150**	**260**
N150HN	SBRL	465-42
N150HR	C550	129
N150HR	WW24	170
N150HR	WW24	71
N150JP	C650	7010
N150JP	FA50	44
N150JT	FA50	40
N150JT	FA50	53
N150K	FA50	108
N150KM	**G150**	**206**
N150LR	**HS25**	**259050**
N150MH	CL61	3021
N150MJ	C52B	0280
N150MJ	**FA50**	**121**
N150MS	**LJ55**	**049**
N150NC	HS25	258293
N150NE	**EA50**	**550-1002**
N150NE	LJ55	123
(N150NW)	FA50	13
N150PG	**G150**	**305**
N150PG	GLF4	1154
N150PU	G150	225
N150QS	**GLEX**	**9657**
N150QX	GLF3	318
N150RD	C550	158
(N150RH)	HS25	257083
N150RJ	**FA50**	**324**
N150RK	GLF3	318
N150RM	**C500**	**451**
N150RS	LJ25	162
N150RT	G150	201
N150S	C560	0476
N150SA	HS25	25265
N150SB	**HS25**	**258197**
N150TF	BE40	RK-240
(N150TF)	BE40	RK-9
N150TJ	C500	422
N150TT	**C500**	**176**
N150TX	**FA50**	**13**
N150UC	FA50	86
N150WC	C56X	5150
N150WC	FA50	47
N150WL	LJ24	011
N150WW	LJ25	147
N150YB	HS25	257116
N151A	GLF4	1026
N151AE	F2TH	39
N151AE	HS25	257089
N151AG	LJ24	137
N151AG	LJ24	298
N151AS	C500	183
N151CC	C500	151
N151CC	CL61	5167
N151CG	FA20	15
N151CM	**F2TH**	**151**
N151CR	WW24	33
N151CS	C525	0529
(N151DC)	FA10	181
N151DD	C555	0001
N151DR	**C650**	**0147**
(N151EC)	C560	0441
N151EW	**C525**	**0529**
N151EX	F2EX	151
N151FD	C550	550-1087
N151FJ	FA10	67
N151G	GLF4	1150
N151GA	G280	2051
N151GA	GLF4	4251
N151GR	F2TH	151
N151GS	FA10	181
N151GX	GLF4	1154
N151JC	C550	477
N151KD	C52B	0268
N151KD	PRM1	RB-16
N151KV	C56X	5320
N151MZ	GLF3	426
N151NS	FA7X	151
N151PJ	LJ55	074
(N151PR)	C550	191
N151PW	**G150**	**310**
N151Q	C555	0151
N151QS	C555	0151
N151QS	BE40	RK-422
N151SD	GLF2	81
N151SD	**GLF4**	**1249**
N151SG	HS25	25035
N151SP	**C500**	**384**
N151SP	MU30	A046SA
(N151SR)	CL60	1034
N151ST	GLF4	1151
N151TB	SBRL	380-11
N151TC	HS25	258211
N151TM	C550	550-1063
(N151TT)	C525	0151
N151VA	LJ40	2034
N151VP	C560	0351
N151WC	FA10	163
N151WW	LJ24	170
N151XL	**C56X**	**6151**
N151YD	**C680**	**0197**
N152A	GLF4	1036
N152AE	HS25	257164
N152AG	LJ24	068
N152CC	C500	152
N152CS	C525	0539

N152CZ	C52C	0152
N152DJ	EA50	000071
N152FJ	FA10	68
N152FJ	**FA50**	**152**
N152GA	C550	006
N152GA	GALX	152
N152GA	GLF4	4152
N152GA	GLF5	5352
N152GS	JSTR	5061/48
N152JC	C550	433
N152JH	C560	0442
N152JH	**C560**	**0615**
(N152JQ)	C550	433
N152KB	GLF4	1149
N152KC	C525	0152
N152KV	**C525**	**0152**
N152NS	HS25	258191
N152QS	BE40	RK-440
N152RG	GLF2	45
N152RJ	BE40	RK-421
N152SM	CL60	1077
N152SV	C680	0152
N152SV	BE40	RK-152
N152TJ	LJ35	243
N152TS	CL60	1052
N152TS	GLF4	1052
N152UT	LJ40	2101
N152VP	C550	550-1052
(N152VP)	C650	0152
N152WC	C560	0324
N152WJ	FA10	152
N152WR	C525	0520
N153AG	LJ24	058
N153BJ	BE40	RK-153
N153BR	LJ24	153
N153CJ	**C52A**	**0153**
N153CS	C525	0548
N153DJ	EA50	000072
(N153EC)	C560	0444
N153FJ	F900	153
N153FJ	FA10	69
N153G	SBRL	282-26
(N153G)	SBRL	282-48
N153H	LJ24	151
N153JP	C500	153
N153MR	C525	0153
N153NP	LJ31	153
N153NS	CL61	5056
N153Q	BE40	RK-490
N153QS	CS55	0153
N153QS	BE40	RK-490
N153RA	GLF4	1050
N153RB	**LJ31**	**153**
N153SG	C550	550-1088
N153SG	C56X	5231
N153SG	**C680**	**0101**
N153SR	CL60	1034
N153TH	C550	695
N153TW	LJ25	053
(N153VP)	C560	0153
N153WB	C500	153
N153XP	HS25	HA-0153
N154	HS25	25236
N154AG	LJ24	034
N154AK	**LJ60**	**114**
N154BA	CL61	5154
N154C	GLF2	253
N154C	**GLF4**	**1493**
N154CC	C500	687
N154CC	C650	0154
N154DD	ASTR	029
N154FJ	FA10	72
N154FJ	**HS25**	**257110**
N154FV	**GLF4**	**4318**
N154G	C500	110
N154G	**GLF4**	**1044**
N154GA	MU30	A045SA
N154GV	C52C	0154
N154JC	HS25	25249
(N154JC)	CL64	5347
N154JD	HS25	257032
N154JH	**C560**	**0555**
N154JK	**C560**	**0128**
N154JS	C560	0540
N154JS	HS25	257032
N154LA	**FA50**	**127**
N154NS	CL61	5169
N154PA	FA50	154
N154QS	BE40	RK-509
N154RA	C525	0304
N154RP	**C525**	**0903**
N154RR	**HS25**	**258375**
N154RT	**LJ31**	**154**
N154SC	**C500**	**558**
(N154SV)	C560	0154
N154TR	HS25	25084
N154VP	C560	0154
N154X	GLF2	12
N154X	**HS25**	**HA-0151**
N154XL	C56X	5154
N154XP	HS25	HA-0154
N155AC	C550	573
N155AD	**GLF5**	**5029**
N155AG	LJ25	037
(N155AJ)	LJ55	013
N155AM	**LJ35**	**131**
N155AN	GLF5	5029
N155AN	GLF5	5421
N155AN	GLF6	6187
N155AU	LJ25	218
N155AV	JSTR	5104/6
N155BC	LJ55	115
N155BT	C550	170
N155BT	LJ24	168
N155CA	C500	191
(N155CD)	LJ55	030
N155CJ	C525	0155
N155CS	LJ55	033
N155DB	**LJ55**	**141**
N155DD	LJ55	004
N155DH	BE40	RK-36
N155EC	**C525**	**0024**
N155EC	SBRL	306-20
N155ER	**LJ55**	**098**
N155EX	F2EX	155
(N155FF)	C550	175
N155FJ	F900	155
N155FJ	FA10	73
N155FS	**C56X**	**5168**
N155GA	GLF5	5355
N155GB	CS55	0155
N155GD	PRM1	RB-5
N155GM	LJ55	022
N155GM	SBRL	282-90
N155GS	LJ55	088
N155HM	LJ55	036
N155J	LJ24	182
N155JC	LJ55	071
N155JC	LJ55	076
(N155JC)	LJ55	055
N155JH	C560	0568
N155JK	C550	208
N155JT	LJ55	107
N155LJ	LJ55	133
N155LP	LJ55	055
N155LR	LJ55	074
N155ME	WW24	391
N155MK	**C500**	**155**
N155MM	**C510**	**0452**
N155MM	GLF3	325
N155MP	LJ55	014
N155NK	FA20	107
N155NS	**HS25**	**258549**
N155PJ	LJ55	004
N155PJ	LJ55	041
N155PL	LJ55	133
N155PS	LJ55	136
N155PT	C550	170
N155PT	**C560**	**0257**
N155PX	**FA10**	**189**
N155QS	CS55	0155
N155RB	LJ55	117
N155RD	LJ35	477
N155RJ	GLF4	1347
N155RM	PRM1	RB-6
N155RW	**C56X**	**5570**
N155SB	LJ55	013
N155SC	LJ55	121
N155SJ	**LJ55**	**102**
N155SL	**CL30**	**20187**
N155SM	**C56X**	**6058**
N155SP	LJ55	137
N155T	HS25	258149
N155TA	C550	204
N155TD	LJ35	335
N155TJ	C550	175
N155TJ	JSTR	5104/6
N155TS	LJ55	102
(N155UT)	LJ55	071
N155V	LJ55	073
N155VP	C560	0155
N155VW	WW24	123
N155WL	LJ35	326
N155XP	HS25	HA-0155
(N156AG)	LJ24	065A
N156AV	LJ45	156
N156BA	C650	7038
N156BA	LJ35	287
N156BE	FA10	87
(N156BE)	LJ60	266
N156BF	**CL65**	**5912**
N156BF	FA10	87
N156BF	LJ60	266
N156CB	LJ25	101
N156CW	WW24	204
N156DB	FA50	40
N156DG	GLEX	9156
N156DH	**LJ60**	**091**
N156DH	BE40	RK-36
N156DJ	EA50	000073
(N156DT)	C650	0066
N156EC	LJ31	060
(N156EC)	C560	0445
N156FJ	F2EX	156
N156FJ	FA10	74
N156GA	MU30	A056SA
N156GW	**C550**	**550-0982**
N156JC	LJ55	056
N156JH	C560	0575
N156JS	LJ31	033A
(N156K)	HS25	257121
N156ML	**C525**	**0156**
N156N	C550	093
N156NS	**HS25**	**258668**
N156PB	LJ45	027
N156PH	**C680**	**0031**
N156PH	LJ45	027
N156QS	CS55	0156
N156RC	**CL64**	**5446**
N156RE	**FA50**	**156**
N156SC	LJ31	060
N156TE	EA50	000056
N156TS	GLF4	1156
N156TW	C52B	0056
N156VP	**C750**	**0056**
N156WC	FA50	89
N156WC	GLF4	4004
N156WJ	**GLF4**	**1347**
N156X	FA10	30
N156XL	**C56X**	**6056**
N156XP	HS25	HA-0156
N157AE	C56X	5017
N157AF	**E55P**	**50500187**
N157AG	**LJ24**	**252**
N157AK	LJ35	019
N157AL	**F2EX**	**110**
(N157AT)	SBRL	282-102
N157BM	CS55	0157
(N157BP)	LJ24	157
N157BR	FA7X	57
N157CA	LJ25	157
N157CB	LJ28	28-003
N157CM	C650	7057
N157DJ	LJ35	157
N157DW	C550	295
N157EA	FA10	157
N157EC	LJ31	147
N157EX	F2EX	157
N157FJ	F900	157
N157FJ	FA10	75
N157FQ	GLF4	1157
N157G	**LJ25**	**112**
N157GA	**ASTR**	**015**
N157H	GLF4	1209
N157H	HS25	258033
(N157JA)	FA10	157
N157JF	JSTR	5149/11
N157JF	WW24	8
N157JH	C560	0581
N157JL	**C52B**	**0157**
N157JS	LJ31	033D
N157LH	GLF2	228
N157MW	**LJ45**	**456**
N157NS	**CL65**	**5859**
N157PB	**LJ45**	**030**
N157PH	**C680**	**0035**
N157PH	LJ45	030
N157QP	JSTR	5149/11
N157QS	CS55	0157
N157QS	BE40	RK-520
(N157RP)	HS25	256067
N157SP	ASTR	057
N157SP	FA50	176
N157TF	**C560**	**0157**
N157TW	LJ24	157
N157WH	**BE40**	**RK-157**
N157WW	**C550**	**550-0896**
N157XL	**C56X**	**6157**
N157XP	HS25	HA-0157
N158AF	GLF5	506
N158AG	HS25	25155
N158CG	JSTR	5014
N158CJ	C52A	0158
N158DJ	EA50	000074
N158DP	JSTR	5013
N158EC	**LJ45**	**186**
N158EC	LJ45	191
N158EX	F2EX	58
N158FJ	F900	158
N158FJ	FA10	77
N158FM	G280	2023
N158GL	LJ25	158
N158HB	HA4T	RC-58
N158JA	F900	131
N158JA	F9EX	20
(N158JJ)	GLF5	534
(N158JP)	LJ60	147
N158JS	**C560**	**0540**
N158JS	LJ31	033C
(N158JS)	HS25	257032
N158LC	ASTR	158
N158M	FA50	273
N158M	FA50	351
N158MJ	LJ24	033
N158MJ	LJ35	158
N158NE	LJ35	158
N158PD	LJ45	047
N158PH	**C680**	**0049**
N158PH	LJ45	047
N158QS	CS55	0158
N158R	LJ31	189
(N158RA)	GLF5	522
N158SG	C550	550-1088
N158SN	BE40	RK-158
N158SV	C680	0158
N158TE	**EA50**	**000058**
(N158TJ)	C500	158
N158TN	HS25	258158
N158TW	**FA20**	**158/449**
N158XP	HS25	HA-0158
N159AK	BE40	RK-120
N159AK	BE40	RK-439
N159AL	BE40	RK-439
N159B	GLF2	190
N159B	GLF3	380
N159B	JSTR	5011/1
N159CJ	**C52C**	**0159**
(N159DA)	GLF2	93
(N159DJ)	GLF2	156/31
N159DP	WW24	52
N159EA	EA50	000261
N159EC	**LJ45**	**229**
N159FC	FA20	45
N159FJ	FA10	78
N159FJ	FA7X	159
N159FM	**HS25**	**258651**
N159H	**C52C**	**0195**
N159J	LJ24	153
N159JA	**GLF5**	**5062**
N159JH	C560	0270
N159JH	GALX	159
N159JS	**C52B**	**0038**
N159KC	**C500**	**159**
N159LC	C500	488
N159M	C650	0130
N159M	FA50	276
N159M	HS25	HA-0082
N159M	**LEG5**	**55000038**
N159MN	**HS25**	**258841**
N159MP	WW24	52
N159MR	C650	0130
N159MV	FA20	59
N159NB	**GLF2**	**140/40**
N159RA	HS25	258155
N159RA	**LJ35**	**024**
(N159RA)	FA20	349
N159SC	LJ60	059
N159TE	EA50	000059
N159TF	C680	0159
N159TS	CL61	5159
N159VP	C550	550-1059
N159WG	**C52C**	**0216**
N159YC	WW24	52
N160AF	FA50	188
N160AG	**HS25**	**25160**
N160AJ	LJ60	005
N160AN	LJ60	126
N160AT	LJ35	031
N160BA	HS25	259035
N160BG	LJ60	294
N160BL	LJ60	104
N160BP	**LJ60**	**138**
N160BR	**C52B**	**0454**
N160BS	**LJ60**	**112**
N160CF	**LJ31**	**160**
N160CF	SBRL	306-3
N160CT	ASTR	152
N160CT	HS25	258331
N160D	C550	162
N160DJ	EA50	000077
(N160EC)	C560	0451
N160EE	**LJ60**	**093**
N160EM	**LJ60**	**149**
N160FF	**EA50**	**000210**
N160FJ	FA10	160
N160FJ	FA10	79
N160GC	**LJ36**	**030**
(N160GC)	LJ24	295
N160GG	**LJ60**	**113**
N160GH	LJ60	129
N160H	MU30	A084SA
(N160H)	HS25	258234
N160HA	GALX	013
N160J	LJ25	076
N160JA	LJ60	283
N160JD	LJ60	068
N160JS	C500	250
N160LC	CL60	1068
N160MG	**LJ60**	**244**
N160NE	EA50	550-1003
N160NE	LJ55	147
N160NW	HS25	258160
N160QS	**GLEX**	**9475**
N160RC	**BE40**	**RK-333**
N160RM	LJ60	147
N160RW	SBRL	306-16
N160S	MU30	A084SA
N160SB	**CL30**	**20293**
N160SP	C550	660
N160TC	SBRL	282-83
N160TG	LJ60	339
N160TJ	FA10	107
N160TL	LJ55	042
N160TM	**GLF4**	**1526**
N160VE	C550	281
N160W	**SBRL**	**282-101**
N160WC	**CL30**	**20305**
N160WC	FA20	140
N160WC	GLF2	12
N160WC	HS25	258069
N160WC	WW24	141
(N160WC)	HS25	257090
N160WS	F2TH	28
N160XP	HS25	HA-0160
N161AC	LJ25	230
N161AK	GLF4	1061
N161AV	LJ45	161
N161BA	HS25	259036
N161BB	**EA50**	**000222**
N161BH	C550	048
N161CB	C500	595
N161CC	C500	161
N161CC	C650	0161
N161CE	**E50P**	**50000274**
N161CM	SBRL	306-5
N161DJ	EA50	000078
(N161EC)	C560	0455
N161EU	FA20	485
N161FJ	FA10	80
N161G	HS25	257151
N161GF	**GLEX**	**9704**
N161GS	JSTR	5061/48
N161JG	**CL61**	**5028**
(N161KK)	C500	219
N161LM	JSTR	5005
N161LM	JSTR	5083/49
N161MA	LJ35	610
N161MD	CL64	5416
N161MM	CL64	5416
N161MM	**GLF4**	**1511**
N161MM	HS25	257151
N161MM	HS25	258061
N161MN	CL64	5416
N161PA	**E50P**	**50000169**
N161PB	CL61	5069
N161PE	F900	161
N161PL	**E50P**	**50000259**
N161QS	BE40	RK-435
N161RB	LJ25	294
N161SD	**C650**	**7066**
N161SM	C525	0369
N161SV	C680	0161
N161TM	**C550**	**550-0867**
N161VP	C550	550-1061
N161WC	C500	117
N161WC	GLEX	9006
N161WC	HS25	257090
N161WT	FA20	478
N161X	WW24	133
N161X	WW24	234
N161XP	HS25	HA-0161
N162A	HS25	25183
N162A	HS25	257012
(N162AC)	LJ25	126
N162BA	HS25	258236
N162CC	C550	162
N162CT	FA20	162/451
N162D	HS25	25183
N162DJ	**EA50**	**000079**
N162DS	**C650**	**0164**
N162DW	C550	131
N162E	WW24	229
N162EC	**C52B**	**0026**
N162EM	LJ35	658
N162F	FA20	387
N162FJ	F900	162
N162FJ	FA10	81
N162G	GLF4	1206
N162G	HS25	258893
N162GA	LJ55	003
N162GB	**GALX**	**117**
N162J	LJ24	336
N162JB	**HS25**	**258509**
N162JB	SBRL	306-62
N162JC	GLF3	373
N162JC	**GLF5**	**539**
(N162JG)	LJ55	126
N162LJ	LJ31	162
N162NS	F2EX	162
N162QS	GLEX	9484
N162QS	BE40	RK-438
N162RU	**G150**	**245**
N162TF	C560	0573
N162TJ	**C550**	**550-0888**
(N162TJ)	FA10	162
N163A	LJ35	073
N163AF	C650	0163
N163AG	HS25	25169
N163AL	**LJ31**	**053**
N163AV	FA10	163
N163BA	HS25	258238
N163BA	LJ60	141
N163BB	**EA50**	**000250**
N163BJ	BE40	RK-163
N163C	**CS55**	**0122**
N163CB	C550	234
N163CH	FA10	163
N163CK	**LJ35**	**163**
N163DA	C550	190
N163DC	WW24	89
N163DE	HA4T	RC-18
N163DJ	EA50	000081
N163DK	HA4T	RC-18
N163DK	**HA4T**	**RC-19**
N163DL	WW24	163
N163EB	**F2EX**	**36**
(N163EC)	C560	0460
N163EG	CL60	1035
N163EG	**GLF4**	**1040**
N163ET	**CL60**	**1035**
N163F	FA10	163
N163FJ	F900	163
N163FJ	FA10	83
N163FJ	**FA7X**	**163**
N163GA	G280	2063

N163J	F2TH	163
N163JD	LJ31	095
N163JM	**C650**	**0163**
N163L	C560	0374
(N163L)	C560	0163
N163M	**C52C**	**0035**
N163M	CL61	5113
N163M	GLF4	1193
(N163ME)	LJ24	277
N163MJ	**FA10**	**163**
N163MR	CL61	5113
N163PA	**GLF3**	**249**
N163PB	C52A	0033
N163RK	BE40	RK-63
N163TC	**C510**	**0039**
(N163W)	WW24	162
N163WC	WW24	141
N163WC	**WW24**	**217**
N163WG	**CL61**	**3057**
N163WS	WW24	141
N163WW	FA50	52
N163XP	HS25	HA-0163
N164AF	C650	0164
N164AL	**LJ31**	**134**
N164AS	C56X	5192
N164BA	HS25	258239
N164CB	C500	510
N164CB	C500	571
N164CC	C500	164
N164CC	C550	211
N164CC	CL61	5164
N164CJ	C52A	0164
N164CV	C560	0164
N164DA	SBRL	282-112
N164DN	SBRL	282-112
N164DW	C560	0018
(N164EC)	C560	0471
N164FJ	FA10	84
N164FJ	FA50	164
N164GA	G280	2064
N164GA	GALX	164
N164GB	**FA50**	**164**
N164GD	**G280**	**2063**
(N164GJ)	C500	164
N164M	C750	0024
(N164M)	C750	0021
N164MA	FA50	164
N164MW	**EA50**	**000122**
N164NW	FA20	164
N164PA	LJ60	030
N164RJ	GLF3	482
N164SB	LJ31	164
N164TC	C560	0174
N164WC	HS25	257144
N164WC	**HS25**	**258072**
N165A	GLF2	70/1
N165AA	**LJ25**	**152**
N165AG	HS25	25206
(N165AG)	HS25	25043
(N165AG)	HS25	25208
N165AL	**LJ31**	**137**
N165BA	C500	159
N165BA	HS25	258091
N165BA	HS25	258241
N165CA	**C525**	**0451**
N165CB	C500	353
N165CM	**LJ24**	**355**
N165DJ	EA50	000199
N165DL	**EA50**	**000218**
N165DL	HS25	257174
N165DS	**C56X**	**6175**
N165F	BE40	RJ-16
N165FJ	F9EX	165
N165FJ	FA10	85
N165FJ	FA50	166
(N165FJ)	FA50	163
N165G	**GLF3**	**414**
N165GA	GLF4	4005
N165GA	MU30	A065SA
N165GD	GLF4	1265
N165HB	BE40	RK-90
N165JB	C56X	5032
N165JB	C555	0009
N165JF	**GLF4**	**1251**
N165L	HS25	258432
N165MC	C550	195
N165NA	C500	557
N165NA	SBRL	465-68
N165PA	FA20	360
N165PA	**GLF2**	**87/775/6**
N165RD	**C550**	**342**
N165SC	CL61	5165
N165ST	GLF3	414
N165ST	GLF4	1053
N165TW	FA20	65
N165U	GLF2	66
N165W	GLF2	66
N165WC	FA20	140
N165XP	HS25	HA-0165
N166A	CL61	5170
(N166AA)	LJ31	050
N166AC	JSTR	5029/38
(N166AG)	LJ35	145
N166AN	**PRM1**	**RB-227**
N166BA	HS25	258244
N166BA	LJ31	086
N166CB	C500	532
N166CF	C550	180
N166CJ	C510	0266
N166CK	**FA7X**	**177**
N166CL	CL30	20166
N166DJ	EA50	000200
N166DT	LJ31	166
N166EA	**EA50**	**000169**
(N166EC)	C560	0483
N166FA	**C500**	**559**
N166FB	F9EX	18
N166FJ	F900	166
N166FJ	FA10	86
N166FJ	FA50	167
N166GA	GLF4	4006
N166HE	LJ35	235
N166HL	LJ35	235
N166HL	**LJ60**	**041**
N166J	GLEX	9166
N166JV	C560	0166
N166KB	C560	0374
N166MA	C550	151
N166MB	C56X	5005
N166MC	**C560**	**0523**
N166MC	C650	0003
N166MK	**GLEX**	**9212**
N166MS	**LJ60**	**255**
N166MS	LJ60	267
N166PC	**LJ25**	**166**
N166QS	BE40	RK-439
N166RA	**FA20**	**449**
N166RD	**C56X**	**5740**
N166RM	**ASTR**	**047**
N166RM	LJ35	336
N166RS	FA20	157
(N166SS)	FA10	166
N166ST	**C560**	**0606**
(N166TM)	C550	550-1063
N166VP	C550	180
N166WC	**CL30**	**20214**
N166WC	GLF3	413
N166WC	HS25	258119
N166XP	HS25	HA-0166
N167A	GLF2	53
N167AA	**GLF4**	**1096**
N167AC	FA10	167
N167AD	**GLF4**	**4197**
N167BA	HS25	259038
N167BA	LJ31	087
N167BD	**F900**	**174**
N167BD	FA50	42
N167BR	**FA50**	**42**
N167BS	F900	174
N167C	WW24	261
N167CB	C500	542
N167DD	HS25	258068
N167DF	**HS25**	**258500**
N167DJ	EA50	000201
N167DP	**PRM1**	**RB-67**
N167EA	C550	667
N167EX	F2EX	167
N167EX	F9EX	167
N167FJ	F900	168
N167FJ	FA10	87
N167FJ	FA50	168
N167G	JSTR	5212
N167G	SBRL	282-11
N167GH	C52A	0217
N167GX	GLEX	9167
N167H	C52C	0167
N167H	SBRL	282-11
N167H	SBRL	306-119
N167J	HS25	25020
N167J	LJ25	011
N167J	WW24	265
N167JB	**WW24**	**425**
N167JN	**C56X**	**6100**
N167LJ	LJ31	167
N167MA	C550	303
N167QS	BE40	RK-529
N167R	JSTR	5204
N167RD	**CL30**	**20363**
N167SC	CL60	1012
(N167SG)	HS25	258110
N167TV	**GLF4**	**1533**
N167WE	C560	0087
(N167WE)	C550	386
(N167WE)	C560	0167
N167XP	HS25	HA-0167
N167XX	LJ60	167
N168AM	C550	175
N168AM	F2EX	138
N168AS	C500	328
N168BA	HS25	258209
N168BB	**GLF4**	**1330**
N168BF	**HS25**	**258373**
N168BG	C56X	5162
N168CB	C550	150
N168CE	F2EX	95
N168CE	**GLF5**	**568**
N168CV	C560	0168
N168D	SBRL	282-21
(N168D)	GLF6	6079
N168DA	GLF2	112
N168DB	JSTR	5074/22
N168DB	WW24	202
N168DJ	**FA20**	**168**
(N168DN)	FA10	113
N168EA	C500	568
N168EA	**C560**	**0168**
N168EC	GALX	038
(N168EC)	C560	0486
N168ES	**C550**	**706**
N168FG	E50P	50000012
N168FJ	FA10	82
N168GW	C56X	6189
N168H	SBRL	282-21
N168H	SBRL	306-122
(N168H)	HS25	257171
N168HC	C555	0081
N168HH	HS25	258398
(N168HH)	GLEX	9477
N168HT	F900	182
N168J	**E55P**	**50500243**
N168JC	**E55P**	**50500334**
N168JC	FA50	119
N168JH	GLEX	9458
N168JW	GLF2	168
N168KS	**LJ60**	**395**
N168LA	CL61	5179
N168LJ	LJ31	168
N168MC	**C56X**	**5355**
N168NB	GLF5	667
N168NJ	**GLF5**	**5359**
N168NJ	GLF5	667
N168NQ	**CL64**	**5531**
(N168NS)	F2EX	168
N168PJ	BE40	RK-347
N168PK	**GLF4**	**1053**
N168PX	**C680**	**0002**
N168RL	C500	271
N168RR	**GALX**	**217**
N168RT	**GLF4**	**1316**
(N168TE)	EA50	000079
N168TR	GLF4	1113
N168TR	**LJ35**	**068**
N168TS	CL61	5179
"N168TS"	CL60	1052
N168TT	EA50	000042
N168TY	**C510**	**0297**
N168VA	GLF2	112
N168W	**SBRL**	**282-33**
N168WC	GLF4	1002
N168WC	**BE40**	**RK-198**
N168WM	**GLF4**	**1002**
N168WU	HS25	259009
(N168WU)	HS25	257157
N168ZZ	**LJ60**	**078**
N169AC	SBRL	306-98
N169B	GLF2	190
N169B	HS25	256061
N169BA	HS25	259039
N169CA	GLF4	1241
N169CA	GLF5	563
N169CC	C650	0169
N169CJ	C525	0069
N169CP	C560	0230
(N169CP)	C550	018
(N169DA)	C550	191
N169DJ	EA50	000202
N169DT	GLEX	9287
(N169DT)	PRM1	RB-138
N169EA	GLF2	169
N169F	FA20	388
N169FJ	F9EX	169
N169FJ	FA10	88
N169FJ	FA50	170
N169HM	**GLF2**	**13**
N169JC	GLF4	1250
N169JM	C550	191
N169LL	GLEX	9397
N169LL	GLF5	673
N169LS	**FA10**	**115**
N169MM	**GLF2**	**225**
N169P	GLF2	169
(N169PG)	GLF5	563
N169RF	SBRL	306-45
(N169SC)	LJ31	069
N169SD	GLF5	5206
N169SD	**GLF5**	**5455**
N169SM	C56X	5749
N169TA	CL61	3041
N169TA	CL65	5790
N169TA	**GLF4**	**4337**
N169TA	HS25	257114
N169TD	CL61	3041
N169TT	GLF4	1113
N169US	**LJ24**	**298**
N170AL	SBRL	282-29
N170AP	**E50P**	**50000170**
N170AR	C550	097
N170BA	HS25	258097
N170BG	C525	0170
N170CC	C550	170
N170CC	C650	0170
N170CC	SBRL	465-3
N170CS	FA10	58
N170CV	C560	0170
N170DC	**HS25**	**HA-0001**
N170DD	SBRL	282-29
N170EA	C500	573
N170EA	**EA50**	**000170**
(N170EP)	LJ25	170
N170EV	LJ25	170
N170FA	HS25	HB-1
N170FJ	FA10	90
N170FJ	FA50	171
N170FJ	FA50	172
N170FL	CL61	5041
N170GT	LJ25	117
N170HL	C500	683
N170HL	C650	0125
N170HL	C750	0100
N170JL	SBRL	282-29
N170JL	SBRL	465-3
N170JS	C500	570
N170L	LJ35	156
N170LD	LJ35	287
N170LS	**LJ45**	**029**
(N170LX)	F2EX	170
N170MD	C500	088
N170MK	C500	668
N170MK	FA10	162
N170MK	LJ60	002
N170MR	**C52A**	**0170**
N170MU	**C525**	**0170**
N170NE	EA50	550-1004
N170PF	F9EX	17
N170RD	C555	0148
N170RL	LJ25	117
N170SD	**C56X**	**5091**
(N170SK)	HS25	258582
N170SW	**GLEX**	**9042**
N170TC	C550	619
N170TM	**C52A**	**0100**
N170TY	CL65	5702
N170VE	LJ55	089
N170VP	C52A	0170
N171AA	**C510**	**0412**
N171AM	**GLF3**	**437**
N171AR	**LJ31**	**171**
(N171AV)	HS25	25171
N171CB	C550	275
(N171CB)	C550	011
N171CC	C500	171
N171CC	JSTR	5127
N171CL	**CL65**	**5934**
N171DP	LJ45	171
N171EX	**FA7X**	**24**
N171FJ	FA10	94
N171FJ	FA50	171
N171GA	HFB3	1039
N171JC	**GLF4**	**1222**
N171JJ	GLEX	9209
N171JL	JSTR	5074/22
N171L	C650	0039
N171L	LJ24	182
N171LE	C550	352
N171MC	FA10	30
N171MD	**HS25**	**258251**
N171PF	FA20	117
(N171RH)	GLF4	1529
N171SG	JSTR	5227
N171TG	**FA50**	**251**
N171TS	HS25	256071
N171TV	GLF3	422
N171UT	**C510**	**0434**
(N171VP)	C550	188
N171W	C525	0292
N171WH	LJ35	171
N171WJ	**C500**	**574**
N171WW	LJ25	171
N171XP	HS25	HA-0171
N172CB	C550	285
N172CC	C500	172
N172CJ	C525	0172
N172CJ	C52A	0017
N172CP	FA10	172
N172CV	C560	0172
N172DH	C52B	0012
N172EX	**GALX**	**172**
N172FJ	**F2EX**	**72**
N172FJ	FA10	92
N172FJ	FA50	173
N172L	JSTR	5015
N172MA	C500	110
(N172MV)	FA20	72/413
N173A	SBRL	306-41
N173A	**SBRL**	**465-20**
N173A	WW24	80
N173AA	**C550**	**189**
N173AR	WW24	80
(N173BF)	GALX	009
N173CA	C525	0366
N173CN	**FA7X**	**173**
N173CX	C750	0173
N173DS	**LJ40**	**2092**
N173DX	**LJ45**	**533**
(N173EC)	C560	0493
N173EL	GLF2	173
N173F	FA20	390
N173FJ	FA10	95
N173GA	HFB3	1052
N173GH	**E50P**	**50000173**
N173HH	C500	082
N173J	LJ25	112
N173JA	LJ36	007
N173JM	**GALX**	**122**
N173KR	**LJ60**	**099**
N173LC	LJ31	173
N173LP	C650	0055
N173LP	GLF4	1033
N173LP	LJ24	196
N173LP	LJ25	163
(N173LP)	GLF3	310
N173LR	C650	0055
N173LR	LJ25	163
N173MC	WW24	150
N173NL	C52C	0173
N173PA	**GLF3**	**313**
N173PD	**EA50**	**000173**
N173PS	LJ31	009
N173SK	C500	381
N173TE	EA50	000073
N173TR	HS25	258039
N173VP	**C650**	**0173**
N173W	ASTR	073
N173WF	C750	0112
N173XP	HS25	HA-0173
N174A	HS25	258174
N174AB	BE40	RK-174
N174B	**FA10**	**142**
N174B	MU30	A031SA
N174BD	FA20	174/457
N174BL	**LJ60**	**174**
N174CB	C500	647
N174CF	**C500**	**524**
(N174CF)	C500	579
N174CH	**C750**	**0174**
N174CP	LJ35	177
N174CX	C750	0174
N174DR	**C550**	**069**
N174FJ	FA10	96
N174GA	FA20	27
N174GA	GLF5	5274
(N174GM)	C525	0275
N174JF	**ASTR**	**143**
N174JS	C560	0074
N174JS	**C560**	**0572**
N174LM	GLF4	1174
N174LX	F2EX	174
N174NW	HS25	258174
N174RD	**LJ24**	**319**
N174SA	MU30	A072SA
N174SJ	**C52B**	**0174**
N174SJ	GLF4	1174
N174TM	C680	0021
N174TS	LJ31	074
N174VP	C650	7004
N174WC	**HS25**	**258593**
N174XP	HS25	HA-0174
N175BA	LJ24	038
N175BA	LJ60	060
N175BC	F2TH	32
N175BC	**F9EX**	**243**
N175BC	FA10	128
(N175BC)	FA20	403
N175BG	**GLF3**	**396**
N175BJ	**BE40**	**RK-175**
N175BL	FA10	168
N175BL	**GLF4**	**4233**
N175CC	C500	175
N175CJ	**FA10**	**175**
N175CP	C525	0175
N175CW	C550	550-1065
N175DP	C650	7116
N175DP	**CL30**	**20506**
(N175EC)	C560	0496
N175EM	**E50P**	**50000106**
N175EW	E50P	50000006
N175EX	F2EX	175
N175F	FA20	391
N175FF	LJ31	175
N175FJ	FA10	97
N175FS	LJ24	031
N175GA	FA20	45
N175GA	GLF4	4173
N175GA	GLF6	6175
N175J	**C650**	**0168**
N175J	LJ35	005
(N175J)	C650	0175
N175JE	**EA50**	**000111**
N175MC	**E55P**	**50500098**
N175MC	HS25	257178
N175MD	JSTR	5215
N175MX	**LJ45**	**497**
N175PC	LJ60	175
N175PS	C525	0087
N175PS	BE40	RK-213
N175QS	BE40	RK-574
N175SB	C525	0371
(N175SP)	ASTR	075
N175SR	**C650**	**0175**
N175ST	CL60	1084
N175ST	CL61	5023
N175TM	HS25	258496
(N175TN)	C550	181
N175TP	C56X	6183
N175U	HS25	258175
N175VB	C550	230
N175VP	C680	0175
N175WS	C56X	5327
N175WS	C680	0151
N176AF	C650	0176
N176AK	WW24	154
N176AN	JSTR	5103
N176BN	FA20	69
N176BN	JSTR	5103
N176BN	JSTR	5207

N176CA	LJ40	2045
N176CF	F900	160
N176CG	**F2EX**	**92**
N176CL	F9EX	110
N176CP	LJ24	204
N176CR	**PRM1**	**RB-154**
N176DC	SBRL	380-54
N176DL	**C56X**	**5192**
N176DT	**WW24**	**154**
(N176EC)	C560	0510
N176EX	F9EX	176
N176F	FA20	393
N176FB	C500	650
N176FJ	FA10	99
N176G	GLF4	1176
N176G	LJ25	088
N176GA	GLF4	4276
N176GA	HFB3	1053
N176GS	C56X	5278
N176HS	**GLEX**	**9531**
(N176HT)	GLEX	9531
N176JE	LJ35	176
N176KS	LJ60	066
N176L	C650	0176
N176LG	JSTR	5005
N176MB	LJ60	176
N176MG	**GLF4**	**1501**
N176MG	LJ45	383
N176NP	FA20	69
N176P	GLF2	176
N176QS	BE40	RK-583
N176RS	HS25	257162
N176SB	GLF2	176
N176TG	**LJ45**	**512**
N176TK	LJ45	176
N176TL	**HS25**	**258176**
N176TS	HS25	25176
N176VP	C560	0176
N176WA	HS25	258176
N176WS	LJ31	176
N176XP	HS25	HA-0176
N177A	SBRL	282-1
N177A	SBRL	306-3
N177A	WW24	16
N177AM	LJ55	147
N177BB	**GLF4**	**1073**
N177BC	FA10	25
N177CJ	C550	177
N177CK	**EA50**	**000182**
(N177CM)	C550	247
N177E	**C56X**	**5699**
N177EA	EA50	000177
(N177EC)	C560	0519
N177EL	C750	0177
N177FF	**CL65**	**5878**
N177FJ	F900	172
N177FJ	FA10	100
N177FJ	FA50	175
N177FL	**CL61**	**3032**
N177GP	HS25	25111
N177HB	WW24	141
N177HH	C550	043
N177HN	**C52B**	**0357**
N177JB	C525	0182
N177JB	**LJ31**	**161**
N177JC	WW24	77
N177JE	**C560**	**0678**
N177JF	**C525**	**0182**
N177JW	HS25	257110
N177KS	LJ60	109
N177LD	**LJ35**	**287**
N177MJ	**FA50**	**177**
N177NC	JSTR	5070/52
N177NC	SBRL	380-52
N177NQ	SBRL	380-52
(N177NS)	F2EX	177
N177PC	WW24	141
N177RE	C525	0030
(N177RE)	C52A	0013
N177RJ	**C550**	**550**
(N177SB)	LJ35	401
N178AM	**LJ55**	**144**
(N178AT)	C750	0080
N178AX	HS25	258178
N178B	**GLF2**	**125/26**
N178BH	**HS25**	**258538**
N178BR	**C56X**	**5354**
N178CC	C650	0178
N178CP	**LJ35**	**005**
N178DA	**CS55**	**0004**
N178EX	F9EX	178
N178F	FA20	394
N178FJ	FA10	102
N178FJ	FA50	176
N178GA	FA20	163
N178GA	GLF4	4176
N178GA	GLF4	4278
N178HH	C500	082
N178HH	C550	190
N178HH	GLF3	448
N178HH	WW24	347
N178HL	**C650**	**0125**
N178JC	**C56X**	**5758**
N178MH	GLF4	1121
N178MM	**LJ60**	**178**
N178NP	LJ31	178
N178PC	HS25	25264

N178PT	**GLF4**	**1204**
N178RH	**C680**	**0178**
N178SD	**GLF4**	**4111**
N178SF	**C510**	**0128**
N178TJ	FA10	78
N178TM	GALX	167
N178TM	**LJ45**	**487**
N178W	SBRL	306-4
N178WB	HS25	257178
N178WG	C52A	0342
N178WS	C56X	5327
N178XP	HS25	HA-0178
N179AE	GALX	068
N179AG	FA10	176
N179AP	GLF2	37
N179AR	GLF2	37
N179CJ	C525	0079
N179CJ	C52B	0179
N179CJ	**FA20**	**176/458**
(N179CJ)	C560	0179
N179DC	ASTR	128
(N179DE)	GLF2	86/16
N179DV	C52A	0172
N179EA	C500	179
N179EX	F2EX	179
N179F	FA20	396
N179FJ	F900	178
N179FJ	FA10	104
N179FJ	FA50	178
N179FZ	C52A	0179
N179GA	FA20	100
N179GV	C52C	0179
(N179HB)	HA4T	RC-79
N179JA	**GALX**	**088**
N179LF	**LJ60**	**101**
N179MR	**LJ45**	**179**
N179PG	**C680**	**0519**
N179PH	**E50P**	**50000179**
N179QS	BE40	RK-578
N179RP	C560	0768
N179S	SBRL	380-50
N179T	GLF2	86/16
N179TD	**EA50**	**000074**
N179TS	CL61	5179
N179WC	**C52B**	**0025**
N180AR	FA50	216
N180AR	**GLF2**	**148/5**
N180AR	SBRL	306-77
N180B	**C560**	**0278**
N180CC	C500	180
N180CH	CL60	1005
N180CH	**GLF4**	**1192**
N180CH	HS25	257076
(N180CH)	GLF5	563
N180CP	**LJ60**	**081**
N180EG	**HS25**	**258188**
N180FJ	FA10	105
N180FJ	FA50	179
N180FW	C550	403
N180FW	C560	0260
N180FW	C56X	5072
N180GC	LJ36	004
N180HL	**C560**	**0188**
(N180JS)	WW24	180
N180KT	CL61	5004
N180MC	LJ25	261
N180MC	LJ35	212
N180ML	HS25	25115
N180NA	SBRL	380-51
N180NE	**HS25**	**258100**
N180NL	**FA50**	**352**
N180PF	C500	047
N180QS	BE40	RK-569
N180TA	ASTR	129
N180TJ	WW24	106
N180UF	C500	314
N180VP	C500	593
N180YA	**C52A**	**0099**
N180YA	LJ25	136
N181AP	CL61	5010
N181AR	SBRL	306-90
N181BR	C650	7082
N181BR	C750	0181
N181BS	F900	39
N181CA	LJ24	277
N181CA	**LJ35**	**420**
N181CB	FA20	436
N181CC	C500	181
(N181CC)	C650	0181
N181CJ	C510	0281
N181CJ	C525	0181
N181CL	**GLEX**	**9572**
N181CN	**C52C**	**0040**
N181CR	**GLF4**	**1001**
N181CW	GLF4	1001
N181EA	C52B	0380
N181EB	**C550**	**431**
N181EF	**LJ35**	**190**
N181EF	LJ55	090
N181EX	F9EX	181
N181FH	**HS25**	**258098**
N181FJ	F900	187
N181FJ	FA10	106
N181FJ	FA50	181
N181G	**CS55**	**0006**
N181GA	GLF4	4181
N181GA	GLF5	5181

(N181GL)	LJ35	405
N181HB	**C52C**	**0071**
N181J	CL64	5433
N181JC	CL61	5173
N181JT	C525	0081
(N181JT)	PRM1	RB-170
N181MA	MU30	001SA
N181MC	FA50	279
N181MG	**C650**	**0119**
N181PA	LJ25	346
N181PA	LJ31	156
N181RB	FA20	66
N181RK	**FA20**	**515**
(N181RW)	LJ24	277
N181SG	**C560**	**0181**
(N181SM)	CL61	3031
N181SV	WW24	110
N181VP	C550	550-1081
N181WT	FA20	478
N181XP	**HS25**	**HA-0181**
N182AR	SBRL	306-93
N182FJ	FA10	107
N182FJ	FA50	182
N182GA	FA20	146
N182GX	GLEX	9182
N182K	LJ35	293
N182PA	C650	7049
N182U	C550	373
N183AB	C550	628
N183AJ	C550	628
N183AJ	C560	0276
N183AP	LJ25	271
N183AR	SBRL	282-127
(N183B)	FA50	118
N183BX	**LJ60**	**285**
N183CC	C500	183
N183CM	**LJ45**	**133**
N183CW	GLF5	649
N183DT	LJ31	183
N183F	FA20	398
N183FD	LJ35	183
N183FJ	F2EX	183
N183FJ	FA10	109
N183FJ	FA50	184
N183FM	HS25	258183
N183GA	FA20	147/444
N183GA	**GLF6**	**6183**
N183JC	LJ35	363
(N183JN)	C550	576
N183JS	C56X	5322
N183MK	FA7X	183
N183ML	LJ31	183
N183PA	GLF2	108
N183PA	**GLF3**	**385**
N183RD	HS25	256009
"N183RM"	HS25	256009
N183SC	GLF2	91
N183SD	LJ55	032
N183SR	FA10	183
N183TS	FA20	313
N183TS	**LJ45**	**273**
N183TX	**C52A**	**0183**
N183V	GLF2	165/37
N183WW	**F900**	**165**
N183XP	HS25	HA-0183
N183YS	**C56X**	**5322**
N184AL	LJ24	246
N184AR	**BE40**	**RK-34**
N184BK	**CL30**	**20209**
N184CD	**C52A**	**0184**
N184CW	GLF4	1004
N184F	FA20	399
N184FJ	F900	184
N184FJ	FA10	110
N184FJ	FA50	185
N184G	C56X	5050
N184G	C680	0039
N184G	**F2TS**	**730**
N184GA	FA20	266/490
N184GP	**C650**	**0236**
N184GP	JSTR	5064/51
N184HA	HS25	HA-0184
N184J	LJ25	063
N184LJ	LJ60	184
N184NA	C500	184
N184PA	**GLF3**	**318**
N184PC	SBRL	380-6
N184R	CL30	20024
N184R	LJ45	082
(N184RM)	LJ31	026
N184SC	MU30	A067SA
(N184SC)	C500	677
N184TB	**GALX**	**211**
N184TB	HS25	257084
N184TB	HS25	258671
N184TR	**HS25**	**258671**
N184TS	FA20	313
N184TS	LJ35	084
N184VP	C550	550-1084
N184WW	**FA20**	**352**
N184XL	C56X	5184
N184XP	HS25	HA-0184
N185BA	FA50	42
N185BA	LJ35	025
(N185BR)	WW24	365
N185CC	C550	185
N185CX	C750	0185

N185FJ	FA10	111
N185FJ	FA50	163
(N185FN)	BE40	RK-185
N185FP	LJ35	360
N185G	F2EX	36
N185G	WW24	161
N185GA	GLF4	4007
N185GA	**GLF5**	**5185**
(N185GA)	MU30	A066SA
N185GV	C52C	0185
N185GX	GLEX	9185
N185HA	LJ35	605
N185MB	WW24	365
N185S	FA20	56
N185SF	CS55	0029
N185VP	C650	0185
N186CJ	C525	0186
N186CJ	C52B	0186
N186CP	**C500**	**186**
N186CW	**GALX**	**081**
N186DC	GLF3	447
N186DL	**C525**	**0803**
N186DS	GLF3	447
N186DS	**GLF4**	**1154**
N186EX	F9EX	186
N186FJ	FA10	112
N186G	HS25	258011
N186G	WW24	282
N186G	WW24	43
N186HG	FA50	167
N186MT	CS55	0072
N186MW	C500	186
N186NM	HS25	25186
N186PA	**GLF3**	**317**
N186RW	**G280**	**2054**
N186S	FA20	195
N186S	FA50	113
N186SC	C500	186
N186ST	LJ60	186
N186TJ	FA10	186
N186TW	**C525**	**0416**
N186VP	C650	0186
(N186VP)	C550	550-1089
(N186WS)	C56X	5179
N186XL	**C56X**	**5186**
N186XP	HS25	HA-0186
N187AA	**F2TH**	**156**
N187AP	CL60	1035
(N187AP)	C500	096
N187CA	**LJ25**	**187**
N187CJ	C52C	0187
N187CM	C650	0187
N187CP	C650	0003
N187CR	**C750**	**0119**
N187DL	C525	0316
(N187DY)	LJ25	342
N187EA	**EA50**	**000187**
N187EC	WW24	434
N187F	FA20	402
N187FJ	FA10	114
N187G	WW24	41
N187GA	GLF4	4187
N187GA	GLF5	5187
N187H	F900	16
N187HF	ASTR	054
(N187HF)	C550	704
(N187HG)	F900	16
N187JN	C550	365
N187MC	**C525**	**0276**
N187MG	C52A	0187
N187MW	C500	187
N187MZ	LJ36	023
(N187PA)	GLF2	218
N187PH	GLF2	218
N187PN	**FA50**	**187**
N187S	C560	0353
N187S	F900	136
N187S	FA50	18
N187TA	C550	280
N187TJ	**WW24**	**187**
(N187TS)	WW24	187
N187XP	HS25	HA-0187
N188AF	**HS25**	**258238**
N188AJ	**GALX**	**049**
N188AK	**ASTR**	**121**
N188BC	LJ25	078
N188CA	**LJ25**	**208**
N188CJ	C525	0088
(N188CJ)	C560	0188
N188DC	GLF2	188
N188DH	FA10	188
N188DM	FA50	327
(N188DR)	C500	155
N188DX	**GLF4**	**4188**
N188ES	**GLF5**	**629**
N188FC	LJ25	006
N188FJ	FA10	115
N188FJ	**FA50**	**188**
N188FJ	FA50	88
N188G	WW24	139
(N188G)	CS55	0017
N188GA	GLF4	4188
N188GA	GLF5	5188
N188GS	**C510**	**0368**
N188HA	**BE40**	**RK-164**
N188J	**GLEX**	**9383**
(N188JA)	LJ35	025

N188JB	C52A	0216
N188JF	**BE40**	**RK-446**
N188JR	C52A	0188
N188JS	GLF2	29
N188K	HS25	25057
N188KA	HS25	257132
N188ML	GALX	024
N188MP	**C52A**	**0483**
N188MR	**E50P**	**50000357**
N188MR	GLF2	218
N188PR	**LJ25**	**371**
N188PS	SBRL	282-122
N188R	LJ25	305
N188SB	**C525**	**0879**
N188SF	C550	216
N188SG	**LJ45**	**142**
N188ST	C56X	6138
N188ST	MU30	A040SA
N188SW	**FA7X**	**23**
N188TA	LJ25	276
N188TC	GLF3	492
N188TC	LJ25	276
N188TC	LJ60	078
N188TG	LJ60	078
N188TJ	GLF3	399
N188TL	**C680**	**0257**
N188TM	**E50P**	**50000124**
N188TQ	LJ25	276
N188TS	**BE40**	**RK-244**
N188TW	**C525**	**0326**
N188VP	C550	550-1088
N188WP	WW24	90
N188WR	**GLF5**	**5178**
N188WS	**C56X**	**5179**
N188XP	HS25	HA-0188
N189AR	SBRL	282-77
N189B	HS25	25224
N189B	HS25	256061
N189B	HS25	258075
N189CC	C500	189
N189CJ	C525	0089
N189CM	**C525**	**0189**
N189CV	C560	0189
N189F	FA20	403
N189FJ	F900	189
N189FJ	FA10	116
N189G	WW24	35
N189GA	GLF5	5189
N189GA	BE40	RK-18
N189GE	HS25	257001
N189H	**C560**	**0004**
N189J	**GLF4**	**1068**
N189JM	FA10	189
N189JW	FA10	9
N189K	CL61	5083
N189K	**PRM1**	**RB-248**
N189LJ	LJ60	189
N189MM	C52C	0160
N189MM	FA20	453
N189MS	**C52A**	**0189**
N189PA	**GLF2**	**108**
N189PP	**LJ45**	**264**
N189RB	**FA20**	**262**
N189RR	HS25	25248
N189SC	GLF5	552
N189TA	**CL65**	**5790**
N189TA	HS25	258814
N189TC	GLF2	140/40
N189TC	LJ35	206
(N189TC)	LJ35	189
N189TM	**HS25**	**258196**
N189VP	**C550**	**550-1089**
(N189WJ)	GLF4	1068
N189WS	GLF2	228
N189WT	**C560**	**0613**
N189WW	**C56X**	**5069**
(N189WW)	C550	570
N189XP	HS25	HA-0189
N190AB	C500	157
N190AR	LJ25	190
N190AS	LJ60	002
N190BD	FA20	8
N190BP	LJ24	190
N190BW	**E50P**	**50000028**
N190CC	C500	190
N190CK	EA50	000190
N190CS	**GLF2**	**190**
N190DA	LJ35	156
(N190DB)	FA10	11
(N190DB)	LJ24	190
N190EB	LJ35	156
N190EK	CL61	5190
N190ES	GLF4	1135
N190EX	F2EX	90
N190FJ	F9EX	190
N190FJ	FA10	117
N190GC	LJ35	014
N190GG	CL61	5051
N190H	FA10	71
N190H	GLEX	9210
N190HL	E50P	50000124
N190HS	**HS25**	**HA-0063**
N190JH	C560	0303
N190JJ	C650	0190
N190JK	**C560**	**0303**
N190K	C500	369
N190K	C500	590

N190K	**C560**	**0279**
N190KL	C560	0380
N190L	FA10	190
(N190LH)	WW24	180
N190LJ	LJ60	190
N190M	WW24	232
N190MC	**F2TH**	**45**
N190MC	FA50	26
N190MD	SBRL	306-142
(N190MD)	FA10	47
(N190MM)	LJ31	112
N190MP	CL61	5161
N190MQ	**FA50**	**26**
N190NC	HS25	258551
N190NE	**EA50**	**550-1005**
N190PA	**GLF3**	**320**
N190PR	**C56X**	**5165**
N190RP	GLF2	136
N190SB	CL61	5051
N190SC	LJ24	190
N190SW	**HS25**	**HA-0079**
N190VE	LJ35	301
N190VP	**C52B**	**0190**
N190WC	HS25	257182
N190WP	GLEX	9104
N190WW	WW24	190
N190XP	HS25	HA-0190
N191AB	C500	167
N191AE	**F9EX**	**191**
N191BA	CL64	5410
N191BA	HS25	258188
N191BE	CL61	5191
N191C	FA20	195
N191CA	HS25	258672
N191CM	C650	0191
N191CP	**FA50**	**351**
N191CP	G150	249
N191DA	LJ24	157
N191DA	LJ25	012
N191FJ	FA10	119
N191GH	**HS25**	**258318**
N191GS	MU30	A030SA
N191JT	C650	7069
N191KL	C560	0659
N191LJ	LJ45	191
N191MC	FA10	30
N191MC	**FA50**	**282**
N191MD	**FA7X**	**180**
N191NC	BE40	RK-143
N191NQ	BE40	RK-143
N191PB	C56X	5013
N191PP	C525	0487
N191ST	**FA7X**	**6**
N191TD	**LJ45**	**298**
N191TF	**C550**	**567**
N191VB	C560	0627
N191VE	**C560**	**0150**
N191VF	C560	0150
N191VF	**C560**	**0627**
N191XP	HS25	HA-0191
N192A	HS25	257180
N192AB	C500	177
N192AT	HFB3	1038
N192BG	GLF5	5038
N192BH	GLF5	5038
N192CK	**FA20**	**192**
N192CN	C680	0137
N192DM	**E55P**	**50500126**
N192DW	C550	214
N192F	FA50	277
N192FG	GLF2	192
N192FJ	F900	192
N192FJ	FA10	120
N192FJ	FA7X	192
N192G	C500	163
N192JS	HS25	258251
N192LH	WW24	180
N192LW	F900	192
(N192LX)	F2EX	192
N192MB	LJ24	214
N192MC	FA10	84
N192MG	C52A	0145
N192MH	LJ24	214
N192MH	LJ25	239
N192N	GLF4	1286
N192NC	GLF4	1286
N192NC	**GLF4**	**4126**
N192NC	HS25	258476
N192R	FA20	192
N192RS	C555	0108
N192RS	**FA50**	**207**
N192RW	**C56X**	**5066**
N192SA	**HS25**	**HA-0192**
N192SJ	HS25	258192
N192SW	**G150**	**216**
N192TD	**LJ45**	**397**
N192W	**C56X**	**5239**
N192WF	GLF2	192
N192XL	C56X	5192
N192XP	HS25	HA-0192
N193AF	LJ60	193
N193AT	SBRL	282-124
N193BJ	**BE40**	**RK-193**
N193BK	**HS25**	**HA-0193**
N193CF	C52C	0193
N193CJ	C525	0193
N193CK	GLF2	168

N193CS	**PRM1**	**RB-115**
N193DB	**LJ24**	**193**
N193DQ	CL60	1041
(N193DR)	LJ25	129
N193EA	EA50	000193
N193F	F9EX	147
N193FJ	F900	193
N193FJ	FA10	122
N193G	C560	0137
N193JF	LJ24	193
N193LA	GLEX	9255
N193LA	**GLEX**	**9524**
N193LC	GLEX	9524
N193PC	**C550**	**550-1081**
N193PP	**C52A**	**0192**
N193RC	HS25	257081
N193SB	C560	0229
N193SB	C56X	6019
N193SE	**C560**	**0229**
N193SS	C550	572
N193TA	HS25	257001
N193TR	F900	9
N193TR	FA50	112
N193TR	HS25	258039
N193TR	BE40	RJ-29
N193XP	HS25	HA-0193
N193ZP	C750	0090
N194	GLF3	391
N194AL	LJ60	004
N194AT	C500	146
(N194AT)	C500	152
N194B	C750	0194
N194BJ	BE40	RK-194
N194CV	C560	0194
N194CX	C750	0194
N194DC	C650	0074
N194ER	**C510**	**0432**
N194FJ	FA10	123
(N194JM)	C550	297
N194JS	HS25	258251
N194K	FA50	194
N194LE	CL30	20194
N194MC	FA20	135
N194MF	**GLF5**	**510**
N194MG	**C525**	**0357**
N194RC	C500	545
N194SA	**C560**	**0238**
N194SF	C525	0821
N194SJ	C52A	0194
N194SR	**C750**	**0112**
N194SS	**C52C**	**0171**
N194SW	**G150**	**295**
N194TS	C500	194
N194VP	C750	0194
(N194VP)	C525	0194
N194WA	GLF2	194
N194WC	HS25	257144
N194WM	CL64	5340
N194WM	**GLEX**	**9277**
N194XP	HS25	HA-0194
N195AR	GLF2	195
N195AS	FA20	71
N195CR	**F900**	**147**
N195FC	ASTR	036
N195FJ	F900	195
N195FJ	FA10	125
N195GA	GLF5	5395
N195GX	GLEX	9195
N195JH	BE40	RJ-64
N195KA	BE40	RJ-53
N195KC	HS25	258189
N195KC	BE40	RJ-53
N195L	HS25	259008
N195MC	**E55P**	**50500095**
N195ME	**C525**	**0110**
(N195ML)	WW24	195
N195MP	FA20	195
N195SV	FA50	236
N195SV	**FA50**	**293**
(N195VP)	C550	550-1095
N195WM	GLEX	9041
N195WS	GLF4	1050
N195XP	HS25	257023
N195XP	HS25	HA-0195
N196AF	LJ24	196
N196AT	**LJ45**	**344**
N196CC	**GLF3**	**463**
N196CF	LJ24	186
N196CM	C650	0196
N196CT	LJ45	318
N196CT	BE40	RK-151
N196CV	C560	0196
(N196DR)	C525	0256
N196DT	LJ35	171
N196EC	E50P	50000151
N196EX	F9EX	196
N196FJ	F900	196
N196FJ	FA10	131
N196FJ	FA50	196
(N196FJ)	FA10	126
N196GA	GALX	096
N196GA	GLF5	5196
N196GA	HS25	258126
N196HA	C525	0256
N196HA	C550	196
N196HA	LJ31	084
N196HR	C550	196

N196JH	**C52B**	**0395**
N196JH	BE40	RJ-52
N196JP	**C560**	**0809**
N196JS	C550	219
N196KC	**F2TH**	**195**
N196KC	HS25	25180
N196KC	JSTR	5231
N196KC	WW24	68
N196KC	BE40	RJ-52
N196KQ	HS25	25180
(N196KQ)	BE40	RJ-52
N196MC	HS25	258081
N196MG	**HS25**	**258081**
N196MR	C52B	0297
N196PH	LJ45	056
N196RG	F2TH	135
N196RJ	**C550**	**234**
N196SA	C560	0384
N196SB	**C56X**	**5513**
N196SD	C650	0093
N196SD	LJ35	414
N196SG	C650	0093
N196SP	LJ35	414
N196SV	FA50	236
N196TB	**LJ24**	**196**
N196TS	FA20	196
(N196V)	CL60	1030
N196X	**GALX**	**196**
N197AR	**EA50**	**000114**
N197BE	**BE40**	**RK-33**
N197CC	C650	0197
N197CF	**LJ25**	**197**
N197CJ	C52A	0197
N197CV	C560	0197
N197DA	SBRL	282-28
N197EC	**LJ45**	**197**
N197EX	F9EX	197
N197FJ	F900	197
N197FJ	FA10	128
N197FS	C500	524
"N197FT"	HS25	257016
(N197GH)	C550	704
N197GL	LJ24	070
N197HF	C550	704
N197HF	**G150**	**220**
N197JH	C560	0267
N197JK	F2EX	182
N197JS	**CL30**	**20155**
N197JS	JSTR	5069/20
(N197JS)	CL30	20115
N197KA	F2EX	182
N197LS	LJ25	363
N197MJ	**FA10**	**197**
N197PA	**GLF3**	**329**
N197PF	BE40	RK-33
N197PH	LJ31	169
N197PH	LJ31	172
N197PR	**C550**	**704**
N197RJ	C525	0660
N197SD	BE40	RK-126
(N197SL)	MU30	A069SA
N197SW	**GLF4**	**1413**
(N197VP)	C650	0197
N197WC	LJ25	197
N197XL	**C56X**	**6197**
N197XP	HS25	HA-0197
N198AV	GLF2	98/38
N198CC	CL60	1018
N198CM	C650	0198
N198CT	BE40	RK-151
N198CV	C560	0198
N198D	C650	0209
N198D	CL64	5550
N198DC	CL64	5481
N198DF	C550	630
N198DF	C56X	5337
N198DF	C650	0209
N198DL	JSTR	5083/49
N198FJ	F900	198
N198FJ	FA10	132
N198GB	SBRL	380-32
N198GH	WW24	364
N198GJ	**LJ35**	**198**
N198GS	**GLF4**	**1098**
N198GT	HS25	257123
N198HB	**LJ60**	**198**
N198HE	WW24	364
N198HF	ASTR	054
N198HF	WW24	364
N198JA	**LJ25**	**198**
N198JH	**C525**	**0265**
N198KF	LJ31	147
N198M	FA50	149
N198M	**FA50**	**273**
N198M	FA50	277
N198MA	LJ25	110
N198MM	C560	0031
N198MR	FA50	149
N198ND	C550	630
N198NS	C550	148
N198RG	C525	0198
(N198SD)	CL60	1009
N198SL	C550	550-0835
N198ST	C555	0046
N198T	LJ35	074
N198TX	C650	7047
N198VP	C500	602

(N198VP)	C560	0198
N198XP	HS25	HA-0198
N199B	HS25	25224
N199BA	CL64	5410
N199BA	E50P	50000179
N199BA	**E55P**	**50500290**
N199BB	C550	550-0895
N199BP	**PRM1**	**RB-261**
N199BT	LJ25	311
N199CJ	LJ35	071
N199CK	C500	216
N199D	C750	0194
N199D	CL60	1081
N199DF	HS25	258713
N199DJ	**C500**	**571**
N199FG	**FA50**	**231**
N199FJ	F900	199
N199FJ	F9EX	199
N199FJ	FA10	135
N199FJ	FA7X	99
N199FJ	**HS25**	**HA-0199**
N199GA	G150	299
N199GA	GLF4	4099
N199GD	**CL64**	**5630**
N199GH	ASTR	027
N199GH	WW24	364
N199HE	**ASTR**	**027**
N199HF	ASTR	027
N199HF	**G280**	**2051**
N199HF	GALX	028
N199JK	**C500**	**199**
N199LA	GLEX	9255
N199LA	JSTR	5098/28
(N199LX)	GLF4	1004
N199ML	**C510**	**0002**
N199NP	C750	0078
(N199PZ)	GLF4	1203
N199Q	C550	003
N199QS	GLF4	1099
N199RM	**PRM1**	**RB-99**
N199SA	FA10	78
N199SC	**G280**	**2087**
N199SC	LJ60	114
N199SG	HS25	256038
N199SP	C500	199
N199WT	C750	0018
N199WW	GLF4	1059
N199WW	WW24	199
N199XL	C56X	6199
N199XP	**C750**	**0019**
N200A	GLEX	9077
N200A	GLEX	9203
N200A	GLF2	94
N200A	GLF3	370
N200A	GLF3	372
N200A	GLF4	1138
N200A	**GLF5**	**5341**
N200A	JSTR	5081
N200A	SBRL	282-52
N200AB	GLF2	71
N200AB	**GLF3**	**393**
(N200AF)	FA10	87
N200AL	JSTR	5081
N200AP	C750	0003
N200AQ	GLF2	32/2
N200AS	**C550**	**550-0934**
N200AX	GALX	009
N200AX	GALX	022
N200BA	**GALX**	**076**
N200BA	LJ55	011
(N200BA)	C500	250
N200BC	LJ25	095
N200BE	GLF2	196
N200BF	**E55P**	**50500283**
N200BH	**GALX**	**013**
N200BL	BE40	RK-23
N200BN	GALX	221
(N200BN)	FA50	240
N200BP	GLF2	115
N200BP	WW24	117
N200BP	WW24	46
N200CC	GLF2	31
N200CC	HS25	25179
N200CC	HS25	25265
N200CC	JSTR	5033/56
N200CC	JSTR	5150/37
N200CD	**F2TH**	**40**
N200CE	SBRL	306-87
N200CG	**C500**	**230**
N200CG	FA20	191
N200CG	JSTR	5033/56
N200CG	JSTR	5150/37
N200CH	F2EX	4
N200CH	LJ31	222
N200CK	ASTR	021
N200CK	C560	0298
N200CK	JSTR	5039
(N200CK)	SBRL	282-111
N200CN	CL60	1032
N200CP	C560	0055
N200CP	**FA20**	**275**
N200CP	FA20	410
N200CQ	C750	0245
N200CU	**FA20**	**499**
N200CV	**C750**	**0245**
N200CV	C555	0064
N200CX	C555	0064

N200CX	FA20	112
N200CX	SBRL	306-93
N200DE	CL61	5015
N200DE	**CL64**	**5390**
N200DE	FA20	191
N200DE	FA20	368
N200DE	GLF3	358
N200DE	WW24	148
N200DF	WW24	148
N200DH	LJ24	170
N200DL	WW24	189
N200DM	LJ24	065
N200DV	**SJ30**	**008**
N200DW	JSTR	5058/4
N200E	C550	399
N200E	SBRL	282-124
N200E	SBRL	282-135
N200EC	LJ35	094
N200EL	GLF2	71
N200EL	GLF3	393
N200ES	C500	502
N200ES	GLEX	9245
N200ET	FA20	498
N200FJ	FA10	137
N200FJ	FA20	401
N200FJ	**FA20**	**408**
N200FJ	FA20	479
N200FJ	FA20	491
N200FJ	FA20	494
N200FJ	FA20	507
N200FT	**C52A**	**0200**
N200FT	FA20	100
(N200FX)	FA20	479
N200G	LJ24	064
N200G	LJ25	048
(N200G)	C550	030
N200GA	GALX	013
N200GA	GALX	048
N200GA	GALX	054
N200GA	GALX	088
N200GA	GALX	122
N200GA	GALX	151
N200GA	GALX	173
"N200GA"	GALX	106
(N200GA)	GALX	034
N200GB	BE40	RK-53
N200GF	C500	679
N200GF	C550	556
N200GH	FA20	181
N200GH	GLF2	108
N200GL	FA20	181
(N200GL)	GLF2	108
N200GM	C500	142
N200GM	C52B	0016
N200GN	F2TH	68
N200GN	FA20	339
N200GN	GALX	120
N200GN	GLF2	110
N200GN	GLF3	312
N200GP	LJ24	134
N200GP	**BE40**	**RK-172**
N200GP	BE40	RK-53
(N200GP)	C550	022
N200GT	FA20	137
N200GT	WW24	46
N200GV	GALX	167
N200GX	GALX	133
N200GX	HS25	257033
N200GX	HS25	258202
(N200GX)	FA20	339
N200GY	HS25	257033
N200HA	PRM1	RD-1
N200HR	WW24	182
N200HR	WW24	268
N200HW	PRM1	RD-2
N200J	FA20	410
N200JB	**CL30**	**20353**
N200JB	GALX	164
N200JE	FA20	133
N200JJ	GLF3	312
N200JP	CL64	5421
N200JP	HS25	257053
N200JR	C550	239
N200JR	C560	0576
N200JR	C56X	5550
N200JR	LJ24	259
N200JW	**F2TH**	**128**
N200JW	FA20	64
N200KB	**LJ31**	**098**
N200KC	C500	104
N200KC	HS25	25249
N200KC	WW24	319
N200KF	HS25	258039
N200KJ	**LJ40**	**2057**
N200KN	**GALX**	**177**
N200KP	C510	0135
N200KP	C52A	0004
N200KP	**LJ45**	**025**
N200KQ	C500	104
N200L	F9EX	2
(N200L)	FA7X	6
N200LB	**PRM1**	**RB-116**
N200LC	**GLF4**	**1067**
N200LF	WW24	47
N200LH	C650	0100
N200LH	**C650**	**7005**
N200LH	WW24	312

(N200LH)	WW24	309
N200LJ	LJ35	200
N200LL	C650	0100
N200LP	**MU30**	**A006SA**
N200LR	**G150**	**279**
N200LS	**CL65**	**5911**
N200LS	FA20	479
N200LS	GLF2	227
N200LS	GLF4	1182
N200LS	GLF4	1449
N200LS	HS25	258095
N200LS	WW24	400
(N200LS)	GLEX	9227
N200LV	GALX	115
N200LX	CS55	0061
N200M	WW24	120
N200M	WW24	132
N200M	WW24	44
N200MH	LJ25	083
N200MK	FA20	355
N200MM	C560	0036
N200MP	**GALX**	**236**
N200MP	SBRL	282-36
N200MP	WW24	95
(N200MR)	C550	200
N200MT	CRVT	40
N200MT	**LJ60**	**150**
N200MW	C500	200
N200MZ	WW24	95
N200NA	BE40	RK-200
N200NC	**C550**	**142**
N200NE	**EA50**	**550-1006**
N200NE	F2TH	22
N200NG	C560	0190
N200NK	C560	0511
N200NK	CS55	0095
N200NP	FA20	488
N200NR	LJ24	142
N200NR	LJ25	328
N200NV	CS55	0095
N200P	FA20	54
N200P	GLF2	121
N200PB	GLF2	110
N200PB	HS25	25121
N200PB	JSTR	5161/43
N200PC	LJ55	058
N200PF	C56X	5098
N200PF	HS25	25121
N200PM	GLF4	1147
N200PR	PRM1	RB-79
N200QC	C500	023
N200QM	LJ25	084
N200QS`	**CL65**	**6052**
N200RC	WW24	140
N200RG	GLF2	216
N200RG	**HS25**	**HB-31**
N200RM	WW24	46
N200RN	C550	419
N200RT	C550	419
N200RT	C650	0025
N200RT	FA20	489
N200RT	FA20	490
N200RT	FA50	126
N200RT	FA50	175
N200RT	FA50	24
(N200SA)	FA20	479
N200SC	C560	0326
N200SC	C56X	5148
N200SF	GLF3	390
N200SF	LJ25	084
N200SG	**FA50**	**239**
N200SK	**GLF3**	**319**
N200SL	**C525**	**0461**
N200SR	FA20	195
(N200SS)	FA20	91
N200ST	ASTR	061
N200ST	**PRM1**	**RB-102**
N200SX	LJ35	286
N200TC	LJ24	134
N200TC	LJ35	423
N200TJ	C550	051
N200TJ	FA20	501
N200TJ	LJ31	120
N200TW	**LJ35**	**397**
(N200UJ)	GLF2	200
N200UL	CL64	5316
(N200UN)	SBRL	380-1
N200UP	FA50	55
(N200UP)	FA20	513
N200V	FA50	175
N200VR	**GALX**	**133**
N200VT	C550	210
N200VT	HS25	25249
N200WC	WW24	153
N200WD	FA20	479
(N200WF)	FA20	144
N200WK	**FA20**	**261**
N200WN	C500	252
(N200WN)	WW24	38
N200WY	FA20	509
(N200XJ)	WW24	281
N200XR	HS25	256058
N200XT	E50P	50000029
N200Y	**C680**	**0030**
N200Y	LJ24	003
N200Y	LJ25	083
N200Y	LJ36	014

N200YB	GALX	075
N200YM	C550	409
N200YM	FA10	114
N201BA	LJ24	013
N201BR	**FA20**	**166**
N201CC	C550	201
(N201CP)	C560	0055
N201CR	**F2TH**	**2**
N201EA	**EA50**	**000201**
N201GA	GALX	101
N201GA	GLF4	1511
N201GF	**FA20**	**284**
N201H	HS25	25109
N201HR	**C750**	**0024**
N201LS	**HS25**	**258777**
N201PG	C680	0336
N201PG	**F2EX**	**216**
N201PM	HS25	257192
"N201QS"	CL65	6053
N201RC	C680	0094
N201RC	**C680**	**0256**
N201S	WW24	85
N201SU	**C560**	**0586**
N201U	C550	215
N201UD	LJ60	387
N201WL	LJ24	215
N201WR	**F2TH**	**201**
N202A	GLF2	94
N202AR	**FA20**	**496**
N202AT	FA20	509
N202AV	**C650**	**7108**
N202BA	LJ24	031
N202BD	LJ35	041
N202BG	C525	0089
N202BP	PRM1	RB-202
N202BT	LJ24	195
N202BT	LJ25	132
N202BT	LJ35	041
N202BT	LJ35	483
N202CE	C550	104
N202CE	F2TH	22
N202CF	C500	436
N202CH	HS25	257084
N202CJ	C525	0102
N202CJ	C525	0202
N202CJ	C52A	0202
N202CP	FA50	202
(N202CV)	C560	0202
(N202CV)	C650	0202
N202CW	**C56X**	**5067**
N202CW	C650	7061
N202DD	FA50	54
N202DD	WW24	202
N202DF	**C680**	**0098**
N202DH	**CL30**	**20117**
N202DN	FA10	202
(N202DR)	LJ25	253
N202EA	**EA50**	**000202**
N202ES	JSTR	5204
N202EX	**F2EX**	
N202FJ	**F900**	**156**
N202FJ	FA10	134
N202FJ	FA20	484
N202GA	ASTR	101
N202GA	**G280**	**2002**
N202GA	G280	2020
N202GA	GLF2	152
N202GA	GLF2	187
N202GA	GLF2	26
N202GA	GLF4	1502
N202GA	GLF4	4202
(N202GJ)	GALX	133
(N202GP)	LJ24	134
N202HG	CL61	5017
N202HM	**C500**	**260**
(N202JG)	EA50	000270
N202JK	**C650**	**0100**
(N202JR)	LJ45	014
N202JS	**LJ24**	**278**
N202JW	LJ25	347
N202KC	**C750**	**0202**
N202KH	FA20	45
N202LC	LJ31	147
N202LJ	LJ60	202
N202LS	GLF4	1182
(N202LX)	C525	0116
N202MW	C500	202
N202MW	WW24	255
N202N	**LJ60**	**258**
N202PB	C550	029
N202PH	CL61	3011
(N202PV)	FA10	71
N202PX	GLF2	17
N202QS	**CL65**	**6053**
(N202RA)	BE40	RK-86
N202RB	C650	0162
N202RL	**C56X**	**5117**
N202SJ	LJ60	311
N202SW	C550	470
N202TA	FA20	59
(N202TA)	BE40	RK-388
N202TH	F2TH	130
N202TJ	C650	0202
N202TS	C550	295
N202TT	**BE40**	**RK-504**
N202VP	C500	607
N202VS	C500	096

N202VS	LJ35	190
N202VV	C500	096
N202VZ	GLF4	1289
N202VZ	**GLF4**	**4158**
N202W	CL61	5035
N202WC	CS55	0077
N202WM	LJ25	355
N202WR	**F900**	**24**
N202WR	LJ35	190
N202XT	**CL30**	**20198**
N202XT	GLF2	170
N202Y	LJ24	024
N203	**CL64**	**5374**
N203A	GLF2	89
N203A	GLF5	5169
N203AF	**F2TH**	**3**
(N203AL)	LJ35	483
N203BA	BE40	RJ-3
N203BE	C550	149
N203BG	**C525**	**0378**
N203BP	**PRM1**	**RB-203**
N203BT	FA50	22
(N203CD)	C650	0203
(N203CJ)	C525	0103
N203CK	F2TH	215
N203CK	LJ24	203
(N203CV)	C560	0203
N203CW	F900	33
(N203DD)	F2TH	180
N203DF	**BE40**	**RK-203**
N203DN	**C680**	**0203**
N203FJ	**F9EX**	**203**
N203FJ	FA10	138
N203FJ	FA20	489
N203FL	BE40	RK-123
N203G	CL60	1069
N203G	CL61	5189
N203GA	G150	303
N203GA	G280	2083
N203GA	GALX	103
N203GA	GALX	231
N203GA	GLF2	113
N203GA	GLF2	124
N203GA	GLF5	5203
N203JD	CL61	5099
N203JE	CL61	5099
N203JE	GLEX	9019
N203JE	**GLEX**	**9467**
N203JK	SBRL	465-39
N203JL	LJ24	203
N203JZ	GLEX	9019
N203LH	C500	384
N203LX	F2EX	203
(N203LX)	C525	0131
N203M	C560	0166
N203M	WW24	120
N203MH	CL65	5852
N203NC	**FA50**	**203**
N203NM	**C560**	**0609**
N203PM	C550	578
(N203PV)	FA10	71
N203QS	**F2TH**	**198**
N203R	**CL64**	**5386**
N203R	HS25	258119
N203RK	BE40	RK-203
N203RW	LJ35	203
N203TA	CL64	5316
N203TA	FA20	442
N203TM	**HS25**	**258653**
(N203TR)	HS25	258653
N203VS	**LJ25**	**347**
N203WB	F2TH	144
N203WS	**C560**	**0785**
N203XP	HS25	HA-0203
N203XP	BE40	RK-503
N203XX	GLEX	9203
N204A	CS55	0008
N204A	GLF2	79
N204A	LJ25	014
N204AB	C550	365
N204AB	GALX	037
N204AB	WW24	342
N204AN	**FA20**	**102**
N204BG	**C560**	**0503**
N204BP	PRM1	RB-204
(N204BX)	LJ60	007
N204C	GLF2	143
N204CA	**C500**	**429**
N204CE	**F2EX**	**165**
N204CF	**C550**	**233**
N204CW	F2EX	101
N204DD	FA20	494
N204DD	FA50	54
N204DD	**GALX**	**139**
N204DH	**BE40**	**RK-290**
N204ED	**FA20**	**315/517**
N204FJ	F9EX	4
N204FJ	FA10	139
N204FJ	FA20	490
N204FX	LJ60	007
N204G	SBRL	306-91
N204GA	GLF2	167
N204GA	GLF2	74
N204HC	FA50	136
N204J	**C525**	**0164**
N204JC	HS25	258175
N204JK	**CL61**	**5015**

N204JP	FA20	24
N204KR	BE40	RK-204
(N204LX)	C525	0154
N204MC	C550	017
N204MK	LJ45	204
N204N	HS25	257113
N204PG	LJ40	2107
N204PM	**C550**	**343**
N204QS	**F2TH**	**104**
N204R	HS25	257113
N204R	HS25	259017
N204R	SBRL	306-91
N204RC	GLF2	34
N204RP	C52B	0289
N204RP	C680	0093
N204RT	**LJ31**	**204**
N204SM	HS25	258135
N204TM	SBRL	282-56
N204TM	WW24	320
N204TW	**FA20**	**204**
N204WS	**FA10**	**181**
N204XP	HS25	HA-0204
N204XP	BE40	RK-504
N204Y	C500	204
N204Y	LJ24	113
N204ZQ	**EA50**	**000186**
(N205A)	CL60	1029
N205AJ	WW24	205
(N205B)	WW24	391
N205BC	C560	0010
N205BC	**PRM1**	**RB-69**
N205BE	C550	647
N205BL	GLF2	205
N205BN	**C525**	**0050**
N205BS	HS25	257048
N205CM	**C560**	**0250**
N205CW	F2EX	45
N205EE	CL61	3011
N205EE	CL64	5347
(N205EF)	LJ55	053
N205EL	CL60	1067
N205EL	CL61	3011
N205EL	CL64	5347
N205EL	**GLEX**	**9201**
N205EL	LJ35	283
N205EL	LJ55	053
N205EX	GLEX	9205
N205FH	C525	0355
N205FJ	F9EX	5
N205FJ	FA10	140
N205FJ	FA20	120
N205FJ	FA20	491
(N205FJ)	FA20	142
N205FL	LJ35	283
N205FM	C500	264
N205FP	**CL30**	**20220**
N205FX	LJ60	005
N205GP	GALX	205
N205GY	PRM1	RB-205
N205JA	**FA50**	**274**
N205JC	FA20	440
N205K	FA20	319
N205K	GLF2	231
N205LX	F2EX	205
(N205LX)	C525	0199
N205M	GLF2	18
N205MM	CL60	1044
N205MM	HFB3	1039
(N205NP)	C525	0205
N205PC	C560	0010
N205QS	**CL65**	**6054**
N205R	BE40	RK-30
N205RJ	LJ24	041
N205SA	LJ25	041
N205SC	C550	176
N205SC	FA20	155
N205SC	LJ25	041
(N205SE)	FA20	155
N205SG	C550	176
N205ST	LJ60	205
(N205TS)	FA20	54
N205TW	**HS25**	**257025**
N205VP	C560	0205
N205VR	**F2TH**	**205**
N205WM	FA20	306/512
N205WP	**FA20**	**306/512**
N205X	FA10	44
N205X	GLF4	1080
N205XP	HS25	HA-0205
N205YY	**C52A**	**0205**
N205ZZ	**FA20**	**379**
N206AG	C550	330
N206AH	**E50P**	**50000059**
N206CK	**LJ45**	**047**
N206CX	C56X	5206
N206EC	LJ25	206
N206EC	LJ35	487
N206EQ	LJ25	206
N206EX	F9EX	206
N206FC	LJ35	487
N206FJ	FA10	14
(N206FJ)	FA20	487
N206FS	**G280**	**2031**
N206FX	LJ60	028
N206HY	**LJ60**	**028**
N206LX	C525	0205
N206MD	GLF2	22

N206PC	C750	0016
N206PC	HS25	258038
N206QS	**CL65**	**6055**
N206TC	C550	465
N206WC	HS25	258038
N206XP	HS25	HA-0206
N207AA	**GLF4**	**1456**
N207AH	**PRM1**	**RB-207**
N207AP	C550	104
N207AW	**LJ60**	**282**
N207BA	C550	234
N207BA	BE40	RJ-7
N207BC	**ASTR**	**093**
N207BG	**C52A**	**0326**
N207BS	C525	0241
N207BS	**C525**	**0445**
N207BS	C52A	0055
N207BX	LJ60	050
N207CA	**FA20**	**153**
N207CC	C650	0207
(N207CF)	C500	610
N207CJ	**C52C**	**0207**
N207CV	C560	0207
N207EA	**EA50**	**000207**
N207EM	F2TH	207
N207FJ	F900	200
N207FJ	FA10	142
N207FJ	FA20	401
N207FX	LJ60	050
N207G	C500	647
N207GA	GLF2	136
N207HF	LJ25	230
N207JB	**CL61**	**5194**
N207JC	LJ25	207
N207JF	C500	610
N207JS	**FA20**	**117**
N207K	**HS25**	**259045**
N207L	JSTR	5050/34
N207L	JSTR	5067
N207L	JSTR	5100/41
(N207L)	C500	038
N207LJ	**LJ60**	**207**
(N207LX)	C525	0218
N207MJ	**MS76**	**002**
N207MM	**C52A**	**0084**
N207PC	C56X	5008
N207PC	HS25	257197
N207PC	HS25	258185
N207QS	F2TH	70
N207R	**CL65**	**5882**
N207R	HS25	259045
N207RC	HS25	257197
(N207RC)	HS25	258185
N207RG	LJ24	339
N207RT	**C52C**	**0202**
N207TB	**EA50**	**000179**
N207TR	FA7X	35
N207TT	**HS25**	**259008**
N207US	FA10	207
(N207VC)	LJ60	207
N207WM	EA50	000247
N207WW	WW24	207
N208BC	C560	0050
N208BG	**C52A**	**0414**
N208BG	HS25	258208
N208BH	**LJ60**	**208**
N208BP	PRM1	RB-208
N208BX	LJ60	059
N208CV	C560	0208
N208D	BE40	RJ-14
N208DX	**E50P**	**50000097**
N208EA	C500	612
N208F	MU30	A016SA
(N208FC)	C550	550-0908
N208FJ	FA10	144
N208FJ	FA20	493
N208FX	LJ60	059
N208GA	G150	208
N208GA	G150	288
N208GA	G150	308
N208GA	G280	2008
N208GA	G280	2085
N208H	HS25	25141
N208H	HS25	25163
N208HP	PRM1	RB-232
N208JV	C525	0208
N208L	HS25	259011
N208L	JSTR	5050/34
N208L	JSTR	5083/49
N208LT	CL64	5440
(N208LX)	C525	0247
N208MD	WW24	208
(N208MD)	FA20	315/517
N208MF	**C680**	**0233**
N208MM	HFB3	1039
N208MM	**PRM1**	**RB-232**
N208N	C500	021
N208PC	C560	0050
N208PC	C56X	5005
N208QS	**CL65**	**6056**
N208QS	F2TH	206
N208R	CL64	5316
N208R	HS25	259011
N208R	BE40	RJ-14
(N208RT)	FA20	490
N208ST	WW24	208
N208TC	C550	327

N208VP	**C560**	**0208**
N208W	C500	421
(N208WR)	LJ35	190
N209A	C650	0156
N209AM	**C52A**	**0365**
N209BA	BE40	RJ-9
N209BK	**BE40**	**RK-137**
N209BP	PRM1	RB-209
N209BS	C525	0241
N209CA	FA20	71
N209CJ	C510	0209
N209CP	C560	0055
N209CQ	**F9EX**	**98**
(N209CR)	C680	0069
N209CV	**C560**	**0209**
N209EA	**EA50**	**000209**
N209EX	F9EX	209
(N209EX)	F2EX	9
N209FJ	F2TH	9
N209FJ	F9EX	2
N209FJ	FA10	145
N209FJ	FA20	494
N209FS	F2TH	209
N209FS	**G280**	**2018**
N209FX	LJ60	060
N209G	C550	558
N209GA	G150	309
N209GA	G280	2009
N209GA	G280	2090
N209GA	GLF2	9/33
N209HP	**HS25**	**HB-26**
N209HR	LJ31	209
N209KM	LJ45	209
N209LS	GLF4	1449
(N209LX)	C525	0253
(N209LX)	F2EX	209
N209MD	**LJ40**	**2127**
N209MG	**GLF5**	**545**
N209MW	C500	209
N209NC	HS25	25190
N209QS	**CL65**	**6057**
N209RR	WW24	127
N209SU	F2EX	163
N209TM	F2TH	209
N209TS	**HS25**	**257014**
(N209WE)	CL60	1034
N209WF	CL60	1034
N209XP	HS25	HA-0209
N210A	GLEX	9203
N210CJ	C525	0010
N210CJ	C525	0210
N210CM	**C560**	**0369**
N210EK	JSTR	5117/35
N210EM	FA10	210
N210F	C650	0067
N210F	SBRL	306-25
N210FE	WW24	95
N210FF	**E50P**	**50000088**
N210FJ	F900	201
N210FJ	**F9EX**	**210**
N210FJ	FA10	13
N210FJ	FA20	495
N210FP	LJ24	155
N210FX	LJ60	064
N210GA	GLF2	102/32
N210GK	GLF3	875
N210GP	LJ24	020
N210HV	LJ60	064
N210KP	PRM1	RB-210
N210M	HS25	25103
N210MJ	C550	108
(N210MJ)	FA10	113
(N210MJ)	FA10	178
N210MT	C550	210
N210NC	LJ25	154
N210PC	LJ24	036
N210PM	**C510**	**0301**
N210QS	**F2TH**	**211**
N210RK	**HS25**	**257073**
N210RS	FA20	18
(N210ST)	HS25	256009
N210VS	**C56X**	**5093**
N210WL	LJ35	210
N211BC	LJ55	145
N211BL	GLF2	113
N211BL	LJ24	150
N211BR	**SBRL**	**282-99**
N211BR	SBRL	306-85
N211BX	LJ60	076
N211BY	LJ35	227
(N211BY)	LJ55	059
N211CC	C650	0211
N211CC	**C680**	**0034**
N211CD	LJ25	275
N211CN	FA10	173
N211CN	FA50	31
N211CQ	C650	0211
N211DB	C500	174
N211DB	WW24	405
N211DG	C560	0167
N211DH	GLF2	236
N211DH	**GLF4**	**1432**
N211DH	LJ35	253
N211DK	**GLF4**	**1078**
N211EC	**FA10**	**166**
N211EF	C500	434
N211EF	FA50	123
N211EF	LJ55	101
N211FJ	FA10	146
N211FJ	FA20	347
N211FX	LJ60	076
N211FZ	GLF4	4013
N211GA	**MU30**	**A011SA**
(N211GA)	GLF2	36/3
N211GM	**C525**	**0208**
N211GS	CL65	5965
N211GS	**LJ55**	**021**
N211HF	FA20	289
N211HF	FA20	474
N211HJ	LJ24	150
N211HS	GLF5	5206
N211HS	**GLF6**	**6003**
N211JA	F900	63
N211JB	LJ25	249
N211JC	LJ25	310
(N211JE)	LJ25	310
N211JH	**C525**	**0386**
N211JL	**FA10**	**180**
N211JN	**HS25**	**258104**
N211JS	C550	105
N211LM	**CL61**	**3024**
(N211LX)	C525	0326
N211MA	C560	0022
N211MA	GLF4	1247
(N211MA)	C650	0219
N211MB	LJ25	059
N211MT	**C550**	**105**
N211MT	GLF2	52
N211PA	JSTR	5227
N211PB	**GLEX**	**9378**
N211PD	LJ25	310
N211QS	**CL65**	**6058**
N211QS	CS55	0011
N211RG	**CL61**	**5107**
N211RN	**LJ31**	**072**
N211RR	C650	0079
N211SF	SBRL	282-136
N211SJ	GLF2	75/7
N211SP	C550	337
N211SR	FA10	115
N211ST	**WW24**	**303**
N211TB	CL30	20117
N211TJ	FA10	11
N211TS	LJ24	066
N211VP	CS55	0002
N211VR	C52B	0201
(N211WC)	C560	0311
N211WG	**F900**	**142**
N211WH	LJ35	269
N211WZ	HS25	257017
N211X	C500	434
N211XP	HS25	HA-0011
N211XP	HS25	HA-0211
N212AD	GLF3	492
N212AP	JSTR	5147
N212AT	C500	403
N212AT	GLF3	492
N212AT	GLF4	1204
N212AW	GLF4	1240
N212BA	**GLF3**	**353**
N212BD	C560	0309
N212BH	C550	550-1020
N212BW	C560	0038
N212BX	LJ60	099
N212C	C510	0060
N212C	FA20	155
N212CE	**C56X**	**5639**
N212CP	WW24	340
N212CT	CL61	5104
N212CW	WW24	75
N212EA	**EA50**	**000212**
N212EX	F9EX	212
N212F	SBRL	306-25
N212FH	BE40	RK-448
N212FJ	FA10	147
N212FJ	FA20	497
N212FX	LJ60	077
N212FX	LJ60	099
(N212FX)	LJ60	007
N212GA	GLF2	140/40
N212GA	LJ35	354
N212GB	C52B	0478
(N212GW)	LJ25	203
N212H	C550	105
N212H	FA20	259
N212HF	**C56X**	**6190**
N212JA	**LJ60**	**010**
N212JE	**GLF4**	**1085**
N212JP	FA50	94
N212JP	LJ55	006
N212JW	JSTR	5131
N212K	FA50	89
N212K	GLF2	195
N212K	GLF4	1192
N212KM	FA50	89
N212LD	ASTR	020
N212LE	GLEX	9607
N212LE	GLF4	4139
N212LF	**GLEX**	**9607**
N212LF	GLF4	4139
N212LF	GLF6	6090
N212LF	LJ24	216
N212LM	CL61	5037
N212LP	**C560**	**0483**
(N212LX)	C525	0339
N212M	**C500**	**415**
N212MP	GALX	033
N212N	FA10	150
N212N	FA50	202
N212NC	FA10	150
N212NE	LJ25	212
(N212PA)	MU30	A038SA
N212PB	FA20	313
N212Q	FA50	179
N212QS	**CL65**	**6066**
N212QS	F2TH	213
N212R	FA20	212
N212RG	HS25	258073
N212RH	**C525**	**0636**
N212RR	CL64	5336
N212SL	GALX	055
N212T	**ASTR**	**110**
N212T	F2TH	52
N212T	FA20	273
N212T	FA50	192
N212TC	FA20	273
N212TG	FA20	273
N212TJ	GLF2	12
N212U	**GALX**	**164**
N212US	F2TH	40
N212VZ	GLF4	1531
N212VZ	**GLF4**	**4325**
N212WW	WW24	212
N212WZ	GLF4	1489
N212XX	**HS25**	**257093**
N213AP	JSTR	5122
N213AR	LJ31	107
N213BA	**GLF3**	**453**
(N213BE)	SBRL	306-123
N213BK	**BE40**	**RK-216**
N213BM	SBRL	282-111
N213BP	PRM1	RB-213
N213BR	LJ31	103
N213C	HS25	257213
N213CA	LJ25	241
N213CC	**C550**	**250**
(N213CE)	C500	213
N213CF	C550	124
N213CJ	C52A	0213
N213CJ	**C52C**	**0213**
(N213DC)	GLF2	19
N213EX	F9EX	213
N213F	**C52B**	**0184**
(N213FC)	FA20	213
N213FJ	FA10	148
N213FJ	FA20	499
(N213FX)	LJ60	086
N213GA	GLF5	5413
N213GS	CL61	5101
N213GS	**CL65**	**5965**
N213H	HS25	25119
N213HP	**C650**	**0133**
N213JS	**C550**	**597**
N213JT	**C525**	**0492**
N213LG	MU30	A079SA
N213LS	FA20	107
(N213LX)	C525	0348
N213MC	CL61	5171
N213MF	LJ31	213
N213NU	LJ31	213
N213PA	LJ31	013
N213PC	PRM1	RB-173
N213PC	**PRM1**	**RB-288**
N213PC	PRM1	RB-75
N213PQ	**PRM1**	**RB-75**
N213QS	**F2TH**	**113**
N213RG	**HS25**	**258073**
N213RQ	PRM1	RB-173
N213TG	**GLF4**	**4219**
N213TS	**CL61**	**3013**
N213VU	**PRM1**	**RB-197**
N213WW	WW24	213
N213X	**GLF2**	**213**
N214AM	C550	312
N214AS	**FA20**	**501**
N214BL	CL30	20214
N214BM	GLF4	1050
(N214BM)	C750	0032
N214BX	LJ60	046
N214CA	C500	214
N214CC	C500	214
N214CC	WW24	197
(N214CP)	C550	635
N214DV	FA50	289
N214DV	**FA50**	**350**
N214EE	**LEG5**	**55010007**
N214FJ	F2TH	214
N214FJ	FA10	149
N214FJ	FA20	500
(N214FJ)	FA50	214
N214FT	**FA50**	**300**
N214FW	CL61	3008
N214FX	LJ60	046
N214GA	G280	2014
N214GA	G280	2041
N214GA	GALX	114
N214GA	GLF2	160
N214GA	GLF4	4214
(N214GA)	FA50	105
N214GP	GLF2	3
N214HT	C510	0097
N214JP	FA20	296/507
N214JR	HS25	25070
N214JR	HS25	25146
N214JT	**C550**	**417**
N214L	C560	0381
N214LD	**F2TH**	**41**
N214LF	LJ45	214
N214LJ	LJ25	214
N214LS	LJ35	096
(N214LS)	C560	0190
(N214LS)	LJ35	229
N214LV	**C680**	**0096**
(N214LX)	C525	0026
N214MD	C550	273
N214MD	CL61	3016
N214MD	**GLEX**	**9152**
N214ME	LJ25	214
N214MJ	LJ24	214
N214MS	**EA50**	**000252**
N214NW	GLF2	214
N214PC	**E50P**	**50000298**
N214PG	MU30	A082SA
N214PN	CS55	0038
N214PW	CL30	20119
N214PW	LJ31	219
N214PW	LJ60	264
N214QS	CS55	0014
(N214RG)	HS25	258073
N214RT	**C525**	**0852**
N214RV	**FA10**	**217**
N214RW	C550	478
N214RW	CL30	20119
N214RW	**CL30**	**20308**
N214RW	LJ31	219
N214RW	LJ60	264
N214SG	**CL30**	**20004**
N214TC	HS25	25146
N214TD	**HS25**	**258332**
N214TJ	C550	550-0900
N214TS	GLF4	1121
N214WM	BE40	RK-197
N214WT	**C750**	**0032**
N214WW	WW24	214
N214WY	GLF3	441
(N214XP)	HS25	HA-0214
N215BB	**HS25**	**258630**
N215BL	CL30	20215
N215BR	PRM1	RB-215
N215BX	LJ60	101
N215C	WW24	206
N215CC	C500	215
N215CJ	**C52C**	**0215**
N215CM	C650	0215
N215CW	C550	175
N215CX	C750	0215
N215DA	**CL30**	**20304**
N215DH	WW24	215
N215DL	JSTR	5215
N215EF	**F9EX**	**280**
N215EX	F2EX	15
N215FJ	F2EX	215
N215FJ	FA10	150
N215FJ	FA20	498
N215FX	LJ60	101
N215G	HS25	25058
N215G	HS25	257095
N215G	WW24	206
N215GA	G150	215
N215GA	G280	2015
N215GA	GLF2	93
N215H	**C560**	**0352**
(N215HZ)	JSTR	5215
N215J	LJ24	134
N215JW	LJ35	223
N215KH	F2TH	197
N215KM	LJ60	109
(N215LX)	C525	0114
N215M	WW24	206
N215NA	**C500**	**622**
N215NJ	C510	0307
N215QS	**F2TH**	**214**
N215RB	**C525**	**0031**
N215RE	**F2TH**	**215**
N215RL	CL60	1068
N215RL	GLF2	45
N215RL	LJ36	012
N215RS	**HS25**	**257023**
N215RX	C750	0225
N215SC	WW24	243
N215SP	HS25	258316
N215TM	GLF4	1400
N215TP	**BE40**	**RJ-64**
N215TS	JSTR	5215
N215TT	LJ31	076
(N215WC)	C560	0315
N215WS	**C680**	**0316**
N215Z	LJ24	246
N215Z	LJ25	020
N216BG	FA20	196
N216BX	LJ60	103
N216CA	FA20	11
(N216CC)	C500	216
N216CJ	C525	0016
N216CJ	C52B	0216
N216CW	C525	0116
N216FB	F900	65
N216FJ	FA10	152
N216FJ	FA20	502
N216FP	F900	146
N216FP	F900	65
N216FX	LJ60	103
N216GA	G150	216
N216GA	G280	2016
N216GA	GALX	116
N216GA	GLF4	4116
N216GA	GLF4	4216
N216HB	LJ24	275
N216HE	GLF2	113
N216KH	HS25	257038
(N216MF)	GLF2	113
N216PA	GLEX	9282
N216R	SBRL	282-94
N216RG	LJ24	066
N216RL	C500	467
N216RR	GLF2	22
N216SA	FA20	16
N216SA	LJ25	216
(N216SA)	LJ24	082
N216SC	WW24	216
N216TM	**C52B**	**0387**
N216TW	FA20	16
(N216VP)	C550	017
N216WD	**FA50**	**112**
(N216XP)	HS25	HA-0216
(N216YM)	GALX	034
N217A	HS25	256030
N217A	SBRL	282-103
N217A	SBRL	306-85
(N217AH)	GLF2	197
N217AJ	FA20	171
N217AJ	**LJ24**	**345**
N217AL	C750	0217
N217AL	HS25	258177
N217AL	WW24	38
N217AT	LJ24	217
N217BA	**GALX**	**144**
N217BL	WW24	284
N217BM	WW24	409
N217BX	LJ60	105
N217CA	FA20	75
N217CB	**E55P**	**50500305**
N217CC	C500	217
N217CJ	C525	0117
N217CJ	**C52C**	**0217**
N217CK	**LJ35**	**217**
N217CM	C650	0217
(N217CP)	FA10	100
N217CS	LJ35	062
N217CS	LJ36	039
N217CX	C750	0217
(N217DA)	GLF2	17
N217E	SBRL	282-103
N217EC	**BE40**	**RK-356**
N217EM	GLF4	1045
N217EX	F2EX	17
N217F	HS25	25175
N217F	WW24	321
N217FJ	FA10	151
N217FJ	FA20	504
N217FS	C550	308
N217FX	LJ60	105
N217GA	G150	217
N217GA	G150	297
N217GA	GALX	117
N217GA	GLF2	17
N217GA	GLF5	5227
N217GH	**CL30**	**20248**
N217GL	**C560**	**0076**
(N217JC)	GLEX	9079
N217JD	GLF2	14
N217JS	GLF2	113
N217JS	LJ24	345
N217LG	C550	304
N217MB	BE40	RK-217
N217MJ	**LJ45**	**217**
N217MS	**G150**	**217**
N217MW	**C560**	**0361**
N217PM	WW24	16
N217PM	WW24	38
N217PT	ASTR	105
N217RJ	C650	0079
N217RM	CL60	1054
N217RM	HS25	258017
N217RM	SBRL	306-94
N217RM	WW24	409
N217RN	SBRL	306-94
N217RR	C500	643
N217RR	C650	0079
N217RR	GLF2	22
N217RR	GLF4	1042
N217RT	LJ35	379
N217S	C500	217
N217SA	**C550**	**263**
N217SC	WW24	217
N217SQ	WW24	217
N217TA	**LJ35**	**289**
N217TE	SBRL	282-103
(N217TE)	GLF2	33
N217TH	**C560**	**0390**
N217TL	GLF2	33
N217W	C52A	0022
N217WC	C560	0317
N217WC	WW24	217
N217WM	LJ25	217

(N217XP)	HS25	HA-0217
N218AC	HS25	256013
N218AD	**HS25**	**258139**
N218AL	**GLEX**	**9260**
N218AM	C500	626
N218AM	C56X	5218
N218BA	FA10	218
N218BR	C560	0218
N218BX	LJ60	098
N218CA	**FA20**	**218**
N218CC	C650	0218
(N218CC)	C500	218
(N218CP)	GLF5	656
(N218CR)	LJ35	258
N218DF	C560	0218
N218DJ	WW24	218
N218EC	GLF5	656
N218EE	**GLF3**	**489**
N218EX	F2EX	22
N218FJ	FA10	153
N218FJ	FA20	503
N218FX	LJ60	098
N218G	**EA50**	**000197**
(N218G)	C550	550-0888
N218GA	G150	218
N218GA	GLF2	218
N218GA	GLF4	1518
N218GA	GLF4	4218
N218H	C550	430
N218JG	**C500**	**626**
N218JL	**LJ45**	**131**
N218JT	**EA50**	**000047**
N218KD	**GLF4**	**1164**
N218KF	**CL30**	**20438**
N218LX	F2EX	218
N218MB	**C52C**	**0117**
N218MD	**GLF3**	**467**
N218NB	LJ25	361
N218NB	**LJ31**	**146**
N218NR	LJ25	361
N218PH	**F2TH**	**218**
N218PM	WW24	218
N218QS	**F2TH**	**118**
N218R	LJ25	365
N218RG	**E50P**	**50000172**
N218RG	BE40	RJ-45
N218S	FA20	32
N218SC	WW24	271
N218SE	C560	0086
N218SE	GLF2	116
N218SV	**C680**	**0218**
N218TJ	**HS25**	**25018**
(N218UB)	SBRL	380-45
N218US	FA20	51
N218US	SBRL	380-45
N218WA	FA50	218
N218WW	GLF4	4058
N218WW	WW24	218
(N218XP)	HS25	HA-0218
N219AX	GALX	019
N219CA	FA20	193
N219CC	C500	219
N219CC	C650	0219
N219CJ	C525	0219
N219CM	**C52A**	**0045**
N219CQ	**C52A**	**0182**
N219CS	C550	374
N219DC	LJ60	061
N219DC	BE40	RK-518
(N219DC)	HS25	258327
N219EA	**EA50**	**000219**
N219EC	HS25	25219
N219EX	F2EX	20
N219F	C52B	0091
N219FJ	F2TH	219
N219FJ	FA10	154
N219FJ	FA20	508
N219FL	C52A	0111
N219FX	LJ60	007
N219GA	G150	219
N219GA	GALX	019
N219GA	GLF2	91
N219GA	GLF5	5419
N219GR	C525	0893
N219JA	HS25	257013
(N219JA)	HS25	258005
N219JL	**LJ45**	**267**
N219JW	FA10	219
N219L	C52B	0091
N219L	**C52C**	**0023**
N219LC	C550	550-1020
N219LC	**C680**	**0249**
N219MF	JSTR	5219
N219MS	**C550**	**193**
N219RB	LJ25	255
N219RB	**LJ40**	**2058**
N219RR	**LJ25**	**255**
N219RW	CL30	20308
N219SC	C550	374
N219SJ	BE40	RK-219
N219ST	HS25	256009
N219TF	**HS25**	**HB-41**
N219TS	HS25	257026
N219TT	SBRL	380-24
(N219XP)	HS25	HA-0219
N219YY	**CL61**	**5055**
N220AB	C550	630
N220AB	**F2TH**	**170**
N220AJ	ASTR	077
N220AR	LJ45	067
(N220AR)	LJ25	097
N220AZ	**LJ60**	**418**
N220BA	**C52C**	**0047**
N220BJ	BE40	RK-220
N220BP	**C555**	**0034**
N220BW	EA50	000179
N220CA	C555	0085
N220CA	FA20	220
N220CC	C500	118
N220CC	C550	040
N220CC	C550	457
N220CC	C650	0140
N220CJ	C525	0220
N220CK	LJ35	120
N220CM	C560	0048
N220CM	**C650**	**0160**
N220CM	FA20	11
N220CV	**FA10**	**220**
N220DF	**F2TH**	**69**
N220DH	**C550**	**550-0860**
N220DH	WW24	440
N220DK	**C510**	**0150**
N220EJ	F2TH	105
N220EJ	F2TH	69
(N220ES)	JSTR	5204
N220FJ	FA20	313
N220FJ	FA20	507
(N220FJ)	FA10	155
N220FL	GLF2	50
N220FL	HS25	257117
N220FX	LJ60	108
N220GA	G150	220
N220GA	GALX	120
N220GA	GLF2	184
N220GA	GLF4	1042
(N220GA)	GLF2	234
N220GH	LJ35	220
N220GS	**LJ35**	**220**
N220GV	**C52C**	**0220**
N220HM	**C500**	**583**
N220HS	LJ25	220
N220JC	LJ55	050
N220JD	C52A	0120
N220JJ	**HS25**	**258475**
N220JL	**C525**	**0020**
N220JM	F2TH	47
N220JM	F2TH	85
(N220JM)	C525	0493
(N220JM)	F2TH	46
(N220JM)	F2TH	69
N220JN	F2TH	69
N220JP	FA50	22
N220JR	GLF2	50
N220JT	C560	0272
N220KP	WW24	117
N220KS	**FA10**	**71**
N220LA	C550	144
N220LA	**FA20**	**296/507**
N220LC	C52B	0251
N220LC	C560	0315
N220LC	CL60	1071
N220LC	**CL61**	**5006**
(N220LC)	CL61	5038
N220LE	C550	722
N220LH	GLF4	1054
N220LJ	LJ31	220
N220M	FA10	34
(N220MR)	F2TH	69
N220MT	C500	135
N220MT	CRVT	40
N220N	M220	1
N220NJ	LJ25	220
N220NJ	LJ35	021
N220PA	FA10	113
N220PK	HS25	258808
N220PM	LJ24	158
(N220PX)	LJ60	108
N220RT	FA20	142
N220S	C500	192
N220SC	**C560**	**0326**
N1220SC	FA10	158
N220ST	WW24	46
N220T	HS25	25201
N220TE	EA50	000020
N220TG	LJ25	370
N220TS	HS25	256021
N220TV	C650	0060
N220TW	C650	0060
N220TW	CL61	5067
N220VE	LJ55	108
N220W	C500	025
N220WC	C560	0321
N220WE	**FA20**	**349**
N221AA	E50P	50000293
N221AC	C500	392
N221AE	C56X	250
N221AL	ASTR	154
(N221AL)	C750	0217
N221AM	C500	109
N221AM	C56X	6044
N221AP	LJ25	290
N221B	FA20	12
N221BJ	BE40	RK-221
N221BR	FA20	74
N221BS	GALX	110
N221BW	**CL61**	**5188**
(N221BW)	C550	271
N221CC	C500	118
N221CC	C500	221
N221CE	C560	0557
N221CF	WW24	93
N221CM	**GLF3**	**343**
N221CR	JSTR	5214
N221DA	**C500**	**201**
N221DG	GLF5	5020
N221DG	**GLF6**	**6061**
N221DT	ASTR	016
N221EA	**GLF4**	**1476**
N221EB	C500	643
N221EJ	F2TH	85
N221EJ	**LJ31**	**203**
N221EL	LJ25	290
N221EX	F2EX	21
N221EX	F9EX	221
N221FJ	FA10	156
N221FJ	FA20	505
N221FX	LJ60	111
N221GA	C550	135
N221GA	C550	441
N221GA	**G150**	**321**
N221GA	GALX	125
N221GA	GLF4	1521
N221GA	GLF5	5221
N221GA	GLF6	6021
N221H	**FA20**	**461**
N221HB	HS25	258052
N221HJ	**FA7X**	**19**
(N221JB)	C500	392
(N221JS)	C550	317
N221LC	C52B	0103
N221LC	C56X	5077
N221LC	**C680**	**0228**
N221LC	CL61	5066
(N221LC)	C550	383
N221LV	LJ25	235
N221MC	LJ35	407
N221MJ	WW24	160
N221MJ	WW24	204
N221NB	GLF4	4059
N221PA	ASTR	016
N221PB	**HS25**	**258623**
N221PF	SBRL	306-15
N221PH	SBRL	282-55
N221PH	SBRL	306-15
N221PH	SBRL	380-49
(N221PX)	SBRL	282-55
N221QS	**F2EX**	**54**
N221RE	HS25	258119
N221RJ	WW24	160
N221SG	LJ35	182
N221TC	LJ25	136
N221TR	LJ35	221
N221TW	**FA20**	**221**
N221UE	LJ35	042
N221VP	C560	0585
N221WR	**GLF3**	**381**
(N221XP1)	HS25	HA-0221
N221Z	LJ55	059
N222	GLF4	1142
N222AD	GLF4	1057
N222AG	C550	163
N222AK	LJ25	127
N222AP	LJ24	211
N222AP	LJ25	225
(N222AP)	GLF3	391
N222AW	LJ36	012
N222B	LJ25	047
N222BE	LJ35	180
N222BE	LJ35	489
N222BG	LJ35	448
N222BK	LJ35	180
N222BN	F2TH	135
N222BN	LJ24	296
N222BR	LJ60	310
N222BW	GLF3	440
N222CC	C500	222
N222CD	C650	0222
N222CX	C750	0222
N222D	C550	027
N222DE	C550	027
N222FA	C550	725
N222FJ	FA10	157
N222FJ	FA20	509
N222FJ	WVII	001
N222FX	LJ60	008
N222G	GLF3	422
N222G	HS25	25064
N222GH	LJ24	026
N222GL	WW24	47
N222GP	E50P	50000218
N222GT	C650	0093
N222GY	**GLF4**	**1142**
N222HL	HS25	257088
N222HM	WW24	47
N222HV	LJ60	008
N222JE	**BE40**	**RK-4**
N222KC	GLF3	366
N222KC	WW24	434
N222KN	JSTR	5118
N222KW	C500	080
N222LB	C500	212
N222LB	C550	093
N222LH	CL60	1052
N222LH	WW24	209
N222LM	**CL60**	**1052**
N222LR	**G150**	**238**
N222LW	LJ25	299
N222LX	**GLF5**	**633**
N222MC	**CL64**	**5329**
N222MC	FA50	179
N222MC	LJ25	076
N222MC	LJ55	061
N222MC	LJ55	108
(N222MC)	FA50	141
(N222MC)	GLF4	1382
N222MF	JSTR	5229
N222MJ	C550	154
N222MQ	LJ25	076
N222MS	C500	018
N222MS	**HS25**	**258132**
N222MU	**FA10**	**164**
N222MW	**LJ45**	**110**
N222MW	WW24	255
(N222MZ)	CL64	5329
N222NB	GLF2	245/30
N222NB	GLF4	4059
N222NB	**GLF4**	**4229**
N222NF	**C52A**	**0074**
N222NG	HS25	25016
N222NP	**GLF2**	**245/30**
N222PV	GLF2	234
N222Q	MU30	A021SA
N222QA	JSTR	5116
N222QS	**F2TH**	**122**
(N222R)	JSTR	5016
N222RA	**GLF4**	**1375**
N222RB	HS25	25224
N222RB	HS25	257004
N222RB	LJ24	136
N222RG	HS25	25224
N222SG	C550	122
N222SL	C500	096
N222SL	LJ35	162
N222SR	WW24	194
N222TG	C550	098
N222TW	**LJ24**	**161**
N222VR	**C52B**	**0155**
N222VV	C500	310
N222VV	C550	151
N222WA	**C500**	**360**
N222WL	C550	241
N222Y	JSTR	5006/40
N222YJ	**BE40**	**RJ-15**
N223AF	HA4T	RC-46
N223AM	C56X	5018
(N223AM)	GALX	011
N223AS	C500	212
N223B	FA20	102
N223BG	**FA20**	**250**
(N223BX)	LJ60	124
N223CC	C500	223
N223CF	**C525**	**0403**
N223CV	C560	0223
N223DD	FA50	128
(N223DK)	BE40	RK-142
N223EX	F2EX	23
N223EX	F9EX	223
N223F	FA50	328
N223F	PRM1	RB-22
N223FA	HS25	258559
N223FJ	FA10	158
N223FJ	FA20	510
N223FX	LJ60	124
N223G	HS25	25170
N223GA	ASTR	141
N223GA	GALX	123
N223GA	**GLF5**	**538**
N223GB	**C52B**	**0476**
N223GC	C500	570
N223HD	FA50	283
N223HS	FA10	160
N223J	C550	410
N223JF	**C525**	**0223**
N223JV	**C560**	**0131**
N223LB	C500	212
N223LB	SBRL	465-23
N223LC	C500	425
N223LP	SBRL	380-5
N223LX	F2EX	223
N223MC	C500	212
N223MD	GLF5	665
N223P	C500	223
N223PA	WW24	171
N223PW	**C510**	**0314**
N223QS	**F2EX**	**86**
(N223RE)	C500	486
N223RR	**HS25**	**25282**
N223S	C500	233
N223S	MU30	A033SA
(N223SS)	GLF5	572
N223SV	C680	0223
N223TE	EA50	000023
N223TG	LJ25	370
N223TV	**CL30**	**20151**
N223TW	**FA20**	**123**
N223VP	C560	0223
N223WA	WW24	423
N223WW	WW24	153
N223XP	BE40	RK-423
N224BA	**C525**	**0669**
N224BH	**GLF4**	**4241**
N224BP	FA10	159
N224CC	C550	224
N224CC	FA10	36
(N224CC)	C500	224
N224CD	C650	0224
N224CJ	**C525**	**0224**
N224CV	C560	0224
N224DJ	LJ55	024
N224EA	**HS25**	**257088**
N224EX	F2EX	24
N224F	CL61	3064
N224F	CL61	5163
N224FD	**BE40**	**RK-324**
N224FJ	FA10	159
N224FJ	FA20	512
N224FL	BE40	RK-324
N224FX	LJ60	126
N224GP	C500	499
N224GP	**C560**	**0079**
N224GP	WW24	372
N224GX	GLEX	9224
N224HD	FA50	336
(N224HF)	CL61	3064
N224JB	LJ24	321
N224JV	C56X	6120
N224JW	**C56X**	**6120**
N224KC	**C555**	**0104**
N224KL	**GLF3**	**409**
N224KT	LJ24	161
N224LJ	LJ31	224
N224MC	**BE40**	**RK-165**
N224MD	E50P	50000057
N224MF	JSTR	5229
N224N	CL61	3064
N224N	CL61	5108
N224N	**CL64**	**5661**
N224NS	CL64	5661
N224PA	**WW24**	**411**
N224PG	C650	0054
N224QS	**F2TH**	**124**
N224RP	C500	632
N224RP	FA10	159
N224SC	LJ24	100
(N224TS)	GLF2	24
N224U	CL61	3064
(N224WC)	C560	0466
N224WD	C52A	0122
N224WE	**FA20**	**272**
N224ZQ	**EA50**	**000162**
N225AC	LJ25	139
N225AC	LJ25	280
N225AD	C550	118
N225AL	ASTR	075
N225AR	CL30	20166
N225AR	CL64	5500
(N225AR)	CL65	5702
N225AS	**E50P**	**50000239**
N225BC	C500	274
N225BJ	**HS25**	**257044**
(N225BK)	GLF4	1467
(N225BX)	LJ60	127
N225CC	**FA10**	**225**
N225CC	GLF2	8
N225CC	LJ25	107
N225CC	LJ35	192
N225CF	LJ35	225
N225CJ	C52C	0188
N225CV	C560	0225
(N225CV)	C650	0225
N225CX	GLF4	1467
N225CX	**GLF4**	**4171**
N225DC	C500	148
N225DC	**GLF4**	**1253**
N225DF	**F2EX**	**283**
N225DS	LJ25	025
(N225EA)	LJ25	057
N225EE	**GLF5**	**563**
N225EL	C52A	0065
N225EX	F2EX	25
N225F	LJ35	269
N225FD	F2EX	283
N225FJ	F2EX	225
N225FJ	FA10	160
N225FJ	FA20	513
N225FM	C550	118
N225FX	LJ60	127
N225GD	G280	2025
N225GG	C52A	0047
N225GV	GLF5	672
N225HD	FA50	313
N225HR	HS25	256017
N225HW	LJ25	231
N225J	C550	316
N225JD	**GALX**	**028**
(N225JF)	CL61	5172
N225JL	LJ25	182
N225K	HS25	25026
N225KA	**LJ25**	**004**
N225KJ	HS25	25026
N225KS	F900	105
N225LC	LJ25	127
N225LJ	LJ24	011
N225LJ	LJ40	2025
N225LL	HS25	25026

N225LS	SBRL	282-51
N225LY	CL64	5311
N225MC	LJ35	225
N225MD	**LJ55**	**085**
N225MS	GLF2	8
N225MS	LJ28	28-004
N225N	CL61	5036
N225N	CL61	5100
N225N	**CL64**	**5652**
N225N	WW24	319
N225PB	**HS25**	**258558**
N225QC	LJ35	192
N225RD	C500	194
N225RP	**HS25**	**258311**
N225SB	**BE40**	**RK-510**
N225SE	GLF2	55
N225SF	GLF2	55
N225SF	GLF3	423
N225TJ	**C52B**	**0472**
N225TJ	LJ25	222
N225TR	GLF2	225
N225WT	C550	550-0821
(N225WT)	C500	674
N225WW	C52A	0065
N226AL	GLF4	1057
N226B	C525	0200
N226BR	EA50	000226
N226CC	LJ36	007
N226CF	CL64	5338
N226CK	**FA20**	**226**
N226CP	E50P	50000071
N226CV	**C560**	**0226**
N226CW	C525	0326
N226CX	C750	0226
N226CX	GLF4	1467
N226EC	**CL61**	**5090**
N226EM	C650	0187
N226EW	F2EX	55
N226EX	F2EX	26
N226FJ	FA10	162
N226FJ	FA50	227
N226FX	LJ60	128
N226G	CL61	3012
N226G	FA20	244
N226G	GLF3	434
N226G	GLF4	1122
N226G	HS25	25170
N226GA	G280	2026
N226GA	GLF2	106
N226GC	GLF3	434
N226GL	CL61	3012
N226HD	GLEX	9022
N226JT	**C56X**	**5652**
N226JV	C560	0132
N226KV	**E50P**	**50000071**
N226L	C550	093
N226LJ	LJ31	226
N226MP	**GLF4**	**1300**
N226MY	**CL64**	**5498**
N226N	C550	093
N226N	C560	0248
N226PC	**C550**	**550-0835**
N226QS	**F2TH**	**126**
N226R	FA20	226
N226RM	GLF2	145
N226RS	**GLF4**	**1479**
N226SF	LJ60	092
(N226U)	C560	0248
N226VP	C500	635
N226VP	C680	0226
N226W	C650	7111
N226WC	**BE40**	**RK-248**
N226WW	WW24	226
N227A	LJ55	027
N227AN	ASTR	060
N227BA	C650	0130
N227BA	GLF2	27
N227BX	LJ60	077
N227CC	CL60	1004
N227CC	FA20	59
(N227CC)	C500	227
N227CK	**FA20**	**227**
N227CP	**CL61**	**5097**
(N227CV)	C560	0227
(N227CV)	C650	0227
N227DH	C680	0086
N227DH	HS25	25027
N227DR	C550	254
N227EW	LJ25	227
N227FH	PRM1	RB-102
N227FJ	FA10	163
(N227FJ)	FA50	227
N227FS	C52A	0238
N227FX	LJ60	077
N227G	CL60	1059
N227G	**EA50**	**000124**
N227G	GLF2	76
N227G	GLF4	1045
N227GA	GLF2	76
N227GC	FA20	59
N227GH	GLF4	1045
N227GJ	**FA50**	**182**
N227GL	CL60	1059
N227GL	GLF2	76
N227GM	C500	227
N227GX	GLF2	76
N227H	C500	011
N227HD	F9EX	157
N227HF	HS25	25118
N227HP	C500	227
N227JP	C52B	0265
N227K	JSTR	5006/40
N227KT	LJ31	208
N227LA	C650	0130
N227LA	GLF2	193
N227LA	HS25	25235
(N227LA)	FA20	330
N227LS	**EA50**	**000195**
N227LS	SBRL	282-51
N227LT	HS25	25232
N227MC	**C56X**	**5064**
N227MH	CL65	5943
(N227MJ)	LJ35	227
N227MK	**C500**	**070**
N227MM	**HS25**	**257081**
N227MS	HS25	25227
N227N	ASTR	053
N227N	LJ60	049
N227NL	ASTR	053
N227PC	C550	125
N227PE	CL61	3002
N227QS	**F2TH**	**127**
N227R	FA20	227
N227RE	CL61	5177
N227RH	CL61	5177
N227RH	**GLF4**	**4108**
N227RW	LJ25	201
N227S	SBRL	282-16
N227SE	**C680**	**0332**
N227SV	**GLF4**	**1172**
N227SW	SBRL	282-16
N227TA	FA20	496
(N227TJ)	GLF2	27
N227TS	GLF2	27
(N227UH)	EA50	000227
N227VG	C500	246
N227WE	FA20	344/534
N227WG	**CL61**	**5078**
N227WL	FA20	344/534
N227WS	C560	0676
N228AJ	C500	378
N228AK	C500	378
N228AK	C550	196
N228AM	C550	291
N228BD	C750	0228
N228BL	**F2EX**	**228**
N228CC	C510	148
(N228CC)	C500	228
N228CF	C750	0028
N228CK	FA20	128/436
N228CM	C650	0228
N228CV	C560	0228
N228DB	**C750**	**0228**
N228E	CL64	5589
N228EA	C500	631
N228EA	**HS25**	**25232**
N228EJ	F2TH	128
N228ES	C500	378
N228EX	F9EX	228
N228FJ	FA10	164
N228FJ	**FA50**	**228**
N228FJ	FA50	231
N228FS	C500	378
N228FS	C52A	0238
N228FS	C560	0438
N228FX	LJ60	132
N228G	GLF3	424
N228G	HS25	25021
N228G	HS25	25170
N228G	HS25	258203
(N228G)	C550	583
N228GC	HS25	25284
N228GL	HS25	25021
N228H	GLEX	9040
N228H	LJ45	472
N228KT	**CL30**	**20142**
N228L	C56X	5342
N228L	**CL30**	**20194**
N228L	WW24	331
N228LS	SBRL	465-43
N228MD	HS25	256037
N228MH	**C550**	**196**
N228MN	F2TH	184
N228N	**CL30**	**20060**
N228N	LJ60	031
N228N	WW24	331
N228PC	C560	0310
N228PC	**C56X**	**5600**
N228PG	**C560**	**0310**
N228PK	**CL30**	**20011**
N228PK	CL61	3046
N228PK	HS25	258808
N228PK	LJ55	006
N228RE	**GLF4**	**1438**
N228RH	**C680**	**0128**
N228S	C500	233
N228SJ	FA10	128
N228SW	LJ25	228
N228TM	HS25	258458
N228WH	**C750**	**0233**
N228Y	C56X	5342
N228Y	CL30	20194
N228Y	**CL30**	**20447**
N228Y	JSTR	5066/46
N229AP	LJ25	295
N229AR	**GLF4**	**4317**
N229BK	**LJ45**	**198**
N229BP	**CL30**	**20223**
N229BP	LJ60	320
N229BW	EA50	000004
N229BW	**EA50**	**550-0264**
N229CE	**C750**	**0229**
N229CJ	C525	0129
N229CK	**FA20**	**229**
N229CN	**C52B**	**0223**
N229D	**WW24**	**427**
N229DA	**F2TH**	**75**
N229DK	**F9EX**	**229**
N229EA	**EA50**	**000229**
N229FJ	FA10	165
N229FX	LJ60	137
N229GA	G280	2029
N229GA	GALX	129
N229GA	GLF4	4229
N229GC	CL60	1043
N229GS	**LJ25**	**078**
N229HD	F900	108
(N229J)	C650	0089
N229JB	FA10	71
N229JR	C510	0332
N229KD	LJ31	139
N229LC	C680	0135
N229LJ	**LJ31**	**229**
N229LS	SBRL	306-38
(N229LS)	GLF4	4205
N229MC	**C550**	**255**
N229N	**C560**	**0759**
N229N	WW24	427
(N229N)	C560	0248
N229P	HS25	25115
N229QS	**F2TH**	**129**
N229R	FA20	229
N229RB	PRM1	RB-229
N229RP	**LJ60**	**320**
N229RY	HS25	258229
N229TS	**LJ60**	**226**
N229U	HS25	259009
N229VP	C650	0219
N229WJ	LJ25	229
N229X	LJ35	129
N230A	SBRL	306-38
N230AJ	ASTR	036
N230BF	C510	0122
N230BF	C510	0230
N230BT	FA50	62
(N230BX)	LJ60	138
N230CC	C500	230
N230DP	HS25	257060
N230E	GLF2	34
N230FJ	F2TH	230
N230FJ	FA10	161
N230FX	LJ60	138
N230H	HS25	25064
N230JE	**HA4T**	**RC-23**
N230JK	**C560**	**0647**
N230JK	WW24	279
N230JS	C500	107
N230JS	C550	550-1119
N230JS	WW24	301
N230LC	C680	0141
N230LC	CL64	5489
N230LL	C525	0169
N230PA	HS25	258844
N230QS	**F2EX**	**59**
N230R	HS25	257202
N230R	LJ24	188
N230R	LJ35	130
N230RA	FA20	230
N230RC	WW24	105
N230RS	FA10	24
N230S	FA50	70
N230TL	WW24	279
N230TS	HS25	25134
N231A	SBRL	282-61
N231A	SBRL	306-72
N231CA	SBRL	306-72
N231CE	**GLF5**	**5232**
N231FJ	F9EX	231
N231JH	**FA10**	**176**
(N231LC)	C500	493
N231R	LJ24	134
N231R	LJ35	128
N231TJ	**F2EX**	**273**
N231WC	C560	0331
(N231WJ)	GLF3	331
N231XL	C56X	5231
(N232AV)	HS25	HB-10
N232BC	C550	550-0913
N232BJ	BE40	RK-34
N232CC	C550	496
N232CC	LJ35	367
N232CE	**C650**	**0067**
N232CF	C650	0067
N232CF	**C750**	**0161**
N232CL	**F900**	
N232CS	**HS25**	**HB-22**
N232CW	**C550**	**032**
N232CX	C750	0232
N232DM	C550	087
N232EA	**HS25**	**HA-0107**
N232EH	**HS25**	**258729**
N232F	FA20	502
N232F	PRM1	RB-22
N232FJ	FA10	166
N232FJ	FA50	233
N232FX	LJ35	620
N232HC	GLF3	373
N232JR	C550	550-0855
N232JS	C550	727
N232JS	**C560**	**0584**
(N232JS)	HS25	25198
N232K	**GLF4**	**1232**
N232KS	**C550**	**732**
N232LJ	LJ60	232
N232MC	**CL65**	**5954**
N232MD	LJ25	052
N232PH	**LJ40**	**2044**
N232PR	FA50	179
N232PR	LJ35	394
N232QS	CS55	0032
N232QS	**F2EX**	**115**
N232R	LJ24	005
N232R	LJ24	131
N232R	LJ35	102
N232RA	FA20	232
N232S	ASTR	032
N232SF	**F9DX**	**615**
N232T	SBRL	282-83
N232TN	HS25	257043
N232TW	**FA20**	**32**
N232WC	CS55	0032
N233BC	FA50	241
(N233BJ)	BE40	RJ-33
N233BX	LJ31	233
N233CA	LJ25	133
N233CC	C500	233
N233CC	LJ35	031
N233CJ	C525	0233
N233DB	**C500**	**158**
N233DW	C550	550-0931
N233EH	**F2TH**	**144**
N233EM	F2TH	144
N233FJ	FA10	167
N233FJ	FA50	234
N233FJ	GLEX	9233
(N233FJ)	FA50	233
N233FT	**C52B**	**0075**
N233FX	LJ60	139
N233FX	LJ60	154
N233GA	GLF4	1144
N233GA	GLF5	5433
N233GF	**HS25**	**258096**
N233JJ	**C500**	**233**
N233KC	**F900**	**48**
N233KC	HS25	258052
(N233ME)	C500	312
N233MK	**LJ45**	**052**
N233MM	C52B	0133
N233MT	**EA50**	**000093**
N233MW	**BE40**	**RK-233**
N233QS	**F2EX**	**91**
N233R	LJ24	017
N233R	LJ24	132
N233R	LJ35	048
N233RS	GLF2	233
N233SG	CL61	5104
N233ST	C550	261
N233TM	LJ45	210
N233TW	**LJ24**	**221**
N233U	FA50	14
N233VM	C500	233
N233VP	C52C	0003
(N233VP)	C750	0233
N233VR	**LJ60**	**075**
N233VW	LJ24	011
N233WC	PRM1	RB-233
N233XL	**C56X**	**5233**
N234AQ	**C560**	**0234**
N234AT	**C500**	**240**
N234CA	FA20	17
N234CJ	C525	0134
N234CJ	**C52A**	**0454**
(N234CJ)	C52A	0463
N234CM	LJ24	214
N234DB	GLF2	100
N234DB	GLF4	1000
N234DB	GLF4	1457
N234DB	**GLF5**	**5106**
N234DC	SBRL	306-103
N234DK	**BE40**	**RK-182**
N234DN	GLF4	1457
N234DP	**CL30**	**20040**
N234DT	LJ35	407
N234EA	EA50	000156
(N234EJ)	LJ25	234
N234ES	LJ55	138
N234FJ	**F2TH**	**34**
N234FJ	FA10	168
N234FJ	FA50	236
N234FP	**E50P**	**50000359**
N234FX	LJ60	141
N234FX	LJ60	151
N234G	**WW24**	**28**
N234GF	HS25	258096
N234GF	**HS25**	**HA-0175**
N234GX	GLEX	9234
(N234HM)	C650	0044
N234JW	C500	408
N234KK	LJ25	234
(N234LC)	LJ55	034
N234LR	**GLF3**	**300**
N234MR	LJ24	130
N234MR	**LJ35**	**201**
N234MW	CL60	1073
N234ND	LJ25	043
N234P	**C510**	**0450**
N234Q	LJ24	181
N234QS	F2EX	158
(N234RA)	C550	561
N234RB	LJ25	105
N234RC	WW24	162
N234RG	CL60	1073
N234SA	**F9EX**	**268**
N234SV	LJ25	226
N234TG	LJ45	512
"N234TS"	JSTR	5234
N234U	FA10	29
N234U	SBRL	306-48
N234UM	C500	105
N234WR	LJ24	172
N234WS	C525	0097
N234YP	C650	0074
N235AC	LJ35	676
N235AF	CL30	20190
N235AV	HS25	25235
N235BS	**C550**	**550-0899**
(N235BX)	LJ60	153
N235CA	FA20	139
N235CC	C500	235
N235CG	GLF4	4030
N235CG	LJ60	230
N235CM	C650	0235
N235DB	C550	374
N235DH	LJ35	134
N235DX	GLF4	1493
N235DX	GLF5	5085
N235DX	**GLF5**	**5345**
N235EA	**LJ35**	**061**
N235EE	**E55P**	**50500235**
N235EF	**CL30**	**20434**
(N235EX)	F2EX	235
N235FJ	F9EX	235
N235FJ	FA10	169
N235FX	LJ60	143
N235FX	LJ60	153
N235HR	LJ35	082
N235HR	**LJ55**	**094**
(N235HR)	LJ60	208
N235JL	LJ35	049
N235JS	**LJ35**	**199**
N235JW	LJ25	096
N235JW	LJ35	032
N235KC	HS25	25096
N235KK	C550	436
N235KK	C650	0175
N235KK	**GLF4**	**1458**
N235KS	C52A	0235
N235LC	GALX	142
N235LP	GLF4	1336
N235MC	**LJ35**	**334**
N235PE	GLF5	5272
N235PV	GLF5	5286
N235PZ	GLF4	4191
N235R	LJ24	032
N235SC	LJ35	275
N235SS	C510	0070
N235SV	**C650**	**0235**
N235TS	C550	365
N235U	FA20	364
N235U	GLF3	305
N235UJ	LJ35	477
(N235WL)	GLF4	4191
N235Z	LJ24	146
N236BN	HS25	257051
N236CA	**GLF4**	**1202**
N236CA	LJ25	161
N236CC	C500	236
N236DJ	FA10	138
N236FJ	FA10	170
N236FS	**GLF4**	**4236**
N236FX	LJ60	157
N236HR	LJ55	113
(N236HR)	LJ55	094
N236JP	WW24	116
N236JW	LJ55	036
N236LB	C56X	5023
N236LC	**GALX**	**154**
N236LD	C56X	5023
N236LD	C56X	5236
N236LP	**GLF4**	**4206**
N236MJ	**GLF4**	**1177**
N236N	**CL61**	**5108**
(N236PJ)	LJ55	023
N236QS	**F2TH**	**136**
N236R	LJ55	025
N236TS	C500	236
N236TS	LJ24	236
N236TW	**FA20**	**236**
N236W	WW24	236
N236WJ	LJ24	236
N236Y	SBRL	282-31
N237AF	**LJ35**	**262**
N237BB	**F2EX**	**70**
N237BG	C560	0771
N237CC	MU30	A027SA

N237CJ	C525	0237
N237CJ	**C525**	**0353**
N237CK	**LJ35**	**237**
N237CW	C550	037
N237DG	C525	0141
N237DM	LJ45	058
N237DX	**HS25**	**257148**
N237EE	**C56X**	**6149**
N237FJ	FA10	171
N237FJ	FA50	237
N237FX	LJ60	158
(N237G)	CL64	5400
N237GA	CL61	5019
N237GA	CL64	5400
N237GA	**GLF4**	**4055**
N237GA	LJ35	262
(N237GA)	GLF5	5523
N237JA	**E50P**	**50000066**
N237JF	WW24	117
(N237JM)	PRM1	RB-169
(N237JP)	C500	330
N237LJ	LJ40	2037
(N237LM)	GLF2	101
N237MB	**C550**	**550-0874**
N237MP	**C52A**	**0179**
N237NA	C56X	5195
N237PJ	**LJ55**	**119**
N237PT	**C52A**	**0465**
N237PT	FA20	432
N237R	LJ55	066
N237RA	HS25	258237
N237RF	GLF2	237/43
(N237RG)	HS25	257072
N237SC	C500	640
N237SP	**BE40**	**RK-25**
N237TJ	LJ35	237
N237TW	**LJ24**	**237**
N237VP	**C560**	**0237**
N237WC	**C550**	**145**
N237WR	HS25	257072
N238AJ	HS25	258155
N238BG	**C500**	**644**
N238BX	LJ60	163
N238CA	LJ25	040
N238CV	C560	0238
N238CX	C750	0238
N238DB	**WW24**	**215**
N238DL	FA50	238
N238EJ	**C550**	**550-0812**
N238FJ	CL30	20138
N238FJ	FA10	172
N238FJ	FA50	238
N238FJ	GLF5	564
N238FX	LJ60	163
N238JA	LJ35	134
N238JC	C560	0192
N238JS	C500	649
N238KJ	E50P	50000238
N238LM	**LJ45**	**039**
N238MH	**GLF4**	**4316**
N238MP	LJ25	238
N238PR	LJ35	394
N238R	LJ24	132
N238R	LJ55	085
N238RC	LJ35	061
N238RM	**C52A**	**0453**
N238SM	**C56X**	**5238**
N238SW	**C52B**	**0141**
N238SW	CL64	5423
N238U	FA50	86
N238U	GLF2	63
N238U	JSTR	5106/9
N238Y	FA50	185
N239AX	**F900**	**39**
N239AY	**LJ31**	**189**
N239BD	FA20	239
N239CA	LJ25	149
N239CA	**LJ31**	**126**
N239CC	C500	239
N239CD	C550	242
N239CD	FA20	239
N239CD	**FA20**	**339**
N239CV	C560	0239
N239CW	C525	0339
N239FJ	FA10	173
N239FJ	FA50	239
N239FX	LJ60	166
N239GJ	LJ35	239
N239P	GLF2	63
N239QS	F2TH	193
N239R	FA50	178
N239R	HS25	258119
N239RC	LJ60	046
N239RF	PRM1	RB-139
N239RT	**HS25**	**HA-0120**
N239RT	PRM1	RB-139
N239SR	**LJ40**	**2049**
N239WC	C56X	5139
(N239WJ)	GLF2	239
N239XL	C56X	5239
N240AA	C500	202
N240AA	WW24	82
N240AC	SBRL	282-41
N240AG	LJ24	079
N240AG	LJ25	197
N240AK	CL60	1067
N240AQ	LJ24	079
N240AR	C550	240
N240AT	FA20	240/478
N240B	C56X	5057
N240B	HS25	258358
N240B	**LJ31**	**175**
N240B	LJ35	240
N240BX	LJ60	167
N240CC	C500	240
N240CF	SBRL	282-132
N240CJ	C52B	0240
N240CK	**FA20**	**24**
N240CM	C560	0048
N240CX	GLF2	101
N240CX	GLF4	1370
N240CX	**GLF6**	**6131**
(N240EA)	GLF2	240
N240EX	F2EX	40
N240FJ	FA10	174
N240FJ	FA50	245
N240FX	LJ60	167
N240JA	GLF4	4055
N240JK	**LJ60**	**137**
N240JR	SBRL	282-132
N240JS	LJ35	241
N240LG	**F9EX**	**61**
N240MC	**CL60**	**1075**
N240QS	F2TH	204
N240RP	**LJ40**	**2025**
N240RS	FA20	479
N240S	WW24	309
N240TJ	FA20	24
N240TW	**FA20**	**40**
N240V	**HS25**	**258417**
N240WG	LJ40	2063
N240WW	WW24	240
N240Z	**HS25**	**258565**
N241AG	LJ25	075
N241AG	LJ35	491
N241AQ	LJ25	075
N241BF	**C500**	**621**
N241BJ	BE40	RJ-41
N241BN	LJ24	034
N241BX	LJ60	172
N241CA	**LJ35**	**142**
N241CJ	C52A	0341
N241CJ	**C52B**	**0241**
N241CT	WW24	267
N241CT	**WW24**	**355**
N241CV	C560	0241
N241DE	**E50P**	**50000070**
N241DS	**C555**	**0042**
N241EA	**CL65**	**5945**
N241EP	C525	0247
N241FB	CL61	5102
N241FB	HS25	257129
N241FJ	FA10	175
N241FJ	FA50	242
N241FR	CL61	5102
N241FT	C550	268
N241FX	LJ60	172
N241H	SBRL	465-5
N241JA	LJ24	131
N241JC	FA20	241/479
N241JS	**HS25**	**258652**
N241KA	C52B	0241
(N241KP)	C560	0383
N241LA	C555	0091
N241LJ	**LJ45**	**241**
N241MH	C500	621
N241MH	GLF2	160
N241N	**CL61**	**5100**
N241RH	WW24	187
N241RS	FA10	18
N241RT	HS25	257057
N241RT	LJ35	024
(N241SM)	HS25	258135
N241TR	**BE40**	**RJ-45**
N241WS	C525	0241
N242AC	C560	0177
N242AC	C560	0609
(N242AF)	LJ25	242
N242AG	LJ25	025
N242AL	HS25	257199
N242AS	C52A	0511
N242AS	C52A	0519
N242BG	ASTR	113
N242BS	**C525**	**0230**
N242CK	**CL61**	**5181**
N242CT	FA20	316
N242CV	C560	0242
N242DR	**LJ35**	**242**
N242F	LJ24	045
N242FJ	F2EX	242
N242FJ	FA10	176
N242FX	LJ60	174
N242GB	C525	0151
N242GM	LJ25	242
N242GS	**LJ25**	**242**
(N242JG)	HS25	258187
N242JT	**C56X**	**6131**
N242KV	**C52B**	**0242**
N242LA	C555	0153
N242LB	FA20	121
N242LJ	C525	0242
(N242LT)	C750	0082
(N242MA)	FA20	242
N242ML	**C525**	**0506**
N242MT	LJ35	621
N242PF	LJ25	298
N242RB	LJ55	132
(N242RJ)	FA20	242
N242SR	BE40	RJ-9
N242SW	**C550**	**550-0908**
N242WT	C550	364
N242WT	LJ24	034
N242WT	LJ25	034
N242ZX	LJ60	174
(N243AB)	C500	685
N243BA	**CL64**	**5401**
N243BA	HS25	258365
N243CH	C56X	5243
N243DG	GLF5	5020
N243EE	C500	619
N243F	LJ24	063
N243F	LJ60	175
N243FJ	FA10	177
N243FJ	**FA20**	**430**
N243FJ	FA50	243
N243FJ	FA50	244
N243FX	LJ60	175
N243JB	HS25	25204
N243JP	**CL61**	**5101**
N243K	FA20	105
N243LS	C525	0487
N243MS	C510	0243
N243MW	**GLF3**	**436**
N243PC	**HA4T**	**RC-65**
N243RC	**CL30**	**20243**
(N243RK)	LJ24	306
N243SH	**C500**	**243**
N243SL	**C560**	**0593**
N243TS	HS25	25243
(N243TS)	GLF2	43
N243V	**F2TH**	**152**
N243VP	C560	0243
N244	JSTR	5141
N244A	**FA10**	**145**
N244AD	FA50	162
N244AL	CL60	1005
N244BH	CL61	5027
N244CA	FA20	321
N244CE	**C510**	**0244**
N244CJ	C52A	708
(N244CV)	C560	0244
N244DM	GLF2	21
N244DS	**GLEX**	**9617**
N244DS	GLF4	1248
N244DS	GLF4	1477
N244DS	GLF4	4050
N244FC	LJ35	299
N244FJ	FA10	178
N244FJ	FA20	444
N244FJ	FA50	232
N244FL	**HS25**	**258066**
N244FX	LJ60	178
N244GL	LJ24	227
N244J	**GLF4**	**1451**
N244JM	HS25	258138
N244LJ	**LJ35**	**244**
N244LS	HS25	258569
N244MD	**E50P**	**50000232**
N244RD	LJ24	120
N244RG	**LJ35**	**154**
N244S	**GALX**	**235**
N244SL	C500	650
N244TJ	FA10	44
N244TS	LJ35	244
N244WJ	C500	244
N244WJ	C500	252
N244XL	C56X	5244
(N245BC)	C500	245
(N245BC)	C500	258
N245BD	**GLF5**	**5165**
N245BS	LJ25	214
N245CC	**C550**	**245**
N245CM	**LJ45**	**403**
N245DK	LJ25	245
N245DR	C510	0105
N245FH	LJ45	393
N245FJ	FA10	180
N245FX	LJ60	182
N245GA	GLF2	45
N245GL	LJ24	228
N245J	C56X	5245
N245K	LJ45	076
N245K	**LJ45**	**269**
N245KC	LJ45	150
(N245KK)	LJ25	281
(N245LH)	LJ45	306
(N245MG)	C500	245
N245MS	**LJ55**	**077**
N245MU	**C510**	**0006**
N245QS	**F2TH**	**145**
N245RA	**C52A**	**0374**
N245RS	**HS25**	**256027**
N245S	WW24	336
N245SP	FA10	135
N245TJ	GLF5	548
N245TL	CL61	5001
N245TT	CL61	5001
N245TT	**GLF5**	**5003**
N245TT	GLF5	548
N245TX	HS25	258062
N246AG	F900	112
N246AG	**F9EX**	**135**
N246CB	C550	550-0849
N246CM	LJ24	200
N246CM	LJ35	395
N246CZ	C52B	0246
N246DF	PRM1	RB-182
N246FJ	FA10	108
N246FJ	FA50	246
N246FX	LJ60	183
N246GA	G280	2046
N246GA	MU30	A064SA
N246GS	**C525**	**0446**
(N246GS)	SBRL	282-111
N246JL	**CL60**	**1046**
N246N	HS25	25261
(N246N)	FA10	33
N246NW	C550	336
N246NW	C560	0068
N246RE	**C510**	**0295**
N246RR	C500	167
N246V	F2TH	152
N246V	**GLF4**	**4149**
N246V	HS25	258417
N246VF	HS25	257126
N247AB	GLF2	208
N247AD	GLF2	208
N247BC	FA50	48
N247CJ	**F900**	**122**
N247CJ	FA50	249
N247CK	CL60	1045
N247CN	**C560**	**0173**
N247CP	LJ60	052
N247CS	**SBRL**	**465-27**
N247CW	C525	0247
N247DB	LJ24	247
N247DG	**C560**	**0082**
N247DR	**C510**	**0177**
N247EM	FA50	48
N247EM	GLF4	1045
N247EM	**GLF5**	**5265**
N247FJ	FA10	181
N247FJ	FA50	247
N247FR	**F900**	**184**
N247FS	**CL30**	**20068**
N247FX	LJ60	187
(N247GA)	CL61	5019
N247GW	HFB3	1030
N247JD	CL30	20598
N247JK	**E55P**	**50500033**
N247JM	**C550**	**307**
N247KB	GLF4	1375
(N247LG)	GLF2	43
N247MV	C52B	0105
N247MX	**LJ45**	**452**
N247N	LJ60	049
(N247PJ)	HS25	257065
N247PL	**FA20**	**247**
N247PS	ASTR	069
N247PS	ASTR	127
N247PS	**G150**	**215**
N247PS	G150	252
N247RG	GLF3	252
N247SC	LJ60	270
N247SK	**E50P**	**50000015**
N247SS	CL30	20138
N247TA	**C680**	**0131**
N247TA	LJ35	112
N247VA	VVAN	001
N247VP	C510	0247
N247WE	CL64	5369
N247WE	**GLEX**	**9245**
N247WF	CL64	5369
N248AB	GLF4	1474
N248AG	F900	112
N248BT	**FA50**	**283**
N248CJ	C525	0248
N248CK	**LJ25**	**248**
N248CV	C560	0248
N248CW	C525	0348
N248DA	LJ35	238
N248DV	**F9EX**	**275**
N248EC	**HS25**	**258368**
N248FJ	FA10	182
N248FJ	FA50	249
N248FX	LJ60	188
N248GA	G280	2048
N248H	WW24	374
(N248H)	WW24	214
N248HA	C550	422
N248HM	LJ35	164
N248J	LJ24	220
N248JF	F2TH	11
(N248JH)	HS25	257029
N248L	LJ60	248
N248LA	**LJ60**	**248**
(N248LJ)	LJ25	248
N248LX	**F9EX**	**248**
(N248PA)	BE40	RJ-9
N248PM	**C52B**	**0494**
N248RF	**C52A**	**0199**
N248SE	**C525**	**0847**
N248SF	**C56X**	**5265**
N248SL	ASTR	125
N248SL	G150	211
N248TA	C510	0391
N248TH	GLF2	248
(N248TX)	C750	0124
N248VR	F2TH	148
N248WE	CL64	5369
N249AJ	**CL60**	**1047**
N249AS	C500	514
N249B	LJ35	240
N249BW	HS25	25115
N249CA	**C525**	**0291**
N249CB	C550	550-1049
N249DJ	LJ35	249
N249E	WW24	261
N249FJ	**F2EX**	**49**
N249FJ	FA10	183
N249FJ	FA50	248
N249FX	LJ60	193
N249GA	G280	2049
N249GA	GLF4	4249
N249HP	**LJ24**	**301**
N249LJ	LJ25	249
N249MW	HS25	25115
N249RA	LJ24	249
N249RM	**BE40**	**RK-285**
N249S	LJ60	417
N249SB	BE40	RK-285
N249SC	LJ25	249
N249SR	HS25	258249
N249TX	LJ45	360
(N249TX)	C750	0108
N250AA	C500	200
N250AF	C555	0042
N250AF	**GLF4**	**4261**
N250AJ	**BE40**	**RK-23**
N250AL	**C560**	**0605**
N250AL	C555	0042
N250AS	FA50	182
N250AT	C680	0075
N250BC	C750	0271
N250BC	SBRL	370-5
N250BL	C52A	0403
N250CC	C500	250
N250CC	CL64	5550
N250CC	LJ25	052
N250CF	C550	052
N250CJ	C525	0250
N250CM	C650	0133
N250CM	**C680**	**0170**
N250CV	**SJ50**	**0002**
(N250CV)	C560	0250
N250DH	HS25	25187
N250DL	**F2TH**	**138**
(N250DR)	C550	199
N250DV	**GLF5**	**5066**
N250DV	GLF5	691
N250EA	**G150**	**235**
N250EC	SBRL	282-110
N250EX	**ASTR**	**139**
N250FJ	F9EX	250
N250FJ	FA10	184
N250FJ	FA50	250
N250FX	LJ60	194
N250GA	G280	2050
"N250GA"	G280	2001
"N250GA"	G280	2003
N250GD	GALX	250
N250GM	C500	456
N250GM	C525	0196
N250GM	C550	620
N250GM	C550	679
N250GM	HS25	258290
N250GP	**MU30**	**A069SA**
N250HP	**BE40**	**RK-250**
N250J	GLF4	1144
N250JE	HS25	258237
N250JH	C560	0350
N250JP	WW24	121
N250JP	WW24	196
N250JT	HS25	25053
N250KC	**GLF4**	**1025**
N250KD	BE40	RJ-60
(N250KD)	C550	454
(N250KD)	WW24	250
N250LB	GLF4	1269
N250LB	LJ25	357
N250LC	**LEG5**	**55000041**
N250LG	**FA7X**	**12**
N250LX	F2EX	50
N250MA	FA10	132
N250MB	**HS25**	**258237**
N250MJ	**FA50**	**125**
N250MS	GLF2	45
N250PM	WW24	227
N250QS	F2EX	174
N250RA	FA20	481
N250RA	WW24	280
N250RG	**GLF4**	**1003**
N250RJ	FA50	31
N250SG	LJ60	194
N250SM	C56X	5167
N250SP	C500	588
N250SP	C560	0211
N250SP	HS25	258600
N250SR	C500	588
N250SR	**C560**	**0211**
N250UA	WW24	121
(N250UC)	FA50	42
N250VC	GLF4	1231
N250VC	GLF4	1495
N250VP	**C550**	**270**

N250VZ	GLF4	1231
N250WW	WW24	250
N250YB	**E50P**	**50000349**
N251AB	HS25	25226
N251AF	LJ25	004
N251AL	**LJ25**	**313**
N251CB	**C500**	**479**
N251CB	C550	550-1051
N251CF	C500	479
N251CF	C550	550-0803
N251CM	**C550**	**550-0803**
N251CP	CL64	5524
N251CT	C500	569
N251CT	LJ35	251
N251CV	**SJ50**	**0003**
N251CX	C750	0251
N251DD	C500	088
N251DS	LJ25	218
N251DV	GLF4	1522
N251FJ	F2EX	251
N251FJ	FA10	186
N251FX	LJ60	195
N251GL	LJ25	061
N251GL	LJ25	074
N251GV	**GLF5**	**5251**
N251HR	**GLF4**	**4027**
N251JA	LJ25	150
N251JE	SBRL	465-2
N251JS	GLF2	251
N251KD	**C52A**	**0133**
N251LA	HS25	25101
N251LB	**GALX**	**024**
N251MA	SBRL	306-38
N251MC	**C510**	**0164**
N251MD	LJ25	356
N251MG	C500	250
N251MM	GLF4	1495
N251NG	LJ55	101
N251P	C500	250
N251QS	CS55	0051
N251QS	**F2TH**	**202**
N251SD	**LJ60**	**195**
N251SJ	F900	11
N251SP	**HS25**	**HA-0203**
N251SP	WW24	422
N251TD	**GLF6**	**6116**
N251TJ	LJ24	251
(N251TJ)	HS25	258020
N251TS	**LJ25**	**201**
N251TX	LJ45	362
(N251TX)	C750	0089
N251VG	CL64	5524
N251VG	LJ55	101
N251VP	**GLF4**	**4083**
N251X	HS25	258312
N252BK	LJ25	107
N252C	GLF4	1252
N252CH	GLF4	1204
N252CJ	C525	0052
N252CV	C560	0252
N252CV	**SJ50**	**0004**
N252CX	C750	0252
N252DH	**CL64**	**5419**
N252DH	HS25	258244
(N252DL)	LJ24	124
N252DT	HS25	258244
N252FJ	FA10	187
N252FX	LJ60	196
N252GA	G280	2052
N252GA	GLF4	4252
N252GL	LJ24	230
N252HS	LJ25	370
N252JK	**C525**	**0166**
N252JS	GLF5	525
N252LJ	LJ25	097
N252M	LJ24	140
(N252MA)	HS25	25052
N252PC	C52A	0187
N252R	WW24	21
(N252RD)	LJ60	196
(N252RF)	C550	011
N252RP	**LJ60**	**235**
N252RV	**C525**	**0252**
N252SC	LJ25	006
(N252TJ)	LJ24	252
N252V	HS25	25112
N252WJ	LJ35	349
N252XJ	HS25	258452
N253AF	**BE40**	**RK-276**
(N253CC)	HS25	25253
N253CM	**GLF5**	**610**
N253CV	C560	0253
N253CV	**SJ50**	**0005**
N253CW	**C525**	**0253**
N253CX	**C750**	**0253**
N253DE	G150	253
N253DV	**GLF5**	**5257**
N253EC	**LJ40**	**2053**
N253EJ	LJ25	253
N253EX	FA50	253
N253FJ	FA10	188
N253FX	LJ60	199
N253FX	LJ60	227
N253FX	LJ60	241
N253GA	G280	2053
N253GL	LJ24	233
N253J	LJ25	253
N253K	FA10	10
N253L	FA50	19
N253M	LJ25	253
N253MD	WW24	253
N253MT	HS25	25253
N253MZ	SBRL	306-38
N253QS	CS55	0053
N253QS	**F2TH**	**153**
N253RM	LJ40	2053
N253S	LJ55	053
N253SC	LJ25	253
N253SJ	FA50	107
(N253TX)	C750	0084
N253W	C550	253
N254AB	**C52C**	**0212**
N254AD	**C560**	**0688**
N254AM	C550	090
N254AM	**CL64**	**5361**
N254AR	GLF2	254/41
N254CA	**GLF4**	**1054**
N254CB	C550	550-1054
N254CC	C550	254
N254CL	**LJ25**	**275**
N254CR	GLF2	184
N254CW	C525	0154
N254CX	C750	0254
N254DR	**C560**	**0607**
N254DV	**CL30**	**20262**
N254DV	FA50	85
N254FJ	**F2TH**	**54**
N254FJ	FA10	189
N254FX	LJ60	200
N254FX	LJ60	220
N254FX	LJ60	247
(N254FX)	LJ60	206
N254FY	LJ60	200
N254FZ	LJ60	220
N254GA	G280	2054
N254GA	GLF4	1032
N254GS	G150	254
N254JT	HS25	25053
N254JT	LJ24	181
(N254MC)	WW24	202
N254NA	FA50	148
N254RK	BE40	RK-254
N254SB	**HS25**	**258616**
N254SC	LJ25	102
(N254SC)	GALX	054
N254SD	GLF4	1387
N254SD	GLF4	1522
N254SD	**GLF5**	**5060**
N254SD	GLF5	5120
N254TB	**C510**	**0449**
N254TW	C500	541
N254US	LJ35	254
(N254W)	GLF5	688
N255AG	PRM1	RB-255
N255AH	LJ40	2123
N255AR	LJ24	255
N255BD	LJ60	221
N255BL	LJ55	128
N255CB	HS25	25122
N255CC	C550	588
N255CC	CL61	5156
N255CC	**CL64**	**5302**
N255CM	FA50	255
N255CT	HS25	257011
N255CT	SBRL	282-54
N255CV	C560	0255
N255DA	HS25	258070
N255DG	**MU30**	**A056SA**
N255DV	HS25	258070
N255DV	HS25	258169
N255DV	LJ31	030
N255DX	**HS25**	**258535**
N255DY	LJ31	030
N255EE	E50P	50000255
N255ES	LJ24	082A
N255FJ	F2EX	255
N255FJ	FA10	190
N255FX	LJ60	220
N255FX	LJ60	228
N255GA	G280	2055
N255GA	GLF4	1055
N255GA	**GLF5**	**5555**
N255GL	LJ25	070
N255GM	SBRL	282-45
N255JC	LJ35	326
N255JH	LJ35	055
N255JT	GALX	055
N255LJ	C500	292
N255MB	LJ55	117
N255MV	**C52C**	**0126**
N255PX	**PRM1**	**RB-189**
N255QS	**F2TH**	**155**
(N255QT)	HS25	257011
N255RA	**C52B**	**0065**
N255RB	HS25	258059
N255RB	**HS25**	**258791**
N255RB	WW24	336
N255RC	**C56X**	**5554**
N255RD	C500	069
N255RG	LJ35	055
N255RK	FA20	196
N255RK	LJ60	083
N255RM	**C560**	**0201**
N255SB	GLF3	448
N255SL	**LJ60**	**188**
N255SM	**C56X**	**6194**
N255SP	LJ60	090
N255ST	LJ55	064
N255TC	**C550**	**638**
N255TE	EA50	000055
N255TS	C500	375
N255TS	GLF4	1231
N255TS	LJ55	060
(N255TS)	HS25	25255
N255TT	HS25	257011
(N255TX)	C750	0110
N255UJ	LJ55	032
N255VP	C650	0152
N255WA	C560	0255
N255WT	C550	118
N256A	FA20	438
N256A	**FA50**	**172**
N256AH	LJ40	2042
N256AH	**LJ40**	**2123**
N256BC	HS25	258256
N256CC	C500	256
N256CC	C550	550-0965
N256CJ	C52A	0156
N256CJ	**C52B**	**0256**
N256CP	**CS55**	**0033**
N256CT	SBRL	282-54
N256DA	C52B	0301
N256DP	**EA50**	**000230**
N256DV	C52B	0301
N256DV	F900	20
N256EA	SBRL	282-60
N256EN	FA20	23
N256EN	HS25	257129
N256EN	SBRL	282-60
N256FC	HS25	256003
N256FJ	FA10	191
(N256FS)	HS25	258256
N256FX	LJ60	257
N256GA	G280	2056
N256GA	GLF5	656
N256GL	LJ25	072
N256JB	**C525**	**0284**
N256JC	FA20	496
N256JC	FA50	219
N256LK	GLF5	514
N256M	FA20	274
N256M	GLF2	235
N256M	LJ60	073
N256MA	FA20	23
N256MA	FA20	75
N256MA	LJ35	235
N256MA	SBRL	282-60
N256MA	SBRL	282-69
(N256MA)	HS25	257129
(N256MB)	LJ35	235
N256MH	LJ40	2039
N256MJ	LJ24	256
(N256MT)	SBRL	306-13
N256N	WW24	427
N256P	**C500**	**659**
N256P	LJ25	006
N256PH	**C550**	**550-0840**
N256SD	CL61	3006
N256SP	**C52A**	**0006**
N256TT	**LJ45**	**375**
N256TW	LJ35	218
(N256TX)	C750	0083
N256V	**FA10**	**151**
N256W	C550	026
N256W	C650	7111
N256W	C750	0221
N256W	FA10	151
N256WJ	**HS25**	**256008**
N256WM	LJ24	256
N256WN	C500	019
N257AJ	HS25	257001
N257AK	**EA50**	**000258**
N257AL	C750	0226
N257AL	**F2EX**	**151**
N257AL	LJ35	128
N257AM	HS25	257046
N257AR	C52A	0007
N257CB	MU30	A050SA
N257CB	**BE40**	**RK-207**
N257CM	**C510**	**0257**
N257CW	C550	229
N257DJ	LJ35	257
(N257DP)	LJ35	064
N257DW	**C550**	**316**
N257FX	LJ60	260
N257GA	G280	2057
N257GL	LJ25	071
N257H	GLF2	223
N257H	**GLF4**	**1223**
N257H	HS25	25104
N257H	JSTR	5083/49
N257H	JSTR	5230
N257HA	JSTR	5083/49
N257JC	CS55	0029
N257K	**EA50**	**000257**
N257MV	C525	0548
N257PL	**HS25**	**258167**
N257QS	F2EX	191
N257SD	LJ35	064
N257SJ	**LJ55**	**118**
N257TH	HS25	257007
N257TM	SBRL	282-76
N257V	FA10	119
N257W	C650	7112
N257W	FA10	119
N257WJ	HS25	257007
N258A	FA20	438
N258AF	**BE40**	**RK-129**
N258AH	LJ40	2042
N258AV	WW24	258
N258BJ	BE40	RJ-58
N258CC	C550	258
(N258CF)	WW24	258
N258CW	C550	183
N258FJ	F2EX	258
N258FJ	FA10	192
N258FV	**FA50**	**224**
N258FX	LJ60	263
N258G	LJ25	092
N258G	LJ35	443
N258GA	G280	2058
N258GA	GLF4	4258
N258GL	LJ25	078
N258HH	HS25	258554
N258JS	C550	285
N258KT	HS25	258007
N258LX	F9EX	258
N258MD	LJ25	258
N258MR	**HS25**	**258258**
N258MS	**HS25**	**258405**
N258P	CS55	0022
(N258P)	C550	408
(N258P)	C550	454
(N258P)	C550	493
N258PC	C56X	5763
N258PE	FA20	163
N258QS	**F2TH**	**158**
N258RA	HS25	258273
N258SA	HS25	258235
(N258SC)	LJ31	058
N258SP	HS25	258258
N258SR	HS25	258051
(N258TT)	C550	438
(N258TT)	C56X	5178
N258TX	**BE40**	**RK-443**
N258WC	C510	0096
N259AF	**BE40**	**RK-407**
(N259B)	GLF3	431
N259CA	**C680**	**0505**
N259CA	HS25	HB-43
N259CK	**C680**	**0278**
N259DB	LJ24	064
N259DH	**C500**	**259**
N259EX	F2EX	259
N259FG	**G280**	**2015**
N259FJ	FA10	193
N259FX	LJ60	266
N259FX	LJ60	295
N259GA	G280	2059
N259HA	LJ35	259
(N259JC)	LJ35	259
(N259JH)	C560	0270
(N259JM)	MU30	A059SA
N259JP	**GALX**	**159**
N259QS	**F2TH**	**159**
N259RH	**HS25**	**258529**
N259SK	GLF3	327
N259SP	HS25	258531
N259TX	BE40	RK-410
N259WJ	LJ35	341
N260AJ	**LJ60**	**021**
(N260AL)	E50P	50000260
N260AM	**C525**	**0260**
N260AN	LJ60	124
N260BS	CS55	0080
N260BS	**LJ60**	**238**
N260CA	LJ60	149
N260CC	C500	260
N260CH	GLF4	1072
N260CV	C560	0260
N260CX	C750	0260
N260DB	LJ60	290
N260ER	**FA50**	**67**
N260FJ	FA10	194
(N260FJ)	F2TH	60
N260FX	**LJ60**	**307**
(N260G)	HS25	258782
N260GA	G150	260
N260GA	G280	2006
N260GA	G280	2060
N260GD	**LJ60**	**220**
N260H	**HS25**	**258248**
N260J	C550	249
N260LF	**LJ31**	**015**
N260MB	FA20	274
N260QS	CS55	0060
N260RD	C500	260
N260TB	C550	720
N260TT	**C525**	**0810**
N260TX	BE40	RK-408
N260UJ	LJ60	008
N260V	CL60	1022
N260VP	C650	0152
N260VP	C650	0190
N260Z	**GLF5**	**5522**
N261AH	**C680**	**0261**
N261CC	C500	261
N261CH	**F9EX**	**261**
N261CV	C560	0261
N261DC	**EA50**	**000127**
N261FJ	FA10	195
N261FX	LJ60	319
N261GA	ASTR	143
N261GA	G150	261
N261GA	G280	2061
N261GA	GLF4	4261
N261GA	GLF5	5161
N261GC	**C56X**	**5170**
N261JP	**BE40**	**RK-76**
N261NA	**C680**	**0118**
N261PA	HS25	258587
N261PA	**HS25**	**259003**
N261PC	LJ31	109
N261PC	LJ35	329
N261PC	LJ60	146
N261PG	LJ35	329
N261PQ	LJ31	109
N261PW	**CL65**	**5858**
N261SC	LJ31	061
N261SS	C550	288
N261SV	C680	0261
N261T	SBRL	306-125
N261TD	**EA50**	**000261**
N261TX	BE40	RK-425
N261UH	C560	0261
N261US	JSTR	5211
(N261VP)	C550	288
(N261WB)	C500	674
N261WC	**LJ25**	**261**
N261WD	C500	674
N261WD	CS55	0119
N261WR	C500	674
N261WR	C560	0122
N261WR	**C560**	**0447**
N261WR	CS55	0119
N262BK	**C525**	**0262**
(N262CT)	HS25	258239
N262CV	C560	0262
N262CX	C750	0262
N262DA	C510	0333
N262DA	C510	0351
N262DA	**C525**	**0833**
N262DB	LJ60	286
N262DJ	**EA50**	**000262**
N262EX	FA50	262
N262FJ	FA10	196
N262FX	LJ60	323
N262G	HS25	258354
N262GA	ASTR	144
N262GA	G150	256
N262GA	G280	2062
N262GA	GALX	232
N262GL	LJ24	238
N262HA	LJ24	123
N262JE	LJ25	100
N262MW	F2EX	217
N262NA	**C680**	**0167**
N262PA	GLF2	62
N262PA	BE40	RK-203
N262PC	F2TH	78
N262PF	**E55P**	**50500262**
N262QS	**F2TH**	**162**
N262RB	PRM1	RB-262
N262SP	ASTR	062
N262SV	C680	0262
N262TX	**BE40**	**RK-464**
N262WC	WW24	262
N262WW	WW24	262
N262Y	C550	320
N263AL	C500	263
N263C	GLF3	341
N263CA	**EA50**	**000266**
N263CJ	C52A	0063
N263CT	**C525**	**0263**
(N263EJ)	EA50	550-0263
N263FJ	FA10	198
N263FX	LJ60	334
N263GA	G150	263
N263GA	GALX	025
N263GA	GLF5	5263
N263GL	LJ25	028
N263GL	LJ35	003
N263GL	LJ35	009
N263K	FA20	438
N263MR	**LJ45**	**263**
N263MW	FA20	59
N263PA	BE40	RK-429
N263PW	F900	159
N263R	HS25	259024
N263RA	LJ45	263
N263S	GLF4	1263
N263SV	C680	0263
N263TA	**C680**	**0263**
(N263TN)	HS25	257089
N263XF	**F2EX**	**13**
N264A	C550	429
N264A	**GLEX**	**9064**
N264AG	**E50P**	**50000192**
N264C	**F9EX**	**254**
N264CA	C510	0381
N264CJ	C510	0264
N264CK	**LJ35**	**264**
N264CL	GLF2	227
N264CV	C560	0264
N264DL	**PRM1**	**RB-27**

N264EJ	EA50	550-0264
N264FJ	FA10	199
N264FX	LJ60	340
(N264G)	F9EX	254
N264GA	ASTR	145
N264GA	G150	264
N264GA	GALX	244
N264HB	PRM1	RB-264
N264SC	C56X	5560
N264TC	**HS25**	**HB-13**
N264TN	FA20	264
N264TS	HS25	25264
N264TW	**LJ25**	**232**
N264TX	HS25	258511
N264U	C560	0264
N264WC	HS25	257090
(N264WD)	HS25	25264
N265A	GLF3	440
N265A	SBRL	465-47
(N265AC)	SBRL	282-23
N265C	SBRL	306-120
N265C	SBRL	465-33
(N265CA)	SBRL	465-21
N265CH	SBRL	380-30
N265CM	SBRL	282-76
N265CP	SBRL	465-48
N265DA	C525	0833
N265DC	LJ24	081
N265DE	GLEX	9265
N265DL	HS25	25287
N265DP	SBRL	306-68
N265DP	SBRL	380-30
(N265DR)	SBRL	465-45
N265DS	**SBRL**	**465-45**
N265DW	C52B	0265
N265EA	EA50	550-0265
N265EJ	LJ25	265
N265FJ	FA10	200
N265FT	**SBRL**	**465-46**
N265FX	**LJ60**	**345**
N265G	**FA50**	**214**
N265GA	C510	0407
N265GC	GLF5	5465
N265GL	LJ25	090
N265GM	SBRL	306-84
N265H	**F9EX**	**139**
N265JS	SBRL	465-56
N265K	**CL30**	**20265**
N265KC	**SBRL**	**380-49**
N265LJ	LJ25	265
N265LX	F9EX	265
N265M	SBRL	465-31
N265MK	SBRL	306-90
N265MP	**FA20**	**265**
N265PC	SBRL	465-24
N265QS	**F2TH**	**165**
(N265QS)	C550	293
N265R	SBRL	282-20
N265RW	SBRL	306-125
N265RX	**C750**	**0249**
N265SC	**SBRL**	**282-117**
N265SJ	**GLF4**	**1351**
N265SP	SBRL	465-48
N265SR	SBRL	306-120
N265SR	SBRL	370-5
N265SR	SBRL	380-11
N265ST	GLF4	1179
N265SV	C680	0265
N265TJ	SBRL	306-102
N265TS	C550	550-0942
N265TW	LJ25	265
N265TX	HS25	258499
N265U	SBRL	306-132
N265VP	SBRL	465-33
N265W	SBRL	282-37
N265WB	SBRL	276-39
N265WS	**SBRL**	**465-62**
N266AZ	PRM1	RB-266
N266BS	LJ24	266
N266BS	LJ25	180
N266BS	LJ36	035
N266CJ	**C525**	**0266**
(N266EC)	FA50	266
N266FJ	FA10	201
N266FX	LJ60	348
N266GA	CL64	5400
N266GA	G280	2066
N266GA	GLF4	1466
N266GL	LJ25	064
N266JP	LJ24	037
N266LJ	LJ60	266
N266P	LJ24	186
(N266TS)	HS25	25266
N266TW	**LJ24**	**266**
(N267AD)	JSTR	5067
N267BB	**C550**	**094**
N267BW	CL64	5391
N267BW	F2EX	107
N267BW	**GLEX**	**9192**
N267CW	C550	094
N267DF	**CL64**	**5391**
N267DW	CL64	5391
N267DW	**CL65**	**5852**
N267FJ	FA10	203
N267FX	LJ60	356
N267GA	GLF5	5477
N267GF	JSTR	5074/22
N267GL	LJ25	102
N267H	FA20	267/491
N267JE	HS25	257095
N267L	JSTR	5067
N267LG	**GLF4**	**1266**
N267MP	LJ24	267
N267P	JSTR	5074/22
N267PS	GLF2	8
N267SP	ASTR	067
N267TC	C550	376
N267TG	C550	376
N267TG	C650	0159
N267TS	HS25	257067
N267VP	C560	0267
(N267W)	C650	7112
N267WB	**F2EX**	**141**
N267WG	**C560**	**0267**
N268AA	GLEX	9406
N268CL	CL30	20268
N268CM	**C56X**	**6059**
N268DM	F2EX	146
N268EJ	EA50	550-0268
N268EM	**EA50**	**550-0268**
N268FJ	FA10	204
N268FJ	FA50	268
N268FJ	FA7X	168
N268FX	LJ60	421
(N268FX)	LJ60	366
N268GA	G150	268
N268GA	GALX	070
N268GL	LJ25	101
(N268GM)	C500	323
N268J	C550	268
N268KR	LJ40	2074
N268LX	F2EX	268
N268ND	GLF4	4227
N268PA	BE40	RK-323
N268QS	**F2TH**	**168**
N268RB	**GLF4**	**4281**
N268RJ	GLF3	482
(N268TS)	HS25	25268
N268VT	**GLF4**	**1220**
N268WC	LJ25	268
N268WS	LJ60	268
N269AA	**HS25**	**258800**
N269AJ	WW24	276
(N269AJ)	C550	063
(N269AL)	LJ24	159
N269AS	LJ25	101
N269BK	**FA7X**	**240**
N269CM	C500	546
N269CM	C560	0268
N269EJ	EA50	550-0269
N269FJ	FA10	205
N269FX	LJ60	422
(N269FX)	LJ60	372
N269GA	G280	2069
N269GA	GLF4	1469
N269HM	GLF2	13
N269HM	**GLF4**	**1118**
N269JD	C550	477
N269JH	**LJ60**	**201**
N269JR	C550	477
N269JR	C560	0266
N269JR	C56X	5086
N269JR	C750	0073
N269JR	**LJ35**	**224**
N269LB	**HA4T**	**RC-24**
N269MD	C500	546
N269MD	LJ25	269
N269MH	GLF2	13
N269MJ	**CL30**	**20180**
(N269MT)	CS55	0080
N269QS	**F2TH**	**169**
N269RC	**C500**	**078**
N269SR	FA20	370
N269SW	FA10	125
N269TA	C560	0006
N269TA	**C650**	**7112**
N269TX	GLF5	625
N269TX	HS25	258393
N269WR	**GLF4**	**1378**
N269X	HS25	258129
"N269Y"	SBRL	276-30
N270A	WW24	270
N270AB	**C650**	**7046**
N270AS	LJ55	056
N270AV	HS25	25270
N270BC	**C56X**	**6088**
N270BH	C500	330
(N270BJ)	BE40	RJ-41
N270CF	C550	300
N270CS	LJ35	042
N270CW	**C550**	**570**
N270CX	C750	0270
(N270DT)	WW24	270
(N270EJ)	EA50	550-0270
N270EX	FA50	270
N270F	**GLEX**	**9398**
N270FJ	FA10	206
N270FX	LJ60	423
(N270FX)	FA50	216
N270GA	G280	2070
N270GA	GALX	060
N270GP	**CL30**	**20268**
N270HC	HS25	258020
N270J	C525	0301
N270J	C525	0311
N270JP	**LJ55**	**078**
N270KA	HS25	257154
N270LC	**WW24**	**245**
N270LE	**GLF6**	**6164**
N270MC	**GLF3**	**374**
N270MC	HS25	256067
N270MC	HS25	257154
N270MF	**FA20**	**509**
N270MH	HS25	257152
N270MK	C510	0241
N270MQ	HS25	256067
N270NF	C500	536
N270PM	C500	196
N270PR	**C56X**	**5507**
N270QS	F2TH	210
N270RA	C550	265
N270RA	CL64	5337
N270RA	FA20	446
N270SC	**GLF4**	**1229**
(N270SC)	LJ31	070
N270SF	C500	536
N270TC	LJ24	134
N270TS	GLF2	43
N270TX	HS25	258452
N270V	CL60	1017
N270WS	LJ55	138
(N270WW)	WW24	270
N270X	HS25	258131
(N270X)	HS25	258134
N271AC	C500	218
N271AG	C550	471
N271CA	**C560**	**0071**
N271CG	C550	423
N271CJ	C52A	0171
N271CQ	**C52C**	**0091**
N271CS	**C510**	**0158**
N271CX	C750	0271
N271DU	**F9EX**	**68**
N271DV	F9EX	68
N271DV	**GLF6**	**6133**
N271E	WW24	43
N271EJ	EA50	550-0271
N271FJ	FA10	207
N271FX	LJ60	424
N271GA	G280	2071
N271GA	GALX	061
N271JG	GLF5	582
N271L	LJ60	271
N271MB	CL60	1055
N271MB	MU30	A015SA
N271MB	SBRL	465-24
(N271MB)	SBRL	465-33
(N271MF)	C500	218
N271MP	**C52C**	**0080**
N271PH	**C680**	**0151**
N271PS	**GLF4**	**1059**
N271RA	**GALX**	**104**
N271SC	LJ31	071
N271SC	LJ60	027
N271TX	GLF4	1311
N271V	HS25	259030
N271X	HS25	258134
(N271X)	HS25	258131
N272B	HS25	25175
N272BC	CL30	20286
N272BC	**CL30**	**20600**
N272BC	LJ45	252
N272BC	MU30	A046SA
N272BC	BE40	RK-192
N272BC	BE40	RK-2
N272BC	BE40	RK-325
N272BG	MU30	A046SA
N272BQ	BE40	RK-192
N272BQ	BE40	RK-2
N272CB	G150	262
N272CJ	C52B	0272
N272DJ	LJ60	272
N272DN	**FA10**	**135**
N272EJ	**EA50**	**550-0272**
N272EJ	F2TH	172
N272EJ	LJ25	272
N272EX	FA50	272
N272F	FA50	272
(N272FA)	FA20	272
N272FJ	FA10	209
N272GA	G280	2072
N272GA	GALX	072
N272GA	GLF4	4272
N272GL	LJ24	195
N272HS	LJ35	272
(N272HS)	SBRL	370-7
N272HT	**C52A**	**0061**
N272JC	GALX	054
N272JM	LJ25	272
N272JP	FA20	272
N272JS	GLF3	489
N272MH	C680	0015
N272MW	GALX	058
N272NR	**E55P**	**50500272**
N272P	C560	0815
N272T	LJ35	349
N272TB	LJ55	056
N272TX	**GLF4**	**1322**
N272X	HS25	258154
N272XJ	HS25	258472
N273A	**GLF5**	**5273**
N273CA	LJ25	039
(N273DA)	C500	382
(N273EJ)	EA50	550-0273
N273FJ	FA10	210
N273G	CL61	3002
N273G	GLF3	454
N273GL	LJ24	201
N273JC	F2TH	73
N273JC	**FA7X**	**18**
N273JE	F2TH	73
N273K	FA20	349
N273K	HS25	256041
N273KH	LJ25	315
(N273LB)	C650	0056
N273LF	WW24	44
N273LJ	**LJ35**	**273**
N273LM	LJ45	077
N273LP	C650	0056
N273LP	GLF2	192
N273LP	LJ25	058
N273LP	**LJ45**	**185**
N273LP	WW24	44
N273LR	LJ25	058
N273M	LJ25	315
N273MC	LJ35	149
N273MC	LJ55	119
N273MC	**LJ60**	**181**
N273MG	LJ35	149
N273MG	LJ55	119
N273RA	ASTR	097
N273RC	C500	273
N273S	CL64	5396
N273SW	**F2EX**	**73**
N273TA	LJ45	292
N273TA	**LJ45**	**525**
N273TX	F2TH	77
N273W	C650	0068
N273X	HS25	258156
N274	LJ55	105
N274CA	SBRL	306-31
N274CZ	LJ45	274
N274EJ	EA50	550-0274
N274FD	LJ35	274
N274FJ	FA10	213
N274GA	G280	2074
N274GA	GALX	074
N274GA	GLF4	4274
N274HM	WW24	202
N274HM	WW24	342
N274JC	GALX	034
N274JD	CL30	20597
N274JH	LJ35	274
N274JS	LJ35	274
N274K	WW24	274
N274LJ	LJ25	274
N274MA	**WW24**	**74**
N274PG	CS55	0074
N274QS	CS55	0074
N274SW	**F2EX**	**155**
N274TX	GLF4	4091
N274TX	HS25	258416
N274X	HS25	258158
N274XJ	HS25	258474
N275AL	C500	333
N275BB	C550	550-1075
N275BC	BE40	RK-325
N275BD	C550	675
(N275BH)	C500	275
N275BS	**C680**	**680A0007**
N275CC	C500	508
N275CC	C550	248
N275CQ	C500	508
N275CW	C525	0205
N275DE	**LJ45**	**475**
N275DJ	**GLF4**	**1167**
N275E	**LJ24**	**245**
N275EE	**LEG5**	**55000035**
N275EJ	EA50	550-0275
N275FJ	FA10	214
N275GA	G280	2075
N275GA	GALX	065
N275GA	GLF4	4275
N275GC	C650	0162
N275GC	**CL65**	**5943**
N275GK	C500	275
N275HH	FA50	207
N275HS	MU30	A080SA
N275HZ	**LJ60**	**215**
N275J	LJ35	009
N275JP	**CL60**	**1036**
N275KH	**BE40**	**RK-280**
N275LE	LJ24	245
(N275MB)	C500	275
N275MD	JSTR	5230
N275ML	C52A	0316
N275MT	**CL61**	**3007**
N275NM	C750	0178
(N275PC)	BE40	RK-75
N275QS	F2TH	75
N275RA	ASTR	098
N275RB	HS25	258096
N275SC	G150	227
(N275TA)	C550	550-0988
(N275TX)	BE40	RK-483
(N275VP)	CS55	0075
N275WN	C650	0018
N276A	C56X	5276
N276A	**GLF5**	**5491**
N276AL	C550	017
N276BG	**LJ60**	**276**
N276CC	C500	276
N276EJ	EA50	550-0276
N276FJ	FA10	216
N276GA	G280	2076
N276GA	GALX	066
N276GA	GALX	176
N276GA	GLF5	5276
N276GC	**CL64**	**5431**
N276GR	**CL61**	**5174**
N276JS	LJ35	458
N276LE	LJ25	078
N276MM	BE40	RK-437
N276PS	**LJ31**	**211**
N276RS	PRM1	RB-194
N276TX	BE40	RK-498
(N277A)	C550	083
(N277AG)	GLF4	1026
N277AL	CS55	0013
N277AL	**LJ55**	**104**
(N277AM)	LJ35	204
(N277AT)	FA20	509
N277C	C52C	0076
(N277CB)	HS25	257182
N277CC	C500	277
N277CJ	C525	0277
N277CJ	C550	040
N277CT	HS25	257086
N277CT	SBRL	306-2
N277EJ	EA50	550-0277
N277FJ	FA10	217
N277G	**EA50**	**000102**
N277GA	G280	2077
N277GA	GALX	077
N277GM	**GLF4**	**1124**
N277GR	GLF4	1237
N277GS	**GLF2**	**77**
(N277HG)	C650	0025
N277HM	C550	277
N277JB	**C525**	**0855**
N277JE	C550	635
N277JH	**CL30**	**20593**
N277JM	**C550**	**277**
N277JW	FA50	250
N277JW	HS25	257110
N277LE	LJ25	028
N277MG	WW24	127
N277NS	GLF3	381
N277NS	JSTR	5099/5
N277QS	CS55	0077
N277QS	**F2TH**	**177**
N277RA	**FA20**	**8**
N277RC	**C560**	**0210**
N277RG	LJ25	277
N277RP	GLF4	1026
N277RS	**HS25**	**258693**
(N277RW)	C500	444
N277SF	FA10	44
N277SR	**HS25**	**258819**
N277SS	HS25	258028
N277T	GLF2	209
N277T	JSTR	5105
N277TW	**LJ24**	**277**
N277TX	HS25	258482
N277W	C650	0072
N277WW	WW24	277
N278A	C550	168
N278AP	PRM1	RB-278
(N278CA)	C525	0510
N278CC	C500	278
N278DM	F2EX	147
N278EJ	EA50	550-0278
N278FJ	**F9EX**	**278**
N278FJ	FA50	186
N278GA	**GALX**	**078**
N278GS	F2TH	193
N278GS	**F2TS**	**732**
N278HN	**C56X**	**6132**
(N278JC)	EA50	000278
N278JM	LJ31	221
N278K	**C525**	**0527**
N278KP	C52A	0492
N278KP	**C52B**	**0413**
N278L	**GLF6**	**6038**
N278LE	LJ25	120
N278MS	C510	0278
N278MW	C510	0332
N278NA	**GLF4**	**4278**
N278PC	**CL30**	**20444**
N278PH	**GLF5**	**640**
N278QS	F2TH	77
N278RF	**F9EX**	**180**
(N278S)	C550	571
N278SP	C500	278
(N278SR)	C500	278
N278SV	C680	0278
N278TX	HS25	258486
N278XJ	HS25	258486
N278XL	**C56X**	**5278**
N279AJ	LJ45	279
N279AK	**BE40**	**RK-419**
N279AL	FA20	279/502
(N279AP)	GLF4	1371
N279CF	**HS25**	**258642**
N279CJ	C52B	0279

N279D	**C52B**	**0070**
N279DM	LJ35	214
N279DP	ASTR	020
N279DS	ASTR	040
N279DV	C52B	0070
N279DV	**C52C**	**0052**
N279E	**EA50**	**000241**
N279EJ	EA50	550-0264
N279EJ	**EA50**	**550-0279**
N279FJ	FA50	187
N279GA	G280	2079
N279GA	GALX	069
N279GA	GLF4	4279
N279GS	**F2TH**	**193**
N279LE	LJ25	112
N279PH	**GLF5**	**531**
N279QS	F2TH	178
N279SP	LJ35	452
N279TG	LJ25	265
N279TX	HS25	258545
N280AJ	HS25	257102
N280AJ	BE40	RK-164
N280AT	WW24	247
N280AZ	WW24	247
N280BC	F900	71
N280BC	FA50	109
N280BC	FA50	332
N280BC	**GLF4**	**4222**
N280BD	**FA50**	**332**
N280BG	FA50	109
N280BQ	F900	71
N280C	**G280**	**2077**
N280C	LJ24	082
N280C	LJ25	280
N280CB	**HS25**	**258733**
N280CC	C500	280
N280CC	**G280**	**2005**
(N280CH)	HS25	25190
N280CJ	**SJ50**	**0001**
N280DB	WW24	187
N280DM	C52A	0210
N280DM	C750	0161
N280DX	**G280**	**2011**
N280EJ	EA50	550-0280
N280EU	PRM1	RB-280
N280EX	**G280**	**2039**
N280FJ	FA50	188
N280FR	G280	2007
N280FW	**G280**	**2076**
N280GC	**G280**	**2003**
N280GC	G280	2007
N280GD	**G280**	**2001**
N280GD	G280	2004
N280GT	G280	2003
N280GU	G280	2041
"N280HF"	G280	2051
N280JR	C560	0576
N280JS	C550	400
N280K	CL64	5365
N280KR	**G280**	**2040**
N280LA	LJ25	280
N280LC	LJ25	029
N280LM	WW24	247
N280MH	C550	313
N280PF	**G280**	**2047**
N280PH	**GLF5**	**581**
N280PM	**C550**	**207**
N280PU	**G280**	**2017**
N280QS	**F2TH**	**181**
N280R	LJ24	188
(N280RC)	FA20	28
N280RT	FA50	24
N280SD	**G280**	**2080**
N280TA	**C550**	**226**
N280TD	**G280**	**2061**
N280VC	HS25	257102
(N281AM)	C550	281
N281BC	LJ35	380
N281BT	HS25	257114
N281CC	**G280**	**2006**
N281CD	LJ35	417
N281CW	C525	0131
(N281EJ)	EA50	550-0281
N281FJ	FA50	189
N281FP	LJ24	281
N281GA	G280	2081
N281GA	GLF2	81
N281GA	GLF4	1481
N281GA	GLF4	4281
N281JJ	FA20	281/496
(N281NW)	GLF2	81
N281QS	**F2TH**	**81**
N281R	LJ24	134
N281R	LJ25	026
N281RB	GLF2	200
N281TX	**BE40**	**RK-394**
N281VP	C560	0281
N281VP	C750	0281
N281XP	HS25	258281
N282AC	LJ24	145
(N282AM)	SBRL	282-20
N282C	FA20	282
N282CA	SBRL	282-50
N282CC	C500	282
N282CC	**G280**	**2014**
N282CD	GLF4	1098
N282CJ	C52A	0082

N282CM	**GALX**	**182**
N282CX	C750	0282
N282DA	**C510**	**0333**
N282DF	**PRM1**	**RB-282**
N282DR	**C680**	**0111**
N282EJ	EA50	550-0282
N282FJ	FA50	191
N282GA	G280	2082
N282GA	GALX	082
N282GA	GLF4	4282
N282GA	GLF5	5282
N282GS	**E55P**	**50500041**
N282JG	**C500**	**611**
N282JJ	FA20	282
N282MC	SBRL	282-52
N282NA	SBRL	282-23
(N282PC)	C650	0058
N282Q	GLF3	379
N282Q	**GLF5**	**5090**
N282Q	GLF5	532
N282QA	GLF5	532
N282QS	CS55	0082
N282QT	GLF5	673
(N282QT)	GLF5	532
N282R	LJ24	131
N282R	LJ24	134
N282RH	C560	0055
N282SA	C500	282
N282SM	WW24	432
N282T	**FA10**	**42**
N282TA	LJ45	525
N282TX	HS25	258387
N282U	FA20	305
N282VR	C560	0282
N282WW	SBRL	306-134
(N282XL)	C56X	6082
N283BA	**G280**	**2090**
N283BX	HS25	258283
N283CJ	C52A	0183
N283CW	C550	713
N283DF	**C550**	**456**
N283DJ	**GALX**	**051**
N283DM	CL64	5572
N283DM	**GLEX**	**9320**
N283EJ	EA50	550-0283
N283EM	**G280**	**2089**
N283FJ	FA50	192
N283FJ	FA50	283
N283GA	G150	283
N283GA	GALX	083
N283GA	GLF5	5283
N283HB	PRM1	RB-283
N283K	FA50	87
N283MM	**C56X**	**5512**
N283MM	GLF2	81
N283R	LJ25	026
N283RA	**C52B**	**0283**
N283S	GLEX	9080
N283SA	**FA20**	**83**
N283SL	F2EX	83
N283TX	HS25	258474
N283U	FA50	14
N283U	LJ25	277
(N283XP)	HS25	258283
N284	C550	225
N284AM	C500	028
N284BG	**EA50**	**550-0284**
N284CC	C500	284
N284CC	**GLF5**	**5410**
N284CE	FA20	284
N284CP	**C560**	**0358**
N284DB	HS25	25023
N284DB	HS25	25179
N284DS	GLF4	1477
N284EJ	EA50	550-0284
N284EM	G280	2094
N284FJ	FA50	194
N284GA	G280	2084
N284GA	GALX	084
N284GA	GLF4	4284
N284GA	GLF5	5184
N284HS	**C560**	**0305**
N284JC	CL30	20284
N284JJ	FA20	284
N284L	LJ60	284
N284PC	C500	433
N284PD	E55P	50500031
N284QS	**F2TH**	**185**
N284RJ	C500	357
N284RP	C680	0284
(N284RP)	HS25	258522
N284SD	GLF5	5120
N284TJ	**LJ25**	**284**
N284TX	HS25	258542
N284U	SBRL	306-48
N284VP	C56X	5284
N285AL	HS25	258085
N285AP	FA20	285/504
N285BA	**G280**	**2095**
N285CC	**C560**	**0285**
(N285CC)	C500	285
(N285CF)	CS55	0085
N285CG	GLF4	4030
N285CP	FA50	44
N285CV	C560	0285
N285DH	**LJ55**	**026**
N285DX	**G280**	**2026**

N285EA	EA50	550-0269
N285EB	**PRM1**	**RB-285**
N285ER	C52B	0471
N285FA	**C56X**	**6005**
N285FJ	FA50	196
N285FW	**C52A**	**0424**
N285GA	**G150**	**285**
N285GA	GALX	085
N285GA	GALX	185
N285GA	GLF5	5285
N285GC	**E50P**	**50000285**
N285HR	LJ35	082
N285JE	C52A	0424
N285KR	CL30	20078
N285LM	JSTR	5224
N285MC	**CS55**	**0102**
N285TW	**FA20**	**285/504**
N285TX	GLF5	623
N285TX	HS25	258433
N285U	FA20	364
N285XJ	HS25	258482
N285XL	C56X	5285
N285XP	**HS25**	**258285**
N286AB	LJ36	044
N286CC	C500	286
(N286CP)	LJ35	268
N286CV	C560	0286
N286CW	C525	0026
N286CX	**F2TH**	**102**
N286EC	**CL30**	**20286**
N286FJ	FA50	197
N286G	C550	191
N286GA	G280	2086
N286GA	GALX	086
N286GA	GLF4	1286
N286GA	GLF4	4286
N286GA	GLF5	5186
N286JS	**GLEX**	**9492**
N286KR	GLEX	9141
N286KR	LJ40	2068
N286KR	LJ45	408
N286MC	**C650**	**7076**
N286MG	F2TH	94
N286MJ	**F9EX**	**208**
N286PC	**C500**	**570**
N286RW	**G280**	**2050**
N286SD	**LJ35**	**286**
N286TX	HS25	258528
N286VP	**C52B**	**0286**
N286WL	LJ35	286
N286XJ	HS25	258542
N286ZT	**FA50**	**286**
N287	C550	225
N287AB	C500	287
N287AP	PRM1	RB-287
N287CC	C500	287
N287CD	**C650**	**0179**
N287CD	BE40	RK-171
N287CV	C560	0287
N287DL	**CL60**	**1065**
N287DL	HS25	256040
N287DM	HS25	256040
N287F	F2EX	87
N287FJ	FA50	199
N287GA	G280	2087
N287GA	GALX	087
N287GA	GLF4	4287
N287GA	GLF5	5137
N287KR	CL30	20176
N287MC	C650	7096
N287MC	CS55	0102
N287MF	LJ25	287
N287NA	SBRL	287-1
N287QS	F2TH	87
N287SA	FA20	349
N287TG	**C750**	**0018**
N287TX	GLF4	1304
N287W	FA20	194
N287WM	**EA50**	**000247**
(N287XP)	HS25	258287
N287Z	GLEX	9024
N287Z	GLEX	9228
N288A	**GLF5**	**5307**
N288AG	C525	0288
N288AS	**LJ40**	**2088**
(N288BF)	LJ31	108
N288CB	**LJ45**	**272**
N288CC	C500	288
N288CC	C550	248
N288CC	C650	0079
N288CW	C525	0218
N288CX	C750	0219
N288DF	LJ24	288
N288DG	**GLEX**	**9546**
N288DX	**E50P**	**50000166**
N288EX	FA50	288
N288FF	**LJ31**	**108**
N288FJ	FA50	200
N288G	**C52A**	**0035**
N288GA	G280	2088
(N288GA)	GALX	008
N288HK	**C680**	**0313**
N288HL	**C560**	**0599**
N288J	LJ24	357
N288JA	C680	0288
N288JE	LJ35	288
N288JP	LJ35	288

N288JR	C560	0266
N288JR	**EA50**	**550-0274**
N288K	LJ24	175
N288KA	GLF3	391
N288KR	HS25	HA-0020
(N288KR)	LJ40	2081
N288MB	HS25	HA-0063
N288MM	C500	689
(N288MM)	FA20	380
N288MW	HS25	256018
N288NE	LJ35	288
N288QS	CS55	0088
(N288SJ)	WW24	299
N288SP	C500	241
N288TX	GLF4	1308
N288U	JSTR	5106/9
N288VP	C52B	0288
N288VW	LJ24	117
N288WR	**GLF6**	**6007**
N288WW	WW24	277
N288Z	F900	43
N288Z	GLEX	9024
N288Z	GLEX	9228
N288Z	**GLF6**	**6093**
N289BZ	PRM1	RB-289
N289CA	**FA10**	**111**
N289CA	LJ28	29-003
N289CC	CS55	0159
(N289CC)	CS55	0089
N289CP	**C550**	**331**
(N289CR)	C550	331
N289EE	E50P	50000289
N289FJ	FA50	201
N289G	LJ24	289
N289GA	G280	2089
N289GA	GALX	089
N289GA	GALX	189
N289GA	GLF4	4289
(N289GA)	LJ35	357
N289HB	PRM1	RB-289
(N289HC)	GLF4	4217
N289JP	LJ40	2118
N289K	**CL61**	**5132**
N289K	GLF2	225
N289KR	**C680**	**0193**
N289LJ	LJ35	289
N289MJ	LJ35	289
N289MM	FA20	380
N289MU	GLF4	1289
N289NE	LJ35	289
N289RZ	**E50P**	**50000289**
N289SA	LJ24	289
N289TX	F2TH	98
N289Z	GLEX	9228
N290	LJ25	251
(N290AR)	BE40	RK-320
N290AS	C650	0088
N290BA	C550	304
N290BB	**C560**	**0470**
N290BC	LJ35	064
(N290BC)	FA20	495
N290CA	WW24	216
N290CC	C500	290
N290CK	**LJ35**	**090**
N290CL	**CL30**	**20290**
N290CP	**WW24**	**219**
N290EC	HS25	258172
N290FJ	FA50	202
N290GA	G150	209
N290GA	GALX	049
N290GA	GLF3	875
N290GA	GLF5	5190
N290GA	GLF5	5290
N290GS	**LJ40**	**2038**
N290H	HS25	259034
N290JP	**EA50**	**000254**
N290KR	GLEX	9396
N290KR	LJ60	245
N290LJ	LJ45	029
N290MH	CL65	5842
N290MX	**FA50**	**199**
N290PC	HS25	257149
N290QS	**F2TH**	**190**
N290RA	WW24	390
N290SC	C650	0079
N290SC	C650	0140
N290TJ	FA50	29
N290TX	BE40	RK-422
N290VP	**C550**	**085**
N290W	FA50	90
N290W	WW24	280
N291A	LJ35	212
N291BC	FA50	199
N291BC	LJ24	212
N291BC	LJ35	015
N291BC	LJ35	064
N291BC	LJ35	380
N291BX	LJ35	380
N291CW	C525	0301
N291DS	C500	291
N291DV	**C56X**	**5146**
N291EU	PRM1	RB-291
N291FJ	FA50	205
N291FJ	**FA50**	**291**
N291GA	**G280**	**2091**
N291GA	GALX	050
N291GA	GLF2	91

N291GA	GLF5	5191
N291H	HS25	259016
N291K	LJ35	665
(N291KR)	CL65	5743
N291LJ	**LJ45**	**291**
N291MJ	**F9EX**	**23**
N291SJ	HS25	258291
(N291SL)	GLEX	9325
N291TX	HS25	258355
(N291WK)	ASTR	101
N291XP	HS25	258291
N292BC	FA50	62
N292BC	LJ24	010
N292BC	LJ24	220
N292CS	C680	0292
N292EX	FA50	292
N292FH	FA50	31
N292FJ	FA50	207
N292GA	CL61	3014
N292GA	**G280**	**2092**
N292GA	GLF4	4292
N292GA	HS25	25219
N292H	HS25	259025
N292JC	WW24	292
N292KR	LJ60	317
N292ME	**LJ35**	**292**
N292MU	GLF4	1292
N292PC	**FA50**	**99**
(N292PC)	C650	0058
N292QS	**F2TH**	**93**
N292RC	LJ55	062
(N292RC)	HS25	25219
N292SG	C525	0423
N292ST	**C52C**	**0172**
N292TX	HS25	258472
N293BC	**FA50**	**135**
N293BC	FA50	82
N293BC	LJ24	042
N293BC	LJ24	229
N293EX	FA50	293
N293FJ	FA50	209
N293GA	**G280**	**2093**
N293GA	GALX	051
N293GA	GLF5	5193
(N293GT)	FA20	71
(N293H)	HS25	258266
N293HC	**CL30**	**20330**
N293K	FA50	170
N293KR	CL30	20047
N293MC	**LJ24**	**293**
N293MM	**C510**	**0293**
N293P	**ASTR**	**049**
N293PC	C550	713
N293QS	C560	0293
N293RK	BE40	RK-293
N293RT	CS55	0023
N293S	C500	193
N293S	HS25	258572
N293SA	LJ31	101
N293TX	HS25	258517
N294AT	**C525**	**0294**
N294AW	BE40	RK-1
N294B	WW24	222
N294BC	LJ24	149
N294CA	LJ28	29-004
N294CC	**C52B**	**0294**
N294CV	**HS25**	**258339**
N294CW	**C525**	**0114**
N294DD	**LJ60**	**186**
N294EX	FA50	291
N294FA	BE40	RK-1
N294FJ	FA50	212
N294G	**GLF4**	**1294**
N294GA	**G280**	**2094**
N294GA	GALX	052
N294GA	GLF4	4294
N294GM	**C680**	**0510**
N294H	HS25	258267
(N294KR)	CL64	5413
(N294M)	LJ25	031
N294NW	**LJ25**	**031**
N294RT	**C560**	**0264**
N294S	ASTR	094
N294TX	HS25	258436
(N294VP)	C56X	5294
N294W	FA10	30
N294W	HS25	258014
N294W	WW24	222
N295	**C52A**	**0073**
N295AR	JSTR	5134/50
N295BM	C560	0295
N295CK	**LJ35**	**295**
N295CM	C525	0295
N295CV	C560	0295
N295DJ	LJ25	295
N295DS	**C525**	**0091**
(N295EA)	C550	325
N295FA	BE40	RK-68
N295FJ	FA50	213
N295GA	G280	2095
N295GA	GALX	053
N295GA	GLF5	5125
N295GA	GLF5	5195
N295GA	GLF5	5295
N295H	HS25	258269
N295HB	PRM1	RB-295
N295JL	**CL64**	**5415**

N295JM	**HS25**	**258754**
N295JR	HS25	258168
N295KR	LJ60	212
N295NW	**LJ24**	**295**
N295PJ	**C510**	**0372**
N295PS	LJ31	230
N295SG	CL30	20269
N295SG	LJ40	2105
N295TW	FA20	5
N295TX	GLEX	9017
N295TX	HS25	258564
N295VP	C52B	0295
N295WW	WW24	295
N296AB	C550	011
(N296AP)	PRM1	RB-296
N296AR	JSTR	5055/21
N296BF	C500	296
N296BS	LJ35	296
N296CC	C550	296
N296CF	C550	296
N296CJ	C52B	0296
N296CW	C550	330
N296DC	**C525**	**0296**
N296EX	FA50	296
N296FA	BE40	RK-91
N296FJ	FA50	214
(N296G)	HS25	258507
N296GA	**G280**	**2096**
N296GA	GALX	054
N296GA	GLF4	4296
N296GC	GLF5	5296
N296H	HS25	259047
(N296H)	HS25	259045
N296JA	**LJ45**	**381**
N296KR	CL65	5814
N296L	**LJ60**	**296**
N296NW	WW24	284
N296PH	C550	296
N296PM	C52B	0296
N296QS	**F2TH**	**196**
N296RG	F2TH	222
N296RG	HS25	257131
N296SB	CL30	20157
N296SF	LJ31	166
N296SG	LJ40	2105
N296TS	LJ60	029
N296TX	HS25	258523
N296V	CL60	1006
N296VP	C510	0296
N297A	WW24	267
"N297AG"	FA20	297
N297AP	**F900**	**13**
N297AP	JSTR	5209
N297AR	FA20	24
N297CK	FA20	296/507
N297CP	**C560**	**0422**
N297DD	C650	0071
N297EJ	LJ24	297
N297EJ	LJ25	297
(N297EU)	PRM1	RB-297
N297FF	FA10	56
N297FJ	FA50	215
N297GA	ASTR	091
N297GA	ASTR	101
N297GA	ASTR	111
N297GA	ASTR	130
N297GA	**G280**	**2097**
N297GA	GLF4	4297
(N297GA)	ASTR	113
(N297GA)	ASTR	122
N297GB	**F9EX**	**131**
N297GB	GLF2	185
N297GB	GLF4	1208
N297H	HS25	258270
N297JD	HS25	25235
N297JS	WW24	435
(N297KR)	CL64	5644
N297MC	**CL30**	**20127**
N297MC	GLF4	1393
N297PF	FA10	56
N297PJ	**GLF4**	**1160**
N297QS	F2TH	195
N297RG	F2TH	222
N297RJ	C525	0663
N297S	C500	197
N297SF	**GLEX**	**9210**
N297TX	HS25	258505
N297TX	**HS25**	**HA-0011**
N297W	FA20	194
N297W	FA50	111
N297W	WW24	267
N297XP	HS25	258297
N298A	WW24	318
N298AG	**HS25**	**258014**
(N298AS)	SBRL	282-117
N298BP	HS25	257138
N298CH	LJ31	058
N298CJ	**C52B**	**0298**
N298CJ	C550	298
N298CK	FA20	347
N298CK	**LJ35**	**298**
N298CM	WW24	298
N298DC	CL64	5503
N298DR	LJ25	298
N298EE	LEG5	55000026
N298EF	**LJ60**	**103**
N298EJ	LJ24	298

N298FJ	FA50	216
N298GA	G150	298
N298GA	GALX	056
N298GA	GLF5	5198
(N298GS)	LJ25	295
N298H	HS25	258271
N298H	LJ24	229
N298HM	**WW24**	**240**
(N298KR)	CL65	5707
N298NM	HS25	25278
N298NW	LJ35	298
N298QS	F2TH	98
N298TB	GLF3	875
N298TS	HS25	257138
N298TX	HS25	258463
N298W	F900	33
N298W	F900	45
N298W	FA20	142
N298W	FA50	90
N298W	WW24	318
N298WB	**HS25**	**258009**
N298XJ	HS25	258463
N298XP	HS25	258298
(N299AJ)	GLF4	4009
N299AW	BE40	RK-212
(N299BB)	LJ45	211
N299BW	HS25	256046
N299CS	C52B	0299
N299CT	HS25	257090
N299CW	**C525**	**0199**
N299CX	**C750**	**0299**
N299D	C500	564
N299DB	**C56X**	**6019**
N299DB	FA10	50
N299DB	FA50	274
N299DB	GLF4	1137
(N299DG)	HS25	256046
N299DH	**C560**	**0645**
N299DP	**FA10**	**50**
N299EJ	LJ24	299
N299EX	FA50	299
N299FB	GLF4	1099
N299FB	HS25	257122
N299GA	**G280**	**2099**
N299GA	GALX	057
N299GA	GLF4	4299
N299GA	HS25	256046
N299GS	**HS25**	**256046**
N299H	HS25	258272
N299HS	C550	550-1049
N299JC	**FA20**	**299**
N299JM	**HS25**	**258742**
N299K	**C500**	**438**
N299KR	**CL65**	**5770**
N299LR	LJ35	112
N299LR	SBRL	282-38
N299LS	C52B	0346
N299MV	FA50	299
N299MW	LJ25	299
N299NW	FA20	61
N299PP	**E50P**	**50000151**
N299PR	**FA50**	**299**
N299PS	GALX	136
N299QS	C525	0099
N299RA	FA20	146
N299RK	**C550**	**550-1027**
N299RP	C500	448
N299RR	C56X	6105
N299SC	**GLF4**	**4289**
N299SC	LJ60	025
N299SC	LJ60	112
N299SG	LJ60	025
N299TB	C500	230
N299TJ	HS25	256046
N299TW	LJ24	299
N299VR	C52B	0299
N299W	FA50	21
N299WB	**HS25**	**257092**
N299WV	C500	320
N299XP	HS25	258299
N300A	FA10	59
N300A	FA50	64
N300A	**GLF5**	**5309**
N300AA	LJ45	211
N300AA	**LJ45**	**285**
N300AA	MU30	A041SA
N300AG	JSTR	5056
N300AH	CL30	20195
N300AH	CL30	20423
N300AJ	ASTR	070
N300AK	C550	550-0809
N300AK	C550	612
N300AK	C560	0593
N300AK	**C56X**	**5235**
N300AL	FA20	330
N300AN	CL30	20426
N300AQ	LJ45	211
N300AR	MU30	A041SA
(N300AT)	C750	0003
N300AV	**CL30**	**20092**
N300AY	CL30	20436
N300BA	**FA20**	**142**
N300BB	**C52C**	**0165**
N300BC	**CL30**	**20067**
N300BC	CL64	5563
N300BE	GLF3	332
N300BK	GLF3	409

N300BL	HS25	258155
N300BP	FA20	239
N300BS	HS25	257056
N300BU	CL30	20442
N300BV	**C525**	**0418**
N300BW	HS25	258074
N300BY	CL30	20244
N300BZ	CL30	20030
N300BZ	**CL30**	**20340**
N300CC	FA20	257
N300CC	HS25	25250
N300CC	LJ24	179
N300CC	LJ36	019
N300CF	CL30	20397
N300CF	CL30	20448
N300CF	HS25	25276
N300CH	**C560**	**0080**
N300CH	SBRL	282-26
N300CM	LJ35	381
N300CQ	C525	0300
N300CQ	**HS25**	**258555**
N300CR	CL61	5092
N300CR	FA50	55
N300CR	**GLF4**	**1401**
N300CR	JSTR	5020
N300CS	C550	550-0818
N300CT	FA20	366
N300CV	FA20	322
N300CY	CL30	20353
N300DA	**C56X**	**5270**
N300DA	LJ35	249
N300DG	**CL30**	**20058**
N300DH	**CL30**	**20083**
N300DH	MU30	A010SA
N300DH	WW24	74
N300DK	GLF2	57
N300DK	LJ36	019
N300DL	C525	0148
N300DL	GLF2	57
N300DL	LJ36	019
N300DM	MU30	A003SA
N300DY	CL30	20439
N300EC	C500	339
N300EJ	LJ24	300
N300EL	GLF3	393
N300ER	**CL30**	**20428**
N300ES	CL64	5439
N300ES	FA50	70
N300ES	GLEX	9016
N300ES	**GLF4**	**4209**
N300ES	LJ35	278
N300ET	C52B	0014
N300EU	**CL30**	**20373**
N300FC	**C525**	**0248**
N300FJ	**E55P**	**50500046**
N300FJ	FA20	168
N300FJ	FA20	300/508
N300FL	**E55P**	**50500027**
N300FN	LJ35	447
(N300FN)	GLF2	65
N300FP	**E55P**	**50500277**
N300FS	CL30	20143
N300FS	**F2EX**	**182**
N300FS	GLF3	367
N300GA	G150	300
N300GA	GLF3	249
N300GA	GLF3	300
N300GA	GLF3	303
N300GA	GLF5	5300
N300GB	HS25	25074
N300GB	**BE40**	**RK-262**
N300GC	**C550**	**337**
N300GF	C550	550-0856
N300GF	C550	550-1046
N300GF	**LJ40**	**2119**
N300GH	**C550**	**033**
N300GM	C550	343
N300GM	CL30	20186
N300GM	CL30	20312
N300GN	FA10	59
N300GN	HS25	258057
N300GP	C550	550-0856
N300GP	**CL30**	**20253**
N300GP	GLF2	3
N300GV	**E55P**	**50500104**
N300GX	GLF4	1164
N300HA	FA20	503
N300HB	HS25	257173
N300HC	C500	124
N300HC	C500	348
N300HC	WW24	307
N300HH	LJ24	149
N300HH	MU30	A035SA
N300HJ	**E55P**	**50500204**
N300HK	CL30	20447
N300HQ	C500	124
N300HQ	**CL30**	**20445**
N300HR	WW24	335
N300HW	HS25	25021
N300JA	**GLF4**	**1023**
N300JA	LJ24	282
N300JC	LJ45	209
N300JC	LJ45	340
N300JC	**LJ45**	**510**
N300JD	C750	0202
N300JD	**C750**	**0515**
N300JE	CL30	20398

N300JE	LJ25	234
N300JE	LJ45	094
N300JJ	ASTR	024
N300JJ	FA20	208/468
N300JK	C550	262
N300JK	WW24	369
N300JQ	LJ45	340
N300JZ	**GLF3**	**875**
N300K	GLF4	1266
N300K	GLF5	587
N300KC	**CL30**	**20385**
N300KC	CL61	5051
N300KC	HS25	25118
N300KE	**CL30**	**20336**
N300KH	**CL30**	**20130**
N300KK	**C52C**	**0076**
N300L	GLF2	92
N300L	GLF3	318
N300L	GLF4	1018
N300L	GLF5	507
N300L	JSTR	5097/60
N300LA	MU30	A049SA
N300LB	GLF4	1448
N300LB	LJ24	149
N300LD	HS25	25202
N300LD	HS25	25265
(N300LD)	HS25	257043
N300LE	CL30	20443
(N300LF)	GLF3	318
N300LG	MU30	A090SA
N300LH	WW24	312
N300LJ	CL30	20011
N300LJ	CL30	20213
N300LJ	**E50P**	**50000021**
N300LS	HS25	257173
N300LS	HS25	258098
N300LS	HS25	259032
N300LS	WW24	137
N300LS	WW24	226
N300LS	WW24	400
N300LV	CL30	20129
N300M	GLF3	417
N300M	WW24	124
N300MV	**C52B**	**0148**
N300MY	**CL30**	**20062**
N300NB	**CL30**	**20157**
N300NC	**CL30**	**20440**
N300ND	MS76	009
N300NL	FA20	221
N300NZ	**CL30**	**20397**
N300P	HS25	25226
N300P	JSTR	5052
N300PB	C500	323
N300PB	C500	400
N300PB	C550	007
N300PH	**E55P**	**50500306**
N300PL	LJ25	247
N300PM	HS25	258193
N300PP	LJ25	043
(N300PR)	C550	239
N300PX	C500	140
N300PX	C560	0691
(N300PX)	C56X	5017
N300PY	C550	550-0806
N300QC	HS25	25250
N300QS	C560	0322
N300QS	C680	0164
N300QS	E55P	50500091
N300QS	**E55P**	**50500379**
N300QW	C555	0100
N300R	E55P	50500031
N300R	**G280**	**2012**
N300R	HS25	25043
N300R	HS25	HA-0076
N300R	LJ35	438
N300R	BE40	RK-386
N300RB	HS25	258013
N300RC	SBRL	282-41
N300RC	SBRL	306-111
N300RC	**BE40**	**RK-539**
N300RD	GLF2	3
N300RG	SBRL	282-41
N300RL	**CL30**	**20090**
(N300RN)	C500	517
N300RT	FA20	478
N300RY	CL30	20342
N300RZ	**E55P**	**50500228**
N300S	CL61	3026
N300SB	HFB3	1031
N300SC	LJ25	208
N300SC	**LJ35**	**440**
N300SF	FA20	258
N300SJ	**C56X**	**5107**
(N300SJ)	MU30	A060SA
N300SL	**PRM1**	**RB-110**
N300SM	CL30	20015
N300TA	LJ24	038
N300TB	SBRL	306-24
(N300TB)	C500	230
N300TC	C550	313
N300TC	**WW24**	**241**
N300TE	LJ35	237
N300TE	WW24	201
N300TJ	LJ24	285
(N300TJ)	MU30	A003SA
N300TK	**CL60**	**1077**
N300TK	HS25	257192

(N300TK)	SBRL	282-41
N300TL	LJ25	238
N300TS	**MU30**	**A003SA**
N300TU	**CL30**	**20264**
N300TW	C550	047
N300TW	CL60	1080
N300TW	**CL64**	**5428**
N300TW	HS25	257192
N300TW	LJ35	237
N300U	GLF2	92
N300UJ	**GLF3**	**316**
N300VC	CL30	20430
(N300VP)	C750	0003
N300VR	**E55P**	**50500043**
N300WC	C560	0322
N300WC	C56X	5137
N300WG	LJ25	346
N300WK	C500	374
N300WY	GLF3	427
N300XL	**WW24**	**276**
N300YM	SBRL	306-83
N301AE	**MU30**	**A091SA**
N301AJ	**C510**	**0233**
N301AJ	WW24	48
N301AS	**E55P**	**50500119**
N301AS	LJ31	052
(N301AS)	HS25	257188
N301AT	HFB3	1038
N301CK	HS25	25038
N301DM	MU30	A007SA
N301DN	C510	0301
N301DR	**C500**	**382**
N301EC	GLF2	258
N301EL	C500	544
N301EL	C52A	0109
N301EX	FA50	301
(N301FC)	FA20	335
(N301FP)	GLF2	118
N301GA	GLF3	329
N301GA	GLF3	402
(N301GA)	GLF3	252
N301GT	**C510**	**0076**
N301HA	SBRL	282-23
N301HB	C56X	5607
N301HC	C500	348
N301HC	FA10	77
(N301HC)	WW24	307
N301HR	**C750**	**0062**
N301JJ	C500	551
N301JJ	FA10	24
N301JJ	FA50	161
(N301JJ)	HS25	256040
N301JL	**CL30**	**20351**
N301K	GLF4	1267
N301K	GLF5	591
N301KF	WW24	301
N301KR	CL61	5181
N301KR	LJ45	366
N301L	**C56X**	**6101**
N301L	WW24	98
N301LJ	LJ60	301
(N301LX)	HS25	257188
N301MB	CL30	20287
N301MC	C500	390
N301MC	SBRL	306-146
N301MC	SBRL	465-14
(N301MC)	C500	383
N301MF	CL61	5013
N301MG	C500	390
N301MG	SBRL	306-146
N301MK	**EA50**	**000214**
N301ML	**HS25**	**HA-0094**
N301MT	LJ25	301
N301MY	C500	668
N301NT	SBRL	282-9
N301P	MU30	A030SA
N301PB	HS25	259031
N301PC	SBRL	282-112
N301PC	**WW24**	**377**
(N301PC)	WW24	383
N301PE	**CL30**	**20244**
N301PE	HS25	259031
N301PG	C52A	0301
N301PH	HS25	257121
N301PH	HS25	259031
N301PP	C500	518
N301QS	C560	0038
N301QS	**C680**	**0010**
N301QS	C555	0158
N301R	FA20	3/403
N301RJ	LJ60	054
N301SC	LJ35	143
N301SG	G150	205
N301TG	CL30	20137
N301TG	E55P	50500036
N301TP	LJ35	301
N301TT	FA20	160/450
N301WC	C560	0335
N302A	FA10	59
N302AJ	C500	382
N302AK	GLEX	9181
N302AK	**GLEX**	**9436**
N302AT	WW24	12
N302BG	FA50	305
N302CE	C500	302
N302CJ	C525	0302
N302CJ	**C52A**	**0302**

N302CS	C550	550-0820
N302CZ	C52B	0302
N302DM	C52A	0030
N302DM	MU30	A004SA
N302DP	GLF2	237/43
N302EA	**HS25**	**258269**
N302EC	CL61	5093
N302EJ	C560	0302
N302EJ	LJ24	302
N302EM	CL30	20054
N302FJ	FA50	302
N302GA	GLF3	302
N302GA	GLF3	339
N302GA	GLF3	438
N302GA	GLF3	480
N302GV	**E55P**	**50500322**
N302H	SBRL	306-5
(N302HM)	GALX	039
N302JC	F2TH	63
N302JK	**C52B**	**0493**
N302K	**CL30**	**20267**
N302K	GLF5	597
N302KC	**CL30**	**20389**
N302KR	LJ45	153
N302MB	**CS55**	**0097**
N302MC	GALX	025
N302MT	HS25	258302
N302NT	SBRL	282-81
(N302NT)	SBRL	282-100
N302PC	CL60	1072
N302PC	**CL64**	**5337**
N302PC	CS55	0130
N302PC	HS25	257125
N302PC	LJ25	351
N302PE	**CL30**	**20144**
N302PE	HS25	258693
N302PJ	**HS25**	**258302**
N302QS	C560	0402
N302QS	**E55P**	**50500123**
N302R	**CL30**	**20204**
N302SE	HS25	258269
N302SG	G150	244
N302SG	WW24	379
N302SJ	**C550**	**067**
N302ST	GLF3	302
N302TB	**BE40**	**RK-384**
N302TG	**E55P**	**50500310**
N302TS	ASTR	108
N302TS	C500	382
N302TT	FA20	122
N302WC	**C560**	**0329**
(N302WY)	FA50	290
N302XP	HS25	258302
N303A	**C500**	**478**
N303A	SBRL	282-52
N303A	SBRL	465-32
N303AF	LJ24	144
N303AJ	WW24	149
N303BC	**HS25**	**258324**
N303BX	CL61	3031
(N303BX)	HS25	25249
N303CB	C500	422
N303CB	C560	0190
N303CJ	C52B	0031
N303CL	**F2TH**	**44**
N303CP	**C560**	**0539**
N303CS	C550	550-0814
N303CZ	**CL30**	**20003**
N303DM	MU30	A008SA
N303DT	HS25	258303
(N303E)	WW24	390
N303EC	C550	330
(N303EC)	C550	303
N303EJ	LJ24	303
N303EM	CL30	20068
N303FZ	FA10	218
N303GA	GLF3	303
N303GA	GLF3	357
N303GA	GLF3	462
N303GA	GLF4	4303
N303GA	GLF5	5303
(N303GC)	C550	193
N303H	JSTR	5055/21
N303HB	GLF3	402
N303HC	**C560**	**0460**
N303J	C550	303
N303JH	MU30	A003SA
N303JJ	LJ25	062
N303JW	FA50	140
N303K	GLF5	607
N303KR	CL64	5473
N303LA	WW24	51
N303LC	C525	0068
N303LE	JSTR	5113/25
N303LJ	**LJ45**	**303**
N303MC	GALX	030
N303MW	HS25	256033
N303NT	SBRL	282-29
N303P	MU30	A034SA
N303PC	C500	124
N303PC	C650	0110
N303PC	**C650**	**7098**
N303PC	WW24	223
N303PL	FA10	187
N303PM	**FA50**	**103**
N303PM	LJ55	014
N303QS	C560	0343
N303QS	**E55P**	**50500141**
N303QW	F2EX	66
N303RH	**C500**	**551**
N303SC	LJ25	095
N303SD	**C550**	**416**
N303SE	**HS25**	**258060**
N303SG	WW24	391
N303SQ	LJ25	095
N303ST	**C56X**	**6160**
N303TP	GLF4	1411
N303TS	WW24	416
N303WB	LJ31	056
N303WS	**CL30**	**20045**
N303X	C550	198
N303XP	HS25	258303
N304AC	**C680**	**0024**
N304AF	LJ35	013
N304AT	**HS25**	**258257**
N304AT	LJ35	045
N304AT	LJ55	107
N304BC	CL30	20067
N304BX	CL61	5063
N304CC	C500	304
N304CC	GLEX	9027
N304CK	JSTR	5055/21
N304CS	C550	550-0847
N304CT	**CL61**	**3044**
N304DM	MU30	A005SA
N304E	LJ36	038
N304EJ	LJ24	304
N304EM	**CL30**	**20077**
N304FL	**E55P**	**50500028**
N304FX	CL61	5063
N304GA	GLF3	312
N304GA	GLF3	381
N304GA	GLF3	440
N304GA	GLF3	481
N304HE	**HS25**	**258229**
N304JR	**BE40**	**RK-63**
N304K	GLF5	514
N304K	GLF5	622
N304KC	**CL30**	**20390**
N304KR	**CL65**	**5824**
N304KT	C550	290
N304LP	LJ24	304
N304NT	SBRL	282-2
N304P	HS25	25226
N304PC	**C650**	**0110**
N304PS	**CL30**	**20059**
N304QS	C560	0408
N304QS	**E55P**	**50500143**
N304RJ	HS25	258286
N304SE	BE40	RK-304
N304SG	C525	0840
N304TC	**C52B**	**0478**
(N304TH)	C550	240
N304TS	GLF3	304
N304TT	**CL60**	**1033**
N304TZ	LJ35	045
N304VS	**LJ25**	**354**
N304WW	WW24	304
N305AF	GLF2	17
N305AG	**HS25**	**258013**
N305AJ	WW24	100
N305AK	**C510**	**0080**
N305AR	FA20	378
N305AR	**LJ25**	**314**
N305BB	C500	305
N305BB	WW24	228
(N305BP)	PRM1	RB-305
N305CC	GLEX	9027
N305CC	**GLF6**	**6021**
N305CF	**GLF4**	**1457**
N305CJ	C525	0105
N305CL	CL30	20305
N305CS	C550	550-0825
N305CX	C750	0305
N305DL	**CL30**	**20608**
N305DM	MU30	A009SA
N305EJ	C680	0105
N305EJ	LJ24	305
N305EM	**CL30**	**20098**
N305FL	E55P	50500029
N305FX	CL61	5070
N305GA	G150	305
N305GA	GALX	105
N305GA	GLF3	305
N305GA	GLF3	343
N305GA	GLF3	382
N305GA	GLF4	1305
N305GA	GLF5	5505
N305JA	HS25	258625
N305KN	**GLF6**	**6142**
N305KR	**HS25**	**HA-0166**
N305LM	**GLF4**	**1443**
N305LX	**C56X**	**5049**
N305M	C500	443
(N305M)	CL61	5021
N305MD	GLF3	305
N305MD	**BE40**	**RK-131**
N305NT	SBRL	282-66
N305PB	GLF4	1088
N305PC	CS55	0138
N305PG	E50P	50000319
N305PL	**E50P**	**50000305**
N305QS	C560	0261
N305QS	**C680**	**0088**
N305S	**C500**	**301**
N305SC	HS25	258662
N305SC	LJ35	322
N305SJ	GLF2	119/22
N305TC	GLF3	359
N305TC	**GLF4**	**1116**
N305TH	HS25	257150
N305WM	**CL30**	**20379**
N305XP	HS25	258305
N306AV	**LJ45**	**306**
N306BH	**F2TH**	**220**
N306BP	PRM1	RB-206
N306BX	CL61	5175
N306CF	SBRL	306-13
N306CJ	**C52A**	**0016**
N306CS	C550	550-0881
N306CW	SBRL	282-108
N306DM	MU30	A010SA
N306EC	C525	0084
N306EJ	LJ24	306
N306EM	**CL30**	**20101**
N306ES	FA50	70
N306FL	**E55P**	**50500030**
N306FX	CL61	5175
N306GA	GALX	206
N306GA	GLF3	306
N306GA	GLF3	344
N306GA	GLF3	441
N306GA	GLF3	482
N306GA	GLF4	1506
N306GA	GLF4	4306
N306JA	**LJ24**	**306**
N306JR	C52A	0306
N306KR	LJ60	362
N306L	HS25	25093
N306L	JSTR	5097/60
N306M	LJ35	416
N306MF	**CL30**	**20009**
N306MP	HS25	25017
N306NA	SBRL	306-1
N306NT	SBRL	282-30
N306P	MU30	A009SA
N306PA	**C650**	**0053**
N306PC	SBRL	282-112
N306PT	WW24	306
N306QS	C560	0266
N306QS	**C680**	**0207**
(N306QS)	C650	0006
N306R	LJ60	084
N306SA	SBRL	306-40
N306SC	C550	306
N306SP	LJ35	459
N306TR	C560	0306
N306TT	**GLF4**	**1148**
N307AD	HS25	258307
N307AF	GLF2	219/20
N307AJ	C550	107
N307AJ	LJ25	175
N307BJ	LJ24	307
N307BL	CL30	20119
N307BS	**C525**	**0241**
N307BX	CL61	5179
N307CS	C550	550-0974
N307D	**C500**	**388**
N307D	SBRL	306-31
N307DM	MU30	A011SA
N307EJ	LJ24	307
N307EM	**CL30**	**20283**
N307EW	C500	323
N307FL	**E55P**	**50500032**
N307FT	**ASTR**	**021**
N307FX	CL61	5179
N307G	HS25	25121
N307GA	GALX	207
N307GA	GLF3	331
N307GA	GLF4	1507
N307GA	GLF4	4307
N307HF	LJ25	075
N307JA	LJ55	101
N307JW	**ASTR**	**123**
N307KR	CL64	5343
N307KR	CL65	5758
N307LS	**C680**	**0066**
N307M	GLF2	220
N307MS	C550	550-0974
N307MT	**BE40**	**RK-42**
N307NA	SBRL	306-2
N307NT	SBRL	282-72
N307PE	**C52B**	**0254**
N307PS	**F2EX**	**300**
N307QS	C560	0307
N307QS	**C680**	**0130**
N307RM	**HS25**	**258322**
N307RX	C750	0107
N307SC	CL61	3026
N307SC	**CL61**	**5128**
N307SH	C510	0307
N307ST	HS25	HB-43
N307ST	SBRL	465-46
(N307TC)	C510	0014
(N307TC)	HS25	257007
N307XP	HS25	258307
N308A	**C550**	**703**
N308A	GLF2	155/14
N308AB	GLF4	1496
N308AF	GLF3	351
N308AJ	LJ25	039
(N308AJ)	WW24	149
N308AK	C560	0593
N308AT	C500	537
N308BW	LJ35	438
N308BX	CL61	5110
N308CC	C500	308
N308CJ	C52A	0308
N308CK	C550	117
N308CR	CL61	5092
N308CS	C550	550-0976
N308CX	C750	0308
N308DD	HS25	257069
N308DM	FA50	328
N308DM	MU30	A012SA
N308DT	**C550**	**550-1094**
N308EE	GLF2	68
N308EJ	LJ24	308
N308EL	GLF2	68
N308FX	CL61	5110
N308GA	GLF3	308
N308GA	GLF3	318
N308GA	GLF3	383
N308GA	GLF4	4308
N308GL	**CS55**	**0036**
N308GT	C52A	0004
N308GT	**C52B**	**0236**
N308GW	**HS25**	**HA-0157**
N308HG	GLF3	308
N308JM	C500	097
N308JS	WW24	308
N308KB	**G280**	**2068**
(N308LJ)	LJ24	308
N308MJ	E55P	50500008
N308MM	C560	0145
N308MR	**C650**	**0153**
N308MS	C550	550-0976
N308NT	SBRL	282-90
N308PM	LJ55	014
N308QS	C560	0277
N308QS	**C680**	**0116**
N308R	LJ35	438
N308SG	JSTR	5226
N308SM	LJ24	290
N308TS	WW24	308
N308TW	**C550**	**047**
N308U	**F2EX**	**37**
N308WC	JSTR	5020
N308WY	GLF3	427
N308XP	HS25	258308
N309AJ	LJ25	034
N309AK	BE40	RK-348
N309AT	C550	448
(N309BE)	BE40	RK-348
N309BT	C56X	5067
N309BX	CL64	5306
N309CJ	**C52A**	**0309**
N309CK	WW24	350
N309CQ	**C52C**	**0187**
N309CS	C550	550-0977
N309DM	MU30	A044SA
N309EL	GLF2	250
N309ES	GLEX	9016
N309FX	CL64	5306
N309G	HS25	258108
N309GA	GLF3	328
N309GA	GLF3	388
N309GA	GLF3	446
N309GA	GLF3	483
N309GA	GLF4	1309
N309GA	GLF4	4309
N309KB	**CL64**	**5418**
N309KC	LJ45	412
N309KR	**HS25**	**HA-0067**
N309LJ	LJ25	034
N309MG	LJ60	223
N309MT	**C510**	**0138**
N309NT	SBRL	282-61
N309QS	C560	0509
N309QS	**E55P**	**50500152**
N309SF	**FA50**	**29**
N309SG	GLF4	1449
(N309SM)	CL30	20015
(N309TA)	C650	0129
N309TC	LJ24	309
N309TW	**C52B**	**0470**
N309TX	**C52B**	**0309**
N309WM	HS25	257156
N309XL	C56X	5309
N310	**GLF4**	**1109**
N310AD	JSTR	5051
N310AF	C500	524
N310AS	HS25	258443
N310AV	C550	028
N310BA	LJ35	062
N310BN	C56X	6020
N310BN	**C680**	**0516**
N310BX	CL64	5336
N310CK	JSTR	5117/35
N310EG	**C52B**	**0067**
N310EJ	GLF4	1109
N310EL	GLF4	1021
(N310EN)	GLF4	1021
N310EX	FA50	310
N310FJ	FA10	23
N310FX	CL64	5336
N310GA	G150	310
N310GA	G280	2010
N310GA	GLF3	332
N310GA	GLF3	389
N310GA	GLF3	449
N310GA	GLF3	484
N310GA	GLF4	1405
N310GF	**BE40**	**RK-433**
N310GJ	GLF4	4078
N310KR	LJ24	020
N310LJ	LJ24	309
N310LJ	LJ31	033C
N310LJ	**LJ45**	**031**
N310LV	**C680**	**0209**
N310ME	LJ35	310
N310NT	SBRL	282-77
N310PE	CL60	1012
N310PJ	**LJ35**	**310**
N310QS	C680	0259
N310QS	**E55P**	**50500147**
N310RG	GLF3	321
N310SL	GLF3	496
N310SL	GLF4	1087
N310TK	CL64	5606
N310TK	**GLF5**	**5028**
N310U	C500	194
N310U	**F2EX**	**100**
N310VZ	**CL30**	**20366**
N310XP	HS25	258310
N310ZM	LJ45	218
N311AC	GLF2	74
N311AF	**CS55**	**0051**
N311BD	**GLF2**	**236**
(N311BK)	GLF3	311
N311BN	C680	0516
N311BP	CL64	5405
N311BP	**FA50**	**314**
N311BP	LJ35	311
N311BP	LJ45	010
N311BR	WW24	344
N311BX	CL64	5342
N311CC	LJ25	102
N311CG	GLF5	5108
N311CG	**GLF6**	**6064**
N311CJ	CL30	20343
N311CS	**C550**	**550-0979**
N311CW	C650	0011
N311DB	WW24	208
(N311DB)	C52A	0314
(N311DB)	CL30	20011
N311DF	LJ31	001
N311DG	C560	0167
N311DH	GLF2	236
N311DM	MU30	A019SA
N311EL	**GLF4**	**1095**
N311FL	**E55P**	**50500034**
N311FX	CL64	5342
N311G	CL61	5014
N311GA	G150	311
N311GA	GLF3	311
N311GA	GLF3	394
N311GA	GLF3	474
N311GA	GLF4	1406
N311GA	GLF5	5411
N311GF	**BE40**	**RK-431**
N311GL	BE40	RK-311
N311GX	CL61	5014
N311HA	C52A	0168
N311HS	BE40	RK-296
N311HS	**BE40**	**RK-529**
N311JA	F900	63
N311JA	**F9EX**	**251**
N311JA	HS25	25176
N311JA	HS25	258096
N311JD	HS25	257020
N311JJ	GLF2	3
N311JK	GLF3	434
N311JS	FA20	341
N311JS	**LJ31**	**216**
N311JV	**BE40**	**RK-281**
N311JX	HS25	258096
N311LJ	LJ24	311
N311LJ	LJ31	033A
N311MA	C650	0126
N311MB	**C56X**	**5770**
N311ME	C500	504
N311MG	GLF2	41
(N311MG)	HS25	257119
N311MK	**GALX**	**095**
N311NB	**GLEX**	**9410**
N311NT	SBRL	282-19
N311NW	HS25	257159
N311QS	C560	0311
N311QS	**C680**	**0196**
N311RM	SBRL	306-6
N311RS	**JSTR**	**5222**
N311SL	PRM1	RB-120
N311TK	GLF5	5028
N311TP	**C500**	**597**
N311TS	LJ31	010
N311TT	C550	108
(N311TT)	C500	597
N311VP	**C500**	**600**
N311WK	GALX	107
N312A	FA10	122
N312A	FA50	157
N312AF	**GLEX**	**9551**
N312AL	LJ55	089
N312AL	**LJ60**	**225**

N312AM	**CL64**	**5312**
N312AM	FA10	123
N312AM	FA10	210
N312AN	FA10	123
(N312AR)	FA10	209
N312AT	CL61	5141
N312AT	CL64	5313
N312AT	FA10	122
N312AT	FA10	123
N312AT	FA10	209
N312BL	**EA50**	**000020**
N312BX	CL64	5349
N312CC	LJ31	172
(N312CC)	C550	312
N312CE	LJ35	403
N312CF	C650	0143
N312CF	LJ35	403
N312CJ	C52A	0031
N312CJ	C52B	0312
N312CK	JSTR	5150/37
N312CS	C550	550-0980
N312CT	CL61	5030
N312CT	LJ35	403
N312DC	C550	376
N312DM	MU30	A033SA
N312DM	MU30	A090SA
N312EL	**GLF4**	**1105**
N312FL	**E55P**	**50500037**
N312FX	CL64	5349
N312GA	C550	004
N312GA	GLF3	416
N312GA	GLF3	475
N312GA	GLF4	1407
N312GA	GLF4	4312
N312GK	C500	492
N312GK	LJ25	283
N312GK	**BE40**	**RK-44**
N312GS	BE40	RK-312
(N312GV)	GLF5	582
N312HX	**CL65**	**5865**
N312JS	**BE40**	**RK-19**
N312K	FA20	324
N312K	SBRL	282-105
N312KG	**HS25**	**258704**
N312LG	**LJ35**	**489**
N312LJ	LJ31	033D
N312LR	**HS25**	**258182**
N312NA	LJ24	312
N312NC	**C550**	**304**
N312NT	SBRL	282-32
N312NW	GLF3	312
N312P	F9EX	67
N312P	FA7X	72
N312P	**GLF5**	**5366**
N312PV	**F9EX**	**67**
N312PY	FA7X	72
N312QS	C560	0312
N312QS	C680	0248
N312QS	**E55P**	**50500153**
(N312RD)	C550	550-0881
N312S	WW24	118
N312S	WW24	84
N312SB	C525	0355
N312SB	**C52A**	**0447**
N312SE	C525	0355
N312SL	PRM1	RB-125
N312TL	**LJ31**	**172**
N312VP	C52B	0012
N312W	ASTR	012
N312XP	HS25	258312
N313AR	**LJ60**	**154**
N313AV	**F2TH**	**176**
N313BA	C500	313
N313BH	**LJ45**	**108**
N313BT	C550	113
N313BW	LJ45	108
N313BW	**LJ45**	**322**
N313CC	**F2EX**	**12**
N313CC	HS25	258043
N313CC	HS25	258509
N313CE	C550	358
N313CK	C550	041
N313CQ	HS25	258043
N313CR	**C52A**	**0234**
N313CS	C550	550-0981
N313CV	**C560**	**0313**
N313DM	MU30	A022SA
N313DS	**CL30**	**20183**
N313GH	F2TH	125
N313GH	FA50	228
(N313GH)	FA50	252
N313HC	C560	0603
N313JL	C500	166
N313JS	**JSTR**	**5086/44**
N313K	**FA20**	**404**
N313MU	HS25	258313
N313NT	SBRL	282-94
N313QS	C560	0325
N313QS	C650	0013
N313QS	**C680**	**0140**
(N313RC)	HS25	257087
N313RF	**GLEX**	**9194**
N313RG	GLF3	321
N313RG	**GLF5**	**504**
N313TW	WW24	190
N313V	**CL30**	**20365**
"N313VR"	HS25	257207

N313XP	HS25	258313
N313ZP	**HS25**	**HA-0064**
N314AC	LJ31	140
N314AD	ASTR	072
N314AD	**ASTR**	**128**
N314AD	WW24	394
N314AE	FA20	140
N314AJ	**LJ25**	**260**
N314AM	**FA50**	**205**
N314C	LJ35	412
(N314CC)	C500	314
N314CK	C550	051
N314CM	**LJ60**	**295**
N314CS	C550	550-1004
N314CV	C560	0314
N314DM	MU30	A023SA
N314DT	LJ31	236
N314EB	C500	615
N314ER	HS25	25170
N314EX	FA50	314
N314FL	**E55P**	**50500050**
N314FX	CL64	5372
N314G	C555	0060
N314GA	G150	214
N314GA	GLF3	411
N314GA	GLF3	476
N314GA	GLF4	1114
N314GA	GLF4	1514
N314GA	GLF4	4014
N314GA	GLF4	4314
N314GA	GLF5	5214
N314GS	C500	669
(N314MC)	C550	293
N314MK	LJ31	040
N314NT	SBRL	282-28
N314QS	C560	0441
N314QS	**E55P**	**50500158**
N314RC	**HS25**	**257155**
N314RW	C560	0051
N314SC	LJ31	004
N314SG	**LJ31**	**133**
N314SL	C650	7115
N314TC	C500	216
N314TC	**HS25**	**258400**
N314TL	**BE40**	**RK-181**
N314TM	**C680**	**0529**
N314TP	**GLF5**	**5104**
N314TW	**FA20**	**314/516**
N314XP	HS25	258314
N314XS	LJ31	048
N315AJ	LJ24	108
N315BK	HS25	258410
N315BX	CL64	5377
N315CJ	**C52B**	**0315**
N315CK	C550	075
N315CS	**C560**	**0371**
N315DG	CL64	5386
N315DM	MU30	A015SA
N315DV	FA50	289
N315EJ	**C560**	**0215**
N315ES	C550	459
N315FL	E55P	50500054
N315FW	LJ25	315
N315FX	CL64	5377
(N315FX)	CL61	5063
N315GA	GLF3	315
N315GA	GLF3	398
N315GA	GLF3	443
N315GA	GLF3	485
N315GA	GLF4	1315
N315GA	GLF4	4315
N315GS	GLF3	315
N315HC	**C525**	**0373**
N315JL	**HS25**	**258891**
N315JM	SBRL	306-96
N315JM	WW24	259
N315KP	F9EX	74
N315LJ	CL30	20013
N315MA	GLF4	1032
N315MC	**C52A**	**0068**
N315MC	GLF4	1032
N315MK	CL60	1047
N315MK	**GLF4**	**1206**
(N315ML)	HS25	258891
N315MP	C500	451
N315MR	C500	451
N315MR	C525	0198
N315N	C550	550-0849
(N315N)	C525	0493
N315NT	SBRL	282-20
(N315P)	C500	409
N315PA	FA20	113
N315QS	C560	0315
N315QS	**C680**	**0220**
N315R	**BE40**	**RK-9**
N315RG	**GLF5**	**5262**
N315S	C500	409
(N315S)	ASTR	053
N315SA	WW24	126
(N315SA)	BE40	RJ-22
N315SC	**FA50**	**130**
N315SL	CL61	3054
N315SL	BE40	RK-401
N315TR	WW24	315
N315TS	GLF2	220
N316	LJ35	024
N316	LJ55	062

N316	WW24	3
N316AC	LJ31	190
N316AS	LJ31	150
N316BD	**C52B**	**0316**
N316BG	CL61	5062
N316BG	**E50P**	**50000050**
N316CC	C550	316
N316CF	C550	316
N316CP	**EA50**	**000089**
N316CS	C550	550-1010
N316CS	HS25	258102
N316CW	**C525**	**0828**
N316CW	C650	0016
N316DM	MU30	A024SA
N316E	WW24	3
N316EC	HS25	258102
N316EC	SBRL	380-38
N316EJ	C525	0316
N316EQ	SBRL	380-38
N316EX	FA50	316
N316FA	GLF3	316
N316FL	**E55P**	**50500057**
N316FX	CL64	5387
N316GA	GLF3	316
N316GA	GLF3	386
N316GA	GLF3	445
N316GA	GLF3	486
N316GA	GLF4	1408
N316GA	GLF4	4316
N316GB	**FA10**	**103**
N316GD	GLF5	5316
N316GK	C56X	5106
N316GS	GLEX	9075
N316GS	GLF4	1225
N316GS	**HS25**	**258102**
N316H	C550	316
N316LJ	CL30	20016
N316LJ	LJ31	036
N316LP	MU30	A012SA
N316M	LJ24	061
N316M	LJ24	101
N316M	LJ25	014
N316MA	C550	550-0907
N316MF	**HS25**	**258314**
N316MF	LJ24	101
N316MH	C555	0108
N316MJ	C525	0297
N316MJ	C680	0316
N316MW	**C500**	**197**
N316N	**E50P**	**50000280**
N316NT	SBRL	282-60
N316PA	FA50	166
N316QS	C560	0516
N316QS	**E55P**	**50500161**
N316RS	LJ31	150
N316RS	LJ31	189
N316SR	LJ45	119
N316SR	LJ45	121
N316SS	**F900**	**8**
N316TA	**E55P**	**50500125**
N316TD	**WW24**	**312**
N316TF	**C56X**	**6061**
N316VA	**GLF5**	**5530**
N316WH	C560	0516
N316XP	HS25	258316
(N317AB)	C500	017
N317AF	GLF2	168
N317BG	LJ35	506
N317BH	EA50	000013
N317BR	C52B	0150
N317BX	CL64	5407
N317CC	HS25	258093
N317CC	**HS25**	**258532**
N317CC	MU30	A081SA
N317CJ	C525	0317
N317CQ	HS25	258093
N317CS	C550	550-1019
N317DJ	EA50	000095
N317DM	MU30	A025SA
N317EM	HS25	25115
N317FE	CL60	1074
N317FL	E55P	50500059
N317FX	CL64	5407
N317GA	GLF3	350
N317GA	GLF3	417
N317GA	GLF3	477
N317GA	GLF4	1409
N317GA	GLF4	4317
N317GC	MU30	A081SA
N317HC	C550	228
N317JD	GLF5	549
(N317JD)	LJ35	186
N317JM	C560	0443
N317JM	C56X	5122
(N317JQ)	C500	651
N317JS	**WW24**	**385**
N317K	LJ31	235
N317LJ	LJ31	117
N317M	C650	7055
N317M	**F2TH**	**188**
N317M	GLF4	1122
N317M	GLF4	1191
N317M	GLF4	1446
N317M	WW24	257
N317M	WW24	432
N317MB	C650	7012
N317MB	GLF4	1191

N317MB	WW24	257
N317MB	WW24	432
(N317MG)	CL64	5629
N317MJ	**GLF4**	**1122**
N317ML	C56X	5036
N317ML	**F2TH**	**131**
N317ML	F2TH	144
N317ML	GLF3	460
N317ML	GLF4	1446
N317MN	F2TH	146
N317MQ	C650	7015
N317MQ	F2TH	152
N317MQ	WW24	421
N317MR	F2TH	144
N317MR	GLF4	1191
N317MR	LJ35	176
(N317MR)	LJ24	297
(N317MT)	WW24	432
(N317MV)	WW24	418
N317MX	WW24	418
(N317MX)	C650	7015
N317MZ	C650	7010
N317MZ	C650	7055
N317MZ	F2TH	188
N317N	**E55P**	**50500280**
N317NT	SBRL	282-100
N317PC	**BE40**	**RK-357**
N317QS	C560	0317
N317QS	**C680**	**0160**
N317SA	**EA50**	**550-0277**
N317SK	**FA7X**	**82**
N317SM	C550	162
N317TC	HS25	256007
N317TS	LJ25	317
N317TT	**LJ35**	**317**
N317VP	C500	317
N317VP	C52B	0317
N317VR	C510	0317
N317VS	LJ25	317
N318AG	**GLF5**	**536**
N318CD	HS25	257136
N318CL	**F2EX**	**66**
N318CM	C650	0318
N318CS	C550	550-1029
N318CT	**C560**	**0081**
N318DM	MU30	A034SA
N318DN	**C500**	**575**
N318FL	**E55P**	**50500047**
N318FX	CL64	5415
N318GA	**FA50**	**233**
N318GA	GLF3	355
N318GA	GLF3	421
N318GA	GLF3	478
N318GA	GLF4	1410
(N318GD)	GLF2	170
N318JF	**GALX**	**093**
N318JH	**C525**	**0817**
N318JH	LJ55	026
N318JH	LJ55	106
N318JS	**CL30**	**20137**
N318LJ	LJ31	118
N318MM	C560	0219
N318MM	**C56X**	**5220**
N318MN	C560	0219
N318NW	**LJ35**	**318**
N318PT	**E55P**	**50500312**
N318QS	C560	0418
N318QS	**E55P**	**50500162**
N318RS	MU30	A009SA
N318RW	**C560**	**0051**
N318SA	**LJ45**	**114**
N318SP	GLF2	168
N318XP	HS25	258318
N318XX	GLF5	615
N319AT	HS25	258043
N319BG	WW24	192
N319CH	LJ31	041
N319CS	C550	550-1036
N319DM	MU30	A019SA
N319DM	MU30	A027SA
N319EJ	LJ25	319
N319EX	FA50	319
N319FL	E55P	50500067
N319FX	CL64	5418
N319GA	GLF3	370
N319GA	GLF3	422
N319GA	GLF3	479
N319GA	GLF4	1356
N319GA	GLF4	4319
N319GP	GLF2	150
N319LJ	LJ60	079
N319MF	HS25	256070
N319NW	HS25	257171
N319PP	**GLF5**	**5513**
N319QS	C560	0519
N319QS	**E55P**	**50500164**
N319R	C52A	0176
N319RG	CL30	20019
N319SC	LJ31	131
N319VP	**C52B**	**0019**
N319Z	GLF3	319
N320AF	HFB3	1023
N320AF	HFB3	1061
N320BP	**C52B**	**0143**
N320CB	**C560**	**0207**
N320CC	C500	320
N320CH	MU30	A024SA

N320CL	CL64	5370
N320CS	C550	550-1039
N320DG	C555	0021
N320DM	MU30	A028SA
N320EJ	LJ25	320
N320FE	GLF2	9/33
(N320FJ)	FA20	242
N320FX	CL64	5425
N320GA	GLF3	372
N320GA	GLF3	409
N320GA	GLF3	424
N320GA	GLF4	1366
N320GB	GLEX	9467
N320GP	HS25	257173
(N320GP)	FA10	80
N320GX	**GLEX**	**9116**
N320J	HFB3	1023
N320J	HFB3	1034
N320JJ	HS25	25198
N320JT	**C550**	**303**
N320K	FA50	154
N320K	GLF5	514
N320LA	EA50	000016
N320LV	**GALX**	**032**
N320M	LJ35	320
N320MC	HFB3	1034
N320MD	**WW24**	**366**
N320MP	WW24	432
N320QS	C560	0321
N320QS	**C680**	**0169**
N320RG	C500	236
N320RH	C52B	0320
N320S	C550	138
N320S	C555	0090
N320S	JSTR	5082/36
N320T	MU30	A032SA
N320TM	**C680**	**0136**
N320TR	GLF2	233
N320V	C550	193
N320VA	CL30	20232
N320VP	C560	0320
N320W	WW24	15
N320WE	GLF3	320
N321AF	HFB3	1060
N321AN	LJ35	272
N321AR	C650	0151
N321AS	LJ25	273
N321AU	LJ25	253
N321BN	GLF4	1300
N321CL	**C56X**	**5527**
N321DM	MU30	A029SA
N321EJ	HS25	258515
N321EX	FA50	321
N321F	C550	567
N321FM	C500	687
N321FX	CL64	5427
N321GA	GLF3	321
N321GA	GLF3	426
N321GA	GLF3	459
N321GE	CL61	5128
N321GE	LJ25	289
N321GG	C560	0474
N321GL	CL61	5128
N321GL	LJ24	174
N321GL	LJ25	277
N321GL	LJ25	289
N321GL	LJ31	085
N321GL	LJ31	216
(N321GL)	LJ55	026
N321GN	C550	347
N321GX	**CL30**	**20273**
N321KM	**E50P**	**50000321**
N321KR	C550	035
N321LV	GLF4	4321
N321MS	**HS25**	**258515**
N321PT	GLF4	1013
(N321PT)	GLF4	1251
N321Q	LJ24	177
N321RB	LJ25	290
N321RT	GLF4	1013
N321SD	**C52B**	**0320**
N321SE	C550	347
N321SF	**GALX**	**021**
N321TS	C500	564
N321VA	E50P	50000066
N321VP	C500	668
(N321VP)	C560	0123
(N321WJ)	LJ35	321
N322AD	GALX	022
N322AF	HFB3	1058
N322AU	LJ24	326
N322BC	**HS25**	**257176**
N322BE	MU30	A022SA
N322BH	**EA50**	**550-0276**
N322BJ	**PRM1**	**RB-93**
N322BX	CL64	5434
N322CC	HS25	256070
N322CP	**F900**	**134**
N322CS	C550	344
N322CS	C550	550-1052
N322CS	JSTR	5208
N322CS	SBRL	282-56
N322DM	MU30	A030SA
N322FA	**GLEX**	**9025**
N322FL	**E55P**	**50500074**
N322FX	CL64	5434
N322GA	GLF3	322

N322GA	GLF3	428
N322GA	GLF3	460
N322GA	GLF3	493
N322GA	GLF4	1368
N322GC	**LJ55**	**008**
N322GT	**C550**	**550-1030**
N322JG	EA50	000130
N322K	**GLF5**	**5507**
N322K	JSTR	5013
N322K	JSTR	5133
(N322K)	LJ45	171
N322LA	CL64	5482
N322LA	HS25	258410
N322LA	SPEC	0001
N322LV	**E55P**	**50500117**
N322MA	**C550**	**375**
N322MD	MU30	A022SA
(N322MG)	GLF4	1331
N322PE	HS25	258693
N322PJ	**C52B**	**0322**
N322PL	**EA50**	**000059**
N322QS	C560	0421
N322QS	E55P	50500165
N322RG	C650	7070
N322RR	**FA20**	**514**
N322RS	LJ24	322
N322SB	**C52C**	**0053**
N322ST	**C500**	**402**
N322SW	**GALX**	**184**
(N322TJ)	LJ24	322
N322TP	HS25	25170
N322TS	LJ31	002
(N322TW)	SBRL	465-17
N322VA	**C560**	**0399**
N323AD	**C52B**	**0318**
N323AF	HFB3	1062
(N323AM)	C550	351
N323BD	GLF5	5192
N323BX	CL64	5447
N323CB	C500	563
N323CJ	C550	323
N323CM	**PRM1**	**RB-22**
N323DM	MU30	A032SA
N323EC	SBRL	306-134
N323EG	**F2TH**	**80**
N323EJ	LJ25	323
N323EP	**E55P**	**50500102**
N323EX	FA50	323
N323FX	CL64	5447
N323G	C525	0532
N323G	GLF3	323
N323GA	GLF3	429
N323GA	GLF3	461
N323GA	GLF4	1369
N323GA	GLF4	1414
N323GA	GLF4	4323
N323JA	C525	0116
(N323JB)	C500	468
N323JH	GLF3	434
N323JK	HS25	257048
N323JR	**CS55**	**0129**
N323KM	**PRM1**	**RB-270**
(N323L)	HS25	258212
N323LJ	LJ31	123
N323LM	C525	0230
N323LM	C52A	0020
(N323LM)	C525	0204
N323MK	**GLF3**	**370**
N323MP	HS25	258594
N323MR	WW24	324
N323NE	**C560**	**0442**
N323P	ASTR	049
N323P	**ASTR**	**096**
N323P	JSTR	5099/5
N323PG	**C510**	**0288**
N323QS	C560	0323
N323QS	**C680**	**0134**
N323R	SBRL	306-26
N323SH	**CL64**	**5343**
N323SK	**C52A**	**0134**
N323SL	HS25	258084
N323WA	LJ25	018
N323XP	HS25	258323
N324AF	HFB3	1064
N324AJ	WW24	208
N324AM	PRM1	RB-42
N324B	CL61	5069
N324BD	**C525**	**0674**
N324BG	**HS25**	**258165**
N324C	C500	324
N324CC	C550	431
N324CL	F2TH	32
N324CS	C550	550-1059
N324CX	**GLF5**	**615**
N324DR	**C510**	**0271**
N324EX	FA50	324
N324FL	**E55P**	**50500075**
N324FP	**GLF4**	**1475**
N324FX	CL64	5454
N324GA	GLF3	430
N324GA	GLF3	462
N324GA	GLF3	487
N324GA	GLF4	1330
N324GA	GLF4	1421
N324GA	GLF4	4324
N324GA	GLF5	5424
N324HS	C510	0324
N324JC	**C500**	**324**
N324JT	**C550**	**550-0819**
N324JW	**GLF3**	**324**
N324K	**GLF5**	**5516**
N324K	HS25	257111
N324K	JSTR	5089
N324L	**C500**	**594**
(N324LE)	C56X	5109
N324LX	C56X	5109
N324MM	BE40	RJ-52
N324QS	C560	0423
N324QS	**C680**	**0242**
(N324QS)	C560	0424
N324SA	HS25	258047
N324SM	GLEX	9023
N324SR	F900	14
N324TC	FA20	324
N324TW	**LJ24**	**324**
(N324VP)	C56X	5324
N324WK	GALX	108
N324XP	HS25	258324
N324ZR	SBRL	465-25
N325AF	HFB3	1065
N325AJ	WW24	181
N325AP	**F2EX**	**267**
N325B	**F2EX**	**197**
N325BC	C500	450
N325CJ	**C52B**	**0325**
N325CP	LJ55	112
N325CS	C550	550-1061
N325DA	CL61	5016
N325DM	C525	0438
N325DM	MU30	A006SA
N325EX	FA50	325
N325FL	**E55P**	**50500090**
N325FN	C56X	5350
N325FX	CL64	5457
N325GA	GLF3	433
N325GA	GLF3	466
N325GA	GLF3	488
N325GA	GLF4	1326
N325GA	GLF5	5225
N325GA	GLF5	5525
N325GA	GLF6	6025
N325HS	**C510**	**0325**
N325JB	LJ25	325
N325JG	BE40	RK-190
N325JJ	**CL64**	**5392**
N325JL	LJ25	215
N325K	SBRL	282-63
N325LB	WW24	402
N325LJ	WW24	181
N325LW	WW24	334
(N325MC)	FA20	325
N325MH	CL65	5928
N325NW	**LJ35**	**325**
N325PE	**CL30**	**20409**
(N325PM)	C500	450
N325PT	**LJ45**	**387**
N325QS	C560	0425
N325QS	**E55P**	**50500168**
N325RC	**C52B**	**0021**
N325RC	GLF4	1139
N325RD	**C650**	**7056**
N325RR	C510	0025
N325SJ	LJ25	102
N325TG	**CL30**	**20455**
N325WC	C560	0343
N325WP	**C550**	**550-0933**
N326AJ	WW24	191
N326AZ	GLF4	1262
N326AZ	**GLF4**	**4020**
N326B	C525	0302
(N326BX)	CL64	5464
N326CB	JSTR	5143
N326CM	C510	0326
N326CS	C550	550-1065
N326CW	MU30	A026SA
N326DD	**LJ35**	**173**
(N326DD)	GLF3	326
N326DM	MU30	A036SA
N326EJ	LJ24	326
N326EW	C550	622
N326EW	**F2EX**	**248**
N326EW	F2EX	55
N326EW	F2TH	58
N326EW	FA10	220
N326EW	FA20	392/553
N326FB	FA50	39
N326FL	**E55P**	**50500093**
N326FX	CL64	5464
N326GA	GLF3	434
N326GA	GLF3	473
N326HG	LJ35	501
N326HG	**LJ60**	**163**
N326JD	GLF4	1460
N326JD	**GLF6**	**6109**
N326JK	**C525**	**0511**
N326K	F9EX	36
N326K	F9EX	84
N326K	HS25	257119
N326K	JSTR	5102
N326KE	LJ24	326
(N326LA)	EA50	000136
(N326LM)	GLF4	1460
N326LW	F2EX	55
N326LW	FA10	220
N326LW	FA20	392/553
N326MA	**C56X**	**5159**
N326MM	CL60	1024
N326N	**HS25**	**258140**
N326PZ	C52C	0196
N326QS	C560	0526
N326SM	LJ60	370
N326SU	C750	0015
N326SU	HS25	258249
N326TD	**HS25**	**257178**
N326TF	**C680**	**0326**
(N326VP)	C56X	5326
N326VW	FA20	27
N326XP	HS25	258326
N327AR	LJ60	311
N327BC	FA20	327
(N327BC)	LJ25	327
N327CB	LJ35	483
N327CM	C510	0027
N327CS	C550	550-1070
N327DM	MU30	A037SA
N327EJ	LJ24	327
N327EX	FA50	327
N327F	LJ35	327
N327FL	E55P	50500094
N327FX	**CL64**	**5466**
N327GA	ASTR	127
N327GA	**ASTR**	**157**
N327GA	GLF3	427
N327GA	GLF3	463
N327GA	GLF4	1327
N327GA	GLF4	1527
N327GJ	LJ24	327
N327JA	**C52B**	**0483**
N327JB	SBRL	282-9
N327JJ	GLF3	329
N327K	F900	3
N327K	F9EX	103
N327K	F9EX	37
N327K	GLF2	25
N327LJ	C550	550-0900
N327LJ	HS25	258490
N327LN	C550	550-0900
N327MC	**C52A**	**0093**
N327MP	**HS25**	**HB-72**
N327PD	**C52A**	**0517**
N327QS	C560	0327
N327QS	**E55P**	**50500170**
N327R	C650	0152
N327RD	**C52B**	**0482**
(N327RH)	SBRL	282-9
N327RX	**F2EX**	**274**
N327SA	WW24	428
N327SV	**C680**	**0327**
N327TC	GLF2	33
N327TL	GLF2	33
N327TL	**GLF4**	**1339**
N327VP	**C560**	**0343**
N327XP	HS25	258327
N328AM	CL61	5121
(N328BT)	C650	7046
N328BX	CL64	5328
N328CC	C500	328
N328CC	CL30	20028
(N328CF)	CL30	20328
N328CJ	**C525**	**0328**
N328CL	**C510**	**0328**
N328CS	C550	550-1074
N328DM	MU30	A039SA
N328EW	FA20	392/553
N328EX	FA50	328
N328FL	**E55P**	**50500097**
N328FX	CL64	5474
N328GA	GLF3	444
N328GA	GLF3	489
N328GA	GLF4	1328
N328GA	GLF4	1424
N328GA	GLF4	4328
N328GA	GLF6	6028
N328JK	LJ24	212
N328JR	F900	51
N328JS	SBRL	306-92
N328JW	LJ25	328
N328K	F900	13
N328K	F9EX	38
N328K	GLF2	26
N328MM	**GLF5**	**636**
N328MY	E50P	50000041
N328N	**C680**	**680A0008**
N328NA	**C500**	**568**
N328PC	**WW24**	**328**
N328PT	F9EX	28
N328QS	C560	0428
N328QS	C650	0028
N328QS	**E55P**	**50500175**
N328RC	**C52B**	**0203**
(N328RC)	CL30	20028
N328RR	LJ45	175
N328SA	WW24	425
N328SB	C550	550-1027
(N328SB)	C560	0062
N328TL	LJ24	212
N328XP	HS25	258328
N329BH	**C52B**	**0292**
N329CC	C550	329
N329CF	**C52C**	**0065**
N329CH	**CL30**	**20185**
N329CJ	**C52B**	**0130**
N329CS	**C525**	**0909**
N329CS	C550	550-1077
(N329DM)	MU30	A040SA
N329EX	FA50	329
N329FL	**E55P**	**50500100**
N329FX	CL64	5476
N329FX	CL64	5541
N329GA	GLF3	450
N329GA	GLF4	1329
N329HN	LJ24	230
N329HN	WW24	34
N329J	JSTR	1001
N329JC	**C680**	**0112**
N329JC	CS55	0059
N329JS	JSTR	5206
N329K	F2TH	182
N329K	F900	46
N329K	GLF2	180
N329K	JSTR	1002
N329K	JSTR	5133
N329LN	**PRM1**	**RB-173**
N329MD	JSTR	5215
N329MP	CL60	1072
(N329N)	GLF3	329
N329PK	**GALX**	**092**
N329PV	**C560**	**0140**
N329SH	C52C	0170
N329SH	**C52C**	**0194**
N329SS	SBRL	282-9
N329TJ	LJ24	329
N329TJ	**LJ55**	**120**
N329TL	**CL65**	**5714**
N329XP	HS25	258329
N329Z	**SBRL**	**465-32**
N330AG	E55P	50500078
N330AM	**HS25**	**25235**
N330BC	LJ35	432
N330CC	C500	330
N330CJ	C525	0330
N330DE	HS25	258060
N330DK	**C550**	**296**
N330DM	MU30	A041SA
N330EX	FA50	330
N330FL	**E55P**	**50500105**
N330FX	CL64	5487
N330G	**HS25**	**25087**
N330G	HS25	256033
N330GA	GALX	130
N330GA	GLF3	451
N330GA	GLF4	1350
N330GA	GLF4	1428
N330GA	GLF4	1530
N330GA	GLF4	4330
N330GA	GLF5	5230
N330GA	GLF6	6030
N330GM	CL30	20186
N330GW	**HS25**	**HA-0003**
N330J	LJ24	130
N330K	**F2TH**	**189**
N330K	F900	50
N330KM	C52B	0266
N330L	**LJ25**	**330**
N330LJ	LJ25	330
N330MB	C650	0129
N330MC	F9EX	21
N330MC	FA10	199
N330MC	FA50	175
N330MG	WW24	434
(N330MG)	C550	147
N330PC	FA20	107
N330PC	WW24	207
N330PK	**C52B**	**0351**
N330QS	C560	0329
N330QS	**E55P**	**50500180**
N330R	HS25	HA-0076
N330R	**BE40**	**RK-386**
N330TJ	C650	0101
N330TP	CL61	5142
N330TS	**BE40**	**RK-330**
N330TW	LJ24	330
N330U	SBRL	306-20
N330VP	**C560**	**0330**
N330WJ	**GALX**	**022**
N330WR	**GLF3**	**337**
N330X	HS25	258060
N330XP	HS25	258330
N330XX	E50P	50000317
N331AP	WW24	205
N331BD	**GALX**	**230**
N331BN	**G280**	**2035**
N331BN	GALX	095
N331BN	GALX	230
N331BR	**C560**	**0530**
N331CC	C500	331
N331CC	C560	0044
N331CC	LJ31	003
(N331CG)	HS25	257043
N331CJ	C52B	0131
N331CW	WW24	231
N331DC	CL61	5093
N331DC	F2TH	206
N331DC	**F2TH**	**601**
N331DC	HS25	256061
N331DC	HS25	258112
N331DC	MU30	A028SA
N331DM	**FA20**	**429**
N331DM	MU30	A042SA
N331DP	LJ24	059
N331DP	LJ24	067
N331DQ	CL61	5093
N331EC	C560	0269
(N331EC)	C560	0279
N331EX	FA50	331
N331FP	CL60	1072
N331FX	CL64	5491
N331GA	GLF3	452
N331GA	GLF4	1331
N331GA	GLF4	1430
N331GA	GLF6	6031
(N331GC)	C500	033
N331GW	WW24	231
N331JR	LJ24	072
N331LV	GLF4	1460
N331MC	**F9EX**	**22**
N331MC	FA50	95
N331MS	C525	0330
N331MW	**C560**	**0384**
N331N	**LJ31**	**022**
N331P	GLF2	20
N331P	GLF4	1139
N331PL	LJ60	331
N331PR	**C550**	**550-0831**
N331PS	CL64	5491
N331QS	C560	0331
N331QS	**E55P**	**50500183**
N331SC	HS25	258093
(N331SE)	FA50	331
N331SJ	LJ31	113
N331SK	**ASTR**	**063**
N331TH	CL64	5325
N331TP	CL64	5350
N331US	**LJ31**	**196**
N331WR	LJ24	072
(N331WT)	CL60	1073
N331ZX	LJ31	133
N332AR	C560	0332
N332BN	**C56X**	**6052**
N332CG	**CL30**	**20332**
(N332CM)	C750	0107
N332CS	C550	550-1081
N332DF	WW24	332
N332DM	MU30	A043SA
N332EC	F900	106
N332EX	FA50	332
N332FE	FA20	225/472
N332FG	LJ35	332
N332FL	**E55P**	**50500109**
N332FP	LJ24	126
N332FW	C650	0032
N332FX	**CL64**	**5543**
N332GA	GLF3	453
N332GA	GLF3	490
N332GA	GLF4	1332
(N332GJ)	C500	015
N332H	C500	144
N332J	FA10	29
N332K	LJ45	169
N332LC	C560	0332
N332LS	LJ25	122
N332MC	F900	78
N332MC	FA50	55
(N332MC)	F9EX	22
N332MM	**GLF5**	**5283**
N332MQ	FA50	55
N332MT	**C550**	**550-1105**
N332PC	LJ24	056
N332QS	C560	0523
N332QS	**E55P**	**50500184**
N332SB	C52B	0145
N332SE	**C500**	**332**
N332TA	HS25	256032
N332TM	**GALX**	**201**
(N332VP)	C525	0332
N332WE	HS25	257186
N332XP	HS25	258332
N333AH	**C650**	**0222**
N333AJ	ASTR	080
N333AR	GLF2	189/42
N333AV	FA20	28
N333AW	LJ25	163
N333AX	GLF2	30/4
N333AX	GLF4	1063
N333B	SBRL	282-39
N333BD	**C52A**	**0237**
N333BD	C550	550-0958
N333BF	LJ24	010
N333BG	WW24	98
(N333BG)	C500	482
N333CD	LJ25	258
N333CG	C550	188
N333CG	LJ25	262
N333CG	WW24	339
N333CJ	HS25	25155
N333CR	LJ24	199
N333CZ	ASTR	080
N333DP	HS25	25282
N333DS	CL64	5498
N333EA	**BE40**	**RK-425**
N333EB	**C550**	**550-0893**
N333EC	F900	106
N333EC	**GLF4**	**1414**
N333EC	JSTR	5061/48
N333FJ	FA10	1

N333FX	CL64	5544
N333GA	GLF3	326
N333GA	GLF3	420
N333GA	GLF3	432
N333GA	GLF3	875
N333GA	GLF4	1333
N333GJ	CL61	3042
(N333GJ)	LJ55	132
N333GM	SBRL	282-106
N333GM	SBRL	282-45
N333GU	GLF3	875
N333GW	**GLF4**	**4205**
N333GZ	HS25	25070
N333HK	GLF3	482
N333HP	LJ25	109
N333HS	**C510**	**0370**
N333J	C525	0531
N333JH	C500	292
N333KC	GLF3	366
N333KC	LJ35	037
(N333KC)	GLF3	403
(N333KD)	GLF3	366
N333KE	**FA10**	**14**
N333KG	**C680**	**0189**
N333KG	FA7X	88
N333KK	CL60	1082
N333KK	LJ45	498
N333KN	JSTR	5118
N333KN	JSTR	5202
N333LX	GALX	146
N333LX	GLF3	366
N333M	HS25	25017
N333ME	HS25	25115
N333ME	HS25	257003
N333MF	HS25	25115
N333MG	**C680**	**0055**
N333MG	CL61	5035
N333MS	C500	584
N333MS	HS25	257115
N333MV	**HS25**	**258403**
N333MX	CL61	5151
N333MX	**F2EX**	**120**
N333MY	EA50	000103
N333NC	SBRL	306-76
N333NM	**SBRL**	**282-45**
N333NR	HS25	257167
N333PC	HS25	257008
N333PC	HS25	258277
N333PC	**HS25**	**258669**
N333PC	SBRL	306-76
N333PC	SBRL	465-28
N333PD	C500	382
N333PE	C500	382
N333PP	C500	050
N333PV	GLF4	1240
N333PY	**GLF4**	**1317**
N333QA	JSTR	5118
N333QS	C560	0333
N333QS	**E55P**	**50500186**
N333RB	LJ35	220
(N333RB)	C500	498
N333RL	C650	0019
N333RL	**HS25**	**259027**
N333RP	LJ35	148
N333RS	BE40	RJ-62
N333RU	HS25	259027
N333RW	JSTR	5138
N333RY	LJ24	202
N333SG	LJ25	226
N333SR	FA10	48
(N333ST)	GLF2	57
N333SV	WW24	114
N333SZ	GALX	210
N333SZ	GLF4	4184
N333TS	MU30	A047SA
(N333TS)	CL60	1023
N333TW	**LJ24**	**168**
N333VS	C525	0034
N333WC	C650	0211
N333WF	FA20	113
N333WM	C560	0385
N333X	C550	042
N333X	LJ24	128
N333X	LJ24	251
N333X	LJ35	286
N333XP	HS25	258733
(N333XX)	LJ35	286
N333YJ	**BE40**	**RK-159**
N334	GLF2	143
N334	HS25	258013
N334	WW24	344
(N334AB)	LJ35	334
N334AF	**CL30**	**20359**
N334AF	LJ31	225
N334AF	LJ45	143
N334AM	C550	227
N334BD	C525	0486
(N334BG)	LJ60	334
N334CM	C650	0234
N334CS	C550	550-1089
(N334DB)	C525	0409
N334DM	MU30	A044SA
N334DM	MU30	A045SA
N334EC	**CL30**	**20298**
N334ED	C550	252
N334EX	FA50	333
N334FX	CL64	5545
N334FX	**CL64**	**5586**
N334GA	GLF3	454
N334GA	GLF4	1334
N334GA	GLF4	1431
N334H	C650	0071
N334JC	C500	334
N334JC	GLF4	1134
N334JK	**GALX**	**069**
N334JR	FA20	139
N334JR	HS25	256020
(N334JW)	LJ55	034
N334KC	MU30	A034SA
N334LP	WW24	20
N334LS	LJ25	158
N334MC	F900	108
N334MC	FA50	175
N334MC	GLF4	1289
N334MD	LJ25	334
N334MM	**ASTR**	**044**
N334PS	C500	164
N334PS	HS25	256032
N334QS	C560	0434
N334QS	**C680**	**0164**
N334RC	C500	062
N334RJ	**C550**	**252**
N334RK	MS76	090
N334RK	WW24	5
N334SP	LJ35	334
N334SR	BE40	RK-129
N334WC	C650	0207
N334WM	MU30	A057SA
N334XP	HS25	258334
N335AF	**CL30**	**20190**
N335AF	LJ31	241
N335AF	LJ60	244
N335AJ	FA20	335
N335AS	**E55P**	**50500079**
N335AS	LJ35	170
N335AT	**LJ35**	**009**
N335CC	C550	480
N335CJ	C525	0335
N335CJ	C52B	0335
N335CS	**C550**	**550-1091**
N335CT	C525	0335
N335DJ	LJ35	335
N335DM	MU30	A045SA
N335DM	MU30	A048SA
N335EA	LJ35	614
N335EE	LJ35	335
N335EJ	C560	0235
N335EX	FA50	334
N335FL	**E55P**	**50500115**
N335FX	CL64	5546
N335FX	CL64	5619
N335GA	GLF3	455
N335GA	GLF4	1335
N335GA	GLF4	1432
(N335GA)	LJ35	423
N335H	GLF2	238
N335J	C525	0425
N335JB	PRM1	RB-15
(N335JD)	LJ35	397
N335JJ	**C52A**	**0162**
N335JL	LJ35	015
(N335JR)	LJ24	226
N335JW	LJ24	226
N335K	LJ35	381
(N335K)	SBRL	380-12
N335KB	**LJ35**	**588**
N335L	GLF4	1367
(N335LA)	EA50	000168
N335LL	GLF4	1367
N335LL	**GLF5**	**5107**
N335MB	**C525**	**0211**
N335MC	F900	150
N335MC	FA20	355
N335MC	GLF5	5282
N335MG	LJ35	626
N335MR	**LJ35**	**443**
N335MW	LJ35	472
N335NA	LJ35	170
N335NE	LJ35	335
N335PR	**LJ35**	**647**
N335QS	C560	0335
N335QS	**E55P**	**50500200**
N335RC	**LJ35**	**256**
N335RD	LJ35	216
N335RJ	**C550**	**550-1063**
N335RY	LJ24	226
N335SB	LJ35	656
(N335SJ)	LJ35	443
(N335SS)	LJ35	015
N335TW	**FA20**	**335**
N335UJ	LJ35	492
N335VB	**WW24**	**297**
N335WC	C650	0211
N335WJ	FA20	122
N335WR	FA20	122
N335XL	**C56X**	**5335**
N335XP	HS25	258335
N336AC	HS25	25202
N336AC	HS25	257033
(N336BC)	C56X	5336
N336CC	C500	336
N336CJ	C52A	0336
N336CJ	C52B	0336
N336CS	C550	550-1095
N336DM	MU30	A049SA
(N336EA)	LJ35	336
N336EB	**GLF5**	**5525**
N336FX	CL64	5634
N336GA	GLF3	456
N336MA	**C550**	**036**
N336MA	C56X	5159
N336MB	HS25	25153
N336QS	C560	0336
N336QS	**E55P**	**50500201**
N336RJ	**SBRL**	**465-10**
N336SC	**C550**	**550-1077**
N336SV	WW24	336
N336UB	LJ45	046
N336WR	LJ25	148
N336XL	**C56X**	**5336**
N336XP	HS25	258336
N337AS	**E55P**	**50500267**
N337BG	LJ60	337
N337CC	C560	0810
N337CC	**HS25**	**HA-0155**
N337CS	C550	550-1097
N337FL	E55P	50500135
N337FP	LJ31	020
N337FX	CL64	5647
N337GA	GLF3	457
N337GA	GLF3	491
N337GA	GLF4	4137
N337GA	GLF4	4337
N337GL	LJ25	337
(N337GM)	C650	7062
N337JD	GALX	037
N337MC	F900	152
N337QS	C560	0437
N337QS	**E55P**	**50500202**
N337RB	LJ31	154
N337RE	C550	575
N337RE	**HS25**	**258024**
N337RE	WW24	210
N337TV	C500	236
N337US	JSTR	5107
N337WC	LJ35	337
N337WR	**HS25**	**258273**
N337XP	HS25	258337
N338	HS25	25023
N338	HS25	25134
N338AX	GLF2	30/4
N338B	**C550**	**550-1132**
N338CL	GLF2	199/19
N338CS	C550	550-1084
N338CW	**LJ31**	**038**
N338CZ	C52B	0338
N338DB	FA20	225/472
N338DM	MU30	A038SA
N338DS	LJ24	162
N338EC	JSTR	5061/48
N338FJ	FA50	338
N338FL	E55P	50500139
N338FP	LJ55	138
N338FX	CL64	5656
N338GA	GLF3	458
N338K	LJ45	223
(N338K)	SBRL	380-15
N338KK	LJ24	020
N338MC	C560	0662
N338MM	**GLF4**	**1076**
N338PR	LJ60	338
N338QS	**C680**	**0011**
N338R	**C560**	**0338**
(N338RJ)	GLF3	338
N338TM	**C680**	**0177**
N338TP	GLEX	9073
N338TZ	**GLF4**	**4064**
N338W	WW24	338
N338X	LJ24	251
N339A	GLF3	339
N339B	C525	0339
N339B	**C680**	**0058**
(N339BA)	LJ25	240
N339BC	LJ55	039
(N339BW)	HS25	257010
N339CA	HS25	257019
N339CC	**HS25**	**258277**
N339CS	C550	550-1085
N339DM	MU30	A014SA
N339ES	**C680**	**0339**
N339FX	**CL65**	**5719**
N339GA	GLF2	139/11
N339GA	GLF3	374
N339GA	GLF3	448
N339GA	GLF3	492
N339GA	GLF4	1339
N339GA	GLF5	5239
N339GA	GLF5	5339
N339GW	SBRL	306-18
N339H	GLF2	145
N339HP	**C500**	**472**
(N339K)	SBRL	380-17
N339KC	**C52C**	**0122**
N339MC	C550	325
N339MH	CL65	5782
N339NA	SBRL	282-46
N339PC	CL30	20444
(N339PC)	HS25	258277
N339PM	SBRL	282-38
N339QS	C560	0339
N339QS	**C680**	**0191**
N339RA	HA4T	RC-22
N339RA	**HA4T**	**RC-52**
N339RK	FA20	313
N339SM	**BE40**	**RK-458**
N339TG	FA10	103
N339TG	FA20	198/466
N339W	LJ35	209
N340	GLF3	357
N340	JSTR	5029/38
(N340AC)	C500	621
N340AK	**CL64**	**5405**
N340AS	**E55P**	**50500148**
N340CX	**GLF4**	**1370**
N340DA	C550	263
N340DN	C500	340
N340DR	C560	0094
N340DR	WW24	242
N340DR	WW24	45
N340ER	WW24	45
N340EX	FA50	340
N340FX	**CL65**	**5723**
N340GA	GLF3	340
N340GA	GLF3	373
N340GA	GLF3	464
N340GA	GLF4	1340
N340GA	GLF5	5401
N340GF	GLEX	9340
N340LJ	LJ31	040
N340PM	WW24	340
N340QS	C560	0514
N340QS	**E55P**	**50500189**
(N340RL)	C500	340
N340SP	C52A	0131
(N340TB)	C500	276
N341AG	C550	043
N341AP	**F2EX**	**24**
N341AP	HS25	258204
N341AP	SBRL	282-35
N341AP	SBRL	465-40
N341AR	**C525**	**0341**
N341AR	SBRL	282-35
N341CC	C500	320
N341CS	C550	550-1106
N341CW	C550	330
N341DB	FA10	71
N341DM	MU30	A056SA
N341EC	E55P	50500041
N341ES	**C680**	**0341**
N341FW	LJ25	341
N341FX	CL65	5742
N341GA	GALX	241
N341GA	GLF3	360
N341GA	GLF3	467
N341GA	GLF4	1341
N341GA	GLF4	1441
N341K	FA20	281/496
N341K	JSTR	5223
N341K	**LJ40**	**2132**
N341K	LJ45	157
N341KA	FA20	281/496
N341M	FA50	157
(N341MB)	C650	0020
(N341MM)	GLF6	6152
N341N	JSTR	5038
N341NS	GLF2	64/27
N341NS	JSTR	5038
N341PF	FA20	179
N341QS	C560	0341
N341QS	**C680**	**0225**
N341TS	CL30	20141
N342AA	LJ25	342
N342AC	C525	0342
N342AJ	**C550**	**052**
N342AJ	WW24	342
N342AP	C500	077
N342AP	**GLF4**	**1515**
N342AS	C650	0042
N342BL	**C56X**	**5342**
N342CC	C550	413
N342CC	C680	0342
(N342CC)	C550	431
N342CS	C550	550-1101
N342DA	C550	181
N342DM	MU30	A057SA
N342EX	FA50	342
N342F	**CL65**	**5752**
N342F	FA20	101
N342FL	E55P	50500155
N342FX	CL65	5752
N342G	FA10	52
N342GA	GLF3	377
N342GA	GLF3	468
N342GA	GLF4	1342
N342GA	**GLF5**	**5402**
N342GG	LJ25	342
N342HM	C650	0062
N342JP	**LJ31**	**100**
N342K	FA20	101
N342K	FA20	357
N342K	**LJ40**	**2143**
N342K	LJ45	171
N342KF	FA20	357
N342QS	C560	0324
N342QS	C650	0042
N342QS	**C680**	**0214**
N342SP	**LJ45**	**484**
N342TC	CL61	5155
N342TS	WW24	342
N343AP	**FA7X**	**265**
N343AP	WW24	194
N343AR	**GLF5**	**5343**
N343AT	F2TH	187
N343CA	LJ25	202
N343CC	C550	343
N343CC	C560	0368
N343CC	**C56X**	**6004**
N343CM	**C550**	**259**
N343CV	C560	0343
N343DA	WW24	149
N343DE	**GLEX**	**9206**
N343DF	GLEX	9206
N343DF	**GLEX**	**9702**
N343DF	GLF3	483
N343DF	GLF4	1241
N343DM	MU30	A058SA
N343DP	GLF3	483
N343EC	**LJ60**	**343**
N343EX	FA50	343
N343FL	E55P	50500156
N343FX	CL65	5761
N343GA	GLF3	378
N343GA	GLF3	469
N343GA	GLF4	1343
(N343HM)	CL65	5761
N343K	CL61	5086
N343K	CL64	5476
N343K	GLF2	10
N343K	GLF2	9/33
N343KA	CL61	5086
N343MG	F900	95
N343MG	F9EX	193
N343MG	FA20	491
N343MG	**FA7X**	**249**
N343MG	LJ35	188
N343N	GLF2	10
N343PJ	C525	0166
N343PM	FA50	159
N343PR	PRM1	RB-7
N343QS	C560	0444
N343QS	**E55P**	**50500194**
N343RD	WW24	343
N343RK	**LJ25**	**110**
N343SC	**HS25**	**258365**
N344A	C550	609
N344A	FA10	153
N344AA	GLF2	123/25
N344AA	**GLF4**	**1186**
N344AA	GLF4	1207
N344AB	GLF2	123/25
(N344AB)	GLF4	1207
N344AS	C650	7053
N344BA	CL64	5344
N344BP	**HS25**	**257206**
N344CA	LJ25	203
N344CK	WW24	159
N344CM	FA50	300
N344DA	WW24	12
N344DD	GLF3	344
N344DM	MU30	A059SA
N344EX	FA50	344
N344FJ	FA20	344/534
N344FL	E55P	50500171
N344FX	CL65	5773
N344G	FA20	355
N344GA	GLF3	317
N344GA	GLF3	425
N344GA	GLF3	470
N344GA	GLF4	1344
N344GA	GLF4	1444
N344GA	GLF5	5444
N344GC	F2TH	85
N344GL	C680	0344
N344GW	GLF3	344
N344JR	GLEX	9020
N344K	SBRL	306-97
N344KK	C550	477
N344MC	LJ35	344
N344PL	**E55P**	**50500131**
N344PS	WW24	111
N344QS	C560	0344
N344QS	**E55P**	**50500219**
N344RJ	C500	340
N344RS	**GLF5**	**5444**
N344UP	SBRL	282-45
N344W	PRM1	RB-50
N344WC	LJ24	092
N345	LJ35	355
N345AA	GLF2	123/25
N345AA	GLF4	1186
(N345AA)	GLF5	5006
N345AP	FA50	181
N345AP	FA50	254
N345AW	**LJ45**	**182**
N345BA	CL64	5345
N345BH	**LJ45**	**100**
N345BM	FA20	89
N345BR	HS25	258308
N345BS	WW24	181
N345CC	C555	0095
N345CJ	**C52A**	**0136**
(N345CK)	JSTR	5150/37
N345CP	GLF2	123/25
N345CT	HS25	25116
N345CV	C560	0345

N345DA	HS25	25116
N345DM	MU30	A059SA
N345DM	MU30	A060SA
N345EJ	LJ25	345
N345EX	F2EX	145
N345FF	**LJ45**	**153**
N345FH	FA20	146
N345FJ	FA20	345
(N345FJ)	LJ25	216
N345FL	E55P	50500208
N345FM	**LJ45**	**151**
N345FX	**CL65**	**5901**
N345GA	**F2EX**	**145**
N345GA	GLF3	380
N345GA	GLF4	1345
N345GA	GLF4	4250
N345GC	ASTR	023
N345GL	**GLF2**	**205**
N345GL	HS25	25230
(N345GV)	GLF2	205
(N345HB)	C500	611
N345HC	**BE40**	**RK-421**
N345JR	C550	325
N345K	LJ45	151
N345K	**LJ45**	**310**
N345KB	LJ25	345
N345KC	C500	187
N345KM	**F900**	
N345LC	**GLF4**	**1442**
N345LC	**GLF5**	**5145**
N345LJ	LJ35	345
N345LT	**C52B**	**0345**
N345MA	**LJ45**	**054**
N345MB	C560	0023
N345MC	LJ25	046
N345MG	**C525**	**0372**
N345MP	HS25	258757
N345N	C500	611
N345NF	**C560**	**0695**
N345NT	C52B	0345
N345PA	FA50	36
N345PF	C680	0080
N345PY	E55P	50500074
N345QS	C560	0445
N345QS	**E55P**	**50500230**
N345RJ	LJ55	078
N345RL	LJ45	022
N345RL	**LJ45**	**180**
(N345SF)	LJ24	126
N345SK	C650	0001
N345SK	**F900**	**138**
N345SK	FA50	157
N345SV	**LJ45**	**140**
N345TL	C500	345
N345TR	**WW24**	**345**
N345UP	GLF2	159
N345WB	LJ45	036
N345XB	**CL64**	**5631**
N346BA	CL64	5361
N346CC	C560	0346
N346CM	C550	550-0915
N346CM	LJ40	2098
N346CM	**LJ45**	**471**
N346CN	LJ40	2098
(N346CP)	WW24	434
N346CZ	C52B	0346
N346DM	MU30	A046SA
N346EC	C680	0346
N346EX	FA50	346
N346GA	GLF3	436
N346GA	GLF4	1346
N346GA	GLF5	5406
N346L	**GLEX**	**9449**
N346P	FA10	184
N346PC	**F2EX**	**62**
N346QS	**C680**	**0013**
N346SK	F900	138
(N346SR)	F2TH	69
N346US	**C52A**	**0077**
N346XL	**C56X**	**5346**
N347AC	LJ25	347
N347BA	CL61	5144
N347BC	**C525**	**0431**
N347BD	**FA7X**	**248**
N347BG	C650	0201
(N347CP)	CS55	0094
N347DA	C500	457
(N347DA)	C500	420
N347DM	MU30	A047SA
N347EJ	LJ25	347
N347FX	**E55P**	**50500094**
N347GA	GLF3	403
N347GA	GLF3	471
N347GA	GLF4	1347
N347GA	**WW24**	**347**
N347GS	LJ60	026
N347HS	FA20	347
N347J	LJ24	047
N347JR	**HS25**	**258861**
N347JV	LJ25	347
(N347JW)	LJ25	347
N347K	**CL30**	**20240**
N347K	FA10	37
N347K	FA20	281/496
N347K	FA50	236
N347K	FA50	46
N347MD	LJ25	347
N347MH	**C500**	**564**
N347PP	**E55P**	**50500112**
N347QS	C560	0357
N347QS	**E55P**	**50500257**
N347RL	**C750**	**0276**
N347TC	**HS25**	**257055**
N347TX	**C52B**	**0047**
N347WW	WW24	347
N348BE	**BE40**	**RK-348**
N348BJ	LJ24	141
N348CC	C560	0368
N348CM	**C550**	**550-0915**
(N348D)	CL61	5139
N348DH	WW24	386
N348DM	MU30	A061SA
N348GA	GLF3	405
N348GA	GLF3	472
N348GA	GLF4	1348
N348GA	GLF4	4248
N348HM	LJ55	109
N348K	FA50	205
N348K	LJ45	150
N348KH	C525	0348
N348MC	HS25	258290
N348N	**E50P**	**50000352**
(N348PR)	PRM1	RB-7
N348QS	C560	0348
N348QS	**E55P**	**50500259**
N348RS	**GLF4**	**4030**
N348SJ	WW24	348
N348TS	CL30	20048
N348VL	LJ24	141
N348W	SBRL	306-94
N348WW	WW24	348
N349AK	**HA4T**	**RC-42**
N349AK	HS25	258876
N349AS	HS25	258876
N349BS	LJ24	349
(N349CB)	C525	0117
N349DA	WW24	145
N349DM	MU30	A062SA
N349EJ	LJ25	349
N349GA	GLF3	391
N349GA	GLF4	1349
N349GA	GLF5	5409
N349GA	HS25	258349
N349H	F900	10
N349HP	LJ31	153
(N349HP)	BE40	RK-49
N349JC	**FA10**	**70**
N349JF	**HS25**	**HA-0012**
N349JR	CL61	5130
N349JR	CL64	5603
N349K	F900	10
N349K	FA50	17
N349K	**GLF4**	**1510**
N349KS	FA50	17
N349M	WW24	23
N349MC	**WW24**	**224**
N349MG	FA20	479
N349MR	FA20	360
N349QS	**C680**	**0029**
N349RR	C750	0236
N349SF	**C525**	**0049**
(N349TS)	LJ35	349
N350AD	**CL30**	**20594**
N350AF	FA50	35
N350AG	LJ25	350
N350AJ	CL30	20605
N350AP	**LJ45**	**368**
N350BN	G150	223
N350BV	**C52A**	**0186**
N350C	GLF5	612
N350CC	C500	350
N350CC	C550	350
N350CD	C650	0190
N350CX	**CL30**	**20619**
N350DA	**CL30**	**20611**
N350DA	LJ35	366
N350DH	HS25	257087
N350DH	LJ25	193
N350DM	MU30	A050SA
N350DS	LJ31	002
N350DV	FA50	350
N350E	SBRL	282-76
N350EF	LJ35	385
N350EH	**CL30**	**20613**
N350EJ	**CL30**	**20598**
N350ES	CL64	5439
N350FA	CL30	20616
N350FK	**GLF4**	**4040**
N350GA	GLF3	410
"N350GA"	GLF4	4019
N350GM	C525	0172
N350GS	**CL30**	**20520**
N350HS	**C510**	**0350**
N350JF	LJ35	219
N350JH	LJ25	200
N350JS	**FA50**	**15**
N350KM	**CL30**	**20505**
N350M	C500	499
N350M	C650	0203
N350M	F2TH	128
N350M	WW24	14
N350MB	**CL30**	**20531**
N350MD	LJ35	277
N350MH	HS25	256069
N350MQ	C650	0203
N350MT	SBRL	380-54
N350NC	HS25	25160
N350PH	**CL30**	**20571**
N350PL	**HS25**	**257193**
N350PM	WW24	338
N350PR	**CL64**	**5394**
N350QS	**C680**	**0036**
N350RB	LJ35	334
N350RD	C560	0026
N350RD	C56X	5057
N350RM	**CL30**	**20605**
N350RX	**CL30**	**20582**
N350TG	CL30	20050
N350TS	LJ35	035
N350VJ	**CL30**	**20569**
N350WB	**FA50**	**102**
N350WC	**C560**	**0266**
N350WC	C560	0378
N350WC	C56X	5226
N350WC	HS25	258018
N350WG	HS25	258018
N350X	FA50	108
N350X	WW24	109
N350ZE	CL64	5547
N351AC	**LJ31**	**051**
N351AF	SBRL	465-27
N351AJ	**C52B**	**0370**
N351AJ	LJ35	036
N351AM	**LJ35**	**409**
N351AP	CL64	5595
N351AS	**LJ35**	**146**
N351BC	**C525**	**0159**
N351C	WW24	264
N351CB	PRM1	RB-53
N351CG	**C56X**	**5225**
N351CJ	**C550**	**386**
N351CW	**PRM1**	**RB-53**
N351DM	MU30	A051SA
N351EF	**LJ35**	**125**
N351FJ	GLF3	451
N351GA	G150	251
N351GA	GLF3	397
N351GA	GLF4	1351
N351GA	GLF4	1451
N351GA	GLF4	4051
N351GA	**GLF4**	**4351**
N351GA	GLF5	5251
N351GA	GLF5	5451
N351GL	LJ35	001
(N351JM)	SBRL	282-1
N351JS	FA50	104
N351MH	**LJ24**	**321**
N351N	LJ24	054
N351NR	LJ24	054
N351PJ	**LJ35**	**074**
N351QS	C560	0451
N351QS	**E55P**	**50500237**
N351SB	HS25	258280
N351SE	GLF2	64/27
N351SP	HS25	258280
N351SP	**HS25**	**HA-0004**
N351TC	HS25	258675
N351TC	WW24	351
N351TV	**LJ35**	**368**
N351TX	**LJ35**	**127**
N351V	C510	0351
N351VJ	**CL30**	**20573**
N351WB	LJ24	054
N351WB	LJ35	355
N351WC	C560	0330
N351WC	C56X	5225
N351WC	JSTR	5229
N351WC	LJ24	054
N351XR	LJ45	351
N352AE	CL61	5041
N352AE	F900	172
N352AF	CL61	5041
N352AF	F900	172
N352AF	**GLEX**	**9302**
N352AM	C550	393
N352AP	CL64	5375
N352AP	CL64	5657
N352AS	C510	0201
N352BB	**EA50**	**000123**
N352BH	**GLF4**	**1393**
N352CK	**LJ35**	**313**
N352DA	C550	393
N352DM	MU30	A052SA
N352EF	**LJ31**	**046**
N352GA	ASTR	152
N352GA	G150	252
N352GA	GLF3	401
N352GA	GLF4	1352
N352GA	**GLF4**	**4352**
N352GA	GLF5	5325
N352GA	GLF5	5452
N352GL	LJ35	002
(N352HC)	C525	0373
N352HS	**LJ35**	**596**
N352JM	**CL30**	**20522**
N352JS	FA50	41
N352K	**LJ40**	**2138**
N352K	LJ45	215
N352MD	**LJ24**	**352**
N352PJ	**LJ35**	**530**
N352QS	C560	0352
N352QS	**E55P**	**50500244**
N352RJ	**LJ35**	**188**
N352SC	LJ25	189
N352TC	WW24	394
N352TV	**LJ35**	**410**
N352TX	LJ35	073
N352VJ	**CL30**	**20576**
N352WB	**FA50**	**71**
N352WC	C500	275
N352WC	C560	0194
N352WC	HS25	257095
N352WC	LJ36	013
N352WG	C500	275
(N352WQ)	C560	0194
N352WR	LJ24	126
N352XR	**LJ60**	**352**
(N352XR)	LJ25	352
N353AE	BE40	RK-353
N353AP	LJ45	023
N353CA	SBRL	306-28
N353CK	**LJ35**	**081**
(N353CK)	LJ35	085
N353CP	FA20	461
N353CV	C560	0353
N353DM	MU30	A053SA
N353EF	LJ35	364
N353EJ	LJ25	353
N353FT	C550	397
N353GA	ASTR	153
N353GA	G150	253
N353GA	GLF4	1353
N353GA	GLF5	5453
(N353GA)	GLF3	409
N353H	FA50	301
N353HA	**C650**	**0109**
(N353HA)	C550	189
N353J	LJ24	237
N353K	CL61	5086
N353K	**LJ45**	**459**
N353MA	GLF3	472
N353PC	**CL30**	**20053**
N353PJ	**C500**	**104**
N353QS	C560	0530
N353QS	**E55P**	**50500263**
N353SB	**E50P**	**50000038**
N353TC	CL61	5037
N353VA	GLF3	371
N353VJ	**CL30**	**20609**
N353WB	C500	359
N353WB	SBRL	282-55
N353WC	C750	0008
N353WC	**C750**	**0180**
N353WC	HS25	257032
N353WC	HS25	258123
N353WC	SBRL	282-55
N353WG	HS25	258123
N353Z	C560	0353
(N354AP)	CL64	5621
(N354AP)	LJ45	025
N354AS	MS76	054
N354CA	JSTR	5054/59
N354CJ	C52B	0354
N354CL	**LJ35**	**493**
N354DM	MU30	A054SA
(N354DT)	LJ35	112
N354EF	**LJ35**	**378**
(N354EM)	LJ35	440
N354FX	**E55P**	**50500135**
N354GA	ASTR	154
N354GA	G150	254
N354GA	GLF3	412
N354GA	GLF4	1354
N354GA	GLF4	4254
N354GA	**GLF4**	**4354**
(N354GE)	LJ35	610
(N354GG)	LJ35	610
N354H	FA20	16
N354H	FA20	40
N354JC	LJ35	112
N354JR	**C680**	**0502**
N354K	**LJ45**	**462**
N354LQ	**LJ35**	**055**
N354ME	LJ35	378
N354PM	LJ35	015
N354QS	C560	0356
N354QS	**E55P**	**50500265**
N354RB	**PRM1**	**RB-54**
N354RC	C500	363
N354RX	**E50P**	**50000089**
N354RZ	LJ35	170
N354SH	SBRL	380-39
N354SS	**LJ35**	**112**
N354TC	CL61	5192
N354VJ	**CL30**	**20614**
N354WC	C750	0027
N354WC	**C750**	**0191**
N354WC	FA20	40
N354WC	HS25	257058
N354WC	HS25	258160
N354WG	**CL30**	**20354**
N354WG	HS25	258160
N355AC	HS25	25227
N355AM	LJ25	355
N355AP	LJ60	304
N355BM	**EA50**	**000092**
N355CA	LJ35	597
N355CC	CL64	5302
N355CC	CL64	5393
N355CD	SBRL	306-85
N355CD	**SBRL**	**465-57**
N355CV	C560	0355
N355DB	LJ55	006
N355DF	C550	411
N355DF	C550	550-1004
N355DG	FA20	432
N355DH	LJ55	073
N355DM	MU30	A069SA
N355EJ	C560	0255
N355FA	**HS25**	**258156**
N355FX	**E55P**	**50500139**
N355GA	GLF3	404
N355GA	GLF4	1355
N355GA	**GLF4**	**4355**
N355GA	GLF5	5455
N355GA	LJ35	655
N355H	C500	213
N355JK	WW24	355
N355KM	**GLF2**	**226**
N355MJ	SBRL	282-66
N355PC	LJ35	431
N355PX	**C750**	**0266**
N355RB	HS25	258059
N355RM	**LJ55**	**033**
(N355TR)	GLF3	355
N355TS	GLF3	355
N355UA	**LJ55**	**114**
N355UJ	LJ55	033
N355WB	FA20	44
N355WC	C750	0030
N355WC	C750	0266
N355WC	FA20	44
N355WC	HS25	258181
N355WG	FA20	44
N355WG	HS25	258181
N355WJ	HS25	257172
N355WW	WW24	355
N356AC	LJ35	230
N356AP	CL64	5629
N356AP	GLEX	9054
N356BR	**GLF3**	**356**
N356CG	LJ60	230
N356DC	**C52B**	**0372**
N356DM	MU30	A073SA
N356EJ	C560	0256
N356FX	**E55P**	**50500155**
N356GA	GLF3	406
N356GA	**GLF4**	**4356**
N356GA	GLF5	5356
N356GA	GLF5	5456
N356JB	FA20	80
N356JH	**LJ60**	**356**
N356JM	**CL30**	**20597**
N356JW	LJ35	656
N356K	**LJ40**	**2135**
N356MR	C52B	0138
N356MS	GLEX	9149
N356N	CL61	3064
N356N	**E50P**	**50000335**
N356P	LJ35	006
N356RR	**LJ40**	**2065**
N356SA	**C560**	**0256**
N356SR	HS25	257170
N356SR	**HS25**	**258620**
N356TJ	GLF3	356
N356WA	**LJ60**	**123**
N356WB	FA20	80
N356WC	C560	0432
N356WC	C56X	5270
N356WC	FA20	80
N356WW	**GLF5**	**5025**
N356WW	WW24	356
N357AP	LJ60	377
(N357AP)	CL64	5450
N357AZ	C560	0196
N357BC	WW24	357
N357BE	**C560**	**0663**
N357BV	**C52C**	**0060**
N357CL	FA20	484
N357DM	MU30	A091SA
(N357DM)	MU30	A051SA
N357EA	WW24	357
N357EC	C560	0269
N357EC	C56X	5510
N357EF	**LJ35**	**323**
N357FX	**E55P**	**50500156**
N357GA	GLF3	413
N357GA	GLF4	1357
N357GA	GLF4	1457
N357H	GLF3	472
N357H	JSTR	5234
N357HC	LJ25	032
N357J	C52A	0184
N357JV	C525	0357
N357KM	**GLF3**	**435**
N357LJ	**LJ35**	**357**
(N357MD)	MU30	A091SA
N357MP	C56X	5774
N357PR	**GLF3**	**348**
N357PR	LJ55	073
N357PS	FA20	357
N357PT	**LJ60**	**426**
N357PT	PRM1	RB-250
N357QS	**C680**	**0155**
N357RM	LJ35	007

N357RT	CL60	1033
N357TW	**C56X**	**5669**
N357TX	C500	498
(N357W)	WW24	357
N357WC	C560	0069
N357WC	C56X	5119
N358AC	LJ35	427
N358AP	LJ60	196
N358CC	C500	358
N358CT	WW24	358
N358CV	C560	0358
N358CY	**GLF3**	**358**
N358FX	**E55P**	**50500171**
N358GA	GLF3	414
N358GA	GLF4	1358
N358GA	GLF4	1458
N358HA	**C525**	**0358**
N358JA	**LJ60**	**358**
N358JJ	**C52B**	**0267**
N358JM	**CL30**	**20518**
N358K	C525	0527
N358LL	HS25	258093
N358MH	**FA50**	**209**
N358MY	**CL30**	**20369**
N358P	**LJ60**	**205**
N358PG	LJ35	358
N358PJ	**CL61**	**5141**
(N358PP)	LJ60	205
N358PR	**F2TH**	**26**
N358QS	C560	0455
N358QS	**E55P**	**50500250**
N358WC	**C52A**	**0306**
N358WC	C750	0121
N359AP	LJ60	220
N359AS	**E55P**	**50500354**
N359BC	**HS25**	**258812**
N359BR	**FA20**	**359/542**
(N359C)	WW24	42
N359CC	C56X	5133
N359CF	HS25	258154
N359CJ	C52B	0359
N359CW	C650	0159
N359D	ASTR	102
N359EC	C560	0559
N359EF	**LJ35**	**193**
N359EJ	C560	0559
N359FX	**E55P**	**50500208**
N359GA	GLF4	1359
N359GW	C550	550-1076
N359H	LJ40	2140
N359JR	LJ45	407
N359JS	WW24	335
N359K	GLF2	180
N359K	**LJ40**	**2140**
N359K	LJ45	216
(N359K)	LJ40	2138
N359QS	**C680**	**0126**
N359RA	**LJ31**	**112**
(N359RM)	LJ60	008
N359SK	LJ25	359
N359TJ	C750	0310
N359V	ASTR	039
N359V	ASTR	102
N359V	**CL64**	**5349**
N359V	FA10	120
N359VP	ASTR	039
N359VS	ASTR	039
N359WC	C56X	5129
N359WJ	**SBRL**	**306-1**
N359XP	HS25	258359
N360	**CL61**	**5068**
N360AA	LJ25	123
N360AN	LJ60	137
N360AP	CL61	5151
N360AV	**G150**	**240**
N360AX	**LJ35**	**367**
N360BA	HS25	258052
N360CA	MU30	A009SA
N360CF	SBRL	306-133
N360CH	SBRL	306-146
N360CH	SBRL	306-15
N360CK	**C52B**	**0180**
N360DA	C500	056
N360DE	HS25	258163
(N360DE)	HS25	257042
N360DJ	C500	583
N360E	SBRL	282-80
N360EJ	LJ24	052
N360FF	CL61	5068
N360FX	**E55P**	**50500233**
N360GA	GALX	058
N360GA	GALX	163
N360GA	GLF4	1360
N360GA	GLF4	4160
N360GA	**GLF4**	**4360**
N360GA	GLF5	5360
(N360GL)	LJ35	360
N360HK	WW24	166
N360HP	**GLEX**	**9344**
N360HS	C550	550-0889
N360HS	**C560**	**0808**
N360J	SBRL	282-7
N360JG	LJ25	360
N360KE	**C510**	**0376**
N360LA	**GLEX**	**9087**
N360LJ	LJ35	360
N360LS	LJ36	030
N360M	CS55	0022
N360M	**F2EX**	**68**
N360M	WW24	24
N360MB	**GLF3**	**306**
N360MC	C500	406
N360MC	WW24	24
N360N	C550	072
N360N	HS25	257067
N360N	SBRL	282-81
N360PA	**CL30**	**20202**
N360PJ	PJET	4798E001
N360PK	C52A	0448
N360PK	**C52C**	**0030**
N360PL	**CL64**	**5303**
N360Q	SBRL	282-24
N360QS	C560	0460
N360QS	**E55P**	**50500254**
N360RL	**CL61**	**5089**
N360RP	C550	081
N360SJ	**GALX**	**068**
N360SL	CL61	5089
N360SL	**CL64**	**5456**
N360TD	**C52B**	**0360**
N360UJ	LJ60	053
N360WF	**GLF5**	**5534**
N360X	HS25	257042
N361AA	LJ24	100
(N361AP)	CL64	5611
N361AS	**E55P**	**50500313**
N361AS	BE40	RK-287
N361BA	HS25	258053
(N361CA)	C560	0366
N361CE	**E55P**	**50500176**
N361DA	SBRL	306-8
N361DB	C500	687
N361DB	C550	550-0884
N361DE	**C500**	**687**
N361DJ	C550	037
N361DM	MU30	A065SA
N361EC	C560	0279
N361EC	C56X	5515
N361EE	C650	7057
N361EJ	LJ24	053
N361EV	C52B	0361
N361FX	**E55P**	**50500234**
N361GA	GALX	059
N361GA	GLF4	1361
N361GA	**GLF4**	**4361**
N361GA	GLF5	5361
(N361GA)	GALX	161
N361JR	**C52A**	**0361**
N361K	**F900**	**83**
N361LA	**HS25**	**258562**
N361PJ	**LJ36**	**003**
(N361PJ)	LJ36	017
N361QS	C560	0361
N361QS	**C680**	**0235**
(N361RA)	GLF3	361
N361RB	C525	0361
N361TL	**C52B**	**0061**
N361TS	LJ60	361
N361XL	C56X	5361
N362AA	LJ24	110
N362AP	HS25	258405
N362B	**C510**	**0263**
N362BA	HS25	258057
N362CA	C56X	5662
N362CC	C500	362
N362CJ	C525	0362
N362CP	C550	371
N362DA	SBRL	282-90
N362DJ	C550	052
N362EA	**BE40**	**RK-486**
N362EJ	LJ24	056
N362FL	C525	0362
N362FW	**LJ35**	**362**
N362FX	**E55P**	**50500239**
N362GA	GALX	062
N362GA	GLF4	1362
N362GA	**GLF4**	**4362**
N362GL	LJ36	002
N362JM	C52B	0066
N362KM	BE40	RK-227
N362MD	MU30	A062SA
N362PE	C525	0362
N362PJ	**LJ36**	**017**
N362PT	**FA10**	**73**
N362QS	**C680**	**0051**
N362TA	**C52B**	**0362**
N362TW	**C650**	**0011**
N362XP	**HS25**	**HA-0162**
N362XP	BE40	RK-362
N363AL	**C52B**	**0409**
N363AP	**C680**	**0095**
N363BA	HS25	258059
N363BC	LJ24	241
N363BS	**C510**	**0442**
N363CA	**C550**	**550-1009**
N363CL	**CL30**	**20063**
N363CR	CL61	3025
N363DM	MU30	A063SA
N363EA	BE40	RK-407
N363EJ	LJ24	058
N363FJ	FA20	363/544
N363FX	**E55P**	**50500242**
N363GA	GALX	063
N363GA	GLF4	1363
N363GA	**GLF4**	**4363**
N363GL	LJ36	003
N363HA	LJ25	242
N363JG	**GLF5**	**594**
N363K	C500	110
N363K	BE40	RK-114
N363MF	**GLF5**	**5112**
N363MU	C510	0363
N363NH	**ASTR**	**097**
N363PJ	**LJ36**	**038**
N363QS	C560	0536
N363QS	**E55P**	**50500256**
N363SP	C550	394
N363TD	C500	438
N363VP	**C52A**	**0363**
N363WC	**C550**	**550-1098**
(N363XP)	BE40	RK-363
N364BA	HS25	258060
N364CL	**LJ35**	**383**
N364CW	C650	0164
N364DM	MU30	A064SA
N364EJ	LJ24	059
N364FX	E55P	50500246
N364G	GLF2	125/26
N364G	GLF4	1091
N364G	WW24	5
N364GA	GALX	064
N364GA	GLF4	1364
N364PF	E55P	50500064
N364QS	**C680**	**0062**
(N364VP)	C56X	5364
N364WC	HS25	258069
N364WT	C525	0364
N365AS	LJ36	055
N365AT	HS25	258449
N365BA	HS25	258061
N365CD	FA20	202
N365CJ	**GLEX**	**9077**
N365CM	LJ25	365
N365CX	**GALX**	**075**
N365CX	WW24	425
N365DA	HS25	25271
N365DF	**FA50**	**227**
N365DJ	HS25	25020
N365EA	**C560**	**0107**
N365EG	**C550**	**550-0922**
N365EJ	LJ24	064
N365EJ	LJ24	102
N365FJ	F2EX	47
N365FX	**E55P**	**50500269**
N365G	GLF2	198/35
N365G	GLF4	1101
N365G	WW24	15
N365GA	ASTR	072
N365GA	**G150**	**225**
N365GA	GLF4	1365
N365GC	**GALX**	**203**
N365GL	**LJ31**	**128**
N365JR	HS25	HA-0065
N365KM	**BE40**	**RK-572**
N365LP	**LJ45**	**448**
N365MC	**CL30**	**20108**
N365N	LJ35	300
N365N	SBRL	306-5
N365QS	**C680**	**0057**
(N365QX)	WW24	425
N365RJ	WW24	91
N365SB	HS25	256070
N365SC	**G150**	**268**
N365TB	**C52A**	**0139**
N365TC	GLF2	41
N365WA	**C550**	**358**
N366AA	LJ25	151
N366AC	LJ35	418
N366BA	HS25	258062
N366BR	HS25	25134
N366CJ	C52A	0366
N366CM	LJ45	471
N366DA	SBRL	282-82
N366DM	MU30	A066SA
N366EA	C550	550-1005
N366EA	BE40	RK-193
N366EJ	LJ24	095
N366F	FA50	77
N366F	GLF4	1041
N366FW	C510	0044
N366FX	**E55P**	**50500326**
N366G	C650	0038
N366G	FA20	9
N366GE	C650	0038
N366JA	GLF3	366
N366LJ	LJ25	366
N366LP	**CL61**	**5091**
N366LV	**LJ45**	**366**
N366MH	**CL65**	**5797**
N366MP	HS25	25134
N366N	SBRL	282-8
N366N	SBRL	306-93
N366QS	C560	0466
N366QS	**E55P**	**50500268**
N366TS	LJ31	166
N366TT	LJ35	227
N367BA	HS25	258063
N367BL	**FA20**	**376**
N367BP	C550	550-0970
N367BW	F2EX	107
N367CJ	C52A	0367
N367CM	C510	0367
N367CS	PRM1	RB-234
N367DA	**LJ35**	**599**
N367DM	HS25	258367
N367DM	MU30	A067SA
N367EA	BE40	RK-191
(N367EA)	C550	373
N367EG	GLF2	128
N367EJ	FA20	28
N367ER	**E50P**	**50000159**
N367F	FA10	206
N367G	C650	0053
N367G	FA20	20
N367G	GLF2	125/26
N367GA	FA20	20
N367GA	G150	267
N367GA	G280	2067
N367GA	GALX	067
N367GA	GALX	167
N367GA	GALX	227
N367GA	GLF3	367
N367GA	GLF4	1367
N367HB	C500	611
N367JC	C550	180
N367JC	**C560**	**0069**
N367LJ	**LJ60**	**367**
N367QS	C560	0367
N367QS	**E55P**	**50500273**
(N367TA)	F900	52
N367TP	FA50	181
N367WW	**WW24**	**367**
N368AG	GLF2	167
N368AG	**GLF4**	**1087**
N368AS	**E55P**	**50500341**
N368BA	HS25	258065
N368BE	**C560**	**0546**
N368BG	LJ35	368
N368CC	**PRM1**	**RB-184**
N368CS	PRM1	RB-184
N368CS	**PRM1**	**RB-234**
N368D	LJ25	368
N368DA	SBRL	282-12
N368DM	MU30	A068SA
N368DS	FA20	256
N368DS	GLF2	123/25
N368EA	**BE40**	**RK-57**
N368EE	**LEG5**	**55000032**
N368EJ	FA20	30
N368F	FA10	220
N368FJ	**CL61**	**5049**
N368FK	**F9EX**	**227**
N368G	C650	0057
N368G	CL64	5368
N368G	FA20	29
N368GA	G280	2068
N368GA	GALX	068
N368GA	GALX	168
N368GA	GLF3	368
N368GA	GLF5	5368
N368HK	GLEX	9409
N368HS	**C550**	**550-0889**
N368K	C500	110
N368L	FA20	29
N368M	FA50	277
N368MD	WW24	368
N368MJ	LJ24	043
N368PK	C52A	0448
N368PU	MU30	A068SA
N368QS	**C680**	**0073**
N368S	WW24	271
N368TF	C510	0368
(N368TJ)	GLF3	368
N368XR	LJ60	368
N369AK	**BE40**	**RK-323**
N369AP	GLF2	14
N369B	C750	0030
N369BA	HS25	258066
N369BA	LJ35	312
N369BG	F900	40
N369BG	HS25	258160
N369BG	WW24	304
N369CA	FA20	359/542
(N369CA)	FA50	115
N369CE	FA20	359/542
N369CS	GLF2	2
N369CS	GLF3	384
N369CS	HS25	25214
N369D	LJ25	369
N369DA	C550	327
N369EA	**BE40**	**RJ-2**
(N369EA)	BE40	RK-115
N369EJ	FA20	33
N369EJ	LJ24	081
N369G	C650	0015
N369G	FA20	34
N369G	HS25	257125
N369GA	**GLF4**	**4369**
N369GA	GLF5	5269
N369GC	**C510**	**0248**
N369GM	C52B	0277
N369JB	HS25	25066
N369JH	HS25	25275
N369JK	GALX	190
N369KL	**C52A**	**0471**
N369MJ	LJ25	369
N369MN	**C52B**	**0314**
N369MU	**C510**	**0369**
N369N	SBRL	282-8
N369PA	C510	0211
N369QS	**C680**	**0081**
(N369TC)	C560	0284
N369TS	HS25	256069
N369V	FA10	120
N369WR	FA20	196
N369XL	GLF4	1202
N369XL	LJ35	423
N369XP	BE40	RK-369
N370	FA20	21
N370AC	C550	228
N370AG	FA20	357
N370AS	MS76	030
N370AT	LJ60	139
N370BA	C56X	5525
N370BH	SBRL	370-4
(N370CD)	C550	028
(N370CL)	CL64	5370
N370DE	HS25	258441
N370DM	MU30	A070SA
N370EA	**EA50**	**000125**
N370EC	LJ35	003
N370EJ	**EPC1**	**001**
N370EK	C750	0185
N370EL	**CL30**	**20399**
(N370EU)	FA20	297
N370FC	**BE40**	**RK-378**
N370GA	GALX	170
N370GA	GLF3	494
N370GA	GLF4	1370
N370GA	GLF4	1450
N370GA	**GLF4**	**4370**
N370GA	GLF5	5270
(N370GA)	GLF3	451
N370HF	FA20	370
(N370J)	GLF3	401
N370JJ	C52A	0370
N370JL	**GLF3**	**401**
N370KP	FA50	103
N370L	SBRL	306-64
N370LJ	LJ25	370
N370LN	**C500**	**101**
N370M	C56X	5565
N370M	**C680**	**0307**
N370M	CS55	0128
N370M	HS25	257019
N370M	SBRL	306-71
(N370ME)	FA20	310
N370MR	**C52B**	**0385**
N370P	**EA50**	**000066**
(N370P)	EA50	000068
N370QS	C650	0070
N370QS	**C680**	**0099**
N370RP	**C52A**	**0370**
N370RR	HS25	257019
N370RS	**GLF4**	**1265**
N370SC	LJ31	070
N370SL	SBRL	370-9
(N370SP)	GLF2	168
N370TC	C560	0684
N370TG	C650	0070
N370TP	C500	551
N370TP	**C650**	**0059**
N370TS	CL64	5370
N370V	CL60	1014
N370VS	SBRL	306-54
N370WT	FA20	274
N370Z	**G280**	**2082**
N371AS	**MS76**	**034**
N371CE	PRM1	RB-73
N371CF	PRM1	RB-73
N371CF	**BE40**	**RK-351**
N371CL	CL64	5371
N371CV	C560	0371
N371CW	BE40	RK-371
N371D	HS25	257134
N371DM	MU30	A071SA
N371EA	C550	550-1013
N371FP	**GLF4**	**1371**
N371G	**CL65**	**5741**
N371GA	G150	235
N371GA	GALX	071
N371GA	GLF3	495
N371GA	GLF4	1371
N371GA	GLF5	5371
(N371GA)	C500	407
N371GP	C500	407
N371H	JSTR	5020
N371H	WW24	315
N371HA	**CL30**	**20371**
N371HH	C500	214
N371JC	CL64	5342
N371JC	**GLF5**	**505**
N371K	LJ45	157
N371P	C56X	5371
N371QS	C560	0471
N371QS	**E55P**	**50500279**
N371SF	**C525**	**0814**
N371TS	CL30	20071
N371VP	**C510**	**0371**
(N371W)	C500	214
N372AS	G150	281
N372AS	LJ35	372
N372BC	CL61	3034
N372BC	GLF4	1273
N372BC	HS25	257026

N372BD	HS25	257026
N372BG	CL61	3034
N372BG	GLF4	1273
N372BG	GLF5	5038
N372BG	**GLF5**	**5164**
N372CC	C550	372
N372CM	GLF2	185
N372CM	GLF2	62
N372CM	GLF3	338
N372CM	GLF4	1049
N372CM	GLF4	1451
N372CM	HS25	25073
N372CP	C525	0372
N372CT	C52A	0005
N372CV	C560	0372
N372DM	MU30	A072SA
N372EJ	C560	0272
N372G	CL61	3006
N372G	CL64	5351
N372G	**CL65**	**5867**
N372GA	G150	272
N372GA	GLF3	496
N372GA	GLF4	1372
N372GA	GLF4	1472
N372GA	GLF4	4072
N372GA	GLF4	4273
N372GM	GLF2	185
N372GM	GLF2	62
N372GM	GLF3	338
N372GM	GLF4	1049
N372GM	HS25	25073
N372H	JSTR	5092/58
N372H	JSTR	5228
N372JL	**LJ31**	**142**
(N372N)	CL30	20060
N372PG	CL61	3034
N372Q	WW24	112
N372QS	C560	0372
N372QS	**C680**	**0201**
N372RS	HS25	25066
N372WC	C560	0372
N372WW	WW24	372
N372XP	HS25	258372
N373AB	**C750**	**0243**
N373AF	**C525**	**0308**
N373AG	**C52B**	**0301**
N373AS	MS76	036
(N373CC)	C510	0369
N373CM	WW24	373
N373DH	HS25	25066
N373DJ	C650	0038
N373DN	**FA20**	**324**
N373G	CL61	3009
N373G	CL64	5556
N373G	**CL65**	**5870**
N373GA	G150	273
N373GA	G280	2073
N373GA	GALX	243
N373GA	GLF3	497
N373GA	GLF4	1373
N373GA	GLF4	1473
N373GA	GLF4	4073
N373GS	GLF3	373
N373KC	FA20	264
N373KM	GLF4	1373
N373LB	GLF2	13
N373LP	GLF2	13
(N373LP)	GLF3	310
(N373LP)	LJ35	220
N373MG	**FA20**	**428**
(N373MJ)	C56X	5122
N373ML	**G150**	**204**
N373MM	**PRM1**	**RB-237**
N373QS	C560	0373
N373QS	**E55P**	**50500275**
N373RR	**FA50**	**259**
N373RR	GLF3	373
N373RS	**F9EX**	**291**
N373RS	FA50	259
N373SB	GLEX	9047
N373SC	LJ25	204
N373W	LJ25	032
N373XP	BE40	RK-373
N374AS	**MS76**	**038**
N374BC	CL61	3034
(N374DH)	HS25	25066
N374DM	MU30	A074SA
N374FC	C550	374
N374FS	**GLF6**	**6056**
N374G	CL61	3015
N374G	CL64	5351
N374G	CL64	5368
N374GA	G150	274
N374GA	GLF3	498
N374GA	GLF4	1374
N374GA	GLF4	1474
N374GA	GLF4	1504
N374GA	GLF4	4074
N374GA	GLF4	4237
N374GC	C555	0055
N374GS	C500	634
N374GS	C500	669
N374GS	C555	0055
N374HM	**HS25**	**HA-0112**
(N374LJ)	LJ35	249
N374MV	F9EX	7
N374N	**E50P**	**50000311**
N374PS	GLF2	92
N374QS	C560	0475
N374QS	**E55P**	**50500289**
N374WC	C560	0475
N374XP	BE40	RK-374
N375AS	**MS76**	**044**
N375BC	**HS25**	**258856**
N375BK	FA20	236
N375BW	**LJ60**	**223**
N375CM	C560	0365
N375DM	MU30	A075SA
N375DS	C52A	0506
N375DT	**BE40**	**RK-372**
N375E	C650	7014
N375ET	**EA50**	**000216**
N375G	CL61	3019
N375G	GLEX	9158
N375G	**GLEX**	**9242**
N375GA	G150	275
N375GA	GLF3	375
N375GA	GLF4	1151
N375GA	GLF4	1375
N375GA	GLF4	4075
N375GA	GLF5	5375
N375H	CL61	5093
N375JP	CL61	5029
N375KD	**EA50**	**000006**
N375KH	C525	0375
N375LT	**GLF3**	**375**
N375MD	JSTR	5209
N375MD	JSTR	5227
N375MH	CL30	20155
N375NM	GLF3	375
N375NW	GLF3	375
N375PK	CL60	1018
N375PK	CL61	3054
N375PK	FA20	236
N375PK	GLF2	15
N375QS	C560	0375
N375QS	**C680**	**0230**
N375RF	CL30	20025
N375SC	C650	0027
N375SC	F2TH	23
N375SC	**F9EX**	**215**
N375SC	HS25	258111
N375SH	**EA50**	**000256**
N375TC	GLF4	1133
N375TW	**HS25**	**HA-0097**
N375WB	CL30	20025
N375WB	**GLEX**	**9288**
N375XP	BE40	RK-375
N376BE	WW24	376
(N376CW)	C650	0183
N376D	SBRL	282-115
N376D	SBRL	306-101
N376D	**SBRL**	**465-76**
N376DD	SBRL	282-115
N376DM	MU30	A076SA
N376EJ	GLF3	376
N376G	**GLEX**	**9164**
N376GA	GALX	076
N376GA	GLF4	1376
N376GA	GLF4	4076
N376GA	GLF5	5376
N376HA	LJ35	477
(N376HW)	C650	0025
N376MB	LJ31	234
N376PJ	GLF3	376
N376QS	C560	0276
N376QS	**C680**	**0180**
N376RP	SBRL	282-115
N376RS	**C525**	**0366**
N376SC	C650	0076
N376SC	**F2EX**	**315**
N376SC	F2EX	57
N376SC	F2TH	24
N376SC	FA20	391
N376SC	HS25	258124
N376SC	LJ25	204
N376SF	**F2EX**	**176**
N376WA	WW24	376
N376WC	C560	0276
N377AC	**ASTR**	**109**
N377AG	**F2EX**	**32**
N377BT	FA20	44
N377C	LJ25	257
N377C	LJ35	389
N377DM	MU30	A077SA
N377DP	**CL30**	**20377**
(N377EM)	SBRL	306-26
N377EX	F2EX	77
N377GA	C52B	0247
N377GA	GLF3	487
N377GA	GLF4	1377
N377GA	GLF4	4077
N377GM	F2EX	32
N377GS	C525	0179
N377GS	C52A	0077
N377HS	SBRL	380-36
N377HW	**F900**	**37**
N377HW	FA50	156
N377JC	HS25	258349
N377JE	C650	0013
(N377JW)	LJ55	033
N377KC	C500	388
N377LR	GLF3	377
N377MD	**CL30**	**20149**
N377N	**E55P**	**50500199**
N377P	SBRL	282-70
N377PT	LJ60	426
N377Q	LJ25	257
N377QS	C560	0377
N377QS	**C680**	**0187**
N377RA	C560	0377
N377RA	CL30	20149
N377RP	FA20	377/548
N377RV	**C510**	**0227**
N377RX	GLF3	377
N377SA	**JSTR**	**5229**
N377SC	**F2EX**	**227**
N377SC	F9EX	66
N377SF	C750	0068
N377WC	C560	0377
N378AS	**MS76**	**045**
N378C	FA10	73
N378CC	C500	378
N378CM	**C510**	**0378**
N378D	**SBRL**	**306-101**
N378DB	**FA20**	**378**
N378DM	MU30	A078SA
N378GA	GALX	211
N378GA	GLF4	1378
N378GA	GLF4	1478
N378GA	GLF4	4078
N378HC	GLF3	378
N378L	GLF5	5008
N378L	**GLF5**	**5072**
N378MB	**GLF3**	**336**
N378QS	**C680**	**0103**
N378SE	GLF3	378
(N378VP)	C560	0378
N379AV	WW24	344
N379B	**C52B**	**0212**
N379BC	**C560**	**0642**
(N379BW)	LJ35	454
N379CZ	C510	0379
N379DB	**C52B**	**0191**
N379DM	MU30	A079SA
N379DR	BE40	RK-321
N379G	**GLEX**	**9199**
N379GA	**GALX**	**079**
N379GA	GALX	213
N379GA	GALX	239
N379GA	GLF4	1379
N379GA	GLF4	4079
N379JR	WW24	353
N379LJ	**LJ45**	**379**
N379P	GLF5	581
N379QS	C560	0479
N379QS	**E55P**	**50500294**
N379R	**C52A**	**0421**
N379RH	GLF3	379
N379SM	**C52B**	**0379**
N379TH	WW24	109
N379XX	GLF3	394
N380AA	JSTR	5131
N380AC	**GLF2**	**241**
N380AG	**GLF3**	**376**
N380AK	**C550**	**550-0809**
N380AK	C550	612
N380AR	C52A	0465
N380BA	LJ60	292
N380BC	SBRL	380-17
N380BR	C525	0643
N380CF	SBRL	380-51
N380CF	SBRL	380-54
N380CJ	C52B	0080
N380CJ	FA20	380
N380CM	MU30	A080SA
N380CR	C525	0643
N380CR	C52A	0465
N380CV	C560	0380
N380CW	C650	0030
N380DA	WW24	380
N380DE	HS25	258269
(N380DG)	CL30	20058
N380DJ	SBRL	380-32
N380DM	MU30	A080SA
N380EX	HFB3	1036
N380FP	SBRL	380-54
N380GA	GALX	080
N380GA	GLF4	1380
N380GA	GLF4	4080
N380GA	GLF5	5380
N380GG	HS25	258591
N380GK	SBRL	380-44
N380GP	HS25	258591
N380JR	**BE40**	**RK-411**
N380L	LJ60	380
N380LC	LJ25	030
N380LV	C560	0781
N380M	**C56X**	**5111**
N380MS	C550	480
N380MS	SBRL	380-21
N380N	SBRL	380-72
N380PK	**C56X**	**5019**
N380QS	**C680**	**0089**
N380RA	FA20	54
N380RD	**C560**	**0026**
(N380RS)	SBRL	380-70
N380SE	**GLF6**	**6088**
N380SF	FA20	258
N380SR	SBRL	380-2
N380SR	SBRL	380-53
N380T	SBRL	380-58
N380TJ	FA50	138
N380TT	GLF3	437
N380V	CL60	1008
N380X	HS25	25204
N380X	HS25	258269
N381AA	JSTR	5058/4
N381AL	**LJ31**	**150**
N381BJ	**C500**	**445**
N381CC	C550	381
N381CJ	C525	0380
N381CW	**C650**	**0111**
N381DA	WW24	118
N381DM	MU30	A081SA
(N381EM)	C650	0111
N381GA	GALX	221
N381GA	GLF4	1381
N381GA	GLF4	4081
N381GA	GLF5	5381
N381GX	**GLEX**	**9381**
N381MF	FA10	121
N381MG	MU30	A081SA
(N381MS)	GLEX	9226
N381QS	**C680**	**0097**
N381VP	**C550**	**170**
N381W	WW24	381
N381XP	**BE40**	**RK-381**
N382AA	WW24	56
N382AG	C560	0066
N382AK	GLEX	9181
N382AL	LJ31	142
N382AL	**LJ31**	**192**
N382BL	LJ35	382
N382BP	LJ35	382
N382CA	F2EX	29
(N382DA)	HS25	25218
N382DM	MU30	A082SA
N382E	FA20	382
N382EA	**EA50**	**000082**
N382EM	C525	0496
N382G	GALX	079
N382GA	G150	282
N382GA	GLF4	1382
N382GA	GLF4	4082
N382JP	C500	164
N382KU	**F2TH**	**116**
N382LS	SBRL	380-51
N382MC	SBRL	380-34
N382MU	**C510**	**0382**
N382QS	C560	0382
N382QS	**C680**	**0245**
N382RF	SBRL	282-17
N382TC	**LJ35**	**039**
N383AL	LJ35	495
N383AZ	**GALX**	**248**
N383CF	SBRL	380-9
N383CH	**E55P**	**50500344**
N383CJ	**C52B**	**0383**
N383DM	MU30	A083SA
N383DT	CL64	5383
N383GA	GALX	223
N383GA	GLF4	1383
N383GA	GLF4	4083
N383JA	GLF5	596
N383JR	C52B	0383
N383KK	**GLF4**	**4252**
N383LJ	LJ60	383
N383LS	**GLF5**	**544**
N383MB	CL64	5568
N383MB	LJ60	083
N383MH	F2EX	262
N383MR	HS25	258915
N383QS	C560	0483
N383QS	**E55P**	**50500302**
N383RF	FA20	65
N383SC	C500	341
N383SF	**ASTR**	**083**
N383T	**GLF5**	**5007**
N383TS	SBRL	306-84
N383X	LJ24	128
(N383XX)	GLF4	4252
N384AB	**HS25**	**258097**
N384AF	LJ45	143
N384AJ	**C560**	**0230**
N384AI	WW24	175
N384BB	**GLF3**	**496**
N384CF	**LJ35**	**384**
N384CW	C650	0144
N384DA	C550	048
N384DM	MU30	A058SA
N384EM	**C650**	**0144**
N384GA	GALX	184
N384GA	GLF4	1384
N384GA	GLF4	4084
N384GA	GLF5	5384
N384JK	FA20	384/551
N384JW	LJ35	316
N384JW	**LJ60**	**130**
N384K	FA20	387
N384MP	CL61	5047
N384MS	GLF4	1082
N384PS	**FA20**	**384/551**
N384QS	**C680**	**0110**
N384RV	**CL30**	**20184**
N384TC	**EA50**	**000065**
N384TC	HS25	258138
N384WC	C56X	5084
N385AC	FA20	144
N385CC	C500	385
N385CT	**CL64**	**5592**
N385CW	C650	0145
N385EM	C650	0145
N385FJ	FA20	385
(N385G)	WW24	43
N385GA	GALX	225
N385GA	GLF4	4085
N385GP	GLF4	1049
N385GP	**GLF4**	**1133**
N385J	LJ24	085
N385M	GLF2	77
N385MG	C56X	5556
(N385MG)	LJ35	626
N385PB	**BE40**	**RK-217**
(N385PB)	BE40	RK-522
N385PD	**GLF4**	**1088**
N385QS	**C680**	**0115**
N385RC	**LJ55**	**117**
N385WL	GLF5	5196
N386AG	GLF4	1150
N386AM	C550	163
N386CM	**LJ35**	**283**
N386CW	C650	0186
(N386DA)	C500	460
N386G	WW24	43
N386JC	**CL30**	**20386**
N386JD	**GLF4**	**1460**
(N386JM)	WW24	128
N386K	LJ45	086
(N386K)	CL61	5174
N386MA	C550	069
N386MC	WW24	128
N386MM	**LJ31**	**002**
N386QS	C560	0486
N386QS	**E55P**	**50500309**
N386RF	C525	0386
N386RL	**WW24**	**386**
N386RW	**G280**	**2052**
N386SC	C500	323
N386SF	**C52B**	**0376**
N386SF	C56X	5064
N386TA	**C510**	**0386**
N387A	**C560**	**0240**
N387AT	BE40	RK-256
N387CE	FA20	387
N387CL	CL64	5387
(N387FJ)	FA20	487
N387GA	GALX	187
N387GA	GLF4	4087
N387GA	GLF5	5387
N387H	HS25	258246
N387HA	C550	465
N387HA	**LJ35**	**251**
N387MA	C550	095
N387MB	**E50P**	**50000218**
N387MM	**C560**	**0109A**
N387PA	ASTR	025
N387PA	ASTR	145
N387PC	CL30	20087
N387QS	**C680**	**0119**
N387RE	**C550**	**575**
N387SC	C550	157
N387SV	C560	0759
N387WM	GLEX	9041
N388AC	**GLF5**	**5125**
N388AJ	FA20	56
N388AJ	**GLF4**	**1508**
N388BS	HS25	258423
(N388BS)	HS25	257056
N388CA	**GLF4**	**1034**
N388CJ	C500	388
N388CW	GLF3	489
N388DA	C650	0062
N388DA	BE40	RJ-26
N388DB	CL61	3016
N388DD	CL60	1082
N388FA	C550	633
N388FW	**C525**	**0656**
N388GA	GALX	088
N388GA	GALX	188
N388GA	GLF4	1438
N388GA	GLF4	4088
N388GA	WW24	366
N388GM	C500	323
N388GS	F9EX	55
N388H	HS25	258248
N388JR	C680	680A0010
N388LR	**GLF3**	**388**
N388LS	LJ35	388
N388MA	C550	108
N388MM	**GLF3**	**490**
N388P	LJ24	211
N388PD	LJ35	388
N388PD	**LJ35**	**630**
N388PG	CL61	5152
N388Q	LJ24	065A
N388QS	**C680**	**0113**
N388R	LJ24	020
N388R	LJ24	110
N388RD	C560	0162
N388RF	GLEX	9154
N388RF	GLF6	6106
N388SB	**C550**	**279**
N388TC	FA50	196
N388WM	HS25	25052

N388WS	CL30	20108
N388WW	**WW24**	**388**
N388Z	F900	43
(N389AC)	FA20	162/451
N389AL	C52C	0184
N389AT	**LJ25**	**297**
N389AW	LJ35	157
N389BG	HS25	258160
N389BG	WW24	304
(N389BG)	F900	40
N389CC	C500	389
N389CG	LJ45	389
N389CJ	C525	0389
(N389DA)	HS25	25037
N389GA	GLF4	1389
N389GA	GLF4	1489
N389GA	GLF4	4089
N389GA	GLF5	5389
N389GA	LJ25	289
N389GS	F2TH	20
N389JP	C500	643
N389JV	C560	0389
N389KA	**LJ35**	**389**
N389L	CS55	0013
N389MW	**E50P**	**50000022**
N389QS	C680	0105
N389QS	**C680**	**0149**
N389W	C650	0098
N390AB	**PRM1**	**RB-83**
(N390AB)	LJ45	039
N390AG	FA20	360
N390AJ	C550	369
N390BA	C560	0409
N390BD	**PRM1**	**RB-193**
N390BL	PRM1	RB-30
(N390BP)	PRM1	RB-20
N390BR	**PRM1**	**RB-118**
N390BW	PRM1	RB-12
N390CE	**PRM1**	**RB-40**
N390CG	LJ45	390
N390CK	PRM1	RB-42
N390CL	PRM1	RB-25
N390CM	C510	0390
N390CV	C560	0390
N390DA	C550	434
N390DB	**CL30**	**20131**
N390DE	F9EX	68
N390DP	**PRM1**	**RB-34**
N390EE	E50P	50000310
N390EM	PRM1	RB-9
N390EU	PRM1	RB-242
N390F	F900	127
N390F	GLF2	178
N390GG	LJ45	325
N390GM	PRM1	RB-121
N390GM	**PRM1**	**RB-172**
N390GS	F2TH	21
N390GS	PRM1	RB-231
N390GW	PRM1	RB-201
N390HG	**PRM1**	**RB-283**
(N390HR)	PRM1	RB-26
N390JK	**PRM1**	**RB-39**
(N390JP)	C550	369
N390JV	**PRM1**	**RB-129**
N390JW	**PRM1**	**RB-78**
N390K	**PRM1**	**RB-225**
N390LM	**PRM1**	**RB-95**
N390MB	**PRM1**	**RB-21**
N390MG	PRM1	RB-293
N390ML	**PRM1**	**RB-142**
N390MM	**PRM1**	**RB-266**
N390NS	PRM1	RB-50
N390P	PRM1	RB-12
N390P	**PRM1**	**RB-250**
N390P	PRM1	RB-275
N390P	PRM1	RB-81
N390PL	PRM1	RB-55
N390PR	PRM1	RB-113
N390PT	**PRM1**	**RB-135**
N390QS	C560	0490
N390QS	**E55P**	**50500328**
N390R	PRM1	RB-6
N390RA	PRM1	RB-1
N390RB	PRM1	RB-26
N390RC	PRM1	RB-56
N390RJ	**PRM1**	**RB-220**
(N390S)	C500	290
N390TA	PRM1	RB-12
N390TA	PRM1	RB-86
N390TC	PRM1	RB-3
N390TG	C52B	0075
N390TP	**E50P**	**50000024**
N390VP	C560	0390
N390WC	C560	0490
N391AN	C550	093
N391BC	C550	170
N391BC	**C550**	**550-0909**
N391CV	C560	0391
N391DA	HS25	25029
(N391DH)	C550	620
N391DT	**C550**	**620**
(N391DT)	C550	641
N391GA	G150	291
N391GA	GALX	091
N391GA	GALX	191
N391GA	GLF4	1391
N391GA	GLF4	1440
N391GA	GLF4	4091
N391JP	LJ35	487
N391JR	LJ35	487
N391KC	C550	170
N391KK	**C680**	**0074**
N391QS	C560	0493
N391QS	**E55P**	**50500331**
(N391RB)	PRM1	RB-70
N391SH	GLF3	392
N391TC	HS25	257199
N391TC	HS25	258063
N391VR	E55P	50500091
N391W	**CL30**	**20091**
N391XP	HS25	258391
N391YS	**PRM1**	**RB-6**
N392AS	**E55P**	**50500009**
N392BD	GLF2	120
N392BS	C560	0164
N392DA	C500	541
N392DL	**LJ45**	**351**
N392F	SBRL	282-17
(N392FJ)	FA20	392/553
N392FV	CL61	3032
N392GA	G150	292
N392GA	GLF4	1392
N392GA	GLF4	1492
N392GA	GLF4	4092
N392JP	LJ35	328
N392JT	**CL61**	**5020**
N392MG	**C52B**	**0392**
N392P	PRM1	RD-2
N392PT	CL61	5110
N392QS	C560	0429
N392QS	**E55P**	**50500349**
N392RG	**C525**	**0340**
N392RS	C52B	0392
N392SM	**C525**	**0392**
N392T	LJ24	158
N392T	LJ25	104
N392U	FA50	54
N392X	PRM1	RD-1
N393AC	LJ60	393
N393BB	BE40	RJ-39
N393BB	**BE40**	**RK-542**
N393BD	GLF2	120
N393BD	GLF4	1205
N393BV	**GLEX**	**9385**
N393BZ	**GLEX**	**9022**
N393CF	LJ35	669
N393CM	C510	0393
N393CW	C650	0113
N393DA	C500	584
N393E	**CS55**	**0053**
N393F	FA20	65
N393GA	G150	293
N393GA	GALX	093
N393GA	GLF4	1393
N393GA	GLF4	4093
N393GH	**BE40**	**RK-240**
(N393HC)	C550	336
N393JC	**C650**	**0113**
N393JP	LJ35	320
N393N	C525	0109
N393PJ	C500	551
N393QS	C560	0393
N393QS	**E55P**	**50500356**
N393RC	C550	336
(N393RF)	FA20	65
N393S	FA20	473
N393SC	**LJ35**	**650**
N393TA	LJ60	143
N393U	GLF3	325
N393VP	C52B	0393
N393WB	**MU30**	**A045SA**
N394AG	**C56X**	**5576**
N394AJ	C560	0230
N394AJ	FA50	236
N394AK	**GLF4**	**1470**
N394AM	C550	090
N394AS	**E55P**	**50500035**
N394BB	**BE40**	**RK-364**
N394CK	C560	0270
N394CK	**C680**	**0109**
N394CM	**C510**	**0394**
N394GA	GALX	094
N394GA	GLF4	1394
N394GA	GLF5	5194
N394HA	**CS55**	**0132**
N394JP	LJ35	491
(N394MA)	C550	672
N394PA	LJ35	462
N394QS	C560	0394
N394QS	**E55P**	**50500362**
N394SA	LJ31	034
N394TR	GLF4	1252
N394U	FA50	113
N394WJ	C56X	5086
N394WJ	F900	37
N394XP	HS25	258394
(N395BB)	FA20	395/554
N395BC	**LJ45**	**258**
N395CC	C550	395
N395EJ	GLF3	395
N395EJ	HS25	256060
N395GA	GLF4	1395
N395GA	**SBRL**	**465-65**
N395HE	C550	641
N395HE	**HS25**	**258206**
N395L	F900	133
N395LJ	**LJ31**	**095**
N395MH	**CL64**	**5644**
N395MY	LJ35	395
N395QS	C560	0496
N395QS	**E55P**	**50500365**
(N395QS)	C560	0395
N395R	C560	0188
N395RD	HS25	257064
N395SC	C500	395
N395SD	C525	0439
N395SR	WW24	395
N395TJ	**WW24**	**395**
N395WB	**LJ45**	**009**
N395WB	MU30	A045SA
N395WC	C560	0367
N395WJ	**C56X**	**5330**
N396BB	**C680**	**0123**
N396BC	GLF2	93
N396CF	GLF2	96
N396CJ	C52B	0196
(N396DA)	C550	282
N396DM	C510	0008
N396EG	FA50	207
N396GA	GLF4	1396
N396GA	GLF4	1456
N396GC	LJ45	396
N396KM	**CL60**	**1059**
N396LJ	LJ60	396
N396M	**C550**	**396**
N396NS	**GLF4**	**1395**
N396PB	C550	550-1122
N396QS	C560	0396
N396QS	**C680**	**0240**
N396RC	HS25	257087
N396U	**GLF4**	**1350**
N396U	HS25	257071
N396V	**CL60**	**1009**
N396VP	C560	0396
N396XP	HS25	HA-0196
N397AF	C560	0397
N397AT	LJ45	105
N397AT	BE40	RK-157
N397AT	BE40	RK-256
N397B	JSTR	5075/19
N397BC	**C56X**	**5291**
N397BC	LJ24	144
N397BE	CL60	1053
N397CA	BE40	RK-136
N397CM	**C510**	**0397**
N397CS	C650	0056
N397CW	C650	0107
N397DR	**C650**	**0107**
N397F	GLF2	72
N397GA	GALX	097
N397GA	GLF4	1397
N397GA	GLF4	1497
N397GA	GLF4	4097
N397GA	GLF4	4197
N397GA	GLF5	5397
N397J	CL61	5033
N397J	GLF2	97
N397J	GLF4	1354
N397JJ	**GLF4**	**1354**
N397JK	**LJ60**	**261**
(N397JQ)	CL61	5033
N397L	LJ24	144
(N397L)	GLF2	97
N397LE	GLF2	106
N397MG	**BE40**	**RK-259**
N397Q	CL61	5033
N397QS	C560	0531
N397QS	**C680**	**0144**
N397RD	GLF2	37
N397RJ	C525	0683
N397SC	**C500**	**019**
(N397SL)	MU30	A022SA
(N397WC)	C560	0333
N398AS	LJ60	338
N398AC	FA50	240
N398AC	LJ55	033
N398AG	ASTR	088
N398BB	**BE40**	**RJ-39**
N398CC	C550	398
N398CG	LJ45	398
N398CJ	C525	0398
N398CW	C650	0098
N398DC	FA10	180
N398DL	C650	0098
N398EP	C525	0327
N398GA	GALX	098
N398GA	GALX	198
N398GA	GLF4	1398
N398GA	GLF4	1498
N398GA	GLF4	4098
N398GA	GLF4	4198
N398GA	GLF5	5398
N398LS	**C550**	**550-0853**
N398QS	C560	0522
N398QS	**E55P**	**50500371**
N398RP	C500	316
N398RS	**C56X**	**5009**
N398S	C550	338
N398TA	GLF5	5231
N398W	C650	7038
N399AF	**C560**	**0346**
N399AG	ASTR	090
N399AP	GLF3	399
N399AZ	LJ35	399
(N399AZ)	LJ35	399
N399BA	**LJ35**	**371**
N399BH	GLF3	384
N399CB	GLF2	118
N399CB	GLF3	433
N399CB	GLF4	1261
N399CC	GLF4	1051
N399CF	CL61	5084
(N399CG)	F9EX	55
N399D	WW24	31
N399DH	**C680**	**680A0031**
(N399DJ)	LJ35	399
N399DM	**MU30**	**A008SA**
N399EX	F9EX	222
N399FA	F2TH	101
N399FG	FA20	373
N399FL	**CL60**	**1083**
N399FP	GLF2	118
N399G	**C525**	**0183**
N399GA	G150	225
N399GA	GLF4	1459
N399GA	GLF5	5199
N399GA	GLF5	5399
N399GA	HS25	256004
N399GG	**FA50**	**108**
N399GS	C550	550-0914
N399GS	GLEX	9074
N399HS	C560	0678
N399JC	HS25	258334
(N399JC)	HS25	25224
N399JR	LJ60	103
N399KL	LJ35	362
N399LB	LJ45	429
N399MJ	MU30	A039SA
N399MM	**MU30**	**A017SA**
N399NC	**CL30**	**20347**
N399P	SBRL	282-87
N399PA	C500	327
N399PA	GLF4	1093
N399PV	**C56X**	**5211**
N399QS	C560	0510
N399RA	**BE40**	**RK-200**
N399RL	**LJ55**	**039**
N399RP	MU30	A020SA
N399RV	GLF3	423
N399RW	LJ31	182
N399SC	G150	272
N399SC	GLF3	488
N399SC	LJ60	040
N399SF	C56X	5718
N399SR	SBRL	306-33
N399SW	CL61	5009
N399SW	FA20	197
N399W	C650	0098
N399W	C650	7038
N399W	**C750**	**0171**
N399W	LJ35	209
N399WB	**CL60**	**1025**
(N399WC)	C560	0348
N399WW	CL61	3011
N399WW	GLF3	384
N400	CL64	5572
N400	LJ25	137
N400	LJ31	128
N400	LJ45	217
N400	LJ45	304
N400A	BE40	RK-3
N400A	BE40	RK-34
N400A	BE40	RK-342
N400A	BE40	RK-353
N400A	BE40	RK-66
N400A	BE40	RK-98
(N400A)	BE40	RK-110
N400AA	**GLF3**	**362**
N400AD	LJ35	519
N400AG	HS25	25206
N400AJ	LJ25	038
N400AJ	BE40	RK-137
(N400AJ)	CS55	0156
N400AK	LJ35	520
N400AL	GLF3	343
N400AL	HS25	258009
N400AN	LJ35	521
N400AP	LJ35	522
N400AQ	LJ35	523
N400AS	LJ35	524
N400AT	LJ35	525
N400AT	**LJ55**	**064**
N400AU	LJ35	526
N400AX	LJ35	527
N400AY	LJ35	528
N400AZ	LJ35	529
N400BA	LJ35	530
N400BC	**GLEX**	**9573**
N400BE	BE40	RK-4
N400BF	LJ24	010
N400BH	C500	244
N400BH	HS25	25230
N400BN	LJ35	532
N400BQ	LJ35	533
N400BU	LJ35	534
N400BY	LJ35	535
N400BZ	LJ35	536
N400CC	GLF2	102/32
N400CC	GLF4	1046
N400CC	HS25	25179
N400CC	LJ35	083
N400CD	LJ35	537
N400CE	SBRL	306-87
N400CG	LJ35	538
N400CH	**CL30**	**20051**
N400CH	HS25	257186
N400CH	HS25	258500
N400CJ	LJ35	539
N400CK	**GLF4**	**1376**
N400CK	LJ35	540
N400CP	**ASTR**	**131**
N400CP	WW24	30
N400CQ	LJ35	541
N400CR	LJ35	542
N400CS	LJ24	022
N400CS	SBRL	282-34
N400CT	C560	0104
N400CT	BE40	RK-179
N400CU	LJ35	543
N400CV	**C52A**	**0396**
N400CV	LJ35	544
N400CX	GLF2	100
N400CX	LJ35	545
N400CY	LJ35	546
N400CZ	LJ35	547
N400D	**GLF2**	**100**
N400D	HS25	25216
N400DB	C500	508
N400DB	FA20	193
N400DB	SBRL	370-4
(N400DB)	LJ25	124
N400DD	LJ35	548
N400DH	**CL61**	**5036**
N400DJ	LJ35	549
N400DK	C550	219
N400DL	LJ35	550
N400DN	LJ35	551
N400DP	HS25	25271
N400DQ	LJ35	552
N400DR	LJ35	553
N400DT	C550	102
(N400DT)	BE40	RK-66
N400DU	LJ35	554
N400DV	LJ35	555
N400DW	**BE40**	**RJ-40**
N400DX	LJ35	556
N400DY	LJ35	557
N400DZ	LJ35	558
N400EC	**C550**	**713**
N400EC	LJ35	559
N400EE	LJ35	560
(N400EE)	GLF4	1033
N400EF	LJ35	561
N400EG	LJ35	562
N400EJ	LJ35	563
N400EK	LJ35	564
N400EL	LJ35	565
N400EM	LJ35	566
N400EN	LJ35	567
N400EP	LJ24	116
N400EP	LJ24	215
N400EQ	LJ35	568
N400ER	LJ35	569
N400ES	**CL65**	**5727**
N400ES	LJ35	570
N400ET	**C52C**	**0077**
N400ET	LJ35	571
N400EU	LJ35	572
N400EV	LJ35	573
N400EX	C550	597
N400EX	LJ35	574
N400EY	LJ35	575
N400EZ	LJ35	576
N400FE	HS25	25222
N400FE	LJ35	577
N400FF	LJ35	498
N400FG	LJ35	578
N400FH	LJ35	579
N400FJ	**GLF4**	**1494**
N400FK	LJ35	580
N400FM	LJ35	581
N400FN	LJ35	582
N400FP	LJ35	583
N400FQ	LJ35	548
N400FQ	LJ35	584
N400FR	HS25	25228
N400FR	LJ35	585
N400FT	LJ35	586
N400FT	BE40	RJ-60
N400FT	BE40	RK-101
N400FT	BE40	RK-47
N400FU	LJ35	587
N400FV	LJ35	588
N400FX	**LEG5**	**55000025**
N400FY	LJ35	531
N400GA	GLF4	1001
N400GA	GLF4	1042
N400GA	GLF4	1500
N400GA	GLF4	1516
N400GA	GLF4	4300
N400GB	C500	400
N400GG	C52B	0195
N400GJ	BE40	RJ-23
N400GK	**MU30**	**A019SA**
N400GM	SBRL	282-99

N400GN	FA20	325
N400GN	HS25	258059
N400GP	HS25	25245
N400GP	HS25	25270
N400GR	**BE40**	**RK-335**
N400GX	GLEX	9037
(N400GX)	FA20	325
N400HC	WW24	117
N400HD	**BE40**	**RK-191**
N400HD	BE40	RK-303
N400HF	GLF4	1444
(N400HF)	HS25	25207
N400HG	**GLF4**	**1026**
N400HG	MU30	A091SA
N400HH	**MU30**	**A025SA**
N400HS	BE40	RK-303
N400HS	BE40	RK-314
N400HT	**C52A**	**0208**
N400J	ASTR	014
N400J	GLF2	196
N400J	GLF3	493
N400J	GLF4	1330
N400J	**GLF4**	**4280**
N400JD	C650	0035
N400JD	C750	0235
N400JD	GLF2	67
N400JD	GLF5	524
N400JE	**LJ35**	**120**
N400JF	ASTR	014
N400JH	C650	0226
N400JH	SBRL	306-133
N400JJ	BE40	RK-255
N400JK	HS25	25234
N400JS	LJ25	235
N400JT	LJ55	092
N400K	C500	102
N400K	GLF3	370
N400KC	CL61	5090
N400KC	HS25	25198
N400KC	JSTR	5051
N400KC	JSTR	5210
(N400KC)	CL61	5073
N400KD	HS25	25208
N400KE	FA50	54
N400KG	BE40	RK-221
N400KL	BE40	RK-125
N400KP	BE40	RK-125
N400KP	**BE40**	**RK-308**
N400KS	**C560**	**0041**
N400KV	SBRL	465-69
N400LC	HS25	25216
(N400LC)	FA50	89
N400LH	GLF3	401
N400LR	WW24	48
N400LV	**C56X**	**5780**
N400LV	LJ35	083
N400LX	C500	661
N400LX	C500	666
N400LX	C550	597
N400LX	C560	0453
N400M	GLF2	132
N400M	JSTR	5008
N400MC	C560	0440
N400MC	LJ35	487
(N400MC)	C550	495
(N400MJ)	LJ35	083
N400ML	MU30	A064SA
N400MP	**GLF4**	**1369**
N400MP	JSTR	5228
N400MR	**HA4T**	**RC-12**
N400MR	JSTR	5228
N400MR	BE40	RK-269
(N400MR)	HS25	25241
N400MS	**LJ24**	**246**
(N400MT)	C550	238
N400MV	BE40	RK-269
N400MV	**BE40**	**RK-286**
N400MX	**BE40**	**RK-509**
N400N	SBRL	380-41
N400NE	HS25	256047
N400NE	WW24	240
N400NF	MU30	A091SA
(N400NL)	FA20	70
N400NR	SBRL	380 41
N400NS	BE40	RK-28
N400NU	HS25	257041
N400NW	HS25	25074
N400NW	HS25	256047
N400NW	HS25	257041
N400NW	HS25	258012
N400PC	C500	425
N400PC	C550	051
N400PC	C550	242
N400PC	C650	0057
N400PC	C650	0061
N400PC	FA20	113
N400PC	FA50	89
N400PC	LJ25	235
N400PC	WW24	87
N400PG	C500	425
N400PG	FA20	113
N400PG	LJ24	068
(N400PG)	C500	434
N400PH	HS25	25180
N400PJ	GLF2	183
N400PL	BE40	RJ-42
N400PR	HS25	25203
N400PU	**BE40**	**RK-156**
N400PZ	**E50P**	**50000181**
N400Q	BE40	RK-39
N400Q	BE40	RK-55
(N400Q)	WW24	240
N400QH	HS25	257186
N400QW	BE40	RK-290
N400RB	C750	0076
N400RB	LJ24	064
N400RB	LJ35	011
N400RB	BE40	RK-448
N400RE	**C650**	**0199**
N400RE	CS55	0093
N400RL	C525	0151
N400RM	**C500**	**290**
N400RS	LJ24	138
N400RS	**SBRL**	**380-25**
(N400RV)	LJ35	120
N400RY	**BE40**	**RK-355**
N400SA	C500	223
N400SA	GLF2	8
N400SA	GLF4	1120
N400SF	**BE40**	**RK-221**
N400SH	**BE40**	**RK-100**
N400SJ	GLF2	156/31
N400SJ	GLF2	8
N400SJ	WW24	240
N400SP	FA10	125
N400SR	C500	685
N400T	BE40	RJ-17
N400TB	CL61	5120
N400TB	HS25	258039
N400TB	**BE40**	**RK-91**
N400TC	**BE40**	**RK-225**
N400TE	BE40	RK-187
N400TF	WW24	279
N400TG	**C52B**	**0195**
N400TJ	**CL64**	**5400**
N400TJ	HS25	258531
N400TJ	MU30	A006SA
N400TL	BE40	RK-339
(N400TN)	BE40	RJ-13
N400TX	C550	406
N400UF	**MU30**	**A022SA**
N400UP	GLF4	1054
N400UP	GLF4	1258
N400UW	HS25	25074
N400VC	LJ25	235
(N400VC)	LJ25	267
N400VG	BE40	RK-113
N400VG	BE40	RK-3
N400VK	BE40	RK-3
N400VK	**BE40**	**RK-420**
N400VP	BE40	RK-110
N400VP	**BE40**	**RK-242**
N400VR	HA4T	RC-24
N400WD	**C52A**	**0002**
N400WK	**C650**	**0231**
N400WP	HS25	257152
N400WT	FA20	479
N400WT	HS25	25286
N400WT	WW24	3
N400WY	GLF3	467
(N400XB)	LJ24	326
N400XJ	HS25	25220
N400XP	BE40	RK-356
N400XP	BE40	RK-400
N400XP	BE40	RK-96
N400XS	**ASTR**	**037**
N400XT	BE40	RK-137
N400XT	BE40	RK-93
N400Y	BE40	RK-66
N400YM	WW24	315
N401AB	FA20	66
N401AB	HS25	25222
N401AB	BE40	RK-7
N401AC	LJ25	140
N401AJ	LJ25	171
N401AS	**C56X**	**5757**
N401BP	WW24	260
N401CG	BE40	RJ-43
N401CS	C52B	0030
N401CV	C560	0401
N401CW	BE40	RK-371
(N401CW)	BE40	RK-1
N401DE	**C510**	**0010**
N401DE	WW24	92
N401DP	**LJ25**	**329**
N401EE	LEG5	55000024
N401EE	BE40	RK-6
N401EG	C525	0154
N401EG	**LJ40**	**2021**
N401FF	HS25	259021
(N401FF)	BE40	RK-6
N401FN	**CL30**	**20401**
N401FT	**GLF4**	**1523**
N401FX	**LEG5**	**55000027**
N401G	C500	667
N401GA	GLF2	41
N401GA	GLF4	1136
N401GA	GLF4	1401
N401GA	GLF4	1501
N401GA	GLF4	4041
N401GA	GLF4	4101
N401GA	GLF4	4201
N401GJ	**BE40**	**RJ-26**
N401GN	HS25	257072
N401HB	**GLF5**	**5173**
N401HF	GLF5	5039
N401HR	GLF2	39
(N401HR)	HS25	256046
N401JE	LJ55	041
N401JK	GALX	199
N401JL	GLF4	1283
N401JR	HS25	25191
N401JW	**FA10**	**46**
N401KC	C550	550-0969
N401KH	C560	0304
N401LG	C525	0154
N401LG	**C52A**	**0037**
N401LJ	**LJ40**	**2001**
N401LS	HS25	259032
(N401LX)	BE40	RK-17
N401M	GLF2	158
N401M	GLF2	174
N401MC	C560	0034
N401MM	C560	0114
N401MM	GLF4	1130
N401MS	SBRL	306-17
N401NK	CL64	5409
(N401NK)	CL61	3027
N401NW	**BE40**	**RK-414**
N401NX	BE40	RK-28
N401PG	**C680**	**0221**
N401PJ	GLF3	488
N401PM	GLEX	9679
N401PP	**PRM1**	**RB-130**
N401Q	LJ45	217
N401QS	**GLF4**	**1408**
N401RB	LJ24	064
N401RD	C500	267
N401RJ	CL61	5155
N401RJ	GLF3	488
N401RL	**BE40**	**RK-455**
N401SF	**LJ45**	**247**
N401SR	**GLF4**	**4001**
N401SY	**LJ60**	**256**
(N401TC)	BE40	RK-21
(N401TJ)	BE40	RJ-4
N401TM	**HS25**	**258602**
(N401U)	C550	215
N401V	WW24	30
N401WJ	GLF5	599
N401WT	**ASTR**	**068**
N401WT	GLF4	1338
N401XP	BE40	RK-455
N401XR	**BE40**	**RK-300**
(N401XT)	BE40	RK-28
N402AC	**HS25**	**25103**
N402CB	BE40	RK-399
N402CW	BE40	RK-2
N402DP	LJ25	351
N402DP	LJ35	439
N402EF	**CL30**	**20247**
N402ES	FA10	174
N402FB	BE40	RJ-2
N402FB	**BE40**	**RK-255**
(N402FF)	HS25	259036
N402FG	F900	87
N402FL	**BE40**	**RK-201**
N402FT	**GLF4**	**1527**
(N402FW)	LJ35	256
N402FX	**LEG5**	**55000028**
N402GA	GLF4	1049
N402GA	GLF4	1097
N402GA	GLF4	1137
N402GA	GLF4	1189
N402GJ	HS25	257034
N402GJ	**BE40**	**RK-380**
N402GS	**BE40**	**RK-71**
N402HR	HS25	256046
N402JP	GLF4	1283
N402JW	FA10	120
N402KC	GLF4	1017
N402LM	**GALX**	**082**
(N402LM)	GLF3	404
(N402LX)	BE40	RK-18
(N402NC)	FA20	339
N402PM	**GLEX**	**9683**
(N402QS)	GLF4	1501
(N102QS)	GLF4	1504
N402SE	**HA4T**	**RC-47**
N402SF	**C680**	**0211**
N402ST	C550	058
N402TJ	C550	051
N402TS	ASTR	039
N402TX	**GALX**	**052**
N402XT	BE40	RK-274
(N402Y)	LJ24	113
N403AC	LJ25	140
N403BG	HS25	257003
(N403BL)	C650	7010
N403CB	C650	0099
N403CC	C500	403
N403CH	C52B	0250
N403CM	**C510**	**0003**
N403CT	**HS25**	**258818**
N403CW	BE40	RK-103
N403DP	HS25	257114
N403DP	**LJ35**	**446**
N403ET	**C560**	**0535**
N403FF	HS25	259038
N403FJ	F900	3
N403FW	LJ35	403
N403FX	LEG5	55000029
N403GA	GALX	173
N403GA	GLF4	1003
N403GA	GLF4	1051
N403GA	GLF4	1098
N403GA	GLF4	1138
N403GA	GLF4	1190
N403GA	GLF4	1288
N403GA	GLF4	1403
N403GA	GLF4	1503
N403GA	GLF4	4203
N403HR	F900	10
N403JC	**CL61**	**5059**
N403JP	BE40	RJ-7
N403JW	FA20	102
N403LB	EA50	000004
N403LM	GALX	083
N403LM	GLF3	404
N403LS	**LJ40**	**2124**
(N403LX)	BE40	RK-19
N403M	WW24	132
N403ND	**C52B**	**0250**
N403NW	GLF3	403
N403PM	**GLEX**	**9673**
N403QS	**GLF4**	**1403**
N403SC	C560	0403
N403SR	C560	0590
N403SR	GLF4	4003
N403TB	**GLF4**	**1191**
N403TX	GALX	069
N403W	WW24	403
N403WC	BE40	RK-198
N403WJ	GLF3	403
N403WY	CL60	1059
N404A	F9EX	56
N404AB	CL61	5112
N404AC	GLF2	189/42
N404AC	GLF4	1384
N404AJ	LJ24	026
N404BB	LJ35	404
N404BC	**F900**	**128**
N404BF	C550	066
N404BL	**BE40**	**RK-367**
N404BS	C550	371
N404BS	HS25	258294
N404BT	C56X	5038
(N404BV)	C550	066
N404BY	**C650**	**0152**
N404CB	CL61	5090
N404CB	HS25	257087
N404CB	WW24	245
N404CC	GLF4	1098
N404CC	BE40	RK-55
N404CD	**LJ60**	**277**
N404CE	HS25	257106
N404CE	HS25	258293
N404CF	**C52A**	**0404**
N404CF	HS25	257106
N404CM	**C510**	**0004**
N404CS	C52B	0033
N404CZ	**C510**	**0404**
N404DB	GLF4	1000
N404DB	HS25	258404
N404DB	LJ24	026
(N404DB)	SBRL	370-4
N404DH	**FA20**	**366**
N404DP	LJ35	404
N404E	C550	104
N404E	FA50	154
N404EL	**LJ40**	**2033**
N404F	F900	41
N404F	**F9EX**	**49**
N404F	FA20	404
N404FF	F900	41
N404FJ	F900	5
N404FL	**BE40**	**RK-108**
N404FX	**LEG5**	**55000036**
N404FZ	**FA20**	**473**
N404G	C500	147
N404G	C550	104
N404G	**C560**	**0095**
N404G	CS55	0068
N404GA	GALX	149
N404GA	GLF4	1000
N404GA	GLF4	1101
N404GA	GLF4	1139
N404GA	GLF4	1191
N404GA	GLF4	1244
N404GA	GLF4	1404
N404GA	GLF4	1406
N404HG	**CL61**	**5017**
N404HR	**FA20**	**455**
N404HR	WW24	324
N404HS	GLF4	1404
N404JC	HS25	258400
N404JF	C650	7001
N404JF	FA50	197
N404JM	**PRM1**	**RB-167**
N404JS	LJ35	441
N404JW	FA10	29
(N404JW)	C500	338
N404KA	LJ35	404
N404KK	CS55	0081
N404KS	C550	361
N404LM	GLF4	1130
N404LN	C560	0190
(N404LN)	C650	0106
N404LR	**BE40**	**RK-339**
N404LS	**C550**	**550-1074**
(N404LX)	BE40	RK-22
N404M	GLF2	220
N404M	GLF2	83
N404M	GLF3	404
N404M	GLF4	1110
N404M	GLF4	1366
N404M	GLF5	654
N404MA	C500	126
N404MK	LJ40	2003
N404MM	C560	0491
N404MM	C56X	5161
N404MM	C56X	5737
N404MM	**C56X**	**6200**
N404MM	GLF3	404
N404MS	**BE40**	**RK-283**
N404MU	C560	0270
N404MW	WW24	372
N404MY	GLF4	1110
N404N	F9EX	81
N404NA	**GLEX**	**9356**
(N404PC)	WW24	13
N404PG	WW24	358
(N404PK)	C56X	5336
N404PM	**GLEX**	**9697**
N404PX	**GLF4**	**4033**
N404QS	GLF4	1304
N404R	F900	55
N404R	F9EX	81
N404R	FA20	155
N404R	FA50	154
N404RK	C550	550-0958
N404RP	**C550**	**041**
N404SB	C550	425
N404SB	C56X	5069
N404SJ	**SJ30**	**004**
N404SK	CL61	5058
N404SP	C560	0774
N404SP	GLF4	1243
N404SR	GLF4	4004
N404ST	F900	200
N404TC	GLF4	1411
N404TM	**HS25**	**258848**
N404TR	F900	200
N404UK	F2EX	170
N404UK	F2EX	47
N404VC	F900	158
N404VL	F900	158
N404VL	**GLEX**	**9085**
N404VP	BE40	RK-44
N404W	WW24	404
N404WC	WW24	128
N404XP	BE40	RK-404
N404XT	GLF4	1366
N405AR	**CL61**	**5151**
N405BX	LJ45	026
N405CC	C500	405
N405CJ	C52A	0405
N405CS	C52B	0036
N405CT	HS25	258819
N405CW	BE40	RK-305
(N405CW)	BE40	RK-5
N405CZ	C52B	0405
N405DC	FA50	42
N405DC	**LJ60**	**064**
N405DP	HS25	257130
(N405DP)	CL61	5131
N405DR	GLF5	541
N405DW	HS25	257130
N405EJ	F900	105
N405F	FA20	405
(N405FF)	HS25	259020
N405FJ	F900	6
N405FM	**LJ25**	**280**
N405FX	LJ45	026
N405GA	G150	205
N405GA	GLF2	105
N405GA	GLF4	1017
N405GA	GLF4	1102
N405GA	GLF4	1140
N405GA	GLF4	1214
N405GA	GLF4	1245
N405GA	GLF4	1289
N405GA	GLF4	1505
N405GA	GLF4	4105
N405GA	**GLF5**	**5205**
N405GJ	**LJ35**	**354**
N405HG	**GLF5**	**661**
N405JD	C680	0237
N405JW	FA20	54
N405LA	**HS25**	**258726**
N405LM	GLF5	541
(N405LM)	GLF3	360
N405LS	**C750**	**0013**
(N405LX)	BE40	RK-27
N405MG	**MU30**	**A021SA**
N405MM	C56X	5161
N405MM	GLF2	220
N405MU	**GLF4**	**4051**
(N405MW)	LJ45	115
N405PC	C500	562
N405PC	**LJ35**	**651**
N405PM	**GLEX**	**9698**
N405QS	**GLF4**	**4054**
(N405RH)	C560	0062
N405RS	LJ25	096

N405SD	LJ25	280
N405ST	F2TH	20
N405TC	**CL61**	**5130**
N405TK	**LJ60**	**233**
N405TM	**HS25**	**258667**
N405TP	HS25	257130
N405XP	HS25	258405
N406BJ	**CL30**	**20343**
N406BX	LJ45	089
N406CA	C550	550-1017
N406CH	WW24	372
N406CJ	C500	406
N406CJ	**C650**	**7010**
(N406CJ)	C550	058
N406CL	**CL30**	**20406**
N406CM	**C510**	**0015**
N406CS	C52B	0043
N406CT	**CS55**	**0038**
N406CW	BE40	RK-6
N406F	FA20	407
N406FA	GLF3	406
N406FJ	F900	8
(N406FL)	BE40	RK-295
N406FX	LJ45	089
N406GJ	BE40	RJ-50
N406HR	**WW24**	**324**
N406J	**HS25**	**257131**
N406L	LJ24	148
N406LM	C650	0102
N406LM	GALX	032
(N406LM)	GALX	017
N406LX	**BE40**	**RK-178**
(N406LX)	BE40	RK-30
(N406M)	C650	0102
(N406ML)	BE40	RK-6
N406MM	C650	0102
N406NL	**F2TH**	**67**
N406PW	SBRL	380-2
(N406RH)	C500	589
N406SA	**FA50**	**50**
N406SS	C550	368
(N406ST)	F2TH	25
N406TM	**HS25**	**258578**
N406TS	BE40	RJ-6
N406TX	GALX	085
N406VC	**HS25**	**258221**
N406VJ	**C560**	**0056**
N406W	WW24	406
N406W	WW24	442
N407BS	**LJ31**	**033**
N407CA	GLF3	422
N407CJ	C52A	0407
N407CJ	C52C	0007
N407CW	BE40	RK-307
N407F	FA20	409
N407FJ	F900	10
N407FX	LJ45	090
N407GA	GLF3	407
N407GA	GLF4	1018
N407GA	GLF4	1070
N407GA	GLF4	1119
N407GA	GLF4	1141
N407GA	GLF4	1192
N407GA	GLF4	1246
N407GA	**GLF4**	**4076**
N407GA	GLF5	5407
N407GC	**GLF4**	**1242**
N407GK	**GLF5**	**5068**
N407KT	FA7X	98
N407LM	C650	0103
N407LM	GALX	019
(N407LX)	BE40	RK-180
(N407LX)	BE40	RK-31
(N407M)	C650	0103
N407MM	C650	0103
N407MR	LJ35	407
N407MW	**PRM1**	**RB-86**
N407NS	**GLF4**	**1407**
N407PC	FA20	30
N407QS	GLF4	1407
N407RA	LJ31	103
N407SC	C500	037
N407TR	**GLF5**	**5375**
N407V	LJ24	087
"N407V"	LJ24	034
N407W	**WW24**	**407**
N408AL	HS25	258009
(N408BX)	LJ45	091
N408CA	C500	219
N408CC	SBRL	282-13
N408CS	C52B	0045
N408CS	SBRL	282-13
N408CT	**CS55**	**0055**
N408CW	BE40	RK-108
(N408ER)	FA50	8
N408F	FA20	411
N408FJ	F900	12
N408FX	LJ45	091
N408GA	GLF4	1020
N408GA	GLF4	1105
N408GA	GLF4	1142
N408GA	GLF4	1247
N408GA	GLF4	1290
N408GJ	**BE40**	**RK-382**
N408GR	C525	0408
N408H	**GALX**	**221**
N408J	PRM1	RB-193
N408JC	CL61	5059
N408JD	C650	0035
N408JT	C560	0408
N408LH	BE40	RK-512
N408LM	GALX	036
N408LN	GALX	036
(N408LX)	BE40	RK-32
N408M	GLF3	362
N408M	BE40	RK-6
N408MG	LJ35	328
N408MJ	WW24	408
N408MM	C500	443
N408MM	HS25	258033
N408MW	C500	443
(N408NX)	BE40	RK-108
N408PA	FA20	408
N408PC	FA20	98/434
N408PC	**BE40**	**RK-325**
N408PC	BE40	RK-47
N408QS	GLF4	1308
N408RB	LJ35	011
N408RK	**C525**	**0860**
N408RT	HS25	258440
N408S	SBRL	282-13
N408TB	CL61	5120
N408TR	SBRL	282-4
N408TX	GALX	100
N408U	**HA4T**	**RC-17**
N408W	WW24	408
N408WT	HS25	25286
(N408XT)	BE40	RK-108
N409AC	C500	433
N409AV	**HS25**	**258347**
N409BM	**GALX**	**059**
N409CC	C750	0246
N409CC	CL60	1063
N409CC	GLF4	4035
N409CS	C52B	0050
N409CT	CS55	0095
N409DJ	**C52B**	**0311**
N409ER	FA50	8
N409F	FA20	412
N409F	LJ45	095
N409FJ	F900	13
N409FX	LJ45	095
N409GA	G150	209
N409GA	GALX	109
N409GB	C680	0006
N409GB	**F2EX**	**266**
N409GL	SBRL	282-122
"N409GL"	SBRL	282-122
N409KC	CL60	1052
N409KC	CL61	5075
N409LM	GALX	059
(N409LX)	BE40	RK-35
N409M	GLF2	83
N409M	JSTR	5047
N409MA	GLF2	83
N409MA	JSTR	5047
N409PC	FA20	11
N409S	**C500**	**238**
N409SF	C650	0029
N409ST	**C550**	**559**
N409TX	**GALX**	**060**
N409VP	**C52A**	**0409**
(N409VP)	C560	0409
N409WT	**WW24**	
N409WW	**WW24**	**409**
N410AC	CL61	5166
N410AS	F2TH	102
N410AW	HS25	256039
N410AZ	**FA20**	**410**
N410BA	BE40	RJ-10
N410BD	CL64	5548
N410BD	LJ35	594
N410BT	HS25	258209
N410BX	LJ45	101
N410CC	C550	410
N410CS	C550	486
N410CT	BE40	RK-495
N410CV	C560	0310
N410CW	BE40	RK-310
N410DM	**C560**	**0184**
N410DW	C560	0021
(N410EL)	WW24	410
N410F	FA20	413
N410FJ	F900	14
(N410FJ)	FA20	206
N410FL	**BE40**	**RK-123**
N410FX	LJ45	101
N410GA	GLF4	1071
N410GA	GLF4	1108
N410GA	GLF4	1120
N410GA	GLF4	1143
N410GB	C500	148
N410GS	F2TH	112
N410GS	**F2TS**	**731**
N410J	C560	0147
N410JL	**C52A**	**0007**
(N410JP)	C550	081
N410KA	F900	43
N410KC	FA50	318
N410KD	BE40	RK-496
N410LG	**BE40**	**RK-597**
N410LM	GLF5	578
(N410LR)	GLF2	116
(N410LX)	BE40	RK-195
(N410LX)	BE40	RK-40
N410M	GLEX	9689
N410M	GLF4	1115
N410M	GLF5	575
N410MG	**GLEX**	**9689**
N410ML	BE40	RK-104
N410MT	**C56X**	**5018**
(N410MU)	CL64	5410
(N410MW)	F9EX	85
N410MY	GLF4	1115
N410N	C500	345
N410NA	C500	345
N410NA	C550	085
N410NA	C560	0435
N410NA	WW24	382
N410ND	C500	259
N410PA	HS25	25198
N410PB	LJ24	179
N410PD	LJ24	179
N410PS	**C550**	**550-1124**
N410PT	**C52B**	**0335**
N410QS	GLF4	1210
N410RD	LJ35	647
N410SB	FA20	410
N410SG	**F2EX**	**210**
N410SH	**PRM1**	**RB-251**
N410SP	LJ25	174
N410ST	LJ60	087
N410TG	**C550**	**550-0985**
N410UJ	GLF3	320
N410US	FA20	120
N410US	HS25	258090
N410US	HS25	259005
N410WW	FA10	86
N410WW	FA50	76
N410WW	GLEX	9047
N410WW	GLF4	1203
N411AJ	**LJ40**	**2011**
N411AL	GLF4	1368
N411BA	LJ35	024
N411BB	C650	0037
N411BB	C650	0195
N411BB	CL64	5316
N411BE	C52A	0116
N411BP	C650	0195
N411BW	BE40	A1008SA
N411BX	LJ45	102
N411CC	FA20	159
(N411CJ)	C500	411
N411DJ	**LJ31**	**224**
N411DR	C500	249
N411DS	C500	400
N411EC	**C56X**	**5734**
N411FB	**HS25**	**25074**
N411FG	**LJ45**	**418**
N411FJ	F900	17
N411FX	LJ45	102
N411GA	GLF4	1411
N411GA	HS25	256024
N411GC	C52A	0006
N411GC	FA50	210
N411GL	LJ55	011
N411HB	WW24	419
N411HC	**LJ40**	**2056**
N411KQ	**C56X**	**5226**
N411LC	LJ35	366
N411LL	**GLF4**	**1344**
(N411LX)	BE40	RK-42
N411MD	SBRL	306-83
N411ME	C500	400
(N411MF)	HS25	25155
N411MM	ASTR	080
N411MM	LJ24	353
N411MY	C525	0512
N411NB	**C750**	**0309**
N411PA	**HS25**	**257017**
(N411PB)	C52A	0006
N411QS	GLF4	1311
N411RA	HS25	258177
N411RE	**MU30**	**A016SA**
(N411RJ)	C500	411
N411SC	FA10	50
N411SC	**BE40**	**RK-408**
N411SF	CL30	20031
N411SF	CL30	20509
N411SK	FA50	279
N411SK	LJ60	201
N411SK	BE40	RK-111
N411SK	BE40	RK-28
N411SL	C650	0003
N411SP	LJ24	216
N411SP	MU30	A049SA
N411SS	HS25	257104
N411ST	CL30	20031
N411ST	CL30	20266
N411ST	**CL30**	**20509**
N411ST	LJ60	087
N411ST	LJ60	201
(N411TC)	HS25	256070
N411TE	EA50	000130
N411TF	**HA4T**	**RC-74**
N411TJ	**C52B**	**0269**
N411TJ	CL61	3010
N411TN	**C500**	**275**
N411TP	HS25	256070
N411VE	LJ45	411
N411VP	**EA50**	**000057**
N411VR	**C525**	**0411**
N411VZ	HS25	258313
N411WC	C500	411
N411WW	FA10	86
N411WW	FA50	76
N411WW	GLF2	257/17
N411WW	GLF4	1121
N411WW	GLF4	1203
N411WW	GLF5	5063
N411YF	**F2TH**	**161**
N412AB	**C56X**	**5752**
N412AB	FA20	492
N412AP	**GALX**	**102**
N412AR	C52B	0412
N412BT	**C550**	**550-1134**
N412CC	C56X	6006
N412CS	C52B	0059
N412CW	C560	0412
N412DA	**HS25**	**258061**
N412DP	HS25	257162
(N412EA)	C560	0412
N412ET	C550	550-1041
N412ET	C550	550-1134
N412ET	LJ40	2083
N412F	FA20	414
(N412F)	LJ45	103
N412FJ	F900	16
(N412FL)	BE40	RK-324
N412FX	LJ45	103
N412GA	G150	212
N412GA	GLF4	1008
N412GA	GLF4	1021
N412GA	GLF4	1024
N412GA	GLF4	1075
N412GA	GLF4	1121
N412GA	GLF4	1193
N412GA	GLF4	1266
N412GA	GLF4	1291
N412GA	GLF4	1412
N412GA	GLF5	5412
N412GJ	**BE40**	**RK-412**
N412GL	LJ35	412
N412JT	GLF2	101
N412LJ	LJ45	012
(N412LX)	BE40	RK-45
N412MA	C550	466
N412P	C550	187
N412PD	LJ24	179
N412PE	C550	483
N412PG	**FA50**	**97**
N412SC	WW24	412
N412SE	C500	633
N412SP	LJ25	174
(N412TE)	HA4T	RC-50
N412TF	**HA4T**	**RC-50**
N412TS	**BE40**	**RK-409**
N412W	WW24	412
N412WP	BE40	RK-111
N412WW	**GLF4**	**1203**
N413CA	C550	128
N413CK	C550	041
N413CK	C560	0194
N413CK	C56X	5042
N413CK	**C680**	**0064**
N413CQ	C525	0677
N413CS	C52B	0082
N413CT	**CS55**	**0017**
N413CV	C560	0413
N413F	FA20	415
N413FC	**C52A**	**0405**
N413FJ	F900	18
N413GA	GALX	113
N413GA	GLF4	1034
N413GA	GLF4	1212
N413GA	GLF4	1292
N413GA	GLF4	1315
N413GA	GLF4	1413
N413GA	GLF4	4213
N413GA	GLF4	4313
N413GA	GLF5	5213
N413GH	HS25	25030
N413GK	C560	0194
N413HB	HA4T	RC-13
N413HS	**HS25**	**258119**
N413JP	LJ35	421
(N413KA)	C500	250
N413LC	C560	0003
N413LC	LJ35	659
N413LJ	LJ45	013
(N413LV)	CL64	5372
N413LX	BE40	RK-209
(N413LX)	BE40	RK-50
N413MA	LJ35	413
N413MH	C650	0148
N413QS	**GLF4**	**1521**
(N413SC)	ASTR	013
N413SK	**C56X**	**5793**
N413ST	**C550**	**550-0894**
N413TX	**GALX**	**061**
N413VP	C550	412
(N413VS)	GLF4	1413
N413WF	LJ24	211
N413WW	WW24	413
N414AA	C56X	5701
N414BM	GLF4	1214
N414BX	LJ45	111
N414CB	C500	589
(N414CB)	C500	576
N414CC	C500	414
N414CC	F2TH	206
N414DH	CL30	20188
N414DH	**CL30**	**20516**
N414DH	GALX	023
N414DH	GALX	081
N414DK	GALX	023
N414DY	CL30	20188
N414FJ	F900	19
N414FW	**C52A**	**0081**
N414FX	LJ45	111
N414GC	C550	096
(N414JC)	FA20	369
N414KB	GALX	022
N414KD	C52B	0208
N414KD	GALX	022
N414KD	GALX	084
N414KL	LJ35	595
N414KU	**C52C**	**0175**
(N414LX)	BE40	RK-53
N414PE	**HS25**	**258090**
N414RF	HS25	257060
N414RF	LJ55	033
(N414RK)	BE40	RK-14
N414TB	**LJ55**	**022**
N414TE	**PRM1**	**RB-4**
N414TJ	LJ35	414
N414TR	F2EX	135
N414TW	**EA50**	**000147**
N414VE	LJ45	414
N414VF	LJ45	414
(N414VP)	C550	413
(N414XL)	C56X	5248
N414XP	HS25	258266
N415AJ	**C550**	**600**
(N415BA)	HS25	256017
N415BE	CL30	20415
N415BJ	HS25	258257
N415BS	**ASTR**	**081**
N415CL	LJ45	308
N415CS	C525	0373
N415CS	SBRL	282-76
N415CS	SBRL	465-42
N415CT	BE40	RJ-15
N415DJ	LJ35	415
N415EL	WW24	415
N415F	FA20	416
(N415FC)	C500	145
N415FJ	F900	20
N415FL	**BE40**	**RK-506**
N415FW	C750	0095
N415FX	LJ45	112
N415GA	GLF4	1023
N415GA	GLF4	1059
N415GA	GLF4	1110
N415GA	GLF4	1144
N415GA	GLF4	1194
N415GA	GLF4	1293
N415GA	GLF4	1415
N415GA	GLF4	1515
N415GA	GLF5	5415
N415GS	SBRL	282-76
N415JA	**HS25**	**258516**
N415JW	FA20	369
N415KA	**C52C**	**0205**
N415LJ	LJ24	092
N415LS	LJ35	229
N415LT	**GLF4**	**1367**
N415LX	BE40	RK-225
(N415LX)	BE40	RK-56
N415NG	**CL30**	**20061**
N415NP	**LJ60**	**024**
N415P	**GLF5**	**5312**
(N415P)	GLF4	1260
N415PG	GLF4	1238
N415PR	**GALX**	**017**
N415PT	CL60	1053
N415PT	HS25	258016
N415QS	**GLF4**	**4014**
N415RC	MU30	A015SA
N415RD	HS25	257094
(N415RD)	LJ35	236
N415SE	**GALX**	**101**
N415SG	**LJ60**	**283**
N415SH	GLF4	1125
N415SL	C52A	0051
N415TH	WW24	415
N415TX	**GALX**	**070**
N415VE	LJ45	415
N415VF	GALX	237
N415WW	GLF4	1226
N416AS	FA10	16
N416BA	**C560**	**0359**
N416BB	GLEX	9043
N416BD	CL64	5548
N416BD	GLEX	9043
N416BD	**GLEX**	**9375**
N416BS	**C560**	**0793**
N416CC	**C550**	**415**
N416CG	GLF2	180
N416CM	**C510**	**0016**
N416CS	SBRL	282-81
N416CT	**BE40**	**RJ-43**
N416CW	BE40	RK-16
N416F	FA20	416
N416F	FA20	417

N416FJ	F900	22
N416FJ	FA20	417
N416FX	LJ45	113
N416G	LJ24	325
N416GA	GLF4	1027
N416GA	GLF4	1111
N416GA	GLF4	1145
N416GA	GLF4	1213
N416GA	GLF4	1258
N416GA	GLF4	1294
N416GA	GLF4	1416
(N416H)	C560	0104
N416HC	FA10	16
N416HF	C560	0037
N416K	GLF2	126
N416K	GLF2	41
N416KC	C525	0130
N416KC	**F9DX**	**618**
N416KC	FA50	318
N416KD	GLF2	231
N416KD	JSTR	5153/61
N416LJ	LJ24	093
(N416LX)	BE40	RK-226
(N416LX)	BE40	RK-57
N416MU	C510	0416
(N416NL)	WW24	187
N416NP	GLF3	875
N416QS	GLF4	1316
N416RD	HS25	257062
N416RJ	**GLF5**	**587**
N416RM	FA20	426
N416RM	LJ25	301
N416RP	BE40	RK-7
N416RX	**BE40**	**RK-514**
N416SH	GLF2	15
N416SJ	**JSTR**	**5153/61**
N416TM	BE40	RK-472
N416VP	C560	0416
N416W	WW24	416
N416WM	**GLF3**	**487**
N417AM	LJ55	123
N417BA	**LJ35**	**257**
N417BJ	BE40	RJ-17
N417C	C525	0174
N417C	C525	0385
N417C	C52B	0006
N417C	**C52C**	**0021**
N417CG	**EA50**	**000094**
N417CL	CL61	5107
N417CS	C52B	0090
N417CS	**GLEX**	**9255**
N417CW	BE40	RK-17
N417EK	GLF2	110
N417EL	WW24	417
N417F	FA20	418
N417FJ	F900	24
N417FX	LJ45	114
N417GA	GALX	217
N417GA	GALX	237
N417GA	GLF4	1112
N417GA	GLF4	1146
N417GA	GLF4	1217
N417GA	GLF4	1267
N417GA	GLF4	1295
N417GA	GLF4	1317
N417GA	GLF4	1417
N417GA	GLF4	4117
(N417GA)	GLF2	41
N417GR	**C510**	**0176**
(N417GW)	WW24	417
(N417H)	C560	0170
N417JD	C550	550-1124
N417JD	C56X	5231
N417JD	**C56X**	**6041**
N417JD	LJ24	253
N417JP	C550	550-1124
N417KM	C52B	0103
N417KT	MU30	A083SA
N417KW	C550	550-0933
N417LJ	LJ24	094
N417LJ	LJ45	017
N417LX	**GLEX**	**9620**
N417LX	BE40	RK-230
(N417LX)	BE40	RK-61
N417MD	**FA20**	**417**
N417MH	**C52A**	**0054**
N417NK	GLF4	1203
N417NZ	C750	0010
N417PC	WW24	415
N417PJ	JSTR	5098/28
N417PJ	LJ25	075
N417Q	**C525**	**0385**
(N417Q)	C525	0174
(N417QS)	GLF4	1417
N417RC	C500	606
N417RC	C555	0055
(N417RD)	GLF2	3
N417RQ	C500	606
(N417TF)	HS25	25038
N417TM	**HS25**	**258657**
N417TX	GALX	092
N417WW	LJ24	171
N418AB	GLEX	9029
N418BA	HS25	257057
N418CA	**HS25**	**258218**
N418CA	LJ36	018
N418CG	C550	417
N418CK	C56X	5042
(N418CQ)	C525	0677
N418CS	**C52B**	**0108**
N418CT	**BE40**	**RJ-42**
N418CW	BE40	RK-18
N418DL	**LJ31**	**181**
N418DM	HS25	257069
N418FA	LJ45	120
N418FJ	F900	25
N418FX	LJ45	120
N418GA	GLF4	1318
N418GA	GLF4	1418
N418GA	GLF4	4118
N418GA	GLF4	4180
N418GA	GLF5	5418
N418GJ	**BE40**	**RK-418**
N418KC	**C525**	**0130**
N418KS	LJ25	372
N418KW	**C550**	**550-0959**
N418LJ	LJ24	081
N418LJ	LJ45	018
N418LX	BE40	RK-234
(N418LX)	BE40	RK-62
N418MA	C550	159
N418MG	**BE40**	**RJ-54**
N418MN	**LJ45**	**130**
N418PP	**CL61**	**3041**
N418QA	GLF4	1018
N418R	C500	650
N418R	LJ31	075
N418R	LJ60	047
N418RD	**HS25**	**257015**
N418RM	BE40	RJ-18
N418RT	LJ31	075
N418S	FA20	32
N418S	FA50	64
N418SG	GLF5	5040
N418SG	GLF5	5207
N418SG	**GLF5**	**5316**
N418SG	GLF5	609
N418SM	GLF5	609
N418SP	GLF4	1218
N418TM	**BE40**	**RK-475**
N418TT	GLF4	1118
N418WA	**WW24**	**250**
(N419BL)	LJ25	220
N419CW	BE40	RK-19
N419ET	LJ40	2083
N419F	FA20	419
N419FJ	F900	27
N419FX	LJ45	125
N419GA	GALX	119
N419GA	GLF4	1025
N419GA	GLF4	1052
N419GA	GLF4	1147
N419GA	GLF4	1195
N419GA	GLF4	1296
N419GA	GLF4	1419
N419GA	GLF5	5219
N419GL	LJ25	294
N419HB	HA4T	RC-19
N419K	C500	080
(N419LX)	BE40	RK-68
N419MB	BE40	RK-85
N419MK	**ASTR**	**066**
N419MS	GLF2	81
N419MS	BE40	RK-121
N419MS	BE40	RK-85
N419PJ	**E55P**	**50500281**
N419RD	HS25	257153
N419TK	ASTR	122
N419TM	**BE40**	**RK-495**
N419TX	GALX	066
N419W	WW24	419
N419WC	**ASTR**	**053**
N419WC	FA10	11
N419XP	HS25	258419
N420A	JSTR	5063
N420AG	**GLEX**	**9006**
N420AH	**HDJT**	**42000003**
N420AM	C500	410
N420AZ	**HDJT**	**42000015**
N420BD	**BE40**	**RK-498**
N420BG	**LJ55**	**123**
N420BT	**HDJT**	**42000022**
N420CC	C555	0023
N420CC	GLF4	1164
N420CE	ASTR	139
N420CE	WW24	405
N420CH	C525	0066
N420CH	C52A	0027
N420CH	**C52B**	**0151**
N420CL	FA20	391
N420CL	**FA50**	**10**
N420CR	**C52A**	**0215**
N420CS	C52B	0115
N420CT	**BE40**	**RK-517**
N420DE	HDJT	42000017
N420DH	BE40	RK-326
N420DM	C560	0210
N420DM	C560	0464
N420DP	FA20	391
N420EA	**HDJT**	**42000016**
N420EA	HDJT	42000017
N420EH	**C52A**	**0027**
N420ET	HDJT	42000016
N420EU	HDJT	42000018
N420EX	**HDJT**	**42000011**
N420F	FA20	420
(N420FA)	MU30	A042SA
N420FJ	F900	28
N420FL	**BE40**	**RK-541**
N420FX	LJ45	126
N420G	JSTR	5063
N420GA	GALX	220
N420GA	GLF4	1007
N420GA	GLF4	1045
N420GA	GLF4	1124
N420GA	GLF4	1196
N420GA	GLF4	1297
N420GA	GLF4	1420
N420GA	GLF4	4120
N420GL	FA20	391
N420GT	C650	0020
N420HA	**HDJT**	**P001**
N420HB	HA4T	RC-20
N420HE	HDJT	42000016
N420HE	**HDJT**	**42000017**
N420HJ	**HDJT**	**42000001**
N420HM	**HDJT**	**42000002**
N420J	FA20	369
N420J	WW24	193
N420JB	**HDJT**	**42000028**
N420JC	**GLF3**	**326**
N420JC	HS25	25115
N420JD	FA10	115
N420JM	GLF2	94
N420JM	WW24	193
N420JM	WW24	363
N420JP	LJ60	147
(N420JP)	FA50	168
(N420JP)	LJ60	368
N420JT	GLF2	94
N420KA	**HDJT**	**42000013**
N420KH	**C550**	**403**
N420KK	F9EX	84
N420KM	**LJ60**	**197**
N420KV	LJ60	197
N420L	CL60	1027
N420L	JSTR	5063
N420LJ	LJ31	111
(N420LX)	BE40	RK-91
N420MP	**CL30**	**20420**
N420MP	WW24	418
N420MX	HDJT	42000019
N420NC	**HDJT**	**42000004**
N420P	C550	250
N420P	WW24	6
N420PC	C500	462
N420PC	**C500**	**640**
N420PC	FA10	186
N420PC	LJ35	132
N420PD	**F9EX**	**84**
N420PL	**C56X**	**6180**
N420PR	CL60	1039
N420QS	GLF4	1320
N420RC	C500	462
N420RC	GLF3	354
N420SK	**CL64**	**5590**
N420SL	GLF4	1025
N420SS	C550	469
N420ST	CL61	5027
N420SZ	CL61	5027
N420SZ	GLF4	1025
N420TG	HDJT	42000017
N420TJ	MU30	A042SA
N420TJ	WW24	405
N420TX	CL60	1027
N420W	WW24	420
N420WR	LJ24	130
N421AE	FA50	278
N421AL	**GLEX**	**9051**
N421CJ	C550	421
(N421CP)	C525	0083
N421EK	**HDJT**	**42000030**
N421FJ	F900	29
N421FX	LJ45	127
N421FX	LJ45	145
N421FY	LJ45	127
N421GD	**GLF5**	**5421**
N421GM	GLF3	421
N421L	LJ24	096
N421LT	C560	0311
N421LT	**C56X**	**5370**
(N421LX)	BE40	RK-239
(N421LX)	BE40	RK-93
N421MP	**C52B**	**0328**
N421QL	LJ55	026
N421QS	**GLF4**	**4114**
N421SV	**LJ35**	**660**
N421SZ	CL61	5027
N421SZ	GLEX	9056
N421SZ	GLEX	9239
N421SZ	GLF4	1025
N421SZ	HS25	257146
N421TX	C550	250
N421XR	LJ60	421
N421ZC	FA20	117
N422AB	C56X	5285
N422AJ	**LJ45**	**437**
N422AW	WW24	422
N422B	LJ25	331
N422BC	**C650**	**0024**
N422BC	WW24	302
N422CC	C500	422
N422CP	CL30	20061
N422CP	**CL30**	**20548**
N422CP	LJ60	171
N422CR	CL30	20061
N422CR	LJ60	171
N422CS	**HS25**	**258110**
N422CW	BE40	RK-22
N422D	FA20	498
N422DA	C500	422
N422DV	GLF2	17
N422F	FA20	421
(N422F)	FA20	422
N422FJ	F900	31
N422FL	**BE40**	**RK-346**
N422FX	LJ45	135
N422G	LJ25	285
N422GA	G150	222
N422GA	GALX	122
N422GA	GLF4	1248
N422GA	GLF4	1298
N422GA	GLF4	1422
N422GA	GLF4	4122
N422GA	GLF4	4222
N422GA	GLF4	4322
(N422HB)	HA4T	RC-22
N422HS	PRM1	RB-74
N422JR	LJ24	092
N422JT	C560	0774
N422KS	LJ40	2049
N422L	FA20	498
(N422LX)	BE40	RK-103
N422MJ	C555	0010
N422ML	**C680**	**0068**
N422ML	GLF4	1367
N422MP	**CL30**	**20422**
N422MU	FA20	484
N422PR	CL61	5001
N422QS	GLF4	1322
N422RR	C510	0446
N422TG	**C510**	**0429**
N422TK	**GLF3**	**395**
N422TK	HS25	256060
N422TR	HS25	256060
N422TX	GALX	093
N422U	LJ24	155
N422VP	C525	0422
N422X	**HS25**	**257074**
N422XR	LJ60	422
N423AK	BE40	RK-328
N423BB	**C52B**	**0095**
N423CS	**C52B**	**0121**
N423D	C550	183
N423DC	LJ45	135
N423F	FA20	423
N423FA	LJ45	134
N423FJ	F900	32
N423FX	LJ45	134
N423GA	GLF4	1009
N423GA	GLF4	1044
N423GA	GLF4	1113
N423GA	GLF4	1197
N423GA	GLF4	1249
N423GA	GLF4	1299
N423GA	GLF4	1423
N423GA	GLF4	1523
N423GA	GLF4	4123
N423GA	GLF4	4223
N423GA	GLF5	5423
N423HB	HA4T	RC-23
N423JG	**CL30**	**20266**
N423LM	C56X	6022
(N423LX)	BE40	RK-105
N423RD	C500	227
N423RD	LJ25	027
N423SA	GLF3	429
N423SJ	HS25	258135
N423TT	GLF4	1085
N423TX	CL65	5878
(N423XR)	LJ60	423
N424AD	C500	266
N424BT	**BE40**	**RJ-62**
N424CJ	C52A	0224
N424CJ	C52C	0024
N424CS	**WW24**	**255**
N424CV	C560	0424
N424DA	C500	029
N424DN	LJ35	061
N424F	FA20	424
N424FJ	F900	33
N424FX	LJ45	146
N424GA	G150	224
N424GA	GALX	127
N424GA	GLF4	1004
N424GA	GLF4	4124
N424GA	GLF5	5024
N424GA	GLF5	5442
N424GC	GLF2	115
N424HH	C560	0517
N424HH	**C56X**	**5534**
N424JM	SBRL	465-36
(N424JM)	CL61	3064
N424JP	LJ25	141
N424JR	LJ25	141
N424JR	LJ35	092
N424JR	**WW24**	**405**
N424JX	FA20	23
N424KW	**LJ60**	**153**
N424LB	C650	0076
N424LF	LJ40	2024
N424LJ	LJ60	424
N424LX	BE40	RK-245
(N424LX)	BE40	RK-108
N424ML	**LEG5**	**55000007**
N424MP	ASTR	129
N424MP	CL30	20594
N424MW	**LJ60**	**171**
N424NJ	LJ24	100
N424PX	**GLF4**	**4101**
N424QS	GLF4	1324
N424R	SBRL	306-3
N424R	**SBRL**	**380-15**
N424RD	LJ24	154
N424RD	LJ25	016
(N424RD)	C500	190
N424RJ	HS25	257010
N424RS	**LJ24**	**258**
N424SK	**BE40**	**RK-328**
N424TG	C550	285
N424TG	**LJ45**	**169**
N424TM	CL30	20051
N424TV	**C525**	**0145**
N424VE	LJ45	424
N424W	WW24	424
(N424XR)	LJ60	424
N424XT	**FA20**	**316**
N425A	GLF2	39
N425AS	**LJ35**	**281**
N425BD	CL30	20425
N425BJ	**BE40**	**RJ-25**
N425CS	**C52B**	**0132**
N425CT	**BE40**	**RK-523**
N425CW	BE40	RK-345
N425DC	HS25	25079
N425DN	LJ35	065
N425EJ	LJ24	009
N425F	FA20	425
N425FD	HS25	25079
N425FJ	F900	34
N425FX	**CL30**	**20454**
N425FX	LJ45	147
N425G	**LJ45**	**307**
N425GA	GLF4	1198
N425GA	GLF4	1250
N425GA	GLF4	1425
N425GA	GLF4	1525
N425GA	GLF4	4125
N425GA	GLF4	4215
N425GA	GLF4	4325
N425GA	GLF5	5425
N425GS	**LJ60**	**425**
N425GT	**C550**	**081**
N425JA	FA20	51
N425JF	FA20	51
N425JF	**FA20**	**64**
N425JF	WW24	210
(N425JF)	HS25	25284
N425JL	LJ25	127
N425JR	**FA10**	**162**
N425JS	C500	279
N425JX	LJ25	059
N425K	HS25	25114
N425KG	**HS25**	**257001**
N425LW	LJ45	147
(N425LX)	BE40	RK-145
N425M	**LJ31**	**055**
N425M	LJ35	281
(N425MK)	JSTR	5123/14
N425NA	SBRL	282-95
N425NJ	LJ24	105
N425PQ	**C680**	**0517**
N425QS	**GLF4**	**4010**
N425RA	LJ25	351
N425RD	LJ25	024
N425RH	LJ25	351
N425RJ	FA20	484
N425RJ	HS25	257010
N425RJ	WW24	218
N425SA	**LJ35**	**425**
N425SC	LJ24	097
N425SD	HS25	257018
N425SP	GLF3	425
N425ST	**C550**	**709**
N425SU	**CL61**	**3064**
N425SV	**GLF3**	**360**
N425TS	ASTR	004
"N425TS"	ASTR	004
N425VE	LJ45	425
N425WA	WW24	425
N425WH	**C525**	**0537**
N425WN	CL61	3052
N425WN	HS25	257159
N425WY	C550	669
N425XF	CL30	20454
N426CB	BE40	RK-403
(N426CC)	C500	426
(N426CC)	FA20	205
N426CF	CL64	5338
N426CF	GLEX	9340
N426CH	**C56X**	**5222**
N426CJ	C52A	0426
N426CM	**C750**	**0117**
N426DA	MU30	A062SA
N426EA	**BE40**	**RK-275**

N426ED	**C525**	**0426**
N426EJ	LJ24	014
N426EM	LJ55	040
N426F	FA20	428
N426FJ	F900	36
N426FL	BE40	RK-376
N426FX	LJ45	162
N426GA	GLF4	1010
N426GA	GLF4	1054
N426GA	GLF4	1126
N426GA	GLF4	1215
N426GA	GLF4	1426
N426GA	GLF4	4126
N426GA	GLF4	4226
N426GA	**GLF4**	**4266**
N426GA	GLF4	4326
N426GF	**BE40**	**RK-218**
N426JK	C550	550-0856
N426JK	LJ40	2092
N426JN	LJ60	142
N426LF	C510	0170
N426LW	LJ45	162
(N426LX)	BE40	RK-146
N426MD	BE40	RJ-26
N426MJ	**HS25**	**258759**
N426N	**C510**	**0318**
N426NA	LJ24	292
N426NS	C510	0318
N426NS	**C52B**	**0457**
N426PE	CL61	5046
N426PF	CL61	5046
N426PF	**CL64**	**5547**
N426PS	LJ24	148
N426QS	**GLF4**	**1426**
N426RJ	**WW24**	**218**
(N426SP)	C550	425
N426ST	**FA20**	**426**
N426TA	**LJ24**	**181**
N426TM	**HS25**	**258680**
(N426TM)	MU30	A026SA
N426TT	GLF4	4236
(N426VP)	C52C	0026
N426WW	WW24	426
N426XP	HS25	258426
N427AC	GLF2	95/39
N427BX	LJ45	163
N427CD	C560	0633
N427CJ	FA10	67
N427CS	C52B	0152
N427CW	BE40	RK-27
(N427CW)	BE40	RJ-27
N427DA	HS25	25220
N427DB	**PRM1**	**RB-223**
N427DC	LJ40	2079
N427DJ	BE40	RK-276
N427DM	C500	179
N427EJ	LJ24	021
N427F	FA20	426
N427FJ	F900	37
N427FL	**BE40**	**RK-368**
N427FX	LJ45	163
N427GA	G280	2027
N427GA	GLF4	1016
N427GA	GLF4	1060
N427GA	GLF4	1127
N427GA	GLF4	1148
N427GA	GLF4	1268
N427GA	GLF4	1316
N427GA	GLF4	1427
N427GA	GLF4	4127
N427GA	GLF4	4217
N427GA	GLF4	4327
N427GW	**F2TH**	**20**
N427HG	**GLF5**	**662**
N427JX	LJ24	257
N427KP	**C525**	**0837**
N427LJ	LJ24	100
(N427LX)	BE40	RK-149
N427MD	HS25	257095
N427MG	GLF4	4180
N427MJ	**F2TS**	**717**
N427NJ	LJ24	021
N427PM	**LJ60**	**210**
N427RC	**C510**	**0423**
N427RD	LJ25	082
N427RR	**C650**	**0178**
N427RR	E50P	50000150
N427SA	**GLF4**	**1314**
N427SS	C500	681
N427TL	LJ55	006
N427TM	**HS25**	**258720**
N427WW	WW24	427
N427X	**EA50**	**000253**
N428AS	GLF4	1487
N428AS	HS25	257026
N428AZ	GLF4	1487
N428BB	LJ31	209
N428BR	**C52B**	**0205**
N428CC	**FA50**	**225**
(N428CH)	LJ25	350
N428CJ	C52C	0028
N428CJ	PRM1	RB-137
N428CL	CL61	5108
N428CS	**C52B**	**0165**
N428DA	JSTR	5048
N428EJ	LJ24	022
N428F	FA20	430
N428FJ	F900	39
N428FS	HS25	257026
N428FX	LJ45	164
N428GA	GLF4	1028
N428GA	GLF4	1114
N428GA	GLF4	1199
N428HR	BE40	RK-244
N428JD	**G150**	**210**
N428JD	BE40	RJ-13
N428JF	**C52A**	**0428**
N428JF	WW24	210
N428JM	WW24	193
N428JX	LJ25	103
N428KS	GLF4	1360
N428LX	BE40	RK-264
(N428LX)	BE40	RK-161
N428M	GLF4	1382
N428NG	MU30	A086SA
N428P	C510	0339
N428P	**E55P**	**50500031**
N428PC	C525	0314
(N428PC)	C525	0324
N428QS	GLF4	1328
N428RJ	C500	082
N428SJ	C560	0584
N428SK	C510	0428
N428TT	GLF4	4004
(N428TT)	GLF4	4236
N428W	WW24	428
N428WE	BE40	RK-72
N428WT	GLF5	599
N429AC	HS25	25115
N429AL	GLF4	1061
(N429BA)	HS25	256058
N429CC	**EA50**	**000060**
N429CS	**C52B**	**0177**
N429DA	HS25	25090
N429DD	GLF3	354
N429DD	**GLF4**	**1293**
N429EJ	LJ24	023
N429F	FA20	431
N429FC	**LJ55**	**091**
N429FJ	F900	40
N429FL	**BE40**	**RK-423**
N429FX	LJ45	165
N429GA	GLF4	1029
N429GA	GLF4	1128
N429GA	GLF4	1251
N429GA	GLF4	1319
N429GA	GLF4	1429
N429GA	GLF4	4129
N429GA	GLF4	4219
N429GA	GLF4	4329
N429JG	BE40	RK-67
N429JS	**C56X**	**5249**
N429JX	GLF2	122
N429LX	BE40	RK-265
(N429LX)	BE40	RK-168
N429MR	**C52C**	**0011**
N429PK	C525	0429
N429RC	C500	078
N429SA	F2EX	178
N429SA	GLF3	429
N429SA	GLF4	1314
N429SJ	F2TH	66
(N429TJ)	LJ25	042
N429TM	**HS25**	**258767**
(N429W)	WW24	429
N429WG	CL61	5010
N429WG	**CL64**	**5341**
N430A	WW24	430
N430AC	**FA50**	**146**
N430AM	**C560**	**0542**
N430BB	HS25	258178
N430BC	GLF2	27
N430BJ	WW24	430
(N430BX)	LJ45	166
N430C	WW24	49
N430CS	C52B	0185
N430CW	BE40	RK-30
N430DC	WW24	87
N430DP	GLF2	167
N430EJ	LJ24	027
N430F	FA20	432
N430FJ	F900	41
N430FX	LJ45	166
N430GA	GLF4	1030
N430GA	GLF4	1115
N430GA	GLF4	1149
N430GA	GLF4	1200
N430GR	C525	0430
N430GW	PRM1	RB-208
N430HM	LJ55	043
N430J	LJ24	091
N430JA	LJ24	091
N430JF	**C525**	**0530**
N430JH	C525	0530
N430JH	**C52B**	**0355**
N430JW	LJ24	285
N430LJ	LJ24	103
N430LR	HS25	259030
(N430LX)	BE40	RK-178
N430MB	JSTR	5153/61
N430MB	SBRL	282-113
N430MP	**SBRL**	**282-113**
N430PC	WW24	87
N430PT	**WW24**	**430**
N430QS	**GLF4**	**4021**
N430R	GLF2	6
N430RG	GLF2	235
N430SA	**C650**	**7041**
N430SA	GLF2	92
N430SK	**CL30**	**20030**
N430TB	**E50P**	**50000052**
N430W	WW24	430
N430WC	**CL30**	**20288**
N431AM	WW24	431
N431AS	LJ35	431
N431BC	LJ31	005
N431CA	LJ24	030
N431CB	C550	431
N431CB	C650	0084
N431CB	CL61	5164
N431CC	C500	431
N431CK	**LJ35**	**431**
(N431CQ)	C650	0084
N431CS	**C52B**	**0228**
N431CW	LJ35	431
N431CW	BE40	RK-31
N431DA	**LJ31**	**163**
(N431DA)	SBRL	282-111
N431DC	LJ40	2091
N431DS	C550	324
N431EH	CL30	20431
N431EJ	LJ24	030
N431FJ	F900	42
N431FL	**FA20**	**249**
(N431FL)	BE40	RK-230
N431FX	LJ45	177
N431GA	GLF4	1116
N431GA	GLF4	1201
(N431GA)	GLF4	1039
(N431GH)	F2EX	72
(N431JC)	C550	430
N431JG	GLF3	417
N431JT	GLF3	417
N431JV	C560	0431
N431LC	**C500**	**177**
(N431LX)	BE40	RK-271
N431M	LJ35	132
N431MC	**C52A**	**0091**
N431MS	**C555**	**0127**
N431NA	SBRL	265-16
N431NA	SBRL	285-2
N431RC	**HS25**	**257170**
N431RX	LJ45	207
N431TX	C52C	0131
N431WA	**WW24**	**431**
N431WM	C555	0133
N431YD	C525	0431
N432AC	C750	0231
N432AC	HS25	258150
N432AQ	HS25	258150
N432AS	GLF4	4142
(N432AS)	LJ25	234
N432CC	C550	438
N432CC	**SBRL**	**465-6**
N432CJ	C52A	0043
N432CS	**C52B**	**0244**
N432CW	BE40	RK-32
N432DG	C500	403
N432EJ	LJ24	028A
N432EZ	FA10	130
N432F	FA20	433
N432FJ	F900	44
N432FJ	F9EX	234
N432FX	LJ45	197
N432GA	GLF4	1040
N432GA	GLF4	1125
N432GA	GLF4	1202
N432GA	GLF4	1300
N432GA	GLF4	4232
N432GA	GLF4	4321
N432GA	GLF5	5132
N432HC	**GLF4**	**1262**
N432HS	WW24	432
N432JW	LJ36	043
N432LW	**C52B**	**0003**
(N432LX)	BE40	RK-183
N432MA	C52A	0300
N432MA	**BE40**	**RK-370**
N432MC	CL64	5532
N432NM	**C550**	**083**
N432QS	GLF4	1032
N432RJ	**C550**	**550-0967**
N432SL	LJ25	241
N432TX	**C560**	**0154**
N432XP	HS25	258432
N433CJ	C52A	0433
N433CS	C52B	0257
N433CV	C560	0430
N433DC	CL30	20133
N433DC	**GLEX**	**9262**
N433DD	**LJ35**	**161**
N433EJ	LJ24	040
N433F	FA20	435
N433FJ	F900	45
N433FS	CL64	5433
N433FX	LJ45	192
N433GA	GALX	133
N433GA	GLF4	1041
N433GA	GLF4	1103
N433GA	GLF4	1150
N433GA	GLF4	1252
N433GA	GLF4	1301
N433GA	GLF4	1433
N433GA	GLF4	4133
N433GA	GLF4	4233
N433GA	GLF4	4333
N433GM	WW24	433
N433J	LJ24	038
N433J	LJ24	230
N433JA	LJ24	230
N433JB	LJ24	038
(N433JW)	LJ35	041
N433LF	C650	0027
N433LJ	LJ24	104
(N433LX)	BE40	RK-186
(N433LX)	BE40	RK-273
N433MM	C500	575
N433WR	WW24	433
N433WW	WW24	433
N434AN	JSTR	5050/34
N434CC	C550	434
N434CF	**C52A**	**0434**
(N434CJ)	LJ35	434
N434CS	C52B	0268
N434CS	C52B	0332
N434EJ	LJ24	046
N434F	FA20	436
N434FJ	F900	46
N434FX	LJ45	193
N434FX	LJ45	212
N434GA	GALX	134
N434GA	GLF4	1031
N434GA	GLF4	1203
N434GA	GLF4	1269
N434GA	GLF4	1302
N434GA	GLF4	1434
N434GA	GLF4	1534
N434GA	GLF4	4134
N434GA	GLF4	4234
N434GA	GLF4	4334
N434H	C650	0123
N434HB	HS25	HB-34
N434JM	**G150**	**250**
N434JW	GLF2	2
N434LX	BE40	RK-274
(N434LX)	BE40	RK-189
N434MT	**EA50**	**000061**
N434QS	GLF4	1334
N434SB	**C550**	**425**
N434UM	C500	190
N435AS	LJ24	345
N435CC	C500	435
N435CM	C52B	0411
N435CT	**BE40**	**RK-531**
N435CW	BE40	RK-35
N435DC	**LJ45**	**249**
(N435EC)	LJ35	018
N435F	FA20	437
(N435FA)	LJ45	209
N435FJ	F900	48
N435FX	LJ45	209
N435FX	LJ45	271
N435GA	GALX	135
N435GA	GLF4	1035
N435GA	GLF4	1135
N435GA	GLF4	1204
N435GA	GLF4	1253
N435GA	GLF4	1303
N435GA	GLF4	1435
N435GA	GLF4	1535
N435GA	GLF5	5235
N435GA	GLF5	5435
N435GM	GLF2	137
N435HB	C510	0426
N435HB	**C52C**	**0156**
N435HC	**GLF4**	**1450**
N435HH	**LJ45**	**335**
N435JD	**HS25**	**258298**
N435JF	**F2TH**	**47**
N435JL	LJ35	018
N435JW	LJ35	331
N435K	PRM1	RB-35
N435LX	BE40	RK-276
(N435LX)	BE40	RK-195
N435M	LJ35	086
N435MS	**LJ35**	**054**
N435N	LJ35	435
N435NF	**EA50**	**000189**
N435QS	**GLF4**	**4068**
N435SC	**E50P**	**50000294**
N435T	F2TH	9
N435T	**F9EX**	**63**
N435T	FA20	357
N435T	HS25	25083
N435TM	F2TH	9
N435TP	FA20	357
N435U	GLF3	435
N435UJ	LJ35	025
N435UM	C550	423
(N435W)	WW24	435
N435WW	WW24	435
N436BL	LJ35	436
N436CC	C500	436
N436CC	SBRL	306-36
N436CS	C52B	0274
N436DM	**CL61**	**5116**
N436DM	LJ35	389
N436EP	**C52B**	**0274**
N436FJ	F900	50
N436FL	**BE40**	**RK-279**
N436FX	LJ45	225
N436FX	LJ45	308
N436FX	LJ45	309
N436GA	GALX	136
N436GA	GLF3	436
N436GA	GLF4	1056
N436GA	GLF4	1130
N436GA	GLF4	1254
N436GA	GLF4	1304
N436GA	GLF4	1436
N436GA	GLF4	4136
N436GA	GLF4	4236
N436GA	GLF4	4336
N436JW	GLF2	73/9
N436LJ	LJ24	102
N436LX	BE40	RK-279
(N436LX)	BE40	RK-198
N436MP	FA20	436
N436QS	**GLF4**	**1436**
N436RB	**F9EX**	**91**
N436RB	FA20	436
N436RK	**BE40**	**RK-436**
N436RV	C52C	0036
N436WW	WW24	436
N437CC	C550	437
N437CF	C550	436
N437CS	C52B	0282
N437CW	BE40	RK-237
N437FJ	F900	51
N437FT	CL64	5437
N437FX	LJ45	227
N437FX	**LJ45**	**315**
N437GA	GLF3	396
N437GA	GLF4	1057
N437GA	GLF4	1131
N437GA	GLF4	1206
N437GA	GLF4	1255
N437GA	GLF4	1320
N437GA	**GLF4**	**1437**
N437H	GLF2	258
N437JD	C52A	0325
N437JD	HS25	258757
N437JD	**HS25**	**HA-0117**
(N437JL)	LJ60	367
N437JR	HS25	258757
N437LJ	LJ24	081
N437LJ	LJ45	437
(N437LX)	BE40	RK-201
N437MC	**CL64**	**5537**
N437MR	**C52C**	**0193**
N437SJ	**WW24**	**437**
N437T	HS25	25083
N437WR	**HS25**	**258963**
N437WW	WW24	437
N438	WW24	118
N438AD	C650	0094
N438AM	WW24	438
(N438AM)	MU30	A019SA
N438BC	**BE40**	**RK-438**
N438CC	C500	438
N438CS	C52B	0321
N438DA	BE40	RJ-38
N438DM	LJ25	250
N438E	CL64	5594
N438E	**CL64**	**5646**
N438FJ	F900	53
(N438FS)	WW24	438
N438FX	LJ45	317
N438FX	**LJ45**	**333**
N438GA	GLF4	1038
N438GA	GLF4	1256
N438HB	HA4T	RC-38
N438LJ	LJ24	113
N438LX	**BE40**	**RK-202**
N438MC	C560	0438
N438PM	HS25	257098
N438PM	HS25	258425
N438PM	**HS25**	**258636**
N438SJ	**FA20**	**438**
N438SP	C550	550-0882
N438SP	**C550**	**550-1026**
N438SP	C550	576
N438TA	C52A	0438
(N438W)	WW24	438
N438WR	**HS25**	**258983**
N439CL	CL61	5109
N439CS	C52B	0326
N439CW	BE40	RK-339
N439FJ	F900	55
N439FL	**BE40**	**RK-284**
N439FX	**LJ45**	**341**
N439GA	GLF4	1064
N439GA	GLF4	1118
N439GA	GLF4	1205
N439GA	GLF4	1305
N439GA	GLF4	1439
N439GA	GLF4	4039
N439GA	GLF4	4139
N439GA	GLF4	4239
N439GA	GLF4	4339
N439H	C650	0005
N439HB	HA4T	RC-39
N439LX	BE40	RK-284
(N439LX)	BE40	RK-209
N439ME	LJ35	439

(N439PW)	C525	0513
N439WW	**WW24**	**439**
N440AS	F2TH	102
N440AS	GLF4	4075
N440BC	HS25	25218
N440BM	LJ55	005
N440CE	**C550**	**550-0937**
N440CJ	C525	0440
N440CJ	C52A	0441
N440CP	GLF4	1118
N440CT	**BE40**	**RK-534**
N440CW	**BE40**	**RK-40**
N440CX	**HS25**	**258900**
N440DC	HS25	25079
N440DM	**F9EX**	**104**
N440DM	LJ25	348
N440DM	LJ55	005
N440DM	LJ60	262
N440DN	LJ60	262
N440DR	GLF2	69
N440DS	**BE40**	**RK-8**
N440EZ	C500	195
N440F	LJ25	262
N440FJ	F900	56
N440FL	**BE40**	**RK-289**
N440FX	**LJ45**	**346**
N440GA	GALX	240
N440GA	GLF4	1002
N440GA	GLF4	1216
N440GA	GLF4	4040
N440GA	GLF4	4340
N440HB	HA4T	RC-13
N440HM	LJ35	294
N440JB	LJ35	078
N440JJ	**LJ45**	**021**
N440JR	**BE40**	**RK-326**
N440KM	**CL61**	**5053**
N440KT	LJ24	249
N440LK	PRM1	RB-294
N440LN	**BE40**	**RK-189**
N440LN	BE40	RK-225
N440LX	BE40	RK-289
(N440LX)	BE40	RK-222
N440MB	**GLF4**	**4292**
N440MB	HA4T	RC-33
N440MC	LJ35	495
N440MC	**LJ60**	**301**
N440ML	**C56X**	**5323**
(N440MP)	BE40	RJ-16
N440NE	**EA50**	**000004**
N440PC	C650	0061
(N440PJ)	C550	396
N440QS	**GLF4**	**4025**
N440RC	**BE40**	**RK-269**
N440RD	HS25	25270
N440RM	JSTR	5016
N440SA	C650	7088
N440SC	LJ31	240
N440TC	GLF4	1115
N440TT	GALX	045
N440TX	C550	411
N440WF	**BE40**	**RK-440**
N440WW	WW24	440
N440XT	**BE40**	**RK-230**
N440XX	**E55P**	**50500166**
N441A	GLF3	342
N441A	JSTR	5123/14
N441BC	ASTR	033
N441BP	**C56X**	**5612**
N441CB	**CL30**	**20441**
N441CG	LJ55	014
N441CL	CL64	5441
N441CW	LJ35	410
N441DM	FA10	173
(N441EE)	BE40	RJ-41
N441FA	FA20	284
N441FJ	F900	57
N441FX	**LJ45**	**357**
N441GA	GLF4	1001
N441GA	GLF4	1207
N441GA	GLF4	1306
N441GC	**GLF5**	**5441**
N441JT	C500	601
N441JW	**GALX**	**195**
N441LX	BE40	RK-292
(N441LX)	BE40	RK-230
N441MB	HA4T	RC-33
N441PC	LJ35	441
N441PC	**LJ35**	**668**
N441PG	LJ35	441
N441PJ	**CL61**	**5170**
N441QS	GLF4	1341
N441T	C550	329
N441TC	C500	140
N442A	GLF2	255/18
N442A	SBRL	282-39
N442A	SBRL	306-21
N442AM	FA50	42
N442CJ	C525	0491
N442CW	BE40	RK-42
N442DM	LJ35	405
N442EA	**MU30**	**A058SA**
N442EW	**C680**	**0168**
N442F	FA20	438
N442FJ	F900	59
N442FL	**BE40**	**RK-334**
N442FP	LJ45	364
N442FX	**LJ45**	**364**
N442GA	G150	242
N442GA	GLF4	1065
N442GA	GLF4	1132
N442GA	GLF4	1270
N442GA	GLF4	1442
N442GA	GLF4	4042
N442GJ	**BE40**	**RK-442**
(N442HC)	LJ35	233
N442HM	**GLF4**	**4034**
N442JB	**C500**	**117**
N442JC	BE40	RJ-42
(N442JC)	MU30	A008SA
N442JT	LJ35	021
N442KM	**CS55**	**0060**
N442LF	GLEX	9142
N442LF	LJ45	019
N442LU	C56X	5609
N442LV	**C510**	**0153**
N442LV	C550	550-1028
N442LW	C550	550-1028
N442LW	C56X	5609
N442LW	C680	0168
N442LW	**C680**	**0539**
(N442LX)	BE40	RK-234
N442MA	**HS25**	**258378**
N442ME	C550	442
N442MR	C550	442
N442MS	**HS25**	**258199**
N442NE	LJ35	442
N442NR	C550	550-1078
N442QG	GLF2	133
N442RM	SBRL	306-73
N442RR	C52C	0042
(N442SC)	LJ36	040
N442SR	GLF4	4002
N442SW	C550	550-0840
N442SW	C550	550-0862
N442WE	**C750**	**0303**
N442WJ	C650	7025
N442WJ	C750	0099
N442WP	C750	0233
N442WP	SBRL	282-108
N442WT	C650	7025
N442WT	C750	0099
N442WT	C750	0233
N442WT	C750	0303
N442WT	**C750**	**0514**
N442WT	SBRL	282-108
N442WT	SBRL	465-45
N442WT	WW24	114
N442WT	WW24	77
N442XP	HS25	258442
N443A	WW24	354
N443BB	**E55P**	**50500106**
N443BP	PRM1	RB-243
N443C	BE40	RK-42
N443CJ	C525	0443
N443DB	**CL30**	**20552**
N443EA	**C560**	**0400**
N443F	FA20	439
N443FJ	F900	60
N443FX	LJ45	371
N443GA	G150	243
N443GA	GLF4	1066
N443GA	GLF4	1133
N443GA	GLF4	1208
N443GA	GLF4	1307
N443GA	GLF4	1443
N443GA	GLF4	4043
N443GA	GLF4	4343
N443GA	GLF5	5443
N443HC	C510	0012
N443LJ	LJ24	114
N443LJ	LJ45	443
N443LX	**BE40**	**RK-237**
N443M	**GLF5**	**5199**
N443M	HS25	258519
N443PR	**GLEX**	**9520**
N443PW	**C52B**	**0103**
N443RK	LJ35	023
N443SL	**LJ45**	**061**
N444A	C680	0218
N444A	C680	680A0003
N444AG	C500	434
N444AG	LJ24	208
N444AQ	LJ24	208
N444BC	**C750**	**0025**
N444BF	FA20	189
N444BF	LJ35	391
N444BL	C550	487
N444CC	C550	394
N444CM	LJ35	282
N444CR	FA10	45
N444CW	**C650**	**0064**
(N444CW)	C500	444
N444CX	C750	0125
N444CZ	**CL64**	**5363**
N444DN	**C560**	**0385**
N444EA	**C550**	**550-1079**
(N444EJ)	EA50	000272
N444EP	**WW24**	**436**
N444ET	**CL60**	**1062**
N444ET	MS76	101
N444EX	C650	7056
N444FJ	C550	070
N444FJ	FA20	284
N444FL	**BE40**	**RK-292**
N444FX	**LJ45**	**378**
N444G	**C550**	**232**
N444GA	GLF3	301
N444GA	GLF4	1321
N444GA	GLF4	4144
N444GA	GLF4	4244
N444GA	GLF4	4344
N444GB	C550	216
N444GG	**C560**	**0262**
(N444GV)	GLF4	1444
(N444H)	C525	0106
N444HC	LJ24	199
N444HC	**LJ31**	**064**
N444HC	LJ35	199
(N444HE)	LJ24	246
N444HH	HS25	25191
N444J	C500	179
N444JH	JSTR	5036/42
N444JJ	C550	160
N444KE	C650	7029
N444KM	GLF3	378
N444KM	**LJ40**	**2137**
N444KV	C500	223
N444KW	LJ24	147
(N444L)	C525	0304
N444LP	C500	223
N444LT	GLF4	1114
N444MA	SBRL	306-102
N444MG	HS25	258415
N444MJ	LJ35	444
N444MK	LJ25	252
(N444ML)	GLF2	173
N444MM	C550	317
N444MM	WW24	210
N444MV	C500	401
N444MW	C500	401
N444MW	LJ45	131
N444MW	WW24	372
N444PB	LJ25	227
N444PD	HS25	256001
N444PE	**FA50**	**143**
N444PE	HS25	256001
N444QC	**GLF4**	**1411**
N444QG	GLF2	133
N444QG	**GLF4**	**1453**
N444RF	**C560**	**0559**
"N444RF"	C525	0001
N444RH	C525	0001
N444RH	C52A	0099
N444RL	**EA50**	**000040**
N444RP	C500	250
N444SC	FA20	324
N444SC	LJ24	246
(N444SC)	LJ36	040
(N444SL)	MU30	A041SA
N444SS	PRM1	RB-16
N444TG	**LJ25**	**327**
N444TG	LJ35	469
N444TJ	GLF4	1010
N444TJ	WW24	146
N444TW	LJ24	348
N444WA	CL60	1005
N444WB	**LJ35**	**105**
N444WB	LJ35	318
N444WB	BE40	RJ-42
N444WC	LJ24	047
N444WJ	FA10	64
(N444WJ)	C550	088
N444WL	WW24	48
N444WS	LJ25	038
N444WW	**LJ25**	**283**
N445	WW24	37
N445A	WW24	362
N445AC	CL61	3051
N445AK	**ASTR**	**155**
N445AX	LJ45	206
N445BH	**CL65**	**5758**
N445BH	LJ45	006
N445BJ	**GLF4**	**1254**
N445BL	WW24	382
N445CC	C500	445
N445CC	BE40	RK-45
N445CJ	C525	0445
N445CT	**BE40**	**RK-535**
N445CW	BE40	RK-45
N445DB	**GLEX**	**9400**
N445E	BE40	RK-45
N445F	FA20	441
N445FD	LJ45	445
N445FD	**LJ45**	**455**
N445FJ	F900	63
N445FL	**BE40**	**RK-345**
(N445FX)	LJ45	397
(N445FX)	LJ45	479
N445GA	GLF4	1012
N445GA	GLF4	1077
N445GA	GLF4	1134
N445GA	GLF4	1209
N445GA	GLF4	1322
N445GA	GLF4	1445
N445GA	GLF4	4045
N445GA	GLF4	4245
N445GA	GLF4	4345
N445GA	GLF5	5445
N445LX	BE40	RK-298
(N445LX)	BE40	RK-244
N445MD	**GLF4**	**1366**
N445MU	**C510**	**0445**
N445N	**LJ45**	**202**
N445PK	**BE40**	**RK-45**
N445QS	GLF4	1445
N445QS	**GLF4**	**4037**
N445RM	**LJ45**	**206**
N445SB	LJ45	027
N445SE	**LJ45**	**334**
N445TG	**LJ45**	**332**
N445UC	HS25	257120
N445WF	**LJ45**	**299**
N446	LJ31	010
N446A	WW24	367
(N446BM)	FA10	211
N446CC	**HA4T**	**RC-64**
N446CJ	C52A	0446
N446CJ	**C52C**	**0046**
N446CW	BE40	RK-346
N446D	FA20	446
N446F	FA20	442
N446FJ	F900	64
N446GA	GLF3	488
N446GA	GLF4	1013
N446GA	GLF4	1067
N446GA	GLF4	1152
N446GA	GLF4	1219
N446GA	GLF4	1308
N446GA	GLF4	1446
N446GA	GLF4	4046
N446GA	GLF4	4246
N446GA	GLF4	4346
N446HB	HA4T	RC-46
N446JB	CL65	5794
N446LJ	**LJ45**	**446**
N446LX	BE40	RK-299
(N446LX)	BE40	RK-245
N446M	BE40	RK-199
N446RT	C680	0017
N446RT	**C680**	**0296**
N446TD	**F9EX**	**168**
(N446TW)	HS25	258590
N446U	GLF3	446
N446V	C500	552
N446VG	**GLF5**	**5253**
N447CC	BE40	RJ-38
N447CJ	C52A	0447
(N447CJ)	C550	447
N447CW	BE40	RK-347
N447F	FA20	443
(N447FA)	LJ60	220
N447FJ	F900	65
(N447FM)	C550	007
N447GA	GLF4	1014
N447GA	GLF4	1080
N447GA	GLF4	1211
N447GA	GLF4	1309
N447GA	GLF4	1447
N447GA	GLF4	4047
N447GA	GLF4	4147
N447GA	**GLF4**	**4347**
N447HB	HA4T	RC-47
N447LJ	LJ24	112
N447LX	BE40	RK-248
N447MJ	**C56X**	**5349**
N447SF	**C550**	**550-1020**
N447SP	**HS25**	**258618**
N447TF	PRM1	RB-68
N447TR	**GLF5**	**5438**
N448AS	CL30	20027
N448AS	F2EX	233
N448CC	HS25	259019
N448CJ	**C52C**	**0163**
N448CL	CL30	20027
N448CW	BE40	RK-348
N448CW	BE40	RK-368
N448DC	HS25	25078
N448DC	HS25	25079
N448E	**CL64**	**5601**
N448EA	C525	0448
N448EC	C500	191
N448FJ	F900	67
N448GA	GLF4	1048
N448GA	GLF4	1153
N448GA	GLF4	1210
N448GA	GLF4	1257
N448GA	GLF4	1310
N448GA	GLF4	1448
N448GA	GLF4	4048
N448GA	GLF4	4148
N448GA	**GLF4**	**4348**
(N448GA)	GLF4	1084
N448GC	LJ24	057
N448GC	LJ35	472
N448GG	LJ24	057
N448GL	**LJ60**	**206**
N448GR	**ASTR**	**070**
N448H	C560	0613
N448H	**HS25**	**258907**
N448HB	HA4T	RC-48
N448HC	**EA50**	**000161**
N448HM	LJ60	007
N448JC	C525	0448
N448JM	HS25	258404
N448LX	BE40	RK-305
N448PC	GLF2	226
N448QS	**GLF4**	**4100**
(N448QS)	GLF4	1408
N448RL	**C550**	**550-0990**
N448RT	C680	0017
N448SC	**BE40**	**RK-448**
N448TB	**FA20**	**439**
N448TM	**E55P**	**50500042**
N448W	**SBRL**	**380-63**
N448WC	LJ35	472
N448WG	LJ35	472
N448WT	SBRL	465-45
N448WT	WW24	114
N449A	FA10	49
N449BZ	**C52C**	**0198**
N449CW	BE40	RK-349
N449DT	C500	369
N449EB	HS25	257012
N449F	FA20	445
N449FJ	F900	68
N449GA	GALX	249
N449GA	GLF4	1085
N449GA	GLF4	1220
N449GA	GLF4	1311
N449GA	GLF4	1449
N449GA	GLF4	4049
N449GA	GLF4	4149
N449GA	**GLF4**	**4349**
N449HB	HA4T	RC-49
(N449JS)	LJ24	352
N449LJ	LJ24	115
N449LX	BE40	RK-257
N449MC	CL61	5022
N449ML	CL61	5022
N449ML	GLEX	9055
N449QS	LJ35	449
N449SA	C650	7088
N449SA	**F2EX**	**171**
(N449SA)	C650	7041
N449TM	**BE40**	**RK-573**
N450	LJ25	127
N450AB	**GLF4**	**4043**
N450AF	FA50	36
N450AJ	**C56X**	**5260**
N450AJ	CL60	1075
N450AK	**FA50**	**100**
N450AR	GLF4	1069
N450AR	GLF5	520
(N450AT)	BE40	RK-185
N450BC	**LJ45**	**075**
N450BD	**GLF3**	**412**
N450BE	**GLF4**	**4214**
N450BE	GLF5	554
N450BF	GLF4	1015
N450BK	LJ45	104
N450BM	ASTR	011
N450BV	**C52B**	**0167**
N450CB	GLF3	324
(N450CB)	BE40	RK-330
N450CC	C550	281
N450CE	**GLF4**	**4250**
(N450CE)	SBRL	306-22
N450CH	**LEG5**	**55010004**
N450CL	**FA50**	**76**
N450CM	**C52C**	**0022**
N450CP	**FA20**	**289**
(N450CT)	FA10	157
N450CW	BE40	RK-50
N450DA	HS25	256041
N450DK	CL64	5450
N450DR	FA50	113
(N450DS)	LJ45	142
N450EA	**GLF4**	**4065**
N450EE	**GLF4**	**4163**
N450EF	**GLF4**	**1379**
N450EJ	GLF4	4088
N450FC	**LJ45**	**416**
N450FJ	F900	70
N450FK	**GLF4**	**4031**
N450FX	**GLF4**	**4330**
N450GA	GLF4	4004
N450GA	GLF4	4039
N450GA	GLF4	4091
N450GA	GLF4	4144
N450GA	GLF4	4189
N450GA	GLF4	4275
N450GA	**GLF4**	**4331**
(N450GA)	GLF4	4020
N450GD	GLF4	4065
N450GD	GLF4	4117
N450GD	GLF4	4163
N450GD	GLF4	4225
N450GD	**GLF4**	**4308**
N450GM	C550	150
N450GM	C550	617
(N450GQ)	GLF4	4091
N450HA	**LJ45**	**098**
N450HE	**GLF4**	**4217**
N450JC	**LJ45**	**070**
N450JD	HS25	25148
N450JD	WW24	9
N450JE	GLF4	1233
N450JF	**E50P**	**50000184**
N450JG	LJ45	096
(N450JK)	GLF4	4031
N450JR	GLF4	4218
N450JS	**GLF4**	**4344**
N450K	FA50	186
N450KD	C550	410

N450KD	GLF4	1225
N450KK	**GLF4**	**1225**
N450KK	LJ35	450
N450KP	FA50	82
N450KR	**GLF4**	**4044**
N450L	**GLF4**	**4213**
N450LC	GLF4	4127
N450LV	**GLF4**	**4061**
(N450LX)	BE40	RK-260
N450MA	FA20	158/449
N450MB	**GLF4**	**1295**
N450MC	LJ35	368
N450MH	GLF2	225
(N450MK)	GLF4	4218
N450MM	**C560**	**0119**
N450MQ	**C560**	**0657**
N450MS	**GLF4**	**1055**
N450NE	**EA50**	**550-0280**
N450NS	GLF4	4079
N450PC	MU30	A024SA
N450PG	**GLF4**	**4072**
(N450PG)	GLF4	4056
N450PJ	GLF4	4123
N450PM	ASTR	011
N450PU	**GLF4**	**4095**
N450QS	**GLF4**	**4046**
N450RA	C560	0377
N450RA	WW24	13
N450RB	**EA50**	**000165**
N450RG	**GLF4**	**4038**
N450RS	C650	0061
N450SC	LJ25	127
N450T	C750	0054
N450T	**GLF4**	**4105**
N450TB	HS25	256026
N450TJ	**LJ45**	**012**
N450TJ	MU30	A005SA
N450TL	GLF4	1265
N450TM	**BE40**	**RK-508**
N450TR	**C52A**	**0227**
N450TR	LJ45	093
N450WB	**GLF4**	**4110**
N450WG	**GLF4**	**1328**
N450WH	**BE40**	**RK-119**
N450X	FA50	54
N450XX	**GLF4**	**4062**
N450Z	**GLF4**	**4012**
N451A	**LJ45**	**413**
N451AJ	**C52A**	**0110**
N451BH	**GLF4**	**4157**
N451BW	**LJ45**	**261**
N451C	**GLF4**	**4159**
(N451C)	GLF4	1279
N451CF	FA50	58
N451CF	LJ45	109
N451CG	**HS25**	**HA-0087**
N451CJ	C500	451
N451CL	**FA50**	**223**
N451CL	LJ45	149
N451CM	**GLF4**	**4024**
N451CS	GLEX	9134
N451CS	GLF2	70/1
N451CS	GLF5	570
N451CS	**GLF6**	**6063**
N451DA	**C550**	**108**
N451DC	**GLF4**	**4041**
N451DJ	LJ45	080
N451DP	FA20	249
(N451DZ)	LJ45	080
N451FJ	F900	71
N451FL	**BE40**	**RK-310**
N451FP	**C52A**	**0451**
N451FX	**GLF4**	**4332**
N451GA	**GLF4**	**1221**
N451GL	LJ45	149
N451GP	**C52B**	**0080**
N451GS	GLF2	70/1
N451GV	**GLF5**	**5451**
N451GX	**GLEX**	**9451**
N451HB	HA4T	RC-51
N451HC	LJ45	267
N451JC	GLF4	4152
N451JC	LJ45	218
(N451K)	LJ45	405
N451LC	GLF4	4195
N451LJ	**LJ45**	**259**
N451LX	BE40	RK-310
(N451LX)	BE40	RK-264
N451MM	PRM1	RB-137
N451MP	**C550**	**118**
N451N	**LJ45**	**230**
N451NS	**GLF4**	**4082**
N451PW	**GLF4**	**4312**
N451QS	GLF4	1351
N451QS	GLF4	4141
N451R	G150	227
N451RS	HS25	258748
N451SC	GLF4	4212
(N451SC)	LJ45	201
N451SD	**LJ45**	**411**
N451ST	LJ45	200
N451TM	**BE40**	**RK-576**
N451W	C56X	5232
N451WM	LJ45	091
N451XR	LJ45	319
N452A	LJ45	320
N452A	PRM1	RB-37
N452AC	**GALX**	**160**
N452AC	GLF5	519
N452AC	LJ35	508
N452AJ	C560	0494
(N452AJ)	C550	047
N452AR	**E50P**	**50000269**
N452AS	PRM1	RB-252
N452CF	**FA50**	**104**
N452CJ	C550	452
N452CJ	**LJ45**	**090**
N452CS	GLEX	9134
N452DA	**LJ35**	**452**
N452DP	FA10	11
N452ET	LJ25	152
N452F	FA20	440
N452FJ	F900	73
N452FL	**BE40**	**RK-317**
N452FX	**GLF4**	**4334**
N452GA	GLF4	1222
N452GA	GLF4	1271
N452GA	GLF4	1452
N452GA	GLF4	4052
N452GA	GLF4	4205
N452HB	HA4T	RC-52
(N452K)	LJ45	406
N452LJ	LJ24	118
N452LJ	LJ45	002
N452LX	BE40	RK-317
(N452LX)	BE40	RK-265
N452NS	GLF4	4094
N452QS	GLF4	1352
N452RS	**HS25**	**258799**
N452SB	BE40	RK-317
N452SD	LJ45	428
N452SM	HS25	258136
N452ST	LJ45	201
N452TM	**BE40**	**RK-577**
N452TS	C500	604
N452WU	CL64	5452
N453	LJ24	323
N453A	**LJ45**	**363**
N453AD	CL64	5453
N453AM	**LJ35**	**453**
N453BL	LJ45	022
N453CF	FA50	127
N453CM	HS25	25084
N453CV	C560	0453
N453CW	BE40	RK-53
N453DP	HS25	256044
N453DW	C510	0187
N453EP	HS25	257014
N453F	FA20	444
N453FD	**CL30**	**20453**
N453FJ	F900	74
N453FX	**GLF4**	**4336**
N453GA	GLF4	1223
N453GA	GLF4	1312
N453GA	GLF4	1453
N453GA	GLF4	4053
N453GA	GLF4	4153
N453GA	GLF4	4253
N453GA	**GLF4**	**4353**
N453GS	CL61	3011
N453HB	HA4T	RC-53
N453JE	**HA4T**	**RC-53**
N453JS	F900	144
N453JS	F9DX	605
N453JT	LJ24	033
(N453K)	LJ45	409
N453LJ	LJ24	033
N453LJ	LJ24	119
N453LJ	LJ45	003
(N453LX)	BE40	RK-268
N453MA	LJ25	291
N453S	**C550**	**445**
N453SA	LJ24	119
N453SB	FA20	308
N453SB	FA20	382
N453ST	LJ45	299
N453TM	HS25	258203
N453TM	**BE40**	**RK-581**
N454AC	**C500**	**373**
N454AJ	**F900**	**164**
N454AJ	GLEX	9153
N454AN	**LJ60**	**045**
N454AS	LJ45	038
(N454BE)	GLF3	472
N454CG	LJ45	085
N454DP	**FA10**	**130**
N454DP	HS25	256044
N454DQ	C500	579
N454DR	**E55P**	**50500005**
N454EP	HS25	257017
N454F	FA20	446
N454FJ	F900	76
N454FL	**BE40**	**RK-327**
N454FX	**GLF4**	**4339**
N454GA	GLF4	1224
N454GA	GLF4	1272
N454GA	GLF4	1323
N454GA	GLF4	1454
N454GA	GLF4	4054
N454GA	GLF4	4154
N454GA	GLF5	5354
N454GL	LJ24	121
N454HB	HA4T	RC-54
N454HC	MS76	090
N454JB	GLF3	345
N454JB	HS25	258003
N454JB	JSTR	5205
N454JF	LJ45	329
N454LC	LJ45	123
N454LC	LJ45	296
N454LC	**LJ45**	**419**
N454LJ	LJ24	121
N454LJ	LJ24	226
N454LJ	LJ45	004
N454LP	LJ45	034
N454LX	BE40	RK-327
(N454LX)	BE40	RK-271
N454MF	**C510**	**0454**
N454MK	LJ45	088
N454MM	**C56X**	**5737**
N454N	**LJ45**	**339**
N454QS	**GLF4**	**1454**
N454RJ	**BE40**	**RK-454**
N454RN	LJ24	121
(N454RR)	HA4T	RC-69
(N454RR)	LJ45	038
N454RT	C560	0454
N454SR	WW24	79
N454TH	**GALX**	**096**
N455BE	CL60	1069
N455BK	**HS25**	**257078**
N455BP	HA4T	RC-16
N455CW	BE40	RK-365
N455DE	LJ45	160
N455DG	**LJ45**	**129**
N455DM	C550	095
N455DW	**BE40**	**RJ-20**
N455DX	**F2TH**	**146**
N455EA	**LJ45**	**162**
(N455EC)	LJ55	043
N455EM	LJ55	014
N455F	FA20	447
N455FD	**C500**	**357**
N455FD	BE40	RJ-17
N455FJ	F900	77
N455FX	**GLF4**	**4340**
N455GA	GLF4	1313
N455GA	GLF4	1455
N455GA	GLF4	4055
N455GA	GLF4	4155
N455GA	GLF4	4255
N455H	C500	552
N455JA	LJ24	300
N455JD	**C650**	**0069**
N455LB	SBRL	465-49
N455LJ	LJ45	005
N455LX	BE40	RK-328
(N455LX)	BE40	RK-273
N455NE	LJ45	455
N455PM	LJ45	160
N455QS	**GLF4**	**4074**
N455RH	**LJ55**	**110**
N455RM	LJ35	171
N455S	WW24	367
N455SC	**LJ45**	**474**
N455SF	SBRL	465-49
N455SH	ASTR	017
N455SR	CL60	1032
N455TX	**C52C**	**0055**
(N455UJ)	LJ55	098
N455VP	C52A	0455
N456AB	C550	215
N456AF	C650	0147
N456AL	**GLF3**	**405**
N456AS	GLF2	17
N456AS	LJ45	039
N456BE	**GLF3**	**335**
N456BE	GLF4	1135
N456CE	C500	630
N456CG	**LJ25**	**343**
(N456CG)	CL60	1027
N456CJ	C680	0249
N456CL	**LJ35**	**456**
N456CM	FA10	207
(N456CM)	C550	456
N456CW	BE40	RK-56
N456DK	CL60	1081
N456FB	C560	0009
N456FJ	F900	78
N456FL	**BE40**	**RK-365**
(N456FL)	BE40	RK-146
N456GA	GLF4	4256
N456GA	**GLF5**	**5456**
N456GB	C500	256
N456HC	C56X	5517
N456HK	**CL64**	**5568**
N456JA	**G280**	**2064**
N456JA	LJ24	265
N456JG	BE40	RK-119
N456JN	**LJ31**	**076**
N456JP	SBRL	282-32
N456JW	C560	0266
N456JW	C56X	5033
N456KT	**CL30**	**20100**
N456LG	**LEG5**	**55000020**
N456LJ	LJ45	006
N456LM	LJ45	006
(N456LX)	BE40	RK-274
N456MF	**EA50**	**000050**
N456MS	CL64	5456
N456MS	GLEX	9149
N456MS	LJ35	017
N456N	C550	077
(N456NS)	BE40	RK-119
N456PR	ASTR	116
N456Q	LJ45	282
N456R	C500	472
N456RF	E50P	50000223
N456SC	LJ24	022
N456SL	C56X	5528
N456SM	**C680**	**0038**
N456SR	FA20	299
N456SW	C560	0222
N456SW	GLF3	337
N456SW	**GLF4**	**4304**
N456TM	**BE40**	**RK-585**
N456TX	**C550**	**215**
N456WH	HS25	25244
N457BE	GLF2	248
N457CA	C500	131
N457CF	C550	457
N457CP	**BE40**	**RK-557**
N457CS	C500	578
N457CW	BE40	RK-57
N457DS	**GLF4**	**1077**
N457F	FA20	449
(N457F)	C56X	5563
N457FJ	F900	79
N457GA	G150	257
N457GA	GLF4	1061
N457GA	GLF4	1123
N457GA	GLF4	1157
N457GA	GLF4	1162
N457GA	GLF4	1273
N457GA	GLF4	1324
N457GA	GLF4	4057
N457GA	GLF4	4257
N457GM	LJ24	340
N457H	GLF3	457
N457H	GLF4	1462
N457HB	HA4T	RC-57
N457HL	**CL60**	**1063**
N457J	**HS25**	**258085**
N457JA	LJ24	207
N457JC	**GLF3**	**457**
N457K	PRM1	RB-57
N457LJ	LJ24	120
N457LJ	LJ45	007
N457LJ	LJ45	457
(N457LX)	BE40	RK-276
(N457LX)	BE40	RK-345
N457MD	**C52A**	**0009**
N457SF	GLF3	409
N457ST	GLF3	409
N457ST	GLF4	1345
(N457ST)	GLF5	616
N457SW	GLF2	115
N457TB	**EA50**	**000088**
(N457TB)	EA50	000093
N458A	FA10	58
N458A	LJ45	397
(N458AJ)	CL60	1075
N458BE	GLF3	440
N458BE	**GLF4**	**1012**
N458BN	**GALX**	**071**
N458CC	C550	458
(N458CG)	LJ25	343
N458CK	**C560**	**0160**
N458DA	**C560**	**0458**
N458DP	**LJ45**	**008**
(N458DS)	C550	458
N458F	C550	550-0986
N458F	FA20	450
N458FA	GLF4	1159
N458FJ	F900	75
N458FS	**C56X**	**6011**
N458GA	G150	258
N458GA	GLF4	1058
N458GA	GLF4	1163
N458GA	GLF4	1274
N458GA	GLF4	4058
N458GA	GLF4	4158
N458GA	**GLF4**	**4358**
N458GA	GLF5	5458
(N458H)	C550	377
N458HC	**BE40**	**RJ-58**
N458HW	C550	377
N458J	LJ25	106
N458JA	LJ25	106
N458JA	LJ35	376
N458JW	C560	0266
N458LC	C56X	5109
N458LJ	LJ24	115
N458LM	**E50P**	**50000019**
(N458LX)	BE40	RK-279
N458MS	CL64	5458
N458MT	C525	0316
N458N	**C550**	**077**
(N458N)	C550	061
N458NC	**C560**	**0478**
N458PE	C555	0143
N458RM	**C650**	**7049**
N458SB	**FA20**	**308**
N458SF	**BE40**	**RK-90**
N458SM	C525	0541
N458SW	F2TH	192
N458SW	FA20	68
N458X	**GLF4**	**4138**
N459A	LJ31	137
N459BE	GLF4	1245
N459BE	**GLF5**	**541**
N459BN	**G280**	**2024**
N459BN	GALX	071
N459BN	GALX	195
N459CS	CL64	5546
N459DP	**LJ45**	**011**
N459F	FA20	452
N459FA	GLF4	1161
N459FJ	F900	80
N459GA	GLF4	1069
N459GA	GLF4	1164
N459GA	GLF4	1225
N459GA	GLF4	1275
N459GA	GLF4	1325
N459GA	GLF4	4059
N459GA	GLF4	4159
N459GA	GLF4	4259
N459GA	**GLF4**	**4359**
N459HB	HA4T	RC-59
N459JD	WW24	9
N459LC	**LJ45**	**060**
N459LJ	LJ45	009
N459LX	BE40	RK-365
(N459LX)	BE40	RK-282
N459M	**HS25**	**HA-0163**
N459MB	**C560**	**0438**
N459MT	CL64	5459
N459NA	**C525**	**0459**
N459SB	**FA20**	**382**
N459SF	**LJ60**	**049**
N459VP	**C52A**	**0459**
(N459X)	GLF4	4151
N459XP	BE40	RK-459
N460AN	LJ60	127
N460AS	**PRM1**	**RB-8**
N460BG	LJ60	090
N460CC	C500	460
N460CP	C650	0021
N460D	**F9EX**	**188**
N460DC	LJ45	146
N460F	CL61	5055
N460F	FA20	453
N460F	LJ24	068
N460FJ	F900	83
N460GA	GLF4	1086
N460GA	GLF4	1165
N460GA	GLF4	1226
N460GA	GLF4	1276
N460GA	GLF4	1460
N460GA	GLF4	4060
N460GA	GLF4	4260
N460GA	GLF5	565
N460HB	HA4T	RC-60
N460JD	LJ60	158
(N460JW)	BE40	RK-460
N460KG	**BE40**	**RK-460**
N460L	PRM1	RB-46
N460LX	BE40	RK-366
(N460LX)	BE40	RK-284
N460M	**C555**	**0022**
N460MC	FA20	105
N460MC	**LJ60**	**309**
N460PG	GLF3	460
N460PK	C52C	0030
N460QS	**GLF4**	**1360**
N460RG	**C52C**	**0105**
N460RV	**C52A**	**0203**
N460SB	**LJ35**	**670**
N460SJ	**F2EX**	**168**
N460TM	**BE40**	**RK-516**
N460WF	HS25	258460
N460WJ	CL64	5460
N460XP	BE40	RK-460
N461AR	**GLF3**	**384**
N461AS	FA10	146
N461CJ	C52A	0461
N461CQ	C52A	0468
N461CW	BE40	RK-61
N461EA	**BE40**	**RJ-61**
N461F	FA20	454
N461F	LJ24	116
N461FJ	F900	85
N461FL	**FA20**	**94/428**
N461GA	GALX	181
N461GA	GLF4	1047
N461GA	GLF4	1166
N461GA	GLF4	1260
N461GA	GLF4	1314
N461GA	GLF4	1461
N461GA	GLF4	4061
N461GA	GLF4	4161
N461GA	GLF5	5461
N461GA	GLF5	568
N461GB	**GLF3**	**411**
N461GT	GLF3	411
N464ST	GLF4	4022
N461HB	HA4T	RC-61
N461LJ	LJ24	122
N461LJ	LJ45	461
N461LX	BE40	RK-368
(N461LX)	BE40	RK-289
N461MC	**LJ60**	**284**
N461N	**EA50**	**000234**
N461QS	**GLF4**	**4125**
N461TS	GLF4	1161

N461VP	C560	0461
N461W	HS25	258200
N462B	**C560**	**0016**
N462B	LJ24	155
N462B	LJ24	290
N462B	LJ25	175
N462B	LJ25	331
N462BA	LJ24	155
N462BA	LJ25	175
N462CB	**PRM1**	**RB-136**
N462CC	C500	462
N462CK	GLF4	1462
N462CS	GLF4	1462
N462CW	BE40	RK-62
N462F	FA20	456
N462FJ	F900	87
N462GA	GLF4	1062
N462GA	GLF4	1168
N462GA	GLF4	1277
N462GA	GLF4	1462
N462GA	GLF4	4062
N462GA	GLF4	4162
N462GA	GLF4	4262
N462LJ	LJ24	124
N462LX	BE40	RK-423
N462MK	**GLF5**	**5362**
N462MM	**HS25**	**258202**
N462PG	CL64	5462
N462QS	GLF4	1262
N462ST	F2TH	134
N462XP	BE40	RK-462
N463AG	CL64	5463
N463C	C550	285
(N463CJ)	C500	463
N463DD	**HS25**	**258178**
N463EA	C560	0463
N463F	FA20	457
N463FJ	F900	92
N463G	GLF4	1363
N463GA	GLF4	1087
N463GA	GLF4	1169
N463GA	GLF4	1227
N463GA	GLF4	1463
N463GA	GLF4	4063
N463GA	GLF4	4163
N463GA	GLF4	4263
N463GA	GLF5	563
N463GE	GLF3	463
N463GR	**CL30**	**20316**
N463HK	GLF2	11
N463JD	**FA50**	**281**
N463LJ	LJ25	001
N463LM	GLF3	370
N463LX	BE40	RK-426
(N463LX)	BE40	RK-295
N463MA	**GLF4**	**1108**
N463QS	GLF4	1363
(N464)	C555	0061
N464AC	FA10	54
N464AM	**MU30**	**A090SA**
N464C	C525	0325
N464C	C52A	0118
N464CL	**LJ24**	**096**
N464EC	WW24	305
N464FJ	F900	95
N464GA	GLF4	1088
N464GA	GLF4	1170
N464GA	GLF4	1228
N464GA	GLF4	1278
N464GA	GLF4	1464
N464GA	GLF4	4064
N464GA	GLF4	4164
N464GA	GLF5	5464
N464GR	CL30	20316
N464GR	**GLF5**	**5482**
N464HA	LJ35	304
N464HB	HA4T	RC-64
N464J	LJ24	164
N464KF	**C510**	**0464**
N464LX	BE40	RK-453
(N464LX)	BE40	RK-297
(N464LX)	BE40	RK-434
N464M	FA20	322
N464PG	**EA50**	**000096**
N464QS	GLF4	1264
N464SP	GLF4	1286
N464ST	**GLF4**	**4022**
N464TF	LJ60	185
N464WL	LJ35	464
N465AV	CL64	5465
N465BC	**SBRL**	**465-53**
N465CV	C560	0465
N465D	C550	377
N465F	FA20	458
N465FJ	F900	98
N465FL	**BE40**	**RK-426**
N465GA	G150	265
N465GA	GLF3	465
N465GA	GLF4	1089
N465GA	GLF4	1171
N465GA	GLF4	1229
N465GA	GLF4	1265
N465GA	GLF4	1465
N465GA	GLF4	4065
N465GA	GLF4	4265
N465GA	**GLF4**	**4365**
N465HB	HA4T	RC-65

N465JH	SBRL	306-57
N465LC	SBRL	465-21
N465LX	BE40	RK-444
N465LX	BE40	RK-454
(N465LX)	BE40	RK-301
N465NH	SBRL	465-37
N465NW	**LJ35**	**465**
N465PD	**SBRL**	**465-37**
N465PM	SBRL	465-40
N465QS	**GLF4**	**1463**
N465R	HS25	257029
N465RM	SBRL	465-40
N465S	SBRL	282-59
N465S	SBRL	306-136
N465S	SBRL	465-1
N465SC	**SBRL**	**465-30**
N465SL	SBRL	465-26
N465SP	SBRL	465-72
N465SR	SBRL	465-33
N465T	SBRL	465-2
N465TM	**BE40**	**RK-554**
N465TS	SBRL	465-15
N465VC	HS25	258800
N466AE	C525	0642
N466AE	HS25	258206
N466CJ	**C52A**	**0466**
N466CS	HS25	258206
N466CW	BE40	RK-366
N466F	C525	0119
N466F	**C52B**	**0336**
N466F	FA20	459
N466FJ	F900	101
N466GA	GLF4	1090
N466GA	GLF4	1172
N466GA	GLF4	1279
N466GA	GLF4	4066
N466GA	GLF4	4266
N466GA	**GLF4**	**4366**
N466GA	GLF5	566
N466HB	HA4T	RC-66
N466JB	GLF2	57
N466LM	C56X	5074
N466LX	BE40	RK-445
N466LX	BE40	RK-455
N466LX	BE40	RK-507
(N466LX)	BE40	RK-305
N466MM	**HS25**	**257059**
N466MP	HS25	25155
N466SG	**C550**	**695**
N466SS	**C550**	**626**
N466TS	GLF4	1066
(N466TS)	BE40	RK-159
(N466TT)	C52A	0300
N466XP	BE40	RK-466
N467AM	GLF2	169
N467AM	**GLF3**	**441**
N467AN	GLF2	169
N467CJ	C52A	0467
N467F	C525	0335
N467F	FA20	460
N467FJ	F900	102
N467FL	**BE40**	**RK-468**
(N467FL)	BE40	RK-447
N467GA	GLF4	1091
N467GA	GLF4	1174
N467GA	GLF4	1230
N467GA	GLF4	1467
N467GA	GLF4	4067
N467GA	GLF4	4167
N467GA	GLF4	4267
N467GA	**GLF4**	**4367**
N467GA	GLF5	567
N467H	SBRL	282-3
N467HB	HA4T	RC-67
N467HS	**C550**	**550-0862**
N467LX	BE40	RK-447
(N467LX)	BE40	RK-307
N467MW	ASTR	067
N467MW	**CL30**	**20515**
N467MW	GALX	014
N467MW	WW24	325
(N467MW)	C550	093
N467QS	GLF4	1533
N467RD	CL64	5467
N467RG	BE40	RK-67
N468AB	GLF4	1477
N468AM	**F2TH**	**74**
N468AM	FA50	31
N468CE	C560	0788
N468CE	**C680**	**0315**
N468CF	C560	0788
N468CJ	C52B	0468
N468CJ	C550	468
N468DM	LJ24	156
N468EC	**C52B**	**0468**
N468ES	**C650**	**0185**
N468FJ	F900	104
N468GA	GLF4	1092
N468GA	GLF4	1176
N468GA	GLF4	1280
N468GA	GLF4	1468
N468GA	GLF4	4068
N468GA	GLF4	4168
N468GA	GLF4	4268
N468GA	**GLF4**	**4368**
N468GH	F900	190
N468GH	**GLEX**	**9558**

N468HW	GLF2	157
N468JD	BE40	RJ-13
N468JJ	**GALX**	**123**
N468JM	**LJ60**	**368**
N468KE	CL61	5036
N468KL	CL61	5036
N468KL	**GLEX**	**9279**
N468LM	HS25	25221
N468LM	LJ35	468
N468LX	BE40	RK-468
(N468LX)	BE40	RK-310
N468PD	C500	294
N468QS	**GLF4**	**4146**
N468RB	**SBRL**	**306-133**
N468RW	**C525**	**0468**
N468SA	C680	0122
(N469)	C550	423
(N469)	LJ31	128
N469AL	HS25	258067
N469BB	**LJ35**	**434**
N469BT	**GLF3**	**432**
N469CJ	C52A	0469
N469DE	**C550**	**550-0883**
N469DN	**C560**	**0469**
N469ED	**C56X**	**5688**
N469ES	**C560**	**0311**
N469F	FA20	461
N469FJ	F900	105
N469FL	**BE40**	**RK-463**
N469G	GLF4	1369
N469GA	G150	269
N469GA	GLF4	1095
N469GA	GLF4	1177
N469GA	GLF4	1261
N469GA	GLF4	4069
N469GA	GLF4	4269
N469GA	GLF5	569
N469J	LJ24	165
N469JR	HS25	257174
N469LH	**C52A**	**0469**
N469LX	BE40	RK-463
(N469LX)	BE40	RK-317
N469MW	GALX	014
N469PW	C500	302
N469QS	GLF4	1369
N469RC	CL64	5469
N469RJ	**HS25**	**258067**
N469RS	**C56X**	**5082**
N469SD	**GLF5**	**5206**
N469TB	GLF3	469
N469VP	C52A	0469
N469WC	**WW24**	**202**
N470BC	HS25	258651
N470CT	**BE40**	**RK-536**
(N470CW)	BE40	RK-370
N470D	F2EX	139
N470DP	**C560**	**0291**
N470EM	HS25	258546
N470F	FA20	462
N470FJ	F900	107
N470FJ	**FA20**	**470**
N470FX	**LJ45**	**479**
N470G	FA20	470
N470GA	G150	270
N470GA	GLF4	1178
N470GA	GLF4	1231
N470GA	GLF4	1281
N470GA	GLF4	1470
N470GA	GLF4	4070
N470GA	GLF4	4270
N470GA	GLF5	570
N470HB	HA4T	RC-70
N470LX	BE40	RK-478
(N470LX)	BE40	RK-324
N470MD	**LJ60**	**187**
N470QS	**GLF4**	**4084**
N470R	HS25	25058
N470SK	**C56X**	**5348**
N470TR	LJ24	298
N470TS	HS25	25070
N470XP	BE40	RK-470
N471CJ	C525	0471
N471CR	GLF4	1471
N471CW	BE40	RK-161
N471DG	GLEX	9049
N471F	FA20	463
N471FJ	F900	108
N471FL	**FA20**	**163**
N471FX	**LJ45**	**500**
N471GA	G150	271
N471GA	GLF4	1179
N471GA	GLF4	1232
N471GA	GLF4	1282
N471GA	GLF4	1471
N471GA	GLF4	4071
N471GA	GLF4	4271
N471H	C500	471
N471HH	C500	050
N471LX	BE40	RK-471
N471LX	BE40	RK-506
(N471LX)	BE40	RK-327
N471MD	**C525**	**0122**
N471MH	C500	050
N471MK	CL64	5471
N471MM	C500	050
N471MM	LJ25	169
N471RJ	**CL64**	**5545**

N471SB	CL60	1083
N471SP	CL60	1083
N471SP	CL61	5157
N471TM	WW24	370
N471WR	C550	550-0987
N471XP	**BE40**	**RK-471**
(N472AS)	LJ35	472
N472EJ	LJ24	238
N472EM	**BE40**	**RK-472**
N472F	FA20	464
N472FJ	F900	111
N472FX	**LJ45**	**501**
N472GA	GALX	247
N472GA	GLF4	1180
N472GA	GLF4	1233
N472GA	GLF4	1283
N472GA	GLF5	572
N472J	LJ25	204
N472LX	**BE40**	**RK-481**
(N472LX)	BE40	RK-328
N472MM	**GLF4**	**1072**
N472QS	**GLF4**	**1372**
N472SP	JSTR	5078/3
N472SW	C525	0033
N472TS	GLF4	1172
(N472TS)	CL64	5572
N473	LJ24	101
(N473AC)	LJ45	304
N473BD	LJ40	2047
N473CC	C500	473
N473CJ	**C52A**	**0473**
N473CW	**GLF4**	**1194**
N473EJ	LJ24	101
N473F	FA20	466
N473FJ	F900	112
N473FL	**BE40**	**RK-397**
N473FX	**LJ45**	**502**
N473GA	GLF4	1181
N473GA	GLF5	5473
N473HB	**HA4T**	**RC-73**
N473JE	BE40	RK-121
(N473JF)	GLF2	106
N473K	**F2TH**	**603**
N473KT	GLF3	438
N473LP	C500	276
N473LP	LJ45	196
N473LP	LJ45	201
N473LR	C500	276
N473LX	BE40	RK-518
(N473LX)	BE40	RK-334
N473SB	C560	0473
N473SC	C52C	0073
N473SH	FA20	473
N473TC	**LJ25**	**043**
N473YH	LJ45	082
N474AN	LJ35	295
N474CC	C52B	0474
N474CF	**HS25**	**258662**
N474CV	C560	0474
N474D	GLF4	1445
N474D	**GLF5**	**5083**
N474F	FA20	467
N474FJ	F900	114
N474FX	**LJ45**	**506**
N474HB	HA4T	RC-74
N474KA	**LJ35**	**174**
N474L	C500	323
N474L	C555	0107
N474LX	BE40	RK-541
(N474LX)	BE40	RK-345
N474M	GLF4	4073
N474ME	BE40	RK-474
N474MJ	**GLF5**	**524**
N474PC	**C52A**	**0087**
N474PE	**C560**	**0474**
N474PT	**LJ60**	**245**
N474SP	C550	485
N474TC	**LJ45**	**405**
N474VP	C560	0474
N474VW	SBRL	282-76
N474X	**GLF4**	**1445**
N474XP	BE40	RK-474
N475AD	CL64	5475
N475AT	WW24	270
N475BC	C680	0098
N475BC	BE40	RK-93
N475CC	C500	475
N475CJ	C525	0475
(N475CY)	GLF3	358
N475DH	**C52A**	**0090**
N475DJ	GLF3	358
N475EZ	FA20	475
N475FJ	F900	116
N475FX	**LJ45**	**508**
N475GA	GLF4	1182
N475GA	GLF4	1234
N475GA	GLF4	1284
N475GA	GLF4	1475
N475GA	GLF4	4175
N475GA	GLF5	5475
N475GA	GLF5	575
N475HC	**C550**	**475**
N475HM	**HS25**	**258451**
N475JC	**C560**	**0777**
N475JC	C56X	5517
N475JC	C56X	6095
N475JT	**LJ45**	**473**

N475LC	**GLF4**	**1472**
N475LX	BE40	RK-554
(N475LX)	BE40	RK-346
(N475LX)	BE40	RK-563
N475M	C650	0062
N475M	GLF4	4067
N475MD	JSTR	5112/7
N475PD	**C56X**	**5080**
N475QS	GLF4	1275
N475RS	**HS25**	**258674**
N475TC	**BE40**	**RK-158**
N475TM	**BE40**	**RK-560**
N475WA	C550	475
N476AC	**C650**	**0170**
N476BJ	**BE40**	**RK-176**
N476CA	**LJ45**	**077**
N476CJ	C525	0476
N476CW	BE40	RK-376
N476FJ	F900	117
N476FX	**LJ45**	**511**
N476GA	GLF4	1183
N476GA	GLF4	1476
N476GA	GLF5	5176
N476GA	GLF5	5476
N476GA	GLF5	576
N476HB	HA4T	RC-76
N476JC	**C56X**	**6095**
N476JD	**C52A**	**0426**
(N476JD)	C525	0381
N476LC	**C555**	**0091**
N476LC	C555	0153
N476LX	BE40	RK-376
N476MK	FA50	301
N476RS	**C550**	**441**
N476VC	LJ35	476
N476X	C500	559
N477A	C550	106
N477A	SBRL	282-110
N477AT	CL64	5477
N477BL	LJ24	031
N477BM	LJ60	010
N477CJ	C52A	0477
N477CW	BE40	RK-377
N477DM	CL61	5174
N477DM	CL64	5398
N477DM	LJ60	010
N477F	FA20	470
N477FJ	F900	119
N477FL	**BE40**	**RK-377**
N477FX	**LJ45**	**514**
N477GA	GLF4	1184
N477GA	GLF4	1235
N477GA	GLF4	1285
N477GA	GLF4	1388
N477GA	GLF4	1477
N477GA	GLF4	4277
N477GG	**GLF2**	**155/14**
N477GJ	**BE40**	**RK-477**
(N477HB)	HA4T	RC-77
N477JB	**GLF4**	**1214**
N477JB	LJ24	230
N477JE	C550	620
(N477JM)	SBRL	306-5
(N477JN)	EA50	000199
(N477JR)	C550	477
N477K	LJ24	036
N477KM	C500	607
N477KM	C550	397
N477LC	C555	0091
N477LC	**C555**	**0153**
N477LX	BE40	RK-377
(N477MM)	LJ25	291
(N477MS)	LJ35	477
N477QS	**GLF4**	**1377**
N477RP	GLF4	1247
N477RT	**C680**	**0138**
(N477RW)	HS25	257191
N477SA	**GLF4**	**1529**
N477SJ	GLF3	477
N477TM	**BE40**	**RK-519**
N477TS	GLF4	1077
N477TX	CL64	5477
N477WB	LJ35	477
N477WG	GLF3	477
N477X	SBRL	282-110
N477X	SBRL	306-78
N477XP	BE40	RK-477
N477XR	LJ40	2113
N477YP	**LJ55**	**065**
N478A	F900	95
N478BA	CL64	5478
N478CJ	C52A	0478
(N478CW)	BE40	RK-178
N478DR	**BE40**	**RK-404**
N478DR	BE40	RK-61
N478F	**EA50**	**000228**
N478F	FA20	471
N478FJ	F900	121
N478FX	**LJ45**	**516**
N478GA	GLF4	1185
N478GA	GLF4	1236
N478GA	GLF4	1400
N478GA	GLF4	4178
N478GA	GLF5	5478
N478GS	**GLF4**	**1478**
(N478HB)	HA4T	RC-78
N478JC	C56X	5517

N478LX	BE40	RK-387
N478PA	**C650**	**7069**
N478PM	**C750**	**0014**
N478PM	HS25	258224
N478QS	GLF4	4133
N478SB	**C560**	**0375**
N478U	CL64	5478
(N478WC)	GLF4	4133
N479CC	C500	479
N479DC	**C510**	**0302**
N479DR	**BE40**	**RK-61**
N479FJ	F900	122
N479GA	GALX	179
N479GA	GLF4	1186
N479GA	GLF4	1402
N479GA	GLF4	1479
N479GA	GLF4	4179
N479GA	GLF5	5479
N479JS	C500	479
N479JS	**LJ40**	**2012**
N479KA	CL64	5479
N479LX	BE40	RK-388
N479LX	BE40	RK-397
N479M	**HS25**	**HA-0082**
N479MM	**PRM1**	**RB-87**
N479PF	**LJ60**	**025**
N479PR	**GALX**	**008**
N479TS	GLF4	1079
N479XP	BE40	RK-479
N480BA	**CL30**	**20197**
N480BN	GALX	195
N480CB	**CL30**	**20147**
N480CC	**C52B**	**0326**
N480CC	CS55	0129
(N480CC)	C500	480
N480CF	**F2TH**	**30**
N480CM	C510	0357
N480CT	**BE40**	**RK-544**
(N480CW)	BE40	RK-180
N480D	F2EX	163
N480DG	**C560**	**0015**
N480ES	**LJ40**	**2097**
N480FJ	F900	124
N480FL	**BE40**	**RK-398**
N480GA	GALX	180
N480GA	GLF2	234
N480GA	GLF4	1237
N480GA	GLF4	1286
N480GA	GLF4	1480
N480JD	**C750**	**0235**
N480JE	**HA4T**	**RC-48**
N480JH	C52B	0355
N480JJ	G150	241
N480JJ	**G150**	**270**
N480JJ	LJ31	212
N480LB	CL64	5480
N480LP	F2TH	36
N480LR	HFB3	1054
N480LX	BE40	RK-390
N480LX	BE40	RK-398
N480M	**BE40**	**RK-586**
N480M	BE40	RK-6
N480ME	**LJ31**	**085**
N480QS	GLF4	1380
N480RE	**PRM1**	**RB-286**
N480RL	**C560**	**0109**
N480RW	GLF3	301
N480UP	GLF4	1054
N480VR	**GLF4**	**1380**
N480WB	**C525**	**0807**
N480YA	LJ35	477
N481AM	**C52C**	**0029**
N481CW	BE40	RK-1
N481DH	WW24	139
N481EZ	LJ24	139
N481FB	GLF4	1442
N481FJ	F900	126
N481FL	**FA20**	**27**
N481FM	LJ35	218
N481GA	GLF4	1187
(N481GJ)	BE40	RK-481
N481JJ	LJ31	212
N481JT	CL60	1034
N481KW	CL64	5481
N481LX	BE40	RK-405
N481LX	BE40	RK-581
N481MC	WW24	184
N481MM	**BE40**	**RK-469**
N481NS	**WW24**	**378**
N481QS	GLF4	1281
N481SC	**HS25**	**258438**
N481TM	**BE40**	**RK-532**
N481VP	C52A	0481
N481VP	C550	481
N482BB	CL64	5482
N482CJ	C52C	0082
N482CP	LJ24	230
N482CP	LJ25	331
N482CW	BE40	RK-222
N482DM	**MU30**	**A088SA**
N482ES	LJ40	2002
N482FJ	F900	127
N482G	WW24	98
N482GA	GALX	182
N482GA	GLF4	1188
N482GA	GLF4	1482
N482GA	GLF4	4182
N482GA	GLF5	5482
N482GS	**BE40**	**RK-482**
N482HC	SBRL	282-28
N482JC	F2EX	284
N482LJ	LJ45	482
N482LX	BE40	RK-413
(N482LX)	BE40	RK-282
N482MG	**HS25**	**HA-0202**
N482MS	**BE40**	**RK-264**
N482QS	GLF4	1480
N482RJ	C500	082
N482RK	**BE40**	**RK-222**
N482SG	LJ35	493
N482TM	**BE40**	**RK-538**
N482U	LJ35	482
N482XP	BE40	RK-482
N483A	WW24	283
N483AM	**GALX**	**100**
N483AM	HS25	258648
N483AS	C550	483
N483BA	CL64	5483
N483CC	CL64	5483
N483CM	**GLF4**	**4116**
(N483CW)	BE40	RK-273
N483DJ	**GLF4**	**1100**
N483DM	LJ24	291
N483DM	MU30	A089SA
N483FG	**HS25**	**257094**
N483FJ	F900	129
N483G	C550	325
N483GA	GLF4	1238
N483GA	GLF4	1483
N483GA	GLF4	4183
N483GA	GLF4	4283
(N483H)	GLF3	483
N483LX	BE40	RK-398
N483PA	BE40	RK-483
N483SC	C550	483
N483SC	**LJ45**	**445**
N483TM	**BE40**	**RK-549**
N483TW	**C680**	**0143**
N483VL	**LJ60**	**355**
(N484)	LJ35	480
N484AT	PRM1	RB-141
N484BA	**LJ31**	**156**
N484CA	**C550**	**550-1048**
N484CC	BE40	RJ-27
N484CH	LJ40	2075
N484CJ	C525	0484
N484CJ	**C52B**	**0484**
N484CR	**CL64**	**5316**
(N484CS)	C500	548
N484CT	**C52A**	**0231**
N484CW	C52A	0453
N484CW	BE40	RK-334
(N484CW)	MU30	A004SA
N484DJ	GLF4	1375
N484DM	MU30	A084SA
N484FM	**F900**	**81**
N484GA	G150	284
N484GA	GLF4	1239
N484GA	GLF4	1287
N484GA	GLF4	1484
N484GC	CL64	5484
N484GM	GLF3	387
N484H	C750	0006
N484HB	**C510**	**0426**
N484HB	LJ36	027
N484J	**C525**	**0048**
N484JC	HS25	258644
N484JH	**E50P**	**50000016**
N484JM	**CL65**	**5846**
N484KA	C500	484
N484LC	LJ45	123
N484LC	LJ45	296
N484MA	C550	473
N484MM	**C560**	**0491**
N484RA	HS25	258053
N484SE	**C525**	**0657**
N484SF	**C56X**	**5614**
N484T	C750	0006
N484T	**C750**	**0199**
N484TL	GLF2	93
N484TM	**BE40**	**RK-550**
N484VB	**C510**	**0329**
N484VL	LJ45	088
(N484VS)	MU30	A084SA
N484W	HS25	256063
N485	LJ35	491
(N485)	LJ35	306
N485A	C550	485
N485AC	LJ35	485
N485AK	C550	249
N485AS	**FA10**	**219**
N485CC	C500	485
N485CJ	C52C	0085
N485CL	CL64	5485
N485CT	**BE40**	**RK-545**
N485CW	MU30	A007SA
(N485CW)	BE40	RK-195
N485CZ	**C52B**	**0485**
N485DM	MU30	A085SA
(N485DM)	MU30	A091SA
N485FL	BE40	RK-239
N485FW	**FA20**	**485**
N485GA	G150	285
N485GA	GLF4	1185
N485GA	GLF4	1385
N485GA	GLF4	1485
N485GM	GLF2	137
N485GM	GLF3	387
N485GM	**GLF4**	**1311**
N485HB	C52C	0156
N485LT	HS25	258485
N485LX	BE40	RK-402
N485RP	C500	503
N485S	LJ35	485
N485TX	CL64	5485
(N485VL)	FA50	44
N485XP	BE40	RK-485
(N486)	LJ55	120
N486BG	C560	0549
N486BG	**CL61**	**5133**
(N486BG)	C560	0541
N486CC	C500	486
N486CC	**C525**	**0213**
N486CW	MU30	A026SA
N486DM	MU30	A086SA
N486EJ	CL64	5486
N486G	LJ24	093
N486G	WW24	48
N486GA	G150	286
N486GA	GALX	186
N486GA	GLF4	1240
N486GA	GLF4	1386
N486GA	GLF4	1486
N486GA	GLF4	4086
(N486GA)	GLF4	1286
N486GS	**C510**	**0419**
N486JR	**C52B**	**0486**
(N486LW)	CL65	5707
N486MJ	FA10	199
N486MJ	HS25	257035
N486MJ	JSTR	5217
N486MJ	BE40	RJ-17
N486MJ	BE40	RJ-30
N486QS	**GLF4**	**1386**
N486RW	**GLF5**	**5484**
N486SB	C560	0580
(N486TL)	C52A	0300
N486TT	C525	0213
N486TT	C52A	0300
N486TT	**C56X**	**5635**
N487AV	**C56X**	**6076**
N487C	**FA7X**	**221**
N487CB	**C525**	**0878**
(N487CC)	C550	487
N487CJ	**C525**	**0487**
N487DM	MU30	A087SA
N487DT	**PRM1**	**RB-85**
N487F	CL30	20152
N487F	FA50	160
N487FW	LJ35	487
N487G	WW24	103
N487GA	G150	287
N487GA	GLF4	1241
N487GA	GLF4	1387
N487GA	GLF4	1487
N487HR	C500	487
N487JA	C56X	6076
N487JA	**CL30**	**20075**
N487JD	C52A	0325
N487LD	C550	551
N487LP	**LJ60**	**361**
(N487LP)	LJ35	669
N487LS	C500	487
(N487LW)	CL64	5644
N487MA	F9EX	87
N487QS	GLF4	1287
N487TM	**BE40**	**RK-555**
N487TT	**C52B**	**0022**
N487WF	C525	0487
N487XP	BE40	RK-487
N488A	C550	550-0882
N488AM	**HS25**	**258648**
(N488LW)	LJ24	193
N488CC	C500	488
N488CC	CS55	0129
N488CH	**GLEX**	**9150**
N488CP	**C56X**	**5055**
N488DB	**BE40**	**RK-10**
N488DM	LJ24	291
N488DM	SBRL	465-26
N488EC	JSTR	5061/48
N488GA	GLF4	1488
N488GA	GLF4	4288
N488GB	**F2EX**	**305**
N488GR	JSTR	5051
N488HP	HS25	258488
(N488HW)	GLF2	157
N488J	LJ24	024
N488JD	C560	0815
N488JD	**C56X**	**6015**
N488JS	JSTR	5051
N488JT	C650	0020
N488KF	**FA20**	**488**
N488LW	CL64	5388
N488LX	**BE40**	**RK-183**
N488MR	JSTR	5061/48
N488PC	PRM1	RB-23
N488PC	PRM1	RB-57
N488RC	**GALX**	**228**
N488RC	PRM1	RB-23
N488SB	GLF3	487
N488SR	**C525**	**0488**
N488TM	**BE40**	**RK-556**
N488VC	**CL30**	**20430**
N488VC	HS25	258546
(N489)	LJ35	277
N489B	**BE40**	**RK-489**
N489BA	CL64	5489
N489BB	FA20	489
N489BH	BE40	RK-331
N489BM	**HS25**	**258271**
N489CB	**C525**	**0489**
N489ED	C525	0489
(N489FL)	BE40	RK-268
N489G	WW24	149
N489GA	G150	279
N489GA	G150	289
N489GA	GLF5	5489
N489GM	**CS55**	**0092**
N489H	GLF4	1099
N489HC	**C525**	**0437**
N489JB	GLEX	9147
N489JC	EA50	000044
(N489JC)	C525	0437
N489QS	**GLF4**	**1389**
N489SA	HS25	258053
N489SS	C550	489
N489TK	FA20	489
N489TM	**BE40**	**RK-559**
N489VC	GALX	110
N489VC	HS25	258443
N489XP	BE40	RK-489
(N490A)	FA10	49
N490AJ	CL64	5489
N490AM	**BE40**	**RK-101**
N490BC	LJ35	364
N490CA	**C550**	**550-1043**
N490CC	C550	490
(N490CD)	C550	490
N490CT	**BE40**	**RK-546**
N490DC	**C550**	**129**
N490EA	C500	061
N490FL	**BE40**	**RK-252**
N490GA	G150	290
N490GA	GLF4	1242
N490GA	GLF4	1390
N490GA	GLF4	1490
N490GA	GLF4	4090
N490JC	**BE40**	**RK-373**
N490JP	**LJ35**	**492**
N490MP	HS25	257135
N490QS	**GLF4**	**1488**
(N490QS)	GLF4	1490
N490RM	**C52A**	**0300**
N490S	**F9EX**	**29**
N490SJ	FA20	490
N490TN	BE40	RK-45
N490VP	**C52A**	**0490**
N490WC	C500	518
N491	C500	072
N491AM	**C52B**	**0473**
N491AM	BE40	RK-109
N491AN	**WW24**	**393**
N491BT	C500	102
N491BT	**MU30**	**A054SA**
N491CJ	C525	0491
N491CW	BE40	RK-91
N491DB	CL60	1049
N491EC	**GLF4**	**1491**
N491GA	GLF4	1243
N491GA	GLF4	1491
N491GA	GLF4	4191
N491GA	GLF4	4291
N491HR	**BE40**	**RK-491**
N491HS	LJ35	491
N491J	**C52B**	**0186**
N491JB	C650	0182
N491JL	C52B	0186
N491JL	**C56X**	**6181**
N491LT	C525	0491
N491MB	FA20	491
N491N	C550	360
N491N	C56X	5530
N491N	**F2TS**	**711**
N491PT	**C500**	**102**
(N491SS)	C650	0123
N491TM	**BE40**	**RK-564**
N491TS	CL60	1049
N491XP	BE40	RK-491
N492A	**GLF3**	**425**
N492AM	**BE40**	**RK-35**
N492AT	C550	472
(N492BA)	C650	0142
N492BB	**E55P**	**50500018**
N492BJ	BE40	RK-192
N492CA	**C52C**	**0192**
N492CB	HS25	257056
N492CC	FA20	492
N492CJ	C525	0492
N492CV	C560	0492
N492DD	GLF3	492
N492GA	GALX	092
N492GA	GLF4	4192
N492GA	GLF5	5192
N492GA	GLF5	5392
N492GA	GLF5	5492
N492JR	GLF4	1292
N492JT	GLF2	82
N492LJ	LJ45	492
N492MA	C550	472
N492P	**BE40**	**RK-39**
N492QS	**GLF4**	**1392**
N492RM	LJ35	492
N492ST	C550	249
N492TM	**BE40**	**RK-580**
N492TM	BE40	RK-592
N493CH	LJ35	493
N493CJ	**C52A**	**0493**
N493CW	BE40	RK-93
N493GA	GALX	193
N493GA	GLF4	1493
N493GA	GLF4	4293
N493LX	BE40	RK-244
N493NW	LJ35	493
N493QS	GLF4	1293
N493RP	C56X	5635
N493S	**F2EX**	**64**
N493S	F2TH	134
N493SF	F2EX	64
(N493SV)	F2TH	134
N493TM	**BE40**	**RK-582**
N493TM	BE40	RK-593
N493XP	BE40	RK-493
N494AT	HS25	258103
N494BA	C525	0243
N494BP	WW24	307
N494CC	**BE40**	**RK-30**
N494CJ	C52B	0484
N494CW	BE40	RK-4
N494EC	**GLF4**	**4226**
N494G	C500	147
N494GA	GALX	194
N494GA	GLF4	1494
N494GA	GLF4	4094
N494GA	GLF4	4194
N494GA	GLF5	5394
N494GP	**C550**	**627**
N494JC	CL64	5494
N494LC	CL61	5102
N494PA	LJ35	505
N494PA	LJ60	076
N494RG	HS25	258378
N494TB	**C52A**	**0442**
N495AS	BE40	RK-251
N495BA	CL64	5495
N495BC	CL64	5495
N495CC	C550	495
N495CE	**CL64**	**5495**
N495CM	**C550**	**202**
N495CT	**BE40**	**RK-547**
N495CW	BE40	RK-5
N495EC	**LJ45**	**156**
N495G	HS25	25017
N495GA	F900	55
N495GA	GLF4	1259
N495GA	GLF4	1495
N495GA	GLF4	4095
N495GA	GLF4	4195
N495GA	GLF4	4295
N495GA	GLF5	597
N495JK	**C510**	**0296**
N495MH	C550	550-1020
N495QS	GLF4	1295
N495RJ	**LJ45**	**480**
N495RS	**GLF4**	**1161**
N495XP	BE40	RK-495
N496AC	**FA7X**	**211**
N496AS	BE40	RK-117
N496DB	CL64	5496
N496EE	BE40	RK-40
N496G	HS25	25174
N496GA	GLF4	1262
N496GA	GLF4	1496
N496GA	GLF4	4096
N496GA	GLF5	599
(N496LJ)	LJ35	496
(N496LX)	BE40	RK-301
N496PT	**FA50**	**64**
N496RA	**C650**	**0066**
N496RT	FA20	496
N496SW	LJ35	496
N496TM	**BE40**	**RK-561**
N496WH	**LJ60**	**063**
N496XP	BE40	RK-496
N497	FA20	6
N497AG	**HS25**	**258439**
N497AS	BE40	RK-227
N497CW	BE40	RK-297
N497DC	**F2EX**	**192**
N497DM	CL64	5359
N497EA	C560	0497
N497EC	CL30	20025
N497EC	**GLEX**	**9396**
N497GA	GLF4	1263
N497HA	WW24	336
N497KK	C680	0093
N497PT	HS25	257093
(N497QS)	GLF4	1497
N497RC	**BE40**	**RK-297**
N497SB	**FA50**	**236**
N497TJ	GLF2	61
N497TM	**BE40**	**RK-596**
N497XP	**BE40**	**RK-497**
N498A	F9EX	55
N498AB	**C56X**	**5116**

N498AS	**BE40**	**RK-347**
N498CS	**C650**	**0180**
N498CW	BE40	RK-108
N498DC	**F2TS**	**722**
N498EE	LEG5	55000007
N498JR	LJ35	498
N498LX	**BE40**	**RK-265**
N498QS	**GLF4**	**1398**
N498R	HS25	25225
N498RS	HS25	25225
N498SW	LJ60	017
N498TM	**BE40**	**RK-601**
N498YY	**C525**	**0498**
N499AS	JSTR	5146
N499AS	BE40	RK-220
N499BA	C500	196
N499BS	**LJ25**	**239**
N499CP	GLF5	5005
N499DM	BE40	RJ-10
N499EH	LJ25	239
N499G	LJ35	147
N499G	LJ35	202
N499GA	GALX	099
N499GA	GLF4	1264
N499GA	GLF4	1399
N499GA	GLF4	1499
N499GA	GLF4	4199
N499GA	GLF5	5499
N499GA	HS25	257130
N499GB	**C680**	**0006**
N499GS	C550	550-0914
N499GS	**LJ40**	**2014**
N499HS	**C56X**	**5602**
N499KR	CL64	5499
N499LX	**BE40**	**RK-149**
N499MD	C56X	5776
N499MJ	FA20	57
(N499MW)	ASTR	019
N499NH	**SBRL**	**465-56**
N499P	BE40	RJ-31
N499PA	**HS25**	**258739**
N499PB	JSTR	5063
N499PC	JSTR	5112/7
N499QS	GLF4	1299
(N499QS)	GLF4	1099
N499RC	**CS55**	**0090**
N499SC	GLF4	1238
N499SC	**GLF4**	**4135**
N499SC	HS25	25236
N499SC	HS25	258082
N499SC	LJ55	147
N499TM	**BE40**	**RK-602**
N499TR	WW24	41
N499UM	LJ35	575
N499WJ	LJ35	499
N499WM	**C550**	**550-0869**
N499XP	BE40	RK-499
(N499YK)	LJ35	577
N500	C650	7027
N500	CL64	5419
N500	HS25	257111
N500	LJ60	115
N500	LJ60	306
N500AB	C500	110
N500AD	C500	006
N500AD	C500	091
N500AD	**E55P**	**50500039**
N500AE	C550	269
N500AE	C650	0161
N500AE	FA50	166
N500AF	FA50	166
N500AF	FA50	170
N500AF	FA50	320
N500AG	**GALX**	**158**
N500AG	HS25	25203
N500AG	JSTR	5119/29
(N500AH)	C500	006
N500AJ	ASTR	074
N500AL	CL30	20092
N500AL	GLF3	416
N500AS	**C52B**	**0164**
N500AT	C560	0146
N500AX	WW24	359
N500AZ	C500	185
N500AZ	HS25	258607
N500BE	LJ55	058
N500BF	LJ24	010
N500BG	FA20	121
N500BJ	**WW24**	**242**
N500BK	C500	646
N500BL	F900	32
N500BL	**F9EX**	
N500BL	**FA50**	**66**
(N500BL)	GLF4	1300
N500BN	HS25	258608
N500BR	C550	411
N500CA	LJ25	091
N500CC	C500	669
N500CD	**EA50**	**000045**
N500CD	GLF4	1321
N500CD	LJ25	091
N500CD	LJ35	083
N500CE	**EA50**	**000157**
N500CG	**C750**	**0519**
N500CG	LJ24	304
N500CG	LJ31	068
N500CG	LJ35	238

N500CG	LJ35	620
N500CG	LJ45	009
N500CM	C650	0111
N500CP	C500	087
N500CQ	LJ35	620
(N500CQ)	LJ31	068
N500CU	C560	0500
N500CV	C500	076
N500CV	C500	082
N500CV	C550	186
N500CW	C525	0542
N500CW	**LJ60**	**133**
(N500CX)	C500	300
N500CZ	**PRM1**	**RB-98**
N500DB	C500	056
N500DB	**C500**	**148**
N500DB	JSTR	5219
N500DD	C500	334
N500DD	LJ35	351
N500DE	FA10	64
N500DG	**EA50**	**000129**
N500DG	GLF4	1169
N500DG	BE40	RJ-43
N500DJ	LJ24	296
N500DL	C500	542
N500DL	LJ25	027
N500DN	C500	034
N500DS	FA10	28
N500DS	LJ35	079
N500DW	C560	0199
N500E	C650	0065
N500E	GLEX	9105
N500E	GLF3	372
N500E	GLF4	1072
N500E	GLF4	1235
N500E	SBRL	465-52
N500EA	EA50	EX500-100
"N500EA"	EA50	EX500-101
N500EC	**E55P**	**50500251**
N500ED	**LJ35**	
241(N500EE)		**C550**
269		
N500EF	**GLF3**	**400**
N500EF	HS25	257086
N500EF	LJ35	
272(N500EF)	LJ25	249
N500EL	C500	
173(N500EN)	C500	135
N500EP	GLF4	1235
N500ER	C550	150
N500ES	JSTR	5075/19
N500ET	**C500**	**180**
N500EW	FA20	21
N500EW	LJ25	232
N500EW	LJ31	068
N500EX	C550	298
N500EX	GLF3	372
N500EX	JSTR	5217
N500EX	LJ35	241
N500EX	LJ35	591
(N500EX)	CL60	1047
N500FA	ASTR	011
N500FA	LJ55	092
(N500FA)	LJ55	004
N500FB	**EA50**	**000185**
N500FC	HS25	257011
N500FD	LJ35	241
N500FE	F2EX	13
N500FE	FA20	163
N500FF	FA10	58
N500FG	JSTR	5135
N500FJ	FA50	38
N500FK	C560	0047
N500FM	**HS25**	**257102**
N500FM	LJ24	088
N500FM	LJ24	111
N500FP	C750	0029
N500FR	**C650**	**0208**
N500FX	C550	298
N500FZ	**C560**	**0018**
N500GA	C500	217
N500GA	C500	632
N500GA	GALX	100
N500GA	GLF5	5400
N500GA	GLF5	5500
N500GA	**GLF7**	**72001**
N500GB	C500	098
N500GD	HS25	256018
N500GE	C500	004
N500GF	**GLF3**	**488**
N500GJ	WW24	64
N500GK	WW24	301
N500GM	C550	074
N500GM	FA10	99
N500GM	FA20	195
N500GM	LJ35	211
N500GP	LJ35	241
N500GR	C500	098
N500GR	FA50	323
N500GS	C500	004
N500GS	CL61	5045
N500GS	FA10	132
N500GS	HS25	257162
N500GV	GLF5	506
N500HC	C525	0048
(N500HC)	FA50	136
(N500HD)	FA20	163

N500HF	HS25	258249
N500HG	LJ35	238
(N500HG)	LJ55	083
N500HH	C500	189
N500HK	C500	190
N500HK	FA20	113
N500HY	**BE40**	**RK-153**
N500HZ	LJ35	238
N500J	GLF2	60
N500J	GLF4	4052
N500J	**GLF5**	**5496**
N500J	HS25	258216
N500J	WW24	303
N500JA	LJ25	007
N500JB	C500	185
N500JC	C500	430
(N500JC)	LJ55	043
N500JD	C500	009
N500JD	**F900**	**190**
N500JD	FA20	378
N500JD	FA50	84
N500JD	JSTR	5152
N500JE	**LJ31**	**088**
N500JK	C500	202
N500JR	GLF2	34
N500JR	WW24	65
N500JS	**C650**	**0112**
N500JS	LJ25	020
N500JS	LJ35	169
N500JS	LJ35	404
N500JW	GLF2	14
N500JW	GLF2	234
N500JW	LJ24	005
N500JW	LJ25	054
N500JW	LJ55	043
N500K	C500	500
N500K	LJ24	016
N500KE	**WW24**	**360**
N500KJ	FA50	197
N500KK	LJ35	211
N500KP	C500	095
N500LD	FA20	163
N500LE	C500	602
N500LE	C560	0052
N500LF	C500	007
N500LG	**LJ28**	**28-005**
N500LH	C500	602
(N500LH)	CS55	0119
(N500LH)	LJ24	088
N500LJ	C500	195
N500LJ	**BE40**	**RK-340**
N500LL	LJ24	347
N500LL	**LJ35**	**095**
(N500LL)	HS25	258095
N500LP	C500	251
N500LR	**CL61**	**5012**
N500LS	CL60	1048
N500LS	GLF3	460
N500LS	GLF4	1009
N500LS	HS25	257173
N500LS	WW24	137
N500LS	WW24	226
N500LW	LJ25	232
N500LY	**FA50**	**323**
N500M	ASTR	018
N500M	ASTR	091
N500M	**CL64**	**5480**
N500M	WW24	175
N500M	WW24	300
N500MA	**ASTR**	**094**
N500MA	GLF2	119/22
N500MA	HS25	25237
N500MA	HS25	256064
N500MA	JSTR	5033/56
N500MA	WW24	435
N500MD	WW24	300
(N500MD)	C500	370
N500MF	WW24	34
N500MG	C560	0223
N500MG	C560	0624
N500MH	LJ24	158
N500MJ	LJ25	091
N500MJ	LJ35	348
N500MJ	LJ36	025
N500ML	C500	074
N500ML	WW24	175
N500MM	**EA50**	**000139**
N500MM	GLF3	460
N500MM	GLF4	1135
N500MN	GLF3	460
N500MP	LJ25	208
N500MP	**LJ31**	**198**
N500MQ	ASTR	018
N500MS	LJ24	246
N500MX	C500	006
N500MZ	ASTR	091
N500N	C750	0239
N500N	F2EX	142
N500N	FA50	323
N500N	GLF4	4056
N500N	**GLF4**	**4296**
N500NB	**C52A**	**0339**
(N500NB)	LJ55	100
N500ND	LJ35	351
N500NH	FA20	470
N500NH	LJ24	355
N500NH	LJ55	100

N500NJ	C500	113
N500NL	SBRL	380-8
N500NM	JSTR	5229
N500NT	C500	314
(N500NU)	FA20	21
N500NW	C500	660
(N500NX)	C500	120
N500P	LJ24	077
N500P	LJ24	119
N500PB	C500	017
N500PB	C500	232
N500PB	CL65	5938
N500PC	CL61	3003
N500PC	CL61	5071
N500PC	FA20	19
N500PC	GLF2	65
N500PC	**GLF4**	**1492**
N500PE	CL61	3065
N500PE	CL64	5440
N500PG	CL61	3039
N500PG	**CL64**	**5663**
N500PG	JSTR	5153/61
(N500PJ)	LJ24	119
N500PM	**BE40**	**RK-132**
N500PP	LJ24	119
N500PP	LJ25	121
N500PP	LJ25	208
N500PP	LJ25	248
N500PP	LJ35	390
N500PP	**MU30**	**A061SA**
"N500PP"	LJ25	208
N500PR	JSTR	5204
N500PX	C550	191
N500PX	C560	0178
N500PX	C560	0691
N500PX	C56X	5017
N500PX	**C56X**	**5589**
N500PX	FA20	19
N500QC	JSTR	5205
N500QM	C550	074
N500R	C500	127
N500R	CL60	1077
N500R	F2EX	13
N500R	**F2EX**	**163**
N500R	FA50	323
N500R	GLF2	12
N500R	HS25	256068
N500R	WW24	280
N500RB	**E50P**	**50000334**
N500RD	GLF5	5105
N500RE	FA50	124
N500RE	FA50	156
N500RE	**FA50**	**317**
N500RE	LJ24	193
N500RH	CL60	1069
N500RH	GLF2	80
N500RH	GLF3	451
N500RH	**GLF5**	**558**
"N500RH"	HS25	258013
N500RK	LJ24	296
N500RK	SBRL	282-42
N500RK	SBRL	306-85
(N500RK)	SBRL	306-64
N500RL	GLF2	122
N500RL	**GLF4**	**1513**
N500RP	C650	0187
N500RP	C750	0029
N500RP	**G150**	**306**
N500RP	GLF4	4057
N500RP	LJ24	193
N500RP	LJ24	345
N500RP	LJ35	351
N500RP	LJ55	053
N500RP	LJ60	206
N500RQ	GLF2	122
N500RR	C550	638
N500RR	**F2EX**	**156**
N500RR	FA20	491
N500RR	LJ24	345
N500RR	SBRL	306-33
N500RR	SBRL	465-49
N500RR	WW24	359
N500RW	LJ24	233
N500RW	LJ35	148
N500S	JSTR	5134/50
N500S	JSTR	5209
N500SB	LJ24	166
N500SD	**C52A**	**0132**
N500SJ	C500	231
N500SJ	JSTR	5012
N500SK	**C500**	**129**
N500SQ	LJ24	325
N500SR	LJ24	347
N500SV	C52A	0153
N500SV	**C52C**	**0119**
N500SV	LJ36	040
N500SW	LJ24	325
N500SW	LJ60	017
N500SX	**C560**	**0042**
N500T	GLF2	244
N500T	JSTR	5211
N500TB	CL61	3003
N500TB	**E50P**	**50000168**
(N500TB)	CL61	5120
N500TD	C500	070
N500TD	CL61	3003
N500TF	SBRL	380-19

N500TH	**BE40**	**RK-246**
N500TL	C525	0281
N500TL	LJ25	238
N500TM	C500	112
N500TS	C550	550-0886
N500TS	**FA50**	**179**
N500TS	LJ24	347
N500TW	C500	623
N500UB	C560	0052
N500UJ	**C560**	**0062**
N500UK	**EA50**	**000051**
N500UP	**C56X**	**5294**
N500VA	**C52A**	**0369**
N500VA	C550	550-0987
N500VB	C550	147
N500VC	**C560**	**0144**
N500VF	WW24	115
N500VH	**EA50**	**000211**
N500VJ	**GLEX**	**9552**
N500VK	C500	202
N500VK	EA50	000010
N500VM	F9EX	5
N500VS	GLF3	460
N500VS	GLF4	1009
N500VT	C550	550-0987
N500WD	C52B	0267
N500WD	**C52B**	**0393**
N500WD	SBRL	465-48
N500WH	WW24	215
N500WJ	C500	202
N500WJ	C52B	0267
N500WK	WW24	196
N500WN	C550	404
N500WN	JSTR	5048
N500WN	JSTR	5135
N500WP	C500	185
N500WP	C550	238
N500WR	C500	166
N500WR	LJ31	038
N500WW	GLF3	318
N500WW	LJ25	137
N500WZ	JSTR	5048
(N500XB)	GLF3	416
N500XP	**HS25**	**258455**
N500XP	BE40	RK-465
N500XP	BE40	RK-500
(N500XP)	BE40	RK-492
N500XX	C500	509
N500XY	C500	347
N500XY	HS25	25119
N500Y	C500	110
N500Y	FA20	155
N500YB	HS25	25170
(N500YD)	EA50	000269
(N500YY)	JSTR	5211
(N500YY)	LJ24	028
N500Z	JSTR	5008
N500Z	JSTR	5072/23
N500ZA	LJ24	182
N500ZA	**LJ24**	**350**
N500ZB	**CS55**	**0023**
N500ZB	HS25	257043
N500ZB	JSTR	5102
N500ZC	C500	435
N500ZH	**EA50**	**000158**
N500ZH	LJ24	182
N500ZH	LJ60	115
N501	**C500**	**364**
N501A	**C500**	**422**
N501AA	C550	054
N501AB	**C500**	**460**
N501AD	**C500**	**465**
N501AF	**C500**	**526**
N501AJ	**C500**	**431**
N501AJ	CL64	5501
N501AL	JSTR	5012
N501AR	C500	128
N501AS	FA20	262
N501AT	C500	208
N501AT	**C500**	**376**
N501AZ	**C500**	**452**
N501BA	C500	443
N501BB	**C500**	**474**
(N501BB)	C500	455
N501BE	C500	354
(N501BE)	CS55	0138
(N501BF)	C500	354
N501BG	C500	432
N501BG	BE40	RK-5
N501BK	C500	683
N501BL	C550	028
N501BP	C500	604
N501BW	C500	625
N501BW	WW24	335
N501BW	**BE40**	**RK-167**
N501BZ	**CL30**	**20501**
N501CB	**C500**	**423**
N501CB	WW24	435
N501CC	C500	701
N501CD	**C500**	**432**
N501CE	C500	525
N501CF	**C500**	**522**
N501CG	C500	486
N501CG	LJ45	040
N501CJ	C525	0355
(N501CJ)	C525	0501
N501CM	C500	631

N501CP	**C500**	**401**
(N501CP)	WW24	435
N501CR	C500	614
N501CT	HS25	258512
N501CV	**GLF5**	**639**
N501CW	C500	282
N501CW	C500	477
N501CW	C560	0050
N501CX	C500	432
N501D	C500	511
N501DA	**C500**	**349**
(N501DA)	C500	613
N501DB	**F900**	**196**
(N501DB)	C500	362
N501DD	**C500**	**404**
N501DG	C500	194
N501DG	C500	578
N501DJ	**C52B**	**0185**
N501DK	C550	462
N501DL	C500	375
(N501DL)	C500	613
N501DP	**C500**	**552**
(N501DP)	C500	531
N501DR	C500	270
N501DR	C500	342
N501DR	C500	532
N501DT	WW24	270
N501DV	GALX	192
N501DX	**EA50**	**000110**
N501DY	C500	644
N501DZ	**C500**	**059**
N501E	C500	392
N501E	C500	412
N501E	C560	0231
(N501E)	GLF4	1138
N501EA	**C500**	**419**
N501ED	C500	547
N501EF	C500	441
N501EG	C500	685
N501EJ	**C500**	**119**
N501EK	C500	453
N501EM	C500	516
(N501EM)	C500	382
N501EZ	C500	434
(N501EZ)	C500	649
(N501EZ)	MU30	A069SA
N501F	FA20	269
N501F	HS25	258286
(N501F)	HS25	257167
(N501FB)	C500	386
(N501FF)	C500	165
N501FJ	**C500**	**563**
N501FM	C500	547
N501FP	C500	550
N501FR	C500	683
N501FT	C500	434
N501G	**C500**	**607**
N501GB	**C500**	**231**
N501GF	C500	507
N501GF	HS25	257208
N501GG	C500	532
N501GG	**C550**	**484**
N501GK	C500	507
N501GP	C500	026
N501GR	**C500**	**358**
N501GR	C500	378
N501GS	C500	369
(N501GS)	C500	468
N501GV	GLF5	501
N501GW	C500	578
(N501H)	HS25	256020
N501HC	C500	508
(N501HD)	C500	650
N501HG	C500	643
(N501HH)	C500	679
N501HK	C500	292
N501HM	C500	615
N501HM	**GLF5**	**5001**
N501HP	C500	573
N501HS	**C500**	**480**
N501J	JSTR	5213
N501JC	C500	252
N501JD	**C500**	**512**
N501JE	**C500**	**670**
N501JF	**C500**	**343**
N501JF	C500	382
N501JG	C500	150
N501JG	C500	409
N501JG	**C560**	**0344**
N501JJ	**C500**	**368**
N501JM	**C500**	**635**
N501JP	C500	477
N501JP	C550	730
N501JS	C560	0066
N501JT	ASTR	050
N501JT	GLEX	9265
N501JT	GLEX	9340
N501JV	**GLF2**	**168**
N501KB	C500	446
N501KC	C550	030
N501KC	FA20	401
N501KE	**C52A**	**0430**
N501KG	C500	001
N501KG	C500	279
N501KK	C500	588
N501KM	**C500**	**468**
N501KR	C500	446
N501KR	**C525**	**0033**
N501KT	**LJ45**	**435**
N501KV	**CL61**	**5173**
N501LB	C500	165
N501LC	**C550**	**161**
N501LE	C500	671
(N501LG)	C500	294
N501LH	**C500**	**342**
N501LL	C500	561
N501LM	C500	673
N501LR	HS25	259025
N501LS	C500	482
N501LW	C500	516
N501MB	**C500**	**508**
N501MC	C550	500
N501MD	C500	382
N501MD	FA20	284
(N501MD)	C500	508
(N501MD)	HS25	257121
N501MF	**C500**	**650**
N501MG	C500	535
N501MH	LJ24	314
N501MK	**F9EX**	**108**
N501MM	C500	601
N501MM	HS25	257079
N501MR	**C500**	**421**
N501MR	C500	661
N501MS	C500	674
N501MT	C500	675
N501MX	**C500**	**361**
N501NA	C500	459
N501NB	C555	0018
N501NC	C500	578
N501NC	FA50	11
(N501NP)	C500	518
N501NY	**C500**	**409**
N501NZ	C500	459
N501PC	C500	005
N501PC	CL61	3004
N501PC	CL61	3023
N501PC	**CL64**	**5551**
N501PC	FA50	265
N501PC	GLF4	1298
N501PJ	**C500**	**498**
N501PS	LJ25	153
N501PV	**C500**	**394**
N501Q	C500	653
N501QS	C560	0024
N501QS	**C680**	**680A0037**
N501R	HS25	256068
N501RB	C500	132
N501RB	**GLF4**	**1138**
N501RC	**C500**	**557**
N501RF	C500	671
N501RG	**C500**	**632**
N501RG	C500	666
N501RL	C500	292
N501RL	C500	311
N501RL	**C550**	**601**
N501RM	C500	001
N501RM	C500	465
N501RP	G150	209
N501RP	**G150**	**308**
N501RP	LJ55	053
N501RR	**F2EX**	**200**
N501RS	C500	479
N501RS	**LJ31**	**223**
N501SC	C500	265
N501SC	C500	314
N501SE	C500	010
N501SE	C500	249
N501SE	C500	474
(N501SF)	C500	426
N501SJ	C500	423
N501SJ	**C500**	**446**
N501SJ	C500	474
(N501SK)	C500	388
(N501SK)	C500	459
N501SP	C500	383
N501SP	**C500**	**403**
N501SR	C500	446
N501SS	C500	282
N501SS	**C500**	**455**
N501ST	**C500**	**374**
N501T	C500	650
N501T	C52B	0365
N501T	C560	0136
N501T	GLF2	248
N501T	JSTR	5213
N501TB	**C500**	**510**
N501TB	C500	685
N501TJ	C500	372
N501TK	C500	210
N501TL	**C500**	**207**
N501TP	**C500**	**684**
N501TW	LJ35	612
N501TW	LJ55	101
N501U	C500	408
N501U	WW24	381
N501UP	**C56X**	**5252**
(N501VB)	C500	453
N501VC	C500	575
N501VE	C555	0109
N501VH	C500	044
N501VJ	**GLEX**	**9563**
N501VP	C500	352
N501W	HS25	25136
N501WB	**C500**	**556**
N501WD	**C500**	**666**
N501WJ	C500	353
N501WJ	**C500**	**535**
(N501WK)	C500	353
N501WL	**C500**	**519**
(N501WL)	C500	186
N501WW	C500	044
N501WX	**C500**	**660**
N501X	C500	478
N501X	**C500**	**661**
N501XL	C56X	5209
N501XP	HS25	258701
N501XP	BE40	RK-501
N501ZD	**C500**	**069**
N501ZK	GLF5	5001
N502AL	C550	029
(N502BA)	C500	288
N502BC	**C56X**	**5098**
N502BE	C500	195
N502BG	C550	297
N502BG	**F2TH**	**15**
N502BG	FA10	144
N502BG	FA20	388
N502BG	WW24	372
(N502BH)	EA50	000280
N502CA	**BE40**	**RK-525**
N502CC	C500	001
N502CC	C500	008
N502CC	**C500**	**502**
N502CL	C550	014
N502E	C560	0232
N502EA	**EA50**	**EX500-103**
(N502EA)	EA50	EX500-101
N502EG	**C56X**	**5502**
N502ET	**EA50**	**000052**
N502EZ	FA50	25
N502F	C560	0153
N502F	CL61	5111
N502F	FA20	481
N502G	LJ35	219
N502GF	HS25	257210
N502GM	**GLF4**	**4011**
N502GP	C500	027
N502GS	**GLF7**	**72002**
N502GV	GLF5	502
N502HE	**CL61**	**5111**
N502HR	HS25	258502
N502JB	FA50	115
N502JC	LJ25	264
N502JF	LJ35	490
N502JL	GLEX	9050
N502JM	LJ40	2017
N502JT	GLF4	1212
N502JV	**LJ25**	**311**
N502KA	**GLF5**	**502**
N502LT	EA50	000027
N502MH	LJ25	098
N502N	BE40	RK-386
N502NX	C750	0502
N502P	**GLF4**	**4231**
N502PC	CL61	5121
N502PC	GLF2	170
N502PC	**GLF4**	**1435**
N502PG	**FA10**	**144**
N502PM	**PRM1**	**RB-185**
N502QS	**GLF5**	**601**
(N502R)	HS25	257159
N502RB	LJ60	199
N502RD	C500	043
N502RG	GLF2	178
N502RL	C500	043
N502RP	**G150**	**212**
N502RP	LJ60	199
N502RR	SBRL	282-13
N502S	HS25	257206
N502SU	C550	621
N502SV	**FA20**	**502**
N502T	C560	0153
N502T	C650	7067
N502TF	CL64	5502
N502TN	**C525**	**0505**
N502TS	C560	0157
N502TS	**EA50**	**000097**
N502U	WW24	48
N502UP	**C56X**	**5310**
N502VJ	**GLEX**	**9608**
(N502VP)	C56X	5205
N502XL	C56X	5502
N502XL	C56X	6002
N502XP	BE40	RK-502
N503AS	**C52A**	**0445**
N503BB	C510	0390
N503BC	**LJ60**	**239**
N503BG	**C550**	**413**
N503CC	**C500**	**003**
N503CS	C56X	5205
N503CX	**C750**	**0503**
N503EA	**EA50**	**EX500-108**
N503EB	BE40	RJ-29
N503EZ	FA50	84
N503F	FA20	391
(N503F)	C560	0154
N503G	**GLF7**	**72003**
N503GP	C500	086
N503GV	GLF5	503
N503KJ	**CL30**	**20188**
N503LB	**LJ35**	**232**
N503LC	C52B	0162
(N503LR)	HS25	259003
N503PC	CL61	3021
N503PC	**CL64**	**5503**
N503PC	FA50	263
N503PC	GLF4	1323
N503PQ	**FA50**	**263**
N503QF	**C56X**	**5205**
N503QS	**C680**	**680A0040**
N503QS	HS25	259003
N503RE	LJ60	227
(N503RH)	WW24	260
(N503RJ)	HS25	258218
N503RP	G150	215
N503RP	**G150**	**307**
N503RP	LJ35	070
N503RP	LJ60	227
N503RV	FA20	161
N503SV	**C680**	**0503**
N503T	C560	0154
N503TF	**C52C**	**0062**
N503U	WW24	83
N503UP	**C56X**	**5326**
N503VJ	**GLEX**	**9565**
N503XS	C56X	5503
N504AB	**LJ60**	**067**
N504AC	**GLF5**	**5392**
N504BM	C56X	5004
N504BW	C560	0128
N504CC	C500	004
N504CC	**C560**	**0504**
(N504CL)	FA20	504
N504CR	**LJ45**	**499**
N504CS	C56X	5229
N504CX	**FA50**	**81**
N504D	**C500**	**484**
N504DM	BE40	RJ-4
N504EA	**EA50**	**EX500-109**
N504EX	JSTR	5217
N504F	LJ35	340
N504FJ	FA20	504
N504GP	C500	265
N504GS	**GLF7**	**72004**
N504GV	GLF5	504
N504JC	WW24	277
N504JV	LJ24	350
N504LV	**C56X**	**5369**
N504M	CL61	5099
N504MF	**HS25**	**258286**
N504MK	FA50	205
N504MS	FA50	301
N504PA	**F900**	**43**
N504PA	FA50	94
N504PK	C56X	5369
N504PS	**C52B**	**0466**
N504QS	**C680**	**680A0041**
N504QS	GLF5	613
N504R	**GLEX**	**9634**
N504RP	**C650**	**0176**
N504RS	**EA50**	**000005**
N504ST	FA50	201
N504ST	**GLF4**	**1255**
N504SU	C750	0024
N504SV	C680	0504
N504T	**C650**	**7040**
N504TC	**EA50**	**000141**
N504TF	GLF2	8
N504TS	CL61	5004
N504U	**C560**	**0665**
N504U	WW24	325
N504UP	**C56X**	**5324**
N504VP	C56X	5004
N504VR	**C550**	**550-1104**
N504WE	FA50	55
N504WV	C750	0522
N504WV	**LJ45**	**393**
N504Y	LJ35	282
N504YP	**FA50**	**170**
N505AG	**C550**	**550-0905**
N505AJ	FA20	89
N505AM	C500	340
N505AX	GLF5	505
N505AZ	**C500**	**188**
N505BB	**C500**	**671**
(N505BB)	C500	455
N505BC	C500	367
N505BC	**LJ45**	**361**
N505BC	WW24	278
N505BG	C500	430
N505BG	C500	561
N505BG	**C52A**	**0188**
N505BL	FA50	335
N505BX	CL30	20006
N505C	JSTR	5040
N505C	JSTR	5113/25
N505CC	C500	005
N505CC	C500	638
N505CC	C555	0115
N505CF	**C500**	**517**
N505CL	FA50	38
N505CS	C56X	5252
N505D	**GLF5**	**5323**
N505DH	LJ35	504
N505EA	EA50	EX500-106
N505EB	BE40	RK-17
N505EC	E55P	50500039
(N505EC)	E55P	50500064
N505EE	E55P	50500118
N505EE	**E55P**	**50500338**
N505EE	LJ35	505
N505EH	**LJ55**	**067**
N505FF	**E55P**	**50500226**
N505FX	CL30	20006
N505GA	**GALX**	**005**
N505GD	**GLF7**	**72005**
N505GF	**GLF4**	**1275**
N505GJ	**LJ35**	**505**
N505GL	C550	495
N505GP	C500	272
N505GP	C550	279
N505GP	**E55P**	**50500188**
N505GV	GLF5	505
N505HG	**LJ36**	**009**
N505JC	C500	341
N505JC	GALX	050
N505JD	CL64	5505
N505JH	**C500**	**505**
N505JT	GLF2	46
N505K	C500	004
N505LC	**HS25**	**25248**
N505LR	HS25	259005
N505M	CL61	5100
N505MA	C750	0057
N505PA	HS25	25022
N505PF	LJ24	006
N505PJ	**E55P**	**50500165**
N505PL	**ASTR**	**141**
N505PM	**CL60**	**1051**
N505QS	**C680**	**680A0042**
N505QS	HS25	259005
N505RA	LJ36	009
N505RH	**C560**	**0813**
N505RJ	**C500**	**367**
N505RM	**C52A**	**0041**
N505RP	C550	450
N505RR	**F2TH**	**46**
N505RX	GLF2	219/20
N505RX	GLF5	675
N505SP	C500	505
N505SS	**GLF5**	**608**
N505SV	C680	0505
N505T	JSTR	5015
N505TC	**FA50**	**57**
N505TM	**E55P**	**50500063**
N505U	WW24	196
N505UP	**GLF4**	**1439**
N505VS	GLF4	1414
N505W	HS25	25136
N505W	HS25	256013
N505X	C550	550-0865
N505XP	**BE40**	**RK-505**
N505XX	EA50	000073
N506AB	**LJ60**	**266**
N506AM	C56X	5106
N506BA	CL61	5060
N506BA	**F900**	**160**
N506BA	FA50	230
N506C	LJ35	094
N506CC	C500	006
N506CS	C56X	5267
N506D	JSTR	5061/48
N506E	C560	0236
N506EA	EA50	EX500-107
N506FX	CL30	20007
N506GD	**GLF7**	**72006**
N506GP	LJ35	109
N506GV	GLF5	506
N506HG	**GLF5**	**5400**
N506HL	**LJ35**	**522**
N506KS	**LJ40**	**2055**
N506LG	**LJ35**	**537**
N506MX	C500	006
N506N	HS25	25136
N506QS	**C680**	**680A0043**
N506QS	GLF5	623
N506RD	GLF5	641
N506RL	**C560**	**0114**
N506SA	**GLF5**	**5380**
N506SR	C500	006
N506T	GLF3	484
N506T	JSTR	5061/48
N506TF	C500	006
N506TF	C500	351
N506TN	CL61	5066
N506TS	CL61	5006
N506U	WW24	354
N506UP	**C56X**	**5362**
N507AB	C550	030
N507AS	**C52A**	**0448**
N507AS	FA50	311
N507BW	HS25	258507
N507BX	CL30	20008
N507CC	C500	007
N507CC	CL60	1026
(N507CC)	C555	0002
N507CJ	C555	0002
N507CR	C560	0791
N507CR	C56X	6071
N507CS	C56X	5282
N507CW	MU30	A007SA
N507CZ	CL61	5047
N507D	**C56X**	**5145**
N507DM	BE40	RJ-7

N507DS	C500	403
N507DW	**GLF5**	**507**
N507EC	C550	158
N507F	HS25	257177
N507FG	LJ45	326
N507FX	CL30	20008
N507GA	GLF5	507
N507GA	GLF5	5307
N507GD	**GLF7**	**72007**
N507GP	C550	294
N507HB	BE40	RK-507
N507HC	CL60	1026
N507HF	LJ25	057
N507HP	**C525**	**0395**
N507JC	GLF2	121
N507PD	**C560**	**0596**
N507PG	CL61	3039
N507QS	GLF5	625
N507R	CL60	1077
N507SA	GLF4	1456
N507SF	**C680**	**0507**
N507SV	C680	0507
(N507TE)	GLF4	1383
N507TF	SBRL	306-39
N507U	SBRL	306-93
N507UP	**C56X**	**5542**
N507VP	C56X	5070
N507WM	**BE40**	**RK-507**
(N507WY)	CL60	1026
N508AF	FA50	170
(N508AJ)	C550	620
N508BP	HS25	258419
N508CC	C500	008
N508CC	CL60	1057
(N508CC)	C500	208
N508CJ	C525	0508
N508CK	**HA4T**	**RC-9**
N508CP	**EA50**	**000196**
N508CS	C56X	5294
N508CV	C550	186
N508DM	BE40	RJ-3
N508DW	C550	620
(N508DW)	C560	0245
N508EA	**C52B**	**0187**
N508EJ	FA50	8
N508FX	CL30	20009
N508GA	GALX	108
N508GA	GLF4	1508
N508GA	GLF5	508
N508GA	GLF5	5280
N508GD	**GLF7**	**72008**
N508GP	LJ35	424
N508HC	CL60	1057
N508J	LJ31	088
N508JA	**EA50**	**000001**
(N508JM)	GLF4	1184
N508JP	**EA50**	**000071**
N508KD	**C560**	**0147**
N508KD	C560	0245
(N508L)	FA20	359/542
N508M	LJ24	025
N508ML	E50P	50000196
N508MM	HS25	258055
N508MN	CL65	5882
N508MV	C56X	6006
N508P	GLF5	693
N508P	LJ35	390
N508PB	C500	017
N508PC	**CL64**	**5558**
N508PC	F9EX	111
N508QS	**GLF5**	**631**
N508R	WW24	280
N508RN	**PRM1**	**RB-156**
N508S	C500	192
N508SN	**CL30**	**20269**
N508SR	**LJ24**	**347**
N508SV	C680	0508
N508T	GLF2	232
N508T	JSTR	5119/29
N508TA	JSTR	5119/29
(N508TC)	FA20	408
N508TF	LJ35	508
N508TL	C525	0281
N508TS	FA50	179
N508UJ	C550	550-0922
N508UP	**C56X**	**5546**
N508VM	HS25	256045
N508XJ	**CL30**	**20008**
N508YV	LJ35	573
N509	HS25	257111
N509AB	**LJ31**	**136**
N509AB	SBRL	306-75
N509CC	C500	009
N509CC	CS55	0109
N509CS	C56X	5310
N509CX	**C750**	**0509**
N509DM	C510	0191
N509FX	CL30	20012
N509G	LJ25	054
N509GA	GLF4	1509
N509GA	GLF5	509
N509GA	GLF5	5229
N509GA	GLF5	5309
N509GE	CL64	5573
N509GP	HS25	258077
N509GV	GLF5	509
N509J	JSTR	5222

N509JA	**EA50**	**000084**
(N509MD)	FA50	219
N509MM	CL65	5975
N509P	C500	446
N509PC	CL61	3004
(N509PC)	CL61	3002
N509QC	HS25	257111
N509QS	**GLF5**	**637**
N509RP	**CS55**	**0030**
N509SB	C52B	0353
N509SB	**CL30**	**20580**
N509SD	C52B	0353
N509SE	C525	0058
"N509SM"	HS25	257002
N509T	GLF2	244
N509T	JSTR	5222
N509TC	C550	462
N509TC	FA10	134
(N509TF)	JSTR	5222
(N509TS)	CL64	5309
N509TT	GLF2	244
N509UP	**C56X**	**5551**
N509VE	C560	0509
N509W	CL61	5099
N509WP	FA20	369
N509XP	HS25	258509
N510	CL61	5100
N510AA	SBRL	380-4
N510AB	**LJ31**	**063**
N510AF	**CL30**	**20306**
N510AG	**GLF2**	**159**
N510AJ	C500	395
N510AK	GLF4	4186
N510AT	**C510**	**0331**
N510AZ	**C510**	**0124**
N510BA	**C510**	**0143**
N510BA	HS25	258331
N510BB	SBRL	380-9
N510BC	**MU30**	**A057SA**
N510BD	**C510**	**0249**
N510BE	**C510**	**0211**
N510BG	C560	0615
N510BK	**C510**	**0311**
N510BM	FA20	215
N510BR	C510	0280
N510BT	**C510**	**0336**
N510BW	**C510**	**0098**
N510CA	C550	550-1082
N510CC	C500	010
N510CC	C500	310
(N510CC)	C500	001
N510CE	C510	0001
N510CF	**C510**	**0045**
N510CJ	**C510**	**0173**
N510CL	FA10	9
N510CP	FA10	43
N510CT	**F2EX**	**53**
N510CX	**C750**	**0510**
N510DG	**C510**	**0012**
N510DH	**C510**	**0208**
N510DP	**C510**	**0220**
N510DT	C510	0299
N510DW	**C510**	**0025**
N510EE	**C510**	**0275**
N510EG	C510	0246
N510EM	**C510**	**0414**
N510FD	**C510**	**0420**
N510FF	C510	0007
N510FS	**C56X**	**5133**
N510FX	CL30	20017
N510G	GLF2	85
N510GA	C500	625
N510GA	G150	210
N510GA	GALX	110
N510GA	GALX	210
N510GA	GLF4	1510
N510GA	GLF5	5310
N510GA	GLF5	5510
N510GG	**C510**	**0168**
N510GH	C510	0036
N510GJ	**C510**	**0083**
N510GP	**C550**	**420**
N510GT	**FA50**	**88**
N510GT	WW24	190
N510GW	**LJ40**	**2022**
N510HF	**C56X**	**5331**
N510HS	**C510**	**0320**
N510HS	HS25	257034
N510HW	C510	0290
N510J	C510	0060
(N510JA)	EA50	000277
N510JC	**C550**	**220**
N510JH	C510	0051
N510JL	**C510**	**0250**
N510JM	**C510**	**0051**
N510JN	**C560**	**0295**
N510K	**C510**	**0121**
N510K	C510	0172
(N510KA)	C510	0247
N510KB	**C510**	**0155**
N510KM	**C510**	**0323**
N510KS	C510	0002
N510KZ	**C510**	**0251**
(N510L)	LJ25	280
N510LF	**C510**	**0159**
N510LF	FA20	510
N510LJ	LJ35	025

N510LL	**C510**	**0074**
N510LM	**C510**	**0304**
N510MB	C510	0118
N510MD	**C510**	**0202**
N510MG	**GLF4**	**1349**
N510MP	**FA50**	**140**
N510MS	LJ24	204
N510MT	**C510**	**0447**
N510MT	C560	0122
N510MW	**C510**	**0109**
N510ND	C510	0001
N510ND	LJ24	204
N510NJ	C500	593
(N510NY)	C500	409
N510NZ	**C510**	**0054**
N510PA	LJ24	305
N510PC	CL60	1011
N510PS	C510	0171
N510PS	CL60	1011
N510PT	**C510**	**0114**
N510PX	**C510**	**0359**
N510QS	**GLF5**	**5326**
N510QS	GLF5	642
N510RC	C500	282
N510RC	C52B	0325
N510RC	C56X	6197
N510RH	GLF2	80
N510RR	**F2TH**	**137**
N510SA	**C510**	**0094**
N510SD	**C650**	**0161**
N510SE	GLF2	70/1
N510SG	LJ35	268
(N510SG)	LJ60	062
N510SJ	C500	668
N510SP	**GLF4**	**1183**
N510SR	GLF2	70/1
N510SR	GLF4	1183
N510SR	**GLF5**	**5021**
N510ST	GLF4	1183
N510SV	C510	0154
N510T	GLF2	248
N510TA	SBRL	265-10
N510TB	SBRL	265-86
N510TC	SBRL	276-27
N510TD	SBRL	265-15
N510TL	GLF2	248
N510TL	**BE40**	**RK-13**
(N510TL)	LJ31	012
N510TP	LJ25	353
N510TS	JSTR	5100/41
N510TW	**C510**	**0240**
N510TX	**C510**	**0131**
N510UP	**C56X**	**5572**
N510US	GLF2	223
N510VP	C510	0244
N510VP	C550	710
N510VV	**C510**	**0014**
N510WC	**C510**	**0017**
N510WD	C680	0510
N510WG	**C510**	**0317**
N510WP	C510	0172
N510WS	FA20	292
N510WS	BE40	RJ-24
N510X	HS25	25126
N510XL	C56X	5100
N510XP	BE40	RK-510
N511AB	**C550**	**328**
N511AC	C525	0098
N511AC	**C52C**	**0081**
N511AJ	LJ25	055
N511AK	**GLF4**	**4186**
N511AT	C500	166
N511AT	LJ24	330
N511BA	GLF2	49
N511BB	CS55	0083
N511BK	**HS25**	**259031**
N511BP	**C525**	**0332**
N511BR	CS55	0083
N511BX	HS25	25150
N511C	GLF4	1065
N511CC	C500	011
N511CC	WW24	253
N511CC	WW24	367
(N511CL)	LJ60	094
N511CQ	WW24	253
N511CS	C56X	5324
N511CT	**G150**	**234**
N511CX	C750	0511
N511DB	**GLF6**	**6058**
N511DB	LJ28	28-002
N511DD	**CL61**	**5187**
N511DL	C550	228
N511DN	C56X	5231
(N511DP)	C560	0274
N511DR	C550	228
N511DR	C560	0274
N511ED	EA50	000262
N511FG	**LJ45**	**420**
N511FL	**FA20**	**122**
N511FX	CL30	20021
N511GA	GLF5	511
N511GG	FA50	82
N511GP	HS25	257052
N511HA	C550	550-1039
N511HC	**C500**	**520**
N511JF	BE40	RK-34
N511JP	C550	550-0959

N511JP	BE40	RK-219
N511JP	BE40	RK-34
N511KA	HS25	257052
N511LD	HS25	257188
N511NC	SBRL	465-6
N511PA	GLF2	49
N511PA	**GLF4**	**1111**
N511PK	**GLF2**	**102/32**
N511QS	GLF5	647
N511RG	HS25	257206
N511S	FA10	115
N511S	FA20	96
N511SC	CL64	5510
N511ST	C560	0281
N511SV	C680	0511
N511T	FA20	142
N511TA	FA20	142
N511TC	**C525**	**0074**
N511TD	JSTR	5145
N511TH	**C560**	**0561**
N511TK	C52C	0098
N511TL	GLF2	199/19
N511TP	**C510**	**0407**
N511TS	JSTR	5101/15
N511UP	**C56X**	**5637**
N511VB	BE40	RK-91
N511VP	C52B	0101
N511WA	ASTR	034
N511WC	C550	189
N511WD	HS25	258196
N511WH	LJ24	055
N511WK	**E50P**	**50000103**
N511WM	CL61	5134
N511WM	F900	108
N511WM	HS25	25159
N511WM	HS25	258196
N511WN	CL61	5134
N511WN	HS25	25159
N511WP	FA20	341
N511WP	GLF2	185
N511WP	HS25	25174
N511WP	LJ45	183
N511WR	FA20	341
N511WS	C550	439
N511WV	C560	0138
N511XP	BE40	RK-511
N511YP	HS25	25191
N512AB	**C56X**	**6142**
(N512AC)	CL60	1073
N512BC	CL61	5125
N512BH	GLEX	9512
N512C	GLF4	1428
N512CC	C500	012
N512CC	C500	112
N512CC	WW24	354
N512CS	C56X	5326
N512CX	**C750**	**0512**
N512DG	CL61	5157
N512DR	C56X	5179
N512F	**BE40**	**RK-115**
N512FX	CL30	20022
N512GA	GLF4	1512
N512GA	GLF5	5212
N512GA	GLF5	5512
N512GP	HS25	257182
N512GV	GLF5	512
(N512HR)	HS25	259012
N512JB	**FA50**	**202**
N512JC	**HS25**	**258556**
N512JT	GLF2	101
N512JT	GLF4	4005
N512JT	**GLF5**	**5278**
N512JY	F900	144
N512LR	HS25	259012
N512LT	**GLF4**	**4005**
N512MB	**EA50**	**000175**
(N512MT)	C650	0232
N512NP	**CL64**	**5572**
N512QS	HS25	259012
N512RB	LJ45	062
N512RJ	**GLF4**	**4124**
N512SD	GLF2	130
N512SH	CL64	5512
N512T	FA20	118
N512TB	C52A	0084
N512TB	LJ60	083
N512TF	F9EX	184
N512UP	**C56X**	**5680**
N512VB	GLF2	189/42
N512WC	**HS25**	**258595**
N512WP	BE40	RJ-16
N512WS	BE40	RJ-24
N513AC	**FA20**	**242**
N513AG	FA20	64
N513AN	FA20	64
N513BE	**HS25**	**258471**
N513CC	C500	013
N513CC	C500	513
N513CC	C550	013
N513CC	**C56X**	**5678**
N513DL	**CL65**	**5811**
N513EA	**EA50**	**000009**
N513EF	C560	0412
N513FX	CL30	20023
N513GA	GLF5	513
N513GP	HS25	257072
N513HS	**F9EX**	**175**

N513JK	C500	313
N513LR	**HS25**	**259013**
N513MA	**GLF3**	**464**
N513ML	HS25	258641
N513MW	GLF5	510
N513NN	C52C	0120
N513PN	C52B	0393
N513QS	HS25	259013
(N513RA)	HS25	259013
N513RB	GALX	060
N513RV	**C525**	**0513**
N513SK	C52A	0064
N513SK	C56X	5678
N513SK	**FA50**	**338**
N513SV	C680	0513
N513T	FA20	123
N513TS	**C650**	**7096**
N513UP	**C56X**	**5794**
N513UT	FA20	464
N513VF	FA20	462
N513VP	C56X	5132
N513WT	**C550**	**556**
N513XF	FA20	450
N513XP	**BE40**	**RK-513**
(N513XX)	C56X	5678
N513YF	FA20	445
N513ZF	FA20	466
N514AF	**E50P**	**50000039**
N514AJ	HS25	256033
N514AJ	**PRM1**	**RB-19**
N514B	HS25	257071
N514BB	**ASTR**	**032**
N514BC	C550	550-0947
N514CA	C550	550-1090
N514CC	C500	014
N514CS	C56X	5328
N514DD	**C510**	**0313**
N514DS	**C525**	**0255**
N514EA	EA50	000053
N514FX	CL30	20023
N514GA	GLF5	514
N514GW	**PRM1**	**RB-263**
N514HB	HA4T	RC-14
N514JJ	FA20	168
N514JR	CL61	5147
N514LR	**HS25**	**259014**
N514MB	**FA50**	**168**
N514MH	HS25	256033
N514MM	ASTR	115
N514QS	HS25	259014
N514RB	CL61	5015
N514RD	HS25	256033
N514RV	C525	0514
N514SA	FA20	30
N514SK	HS25	258711
N514T	FA20	130
N514TS	**CL61**	**5014**
N514UP	**C56X**	**5705**
N514V	HS25	25134
N514V	HS25	256023
N514VA	**GLF5**	**5463**
N514VA	HS25	25134
N514X	**C750**	**0065**
N514XP	BE40	RK-514
N515AA	C500	085
N515AJ	JSTR	5078/3
N515AN	**F2EX**	**284**
N515BP	CL60	1006
N515CC	C500	015
(N515CC)	C500	502
N515CF	**F2EX**	**170**
N515CP	**C56X**	**5626**
N515CS	C56X	5335
N515CS	**LJ31**	**185**
N515CY	**LJ55**	**028**
N515DB	FA20	510
N515DC	C500	112
N515DJ	LJ55	015
N515DM	CL64	5515
N515EV	**C52A**	**0211**
N515FX	CL30	20032
(N515FX)	CL30	20024
N515GP	HS25	258289
N515HB	HA4T	RC-15
N515JA	**GLF4**	**1051**
N515JM	**HS25**	**258695**
N515JM	HS25	HA-0208
N515JT	GLF2	135
(N515JT)	GLF2	189/42
N515KA	GLF2	166/15
N515KK	**MU30**	**A086SA**
N515KS	**CL65**	**5853**
N515LF	**CL61**	**3052**
N515LG	WW24	193
N515LP	FA10	87
N515LR	**HS25**	**259015**
(N515M)	C550	433
N515MB	**C650**	**0122**
N515MP	**EA50**	**000015**
N515MW	BE40	RK-38
N515PE	GLF4	1092
N515PE	GLF5	5144
N515PL	GLF4	1092
N515PL	GLF5	5144
N515PL	**GLF6**	**6015**
N515PV	F2TH	192
N515PV	**F2TS**	**702**

N515QS	HS25	259015
N515RW	C560	0219
N515RY	**BE40**	**RK-46**
N515SC	LJ25	152
N515TB	C680	0148
N515TC	LJ25	354
N515TJ	**BE40**	**RK-229**
N515TK	F2TH	102
N515TX	**C52B**	**0123**
N515UJ	GLF4	1051
N515UP	**C56X**	**5726**
N515VC	C650	0055
N515VP	C560	0315
N515VW	LJ25	013
N515WA	**BE40**	**RK-215**
N515WC	LJ24	203
N515WE	C500	208
N515WH	LJ25	142
N515XL	GLF4	1276
N516AB	C500	244
N516AC	WW24	187
N516CC	C500	016
N516CC	**G280**	**2020**
N516CC	GALX	020
N516CC	WW24	394
N516CJ	**FA50**	**16**
N516CM	**C680**	**0549**
N516CX	C750	0516
N516DG	CL64	5516
N516DM	JSTR	5158
N516EA	**EA50**	**000106**
N516FX	CL30	20036
N516GA	GLF4	1516
N516GA	GLF5	516
N516GA	GLF5	5216
N516GA	GLF5	5416
N516GA	GLF5	5516
N516GH	**GLF5**	**553**
N516GP	HS25	258316
N516GW	**PRM1**	**RB-46**
N516LW	SBRL	282-98
N516PL	GLF6	6015
N516QS	**GLF5**	**658**
N516SM	C650	0157
N516SM	CL61	5089
N516SM	FA10	167
N516TH	**HS25**	**258418**
(N516TM)	HS25	258418
N516TR	**GLF3**	**252**
N516TX	**C52B**	**0289**
N516VE	GLF4	4116
N516WC	JSTR	5150/37
N516WP	SBRL	282-98
N517A	C500	375
N517AF	**C550**	**550-0846**
N517AM	LJ55	108
N517BA	C500	400
N517BB	**CL61**	**5047**
N517CC	C500	017
N517CC	**LJ31**	**117**
N517CF	**C750**	**0049**
N517CS	C56X	5346
N517CW	FA50	17
N517DW	**GLF5**	**5417**
N517FX	**CL30**	**20038**
N517GA	GLF4	1517
N517GA	GLF5	517
N517GA	GLF5	5217
N517GA	GLF5	5417
N517GA	GLF5	5517
N517GP	**LJ31**	**152**
(N517KR)	MU30	A014SA
N517LR	**HS25**	**259017**
N517MD	BE40	RK-459
N517ML	**GLF4**	**1050**
N517MT	C650	0232
N517PD	C52A	0517
N517PJ	F2TH	94
N517QS	**GLF5**	**5209**
N517QS	HS25	259017
N517RH	CL64	5517
N517ST	**HS25**	**258069**
N517SV	C680	0517
N517TT	GLEX	9046
N517XL	C56X	5017
N517XP	BE40	RK-517
N518AR	C52A	0481
N518AR	**C52B**	**0412**
(N518AS)	CS55	0013
N518BA	HS25	258075
N518CC	C500	018
N518CC	C500	318
N518CJ	C52B	0318
N518CL	CL61	5180
N518CS	C56X	5354
N518EJ	FA50	18
(N518FE)	GLF2	135
(N518FS)	CL60	1033
N518FX	**CL30**	**20046**
N518GA	GLF5	5018
N518GA	GLF5	518
N518GA	GLF5	5218
N518GA	GLF5	5518
N518GH	**C52B**	**0040**
N518GS	**CL30**	**20132**
N518GS	GLF2	130
N518GS	LJ45	225

N518GT	**WW24**	**190**
N518JC	LJ31	208
N518JG	**CL61**	**5137**
N518JG	LJ25	328
N518JG	LJ31	208
N518JG	LJ31	219
N518JT	GLF2	135
N518L	JSTR	5040
N518M	**HS25**	**258737**
N518MB	**G280**	**2023**
N518ME	C52A	0091
N518MV	**C550**	**267**
N518N	**C550**	**563**
N518PR	LJ35	497
N518QS	**GLF5**	**5075**
N518RC	**C525**	**0516**
(N518RJ)	FA10	139
N518RR	**HS25**	**257108**
N518S	FA10	74
N518S	HS25	257202
N518S	**HS25**	**258074**
N518SA	LJ31	076
N518SA	LJ55	139A
N518SB	**LJ55**	**139A**
N518SS	**F2TH**	**100**
N518SV	C680	0518
N518TG	BE40	RK-518
N518TT	**C52C**	**0016**
N518WA	**WW24**	**223**
N518XP	BE40	RK-518
N519AA	**C550**	**053**
(N519AC)	LJ55	013
N519AF	GLF3	393
N519BA	HS25	258069
N519CC	C500	019
N519CJ	CS55	0019
N519CP	**GLEX**	**9200**
N519CS	C56X	5356
N519CW	FA50	19
N519DB	CL61	5119
N519EJ	**EA50**	**000019**
N519EM	**FA50**	**19**
N519FX	**CL30**	**20055**
N519GA	GLF4	1519
N519GA	GLF5	5119
N519GA	GLF5	5319
N519GA	GLF5	5519
N519GE	LJ35	305
N519L	JSTR	5037/24
N519M	HS25	258747
N519ME	WW24	207
N519MN	HS25	258747
N519MZ	CL64	5519
(N519QS)	GLF5	681
N519RJ	**C550**	**217**
N519RW	**BE40**	**RK-3**
(N519TW)	GLF2	106
N519VP	**C550**	**550-1019**
N520AF	**FA50**	**247**
N520AW	**FA20**	**453**
N520BA	HS25	258070
N520BA	HS25	258317
N520BE	C510	0243
N520BE	**C510**	**0284**
N520BH	C500	535
N520BP	**C560**	**0031**
N520CC	C500	020
N520CC	C500	200
N520CC	**CL30**	**20291**
N520CH	G150	269
N520CH	PRM1	RB-121
N520CH	BE40	RK-162
N520CJ	C525	0520
N520CM	C750	0107
N520CV	C560	0020
N520CX	**C750**	**0520**
N520DB	**MS76**	**101**
N520DF	**C525**	**0154**
N520E	GLEX	9077
N520E	GLF4	1138
N520EP	GLF4	1138
N520FD	FA20	55/410
N520FX	**CL30**	**20056**
N520G	C560	0369
N520G	C56X	5083
N520G	**C680**	**0243**
N520GA	GLF4	1500
N520GA	GLF4	1520
N520GA	GLF5	5220
N520GA	GLF5	650
N520GA	GLF6	6020
N520GB	**C525**	**0388**
N520JF	**HS25**	**258317**
N520JM	**C510**	**0179**
N520JM	C52A	0086
N520JR	CL64	5520
N520KC	**C510**	**0223**
N520LR	**HS25**	**259020**
N520M	HS25	25070
N520M	HS25	257131
N520M	JSTR	5159
N520MP	**WW24**	**421**
N520N	C500	205
N520PA	LJ35	037
N520Q	C56X	5083
N520QS	HS25	259020
N520RB	C500	282

N520RB	**E50P**	**50000290**
N520RM	**C525**	**0469**
N520RP	C500	607
N520RP	**CL30**	**20032**
N520RP	CS55	0115
N520S	JSTR	5084/8
N520S	LJ60	233
N520S	SBRL	282-8
N520SC	**CL65**	**5779**
N520SC	LJ55	087
N520SC	LJ60	233
(N520SC)	C500	208
(N520SH)	G150	269
N520SL	C52A	0520
N520SP	HS25	258669
N520SQ	LJ55	087
N520SR	LJ25	272
N520TC	**FA20**	**319**
N520TJ	FA20	198/466
N520TT	MU30	A033SA
N520WS	**BE40**	**RJ-53**
N521BA	HS25	258071
N521BH	C550	727
N521BH	C650	0185
N521BU	**C680**	**0330**
N521CC	C500	021
N521CD	F2EX	21
N521CH	LJ31	220
N521CH	**LJ40**	**2023**
N521CJ	C525	0521
N521CS	C56X	5362
N521CV	C560	0521
N521DC	**FA50**	**163**
N521EC	E55P	50500021
N521FL	**FA20**	**68**
N521FP	**C750**	**0016**
N521FX	**CL30**	**20057**
N521GA	GLF5	521
N521HN	GLF5	570
N521HN	**GLF6**	**6027**
N521JK	**HS25**	**258262**
N521JP	LJ25	302
N521JP	LJ25	330
(N521JW)	LJ36	043
N521LF	**C560**	**0132**
N521LL	**C560**	**0273**
N521M	HS25	25129
(N521MJ)	LJ31	098
N521N	SBRL	306-1
N521NC	SBRL	306-109
N521PA	LJ35	239
N521PF	**C525**	**0005**
N521RA	C56X	5076
N521RF	**C650**	**7039**
N521RF	CL64	5521
N521TE	EA50	000021
N521TM	**C550**	**705**
N521VP	**C560**	**0312**
N521WH	LJ31	220
N521WM	C550	093
N521XP	BE40	RK-521
N522AC	F900	148
N522AC	GLF4	1108
N522AC	GLF4	1524
N522AG	GLF4	1524
N522AG	JSTR	5219
(N522AG)	LJ35	625
N522AJ	**C525**	**0068**
N522BA	HS25	258072
N522BD	**F2EX**	**84**
N522BP	GLF4	1451
N522BP	**GLF5**	**5135**
N522BR	GLF4	1451
N522BW	HS25	25043
N522C	FA20	495
N522C	HS25	256067
N522CC	C500	022
N522CC	C500	522
N522CC	C550	002
N522CC	C56X	5111
N522CC	C680	0027
N522CC	F2TH	230
N522CS	C56X	5364
N522DD	FA20	74
N522DK	**EA50**	**000105**
(N522EA)	EA50	000263
N522EE	HS25	258621
N522EE	**HS25**	**258764**
N522EE	BE40	RK-342
N522EE	BE40	RK-38
N522EF	HS25	258621
N522EF	BE40	RK-38
N522EL	**BE40**	**RK-342**
N522EP	C52C	0168
N522FJ	C550	619
N522FP	CL64	5522
N522FX	**CL30**	**20064**
N522GA	GLF4	1522
N522GA	GLF5	5122
N522GA	GLF5	635
N522GS	FA50	115
N522GS	LJ25	348
(N522GS)	C650	0025
N522HS	GLF2	253
N522JA	**C560**	**0288**
N522JD	C500	022
N522JP	LJ25	318

N522JS	LJ25	348
(N522KJ)	BE40	RK-22
N522KM	F900	78
(N522KM)	GLEX	9069
N522KN	C52A	0156
N522M	HS25	25156
N522M	HS25	257144
N522MB	**BE40**	**RK-522**
N522ME	HS25	25043
N522N	SBRL	306-109
N522NJ	C52B	0081
N522PA	LJ35	254
(N522QS)	GLF5	5011
N522RA	C56X	5136
N522SB	GLF3	339
N522SC	LJ25	006
N522TA	LJ25	318
N522TE	EA50	000022
N522VR	**GLF4**	**1102**
N522WK	LJ55	088
N522X	HS25	256067
N522XL	C56X	5022
N522XP	BE40	RK-522
N523AC	F900	139
N523AC	GLF4	1528
N523AC	**GLF5**	**5411**
N523AC	JSTR	5013
N523AC	WW24	77
N523AG	GLF5	691
(N523AG)	F900	139
N523AM	**GLF3**	**372**
N523AR	**CL65**	**5839**
N523AS	C525	0092
N523B	CL60	1071
N523BA	HS25	258077
N523BM	LJ45	158
N523BT	C525	0311
N523BT	**C52A**	**0124**
N523CC	C500	023
N523CC	C500	123
N523CC	C500	323
N523CC	C56X	5201
N523CL	CL64	5523
N523CS	C56X	5507
N523CW	FA50	23
N523DG	C52A	0084
N523DM	**E55P**	**50500036**
N523DR	**PRM1**	**RB-50**
N523DV	**C52B**	**0415**
N523FX	**CL30**	**20074**
N523GA	GLF5	5123
N523GA	GLF5	523
N523GA	GLF5	5253
N523GA	**GLF5**	**5523**
N523GA	GLF5	643
N523JD	C500	023
N523JM	**CL61**	**5106**
(N523JP)	LJ25	330
N523KW	C560	0224
N523KW	C56X	5015
N523LM	C52B	0148
N523LR	HS25	259023
N523M	HS25	25245
N523M	HS25	257188
N523MA	HS25	256023
N523MV	LJ60	154
N523N	SBRL	306-7
N523NA	FA20	439
N523PA	LJ35	247
N523PB	FA50	23
(N523PT)	GLF3	336
N523QS	HS25	259023
N523RB	WW24	175
N523SA	LJ25	325
N523SV	C680	0523
N523TS	**C525**	**0363**
(N523TX)	GLF3	336
N523VP	C560	0423
N523W	F2TH	212
(N523W)	HS25	258086
N523WC	**F2TH**	**212**
N523WC	HS25	258086
N523WG	**HS25**	**258086**
N523XP	BE40	RK-523
N524AC	**GLF5**	**5433**
N524AC	GLF5	686
N524AC	JSTR	5004
N524AC	JSTR	5149/11
N524AC	SBRL	282-28
N524AF	C525	0199
N524AG	**GLF5**	**686**
N524AG	SBRL	282-28
N524AN	GLF4	1119
N524BA	HS25	258080
N524CA	C500	024
N524CC	C500	024
N524CJ	C525	0524
N524DW	**LJ25**	**081**
(N524DW)	LJ24	177
N524EA	**GLF6**	**6012**
N524FX	**CL30**	**20095**
N524GA	GLF4	1524
N524GA	GLF5	5124
N524GA	GLF5	524
N524GA	GLF5	5324
N524GA	GLF5	5524
N524GA	GLF5	646

N524HC	**LJ31**	**114**
N524HC	LJ35	358
N524LP	BE40	RK-386
N524LR	**HS25**	**259024**
N524M	HS25	257204
N524MA	**C550**	**029**
N524MM	GLF2	85
N524NA	**FA20**	**411**
N524PA	**LJ35**	**033**
N524PC	CL61	3023
N524QS	HS25	259024
N524RH	WW24	414
N524S	**FA50**	**51**
N524SA	F2TH	60
N524SC	LJ24	153
N524SF	**C525**	**0240**
N524SM	**C510**	**0391**
N524VE	**GLF5**	**5424**
N524X	WW24	92
N524XA	**C550**	**550-0988**
N524XP	BE40	RK-524
N525AC	C500	343
N525AC	GLF5	691
N525AC	LJ31	030
N525AD	C525	0435
N525AD	C525	0600
N525AE	C525	0017
N525AG	GALX	226
N525AJ	C525	0040
N525AJ	C525	0671
N525AJ	**C525**	**0673**
N525AJ	WW24	325
(N525AJ)	C525	0395
N525AK	**WW24**	**260**
N525AL	**C525**	**0011**
N525AM	**C525**	**0538**
N525AP	C525	0045
N525AP	**C52A**	**0460**
N525AR	C525	0395
N525AS	C525	0092
N525AS	C525	0363
N525AU	**C525**	**0900**
N525AW	**C525**	**0369**
N525AW	WW24	129
N525AZ	C52A	0001
N525BA	C560	0417
N525BA	HS25	258081
(N525BA)	C525	0522
N525BE	C525	0299
(N525BE)	C525	0306
N525BF	C525	0191
(N525BL)	C525	0191
N525BP	**C525**	**0479**
N525BR	**C525**	**0444**
N525BT	**C525**	**0161**
N525BW	**C525**	**0409**
N525BY	**C52B**	**0014**
N525CC	C500	025
N525CC	C525	0001
N525CC	C525	0100
N525CC	C52A	0007
N525CC	C52A	0125
N525CD	**C525**	**0360**
N525CE	**C52A**	**0181**
N525CF	C525	0516
N525CF	**C52B**	**0189**
N525CF	HS25	258018
N525CF	LJ60	010
N525CG	**C525**	**0853**
N525CG	C52A	0125
N525CH	**C525**	**0078**
N525CJ	C525	0500
N525CJ	C525	702
N525CJ	C52B	0333
N525CK	C525	0058
N525CK	**C52A**	**0128**
N525CM	**C525**	**0093**
N525CP	C525	0099
N525CP	**C525**	**0228**
N525CP	C525	0378
N525CR	**C52B**	**0238**
N525CU	C525	0292
N525CW	**C52B**	**0465**
N525CW	C560	0225
(N525CY)	C525	0367
N525CZ	C525	0120
N525CZ	C52C	0004
N525DC	**C525**	**0195**
N525DE	C525	0364
N525DE	**C52B**	**0006**
N525DG	C525	0057
N525DG	C52A	0084
N525DG	C52B	0039
N525DJ	C525	0024
N525DL	C525	0364
N525DL	**C52A**	**0050**
N525DM	C525	0314
N525DM	**C52A**	**0516**
N525DP	**C525**	**0318**
N525DR	C525	0308
N525DR	**C52A**	**0330**
N525DR	C52B	0078
N525DT	**C52A**	**0003**
N525DU	**C525**	**0205**
N525DV	C52A	0119
N525DY	C525	0199
N525DY	**C525**	**0306**

N525E	CL64	5525
N525EC	C525	0246
N525EC	E50P	50000159
N525EE	**C52B**	**0081**
(N525EF)	C525	0153
N525EG	**C52A**	**0449**
N525EM	**C52C**	**0007**
N525EP	C52A	0346
N525EP	**C52C**	**0168**
N525ET	C525	0244
N525EZ	C525	0400
N525EZ	C52A	0080
N525EZ	C52B	0089
N525EZ	C52B	0238
N525EZ	C52B	0295
N525EZ	**C52C**	**0096**
N525F	C525	0058
N525FC	**C525**	**0531**
N525FD	C525	0008
N525FF	**C52A**	**0161**
N525FN	**C525**	**0368**
N525FS	C525	0026
N525FT	C525	0367
N525FX	**CL30**	**20112**
N525GA	C500	182
N525GB	C525	0232
N525GB	C525	0380
N525GB	C52B	0104
N525GC	**C525**	**0065**
N525GE	**C525**	**0679**
(N525GF)	GALX	226
N525GG	C525	0041
N525GJ	**C525**	**0217**
N525GK	**C52B**	**0404**
N525GL	**C525**	**0872**
N525GM	C525	0240
N525GM	C52A	0150
N525GM	C52B	0024
N525GM	**C52B**	**0474**
(N525GN)	C52B	0024
N525GP	C525	0203
N525GP	LJ31	155
N525GP	LJ31	162
N525GT	**C52B**	**0104**
N525GV	C525	0001
N525GY	**C52B**	**0024**
N525H	**C525**	**0520**
N525H	C52A	0045
N525H	C52B	0306
N525HA	**C525**	**0081**
N525HB	**C52A**	**0040**
N525HC	**C525**	**0270**
(N525HC)	C525	0273
N525HD	**C52A**	**0301**
N525HG	**C52A**	**0352**
N525HJ	C525	0211
N525HL	**C525**	**0808**
N525HL	C52A	0467
N525HQ	**C525**	**0827**
N525HS	**C525**	**0035**
N525HV	**C525**	**0201**
N525HX	**C525**	**0278**
N525HY	**C525**	**0239**
N525J	**C525**	**0184**
N525JA	**C550**	**294**
N525JD	**C525**	**0819**
N525JD	C52A	0130
N525JH	C525	0124
N525JJ	C525	0141
N525JJ	**C525**	**0497**
N525JL	**C525**	**0407**
N525JM	**C525**	**0134**
N525JN	**C52A**	**0423**
(N525JN)	C525	0635
N525JT	GLF2	156/31
(N525JT)	C525	0440
N525JV	C525	0010
(N525JV)	C52B	0014
N525JW	**C525**	**0162**
N525JZ	**C560**	**0277**
N525KA	**C525**	**0019**
N525KB	C52C	0116
N525KD	C52B	0126
N525KF	GLF4	1315
N525KF	**GLF5**	**5504**
(N525KF)	C525	0090
N525KH	C525	0197
N525KH	**C525**	**0908**
N525KJ	**C52C**	**0155**
N525KK	C525	0056
N525KL	C525	0136
N525KM	**C525**	**0472**
N525KN	**C525**	**0007**
N525KP	**C52A**	**0160**
N525KR	C52A	0160
N525KR	**C52C**	**0086**
N525KS	C52C	0002
N525KT	**C52A**	**0058**
(N525KT)	C525	0029
N525L	**C52B**	**0051**
(N525L)	C52A	0039
N525LA	**C525**	**0422**
N525LB	C525	0388
N525LC	C52A	0009
N525LC	C550	383
N525LD	**C52A**	**0335**
N525LE	**C525**	**0447**

N525LF	**C525**	**0382**
N525LH	**C525**	**0018**
N525LJ	**C525**	**0314**
N525LK	**C525**	**0200**
N525LM	**C525**	**0427**
N525LP	**C525**	**0196**
N525LR	C52A	0176
N525LR	HS25	259035
N525LS	**C525**	**0840**
N525LS	E55P	50500053
N525LW	**C525**	**0082**
N525LX	**C525**	**0058**
N525M	ASTR	102
N525M	**C525**	**0334**
N525MA	**C52A**	**0012**
(N525MA)	FA50	18
N525MB	**C525**	**0036**
N525MC	C525	0018
N525MC	**C52B**	**0288**
N525MD	C525	0367
N525ME	**C52A**	**0032**
N525MF	**C525**	**0313**
N525MH	C525	0388
N525MH	**F900**	**113**
N525ML	**C525**	**0402**
N525ML	WW24	260
N525MM	**C525**	**0815**
N525MN	**E50P**	**50000235**
N525MP	C525	0313
N525MP	C52A	0012
N525MP	**C52B**	**0088**
N525MR	C525	0313
N525MR	**C52A**	**0173**
N525MW	**C525**	**0370**
N525MX	**C525**	**0423**
N525N	SBRL	282-10
N525NA	C525	0048
N525NA	**FA20**	**447**
N525NB	C52C	0003
N525NE	**C52B**	**0295**
N525NG	**C52A**	**0388**
N525NG	C52C	0001
N525NP	C525	0458
N525NT	**C525**	**0440**
N525NY	**C52B**	**0201**
N525P	**C525**	**0165**
N525PB	C525	0232
N525PB	**C52A**	**0172**
N525PC	**C525**	**0616**
N525PC	C52B	0041
N525PC	E55P	50500011
N525PE	C525	0125
N525PE	**C550**	**550-1031**
N525PF	C525	0232
N525PF	**C52A**	**0023**
N525PG	**ASTR**	**152**
N525PH	**C52A**	**0329**
N525PJ	C525	0490
N525PL	**C525**	**0043**
N525PM	**C52A**	**0067**
N525PS	**C525**	**0061**
N525PT	**C525**	**0125**
N525PV	**C500**	**569**
N525PZ	C525	0820
N525PZ	**C52C**	**0196**
N525QS	HS25	259025
N525RA	**C525**	**0167**
N525RC	**C525**	**0178**
N525RC	FA10	116
N525RD	**C560**	**0106**
N525RF	C525	0023
N525RF	C525	0411
N525RF	**C52A**	**0327**
N525RG	C52A	0387
N525RK	**C525**	**0413**
N525RL	C525	0338
N525RL	C525	0524
N525RL	**C52A**	**0494**
N525RM	**C525**	**0225**
N525RN	**C525**	**0522**
N525RP	**C525**	**0023**
N525RU	C52A	0303
N525RW	**C52A**	**0060**
N525RY	**C525**	**0438**
N525RZ	**C525**	**0612**
N525SA	C52A	0089
N525SC	C525	0099
N525SD	**CL61**	**5056**
(N525SE)	C525	0137
N525SJ	**C52C**	**0170**
N525SM	**C52A**	**0175**
(N525SP)	C525	0019
(N525ST)	C525	0195
N525SY	**C525**	**0324**
N525TA	C525	0141
N525TA	C52A	0318
N525TF	**C525**	**0067**
N525TG	**C525**	**0826**
N525TG	C52A	0021
N525TH	**C52B**	**0410**
N525TJ	C52A	0024
N525TK	**C525**	**0355**
N525TK	C52A	0080
(N525TL)	C525	0134
N525TW	**LJ25**	**011**
N525TX	C525	0304
N525U	C52A	0112

N525U	**C52B**	**0012**
N525VG	C525	0239
N525VP	C525	0001
N525VP	C56X	5205
N525VV	C52A	0113
N525WB	**C525**	**0079**
N525WC	**C525**	**0107**
N525WD	**C52A**	**0107**
N525WF	**C525**	**0246**
N525WH	C525	0028
N525WH	C525	0488
N525WL	**C52B**	**0237**
N525WM	C525	0213
N525WR	**C525**	**0034**
(N525WS)	C525	0444
N525WW	**C525**	**0060**
N525XD	**C525**	**0335**
N525XD	C52A	0337
N525XL	GLF2	135
N525XX	WW24	336
N525ZZ	**C52A**	**0055**
N526AC	C550	038
N526AC	**CL30**	**20263**
N526AC	HS25	258169
N526AG	C550	038
N526BA	HS25	258083
N526CA	C525	0033
N526CC	C500	026
N526CC	C500	526
N526CC	FA50	147
N526CF	**LJ45**	**124**
N526CK	C525	0058
N526CP	**C525**	**0099**
N526CW	MU30	A026SA
N526D	FA10	84
N526DG	C52B	0039
N526DM	HS25	257156
N526DV	**C52A**	**0226**
N526EE	GLF4	1110
N526EE	**GLF4**	**1304**
N526EE	GLF4	1406
N526EE	GLF5	519
N526EL	LJ45	327
N526EZ	C525	0400
N526FX	**CL30**	**20118**
N526GA	ASTR	115
N526GA	GLF4	1526
N526GA	GLF5	5126
N526GA	GLF5	5226
N526GA	GLF5	526
N526GA	GLF5	5286
N526GA	GLF5	5426
N526GA	GLF5	5526
N526GP	LJ31	181
N526GX	**GLEX**	**9526**
N526HV	C52A	0139
(N526JC)	HS25	257021
N526LC	C525	0526
N526M	HS25	258032
N526N	SBRL	282-30
N526PS	HS25	HA-0012
N526SM	C56X	5036
N526SM	**FA50**	**201**
N526XP	HS25	258526
N527AC	C550	121
N527AC	HS25	258104
N527AG	C550	121
N527BA	HS25	258084
N527CC	C500	027
N527CC	C550	027
N527CC	GLF3	412
N527CJ	C525	0527
N527CP	C650	0199
(N527DF)	BE40	RK-527
N527DS	C550	317
N527DV	**C52B**	**0327**
N527EA	C550	426
N527EE	**C56X**	**5549**
N527ER	LJ24	096
N527EW	**C500**	**669**
N527FX	**CL30**	**20124**
N527GA	ASTR	116
N527GA	GLF5	5127
N527GA	GLF5	527
N527GA	GLF5	5277
N527GA	GLF5	5527
N527GA	GLF5	653
N527GP	LJ31	182
N527HV	**C52B**	**0213**
N527JA	**CL61**	**5058**
N527JC	**GLF4**	**1179**
N527JG	**GLF4**	**1519**
N527JG	LJ31	125
N527K	GLF2	25
N527M	HS25	258054
N527MW	**HDJT**	**42000021**
N527MW	HDJT	42000025
N527NP	**C750**	**0231**
N527PA	**LJ36**	**019**
N527PM	PRM1	RB-177
N527PM	**BE40**	**RK-304**
N527PN	**PRM1**	**RB-177**
N527SC	C56X	5260
(N527TA)	C500	334
N527WA	HS25	258618
N527XP	**BE40**	**RK-527**
N527Z	LJ35	527

N528AC	**C56X**	**5695**
N528AC	HS25	258070
N528AP	GLF3	399
N528AP	**GLF5**	**5168**
N528BA	HS25	258086
N528BD	F2EX	19
N528BP	HS25	258646
N528BS	**C52B**	**0243**
N528CB	**C525**	**0678**
N528CC	C500	028
N528CE	C52B	0022
N528CJ	C525	0528
N528CJ	C52A	0054
N528DK	CL64	5508
N528DM	**C510**	**0031**
N528DS	**C500**	**615**
N528DT	CL64	5528
N528DV	**C52B**	**0329**
N528EA	**EA50**	**000128**
N528EA	LJ35	024
N528FX	**CL30**	**20125**
N528GA	ASTR	117
N528GA	G150	203
N528GA	GLF4	1528
N528GA	GLF4	4128
N528GA	GLF5	5278
N528GA	GLF5	528
N528GA	GLF5	5528
N528GP	CL64	5401
N528HV	**C52B**	**0469**
N528J	GLEX	9177
N528JC	C52B	0075
N528JD	FA10	76
N528JD	LJ35	024
N528JJ	**LJ45**	**436**
N528JL	**FA10**	**76**
N528JR	F900	51
N528JR	FA50	220
N528JR	GLEX	9177
N528KW	**C560**	**0224**
N528L	LJ35	528
N528LG	**MU30**	**A050SA**
N528LJ	CL61	3050
N528M	GLF5	5072
N528M	HS25	258055
N528MP	**GLEX**	**9307**
N528QS	**GLF5**	**5042**
N528RM	**C500**	**435**
N528RM	C500	613
N528RR	**ASTR**	**042**
N528SM	C56X	5036
N528TM	**E55P**	**50500128**
N528VM	C560	0423
N528VP	C56X	5282
(N528VP)	LJ35	285
N528XL	C56X	5028
N528XP	BE40	RK-528
N528YT	**CL30**	**20382**
N529AK	CL64	5418
N529AK	**HA4T**	**RC-21**
N529AL	GLF4	1123
N529BA	HS25	258087
N529BC	**LJ35**	**471**
N529CC	C500	029
(N529CC)	C525	0009
N529CF	SBRL	306-58
N529CW	FA50	29
N529D	CL61	3025
N529D	CL65	5711
N529DM	CL61	3025
N529DM	CL64	5575
N529DM	CL65	5711
N529DM	**CL65**	**5880**
N529DM	HS25	257156
N529DV	**C52B**	**0358**
N529F	C550	011
N529FX	**CL30**	**20128**
N529GA	ASTR	118
N529GA	GLF4	1529
N529GA	GLF5	5129
N529GA	GLF5	529
N529GA	GLF5	5299
N529GA	GLF5	5529
N529GA	GLF5	655
N529GP	CL64	5412
N529KE	LJ60	064
N529KF	**CL64**	**5477**
N529KF	LJ60	064
N529KT	**C500**	**500**
N529M	HS25	258446
N529MM	FA50	29
N529NM	**C525**	**0268**
N529PC	**C52A**	**0001**
N529QS	**GLF5**	**5156**
N529SC	SBRL	306-58
N529SC	SBRL	465-12
N529SG	**F9EX**	**259**
N529SM	HS25	257002
N529SQ	SBRL	306-58
N529TA	GLF5	529
N529TS	JSTR	5209
N529VP	C56X	5229
N529X	C560	0163
N530AG	C510	0193
N530AG	C525	0409
N530AJ	**C510**	**0234**
N530AQ	C525	0409

N530AR	FA50	175
N530BA	HS25	258089
N530BA	HS25	258244
N530BL	HS25	257002
N530CC	C500	030
(N530CC)	C56X	5111
(N530CM)	ASTR	040
N530DC	LJ25	291
N530DG	FA50	245
N530DL	**WW24**	**287**
N530DW	C52A	0369
N530FX	**CL30**	**20148**
N530G	JSTR	5096/10
N530GA	**GLF2**	**247**
N530GA	GLF5	530
N530GP	**G150**	**203**
N530GV	WW24	213
N530GV	WW24	356
N530J	LJ35	074
N530JD	GLF4	1430
(N530JM)	GLEX	9216
N530L	FA20	84
N530M	JSTR	5214
N530P	C550	333
N530PT	**PRM1**	**RB-51**
N530QS	HS25	259030
N530RD	MU30	A016SA
N530RM	**C510**	**0242**
N530SC	**CL65**	**5908**
N530SM	HS25	258697
N530SW	GLF2	162
N530TC	FA10	69
(N530TE)	HS25	257065
N530TL	C500	342
N530TL	HS25	257065
N530XP	BE40	RK-530
N531A	C550	481
N531AB	SBRL	306-98
N531AC	**LJ45**	**196**
N531AF	GLF5	531
N531AJ	C52B	0451
N531AJ	LJ35	011
N531AT	LJ31	085
N531BA	HS25	258090
N531BJ	C56X	5031
N531BR	C525	0264
N531CC	C500	031
N531CC	C560	0178
N531CC	CS55	0031
N531CM	**C52B**	**0071**
N531CM	CS55	0033
N531CW	LJ25	231
N531EA	**EA50**	**000031**
N531EE	E50P	50000331
N531F	C560	0054
N531FC	**C680**	**0107**
N531FL	**FA20**	**113**
N531FX	**CL30**	**20150**
N531GA	GLF4	1531
N531GA	GLF4	4131
N531GA	GLF5	5131
N531GA	GLF5	531
N531GA	GLF5	5311
N531GA	GLF5	5431
N531GA	**GLF5**	**5531**
(N531GC)	LJ25	245
N531GP	**G150**	**207**
(N531JC)	GLF3	491
N531JF	GLF3	491
N531K	**LJ55**	**053**
N531M	JSTR	5236
N531MB	C560	0027
N531MB	**C56X**	**5014**
N531MD	GLF4	1280
N531MF	C560	0027
N531MU	GLF4	1531
N531NC	SBRL	306-7
N531P	**LJ55**	**093**
N531PM	CS55	0059
N531QS	**GLF5**	**5133**
N531RA	LJ31	106
N531RA	LJ31	192
N531RC	C56X	5184
N531RC	C680	0107
N531RC	**G280**	**2065**
N531RQ	**C56X**	**5184**
N531SK	**LJ31**	**043**
N531TS	LJ31	106
N531VP	C560	0311
N531WB	FA20	514
N532BA	HS25	258092
(N532C)	C650	0167
N532CC	C500	032
N532CC	C56X	5111
N532CC	C650	0167
N532CC	C680	0027
N532CC	CS55	0032
N532CC	**F2EX**	**238**
N532CC	F2TH	230
N532CF	CS55	0032
N532CJ	C525	0032
N532DM	CL64	5532
N532FX	**CL30**	**20154**
N532GA	GLF4	1532
N532GA	GLF4	4132
N532GA	GLF5	5302
N532GA	GLF5	532

N532GA	GLF5	5532
N532GA	GLF5	658
N532GP	**G150**	**221**
N532JF	C650	7077
(N532JF)	C750	0073
N532LW	**C52B**	**0118**
N532M	C550	378
N532MA	C560	0036
N532MT	**C56X**	**6118**
N532PJ	HS25	258448
N532SP	**GLF5**	**632**
N532XP	BE40	RK-532
N533	HS25	25083
N533	HS25	25103
N533	HS25	257114
N533	WW24	356
(N533)	WW24	345
(N533AG)	C510	0193
N533BA	HS25	258093
N533BF	C500	033
N533CC	C500	033
N533CC	C56X	5201
N533CC	C56X	5687
N533CC	**C56X**	**6063**
N533CC	C650	0185
N533CC	CS55	0132
N533CM	**C52B**	**0182**
N533CS	FA10	177
N533DK	CL64	5533
N533DK	**EA50**	**000143**
N533EJ	JSTR	5099/5
N533ES	C56X	5823
N533F	**C52A**	**0489**
N533FX	**CL30**	**20160**
N533GA	GALX	233
N533GA	GLF4	1533
N533GA	GLF5	5133
N533GA	GLF5	533
N533GA	GLF5	5533
N533GA	GLF5	660
N533GT	**EA50**	**000267**
N533HB	BE40	RK-533
N533JF	C525	0247
(N533JF)	C52A	0101
N533LM	**GLEX**	**9574**
N533LR	**HS25**	**259033**
N533M	C550	041
N533MA	C550	083
N533P	HS25	258075
N533QS	HS25	259033
N533SR	**GLF4**	**4253**
N533SV	C680	0533
N533TS	CL65	5733
N533VP	C510	0033
N533XL	C56X	5333
N534	WW24	345
N534A	LJ35	304
N534BA	HS25	258095
N534CC	C500	034
N534CC	C56X	5025
N534CC	C56X	5707
N534CC	**C56X**	**6070**
N534CJ	C52A	0126
N534FX	**CL30**	**20161**
N534GA	G280	2034
N534GA	GALX	234
N534GA	GLF5	5134
N534GA	GLF5	534
N534GA	GLF5	5534
N534GA	GLF5	634
N534H	**C650**	**0196**
N534H	LJ35	304
(N534LL)	C525	0092
N534M	C550	048
(N534M)	C550	612
N534MA	FA50	29
N534MW	C550	067
N534NA	C525	0534
N534QS	**GLF5**	**5103**
N534R	WW24	345
N534RF	CL64	5534
N534TP	LJ60	082
N534TX	C525	0092
N535AF	**LJ35**	**191**
N535BA	HS25	258096
N535BC	**E55P**	**50500120**
N535BC	HS25	258655
N535BC	HS25	258776
N535BC	PRM1	RB-72
N535BP	**C560**	**0646**
N535BR	PRM1	RB-72
N535CC	C500	035
N535CD	**PRM1**	**RB-96**
N535CE	C560	0635
N535CJ	C525	0535
N535CM	C52A	0491
N535CM	C52B	0182
N535CM	**C52B**	**0411**
N535CS	GLF3	464
N535D	WW24	74
N535DL	**C52B**	**0172**
N535DT	**C52B**	**0069**
N535EX	FA50	335
N535F	**C52B**	**0001**
N535FX	**CL30**	**20167**
N535GA	C500	583
N535GA	GLF4	4135
N535GA	GLF5	5135
N535GA	GLF5	5305
N535GA	GLF5	5535
N535GA	GLF5	620
N535GH	**C52B**	**0054**
(N535GV)	GLF5	535
N535JF	**C52A**	**0349**
N535JM	LJ35	401
N535LC	**LJ35**	**021**
N535LR	C525	0128
N535MA	C550	037
N535MC	LJ35	385
N535PC	C550	229
N535PC	LJ35	291
N535PS	**LJ31**	**087**
N535QS	GLF5	5229
N535QS	HS25	259035
N535RF	C525	0411
N535SW	C550	550-0899
N535TA	LJ35	013
N535TF	**C56X**	**5535**
N535TV	C52A	0349
N535V	**GLF5**	**535**
N535VP	C52A	0491
N535WT	**C525**	**0687**
N536BA	HS25	258098
N536BW	**HS25**	**HA-0201**
N536CC	C500	036
N536CS	GLF2	24
(N536EC)	E50P	50000136
N536FX	**CL30**	**20171**
N536GA	GALX	236
N536GA	GLF5	5136
N536GA	GLF5	536
N536GA	GLF5	5386
N536GA	**GLF5**	**5536**
N536GA	GLF5	601
N536KN	**LJ35**	**073**
N536M	C550	144
N536MP	CL64	5536
N536V	C500	032
N536V	BE40	RK-445
N536XJ	**CL30**	**20036**
N537BA	HS25	258099
N537CC	C500	037
N537DF	**BE40**	**RK-537**
N537DR	CL64	5537
N537FX	CL30	20187
N537GA	G150	237
N537GA	GLF4	4037
N537GA	GLF5	5337
N537GA	GLF5	537
N537GA	GLF5	5437
N537GA	**GLF5**	**5537**
N537M	C550	145
N537RB	**PRM1**	**RB-190**
N537VP	C560	0377
N537XJ	**CL30**	**20213**
N537XP	BE40	RK-537
N538	HS25	25083
N538BA	HS25	258100
N538CC	C500	038
N538CC	C650	0185
N538CC	CS55	0138
N538CF	**C52A**	**0381**
N538FX	**CL30**	**20201**
N538GA	GALX	238
N538GA	GLF4	4038
N538GA	GLF5	538
N538GA	**GLF5**	**5538**
N538GA	GLF5	602
(N538JF)	C525	0247
N538LD	HS25	258538
N538M	C550	328
N538RF	CL64	5538
N538TS	CL65	5738
N538WS	E55P	50500025
N538XJ	**CL30**	**20224**
N538XL	C56X	5538
N538XP	BE40	RK-538
N539AB	CL64	5539
N539BA	HS25	258101
N539BA	**LJ31**	**033D**
N539CA	**F9EX**	**181**
N539CC	C500	039
N539CC	C550	330
N539CC	C56X	6135
N539CE	C560	0539
N539CS	CL61	5194
N539FX	CL30	20202
N539GA	GLF5	5139
N539GA	GLF5	539
N539GA	GLF5	5439
N539GA	**GLF5**	**5539**
N539GA	GLF5	603
N539JM	LJ55	039
N539KH	**C52B**	**0231**
N539LB	LJ31	078
N539LR	**HS25**	**259039**
N539PG	SBRL	306-79
N539QS	HS25	259039
N539RM	**EA50**	**000101**
N539TA	E55P	50500039
N539VE	GLF4	4039
N539VP	C560	0339
N539WA	C560	0556
N539WA	**C56X**	**6135**
N539XJ	**CL30**	**20230**
N539XP	BE40	RK-539
N540AS	**C52A**	**0467**
N540B	HS25	257077
N540BA	CL65	5729
N540BA	HS25	258102
N540BA	HS25	258241
N540CC	C500	040
N540CH	**GLEX**	**9055**
N540CH	GLF4	1306
N540CL	LJ24	026
N540CS	C56X	5516
N540CV	C560	0540
N540EA	**GLF2**	**174**
N540FX	**CL30**	**20205**
N540G	JSTR	5009
N540G	JSTR	5075/19
N540GA	**GLF5**	**5540**
N540HP	LJ35	399
N540JB	CS55	0061
N540JW	CL64	5549
N540LH	LJ40	2064
N540LR	**HS25**	**259040**
N540M	GLF5	597
N540M	HS25	258145
N540PA	C560	0027
N540PA	LJ36	019
N540QS	HS25	259040
N540RK	BE40	RK-540
N540VP	C52B	0040
N540W	CL61	5062
N540W	GLF4	1265
N540W	GLF5	5416
N540WY	GLEX	9187
N540XJ	CL30	20238
N541AG	C500	041
N541AL	LJ45	179
N541BA	**CL65**	**6060**
N541BA	HS25	258103
N541CC	C500	041
N541CJ	C525	0454
N541CS	C56X	5521
N541CV	C560	0541
N541CW	MU30	A004SA
N541CX	**C750**	**0036**
N541DE	CL64	5390
(N541FJ)	FA50	41
N541FL	**FA20**	**48**
N541FX	**CL30**	**20211**
N541GA	GLF4	4141
N541GA	GLF5	5141
N541GA	GLF5	5341
N541GA	GLF5	5441
N541GA	**GLF5**	**5541**
N541JG	C550	550-0849
N541LB	**EA50**	**000041**
N541LF	CL65	5712
N541LJ	LJ45	041
N541LR	**HS25**	**259041**
N541M	WW24	48
N541MM	CL60	1044
(N541NC)	C500	205
N541PA	**LJ35**	**053**
N541QS	HS25	259041
N541RL	**ASTR**	**034**
N541RS	**PRM1**	**RB-144**
N541S	**C650**	**0115**
N541SG	WW24	48
N541SV	**C680**	**0541**
(N541TM)	MU30	A004SA
"N541TS"	CL61	5041
N541VP	C560	0341
N541WG	C52B	0188
N541XJ	CL30	20239
N541XJ	**CL30**	**20279**
N541XP	**HS25**	**258541**
N541Z	**F2EX**	**312**
N542AP	**F2EX**	**89**
N542BA	**CL65**	**5737**
N542BA	HS25	258104
N542CC	C500	042
N542CC	**C680**	**0333**
N542CC	CS55	0142
N542CE	C560	0542
N542CS	C56X	5523
N542FX	**CL30**	**20217**
N542GD	**GLF5**	**5542**
N542HB	HA4T	RC-42
N542LF	GLEX	9060
N542LM	**LJ35**	**280**
N542LR	HS25	259042
N542M	**HS25**	**258766**
N542PA	**LJ35**	**030**
N542QS	HS25	259042
N542RK	**C510**	**0373**
(N542S)	SBRL	306-16
N542SA	**LJ35**	**503**
N542TW	JSTR	5113/25
N542XJ	CL30	20242
N542XP	BE40	RK-542
N543BA	**CL65**	**6061**
N543CC	C500	043
N543CM	**LJ45**	**062**
N543GD	**GLF5**	**5543**
N543GL	**GLEX**	**9543**
N543H	**GLF5**	**688**
N543LE	C560	0543
N543LF	**HS25**	**258391**
N543LM	**LJ35**	**426**
N543PA	LJ35	070
N543PD	**C52B**	**0458**
(N543QS)	HS25	259043
N543SC	C650	0130
N543SC	**CS55**	**0144**
N543TX	**C52C**	**0043**
(N543VP)	C560	0143
N543WW	**GALX**	**213**
N543WW	LJ35	332
N543XJ	CL30	20245
N544CC	C500	044
N544CM	**F900**	**152**
N544CM	FA50	173
N544FX	CL30	20240
N544GD	**GLF5**	**5544**
N544JB	**C510**	**0353**
N544KB	C680	0047
N544KK	GLF5	669
N544LF	BE40	RK-428
N544LM	**LJ35**	**500**
N544LR	**HS25**	**259044**
N544MF	**C510**	**0097**
N544MG	HS25	258753
N544PA	**LJ35**	**247**
N544PH	SBRL	465-56
N544PS	C550	550-0847
N544PS	C550	550-1010
N544PS	**HS25**	**258491**
N544QS	HS25	259044
N544RA	FA50	144
N544S	**F2EX**	**255**
N544SV	C680	0544
N544TS	CL64	5544
N544TX	**C52C**	**0044**
N544VP	C560	0544
N544X	FA20	258
N544XJ	CL30	20248
N544XL	**C56X**	**5044**
N545AR	LJ45	423
N545BF	JSTR	5146
N545BP	**C560**	**0756**
N545C	FA20	17
N545C	SBRL	282-57
N545CC	C500	045
N545CC	C500	545
N545CC	GLF5	545
N545CG	**LJ45**	**386**
N545CM	**C510**	**0460**
N545CS	**GLF4**	**1361**
N545DL	**C52A**	**0521**
N545EC	LJ45	199
N545EE	**E55P**	**50500345**
N545ES	C525	0066
N545FX	**CL30**	**20302**
N545G	**PRM1**	**RB-28**
(N545G)	C500	368
N545GA	C500	368
N545GA	C550	040
N545GA	GLF4	4145
N545GA	GLF5	5145
N545GA	GLF5	5405
N545GA	**GLF5**	**5545**
N545GH	**C52C**	**0067**
N545GM	HS25	257039
N545GM	BE40	RJ-31
N545JF	**C52C**	**0027**
N545JS	**C525**	**0524**
N545JT	GLF3	347
N545K	**LJ45**	**244**
(N545K)	LJ45	399
N545KS	LJ45	399
N545LF	LJ60	327
(N545LR)	HS25	259045
N545MA	**EA50**	**000144**
N545PA	**LJ36**	**028**
N545PL	C560	0225
(N545PT)	PRM1	RB-133
N545QS	HS25	259045
N545RA	LJ45	157
(N545RS)	LJ45	099
N545RW	**C525**	**0141**
N545S	HS25	25188
(N545SH)	HS25	257007
N545TC	**BE40**	**RK-213**
N545TG	**C525**	**0545**
N545TP	MU30	A045SA
N545XJ	CL30	20253
N545XJ	**CL30**	**20278**
N545ZT	CL65	5701
N546BC	HS25	257004
N546BW	**EA50**	**000025**
N546BZ	BE40	RK-41
N546CC	C500	046
N546CS	**C56X**	**5524**
N546DH	**LJ45**	**150**
N546EX	FA50	41
N546FX	CL30	20319
N546GD	**GLF5**	**5546**
N546LF	CL61	5124
N546LR	**HS25**	**259046**
N546LS	**ASTR**	**129**
N546MD	**C750**	**0215**
N546MG	**GLF4**	**1153**
N546MG	HS25	258753
N546MM	**G150**	**256**
N546MT	C550	550-0881
N546PA	LJ36	045
N546QS	**GLF5**	**5190**
N546QS	HS25	259046
N546XJ	**CL30**	**20280**
(N546XJ)	CL30	20260
(N547AC)	C52A	0016
N547CC	C500	047
N547CC	C500	547
N547CS	C56X	5542
N547FP	CL61	5047
N547FX	**CL30**	**20341**
N547GA	**GLF5**	**5547**
N547JG	LJ25	264
N547JL	SBRL	380-69
N547K	FA50	46
N547LF	LJ45	288
N547LF	LJ45	361
N547LR	**HS25**	**259047**
N547PA	**LJ36**	**012**
N547QS	HS25	259047
N547ST	C525	0547
N547TW	**C525**	**0547**
N547XJ	**CL30**	**20281**
N548AJ	**C52C**	**0036**
N548BA	**CL65**	**5771**
N548CC	C500	048
N548CC	**CL61**	**5087**
N548EE	**E50P**	**50000348**
N548FX	**CL30**	**20342**
N548GD	**GLF5**	**5548**
N548GX	GLEX	9548
N548KK	**BE40**	**RK-151**
N548LF	CL64	5407
N548LM	**LJ31**	**050**
N548LP	CL64	5548
N548LR	**HS25**	**259048**
(N548ME)	C52A	0091
N548PA	LJ36	038
N548QS	HS25	259048
N548W	CL61	5062
N548WC	LJ60	290
N548XJ	**CL30**	**20301**
N548XL	C56X	5048
N548XP	BE40	RK-548
N549AF	**EA50**	**000049**
N549AS	FA10	87
N549BA	**CL65**	**5775**
N549CC	C500	049
N549CC	C550	456
N549CJ	C525	0549
N549CP	FA50	300
N549CP	**GLF5**	**519**
N549CS	C56X	5546
N549FX	**CL30**	**20374**
N549GA	**GLF5**	**5549**
N549LF	CL64	5420
N549LR	**HS25**	**259049**
N549PA	**LJ35**	**119**
N549QS	HS25	259049
N549XJ	**CL30**	**20322**
N550A	CS55	0009
N550A	**GLF5**	**5207**
N550AA	**GLF5**	**5020**
(N550AA)	GLF5	5006
N550AB	C550	063
N550AB	**C550**	**633**
N550AD	**EA50**	**550-0263**
N550AJ	C550	183
N550AJ	**CS55**	**0141**
N550AK	LJ55	045
N550AL	C550	462
N550AL	FA20	55/410
N550AL	**GLF5**	**5443**
N550AN	GLF5	5181
N550AR	**C550**	**550-1029**
N550AR	C550	661
N550AS	CS55	0020
N550AU	**GLF5**	**5338**
N550AV	C550	403
N550AV	**GLF5**	**5490**
(N550AZ)	C550	570
N550BB	**C550**	**734**
N550BC	**C550**	**550-0804**
N550BD	C525	0209
N550BD	C550	619
N550BF	C550	550-0888
N550BG	CS55	0148
(N550BG)	C550	719
N550BJ	C550	309
N550BM	C550	286
N550BM	GLF5	5171
N550BP	C550	235
N550BP	C550	282
N550BP	C550	731
N550BT	CS55	0085
N550BW	**C52B**	**0464**
N550CA	C550	167
N550CA	C550	303
N550CA	C550	381
N550CB	C550	118
N550CC	C500	021
N550CC	C500	050
N550CC	C550	686
N550CD	C550	320
N550CE	C550	063
N550CE	FA50	8

N550CF	C550	382
N550CG	C550	102
N550CJ	C550	498
(N550CK)	LJ55	083
N550CL	FA50	8
N550CM	**C525**	**0264**
N550CM	C550	285
N550CP	C550	163
N550CP	C550	356
N550CP	**PRM1**	**RB-121**
N550CS	C56X	5551
N550CS	LJ55	005
N550CU	C550	178
N550CW	**CL60**	**1084**
N550CY	C550	550-1118
N550CZ	**C555**	**0128**
N550DA	C550	186
N550DA	C550	246
N550DC	**C560**	**0198**
(N550DD)	C550	285
(N550DD)	LJ55	066
N550DG	C550	727
N550DG	**LJ60**	**348**
(N550DK)	C550	462
N550DL	**C555**	**0155**
N550DR	C550	067
N550DR	**GLF5**	**5413**
N550DS	**C555**	**0154**
N550DU	C56X	5217
N550DV	GLF5	5396
N550DW	C550	074
N550DW	**C550**	**487**
N550DX	**GLF5**	**5517**
N550E	LJ35	100
N550EC	C550	053
N550EK	C550	265
N550EW	C550	103
N550EZ	**C555**	**0158**
N550F	C555	0010
N550F	C555	0056
N550F	**EA50**	**550-1001**
N550FB	C550	285
N550FB	C550	550-0803
(N550FB)	C550	674
N550FG	GLF5	5082
N550FJ	**FA10**	**215**
N550FM	C550	550
N550FP	C550	550-1024
N550FS	C555	0067
N550FX	**CL30**	**20391**
N550G	C550	260
N550GA	GLF5	5002
N550GA	GLF5	5043
N550GA	GLF5	5097
N550GA	GLF5	5155
N550GA	GLF5	5211
N550GA	GLF5	5304
N550GA	GLF5	5418
N550GA	**GLF5**	**5526**
N550GA	GPER	551
(N550GA)	GLF5	5071
N550GB	C550	177
N550GD	GLF5	5125
N550GD	GLF5	5184
N550GD	GLF5	5305
N550GD	GLF5	5477
N550GH	C550	550-0898
N550GH	**GLF5**	**5477**
N550GM	**C550**	**378**
N550GN	**GLF4**	**1340**
N550GP	C550	194
N550GS	GLF5	5368
N550GT	**C550**	**469**
N550GT	C555	0160
N550GV	GLF5	5022
N550GW	**GLF5**	**5006**
N550GX	**C550**	**560**
N550GZ	**C550**	**114**
N550H	HS25	258356
N550HA	C555	0067
N550HB	**ASTR**	**106**
N550HB	C550	250
N550HB	WW24	414
N550HC	**C555**	**0116**
N550HD	**LEG5**	**55000024**
N550HF	C550	287
N550HG	**LJ55**	**083**
N550HH	**C550**	**550-0802**
N550HJ	C550	302
N550HK	**C550**	**550-0816**
N550HM	C550	047
N550HM	**C550**	**718**
N550HP	C550	191
N550HS	MU30	A051SA
N550HT	C555	0107
N550HW	C550	635
N550J	C550	417
N550J	**C550**	**550-0848**
N550JB	C550	177
N550JB	LJ55	013
N550JC	**C550**	**038**
N550JC	C555	0124
N550JD	**GLF5**	**5032**
N550JE	**C555**	**0121**
(N550JE)	GLF5	5211
N550JF	C550	008
N550JF	C550	660
N550JM	C550	255
(N550JN)	C550	550-0847
N550JP	**FA50**	**240**
(N550JP)	HS25	257106
N550JR	C550	356
N550JS	C550	118
N550JT	**C555**	**0020**
N550JU	**GLF5**	**5442**
N550K	C550	229
N550K	WW24	127
N550KA	C550	064
N550KA	**C550**	**166**
N550KC	C550	292
N550KD	**C550**	**125**
N550KE	C550	694
(N550KE)	C550	550-0830
N550KF	GLF5	5095
N550KG	C550	550-0949
N550KH	C550	550-0854
N550KH	C550	550-0886
(N550KH)	C550	550-0859
N550KJ	C550	550-0854
N550KL	**C550**	**550-0844**
N550KM	C555	0081
N550KP	C550	130
(N550KP)	GLF5	5480
N550KR	C52A	0130
N550KR	C550	727
(N550KR)	C550	075
N550KT	**C550**	**364**
N550KW	C550	409
N550L	C500	388
N550L	SBRL	282-61
N550LA	**C550**	**006**
N550LC	C555	0074
N550LD	**C550**	**351**
N550LF	CL30	20042
N550LF	GLEX	9054
N550LG	CL61	5127
N550LH	**C550**	**116**
N550LJ	EA50	550-0263
N550LJ	LJ55	015
N550LJ	LJ55	041
N550LL	SBRL	282-61
N550LP	C550	200
N550LS	**C550**	**086**
N550LT	**C500**	**184**
(N550LX)	FA50	17
N550M	ASTR	061
N550M	FA20	355
N550M	GLF5	5101
N550MC	C525	0205
N550MC	FA20	200
N550MC	**GLF5**	**5440**
N550MD	C550	299
N550MD	C550	354
N550ME	**C550**	**104**
N550MH	C500	668
N550MJ	**C550**	**238**
N550MK	C550	550-1082
N550ML	**C550**	**550-1082**
N550MN	**C550**	**063**
N550MT	C550	330
N550MT	GLF5	5026
N550MT	GLF5	5299
(N550MT)	C550	309
N550MW	C550	481
N550MW	**C550**	**720**
N550MX	**C52B**	**0137**
N550MZ	C550	658
N550MZ	**GLF5**	**5095**
N550NE	C550	230
N550NM	WW24	39
N550NS	C550	635
N550NT	**C550**	**136**
N550PA	C550	213
N550PD	C550	550-0995
N550PF	**C550**	**427**
N550PF	C550	550-0925
N550PF	C550	672
N550PG	C550	240
N550PL	C550	010
N550PL	C555	0130
N550PM	C550	035
N550PM	**GLF5**	**5252**
N550PP	**GLF3**	**345**
N550PR	C550	285
N550PR	GLF5	5121
N550PR	**GLF5**	**5330**
N550PS	C550	124
N550PT	C550	499
N550PT	FA20	391
N550PW	**C550**	**216**
N550QS	**C680**	**680A0015**
N550QS	HS25	259050
N550RA	C550	661
N550RB	C550	129
(N550RB)	C52B	0073
N550RD	C550	421
(N550RD)	C550	145
N550RG	C550	262
N550RH	**GLF5**	**5495**
N550RH	HS25	258038
N550RH	LJ55	014
N550RH	LJ55	041
N550RL	C550	317
(N550RL)	C550	266
N550RM	C550	698
N550RM	**GLF3**	**373**
(N550RN)	GLF5	5029
N550RP	C550	035
N550RP	**GLF5**	**5184**
N550RS	**C500**	**202**
N550RS	C550	439
N550RT	**C550**	**228**
N550RV	C555	0012
N550RZ	**C550**	**550-0817**
N550SA	C550	261
N550SA	GLF5	5301
N550SB	C550	634
N550SC	C550	040
N550SC	LJ55	098
(N550SC)	C550	338
N550SF	**C550**	**122**
N550SG	**C555**	**0070**
N550SG	GLF5	5223
N550SJ	**C555**	**0100**
N550SL	SBRL	306-72
N550SM	C550	286
N550SM	C550	307
N550SM	C550	587
N550SN	**GLF5**	**5195**
N550SP	C555	0151
N550SS	**C550**	**093**
N550ST	C555	0033
N550T	C500	388
N550T	C500	413
N550T	C525	0013
N550T	C52A	0025
N550T	C52B	0040
N550T	**C52B**	**0365**
N550TA	C550	278
N550TA	**C550**	**550-0964**
N550TA	GLF5	5026
N550TB	**C52A**	**0025**
N550TB	C555	0012
N550TB	C555	0019
N550TC	**LJ55**	**034**
N550TE	C550	550-0894
N550TF	**C525**	**0013**
N550TG	C500	378
N550TG	C550	550-0822
N550TH	**F9EX**	**100**
N550TJ	C550	029
N550TJ	C550	143
N550TJ	C550	157
(N550TJ)	C550	080
N550TL	C550	716
N550TM	**C550**	**550-0936**
(N550TM)	C560	0299
N550TP	C550	186
N550TP	C550	296
N550TR	C550	186
N550TR	**C550**	**302**
N550TR	C550	733
N550TT	C550	158
N550TT	C550	296
N550TT	C550	550-1076
N550TW	**C550**	**603**
N550TY	**GLF5**	**5512**
(N550TY)	C550	007
N550U	C500	413
N550UZ	**EA50**	**550-0270**
N550VC	C550	550-0924
N550VE	**GLF5**	**5365**
N550VR	C550	733
(N550VS)	C555	0001
N550VT	**LJ40**	**2071**
N550VW	**C550**	**274**
N550WB	C550	265
N550WB	**C550**	**550-0949**
N550WD	**C555**	**0110**
N550WG	C550	550-0953
N550WJ	C550	309
N550WJ	**C550**	**393**
N550WL	**C550**	**242**
N550WM	**FA50**	**229**
N550WP	GLF2	176
N550WR	C550	400
N550WR	**C550**	**482**
N550WS	**C550**	**550-0845**
N550WV	C550	584
N550WW	C550	584
N550WW	C560	0180
N550WW	**GLF5**	**5214**
N550XJ	**CL30**	**20323**
N550XY	**GLF5**	**5468**
(N550YM)	GLF5	5047
N551AB	C550	173
N551AC	GLF3	467
N551AD	C550	079
N551AM	C750	0155
(N551AM)	LJ55	108
N551AS	C550	348
N551AS	LJ24	229
N551AS	LJ55	083
(N551BA)	HS25	258105
N551BB	C550	246
N551BC	**C550**	**059**
N551BD	LJ60	062
N551BE	C555	0097
N551BP	C550	423
N551BT	CL64	5551
N551BW	C550	272
N551CB	**GLF4**	**1449**
N551CC	C500	051
N551CC	LJ35	017
(N551CC)	C550	001
N551CE	C550	398
N551CF	C52B	0011
N551CF	C550	107
N551CG	LJ55	014
N551CL	**C550**	**191**
N551CS	C56X	5557
N551CS	GLF5	5264
N551CW	FA50	51
N551CZ	**C550**	**028**
N551DA	**C550**	**025**
N551DB	LJ55	052
N551DF	LJ55	001
N551DF	LJ60	55-001
N551DN	**C680**	**0551**
N551DP	LJ25	213
N551DS	C550	023
N551EA	**C550**	**354**
(N551EU)	BE40	RK-551
N551FA	SBRL	465-39
N551FP	**C525**	**0515**
N551FX	**CL30**	**20272**
N551G	C525	0153
N551G	C550	550-0850
N551G	**C550**	**550-0968**
N551GA	GLF5	604
N551GA	GLF5	606
(N551GA)	C550	040
(N551GC)	C550	364
N551GD	**GLF5**	**5551**
N551GE	**C550**	**152**
N551GF	**C550**	**278**
(N551GK)	C550	617
N551GL	LJ55	001
N551GL	LJ60	55-001
(N551GN)	C550	069
N551GR	GLF4	4016
N551GS	**C550**	**430**
N551GT	**GLF5**	**5008**
N551HB	LJ55	038
N551HH	**C550**	**023**
N551HK	C550	266
N551HM	LJ35	612
N551JF	C550	063
N551KF	GLF5	5148
N551KH	C550	550-0859
N551LR	HS25	259051
(N551LX)	FA50	19
N551M	GLF5	682
N551MB	LJ25	007
N551MC	C550	086
N551MD	GLF2	212
N551MD	LJ25	007
N551MD	LJ35	057
(N551MD)	LJ55	085
N551MF	**LJ55**	**015**
N551MS	**C500**	**541**
N551MW	**C550**	**097**
(N551NA)	C550	037
N551NC	FA10	198
N551NH	**C550**	**290**
N551PL	C550	150
N551PM	**GLF5**	**5374**
N551PS	C555	0013
N551Q	C525	0153
N551QS	**C56X**	**5221**
N551QS	HS25	259051
N551R	C550	115
N551RA	**LJ55**	**076**
N551RC	**GLF5**	**5138**
N551RF	C555	0097
N551RM	**C550**	**046**
(N551S)	FA50	51
N551SC	LJ55	008
N551SD	**CL61**	**5016**
(N551SE)	C550	353
N551SR	C550	072
N551SR	C550	266
N551SS	F2TH	186
N551ST	**LJ60**	**048**
N551TG	**GLF5**	**5264**
N551TK	C550	282
N551TP	WW24	419
N551TT	C550	172
N551TW	LJ35	612
N551UT	LJ55	069
N551V	**C550**	**550-0850**
N551VB	C550	550-1038
N551VB	HS25	258617
N551VL	**GLF5**	**5381**
(N551VP)	C550	550-1038
N551WC	LJ25	129
N551WC	LJ35	441
N551WH	**C510**	**0055**
N551WJ	C550	465
N551WL	**C550**	**288**
N551WM	**C52A**	**0243**
N551XJ	**CL30**	**20324**
N551XP	BE40	RK-551
N552AJ	**C500**	**449**
N552AV	**GLF5**	**5497**
N552BA	HS25	258107
(N552BA)	LJ55	050
N552BE	C555	0138
N552CB	C550	550-1026
N552CB	**G150**	**205**
N552CC	C500	052
N552CC	C550	002
N552CC	C552	0001
N552CC	CL64	5552
N552CC	**BE40**	**RK-186**
(N552CF)	C555	0052
N552CJ	C52A	0005
N552CN	**C560**	**0674**
N552EU	BE40	RK-552
N552FJ	C550	619
N552GA	GLF5	5252
N552GA	**GLF5**	**5288**
N552GD	**GLF5**	**5552**
N552GL	LJ55	002
N552GR	**F2EX**	**160**
N552HV	**C560**	**0552**
N552JH	JSTR	5037/24
N552JT	GLF2	135
N552JT	GLF3	305
N552KF	CL30	20204
N552LR	HS25	259052
(N552LX)	FA50	20
N552M	**C510**	**0187**
N552MA	C56X	5198
N552MD	C500	425
N552N	HS25	25124
N552PM	**GLF5**	**5382**
N552QS	**C56X**	**5334**
N552QS	HS25	259052
N552SC	**C56X**	**5144**
N552SC	CL64	5523
N552SD	C555	0130
N552SD	F9EX	105
N552SE	C555	0130
N552SK	**LJ60**	**219**
N552SM	**C550**	**550-0929**
(N552SM)	C555	0125
N552SQ	LJ55	100
N552TC	C560	0674
N552TF	C550	203
N552TL	**LJ55**	**139**
N552TS	CL64	5552
N552UT	LJ55	100
(N552VP)	C56X	5252
N552WF	**GLF4**	**1000**
N552WS	**GLF5**	**552**
N552X	**GLF5**	**5390**
N552XJ	**CL30**	**20329**
N552XP	BE40	RK-552
N553AC	C650	0198
N553BA	HS25	258108
N553BW	HS25	258297
N553BW	**HS25**	**258570**
N553CB	**G150**	**244**
N553CC	C500	053
N553CC	C550	553
N553CC	C555	0046
N553CC	C555	0113
N553CJ	C550	003
N553CS	C56X	5560
N553CW	C560	0253
(N553CW)	CL61	5053
N553DF	CL61	5078
N553DJ	LJ55	003
N553EJ	C525	0289
N553GD	**GLF5**	**5553**
(N553GJ)	LJ55	003
N553GP	LJ55	003
N553GR	**F2TH**	**64**
N553JT	GLF3	305
(N553LX)	FA50	23
N553M	FA50	201
N553M	HS25	258027
N553M	LJ35	141
N553MC	WW24	252
N553MD	GLF2	47
N553MJ	**C550**	**553**
N553PF	BE40	RK-32
N553QS	**C56X**	**5372**
N553SC	C560	0057
N553SD	C555	0107
(N553US)	HS25	258027
N553V	**LJ35**	**141**
N553VP	C56X	5503
N553XP	BE40	RK-553
N554BA	C550	040
N554BA	HS25	258111
(N554BA)	HS25	258109
N554CA	C555	0004
N554CC	C500	054
N554CC	C555	0075
N554CE	**GLF5**	**5188**
N554CL	**LJ55**	**040**
N554CS	C56X	5572
N554DG	**GLF5**	**5196**
N554EJ	C560	0328
(N554EM)	LJ55	014
N554GA	GLF5	5254
N554GA	**GLF5**	**5454**
N554GA	GLF5	605
N554GD	**GLF5**	**5554**
N554GR	**C550**	**321**
N554HD	GLF3	444
N554HD	**LJ40**	**2110**
(N554LX)	FA50	51

N554MB	**C550**	**040**
N554PF	LJ55	087
N554QS	**C56X**	**5520**
N554R	C560	0328
N554SC	CL64	5527
N554SD	C560	0593
N554SR	FA10	173
N554T	C500	477
N554T	**C500**	**528**
N554T	C560	0376
N554T	CS55	0124
N554TS	**C560**	**0376**
(N554UJ)	C560	0328
N554VP	**C560**	**0554**
N555AB	SBRL	282-60
N555AE	SBRL	282-60
N555AE	SBRL	306-102
N555AJ	C500	007
N555BA	HS25	258113
(N555BA)	HS25	258110
N555BC	C550	235
N555BG	**C525**	**0113**
N555BK	**C550**	**550-0916**
N555BS	JSTR	5051
N555BY	WW24	306
N555BY	**BE40**	**RJ-36**
N555CB	HS25	25122
N555CB	HS25	25285
N555CB	HS25	256011
N555CB	HS25	257039
N555CC	C500	039
N555CJ	LJ55	089
N555CK	**LJ45**	**214**
N555CR	HS25	257039
N555CS	GLF2	73/9
N555CS	GLF5	516
N555CW	WW24	295
N555DH	C550	423
N555DH	C650	0016
N555DH	C650	0090
N555DH	CL30	20083
N555DH	FA10	114
N555DH	FA10	186
N555DH	FA10	187
N555DH	WW24	373
(N555DH)	LJ24	153
N555DM	WW24	25
N555DS	**C550**	**356**
N555DW	**GLF3**	**459**
N555DZ	**FA10**	**186**
N555EF	GLEX	9154
N555EH	**LJ60**	**236**
N555EJ	**EA50**	**000183**
N555EW	C500	456
N555EW	C550	303
(N555EW)	C650	0074
(N555EW)	C650	0099
N555FA	MU30	A082SA
N555FD	**C560**	**0113**
N555GB	HS25	256011
N555GB	LJ35	246
N555GE	**CL30**	**20025**
N555GL	GLF3	403
N555GL	LJ55	036
N555GL	LJ55	065
N555GN	GLF5	518
N555GS	**F2TH**	**149**
N555GV	GLF5	518
N555GV	**GLF5**	**5285**
N555HD	**GLEX**	**9328**
N555HD	GLF2	134
N555HD	GLF3	444
N555HD	WW24	341
N555HM	**C550**	**550-0950**
N555HR	C500	643
N555J	WW24	213
N555JA	**C560**	**0781**
N555JE	LJ35	195
N555JK	LJ28	28-003
N555JM	HFB3	1037
N555JR	SBRL	380-72
(N555JS)	LJ31	053
N555KC	GLF3	366
N555KC	GLF4	1342
N555KE	ASTR	017
N555KE	**GLF4**	**1082**
N555KH	GLF2	134
N555KK	BE40	RK-92
N555KT	C550	419
N555KT	**C560**	**0368**
N555KW	**C500**	**443**
N555LA	LJ24	177
N555LB	LJ24	177
N555LG	**C560**	**0421**
N555LG	CL61	5127
N555LG	GLF2	10
N555LJ	**LJ24**	**195**
N555LK	**GLF4**	**1299**
N555LR	**GLF4**	**4189**
(N555LR)	GLF4	4065
N555MB	C680	0337
N555MH	LJ24	213
N555MU	GLF2	188
N555MW	GLF2	188
N555MX	LJ55	142
N555NN	CL65	5718
N555NT	GLF3	322
N555PB	JSTR	5047
N555PG	**C560**	**0102**
N555PG	LJ25	281
N555PT	FA20	426
N555PT	SBRL	282-53
N555PV	LJ24	133
N555QB	C750	0510
N555QB	**C750**	**0516**
N555QS	**C56X**	**5543**
N555RA	FA20	194
N555RB	HS25	257140
N555RE	GLF3	409
N555RR	SBRL	306-60
N555RS	GLF2	3
N555RT	**C550**	**311**
N555RU	HS25	HB-14
N555SD	LJ25	333
N555SG	JSTR	5090
N555SL	SBRL	306-13
(N555SL)	C550	553
N555SR	FA10	173
N555SR	FA20	455
(N555TD)	C550	437
N555TF	CL30	20102
N555TF	FA20	325
N555TF	**GLF4**	**4080**
N555VH	**LJ25**	**214**
N555VR	LJ31	033C
N555VR	**LJ45**	**257**
N555VV	CL64	5555
N555WD	CL60	1047
N555WD	**CL64**	**5355**
N555WE	C56X	5058
N555WF	C560	0190
N555WF	C560	0449
N555WF	C560	0488
N555WF	C56X	5058
N555WF	C56X	5064
N555WF	C56X	5366
N555WH	LJ36	037
N555WK	C560	0449
N555WL	**C560**	**0488**
N555WL	GLF4	1114
N555WV	CS55	0124
N555WZ	**C56X**	**5366**
N555XL	GLF2	189/42
N555XS	GLF3	342
N555ZT	**F9EX**	**55**
N556AF	GLF3	479
N556AR	GLF5	556
N556AT	C500	020
N556BA	HS25	258114
(N556BA)	HS25	258111
N556BG	**C560**	**0499**
N556CC	C500	056
N556CC	C550	095
N556CG	**LJ45**	**237**
N556CS	C56X	5577
N556GA	G150	255
N556GA	GLF4	4056
N556GA	GLF5	636
N556GA	LJ55	028
N556GD	**GLF5**	**5556**
N556HD	**FA50**	**321**
N556HD	LJ31	230
N556HD	LJ40	2110
N556HD	WW24	341
N556HJ	LJ55	028
N556JP	**LJ45**	**010**
N556LS	**C56X**	**5276**
(N556LX)	FA50	73
N556N	WW24	331
N556QS	**C56X**	**5553**
N556RA	C650	7070
(N556SA)	LJ60	056
N556TT	**GLF5**	**5056**
N556VP	C560	0556
N556WD	CL60	1047
N557BA	HS25	258117
N557BK	**LJ31**	**090**
N557CC	C500	057
N557CC	C500	557
N557CC	C550	577
N557CS	**CS55**	**0016**
N557E	GLF5	557
N557EE	**E55P**	**50500357**
N557GA	**G150**	**292**
N557GA	GALX	157
N557GA	GLF5	5154
N557GD	**GLF5**	**5557**
N557H	GLF5	5223
N557HP	**C525**	**0668**
N557JK	**GLF3**	**340**
N557LZ	FA50	220
(N557MG)	CS55	0064
N557MW	**HDJT**	**42000021**
N557PG	**C560**	**0557**
N557PK	**F2TH**	**184**
N557PK	LJ31	090
N557QS	**C56X**	**5559**
N557SV	**C680**	**0557**
N557TC	E50P	50000067
(N557TC)	CS55	0088
N557VB	HS25	258617
N557WY	**GLF4**	**1276**
N557XJ	**CL30**	**20047**
N557XP	BE40	RK-557
N558AC	LJ55	048
N558AG	C550	558
N558AK	C560	0558
N558BA	HS25	258119
N558CB	C550	058
N558CC	C500	058
N558CC	C550	058
N558CG	C560	0558
N558CS	C56X	5585
N558E	LJ35	100
N558GA	GLF5	5258
N558GA	**GLF5**	**5384**
N558GA	GLF5	606
N558GD	**GLF5**	**5558**
N558GG	C560	0558
N558GS	LJ45	225
N558HD	LJ31	230
N558HJ	LJ55	048
N558M	HS25	258027
N558NC	C560	0558
N558QS	**C56X**	**5568**
N558R	C56X	5075
N558R	**C680**	**680A0033**
N558RA	**LJ55**	**086**
N558V	C560	0558
N558VP	C550	558
N558WB	C550	265
N558WW	**C560**	**0180**
N558XP	**BE40**	**RK-558**
N559AK	HA4T	RC-50
N559AM	C650	7107
N559AM	**FA7X**	**206**
(N559BA)	HS25	258121
N559BC	C500	059
N559BC	LJ55	009
N559BM	**C560**	**0259**
N559CC	C500	059
N559CS	C56X	5593
N559DM	**HS25**	**258419**
N559GA	GALX	159
N559GA	GLF5	5359
N559GA	GLF5	5459
N559GA	**GLF5**	**5559**
N559GA	GLF5	607
N559GP	JSTR	5123/14
N559GV	GLF5	559
N559HF	**C52B**	**0406**
N559JA	CL64	5559
(N559K)	LJ45	216
N559L	**GLF2**	**152**
N559LC	GLF2	152
N559LC	**GLF4**	**1259**
N559RA	**LJ55**	**146**
N559SA	CL30	20559
N559VP	**C56X**	**5590**
N559X	**GLF5**	**5489**
N560A	C560	0364
N560AB	C550	603
N560AE	C560	0056
N560AF	**C560**	**0100**
N560AG	C560	0064
N560AG	C560	0301
N560AJ	C550	560
N560AJ	CS55	0094
N560AN	LJ60	138
N560AR	**C56X**	**6026**
N560AT	**C560**	**0521**
N560AV	**C560**	**0321**
N560AW	**C56X**	**5351**
N560BA	C560	0003
N560BA	C560	0102
N560BA	C56X	5585
N560BA	HS25	258122
N560BB	C560	0135
N560BC	**C560**	**0032**
(N560BD)	C560	0172
(N560BD)	C560	0303
N560BG	C560	0198
N560BG	C560	0277
N560BJ	C560	0303
N560BJ	C560	0436
N560BL	C560	0057
N560BL	C560	0566
N560BL	**C560**	**0633**
N560BP	**C560**	**0172**
N560BP	C560	0449
N560BT	**C56X**	**5031**
(N560C)	C560	0007
N560CB	C550	555
N560CC	C500	060
N560CC	C550	001
N560CC	**C560**	**0064**
N560CC	C560	0751
N560CC	C560	550-0001
N560CE	C560	0302
N560CE	**C56X**	**5012**
N560CF	**C560**	**0040**
N560CG	**C56X**	**5121**
N560CH	C560	0611
N560CH	**C560**	**0783**
N560CH	C56X	5091
N560CJ	**C560**	**0086**
N560CK	C560	0207
N560CL	**C560**	**0780**
N560CM	C56X	5277
(N560CP)	C560	0055
N560CR	C560	0662
N560CR	**C56X**	**5229**
N560CR	C56X	5560
N560CS	**C560**	**0549**
(N560CT)	C560	0104
N560CV	**C560**	**0038**
N560CV	C560	560-0001
N560CX	C560	0086
N560CX	**C560**	**0582**
N560CZ	**C560**	**0002**
N560DA	C56X	5107
N560DC	C560	0021
N560DE	C56X	5284
N560DG	**C56X**	**6009**
N560DL	**C560**	**0761**
N560DM	C560	0101
N560DM	C560	0351
N560DM	**GLF5**	**5045**
N560DP	**C56X**	**5212**
N560DR	**C56X**	**5073**
N560DW	**C56X**	**5729**
(N560DW)	C560	0399
N560EA	C560	0062
N560EC	C560	0101
(N560ED)	C560	0150
N560EJ	FA50	60
(N560EJ)	C560	0036
N560EL	**C560**	**0049**
N560EM	C560	0278
N560EM	**C560**	**0497**
N560EP	C560	0101
N560ER	C560	0003
N560ES	**C56X**	**5800**
N560ET	**C560**	**0638**
N560FA	C560	0142
N560FB	C560	0148
N560FC	C56X	5690
N560FF	**C560**	**0477**
N560FH	**C56X**	**5127**
N560FM	**C56X**	**5325**
N560FN	C560	0024
N560FP	**C560**	**0566**
N560FS	**C56X**	**5242**
N560G	**C560**	**0112**
N560GA	C500	217
N560GB	C560	0254
N560GB	C56X	5027
N560GB	**C56X**	**6030**
N560GC	**C56X**	**5089**
N560GD	**GLF5**	**5560**
N560GG	**C560**	**0037**
N560GJ	**C56X**	**6186**
N560GL	C560	0079
N560GM	C560	0099
N560GM	C56X	5021
N560GP	C56X	5027
N560GS	**C560**	**0263**
N560GT	C560	0142
N560GT	**C560**	**0588**
N560H	C560	0017
N560H	**C560**	**0576**
N560HB	C560	0440
(N560HB)	C56X	5607
N560HC	C560	0020
N560HC	**C560**	**0631**
N560HD	**C560**	**0274**
N560HG	C560	0020
N560HJ	C56X	5078
N560HL	**C560**	**0341**
N560HM	**C560**	**0699**
N560HN	**C56X**	**5015**
N560HP	C560	0081
N560HS	**C560**	**0377**
N560HW	**C560**	**0281**
N560HX	**C56X**	**5139**
N560JA	**C550**	**550-0849**
N560JC	C560	0283
N560JC	C56X	5541
N560JD	**C560**	**0174**
N560JE	**C560**	**0581**
N560JF	**C56X**	**5173**
N560JG	C56X	5531
N560JL	**C560**	**0044**
N560JM	**C560**	**0010**
N560JM	C560	0023
N560JP	C560	0431
N560JP	C56X	5136
N560JP	C56X	5222
N560JP	C56X	5284
N560JP	C56X	5311
N560JP	C56X	5337
N560JR	C560	0027
N560JS	C560	0196
N560JS	**C560**	**0322**
N560JT	C560	0167
N560JT	C560	0670
N560JV	C560	0065
N560JV	C56X	6186
N560JW	**C560**	**0560**
N560JZ	**C560**	**0017**
N560KC	LJ35	079
N560KL	C560	0622
(N560KN)	C56X	5055
N560KS	**C56X**	**5151**
N560KT	C56X	5127
N560KW	**C560**	**0751**
N560L	C560	0156
N560L	**C56X**	**5011**
N560L	FA20	132
N560LC	C560	0026
N560LC	C560	0110
N560LC	**C560**	**0296**
N560LF	**C560**	**0662**
N560LM	C560	0068
N560LS	**C56X**	**5660**
N560LT	C560	0275
N560LW	**C560**	**0053**
(N560LW)	C560	0275
N560MC	WW24	24
N560ME	C560	0012
N560MF	**C560**	**0370**
N560MF	C56X	5703
N560MG	**C560**	**0223**
N560MH	**C560**	**0105**
N560ML	**C56X**	**5027**
N560MM	**C560**	**0228**
N560MM	C560	0235
N560MR	C560	0015
N560MR	**C560**	**0594**
N560MT	**BE40**	**RK-235**
N560MU	**C56X**	**5565**
N560MV	C560	0355
N560N	**C56X**	**6212**
N560NS	C560	0408
(N560NS)	C560	0345
N560NV	C560	0429
N560NY	C56X	5198
N560PA	**C560**	**0136**
N560PD	**C56X**	**5311**
N560PE	**C560**	**0379**
N560PH	**C560**	**0199**
N560PJ	C52B	0104
N560PK	**C560**	**0133**
N560PL	C56X	5600
N560PM	**C56X**	**5629**
(N560PM)	C560	0530
N560PS	C560	0120
(N560PS)	C56X	5679
(N560PT)	C560	0106
N560PW	**C560**	**0101**
N560PX	C560	0691
N560PY	C560	0034
N560QG	**C56X**	**5744**
N560R	FA20	313
N560RA	C560	0182
N560RA	FA20	56
N560RB	C56X	5676
(N560RB)	C560	0137
(N560RB)	C560	0239
N560RC	C560	0397
N560RC	HA4T	RC-56
N560RF	C560	0379
N560RG	C560	0198
N560RG	C560	0551
N560RH	**C560**	**0773**
N560RJ	C560	0107
N560RK	**C560**	**0407**
N560RL	C560	0135
N560RM	**C560**	**0658**
N560RN	C560	0309
N560RP	**C560**	**0158**
N560RR	**C560**	**0012**
N560RS	C560	0109A
N560RS	**C56X**	**5288**
N560RS	C56X	5323
N560RV	**C560**	**0417**
N560RV	C560	0558
N560RW	**C560**	**0196**
N560S	C56X	5190
N560SB	HS25	257105
N560SE	C560	0390
N560SH	**GLF3**	**404**
N560SH	WW24	319
N560SJ	**C56X**	**5215**
N560TA	**C560**	**0430**
N560TD	**C56X**	**5711**
N560TE	C560	0595
N560TG	C560	0668
N560TH	C56X	5215
N560TJ	C560	0417
N560TM	C56X	5564
N560TP	**C560**	**0271**
(N560TP)	C560	0668
N560TS	C56X	5144
(N560TS)	CL64	5560
N560TV	**C56X**	**5545**
N560TW	**C56X**	**5585**
N560TX	C560	0206
N560TX	**C560**	**0382**
N560U	**GLEX**	**9366**
N560US	**F2EX**	**233**
N560VH	C56X	5629
N560VP	C560	0002
N560VP	C560	0361
N560VR	C560	0480
N560VR	C56X	5049
N560VS	**C560**	**0124**
N560VU	C560	707
N560W	C560	0030
N560WD	C560	0399
N560WE	C560	0100
N560WF	C560	0045
(N560WF)	C56X	5366
N560WH	**C560**	**0013**
N560WJ	**C560**	**0045**

N560WR	**C560**	**0121**
N560WW	**C560**	**0047**
N560XL	**C56X**	**706**
N560XP	BE40	RK-560
N560ZF	C56X	5189
N561A	C560	0139
N561AC	C560	0218
N561AS	C550	173
N561B	**C560**	**0008**
N561BA	HS25	258123
N561BC	**C525**	**0257**
N561BC	C560	0057
N561BP	C56X	5134
N561CC	C500	061
N561CC	**C560**	**0416**
N561CC	CL64	5561
N561CE	**C56X**	**5206**
N561CF	**C560**	**0003**
N561CM	C560	0443
(N561CM)	F900	82
N561CT	**LJ60**	**376**
N561D	FA10	54
N561DA	**C560**	**0314**
N561DA	C56X	5012
N561EA	**EA50**	**000024**
N561EJ	**C560**	**0035**
N561GA	GLF5	5261
N561GA	GLF5	608
N561GA	GLF5	661
(N561GB)	C560	0254
N561GR	C56X	5109
N561HH	**C56X**	**5161**
N561JL	**C56X**	**5361**
N561JS	**C560**	**0413**
N561JV	C56X	6189
N561LS	**C56X**	**5280**
N561MJ	**EA50**	**000140**
N561MK	**C56X**	**5622**
N561MT	**C560**	**0122**
N561NC	FA10	195
N561PA	**C560**	**0116**
N561PF	**C560**	**0048**
N561PS	CS55	0013
N561PS	**HS25**	**257087**
N561RP	HS25	256001
N561RW	C56X	5323
N561SK	**GLF5**	**5529**
N561SR	**C560**	**0138**
N561ST	GLF3	388
(N561ST)	GLF3	302
N561TC	LJ60	010
N561TS	C560	0057
N561VP	**C560**	**560-0001**
N561WF	**C560**	**0182**
N561XL	C56X	5001
N561XP	HS25	258561
N562BA	CL64	5562
N562BA	HS25	258124
N562CC	C500	062
N562CD	C525	562
N562CL	**C560**	**0768**
N562CS	C56X	5597
N562CV	C560	0002
N562DB	C56X	5108
N562DB	C56X	5532
N562DB	C56X	5604
N562DB	C56X	6005
N562DD	**C56X**	**5108**
N562DL	C56X	5604
N562E	C560	0140
N562EJ	FA50	62
N562GA	GALX	162
N562GA	GLF5	5262
N562GA	GLF5	5362
N562GA	GLF5	642
N562GX	GLEX	9562
N562HC	**C56X**	**5350**
N562JV	C56X	6193
N562LD	**C56X**	**5532**
N562ME	CL64	5562
N562MJ	**EA50**	**000156**
N562MS	SBRL	306-44
N562PA	**C52B**	**0150**
N562PC	**C525**	**0151**
(N562PZ)	C52B	0150
N562R	SBRL	306-37
N562RM	**C550**	**646**
N562SC	C56X	5168
N562SC	C56X	5266
N562TM	**E55P**	**50500059**
N562TS	**C56X**	**5178**
N562VP	**C56X**	**5623**
N562WD	C56X	5226
N562XL	C56X	5002
N562XL	C56X	5313
N562XL	C56X	5501
N563BA	**C750**	**0169**
N563BA	CL64	5563
N563BA	HS25	258125
N563C	C560	0174
N563CC	C500	063
N563CC	C500	563
N563CH	C56X	5182
N563CS	**C56X**	**5563**
N563CS	C56X	5601
N563CV	C560	0003
N563GA	GLF5	5236
N563GA	GLF5	5463
N563JV	C56X	6195
N563M	**C560**	**0550**
(N563M)	C52B	0100
N563MJ	**EA50**	**000027**
N563RJ	**BE40**	**RK-220**
N563TS	CL61	5063
N563WD	**C56X**	**6038**
N563XL	C56X	5003
N563XL	C56X	5601
N563XL	C56X	6003
N563XP	**C56X**	**5617**
N564BA	CL64	5564
N564BA	HS25	258126
N564BR	**HS25**	**257122**
N564CC	C500	064
N564CC	C550	064
N564CH	**C56X**	**6092**
N564CL	**LJ25**	**060**
N564CS	C56X	5612
(N564D)	C560	0175
N564GA	GLF5	5264
N564HV	**C56X**	**6211**
N564M	**C560**	**0569**
N564MG	JSTR	5021
N564QS	GLF5	664
N564RM	WW24	434
N564TJ	**C560**	**0432**
N564TS	CL61	5064
N564VP	C550	564
N564XP	BE40	RK-564
N565	FA50	251
N565A	C680	0024
N565A	FA20	499
N565A	FA20	50
N565A	FA50	174
N565AB	C56X	5072
N565AB	C56X	6050
N565AB	**G150**	**294**
N565AP	C56X	6050
N565AR	**C550**	**550-0919**
(N565B)	LJ55	065
N565BA	C56X	5072
N565BA	HS25	258127
N565CC	**C500**	**065**
N565CJ	C550	565
N565DR	C56X	5168
N565EJ	**C560**	**0099**
N565EU	BE40	RK-565
N565FP	**EA50**	**000081**
N565GA	GALX	165
N565GA	GLF4	4165
N565GA	GLF5	5365
N565GA	GLF5	665
N565GB	GALX	130
N565GG	**LJ35**	**501**
(N565GW)	C500	050
N565JF	C525	0041
N565JM	GLF5	5538
N565JP	C525	0041
N565JP	**C52B**	**0159**
N565JS	C550	565
N565JW	C560	0149
N565KC	GLF2	46
N565KE	**ASTR**	**017**
N565NC	C550	565
N565NC	C560	0490
N565QS	**C56X**	**5818**
N565RS	**GLEX**	**9462**
N565RV	**GLF4**	**1323**
N565RX	CL30	20022
N565SK	**HS25**	**258604**
N565SS	C500	017
N565ST	**GLF5**	**5015**
(N565TW)	C500	065
N565V	**C500**	**365**
N565VV	C500	365
N565VV	C550	152
(N565VV)	C510	0013
N565XP	BE40	RK-565
N566BA	HS25	258128
N566C	GLF3	459
N566CC	C500	066
N566CC	C550	166
N566EE	**E55P**	**50500266**
N566F	**C56X**	**5606**
N566GA	GALX	166
N566GA	GLF5	5366
N566GA	GLF5	5466
N566GA	GLF5	609
N566GA	GLF5	666
N566GA	GLF5	699
N566KB	**C560**	**0325**
N566L	**FA50**	**196**
N566MP	WW24	156
N566N	CL61	3064
N566NA	LJ25	064
N566NS	**GLF6**	**6180**
(N566PG)	WW24	273
N566QS	**C56X**	**5825**
N566RB	LJ24	180
N566TS	CL61	5066
N566TX	C550	227
N566VP	C560	0006
N566VP	C56X	6077
N566VR	**C560**	**0480**
(N566W)	BE40	RK-277
N566YT	FA20	94/428
N567A	GLF2	251
N567BA	HS25	258132
N567BA	**BE40**	**RJ-22**
N567CA	C550	114
N567CC	C500	067
N567CH	C56X	5243
N567CL	**HS25**	**259035**
N567DK	BE40	RK-155
N567DW	SBRL	282-35
N567EA	C500	067
N567F	**C560**	**0171**
N567GA	GLF5	610
N567GA	GLF5	667
N567HB	C52B	0298
N567HB	**CL30**	**20396**
N567JK	MU30	A007SA
N567JP	C52A	0011
N567KS	C56X	5567
N567L	C500	621
N567MC	**C56X**	**5357**
N567ML	CL60	1024
N567NT	CL64	5567
N567RA	**FA10**	**80**
N567RB	**C52B**	**0306**
N567S	C550	429
(N567SC)	LJ55	091
N567T	**PRM1**	**RB-37**
N567WB	C500	491
N567XP	**BE40**	**RK-567**
N567YX	**CL65**	**5907**
N568BA	HS25	258135
N568CC	C500	068
N568CH	C560	0611
N568CM	C500	068
N568CM	**C52B**	**0380**
N568CS	C56X	5637
N568DM	C56X	5325
N568EA	**EA50**	**000168**
N568GA	GLF5	5268
N568GA	GLF5	5468
N568GA	GLF5	611
N568GA	GLF5	668
N568GB	C560	0254
N568JC	**C560**	**0283**
N568JC	GLF5	568
N568L	**F900**	**101**
N568M	**GLEX**	**9069**
N568PA	**LJ35**	**205**
N568PB	**EA50**	**000067**
N568PC	**C550**	**500**
N568Q	FA20	149
N568QS	**C56X**	**5829**
N568R	**C56X**	**5075**
N568RL	C560	0443
N568SD	**BE40**	**RK-36**
N568SP	GLF5	5436
N568ST	**C550**	**565**
N568TN	GLF2	67
N568VA	C510	0107
N568VA	**C680**	**0331**
N568VA	FA50	176
N568WC	C560	0083
N569BA	HS25	258136
N569BW	FA20	259
N569BW	**FA50**	**45**
N569CA	FA50	115
N569CC	C500	069
N569CC	**C550**	**550-1113**
N569CC	FA50	115
N569CJ	C52C	0069
N569CS	HS25	25214
N569CW	GLF4	1145
N569D	FA20	259
N569DM	**C52A**	**0088**
N569DW	FA10	220
N569DW	FA20	259
N569EE	**E55P**	**50500284**
N569GA	GLF4	4169
N569GA	GLF5	5169
N569GA	GLF5	5369
N569GA	GLF5	612
N569GA	GLF5	669
N569GB	C550	650
N569LM	**C560**	**0068**
N569MK	**C56X**	**5006**
N569P	C560	0569
N569RS	C650	7028
N569SC	**LJ31**	**177**
N569TA	**C560**	**0006**
N569VP	C56X	5696
N570AM	**LJ45**	**238**
N570BA	HS25	258137
N570BJ	C560	0030
N570BY	**GLF4**	**1504**
N570CC	C500	070
N570CC	C500	570
N570CC	CS55	0070
N570CF	C56X	5701
N570D	C500	660
N570DC	**GLF4**	**1185**
N570DM	**C525**	**0055**
N570EA	**EA50**	**000070**
N570EJ	C560	0164
N570FT	LJ24	005
N570FX	**CL30**	**20527**
N570GA	GLF4	4170
N570GA	GLF5	5370
N570GA	GLF5	613
(N570JG)	LJ24	221
N570L	FA20	171
N570LT	**C510**	**0441**
N570MC	C500	298
N570MH	C560	0006
N570P	LJ24	221
N570PT	C750	0270
N570R	SBRL	282-3
N570R	**SBRL**	**465-75**
N570RC	CS55	0070
N570RF	**FA7X**	**4**
N570RG	**EA50**	**000048**
N570RZ	C680	0231
N570VP	C550	570
N570VP	C560	0070
N570WD	C550	570
N570XP	BE40	RK-570
N570ZD	**FA20**	**293**
N571AP	**C560**	**0805**
N571BA	CL64	5571
N571BC	**C550**	**599**
N571BJ	GLF2	15
N571CC	C500	071
N571CC	CS55	0071
N571CH	HS25	25284
N571CH	HS25	257071
N571CH	HS25	257078
N571CH	**HS25**	**258540**
N571CS	C56X	5680
N571DU	HS25	256071
N571E	HS25	256071
N571EE	**E55P**	**50500271**
N571FX	**CL30**	**20536**
N571GA	GLF4	4171
N571GA	GLF5	5071
N571GA	GLF5	5471
N571GA	GLF5	614
N571GA	GLF5	671
N571GH	HS25	25284
(N571K)	C500	328
N571KG	**HS25**	**HA-0179**
(N571MC)	WW24	175
N571NA	**CL61**	**5029**
N571NC	SBRL	306-1
N571P	MS76	071
N571TS	CL65	5718
N571TW	BE40	RK-571
N572CC	C500	072
(N572CC)	CS55	0072
N572CV	C560	0072
N572EC	**GLF4**	**1139**
N572EC	GLF5	5072
N572FX	**CL30**	**20521**
N572GA	GLF4	4172
N572GA	GLF5	5072
N572GA	GLF5	5472
N572GA	GLF5	615
N572M	WW24	258
N572MS	CL64	5572
N572MS	**GLF4**	**1352**
N572PB	C550	550-0956
N572R	SBRL	282-74
N573AB	C52C	0107
N573AB	C560	0427
N573AB	C56X	5635
N573AC	CL61	5060
N573AC	FA50	217
N573BA	CL64	5573
N573BB	**C52B**	**0042**
N573BB	C560	0108
N573BB	CS55	0037
N573BC	C52A	0494
N573BC	CL64	5573
(N573BP)	C560	0108
N573CC	C500	073
N573CC	CS55	0007
N573CM	**C525**	**0352**
N573CW	FA50	73
N573E	FA20	502
N573EJ	FA20	28
N573F	C560	0171
N573FX	**CL30**	**20564**
N573J	F900	39
N573J	FA10	196
N573L	C500	435
N573LP	LJ24	196
N573LP	LJ35	153
N573LP	LJ35	658
N573LR	LJ24	196
N573LR	**LJ35**	**153**
N573M	**C550**	**550-1066**
N573P	WW24	257
N573PT	GALX	127
N573QS	**C56X**	**5827**
N573TR	**FA50**	**217**
N573XP	BE40	RK-573
N574AV	C56X	5074
N574BA	LJ31	211
(N574BA)	LJ60	055
N574BB	**C52A**	**0371**
N574BB	C560	0022
N574BP	**C560**	**0022**
N574CC	C500	074
N574CC	C500	657
N574CF	MU30	A079SA
N574CS	C56X	5705
N574DA	LJ31	211
N574DA	LJ60	055
N574DA	LJ60	321
N574F	CL64	5574
N574FX	**CL30**	**20567**
N574GA	GLF4	4174
N574GA	GLF5	5074
N574GA	GLF5	5374
N574GA	GLF5	616
N574JS	**E50P**	**50000046**
N574M	**C550**	**550-0910**
N574QS	**C56X**	**5820**
N574R	SBRL	282-82
(N574U)	MU30	A079SA
N574W	C500	074
N574W	LJ55	011
N575	HS25	25218
N575AG	**CL64**	**5610**
N575AG	LJ45	312
N575AR	**LJ45**	**458**
N575BW	C550	128
N575CC	C500	075
N575CC	C500	475
N575CC	**EA50**	**000075**
N575CF	CL61	5019
N575CF	CL61	5188
N575CT	GLF4	1284
N575DM	C52A	0516
N575DM	**HDJT**	**42000031**
N575DU	HS25	25021
N575DU	HS25	25218
N575E	GLF2	219/20
N575E	GLF4	1007
N575ET	ASTR	042
N575EW	ASTR	042
N575EW	**CS55**	**0140**
N575FM	C550	129
N575FX	**CL30**	**20578**
N575G	LJ24	138
N575GA	GLF5	5075
N575GA	GLF5	5275
N575GA	GLF5	617
N575GD	LJ25	101
N575GH	**LJ55**	**042**
N575HP	**C52B**	**0073**
N575HW	LJ24	068
N575JC	C56X	6005
N575JC	**FA50**	**349**
N575JJ	**F9EX**	**163**
N575JR	HS25	258755
N575JS	**E50P**	**50000051**
N575JT	**E50P**	**50000310**
N575M	C550	550-0911
N575MA	**HS25**	**HA-0016**
(N575MA)	CL61	5061
N575MR	**HS25**	**258255**
N575MW	**CL30**	**20577**
N575NR	C56X	5759
N575PC	C560	0223
N575PK	**GLF5**	**5203**
N575PT	PRM1	RB-133
(N575PT)	PRM1	RB-150
N575QS	**C56X**	**5730**
N575R	SBRL	282-34
N575RB	**BE40**	**RK-99**
N575RD	C500	075
N575RE	**C525**	**0839**
N575SC	F2TH	23
N575SE	GLF2	221
N575SF	C510	0410
N575SF	GLF2	221
N575SF	GLF4	1233
N575SG	**CS55**	**0064**
N575SR	C500	597
N575TM	**C525**	**0838**
N575TP	**C510**	**0022**
N575VP	C560	0375
N575W	C550	008
N575WB	CL30	20075
N575WW	LJ35	043
N575XP	BE40	RK-575
N576CC	C500	076
N576CC	C500	576
N576CC	C550	576
N576CS	C56X	5794
N576EA	**EA50**	**000076**
N576EE	LEG5	55000012
N576FX	**CL30**	**20585**
N576GA	GLF5	5076
N576JS	E50P	50000057
N576LC	WW24	257
N576QS	**C56X**	**5708**
N576R	SBRL	282-7
N576SC	**C52A**	**0224**
N576XP	BE40	RK-576
N577AC	**LJ35**	**448**
N577AN	**ASTR**	**060**
N577CC	C500	077
(N577CC)	LJ45	238
N577CF	**FA7X**	**145**
N577CJ	CL64	5577
N577CS	C56X	5726
N577DA	**CL64**	**5398**
(N577FX)	CL30	20594
N577GA	GLF4	4177
N577GA	GLF5	5077

N577GA	GLF5	5377
N577GA	GLF5	577
N577JC	**C750**	**0122**
N577JF	**FA7X**	**142**
N577JM	**E55P**	**50500301**
N577JT	**C500**	**430**
N577LJ	LJ25	023
N577MC	**C550**	**550-0861**
N577PM	SBRL	282-2
N577PS	**C56X**	**5581**
N577QS	**C56X**	**5735**
N577QT	**F9EX**	**262**
N577R	SBRL	282-2
N577RT	**C52C**	**0133**
N577RT	FA10	80
N577S	FA20	68
(N577SD)	C525	0131
N577SV	C525	0131
N577SW	GLF4	1385
N577SW	SBRL	380-21
(N577SW)	GLF4	1284
N577T	HS25	258149
N577TH	**C52C**	**0034**
N577VM	C500	430
N577VM	**C550**	**550-0863**
N577VM	C550	615
N577VM	SBRL	282-31
N577VN	C550	615
N577VU	GLF4	1385
N577XP	BE40	RK-577
N577XW	**C560**	**0083**
N578AB	**C680**	**0540**
N578AN	C680	0293
N578BB	CS55	0037
N578CC	C500	078
N578CJ	**C52B**	**0282**
N578CM	**C510**	**0292**
N578CS	C56X	5800
N578CT	C510	0342
N578DF	GLF2	126
N578FP	CL61	5078
N578FX	CL30	20601
N578GA	GLF5	5078
N578GA	GLF5	5378
N578GA	GLF5	578
N578GG	**CS55**	**0079**
N578LJ	LJ24	006
N578M	**C550**	**612**
N578QS	C56X	5754
N578VR	**C56X**	**5578**
N578W	C550	082
(N578WB)	C500	095
N578WZ	**C52B**	**0403**
N578XJ	**CL30**	**20078**
N579AT	GLEX	9361
N579BB	**C560**	**0108**
N579BJ	**C560**	**0383**
N579BJ	C56X	5528
N579CC	C500	079
N579CE	C560	0579
N579CL	C56X	5779
N579CS	C56X	5807
N579DN	**FA20**	**388**
N579GA	GLF5	5079
N579GA	GLF5	5279
N579GA	GLF5	5379
N579GA	GLF5	579
N579JS	**E50P**	**50000064**
N579L	C550	579
N579M	**C550**	**550-1133**
N579MH	**C56X**	**5071**
N579QS	**C56X**	**5773**
N579RS	**CL64**	**5473**
N579TG	GLF3	433
N579XP	BE40	RK-579
N580AS	**C52A**	**0468**
N580AV	C550	161
N580AW	**C56X**	**5017**
N580BA	HS25	258139
N580BA	**LJ60**	**292**
N580BC	**C56X**	**5059**
N580BD	**C525**	**0209**
N580CB	**F9EX**	**235**
N580CC	C500	080
N580CE	C560	0302
N580CE	C560	0580
N580CS	C56X	5815
N580EE	**C56X**	**5166**
N580GA	GLF5	5080
N580GA	GLF5	5480
N580GA	GLF5	580
N580GA	GLF5	640
N580GS	FA10	132
N580GV	WW24	213
N580HC	**C56X**	**5707**
N580JH	**E50P**	**50000006**
N580JS	**E50P**	**50000079**
N580JT	C560	0167
N580KF	**GLF4**	**1315**
N580MA	HS25	25237
N580MA	HS25	256064
N580MR	C560	0015
N580NJ	WW24	58
N580QS	**C56X**	**5741**
N580R	C500	127
N580RA	GLF2	117
N580RC	C56X	5166
N580RJ	**HS25**	**HA-0039**
N580RJ	BE40	RK-329
N580RK	**BE40**	**RK-329**
N580SB	CL30	20580
N580SH	C550	550-0994
N580WC	**EA50**	**000080**
N580WE	WW24	123
N580WS	HS25	25047
N580XP	BE40	RK-580
N581AS	LJ35	311
N581BA	HS25	258140
N581CC	C500	081
N581CC	LJ35	083
N581CM	CS55	0033
N581CS	**C56X**	**5817**
N581D	**GLF5**	**5353**
N581EA	CS55	0080
N581FL	**FA20**	**440**
N581GA	GLF5	5081
N581GA	GLF5	5281
N581GA	GLF5	5481
N581GA	GLF5	581
N581GA	GLF5	651
N581GE	HS25	258581
N581GM	**F2EX**	**51**
N581JB	GALX	184
N581JS	**E50P**	**50000110**
N581MB	GLF2	109
N581NC	FA10	196
N581PH	**LJ35**	**083**
N581PJ	C500	666
N581RA	LJ31	106
N581SC	C560	0518
N581SF	**PRM1**	**RB-47**
N581SS	FA20	66
N581TS	**CL64**	**5482**
N581VC	**EA50**	**000095**
N581WD	GLF2	126
N582BA	HS25	258138
N582CC	C500	082
N582CC	C550	082
N582CJ	C680	0282
(N582CP)	HS25	258021
N582D	**GLF5**	**5397**
N582EJ	FA50	82
(N582G)	FA20	23
N582GA	GLF5	5082
N582GA	GLF5	5382
N582GA	GLF5	582
N582GA	GLF5	652
N582GV	GLF5	582
(N582JF)	C650	7077
N582JS	**E50P**	**50000135**
N582MM	**LJ60**	**227**
N582VP	C560	0382
N582WP	**C560**	**0568**
N582XP	BE40	RK-582
N583AJ	**GLF4**	**1184**
N583BA	HS25	258141
N583BS	LJ35	258
N583CC	C500	083
N583CE	**C560**	**0583**
N583CM	HS25	25225
(N583CS)	C56X	6064
N583CW	C560	0123
N583D	**CL30**	**20318**
N583D	GLF3	471
N583FH	LJ45	130
N583GA	GLF5	5083
N583GA	GLF5	5383
N583GA	GLF5	5483
N583GA	GLF5	583
N583JF	**F900**	**63**
N583JS	**E50P**	**50000131**
N583KD	**E55P**	**50500073**
N583LJ	LJ31	151
N583M	C560	0186
N583M	C560	0326
N583MP	C500	477
N583N	C560	0186
N583PS	LJ31	151
N583PS	LJ35	258
N583PS	LJ45	136
N583PS	**LJ45**	**331**
N583QS	**C56X**	**5812**
N583SB	**C52A**	**0307**
N583SD	**C650**	**7034**
N583TA	CL65	5838
N583VC	HS25	258003
(N583VP)	C550	583
N583XP	BE40	RK-583
N584A	**GLF4**	**4341**
N584BA	HS25	258142
N584CC	C500	084
N584CC	C500	584
N584CC	C56X	5025
N584D	**CL30**	**20239**
N584D	GLF4	1065
N584DB	HS25	25023
(N584DM)	GLF2	92
N584GA	GLF5	5084
N584GA	GLF5	5284
N584GA	GLF5	5484
N584GA	GLF5	584
N584GA	GLF5	654
N584JS	**E50P**	**50000140**
N584PS	**C550**	**550-0847**
N584SB	**C52A**	**0358**
N584SC	BE40	RK-584
N585A	GLF2	44
N585A	**GLF5**	**5110**
N585AC	FA20	205
N585BA	HS25	258144
N585BC	E55P	50500106
N585BC	**LEG5**	**55000033**
N585BD	CL64	5585
N585BG	**C500**	**561**
N585BP	F9EX	170
N585CC	C500	085
N585D	**CL30**	**20417**
N585D	GLF4	1258
N585DD	**GALX**	**085**
N585DG	**C525**	**0057**
N585DM	**C525**	**0697**
N585DM	C550	086
N585DW	**GLF5**	**5485**
N585EE	E55P	50500185
N585EP	**C52A**	**0346**
N585G	BE40	RK-94
N585GA	GLF5	5085
N585GA	GLF5	5385
N585GA	GLF5	5485
N585GA	GLF5	585
N585GA	GLF5	618
N585GA	GLF5	685
N585GS	**GLF6**	**6084**
N585JC	**GLF5**	**618**
N585JS	**E50P**	**50000138**
N585KS	**C550**	**550-0945**
N585KT	**C550**	**419**
N585LE	**CL30**	**20191**
N585M	**C750**	**0096**
N585MC	**C525**	**0452**
N585PC	C56X	5366
N585PC	**E55P**	**50500222**
N585PF	E55P	50500106
N585PJ	**CL64**	**5589**
N585PK	C525	0452
N585PK	C52B	0011
N585PS	C550	585
N585QS	C56X	5748
N585RA	**C550**	**585**
N585T	**C750**	**0197**
N585TC	MU30	A060SA
N585TH	C550	550-1035
N585TV	**E55P**	**50500006**
N585UC	CL61	5002
N585UC	FA20	299
N585VC	**HS25**	**258585**
N585VP	C52C	0085
(N585VP)	C560	0585
N585XP	BE40	RK-585
N586	JSTR	5085
N586AL	**CL30**	**20586**
N586BA	HS25	258145
N586C	GLF3	459
N586CC	C500	086
N586CC	C560	0186
N586CC	CS55	0086
N586CC	**LJ40**	**2048**
N586CP	C550	013
N586CS	FA50	260
N586D	GLF4	1439
N586ED	C52A	0324
N586ED	**C52C**	**0087**
N586FD	**C52A**	**0324**
N586G	**GLF5**	**5486**
N586GA	GLF5	5086
N586GA	GLF5	5486
N586GA	GLF5	586
N586GR	**C550**	**013**
N586GV	**GLF5**	**586**
N586JR	HS25	257014
N586JS	**E50P**	**50000183**
N586M	**C750**	**0506**
N586MS	GLF5	5393
N586RE	**C550**	**222**
N586RW	**GLF5**	**5448**
N586SF	C56X	5064
N586SF	**C56X**	**5592**
N586SF	BE40	RK-151
N586XP	BE40	RK-586
N587AG	**C510**	**0113**
N587BA	HS25	258147
N587CC	C500	087
N587CC	CL61	5087
N587DV	**GLF4**	**4345**
N587DZ	**F9EX**	**112**
N587FA	**CL30**	**20587**
N587G	**GLF5**	**5520**
N587GA	GLF5	5087
N587GA	GLF5	5287
N587GA	GLF5	5487
N587GA	GLF5	587
N587GA	GLF5	657
(N587K)	C560	0587
N587MV	C560	0765
N587QS	**C56X**	**5805**
N587S	C650	0188
N587VV	HS25	257046
N587XP	BE40	RK-587
N588AC	**C550**	**550-0912**
N588AL	**CL64**	**5388**
N588AT	GLF4	4020
N588BA	HS25	258150
N588BA	**LJ60**	**023**
N588BF	**LJ60**	**421**
N588CA	C500	471
N588CB	**E55P**	**50500297**
N588CC	C500	088
N588CC	**C56X**	**5687**
N588CG	LJ24	304
N588CT	CS55	0060
N588EE	E55P	50500188
N588FJ	FA50	88
N588G	**GLF5**	**5488**
N588GA	GLF5	5088
N588GA	GLF5	5288
N588GA	GLF5	5388
N588GA	GLF5	5488
N588GA	GLF5	588
N588GS	F9EX	104
N588GV	GLF5	588
N588LQ	**GLEX**	**9606**
N588LS	**GLF4**	**1245**
N588MM	C52C	0026
N588MM	**GLEX**	**9684**
N588PX	**GLF5**	**5467**
N588QS	**C56X**	**5721**
N588R	ASTR	042
N588SS	GLF2	142
N588UC	CL60	1071
N588VA	**C510**	**0107**
N588XP	BE40	RK-588
N588ZJ	**GLEX**	**9679**
N589BA	HS25	258157
N589CC	C500	089
N589CH	LJ45	421
N589CJ	C500	589
N589DC	**FA20**	**45**
N589EJ	FA50	89
(N589FJ)	FA50	289
N589GA	GLF5	5089
N589GA	GLF5	5289
N589GA	GLF5	589
N589GA	GLF5	659
N589GB	**C52C**	**0142**
N589HH	**C550**	**550-1005**
N589HM	GLF2	92
N589HM	GLF4	1153
N589HM	GLF5	554
N589K	**GLF5**	**5235**
N589KM	FA50	54
N589MD	**CL65**	**5952**
N589MD	G150	302
(N589MV)	C560	0765
(N589MV)	E55P	50500167
N589QS	**C56X**	**5810**
N589SJ	C550	589
N589TB	ASTR	037
N589UC	HS25	257137
N589WT	**E50P**	**50000344**
N589XP	BE40	RK-589
N590	LJ35	186
N590A	**C560**	**0029**
N590AK	**C56X**	**5038**
N590AS	C650	0088
N590BA	HS25	258160
N590CC	C500	090
N590CH	GLF2	19
N590CH	HS25	25222
N590CH	LJ24	295
N590CH	LJ45	416
(N590CH)	LJ35	060
N590CL	**F9EX**	**132**
N590CW	FA50	20
N590DA	GLF3	445
N590E	**GLEX**	**9105**
N590EA	C500	072
N590EA	C500	182
N590F	**F900**	**98**
N590FA	**G150**	**224**
N590GA	GALX	190
N590GA	GLF5	5090
N590GA	GLF5	5390
N590GA	GLF5	5490
N590GA	GLF5	590
N590GA	LJ24	139
N590HM	GLF4	1153
N590J	LJ35	336
N590JC	LJ45	059
N590MH	LJ31	058
N590PJ	C52B	0104
N590QS	**C56X**	**5738**
N590RA	**FA50**	**20**
N590RB	C500	090
N590RB	C550	230
N590TA	**ASTR**	**146**
(N590VC)	HS25	258590
N590VP	**C56X**	**5090**
N590XL	C56X	5590
N591BA	HS25	258162
N591CC	C500	091
N591CF	C560	0661
N591CF	**HS25**	**258175**
N591CH	**CL65**	**5717**
N591D	LJ24	115
N591D	LJ35	069
N591DK	**C560**	**0591**
N591DL	LJ24	115
N591ES	C510	0042
N591GA	GLF5	5091
N591GA	GLF5	5291
N591GA	GLF5	5391
N591GA	GLF5	5491
N591GA	GLF5	591
N591GA	LJ24	142
N591KR	LJ25	019
N591M	C560	0085
N591M	C560	0533
N591MA	**C56X**	**5163**
N591MB	C52B	0138
N591MB	**G150**	**253**
N591ME	**C52B**	**0138**
N591SC	LJ55	091
N591XP	BE40	RK-591
N592BA	HS25	258166
N592CC	C500	092
N592CF	**C56X**	**5207**
N592CH	CL65	5718
N592CL	**F9EX**	**152**
N592DC	FA10	26
N592DR	**C52A**	**0028**
N592GA	GLF5	5092
N592GA	GLF5	5292
N592GA	GLF5	592
N592GA	LJ24	143
"N592GA"	GLF5	5250
N592HC	**PRM1**	**RB-92**
N592KR	LJ25	028
N592M	C560	0338
N592M	CS55	0041
N592MA	**C560**	**0372**
N592QS	**C56X**	**5706**
N592SP	CL30	20123
N592UA	LJ35	658
N592VP	**C560**	**0092A**
N592WP	**C500**	**253**
N592XP	BE40	RK-592
N593BA	HS25	258168
N593BW	**C500**	**675**
N593CC	C500	093
N593CC	CS55	0093
(N593CC)	C500	593
N593CH	CL65	5745
N593CW	C560	0223
N593DC	FA10	180
N593DS	C500	593
N593EM	C550	714
N593GA	GLF5	5093
N593GA	GLF5	535
N593GA	GLF5	5393
N593GA	GLF5	5493
N593GA	GLF5	593
N593GA	LJ24	144
N593HR	**CL30**	**20143**
N593HR	HS25	258089
N593KR	LJ24	140
N593LR	LJ35	593
N593M	C560	0237
N593M	C560	0525
N593M	CS55	0021
N593M	**BE40**	**RK-53**
N593MD	C560	0074
N593PN	LJ35	593
(N593WH)	HS25	258045
N593XL	C56X	5593
N593XP	BE40	RK-593
N594BA	HS25	258170
N594CA	**CL30**	**20082**
N594CC	C500	094
N594CC	CS55	0094
N594CH	CL65	5749
N594G	C550	482
N594GA	GLF5	5094
N594GA	GLF5	525
N594GA	GLF5	5294
N594GA	GLF5	5494
N594GA	GLF5	594
N594JB	C525	0067
N594KR	JSTR	5099/5
N594M	C560	0279
N594QS	**C56X**	**5697**
N594RJ	CL61	5029
N594SF	CL64	5594
(N594VP)	C560	0094
N594WP	**C550**	**693**
N594XP	BE40	RK-594
N595A	C56X	5160
N595A	**GLF5**	**5117**
N595AB	C56X	6050
N595B	**GLF5**	**597**
N595BA	HS25	258171
N595BA	**LJ35**	**230**
N595CB	**CL30**	**20326**
N595CC	C500	095
N595CC	CS55	0091
N595CH	**C52A**	**0401**
N595CL	C56X	5795
N595CM	CS55	0091
(N595CW)	FA50	15
N595DC	**C500**	**265**
N595DC	FA20	500
N595DM	C525	0697
N595DM	**C52A**	**0478**
N595E	**GLEX**	**9075**
N595E	GLF4	1025
N595E	GLF5	597

N595EU	BE40	RK-595
N595G	**C56X**	**5224**
N595GA	G150	295
N595GA	GALX	095
N595GA	GALX	195
N595GA	GLF5	5095
N595GA	GLF5	522
N595GA	GLF5	5495
N595GA	GLF5	595
N595GA	LJ24	147
(N595GV)	GLF5	595
N595JJ	C560	0680
N595JS	FA50	200
N595KW	**C560**	**0595**
N595LA	**LJ45**	**294**
N595MA	C560	0680
N595PA	LJ31	150
N595PC	**C550**	**550-0826**
N595PD	**HS25**	**258526**
N595PE	**GLF4**	**1373**
N595PL	**F900**	**97**
N595PL	HS25	258526
N595PL	LJ35	448
N595PT	BE40	RJ-18
N595QS	C56X	5712
N595S	C56X	6012
N595SA	LJ31	203
N595SY	C680	0091
N595US	**HS25**	**258131**
N595VR	C550	550-1099
N595XP	BE40	RK-595
N596A	F2TH	28
N596BA	HS25	258172
N596CC	C500	096
N596CH	CL64	5392
N596DA	FA20	273
N596DC	**GLF4**	**4129**
N596GA	GLF5	520
N596GA	GLF5	5396
N596GA	GLF5	5496
N596GA	GLF5	596
N596GA	LJ24	150
N596HF	LJ24	150
N596MC	**CL30**	**20027**
N596MC	LJ60	226
N596MG	LJ60	226
N596SW	HS25	258096
N596VP	C560	0396
N596XP	HS25	258596
N596XP	BE40	RK-596
N597AF	**C650**	**7057**
N597BA	HS25	258174
N597BJ	**C56X**	**5742**
N597BL	LJ35	597
N597CC	C500	097
N597CS	C500	481
N597DA	CL64	5359
N597DC	**GLF4**	**4167**
N597DM	CL64	5398
N597FJ	CL61	3061
N597FJ	FA50	97
N597GA	GLF5	5097
N597GA	GLF5	519
N597GA	GLF5	5197
N597GA	GLF5	5497
N597GA	LJ24	152
N597JA	CL64	5597
N597JT	LJ35	597
(N597JV)	C500	597
N597KC	C560	0597
(N597N)	BE40	RJ-29
N597TB	**E55P**	**50500327**
N597TX	C56X	5097
N597U	C750	0004
N597XP	HS25	258597
N597XP	BE40	RK-597
N598AW	C650	0112
N598BA	HS25	258175
N598C	C650	0112
N598CA	C550	198
N598CC	C500	098
N598CH	**GLEX**	**9151**
N598CW	C560	0198
N598DA	CL64	5498
N598DB	LEG5	55000007
N598DR	**BE40**	**RK-478**
N598EA	**EA50**	**000098**
N598EU	BE40	RK-598
N598F	GLF5	598
N598GA	GLF5	5098
N598GA	GLF5	510
N598GA	GLF5	5298
N598GA	GLF5	5498
N598GA	GLF5	598
N598GA	LJ24	155
N598GS	GLF2	85
N598GS	GLF3	469
N598GS	**GLF4**	**1258**
N598HR	**HS25**	**258089**
N598JC	FA10	112
N598JL	BE40	RJ-19
N598JM	**WW24**	**222**
N598KW	**CS55**	**0098**
N598KZ	**GLF5**	**582**
N598LG	**E50P**	**50000360**
N598MT	CL64	5502
N598TB	E55P	50500179

N598TP	**E55P**	**50500179**
N598WC	**CL64**	**5511**
N598WC	CS55	0098
(N598WW)	LJ35	332
N599AK	HS25	258630
N599BA	HS25	258173
N599BR	C500	664
N599CB	CS55	0054
N599CC	C500	099
N599CH	**GLEX**	**9515**
N599CN	GLF4	1065
N599CS	**C56X**	**6083**
N599CT	LJ31	200
N599DA	CL64	5498
N599DA	GLF3	445
N599DP	WW24	318
N599EC	HS25	258183
N599EC	LJ55	018
N599FW	C550	599
N599GA	GLF5	515
N599GA	LJ24	156
N599GB	**C680**	**0146**
N599H	**GLF5**	**5016**
N599HA	**CL30**	**20599**
N599JL	BE40	RJ-14
N599KC	WW24	42
N599LP	C560	0085
N599LP	**HS25**	**HB-71**
N599LR	C560	0085
N599QS	**C56X**	**5714**
N599RR	FA20	325
N599SC	C560	0051
N599SC	FA50	242
N599SC	LJ35	670
N599SC	LJ60	113
N599SG	C560	0051
N599TA	**LJ45**	**212**
N599TC	**LJ55**	**082**
N599XP	BE40	RK-599
N599ZM	FA20	481
N600AE	HS25	256068
N600AE	LJ35	149
N600AG	HS25	256069
N600AJ	**LJ60**	**199**
N600AK	**GLEX**	**9033**
N600AL	**C525**	**0383**
N600AL	HS25	256051
N600AM	CL64	5345
N600AN	CRVT	10
N600AN	LJ31	242
(N600AP)	FA10	187
N600AR	GLF4	1419
N600AR	**GLF4**	**4098**
N600AS	E50P	50000018
N600AS	**E50P**	**50000246**
N600AS	F9EX	17
N600AS	FA50	90
N600AS	LJ60	040
N600AT	**C550**	**551**
N600AV	HS25	256015
N600AW	**C750**	**0181**
N600AW	HS25	256018
N600AW	LJ31	017
N600AW	LJ31	242
N600AW	LJ35	149
N600B	GLF2	82
N600B	GLF3	459
N600B	SBRL	306-33
N600BD	CL60	1020
N600BE	LJ35	348
N600BG	GLF3	430
N600BG	GLF4	1268
N600BJ	C56X	5017
N600BL	F2EX	56
N600BL	GLF3	482
N600BP	CL60	1004
N600BP	CL60	1073
N600BP	SBRL	282-53
N600BS	**C56X**	**5162**
N600BT	FA10	6
N600BT	GLF2	82
N600BW	C560	0087
N600BW	**C560**	**0671**
N600BZ	CL60	1028
N600C	**LJ55**	**047**
N600CB	**C56X**	**6129**
N600CC	CL60	1056
N600CC	GLEX	9019
N600CC	BE40	RK-6
(N600CC)	GLF4	1321
(N600CC)	LJ35	083
(N600CC)	BE40	RK-45
N600CD	**FA20**	**377/548**
N600CD	GLF2	221
N600CD	LJ25	274
N600CD	WW24	10
N600CF	**C56X**	**5202**
N600CF	CL60	1049
N600CF	CL60	1078
N600CG	MU30	A055SA
N600CH	FA50	181
N600CK	**GLF4**	**1169**
N600CL	CL60	1005
N600CL	**LJ60**	**110**
N600CN	LJ35	235
N600CN	**LJ60**	**040**
N600CP	CL60	1075

N600CR	C550	401
N600CS	**E50P**	**50000084**
N600CS	GLF2	75/7
N600CS	GLF4	1020
N600DE	**C510**	**0005**
N600DH	CL61	5176
(N600DH)	C500	576
N600DL	CL60	1078
N600DP	**CL60**	**1070**
(N600DP)	HS25	25202
N600DR	CL61	5176
N600DR	GLF4	1356
N600DT	**LJ35**	**017**
(N600DT)	JSTR	5058/4
N600DW	GLF4	1169
N600EA	**CS55**	**0015**
(N600EC)	CL60	1073
N600EF	C560	0376
N600EF	**LJ60**	**182**
N600EG	HS25	25075
N600ER	WW24	84
N600ES	CL64	5439
N600ES	GLF3	322
N600EZ	C550	228
N600FF	CL60	1019
N600FL	HS25	256034
N600G	HS25	256066
N600G	LJ24	025
N600G	LJ35	352
N600GA	**CL61**	**3046**
N600GA	LJ60	021
(N600GE)	SBRL	306-24
N600GG	**LJ60**	**115**
N600GH	C550	717
N600GH	C650	0029
N600GK	**C525**	**0297**
N600GL	SBRL	306-24
N600GM	FA10	25
N600GM	**LJ25**	**290**
N600GP	LJ35	236
(N600GP)	HS25	256055
N600GW	**MU30**	**A044SA**
N600HA	CL60	1071
N600HC	HS25	257036
N600HD	LJ25	101
N600HL	FA10	19
N600HR	**C525**	**0038**
N600HS	C525	0089
N600HS	HS25	256033
N600HS	HS25	258029
N600HT	**E50P**	**50000036**
N600HT	LJ25	101
N600HW	**C550**	**479**
N600J	GLF5	5138
N600J	**GLF5**	**5499**
N600J	HS25	258217
N600J	JSTR	5039
N600J	JSTR	5086/44
N600J	WW24	302
N600JA	HS25	25187
N600JB	**C550**	**691**
N600JC	FA20	7
N600JC	LJ24	246
N600JD	C650	0236
N600JD	GLF5	640
N600JJ	**CL60**	**1022**
N600JM	**F9EX**	
N600JM	**FA50**	**124**
N600JS	SBRL	282-44
N600JT	LJ25	291
(N600JT)	JSTR	5213
N600JV	**GLEX**	**9664**
N600JW	CL60	1061
N600K	WW24	148
N600KC	CL60	1012
N600KC	FA20	58
N600KC	HS25	258207
N600KE	**WW24**	**416**
N600KM	CS55	0008
N600L	HS25	25187
N600L	LJ60	020
N600L	**LJ60**	**259**
N600LC	LJ35	211
N600LC	LJ60	021
N600LC	LJ60	265
N600LE	LJ35	149
N600LE	WW24	425
N600LF	C560	0376
N600LF	C560	0569
N600LF	F9EX	74
N600LF	LJ35	654
N600LG	CL60	1052
N600LG	LJ60	021
N600LG	**LJ60**	**230**
N600LJ	**LJ60**	**047**
N600LL	LJ35	438
N600LN	LJ35	332
N600LN	LJ60	082
N600LN	**LJ60**	**424**
N600LP	HS25	25187
N600LS	CL30	20134
N600LS	CL60	1048
N600LS	**CL65**	**5913**
N600LS	HS25	258114
N600LS	HS25	259019
(N600LS)	CL30	20147
(N600LX)	CL61	3008

N600LY	GLF4	1122
N600MB	GLF2	108
N600MB	HS25	256044
N600MC	**C525**	**0194**
N600ME	**F900**	**163**
N600MG	CL60	1020
N600MK	CL60	1050
N600MK	HS25	256004
N600ML	GLF4	1104
N600ML	LJ60	217
N600MS	CL61	3041
N600MS	CL64	5333
N600MS	MU30	A055SA
N600MT	C500	070
N600MV	**HS25**	**259036**
N600N	**FA50**	**256**
N600NG	HS25	258537
N600NM	LJ60	182
N600NP	CL61	3002
N600NY	**WW24**	**231**
N600PB	E50P	50000130
N600PB	FA10	189
N600PC	LJ24	292
N600PC	LJ25	116
N600PD	CL60	1020
N600PH	**LJ60**	**074**
N600PJ	LJ60	004
N600PM	GLF3	333
N600PM	GLF4	1255
N600PY	**C56X**	**5253**
N600QJ	SBRL	465-54
N600QS	**C56X**	**5664**
N600R	SBRL	282-6
N600RA	CRVT	36
N600RE	CL60	1079
N600RH	GLF3	451
N600RH	GLF5	558
N600RM	C500	424
N600SB	HS25	256034
N600SB	BE40	RK-283
N600SJ	SBRL	306-15
N600SN	HS25	256064
N600SR	C500	236
N600SR	C500	275
N600SS	C500	623
N600ST	C550	383
N600ST	C550	550-1054
N600ST	CL60	1028
N600ST	CL60	1082
N600ST	CL60	1085
(N600ST)	BE40	RK-600
N600SV	HS25	25159
N600SZ	C550	383
N600TC	WW24	299
N600TD	**LJ60**	**084**
N600TD	WW24	254
N600TD	WW24	84
N600TE	CL60	1056
N600TF	CS55	0118
N600TG	SBRL	465-65
N600TH	HS25	258030
(N600TH)	HS25	258029
N600TJ	WW24	198
N600TN	CL60	1029
N600TP	JSTR	5058/4
N600TP	WW24	84
N600TT	CL60	1048
N600TT	HS25	256047
N600TT	JSTR	5058/4
(N600TT)	C500	075
N600TW	**FA10**	**153**
N600UD	C650	0236
(N600US)	F9EX	210
N600VC	GLF4	1227
(N600VE)	CS55	0019
N600VM	**C525**	**0804**
N600WD	**FA20**	**300/508**
N600WG	**FA50**	**98**
N600WJ	**CL60**	**1007**
N600WJ	HS25	256017
N600WJ	LJ35	466
N600WM	C500	040
N600WM	**BE40**	**RK-417**
N600WT	LJ35	037
N600XJ	LJ24	190
N600XT	**C525**	**0375**
N600YB	GALX	096
N600YY	CL60	1033
N600YY	GLF3	304
N601A	CL61	5166
N601AA	CL61	3061
N601AB	C560	0158
N601AB	C650	7098
N601AB	GALX	047
N601AD	**CL61**	**5186**
N601AE	CL61	3050
N601AF	**CL61**	**5045**
N601AG	CL61	3001
N601AG	CL61	3011
N601AN	CRVT	13
(N601AV)	GALX	053
N601BA	HS25	256040
N601BA	HS25	258082
N601BC	**C550**	**121**
N601BD	CL61	3010
N601BE	**CL61**	**5103**
N601BF	CL61	5065

N601BH	CL61	5043
N601BW	CL61	5150
(N601BX)	HS25	258082
N601CB	CL61	5090
N601CC	C500	101
N601CC	CL61	5008
N601CC	CL61	5087
N601CC	CL64	5324
N601CD	CL61	5088
N601CH	CL61	5093
(N601CH)	FA50	47
N601CJ	C525	0601
N601CJ	CL61	5023
N601CL	CL61	3001
N601CL	CL61	3003
N601CL	CL61	3016
N601CM	CL60	1079
N601CM	JSTR	5214
N601CN	**LJ60**	**087**
(N601CR)	CL60	1051
N601CT	**CL60**	**1049**
N601CV	**CL61**	**5144**
N601CV	CRVT	40
N601DB	CL61	5080
N601DL	**C750**	**0140**
N601DR	HS25	258299
N601DR	WW24	434
(N601DR)	CL61	5018
N601DS	**CL61**	**5148**
N601DT	CL61	5024
N601DV	GALX	102
N601DW	CL61	5099
(N601EA)	CL61	5028
N601EB	CL61	5153
N601EC	CL61	5064
N601EG	CL61	5008
N601ER	CL61	5032
N601ER	**CL61**	**5062**
N601ER	CL61	5141
N601FB	CL61	5152
N601FJ	CL61	3023
N601FM	**C52C**	**0148**
N601FR	**CL61**	**5003**
N601FR	CL61	5175
N601FS	CL61	5119
N601FS	CL61	5172
N601GA	GLF6	6051
N601GA	GLF6	6150
N601GB	CL61	3044
N601GB	CL61	5130
N601GD	GLF6	6001
N601GD	GLF6	6100
(N601GF)	CL61	3052
N601GG	**LJ60**	**192**
N601GL	CL61	3026
N601GL	SBRL	306-50
N601GN	C500	214
N601GR	CL61	5149
(N601GR)	CL61	5018
N601GS	CL61	5018
N601GT	CL61	3062
N601GT	**CL64**	**5524**
N601HC	CL61	5055
N601HC	CL61	5088
N601HF	CL61	5183
N601HH	CL61	5018
N601HJ	CL61	3046
(N601HJ)	CL61	5193
N601HP	CL61	3062
N601HW	**CL61**	**5154**
N601J	LJ25	118
N601JA	HS25	256051
N601JE	CL61	5086
N601JG	**CL61**	**3006**
N601JJ	HS25	25173
N601JJ	HS25	256051
N601JJ	JSTR	5102
N601JL	**C52C**	**0208**
N601JM	CL61	3048
N601JP	CL61	3065
N601JP	CL61	5141
N601JR	CL60	1011
(N601JR)	HS25	257087
N601KE	CL61	3023
N601KF	CL61	3023
N601KF	CL61	5175
N601KJ	CL61	5187
N601KK	C550	030
N601KK	**CL60**	**1061**
N601KK	HS25	25224
N601KR	CL61	5015
N601LJ	**LJ60**	**001**
N601LS	CL60	1048
N601MC	LJ35	306
N601MD	CL61	5078
N601MD	GLF5	538
N601MG	CL61	5078
N601MG	SBRL	306-73
N601MU	**CL61**	**5160**
N601NB	CL61	5024
N601NP	CL61	3026
N601PR	**CL61**	**3045**
N601PR	CL61	3054
(N601PR)	CL61	5106
N601PS	HS25	256051
N601QA	**CL61**	**5041**
N601QS	**C56X**	**5301**

N601R	CL61	5194
N601RC	**CL61**	**3055**
N601RC	CRVT	36
N601RL	CL61	5028
N601RP	CL61	3045
N601RS	HS25	258018
N601RS	HS25	258403
N601S	**CL61**	**3060**
N601SA	CL60	1013
N601SA	CL60	1079
(N601SN)	CL61	3060
N601SQ	CL61	3010
N601SR	CL60	1051
N601SR	CL61	3002
N601SR	CL61	5130
N601ST	**CL61**	**5081**
N601TG	CL61	3013
N601TJ	CL61	3033
N601TJ	CL61	3046
N601TL	CL61	5028
N601TM	CL61	5141
N601TP	CL61	3054
N601TP	**CL61**	**5156**
N601TX	CL61	3005
N601UC	CL61	5177
N601UP	CL61	5123
N601UT	CL61	3010
N601UU	HS25	25103
N601UU	HS25	258005
(N601UU)	HS25	257041
N601VC	HS25	258267
N601VF	CL61	5154
N601VH	**CL61**	**5043**
N601WG	**CL61**	**5010**
N601WJ	CL60	1065
N601WM	CL61	5026
N601WT	C500	568
(N601WT)	LJ35	218
N601WW	CL60	1047
N601WW	CL60	1076
N601WY	**CL61**	**5117**
N601XP	BE40	RK-601
N601Z	CL60	1079
N601Z	CL61	5075
N601ZT	CL61	3054
N602AB	C560	0217
N602AB	C650	7101
N602AB	GALX	048
(N602AG)	GLF4	1402
N602AJ	**CL60**	**1020**
N602AN	CRVT	31
(N602AN)	CL61	5178
N602AS	CL60	1054
N602AT	**C550**	**606**
(N602AV)	GALX	059
N602BC	C500	190
N602BD	CL61	5019
N602BW	C550	550-0884
N602CA	**C525**	**0026**
N602CC	CL61	3065
N602CC	CL61	5029
N602CC	CL61	5150
(N602CC)	C500	102
(N602CC)	C500	602
N602CF	HS25	256057
N602CJ	C525	0602
N602CL	CL60	1020
(N602CM)	GLF2	153
(N602CN)	CL61	5038
N602CS	C680	0003
N602CV	**F9EX**	**25**
N602CW	CL61	3002
N602D	CL61	5181
N602DM	FA10	162
(N602DM)	LJ60	002
N602DP	CL61	5154
N602DS	C650	7101
N602DV	PRM1	RB-121
N602EE	E50P	50000246
N602GA	GLF6	6052
N602GA	**GLF6**	**6205**
N602GA	HFB3	1041
N602GD	GLF6	6002
N602GD	**GLF6**	**6222**
N602GV	GLF5	602
N602HJ	CL61	3047
N602JB	CL61	5131
N602JC	**BE40**	**RK-256**
(N602JF)	LJ24	343
(N602JJ)	HS25	257017
N602JR	**HS25**	**25229**
N602KB	SBRL	306-109
(N602KF)	GLF4	1402
N602LJ	LJ60	002
N602LP	**F2TH**	**36**
N602LP	FA20	381/549
(N602LX)	CL61	3013
N602MA	C56X	5660
N602MC	CL61	5177
N602MJ	**C52B**	**0066**
N602MM	HS25	256002
N602N	LJ25	274
N602NC	FA10	82
N602NC	LJ25	274
N602NP	**CL61**	**5121**
N602PL	GLF4	1402
N602PM	GLF4	1402
N602QS	**C56X**	**5518**
N602RF	GALX	146
(N602SA)	C560	0302
N602SC	LJ60	095
N602TJ	CL61	3047
N602TS	**CL61**	**5002**
(N602TS)	CL61	3057
N602UK	CL61	5011
N602VC	GALX	038
N602WA	CL61	5068
N602XP	BE40	RK-602
(N603AF)	CL61	5129
(N603AG)	GLF4	1452
N603AT	C650	0178
N603CC	CL61	5011
N603CC	CL61	5067
N603CC	CL64	5333
N603CC	CL64	5420
(N603CC)	C500	103
N603CJ	C550	603
N603CL	CL60	1019
N603CS	GLF4	1257
N603CV	C560	0603
N603D	**G280**	**2034**
N603GA	GLF4	4103
N603GA	GLF6	6034
(N603GA)	HFB3	1042
N603GD	GLF6	6003
N603GD	GLF6	6103
N603GJ	CL61	3012
N603GP	LJ60	241
N603GP	**LJ60**	**416**
N603GR	**LJ60**	**241**
N603GY	HS25	257028
N603HC	**C560**	**0061**
N603HC	C650	0130
N603HC	C650	7077
N603HD	C650	7077
N603HJ	CL61	3052
N603HP	C650	0130
(N603JC)	C525	0053
N603JM	CL64	5402
N603KE	GLF4	1452
N603KF	GLF4	1452
N603KS	CL61	5130
N603LJ	LJ31	033
(N603LX)	CL61	3027
N603MA	**HS25**	**258282**
N603MA	SBRL	465-16
N603PM	GLF4	1452
N603QS	C56X	5203
N603RF	**GALX**	**147**
N603SC	**LJ60**	**096**
N603TS	HS25	256041
"N603TS"	CL61	3065
N603WM	**E55P**	**50500295**
N603WS	**C510**	**0215**
N603XP	BE40	RK-603
N604AB	CL64	5306
N604AC	CL60	1012
N604AC	CL61	5102
N604AC	CL64	5470
N604AF	**CL64**	**5444**
N604AG	CL64	5414
(N604AG)	CL64	5354
N604AK	**CL64**	**5623**
N604AN	CRVT	18
N604AS	**LJ25**	**292**
N604AU	**CL64**	**5434**
N604AV	**CL64**	**5437**
N604AX	CL64	5342
N604AZ	CL64	5328
N604B	CL64	5305
N604B	**CL64**	**5335**
N604BA	CL61	5153
N604BA	**CL64**	**5476**
N604BA	CL64	5546
N604BA	CL64	5571
(N604BA)	CL64	5307
N604BB	CL64	5316
N604BB	**CL64**	**5582**
N604BC	**CL64**	**5563**
N604BD	CL64	5303
N604BD	CL64	5489
N604BG	CL64	5509
N604BK	**LJ60**	**262**
N604BL	**CL64**	**5301**
N604BL	LJ35	604
N604BM	CL64	5354
N604BS	**CL64**	**5560**
N604CA	**CL64**	**5304**
N604CA	CL64	5379
N604CB	CL64	5448
N604CB	CL64	5526
N604CC	CL61	5016
N604CC	CL61	5032
N604CC	CL61	5101
N604CC	CL64	5301
N604CC	CL64	5376
N604CC	CL64	5488
N604CC	CL64	5560
N604CC	**CL64**	**5633**
"N604CC"	CL64	5991
(N604CC)	C500	104
(N604CC)	CL61	5179
N604CD	CL64	5376
N604CD	**CL64**	**5402**
N604CD	CL64	5591
N604CE	CL64	5446
N604CF	CL61	5020
N604CG	CL64	5632
N604CH	CL64	5394
N604CL	CL60	1015
N604CL	CL60	1030
N604CL	CL61	3053
N604CL	CL64	5322
N604CL	**CL64**	**5570**
N604CM	CL64	5652
N604CP	CL64	5321
N604CR	CL64	5376
N604CR	CL64	5418
N604CR	CL64	5424
N604CS	C680	0007
N604CT	CL64	5314
N604CU	CL64	5339
N604CW	**CL64**	**5455**
N604D	CL61	5193
N604D	CL64	5488
N604D	CL65	5713
N604D	**G280**	**2046**
(N604D)	G280	2043
N604DC	CL64	5365
N604DC	CL64	5403
N604DD	CL64	5366
N604DE	CL64	5380
N604DE	CL64	5471
N604DF	**CL64**	**5451**
N604DH	**CL64**	**5344**
N604DR	**C52C**	**0201**
N604DS	C550	647
N604DS	CL64	5323
N604DT	**CL64**	**5627**
N604DW	CL64	5470
N604ED	**LJ60**	**304**
N604EF	**CL60**	**1068**
N604EG	CL64	5635
N604EM	**CL64**	**5492**
N604EP	**CL64**	**5462**
N604FJ	**CL61**	**5001**
N604FK	LJ55	102
N604FM	**CL64**	**5488**
N604FS	CL64	5357
N604FS	**CL64**	**5465**
N604GA	GLF5	5304
N604GA	GLF6	6044
N604GA	HFB3	1037
N604GD	CL64	5490
N604GD	CL64	5624
N604GD	GLF6	6004
N604GD	GLF6	6042
N604GG	CL64	5407
N604GJ	**LJ60**	**185**
(N604GJ)	CL64	5401
N604GM	CL64	5399
N604GR	CL64	5478
N604GS	**LJ35**	**604**
N604GT	CL64	5449
N604GW	**CL64**	**5424**
N604HC	CL64	5555
N604HD	CL64	5445
N604HF	CL64	5575
N604HJ	CL61	5024
N604HJ	CL64	5382
N604HM	**CL64**	**5555**
N604HP	CL64	5375
N604HS	**CL64**	**5311**
N604HT	**CL64**	**5638**
N604JA	CL64	5426
N604JC	CL64	5372
N604JC	CL64	5568
N604JC	CL64	5609
N604JE	CL64	5389
N604JE	CL64	5549
N604JJ	CL64	5411
N604JJ	**CL64**	**5635**
N604JP	CL64	5346
N604JP	CL64	5421
N604JR	CL64	5449
N604JS	CL64	5311
N604JW	CL64	5325
N604KB	CL64	5565
N604KC	CL64	5312
N604KG	CL64	5390
N604KJ	**CL64**	**5554**
N604KM	CL64	5429
N604KR	CL64	5319
N604KS	CL64	5308
N604KS	CL64	5558
N604KT	**LJ60**	**315**
N604LA	CL64	5436
N604LA	**CL64**	**5497**
N604LC	**CL64**	**5373**
N604LE	CL64	5456
N604LJ	**C52A**	**0180**
N604LJ	LJ31	034
N604LL	CL64	5548
(N604LM)	CL64	5309
N604LS	CL64	5315
N604LV	**CL64**	**5395**
(N604LX)	CL61	3051
N604M	**CL64**	**5409**
N604M	GLF4	1132
(N604MA)	CL64	5430
N604MB	**CL61**	**5115**
N604MC	CL61	5013
N604MC	CL64	5581
N604ME	CL61	5112
N604MG	CL64	5416
N604MG	CL64	5638
N604MG	CL64	5654
N604MH	CL60	1042
N604MJ	CL64	5320
N604MK	SBRL	306-15
N604MM	**CL64**	**5381**
N604MU	CL64	5406
N604NB	C560	0091
N604NC	CL64	5348
N604NG	CL64	5513
N604PA	CL64	5391
N604PA	**CL64**	**5566**
N604PC	CL64	5425
N604PH	CL64	5578
N604PJ	**C550**	**459**
N604PL	CL64	5338
N604PM	CL64	5354
N604PN	CL64	5435
N604PS	CL64	5442
N604PS	**CL64**	**5447**
N604PT	**FA20**	**202**
N604PV	**CL64**	**5478**
N604QS	**C56X**	**5204**
N604RB	CL64	5377
N604RB	**CL64**	**5513**
N604RC	CL64	5334
N604RF	**CL30**	**20026**
N604RM	**CL64**	**5441**
N604RP	CL64	5473
N604RR	CL64	5377
N604RR	**CL64**	**5504**
N604RS	CL64	5551
N604RT	CL64	5497
N604S	CL64	5400
N604S	**LJ35**	**597**
N604SA	CL64	5341
N604SA	**CL64**	**5408**
N604SB	**CL64**	**5569**
N604SC	CL64	5385
N604SC	CL64	5593
N604SF	CL64	5589
N604SG	CL64	5615
N604SH	**CL60**	**1008**
N604SH	CL64	5396
N604SJ	CL60	1042
N604SL	CL64	5635
N604SL	**LJ60**	**060**
N604SN	C56X	5181
N604SR	CL64	5558
N604ST	CL64	5479
N604SX	CL64	5492
N604TB	**CL64**	**5471**
N604TB	CL64	5663
N604TC	**CL64**	**5323**
N604TF	**CL64**	**5655**
N604TH	CL64	5496
N604TS	CL64	5308
N604TS	CL64	5411
N604TS	CL64	5420
N604TS	CL64	5544
(N604TS)	CL61	5104
(N604TS)	CL64	5304
(N604TS)	CL64	5323
N604TX	CL64	5510
(N604UC)	CL64	5587
N604UP	CL64	5496
N604VF	CL64	5444
N604VG	**CL64**	**5562**
N604VK	CL64	5493
N604VM	CL64	5304
N604W	CL64	5421
N604WB	CL61	5125
N604WB	**CL64**	**5306**
N604WC	**LJ60**	**364**
N604WF	CL64	5561
N604WS	CL64	5471
N604WW	**CL64**	**5406**
N604XP	BE40	RK-604
(N604YZ)	CL60	1061
N604Z	**CL64**	**5496**
N604ZH	CL64	5376
N605AB	CL65	5792
N605AB	CL65	5912
N605AG	CL65	5739
(N605AG)	CL61	5115
(N605AG)	CL64	5356
N605AH	CL65	5939
N605AJ	CL65	5867
N605AK	CL65	5851
N605AM	**CL64**	**5596**
N605AM	CL65	5957
N605AS	**E50P**	**50000025**
N605AT	C560	0242
N605AT	CL65	5750
N605AZ	CL65	5827
N605BA	CL61	5152
N605BA	CL65	5707
N605BA	**CL65**	**5925**
(N605BA)	CL64	5543
N605BB	**CL65**	**5864**
N605BD	CL65	5980
(N605BE)	CL65	5950
N605BF	CL65	5935
(N605BK)	CL65	5951
N605BL	CL65	5781
N605BL	CL65	5956
N605BR	CL65	5893
N605BS	**CL65**	**5950**
N605BT	CL65	5789
N605BX	CL65	5815
N605BX	**LJ40**	**2004**
N605CB	CL65	5708
N605CC	CL61	5113
N605CC	CL61	5174
N605CC	CL64	5320
N605CC	CL65	5702
N605CE	C560	0605
N605CH	**GLF5**	**5263**
N605CH	GLF5	621
N605CJ	CL65	5759
N605CK	CL61	5112
N605CL	CL60	1057
N605CL	CL61	3054
N605CL	CL64	5605
N605CL	**CL65**	**5909**
N605CM	CL65	5890
N605CM	**GLF4**	**1137**
N605CR	CL65	5855
N605CS	C680	0001
N605DA	**CL65**	**5930**
N605DC	CL64	5422
N605DJ	CL65	5870
N605DS	C650	0178
N605DX	CL65	5735
N605FA	CL65	5806
N605FH	CL65	5765
N605FH	CL65	5767
N605FJ	F9DX	605
N605FR	CL65	5839
N605FX	LJ40	2004
N605GA	HFB3	1038
N605GA	LJ24	119
N605GB	CL65	5755
N605GD	GLF6	6005
N605GD	GLF6	6050
N605GD	GLF6	6165
N605GF	**CL65**	**5766**
N605GG	CL65	5728
N605GL	CL65	5747
N605GN	**CL65**	**5712**
N605GS	**CL65**	**5939**
N605H	CL65	5767
N605HC	**CL65**	**5720**
N605HG	CL65	5721
N605HJ	CL61	5025
N605HP	C525	0304
N605JA	**CL64**	**5369**
N605JA	CL64	5443
N605JA	CL65	5751
N605JD	CL65	5891
N605JF	**CL61**	**5172**
N605JK	CL65	5817
N605JM	CL65	5716
N605JM	**CL65**	**5935**
N605JP	CL65	5726
N605JS	**CL65**	**5860**
N605KA	**CL65**	**5718**
N605KB	**CL65**	**5701**
N605KC	CL64	5313
N605KR	CL65	5822
N605KS	CL65	5701
N605L	**CL65**	**5794**
N605LC	**CL65**	**5740**
N605LD	CL65	5730
N605LT	**CL65**	**5923**
N605M	CL65	5981
(N605M)	GLF5	621
N605ML	**HS25**	**HB-68**
N605MM	**CL65**	**5769**
N605MP	CL64	5417
N605MP	CL65	5960
N605MS	CL65	5821
N605MX	CL65	5954
N605NA	**LJ24**	**049**
N605NE	LJ25	139
N605NP	**CL65**	**5895**
N605PA	CL64	5397
N605PA	**CL65**	**5753**
N605PM	CL64	5356
N605PR	**C560**	**0436**
N605PS	**CL65**	**5795**
N605PW	CL65	5858
N605PX	CL65	5859
N605QS	**C56X**	**5321**
N605RA	GLF2	57
N605RA	**GLF4**	**1028**
N605RC	**CL65**	**5800**
N605RF	**CL30**	**20089**
N605RG	SBRL	306-116
N605RJ	CL65	5763
N605RK	CL65	5875
N605RP	CL61	5184
N605RP	**CL65**	**5801**
N605RP	FA20	100
N605RT	**CL65**	**5917**
N605RZ	CL65	5798
N605S	**CL65**	**5788**
N605SA	C650	0152
N605SB	**LJ60**	**156**
N605SE	LJ45	317

N605T	**CL61**	**5191**
N605T	FA10	189
N605TA	CL65	5790
N605TC	**PRM1**	**RB-52**
N605TS	CL60	1005
N605TX	CL65	5766
N605UK	CL30	20142
N605V	WW24	100
N605VF	GLEX	9152
N605W	HS25	25136
N605WF	**CL65**	**5703**
N605WV	CL65	5899
N605XP	BE40	RK-605
N605Y	SBRL	465-63
N605ZH	**CL65**	**5738**
N605ZK	CL65	5983
N606	**HS25**	**258068**
N606	LJ35	200
N606AB	WW24	268
(N606AG)	CL64	5360
N606AM	**FA10**	**205**
N606AT	C650	0225
N606BA	CL61	3006
N606BR	LJ60	006
N606CC	C500	106
N606CC	CL61	5018
N606CC	CL61	5035
N606CC	CL61	5117
N606CC	CL64	5340
N606CC	CL64	5395
N606CC	CL64	5606
N606CE	C560	0606
N606CH	GLF4	4089
N606CL	CL60	1009
N606CS	C680	0061
N606DH	GLF3	445
N606DR	F9EX	40
N606ES	GLF3	322
N606FX	LJ40	2005
N606GA	GALX	106
N606GA	GLF4	4106
N606GA	**GLF6**	**6031**
N606GA	GLF6	6066
N606GB	**LJ25**	**245**
N606GD	GLF6	6006
N606GG	CL64	5500
N606HC	**C525**	**0087**
N606JF	**HS25**	**258337**
N606JL	**CL64**	**5332**
N606JM	MU30	A044SA
N606JM	WW24	149
N606JR	C525	0231
(N606JR)	PRM1	RB-161
(N606KF)	GLF4	1512
N606KG	**C680**	**0554**
N606KK	C500	306
N606KK	**C550**	**225**
N606KR	**C500**	**306**
N606L	**LJ60**	**020**
(N606LX)	CL61	3064
N606MA	**WW24**	**196**
N606MC	**C52C**	**0121**
N606MG	C525	0231
N606MH	**GLF4**	**1107**
N606MM	C525	0104
(N606MM)	C52A	0051
N606PM	CL64	5360
N606PM	GLF4	1512
N606PS	**GLF4**	**1477**
N606PT	GLF3	308
N606Q	C56X	5323
N606QS	C56X	5323
N606QS	**C56X**	**5338**
N606RP	CL64	5578
N606RP	FA20	265
N606SB	**LJ60**	**184**
N606SG	**F9EX**	**202**
N606SM	**LJ25**	**185**
N606SV	C680	0206
N606TJ	F2EX	155
N606TJ	**FA7X**	**235**
N606TS	HS25	256006
N606TS	LJ60	006
N606US	F9EX	218
N606XG	C52A	0015
N606XT	**CL30**	**20052**
(N607AW)	GALX	122
N607AX	CL61	5075
N607BF	FA50	206
N607BF	**LJ45**	**016**
N607BF	LJ55	056
(N607BH)	CL60	1007
N607BR	LJ55	056
(N607CC)	C500	107
N607CF	**SBRL**	**306-118**
N607CH	**GLF5**	**5159**
N607CJ	C500	607
N607CL	CL60	1071
N607CL	CL61	3031
N607CL	CL61	5007
N607CV	F9EX	25
N607CV	**GLF5**	**5035**
(N607CZ)	CL61	5007
N607DB	**C525**	**0269**
(N607DX)	F9DX	607
N607FG	LJ45	344
N607FX	LJ40	2012
N607GA	GLF4	4107
N607GA	GLF5	5207
N607GA	GLF6	6027
N607GD	GLF6	6007
N607HB	HA4T	RC-6
N607HM	C560	0322
N607KF	GLF4	1509
N607LC	CL64	5607
N607LM	**EA50**	**000204**
N607MH	**GLF4**	**1289**
N607PH	CL61	5184
N607PM	CL64	5362
N607PM	GLF4	1509
N607PM	GLF5	5146
N607QS	**C56X**	**5340**
N607RJ	C560	0370
N607RJ	**FA50**	**206**
N607RP	**CL30**	**20349**
N607RP	CL61	5184
N607RP	FA20	470
N607S	FA20	7
N607SB	**LJ60**	**086**
N607SG	FA50	317
N607SR	SBRL	306-118
N607TC	FA10	77
N607TN	**C525**	**0662**
N607VP	C56X	6071
N607X	FA7X	6
(N608AG)	GLF4	1486
N608AM	C550	608
N608AR	SBRL	282-77
N608BC	**C560**	**0235**
N608BG	**GLF3**	**430**
N608CC	CL61	5023
N608CC	CL61	5037
N608CC	CL61	5179
N608CC	CL64	5301
N608CE	**C560**	**0608**
N608CH	GLF4	4098
N608CL	CL61	3040
N608CL	**GLF4**	**1193**
N608CM	GLF2	95/39
N608CS	C680	0063
N608CT	**C560**	**0065**
N608CW	CL61	3008
N608CW	**PRM1**	**RB-162**
N608D	**GLF4**	**4152**
N608DB	**C525**	**0179**
N608DC	**ASTR**	**095**
N608FX	LJ40	2014
N608GA	GLF4	4008
N608GA	GLF4	4108
N608GA	GLF4	4208
N608GA	GLF5	619
N608GA	GLF6	6080
N608GD	GLF6	6008
N608GF	LJ35	477
N608JA	LJ60	325
N608JR	**C550**	**591**
(N608KF)	GLF4	1486
N608LB	CS55	0029
N608LJ	LJ60	008
N608MD	GLF2	197
N608MM	**C525**	**0104**
N608PM	GLF4	1486
N608QS	**C56X**	**5308**
N608RP	**CL30**	**20372**
N608RP	CL61	3055
N608S	SBRL	282-77
N608SG	**C52B**	**0249**
N608VP	C550	608
N608W	**LJ31**	**165**
N608WB	GLF5	608
N609AM	HS25	257002
N609BD	CL64	5303
N609CC	CL61	5068
N609CC	CL64	5327
N609CC	CL64	5438
N609CH	F2TH	22
N609CL	CL61	3043
N609CL	CL61	3066
(N609CR)	CL64	5418
N609FX	LJ40	2022
N609GA	GLF4	4109
N609GA	GLF5	5209
N609GA	GLF6	6019
N609GD	GLF6	6009
N609K	CL61	5072
(N609KF)	GLF4	1510
(N609LC)	LJ60	075
N609LS	**CL30**	**20134**
N609LS	F2EX	176
(N609PA)	GLF2	206
N609PM	GLF4	1510
N609PM	GLF5	5086
N609QS	**C56X**	**5522**
(N609RM)	GLF4	1510
N609SG	F900	136
N609SM	**C525**	**0247**
N609TC	C510	0142
N609TC	C550	609
N609TF	LJ35	609
N609TJ	F2EX	155
N609TS	CL64	5309
N610AB	**GLF3**	**398**
N610AS	E50P	50000044
N610AS	F2TH	8
N610BA	HS25	258179
(N610BA)	HS25	258176
N610BD	**C500**	**391**
N610BK	C560	0809
N610BL	C550	610
N610CB	**C550**	**550-1014**
N610CC	FA20	373
N610CC	GLF2	56
N610CC	GLF3	412
(N610CC)	C500	110
N610CL	CL61	3049
N610CM	C650	0210
(N610CM)	GLF5	610
N610CR	**LJ60**	**339**
N610CS	C680	0092
N610CX	**F900**	**104**
N610DB	CL61	5132
N610ED	C500	241
N610ED	C550	338
N610EG	BE40	RK-13
N610F	C680	0329
N610FX	LJ40	2027
N610GA	GLF4	4110
N610GA	GLF5	5210
N610GA	GLF6	6110
N610GA	LJ35	073
N610GD	C500	551
N610GD	**C560**	**0547**
N610GD	CS55	0034
N610GE	LJ35	338
N610GE	LJ36	036
N610GG	**C500**	**573**
N610GR	C750	0163
N610HC	ASTR	012
N610HC	**C750**	**0054**
N610HC	HS25	25253
N610HC	LJ35	255
N610HC	WW24	346
N610HC	WW24	361
(N610HC)	HS25	25173
N610J	WW24	1
(N610J)	FA10	139
N610JA	WW24	298
N610JB	C550	610
N610JB	LJ25	370
N610JC	**C550**	**292**
N610JL	**C510**	**0379**
N610JR	LJ25	370
N610JR	LJ35	402
N610JR	**LJ55**	**125**
N610L	**CL64**	**5607**
N610LJ	**LJ35**	**610**
N610LM	LJ25	301
N610LS	CL30	20139
(N610LX)	CL61	5009
N610MC	GLF2	196
N610MC	GLF4	1368
N610MS	CL61	3041
N610PR	BE40	RK-441
N610PR	BE40	RK-466
N610PT	**C510**	**0172**
(N610PW)	EA50	000274
N610QS	**C56X**	**5210**
N610R	LJ35	622
N610RA	SBRL	306-54
N610RL	**F900**	**68**
N610RP	C650	0206
N610RT	C750	0167
N610RT	C750	0283
N610RW	**C750**	**0167**
N610SA	CL64	5510
N610SE	**WW24**	**346**
N610SF	**C52A**	**0015**
N610SM	**ASTR**	**101**
N610TM	**CL64**	**5377**
N610TM	LJ60	005
N610TS	LJ60	010
(N610TS)	CL60	1023
N610TT	C500	573
(N610VP)	C650	0010
N611AB	**CL64**	**5324**
N611AC	CRVT	7
N611AG	MU30	A091SA
N611AT	C500	490
N611BA	HS25	258178
(N611CA)	LJ24	077
N611CC	CL61	5185
N611CF	C550	244
N611CG	GLF5	5108
N611CL	CL61	3030
N611CL	CL61	5002
N611CM	LJ35	253
N611CR	C550	260
(N611CR)	HS25	258061
N611CS	**C52B**	**0063**
N611CS	C560	0670
N611DB	**LJ24**	**318**
(N611DT)	FA20	471
N611EC	**E50P**	**50000265**
(N611EL)	HS25	257080
N611ER	C550	260
N611FX	LJ40	2037
N611GA	FA20	9
N611GA	GLF6	6101
N611GD	GLF6	6011
N611GD	GLF6	6111
N611GD	**GLF6**	**6211**
N611GS	CL61	5082
N611JC	WW24	2
N611JM	**GLF4**	**1178**
N611JW	CL61	5063
N611JW	F900	162
(N611LX)	CL61	5053
N611MC	**HS25**	**257080**
N611MH	CL61	5011
N611MM	HS25	258061
N611MP	**C560**	**0611**
N611MR	C560	0611
N611MR	**C56X**	**5514**
N611MW	**C510**	**0028**
N611NC	**G150**	**223**
N611NJ	**C680**	**0156**
N611NM	C550	616
N611NS	**C650**	**7055**
N611NT	CL61	5082
N611PA	BE40	RK-78
N611QS	**C56X**	**5548**
(N611RR)	C550	161
N611SH	LJ35	253
N611ST	C560	0123
N611SW	C500	093
N611TA	**LJ35**	**439**
N611TG	**BE40**	**RJ-27**
N611TJ	GLF2	11
N611TK	C52B	0299
N611TK	**C52C**	**0098**
N611TS	LJ60	011
N611TW	LJ35	611
N611VT	GLEX	9219
N611WM	BE40	RK-249
N611WV	WW24	313
N611XP	BE40	RK-411
N612AB	C650	7101
(N612AB)	C650	7098
N612AC	**C56X**	**5676**
N612AC	CRVT	9
N612AC	GLF4	1059
N612AF	**GLF4**	**4069**
N612BA	HS25	258181
N612BH	F900	122
(N612CA)	C500	216
N612CC	C550	344
N612CC	CL61	5063
N612CC	CL61	5186
N612CL	CL61	3056
N612DG	LJ35	326
N612DS	C500	469
(N612EL)	HS25	257168
N612EM	**C750**	**0100**
N612EQ	LJ55	003
N612FG	**GLEX**	**9490**
N612FX	LJ40	2039
N612G	HS25	25139
N612GA	FA20	8
N612GA	GALX	212
N612GA	GLF4	4112
N612GA	GLF6	6102
N612GD	GLF6	6012
N612GD	GLF6	6112
N612GD	**GLF6**	**6212**
N612HT	**F2EX**	**107**
N612J	WW24	3
N612JC	WW24	50
N612JD	**C52A**	**0366**
N612JN	**CL30**	**20297**
N612KB	**EA50**	**000026**
N612KC	LJ35	105
(N612LX)	CL61	5139
(N612M)	WW24	389
N612MC	HS25	257168
N612MH	**GALX**	**019**
N612NL	F900	113
N612QS	**C56X**	**5312**
N612SQ	LJ35	472
N612ST	CS55	0065
N612VR	**C550**	**115**
N612XP	HS25	258612
N613AC	CRVT	11
N613AL	C525	0661
N613BA	HS25	258183
N613BB	**C56X**	**5528**
N613BR	LJ24	082A
N613BR	SBRL	306-8
N613BS	FA20	489
(N613CC)	C500	113
N613CF	**HS25**	**258256**
N613CK	GLF2	150
N613CL	**C680**	**680A0013**
N613CL	CL61	3042
N613CL	CL61	5005
(N613E)	SBRL	306-25
(N613EL)	HS25	257151
N613GA	FA20	77/429
N613GA	G150	213
N613GD	GLF6	6013
N613GD	GLF6	6113
N613GD	**GLF6**	**6213**
N613GH	F2EX	72
N613GL	LJ25	329
N613GY	C56X	5300
N613H	LJ60	313
N613J	WW24	12
N613JG	**C525**	**0342**
N613JT	C56X	6115
N613KS	C56X	5300
N613LB	**C52A**	**0174**
(N613LX)	CL61	5141
N613MC	HS25	257151
N613ML	**C510**	**0190**
N613PB	FA20	489
N613PD	**FA50**	**82**
N613PJ	**CL61**	**5123**
N613QS	**C56X**	**5599**
N613R	**E55P**	**50500205**
N613R	LJ60	044
N613RR	LJ35	276
N613SA	LJ31	167
N613SB	CL61	5088
N613SZ	LJ25	156
N613SZ	LJ31	040
N613W	LJ24	013
N613WE	**GLEX**	**9128**
N613WF	GLEX	9005
N613WF	GLEX	9128
N613WF	**GLF5**	**5535**
N613WM	**C56X**	**6115**
N613XL	C56X	5613
N614AC	CRVT	17
N614AF	**CL61**	**5171**
N614AF	HS25	258057
N614AJ	**HS25**	**258019**
N614AP	**HS25**	**258057**
N614B	**C52B**	**0017**
N614BA	**CL64**	**5614**
N614BA	HS25	258185
N614BG	HS25	258704
N614CC	CL61	5056
N614CC	CL61	5188
(N614CC)	C500	114
N614CL	CL61	3059
N614CM	**GLF5**	**614**
(N614DD)	C500	576
N614DJ	**HA4T**	**RC-33**
N614EP	C56X	5713
N614FX	LJ40	2041
N614GA	FA20	94/428
N614GA	**GALX**	**214**
N614GA	GLF4	4114
(N614GA)	C550	399
N614GD	GLF6	6014
N614GD	GLF6	6114
N614GD	**GLF6**	**6214**
N614HF	GLF4	1119
N614J	WW24	26
N614JA	CL64	5614
N614JC	WW24	26
N614JH	LJ60	201
N614JK	**CS55**	**0018**
N614MH	WW24	95
(N614MJ)	CL64	5420
N614MM	SBRL	306-41
N614QS	**C56X**	**5580**
N614RD	**GLF4**	**1006**
N614SJ	C550	248
N614TH	E55P	50500088
N614TH	**LEG5**	**55000012**
N614TS	LJ60	104
N614TX	**C680**	**0114**
N614XL	C56X	5614
N615AC	CRVT	18
N615AK	**C525**	**0367**
N615AT	C560	0245
N615BA	HS25	258187
N615CG	**LJ45**	**208**
N615DM	**E50P**	**50000358**
(N615DM)	WW24	196
N615DS	**C500**	**337**
N615EA	C550	615
N615EC	**C56X**	**5158**
N615FX	**LJ40**	**2051**
N615GA	G150	215
N615GA	GALX	115
N615GA	GLF5	5215
N615GA	GLF6	6105
N615GA	**GLF6**	**6215**
N615GD	GLF6	6015
N615GD	**GLF6**	**6115**
N615HB	**LJ35**	**444**
N615HP	LJ35	444
N615HP	BE40	RK-172
N615HP	**BE40**	**RK-231**
N615HR	**C560**	**0309**
N615J	WW24	29
N615L	C560	0386
N615L	**CL61**	**5159**
N615ME	F900	25
N615MS	F900	25
N615MS	**F9EX**	**160**
N615PL	**C52C**	**0006**
N615QS	**C56X**	**5360**
N615RG	**C56X**	**5016**
N615RH	**EA50**	**000068**
(N615SA)	CL61	5052
N615SM	**E50P**	**50000223**
N615SR	**FA50**	**298**
(N615TJ)	HS25	256015
N615TL	CL64	5393
N615WP	**C52A**	**0342**
N615XP	HS25	258615
N616AC	CRVT	20
N616AT	C650	0230

N616BA	HS25	258188
N616BM	C525	0251
N616CC	CL61	5045
N616CC	CL61	5144
N616CC	**GLF4**	**1455**
N616CE	C560	0616
N616CS	C680	0016
N616DC	GLEX	9025
N616DC	**GLEX**	**9296**
N616DC	GLF4	1349
N616DF	CL60	1038
N616DG	GLF4	1349
N616DJ	LJ36	016
N616EA	HA4T	RC-36
N616FX	LJ40	2047
N616FX	LJ40	2057
N616GA	GALX	216
N616GA	GLF6	6016
N616GA	GLF6	6116
N616GA	**GLF6**	**6216**
(N616GB)	CS55	0100
N616GD	GLF6	6106
N616GX	GLEX	9616
N616HC	LJ35	255
(N616KF)	GLF4	1534
N616KG	GLF4	1534
N616KG	GLF5	5361
N616KG	**GLF6**	**6145**
N616LJ	LJ35	616
N616MM	MU30	A062SA
N616NA	**LJ25**	**035**
N616PA	HS25	256051
N616PS	LJ24	088
N616QS	**C56X**	**5345**
N616RK	**GLF5**	**5361**
N616SC	LJ24	100
N616TD	**C560**	**0405**
N616TG	CS55	0119
N616TR	**SBRL**	**306-23**
N616WG	**HS25**	**258030**
N617AC	CRVT	22
N617BA	HS25	258189
N617BD	LJ45	281
N617BG	MU30	A067SA
N617CB	C52A	0356
N617CC	C500	117
N617CC	C500	617
N617CM	C550	617
N617CS	C680	0102
N617EA	**GLF5**	**693**
N617FX	LJ40	2065
N617GA	FA20	88
N617GA	GLF6	6017
N617GA	GLF6	6117
N617GA	**GLF6**	**6217**
N617GD	GLF6	6107
N617JN	**GLEX**	**9004**
(N617JS)	GLF5	646
N617PD	C560	0075
N617PD	**C56X**	**5273**
N617QS	**C56X**	**5509**
N617RA	**ASTR**	**113**
N617RX	**LJ45**	**201**
N617SA	C56X	6171
N617TM	HS25	258411
N617VP	C525	0617
N617WM	**GLF4**	**1419**
N617XP	HS25	258617
N617XT	**GLF4**	**4295**
N618AC	CRVT	26
N618AJ	CL60	1018
N618AR	HS25	258645
N618BA	HS25	258191
N618BR	LJ24	082A
N618CC	C650	0008
N618CC	CL61	5085
N618CC	CL61	5166
(N618CC)	C500	118
N618CF	LJ35	618
N618CW	**LJ45**	**430**
N618DB	C550	340
N618DB	CL61	5018
N618DC	CL61	5004
N618DC	CL64	5365
N618DM	LJ35	618
N618FX	LJ40	2067
N618FX	**LJ40**	**2076**
N618GA	FA20	211
N618GA	GALX	218
N618GA	GLF4	4018
N618GA	GLF6	6018
N618GA	GLF6	6118
N618GA	**GLF6**	**6218**
N618GD	GLF6	6108
N618GH	FA20	236
N618GH	FA20	513
N618GR	C750	0163
N618GX	GLEX	9618
N618HC	ASTR	012
N618JC	WW24	105
N618JC	WW24	51
N618JL	HS25	258224
N618KA	C525	0618
N618KG	**CL30**	**20093**
N618KM	GLF3	487
N618KR	HS25	257008
(N618KS)	C56X	5300
N618L	**LJ60**	**267**
N618LT	**BE40**	**RK-257**
N618P	LJ25	360
(N618P)	LJ60	044
N618QS	**C56X**	**5506**
N618R	CL30	20045
N618R	LJ24	225
N618R	LJ25	139
N618R	LJ25	360
N618R	LJ31	035
N618R	LJ60	044
N618RF	LJ31	035
N618RL	CL60	1018
N618RR	**CL61**	**5022**
N618S	FA10	156
N618SA	GLF4	1367
N618SR	EA50	000254
N618TH	**E55P**	**50500088**
N618VH	**C560**	**0214**
N618WA	WW24	236
N618WF	**GLEX**	**9005**
N618XL	C56X	5618
N618XP	HS25	258618
N618XP	BE40	RK-418
N619A	**GLF4**	**1123**
N619AT	**C750**	**0017**
N619BA	HS25	258193
(N619BA)	C550	619
N619BD	F900	16
N619CC	C500	119
N619CC	CL61	5081
N619EA	C500	220
N619FE	CL61	5054
N619FL	**GLF4**	**1312**
N619FX	LJ40	2059
N619FX	**LJ40**	**2082**
N619G	**BE40**	**RK-196**
N619GA	FA20	215
N619GA	GALX	219
N619GA	GLF6	6109
N619GA	BE40	RK-196
N619GA	**GLF6**	**6219**
N619GD	GLF6	6119
N619JC	WW24	93
N619JM	C550	550-0889
N619KK	GLF4	1062
N619KS	**GALX**	**151**
N619MC	GLF2	196
N619MJ	LJ55	021
N619ML	**GLF4**	**1062**
(N619MS)	C550	193
N619MW	FA20	312
(N619PD)	C560	0075
N619QS	**C56X**	**5562**
N619RJ	**EA50**	**000231**
N619SM	**F2EX**	**112**
N619TC	**C525**	**0698**
N619TD	HS25	257118
N619TS	**CL60**	**1019**
N619XP	BE40	RK-419
N620A	FA20	412
N620AC	CL60	1052
N620AS	**E50P**	**50000045**
N620AS	F2TH	97
N620AT	C560	0520
N620BA	F2TH	220
N620BB	**C525**	**0467**
N620CC	FA20	373
(N620CC)	C500	120
(N620CC)	HS25	257159
N620CJ	C525	0620
N620CM	**C510**	**0206**
N620DS	GLF4	1040
N620DX	**F9DX**	**620**
N620EM	LJ35	620
N620FX	**LJ40**	**2085**
N620GB	C52A	0112
N620GB	**C52C**	**0130**
N620GD	GLF6	6120
N620GD	**GLF6**	**6200**
N620GS	C56X	5053
N620GS	**GLF6**	**6220**
N620GX	GLEX	9620
N620HF	CL61	5021
(N620HF)	GLF4	1286
N620J	LJ35	193
N620JA	GLF3	387
N620JB	JSTR	5143
N620JC	C525	0335
N620JE	**GALX**	**118**
N620JF	CL30	20059
N620JF	**GLF5**	**5086**
N620JF	LJ60	074
N620JH	GLF3	387
N620JH	**GLF4**	**1272**
N620JM	LJ35	207
N620JW	**C525**	**0601**
N620K	GLEX	9052
N620K	GLF2	64/27
N620K	GLF4	1193
N620K	SBRL	282-9
N620KA	GLF4	1193
N620KE	**ASTR**	**137**
N620M	GLF4	1473
N620M	HS25	257005
N620M	SBRL	282-9
N620MJ	**LJ35**	**676**
N620MS	**F2EX**	**31**
N620PJ	**CL61**	**5169**
N620RB	FA20	161
N620RM	HS25	258124
N620S	**CL60**	**1031**
N620SB	CL60	1025
N620TC	**C525**	**0014**
N620TM	**CL64**	**5440**
N620V	**F2EX**	**249**
N620VP	C56X	6020
N620WB	**C510**	**0162**
N620XP	HS25	258620
N620XP	BE40	RK-420
N621AB	C650	7098
N621AB	**GALX**	**199**
(N621AB)	C650	7101
(N621AC)	C560	0251
N621AD	**C525**	**0621**
N621BA	HS25	256040
N621CD	C560	0192
N621CF	CL61	5021
N621CF	CL61	5090
N621CH	HS25	258303
N621CS	**C680**	**0120**
N621FP	**C750**	**0045**
N621FX	**LJ40**	**2089**
N621GA	**C52B**	**0126**
N621GA	GLF4	4021
N621GA	GLF5	621
N621GD	GLF6	6121
N621GD	**GLF6**	**6201**
N621GS	**GLF6**	**6221**
N621HB	HA4T	RC-21
N621JA	GLF3	387
N621JA	GLF4	1272
N621JA	HS25	257099
N621JH	GLF3	387
N621JH	GLF4	1272
N621JH	**GLF4**	**1423**
N621JH	HS25	257099
N621JS	FA20	356
N621KB	GALX	044
N621KD	ASTR	127
N621KD	GALX	044
N621KD	GLF5	5001
N621KM	**C550**	**550-0842**
N621KR	C550	550-0842
N621L	HS25	25205
N621LA	C680	680A0021
N621LJ	LJ60	121
N621MT	HS25	258036
N621QS	C56X	5280
N621RB	LJ35	211
N621S	GLF3	381
N621S	HS25	25205
N621S	HS25	257178
N621SC	GLF4	1481
N621ST	HS25	25014
N621SV	C680	0021
N621TF	**HA4T**	**RC-69**
N621VS	**BE40**	**RK-128**
N621WH	**HS25**	**258369**
N621WP	**HS25**	**258033**
(N621XP)	HS25	258621
N622AB	CL61	5016
N622AB	GLEX	9022
N622AB	HS25	257012
N622AB	HS25	258223
N622AD	HS25	257012
N622AD	HS25	258223
(N622AD)	CL61	5016
N622AT	**C500**	**252**
N622CS	**C680**	**0124**
N622EX	C550	679
(N622EX)	C550	635
N622FX	LJ40	2095
N622GA	GLF4	4022
N622GA	GLF4	4225
N622GA	GLF5	5222
N622GA	GLF5	622
N622GA	GLF6	6122
N622GB	C52C	0130
N622GD	**GLF6**	**6202**
N622JK	**PRM1**	**RB-59**
N622LJ	LJ60	122
N622PC	C56X	5024
N622PC	**C680**	**0310**
N622PG	**C550**	**037**
N622PL	**C56X**	**5024**
N622PM	**C650**	**7027**
N622QS	**C56X**	**5286**
N622QW	F2TH	134
N622R	FA20	15
N622R	FA20	86
N622RB	LJ35	064
N622RR	GLF2	12
N622SF	**G150**	**317**
N622SL	**C525**	**0622**
(N622SS)	C500	372
N622SV	**GALX**	**015**
N622VH	C550	635
N622VL	HS25	258531
N622WG	LJ35	611
N622WM	CL61	5084
N622WM	**F9EX**	**147**
N622WZ	CL61	5084
N622XL	C56X	6022
N622XP	HS25	258622
N623AR	C550	550-1086
N623BG	**CS55**	**0105**
N623BM	CL61	5159
N623BM	GLF2	205
N623CL	C56X	6023
N623CT	**F2EX**	**142**
N623CW	CL61	5023
N623CX	GLF2	101
N623DS	C550	662
N623DT	**E50P**	**50000148**
N623FX	LJ40	2099
N623GA	GLF4	4023
N623GA	GLF5	5223
N623GA	GLF5	623
N623GA	GLF6	6023
N623GA	GLF6	6123
N623GA	**GLF6**	**6223**
N623GD	**GLF6**	**6203**
N623HA	CL64	5623
N623HD	**F2TH**	**35**
N623JL	C550	662
N623KC	C560	0076
(N623KC)	C550	471
N623KM	**LJ35**	**307**
N623LB	C500	465
N623MS	**GLF3**	**351**
N623MW	GLF2	94
N623N	C550	550-0849
N623NP	GLF3	357
N623PM	**C650**	**7018**
N623QS	**C56X**	**5299**
N623QW	F2TH	44
N623QW	FA50	278
N623RC	LJ24	173
N623RM	C500	623
N623SA	**C56X**	**6203**
N623TS	CL64	5323
N623XP	HS25	258623
N624AT	C56X	5174
N624B	BE40	RK-369
N624BP	**GLEX**	**9236**
N624BP	GLF3	320
N624BP	GLF4	1093
N624BR	GLEX	9236
N624CC	C650	0123
N624CS	C680	0131
N624DS	SBRL	465-2
N624EC	CL65	5758
N624EC	LJ45	406
N624FA	SBRL	306-53
N624FX	**LJ40**	**2104**
N624GA	GLF4	4024
N624GA	GLF5	5224
N624GA	GLF5	624
N624GA	GLF6	6024
N624GA	GLF6	6124
N624GD	**GLF6**	**6204**
N624GF	**C56X**	**5525**
N624GJ	**GLF4**	**1267**
N624GS	**GLF6**	**6224**
N624KM	**WW24**	**227**
N624MH	GLF4	1289
N624MP	**HS25**	**25234**
N624N	**GLF5**	**681**
N624PD	HS25	25234
N624PL	C52A	0357
N624PP	GLF3	320
N624QS	**C56X**	**5302**
N624RL	**C550**	**366**
N624VP	C650	0024
N624WP	**C56X**	**5174**
N624XP	HS25	258624
N625AC	**C560**	**0251**
N625AT	**C56X**	**5175**
N625AU	LJ25	340
N625BE	**ASTR**	**125**
N625BL	LJ35	625
N625CC	C650	7058
N625CH	C500	625
N625CJ	C525	0625
N625CR	FA50	55
N625CY	**LJ35**	**625**
N625EA	C550	625
N625EL	**CL30**	**20331**
N625EL	E50P	50000171
N625FX	LJ40	2109
N625FX	**LJ40**	**2116**
N625G	C650	7059
N625GA	C500	217
N625GA	GLF5	625
N625GD	GLF6	6125
N625GD	**GLF6**	**6225**
N625GN	**GLF5**	**575**
N625J	C500	625
N625JK	GLF5	5355
N625LR	**CL61**	**5075**
N625MM	ASTR	125
N625PG	**C525**	**0282**
N625PZ	**C525**	**0820**
N625QS	**C56X**	**5319**
N625SC	GLEX	9108
N625SC	**GLEX**	**9647**
N625SG	GLEX	9108
N625TF	**GLF5**	**547**
N625TX	**C510**	**0219**
N625VP	C650	0025
N625W	**BE40**	**RK-106**
N625WA	**C560**	**0027**
N625XP	HS25	258625
N626AT	C56X	5239
N626BM	LJ35	634
N626BS	**HS25**	**HB-2**
N626CC	C650	0062
N626CC	F9EX	27
(N626CC)	C500	126
N626CG	**HS25**	**258041**
N626CS	**C680**	**0188**
N626CV	**C525**	**0626**
N626DJ	GLEX	9152
N626EK	F900	157
N626FX	LJ40	2120
N626GA	GALX	226
N626GA	GLF4	4026
N626GA	GLF5	626
N626GA	GLF6	6026
N626GA	GLF6	6126
N626GA	**GLF6**	**6226**
N626GD	**GLF6**	**6206**
N626HJ	**FA50**	**180**
N626JE	**GLF5**	**642**
(N626JP)	CL61	3050
N626JS	**GLEX**	**9599**
N626JS	GLF4	1334
N626JS	GLF5	642
N626JS	LJ35	394
(N626JW)	CL64	5512
N626KM	LJ60	012
N626LA	**C680**	**680A0026**
N626LJ	GLF4	1334
N626LJ	LJ60	119
N626NT	**F2EX**	**35**
N626P	C500	267
(N626PM)	HS25	259043
N626PS	**CL30**	**20276**
N626QS	C56X	5126
N626RB	**C560**	**0221**
N626SG	**C56X**	**6126**
N626SL	C560	0118
N626TC	GLF2	129
N626TC	GLF4	1227
N626TC	MS76	088
N626TG	GLF4	1227
N626TM	**C525**	**0010**
N626TN	**C56X**	**5254**
N626UT	**GLF5**	**648**
N626VP	C550	626
N626XP	HS25	258626
N627AF	**CL64**	**5548**
N627AF	LJ60	193
N627AK	HS25	258723
N627AT	C560	0527
(N627BB)	C52B	0003
N627BC	**C550**	**550-0868**
N627CM	C510	0127
N627CR	**F9EX**	**48**
N627CR	HS25	25160
N627CW	CL61	3027
N627DB	**E50P**	**50000118**
N627E	**C500**	**513**
N627ER	LJ24	290
(N627FX)	LJ40	2124
N627GA	GALX	227
N627GA	GLF4	4027
N627GA	GLF4	4227
N627GA	GLF5	627
N627GA	GLF6	6127
N627GA	**GLF6**	**6227**
N627GD	**GLF6**	**6207**
N627HS	**CS55**	**0072**
N627HS	HS25	256013
N627JG	FA20	267/491
N627JJ	LJ24	340
N627JW	**GLEX**	**9550**
N627KR	CL61	5059
N627L	C500	513
N627L	C550	550-0843
N627MW	**C525**	**0627**
N627MZ	**HS25**	**258531**
N627QS	**C56X**	**5227**
N627R	C650	0152
N627R	C750	0132
N627RP	C52C	0014
N627RP	**C52C**	**0149**
N627RP	BE40	RK-155
N627RR	**C52C**	**0014**
N627TA	C550	051
N627TF	**HS25**	**HA-0172**
N627V	C52B	0309
N627WS	LJ25	170
N627X	CS55	0018
N627XL	**C56X**	**5149**
N627XP	HS25	258627
N628BD	**GLF5**	**628**
N628BL	LJ35	628
N628BS	**C500**	**045**
N628CB	**C52B**	**0049**
N628CB	C550	550-0991
N628CC	C650	0128
N628CC	**F2TH**	**95**
N628CH	C500	628
N628CK	C560	0194
N628CM	**CL61**	**3062**
N628DB	LJ35	246

N628DC	LJ35	628
N628DS	**E55P**	**50500151**
(N628FS)	C500	045
N628GA	G150	228
N628GA	GLF4	4028
N628GA	GLF5	628
N628GA	**GLF6**	**6228**
N628GB	**C550**	**550-0991**
N628GD	GLF6	6128
N628GD	**GLF6**	**6208**
N628GZ	LJ35	628
N628HC	GLF2	134
(N628JG)	GLF3	398
N628KM	WW24	308
(N628NP)	GLF4	1094
N628PT	LJ55	089
N628QS	**C56X**	**5305**
(N628RC)	GALX	065
N628SA	F2TH	128
N628TS	**GLF6**	**6177**
N628VK	CL61	5049
(N628WC)	CL61	3048
N628WJ	LJ35	628
N628XP	HS25	258628
N628ZG	C500	444
N629AS	E50P	50000067
N629CS	C680	0165
N629DM	C525	0369
N629DR	C525	0667
N629EC	**C56X**	**5815**
N629EE	C52B	0129
N629EP	**C560**	**0490**
N629GA	GALX	229
N629GA	GLF4	4029
N629GA	GLF5	629
N629GA	GLF6	6029
N629GA	GLF6	6129
N629GA	**GLF6**	**6229**
N629GB	CL30	20144
N629GD	**GLF6**	**6209**
N629JJ	**E50P**	**50000157**
N629KD	**GLEX**	**9141**
N629LJ	LJ60	129
N629MD	**C650**	**0096**
N629P	HS25	25179
N629PA	C52A	0015
N629QS	**C56X**	**5306**
N629RA	CS55	0093
N629RM	C650	0096
N629TD	GLF2	92
N629TG	**F2TH**	**68**
N629TS	CL61	3029
N629TS	HS25	256029
N629WH	WW24	305
N629WH	**WW24**	**409**
N630AB	**HS25**	**HA-0205**
N630AR	**CL61**	**5140**
N630AS	**E50P**	**50000228**
N630BA	HS25	258195
N630BB	CL60	1030
N630BB	LJ45	265
N630CC	**C550**	**169**
N630CE	C500	630
N630CS	C680	0170
N630DB	**C510**	**0130**
N630EE	E50P	50000041
N630GA	CL65	5934
N630GA	G150	230
N630GA	GALX	230
N630GA	GLF4	4030
N630GA	GLF5	630
N630GD	GLF6	6130
N630GD	**GLF6**	**6230**
N630GS	**HS25**	**258769**
N630JS	C550	550-1119
N630JS	**HS25**	**HA-0030**
N630L	FA50	130
N630LJ	LJ60	130
N630M	C750	0021
N630M	CL60	1023
N630M	CL61	5060
N630M	SBRL	282-73
(N630MT)	CL30	20020
N630N	SBRL	282-73
N630PA	C52A	0385
N630PM	GLF2	236
N630QS	C56X	5130
N630S	**ASTR**	**046**
N630SJ	LJ35	344
N630SR	FA50	227
N630TF	**C52A**	**0022**
N630TK	**C560**	**0155**
N630TS	**F2TH**	**71**
N630TX	C680	0330
N630XP	HS25	258630
N631AT	LJ31	191
N631BA	HS25	258196
N631CB	**C680**	**0227**
N631CC	C550	631
N631CC	C650	0031
N631CC	**LJ31**	**104**
(N631CF)	CL61	3031
(N631CK)	GLF2	150
N631CS	C680	0197
N631CW	LJ25	313
N631CW	LJ35	302
N631DV	**GALX**	**166**
N631EA	C550	631
N631EC	C525	0631
N631GA	G150	241
N631GA	G150	281
N631GA	GALX	231
N631GA	GLF4	4031
N631GA	GLF5	631
N631GA	GLF6	6131
N631GD	**GLF6**	**6231**
N631HH	**C56X**	**5693**
N631JD	**C56X**	**5631**
N631KA	FA10	120
(N631LA)	LJ31	019
N631LJ	LJ60	131
N631M	C560	0383
N631PP	BE40	RK-155
N631QS	C56X	5131
N631RP	C56X	5254
N631RP	C680	0037
N631RP	C680	0256
N631RP	**CL30**	**20603**
N631RP	BE40	RK-155
N631RP	BE40	RK-7
(N631RR)	BE40	RK-7
N631SC	GLF2	224
N631SC	HS25	25065
N631SC	HS25	256002
N631SF	LJ31	075
N631SF	**LJ31**	**210**
N631SQ	HS25	25065
N631SQ	HS25	256002
N631TJ	**C52C**	**0031**
N631TS	**C550**	**631**
N631XP	HS25	258631
N632BA	HS25	258199
N632BE	**ASTR**	**132**
N632BL	C56X	5171
N632BL	C56X	5550
N632BL	**C680**	**680A0006**
(N632CC)	C500	132
N632CS	C680	0222
N632FW	**CL30**	**20195**
N632FW	HS25	258294
N632GA	GALX	232
N632GA	GLF4	4032
N632GA	GLF5	5322
N632GA	GLF5	632
N632GA	GLF6	6132
N632GA	**GLF6**	**6232**
N632KA	FA20	273
N632PB	FA20	206
N632PB	**FA20**	**355**
N632PB	HS25	25058
N632PB	LJ31	033
N632PE	HS25	25058
N632QS	C56X	5132
N632SC	C500	344
N632SC	C550	379
(N632VP)	C650	0032
N632XL	**C56X**	**5632**
N632XP	HS25	258632
N633AB	**CL65**	**5841**
N633AC	LJ55	115
N633AT	**C500**	**087**
N633BA	HS25	258200
N633CC	C650	0133
N633CS	C680	0236
N633CW	CL61	3013
N633DS	LJ35	362
N633EE	CS55	0058
N633GA	ASTR	112
N633GA	G150	233
N633GA	GLF4	4033
N633GA	GLF5	5313
N633GA	GLF5	633
N633GA	GLF6	6033
N633GA	GLF6	6133
N633GA	**GLF6**	**6233**
N633J	LJ24	120
N633KA	**FA20**	**399**
N633L	FA50	223
N633NJ	LJ24	120
N633P	GLF3	452
N633PC	**C550**	**550-1085**
N633QS	**C56X**	**5526**
N633RP	C56X	5501
N633RP	C56X	5669
N633RP	**C680**	**0172**
N633RT	**C550**	**588**
N633SA	C560	0235
N633SF	**LJ31**	**241**
N633SL	**SBRL**	**306-33**
N633W	FA50	184
N633WM	**CL65**	**5951**
N633WW	FA10	59
N633WW	LJ35	654
N633XP	HS25	258633
N634BA	HS25	258202
N634BE	**C56X**	**6034**
N634CJ	C525	0634
N634CS	C680	0244
N634GA	GALX	011
N634GA	GLF4	4034
N634GA	GLF6	6134
N634GA	**GLF6**	**6234**
N634H	FA50	178
N634H	LJ35	292
N634KA	**FA50**	**129**
N634QS	**C56X**	**5558**
N634S	GLF4	1249
N634VP	C56X	5634
N634XJ	CL65	5834
N635AV	GLF2	168
N635AV	GLF4	1185
N635BA	HS25	258203
N635CJ	C56X	6035
N635CS	C680	0275
N635E	**F2TH**	**106**
N635GA	ASTR	120
N635GA	G150	235
N635GA	GLF4	4035
N635GA	GLF6	6035
N635GA	GLF6	6135
N635GA	**GLF6**	**6235**
"N635PA"	HS25	256035
N635QS	**C56X**	**5358**
N635S	**CL61**	**5035**
N635XJ	**CL65**	**5835**
N635XP	HS25	258635
N636	JSTR	5127
N636	JSTR	5135
N636	SBRL	306-140
N636BA	HS25	258204
N636BC	**ASTR**	**039**
N636BC	**C680**	**0239**
N636C	JSTR	5127
N636CC	C500	636
N636CN	**GALX**	**171**
N636DS	**C52C**	**0127**
N636EJ	**C56X**	**5304**
N636GA	GALX	183
N636GA	GLF4	1336
N636GA	GLF6	6136
N636GA	**GLF6**	**6236**
N636GD	GLF4	1012
N636GD	GLF6	6036
N636GS	C56X	5074
N636HC	CL64	5636
N636JS	**GLEX**	**9325**
(N636MA)	C550	108
N636MC	SBRL	306-140
(N636MC)	JSTR	5127
N636MF	GLF2	150
N636MF	GLF4	1012
N636MF	GLF5	5112
N636MF	GLF5	512
N636MF	**GLF5**	**5351**
N636N	**C500**	**441**
N636QS	C56X	5304
N636SC	C500	222
N636SC	FA10	115
N636SD	**E50P**	**50000117**
N636SE	C560	0636
N636SE	**LJ31**	**075**
N636SF	**G150**	**277**
N636SF	LJ31	075
(N636TS)	CL64	5636
N636VP	C525	0636
N636XJ	CL65	5836
N636XP	HS25	258636
N637AS	**E50P**	**50000133**
N637BA	HS25	258205
N637CJ	C525	0637
N637EH	C550	371
N637GA	GLF4	1337
N637GA	GLF5	5037
N637GA	GLF5	637
N637GA	GLF6	6037
N637GA	GLF6	6137
N637GA	**GLF6**	**6237**
N637LJ	LJ60	037
N637ML	CL60	1024
N637QS	C56X	5137
N637RP	C56X	5669
N637SF	**G150**	**248**
N637SV	**C680**	**0037**
N637TF	**CL64**	**5637**
N637XP	HS25	258637
N638AH	**C510**	**0167**
N638BA	HS25	258206
N638GA	GLF4	1338
N638GA	GLF5	5138
N638GA	GLF5	5308
N638GA	GLF5	638
N638GA	GLF6	6138
N638GA	**GLF6**	**6238**
N638GD	GLF6	6038
N638JS	HS25	HA-0030
N638LJ	LJ60	038
N638MA	HS25	HA-0194
N638MF	GLF2	150
(N638PB)	LJ31	033
(N638Q)	C56X	5330
N638QS	C56X	5330
N638QS	**C56X**	**5363**
N638SF	**LJ31**	**219**
N638XP	HS25	258638
N639AS	**E50P**	**50000044**
N639AS	E50P	50000075
N639AT	WW24	308
N639BA	HS25	258207
N639CL	CL61	3039
N639CV	C560	0639
N639GA	G150	239
N639GA	GLF5	639
N639GA	GLF6	6039
N639GA	GLF6	6139
N639GA	**GLF6**	**6239**
N639J	WW24	337
N639M	**F2TS**	**733**
N639QS	C56X	5139
N639RA	**HA4T**	**RC-22**
N639SF	**G150**	**297**
N639TC	**C52A**	**0484**
N639TS	**CL61**	**5139**
N639VP	C56X	5639
N639XP	HS25	258639
N640AC	BE40	RK-3
N640BA	**LJ35**	**664**
N640BS	C500	640
N640CE	C560	0640
N640CH	CL64	5428
N640GA	GALX	140
N640GA	GLF5	540
N640GA	GLF6	6040
N640GA	LJ24	157
N640GA	**GLF6**	**6240**
N640GD	GLF6	6140
N640M	HS25	25228
N640PM	HS25	257167
N640PN	CL64	5640
N640QS	**C56X**	**5240**
N640TS	CL60	1004
N640W	**GLF5**	**5416**
N640XP	HS25	258640
N641CA	CL64	5441
N641CL	CL61	5041
N641DA	CL64	5641
N641FG	WW24	370
N641GA	GALX	141
N641GA	GLF4	4241
N641GA	GLF5	541
N641GA	GLF5	641
N641GA	GLF6	6104
N641GA	LJ25	004
N641GA	**GLF6**	**6241**
N641GD	GLF6	6041
N641GD	GLF6	6141
N641K	LJ40	2132
N641L	C550	550-0961
N641MS	**C650**	**0056**
N641QS	**C56X**	**5295**
N641RP	**HS25**	**258858**
N641XP	HS25	258641
N642AC	**BE40**	**RK-224**
N642BB	C550	339
N642BJ	C500	388
N642CC	C550	038
(N642CT)	C500	262
N642GA	GLF5	542
N642GA	LJ24	158
(N642GG)	LJ31	113
N642GS	**GLF6**	**6242**
N642JA	CL64	5642
N642JC	F900	71
N642LF	C560	0642
(N642LJ)	LJ60	142
N642LR	SBRL	282-83
N642QS	**C56X**	**5561**
N642RP	SBRL	306-46
N642TA	F2EX	89
N642TS	SBRL	380-2
N642WW	**C52A**	**0418**
N642XL	C56X	5642
N642XP	HS25	258642
N643CC	C650	0043
N643CR	C650	0024
N643CR	CL60	1055
N643CT	CL64	5643
N643GA	GLF5	5143
N643GA	GLF5	543
N643GA	GLF6	6043
N643GA	GLF6	6143
N643GA	**GLF6**	**6243**
N643JL	HS25	25208
N643MC	C500	643
N643MC	C550	643
N643MJ	LJ35	643
N643QS	C56X	5331
N643QS	**C56X**	**5588**
N643RF	C525	0643
N643RT	C500	639
N643RT	C560	0010
N643RT	**C560**	**0019**
N643TD	C550	437
(N643VP)	C500	643
N644CC	C650	0144
(N644CC)	C500	144
N644GA	GLF4	4044
N644GA	GLF5	5144
N644GA	GLF5	544
N644GA	GLF5	644
N644GA	GLF6	6144
N644GA	LJ25	007
N644GA	**GLF6**	**6244**
N644JL	HS25	258012
N644JP	**BE40**	**RJ-7**
N644JW	JSTR	5223
N644QS	**C56X**	**5582**
N644RM	**E50P**	**50000061**
(N644RP)	E50P	50000061
N644RV	**F2TH**	**22**
N644VP	C560	0644
N644X	FA20	36
N644X	SBRL	306-26
N644XP	HS25	258644
N645AM	**LJ35**	**645**
N645AS	**E50P**	**50000114**
N645B	**E55P**	**50500238**
N645CC	SBRL	306-49
N645FD	**LJ45**	**227**
N645G	LJ24	160
N645G	**LJ35**	**056**
N645GA	GALX	145
N645GA	GLF5	545
N645GA	GLF5	645
N645GA	GLF6	6045
N645GA	GLF6	6145
N645GA	**GLF6**	**6245**
N645HA	**LJ31**	**129**
N645HJ	LJ45	087
N645KM	LJ45	133
N645L	LJ25	008
N645M	C560	0350
N645MD	LJ60	247
N645MS	**HS25**	**258044**
N645PM	**GALX**	**105**
N645Q	C56X	5145
N645QS	C56X	5145
N645TL	CL64	5393
N645TS	**C500**	**371**
N645XP	HS25	258645
N646AM	HS25	257201
N646AS	**E50P**	**50000149**
N646CC	C650	0146
N646EA	LJ35	646
N646G	LJ55	016
N646GA	ASTR	146
N646GA	GLF5	5146
N646GA	GLF5	546
N646GA	GLF6	6046
N646GA	LJ25	005
N646GD	GLF6	6146
N646JC	CL64	5646
N646QS	**C56X**	**5246**
N646RH	**C56X**	**6046**
N646S	PRM1	RB-142
N646TG	C52A	0190
N646TG	E50P	50000179
N646VP	C525	0646
N646WT	**EA50**	**000225**
N646XP	HS25	258646
N647AS	**E50P**	**50000067**
N647CC	C550	647
N647CE	C560	0647
N647CM	C650	7047
N647EF	LJ60	047
N647GA	ASTR	147
N647GA	GLF4	4247
N647GA	GLF5	5147
N647GA	GLF5	547
N647GA	GLF5	647
N647GA	GLF6	6147
N647GA	LJ24	159
N647GD	GLF6	6047
N647JP	FA20	120
N647JP	FA20	359/542
N647JP	FA20	70
N647JP	SBRL	380-21
N647MK	**C56X**	**5188**
N647QS	**C56X**	**5547**
(N647SA)	FA20	70
(N647TJ)	LJ35	647
N647TS	LJ60	047
N648DX	**E50P**	**50000176**
N648GA	ASTR	148
N648GA	GLF5	5148
N648GA	GLF5	548
N648GA	GLF5	648
N648GA	GLF6	6048
N648GA	GLF6	6148
N648GA	LJ25	008
N648HE	**C525**	**0219**
N648J	LJ35	648
N648JW	LJ25	350
N648JW	LJ35	648
N648LJ	LJ60	048
N648QS	**C56X**	**5574**
N648TS	LJ60	148
N648VP	C560	0648
N648WW	C550	477
N648WW	HS25	257004
(N649AF)	C650	0109
N649CC	C650	0149
N649DA	C550	649
N649DX	**E50P**	**50000194**
N649G	LJ24	161
N649GA	GLF5	5149
N649GA	GLF5	549
N649GA	GLF5	649
N649GA	GLF6	6049
N649GA	GLF6	6149
N649JA	CL64	5649
N649JR	**C510**	**0247**
N649SP	**LJ60**	**390**
N649TT	F900	82
N649TT	**FA50**	**342**
N649WW	C550	477

N649XP	HS25	258649
N650	C650	697
N650AB	C650	7053
N650AB	**GLF6**	**6100**
N650AC	C500	364
N650AE	C650	0152
N650AF	C650	0120
N650AF	C650	0125
N650AF	C650	0145
N650AF	**GLF6**	**6089**
(N650AF)	C650	0113
N650AH	**C650**	**0139**
N650AJ	C650	0068
N650AL	FA50	49
(N650AN)	C650	0049
N650AS	**C650**	**0002**
N650AS	C650	7053
(N650AS)	FA50	171
(N650AS)	FA50	90
N650AT	C650	0063
N650AT	**C650**	**7035**
N650AT	C650	7053
(N650AT)	C650	0109
(N650AT)	LJ24	157
N650BA	C650	0178
N650BC	**C500**	**590**
N650BC	C650	0198
(N650BG)	C650	0002
N650BP	C550	131
(N650BP)	C650	0017
N650BS	C650	0036
N650BW	C650	0028
(N650BW)	C650	0198
N650C	SBRL	306-137
N650CA	LJ24	050
N650CB	**C650**	**0084**
N650CC	C650	0156
N650CC	C650	0193
N650CC	C650	696
N650CD	C650	0066
N650CE	C650	0106
N650CE	C650	0211
N650CF	C650	0104
N650CG	**C650**	**0023**
N650CH	**C650**	**0154**
N650CJ	C500	650
N650CJ	C650	0014
N650CJ	**C650**	**7044**
N650CK	GLF6	6041
N650CM	**C560**	**0177**
N650CM	C650	0200
N650CN	C650	0047
N650CN	C650	0062
N650CP	C650	7016
(N650CP)	GLF6	6039
N650CZ	**C650**	**7050**
N650DA	C650	0085
N650DA	C650	0114
N650DA	**GLF6**	**6057**
N650DD	**C650**	**0114**
N650DD	C650	7047
N650DF	C650	0136
N650DH	C650	7043
N650DR	C650	0181
(N650DW)	C650	0184
N650DX	GLF6	6039
N650ER	GLF6	6084
N650ER	GLF6	6210
N650EW	**GLF6**	**6069**
(N650FA)	C650	0231
N650FC	**C650**	**0146**
N650FJ	**GLF6**	**6175**
N650FP	C650	0188
N650G	WW24	233
N650GA	GLF5	550
N650GA	GLF5	600
N650GA	GLF6	6001
N650GA	GLF6	6087
N650GA	**GLF6**	**6161**
(N650GA)	C650	0198
N650GC	**C650**	**0215**
N650GD	GLF6	6004
N650GD	**GLF6**	**6149**
N650GE	ASTR	064
N650GE	G150	210
N650GE	WW24	233
N650GF	ASTR	064
N650GH	C650	0034
(N650GJ)	C650	0165
N650GL	**GLF6**	**6054**
N650GT	C650	0004
N650GU	**GLF6**	**6067**
N650GX	**GLF6**	**6001**
N650GY	**GLF6**	**6144**
N650HC	C650	0124
N650HC	GLF6	6022
N650HC	**GLF6**	**6097**
(N650HE)	GLF6	6022
N650HF	**GLF6**	**6117**
N650HG	**C650**	**0083**
N650HH	GLF6	6127
N650HM	C650	0119
N650HR	C650	0101
N650HS	C650	0185
N650HW	**C650**	**7077**
N650J	C650	0022
N650JA	C650	0073
N650JA	**C650**	**0090**
N650JB	C650	7113
N650JC	C650	0089
N650JC	**C680**	**0161**
N650JF	**CL65**	**6064**
N650JG	C650	0107
N650JH	GLF6	6076
N650JK	**GLF6**	**6046**
N650JL	C650	0019
N650JL	**C650**	**7101**
(N650JP)	C550	730
N650JS	C560	0190
N650JS	**FA50**	**216**
N650JS	HS25	258537
(N650JS)	C650	0058
N650JV	C650	0138
N650K	C650	7034
N650KA	GLF2	50
N650KB	**C650**	**0078**
N650KC	C650	0215
N650KD	C650	7047
(N650KG)	GLF6	6068
N650KK	**C650**	**0018**
N650KM	C650	0144
N650KP	**C650**	**0095**
N650KS	CL64	5660
N650L	C650	0209
N650LA	C650	0004
N650LG	CL61	5126
N650LR	LJ35	650
N650LW	C650	0010
N650M	C650	0044
N650M	WW24	67
N650MC	C650	0237
N650MD	C650	0035
N650MG	C650	0007
N650MG	**FA20**	**387**
(N650MG)	C650	0185
N650MK	C650	7006
N650MM	C650	0048
N650MP	C650	0107
N650MP	G150	289
N650MP	**G280**	**2060**
N650MS	C650	0019
N650MT	**GLF6**	**6030**
(N650MT)	C650	0122
N650MW	C500	593
N650NL	LJ35	154
N650NV	**C560**	**0429**
N650NY	C650	0027
N650NY	**GLF6**	**6079**
N650PA	**GLF6**	**6138**
N650PD	C650	7088
N650PE	**GLF6**	**6050**
N650PF	C650	0095
N650PF	GLF2	118
N650PH	GLF6	6013
N650PJ	**C650**	**7059**
N650PL	GLF5	5148
N650PM	HS25	258081
N650PP	**CL65**	**6051**
N650PR	GLF6	6050
N650PT	C650	0160
N650PT	**C650**	**0169**
N650PW	**GLF4**	**1530**
(N650PW)	GLF4	1534
(N650QF)	C650	0238
N650QS	C56X	5150
N650RA	**C650**	**7047**
N650RB	C650	0079
N650RF	**C650**	**7081**
N650RG	**GLF6**	**6004**
(N650RJ)	C56X	5152
(N650RJ)	C650	0111
(N650RJ)	C650	7003
N650RL	C650	7029
N650RL	**CL65**	**6074**
N650RP	**C650**	**0157**
N650RP	C650	7016
N650RR	**GLF6**	**6019**
N650SB	C650	0018
N650SC	C650	0030
N650SF	**C650**	**0034**
N650SG	**C650**	**0191**
N650SL	C650	0024
N650SP	C650	0094
N650SS	C650	0021
N650SS	GLF6	6036
(N650SS)	C650	0140
(N650ST)	C560	0014
N650TA	**C650**	**0088**
N650TC	C650	0061
N650TC	C650	0064
N650TC	FA50	126
N650TC	**HS25**	**257126**
N650TF	C500	142
N650TJ	C650	0191
N650TL	**CL60**	**1050**
N650TP	C650	0061
N650TP	**GLF6**	**6051**
N650TS	C650	0006
N650TS	C650	0219
N650TT	C650	0046
N650TT	C650	0122
N650UA	**C650**	**7065**
N650VM	**C525**	**0921**
N650VP	C650	0025
N650W	**C650**	**0237**
N650W	C650	7065
N650WB	C650	0020
N650WC	C550	007
N650WC	C550	627
N650WE	**C650**	**0040**
N650WG	C550	007
N650WJ	C650	0078
N650WL	C650	0078
N650WT	**C650**	**7094**
N650X	FA50	69
N650XA	GLF6	6201
N650XP	HS25	258650
N650XP	BE40	RK-450
N650XY	**GLF6**	**6071**
N650Z	C650	0108
N650ZK	GLF6	6117
(N651AC)	CL61	3009
N651AF	C650	0114
N651AP	C650	0082
(N651AP)	C650	0001
N651AR	C650	0212
N651AT	**C650**	**0063**
N651AV	GLF6	6133
N651AY	**LJ45**	**288**
N651BH	C650	0051
N651BP	**C650**	**0017**
N651CC	C650	0001
N651CC	**C650**	**7119**
N651CC	C555	0010
N651CG	C650	0001
N651CH	**GLF6**	**6060**
N651CJ	**C525**	**0365**
N651CN	C650	0072
N651CV	**C650**	**0036**
N651CW	CL61	3051
N651DH	G150	319
N651E	WW24	406
N651EJ	**C650**	**0241**
N651EM	**C650**	**0030**
(N651ES)	WW24	406
N651FC	EA50	000012
N651GA	GALX	151
N651GA	GLF4	4151
N651GA	GLF5	551
N651GA	GLF6	6151
N651GL	SBRL	465-36
N651GS	GLEX	9260
N651GV	GLF5	651
N651J	LJ24	181
N651JC	CL64	5651
N651JM	C650	0241
N651JP	**CL61**	**5050**
N651LJ	LJ24	125
N651LS	**CL64**	**5413**
N651MK	**SBRL**	**465-73**
(N651NA)	GLF2	118
N651PW	C650	0090
N651QS	**C56X**	**5251**
N651RS	C650	0094
N651S	SBRL	465-14
(N651SB)	FA50	70
N651SD	**C52B**	**0105**
N651SD	FA20	256
N651TC	C650	0090
N651TK	C56X	6051
N651TW	**C52B**	**0217**
N651WE	**GLF6**	**6141**
N651XP	HS25	258651
N652AL	FA50	112
N652BA	**GLF6**	**6130**
N652BL	CL65	5843
N652CC	C650	0002
N652CC	C650	0078
N652CC	**C650**	**7107**
(N652CC)	SBRL	465-6
N652CH	**GLF6**	**6074**
N652CN	CL61	5040
N652CV	C650	0055
N652CW	CL61	5052
N652FC	**EA50**	**000188**
N652GA	GLF5	5152
N652GA	GLF5	552
N652GD	GLF6	6002
N652GD	GLF6	6152
N652J	LJ24	018
N652JM	C650	0113
N652KZ	**LJ35**	**652**
N652MC	CL64	5662
N652MK	SBRL	465-36
N652ND	C500	277
N652NR	C560	0652
N652PC	F2TH	10
N652QS	C56X	5152
N652SA	LJ35	652
N652XP	HS25	258652
N653AC	CL61	5153
N653CC	C650	0003
N653CC	C650	0089
N653CC	C650	0153
N653CC	**C650**	**7116**
N653CW	CL61	5053
N653DR	C500	561
N653EJ	C650	7057
N653F	C500	638
N653FC	EA50	000205
N653FJ	**FA10**	**110**
N653GA	GALX	153
N653GA	GLF5	553
N653GA	GLF6	6053
N653GA	GLF6	6153
N653GD	GLF6	6003
(N653J)	WW24	161
N653LJ	LJ24	126
N653MF	FA20	185/467
N653MK	**GLF5**	**5211**
N653XP	HS25	258653
N654	LJ25	082
N654AN	**LJ60**	**065**
N654AP	BE40	RK-88
(N654AR)	C650	0004
N654AT	LJ45	136
N654AT	**LJ45**	**371**
N654AT	BE40	RK-88
N654CC	C650	0001
N654CE	**C560**	**0654**
N654CM	**CL61**	**5009**
N654CN	F900	127
N654CP	**FA50**	**113**
N654DN	LJ24	019
N654E	FA20	164
N654E	SBRL	282-70
N654EA	C510	0010
N654EJ	C650	7070
N654EL	C56X	5024
N654FC	**EA50**	**000227**
N654GA	GLF5	5154
N654GA	GLF5	554
N654GA	GLF6	6054
N654GA	GLF6	6154
N654GC	C650	0004
(N654GV)	GLF5	654
N654JC	LJ24	127
N654LD	LJ24	127
N654LJ	LJ24	127
N654PC	FA10	131
N654QS	**C56X**	**5611**
N654WW	**C525**	**0053**
N654XP	HS25	258654
N654YS	**SBRL**	**465-60**
N655AL	LJ55	129
N655AT	**C500**	**390**
N655CC	C650	0105
(N655CC)	C500	155
N655CM	**BE40**	**RJ-17**
N655CN	CL61	5069
(N655DB)	FA10	28
N655EW	C550	303
N655GA	GLF5	555
N655GA	GLF6	6005
N655GA	GLF6	6055
N655GA	GLF6	6155
N655GP	LJ55	128
N655JH	**LJ35**	**655**
(N655JH)	GLF2	22
N655JS	**C560**	**0190**
N655LJ	LJ24	128
N655MM	**C680**	**0063**
N655NC	**LJ55**	**061**
N655PC	C550	134
N655PE	**FA10**	**199**
N655QS	**C56X**	**5655**
N655TC	**F900**	**195**
N655TH	CL61	5022
N655TH	LJ60	141
N655TJ	GLF2	5
N655TR	**LJ55**	**006**
N655TS	CL64	5505
N655XP	HS25	258655
N656CC	C650	0006
(N656CC)	C650	0026
N656FP	**EA50**	**550-0265**
N656GA	GALX	156
N656GA	GLF4	4156
N656GA	GLF5	556
N656GA	GLF6	6056
N656GD	GLF6	6156
N656JG	**C560**	**0298**
(N656LE)	C650	0237
N656LJ	LJ24	129
N656PC	FA10	99
N656PS	**C550**	**009**
N656QS	**C56X**	**5732**
(N656QS)	C56X	5672
N656SM	**C52B**	**0117**
N656XP	HS25	258656
N656Z	**C560**	**0656**
N657AT	**GLF6**	**6041**
N657BM	**LJ25**	**331**
N657CC	C650	0007
N657CC	C650	0157
N657CT	**CL64**	**5665**
N657DB	**F2TS**	**724**
N657DM	**C560**	**0810**
N657ER	C650	7027
N657GA	GLF4	4157
N657GA	GLF5	5157
N657GA	GLF5	557
N657GA	GLF6	6057
N657GD	GLF6	6157
N657GF	E55P	50500104
N657GF	**LEG5**	**55000011**
N657JW	C650	7110
(N657K)	HS25	25032
N657LJ	LJ24	130
N657MC	FA20	148
N657MP	**LJ40**	**2005**
N657NG	**PRM1**	**RB-113**
N657P	MS76	057
N657PP	**LJ45**	**340**
N657QS	**C56X**	**5636**
N657RB	C525	0409
N657RH	**C560**	**0757**
N657T	**C650**	**7042**
N657XP	HS25	258657
N658AT	LJ24	219
N658CC	C650	0046
N658CF	CL60	1058
N658CJ	C650	0158
N658DM	**HS25**	**258901**
N658FM	F2TH	17
N658GA	GALX	158
N658GA	GLF5	558
N658GA	GLF6	6058
N658GD	GLF6	6158
N658HC	**GLF6**	**6022**
N658JC	CL64	5658
N658KA	HS25	256058
N658KS	**LJ60**	**071**
N658L	LJ24	017
N658LJ	LJ24	132
N658MA	C650	0023
N658MB	**E50P**	**50000343**
N658PC	GLF2	157
N658QS	**C56X**	**5665**
N658TC	LJ25	044
N658TS	HS25	256058
N658XP	HS25	258658
N659AT	LJ24	157
N659AT	**LJ45**	**136**
N659BX	**LJ31**	**169**
N659CJ	C525	0659
N659FM	**F2EX**	**45**
N659FM	F2TH	17
N659GA	GLF5	5059
N659GA	GLF5	5159
N659GA	GLF5	559
N659GA	GLF6	6059
N659GD	GLF6	6159
N659HX	LJ25	179
N659HX	LJ25	300
N659JF	CL30	20059
N659LJ	LJ24	131
N659NR	**CL30**	**20555**
N659PC	GLF2	204
N659QS	C56X	5355
N659QS	**C56X**	**5359**
(N659SA)	C560	0559
N659TS	CL61	5159
N659WL	**GLF2**	**204**
N659XP	HS25	258659
N660A	LJ24	155
N660AA	C500	480
N660AA	C650	0059
(N660AC)	C550	158
N660AF	C650	0151
N660AF	**CL61**	**5025**
N660AF	GLF2	70/1
N660AH	LJ60	017
(N660AH)	FA50	290
N660AJ	C555	0154
N660AL	**CL30**	**20129**
(N660AN)	LJ60	128
N660AS	**C56X**	**6150**
N660AS	LJ60	040
N660AS	LJ60	191
N660BC	LJ60	063
N660BD	F900	25
(N660BW)	SBRL	306-33
N660CB	LJ60	055
N660CC	**BE40**	**RK-319**
N660CJ	LJ35	079
N660CJ	**LJ60**	**126**
N660EG	F900	152
N660GA	GLF5	5160
N660GA	GLF5	560
N660GA	GLF6	6060
N660GA	GLF6	6160
N660HC	**C680**	**0553**
N660HC	HS25	258624
N660HC	LJ45	058
N660KC	C500	480
N660KS	LJ60	219
N660L	LJ35	660
N660LJ	LJ24	133
N660LT	C560	0564
N660P	FA20	430
N660PA	**C650**	**0230**
N660Q	C650	0162
N660QS	**C56X**	**5647**
N660RM	CL60	1054
N660RM	SBRL	306-91
N660RW	WW24	128
N660S	**C52A**	**0305**
N660SA	LJ35	469
N660SB	C560	0433
N660TC	HS25	256060
N660TC	LJ25	317
N660TJ	C650	0060
N660W	WW24	58
N660XP	HS25	258660

N661AA	C500	357
N661AA	LJ36	049
N661AC	C500	121
N661AJ	C560	0176
N661BP	**C525**	**0832**
N661BS	LJ24	108
N661CL	CL61	5061
N661CP	GLF5	5104
N661CP	LJ24	108
N661CP	LJ24	174
N661CP	WW24	210
N661EP	**E50P**	**50000123**
N661FS	LJ24	018
N661GA	GLF5	561
N661GA	GLF6	6061
N661GA	GLF6	6161
N661GL	FA10	3
N661HS	**LEG5**	**55000034**
N661J	FA20	81
N661JB	CL60	1073
N661JB	FA20	275
N661JB	FA20	81
N661JB	HS25	257106
N661JB	LJ24	159
N661JB	WW24	209
N661JG	LJ24	174
N661JN	HS25	258209
N661LJ	LJ25	002
N661MP	LJ25	162
N661MP	WW24	176
N661MS	**LJ35**	**454**
N661P	SBRL	282-41
N661QS	**C56X**	**5677**
N661R	GLF4	1092
N661SS	LJ24	108
N661TS	CL60	1061
N661TV	C500	661
N661TW	C500	661
N661WD	**BE40**	**RK-94**
N661XP	HS25	258661
N662AA	LJ35	315
(N662AA)	C550	183
N662AJ	C550	624
N662BM	**C510**	**0408**
N662CB	**C550**	**550-1062**
N662CC	C500	277
N662CC	**C510**	**0178**
N662CG	C500	277
N662CP	GLF5	5107
N662D	FA10	200
N662D	FA10	87
N662EP	**ASTR**	**158**
N662F	SBRL	306-6
N662G	GLF2	188
N662GA	GLF4	1362
N662GA	GLF5	5162
N662GA	GLF5	562
N662GA	GLF5	662
N662GA	GLF6	6062
N662GA	GLF6	6162
N662JB	HS25	257018
N662JB	WW24	209
N662JB	WW24	210
N662JN	**HS25**	**258837**
N662K	WW24	418
N662P	F9EX	30
N662P	FA20	378
N662P	FA50	320
N662P	**GLF5**	**5403**
N662P	SBRL	306-6
(N662PP)	FA20	378
N662QS	**C56X**	**5262**
N662XP	HS25	258662
N663AJ	BE40	RK-148
N663B	GLF2	14
N663CA	LJ35	063
N663CP	GLF4	4044
N663GA	GLF5	5163
N663GA	GLF5	663
N663GA	GLF6	6063
N663GA	GLF6	6163
N663JB	LJ25	162
N663JB	WW24	209
N663L	LJ24	140
N663LB	LJ40	2114
N663LJ	LJ24	140
N663LS	E50P	50000118
N663MK	F9EX	94
N663MN	FA50	249
N663P	GLF2	14
N663P	GLF4	1434
N663PD	GLF2	139/11
N663PD	**GLF4**	**1022**
N663QS	**C56X**	**5263**
N663TW	**LJ35**	**662**
N663XP	HS25	258663
N664AC	**HS25**	**258566**
N664AF	**C56X**	**6064**
N664AJ	**C550**	**613**
N664B	FA20	95
N664B	FA50	200
N664CC	C500	664
N664CE	**C560**	**0664**
N664CJ	C525	0664
N664CL	LJ24	151
N664CL	LJ24	167
N664CP	GLF4	4047
N664CW	CL61	3064
N664D	**CL64**	**5505**
N664DF	**C550**	**550-1007**
N664GA	GLF5	564
N664GA	GLF5	664
N664GA	GLF6	6064
N664GA	GLF6	6164
N664GL	LJ24	151
N664J	C550	025
N664JB	C550	025
N664JB	FA10	162
N664JB	HS25	257106
N664JC	CL64	5663
N664JN	**GLF4**	**1396**
N664LJ	LJ24	136
N664P	FA20	95
N664P	FA50	200
N664P	GLF3	343
N664QS	**C56X**	**5264**
(N664RB)	C650	0014
N664S	GLF3	343
N664SS	C550	458
N664XP	HS25	258664
(N665AJ)	C525	0120
N665AS	**E50P**	**50000018**
N665AS	E50P	50000157
N665B	FA20	88
N665CH	**C525**	**0504**
N665CJ	C525	0665
N665CP	GLF4	4049
N665CT	CL64	5665
N665DP	C525	0028
N665JB	C500	357
N665JN	**GLF5**	**5126**
N665MC	C550	665
N665MM	**C550**	**631**
N665P	FA20	444
N665P	FA20	88
N665P	GLF4	4049
N665QS	C56X	5165
N665SF	**GLF2**	**94**
N665XP	HS25	258665
N666AE	HS25	25046
N666AG	C500	101
N666AJ	C550	095
(N666BC)	HS25	258524
N666BE	F2EX	32
(N666BG)	LJ45	121
(N666BK)	C680	0087
N666BP	WW24	122
N666BR	SBRL	306-2
N666BS	C500	045
N666BT	FA20	7
N666CC	LJ24	214
N666CC	LJ35	254
N666CP	WW24	347
N666CT	**CL61**	**5007**
N666DA	FA20	129
N666DC	WW24	61
N666DJ	F900	195
N666ES	C500	045
N666FH	C680	0125
N666HA	**ASTR**	**059**
N666JC	**HS25**	**258115**
N666JD	WW24	39
N666JJ	C500	537
N666JM	C650	0241
N666JM	WW24	133
N666JM	WW24	149
N666JM	WW24	184
N666JM	WW24	283
N666JR	LJ35	074
N666JT	C550	272
N666JT	GLF2	162
N666JT	HS25	25186
N666K	ASTR	040
N666K	**ASTR**	**134**
N666K	WW24	207
N666K	WW24	321
N666KK	LJ25	285
N666KK	LJ35	481
N666KL	**ASTR**	**040**
N666KL	WW24	321
N666KQ	GLF6	6036
N666LC	HFB3	1039
N666LC	HS25	256064
N666LN	C555	0005
N666LP	LJ25	185
N666LQ	HFB3	1039
N666M	HS25	25075
N666MP	LJ24	041
(N666MP)	WW24	156
N666MW	LJ24	305
N666MX	C56X	5292
N666NF	HS25	HB-27
N666PE	LJ25	359
N666RB	LJ25	291
N666RB	LJ35	393
N666RC	C550	044
N666RE	LJ25	359
N666RE	LJ31	016
N666RE	LJ31	055
N666SA	C500	031
N666SA	**GLF2**	**130**
N666SC	HS25	25098
N666TB	LJ36	012
N666TF	CL64	5309
N666TK	**LJ55**	**038**
N666TM	**EA50**	**000221**
N666TR	CL64	5309
N666TR	C555	0106
N666TR	**F2EX**	**279**
N666TR	F900	195
N666TS	C500	446
N666TV	LJ55	012
N666TW	LJ25	116
N666WL	LJ25	017
N666WL	SBRL	306-75
N666WW	C550	201
(N666WW)	C550	445
N666ZW	**GLF4**	**4311**
N667BB	**GLEX**	**9618**
N667CC	C650	0167
N667CC	CL61	5032
N667CG	C550	365
N667CX	GLF2	10
N667GA	GLF6	6067
N667GD	GLF6	6167
N667H	HS25	258276
N667HS	**GLF4**	**4131**
N667LC	CL61	5032
N667LC	CL64	5324
N667LC	CL65	5740
N667LC	**GLF4**	**4118**
N667LQ	CL64	5324
N667LQ	CL65	5740
N667MB	**LJ55**	**073**
N667MC	**LJ45**	**409**
N667P	FA20	432
N667P	GLF4	1447
N667P	**GLF5**	**5502**
N667QS	**C56X**	**5365**
N667XP	HS25	258667
N668AJ	**C550**	**442**
N668AS	E50P	50000168
N668CB	**C550**	**550-1068**
N668CM	C550	668
N668EA	C550	667
N668EM	**GLF4**	**4299**
N668GA	GLF5	5168
N668GA	GLF6	6068
N668GA	**GLF6**	**6168**
N668H	HS25	258287
N668JF	**HS25**	**258124**
N668JH	LJ60	393
N668JP	**C510**	**0377**
N668JT	GLF2	162
N668JT	HS25	25186
N668MC	LJ24	214
N668P	FA20	308
N668P	FA50	315
N668P	**GLF5**	**5229**
N668QS	**C56X**	**5268**
N668RC	LJ60	044
N668S	**C500**	**314**
N668S	FA20	308
N668VB	C525	0228
N668VP	C525	0228
N668VP	LJ31	232
N668XP	HS25	258668
N668Z	**PRM1**	**RB-247**
(N669AC)	FA20	299
N669AJ	C560	0021
N669AS	**E50P**	**50000182**
N669B	C550	550-1060
N669BJ	**GLF4**	**1397**
N669CC	C56X	5512
N669CC	**HS25**	**258814**
N669CM	EA50	000165
N669DB	C525	0228
(N669DM)	C500	669
N669GD	GLF6	6069
N669GD	GLF6	6169
N669H	HS25	258289
N669HP	**F2EX**	**83**
N669LJ	LJ35	669
N669MA	C550	128
N669PG	F2EX	126
N669QS	**C56X**	**5689**
(N669SB)	WW24	435
N669SC	HS25	256024
N669TT	**C56X**	**5684**
N669W	C650	0045
N669W	C650	7066
N669XP	HS25	258669
N670AC	**SBRL**	**465-31**
N670AG	**GLEX**	**9056**
N670AS	E50P	50000188
N670AS	**E50P**	**50000267**
N670AS	SBRL	465-58
N670BA	HS25	258209
N670BB	C56X	5349
N670C	SBRL	370-7
N670CE	C560	0670
N670CL	CL60	1070
N670CM	CL64	5488
N670CP	**CL30**	**20313**
N670DD	**C555**	**0019**
N670GA	GLF5	670
N670GA	GLF6	6070
N670GA	GLF6	6170
N670H	HS25	258290
N670H	**SBRL**	**465-58**
N670JD	C555	0019
N670JD	**F900**	**45**
N670LJ	LJ25	009
N670MF	LJ24	062
N670MW	**C56X**	**5511**
N670QS	C56X	5170
N670RW	GALX	160
(N670WJ)	LJ35	670
N670XL	C56X	5670
N670XP	HS25	258670
N671AF	**GLF4**	**1205**
N671B	C550	271
N671BA	HS25	258216
N671BA	LJ35	671
N671BP	**GALX**	**031**
N671BX	LJ35	671
N671CB	**LJ60**	**257**
N671EA	C550	671
N671GA	GALX	171
N671GA	GLF5	571
N671GA	GLF6	6071
N671GA	GLF6	6171
N671LB	GLF5	671
N671LE	**GLF5**	**5130**
N671LE	GLF5	671
N671LW	**GLF2**	**90**
N671MD	**C680**	**0524**
N671PB	F2EX	114
N671PP	**F2EX**	**114**
N671PP	GALX	031
N671QS	C56X	5071
N671RR	**HS25**	**258244**
N671RW	GLF5	5131
N671RW	HS25	258244
N671SR	CL60	1071
N671SR	FA20	56
N671TS	LJ35	671
N671WB	**FA7X**	**29**
N671WM	**F2TH**	**194**
N671WM	LJ25	010
N671XP	HS25	258671
N672AT	BE40	RJ-14
N672BA	HS25	258217
N672BP	CL30	20258
N672CA	C550	591
N672CC	C650	0172
N672DK	LJ35	672
N672GA	GALX	172
N672GA	GLF5	672
N672GA	GLF6	6072
N672GA	**GLF6**	**6172**
N672H	HS25	258291
N672JM	**C525**	**0485**
N672LJ	LJ24	146
N672M	JSTR	5103
N672PP	**C680**	**0083**
N672PS	**GALX**	**010**
N672QS	**C56X**	**5663**
N672RW	HS25	258289
N672SA	C560	0272
N672WM	**F9EX**	**234**
N672XP	HS25	258672
N672XP	HS25	258772
N673BA	F2TH	173
N673BA	HS25	258218
(N673BH)	CL60	1073
N673CA	C550	590
N673DC	**E50P**	**50000010**
N673FH	SBRL	380-49
N673GA	GALX	073
N673GA	GLF5	5073
N673GA	GLF5	5173
N673GA	GLF5	573
N673GA	GLF6	6073
N673GD	GLF6	6173
N673H	HS25	258292
N673HA	**GLF6**	**6018**
N673JS	C650	0073
N673LB	LJ45	222
N673LJ	LJ24	147
N673LP	C500	503
N673LP	C550	192
N673LP	LJ45	222
N673LR	C500	503
N673LR	**C550**	**192**
N673M	LJ35	008
N673MG	**C56X**	**5821**
N673MM	**GLF5**	**5139**
N673P	**GLF5**	**673**
N673QS	**C56X**	**5651**
N673RW	**HS25**	**258331**
N673SH	SBRL	380-49
N673TM	HS25	258033
N673TS	CL60	1073
N673VP	C560	0673
N673W	**C56X**	**5122**
N673WM	LJ24	040
N673XP	HS25	258673
N673YS	CL60	1073
N674AC	MU30	A024SA
N674AS	C52A	0307
N674BA	HS25	258220
N674BP	LJ60	074
N674CA	C550	564
N674CC	C650	0174
N674CW	CL60	1074
N674DJ	**BE40**	**RK-232**
N674G	**C550**	**434**
N674GA	GALX	174
N674GA	GLF5	574
N674GA	GLF5	674
N674GA	GLF6	6074
N674GA	GLF6	6174
N674JM	C525	0485
N674JM	**C52A**	**0458**
N674JM	C555	0127
N674LJ	LJ24	178
N674LJ	LJ35	674
N674ND	C550	550-0852
N674RW	GLF5	5234
N674RW	GLF5	524
N674SF	BE40	RK-232
N674TB	**CL60**	**1074**
N674XP	HS25	258674
N675AB	**C52A**	**0522**
N675BA	HS25	258221
N675BP	**CL64**	**5336**
N675BP	LJ60	321
N675CF	CL61	5094
N675CS	**C750**	**0163**
(N675DM)	C550	608
N675GA	GALX	175
N675GA	GLF5	675
N675GA	GLF6	6075
N675L	LJ24	172
N675LJ	LJ60	075
N675M	LJ55	075
N675QS	**C56X**	**5275**
N675RW	GLF2	191
N675RW	GLF5	526
(N675RW)	HS25	258181
N675SS	**C550**	**550-1123**
N675SS	C550	576
N675XP	HS25	258675
N676AH	**HS25**	**258831**
N676AS	**GLF5**	**5407**
N676BA	F2TH	176
N676BA	HS25	259020
N676BB	C550	550-0923
N676BB	C56X	5349
N676BB	**C56X**	**6112**
N676CC	**C500**	**676**
N676CM	**C550**	**197**
N676CW	C500	169
N676DG	**C500**	**256**
N676DW	FA20	387
N676GA	GLF5	676
N676GA	GLF6	6076
N676GA	GLF6	6176
N676GH	**HS25**	**258676**
N676JB	**HS25**	**258619**
N676LJ	LJ24	183
N676PB	C550	550-0923
N676PC	FA10	36
N676PC	HS25	25153
N676QS	**C56X**	**5176**
N676RW	GLF3	355
N676RW	GLF4	1253
N676RW	GLF5	5126
N676TC	ASTR	044
N676TC	ASTR	128
(N676WE)	C500	169
N676XP	HS25	258676
N677AS	PRM1	RB-33
N677BA	HS25	258223
N677BM	FA20	57
N677CC	C650	0077
N677CT	LJ35	307
(N677DC)	PRM1	RB-226
N677F	**GLF5**	**677**
N677FP	**GLF5**	**529**
N677FR	GLF4	1289
N677GA	GALX	177
N677GA	GLF5	677
N677GD	GLF6	6077
N677GD	GLF6	6177
N677GS	C550	669
N677JM	C500	427
N677LJ	LJ60	077
N677LM	C650	0083
N677LM	CL60	1080
N677MS	**E50P**	**50000299**
N677QS	**C56X**	**5367**
N677RP	GLF4	1085
N677RW	GLF2	191
N677RW	GLF2	192
N677RW	GLF4	1177
N677RW	HS25	257191
N677S	GLF2	115
(N677SC)	F9EX	66
N677SL	C52A	0418
N677SW	FA20	27
N677SW	GLF4	1269
N677SW	LJ24	356
N677TW	**C510**	**0367**
N677V	GLF2	120
N677VU	GLF4	1269
N677XP	HS25	258677
N678AB	C510	0413
N678AM	**PRM1**	**RB-194**
N678AM	SBRL	465-22
N678BA	HS25	258230
N678BC	JSTR	5109/13
N678BM	FA20	345
N678BM	FA20	57

N678CA	C550	060
N678CF	C500	678
N678CG	CL60	1027
N678CH	F900	47
N678DG	C500	625
(N678DG)	C500	652
N678EQ	C650	7008
N678GA	GALX	178
N678GA	GLF5	678
N678GA	GLF6	6078
N678GA	**GLF6**	**6178**
N678GS	**C550**	**710**
N678HB	**CL30**	**20622**
N678JD	C500	452
(N678JG)	C500	452
N678MA	**FA50**	**116**
N678MB	**C510**	**0348**
N678ML	CL60	1011
N678PC	MU30	A021SA
N678PS	**EA50**	**000191**
N678QS	C56X	5353
N678QS	C56X	5369
N678QS	**C56X**	**5616**
N678RC	**GLEX**	**9454**
N678RF	C525	0537
N678RW	GLF2	13
N678RW	GLF2	192
N678RW	GLF4	1017
N678RZ	GLF2	13
N678S	LJ35	342
N678SB	HS25	259016
N678SC	GLF5	5224
N678SP	LJ24	354
N678SV	C680	0078
N678W	HS25	257147
N678XP	HS25	258678
N679BA	HS25	259023
N679BC	C550	589
N679CC	C500	679
N679CC	C650	0179
N679CF	C56X	5679
N679GA	GLF5	679
N679GA	GLF6	6079
N679GA	**GLF6**	**6179**
N679H	HS25	258293
N679H	HS25	259049
N679JB	GLEX	9323
N679LG	**C56X**	**6195**
N679QS	**C56X**	**5279**
N679RE	FA20	150/445
N679RW	GALX	072
N679RW	GLF2	109
N679RW	GLF2	191
N679RW	GLF4	1131
N679RW	JSTR	5062/12
N679SJ	**BE40**	**RK-168**
N679TC	**C52C**	**0189**
N679XP	HS25	258679
N680AB	C680	0319
N680AF	LJ31	068
N680AJ	**C680**	**0285**
N680AK	**C680**	**0283**
N680AR	C680	0025
N680AR	CL61	5140
N680AT	**C56X**	**5129**
N680BA	C680	0316
N680BA	HS25	259014
N680BC	C650	0087
N680BC	LJ25	200
N680BD	C680	0171
N680BF	**C680**	**0244**
N680CF	**C680**	**0117**
N680CG	**C680**	**0044**
N680CJ	LJ24	211
N680CM	**C680**	**0194**
N680CS	**C680**	**709**
N680CT	**C680**	**680A0012**
N680DF	**F2TH**	**180**
N680DJ	**C680**	**680A0030**
N680EV	**C680**	**0087**
(N680FA)	CL61	3003
N680FD	**C680**	**0289**
N680FM	GLF3	371
N680G	**C680**	**0280**
N680GA	GLF5	680
N680GD	GLF6	6180
N680GG	C680	0104
N680GR	**C680**	**0210**
N680GT	**C680**	**0075**
N680GW	C560	0369
N680HA	**C680**	**0504**
N680HB	C680	0338
N680HC	C680	0079
N680J	LJ25	063
N680JB	C52A	0190
N680JC	LJ25	319
N680JG	C680	0250
N680K	WW24	173
N680KG	**C750**	**0513**
N680KH	**C525**	**0680**
N680KJ	**C680**	**0521**
N680KT	**FA50**	**77**
N680LK	C680	0340
N680LN	C680	0236
N680M	CL60	1023
N680MB	C680	0310
N680MC	**C680**	**0515**

N680ME	**WW24**	**423**
N680NA	**C680**	**0526**
N680NY	**C680**	**0226**
N680PA	C680	0255
N680PB	**C680**	**0145**
N680PG	**C680**	**0108**
N680PH	C680	0030
N680RB	**C680**	**0349**
N680RC	**C680**	**0192**
N680RH	**C680**	**0545**
N680RP	C680	0239
N680RW	GALX	163
N680RW	GLF2	191
N680RW	GLF2	4/8
N680RZ	GLF2	4/8
N680SB	**C52A**	**0220**
N680SB	C680	0039
N680SC	**C680**	**0513**
N680SE	**C680**	**0078**
N680SG	C680	0343
N680SV	C680	0056
N680SV	**C680**	**0520**
N680SW	C680	0044
N680SW	LJ31	242
N680TG	**C680**	**0175**
N680TR	**C680**	**0560**
N680TT	JSTR	5108
N680UT	**C680**	**0153**
N680VP	C680	0012
N680VR	C56X	5049
N680VR	C680	0108
N680WC	**C680**	**0102**
N680XP	HS25	258680
N681AF	LJ31	102
N681AR	GLF2	81
N681CE	**C560**	**0681**
N681CL	**C680**	**680A0001**
N681CS	C680	0001
N681FM	GLF2	167
N681FM	GLF3	371
N681GD	GLF6	6081
N681GD	**GLF6**	**6181**
N681GF	**C680**	**0501**
N681HS	**C680**	**0287**
N681LF	C680	0151
N681LJ	LJ60	081
(N681MR)	C680	0255
N681P	**LJ45**	**426**
N681QS	C56X	5181
N681RP	C56X	5254
N681RP	C680	0037
N681SV	C680	0117
(N681TS)	CL60	1081
N681WA	C56X	6098
N681WD	C750	0052
N681WD	BE40	RK-94
N681XP	HS25	258681
N682A	**C680**	**680A0002**
N682AB	C680	0328
N682B	HS25	258144
N682BA	HS25	258225
N682BF	**C500**	**682**
N682BL	C56X	5550
N682CC	C650	0182
N682CE	**C560**	**0661**
N682CJ	C550	682
N682CM	C550	682
N682CS	C680	0002
N682D	C560	0021
N682D	FA10	87
N682D	**HS25**	**258144**
(N682D)	FA10	200
N682DB	**C680**	**0009**
N682DC	C500	682
N682DG	**C560**	**0673**
N682DK	HS25	258682
N682FM	GLF2	167
N682FM	GLF3	305
N682GA	**GALX**	**202**
N682GA	GLF5	682
N682GD	GLF6	6082
N682GD	**GLF6**	**6182**
N682H	HS25	258294
N682HC	C500	682
N682HS	**C680**	**0291**
N682JB	FA20	488
N682LJ	LJ24	218
N682LJ	LJ60	082
N682QS	**C56X**	**5654**
N682SS	C680	0502
N682SV	C680	0002
N682TM	**HDJT**	**42000023**
N682XP	HS25	258682
N683AB	C680	0514
N683BA	HS25	258229
N683CF	C555	0085
N683CL	**C680**	**680A0003**
N683E	HS25	258113
N683EC	GLF2	157
N683EF	LJ35	614
N683EL	LJ35	614
N683F	**HS25**	**258113**
N683FM	GLF2	167
N683FM	GLF2	22
N683GA	G150	283
N683GA	GALX	203
N683GA	**GLEX**	**9134**

N683GA	GLF5	683
N683GD	GLF6	6083
N683H	HS25	258295
N683JB	GLEX	9470
N683LJ	LJ25	035
N683LJ	LJ60	083
N683MB	C650	0159
N683MB	C555	0085
N683PF	C555	0083
N683QS	**C56X**	**5643**
N683RP	C56X	5501
N683SL	**C680**	**0219**
N683SV	**C680**	**0003**
N683UF	CL61	5083
N683UF	**CL65**	**5734**
N683WS	FA10	51
N684AB	C680	0535
N684AT	GLF3	339
N684BA	HS25	259033
N684BM	C560	0684
N684C	HS25	258063
N684CE	C560	0684
N684CL	C680	680A0004
N684DB	**C680**	**680A0016**
N684DK	**HS25**	**258684**
N684GA	GLF5	684
N684GA	GLF6	6084
N684GA	**GLF6**	**6184**
N684H	C500	113
N684HA	C500	113
N684HA	LJ35	113
N684JB	LJ40	2027
N684KF	**F2TH**	**213**
N684LA	LJ35	113
N684LJ	LJ60	084
N684QS	C56X	5084
N684SC	**C525**	**0384**
N684SW	CL61	5032
N684TA	BE40	RK-334
N684TS	**CL64**	**5384**
N684TS	CL64	5484
N685AS	**E50P**	**50000041**
N685BA	HS25	258231
N685CL	**C680**	**680A0005**
N685CS	C680	0142
N685DC	**F9EX**	**232**
N685EM	HS25	257026
N685FF	HS25	25121
N685FM	HS25	257026
N685GD	**GLF6**	**6185**
N685H	HS25	258296
N685JF	**G150**	**298**
N685LJ	LJ60	085
N685LM	**PRM1**	**RB-186**
N685MF	**GLF4**	**1056**
N685QS	**C56X**	**5650**
N685RC	LJ31	149
N685RC	LJ45	053
N685SF	GLF2	94
N685SF	GLF4	1056
N685TA	GLF2	31
N685TA	GLF4	1003
N685TA	GLF5	685
N685VP	C680	0050
N686AB	**LJ31**	**239**
N686BA	HS25	258232
N686BC	ASTR	039
N686CB	**CL30**	**20604**
N686CF	HS25	258060
N686CG	GLF4	1171
N686CP	**HS25**	**258059**
N686FG	HS25	257207
N686GA	GLF5	686
N686GD	GLF6	6086
N686GD	**GLF6**	**6186**
N686HC	C680	0101
N686HC	**C680**	**0266**
N686LJ	LJ60	086
N686MC	C555	0072
N686QS	**C56X**	**5661**
N686RC	**C550**	**437**
N686SC	**BE40**	**RK-211**
N686SG	HS25	257207
N686T	**C750**	**0211**
N686TA	BE40	RK-328
N686TR	BE40	RK-127
N687AC	HS25	258581
N687CJ	C525	0687
N687DS	**C52B**	**0087**
N687GA	GLF5	687
N687GA	GLF6	6087
N687GD	**GLF6**	**6187**
N687HS	**F900**	**47**
N687LJ	LJ25	040
N687LJ	LJ60	087
N687QS	C56X	5187
N687TA	BE40	RK-322
N687VP	C650	0087
(N687VP)	C680	0007
N688AG	C56X	5056
N688AJ	**GALX**	**242**
N688AT	**C555**	**0083**
N688CB	**GLF5**	**5172**
N688CC	HS25	25142
N688CF	C500	147
N688CK	C52B	0216
N688CP	**F2EX**	**241**

N688DB	C52A	0192
N688DB	**LJ60**	**097**
(N688DP)	C52A	0192
N688G	HS25	258688
N688GA	GLF5	688
N688GA	GLF6	6088
N688GA	**GLF6**	**6188**
N688GS	**LJ25**	**123**
N688H	GLF4	1062
N688JD	C550	550-0902
N688JG	**C680**	**0301**
N688JH	CL65	5827
N688JR	**GLF6**	**6173**
N688LJ	LJ60	088
N688LS	**GLF4**	**1280**
N688MC	FA20	175
N688MC	GLEX	9203
N688MC	GLEX	9320
N688MC	**GLEX**	**9444**
N688MC	GLF2	81
(N688NY)	CL64	5622
N688QS	C56X	5188
N688SF	**CL65**	**5716**
N688TA	BE40	RK-321
N688TF	GLF4	1220
N688TT	GLF4	1220
N688TY	GLF5	536
(N688WS)	SBRL	465-60
N688ZJ	**GLEX**	**9688**
N689AK	BE40	RK-462
N689AM	**HS25**	**258665**
N689CC	C500	689
N689GA	GLF5	689
N689GA	GLF6	6089
N689GA	**GLF6**	**6189**
N689H	HS25	258300
N689HC	**C525**	**0894**
N689JB	LJ40	2037
N689JE	**GLF2**	**258**
N689QS	**C56X**	**5659**
N689TA	BE40	RK-319
N689TA	BE40	RK-327
N689VP	**C550**	**689**
N689W	**C650**	**0045**
N689WC	FA10	123
N689WM	**GLEX**	**9265**
N690	LJ24	339
N690AN	C550	674
N690DM	C500	592
N690EA	C500	201
N690EC	**FA20**	**484**
N690ES	**C560**	**0336**
N690EW	**C550**	**119**
N690GA	GLF5	690
N690GA	GLF6	6090
N690GA	**GLF6**	**6190**
N690J	LJ24	145
N690JC	**LJ25**	**320**
N690LJ	LJ24	078
N690MC	C500	388
N690PC	GLF2	56
N690QS	C56X	5090
N690RB	**CL30**	**20421**
N690WY	**C500**	**592**
N690XL	**C56X**	**5690**
N690XS	C56X	6090
N691AC	GLF3	316
N691CC	**CL61**	**5126**
N691CJ	C525	0691
(N691DE)	C650	0204
N691ES	**C560**	**0402**
N691GA	GLF5	691
N691GA	GLF6	6091
N691GD	**GLF6**	**6191**
N691H	HS25	258321
N691HM	GLF2	92
N691LC	GLF6	6085
(N691NS)	LJ35	208
N691QS	**C56X**	**5290**
N691RC	GLF2	43
N691RC	GLF4	1079
N691RC	GLF5	605
N691SC	GLF4	1481
N691TA	BE40	RK-317
N692BE	**C650**	**0092**
N692CC	C650	0092
N692EB	GLF2	87/775/6
N692FC	HS25	25032
N692FC	LJ25	052
N692FG	LJ25	052
N692G	FA20	44
N692GA	GALX	192
N692GA	GLF5	692
N692GA	GLF6	6092
N692GA	**GLF6**	**6192**
N692JB	CL65	5845
N692JM	C52A	0004
N692JM	C52A	0109
N692LJ	LJ24	222
N692M	C555	0041
N692PC	LJ60	010
N692QS	C56X	5092
(N692SH)	F900	43
N692TA	BE40	RK-307
N692TT	C550	692
N692TV	GLF3	397
N692US	**FA10**	**79**

(N692VP)	C680	0092
N693BA	C650	0005
N693C	HS25	258209
(N693CC)	C650	0093
N693EA	C56X	5693
N693GA	GLF4	4193
N693GA	GLF5	693
N693GA	GLF6	6093
N693GD	**GLF6**	**6193**
N693GS	**BE40**	**RK-171**
N693LJ	LJ24	231
N693M	C555	0021
N693PB	GLF3	451
N693QS	**C56X**	**5657**
N693SH	F900	43
N693SV	C550	550-1059
N693TA	BE40	RK-305
N693TJ	HS25	256027
N693XP	HS25	258693
N694BD	HS25	258777
N694CC	C650	0090
N694CM	C550	694
N694ES	**HS25**	**258694**
N694FJ	HS25	258694
N694GA	GLF6	6094
N694GA	**GLF6**	**6194**
N694HC	LJ60	385
N694JC	CL60	1026
N694JC	HS25	25107
N694JP	F9EX	59
N694LM	C500	363
N694LP	LJ45	384
N694PD	**CL30**	**20257**
N694PD	HS25	258777
N694PG	CL60	1026
(N694PG)	LJ35	041
N694PW	C500	315
N694QS	**C56X**	**5194**
(N694SC)	LJ45	293
N694SH	LJ45	398
N694TX	C680	0094
N695BD	LJ40	2059
N695BK	BE40	RK-235
N695CC	C500	593
N695GA	GLF6	6095
N695GA	**GLF6**	**6195**
N695GL	LJ45	177
N695JB	**FA50**	**272**
N695LJ	LJ25	060
N695PA	**C525**	**0158**
N695QE	**C56X**	**5277**
N695QS	**C56X**	**5293**
N695ST	FA50	40
N695ST	GLF2	28
N695TA	**C550**	**106**
N695TA	BE40	RK-303
N695TA	BE40	RK-310
N695V	C560	0695
N695VP	C550	695
N695XP	HS25	258695
N696A	C550	363
N696CM	C550	550-0978
N696GA	GALX	196
N696GA	GLF5	5096
N696GA	GLF6	6096
N696GA	**GLF6**	**6196**
N696GW	WW24	52
N696HC	C650	0154
N696HC	C680	0101
N696HC	C680	0266
N696HC	FA50	250
N696HC	FA50	316
N696HC	**G280**	**2078**
N696HQ	FA50	250
N696HQ	FA50	316
N696HS	**CL65**	**5819**
(N696JH)	HS25	257055
(N696JH)	LJ35	084
N696JM	**F900**	**28**
N696M	**C56X**	**5181**
N696MJ	GLF2	165/37
N696MM	C525	0854
N696NA	EA50	000123
N696PA	LJ31	060
N696QS	**C56X**	**5296**
(N696RB)	LJ31	145
N696RG	**WW24**	**311**
N696RV	WW24	118
N696SB	**F2EX**	**206**
N696SC	LJ35	018
(N696SC)	LJ35	179
N696ST	C525	0187
N696TA	BE40	RK-301
N696TR	BE40	RK-127
N696US	SBRL	465-18
N696VP	**C550**	**696**
N697A	C550	034
N697A	GLF2	16/13
N697A	GLF5	662
N697AH	**CL30**	**20166**
N697AS	**E55P**	**50500056**
N697BA	C550	697
N697BH	FA20	239
N697BJ	GLF3	370
N697CC	**G280**	**2058**
N697CE	C560	0697
N697EA	C550	697

N697FF	**C56X**	**5026**
N697GA	GLF6	6097
N697GA	**GLF6**	**6197**
N697MB	C500	224
N697MC	C650	0097
N697NP	HS25	257052
N697QS	C56X	5197
N697SD	**C56X**	**5197**
N697TA	BE40	RK-299
N697US	**SBRL**	**465-49**
N697XP	HS25	258697
N698CW	CL61	3008
N698DC	HS25	259043
N698GA	GALX	150
N698GA	GLF6	6098
N698GD	**GLF6**	**6198**
N698GS	GLF3	469
N698MM	LJ31	142
N698PW	BE40	RK-114
N698QS	**C56X**	**5653**
N698RS	CL61	3014
N698RS	**CL64**	**5460**
N698RT	CL61	3014
N698TA	BE40	RK-298
N698VP	C56X	5698
N699AK	**HA4T**	**RC-16**
N699BA	LJ35	463
N699BC	C56X	5123
N699BG	**F900**	**82**
N699CC	C560	0351
N699CJ	**C525**	**0699**
N699CP	LJ31	060
N699CW	CL61	5009
N699DA	LJ60	237
N699EC	HS25	258193
N699GA	FA20	401
N699GA	GLF5	5099
N699GA	GLF5	666
N699GA	GLF5	699
N699GA	GLF6	6099
N699GA	**GLF6**	**6199**
N699GG	**LJ31**	**182**
N699HH	GLF4	1239
(N699JM)	C52A	0004
N699MC	ASTR	076
N699MC	F2EX	25
N699MG	**C650**	**0094**
N699MQ	ASTR	076
N699PM	**BE40**	**RK-67**
N699QS	**C56X**	**5199**
N699RD	SBRL	306-53
N699SC	FA50	70
N699SC	HS25	256026
N699SC	LJ60	041
N699ST	LJ35	441
N699TA	BE40	RK-297
N699TS	**HS25**	**256001**
N699TW	**FA20**	**50**
N699XL	C56X	5699
N699XP	**HS25**	**258699**
N700AA	HS25	257149
(N700AB)	HS25	25033
N700AC	HS25	257126
N700AD	GLEX	9058
N700AH	GLEX	9016
N700AH	GLEX	9078
N700AJ	A700	0001
N700AJ	A700	0004
N700AJ	**E50P**	**50000029**
N700AL	**FA10**	**55**
N700AP	GLEX	9079
N700AQ	GLEX	9025
N700AR	HS25	257053
N700AS	C550	014
N700AU	GLEX	9083
N700AU	**SBRL**	**306-112**
N700AY	GLEX	9082
N700BA	HS25	257032
N700BA	HS25	257058
N700BA	HS25	257131
N700BA	HS25	257185
N700BA	HS25	257189
N700BB	HS25	257041
N700BB	HS25	257148
N700BD	FA10	81
N700BD	GLEX	9063
N700BF	WW24	137
N700BH	GLEX	9024
N700BH	GLF2	115
N700BJ	LJ25	257
N700BK	GLEX	9067
N700BP	GLEX	9044
N700BQ	GLEX	9087
N700BU	GLEX	9043
N700BV	GLEX	9046
N700BW	HS25	25263
N700BW	HS25	257123
N700BX	**GLEX**	**9068**
N700BY	GLEX	9048
N700C	LJ24	123
N700C	LJ24	144
N700C	WW24	44
N700CB	WW24	44
N700CC	HS25	25202
N700CE	GLEX	9098
N700CE	**HS25**	**257213**
N700CF	SBRL	282-109
N700CH	**F2TH**	**147**
N700CH	LJ60	056
N700CJ	**C525**	**0027**
N700CJ	GLEX	9062
N700CJ	HS25	257178
N700CL	CL60	1035
N700CN	GLF3	488
N700CN	GLF4	1133
N700CN	HS25	257102
(N700CQ)	GLF2	228
N700CS	C650	0036
N700CU	GLEX	9099
N700CU	HS25	257081
N700CV	GLEX	9065
N700CW	C500	205
N700CX	GLEX	9100
N700CY	GLEX	9102
N700CZ	GLEX	9103
N700DA	HS25	257135
N700DA	LJ25	302
(N700DA)	SBRL	306-142
N700DD	HS25	257152
N700DE	HS25	257105
N700DK	FA10	191
N700DQ	GLEX	9052
N700DU	GLEX	9056
N700DU	GLEX	9109
N700DW	FA10	205
N700DZ	GLEX	9051
(N700E)	HS25	257101
(N700EA)	C550	072
N700EC	GLEX	9105
N700EC	WW24	182
N700EG	GLEX	9059
N700EK	GLEX	9108
N700EL	GLEX	9110
N700ER	C500	542
N700ER	HS25	257010
(N700ET)	LJ24	123
N700EW	GLEX	9116
N700EW	GLEX	9142
N700EX	GLEX	9057
N700EY	GLEX	9117
N700EZ	GLEX	9118
N700FA	**G150**	**278**
N700FA	HS25	25229
N700FA	BE40	RK-399
N700FC	LJ25	082
N700FE	GLEX	9119
N700FE	HS25	257108
N700FG	GLEX	9120
N700FG	GLEX	9163
N700FH	**FA10**	**158**
N700FJ	GLEX	9050
N700FL	F2TH	29
N700FL	**F9EX**	**170**
N700FN	GLEX	9121
N700FQ	GLEX	9122
N700FR	GLEX	9125
N700FR	HS25	257130
N700FS	GLF2	108
N700FS	GLF3	367
N700FS	**GLF4**	**1400**
N700FS	HS25	257012
N700FW	HS25	257008
N700FY	GLEX	9128
N700FZ	GLEX	9129
(N700GA)	WW24	137
N700GB	**GLEX**	**9124**
N700GB	HS25	257050
N700GB	LJ35	082
N700GB	BE40	RK-26
N700GD	C510	0244
N700GD	**C52B**	**0363**
N700GD	GLF4	1104
N700GG	HS25	257154
N700GG	LJ36	038
N700GK	GLEX	9020
N700GM	BE40	RK-34
(N700GN)	FA20	325
N700GQ	GLEX	9085
N700GR	GLEX	9366
N700GS	LJ60	026
N700GT	GLEX	9039
N700GU	GLEX	9084
N700GW	C525	0275
N700GX	**GLEX**	**9014**
N700HA	**GLF5**	**634**
N700HA	HS25	257143
N700HA	HS25	257149
N700HB	HS25	257146
N700HB	WW24	135
N700HE	GLEX	9032
N700HF	GLEX	9034
N700HG	GLEX	9022
N700HH	HS25	257045
N700HM	**GLEX**	**9330**
(N700HM)	BE40	RJ-19
N700HS	HS25	257002
N700HS	HS25	257012
N700HS	HS25	257072
N700HS	HS25	257150
N700HW	HS25	257173
N700HX	GLEX	9005
N700JA	C500	379
N700JC	**SBRL**	**465-74**
N700JD	C500	009
N700JD	**FA50**	**84**
N700JE	HA4T	RC-7
N700JE	LJ55	091
N700JE	LJ60	210
N700JJ	A700	0001
N700JP	GLF2	77
N700JR	C500	379
N700JR	C550	554
N700JR	C560	0666
N700JR	SBRL	306-138
N700K	HS25	257102
N700KB	PRM1	RB-103
N700KC	CL61	5017
N700KG	HS25	257201
N700KG	**LJ40**	**2017**
N700KJ	GLEX	9011
N700KK	CL60	1082
N700KK	HS25	257155
N700KL	**HS25**	**257105**
N700KS	GLEX	9015
N700KS	**GLEX**	**9109**
N700LA	GLEX	9054
N700LB	C550	366
N700LD	GLEX	9069
N700LH	**C750**	**0148**
N700LJ	A700	0002
N700LJ	GLEX	9053
N700LK	GLEX	9192
N700LL	HS25	257157
N700LN	GLEX	9072
N700LP	**C560**	**0194**
N700LP	HS25	257159
N700LP	MU30	A005SA
N700LP	BE40	RJ-28
N700LS	GLEX	9217
N700LS	**GLEX**	**9519**
N700LS	GLF4	1009
N700LS	GLF4	1180
N700LS	GLF4	1412
N700LS	HS25	257041
N700LW	C500	279
N700LW	C500	400
N700LX	C750	0038
N700M	HS25	25123
N700MB	**LJ40**	**2106**
N700MD	**WW24**	**212**
(N700MD)	LJ36	045
N700MG	HS25	258540
N700MH	**C650**	**0127**
N700MH	SBRL	306-142
(N700MJ)	JSTR	5138
N700MK	CL61	3011
N700MK	**GLF5**	**5224**
N700MK	HS25	257156
N700ML	GLEX	9043
N700ML	GLEX	9258
N700MM	WW24	311
N700MP	C500	198
N700MP	**FA50**	**70**
N700MV	**GLF4**	**1233**
N700NB	HS25	257131
N700NH	HS25	257148
N700NK	**C560**	**0700**
N700NN	HS25	257162
N700NP	**HS25**	**257207**
N700NP	HS25	257213
(N700NP)	LJ24	082
N700NT	HS25	257056
N700NW	**HS25**	**257063**
N700NW	LJ35	331
N700NY	GLF4	1468
N700NY	HS25	257002
N700NY	HS25	257140
N700PD	HS25	257029
(N700PD)	FA10	55
(N700PG)	HS25	25202
N700PL	GLEX	9064
N700PL	HS25	25229
N700PM	GLF2	207/34
N700PM	HS25	258081
N700PP	**GLF4**	**1248**
N700PP	HS25	257167
N700QA	**HS25**	**257052**
N700QG	SBRL	465-16
N700QS	GALX	052
N700R	HS25	256001
N700R	HS25	258692
N700R	LJ55	133
N700R	LJ60	113
N700R	SBRL	282-31
N700R	WW24	149
N700R	WW24	222
N700RD	HS25	25136
(N700RD)	C650	0036
N700RG	HS25	25136
N700RH	**C750**	**0205**
N700RJ	HS25	257004
N700RM	**JSTR**	**5224**
N700RR	C650	0025
N700RR	C650	7020
N700RR	**HS25**	**257024**
N700RR	HS25	257161
N700RY	C500	087
N700RY	C650	0005
N700SA	HS25	257141
N700SA	HS25	257145
N700SB	GLF3	334
N700SB	HS25	257121
N700SF	HS25	257061
N700SJ	LJ35	082
(N700SM)	HS25	256066
N700SP	C500	528
N700SR	**LJ55**	**079**
N700SS	HS25	257061
N700SS	HS25	257168
N700ST	GLF2	28
N700SV	C555	0119
N700SV	HS25	257001
N700SW	C650	0096
N700SW	**C750**	**0142**
N700SW	C555	0119
N700TF	C560	0011
N700TG	LJ55	021
N700TL	HS25	257028
N700TR	HS25	25220
N700TT	FA10	49
N700UJ	**HS25**	**257086**
N700UK	HS25	257051
N700UR	HS25	257057
(N700UU)	HS25	25103
N700VA	GLF3	300
N700VC	**C500**	**011**
N700VN	GLEX	9031
N700VP	C650	7011
N700VT	HS25	257158
N700WB	GLF4	1125
N700WC	HS25	257022
N700WE	WW24	417
N700WH	HS25	257010
N700WH	**BE40**	**RJ-60**
N700WJ	LJ35	393
(N700WJ)	LJ35	466
N700WL	GLEX	9042
N700WL	LJ35	003
N700WM	WW24	319
N700WR	GLEX	9402
N700WS	SBRL	306-133
N700WY	**HS25**	**HA-0029**
N700XF	HS25	257101
N700XJ	HS25	256015
N700XM	GLEX	9091
N700XN	GLEX	9073
N700XR	GLEX	9070
N700XT	GLEX	9076
N700XY	GLEX	9077
N700YM	C550	139
N700YY	**C510**	**0148**
N701A	HS25	256022
N701AG	C650	0077
N701AL	**C52C**	**0169**
N701AP	LJ24	163
N701AP	WW24	52
(N701AR)	LJ36	008
N701AS	C500	127
N701AS	LJ35	047
N701AT	C500	127
N701BG	**C555**	**0142**
N701BR	C500	191
N701CD	C650	7001
N701CF	HS25	257057
N701CP	**BE40**	**RK-272**
N701CR	C560	0469
N701CR	C56X	5141
N701CR	**C680**	**0176**
N701CW	HS25	257001
N701DA	**LJ35**	**180**
N701DB	**GLF4**	**1036**
N701DB	LJ55	074
N701DF	PRM1	RB-59
N701DK	C560	0221
N701DK	C560	0544
N701FW	SBRL	306-57
N701FW	**SBRL**	**465-21**
N701GA	CL60	1066
N701GP	C560	0536
N701HA	**C650**	**7001**
N701HB	GALX	042
N701JA	GLF2	7
N701JH	JSTR	5230
N701KB	**C56X**	**6191**
N701KB	PRM1	RB-103
N701KB	PRM1	RB-110
N701KB	PRM1	RB-211
N701KB	PRM1	RB-257
N701KD	PRM1	RB-211
N701KR	C56X	6191
N701KR	PRM1	RB-257
N701LP	BE40	RJ-61
N701LX	C750	0114
N701MG	FA20	196
N701MS	HS25	256061
N701NA	LJ24	049
N701NB	C560	0244
N701NC	SBRL	282-79
N701NW	HS25	257009
N701QS	CL60	1066
N701QS	GALX	141
N701QS	GLF4	1059
N701RH	GLF5	5010
N701RM	C550	242
N701RZ	LJ24	042
N701S	GLF2	69
N701SC	**LJ24**	**235**
N701SF	**C52A**	**0071**
N701TA	HS25	257073
N701TF	C525	0190
N701TF	C52A	0112
N701TP	C525	0190
N701TS	HS25	257002
N701US	LJ35	062
N701VF	C500	650
N701VV	**C550**	**550-1033**
N701W	WW24	274
N701WC	F2TH	48
N701WC	FA50	333
N701WC	**GLF4**	**4224**
N701WG	F2TH	48
N701WH	GLEX	9010
N701WQ	FA50	333
N701Z	HS25	25234
N701Z	HS25	256022
N701Z	HS25	256058
N701Z	WW24	274
N702A	**HS25**	**HA-0146**
N702AB	**C680**	**0258**
N702AC	C56X	5678
N702AM	C560	0702
N702BA	HS25	257059
(N702BC)	C550	252
N702BV	**G280**	**2055**
N702CA	FA20	429
N702CM	C650	7002
N702CS	**HS25**	**HA-0077**
N702CS	BE40	RK-381
N702D	HS25	25210
N702DA	LJ25	302
N702DD	FA20	74
N702DM	FA20	74
N702DM	**GLF3**	**428**
N702DR	**GLEX**	**9184**
N702E	HS25	257198
N702FJ	F2TS	702
N702FL	**C750**	**0076**
N702FM	**C52A**	**0212**
N702GA	G150	302
N702GA	GALX	102
N702GA	GLF4	4102
N702GA	GLF5	5002
N702GA	GLF5	5502
(N702GA)	HS25	25158
N702GH	**GLF4**	**1497**
N702H	GLF2	229
N702HC	HS25	256023
N702JA	GLF2	180
N702JF	GLF4	1528
N702JH	MU30	A035SA
N702JR	SBRL	306-138
N702KH	C550	290
N702LK	**GLEX**	**9474**
N702LP	**BE40**	**RK-444**
N702LP	BE40	RK-87
N702LX	C750	0076
N702M	HS25	25241
N702M	HS25	257195
N702MA	HS25	25241
N702NC	C500	579
N702NC	FA10	220
N702NC	FA10	55
N702NG	FA10	55
N702NV	BE40	RK-120
N702NW	HS25	257098
N702NY	C500	579
N702P	HS25	25212
N702PC	CL61	5121
N702PE	HS25	258155
N702QS	GALX	070
(N702QS)	GALX	058
N702R	C550	015
N702R	LJ60	113
N702RH	GLF4	1529
(N702RK)	LJ24	024
N702RT	**C500**	**683**
N702RV	CL61	5078
N702S	HS25	25200
N702SB	FA20	504
N702SC	FA20	321
N702SS	**C650**	**0135**
N702SS	HS25	25200
N702SW	C650	0096
(N702TJ)	HS25	257144
N702TR	**GLF4**	**4259**
N702TY	**GLF5**	**621**
N702W	HS25	257199
N703A	**HS25**	**HA-0147**
N703AJ	A700	0003
N703AW	FA50	284
N703CD	**HS25**	**HA-0026**
N703CL	GLEX	9112
N703DC	LJ24	067
N703DJ	**LJ35**	**155**
N703DM	**C750**	**0080**
N703GA	G280	2103
N703GA	GLF5	5003
N703GA	GLF5	5373
N703GA	GLF5	5503
N703HA	**G150**	**202**
N703J	LJ24	256
N703JA	GLF3	426
N703JH	MU30	A010SA
N703JN	HS25	257031
N703JP	HS25	257140

N703JS	FA10	157
N703LH	GLF4	4112
N703LP	BE40	RK-20
N703LX	C750	0074
N703MA	LJ35	003
(N703MJ)	HS25	257213
N703QS	GALX	060
N703RB	C650	7046
(N703RE)	HS25	258587
N703RJ	GLEX	9297
N703RK	**GLF5**	**671**
N703RK	HS25	258587
N703RT	**C500**	**114**
N703SC	FA20	24
N703SM	**HS25**	**258204**
N703TM	**FA50**	**218**
N703TS	HS25	257031
(N703VP)	C650	7030
N703VZ	**CL30**	**20199**
N703VZ	HS25	258108
N704CD	C550	704
N704CW	HS25	257004
N704DA	**C550**	**230**
N704GA	GLF4	4104
N704J	LJ36	009
N704JA	GLF3	432
N704JM	**HS25**	**258367**
N704JW	C550	550-0863
N704JW	C56X	5138
N704JW	GALX	088
N704JW	**GLF4**	**4003**
N704LX	C750	0091
N704MF	**GLEX**	**9065**
N704R	F900	55
N704SC	BE40	RK-104
N704T	PRM1	RB-2
N704TP	**C510**	**0437**
N705AC	**WW24**	**209**
N705AM	**CL65**	**5889**
N705BB	**HS25**	**258015**
N705CC	HS25	257027
N705EA	HS25	25142
N705FJ	FA7X	5
N705JA	GLF3	360
N705JH	HS25	257029
(N705JT)	C550	554
N705KU	**BE40**	**RK-305**
N705LP	BE40	RK-251
N705LX	C750	0082
N705MA	ASTR	011
N705NA	LJ24	102
N705PC	GLF4	1240
N705PT	**EA50**	**000014**
N705QS	GALX	061
N705SG	**C56X**	**5142**
N705SP	**C555**	**0048**
N705TX	C56X	5705
N705US	LJ35	144
N705WL	**C56X**	**5036**
N706A	SBRL	282-7
N706AM	**HS25**	**257009**
N706CJ	LJ60	168
N706CJ	LJ60	207
N706CP	C550	550-0909
N706CP	C550	550-0943
N706CR	LJ60	168
(N706CW)	HS25	258782
N706DC	C500	651
N706HB	**C650**	**0047**
N706JA	GLF3	322
N706JH	MU30	A016SA
N706L	LJ24	026
N706LP	**BE40**	**RK-336**
N706LX	C750	0073
N706M	HS25	25123
N706NA	C550	706
(N706PL)	BE40	RK-336
N706PT	**EA50**	**000107**
N706QS	GALX	131
(N706QS)	GALX	064
(N706QS)	GALX	071
N706RJ	GLEX	9283
N706RM	**BE40**	**RK-161**
N706RT	**C52B**	**0039**
N706SA	LJ31	026
N706SB	CS55	0139
N706SB	**FA20**	**383/550**
N706TF	C52A	0172
N706TJ	GLF2	212
N706TS	GLF2	254/41
N706VA	**GLF4**	**1528**
N706VP	C750	0006
(N706VP)	C650	7006
N706XJ	**C750**	**0006**
N706XP	HS25	258706
N707AM	**FA10**	**159**
N707AM	FA10	26
N707BC	ASTR	093
N707BC	**GALX**	**107**
N707BC	WW24	366
(N707BJ)	LJ35	077
N707CA	LJ25	342
N707CG	FA10	165
N707CS	LJ60	324
N707CV	C560	0095
N707CW	**GLF4**	**1252**
N707CW	MU30	A007SA

N707CX	FA10	135
N707CX	**FA10**	**216**
N707DB	SBRL	306-97
N707DC	FA10	159
N707DS	HS25	257148
N707EA	C550	707
N707EA	**GLF4**	**1284**
N707EL	**C52A**	**0109**
N707ES	**EA50**	**000232**
N707EZ	HS25	25231
N707EZ	JSTR	5055/21
N707FH	SBRL	282-74
N707GG	**C500**	**495**
N707GG	CL61	5037
(N707GP)	SBRL	306-141
N707GW	GLF5	629
N707HD	**HS25**	**259016**
N707HJ	C650	0177
N707HP	C550	550-1096
N707JA	GLF3	447
N707JC	**CL30**	**20378**
N707JC	FA20	335
N707JC	HS25	258703
N707JM	SBRL	282-41
N707JQ	**HS25**	**258703**
(N707JZ)	FA20	335
N707KD	GLF2	214
N707LL	**C52A**	**0046**
N707LM	**C550**	**338**
N707LX	C750	0078
N707MM	F2TH	131
N707MN	F2TH	131
N707MS	C650	0019
N707MT	C56X	5576
N707MT	**F2EX**	**57**
N707NV	LJ31	063
N707PE	C550	452
N707PE	HS25	258171
N707PF	**C550**	**452**
N707QS	GALX	066
N707RG	**LJ35**	**169**
N707RK	PRM1	RB-283
N707RX	GLF3	377
N707SB	CS55	0141
N707SC	LJ24	065
N707SG	**GALX**	**087**
N707SG	LJ60	062
N707SG	LJ60	109
N707SH	GLF2	77
N707SH	HS25	25231
N707SQ	LJ60	062
N707TA	HS25	258296
N707TE	**GLF4**	**1383**
N707TE	WW24	137
N707TE	WW24	155
N707TF	**WW24**	**155**
N707TG	SBRL	282-74
(N707TP)	LJ25	005
N707TR	LJ25	005
N707US	C500	339
N707W	C500	475
N707W	**C560**	**0556**
N707WB	F900	132
N707WB	**F9EX**	**233**
N707WB	HS25	256061
N707WB	JSTR	5210
N707WF	C500	661
N707WF	C550	452
N707XP	HS25	258707
N708BG	**C680**	**0325**
N708BW	HS25	25263
N708CF	C650	0185
N708CF	**LJ60**	**212**
(N708CM)	C650	7008
N708CT	C650	0185
N708CT	C650	7004
N708FL	**C750**	**0109**
N708GP	**C52A**	**0154**
N708JR	**C560**	**0666**
N708KS	GLEX	9015
N708LX	C750	0109
N708M	C56X	5194
N708QS	GALX	069
N708RJ	**GLEX**	**9246**
N708SC	CL64	5391
N708SC	GLEX	9066
N708SP	**LJ45**	**014**
N708TA	BE40	RK-178
N708TF	C525	0190
N708TR	LJ25	015
N708VP	C750	0008
N709AA	**GLF5**	**635**
N709AB	SBRL	306-75
N709CB	**C52C**	**0186**
N709CC	C550	709
(N709CM)	C650	7009
N709DS	**GLEX**	**9278**
N709DW	GLF5	5082
N709EA	HS25	258226
N709EL	**BE40**	**RK-52**
(N709EW)	BE40	RK-52
N709FG	**GLEX**	**9300**
N709FL	**C750**	**0145**
N709JB	SJ30	004
N709JB	BE40	RK-52
N709JB	BE40	RK-72
N709JM	CL61	5163

N709JW	C550	550-0863
N709LS	GLEX	9217
N709LS	GLF4	1180
N709LS	GLF4	1412
N709LX	C750	0145
N709PG	C52B	0107
N709Q	SBRL	282-30
N709Q	WW24	95
N709QS	C650	7109
N709R	HS25	256001
N709RJ	GLEX	9204
N709RS	C550	709
N709TA	BE40	RK-180
N709TB	C500	214
N709VP	C550	709
N709VP	C650	7009
N709XP	HS25	258709
N710A	HS25	258110
N710AF	HS25	257126
N710AG	HS25	257193
N710AN	**CL61**	**5150**
N710AT	LJ35	337
N710AW	C750	0033
N710BA	HS25	257191
N710BB	**C650**	**7016**
N710BC	HS25	257186
N710BD	HS25	257183
N710BF	HS25	257182
N710BG	FA50	305
N710BG	**G280**	**2036**
N710BG	HS25	257180
N710BJ	HS25	257177
N710BL	HS25	257174
N710BN	HS25	257173
N710BP	HS25	257171
N710BQ	FA50	305
N710BQ	HS25	257210
N710BR	HS25	257208
N710BS	HS25	257207
N710BT	HS25	257206
N710BU	HS25	257202
N710BV	HS25	257201
N710BW	HS25	257199
N710BX	HS25	257198
N710BY	HS25	257195
N710BZ	HS25	257193
N710CF	**GLF3**	**448**
N710DC	WW24	112
N710DL	**CL30**	**20282**
N710EB	C510	0107
N710EC	FA20	102
N710EC	GLF3	315
N710EC	**GLF4**	**1502**
(N710EG)	FA20	102
N710ET	**F2TH**	**38**
N710FL	**C750**	**0038**
N710GA	CL61	3008
N710GD	C52B	0363
N710GS	**LJ35**	**032**
N710HL	CL60	1050
N710HM	CL61	5160
N710HM	HS25	HA-0077
(N710JA)	JSTR	5150/37
N710JC	FA10	120
N710JL	GLF2	169
N710JW	WW24	35
N710K	MS76	112
N710LC	**C560**	**0058**
N710LM	CL61	5037
N710LX	**GLF4**	**1297**
N710MB	MU30	A078SA
N710ML	**C560**	**0254**
N710MP	GLF2	148/5
N710MR	FA20	59
N710MR	GLF2	148/5
N710MR	SBRL	306-123
N710MS	**C680**	**0162**
N710MT	C550	057
N710MT	C560	0254
N710MT	**C56X**	**5332**
N710MT	FA20	59
N710MW	FA20	59
N710PT	**C52B**	**0346**
N710QS	C650	7100
N710R	**LJ45**	**359**
N710RA	**BE40**	**RK-543**
N710RM	**JSTR**	**5213**
N710SA	**WW24**	**296**
N710SG	**LJ60**	**191**
N710SG	LJ60	311
N710SG	LJ60	322
N710TA	BE40	RK-183
(N710TF)	LJ60	046
N710TJ	LJ24	197
N710TP	LJ60	046
(N710TP)	CL61	5031
N710TS	CL65	5710
N710TV	**LJ24**	**159**
(N710TX)	C750	0071
N710VF	CL61	5050
N710VL	**C500**	**302**
N710VP	**C650**	**7100**
N710WB	FA20	102
N710WJ	**GLF4**	**1007**
N710WL	LJ35	485
N711	LJ24	098
N711	LJ24	197

N711	LJ35	012
N711	LJ35	207
N711A	SBRL	380-21
N711AE	LJ24	098
(N711AE)	C500	477
N711AF	LJ35	029
N711AG	HS25	256001
N711AG	JSTR	5086/44
N711AJ	PRM1	RB-18
(N711AJ)	CL60	1063
N711AQ	HS25	25173
N711BC	FA20	36
N711BE	C525	0299
N711BE	C52A	0116
N711BE	C52B	0212
N711BE	LJ35	274
N711BF	LJ25	324
N711BH	LJ35	041
N711BP	C550	036
N711BP	HS25	25218
N711BT	C500	644
N711BX	C525	0299
N711BY	SBRL	380-51
N711C	**C525**	**0630**
N711CA	LJ25	076
N711CC	C550	426
N711CD	LJ35	456
N711CE	LJ24	219
N711CH	LJ35	032
N711CJ	WW24	289
N711CN	C550	711
N711CN	LJ24	197
N711CR	C500	016
N711CU	HS25	257081
N711CW	LJ24	055
N711DB	CL60	1071
N711DB	LJ24	216
N711DB	LJ24	253
N711DB	LJ25	032
N711DP	GLF2	82
N711DS	GLF2	129
N711DS	LJ24	189
N711DS	LJ25	170
N711DS	LJ35	209
N711DX	LJ24	189
N711DZ	JSTR	5201
N711EC	**LJ35**	**311**
N711EC	BE40	RJ-53
N711EC	BE40	RK-167
N711EG	GLF3	349
N711EG	**GLF4**	**1473**
(N711EG)	C500	662
N711EJ	FA10	149
N711EV	GLF2	129
N711EV	LJ25	016
(N711EV)	LJ35	377
N711FC	BE40	RJ-55
N711FG	**LJ31**	**092**
N711FG	BE40	RJ-55
N711FJ	**F900**	**71**
N711FJ	FA10	149
N711FJ	FA20	347
N711FS	**C680**	**0548**
N711FW	GLF4	1033
N711FW	GLF4	4085
(N711FW)	C500	196
N711GA	CL60	1025
N711GA	G280	2011
N711GA	GLF4	4211
N711GA	GLF5	5211
N711GD	**HA4T**	**RC-7**
N711GD	HS25	258612
N711GD	SBRL	380-6
N711GD	BE40	RK-311
N711GF	C560	0068
N711GF	**C650**	**7075**
N711GL	C500	519
N711GL	FA20	396
N711GL	**GLF4**	**1130**
N711GL	SBRL	380-6
N711GL	BE40	RK-311
N711GW	WW24	12
N711HA	C550	550-1039
N711HA	C56X	5260
N711HA	**C56X**	**5648**
N711HE	C750	0078
N711HE	F2EX	47
N711HE	GLF4	1217
N711HF	**FA10**	**213**
N711HH	LJ35	162
N711HL	C500	503
N711HL	HS25	25232
N711HQ	C750	0078
N711HT	**FA50**	**66**
N711JC	FA10	69
N711JG	ASTR	017
N711JG	CS55	0035
N711JG	GALX	004
N711JN	CS55	0035
N711JQ	ASTR	017
(N711JQ)	GALX	004
N711JS	JSTR	5153/61
N711JT	LJ25	243
N711JT	WW24	91
(N711JU)	GALX	004
N711KE	**WW24**	**288**
N711KG	FA20	57

N711KT	**C550**	**550-0851**
N711KT	FA50	125
N711KU	**FA20**	**396**
N711L	LJ24	164
N711L	LJ24	252
N711L	LJ35	151
N711LD	LJ24	252
N711LS	GLEX	9035
N711LS	GLEX	9155
N711LS	**GLEX**	**9476**
N711LS	GLF2	76
N711LT	**C650**	**0232**
N711LT	GLF3	327
N711LV	**C56X**	**5597**
N711LV	C650	0232
N711MA	LJ35	032
N711MB	WW24	282
N711MC	GLEX	9002
N711MC	**GLEX**	**9121**
N711MC	GLF2	48/29
N711MC	GLF4	1217
N711MD	**CS55**	**0066**
N711MM	GLF2	61
N711MN	GLEX	9002
N711MQ	GLF2	189/42
N711MR	LJ24	045
N711MR	SBRL	306-118
N711MR	WW24	191
N711MT	**C500**	**316**
N711MT	FA10	105
N711MT	FA10	207
N711MT	GLF2	16/13
N711MT	GLF2	52
N711NA	CL30	20289
N711NB	**C650**	**7009**
N711NF	LJ35	626
N711NK	C56X	5533
N711NK	C680	0095
N711NK	**CL30**	**20289**
(N711NL)	C680	0095
N711NM	LJ25	224
N711NR	C500	387
N711NR	C56X	5533
N711NV	**C550**	**557**
N711P	**BE40**	**RK-578**
N711PC	LJ24	327
N711PD	CL61	5013
N711PD	LJ24	353
N711PD	LJ25	138
N711PE	**F2TH**	**105**
N711PE	HS25	258155
(N711PE)	GLF4	1217
N711PJ	LJ24	011
N711PR	LJ35	501
(N711QH)	LJ35	032
N711QS	GALX	129
N711R	GLF2	45
N711R	LJ35	035
N711R	**LJ45**	**049**
N711RA	**FA50**	**80**
N711RL	GLF2	25
N711RL	GLF5	5010
N711RL	GLF5	629
N711RL	**GLF6**	**6072**
N711RL	HS25	257146
N711RP	C500	639
N711RQ	GLF5	629
(N711RQ)	LJ35	035
(N711RT)	FA20	242
(N711RT)	GLF2	26
N711RZ	GLF2	25
N711RZ	**GLF5**	**5010**
N711S	GLF2	67
N711S	SBRL	306-92
N711SB	GLF2	70/1
N711SC	FA50	168
N711SC	GLF2	70/1
N711SC	LJ25	345
(N711SC)	HS25	25169
(N711SC)	LJ24	283
N711SD	HS25	25233
N711SD	LJ35	078
N711SE	C500	261
N711SE	**LJ60**	**015**
N711SE	WW24	329
N711SF	C500	261
N711SJ	CL61	3021
N711SK	**GLF4**	**1364**
(N711SP)	CL61	3021
N711SQ	LJ25	005
(N711SQ)	GLEX	9065
N711SR	CL61	3007
N711ST	CL61	3024
N711ST	SBRL	306-129
N711SW	GLEX	9065
N711SW	GLF2	71
N711SW	GLF3	311
N711SW	GLF4	1033
N711SW	GLF4	1170
N711SW	GLF4	4085
N711SW	GLF5	523
N711SW	GLF6	6007
N711SW	**GLF6**	**6087**
N711SW	HS25	25146
N711SW	LJ35	078
N711SX	CL61	3007
N711SX	CL64	5492

N711SX	**GLEX**	**9125**
N711SZ	CL61	3007
N711SZ	LJ60	015
(N711SZ)	GLF4	4085
N711T	**F9EX**	
N711T	**FA50**	**176**
N711T	SBRL	282-67
(N711T)	F900	20
N711TE	C500	342
N711TE	GLF2	105
N711TF	FA10	52
N711TG	HS25	257177
N711TG	LJ25	298
N711TJ	LJ24	011
N711TQ	LJ25	298
N711TU	FA50	124
N711TW	SBRL	306-33
N711UC	SBRL	282-32
N711UF	GLF3	421
N711UR	LJ24	197
N711VF	C500	642
(N711VF)	C500	650
N711VH	C56X	5260
N711VH	C650	0047
N711VJ	**C750**	**0101**
N711VJ	LJ60	045
N711VK	LJ25	292
(N711VK)	WW24	7
N711VL	**GLF2**	**120**
N711VP	**C750**	**0283**
N711VR	C550	260
N711VT	C750	0101
N711VT	C750	0283
N711VT	**G280**	**2033**
N711VT	HS25	25249
N711VT	LJ25	292
N711VT	LJ60	045
N711VZ	C650	0047
N711WD	LJ25	196
N711WD	LJ25	241
N711WD	LJ25	282
N711WE	LJ25	105
N711WG	**C525**	**0424**
N711WJ	HS25	25021
N711WK	ASTR	101
N711WK	SBRL	306-40
(N711WK)	F900	50
N711WM	C550	387
N711WM	HS25	25020
N711WM	HS25	257087
N711WU	WW24	313
N711WV	**F900**	**166**
N711WV	FA20	396
N711WV	WW24	313
N711XR	C555	0121
N711YP	HS25	25265
N711YP	HS25	257048
N711YR	HS25	25265
N711Z	C550	435
N711Z	JSTR	1002
N711Z	JSTR	5023
N711Z	JSTR	5067
N711Z	JSTR	5078/3
N711Z	JSTR	5093
N711Z	JSTR	5141
N711Z	JSTR	5149/11
N711Z	JSTR	5151
N711Z	JSTR	5155/32
N711Z	JSTR	5201
(N711Z)	C560	0326
N711ZC	C550	711
N712AS	**GLF3**	**423**
N712BD	**C550**	**550-1025**
N712BG	C550	550-1025
N712BG	C56X	5260
N712BS	**HS25**	**HA-0105**
N712BW	LJ25	241
(N712CB)	LJ25	298
N712CC	GLF4	1028
N712CG	**C56X**	**5182**
N712CM	C650	7012
N712CW	GLF4	1028
N712DA	GLF5	5134
N712DC	LJ25	032
N712DG	CL64	5328
N712DH	C56X	6028
(N712DH)	C56X	5527
(N712DM)	LJ35	231
N712DP	LJ25	319
N712EJ	LJ31	231
N712FL	**C750**	**0082**
N712G	C500	060
N712GA	GLF4	4221
N712GC	C56X	5182
N712GF	C560	0068
N712GK	**C56X**	**5106**
N712GK	BE40	RK-44
(N712GM)	WW24	118
N712GW	JSTR	5016
N712HL	CL60	1056
N712J	C500	060
N712J	C500	270
N712J	C550	404
N712JA	LJ25	134
N712JB	LJ35	646
N712JC	C750	0052
N712JE	LJ36	012
N712KC	C56X	5311
N712KC	**C750**	**0255**
N712KM	**C500**	**348**
N712KT	GLF5	5134
N712KT	**GLF6**	**6035**
N712L	C560	0365
N712L	LJ35	256
N712MB	**C500**	**120**
N712MC	LJ55	022
N712ME	FA20	355
N712MG	**C555**	**0080**
N712MQ	GLF2	104/10
N712MR	SBRL	306-113
N712N	C500	270
N712PD	C550	063
N712PR	**CL64**	**5313**
N712QS	GALX	073
N712R	LJ24	156
N712RD	JSTR	5005
N712RW	LJ25	296
N712S	C555	0035
N712SD	CL61	5024
N712SJ	LJ25	296
N712TA	BE40	RK-186
N712TE	JSTR	5070/52
N712TX	C750	0012
N712US	C500	044
N712US	FA10	110
(N712VE)	C500	640
N712VF	C500	640
N712VP	C750	0012
N712VS	HS25	25174
N712WB	**C750**	**0088**
N712WG	**EA50**	**000180**
(N713AG)	C56X	6032
N713AK	**HA4T**	**RC-72**
N713AL	C500	576
N713AZ	**PRM1**	**RB-111**
N713B	LJ25	201
N713DA	C560	0416
N713DF	C56X	5144
N713DH	C560	0376
N713DH	C560	0416
N713DH	C560	0549
N713DH	C56X	5144
N713DH	C56X	5527
N713DH	C56X	5700
N713DH	C56X	6050
N713DH	C555	0107
N713DJ	LJ25	355
N713FL	**C750**	**0074**
(N713G)	FA10	162
N713HC	**CL64**	**5308**
N713HC	HS25	258040
(N713HG)	CL64	5308
N713HH	C560	0192
N713HH	C555	0138
(N713HH)	C560	0092A
N713JD	**C500**	**450**
N713JL	**C52A**	**0004**
N713K	HS25	257094
N713KM	GLF3	432
N713KM	HS25	257094
N713L	**FA7X**	**13**
(N713L)	PRM1	RB-25
N713LJ	LJ25	241
N713M	LJ55	113
N713MC	**FA20**	**392/553**
N713MD	C510	0274
N713MR	SBRL	282-82
(N713PE)	FA20	113
N713Q	LJ25	105
N713QS	C650	7103
N713R	JSTR	5205
N713RJ	GLEX	9268
N713RL	HS25	257146
N713RR	LJ25	241
N713RX	LJ45	195
N713SA	C500	132
N713SC	ASTR	013
N713SC	**HS25**	**258712**
N713SD	**C525**	**0218**
N713SN	FA50	182
N713SS	HS25	25174
N713US	LJ25	015
(N713VL)	GLF4	1012
N713VP	C650	7103
(N713VP)	C650	7013
N713VT	GLF4	1012
N713WD	C52C	0117
N713WD	C560	0765
N713WD	**E55P**	**50500167**
N713WH	C525	0606
N713XP	HS25	258713
N714JS	**C52A**	**0213**
N714K	**FA7X**	**100**
N714K	LJ25	150
N714K	LJ35	230
N714KP	LJ25	150
N714RK	**F2TS**	**714**
N714RM	**C550**	**550-1057**
N714S	LJ35	367
N714TS	**LJ60**	**340**
(N714TS)	CL61	5014
N714US	C500	040
(N714VP)	C650	7014
N714X	LJ24	103
N715AB	C550	715
N715BC	C650	0018
N715BC	LJ24	029
(N715BD)	CL61	5091
N715BG	CL61	5164
N715CB	**FA50**	**301**
N715CG	**CL30**	**20537**
N715CG	LJ45	208
N715CJ	**HA4T**	**RC-8**
N715CX	C750	0015
N715DE	**E55P**	**50500191**
(N715DG)	C500	400
N715DL	**C52A**	**0481**
N715EK	C500	367
N715FJ	**FA7X**	**215**
N715GA	GALX	215
N715GB	**C680**	**0544**
(N715GW)	WW24	187
N715JC	**FA10**	**99**
N715JF	LJ25	132
(N715JM)	C500	367
N715JS	C500	001
N715JS	**C52A**	**0129**
N715LA	**HS25**	**258441**
N715MH	LJ25	132
N715MM	C56X	5528
N715MR	SBRL	282-40
N715MS	E55P	50500040
N715PH	HS25	258715
N715PS	C560	0055
(N715PS)	C550	118
N715QS	C650	7105
N715TA	BE40	RK-189
N715VP	C750	0015
(N715VP)	C650	7015
N715WE	**C680**	**0286**
N715WG	G150	205
N715WG	**GALX**	**186**
N715WG	HS25	258386
N715WS	**FA20**	**305**
N715WT	HS25	258386
N715XP	HS25	258715
N716AS	**GLF4**	**1119**
N716BB	HS25	258048
N716BB	WW24	118
N716BD	**LJ31**	**093**
N716BG	LJ60	236
N716CB	C500	055
N716CG	F2EX	174
N716CG	**FA7X**	**255**
N716CQ	**F2EX**	**174**
N716DB	C555	0120
N716DB	**HS25**	**258048**
N716DD	**C555**	**0120**
N716DV	**C52C**	**0049**
N716FJ	F2TS	716
N716FL	**C750**	**0073**
N716GA	C500	210
N716GC	C680	0197
N716GC	**F2EX**	**154**
N716GS	**PRM1**	**RB-199**
N716HP	CL61	3026
(N716JC)	FA10	113
N716JN	C56X	6079
N716JS	**C52A**	**0083**
N716LD	**C56X**	**5255**
N716LT	**C500**	**034**
N716MB	**C52B**	**0251**
N716NC	LJ25	264
(N716PT)	ASTR	032
N716QS	C650	7106
N716QS	GALX	148
(N716QW)	C555	0120
N716RD	CL61	5048
N716RD	JSTR	5005
N716RD	JSTR	5218
N716RJ	LJ60	403
N716S	**C560**	**0473**
N716SC	LJ45	016
N716SN	C525	0528
N716SX	C560	0281
N716TE	GLF2	116
N716US	LJ24	297
N716W	ASTR	016
N716WW	**CL30**	**20179**
N716XP	HS25	258716
N717	GLF3	401
N717	JSTR	5009
N717	JSTR	5202
N717A	GLF3	308
N717AF	HS25	257059
N717AJ	**LJ35**	**183**
N717AL	GLEX	9322
N717AL	**GLF4**	**1484**
N717AM	**LJ55**	**100**
N717AN	LJ25	272
N717BK	**LJ60**	**129**
N717BN	**CL65**	**5960**
N717CB	**C550**	**550-0830**
N717CB	C550	550-1007
N717CD	**C56X**	**5104**
N717CF	MU30	A033SA
N717CF	BE40	RK-177
N717CH	**C550**	**550-0825**
(N717CH)	BE40	RK-164
N717CP	ASTR	053
N717CW	LJ25	362
N717D	**C560**	**0275**
(N717DA)	C525	0087
N717DB	LJ24	179
N717DD	**E55P**	**50500019**
N717DD	BE40	RK-18
N717DD	BE40	RK-207
N717DD	BE40	RK-389
N717DF	MU30	A033SA
N717DM	C550	435
N717DS	LJ35	302
N717DT	C550	182
N717DW	BE40	RK-18
N717DX	GLF4	1493
N717DX	**GLF4**	**4107**
N717EA	WW24	305
N717EA	BE40	RK-354
N717EB	**LJ55**	**016**
N717EH	**C56X**	**6008**
N717EL	LJ60	410
N717EP	G150	222
N717EP	LJ25	255
N717EP	LJ55	016
N717EP	**LJ60**	**410**
N717ET	**C510**	**0443**
N717FF	**LJ60**	**213**
N717FH	C56X	6008
N717FH	**C680**	**680A0004**
(N717GF)	HS25	25047
N717GK	**C550**	**550-0971**
N717HA	**C52A**	**0079**
N717HB	LJ24	295
N717HB	**LJ55**	**066**
N717HD	**EA50**	**000113**
N717HE	LJ24	295
N717JB	LJ35	229
N717JB	LJ35	646
N717JB	LJ55	128
N717JB	LJ60	093
N717JJ	**CL30**	**20152**
N717JL	C500	527
N717JM	**C650**	**0138**
N717JM	JSTR	5009
N717KQ	C550	550-0971
N717KV	**HS25**	**258449**
N717LA	**F9EX**	**35**
N717LA	FA50	32
N717LA	WW24	305
N717LC	**C550**	**269**
N717LF	**FA50**	**32**
N717LK	**EA50**	**000064**
N717LS	C555	0054
N717LS	GLEX	9155
N717MB	C560	0007
N717MB	C56X	5114
N717MB	**C680**	**0084**
N717MK	**GLEX**	**9155**
N717MS	GLF3	335
N717MT	**HS25**	**258163**
N717NA	C525	0437
N717NB	**C56X**	**5694**
N717PC	C550	366
N717RA	C550	550-0825
N717RB	C500	449
N717TF	C550	550-0825
N717TF	GLEX	9028
N717TG	**BE40**	**RK-320**
N717TR	**C550**	**435**
N717TR	GLF3	418
N717VA	BE40	RK-21
N717VB	C52A	0137
N717VF	C550	550-1108
N717VL	C550	550-1108
N717VL	**C560**	**0788**
N717VL	MU30	A073SA
N717VL	BE40	RK-21
N717W	LJ35	147
N717WW	ASTR	017
N717X	JSTR	5009
N717X	JSTR	5202
N717XJ	**C750**	**0217**
N717XP	HS25	258717
N718AK	**F9EX**	**201**
N718AL	**C52A**	**0118**
N718AN	LJ60	065
N718CA	FA10	64
N718CG	CL30	20537
N718CK	**C550**	**402**
N718DW	FA50	81
N718DW	GLF4	1442
N718EA	LJ35	229
N718EC	GLF3	315
N718EJ	LJ40	2108
N718GA	GLF4	4318
N718GA	GLF5	5318
N718GM	GLF4	1294
N718HC	**HS25**	**258040**
N718JA	GLF2	66
N718JS	GLF2	66
N718JS	**GLF4**	**4164**
N718KS	F2TH	216
N718MC	**GLF5**	**5061**
N718MC	GLF5	549
N718MD	GLF5	549
N718MM	**F9EX**	**179**
N718MN	C680	0043
N718MV	**C52C**	**0041**
N718P	CL61	5127
N718PM	**F2TH**	**192**
N718QS	**GALX**	**136**
N718R	CL61	5127
N718R	JSTR	5147
N718R	JSTR	5205
N718RA	**LEG5**	**55000026**
N718RJ	GLEX	9586
N718RJ	LJ60	405
N718SA	C500	589
N718SJ	**HS25**	**258718**
N718SW	LJ35	179
N718TA	BE40	RK-195
N718US	LJ36	019
N718VA	C500	148
N718VA	C550	029
N718VP	C650	7018
N718XP	HS25	258718
N719A	GLF3	310
N719AL	FA10	25
N719CC	**WW24**	**290**
N719CG	LJ45	208
N719D	C525	0075
N719D	**PRM1**	**RB-25**
N719DW	FA50	308
N719EH	C550	572
N719EL	**BE40**	**RK-488**
N719GA	GLF2	79
N719HG	C650	0007
N719HG	**HS25**	**258488**
N719JB	LJ35	166
N719JB	**LJ60**	**288**
N719JE	LJ36	019
N719L	C525	0075
N719L	**C52C**	**0084**
N719L	PRM1	RB-25
N719QS	**GALX**	**162**
N719RM	**C560**	**0092**
N719SA	GLF2	154/28
N719SA	**GLF4**	**1155**
N719SH	**F9EX**	**119**
N719SQ	GLF2	154/28
N719TT	**C56X**	**5516**
N719US	LJ35	135
N719UW	**CL61**	**5046**
(N719WD)	C560	0765
N719WP	C52A	0202
N719XJ	**C750**	**0179**
N720AS	CL64	5653
N720AS	LJ25	017
N720BA	GLF4	1335
N720C	C500	073
N720CC	C550	720
N720CC	**C750**	**0050**
N720CC	LJ45	072
N720CH	**GLEX**	**9100**
N720CH	GLF4	1118
N720DF	**FA10**	**26**
N720DR	**GLF2**	**209**
N720E	GLF2	65
N720F	GLF2	66
N720G	GLF2	119/22
N720GB	**LJ45**	**072**
(N720GH)	LJ35	105
N720GL	LJ35	087
N720GM	C525	0350
N720HC	FA20	497
N720HG	CL65	5720
N720HW	**C680**	**0069**
N720J	SBRL	282-24
N720JC	FA20	273
N720JC	**HS25**	**257065**
N720JS	**GLF5**	**5114**
N720JW	GLF2	178
N720LF	GLF6	6197
N720LH	**GLF2**	**233**
N720LH	GLF4	1063
N720LM	CL61	5104
N720M	FA50	18
N720M	LJ35	183
N720M	LJ55	020
N720MC	LJ45	103
N720MC	WW24	358
N720ME	C650	0016
N720ME	F9EX	115
N720ME	FA50	48
N720ME	FA50	245
N720ML	C650	0016
N720ML	F9EX	115
N720ML	**F9EX**	**231**
N720ML	FA10	48
N720ML	FA20	262
N720ML	FA50	245
N720ML	WW24	147
N720MV	**E50P**	**50000180**
N720NP	F2TS	720
N720PT	**HS25**	**257032**
N720Q	GLF2	58
N720QS	GALX	085
N720R	SBRL	282-27
N720RA	LJ35	156
N720SJ	C560	0386
N720SL	C52A	0150
N720TA	HS25	258320
N720UA	LJ24	067
N720WC	C550	708
N720WS	**GLEX**	**9176**

N720WW	**LJ35**	**254**
N720WY	**F2EX**	**189**
N720XP	HS25	258720
N720XP	**BE40**	**RK-315**
N721AH	**LJ55**	**145**
N721AS	LJ35	101
N721AS	WW24	58
N721BS	F2TH	11
N721BS	GALX	110
N721BS	**GLF4**	**1516**
N721BS	LJ45	227
N721BW	CL61	5049
N721CC	C550	721
(N721CC)	C500	183
(N721CG)	C500	543
N721CJ	**GALX**	**047**
N721CM	LJ35	210
N721CN	**GLF2**	**206**
N721CP	GLF2	46
N721CP	LJ45	006
N721CR	JSTR	5150/37
N721CW	GLF3	485
(N721DG)	C56X	5297
N721DP	FA10	64
N721DR	C550	211
N721EC	**LJ35**	**355**
N721EE	**LEG5**	**55000046**
N721ES	**C52A**	**0452**
N721EW	CL61	5049
N721FA	BE40	RJ-21
N721FF	GLEX	9354
N721FF	GLF3	421
N721FF	GLF4	1484
N721FL	**C750**	**0091**
N721G	**CL61**	**5109**
N721GB	LJ24	005
N721GB	WW24	135
N721GB	WW24	71
N721GL	LJ24	335
(N721GS)	LJ55	021
N721HM	**F900**	**158**
N721HW	LJ24	005
(N721HW)	C500	324
N721J	CL64	5590
N721J	FA20	255/487
N721J	LJ24	200
(N721J)	LJ24	205
N721JA	LJ24	200
(N721JJ)	FA20	509
(N721KE)	HS25	258313
N721KJ	**GLF4**	**1534**
N721KY	HS25	258313
(N721KY)	CL61	5057
N721LH	HS25	256025
N721LR	CS55	0118
N721MA	C52B	0042
N721MA	C52B	0288
N721MA	**C52C**	**0107**
N721MA	EA50	000178
N721MC	CL61	5031
N721MC	GLF4	1110
N721MC	**GLF5**	**691**
N721MD	CL61	5031
(N721MD)	LJ24	195
N721MJ	**GLF4**	**4263**
N721MJ	LJ31	098
N721MJ	LJ60	159
N721MM	**GLF5**	**5370**
N721MM	GLF5	613
N721NA	EA50	000178
N721NB	**C560**	**0659**
N721PA	JSTR	5054/59
N721PL	GLF2	121
N721PP	**CL30**	**20579**
N721QS	GALX	092
(N721QS)	GALX	088
N721RB	GLF3	311
N721RL	GLF2	121
N721RL	**GLF4**	**1394**
N721RM	**HS25**	**256053**
N721RN	**C56X**	**5785**
N721S	CL61	5109
N721S	**GLF5**	**668**
N721SC	**C52A**	**0210**
N721SE	**LJ60**	**168**
N721SF	LJ24	325
N721SS	BE40	RK-34
N721ST	C650	0158
N721ST	CL60	1030
N721SW	CL60	1066
N721SW	CL61	5049
N721SW	GLF2	2
N721T	**C550**	**550-0993**
(N721TB)	C500	281
N721US	C500	579
N721US	C550	391
N721V	**GLF5**	**5412**
(N721V)	GLF5	5206
N721VT	C750	0167
N722A	HS25	258200
N722AW	WW24	154
N722AZ	ASTR	132
N722AZ	**FA7X**	**99**
N722AZ	WW24	351
N722CC	HS25	258008
N722CM	C650	7022
(N722CX)	C750	0022

N722DJ	**CL60**	**1029**
(N722DM)	LJ24	224
(N722ED)	SBRL	282-56
N722EM	LJ25	372
N722FD	SBRL	282-56
N722FS	FA50	216
N722GA	GALX	222
N722GA	GLF6	6022
N722GL	LJ35	092
N722HP	CL60	1039
N722HP	CL61	3054
N722JB	**F2TH**	**13**
N722JS	LJ31	109
N722KS	FA20	130
N722MK	**FA50**	**222**
N722MM	GLF4	1052
N722MM	GLF4	4086
N722MN	GLF4	4086
N722NB	**PRM1**	**RB-280**
N722NK	BE40	RK-230
N722Q	**MS76**	**009**
N722QS	GALX	093
N722SG	**C525**	**0088**
N722SM	**C52A**	**0338**
N722ST	SBRL	282-56
N722SW	**G150**	**230**
N722TA	HS25	258322
N722TD	**EA50**	**000224**
N722TP	GLF2	92
N722TS	**C52A**	**0138**
N722US	C500	253
N722W	WW24	159
(N722W)	WW24	306
N722XJ	**C750**	**0222**
N723AB	**GLEX**	**9207**
N723BH	C650	0127
N723CC	**LJ55**	**036**
N723GB	**E50P**	**50000111**
N723GL	LJ35	107
N723H	LJ55	090
N723HA	CL61	5165
N723HA	CL65	5718
N723HC	**LJ60**	**420**
N723HH	CL61	5165
N723HH	GLEX	9325
N723HH	**GLEX**	**9508**
N723HH	HS25	258232
N723J	GLF2	87/775/6
N723JA	CL30	20088
N723JB	WW24	37
N723JM	C500	563
N723JM	**CL30**	**20418**
(N723JM)	WW24	363
N723JR	**C500**	**584**
N723JW	LJ24	142
N723JW	LJ24	178
N723K	WW24	330
N723L	WW24	349
N723LF	LJ25	087
N723LK	**HS25**	**258155**
N723LL	LJ24	216
N723LL	LJ28	29-002
N723LL	LJ35	277
N723M	WW24	237
N723MC	**CL30**	**20123**
N723MM	GLF3	357
N723MM	**GLF4**	**4077**
N723QS	GALX	099
N723R	SBRL	306-11
N723R	WW24	272
N723RE	C550	550-0944
N723SG	**C52B**	**0368**
N723ST	JSTR	5023
N723TA	HS25	258349
N723TS	HS25	25191
N723US	LJ35	311
N723XP	HS25	258723
N724AA	BE40	RJ-22
N724AF	**GLEX**	**9031**
N724AG	**GLF5**	**656**
N724AS	FA10	83
N724B	**HS25**	**257006**
N724BP	C52B	0303
N724CC	C750	0062
(N724CC)	C500	203
N724CJ	LJ60	322
N724CP	FA20	319
N724CP	**BE40**	**RK-263**
N724CV	C52B	0259
N724DB	GLF3	372
N724DB	GLF4	1209
N724DB	**GLF4**	**1420**
N724DD	GLF3	372
N724DD	GLF4	1209
N724DL	**C510**	**0078**
N724DS	FA10	92
N724DS	**FA20**	**198/466**
N724EA	C500	387
N724EA	**HS25**	**257090**
N724EB	C550	550-1113
N724EB	LJ60	346
N724EF	**LJ60**	**388**
N724EH	C550	550-1113
N724EH	CL30	20613
N724EH	LJ60	346
N724EH	LJ60	388
N724FS	C525	0387

N724FS	**LJ31**	**231**
N724GL	LJ24	347
N724HB	BE40	RJ-55
N724J	LJ55	092
N724JC	FA20	310
N724JK	**CS55**	**0115**
N724JS	LJ60	168
(N724JS)	FA20	379
N724KW	BE40	RK-263
N724LG	LJ24	143
N724MF	CL64	5631
N724MF	**GLEX**	**9457**
N724MH	**E55P**	**50500221**
N724MH	BE40	RK-263
N724ML	EA50	000220
N724MV	**GLEX**	**9117**
N724PB	**C52B**	**0303**
N724QS	GALX	100
N724RM	**C680**	**0314**
N724RN	**E50P**	**50000146**
N724SC	**CL30**	**20072**
N724SJ	**CL30**	**20039**
N724TN	LJ25	216
N724TS	**HS25**	**25192**
N724XP	HS25	258724
N725AF	GLF5	5330
(N725AF)	GLF5	5305
N725AT	**C52A**	**0332**
N725BA	C550	431
N725BF	C550	431
N725BH	**LJ40**	**2101**
N725CC	**C550**	**725**
N725CC	HS25	257027
N725CF	C525	0141
N725CF	CL30	20186
N725CG	**C525**	**0869**
N725CJ	**FA10**	**25**
N725CS	HS25	258758
N725DM	**FA10**	**184**
N725DM	LJ25	328
(N725DM)	C500	131
(N725DM)	LJ24	305
N725DS	**C550**	**550-0822**
N725DT	**C750**	**0023**
N725DW	HS25	25134
N725EE	**LEG5**	**55000021**
N725FL	C550	431
N725GL	LJ24	348
N725JA	HS25	258297
N725JB	**C510**	**0030**
N725JG	FA20	416
N725JS	**LJ25**	**156**
N725K	LJ55	093
N725L	C525	0140
N725LB	FA50	46
N725LB	GLEX	9129
N725LB	GLF4	1296
N725MK	**JSTR**	**5123/14**
N725MM	GLF5	5161
N725MN	**GLF5**	**5161**
N725MW	E50P	50000084
N725N	**CL30**	**20292**
N725P	FA10	169
N725P	FA20	72/413
N725P	LJ35	167
(N725P)	FA20	306/512
N725PA	FA10	155
N725PA	FA50	104
N725PA	FA50	204
N725PA	FA50	23
N725PA	FA50	236
N725QS	GALX	105
N725RH	C550	006
N725RH	**C650**	**0106**
(N725RH)	C500	503
N725SC	LJ60	083
N725ST	LJ35	285
N725T	BE40	RK-273
N725TA	HS25	258297
N725TM	**C52B**	**0488**
N725WH	C650	0097
N725WH	HS25	25042
(N725WH)	HS25	257015
N725XL	**C56X**	**5725**
N726AF	**GLEX**	**9352**
N726AG	**C52B**	**0029**
N726AM	C550	726
(N726BB)	C500	517
N726BM	C550	726
N726CC	HS25	25116
N726CL	C525	0420
N726DC	**F2EX**	**50**
N726DC	GALX	058
N726DR	**GALX**	**058**
N726EL	LJ45	327
N726EP	HS25	258139
N726GL	LJ25	222
N726JG	FA50	258
N726JR	SBRL	370-4
N726L	LJ55	098
N726MF	**CL65**	**5902**
N726MP	LJ31	233
N726MR	FA10	35
N726PG	**BE40**	**RK-337**
N726QS	**GALX**	**108**
N726R	SBRL	282-83
N726RK	F2TS	726

N726RP	**C52A**	**0114**
N726RW	**GLF4**	**1039**
N726SC	**C525**	**0051**
N726TA	HS25	258363
N726TM	**C525**	**0414**
N726WR	**LJ25**	**007**
N726XJ	**C750**	**0226**
(N726XL)	C56X	5726
N726XP	HS25	258726
(N727AL)	CS55	0043
N727AT	**WW24**	**284**
N727AW	**C650**	**0132**
N727AW	LJ25	313
N727BG	**LJ60**	**218**
N727BT	LJ31	082
N727C	C550	368
N727C	C550	485
N727CM	C550	727
N727CP	LJ31	009
N727CS	LJ25	313
N727CW	**EA50**	**000159**
N727EE	C500	048
N727EF	**CS55**	**0043**
N727FJ	**CL30**	**20088**
N727GL	LJ35	127
N727GW	**F900**	**169**
N727HD	**EA50**	**000115**
N727HE	ASTR	036
N727JP	LJ35	189
N727KG	PRM1	RB-113
N727KG	PRM1	RB-143
N727KG	**BE40**	**RK-260**
N727LE	C500	048
(N727LG)	LJ24	143
N727LJ	LJ25	028
N727LM	**LJ25**	**308**
N727MC	C500	677
N727MG	LJ35	320
N727MH	C56X	5549
N727MH	PRM1	RB-158
N727ML	**PRM1**	**RB-158**
N727NA	CS55	0043
N727PR	**GLF5**	**613**
N727QS	GALX	113
N727R	SBRL	282-42
N727S	CL61	5062
N727S	FA50	17
N727SJ	CL30	20039
N727SJ	LJ60	147
N727TA	HS25	257003
N727TE	**GLF5**	**5223**
N727TK	**C500**	**141**
N727TS	FA10	76
N727TX	**C650**	**0118**
N727US	SBRL	380-61
N727YB	**C52B**	**0171**
N727YB	C56X	5332
N728AZ	ASTR	132
N728AZ	WW24	351
N728C	SBRL	465-71
N728CC	C550	728
N728CL	**LJ31**	**109**
N728CM	C650	7028
N728CP	GLF3	875
N728CX	C750	0028
N728EC	C56X	5815
N728EC	**GLF5**	**5439**
N728EF	**BE40**	**RK-598**
N728FJ	**F2TS**	**728**
N728GH	F900	3
N728GL	LJ35	133
N728JC	FA20	399
N728JP	CL64	5553
N728JP	GLF4	1297
N728JR	**CL65**	**5847**
N728JW	HS25	257129
N728KA	HS25	25224
N728L	WW24	349
N728LB	FA50	46
N728LB	**GLF4**	**1296**
N728LM	WW24	341
N728LW	**FA50**	
N728LW	**WW24**	**341**
N728MB	**WW24**	**419**
N728MC	C500	507
N728MC	WW24	147
N728MG	LJ55	004
N728MM	GLF4	4147
N728MN	**GLF4**	**4147**
N728MP	LJ35	481
N728PX	JSTR	5112/7
N728QS	GALX	116
(N728RX)	C500	194
(N728SA)	FA10	71
N728SB	LJ45	254
N728T	GLF2	82
N728TA	**HS25**	**258364**
N728TG	**WW24**	**420**
N728US	C500	171
N728VG	**LJ45**	**274**
N728XP	HS25	258728
N729AG	HS25	258729
N729AT	**HS25**	**258402**
N729DM	CL65	5711
N729EZ	HS25	258171
N729GL	LJ24	338
N729HS	LJ35	481

N729HZ	CL61	5107
N729HZ	**CL65**	**5749**
N729HZ	HS25	258171
N729JE	E55P	50500081
N729JF	E55P	50500081
N729JF	**HA4T**	**RC-32**
N729JM	**CL30**	**20121**
N729JM	LJ45	380
N729JV	LJ45	380
N729KF	CL64	5513
N729KF	GLEX	9172
N729KF	**GLEX**	**9452**
N729KG	PRM1	RB-143
N729KP	CL64	5513
N729KP	GLEX	9172
N729LJ	LJ60	298
N729MJ	C550	303
(N729MJ)	C550	151
N729MM	**LEG5**	**55000031**
N729PX	C500	433
N729QS	GALX	118
N729S	FA20	173
N729SB	CL30	20208
N729SB	LJ45	254
N729TA	C550	483
N729TA	HS25	258374
N729TY	**GLF4**	**1141**
N729VP	**C750**	**0029**
N729XP	HS25	258729
(N730AA)	HS25	257061
(N730AS)	CL64	5606
N730BA	GLF4	1290
(N730BG)	HS25	258191
N730BR	C550	730
N730CA	SBRL	282-103
N730CA	SBRL	306-145
N730CA	**WW24**	**295**
N730CJ	**HS25**	**259019**
N730CP	SBRL	282-103
N730DF	**ASTR**	**067**
N730EA	**GLF5**	**5449**
N730FL	**C750**	**0078**
N730GA	**C52B**	**0396**
N730GA	GLF4	4230
N730GL	LJ36	025
N730H	HS25	257150
N730HB	HS25	HB-30
N730LM	**F9EX**	**101**
N730M	LJ60	048
N730MS	PRM1	RB-103
N730PV	FA10	106
N730PV	WW24	36
N730QS	GALX	120
N730R	SBRL	282-43
N730RA	**FA20**	**347**
N730RJ	C500	143
N730S	FA20	247
N730SA	F900	155
N730TA	HS25	258383
(N730TC)	C550	333
N730TK	GLF2	140/40
N730TL	CL60	1084
N730TS	HS25	25201
N730V	FA20	319
(N730VP)	C550	730
N731A	JSTR	5011/1
N731AE	GLF4	1173
N731AE	GLF5	634
(N731AE)	FA20	344/534
N731AG	JSTR	5070/52
N731AS	FA20	344/534
(N731BF)	CL30	20073
N731BP	**C56X**	**5802**
N731BW	HS25	25075
N731CW	LJ25	117
N731DC	CL30	20073
N731DD	FA50	64
N731DL	HS25	257048
N731F	FA20	113
N731F	FA50	45
(N731F)	FA20	344/534
N731FJ	F9EX	160
N731FJ	F9EX	163
N731FJ	FA10	3
N731G	FA20	267/491
N731G	HS25	25153
N731G	HS25	25195
N731GA	C650	0076
N731GA	**LJ31**	**024**
N731GA	LJ35	001
N731GA	LJ35	003
N731GA	LJ36	028
(N731GA)	HS25	257122
N731H	HS25	25278
N731HS	HS25	25214
N731HS	HS25	25229
N731HS	HS25	25253
N731JR	HS25	25286
N731JR	HS25	258183
N731JS	JSTR	5006/40
N731KC	HS25	25118
N731L	JSTR	5095/30
N731MS	HS25	25239
N731PS	BE40	RK-543
N731QS	GALX	123
N731RA	LJ31	102
N731RA	**LJ35**	**328**

N731RG	FA20	168
N731RG	FA20	388
(N731RG)	FA20	113
N731RJ	LJ60	406
N731SR	**F9EX**	**94**
N731TA	BE40	RK-273
N731TC	**HS25**	**258039**
(N731TC)	HS25	256024
N731TH	HS25	HB-31
N731TR	**C560**	**0411**
N731UG	PRM1	RB-70
(N731WB)	HS25	25264
N731WH	**C52B**	**0112**
N731WL	JSTR	5070/52
N731X	HS25	25244
N732AA	**HS25**	**258243**
N732AC	**E55P**	**50500070**
N732AM	**FA50**	**278**
N732FL	**C750**	**0114**
N732GA	GALX	132
N732GA	GLF5	5320
N732GA	GLF5	5432
N732HB	HS25	HB-32
N732JR	C56X	5503
N732JR	**C56X**	**6099**
N732LH	LJ60	021
N732M	**C525**	**0685**
N732M	JSTR	5084/8
N732PA	**CL65**	**5916**
N732RJ	**LJ60**	**407**
N732S	FA20	272
N732TS	HS25	25203
N732WB	**BE40**	**RK-403**
N733A	C650	0234
N733A	CL61	3008
N733A	**F2EX**	**235**
N733A	F900	126
N733A	HS25	258687
N733AU	C650	0234
N733CF	**C510**	**0458**
N733CF	CL60	1041
N733CF	CL61	5057
N733CJ	**C52B**	**0057**
N733DB	**HS25**	**HA-0033**
N733E	FA50	128
N733E	**LJ55**	**057**
N733EX	CL61	5113
N733EY	CL61	5113
N733EY	LJ55	057
(N733EY)	GLEX	9063
N733FL	**C750**	**0027**
N733G	**FA50**	**340**
N733GA	GLF5	5233
N733H	C550	081
N733H	C560	0137
N733H	C650	0210
N733H	**F2EX**	**219**
N733H	HS25	257018
N733H	HS25	258590
N733HL	F900	126
N733JB	**FA20**	**256**
N733K	C650	0222
N733K	CL60	1041
N733K	FA50	242
N733K	HS25	25285
N733K	HS25	258137
N733K	HS25	258645
N733L	HS25	258645
N733LX	FA7X	133
N733M	C560	0249
N733M	FA50	242
N733M	**FA50**	**343**
N733M	HS25	257092
N733MK	BE40	RK-107
N733N	FA50	242
N733R	SBRL	282-51
N733S	FA20	292
N733SW	**LJ60**	**007**
N733TA	HS25	258337
N734	LJ55	051
(N734)	LJ55	048
N734AK	HS25	25014
N734DB	**C560**	**0143**
N734DB	FA20	500
N734S	FA10	13
N734S	FA20	316
(N734S)	FA20	299
N734TJ	**GLF3**	**392**
N735A	LJ35	323
(N735A)	C650	0234
N735GA	GLF4	4235
N735GA	BE40	RJ-42
N735HC	C650	0158
N735TA	BE40	RK-274
N735XL	**C56X**	**5733**
N735XP	HS25	HB-35
N736FL	**C750**	**0039**
N736LB	C52A	0203
N736LE	HS25	25207
N736R	SBRL	282-82
(N736US)	WW24	192
N737CC	C650	7037
N737D	**C56X**	**5638**
N737E	SBRL	282-26
N737EF	LJ25	037
N737FL	**C750**	**0103**
N737FN	LJ24	171

N737KB	C680	0047
N737MM	**C650**	**7113**
N737MM	BE40	RJ-35
N737QS	GALX	127
N737R	SBRL	282-33
N737R	SBRL	282-66
N737RJ	**C500**	**649**
N737X	HS25	257052
N738DC	C510	0151
N738E	**CL30**	**20410**
N738GL	LJ25	038
N738K	C650	0222
N738QS	**GALX**	**204**
N738R	SBRL	282-40
N738RH	FA20	24
N738RJ	**LJ60**	**409**
N738TS	GLEX	9038
N739CX	C750	0038
N739E	**CL30**	**20446**
N739LN	**C525**	**0541**
N739QS	**GALX**	**198**
N739R	SBRL	282-78
N739TA	BE40	RK-199
N739TA	BE40	RK-257
N739XP	HS25	258739
N740AC	**FA7X**	**52**
N740AC	LJ55	084
N740AK	**C52C**	**0032**
N740BA	GLF5	516
N740DM	**EA50**	**000205**
N740E	LJ24	222
N740E	LJ31	061
N740E	LJ45	023
N740EJ	LJ24	222
N740F	LJ24	222
N740F	LJ31	061
N740GA	GLF4	4140
N740GA	GLF5	5140
N740GA	GLF5	5340
N740GL	LJ24	353
N740J	LJ24	077
N740JA	GLF4	1074
N740JB	C550	353
(N740JB)	C525	0182
N740JS	**C52A**	**0207**
N740JV	C525	0252
N740K	GLF4	1094
N740K	LJ25	302
N740KD	**LJ40**	**2083**
N740KG	**LJ40**	**2063**
N740L	FA20	7
N740LM	**F9EX**	**74**
N740QS	**GALX**	**194**
N740R	FA50	247
N740R	SBRL	282-47
N740R	SBRL	306-112
N740R	SBRL	465-14
N740RC	SBRL	306-112
(N740SG)	LJ45	023
N740SS	GLF3	369
N740SS	**GLF5**	**532**
N740TA	BE40	RK-123
N740TF	**LJ45**	**074**
N740VC	**GLF3**	**454**
N740VP	C750	0040
N740XP	HS25	258740
N741AK	**WW24**	**292**
N741AM	JSTR	5236
N741C	WW24	292
N741CC	**C525**	**0227**
N741E	LJ25	036
N741E	LJ25	100
N741E	LJ31	070
N741E	LJ35	508
N741E	LJ45	011
N741E	**LJ45**	**367**
N741ED	LJ25	036
N741F	LJ25	100
N741F	LJ31	070
N741F	LJ35	508
N741F	LJ45	011
N741FJ	FA7X	41
N741GL	LJ24	350
N741JB	C500	213
N741JC	C550	346
N741MR	FA20	312
N741MT	SBRL	276-34
N741PC	**C52A**	**0066**
N741PP	C550	550-0965
N741QS	GALX	212
N741R	SBRL	306-143
N741R	SBRL	306-28
N741R	SBRL	465-24
N741RC	SBRL	306-143
N741RD	BE40	RK-432
N741RL	SBRL	306-28
N741SP	**F2EX**	**207**
N741T	**C550**	**394**
N741TA	BE40	RK-201
N741TS	CL65	5741
N741VR	**HS25**	**258741**
N741WY	**C525**	**0875**
N742AR	**C52B**	**0074**
N742AW	**C680**	**0511**
N742E	**CL30**	**20231**
N742E	LJ25	096
N742E	LJ31	071

N742E	LJ35	630
N742E	LJ45	025
N742F	LJ31	071
N742F	LJ45	025
N742GA	G280	2042
N742GA	GLF4	4142
N742GL	LJ35	140
N742JS	**C52A**	**0241**
N742K	C500	236
N742K	SBRL	306-45
N742P	LJ35	630
N742QS	GALX	227
N742R	FA50	243
N742R	SBRL	306-142
N742R	SBRL	306-45
N742R	SBRL	465-28
N742RC	SBRL	306-142
N742TA	BE40	RK-202
N742TS	GLF2	142
N742XP	HS25	258742
N742Z	LJ25	096
N743CC	C650	0181
N743DB	C560	0479
N743DB	**C560**	**0622**
N743E	LJ25	169
N743E	LJ31	068
N743E	LJ45	016
N743E	**LJ45**	**370**
N743F	LJ25	169
N743F	LJ31	068
N743F	LJ45	016
N743GL	LJ35	141
N743HB	HS25	HB-43
N743JA	**C56X**	**6032**
N743JG	**C52A**	**0056**
N743PB	**WW24**	**286**
N743QS	**GALX**	**216**
N743R	SBRL	306-11
N743TA	BE40	RK-271
N743UP	SBRL	306-22
(N743UP)	HS25	258069
N743UT	HS25	25118
N744AT	**C550**	**021**
N744C	BE40	RK-331
N744CC	FA20	313
N744CC	FA20	347
N744CC	HS25	25142
N744CF	LJ24	082A
N744DB	LJ60	053
N744DC	C550	009
N744DC	HS25	257146
N744E	LJ31	069
N744E	LJ35	203
N744E	**LJ45**	**348**
N744GA	G150	244
N744GA	G280	2044
N744GA	GLF5	5244
N744GL	LJ35	126
N744JC	CL65	5744
N744JC	LJ24	323
N744JR	WW24	198
N744LC	LJ25	232
N744MC	LJ25	120
N744N	**LJ31**	**069**
N744P	LJ35	203
N744R	C560	0291
N744R	SBRL	282-72
N744RD	**LJ60**	**053**
N744SD	GLEX	9173
N744SW	C550	009
N744TA	BE40	RK-245
N744UT	JSTR	5147
N744W	LJ25	008
N744WW	C560	0143
N744X	FA50	58
N744XP	**HS25**	**258744**
(N745BD)	C680	0241
N745CC	C550	550-1051
(N745CW)	C750	0145
N745DB	C680	0241
N745DM	C500	131
N745DM	JSTR	5201
N745E	LJ35	294
N745E	LJ45	008
N745E	**LJ45**	**356**
(N745EA)	C650	0158
N745F	LJ24	077
N745F	LJ35	294
N745GA	G150	245
N745GA	GLF5	5450
N745GL	LJ36	032
(N745HG)	HS25	25084
N745K	**LJ45**	**245**
(N745K)	LJ45	402
N745KD	**LJ45**	**384**
N745QS	**GALX**	**170**
N745RP	**C750**	**0517**
N745RS	GLF4	1063
N745SA	LJ45	052
N745TA	BE40	RK-145
N745TC	**LJ45**	**260**
N745TH	HS25	257095
N745TM	F9EX	64
N745TS	HS25	25220
N745TT	**LJ45**	**099**
N745UP	GLF4	1054
N745UP	**HS25**	**258336**

N745UP	SBRL	306-39
(N745UP)	HS25	258072
N745UR	GLF4	1054
N745US	C500	025
N745VP	C650	7045
N745W	LJ24	108
N745W	LJ25	030
N745W	LJ25	177
(N745WG)	HS25	25236
N745XP	HS25	258745
N746BC	HS25	257004
N746BR	C650	7046
N746CM	C650	7046
N746CX	**C52A**	**0064**
N746CX	C750	0046
N746E	**CL30**	**20207**
N746E	LJ35	297
N746F	LJ35	297
N746GA	G150	259
N746GL	LJ35	157
(N746JB)	C525	0404
N746PC	**C56X**	**6192**
N746TA	BE40	RK-146
N746TS	HS25	257046
N746UP	HS25	258069
N746UP	HS25	258522
N746UP	SBRL	306-22
N746UT	JSTR	5225
N747	CL64	5305
N747	FA50	146
N747	FA50	50
N747	SBRL	282-22
N747AC	**C525**	**0202**
N747AC	FA10	166
N747AE	GLF5	5065
N747AH	**C525**	**0304**
N747AN	LJ25	272
N747AN	LJ55	121
N747BK	PRM1	RB-29
(N747BL)	C500	306
N747BW	**LJ35**	**594**
N747CC	C680	0056
N747CP	C555	0077
N747CP	**LJ35**	**502**
N747CR	C550	643
N747CX	**FA20**	**442**
N747DP	**LJ60**	**251**
N747E	SBRL	282-22
N747G	GLF2	49
N747G	GLF3	381
N747GB	JSTR	5141
N747GL	LJ35	171
N747GM	LJ35	308
(N747GP)	C555	0077
N747GV	**C560**	**0367**
N747HN	C52A	0099
(N747HR)	C52C	0002
N747HS	C52C	0002
N747JB	C550	617
N747JJ	**C52A**	**0314**
N747JX	**GLF2**	**33**
N747KE	**C52B**	**0015**
N747KL	C555	0010
N747KL	**F2EX**	**175**
(N747KL)	C500	345
N747KR	C52B	0015
N747KR	C52C	0002
N747KS	**C510**	**0280**
N747LA	**C52C**	**0110**
N747LB	WW24	55
N747LG	**EA50**	**000235**
N747LV	CL61	3034
N747NB	GLF2	20
N747NB	GLF2	33
N747NG	HS25	258417
N747NL	C510	0427
N747R	SBRL	282-48
N747RC	C680	0002
N747RC	SBRL	306-34
N747RL	C500	345
N747RL	C560	0554
N747RL	C680	0002
N747RL	C555	0010
N747RL	F2EX	175
N747RL	**FA7X**	**158**
(N747RL)	LJ35	308
N747RR	**BE40**	**RK-95**
(N747RT)	C550	588
N747RX	**C750**	**0508**
N747RY	**LJ35**	**243**
N747SC	GLF6	6089
N747SC	LJ24	019
N747SG	LJ60	109
(N747SG)	GALX	087
N747T	FA20	81
N747TS	CL61	3057
N747TS	CL64	5347
N747TX	C650	7046
N747UP	HS25	258072
N747UP	SBRL	282-45
N747UP	SBRL	306-39
N747V	FA20	461
N747W	FA20	5
N747WA	C500	301
N747XJ	**C750**	**0247**
N747Y	CL64	5305

N747Y	FA50	50
N748CX	**C52B**	**0005**
N748DC	C550	136
(N748DC)	C560	0054
N748FB	HS25	257129
N748FJ	FA7X	48
N748GA	GLF5	5248
N748GL	LJ35	172
N748GM	LJ24	311
N748JX	**GLF3**	**377**
N748MN	**GLF2**	**215**
N748QS	**GALX**	**157**
N748RB	C56X	6008
N748RE	C52A	0215
N748RE	C56X	6008
N748RE	**F2TS**	**708**
N748RF	C52A	0215
N748RM	C52B	0056
N748T	GLF3	388
N748TA	BE40	RK-222
N748TS	**HS25**	**25224**
N748VA	C500	148
N748W	**C56X**	**5531**
N748XP	HS25	258748
N749BA	CL65	5749
N749CM	C650	7049
N749CP	C525	0158
N749CP	C650	0163
N749CP	FA50	200
N749CP	FA50	300
N749CP	**GLF5**	**646**
N749DC	C560	0370
N749DC	C650	0169
N749DX	C750	0046
N749DX	C750	0173
N749FB	C550	550-0952
N749FF	C550	550-0952
N749GA	**ASTR**	**149**
N749GL	LJ25	242
N749GP	F2TH	52
N749MC	WW24	8
N749MP	WW24	8
N749P	**C750**	**0046**
N749QS	**GALX**	**165**
N749RH	BE40	RK-326
N749RL	C560	0554
N749SS	**LJ60**	**252**
N749SS	BE40	RK-240
N749TA	BE40	RK-149
N749TT	**C560**	**0248**
N749UP	SBRL	306-129
N750AB	BE40	RK-50
N750AC	GLF3	422
(N750AG)	C750	0022
N750AJ	**BE40**	**RK-278**
N750BA	GLF5	558
N750BL	**C750**	**0178**
N750BM	CL60	1012
N750BP	**C750**	**0111**
N750BR	**FA50**	**131**
N750CC	SBRL	465-37
N750CK	**C650**	**7015**
N750CR	**LJ45**	**123**
(N750CR)	C750	0248
N750CS	SBRL	465-37
N750CT	**C750**	**E750-716001**
N750CW	**C750**	**0008**
N750CX	**C750**	**703**
(N750D)	HS25	25015
N750DD	**C750**	**0185**
N750DF	FA50	140
N750DM	C750	0146
N750DX	**C750**	**0263**
N750EA	**C750**	**0188**
N750EC	**C750**	**0007**
N750EL	**HS25**	**HB-18**
N750FA	HS25	HB-9
N750FB	C650	7049
N750FJ	FA50	218
N750FL	**C560**	**0268**
N750GA	ASTR	150
N750GA	GLF5	5350
N750GA	**GLF5**	**5550**
N750GB	**C750**	**0504**
N750GF	**C750**	**0244**
N750GL	LJ35	173
N750GM	**C750**	**0066**
N750GM	HS25	25075
N750GM	HS25	257058
N750GS	**C750**	**0152**
N750GT	CL61	3002
N750H	**FA50**	**171**
N750HB	HS25	HB-1
N750HH	**C750**	**0284**
N750HM	**HS25**	**HB-35**
N750HS	C750	0103
N750J	C750	0051
N750JB	C750	0063
N750JC	FA50	162
N750JJ	C750	0065
N750JM	**C555**	**0045**
N750JT	**C750**	**0302**
N750KH	**HS25**	**HB-12**
(N750KP)	BE40	RJ-58
N750LA	C500	398
N750LA	C500	570

N750LC	E55P	50500290
N750LG	**CL61**	**5192**
N750LM	C750	0039
N750LQ	FA50	162
N750MC	FA50	202
N750MD	C750	0150
N750ME	**C750**	**0248**
N750ME	FA20	262
N750ML	**C560**	**0247**
N750NA	**C750**	**0104**
N750NS	C750	0172
(N750PB)	HS25	258187
N750PM	CL60	1012
N750PP	C500	686
N750PT	**C750**	**0068**
N750PT	C750	0109
N750PT	C750	0222
(N750QK)	LJ24	065
N750QS	**GALX**	**185**
N750R	FA20	187
N750RA	**GLF2**	**117**
N750RB	**C750**	**0059**
N750RL	C750	0025
N750RM	LJ35	019
N750RT	C750	0140
N750RV	HS25	258187
N750SB	HFB3	1031
(N750SB)	WW24	198
N750SC	**E55P**	**50500299**
N750SG	**HS25**	**HB-63**
N750SL	**C52A**	**0150**
N750SL	C550	554
N750SP	WW24	198
N750SS	FA20	6
N750SW	**GLF3**	**338**
N750T	BE40	RK-70
N750TA	**BE40**	**RK-226**
N750TB	**C550**	**579**
N750TJ	MU30	A006SA
N750TJ	MU30	A081SA
N750TX	**C750**	**0150**
N750VM	**HS25**	**HB-69**
N750VP	**C750**	**0022**
N750VR	C750	0050
(N750WC)	HS25	25115
N750WJ	LJ24	065
N750WM	C750	0230
N750WR	**C750**	**0172**
N750WS	**C750**	**0234**
(N750XB)	C750	0058
N750XJ	**C750**	**0250**
N750XX	C750	0094
N750XX	**C750**	**0192**
N751AC	**LJ35**	**101**
N751AJ	C750	0143
N751BC	GALX	049
N751BC	**GALX**	**132**
N751BG	**C680**	**0181**
N751BH	C750	0059
N751BP	LJ31	208
N751CA	LJ25	122
N751CC	C500	266
N751CF	C560	0274
N751CR	WW24	88
N751CT	**C750**	**0501**
N751CX	C750	0001
N751DB	CL60	1075
N751EL	C750	0061
N751EM	**C750**	**0254**
N751GA	ASTR	151
N751GA	GLF5	5351
N751GA	GLF5	5501
N751GL	LJ35	162
N751GM	**C750**	**0207**
N751JC	FA50	129
N751JC	**LJ45**	**134**
N751LJ	**LJ45**	**503**
N751MM	**C750**	**0146**
N751MT	**HS25**	**258751**
N751MZ	GLF3	426
N751NS	**HS25**	**HB-23**
(N751NS)	HS25	HB-1
(N751NS)	HS25	HB-2
N751PJ	MS76	051
N751PL	**C56X**	**5237**
N751PT	C750	0247
N751TA	BE40	RK-225
N752AC	LJ35	121
N752AR	**HS25**	**HA-0024**
N752BA	GLF5	640
N752BP	LJ60	184
N752CA	LJ25	137
N752CC	C550	
019		
N752CE	**C560**	**0752**
N752CK	**C500**	**255**
N752CM	C650	7052
N752CM	**HS25**	**257082**
N752CS	**HS25**	**258323**
N752CX	C750	0002
N752DS	GLEX	9052
N752EA	**LJ25**	**137**
(N752EL)	C750	0047
N752GL	LJ25	251
N752GM	C750	0276
N752GS	C550	285
N752HB	HS25	HB-2
N752JC	**FA50**	**28**
N752JH	C560	0442
N752KP	C52C	0091
(N752LX)	HS25	258397
N752M	**CL30**	**20210**
N752MT	**HS25**	**258752**
N752NS	**HS25**	**HB-28**
N752NS	HS25	HB-3
(N752NS)	HS25	HB-2
N752PT	C750	0250
N752QS	**GALX**	**152**
N752R	**LJ45**	**485**
N752RT	C550	070
N752S	**F2TH**	**82**
N752SC	HS25	HA-0175
N752TA	HS25	258397
N752TX	**C750**	**0511**
(N752VP)	C750	0002
N753A	**LJ45**	**528**
(N753BB)	C560	0306
N753BC	GALX	049
N753BD	C560	0306
N753BD	C750	0118
N753BP	LJ60	238
N753CA	LJ25	136
N753CC	C550	120
N753CE	C560	0753
N753CJ	C52B	0001
N753G	HS25	258162
N753GA	GLF5	5372
N753GJ	**C560**	**0306**
N753GL	LJ35	186
(N753GL)	C560	0306
N753JC	FA50	25
N753JL	**C56X**	**5274**
N753MB	**C560**	**0028**
N753MS	**C680**	**0267**
N753NS	**HS25**	**HB-29**
(N753NS)	HS25	HB-7
N753PT	C750	0256
N753S	F2TH	88
N753TA	BE40	RK-230
N753TW	SBRL	380-45
N753XJ	**C750**	**0053**
N754AA	C550	200
N754AE	HS25	258754
N754AE	**HS25**	**HA-0171**
N754AF	HS25	258754
N754BA	GLF5	5007
N754CA	LJ25	090
(N754CM)	C650	7054
N754CX	C750	0004
N754DB	LJ25	014
N754G	HS25	258171
N754GL	LJ35	197
N754JB	GLF2	105
N754M	LJ24	185
N754PT	C750	0257
N754RL	**C52C**	**0173**
N754S	FA50	39
N754SE	C750	0001
N754TA	HS25	258406
N754TS	GLEX	9254
N754V	C56X	5544
N754WS	LJ35	197
N755A	**ASTR**	**103**
N755BB	F2TH	163
N755BP	C550	361
N755CL	**LJ55**	**074**
N755CM	C550	033
N755CM	C650	7055
N755CM	WW24	257
(N755CS)	GLF4	1331
N755FL	**F2TH**	**96**
N755GL	LJ35	187
N755GW	HS25	25233
N755LL	**C680**	**0039**
N755PA	ASTR	015
N755PA	**GALX**	**042**
N755PT	C750	0258
N755QS	**GALX**	**168**
N755RA	**GLEX**	**9468**
N755RV	CL64	5370
N755S	GLF2	20
N755TA	HS25	258410
N755TA	BE40	RK-311
N755TA	BE40	RK-324
(N755TS)	HS25	257055
N755VE	**GLF5**	**5055**
N755VT	**LJ55**	**142**
N755WJ	HS25	25233
N756	FA20	388
N756	HS25	25102
N756	JSTR	5154
N756M	HS25	25102
N756N	HS25	25161
N756N	HS25	257182
N756S	GLF3	348
N756XJ	**C750**	**0256**
N757AL	LJ35	130
N757AL	WW24	72
N757BD	ASTR	036
N757BL	**HS25**	**258088**
N757C	HS25	257017
N757CE	BE40	RK-86
N757CK	C560	0028
N757CP	**C52A**	**0069**
N757CX	FA20	408
N757E	SBRL	282-50
N757EG	C680	0017
N757EM	C52A	0422
N757GA	G150	211
N757GA	GLF5	5357
N757GS	**HS25**	**258624**
N757M	HS25	256022
N757M	HS25	257017
N757M	**HS25**	**258101**
N757MB	C650	7035
N757MC	CL60	1016
N757MC	CL61	5177
N757MC	**GLF4**	**1498**
N757P	HS25	256022
N757PC	**C52B**	**0188**
N757PL	**GLF5**	**5249**
N757R	SBRL	282-49
N757T	C750	0014
N757TR	**C560**	**0598**
N757WS	BE40	RK-169
N757XJ	**C750**	**0257**
N757XP	HS25	258757
N758CC	**CL64**	**5353**
N758CP	**C56X**	**5577**
N758CX	**C750**	**0058**
N758GA	GLF5	5358
N758JA	**LJ35**	**497**
(N758PM)	C560	0208
N758QS	**GALX**	**178**
N758S	C550	401
N758SL	**C550**	**554**
N758XJ	**C750**	**0258**
N758XL	C56X	5758
N759A	GLF2	131/23
(N759FS)	LJ31	231
N759G	**C52A**	**0513**
N759R	C525	0524
N759R	C52A	0086
N759R	C52A	0513
N759R	**C52C**	**0203**
(N759R)	C52A	0506
N759SB	**C510**	**0403**
N759SH	**LJ60**	**143**
N759WR	GLF5	5063
N760	C550	302
N760	**F9EX**	
N760A	**GLF3**	**428**
(N760A)	LJ25	051
N760AA	LJ60	423
N760AC	GLF3	377
N760AC	LJ55	017
N760AC	LJ60	017
N760AG	GLEX	9358
N760AQ	LJ55	017
N760AR	**MS76**	**108**
N760BP	C750	0025
N760C	GLF3	430
N760C	MS76	043
N760C	WW24	174
N760CC	GLF5	5100
N760CF	LJ60	007
N760CG	GLF5	5100
N760DE	JSTR	5101/15
N760DE	JSTR	5214
N760DL	JSTR	5101/15
N760DL	JSTR	5214
N760DL	LJ35	155
(N760DL)	FA50	41
N760E	MS76	102
N760ED	**C56X**	**5201**
N760EW	C650	0056
N760F	**MS76**	**058**
N760FB	**MS76**	**069**
N760FM	MS76	111
N760FR	MS76	072
N760G	GLF3	428
N760G	GLF4	4039
N760G	LJ55	107
N760GA	GLF5	5460
N760GL	LJ35	206
N760H	MS76	005
N760J	MS76	006
N760JR	**ASTR**	**111**
N760JS	**MS76**	**088**
N760LB	**C650**	**0076**
(N760LB)	MS76	005
N760LP	LJ35	155
N760M	**C550**	**635**
N760M	MS76	049
N760MM	MS76	002
N760N	MS76	103
N760NB	CS55	0046
N760NE	**EA50**	**000034**
N760NS	HS25	HB-34
N760P	MS76	104
N760PJ	**MS76**	**027**
N760PJ	MS76	101
N760PT	C750	0260
N760Q	MS76	105
N760R	MS76	104
N760RA	**FA20**	**432**
(N760RE)	C56X	5201
N760S	**MS76**	**043**
(N760SA)	SBRL	306-76
N760T	MS76	103
N760TA	HS25	258413
N760U	GLF2	75/7
N760WF	**C560**	**0760**
N760X	**MS76**	**028**
N760XJ	**C750**	**0260**
N761A	LJ36	022
N761JP	C510	0045
N761JS	MS76	082
N761KG	C52A	0227
N761LE	**GLF6**	**6108**
N761NS	HS25	HB-43
N761PA	**C510**	**0374**
N761QS	**GALX**	**176**
N761TA	BE40	RK-161
N761X	**MS76**	**030**
N761XP	**HS25**	**258761**
N762BG	BE40	RK-57
N762CC	**LEG5**	**55000006**
N762DL	**EA50**	**000215**
N762EL	**LJ45**	**107**
N762GA	GLF5	5462
N762GL	LJ36	026
N762GS	GLF3	413
N762JP	**HS25**	**HA-0032**
N762L	LJ36	033
(N762L)	LJ36	026
N762MS	**GLF6**	**6008**
N762PF	C550	247
N762QS	**CL30**	**20502**
N762XP	HS25	258762
N762XP	HS25	HB-62
N763AJ	**BE40**	**RK-21**
N763CJ	C52B	0002
N763D	C560	0007
N763DB	**GLF4**	**1114**
N763F	C510	0276
N763FJ	FA7X	63
N763GA	GLF5	5363
N763GL	LJ35	113
N763J	GLF3	304
N763JA	**C680**	**680A0024**
N763JJ	GLF4	4064
N763JS	**MS76**	**092**
N763MT	**CL30**	**20206**
(N763PD)	GLF2	139/11
N763QS	**CL30**	**20510**
N763R	LJ36	034
N763RR	ASTR	024
N764C	C525	0325
N764CE	C560	0764
N764G	LJ35	406
N764GA	GLF5	5164
N764GA	GLF5	5364
N764JA	**C56X**	**6122**
N764JS	MS76	093
N764KF	LJ25	234
N764LA	FA20	211
N764PT	C750	0264
N764QS	**CL30**	**20517**
N764RH	LJ25	210
N764XJ	**C750**	**0264**
N764XP	HS25	258764
N765A	**ASTR**	**011**
N765A	GLF2	111
N765A	GLF4	1069
N765CT	C52A	0002
N765DF	**C52C**	**0075**
N765F	**C560**	**0771**
N765JS	MS76	094
N765KC	**MU30**	**A079SA**
N765M	**GALX**	**124**
N765PT	C750	0265
N765QS	**CL30**	**20523**
N765RM	**GLF4**	**1170**
N765SG	GLF5	665
N765TS	**HS25**	**25263**
(N765W)	C650	7065
N765WG	**C560**	**0461**
N765WM	**GALX**	**115**
N765WS	**GALX**	**161**
N765WT	**CL61**	**5039**
N765XJ	**C750**	**0265**
N766	JSTR	5154
N766AB	BE40	RK-208
N766AE	C550	231
(N766AF)	C550	231
N766AJ	LJ31	103
N766CE	C560	0766
N766CG	C650	7066
(N766CH)	HS25	258543
N766DD	GLF3	483
N766FT	C500	014
N766GA	**GLF6**	**6166**
N766HK	**FA50**	**161**
N766LF	**C52B**	**0461**
N766MH	**C650**	**0015**
N766NB	CS55	0156
N766NW	FA20	66
N766QS	**CL30**	**20526**
N766R	SBRL	282-1
N766RA	**FA20**	**360**
N766WC	GLF3	413
N767AC	FA20	349
N767AC	WW24	356
N767AG	FA20	349
N767AG	FA20	479
N767AZ	LJ55	136
N767BS	**C56X**	**5191**
N767CB	**GLF3**	**397**
N767CF	F900	105
(N767CJ)	HS25	259036
N767CS	PRM1	RB-142
N767CW	**GLF5**	**520**
N767DT	GLF4	4065
N767DX	GLF4	4065
N767EL	GLF4	1141
N767FL	GLF2	50
N767FL	GLF4	
1141		
N767FL	**GLF5**	**503**
N767GA	GLF5	5367
N767HB	HS25	HB-67
N767JH	SBRL	282-98
N767KC	**C560**	**0517**
(N767LC)	HS25	
25170		
N767LD	**C560**	**0222**
N767NY	LJ55	136
N767PC	C500	080
N767PJ	**FA20**	**512**
(N767PW)	EA50	000265
N767QS	**CL30**	**20533**
N767RA	LJ36	023
N767SA	LJ25	216
N767SB	BE40	RK-355
N767SC	LJ25	023
(N767TR)	C550	401
N767W	C52A	0168
(N767W)	FA50	82
N767WB	**F900**	**132**
N767XJ	**C750**	**0067**
N767XP	HS25	258767
N767Z	JSTR	5009
N767Z	JSTR	5023
N768DV	SBRL	306-79
N768E	**CL64**	**5603**
N768HB	HS25	HB-68
N768J	FA20	440
N768J	GLF3	304
N768J	GLF4	
1119		
N768JF	**EA50**	**000030**
N768JJ	GLF4	4064
N768JJ	**GLF5**	**5217**
N768JW	F2TH	72
N768LP	C56X	6110
N768LP	**C56X**	**6124**
N768LR	C56X	6110
N768NB	C650	0180
N768QS	**CL30**	**20534**
N768R	C525	0471
N768TA	BE40	RK-168
N768TX	**C56X**	**5768**
(N768V)	FA20	440
N768XP	HS25	258768
N769BH	FA10	60
N769CA	**LJ28**	**28-004**
N769CC	CL65	5769
(N769CM)	C650	7069
N769CP	FA50	200
N769CS	**C560**	**0769**
N769DS	LJ60	052
(N769EG)	SBRL	465-9
(N769EW)	C500	669
N769H	C550	183
N769HB	HS25	HB-69
N769JW	**F2EX**	**205**
N769JW	F2TH	72
N769K	C500	228
N769KC	SBRL	465-9
N769M	**WW24**	**344**
N769MS	G150	252
N769MS	**GALX**	**190**
N769MS	WW24	344
N769PT	C750	0269
N769QS	**CL30**	**20539**
N769SC	FA10	7
N769XJ	**C750**	**0269**
N769XP	HS25	258769
N770AC	GLF2	57
N770AC	LJ25	209
N770AF	**C500**	**208**
N770AF	C650	0119
N770AG	GLEX	9355
N770AQ	LJ25	209
N770AZ	**HS25**	**257046**
N770BB	C550	606
N770BC	**CL64**	**5352**
N770BC	LJ60	203
(N770BC)	HS25	25078
N770BG	LJ60	203
N770BM	**LJ35**	**654**
N770BM	**LJ60**	**289**
N770BQ	CL64	5352
N770BR	**E50P**	**50000077**
N770BX	C525	0524
N770CA	CL60	1042
N770CC	HS25	257108
N770CC	**HS25**	**258587**
N770CC	LJ31	058
N770CH	LJ31	222
N770CK	**C56X**	**5257**
N770DA	HS25	25142
N770DR	JSTR	5219
N770DS	LJ45	077

N770E	FA50	21
N770EC	E50P	50000077
N770FF	ASTR	054
N770FF	**CL64**	**5469**
N770FG	**FA20**	**116**
N770GA	GLF3	470
N770GA	GLF5	5170
N770GE	CL61	5113
N770GF	C650	0013
N770GS	**HS25**	**HB-3**
N770HB	HS25	HB-70
N770HS	HS25	257191
(N770JB)	LJ60	225
N770JC	CL60	1061
N770JD	**FA50**	**148**
N770JJ	WW24	296
N770JM	C550	072
N770JM	C550	550-0902
N770JM	C56X	5370
N770JM	LJ55	039
N770JP	**LJ35**	**210**
N770JR	JSTR	5037/24
N770JT	**HS25**	**258254**
N770KS	**GLF4**	**1093**
N770LE	**C52C**	**0095**
N770LM	**FA7X**	**262**
N770MC	FA20	330
N770MD	**SBRL**	**465-26**
N770MH	C500	364
N770MP	C650	0118
N770MP	**F2TH**	**99**
N770MP	FA50	161
N770MR	C650	0118
N770MS	**CL64**	**5491**
N770PA	GLF2	175
(N770PA)	LJ25	209
N770PC	**LJ60**	**318**
N770PC	MU30	A080SA
N770PJ	HS25	257077
N770QS	**CL30**	**20543**
N770RG	**HS25**	**259025**
N770RR	FA20	272
N770SC	**ASTR**	**054**
N770SC	GLF4	1056
N770SW	**CL64**	**5309**
N770SW	HS25	258131
N770TB	C550	471
(N770TB)	BE40	RJ-14
N770TE	EA50	000013
N770TJ	HS25	257175
N770UM	C550	550-0902
N770UP	ASTR	120
(N770VP)	C650	7070
N770VR	C560	0770
N770WL	WW24	57
N770X	**LJ60**	**336**
N770XB	**GLF4**	**4117**
N770XJ	**C750**	**0270**
N771A	C550	034
N771A	LJ35	303
N771AA	C550	317
(N771AC)	WW24	191
N771AT	F2TH	217
N771AV	**GLF4**	**1197**
N771B	WW24	258
N771CB	LJ25	326
N771CP	ASTR	077
N771DE	**C56X**	**5591**
N771DM	**C52B**	**0210**
N771DV	**F2EX**	**106**
N771EL	BE40	RK-4
N771EM	**C52A**	**0217**
N771ES	**C510**	**0344**
N771GA	GALX	131
N771GD	CL60	1023
N771HB	HS25	HB-71
N771HM	**FA50**	**318**
N771HR	C500	206
N771JB	C650	0214
(N771JG)	GLF4	1013
N771JT	**GLF5**	**5089**
N771KB	**C510**	**0351**
N771LD	FA20	59
N771MT	**EA50**	**550-0273**
N771PM	**C56X**	**5799**
(N771R)	C550	163
N771RS	FA7X	162
N771SB	LJ35	401
N771ST	C550	021
N771SV	HS25	258391
N771TF	GLEX	9175
N771WB	SBRL	306-29
N771WW	CL60	1018
N771WW	SBRL	306-29
N771WY	C550	292
N771XJ	C750	0071
N772AA	C560	0136
(N772AC)	C550	106
N772AV	**GLF4**	**1015**
N772C	C500	180
N772CS	**C560**	**0772**
N772GA	GLF5	5272
N772GA	GLF5	5327
N772HB	HS25	HB-72
N772HP	C550	262
N772JS	**CL30**	**20153**
(N772KC)	C560	0072
N772M	CS55	0041
N772MC	**F2EX**	**150**
N772MC	F2TH	79
N772PP	**LJ60**	**293**
N772PT	C750	0272
N772QS	**CL30**	**20551**
N772SB	**C550**	**498**
N772TA	HS25	258428
N772XJ	**C750**	**0272**
N773A	CL61	5169
N773AA	HS25	25175
N773AJ	GLF4	1225
N773AJ	GLF5	5232
N773AW	WW24	232
N773CA	C550	550-0840
N773DL	LJ35	174
N773EJ	WW24	153
N773FR	C500	410
N773HA	**C650**	**7082**
N773HB	HS25	HB-73
N773HR	HS25	258836
(N773HS)	FA20	44
N773JC	CL61	3029
N773JC	GLF4	1066
N773JC	HS25	256001
N773LP	C500	450
N773LP	C550	399
N773LP	LJ35	362
N773LR	C500	450
N773M	C650	0093
N773MJ	GLF4	1225
N773MJ	GLF5	5232
N773MJ	**GLF6**	**6048**
N773RC	**CL30**	**20448**
N773RS	LJ40	2046
N773SW	**LJ60**	**254**
N773TA	BE40	RK-279
N773V	FA20	264
N773VP	C550	730
N773W	SBRL	380-20
N773WB	WW24	112
N774AB	LJ36	025
N774AK	GLF3	339
N774AR	**C510**	**0077**
N774CA	C525	0141
N774CC	C560	0774
N774CC	LJ45	380
N774CZ	C750	0074
N774EC	HS25	25281
N774GE	**C525**	**0457**
N774GF	HS25	257207
N774HB	HS25	HB-74
N774KD	C550	550-0820
N774KD	**PRM1**	**RB-188**
N774KK	GLEX	9290
N774MB	GLF3	339
N774MC	F2TH	79
N774MC	**LJ45**	**032**
N774PC	CL61	5094
N774QS	**CL30**	**20554**
N774RC	**HDJT**	**42000020**
N774SB	**C560**	**0684**
N774ST	**C510**	**0245**
N774TS	**HS25**	**25281**
N774W	SBRL	380-37
N774WF	**HS25**	**258774**
N774XJ	**C750**	**0274**
N774XP	HS25	258774
N775CM	**PRM1**	**RB-279**
N775DF	ASTR	132
(N775JC)	WW24	205
N775M	**C650**	**7017**
N775QS	**CL30**	**20557**
(N775RB)	HS25	258636
N775RP	**CL65**	**5821**
N775ST	**F2TH**	**43**
N775TA	BE40	RK-276
N775TB	**C525**	**0075**
N775TF	**C52A**	**0393**
N775TM	F2TS	711
N775US	GLF5	535
N776BG	**LJ35**	**659**
N776DF	**C525**	**0111**
N776DS	FA20	76
N776GM	**C650**	**0124**
N776JB	**GLF4**	**4042**
(N776JK)	MS76	043
N776JM	JSTR	5036/42
N776JS	**ASTR**	**138**
N776JS	LJ35	476
(N776JS)	C500	227
N776K	MS76	043
N776LB	C52A	0191
N776MA	GLF2	166/15
N776MA	GLF3	447
N776MA	**GLF4**	**1257**
N776PH	LJ31	201
N776PT	C750	0276
N776QS	**CL30**	**20558**
N776RB	**GLF5**	**585**
N776RS	**HS25**	**258776**
(N776TS)	HS25	257076
N776US	GLF4	1146
N776VP	**C56X**	**5776**
N776WR	**C560**	**0459**
N776XJ	C750	0276
N777	**FA50**	**260**
N777AG	**C52A**	**0238**
N777AJ	C500	495
N777AL	**C650**	**0201**
N777AM	**ASTR**	**038**
N777AM	CS55	0014
N777AN	C500	027
N777AT	C56X	5792
N777AX	**CS55**	**0149**
N777AY	JSTR	5201
N777BF	E50P	50000041
(N777CB)	LJ60	086
N777CF	WW24	231
N777CJ	C52A	0182
N777CJ	WW24	177
(N777CR)	SBRL	306-27
N777CX	**C750**	**0072**
N777DB	**CL64**	**5502**
N777DB	HS25	258551
N777DC	FA20	91
N777DC	MU30	A045SA
N777DC	MU30	A072SA
N777DC	**WW24**	**410**
N777DM	LJ35	297
N777DY	C52A	0189
N777DY	**C680**	**0247**
N777EG	FA20	146
N777EH	**HS25**	**257020**
N777EN	C560	0777
N777EP	JSTR	5004
N777EW	C52B	0359
N777FA	FA20	7
N777FB	C550	443
N777FC	C500	038
N777FC	**FA20**	**508**
N777FD	CS55	0099
N777FE	C500	498
N777FE	C550	443
N777FE	C560	0076
N777FE	**BE40**	**RJ-30**
N777FF	**CL64**	**5463**
N777FH	C560	0076
N777FH	C56X	5148
N777FJ	FA10	154
N777FL	ASTR	124
N777FL	C550	064
N777FL	**G150**	**214**
N777FL	BE40	RK-223
N777FL	BE40	RK-4
N777FN	C560	0076
(N777FN)	CL64	5463
N777FZ	**ASTR**	**124**
N777G	**BE40**	**RK-540**
N777GA	**CL60**	**1056**
N777GA	HS25	25146
N777GC	BE40	RK-86
N777GD	C680	0334
N777GD	CL60	1023
N777GD	HS25	25186
N777GF	CS55	0090
N777GG	C500	495
N777GG	CS55	0012
N777GG	GLF2	8
N777GU	**CL61**	**5084**
N777GV	GLF5	508
N777GX	GLEX	9036
N777GZ	**GLEX**	**9143**
N777HD	**WW24**	**397**
N777HN	C52A	0099
N777HN	C52B	0357
N777HN	**C56X**	**6204**
(N777HN)	CS55	0111
N777J	**CL64**	**5433**
(N777JA)	LJ24	163
N777JE	C550	723
N777JF	FA20	18
N777JF	FA20	249
N777JF	**PRM1**	**RB-105**
N777JJ	**C500**	**056**
N777JJ	FA10	35
N777JJ	MU30	A006SA
N777JM	C500	056
N777JQ	**E50P**	**50000072**
N777JS	GLF2	77
N777JV	C56X	5342
N777KK	CL60	1082
N777KK	**GLF4**	**1429**
N777KY	C560	0108
N777KZ	CL60	1082
N777LB	**C52B**	**0369**
N777LB	LJ24	216
N777LB	LJ35	473
N777LB	LJ35	476
N777LD	**LJ35**	**314**
N777LF	C650	0034
N777LF	LJ25	087
N777LF	LJ35	449
N777LU	WW24	350
N777LX	**C56X**	**5736**
N777MC	LJ24	217
N777MC	LJ35	125
N777MC	LJ55	081
N777MC	**LJ60**	**180**
N777MG	PRM1	RB-20
N777MH	WW24	34
N777MJ	FA50	115
N777MJ	MU30	A085SA
N777MN	F2TH	147
N777MQ	LJ24	217
N777MQ	LJ55	081
N777MQ	PRM1	RB-20
N777MR	LJ24	142
N777MS	**CL30**	**20168**
(N777MS)	C650	7098
N777MW	GLF3	485
N777MX	**C650**	**0051**
N777ND	BE40	RK-71
(N777ND)	FA10	130
N777NG	C550	550-0992
N777NJ	C52B	0009
N777NJ	**C52B**	**0099**
N777NJ	LJ25	173
(N777NJ)	C550	394
N777NQ	LJ35	125
(N777NZ)	GLF4	1212
N777PD	LJ25	138
N777PQ	HFB3	1050
N777PS	HFB3	1050
N777PV	FA20	137
N777PV	HFB3	1050
N777PY	GLF5	508
N777PZ	HFB3	1050
N777PZ	JSTR	5128/16
(N777QE)	C500	302
N777QG	F9EX	245
N777QL	**LJ45**	**216**
N777QP	C52A	0241
N777QS	**CL30**	**20562**
N777QX	**CL65**	**5761**
N777RA	LJ25	005
N777RA	LJ35	285
N777RB	**C560**	**0052**
N777RF	**FA10**	**179**
N777RN	**HS25**	**25027**
N777RW	**GLF2**	**184**
N777RY	GLF3	327
N777RZ	GLF3	398
N777SA	GLF4	1081
N777SA	GLF4	1138
N777SA	HS25	25224
N777SA	HS25	256015
N777SA	HS25	256055
N777SA	LJ24	228
N777SA	LJ25	201
(N777SA)	F9EX	165
(N777SC)	C500	140
N777SG	JSTR	5074/22
(N777SG)	E50P	50000014
N777SJ	**CL30**	**20436**
N777SK	SBRL	465-24
N777SL	**C500**	**307**
N777SL	SBRL	282-135
(N777SL)	GLF3	252
N777SN	FA10	13
(N777ST)	SBRL	282-82
N777SW	GLEX	9037
N777SW	GLF2	81
N777SW	GLF3	306
N777SW	GLF4	1014
N777SW	GLF4	1149
N777SW	GLF5	514
N777TC	GLF4	1137
N777TE	FA20	500
N777TE	LJ24	031
N777TF	LJ24	031
N777TK	HS25	256015
N777TX	FA20	365
N777TX	**LJ25**	**084**
(N777TX)	GLF2	62
N777TY	GLF5	508
N777UE	GLF4	1146
N777UT	**C680**	**0048**
N777UU	C550	550-1003
N777UV	**FA50**	**176**
N777V	FA20	264
N777V	GLF2	120
N777V	SBRL	282-69
N777V	WW24	12
N777VC	CL30	20016
N777VC	HS25	259031
N777VC	LJ60	207
N777VC	LJ60	318
N777VE	EA50	000011
N777VE	**EA50**	**550-0283**
N777VG	PRM1	RB-208
N777VQ	LJ60	207
N777VU	GLEX	9037
N777VW	**HS25**	**258169**
N777VZ	SBRL	282-69
N777WJ	FA20	142
N777WJ	FA20	65
N777WJ	JSTR	5215
N777WJ	WW24	72
N777WL	FA20	65
N777WY	C550	292
N777WY	**C560**	**0525**
N777XS	**C650**	**0008**
N777XX	CL60	1017
N777XX	CL61	5104
N777XX	CL61	5152
N777XX	FA20	150/445
N777XY	**F900**	**27**
N777XY	FA50	176
N777YC	LJ55	120
N777YG	CL61	5172
(N777YL)	LJ31	033D
N777YY	**LJ60**	**054**
N777ZA	E50P	50000117
N777ZC	C650	0153
N777ZL	**FA50**	**46**
N777ZY	**EA50**	**000109**
N778BC	**C510**	**0380**
N778BC	C560	0657
N778BC	C56X	5517
N778BS	C52B	0327
N778C	C550	169
(N778CC)	HS25	258587
N778CR	**GLF4**	**4056**
N778EC	C525	0806
N778FW	C560	0442
N778GA	GLF5	5328
N778GA	LJ24	143
N778GM	LJ25	078
(N778HS)	HS25	257191
N778JA	**HS25**	**25285**
N778JC	**C550**	**363**
N778JC	LJ25	078
N778JE	**C510**	**0236**
N778JM	C550	072
N778LC	C510	0380
N778LC	C525	0806
N778LC	**C52B**	**0460**
N778MA	C52A	0222
N778MT	GLF4	1108
N778PT	C750	0278
N778QS	**CL30**	**20563**
N778S	HS25	25179
N778SC	**C680**	**680A0029**
N778SM	HS25	25047
(N778T)	LJ45	259
N778TC	**EA50**	**000085**
N778VW	**EA50**	**000063**
N778W	GLF3	413
N778W	GLF4	1023
(N778W)	GLF4	1146
N778XJ	**C750**	**0278**
N778XX	CL61	3017
N778XX	CL61	5003
(N778XX)	CL60	1077
N778YY	CL61	3017
N778YY	CL61	3023
N779AF	C650	0136
N779AZ	C650	0136
N779AZ	CL61	5176
N779AZ	**GLF4**	**4089**
N779CF	**LJ40**	**2087**
N779CM	**LJ36**	**018**
N779CS	GLF4	4076
N779CS	**SBRL**	**465-29**
N779DC	**MU30**	**A072SA**
N779DD	C550	333
N779JS	**C52B**	**0036**
N779KD	**C550**	**550-0820**
N779LC	**GLF2**	**88/21**
N779P	FA20	122
N779QS	C650	7079
N779QS	**CL30**	**20566**
N779RB	C525	0637
N779RK	**C560**	**0779**
N779SG	F900	46
N779SW	GLF4	1014
N779VP	C650	7079
N779WA	**GLF5**	**511**
N779WG	CL64	5356
N779XJ	**C750**	**0279**
N779XX	CL61	3018
N779YY	CL61	3032
N779YY	CL61	5043
N780A	HS25	258084
N780A	LJ25	056
N780A	LJ35	302
N780AB	**C525**	**0073**
N780AC	LJ25	173
(N780AJ)	C525	0073
N780AQ	LJ25	173
N780BF	C560	0207
N780CC	C56X	5597
N780CE	C560	0780
N780CF	**C550**	**015**
N780CS	C56X	5168
N780DC	**C525**	**0910**
N780E	GLF4	1165
N780E	**GLF5**	**5258**
N780F	FA50	240
N780F	**GLF5**	**5261**
N780F	GLF5	530
N780GT	C550	015
N780GT	C650	0222
N780GT	BE40	RJ-55
N780HC	CL61	5070
N780JS	**C52B**	**0043**
N780LS	GLF4	1009
N780N	GLF4	1165
(N780PM)	GLF2	207/34
N780PT	C750	0280
N780PV	WW24	36
N780QS	C650	7080
N780QS	**CL30**	**20568**
N780RA	GLF3	472
N780RH	GLF3	472
N780RH	GLF4	1498
N780RH	JSTR	5095/30

(N780SC)	HS25	256018
N780SP	**F900**	**93**
N780TA	HS25	258437
N780TP	BE40	RK-136
N780W	**GLF5**	**530**
N780XJ	**C750**	**0280**
N781AJ	FA20	98/434
N781B	FA50	116
N781CE	C560	0781
N781EX	F2EX	187
N781JR	HS25	25286
N781JS	**C52B**	**0045**
N781KB	PRM1	RB-103
N781L	C500	355
N781QS	C650	7081
N781QS	**CL30**	**20570**
N781RS	LJ35	218
N781RX	**LJ45**	**015**
N781SC	C550	398
N781SC	LJ60	336
N781TA	HS25	258281
N781TP	BE40	RK-231
N781W	FA20	257
N782BJ	**CL30**	**20164**
N782CC	**C650**	**7030**
N782GA	GLF5	5182
N782JR	LJ35	336
(N782JR)	LJ25	316
N782JS	**C52B**	**0059**
(N782NA)	C550	376
N782PC	WW24	339
N782PT	C750	0282
N782QS	C650	7082
N782QS	**CL30**	**20561**
N782RP	**F900**	**116**
N782SF	**GLEX**	**9392**
N782ST	**C550**	**679**
N782TA	HS25	258282
N782TP	**BE40**	**RK-243**
N782VP	C650	7082
N782XJ	**C750**	**0282**
N782XP	HS25	258782
N783A	CL61	3008
N783DM	CL61	3005
N783FS	**F2TH**	
N783FS	**WW24**	**319**
N783H	C550	081
N783H	C650	0210
N783JS	**C52B**	**0033**
N783KK	**C500**	**350**
N783M	HS25	257092
N783MB	**GLF5**	**602**
N783QS	**CL30**	**20574**
N783SL	**FA7X**	**169**
N783TA	BE40	RK-234
N783XJ	**C750**	**0083**
N783XL	C56X	5783
N784A	C550	465
N784AE	HS25	25084
N784AM	**LJ31**	**106**
N784B	FA50	118
N784BX	**F2TH**	**56**
N784CC	**LJ40**	**2052**
N784CE	FA10	78
N784JP	**E50P**	**50000074**
N784JS	**C52B**	**0050**
N784KS	**E50P**	**50000178**
(N784LB)	LJ31	215
N784MA	**PRM1**	**RB-141**
N784PT	C750	0284
N784QS	**CL30**	**20575**
N784TA	BE40	RK-237
N784XJ	**C750**	**0084**
N784XJ	C750	0284
N784XP	HS25	258784
N785AD	**F2EX**	**146**
N785B	LJ55	043
N785BC	**LJ40**	**2129**
N785CA	C550	184
N785CA	HS25	258001
N785CC	C650	7085
N785DR	LJ60	289
N785DW	**C56X**	**5137**
N785JM	LJ35	655
N785JS	**C52B**	**0082**
N785MT	**C52A**	**0419**
N785QS	C650	7085
N785QS	**GLF5**	**5157**
N785RC	**C680**	**0040**
N785TA	BE40	RK-239
N785VC	**HS25**	**258785**
N785XP	HS25	258785
N786AC	**C52A**	**0312**
N786AD	F2EX	147
N786AF	**C510**	**0273**
N786CC	**LJ45**	**095**
N786CM	**GLF4**	**1176**
N786CS	**FA7X**	**31**
(N786CW)	GLF5	520
N786FG	CL30	20142
N786JB	GLF4	1092
N786JS	**C52B**	**0030**
N786MS	LJ25	033
N786QS	**CL30**	**20590**
N786SC	LJ60	347
N786TA	BE40	RK-248
N786TT	**C56X**	**5786**
N786TX	C56X	5786
N786XJ	**C750**	**0286**
N786YA	LJ31	215
N786ZS	HA4T	RC-32
N787AD	**FA7X**	**73**
(N787AF)	GLF4	1414
N787BA	C500	143
N787BN	**G150**	**231**
N787CA	**HS25**	**HB-43**
N787CH	**LJ45**	**266**
N787CM	HS25	258271
N787CV	**C650**	**7037**
N787CW	C560	0779
(N787CW)	C750	0147
N787EJ	LJ45	190
N787EV	**C52B**	**0397**
N787FF	HS25	HB-2
N787GT	**LJ55**	**128**
N787JC	HS25	258727
N787JD	C550	589
N787JJ	**C52C**	**0010**
N787LC	LJ60	398
N787LD	LJ60	248
N787LG	**CL64**	**5626**
N787LP	LJ35	670
N787LP	LJ60	087
N787LP	LJ60	248
N787LP	**LJ60**	**398**
N787PJ	**E50P**	**50000258**
N787PR	GALX	138
N787QS	C650	7087
N787QS	**CL30**	**20595**
N787R	SBRL	282-76
N787R	SBRL	306-16
N787R	SBRL	306-77
(N787RA)	F2TH	11
N787RP	WW24	358
N787TA	BE40	RK-260
N787WB	JSTR	5210
N787WC	C550	471
N787X	HS25	25037
N787XJ	C750	0287
N788AC	GLF6	6046
N788BA	C650	0116
N788C	GLF2	165/37
N788CE	C560	0788
N788CG	**F9EX**	**79**
(N788CW)	C750	0038
N788DR	LJ24	084
N788FS	**WW24**	**319**
N788JB	**C52A**	**0080**
N788JS	**C52A**	**0216**
(N788JS)	JSTR	5231
N788MA	WW24	311
N788MM	**CL30**	**20105**
N788MM	LJ60	016
N788MP	C525	0645
N788NB	C650	0155
N788QC	LJ35	609
N788QS	**CL30**	**20607**
N788R	SBRL	282-68
N788S	GLF2	30/4
N788S	JSTR	5110/47
N788SC	CL64	5391
N788SS	C500	433
N788WG	CL60	1069
N788WG	HS25	257026
N788ZJ	**GLEX**	**9716**
N789A	ASTR	092
N789AA	LJ24	309
(N789AA)	C500	445
N789AH	LJ40	2002
N789AT	GALX	004
N789BA	**HS25**	**257168**
N789BR	C550	036
N789CA	**ASTR**	**074**
N789CN	C56X	5070
N789DD	C500	560
N789DD	MU30	A015SA
(N789DD)	C500	249
(N789DD)	C550	137
(N789DD)	WW24	187
N789DJ	**MU30**	**A015SA**
N789DK	C500	560
N789DK	GLF4	1054
N789DR	CL61	3001
N789DT	**PRM1**	**RB-176**
N789FF	GLF2	31
N789H	**C680**	**0041**
(N789H)	LJ45	003
N789HU	**C56X**	**6081**
N789JC	FA50	66
N789KG	**C56X**	**5538**
N789KW	LJ35	222
N789LB	HS25	258248
N789LR	**GLF5**	**5100**
N789LT	HS25	258071
N789MA	C555	0067
N789MB	CL30	20020
N789ME	FA50	276
N789MS	G150	252
N789MS	**LJ60**	**094**
N789PF	LJ55	089
N789PR	GALX	050
N789QS	C650	7089
N789QS	**CL30**	**20617**
N789RR	GALX	050
N789RR	**GLEX**	**9387**
N789RR	GLF4	1509
N789RR	GLF5	5045
(N789RR)	C550	036
N789SB	**GALX**	**146**
N789SG	SBRL	306-121
N789SM	**CL64**	**5621**
N789SR	**LJ31**	**083**
N789SS	C550	087
N789TA	BE40	RK-268
N789TE	WW24	241
N789TN	**GLF4**	**1240**
N789TP	GLEX	9065
N789TP	GLF3	405
N789TR	GLF3	405
N789TS	**C510**	**0395**
N789TT	**C550**	**391**
N789VP	C650	7089
N789XJ	**C750**	**0289**
N789XP	HS25	258789
N789ZZ	**F9EX**	**174**
N790AL	**C555**	**0024**
N790BR	CL64	5572
N790D	C550	023
N790DC	**F2EX**	**33**
N790EA	C500	251
N790FH	**ASTR**	**056**
N790FH	FA10	158
N790GA	GALX	090
N790GA	GLF4	4190
N790JC	F900	17
N790JR	**WW24**	**424**
N790L	F2TH	15
N790M	**F2TH**	**19**
N790MC	GLF5	523
N790PS	C560	0272
N790QS	C650	7090
N790R	**F2EX**	**225**
N790SS	**BE40**	**RK-363**
N790SU	**LJ60**	**146**
N790T	**F9DX**	**621**
N790TA	BE40	RK-252
N790TX	**C56X**	**5790**
N790US	FA10	91
N790VP	C650	7090
N790XJ	**C750**	**0070**
N790XP	HS25	258790
N790Z	**F2TH**	**31**
N790Z	HS25	257197
N790ZK	**C56X**	**6111**
N791BR	CL64	5417
N791CP	**FA10**	**54**
(N791CW)	C750	0091
N791DM	C52A	0314
N791JF	**C500**	**456**
N791JK	**C52A**	**0152**
N791MA	C500	309
N791QS	C650	7091
N791TA	HS25	258291
N791VP	C650	7091
N792A	HS25	25248
N792AA	JSTR	5098/28
N792CB	**C52A**	**0461**
N792CC	C650	7092
N792CT	CL61	5148
(N792DL)	EA50	000215
N792GA	GLF5	5297
N792H	HS25	259019
N792MA	C550	329
N792QS	C650	7092
N792TA	BE40	RK-264
(N792VP)	C650	7092
N792XJ	**C750**	**0292**
N792XP	HS25	258792
N793A	ASTR	086
N793AA	**C500**	**501**
N793BG	WW24	392
N793CG	**F9EX**	**121**
N793CJ	**C525**	**0021**
N793CP	**GLF5**	**5473**
N793CS	C560	0793
N793CT	CL61	5148
N793CT	**CL64**	**5643**
N793ES	**LJ45**	**318**
N793JR	WW24	365
N793KK	**C680**	**0159**
N793QS	C650	7093
N793RC	**HS25**	**258550**
N793TA	BE40	RK-244
N793WF	**F2TH**	**66**
N793XJ	**C750**	**0093**
N793XP	HS25	258793
N794EZ	C500	397
N794GC	LJ35	446
N794ME	**GLF3**	**483**
N794MH	**GLF4**	**1079**
N794PF	**C525**	**0649**
N794QS	C650	7094
N794RC	**CL30**	**20193**
N794SB	**CL61**	**5082**
N794SB	GLF2	12
N794SB	GLF2	176
(N794SB)	FA20	24
N794SC	GLF2	176
N794SE	**F9EX**	**32**
(N794SM)	BE40	RK-60
N794TA	BE40	RK-282
N794TK	**WW24**	**373**
N794VP	C650	7094
(N794WB)	C500	621
N794XJ	**C750**	**0294**
N795A	HS25	257127
N795AB	FA20	262
N795AJ	C560	0522
N795BA	**GLF5**	**5031**
N795BM	C525	0481
N795BM	C52B	0246
N795CP	**GLF5**	**5474**
N795FM	**WW24**	**228**
N795HA	LJ55	132
N795HB	ASTR	084
(N795HC)	C750	0053
N795HE	HS25	257149
N795HG	C750	0053
N795HG	**C750**	**0308**
(N795HL)	HS25	257149
N795HP	ASTR	084
N795J	HS25	25121
N795MA	C500	615
N795PH	HS25	258139
N795QS	C650	7095
N795T	**C510**	**0357**
N795TA	BE40	RK-284
N795VP	C650	7095
N795W	**E55P**	**50500296**
N795XJ	**C750**	**0295**
N796A	FA50	238
N796AC	**CL30**	**20435**
N796BM	C525	0481
N796CH	**HS25**	**258049**
N796HP	ASTR	085
N796HR	**ASTR**	**085**
N796MA	**C550**	**550-0941**
N796MA	FA10	162
N796MA	GLF4	4076
N796QS	C650	7096
N796RM	**HA4T**	**RC-61**
N796SF	FA10	75
N796TA	BE40	RK-289
N796XP	HS25	258796
N797BD	GLF3	388
N797CB	**CL30**	**20158**
N797CB	LJ60	086
N797CC	**C650**	**7097**
N797CD	GLF4	1145
N797CH	LJ45	016
N797CM	**F2TH**	**51**
N797CM	GLF4	1064
N797CP	**GLF5**	**5479**
N797CP	LJ60	086
N797CS	LJ55	018
N797CS	**LJ60**	**324**
N797CT	**GLEX**	**9435**
N797CW	**C550**	**284**
N797CX	**C750**	**0297**
(N797EM)	HS25	257193
N797EP	HS25	258139
N797ES	LJ45	318
N797FA	HS25	257193
N797HD	**F2TH**	**135**
N797HT	F2TH	171
N797KB	LJ31	098
N797KK	**GLEX**	**9290**
N797M	**GALX**	**179**
N797MM	**C560**	**0078**
N797PA	LJ60	098
N797QS	C650	7097
N797R	SBRL	282-79
N797SA	**CL61**	**5033**
N797SA	GLF4	1081
N797SC	LJ25	042
N797SE	**C500**	**546**
N797SF	C500	546
N797SF	C550	225
N797SM	F2TH	140
N797T	C650	0197
N797TA	BE40	RK-265
N797TE	**C550**	**550-0962**
N797TJ	C555	0048
N797VS	**C650**	**0151**
N797WB	LJ31	200
N797WC	C550	471
N797WC	**F2TH**	**140**
N797WC	JSTR	5216
N797WQ	**JSTR**	**5216**
N797XJ	C750	0077
N797XJ	C750	0297
(N798AC)	FA50	240
(N798CW)	C750	0098
N798KG	**HS25**	**258443**
N798PA	**HS25**	**258070**
N798QS	C650	7098
N798RS	**CL65**	**5985**
N798S	C52B	0273
N798TA	BE40	RK-198
(N798W)	F900	45
N798XP	HS25	258798
N799AG	**HS25**	**HA-0027**
N799AZ	CL61	5176
N799BC	F2TH	138
N799CP	**GLF4**	**1402**
(N799FL)	HS25	257111
N799G	FA20	81
(N799HF)	CL60	1007
N799JC	HS25	258544
N799JL	C550	550-1019
N799MJ	**C680**	**0205**
N799MW	**SBRL**	**465-42**
N799RM	**HS25**	**258708**
N799S	HS25	258019
N799S	**HS25**	**258588**
N799SC	HS25	257068
N799SC	HS25	258019
N799SC	LJ60	067
N799SM	BE40	RK-220
N799TA	BE40	RK-209
N799TD	**LJ35**	**187**
N799TG	C750	0136
(N799TS)	GLEX	9199
N799WW	GLEX	9092
N799WW	GLF4	1059
N800AB	C500	130
N800AB	C550	550-0875
N800AB	CL60	1067
N800AB	**LJ45**	**137**
N800AF	HS25	25207
N800AF	**HS25**	**258158**
N800AF	JSTR	5101/15
N800AH	HS25	258679
N800AJ	ASTR	081
N800AJ	C525	0131
N800AK	C550	550-0809
N800AL	GLF4	1340
N800AL	**GLF4**	**4087**
N800AM	**C56X**	**5195**
N800AR	GLF3	362
N800AR	**GLF4**	**1496**
N800AV	C500	209
N800AW	LJ35	149
N800AZ	**EA50**	**000153**
N800BA	HS25	258003
N800BA	HS25	258046
N800BA	HS25	258124
N800BA	HS25	258157
N800BA	HS25	258195
N800BA	HS25	258223
N800BA	HS25	258225
"N800BA"	HS25	258001
N800BD	**CL30**	**20270**
N800BD	FA50	161
N800BD	FA50	224
N800BD	FA50	35
N800BF	C500	457
N800BG	GLF3	488
N800BG	GLF4	1034
(N800BG)	F2TH	38
N800BH	C500	403
(N800BJ)	HS25	258206
N800BL	F2TH	47
N800BL	F900	32
N800BL	LJ36	025
N800BM	HS25	258155
N800BN	CL64	5600
N800BP	HS25	258080
N800BQ	GLF4	1034
N800BS	HS25	258014
N800BT	**CL60**	**1044**
N800BV	HS25	258097
N800BW	**C560**	**0640**
N800CB	HS25	25179
N800CB	HS25	257016
N800CC	CL60	1080
N800CC	GLF3	472
N800CC	GLF4	1052
N800CC	**HS25**	**258266**
N800CD	LJ35	335
N800CD	**SBRL**	**380-23**
N800CF	FA20	191
N800CF	FA20	242
N800CF	FA20	368
N800CH	LJ31	223
N800CH	LJ35	335
N800CH	**LJ45**	**489**
N800CJ	C500	330
N800CJ	HS25	258225
N800CJ	HS25	258244
N800CK	**LJ31**	**157**
N800CL	**HS25**	**258912**
N800CQ	HS25	258636
N800CR	**GLF4**	**1334**
N800CS	**E55P**	**50500169**
N800CS	PRM1	RB-62
N800CS	SBRL	282-64
N800CU	**C52B**	**0246**
N800CU	C550	190
N800CU	SBRL	465-24
N800CV	C560	0800
N800CV	**HS25**	**258386**
N800CZ	**C525**	**0800**
N800DA	**HS25**	**25047**
N800DC	C500	403
N800DC	FA20	74
N800DC	FA20	75
N800DC	SBRL	282-102
N800DJ	GLF2	159
N800DL	C560	0015
N800DL	**GLF5**	**5244**
N800DM	GLF2	159
N800DN	HS25	258183
N800DN	HS25	258202
N800DP	HS25	258024

N800DR	HS25	258202
N800DR	HS25	258478
N800DR	LJ25	353
N800DT	C500	602
N800DT	**C525**	**0092**
N800DW	C500	564
N800DW	**F900**	**79**
N800DW	FA20	135
N800DW	FA50	49
N800DW	HS25	258394
N800E	HS25	257045
N800EA	**HS25**	**258582**
N800EC	C550	219
N800EC	HS25	258114
N800EE	HS25	258004
N800EG	FA20	495
N800EH	BE40	RK-322
N800EJ	**EA50**	**000134**
N800EL	C550	343
N800EL	HS25	258622
N800EL	BE40	RK-322
N800EM	HS25	258456
N800EM	**HS25**	**258649**
N800ER	HS25	258394
N800EX	HS25	258049
N800FD	HS25	258390
N800FF	**FA20**	**406/557**
N800FH	HS25	258006
N800FJ	HS25	258090
N800FJ	**HS25**	**258138**
N800FJ	HS25	258492
N800FK	HS25	258133
N800FL	GLF2	47
N800FL	GLF2	50
N800FL	**HS25**	**258005**
N800FM	**C52B**	**0305**
N800FM	FA50	28
N800FN	HS25	258090
N800FR	PRM1	RB-165
N800FT	BE40	RJ-9
N800FZ	**C510**	**0444**
N800GA	GLF2	197
N800GA	**LJ28**	**28-003**
(N800GC)	MU30	A030SA
N800GD	JSTR	5100/41
N800GD	**JSTR**	**5219**
N800GE	**HS25**	**25206**
N800GF	**C52A**	**0038**
N800GF	BE40	RK-96
N800GG	HS25	258005
N800GG	LJ25	008
N800GH	**F2TH**	**89**
N800GJ	LJ35	352
N800GK	BE40	RK-96
N800GM	**C650**	**0077**
N800GN	HS25	258057
N800GN	**HS25**	**258372**
N800GP	LJ35	158
N800GR	BE40	RK-356
(N800GT)	HS25	258266
N800GV	**BE40**	**RK-271**
N800GW	C525	0276
N800GX	HS25	258195
N800HH	CL60	1074
N800HM	FA20	495
N800HM	BE40	RJ-19
N800HS	C525	0051
N800HS	C525	0100
N800HS	HS25	258026
(N800HS)	HS25	258083
N800HT	BE40	RK-356
N800HT	BE40	RK-455
N800HW	**C555**	**0057**
N800J	GLF3	359
N800J	GLF4	1333
N800J	**GLF5**	**5419**
N800J	JSTR	5087/55
N800JA	LJ24	039
N800JA	LJ25	042
(N800JA)	HS25	258598
(N800JA)	LJ25	118
N800JC	HS25	25201
N800JD	C500	022
N800JH	F2TH	63
N800JH	GLF3	312
N800JH	**GLF5**	**5073**
N800JJ	WW24	290
N800JM	**HS25**	**258001**
N800JP	HS25	256066
N800JR	**EA50**	**000167**
(N800JS)	ASTR	017
N800JT	HS25	25272
N800KC	C500	083
N800KC	CL61	5157
(N800KC)	C550	716
N800KR	FA20	144
N800KV	**C56X**	**6104**
N800L	LJ25	249
N800LA	C550	325
N800LA	HS25	258679
N800LE	MU30	A064SA
N800LF	HS25	258492
N800LJ	**LJ55**	**009**
N800LL	HS25	258017
N800LL	**HS25**	**258079**
N800LM	**HS25**	**257140**
N800LQ	**HS25**	**258551**
N800LR	HS25	258029
N800LR	HS25	258415
N800LS	FA20	144
(N800LV)	HS25	258155
(N800LX)	HS25	258010
(N800LX)	HS25	258282
N800M	SBRL	282-23
N800M	SBRL	306-143
N800M	**SBRL**	**465-41**
(N800M)	C500	404
N800MA	LJ45	064
N800MA	LJ45	189
N800MA	WW24	358
N800MC	C650	0195
N800MC	FA20	74
N800MC	GLF2	61
N800MD	HS25	258074
N800MJ	HS25	258226
N800MK	ASTR	106
N800MK	GLF3	396
N800MM	HS25	258014
N800MN	HS25	258074
N800MP	HS25	257152
N800MT	**C550**	**550-0981**
N800MT	C550	647
(N800MT)	WW24	372
N800N	HS25	258003
N800NB	**C525**	**0212**
(N800NE)	HS25	258300
N800NJ	HS25	258314
N800NM	HS25	256027
N800NP	HS25	25239
N800NS	HS25	258633
(N800NW)	HS25	258019
N800NY	HS25	258254
N800PA	FA20	74
N800PA	**HS25**	**258162**
N800PB	HS25	258441
N800PC	HS25	258369
N800PC	LJ24	292
N800PE	HS25	258441
N800PE	**HS25**	**258508**
N800PF	**C525**	**0605**
N800PJ	**GALX**	**026**
N800PL	C500	102
N800PL	**HS25**	**258696**
N800PM	GLF2	224
N800PM	**GLF5**	**599**
N800PM	HS25	258027
N800PP	FA20	44
N800PP	HS25	258018
N800PW	ASTR	079
N800QB	HS25	25179
N800QC	HS25	258174
N800QS	C560	0598
N800R	C650	0197
N800R	HS25	258694
N800R	LJ60	146
N800RC	**HS25**	**258660**
N800RD	HS25	258311
N800RD	LJ35	213
N800RD	MU30	A027SA
N800RF	**LJ25**	**281**
N800RG	**HS25**	**258230**
N800RK	C525	0158
N800RL	C525	0158
N800RL	C52A	0220
N800RL	**C52C**	**0094**
N800RM	HS25	258001
N800RM	SBRL	306-138
N800RR	C550	088
N800RT	GLF2	47
N800RY	HS25	258002
N800S	HS25	258006
N800S	HS25	258082
N800S	HS25	258093
N800SB	C550	343
N800SB	FA10	104
N800SD	**BE40**	**RK-270**
N800SE	HS25	258137
(N800SG)	HS25	258390
N800SN	HS25	258043
N800SV	**HS25**	**258217**
N800TA	**FA50**	**220**
N800TD	**GLF3**	**452**
N800TE	**EA50**	**000021**
(N800TE)	GLF2	22
N800TF	HS25	258045
N800TG	HS25	25287
N800TJ	HS25	258236
N800TJ	MU30	A022SA
N800TK	GLEX	9101
N800TL	**HS25**	**258394**
N800TR	HS25	258038
N800TR	HS25	258087
N800TR	HS25	258111
N800TS	JSTR	5215
(N800TS)	BE40	RJ-34
N800TT	HS25	258012
N800TV	C550	187
N800TW	C500	520
N800TW	SBRL	465-4
N800UA	LJ45	064
N800UK	**HS25**	**258577**
N800UP	HS25	258096
N800UW	**HS25**	**258395**
N800VA	**C550**	**550-0956**
N800VA	HS25	258425
N800VC	HS25	258122
N800VF	HS25	258300
N800VJ	C550	343
N800VL	C525	0001
(N800VL)	LJ35	127
N800VR	**HS25**	**258016**
N800VT	C525	0001
N800VT	C52A	0103
N800VV	HS25	258011
N800W	C500	014
N800W	C750	0122
N800WA	**HS25**	**258121**
N800WC	C52A	0006
N800WC	GLF3	392
N800WC	GLF4	1289
N800WC	LJ45	094
N800WC	BE40	RK-407
N800WD	**HS25**	**259052**
N800WF	**HS25**	**258728**
N800WG	HS25	258152
N800WH	**HS25**	**258080**
N800WJ	**HS25**	**258437**
N800WJ	LJ35	356
N800WP	**HS25**	**258459**
N800WS	ASTR	106
N800WS	WW24	253
N800WT	HS25	258178
(N800WT)	C560	0105
N800WV	BE40	RJ-24
N800WW	HS25	258006
N800WW	HS25	258459
N800WW	**HS25**	**258661**
N800WW	WW24	253
N800WW	BE40	RJ-24
N800WY	HS25	258556
N800WZ	**HS25**	**25201**
(N800XC)	GLF2	24
(N800XJ)	C750	0300
N800XL	GLF2	24
N800XL	WW24	276
N800XM	**HS25**	**258414**
N800XP	HS25	258266
N800XP	HS25	258414
N800XP	HS25	258541
(N800XP)	HS25	258285
(N800XZ)	HS25	258301
N800Y	SBRL	282-31
N800Y	WW24	198
N800YB	CL61	5175
N800YY	**CL61**	**5112**
N800YY	HS25	258334
N800ZZ	ASTR	028
N800ZZ	HS25	258020
N801	GLF2	160
N801	JSTR	5132/57
N801	JSTR	5138
N801AB	C560	0158
N801AB	HS25	258135
N801AR	**GLF5**	**578**
N801AS	**GLF5**	**5097**
N801BB	**C550**	**550-0801**
N801BC	HS25	256032
N801BP	PRM1	RB-201
N801CC	C650	0064
N801CC	GLF4	1254
(N801CC)	C555	0038
N801CE	HS25	258253
N801CF	**HS25**	**258185**
N801CR	HS25	258001
N801CT	LJ31	017
N801CW	HS25	258012
N801DE	F2EX	203
N801DL	FA50	206
N801EE	**LEG5**	**55010005**
N801EL	C500	544
N801EL	**CL30**	**20241**
N801F	FA20	4
N801FL	CL61	5063
N801FT	**SBRL**	**380-16**
N801G	ASTR	081
N801G	C550	110
N801G	HS25	258017
N801GA	GLF2	1
N801GA	GLF2	103
N801GA	GLF2	108
N801GA	GLF2	173
N801GA	GLF2	2
(N801GA)	GLF2	241
N801GC	CL61	3052
N801GE	C510	0112
N801GJ	**LJ55**	**116**
N801HB	HS25	258327
N801JA	LJ24	076
N801JP	C550	046
N801JT	HS25	258296
N801K	C500	236
N801K	LJ35	462
N801KB	**CL30**	**20503**
N801KF	**GLEX**	**9073**
N801KT	C500	167
N801L	C500	236
N801L	C500	606
N801L	LJ24	001
(N801L)	C550	110
N801LM	**HS25**	**258111**
(N801LX)	HS25	258012
(N801LX)	HS25	258320
N801MB	HS25	258067
N801MB	HS25	258440
(N801MD)	FA20	284
N801MJ	GLF3	450
N801MM	HS25	258067
N801MS	SBRL	282-30
N801MS	WW24	421
N801NC	SBRL	282-68
N801NM	WW24	122
N801NW	HS25	258124
N801P	CL61	5099
N801P	CL64	5335
N801P	HS25	258017
N801P	**HS25**	**258191**
(N801PA)	CL61	3044
N801PF	LJ35	179
N801PH	**CL30**	**20081**
N801PJ	C525	0092
N801PN	**GLEX**	**9062**
N801QS	C560	0601
N801R	CL61	5099
(N801R)	HS25	258017
N801RA	HS25	257100
N801RJ	HS25	258135
N801RM	**HS25**	**258011**
N801RR	HS25	258759
N801RS	**ASTR**	**084**
N801SA	HS25	258192
N801SA	PRM1	RB-205
N801SC	FA20	206
N801SG	HS25	258762
N801SM	WW24	297
N801SS	**HS25**	**258291**
N801SS	SBRL	465-40
N801ST	HS25	258103
(N801TA)	C550	489
N801TK	CL64	5610
N801TK	GLEX	9007
N801TM	**GLF5**	**5222**
N801WB	HS25	258287
N801WC	**F2EX**	**21**
N801WC	GLF2	183
N801WC	GLF3	392
N801WJ	**HS25**	**258281**
N801WM	HS25	258503
N801WW	F2EX	21
N801WW	**F2EX**	**226**
N801WZ	**E55P**	**50500144**
N802AB	**C560**	**0217**
N802AG	**GLF5**	**5245**
N802AK	**LJ40**	**2128**
N802CA	**C550**	**550-1034**
N802CB	C550	550-0802
N802CB	**GLEX**	**9041**
(N802CB)	F9EX	89
N802CC	**GLF2**	**187**
N802CC	LJ35	289
N802CE	HS25	258270
N802CF	**HS25**	**258425**
N802CJ	F9EX	89
(N802CW)	HS25	258002
N802D	HS25	258024
N802DB	**C650**	**0080**
N802DC	HS25	258024
N802DC	HS25	258257
N802DC	HS25	258562
N802DR	HS25	258667
(N802EC)	LJ35	453
N802F	FA20	17
N802F	FA20	26
N802F	FA20	95
N802FT	**SBRL**	**380-33**
N802GA	GLF2	2
N802GA	GLF3	357
N802GJ	LJ55	041
N802H	HS25	259048
N802HH	**HA4T**	**RC-2**
N802JA	LJ24	180
N802JD	**C510**	**0431**
N802JH	C525	0376
N802JT	HS25	258304
N802JW	LJ35	453
N802L	LJ24	002
(N802LX)	HS25	258033
N802MM	HS25	258073
N802PA	CL61	3050
(N802PF)	GLEX	9041
N802Q	CL60	1010
N802Q	**C555**	**0157**
N802QS	C560	0606
N802QS	**C560**	**0706**
N802RC	HS25	257125
N802RM	HS25	258013
N802RR	G150	260
N802RR	**G150**	**263**
N802SA	HS25	258045
(N802SJ)	HS25	258167
N802TA	HS25	258453
N802TA	HS25	258454
(N802TK)	CL64	5413
N802W	C750	0167
N802W	LJ24	128
N802WC	GLF4	1289
N802WJ	**HS25**	**258008**
N802WM	HS25	258307
N802WM	HS25	258503
N802X	HS25	258125
N803AC	**FA50**	**210**
N803AG	**GLF4**	**4194**
(N803AU)	WW24	149
N803BA	HS25	258003
N803BF	HS25	257178
N803BG	HS25	258064
N803CC	GLF3	378
N803CE	HS25	258271
N803CJ	C560	0803
(N803CW)	HS25	258603
N803D	HS25	HA-0106
N803E	BE40	RJ-16
(N803EA)	C560	0080
N803F	FA20	12
N803F	FA20	492
N803FL	HS25	258455
N803GA	GLF2	150
N803GA	GLF2	47
N803GE	HS25	258003
N803GJ	**LJ55**	**115**
N803H	HS25	258273
N803HH	HA4T	RC-3
N803JA	LJ24	024
N803JL	HS25	258160
N803JT	HS25	258309
N803JW	ASTR	038
N803L	LJ24	003
N803L	LJ24	195
N803LC	FA20	18
N803LJ	LJ24	028A
N803LJ	LJ24	045A
(N803LL)	HS25	256045
(N803LX)	HS25	258045
(N803MM)	FA20	272
N803NA	GLF3	309
N803PF	C56X	5085
N803PF	LJ25	213
N803QS	**C560**	**0775**
N803QS	HS25	258603
(N803RA)	FA10	80
N803RK	**HS25**	**258003**
N803RR	CL61	5073
N803SA	HA4T	RC-8
N803SC	**C550**	**615**
(N803SR)	FA10	139
N803TA	HS25	258455
(N803TG)	GLF5	5243
N803TJ	HS25	258003
N803TK	CL61	5175
N803TM	**GLF5**	**5226**
N803WC	FA20	355
N803X	HS25	258127
N804AC	HS25	258368
N804AC	**HS25**	**HA-0189**
N804AG	**GLF4**	**4199**
N804AQ	HS25	258368
N804AS	GLEX	9141
N804BC	C550	627
N804BC	C560	0573
N804BG	**C560**	**0573**
N804BH	**HS25**	**258596**
N804CB	C550	550-0804
N804CB	CL64	5526
N804CC	LJ35	093
N804CC	**WW24**	**305**
N804CS	HS25	257093
N804CV	**C560**	**0804**
N804CW	HS25	257004
N804D	HS25	HA-0110
N804F	FA20	14
N804F	FA20	30
N804F	FA20	5
N804F	FA20	50
N804FF	HS25	257004
N804GA	GALX	204
N804GA	GLF2	151/24
N804GA	GLF2	172
N804GA	GLF2	187
N804GA	GLF2	87/775/6
N804H	HS25	258274
N804HB	HS25	HB-4
N804HH	**HA4T**	**RC-4**
N804JA	LJ24	088
N804JD	LJ60	332
N804JH	F2TH	63
N804JJ	**FA10**	**105**
N804JM	**HS25**	**258467**
N804JT	HS25	258311
N804JW	ASTR	069
N804LJ	LJ24	004
N804LJ	LJ24	015A
(N804LX)	HS25	258051
(N804LX)	HS25	258364
N804MR	**HS25**	**258012**
N804NA	**GLF3**	**344**
N804PA	**SBRL**	**465-4**
N804PH	LJ25	361
N804QS	**C560**	**0610**
N804RH	LJ25	361
N804RM	HS25	258042
N804ST	**C500**	**545**
N804SW	**E55P**	**50500346**
N804TA	HS25	258461
N804TF	**LJ35**	**404**
N804TK	GLEX	9060
N804WA	C560	0277

N804WC	GLF4	1289
N804WJ	HS25	257199
N804X	HS25	258128
(N805AF)	HS25	258083
N805BB	C500	305
N805C	CL60	1037
N805C	FA20	492
N805CC	FA20	83
N805CC	GLF2	123/25
N805CD	HS25	257209
N805CJ	**C525**	**0603**
N805CW	HS25	258145
N805D	**HS25**	**HA-0113**
N805DB	CL61	5161
N805DB	**F2EX**	**143**
N805DW	**FA50**	**49**
N805F	FA20	32
N805F	FA20	6
N805F	FA20	60
N805GA	GALX	205
N805GA	GLF2	157
N805GA	GLF2	174
N805GA	GLF2	220
N805GA	GLF4	4305
N805GA	GLF5	5005
N805GT	C650	0212
N805H	HS25	258264
(N805HD)	SBRL	380-39
N805HH	HA4T	RC-5
N805JA	LJ24	082
N805JD	LJ60	333
N805JL	**HS25**	**258203**
(N805JM)	GLF4	1184
N805JW	ASTR	070
N805KK	**C525**	**0198**
N805LC	**C550**	**581**
N805LJ	LJ24	010
N805LJ	LJ24	048
N805LX	**HS25**	**258374**
(N805LX)	HS25	258061
N805M	HS25	257129
N805M	HS25	258753
N805NA	**GLF2**	**221**
N805NA	LJ24	102
N805P	**C525**	**0701**
N805PC	**LJ55**	**018**
N805PG	**E55P**	**50500287**
N805QS	HS25	258505
N805RG	SBRL	380-48
(N805SA)	WW24	145
N805SM	WW24	145
N805TA	HS25	258466
N805VC	**C525**	**0076**
N805VZ	CL64	5410
N805WB	GLEX	9530
N805WC	GLF3	392
N805WD	**HS25**	**25276**
N805WM	F9EX	104
N805WM	**GLEX**	**9530**
N805X	HS25	258205
N805Y	GLF2	56
N806AC	GLF5	5097
N806AC	GLF5	622
N806AD	**C56X**	**5743**
N806AS	**GLEX**	**9511**
N806C	C550	010
N806CB	HS25	25038
N806CC	GLF2	134
N806CC	GLF2	204
N806CC	GLF2	46
N806CC	GLF3	472
N806CJ	C52A	0423
N806DB	F2EX	143
N806DE	**C56X**	**5823**
N806F	FA20	15
N806F	FA20	31
N806F	FA20	490
N806F	FA20	64
N806F	FA20	8
N806GA	G150	206
N806GA	G150	306
N806GA	GLF2	156/31
N806GA	GLF2	176
N806GA	GLF2	209
N806GA	GLF2	232
N806GA	GLF5	5206
N806GG	BE40	RK-343
N806H	HS25	258265
(N806HH)	HA4T	RC-6
N806JD	LJ60	359
N806JH	F2TH	63
N806JK	**G280**	**2069**
N806LJ	LJ24	011
N806LJ	**LJ24**	**073**
N806LX	HS25	258383
(N806LX)	HS25	258062
N806MN	C52A	0194
N806MN	C56X	5587
N806MN	C680	0199
N806PH	**CL30**	**20086**
N806QS	**C560**	**0614**
N806TA	HS25	258478
N806TA	HS25	258543
N806TM	**HS25**	**258486**
N806WC	C560	0598
N806WC	GLF2	183
N806XM	HS25	258418
N807AD	**C56X**	**6103**
N807BC	**GLF4**	**4207**
N807BF	**WW24**	**194**
N807CC	GLF2	212
N807CE	C560	0807
N807CH	CL60	1085
N807CT	**C550**	**550-1078**
(N807CW)	HS25	257001
N807DC	**GLEX**	**9314**
N807DD	**CL61**	**5161**
N807F	FA10	114
N807F	FA20	16
N807F	FA20	33
N807F	FA20	7
N807F	FA20	71
N807G	HS25	25121
N807GA	G150	207
N807GA	GLF2	105
N807GA	GLF2	212
N807GA	GLF2	233
N807GA	GLF5	5507
N807H	HS25	258286
N807HB	HS25	HA-0007
(N807HH)	HA4T	RC-7
N807JD	CL30	20200
N807JD	CL65	5839
N807JW	ASTR	100
N807LJ	LJ24	018
N807LX	HS25	258413
(N807LX)	HS25	258067
N807MB	**C550**	**694**
N807MC	**HS25**	**258114**
N807MM	**CL61**	**3014**
N807PA	FA20	71
N807QS	**C560**	**0617**
N807RH	CL64	5626
N807TA	HS25	258483
N807TC	HS25	257008
N807Z	CL61	5040
N808AC	**C560**	**0323**
N808AK	**LJ45**	**312**
(N808AL)	HS25	258373
N808BC	C500	403
N808BL	HS25	258634
N808CC	HS25	25286
N808CH	**CL60**	**1017**
N808CK	FA20	108/430
N808CS	**PRM1**	**RB-62**
N808CZ	C750	0010
N808D	LJ24	138
N808DM	C550	093
N808DP	LJ24	138
N808DP	LJ25	043
N808DS	LJ25	225
N808EB	SBRL	380-51
N808F	FA20	11
N808F	FA20	34
N808F	FA20	86
N808G	**CL61**	**5098**
N808GA	GLF2	106
N808GA	GLF2	193
N808GA	GLF2	208
N808GA	GLF2	231
N808GA	GLF2	234
N808GG	**C750**	**0033**
N808H	CL61	5155
N808H	HS25	258285
N808HG	CL61	5157
(N808HH)	HA4T	RC-8
N808HS	C525	0051
(N808HS)	C525	0100
N808HT	BE40	RK-356
N808JA	LJ24	050A
N808JG	**GLF5**	**598**
N808JN	C52B	0072
N808JW	GALX	010
(N808KD)	EA50	000185
N808KS	LJ45	305
N808L	FA10	200
N808L	**PRM1**	**RB-244**
N808LJ	LJ24	050A
(N808LX)	HS25	258077
(N808LX)	HS25	258428
N808MF	**GLF4**	**1448**
N808ML	LJ60	003
N808MN	**C56X**	**5587**
N808MV	C550	550-0812
N808NA	HS25	258664
N808PL	**C560**	**0798**
N808QS	**C560**	**0619**
N808RD	**C510**	**0086**
N808RP	HS25	256041
N808RP	JSTR	5215
N808RT	CL30	20162
N808SD	**C52B**	**0341**
N808SK	**LJ60**	**008**
N808T	GLF3	463
N808T	**GLF4**	**1342**
N808TA	HS25	258494
N808TA	HS25	258548
N808TC	**GLF5**	**5154**
(N808TC)	GLF4	1411
N808TH	C560	0378
N808TM	CL60	1020
N808TM	**HS25**	**258482**
N808V	HS25	25238
N808V	**PRM1**	**RB-5**
N808VA	C650	7057
N808W	C56X	6006
N808W	LJ31	165
N808W	**LJ45**	**423**
N808W	PRM1	RB-25
N808WA	C525	0290
N808WC	C680	0030
N808WG	LJ60	112
N808XR	C52B	0341
N808XT	**CL30**	**20285**
N808YY	**HS25**	**258334**
N809BA	HS25	258388
N809C	GLF4	1450
N809F	FA10	182
N809F	FA20	35
N809F	FA20	393
N809F	FA20	9
N809GA	GALX	209
N809GA	GLF2	107
N809GA	GLF2	47
N809H	HS25	258268
N809HB	HS25	HA-0009
(N809HH)	HA4T	RC-9
N809JC	WW24	298
N809JW	**ASTR**	**135**
N809LJ	LJ24	055
N809LS	GLF2	47
N809LX	HS25	258432
(N809LX)	HS25	258124
N809M	HS25	257081
N809P	FA20	35
N809PT	GLEX	9575
N809QS	**C560**	**0698**
N809QS	HS25	258611
N809R	LJ60	146
N809RM	PRM1	RB-45
N809SD	GLEX	9133
N809SD	LJ60	360
N809TA	HS25	258388
N809TA	HS25	258498
(N809TP)	HS25	258388
N809VC	WW24	264
N810AA	GALX	063
N810AA	HS25	258023
N810AF	**HS25**	**258589**
N810BA	HS25	258010
N810BE	**C560**	**0066**
N810BG	HS25	258010
N810CC	LJ35	486
N810CC	**WW24**	**264**
N810CM	**C525**	**0339**
N810CR	HS25	25241
N810CR	HS25	257071
N810CV	C560	0810
N810CW	HS25	258010
N810D	CL61	5075
N810D	**CL64**	**5331**
N810E	FA10	60
N810ET	**F2EX**	**190**
N810F	FA20	10
N810F	FA20	151
N810F	FA20	36
N810GA	GLF2	108
N810GA	GLF2	165/37
N810GA	GLF2	191
N810GA	GLF2	224
N810GS	HS25	257061
N810GT	**CL64**	**5600**
N810GW	**C52C**	**0139**
(N810HH)	HA4T	RC-10
N810HS	HS25	25271
(N810J)	FA10	139
N810JB	**C56X**	**5113**
N810JK	**LJ40**	**2098**
N810JT	C550	289
N810JW	ASTR	138
N810KB	**HS25**	**257118**
N810LG	**C500**	**664**
N810LP	**GLF4**	**1260**
N810LX	HS25	258145
N810M	HS25	257102
(N810M)	F9EX	33
(N810MB)	CL61	3026
N810MC	C550	225
N810MC	HS25	25201
N810ME	WW24	372
(N810MG)	C550	225
(N810MK)	FA10	73
N810MT	CL60	1024
N810MT	CL61	3026
N810MT	WW24	372
(N810MY)	GLF2	134
N810N	HS25	258460
N810PA	FA20	151
N810PF	**C52A**	**0399**
N810QS	**C560**	**0625**
N810RA	FA20	81
N810RJ	C500	067
N810SC	C500	076
N810SC	C550	032
N810SC	HS25	257179
N810SC	**HS25**	**258464**
N810SD	LJ60	364
N810SG	C500	076
N810SG	C550	032
N810SS	**C525**	**0137**
N810TA	HS25	258510
N810TK	**CL64**	**5606**
N810TM	**GLF4**	**1483**
N810TS	**GLEX**	**9622**
N810U	**F2EX**	**126**
N810US	FA10	53
N810V	C555	0149
N810V	HS25	257058
N810V	HS25	258224
N810V	LJ55	133
N810VC	WW24	321
N810WT	**PRM1**	**RB-122**
N810X	C750	0081
N810Y	LJ60	183
N810YS	LJ45	102
N810YS	**LJ60**	**397**
(N811)	JSTR	5227
N811AA	**FA20**	**187**
N811AA	HS25	258024
N811AG	F2TH	71
N811AM	**HS25**	**258172**
N811AV	F2TH	71
N811AV	F9EX	74
N811BB	CL61	5039
N811BB	CL64	5333
N811BP	CL61	5039
N811BP	CL64	5405
N811BP	LJ45	010
N811BR	CL61	5039
N811CC	HS25	258267
N811CP	LJ31	168
N811CW	HS25	258011
N811DD	LJ35	384
N811DE	**GLF2**	**244**
N811DF	GLF2	244
N811DF	GLF4	1306
N811DF	LJ35	384
N811DJ	MU30	A022SA
N811GA	GLF2	109
N811GA	GLF2	166/15
N811GA	GLF2	192
N811GA	**GLF5**	**5011**
N811HL	C500	503
N811JA	**C550**	**550-0952**
N811JA	HS25	25176
N811JK	GLF3	434
N811JK	GLF4	1030
N811JK	GLF4	1140
N811JT	C650	0204
N811JW	ASTR	140
N811JW	CL61	5063
(N811LX)	HS25	258282
N811MB	C560	0479
N811MB	**C56X**	**5728**
(N811ML)	LJ35	256
N811MT	CL60	1024
N811NC	**CL61**	**5064**
N811PA	FA20	196
N811PD	LJ25	138
N811PS	LJ31	166
N811QS	**HS25**	**258614**
N811RA	**LJ60**	**264**
N811RC	C52A	0058
N811RG	C555	0061
N811SD	LJ60	373
N811ST	C56X	5193
(N811SW)	GLF4	1170
N811TA	HS25	258516
N811TY	F2TH	71
N811VC	C550	062
N811VC	WW24	331
N811VG	**C550**	**062**
N811WE	**C560**	**0811**
N811WV	FA20	396
N811WW	GLF4	1121
N812AA	FA20	57
N812AA	HS25	258027
N812AM	FA10	210
N812AM	**HS25**	**258147**
N812BR	**LJ45**	**505**
N812CV	C560	0812
N812DC	C560	0541
N812FT	GALX	019
N812G	**CL64**	**5330**
N812G	WW24	389
N812GA	GLF2	168
N812GA	GLF2	236
N812GA	GLF4	4012
N812GA	GLF5	5012
N812GJ	**HS25**	**258112**
N812GR	**LJ60**	**298**
N812GS	CL61	5098
N812HA	**C555**	**0054**
N812HF	C52B	0262
N812J	**C510**	**0435**
N812JM	**C52B**	**0102**
N812KC	**CL30**	**20457**
N812KC	FA10	189
N812KD	C750	0246
N812LJ	LJ24	038
N812LJ	LJ24	077
N812LX	HS25	258437
(N812LX)	HS25	258296
N812M	HS25	25052
N812M	HS25	257081
N812M	WW24	389
N812MG	**C500**	**330**
N812MJ	EA50	000108
N812MM	LJ25	357
N812N	HS25	25052
N812PA	FA20	125
N812PJ	**C52A**	**0176**
N812QS	**C560**	**0628**
N812RS	GLF2	98/38
N812RX	**F2EX**	**295**
N812SD	**GLEX**	**9235**
N812SD	LJ60	386
(N812SS)	CL30	20138
N812TA	HS25	258522
N812TT	HS25	25046
N812VP	C560	0812
N812WN	SBRL	465-25
(N812XL)	CL60	1016
N812XP	HS25	258812
N812XP	HS25	HA-0212
N813A	C550	562
N813AA	FA20	25/405
N813AA	HS25	258029
N813AC	**HS25**	**258105**
N813AK	**C550**	**550-0944**
N813AS	LJ35	167
N813AV	FA10	28
N813BR	SBRL	306-8
N813CB	C550	550-0813
N813CJ	C560	0813
N813CW	HS25	258413
N813CZ	**C510**	**0339**
N813DH	C550	142
N813DH	C56X	5700
N813DH	**CL30**	**20426**
N813FM	**C525**	**0884**
N813GH	F2TH	125
N813H	HS25	257009
N813JD	**C550**	**550-0838**
N813JW	LJ25	038
N813LS	FA20	185/467
N813LS	**GLF3**	**443**
N813LX	HS25	258454
(N813LX)	HS25	258320
N813M	LJ35	151
N813MK	FA20	272
N813MK	GLF3	407
N813NA	**HS25**	**257158**
N813P	FA20	121
N813P	JSTR	5222
N813PA	FA20	121
N813PD	**GLF4**	**1069**
N813PR	HS25	25137
N813QS	C560	0631
N813QS	**GLF5**	**5160**
N813RR	LJ35	391
N813SQ	GLEX	9009
N813TA	**CL61**	**3016**
N813TA	HS25	258527
N813TS	F900	133
N813VC	**HS25**	**257013**
N813VZ	CL61	5160
N813WP	GLF5	555
N814AA	FA20	31
(N814AA)	FA10	157
N814AM	C550	413
N814BP	PRM1	RB-214
N814BR	**C56X**	**5003**
N814CC	C555	0018
N814CE	JSTR	5217
N814CM	C560	0170
N814CP	**GLF4**	**4191**
N814D	HS25	25237
N814DM	**C525**	**0376**
N814ER	C500	280
N814ER	**FA20**	**66**
N814ER	HS25	25170
N814GA	GLF2	110
N814GA	GLF2	44
N814GA	GLF5	5414
N814GF	**LJ60**	**085**
N814HH	LJ24	202
(N814HP)	LJ24	276
N814JR	LJ24	202
N814K	JSTR	5204
N814K	WW24	106
N814L	LJ24	014
N814LC	**C550**	**692**
N814LG	**C525**	**0534**
N814LJ	LJ24	069
(N814LX)	HS25	258322
N814M	F900	155
N814M	HS25	25196
N814M	LJ35	077
N814NA	JSTR	5003
N814P	HS25	25148
N814PA	FA20	202
N814PE	**C56X**	**6069**
(N814PJ)	FA10	225
N814PS	CL61	5159
N814PS	CL64	5309
N814PS	**CL64**	**5544**
N814QS	C560	0644
N814QS	**C560**	**0776**
(N814QS)	C560	0638
N814RR	**GLF4**	**1468**
N814SP	**C525**	**0510**
N814ST	**HS25**	**258272**
N814T	**WW24**	**106**
N814TA	HS25	258529

N814TP	**FA7X**	**234**
N814TS	**LJ60**	**319**
N814TX	C560	0814
N814WS	**C510**	**0032**
N815A	LJ31	118
N815A	LJ35	142
N815A	LJ45	074
N815AA	FA20	205
N815AA	HS25	258032
N815AC	FA20	206
N815BC	WW24	301
(N815BS)	BE40	RJ-30
N815CA	FA50	6
N815CC	HS25	258100
N815CE	C550	239
N815CJ	C560	0815
N815CM	**C560**	**0104**
N815DD	**LJ35**	**414**
N815E	LJ31	118
N815GA	GLF2	111
N815GA	GLF2	45
N815GA	GLF4	4115
N815GK	C550	228
N815H	C555	0146
N815HC	C500	005
N815J	LJ25	045
N815JW	**GALX**	**053**
N815L	LJ35	142
N815LC	FA10	46
N815LJ	LJ24	067
N815LP	C52B	0307
N815LT	**C560**	**0202**
(N815LX)	HS25	258337
N815MA	C550	398
N815MC	**C525**	**0142**
N815PA	CL64	5511
N815PA	**GLEX**	**9305**
N815QS	**HS25**	**258705**
N815RA	CL64	5511
N815RB	LJ35	647
N815RC	JSTR	5226
N815RC	WW24	301
N815RK	WW24	416
(N815RK)	HS25	258787
N815TA	HS25	258534
N815TK	C650	7111
N815TR	**HS25**	**257104**
N815WT	**EA50**	**000119**
N816AA	FA20	290
N816AA	HS25	258035
N816BD	LJ45	264
N816BG	**HS25**	**258168**
N816BL	**C52B**	**0467**
N816CC	CL64	5451
N816CC	CL65	5816
N816CC	GALX	020
N816CS	**C56X**	**5153**
N816CW	**C510**	**0079**
N816CW	HS25	258016
N816DC	GLEX	9025
N816DK	**BE40**	**RK-291**
N816DV	C52C	0049
N816FC	C525	0059
N816FC	**C52B**	**0096**
N816GA	GLF2	112
N816GA	GLF2	215
N816GA	GLF2	237/43
N816GA	GLF4	4016
N816GS	GLF4	1225
N816H	HS25	258288
N816H	WW24	323
N816HB	ASTR	028
N816JA	LJ35	394
N816JA	WW24	328
(N816JA)	LJ25	091
N816JM	**HS25**	**257011**
N816JW	**GALX**	**097**
N816KD	**EA50**	**000003**
N816LC	**WW24**	**291**
N816LJ	LJ24	088
N816LL	C500	411
N816LP	LJ45	327
N816LS	**HDJT**	**42000029**
N816LX	**HS25**	**258363**
N816M	FA50	99
N816M	HS25	25052
N816M	LJ35	030
N816MC	HS25	25052
N816MC	LJ55	035
N816MG	**GLF5**	**5187**
N816PD	CL60	1069
N816QS	HS25	258416
N816RD	JSTR	5218
N816S	WW24	360
(N816S)	MU30	A022SA
N816SE	HS25	HA-0055
N816SG	GLEX	9106
N816SP	CL61	5030
N816SP	**GLF4**	**1452**
N816SQ	CL61	5030
N816SQ	GLEX	9009
N816SQ	GLEX	9106
N816SR	GLEX	9009
N816ST	WW24	360
N816TA	HS25	258538
N816TR	HS25	258816
N816V	C555	0149
N817AA	FA20	233
N817AA	HS25	258036
N817AF	**CL65**	**5931**
N817AM	**LJ55**	**069**
N817AM	LJ55	082
N817BD	JSTR	5083/49
N817BD	LJ31	094
N817BD	LJ45	281
N817BF	**C525**	**0635**
N817BT	C525	0635
N817BT	**C52C**	**0109**
N817CB	C550	550-0817
N817CJ	C525	0174
N817CJ	C52C	0021
N817CK	CL60	1069
N817EM	**LJ35**	**486**
N817GA	G150	317
N817GA	G280	2017
N817GA	GLF2	113
N817GA	GLF2	222
N817GR	**MU30**	**A062SA**
N817GS	**GLF6**	**6111**
N817H	HS25	258279
N817JS	FA20	181
N817LF	**C56X**	**5150**
N817LS	GLEX	9035
N817LX	HS25	258516
(N817LX)	HS25	258364
N817M	FA50	24
N817MB	**C650**	**7012**
N817ME	**GLF4**	**1446**
N817MF	**GLF3**	**466**
N817MQ	C650	7015
N817MZ	C650	7055
N817PD	**C560**	**0075**
N817QS	HS25	258517
N817RA	**GLF4**	**1324**
N817TA	HS25	258552
N817W	**PRM1**	**RB-107**
N817X	**FA7X**	**208**
N817X	FA7X	51
N818	HS25	257020
N818AA	FA20	36
N818AA	HS25	258039
N818AC	**CL65**	**5799**
N818AF	**LJ45**	**380**
N818AJ	C550	550-0818
N818BA	**GLF4**	**1017**
N818BD	**LJ45**	**277**
N818BF	**C560**	**0317**
N818BH	F2EX	57
N818BK	**GLF4**	**1094**
N818BL	C560	0317
N818BL	**C56X**	**5328**
N818CD	C500	311
(N818CD)	C500	297
N818CH	LJ45	394
N818CH	LJ45	398
N818CK	**LJ25**	**118**
N818CP	FA20	71
N818CR	GALX	024
N818DA	GLF2	208
N818DA	GLF5	520
N818DD	GLF3	455
N818DE	**C650**	**0121**
N818DW	SBRL	380-30
(N818E)	CL60	1069
N818EC	**GLF3**	**399**
N818EE	**C525**	**0128**
N818ER	**GALX**	**111**
(N818ER)	C525	0503
N818FC	**C525**	**0059**
N818FH	GLEX	9180
N818G	GLF4	4070
N818G	HS25	258186
N818GA	GLF2	114
N818GA	GLF2	227
(N818GY)	LJ25	116
N818HK	**GLF5**	**5109**
N818JH	**WW24**	**341**
N818JW	**GALX**	**121**
N818KC	CL30	20043
N818KC	HS25	257009
N818KE	**GLF4**	**4204**
N818KF	**FA50**	**277**
N818LD	**HS25**	**257192**
N818LD	SBRL	380-30
N818LF	**GLF5**	**5311**
N818LJ	LJ24	028
N818LJ	**LJ31**	**019**
N818LK	GLF5	5311
N818LS	CL60	1047
N818LS	CL61	5090
N818LS	CL64	5315
N818LS	FA20	185/467
N818LS	GLEX	9035
N818LX	**HS25**	**258534**
(N818LX)	HS25	258374
N818ME	**GLF4**	**1431**
N818MV	HS25	258186
N818NX	**CL30**	**20612**
N818QS	**C560**	**0778**
N818R	C500	170
N818RC	**CL30**	**20165**
N818RF	GLF5	5018
N818RJ	C550	085
N818RU	**C560**	**0443**
N818SE	**C650**	**0207**
N818SH	FA20	71
(N818SL)	CL64	5391
N818SS	GLF3	342
N818SS	GLF4	1302
N818SS	**GLF4**	**4257**
N818TB	C550	460
N818TG	HS25	258018
N818TH	CL60	1069
N818TH	CL61	5046
N818TH	CL61	5090
N818TH	**CL64**	**5315**
N818TJ	GLF3	384
N818TM	**HS25**	**258463**
N818TP	C550	460
N818TP	HS25	256026
(N818TP)	C650	0120
N818TS	GALX	158
N818TS	GLEX	9018
N818TS	**GLF4**	**4208**
N818TY	CL61	5046
N818VB	GLF3	302
N818WF	**ASTR**	**091**
N818WM	HS25	258126
N818WS	LJ35	285
N819AA	FA20	26
N819AA	HS25	258041
N819AB	HS25	258559
N819AM	**G150**	**272**
N819AP	GALX	109
N819AP	**GALX**	**191**
N819AP	HS25	258559
N819CH	ASTR	098
N819CW	**C52B**	**0331**
N819DM	HS25	257144
N819EK	**C555**	**0009**
N819GA	**G150**	**319**
N819GA	GLF2	115
N819GA	GLF2	17
N819GA	GLF2	178
N819GA	GLF2	228
N819GA	GLF4	4119
N819GF	LJ24	230
N819GY	LJ25	116
N819GY	SBRL	380-66
N819H	C500	263
N819JA	WW24	328
N819JE	LJ35	077
"N819JF"	GLF4	1414
N819JR	**HS25**	**HA-0065**
N819KR	**C550**	**126**
N819LX	HS25	258543
(N819LX)	HS25	258383
N819M	HS25	257170
(N819P)	HS25	25148
N819QS	**C560**	**0786**
N819R	**C525**	**0871**
N819RC	**WW24**	**192**
N819SS	**GLF4**	**1302**
N819VE	**GALX**	**109**
N819WG	HS25	257010
N819Y	C550	311
N820	C500	310
N820	C550	239
N820AA	FA20	118
N820AA	HS25	258042
N820AT	**LJ45**	**270**
(N820AT)	LJ31	133
N820AV	**GLF4**	**4002**
N820BA	GLF3	422
N820CB	C550	550-0820
N820CE	C525	0368
N820CE	FA10	111
N820CK	**FA20**	**120**
N820CT	**HS25**	**257041**
N820DY	SBRL	380-40
N820EC	**F2EX**	**135**
N820F	C555	0118
(N820F)	C650	0183
N820FJ	C500	310
N820FJ	C550	299
N820FJ	**C650**	**0183**
N820FJ	C555	0118
N820GA	GLF4	4200
N820GA	GLF4	4320
N820GA	GLF5	5100
N820GA	HS25	258011
N820HB	GLF4	1024
N820HB	**GLF5**	**570**
N820JM	C550	550-0856
N820JM	C550	550-0885
N820JR	SBRL	282-135
N820JT	**C510**	**0332**
N820L	**LJ24**	**020**
(N820LX)	HS25	258397
N820M	**F900**	**192**
N820M	HS25	258774
N820M	LJ25	342
N820MC	**C550**	**117**
N820MC	HS25	25211
N820MG	HS25	25211
(N820MQ)	C550	117
N820MS	**GLF4**	**1147**
N820MT	LJ31	171
N820NC	**C52B**	**0356**
N820QS	C560	0648
N820QS	**C560**	**0650**
N820RP	LJ35	410
(N820RT)	LJ25	023
(N820RT)	WW24	157
N820SA	C550	299
N820TA	HS25	258555
N820TM	GLF4	1508
N820TM	**HS25**	**258472**
N821AA	FA20	203
N821AA	FA20	67/414
N821AA	HS25	258044
N821AM	**GLEX**	**9183**
N821AV	GLF4	4003
N821AW	LJ25	101
N821BS	FA50	23
N821BS	LJ45	227
N821CC	LJ60	208
N821CN	WW24	181
N821DF	**LJ60**	**042**
N821DG	C56X	5206
N821DG	C56X	5297
N821G	C550	604
N821GA	GLF2	116
N821GA	GLF2	229
N821GA	GLF2	250
N821GA	GLF4	4121
N821GA	GLF5	5101
N821H	WW24	268
N821LB	**HS25**	**258650**
N821LC	**LJ45**	**406**
N821LG	FA10	170
N821LG	WW24	430
(N821LL)	LJ24	216
N821LM	LJ25	317
N821LX	HS25	258406
N821MD	JSTR	5211
N821MP	**HS25**	**258043**
(N821MS)	LJ25	121
N821ND	C510	0038
N821P	C525	0354
N821PA	GLF2	183
N821PC	LJ35	486
N821PP	**C52A**	**0476**
N821QS	**HS25**	**258709**
N821VP	C560	0121
N822A	**GLF4**	**1447**
N822AA	**FA20**	**195**
N822AA	HS25	258045
N822BD	HS25	256067
N822BL	HS25	256067
N822BL	**HS25**	**258022**
N822CA	GLF2	99
N822CA	LJ35	591
N822CA	LJ45	215
N822CA	LJ45	224
N822CB	C550	550-0822
N822CC	**C525**	**0822**
N822CC	HS25	25142
N822CP	LJ35	591
N822DS	C680	0121
N822GA	GLF2	117
N822GA	GLF2	257/17
N822GA	GLF4	4228
N822GA	GLF5	5102
N822GA	GLF5	5522
N822GA	LJ45	224
N822HA	**C550**	**464**
N822LJ	LJ24	080
(N822LX)	HS25	258413
N822MC	LJ55	018
N822MJ	C56X	5023
N822QL	**WW24**	**441**
N822QS	**C560**	**0789**
N822QS	HS25	258422
(N822SF)	LJ35	590
N822ST	F2EX	66
N822TM	**HS25**	**258433**
N822TP	F2TH	20
N822WW	**F9EX**	**136**
N822XP	HS25	258822
N823A	**GLF4**	**4032**
N823AA	FA20	228/473
N823AA	HS25	258046
N823BJ	F900	107
N823CA	LJ35	600
N823CA	**LJ45**	**221**
(N823CB)	C550	550-0823
N823CE	C560	0823
N823CP	LJ35	600
N823CR	**E50P**	**50000316**
N823CT	C550	650
(N823CW)	HS25	258623
N823DF	**GLEX**	**9066**
N823DT	C52A	0086
N823DT	**C56X**	**5634**
N823ES	C525	0066
N823ET	**BE40**	**RK-360**
N823GA	GLF2	118
N823GA	GLF2	188
N823GA	GLF2	258
N823GA	GLF2	75/7
N823GA	GLF4	1005
N823HM	**BE40**	**RK-461**
N823J	LJ35	171
N823L	**C52A**	**0020**
N823LJ	LJ24	082A
N823LT	**C52B**	**0011**
(N823LX)	HS25	258428
(N823LX)	HS25	258648
N823M	**C510**	**0228**
N823M	LJ24	050
N823NA	C550	260
N823PM	**C550**	**550-1064**
N823QS	**C560**	**0794**
N823TR	LJ60	068
N823TT	BE40	RK-278
N823WB	C560	0124
N823XP	HS25	258823
N824AA	HS25	258047
N824CA	GLF4	1010
N824CA	GLF4	1309
N824CB	C550	550-0824
N824CC	**LJ55**	**024**
N824CK	**C560**	**0245**
N824CT	C550	650
N824CW	HS25	258124
N824D	BE40	RK-141
N824DH	**CL61**	**3047**
N824DM	**C52B**	**0270**
N824DM	BE40	RK-141
N824DP	**CL30**	**20507**
N824DS	**FA10**	**92**
N824DW	MU30	A075SA
N824ES	**C525**	**0066**
(N824FL)	HS25	258740
N824GA	GALX	224
N824GA	GLF2	119/22
N824GA	GLF2	77
N824GA	GLF5	5104
N824GA	LJ24	342
N824GB	BE40	RK-371
N824HG	**BE40**	**RK-143**
N824HH	**C56X**	**6077**
N824JK	CL61	5118
N824JM	BE40	RK-96
N824K	HS25	257111
N824LA	FA10	53
N824LJ	LJ24	083
N824LX	**HS25**	**258740**
(N824LX)	HS25	258432
N824MG	**LJ55**	**106**
N824MT	C525	0824
N824QS	HS25	258523
N824R	FA50	121
N824SS	BE40	RJ-18
N824TJ	HS25	25179
N825A	LJ25	111
N825AA	HS25	258049
N825AA	LJ24	147
N825AC	LJ31	058
N825AM	LJ24	340
N825AV	**C52B**	**0152**
N825CA	LJ35	605
N825CA	**LJ45**	**220**
N825CP	**HS25**	**258329**
N825CT	**CL30**	**20162**
N825CT	HS25	257041
N825CT	HS25	258497
N825D	LJ25	263
N825DA	HS25	258167
N825DM	LJ24	237
(N825EC)	WW24	403
N825FL	HS25	258767
N825GA	C525	0027
N825GA	C750	0143
N825GA	GLF2	119/22
N825GA	GLF2	120
N825GA	GLF2	198/35
N825HL	C500	657
N825HL	C555	0088
N825JL	WW24	307
N825JV	C550	296
N825JW	C550	296
N825JW	C650	0082
N825LH	C550	660
N825LJ	LJ24	008
N825LJ	LJ24	085
N825LJ	**LJ35**	**496**
N825LM	**GLF5**	**655**
(N825LM)	GLF4	1460
N825LX	HS25	258767
(N825LX)	HS25	258437
N825MG	LJ55	055
N825MS	HS25	257151
N825MT	**C525**	**0825**
N825PS	**C500**	**630**
N825PS	HS25	258117
N825QS	**C560**	**0655**
N825QT	**HS25**	**258497**
N825SA	**CL65**	**5869**
N825SB	SBRL	282-92
N825T	**GLF4**	**1535**
N825TB	**CL30**	**20234**
N825TC	FA20	52
N825UW	**C650**	**0082**
N825XP	HS25	258425
N826AA	**FA20**	**67/414**
N826AA	HS25	258051
N826AC	**C560**	**0242**
N826AG	**C510**	**0400**
N826AG	C56X	6029
N826AG	GLF2	166/15
N826BM	**C52C**	**0111**
N826CA	LJ35	596
N826CA	**LJ45**	**222**

N826CM	C510	0126
N826CP	LJ35	596
N826CS	**C52B**	**0229**
N826CT	HS25	258117
N826CW	HS25	258026
N826E	E50P	50000338
N826EP	**LJ45**	**439**
N826ES	**EA50**	**550-0282**
N826EW	C550	622
N826EW	**F2TH**	**58**
N826GA	GLF2	166/15
N826GA	GLF2	200
N826GA	GLF2	79
N826GA	**HA4T**	**RC-67**
N826GA	HS25	258263
N826GC	**HS25**	**258263**
N826GW	GLF2	210
N826HS	C525	0305
N826JH	MU30	A050SA
N826JH	BE40	RK-70
N826JM	**BE40**	**RK-199**
N826JP	CL61	5050
N826JS	CL64	5587
N826K	**F9EX**	**36**
N826K	HS25	257119
N826KR	**F2TH**	**182**
N826L	LJ24	007
N826LJ	**LJ60**	**145**
N826LX	HS25	258826
(N826LX)	HS25	258454
N826QS	**C560**	**0782**
N826RD	C500	290
N826RD	LJ35	509
N826RP	C650	0206
N826RP	**GLF4**	**1507**
N826RT	**C550**	**312**
N826SR	LJ60	230
N826SS	LJ60	015
(N826SU)	HS25	258249
N826TG	**PRM1**	**RB-258**
N827AA	**FA20**	**298**
N827BT	C52C	0109
N827CA	LJ35	590
N827CR	LJ35	332
N827CT	**FA50**	**245**
N827DC	C680	0027
N827DC	**GLF6**	**6174**
(N827DC)	GLF5	5011
N827DK	C510	0018
N827DP	C550	660
N827DP	**C560**	**0380**
N827G	GLF3	398
N827GA	GLF2	80
N827GA	GLF3	398
N827GA	**GLF4**	**1391**
N827JB	C550	577
N827JB	C550	604
(N827JK)	GLF4	1140
N827JM	GLF4	1140
N827K	GLF2	221
N827K	GLF4	1180
N827LX	HS25	258848
(N827LX)	HS25	258455
N827NS	HS25	258409
N827QS	**C560**	**0801**
N827RH	HS25	258224
N827SA	HS25	258438
N827SB	**BE40**	**RK-2**
N827SL	**C750**	**0225**
N827SL	SBRL	380-53
(N827TV)	C560	0684
N828AA	FA20	149
N828AF	CS55	0067
N828AN	HS25	257046
N828B	C550	346
N828C	ASTR	055
N828CA	**LJ45**	**159**
N828CC	**GLEX**	**9209**
N828CK	C56X	5201
N828CW	HS25	258428
N828DR	**C56X**	**5774**
N828G	C650	0138
N828GA	G280	2028
N828GA	GLF2	247
N828GA	GLF5	5108
N828GA	GLF5	5228
N828GA?	GLF2	81
N828KC	HS25	257009
N828KD	**CL64**	**5584**
N828KW	FA10	52
N828LX	HS25	258461
N828M	LJ24	050
N828M	LJ35	063
N828MG	GLF3	409
N828MT	C525	0828
N828MW	LJ24	050
N828NS	HS25	258464
N828PA	**EA50**	**000237**
N828PJ	**HS25**	**257005**
N828QA	LJ25	052
N828QS	HS25	258528
(N828SA)	HS25	257002
(N828SH)	C550	275
N828SK	CL30	20020
N828SK	**CL30**	**20258**
N828SK	CL61	5018
N828SS	C550	181
N828UM	**CL64**	**5427**
N828WB	CS55	0097
N829AA	LJ25	100
(N829AM)	F2TH	74
N829BC	**C510**	**0365**
N829CA	LJ35	459
N829CB	**C550**	**550-0829**
N829CR	HS25	258043
N829CS	GLF4	1049
N829GA	GLF2	199/19
N829GA	GLF2	245/30
N829GA	GLF5	5109
N829GA	GLF5	5293
N829GL	**GLF2**	**196**
N829JC	C56X	5291
N829JC	C680	0112
N829JC	CS55	0059
N829JC	**G280**	**2071**
N829JM	C550	215
N829JQ	C56X	5291
N829JV	**GLF6**	**6044**
N829LC	**C56X**	**5300**
N829LX	HS25	258466
N829MB	**C500**	**534**
N829MG	GLF3	327
N829NL	C550	037
N829NL	GLF2	128
N829NS	HS25	258475
N829QS	**C560**	**0796**
N829RA	**GLEX**	**9029**
N829SE	HS25	257095
N829TG	**CS55**	**0010**
N829TS	FA20	359/542
N830	**HS25**	**258782**
N830	WW24	406
N830	WW24	442
N830AA	FA20	55/410
N830BA	HS25	258122
N830BH	GLF2	49
N830C	**WW24**	**442**
N830CB	C650	0160
N830CB	CL61	5057
N830CB	CS55	0004
N830CB	GLF4	1263
N830CD	CL61	5057
N830DB	ASTR	099
N830DB	G150	206
N830DT	**GALX**	**083**
N830EC	**CL30**	**20300**
N830EC	GLF4	1229
N830EF	GLF4	1023
N830FL	**HS25**	**258483**
N830G	GLF2	44
N830GA	G280	2030
N830GA	GLF2	241
N830GA	GLF5	5030
N830GA	GLF5	5330
N830GA	GLF5	5530
(N830GB)	C650	0160
N830GS	**C680**	**0200**
N830JB	**C560**	**0164**
N830KE	C550	550-0830
(N830LR)	HS25	257078
N830LX	HS25	258483
N830MA	WW24	358
N830MF	FA20	112
N830MG	**C650**	**0209**
N830NF	**E50P**	**50000188**
N830NS	HS25	258476
N830QS	**C560**	**0784**
N830RA	FA20	66
(N830SR)	FA10	149
N830SU	**GLF3**	**321**
N830TA	C550	550-1119
N830TE	GLF2	49
N830TL	GLF2	35
N830TL	GLF2	49
N830TM	**HS25**	**258355**
N830TS	**HA4T**	**RC-30**
N830VL	C550	410
(N830WM)	LJ25	355
N831BG	**GALX**	**226**
N831CB	C500	640
N831CB	C650	0160
N831CJ	CL61	5050
N831CJ	LJ35	166
(N831CJ)	HS25	257074
N831CW	C500	159
N831CW	**LJ35**	**390**
N831DC	F2TH	206
N831DC	HS25	258112
N831DF	HS25	25231
N831ET	CL64	5451
N831FC	C52B	0155
N831FJ	**CL30**	**20425**
N831GA	C650	0194
N831GA	**C680**	**0347**
N831GA	GLF2	238
N831GA	GLF2	3
N831HG	FA20	310
N831HS	**C52B**	**0216**
N831HS	C550	550-1028
N831J	LJ35	166
N831JP	**LJ55**	**048**
N831LC	HS25	25095
N831LH	LJ25	244
N831LX	**HS25**	**258510**
N831MF	**C510**	**0118**
N831MM	C560	0362
N831NW	HS25	25231
N831QS	**C560**	**0792**
N831RA	LJ24	164
N831S	C525	0031
(N831TJ)	MU30	A018SA
N831V	C52B	0013
N831VP	**C650**	**0194**
N831WM	LJ25	076
N832CB	C560	0110
N832CB	**C650**	**7020**
N832CC	C650	0167
N832CW	HS25	258432
N832GA	G280	2032
N832GA	GLF2	122
N832GA	GLF2	4/8
N832GA	GLF4	4332
N832GA	GLF5	5112
N832JP	LJ55	051
N832LX	HS25	258281
(N832LX)	HS25	258516
(N832MB)	HS25	25231
N832MG	C52A	0302
N832MJ	HS25	258040
N832MR	HS25	25231
N832MR	HS25	258040
N832QB	C560	0110
N832QS	**HS25**	**258683**
N832R	**C560**	**0585**
N832SC	**CL64**	**5461**
N832UJ	C550	550-0832
N833	C500	416
N833AV	F900	181
N833BA	GALX	114
N833BD	C550	550-0958
N833CL	**E55P**	**50500029**
N833CW	HS25	258033
N833E	**GLF5**	**557**
N833GA	G280	2033
N833GA	GLF2	103
N833GA	GLF2	8
N833GA	GLF4	4331
N833GA	GLF5	5113
N833GA	GLF5	5333
N833GA	LJ24	155
N833JL	C500	416
N833JP	**C550**	**340**
N833JP	HS25	258044
N833LX	HS25	258291
(N833LX)	HS25	258534
N833PA	C550	550-0833
N833PS	**PRM1**	**RB-18**
N833QS	HS25	258433
N833RL	C650	0019
N833TM	**HS25**	**258474**
(N833WM)	C560	0385
N834AF	**LJ31**	**225**
N834CB	C550	550-0834
N834DC	**CS55**	**0035**
N834FW	C525	0834
N834GA	GLF2	124
N834GA	GLF2	6
N834GA	GLF2	62
N834GA	GLF5	5114
N834GA	GLF5	5314
N834GA	GLF5	5434
N834H	C650	0177
N834LX	HS25	258552
(N834LX)	HS25	258543
N834QS	**C560**	**0669**
N835AA	**GLF4**	**1065**
N835AC	LJ24	162
N835AC	LJ35	158
N835AF	LJ60	244
N835AG	LJ24	162
N835CB	**C52B**	**0284**
N835CB	C550	550-0835
N835CW	HS25	258035
N835DM	C52B	0079
N835F	FA10	135
N835GA	G280	2035
N835GA	GLF2	11
N835GA	GLF2	63
N835GA	**GLF4**	**4335**
N835GA	GLF5	5115
N835GA	GLF5	5315
N835GA	LJ35	087
(N835GM)	LJ25	027
N835KK	C650	0175
(N835LX)	HS25	258548
(N835MA)	SBRL	380-36
N835MC	LJ35	673
N835QS	HS25	258435
N835QS	HS25	258505
N835TB	**BE40**	**RK-393**
N835TM	**HS25**	**258387**
N835TS	HS25	258035
(N835VP)	C550	550-0835
N835WB	LJ25	027
N835ZP	HS25	HA-0164
N835ZT	**PRM1**	**RB-180**
N836CM	**CL61**	**5079**
N836GA	G280	2036
N836GA	GLF2	64/27
N836GA	GLF5	5116
N836GA	GLF5	5306
N836GA	LJ36	027
(N836LX)	HS25	258552
N836ME	GLF2	95/39
N836MF	GLF2	154/28
N836MF	GLF2	95/39
N836MF	GLF3	351
N836MF	GLF4	1012
N836QS	HS25	258436
N836UC	FA20	181
N837AC	C525	0537
N837AC	C52A	0188
N837BA	**GLF5**	**5122**
N837CS	LJ25	351
N837F	FA10	137
N837GA	GLF2	65
N837JM	PRM1	RB-169
(N837LX)	HS25	258647
N837MA	C500	096
N837QS	**C560**	**0685**
N837RE	**HA4T**	**RC-54**
N837RE	HS25	258526
N837RF	HS25	258526
N837WM	GLEX	9292
N838BA	**GLF5**	**5140**
N838BB	**FA50**	**126**
N838CC	**C56X**	**6164**
N838CT	**C56X**	**6146**
N838DB	ASTR	099
N838DB	CL64	5427
N838DB	FA50	265
N838GA	GLF2	18
N838GA	GLF2	66
N838GA	GLF4	4338
N838GA	GLF5	5118
N838GA	GLF5	5238
N838JL	**HS25**	**258270**
N838KE	**GLF5**	**5398**
N838LJ	**CL64**	**5327**
N838LJ	HS25	HA-0026
N838LM	**GLF5**	**5115**
N838MA	LJ60	158
N838MF	GLF4	1012
N838MF	GLF5	512
N838MF	**GLF6**	**6042**
N838QS	HS25	258338
N838RC	LJ60	276
N838RT	C56X	5047
N838SB	**EA50**	**000056**
N838SC	**GLEX**	**9035**
N838TH	LJ45	027
N838WC	HS25	258338
N839AC	C525	0537
N839DM	**C52B**	**0248**
N839DW	C550	550-0839
N839F	FA50	55
N839GA	GLF2	19
N839GA	GLF2	67
N839LX	HS25	258657
N839QS	**C560**	**0690**
N839RM	F900	40
N839RM	FA50	159
N840AA	**C560**	**0433**
N840AR	WW24	121
N840CC	**C56X**	**5040**
N840CE	**HS25**	**258677**
N840CT	**C560**	**0236**
N840DP	**FA20**	**381/549**
N840ER	**GLF4**	**1049**
N840F	FA20	18
N840FJ	FA50	223
N840FL	HS25	258666
N840GA	G280	2040
N840GA	GLF5	5240
N840GL	FA10	109
N840GL	LJ35	210
N840H	HS25	25230
N840JM	**LJ45**	**289**
N840JM	BE40	RK-492
N840LX	HS25	258666
N840MA	SBRL	380-21
N840MC	C550	426
(N840MC)	C500	448
N840MQ	C550	426
N840QS	HS25	258340
N840R	C650	0197
N840RG	GLF2	235
N840SP	**C500**	**001**
N840SW	**LJ31**	**084**
N840TJ	MU30	A084SA
N840TM	**HS25**	**258393**
N840WC	HS25	258340
N841AM	**C52B**	**0084**
N841CW	C500	516
N841DW	**C56X**	**5177**
N841F	FA20	19
N841F	FA50	63
(N841FJ)	FA50	41
N841G	C650	0136
N841G	LJ24	162
N841GA	GLF4	4341
N841GA	GLF5	5041
N841GA	GLF5	5241
N841GL	LJ35	235
N841LC	LJ24	167
N841LX	HS25	258702
N841MA	C500	532
N841PA	GLF4	1034
N841PC	CL61	5116
N841QS	**C560**	**0799**
N841TC	C525	0339
N841TC	**HS25**	**258874**
N841TF	**LJ35**	**416**
N841TT	LJ35	416
N841TT	**LJ60**	**031**
N841W	C550	550-0841
N841WS	C550	550-0841
N841WS	**GLF4**	**4099**
N841WS	HS25	258674
N842A	**C56X**	**5042**
N842AW	**C525**	**0873**
N842CB	C550	550-0842
(N842CC)	C550	038
N842DW	C56X	5589
N842F	FA20	20
N842F	FA20	38
N842FL	HS25	258428
N842GA	GALX	142
N842GA	GALX	242
N842GA	GLF5	5242
N842GA	GLF5	5422
N842GL	LJ25	270
N842HS	C52A	0039
N842PA	**GLF4**	**1057**
N842PM	PRM1	RB-4
N842QS	HS25	258542
N843B	HS25	25214
N843CA	C52C	0167
N843CP	HS25	257014
N843CP	**LJ60**	**011**
N843CW	HS25	258543
N843DF	GLF4	1241
N843DW	C680	0219
N843F	FA20	21
N843F	FA20	39
N843G	C650	0173
N843G	CS55	0152
N843GA	ASTR	121
N843GA	GLF4	4143
N843GA	GLF5	5343
N843GA	LJ25	009
N843GL	LJ35	237
N843GS	**CL61**	**5184**
N843HS	C560	0582
N843HS	GLF3	496
N843JS	C56X	5343
N843LX	HS25	258297
N843M	**E55P**	**50500285**
N843MG	**F9EX**	**193**
N843MG	FA20	491
N843QS	**C560**	**0790**
N843RH	**BE40**	**RK-88**
N843TE	**EA50**	**000072**
(N843TS)	HS25	258643
N844AV	F2TH	146
N844CB	GLF4	4350
N844DR	C550	550-0860
N844F	**FA10**	**201**
N844F	FA20	23
N844GA	ASTR	044
N844GA	GALX	004
N844GA	GALX	148
N844GA	LJ24	165
N844GF	GLF4	1107
N844GF	**GLF4**	**4160**
N844GL	LJ35	238
N844GS	GLF4	1107
N844HS	C560	0596
N844HS	GLF4	1289
(N844J)	FA50	56
N844JD	**HS25**	**HA-0174**
N844L	LJ35	014
N844MM	**C525**	**0844**
N844NX	FA50	147
N844QS	**C560**	**0629**
N844RC	**GALX**	**007**
N844S	**LJ60**	**417**
N844SL	FA20	77/429
N844TM	**C560**	**0660**
N844UP	**F2EX**	**287**
N844UP	F2TH	156
N844UR	F2TH	156
N844X	FA50	93
N845BA	LJ45	435
(N845CA)	CL30	20294
N845CW	HS25	258045
N845F	FA20	24
N845FP	**C650**	**7115**
N845FW	C650	0153
N845FW	GLF3	875
N845G	**GLF4**	**4053**
N845GA	**G280**	**2045**
N845GA	GALX	012
N845GA	GLF2	74
N845GA	GLF5	5245
N845GL	LJ35	221
N845HS	GLF5	568
N845HS	GLF5	665
N845JS	**C56X**	**5180**
N845QS	HS25	258545
N845RL	LJ45	022
N845SC	LJ45	084
N845TM	**HS25**	**258436**
N845TX	**C750**	**0011**
N845UP	CL30	20081

N845UP	**F2TS**	**727**
N845UR	CL30	20081
N846BA	LJ45	450
N846F	FA20	26
N846FL	HS25	258461
N846GA	GLF5	5246
N846GA	LJ25	010
N846GL	LJ35	242
N846HC	LJ25	010
N846HS	C550	669
N846JS	**C56X**	**5352**
(N846L)	C550	477
N846MA	C560	0046
N846QM	**GLF5**	**626**
N846QS	C560	0646
N846QS	**C560**	**0797**
N846UP	CL30	20086
N846UP	**F2TS**	**729**
N846UR	CL30	20086
N846YC	LJ25	012
N846YT	LJ25	012
N847A	**C56X**	**5047**
N847C	C555	0003
N847CA	CL30	20039
N847CW	HS25	258647
N847F	FA20	27
(N847FL)	HS25	258647
N847G	C650	0101
N847G	**C555**	**0003**
N847GA	GALX	007
N847GA	GLF5	5247
N847GA	LJ24	167
N847GL	LJ35	239
N847HS	C550	661
N847HS	C560	0609
(N847JA)	C550	550-1005
N847JJ	C525	0520
N847JJ	C550	550-1005
N847JL	C525	0520
N847JS	**C56X**	**5320**
N847NG	**C52B**	**0144**
N847RC	**GLF4**	**4215**
N847RH	HS25	258224
N848AB	JSTR	5214
N848AG	**LJ45**	**401**
N848AM	**E55P**	**50500316**
N848C	WW24	54
N848C	**BE40**	**RJ-63**
N848CA	LJ45	401
N848CC	CL64	5367
N848CC	**CL64**	**5660**
N848CS	**CL30**	**20139**
N848CW	HS25	258648
N848D	C550	039
N848DM	**C56X**	**5329**
N848F	FA20	28
N848FL	HS25	258648
(N848FP)	C650	7115
N848G	**C560**	**0465**
N848G	C555	0152
N848GA	ASTR	111
N848GA	GALX	248
N848GF	GLF4	1107
N848GL	LJ35	488
N848HS	C550	720
N848JA	**GLF5**	**5047**
N848JS	**C56X**	**5292**
(N848K)	FA50	205
(N848K)	LJ45	150
N848MP	FA10	118
N848N	**HS25**	**258371**
N848PF	BE40	RK-288
N848QS	**HS25**	**HA-0031**
N848RJ	GLF3	492
N848TC	**BE40**	**RK-7**
N848US	C650	0060
N848W	HS25	256044
N849AC	**C650**	**0073**
N849BA	LJ45	454
(N849CB)	C550	550-0849
N849F	FA20	29
N849GA	GALX	009
N849GA	GLF5	5249
N849GA	GLF5	5429
N849GL	LJ24	279
N849HS	WW24	344
N849WC	**LJ60**	**211**
N850BA	C550	134
N850BA	C560	0322
N850BA	FA50	115
N850BL	HS25	259033
N850BM	HS25	258142
N850C	**BE40**	**RK-31**
N850CA	FA50	75
N850CC	**SBRL**	**465-38**
N850CS	SBRL	465-38
N850CT	HS25	258677
N850DG	C525	0268
N850DP	**HS25**	**258468**
N850DS	LJ60	047
N850EC	**HS25**	**258789**
N850EJ	CL30	20005
N850EM	HS25	258876
N850EN	**FA50**	**326**
N850EP	**FA50**	**39**
N850EZ	HS25	258799
N850FB	CL61	5162
N850FC	HS25	259032
N850FL	CL61	5162
N850GA	G150	250
N850GA	GLF2	98/38
N850GA	GLF4	4050
N850GA	**GLF4**	**4350**
N850GA	GLF5	5430
N850GM	C525	0366
N850GM	C550	550-0906
N850HB	HS25	258900
N850HS	**HS25**	**258390**
N850J	HS25	258311
N850JA	**HS25**	**259006**
N850JD	C510	0317
N850JL	HS25	258548
N850K	F2TH	210
N850KE	HS25	258796
N850KE	**HS25**	**258961**
N850LA	HS25	258008
N850LG	**GLF4**	**1310**
N850MA	C500	481
N850MA	**C560**	**0514**
N850MC	C650	0090
N850MC	FA50	97
N850ME	HS25	258861
N850MM	LJ35	596
N850MX	LJ25	286
N850NS	HS25	258789
(N850PA)	LJ55	106
N850PE	**HS25**	**258808**
N850PG	**GLF3**	**445**
N850PM	C550	247
(N850PT)	C750	0222
N850RC	**HS25**	**258784**
N850RG	HS25	258622
(N850RG)	BE40	RK-67
N850SC	LJ25	023
N850SM	HS25	258074
N850TC	**F2TH**	**92**
N850TC	HS25	259032
N850TJ	MU30	A054SA
N850TM	**HS25**	**258798**
N850TR	**GLEX**	**9027**
N850VP	**HS25**	**258768**
N850VR	HS25	258656
N850WC	C560	0378
N850WW	WW24	338
N850ZH	HS25	258798
(N850ZH)	HS25	258816
N851AB	**E55P**	**50500241**
N851AC	C52C	0081
N851AC	**C56X**	**5575**
N851BA	LJ24	194
N851BC	C500	514
N851C	**MU30**	**A077SA**
N851CB	**GLF4**	**4132**
N851CC	**HS25**	**258787**
N851CC	LJ24	339
N851CW	HS25	258051
N851DB	**C525**	**0054**
N851E	WW24	379
N851EL	GLF4	1515
N851GA	GLF2	99
N851GA	GLF5	5051
N851GA	GLF5	5511
N851GG	**GLF4**	**4120**
N851HS	**C550**	**550-1028**
N851JH	LJ24	207
N851L	**LJ35**	**114**
N851LE	GALX	106
N851LJ	**LJ85**	**3001**
N851QS	**HS25**	**258686**
N851RG	**HS25**	**258634**
N851RV	**E50P**	**50000260**
N851SC	GALX	174
N851TM	**PRM1**	**RB-211**
N851VR	**HS25**	**258673**
N851WC	C560	0330
N851WC	JSTR	5229
N852A	**HS25**	**258083**
N852AC	C560	0692
N852BA	**LJ45**	**292**
N852CA	F9EX	155
N852CC	HS25	HA-0012
N852E	**FA20**	**486**
N852GA	GLF2	100
N852GA	HS25	256048
N852GA	LJ24	173
N852HA	**C550**	**172**
N852K	**LJ45**	**215**
N852L	C525	0625
(N852LJ)	LJ85	3002
N852LX	HS25	258397
N852PA	LJ55	055
N852QS	HS25	258452
N852QS	**HS25**	**258714**
N852SB	C550	172
N852SC	LJ25	006
N852SP	**C52B**	**0092**
N852SP	C550	172
N852WC	C560	0194
N852WC	HS25	257095
(N852WC)	LJ36	013
N852WR	C550	151
N853AC	**C560**	**0774**
N853CC	**HS25**	**258803**
N853CR	**C560**	**0324**
N853DC	**PRM1**	**RB-255**
N853DS	LJ25	012
N853GA	GLF2	101
N853GA	GLF5	5335
N853GA	GLF5	5513
N853GA	LJ25	012
N853JA	C56X	6031
N853JL	C510	0113
N853JL	C52B	0048
N853KB	C500	637
(N853LJ)	LJ85	3003
N853M	ASTR	146
N853QS	HS25	258535
N853QS	**HS25**	**258721**
N853SD	**C525**	**0672**
N853SP	ASTR	053
N853TC	**EA50**	**000245**
N853WC	C750	0008
N853WC	HS25	257032
N854AN	**C56X**	**5713**
N854FL	**HS25**	**258454**
N854GA	FA20	279/502
N854GA	GLF2	102/32
N854GA	GLF5	5342
N854GA	GLF5	5514
N854GA	LJ24	174
(N854GA)	LJ55	056
N854JA	**C550**	**550-0920**
(N854LJ)	LJ85	3004
N854QS	**HS25**	**258725**
N854RB	SBRL	282-106
N854SD	GLF4	1387
N854SD	**GLF4**	**1522**
N854SM	**HS25**	**25265**
(N854W)	FA50	163
N854WC	C750	0027
N854WC	FA20	40
N854WC	HS25	257058
N855A	**G280**	**2044**
N855BB	**C525**	**0381**
N855BC	**HS25**	**258055**
N855CD	SBRL	306-85
N855DB	LJ55	062
N855DG	**F2EX**	**97**
N855DG	FA20	432
(N855DH)	C650	0014
N855ED	**C525**	**0850**
(N855ER)	HS25	258331
N855FC	**HS25**	**HA-0008**
N855FC	BE40	RK-141
N855G	**GLF5**	**5118**
N855GA	GLF2	103
N855GA	**HS25**	**258211**
N855GA	LJ24	158
N855JB	**PRM1**	**RB-104**
(N855LJ)	LJ85	3005
N855MS	**EA50**	**000121**
N855MW	**HS25**	**258241**
N855NC	**LJ55**	**108**
N855PT	**LJ55**	**046**
N855QS	HS25	258355
N855QS	**HS25**	**258730**
N855RA	**BE40**	**RK-114**
N855RB	GLF5	509
N855RM	**PRM1**	**RB-174**
N855SA	**GLF3**	**363**
N855SC	**C56X**	**5763**
N855TJ	**F2EX**	**19**
N855TM	**HS25**	**258457**
N855W	LJ24	159
N855W	LJ24	191
N855W	LJ24	199
N856AF	GLF4	1276
N856AF	HS25	258140
N856BB	C525	0381
N856BB	**C52B**	**0207**
N856CW	C560	0432
N856F	F2TH	138
N856G	LJ25	013
N856GA	GLF2	104/10
N856GA	GLF5	5256
N856GA	GLF5	5506
N856JB	**LJ24**	**052**
N856JM	CL61	5094
(N856LJ)	LJ85	3006
N856MA	SBRL	306-41
N856RR	LJ35	496
N856T	**GALX**	**112**
N856TD	GLF5	646
N856W	GLF2	104/10
N856W	GLF3	484
N857AA	**C550**	**550-0901**
N857BL	C560	0381
(N857BT)	C550	231
N857C	**BE40**	**RK-17**
(N857CW)	HS25	258657
N857DN	**C650**	**0181**
N857GA	LJ25	014
N857PR	LJ55	073
N857QS	HS25	HA-0132
(N857SC)	LJ25	006
N857ST	**GLF4**	**1345**
N857W	SBRL	465-72
N857WC	C560	0069
N858CB	**C52B**	**0490**
N858CV	**CL65**	**5772**
N858DN	**GALX**	**038**
N858EE	**E55P**	**50500352**
N858EZ	BE40	RK-425
N858GM	LJ25	015
N858GS	**EA50**	**000039**
N858JR	HS25	257100
N858KE	HS25	258796
N858ME	**C560**	**0253**
N858MK	**LJ45**	**141**
N858PJ	**CL60**	**1028**
N858Q	**PRM1**	**RB-269**
N858QS	HS25	258691
N858RM	**C550**	**550-0914**
N858SD	C525	0672
N858SD	**C52A**	**0475**
(N858SH)	JSTR	5117/35
N858SP	**FA10**	**11**
N858TH	**C750**	**0312**
N858TM	LJ35	409
(N858TS)	GLEX	9158
N858W	GLF2	104/10
N858WW	**ASTR**	**064**
N858WZ	ASTR	102
N858XL	HS25	258140
N858XP	**HS25**	**258758**
N859AE	C56X	5695
N859AG	**CL65**	**5831**
N859BA	**CL65**	**5743**
N859GA	GLF2	180
N859GM	LJ24	175
N859L	LJ24	175
N859QS	HS25	HA-0122
(N859RP)	HS25	258331
N859XP	HS25	258859
N860AA	**GLF5**	**5079**
(N860AH)	LJ60	017
N860AP	**HA4T**	**RC-60**
N860BA	**FA50**	**142**
N860CR	**C560**	**0500**
N860DB	C525	0271
N860DB	**C525**	**0434**
N860DD	C525	0271
N860DD	C525	0434
N860DD	C52B	0046
N860DD	**C52B**	**0375**
N860E	FA10	52
N860FJ	F9EX	30
N860GA	GLF2	181
(N860J)	C550	550-
0860 N860JB	GLF4	1054
N860JH	C550	550-0860
N860JL	HS25	258548
N860MX	LJ25	109
N860PD	**LJ60**	**073**
N860PM	GLF2	224
(N860Q)	C560	0633
N860QS	**HS25**	**258698**
N860S	LJ35	086
N860SB	**CL30**	**20307**
(N860SC)	C52A	0009
N860SM	**C680**	**0255**
N860ST	F900	60
N860TM	**HS25**	**258479**
N860W	**C650**	**7086**
N861BB	C550	550-0861
N861CE	C560	0273
N861CE	HS25	258006
N861CE	HS25	258181
(N861CF)	C560	0273
N861CW	HS25	258061
N861GA	GLF2	184
N861GA	LJ25	018
N861GS	WW24	356
N861HA	**C52B**	**0366**
(N861L)	LJ25	023
N861ME	HS25	258861
N861PA	LJ60	015
N861PD	C525	0027
N861QS	HS25	258361
N861RD	C525	0027
N861SS	SBRL	465-40
N861WC	HS25	258361
(N862BD)	LJ35	087
N862CE	C56X	5021
N862CE	GLF2	109
N862CE	GLF3	306
N862CE	HS25	258089
N862CE	HS25	258244
N862CF	C56X	5021
N862CW	HS25	258062
N862G	GLF2	188
N862G	GLF3	329
N862GA	GLF2	185
N862GA	GLF2	22
N862GA	GLF3	338
N862GS	**C510**	**0406**
(N862JA)	HS25	258362
N862KM	BE40	RK-227
N862LG	**E55P**	**50500163**
N862MT	C525	0862
N862PA	**LJ60**	**014**
N862PD	LJ35	087
N862QS	HS25	258362
N862VP	**CL30**	**20012**
N862WC	HS25	258362
(N863A)	GLF3	361
N863AB	WW24	196
N863BA	**GLEX**	**9360**
N863BD	FA50	161
N863CA	LJ45	160
N863CA	LJ45	179
N863CE	GLF3	306
N863CE	HS25	258289
N863DD	C52B	0375
N863GA	GLF2	23
N863GJ	**HS25**	**258663**
N863JB	**C560**	**0260**
N863LB	**LJ45**	**160**
N863MF	**GLF5**	**512**
N863PA	LJ60	004
N863QS	HS25	258463
N863RD	**C560**	**0287**
N863TM	F2TH	217
(N863TS)	F2TH	63
N863VP	CL30	20311
N864BA	**CL65**	**5707**
N864CB	C550	550-0864
N864CC	C56X	5067
N864CE	GLF4	1085
N864CE	HS25	258331
N864CL	LJ24	229
N864D	C550	313
N864DC	**HS25**	**258647**
N864EC	C650	7014
N864KB	**LJ31**	**048**
N864MM	**C750**	**0071**
N864PA	LJ60	017
N864QS	HS25	258564
(N864TT)	C500	477
N864YC	GLF4	1003
N864YD	GLF2	156/31
N865AA	**GLF2**	**48/29**
N865AM	**BE40**	**RK-358**
N865BB	**E55P**	**50500217**
N865CA	**LJ45**	**193**
N865CE	C56X	5017
N865EC	**C680**	**0028**
(N865EC)	C650	7014
N865JM	**GLF4**	**4078**
N865JM	HS25	HA-0087
N865JT	HS25	258800
N865LS	HS25	HA-0037
N865M	C560	0179
N865M	C560	0550
N865M	C560	0803
N865M	**C56X**	**6091**
N865MK	**C52B**	**0463**
N865MT	**C525**	**0865**
N865PC	**FA50**	**271**
N865R	**GLF4**	**4050**
N865SM	HS25	258365
N865SP	**LJ35**	**544**
N865TM	**HS25**	**258505**
N865VP	C525	0356
N865VP	FA20	360
N866AB	**GLF5**	**579**
N866AV	F2TH	146
N866BB	**GLF5**	**5466**
N866BB	BE40	RK-98
N866CA	**LJ45**	**184**
N866CB	C550	550-0866
N866CW	HS25	258466
N866DB	LJ24	018
N866DH	WW24	78
N866FP	FA50	22
N866G	ASTR	062
N866G	**GALX**	**025**
N866JM	WW24	184
N866JS	LJ24	018
N866MM	FA20	175
N866Q	ASTR	062
N866QS	C560	0633
N866RA	LJ45	210
N866RB	HS25	258405
N866RR	HS25	258405
N866RR	HS25	258624
N866ST	**C525**	**0866**
N866TC	**C560**	**0802**
N866TM	**CL30**	**20066**
N866VP	**C560**	**0704**
(N866VP)	C550	668
N867CE	GLF4	1195
N867CW	C550	094
N867CW	HS25	258067
N867GA	GLF5	5267
N867GA	GLF5	5467
N867JC	**C550**	**180**
N867JS	LJ31	086
N867K	**EA50**	**000239**
N867QS	**HS25**	**258576**
N867W	**C56X**	**5601**
N868AG	GLF2	167
N868BB	GLF4	4051
N868BT	**FA50**	**93**
N868CC	**CL64**	**5662**
N868CE	CL61	5016
(N868CE)	GLF3	306
N868CP	WW24	341
N868D	GLF5	5183
(N868D)	C500	338
N868DB	**FA50**	**265**
N868DS	FA20	256
N868DS	GLF2	123/25
N868EM	C52B	0081
N868EM	**C680**	**0282**

(N868GB)	HS25	259017
N868GM	C680	0090
N868HC	**C52C**	**0008**
N868J	C56X	5089
N868J	C56X	5180
N868J	LJ24	077
N868JB	C56X	5048
N868JB	C56X	5089
N868JB	C56X	5180
N868JB	C56X	6014
N868JL	BE40	RK-239
N868JS	LJ31	087
N868JT	C560	0310
N868MJ	**C680**	**680A0022**
N868MJ	C680	680A0024
(N868NB)	FA50	283
N868QS	**HS25**	**258765**
N868RB	**C56X**	**6057**
(N868SB)	EA50	000056
N868SC	GLEX	9352
N868SM	**GLF2**	**254/41**
N868WC	HS25	258178
N868XL	**C56X**	**5603**
N869AC	**C52A**	**0103**
N869AV	**LJ60**	**306**
N869AW	**EA50**	**000233**
N869B	LJ24	089
N869CB	**C525**	**0453**
N869CS	GLF2	2
N869DL	**LJ45**	**113**
(N869EG)	SBRL	465-33
N869GA	GLF2	29
N869GR	**C525**	**0478**
N869GS	C525	0478
N869JS	LJ60	005
N869K	C500	077
N869KA	**C52C**	**0074**
N869KC	SBRL	465-33
N869KM	HS25	257165
N869MD	**GLF4**	**1363**
N869QS	**HS25**	**258771**
N869QS	HS25	HA-0075
(N869QS)	HS25	HA-0122
N870	FA50	251
N870AJ	C560	0048
N870AM	MU30	A087SA
N870BA	**WW24**	**412**
N870BB	BE40	RK-22
N870CA	HS25	258111
N870CK	**LJ35**	**170**
N870CM	CL64	5488
N870CM	**GLF5**	**5076**
N870F	FA20	40
N870GA	GLF2	125/26
N870GA	GLF2	30/4
N870GA	GLF5	5070
N870GA	GLF5	5470
N870HY	C510	0166
N870JS	LJ60	028
N870MH	C550	475
N870P	MU30	A015SA
N870P	BE40	RK-20
N870PT	C550	383
N870QS	**HS25**	**258732**
N870R	SBRL	282-137
N870SB	**C56X**	**5567**
N870TM	**HS25**	**258517**
N870WC	C550	695
N871CB	C550	550-0871
N871D	GLF2	145
N871D	GLF2	245/30
N871D	HS25	257134
N871D	JSTR	5067
N871E	GLF2	145
N871F	FA20	42
N871FR	**GLF6**	**6013**
N871GA	GLF2	129
N871GA	GLF2	49
N871HB	HA4T	RC-71
(N871MA)	HS25	25233
N871MM	F9EX	89
N871QS	**HS25**	**258763**
N871RF	**C56X**	**5219**
N872AT	**HS25**	**258278**
N872BC	**CL64**	**5479**
N872BC	HS25	258524
N872D	HS25	25275
N872E	GLF2	257/17
N872EC	C650	0113
N872EC	F2TH	143
N872F	FA20	43
N872G	**C510**	**0307**
N872GA	GLF2	130
N872HB	HA4T	RC-72
N872J	**C52B**	**0477**
N872JR	LJ24	173
N872MK	**BE40**	**RK-195**
N872QS	HS25	258472
N872RD	C550	262
N872RT	C550	262
N872XP	HS25	258872
N873	WW24	137
N873D	C500	337
N873D	HS25	25160
N873DB	C560	0184
N873E	GLF3	320
N873EJ	WW24	167
N873F	FA20	44
N873G	CL61	3009
N873G	HS25	25160
N873GA	GLF2	132
N873GA	GLF5	673
N873LP	LJ35	104
N873LP	LJ35	220
N873LP	LJ35	659
N873LR	LJ35	220
N873QS	**HS25**	**258573**
"N873QS"	HS25	258570
N874A	GLF4	1285
N874AJ	SBRL	282-70
N874C	**GLF4**	**1219**
(N874CW)	HS25	258374
N874G	C650	0137
N874GA	GLF2	136
N874JD	HS25	258589
N874JD	LJ35	457
N874JD	BE40	RK-141
N874JM	C555	0127
N874PT	C750	0274
N874PW	**C510**	**0392**
N874QS	HS25	258474
N874RA	GLF3	361
(N874RR)	GLF3	361
N874VT	**F900**	**161**
N874WD	ASTR	062
N874WD	**CL30**	**20186**
N874XP	HS25	258874
N875BC	**HS25**	**258524**
N875CA	**LJ60**	**286**
N875CA	SBRL	465-42
(N875E)	GLF2	119/22
(N875E)	GLF3	361
N875F	FA20	47
(N875F)	F9EX	101
N875G	CL61	3019
N875GA	GALX	075
N875GA	GLF2	137
N875GA	GLF2	55
N875H	CL61	5093
N875HB	**HA4T**	**RC-75**
N875HS	WW24	370
N875LP	**HS25**	**258308**
N875MT	C525	0875
N875NA	EA50	000018
N875P	**WW24**	**370**
N875PK	CL60	1018
N875QS	HS25	258375
N875SC	C650	0027
N875SC	HS25	258111
N875TM	**HS25**	**258523**
N875WP	HS25	258524
N876AM	**C510**	**0282**
N876BB	**C550**	**550-1087**
N876BC	LJ45	252
N876C	**F9EX**	**162**
N876C	LJ35	616
N876CB	C550	550-0876
N876CS	LJ35	616
N876CS	**LJ60**	**263**
N876CW	HS25	258666
N876DG	**CL30**	**20222**
N876F	FA20	45
N876G	**C650**	**7062**
N876GA	ASTR	106
N876GA	GLF2	57
N876H	CL64	5542
N876H	HS25	258303
N876JC	**E50P**	**50000075**
N876JC	HS25	257055
N876MA	FA10	63
N876MA	**LJ60**	**193**
N876MC	**LJ24**	**217**
N876MS	**C525**	**0876**
N876QS	**HS25**	**258586**
N876RA	**C56X**	**5231**
N876RW	GLF3	355
N876SC	C650	0076
N876SC	F2TH	24
N876SC	FA20	391
N876SC	HS25	258124
N876SF	**LJ60**	**100**
N876UC	**C52A**	**0147**
N876WB	C500	347
N877A	**GLF4**	**1461**
N877AB	GLEX	9167
N877B	C550	550-1096
N877B	C550	550-1110
N877BP	C500	255
N877C	C500	376
N877CM	C650	7077
N877CW	HS25	258077
N877D	ASTR	102
N877DF	FA50	25
N877DM	CL61	5174
N877DM	HS25	258279
N877FL	**BE40**	**RK-223**
N877G	C650	7063
(N877GB)	C550	232
N877GS	C525	0179
N877H	**CL64**	**5445**
N877J	**BE40**	**RK-69**
N877JG	**FA20**	**325**
N877LC	**GLF4**	**1165**
N877PM	**EA50**	**000260**
N877QS	**HS25**	**HA-0066**
N877RB	C560	0318
N877RF	C560	0318
N877RF	C56X	5219
N877RF	CL30	20306
N877RP	HS25	258084
N877RW	**C56X**	**5114**
N877S	HS25	258323
N877S	HS25	258560
N877S	MU30	A055SA
N877S	BE40	RJ-17
N877S	BE40	RK-17
N877S	BE40	RK-420
N877S	BE40	RK-69
(N877S)	HS25	258562
N877SD	C550	550-0875
N877SL	HS25	258323
N877T	MU30	A055SA
N877TM	**HS25**	**258542**
N877W	**LJ45**	**496**
N877W	PRM1	RB-107
N877XP	HS25	258777
N877Z	BE40	RK-17
N878AG	C550	550-0941
N878BW	**EA50**	**000013**
N878CC	**CL65**	**5777**
N878CS	GALX	027
N878DB	**GLF5**	**5167**
N878DE	LJ24	153
N878DN	GALX	046
N878EE	LEG5	55000008
N878EE	**LEG5**	**55000017**
N878F	FA20	48
N878G	**GALX**	**209**
N878G	GLF4	1331
N878GA	GLF2	58
(N878H)	CL65	5846
N878HL	**GLEX**	**9261**
N878J	**C525**	**0608**
N878JP	**C52A**	**0105**
(N878LP)	LJ35	659
N878MA	LJ31	031
N878MB	**HS25**	**258603**
N878ME	LJ25	351
N878MM	**C510**	**0188**
N878MT	C525	0878
N878PR	**C510**	**0362**
N878QS	**HS25**	**HA-0054**
N878RG	**LJ60**	**027**
N878RM	CL61	3012
N878SC	**GLEX**	**9614**
N878SM	**GLF4**	**1319**
N878SP	C510	0188
N878W	LJ24	207
N879F	FA20	50
N879GA	GLF2	59
N879PT	C750	0279
N879QS	HS25	258379
N879RA	JSTR	5023
N879WC	HS25	258379
N880A	GLF2	38
N880AF	**HS25**	**258279**
N880CA	ASTR	055
N880CC	**CL65**	**5949**
N880CH	ASTR	045
N880CH	LJ35	335
N880CK	SBRL	306-121
N880CM	C500	398
N880CM	C550	550-1032
N880CM	**CL65**	**5818**
N880CR	CL64	5356
(N880CR)	HS25	257177
(N880EF)	C560	0147
N880ET	**CL64**	**5514**
N880F	FA20	51
N880F	FA50	3
N880G	GLF4	1286
N880GA	GLF2	139/11
N880GA	GLF2	86/16
N880GC	GLF4	1016
N880GM	GLF2	42/12
N880GP	**ASTR**	**086**
N880HK	**CL65**	**5793**
(N880HL)	SBRL	282-72
N880HM	BE40	RJ-19
N880KC	SBRL	306-121
N880LJ	LJ45	180
N880LT	**HS25**	**259051**
N880M	C500	524
N880M	HS25	258027
N880MD	GLF6	6035
N880MG	**BE40**	**RK-83**
N880MR	**C52B**	**0226**
N880MS	LJ40	2093
(N880NE)	GLEX	9043
N880P	**C56X**	**5364**
N880P	FA20	51
N880PC	**F2EX**	**138**
N880PF	C52B	0317
N880QS	HS25	258570
N880QS	HS25	258580
N880RG	**HS25**	**257107**
N880RJ	**F2EX**	**26**
N880RJ	GLF2	159
N880RL	C52A	0220
N880SC	HS25	256018
N880SP	HS25	258298
N880TD	**FA50**	**14**
N880TM	**HS25**	**258528**
N880WC	**C525**	**0885**
N880WD	GLF2	217
N880WD	GLF4	1170
N880WE	GLF2	217
N880WW	HS25	258019
N880WW	WW24	195
N880XP	HS25	258800
N880YY	**HS25**	**258546**
N880Z	**LJ35**	**591**
N880Z	WW24	203
N881A	**C555**	**0139**
N881AA	**PRM1**	**RB-12**
N881AF	**HS25**	**258289**
(N881BA)	C650	0081
N881CA	C500	132
N881CA	LJ35	508
N881CJ	CL61	5050
N881CW	HS25	258461
N881DM	SBRL	282-137
N881E	GLF4	4028
N881F	FA20	52
N881FC	LJ24	175
N881G	C750	0101
N881G	F900	104
N881G	FA20	399
N881GA	GALX	081
N881GA	GLF2	140/40
N881GA	GLF2	153
N881GA	GLF2	88/21
N881HS	**GLF5**	**603**
N881J	FA20	396
N881J	LJ25	294
(N881J)	FA50	92
N881JG	**C550**	**669**
N881JT	C500	159
N881JT	FA20	513
(N881JT)	HS25	259043
(N881K)	FA50	79
N881KS	C525	0300
(N881L)	FA50	105
N881M	FA50	83
(N881M)	C500	073
N881MC	SBRL	282-19
N881MC	SBRL	306-100
N881MD	SBRL	282-19
N881MJ	**LJ45**	**076**
N881P	F900	146
N881P	FA10	33
N881P	LJ25	302
N881Q	**F2EX**	**278**
N881Q	F9EX	80
N881QS	**HS25**	**HA-0050**
N881S	HS25	257042
N881SA	C550	617
N881ST	**GALX**	**210**
N881TS	**GLEX**	**9247**
N881TW	CL64	5348
N881VP	**C56X**	**6018**
N881W	LJ35	269
N881WR	**GLF5**	**5327**
N881WT	**GLEX**	**9002**
N882AA	**PRM1**	**RB-41**
N882C	CL61	5065
N882CA	C500	296
N882CA	**LJ45**	**155**
N882CB	**CL65**	**5927**
N882CW	HS25	258002
N882ET	**GALX**	**044**
N882F	FA20	56
N882GA	**ASTR**	**082**
N882GA	GLF2	142
N882GA	GLF2	89
N882JD	LJ31	109
N882KB	C650	0095
N882KB	**C750**	**0216**
N882KB	C555	0075
N882LT	**G280**	**2075**
N882LT	GALX	044
N882QS	HS25	258482
N882RB	**C555**	**0075**
N882SB	LJ25	227
N882SC	**LJ35**	**590**
N882SG	**GALX**	**084**
N882SS	**F900**	**80**
N882W	GLF2	109
N882WF	**C550**	**550-0882**
N882WT	**GLF5**	**516**
N883A	GLF3	416
N883A	**GLF5**	**5175**
N883BS	LJ45	136
N883CW	HS25	258643
N883EJ	HS25	258183
N883ES	GLF2	98/38
N883F	FA20	57
N883GA	GLF2	143
N883GA	GLF2	90
N883KB	C650	0095
(N883KF)	GLF2	92
N883LC	**EA50**	**000203**
N883LS	**GLF4**	**1110**
N883MT	**C525**	**0883**
N883PA	GLF3	385
N883PF	C52B	0317
N883PF	C56X	5085
N883PF	**C56X**	**6053**
N883PF	C555	0083
(N883PP)	C52B	0317
N883QS	**HS25**	**258773**
N883RA	FA50	338
N883RA	**LJ60**	**389**
N883RA	SBRL	465-22
N883RP	**C56X**	**5501**
N883RT	C560	0260
N883RW	FA50	338
N883SC	**C56X**	**5124**
N883XL	C500	177
N884AM	**EA50**	**000164**
N884B	**C56X**	**5140**
N884BB	C56X	5036
N884BB	**F900**	**17**
N884CF	HS25	258084
(N884DR)	C500	242
N884F	FA20	58
N884GA	GLF2	92
N884JG	**C525**	**0700**
(N884JL)	C750	0143
N884JW	LJ35	316
N884L	GLF4	1212
(N884MF)	C510	0078
N884QS	**HS25**	**258734**
N884RS	C680	0189
N884TM	**C510**	**0180**
N884TW	LJ60	244
N884VC	HS25	258584
N884WE	**GLF4**	**4143**
N884WT	GLF4	4143
N884WY	F2TH	178
N885	**F900**	**6**
N885A	**F2EX**	**265**
N885AR	GALX	055
N885AR	**GLF4**	**4009**
(N885AR)	GLF5	5219
N885B	**F9EX**	**169**
N885BB	**C56X**	**5135**
N885BH	FA20	272
N885BT	**C52B**	**0058**
N885CA	ASTR	039
N885CA	C500	255
N885DR	WW24	279
N885F	FA20	60
N885FJ	F2EX	223
N885G	GLF5	518
N885GA	GLF2	93
N885GA	GLF4	4285
N885JF	**C52B**	**0342**
N885KT	**GLF5**	**699**
N885LA	**C52B**	**0085**
N885LS	**HS25**	**258428**
N885M	C560	0179
N885M	**C680**	**0508**
N885M	HS25	258410
N885QS	**HS25**	**258743**
N885RR	GALX	055
(N885RR)	GLF4	4009
N885RS	**C510**	**0389**
N885TA	GLF4	1003
N885TM	**HS25**	**258564**
N885TW	**CL30**	**20037**
N885TW	LJ31	165
(N885VC)	HS25	258585
N885WT	**GLF5**	**5237**
N886AT	C550	166
N886BB	F9DX	611
N886BH	**C56X**	**5717**
N886CA	C500	258
N886CA	C52C	0167
N886CA	LEG5	55000017
N886CA	LJ45	154
N886CE	**F2EX**	**79**
N886CS	LJ35	023
N886CW	HS25	258006
N886DC	**F900**	**177**
N886DT	GLF3	463
N886DT	GLF5	636
N886DT	JSTR	5223
N886EM	**C525**	**0651**
N886EP	**BE40**	**RK-117**
(N886ER)	BE40	RK-117
N886F	FA20	54
N886G	**GALX**	**057**
N886GA	GLF2	94
N886GB	HS25	257002
(N886GW)	HS25	258006
N886LS	**GLF4**	**1341**
N886MJ	FA10	199
N886MT	C525	0886
N886QS	HS25	258486
N886R	**LJ35**	**269**
N886RP	C555	0158
N886S	HS25	257025
N886WC	LJ24	213
N886WC	LJ35	023
N886WT	**GLF6**	**6017**
N886YS	**C550**	**550-1013**
N887AG	GLF5	5175
N887BB	C550	550-0887
N887CE	F2EX	95
N887CS	**C560**	**0787**
(N887CW)	HS25	258397
(N887DM)	C500	476
N887DR	**FA20**	**369**
N887DT	JSTR	5223

N887F	FA20	61
N887GA	GLF2	95/39
N887PA	ASTR	025
N887PC	ASTR	015
N887PC	**HS25**	**HA-0095**
N887PL	WW24	195
N887QS	HS25	258387
N887SA	C550	604
N887SB	**C525**	**0887**
N887SG	**LJ45**	**174**
N887TM	**GLF5**	**5294**
N887WM	GLEX	9041
N887WM	**GLEX**	**9292**
N887WS	GLEX	9120
N887WT	**GLF6**	**6124**
N887X	**FA7X**	**150**
N887XF	**FA7X**	**88**
N888AC	C500	349
N888AR	FA20	33
N888AZ	CL61	3024
N888B	LJ24	167
N888BH	C500	526
N888BL	LJ35	140
N888BS	LJ35	409
N888BY	BE40	RK-171
N888CE	**F2EX**	**124**
N888CF	GLF2	10
N888CF	JSTR	5070/52
N888CJ	HS25	25084
N888CN	C750	0086
N888CN	CL30	20062
N888CP	**LJ31**	**003**
N888CR	HS25	25180
N888CS	GLF2	98/38
N888CW	GLF3	489
N888CW	GLF5	545
N888CX	LJ45	044
N888DB	LJ25	073
N888DC	**GLF4**	**4256**
N888DE	LJ35	010
N888DF	LJ25	189
N888DH	CL61	5014
N888DH	**CL64**	**5305**
N888DH	HS25	258051
N888DH	LJ25	109
N888DH	LJ35	010
N888DJ	LJ35	067
N888DL	HFB3	1051
N888DS	C500	449
N888DS	LJ24	013
(N888DT)	LJ35	187
N888DV	LJ25	370
N888DZ	EA50	000198
N888EB	C550	350
N888ES	GLF2	98/38
N888ES	**GLF4**	**1120**
N888FA	LJ24	257
N888FC	**F2TH**	**48**
N888FG	**C550**	**324**
N888FJ	**CL61**	**5178**
N888FJ	FA10	4
(N888FK)	LJ55	108
N888FL	C500	371
N888FR	**GLF4**	**1041**
N888FW	CL60	1079
N888G	FA10	197
N888GA	C500	132
N888GA	GLF2	96
N888GC	LJ25	258
N888GJ	**HS25**	**259042**
N888GL	**C52A**	**0201**
N888GN	**HS25**	**257154**
N888GQ	GALX	167
N888GS	**C510**	**0209**
N888GX	**GLEX**	**9248**
N888GZ	C500	349
N888HE	GLF5	638
N888HH	**GLF4**	**4029**
N888HK	**GLF5**	**5213**
(N888HK)	GLF5	638
N888HS	C550	550-0862
N888HW	C550	108
N888HZ	**GLF5**	**5197**
N888JA	CL61	5049
(N888JA)	LJ25	301
N888JD	C500	132
(N888JE)	GLF4	4256
(N888JK)	MS76	043
N888JL	C500	242
N888JR	FA20	144
N888KG	**C52C**	**0125**
N888KG	C650	0119
N888KJ	**C52C**	**0209**
N888KJ	GLF4	4208
N888KL	C52A	0102
N888KL	**LJ60**	**141**
N888KS	CL60	1073
N888KU	C525	0068
N888L	FA20	144
N888LB	**C52C**	**0167**
N888LD	PRM1	RB-95
(N888LF)	GLF4	1362
N888LG	**F900**	**201**
N888LG	GLF4	1125
N888LJ	**LJ60**	**216**
N888LK	GLF4	1125
N888LK	GLF4	1362

N888LK	GLF5	5012
N888LR	LJ25	171
N888LV	GLF3	347
N888LW	CL60	1025
N888MC	GLF2	247
N888MC	GLF3	351
N888MC	GLF4	1086
N888MC	LJ24	106
N888MC	SBRL	306-39
N888ME	FA50	41
N888MF	FA50	41
N888MF	**GLF4**	**1268**
N888MJ	C500	097
N888MN	**PRM1**	**RB-153**
(N888MP)	WW24	147
N888MQ	C525	0888
N888MV	LJ35	362
N888MW	C550	028
N888MX	**F2EX**	**148**
N888MX	GLF4	1110
N888NA	**F2TH**	**77**
(N888NA)	C550	723
N888ND	**GLF4**	**4343**
N888NS	**GALX**	**114**
N888NS	LJ24	106
N888NX	F2EX	40
N888PA	C560	0270
(N888PA)	C500	242
N888PM	GLF3	435
N888PM	**GLF4**	**1195**
N888PM	HS25	256041
N888PM	SBRL	282-12
N888PN	**C500**	**457**
N888PS	C525	0492
N888PS	C52B	0263
N888PT	**E50P**	**50000143**
N888PT	LJ35	391
N888PY	C525	0492
N888QS	**HS25**	**HA-0042**
N888R	WW24	254
N888RA	**C525**	**0135**
N888RB	LJ25	150
N888RE	C560	0260
N888RF	C550	108
N888RF	FA20	272
N888RK	C525	0331
N888RK	C52B	0097
N888RK	**C52C**	**0183**
N888RL	**C550**	**275**
N888RP	**C56X**	**5152**
N888RT	C550	275
N888RT	C560	0260
N888RT	C56X	5047
N888RT	**C56X**	**6033**
N888RT	CL30	20162
N888RW	JSTR	5040
N888SF	C525	0480
N888SF	**C680**	**0154**
N888SM	**GLF3**	**367**
N888SQ	GLF4	1305
N888SS	HS25	258106
N888SV	C560	0442
N888SW	GLF2	117
N888SW	HS25	257134
(N888TD)	F900	51
N888TF	C510	0023
N888TF	C525	0823
N888TF	**C52B**	**0481**
N888TJ	HS25	25250
(N888TN)	LJ36	026
N888TW	**LJ24**	**292**
N888TX	**C650**	**7003**
(N888UD)	CL30	20142
N888UE	GLF4	1032
N888UP	**SBRL**	**465-68**
N888VS	GLF3	450
N888VS	**GLF5**	**5313**
N888WE	**GLF3**	**394**
(N888WJ)	FA10	89
N888WK	HS25	25141
N888WL	**F2EX**	**69**
N888WL	GLF3	471
N888WL	SBRL	306-27
N888WS	CL61	5170
N888WS	E50P	50000260
N888WS	FA20	148
N888WT	JSTR	5070/52
(N888WW)	JSTR	5061/48
N888WY	**HS25**	**258921**
(N888WZ)	GLF3	397
N888XL	C500	177
N888XL	**C550**	**598**
N888XP	HS25	HA-0200
N888XS	**GLF5**	**5344**
N888XY	**GLF5**	**509**
N888YC	**G150**	**266**
N888YV	**G150**	**302**
N888YZ	**GLF2**	**92**
N888ZF	**GLF4**	**1466**
N888ZJ	**GLEX**	**9071**
N888ZP	**GLEX**	**9104**
N888ZY	**EA50**	**000213**
N888ZZ	**HS25**	**258017**
N889AB	**FA7X**	**170**
N889B	**C550**	**550-1047**
N889BW	**EA50**	**000248**
N889CA	**LJ45**	**132**

N889CG	GLF4	1386
N889CM	**EA50**	**000035**
N889CP	GLEX	9104
N889DF	**C680**	**0018**
N889DF	GLF2	95/39
N889DH	HS25	258051
N889DT	**PRM1**	**RB-77**
N889DW	**LJ60**	**117**
N889F	FA20	64
N889FA	C550	162
N889G	C650	0023
N889G	GALX	046
N889GA	GLF2	97
N889H	**F9EX**	**126**
N889JA	**GLEX**	**9148**
N889JC	GLF2	158
(N889JC)	GLEX	9068
N889JF	LJ24	019
N889MB	**HS25**	**258228**
N889MC	**F2TH**	**29**
N889MR	**GALX**	**074**
N889MU	**F2TH**	**160**
N889QS	HS25	HA-0019
N889QS	**HS25**	**HA-0021**
N889RA	SBRL	465-22
N889RP	C555	0158
N889SH	**C500**	**681**
N889ST	**GLEX**	**9610**
N889SW	**C52A**	**0504**
N889TA	F9EX	171
N889TC	GLF4	1042
N889TD	F900	94
N889TD	**F9EX**	**171**
N889TF	**C525**	**0823**
N889TR	**F900**	**94**
N889WF	LJ24	060
N889WF	LJ24	237
N890A	GLF2	16/13
N890A	GLF3	325
N890A	GLF4	1396
N890A	**GLF5**	**5371**
N890A	HS25	258071
N890AC	**LJ55**	**092**
N890BA	**WW24**	**301**
N890BB	**F9DX**	**611**
N890BH	BE40	RK-208
N890BJ	**LJ25**	**229**
N890CM	**CL65**	**5862**
N890CW	HS25	258510
(N890E)	FA10	53
N890F	FA20	65
N890FH	F9EX	99
N890FH	FA50	31
N890GA	FA50	89
N890GA	GLF4	4290
N890HJ	HFB3	1026
(N890K)	LJ25	089
N890LE	**C56X**	**5628**
N890LJ	**LJ35**	**487**
N890LR	LJ35	487
N890MC	C650	0199
(N890MC)	JSTR	5033/56
N890MT	**C525**	**0890**
N890PT	LJ24	236
N890QS	**HS25**	**HA-0010**
N890RC	HS25	25084
N890SP	HS25	258530
N890TJ	GLF2	23
N890TM	**HS25**	**258545**
(N890VC)	HS25	258590
N890WW	WW24	190
N891CA	**C500**	**168**
N891CQ	FA10	53
N891E	**GLF5**	**5321**
N891F	FA20	66
N891FV	**C560**	**0427**
N891HJ	HFB3	1036
N891M	C560	0085
N891MG	GLF3	357
N891NY	**C510**	**0421**
N891P	**LJ25**	**340**
N891QS	**HS25**	**258788**
N891SH	**C650**	**0210**
N891WW	GLF6	6192
N892AB	C52B	0372
N892AB	**C52C**	**0131**
(N892AC)	LJ35	155
(N892BP)	HS25	258188
N892CA	C500	044
N892F	FA20	68
N892GA	GLF2	60
N892HJ	HFB3	1037
N892PB	C550	064
N892QS	**HS25**	**258592**
N892S	FA20	379
N892SB	C560	0208
N892SB	**C56X**	**5686**
N892SB	FA20	379
N892SB	GALX	072
N892TM	GLF2	121
N892VR	HS25	258592
N892Z	**C56X**	**6007**
N893A	**C525**	**0893**
N893AC	CL61	5018
N893AC	LJ35	644
N893CA	C500	374
N893CF	LJ35	669

N893CM	C560	0226
N893CW	HS25	258603
N893EJ	HS25	258193
N893F	FA20	69
N893FL	HS25	258603
N893HJ	HFB3	1039
N893M	C560	0237
N893MW	E50P	50000142
N893QS	HS25	258393
N893WA	LJ25	169
N894C	**C52A**	**0013**
N894CA	FA10	36
N894CA	HS25	258366
N894CJ	**LJ24**	**335**
N894F	FA20	133
N894GA	GLF2	145
N894HJ	HFB3	1045
N894JH	**E55P**	**50500138**
N894KS	**C56X**	**5662**
N894MA	**C56X**	**5307**
N894Q	C525	0253
N894QS	**HS25**	**HA-0005**
N894TW	**WW24**	**354**
N895BB	**CL30**	**20156**
N895CB	**C52B**	**0398**
(N895CB)	C525	0680
N895CC	CL60	1039
N895CC	**CL61**	**5177**
N895CC	HS25	257072
N895CP	**BE40**	**RK-59**
N895DM	**LJ31**	**199**
N895EE	**LEG5**	**55000014**
N895F	FA20	134
N895HE	C550	641
N895HJ	HFB3	1051
N895J	LJ24	213
N895JH	**E55P**	**50500174**
N895LD	C560	0034
N895QS	HS25	258597
N895QS	**HS25**	**258606**
(N895QS)	HS25	258618
N895TM	**HS25**	**258416**
N896AC	**GLF4**	**1374**
N896BB	**CL30**	**20177**
N896C	BE40	RK-53
N896CG	**C550**	**550-1055**
N896CW	HS25	258516
N896DA	**FA50**	**117**
N896EC	C650	0196
N896GA	GLF2	149
N896GA	GLF5	5296
N896HJ	HFB3	1054
N896JH	**E55P**	**50500215**
N896LS	**E55P**	**50500071**
N896MA	C500	290
N896MA	C550	134
N896MA	**C550**	**550-1065**
N896MB	C500	290
N896P	**C52A**	**0379**
N896QS	HS25	258596
N896QS	HS25	258618
N896QS	**HS25**	**258640**
(N896QS)	HS25	258612
N896R	LJ60	091
N896RJ	C650	0178
N896RJ	**C750**	**0271**
(N896TW)	FA50	117
N897A	**HS25**	**258326**
N897AT	GLF5	5063
N897AT	BE40	RK-157
N897AW	**GLF5**	**5063**
N897CW	**HS25**	**258077**
N897D	FA20	134
N897DM	FA20	134
N897GA	GLF2	146
N897HJ	HFB3	1055
N897JH	**E55P**	**50500318**
N897MC	C550	550-0914
N897NC	**GLF5**	**5234**
N897QS	**HS25**	**HA-0014**
N897R	LJ60	097
N897SC	C550	550-0897
N897SS	C56X	6154
N898AK	**CL61**	**5040**
N898AN	CL64	5408
N898AW	**GLF4**	**1283**
N898BA	**C550**	**550-0902**
N898CB	C560	0097
N898CC	CL64	5367
N898CC	**GLEX**	**9696**
N898CE	**GLF5**	**5230**
N898CT	**F2TH**	**60**
N898DD	HS25	258704
N898DL	**CL65**	**5897**
N898DV	C525	0898
N898EW	CL61	5134
N898GA	GLF2	147
N898GF	C560	0121
N898MC	C56X	5244
N898MP	C56X	5512
N898MW	**E55P**	**50500048**
N898NC	**GLF6**	**6125**
N898PA	**LJ60**	**111**
N898PP	**C56X**	**5244**
(N898PR)	LJ60	111
N898QS	HS25	258593
(N898QS)	HS25	258602

N898R	CL64	5408
N898SC	GLEX	9066
N898SR	WW24	224
N898TA	BE40	RK-295
N898TS	**F900**	**95**
N898WS	**GLEX**	**9271**
N899AB	**HS25**	**257042**
N899AK	**HA4T**	**RC-20**
N899AL	GLF4	1495
N899AU	GALX	149
N899B	**C550**	**550-1073**
N899BC	C56X	5030
N899BC	**F2EX**	**132**
N899CH	**GLEX**	**9390**
N899CS	LJ31	052
N899DC	C550	550-0899
N899DM	HS25	257028
N899DX	**E50P**	**50000216**
N899EE	**E55P**	**50500154**
N899FS	**GLF4**	**4338**
N899GA	GLF2	43
N899GM	GLF5	508
N899JC	E50P	50000029
N899JF	**C680**	**0122**
N899KK	**CL65**	**5875**
N899MA	C52B	0073
N899MA	C550	134
N899N	C500	114
N899NB	C52C	0145
N899NC	**GLF5**	**5401**
N899NH	C52B	0242
N899NH	**C52C**	**0145**
N899QS	HS25	258399
N899QS	**HS25**	**HA-0019**
N899QS	HS25	HA-0021
N899RJ	**C550**	**450**
N899RR	C52B	0020
N899S	WW24	101
(N899SA)	HS25	25146
N899SC	HS25	258602
N899SC	LJ60	040
N899SR	GLF5	5231
N899ST	**CL65**	**5791**
N899TA	BE40	RK-292
N899TG	SBRL	282-13
N899TM	**HS25**	**258452**
N899U	F2TH	199
N899WA	LJ35	049
N899WW	CL61	3011
N899WW	GLEX	9092
N899XP	HS25	HA-0199
N899YF	**GLF6**	**6127**
N900AD	HS25	25275
N900AF	C550	022
N900AJ	LJ25	027
N900AK	GLF2	108
N900AL	GLF4	1097
N900AL	GLF4	4048
N900AL	**GLF5**	**5500**
N900AP	**GLF4**	**1097**
(N900AR)	FA10	157
N900BA	C550	242
N900BD	LJ24	143
N900BF	GLF2	206
N900BF	**HS25**	**HA-0022**
N900BF	WW24	382
(N900BF)	F900	39
(N900BF)	F900	71
N900BJ	**LJ35**	**123**
N900BK	**F900**	**187**
N900BL	HS25	257185
(N900BM)	C550	126
N900BR	GLF2	111
N900BT	**C525**	**0377**
N900BT	MU30	A046SA
N900BZ	F9EX	37
N900CC	C500	310
N900CC	CL61	3042
N900CC	F900	183
N900CC	**GLF4**	**1517**
N900CC	HS25	257043
N900CD	HS25	25111
N900CE	GLF2	10
N900CH	**F2EX**	
N900CH	**FA20**	**383/550**
N900CH	FA50	264
N900CJ	LJ25	020
N900CL	CL61	5031
N900CL	CL61	5122
N900CM	C650	0017
N900CM	**F9EX**	**80**
N900CM	FA50	321
N900CP	HS25	257066
N900CQ	**F9EX**	**30**
N900CQ	HS25	257066
N900CR	JSTR	5036/42
N900CS	F900	104
N900CS	SBRL	282-17
N900CS	WW24	212
N900CX	F9EX	19
N900CZ	F900	14
N900D	**F900**	**131**
N900D	FA10	141
N900DA	F900	170
N900DB	FA20	327
N900DB	**JSTR**	**5225**
(N900DG)	LJ35	378

N900DH	C500	576
N900DH	**GLF2**	**111**
N900DL	ASTR	030
N900DL	C500	576
N900DL	LJ24	109
N900DM	C500	421
N900DM	CS55	0067
N900DM	**WW24**	**358**
N900DP	ASTR	152
N900DP	CL60	1036
N900DS	**C525**	**0032**
N900DS	HS25	25187
(N900DU)	F900	97
N900DV	F900	148
N900DW	F900	179
N900DW	**FA7X**	**39**
N900DW	MU30	A026SA
N900E	**C560**	**0206**
N900EB	C52A	0008
N900EB	**C680**	**0008**
N900EC	LJ35	236
N900EF	**F9EX**	**59**
N900EF	BE40	RK-68
(N900EF)	BE40	RJ-47
N900EG	**GLF4**	**1101**
N900EJ	C750	0109
N900EJ	**F900**	**110**
N900EL	HS25	25222
N900EL	**LJ31**	**200**
N900EM	LJ35	185
N900ER	**HS25**	**HA-0191**
N900ES	CL64	5381
N900ES	GLF2	174
N900ES	**GLF5**	**5322**
N900EX	F9EX	103
N900EX	F9EX	114
N900EX	F9EX	12
N900EX	F9EX	120
N900EX	F9EX	159
N900EX	F9EX	178
N900EX	F9EX	201
N900EX	F9EX	27
N900EX	F9EX	40
N900EX	F9EX	63
N900EX	F9EX	84
(N900EX)	F9EX	117
(N900EX)	F9EX	140
N900FA	LJ55	024
N900FC	CL60	1045
N900FG	HS25	HA-0105
N900FH	F9EX	6
N900FJ	F900	10
N900FJ	F900	116
N900FJ	F900	126
N900FJ	F900	131
N900FJ	F900	147
N900FJ	F900	158
N900FJ	F900	166
N900FJ	F900	179
N900FJ	F900	31
N900FJ	F900	42
N900FJ	F900	60
N900FJ	F900	79
N900FJ	F900	98
N900FJ	F9EX	233
N900FJ	**F9EX**	**37**
N900FL	C650	7049
N900FN	CL61	5118
N900FR	FA20	223
N900FS	C56X	6049
N900FS	**F2EX**	**177**
N900FS	WW24	191
N900FU	HS25	HA-0105
N900G	**C500**	**268**
N900GA	GALX	164
N900GB	GLF4	1025
N900GC	C500	298
N900GF	**C550**	**550-1046**
N900GG	LJ24	216
N900GW	**C525**	**0323**
N900GX	**GLEX**	**9298**
N900H	**CL61**	**5080**
N900H	JSTR	5135
N900H	WW24	388
N900HA	**C52A**	**0039**
N900HC	F900	68
N900HC	F9EX	127
N900HD	**F9EX**	**103**
N900HE	F900	68
N900HG	**F9EX**	**1**
N900HT	**E55P**	**50500061**
N900HW	F900	68
N900JA	LJ24	108
N900JB	FA50	113
N900JB	FA50	59
N900JB	LJ55	088
N900JC	LJ35	178
N900JD	C500	023
N900JD	C650	0213
N900JD	C680	0109
N900JD	C750	0503
N900JD	**C750**	**0507**
N900JD	LJ25	020
(N900JD)	C650	0199
(N900JD)	C650	0215
N900JE	LJ35	123
N900JE	LJ35	674

N900JF	WW24	191
(N900JF)	F9EX	168
N900JG	F9EX	168
N900JG	**FA7X**	**115**
(N900JG)	HS25	257069
N900JL	FA20	171
N900JL	WW24	80
N900JQ	F9EX	168
N900JS	**F900**	**115**
N900JT	**HS25**	**257147**
(N900JV)	LJ35	091
N900KC	C500	055
N900KC	HS25	25191
N900KC	HS25	257021
N900KC	HS25	258232
(N900KC)	HS25	25038
N900KD	**C56X**	**5523**
N900KD	F900	131
N900KE	**FA50**	**52**
N900KJ	**F900**	**199**
N900KK	LJ60	052
N900KM	**C750**	**0089**
N900KM	F9EX	177
N900KR	**F900**	**146**
N900KS	**GLF6**	**6163**
N900KX	F9EX	98
N900LA	GLF3	379
N900LC	C550	040
N900LC	**F900**	**186**
N900LC	FA20	122
N900LD	HS25	HA-0008
N900LD	**HS25**	**HA-0213**
N900LF	GLEX	9015
N900LG	CL60	1036
N900LH	MU30	A018SA
N900LJ	C550	011
(N900LK)	F9EX	128
(N900LL)	C500	499
N900LM	**CS55**	**0145**
N900LM	WW24	373
N900LP	**F900**	**20**
N900LS	GLEX	9216
N900LS	**GLEX**	**9522**
N900LS	GLF4	1178
N900LS	GLF4	1401
N900MA	F900	67
N900MC	C500	427
N900MC	**F2TH**	**228**
N900MD	HS25	257107
N900MD	HS25	258019
N900MD	LJ36	045
N900MF	C550	074
N900MF	F9EX	112
N900MG	F900	67
N900MJ	F900	48
N900MJ	F9EX	57
N900MJ	**HS25**	**HA-0038**
N900MK	**F900**	**40**
N900MK	F9EX	29
N900MM	C500	522
N900MN	C650	7027
N900MP	C500	055
N900MP	GLF2	99
N900MR	HS25	257072
N900MT	F9EX	57
N900MV	F9EX	131
N900NA	**LJ24**	**111**
N900NB	F900	190
N900NB	F9EX	169
N900NB	**FA7X**	**74**
N900NE	F900	83
N900NF	F9EX	169
N900NH	**F2TH**	**206**
N900NM	CL61	5057
N900NS	F9EX	150
N900NW	WW24	337
N900P	C525	0234
N900P	FA20	36
N900P	LJ25	049
N900P	LJ31	199
N900P	LJ35	457
N900P	LJ45	173
N900P	**LJ60**	**366**
N900P	SBRL	306-12
N900PA	WW24	400
N900PB	**C550**	**566**
N900PE	**HS25**	**HA-0057**
N900PF	HS25	HA-0022
N900PF	**HS25**	**HA-0209**
N900PJ	LJ55	064
N900PJ	WW24	135
N900PL	F9EX	44
N900PS	C500	362
N900PS	**C560**	**0118**
N900PY	**GLF4**	**4298**
N900Q	F900	93
N900Q	F9EX	10
N900Q	LJ25	049
N900QC	**HS25**	**HA-0143**
N900QM	C650	0017
N900QS	**C750**	**0123**
N900R	**HS25**	**HA-0013**
N900R	LJ31	101
N900R	LJ35	488
N900RA	**FA20**	**59**
N900RB	C500	664
N900RB	CS55	0086

N900RD	C500	664
N900RD	LJ35	261
(N900RF)	F9EX	209
(N900RG)	CS55	0065
N900RL	**GLF4**	**1150**
N900RL	HS25	258090
N900RN	F900	26
N900RX	**F900**	**183**
N900SA	JSTR	5148
N900SB	F900	14
N900SB	**F9EX**	**26**
(N900SB)	F9EX	12
N900SE	C550	074
N900SF	**F900**	**16**
N900SF	GLF2	167
N900SG	F9EX	159
N900SJ	F900	19
N900SJ	**F9EX**	
N900SK	**HS25**	**258777**
N900SM	**C560**	**0014**
N900SM	F900	176
N900SN	**F9EX**	**117**
N900SQ	BE40	RK-416
N900SS	C550	550-0941
N900SS	CL61	5047
N900SS	**FA50**	**284**
N900SS	HS25	258616
N900ST	**HA4T**	**RC-58**
N900ST	HS25	258777
N900ST	BE40	RK-416
N900SX	**F900**	**139**
N900T	C500	135
N900T	FA10	134
N900TA	C500	182
N900TA	F900	50
(N900TE)	C550	203
N900TF	C550	203
N900TG	F900	155
N900TJ	C550	203
N900TJ	GLF2	199/19
N900TN	C550	430
N900TN	WW24	400
N900TP	GLF2	160
N900TR	F900	170
N900TR	F900	9
N900TR	**GLEX**	**9226**
N900TV	**C56X**	**5097**
N900TW	C500	563
(N900TW)	C525	0455
N900UC	**CL64**	**5519**
N900UC	FA10	33
N900UD	C650	0213
N900UT	F900	140
N900VA	**HS25**	**HA-0020**
N900VE	**F9EX**	**111**
N900VG	F900	148
N900VG	F9EX	178
N900VG	**F9EX**	**286**
(N900VH)	F900	148
N900VL	F900	60
N900VL	**F9DX**	**609**
N900VL	GLF2	99
N900VM	F9EX	64
N900VP	WW24	289
N900VQ	F9EX	178
N900VT	F900	131
N900W	C500	014
N900W	FA50	60
N900WA	LJ25	248
N900WB	FA20	139
N900WF	F900	117
N900WG	F900	83
N900WG	**F9EX**	**33**
N900WG	HS25	25236
N900WJ	GLF2	190
N900WJ	MU30	A028SA
N900WK	F900	57
N900WL	**C56X**	**5037**
(N900WP)	F900	183
N900WR	**GLF4**	**1416**
N900WS	E50P	50000294
N900WS	**HS25**	**258893**
N900WW	WW24	321
N900WY	**CL30**	**20035**
N900XL	**C56X**	**5544**
N900XP	**HS25**	**HA-0062**
N900Y	LJ24	111
N900Y	LJ36	014
N900YB	F900	18
N900YG	**F9EX**	**246**
N900YP	**F9EX**	**114**
N900ZA	F9EX	96
N900ZM	F9EX	88
N901AB	**C560**	**0302**
N901AG	**HS25**	**HA-0083**
N901AS	GLF2	88/21
N901B	F900	24
N901BB	F900	42
N901BM	CL61	5044
N901BM	GLF2	120
N901C	JSTR	5218
N901CD	SBRL	465-39
N901CJ	C525	0278
N901CR	**C56X**	**5141**
N901DK	C560	0544
N901DK	**C56X**	**5505**
N901EB	**C52A**	**0008**

N901EH	**GLF3**	**333**
N901EH	JSTR	5230
N901FH	C56X	5160
N901FH	**F2EX**	**203**
N901FH	GLF3	333
N901FH	JSTR	5230
N901FJ	F900	79
(N901FJ)	F900	147
N901FR	FA20	270
N901G	C680	0065
N901GA	GALX	201
N901GA	GLF3	249
N901GA	**GLF4**	**4301**
N901GA	GLF5	5001
N901GA	GLF5	5301
N901GG	**C525**	**0901**
N901GW	**C525**	**0470**
N901GX	GLEX	9001
N901H	JSTR	5092/58
N901HB	SJ30	006
N901JC	LJ55	088
(N901JF)	GLF3	315
N901JL	WW24	38
N901K	GLF2	36/3
N901K	GLF4	1075
N901K	HS25	258329
N901K	HS25	HA-0009
N901KB	GLF2	36/3
N901LB	**C560**	**0218**
N901LK	**C650**	**7064**
N901MD	F9EX	38
N901MH	FA10	110
N901MJ	**HS25**	**HA-0101**
N901MK	FA50	157
N901MM	**F9EX**	**21**
(N901MS)	LJ35	360
N901MT	**PRM1**	**RB-119**
N901MV	C52B	0114
N901NB	C500	661
N901P	LJ31	199
N901P	BE40	RJ-20
N901PM	LJ25	280
N901PM	**LJ60**	**404**
N901PV	CS55	0156
N901QS	C750	0101
N901QS	**C750**	**0102**
N901RD	HS25	HA-0018
N901RH	**C650**	**0130**
N901RL	HS25	258090
N901RM	C550	242
N901RM	C560	0116
N901RP	HS25	258090
N901S	**C680**	**0065**
N901SB	C650	7008
N901SB	F900	33
N901SB	**F9EX**	**122**
N901SB	FA20	446
N901SB	FA20	493
N901SC	**HS25**	**258561**
N901SG	**CL64**	**5399**
N901SG	HA4T	RC-29
N901SG	HS25	258762
N901SS	F900	187
N901SS	**G150**	**254**
N901TA	CL61	5141
N901TC	FA20	335
N901TC	HS25	25108
N901TF	**FA50**	**285**
N901TG	HS25	25108
N901TX	F900	170
(N901VB)	G150	202
N901WG	GLF2	126
N901XP	HS25	HA-0201
N901YP	FA20	360
N902	GLF2	11
N902	GLF4	1310
N902AB	LJ24	068
N902AG	**CL64**	**5512**
N902AR	LJ24	068
N902AR	LJ24	237
N902AU	**ASTR**	**025**
(N902AV)	C560	0326
N902BE	**HS25**	**HA-0070**
(N902BE)	HS25	HA-0081
N902BW	**CL61**	**5005**
N902C	GLF3	388
N902CG	CL64	5427
N902DD	C500	126
N902DK	C550	732
N902DP	C525	0644
N902DW	**F900**	**179**
N902F	**C650**	**7022**
N902FH	**C56X**	**5160**
N902FR	FA20	132
N902G	ASTR	030
N902GA	G280	2102
N902GA	GLF2	11
N902GA	GLF4	4302
N902GT	GLF2	2
N902GW	**C525**	**0553**
N902H	GLF4	1310
N902JC	LJ35	227
N902K	GLF3	386
N902K	GLF4	1113
N902K	JSTR	5104/6
N902KB	GLF3	386
N902KB	JSTR	5104/6

N902L	GLF4	1504
N902LG	**C510**	**0066**
N902M	F900	152
N902MC	**F2TH**	**130**
N902MK	F900	152
(N902MK)	GLF2	241
N902MM	GLEX	9097
N902MP	**CL64**	**5559**
N902MP	GLF2	241
N902MS	**HS25**	**HA-0196**
N902MY	**GLEX**	**9616**
N902MZ	**C525**	**0902**
N902NC	F900	97
N902P	BE40	RJ-15
N902PC	FA10	106
(N902PC)	BE40	RK-28
N902PM	HS25	257036
N902QS	C750	0002
N902RD	C525	0453
N902RD	PRM1	RB-74
N902RL	LJ55	087
N902RM	C650	7022
N902RM	HS25	257036
N902SB	C650	7008
N902SB	**F9EX**	**167**
N902SB	FA20	504
N902SB	FA50	308
N902SS	**C52B**	**0273**
N902T	C500	135
N902TA	CL61	5139
N902TF	**FA50**	**303**
N902VP	C650	0209
N902VP	**C750**	**0002**
N902WJ	LJ36	040
N902XP	HS25	HA-0202
N902YP	**F9EX**	**92**
N903AG	**CL65**	**5961**
N903AG	GLF2	172
N903AG	LJ60	045
N903AL	LJ35	084
N903AM	LJ60	104
N903AM	**LJ60**	**269**
N903BH	C560	0295
N903BT	**LJ45**	**353**
N903CG	BE40	RK-333
N903CS	**FA50**	**138**
N903DD	**CL60**	**1038**
N903DK	C56X	5093
N903EX	F9EX	33
N903FH	C56X	5160
N903FJ	F9EX	3
(N903FJ)	F900	98
N903FR	FA20	20
N903G	GLF2	172
N903G	GLF3	422
N903G	**GLF4**	**4183**
N903G	SBRL	282-60
N903GA	GLF2	172
(N903GL)	GLF3	422
N903GS	**F2TH**	**183**
N903GW	**C525**	**0676**
N903HC	LJ35	440
N903HC	LJ45	010
N903JC	LJ55	081
(N903JF)	GLF4	1051
N903JP	**C510**	**0102**
N903JS	**FA50**	**95**
N903K	HS25	258329
N903K	SBRL	282-33
N903K	SBRL	465-57
N903KB	SBRL	282-33
(N903KP)	GLF4	1051
N903LJ	LJ31	242
N903MC	**C52B**	**0272**
N903MM	WW24	235
N903MT	**PRM1**	**RB-24**
N903QS	**C750**	**0162**
N903RL	LJ45	227
N903SB	C650	7061
N903SB	FA20	335
N903SB	FA50	309
N903SC	HS25	257004
N903TA	CL61	5080
N903TC	CL30	20083
N903TC	GLF3	454
N903TC	**GLF4**	**4320**
N903TF	GLEX	9097
N903VP	C550	550-0903
N903WJ	LJ35	380
N903XP	HS25	HA-0003
N903XP	HS25	HA-0213
N904AM	C52A	0020
(N904AM)	C525	0230
N904BB	**C550**	**550-0904**
N904BW	**HS25**	**258042**
N904DP	C525	0503
N904DS	**GLEX**	**9118**
N904FR	FA20	151
(N904FR)	FA20	223
N904G	**GLF5**	**5101**
N904GA	GLF4	4204
N904GA	GLF5	5004
N904GA	GLF5	5404
N904GA	GLF5	5504
N904GP	HS25	258179
N904GR	**HS25**	**258179**
N904GW	**C525**	**0681**

N904H	HS25	258239
N904H	HS25	259040
N904HD	**LJ45**	**149**
N904JC	HS25	258904
N904JK	**CL64**	**5615**
N904JR	**HS25**	**258018**
N904JY	**F9EX**	**187**
N904K	SBRL	282-42
N904K	SBRL	465-23
N904KB	SBRL	282-42
(N904KB)	SBRL	465-23
N904LR	**C560**	**0163**
N904M	F900	40
N904MT	**C525**	**0904**
N904QS	**C750**	**0210**
N904RS	F900	86
N904SB	FA20	446
N904SB	FA50	284
N904SB	HS25	258016
N904SJ	**C550**	**604**
(N904SR)	C560	0163
N904TC	GLF4	1444
N904TC	**GLF4**	**4327**
N904TF	**F2EX**	**71**
N904TS	GLF4	4347
(N904VA)	CS55	0059
N904XP	HS25	HA-0004
N905AC	**C56X**	**5196**
N905B	**F2TH**	**132**
N905BA	CL30	20257
N905BG	SBRL	306-30
N905CK	**LJ36**	**005**
N905CW	C550	072
N905EM	C550	032
N905EX	F9EX	5
N905FJ	**F900**	
N905FR	**FA20**	**213**
N905G	**G280**	**2067**
N905GW	**C525**	**0682**
N905H	HS25	258275
N905K	SBRL	282-49
N905K	SBRL	465-17
N905KB	SBRL	282-49
N905LC	C550	581
N905LC	**C560**	**0334**
N905LC	LJ35	320
N905LD	LJ35	320
N905LP	**GLF4**	**1321**
N905M	SBRL	282-12
N905MG	HS25	258430
N905MH	**C550**	**454**
N905MP	**CL60**	**1039**
N905MT	**CL30**	**20020**
N905MT	HS25	258430
N905MW	HFB3	1027
N905MZ	**C525**	**0905**
N905P	SBRL	306-62
N905QS	**C750**	**0105**
N905R	SBRL	306-30
N905R	SBRL	306-62
N905R	SBRL	306-99
N905RL	LJ55	074
N905SA	**CL65**	**5957**
N905SB	FA20	360
N905SB	FA50	348
(N905SB)	CL64	5312
N905ST	**LJ40**	**2109**
N905T	**GLEX**	**9179**
N905TF	**F2EX**	**262**
N905TS	F900	5
N905WJ	LJ25	105
N905WS	**C680**	**0141**
(N905Y)	HS25	25199
N906AC	**C56X**	**5596**
N906AS	C560	0547
N906AS	**HS25**	**258569**
N906BL	**HS25**	**258806**
(N906BL)	HS25	258801
N906BP	**CL30**	**20338**
N906CM	**F900**	**102**
N906D	**F9DX**	**624**
N906DK	**C56X**	**6016**
(N906EA)	C500	490
N906FM	PRM1	RB-176
N906FR	FA20	214
N906FS	**GLF5**	**5521**
N906GA	GLF4	1181
N906GA	GLF4	4206
N906GA	GLF5	5006
N906GW	**C52B**	**0408**
N906GX	GLEX	9006
N906JC	**GLF4**	**4026**
N906JW	GLEX	9110
N906KW	F900	151
N906MC	**C52B**	**0352**
N906MS	**C550**	**550-0906**
N906MT	**C525**	**0906**
N906NB	F900	190
N906NB	FA7X	74
(N906NB)	F9EX	169
N906P	**LJ45**	**173**
N906QS	**C750**	**0206**
N906SB	C560	0092A
N906SB	CL64	5313
N906SB	CS55	0139
N906SB	F900	14
N906SB	FA50	349
N906SB	**FA7X**	**75**
N906SB	HS25	258016
N906SU	LJ25	123
N906TC	CL30	20083
N906TF	CL64	5366
N906TF	**FA7X**	**146**
N906WK	F900	102
N907CR	C56X	6071
N907CS	LJ24	137
N907DF	**C650**	**0120**
N907DK	**C525**	**0338**
N907DP	**ASTR**	**100**
N907DX	F9DX	607
(N907EA)	C560	0104
N907EX	F9EX	207
N907FJ	F9EX	7
N907FR	FA20	224
(N907FR)	FA20	270
N907GA	G150	307
N907GA	GLF4	4207
N907GA	GLF5	5007
N907GX	GLEX	9007
N907JE	**BE40**	**RK-107**
N907KH	C500	599
N907LW	**C525**	**0868**
N907M	FA50	35
N907MC	**HS25**	**258340**
N907MT	**C525**	**0907**
N907PJ	**HS25**	**HA-0009**
N907QS	**C750**	**0201**
N907R	LJ35	488
N907R	SBRL	306-40
(N907RM)	C650	0103
N907RT	C500	255
N907SB	C560	0109A
N907SB	CS55	0141
N907SB	FA7X	13
N907SF	**C52C**	**0028**
N907SK	LJ60	092
N907SW	GLF2	71
N907TF	**FA10**	**107**
N907TP	**ASTR**	**151**
N907WC	**CL61**	**5048**
N907WL	**C525**	**0658**
N907WS	CL61	5048
N907WS	**CL64**	**5571**
N907XP	HS25	HA-0207
N907YB	**C525**	**0490**
N908AS	C560	0547
N908BX	GLEX	9084
N908CA	**F900**	**151**
N908CE	GLF2	70/1
N908CH	FA20	383/550
N908CL	CL61	5031
N908CL	CL61	5122
N908DG	**CL61**	**5018**
N908DH	GLF4	1040
N908EF	FA50	46
N908EJ	GLF2	70/1
N908FR	FA20	207
N908G	CL64	5326
N908GA	GLF5	5008
N908GA	GLF5	5208
N908GA	GLF5	5408
N908GA	GLF5	5508
N908HC	LJ35	440
N908JB	**F900**	**112**
N908JE	GLF2	151/24
N908JE	HS25	257087
N908JP	**C525**	**0148**
N908NR	**HS25**	**258600**
N908QS	C750	0108
N908R	SBRL	306-18
N908R	SBRL	306-23
N908R	SBRL	306-55
N908R	BE40	RK-44
N908RF	FA10	46
N908SB	C650	7061
N908SB	**F9EX**	**81**
(N908SB)	FA10	46
N908TE	GLEX	9097
N908TF	**FA10**	**102**
N908VR	C750	0108
N908VZ	GLF4	4051
N908VZ	**GLF4**	**4329**
N908VZ	HS25	258313
N908XP	HS25	HA-0208
N909AS	F900	127
N909B	HS25	25082
N909BK	**E55P**	**50500293**
(N909CA)	C550	550-0909
N909CF	**F2EX**	**4**
N909CK	**F9EX**	**42**
(N909DD)	LJ45	025
N909DP	**C525**	**0503**
N909EC	C52B	0042
N909EC	C52C	0028
(N909ES)	CL64	5381
(N909F)	C525	0249
N909FJ	F9EX	9
N909FK	GLF2	241
N909FR	FA20	209
N909GA	GLF4	4009
N909GA	GLF4	4209
N909GA	GLF5	5009
N909GA	GLF5	5509
N909GA	MU30	A009SA
N909JE	GLF2	151/24
N909JM	**FA50**	**304**
N909JS	LJ60	206
N909L	GLF2	112
N909LA	**C56X**	**5021**
N909LB	**C560**	**0519**
N909LS	GLF4	1178
N909M	**C525**	**0249**
N909MG	CL60	1010
N909MK	GLF2	241
N909MM	**F2EX**	**38**
N909MM	F9EX	88
N909MN	**C52A**	**0351**
N909PM	**F900**	**176**
N909PS	**C500**	**362**
N909QS	C750	0009
(N909RG)	CS55	0065
N909RR	GLF3	332
N909RX	GLF4	1239
N909SB	C650	7008
N909SB	**F9EX**	**56**
N909SK	LJ60	060
(N909SP)	GLF4	1210
N909ST	BE40	RK-194
N909TF	**FA10**	**51**
N909VJ	**FA50**	**69**
N909VT	F900	129
N910A	GLF3	369
(N910A)	GLF3	367
N910AF	GLF4	1312
N910B	GLF4	1102
N910BD	LJ45	264
N910BH	SBRL	380-54
(N910BH)	C52B	0130
N910CF	**HS25**	**258267**
N910CL	**CL30**	**20099**
N910CN	**FA50**	**59**
N910CS	C56X	5036
N910CS	**F2TH**	**87**
N910CS	F900	126
N910DC	GLF5	544
N910DF	**C650**	**0081**
N910DP	C650	0081
N910DP	**C750**	**0239**
N910DS	CS55	0154
N910E	**C750**	**0121**
N910E	JSTR	5084/8
N910E	SBRL	282-29
N910EX	**F9EX**	**10**
N910F	C650	0051
N910FJ	F9EX	10
(N910FJ)	F900	10
N910FR	FA20	280/503
N910G	**C500**	**462**
N910G	C550	575
N910G	JSTR	5112/7
N910GA	GALX	200
N910GA	GLF4	4010
N910GA	GLF5	5010
N910GA	GLF5	5410
N910GF	**C510**	**0425**
N910H	C550	691
N910HM	C550	674
N910HM	**C560**	**0318**
N910J	**CL64**	**5640**
N910JB	LJ25	213
N910JD	HS25	258258
N910JD	**HS25**	**258420**
N910JN	HS25	258258
N910JW	**F900**	**31**
N910KB	CL61	3007
N910KS	**HS25**	**257180**
N910L	FA20	191
N910LA	F2TH	69
N910LJ	**LJ45**	**088**
N910M	C650	0069
N910M	JSTR	5069/20
N910MH	WW24	45
N910MT	C550	057
N910MW	F9EX	85
N910N	C500	158
N910N	C550	550-1032
N910PC	C560	0273
N910Q	F900	156
N910QS	C750	0110
N910R	GLF2	234
N910RB	**C550**	**297**
(N910RL)	C750	0112
N910S	GLF2	234
N910S	GLF4	1155
N910SD	**F900**	**172**
N910SH	BE40	RK-72
N910SS	**C52C**	**0180**
N910SY	**C510**	**0009**
N910TF	**C560**	**0440**
(N910TS)	GLEX	9120
N910U	FA20	39
N910V	C560	0165
N910V	GLF5	636
N910VP	**C750**	**0110**
(N910VP)	HS25	258085
N910W	FA20	192
N910XP	HS25	HA-0210
N910Y	C500	158
N910Y	FA20	48
(N911A)	C500	087
N911AE	LJ35	109
N911AJ	**LJ25**	**163**
N911AS	HS25	25039
N911BB	CS55	0128
N911CB	C550	662
N911CB	C560	0604
(N911CB)	C560	0634
(N911CJ)	C500	087
N911CR	JSTR	5150/37
N911CR	SBRL	380-59
N911CU	**WW24**	**246**
N911DB	GLF2	100
N911DB	LJ35	231
N911DG	FA20	162/451
N911DT	FA20	471
N911DX	LJ35	499
N911EK	C56X	5742
N911EM	LJ25	319
N911FC	LJ55	091
N911FR	FA20	295/500
N911GM	**C500**	**048**
N911GU	**WW24**	**343**
N911HB	FA50	157
N911HJ	GLF3	349
N911JD	C500	082
N911JG	LJ25	147
(N911JJ)	MU30	A020SA
(N911JJ)	MU30	A085SA
N911KB	LJ24	128
N911KT	GLF3	438
N911LM	LJ25	070
N911MG	LJ25	212
N911ML	LJ35	256
N911MM	C500	390
(N911MU)	C500	390
N911MX	**EA50**	**000099**
(N911NJ)	C550	240
N911NP	**C525**	**0273**
N911Q	**C525**	**0220**
N911Q	SBRL	282-17
N911QB	C550	662
N911RD	**HS25**	**25253**
N911RF	F900	20
N911RF	FA10	46
N911RF	FA50	46
N911RF	LJ25	138
N911RG	FA20	144
N911SB	FA20	360
N911SH	F2TH	125
N911SP	**WW24**	**244**
N911TR	FA20	242
N911TR	LJ24	134
N911UM	**C560**	**0562**
N911UN	FA10	122
N911WT	FA20	203
N911WW	GLF2	257/17
N911WX	LJ35	439
N911YA	**E50P**	**50000300**
N912AS	HS25	25124
N912BD	C550	580
N912BD	LJ45	277
N912BD	LJ45	517
N912DA	**WW24**	**147**
N912DP	**C560**	**0575**
N912EL	C56X	6051
N912EX	F9EX	12
N912GG	GLF6	6193
N912GW	**C52A**	**0304**
N912JD	**C510**	**0453**
N912MM	LJ55	064
N912MT	F2EX	94
N912MT	**GLEX**	**9699**
N912PM	WW24	250
N912QS	C750	0012
N912SH	BE40	RK-128
N912TB	LJ31	024
N912VV	**F2EX**	**94**
N913BJ	**C560**	**0011**
N913CK	**LJ35**	**013**
N913CL	**C56X**	**5718**
N913CS	**C56X**	**5625**
N913CW	**WW24**	**332**
N913DC	**C52A**	**0157**
N913FJ	F9EX	12
N913GA	G150	313
N913GA	G280	2013
N913GA	GLF4	4013
N913GA	GLF4	4113
N913GA	GLF5	5013
N913HB	WW24	40
N913JB	CL64	5338
N913KZ	**C56X**	**5533**
N913MC	BE40	RJ-22
N913MK	FA20	272
N913MK	GLF3	407
N913MK	**GLF4**	**4075**
N913PD	GLF3	354
N913QS	**C750**	**0113**
N913RC	C500	059
N913SC	**HS25**	**258125**
(N913SC)	GLF4	1305
N913SF	BE40	RJ-22
N913SH	**FA20**	**368**
N913SN	F9EX	35
N913SQ	C650	7004
N913SQ	GLF4	1430
N913V	FA10	104
N913V	HS25	257207
N913VL	FA10	104
N913VS	FA10	106
N914BA	**GLEX**	**9484**
N914BA	LJ24	128
N914BB	CL61	3045
N914BD	CL61	3045
N914BD	F900	80
N914BD	GLF5	690
N914BD	**GLF6**	**6005**
N914BD	HS25	25229
N914BS	GLF2	157
N914CD	**C500**	**150**
N914CE	HS25	258841
N914CF	GLF2	190
N914DD	F900	80
N914DM	**WW24**	**357**
N914DT	GLEX	9145
N914DZ	GLF2	190
N914EG	GLF4	1174
N914FF	C52B	0184
N914G	**C510**	**0239**
N914GA	G150	314
N914GA	GLF5	5014
N914GS	**CL30**	**20437**
N914GW	**C510**	**0146**
N914H	HS25	258281
N914J	F900	44
N914J	F9EX	15
N914J	GLF5	615
(N914JC)	SBRL	380-56
N914JH	FA50	140
N914JL	F900	44
N914JL	F9EX	15
N914KA	GLF2	214
N914KB	GLF2	214
N914LJ	E55P	50500004
N914MH	GLF2	91
N914MM	WW24	250
N914P	JSTR	5080
N914QS	**C750**	**0296**
(N914RA)	LJ25	123
N914SB	LJ25	014
N914SH	BE40	RK-193
N914SP	C680	0020
N914TQ	**E50P**	**50000323**
N914X	CL60	1021
N914X	CL61	5185
N914X	**GLF5**	**5503**
N914X	JSTR	5080
N914XA	CL60	1021
N914Y	**CL61**	**5185**
N915AM	GLF4	4179
N915AM	HS25	258574
N915AP	**HS25**	**258574**
N915AV	GLEX	9115
N915BB	C550	550-0915
N915BB	CL61	5019
N915BD	CL61	5019
N915BD	CL61	5091
N915BD	GLF4	4028
N915BD	**GLF5**	**690**
N915C	GLF2	253
N915DK	**C560**	**0600**
N915EX	F9EX	15
N915FB	**FA10**	**77**
N915FG	**C680**	**0056**
N915G	GLF4	1186
N915GA	G150	315
N915GA	GLF4	4015
N915GA	GLF5	5015
N915JT	HS25	256002
N915KH	**CL60**	**1054**
N915MP	**C52A**	**0024**
(N915MT)	HS25	258574
N915QS	C750	0015
N915R	SBRL	306-42
N915RB	**C750**	**0042**
N915RB	LJ35	647
N915RJ	C52A	0170
N915RP	C500	270
N915RP	C525	0608
N915RT	**LJ55**	**029**
N915SA	FA20	205
N915ST	**C525**	**0301**
N915TB	**HS25**	**258822**
N915TB	BE40	RK-455
N915US	LJ24	189
N915XP	HS25	HA-0015
(N915XP)	HS25	HA-0215
N916AN	FA20	64
N916BD	LJ31	093
N916BD	LJ45	264
N916BD	LJ45	435
(N916BD)	LJ31	094
N916BG	ASTR	045
N916BG	LJ60	206
N916BG	LJ60	236
N916CG	**ASTR**	**045**
N916CG	C560	0400
N916CS	C560	0400
N916CS	C56X	5153
N916CS	C56X	5625
N916CS	**C56X**	**6062**
N916DD	**LJ45**	**520**
N916DJ	**C500**	**227**
N916DK	**C56X**	**5700**
N916EX	F9EX	16

N916GA	G150	316
N916GA	GLF5	5016
N916GA	GLF5	5316
N916GB	**GALX**	**067**
N916GR	GALX	067
N916GR	**GALX**	**126**
N916GR	BE40	RK-102
N916H	HS25	258282
N916JB	**HS25**	**HA-0150**
N916PT	HS25	258103
N916QS	**C750**	**0116**
N916RC	C500	061
N916RC	C550	211
N916RC	JSTR	5078/3
(N916RG)	JSTR	5078/3
N916SB	**BE40**	**RK-14**
N916WJ	C550	561
N917AP	**C525**	**0917**
N917BB	**C550**	**483**
N917BC	**F900**	**193**
N917BD	LJ31	094
N917BD	LJ45	281
N917BD	LJ45	450
N917BD	**LJ45**	**517**
(N917BD)	LJ31	093
N917BE	**LJ45**	**143**
N917BE	WW24	291
N917BF	LJ24	293
N917BF	WW24	291
N917DP	**GALX**	**018**
N917EA	**BE40**	**RK-369**
N917EE	C56X	5158
N917EE	C56X	5533
N917GA	GLF4	4017
N917GA	GLF5	5017
N917GA	**GLF5**	**5317**
N917GL	GLEX	9117
N917GP	**C555**	**0067**
N917J	JSTR	5082/36
N917JC	**F2EX**	**224**
N917JC	FA20	490
N917JC	FA50	250
N917JG	FA20	490
N917JG	FA50	250
N917K	HS25	256015
N917LE	**WW24**	**400**
N917LH	LJ45	042
N917LH	WW24	400
N917LJ	E50P	50000116
N917LJ	**E55P**	**50500004**
N917MC	LJ31	012
N917MM	**E50P**	**50000142**
N917MS	**GLF4**	**1241**
(N917ND)	GLF5	518
N917NS	**E50P**	**50000248**
N917R	**GLEX**	**9008**
N917R	GLF2	17
N917RG	**C52B**	**0010**
N917S	LJ55	033
N917SB	FA50	14
N917SC	ASTR	020
N917SC	LJ35	440
N917SC	**LJ60**	**125**
N917SL	**C52A**	**0059**
N917SM	**ASTR**	**099**
N917TF	HS25	257138
N917TL	**C560**	**0812**
N917VZ	GLF4	1292
N917VZ	**GLF4**	**4198**
N917W	**GLF4**	**1158**
N917XP	HS25	HA-0017
N918A	C500	168
N918AM	**C525**	**0508**
N918BD	C560	0173
N918BD	LJ45	277
N918BD	LJ45	454
N918BD	**LJ45**	**518**
N918BG	GLF3	300
N918BH	C650	0130
N918CC	GLF4	1335
N918CC	**GLF4**	**4052**
N918CG	F2TH	57
N918CW	C525	0342
N918DD	LJ45	518
N918DG	E55P	50500054
N918DG	**LJ45**	**251**
N918DG	LJ45	394
N918E	**GLF4**	**4049**
N918EG	**LJ45**	**154**
N918EX	F9EX	18
N918GA	C550	726
N918GA	**G150**	**318**
N918GA	G280	2018
N918H	HS25	258283
N918HM	C550	674
N918JL	**HS25**	**HA-0037**
N918JM	**F9EX**	**199**
N918JM	FA50	304
(N918JT)	GALX	091
N918LL	**GLF4**	**4177**
N918MJ	ASTR	073
N918MJ	**F2EX**	**270**
N918MJ	G150	250
N918MK	ASTR	089
N918MM	JSTR	5069/20
N918MV	**F900**	**156**
(N918PC)	FA10	106
N918QS	**C750**	**0223**
N918R	SBRL	306-19
N918R	SBRL	306-36
N918RD	**FA50**	**328**
N918RZ	**C56X**	**6130**
N918SM	**GLF5**	**5012**
N918SS	**WW24**	**263**
N918ST	**C510**	**0135**
N918TA	**GLEX**	**9465**
N918TB	**GLEX**	**9613**
N918TB	GLF4	1499
N918TD	**GLF4**	**1499**
N918TD	LJ25	166
N918TT	BE40	RK-529
N918WA	**C510**	**0237**
N919AM	**GLF4**	**4179**
(N919AT)	C500	209
N919BA	F2EX	239
N919BT	WW24	434
N919CH	**ASTR**	**098**
N919CT	GLF4	1051
N919DS	**ASTR**	**127**
N919DW	**HS25**	**HA-0055**
N919EX	F9EX	19
N919G	GLF2	29
N919GA	G280	2019
N919GA	GLF5	5019
(N919GA)	FA50	233
N919H	HS25	258284
N919JH	WW24	154
N919K	LJ24	162
(N919MA)	LJ24	291
N919MB	C510	0304
N919MC	**C525**	**0600**
N919P	HS25	258147
N919PE	**GLF5**	**5113**
N919QS	**C750**	**0224**
N919RS	LJ60	025
N919RT	HS25	258607
N919S	LJ25	063
N919SA	**F9EX**	**124**
N919SB	**GLF6**	**6026**
N919SF	HS25	258635
N919SS	HS25	258221
N919SV	**C52B**	**0384**
N919TG	GLF2	160
(N919TX)	C550	550-0919
N919WG	C56X	5168
N919YC	**GLF5**	**682**
(N920AD)	WW24	195
N920C	LJ35	283
N920CC	LJ25	136
N920CC	SBRL	465-16
N920CF	FA20	388
N920CG	C56X	6133
N920CL	**C680**	**680A0020**
N920DB	F900	20
N920DC	GLF5	534
N920DG	JSTR	5234
(N920DG)	SBRL	465-50
N920DS	CL60	1023
N920DS	GLEX	9113
N920DS	GLF2	73/9
N920DS	GLF4	1254
(N920DS)	CL65	5824
N920DY	JSTR	5234
N920DY	SBRL	380-40
N920DY	SBRL	465-50
N920E	C550	317
N920EA	LJ25	057
N920EX	F9EX	20
N920FF	LJ24	179
N920G	FA20	352
N920G	SBRL	306-74
N920G	WW24	87
N920GA	GLF4	4220
N920GA	GLF5	5020
N920GA	GLF5	5120
N920GB	**EA50**	**000150**
N920GL	LJ28	29-002
N920GP	WW24	87
N920JS	F9EX	181
N920K	FA50	154
(N920KP)	WW24	144
N920L	FA20	192
N920MS	C525	0089
N920MZ	**C525**	**0920**
N920NL	**C52A**	**0112**
N920PM	C560	0182
N920QS	**C750**	**0120**
N920R	WW24	45
N920RV	**CL60**	**1016**
N920S	LJ25	025
N920SA	**F900**	**49**
N920SA	BE40	RK-41
N920TB	GLF4	1254
N920TM	**LJ35**	**211**
N920US	LJ25	136
N920W	C500	155
N920XP	HS25	HA-0020
(N920XP)	HS25	HA-0220
N921AP	**C52A**	**0137**
N921AS	GLF3	332
N921BA	**GALX**	**116**
N921BE	**C500**	**579**
N921CC	**SBRL**	**465-67**
N921CG	**C56X**	**6174**
N921CH	**LJ35**	**228**
N921DG	C56X	5206
N921DT	WW24	372
N921EC	FA50	313
N921EW	**FA50**	**31**
N921FF	GLF3	421
N921FP	LJ55	103
N921GA	G280	2021
N921GA	GLF5	5021
N921GA	GLF5	5121
N921GA	GLF5	5151
N921GA	GLF5	5321
N921GA	GLF5	5521
N921GS	FA10	130
(N921HA)	HA4T	RC-30
N921JG	SBRL	282-105
N921JG	SBRL	282-38
N921K	CL61	3044
N921MB	SBRL	306-135
N921MG	**GLF3**	**308**
N921ML	**FA20**	**99**
N921MW	**C56X**	**5646**
N921PP	C510	0139
N921QS	C750	0225
N921QS	**C750**	**0241**
N921RD	HS25	256032
N921RD	HS25	257199
N921SA	**F2TH**	**148**
N921TH	**GALX**	**048**
N921TM	**LJ35**	**064**
N921TX	**C510**	**0071**
N921WC	F9EX	92
N921WC	**GLF5**	**5026**
N921XT	**C525**	**0877**
N922AC	**C560**	**0187**
(N922BA)	C500	137
N922CB	**GLF4**	**4169**
N922CK	WW24	299
N922CP	WW24	99
N922CR	HS25	256014
N922CR	WW24	299
N922CR	WW24	99
N922DS	FA20	373
N922EB	**WW24**	**372**
N922EH	**C550**	**084**
N922GA	G280	2022
N922GA	GLF4	4212
N922GA	GLF5	5022
N922GK	HS25	25195
N922GL	LJ35	266
N922GR	HS25	256014
N922H	F2TH	97
N922H	GLF4	4036
N922H	**GLF6**	**6020**
N922J	F2TH	97
N922JW	**F900**	**36**
N922KG	**C560**	**0167**
N922KM	LJ45	340
N922LJ	**F900**	**25**
N922ML	FA20	380
N922MR	**GLF2**	**93**
N922MS	JSTR	5097/60
N922N	GLF4	4036
N922QS	**C750**	**0293**
N922RA	ASTR	033
N922RA	C550	397
N922RR	HS25	25195
N922RT	C550	397
N922RV	**C550**	**271**
N922SL	**C550**	**034**
N922TR	**BE40**	**RJ-44**
N922WC	**GLF4**	**4139**
N922XP	HS25	HA-0022
N923AL	LJ55	041
N923AL	**LJ60**	**316**
N923AR	C525	0055
N923CL	**GLF4**	**1471**
N923DS	FA10	117
N923GA	G280	2023
N923GA	GLF5	5023
N923GA	GLF5	5103
N923GA	GLF5	5153
N923GA	GLF5	5323
N923GL	LJ25	298
N923GS	**C52A**	**0439**
N923HB	FA10	99
(N923HE)	FA10	99
N923JA	WW24	146
N923JE	**F2TH**	**94**
N923JH	**C550**	**708**
N923JP	**C510**	**0103**
N923JR	**HS25**	**258666**
N923KB	**CL64**	**5410**
N923ML	GLF2	219/20
N923PC	C56X	5169
N923QS	C750	0023
N923RL	C550	426
N923S	C555	0092
N923SG	**GLEX**	**9354**
N923SK	LJ60	050
N923SL	**CL61**	**3042**
N923VP	C750	0023
N923WC	**GLF6**	**6009**
N923XP	HS25	HA-0023
N924AM	LJ35	188
N924AS	C500	294
N924BC	F2EX	33
N924BW	LJ24	164
N924BW	**LJ25**	**158**
N924DS	GLF2	181
N924ED	LJ24	104
N924EJ	C750	0024
N924GA	G280	2024
N924GA	GLF4	4224
N924GA	GLF5	5024
N924GA	GLF5	5243
N924GL	LJ35	361
N924JE	C56X	5138
N924JM	HS25	258312
N924JM	BE40	RK-96
N924KW	**LJ60**	**322**
N924ML	GLF4	1234
N924PS	**LJ60**	**050**
N924QS	C750	0124
N924S	**F900**	**149**
N924S	F900	40
N924TC	C52B	0371
N924TC	**CL30**	**20087**
N924TD	**C52B**	**0371**
N924WJ	**FA50**	**141**
N924XP	HS25	HA-0024
N925AJ	**F2TH**	
N925AK	**F2EX**	**123**
N925AK	**F2TH**	**111**
N925BC	**F2EX**	**74**
N925BC	FA50	257
N925BE	FA20	80
(N925BH)	HS25	256002
N925BL	SBRL	282-104
N925CA	LJ35	605
N925CT	HS25	25066
N925DC	**GLF4**	**1279**
N925DD	CL61	5170
N925DM	LJ35	486
N925DP	HS25	257132
N925DS	FA10	116
N925DS	GLF2	98/38
N925DW	LJ25	213
N925EX	F9EX	25
N925GA	GLF5	5025
N925GL	LJ35	277
N925GS	FA50	90
N925HB	WW24	53
N925JF	HS25	258423
N925JS	**GLF4**	**1269**
N925MJ	**MU30**	**A065SA**
N925MW	**LJ45**	**451**
N925QS	C750	0299
N925R	SBRL	306-41
N925R	WW24	80
N925ST	**LJ45**	**442**
N925WC	**HS25**	**257100**
N925WC	HS25	257132
N925WC	MU30	A080SA
N925WG	HS25	257132
(N925WL)	SBRL	465-65
N925WP	LJ25	022
N925Z	SBRL	306-3
N925Z	WW24	307
N926AG	CL30	20102
N926CB	C650	0008
N926CB	**C650**	**7114**
N926CC	**C525**	**0491**
N926CE	**C560**	**0763**
N926CH	C525	0087
N926CJ	**F900**	**26**
N926CR	C650	0008
N926DR	C56X	5612
N926DS	WW24	189
N926EC	C550	550-1016
N926EC	**CL65**	**5832**
N926ED	C550	550-1016
N926G	HS25	25038
N926GA	GLF5	5026
N926GA	GLF5	5266
N926GL	LJ35	306
N926HC	C650	0094
N926HL	**C56X**	**5216**
N926JJ	**C52A**	**0310**
N926JK	**E50P**	**50000107**
N926JM	WW24	146
N926JR	**CL30**	**20103**
(N926JR)	HS25	258666
N926LR	FA20	139
N926LR	HS25	25098
N926MC	**HS25**	**257021**
N926NC	**C560**	**0328**
N926NY	GLF2	33
N926PY	**C52A**	**0450**
N926QS	C750	0026
N926RM	C550	567
N926RR	**GLF4**	**4081**
N926SS	**CL64**	**5436**
N926TC	HS25	257021
N926TF	C525	0519
N926TF	**C52C**	**0018**
N926TT	GLF4	1372
N926VP	C750	0026
N926VR	**C750**	**0026**
N926ZT	HS25	257021
N927A	CL61	3026
N927AA	**C525**	**0895**
N927AA	LJ24	169
N927AA	SBRL	465-22
N927CC	C525	0422
(N927CC)	C52B	0109
N927DJ	LJ31	210
(N927DS)	FA10	116
(N927EM)	GLF4	4024
N927EX	F9EX	27
N927FW	**LJ25**	**203**
N927GA	GLF5	5027
N927GA	GLF5	5273
N927GA	GLF5	5427
N927GL	LJ35	315
N927LL	**HS25**	**257135**
N927LT	C680	0070
N927LT	**G280**	**2043**
N927MC	**GLF6**	**6052**
N927MM	**C550**	**550-1060**
N927PK	**C560**	**0551**
N927QS	**C750**	**0290**
N927R	SBRL	306-47
N927S	WW24	82
N927SK	**LJ45**	**051**
N928AL	**LJ55**	**041**
N928BC	C52B	0335
N928CB	**C550**	**550-0928**
N928CD	LJ60	010
N928CD	LJ60	110
(N928DA)	C550	550-0928
(N928DJ)	LJ31	210
N928DS	C550	276
N928G	WW24	381
N928GA	GALX	228
N928GA	GLF5	5028
N928GA	GLF5	5128
N928GA	GLF5	5428
N928GC	GLF4	1513
N928GC	**GLF5**	**5239**
(N928GC)	F2EX	181
N928GD	LJ60	010
N928GF	GLF2	119/22
N928GV	WW24	381
N928HR	**WW24**	**415**
N928JA	**ASTR**	**075**
N928JK	**C680**	**0104**
N928KG	**C510**	**0337**
(N928KH)	HS25	258001
(N928MC)	CL30	20100
N928PS	**C650**	**0116**
N928QS	**C750**	**0288**
N928R	SBRL	282-90
N928R	SBRL	306-51
N928RD	C500	204
N928S	LJ25	025
N928ST	**G150**	**232**
N928ST	GLF4	1025
N928SZ	GLEX	9056
N928SZ	**GLEX**	**9239**
N928SZ	GLF4	1025
N928VC	C525	0453
N928WG	**ASTR**	**079**
N928WK	**F2EX**	**183**
N928WK	FA50	279
N929A	C500	207
N929AK	HS25	258409
N929AK	**HS25**	**258627**
N929AL	HS25	258409
N929AW	**GALX**	**192**
N929BA	**GALX**	**141**
N929BC	C52A	0333
N929BC	C52B	0335
N929BC	**C52C**	**0070**
N929CA	C500	046
N929CG	**SBRL**	**380-52**
N929DS	C550	284
N929DS	C650	0007
N929EJ	C750	0029
N929GA	**GALX**	**029**
N929GA	GLF5	5029
N929GC	SBRL	380-52
N929GL	LJ28	29-001
N929GV	GLF2	258
N929GV	LJ60	165
N929GV	WW24	356
N929GV	WW24	381
N929GV	WW24	48
N929GW	LJ60	165
N929GW	**LJ60**	**427**
N929GX	LJ60	427
N929HF	LJ24	243
N929HG	F2TH	79
N929JH	**LJ31**	**132**
N929KD	**EA50**	**000240**
N929MC	**LJ24**	**243**
N929ML	FA50	92
N929MM	**C525**	**0692**
N929QS	**C750**	**0129**
N929RW	C500	046
(N929SF)	C52B	0001
N929SL	LJ35	287
N929SR	LJ35	287
N929SR	**LJ60**	**144**
N929SS	**PRM1**	**RB-15**
N929ST	**C510**	**0352**
N929T	**FA50**	**24**
N929TS	GLEX	9029
N929VC	C525	0453
N929VC	**C52A**	**0353**
N929WC	**GALX**	**181**

N929WD	GALX	056
N929WG	GALX	056
N929WG	**GALX**	**239**
N929WG	HS25	258196
N929WG	MU30	A032SA
N929WQ	HS25	258196
N929WT	**FA50**	**119**
N929WT	GLF4	1317
N930BS	C550	087
N930BS	GLF2	29
N930DC	GLF4	1254
N930DC	**GLF4**	**4063**
N930EN	**GLEX**	**9040**
N930GL	LJ35	330
N930JG	**FA50**	**230**
N930L	FA20	193
N930LS	GLF2	133
N930LS	**GLF4**	**1135**
N930M	JSTR	5114/18
N930MG	C650	0209
N930MG	**C680**	**0152**
N930MG	BE40	RJ-52
N930MT	JSTR	5114/18
N930PJ	LJ24	305
N930PT	**HS25**	**258404**
N930QS	**C750**	**0130**
N930RA	SBRL	465-68
N930SC	ASTR	038
N930SD	F2TH	90
N930SD	GLF2	97
N930TC	**LJ45**	**040**
N930UC	ASTR	038
N930XP	HS25	HA-0030
N931BA	LJ35	003
N931BR	PRM1	RB-66
N931CA	C500	174
N931CC	FA50	31
N931CW	GLF2	85
N931DC	**GLF4**	**4013**
N931DW	CL61	5025
N931ED	**LJ31**	**124**
(N931EJ)	FA50	31
N931FD	LJ31	124
N931FL	**GLF5**	**5515**
N931G	FA50	126
N931GA	GLF4	4231
N931GA	GLF4	4311
N931GA	GLF5	5031
N931GL	LJ35	392
N931MA	**MU30**	**A010SA**
N931QS	C750	0064
N931RS	**LJ31**	**184**
N931SB	F900	33
N932BA	GALX	105
N932BC	HS25	HA-0032
N932DM	**E55P**	**50500142**
N932EA	**BE40**	**RK-32**
N932ED	LJ31	187
N932FD	LJ31	187
N932GA	GLF5	5032
N932GA	GLF5	5232
N932GA	GLF6	6032
N932GL	LJ35	393
N932HA	C500	220
N932JC	LJ45	032
N932LM	C550	297
N932MA	**E50P**	**50000105**
N932QS	C750	0032
N932S	FA20	56
N932XL	C56X	6032
N933	HS25	25186
N933AC	**BE40**	**RJ-5**
N933BB	C550	550-1033
N933CY	JSTR	5115/39
N933DB	C650	0009
N933EX	F9EX	33
N933EY	**GLEX**	**9063**
N933GA	GLF5	5033
N933GL	LJ35	377
N933H	**GLF5**	**5077**
N933H	HS25	258249
N933JC	SBRL	380-72
N933JJ	GLF4	1347
N933LC	JSTR	5115/39
N933MA	**E50P**	**50000012**
N933ML	CL65	5705
N933ML	**GLEX**	**9504**
(N933N)	LJ24	049
N933NA	LJ24	049
N933PA	GLF3	367
N933PB	**C560**	**0618**
(N933PG)	CL61	5152
N933QS	**C750**	**0133**
N933RD	GLF2	251
N933SC	**C680**	**0077**
N933SH	C650	0009
N933SP	**C560**	**0007**
(N933TS)	FA10	33
N933XP	HS25	HA-0033
N934AM	C525	0230
N934BD	C750	0152
N934CT	**C52B**	**0263**
N934DF	GLF4	1255
N934GA	GLF4	4304
N934GA	GLF5	5034
N934GA	GLF5	5234
N934GA	GLF5	5334
N934GL	LJ35	417
N934H	C550	188
N934H	C650	0172
N934H	LJ24	290
N934QS	C750	0034
N934RD	**HS25**	**258296**
N934ST	F2EX	68
N934TQ	**CL65**	**5845**
N935AC	**C510**	**0338**
N935BD	LJ35	094
N935DH	GLF3	455
N935GA	C500	084
N935GA	GALX	235
N935GA	GLF5	5035
N935GA	GLF5	5105
N935GA	GLF5	5155
N935GB	**G150**	**293**
N935GL	LJ35	419
N935H	**HS25**	**258225**
(N935NA)	LJ35	213
(N935PC)	SBRL	380-59
N935QS	**C750**	**0135**
N935R	SBRL	306-56
N935SH	GLF4	1223
N935SS	G150	279
N936AA	WW24	401
N936BR	**C555**	**0058**
N936EA	**C56X**	**5670**
(N936EA)	BE40	RK-35
N936GA	GLF4	4036
N936GA	GLF5	5036
N936GA	GLF5	5156
N936GA	GLF5	5336
N936GA	GLF5	5436
N936H	HS25	259041
N936MP	**GLF4**	**4173**
N936NW	FA20	236
N936QS	C750	0036
N936SM	E50P	50000056
N937BC	HS25	258043
N937BG	**GLF4**	**4039**
N937D	FA10	75
N937DM	E50P	50000136
N937GA	GLF5	5107
N937GA	GLF5	5237
N937GC	FA20	76
N937GL	LJ25	337
N937H	HS25	258251
(N937H)	HS25	259041
N937J	FA10	19
N937M	GLF2	42/12
N937QS	**C750**	**0137**
N937R	SBRL	306-57
N937RV	**BE40**	**RK-296**
N937TC	C650	7049
N937US	GLF2	204
N937US	GLF4	1092
N938AM	**C550**	**550-0938**
N938CC	C750	0038
N938D	C550	454
N938EJ	C750	0038
N938GA	GLF4	4238
N938GA	GLF5	5038
N938GA	GLF5	5438
N938GL	LJ35	396
N938GR	C560	0214
N938H	HS25	258252
N938LN	**C52C**	**0150**
N938QS	**C750**	**0183**
(N938QS)	C750	0038
N938R	SBRL	306-20
N938R	SBRL	306-48
N938W	C550	448
(N938WF)	GLEX	9005
N938WH	CL60	1068
N938WH	WW24	209
N939AM	**C52C**	**0206**
N939AP	**GLEX**	**9180**
(N939BB)	C550	550-0939
N939BC	**C52A**	**0333**
N939CC	**CL61**	**5124**
(N939CG)	CL60	1042
N939CK	**FA20**	**317**
N939EX	F9EX	39
N939GA	GLF5	5039
N939GP	**BE40**	**RK-125**
N939GS	**GLEX**	**9663**
N939JC	C510	0108
N939KM	**GLF3**	**492**
N939KS	C500	289
N939LE	HS25	258459
N939MC	**ASTR**	**012**
N939ML	GLEX	9330
N939PG	**GLF4**	**1212**
N939QS	**C750**	**0193**
N939RR	**GLF3**	**332**
N939RT	**C650**	**0061**
N939SA	**C550**	**360**
N939SG	CL30	20397
N939SR	C500	121
N939SS	**F900**	**155**
N939TT	**HS25**	**258205**
N939TW	**C560**	**0185**
N940AJ	**GLF5**	**565**
N940BS	GLF2	157
N940BS	GLF2	64/27
N940CC	SBRL	282-34
N940CL	**F9EX**	**31**
N940DC	GLF4	1052
N940DC	GLF5	5128
(N940DH)	CL60	1077
N940EX	F9EX	140
N940EX	F9EX	40
N940EX	FA7X	101
N940GA	GLF4	4240
N940GA	GLF5	5040
N940GA	GLF5	5110
N940GA	GLF5	5440
N940GA	BE40	RJ-18
N940HC	HS25	258195
N940JM	**BE40**	**RK-492**
N940K	LJ45	410
N940P	LJ60	071
N940QS	**C750**	**0285**
(N940RL)	LJ60	142
(N940SJ)	F900	40
N940SW	**C525**	**0071**
N940VA	**BE40**	**RK-197**
(N941AA)	C56X	6021
N941AM	C52B	0252
N941AM	GLF4	1499
N941BB	**C550**	**214**
N941CC	FA50	138
N941CE	**HS25**	**257083**
N941CW	GLF2	29
N941GA	LJ25	020
N941H	HS25	259042
N941HC	HS25	258195
N941JC	C500	310
N941JP	**C550**	**336**
N941JR	**CL30**	**20022**
N941KA	**C56X**	**5510**
N941KA	C650	0095
N941KN	**C52C**	**0005**
N941NC	**EA50**	**000008**
N941QS	**C750**	**0141**
N941RM	**C560**	**0476**
N941SC	**C550**	**590**
N941TS	GLEX	9241
N942B	C500	044
N942B	FA10	105
N942BY	LJ31	005
N942C	FA10	11
N942CC	SBRL	380-64
N942CJ	C52A	0094
N942CK	F9EX	42
N942DS	HS25	25032
N942EB	**C550**	**550-1090**
N942EB	WW24	372
N942EX	F9EX	42
N942FA	WW24	257
N942FK	**LJ45**	**145**
N942GA	GLF4	4242
N942GA	GLF4	4342
N942GA	GLF5	5042
N942GA	LJ25	021
N942H	HS25	258253
N942JT	**GLF5**	**5487**
(N942M)	FA10	138
N942QB	C750	0024
N942QS	C750	0024
N942RC	**LJ31**	**107**
N942TS	GLEX	9242
N942WC	**WW24**	**383**
N942WN	HS25	25079
N942Y	HS25	25079
N942Y	JSTR	5098/28
N943CC	SBRL	380-66
N943CE	**HS25**	**257141**
(N943CL)	WW24	187
N943EL	**C750**	**0043**
N943GA	G280	2043
N943GA	GLF4	4243
N943GA	GLF5	5043
N943GA	LJ25	022
N943H	HS25	258254
N943JB	F2EX	18
N943JL	WW24	206
N943LL	C500	615
N943LL	C550	442
N943LL	WW24	206
N943QS	C750	0043
N943RC	C500	615
N943RL	FA50	88
N943RM	LJ60	333
N944AD	F900	17
N944AF	C550	573
N944AH	**C56X**	**5008**
N944AL	GLF4	4124
N944AM	GLEX	9161
N944B	C500	318
N944BB	**HS25**	**258611**
N944CA	C650	0083
N944D	C750	0011
N944GA	GLF5	5044
N944GA	GLF5	5344
N944GA	GLF5	5449
N944GX	GLEX	9444
N944H	C650	0083
N944H	C650	7007
N944H	C750	0011
N944H	GLF2	251
N944H	GLF5	5016
N944JD	C500	424
N944KM	LJ24	334
N944KR	**HS25**	**258688**
N944L	C650	7007
N944M	WW24	364
N944NA	GLF2	144
(N944PP)	HS25	258611
N944QS	**C750**	**0144**
N944RS	**ASTR**	**062**
N944TB	**HS25**	**257177**
N944TC	GLF4	1444
N944TG	C500	365
N944XP	HS25	HA-0044
N945AA	C500	432
N945AC	**CL30**	**20442**
N945BC	C500	666
N945CC	SBRL	465-13
N945CE	**HS25**	**257137**
N945EJ	**LJ40**	**2108**
N945ER	**C555**	**0021**
N945FD	**LJ45**	**122**
N945G	**LJ60**	**106**
N945GA	GALX	245
N945GA	GLF5	5045
N945GA	LJ24	182
N945GS	**GLF4**	**1384**
N945GS	LJ60	106
N945HC	**LJ45**	**109**
N945K	**LJ45**	**402**
N945LC	**PRM1**	**RB-205**
N945MC	FA10	37
N945NA	**GLF2**	**118**
N945PK	**GLF2**	**165/37**
N945QS	C750	0029
N945R	SBRL	306-59
N945SK	**C650**	**0001**
N945SL	HS25	258626
N945TM	F900	104
N945TM	**F9EX**	**64**
N945W	**LJ35**	**301**
N946BA	**GALX**	**131**
N946CC	C500	206
N946CM	C510	0046
N946EJ	C750	0046
N946EX	F9EX	46
N946FP	LJ55	056
N946FS	HS25	25134
N946GA	GLF5	5046
N946GA	GLF5	5346
N946GM	WW24	215
N946H	HS25	258255
N946JB	**GLF6**	**6157**
N946JR	SBRL	306-10
N946NA	GLF2	146
N946PC	C56X	5728
N946QS	**C750**	**0195**
N946RM	**C52B**	**0008**
N946TC	C56X	5331
N946TC	**FA50**	**94**
N946TS	**C560**	**0765**
N947AS	**E55P**	**50500288**
N947CB	C550	550-0947
N947CC	C500	123
N947CE	**HS25**	**257128**
N947EL	**C750**	**0047**
N947GA	G280	2047
N947GA	GLF5	5047
N947GS	**LJ35**	**250**
N947H	HS25	258256
N947KK	**CL61**	**3054**
N947LF	F9EX	44
N947NA	GLF2	147
N947QS	C750	0047
N947R	SBRL	282-39
N947R	SBRL	306-60
N947TC	**LJ25**	**233**
N947WK	**CL30**	**20392**
(N948AV)	GLF4	1474
N948DC	C550	136
N948GA	GLF5	5048
N948GA	GLF5	5348
N948H	HS25	259043
N948LM	ASTR	139
N948N	C500	354
N948NA	GLF2	222
N948QS	**C750**	**0149**
N948R	SBRL	306-21
N948R	SBRL	306-50
(N949AV)	GLF4	1477
N949BC	**CL61**	**5162**
N949CC	**WW24**	**280**
N949CE	**HS25**	**257204**
N949CV	HS25	25195
N949CW	HS25	25195
N949EB	HS25	257028
N949EX	F9EX	49
N949GA	GLF5	5049
N949GA	GLF5	5349
N949GP	GLEX	9049
N949JA	**HS25**	**258362**
N949JB	**C510**	**0218**
N949LL	C52B	0306
N949LL	C56X	6035
N949NA	GLF2	221
N949QS	C750	0049
N949SA	C550	360
N949SA	**C650**	**0074**
(N949SA)	C500	067
N950AM	C500	095
N950AV	GLF4	1464
N950AV	**GLF4**	**4048**
N950BA	**C56X**	**5200**
N950BD	**FA50**	**144**
N950BS	GLF2	64/27
N950CL	**FA50**	**149**
N950CM	GLF4	1315
N950CM	**GLF5**	**592**
N950CS	LJ35	364
N950CS	SBRL	465-43
N950DB	**C52A**	**0377**
N950DM	GLF4	1010
N950DM	**GLF4**	**1239**
N950DP	**HS25**	**258154**
N950F	**FA50**	**191**
N950FB	CL61	5013
(N950FC)	C550	401
N950G	LJ36	032
N950GA	GLF4	4150
N950GA	GLF5	5050
N950GA	LJ24	184
N950H	**FA50**	**307**
N950HB	GLF4	1464
N950HB	HA4T	RC-50
N950JB	**F9DX**	**602**
N950JK	**PRM1**	**RB-252**
N950L	FA20	189
N950LG	**GLF4**	**1441**
N950M	**C750**	**0311**
N950MA	C56X	5199
N950N	G150	244
N950NA	**GLF2**	**185**
N950P	**C525**	**0234**
N950PC	**HS25**	**258300**
N950PG	**CL64**	**5575**
N950QS	C750	0050
N950RA	FA20	95
N950RD	**F9EX**	**16**
N950RG	**C52C**	**0146**
N950RJ	CL65	5742
N950RL	**F2TH**	**221**
N950S	FA50	115
N950SF	**F900**	**50**
N950SP	**LJ35**	**450**
N950SW	CL61	5032
N950SW	**GLF4**	**4109**
N950TC	C560	0384
N950WA	C560	0082
N950X	**FA7X**	**131**
N950XP	HS25	258750
N950XP	HS25	HA-0150
N951BA	GALX	148
N951CM	**C510**	**0327**
N951DB	WW24	195
N951DH	**C525**	**0881**
N951DJ	**FA50**	**38**
N951DP	**HS25**	**258338**
N951FM	**LJ40**	**2077**
N951GA	LJ25	030
N951H	HS25	258257
N951QS	**C750**	**0151**
N951RK	GLF2	191
N951RM	CL61	3042
N951XF	GLF3	451
N951XP	HS25	HA-0051
N952	LJ25	291
N952B	HS25	25100
N952CH	C550	550-0952
N952DP	**HS25**	**258135**
N952GA	GLF5	5052
N952GA	GLF5	5250
N952GA	GLF5	5520
N952GA	LJ24	194
N952GD	F900	79
N952GL	LJ35	592
N952GL	**PRM1**	**RB-213**
N952GL	PRM1	RB-87
N952GM	PRM1	RB-87
N952HF	WW24	279
N952QS	**C750**	**0200**
N952R	**EPC1**	**002**
N952RB	**C56X**	**6006**
N952SP	C525	0447
N952SP	**PRM1**	**RB-260**
(N952TC)	FA10	31
N952VS	LJ31	168
(N952XP)	HS25	HA-0052
N953C	C560	0163
(N953DC)	FA20	300/508
N953DP	**HS25**	**258134**
N953EX	F9EX	53
N953F	**C560**	**0005**
N953FA	CL61	5041
N953FF	**C52C**	**0141**
N953FT	C550	295
N953GA	GLF5	5053
N953GA	GLF5	5353
N953GA	LJ24	197
N953GM	C550	550-0953
(N953H)	HS25	258258
N953HC	**C500**	**606**
N953JB	**EA50**	**000126**
N953JF	**C650**	**0043**
N953QS	**C750**	**0153**
N953SL	C500	606
N953TJ	**C750**	**0310**

N954AM	**FA50**	**162**
N954BA	**CL61**	**5054**
N954DP	FA50	54
N954FA	LJ25	034
N954FJ	F900	54
N954GA	GLF5	5054
N954GA	GLF5	5345
N954GA	LJ25	034
N954H	**HS25**	**258259**
N954L	CL64	5607
N954L	**GLEX**	**9340**
N954ME	FA50	244
N954Q	C750	0211
N954QS	C750	0211
N954RM	C52A	0093
N954S	LJ24	136
N954SC	F2TH	6
(N954SC)	LJ24	019
N954SG	**FA50**	**54**
N954SP	F2EX	56
N954TW	BE40	RK-132
N954WS	**LJ60**	**271**
N955CC	GLF2	54/36
(N955CE)	CL64	5436
N955CP	GLF3	375
N955DB	CL61	3044
N955DP	**HS25**	**258117**
N955E	FA50	14
N955E	GLF4	1383
N955EA	**LJ24**	**279**
N955EX	F9EX	155
N955FD	LJ55	009
(N955FJ)	F900	55
N955GA	GLF5	5055
N955GA	GLF5	5255
N955GA	GLF5	5515
N955GH	**C750**	**0106**
N955H	**CL30**	**20109**
N955H	GLF2	98/38
N955H	GLF3	378
N955H	GLF4	1081
N955H	GLF4	1383
N955H	JSTR	5126
(N955HC)	GLF4	1081
N955HG	**C650**	**0057**
N955HL	JSTR	5126
N955JS	**LJ31**	**228**
N955KC	C680	0244
N955LS	LJ55	009
N955MC	HS25	258384
N955MD	LJ55	009
N955NC	LJ55	087
N955PM	**CL65**	**5883**
N955PR	SBRL	465-43
N955QS	**C750**	**0055**
N955R	SBRL	306-52
N955SE	**HS25**	**HA-0102**
N955SL	**F2TH**	**52**
(N955WP)	C500	528
N956	SBRL	282-50
N956CC	SBRL	282-50
N956DP	**FA50**	**41**
N956EX	F9EX	56
N956GA	**C52B**	**0233**
N956GA	GLF5	5056
N956GA	LJ25	036
N956H	HS25	259044
N956HC	**C52A**	**0187**
N956J	LJ25	036
(N956M)	SBRL	277-7
N956MB	**C680**	**0538**
(N956MJ)	GLF2	234
N956P	MS76	056
N956PP	ASTR	029
N956PP	**CL64**	**5483**
N956PP	MU30	A031SA
N956QS	**C750**	**0156**
N956RA	**HS25**	**258129**
N956RS	LJ60	407
N956S	C500	056
N957	SBRL	282-71
N957BJ	**C56X**	**5086**
N957CC	SBRL	282-71
N957CP	**F2TS**	**703**
N957DP	**CL61**	**3010**
N957DT	**CL30**	**20429**
N957E	LJ24	204
N957EC	**FA10**	**146**
N957F	ASTR	104
N957GA	**GLF4**	**4357**
N957GA	GLF5	5057
N957GA	GLF5	5257
N957GA	GLF5	5457
N957GA	LJ24	204
N957H	**HS25**	**258260**
(N957M)	SBRL	285-1
N957MB	**HS25**	**256015**
N957P	ASTR	104
N957P	GALX	062
N957PH	C550	550-0957
N957R	SBRL	306-53
N957RC	WW24	58
N957SC	LJ24	065
N957TH	FA20	38
N958AP	**C56X**	**5074**
(N958AV)	GLF5	666
(N958AV)	GLF5	699

N958BX	**GLF4**	**1227**
N958CR	**CL30**	**20565**
N958DM	F9EX	119
N958DM	LJ25	042
N958DP	CL61	3005
N958EX	F9EX	58
N958GA	GLF5	5058
N958GA	LJ25	042
N958GB	**C560**	**0680**
N958GC	**C550**	**550-1016**
N958H	HS25	258261
N958M	SBRL	282-85
N958MG	**C525**	**0805**
N958PP	MU30	A031SA
N958QS	**C750**	**0158**
N958R	SBRL	306-24
N958R	SBRL	306-9
N958TB	**GLF4**	**1512**
N959AT	LJ35	019
N959C	SBRL	465-50
N959CC	**C56X**	**5759**
N959CR	BE40	RK-387
N959DM	**FA50**	**252**
N959EN	**HDJT**	**42000012**
N959EX	F9EX	159
N959EX	F9EX	59
N959GA	GLF5	5059
N959GA	GLF5	5259
N959GA	LJ25	039
N959H	HS25	258262
N959KW	HS25	25020
(N959M)	SBRL	277-6
N959P	MS76	059
N959PP	**ASTR**	**029**
N959QP	**GLF2**	**176**
(N959RB)	LJ40	2100
N959RC	**LJ40**	**2136**
N959RE	LJ25	039
N959RP	**LJ40**	**2100**
N959SA	LJ35	076
N959SC	LJ24	045A
N959WC	LJ55	030
N960AA	**FA20**	**144**
N960AA	LJ35	003
(N960AJ)	BE40	RK-23
N960AS	**LJ45**	**408**
N960AV	GLF5	654
(N960BM)	C560	0643
N960CB	C550	550-0960
N960CD	C560	0121
N960CL	F900	94
N960CP	C550	336
N960CR	C560	0500
N960CR	**CL30**	**20080**
N960DC	GLF3	378
N960DP	**GLF4**	**1157**
N960DT	G280	2096
N960E	LJ55	033
N960ES	E55P	50500033
N960EX	F9EX	60
N960FA	WW24	348
N960GA	GLF5	5060
N960GA	GLF5	5260
N960GA	LJ25	041
N960H	LJ60	015
(N960H)	LJ60	013
N960HD	**C56X**	**5077**
(N960HL)	LJ60	015
N960JA	BE40	RK-191
N960JH	C560	0643
(N960JH)	C560	0754
N960JJ	BE40	RK-191
N960JJ	BE40	RK-255
N960KC	C750	0011
N960M	**C560**	**0691**
(N960M)	SBRL	277-2
N960PT	**C510**	**0238**
N960QS	**C750**	**0160**
N960S	**FA50**	**86**
N960SC	C550	550-0961
N960SF	**F9EX**	**62**
N960TC	**HS25**	**258297**
N960TT	LJ60	145
N960TX	**FA20**	**403**
N961AA	**FA20**	**205**
N961AS	**LJ45**	**404**
N961BB	C550	550-0961
N961EX	F9EX	61
N961GA	GLF5	5061
N961H	HS25	258263
N961JC	HS25	258062
N961JC	WW24	208
(N961JD)	WW24	208
N961JE	WW24	208
(N961M)	SBRL	285-25
N961MR	LJ60	003
N961P	MS76	061
N961QS	C750	0061
N961R	SBRL	306-61
N961RA	C525	0245
N961SV	GLF4	1395
N961TC	C680	0077
N961TC	**CL65**	**5928**
N961V	**GLF4**	**1298**
N962	LJ25	102
N962A	**ASTR**	**031**
N962AA	**FA20**	**75**

(N962DP)	HS25	258062
N962EX	F9EX	162
N962FM	**LJ31**	**237**
N962GA	GLF5	5062
N962GA	LJ25	044
N962H	HS25	259046
(N962HA)	C550	248
N962J	**C550**	**453**
N962JC	C550	453
N962JC	C560	0006
N962KC	**C560**	**0670**
N962MV	WW24	385
N962QS	**C750**	**0126**
N962RA	**C52A**	**0242**
N962SS	**GLF4**	**1121**
N962TS	GLEX	9262
N963CH	**G150**	**316**
N963EC	**CL30**	**20119**
N963EX	F9EX	63
N963FF	**C510**	**0096**
N963GA	GLF5	5063
N963GA	LJ25	045
N963H	HS25	259017
N963JB	**HS25**	**HA-0210**
N963JF	**FA50**	**18**
N963JG	**EA50**	**000028**
N963JN	**FA50**	**90**
N963RB	CL30	20121
N963RS	CL30	20121
N963RS	F900	127
N963RS	**F9EX**	**97**
N963U	C650	7059
N963U	**FA50**	**331**
N963WA	SBRL	306-53
N963WL	SBRL	306-53
N963WL	SBRL	465-65
N963WM	WW24	88
(N963Y)	JSTR	5098/28
(N963Y)	LJ31	005
N963YA	HS25	25079
N964C	**SBRL**	**465-66**
N964CL	LJ35	152
N964EJ	C750	0064
N964EL	**C750**	**0064**
N964GA	GLF4	4264
N964GA	**GLF4**	**4364**
N964GA	GLF5	5064
N964GA	LJ25	046
N964H	CL64	5363
N964J	C550	448
N964JC	C550	448
N964JC	C560	0007
N964JD	**BE40**	**RK-451**
N964JG	**EA50**	**000172**
N964M	FA20	146
N964M	JSTR	5148
(N964MP)	GLF3	400
N964QS	C750	0064
N964QS	**C750**	**0164**
N964RS	F900	127
N964S	**EA50**	**000132**
N964XP	HS25	HA-0164
N965BB	C550	550-0965
N965BC	FA20	107
N965CC	GLF2	165/37
N965EC	C525	0462
N965EX	F9EX	65
N965GA	G280	2065
N965GA	GLF5	5065
N965GA	GLF5	5165
N965GA	GLF5	5265
N965GA	GLF6	6065
N965GA	LJ25	048
N965JC	C650	7051
N965JC	HS25	257084
N965LC	C525	0462
N965LC	**C56X**	**6107**
N965M	F9EX	65
(N965QS)	C750	0065
N965R	SBRL	306-61
N966E	F9EX	126
N966F	FA20	70
N966GA	GLF5	5066
N966GA	GLF5	5166
N966GA	LJ25	049
N966H	C650	7006
N966H	C750	0012
N966H	F9EX	101
N966H	F9EX	126
N966H	**FA7X**	**89**
N966H	GLF2	150
N966H	GLF3	411
N966JM	C560	0240
N966JM	C56X	5143
N966JM	**C680**	**0027**
N966K	C650	7006
N966K	HS25	258702
N966L	CL61	3021
N966L	FA20	181
(N966L)	HS25	258259
N966MT	C56X	5046
N966QS	**C750**	**0166**
N966RJ	**HS25**	**257129**
N966SW	**C560**	**0284**
N967A	WW24	205
N967B	**C500**	**550**
N967CB	C550	550-0967

N967CM	C510	0067
N967EX	F9EX	67
N967F	FA20	71
N967F	**PRM1**	**RB-133**
N967GA	GLF5	5067
N967GA	GLF5	5117
N967GA	GLF5	5167
N967L	CL61	3004
N967L	CL61	3021
N967L	CL61	3023
N967L	HS25	258273
N967L	WW24	37
N967NX	**GLEX**	**9675**
N967PC	**GALX**	**110**
N967QS	C750	0067
N967R	SBRL	306-16
N967R	SBRL	306-62
N967TC	**C52A**	**0319**
N968AG	C680	680A0018
N968BN	JSTR	5109/13
N968BS	**C56X**	**5193**
N968BX	**GLEX**	**9694**
N968CM	C510	0068
N968DM	C500	610
N968DS	GLEX	9386
N968DW	GLEX	9678
N968DX	GLEX	9687
N968DZ	GLEX	9685
N968EX	GLEX	9643
N968F	FA20	74
N968FA	**GLF6**	**6150**
N968GA	GLF5	5068
N968GN	JSTR	5109/13
N968GX	GLEX	9668
N968HX	**GLEX**	**9707**
N968L	CL61	5089
N968R	SBRL	306-2
N969	LJ31	086
N969AR	**LJ25**	**220**
N969B	LJ24	089
N969DW	C560	0399
(N969EG)	WW24	221
N969EX	F9EX	69
N969F	FA10	135
N969F	FA20	75
N969GA	GLF5	5069
N969GA	GLF5	5469
N969GB	**C560**	**0225**
N969GC	**E55P**	**50500223**
N969J	LJ24	106
N969JD	LJ60	154
N969JJ	**HS25**	**258313**
N969KC	WW24	221
N969MC	CS55	0001
N969MC	LJ35	590
N969MQ	CS55	0001
N969MT	C550	072
N969MT	LJ35	459
N969PW	WW24	221
N969RE	**PRM1**	**RB-14**
N969SE	C500	069
N969SG	GLF4	1197
N969SS	LJ25	317
N969WR	**G150**	**218**
N969XX	**C56X**	**5343**
(N969ZS)	C500	196
N970BA	**GALX**	**120**
N970CC	**F9EX**	**2**
N970DM	**C52B**	**0168**
N970DX	GLEX	9663
N970EX	F9EX	70
N970F	FA20	76
N970F	LJ55	055
N970GA	FA20	246/482
N970GA	LJ24	209
N970GW	**C650**	**0019**
N970H	LJ55	055
N970KG	**GLF4**	**1356**
N970MM	**C525**	**0867**
N970NX	**GLEX**	**9671**
N970QS	C750	0070
N970RC	C680	0012
N970RJ	F9EX	97
N970RP	**C500**	**270**
N970RP	C525	0608
N970S	**FA50**	**238**
N970SF	**F9EX**	**194**
N970SG	**GLF5**	**5149**
N970SJ	GLF4	1146
N970SJ	**GLF5**	**562**
N970SK	**C750**	**0186**
N970SU	C525	0173
N970SY	**GLF4**	**1146**
N970WJ	**LJ25**	**324**
N970XP	HS25	HA-0170
N970ZG	**C52A**	**0086**
(N971AB)	C500	232
N971AS	JSTR	5007/45
N971DM	C525	0510
N971EC	GLF2	32/2
N971EC	GLF4	1000
N971EC	LJ55	033
N971EQ	GLF2	32/2
(N971EX)	F9EX	71
N971F	FA20	59
N971F	LJ35	095
N971GA	GLF5	5171

N971GA	GLF5	5271
N971GA	LJ24	215
N971H	LJ35	095
N971K	LJ35	373
N971L	GLF4	1116
N971MD	C680	0347
N971QS	C750	0071
N971TB	C52A	0111
N971TB	C52A	0118
N971TB	**C52B**	**0353**
N971TE	C52A	0118
N972	LJ24	252
N972AB	**C500**	**140**
N972D	HS25	25275
N972F	FA20	80
N972G	GLF3	457
N972GA	GLF5	5172
N972GW	C500	118
N972H	LJ24	322
N972H	LJ25	370
N972JD	C500	118
N972LM	HS25	257098
N972MS	**GLF4**	**1285**
N972NR	**SBRL**	**380-65**
N972PF	**PRM1**	**RB-38**
N972TF	WW24	138
N972VZ	C650	0212
N972W	**HS25**	**257111**
N972XP	HS25	HA-0172
N973	LJ25	254
N973AC	C680	0195
N973EJ	WW24	168
N973F	FA20	81
N973GA	LJ25	051
N973HR	**LJ60**	**260**
N973JD	LJ25	123
N973M	F9EX	73
(N973ME)	E55P	50500005
(N973MV)	GLF3	301
N973MW	GLF3	301
N973MW	**GLF4**	**1145**
N974BK	**F900**	**105**
N974D	LJ24	095
N974F	FA20	83
N974GA	GLF5	5174
N974GA	GLF5	5474
N974GA	LJ25	053
N974HR	**F2TH**	**33**
N974JD	**GLF4**	**1301**
N974JD	HA4T	RC-11
N974JD	HS25	258589
N974JD	LJ24	205
N974JD	LJ25	106
N974JD	LJ35	457
N974JD	LJ35	648
N974JD	BE40	RK-141
(N974JD)	HA4T	RC-5
N974M	LJ25	053
N974SC	**E55P**	**50500282**
N974TS	GLEX	9274
N975AA	LJ35	012
N975AD	LJ35	012
N975AR	EPC1	002
N975BD	**BE40**	**RK-553**
N975CM	BE40	RK-166
N975DM	C52A	0083
N975DM	**LJ40**	**2073**
N975DN	C52A	0083
N975EE	C500	135
N975F	FA20	84
N975GA	GLF2	26
N975GA	GLF5	5175
N975GR	GLF4	4154
N975GR	MU30	A077SA
N975HM	C550	550-0975
N975LV	**LJ60**	**128**
N975P	**MS76**	**075**
N975QS	**C750**	**0175**
N975RD	BE40	RK-390
N975RG	**GLF3**	**471**
N975RR	**BE40**	**RK-349**
N975SC	**E55P**	**50500298**
N975XP	HS25	HA-0175
(N975XP)	HS25	HA-0075
N976AM	**CL64**	**5372**
N976B	GLF2	32/2
N976BS	LJ25	016
N976CB	**GLEX**	**9428**
N976EE	C500	025
N976F	FA20	86
N976GA	**C550**	**179**
N976M	FA10	63
N976PW	F900	125
N976SR	SBRL	465-29
N977AE	C750	0125
N977AE	**G280**	**2057**
N977AF	**C750**	**0125**
N977AR	LJ31	134
(N977AR)	LJ45	217
N977AV	**HS25**	**258559**
N977BA	**GALX**	**127**
N977CB	**GLF4**	**1217**
N977CC	HS25	257010
N977CP	**F2EX**	**17**
N977DM	C525	0338
N977DM	**C560**	**0494**
N977DT	**C560**	**0579**

N977EE	C500	140
N977F	FA20	88
N977GA	GLF5	5177
N977GA	GLF5	596
N977GA	LJ24	219
N977GA	LJ24	221
(N977GR)	HS25	258344
N977GS	**FA7X**	**202**
N977HG	**HS25**	**HA-0184**
N977HS	**GLF5**	**5385**
N977JK	**E55P**	**50500124**
N977JP	**LJ31**	**140**
N977KG	**FA50**	**25**
N977LC	**HS25**	**258977**
N977LP	F9EX	77
N977MR	**C560**	**0623**
N977QS	C750	0077
N977RJ	**LJ45**	**478**
N977SA	**GLF5**	**593**
N977SD	**C56X**	**5013**
N977SS	LJ60	257
N977TW	FA20	13
(N977TX)	C750	0077
N977VH	**EA50**	**000206**
N977XP	HS25	HA-0177
N978BE	**C680**	**0070**
N978CC	**GLF4**	**1335**
N978DB	**C750**	**0009**
N978E	LJ36	024
N978EE	C500	018
N978F	FA20	89
N978FL	GLF3	397
N978GA	G280	2078
N978GA	GLF5	5178
N978PC	C510	0199
N978PC	**E55P**	**50500330**
N978PW	F900	125
N978PW	**F9EX**	**155**
N978QS	**C750**	**0187**
N978R	SBRL	306-1
N978R	SBRL	306-27
N978R	SBRL	306-63
N978W	FA50	49
N979BK	F900	105
N979C	C550	504
N979C	C560	0263
N979CB	GLEX	9428
N979CB	**GLEX**	**9561**
N979CB	GLF4	1217
N979CF	**HS25**	**HA-0195**
N979CM	**BE40**	**RK-570**
N979CM	BE40	RK-571
N979DR	**LJ45**	**158**
N979EE	C500	015
N979EL	C750	0079
N979F	FA20	91
N979G	C550	504
N979GA	GLF2	151/24
N979GA	GLF5	5179
N979JB	HS25	258399
N979JC	FA50	218
N979KC	**CL30**	**20610**
N979PC	**C510**	**0199**
N979QS	C750	0079
N979RA	GLF2	151/24
N979RA	GLF4	1191
N979RA	JSTR	5023
N979RD	LJ55	025
N979RF	**LJ35**	**376**
N979TB	**HS25**	**HA-0075**
N979TM	**HA4T**	**RC-28**
N979TM	HS25	HA-0075
(N979TM)	HS25	HA-0082
(N979TX)	C52B	0139
N979WC	**C550**	**584**
N979XP	HS25	HA-0179
N979XP	BE40	RK-379
N980A	LJ25	340
N980AG	**C560**	**0348**
N980AW	WW24	414
N980BA	GALX	129
(N980CM)	GLF4	4005
N980DC	HS25	258267
N980DK	C56X	5019
N980DM	C500	421
N980EE	C500	034
(N980EF)	GLF2	124
N980F	FA20	95
N980GA	G150	280
N980GA	G280	2080
N980GA	GLF4	4280
N980GA	GLF5	5180
N980GG	GLEX	9009
N980GG	**GLEX**	**9439**
N980HC	CL61	5070
N980HC	CL61	5163
N980JC	**CL30**	**20419**
N980MB	C525	0686
N980ML	ASTR	033
(N980ML)	GLF4	1193
N980R	FA20	98/434
N980S	**FA50**	**249**
N980S	WW24	401
N980SF	**F9EX**	**224**
N980SK	CL65	5701
N980VP	**C525**	**0098**
N980XP	HS25	HA-0180
N981	F2TH	53
N981AG	**C560**	**0466**
N981CE	**HS25**	**258563**
N981EE	C500	005
N981F	FA20	96
N981GA	GLF5	5111
N981GA	GLF5	681
N981HC	GLF4	1217
N981LB	C525	0546
N981SW	GLF4	1001
N981TH	LJ35	364
N981TS	**GLEX**	**9281**
N981WA	C52A	0473
N981WA	E50P	50000050
N982AR	**BE40**	**RK-206**
N982B	GLF2	98/38
N982BZ	**C52B**	**0364**
N982EX	F9EX	82
N982F	FA20	99
N982HC	GLF4	1242
N982J	CL64	5308
N982JC	**CL30**	**20380**
N982LC	**HS25**	**259005**
(N982LC)	C550	376
N982MC	FA10	114
N982NA	**C550**	**376**
N982QS	**C750**	**0182**
N982RK	GLF3	310
N982XP	HS25	258982
N983AG	C550	413
N983AJ	FA20	11
(N983AJ)	C550	369
N983CC	FA10	163
N983CE	**HS25**	**258446**
N983CE	HS25	258509
(N983CE)	CL61	5102
(N983EC)	HS25	258446
N983F	FA20	100
N983GA	GLF5	5183
N983GA	GLF5	5403
N983GT	HS25	257086
N983J	**GLEX**	**9072**
N983QS	C750	0083
N984BD	LJ60	378
N984BH	**LJ45**	**469**
N984BK	**C550**	**550-0857**
N984BX	**F9EX**	**127**
N984EP	E50P	50000313
N984EX	F9EX	84
N984F	FA20	101
N984GA	C560	0328
N984GA	GLF4	4184
N984GB	C550	550-1122
N984GC	HS25	258377
N984GC	LJ45	009
(N984H)	C550	188
(N984H)	F9EX	210
N984HF	HS25	25183
N984HM	HS25	258229
N984JC	HA4T	RC-32
N984JC	HA4T	RC-56
N984JD	LJ25	342
N984JD	LJ31	001
N984JD	LJ55	139A
N984JW	**GLF4**	**1091**
N984MS	HS25	258984
N984QS	C750	0084
N984SA	MU30	A063SA
N984TS	GLEX	9084
(N984VP)	C550	550-0984
N984XP	HS25	HA-0084
N984XR	**LJ45**	**373**
N985AS	EA50	000261
N985BA	C550	043
N985BB	GLF2	250
N985BC	C56X	6144
N985BC	**C680**	**680A0009**
N985CE	**HS25**	**258490**
N985EL	**GLEX**	**9337**
N985EX	F9EX	85
N985F	FA20	102
N985FM	**CL30**	**20113**
N985GA	GLF4	4185
N985GA	GLF6	6085
N985JC	GLF5	5083
N985M	C650	0068
(N985QS)	C750	0085
N985RM	HS25	HA-0085
N985XP	HS25	HA-0185
N986AH	GLF4	1003
N986BA	**GLEX**	**9498**
N986BL	**LJ45**	**449**
N986DS	**C500**	**668**
N986DV	F2TH	74
N986EX	F9EX	86
N986F	FA20	105
N986GA	GLF4	4186
N986GA	GLF5	5106
N986H	HS25	257009
N986JB	SBRL	282-72
N986JC	**HA4T**	**RC-35**
N986M	C650	0048
N986MA	**LJ31**	**080**
N986PA	C550	550-0986
(N986PA)	FA50	126
N986PB	**PRM1**	**RB-290**
N986PR	**C525**	**0886**
N986QS	**C750**	**0086**
N986SA	**LJ35**	**609**
N986ST	**C52C**	**0181**
N986WC	LJ24	213
N986WC	LJ35	023
N986WC	LJ55	030
N986XP	HS25	HA-0086
N987A	ASTR	099
N987AB	FA20	368
N987AC	GLF4	1156
N987AL	F9EX	194
N987AR	GLF4	1156
N987CE	**HS25**	**258557**
N987CJ	**C555**	**0152**
N987CM	**C510**	**0140**
(N987DK)	LJ35	360
N987F	FA20	106
N987F	**FA50**	**124**
N987G	ASTR	031
N987GA	GLF5	5347
N987GK	ASTR	031
N987GK	F900	88
N987GR	C550	550-0987
N987HP	**CL30**	**20069**
(N987JJ)	GLEX	9451
N987LP	LJ35	670
N987QK	F900	88
N987QS	C750	0087
N987RC	FA50	31
N987SA	GLF2	172
N988AA	LJ25	185
N988AA	**LJ25**	**348**
N988AC	LJ25	185
(N988AC)	C500	349
N988AG	**HS25**	**HA-0088**
N988AK	**F900**	**22**
N988AL	GLF4	4128
N988AS	LJ25	257
N988BC	**E50P**	**50000139**
N988DB	LJ25	185
N988DS	GLF2	98/38
(N988DT)	HA4T	RC-16
N988DV	**F2EX**	**211**
N988DV	F2TH	74
N988F	FA20	107
N988GA	GLF5	5338
(N988GA)	HS25	257057
N988GC	**FA50**	**337**
N988GG	**GLEX**	**9009**
N988H	C650	0087
N988H	**F9EX**	**125**
N988H	GLF2	150
N988H	GLF2	98/38
N988H	GLF4	1347
N988HL	C650	0087
N988JC	**CL65**	**5942**
N988JE	HS25	257087
(N988JE)	GLF2	151/24
N988JG	BE40	RK-255
N988KD	GALX	196
N988LS	**GLF4**	**1290**
N988MC	**LJ45**	**352**
N988MM	**C52B**	**0401**
N988MT	SBRL	276-32
N988MW	JSTR	5231
N988NA	WW24	372
N988NW	**FA7X**	**174**
N988P	LJ60	366
N988PA	LJ45	076
N988PG	**C560**	**0644**
N988QC	**LJ35**	**455**
N988R	SBRL	306-17
N988RC	**LJ45**	**190**
N988RS	C550	568
N988RS	**HS25**	**258598**
N988S	**F2TH**	**173**
N988SA	LJ24	037
N988SB	FA50	174
N988T	**F900**	**65**
N988T	FA50	130
N988TM	**C680**	**0021**
N988WH	WW24	209
(N989AB)	HS25	25286
N989AL	**LJ35**	**212**
N989AR	**GLF5**	**5339**
N989BA	CL65	5850
N989BC	**CL61**	**5021**
N989CJ	**C52C**	**0089**
(N989DH)	CL64	5311
N989EX	F9EX	91
N989F	FA20	110
N989GA	GLF4	4019
N989GA	GLF4	4189
N989H	C680	0506
N989JC	**GLF5**	**5318**
N989JN	JSTR	5132/57
N989PA	LJ45	071
N989PT	**C650**	**0129**
N989QS	C750	0089
N989RF	**EA50**	**000238**
N989RJ	**GLEX**	**9224**
N989RS	**C52B**	**0459**
N989SA	LJ24	100
N989SC	C500	148
N989SE	**ASTR**	**120**
N989SF	**GLEX**	**9234**
N989ST	**HS25**	**258478**
N989TL	**LJ24**	**160**
N989TV	C550	305
N989TW	C550	305
N989TW	C560	0185
N989TW	C56X	5014
N989VR	C750	0089
N989WS	GLF4	4033
N990AC	SBRL	306-24
N990AE	LJ31	240
N990AK	CL64	5337
N990AL	**C500**	**033**
N990BB	**F900**	**42**
N990CB	C500	211
N990CH	JSTR	5225
N990CH	**LJ55**	**136**
N990DF	BE40	RK-430
N990DK	C56X	5019
N990DW	**C56X**	**6022**
N990EA	**GLF4**	**1388**
N990EX	F9EX	89
N990F	FA20	111
N990FL	**F9EX**	**190**
N990FV	**C525**	**0863**
N990GA	GLF4	4020
N990GA	GLF5	5200
N990GC	**LJ31**	**033A**
N990H	C52C	0003
N990H	**C680**	**0506**
N990H	F9EX	17
N990HC	**HS25**	**258412**
(N990HP)	C555	0064
N990JH	**C560**	**0754**
(N990JH)	C560	0643
N990JM	C550	550-0990
N990JT	**GALX**	**091**
N990JT	LJ40	2007
N990L	FA20	43
N990LC	**LJ35**	**483**
N990LT	**F900**	**60**
N990M	**C550**	**608**
N990MC	F900	65
N990MC	F9EX	123
N990MF	**C56X**	**5052**
N990ML	F9EX	123
N990ML	GLF3	400
N990MM	C550	288
N990MM	**FA50**	**105**
(N990MQ)	F900	65
N990MR	**C550**	**488**
N990NA	**EA50**	**000086**
N990NB	GLF4	1428
N990NB	**GLF5**	**5192**
N990PA	**SBRL**	**306-114**
(N990PJ)	GLF4	1134
N990PM	GLF4	1134
N990PT	FA20	391
N990PT	GLF4	1134
N990PT	GLF4	4116
N990PT	LJ24	236
N990PT	SBRL	306-114
N990QS	**C750**	**0190**
N990S	**WW24**	**322**
(N990TB)	HS25	259005
N990TC	**C550**	**550-0963**
N990TM	LJ24	051
(N990UH)	GLF4	1247
N990WA	**LJ40**	**2122**
N990WC	GLF3	405
N990WC	GLF4	1268
N990WM	**F9EX**	**40**
(N990Y)	C550	311
N991	JSTR	5139/54
N991AL	**LJ35**	**216**
N991AS	F900	12
N991BB	**C510**	**0256**
N991BM	C550	126
N991CA	**E50P**	**50000122**
N991CE	**F2TH**	**163**
N991CH	LJ55	091
N991CX	C750	0091
N991DB	**LJ60**	**177**
N991EA	GALX	180
N991EJ	C750	0091
N991EJ	F900	91
N991F	FA20	112
N991F	JSTR	5139/54
N991GA	GLF2	170
N991GA	GLF5	5011
N991GA	GLF5	5201
N991GS	CL30	20099
N991GS	LJ45	489
N991L	C560	0350
N991LB	**FA50**	**213**
N991LF	GLF5	576
N991ML	**PRM1**	**RB-254**
N991NB	**GLF4**	**1428**
N991PC	C560	0043
N991PC	C560	0364
N991PS	**HS25**	**HA-0084**
N991RF	F900	3
N991RL	**GALX**	**148**
N991RV	ASTR	011
N991RV	FA10	24
N991RW	**C56X**	**5053**
N991SA	C500	194
N991TD	LJ24	124
N991TW	**CL64**	**5333**
N991WC	GLF3	405
N992	FA50	77
N992	JSTR	5070/52
N992	SBRL	306-88
N992AB	**C680**	**680A0028**
N992AS	**C550**	**074**
N992DC	**CL30**	**20423**
N992FJ	F9EX	92
N992GA	GLF5	5202
N992GA	GLF5	5332
N992GA	BE40	RJ-22
N992HE	**C550**	**550-1006**
(N992HG)	C500	132
N992MS	**GLF4**	**1309**
N992NA	**GLF3**	**309**
(N992NW)	C500	660
(N992QS)	C750	0029
N992SC	**PRM1**	**RB-191**
N992SF	HS25	256044
N992TD	LJ24	035
N993	FA50	38
N993AC	G150	265
N993AM	**F9EX**	**265**
N993DS	WW24	356
N993EX	F9EX	93
N993F	FA20	113
N993GH	**F2EX**	**85**
N993GL	**C525**	**0509**
N993GT	F9EX	93
N993H	BE40	RK-241
N993JL	**CL30**	**20312**
N993KL	LJ24	166
N993LC	**C650**	**0027**
N993MC	CL30	20186
N993QS	C750	0093
N993SA	**CL61**	**5127**
N993SA	HS25	258377
N993SJ	**HS25**	**258377**
N993TD	LJ24	166
N994	SBRL	465-33
N994CE	**C550**	**448**
N994CF	C550	448
(N994CF)	C560	0120
N994CR	LJ35	492
N994CT	CL61	5161
N994EA	**LJ35**	**460**
N994EX	F9EX	94
N994F	FA20	116
N994GA	G150	294
N994GC	GLF2	77
N994GC	GLF4	1435
N994GG	GLF2	77
N994GP	F2EX	105
N994HP	**C560**	**0507**
N994JD	GLF2	37
N994JD	GLF2	92
N994JD	LJ55	139A
N994JG	C525	0685
N994JR	PRM1	RB-183
N994MP	C52B	0328
N994SA	LJ24	005
N994SA	LJ24	119
N994TA	CL60	1077
N994TD	LJ24	179
N994U	C650	0099
(N994W)	SBRL	306-132
N995	SBRL	306-29
N995AU	**C510**	**0198**
(N995AU)	C500	385
N995AW	LJ31	063
N995BA	**CL61**	**5095**
N995BC	GLF3	432
N995BE	HA4T	RC-24
N995CK	**FA20**	**95**
N995CR	LJ35	304
N995DC	C555	0065
N995DP	**LJ35**	**600**
N995DR	LJ24	285
N995F	FA20	117
N995G	**F2TS**	**734**
N995GA	ASTR	158
N995GA	GALX	111
N995GG	**GLF4**	**1074**
N995GH	F2EX	72
N995JP	**C500**	**481**
N995LP	**E55P**	**50500321**
N995MA	CL64	5362
N995ML	**GLEX**	**9322**
(N995P)	F900	117
N995PA	C500	649
N995PT	FA20	391
N995RD	**SBRL**	**380-9**
(N995RD)	LJ24	285
(N995RD)	SBRL	306-24
N995SA	HS25	257035
N995SK	F900	166
N995SK	HS25	257035
(N995SL)	HS25	257035
N995TD	LJ24	149
N995TE	EA50	000095
N996AC	**C550**	**641**
N996AG	F2TH	64
N996AL	LJ40	2029
N996BP	LJ45	301
N996CM	C510	0096
N996CR	LJ55	060
(N996DR)	MU30	A032SA

N996EX	F9EX	99
N996F	FA20	118
N996GA	ASTR	156
N996GA	G150	296
N996GA	GLF4	4196
N996GA	**GLF5**	**596**
N996JP	ASTR	017
N996JR	C525	0147
N996JS	**LJ31**	**119**
N996LF	**E50P**	**50000213**
N996LP	E50P	50000213
N996MS	**FA7X**	**149**
N996PE	**C52B**	**0170**
N996QS	**C750**	**0196**
N996RP	HS25	257131
N996TD	LJ24	320
N996UA	**C680**	**680A0023**
N996W	SBRL	465-22
N996XP	HS25	HA-0096
N997AG	GLF4	1440
N997BC	GLF4	1170
N997BX	**HS25**	**258909**
N997C	**C680**	**0216**
N997CA	C500	198
N997CB	**C56X**	**5102**
N997CM	GLF3	432
(N997CT)	CL61	5161
N997EA	**C560**	**0178**
N997EX	F9EX	100
N997GA	ASTR	107
N997GC	CL61	3025
(N997HM)	GLF3	432
N997HT	C550	550-0848
N997ME	SBRL	306-40
N997MX	**MU30**	**A036SA**
N997QS	**C750**	**0208**
N997RS	**BE40**	**RK-388**
(N997S)	C500	179
N997SS	C52A	0469
N997SS	**C56X**	**6154**
N997T	**C510**	**0436**
N997TD	LJ24	247
N997TT	FA20	485
N998AA	C500	310
N998AB	LJ40	2144
(N998AB)	LJ40	2130
N998AL	LJ31	240
N998AL	LJ40	2029
N998AL	LJ40	2130
N998AL	**LJ40**	**2144**
(N998AL)	LJ40	2105
N998AM	GLEX	9009
N998AQ	**LJ40**	**2029**
N998BC	**C550**	**665**
N998BM	**FA20**	**474**
N998CK	**FA20**	**98/434**
N998CX	**C750**	**0098**
(N998DJ)	LJ35	098
N998EA	**C500**	**492**
N998EJ	C750	0098
N998EX	F9EX	98
N998FA	**GLF5**	**5450**
N998FF	**BE40**	**RK-37**
N998G	GALX	008
N998GA	ASTR	108
N998GA	**G280**	**2098**
N998GA	GLF4	4025
N998GA	GLF4	4298
N998GA	GLF5	5158
N998GC	LJ35	343
N998GP	ASTR	108
N998GP	C550	363
N998GP	BE40	RK-32
N998JB	GLF3	491
N998JL	**C560**	**0604**
N998JP	LJ35	211
N998JR	CL61	3045
N998M	LJ24	249
(N998M)	LJ35	098
N998NJ	**LJ40**	**2130**
N998PA	HS25	258070
N998PA	**PRM1**	**RB-70**
N998PB	**GLF6**	**6104**
(N998PS)	HS25	25229
N998QS	**C750**	**0198**
N998R	SBRL	306-9
N998RD	WW24	103
N998RL	LJ24	087
N998SA	**C560**	**0485**
N998SR	C550	550-1136
N998SS	**FA7X**	**250**
N998TS	**C550**	**550-0987**
N998TW	**C560**	**0362**
N999AA	**GLF4**	**1286**
N999AD	C560	0136
(N999AH)	FA10	152
N999AM	**C500**	**232**
N999AU	C550	181
N999AU	LJ31	074
N999AZ	WW24	343
N999BE	F2EX	32
N999BE	F2TH	147
N999BE	**FA7X**	**8**
(N999BG)	FA20	275
N999BH	LJ25	318
N999BL	ASTR	024
N999BL	C550	131
N999BL	WW24	382
N999BS	SBRL	282-53
N999CA	**C680**	**0555**
N999CA	WW24	111
N999CB	C500	211
N999CB	**C560**	**0692**
N999CB	CS55	0054
(N999CB)	C500	631
N999CM	C500	158
N999CM	**LJ55**	**005**
N999CV	C500	211
N999CX	**C550**	**550-0841**
N999CX	C750	0073
N999CY	HS25	257086
N999DC	FA20	322
N999DC	SBRL	306-95
N999EA	CS55	0077
N999EB	C525	0210
N999EB	C525	0616
N999EH	**F900**	**15**
N999EK	**LJ40**	**2060**
N999EQ	FA20	275
N999F	FA10	29
N999FA	LJ35	386
N999FB	WW24	61
N999FH	**GLF5**	**5372**
N999GC	**E55P**	**50500008**
N999GH	C550	496
N999GH	LJ31	216
(N999GL)	CS55	0030
N999GP	ASTR	062
N999GP	ASTR	108
N999GP	C550	363
N999GP	**GLF4**	**1061**
N999GP	GLF4	1422
N999GP	BE40	RK-32
N999GR	C550	104
N999GY	**C750**	**0063**
N999HC	CS55	0030
N999HG	LJ25	178
(N999HY)	GLEX	9694
N999HZ	**GLF5**	**5383**
(N999JA)	LJ35	352
N999JB	C500	114
N999JD	**C510**	**0036**
N999JF	HS25	257016
N999JF	HS25	258220
N999JF	HS25	258380
N999JF	LJ35	188
N999JF	BE40	RK-98
N999JR	CL61	3061
N999JR	LJ24	174
N999JS	**LJ35**	**277**
N999KG	SBRL	306-53
N999LB	C52B	0057
N999LB	LJ45	429
N999LB	**LJ45**	**460**
N999LC	WW24	402
N999LF	HS25	25155
(N999LG)	SBRL	306-53
N999LJ	LJ60	314
N999LL	FA10	152
(N999LL)	C550	106
N999LR	**GLF5**	**5481**
N999LX	GLF4	1099
N999LX	**GLF5**	**665**
N999M	LJ24	114
N999M	LJ24	249
N999M	LJ25	030
N999M	LJ25	102
N999M	LJ25	178
N999M	LJ25	231
N999M	LJ35	045
N999M	SBRL	380-54
N999MC	WW24	412
N999ME	LJ25	231
N999MF	LJ24	202
N999MF	**LJ25**	**050**
N999MH	FA10	6
N999MK	C550	290
N999MK	LJ25	030
N999ML	LJ25	102
N999MS	**C500**	**638**
N999MS	WW24	199
N999MV	LJ25	178
N999MY	**CL65**	**5959**
N999NB	**GLF4**	**1234**
N999ND	**CL30**	**20250**
N999ND	LJ35	112
(N999NM)	HS25	25186
N999NN	GLF6	6040
N999PJ	**MS76**	**089**
N999PM	F900	128
N999PM	F900	20
N999PM	**F9EX**	**70**
(N999PN)	F900	128
N999PW	**C500**	**549**
N999PX	**CL64**	**5387**
N999QE	C52A	0366
N999QH	**CS55**	**0077**
N999QS	**C750**	**0203**
N999RA	LJ24	213
(N999RA)	WW24	93
N999RB	C500	369
N999RB	LJ35	301
(N999RB)	C500	578
N999RC	C550	479
N999RN	**E50P**	**50000053**
N999RW	HS25	25236
N999RZ	**HS25**	**258361**
N999SA	HS25	25146
N999SF	C500	055
N999SM	**C52B**	**0052**
N999SR	CL60	1042
(N999SW)	CL61	3008
N999TC	C500	120
N999TF	CL60	1042
N999TH	FA20	512
N999TH	LJ25	293
N999TH	LJ35	621
N999TJ	C750	0254
N999TJ	CS55	0048
N999TN	**E50P**	**50000270**
N999TN	LJ35	621
N999U	LJ24	253
N999U	WW24	178
N999UB	C52B	0057
N999VK	**CL64**	**5499**
N999VT	SBRL	282-38
N999WA	C550	051
N999WA	LJ24	242
N999WC	**C52C**	**0051**
N999WE	C52A	0126
N999WJ	FA10	216
N999WS	**C500**	**581**
N999WW	BE40	RK-520
N999YA	GLEX	9114
N999YB	**BE40**	**RK-98**
N999YC	LJ60	353
N999YX	GLEX	9240
N999YY	GLEX	9114
N999YY	**GLEX**	**9240**
N999ZG	PRM1	RB-182
N1000	GLF2	205
N1000	GLF2	75/7
N1000E	C525	0077
N1000E	**C550**	**550-1011**
N1000E	HS25	259015
N1000E	SBRL	282-19
N1000U	HS25	259006
N1000W	C560	0204
N1000W	CS55	0079
N1001A	LJ24	071
N1001G	SBRL	306-3
N1001L	LJ35	357
"N1001L"	LJ35	155
N1002B	LJ24	038
N1004T	GLF2	35
N1005	GLF5	5253
N1006F	C525	0112
N1007	JSTR	5057
N1008	**C500**	**616**
N1008S	**LJ24**	**118**
N1008U	**E50P**	**50000283**
N1010A	LJ36	017
N1010F	FA20	360
N1010G	LJ36	043
N1010H	LJ36	044
N1012B	JSTR	5012
N1013	**CL30**	**20229**
N1013F	FA20	364
N1014X	C750	0008
N1015B	C525	0151
N1015G	E50P	50000290
N1015J	E50P	50000293
N1016M	E50P	50000299
N1018F	FA20	365
N1018S	E50P	50000302
N1019K	LJ45	246
N1019K	WW24	180
N1019L	E50P	50000304
N1019Q	E50P	50000305
N1020F	FA20	366
N1020G	E50P	50000311
N1020P	SBRL	306-54
N1021B	LJ24	086
N1021T	C500	413
N1022G	LJ35	650
N1024G	SBRL	306-64
N1025C	HS25	25108
(N1026)	HFB3	1026
N1027S	BE40	RK-141
N1028Y	SBRL	306-71
N1036F	FA20	368
N1036N	LJ25	121
N1037F	FA20	369
N1038F	FA20	370
N1039	GLF2	40
N1039F	FA20	371
N1039L	LJ55	139
N1039V	E55P	50500118
N1040	GLF2	40
N1040	GLF3	314
N1040	GLF4	1044
N1040	GLF4	1206
N1040	**GLF5**	**650**
N1041B	HS25	25111
N1041F	FA20	373
N1043B	LJ35	644
N1045F	FA20	374
N1045J	LJ35	648
N1045T	C500	131
N1045X	CL60	1038
N1045X	LJ55	096
N1047T	FA20	126/438
N1048X	LJ36	063
N1055C	LJ55	135
(N1058G)	CS55	0105
N1058X	SBRL	465-4
N1061	HS25	258134
N1061D	CL61	5140
N1062	SBRL	282-15
N1064	SBRL	265-52
N1066W	C560	0374
N1069L	BE40	TX-9
N1072	SBRL	282-18
N1075X	LJ55	082
N1080Q	FA10	80
N1082A	GLF4	1082
N1083Z	BE40	RK-131
N1084D	BE40	RK-114
N1086	**GLF4**	**1086**
N1087T	LJ25	289
N1087T	LJ35	589
N1087T	LJ36	052
N1087T	LJ55	096
N1087T	LJ55	128
N1087Y	LJ35	274
N1087Y	LJ35	491
N1087Y	LJ35	641
N1087Y	LJ55	102
N1087Y	LJ55	116
N1087Z	LJ35	427
N1087Z	LJ35	490
N1087Z	LJ35	503
N1087Z	LJ35	660
N1087Z	LJ36	054
N1087Z	LJ36	059
N1087Z	LJ55	073
N1087Z	BE40	RK-132
N1088A	LJ25	368
N1088A	LJ35	271
N1088A	LJ35	431
N1088A	LJ35	655
N1088A	LJ36	060
N1088A	LJ55	068
N1088A	LJ55	131
N1088C	LJ25	292
N1088C	LJ25	310
N1088C	LJ35	594
N1088C	LJ35	644
N1088C	LJ55	065
N1088C	LJ55	094
N1088D	LJ25	291
N1088D	LJ25	366
N1088D	LJ31	004
N1088D	LJ35	342
N1088D	LJ35	463
N1088D	LJ35	495
N1088D	LJ35	605
N1088R	**C56X**	**6156**
N1090X	CL64	5576
N1090X	BE40	RK-110
N1094D	BE40	RK-134
N1094L	**C56X**	**5094**
N1094N	BE40	RK-140
N1099S	BE40	RK-139
(N1100A)	GLF4	4244
N1100D	WW24	169
N1100M	WW24	86
N1101A	**CL64**	**5354**
N1101G	SBRL	282-58
N1102	C650	0047
N1102	GLF2	231
N1102A	FA50	18
N1102B	**CL64**	**5376**
N1102B	BE40	RK-122
N1102D	SBRL	282-7
N1102U	HS25	258343
N1103	C650	0054
N1103	HS25	257060
N1103R	LJ25	135
N1103U	HS25	258306
N1105U	BE40	RK-125
N1105Z	HS25	258301
N1107M	FA20	38
N1107M	JSTR	5122
N1107Z	C750	0112
N1107Z	CL61	3016
N1107Z	JSTR	5023
N1107Z	JSTR	5122
N1108T	BE40	RK-148
N1108Y	BE40	RK-128
N1109	C550	433
(N1109)	C650	0047
N1110S	LJ35	306
N1112N	HS25	258325
N1115	SBRL	380-17
N1115G	HS25	258347
N1115V	C525	0157
N1116A	SBRL	306-30
N1116R	**BE40**	**RK-116**
N1117S	BE40	RK-117
N1117Z	BE40	RK-137
N1118Y	BE40	RK-118
N1119C	GLF3	417
N1119C	BE40	RK-119
N1121	LJ25	004
N1121A	WW24	123
(N1121B)	WW24	129
N1121C	LJ25	004
N1121C	WW24	76
N1121E	WW24	149
N1121E	WW24	20
N1121E	WW24	78
N1121E	WW24	90
N1121F	WW24	150
N1121G	WW24	52
N1121G	WW24	67
N1121M	WW24	111
N1121M	WW24	36
N1121N	WW24	110
N1121N	WW24	125
N1121N	WW24	135
N1121N	WW24	98
N1121R	WW24	121
N1121R	**WW24**	**125**
N1121R	WW24	75
N1121S	WW24	103
N1121U	WW24	128
N1121X	WW24	121
N1121X	WW24	77
N1121Z	WW24	108
N1121Z	BE40	RK-121
N1122K	**C56X**	**5283**
N1123E	WW24	151
N1123E	WW24	159
N1123G	GLF2	160
N1123G	WW24	158
N1123H	WW24	156
N1123H	WW24	167
N1123H	WW24	172
N1123Q	WW24	157
N1123Q	WW24	173
N1123Q	WW24	182
N1123R	WW24	160
N1123R	WW24	165
N1123R	WW24	175
N1123R	WW24	186
N1123S	WW24	162
N1123T	WW24	163
N1123T	WW24	176
N1123T	WW24	184
N1123U	WW24	169
N1123U	WW24	177
N1123U	WW24	185
N1123W	WW24	160
N1123W	WW24	170
N1123X	WW24	174
N1123Y	WW24	179
N1123Z	WW24	159
N1123Z	WW24	178
N1123Z	BE40	RK-123
N1124E	WW24	196
N1124E	WW24	235
N1124F	WW24	281
N1124G	WW24	188
N1124G	WW24	203
N1124G	WW24	216
N1124G	WW24	220
N1124G	WW24	243
N1124K	WW24	307
N1124K	WW24	388
N1124L	WW24	340
N1124L	WW24	405
N1124N	WW24	187
N1124N	WW24	201
N1124N	WW24	214
N1124N	WW24	259
N1124N	WW24	321
N1124N	WW24	346
N1124N	WW24	396
N1124P	WW24	199
N1124P	WW24	207
N1124P	WW24	223
N1124P	WW24	245
N1124P	WW24	341
N1124P	WW24	376
N1124Q	WW24	201
N1124Q	WW24	232
N1124Q	WW24	288
N1124U	WW24	225
N1124U	WW24	286
N1124X	WW24	200
N1124X	WW24	233
N1124Z	WW24	234
N1124Z	WW24	410
N1124Z	BE40	RK-124
N1125	ASTR	021
N1125	ASTR	062
N1125	ASTR	076
N1125	HS25	25023
N1125	HS25	258101
N1125A	ASTR	012
N1125A	ASTR	021
N1125A	ASTR	032
N1125A	**ASTR**	**051**
N1125E	ASTR	058
N1125E	HS25	25149
N1125E	LJ24	196
N1125G	ASTR	076
N1125G	HS25	25019
N1125G	HS25	25033
N1125G	HS25	25084
N1125G	WW24	247
N1125J	**ASTR**	**078**
N1125K	**ASTR**	**035**
N1125L	ASTR	072

N1125M	LJ55	065
N1125S	ASTR	021
N1125S	ASTR	134
N1125V	ASTR	048
N1125V	ASTR	132
N1125Y	ASTR	049
N1125Z	ASTR	055
N1125Z	ASTR	068
N1126G	WW24	279
N1126V	BE40	RK-151
N1127G	C650	7084
N1127K	C525	0278
N1127K	C525	0293
N1127M	LJ35	226
N1127M	LJ55	120
N1127M	**LJ60**	**253**
N1127P	C560	0349
N1127U	BE40	RK-127
N1128B	C650	0184
N1128B	**F2TH**	**83**
N1128G	C525	0304
N1128J	LJ35	426
N1128M	**LJ60**	**222**
N1128V	C750	0159
N1129E	C56X	5112
N1129L	C560	0507
N1129M	LJ35	360
N1129M	LJ55	101
N1129X	GLF4	1129
N1129X	BE40	RK-129
N1130B	**F9EX**	**281**
N1130B	BE40	RK-130
N1130G	C56X	5213
N1130N	C650	7071
N1130X	C56X	5683
(N1131K)	C550	651
N1132D	PRM1	RB-32
N1133G	C525	0347
N1133N	HS25	258366
N1133T	BE40	RK-133
N1135A	HS25	258345
N1135A	BE40	RK-135
N1135K	HS25	25019
N1135U	BE40	RK-150
N1136Q	BE40	RK-136
N1140A	LJ35	045
N1141G	WW24	275
(N1149E)	GLF3	358
N1151K	JSTR	5115/39
N1159B	**GLF2**	**257/17**
N1159K	GLF2	101
N1161G	**HS25**	**258547**
N1164A	GLF2	42/12
N1166Z	WW24	18
(N1169D)	HS25	258002
N1172L	WW24	11
N1172Z	WW24	11
N1172Z	WW24	133
N1173Z	WW24	7
(N1175B)	GLF4	1175
N1178	C550	433
N1180Z	WW24	33
N1181G	FA50	72
N1183	C650	0054
N1183	HS25	257060
(N1184L)	HFB3	1050
N1188A	ASTR	018
N1189A	JSTR	5139/54
N1190Z	WW24	28
N1194Z	WW24	70
N1195N	WW24	89
N1196Z	WW24	61
N1198V	C56X	5692
N1199G	HS25	25174
N1199M	FA20	121
N1199M	HS25	25174
(N1199V)	C510	0045
N1200N	C550	681
N1202D	C560	0403
N1202T	C550	707
N1203	LJ24	008
N1203D	C550	709
N1203N	C550	710
N1203S	C550	711
N1204A	C550	715
N1205A	C550	716
(N1205M)	C550	717
(N1207A)	C550	720
N1207B	C550	721
N1207C	C550	722
N1207D	C550	723
N1207F	C550	724
N1207Z	C550	725
N1207Z	JSTR	5108
N1209T	C550	726
N1209T	C560	0002
(N1209X)	C550	727
(N1209X)	C560	0003
N1210	SBRL	306-4
N1210	WW24	34
N1210G	WW24	34
N1210M	LJ35	410
(N1210N)	C550	728
(N1210N)	C560	0004
N1210V	C550	729
(N1210V)	C560	0005
N1211M	C550	730
(N1211M)	C560	0006
N1212G	WW24	229
N1212H	C550	219
N1213S	C550	732
(N1213S)	C560	0008
N1213Z	C550	733
(N1213Z)	C560	0009
(N1214D)	C550	391
N1214H	C550	392
(N1214J)	C550	393
(N1214J)	C550	734
(N1214J)	C560	0010
N1214S	C550	394
(N1214Z)	C550	395
(N1214Z)	C560	0011
(N1215A)	C550	398
N1215G	C550	399
(N1215S)	C550	401
(N1216A)	C550	405
(N1216A)	C560	0003
N1216H	C550	406
N1216J	C550	407
(N1216J)	C560	0004
N1216K	C525	0199
N1216K	C550	408
N1216K	C550	454
N1216K	FA7X	172
(N1216K)	C560	0005
N1216N	C525	0226
N1216N	C550	409
(N1216N)	C560	0006
N1216Q	C550	410
(N1216Q)	C560	0007
N1216Z	C560	0454
(N1216Z)	C550	411
(N1216Z)	C560	0008
N1217D	C550	416
N1217H	C550	417
N1217H	C560	0376
(N1217H)	C560	0011
N1217N	C550	418
N1217N	C560	0012
N1217P	C550	419
(N1217P)	C560	0013
N1217S	C550	420
N1217S	C560	0014
N1217V	C550	421
N1217V	C560	560-0001
N1218A	C550	424
N1218C	**GLF2**	**99**
N1218F	C550	425
N1218F	**CL64**	**5658**
N1218K	C550	426
(N1218P)	C550	427
(N1218P)	C560	0017
N1218S	C550	428
N1218T	C550	429
N1218V	C550	430
N1218Y	C550	431
N1218Y	C560	0407
(N1218Y)	C560	0018
N1219D	C550	432
(N1219D)	C560	0019
(N1219G)	C550	433
(N1219G)	C560	0020
N1219L	**CL61**	**3050**
N1219M	**C56X**	**5171**
(N1219N)	C550	434
N1219P	C550	435
N1219Z	C550	436
N1220A	C550	439
(N1220D)	C550	440
N1220J	C550	441
(N1220N)	C550	442
N1220S	C550	443
N1220S	CL65	5808
N1220W	**C52A**	**0146**
N1221G	**GALX**	**045**
N1221J	**LJ60**	**209**
N1222P	**GLF5**	**606**
(N1223A)	C560	0017
N1223N	C650	0120
N1223N	CS55	0053
(N1226X)	C560	0019
N1227W	**FA7X**	**244**
N1228N	C56X	5030
(N1228N)	C560	0020
N1228V	C560	0021
(N1228Y)	C560	0022
(N1229A)	C560	0028
(N1229C)	C560	0029
(N1229D)	C560	0030
N1229F	C560	0031
N1229M	C560	0032
N1229N	C560	0033
(N1229Q)	C560	0034
N1229Z	C560	0035
N1230	WW24	53
N1230A	HS25	257026
(N1230A)	C560	0039
N1230B	HS25	25088
N1230D	WW24	53
N1230F	C56X	5679
N1230G	HS25	25091
(N1230G)	C560	0040
N1230R	JSTR	5049
N1230V	HS25	25043
(N1234F)	C500	501
N1234X	C500	394
(N1236P)	C500	358
N1239L	C650	0134
N1241K	C56X	5118
N1241N	C525	0185
(N1242A)	C550	609
N1242B	C550	610
N1242K	C560	0624
(N1242K)	C550	611
N1243C	C56X	5013
N1244V	C550	612
N1245	**C510**	**0204**
N1247V	C560	0535
N1248B	C560	0417
(N1248G)	C550	444
N1248K	C550	445
"N1248K"	C550	447
N1248N	C550	446
N1249B	C550	448
N1249H	C550	449
N1249K	C550	450
N1249P	**C550**	**451**
(N1249T)	C550	452
N1249V	C550	453
N1250	**LJ45**	**027**
N1250B	C550	455
N1250C	C550	456
N1250L	C550	457
N1250P	C550	458
N1250P	C550	613
N1250V	**C550**	**439**
N1251B	C550	463
N1251D	C550	464
N1251H	C550	465
N1251K	C550	466
N1251K	HS25	258372
N1251K	HS25	258377
N1251N	C550	467
(N1251P)	C550	468
(N1251P)	C550	614
N1251V	C550	469
(N1251V)	C550	614
N1251Z	C550	470
N1252B	C550	475
N1252D	**C550**	**476**
N1252J	C550	477
N1252N	C550	478
N1252P	C550	479
N1253D	C550	481
N1253G	C550	482
(N1253K)	C550	483
(N1253K)	C550	616
N1253N	C550	484
N1253P	C550	485
N1253Y	C550	486
(N1253Y)	C550	617
N1254C	C550	490
N1254C	C550	618
N1254C	C650	7098
(N1254D)	C550	491
(N1254D)	C550	619
N1254G	C550	620
(N1254G)	C550	492
N1254P	C550	493
N1254X	C550	494
(N1254Y)	C550	495
N1255D	C550	502
(N1255D)	C550	498
N1255G	C550	503
(N1255G)	C550	499
N1255J	C52A	0101
N1255J	**C52B**	**0109**
N1255J	C550	500
(N1255J)	C550	504
(N1255J)	C550	622
N1255K	**C550**	**505**
(N1255L)	C550	623
(N1255L)	CS55	0001
N1255Y	C550	624
(N1255Y)	CS55	0002
N1256B	CS55	0004
(N1256G)	C550	626
(N1256G)	CS55	0005
(N1256N)	C550	627
(N1256N)	CS55	0006
(N1256P)	C550	628
(N1256P)	CS55	0007
N1256T	C550	629
(N1256T)	CS55	0008
N1256Z	CS55	0009
N1257B	**C550**	**497**
N1257K	C550	630
(N1257K)	CS55	0010
(N1257M)	C550	631
(N1257M)	CS55	0011
N1258B	C550	550-1037
(N1258B)	C550	634
N1258H	C550	635
N1258M	C550	636
(N1258U)	C550	637
(N1258U)	CS55	0015
N1259B	C550	550-0819
N1259B	C650	7001
(N1259B)	C550	639
(N1259B)	CS55	0016
N1259G	CS55	0017
N1259K	C650	7002
N1259K	HS25	25170
(N1259K)	C550	640
(N1259K)	CS55	0018
(N1259M)	CS55	0019
N1259N	C650	7003
(N1259N)	C550	641
N1259R	C650	7004
(N1259R)	C550	642
(N1259R)	CS55	0020
N1259S	C650	7005
(N1259S)	C550	643
(N1259S)	CS55	0021
N1259Y	C525	0449
(N1259Y)	C550	644
(N1259Y)	C650	7006
(N1259Y)	CS55	0022
N1259Z	C650	7007
(N1259Z)	C550	645
(N1259Z)	CS55	0023
N1260G	C550	648
N1260G	C650	7010
(N1260G)	CS55	0026
N1260K	CS55	0027
(N1260L)	CS55	0028
N1260N	C650	7011
(N1260N)	CS55	0029
N1260V	C650	7012
(N1260V)	CS55	0030
N1261A	C650	7014
(N1261A)	CS55	0032
N1261K	C650	7015
(N1261K)	CS55	0033
N1261M	C650	7016
(N1261M)	C650	7017
(N1261M)	CS55	0034
(N1261P)	C650	7018
(N1261P)	CS55	0035
N1262A	C650	7020
N1262B	C650	7021
N1262E	C650	7022
N1262G	C650	7023
N1262Z	C650	7024
N1263B	C650	7025
N1263G	C650	7026
N1263P	C650	7027
(N1263V)	C650	7028
(N1263Y)	C650	7029
N1263Z	C650	7030
N1264B	C650	7033
N1264E	C650	7034
N1264M	C650	7035
N1264P	C650	7036
N1264V	C525	0126
(N1264V)	C650	7037
N1265B	C650	7040
N1265C	C650	7041
N1265K	C650	7042
N1265P	C650	7043
N1265U	C650	7044
N1267B	C52A	0207
N1268D	C56X	5273
N1268F	C750	0216
N1268G	LJ35	661
N1269B	C525	0534
(N1269D)	CS55	0040
(N1269E)	CS55	0041
(N1269J)	CS55	0042
(N1269N)	CS55	0043
N1269P	C560	0638
(N1269P)	CS55	0044
N1269Y	CS55	0045
N1270D	CS55	0048
N1270F	FA20	72/413
N1270K	C500	133
N1270K	CS55	0049
N1270S	CS55	0050
N1270Y	CS55	0051
N1271A	CL61	5038
N1271A	CS55	0055
N1271B	C550	550-1079
(N1271B)	CS55	0056
N1271D	CS55	0057
N1271E	CS55	0058
(N1271N)	CS55	0059
(N1271T)	CS55	0060
(N1272G)	CS55	0064
(N1272N)	CS55	0065
N1272P	CS55	0066
(N1272V)	CS55	0067
N1272Z	CS55	0068
N1273A	CS55	0072
(N1273E)	CS55	0073
(N1273G)	GLF2	99
N1273J	CS55	0074
(N1273N)	CS55	0075
N1273Q	C550	550-0858
(N1273Q)	CS55	0076
N1273R	C560	0318
(N1273R)	CS55	0077
N1273X	CS55	0078
(N1273Z)	CS55	0079
(N1274B)	CS55	0081
N1274D	CS55	0082
N1274K	CS55	0083
N1274N	CS55	0084
N1274P	CS55	0085
(N1274X)	CS55	0086
N1274Z	CS55	0087
(N1275A)	CS55	0092
N1275B	CS55	0093
(N1275D)	CS55	0094
N1275H	CS55	0095
(N1275N)	CS55	0096
N1275T	C56X	5702
N1276A	C550	550-1102
N1276J	C525	0200
N1276L	C680	0021
N1276Z	C550	550-1103
N1277E	**C52A**	**0076**
N1278	C550	429
N1278D	C52B	0006
N1279A	C525	0551
N1279V	C525	0552
N1279Z	C560	0175
N1280A	C525	0177
N1280A	C560	0178
N1280D	C560	0179
N1280K	C560	0180
N1280R	C560	0181
N1280S	C525	0281
(N1280S)	C560	0182
N1281A	C550	550-1109
N1281A	C560	0184
N1281K	C560	0185
N1281N	C560	0186
N1281N	C56X	5559
N1281R	C56X	5704
(N1282D)	C560	0192
N1282K	C560	0193
(N1282M)	C560	0194
N1282N	C560	0195
N1283F	C560	0198
(N1283K)	C560	0199
N1283M	C560	0200
N1283M	CS55	0120
N1283N	C560	0201
N1283V	C560	0202
N1283X	C560	0203
N1283Y	C560	0204
N1284A	C560	0206
(N1284B)	C560	0207
N1284D	C525	0463
(N1284D)	C560	0208
(N1284F)	C560	0209
N1284N	C560	0210
N1284P	C525	0464
(N1284P)	C560	0211
N1284X	C560	0212
(N1285D)	C560	0214
(N1285G)	C560	0215
N1285N	C560	0216
N1285P	C525	0465
N1285P	C560	0217
N1285V	C560	0218
(N1286A)	C560	0221
N1286C	C560	0222
N1286N	C560	0223
N1287B	C525	0555
N1287B	C560	0224
N1287C	C560	0225
N1287D	C52B	0027
N1287D	C560	0226
N1287F	C525	0557
N1287F	C560	0227
N1287G	C560	0228
N1287K	C560	0229
N1287N	C560	0230
N1287Y	C560	0231
N1288A	C560	0233
N1288B	C560	0234
N1288B	C750	0168
N1288D	C560	0235
N1288N	C525	0558
N1288N	C560	0236
N1288P	C525	0550
N1288P	C560	0237
N1288T	C560	0238
N1288Y	C560	0239
N1289G	C560	0240
N1289G	C750	0242
N1289M	GLF4	1441
N1289N	C560	0241
N1289Y	C560	0242
N1290B	CS55	0097
N1290E	CS55	0098
N1290G	CS55	0099
N1290N	C525	0554
N1290N	C560	0246
(N1290N)	CS55	0100
N1290Y	C52A	0238
(N1290Y)	CS55	0101
N1290Z	CS55	0102
N1291E	CS55	0107
N1291K	C560	0249
(N1291K)	C560	0250
(N1291K)	CS55	0108
N1291P	CS55	0109
N1291V	CS55	0110
N1291Y	C560	0250
(N1291Y)	CS55	0111
N1292A	CS55	0114
N1292B	C560	0253
(N1292B)	CS55	0115

N1292K	C555	0116
N1292N	C555	0117
N1293A	C555	0123
N1293E	C560	0257
(N1293E)	C555	0124
N1293G	C525	0204
N1293G	C555	0125
N1293K	C555	0126
N1293N	C555	0127
N1293V	C555	0128
N1293X	C555	0129
N1293Y	C560	0258
N1293Z	C560	0259
(N1293Z)	C555	0130
N1294B	C560	0260
(N1294D)	C555	0132
N1294K	C560	0261
(N1294K)	C555	0133
N1294M	C555	0134
N1294N	C560	0262
(N1294N)	C555	0135
(N1294P)	C560	560-0001
(N1294P)	C555	0136
N1295A	C560	0264
(N1295A)	C555	0138
N1295B	C560	0518
(N1295B)	C555	0139
N1295G	C560	0266
(N1295G)	C555	0140
N1295J	C560	0267
(N1295J)	C555	0141
N1295M	C560	0268
(N1295M)	C555	0142
N1295N	C560	0269
N1295N	C560	0292
(N1295N)	C555	0143
N1295P	C560	0265
(N1295P)	C555	0144
N1295Y	C560	0270
N1295Y	C560	0294
(N1295Y)	C555	0145
N1296B	C555	0146
N1296N	C560	0271
N1296N	C560	0297
N1296N	C555	0147
N1296Z	C555	0148
(N1297B)	C555	0150
N1297V	C560	0275
N1297V	C560	0300
N1297Y	C550	554
N1297Z	C550	555
N1298	SBRL	306-9
N1298C	C550	557
N1298G	C750	0248
(N1298G)	C550	558
(N1298H)	C550	559
N1298J	C550	560
N1298K	C550	561
(N1298N)	C550	562
N1298P	C550	550-1127
N1298P	C550	563
N1298X	C550	564
N1298X	C560	0502
N1298Y	C550	550-1114
N1298Y	C550	565
N1299B	C550	550-0808
(N1299B)	C550	566
N1299H	C56X	5578
(N1299H)	C550	567
N1299K	C550	568
N1299K	C56X	5586
N1299N	C550	550
N1299P	C550	569
(N1299T)	C550	570
(N1300G)	C550	576
N1300J	C56X	5621
(N1300J)	C550	577
N1300M	WW24	124
N1300N	C550	578
N1301A	C650	0221
(N1301A)	C550	582
N1301B	C550	583
N1301D	C550	584
N1301D	C650	0223
N1301K	C550	585
N1301N	C550	586
N1301P	JSTR	5138
N1301S	C550	587
N1301V	C550	588
N1301Z	C550	589
N1301Z	C650	0225
N1302A	C650	0226
N1302C	C650	0227
N1302N	C550	592
N1302V	C550	593
N1302V	C650	0228
N1302X	C550	594
N1302X	C650	0229
N1303A	C650	0232
N1303H	C550	600
N1303H	C650	0233
N1303M	C650	0236
(N1303M)	C550	601
N1303V	C650	0235
N1304B	C650	0238
N1304G	C650	0239
N1305C	C550	550-0925
(N1305C)	C650	0009
N1305N	C650	0230
(N1305N)	C650	0010
N1305U	C650	0011
N1305V	C650	0012
N1306B	C650	0237
(N1306B)	C650	0014
(N1306F)	C650	0015
N1306V	C56X	5054
N1306V	C650	0016
N1306V	C650	0234
N1307A	C650	0017
(N1307A)	C650	0235
(N1307C)	C650	0018
(N1307C)	C650	0236
(N1307D)	C650	0019
(N1307D)	C650	0237
N1307G	C650	0020
N1308L	C52B	0004
N1308V	C550	640
N1309A	C550	641
(N1309A)	C650	0033
N1309B	**C550**	**550-1121**
N1309K	C550	642
N1309V	C525	0613
(N1310B)	C550	644
(N1310B)	C650	0043
N1310C	C550	645
(N1310G)	C550	646
N1310H	**HS25**	**258253**
(N1310Q)	C550	648
(N1310Z)	C550	649
(N1311A)	C550	650
(N1311A)	C650	0049
(N1311K)	C650	0050
(N1311P)	C550	652
(N1311P)	C650	0051
N1312D	C650	0160
(N1312D)	C650	0054
N1312K	C56X	5624
(N1312K)	C650	0161
N1312Q	C650	0162
N1312T	C56X	5635
N1312T	C56X	5710
N1312T	C650	0163
N1312V	C650	0164
N1312V	C680	0075
N1312X	C650	0165
N1313G	C650	0059
N1313J	C650	0166
(N1313J)	C650	0060
(N1313T)	C650	0061
N1314H	C525	0632
N1314H	C650	0168
(N1314H)	C650	0064
N1314T	C680	0129
(N1314T)	C650	0065
N1314V	C52B	0164
N1314V	C650	0170
(N1314V)	C650	0066
(N1314X)	C650	0067
(N1314X)	C650	0068
(N1315A)	C650	0070
(N1315B)	C650	0071
N1315C	C560	0569
(N1315C)	C650	0072
N1315D	C56X	5711
(N1315D)	C650	0073
N1315G	C680	0173
(N1315G)	C650	0074
N1315T	C650	0075
N1315V	C650	0076
N1315Y	C680	0069
(N1315Y)	C650	0077
(N1316A)	C650	0079
N1316E	C650	0080
(N1316N)	C650	0081
N1317G	C650	0085
N1317X	C52A	0311
(N1317X)	C650	0086
N1317Y	C525	0619
(N1317Y)	C650	0087
(N1318A)	C650	0090
N1318E	C650	0091
(N1318E)	SBRL	306-96
(N1318L)	C650	0092
(N1318M)	C650	0093
(N1318P)	C650	0094
(N1318Q)	C650	0095
N1318X	C680	0143
(N1318X)	C650	0096
N1318Y	C550	550-0884
(N1318Y)	C650	0097
N1319B	C650	0099
N1319D	C560	0319
(N1319D)	C650	0100
N1319M	C650	0101
N1319X	C56X	5640
(N1319X)	C650	0102
(N1320B)	C650	0105
(N1320K)	C650	0106
N1320P	C56X	5648
(N1320P)	C650	0107
N1320U	HFB3	1023
(N1320U)	C650	0108
(N1320V)	C650	0109
(N1320X)	C650	0110
N1321A	C650	0112
N1321C	C650	0113
(N1321J)	C650	0114
N1321K	C650	0115
(N1321L)	C650	0116
N1321N	C650	0117
N1322D	C650	0121
(N1322K)	C650	0122
(N1322X)	C650	0123
(N1322Y)	C650	0124
(N1323A)	C650	0126
N1323D	C650	0127
(N1323K)	C650	0128
(N1323N)	C650	0129
(N1323Q)	C650	0130
(N1323R)	C650	0131
N1323V	C650	0132
N1323X	C650	0133
(N1323Y)	C650	0134
N1324	GLF2	33
N1324B	C56X	5051
N1324B	LJ55	026
(N1324B)	C650	0135
(N1324D)	C650	0136
(N1324G)	C650	0137
N1324P	LJ55	098
(N1324R)	C650	0138
(N1325D)	C650	0140
N1325E	C650	0141
(N1325L)	C650	0142
N1325X	C650	0143
N1325Y	C650	0144
N1325Z	C650	0145
N1326A	**C56X**	**5272**
N1326A	C650	0148
N1326B	C525	0002
N1326B	C650	0149
N1326D	C525	0003
N1326D	C650	0150
(N1326D)	C525	0005
N1326G	C525	0004
N1326G	C650	0151
N1326H	C525	0005
(N1326H)	C650	0152
N1326K	C650	0153
N1326P	C525	0006
N1326P	C525	0385
(N1326P)	C650	0154
N1327A	C650	0157
N1327B	C650	0158
(N1327E)	C525	0007
N1327G	C525	0008
N1327J	**C525**	**0009**
(N1327K)	C525	0010
(N1327N)	C525	0011
(N1327Z)	C525	0012
N1328A	C525	0013
N1328D	C525	0014
(N1328K)	C525	0015
N1328M	C525	0016
N1328M	GLEX	9316
(N1328Q)	C525	0017
(N1328X)	C525	0018
(N1328Y)	C525	0019
N1329D	C525	0020
N1329G	**C525**	**0146**
(N1329G)	C525	0021
N1329K	JSTR	5106/9
N1329L	JSTR	5161/43
N1329N	C525	0022
(N1329T)	C525	0023
(N1330D)	C525	0025
(N1330G)	C525	0026
N1330N	C525	0027
N1330S	C525	0028
N1331X	C525	0030
N1333Z	C550	273
N1348T	C525	0350
N1348T	LJ40	2035
N1354G	C500	539
N1354G	C500	622
N1354G	C525	0033
N1354G	C650	0171
N1363G	GLF4	1363
N1367D	C525	0655
N1368M	**GLEX**	**9536**
N1382C	C500	309
N1382N	C52B	0193
N1387E	C56X	5769
N1388J	C680	0209
N1393	HS25	25190
N1397A	C56X	5629
N1400M	**C650**	**0140**
N1401L	C500	436
N1401L	**C56X**	**6113**
(N1406)	JSTR	5029/38
N1406S	C680	0205
N1411S	LJ25	325
N1414P	**C52A**	**0315**
N1415N	**GLEX**	**9202**
N1419J	C650	0115
N1419J	C650	0201
(N1419J)	C750	0051
(N1420)	LJ24	116
N1424	WW24	345
N1424	WW24	94
N1424Z	WW24	94
N1433B	LJ25	255
N1440W	**C52C**	**0099**
N1441M	**LJ35**	**288**
N1450B	LJ25	212
N1450B	LJ35	182
N1450B	LJ35	354
N1450B	LJ35	497
N1450B	LJ55	113
(N1450B)	LJ55	053
N1451B	LJ35	102
N1451B	LJ35	244
N1451B	LJ35	457
N1451B	LJ35	590
N1451B	LJ35	620
N1451B	LJ55	045
N1451B	LJ55	087
N1454	GLF3	350
N1454H	GLF3	350
N1454H	GLF5	619
N1454H	**GLF6**	**6105**
N1459A	**GLF4**	**1459**
N1461B	LJ25	358
N1461B	LJ35	045
N1461B	LJ35	177
N1461B	LJ35	211
N1461B	LJ35	632
N1461B	LJ55	088
N1461B	LJ55	111
N1462B	LJ25	265
N1462B	LJ35	037
N1462B	LJ35	184
N1462B	LJ35	221
N1462B	LJ35	265
N1462B	LJ35	451
N1462B	LJ35	604
N1462B	LJ35	634
N1462B	LJ36	036
N1462B	LJ55	042
N1462B	LJ55	092
N1465B	LJ35	193
N1465B	LJ35	273
N1465B	LJ35	428
N1465B	LJ35	500
N1465B	LJ35	642
N1465B	LJ55	080
N1466B	LJ25	236
N1466B	LJ25	314
N1466B	LJ35	204
N1466B	LJ35	481
N1466B	LJ35	615
N1466B	LJ55	107
N1466K	LJ35	394
(N1466K)	C550	055
N1468B	LJ25	205
N1468B	LJ25	252
N1468B	LJ25	371
N1468B	LJ31	014
N1468B	LJ35	222
N1468B	LJ35	355
N1468B	LJ35	472
N1468B	LJ35	621
N1468B	LJ55	081
N1471B	LJ35	195
N1471B	LJ35	441
N1471B	LJ35	505
N1471B	LJ35	603
N1471B	LJ35	635
N1471B	LJ55	070
N1473B	LJ25	365
N1473B	LJ35	134
N1473B	LJ35	164
N1473B	LJ35	239
N1473B	LJ35	338
N1473B	LJ35	489
N1473B	LJ35	596
N1473B	LJ35	610
N1473B	LJ35	657
N1476B	LJ25	222
N1476B	LJ35	229
N1476B	LJ35	278
N1476B	LJ35	288
N1476B	LJ35	494
N1476B	LJ35	502
N1476B	LJ35	636
N1476B	LJ55	115
N1479G	GLF4	1479
N1482B	**C525**	**0888**
N1492J	**C52C**	**0166**
N1498G	**LJ60**	**035**
N1500	CL60	1078
N1500	**CL65**	**5830**
N1500	FA20	8
N1500	LJ35	339
N1500B	LJ24	051
N1500B	LJ25	055
N1500C	WW24	169
N1500C	WW24	46
N1500E	LJ35	124
N1500G	LJ24	051
N1500M	JSTR	5058/4
N1500M	WW24	71
N1501	FA20	15
N1502	FA20	15
N1502	LJ35	328
N1503	FA20	42
N1503	LJ35	316
(N1504)	CL60	1078
N1505P	E55P	50500112
N1505P	**E55P**	**50500248**
N1507	LJ35	316
(N1513)	GLF2	177
N1515E	HS25	25035
N1515P	C550	477
N1515P	FA10	43
N1515P	HS25	25035
N1515P	HS25	256022
N1526L	C650	0176
N1526L	LJ35	245
N1526M	GLF3	409
N1526M	GLF4	1118
N1526R	GLF3	409
N1540	GLF3	314
N1540	GLF4	1044
N1540	**GLF5**	**580**
N1545N	BE40	RK-91
N1546T	BE40	RJ-46
N1547B	**BE40**	**RJ-47**
N1548D	BE40	RJ-48
N1549J	BE40	RJ-49
N1549W	BE40	RK-88
N1550Y	BE40	RJ-50
N1551B	BE40	RJ-51
N1551B	BE40	RK-1
N1554R	BE40	RJ-54
N1555P	BE40	RJ-55
N1556W	BE40	RJ-56
N1557D	BE40	RJ-57
N1558F	BE40	RJ-58
N1559U	BE40	RJ-59
N1560G	BE40	RK-89
N1560T	BE40	RJ-60
N1561B	BE40	RJ-61
N1563V	BE40	RK-86
N1564B	BE40	RJ-64
N1565B	BE40	RJ-65
N1567L	BE40	RK-87
N1570B	BE40	RK-100
N1570L	BE40	RK-90
N1618L	C510	0314
(N1618R)	LJ60	044
N1620	CL61	3025
N1620	**G280**	**2028**
N1620	GLF4	1206
N1620	HS25	257155
N1620	HS25	258893
N1620	JSTR	5033/56
N1620	JSTR	5132/57
N1620N	JSTR	5132/57
N1621	GLF2	31
N1621	WW24	275
N1622	CL60	1030
N1622	CL61	5077
N1622	JSTR	5036/42
N1622D	JSTR	5036/42
N1623	CL61	3065
N1624	GLF2	33
N1624	GLF4	1318
N1625	GLF2	154/28
N1625	GLF4	1013
N1625	**GLF4**	**1358**
N1625	WW24	229
N1629	WW24	363
N1630	**G280**	**2029**
N1630	HS25	258557
N1630	HS25	258561
N1638	HS25	258557
N1640	**G280**	**2019**
N1640	GLF3	314
N1640	HS25	258376
N1645	**HS25**	**258376**
N1650	HS25	258432
N1693L	C510	0026
(N1700)	LJ35	258
N1700A	ASTR	018
N1707Z	GLF2	213
N1710E	C500	540
N1710E	C500	623
N1710E	C500	673
N1715G	MU30	A073SA
N1717L	C550	638
N1726M	**F900**	**162**
N1728E	C500	541
N1730M	HS25	258583
N1735J	LJ35	606
N1744P	LJ55	063
N1744Z	**C510**	**0345**
N1749L	C510	0054
N1758E	C500	542
N1758E	C500	624
N1758E	C500	674
(N1759)	GLF5	5128
N1759C	**GLF5**	**5128**
N1761B	GLF3	358
N1761B	GLF4	1043
N1761B	GLF4	1155
N1761D	GLF3	364
N1761D	GLF3	423
N1761D	GLF4	1046
N1761D	GLF4	1109
N1761D	GLF4	1154
N1761J	GLF3	365
N1761J	GLF4	1047
N1761J	GLF4	1117
N1761K	GLF3	385

N1761K	GLF4	1048
N1761K	GLF4	1156
N1761P	GLF3	394
N1761P	GLF4	1055
N1761Q	GLF3	395
N1761Q	GLF4	1083
N1761S	GLF3	396
N1761S	GLF4	1084
N1761W	GLF3	303
N1772E	C500	625
N1772E	C525	0034
(N1772E)	C500	543
(N1772E)	C650	0172
N1776A	HS25	258750
N1776C	**HS25**	**HA-0002**
N1776E	HS25	257036
N1776F	WW24	38
N1776H	**HS25**	**258091**
N1776N	HS25	258670
N1777M	**GLF6**	**6094**
(N1777R)	FA20	35
N1777T	WW24	62
N1779E	C525	0035
(N1779E)	C500	544
(N1779E)	C650	0173
N1782E	C525	0036
(N1782E)	C500	545
(N1782E)	C650	0174
N1800C	CL61	5115
N1806P	GLF2	200
N1807Z	GLF2	27
N1812C	CL60	1018
N1812C	CL61	5010
N1812C	GLEX	9075
N1812C	**GLEX**	**9529**
N1812U	GLEX	9075
N1818C	GLF4	1385
N1818C	**GLF4**	**4151**
N1818S	F900	136
N1818S	F900	39
N1818S	**F9EX**	**153**
N1818S	FA20	149
N1820E	C525	0037
N1820E	C650	0175
(N1820E)	C500	546
N1821U	**CL64**	**5506**
N1823A	FA20	129
N1823B	C500	373
N1823B	C550	196
N1823B	C550	498
N1823C	C550	234
N1823D	GLF2	59
N1823F	FA20	129
N1823S	C560	0094
N1823S	C560	0225
N1823S	C650	0090
N1824S	C560	0120
N1824S	**F2TS**	**709**
N1824T	CL61	3029
N1824T	HS25	257182
N1827S	C560	0094
N1828S	C650	7047
N1828S	**F9EX**	**182**
N1829S	FA50	280
N1836S	C56X	5143
N1836S	**F9EX**	**178**
N1836S	FA50	352
(N1836S)	F900	136
N1837S	**C56X**	**5155**
N1838S	C56X	5322
N1838S	FA50	316
N1839S	FA50	317
N1839S	FA50	331
N1841D	GLF2	227
N1841D	GLF3	438
N1841D	SBRL	380-15
N1841F	FA50	152
N1841F	SBRL	380-15
N1841L	GLF2	227
N1843A	MU30	A025SA
N1843S	HS25	257155
N1843S	MU30	A025SA
N1844S	JSTR	5123/14
N1845T	LJ45	464
N1846	FA20	47
N1847B	C550	365
N1847B	FA20	493
N1847P	C550	365
N1848T	C525	0350
N1848T	LJ40	2035
N1848T	**LJ45**	**464**
N1848U	CL64	5316
N1848U	FA50	227
N1851D	C550	022
N1851N	C500	310
N1851T	C500	310
N1851T	C550	022
N1851T	FA20	508
N1851T	FA20	74
N1852	LJ55	087
N1852B	**GLF5**	**5146**
N1853	**BE40**	**RK-251**
N1857B	FA20	203
N1857W	WW24	258
N1863T	SBRL	282-62
N1865C	**C525**	**0647**
N1865K	**C56X**	**6172**

N1865M	CS55	0071
(N1865S)	C560	0225
N1867M	**C56X**	**5303**
N1867M	C650	7073
N1867W	CS55	0124
N1868M	CL60	1039
N1868M	CL61	5012
N1868M	F900	157
N1868M	FA20	139
N1868M	GLEX	9069
N1868M	**GLEX**	**9316**
N1868M	HS25	257021
N1868N	FA20	139
N1868S	CL60	1039
N1868S	F900	157
N1868S	HS25	257021
N1870G	**CL30**	**20041**
N1871P	LJ24	130
N1871P	LJ36	023
N1871R	C560	0580
N1871R	C56X	5297
N1871R	FA10	128
N1871R	FA50	6
N1871R	GLF3	381
N1871R	LJ24	130
N1871R	LJ36	023
N1873	C560	0353
N1873	**C750**	**0128**
N1874E	C525	0038
N1874E	C650	0176
(N1874E)	C500	547
N1874M	GLF4	1390
N1875P	GLF2	137
N1878C	**LJ45**	**519**
N1878C	BE40	RK-33
N1879W	C550	668
N1880F	C550	372
N1880S	C500	183
N1881Q	**FA20**	**414**
N1881W	BE40	RK-21
N1883	C550	467
N1883M	C550	674
N1884	CL60	1032
N1884	HS25	256067
N1884Z	WW24	150
N1886G	C550	722
N1886X	**C52C**	**0162**
N1887B	**E55P**	**50500210**
N1887M	C650	7073
N1887S	FA10	190
N1888M	C550	674
N1892	GLF5	524
N1892S	FA20	376
N1893N	**LJ45**	**172**
N1895C	C525	0647
N1895C	**C52A**	**0488**
N1896F	FA50	127
N1896F	HS25	257162
N1896T	FA50	127
N1896T	FA50	262
N1896T	HS25	257162
N1897A	C56X	5629
N1897A	**CL30**	**20319**
N1897A	HS25	258326
N1897S	**F2EX**	**239**
N1897S	FA20	376
N1899	LJ45	264
N1899	PRM1	RB-248
(N1899)	C500	091
N1899K	HS25	258424
N1900A	**ASTR**	**026**
N1900W	GLF4	1124
N1901	**C52A**	**0122**
N1901	C680	0022
N1901M	GLF4	1039
N1901W	**CL30**	**20398**
N1901W	BE40	RK-19
(N1902)	C650	7010
N1902J	CL61	5135
N1902L	GLF2	226
N1902P	CL61	5135
N1902P	GLF2	226
N1902P	**GLF4**	**4192**
N1902W	FA20	269
N1902W	FA50	209
N1902W	BE40	RK-2
N1903G	CL61	5051
N1903G	**CL64**	**5326**
N1903P	HS25	258142
N1903W	**F2EX**	**208**
N1903W	FA50	129
N1903W	SBRL	282-36
N1904G	WW24	436
N1904P	CL61	5116
N1904S	LJ31	149
N1904S	**LJ45**	**053**
N1904W	FA50	149
N1904W	**GLF4**	**1237**
N1904W	BE40	RK-21
N1905H	LJ31	051
N1905W	**GLF5**	**5432**
N1907M	**C56X**	**6201**
N1908W	SBRL	282-36
N1909D	SBRL	282-57
N1909R	SBRL	282-57
N1909R	SBRL	306-41
N1909R	SBRL	465-54

N1910A	HS25	258188
N1910A	**HS25**	**258711**
N1910H	HS25	258023
N1910H	HS25	258318
N1910H	**HS25**	**HA-0190**
N1910J	HS25	258023
N1911W	**GLF5**	**5328**
N1918W	LJ36	004
N1919G	LJ24	157
N1919W	LJ24	118
N1919W	LJ24	157
N1919W	LJ24	192
N1920	**G150**	**291**
N1920	BE40	RK-21
N1923G	HS25	25095
N1923M	HS25	25031
N1924D	**G150**	**286**
N1924G	JSTR	5224
N1924L	HS25	25237
N1924V	FA10	24
N1924V	JSTR	5077
N1925B	**LJ45**	**199**
N1925M	**GLF4**	**1282**
N1925P	LJ45	199
N1926S	**LJ31**	**180**
N1927G	F2TH	35
N1929P	SBRL	276-48
N1929S	LJ35	388
N1929Y	**F2TH**	**84**
N1929Y	GLF2	19
N1930E	C650	0177
(N1930E)	C500	548
(N1931P)	GLF4	1514
N1932K	**LJ31**	**099**
N1932P	C750	0090
N1932P	GLF4	1514
N1932P	**GLF5**	**5256**
N1932P	LJ31	099
N1933G	**F2EX**	**123**
N1940	LJ60	002
N1944P	WW24	142
N1949B	C550	414
N1949M	C550	414
N1951E	C500	160
N1951E	C500	549
N1955E	C500	550
N1955E	C550	059
N1955M	GLEX	9185
N1955M	GLEX	9444
N1955M	**GLEX**	**9645**
N1955M	GLF4	1276
N1956A	**C510**	**0305**
N1956M	GLF3	469
N1956M	**GLF5**	**675**
(N1957S)	HS25	258289
N1958E	C500	626
N1958E	C500	676
N1958E	C525	0039
N1958E	C550	060
N1958E	C650	0178
(N1958E)	C500	551
(N1958E)	C500	677
N1958N	CS55	0073
N1959E	C500	552
N1959E	C500	627
N1959E	C525	0040
N1959E	C550	061
N1959E	C650	0179
N1961S	**C550**	**550-0890**
N1962	**C52A**	**0130**
(N1962)	BE40	RK-21
N1962J	C550	550-0862
N1962J	**C750**	**0240**
N1962J	JSTR	5113/25
N1963A	LJ24	097
N1963N	**GLF4**	**4268**
N1965L	**LJ24**	**012**
N1966G	LJ35	5065
N1966J	WW24	66
N1966K	LJ24	011
N1966L	LJ24	108
N1966W	LJ24	076
N1967G	**C560**	**0641**
N1967G	JSTR	5098/28
N1967J	C550	550-0862
(N1967J)	JSTR	5113/25
N1967L	LJ24	012
N1967M	CL30	20040
N1967M	CL30	20268
N1967M	**CL65**	**5910**
N1967M	GLF4	1368
N1967W	LJ24	096
N1968A	LJ24	097
N1968A	LJ35	171
N1968A	LJ55	035
N1968T	LJ35	171
N1968W	LJ24	089
N1969H	LJ24	110
N1969L	LJ24	012
N1969W	LJ25	005
N1971R	FA20	312
N1971R	FA20	322
N1971R	FA50	149
N1972G	LJ24	242
N1972H	**LJ60**	**423**
N1972L	LJ24	096
N1972N	**GLF5**	**5121**

N1972W	WW24	91
N1973L	LJ24	096
N1976L	LJ24	070
N1976L	LJ25	080
N1976L	LJ35	053
N1976S	LJ25	008
N1978G	**FA50**	**327**
N1978L	LJ25	080
N1978L	LJ35	162
N1978X	**F2EX**	
N1980M	**C56X**	**5289**
N1980Z	**CL30**	**20049**
N1982C	GLF3	384
N1982G	HS25	257116
N1982U	CS55	0038
N1983Y	LJ55	079
N1987	CL30	20515
N1987	CL64	5550
N1989D	**HS25**	**258580**
N1990C	GLEX	9166
N1990C	GLF4	1276
N1993	**FA10**	**195**
(N1996E)	HS25	257177
N1996F	HS25	257177
N1999	F2TH	219
N1999E	**C525**	**0077**
N2000	**GLF2**	**56**
N2000	SBRL	282-52
N2000	SBRL	465-7
N2000A	F2EX	119
N2000A	F2EX	151
N2000A	F2EX	170
N2000A	F2EX	235
N2000A	F2EX	255
N2000A	F2TH	112
N2000A	F2TH	141
N2000A	F2TH	182
N2000A	F2TH	189
N2000A	F2TH	192
N2000A	F2TH	26
N2000A	F2TH	3
N2000A	F2TH	44
N2000A	F2TH	63
N2000A	F2TH	89
(N2000A)	F2EX	306
N2000C	CL61	3032
N2000C	CL61	5188
N2000L	**F2TH**	**109**
N2000L	F2TH	92
N2000M	C560	0146
N2000M	LJ24	065
N2000M	LJ25	084
N2000M	LJ35	396
N2000M	LJ36	009
N2000T	HS25	257177
N2000X	C560	0144
N2000X	**C560**	**0249**
N2000X	CS55	0064
N2002P	GLF4	1279
N2003J	C56X	5744
N2004	F2TH	13
N2004	SBRL	282-52
N2004D	C52C	0092
N2004G	CL61	5048
N2005	FA20	54
N2006	SBRL	282-124
N2006	SBRL	282-135
N2007	SBRL	282-55
N2008	C550	399
N2008	LJ24	003
N2009	SBRL	282-14
N2009A	C56X	6055
N2011Z	C56X	6013
N2012C	**GLEX**	**9074**
N2013M	GLF2	51
N2015M	HS25	257192
N2015M	HS25	258254
N2015M	LJ35	072
N2016A	**FA7X**	
N2019V	**C500**	**245**
N2020	HS25	25203
N2020Q	**GLEX**	**9685**
N2022L	LJ35	290
N2022R	LJ25	200
N2028	F2TH	29
N2029E	C550	550-0822
N2032	F2TH	31
N2032	HS25	258175
N2033	**HS25**	**258093**
N2034	F2TH	14
N2035	F2TH	17
N2036	F2TH	23
N2039	F2TH	24
N2040E	C52A	0386
N2042	F2TH	25
N2044S	C52A	0425
N2046	F2TH	26
N2046D	C52A	0430
N2051A	C52A	0436
N2052A	C500	553
N2052A	C500	628
N2052A	C500	678
N2052A	C550	062
N2056	F900	155
N2056E	BE40	RK-156
N2057H	**C550**	**310**
N2060V	C56X	5761

N2061	F2TH	39
N2064M	C52A	0442
N2065X	C56X	5766
N2067E	C52A	0446
N2067V	C56X	5808
N2068G	C750	0291
N2069A	C500	554
N2069A	C550	063
N2070K	C500	133
N2072A	C500	555
N2072A	C500	629
N2072A	C550	064
N2073	F2TH	41
N2074	F2TH	44
N2074H	C52B	0277
(N2077)	F2TH	43
N2079A	C500	431
N2080	F2TH	46
N2087K	C56X	5824
N2089	F2TH	48
N2093	F2TH	101
N2093A	LJ24	194
N2093P	SBRL	380-39
N2094L	**LJ25**	**095**
N2098A	C500	432
N2098A	C525	0041
N2098A	C650	0180
(N2099)	F2TH	99
N2100J	SBRL	380-32
N2100X	WW24	23
N2101J	SBRL	306-109
N2102J	SBRL	380-38
N2103J	SBRL	306-110
N2104J	SBRL	380-34
N2105	**CL60**	**1010**
N2105J	SBRL	380-36
N2106J	SBRL	306-111
N2107J	SBRL	306-112
N2107Z	**GLF4**	**1211**
N2108J	SBRL	306-113
N2109J	SBRL	306-114
N2110J	SBRL	380-39
N2111P	F900	117
N2111W	C52B	0278
N2112J	SBRL	380-40
N2112L	F2TH	112
N2112X	C56X	5830
N2113J	SBRL	380-41
N2114E	HS25	256022
N2114J	SBRL	380-42
N2115J	SBRL	380-43
N2116J	SBRL	380-44
N2116N	C56X	5821
N2117J	SBRL	380-45
N2118J	SBRL	306-115
N2119J	SBRL	306-116
N2120J	SBRL	306-117
N2120Q	WW24	107
N2121	GLF4	1117
N2122J	SBRL	306-118
N2123J	SBRL	306-119
N2124J	SBRL	306-120
N2125	HS25	25082
N2125J	SBRL	380-46
N2126J	SBRL	380-47
N2127E	LJ25	145
N2127J	SBRL	380-48
N2128J	SBRL	380-49
N2129	**GLF4**	**1117**
N2129J	SBRL	380-50
N2130J	SBRL	306-121
N2131A	C500	433
N2131A	C650	0181
N2131J	SBRL	306-122
N2132	F2TH	57
N2132J	SBRL	306-123
N2133	F2TH	58
N2133J	SBRL	306-124
N2134J	SBRL	306-125
N2135J	SBRL	380-51
N2136J	SBRL	380-52
N2137J	SBRL	380-53
N2138J	SBRL	380-54
N2138T	LJ25	091
N2139J	SBRL	380-55
N2140L	C550	554
N2141J	SBRL	306-126
N2142J	SBRL	306-127
N2143J	SBRL	306-128
N2144J	SBRL	306-129
N2145J	SBRL	306-130
N2146	F2TH	59
N2146J	SBRL	380-56
N2147	F2TH	60
N2147J	SBRL	380-57
N2148J	SBRL	380-58
N2148R	HS25	25070
N2149J	SBRL	306-131
N2150H	**WW24**	**210**
N2150J	SBRL	306-132
N2151J	SBRL	306-133
N2151Q	C52A	0391
N2152J	SBRL	306-134
N2155	F2TH	63
N2155P	HS25	25273
N2157D	C680	0241
N2158U	**C500**	**476**

N2159P	BE40	RK-159
N2159X	HS25	258313
N2160N	C550	249
N2164Z	BE40	RK-164
N2168	F2TH	70
N2168G	BE40	RK-168
N2169	F2TH	72
N2169X	HS25	258315
N2170J	C500	040
N2173X	HS25	258317
N2175W	HS25	258348
N2176	F2TH	73
N2183N	CL61	3062
N2189	F2TH	89
N2191	F2TH	92
N2194	F2TH	110
N2197	F2TH	112
N2200A	SBRL	380-26
N2200M	FA20	11
N2200M	JSTR	5062/12
N2200R	C500	095
N2200T	LJ24	112
N2201J	BE40	RK-171
N2201U	C500	217
N2204J	BE40	RK-174
N2208L	C680	0211
N2213T	LJ25	369
N2216	F2TH	116
N2217	F2TH	117
N2217Q	LJ35	243
N2218	F2TH	109
N2220G	MU30	A031SA
N2222R	JSTR	5016
N2224G	C52A	0402
N2225J	MU30	A064SA
N2225Y	BE40	RK-165
N2227	F2TH	141
N2230	F2TH	143
(N2231B)	C550	026
N2232B	SBRL	282-65
N2233B	SBRL	282-66
N2234B	SBRL	282-67
N2235	CS55	0135
N2235	F2TH	149
N2235B	SBRL	282-68
N2235V	BE40	RK-181
N2236	HS25	258073
N2236B	SBRL	282-69
N2236C	SBRL	282-70
N2237X	**FA7X**	**241**
N2239B	SBRL	282-71
N2241B	SBRL	282-74
N2241C	SBRL	282-75
N2242B	SBRL	282-76
N2242P	LJ35	012
N2243	**C500**	**619**
N2243W	C510	0011
N2244B	SBRL	282-77
N2246	HS25	25099
N2248C	SBRL	282-79
N2249B	SBRL	282-80
N2250B	SBRL	282-81
N2250G	C52A	0047
N2250G	**C52C**	**0020**
N2252Q	BE40	RK-152
N2254B	SBRL	282-84
N2254S	FA50	180
N2255B	SBRL	282-85
N2255Q	FA20	24
N2258	F2TH	175
(N2259)	F2TH	166
N2259D	C525	0688
N2259V	SBRL	265-1
N2260	F2TH	180
N2261	F2TH	184
N2264	F2TH	182
N2265	F2TH	183
N2265Z	SBRL	380-43
N2267	F2TH	189
N2267B	BE40	RK-167
N2267Z	LJ36	012
N2270	F2TH	186
N2272K	BE40	RK-172
(N2273G)	LJ25	040
N2273Z	BE40	RK-173
N2274B	C500	295
N2277G	BE40	RK-177
N2277T	JSTR	5105
N2279K	BE40	RK-179
N2282	G150	282
N2283T	BE40	RK-196
N2286B	**C52C**	**0214**
N2286D	LJ35	482
N2286U	HS25	258336
N2288	F2TH	188
N2289	F2TH	192
N2289	G150	289
N2289B	BE40	RK-170
N2290	F2TH	197
N2290F	BE40	RK-190
N2291T	BE40	RK-191
N2291X	HS25	258319
N2293V	BE40	RK-233
N2293V	BE40	RK-250
N2295	F2TH	199
N2296C	SBRL	265-5
N2296S	C500	621
N2296S	C560	0038
N2297B	LJ35	033
(N2297G)	LJ36	002
N2297X	C52A	0410
N2298L	BE40	RK-185
N2298S	C500	621
N2298S	BE40	RK-187
N2298W	BE40	RK-188
N2299T	BE40	RK-166
N2314F	BE40	RK-184
N2317	F2TH	204
N2319	F2TH	206
N2320J	HS25	258342
N2321S	HS25	258352
N2321V	HS25	258353
N2321Z	HS25	258357
N2322	F2TH	212
N2322B	BE40	RK-182
N2322B	BE40	RK-242
N2322X	HS25	258320
N2325	F2TH	210
N2329N	BE40	RK-169
N2345M	JSTR	5075/19
N2349V	BE40	RK-236
"N2351M"	HS25	258341
N2354B	BE40	RK-154
N2355N	BE40	RK-232
N2355T	BE40	RK-155
N2357K	BE40	RK-204
N2358X	BE40	RK-158
N2359W	BE40	RK-203
N2360F	BE40	RK-160
N2362G	BE40	RK-162
N2363A	BE40	RK-163
N2366Y	LJ24	055
N2366Y	LJ25	058
N2369R	**CL61**	**5134**
N2370S	C56X	6042
N2384K	C56X	6047
N2401X	C56X	6053
N2408	LJ40	2008
N2409W	CL64	5391
N2411A	**C650**	**0103**
N2418F	C750	0074
N2418N	C750	0074
N2418Y	C750	0074
(N2422J)	LJ35	263
N2425	C680	0054
N2425	**CL30**	**20413**
N2425	F9EX	32
N2425	FA50	237
(N2425)	GLF4	1310
N2426	C560	0815
N2426	C680	0034
N2426	FA10	186
N2426	HS25	25013
N2426	HS25	25107
N2426	HS25	258272
N2426	LJ25	216
N2426	**LJ45**	**441**
N2426G	FA10	186
N2427F	FA10	187
N2427F	LJ25	157
N2427N	C510	0019
"N2427N"	FA10	187
N2428	C680	0046
N2428	**CL30**	**20414**
N2428	CL60	1013
N2428	HS25	258274
N2437	**GLF6**	**6171**
N2440C	SBRL	306-30
N2440C	SBRL	380-2
N2440G	SBRL	306-30
N2440G	SBRL	380-2
N2440G	SBRL	380-44
N2451Y	LJ45	076
N2454M	WW24	314
N2465N	C680	0272
N2475	**C680**	**0054**
N2476	LJ45	441
N2478	**C680**	**0046**
(N2478)	FA50	48
N2486B	**EA50**	**000090**
N2488L	ASTR	125
N2500B	C560	0386
N2500D	C560	0365
N2500N	C560	0350
N2500W	HS25	25208
N2501E	SBRL	306-136
N2501E	SBRL	465-1
N2503L	LJ24	047
N2504	HS25	25021
N2506E	SBRL	306-137
N2508E	SBRL	306-138
N2513E	SBRL	465-15
N2518M	WW24	337
N2519E	SBRL	306-144
N2521E	SBRL	380-60
N2522E	SBRL	380-61
N2525	FA20	321
N2525	HS25	25112
N2528E	SBRL	380-67
N2531K	**C550**	**594**
N2535E	SBRL	306-135
N2536E	SBRL	380-66
N2537E	SBRL	465-17
N2538E	SBRL	380-68
N2539E	SBRL	465-48
N2542E	SBRL	380-69
N2544E	SBRL	465-20
N2545E	SBRL	465-24
N2548E	SBRL	465-26
N2549E	SBRL	465-28
N2550E	SBRL	465-31
N2551E	SBRL	465-39
N2556E	SBRL	465-41
N2561E	SBRL	465-42
N2568	FA20	75
N2568S	SBRL	282-61
N2569B	SBRL	282-90
N2570E	SBRL	465-50
N2574E	SBRL	465-55
N2579E	SBRL	465-54
N2579E	WW24	21
N2580E	SBRL	465-60
N2581E	SBRL	465-75
N2586E	SBRL	465-21
N2590E	SBRL	465-35
N2600	GLF2	88/21
N2600	GLF3	315
N2600	GLF4	1088
N2600	JSTR	5037/24
N2600	JSTR	5110/47
N2600J	GLF4	1088
N2600S	LJ31	033B
N2600Z	GLF3	315
N2600Z	LJ31	060
N2601	GLF2	30/4
N2601	GLF3	316
N2601	HS25	25060
N2601	JSTR	5110/47
N2601B	LJ36	061
N2601G	LJ35	674
N2601K	LJ31	080
N2601V	LJ60	024
N2602M	LJ35	675
N2602Y	LJ31	070
N2602Z	LJ60	022
N2603G	LJ31	054
N2603Q	LJ31	086
N2603S	LJ31	033A
N2603X	LJ31	068
N2604	C650	0021
N2605	C650	0144
N2605	FA20	312
N2606	C650	0194
N2607	C500	307
N2607	GLF2	30/4
N2610	GLF3	302
N2610	GLF4	1094
(N2610)	C500	340
N2611Y	C500	556
N2611Y	C500	630
N2611Y	C500	679
N2612N	C500	557
N2612N	C500	631
N2613	C500	307
N2613	FA20	293
N2613C	C500	558
N2613C	C500	632
N2614	FA20	376
N2614C	C500	559
N2614C	C500	633
N2614C	C500	680
N2614H	C500	560
N2614H	C500	634
N2614K	C500	561
N2614Y	C650	0183
(N2614Y)	C500	634
N2615	FA20	293
N2615	GLF2	148/5
N2615	GLF4	1214
N2615B	GLF4	1214
N2615D	C650	0184
(N2615D)	C500	635
N2615L	C650	0185
(N2615L)	C500	636
N2615S	CL64	5336
N2616C	C500	637
N2616G	C500	562
N2616G	C500	638
N2616G	C500	681
(N2616G)	C500	637
N2616H	FA20	376
N2616L	C525	0043
N2616L	C650	0186
(N2616L)	C500	563
N2617B	C500	564
N2617B	C500	639
N2617B	C500	682
(N2617B)	C500	638
N2617K	C500	565
N2617K	C525	0044
N2617K	C650	0187
(N2617K)	C500	640
N2617P	C525	0045
N2617P	C650	0188
N2617U	C500	566
N2617U	**C500**	**641**
N2619M	C550	142
N2621U	C525	0047
(N2621U)	C650	0190
N2621Z	C525	0048
(N2621Z)	C650	0191
N2622C	C650	0192
N2622M	FA20	242
N2622Z	C650	0193
N2623B	C500	646
N2624L	C650	0198
(N2624L)	C500	647
N2624M	C650	0021
N2624M	FA20	376
N2624Z	C500	648
(N2625C)	C650	0196
N2625Y	C650	0197
N2626A	C500	649
N2626J	C500	650
N2626M	SBRL	306-113
(N2626X)	C650	0199
N2626Z	C500	651
(N2626Z)	C650	0200
N2627A	C500	434
N2627A	C650	0202
N2627M	SBRL	306-123
N2627N	C500	654
N2627U	C500	655
N2628B	C500	656
N2628Z	C500	657
N2629Z	C500	658
N2630	C500	340
N2630	HS25	257161
N2630B	C650	0204
N2630N	C650	0205
N2630U	C650	0206
N2631N	C500	659
N2631N	C550	143
N2631V	C500	660
N2631V	C550	144
N2632Y	C550	145
(N2632Y)	C650	0207
N2633N	C500	662
N2633N	C550	146
N2633Y	C525	0049
N2633Y	C550	147
(N2634B)	HS25	257020
N2634E	C525	0050
(N2634E)	CS55	0151
N2634Y	C550	148
N2634Y	CL60	1034
N2635D	C550	149
N2635M	SBRL	306-118
N2636N	CL60	1025
N2637M	GLF2	88/21
N2637R	C525	0051
(N2637R)	CS55	0153
N2637Z	LJ35	413
N2638A	C525	0053
N2638A	C550	152
(N2638A)	CS55	0155
N2638U	C525	0054
(N2638U)	CS55	0156
N2639N	CS55	0157
N2639Y	C525	0055
(N2639Y)	CS55	0158
N2640	HS25	257157
N2642F	CL60	1033
N2642Z	CS55	0160
N2646X	C525	0056
N2646X	C550	153
(N2646X)	C500	486
(N2646X)	CS55	0159
N2646Y	C500	487
N2646Y	C550	154
N2646Z	C550	155
(N2646Z)	C500	488
(N2647U)	C500	490
N2647Y	C525	0058
(N2647Y)	C500	491
N2647Z	C525	0059
(N2647Z)	C500	492
N2648X	**C500**	**493**
N2648Y	C525	0060
(N2648Y)	C500	494
N2648Z	C550	157
(N2648Z)	C500	495
N2649	FA10	219
N2649D	C500	498
N2649D	C500	667
N2649D	C550	158
N2649E	C500	499
N2649E	C550	159
N2649H	C500	500
N2649J	C525	0063
(N2649J)	C500	501
N2649S	C525	0064
(N2649S)	C500	502
N2649Y	C500	503
N2649Y	C525	0065
N2649Z	C500	504
N2650	C500	341
N2650C	C500	513
N2650M	C500	514
N2650N	C500	515
N2650S	C500	516
N2650V	C525	0068
(N2650V)	C500	517
N2650X	C500	518
N2650Y	C500	519
N2650Y	C500	670
N2651	C500	565
N2651B	C500	526
N2651B	C500	671
N2651G	C500	527
N2651J	C500	528
N2651J	C500	672
N2651R	C525	0072
(N2651R)	C500	529
N2651S	C500	530
(N2651Y)	C500	531
N2652U	C500	536
N2652Y	C500	537
N2652Z	C500	538
N2653R	C550	160
N2656G	C525	0073
(N2661H)	C550	072
(N2661N)	C550	073
N2661P	C550	162
(N2661P)	C550	074
(N2662A)	C550	082
(N2662B)	C550	083
(N2662F)	C550	084
N2662Z	C550	085
N2663B	C550	094
(N2663B)	C560	0036
N2663F	C550	095
N2663G	C550	096
N2663J	C500	669
N2663J	C550	097
N2663N	C550	098
(N2663X)	C550	099
(N2663X)	C560	0037
N2663Y	**C550**	**602**
(N2663Y)	C550	100
(N2663Y)	C560	0038
N2664F	C550	108
N2664L	C550	109
N2664T	C550	110
(N2664U)	C550	111
(N2664U)	C560	0040
N2664Y	C550	112
N2665A	C550	117
N2665D	C550	118
(N2665F)	C550	119
(N2665F)	C560	0043
N2665N	C550	120
N2665S	C560	0044
(N2665S)	C550	121
N2665Y	C560	0045
(N2665Y)	C550	122
N2666A	C550	125
N2666A	C560	0047
N2667M	GLF2	140/40
N2667X	C560	0048
N2668A	C550	165
(N2672X)	C560	0049
N2675W	HFB3	1050
N2676B	SBRL	282-92
N2677S	CL60	1004
N2680A	C560	0051
N2680D	C560	0052
(N2680X)	C560	0053
N2681F	C560	0055
N2682F	C560	0056
(N2683L)	C560	0057
(N2686Y)	C560	0058
(N2687L)	C560	0059
(N2689B)	C560	0060
N2690M	C500	546
N2694C	HS25	25285
(N2697X)	C560	0061
N2697Y	C560	0060
N2700	**SBRL**	**465-7**
N2701J	C560	0061
(N2701J)	C560	0063
N2707	GLEX	9398
N2707	**GLEX**	**9489**
(N2707)	HS25	258776
N2707T	CL60	1055
N2710T	SBRL	306-2
N2711B	FA50	84
N2711H	EA50	000142
N2711M	GLF2	137
N2716G	C560	0062
N2717X	C560	0064
N2720B	CL60	1049
N2721F	C560	0065
N2721U	LJ25	308
N2722F	C560	0067
N2722H	C560	0068
N2724K	FA20	255/487
(N2724R)	C560	0069
(N2725A)	C560	0070
(N2725X)	C560	0071
N2726J	C560	0072
(N2726X)	C560	0073
N2727F	C560	0074
N2728	HS25	25060
N2728N	C560	0071A
N2734K	C550	595
N2741A	C500	435
N2741Q	CL60	1047
N2743T	LJ35	193
N2745G	C550	126
N2745L	C550	127
(N2745L)	C560	0075
N2745M	C550	128
(N2745M)	C560	0076
N2745R	C550	129

N2745R	C560	0077
N2745T	C550	130
N2745X	C550	131
N2746B	C550	133
N2746C	C550	134
(N2746C)	C560	0079
N2746E	C550	135
N2746E	C560	0080
N2746F	C550	136
(N2746F)	C560	0081
N2746U	C550	137
(N2746U)	C560	0082
N2746Z	C550	138
(N2747R)	C550	139
(N2747R)	C560	0083
N2747U	C550	140
(N2747U)	C560	0084
N2748B	C560	0078
(N2748F)	C560	0085
(N2748V)	C560	0086
N2749B	C560	0087
N2756T	WW24	224
N2757A	C500	436
N2758W	**LJ40**	**2066**
N2762J	C560	0381
N2768A	C500	437
N2782D	C500	152
N2792B	BE40	RK-63
N2796	**C52A**	**0169**
N2800	SBRL	465-7
N2801L	C500	236
N2815	GLF2	148/5
N2815	LJ35	334
N2830	HS25	257161
N2830B	BE40	TT-82
N2841A	C500	438
N2842B	BE40	RK-10
N2843B	BE40	RK-11
N2844	LJ35	424
N2855	LJ55	076
(N2855)	LJ55	079
N2868B	BE40	TT-8
N2872B	BE40	TT-6
N2876B	BE40	TT-5
N2886B	BE40	TT-1
N2887A	C500	439
N2887B	BE40	TT-2
N2888A	C500	440
N2892B	BE40	TT-3
N2896B	BE40	TT-7
N2904	**C500**	**406**
N2906A	C500	441
N2909W	LJ24	243
N2920	BE40	RK-21
N2920C	LJ24	010
N2929	**GLF5**	**5053**
N2932C	LJ24	042
N2937L	C500	335
(N2944M)	BE40	RK-477
N2945C	LJ24	149
N2951P	LJ35	215
N2954T	FA20	58
N2959A	C500	442
N2972Q	LJ36	047
N2979	FA20	183
N2989	FA20	112
N2989	HS25	257167
N2991A	C500	443
N2991Q	GLF2	119/22
N2992	LJ55	099
N2997	SBRL	282-38
N2998	GLF2	236
N3000	SBRL	306-29
N3000	SBRL	465-11
N3000S	LJ45	161
N3000W	C555	0100
N3001H	LJ31	224
N3003S	LJ31	225
N3005P	GLF2	96
N3006J	LJ60	223
N3007	HS25	25043
N3007	HS25	256007
N3007	HS25	258092
N3007	**HS25**	**258487**
N3008	**HS25**	**258092**
N3008	SBRL	306-29
N3008P	LJ45	154
N3011F	LJ60	226
N3013Q	LJ45	152
N3014R	LJ60	114
N3014R	BE40	RK-206
N3015F	LJ60	115
N3015F	BE40	RK-207
N3015M	LJ60	231
N3016X	LJ31	161
N3017F	LJ45	156
N3018C	LJ60	118
N3018P	LJ31	228
N3019S	LJ31	151
N3019T	LJ45	158
N3025T	BE40	RJ-25
N3026U	BE40	RJ-26
N3028U	BE40	RK-211
N3029F	BE40	RK-212
N3030	JSTR	5094
N3030	JSTR	5212
N3030	SBRL	465-11
N3030C	C500	104
N3030C	C550	193
N3030D	BE40	RK-205
N3030T	C550	193
N3031	JSTR	5154
N3031	WW24	269
(N3031)	C550	081
(N3031)	WW24	95
N3032	C550	081
N3032	WW24	97
N3033A	BE40	RK-213
N3034B	LJ24	176
N3035T	BE40	RJ-35
N3038V	BE40	RK-93
N3038W	BE40	RK-215
N3039G	PRM1	RB-139
N3043F	C52B	0355
N3045	CL61	3045
N3050	**GLF5**	**5096**
N3050P	BE40	RK-216
N3051S	BE40	RK-94
N3056R	C500	138
N3056R	LJ35	264
N3059H	BE40	RK-219
N3060	HS25	25017
N3060	JSTR	5037/24
N3060F	HS25	25017
N3062A	C500	444
N3068M	BE40	RK-218
N3079S	BE40	RK-256
N3080	JSTR	5094
N3082B	WW24	97
N3088A	HS25	HA-0058
N3088R	C680	0537
N3093T	HS25	HB-13
N3097N	HMH2	001
N3099	**C680**	**0306**
N3099	LJ60	375
N3100X	FA10	12
N3101B	BE40	RK-208
N3101N	**C56X**	**6184**
N3103D	C56X	6188
N3103L	C56X	6177
N3104M	C500	445
N3104R	C56X	6176
N3105M	C500	446
N3106Y	BE40	RK-251
N3110M	C500	447
N3112B	BE40	RJ-12
N3112K	BE40	RJ-12
N3113B	BE40	RJ-13
N3114B	BE40	RJ-14
N3114X	BE40	RK-95
N3115B	BE40	RJ-15
(N3115U)	FA50	166
N3115Y	HS25	258915
N3117M	C500	448
N3118M	C500	449
N3118M	HS25	25199
N3119H	BE40	RK-6
N3119W	BE40	RJ-19
N3120M	C500	450
N3120Y	BE40	RJ-20
N3121B	BE40	RJ-21
N3122B	BE40	RJ-22
N3122M	C500	451
N3123T	BE40	RJ-23
N3124M	BE40	RJ-24
(N3124M)	C500	452
N3125B	HS25	25110
(N3127M)	C500	453
N3127R	BE40	RJ-27
N3129E	BE40	RJ-29
N3129X	BE40	RK-229
N3130T	BE40	RJ-30
N3131G	LJ25	274
N3132M	C500	454
N3134N	BE40	RJ-34
N3137	**LJ24**	**123**
N3141G	BE40	RJ-41
N3141M	C500	455
N3142E	BE40	RJ-42
N3143T	BE40	RJ-43
N3144A	BE40	RJ-44
N3144M	C500	456
N3145F	BE40	RJ-45
N3145M	C500	457
N3146M	C500	458
N3147M	C500	459
N3150C	**GLF4**	**1013**
N3150M	C500	460
N3151W	PRM1	RB-251
N3155B	LJ35	117
N3156M	C500	461
N3158M	C500	462
N3159U	SBRL	282-117
N3160M	C500	463
N3161M	C500	464
N3163M	C500	465
N3165M	C500	466
N3166Q	BE40	RK-266
N3170A	C500	467
N3170B	C550	162
N3170B	**C650**	**0136**
N3170M	C500	468
N3172M	C500	469
N3173M	C500	470
(N3175M)	C500	471
N3175S	ASTR	057
N3175T	ASTR	056
N3180M	C500	472
N3180T	BE40	RJ-18
(N3181A)	C500	473
(N3183M)	C500	474
(N3184V)	C550	247
N3184Z	C650	0032
(N3184Z)	C550	123
N3185G	HA4T	RC-25
N3185G	BE40	RK-285
N3185K	BE40	RK-318
N3186B	BE40	RK-556
N3186C	PRM1	RB-236
N3186N	HA4T	RC-26
N3187G	PRM1	RB-247
N3187N	HA4T	RC-27
N3188V	PRM1	RB-248
N3188X	HS25	258980
N3189H	HS25	258360
N3189M	C500	475
N3190C	BE40	RK-590
N3191L	BE40	RK-291
N3193B	HS25	258963
N3193L	HS25	HA-0053
N3194F	HA4T	RC-34
N3194M	C500	476
N3194Q	HS25	HB-14
N3194R	PRM1	RB-249
N3195F	HS25	258895
N3195K	BE40	TX-4
N3195M	C500	477
N3195Q	BE40	TX-5
N3195X	BE40	TX-6
N3196N	BE40	RK-96
N3197A	BE40	RK-197
N3197H	HA4T	RC-37
N3197K	HS25	HB-29
N3197K	BE40	RK-227
N3197M	C500	478
N3197P	PRM1	RB-257
N3197Q	BE40	RK-97
N3198C	HS25	HA-0068
N3198M	C500	479
N3198N	PRM1	RB-238
N3198V	HS25	HA-0069
N3198Z	HS25	HB-8
N3199Q	BE40	RK-99
N3199Z	BE40	RK-245
N3200X	PRM1	RB-250
N3201K	HS25	HB-21
N3201P	HS25	258961
N3201T	HS25	258901
N3202A	C500	480
N3202A	LJ35	469
N3202M	C500	481
N3203L	PRM1	RB-223
N3204M	C500	482
N3204P	PRM1	RB-224
N3204Q	BE40	RK-584
N3204T	HS25	258904
N3204W	HS25	HA-0074
N3205M	C500	483
N3205W	PRM1	RB-225
N3206K	BE40	RK-566
N3206M	C500	484
N3206V	HS25	HB-6
(N3207M)	C500	485
N3207T	HS25	258907
N3207V	HS25	HB-7
N3207Y	HS25	HA-0070
N3208M	C550	013
N3210M	C550	014
N3210N	HS25	HB-10
N3210X	BE40	RK-98
N3211G	HS25	HB-11
N3211Q	LJ45	053
N3212H	HS25	HB-12
N3212M	C550	015
N3215J	HS25	HB-15
N3215J	BE40	RK-315
(N3215K)	LJ35	589
N3215M	HS25	258575
N3216G	PRM1	RB-216
N3216L	PRM1	RB-246
N3216M	C550	016
N3216P	PRM1	RB-27
N3216R	HS25	HB-16
N3216X	BE40	RK-316
N3217D	HS25	HB-17
N3217G	**HS25**	**HA-0081**
N3217H	HS25	HA-0067
N3217P	PRM1	RB-217
N3218L	BE40	RK-108
N3220K	HS25	HB-20
N3221M	C550	017
N3221T	BE40	RK-101
"N3221Z"	BE40	TX-10
N3222S	HS25	HB-22
N3222W	HS25	HA-0082
N3223G	PRM1	RB-253
N3223M	C550	018
N3223R	BE40	RK-223
N3224N	BE40	RK-224
N3224X	BE40	RK-104
(N3225M)	C550	019
N3226B	BE40	RK-126
N3226Q	BE40	RK-226
N3227A	C550	020
N3227X	BE40	RK-107
N3228M	PRM1	RB-228
N3228M	BE40	TX-7
N3228V	BE40	RK-228
N3228V	BE40	TX-8
N3230M	C550	021
N3231H	BE40	RK-270
N3231K	PRM1	RB-31
N3232M	C550	022
N3232U	BE40	RK-102
N3234S	HS25	257087
N3235U	BE40	RK-105
N3236M	C550	023
N3236Q	BE40	RJ-36
N3237H	BE40	RK-272
N3237M	C550	024
N3237S	CL60	1070
N3238K	LJ55	013
N3238K	BE40	RJ-38
N3239A	LJ36	002
N3239A	BE40	RK-309
N3239K	BE40	RJ-39
N3239M	C550	025
N3240J	BE40	RK-240
N3240J	BE40	RK-92
N3240M	C550	026
N3240M	BE40	RJ-40
N3241G	PRM1	RB-241
N3241Q	BE40	RK-241
N3245M	C550	027
N3246H	BE40	RK-106
(N3246M)	C550	028
(N3247M)	C550	029
(N3249M)	C550	030
N3250	LJ35	250
N3250M	C550	031
N3251H	C550	397
N3251M	C550	032
N3251M	HS25	258341
N3252J	WW24	115
(N3252M)	C550	033
N3254G	C550	265
N3254P	BE40	RK-254
N3255B	BE40	RK-255
N3258M	C550	034
N3259Z	BE40	RK-259
N3260J	HS25	HA-0060
N3261A	BE40	RK-261
N3261L	LJ35	395
(N3261M)	C550	035
N3261Y	HS25	258333
N3261Y	BE40	RK-120
N3262M	C550	652
(N3262M)	C550	036
N3263E	HS25	258367
N3263N	BE40	RK-113
N3265A	BE40	RK-115
(N3268M)	C550	037
N3269A	BE40	RK-109
N3270X	HS25	258373
(N3271M)	C550	038
N3272L	BE40	RK-112
N3273H	C650	7035
(N3273M)	C550	039
(N3274M)	C550	040
N3274Q	HS25	25102
N3276L	HS25	HB-26
N3276M	C550	041
N3278	SBRL	306-32
N3278M	C550	042
N3279M	C550	043
N3280E	LJ36	013
N3280G	SBRL	282-70
N3283M	C550	044
N3283M	LJ24	356
N3283V	HS25	HA-0073
N3284M	C550	045
N3285M	C550	046
N3285N	HS25	HA-0045
N3285Q	HS25	HB-25
N3286M	C550	047
N3288M	C550	048
N3289H	PRM1	RB-239
N3289N	HS25	258909
N3289R	BE40	RK-559
N3291M	C550	049
(N3292M)	C550	050
N3296M	C550	051
N3298D	SBRL	282-20
(N3298M)	C550	052
N3298W	PRM1	RB-258
N3300	**E55P**	**50500076**
N3300L	C550	286
N3300M	C500	338
(N3300M)	C550	053
(N3301M)	C550	054
(N3308M)	C550	055
N3312T	C500	621
N3313C	**LJ35**	**297**
N3313M	C550	056
N3314M	C550	057
N3319M	C550	058
N3320G	WW24	363
(N3330)	C500	104
N3330L	CL60	1052
N3330M	CL60	1052
N3330S	PRM1	RB-230
N3332C	PRM1	RB-132
N3337H	CL30	20337
N3337J	**CL30**	**20337**
N3337J	BE40	RK-159
N3338	**GLEX**	**9569**
N3338	GLF3	402
N3338	GLF4	1006
N3338	HS25	25253
N3344T	PRM1	RB-244
N3350	LJ24	093
N3350M	FA20	140
N3352W	PRM1	RB-252
N3354S	PRM1	RB-254
N3355D	PRM1	RB-255
N3363U	HS25	HA-0063
N3371D	HS25	HA-0071
N3378M	HS25	HA-0078
N3378M	PRM1	RB-178
N3386A	HS25	HA-0056
N3389H	**GLEX**	**9154**
N3395H	PRM1	RB-259
N3396P	PRM1	RB-256
N3399P	HS25	257010
N3400D	HS25	HA-0059
N3400S	**HS25**	**258959**
N3400X	PRM1	RB-260
N3400Y	PRM1	RB-240
N3402	LJ35	402
N3415A	PRM1	RB-245
N3417F	HS25	HB-24
N3418C	HS25	HB-18
N3433D	HS25	HB-23
N3433T	HA4T	RC-33
N3438	**BE40**	**RK-569**
N3441A	PRM1	RB-261
N3444B	C550	661
N3444B	C560	0192
N3444B	**C56X**	**5023**
N3444G	FA20	21
N3444H	HS25	257122
N3444P	C550	661
N3456B	SBRL	306-35
N3456F	FA50	17
N3456L	LJ36	050
N3468D	BE40	RK-568
N3481V	PRM1	RB-141
N3482Y	HS25	258982
N3488P	HS25	HB-28
N3490L	C500	128
N3491F	HS25	HB-19
N3497J	HS25	HB-27
N3500R	BE40	RK-550
N3501M	BE40	RK-561
N3501Q	HS25	HB-9
N3502N	HA4T	RC-32
N3502T	BE40	RK-572
N3503F	LJ35	075
(N3504)	SBRL	265-32
N3513F	LJ25	207
N3514F	LJ25	211
N3523F	LJ35	081
N3524F	LJ36	021
N3526	C550	047
N3533	SBRL	306-34
N3540R	PRM1	RB-140
N3545F	LJ35	088
N3546	**GLF5**	**672**
N3547F	LJ35	089
N3556F	LJ25	216
N3600X	FA10	88
N3600X	SBRL	306-46
N3616	**C560**	**0571**
N3643	GLF2	125/26
N3652	GLF2	198/35
N3663T	**HA4T**	**RC-55**
N3668	FA20	9
N3683G	C500	684
N3690	FA20	34
N3699T	HS25	25086
N3711H	WW24	106
N3711L	HS25	25173
N3722Z	PRM1	RB-122
N3723A	PRM1	RB-123
N3725F	PRM1	RB-125
N3725L	**PRM1**	**RB-155**
N3725Z	HS25	258825
N3726	**CL64**	**5351**
N3726G	PRM1	RB-126
N3726T	PRM1	RB-156
N3727H	PRM1	RB-127
(N3728)	CL61	3006
N3732Y	PRM1	RB-152
N3733J	PRM1	RB-133
N3734C	PRM1	RB-134
N3735U	BE40	RK-515
N3735V	PRM1	RB-135
N3736	CL64	5556
N3746	CL64	5368
N3759C	LJ35	049
N3765L	**C680**	
		E68A-719001
N3771U	C500	139
N3788B	**GLF5**	**5389**
N3793D	LJ35	391

N3793P	LJ35	407
N3793X	LJ25	316
N3794B	LJ55	021
N3794C	LJ55	028
N3794M	LJ35	362
N3794P	LJ25	352
N3794U	LJ35	455
N3794W	LJ35	454
N3794Z	LJ35	364
N3795U	LJ25	354
N3795Y	LJ55	034
N3796B	LJ55	023
N3796C	LJ55	049
N3796P	LJ35	473
N3796Q	LJ35	467
N3796U	LJ55	042
N3796X	LJ55	027
N3796Z	LJ55	048
N3797A	LJ35	398
N3797B	LJ35	477
N3797C	LJ55	044
N3797K	LJ35	475
N3797L	LJ25	343
N3797N	LJ35	327
N3797S	LJ35	357
N3797U	LJ25	357
N3798A	LJ25	315
N3798B	LJ35	348
N3798D	LJ25	339
N3798L	LJ25	344
N3798P	LJ35	408
N3798V	LJ25	346
N3799B	LJ25	329
N3799C	LJ35	442
N3802G	LJ24	320
N3802G	LJ25	261
N3802G	LJ31	021
N3802G	LJ35	123
N3802G	LJ35	183
N3802G	LJ35	341
N3802G	LJ35	445
N3802G	LJ35	507
N3802G	LJ36	056
N3802G	LJ55	040
N3802G	LJ55	112
N3803G	LJ25	131
N3803G	LJ25	135
N3803G	LJ31	011
N3803G	LJ35	125
N3803G	LJ35	212
N3803G	LJ35	346
N3803G	LJ35	437
N3803G	LJ35	496
N3803G	LJ35	591
N3803G	LJ35	606
N3803G	LJ55	036
N3807G	LJ24	150
N3807G	LJ24	152
N3807G	LJ25	202
N3807G	LJ25	266
N3807G	LJ35	114
N3807G	LJ35	328
N3807G	LJ35	616
N3807G	LJ36	035
N3807G	LJ55	071
N3807G	LJ55	100
N3807G	LJ55	117
N3810G	LJ25	119
N3810G	LJ25	337
N3810G	LJ35	112
N3810G	LJ35	191
N3810G	LJ35	470
N3810G	LJ35	592
N3810G	LJ35	628
N3810G	LJ35	656
N3810G	LJ55	091
N3811G	LJ25	203
N3811G	LJ35	143
N3811G	LJ35	189
N3811G	LJ35	248
N3811G	LJ35	462
N3811G	LJ35	493
N3811G	LJ55	121
N3811G	LJ55	136
N3812G	LJ24	263
N3812G	LJ35	131
N3812G	LJ35	243
N3812G	LJ35	612
N3812G	LJ35	646
N3812G	LJ55	077
N3812G	LJ55	106
N3815G	LJ25	234
N3815G	LJ35	111
N3815G	LJ35	478
N3815G	LJ35	498
N3815G	LJ35	595
N3815G	LJ35	614
N3816G	LJ24	202
N3816G	LJ35	011
N3816G	LJ35	479
N3816G	LJ35	501
N3816G	LJ35	640
N3816G	LJ55	119
N3818G	LJ24	271
N3818G	LJ24	336
N3818G	LJ35	200
N3818G	LJ35	345
N3818G	LJ35	444
N3818G	LJ35	476
N3818G	LJ35	499
N3818G	LJ35	601
N3818G	LJ35	631
N3819G	LJ25	221
N3819G	LJ25	373
N3819G	LJ31	007
N3819G	LJ35	137
N3819G	LJ35	180
N3819G	LJ35	216
N3819G	LJ35	353
N3819G	LJ35	480
N3819G	LJ35	506
N3831C	SBRL	282-90
N3838J	WW24	350
N3848U	FA20	380
N3854B	CL60	1082
N3857N	LJ35	268
N3865M	C560	0550
N3871J	LJ24	201
N3871J	LJ24	274
N3877	**GLEX**	**9304**
N3901A	PRM1	RB-102
N3904	LJ35	266
N3914L	FA10	47
N3918Y	**GLF4**	**4112**
N3933A	HS25	25226
N3937E	C560	0396
N3950N	FA50	95
N3951	C500	682
N3951Z	C550	181
N3952B	C550	016
N3975A	**CL30**	**20170**
N3979P	LJ24	270
N3982A	JSTR	5141
N3986G	C550	657
N3999B	LJ36	048
N3999H	C550	133
N4000K	**C56X**	**5081**
N4000R	HA4T	RC-1
N4000X	CL60	1058
N4000X	GLF2	100
N4001G	LJ40	2011
N4001G	LJ40	2043
N4001G	LJ40	2135
N4001G	LJ40	2144
N4001G	LJ45	086
N4001G	LJ45	130
N4001G	LJ45	404
N4001G	LJ45	414
N4001G	LJ60	331
N4001G	LJ60	413
N4001M	BE40	RK-300
N4002P	LJ40	2138
N4002P	LJ45	110
N4002P	LJ45	267
N4002P	LJ45	291
N4002P	LJ45	321
N4002P	LJ45	376
N4002P	LJ45	418
N4002P	LJ45	437
N4002P	LJ45	502
N4002P	LJ60	273
N4002P	LJ60	377
N4002Y	C550	550-1115
N4003K	LJ31	201
N4003K	LJ40	2072
N4003K	LJ40	2090
N4003K	LJ40	2102
N4003K	LJ45	219
N4003K	LJ45	296
N4003K	LJ45	419
N4003K	LJ45	438
N4003K	LJ45	483
N4003K	LJ45	511
N4003K	LJ60	274
N4003K	LJ60	286
N4003K	LJ60	371
N4003L	LJ31	202
N4003L	LJ40	2105
N4003L	LJ45	375
N4003L	LJ45	428
N4003L	LJ45	513
N4003L	LJ60	287
N4003L	LJ60	313
N4003L	LJ60	333
N4003L	LJ60	380
N4003Q	LJ45	124
N4003Q	LJ45	334
N4003Q	LJ45	512
N4003Q	LJ60	261
N4003Q	LJ60	291
N4003Q	LJ60	352
N4003Q	LJ60	381
N4003Q	LJ60	408
N4003Q	LJ60	426
N4003W	LJ40	2086
N4003W	LJ40	2123
N4003W	LJ45	129
N4003W	LJ45	242
N4003W	LJ45	269
N4003W	LJ45	292
N4003W	LJ45	368
N4003W	LJ45	484
N4003W	LJ45	518
N4003W	LJ60	262
N4003W	LJ60	417
N4004Q	LJ40	2046
N4004Q	LJ40	2117
N4004Q	LJ40	2142
N4004Q	LJ45	134
N4004Q	LJ45	243
N4004Q	LJ45	270
N4004Q	LJ45	429
N4004Q	LJ45	520
N4004Q	LJ60	249
N4004Y	LJ45	135
N4004Y	LJ45	248
N4004Y	LJ45	271
N4004Y	LJ45	295
N4004Y	LJ45	521
N4004Y	LJ60	336
N4004Y	LJ60	365
N4004Y	LJ60	427
N4005G	C56X	5136
N4005G	LJ31	085
N4005Q	LJ40	2062
N4005Q	LJ45	143
N4005Q	LJ45	273
N4005Q	LJ45	348
N4005Q	LJ45	370
N4005Q	LJ45	408
N4005Q	LJ45	485
N4005Q	LJ45	523
N4005Q	LJ60	415
N4005S	LJ25	026
N4005T	C750	0205
N4006G	LJ31	096
N4007J	C56X	5539
N4007J	LJ60	038
N4008G	LJ40	2118
N4008G	LJ45	230
N4008G	LJ45	253
N4008G	LJ45	279
N4008G	LJ45	302
N4008G	LJ45	355
N4008G	LJ45	490
N4008G	**LJ45**	**531**
N4008G	LJ60	204
N4008G	LJ60	419
N4008S	C56X	5540
N4009	LJ45	304
N4009F	C510	0040
N4009F	**C510**	**0468**
N4009F	C525	0801
N4010K	LJ60	042
N4010N	LJ31	104
N4016G	LJ60	018
N4016M	JSTR	5224
N4017L	C525	0608
N4017R	C56X	5594
N4017X	C680	0059
N4018S	C560	0694
N4021E	C510	0041
N4021E	C510	0259
N4021E	C525	0907
N4021M	JSTR	5225
N4021Z	HS25	258514
N4022X	LJ31	082
N4026M	JSTR	5226
N4026Z	LJ60	026
N4027K	LJ31	094
N4027S	LJ60	027
N4029P	LJ60	029
N4030W	C510	0043
N4030W	C510	0260
N4030W	C525	0908
N4030W	LJ60	030
N4031A	LJ60	033
N4031K	LJ31	093
N4031L	LJ60	031
N4033M	JSTR	5227
N4034H	LJ31	084
N4034M	JSTR	5228
N4037A	LJ60	037
N4038M	JSTR	5229
N4041T	C510	0120
N4042H	C525	0910
N4042M	JSTR	5230
N4043M	JSTR	5231
N4046M	JSTR	5232
N4047W	C510	0205
N4048M	JSTR	5233
N4049	CS55	0068
N4049M	JSTR	5234
N4053T	**BE40**	**RK-253**
N4055M	JSTR	5235
N4056M	JSTR	5236
N4056V	BE40	RK-306
N4058A	C510	0264
N4058A	**C510**	**0470**
N4058M	JSTR	5237
N4059H	C510	0029
N4059H	C510	0286
N4059H	**C510**	**0472**
N4059H	C525	0818
N4059H	C525	0869
N4060K	NUTX	246-1
N4060Y	C550	550-1116
N4062M	JSTR	5238
N4063M	JSTR	5239
N4065M	JSTR	5240
N4073S	C510	0287
N4073S	C525	0819
N4073S	C525	0920
N4074M	C510	0288
N4074M	C510	0409
N4074M	C525	0820
N4074M	C525	0871
N4074M	C525	0921
N4074Z	C510	0289
N4074Z	C525	0821
N4074Z	**C525**	**0922**
N4075L	C510	0290
N4075L	C510	0411
N4075L	C525	0822
N4075L	C525	0872
N4075L	**C525**	**0923**
N4075X	C510	0412
N4075X	**C510**	**0473**
N4075X	C525	0823
N4075X	C525	0873
N4075Z	C510	0291
N4076A	**C525**	**0912**
N4076J	C510	0106
N4076J	C510	0186
N4076J	**C525**	**0913**
N4076Z	C510	0414
N4076Z	**C525**	**0925**
N4077P	C510	0294
N4077P	C510	0415
N4077P	C525	0876
N4077P	**C525**	**0926**
N4078A	**C510**	**0474**
N4078L	C510	0297
N4078L	C510	0418
N4078L	**C525**	**0928**
N4078M	C510	0298
N4078M	C510	0419
N4078M	C525	0830
N4078T	C510	0420
N4079L	C510	0301
N4079L	C525	0833
N4079L	C525	0881
N4079S	C510	0302
N4079S	C510	0423
N4079S	C525	0882
N4080M	C525	0883
N4081C	C510	0426
N4081C	C525	0839
N4081C	C525	0884
N4081L	BE40	RK-281
N4081M	C510	0368
N4081M	C510	0427
N4081M	C510	0463
N4082H	C510	0428
N4082U	C510	0146
N4082U	C510	0308
N4082U	C510	0429
N4082U	C525	0886
N4082Y	C510	0232
N4082Y	C525	0887
N4083J	C510	0310
N4083J	C525	0888
N4083N	BE40	RK-283
N4084A	C510	0075
N4084A	C510	0311
N4085A	C510	0076
N4085A	C525	0889
N4085C	C510	0239
N4085C	C510	0313
N4085C	C525	0843
N4085D	C510	0152
N4085D	C525	0891
N4085S	C510	0153
N4085S	C510	0315
N4085S	C510	0464
N4085S	C525	0892
N4085Y	C510	0316
N4085Y	C525	0845
N4085Y	C525	0893
N4085Z	C510	0155
N4085Z	C525	0846
N4085Z	C525	0894
N4086H	C510	0441
N4086H	C525	0896
N4086L	C510	0080
N4086L	C510	0375
N4086L	C510	0442
N4086L	C525	0897
N4086L	C56X	5638
N4087B	C510	0324
N4087B	C525	0899
N4087B	C680	0084
N4087F	C510	0325
N4087F	C525	0900
N4088H	**C525**	**0914**
N4088P	C510	0327
N4088P	C510	0467
N4088T	C525	0902
N4088U	C510	0328
N4088U	C525	0903
N4088Z	C525	0904
N4089Y	C510	0022
N4089Y	C525	0905
(N4090P)	C500	267
N4092E	C510	0027
N4092E	**C510**	**0471**
N4092E	C525	0864
N4095H	C510	0190
N4095H	C510	0388
N4095H	**C525**	**0916**
N4101Z	C750	0212
N4107D	C510	0032
N4107D	C510	0192
N4107D	C525	0867
N4107D	C525	0917
N4107V	C56X	5256
N4107W	C56X	5530
N4108E	**C525**	**0410**
N4109E	HS25	258509
N4110C	C550	085
N4110S	C500	247
N4110S	C550	085
N4110S	C560	0112
N4110T	C510	0033
N4110T	**C525**	**0918**
N4115B	FA20	266/490
N4115H	C52B	0183
N4115Q	C52A	0013
N4115W	C510	0038
N4115W	C510	0346
N4118K	C56X	5515
N4119S	C750	0275
N4123S	C525	0674
N4154G	FA50	80
N4155B	C510	0034
N4159Z	C510	0039
N4159Z	C510	0401
N4165Y	C750	0167
N4190A	C550	550-0991
N4191G	C550	065
N4196T	C500	369
N4200	E50P	50000205
N4200	F2TH	87
N4200K	**C560**	**0354**
N4202M	C510	0035
N4202M	C510	0199
"N4203S"	HS25	256047
N4203Y	HS25	256047
N4209K	C500	164
N4224H	HS25	258524
N4224Y	HS25	256040
N4227N	SBRL	306-126
N4227Y	FA20	237/476
N4228A	SBRL	306-48
N4230S	LJ60	027
N4234K	C500	346
N4238X	C500	270
N4242	HS25	258187
N4246A	C500	580
N4246N	LJ35	061
N4246R	FA20	175
N4246Y	C500	290
N4247C	CL60	1017
N4248Z	JSTR	5155/32
N4249K	BE40	RK-249
N4251D	PRM1	RB-51
N4251H	WW24	281
N4253A	HS25	256005
N4257R	HS25	258022
N4258P	JSTR	5016
N4260K	SBRL	380-60
N4263X	C500	514
N4275K	BE40	RK-275
N4286A	FA20	429
N4289U	LJ31	017
N4289U	LJ35	484
N4289U	LJ35	523
N4289U	LJ35	627
N4289U	LJ55	089
N4289X	LJ35	511
N4289X	LJ35	526
N4289X	LJ35	613
N4289X	LJ55	050
N4289X	LJ55	139A
N4289Y	LJ35	487
N4289Y	LJ35	518
N4289Y	LJ35	533
N4289Y	LJ35	625
N4289Z	LJ35	514
N4289Z	LJ35	528
N4289Z	LJ35	617
N4289Z	LJ55	052
N4290C	LJ35	485
N4290C	LJ35	535
N4290C	LJ35	622
N4290C	LJ55	097
N4290J	LJ35	512
N4290J	LJ35	527
N4290J	LJ35	609
N4290J	LJ36	051
N4290J	LJ36	058
N4290K	LJ35	515
N4290K	LJ35	530
N4290K	LJ35	619
N4290K	LJ35	654
N4290X	GLF2	122
N4290Y	LJ35	522
N4290Y	LJ35	537
N4290Y	LJ35	659
N4290Y	LJ55	057
N4290Y	LJ55	129
N4290Z	LJ55	053
N4291G	LJ24	190
N4291G	LJ35	486
N4291G	LJ35	513

N4291G	LJ35	529
N4291G	LJ55	126
N4291G	LJ55	138
N4291K	LJ25	361
N4291K	LJ31	016
N4291K	LJ35	516
N4291K	LJ35	531
N4291K	LJ55	132
N4291N	LJ35	521
N4291N	LJ36	062
N4291N	LJ55	130
N4292G	LJ24	228
N4293K	BE40	RK-293
N4294A	C500	095
N4300L	LJ25	182
N4305U	LJ24	271
N4308G	C550	066
N4309N	BE40	RK-339
N4313V	SBRL	265-76
N4314B	SBRL	276-8
N4320P	C550	649
N4330B	BE40	RK-330
N4333W	C560	0033
N4340F	FA20	120
N4341F	FA20	121
N4341S	ASTR	059
N4342F	FA20	122
N4343	SBRL	380-51
N4343F	FA20	123
N4344F	FA20	125
N4345F	FA20	127
N4346F	FA20	129
N4347F	C550	733
N4347F	FA20	130
N4348F	FA20	132
N4349F	FA20	133
N4350F	FA20	134
N4350M	FA20	140
N4350M	FA50	142
N4351F	FA20	135
N4351M	FA20	11
N4351M	FA20	457
N4351M	FA50	90
N4351N	FA20	11
N4352F	FA20	137
N4353F	FA20	139
N4354F	FA20	140
N4355F	FA20	142
N4356F	FA20	144
N4357F	FA20	146
N4357H	BE40	RK-343
N4358F	FA20	148
N4358N	LJ35	065
N4359F	FA20	149
N4360F	FA20	151
N4360S	C650	7034
N4361F	FA20	153
N4361Q	HS25	258121
N4362F	FA20	155
N4362M	FA20	457
N4363F	FA20	157
N4364F	FA20	159
N4365F	FA20	161
N4366F	FA20	163
N4367F	FA20	164
N4368F	FA20	166
N4368F	FA20	261
N4369F	FA20	168
N4370F	FA20	169
N4371F	FA20	171
N4372F	FA20	218
N4373F	FA20	175
N4374F	FA20	177
N4375F	FA20	179
N4376F	FA20	181
N4377	**GLF5**	**619**
N4377F	FA20	183
N4378F	FA20	203
N4378P	BE40	RK-278
N4379F	FA20	187
N4380F	FA20	189
N4381F	FA20	191
N4382F	FA20	192
N4383F	FA20	193
N4384F	FA20	194
N4385F	FA20	195
N4386F	FA20	196
N4387	GLF4	1387
N4387F	FA20	197
N4388F	FA20	199
N4389F	FA20	200
N4390F	FA20	213
N4391F	FA20	202
N4392F	FA20	204
N4393F	FA20	205
N4394F	FA20	206
N4395D	PRM1	RB-65
N4395F	FA20	207
N4396F	FA20	209
N4397F	FA20	210
N4398F	FA20	211
N4399F	FA20	212
N4400E	HS25	25026
N4400F	FA20	214
N4401	LJ35	434
N4401F	FA20	215
N4402	HS25	258199
N4402	LJ25	117
N4402F	FA20	216
N4403	C500	271
N4403	**HS25**	**258480**
N4403F	FA20	217
N4404F	FA20	220
N4405	C550	550-1023
N4405	LJ25	117
N4406F	FA20	221
N4407F	FA20	223
N4408F	FA20	224
N4409F	FA20	226
N4410F	FA20	227
N4411	GLF2	48/29
N4411F	FA20	229
N4412F	FA20	230
N4413F	FA20	232
N4413N	FA50	66
N4414F	FA20	233
N4415D	CL61	3051
N4415F	FA20	235
N4415M	LJ35	072
N4415S	LJ35	021
N4415S	LJ35	232
N4415W	LJ35	229
N4416F	FA20	256
(N4416F)	FA20	236
N4417F	FA20	239
N4418F	FA20	242
N4418F	FA20	259
N4419F	FA20	247
N4420E	ASTR	049
N4420F	FA20	244
N4421F	FA20	249
N4422F	FA20	250
N4423F	FA20	254
(N4424)	HS25	258907
N4424P	CL60	1053
N4425	F9EX	32
N4425F	FA20	257
N4425R	HS25	258525
N4426	HS25	258272
N4426F	FA20	258
N4426Z	WW24	409
N4427F	FA20	262
N4428	HS25	258274
N4428F	FA20	264
N4429F	FA20	265
N4430F	FA20	269
N4431F	FA20	272
N4432F	FA20	273
N4433F	FA20	274
N4434F	FA20	275
N4434W	C500	082
N4435F	FA20	270
N4436F	FA20	282
N4436S	JSTR	5141
N4437F	FA20	284
N4438F	FA20	287
N4439F	FA20	289
N4440F	FA20	290
N4441F	FA20	292
N4442F	FA20	293
N4443F	FA20	297
N4444F	FA20	298
N4444J	HS25	258171
N4444U	WW24	163
N4445F	FA20	303
(N4445J)	LJ24	309
N4445N	C550	024
N4445Y	LJ35	432
N4445Y	BE40	RK-345
N4446F	FA20	305
N4446P	C500	373
N4447F	FA20	308
N4447P	LJ25	338
N4447T	WW24	286
N4448F	FA20	312
N4448Y	LJ36	046
N4449F	CL61	3002
N4449F	FA20	313
N4450F	FA20	310
N4451F	FA20	316
N4452F	FA20	317
N4453F	FA20	319
N4454F	FA20	321
N4455F	FA20	322
N4456F	FA20	324
N4457A	C550	035
N4457F	FA20	325
N4458F	FA20	327
N4459F	FA20	335
(N4459F)	FA20	328/522
N4460F	FA20	330
N4461F	FA20	339
N4462F	FA20	341
N4463F	FA20	345
N4464F	FA20	347
N4465F	FA20	349
N4465M	HS25	258565
N4465N	HS25	25053
N4466F	FA20	352
N4466Z	HS25	258566
N4467E	BE40	RK-287
N4467F	FA20	355
N4467X	BE40	RK-267
N4468F	FA20	356
N4468K	HS25	258568
N4469B	HS25	258502
N4469E	BE40	RK-320
N4469F	FA20	357
N4469F	HS25	258531
N4469F	SBRL	282-43
N4469M	HS25	258563
N4469M	SBRL	282-48
N4469N	HS25	258547
N4469N	SBRL	282-68
N4469U	HS25	258520
N4469X	HS25	258569
N4471N	HS25	258571
N4471P	PRM1	RB-71
N4477X	BE40	RK-277
(N4477X)	HS25	257104
N4480W	BE40	RK-280
N4483W	BE40	RK-313
N4485B	PRM1	RB-85
N4488F	PRM1	RB-88
N4488W	LJ25	367
(N4492V)	SBRL	282-39
N4493S	JSTR	5141
N4500X	GLF3	416
N4500X	GLF4	4004
N4545	LJ45	045
N4550E	WW24	83
N4554E	WW24	85
N4555E	HS25	257001
N4557P	FA10	104
N4557W	C550	137
N4562Q	CL61	3016
N4564P	C550	319
(N4564S)	LJ35	365
N4567	SBRL	282-44
N4570X	**GLF4**	**4004**
N4576T	LJ24	227
N4577Q	LJ35	263
N4578F	C550	023
N4581R	FA10	151
N4581Y	C550	375
N4612	C650	0203
(N4612S)	C650	0203
N4612Z	C650	0203
N4614N	C550	659
N4620G	C550	067
N4621G	C550	068
N4641J	LJ24	019
N4644E	WW24	97
N4646S	C500	051
N4646S	HS25	25013
N4661E	WW24	99
N4663E	WW24	100
N4674E	WW24	104
N4679T	FA50	17
N4690E	WW24	106
N4691E	WW24	107
N4701N	SBRL	282-93
N4703N	SBRL	282-94
N4704N	SBRL	282-95
N4705N	SBRL	282-96
N4706N	SBRL	282-97
N4707N	SBRL	282-98
N4709N	SBRL	306-4
N4712N	SBRL	306-6
N4715N	SBRL	306-7
N4716E	WW24	110
N4716N	SBRL	306-8
N4717N	SBRL	306-9
N4720N	SBRL	306-10
N4720T	C550	256
N4721N	SBRL	306-11
N4722R	SBRL	306-12
N4723N	SBRL	306-13
N4724N	SBRL	306-14
N4725N	SBRL	306-15
N4726N	SBRL	306-16
N4727N	SBRL	306-17
N4728N	SBRL	306-18
N4729N	SBRL	306-19
N4730E	WW24	112
N4730N	SBRL	306-20
N4731N	SBRL	306-21
N4732E	WW24	113
N4732N	SBRL	306-22
N4733N	SBRL	306-23
N4734E	WW24	114
N4734N	SBRL	306-24
N4735N	SBRL	306-25
N4736N	SBRL	306-26
N4737N	SBRL	306-27
N4741N	SBRL	306-29
N4742N	SBRL	306-30
N4743E	WW24	116
N4743N	SBRL	306-32
N4745N	SBRL	306-33
N4746N	SBRL	306-34
N4748N	SBRL	306-35
N4749N	SBRL	306-36
N4750N	SBRL	306-37
N4751	**C52C**	**0157**
N4751N	SBRL	306-38
N4752N	SBRL	306-39
N4753	GLF4	1197
N4753N	SBRL	306-40
N4754G	C550	069
N4754N	SBRL	306-41
N4755N	SBRL	306-42
N4757N	SBRL	306-43
N4759D	HS25	25272
N4760N	SBRL	306-44
N4763N	SBRL	306-45
N4764N	SBRL	306-46
N4765N	SBRL	306-47
N4767M	HS25	25159
N4791C	LJ24	160
N4818C	**GLF4**	**1385**
N4868	**CL65**	**5746**
N4875	FA10	54
N4886	HS25	25046
N4895Q	C560	0199
N4903W	FA50	129
N4911	**FA50**	**316**
N4940E	WW24	122
N4943A	SBRL	282-66
N4960S	FA20	296/507
N4981	LJ25	062
N4983E	WW24	126
N4990D	JSTR	5146
N4995A	LJ35	192
N4995N	WW24	230
N4997	**C525**	**0880**
N4997E	HS25	25016
N4998Z	LJ36	039
N4999G	SBRL	265-2
N4999H	C500	329
N4999H	SBRL	265-55
N5000B	JSTR	5093
N5000B	LJ35	074
N5000C	C650	0002
N5000C	JSTR	5093
N5000C	JSTR	5205
N5000E	LJ31	031
N5000E	LJ31	206
N5000E	LJ31	214
N5000E	LJ40	2064
N5000E	LJ45	020
N5000E	LJ45	207
N5000E	LJ45	233
N5000E	LJ45	298
N5000E	LJ45	471
N5000E	LJ45	495
N5000E	**LJ45**	**548**
N5000E	LJ60	276
N5000E	LJ60	284
N5000E	LJ60	328
N5000E	LJ60	354
N5000E	LJ60	374
N5000E	LJ60	395
N5000G	GLF2	110
N5000P	**GLEX**	**9655**
N5000R	C52A	0312
N5000R	C52A	0465
N5000R	C52B	0228
N5000R	C52C	0096
N5000R	C52C	0131
N5000R	C52C	0214
N5000R	C550	550-0879
N5000R	C550	550-0928
N5000R	C560	0445
N5000R	C560	0566
N5000R	C56X	5228
N5000R	C56X	5314
N5000R	C56X	5826
N5000R	C680	0131
N5000R	C750	0023
N5000R	C750	0052
N5000R	C750	0252
N5000X	**GLF5**	**611**
N5001G	HS25	25095
N5001J	LJ45	159
N5001S	HS25	258501
N5001X	LJ31	100
N5002D	LJ31	102
N5002G	BE40	RK-302
N5003F	LJ31	103
N5003G	BE40	RK-323
N5003U	LJ60	063
N5003X	LJ60	039
N5004B	HS25	258504
N5004J	LJ60	232
N5004Y	LJ60	041
N5004Y	BE40	RK-304
N5004Z	LJ31	230
N5005	C500	004
N5005	EA50	000225
N5005K	LJ31	105
(N5005M)	LJ31	115
N5005Q	LJ31	231
N5005X	LJ31	233
N5005X	LJ60	095
N5006G	LJ60	046
N5006K	LJ60	066
N5006T	LJ60	062
N5006V	LJ60	065
N5007	LJ31	156
N5007P	LJ60	047
N5008F	LJ60	233
N5008S	HS25	258508
N5008S	LJ31	232
N5008Z	LJ60	048
N5009	LJ60	306
N5009L	LJ31	089
N5009T	LJ31	220
N5009T	LJ35	665
N5009T	LJ40	2017
N5009T	LJ40	2091
N5009T	LJ40	2108
N5009T	LJ45	021
N5009T	LJ45	096
N5009T	LJ45	234
N5009T	LJ45	306
N5009T	LJ45	454
N5009T	LJ45	472
N5009T	LJ45	494
N5009T	LJ60	018
N5009T	LJ60	283
N5009T	LJ60	285
N5009T	LJ60	404
N5009V	LJ31	043
N5009V	LJ31	066
N5009V	LJ31	096
N5009V	LJ31	213
N5009V	LJ40	2040
N5009V	LJ45	012
N5009V	LJ45	084
N5009V	LJ45	208
N5009V	LJ45	210
N5009V	LJ45	244
N5009V	LJ45	268
N5009V	LJ45	330
N5009V	LJ45	372
N5009V	LJ45	421
N5009V	LJ45	449
N5009V	LJ45	473
N5009V	LJ45	493
N5009V	LJ60	267
N5009V	LJ60	383
N5010J	LJ31	101
N5010U	LJ31	032
N5010U	LJ40	2055
N5010U	LJ45	013
N5010U	LJ45	204
N5010U	LJ45	245
N5010U	LJ45	261
N5010U	LJ45	381
N5010U	LJ45	412
N5010U	LJ45	433
N5010U	LJ45	478
N5010U	LJ45	509
N5010U	LJ60	197
N5010U	LJ60	321
N5010U	LJ60	339
(N5010U)	LJ60	057
N5010X	PRM1	RB-10
N5011J	HS25	258511
N5011L	LJ35	668
N5011L	LJ45	052
N5011L	LJ45	144
N5011L	LJ45	205
N5011L	LJ45	256
N5011L	LJ45	322
N5011L	LJ45	342
N5011L	LJ45	407
N5011L	LJ45	450
N5011L	LJ45	481
N5011L	LJ45	508
N5011L	LJ60	005
N5011L	LJ60	268
N5011L	LJ60	292
N5011L	LJ60	350
N5011L	LJ60	405
N5012G	LJ40	2068
N5012G	LJ45	022
N5012G	LJ45	246
N5012G	LJ45	416
N5012G	LJ45	467
N5012G	LJ60	217
N5012G	LJ60	297
N5012G	LJ60	360
N5012G	LJ60	416
N5012H	LJ31	033
N5012H	LJ31	098
N5012H	LJ31	107
N5012H	LJ40	2128
N5012H	LJ40	2141
N5012H	LJ45	030
N5012H	LJ45	257
N5012H	LJ45	281
N5012H	LJ45	360
N5012H	LJ45	384
N5012H	LJ45	426
N5012H	LJ45	451
N5012H	LJ45	516
N5012H	LJ60	010
N5012H	LJ60	062
N5012H	LJ60	212
N5012H	LJ60	252
N5012H	LJ60	269
N5012H	LJ60	302
N5012K	LJ35	670
N5012K	LJ40	2049
N5012K	LJ45	329
N5012K	LJ45	430
N5012K	LJ45	497
N5012K	LJ60	190
N5012K	LJ60	253
N5012K	LJ60	270
N5012K	LJ60	278
N5012K	LJ60	290
N5012K	LJ60	341

N5012K	LJ60	367
N5012K	LJ60	425
(N5012P)	HS25	25095
N5012U	BE40	RK-312
N5012V	LJ45	167
N5012Z	LJ31	083
N5012Z	LJ35	676
N5012Z	LJ40	2115
N5012Z	LJ45	228
N5012Z	LJ45	285
N5012Z	LJ45	455
N5012Z	LJ45	475
N5012Z	LJ45	500
N5012Z	LJ60	053
N5012Z	LJ60	211
N5012Z	LJ60	317
N5012Z	LJ60	347
N5012Z	LJ60	406
N5013D	LJ45	169
N5013D	LJ60	032
N5013E	LJ45	170
N5013J	LJ60	234
N5013L	LJ31	033C
N5013N	LJ31	130
N5013N	LJ60	235
N5013U	LJ31	222
N5013U	LJ40	2008
N5013U	LJ40	2021
N5013U	LJ45	035
N5013U	LJ45	289
N5013U	LJ45	373
N5013U	LJ45	464
N5013U	LJ45	501
N5013U	LJ60	011
N5013U	LJ60	255
N5013U	LJ60	281
N5013U	LJ60	312
N5013U	LJ60	332
N5013U	LJ60	382
N5013U	LJ60	399
N5013Y	LJ31	085
N5013Y	LJ31	211
N5013Y	LJ40	2022
N5013Y	LJ45	029
N5013Y	LJ45	083
N5013Y	LJ45	287
N5013Y	LJ45	457
N5013Y	LJ45	503
N5013Y	LJ60	056
N5013Y	LJ60	256
N5013Y	LJ60	282
N5013Y	LJ60	306
N5013Y	LJ60	325
N5013Y	LJ60	351
N5013Y	LJ60	384
N5014E	LJ31	134
N5014E	LJ40	2026
N5014E	LJ45	028
N5014E	LJ45	152
N5014E	LJ45	294
N5014E	LJ45	398
N5014E	LJ45	417
N5014E	LJ45	477
N5014E	LJ45	504
N5014E	LJ60	036
N5014E	LJ60	055
N5014E	LJ60	335
N5014E	LJ60	361
N5014E	LJ60	411
N5014F	CL30	20006
N5014F	LJ31	082
N5014F	LJ35	669
N5014F	LJ35	673
N5014F	LJ45	093
N5014F	LJ45	288
N5014F	LJ45	310
N5014F	LJ45	340
N5014F	LJ45	374
N5014F	LJ45	462
N5014F	LJ45	505
N5014F	LJ60	169
N5014F	LJ60	322
N5014F	LJ60	409
N5014G	BE40	RK-314
N5014H	LJ60	012
N5015B	BE40	RK-335
N5015T	LJ60	236
N5015U	LJ31	034
N5015U	LJ40	2032
N5015U	LJ40	2050
N5015U	LJ40	2077
N5015U	LJ45	258
N5015U	LJ45	385
N5015U	LJ45	405
N5015U	LJ45	421
N5015U	LJ45	431
N5015U	LJ45	454
N5015U	LJ45	459
N5015U	LJ60	063
N5015U	LJ60	254
N5015U	LJ60	343
N5016P	C500	358
N5016S	LJ45	176
N5016V	LJ31	038
N5016V	LJ40	2044
N5016V	LJ40	2127
N5016V	LJ45	031
N5016V	LJ45	092
N5016V	LJ45	119
N5016V	LJ45	216
N5016V	LJ45	264
N5016V	LJ45	383
N5016V	LJ45	427
N5016V	LJ45	453
N5016V	LJ45	479
N5016V	LJ45	519
N5016V	LJ60	058
N5016V	LJ60	338
N5016Z	LJ40	2061
N5016Z	LJ40	2093
N5016Z	LJ40	2125
N5016Z	LJ45	072
N5016Z	LJ45	078
N5016Z	LJ45	217
N5016Z	LJ45	240
N5016Z	LJ45	435
N5016Z	LJ45	470
N5016Z	LJ45	492
N5016Z	LJ60	214
N5016Z	LJ60	296
N5016Z	LJ60	327
N5016Z	LJ60	392
N5017J	LJ31	058
N5017J	LJ40	2126
N5017J	LJ45	097
N5017J	LJ45	237
N5017J	LJ45	265
N5017J	LJ45	345
N5017J	LJ45	436
N5017J	LJ45	463
N5017J	LJ45	515
N5017J	LJ60	037
N5017J	LJ60	316
N5017J	LJ60	353
N5017J	LJ60	393
N5017T	PRM1	RB-17
N5018G	LJ35	667
N5018G	LJ40	2013
N5018G	LJ40	2018
N5018G	LJ40	2034
N5018G	LJ40	2053
N5018G	LJ45	077
N5018G	LJ45	138
N5018G	LJ45	188
N5018G	LJ45	215
N5018G	LJ45	236
N5018G	LJ45	496
N5018G	LJ60	326
N5018G	LJ60	359
N5018G	LJ60	390
N5018G	LJ60	412
N5018L	LJ45	424
N5018L	LJ60	373
N5018L	LJ60	423
N5018U	LJ60	238
N5019R	LJ60	239
N5019V	LJ60	240
N5019Y	LJ31	091
N5020J	C510	0178
N5020Y	LJ31	120
N5021G	LJ45	525
N5022C	LJ60	052
N5023D	LJ31	033D
N5023J	HS25	258523
N5023U	LJ45	179
N5024E	LJ45	181
N5024J	PRM1	RB-24
N5024U	BE40	RK-324
N5025K	LJ45	183
N5026	C52A	0159
N5026Q	C52A	0438
N5026Q	C52B	0251
N5026Q	C52C	0073
N5026Q	C56X	5692
N5026Q	C56X	6146
N5026Q	C680	0298
N5026Q	**C680**	**680A0050**
N5026Q	C750	0520
N5026Q	LJ60	241
N5027Q	LJ60	242
N5028E	LJ31	234
N5028J	BE40	RK-328
N5029F	LJ31	109
N5030	JSTR	5212
N5030J	LJ45	187
N5030N	LJ45	189
N5030U	C52A	0502
N5030U	C52B	0126
N5030U	C52B	0323
N5030U	C56X	5770
N5030U	C680	0149
N5030V	PRM1	RB-130
N5031D	BE40	RK-331
N5031E	C52B	0133
N5031E	C52B	0353
N5031E	C56X	6148
N5031E	C680	0260
N5031E	C750	0279
N5031R	LJ60	244
N5031T	**BE40**	**RK-590**
N5032E	WW24	129
N5032H	BE40	RK-332
(N5032H)	CL61	5071
N5032K	C52A	0368
N5032K	C680	0307
N5032K	C680	0510
N5032K	C750	0290
N5032K	C750	0306
N5034J	BE40	RK-334
N5034Z	LJ60	034
N5035F	LJ60	246
N5035R	LJ60	070
N5036Q	C52B	0190
N5036Q	C560	0761
N5036Q	C56X	6100
N5036Q	C680	0233
N5036Q	C680	0286
N5037F	C525	0665
N5037F	C52B	0177
N5037F	C52B	0359
N5037F	C52B	0393
N5037F	C56X	6057
N5037L	BE40	RK-337
N5038E	WW24	130
N5038N	LJ60	248
N5038V	BE40	RK-338
N5039E	WW24	131
(N5040)	GLF2	40
N5040E	C52A	0509
N5040E	C52B	0368
N5040E	C56X	5747
N5040E	C56X	6003
N5040E	C680	0155
N5040E	C680	680A0020
N5040W	LJ45	194
N5040Y	LJ45	195
N5041E	WW24	133
N5042A	LJ45	206
N5043D	LJ60	043
N5043E	WW24	135
N5044E	WW24	136
N5044N	LJ60	044
N5044V	C510	0144
N5044X	PRM1	RB-44
N5045E	WW24	137
N5045S	LJ60	045
N5045W	C52B	0362
N5045W	C52C	0143
N5045W	**C56X**	**6215**
N5045W	C680	0172
N5046E	WW24	138
N5047E	WW24	139
N5048K	LJ45	198
N5048Q	LJ45	202
N5048U	C52A	0399
N5048U	C52A	0429
N5048U	C52C	0065
N5048U	C52C	0126
N5049J	LJ31	099
N5049U	PRM1	RB-49
N5050G	LJ45	208
N5050J	C550	001
N5051A	LJ60	262
N5051X	LJ60	051
N5051X	LJ60	252
N5052K	LJ45	205
N5052U	FA20	65
N5053R	C525	0671
N5053R	C525	0683
N5053R	C680	0125
N5053R	C750	0313
N5053Y	LJ60	053
N5055F	LJ60	055
N5057E	C52B	0131
N5057F	C525	0660
N5057F	C525	0697
N5057F	C52A	0454
N5057F	C52B	0347
N5057F	C680	0234
N5057F	C680	0340
N5057F	**C680**	**0565**
N5057Z	BE40	RK-357
N5058J	C525	0510
N5058J	C52B	0132
N5058J	C52B	0483
N5058J	C52C	0145
N5058J	C550	550-0828
N5058J	C550	550-0901
N5058J	C56X	5182
N5058J	C56X	5270
N5058J	C680	0049
N5058J	C680	0211
N5058J	C750	0028
N5058J	C750	0051
N5058J	C750	0136
N5059J	LJ60	059
N5059X	C52B	0135
N5059X	C52B	0358
N5059X	C56X	5767
N5059X	C56X	6028
N5059X	C680	680A0028
N5060H	CL61	5060
N5060K	C525	0516
N5060K	C52B	0373
N5060K	C56X	5002
N5060K	C56X	5274
N5060K	C56X	5808
N5060K	C680	0058
N5060K	C680	0133
N5060K	**C680**	**0566**
N5060K	C750	0097
N5060K	C750	0170
N5060K	C750	0285
N5060P	C550	550-0825
N5060P	C560	0246
N5061F	C525	0674
N5061F	C52A	0358
N5061F	C52B	0304
N5061F	C52B	0354
N5061F	C52B	0377
N5061F	C680	0197
N5061F	C680	0219
N5061P	C525	0667
N5061P	C525	0680
N5061P	C52A	0507
N5061P	C52C	0198
N5061P	C550	550-0927
N5061P	C56X	5177
N5061P	C56X	5238
N5061P	C56X	5298
N5061P	C56X	5684
N5061P	C56X	6095
N5061P	C680	0071
N5061P	**C680**	**680A0045**
N5061P	C750	0053
N5061P	C750	0091
N5061W	C52B	0166
N5061W	C52B	0222
N5061W	C52C	0007
N5061W	C52C	0074
N5061W	C550	550-1121
N5061W	C560	0398
N5061W	C560	0513
N5061W	C56X	5184
N5061W	C56X	5237
N5061W	C56X	5341
N5061W	C56X	5686
N5061W	C56X	6013
N5061W	C750	0031
N5061W	C750	0125
N5062H	HS25	258562
N5062S	C52A	0485
N5062S	C52B	0183
N5062S	C52B	0238
N5062S	C52B	0287
N5062S	C52B	0341
N5062S	C56X	6136
N5062S	C680	0128
N5063P	C52A	0337
N5063P	C52B	0399
N5063P	C56X	5744
N5063P	C56X	6091
N5063P	C680	0272
N5064M	C560	0807
N5064M	C56X	6108
N5064M	C680	680A0042
N5064M	C750	0282
N5064M	C750	0505
N5064Q	C52A	0341
N5064Q	C56X	5768
N5064Q	C56X	6097
N5064Q	C56X	6129
N5064Q	C680	0280
N5064Q	**C680**	**0559**
N5065S	C56X	6126
N5065S	C680	0264
N5065S	C680	0318
N5065S	C680	0522
N5065S	C680	0548
N5066F	C52B	0204
N5066F	C52B	0286
N5066F	C52B	0330
N5066F	C52B	0376
N5066F	C750	0269
N5066U	C525	0521
N5066U	C525	0636
N5066U	C52A	0427
N5066U	C52B	0058
N5066U	C550	550-0930
N5066U	C56X	5264
N5066U	C56X	5769
N5066U	C56X	6125
N5066U	C680	0317
N5066U	C680	0521
N5066U	C750	0026
N5066U	C750	0041
N5066U	C750	0092
N5066U	C750	0172
N5067U	C52C	0134
N5067U	C56X	5745
N5067U	C56X	6068
N5067U	C56X	6112
N5068F	C52A	0446
N5068F	C52B	0230
N5068F	C52C	0135
N5068F	C56X	5687
N5068F	**C680**	**680A0032**
N5068F	LJ60	078
N5068R	C525	0142
N5068R	C52C	0120
N5068R	C550	550-0882
N5068R	C550	550-1085
N5068R	C550	550-1134
N5068R	C56X	5166
N5068R	C56X	5223
N5068R	C56X	5294
N5068R	C56X	5771
N5068R	C56X	6065
N5068R	C56X	6104
N5068R	C680	0256
N5068R	C750	0027
N5068R	C750	0055
N5068R	C750	0141
N5069E	C525	0656
N5069E	C52C	0059
N5069E	C56X	5693
N5069E	C56X	5777
N5069E	**C680**	**0568**
N5069P	CL61	3021
N5070L	JSTR	5143
N5070W	PRM1	RB-70
N5071L	SBRL	306-9
N5071M	C750	0035
N5072E	C500	043
N5072L	C500	043
N5072L	C500	379
N5072L	HS25	258572
N5072L	LJ60	072
N5072X	C52A	0406
N5072X	C52B	0360
N5072X	C52C	0136
N5072X	C56X	5694
N5072X	C56X	6045
N5072X	**C56X**	**6219**
N5072X	C680	0176
N5072X	PRM1	RB-72
N5073	CL61	5073
N5073F	C52C	0075
N5073F	C680	680A0029
N5073G	C52A	0242
N5073G	C52B	0021
N5073G	C52B	0136
N5073G	C52B	0200
N5073G	C550	550-0850
N5073G	C550	550-0893
N5073G	C550	550-0921
N5073G	C560	0423
N5073G	C560	0637
N5073G	C56X	5189
N5073G	C56X	5273
N5073G	C650	7088
N5073G	C680	0338
N5073G	C680	680A0019
N5075L	SBRL	306-16
N5076J	C525	0160
N5076J	C52A	0348
N5076J	C52B	0089
N5076J	C52B	0343
N5076J	**C52B**	**0495**
N5076J	C550	550-0817
N5076J	C550	550-0830
N5076J	C550	550-0852
N5076J	C550	550-0909
N5076J	C550	550-0951
N5076J	C56X	5207
N5076J	C56X	5234
N5076J	C56X	5583
N5076J	C56X	5772
N5076J	C56X	6027
N5076J	C56X	6098
N5076J	C56X	6130
N5076K	C525	0075
N5076K	C525	0161
N5076K	C525	0666
N5076K	C525	0679
N5076K	C52A	0174
N5076K	C52B	0185
N5076K	C52B	0284
N5076K	C52C	0063
N5076K	C52C	0137
N5076K	C52C	0205
N5076K	C550	550-0847
N5076K	C550	550-0899
N5076K	C550	550-0939
N5076K	C550	550-1124
N5076K	C560	0431
N5076K	C560	0440
N5076K	C560	0693
N5076K	C56X	5211
N5076K	C56X	5277
N5076K	C680	0053
N5076K	C680	0134
N5076K	C750	0126
N5076L	C525	0640
N5076L	C52A	0430
N5076L	C52C	0047
N5076L	C52C	0115
N5076L	C56X	5749
N5076L	C680	0555
N5076P	C52B	0187
N5076P	C52B	0239
N5076P	C52B	0288
N5076P	C52B	0474
N5076P	C56X	6105
N5076P	C680	0304
N5079H	C56X	5219
N5079V	C525	0076
N5079V	C52A	0355
N5079V	C52C	0056
N5079V	C550	550-0843
N5079V	C550	550-0897
N5079V	C550	550-0954
N5079V	C560	0677
N5079V	C560	0694
N5079V	C560	0791

N5079V	C560	707
N5079V	C56X	5217
N5079V	C56X	5272
N5079V	C56X	5360
N5079V	C650	7078
N5079V	C750	0261
N5082S	LJ31	112
N5084U	BE40	RK-354
N5085E	C525	0078
N5085E	C52A	0209
N5085E	C52B	0028
N5085E	C550	550-1067
N5085E	C560	0477
N5085E	C560	0508
N5085E	C560	0768
N5085E	C56X	5230
N5085E	C56X	5300
N5085E	C56X	5779
N5085E	C56X	6023
N5085E	C56X	6070
N5085E	C56X	6197
N5085E	C680	0330
N5085E	C680	0514
N5085E	C750	0015
N5085E	C750	0036
N5085E	C750	0115
N5085E	C750	0147
N5085J	C550	550-0877
N5086W	C525	0079
N5086W	C525	0151
N5086W	C52A	0340
N5086W	C52C	0150
N5086W	C550	550-0840
N5086W	C550	550-0841
N5086W	C550	550-0853
N5086W	C550	550-0929
N5086W	C560	0436
N5086W	C560	0465
N5086W	C560	0521
N5086W	C560	0685
N5086W	C56X	5172
N5086W	C56X	5235
N5086W	C56X	5291
N5086W	C56X	5514
N5086W	C56X	5811
N5086W	C56X	6090
N5086W	C650	7082
N5086W	C680	0166
N5086W	C680	0343
N5086W	C680	680A0041
N5086W	C750	0107
N5087B	LJ45	067
N5090A	C525	0080
N5090A	C525	0124
N5090A	C525	0535
N5090A	C52A	0417
N5090A	C52A	0452
N5090A	C52A	0468
N5090A	C550	550-1071
N5090A	C560	0378
N5090A	C560	0417
N5090A	C560	0549
N5090A	C56X	5191
N5090A	C56X	5244
N5090A	C56X	5311
N5090A	C56X	5574
N5090A	C56X	6162
N5090A	**C56X**	**6213**
N5090A	C680	0132
N5090A	C750	0042
N5090A	C750	0099
N5090A	C750	0257
N5090A	C750	0293
N5090V	C525	0081
N5090V	C525	0125
N5090V	C525	0150
N5090V	C525	0153
N5090V	C52A	0364
N5090V	C52A	0467
N5090V	C550	550-0925
N5090V	C56X	5183
N5090V	C56X	5241
N5090V	C56X	5824
N5090V	C680	0042
N5090V	C680	0080
N5090V	C750	0029
N5090V	C750	0098
N5090Y	C525	0082
N5090Y	C525	0126
N5090Y	C52B	0346
N5090Y	C550	550-0884
N5090Y	C550	550-0924
N5090Y	C56X	5212
N5090Y	C56X	5540
N5090Y	C680	0086
N5090Y	C680	0209
N5090Y	C750	0043
N5090Y	C750	0060
N5091J	C525	0083
N5091J	C525	0127
N5091J	C52A	0154
N5091J	C52B	0270
N5091J	C52B	0312
N5091J	C52C	0146
N5091J	C560	0524
N5091J	C560	0545
N5091J	C560	0783
N5091J	C56X	5215
N5091J	C56X	5261
N5091J	C56X	5372
N5091J	C56X	5698
N5091J	C750	0018
N5091J	C750	0047
N5092	**GLF5**	**5386**
N5092B	C560	0389
N5092D	C525	0128
N5092D	C550	550-0819
N5092D	C560	0391
(N5092D)	C525	0084
N5092R	LJ60	092
N5093D	C525	0085
N5093D	C525	0129
N5093D	C525	0158
N5093D	C52A	0432
N5093D	C52B	0012
N5093D	C52B	0476
N5093D	C52C	0039
N5093D	C560	0473
N5093D	C560	0697
N5093D	C56X	5142
N5093D	C56X	5243
N5093D	C56X	5309
N5093D	C680	0136
N5093D	C680	0171
N5093D	C750	0033
N5093D	C750	0173
N5093D	C750	0262
N5093L	C525	0130
N5093L	C52B	0056
N5093L	C52B	0252
N5093L	C52B	0392
N5093L	C550	550-0814
N5093L	C550	550-0872
N5093L	C550	550-0891
N5093L	C550	550-0981
N5093L	C560	0390
N5093L	C560	0542
N5093L	C56X	5224
N5093L	C56X	5334
N5093L	C56X	5559
N5093L	C680	0137
N5093L	C680	0306
N5093L	C680	0542
N5093L	**C680**	**680A0036**
(N5093L)	C525	0086
N5093Y	C525	0131
N5093Y	C52C	0040
N5093Y	C550	550-0821
N5093Y	C550	550-0904
N5093Y	C550	550-0941
N5093Y	C550	550-1069
N5093Y	C560	0394
N5093Y	C560	0395
N5093Y	C560	0525
N5093Y	C560	0770
N5093Y	C56X	5209
N5093Y	C680	0087
N5093Y	C680	0215
N5093Y	C680	680A0030
(N5093Y)	C525	0087
N5094B	C560	0272
N5094B	WW24	105
N5094D	C52A	0315
N5094D	C52A	0401
N5094D	C52C	0101
N5094D	C56X	5221
N5094D	C56X	5282
N5094D	C56X	5338
N5094D	C56X	5368
N5094D	C650	7084
N5094D	C680	0117
N5094D	C680	0168
N5094D	C680	0277
N5094E	BE40	RK-294
N5095N	C525	0615
N5095N	C52C	0100
N5095N	C550	550-0902
N5095N	C550	550-0942
N5095N	C560	0273
N5095N	C560	0478
N5095N	C560	0507
N5095N	C560	0753
N5095N	C56X	5155
N5095N	C56X	5202
N5095N	C56X	5250
N5095N	C56X	5315
N5095N	C56X	5750
N5095N	C750	0030
N5096F	FA20	157
N5096S	C52A	0314
N5096S	C52A	0512
N5096S	C52B	0157
N5096S	C52B	0260
N5096S	C550	550-0813
N5096S	C550	550-0829
N5096S	C550	550-0913
N5096S	C560	0274
N5096S	C560	0467
N5096S	C56X	5143
N5096S	C56X	5201
N5096S	C56X	5249
N5096S	C56X	5316
N5096S	C56X	6047
N5096S	C56X	6087
N5096S	C680	0221
N5096S	C750	0251
N5097H	C52B	0010
N5097H	C52B	0488
N5097H	C52C	0151
N5097H	C550	550-0818
N5097H	C560	0376
N5097H	C560	0472
N5097H	C560	0529
N5097H	C560	0548
N5097H	C560	0809
N5097H	C56X	5283
(N5097H)	C560	0275
(N5097H)	C560	0323
N5098F	FA20	197
N5098G	JSTR	5098/28
N5098H	FA20	225/472
N5100J	C525	0146
N5100J	C52A	0161
N5100J	C52B	0486
N5100J	C550	550-0917
N5100J	C560	0276
N5100J	C560	0324
N5100J	C560	0448
N5100J	C560	0754
N5100J	C56X	5150
N5100J	C56X	5205
N5100J	C56X	5265
N5100J	C56X	6040
N5100J	C56X	6127
N5100J	C680	0216
N5100J	C680	0319
N5100J	C750	0068
N5100J	C750	0100
N5101	GLF2	84
N5101	GLF5	550
N5101J	C52A	0354
N5101J	C52A	0519
N5101J	C52B	0111
N5101J	C52B	0243
N5101J	C52B	0290
N5101J	**C52B**	**0497**
N5101J	C52C	0016
N5101J	C52C	0076
N5101J	C550	550-0846
N5101J	C550	550-0905
N5101J	C550	550-0936
N5101J	C560	0379
N5101J	C560	0426
N5101J	C56X	5152
N5101J	C56X	5206
N5101J	C56X	5292
N5101J	C56X	5351
N5101J	C56X	5356
N5101J	C56X	5605
(N5101J)	C560	0277
(N5101J)	C560	0325
N5101T	GLF2	84
N5102	GLF2	85
N5102	GLF5	551
N5102G	LJ60	330
N5103	GLF3	440
(N5103)	GLF3	445
N5103J	C52A	0372
N5103J	C52A	0403
N5103J	C52A	0404
N5103J	C52B	0363
N5103J	C550	550-0932
N5103J	C560	0278
N5103J	C560	0326
N5103J	C560	0380
N5103J	C56X	5216
N5103J	C56X	5271
N5103J	C56X	5553
N5103J	C56X	5608
N5103J	C56X	6020
N5103J	C680	0301
N5103J	C680	0517
N5103J	C680	680A0008
N5103J	C750	0044
N5103J	C750	0085
N5104	GLF3	443
N5104G	PRM1	RB-104
(N5104Z)	C560	0328
N5105	GLF3	445
N5105	SBRL	380-4
N5105A	PRM1	RB-105
N5105F	C525	0551
N5105F	C52C	0030
N5105F	C550	550-0881
N5105F	C550	550-0914
N5105F	C560	0329
N5105F	C560	0427
N5105F	C56X	5153
N5105F	C56X	5229
N5105F	C56X	5289
N5105F	C56X	5696
N5105F	C56X	6036
N5105F	C56X	6152
N5105F	**C56X**	**6217**
N5105F	C680	0074
N5105F	C680	0227
N5105F	C750	0056
(N5105F)	C560	0281
N5106	SBRL	380-6
N5107	**FA50**	**109**
N5107	SBRL	380-8
N5108	SBRL	380-9
N5108G	C52A	0343
N5108G	C52A	0374
N5108G	C52B	0322
N5108G	C550	550-0871
N5108G	C560	0284
N5108G	C560	0387
N5108G	C560	0447
N5108G	C560	0539
N5108G	C56X	5144
N5108G	C56X	5213
N5108G	C56X	5816
N5108G	C680	0036
N5108G	C750	0059
N5108G	**C750**	**0528**
(N5108G)	C560	0332
N5109	C650	0135
N5109	SBRL	380-11
N5109R	C52B	0364
N5109R	C550	550-0873
N5109R	C550	550-0918
N5109R	C550	550-0945
N5109R	C560	0385
N5109R	C560	0416
N5109R	C56X	5200
N5109R	C56X	5248
N5109R	C56X	5562
N5109R	C56X	5773
N5109R	C680	0220
N5109R	C680	0284
N5109R	C750	0045
N5109R	C750	0061
N5109R	C750	0231
N5109R	C750	0249
(N5109R)	C560	0285
(N5109R)	C560	0333
N5109T	SBRL	380-11
N5109W	C52A	0501
N5109W	C52B	0022
N5109W	C52B	0248
N5109W	C52C	0167
N5109W	C550	550-0885
N5109W	C550	550-0920
N5109W	C550	550-1094
N5109W	C550	550-1120
N5109W	C560	0334
N5109W	C56X	5165
N5109W	C56X	5208
N5109W	C56X	5284
N5109W	C56X	5648
N5109W	C750	0019
N5109W	C750	0046
N5109W	C750	0274
N5109W	C750	0304
(N5109W)	C560	0286
N5111	C650	7011
N5111H	JSTR	5111
N5112	C650	7012
N5112	C650	7064
N5112	C750	0010
N5112K	C525	0152
N5112K	C525	0550
N5112K	C525	0613
N5112K	C52B	0303
N5112K	C52C	0066
N5112K	C52C	0127
N5112K	C550	550-0880
N5112K	C560	0418
N5112K	C560	0534
N5112K	C560	0752
N5112K	C56X	5220
N5112K	C56X	5285
N5112K	C650	7085
N5112K	C680	0205
N5112K	C750	0140
(N5112K)	C560	0287
N5112S	C750	0010
N5113	C650	7013
N5113	C750	0013
N5113	GLF4	4013
N5113H	GLF2	107
N5113H	JSTR	5142
N5113S	C750	0013
N5114	C650	0094
N5114	C650	7018
N5114	C750	0017
N5114	GLF4	4016
N5114G	LJ35	181
N5115	C650	0095
N5115	C650	7015
N5115	C750	0018
N5115	GLF4	4019
N5116	C650	0096
N5116	C750	0019
N5116	**GLF4**	**4023**
(N5116)	C750	0022
N5117	C650	7064
N5117	GLF4	4026
N5117F	HS25	258617
N5117H	GLF2	197
N5117U	C525	0626
N5117U	C52A	0207
N5117U	C52A	0238
N5117U	C52B	0223
N5117U	C52B	0378
N5117U	C52C	0211
N5117U	C550	550-0820
N5117U	C550	550-0868
N5117U	C550	550-0912
N5117U	C550	550-0943
N5117U	C550	550-1105
N5117U	C56X	5225
N5117U	C56X	5288
N5117U	C650	7047
N5117U	C650	7069
N5117U	C650	7089
N5117U	C680	0145
N5117U	C680	0303
N5117U	C750	0167
N5118	C650	7013
N5118J	PRM1	RB-138
N5119	C650	7015
N5119	HS25	258177
N5120U	C525	0202
N5120U	C525	0400
N5120U	C525	0447
N5120U	C525	0676
N5120U	C52A	0072
N5120U	C52A	0239
N5120U	C52A	0383
N5120U	C52A	0488
N5120U	C52B	0305
N5120U	C560	0449
N5120U	C56X	6139
N5120U	C650	7049
N5120U	C650	7071
N5120U	C680	0100
N5120U	C750	0058
N5120U	C750	0232
N5121N	C550	550-0824
N5121N	C650	7050
N5121P	PRM1	RB-11
N5122X	C525	0162
N5122X	C525	0203
N5122X	C750	0011
N5123	**FA50**	**123**
N5124F	C525	0382
N5124F	C525	0406
N5124F	C525	0623
N5124F	C52A	0189
N5124F	C52B	0046
N5124F	C52B	0320
N5124F	C52B	0475
N5124F	C560	0392
N5124F	C560	0451
N5124F	C56X	6177
N5124F	C680	0180
N5124F	C680	0511
N5124F	C750	0086
N5125J	C525	0405
N5125J	C525	0542
N5125J	C52A	0062
N5125J	C52A	0074
N5125J	C52A	0511
N5125J	C52B	0164
N5125J	C550	550-1130
N5125J	C560	0479
N5125J	C560	0484
N5125J	C56X	5092
N5125J	C56X	6200
N5125J	C680	0297
N5125J	C680	0325
N5125J	C750	0020
N5125J	C750	0024
N5125J	C750	0291
N5129U	BE40	RK-329
N5130J	C525	0187
N5130J	C525	0365
N5130J	C525	0391
N5130J	C52A	0120
N5130J	C52A	0420
N5130J	C52A	0479
N5130J	C52C	0008
N5130J	C52C	0163
N5130J	C52C	0213
N5130J	C560	0452
N5130J	C56X	5690
N5130J	C56X	6008
N5130J	C680	0037
N5130J	C680	0183
N5130J	C750	0088
N5131M	C750	0021
N5132D	PRM1	RB-32
N5132T	C525	0155
N5132T	C525	0193
N5132T	C525	0394
N5132T	C52A	0029
N5132T	C52A	0086
N5132T	C52A	0148
N5132T	C52A	0323
N5132T	C550	550-1098
N5132T	C560	0453
N5132T	C56X	6101
N5132T	C56X	6141
N5132T	C680	0271
N5132T	C750	0090
N5132T	C750	0273
N5133E	C525	0204
N5133K	C500	299
N5135A	C525	0196
N5135A	C525	0399
N5135A	C525	0451
N5135A	C52A	0063
N5135A	C52A	0122

N5135A	C52C	0077
N5135A	C52C	0200
N5135A	C550	550-0876
N5135A	C56X	5095
N5135A	C56X	5587
N5135A	C56X	5658
N5135A	C680	0010
N5135A	C680	0187
N5135A	C680	0226
N5135A	C680	0295
N5135A	C680	0533
N5135A	C750	0048
N5135K	C525	0089
N5135K	C525	0378
N5135K	C52A	0023
N5135K	C52A	0080
N5135K	C52B	0105
N5135K	C52C	0052
N5135K	C550	550-0801
N5135K	C550	550-0878
N5135K	C560	0454
N5135K	C560	0816
N5135K	C56X	5595
N5135K	**C56X**	**6218**
N5135K	C680	0011
N5135K	C680	0186
N5135K	C680	0225
N5135R	C550	550-0802
N5136J	C525	0090
N5136J	C525	0206
N5136J	C525	0316
N5136J	C525	0346
N5136J	C525	0385
N5136J	C525	0443
N5136J	C52A	0065
N5136J	C52A	0108
N5136J	C52A	0230
N5136J	C52A	0424
N5136J	C52A	0456
N5136J	C52C	0034
N5136J	C52C	0202
N5136J	C56X	5697
N5136J	C680	0013
N5136J	C680	0095
N5136J	C680	0191
N5136J	C680	0344
N5136J	C750	0511
N5136T	BE40	RK-336
N5138F	C525	0091
N5138F	C525	0163
N5138F	C525	0195
N5138J	C52A	0188
N5139W	LJ35	396
N5141F	C525	0436
N5141F	C525	0624
N5141F	C52A	0067
N5141F	C52A	0136
N5141F	C52A	0190
N5141F	C52A	0412
N5141F	C560	0288
N5141F	C56X	5006
N5141F	C56X	5111
N5141F	C56X	5535
N5141F	C56X	5612
N5141F	C56X	6161
N5141F	C650	7072
N5141F	C650	7099
N5141F	C750	0275
N5141T	C52C	0182
N5144	C650	7012
N5144	C750	0017
N5145J	C52B	0109
N5145P	C525	0191
N5145P	C525	0318
N5145P	C525	0347
N5145P	C525	0370
N5145P	C525	0404
N5145P	C52B	0030
N5145P	C52B	0153
N5145P	C550	550-0831
N5145P	C550	550-0833
N5145P	C560	0290
N5145P	C56X	5782
N5145P	C680	0273
N5145P	C680	0308
N5145P	C680	0331
N5145P	C680	0515
N5145U	C52B	0477
N5145V	C525	0278
N5145V	C52A	0506
N5145V	C52B	0156
N5145V	C560	0517
N5145V	C560	0553
N5145V	C56X	5252
N5145V	C56X	5343
N5145V	C56X	5586
N5145V	C56X	5787
N5145V	C56X	6092
N5145V	C680	0281
N5145V	C750	0128
N5147B	C52A	0329
N5147B	**C52C**	**0219**
N5147B	C550	550-0979
N5147B	C56X	5151
N5147B	C56X	6041
N5147B	C56X	6191
N5147B	C680	0055
N5147B	C680	0229
N5147B	C680	0320
N5147B	C750	0104
N5147B	C750	0179
N5147Y	PRM1	RB-47
N5148B	C525	0165
N5148B	C525	0194
N5148B	C525	0384
N5148B	C525	0652
N5148B	C52A	0106
N5148B	C52A	0331
N5148B	C52A	0397
N5148B	C550	550-0832
N5148B	C550	550-1072
N5148B	C550	550-1097
N5148B	C560	0291
N5148B	C650	7104
N5148B	C680	0063
N5148B	C680	680A0024
N5148B	C750	0512
N5148N	C525	0166
N5148N	C525	0319
N5148N	C525	0698
N5148N	C52A	0003
N5148N	C52A	0018
N5148N	C52A	0047
N5148N	C52A	0077
N5148N	C52B	0051
N5148N	C52B	0371
N5148N	C52C	0109
N5148N	C52C	0187
N5148N	**C52C**	**0218**
N5148N	C560	0292
N5148N	C560	0357
N5148N	C56X	5004
N5148N	C56X	5699
N5150K	C560	0403
N5151D	C525	0280
N5151D	C525	0642
N5151D	C52A	0163
N5151D	C52B	0055
N5151D	C52B	0236
N5151D	C52B	0395
N5151D	C560	0546
N5151D	C560	0589
N5151D	C560	0664
N5151D	C56X	5158
N5151D	C56X	6093
N5151S	C525	0093
N5151S	C525	0167
N5151S	C525	0197
N5151S	C560	0349
N5152	FA20	440
N5152	GLF2	22
N5152K	C680	0543
N5152X	C525	0648
N5152X	C52A	0199
N5152X	C52A	0394
N5152X	C52C	0129
N5152X	C52C	0220
N5152X	C560	0492
N5152X	C560	0808
N5152X	C56X	5537
N5152X	C56X	5593
N5152X	C56X	5639
N5152X	C650	7119
N5152X	C680	0545
N5152X	C750	0146
N5152X	C750	0178
N5152X	C750	0207
N5153J	C525	0346
N5153K	C525	0095
N5153K	C525	0169
N5153K	C525	0199
N5153K	C525	0330
N5153K	C525	0449
N5153K	C52A	0221
N5153K	C52A	0345
N5153K	C52A	0389
N5153K	C52C	0044
N5153K	C52C	0108
N5153K	C52C	0155
N5153K	C560	0351
N5153K	C560	0481
N5153K	C56X	5102
N5153K	C56X	5581
N5153K	C56X	6025
N5153K	C750	0049
N5153X	C525	0096
N5153X	C525	0170
N5153X	C525	0208
N5153X	C560	0352
N5153Z	C525	0171
N5153Z	C525	0200
N5153Z	C560	0356
(N5153Z)	C525	0097
N5154J	C525	0281
N5154J	C525	0314
N5154J	C525	0646
N5154J	C52A	0228
N5154J	C52A	0395
N5154J	C52B	0366
N5154J	C52C	0049
N5154J	C550	550-0926
N5154J	C550	550-0990
N5154J	C560	0552
N5154J	C560	0554
N5154J	C56X	5253
N5154J	C56X	6149
N5154J	C680	0266
N5154J	**C680**	**0570**
N5154J	C750	0214
N5155G	C525	0612
N5155G	C52A	0425
N5155G	C52A	0492
N5155G	C52C	0015
N5155G	C550	550-0907
N5155G	C550	550-1009
N5155G	C550	550-1051
N5155G	C560	0555
N5155G	C56X	5156
N5155G	C56X	5649
N5155G	C56X	5766
N5155G	C680	0035
N5155G	C750	0131
N5156B	C525	0172
N5156B	C560	0361
N5156D	C525	0098
N5156D	C525	0201
N5156D	C525	0335
N5156D	C525	0360
N5156D	C525	0389
N5156D	C525	0408
N5156D	C525	0450
N5156D	C52A	0076
N5156D	C52B	0374
N5156D	**C52B**	**0499**
N5156D	C52C	0111
N5156D	C560	0482
N5156D	C560	0651
N5156D	C56X	5547
N5156D	C56X	5761
N5156D	C750	0050
N5156D	C750	0301
N5156V	C525	0099
N5156V	C525	0205
N5156V	C560	0393
N5157E	C525	0174
N5157E	C525	0210
N5157E	C525	0467
N5157E	C525	0554
N5157E	C52A	0070
N5157E	C52A	0313
N5157E	C52A	0361
N5157E	C52A	0472
N5157E	C52B	0380
N5157E	C52B	0489
N5157E	C52C	0164
N5157E	C560	0354
N5157E	C560	0460
N5157E	C56X	5115
N5157E	C56X	5515
N5157E	C56X	5798
N5157E	C56X	6051
N5157E	C650	7101
(N5157E)	C525	0101
N5158B	PRM1	RB-58
N5158D	BE40	RK-358
N5159Y	GLF3	451
N5161J	C525	0176
N5161J	C525	0332
N5161J	C525	0363
N5161J	C525	0412
N5161J	C525	0609
N5161J	C525	0670
N5161J	C52A	0054
N5161J	C52A	0453
N5161J	C52C	0141
N5161J	C560	0294
N5161J	C560	0367
N5161J	C560	0458
N5161J	C560	0497
N5161J	C560	0684
N5161J	C56X	5357
N5161J	C56X	5655
N5161J	C56X	5814
N5161J	C680	680A0040
N5161R	JSTR	5161/43
N5162W	C525	0209
N5162W	C525	0388
N5162W	C52A	0017
N5162W	C52A	0078
N5162W	C52A	0198
N5162W	C52A	0396
N5162W	C52B	0398
N5162W	C550	550-1075
N5162W	C560	0459
N5162W	C560	0661
N5162W	C56X	5609
N5162W	C56X	6066
N5162W	C650	7096
N5162W	C680	0246
(N5162W)	C560	0295
N5162X	C52C	0068
N5163C	C525	0177
N5163C	C525	0324
N5163C	C525	0397
N5163C	C525	0526
N5163C	C52A	0055
N5163C	C52A	0118
N5163C	C52A	0431
N5163C	C52B	0249
N5163C	C560	0358
N5163C	C56X	5538
N5163C	C56X	6193
N5163C	C650	7087
N5163C	C680	0075
N5163C	C750	0065
N5163C	C750	0280
N5163C	C750	0508
(N5163C)	C560	0296
N5163G	C56X	5157
N5163K	C525	0633
N5163K	C52B	0015
N5163K	C52B	0042
N5163K	C52B	0267
N5163K	C52B	0310
N5163K	C52C	0069
N5163K	C52C	0130
N5163K	C56X	5159
N5163K	C680	0178
N5163K	C750	0188
N5165P	C52A	0410
N5165P	C52B	0479
N5165P	C550	550-0998
N5165P	C550	550-1111
N5165P	C550	550-1132
N5165P	C560	0556
N5165P	C56X	5336
N5165P	C56X	5534
N5165P	C680	0508
N5165P	C750	0270
N5165P	C750	0310
N5165T	C525	0340
N5165T	C525	0371
N5165T	C525	0392
N5165T	C52A	0022
N5165T	C52A	0073
N5165T	C52A	0243
N5165T	C52A	0316
N5165T	C52A	0414
N5165T	C52A	0437
N5165T	C560	0297
N5165T	C56X	5003
N5165T	C56X	5087
N5165T	C56X	5543
N5165T	C56X	5722
N5165T	C56X	6079
N5165T	C680	0348
N5165T	C750	0080
N5166T	C52A	0196
N5166T	C52B	0083
N5166T	C550	550-0906
N5166T	C550	550-1020
N5166T	C560	0494
N5166T	C560	0590
N5166T	C560	0692
N5166T	C56X	5163
N5166T	C56X	5695
N5166T	C680	0224
N5166T	C750	0217
N5166U	C525	0179
N5166U	C525	0215
N5166U	C52B	0490
N5166U	C52C	0140
N5166U	C550	550-1013
N5166U	C560	0298
N5166U	C560	0359
N5166U	C56X	5164
N5166U	C56X	5554
N5166U	C680	0069
N5166U	C750	0222
N5168F	C525	0180
N5168F	C525	0213
N5168F	C560	0299
N5168F	C560	0360
N5168Y	C52A	0380
N5168Y	C52B	0147
N5168Y	C52C	0104
N5168Y	**C52C**	**0222**
N5168Y	C550	550-0958
N5168Y	C550	550-0976
N5168Y	C550	550-1022
N5168Y	C56X	5548
N5168Y	C680	0054
N5168Y	C750	0294
N5171M	C550	550-1086
N5172M	C525	0540
N5172M	C52B	0171
N5172M	C550	550-0959
N5172M	C550	550-0977
N5172M	C550	550-1025
N5172M	C560	0695
N5172M	C650	7111
N5172M	C680	0079
N5172M	C680	0135
N5172M	C680	0299
N5172M	C680	0349
N5172M	C750	0142
N5172M	C750	0522
N5173F	C56X	5173
N5174	C650	7018
N5174W	C52A	0227
N5174W	C52B	0235
N5174W	C52B	0281
N5174W	C52B	0456
N5174W	C52C	0098
N5174W	C550	550-0988
N5174W	C550	550-1021
N5174W	C560	0558
N5174W	C560	0764
N5174W	C650	7112
N5174W	C680	0181
N5174W	C680	680A0033
N5174W	C750	0145
N5180C	C52A	0155
N5180C	C52A	0405
N5180C	C52A	0459
N5180C	C52B	0472
N5180C	C52C	0216
N5180C	C550	550-1037
N5180C	C550	550-1082
N5180C	C550	550-1099
N5180C	C550	550-1135
N5180C	C560	0560
N5180C	C560	0592
N5180C	C56X	5594
N5180C	C680	0167
N5180C	C680	0323
N5180K	C525	0181
N5180K	C525	0533
N5180K	C52A	0306
N5180K	C52A	0450
N5180K	C52B	0158
N5180K	C52B	0208
N5180K	C52B	0259
N5180K	C52C	0070
N5180K	C550	550-1026
N5180K	C560	0301
N5180K	C560	0363
N5180K	C560	0562
N5180K	C560	0630
N5180K	C56X	5677
N5180K	C56X	6143
N5181U	C52A	0369
N5181U	C52B	0255
N5181U	C52B	0349
N5181U	C52B	0466
N5181U	C52C	0061
N5181U	C550	550-0961
N5181U	C550	550-1008
N5181U	C550	550-1108
N5181U	C560	0537
N5181U	C56X	5596
N5181U	C56X	5642
N5181U	C680	680A0037
N5181U	C750	0205
N5183U	C525	0182
N5183U	C525	0326
N5183U	C525	0361
N5183U	C525	0395
N5183U	C525	0420
N5183U	C525	0604
N5183U	C52A	0048
N5183U	C52A	0193
N5183U	C560	0362
N5183U	C560	0462
N5183U	C56X	5668
N5183U	C650	7052
N5183U	C680	0314
N5183U	C680	0505
N5183U	**C680**	**0564**
N5183U	C750	0238
N5183V	C525	0216
N5183V	C525	0254
N5183V	C525	0398
N5183V	C525	0455
N5183V	C52A	0082
N5183V	C52A	0433
N5183V	C52B	0043
N5183V	C560	0469
N5183V	C56X	5091
N5183V	C56X	5652
N5183V	C650	7074
N5183V	C680	0029
N5183V	C680	0302
N5183V	C750	0287
(N5183V)	C650	7053
N5184U	**EA40**	**SE-400-001**
N5185J	C525	0183
N5185J	C525	0333
N5185J	C525	0368
N5185J	C525	0381
N5185J	C525	0413
N5185J	C525	0456
N5185J	C52A	0085
N5185J	C52A	0464
N5185J	C52B	0180
N5185J	C52B	0229
N5185J	C550	550-0837
N5185J	C56X	5633
N5185J	C650	7054
N5185J	C680	0247
N5185J	C680	0328
N5185J	C680	0512
N5185V	C525	0184
N5185V	C525	0345
N5185V	C525	0352
N5185V	C525	0437
N5185V	C525	0460
N5185V	C52B	0143
N5185V	C52B	0327
N5185V	C52C	0058
N5185V	C560	0461
N5185V	C560	0779
N5185V	C56X	5105
N5185V	C650	7055
N5187B	C525	0185

N5187Z	C525	0442
N5188A	C525	0379
N5188A	C525	0425
N5188A	C525	0458
N5188A	C525	0605
N5188A	C52A	0320
N5188A	C52A	0521
N5188A	C52B	0213
N5188A	C52C	0093
N5188A	C550	550-0854
N5188A	C560	0471
N5188A	C560	0686
N5188A	C560	0805
N5188A	C650	7106
N5188A	**C680**	**680A0025**
N5188N	C525	0239
N5188N	C525	0546
N5188N	C52A	0308
N5188N	C52B	0103
N5188N	C52B	0176
N5188N	C52C	0080
N5188N	C52C	0117
N5188N	C56X	5167
N5188N	C680	0019
N5188N	C680	0121
N5188N	C680	0300
N5188N	C750	0186
N5188W	C52A	0147
N5188W	C680	0214
"N5188W"	C52A	0204
"N5188W"	C52B	0027
"N5188W"	C56X	5640
N5192E	C52B	0104
N5192E	C52C	0191
N5192E	C550	550-0997
N5192E	C560	0559
N5192E	C56X	5667
N5192E	C56X	5727
N5192E	C56X	6048
N5192E	C56X	6107
N5192E	C650	7113
N5192E	C680	0309
N5192E	C680	680A0043
N5192E	C750	0194
N5192E	C750	0219
N5192E	C750	0506
N5192U	C52A	0380
N5194B	C52A	0240
N5194B	C52B	0269
N5194B	C52B	0311
N5194B	C52B	0467
N5194B	C52C	0215
N5194B	C550	550-0874
N5194B	C550	550-1000
N5194B	C56X	5256
N5194B	C56X	5526
N5194B	C56X	5572
N5194B	C56X	6085
N5194B	C56X	6124
N5194B	C56X	6156
N5194B	C650	7114
N5194B	C680	0182
N5194J	C525	0270
N5194J	C52A	0010
N5194J	C52A	0027
N5194J	C52A	0053
N5194J	C52B	0125
N5194J	C52B	0233
N5194J	C52B	0348
N5194J	C560	0368
N5194J	C56X	5064
N5194J	C56X	5320
N5194J	C680	0254
N5194J	C680	680A0006
N5194J	C750	0242
N5196U	C525	0634
N5196U	C52B	0375
N5196U	C52B	0460
N5196U	C560	0806
N5196U	C56X	5226
N5196U	C56X	5257
N5196U	C56X	5322
N5196U	C56X	5565
N5196U	C680	680A0031
N5196U	C750	0075
N5196U	C750	0139
N5197A	C525	0219
N5197A	C525	0260
N5197A	C525	0426
N5197A	C525	0462
N5197A	C52A	0356
N5197A	C52A	0462
N5197A	C52B	0090
N5197A	C52B	0189
N5197A	C52B	0280
N5197A	C560	0401
N5197A	C560	0622
N5197A	C56X	5062
N5197A	C56X	5119
N5197A	C56X	5369
N5197A	C56X	5568
N5197M	C52A	0363
N5197M	C52B	0351
N5197M	C52C	0062
N5197M	C52C	0153
N5197M	C560	0561
N5197M	C56X	5227
N5197M	C56X	5557
N5197M	C56X	5590
N5197M	C56X	5626
N5197M	C680	0202
N5197M	C680	0268
N5197M	C750	0076
N5197M	C750	0204
N5197M	C750	0237
N5197M	C750	0241
N5200	C560	0369
N5200	**F2TH**	**90**
N5200R	C525	0144
N5200R	C525	0441
N5200R	C525	0479
N5200R	C525	0669
N5200R	C52A	0434
N5200R	C52C	0026
N5200R	C560	0665
N5200R	C56X	5007
N5200R	C56X	5061
N5200R	C56X	6110
N5200R	C680	0091
N5200R	C750	0272
N5200R	C750	0504
N5200U	C525	0369
N5200U	C525	0463
N5200U	C525	0487
N5200U	C525	0543
N5200U	C52B	0054
N5200U	C52C	0071
N5200U	C560	0402
N5200U	C56X	5063
N5200U	C56X	5135
N5200U	C56X	6006
N5200U	C56X	6144
N5200U	C56X	6185
N5200U	C680	0041
N5200Z	C525	0439
N5200Z	C525	0466
N5200Z	C525	0499
N5200Z	C52A	0344
N5200Z	C52B	0493
N5200Z	C52C	0045
N5200Z	C560	0814
N5200Z	C56X	5110
N5200Z	C56X	5355
N5200Z	C56X	5792
N5200Z	C680	0021
N5200Z	C680	0096
N5200Z	C680	0179
N5201J	C525	0267
N5201J	C525	0423
N5201J	C525	0498
N5201J	C52B	0025
N5201J	C52B	0160
N5201J	C52B	0215
N5201J	C52B	0274
N5201J	C52B	0350
N5201J	C52C	0099
N5201J	C560	0403
N5201J	C56X	5060
N5201J	C56X	5123
N5201J	C56X	5541
N5201J	C56X	5617
N5201J	C680	0278
N5201J	C750	0510
N5201M	C525	0116
N5201M	C525	0473
N5201M	C525	0639
N5201M	C525	0695
N5201M	C52A	0013
N5201M	C52B	0218
N5201M	C52B	0381
N5201M	C52C	0014
N5201M	C52C	0225
N5201M	C550	550-1083
N5201M	C550	550-1133
N5201M	C560	0404
N5201M	C56X	5026
N5201M	C56X	5069
N5201M	C680	0251
N5201M	C750	0266
N5201M	C750	0514
N5201M	C750	0518
N5202D	C525	0217
N5202D	C525	0427
N5202D	C525	0524
N5202D	C52A	0056
N5202D	C52A	0482
N5202D	C52A	0514
N5202D	C52B	0195
N5202D	C550	550-1112
N5202D	C560	0405
N5202D	C56X	5027
N5202D	C56X	5096
N5202D	C56X	5669
N5202D	C56X	6038
N5202D	C650	0241
N5202D	C680	0085
N5202D	**C680**	**0567**
N5203B	C525	0417
N5203J	C525	0117
N5203J	C525	0258
N5203J	C525	0428
N5203J	C525	0493
N5203J	C52B	0396
N5203J	C560	0678
N5203J	C56X	5028
N5203J	C56X	5078
N5203J	C56X	5809
N5203J	C56X	6094
N5203J	C650	7077
N5203J	C680	0052
N5203J	C680	0282
N5203J	C750	0278
N5203S	C525	0118
N5203S	C525	0221
N5203S	C525	0238
N5203S	C52A	0026
N5203S	C52A	0123
N5203S	C52A	0200
N5203S	C52B	0124
N5203S	C52B	0178
N5203S	C52C	0139
N5203S	C550	550-1100
N5203S	C560	0406
N5203S	C56X	5029
N5203S	C56X	5093
N5203S	C680	0045
N5203S	C680	0067
N5203S	C680	0196
N5203S	C680	0265
N5204B	C525	0134
N5204D	C525	0103
N5204D	C525	0481
N5204D	C52A	0006
N5204D	C52A	0031
N5204D	C52A	0128
N5204D	C52C	0149
N5204D	C560	0407
N5204D	**C560**	**0682**
N5204D	C560	0810
N5204D	C56X	5008
N5204D	C56X	5065
N5204D	C56X	5780
N5204D	C680	0151
N5204D	C680	0342
N5206T	C525	0631
N5206T	C52B	0334
N5206T	C52B	0470
N5206T	C550	550-1041
N5206T	C560	0602
N5206T	C56X	5614
N5206T	C680	0255
N5206T	C680	0530
N5206T	C750	0154
N5207A	C525	0104
N5207A	C525	0135
N5207A	C525	0461
N5207A	C525	0684
N5207A	C52A	0016
N5207A	C52A	0142
N5207A	C52A	0463
N5207A	C52B	0004
N5207A	C52B	0076
N5207A	C52B	0115
N5207A	C560	0408
N5207A	C560	0438
N5207A	C560	0617
N5207A	C560	0773
N5207A	C56X	5070
N5207A	C56X	5124
N5207A	C56X	6147
N5207A	C680	0060
N5207A	C750	0521
N5207V	C52B	0295
N5207V	C52C	0053
N5207V	C52C	0206
N5207V	C550	550-0910
N5207V	C560	0577
N5207V	C560	0687
N5207V	C56X	5672
N5207V	C56X	6151
N5207V	C680	0195
N5208F	C52A	0063
N5208J	C52B	0480
N5209E	C525	0295
N5209E	C560	0532
N5211A	C525	0106
N5211A	C525	0137
N5211A	C525	0446
N5211A	C525	0486
N5211A	C525	0531
N5211A	C52A	0127
N5211A	C52A	0231
N5211A	C52A	0311
N5211A	C52B	0120
N5211A	C52B	0179
N5211A	C52B	0227
N5211A	C560	0410
N5211A	C560	0565
N5211A	C56X	5084
N5211A	C56X	6015
N5211A	C56X	6081
N5211A	**C56X**	**6216**
N5211F	C525	0107
N5211F	C525	0138
N5211F	C525	0225
N5211F	C525	0364
N5211F	C525	0484
N5211F	C52A	0034
N5211F	C52A	0132
N5211F	C52A	0217
N5211F	C52A	0377
N5211F	C52A	0411
N5211F	C52C	0195
N5211F	C56X	5122
N5211F	C56X	5571
N5211F	C56X	6114
N5211Q	C525	0108
N5211Q	C525	0223
N5211Q	C525	0353
N5211Q	C525	0453
N5211Q	C525	0482
N5211Q	C525	0527
N5211Q	C525	0547
N5211Q	C52A	0135
N5211Q	C52C	0005
N5211Q	C52C	0082
N5211Q	**C52C**	**0229**
N5211Q	C550	550-1122
N5211Q	C560	0775
N5211Q	C56X	5033
N5211Q	C56X	5120
N5211Q	C56X	5662
N5211Q	C56X	5789
N5211Q	C680	680A0015
N5212M	C525	0409
N5212M	C525	0511
N5212M	C52A	0494
N5212M	C52B	0117
N5212M	C550	550-0962
N5212M	C550	550-1006
N5212M	C550	550-1109
N5212M	C550	550-1123
N5212M	C560	0662
N5212M	C56X	6067
N5212M	C56X	6133
N5212M	C650	7098
N5212M	C680	0174
N5212M	C680	0259
N5213K	C52B	0277
N5213S	C525	0110
N5213S	C525	0356
N5213S	C52A	0007
N5213S	C52A	0305
N5213S	C52B	0102
N5213S	C56X	5035
N5213S	C56X	5567
N5213S	C56X	6111
N5213S	C56X	6190
N5213S	C56X	6211
N5213S	C650	7076
N5214J	C525	0112
N5214J	C525	0226
N5214J	C525	0245
N5214J	C525	0357
N5214J	C52A	0061
N5214J	C52A	0378
N5214J	C52B	0091
N5214J	C52B	0254
N5214J	C52B	0389
N5214J	C52B	0405
N5214J	**C52C**	**0226**
N5214J	C550	550-0804
N5214J	C56X	5037
N5214J	C56X	5129
N5214J	C680	0059
N5214J	C750	0243
N5214K	C525	0113
N5214K	C525	0227
N5214K	C525	0641
N5214K	C525	0693
N5214K	C52A	0117
N5214K	C52A	0210
N5214K	C52A	0490
N5214K	C52A	0516
N5214K	C52B	0095
N5214K	C52B	0234
N5214K	C52B	0276
N5214K	C550	550-0805
N5214K	C56X	5038
N5214K	C56X	5073
N5214K	C56X	5125
N5214K	C56X	6199
N5214K	C750	0246
N5214L	C525	0114
N5214L	C525	0249
N5214L	C525	0362
N5214L	C525	0555
N5214L	C52A	0045
N5214L	C52A	0466
N5214L	C52A	0486
N5214L	C52B	0072
N5214L	C52B	0192
N5214L	C52B	0485
N5214L	C550	550-0822
N5214L	C550	550-1102
N5214L	C560	0374
N5214L	C560	0639
N5214L	C560	0657
N5214L	C560	0668
N5214L	C560	0798
N5214L	C56X	5040
N5214L	C56X	5118
N5214L	C56X	6137
N5214L	C680	0064
N5216A	C525	0228
N5216A	C525	0342
N5216A	C525	0477
N5216A	C525	0548
N5216A	C52A	0024
N5216A	C52A	0093
N5216A	C52B	0097
N5216A	C52B	0104
N5216A	C52B	0296
N5216A	C52C	0022
N5216A	C550	550-0808
N5216A	C560	0669
N5216A	C560	0698
N5216A	C560	0777
N5216A	C56X	5013
N5216A	C56X	5101
N5216A	C56X	5366
N5216A	C650	7057
N5216A	C680	0519
N5218R	C525	0149
N5218R	C525	0229
N5218R	C525	0488
N5218R	C52A	0103
N5218R	C52A	0166
N5218R	C52A	0384
N5218R	C52B	0266
N5218R	C52B	0309
N5218R	C550	550-1113
N5218R	C560	0755
N5218R	C56X	5043
N5218R	C56X	5103
N5218R	C56X	6076
N5218R	C650	7059
N5218R	C680	0333
N5218R	C680	0525
N5218T	C525	0230
N5218T	C525	0489
N5218T	C525	0607
N5218T	C52A	0028
N5218T	C52A	0181
N5218T	C52A	0495
N5218T	C52B	0106
N5218T	C52B	0108
N5218T	C52C	0029
N5218T	C550	550-0810
N5218T	C560	0690
N5218T	C56X	5044
N5218T	C56X	5079
N5218T	C56X	6034
N5218T	C56X	6171
N5218T	C650	7060
N5218T	C680	0162
N5218T	C680	680A0010
N5219T	C525	0269
N5220J	C500	220
N5221Y	C52A	0037
N5221Y	C52A	0095
N5221Y	C52B	0024
N5221Y	C52B	0045
N5221Y	C52B	0074
N5221Y	C52C	0036
N5221Y	**C52C**	**0228**
N5221Y	C550	550-0811
N5221Y	C56X	5014
N5221Y	C56X	5045
N5221Y	C56X	5106
N5221Y	C56X	5681
N5221Y	C56X	5742
N5221Y	C56X	6192
N5221Y	C650	7061
N5221Y	C680	0245
N5221Y	C750	0283
N5223D	C525	0231
N5223D	C525	0433
N5223D	C52A	0096
N5223D	C52B	0384
N5223D	C560	0776
N5223D	C56X	5015
N5223D	C56X	5046
N5223D	C56X	5104
N5223D	C56X	5790
N5223D	C680	0066
N5223D	C680	0114
N5223D	C680	0276
N5223D	**C680**	**680A0051**
N5223D	C750	0003
N5223D	C750	0225
N5223F	C510	0135
N5223J	C500	188
N5223J	C56X	6075
N5223K	C525	0498
N5223P	C525	0123
N5223P	C525	0253
N5223P	C525	0414
N5223P	C525	0496
N5223P	C52A	0039
N5223P	C52A	0099
N5223P	C52A	0229
N5223P	C52A	0326
N5223P	C550	550-0812
N5223P	C56X	5047
N5223P	C56X	5114
N5223P	C56X	5342
N5223P	C56X	5646
N5223P	C56X	6201
N5223P	C680	0031
N5223P	C680	0153
N5223P	C680	0201
N5223P	C750	0004
(N5223P)	C525	0252
N5223X	C550	550-1032

N5223X	C550	550-1115
N5223X	C560	0778
N5223X	C56X	5174
N5223X	C56X	5645
N5223X	C56X	6021
N5223X	C56X	6071
N5223X	C650	7102
N5223X	C750	0119
N5223X	C750	0185
N5223X	C750	0218
N5223Y	C525	0232
N5223Y	C525	0366
N5223Y	C525	0480
N5223Y	C52A	0030
N5223Y	C52A	0098
N5223Y	C52A	0483
N5223Y	C52A	0515
N5223Y	C52B	0261
N5223Y	C550	550-1114
N5223Y	C56X	5049
N5223Y	C56X	5121
N5223Y	C56X	5504
N5223Y	C56X	6033
N5223Y	**C680**	**680A0048**
N5223Y	C750	0009
(N5223Y)	C560	0302
N5225G	FA20	181
N5225J	C500	225
N5225K	C525	0339
N5225K	C525	0354
N5225K	C525	0375
N5225K	C525	0454
N5225K	C525	0508
N5225K	C52A	0407
N5225K	C52A	0415
N5225K	C550	550-0816
N5225K	C560	0303
N5225K	C56X	5050
N5225K	C56X	5132
N5225K	C56X	5637
N5225K	C56X	6132
N5225K	C680	0116
N5225K	C680	0523
N5225K	C750	0010
N5225K	C750	0309
N5226B	C525	0434
N5226B	C525	0492
N5226B	C52A	0212
N5226B	C52A	0327
N5226B	C52B	0063
N5226B	C52B	0241
N5226B	C52B	0289
N5226B	C52B	0318
N5226B	C560	0304
N5226B	C560	0411
N5226B	C560	0442
N5226B	C56X	5051
N5226B	C56X	5097
N5226B	C56X	5563
N5226B	C56X	6084
N5226B	C56X	6123
N5226B	C56X	6155
N5226B	C680	0157
N5226J	C500	226
N5227G	C52B	0006
N5227G	C52B	0242
N5227G	C52C	0201
N5227G	C550	550-0984
N5227G	C550	550-1131
N5227G	C56X	5709
N5227G	C56X	6074
N5227G	C56X	6121
N5227G	C680	0261
N5228J	C52B	0173
N5228J	C52C	0042
N5228J	C52C	0106
N5228J	C550	550-0969
N5228J	C550	550-1010
N5228J	C560	0632
N5228J	C56X	5597
N5228J	C56X	5651
N5228J	C56X	5822
N5228J	C680	0551
N5228J	C750	0237
N5228Z	C525	0380
N5228Z	C525	0643
N5228Z	C52A	0139
N5228Z	C52A	0324
N5228Z	C52B	0013
N5228Z	C52B	0209
N5228Z	C52B	0273
N5228Z	C52C	0018
N5228Z	C560	0305
N5228Z	C560	0412
N5228Z	C560	0443
N5228Z	C56X	5052
N5228Z	C56X	5128
N5228Z	C56X	6122
N5228Z	C680	680A0023
N5230J	C500	230
(N5231J)	C500	231
N5231S	C525	0383
N5231S	C525	0424
N5231S	C52A	0330
N5231S	C52B	0069
N5231S	C550	550-1019
N5231S	C550	550-1047
N5231S	C560	0306
N5231S	C560	0384
N5231S	C560	0433
N5231S	C56X	5053
N5231S	C56X	5552
N5231S	C56X	6064
N5231S	C680	0184
N5231S	C680	0250
N5231S	C680	0334
N5232J	C500	232
N5233J	C500	233
N5233J	C525	0440
N5233J	C525	0478
N5233J	C52A	0116
N5233J	**C52B**	**0498**
N5233J	C550	550-1126
N5233J	C550	660
N5233J	C560	0307
N5233J	C560	0413
N5233J	C560	0419
N5233J	C56X	5054
N5233J	C56X	5117
N5233J	C56X	5765
N5233J	C56X	6019
N5233J	C680	0004
N5233J	C680	0043
N5233J	C680	0124
N5233J	C750	0502
N5233P	C52A	0153
(N5234J)	C500	234
N5235G	C525	0233
N5235G	C525	0259
N5235G	C525	0497
N5235G	C52A	0005
N5235G	C52A	0009
N5235G	C52A	0038
N5235G	C52A	0400
N5235G	C52A	0444
N5235G	C52A	0500
N5235G	C560	0308
N5235G	C560	0365
N5235G	C560	0414
N5235G	C56X	5058
N5235G	C56X	5358
N5235G	C680	0107
N5235G	C680	0156
N5235G	C680	0316
N5235G	**C680**	**680A0039**
N5235J	C500	235
N5236J	C500	236
N5236L	C525	0625
N5236L	C52A	0233
N5236L	C52B	0404
N5236L	C52C	0083
N5236L	C560	0603
N5236L	C56X	5171
N5236L	C56X	5719
N5236M	C680	0540
(N5237J)	C500	237
N5237R	**E50P**	**50000314**
(N5238J)	C500	238
N5239J	C52A	0307
N5239J	C52B	0007
N5239J	C52B	0057
N5239J	C52B	0181
N5239J	C52C	0085
N5239J	C550	550-0971
N5239J	C550	550-1054
N5239J	C560	0601
N5239J	C680	680A0014
(N5239J)	C500	239
N5240J	C500	240
N5241J	C500	241
N5241R	C525	0635
N5241R	C52A	0513
N5241R	C52B	0458
N5241R	C560	0564
N5241R	C56X	5664
N5241R	C56X	5758
N5241R	C56X	6030
N5241R	C56X	6088
N5241R	C680	0024
N5241R	C680	0040
N5241R	**C680**	**680A0034**
N5241R	C750	0195
N5241Z	C525	0337
N5241Z	C525	0377
N5241Z	C525	0673
N5241Z	C52A	0044
N5241Z	C52A	0205
N5241Z	C52A	0382
N5241Z	C52A	0471
N5241Z	C52B	0292
N5241Z	C52B	0372
N5241Z	C52C	0110
N5241Z	C560	0310
N5241Z	C560	0691
N5241Z	C560	0769
N5241Z	C750	0013
N5241Z	C750	0138
N5242J	C500	242
N5243J	C500	243
N5243K	C52A	0165
N5243K	C52B	0033
N5243K	C52B	0182
N5243K	C52B	0219
N5243K	C52C	0086
N5243K	C550	550-0970
N5243K	C560	0588
N5243K	C560	0670
N5243K	C680	680A0018
N5244F	C525	0343
N5244F	C525	0435
N5244F	C525	0491
N5244F	C525	0530
N5244F	C525	0661
N5244F	C52B	0036
N5244F	C52B	0247
N5244F	**C52B**	**0496**
N5244F	C52C	0094
N5244F	C52C	0197
N5244F	C560	0772
N5244F	C56X	5021
N5244F	C56X	5098
N5244F	C56X	5623
N5244F	C680	0310
N5244F	C750	0014
N5244F	C750	0303
(N5244F)	C560	0311
(N5244J)	C500	244
N5244W	C525	0663
N5244W	C52A	0213
N5244W	C52B	0116
N5244W	C52B	0264
N5244W	C52C	0050
N5244W	C52C	0123
N5244W	C52C	0169
N5244W	C550	550-0993
N5244W	C560	0571
N5244W	C56X	5603
N5245D	C52A	0232
N5245D	C52A	0300
N5245D	C52A	0476
N5245D	C52B	0397
N5245D	C56X	5266
N5245D	C56X	5352
N5245D	C56X	5625
N5245D	C56X	6099
N5245D	C56X	6142
N5245D	C56X	6187
N5245D	C680	0189
N5245D	C750	0159
N5245J	C500	245
N5245L	C52A	0451
N5245L	C52A	0497
N5245L	C52C	0009
N5245L	C560	0680
N5245L	C560	0760
N5245L	C56X	6173
N5245L	C750	0161
N5245L	C750	0199
N5245L	C750	0286
N5245U	C525	0682
N5245U	C52B	0250
N5245U	C52C	0121
N5245U	C550	550-0973
N5245U	C550	550-1057
N5245U	C560	0606
N5245U	C560	0673
N5245U	C560	0765
N5245U	C56X	5576
N5245U	C680	0020
N5245U	C680	0093
N5245U	C680	0305
(N5246J)	C500	246
N5246Z	C525	0140
N5246Z	C525	0235
N5246Z	C525	0351
N5246Z	C525	0495
N5246Z	C52A	0036
N5246Z	C52C	0207
N5246Z	C560	0313
N5246Z	C56X	5020
N5246Z	C56X	5116
N5246Z	C56X	5267
N5246Z	C56X	5619
N5246Z	C56X	5748
N5246Z	C680	0241
N5246Z	C750	0236
N5246Z	C750	0312
(N5247J)	C500	247
N5247U	C52A	0186
N5247U	C52A	0219
N5247U	C52A	0508
N5247U	C52B	0231
N5247U	C52B	0367
N5247U	C550	550-1005
N5247U	C560	0767
N5247U	C560	0803
N5247U	C56X	5660
N5247U	C680	0289
N5247U	C750	0211
N5248B	C560	0688
(N5248J)	C500	248
N5248V	C525	0602
N5248V	C52A	0408
N5248V	C560	0648
N5248V	C560	0704
N5248V	C56X	6046
N5248V	C56X	6086
N5248V	C56X	6106
N5248V	C56X	6194
N5248V	C680	0017
N5248V	**C680**	**680A0044**
N5248V	C750	0169
N5248V	C750	0507
N5249J	C500	249
N5250E	C525	0141
N5250E	C525	0415
N5250E	C525	0483
N5250E	C525	0557
N5250E	C525	0678
N5250E	C52A	0032
N5250E	C52B	0216
N5250E	C560	0314
N5250E	C56X	5018
N5250E	C56X	5353
N5250E	C56X	5703
N5250E	C680	0084
(N5250E)	C56X	5134
(N5250J)	C500	250
N5250K	C560	0264
(N5250K)	C560	0315
N5250P	C525	0701
N5250P	C52B	0060
N5250P	C52B	0169
N5250P	C52B	0224
N5250P	C52C	0105
N5250P	C560	0598
N5250P	C56X	6032
N5250P	C680	0115
N5251F	C510	0294
N5251J	C500	251
(N5251Y)	C560	0316
N5252	C52A	0002
N5252C	C550	661
N5252J	C500	252
N5253A	C500	304
N5253A	GLF2	222
N5253A	HS25	256061
N5253E	C500	304
N5253G	C560	0672
N5253J	C500	253
N5253S	C52C	0038
N5253S	C550	550-1015
N5253S	C550	550-1048
N5253S	C56X	5579
N5253S	C56X	5707
N5253S	C56X	6004
N5253S	C750	0163
N5253Z	C52C	0096
N5254C	**C52C**	**0063**
N5254J	C500	254
N5254Y	C52C	0122
N5254Y	C550	550-1024
N5254Y	C560	0585
N5254Y	C560	0634
N5254Y	C56X	5527
N5254Y	C56X	5710
N5254Y	C56X	6062
N5254Y	C680	0072
N5255B	**C525**	**0231**
N5255J	C500	255
N5256Z	C56X	5683
N5257C	C560	0575
N5257C	C560	0605
N5257C	C560	0635
N5257C	C560	0785
N5257C	C56X	5653
N5257C	C680	0143
N5257C	C680	0262
N5257C	C750	0247
N5257J	C500	257
N5257V	C52A	0185
N5257V	C52A	0436
N5257V	C52B	0119
N5257V	C52B	0345
N5257V	C560	0624
N5257V	C56X	6120
N5257V	C56X	6206
N5257V	C680	0050
N5257V	C680	0193
N5257V	C750	0165
(N5258J)	C500	258
N5259J	C500	259
N5259Y	C525	0065
N5259Y	C52A	0236
N5259Y	C52B	0093
N5259Y	C550	550-1018
N5259Y	C560	0579
N5259Y	C560	0788
N5259Y	C56X	5685
N5259Y	C56X	5788
N5259Y	C680	0341
(N5260J)	C500	260
N5260M	C52A	0303
N5260M	C52B	0325
N5260M	C52C	0088
N5260M	C560	0593
N5260M	C560	0627
N5260M	C56X	5723
N5260M	C680	0046
N5260M	C680	0119
N5260U	C52B	0370
N5260U	C52B	0394
N5260U	C550	550-0982
N5260U	C560	0612
N5260U	C560	0646
N5260U	C56X	5725
N5260U	C56X	5785
N5260U	C680	0034
N5260Y	C52A	0350
N5260Y	C52B	0201
N5260Y	C52B	0308
N5260Y	C52C	0046
N5260Y	C550	550-0934
N5260Y	C560	0364
N5260Y	C560	0650
N5260Y	C56X	6167
N5260Y	C680	0026
N5260Y	C750	0103
N5260Y	C750	0260
N5261J	C500	261
N5261R	C525	0537
N5261R	C52A	0524
N5261R	C52B	0149
N5261R	C560	0318
N5261R	C56X	5578
N5261R	C56X	5629
N5261R	C56X	6042
N5261R	C56X	6205
N5261R	C680	0335
N5262	**CL30**	**20122**
N5262B	C52B	0152
N5262B	C52B	0193
N5262B	C52B	0265
N5262B	C52B	0385
N5262B	C560	0320
N5262B	C560	0370
N5262J	C500	262
N5262W	C52A	0169
N5262W	C52B	0207
N5262W	C52B	0258
N5262W	C52C	0144
N5262W	C560	0321
N5262W	C560	0570
N5262W	C56X	5589
N5262W	C56X	5632
N5262W	C56X	6058
N5262W	C56X	6212
N5262W	C680	0287
N5262W	C680	0546
N5262W	C750	0268
N5262X	C52A	0347
N5262X	C52B	0197
N5262X	C550	550-0933
N5262X	C550	550-1125
N5262X	C560	0322
N5262X	C560	0371
N5262X	C56X	5529
N5262X	C750	0226
N5262Z	C56X	6059
N5262Z	**C56X**	**6221**
N5262Z	C650	7062
N5262Z	C680	680A0017
N5262Z	C750	0265
N5263	**C560**	**0435**
N5263D	C525	0689
N5263D	C52A	0475
N5263D	C52C	0064
N5263D	C550	550-1093
N5263D	C56X	5802
N5263D	C56X	6164
N5263D	C650	7066
N5263D	C650	7117
N5263D	C680	0094
N5263D	C680	0169
N5263D	C750	0519
N5263S	C52B	0064
N5263S	C52B	0361
N5263S	C550	550-0940
N5263S	C560	0638
N5263S	C56X	5679
N5263S	C56X	5774
N5263S	C680	0558
N5263S	C750	0005
(N5263S)	C650	7067
N5263U	C525	0507
N5263U	C52A	0237
N5263U	C52A	0402
N5263U	C52B	0113
N5263U	C52C	0032
N5263U	C56X	5724
N5263U	C56X	6153
N5263U	C750	0006
N5263U	C750	0016
N5264A	C52A	0481
N5264A	C550	550-0935
N5264A	C560	0377
N5264A	C56X	5525
N5264A	C56X	5598
N5264A	C56X	5728
N5264A	C56X	5793
N5264A	C680	0279
N5264A	C750	0111
N5264E	C550	550-0948
N5264E	C56X	5620
N5264E	C56X	5691
N5264E	C680	0028
N5264E	C680	0311
N5264E	C750	0295
(N5264E)	C525	0119
N5264J	C500	264
N5264M	C525	0120
N5264M	C52A	0503
N5264M	C550	550-0908
N5264M	C560	0660
N5264M	C56X	5784

N5264M	C56X	6207
N5264N	C525	0627
N5264N	C52A	0224
N5264N	C52A	0487
N5264N	C560	0578
N5264N	C560	0643
N5264N	C56X	5729
N5264N	C56X	5823
N5264N	C56X	6138
N5264N	C680	0552
N5264N	C750	0258
N5264S	C525	0121
N5264S	C52A	0520
N5264S	C56X	5654
N5264S	C680	0027
N5264S	C680	0073
N5264S	C680	0231
N5264S	C680	0285
N5264U	C525	0122
N5264U	C52B	0088
N5264U	C550	550-1101
N5264U	C56X	5701
N5264U	C56X	6055
N5264U	C650	7118
N5264U	C680	0006
N5264U	C680	0228
N5265B	C52A	0421
N5265B	C52A	0447
N5265B	C52B	0407
N5265B	C550	550-1087
N5265B	C560	0336
N5265B	C560	0681
N5265B	C56X	5613
N5265B	C56X	5756
N5265B	C56X	6208
N5265J	C500	265
N5265N	C52A	0418
N5265N	C52A	0484
N5265N	C52B	0413
N5265N	C52C	0208
N5265N	C550	550-0916
N5265N	C560	0337
N5265N	C560	0653
N5265N	C56X	5138
N5265N	C56X	5676
N5265N	C56X	6135
N5265S	C52B	0487
N5266F	C525	0659
N5266F	C525	0681
N5266F	C525	0692
N5266F	C525	0699
N5266F	C52A	0226
N5266F	C52B	0246
N5266F	C560	0663
N5266F	C56X	5615
N5266F	C56X	5675
N5266F	**C56X**	**6214**
N5266F	C750	0008
N5266F	C750	0118
N5266J	C500	266
N5267D	C525	0651
N5267D	C52B	0473
N5267D	C52C	0113
N5267D	C560	0535
N5267D	C56X	5786
N5267D	C680	0274
N5267G	C525	0662
N5267G	C52A	0310
N5267G	C52A	0461
N5267G	C52C	0027
N5267G	C550	550-1049
N5267G	C560	0580
N5267G	C56X	5524
N5267G	C56X	5819
N5267G	C680	0047
N5267G	C680	0336
N5267G	**C680**	**680A0046**
N5267G	C750	0191
N5267G	C750	0267
N5267J	C500	267
N5267J	C550	550-0944
N5267J	C56X	5575
N5267J	C56X	5801
N5267J	C680	0163
N5267J	C680	0288
N5267J	C680	0337
N5267J	C750	0227
N5267K	C52B	0163
N5267K	C550	550-1061
N5267K	C56X	5542
N5267K	C56X	5577
N5267K	C56X	5624
N5267K	C650	7115
N5267T	C52A	0388
N5267T	C52B	0165
N5267T	C52B	0324
N5267T	C52C	0057
N5267T	C560	0340
N5267T	C560	0342
N5267T	C560	0649
N5267T	C56X	5616
N5267T	C56X	6189
N5267T	**C56X**	**6210**
N5268A	C52B	0127
N5268A	C52C	0097
N5268A	C560	0343
N5268A	C560	0567
N5268A	C560	0812
N5268A	C56X	5791
N5268A	C680	0165
N5268A	C680	680A0013
N5268A	C750	0229
N5268A	C750	0248
N5268A	C750	0256
N5268E	C550	550-1050
N5268E	C550	550-1079
N5268E	C560	0345
N5268E	C560	0700
N5268E	C56X	5663
N5268E	C56X	5796
N5268E	C56X	6116
N5268E	C680	0170
N5268E	C680	0291
N5268E	C680	680A0016
N5268J	C500	268
N5268M	C52A	0387
N5268M	C52B	0161
N5268M	C52C	0089
N5268M	C560	0344
N5268M	C56X	5544
N5268M	C56X	5601
N5268M	C56X	6073
N5268M	C650	7116
N5268M	**C680**	**680A0035**
N5268M	C750	0297
N5268V	C52A	0318
N5268V	C52A	0457
N5268V	C52B	0355
N5268V	C52B	0494
N5268V	C550	550-0952
N5268V	C550	550-1063
N5268V	C560	0347
N5268V	C560	0532
N5268V	C56X	6195
N5268V	C680	0161
N5268V	C750	0239
N5268V	C750	0253
N5269A	C52B	0062
N5269A	C52C	0054
N5269A	C52C	0125
N5269A	C560	0346
N5269A	C560	0388
N5269A	C560	0645
N5269A	C56X	5520
N5269A	C56X	6061
N5269A	C650	7109
N5269A	C750	0245
N5269J	C500	269
N5269J	C52B	0065
N5269J	C550	550-0985
N5269J	C56X	5317
N5269J	C56X	5545
N5269J	C56X	5673
N5269X	C52A	0498
N5269Z	C52A	0499
N5269Z	C52B	0068
N5269Z	C52C	0004
N5269Z	C560	0581
N5269Z	C560	0609
N5269Z	C56X	5671
N5269Z	C680	0206
N5269Z	C680	0248
N5269Z	C680	0554
N5269Z	C750	0228
N5270E	C525	0675
N5270E	C525	0688
N5270E	C52A	0157
N5270E	C52A	0373
N5270E	C52B	0005
N5270E	C52B	0098
N5270E	C52C	0217
N5270E	C550	550-0989
N5270E	C550	550-0999
N5270E	C56X	5532
N5270E	C680	0313
N5270E	C680	0504
N5270J	C500	270
N5270J	C52A	0379
N5270J	C52A	0409
N5270J	C52A	0517
N5270J	C52B	0096
N5270J	C52B	0481
N5270J	C550	550-0991
N5270J	C550	550-1029
N5270J	C560	0641
N5270J	C56X	5530
N5270J	C680	0290
N5270K	C525	0622
N5270K	C52A	0398
N5270K	C52B	0386
N5270K	C52C	0020
N5270K	C560	0265
N5270K	C560	0587
N5270K	C560	0607
N5270K	C560	0644
N5270K	C56X	6202
N5270K	C680	0014
N5270M	C52B	0263
N5270M	C52B	0387
N5270M	**C52C**	**0224**
N5270M	C56X	5350
N5270M	C56X	6049
N5270M	C680	0076
N5270M	C680	0126
N5270M	C750	0174
"N5270M"	C560	0268
N5270P	C52A	0386
N5270P	C52A	0478
N5270P	C52B	0329
N5270P	C52B	0403
N5270P	C52C	0174
N5270P	C550	550-0996
N5270P	C56X	5370
N5271J	C500	271
N5272J	C500	272
N5273J	C500	273
N5274G	C510	0255
(N5274J)	C500	274
N5274K	C510	0258
N5274M	C510	0267
N5274U	HS25	25068
(N5275J)	C500	275
(N5276J)	C500	276
(N5277J)	C500	277
(N5278J)	C500	278
(N5279J)	C500	279
(N5280J)	C500	280
N5281J	C500	281
(N5282J)	C500	282
N5283J	C500	283
(N5284J)	C500	284
N5285J	C500	285
N5286J	C500	286
(N5287J)	C500	287
(N5288J)	C500	288
N5289J	C500	289
(N5290J)	C500	290
N5291J	C500	291
N5292J	C500	292
(N5293J)	C500	293
N5294C	C550	662
N5294J	C500	294
N5295J	C500	295
(N5296J)	C500	296
N5296X	C52B	0225
N5296X	C550	550-1070
N5296X	C550	550-1128
N5296X	C560	0584
N5296X	C560	0614
N5296X	C56X	5528
N5296X	C56X	5561
N5296X	C680	0252
N5296X	C680	0553
N5297J	C500	297
N5298J	C500	298
N5299J	C500	299
(N5300J)	C500	300
N5301J	C500	067
N5301J	C500	301
N5302J	C500	302
(N5303J)	C500	303
N5304J	C500	304
(N5305J)	C500	305
N5306J	C500	306
N5307J	C500	307
(N5308J)	C500	308
N5309J	C500	309
(N5310J)	C500	310
N5311J	C500	311
N5312J	C500	312
(N5313J)	C500	313
N5314J	C500	314
N5314J	C550	663
N5315J	C500	315
N5315J	C550	664
N5316J	C500	316
N5318J	C500	318
N5319	CL64	5319
N5319J	C500	319
(N5320J)	C500	320
N5321J	C500	321
N5322	**FA50**	**322**
N5322J	C500	322
N5323J	C500	323
(N5324J)	C500	324
(N5325J)	C500	325
N5326J	C500	326
N5327J	C500	327
(N5328J)	C500	328
N5329J	C500	329
(N5330J)	C500	330
(N5331J)	C500	331
N5332J	C500	332
(N5333J)	C500	333
N5334J	C500	334
N5335J	C500	335
(N5336J)	C500	336
N5337J	C500	337
N5338J	C500	338
(N5339J)	C500	339
(N5340J)	C500	340
(N5341J)	C500	341
N5342J	C550	070
(N5342J)	C500	342
(N5343J)	C500	343
(N5344J)	C500	344
(N5345J)	C500	345
N5346C	C500	685
N5346J	C500	346
(N5347J)	C500	347
N5348J	C550	071
N5348J	C550	665
(N5348J)	C500	348
N5349	CL64	5349
(N5349J)	C500	349
N5350J	C500	350
N5351J	C500	351
N5352J	C500	352
N5352J	CL64	5352
N5353J	C500	353
(N5353J)	C500	139
N5354J	C500	354
N5355J	C500	355
N5356J	C500	356
N5357J	C500	357
(N5358J)	C500	358
(N5359J)	C500	359
N5360J	C500	360
N5361J	C500	361
N5362J	C500	362
(N5363J)	C500	363
(N5364U)	C500	032
N5366J	C500	366
N5368J	C500	368
N5373D	C560	0381
N5373U	CL61	3026
N5379W	SBRL	306-100
N5400G	GLF2	36/3
N5402X	CL61	3027
N5408G	C550	666
N5410	WW24	123
N5411	**C500**	**633**
N5412	WW24	95
N5415	SBRL	306-16
N5415	WW24	62
N5418	WW24	6
N5419	SBRL	306-24
N5419	SBRL	306-55
N5420	SBRL	306-43
N5420	WW24	92
(N5425)	FA50	237
N5428G	C550	346
N5430G	C550	347
N5450	FA20	17
N5450M	BE40	RJ-31
N5451G	C550	348
N5465M	**GLF5**	**5465**
N5474G	C550	349
N5474G	LJ35	093
N5491V	CL61	3029
N5492G	C550	350
N5498G	**CL61**	**3019**
N5500F	C550	138
N5500L	JSTR	5136
N5500S	C500	048
N5501L	JSTR	5137
N5502L	JSTR	5138
N5503L	JSTR	5139/54
N5504L	JSTR	5140
N5505L	JSTR	5141
N5506L	JSTR	5142
N5507L	JSTR	5143
N5508L	JSTR	5144
N5509L	JSTR	5145
N5510	C510	0339
N5510L	JSTR	5146
N5511A	HS25	257113
N5511A	SBRL	282-137
N5511A	SBRL	282-91
N5511A	SBRL	465-39
N5511L	JSTR	5147
N5511Z	SBRL	282-91
N5512A	SBRL	282-137
N5512L	JSTR	5148
N5513L	JSTR	5149/11
N5514L	JSTR	5150/37
N5515L	JSTR	5151
N5516L	JSTR	5152
N5517L	JSTR	5153/61
N5518L	JSTR	5154
N5519C	GLF2	235
N5519L	JSTR	5155/32
N5520L	JSTR	5156
N5521L	JSTR	5157
N5522L	JSTR	5158
N5523L	JSTR	5159
N5524L	JSTR	5160
N5525L	JSTR	5161/43
N5526L	JSTR	5162
N5527L	JSTR	5201
N5528L	JSTR	5202
N5529L	JSTR	5203
N5530L	JSTR	5204
N5531L	JSTR	5205
N5532L	JSTR	5206
N5533L	JSTR	5207
N5534L	JSTR	5208
N5535	C56X	5265
N5535L	JSTR	5209
N5536L	JSTR	5210
N5537L	JSTR	5211
N5538L	JSTR	5212
N5539L	JSTR	5213
N5540L	JSTR	5214
N5541L	JSTR	5215
N5542L	JSTR	5216
N5543G	LJ55	043
N5543L	JSTR	5217
N5544L	JSTR	5218
N5545L	JSTR	5219
N5546L	JSTR	5220
N5547L	JSTR	5221
N5548L	JSTR	5222
N5549L	JSTR	5223
N5555U	FA20	39
N5565	SBRL	282-119
N5569	**GLF5**	**5169**
N5572	**LJ55**	**072**
N5574	LJ55	074
N5585	**GLF5**	**5085**
N5591A	C500	289
N5594U	HS25	25219
N5598Q	BE40	RK-18
(N5599)	LJ55	099
N5600M	C500	191
N5601T	**C560**	**0564**
N5602	HFB3	1045
N5616	**GLF5**	**616**
N5627	HFB3	1038
N5680Z	BE40	RK-11
N5685X	BE40	RK-38
N5695H	LJ24	278
(N5703C)	C550	351
(N5703C)	C550	666
N5704	C560	0157
N5731	F900	8
N5732	FA20	502
N5732	FA50	217
N5732	HS25	258467
N5733	F900	39
N5733	FA50	156
N5733	GLF5	609
N5734	C560	0157
N5734	FA10	196
N5734	**HS25**	**258304**
N5735	C560	0171
N5735	HS25	257044
N5735	HS25	258309
N5736	FA10	195
N5736	HS25	258471
N5737	C500	435
N5737	F9EX	41
N5738	FA10	198
N5739	FA50	11
N5739	SBRL	465-11
N5794J	HS25	259021
N5810B	CL65	5810
N5852K	**C550**	**550-1056**
N5861	JSTR	5085
N5867	C500	015
N5867	LJ35	016
N5873C	C550	352
N5878	MS76	106
N5878D	JSTR	5143
N5879	**MS76**	**107**
N5895K	**BE40**	**RK-62**
N5901D	C56X	6099
N5942P	C500	612
N5950C	**G150**	**213**
N5956B	**GLF4**	**1469**
N5997K	GLF2	105
N6000J	C650	0118
N6000J	LJ35	079
N6000J	SBRL	465-54
N6001H	HS25	256011
N6001L	C550	185
N6004N	E50P	50000283
N6004N	E50P	50000321
N6005V	HA4T	RC-45
N6005Y	E50P	50000302
N6013X	E55P	50500176
N6013X	E55P	50500326
N6014A	E50P	50000290
N6015Y	PRM1	RB-115
N6026T	C680	0297
N6032F	E50P	50000299
N6032F	E55P	50500155
N6033	HS25	256033
N6033R	C52A	0470
N6034F	C500	239
N6046J	HS25	258746
N6048F	BE40	RK-66
N6051C	BE40	RK-351
N6051D	E50P	50000293
N6051D	E50P	50000314
N6052U	**BE40**	**RK-352**
N6053C	WW24	207
N6053C	WW24	361
N6055K	BE40	RK-355
N6056M	BE40	RK-356
N6060	GLF2	105
N6060S	C52B	0384
N6061U	C52A	0500
N6061Z	C52B	0382
N6062M	C52B	0381
N6064A	C52C	0139
N6068	MS76	050
N6076Y	PRM1	RB-76
N6087	SBRL	282-26
N6100	**EA50**	**000046**
N6100	LJ60	100
N6110	**C650**	**7023**
(N6111)	C650	7011
N6111F	PRM1	RB-111
N6114	C650	0094

N6115	C650	0095
N6117G	PRM1	RB-117
N6118C	PRM1	RB-118
N6119C	PRM1	RB-119
N6120U	PRM1	RB-120
N6124W	PRM1	RB-124
N6128Y	PRM1	RB-128
N6129U	PRM1	RB-129
N6132U	C52B	0323
N6135H	HS25	258735
N6137U	PRM1	RB-137
N6137Y	BE40	RK-457
N6142Y	PRM1	RB-142
N6144S	BE40	RK-344
N6145Q	C500	058
N6146J	PRM1	RB-146
N6148Z	PRM1	RB-148
N6150B	C650	7050
N6150Y	PRM1	RB-150
N6151C	HS25	HA-0121
N6160D	PRM1	RB-60
N6162V	BE40	RK-362
N6162Z	PRM1	RB-62
N6163T	PRM1	RB-63
N6164U	PRM1	RB-64
(N6164Z)	GLF3	367
N6165C	CL61	3012
N6167D	PRM1	RB-67
N6170C	C550	669
N6171U	HS25	258771
N6172V	BE40	RK-372
N6173K	HS25	HB-63
N6174Q	PRM1	RB-274
N6177A	PRM1	RB-77
N6177Y	LJ24	151
N6178X	PRM1	RB-157
N6182F	PRM1	RB-102
N6183G	PRM1	RB-83
N6183Q	C510	0062
N6187Q	PRM1	RB-87
N6193D	BE40	RK-363
N6193S	C510	0069
N6194N	PRM1	RB-94
N6195S	PRM1	RB-95
N6196M	C510	0091
N6197D	**C510**	**0088**
N6197F	PRM1	RB-97
N6198P	HS25	HA-0098
N6200C	C510	0087
N6200D	BE40	RK-360
N6200H	**HS25**	**258087**
N6201A	PRM1	RB-101
N6202W	C510	0100
N6203C	C510	0095
N6206W	C510	0133
N6207Z	C510	0145
N6218	HS25	25205
N6242R	C680	0273
N6243M	C52B	0066
N6245J	C52A	0458
N6248J	PRM1	RB-278
N6262T	LJ24	071
N6273X	HS25	HA-0143
N6307H	LJ25	359
N6307H	LJ35	519
N6307H	LJ35	534
N6307H	LJ35	652
N6307H	LJ55	125
N6317V	LJ35	509
N6317V	LJ35	524
N6317V	LJ35	639
N6317V	LJ55	049
N6324L	C510	0090
N6325U	C510	0092
N6331V	LJ31	006
N6331V	LJ35	510
N6331V	LJ35	525
N6331V	LJ55	060
N6331V	LJ55	123
N6332K	C510	0093
N6340T	HS25	HA-0140
N6340T	LJ25	360
N6340T	LJ35	517
N6340T	LJ35	532
N6340T	LJ36	063
N6340T	LJ55	127
N6351Y	HS25	HA-0151
N6354N	LJ25	336
N6358C	SBRL	282-4
N6360C	SBRL	282-6
N6361C	SBRL	282-7
N6361C	WW24	42
N6362C	SBRL	282-8
(N6362D)	LJ35	277
N6363C	SBRL	282-9
N6364C	SBRL	282-10
N6364U	LJ55	060
N6365C	C500	228
N6365C	SBRL	282-11
N6366C	SBRL	282-12
(N6366W)	FA10	57
N6367C	SBRL	282-13
N6368C	SBRL	282-14
N6368D	HS25	HA-0168
N6369C	SBRL	282-15
N6370C	SBRL	282-16
N6371C	SBRL	282-17
N6372C	SBRL	282-18
N6373C	SBRL	282-19
N6374C	SBRL	282-20
N6375C	SBRL	282-21
N6376C	SBRL	282-22
N6377C	SBRL	282-23
N6378C	SBRL	282-24
N6379C	SBRL	282-25
N6380C	SBRL	282-26
N6380H	HA4T	RC-63
N6381C	SBRL	282-27
N6382C	SBRL	282-28
N6383C	SBRL	282-29
N6384C	SBRL	282-30
N6389C	SBRL	282-34
N6390C	SBRL	282-35
N6391C	SBRL	282-36
N6392C	SBRL	282-37
N6393C	SBRL	282-38
N6394C	SBRL	282-39
N6395C	SBRL	282-40
N6396C	SBRL	282-41
N6397C	SBRL	282-42
N6398C	SBRL	282-43
N6399C	SBRL	282-44
N6403N	HS25	HA-0103
N6405K	HS25	HB-65
N6408F	HS25	HA-0108
N6409A	HS25	HA-0159
N6412	WW24	95
N6430S	C56X	5331
N6434R	HS25	HA-0104
N6452L	HS25	HA-0102
N6452S	HS25	HA-0152
N6453	F2EX	26
N6453	GLF3	349
N6453	GLF4	1033
N6453	GLF5	574
N6453	**GLF6**	**6078**
N6455T	HA4T	RC-55
N6458	F2EX	26
N6458	GLF3	349
N6458	GLF4	1033
N6458	**GLF5**	**574**
(N6462)	LJ24	127
N6465W	PRM1	RB-265
N6469X	PRM1	RB-277
N6470P	PRM1	RB-270
N6471N	PRM1	RB-271
N6504V	WW24	35
N6505V	WW24	39
N6510V	WW24	41
N6511V	WW24	42
N6512V	WW24	64
N6513V	WW24	47
N6513X	GLF3	310
N6516V	C555	0144
N6518V	WW24	43
N6521F	C560	0632
N6523A	C550	460
N6525B	**C52B**	**0004**
N6525J	C500	308
N6527V	WW24	69
N6534V	WW24	54
N6538V	WW24	59
N6544V	WW24	57
N6545V	WW24	60
N6546V	WW24	63
(N6550)	CL64	5400
N6550V	WW24	56
N6550W	FA50	136
N6552C	SBRL	282-45
N6552R	SBRL	276-6
N6553C	SBRL	282-46
N6555C	FA20	78/412
N6555C	SBRL	282-48
N6555L	FA20	85/425
N6556C	SBRL	282-49
N6557C	SBRL	282-50
N6563C	C500	012
N6563C	C500	014
N6563C	C500	551
N6565A	FA20	39
N6565A	SBRL	282-28
N6565C	C550	174
N6565K	SBRL	282-28
N6566C	C550	175
N6567C	C550	176
N6567G	HS25	256048
N6581E	SBRL	265-82
N6596R	LJ25	286
N6610V	WW24	74
N6611V	WW24	75
N6612S	SBRL	276-48
N6612V	WW24	76
N6613V	WW24	78
N6617B	LJ36	026
N6617V	WW24	81
(N6621)	FA20	378
N6637G	C550	670
N6666A	LJ31	150
N6666A	LJ60	143
N6666K	LJ25	285
N6666K	LJ35	481
N6666K	LJ55	115
N6666P	F9EX	102
N6666R	F9EX	102
N6666R	FA50	124
N6666R	LJ25	285
N6666R	LJ31	150
N6666R	LJ31	153
N6666R	LJ35	412
N6666R	LJ55	115
N6666R	LJ60	143
N6701	FA20	177
N6702	HS25	25241
N6707L	C650	0134
N6709	HS25	25239
N6745	**E50P**	**50000091**
N6757M	CL64	5545
(N6761L)	C550	671
N6763C	C550	672
N6763L	C550	673
N6763M	C500	686
(N6770S)	C550	674
N6773P	C550	675
N6775C	C550	677
N6775U	C550	678
(N6776P)	C550	679
N6776T	C550	680
(N6776Y)	C550	681
N6777V	C500	567
(N6777X)	C500	568
N6778C	C500	569
N6778L	C550	684
(N6778L)	C500	570
N6778T	C500	571
(N6778V)	C500	572
N6778Y	C550	687
(N6778Y)	C500	573
N6779D	C500	576
N6779D	C56X	5568
N6779L	C500	577
N6779P	C500	578
N6779Y	C500	579
(N6780)	LJ55	083
N6780A	C560	0360
(N6780A)	C500	581
N6780C	C500	582
N6780C	C550	690
N6780J	C500	583
(N6780M)	C500	584
N6780Y	C500	585
N6780Z	C500	586
N6781C	C500	588
N6781C	C650	7056
(N6781D)	C500	589
(N6781G)	C500	590
N6781L	C500	591
N6781R	C500	592
(N6781T)	C500	593
N6781Z	C500	594
N6782B	C500	597
N6782F	C500	598
(N6782P)	C500	599
N6782T	C550	695
(N6782T)	C500	600
N6782X	C500	601
N6783C	C500	604
N6783L	C500	605
N6783U	C500	606
N6783V	C500	607
N6783X	C500	608
(N6783X)	C560	0088
N6784L	C500	611
N6784P	C500	612
N6784P	C560	0091
N6784T	C500	613
N6784X	C500	614
N6784X	C560	0092
N6784Y	C500	615
N6784Y	C500	645
N6784Y	C560	0092A
N6785C	C500	617
(N6785C)	C560	0093
N6785D	C500	618
N6785D	C560	0094
N6785L	C500	619
N6788P	C560	0095
N6789	LJ55	083
N6789	SBRL	282-112
N6789D	SBRL	282-112
(N6790L)	C560	0097
(N6790P)	C560	0098
(N6792A)	C560	0100
N6798Y	C550	219
N6798Z	C550	220
N6799C	C550	226
N6799C	C550	355
N6799E	C550	227
N6799L	C550	228
N6799L	C550	356
(N6799L)	C560	0104
N6799T	C550	229
N6799T	C550	357
N6799Y	C550	230
N6800C	C550	234
N6800C	C550	360
(N6800C)	C560	0105
N6800J	C550	235
N6800S	C550	236
N6800S	C550	361
N6800Z	C550	237
N6801H	C560	0106
(N6801H)	C550	239
N6801L	C550	240
N6801L	C550	383
(N6801L)	C560	0107
N6801P	C550	241
(N6801P)	C560	0108
N6801Q	C550	242
N6801Q	C550	389
(N6801Q)	C560	0109
N6801R	C550	243
N6801T	C550	244
N6801V	C560	0109
(N6801V)	C550	245
N6801Z	C550	246
N6801Z	C550	390
N6802S	C550	248
N6802S	C550	368
(N6802S)	C560	0110
N6802T	C550	249
N6802T	C550	369
(N6802T)	C560	0111
N6802X	C550	250
N6802Y	C550	251
N6802Y	C550	370
N6802Z	C550	252
N6803E	C550	255
N6803L	C550	256
N6803L	C550	372
N6803L	C560	0113
(N6803T)	C550	257
(N6803T)	C560	0114
N6803Y	C560	0115
(N6803Y)	C550	258
N6804C	C550	261
N6804F	C550	262
N6804F	C550	374
(N6804F)	C560	0117
N6804L	C550	263
N6804L	C550	375
N6804L	C560	0118
N6804L	LJ25	006
N6804M	C550	264
(N6804N)	C550	265
(N6804N)	C560	0119
N6804S	C550	266
N6804Y	C550	267
N6804Y	C550	376
N6804Y	C560	0153
(N6804Y)	C560	0120
N6804Z	C550	268
N6805T	C550	269
N6805T	C550	377
N6805T	C560	0154
N6806X	C550	378
(N6806X)	C560	0120
(N6806Y)	C550	378
N6808C	C550	379
N6808C	C560	0121
(N6808Z)	C560	0122
(N6809G)	C560	0123
(N6809T)	C560	0124
N6809V	C560	0125
N6810J	FA20	125
(N6810L)	C560	0127
(N6810N)	C560	0128
(N6811F)	C560	0129
(N6811T)	C560	0130
(N6811X)	C560	0131
N6811Z	C560	0132
N6812D	C560	0134
(N6812D)	C650	0207
N6812L	C650	0208
(N6812L)	C560	0135
(N6812Z)	C560	0136
(N6812Z)	C650	0209
N6820J	FA20	135
N6820T	C650	0211
(N6820Y)	C650	0212
(N6823L)	C650	0213
(N6824G)	C650	0215
N6825X	C550	364
N6826U	C550	380
(N6828S)	C650	0217
N6829X	C650	0218
N6829Y	C550	365
N6829Z	C650	0219
N6830T	C650	0220
N6830X	C550	366
N6830Z	C550	367
N6846T	C550	625
N6851C	C550	697
N6860A	C550	271
N6860C	C550	272
N6860L	C550	273
N6860R	C550	274
N6860S	C550	275
N6860T	C550	276
N6860U	C550	277
N6860Y	C550	278
N6861D	C550	281
N6861E	C550	282
N6861L	C550	283
N6861P	C550	284
N6861S	C550	285
N6861X	C550	286
N6862C	C550	290
N6862D	C550	291
N6862L	C550	292
N6862Q	C550	293
N6862R	C550	294
N6863B	C550	300
N6863C	C550	301
N6863G	C550	302
N6863J	C550	303
N6863L	C550	304
N6863T	C550	305
"N6864"	C560	0162
N6864B	C550	309
N6864C	C550	310
N6864L	C550	311
N6864X	C550	312
N6864Y	C550	313
N6864Z	C550	314
N6865C	C550	319
(N6868P)	C650	0210
(N6871L)	C560	0135
N6872T	C560	0155
(N6872T)	C560	0136
N6874Z	C560	0137
(N6876Q)	C560	0140
N6876S	C560	0141
N6876Z	C560	0142
N6877C	C560	0143
N6877G	C560	0144
N6877L	C52A	0060
(N6877L)	C560	0145
(N6877Q)	C560	0146
(N6877R)	C560	0147
(N6879L)	C560	0150
N6881Q	**C560**	**0151**
N6882R	C560	0152
N6885L	C560	0156
N6885V	C560	0157
(N6885Y)	C560	0158
N6886X	C560	0160
N6887M	C500	620
N6887R	C500	621
N6887T	C550	320
(N6887T)	C560	0164
N6887X	C550	321
(N6887X)	C560	0165
N6887Y	C550	322
N6888C	C550	326
N6888C	C560	0169
N6888D	C550	327
N6888L	C550	328
N6888L	C560	0170
N6888T	C550	329
(N6888T)	C560	0171
N6888X	C550	330
(N6888X)	C560	0172
N6888Z	C550	331
N6889E	C550	335
N6889E	C560	0174
N6889K	C550	336
N6889L	C550	337
N6889T	C550	338
N6889Y	C550	339
N6889Z	C550	340
(N6890C)	C550	342
(N6890D)	C550	343
(N6890E)	C550	344
N6890G	C550	345
(N6940P)	F9EX	59
(N6960)	HS25	257024
(N6972Z)	CL60	1006
N7000C	**CL30**	**20225**
N7000C	GLF2	165/37
N7000C	GLF3	344
N7000G	C650	0114
N7000G	FA20	440
N7000G	GLF2	156/31
N7000G	LJ25	027
N7000G	SBRL	465-16
N7000K	LJ24	029
N7004	C550	427
N7004T	GLF2	28
N7005	C650	7044
N7005	HS25	257024
N7005	JSTR	5105
N7006	HS25	257024
N7007Q	C555	0030
N7007Q	HA4T	RC-7
N7007V	C555	0030
N7007V	LJ35	594
N7007X	HS25	257034
N7008	CL60	1054
N7008	CL61	5164
N7008	JSTR	5101/15
N7008J	JSTR	5101/15
N7010R	C560	0469
N7011	FA50	144
N7011H	CL61	3032
N7028F	WW24	131
N7028U	C550	290
N7035C	LJ25	352
(N7038Z)	MS76	101
N7043U	SBRL	265-12
N7046J	CL61	5122
N7047K	C555	0133
N7050V	MU30	A058SA
N7051J	WW24	409
N7055	HS25	25142
N7059U	C650	0210

N7062B	HS25	257062
N7070A	**CS55**	**0068**
N7074X	LJ24	223
N7077S	HS25	258827
N7079N	GLF2	211
N7079N	PRM1	RB-179
N7081V	PRM1	RB-181
N7082V	PRM1	RB-182
N7085V	PRM1	RB-185
N7088S	PRM1	RB-188
N7090	SBRL	282-30
N7090	SBRL	306-16
N7090	SBRL	306-5
N7090	SBRL	306-62
N7090	WW24	95
N7092C	LJ35	184
N7096B	GLF4	1162
N7096E	GLF3	498
N7096G	GLF3	497
N7100C	**CL30**	**20254**
N7101Z	HS25	258801
N7102U	PRM1	RB-172
N7102Z	HS25	258802
N7105	JSTR	5078/3
N7110K	C500	016
N7111H	C500	595
(N7113Z)	BE40	RK-51
N7117	LJ35	462
N7118A	CS55	0065
N7121K	LJ24	230
N7125	LJ35	035
N7125J	HS25	25013
N7125J	HS25	25107
N7128T	HS25	258828
N7134E	GLF3	423
N7143N	SBRL	265-70
N7145D	**C750**	**0522**
N7145V	JSTR	5001/53
N7146D	**C56X**	**6208**
N7146T	**C56X**	**6207**
N7148J	**C56X**	**6206**
N7148J	SBRL	380-33
N7153X	C550	407
N7155P	GLF2	169
N7158Q	HFB3	1040
N7163E	PRM1	RB-163
N7165X	PRM1	RB-165
N7170J	HS25	25276
N7170Y	**PRM1**	**RB-170**
N7171	HS25	25264
N7176J	PRM1	RB-176
N7187J	PRM1	RB-187
N7189J	PRM1	RB-189
N7191K	PRM1	RB-191
N7192M	PRM1	RB-192
N7193W	PRM1	RB-193
N7198H	PRM1	RB-198
N7200K	LJ24	099
N7220L	C560	0142
N7226P	BE40	RK-526
N7228K	FA50	146
N7235R	HS25	258835
N7236L	HS25	258836
N7243U	C650	7054
N7244W	LJ55	028
N7255U	HS25	258855
N7256C	HS25	258856
N7257U	PRM1	RB-197
N7259J	LJ35	505
N7260C	LJ25	365
N7260E	LJ35	615
N7260G	LJ55	111
N7260H	LJ35	622
N7260J	LJ55	126
N7260K	LJ55	131
N7260Q	LJ35	623
N7260T	LJ35	627
N7261B	LJ25	366
N7261D	LJ55	134
N7261H	LJ35	641
N7261R	LJ35	626
N7262A	LJ25	367
N7262M	LJ55	113
N7262X	LJ35	642
N7262Y	LJ31	002
N7263C	LJ35	509
N7263D	LJ35	510
N7263E	LJ35	511
N7263F	LJ35	512
N7263H	LJ35	513
N7263K	LJ35	514
N7263L	LJ35	515
N7263N	LJ35	516
N7263R	LJ35	517
N7263X	LJ35	518
N7268M	PRM1	RB-168
N7269Z	PRM1	RB-169
N7274A	C560	0386
N7277	C525	0666
N7277X	MS76	112
N7281Z	C500	047
N7294E	PRM1	RB-194
(N7300G)	LJ24	186
N7300K	LJ24	186
N7301	F9EX	19
N7302P	HS25	258852
N7325	**GLF5**	**5176**

N7337F	C56X	5342
N7338	C560	0137
N7374	HS25	258524
(N7379M)	LJ36	018
N7402	**C680**	**0082**
N7403	**C680**	**0222**
N7418F	C750	0074
N7440C	HS25	25142
N7465T	HS25	257046
N7490A	**HS25**	**257173**
N7500	GLF2	117
N7500	JSTR	5102
N7500K	LJ24	065
N7502V	SBRL	282-52
N7503V	SBRL	282-53
N7504V	SBRL	282-54
N7505V	SBRL	282-55
N7506V	SBRL	282-56
N7507V	SBRL	282-57
N7508V	SBRL	282-58
N7509V	SBRL	282-59
N7510V	SBRL	282-60
N7513D	C560	0124
N7513H	**GLF3**	**493**
N7514V	SBRL	282-64
N7519N	SBRL	306-48
N7522N	SBRL	306-49
N7529N	SBRL	306-50
N7531N	SBRL	306-51
N7543H	C500	266
N7547P	C560	0365
N7567T	**HA4T**	**RC-10**
N7571N	SBRL	306-52
N7572N	SBRL	370-1
N7573N	SBRL	306-53
N7574N	SBRL	306-54
N7575N	SBRL	306-55
N7576N	SBRL	306-56
N7577N	SBRL	306-57
N7578N	SBRL	306-58
N7584N	SBRL	282-107
N7585N	SBRL	370-2
N7586N	SBRL	370-3
N7587N	SBRL	370-4
N7588N	SBRL	370-5
N7589N	SBRL	370-6
N7590N	SBRL	370-7
N7591N	SBRL	370-8
N7592N	SBRL	370-9
N7593N	SBRL	380-1
N7594N	SBRL	282-99
N7595N	SBRL	282-106
N7596N	SBRL	282-101
N7596N	SBRL	282-108
N7597N	SBRL	282-102
N7597N	SBRL	282-110
N7598N	SBRL	282-103
N7600	JSTR	5054/59
N7600	**BE40**	**RK-395**
N7600G	**C750**	**0159**
(N7600J)	JSTR	5054/59
N7600K	LJ25	135
N7600P	**F9EX**	**226**
N7600S	**F9EX**	**173**
N7601	GLF4	1245
(N7601)	GLF2	32/2
N7601B	EA50	000093
N7601R	MS76	060
N7602	GLF2	32/2
(N7602)	GLF4	1245
N7638S	WW24	134
N7654F	FA20	489
N7662N	SBRL	282-111
N7667N	SBRL	282-112
N7670B	**CL30**	**20299**
N7671G	C56X	6143
(N7682V)	SBRL	306-79
(N7684X)	HFB3	1042
(N7685T)	HFB3	1055
N7700L	C560	0203
N7700T	C500	662
N7701L	**LJ24**	**288**
N7707X	**FA7X**	**16**
N7711B	**C510**	**0230**
N7715X	C525	0387
N7715X	C525	0653
N7715X	C52A	0178
N7715Y	C525	0387
N7717B	**C650**	**0214**
N7725D	C52B	0218
N7725D	C550	550-1041
N7728	HS25	257028
N7728T	C560	0374
N7734T	**LJ60**	**139**
N7735A	LJ35	138
N7765D	C550	550-1041
N7766Z	GLF2	174
N7773A	C52A	0004
N7773J	C52B	0223
N7775	HS25	258275
N7775	JSTR	5073
N7776	GLF4	1121
N7777B	C650	0214
N7777B	C680	0020
N7777B	**C680**	**0312**
N7777B	HS25	25174
N7777B	LJ35	079

N7777B	LJ35	508
N7777N	**GLF4**	**4245**
N7777U	**GLEX**	**9591**
N7778L	SBRL	282-135
N7780	GLF6	6080
N7781	FA10	141
N7782	HS25	257025
N7782	JSTR	5066/46
N7784	LJ55	023
N7784	WW24	63
N7788	CL61	3011
N7788	HS25	257073
N7788	JSTR	5107
N7789	GLF2	90
N7798D	C550	333
N7799T	**GLF4**	**1474**
N7800	GLF4	1098
N7801L	LJ25	355
N7810W	LJ25	117
N7814	**C52B**	**0166**
N7818S	F9EX	153
N7820C	SBRL	282-1
N7824M	FA20	42
N7851M	C550	695
N7864J	C550	427
N7867T	**C560**	**0020**
N7876C	**C510**	**0229**
N7877D	C56X	6017
N7877T	**C52B**	**0077**
N7895Q	**C525**	**0405**
N7895Q	C560	0199
N7895Q	C560	0564
N7913M	**E50P**	**50000333**
(N7922)	FA20	37/406
N7953S	JSTR	5108
N7954S	JSTR	5109/13
N7955S	JSTR	5110/47
N7956S	JSTR	5111
N7957S	JSTR	5112/7
N7958S	JSTR	5113/25
N7959S	JSTR	5114/18
N7961S	JSTR	5116
N7962S	JSTR	5117/35
N7963S	JSTR	5118
N7964S	JSTR	5119/29
N7965S	JSTR	5120/26
N7966S	JSTR	5121
N7967S	JSTR	5122
N7967S	JSTR	5141
N7968S	JSTR	5123/14
N7969S	JSTR	5124
N7970S	JSTR	5125/31
N7971S	JSTR	5126
N7972S	JSTR	5127
N7973S	JSTR	5128/16
N7974S	JSTR	5129
N7975S	JSTR	5130
N7976S	JSTR	5131
N7977S	JSTR	5132/57
N7978S	JSTR	5133
N7979S	JSTR	5134/50
N7980S	JSTR	5135
(N7981M)	BE40	RK-119
N7996	HS25	258019
N8000	CL60	1076
N8000	GLF2	39
N8000	SBRL	306-68
N8000E	**FA7X**	**25**
N8000J	GLF2	42/12
N8000U	**C56X**	**5746**
N8000U	C650	0107
N8000U	FA20	436
N8000U	SBRL	306-19
N8000U	SBRL	465-24
N8000Z	HS25	256012
N8005	C56X	5006
N8005Y	LJ25	121
N8008F	C550	496
N8010X	CL60	1038
N8010X	LJ55	096
N8014Q	BE40	RK-37
N8025X	SBRL	306-84
N8029Z	HS25	258129
N8030F	HS25	258131
N8040A	LJ35	048
N8041R	C560	0413
(N8051H)	BE40	RK-45
N8052V	SBRL	265-18
N8053V	BE40	RK-47
N8060V	BE40	RK-48
N8060Y	BE40	RK-49
N8062L	HA4T	RC-62
N8064A	LJ35	324
N8064K	LJ31	223
N8064Q	HS25	258158
N8066P	LJ31	126
N8067Y	LJ60	097
N8068V	GLF5	581
N8070Q	BE40	RK-73
N8070U	WW24	124
N8071J	LJ60	039
N8071L	LJ60	091
N8073R	BE40	RK-24
N8073Y	LJ31	133
N8074W	LJ60	074
N8079Q	LJ31	129
N8079R	PRM1	RB-279

N8080W	LJ60	080
N8082B	LJ60	102
N8082J	LJ31	128
N8083N	BE40	RK-62
N8084J	LJ60	218
N8084R	LJ45	148
N8084U	PRM1	RB-284
N8085T	**BE40**	**RK-51**
N8086L	LJ60	096
N8088U	LJ60	222
N8089Y	LJ60	089
N8090	HS25	258090
N8090P	LJ60	090
N8092F	PRM1	RB-292
N8094U	LJ24	297
N8097V	BE40	RK-26
N8100E	F900	34
N8100E	**F9EX**	
N8100E	**FA10**	**52**
N8100E	FA10	53
N8100E	FA50	33
N8106V	**C52B**	**0072**
N8110N	PRM1	RB-290
N8113Q	PRM1	RB-293
N8114G	C500	129
N8115N	GLF3	404
N8125J	HS25	25148
N8130S	C560	0631
N8138M	BE40	RK-84
N8139T	HA4T	RC-69
N8144D	PRM1	RB-294
N8146J	BE40	RK-74
N8148U	PRM1	RB-288
N8152H	BE40	RK-9
N8157H	BE40	RK-57
N8163G	BE40	RK-16
N8164M	BE40	RK-64
N8166A	BE40	RK-76
N8167G	BE40	RK-81
N8167Y	BE40	RK-67
N8169Q	BE40	RK-69
N8180Q	BE40	RK-80
N8186	HS25	258186
N8186	HS25	258604
N8189	LJ35	654
N8189J	C500	537
N8200E	**F900**	**34**
N8200E	FA10	111
N8200E	FA50	150
N8202Q	C500	002
N8203K	GLF4	1205
N8206S	CL64	5335
N8210W	BE40	RK-72
N8216Q	LJ35	370
N8216Z	LJ35	309
(N8217W)	LJ25	299
N8220F	GLF3	371
N8221M	MU30	A076SA
N8226M	GLF3	413
N8227P	LJ55	086
N8227V	FA20	150/445
N8228N	**GLF5**	**5057**
N8228P	LJ35	263
N8239E	BE40	RK-46
N8249Y	BE40	RK-44
N8252J	BE40	RK-40
(N8252J)	BE40	RK-105
N8253A	HS25	256061
N8253Y	BE40	RK-42
N8260D	CL60	1063
N8260L	BE40	RK-60
N8265Y	BE40	RK-41
N8267D	SBRL	380-58
N8270	LJ60	063
N8271	LJ60	066
N8277Y	BE40	RK-77
N8278Z	BE40	RK-78
N8279G	BE40	RK-79
N8280	LJ25	052
N8280	LJ35	310
N8280J	BE40	RK-68
N8281	LJ35	232
N8282E	BE40	RK-82
N8283C	BE40	RK-83
N8288R	C525	0090
N8288R	**C525**	**0348**
N8299Y	BE40	RK-85
N8300	WW24	12
N8300E	**FA50**	**33**
N8300E	JSTR	5115/39
N8311N	SBRL	282-113
N8333N	SBRL	282-115
N8338N	SBRL	282-117
N8339N	SBRL	282-118
N8341C	**C525**	**0150**
N8341N	SBRL	282-119
N8344M	**C550**	**577**
N8345K	SBRL	282-76
N8349N	SBRL	282-121
N8350N	SBRL	282-123
N8356N	SBRL	282-125
N8357N	SBRL	306-64
N8364N	SBRL	306-65
N8365N	SBRL	306-66
N8400B	SBRL	282-23
N8400E	**FA50**	**150**
N8400E	HS25	257202

N8417B	C550	042
N8418B	C550	043
N8445N	SBRL	380-2
N8447A	FA10	84
N8463	FA10	152
N8467N	SBRL	380-3
N8482B	LJ24	148
N8484P	ASTR	014
N8486	C560	0554
N8490P	GLF2	4/8
N8494	FA10	201
(N8494C)	C650	7072
(N8495B)	FA20	509
N8499B	C500	338
N8500	**SBRL**	**282-108**
N8500	SBRL	465-59
N8508Z	C500	284
N8514Y	WW24	231
N8516Z	FA50	7
N8520J	C550	151
N8526A	SBRL	380-53
N8534	WW24	113
N8535	WW24	139
N8536	WW24	148
N8536Y	LJ24	217
N8537B	LJ35	236
N8550A	FA50	263
N8562W	LJ35	462
N8562Y	LJ35	483
N8563A	LJ35	480
N8563B	LJ25	360
N8563E	LJ55	056
N8563G	LJ35	488
N8563M	LJ55	077
N8563N	LJ35	491
N8563P	LJ55	063
N8563Z	LJ55	075
N8564K	LJ35	496
N8564M	LJ35	493
N8564P	LJ35	498
N8564X	LJ55	089
N8564Z	LJ55	087
N8565H	LJ55	026
N8565J	LJ35	479
N8565K	LJ55	065
N8565N	LJ35	497
N8565X	LJ35	502
N8565Y	LJ25	364
N8565Z	LJ55	095
N8566B	LJ35	492
N8566F	LJ55	091
N8566Q	LJ55	097
N8566X	LJ35	500
N8566Z	LJ25	369
N8567A	LJ35	503
N8567J	LJ25	368
N8567K	LJ35	589
N8567R	LJ35	597
N8567T	LJ35	598
N8567X	LJ55	117
N8567Z	LJ35	591
N8567Z	LJ35	608
N8568B	LJ35	504
N8568D	LJ35	612
N8568J	LJ55	121
N8568P	LJ55	122
N8568Q	LJ35	616
N8568V	LJ35	619
N8568Y	LJ35	640
(N8570)	CL64	5488
N8572	F900	105
N8575J	FA50	196
N8608	**C680**	**0292**
N8701L	C550	550-1075
N8701L	**C56X**	**5751**
N8762	GLEX	9491
N8762M	GLEX	9113
N8762M	**GLEX**	**9491**
N8762W	GLEX	9113
(N8777N)	C550	171
N8778	**HS25**	**258560**
N8783	**LJ60**	**006**
N8785R	GLF2	93
N8796J	GLF4	1134
N8805	FA50	3
N8810	**GLF5**	**5231**
N8811A	**LJ60**	**119**
N8821C	**G150**	**226**
N8833	**GLF6**	**6059**
N8841C	**G150**	**229**
(N8875)	GLF4	4004
N8880D	**C52B**	**0208**
N8881J	**HS25**	**258219**
N8881N	C550	190
N8888	**F2TH**	**28**
N8888	LJ60	128
(N8888D)	LJ35	661
N8888G	**CL65**	**5773**
N8888H	**HS25**	**259043**
N8889	GLF5	5231
N8889	LJ60	128
N8892D	C550	550-0976
N8900M	C500	675
(N8909R)	SBRL	306-41
N8940	C525	0253
N8940	C52A	0013
N8940	C52A	0091

N8989N	**GLF4**	**1090**
N8996	**C560**	**0252**
N8998K	**GLEX**	**9541**
N8999A	FA20	137
N9000F	FA50	172
N9000F	FA50	242
N9000F	SBRL	465-25
N9000S	SBRL	282-64
N9000V	SBRL	282-64
N9000V	SBRL	306-10
N9001V	SBRL	306-10
N9002D	C510	0288
N9003	C525	0257
N9008	CL60	1054
N9008	GLEX	9008
N9008U	C510	0312
(N9011P)	PRM1	RB-74
N9011R	C500	210
N9012H	LJ60	179
N9013S	C500	288
N9014S	C550	025
N9021H	C680	0307
N9022D	C680	0290
N9023F	C510	0316
N9023W	WW24	10
N9026	HS25	259026
N9033X	LJ24	169
N9035Y	MS76	086
N9040	GLF2	82
N9040	HS25	25142
N9040N	WW24	140
N9041N	WW24	141
N9042N	WW24	142
N9043L	C510	0347
N9043N	WW24	143
N9043U	HS25	256058
N9044N	WW24	144
N9045N	WW24	145
N9046F	JSTR	5015
N9046N	WW24	146
N9047N	WW24	147
N9048K	C510	0326
N9048N	WW24	148
N9049N	WW24	149
N9050N	WW24	150
N9060Y	C500	241
N9065J	C500	247
N9071M	CL60	1019
N9072U	**CS55**	**0106**
N9099	**LJ35**	**618**
N9099H	**GLEX**	**9557**
N9102	**GLF5**	**551**
N9106	**GLF4**	**1434**
N9108Z	LJ36	005
N9113F	LJ35	259
N9113J	HS25	257067
N9114S	WW24	164
N9124N	HS25	25075
N9125M	LJ55	146
N9130F	LJ35	664
N9132Z	LJ31	031
N9134Q	WW24	220
N9138	HS25	25216
N9138Y	F900	33
N9140Y	LJ35	672
N9141N	LJ35	671
N9143F	LJ31	055
N9146Z	BE40	RK-120
(N9147F)	FA10	42
N9147Q	LJ31	057
N9149	HS25	25161
N9152R	LJ31	051
N9152X	LJ31	061
N9155Z	LJ60	025
N9160T	C510	0320
N9161X	C510	0309
N9166N	C510	0346
N9166Y	SBRL	265-80
N9168Q	LJ35	668
N9168Y	C510	0302
N9173G	LJ35	673
N9173L	LJ31	029
N9173M	LJ31	067
N9173N	LJ31	071
N9173Q	LJ31	053
N9173R	LJ60	017
N9173T	LJ31	087
N9173V	LJ31	069
N9173X	LJ31	090
N9180K	C525	0342
N9180K	C52A	0345
N9192W	**C750**	**0281**
N9200M	LJ60	132
N9201R	JSTR	5001/53
N9202R	JSTR	5002
N9203R	JSTR	5003
N9204R	JSTR	5004
N9205R	JSTR	5007/45
N9206R	JSTR	5009
N9207R	JSTR	5020
N9208R	JSTR	5101/15
N9210R	JSTR	5016
N9211R	JSTR	5037/24
N9212R	JSTR	5038
N9214R	JSTR	5047
N9215R	JSTR	5048
N9216R	JSTR	5049
N9217R	JSTR	5051
N9218R	JSTR	5052
N9219R	JSTR	5053/2
N9220R	JSTR	5054/59
N9221R	JSTR	5023
N9222R	JSTR	5055/21
N9223R	JSTR	5056
N9225R	JSTR	5060
N9226R	JSTR	5061/48
N9228R	JSTR	5063
N9229R	JSTR	5065
N9230R	JSTR	5066/46
N9231R	JSTR	5068/27
N9233R	JSTR	5072/23
N9234R	JSTR	5074/22
N9235R	JSTR	5076/17
N9235R	JSTR	5102
N9236R	JSTR	5077
N9238R	JSTR	5079/33
N9240R	JSTR	5084/8
N9241R	JSTR	5085
N9242R	JSTR	5086/44
N9243R	JSTR	5087/55
N9244R	JSTR	5088
N9245R	JSTR	5089
N9246R	JSTR	5090
N9247R	JSTR	5091
N9248R	JSTR	5092/58
N9249R	JSTR	5093
N9250R	JSTR	5094
N9251N	SBRL	282-131
N9251R	JSTR	5095/30
N9252N	SBRL	282-132
N9252R	JSTR	5096/10
N9253R	JSTR	5097/60
N9253V	**GLEX**	**9024**
N9253V	GLF4	1176
N9254R	JSTR	5098/28
N9255R	JSTR	5099/5
N9256R	JSTR	5100/41
N9258U	FA10	132
N9260A	LJ24	047
N9272K	GLF2	46
N9280R	JSTR	5006/40
N9282R	JSTR	5011/1
N9282R	JSTR	5046
N9282Y	HS25	256044
N9283R	JSTR	5012
N9284R	JSTR	5013
N9286R	JSTR	5017
N9287R	JSTR	5018
N9288R	JSTR	5019
N9292X	**HS25**	**258315**
N9300	E55P	50500159
N9300	GLF2	7
N9300	GLF4	1020
N9300	HS25	25051
N9300C	FA50	106
N9300C	HS25	25051
N9300C	HS25	25169
N9300M	FA20	106
(N9300P)	HS25	25169
N9308Y	HS25	25058
N9311	FA50	121
N9312	FA50	126
N9313	FA50	128
N9314	FA50	130
(N9366Q)	JSTR	5214
N9395Y	HS25	257059
N9410P	C525	0077
N9474L	C510	0433
N9488B	C510	0438
N9500B	SBRL	282-91
N9503Z	SBRL	282-10
N9506G	GLEX	9506
N9517	CL61	5117
N9542G	C52C	0110
N9550A	FA50	265
N9611Z	G150	231
N9634	GLEX	9634
N9641	GLEX	9641
N9653	GLEX	9653
N9654N	FA20	380
N9661S	C680	0247
N9671A	LJ25	092
(N9680N)	CL61	3050
N9680Z	CL61	3050
N9688R	**E55P**	**50500311**
N9700T	**C560**	**0203**
N9700X	CL61	5186
(N9707X)	FA7X	9
N9708N	CL61	3061
N9711N	GLF3	358
N9712T	C500	397
(N9718P)	GLF3	405
N9739B	JSTR	5052
N9771C	**CL61**	**5063**
N9867	**HS25**	**258678**
N9871R	C500	121
N9871R	**F2EX**	**43**
(N9876S)	LJ35	277
N9881S	GPER	551
N9889	**GALX**	**009**
N9895	**F2EX**	**184**
N9900R	**EA50**	**000176**
N9921	JSTR	5070/52
N9922F	**EA50**	**000100**
N9930B	**PRM1**	**RB-241**
N9932	WW24	82
N9939T	**GLF4**	**4134**
N9990M	**E50P**	**50000186**
N9990P	ASTR	062
N9990S	HS25	258209
N9997X	**FA7X**	**51**
N9999E	FA20	135
N9999M	GLF4	1090
N9999V	HS25	257155
N10108	C500	035
N10121	HS25	25098
N10122	HS25	25029
N10122	WW24	182
N10123	**GLF2**	**107**
N10123	JSTR	5012
N10139	E55P	50500333
N10153	E50P	50000286
N10160	E50P	50000295
N10163	E55P	50500347
N10193	E55P	50500320
N10200	E50P	50000306
N10204	E55P	50500335
N10461	JSTR	5011/1
N10580	SBRL	465-7
N10581	SBRL	465-8
N10726	FA20	54
N10855	HS25	258159
N10855	HS25	259002
N10857	HS25	258213
N10870	LJ35	268
N10870	LJ35	331
N10870	LJ35	430
N10870	LJ35	649
N10870	LJ40	2140
N10870	**LJ45**	**537**
N10870	LJ55	103
N10870	LJ55	122
N10870	LJ60	362
N10870	LJ60	410
N10871	LJ35	270
N10871	LJ35	317
N10871	LJ35	504
N10871	LJ35	618
N10871	LJ36	055
N10871	LJ45	446
N10871	**LJ45**	**538**
N10871	LJ55	143
N10871	LJ60	385
N10872	LJ25	369
N10872	LJ35	275
N10872	LJ45	425
N10872	LJ45	468
N10872	**LJ45**	**540**
N10872	LJ55	013
N10872	LJ60	368
N10873	LJ25	315
N10873	LJ25	364
N10873	LJ31	003
N10873	LJ35	475
N10873	LJ35	602
N10873	LJ45	402
N10873	LJ45	480
N10873	**LJ45**	**541**
N10873	LJ60	369
N10873	LJ60	420
N10972	LJ35	038
N11084	C680	0114
N11111	LJ24	098
N11288	**C650**	**0184**
N11382	LJ35	002
N11697	FA10	40
N11827	FA20	26
N11887	**SBRL**	**380-4**
N11963	C56X	5685
N12001	C550	689
N12003	C550	698
N12012	C560	0268
N12022	C550	708
(N12030)	C550	712
N12033	C550	713
N12035	C550	714
N12058	C552	0004
N12060	C550	718
N12065	C552	0011
N12068	C550	719
N12109	LJ35	410
N12117	C550	731
(N12117)	C560	0007
N12121	JSTR	5005
N12142	C550	396
(N12149)	C550	397
(N12155)	C550	402
N12157	C550	403
(N12159)	C550	404
N12160	C550	412
(N12160)	C560	0009
N12162	C550	413
(N12162)	C560	0010
N12164	C550	414
N12167	C550	415
N12171	C550	422
N12171	C560	0015
N12173	C560	0016
(N12173)	C550	423
N12190	C550	437
(N12191)	C550	438
N12225	HS25	25122
N12241	JSTR	5141
(N12249)	C560	0018
N12269	C552	0015
(N12283)	C560	0023
(N12284)	C560	0024
(N12285)	C560	0025
(N12286)	C560	0026
(N12289)	C560	0027
N12295	C650	7075
(N12295)	C560	0036
(N12297)	C560	0037
(N12298)	C560	0038
N12315	LJ24	154
N12373	LJ25	054
N12378	C550	550-1040
N12403	C560	0040
N12419	C550	608
N12482	C550	447
N12490	C550	454
N12500	C550	459
N12505	C550	460
N12507	C550	461
N12508	C550	462
N12510	C550	471
N12511	C550	472
N12513	C550	473
N12514	C550	474
N12522	C550	615
(N12522)	C550	480
N12532	C550	487
N12536	C550	488
N12539	C550	489
N12543	C550	621
(N12543)	C550	496
N12549	**C550**	**501**
(N12549)	C550	497
(N12554)	C550	625
(N12554)	CS55	0003
N12557	C552	0003
N12564	C552	0010
N12566	C552	0012
N12568	C552	0014
N12570	C550	632
(N12570)	CS55	0012
N12576	C550	633
(N12576)	CS55	0013
(N12582)	C550	638
(N12583)	CS55	0014
N12593	C650	7008
(N12593)	C550	646
(N12593)	CS55	0024
N12596	C650	7009
(N12596)	C550	647
(N12596)	CS55	0025
N12605	C650	7013
(N12605)	CS55	0031
(N12615)	CS55	0036
N12616	C650	7019
(N12616)	CS55	0037
N12632	C650	7030
N12636	C650	7031
N12637	C650	7032
N12642	C650	7038
N12643	C650	7039
N12652	C650	7045
N12659	SBRL	380-16
N12660	C552	0006
N12686	C56X	5368
N12688	C560	0488
(N12690)	CS55	0046
N12695	CS55	0047
N12703	CS55	0052
N12705	CS55	0053
N12709	CS55	0054
(N12712)	CS55	0061
N12715	CS55	0062
(N12717)	CS55	0063
(N12720)	CS55	0069
(N12722)	CS55	0070
(N12727)	CS55	0071
N12730	CS55	0080
N12742	C52A	0359
(N12744)	CS55	0088
N12745	CS55	0089
N12746	CS55	0090
(N12747)	CS55	0091
N12756	C552	0002
N12761	C552	0007
N12762	C552	0008
N12763	C552	0009
N12778	C56X	5553
N12798	C560	0176
N12799	C560	0177
N12807	C560	0183
N12812	C560	0187
N12813	C560	0188
N12815	C560	0189
N12816	C560	0190
N12817	C560	0191
N12824	C560	0196
N12826	C560	0197
N12838	C560	0205
N12845	C560	0213
N12850	C560	0219
N12852	C560	0220
N12855	C552	0001
N12859	C552	0005
(N12879)	C560	0232
N12890	C560	0243
(N12895)	C560	0244
N12896	C560	0245
N12900	CS55	0103
N12903	CS55	0104
N12907	C560	0247
(N12907)	CS55	0105
N12909	C560	0248
(N12909)	C650	7110
(N12909)	CS55	0106
N12910	C560	0251
(N12910)	CS55	0112
N12911	C560	0252
(N12911)	CS55	0113
N12920	CS55	0118
N12921	C560	0254
N12922	C560	0255
(N12922)	CS55	0119
N12924	CS55	0120
N12925	C680	0052
(N12925)	CS55	0121
N12929	C560	0256
N12929	CS55	0122
N12934	CS55	0131
N12945	C560	0263
(N12945)	CS55	0137
N12967	C552	0013
(N12979)	C550	556
N12990	C550	571
N12990	C56X	5598
N12992	C550	572
N12993	C550	550-1126
(N12993)	C550	573
N12998	C550	574
N12999	C550	575
N13001	C52B	0083
(N13001)	C550	579
(N13006)	C550	580
(N13007)	C550	581
N13027	C550	597
N13028	C550	598
(N13047)	C650	0007
(N13049)	C650	0008
N13052	C650	0231
(N13052)	C650	0013
N13087	C52A	0244
N13091	C550	643
N13092	**C560**	**0707**
(N13092)	C550	644
N13113	C650	0159
N13138	C650	0063
(N13142)	C650	0069
(N13150)	C650	0078
(N13162)	C650	0082
N13166	C650	0083
(N13168)	C650	0084
(N13170)	C650	0088
(N13175)	C650	0089
(N13189)	C650	0098
(N13194)	C650	0103
N13195	C52A	0321
N13195	C650	0104
(N13204)	C650	0111
(N13210)	C650	0118
(N13217)	C650	0119
N13218	C56X	5633
N13218	C650	0120
(N13222)	C650	0125
(N13242)	C650	0139
N13256	C650	0146
N13259	C650	0147
N13264	C650	0155
N13267	C650	0156
N13291	C525	0024
N13304	JSTR	5004
N13308	C525	0029
(N13312)	C525	0031
(N13313)	C525	0032
N13474	C52A	0360
N13606	LJ24	254
N13616	C510	0049
N13627	C550	147
N14456	GLF4	1430
N15019	GLF5	5019
N15693	BE40	RK-29
N16200	JSTR	5033/56
(N16251)	GLF4	1013
N16300	HS25	258561
N16777	HS25	25083
N17005	JSTR	5105
(N17401)	FA20	62/409
N17581	GLF2	127
N17581	GLF2	163
N17581	GLF2	183
N17581	GLF2	211
N17581	GLF2	235
N17581	GLF2	256
N17581	GLF3	346
N17581	GLF3	399
N17581	GLF3	435
N17581	GLF4	1001
N17581	GLF4	1011
N17581	GLF4	1059
N17581	GLF4	1107
N17581	GLF4	1157

N17582	GLF2	131/23
N17582	GLF2	164
N17582	GLF2	186
N17582	GLF2	239
N17582	GLF3	252
N17582	GLF3	326
N17582	GLF3	376
N17582	GLF3	415
N17582	GLF4	1005
N17582	GLF4	1061
N17582	GLF4	1096
N17582	GLF4	1158
N17583	GLF2	133
N17583	GLF2	167
N17583	GLF2	187
N17583	GLF2	43
N17583	GLF3	304
N17583	GLF3	347
N17583	GLF3	418
N17583	GLF3	466
N17583	GLF4	1015
N17583	GLF4	1062
N17583	GLF4	1159
N17584	GLF2	141
N17584	GLF2	169
N17584	GLF2	194
N17584	GLF2	224
N17584	GLF2	244
N17584	GLF3	307
N17584	GLF4	1019
N17584	GLF4	1026
N17584	GLF4	1063
N17584	GLF4	1108
N17584	GLF4	1160
N17585	GLF2	144
N17585	GLF2	171
N17585	GLF2	201
N17585	GLF2	214
N17585	GLF2	225
N17585	GLF2	78
N17585	GLF3	311
N17585	GLF3	345
N17585	GLF3	400
N17585	GLF4	1032
N17585	GLF4	1068
N17585	GLF4	1129
N17585	GLF4	1161
N17586	GLF2	149
N17586	GLF2	175
N17586	GLF2	202
N17586	GLF2	230
N17586	GLF2	91
N17586	GLF3	352
N17586	GLF3	379
N17586	GLF3	439
N17586	GLF3	465
N17586	GLF4	1072
N17586	GLF4	1076
N17586	GLF4	1167
N17587	GLF2	152
N17587	GLF2	177
N17587	GLF2	203
N17587	GLF2	246
N17587	GLF3	324
N17587	GLF3	393
N17587	GLF3	442
N17587	GLF4	1074
N17587	GLF4	1173
N17588	GLF2	179
N17588	GLF2	204
N17588	GLF3	367
N17588	GLF4	1037
N17588	GLF4	1175
N17589	GLF2	161
N17589	GLF2	182
N17589	GLF2	248
N17589	GLF3	368
N17589	GLF4	1078
N17603	GLF3	407
N17603	GLF4	1038
N17603	GLF4	1079
N17608	GLF3	356
N17608	GLF3	408
N17608	GLF4	1042
N17608	GLF4	1106
N18243	HS25	257182
N18328	C500	373
N18650	**C52B**	**0343**
N18860	C500	653
N19537	C52B	0486
N19539	C56X	6206
N20373	FA10	33
N20669	C52A	0444
N20768	C750	0298
N21066	GLF2	69
N21076	C56X	5828
N21092	SBRL	265-42
N21654	C680	0258
N21671	**HDJT**	**42000026**
(N22265)	JSTR	5005
(N22508)	C500	474
N22511	C550	089
N22976	WW24	133
N23204	HS25	258346
N23207	HS25	258350
N23208	HS25	258351
N23263	BE40	RK-290

N23395	HS25	258339
N23451	HS25	258382
N23455	HS25	258384
N23466	HS25	258385
N23479	HS25	258386
N23488	HS25	258388
N23493	HS25	258389
N23509	HS25	258390
N23525	BE40	RK-238
N23550	HS25	258403
N23555	FA20	46
N23556	HS25	258370
N23566	HS25	258381
N23569	HS25	258392
N23577	HS25	258395
N23585	HS25	258396
N23592	HS25	258401
N24237	C650	0102
N24329	**C510**	**0020**
N24480	SBRL	276-33
N25685	LJ31	056
N25853	HS25	258538
N25997	LJ31	062
N25999	LJ31	059
N26002	LJ31	077
N26005	LJ31	065
N26006	LJ31	066
N26008	LJ24	026
N26011	HS25	25060
N26011	LJ60	013
N26018	GLF3	316
N26018	LJ31	058
N26029	LJ60	009
N26105	C525	0042
N26105	C650	0182
N26174	C525	0046
N26174	C650	0189
N26178	**C550**	**141**
N26227	C500	642
N26228	C650	0194
(N26228)	C500	643
N26229	C550	093
N26232	C500	644
N26233	C650	0195
N26263	C500	652
N26264	C500	653
(N26264)	C650	0201
N26271	C650	0203
N26369	C550	150
N26369	C555	0152
N26379	C525	0052
N26379	C555	0154
N26461	C500	489
N26461	C550	156
N26481	C525	0061
(N26481)	C500	496
N26486	C525	0062
(N26486)	C500	497
N26492	C500	505
N26493	C500	506
N26494	C500	507
N26494	**C550**	**605**
N26495	C525	0066
(N26495)	C500	508
N26496	**C550**	**607**
(N26496)	C500	509
N26497	C500	510
N26498	C500	511
N26499	C525	0067
(N26499)	C500	512
N26502	C525	0069
(N26502)	C500	520
N26503	C500	521
N26504	C525	0070
(N26504)	C500	522
N26506	C500	523
N26507	C500	524
N26509	C525	0071
(N26509)	C500	525
N26510	C500	532
N26514	C500	533
N26517	C500	534
N26523	C500	535
(N26540)	C500	507
N26581	C525	0074
N26583	LJ35	433
N26610	C550	075
N26610	C550	161
N26613	C550	076
(N26614)	C550	077
(N26615)	C550	078
(N26616)	C550	079
N26617	C550	080
N26619	C550	081
N26619	GLF3	353
N26621	**C550**	**593**
(N26621)	C550	086
(N26622)	C550	087
(N26623)	C550	088
(N26624)	C550	089
N26626	C550	090
N26627	C550	091
N26628	C550	092
(N26630)	C550	101
(N26630)	C560	0039
N26631	C550	102
N26632	C550	103

N26634	C550	104
(N26635)	C550	105
N26638	C550	106
N26639	C550	107
N26640	C550	113
N26640	CL60	1039
N26643	C560	0041
(N26643)	C550	114
(N26648)	C550	115
(N26648)	C560	0042
N26649	C550	116
N26652	C550	123
(N26656)	C550	124
(N26656)	C560	0046
N26674	CRVT	27
(N26771)	C560	0050
(N26804)	C560	0054
N26863	C550	139
N26895	CL60	1056
N27052	**EA50**	**000120**
(N27216)	C560	0066
N27341	CL60	1051
N27369	**C510**	**712**
N27457	C550	132
N28357	**G280**	**2022**
N28686	HS25	25152
N28968	C550	074
N29019	SBRL	370-6
N29134	**BE40**	**RK-484**
N29687	CL60	1048
N29858	C500	112
N29966	FA10	17
N29977	HS25	25028
N29984	CL60	1060
N29991	C500	254
N29995	WW24	250
N30046	LJ31	146
N30046	BE40	RK-206
N30050	LJ31	218
N30051	LJ31	215
N30054	LJ31	227
N30111	LJ31	153
N30137	LJ45	153
N30154	LJ60	191
N30156	WW24	165
N30170	LJ60	225
N30289	HS25	258404
N30319	HS25	258408
N30337	HS25	258409
N30355	HS25	258725
N30423	C56X	6067
N30438	GLF2	30/4
N30501	**GLF3**	**383**
N30562	HS25	258407
N30682	HS25	258412
N30742	HS25	258414
N30884	C680	0536
N31001	GLF4	1001
N31016	HS25	258415
N31031	**C56X**	**6182**
N31046	HS25	258418
N31079	C500	180
N31088	C500	079
N31112	CL30	20083
N31240	CL60	1063
N31340	HS25	258420
N31403	SBRL	276-4
N31428	BE40	RJ-28
N31432	BE40	RJ-32
N31437	BE40	RJ-37
N31496	BE40	RK-396
N31542	BE40	RJ-42
N31590	HS25	258430
N31596	HS25	258439
N31624	HS25	HA-0034
N31685	HS25	HB-5
N31733	BE40	RJ-33
N31820	HS25	258421
N31833	HS25	258427
N31842	HS25	HA-0080
N31921	PRM1	RB-221
N31946	HS25	HA-0046
N31958	HS25	HA-0028
N31959	HS25	HA-0049
N31964	HS25	HA-0064
N31975	BE40	RK-555
N31991	HS25	258891
N32010	SBRL	265-83
N32012	HS25	258912
N32022	PRM1	RB-222
N32051	BE40	RK-541
N32061	HS25	258921
N32185	HS25	HA-0055
N32212	BE40	TX-10
N32287	LJ24	230
N32290	SBRL	465-17
N32508	SBRL	285-17
N32654	SBRL	282-111
N32862	HS25	HA-0062
N32926	HS25	HA-0026
N33055	HS25	HA-0025
N33062	BE40	RK-562
N33235	HS25	HA-0035
N33527	HS25	HA-0027
N33612	HS25	HA-0072
N33805	PRM1	RB-235
N33837	PRM1	RB-237

N34249	BE40	RK-549
N34441	HS25	HA-0041
N34451	HS25	HA-0061
N34548	HS25	HA-0048
N34820	PRM1	RB-220
N34838	HS25	HA-0038
N34859	PRM1	RB-219
N34956	HS25	HA-0036
N35004	HA4T	RC-24
N35403	C550	150
N36050	SBRL	282-80
N36065	SBRL	282-81
N36204	LJ25	138
N36578	HS25	258778
N36607	BE40	RK-407
N36621	HS25	258721
N36632	BE40	RK-472
N36636	PRM1	RB-136
N36646	BE40	RK-443
N36669	HS25	258749
N36672	HS25	258712
N36685	HS25	258685
N36689	HS25	258689
N36690	HS25	258690
N36701	BE40	RK-401
N36726	HS25	258776
N36731	PRM1	RB-131
N36752	BE40	RK-452
N36758	PRM1	RB-158
N36764	BE40	RK-464
N36792	BE40	RK-392
N36803	BE40	RK-403
N36820	HS25	258720
N36826	HS25	258806
N36841	HS25	258741
N36842	C500	364
N36846	C500	365
N36846	BE40	RK-476
N36848	C500	366
N36850	C500	367
N36854	C500	368
N36854	C550	653
N36858	C500	369
N36859	C500	370
N36860	C500	371
N36861	C500	372
N36862	C500	373
N36863	C500	374
N36864	C500	375
N36864	PRM1	RB-164
N36866	**PRM1**	**RB-166**
N36869	C500	376
N36870	C500	377
N36871	C500	378
N36872	C500	379
N36873	C500	380
N36873	PRM1	RB-153
N36878	HS25	258807
N36880	C500	381
N36880	BE40	RK-480
N36881	C500	382
N36882	C500	383
N36883	C500	384
N36884	C500	385
N36885	C500	386
N36886	C500	387
N36886	C550	654
N36887	C500	388
N36888	C500	389
N36890	C500	390
N36890	PRM1	RB-160
N36891	C500	391
N36892	C500	392
N36893	C500	393
N36894	HS25	258694
N36895	C500	394
N36896	C500	395
N36896	HS25	258696
N36897	C500	396
N36898	C500	397
N36901	C500	398
N36906	C500	399
N36907	BE40	RK-417
N36908	C500	400
N36911	C500	401
N36912	C500	402
N36914	C500	403
N36915	C500	404
N36916	C500	405
N36918	C500	406
N36919	C500	407
N36922	C500	408
N36923	C500	409
N36943	C500	423
N36949	C500	428
N36964	PRM1	RB-154
N36970	HS25	258770
N36979	PRM1	RB-149
N36986	HS25	258786
N36997	BE40	RK-397
N37009	HS25	258799
N37010	HS25	258710
N37019	PRM1	RB-177
N37054	HS25	258754
N37056	HS25	258756
N37059	PRM1	RB-159
N37060	HS25	258730

N37061	HS25	258731
N37070	HS25	258780
N37071	PRM1	RB-151
N37079	BE40	RK-469
N37086	PRM1	RB-186
N37092	HS25	258692
N37105	HS25	258775
N37108	BE40	RK-408
N37115	BE40	RK-415
N37146	HS25	258783
N37158	HS25	258758
N37160	HS25	258760
N37165	BE40	RK-465
N37170	HS25	258817
N37179	HS25	258779
N37201	C550	655
N37204	BE40	RK-404
N37211	HS25	258711
N37245	PRM1	RB-145
N37261	HS25	258781
N37295	HS25	258795
N37310	BE40	RK-410
N37312	BE40	RK-412
N37322	HS25	258722
N37325	BE40	RK-425
N37337	BE40	RK-437
N37339	BE40	RK-512
N37346	PRM1	RB-196
N37489	C500	317
N37516	HS25	25271
N37594	LJ24	128
N37643	C500	255
N37931	LJ35	342
N37943	LJ25	344
N37947	LJ35	449
N37949	LJ25	348
N37951	LJ55	011
N37962	LJ35	446
N37965	LJ35	399
N37966	LJ35	403
N37971	**LJ25**	**358**
N37973	LJ25	359
N37975	HS25	257004
N37975	LJ35	474
N37980	LJ35	412
N37984	LJ35	384
N37988	LJ35	436
N38328	LJ25	314
N38788	LJ24	262
N39142	C550	235
N39292	LJ35	189
N39293	LJ35	188
N39300	C500	571
N39301	C500	353
N39391	LJ25	311
N39391	LJ35	118
N39391	LJ36	042
N39391	LJ55	078
N39391	LJ55	105
N39391	LJ55	124
N39391	LJ55	139
N39394	LJ28	28-004
N39394	LJ35	145
N39394	LJ35	597
N39394	LJ36	057
N39394	LJ55	082
N39398	LJ25	245
N39398	LJ25	362
N39398	LJ35	144
N39398	LJ35	272
N39398	LJ35	316
N39398	LJ35	626
N39398	LJ55	095
N39398	LJ55	114
N39399	LJ25	370
N39399	LJ31	025
N39399	LJ35	151
N39399	LJ35	492
N39399	LJ35	607
N39399	LJ55	134
N39404	LJ28	28-002
N39404	LJ35	624
N39404	LJ35	658
N39404	LJ55	079
N39404	LJ55	104
N39412	LJ25	346
N39412	LJ28	29-004
N39412	LJ35	179
N39412	LJ35	217
N39412	LJ35	329
N39412	LJ35	638
N39412	LJ55	067
N39412	LJ55	110
N39413	LJ25	260
N39413	LJ35	259
N39413	LJ35	313
N39413	LJ35	474
N39413	LJ35	611
N39413	LJ55	015
N39413	LJ55	084
N39413	LJ55	137
N39415	LJ25	229
N39415	LJ25	347
N39415	LJ31	005
N39415	LJ35	161
N39415	LJ35	201
N39415	LJ35	598

N39415	LJ55	075
N39415	LJ55	101
N39416	LJ25	238
N39416	LJ25	287
N39416	LJ25	363
N39416	LJ35	219
N39416	LJ35	433
N39416	LJ35	469
N39416	LJ35	633
N39416	LJ55	118
N39418	LJ35	205
N39418	LJ35	230
N39418	LJ35	267
N39418	LJ35	643
N39418	LJ36	053
N39418	LJ55	039
N39418	LJ55	120
N39461	FA50	98
N39515	FA10	37
N40012	LJ31	223
N40012	LJ40	2074
N40012	LJ45	104
N40012	LJ45	266
N40012	LJ45	403
N40012	LJ45	413
N40012	LJ45	465
N40012	LJ60	231
N40012	LJ60	298
N40012	LJ60	349
N40012	LJ60	414
N40027	HS25	258434
N40031	LJ31	242
N40043	LJ31	242
N40043	LJ40	2098
N40043	LJ45	272
N40043	LJ45	303
N40043	LJ45	394
N40043	LJ45	460
N40043	LJ45	522
N40043	LJ60	205
N40043	LJ60	400
N40049	C510	0096
N40049	C510	0174
N40049	C525	0800
N40049	C525	0906
N40050	LJ40	2035
N40050	LJ40	2112
N40050	LJ40	2143
N40050	LJ45	140
N40050	LJ45	250
N40050	LJ45	347
N40050	LJ45	440
N40050	LJ45	527
N40050	LJ60	260
N40050	LJ60	305
N40073	LJ31	227
N40073	LJ40	2029
N40073	LJ45	231
N40073	LJ45	251
N40073	LJ45	305
N40073	LJ45	336
N40073	LJ45	382
N40073	LJ45	422
N40073	LJ45	466
N40073	LJ45	528
N40073	LJ60	191
N40073	LJ60	342
N40075	LJ31	215
N40075	LJ40	2113
N40075	LJ40	2131
N40075	LJ45	148
N40075	LJ45	249
N40075	LJ45	274
N40075	LJ45	362
N40075	LJ45	524
N40075	LJ60	259
N40075	LJ60	303
(N40075)	LJ60	431
N40076	LJ40	2030
N40076	LJ40	2080
N40076	LJ45	232
N40076	LJ45	252
N40076	LJ45	441
N40076	LJ45	486
N40076	LJ45	526
N40076	LJ60	206
N40076	LJ60	304
N40076	LJ60	344
N40076	LJ60	364
N40076	LJ60	386
N40077	LJ31	216
N40077	LJ40	2015
N40077	LJ40	2048
N40077	LJ40	2071
N40077	LJ45	220
N40077	LJ45	354
N40077	LJ45	409
N40077	LJ45	488
N40077	**LJ45**	**539**
N40077	LJ60	288
N40077	LJ60	355
N40077	LJ60	418
N40078	LJ31	217
N40078	LJ40	2016
N40078	LJ40	2097
N40078	LJ45	284
N40078	LJ45	311
N40078	LJ45	388
N40078	LJ45	442
N40078	LJ45	489
N40078	LJ45	530
N40078	LJ60	387
N40079	LJ40	2078
N40079	LJ40	2094
N40079	LJ40	2133
N40079	LJ45	229
N40079	LJ45	280
N40079	LJ45	397
N40079	LJ45	469
N40079	LJ45	510
N40079	LJ60	213
N40079	LJ60	277
N40081	LJ40	2121
N40081	LJ45	117
N40081	LJ45	223
N40081	LJ45	255
N40081	LJ45	328
N40081	LJ45	358
N40081	LJ45	461
N40081	**LJ45**	**532**
N40081	LJ60	300
N40082	LJ40	2004
N40082	LJ40	2079
N40082	LJ40	2119
N40082	LJ45	082
N40082	LJ45	275
N40082	LJ45	369
N40082	LJ45	411
N40082	LJ45	443
N40082	LJ45	487
N40082	LJ45	533
N40083	LJ40	2005
N40083	LJ40	2073
N40083	LJ40	2096
N40083	LJ40	2114
N40083	LJ45	507
N40083	LJ60	215
N40083	LJ60	289
N40083	LJ60	402
(N40083)	LJ60	432
N40084	LJ45	276
N40084	LJ45	331
N40084	LJ45	448
N40084	**LJ45**	**534**
N40084	LJ60	208
N40084	LJ60	264
N40084	LJ60	394
N40085	LJ40	2031
N40085	LJ40	2105
N40085	LJ40	2134
N40085	LJ45	226
N40085	LJ45	325
N40085	LJ45	400
N40085	**LJ45**	**535**
N40085	LJ60	209
N40085	LJ60	403
N40086	LJ45	277
N40086	LJ45	304
N40086	LJ45	391
N40086	LJ45	536
N40086	LJ60	210
N40086	LJ60	265
N40086	LJ60	398
N40086	LJ60	422
N40113	HS25	258438
N40130	LJ31	110
N40144	LJ24	342
N40144	LJ25	283
N40144	LJ31	018
N40144	LJ35	165
N40144	LJ35	199
N40144	LJ35	253
N40144	LJ35	483
N40144	LJ35	508
N40144	LJ35	599
N40144	LJ35	629
N40144	LJ45	392
N40144	LJ45	423
N40144	LJ45	444
N40144	**LJ45**	**542**
N40144	LJ55	014
N40146	LJ25	349
N40146	LJ35	099
N40146	LJ35	178
N40146	LJ35	207
N40146	LJ35	593
N40146	LJ36	032
N40146	LJ45	393
N40146	**LJ45**	**543**
N40146	LJ55	063
N40146	LJ55	090
N40146	LJ60	401
N40146	LJ60	430
N40149	LJ25	357
N40149	LJ25	372
N40149	LJ35	101
N40149	LJ35	208
N40149	LJ35	344
N40149	LJ35	442
N40149	LJ35	623
N40149	LJ45	395
N40149	LJ45	406
N40149	LJ45	445
N40149	**LJ45**	**544**
N40149	LJ55	083
N40149	LJ60	376
N40162	LJ25	246
N40162	LJ25	263
N40162	LJ35	477
N40162	LJ35	608
N40162	LJ40	2122
N40162	LJ40	2137
N40162	LJ45	415
N40162	**LJ45**	**545**
N40162	LJ55	086
N40162	LJ60	421
N40166	C560	0692
N40180	FA10	93
N40202	HS25	258442
N40215	BE40	RK-258
N40252	BE40	RK-247
N40255	HS25	258095
N40280	LJ31	078
N40310	HS25	258447
N40323	LJ60	023
N40339	C510	0334
N40339	**C510**	**0469**
N40339	LJ31	076
N40349	LJ31	079
N40363	LJ31	083
N40366	C525	0909
N40366	LJ60	019
N40435	C550	550-1008
N40488	HS25	258440
N40489	HS25	258444
N40512	C510	0406
N40512	**C525**	**0919**
N40577	C56X	5157
N40593	WW24	41
N40595	C525	0809
N40595	C525	0911
N40708	HS25	258445
N40753	C510	0292
N40753	C525	0824
N40753	**C525**	**0924**
N40770	C510	0059
N40770	C510	0361
N40770	C525	0827
N40770	C525	0877
N40770	**C525**	**0927**
N40780	C510	0300
N40780	C525	0832
N40805	C510	0425
N40805	C510	0462
N40851	C510	0465
N40854	C510	0440
N40854	C525	0895
N40863	C525	0898
N40864	C510	0252
N40864	**C510**	**0466**
N40878	C510	0326
N40878	C510	0379
N40878	C510	0447
N40878	C525	0901
N40933	HS25	258493
N40938	**C525**	**0915**
N40994	FA20	289
N41093	HS25	258454
N41118	C56X	5510
N41154	FA20	147/444
N41159	C525	0652
N41174	C52A	0373
N41184	C52A	0378
N41196	C525	0675
N41199	C680	0228
N41203	C52B	0266
N41212	C52A	0424
N41221	C680	0270
N41222	C680	0274
N41225	C680	0263
N41226	C52B	0309
N41227	C510	0195
N41233	C56X	5804
N41237	C56X	5816
N41280	HS25	258448
N41283	BE40	RK-266
N41297	C510	0196
N41431	HS25	258449
N41441	HS25	258450
N41534	HS25	258451
N41762	HS25	258456
N41953	HS25	25268
N41964	HS25	258464
N41984	HS25	258457
N42137	CL60	1011
N42622	HS25	256011
N42685	HS25	258458
N42799	SBRL	380-30
N42825	LJ25	314
N42830	HS25	258470
N42905	LJ31	020
N42905	LJ35	520
N42905	LJ35	536
N42905	LJ35	630
N42905	LJ55	054
N43079	HS25	258469
N43182	HS25	258482
N43230	HS25	258462
N43259	HS25	258459
N43265	HS25	258465
N43310	HS25	258467
N43436	HS25	258468
N43642	HS25	258471
N43675	HS25	258475
N43783	LJ25	260
N43926	HS25	258481
N44200	GLF3	324
N44515	HS25	258485
N44648	HS25	258478
N44676	HS25	258476
N44695	LJ35	444
N44722	HS25	258472
N44759	HS25	258551
N44767	HS25	258477
N44779	HS25	258479
N44883	HS25	258483
N44888	HS25	258588
N44982	GLF5	581
N45500	HS25	257108
N45678	C550	550-1056
N45793	HS25	25152
N45811	LJ24	108
N45824	LJ24	217
N45826	LJ25	283
N45862	LJ24	291
N46032	LJ24	267
N46106	C500	382
N46190	HS25	25108
N46253	C500	454
N46386	ASTR	067
N46452	LJ24	095
N46901	HS25	257014
N46931	LJ35	092
N47449	GLF3	420
N48172	HS25	25028
N49566	HS25	257094
N49968	WW24	202
N50005	HS25	258505
N50005	LJ31	229
N50031	LJ60	230
N50034	HS25	258554
N50050	LJ60	057
N50054	C525	0630
N50054	C52A	0455
N50054	C56X	5726
N50054	C680	0235
N50054	C680	0315
N50054	C680	0506
N50054	C680	0547
N50054	**C680**	**0562**
N50078	PRM1	RB-109
N50088	LJ31	088
N50088	LJ31	192
N50088	LJ45	168
N50111	LJ31	035
N50111	LJ40	2006
N50111	LJ40	2019
N50111	LJ40	2054
N50111	LJ45	058
N50111	LJ45	116
N50111	LJ45	212
N50111	LJ45	401
N50111	LJ45	439
N50111	LJ45	474
N50111	LJ45	499
N50111	LJ60	329
N50111	LJ60	357
N50111	LJ60	391
N50114	LJ31	111
N50126	LJ31	207
N50126	LJ40	2007
N50126	LJ40	2124
N50126	LJ45	213
N50126	LJ45	262
N50126	LJ45	286
N50126	LJ45	324
N50126	LJ45	326
N50126	LJ45	452
N50126	LJ45	476
N50126	LJ45	514
N50126	LJ60	152
N50126	LJ60	324
N50126	LJ60	396
N50127	JSTR	5214
"N50127"	LJ60	280
N50138	WW24	142
N50145	LJ31	178
N50145	LJ40	2107
N50145	LJ45	037
N50145	LJ45	100
N50145	LJ45	145
N50145	LJ45	211
N50145	LJ45	235
N50145	LJ45	316
N50145	LJ45	399
N50145	LJ45	456
N50145	LJ45	498
N50145	LJ60	279
N50145	LJ60	363
N50145	LJ60	397
N50153	LJ31	065
N50153	LJ31	205
N50153	LJ40	2020
N50153	LJ40	2145
N50153	LJ45	059
N50153	LJ45	327
N50153	LJ45	350
N50153	LJ60	016
N50153	LJ60	019
N50153	LJ60	299
N50153	LJ60	372
N50153	LJ60	389
N50153	LJ60	429
N50154	LJ36	061
N50154	LJ40	2027
N50154	LJ40	2066
N50154	LJ45	108
N50154	LJ45	170
N50154	LJ45	247
N50154	LJ45	297
N50154	LJ45	379
N50154	LJ45	432
N50154	LJ45	506
N50154	LJ60	039
N50154	LJ60	170
N50154	LJ60	379
N50154	LJ60	428
N50157	LJ31	171
N50157	LJ40	2110
N50157	LJ45	069
N50157	LJ45	263
N50157	LJ45	323
N50157	LJ45	420
N50157	LJ45	434
N50157	LJ45	482
N50157	LJ45	517
N50157	LJ60	017
N50157	LJ60	046
N50157	LJ60	218
N50157	LJ60	257
N50157	LJ60	272
N50157	LJ60	301
N50157	LJ60	323
N50157	LJ60	376
N50159	LJ31	045
N50162	LJ45	033
N50162	LJ60	061
N50163	LJ31	044
N50163	LJ40	2010
N50163	LJ40	2023
N50163	LJ45	070
N50163	LJ45	118
N50163	LJ45	218
N50163	LJ45	377
N50163	LJ45	491
N50163	LJ60	294
N50163	LJ60	378
N50163	LJ60	407
N50163	LJ60	424
N50166	HS25	258506
N50175	**C680**	**680A0052**
N50182	HS25	258582
N50185	LJ40	2130
N50185	LJ40	2136
N50185	LJ45	447
N50185	**LJ45**	**547**
N50207	LJ31	097
N50207	LJ45	178
N50231	C52C	0023
N50248	LJ45	182
N50275	C52B	0159
N50275	C52C	0031
N50275	C52C	0090
N50275	C52C	0132
N50275	C56X	5689
N50275	C56X	6037
N50275	C680	0185
N50275	**C680**	**0569**
N50280	PRM1	RB-80
N50282	C52A	0332
N50282	C52A	0445
N50282	C52C	0043
N50282	C52C	0107
N50282	C52C	0157
N50282	C680	0203
N50285	HS25	258585
N50287	LJ60	243
N50298	LJ60	028
N50298	LJ60	049
N50302	LJ31	092
N50309	HS25	258579
N50321	C525	0644
N50321	C52A	0504
N50321	C56X	5799
N50321	C56X	6024
N50324	LJ60	069
N50330	LJ60	245
N50353	LJ45	196
N50353	LJ60	035
N50360	C680	0509
N50378	HS25	258578
N50378	LJ31	098
N50422	LJ60	249
N50433	LJ60	250
N50440	HS25	258540
N50441	HS25	258541
N50445	HS25	258545
N50446	FA20	21
N50450	LJ60	050
N50453	PRM1	RB-53
N50458	LJ60	251
N50459	HS25	258559
N50459	LJ31	095
N50461	HS25	258546
N50468	PRM1	RB-81

N50490	HS25	258490
N50490	LJ45	211
N50512	BE40	TX-12
N50513	HS25	258513
N50521	HS25	258521
N50522	C52A	0441
N50522	C52A	0474
N50522	C56X	5775
N50522	C56X	6118
N50522	C680	0129
N50522	HS25	258612
N50543	C52A	0505
N50543	C52B	0170
N50543	C52B	0226
N50543	BE40	TX-13
N50549	C525	0686
N50549	C52C	0133
N50549	C56X	5682
N50549	C56X	6204
N50549	C680	0208
N50552	BE40	RK-342
N50553	HS25	258703
N50558	LJ60	267
N50561	BE40	TX-11
N50579	LJ45	240
N50586	PRM1	RB-66
N50600	HS25	258500
N50602	C500	083
N50602	LJ60	060
N50612	C525	0528
N50612	C550	550-0870
N50612	C550	550-0953
N50612	C550	550-1103
N50612	C560	0439
N50612	C560	0463
N50612	C560	0763
N50612	C56X	5215
N50612	C56X	6050
N50612	C680	0083
N50612	C680	0207
N50612	C680	0321
N50612	C680	0347
N50612	C750	0025
N50612	C750	0117
N50612	**C750**	**0524**
N50626	HS25	258526
N50639	C56X	5688
N50639	C56X	6078
N50639	C750	0281
N50639	C750	0300
N50648	PRM1	RB-68
N50655	C680	0199
N50657	HS25	258587
N50661	HS25	258581
N50667	HS25	258567
N50670	HS25	258570
N50715	C525	0632
N50715	C52B	0391
N50715	C52B	0462
N50715	C52C	0033
N50715	C550	550-0823
N50715	C550	550-0955
N50715	C560	0397
N50715	C560	0696
N50715	C56X	5746
N50715	C56X	5803
N50715	C56X	6054
N50715	C750	0213
N50727	BE40	RK-389
N50733	HS25	258533
N50736	C52A	0365
N50736	C52A	0510
N50736	C52B	0237
N50736	C52B	0278
N50736	C52B	0319
N50736	C52B	0369
N50736	C560	0811
N50736	C56X	5705
N50736	C680	0560
N50740	HS25	258560
N50756	C52A	0491
N50756	C52B	0141
N50756	C56X	5760
N50756	C56X	6039
N50758	LJ60	098
N50761	LJ60	073
N50776	C52B	0203
N50776	C52B	0245
N50776	C52B	0291
N50776	**C56X**	**6220**
N50776	C680	0322
N50776	C680	680A0012
N50776	LJ60	146
N50788	HS25	258488
N50812	C500	036
N50820	C525	0077
N50820	C525	0529
N50820	C52A	0357
N50820	C52A	0385
N50820	C52B	0016
N50820	C52B	0047
N50820	C52B	0100
N50820	C52B	0337
N50820	C560	0487
N50820	C560	0506
N50820	C56X	5192
N50820	C56X	5245
N50820	C56X	5295
N50820	C56X	5340
N50820	C56X	6096
N50820	C56X	6128
N50820	C650	7083
N50820	C750	0114
N50843	PRM1	RB-33
N50858	BE40	RK-458
"N50904"	C525	0687
N50910	HS25	258590
N50928	CL60	1067
N50938	C525	0132
N50938	C560	0396
(N50938)	C525	0088
N50944	C56X	6080
N50983	HS25	258583
N51001	LJ40	2011
N51008	BE40	RK-308
N51027	HS25	258577
N51038	C52A	0518
N51038	C52B	0328
N51038	C52C	0055
N51038	C52C	0203
N51038	C550	550-0815
N51038	C550	550-0938
N51038	C550	550-1090
N51038	C560	0383
N51038	C560	0446
N51038	C56X	5190
N51038	C56X	5196
N51038	C56X	5247
N51038	C56X	5628
N51038	C56X	5755
N51038	C56X	5821
N51038	C680	0127
N51038	C750	0063
N51038	C750	0094
N51038	C750	0123
N51038	WW24	142
(N51038)	C560	0279
(N51038)	C560	0327
N51042	C52B	0137
N51042	C550	550-0827
N51042	C560	0468
N51042	C560	0515
N51042	C560	0683
N51042	C56X	5185
N51042	C56X	5242
N51042	C56X	5631
N51042	C56X	5754
N51042	C56X	6063
N51042	C680	0237
N51042	C680	0326
N51042	C750	0121
N51042	C750	0221
(N51042)	C560	0280
N51053	LJ40	2132
N51054	LJ31	105
N51054	LJ40	2083
N51054	LJ60	379
N51055	C52A	0375
N51055	C52B	0023
N51055	C52B	0070
N51055	C52B	0144
N51055	C52C	0051
N51055	C52C	0124
N51055	C550	550-0875
N51055	C550	550-0903
N51055	C550	550-0983
N51055	C560	0282
N51055	C56X	5240
N51055	C56X	5344
N51055	C750	0039
N51055	C750	0069
N51055	C750	0132
(N51055)	C560	0330
N51057	LJ31	061
N51058	HS25	258558
N51072	C52C	0138
N51072	C52C	0177
N51072	C550	550-0826
N51072	C550	550-1119
N51072	C560	0331
N51072	C560	0520
N51072	C560	0550
N51072	C560	0576
N51072	C56X	5236
N51072	C56X	5307
N51072	C680	0101
N51072	C680	0148
N51072	C680	0198
N51072	C680	0263
N51072	**C680**	**680A0038**
N51072	C750	0017
N51072	C750	0112
(N51072)	C560	0283
N51099	HS25	258499
(N51099)	C500	203
N51140	PRM1	RB-40
N51143	C525	0603
N51143	C52B	0118
N51143	C52C	0060
N51143	C52C	0212
N51143	C550	550-0849
N51143	C550	550-0915
N51143	C560	0432
N51143	C560	0538
N51143	C56X	5195
N51143	C56X	5286
N51143	C56X	5339
N51143	C56X	5733
N51143	C650	0240
N51143	C650	7067
N51149	HS25	258549
N51160	C52A	0371
N51160	C52B	0067
N51160	C52B	0240
N51160	C52B	0279
N51160	C52C	0067
N51160	C52C	0128
N51160	C550	550-0894
N51160	C550	550-0923
N51160	C560	0474
N51160	C560	0666
N51160	C56X	5154
N51160	C56X	5269
N51160	C56X	5674
N51160	C56X	6060
N51160	C56X	6203
N51160	C650	7046
N51160	C650	7068
N51160	C750	0037
N51160	C750	0078
N51160	C750	0171
N51169	HS25	258599
N51176	C525	0185
N51176	C525	0212
N51176	C650	7048
N51176	C650	7070
N51176	C750	0038
N51191	HS25	258491
N51192	HS25	258492
N51197	HS25	258497
N51239	HS25	258539
N51241	BE40	RK-341
N51245	C56X	6176
N51246	C525	0154
N51246	C525	0186
N51246	C525	0401
N51246	C525	0523
N51246	C52A	0046
N51246	C52A	0075
N51246	C52A	0216
N51246	C52B	0110
N51246	C550	550-0857
N51246	C560	0447
N51246	C560	0450
N51246	C560	0480
N51246	C56X	5090
N51246	C56X	5757
N51246	C680	0060
N51246	C750	0311
N51246	**C750**	**0529**
N51274	HS25	258574
N51289	HS25	258589
N51313	C750	0022
N51335	HS25	258535
N51336	HS25	258536
N51342	C525	0188
N51342	C525	0432
N51342	C525	0638
N51342	C525	0700
N51342	C52A	0081
N51342	C52B	0379
N51342	C52C	0192
N51342	C56X	5107
N51342	C56X	5584
N51342	C56X	5641
N51342	C56X	5776
N51342	C56X	6031
N51342	C650	7086
N51384	HS25	258584
N51387	HS25	258487
N51396	C525	0092
N51396	C525	0190
N51396	C525	0355
N51396	C525	0390
N51396	C52A	0025
N51396	C52A	0066
N51396	C52A	0130
N51396	C52A	0428
N51396	C52B	0211
N51396	C52C	0028
N51396	C52C	0102
N51396	C560	0455
N51396	C560	0527
N51396	C56X	5585
N51396	C56X	5627
N51444	C525	0164
N51444	C525	0192
N51444	C525	0317
N51444	C525	0350
N51444	C525	0418
N51444	C52A	0068
N51444	C52A	0376
N51444	C52C	0162
N51444	C560	0289
N51444	C560	0456
N51444	C56X	5100
N51444	C650	7073
N51444	C680	0092
N51444	C680	0232
N51444	C680	0294
N51453	HS25	258553
N51457	HS25	258557
N51478	C680	0346
N51480	PRM1	RB-48
N51495	HS25	258495
N51511	C525	0650
N51511	C52A	0214
N51511	C52B	0035
N51511	C52B	0071
N51511	C52C	0092
N51511	C52C	0188
N51511	C56X	5162
N51511	C680	0204
N51511	C680	0269
N51511	C750	0180
N51522	C525	0168
N51522	C525	0198
N51522	C560	0350
(N51522)	C525	0094
N51540	BE40	RK-340
N51556	HS25	258556
N51564	C525	0100
N51564	C525	0173
N51564	C525	0336
N51564	C525	0358
N51564	C525	0387
N51564	C525	0538
N51564	C525	0552
N51564	C525	0614
N51564	C52A	0035
N51564	C52A	0069
N51564	C52A	0131
N51564	C52A	0362
N51564	C52C	0021
N51564	C52C	0078
N51564	C52C	0194
N51564	C560	0353
N51564	C560	0457
N51564	C560	0491
N51564	C680	0200
N51564	C680	0267
N51575	C525	0338
N51575	C525	0396
N51575	C525	0411
N51575	C52A	0049
N51575	C52A	0071
N51575	C52A	0112
N51575	C52A	0322
N51575	C560	0293
N51575	C560	0355
N51575	C56X	5005
N51575	C56X	5077
N51575	C680	0032
N51575	C680	0061
N51612	C525	0303
N51612	C525	0553
N51612	C525	0655
N51612	C52B	0140
N51612	C52C	0079
N51612	C52C	0159
N51612	C550	550-0968
N51612	C56X	5297
N51612	C56X	5630
N51612	C56X	5634
N51612	C56X	5806
N51612	C56X	6083
N51612	**C56X**	**6209**
N51612	C750	0233
N51666	C525	0286
N51666	C52B	0388
N51666	C550	550-0937
N51666	C550	550-0956
N51666	C550	550-0980
N51666	C550	550-1017
N51666	C56X	5764
N51666	C56X	6016
N51666	C750	0210
N51666	C750	0240
N51666	C750	0255
N51666	C750	0308
N51684	C525	0696
N51741	GLF2	45
N51743	C525	0214
N51743	C52A	0489
N51743	C550	550-1003
N51743	C550	550-1136
N51743	C560	0300
N51743	C56X	5173
N51743	C56X	5244
N51743	C56X	5318
N51743	C56X	6140
N51743	C750	0276
N51743	C750	0292
N51744	C525	0291
N51744	C52B	0084
N51744	C52C	0048
N51744	C52C	0116
N51744	C52C	0156
N51744	C550	550-1107
N51744	C56X	5711
N51744	C680	0258
N51744	C750	0108
N51744	C750	0143
N51744	C750	0152
N51744	C750	0212
N51780	C52B	0172
N51780	C52B	0400
N51780	C52C	0024
N51780	C52C	0204
N51780	C550	550-0957
N51780	C550	550-0987
N51780	C550	550-1011
N51780	C560	0541
N51780	C56X	5549
N51780	C56X	5600
N51780	C56X	5666
N51780	C56X	5762
N51780	C56X	6018
N51780	C750	0134
N51806	C525	0649
N51806	C52A	0167
N51806	C52B	0009
N51806	C52B	0401
N51806	C550	550-0966
N51806	C56X	5635
N51806	C56X	6002
N51806	C56X	6043
N51806	C680	680A0026
N51806	C750	0176
N51817	C525	0157
N51817	C525	0403
N51817	C525	0610
N51817	C52B	0199
N51817	C550	550-0845
N51817	C560	0518
N51817	C56X	5086
N51817	C56X	6082
N51817	C56X	6113
N51817	C650	7051
N51817	C680	0142
N51817	C750	0192
N51817	C750	0216
N51817	C750	0509
N51869	C52A	0493
N51869	C52C	0199
N51869	C550	550-1042
N51869	C560	0597
N51869	C56X	5160
N51869	C56X	5555
N51869	C56X	5763
N51869	C56X	6069
N51869	C680	0070
N51869	C680	0106
N51869	C680	0160
N51869	C680	0253
N51869	**C680**	**680A0047**
N51872	C525	0159
N51872	C525	0207
N51872	C525	0334
N51872	C525	0367
N51872	C525	0407
N51872	C52A	0079
N51872	C52A	0141
N51872	C52C	0041
N51872	C550	550-0836
N51872	C550	550-1076
N51872	C56X	5522
N51872	C680	0057
N51872	C680	0078
N51872	C680	0104
N51872	C680	0159
N51881	C525	0218
N51881	C525	0422
N51881	C525	0502
N51881	C52A	0011
N51881	C52A	0052
N51881	C52B	0085
N51881	C52B	0302
N51881	C52C	0119
N51881	C560	0399
N51881	C56X	5071
N51881	C56X	5546
N51881	C56X	5573
N51881	C56X	5713
N51881	C56X	6103
N51881	C680	0188
N51881	C680	0218
N51896	C525	0606
N51896	C52A	0352
N51896	C52A	0393
N51896	C52B	0018
N51896	C52B	0202
N51896	C550	550-0922
N51896	C560	0501
N51896	C56X	6056
N51896	C680	0243
N51896	C680	0556
N51896	C750	0150
N51896	C750	0184
N51933	C56X	5023
N51942	C525	0438
N51942	C52A	0019
N51942	C52A	0195
N51942	C52B	0038
N51942	C52B	0138
N51942	C52C	0118
N51942	C52C	0209
N51942	C560	0400
N51942	C560	0420
N51942	C560	0795
N51942	C560	0813
N51942	C56X	5089
N51942	C56X	5337
N51942	C56X	6102
N51984	C56X	5179

N51984	C56X	5560
N51984	C56X	5781
N51984	C56X	6117
N51984	C680	0138
N51984	C750	0189
N51990	WW24	183
N51993	C525	0143
N51993	C525	0386
N51993	C525	0431
N51993	C525	0558
N51993	C525	0637
N51993	C52A	0370
N51993	C52B	0086
N51993	C560	0623
N51993	C56X	5056
N51993	HS25	25249
N51995	C525	0549
N51995	C52B	0073
N51995	C52C	0017
N51995	**C52C**	**0223**
N51995	C550	550-1007
N51995	C560	0543
N51995	C560	0547
N51995	C560	0563
N51995	C560	0618
N51995	C56X	5731
N51995	C56X	5830
N51995	C56X	6196
N51995	C680	0332
N51995	C680	0516
N51995	C750	0102
N52002	C52A	0043
N52035	C52A	0058
N52035	C680	0544
N52038	C525	0102
N52038	C525	0133
N52038	C525	0222
N52038	C525	0224
N52038	C525	0469
N52038	C52A	0125
N52038	C52B	0020
N52038	C52B	0321
N52038	C56X	5030
N52038	C56X	5607
N52038	C680	0120
N52038	**C680**	**0561**
N52038	C680	680A0027
N52059	C52A	0480
N52059	C52B	0003
N52059	C52B	0139
N52059	C52B	0300
N52059	C52C	0189
N52059	C550	550-1129
N52059	C560	0503
N52059	C560	0608
N52059	C560	0689
N52059	C56X	5147
N52059	C56X	5166
N52059	C680	0210
N52061	C56X	5797
N52069	C52B	0198
N52071	C525	0672
N52081	C525	0105
N52081	C525	0136
N52081	C525	0241
N52081	C525	0266
N52081	C525	0430
N52081	C525	0504
N52081	C52A	0241
N52081	C52A	0392
N52081	C52A	0435
N52081	C52B	0079
N52081	C560	0409
N52081	C56X	5068
N52081	C56X	5088
N52081	C56X	5255
N52081	C56X	6115
N52081	C680	0007
N52081	C680	0139
N52081	C750	0157
N52086	C52A	0244
N52086	C52A	0413
N52086	C52A	0440
N52086	C52B	0151
N52086	C52B	0206
N52086	C52C	0081
N52086	C550	550-0965
N52086	C550	550-0992
N52086	C550	550-1034
N52086	C680	0534
N52086	C680	680A0022
N52113	C525	0109
N52113	C525	0475
N52113	C525	0534
N52113	C52B	0101
N52113	C52B	0365
N52113	C550	550-0803
N52113	C560	0369
N52113	C56X	5009
N52113	C56X	5034
N52113	C56X	5085
N52113	C56X	5130
N52113	C56X	5566
N52113	C56X	5783
N52113	C680	0152
N52113	C680	0532
N52114	C52A	0477
N52114	C52B	0210
N52114	C52B	0402
N52114	C52B	0482
N52114	C550	550-0963
N52114	C550	550-1033
N52114	C560	0616
N52114	C56X	5175
N52114	C680	0003
N52114	C680	0033
N52114	C750	0259
N52114	C750	0298
N52135	C560	0619
N52136	C525	0111
N52136	C525	0444
N52136	C525	0485
N52136	C525	0514
N52136	C52A	0004
N52136	C52B	0220
N52136	C52C	0142
N52136	C560	0802
N52136	C56X	5036
N52136	C56X	5131
N52136	C56X	5618
N52136	C56X	6072
N52136	C56X	6186
N52136	**C680**	**0571**
N52136	C750	0012
N52136	C750	0040
N52141	C525	0115
N52141	C525	0145
N52141	C525	0490
N52141	C525	0515
N52141	C52A	0008
N52141	C52A	0020
N52141	C52A	0439
N52141	C52C	0003
N52141	C550	550-0806
N52141	C550	550-1084
N52141	C560	0757
N52141	C56X	5011
N52141	C56X	5041
N52141	C56X	5080
N52141	C56X	5778
N52141	C56X	6109
N52141	C750	0503
N52144	C525	0148
N52144	C525	0410
N52144	C52B	0271
N52144	C52C	0072
N52144	C550	550-0807
N52144	C550	550-1104
N52144	C560	0703
N52144	C56X	5012
N52144	C56X	5083
N52144	C56X	5502
N52144	C56X	6145
N52144	C650	7056
N52144	C680	0175
N52144	**C680**	**680A0049**
N52178	C525	0118
N52178	C525	0147
N52178	C525	0452
N52178	C52C	0037
N52178	C52C	0103
N52178	C56X	5010
N52178	C56X	5042
N52178	C56X	5072
N52178	C56X	5113
N52178	C56X	5539
N52178	C650	7058
N52178	C680	0098
N52178	C680	0130
N52178	C680	0242
N52178	C680	0296
N52178	C750	0277
N52178	C750	0284
N52229	C525	0608
N52229	C52B	0121
N52229	C52B	0294
N52229	C52B	0382
N52229	C52C	0010
N52229	C550	550-0946
N52229	C550	550-0960
N52229	C560	0505
N52229	C560	0582
N52229	C56X	5531
N52229	C56X	5736
N52229	C56X	5795
N52229	C680	0005
N52229	C750	0209
N52230	C56X	6077
N52234	C52B	0114
N52234	C550	550-0964
N52234	C560	0658
N52234	C56X	5148
N52234	C680	0154
N52234	C680	0329
N52234	C680	0513
N52234	C680	680A0007
N52235	C52A	0458
N52235	C52B	0212
N52235	C52B	0383
N52235	C52C	0172
N52235	C550	550-1043
N52235	C560	0596
N52235	C56X	5141
N52235	C56X	5180
N52235	C56X	5602
N52235	C56X	5700
N52235	C56X	5828
N52235	C650	7110
N52235	C680	0023
N52334	C56X	5258
N52338	C510	0195
N52352	C525	0376
N52352	C52A	0042
N52352	C52A	0328
N52352	C52B	0080
N52352	C52B	0272
N52352	C52B	0314
N52352	C52C	0035
N52352	C560	0309
N52352	C560	0366
N52352	C560	0435
N52352	C56X	5134
N52352	C56X	5510
N52352	C680	0190
N52352	C680	0345
N52352	C680	0550
N52369	C525	0536
N52369	C52A	0473
N52369	C52B	0040
N52369	C550	550-1044
N52369	C560	0600
N52369	C56X	5656
N52369	C56X	5717
N52369	C680	0212
N52369	C680	0283
"N52391"	C52A	0391
N52397	C52B	0148
N52397	C52C	0084
N52397	C550	550-0967
N52397	C550	550-1002
N52397	C550	550-1030
N52397	C56X	5325
N52397	C56X	5361
N52397	C56X	5720
N52397	C680	0213
N52433	C525	0628
N52433	C52B	0032
N52433	C52B	0077
N52433	C52B	0214
N52433	C560	0569
N52433	C56X	5512
N52433	C56X	6053
N52433	C680	0032
N52433	C680	0339
N52446	C52A	0448
N52446	C52A	0496
N52446	C52B	0034
N52446	C550	550-1040
N52446	C550	550-1086
N52446	C560	0594
N52446	C56X	6172
N52446	C680	0112
N52446	C680	0177
N52446	C680	0217
N52446	C680	680A0011
N52457	C525	0139
N52457	C525	0262
N52457	C52B	0081
N52457	C52B	0356
N52457	C550	550-1116
N52457	C560	0415
N52457	C560	0671
N52457	C56X	5057
N52457	C56X	5112
N52457	C56X	6198
N52457	C750	0289
(N52457)	C560	0312
N52462	C550	550-0972
N52462	C560	0667
N52462	C560	0699
N52462	C680	0147
N52462	C750	0264
N52475	C525	0621
N52475	C550	550-0978
N52475	C550	550-1014
N52475	C56X	6119
N52475	C680	0025
N52475	C680	0173
N52475	**C680**	**0563**
N52484	**HS25**	**258293**
N52498	C510	0261
N52526	C525	0653
N52526	C560	0574
N52526	C56X	5259
N52526	C680	0122
N52526	C680	0194
N52526	C750	0223
N52526	C750	0225
N52526	C750	0234
N52526	C750	0250
(N52526)	C560	0317
N52582	C680	0123
N52591	C525	0513
N52591	C52C	0114
N52591	C550	550-1117
N52591	C560	0583
N52591	C56X	5813
"N52594"	C525	0657
N52601	C550	550-0919
N52601	C550	550-1056
N52601	C560	0372
N52601	C560	0674
N52601	C56X	5665
N52601	C56X	6131
N52601	C56X	6157
N52601	C680	0048
N52601	C750	0149
N52601	C750	0307
N52609	C525	0694
N52609	C52A	0301
N52609	C52A	0349
N52609	C52C	0013
N52609	C52C	0087
N52609	**C52C**	**0221**
N52609	C56X	5511
N52609	C56X	5558
N52609	C56X	6005
N52609	C750	0263
N52609	C750	0513
N52613	C525	0668
N52613	C52B	0317
N52613	C52B	0406
N52613	C52C	0095
N52613	C560	0319
N52613	C56X	5610
N52613	C56X	5678
N52613	C56X	5743
N52613	C650	7075
N52613	C750	0220
N52623	C525	0691
N52623	C52C	0091
N52623	C550	550-1127
N52623	C56X	5739
N52623	C56X	6154
N52623	C650	7063
N52623	C680	0044
N52623	C680	0240
N52626	C525	0517
N52626	C525	0601
N52626	C52B	0150
N52626	C52B	0191
N52626	C52B	0390
N52626	C52C	0173
N52626	C550	550-1096
N52626	C56X	5644
N52626	C56X	5804
N52626	C56X	6052
N52626	C650	7064
N52627	C525	0690
N52627	C52A	0381
N52627	C52B	0008
N52627	C52B	0256
N52627	C650	7065
N52627	C680	0164
N52627	C680	0312
N52627	C680	0503
N52627	C680	680A0021
N52627	C750	0254
N52639	C52A	0390
N52639	C52B	0184
N52639	C52B	0342
N52639	**C52B**	**0492**
N52639	C560	0568
N52639	C560	0705
N52639	C56X	5136
N52639	C56X	5517
N52639	C56X	5592
N52639	C56X	6026
N52639	C680	0327
N52639	C680	0507
N52639	C750	0022
N52639	C750	0127
N52642	C525	0129
N52642	C750	0106
(N52642)	C525	0123
N52645	C525	0611
N52645	C52A	0443
N52645	C52B	0194
N52645	C52C	0025
N52645	C52C	0210
N52645	C550	550-1092
N52645	C560	0338
N52645	C560	0756
N52645	C56X	5145
N52645	C56X	6134
N52645	C56X	6169
N52653	C52B	0037
N52653	C52B	0092
N52653	C52B	0454
N52653	C52C	0011
N52653	**C52C**	**0227**
N52653	C560	0654
N52653	C56X	5753
N52653	C56X	6017
N52653	C680	0118
N52653	C750	0168
N52655	C52A	0178
N52655	C52A	0360
N52655	C52A	0419
N52655	C52A	0442
N52655	C52B	0409
N52655	C52C	0019
N52655	C550	550-0911
N52655	C56X	5140
N52655	C56X	5519
N52655	C56X	5670
N52655	C750	0007
N52655	C750	0244
N52670	C560	0551
N52682	C52A	0359
N52682	C52B	0205
N52682	C52B	0232
N52682	C560	0348
N52682	C56X	5621
N52682	C750	0024
N52690	C52A	0302
N52690	C52B	0217
N52690	C52B	0275
N52690	C52B	0316
N52690	C52B	0484
N52690	C550	550-0986
N52690	C550	550-1045
N52690	C560	0599
N52690	C56X	5680
N52690	C56X	6089
N52691	C525	0654
N52691	C52B	0134
N52691	C52B	0352
N52691	C550	550-1027
N52691	C550	550-1058
N52691	C560	0586
N52691	C56X	5622
N52691	C56X	6022
N52691	C56X	6170
N52691	C680	0552
N52691	C680	680A0009
N52699	C52A	0304
N52699	C52A	0334
N52699	C52B	0491
N52699	C52C	0112
N52699	C52C	0190
N52699	C560	0610
N52699	C56X	5518
N52699	C680	0270
N52699	C680	0324
N52733	C510	0225
N52905	C510	0286
N53584	C500	128
N53650	LJ35	054
N54531	C500	078
N54555	HS25	257023
N54754	LJ35	026
N54784	SBRL	306-96
(N54888)	LJ25	258
N55922	GLF2	225
N56327	BE40	RK-36
N56356	BE40	RK-58
N56400	BE40	RK-43
N56423	BE40	RK-45
N56576	BE40	RK-6
N56616	BE40	RK-22
N58025	SBRL	282-76
N58521	HS25	258521
N58966	SBRL	380-29
N59019	C500	080
N60055	CL64	5400
N60089	HS25	HA-0089
N60099	HS25	HA-0099
N60126	E50P	50000286
N60126	E50P	50000310
N60143	HA4T	RC-43
N60144	LJ60	144
N60159	HS25	258609
(N60181)	C500	047
N60231	E50P	50000291
N60231	E50P	50000296
N60237	E50P	50000295
N60270	BE40	RK-370
N60280	C680	0299
N60286	C680	0298
N60298	E50P	50000294
N60298	E55P	50500324
N60312	E50P	50000270
N60312	E50P	50000311
N60318	E50P	50000272
N60318	E50P	50000298
N60318	E50P	50000315
N60322	PRM1	RB-112
N60506	HS25	258606
N60507	HS25	258607
N60664	HS25	258604
N60669	PRM1	RB-269
N60724	HS25	258824
N60820	HS25	HA-0120
N61101	HS25	258601
N61161	PRM1	RB-61
N61198	HS25	258598
N61216	HS25	258616
N61256	BE40	RK-456
N61285	HS25	258765
N61320	HS25	258610
N61343	HS25	258683
N61391	HS25	HA-0091
N61407	HA4T	RC-17
N61442	C56X	6048
(N61442)	C550	152
N61474	PRM1	RB-74
N61495	HS25	258595
N61500	HS25	258600
N61515	HS25	258615
N61572	C500	504
N61589	PRM1	RB-89
N61661	BE40	RK-361
N61675	BE40	RK-475
N61678	PRM1	RB-147

N61681	HS25	258621
N61702	HS25	258602
N61706	C510	0065
N61706	PRM1	RB-106
N61708	HS25	258608
N61717	PRM1	RB-107
N61719	HS25	258619
N61729	HS25	258629
N61746	HS25	258686
N61754	PRM1	RB-54
N61784	PRM1	RB-84
N61791	HS25	258591
N61805	HS25	258605
N61826	LJ25	214
N61850	BE40	RK-350
(N61850)	C56X	5020
N61855	C680	0285
N61882	PRM1	RB-82
N61904	HS25	258594
(N61905)	LJ35	535
N61908	**PRM1**	**RB-108**
N61920	HS25	258620
N61930	PRM1	RB-103
N61944	HS25	258714
N61948	PRM1	RB-143
N61959	BE40	RK-359
N61987	HS25	258687
N61998	PRM1	RB-98
N62076	C510	0117
N62276	WW24	432
N62297	HS25	HA-0097
(N62452)	HFB3	1041
N62570	FA20	379
N62783	HS25	258983
N62864	C500	644
N62895	HS25	HA-0095
N62914	HS25	HA-0114
N62991	HS25	HB-41
N63007	**E50P**	**50000145**
N63223	C510	0089
N63357	WW24	99
N63537	FA50	20
N63600	HS25	258843
(N63602)	LJ35	306
N63611	SBRL	276-21
N63633	HS25	HB-33
N63744	HA4T	RC-44
N63768	PRM1	RB-268
N63810	HS25	256037
N63811	SBRL	276-44
N63812	HS25	HA-0112
N63890	HS25	HA-0090
N63984	HS25	258984
N64292	HS25	HA-0092
N64312	PRM1	RB-272
N64373	PRM1	RB-273
N64467	PRM1	RB-267
N64688	HS25	257003
N64769	FA20	359/542
(N64792)	C500	087
N65218	MS76	112
N65229	C560	0069
N65311	FA20	6
N65339	LJ24	163
N65357	CL61	5075
N65618	SBRL	276-42
N65733	SBRL	380-4
N65740	SBRL	282-133
N65741	SBRL	380-6
N65744	SBRL	380-7
N65745	SBRL	306-73
N65749	SBRL	380-8
N65750	SBRL	306-76
N65751	SBRL	306-77
N65752	SBRL	306-78
N65756	SBRL	306-80
N65758	SBRL	380-12
N65759	SBRL	306-82
N65761	SBRL	380-13
N65762	SBRL	306-84
N65763	SBRL	282-137
N65764	SBRL	306-85
N65765	SBRL	306-86
N65766	SBRL	380-15
N65767	SBRL	306-87
N65768	SBRL	380-17
N65769	SBRL	306-88
N65770	SBRL	306-89
N65771	SBRL	380-19
N65772	SBRL	306-90
N65773	SBRL	380-21
N65774	SBRL	306-91
N65775	SBRL	306-92
N65776	SBRL	380-23
N65777	SBRL	306-93
N65778	SBRL	306-94
N65783	SBRL	306-95
N65784?	SBRL	306-96
N65785	SBRL	306-97
N65786	SBRL	306-98
N65787	SBRL	380-27
N65789	SBRL	306-99
N65790	SBRL	306-100
N65791	SBRL	306-101
N65792	SBRL	306-102
N65793	SBRL	380-30
N65794	SBRL	306-103

N65795	SBRL	306-104
N65796	SBRL	306-105
N65797	SBRL	306-106
N65798	SBRL	306-107
N65799	SBRL	306-108
N67201	SBRL	282-53
N67741	C550	676
N67780	C500	574
N67786	C500	575
N67799	C500	580
N67805	C500	587
N67814	C500	595
N67815	C500	596
N67822	C500	602
N67829	C500	603
N67830	C500	609
N67830	C560	0089
N67839	C500	610
(N67839)	C560	0090
N67848	C500	616
N67890	C560	0096
(N67905)	C560	0099
(N67980)	C550	221
(N67980)	C560	0101
N67983	C550	222
N67983	C550	353
(N67983)	C550	400
N67986	C550	223
N67988	C550	224
N67988	C550	354
(N67988)	C560	0102
N67989	C550	225
(N67989)	C560	0103
N67990	C550	231
N67990	C550	358
N67997	C550	232
N67999	C550	233
N67999	C550	359
N68003	C550	238
N68003	C550	362
N68005	**GLEX**	**9010**
N68018	C550	247
(N68018)	C560	0109A
N68026	C550	253
N68027	C550	254
N68027	C550	371
(N68027)	C560	0112
N68032	C550	259
N68032	C550	373
N68032	C560	0116
N68033	C550	260
N68097	C560	0126
(N68118)	C560	0133
N68231	C650	0214
N68269	C650	0216
N68321	C550	387
N68599	C550	270
N68607	C550	279
N68609	C550	280
N68615	C550	287
N68616	C550	288
N68617	C550	289
N68621	C550	295
N68622	C550	296
N68624	C550	297
N68625	C550	298
N68629	C550	299
N68631	C550	306
N68633	C550	307
N68637	C550	308
N68644	C550	315
(N68646)	C550	316
N68648	C550	317
N68649	C550	318
(N68746)	C560	0138
(N68753)	C560	0139
N68770	C560	0148
(N68786)	C560	0149
(N68854)	C560	0159
N68860	C560	0161
N68864	C560	0162
N68869	C560	0163
N68872	C550	323
N68872	C560	0166
N68873	C550	324
(N68873)	C560	0167
N68876	C550	325
(N68876)	C560	0168
N68881	C550	332
N68881	C560	0173
N68887	C550	333
N68888	C550	334
N68888	**CL65**	**5774**
N68889	**GLEX**	**9568**
N68891	C550	341
N68989	**GLF5**	**5509**
N69566	C500	100
N70040	HS25	258840
N70050	GLF3	318
N70158	BE40	RK-508
N70214	HS25	258814
N70224	C550	473
N70338	HS25	25281
N70409	HS25	258809
N70431	HS25	258841
N70451	C500	063
N70454	C500	279

N70467	C500	667
N70606	LJ25	163
N70703	C500	025
N70704	C500	267
N70708	HS25	258808
N70791	HS25	258791
N70830	FA20	281/496
N70841	C500	018
N70890	PRM1	RB-190
N71010	HS25	258810
N71025	HS25	258805
N71167	PRM1	RB-167
N71273	C750	0521
N71325	SBRL	282-100
N71460	SBRL	380-5
N71543	SBRL	380-29
N71761	PRM1	RB-161
N71794	HS25	258794
N71865	PRM1	RB-175
N71874	PRM1	RB-174
N71881	HS25	258811
N71904	HS25	258804
N71907	HS25	258797
N71934	HS25	258834
N71938	HS25	258838
N71944	HS25	258844
N71956	**HA4T**	**RC-39**
N71956	HS25	HA-0006
N71958	HS25	258858
N72028	SBRL	380-14
N72233	HS25	258833
N72335	LJ24	208
N72442	LJ24	103
N72505	HS25	257016
N72520	HS25	258830
N72539	BE40	RK-519
N72594	BE40	RK-494
N72596	LJ35	594
N72600	LJ25	370
N72603	LJ25	371
N72606	LJ25	372
N72608	LJ55	114
N72612	LJ35	596
N72613	LJ55	119
N72614	LJ35	607
N72616	LJ55	140
N72617	HS25	258787
N72626	LJ35	591
N72629	LJ55	120
N72630	LJ35	630
N72645	HS25	258845
N72787	C500	561
N72787	WW24	240
N73535	WW24	91
N73721	HS25	258821
N73729	HS25	258829
N73736	PRM1	RB-173
(N73741)	HS25	258524
N73793	HS25	258813
N74065	PRM1	RB-195
N74116	BE40	RK-516
N74142	HS25	258832
N74155	HS25	258815
N74166	HS25	258816
N74196	FA20	198/466
N74476	HS25	258847
(N75471)	C500	482
N76662	FA20	306/512
N77058	CL61	5017
(N77111)	C500	674
N77215	C525	0149
(N77511)	LJ60	139
N77617	HS25	25146
N77702	LJ45	224
N77709	**G150**	**236**
N77711	C560	0065
N77773	**C680**	**0020**
N77778	C680	0312
N77794	C525	0073
N77797	C550	550-0821
(N78499)	CL60	1012
N80169	LJ40	2048
N80170	LJ60	400
N80172	LJ60	326
N80177	LJ60	306
N80364	C500	299
N80506	FA20	83
N80513	C550	248
N80544	BE40	RK-59
N80631	LJ31	131
N80639	C500	258
N80645	LJ31	135
N80667	LJ60	150
N80683	LJ60	093
N80701	LJ60	148
N80727	LJ31	127
N80775	LJ24	093
N80857	LJ60	220
N80938	BE40	RK-54
N81110	C52B	0388
N81239	HS25	HA-0169
N81366	JSTR	5097/60
N81458	LJ35	230
N81491	PRM1	RB-281
N81516	PRM1	RB-286
N81661	BE40	RK-35
N81709	BE40	RK-14

N81728	GLF2	217
N81863	LJ35	243
N81883	C500	031
N81918	BE40	RK-25
N82025	LJ25	075
N82161	**E55P**	**50500054**
N82197	SBRL	306-39
N82204	GLF2	167
N82283	LJ35	174
N82378	BE40	RK-61
N82400	BE40	RK-75
N82412	BE40	RK-63
N82497	BE40	RK-71
N82628	BE40	RK-20
N82679	LJ55	013
N82824	**C510**	**0279**
N82884	BE40	TX-1
N82885	BE40	TX-2
N82886	BE40	TX-3
N85031	SBRL	380-38
N85351	LJ35	149
N85594	HS25	258551
N85631	LJ55	081
N85632	LJ55	080
N85643	LJ55	084
N85645	LJ35	499
N85653	LJ55	053
N85654	LJ25	363
N87011	C550	550-1075
N87185	C500	410
N87253	C500	411
N87258	C500	412
N87496	C500	413
N87510	C500	414
(N87683)	C550	564
N87878	**CL65**	**5709**
N87950	HFB3	1055
N88692	C550	212
N88707	C550	213
N88716	C550	214
N88718	C550	215
(N88721)	C550	216
N88723	C550	217
(N88727)	C550	218
N88731	C550	180
N88732	C550	181
N88737	C550	182
N88738	C550	183
N88740	C550	184
(N88743)	C550	185
N88791	C550	186
N88795	C550	187
(N88797)	C550	188
N88798	C550	189
(N88798)	C525	0400
N88822	C550	191
N88824	C550	192
N88825	C550	193
N88826	C550	194
N88830	C550	195
(N88838)	C550	166
N88840	C550	167
(N88842)	C550	168
N88845	C56X	5101
(N88845)	C550	169
(N88848)	C550	170
N88879	F900	149
N88906	GLF2	133
N89888	**GLF4**	**1306**
N90005	FA50	40
N90005	GLF3	487
N90005	GLF4	1103
(N90005)	GLEX	9008
N90082	C510	0319
N90237	C500	170
N90298	C510	0343
N90532	LJ24	103
N90573	C510	0358
(N90583)	LJ55	045
N90658	JSTR	5142
N90658	LJ24	077
N90797	LJ24	227
N91164	LJ31	026
N91201	LJ31	027
N91452	LJ35	669
N91480	LJ35	663
N91566	LJ35	667
N91639	C510	0308
N91665	C510	0356
N91669	WW24	17
N91703	C510	0365
N91772	LJ60	053
N91884	HS25	256071
N92045	HFB3	1041
(N92047)	HFB3	1036
N92565	LJ24	287
N92958	C510	0383
N93564	C510	0405
N94124	GLF5	5255
N94731	C510	0431
N94749	C510	0434
N94811	C510	0435
N94817	C510	0436
N94818	C510	0437
N94924	**GLF5**	**5255**
N94924	GLF6	6166
N94970	C510	0440

N94972	C525	0813
N94979	C510	0448
N94980	C525	0844
(N95591)	FA20	150/445
N96757	**GLF3**	**379**
N97315	**C550**	**159**
N97941	CL60	1014
N98386	LJ24	040
N98403	C550	196
N98418	C550	197
N98432	C550	198
N98436	C550	199
N98449	C500	415
N98468	C500	416
N98468	C550	200
N98510	C500	417
(N98510)	C550	201
N98528	C500	418
(N98528)	C550	202
N98563	C500	419
N98563	C550	203
N98586	C500	420
N98599	C500	421
N98599	C550	204
N98601	C500	422
N98601	C550	205
N98630	C550	206
N98675	C500	424
N98675	C550	207
N98682	C500	425
N98682	C550	208
N98688	C500	426
N98715	C500	427
N98715	C550	209
(N98715)	C550	172
N98718	C550	210
(N98718)	C500	428
(N98718)	C550	173
N98749	C500	429
(N98749)	C550	174
N98751	C500	430
(N98751)	C550	001
N98753	C550	002
N98784	C550	003
N98784	C550	176
N98786	C550	004
N98796	LJ25	170
N98817	C550	005
N98820	C550	006
N98830	C550	007
N98840	C550	008
N98853	C550	009
N98858	C550	010
N98871	C550	011
N98871	C550	179
N99114	SBRL	282-128
N99606	LJ24	224
N99786	LJ35	045
(N99876)	C550	012

NASA

NASA4	JSTR	5015
NASA14	JSTR	5003
NASA650	GLF2	118
NASA701	LJ24	049

Peru

(OB-....)	LJ24	112
OB-1195	C550	134
OB-1280	C500	019
OB-1313	LJ25	328
OB-1319	SBRL	282-127
OB-1429	LJ25	159
OB-1430	LJ25	164
OB-1431	**LJ36**	**051**
OB-1432	**LJ36**	**052**
OB-1433	FA20	434
OB-1550	SBRL	306-25
OB-1626	C560	0124
OB-1703	ASTR	004
OB-1792	C555	0086
OB-1792-T	C555	0086
OB-1824	**C56X**	**5605**
OB-1951-P	G150	227
OB-2017-P	GLF4	4212
OB-2023	**GALX**	**034**
OB-2108-P	**ASTR**	**004**
OB-M-1004	LJ25	195
OB-M-1171	C550	056
OB-M-1195	C550	134
OB-R-1313	LJ25	328
OB-S-1280	C500	019
OB-T-1319	SBRL	282-127

Lebanon

OD-APA	BE40	RK-483
OD-BBF	HS25	257054
OD-BOY	**HS25**	**257109**
OD-CXJ	**LEG5**	**55000037**
OD-DTW	**BE40**	**RK-179**
OD-EAS	**HS25**	**258410**
OD-EKF	**HS25**	**258710**
OD-FAF	HS25	257124
OD-FNF	HS25	257124
OD-HHF	HS25	257054
OD-KMI	JSTR	5233
OD-LEA	**HS25**	**258792**

OD-MAF	**HS25**	**258631**
OD-MAS	**HS25**	**257115**
OD-MHA	LJ60	326
OD-MIG	**HS25**	**HA-0148**
OD-MIK	**F9DX**	**610**
OD-ONE	F2TH	121
OD-PAL	FA20	395/554
OD-PWC	LJ31	203
OD-SAS	C500	165
OD-SKY	HS25	258804
OD-STW	BE40	RK-366
OD-TSW	**HS25**	**258319**

Austria

(OE-...)	CL61	5023
(OE-...)	FA10	85
(OE-...)	LJ45	012
OE-FAD	C550	496
OE-FAG	**C52A**	**0229**
OE-FAJ	C510	0264
OE-FAM	E50P	50000100
OE-FAN	C500	289
OE-FAP	C500	300
OE-FAP	PRM1	RB-215
OE-FAU	C500	150
OE-FBA	C500	615
OE-FBD	**C510**	**0303**
OE-FBS	C550	574
OE-FCA	C525	0354
OE-FCB	**C510**	**0044**
OE-FCM	C500	294
OE-FCP	**C510**	**0019**
OE-FCU	C52A	0210
OE-FCW	**C525**	**0292**
OE-FCY	C52A	0204
OE-FCZ	**C52A**	**0427**
OE-FDB	PRM1	RB-263
OE-FDM	C500	529
OE-FDP	C500	139
OE-FDT	**C510**	**0156**
(OE-FEB)	C52A	0239
OE-FEM	C525	0291
OE-FET	**C525**	**0421**
OE-FFB	**C510**	**0065**
OE-FFK	C500	515
OE-FFK	**C525**	**0393**
OE-FGB	C52A	0362
OE-FGD	C525	0020
(OE-FGG)	C525	0146
OE-FGI	**C525**	**0254**
OE-FGK	**C525**	**0331**
OE-FGL	C52A	0082
OE-FGN	**C500**	**291**
OE-FGP	C500	006
OE-FGR	E50P	50000122
OE-FGV	E50P	50000193
OE-FHA	**C510**	**0081**
OE-FHB	C52A	0049
OE-FHC	**C52A**	**0415**
OE-FHH	C500	654
OE-FHK	**C510**	**0315**
OE-FHO	E50P	50000185
OE-FHP	C500	668
OE-FHT	E50P	50000179
OE-FHW	C500	523
OE-FID	**C510**	**0040**
OE-FII	C52A	0321
OE-FIM	PRM1	RB-196
OE-FIN	C52A	0239
OE-FIW	C500	511
OE-FIX	**C525**	**0480**
(OE-FJR)	C52A	0213
OE-FJU	C525	0295
OE-FKH	C525	0223
OE-FKK	PRM1	RB-211
OE-FKO	**C52A**	**0390**
OE-FKW	PRM1	RB-77
OE-FLA	C52A	0365
OE-FLA	**C52A**	**0499**
OE-FLB	C52A	0369
OE-FLG	**C525**	**0103**
OE-FLP	C52A	0011
OE-FLR	C510	0082
OE-FLY	C500	660
OE-FMA	**C525**	**0188**
OE-FMC	PRM1	RB-41
OE-FMD	**C525**	**0614**
OE-FMI	**C525**	**0315**
OE-FMK	**C500**	**536**
OE-FML	**C500**	**396**
OE-FMO	**EA50**	**550-1003**
OE-FMS	C500	510
OE-FMT	C525	0217
OE-FMU	**C525**	**0040**
(OE-FMU)	C525	0614
OE-FMY	C510	0106
OE-FMZ	C510	0116
OE-FNA	C525	0659
OE-FNB	C52A	0398
OE-FNG	C500	301
OE-FNL	C500	100
OE-FNP	C500	100
OE-FNP	**C510**	**0185**
OE-FOA	**C52A**	**0354**
OE-FOE	C52A	0375
OE-FOI	C525	0477
OE-FOM	E50P	50000092

OE-FPA	C550	552
OE-FPH	C500	572
OE-FPK	**C52A**	**0437**
OE-FPM	**C52A**	**0433**
OE-FPO	C500	353
OE-FPO	C525	0645
OE-FPP	**C510**	**0186**
OE-FPS	C52A	0142
OE-FRA	C52A	0150
OE-FRC	PRM1	RB-57
OE-FRF	C525	0539
OE-FRJ	PRM1	RB-12
OE-FRM	C510	0349
OE-FRR	C525	0124
OE-FRS	**C52A**	**0029**
OE-FSG	C52A	0203
OE-FSR	**C525**	**0634**
OE-FSS	**C525**	**0226**
OE-FTF	E50P	50000180
OE-FTR	C510	0053
OE-FTS	**C510**	**0281**
OE-FUJ	C525	0544
OE-FUX	**C52A**	**0106**
OE-FVB	C52A	0229
OE-FVJ	**C525**	**0450**
OE-FWD	**C510**	**0049**
OE-FWF	**C510**	**0048**
OE-FWH	**C510**	**0104**
OE-FWM	C525	0177
OE-FWW	PRM1	RB-131
(OE-FWW)	C510	0106
OE-FXE	**C52A**	**0017**
OE-FXM	**C52A**	**0341**
OE-FXX	C52A	0326
OE-FYC	C500	610
OE-FYF	C500	501
OE-FYH	C52A	0176
OE-FYP	C52A	0176
OE-FZA	**C510**	**0144**
OE-FZB	**C510**	**0145**
OE-FZC	**C510**	**0196**
OE-FZD	**C510**	**0216**
OE-FZE	**C510**	**0217**
OE-FZG	**C510**	**0349**
OE-GAA	C560	0111
OE-GAC	C56X	5564
"OE-GAC"	C680	0186
OE-GAD	C550	066
OE-GAE	C650	0149
OE-GAF	LJ35	382
OE-GAG	FA10	151
OE-GAG	BE40	RK-448
OE-GAH	C550	550-0922
OE-GAK	C680	0186
OE-GAL	**C550**	**550-0974**
(OE-GAL)	C56X	5573
OE-GAM	ASTR	111
OE-GAP	C56X	5004
OE-GAP	CS55	0034
OE-GAR	LJ35	309
OE-GAR	LJ45	148
OE-GAS	**G150**	**242**
OE-GAU	C550	028
OE-GAV	LJ35	185
OE-GBA	C550	100
OE-GBC	**C52B**	**0219**
OE-GBC	C550	717
OE-GBD	**ASTR**	**133**
OE-GBE	**ASTR**	**107**
OE-GBE	ASTR	153
OE-GBG	HS25	HB-34
OE-GBO	C52B	0215
OE-GBR	**C56X**	**5749**
OE-GBR	LJ35	088
OE-GBY	C680	0066
OE-GCA	**C56X**	**5157**
OE-GCB	C560	0517
OE-GCC	C560	0125
OE-GCD	C560	0497
OE-GCE	**HS25**	**258536**
OE-GCF	LJ55	136
OE-GCG	**C56X**	**5316**
OE-GCH	C550	304
OE-GCH	C650	7006
OE-GCI	C550	043
OE-GCJ	FA20	184/462
OE-GCM	C56X	5538
OE-GCN	C650	0014
OE-GCO	C650	0012
OE-GCP	C550	351
OE-GCP	C560	0214
OE-GCR	FA20	191
OE-GCS	FA20	364
OE-GDA	C560	0200
OE-GDA	**C56X**	**5801**
OE-GDF	**E55P**	**50500325**
OE-GDF	LJ60	276
OE-GDI	LJ45	037
OE-GDM	C550	707
OE-GDM	**C560**	**0814**
OE-GDP	C560	0023
OE-GDP	**E55P**	**50500062**
OE-GDP	FA20	302/510
OE-GDR	FA20	203
OE-GEA	HS25	258520
OE-GEC	C550	296
OE-GEC	**LJ45**	**491**

OE-GEG	C56X	5529
OE-GEH	C56X	5755
OE-GEJ	C560	0665
OE-GEM	**C680**	**0033**
(OE-GEM)	C56X	5822
OE-GEN	C550	550-1122
OE-GEO	HS25	258477
OE-GEP	C550	010
OE-GER	LJ35	143
OE-GES	C550	421
OE-GES	**C56X**	**6036**
OE-GET	C52B	0277
OE-GFA	LJ60	214
OE-GFB	BE40	RK-84
OE-GFF	LJ45	243
OE-GGB	LJ40	2018
OE-GGC	**LJ40**	**2015**
OE-GGG	**C56X**	**6013**
OE-GGK	**C56X**	**5058**
OE-GGL	LJ60	287
OE-GGP	**C56X**	**5701**
OE-GHA	C56X	5760
OE-GHA	FA10	221
OE-GHB	**C56X**	**5569**
OE-GHF	**LJ40**	**2091**
OE-GHG	C52B	0150
OE-GHL	LJ25	295
OE-GHM	BE40	RK-148
OE-GHP	C550	139
OE-GHP	C550	550-0998
OE-GHS	HS25	258078
OE-GHU	HS25	258335
OE-GIA	HS25	256027
OE-GID	C560	0081
OE-GIE	**C52B**	**0348**
OE-GII	LJ60	169
OE-GIL	C550	075
OE-GIN	C550	063
(OE-GIS)	HS25	HA-0048
OE-GIW	C550	008
OE-GJA	HS25	258810
(OE-GJA)	LJ60	302
(OE-GJA)	LJ60	303
OE-GJC	LJ45	068
OE-GJF	C52B	0231
OE-GJL	HS25	HA-0210
OE-GJM	C680	0282
OE-GJP	**C52B**	**0255**
OE-GKA	**G150**	**300**
OE-GKE	**C56X**	**5642**
OE-GKK	C550	550-0872
OE-GKM	**C56X**	**5811**
OE-GKN	LJ55	027
OE-GKP	C550	005
OE-GKP	LJ60	280
OE-GKW	**ASTR**	**150**
OE-GKZ	C680	0200
OE-GLA	LJ25	079
OE-GLF	FA20	323/520
OE-GLF	**G150**	**261**
OE-GLG	**C550**	**550-0977**
OE-GLG	FA10	96
OE-GLL	**C550**	**550-1069**
OE-GLL	FA20	307/513
(OE-GLM)	C550	550-0977
OE-GLP	C680	0080
OE-GLP	LJ36	025
OE-GLS	C550	300
OE-GLS	**C650**	**7110**
OE-GLX	LJ60	332
OE-GLY	LJ60	333
OE-GLZ	C550	690
OE-GMA	LJ35	111
OE-GMA	**LJ60**	**270**
OE-GMC	BE40	RK-162
OE-GMD	LJ36	047
OE-GMD	**LJ60**	**305**
OE-GME	C56X	5113
OE-GMG	**C650**	**7102**
OE-GMI	C560	0362
OE-GMI	**HS25**	**258748**
OE-GMJ	LJ35	504
OE-GML	C550	550-0976
OE-GMM	**C680**	**0005**
OE-GMP	LJ35	122
OE-GMR	LJ60	248
OE-GMS	LJ35	341
OE-GMV	C550	550-1136
OE-GMZ	C52B	0318
OE-GNA	**C52B**	**0275**
OE-GNB	C680	0055
OE-GNF	LJ60	304
OE-GNI	LJ60	236
OE-GNK	C650	0147
OE-GNK	LJ55	013
OE-GNL	LJ36	055
OE-GNL	LJ60	032
OE-GNN	FA20	298
OE-GNP	**C56X**	**6017**
OE-GNP	LJ35	347
OE-GNS	CS55	0083
OE-GNW	C56X	5339
OE-GNY	HS25	258859
OE-GOA	HS25	HA-0180
OE-GPA	C560	0099
OE-GPA	C56X	5265
OE-GPC	C560	0064

OE-GPD	C52B	0314
OE-GPD	CS55	0135
OE-GPG	ASTR	115
OE-GPH	C560	0590
OE-GPI	LJ35	341
OE-GPK	**C52B**	**0312**
OE-GPN	C56X	5169
OE-GPN	LJ35	311
OE-GPO	C52B	0125
OE-GPS	**C550**	**550-0837**
OE-GPS	C560	0114
OE-GPZ	C56X	5067
OE-GRA	**C52B**	**0135**
OE-GRB	C550	550-1039
OE-GRD	C550	707
OE-GRF	HS25	258813
OE-GRI	**C56X**	**5315**
OE-GRM	C550	550-0865
OE-GRO	LJ55	122
OE-GRR	LJ55	059
OE-GRS	HS25	258804
OE-GRU	**C52B**	**0222**
OE-GRU	FA20	228/473
OE-GRW	C560	0019
OE-GRZ	C52B	0219
OE-GSC	FA10	122
OE-GSC	LJ60	322
OE-GSG	BE40	RK-402
OE-GSK	G150	245
OE-GSP	C56X	5756
OE-GSR	C56X	5695
OE-GST	C550	299
OE-GSU	LJ60	317
OE-GSV	**LJ60**	**300**
OE-GSW	C560	0088
OE-GSZ	C56X	5763
OE-GTA	LJ31	191
OE-GTF	LJ60	281
OE-GTI	**C52C**	**0100**
OE-GTI	C56X	5037
OE-GTK	C56X	5007
OE-GTM	BE40	RK-343
OE-GTO	LJ60	303
"OE-GTS"	LJ60	281
OE-GTT	C680	0153
OE-GTZ	C550	550-0864
OE-GUK	BE40	RK-124
OE-GUN	**C56X**	**5061**
OE-GUP	C680	0066
OE-GUS	FA20	36
OE-GVA	LJ40	2079
OE-GVB	C52B	0339
OE-GVB	LJ60	167
OE-GVD	LJ60	373
OE-GVE	LJ60	386
OE-GVF	LJ60	401
OE-GVG	LJ60	403
OE-GVH	LJ60	405
OE-GVI	LJ40	2026
OE-GVJ	LJ60	359
OE-GVL	C56X	5772
OE-GVM	LJ45	084
OE-GVN	LJ60	406
OE-GVO	C680	0145
OE-GVP	LJ60	407
OE-GVQ	LJ60	409
OE-GVR	C550	550-0988
OE-GVT	LJ60	360
OE-GVV	LJ60	364
OE-GVX	LJ40	2097
OE-GWB	C52C	0043
OE-GWH	**C56X**	**6029**
OE-GWP	HS25	258811
OE-GWS	**C56X**	**6020**
OE-GWV	**C56X**	**5826**
OE-GXB	C52C	0055
OE-GXL	**C56X**	**5154**
OE-GXX	**LJ40**	**2112**
OE-GYB	HS25	HA-0161
OE-GYG	LJ60	197
OE-GYP	HS25	HA-0107
OE-GYR	BE40	RK-428
OE-GYX	C56X	5029
OE-GZK	**C56X**	**5668**
OE-HAA	CL30	20232
OE-HAB	**CL30**	**20227**
OE-HAC	C750	0232
OE-HAF	F2TH	223
OE-HAG	**GALX**	**065**
OE-HAK	C750	0300
OE-HAL	C750	0259
OE-HAM	F2EX	245
OE-HAP	CL30	20226
OE-HAS	**GALX**	**206**
OE-HAZ	GALX	102
OE-HBA	**CL30**	**20317**
OE-HBG	**F2TH**	**207**
OE-HCA	**CL30**	**20274**
OE-HCB	**F2EX**	**78**
OE-HCL	CL61	3045
OE-HCS	FA50	42
OE-HCZ	**CL30**	**20449**
OE-HDC	**CL30**	**20310**
OE-HDD	CL30	20065
OE-HDI	**CL30**	**20357**
OE-HDT	CL30	20357
OE-HDU	**CL30**	**20094**

OE-HDV	CL30	20261
(OE-HEC)	C750	0277
OE-HEM	F2TH	207
OE-HEO	CL30	20179
(OE-HEP)	CL30	20284
OE-HET	CL60	1085
OE-HEY	**F2EX**	**260**
OE-HFA	F2TH	216
OE-HFC	GALX	050
OE-HFE	C750	0179
OE-HGE	GALX	240
OE-HGG	C750	0214
OE-HGL	**CL30**	**20335**
OE-HGM	**F2EX**	**11**
OE-HGO	GALX	238
OE-HHH	**CL30**	**20314**
OE-HHH	FA50	297
OE-HII	**CL30**	**20111**
OE-HIT	FA50	222
(OE-HIX)	CL30	20289
OE-HJA	C750	0261
OE-HKK	**F2EX**	**10**
OE-HKY	F2TH	226
OE-HLE	CL61	3047
OE-HLL	**CL30**	**20294**
OE-HMA	**GALX**	**245**
OE-HMK	CL30	20276
OE-HMR	**F2EX**	**152**
OE-HNG	**GALX**	**231**
OE-HNL	CL30	20039
OE-HNM	F2EX	8
OE-HOO	**CL30**	**20079**
OE-HOT	F2EX	88
OE-HPG	**CL30**	**20251**
OE-HPH	**F2TH**	**209**
OE-HPK	CL30	20004
OE-HPS	FA50	334
OE-HPZ	CL30	20047
OE-HRA	F2EX	8
OE-HRM	CL30	20222
OE-HRR	**CL30**	**20033**
OE-HRS	**CL30**	**20504**
OE-HSB	GALX	223
OE-HSG	GALX	065
OE-HSN	**GALX**	**225**
OE-HTI	GALX	089
OE-HTO	F2EX	199
OE-HTR	**F2EX**	**276**
OE-HUB	**C750**	**0273**
OE-HUG	**CL30**	**20547**
OE-HVA	F2TH	217
OE-HVJ	CL30	20200
OE-HVV	CL30	20214
(OE-HYN)	HA4T	RC-63
OE-HZP	CL30	20338
OE-IAA	**CL64**	**5618**
OE-IAG	GLF4	4130
OE-IAH	**CL64**	**5475**
OE-IAK	GLEX	9204
OE-IBC	**GLEX**	**9269**
OE-IBN	**F9EX**	**176**
OE-ICA	**GLEX**	**9542**
OE-ICF	F900	22
OE-ICH	GLF4	4104
OE-ICL	CL64	5523
OE-ICN	GLEX	9256
OE-IDG	**CL64**	**5654**
OE-IDM	**F9EX**	**51**
OE-IDO	**GLEX**	**9280**
OE-IDV	CL65	5838
OE-IDX	F9DX	604
OE-IEL	**GLEX**	**9099**
OE-IEN	**F2EX**	**102**
OE-IEO	**GLEX**	**9496**
OE-IEX	F9EX	111
OE-IFB	CL65	5704
OE-IFG	GLEX	9182
(OE-IFH)	GLEX	9120
OE-IGG	**GLEX**	**9251**
OE-IGJ	CL64	5598
OE-IGL	**GLEX**	**9672**
OE-IGO	**GLF5**	**5434**
OE-IGS	**GLEX**	**9044**
OE-IHK	**CL64**	**5422**
OE-IIA	GLF5	641
OE-IIE	**GLF4**	**4307**
OE-IIH	**GLF6**	**6134**
OE-III	GLEX	9401
(OE-III)	CL65	5732
OE-IIS	**GLF5**	**572**
OE-IJA	GLF4	1157
OE-IKM	GLEX	9112
OE-IKP	CL64	5599
OE-ILM	FA7X	125
OE-ILS	F900	58
OE-IMA	F9EX	87
OE-IMA	GLEX	9243
OE-IMB	CL64	5585
OE-IMC	F9EX	165
OE-IMF	**FA7X**	**125**
OE-IMI	F900	147
OE-IMI	**F9EX**	**87**
OE-IMK	**CL64**	**5664**
OE-IMZ	**GLF4**	**4121**
OE-INA	CL65	5782
OE-INB	F9EX	189
OE-INC	**GLEX**	**9168**

OE-IND	CL65	5797
OE-INE	CL65	5842
OE-INF	CL64	5303
OE-ING	CL65	5845
OE-INH	CL65	5852
OE-INI	CL64	5595
OE-INJ	**CL64**	**5435**
OE-INK	**CL65**	**5825**
OE-INL	**GLEX**	**9427**
OE-INM	CL65	5878
OE-INN	CL65	5743
OE-INP	CL65	5745
OE-INS	CL65	5707
OE-INT	CL65	5758
OE-INU	CL65	5749
OE-INX	CL64	5629
OE-INY	CL64	5644
OE-IOD	F900	86
OE-IOE	**F9EX**	**214**
OE-IOK	GLF4	4260
OE-IOO	**GLEX**	**9301**
OE-IPA	GLEX	9286
OE-IPD	CL64	5608
OE-IPE	**GLF5**	**5420**
OE-IPG	CL64	5589
OE-IPH	HS25	258778
OE-IPK	CL64	5612
(OE-IPR)	CL65	5712
OE-IPW	**FA7X**	**238**
OE-IPZ	CL65	5808
OE-IRA	**GLEX**	**9237**
OE-IRE	**GLF4**	**4291**
OE-IRG	GLF5	5139
(OE-IRJ)	CL64	5464
OE-IRL	F9EX	118
OE-IRM	GLEX	9319
OE-IRN	**GLEX**	**9291**
OE-IRP	**GLEX**	**9106**
OE-IRR	**FA7X**	**196**
OE-IRS	**GLEX**	**9507**
OE-IRT	**GLEX**	**9455**
OE-ISM	F9DX	617
OE-ISN	**GLF5**	**5379**
OE-ISS	GLF5	5022
OE-ISU	**CL65**	**5764**
OE-ITH	**CL64**	**5636**
OE-ITN	**GLEX**	**9159**
OE-IVA	FA7X	42
(OE-IVB)	CL65	5715
OE-IVE	CL64	5620
OE-IVG	**GLEX**	**9081**
OE-IVK	F9EX	138
OE-IVV	GLF5	5054
OE-IVY	**GLF5**	**687**
OE-IWG	F9EX	141
OE-IXX	**GLEX**	**9528**
OE-IYA	CL64	5435
OE-IZI	**GLF5**	**5302**
OE-IZK	**GLF4**	**4200**
OE-IZM	**GLF5**	**5177**
OE-LAA	**GLEX**	**9170**
OE-LAF	GLEX	9234
OE-LAI	**GLF4**	**4237**
OE-LAR	**GLF4**	**4119**
OE-LCY	**GLF5**	**5524**
OE-LGX	GLEX	9323
OE-LII	**GLEX**	**9609**
OE-LLL	FA7X	55
(OE-LNX)	GLEX	9167
(OE-LNY)	GLEX	9237
OE-LOK	**GLF5**	**5462**
OE-LPN	**GLF5**	**5395**
OE-LPZ	**GLEX**	**9495**
OE-LUB	**GLEX**	**9208**
OE-LXR	GLEX	9235
OE-LXX	GLEX	9429
OE-LZM	**GLF6**	**6073**

Finland

OH-ADM	**CL30**	**20525**
OH-AEM	LJ60	300
OH-AMB	FA10	193
OH-ANS	CL65	5785
OH-BAP	HS25	257212
OH-BZM	CL64	5626
OH-CAR	C500	144
OH-CAT	C550	133
OH-CIT	C500	551
OH-COC	C500	223
OH-COL	C500	311
OH-CUT	C550	414
OH-CXO	C750	0022
OH-DDI	C750	0227
OH-EPA	**E50P**	**50000190**
OH-EPB	**E50P**	**50000201**
OH-FEX	F2EX	27
OH-FFA	FA20	178/459
OH-FFB	FA10	17
OH-FFC	F9EX	23
OH-FFD	FA7X	20
OH-FFE	F9EX	220
OH-FFF	FA7X	66
OH-FFI	FA7X	69
OH-FFJ	FA20	225/472
OH-FFV	FA20	248/483
OH-FFW	FA20	243/480
OH-FIX	F2TH	179
OH-FLM	CL30	20155
OH-FOX	F2EX	67
OH-FPC	FA20	345
OH-GIV	GLF4	4243
OH-GLA	LJ24	273
OH-GLB	LJ24	262
OH-GPE	F9EX	252
OH-GVA	GLF5	5408
OH-GVE	LJ60	281
OH-GVI	**CL65**	**5849**
(OH-GVI)	LJ60	303
(OH-GVI)	LJ60	317
OH-GVV	GLF6	6006
OH-III	LJ60	303
OH-IPJ	LJ45	104
OH-IPP	LJ55	056
OH-IVS	LJ60	355
OH-JET	HS25	257136
OH-JOT	HS25	258001
OH-JVA	GLF4	4265
OH-KNE	MU30	A014SA
OH-MAL	GLEX	9353
OH-MOL	CL64	5658
OH-MPL	GLEX	9553
(OH-NEM)	CL64	5658
OH-ONE	C56X	5157
OH-PPI	C750	0115
OH-PPJ	C750	0152
OH-PPR	F9EX	118
OH-PPS	GLEX	9237
(OH-PPS)	GLEX	9242
OH-PPT	GLEX	9291
OH-RBX	**C56X**	**5056**
OH-RIF	BE40	RK-79
OH-STP	CL30	20334
OH-SWI	**C52A**	**0408**
OH-SWJ	**C52A**	**0443**
OH-TNF	GLEX	9332
OH-TNR	GLEX	9159
OH-TRA	GLEX	9515
OH-VIV	LJ60	305
OH-VMF	LJ60	312
OH-WIA	**C680**	**0215**
(OH-WIA)	CL64	5658
OH-WIC	**CL64**	**5452**
OH-WIF	FA20	461
OH-WIH	CL60	1029
OH-WII	**CL64**	**5642**
OH-WIN	FA20	481
OH-WIP	FA20	359/542
OH-WIX	**FA7X**	**231**
OH-ZET	**PRM1**	**RB-120**
(OH-ZIP)	CL30	20209

Czech Republic

OK-ACH	C550	550-1111
OK-AJA	**C510**	**0272**
OK-AJD	LJ31	095
OK-AML	**C510**	**0116**
OK-BEE	**BE40**	**RK-293**
OK-BII	**BE40**	**RK-318**
OK-BYA	CL61	5105
OK-CAA	**C56X**	**5183**
OK-DSJ	**C525**	**0351**
OK-EAS	**BE40**	**RK-180**
OK-EEH	FA10	27
OK-EMA	**C680**	**0279**
OK-ESC	**BE40**	**RK-295**
OK-FCY	**C52A**	**0204**
OK-FKA	C500	260
OK-FTR	**C510**	**0053**
OK-GLF	**GALX**	**167**
OK-GLX	**GALX**	**238**
OK-HWK	**HS25**	**HA-0018**
OK-ILA	C52A	0462
OK-ILA	**C52C**	**0085**
OK-ILC	C52A	0462
OK-ILE	**GLF4**	**4122**
OK-IMO	**BE40**	**RK-313**
OK-IRI	C56X	5723
OK-JDM	**LJ60**	**330**
OK-JRT	**C680**	**0558**
OK-JUR	**C680**	**0265**
OK-KAZ	HS25	HA-0034
OK-KKF	**GLF5**	**5426**
OK-KUK	**C510**	**0270**
OK-LEO	C510	0252
OK-LNZ	C510	0368
OK-MAR	**C52A**	**0455**
OK-MYS	**C510**	**0268**
OK-NKN	C650	0010
OK-OBR	**C510**	**0289**
(OK-ONE)	GLF5	680
OK-PBS	**C525**	**0029**
OK-PBT	**C52A**	**0223**
OK-PHE	E55P	50500062
OK-PMI	BE40	RK-162
OK-PPC	C510	0019
OK-PPP	**BE40**	**RK-385**
OK-RHM	BE40	RJ-56
OK-SLA	C525	0310
OK-SLS	**C560**	**0088**
OK-SLX	**C56X**	**5243**
OK-UGJ	**C680**	**0324**
OK-UNI	**C680**	**0139**
OK-UZI	BE40	RJ-56
OK-VAN	**E50P**	**50000134**
OK-VPI	**GLF5**	**5189**
OK-VSZ	C550	550-1040
OK-XLS	**C56X**	**6060**
(OK-YXY)	LJ60	376

Slovakia

OM-AES	C510	0270
OM-ATM	C560	0665
OM-ATN	**C550**	**550-1040**
OM-ATS	**C550**	**550-0865**
OM-BJB	**C52A**	**0321**
OM-FTS	**C52A**	**0239**
OM-GLE	**PRM1**	**RB-195**
OM-HLY	C525	0393
OM-HLZ	C525	0223
OM-IGQ	F2EX	9
OM-LBG	C52B	0067
OM-OIG	**HS25**	**258612**
OM-OLI	C525	0477
OM-OPA	C52B	0269
OM-OPE	C52A	0239
OM-OPF	F2TH	207
OM-OPR	**C525**	**0101**
OM-PTT	**C550**	**352**
OM-RAH	**BE40**	**RK-413**
OM-SKY	HS25	258314
OM-SYN	C52B	0343
OM-TAA	**PRM1**	**RB-149**
OM-TAB	**C525**	**0477**
OM-USS	HS25	258720
OM-USS	HS25	HA-0151
OM-VOV	C500	489
OM-VPB	PRM1	RB-256
OM-VPT	C52B	0217

Belgium

OO-AAA	FA7X	57
(OO-AAM)	FA7X	207
OO-ABC	**FA7X**	**166**
OO-ACC	**C52A**	**0431**
OO-ACO	**C510**	**0260**
OO-ACT	F900	194
(OO-ADA)	FA20	73/419
OO-ADH	LJ60	344
OO-AIE	C56X	5733
OO-ALX	**C680**	**0271**
OO-AMR	**C52A**	**0495**
OO-ATS	C500	044
OO-CEH	**C56X**	**6003**
OO-CEJ	**C525**	**0172**
OO-CIV	**C52A**	**0206**
OO-CLX	C560	0537
OO-DCM	C500	182
OO-DDA	**C52A**	**0164**
OO-DDD	FA20	11
OO-DFG	**F2EX**	**140**
OO-DOK	FA20	162/451
(OO-EBA)	MU30	A048SA
OO-EBE	C56X	6025
(OO-ECT)	C500	542
OO-EDV	**C52B**	**0200**
(OO-EEF)	FA20	95
OO-EJA	**FA7X**	**124**
OO-ENZ	LJ31	202
OO-EPU	LJ45	291
(OO-FAY)	C500	088
OO-FBY	C500	093
OO-FDG	**F2EX**	**61**
OO-FFE	**F9EX**	**220**
OO-FLN	C52A	0179
OO-FNL	C525	0332
OO-FOI	F9EX	121
OO-FPA	C56X	5248
OO-FPB	**C550**	**550-1117**
OO-FPC	**C52B**	**0147**
(OO-FPD)	C52B	0158
OO-FPE	**C52B**	**0158**
OO-FTS	**C56X**	**5318**
OO-FYG	C550	550-1027
OO-FYS	**C52B**	**0197**
OO-GBL	LJ35	284
OO-GFD	F2TH	101
OO-GHE	**F2EX**	**243**
OO GJP	E50P	50000147
OO-GML	F2EX	75
OO-GPE	**F9EX**	**252**
OO-GPN	C500	225
(OO-HFW)	LJ25	231
OO-HPG	E50P	50000187
OO-IAR	F2EX	8
OO-IBC	SBRL	465-68
OO-IBI	C500	238
OO-IBS	SBRL	306-5
OO-IDE	**C525**	**0037**
OO-IDY	**FA7X**	**120**
OO-IIG	C550	550-1018
OO-JBA	LJ31	009
OO-JBB	FA20	116
OO-JBS	LJ35	669
OO-JDK	**C525**	**0250**
OO-JPC	PRM1	RB-228
OO-KJD	LJ45	404
OO-KJG	LJ35	149
OO-KOR	**C52A**	**0485**
OO-KRC	CL64	5577
OO-LCM	C500	036
OO-LFA	LJ24	248
OO-LFN	LJ45	250
OO-LFQ	F900	62
OO-LFR	LJ25	320
OO-LFS	LJ45	018
OO-LFT	FA50	42
"OO-LFU"	C525	0020
OO-LFV	LJ35	481
(OO-LFW)	LJ25	231
(OO-LFX)	C550	067
(OO-LFX)	LJ35	135
OO-LFY	LJ35	200
OO-LFZ	LJ25	118
OO-LIE	**C52B**	**0173**
OO-LMG	**FA7X**	**152**
OO-LMS	**F9EX**	**285**
OO-MAS	E50P	50000196
OO-MCV	E50P	50000177
(OO-MDN)	FA20	262
OO-MLG	**C56X**	**5028**
OO-MMJ	C555	0007
OO-MMP	C550	559
OO-MRA	CRVT	15
OO-MRC	CRVT	30
OO-MRE	CRVT	15
OO-NAD	**FA7X**	**41**
OO-NEY	**LEG5**	**55010003**
OO-NOA	E50P	50000095
OO-OFP	F2EX	132
(OO-OIL)	C56X	6077
OO-OOO	FA20	56
OO-OSA	C555	0147
OO-OSD	C52A	0229
OO-OSG	GALX	065
OO-OTU	E50P	50000243
OO-PAP	F2EX	123
OO-PAR	**C52B**	**0287**
OO-PGG	**C56X**	**5230**
OO-PHI	**C525**	**0115**
OO-PJB	FA20	145/443
OO-PKX	**C750**	**0313**
(OO-PPP)	FA20	56
OO-PRM	**C510**	**0125**
OO-PSD	FA20	384/551
OO-PSE	**F2EX**	**162**
OO-RAM	C510	0317
OO-RJE	C550	421
OO-RJT	C550	023
(OO-RJX)	FA20	73/419
OO-RRR	FA20	98/434
(OO-RSA)	SBRL	465-72
(OO-RSB)	SBRL	465-72
OO-RSE	SBRL	465-72
OO-RST	C500	063
(OO-RYB)	FA20	262
OO-SAV	C56X	5189
OO-SEL	C500	133
(OO-SIN)	C680	0078
OO-SKA	C52A	0054
OO-SKJ	HS25	25089
OO-SKP	C555	0007
OO-SKS	C550	079
OO-SKV	C560	0153
OO-SKY	**C52A**	**0197**
OO-SLM	**C56X**	**5781**
OO-STE	**C525**	**0495**
OO-STE	FA20	218
OO-STF	FA20	220
OO-TME	LJ60	255
OO-TOI	FA7X	213
(OO-TTL)	CRVT	28
(OO-VIZ)	C56X	5284
OO-VMB	F2TH	74
OO-VMI	**F9DX**	**603**
OO-VPQ	FA20	315/517
OO-VRO	**F2EX**	**196**
OO-WTB	FA20	162/451
OO-XLS	**C56X**	**6162**

Denmark

(OY-...)	C550	469
OY-AGZ	LJ24	183
OY-AJV	C500	279
OY-AKL	LJ25	054
OY-AKZ	LJ25	062
OY-APM	CL61	5153
OY-APM	**GLF4**	**4305**
OY-APM	HS25	25253
OY-ARA	CRVT	32
OY-ARB	CRVT	34
OY-ARP	C500	040
OY-ARW	C500	130
OY-ASD	C500	288
(OY-ASK)	LJ25	097
OY-ASO	LJ35	119
OY-ASP	LJ25	171
OY-ASR	C500	194
OY-ASV	C550	067
OY-AZT	FA20	98/434
OY-BDS	FA20	180/460
OY-BFC	LJ25	112
OY-BIZ	LJ24	281
OY-BLG	LJ35	022
OY-BPC	MU30	A023SA
OY-BPI	MU30	A070SA
OY-BZT	**C550**	**289**
OY-CCB	MU30	A037SA
OY-CCG	C650	0003
OY-CCJ	**LJ35**	**468**
OY-CCO	LJ35	670
OY-CCT	LJ35	144
OY-CCU	C550	127
OY-CDK	MU30	A065SA
OY-CEV	**C500**	**329**
OY-CGO	C500	287
OY-CJN	BE40	RK-530
OY-CKE	C650	7070
OY-CKF	F2TH	163
OY-CKH	F2EX	160
(OY-CKH)	FA50	134
OY-CKI	F2TH	154
OY-CKJ	C560	0114
OY-CKK	C56X	5757
OY-CKK	**F2EX**	**281**
OY-CKK	F900	110
OY-CKN	**F2TH**	**76**
(OY-CKO)	CL60	1025
OY-CKT	C560	0078
OY-CKW	F2TH	166
OY-CKY	FA20	293
OY-CLD	CL61	5070
(OY-CLE)	CL64	5303
OY-CLN	F2EX	35
OY-CLP	**C650**	**7093**
OY-CLS	**FA7X**	**155**
OY-CPK	C500	267
OY-CPW	C500	487
OY-CVS	GLEX	9139
OY-CYD	C500	550
OY-CYT	C550	443
OY-CYV	**C550**	**440**
OY-DKP	HS25	25132
OY-DVL	C500	036
(OY-EBD)	C500	299
OY-EDP	**C650**	**0014**
OY-EGE	LJ24	124
OY-EJD	F2EX	63
OY-EJD	**FA7X**	**236**
OY-EKC	C56X	5217
OY-EKC	**FA7X**	**121**
OY-EKS	CL30	20251
OY-ELY	C550	154
(OY-ERY)	C550	469
OY-EVO	**C550**	**550-1050**
(OY-FCE)	C525	0165
OY-FCG	HS25	258541
OY-FFB	**C500**	**603**
OY-FFC	C500	551
OY-FFI	**FA7X**	**69**
OY-FFV	C560	0138
OY-FIT	**GLEX**	**9186**
OY-FLK	LJ55	050
OY-FLW	**PRM1**	**RB-278**
(OY-FPN)	F2EX	103
OY-FRM	FA10	56
OY-FWO	**FA7X**	**198**
OY-FYN	**MU30**	**A014SA**
OY-GBB	CL65	5732
(OY-GDA)	FA50	54
OY-GGG	C650	7039
OY-GGR	C52A	0216
OY-GIP	HS25	258367
OY-GKC	C550	100
OY-GKC	C56X	5189
OY-GKC	C56X	6109
OY-GKJ	**F2EX**	**195**
OY-GKL	C650	0043
OY-GLA	GLEX	9094
OY-GLF	GLF6	6040
OY-GLO	C52A	0303
(OY-GLO)	F2EX	192
(OY-GMB)	C550	066
OY-GMC	C550	025
OY-GMJ	C555	0134
OY-GMK	C550	066
OY-GRC	C550	255
(OY-GSE)	CL61	5137
OY-GVG	GLEX	9470
OY-GVG	GLF4	4066
OY-GVI	GLEX	9458
OY-GWK	**F2TS**	**715**
OY-ICE	F2TH	26
OY-ILG	GLEX	9163
OY-INI	C500	559
OY-INV	C525	0223
OY-IVK	F9EX	138
(OY-IZM)	GLF6	6062
OY-JAI	**C500**	**193**
OY-JAT	BE40	RJ-22
OY-JBJ	**HS25**	**258358**
OY-JDE	FA7X	54
OY-JET	C500	644
OY-JET	C52A	0089
(OY-JET)	C560	0138
(OY-JET)	C680	0067
OY-JEV	**C550**	**243**
OY-JEY	C500	600
OY-JJA	**HS25**	**258496**
OY-JJC	**HS25**	**258637**
(OY-JJC)	HS25	258496
OY-JJD	**BE40**	**RK-133**
OY-JJE	**BE40**	**RK-29**
OY-JJJ	**HA4T**	**RC-57**
OY-JJN	**C500**	**657**
OY-JJO	BE40	RK-267

OY-JKH	LJ60	141
OY-JMC	**C525**	**0277**
OY-JPJ	**C650**	**0060**
OY-JPJ	HS25	257015
OY-JSW	C510	0171
OY-KLG	**C560**	**0401**
"OY-KPV"	LJ40	2064
OY-KVP	**LJ40**	**2064**
OY-KYS	LJ60	369
(OY-LEG)	C56X	5217
OY-LGI	**GLEX**	**9433**
OY-LGI	LJ60	243
OY-LIN	FA50	230
OY-LJA	LJ35	594
OY-LJB	LJ31	086
OY-LJC	LJ31	087
OY-LJD	LJ60	005
OY-LJE	LJ60	011
OY-LJF	LJ60	173
OY-LJG	LJ45	083
OY-LJH	LJ60	051
OY-LJI	LJ31	104
OY-LJJ	LJ45	116
OY-LJK	LJ60	256
(OY-LJK)	LJ60	200
OY-LJL	LJ31	133
OY-LJM	LJ60	060
(OY-LJN)	LJ31	170
OY-LKG	HS25	258345
OY-LKS	C750	0212
OY-LLA	C52A	0005
OY-LNA	**GLEX**	**9331**
OY-LPU	C510	0022
OY-LUK	GLEX	9267
OY-MCL	HS25	258099
OY-MFL	HS25	257103
OY-MGA	**F2EX**	**311**
OY-MGO	F2EX	161
OY-MHA	F2EX	156
OY-MHM	**F9EX**	**273**
OY-MIR	LJ60	322
OY-MKS	CL64	5624
OY-MMM	CL64	5430
OY-MPA	HS25	257127
OY-MSI	**GLEX**	**9032**
OY-MUS	**C525**	**0857**
OY-NDP	**C52A**	**0372**
OY-NLA	**C650**	**0070**
OY-NUD	C560	0064
OY-OAA	HS25	258645
OY-OCV	LJ45	306
OY-OKK	F9EX	128
OY-ONE	C500	535
OY-OYO	**BE40**	**RK-354**
OY-PCW	C500	278
OY-PDN	C550	412
OY-PHN	FA10	209
OY-PNO	F2EX	103
OY-PWO	E55P	50500102
OY-RAA	**HS25**	**258235**
OY-RAC	HS25	258335
OY-RAK	GALX	051
OY-RAW	**C525**	**0892**
OY-RDD	C550	621
OY-RED	LJ40	2096
OY-REN	C52A	0331
OY-RGG	C525	0495
OY-RYA	LJ24	109
OY-SBR	CRVT	23
OY-SBS	CRVT	21
OY-SBT	CRVT	33
OY-SGC	GLEX	9343
OY-SGM	CL64	5596
OY-SIR	F2TH	173
OY-SIS	BE40	RK-162
OY-SKL	F2EX	225
OY-SLS	F9EX	264
OY-SML	**C525**	**0258**
OY-SMS	**CL30**	**20602**
OY-SNK	**F2TH**	**223**
OY-SNZ	**FA7X**	**95**
OY-SPB	**CL30**	**20334**
OY-SUJ	C500	121
OY-SVL	C500	420
OY-SWO	**F2TS**	**725**
OY-TAM	C500	158
(OY-TCG)	LJ60	200
OY-TJF	F2TH	166
OY-TKI	C500	299
OY-TMA	**C550**	**457**
OY-TNF	CL64	5303
OY-TSA	**C52B**	**0198**
OY-TSS	**FA7X**	**98**
OY-UCA	**C52A**	**0209**
(OY-VIA)	CL60	1025
(OY-VIA)	HS25	257105
OY-VIK	**FA7X**	**85**
(OY-VIK)	F9EX	138
OY-VIP	C500	294
(OY-VIP)	C500	311
OY-VIS	C550	672
OY-VIZ	**GLEX**	**9544**
OY-WET	**C680**	**0067**
OY-WIN	GLEX	9280
OY-WWW	**C52B**	**0194**
OY-YAM	ASTR	111
OY-ZAN	LJ40	2071
OY-ZWO	F2EX	196
(OY-ZWO)	F2EX	228

Netherlands

PH-ABO	CL61	5085
PH-ABU	LJ55	107
PH-AJX	**FA7X**	**102**
PH-ANO	**C56X**	**5745**
PH-APV	FA20	490
PH-BAG	FA20	126/438
(PH-BBC)	BE40	RK-313
PH-BPS	FA20	321
PH-CHT	F2EX	40
PH-CIJ	C680	0185
PH-CJI	**C56X**	**5128**
PH-CMW	**C525**	**0613**
PH-CSA	C550	630
PH-CTA	C500	088
PH-CTB	C500	093
PH-CTC	C500	098
PH-CTD	C500	157
PH-CTE	C500	167
PH-CTF	C500	177
PH-CTG	C500	234
PH-CTH	**F2EX**	**194**
PH-CTR	**C680**	**0525**
(PH-CTW)	C500	269
PH-CTX	C550	338
PH-CTY	C500	044
PH-CTZ	C550	067
(PH-DEQ)	ASTR	115
PH-DEZ	**C500**	**407**
PH-DRK	C56X	5258
PH-DRS	C56X	5792
PH-DTP	BE40	RK-313
PH-DYE	C550	550-0927
PH-DYN	C550	550-0928
(PH-DYX)	C56X	5209
PH-EBR	F900	30
PH-ECI	**C525**	**0321**
PH-ECL	C52A	0054
PH-EDM	F900	188
(PH-EEJ)	C525	0291
(PH-EER)	C56X	6097
(PH-EFA)	F900	163
(PH-EFB)	F2TH	49
(PH-ERB)	F900	30
PH-ERP	F9EX	1
(PH-EVY)	C650	0134
PH-FIS	**C525**	**0514**
PH-FJK	**C52B**	**0291**
PH-FJP	GLF2	78
PH-HES	C550	023
PH-HET	C550	323
PH-HFA	HFB3	1032
PH-HFB	HFB3	1033
PH-HFC	HFB3	1035
PH-HGT	**C680**	**0530**
PH-HMA	C550	550-0972
(PH-HMA)	C555	0145
(PH-HMC)	C555	0145
(PH-HRA)	C56X	6097
PH-HRM	**C56X**	**6097**
PH-HWM	**CL65**	**5937**
PH-ILA	C560	0078
PH-ILC	F900	161
(PH-ILC)	F900	9
PH-ILD	FA50	23
PH-ILF	FA20	147/444
PH-ILI	C560	0114
PH-ILO	C560	0362
PH-ILR	FA50	15
PH-ILT	FA10	1
PH-ILX	FA20	266/490
PH-ILY	FA20	326/521
PH-ILZ	C560	0145
PH-INJ	F2TH	36
PH-JAY	C510	0303
PH-JCI	PRM1	RB-122
PH-JND	C56X	5618
PH-JNE	C52A	0242
PH-JNL	FA50	268
PH-JNX	C56X	5641
(PH-JOB)	C500	511
PH-JSB	CRVT	26
PH-JSC	CRVT	35
PH-JSD	CRVT	36
(PH-JSL)	MU30	A087SA
PH-KOM	C525	0331
PH-LAB	**C550**	**712**
PH-LAU	**F9EX**	**54**
PH-LBA	F900	173
PH-LCG	F900	143
PH-LEM	FA50	28
(PH-LEN)	FA20	263/489
PH-LPS	FA20	63/411
PH-LSV	FA50	315
PH-MBX	C550	180
PH-MCX	C550	564
PH-MDC	C560	0280
PH-MDX	C550	634
PH-MED	LJ55	136
PH-MEX	C650	0217
PH-MFX	**C650**	**0240**
PH-MGT	C525	0042
PH-MHM	C56X	5781
PH-MKL	C550	347
PH-MSR	MS76	102
PH-MSS	MS76	103
PH-MST	MS76	104
PH-MSU	MS76	105
PH-MSV	MS76	106
PH-MSW	MS76	107
PH-MSX	C650	0134
PH-MSX	MS76	108
PH-MYX	**C650**	**7117**
PH-NDK	**F900**	**175**
PH-OLI	F900	35
PH-OMC	FA20	239
PH-ORJ	C510	0025
PH-PBM	C560	0100
PH-PKD	C56X	6077
PH-PKF	**F2EX**	**298**
PH-PKX	C750	0313
PH-PST	**E50P**	**50000132**
PH-RID	**C680**	**0212**
PH-RLG	**C680**	**0531**
PH-RMA	C555	0145
PH-RSA	**C56X**	**5110**
PH-SAW	C500	225
(PH-SDL)	FA50	66
PH-SOL	C525	0417
PH-STB	**F900**	**194**
PH-SVZ	**C550**	**133**
(PH-TEU)	C500	086
PH-TEV	C500	086
PH-TLP	**FA7X**	**259**
PH-TXA	**C510**	**0111**
(PH-TXA)	C510	0088
(PH-TXB)	C510	0111
(PH-TXB)	C510	0133
(PH-TXC)	C510	0131
PH-TXI	C510	0050
PH-VBG	**F2EX**	
PH-VLG	**C560**	**0271**
PH-WMS	FA20	285/504
(PH-WOL)	F2TH	36
(PH-WOL)	HS25	258235
PH-YMA	GALX	034

Philippines

PI-C1747	LJ24	264
(PI-C7777)	C500	123

Netherlands Antilles

PJ-ABA	GLF2	163
PJ-ARI	GLF2	8
PJ-AYA	FA10	47
PJ-DOM	**C510**	**0316**
PJ-MAR	C650	0049
PJ-SLB	HS25	25223
PJ-SOL	BE40	RJ-19
PJ-TOM	**C560**	**0414**

Indonesia

PK-...	**LJ31**	**213**
PK-ASB	**PRM1**	**RB-143**
PK-BKS	**C56X**	**5804**
PK-BND	GLF3	316
PK-BSW	**E55P**	**50500078**
PK-CAG	FA20	408
PK-CAH	**LJ31**	**066**
PK-CAJ	**LJ31**	**077**
(PK-CAJ)	FA20	408
PK-CAP	GLF3	316
PK-CAR	**HS25**	**HA-0200**
PK-CIR	FA20	90/426
PK-CTA	HS25	257153
PK-CTC	HS25	257099
PK-CTP	GLF3	431
PK-DJW	HS25	25147
PK-DPD	**C56X**	**6035**
PK-EJR	**HS25**	**258591**
PK-ELI	**BE40**	**RK-111**
PK-ELX	**BE40**	**RK-194**
PK-ERA	BE40	RJ-40
PK-HMG	HS25	256029
PK-HMK	CL61	5073
PK-IJS	JSTR	5046
PK-ILA	C56X	5598
PK-JBB	**HS25**	**HA-0188**
PK-JBH	**HS25**	**HA-0071**
PK-JCO	**E55P**	**50500026**
PK-JKM	**CL61**	**5120**
PK-KIG	C650	0151
PK-LRT	**HS25**	**HA-0207**
PK-LRU	**HS25**	**HA-0212**
PK-NSP	GLF4	1077
PK-NZK	GLF4	1219
PK-OCN	GLF3	305
PK-PJA	GLF3	395
PK-PJD	HS25	256017
PK-PJE	HS25	256029
PK-PJG	GLF2	45
PK-PJH	JSTR	5011/1
PK-PJR	HS25	25147
PK-PJS	JSTR	5011/1
PK-PJZ	GLF2	26
(PK-RGE)	C56X	6138
PK-RGM	HS25	258106
PK-RJB	C650	7073
PK-RJD	**E55P**	**50500080**
PK-RJT	**C56X**	**5598**
PK-RSO	**C650**	**7073**
PK-TIR	FA20	297
PK-TMI	**GLF4**	**4028**
PK-TRI	**FA20**	**173**
PK-TRJ	C650	0078
PK-TRP	F900	71
PK-TRV	C550	287
PK-TSM	C650	0144
PK-TVO	**HS25**	**258579**
PK-TWL	PRM1	RB-56
PK-TWY	**GLF4**	**1381**
PK-WSE	C650	0078
PK-WSG	C550	650
PK-WSJ	HS25	258106
PK-WSO	C550	287
PK-YGK	**BE40**	**RK-383**
PK-YRL	C650	7073

Brazil

PP-...	**WW24**	**181**
PP-AAA	C750	0234
PP-AAD	**C680**	**0260**
PP-AAF	F2EX	16
(PP-AAH)	FA50	338
PP-AAO	**BE40**	**RK-565**
(PP-AAW)	BE40	RK-518
PP-ABV	**E55P**	**50500045**
PP-ACP	**HS25**	**258133**
PP-ACV	**C680**	**0091**
PP-ADD	**C56X**	**5822**
PP-ADZ	GLF6	6190
PP-AFM	E50P	50000049
(PP-AHT)	GLEX	9351
PP-AHW	**E50P**	**50000328**
(PP-AHW)	E50P	50000327
PP-AIO	C650	0087
(PP-AKT)	FA7X	98
PP-AMK	**F2EX**	**252**
PP-AML	**BE40**	**RK-390**
PP-ANA	HS25	258637
PP-ARG	**HS25**	**HA-0078**
PP-ASV	**LJ40**	**2018**
PP-AUL	**F2EX**	**178**
PP-AVX	C52B	0101
PP-BBL	**C56X**	**6152**
PP-BBS	**C52A**	**0325**
PP-BED	**LJ60**	**310**
PP-BGG	**E50P**	**50000233**
PP-BIA	CL64	5539
PP-BIC	**CL30**	**20208**
PP-BIN	LJ60	290
PP-BIO	**E50P**	**50000227**
PP-BIR	CL30	20178
PP-BMG	**C550**	**550-1045**
PP-BPS	**E55P**	**50500160**
(PP-BRP)	LJ60	321
PP-BRS	C56X	5544
PP-BSP	**C525**	**0056**
PP-BST	**C680**	**0184**
PP-CFF	**F2TH**	**110**
PP-CFJ	**FA7X**	**171**
(PP-CFO)	C52C	0056
PP-CGG	**E55P**	**50500113**
PP-CIT	C52A	0471
PP-CMG	C550	630
PP-CMJ	**E55P**	**50500114**
PP-CML	C52A	0119
(PP-CMN)	C525	0008
PP-CMP	**C52C**	**0059**
(PP-CMP)	C52B	0376
PP-CNS	**HS25**	**258816**
PP-COA	**CL65**	**5823**
PP-COR	**E50P**	**50000234**
PP-CPN	**LJ45**	**116**
PP-CRC	**LJ40**	**2117**
PP-CRS	**C525**	**0346**
PP-CRT	**LJ35**	**363**
PP-CRV	**LJ40**	**2107**
(PP-CSC)	FA7X	257
PP-CST	**C550**	**249**
PP-CSW	GLF4	1413
PP-CTA	**LJ31**	**168**
PP-CTC	**E50P**	**50000033**
PP-CTP	LJ60	343
PP-CTS	**E55P**	**50500236**
PP-CTU	**C56X**	**5771**
PP-DBS	**FA7X**	**237**
PP-DDR	**BE40**	**RK-170**
PP-DLC	**C510**	**0261**
PP-DSS	**BE40**	**RK-439**
PP-EEM	HS25	25197
PP-EIF	**C500**	**680**
PP-EIW	LJ24	294
PP-ELE	**E50P**	**50000060**
PP-ELT	**MU30**	**A089SA**
PP-EMB	**E50P**	**50000309**
PP-EMO	**E55P**	**50500110**
"PP-EMS"	GLF2	21
PP-EPH	**E55P**	**50500145**
PP-ERR	**LJ35**	**008**
PP-ESC	**C550**	**618**
PP-ESV	**G150**	**301**
PP-EVG	**C510**	**0101**
PP-FCC	**GLEX**	**9556**
PP-FMA	**C650**	**0102**
PP-FMW	LJ40	2068
PP-FMX	LJ24	090
PP-FOH	FA20	113
PP-FRI	**C52A**	**0472**
PP-FXB	C500	049
PP-GSM	C52A	0004
PP-GUL	**GLEX**	**9447**
PP-HSI	LJ45	237
PP-HUC	**E55P**	**50500157**
PP-HVD	**HS25**	**HA-0049**
PP-IBR	**E55P**	**50500213**
PP-IME	**E50P**	**50000073**
PP-IMP	**C510**	**0399**
PP-INT	**C525**	**0532**
PP-IPR	**F900**	**14**
PP-ISJ	**C560**	**0258**
PP-ITU	E55P	50500038
PP-IVA	**C56X**	**5792**
PP-IVN	**E50P**	**50000339**
(PP-IVN)	E50P	50000340
PP-IZA	**C525**	**0283**
PP-JAA	LJ36	055
PP-JAE	**LJ60**	**325**
PP-JAS	**C550**	**722**
PP-JAW	**LJ45**	**125**
(PP-JBE)	E55P	50500201
PP-JBS	**C525**	**0408**
PP-JCF	**BE40**	**RK-479**
PP-JCG	**C510**	**0430**
PP-JCP	**MU30**	**A049SA**
PP-JDB	**E55P**	**50500249**
(PP-JDB)	E55P	50500255
PP-JDF	C525	0905
PP-JEL	**E50P**	**50000322**
PP-JET	C525	0384
PP-JFH	GLF5	5339
PP-JFM	**C56X**	**5045**
PP-JFZ	**HS25**	**258844**
PP-JGV	**C56X**	**5105**
PP-JJA	**LEG5**	**55000004**
PP-JJB	**E50P**	**50000261**
PP-JJK	WW24	202
PP-JJZ	**C525**	**0356**
PP-JLS	E50P	50000287
PP-JLY	LJ45	197
PP-JMJ	**C750**	**0304**
PP-JMS	**BE40**	**RK-568**
PP-JMT	**C680**	**0534**
PP-JNY	**LJ31**	**118**
PP-JQM	C750	0056
PP-JRA	C650	7113
PP-JSR	C56X	6061
(PP-JSR)	C680	0307
PP-JSZ	**E50P**	**50000325**
(PP-KCB)	E55P	50500305
PP-KIK	**BE40**	**RJ-55**
PP-KKA	**E50P**	**50000126**
PP-KPL	**E50P**	**50000104**
PP-KYK	**C52A**	**0463**
PP-LAR	**C750**	**0010**
PP-LBM	**C680**	**0537**
PP-LBQ	E50P	50000232
PP-LBW	E50P	50000233
PP-LBX	E50P	50000234
PP-LCE	**C550**	**550-1061**
PP-LDW	**C510**	**0060**
(PP-LEM)	C500	171
PP-LFS	**F2TH**	**217**
PP-LFV	**LJ31**	**010**
PP-LGD	**E55P**	**50500052**
PP-LGT	**E50P**	**50000031**
PP-LJA	**E55P**	**50500211**
PP-LJR	C525	0487
PP-LMH	**E55P**	**50500278**
PP-LMR	**E55P**	**50500177**
PP-LRJ	**LJ40**	**2079**
PP-LRR	LJ60	267
(PP-LUA)	BE40	RK-258
(PP-LUG)	PRM1	RB-224
PP-LVY	FA50	338
PP-MAO	**G280**	**2059**
(PP-MAS)	E50P	50000231
PP-MCG	**E55P**	**50500196**
PP-MCL	**E55P**	**50500022**
(PP-MCL)	E55P	50500024
PP-MCO	BE40	RK-518
PP-MDA	**E55P**	**50500086**
PP-MDB	**C56X**	**5552**
PP-MEO	**C52A**	**0337**
PP-MFL	**BE40**	**RK-520**
PP-MID	C510	0288
PP-MIS	**C510**	**0043**
PP-MJC	**F2EX**	**99**
PP-MKB	**E50P**	**50000346**
PP-MLA	**C525**	**0008**
PP-MMF	**F2EX**	**202**
(PP-MMP)	E55P	50500164
PP-MMX	**LJ45**	**192**
PP-MOR	**E50P**	**50000164**
PP-MPB	**E55P**	**50500136**
PP-MPJ	**LJ45**	**177**
PP-MPP	**C52B**	**0297**
PP-MQS	**CL30**	**20311**
PP-MRV	**E50P**	**50000086**
PP-MRX	**C52B**	**0480**
PP-MTG	**C510**	**0046**
PP-MTT	**C510**	**0193**
PP-NBB	**E55P**	**50500245**
PP-NEF	**E55P**	**50500193**
PP-NIV	**E50P**	**50000256**

PP-NMM	E55P	50500129
PP-NNN	C510	0041
PP-NOB	FA50	335
PP-NOC	CL30	20039
PP-NPC	C650	0039
PP-NPP	F2EX	247
PP-NRN	E55P	50500182
(PP-NYV)	LJ31	115
PP-OAA	C550	550-0954
PP-OAC	E55P	50500012
(PP-OAS)	C750	0513
PP-OEG	C525	0849
PP-OGX	E55P	50500049
PP-OLY	E50P	50000284
(PP-ONA)	C550	616
PP-ONE	LJ60	354
PP-ORM	C550	550-0930
PP-OSA	CL64	5411
PP-OSM	FA7X	187
PP-OVD	E55P	50500055
(PP-PFA)	E55P	50500052
PP-PFD	C510	0276
PP-PIM	C525	0548
(PP-PMR)	C510	0087
PP-PMV	FA50	299
PP-PPA	F900	35
PP-PPN	F2EX	164
PP-PRB	C525	0845
PP-PRP	E55P	50500126
PP-PRR	C56X	5823
PP-PRV	C510	0197
PP-PVB	E55P	50500014
PP-RAA	C56X	5034
PP-RCA	C52B	0266
PP-RFA	FA7X	162
PP-RGL	C510	0154
PP-RST	C56X	5579
PP-SBR	C56X	5544
PP-SCB	CL65	5714
PP-SCE	LJ45	353
PP-SCN	E55P	50500137
PP-SDW	WW24	440
PP-SDY	C525	0242
PP-SED	SBRL	282-121
PP-SFY	C56X	6084
PP-SGF	E50P	50000005
PP-SGM	C680	0007
PP-SGP	GLEX	9199
PP-SJJ	BE40	RK-204
PP-SKD	E50P	50000066
PP-SKI	BE40	RK-435
PP-SVG	C680	0321
PP-TDT	E55P	50500050
PP-UBS	E50P	50000221
PP-UQF	BE40	RK-379
PP-URA	E55P	50500121
PP-USA	C650	0028
PP-UTC	C680	0237
PP-UTI	E55P	50500072
PP-VDP	E55P	50500109
PP-VDR	GLEX	9312
PP-VEL	FA7X	205
PP-VFV	E55P	50500291
PP-VIP	E50P	50000134
PP-VRL	E50P	50000326
PP-VYV	C56X	6012
PP-WAJ	E50P	50000186
(PP-WAJ)	E50P	50000185
PP-WAV	HS25	HA-0199
PP-WBP	C525	0667
PP-WEB	C510	0402
PP-WEE	C56X	6158
PP-WGS	C510	0099
PP-WIN	LJ60	159
PP-WJB	GLF4	1348
PP-WLP	E55P	50500092
PP-WMA	C52C	0090
PP-WPM	E50P	50000351
PP-WRV	BE40	RK-258
(PP-WSC)	GLEX	9047
PP-WSR	GLF6	6139
PP-WTR	C525	0364
PP-XOG	E50P	50000004
PP-XOH	E50P	50000003
PP-XOJ	E50P	50000002
PP-XOM	E50P	50000001
PP-XON	E50P	50000005
PP-XOO	E50P	50000006
PP-XOQ	E50P	50000007
PP-XOR	E50P	50000008
PP-XPD	E50P	50000009
PP-XPE	E50P	50000010
PP-XPF	E50P	50000011
PP-XPG	E50P	50000012
PP-XPH	E50P	50099801
PP-XUM	MS76	097
PP-XVI	E55P	50599801
PP-XVJ	E55P	50500001
PP-XVK	E55P	50500002
PP-XVL	E55P	50500003
PP-XVM	E55P	50500004
PP-YOF	C525	0356
PP-ZZC	E55P	50500011
PP-ZZD	E55P	50500012
(PP-ZZE)	E55P	50500013
PR-AAA	C56X	5120
PR-ABP	LJ35	621
PR-ABV	C525	0428
PR-ACC	C56X	5274
PR-ADB	CL30	20325
PR-ADL	C52B	0278
PR-ADQ	E50P	50000101
PR-AEG	C525	0187
PR-AEX	BE40	RK-65
PR-AFA	C56X	6066
PR-AGC	C52A	0403
PR-AGP	C680	0259
PR-AIC	C52A	0385
PR-AJG	C650	7111
PR-AJN	E55P	50500192
PR-AJP	C56X	6068
PR-ALC	C52B	0124
(PR-ALL)	C560	0637
PR-ALS	F2EX	236
PR-ALU	E55P	50500024
PR-ALV	C52B	0129
PR-ALY	BE40	RK-6
PR-AMA	PRM1	RB-21
PR-ANP	C56X	5750
PR-ARA	C525	0441
PR-ARB	C525	0430
PR-ARR	E50P	50000225
PR-ARS	C52A	0392
PR-AUR	GALX	140
PR-AVM	LJ31	005
(PR-AWB)	WW24	363
PR-BBD	GALX	218
PR-BBP	C680	0241
PR-BCC	LJ40	2093
PR-BCK	BE40	RK-595
PR-BCO	C680	0171
PR-BEB	E55P	50500247
PR-BED	BE40	RK-430
PR-BEE	C560	0356
PR-BER	PRM1	RB-40
PR-BET	E50P	50000163
PR-BFM	LJ45	162
PR-BHV	C52B	0350
PR-BIR	C52B	0128
PR-BJA	E55P	50500178
PR-BJM	C525	0458
PR-BLG	BE40	RK-428
PR-BNP	C680	0217
(PR-BOI)	LJ31	242
PR-BPL	BE40	RK-599
PR-BPT	GLEX	9582
PR-BRS	C680	0241
PR-BSA	C510	0062
PR-BSK	C525	0316
PR-BSN	CL30	20015
PR-BTG	FA7X	106
PR-BVO	C550	550-1108
PR-CAN	C525	0233
PR-CAO	LJ45	320
PR-CBA	G150	304
PR-CBK	GLF4	4342
PR-CBT	BE40	RK-490
PR-CCA	EA50	000037
PR-CCC	F9EX	162
PR-CCV	C560	0130
PR-CDF	FA10	126
PR-CFC	C52A	0241
PR-CGI	GLF5	5457
PR-CIM	PRM1	RB-32
PR-CIP	GLF5	5332
PR-CLB	C525	0191
PR-CMQ	E50P	50000320
PR-CNP	C52A	0226
PR-CON	C56X	5583
PR-CPC	E50P	50000125
(PR-CPD)	GLF5	5022
PR-CPT	C510	0142
PR-CRC	G280	2066
PR-CSE	FA7X	55
PR-CSM	LJ45	329
(PR-CSP)	HS25	258559
PR-CSW	E50P	50000048
PR-CTA	C750	0010
PR-CTB	C560	0760
PR-CVC	C52B	0199
PR-CYJ	C525	0912
PR-DAY	E50P	50000065
PR-DBB	HS25	258284
PR-DBD	HS25	HA-0089
PR-DCE	C525	0251
PR-DCJ	E50P	50000027
PR-DDO	E50P	50000007
PR-DDS	BE40	RK-241
PR-DEA	GALX	250
PR-DFC	E50P	50000120
PR-DFG	PRM1	RB-32
PR-DHC	E50P	50000034
PR-DHP	E55P	50500007
PR-DIA	PRM1	RB-287
PR-DIB	LJ40	2081
PR-DIF	BE40	RK-445
PR-DIO	C650	0022
PR-DIS	BE40	RK-422
PR-DLM	E50P	50000098
PR-DLN	E55P	50500227
PR-DLX	F2EX	223
PR-DNZ	FA7X	22
PR-DOT	BE40	RK-104
PR-DPD	HS25	HA-0205
PR-DRC	E50P	50000054
PR-DRI	C510	0063
PR-DRJ	E55P	50500218
PR-DRP	C52B	0386
PR-EAT	E50P	50000297
PR-EBD	C52B	0047
PR-EBK	E50P	50000287
PR-EDB	C52B	0405
PR-EFT	E55P	50500132
PR-EGB	FA10	45
PR-EGF	C525	0336
PR-EGS	C680	0237
PR-EKR	BE40	RK-437
PR-EMD	E55P	50500039
PR-EMS	C56X	5223
PR-EMX	C525	0632
PR-ENE	LJ31	151
(PR-ENY)	E50P	50000224
PR-EOB	C525	0483
PR-ERE	E55P	50500060
PR-ERP	C550	550-0903
PR-ERR	LJ55	137
PR-EST	GALX	183
PR-ETE	GLF4	4065
PR-ETY	F2EX	187
PR-EUF	LEG5	55000005
(PR-EVC)	C550	174
(PR-EVS)	GLF5	5280
PR-EXP	C525	0482
PR-FAC	C510	0129
PR-FAF	HS25	258762
PR-FAP	HS25	258559
PR-FBS	E50P	50000042
PR-FBU	E50P	50000318
PR-FDE	FA10	160
PR-FEP	C550	550-0833
PR-FGA	GLF5	5280
PR-FHI	C525	0843
PR-FIL	E50P	50000197
PR-FIS	GLEX	9653
PR-FJA	C56X	5739
PR-FJL	FA50	87
"PR-FJU"	C56X	5739
PR-FKK	GALX	009
PR-FMA	C500	091
(PR-FMP)	C510	0087
PR-FMW	CL30	20339
PR-FNE	HS25	258762
PR-FNP	C750	0028
PR-FOL	BE40	RK-187
PR-FOR	C680	0300
PR-FRC	C525	0841
PR-FRT	G280	2056
PR-FRU	F9EX	181
PR-FRZ	C510	0422
PR-FSA	C52A	0356
PR-FSB	C525	0606
PR-FSN	G150	235
PR-FTR	CL65	5915
PR-FYB	E50P	50000324
PR-GAM	C56X	5256
PR-GBN	LJ31	166
(PR-GBO)	GLEX	9025
PR-GCA	PRM1	RB-65
PR-GCL	LJ60	283
PR-GCR	E55P	50500077
(PR-GEX)	GLEX	9025
PR-GFS	C525	0663
(PR-GFV)	GLF5	5022
PR-GJC	LJ31	203
PR-GJS	FA50	258
PR-GML	C52C	0056
PR-GMV	GLF5	5022
PR-GNL	C525	0512
PR-GPA	F9EX	82
PR-GPE	C550	550-1122
PR-GPW	HS25	258338
PR-GQG	C560	0704
PR-GRD	C750	0112
(PR-GRN)	C525	0478
PR-HAL	C52A	0317
PR-HAP	C525	0185
PR-HAW	BE40	RK-65
PR-HBH	C52A	0168
(PR-HBO)	C52A	0168
PR-HCA	C550	550-1044
PR-HET	GLEX	9025
PR-HFW	HS25	258226
PR-HIC	GLEX	9047
PR-HIL	LEG5	55000019
PR-HIP	C525	0220
PR-HJH	C525	0415
PR-HJM	E55P	50500140
PR-HLW	C680	0182
PR-HMV	C52B	0321
PR-HNG	CL30	20542
PR-HNZ	E50P	50000327
PR-HOF	C56X	5696
PR-HOT	C510	0195
PR-HRO	E55P	50500320
(PR-HUC)	E55P	50500200
PR-HVN	LJ45	422
PR-IDB	CL30	20168
PR-IEI	E50P	50000085
PR-IER	C510	0328
PR-IJE	BE40	RK-121
(PR-IMP)	F900	14
PR-IMR	E50P	50000257
PR-IND	BE40	RK-470
PR-ITN	C650	0171
PR-IVI	E50P	50000032
(PR-IZB)	GLEX	9492
(PR-IZB)	GLEX	9541
PR-JAJ	E50P	50000083
PR-JAP	C650	7038
PR-JAQ	C750	0060
PR-JBS	LJ40	2048
PR-JEC	LJ40	2105
PR-JET	C52A	0042
PR-JIE	E50P	50000350
PR-JIP	E50P	50000167
PR-JJA	C680	0202
PR-JJD	E50P	50000156
PR-JJR	F2EX	218
PR-JJV	LJ31	149
PR-JNW	C525	0028
PR-JOF	LJ40	2002
PR-JPK	BE40	RK-155
PR-JPP	GALX	234
PR-JRR	PRM1	RB-84
PR-JRV	C52B	0394
PR-JSR	C56X	6051
PR-JST	C52A	0044
PR-JTS	MU30	A066SA
PR-JVF	C52A	0376
PR-KKA	C650	0213
PR-KRT	C52A	0509
PR-KYK	C52A	0440
PR-LAM	C560	0600
PR-LAT	C750	0052
PR-LBP	BE40	RK-448
PR-LDF	LJ60	242
PR-LEB	LJ45	157
PR-LFH	E55P	50500257
PR-LFJ	E55P	50500259
PR-LFK	E55P	50500261
PR-LFL	E50P	50000349
PR-LFO	LEG5	55000006
PR-LFQ	LEG5	55000008
PR-LFT	C56X	5619
PR-LFW	LEG5	55000007
PR-LGL	LEG5	55000010
PR-LGO	LEG5	55000011
PR-LGQ	LEG5	55000012
PR-LGV	LEG5	55000020
PR-LGW	LEG5	55000014
PR-LGY	LEG5	55000016
PR-LGZ	LEG5	55000017
PR-LHE	LEG5	55000015
PR-LHG	LEG5	55000019
PR-LHJ	LEG5	55000018
PR-LHK	LEG5	55000021
PR-LHL	LEG5	55000022
PR-LHM	LEG5	55000023
PR-LHO	LEG5	55000024
PR-LHS	LEG5	55000025
PR-LHT	LEG5	55000026
PR-LHW	GLF4	4235
PR-LHX	LEG5	55000027
PR-LHY	LEG5	55000028
PR-LIC	LEG5	55000029
PR-LIE	LEG5	55000030
PR-LIG	C550	057
PR-LIJ	LEG5	55000031
PR-LIK	LEG5	55000032
PR-LIQ	E50P	50000282
PR-LIR	LEG5	55000033
PR-LIU	LEG5	55000034
PR-LIW	LEG5	55000035
PR-LIX	LEG5	55000036
PR-LIY	LEG5	55000037
PR-LJB	LEG5	55000038
PR-LJD	LEG5	55000039
PR-LJG	LJ40	2102
PR-LJH	LEG5	55010003
PR-LJJ	C550	485
PR-LJK	LEG5	55010004
PR-LJM	C525	0456
PR-LJN	LEG5	55000003
PR-LJO	LEG5	55000040
PR-LJU	LEG5	55000041
PR-LJW	LEG5	55000042
PR-LJY	LEG5	55000043
PR-LJZ	LEG5	55010005
PR-LKB	LEG5	55000044
PR-LKE	LEG5	55000045
PR-LKF	LEG5	55000046
PR-LKG	LEG5	55010006
PR-LKI	LEG5	55010007
PR-LKL	LEG5	55000048
PR-LKM	LEG5	55000049
PR-LKN	LEG5	55010008
PR-LKO	LEG5	55000047
PR-LKP	LEG5	55000051
PR-LKQ	LEG5	55000050
PR-LKT	LEG5	55000052
PR-LKU	LEG5	55010009
PR-LKV	LEG5	55010010
PR-LMP	E50P	50000094
PR-LPG	C56X	5095
PR-LRJ	LJ31	158
PR-LRR	LJ31	017
PR-LTA	HS25	258025
PR-LUG	HS25	258553
PR-LUZ	C750	0004
PR-MCL	C510	0057
PR-MCN	C555	0081
PR-MDB	F2EX	254
(PR-MDB)	CL30	20168
PR-MDE	C510	0231
PR-MEN	GALX	046
PR-MFJ	C525	0542
PR-MFX	LJ40	2075
PR-MGB	C550	550-1128
PR-MGD	BE40	RK-521
PR-MGT	C550	576
(PR-MIS)	LJ45	166
PR-MJC	C750	0237
PR-MJD	E50P	50000096
PR-MJM	C52C	0103
PR-MKB	LJ31	178
PR-MLA	LJ35	072
PR-MLJ	GLEX	9258
PR-MLR	LJ60	357
PR-MMG	BE40	RK-20
PR-MMP	GALX	130
PR-MMS	BE40	RK-457
PR-MMV	C56X	5744
PR-MON	C52B	0324
PR-MPF	C650	0087
PR-MPM	C510	0080
PR-MRE	C52C	0036
PR-MRG	C52B	0187
PR-MSZ	C52A	0515
PR-MTQ	C52B	0277
PR-MUR	LJ31	233
PR-MVB	BE40	RK-350
PR-MVF	LJ31	213
PR-NAK	FA7X	214
PR-NBR	C56X	5289
PR-NCJ	HS25	HB-15
PR-NFT	C550	265
PR-NGM	E55P	50500190
PR-NGT	C52A	0345
PR-NJR	C52C	0050
PR-NJT	WW24	198
PR-NNP	C52A	0316
PR-NOC	GLF5	5144
PR-NPP	E50P	50000043
PR-NRN	C510	0119
PR-NTO	E50P	50000095
PR-NTR	G150	293
PR-NTX	C52A	0228
PR-NXG	F2EX	157
(PR-NYM)	GLF5	5047
PR-NYV	LJ31	115
PR-NZV	GLF5	5505
PR-OBE	F2EX	179
PR-OEC	BE40	RK-524
PR-OFF	C56X	6117
PR-OFP	E50P	50000108
PR-OFT	GALX	027
PR-OGX	GLF5	5253
PR-OJL	C525	0243
PR-OLB	C550	616
PR-OLD	F2EX	223
(PR-OLD)	F9EX	194
PR-OMX	WW24	363
PR-ONE	LJ40	2020
PR-OOF	GLEX	9048
PR-OPF	LJ45	146
PR-OPP	HS25	258547
PR-OSF	LJ45	164
PR-OTA	LJ45	242
PR-OUD	C525	0660
PR-OUR	C56X	5371
PR-OVD	E50P	50000127
(PR-PAA)	E50P	50000318
PR-PAB	C550	550-1015
PR-PAE	E50P	50000365
PR-PAE	E55P	50500134
PR-PAH	E55P	50500135
PR-PAK	LJ45	312
PR-PAL	E55P	50500139
PR-PAO	E50P	50000320
PR-PAP	E50P	50000322
PR-PAU	E55P	50500141
PR-PAY	E55P	50500145
(PR-PAY)	E55P	50500037
PR-PBD	E55P	50500143
PR-PBD	E55P	50500180
PR-PBG	E55P	50500146
PR-PBH	E50P	50000323
PR-PBI	E55P	50500147
PR-PBI	E55P	50500183
PR-PBJ	E55P	50500150
PR-PBJ	E55P	50500184
PR-PBK	E55P	50500152
PR-PBK	E55P	50500186
PR-PBL	E55P	50500153
PR-PBL	E55P	50500195
PR-PBM	E50P	50000333
PR-PBM	E55P	50500157
PR-PBN	E55P	50500158
PR-PBN	E55P	50500198
PR-PBO	E55P	50500161
PR-PBP	E55P	50500162
PR-PBQ	E55P	50500165
PR-PBT	E50P	50000325
PR-PBU	E55P	50500168
PR-PBV	E55P	50500170

(PR-PBV)	C550	576
PR-PBW	E55P	50500175
PR-PBX	E55P	50500173
PR-PBZ	E55P	50500202
PR-PCB	E55P	50500204
PR-PCD	E55P	50500206
PR-PCE	E55P	50500208
PR-PCF	E55P	50500216
PR-PCG	E50P	50000338
PR-PCH	E50P	50000340
PR-PCI	E50P	50000342
PR-PCJ	E55P	50500218
PR-PCK	E55P	50500223
PR-PCM	**E50P**	**50000152**
PR-PCN	E50P	50000341
PR-PCO	E55P	50500236
PR-PCP	E50P	50000343
PR-PCQ	E50P	50000344
PR-PCR	E50P	50000345
PR-PCS	E55P	50500232
PR-PCT	FA7X	146
PR-PCU	E55P	50500238
PR-PCV	E55P	50500240
PR-PCW	E55P	50500241
PR-PCX	E55P	50500243
PR-PCY	E50P	50000347
PR-PEE	E55P	50500251
PR-PEF	E55P	50500253
PR-PEH	E55P	50500255
PR-PEI	E50P	50000350
PR-PEJ	E50P	50000351
PR-PEK	E55P	50500273
PR-PEN	E55P	50500262
PR-PEO	E55P	50500263
PR-PEQ	E55P	50500265
PR-PER	**E50P**	**50000242**
PR-PEU	E55P	50500267
PR-PEV	E55P	50500269
PR-PEW	E50P	50000352
PR-PEY	E55P	50500274
PR-PEZ	E55P	50500276
PR-PFA	E55P	50500272
PR-PFB	E55P	50500278
PR-PFF	E50P	50000353
PR-PFH	**E50P**	**50000355**
PR-PFI	E50P	50000354
PR-PFJ	E55P	50500281
PR-PFK	E55P	50500284
PR-PFL	E50P	50000356
PR-PFM	E55P	50500286
PR-PFO	E55P	50500290
PR-PFS	E50P	50000357
PR-PFT	E50P	50000358
PR-PFU	E55P	50500291
PR-PFV	E55P	50500295
PR-PFW	E50P	50000360
PR-PFY	E55P	50500299
PR-PFZ	E55P	50500301
PR-PGA	E55P	50500303
PR-PGB	E55P	50500305
PR-PGD	E55P	50500308
PR-PGE	**E50P**	**50000361**
PR-PGG	E55P	50500313
PR-PGH	E55P	50500315
PR-PGI	E50P	50000362
PR-PGJ	**E50P**	**50000363**
PR-PGK	**E50P**	**50000366**
(PR-PGK)	E50P	50000364
PR-PGN	E55P	50500325
PR-PGO	E55P	50500329
PR-PGP	**E50P**	**50000367**
PR-PGQ	E55P	50500334
PR-PGR	E55P	50500341
PR-PGT	E55P	50500343
PR-PGU	E55P	50500346
PR-PGV	**E50P**	**50000369**
PR-PGW	**E55P**	**50500350**
PR-PGX	E55P	50500352
PR-PGY	**E50P**	**50000371**
PR-PGZ	**E50P**	**50000373**
PR-PHC	E55P	50500358
PR-PHD	**E50P**	**50000160**
PR-PHE	**E50P**	**50000175**
PR-PHF	**E50P**	**50000374**
PR-PHG	**E55P**	**50500366**
PR-PHH	**E55P**	**50500373**
PR-PHJ	**E55P**	**50500374**
PR-PHK	**E50P**	**50000375**
PR-PHN	**E55P**	**50500376**
PR-PHX	**E50P**	**50000337**
(PR-PHX)	E50P	50000339
PR-PJD	**LJ31**	**214**
PR-PLM	**LJ31**	**105**
PR-PLO	**E50P**	**50000340**
PR-PLR	**E50P**	**50000341**
PR-PLU	**C52B**	**0218**
PR-PMK	**E50P**	**50000345**
PR-PMV	**F9EX**	**207**
PR-PNM	**E50P**	**50000144**
PR-PPG	**LJ40**	**2035**
PR-PPN	F2EX	40
PR-PRA	**PRM1**	**RB-169**
PR-PRC	**PRM1**	**RB-231**
PR-PRE	**PRM1**	**RB-139**
PR-PSE	**GLF5**	**5308**
PR-PTA	E50P	50000077
PR-PTL	C650	7038
PR-PTR	**LJ40**	**2086**
PR-PVI	**LJ40**	**2114**
PR-RAA	C56X	5105
PR-RAQ	C52A	0007
PR-RAR	C52C	0042
PR-RAV	C56X	5517
PR-RBO	**C52B**	**0310**
PR-RBZ	**CL30**	**20394**
PR-RCB	**C680**	**0090**
PR-RCN	**C56X**	**6145**
PR-RDM	**C510**	**0084**
PR-REG	**C52A**	**0075**
PR-REV	**E50P**	**50000266**
PR-REX	**E50P**	**50000199**
PR-RHB	**E50P**	**50000219**
PR-RHG	**C52A**	**0303**
PR-RIY	**C525**	**0846**
PR-RJN	**C52A**	**0417**
(PR-RJZ)	F9EX	235
PR-RLM	**E50P**	**50000336**
PR-RMC	C56X	6034
PR-RMT	C52B	0362
PR-RNF	LJ40	2133
PR-RNY	**F2EX**	**209**
PR-ROD	C510	0280
PR-ROZ	F9EX	235
PR-RRN	PRM1	RB-237
(PR-RSI)	CL65	5721
PR-RSN	**PRM1**	**RB-240**
PR-RTJ	C680	0267
PR-RTS	C56X	6046
PR-RVW	**C650**	**7008**
PR-SAD	**E55P**	**50500220**
PR-SBH	**C510**	**0087**
PR-SCB	LJ31	100
PR-SCE	**BE40**	**RK-466**
PR-SCF	**C52B**	**0239**
PR-SCP	**C550**	**550-1118**
PR-SCR	**C560**	**0653**
PR-SDD	EA50	000232
PR-SEA	F900	192
PR-SFA	**LJ31**	**023**
PR-SFB	**F2TH**	**167**
PR-SHC	**C52B**	**0253**
PR-SIR	**GLEX**	**9043**
PR-SKB	**BE40**	**RK-144**
(PR-SKD)	E50P	50000066
PR-SKW	**C525**	**0289**
PR-SMJ	**C525**	**0285**
PR-SMK	**C680**	**0252**
PR-SMT	FA20	509
PR-SNV	**C550**	**723**
PR-SOL	HS25	258133
PR-SOV	C680	0069
PR-SPJ	**E50P**	**50000076**
PR-SPO	C52B	0028
PR-SPR	C680	0132
PR-SRB	**BE40**	**RK-169**
PR-STA	**E55P**	**50500051**
PR-STJ	**WW24**	**300**
PR-SUL	**FA20**	**129**
PR-SUN	**C680**	**0060**
PR-SVG	C680	0175
PR-SVR	**C680**	**0204**
PR-SZA	**LJ45**	**045**
PR-TAP	**C52A**	**0185**
PR-TAQ	**C56X**	**6105**
PR-TBL	**C52B**	**0245**
PR-TDM	**E50P**	**50000332**
PR-TDV	**E50P**	**50000244**
PR-TED	**E50P**	**50000202**
(PR-TED)	E50P	50000201
PR-TEN	**C56X**	**5778**
(PR-TGA)	BE40	RK-75
PR-TGM	**BE40**	**RK-75**
PR-TLS	**E50P**	**50000236**
PR-TNP	**C510**	**0037**
PR-TOP	C52A	0061
PR-TPA	**E50P**	**50000155**
PR-TRJ	**C56X**	**5644**
PR-TRT	**C525**	**0496**
PR-TUB	CL64	5381
PR-TUC	**C56X**	**6155**
PR-UUT	**E50P**	**50000093**
(PR-VBS)	E50P	50000236
PR-VCO	**GLF4**	**4091**
PR-VDL	**C510**	**0085**
PR-VDR	**GLEX**	**9018**
PR-VEL	**E50P**	**50000068**
PR-VEN	**F2EX**	**309**
PR-VFC	**E50P**	**50000231**
PR-VGD	**C525**	**0120**
PR-VHB	**BE40**	**RK-496**
PR-VII	**C650**	**7006**
PR-VIR	**C550**	**623**
PR-VLJ	C550	623
PR-VMD	**PRM1**	**RB-246**
PR-VNA	**C52B**	**0337**
PR-VOG	E50P	50000307
PR-VON	C52C	0036
PR-VPJ	**E50P**	**50000158**
PR-VPO	LJ45	383
PR-VPP	**PRM1**	**RB-224**
PR-VRD	C56X	5211
PR-VTO	**C56X**	**6163**
PR-VZN	**C52C**	**0072**
PR-WAT	**C52A**	**0406**
PR-WBW	**LJ60**	**237**
PR-WDM	C680	0312
PR-WIN	**E55P**	**50500107**
PR-WMA	**LJ31**	**131**
PR-WNA	**LJ40**	**2040**
PR-WOB	**C52A**	**0089**
PR-WQT	F2EX	22
PR-WQY	**GLF5**	**5105**
PR-WRI	F9EX	44
PR-WRM	FA7X	6
PR-WRO	**GLF5**	**5236**
PR-WRR	**BE40**	**RK-462**
PR-WRT	E55P	50500041
PR-WSB	**LJ40**	**2006**
PR-WSC	CL30	20012
PR-WSM	F2TH	6
PR-WSW	**HS25**	**258084**
PR-WTR	**GALX**	**004**
PR-WTZ	**MU30**	**A034SA**
PR-WYW	**FA50**	**234**
PR-XDN	GLEX	9190
PR-XDY	C750	0118
PR-XJS	**LJ60**	**189**
PR-XLS	**C56X**	**5607**
PR-XPI	**C510**	**0278**
PR-XSX	**C510**	**0058**
PR-YOU	CL30	20443
PR-YVL	**FA7X**	**165**
(PT-...)	C550	460
(PT-...)	C550	598
(PT-...)	C56X	5029
(PT-...)	FA10	224
(PT-...)	HS25	258208
PT-AAC	GLF3	450
PT-AAF	FA50	234
PT-ACC	LJ36	018
PT-ALK	GLF3	418
PT-AMU	**C510**	**0401**
PT-ASJ	FA10	95
PT-ASX	**C52A**	**0123**
PT-BBB	LJ31	103
PT-CBA	**PRM1**	**RB-222**
(PT-CBT)	BE40	RK-490
PT-CMY	LJ25	108
PT-CXJ	LJ24	176
PT-CXK	LJ24	122
PT-DTY	HS25	25243
PT-DUO	LJ25	061
PT-DVL	LJ25	077
PT-DZU	LJ24	244
PT-FAF	LJ25	099
PT-FAT	LJ35	361
PT-FBM	**C525**	**0119**
PT-FCC	**E50P**	**50000099**
PT-FCS	**F2EX**	**131**
PT-FGV	**BE40**	**RK-322**
PT-FIS	C680	0293
PT-FJA	**C525**	**0337**
(PT-FKK)	GLF4	4031
PT-FKY	**F2EX**	**280**
(PT-FKY)	F2EX	284
PT-FLB	**C52A**	**0523**
PT-FLC	**C510**	**0147**
PT-FLE	**LJ45**	**081**
PT-FLO	**C510**	**0056**
PT-FLX	**E50P**	**50000174**
(PT-FLX)	F2EX	157
PT-FNP	**C525**	**0319**
PT-FOH	FA20	113
PT-FPG	**C56X**	**6043**
PT-FPM	**HS25**	**258826**
PT-FPP	C56X	5003
(PT-FQA)	E50P	50000127
PT-FQB	E50P	50000128
PT-FQC	E50P	50000129
PT-FQD	E50P	50000130
PT-FQE	E50P	50000131
PT-FQF	E50P	50000132
PT-FQG	E50P	50000133
PT-FQH	E50P	50000134
PT-FQI	E50P	50000135
PT-FQJ	E50P	50000136
PT-FQK	E50P	50000137
PT-FQL	E50P	50000138
PT-FQM	E50P	50000139
PT-FQN	E50P	50000140
PT-FQO	E50P	50000141
PT-FQP	E50P	50000142
PT-FQQ	E50P	50000143
PT-FQR	E50P	50000144
PT-FQS	E50P	50000145
PT-FQT	E50P	50000146
PT-FQU	E50P	50000147
PT-FQV	E50P	50000148
PT-FQW	E50P	50000149
PT-FQX	E50P	50000150
PT-FQY	E50P	50000151
PT-FQZ	E50P	50000152
PT-FRD	**LJ40**	**2034**
PT-FSF	**E50P**	**50000276**
PT-FTB	**C560**	**0060**
PT-FTC	**C52A**	**0048**
PT-FTE	**C52A**	**0053**
PT-FTG	**C52A**	**0117**
PT-FTR	C52A	0141
PT-FUA	E50P	50000153
PT-FUB	E50P	50000154
PT-FUC	E50P	50000155
PT-FUD	E50P	50000156
PT-FUE	E50P	50000157
PT-FUF	E50P	50000158
PT-FUG	E50P	50000159
PT-FUH	E50P	50000160
PT-FUI	E50P	50000161
PT-FUJ	E50P	50000162
PT-FUK	E50P	50000163
PT-FUL	E50P	50000164
PT-FUM	E50P	50000165
PT-FUN	E50P	50000166
PT-FUO	E50P	50000167
PT-FUP	E50P	50000168
PT-FUQ	E50P	50000169
PT-FUR	E50P	50000170
PT-FUS	E50P	50000171
PT-FUT	E50P	50000172
PT-FUU	E50P	50000173
PT-FUV	E50P	50000174
PT-FUW	E50P	50000175
PT-FUX	E50P	50000176
PT-FUY	E50P	50000177
PT-FUZ	E50P	50000178
PT-FXB	C500	049
PT-FYA	E50P	50000179
PT-FYB	E50P	50000180
PT-FYC	E50P	50000181
PT-FYD	E50P	50000182
PT-FYE	E50P	50000183
PT-FYF	E50P	50000184
PT-FYG	E50P	50000185
PT-FYH	E50P	50000186
PT-FYI	E50P	50000187
PT-FYJ	E50P	50000188
(PT-FYK)	E50P	50000189
PT-FYL	E50P	50000190
(PT-FYM)	E50P	50000191
PT-FYN	E50P	50000192
PT-FYO	E50P	50000193
PT-FYP	E50P	50000194
(PT-FYQ)	E50P	50000195
PT-FYR	E50P	50000196
PT-FYS	E50P	50000197
(PT-FYT)	E50P	50000198
(PT-FYU)	E50P	50000200
PT-FYV	E50P	50000201
PT-FYW	E50P	50000203
PT-FYX	E50P	50000204
PT-FYY	E50P	50000205
PT-FYZ	E50P	50000206
PT-FZA	LJ31	214
PT-GAF	**HS25**	**258261**
PT-GAP	LJ35	589
PT-GBF	**C52B**	**0390**
PT-GCP	**E50P**	**50000161**
PT-GMN	LJ55	139
PT-GMU	**C52B**	**0389**
(PT-GPX)	E55P	50500100
PT-HRI	**E50P**	**50000273**
PT-IBR	LJ25	072
PT-IDW	HFB3	1052
PT-IIQ	**LJ25**	**089**
PT-IKR	LJ25	099
PT-ILJ	C500	057
PT-IOB	HFB3	1053
PT-IQL	C500	069
PT-ISN	LJ25	113
PT-ISO	**LJ25**	**115**
PT-JAA	**HS25**	**258190**
PT-JBQ	LJ25	119
PT-JDX	LJ25	131
PT-JGU	LJ24	276
PT-JKQ	**LJ24**	**284**
PT-JKR	LJ24	278
PT-JMJ	**C500**	**134**
PT-JNJ	SBRL	282-118
PT-JQM	BE40	RK-63
PT-JXS	C500	162
PT-KAP	LJ25	156
PT-KBC	LJ25	165
PT-KBD	LJ25	166
PT-KBR	C500	156
PT-KIR	C500	103
PT-KIU	C500	172
PT-KKV	LJ25	172
PT-KOT	SBRL	306-80
PT-KOU	SBRL	306-84
PT-KPA	C500	181
PT-KPB	C500	188
PT-KPE	LJ24	315
PT-KQT	LJ36	011
PT-KTO	FA10	63
PT-KTU	LJ36	018
PT-KXZ	C500	043
PT-KYR	LJ25	266
PT-KZR	**LJ35**	**252**
PT-KZY	LJ25	204
PT-LAA	LJ35	295
PT-LAS	LJ35	326
PT-LAU	LJ24	239
(PT-LAW)	C500	091
PT-LAX	C500	194
PT-LAY	C500	068
PT-LAZ	C500	180
PT-LBL	**E50P**	**50000230**
PT-LBM	E50P	50000226
PT-LBN	**C500**	**079**
PT-LBR	E50P	50000227
PT-LBS	E50P	50000228
PT-LBS	LJ35	361
PT-LBV	E50P	50000229
PT-LBW	**LJ25**	**056**
PT-LBY	LJ35	411
PT-LBZ	E50P	50000231
(PT-LBZ)	C500	608
PT-LCC	**C500**	**608**
PT-LCD	**LJ35**	**103**
PT-LCN	LJ24	287
PT-LCO	FA10	154
PT-LCR	C550	157
PT-LCV	**LJ24**	**254**
PT-LCW	C550	358
PT-LDH	C500	049
PT-LDI	**C500**	**335**
PT-LDM	**LJ35**	**494**
PT-LDN	LJ35	436
PT-LDR	LJ55	028
PT-LDR	**LJ55**	**134**
PT-LDY	**WW24**	**251**
PT-LEA	**LJ25**	**155**
PT-LEB	LJ35	474
PT-LEL	LJ55	013
PT-LEM	LJ24	270
PT-LEN	**LJ25**	**093**
PT-LET	**LJ55**	**080**
PT-LFR	C500	680
PT-LFS	LJ35	008
PT-LFT	LJ35	473
PT-LGD	MU30	A072SA
PT-LGF	LJ35	019
PT-LGI	C555	0024
PT-LGJ	C555	0025
PT-LGM	C550	128
PT-LGR	LJ35	009
PT-LGS	LJ35	299
PT-LGT	C650	0081
PT-LGW	**LJ35**	**598**
PT-LGZ	C650	0088
PT-LHA	C650	0059
PT-LHB	**HS25**	**258031**
PT-LHC	**C650**	**0086**
PT-LHD	C555	0059
PT-LHK	HS25	25197
PT-LHR	**LJ55**	**044**
PT-LHT	**LJ35**	**479**
PT-LHU	LJ25	099
PT-LHX	LJ35	464
PT-LHY	C550	426
PT-LIG	LJ55	111
PT-LIH	LJ35	433
PT-LII	LJ35	499
PT-LIJ	LJ35	607
PT-LIP	WW24	418
PT-LIV	**C550**	**499**
PT-LIX	**C500**	**171**
PT-LIY	C500	219
PT-LIZ	C500	639
PT-LJA	C550	154
PT-LJC	C650	0115
PT-LJF	**C550**	**272**
PT-LJI	FA50	173
PT-LJJ	C550	276
PT-LJK	**LJ35**	**372**
PT-LJL	**C555**	**0084**
PT-LJQ	**C555**	**0113**
PT-LJT	C550	339
PT-LKD	**LJ24**	**356**
PT-LKQ	LJ24	038
PT-LKR	C550	378
PT-LKS	**C555**	**0114**
PT-LKT	C555	0117
PT-LLF	LJ35	644
PT-LLK	LJ31	010
PT-LLL	LJ25	258
PT-LLN	**LJ25**	**176**
PT-LLQ	C550	495
PT-LLS	**LJ35**	**303**
PT-LLT	**C550**	**349**
PT-LLU	**C550**	**147**
PT-LMA	LJ24	353
PT-LME	C550	204
PT-LMF	LJ24	120
PT-LML	C550	016
PT-LMM	**LJ25**	**323**
PT-LMO	FA10	49
PT-LMS	**LJ24**	**296**
PT-LMY	**LJ35**	**627**
PT-LNC	**C550**	**237**
PT-LND	C550	254
PT-LNE	LJ24	114
PT-LNK	LJ24	294
PT-LNN	MU30	A048SA
PT-LNV	C500	568
PT-LOC	C550	550
PT-LOE	**LJ35**	**393**
PT-LOF	LJ55	028
PT-LOG	**C500**	**284**
PT-LOJ	LJ24	303
PT-LOS	C500	239
PT-LOT	**LJ35**	**093**
PT-LPF	C500	249
PT-LPH	**LJ24**	**275**
PT-LPK	**C550**	**010**

PT-LPN	**C550**	**323**
PT-LPP	**C550**	**199**
PT-LPT	LJ25	051
PT-LPV	WW24	441
PT-LPX	LJ24	158
PT-LPZ	**C500**	**015**
PT-LQF	LJ35	616
PT-LQG	C500	271
PT-LQI	CS55	0154
PT-LQJ	C550	578
PT-LQK	**LJ24**	**333**
PT-LQP	**HS25**	**258116**
PT-LQQ	C500	512
PT-LQR	**C500**	**246**
PT-LQW	C550	158
PT-LSD	LJ25	243
PT-LSF	C500	328
PT-LSJ	**LJ35**	**181**
PT-LSN	C650	0049
PT-LSR	C550	600
PT-LSW	LJ35	286
(PT-LTA)	HS25	258284
PT-LTB	**C650**	**0166**
PT-LTI	**C500**	**226**
PT-LTJ	**C550**	**258**
PT-LTL	C550	608
PT-LUA	**C500**	**346**
PT-LUE	**C650**	**0091**
PT-LUG	**LJ35**	**356**
PT-LUK	LJ55	086
PT-LUO	C650	0129
PT-LUZ	**LJ25**	**335**
PT-LVB	C500	613
PT-LVD	**FA10**	**223**
PT-LVF	C650	0171
PT-LVO	LJ31	002
PT-LVR	LJ31	013
PT-LXG	C550	618
PT-LXH	**C500**	**133**
PT-LXJ	FA10	225
PT-LXO	LJ55	135
PT-LXS	LJ25	111
PT-LXW	CL60	1063
PT-LXX	**LJ31**	**007**
PT-LYA	C550	620
PT-LYE	LJ24	354
PT-LYF	LJ35	650
PT-LYL	LJ24	291
PT-LYN	C550	625
PT-LYS	C550	624
PT-LZO	C550	215
PT-LZP	**LJ35**	**339**
PT-LZQ	C560	0045
PT-LZS	LJ55	139
PT-MAC	BE40	RK-151
PT-MAH	**E50P**	**50000026**
PT-MBZ	**ASTR**	**022**
PT-MCB	LJ31	100
PT-MFR	LJ35	655
PT-MGS	**C650**	**7021**
PT-MIA	**HS25**	**HA-0206**
PT-MIL	**C525**	**0086**
PT-MJC	**C525**	**0085**
PT-MKO	CL64	5347
PT-MLJ	**E55P**	**50500010**
PT-MML	F2TH	43
PT-MMN	**C750**	**0003**
PT-MMO	**C550**	**455**
PT-MMP	**E50P**	**50000264**
PT-MMV	**C550**	**550-0811**
PT-MPE	**C525**	**0015**
"PT-MPE"	C525	0030
PT-MPL	BE40	RK-158
PT-MPP	**C52C**	**0057**
(PT-MPP)	C52B	0375
PT-MSK	**C56X**	**5087**
PT-MSM	LJ55	072
PT-MSP	**C525**	**0259**
PT-MTG	C560	0121
PT-MTP	**GLF4**	**4294**
(PT-MTU)	C525	0295
PT-MVI	LJ31	082
PT-OAA	C550	635
PT-OAC	C550	613
PT-OAF	C550	369
PT-OAG	**C550**	**379**
PT-OAK	C650	0186
PT-OBD	LJ24	228
PT-OBR	LJ55	037
PT-OBS	LJ55	048
PT-OBT	HS25	258112
PT-OBX	C650	0181
PT-OCA	LJ55	140
PT-OCZ	**LJ35**	**361**
PT-ODC	**C500**	**678**
PT-ODL	**C550**	**640**
PT-ODW	C550	643
PT-ODZ	**C550**	**645**
PT-OEF	LJ35	102
PT-OER	C550	390
PT-OEX	**F900**	**92**
PT-OFJ	LJ31	014
PT-OFK	LJ31	017
PT-OFL	LJ31	019
PT-OFW	LJ35	621
PT-OHB	HS25	258190
PT-OHD	LJ25	296
PT-OHM	FA10	50
PT-OHU	LJ55	029
PT-OIC	FA10	171
PT-OIG	**C500**	**005**
PT-OJC	HS25	258177
PT-OJF	C500	131
PT-OJG	**C550**	**676**
PT-OJH	LJ55	144
PT-OJK	C550	675
PT-OJO	C650	0202
PT-OJT	C550	562
PT-OKM	C550	573
PT-OKP	**C550**	**460**
PT-OKV	C650	0206
PT-OLN	WW24	340
PT-OLV	C560	0142
PT-OMB	C550	672
PT-OMC	HS25	258206
PT-OMS	**C500**	**251**
PT-OMT	**C500**	**179**
PT-OMU	**C650**	**0205**
PT-OMV	C650	0200
PT-ONK	LJ35	472
PT-OOA	C550	641
PT-OOF	C500	074
PT-OOI	HS25	258214
PT-OOK	C500	039
PT-OOL	**C500**	**060**
PT-OOM	C550	479
PT-OOO	**C52B**	**0285**
PT-OOR	C560	0176
PT-OOW	LJ55	033
PT-OPJ	**LJ35**	**396**
PT-OQD	**C500**	**244**
PT-OQG	FA20	514
PT-ORA	LJ55	146
PT-ORC	**C560**	**0195**
PT-ORD	C550	154
PT-ORE	C560	0131
PT-ORH	HS25	258035
PT-ORJ	HS25	257145
PT-ORM	C56X	5535
PT-ORO	C550	303
PT-ORS	FA10	219
PT-ORT	C560	0191
PT-OSA	CL61	5075
PT-OSB	HS25	258211
PT-OSD	**C500**	**325**
PT-OSK	C550	633
PT-OSL	CS55	0127
PT-OSM	CS55	0160
PT-OSW	**HS25**	**258184**
PT-OTC	**HS25**	**258194**
PT-OTH	HS25	258229
PT-OTN	C550	715
PT-OTQ	**C500**	**046**
PT-OTS	**C560**	**0213**
PT-OTT	C560	0215
PT-OUG	LJ55	060
PT-OVC	LJ35	399
PT-OVI	LJ60	008
PT-OVK	C500	027
PT-OVM	MU30	A091SA
PT-OVU	**C650**	**7033**
PT-OVV	C550	616
PT-OVZ	**LJ31**	**037**
PT-OXB	FA10	199
PT-OXT	**MU30**	**A039SA**
PT-OYA	C500	072
PT-OYP	C550	561
PT-OZB	C560	0258
PT-OZT	C500	256
PT-OZX	C500	299
PT-PCH	**E55P**	**50500229**
(PT-PMV)	LJ35	299
PT-POK	**LJ35**	**619**
(PT-PPP)	LJ31	112
PT-PRR	C525	0403
PT-PTL	C750	0080
PT-PTR	**CL30**	**20528**
(PT-PTR)	CL30	20524
(PT-PTT)	E55P	50500117
PT-PUB	E55P	50500044
PT-PUC	E55P	50500045
PT-PUE	E55P	50500046
PT-PUF	E55P	50500047
PT-PVA	E55P	50500007
PT-PVC	**E55P**	**50500224**
(PT-PVC)	E55P	50500015
(PT-PVC)	E55P	50500227
PT-PVD	E55P	50500016
PT-PVE	E55P	50500017
PT-PVF	E55P	50500018
PT-PVG	E55P	50500019
PT-PVH	**E55P**	**50500020**
PT-PVI	E55P	50500021
PT-PVJ	E55P	50500022
PT-PVK	E55P	50500029
PT-PVL	E55P	50500023
PT-PVN	E55P	50500024
(PT-PVN)	E55P	50500025
PT-PVO	E55P	50500026
PT-PVP	E55P	50500027
PT-PVQ	E55P	50500028
PT-PVR	E55P	50500030
PT-PVS	E55P	50500031
PT-PVT	E55P	50500032
PT-PVU	E55P	50500033
PT-PVV	E55P	50500034
PT-PVW	E55P	50500035
PT-PVX	E55P	50500036
PT-PVY	E55P	50500004
PT-PVZ	E55P	50500037
(PT-PVZ)	E55P	50500025
(PT-PYA)	E50P	50000207
(PT-PYB)	E50P	50000208
(PT-PYC)	E50P	50000209
PT-PYD	E50P	50000210
(PT-PYE)	E50P	50000211
(PT-PYF)	E50P	50000212
PT-PYG	E50P	50000213
PT-PYH	E50P	50000214
PT-PYI	E50P	50000215
PT-PYJ	E50P	50000216
(PT-PYK)	E50P	50000217
PT-PYL	E50P	50000218
PT-PYM	E50P	50000219
PT-PYN	E50P	50000220
PT-PYO	E50P	50000221
PT-PYP	E50P	50000222
PT-PYQ	E50P	50000223
PT-PYR	E55P	50500038
PT-PYS	E55P	50500040
PT-PYT	E55P	50500041
PT-PYU	E55P	50500042
PT-PYV	E55P	50500043
PT-PYW	E55P	50500039
(PT-RAB)	E55P	50500080
PT-RMB	**C650**	**7111**
PT-RMI	**E50P**	**50000330**
PT-SAF	**LJ45**	**412**
PT-SBC	E55P	50500041
PT-SBF	**PRM1**	**RB-210**
PT-SMO	LJ35	414
PT-SRU	F2TH	187
PT-STK	**C525**	**0300**
PT-STM	**C52A**	**0505**
PT-STR	**E50P**	**50000279**
PT-STU	**CL30**	**20387**
(PT-TAN)	E50P	50000284
PT-TAR	E50P	50000288
PT-TAS	E50P	50000292
(PT-TAS)	E55P	50500128
PT-TAT	**E50P**	**50000275**
PT-TAU	E55P	50500112
PT-TAY	E55P	50500113
PT-TAZ	E55P	50500114
PT-TBI	E55P	50500115
PT-TBM	E55P	50500116
PT-TBO	E50P	50000300
PT-TBP	E55P	50500120
PT-TBR	C750	0140
(PT-TBT)	E55P	50500129
PT-TBU	E55P	5050011
PT-TBW	E55P	5050011
PT-TBX	E55P	50500123
(PT-TBY)	E55P	50500131
PT-TCJ	E55P	50500124
(PT-TCU)	E55P	50500130
PT-TDI	E55P	50500048
PT-TDJ	E50P	50000235
PT-TDJ	E55P	50500133
PT-TDL	E50P	50000237
PT-TDL	E55P	50500127
PT-TDM	E50P	50000238
PT-TDM	E55P	50500125
PT-TDN	E50P	50000239
PT-TDN	E55P	50500128
PT-TDO	E55P	50500129
(PT-TDO)	E50P	50000240
PT-TDP	E50P	50000241
PT-TDP	E55P	50500131
PT-TDQ	E50P	50000242
PT-TDQ	**E55P**	**50500130**
PT-TDR	E50P	50000243
PT-TDS	E50P	50000244
PT-TDU	E55P	50500051
PT-TDV	E55P	50500053
PT-TDW	E55P	50500054
PT-TES	E50P	50000245
PT-TFA	E50P	50000025
PT-TFB	E50P	50000026
PT-TFC	E50P	50000027
PT-TFD	E50P	50000028
PT-TFE	E50P	50000029
PT-TFF	E50P	50000030
PT-TFG	E50P	50000031
PT-TFH	E50P	50000032
PT-TFI	E50P	50000033
PT-TFJ	E50P	50000034
PT-TFK	E50P	50000035
PT-TFL	E50P	50000036
PT-TFM	E50P	50000037
PT-TFN	E50P	50000038
PT-TFO	E50P	50000039
PT-TFP	E50P	50000040
PT-TFQ	E50P	50000041
PT-TFR	E50P	50000042
PT-TFS	E50P	50000043
PT-TFT	E50P	50000044
PT-TFU	E50P	50000045
PT-TFV	E50P	50000046
PT-TFW	E50P	50000047
PT-TFX	E50P	50000048
PT-TFY	E50P	50000049
PT-TFZ	E50P	50000050
PT-TGA	E50P	50000051
PT-TGB	E50P	50000052
PT-TGC	E50P	50000053
PT-TGD	E50P	50000054
PT-TGE	E50P	50000055
PT-TGF	E50P	50000056
PT-TGG	E50P	50000057
PT-TGH	E50P	50000058
PT-TGI	E50P	50000059
PT-TGJ	E50P	50000060
PT-TGK	E50P	50000061
PT-TGL	E50P	50000062
PT-TGM	E50P	50000063
PT-TGN	E50P	50000064
PT-TGO	E50P	50000065
PT-TGO	E50P	50000247
PT-TGP	E50P	50000066
PT-TGP	E50P	50000248
PT-TGQ	E50P	50000067
PT-TGR	E50P	50000068
PT-TGS	E50P	50000069
PT-TGT	E50P	50000070
PT-TGU	E50P	50000071
PT-TGV	E50P	50000072
PT-TGW	E50P	50000073
PT-TGX	E50P	50000074
PT-TGY	E50P	50000075
PT-TGZ	E50P	50000076
PT-THA	E50P	50000077
(PT-THB)	E50P	50000078
PT-THC	E50P	50000079
PT-THD	E50P	50000080
PT-THE	E50P	50000081
PT-THF	E50P	50000082
PT-THG	E50P	50000083
PT-THH	E50P	50000084
PT-THI	E50P	50000085
PT-THJ	E50P	50000086
PT-THK	E50P	50000087
PT-THL	E50P	50000088
PT-THM	E50P	50000089
PT-THN	E50P	50000090
PT-THO	E50P	50000091
PT-THP	E50P	50000092
PT-THQ	E50P	50000093
PT-THR	E50P	50000094
PT-THS	E50P	50000095
PT-THT	E50P	50000096
PT-THT	E55P	50500056
PT-THU	E50P	50000097
PT-THV	E50P	50000098
PT-THW	E50P	50000099
PT-THX	E50P	50000100
PT-THY	E50P	50000101
PT-THZ	E50P	50000102
(PT-TIC)	E55P	50500041
(PT-TIC)	E55P	50500067
PT-TIH	E50P	50000103
PT-TII	E50P	50000104
PT-TIJ	E50P	50000105
PT-TIK	E50P	50000106
PT-TIL	E50P	50000107
PT-TIM	E50P	50000108
PT-TIN	E50P	50000109
PT-TIO	E50P	50000110
PT-TIP	E50P	50000111
PT-TIQ	E50P	50000112
PT-TIR	E50P	50000113
PT-TIS	E50P	50000114
PT-TIT	E50P	50000115
PT-TIU	E50P	50000116
PT-TIV	E50P	50000117
PT-TIW	E50P	50000118
(PT-TIX)	E50P	50000119
PT-TIY	E50P	50000120
PT-TIZ	E50P	50000121
PT-TJB	LJ45	022
(PT-TJG)	E50P	50000324
(PT-TJH)	E55P	50500137
PT-TJJ	E55P	50500057
PT-TJK	E50P	50000250
PT-TJL	E50P	50000252
PT-TJM	E50P	50000253
(PT-TJN)	E50P	50000254
PT-TJO	E50P	50000257
PT-TJP	E50P	50000258
PT-TJQ	E50P	50000259
PT-TJR	E55P	50500058
PT-TJS	**C52B**	**0136**
PT-TJT	E55P	50500059
(PT-TJU)	E55P	50500060
PT-TJV	E55P	50500061
PT-TJW	E55P	50500062
PT-TKL	E55P	50500063
PT-TLW	E55P	50500064
PT-TNA	E55P	50500065
PT-TNB	E55P	50500066
PT-TNC	E55P	50500067
PT-TND	E55P	50500068
PT-TNE	C680	0145
PT-TNF	E55P	50500069
PT-TNH	E55P	50500070
PT-TNI	E55P	50500071
PT-TNJ	E50P	50000269
(PT-TNJ)	E55P	50500072
PT-TNK	E55P	50500073
PT-TNL	E55P	50500074
PT-TNM	E55P	50500075
PT-TNO	E50P	50000260
PT-TNP	E50P	50000261
(PT-TNQ)	E50P	50000262
PT-TNR	E50P	50000263
PT-TNS	E55P	50500077
(PT-TNS)	E50P	50000264
(PT-TNT)	E50P	50000265
PT-TNU	E55P	50500079
(PT-TNU)	E50P	50000266
PT-TNV	E55P	50500083
(PT-TNV)	E50P	50000267
PT-TNW	E50P	50000268
PT-TOA	E55P	50500104
(PT-TOA)	E50P	50000270
PT-TOB	E55P	50500106
PT-TOC	E55P	50500107
PT-TOD	E55P	50500108
PT-TOF	LJ31	103
PT-TOG	E55P	50500109
PT-TOH	E55P	50500110
PT-TOI	E55P	50500111
PT-TOJ	E50P	50000282
PT-TOP	**C510**	**0123**
PT-TPM	E55P	50500085
PT-TPX	E50P	50000271
PT-TPY	E50P	50000273
PT-TPZ	E50P	50000275
PT-TRA	**BE40**	**RK-307**
PT-TRD	E50P	50000276
PT-TRE	E55P	50500097
PT-TRF	E55P	50500099
PT-TRG	E50P	50000278
PT-TRH	E55P	50500076
PT-TRJ	E55P	50500101
PT-TRJ	**F2TS**	**712**
PT-TRK	E55P	50500078
PT-TRN	E55P	50500082
PT-TRO	E55P	50500102
PT-TRP	E55P	50500084
PT-TRP	E55P	50500103
PT-TRQ	E55P	50500087
PT-TRR	E55P	50500089
PT-TRS	E55P	50500091
PT-TRT	E55P	50500088
PT-TRU	E55P	50500105
PT-TRV	E55P	50500090
PT-TRW	E55P	50500092
PT-TSS	E55P	50500093
PT-TST	E55P	50500094
PT-TSU	E55P	50500095
PT-TSV	E55P	50500096
PT-TSW	E55P	50500098
PT-TSX	E50P	50000279
PT-TUA	E50P	50000281
(PT-TVN)	E55P	50500081
PT-TYA	E50P	50000122
PT-TYB	E50P	50000123
PT-TYC	E50P	50000124
PT-TYD	E50P	50000127
PT-WAB	C500	047
PT-WAL	**HS25**	**258198**
PT-WAN	FA50	188
PT-WAR	LJ35	230
PT-WAU	HS25	258133
(PT-WAW)	HS25	258184
PT-WBC	ASTR	086
PT-WBV	C550	485
PT-WBY	**C500**	**008**
PT-WEW	**LJ24**	**158**
PT-WFC	C650	7054
PT-WFD	**C560**	**0308**
PT-WFT	C500	154
(PT-WGB)	LJ60	046
PT-WGD	C525	0120
PT-WGF	**LJ35**	**322**
PT-WGM	LJ36	048
PT-WHB	**BE40**	**RK-73**
PT-WHC	**BE40**	**RK-58**
PT-WHD	**BE40**	**RK-77**
PT-WHE	**BE40**	**RK-81**
PT-WHF	**BE40**	**RK-82**
PT-WHG	**BE40**	**RK-54**
PT-WHH	HS25	258282
PT-WHZ	C500	287
PT-WIA	HS25	258035
PT-WIB	**CS55**	**0137**
PT-WIV	**LJ31**	**110**
PT-WJS	**BE40**	**RK-122**
PT-WJZ	**C550**	**339**
PT-WKL	**LJ24**	**294**
PT-WKQ	**C550**	**675**
PT-WKS	C560	0397
PT-WLC	C650	7035
PT-WLM	BE40	RK-28
PT-WLO	**LJ31**	**122**
PT-WLX	C525	0176
PT-WLY	C650	7074
PT-WLZ	CL61	5189
PT-WMA	**HS25**	**258301**
PT-WMD	HS25	258312
PT-WMG	HS25	258310
PT-WMO	LJ60	090
PT-WMQ	C560	0405
PT-WMZ	**C560**	**0406**

PT-WNE	C560	0411
PT-WNF	C560	0412
PT-WNH	C550	550-0814
PT-WNO	HS25	258284
PT-WOA	C560	0408
PT-WOD	C500	340
PT-WOM	C560	0176
PT-WON	C550	641
PT-WPC	C560	0142
PT-WPF	HS25	258409
(PT-WQE)	C560	0438
(PT-WQG)	C550	154
PT-WQH	C650	7083
PT-WQI	**C525**	**0238**
(PT-WQJ)	C525	0239
PT-WQM	F900	5
PT-WQS	F9EX	53
PT-WRC	GLF3	492
PT-WRR	C560	0389
PT-WSB	**LJ31**	**135**
PT-WSC	FA50	253
PT-WSF	**FA10**	**169**
PT-WSN	C560	0440
PT-WSO	C550	550-0832
PT-WSS	LJ55	102
PT-WUF	BE40	RK-171
PT-WUM	**C750**	**0092**
PT-WUV	FA20	129
PT-WVC	C550	550-0833
PT-WVG	HS25	258395
PT-WVH	C560	0409
PT-WXL	CL64	5321
PT-WYC	**F2TH**	**59**
PT-WYU	**C56X**	**5060**
(PT-WZO)	C56X	5003
PT-WZW	C560	0431
PT-XAC	**C525**	**0280**
PT-XCF	**C560**	**0450**
PT-XCL	C56X	5020
PT-XDB	**C525**	**0274**
PT-XDN	**LJ40**	**2062**
PT-XDY	HS25	258442
PT-XFG	C650	7099
PT-XFS	**LJ60**	**121**
PT-XGS	**LJ60**	**164**
PT-XIB	**C56X**	**5043**
(PT-XIT)	LJ31	148
PT-XJS	C525	0239
(PT-XLF)	LJ45	093
PT-XLI	LJ35	299
PT-XLR	**LJ45**	**048**
PT-XMM	**C525**	**0267**
PT-XPP	**LJ31**	**148**
PT-XSC	F9EX	60
PT-XSX	**C550**	**550-0873**
PT-XTA	**LJ31**	**013**
PT-XVA	LJ45	077
PT-XYW	CL64	5484
(PT-YVL)	FA7X	201
PT-ZAA	HS25	258031
PT-ZEX	**LEG5**	**55000001**
PT-ZEY	**LEG5**	**55000002**
PT-ZFV	LEG5	55000003
PT-ZHY	LEG5	55000004
PT-ZIJ	**LEG5**	**55000009**
PT-ZJF	LEG5	55000005
PT-ZXS	E55P	50500005
PT-ZXT	E55P	50500006
PT-ZXW	E55P	50500007
PT-ZXX	E55P	50500008
PT-ZXY	E55P	50500009
PT-ZXZ	E55P	50500010
PT-ZYA	E50P	50000013
PT-ZYB	E50P	50000014
PT-ZYC	E50P	50000015
PT-ZYD	E50P	50000016
PT-ZYE	E50P	50000017
PT-ZYF	E50P	50000018
PT-ZYG	E50P	50000019
PT-ZYH	E50P	50000020
PT-ZYI	E50P	5000021
PT-ZYL	E50P	50000024
PT-ZYT	E50P	50000022
PT-ZYX	E50P	50000023

Papua New Guinea

P2-ANW	**F9EX**	**218**
P2-BCM	WW24	317
P2-EUV	**C550**	**268**
P2-JMK	C550	299
P2-MBD	C550	099
P2-MBN	C550	160
P2-MEH	**C52B**	**0027**
P2-PNF	GLF2	103
P2-PNG	GLF2	103
P2-RDZ	C550	021
P2-SOS	C550	669
P2-TAA	C550	160

Aruba

P4-...	**WW24**	**135**
P4-AAA	GLEX	9136
P4-ABC	CL64	5628
P4-ADD	**GALX**	**200**
P4-AEA	GLF3	431
P4-AGL	**CL30**	**20596**
(P4-AGL)	CL30	20537
P4-AIM	**CL65**	**5886**
P4-ALA	HS25	HA-0020
P4-ALE	HS25	258359
P4-ALM	C56X	5218
P4-AMB	HS25	25252
P4-AMF	HS25	258201
P4-AMH	HS25	257070
P4-AMR	**CL30**	**20295**
P4-AND	**C750**	**0075**
P4-ANG	**HS25**	**HA-0025**
P4-AOB	HS25	25222
P4-AOC	HS25	25079
P4-AOD	HS25	257153
P4-AOE	HS25	257136
P4-AOF	HS25	257015
P4-AOH	HS25	257013
P4-AVJ	CL64	5519
P4-AVM	LJ60	197
P4-AVN	FA10	128
P4-AZG	GLF6	6147
P4-BAK	FA50	130
P4-BAZ	LJ60	272
P4-BFL	**GLF4**	**4066**
P4-BFS	**LJ45**	**265**
P4-BFY	**GLF5**	**5418**
P4-BOB	HS25	258115
P4-BTA	CL64	5649
P4-BUS	C750	0271
P4-CBA	GLEX	9220
P4-CBG	JSTR	5202
P4-CBJ	JSTR	5082/36
P4-CEO	**CL65**	**5732**
P4-CHV	CL64	5580
P4-CMP	HS25	257214
P4-DBB	**F2EX**	**264**
P4-DDA	GLF4	1425
P4-EPI	CL61	5125
P4-EXG	LJ60	347
P4-FAY	CL64	5508
P4-FAZ	GLF5	572
P4-GEM	**F9EX**	**239**
P4-GIS	**FA7X**	**139**
P4-GMS	**GLEX**	**9426**
P4-HBS	HS25	HA-0097
P4-HER	GLEX	9186
P4-IKF	**F2TH**	**227**
P4-IKR	F2TH	70
P4-JCC	HS25	258115
P4-JET	FA50	295
P4-KIS	LJ35	341
P4-KMK	CL65	5799
(P4-LGM)	F2EX	143
P4-LJG	C750	0227
P4-LSM	GLF6	6140
P4-LVF	HS25	257040
P4-MAA	**C750**	**0048**
P4-MAF	HS25	259026
P4-MLC	GLEX	9098
P4-MMM	GLEX	9430
P4-MVP	**GLF4**	**4247**
P4-NAN	F900	159
P4-NAV	**G280**	**2042**
P4-NMD	**GLF4**	**1425**
P4-NUR	HS25	258982
P4-OBE	HS25	257142
P4-PET	HS25	HA-0035
P4-PIF	**GLEX**	**9346**
P4-PPP	GLF5	5193
P4-PRT	**HS25**	**258682**
P4-SAI	CL64	5553
P4-SAT	**CL65**	**5762**
P4-SBR	GLF5	607
P4-SCM	F9EX	152
P4-SCM	**FA7X**	**245**
P4-SEN	**HS25**	**258617**
P4-SKY	HS25	257013
P4-SNS	FA50	348
P4-SNT	HS25	258538
P4-SSV	LJ60	325
P4-TAK	GLF4	1425
P4-TAM	CL61	3006
P4-TAT	CL64	5567
P4-TID	**LJ35**	**200**
P4-TPS	GLF5	5193
P4-UNI	CL65	5751
P4-VJR	HS25	256049
P4-VVF	GLEX	9147
P4-WIN	**HS25**	**258859**
P4-XZX	HS25	257136
(P4-ZAW)	HS25	25018

Russia

RA-01809	PRM1	RB-256
RA-02771	**HS25**	**257214**
RA-02772	**HS25**	**258126**
RA-02773	**HS25**	**258192**
RA-02775	**HS25**	**257058**
RA-02800	HS25	257007
RA-02801	**HS25**	**257097**
RA-02802	HS25	257054
RA-02802	**HS25**	**257142**
RA-02803	**HS25**	**257139**
RA-02804	HS25	25281
RA-02804	**HS25**	**257175**
RA-02805	HS25	25219
RA-02806	HS25	257017
RA-02806	**HS25**	**258106**
RA-02807	HS25	258076
RA-02808	**HS25**	**257184**
RA-02809	**HS25**	**257022**
RA-02809	HS25	257062
RA-02810	**HS25**	**257012**
RA-02811	**HS25**	**257200**
RA-02850	**HS25**	**257112**
RA-09000	**F900**	**118**
RA-09001	**F900**	**123**
RA-09003	**F9EX**	**223**
RA-09003	FA20	183
RA-09004	FA20	170/455
RA-09005	FA20	293
RA-09006	**F9EX**	**164**
RA-09007	FA20	136/439
RA-09007	**FA7X**	**20**
RA-09008	**F9EX**	**142**
RA-09009	FA7X	47
RA-09010	**FA7X**	**71**
RA-09600	**F9EX**	**240**
RA-09601	**FA7X**	**253**
RA-09602	**FA7X**	**256**
RA-09616	**FA7X**	**191**
RA-2058G	**FA20**	**494**
RA-2400G	**C500**	**097**
RA-3077K	SBRL	306-13
RA-10201	**GLF4**	**1465**
RA-10202	**GLF5**	**5119**
RA-10203	**GLF5**	**5378**
RA-10204	**GLF6**	**6170**
RA-10205	**GLF6**	**6114**
RA-67172	**C525**	**0303**
RA-67216	**CL64**	**5567**
RA-67217	**CL30**	**20173**
RA-67221	**CL30**	**20235**
RA-67222	CL64	5596
RA-67223	**CL30**	**20172**
RA-67224	**CL30**	**20065**
RA-67225	**GLEX**	**9376**
RA-67227	**CL65**	**5803**
RA-67228	**CL64**	**5613**
RA-67238	**CL65**	**5924**
RA-67241	**GLEX**	**9700**
RA-67428	**C525**	**0305**
RA-67431	**C525**	**0349**
RA-67433	**C525**	**0484**
RA-67705	**C525**	**0652**
RF-14423	**SBRL**	**306-13**

Croatia

RC-BLY	SBRL	380-65
RC-BPU	C550	144

Philippines

RP-57	JSTR	5062/12
RP-57	LJ35	244
RP-9363	GLEX	9363
RP-C57	LJ35	244
RP-C59	WW24	254
RP-C102	C500	123
RP-C111	HS25	25256
RP-C125	HS25	25033
RP-C235	HS25	257130
RP-C237	C500	514
RP-C296	C550	031
RP-C390	**PRM1**	**RB-204**
RP-C400	LJ25	289
RP-C525	**C525**	**0288**
RP-C550	C550	031
RP-C581	C550	167
RP-C602	**HS25**	**257212**
RP-C610	LJ35	338
RP-C629	**LJ45**	**513**
RP-C648	LJ35	648
RP-C648	LJ60	093
RP-C650	C650	7110
RP-C653	C550	194
RP-C689	C550	159
(RP-C717)	C525	0177
RP-C718	**C510**	**0246**
RP-C754	FA50	82
RP-C848	**LJ24**	**072**
RP-C850	**HS25**	**258805**
RP-C1180	C550	658
RP-C1261	LJ25	352
RP-C1290	**C56X**	**6078**
RP-C1299	C500	259
RP-C1404	LJ35	441
RP-C1426	LJ35	426
RP-C1432	**LJ31**	**186**
RP-C1500	C500	225
RP-C1600	HS25	256037
RP-C1714	HS25	257085
RP-C1747	LJ24	264
RP-C1911	**FA10**	**174**
RP-C1926	HS25	258226
RP-C1937	CL64	5366
RP-C1944	LJ45	058
RP-C1958	LJ45	100
RP-C1964	C500	242
RP-C1980	FA20	400/556
RP-C2324	LJ24	182
RP-C2424	**LJ24**	**226**
RP-C2480	WW24	364
RP-C2910	**C680**	**0536**
RP-C2956	LJ60	273
RP-C3110	**LJ40**	**2031**
RP-C3958	**C500**	**327**
RP-C4121	LJ25	287
RP-C4654	C550	707
RP-C5128	LJ36	037
RP-C5168	**G150**	**259**
RP-C5354	**LJ35**	**185**
RP-C5505	**CL60**	**1073**
RP-C5538	**C550**	**658**
RP-C5610	CL64	5402
RP-C5808	**HS25**	**257188**
RP-C5880	**WW24**	**353**
RP-C5988	**WW24**	**254**
RP-C5998	**HS25**	**257166**
RP-C6003	LJ60	254
RP-C6038	**C56X**	**6147**
RP-C6153	LJ31	153
RP-C6178	LJ31	178
RP-C6188	**C56X**	**6188**
RP-C6610	LJ25	289
RP-C7272	LJ35	338
RP-C7513	**C52C**	**0120**
RP-C7777	C500	123
RP-C7808	F900	125
RP-C7979	C510	0326
RP-C8008	**HS25**	**258212**
RP-C8082	**HS25**	**258064**
RP-C8101	**HS25**	**257151**
RP-C8108	HS25	257008
RP-C8150	**G150**	**315**
RP-C8215	**CL30**	**20215**
(RP-C8288)	C525	0185
RP-C8338	LJ45	381
RP-C8346	**GLF4**	**1346**
RP-C8568	**C56X**	**6050**
RP-C8576	**HS25**	**258571**
RP-C8818	C560	0417
RP-C8822	**LJ31**	**041**
RP-C9018	**F9EX**	**17**
RP-C9121	**F900**	**121**
RP-C9215	**F2EX**	**215**
RP-C9808	**HS25**	**257209**
RP-C9999	FA10	151

Sweden

SE-DCK	WW24	51
SE-DCO	FA20	241/479
SE-DCU	LJ24	124
SE-DCW	LJ24	109
SE-DCY	WW24	136
SE-DCZ	WW24	137
SE-DDE	C500	063
SE-DDF	FA10	27
SE-DDG	LJ35	172
SE-DDH	LJ36	013
SE-DDI	LJ35	266
SE-DDM	C500	244
SE-DDN	C500	256
SE-DDO	C500	180
SE-DDW	MU30	A023SA
SE-DDX	C500	292
SE-DDY	**C550**	**127**
SE-DDZ	FA20	482
SE-DEA	LJ35	051
SE-DED	CRVT	32
SE-DEE	CRVT	34
SE-DEF	C550	421
SE-DEG	C500	276
SE-DEK	FA10	156
SE-DEL	FA10	14
SE-DEM	LJ35	317
SE-DEN	CRVT	15
SE-DEO	C500	442
SE-DEP	C500	377
SE-DER	LJ35	373
SE-DES	C500	600
SE-DET	C500	603
SE-DEU	C500	036
SE-DEV	C550	136
SE-DEX	C500	279
SE-DEY	C500	396
SE-DEZ	C500	407
SE-DFA	LJ24	283
SE-DFB	LJ24	281
SE-DFC	LJ25	163
SE-DHE	LJ35	368
SE-DHH	HS25	25160
SE-DHK	FA20	259
SE-DHL	C650	0030
SE-DHO	**LJ35**	**195**
SE-DHP	**LJ35**	**075**
SE-DJA	F9EX	171
SE-DJB	F9EX	179
SE-DJC	**FA7X**	**78**
SE-DJD	**FA7X**	**129**
SE-DJH	C550	550-1022
SE-DJK	**FA7X**	**59**
SE-DJL	**FA7X**	**40**
SE-DJM	F9EX	106
SE-DKA	FA20	308
SE-DKB	FA10	132
SE-DKC	FA10	123
SE-DKD	FA10	60
SE-DKF	HS25	256038
SE-DKI	C555	0008
SE-DKM	C500	309
SE-DLB	FA10	183
SE-DLI	C560	0078
SE-DLK	WW24	197
SE-DLL	WW24	205
SE-DLY	C550	306
SE-DLZ	**C500**	**645**
(SE-DMM)	C500	244
SE-DPG	C560	0086
SE-DPK	FA10	152
SE-DPL	C500	037
SE-DPT	WW24	325
SE-DPY	HS25	257035
SE-DPZ	HS25	257015
SE-DRS	BE40	RK-37
SE-DRT	C500	311
SE-DRV	HS25	258079
SE-DRZ	C500	315
SE-DSA	FA20	339
SE-DUZ	C500	143
SE-DVA	C500	551
SE-DVB	C500	294
SE-DVD	HS25	258339
SE-DVE	F9EX	23
SE-DVG	FA50	104
SE-DVK	FA50	249
SE-DVL	FA50	238
SE-DVP	FA10	224
SE-DVS	HS25	25225
SE-DVT	C550	634
SE-DVV	C550	307
SE-DVY	C650	7011
SE-DVZ	C550	550-0808
SE-DYB	FA10	216
SE-DYE	HS25	258382
SE-DYO	C555	0134
SE-DYR	C550	097
SE-DYV	HS25	258385
SE-DYX	C56X	5029
(SE-DYY)	C550	707
SE-DYZ	C560	0153
(SE-DZX)	C750	0075
SE-DZZ	**LJ35**	**415**
SE-RBB	C56X	5005
SE-RBC	C56X	5008
SE-RBD	C550	388
SE-RBK	C550	340
SE-RBM	C550	717
SE-RBO	BE40	RK-303
(SE-RBV)	F2EX	10
SE-RBX	C56X	5056
SE-RBY	**C550**	**550-1038**
(SE-RBY)	C550	550-0917
SE-RBZ	C500	436
SE-RCA	**LJ35**	**175**
SE-RCI	C550	678
SE-RCK	LJ55	011
SE-RCL	C56X	5217
SE-RCM	**C56X**	**5624**
(SE-RCX)	C550	329
(SE-RCX)	C555	0148
SE-RCY	C550	329
(SE-RCY)	C555	0148
SE-RCZ	C550	187
(SE-RDA)	C500	278
SE-RDX	GLF5	5019
SE-RDY	**GLF5**	**5080**
SE-RDZ	GLF5	5153
SE-RFH	**C680**	**0059**
SE-RFI	C680	0114
SE-RFJ	C680	0205
SE-RFK	C680	0228
SE-RGB	**GLEX**	**9264**
SE-RGN	C500	392
SE-RGS	C56X	5807
SE-RGU	LJ55	087
SE-RGX	**C525**	**0502**
SE-RGY	C560	0414
SE-RGZ	C560	0607
SE-RHD	**C56X**	**6185**
SE-RHJ	**C56X**	**5078**
SE-RHP	C550	672
SE-RIC	C750	0212
SE-RIK	C550	133
SE-RIL	**C56X**	**5777**
SE-RIM	**C550**	**066**
SE-RIN	**C52A**	**0190**
SE-RIO	C525	0181
(SE-RIS)	HS25	258458
SE-RIT	C560	0773
SE-RIX	C525	0671
SE-RIZ	**C56X**	**5529**
SE-RKL	**GLF5**	**5260**
SE-RKM	**C52A**	**0435**
SE-RKS	C52A	0202
SE-RKY	LJ45	161
(SE-RKZ)	C500	235
SE-RLP	**C52B**	**0016**
SE-RLU	**C560**	**0537**
SE-RLX	**HS25**	**258458**
SE-RMA	**CL30**	**20136**
SE-RMB	**C52B**	**0119**
SE-RMJ	**C52B**	**0183**
SE-RMO	**LJ45**	**372**
SE-RMR	**C56X**	**5727**
SE-RMT	**GLEX**	**9624**
SE-RMY	**GLEX**	**9714**

Slovenia

SL-BAA	LJ35	618

SL-BAB	LJ24	320
SL-BAC	C550	480

Poland

SP-AAW	**LJ45**	**490**
SP-ARG	F2TS	718
SP-ARK	C56X	6024
SP-ARK	**F2TS**	**718**
SP-AVP	**E50P**	**50000055**
SP-CEO	**HS25**	**HB-70**
SP-CEZ	**LJ60**	**342**
SP-CON	CL30	20295
SP-DLB	C52A	0428
SP-DLV	**C525**	**0279**
SP-EAR	**C680**	**0213**
SP-FCP	FA20	136/439
SP-FOA	CRVT	14
(SP-GHM)	BE40	RK-343
SP-IAF	**E50P**	**50000368**
SP-KBM	**C500**	**269**
SP-KCK	**C52A**	**0158**
SP-KCL	C525	0526
SP-KCS	**C56X**	**5649**
SP-KHI	**CL30**	**20508**
SP-KHK	**C510**	**0189**
SP-KKA	C525	0550
SP-KKB	C52A	0151
(SP-KTB)	BE40	RK-295
SP-MRD	**PRM1**	**RB-7**
SP-NVM	**G280**	**2088**
SP-OHM	BE40	RK-322
SP-RDW	**PRM1**	**RB-233**
SP-TBF	**G150**	**283**
(SP-VVV)	PRM1	RB-276
SP-WOI	**GLEX**	**9110**
(SP-WOY)	GLEX	9110
SP-ZAK	**GLEX**	**9219**
SP-ZSZ	**CL30**	**20044**

Sudan

ST-FSA	**JSTR**	**5236**
ST-JRM	JSTR	5025
ST-PRE	JSTR	5071
ST-PRM	JSTR	5121
ST-PRS	**FA20**	**372/546**
ST-PSA	**F900**	**84**
ST-PSR	**FA50**	**114**

Egypt

SU-AXN	**FA20**	**294/506**
SU-AYD	**FA20**	**361/543**
SU-AZJ	**FA20**	**358/541**
SU-BGM	**GLF4**	**1048**
SU-BGU	**GLF3**	**439**
SU-BGV	**GLF3**	**442**
SU-BNC	**GLF4**	**1329**
SU-BND	**GLF4**	**1332**
SU-BNL	LJ60	149
SU-BNO	**GLF4**	**1424**
SU-BNP	**GLF4**	**1427**
SU-BPE	**GLF4**	**1506**
SU-BPF	**GLF4**	**1518**
SU-BQF	**C510**	**0225**
SU-BQG	**C510**	**0255**
SU-BQH	**C510**	**0258**
SU-BQI	**C510**	**0267**
SU-BRF	**C680**	**0269**
SU-BRG	**C680**	**0295**
SU-DAF	JSTR	5025
SU-DAG	JSTR	5121
SU-DAH	JSTR	5071
SU-EWA	C560	0201
SU-EWB	C56X	5171
SU-EWC	C56X	5042
SU-EWD	**C680**	**0026**
SU-EZI	LJ60	149
SU-HEC	C550	550-1018
SU-MAN	**HS25**	**258832**
SU-MSG	LJ45	069
SU-OAE	FA20	175
SU-PIX	HS25	257184
SU-SMA	C680	0118
SU-SMB	C680	0167
SU-SMC	**C680**	**0246**
SU-SMD	**C680**	**0270**
SU-SME	**C680**	**0274**
(SU-SMF)	C680	0283
SU-ZBB	BE40	RK-480

Greece

SX-ABA	FA20	245/481
SX-ADK	C56X	5608
SX-AHF	LJ36	007
SX-ASO	LJ25	074
SX-BFJ	LJ35	172
SX-BMI	C680	0204
SX-BMK	**C550**	**550-0907**
SX-BNR	**LJ60**	**231**
SX-BNS	LJ55	072
SX-BNT	LJ35	228
SX-BSS	HS25	25116
SX-BTV	LJ55	124
SX-BTX	GLF2	171
SX-CBM	LJ25	094
SX-CRC	FA50	226
SX-DCA	F2EX	29
SX-DCD	C56X	5662
SX-DCE	C56X	5288
SX-DCF	F2TH	134
SX-DCI	C560	0366
SX-DCM	C56X	5051
SX-DCV	FA7X	111
SX-DKI	FA20	275
SX-ECH	F900	26
SX-ECI	**C750**	**0262**
(SX-EDP)	C52B	0193
SX-FAR	HS25	258495
SX-FCA	**PRM1**	**RB-262**
SX-FDA	**C550**	**707**
SX-FDB	**C500**	**392**
SX-FDK	**C650**	**0192**
SX-GAB	**GLF4**	**4172**
SX-GJJ	**GLF5**	**5350**
SX-GJN	GLEX	9260
SX-GRC	**FA7X**	**109**
SX-GSB	**GLF6**	**6092**
SX-IDA	GALX	149
SX-IFB	GALX	063
(SX-IFB)	GALX	149
SX-IRP	GALX	142
SX-JET	**FA7X**	**184**
SX-KFA	**CL64**	**5359**
SX-KMA	**CL64**	**5585**
(SX-MAD)	GALX	065
SX-MAJ	GALX	207
SX-MAW	GLF4	4180
SX-MFA	GLF5	5197
SX-MLA	F2EX	200
SX-NSS	E50P	50000035
SX-ONE	GALX	065
SX-PAP	C52B	0193
SX-SEA	GALX	163
SX-SEE	GLF4	4115
SX-SEM	**LJ35**	**265**
(SX-SEN)	LJ35	429
SX-SHC	**CL65**	**5722**
SX-SMG	GALX	159
SX-SMH	C52A	0229
SX-SMR	C56X	5631
SX-TAJ	GALX	215
(SX-TFA)	CL64	5398
SX-ZHT	F9DX	616

Seychelles

SY-AAP	C560	0003

Bangladesh

S2-AHS	**HS25**	**258200**

Slovenia

S5-ABR	F2EX	15
S5-ADA	CL65	5712
S5-ADB	CL65	5715
S5-ADC	GLF4	4027
S5-ADD	**CL65**	**5754**
S5-ADE	**CL30**	**20236**
(S5-ADE)	GLEX	9336
S5-ADF	**CL65**	**5757**
S5-ADG	F2EX	8
S5-ADK	**CL65**	**5855**
S5-AFR	**HS25**	**258385**
S5-BAA	LJ35	618
S5-BAB	LJ24	320
S5-BAC	C550	480
S5-BAJ	C525	0394
S5-BAR	C52A	0423
S5-BAS	C52A	0348
S5-BAV	C56X	5660
S5-BAW	C52B	0016
S5-BAX	C555	0028
S5-BAY	C525	0315
S5-BAZ	C56X	5236
S5-BBA	C650	7080
S5-BBB	C52A	0019
S5-BBD	C56X	5058
S5-BBG	**C550**	**388**
S5-BBL	**C550**	**550-0972**
S5-BDC	C56X	5209
S5-BDG	C56X	5215
S5-CMT	C510	0186
S5-CWA	**F2TH**	**216**
S5-FUN	CL30	20401
S5-GMG	GLEX	9409
S5-ICR	**C56X**	**5236**
S5-JVA	**GLF4**	**4265**
S5-SAD	**GLEX**	**9553**
S5-ZFL	**GLEX**	**9466**

Seychelles

S7-AAP	C560	0003

Sao Tome

S9-CRH	GLF2	8
S9-CRH	LJ36	055
S9-DBG	HS25	256021
S9-GOT	GLF2	8
S9-NAD	JSTR	5065
S9-NAE	JSTR	5085
S9-PDG	**HS25**	**256021**
S9-PDH	**HS25**	**25132**

Turkey

(TC-...)	F9EX	219
(TC-...)	FA20	489
TC-ABN	**CL65**	**5956**
TC-ACL	HS25	HA-0051
TC-ADO	**HS25**	**258738**
TC-AEH	**G150**	**284**
TC-AEK	**LJ60**	**401**
TC-AFF	**CL30**	**20126**
TC-AGR	**C510**	**0356**
TC-AHE	**C550**	**550-1107**
TC-AHS	HS25	258504
TC-AKE	**F9EX**	**263**
TC-AKH	HS25	259043
TC-AKK	F900	171
TC-ANA	GLF4	1043
TC-ANC	HS25	258208
TC-AND	FA10	89
TC-ANG	PRM1	RB-286
TC-ANT	C650	0229
TC-AOM	F9EX	283
TC-ARB	**CL30**	**20181**
TC-ARC	LJ60	094
TC-ARD	**CL64**	**5611**
TC-ARI	C560	0212
TC-ARK	FA10	218
TC-ASE	BE40	RK-18
TC-ASF	WW24	195
TC-ASH	**HS25**	**HA-0051**
TC-ASL	**CL64**	**5595**
TC-ATA	GLF4	1043
TC-ATA	**GLF5**	**5346**
TC-ATC	C650	7043
TC-ATC	F2EX	136
TC-ATI	FA10	132
TC-ATP	**C680**	**0232**
TC-ATS	**EA50**	**000190**
TC-ATV	C750	0001
TC-AZR	F9EX	236
TC-BAY	C550	316
TC-BHD	HS25	258415
TC-BHO	FA50	271
TC-BNT	FA50	305
TC-BOR	C560	0216
TC-BYD	BE40	RK-254
TC-CAG	F900	142
TC-CAO	C650	0060
TC-CBK	**GLF5**	**5254**
TC-CEA	**CL64**	**5594**
TC-CEN	FA20	326/521
TC-CEY	C650	0214
TC-CIN	F2TH	26
TC-CLG	**HS25**	**HA-0098**
TC-CLH	**CL65**	**5763**
TC-CLK	HS25	258808
TC-CMB	**LJ45**	**007**
TC-CMK	CL30	20233
TC-CMK	**CL65**	**5767**
TC-CMY	C650	0141
TC-COS	HS25	256048
TC-COY	C550	347
TC-CRO	C525	0102
TC-CTN	**F2TH**	**157**
TC-CYL	F2TH	56
TC-DAG	**C56X**	**5769**
TC-DAK	**C56X**	**6048**
TC-DAP	**GLF5**	**5212**
TC-DEM	FA20	489
TC-DGC	F2TH	166
TC-DGN	**F2EX**	**104**
TC-DGS	F2TH	133
TC-DHB	CL61	5094
TC-DHE	CL64	5358
(TC-DHE)	CL64	5318
TC-DHF	LJ60	184
(TC-DHG)	GLEX	9057
TC-DHH	CL64	5448
TC-DLZ	**C56X**	**5824**
TC-DMR	**HS25**	**HA-0170**
TC-DOU	**C510**	**0330**
TC-DOY	HS25	258801
TC-DYO	GLF4	4212
TC-EES	C650	0077
TC-ELL	LJ60	030
TC-EMA	C525	0121
TC-ENK	**HS25**	**HA-0086**
TC-EYE	FA50	161
TC-EZE	FA20	299
TC-FAL	C550	351
TC-FBS	LJ55	138
TC-FIB	**CL65**	**5747**
TC-FIN	HS25	258742
TC-FMB	C550	351
TC-FNS	HFB3	1026
TC-FRK	**GLEX**	**9153**
TC-FTG	**F9EX**	**161**
TC-GAP	GLF3	487
TC-GAP	GLF4	1027
TC-GAP	**GLF4**	**4240**
TC-GEM	LJ35	185
TC-GGG	**FA20**	**326/521**
TC-GMM	FA7X	28
TC-GNC	**F2TH**	**133**
TC-GRS	**C680**	**680A0021**
TC-GSA	HFB3	1055
TC-GSB	HFB3	1042
TC-GUR	C52B	0309
TC-GVA	**GLF4**	**1043**
TC-GVB	**GLF4**	**1027**
TC-IBO	**BE40**	**RK-303**
TC-ICK	**CL64**	**5523**
TC-ICT	**C680**	**0290**
TC-IHS	JSTR	5225
TC-ILY	HS25	258748
TC-IPK	**GLF4**	**4239**
(TC-IRR)	F9EX	271
TC-ISR	CL30	20138
TC-IST	C680	0159
TC-KAM	FA50	95
TC-KAR	CL30	20149
TC-KEA	**EA50**	**000007**
TC-KEH	E55P	50500099
TC-KHA	**HS25**	**HA-0046**
TC-KHB	**GLF4**	**4175**
TC-KHD	**G280**	**2037**
TC-KHE	HFB3	1043
TC-KHG	**GLF5**	**5459**
TC-KIP	**C56X**	**6143**
TC-KJA	**BE40**	**RK-502**
TC-KLE	**CL65**	**5964**
TC-KLS	C650	0191
TC-KMR	**FA7X**	**254**
TC-KOC	C650	7006
TC-KON	**C650**	**7084**
TC-KOP	GLF5	5241
TC-KRM	**GLEX**	**9318**
TC-LAA	**C560**	**0212**
TC-LAB	**C560**	**0216**
TC-LAC	**C56X**	**5779**
TC-LAD	**C56X**	**5795**
TC-LEY	HFB3	1042
TC-LEY	HFB3	1043
TC-LIA	**F2EX**	**221**
TC-LIM	C525	0226
TC-LLL	**C56X**	**5722**
TC-LMA	C56X	5242
TC-LNS	C56X	5693
TC-MAA	F2EX	230
TC-MAN	**HS25**	**258836**
TC-MCX	BE40	RK-170
TC-MDB	BE40	RK-164
TC-MDC	HS25	258384
TC-MDG	CL61	5110
TC-MDJ	BE40	RK-120
TC-MEK	LJ35	441
TC-MEK	LJ55	138
TC-MEK	LJ60	016
TC-MEN	**LJ60**	**335**
TC-MET	C560	0497
TC-MHS	PRM1	RB-77
TC-MJA	**GLEX**	**9408**
TC-MJB	**CL64**	**5625**
TC-MKA	**C550**	**550-0960**
TC-MKR	**F9EX**	**257**
TC-MLA	**LEG5**	**55000016**
TC-MMG	F9EX	161
TC-MMM	**FA7X**	**227**
TC-MOH	**HS25**	**HA-0114**
TC-MRK	**F2EX**	**193**
TC-MSA	BE40	RK-124
TC-MSB	BE40	RK-170
TC-MZA	**GLF4**	**4249**
TC-NEO	**BE40**	**RK-130**
TC-NEU	**BE40**	**RK-548**
TC-NKB	C550	053
TC-NMC	C555	0072
TC-NNK	BE40	RK-211
TC-NOA	JSTR	5220
TC-NRN	**HA4T**	**RC-44**
TC-NRY	**HS25**	**HA-0092**
TC-NSU	HFB3	1046
TC-NTA	**C680**	**0343**
TC-NUB	HS25	258874
(TC-OHY)	C56X	5722
TC-OIL	**FA7X**	**190**
TC-OKN	HS25	258388
TC-OMR	HFB3	1047
TC-OMR	JSTR	5082/36
TC-ORM	FA10	33
TC-OVA	CL61	5094
TC-OYD	**C680**	**0344**
TC-PLM	F2TH	160
TC-PRK	F2TH	191
TC-RAM	C650	0178
TC-REA	**CL64**	**5528**
TC-REC	**GLF4**	**4246**
TC-RED	**C680**	**0272**
TC-RKS	LJ60	282
TC-RMK	F2TH	157
TC-ROT	C560	0454
TC-RSN	F2TH	166
TC-RZA	**CL30**	**20284**
TC-SAB	**CL65**	**5730**
TC-SAM	C555	0007
TC-SBH	C650	0234
TC-SBL	**HS25**	**258793**
TC-SCR	CL30	20136
TC-SEN	HFB3	1042
TC-SES	C550	717
TC-SGO	**F2EX**	**180**
TC-SHE	**HS25**	**258872**
TC-SHU	**F9DX**	**617**
TC-SIS	C650	0077
TC-SMB	BE40	RK-148
TC-SMC	**F2EX**	**294**
TC-SMZ	CL64	5415
TC-SNK	**F2TH**	**229**
TC-SPL	**CL30**	**20424**
TC-SSH	C56X	6055
TC-SSS	**JSTR**	**5226**
TC-STA	**BE40**	**RK-476**
TC-STB	HS25	258793
TC-STD	HS25	258845
TC-STO	**C650**	**7091**
TC-STR	HS25	258415
TC-SZA	**FA7X**	**225**
TC-TAI	**C510**	**0312**
TC-TAJ	**C510**	**0319**
TC-TAN	CL64	5459
TC-TAV	**HS25**	**258736**
TC-TEK	HS25	258229
(TC-THY)	CL30	20190
TC-TKC	**HS25**	**258790**
TC-TKN	**C680**	**0174**
TC-TMO	**C56X**	**5051**
TC-TOP	C650	0083
TC-TOS	**F2TS**	**704**
TC-TPE	C550	550-0951
TC-TRB	**CL64**	**5494**
TC-TSH	HS25	HA-0092
TC-TSY	**C56X**	**6040**
TC-TTC	**GLF5**	**5284**
TC-TVA	C680	0263
TC-TVH	**C680**	**680A0018**
TC-VGP	**F2TS**	**723**
TC-VIN	BE40	RK-188
TC-VPG	**CL30**	**20218**
TC-VSC	HS25	258398
TC-VYN	C52A	0236
TC-VZR	C750	0150
TC-YAA	GLEX	9365
TC-YHK	**FA7X**	**9**
TC-YIB	**MU30**	**A051SA**
(TC-YIL)	GLEX	9058
TC-YRT	BE40	RK-190
TC-YSR	FA50	246
TC-YYA	**GLEX**	**9365**
TC-YZB	C550	351

Iceland

TF-JET	C550	235

Guatemala

TG-ABY	LJ45	293
TG-AIR	LJ31	067
TG-AIR	**LJ60**	**377**
TG-BAC	C550	550-0875
(TG-FIL)	C525	0072
TG-GGA	FA20	25/405
TG-JAY	LJ35	225
TG-KIT	C500	633
TG-LAR	MU30	A062SA
TG-MIL	C500	633
TG-MYS	**LJ31**	**067**
TG-OMF	WW24	34
TG-OZO	C500	204
(TG-PIB)	C550	550-0944
TG-RBW	FA20	150/445
TG-RIE	**C500**	**624**
TG-RIF	C500	624
TG-RIF	**C525**	**0072**
TG-SHV	**LJ31**	**130**
TG-VOC	LJ25	251
TG-VWA	WW24	109

Costa Rica

(TI-ACB)	C500	187
TI-AFB	C500	258
(TI-AHE)	C500	245
TI-AHH	C500	245
TI-APZ	C550	273
TI-AZX	C500	227
TI-BFT	**C650**	**0098**
(TI-BFY)	C650	0098

Cameroon

TJ-...	**HS25**	**256040**
(TJ-...)	GLF3	487
TJ-AAK	GLF2	93
TJ-AAW	**GLF3**	**486**
TJ-AHR	CRVT	12
TJ-ROA	**C550**	**550-0864**
TJ-TRI	F9EX	17

Central African Republic

TL-AAW	C500	078
TL-AAY	FA20	174/457
TL-ABD	LJ35	062
TL-ADK	HS25	25258
TL-AJK	FA20	32
TL-KAZ	FA20	174/457
TL-RCA	CRVT	39
TL-SMI	CRVT	39

Congo

TN-ADB	CRVT	22
TN-ADI	CRVT	9
TN-AJE	**HS25**	**258209**
TN-AJN	**FA50**	**226**
TN-ELS	**FA7X**	**232**

Gabon

TR-...	**FA10**	**221**
TR-...	**FA50**	**151**

TR-AAG	**CL61**	**5071**
TR-AFJ	**F900**	**46**
TR-AFR	**F900**	**59**
TR-CHB	**FA50**	**155**
TR-KGM	**GLF6**	**6137**
TR-KHA	FA20	225/472
TR-KHB	GLF2	127
TR-KHC	GLF3	326
TR-KHD	GLF4	1327
TR-KSP	**GLF4**	**1327**
TR-LAH	CRVT	30
TR-LAI	FA50	78
TR-LAU	HS25	256052
TR-LCJ	F900	7
TR-LDB	HS25	258192
TR-LEX	**F9EX**	**24**
TR-LFB	HS25	25130
TR-LGV	**FA50**	**89**
TR-LGY	**FA50**	**9**
TR-LGZ	**FA20**	**391**
TR-LOL	FA20	13
TR-LQU	HS25	25250
TR-LRU	FA20	225/472
TR-LTI	C500	210
TR-LUW	FA20	309/514
TR-LWY	CRVT	11
TR-LXO	HS25	25130
TR-LXP	LJ35	005
TR-LYB	LJ24	105
TR-LYC	LJ35	174
TR-LYE	C550	033
TR-LYM	CRVT	12
TR-LZI	LJ35	313
TR-LZT	CRVT	20

Tunisia

TS-IAM	**CL64**	**5412**
TS-IAM	FA10	195
TS-IBT	CL64	5628
TS-INV	CL64	5628
TS-IRS	FA20	117
TS-JAM	FA50	125
TS-JBT	FA50	119
TS-JSM	**F900**	**111**

Tchad

TT-AAI	**GLF2**	**240**
TT-ABF	**HS25**	**HA-0048**
TT-DIT	**F900**	**62**

Ivory Coast

TU-...	**GLF5**	**5533**
TU-VAC	GLF2	218
TU-VAD	FA20	98/434
TU-VAD	**GLF4**	**1019**
TU-VAF	GLF2	119/22
TU-VAF	GLF3	303
TU-VAF	**GLF3**	**462**
TU-VAR	GLF5	5029

Benin

TY-AOM	F900	33
TY-BBK	CRVT	29
TY-BBM	FA50	17
TY-SAM	HS25	257195
TY-VLT	HS25	258632

Mali

TZ-PBF	CRVT	19

San Marino

T7-AAA	**GLEX**	**9283**
T7-AAB	**CL30**	**20133**
T7-AAK	**E55P**	**50500329**
T7-AAS	**CL65**	**5813**
T7-AEA	**EA50**	**000226**
T7-AEB	**EA50**	**000198**
T7-ALM	**FA20**	**240/478**
T7-ANA	**E55P**	**50500261**
T7-ANB	**E55P**	**50500315**
(T7-ANC)	E55P	50500366
T7-APP	**C52A**	**0457**
T7-ARG	**GLF5**	**5142**
T7-AWO	**FA50**	**178**
T7-AZG	**GLF6**	**6147**
T7-BCH	**CL65**	**5822**
T7-CBG	**FA7X**	**219**
T7-DFX	**FA50**	**185**
T7-DFZ	**C510**	**0090**
T7-DMA	**CL65**	**5975**
T7-DRM	**GLF4**	**1337**
T7-EAA	**CL64**	**5649**
T7-FAY	**C56X**	**5218**
T7-FGD	FA50	92
T7-FOZ	**C525**	**0851**
T7-FRA	C525	0628
T7-GFA	**CL61**	**3025**
T7-HOT	C510	0190
T7-ISH	**LJ60**	**369**
T7-JET	**C550**	**348**
T7-KAA	**LJ45**	**305**
T7-KBS	**HS25**	**HA-0017**
T7-MJB	F9EX	28
T7-MND	**C525**	**0089**
T7-NES	**PRM1**	**RB-187**
T7-NIK	F2TH	25
T7-OKA	**PRM1**	**RB-57**
T7-OSB	**F900**	**67**
T7-PRM	**GALX**	**215**
T7-RSN	**F2TH**	**166**
T7-SAM	**LJ24**	**339**
T7-SCI	**LJ45**	**033**
T7-SCR	**C525**	**0519**
T7-SIS	**CL30**	**20141**
T7-SOV	**LJ60**	**160**
T7-TAN	**C750**	**0261**
T7-TIL	GLF5	529
T7-TLM	**C500**	**477**
T7-TUN	**HS25**	**258915**
T7-VIG	**C510**	**0069**
T7-VII	C650	7090
T7-VYT	**E50P**	**50000319**
T7-XXV	C550	174
T7-YES	**CL65**	**5966**
T7-ZOR	**F9EX**	**18**

Bosnia

T9-BIH	CS55	0045
T9-BKA	C500	415
T9-SBA	C500	554
T9-SMS	C525	0666

Kazakhstan

UN-09002	F900	11
UN-P1001	PRM1	RB-120
UP-CL6001	CL64	5649
UP-CS301	**C52B**	**0259**
UP-CS302	**C52B**	**0323**
UP-CS401	**C650**	**0202**
UP-CS501	C750	0277
UP-EM009	**E55P**	**50500082**
UP-HA001	**HS25**	**HA-0197**
UP-LJ001	LJ60	347
UP-P1001	PRM1	RB-120
UP-P1002	**PRM1**	**RB-274**
UP-P1003	**PRM1**	**RB-287**
UP-P1004	**PRM1**	**RB-292**

Ukraine

(UR-ACA)	FA50	235
UR-ALA	**E50P**	**50000253**
UR-ALB	E50P	50000250
UR-ALD	E55P	50500117
(UR-BCA)	FA20	141/441
UR-CCA	FA20	256
UR-CCB	FA20	141/441
UR-CCC	FA50	235
UR-CCD	FA20	112
UR-CCF	**FA50**	**212**
UR-CHH	LJ60	016
UR-CLD	FA20	315/517
UR-CLE	**FA20**	**279/502**
UR-CLF	FA20	293
UR-CLG	FA20	52
UR-CRD	F900	202
UR-DWH	C52B	0322
UR-DWL	C52B	0361
UR-EFA	FA20	55/410
UR-EFB	FA20	75
UR-FDB	PRM1	RB-263
UR-ISH	LJ60	369
UR-KAS	G150	242
UR-KKA	FA20	389/552
UR-LDB	C680	0326
UR-MOA	FA20	237/476
UR-NAC	**LJ60**	**016**
UR-NIK	FA20	112
UR-NOA	**FA20**	**345**
UR-NST	**PRM1**	**RB-284**
UR-PME	C52B	0320
UR-PRM	GALX	215
UR-SBS	FA20	141/441
UR-UQA	C56X	6140
UR-USA	**PRM1**	**RB-235**
UR-USB	**PRM1**	**RB-181**
UR-WIG	F9EX	152

Australia

(VH-...)	HS25	259023
(VH-...)	BE40	RJ-55
VH-ACE	F900	37
VH-ACE	HS25	HA-0049
VH-AJG	WW24	281
VH-AJJ	WW24	248
VH-AJK	WW24	256
VH-AJP	WW24	238
VH-AJQ	WW24	281
VH-AJS	LJ35	188
VH-AJS	WW24	221
VH-AJV	LJ35	189
VH-AJV	WW24	282
(VH-ALH)	LJ35	480
VH-ANE	C525	0521
VH-ANE	C52B	0196
VH-ANI	LJ35	468
VH-ANQ	C500	283
VH-APJ	**C525**	**0281**
VH-APU	WW24	395
VH-AQR	C500	263
VH-AQS	C500	263
(VH-ARJ)	HS25	256037
VH-ARZ	C52B	0027
VH-ASG	GLF2	95/39
VH-ASM	CL61	5033
VH-ASM	GLF2	91
VH-ASQ	GLF4	1205
VH-ASR	WW24	316
VH-AYI	WW24	317
VH-BBJ	HS25	25169
VH-BBJ	BE40	RK-26
VH-BCL	WW24	315
VH-BGF	F900	5
VH-BGL	FA20	495
VH-BGV	F900	32
VH-BIB	LJ36	035
VH-BIZ	FA20	73/419
VH-BJC	BE40	RK-154
VH-BJD	BE40	RK-35
VH-BJQ	LJ35	219
VH-BLJ	LJ25	180
VH-BLM	**CL64**	**5407**
VH-BMW	**HS25**	**258895**
VH-BNK	C500	574
VH-BQR	LJ35	471
VH-BRG	CL61	5064
VH-BRR	FA20	208/468
VH-BRX	C550	338
VH-BSJ	LJ24	266
VH-BZL	**BE40**	**RK-139**
VH-CAO	HS25	25015
VH-CCA	GLF4	1175
VH-CCC	GLF4	1083
VH-CCC	GLF5	581
(VH-CCC)	HS25	258002
VH-CCD	**GLEX**	**9297**
VH-CCJ	C500	471
VH-CCJ	C510	0033
VH-CCJ	**C550**	**550-0953**
VH-CCO	GLF4	1107
VH-CCV	**GLEX**	**9133**
VH-CCX	**GLEX**	**9225**
VH-CDG	**C525**	**0163**
VH-CFO	C550	669
VH-CGF	**GLF4**	**1083**
VH-CIR	FA20	90/426
VH-CIT	C525	0100
VH-CMS	LJ36	032
VH-CPE	FA20	504
VH-CPH	LJ35	400
(VH-CPQ)	LJ35	400
VH-CRM	C500	130
VH-CRQ	F2EX	58
VH-CRQ	GLF5	603
VH-CRW	F2EX	58
VH-CRW	**FA7X**	**217**
VH-CSP	**C500**	**471**
VH-CXJ	**LJ45**	**152**
VH-DAA	**C525**	**0138**
VH-DBT	GLF4	1363
VH-DHN	**C650**	**7011**
VH-DJT	FA10	169
VH-DNK	GLEX	9311
VH-DRM	C500	112
VH-DWA	FA20	72/413
VH-ECD	C500	123
VH-ECE	HS25	25062
VH-ECF	HS25	25069
VH-ECG	FA20	493
VH-EEE	**C550**	**370**
VH-EGK	C500	051
VH-EIG	**BE40**	**RK-406**
VH-EJK	LJ45	007
VH-EJL	HS25	258295
VH-EJT	**C510**	**0214**
VH-EJY	**C550**	**156**
VH-ELC	LJ35	428
VH-ELJ	HS25	258281
VH-ELJ	LJ35	038
VH-EMM	C500	051
VH-EMO	**CS55**	**0063**
VH-EMP	LJ35	345
VH-ESM	**LJ35**	**611**
VH-ESW	**LJ35**	**071**
VH-EUV	C550	268
VH-EVF	**HS25**	**HA-0044**
VH-EVJ	**CL64**	**5370**
VH-EXA	C680	0027
VH-EXB	BE40	RK-154
VH-EXG	**C680**	**0072**
VH-EXJ	LJ60	273
VH-EXM	C550	252
VH-EXQ	**C680**	**0129**
VH-EYJ	**C550**	**550-1051**
VH-FAI	**FA20**	**380**
VH-FAX	FA20	247
VH-FCP	F900	37
VH-FCS	**C500**	**486**
VH-FFB	FA10	17
VH-FGJ	**GLEX**	**9163**
VH-FGK	C550	550-0852
VH-FHJ	C560	0278
VH-FHR	F900	138
VH-FIS	ASTR	045
VH-FJO	**F2TH**	**27**
VH-FJP	**E50P**	**50000237**
VH-FJZ	FA20	442
VH-FLJ	LJ24	349
VH-FMG	**GLEX**	**9015**
VH-FOJ	**C550**	**073**
VH-FOL	**FA50**	**159**
VH-FOX	LJ35	427
(VH-FRM)	C500	183
VH-FSA	C500	237
VH-FSQ	C500	225
VH-FSU	LJ35	463
VH-FSW	LJ35	463
VH-FSX	LJ35	046
VH-FSY	LJ35	221
VH-FSZ	LJ35	242
VH-FUM	**C500**	**582**
VH-FWO	FA20	110
VH-FYP	**C550**	**167**
VH-HEY	C560	0009
VH-HFJ	FA20	306/512
VH-HIF	FA20	255/487
VH-HKR	GLF2	69
VH-HKX	**C500**	**050**
VH-HOF	LJ35	165
VH-HPF	FA20	391
VH-HPJ	FA20	491
VH-HSP	HS25	257215
VH-HSS	HS25	257169
VH-HVH	C500	349
VH-HVM	C500	349
VH-HVM	**C550**	**550-0984**
VH-ICN	C500	024
(VH-ICT)	C550	184
VH-ICV	**GLEX**	**9393**
VH-ICX	C500	051
VH-IEJ	**GLEX**	**9680**
VH-IER	**WW24**	**359**
VH-III	HS25	258002
VH-IMP	BE40	RK-26
VH-ING	C550	156
VH-ING	**C650**	**7104**
VH-INT	**C550**	**112**
VH-INX	C550	156
VH-IPG	BE40	RK-222
VH-IQR	**GLEX**	**9230**
VH-IWJ	WW24	371
VH-IWU	CS55	0118
VH-IWW	WW24	314
VH-IXL	HS25	258040
VH-IYG	**C52A**	**0236**
VH-JBH	C550	304
VH-JCC	HS25	257046
VH-JCG	C550	112
VH-JCR	**LJ35**	**231**
VH-JCX	**LJ36**	**057**
VH-JDW	FA10	216
VH-JEP	MU30	A048SA
VH-JFT	HS25	257064
VH-JIG	LJ35	400
VH-JJA	WW24	409
VH-JLU	**CS55**	**0076**
VH-JMK	**C550**	**299**
VH-JMM	**C550**	**162**
VH-JPG	C550	112
VH-JPK	C550	307
(VH-JPL)	WW24	386
VH-JPQ	**CL60**	**1012**
VH-JPW	WW24	317
VH-JSO	**C525**	**0670**
VH-JSX	FA20	78/412
VH-JSY	FA20	85/425
VH-JSZ	FA20	90/426
VH-JVS	C550	418
VH-KDI	C550	235
VH-KDP	C550	289
VH-KEF	HS25	258295
VH-KJG	C510	0398
VH-KNJ	WW24	381
VH-KNR	**WW24**	**340**
VH-KNS	WW24	323
VH-KNU	WW24	317
VH-KRW	F2EX	58
VH-KTG	GLEX	9275
VH-KTI	C650	0144
VH-KTI	LJ35	239
VH-KTK	C550	370
VH-KXL	**C525**	**0100**
VH-KXM	**C510**	**0387**
VH-LAL	F900	192
VH-LAL	**GLF5**	**5259**
VH-LAM	CL64	5353
VH-LAT	HS25	258295
VH-LAW	F900	192
VH-LAW	**GLEX**	**9299**
VH-LAW	HS25	258295
VH-LAW	BE40	RK-35
VH-LCL	C500	538
VH-LDH	C525	0670
VH-LEF	**CL64**	**5577**
VH-LEP	GLEX	9007
VH-LEP	GLEX	9346
VH-LEP	**GLEX**	**9654**
VH-LEQ	LJ35	239
VH-LGH	LJ35	342
VH-LGH	LJ55	048
VH-LGL	C500	206
VH-LJA	**LJ35**	**649**
VH-LJB	LJ25	180
VH-LJG	C500	471
VH-LJG	**LJ35**	**121**
VH-LJJ	**LJ35**	**324**
VH-LJK	C550	184
VH-LJL	C500	123
VH-LJL	LJ35	046
VH-LJQ	**LJ45**	**286**
VH-LJX	**LJ45**	**056**
VH-LKV	HS25	258019
VH-LLW	WW24	253
VH-LLX	WW24	259
VH-LLY	WW24	272
VH-LMP	HS25	257178
VH-LMP	**HS25**	**259022**
VH-LOF	WW24	366
VH-LPJ	**LJ35**	**593**
VH-LRH	HS25	257046
VH-LRX	**LJ35**	**192**
VH-LSW	C550	099
VH-LUL	F900	192
VH-LUY	GLF6	6086
VH-LVH	**CL65**	**5814**
VH-LWZ	**E50P**	**50000306**
VH-LYG	HS25	257001
VH-LYM	**C650**	**7095**
VH-LZP	**GLEX**	**9007**
VH-MAY	C550	021
VH-MBP	**GLF4**	**4185**
VH-MBP	HS25	258712
VH-MCG	CL60	1061
VH-MCX	FA10	134
VH-MEI	FA10	50
VH-MEP	HS25	258712
VH-MGC	C550	550-0810
VH-MGC	**BE40**	**RK-97**
VH-MHO	**C510**	**0363**
VH-MIE	LJ35	459
VH-MIF	**C52B**	**0078**
VH-MIQ	FA20	255/487
VH-MIQ	LJ35	202
VH-MMC	C500	471
VH-MMC	**C560**	**0332**
VH-MOJ	C525	0138
VH-MOR	**C52A**	**0063**
VH-MQK	F9EX	159
VH-MQK	FA7X	183
VH-MQR	F9EX	159
VH-MQY	**HS25**	**258807**
VH-MSU	**C510**	**0300**
VH-MXD	**C560**	**0807**
VH-MXJ	C560	0320
VH-MXK	**CL61**	**3003**
VH-MXK	CL64	5456
VH-MXX	CL60	1061
VH-MYE	**C525**	**0638**
VH-MZL	CL61	3054
VH-MZL	CL64	5561
VH-MZL	LJ35	285
VH-MZL	LJ60	270
VH-MZL	BE40	RK-139
VH-NCF	FA20	368
VH-NCP	GLF4	1108
VH-NEQ	**C510**	**0029**
VH-NEW	C500	268
VH-NGA	WW24	387
VH-NGF	FA20	505
VH-NGH	C56X	5727
VH-NHJ	C560	0108
(VH-NIJ)	WW24	317
VH-NJA	HS25	256037
VH-NJM	HS25	258002
VH-NJW	WW24	315
VH-NKD	**GLF4**	**4086**
VH-NKD	HS25	HA-0064
VH-NKS	CL60	1073
VH-NMN	FA20	327
VH-NMR	HS25	258058
VH-NMW	C500	279
VH-NNE	**C52B**	**0196**
VH-NOU	**C500**	**602**
VH-NPP	**LJ60**	**158**
VH-NSB	C550	330
VH-NSB	**CL61**	**5074**
VH-NTH	C560	0041
VH-NTX	BE40	RK-584
VH-OCV	CL64	5625
VH-OCV	**GLEX**	**9326**
VH-OCV	LJ60	273
(VH-ODJ)	C525	0625
VH-OHE	**C560**	**0320**
VH-OIL	C500	225
VH-ORE	C550	035
VH-OSW	GLF4	1441
VH-OVB	**LJ35**	**400**
VH-OVE	**HS25**	**258366**
VH-OVS	LJ25	120
VH-OVS	**BE40**	**RK-239**
VH-OVX	**LJ31**	**033C**
VH-OYC	C550	112
VH-OYW	C550	054
VH-OZI	C650	0037
(VH-OZZ)	CL60	1057
VH-PAB	HS25	25265
VH-PDJ	FA20	491
VH-PDJ	FA50	176
VH-PFA	LJ35	661
VH-PFL	**GLF5**	**5287**
VH-PFS	**LJ45**	**168**
VH-PFV	**G150**	**233**
VH-PNF	HS25	258844
VH-PNL	BE40	RK-139
VH-PNM	**E50P**	**50000206**
VH-PNY	**FA20**	**357**

VH-POZ	C500	370
VH-PPD	**F900**	**185**
VH-PPF	FA50	187
VH-PPF	LJ35	593
VH-PSM	C550	054
VH-PSU	**C560**	**0515**
VH-PWX	**C510**	**0269**
VH-PYN	**C680**	**0262**
VH-QQZ	**C550**	**099**
VH-RAM	F2EX	162
VH-RAM	HS25	258844
VH-RCA	C750	0012
VH-RHQ	LJ35	400
VH-RIO	**HS25**	**258594**
VH-RIU	**HS25**	**258723**
VH-RJB	**C52A**	**0094**
VH-RRC	FA20	325
VH-SBC	LJ24	279
VH-SBJ	LJ35	193
VH-SBU	C650	0109
VH-SBU	LJ60	304
VH-SCC	**C550**	**550-1058**
VH-SCD	C550	370
VH-SCY	HS25	258328
VH-SDN	LJ35	342
VH-SFJ	FA50	123
VH-SGY	HS25	258019
VH-SGY	HS25	258328
VH-SGY	**HS25**	**258780**
VH-SGY	WW24	395
VH-SIY	**C525**	**0002**
VH-SJP	C510	0033
VH-SJP	C560	0332
(VH-SJP)	C510	0011
VH-SLD	LJ35	145
VH-SLE	LJ35	428
VH-SLF	LJ36	049
VH-SLJ	LJ35	046
VH-SLJ	LJ36	014
VH-SMF	C560	0320
(VH-SOA)	HS25	257169
VH-SOU	**C500**	**333**
VH-SPJ	**C650**	**0101**
VH-SQD	LJ45	033
VH-SQH	WW24	366
VH-SQJ	C510	0347
VH-SQM	**C555**	**0086**
VH-SQM	LJ45	035
VH-SQR	LJ45	195
VH-SQV	LJ45	207
VH-SQW	**C510**	**0294**
VH-SQY	**C510**	**0343**
VH-SSZ	**C650**	**0158**
VH-SWC	C500	494
VH-SWL	C550	207
VH-TEN	C750	0215
VH-TFQ	C550	160
VH-TFW	**C525**	**0442**
VH-TFY	C550	099
VH-TGG	GLEX	9143
VH-TGG	**GLEX**	**9368**
VH-TGG	GLF4	1156
VH-TGQ	GLEX	9143
VH-TGQ	PRM1	RB-225
VH-THG	LJ60	352
VH-TLJ	LJ35	091
VH-TMA	PRM1	RB-137
VH-TNN	LJ25	181
VH-TNP	C550	184
VH-TNX	HS25	258814
VH-TOM	HS25	25242
VH-TPR	LJ35	400
VH-TSL	**GLF4**	**1487**
VH-TXS	**GLF4**	**1115**
VH-UCC	C500	142
(VH-UDC)	LJ35	038
VH-ULT	LJ35	463
VH-UOH	C550	130
VH-UPB	LJ35	215
VH-URR	**CL64**	**5439**
VH-UUZ	WW24	317
VH-VBK	C550	669
(VH-VCJ)	C525	0002
VH-VDF	**C550**	**649**
VH-VDX	**GLEX**	**9101**
VH-VFP	C550	550-0882
VH-VGX	**GLEX**	**9079**
VH-VHP	**PRM1**	**RB-175**
VH-VIW	F900	70
VH-VLA	GLEX	9344
VH-VLC	CL64	5456
VH-VLI	HS25	258372
VH-VLJ	**LJ35**	**432**
VH-VLZ	C550	690
VH-VLZ	**CL64**	**5573**
VH-VPL	C560	0703
VH-VPL	**C680**	**0250**
VH-VPM	**C500**	**613**
VH-VRC	C650	7089
VH-VRC	HS25	258295
VH-VRE	**CL64**	**5561**
VH-VRL	**C560**	**0703**
VH-VSQ	**C510**	**0358**
VH-VSZ	**CL64**	**5411**
VH-VVI	**LJ45**	**262**
VH-WFE	**C560**	**0335**
VH-WFE	LJ35	221
VH-WFJ	LJ35	242
VH-WFP	LJ35	466
VH-WGJ	C550	054
VH-WII	F900	73
VH-WIM	F900	77
VH-WIO	F2EX	183
VH-WIO	**F2EX**	**259**
VH-WIZ	F900	74
VH-WIZ	F900	76
VH-WJW	FA10	134
VH-WLH	FA20	262
VH-WMY	**C525**	**0856**
VH-WNP	C550	112
VH-WNZ	C550	073
VH-WRM	C500	150
VH-WSM	ASTR	123
VH-WWY	WW24	325
VH-WXK	GLF4	1265
VH-XBP	**C550**	**550-0810**
VH-XCJ	C550	550-0810
VH-XCJ	C56X	5673
VH-XCJ	**C750**	**0015**
VH-XCU	**C56X**	**5673**
VH-XDD	C550	099
VH-XGG	GLF4	1156
VH-XMO	HS25	258243
VH-XNC	**CL64**	**5619**
VH-XND	**CL64**	**5634**
VH-XPN	**LJ60**	**290**
VH-XTT	C560	0417
VH-YDZ	C510	0070
VH-YNE	**C525**	**0521**
VH-YPT	**LJ35**	**366**
VH-YRC	BE40	RK-222
VH-YUL	**C560**	**0553**
VH-YXY	C550	550-1125
VH-YYT	E50P	50000029
VH-ZEK	**C680**	**0012**
VH-ZGP	C52A	0054
VH-ZLE	**C550**	**380**
VH-ZLT	**C550**	**550-0878**
VH-ZMD	C500	263
VH-ZSU	**CL60**	**1078**
VH-ZUH	HS25	258366
VH-ZXH	GLEX	9173
VH-ZXH	GLEX	9310
(VH-ZXH)	GLEX	9213
VH-ZYH	**WW24**	**376**
VH-ZZH	CL64	5456
VH-ZZH	GLEX	9167
VH-ZZH	LJ45	204

Bahamas

VP-BDH	HS25	25206
VP-BDH	HS25	256028
VP-BDM	LJ25	008

Bermuda

VP-B..	**GLF6**	**6176**
(VP-B..)	LJ31	074
VP-BAB	GLF3	373
VP-BAC	CL64	5309
VP-BAC	GLF5	588
VP-BAE	GLF4	4119
VP-BAE	PRM1	RB-66
VP-BAF	FA10	210
VP-BAH	**GLEX**	**9223**
"VP-BAH"	F2EX	133
VP-BAK	F2EX	110
VP-BAK	**GLF4**	**4310**
VP-BAM	GLEX	9157
VP-BAR	FA7X	11
VP-BAS	HS25	258702
VP-BAW	HS25	258237
VP-BAW	LJ31	203
VP-BBD	FA50	226
VP-BBE	C500	278
VP-BBF	CL61	3033
VP-BBF	**GLF6**	**6110**
VP-BBH	HS25	257118
VP-BBK	**GLEX**	**9122**
VP-BBO	**GLF5**	**5123**
VP-BBP	F2TH	160
VP-BBQ	PRM1	RB-181
VP-BBV	FA10	22
VP-BBW	HS25	256037
VP-BBX	GLF5	622
VP-BBZ	LJ60	328
VP-BCA	CL64	5391
VP-BCB	CL64	5397
VP-BCC	CL61	5162
VP-BCC	**GLF5**	**5148**
VP-BCD	FA50	134
VP-BCF	HS25	257214
VP-BCH	FA10	70
VP-BCI	CL61	5193
VP-BCM	HA4T	RC-14
VP-BCM	HS25	258404
VP-BCN	HS25	256035
VP-BCO	CL64	5420
VP-BCO	GLF5	5177
VP-BCO	**GLF6**	**6159**
VP-BCP	JSTR	5222
VP-BCT	GLF3	302
VP-BCT	**GLF6**	**6169**
VP-BCV	F2TH	187
VP-BCW	**HS25**	**258719**
VP-BCX	F900	193
VP-BCY	**GLEX**	**9666**
VP-BCY	LJ60	215
VP-BCZ	FA50	107
VP-BDB	C560	0503
VP-BDD	GLEX	9017
VP-BDL	F2TH	111
VP-BDS	**C525**	**0180**
VP-BDU	**GLEX**	**9057**
VP-BDV	F2EX	22
VP-BDX	CL64	5402
VP-BDY	CL64	5539
VP-BDZ	F9EX	53
VP-BEA	FA50	286
VP-BEB	GLEX	9115
VP-BEB	**GLEX**	**9369**
VP-BEC	F900	165
VP-BEE	F9EX	109
VP-BEF	F2TH	49
VP-BEF	**F9EX**	**130**
VP-BEF	FA50	283
VP-BEG	F9EX	17
VP-BEH	F900	163
VP-BEH	F9EX	75
VP-BEH	**FA7X**	**21**
VP-BEJ	**CL61**	**5061**
VP-BEK	CL30	20176
VP-BEK	HS25	257175
VP-BEM	GLEX	9036
VP-BEN	GLEX	9020
VP-BEP	GLF5	636
VP-BER	F2EX	10
VP-BES	CL65	5770
VP-BEZ	F9EX	86
VP-BEZ	LJ60	149
VP-BFC	C52A	0031
(VP-BFD)	GLF5	682
VP-BFF	GLF2	186
VP-BFH	F900	173
VP-BFM	F9EX	131
VP-BFM	**F9EX**	**282**
VP-BFM	FA50	124
VP-BFS	CL61	5149
VP-BFU	PRM1	RB-220
VP-BFV	F9EX	111
VP-BFW	FA10	54
VP-BFW	GLF4	1233
VP-BGB	LJ60	005
VP-BGC	F900	169
VP-BGD	FA10	113
VP-BGE	C500	287
VP-BGF	F900	154
VP-BGG	FA7X	5
VP-BGG	GLEX	9018
VP-BGI	F2EX	126
VP-BGL	GLF5	5043
VP-BGM	**CL65**	**5748**
VP-BGN	GLF5	5011
VP-BGO	CL64	5404
VP-BGO	**CL65**	**5851**
VP-BGS	**GLEX**	**9681**
VP-BGS	LJ60	289
VP-BGT	**CL65**	**5876**
VP-BGT	GLF2	211
VP-BHA	CL64	5307
VP-BHB	HS25	258221
VP-BHC	F2TH	26
VP-BHD	F2TH	167
VP-BHG	GLF4	1017
VP-BHH	**CL64**	**5448**
VP-BHI	C500	664
VP-BHJ	F900	138
VP-BHL	HS25	258349
VP-BHO	C500	610
VP-BHR	GLF3	346
VP-BHS	CL64	5505
VP-BHT	**LJ40**	**2050**
VP-BHW	HS25	257209
VP-BHZ	HS25	258438
VP-BID	F9EX	39
VP-BIE	CL61	3016
VP-BIH	CL61	5193
VP-BIL	FA7X	3
VP-BIP	GLF5	5109
VP-BIS	GLF4	1150
VP-BIV	GLF4	1103
VP-BIV	GLF4	1381
VP-BIV	GLF4	4092
VP-BJA	CL64	5639
VP-BJA	F900	154
VP-BJD	GLF4	1134
VP-BJD	**GLF5**	**5064**
VP-BJD	GLF5	672
VP-BJE	**CL64**	**5605**
VP-BJH	CL64	5397
VP-BJI	**GLEX**	**9276**
VP-BJJ	GLEX	9011
VP-BJK	GLF5	5200
VP-BJM	**CL64**	**5593**
VP-BJN	**GLEX**	**9273**
VP-BJR	C52A	0147
VP-BJR	**C56X**	**6073**
"VP-BJR"	C52B	0198
VP-BJS	LJ35	464
VP-BJT	**CL30**	**20255**
VP-BJV	GLF2	186
VP-BKA	CL65	5856
VP-BKA	F900	170
VP-BKB	HS25	258491
VP-BKR	HS25	258539
VP-BKG	FA50	147
VP-BKH	GLF4	1029
VP-BKI	GLF4	1029
VP-BKI	GLF4	1255
VP-BKK	HS25	25238
VP-BKM	**CL65**	**5976**
VP-BKP	C500	555
VP-BKT	GLF4	1074
VP-BKY	HS25	25150
VP-BKZ	GLF5	602
VP-BLA	CL61	3013
VP-BLA	GLF5	5024
VP-BLA	GLF5	654
VP-BLB	F900	49
VP-BLC	LJ60	311
VP-BLD	JSTR	5117/35
VP-BLF	C500	679
VP-BLF	**GLF6**	**6086**
VP-BLH	GALX	029
VP-BLM	**F900**	**72**
VP-BLN	GLF3	402
VP-BLP	F900	14
VP-BLQ	**GLEX**	**9715**
VP-BLR	GLF5	5059
VP-BLT	WW24	337
VP-BLV	C500	344
VP-BLW	**GLF5**	**5129**
VP-BMA	ASTR	092
VP-BMA	G150	228
VP-BMB	F900	51
VP-BMD	HS25	257200
VP-BME	GLF4	1058
VP-BMF	FA50	206
VP-BMG	CL64	5460
VP-BMG	**GLEX**	**9575**
VP-BMH	**HS25**	**258180**
VP-BMI	FA50	286
VP-BMJ	F2EX	1
VP-BML	CL65	5703
VP-BML	LJ31	140
VP-BMM	CL65	5928
VP-BMM	HS25	258841
VP-BMM	LJ60	054
VP-BMP	FA50	345
VP-BMP	**GLF6**	**6136**
VP-BMR	BE40	RK-133
VP-BMS	F9EX	42
VP-BMT	ASTR	144
VP-BMU	HS25	257212
VP-BMV	F900	202
VP-BMV	**GLF4**	**4150**
VP-BMW	ASTR	146
VP-BMX	**HS25**	**259012**
VP-BMX	LJ31	160
VP-BMY	GLF3	463
VP-BMY	GLF4	4096
VP-BNB	GLF4	1234
VP-BND	GLF2	199/19
VP-BNE	**GLF5**	**5051**
VP-BNF	CL64	5332
VP-BNG	CL61	5119
VP-BNG	CL64	5456
VP-BNJ	F900	120
VP-BNK	HS25	258625
VP-BNL	GLF5	607
VP-BNN	GLF4	1255
VP-BNO	GLF5	5050
VP-BNP	CL64	5657
VP-BNR	**GLF5**	**5033**
VP-BNS	C550	550-0939
VP-BNS	CL64	5384
VP-BNS	F9DX	609
VP-BNT	F2TH	121
VP-BNW	HS25	256057
VP-BNW	**HS25**	**258855**
VP-BNX	GLEX	9246
VP-BNY	GLF4	1208
VP-BNZ	GLF3	452
VP-BNZ	GLF4	1406
VP-BNZ	GLF5	509
VP-BOA	CL61	5114
VP-BOD	LJ60	220
(VP-BOE)	F2EX	128
VP-BOJ	HS25	257103
VP-BOK	GLEX	9101
VP-BOK	**GLEX**	**9505**
VP-BOK	GLF3	390
VP-BOL	GLF4	1266
VP-BOL	LJ55	022
VP-BON	ASTR	060
VP-BOO	HS25	258477
VP-BOR	**CL65**	**5918**
VP-BOR	GLF3	484
VP-BOS	GLEX	9165
VP-BOT	GLF4	1212
VP-BOW	GLEX	9141
VP-BOY	HS25	257109
VP-BOZ	F9EX	174
VP-BPA	FA50	266
VP-BPC	F900	142
VP-BPE	HS25	257040
VP-BPH	**GALX**	**187**
VP-BPI	F900	149
VP-BPO	PRM1	RB-138
VP-BPW	F900	135
VP-BPW	**F9EX**	**225**
VP-BQN	**CL65**	**5922**
VP-BRA	**F2EX**	**133**
VP-BRF	GLF4	1015
VP-BRJ	C525	0351
VP-BRJ	C52B	0198
VP-BRL	C52A	0435
VP-BRL	JSTR	5155/32
VP-BRO	F9EX	13
VP-BSA	FA50	196
VP-BSA	**GLF4**	**4115**
VP-BSC	GLEX	9142
VP-BSD	C56X	5088
VP-BSE	GLEX	9028
VP-BSF	GLF4	1058
VP-BSF	GLF4	1098
VP-BSF	LJ45	374
VP-BSG	**GLEX**	**9204**
VP-BSH	GLF4	1466
VP-BSH	JSTR	5117/35
VP-BSI	**GLF5**	**5084**
VP-BSI	HS25	258073
VP-BSJ	GLF5	555
VP-BSK	F900	125
VP-BSK	GLEX	9379
VP-BSK	HS25	258409
VP-BSL	FA50	209
VP-BSM	GLF5	555
VP-BSN	GLF5	648
VP-BSO	**F9EX**	**144**
VP-BSP	F9EX	151
VP-BSQ	GLF4	4246
VP-BSR	**GLF4**	**4161**
VP-BSS	CL64	5626
VP-BSS	GLF4	1001
VP-BST	CL64	5620
VP-BST	FA50	258
VP-BSX	**HS25**	**HB-34**
VP-BTB	**GLF4**	**4103**
VP-BTC	GLF5	5176
(VP-BTD)	GLEX	9518
VP-BTM	HS25	258233
VP-BTR	C550	693
VP-BTZ	HS25	257109
VP-BUC	FA50	107
VP-BUG	C52B	0160
VP-BUL	C560	0102
VP-BUS	GLF4	1127
VP-BVG	**GLEX**	**9193**
VP-BVK	C500	555
VP-BVM	**GLEX**	**9512**
VP-BVP	F2EX	45
VP-BVT	GLF4	1419
VP-BVV	C550	307
VP-BVV	F2EX	125
VP-BVY	FA7X	9
VP-BWB	CL61	5151
VP-BWB	**GLEX**	**9161**
(VP-BWC)	C56X	5690
VP-BWS	F900	124
VP-BXP	HS25	258494
(VP-BXX)	GLEX	9059
VP-BYS	GLF4	1381
VP-BYY	GLEX	9030
VP-BZA	GLF4	1381
VP-BZB	F900	143
VP-BZC	GLF5	5179
VP-BZE	FA50	144
VP-BZE	**FA7X**	**14**
VP-BZI	CL61	5149
VP-BZM	CL64	5626
VP-BZT	CL61	5094
VP-BZZ	C525	0235

Cayman Islands

(VP-C..)	GLEX	9061
(VP-C..)	GLF4	1228
VP-CAB	F900	101
VP-CAB	**F900**	**171**
VP-CAD	C525	0297
VP-CAE	GLF4	4031
VP-CAF	**GLEX**	**9686**
VP-CAF	HS25	258267
VP-CAG	**CL30**	**20388**
VP-CAG	HS25	HA-0166
(VP-CAH)	GLEX	9213
VP-CAI	**C56X**	**5048**
VP-CAK	**GLEX**	**9222**
VP-CAM	CL61	5090
VP-CAM	F2EX	234
VP-CAM	F2EX	89
VP-CAN	CL64	5335
VP-CAO	CL30	20100
VP-CAP	C500	583
VP-CAP	CL64	5415
VP-CAR	ASTR	133
VP-CAR	C650	0135
VP-CAR	**GLF5**	**577**
VP-CAS	**CL64**	**5500**
VP-CAS	F2TH	1
VP-CAS	GALX	029
VP-CAS	HS25	258167
VP-CAT	C500	637
VP-CAU	GLEX	9231
VP-CAV	**C680**	**0202**
VP-CAX	F900	62

VP-CAX	**GLF4**	**4314**
VP-CAZ	PRM1	RB-202
VP-CBB	GLF4	1250
VP-CBC	F2EX	61
VP-CBD	F900	16
VP-CBE	C550	119
VP-CBF	FA50	311
VP-CBF	**GLEX**	**9584**
VP-CBG	FA7X	219
VP-CBG	SBRL	465-33
VP-CBH	JSTR	5202
VP-CBK	CL64	5621
VP-CBM	C550	729
VP-CBM	**GLEX**	**9394**
VP-CBO	LJ60	350
VP-CBR	CL64	5520
VP-CBS	**CL61**	**5044**
VP-CBT	**F9DX**	**616**
VP-CBT	FA50	256
VP-CBU	HS25	HA-0095
VP-CBV	CL65	5798
VP-CBW	GLF4	1096
VP-CBX	GLF5	511
VP-CBY	**FA7X**	**204**
VP-CCC	C525	0040
VP-CCD	C500	547
VP-CCD	**LJ60**	**312**
VP-CCE	**CL64**	**5622**
VP-CCF	CL61	3031
VP-CCH	HS25	258103
VP-CCK	**GLEX**	**9115**
VP-CCL	**FA20**	**482**
VP-CCM	C550	310
VP-CCN	**GLEX**	**9362**
VP-CCO	C550	347
VP-CCP	C550	550-0857
VP-CCP	CL64	5449
VP-CCP	FA20	502
VP-CCR	CL61	5079
VP-CCV	C560	0320
VP-CCW	**GLF6**	**6122**
VP-CCX	C52B	0352
VP-CDA	F900	164
VP-CDE	HS25	258234
VP-CDE	**HS25**	**258755**
VP-CDF	**GLEX**	**9093**
VP-CDG	**FA50**	**184**
VP-CDM	C500	463
VP-CDR	ASTR	055
VP-CDV	**CL30**	**20140**
VP-CDW	C650	7034
VP-CDY	**FA7X**	**141**
VP-CEA	GLF5	5181
VP-CEA	HS25	258520
VP-CEB	GLEX	9083
VP-CED	C550	550-0870
VP-CEF	FA50	283
VP-CEG	C750	0277
VP-CEI	CL61	5125
VP-CEK	GALX	114
VP-CEK	HS25	257175
VP-CEM	**GLF5**	**5147**
VP-CEO	CL64	5539
VP-CEO	**GLEX**	**9416**
VP-CEP	G150	280
VP-CES	**GLEX**	**9311**
VP-CES	GLF5	669
VP-CET	**GLF4**	**4166**
VP-CEW	**GLEX**	**9652**
VP-CEZ	F9EX	134
VP-CEZ	FA50	138
VP-CFB	GLF4	4137
VP-CFB	LJ31	205
VP-CFD	CL64	5616
VP-CFF	C500	456
VP-CFF	GLF4	1265
VP-CFG	C500	577
VP-CFI	FA50	278
VP-CFI	HS25	257054
VP-CFJ	**HS25**	**257124**
VP-CFL	F900	164
VP-CFL	GLF4	1282
VP-CFM	C56X	5218
VP-CFO	**GLEX**	**9635**
VP-CFP	C525	0126
VP-CFP	C680	0039
VP-CFP	**C750**	**0021**
VP-CFR	F9EX	134
VP-CFS	HS25	258582
VP-CFS	**HS25**	**HA-0090**
VP-CFT	CL61	5067
VP-CFW	PRM1	RB-189
VP-CFZ	C750	0251
VP-CGA	F2TH	100
VP-CGB	F900	145
VP-CGC	F2TH	107
VP-CGD	**F9EX**	**65**
VP-CGE	C650	7077
VP-CGE	**F9EX**	**73**
VP-CGG	C56X	5361
VP-CGH	**JSTR**	**5220**
VP-CGI	GLF5	5149
VP-CGK	C650	0048
VP-CGL	C550	550-0884
VP-CGM	F2TH	160
VP-CGM	**GLEX**	**9372**
VP-CGN	GLF5	5149

VP-CGN	**GLF6**	**6112**
VP-CGO	**GLEX**	**9171**
VP-CGP	F900	163
VP-CGP	FA50	204
(VP-CGR)	F900	193
VP-CGS	**FA7X**	**210**
VP-CGS	GLEX	9102
VP-CGY	GLEX	9076
VP-CHA	F9DX	614
VP-CHE	C525	0364
VP-CHF	BE40	RK-203
VP-CHG	**F9EX**	**266**
VP-CHG	FA50	259
VP-CHH	C500	083
VP-CHH	CL65	5716
VP-CHH	GLF4	4270
VP-CHI	**GLF5**	**5415**
VP-CHK	CL61	5102
VP-CHL	CL64	5597
VP-CHL	**GLEX**	**9391**
VP-CHT	LJ25	075
VP-CHU	CL64	5510
VP-CHU	LJ60	393
VP-CHV	C525	0264
VP-CHW	GALX	004
VP-CIC	**CL61**	**5011**
VP-CID	F900	130
VP-CIF	**CL65**	**5807**
VP-CIF	GLF5	5048
VP-CIG	**FA7X**	**122**
VP-CIM	GALX	223
VP-CIO	**LJ60**	**350**
VP-CIP	GLF4	1371
VP-CIP	**GLF5**	**5048**
VP-CIS	C525	0252
VP-CIS	HS25	HA-0084
VP-CIT	F9DX	610
VP-CJA	**F2TH**	**18**
VP-CJB	C500	564
VP-CJB	CL64	5623
VP-CJC	GLEX	9271
VP-CJC	**GLEX**	**9532**
VP-CJF	F900	26
VP-CJF	LJ25	075
VP-CJI	**C525**	**0526**
VP-CJJ	**GLF6**	**6123**
VP-CJK	**GLEX**	**9611**
VP-CJL	GLF5	5216
VP-CJL	GLF5	5324
VP-CJM	**GLF5**	**5181**
VP-CJP	CL61	5022
VP-CJP	HS25	25258
VP-CJR	C550	388
VP-CJS	F2EX	242
VP-CJS	**FA7X**	**220**
VP-CJT	**GLEX**	**9374**
VP-CKB	**GLF6**	**6068**
VP-CKC	**GLF5**	**5111**
VP-CKD	GLF4	4088
VP-CKG	ASTR	096
VP-CKG	GLF5	5327
VP-CKK	BE40	RK-200
VP-CKM	C560	0413
VP-CKM	**GLEX**	**9445**
VP-CKN	HS25	258615
VP-CKR	CL64	5597
VP-CKR	**GLEX**	**9310**
(VP-CKR)	GLEX	9170
VP-CLA	GLF4	1402
VP-CLB	**F9EX**	**34**
VP-CLD	C550	351
VP-CLD	FA50	134
VP-CLE	CL61	3066
VP-CLI	**GLF4**	**4255**
VP-CLJ	**CL65**	**5776**
VP-CLK	**GLF5**	**5511**
VP-CLN	FA50	251
VP-CLO	**F9EX**	**90**
VP-CLP	**GLEX**	**9267**
VP-CLS	**FA7X**	**226**
VP-CLT	LJ35	016
VP-CLU	HS25	257058
VP-CLV	CL30	20041
VP-CLX	HS25	257091
VP-CLY	GLEX	9071
VP-CLZ	**CL61**	**5193**
VP-CMA	C500	547
VP-CMA	**GLEX**	**9243**
VP-CMA	HS25	258835
VP-CMB	CL64	5618
VP-CMB	HS25	258475
VP-CMB	LJ25	118
VP-CMC	CL61	5044
VP-CMC	**GLF4**	**4269**
VP-CMD	C550	726
VP-CMD	F2EX	82
VP-CMF	GLF4	1062
VP-CMG	**GLF4**	**4093**
VP-CMG	GLF5	519
VP-CMH	C680	0171
VP-CMI	F2EX	113
VP-CMM	**GLF6**	**6152**
VP-CMO	C500	070
VP-CMP	HS25	257214
VP-CMR	GLF4	1117
VP-CMS	C560	0457
VP-CMS	**CL64**	**5581**

VP-CMW	**FA7X**	**267**
VP-CMX	FA7X	108
VP-CMY	**GLF4**	**4203**
VP-CMZ	HS25	259021
VP-CNA	**GLEX**	**9341**
VP-CNF	C525	0153
VP-CNJ	GLF3	426
VP-CNK	CL64	5621
(VP-CNK)	CL65	5843
VP-CNM	C550	550-0857
VP-CNM	C56X	5070
VP-CNP	GLF3	496
VP-CNP	**GLF5**	**5461**
VP-CNR	GLF5	5113
VP-CNR	**GLF6**	**6034**
VP-CNY	**GLEX**	**9270**
VP-CNZ	F9EX	74
VP-COD	CL64	5562
VP-COD	HS25	258816
VP-COJ	CL61	5152
VP-COJ	CL64	5367
VP-COJ	GLEX	9526
VP-COK	CL61	3024
VP-COK	HS25	257028
VP-COM	**C500**	**318**
VP-CON	C500	238
VP-COO	**CL65**	**5781**
VP-COO	LJ60	350
VP-COP	**CL64**	**5552**
VP-COP	GLEX	9050
VP-COR	**GLF6**	**6040**
VP-COU	GLEX	9084
VP-CPA	GLF2	204
VP-CPC	C56X	5215
(VP-CPC)	GLEX	9005
VP-CPF	**CL30**	**20256**
VP-CPH	**BE40**	**RK-188**
VP-CPO	CL61	5165
VP-CPT	**GLEX**	**9509**
VP-CPT	HS25	259004
VP-CPY	**GLF5**	**5324**
VP-CQQ	**GLF4**	**4282**
VP-CRA	C550	585
VP-CRA	HS25	257118
VP-CRB	LJ60	125
VP-CRC	GLEX	9196
VP-CRD	PRM1	RB-57
VP-CRF	FA50	61
VP-CRH	C680	0226
"VP-CRH"	C500	083
VP-CRK	**CL64**	**5362**
VP-CRO	**GLF5**	**5270**
VP-CRR	**CL61**	**5129**
VP-CRS	CL65	5739
VP-CRS	**FA7X**	**268**
VP-CRS	GALX	008
VP-CRS	HS25	258520
VP-CRT	FA50	88
VP-CRX	CL61	3052
VP-CRY	GLF4	1176
VP-CRZ	**GLF6**	**6085**
VP-CSA	**GALX**	**249**
VP-CSB	**GLEX**	**9263**
VP-CSC	C560	0439
VP-CSD	HS25	HA-0177
VP-CSF	GLF4	1390
VP-CSG	FA7X	106
(VP-CSG)	GALX	159
VP-CSH	GLF4	4202
VP-CSI	CL65	5847
VP-CSJ	FA7X	113
VP-CSM	**JSTR**	**5092/58**
VP-CSN	C560	0401
VP-CSP	C500	165
VP-CSP	**HS25**	**258210**
VP-CSS	**C56X**	**6055**
VP-CST	**CL64**	**5520**
VP-CSW	**FA7X**	**143**
VP-CSX	**FA7X**	**147**
VP-CTA	C525	0172
VP-CTA	**GLF5**	**5275**
VP-CTB	C500	432
VP-CTE	C550	716
VP-CTE	**GLF5**	**5304**
VP-CTF	C550	716
VP-CTG	**FA7X**	**104**
VP-CTH	**GLF4**	**4248**
VP-CTJ	C550	068
(VP-CTN)	C525	0399
VP-CTP	**GLEX**	**9335**
VP-CTR	GLF4	1379
VP-CTS	**GLF6**	**6082**
VP-CTS	HS25	25243
VP-CTT	**F2EX**	**139**
VP-CTT	F900	161
VP-CTY	LJ55	035
VP-CUA	**GLF5**	**5409**
VP-CUB	GLF2	207/34
VP-CUC	LJ55	035
VP-CUH	**FA7X**	**201**
VP-CUP	**CL64**	**5403**
VP-CUT	ASTR	080
VP-CVH	**G280**	**2072**
VP-CVI	GLF5	5092
VP-CVI	**GLF6**	**6121**
VP-CVK	CL61	5049
VP-CVK	**GLF5**	**5092**

VP-CVL	LJ45	059
VP-CVP	BE40	RK-300
VP-CVT	**GLF5**	**5102**
VP-CVU	GLEX	9257
VP-CVV	GLEX	9272
VP-CWI	FA50	159
VP-CWM	C550	667
VP-CWM	C56X	5136
VP-CWN	**GLEX**	**9321**
VP-CWQ	**GLEX**	**9501**
VP-CWW	C525	0124
VP-CWW	**GLEX**	**9432**
VP-CWW	PRM1	RB-74
VP-CXP	HS25	258728
VP-CXX	HS25	259032
VP-CYA	**GLEX**	**9628**
VP-CYK	C750	0097
VP-CYL	GLF6	6122
(VP-CYL)	FA7X	165
VP-CYM	GLF4	1090
VP-CYT	**GLEX**	**9361**
VP-CYY	**GLEX**	**9030**
VP-CZA	**GLF6**	**6016**
VP-CZB	**GLF6**	**6129**
VP-CZJ	**GLEX**	**9705**
VP-CZK	GLEX	9244
VP-CZL	**GLEX**	**9540**
VP-CZS	**FA7X**	**257**
VP-CZZ	**GLF6**	**6025**

British Virgin Islands

(VP-LV.)	HS25	258409

Zimbabwe

VP-WKY	LJ25	160

Bermuda

VQ-BAA	**FA7X**	**46**
VQ-BAM	GLEX	9139
VQ-BCC	**GLEX**	**9646**
VQ-BCE	**GLF4**	**4148**
VQ-BDG	CL65	5765
VQ-BDK	**PRM1**	**RB-216**
VQ-BDS	**GALX**	**220**
VQ-BEB	GLEX	9283
VQ-BEP	**PRM1**	**RB-125**
VQ-BFN	**FA7X**	**27**
VQ-BFT	C555	0144
VQ-BGA	**GLF4**	**4092**
VQ-BGG	**FA7X**	**93**
VQ-BGN	**GLF5**	**5218**
VQ-BGS	**GLEX**	**9254**
VQ-BHA	**FA7X**	**84**
VQ-BHP	**GLF5**	**5268**
VQ-BHY	GLEX	9151
VQ-BIH	GLEX	9393
VQ-BIJ	**F2EX**	**214**
VQ-BIL	BE40	RK-480
VQ-BIS	GLEX	9213
VQ-BJA	GLEX	9268
VQ-BJW	F9EX	250
VQ-BKI	**GLEX**	**9342**
VQ-BLA	**GLF5**	**5215**
VQ-BLP	**FA7X**	**132**
VQ-BLV	GLF5	5221
VQ-BLY	**GLF5**	**5221**
VQ-BMC	GLF5	5266
VQ-BMJ	CL30	20126
(VQ-BMJ)	CL65	5832
VQ-BMM	**GLEX**	**9198**
VQ-BMT	**GLF4**	**1362**
VQ-BMZ	**GLF6**	**6102**
VQ-BNH	**F9EX**	**258**
VQ-BNJ	**BE40**	**RK-84**
VQ-BNP	**GLEX**	**9339**
VQ-BNT	**FA7X**	**135**
VQ-BNZ	GLF6	6009
VQ-BNZ	**GLF6**	**6158**
VQ-BOK	GLEX	9396
VQ-BPG	GLEX	9568
VQ-BPH	**HS25**	**HA-0108**
VQ-BRI	HA4T	RC-57
VQ-BRL	GLEX	9385
VQ-BRZ	**CL64**	**5350**
VQ-BSC	GLEX	9297
VQ-BSF	**FA7X**	**113**
VQ-BSN	**FA7X**	**58**
VQ-BSO	**FA7X**	**64**
VQ-BSP	**FA7X**	**83**
VQ-BTV	**FA7X**	**175**
VQ-BUX	**CL64**	**5393**
VQ-BVA	**HS25**	**258813**
VQ-BVS	**FA7X**	**48**
VQ-BYT	**F9EX**	**28**
VQ-BZB	CL65	5763
VQ-BZB	**GLEX**	**9253**
VQ-BZM	**GLF4**	**4123**
VQ-BZZ	F900	87

Swaziland

VQ-ZIL	HS25	25080

Bermuda

(VR-B..)	FA50	175
(VR-B..)	FA50	231
(VR-B..)	FA50	66
(VR-B..)	HS25	258182
VR-BAA	CL61	5156
VR-BAB	GLF3	373
VR-BAC	CL64	5309
(VR-BBP)	CL60	1073
VR-BBY	C500	433
VR-BCC	CL61	5162
VR-BCF	HS25	257214
VR-BCF	LJ24	038
VR-BCG	FA20	3/403
VR-BCH	FA10	70
VR-BCI	CL61	5193
VR-BCJ	FA20	55/410
VR-BCY	C560	0376
VR-BDC	GLF4	1183
VR-BDK	FA20	198/466
VR-BEM	LJ25	098
VR-BES	ASTR	017
VR-BFF	FA10	7
VR-BFR	LJ36	012
VR-BFV	LJ25	094
VR-BFW	FA10	54
VR-BFX	LJ35	054
VR-BGB	C650	0077
VR-BGD	HS25	25157
VR-BGF	LJ25	098
VR-BGL	GLF2	124
VR-BGO	GLF2	124
VR-BGS	HS25	256011
VR-BGT	GLF2	211
VR-BHA	CL64	5307
VR-BHA	GLF2	45
VR-BHB	LJ36	007
VR-BHC	LJ24	267
VR-BHD	GLF2	231
VR-BHE	HS25	257020
VR-BHF	JSTR	5062/12
VR-BHG	C550	273
VR-BHG	GLF4	1017
VR-BHH	HS25	257140
VR-BHI	C500	664
VR-BHJ	F900	138
VR-BHJ	FA10	104
VR-BHL	FA20	429
VR-BHR	GLF2	165/37
VR-BHV	LJ55	045
VR-BHW	HS25	257209
VR-BHX	FA50	140
VR-BHY	FA20	496
VR-BHZ	FA20	492
VR-BIZ	C550	469
VR-BJA	F900	154
VR-BJA	FA50	110
VR-BJB	FA20	244
VR-BJD	GLF2	219/20
VR-BJD	GLF4	1134
VR-BJD	LJ36	008
VR-BJE	GLF3	347
VR-BJG	GLF2	112
VR-BJH	JSTR	5215
VR-BJI	JSTR	5149/11
VR-BJJ	FA20	401
VR-BJJ	FA50	228
VR-BJK	C500	372
VR-BJN	C500	532
VR-BJO	LJ36	008
VR-BJQ	GLF2	140/40
VR-BJS	C650	0119
VR-BJT	GLF2	137
VR-BJV	GLF2	186
VR-BJW	C500	674
VR-BJX	F900	4
VR-BJY	C650	0040
VR-BJZ	GLF4	1005
VR-BKA	MU30	A058SA
VR-BKB	LJ35	370
VR-BKE	GLF4	1037
VR-BKG	FA50	147
VR-BKH	FA20	237/476
VR-BKI	GLF4	1029
VR-BKJ	CL60	1016
VR-BKK	HS25	25238
(VR-BKL)	GLF4	1048
VR-BKN	HS25	25240
VR-BKP	C500	555
VR-BKR	FA20	133
VR-BKS	GLF3	390
VR-BKT	GLF4	1074
VR-BKU	GLF4	1046
VR-BKV	GLF4	1055
VR-BKY	HS25	25150
VR-BKZ	HS25	257199
VR-BLA	CL61	3013
VR-BLB	F900	49
VR-BLC	GLF4	1093
VR-BLD	CL60	1035
VR-BLF	C500	679
(VR-BLG)	BE40	RJ-22
VR-BLH	GLF4	1008
VR-BLJ	GLF2	40
VR-BLL	FA50	136
VR-BLM	F900	72
VR-BLN	GLF3	402
VR-BLO	GLF3	390
VR-BLP	HS25	258139
VR-BLQ	HS25	258175
VR-BLR	GLF4	1127
VR-BLT	F900	88

VR-BLU	LJ35	389
VR-BLV	C500	344
VR-BLW	C500	442
VR-BMA	CL61	3012
VR-BMB	HS25	25240
VR-BMD	HS25	257200
VR-BME	ASTR	041
VR-BMF	FA50	206
VR-BMG	C650	0185
VR-BMK	CL61	5029
VR-BML	GLF2	70/1
VR-BMN	LJ24	267
VR-BMO	C500	083
VR-BMQ	GLF2	42/12
VR-BMT	C500	083
VR-BMY	GLF3	463
VR-BNB	HS25	257002
VR-BND	GLF2	199/19
(VR-BND)	HS25	258164
VR-BNE	GLF2	51
VR-BNF	CL61	5069
VR-BNG	CL61	5119
VR-BNI	LJ35	620
VR-BNJ	F900	120
VR-BNO	GLF3	308
VR-BNT	FA10	73
VR-BNV	BE40	RJ-36
VR-BNW	HS25	256057
VR-BNX	GLF3	320
VR-BNY	GLF4	1208
VR-BNZ	GLF3	452
VR-BOA	CL61	5114
VR-BOB	GLF3	375
VR-BOB	GLF4	1120
VR-BOJ	HS25	257103
VR-BOK	GLF3	390
VR-BOL	LJ55	022
VR-BON	ASTR	060
VR-BOS	GLF2	13
VR-BOT	GLF4	1212
VR-BOY	GLF4	1009
(VR-BPA)	HS25	258139
(VR-BPB)	HS25	258175
VR-BPE	HS25	257040
VR-BPF	C550	599
VR-BPG	HS25	258165
VR-BPI	F900	149
VR-BPM	HS25	258186
VR-BPN	HS25	258239
VR-BPT	HS25	257109
VR-BPW	F900	135
VR-BQA	CL61	5130
VR-BQB	C560	0301
VR-BQF	LJ55	039
(VR-BQG)	JSTR	5155/32
(VR-BQH)	HS25	258233
VR-BRF	GLF4	1015
VR-BRJ	FA20	275
VR-BRL	JSTR	5155/32
VR-BRM	GLF2	194
VR-BRM	GLF2	91
VR-BRS	HS25	256004
VR-BSH	JSTR	5117/35
VR-BSI	HS25	258073
VR-BSK	F900	125
VR-BSL	GLF3	304
VR-BSS	GLF4	1001
VR-BST	LJ60	035
VR-BTM	HS25	258233
VR-BTQ	C500	340
VR-BTR	C550	693
VR-BTT	FA50	32
VR-BTZ	HS25	257109
VR-BUB	C500	345
VR-BUC	FA50	107
VR-BUL	C560	0102
VR-BUS	GLF4	1127
VR-BVI	HS25	25278
VR-BVV	C550	307
VR-BWB	CL61	5151
VR-BWS	F900	124
VR-BYE	C550	599
VR-BZE	FA50	144

Cayman Islands

(VR-C..)	FA20	150/445
(VR-C..)	LJ35	356
VR-CAC	WW24	285
VR-CAD	LJ35	432
VR-CAD	WW24	276
VR-CAE	FA50	228
VR-CAG	GLF2	231
VR-CAR	CL61	3017
VR-CAR	FA20	440
VR-CAS	GLF2	4/8
VR-CAS	HS25	258167
VR-CAT	C500	637
VR-CAU	WW24	72
VR-CAW	JSTR	5133
VR-CBB	GLF4	1250
VR-CBB	WW24	350
VR-CBC	GLF2	167
VR-CBD	HS25	256041
VR-CBK	WW24	285
VR-CBL	FA50	95
VR-CBL	GLF4	1243
VR-CBM	C550	729
VR-CBM	GLF2	34
VR-CBO	FA50	98
"VR-CBP"	CL60	1067
VR-CBR	FA50	9
VR-CBT	FA20	237/476
VR-CBU	LJ35	396
VR-CBW	GLF4	1096
VR-CCC	C650	0023
(VR-CCC)	JSTR	5006/40
VR-CCE	C550	441
VR-CCF	FA20	285/504
VR-CCH	LJ25	091
VR-CCI	C550	046
VR-CCL	FA20	482
VR-CCN	GLF3	345
VR-CCP	C500	083
VR-CCQ	FA20	515
VR-CCQ	FA50	208
VR-CCQ	FA50	73
VR-CCR	CL61	5079
VR-CCV	C560	0320
VR-CCV	CL61	5075
VR-CCX	HS25	258214
VR-CCY	JSTR	5085
(VR-CDA)	BE40	RK-25
VR-CDB	FA20	305
VR-CDE	HS25	258234
VR-CDF	FA50	111
VR-CDG	HS25	256013
VR-CDH	LJ25	213
VR-CDI	LJ35	264
VR-CDK	LJ55	138
VR-CDM	C500	463
VR-CDN	C525	0085
VR-CDT	FA20	341
VR-CEB	C500	094
VR-CEE	SBRL	465-22
VR-CEG	CL61	5104
VR-CEJ	HS25	258021
VR-CES	F900	140
VR-CEZ	FA50	138
VR-CFG	C500	577
VR-CFI	FA50	176
VR-CFL	GLF4	1282
VR-CGB	F900	145
VR-CGD	LJ25	075
VR-CGP	FA50	204
VR-CGP	FA50	63
VR-CGS	LJ31	040
VR-CHA	CL61	5153
VR-CHB	C550	559
VR-CHC	FA20	515
VR-CHF	C500	637
VR-CHH	C500	083
VR-CHJ	LJ31	040
VR-CHK	CL61	5102
VR-CHT	LJ25	075
(VR-CIA)	C500	577
VR-CIC	CL61	5011
VR-CID	F900	130
VR-CIL	WW24	289
VR-CIM	C650	7035
VR-CIT	C550	407
(VR-CJA)	LJ55	033
VR-CJB	C500	564
VR-CJJ	CL61	5142
VR-CJP	HS25	25258
VR-CJR	C550	388
(VR-CKC)	CL61	5073
VR-CKK	CL60	1033
VR-CKP	HS25	257159
VR-CLA	FA10	203
VR-CLD	FA50	134
VR-CLE	CL61	3066
VR-CLI	CL60	1054
VR-CLN	FA50	251
VR-CMC	CL61	5044
(VR-CMC)	GLF3	423
VR-CMF	GLF3	374
VR-CMF	GLF4	1062
VR-CMG	ASTR	034
VR-CML	LJ55	033
VR-CMO	C500	070
VR-CMS	C500	511
VR-CMZ	HS25	259021
VR-CNJ	GLF3	426
VR-CNM	JSTR	5229
VR-CNS	C560	0177
VR-CNV	FA50	224
VR-COG	BE40	RK-7
VR-COJ	CL61	5043
VR-COJ	CL61	5104
VR-COJ	CL61	5152
VR-COM	C500	318
VR-CPA	GLF2	204
VR-CPO	CL61	5165
VR-CPT	HS25	259004
VR-CQZ	FA50	168
VR-CRT	FA50	88
VR-CSA	F900	61
VR-CSF	HS25	256065
VR-CSM	JSTR	5092/58
VR-CSP	C500	165
VR-CSS	C550	030
VR-CTA	F900	16
VR-CTA	GLF4	1278
VR-CTB	C500	432
VR-CTE	C550	716
VR-CTG	GLF3	450
VR-CTL	C560	0023
VR-CUB	GLF2	207/34
VR-CUC	LJ35	203
VR-CVD	HS25	257107
VR-CVK	CL61	5049
VR-CVP	C650	0210
VR-CWI	FA50	159
VR-CWM	C550	667
VR-CWW	C500	044
VR-CXX	HS25	259032
VR-CYM	GLF4	1090
VR-CYR	HFB3	1057

Hong Kong

VR-HIM	HS25	257001
VR-HIN	HS25	257025
VR-HSS	HS25	257169

India

VT-...	**BE40**	**RK-400**
(VT-...)	C56X	5711
VT-AAA	HS25	257161
VT-AAT	**F2TH**	**225**
VT-ABG	**HS25**	**258716**
(VT-ADA)	GLF5	5205
VT-AGP	**HS25**	**258835**
VT-AHI	**GLEX**	**9651**
VT-AJI	**E50P**	**50000205**
VT-AJJ	**E55P**	**50500159**
VT-AJM	**HS25**	**HA-0085**
VT-AKU	**F9EX**	**177**
VT-AMA	GLF4	1060
VT-ANF	**PRM1**	**RB-128**
VT-AON	**C56X**	**5724**
VT-APF	**CL30**	**20395**
VT-APL	**CL65**	**5787**
VT-ARA	**C56X**	**5115**
VT-ARF	**F2TH**	**143**
VT-ARR	HS25	258819
VT-ARV	**GALX**	**098**
VT-AUV	**CL65**	**5706**
VT-AVH	**F2TH**	**103**
VT-AVS	**E50P**	**50000204**
VT-AVV	**C56X**	**5259**
VT-AYV	**F2EX**	**153**
VT-BAJ	**GLEX**	**9149**
VT-BAV	ASTR	143
VT-BIP	**C52A**	**0235**
VT-BIR	**C56X**	**6106**
VT-BJA	C52A	0170
(VT-BJC)	C52A	0430
(VT-BJD)	C52A	0436
VT-BKG	PRM1	RB-225
VT-BKL	**HS25**	**HA-0103**
VT-BNF	**C550**	**550-1096**
VT-BPS	**C52A**	**0410**
VT-BRK	**F2EX**	**169**
VT-BRS	**GLF5**	**5162**
VT-BRT	**C52A**	**0373**
VT-BSL	**C56X**	**5816**
VT-BTA	HS25	258904
VT-BTB	HS25	258909
VT-BTC	HS25	258912
VT-CAP	F9EX	205
VT-CLA	**C56X**	**5010**
VT-CLB	**C550**	**661**
VT-CLC	**C550**	**698**
VT-CLD	**C550**	**727**
VT-CMO	**HS25**	**HB-30**
VT-COT	F2TH	36
VT-CPA	**GLF5**	**5427**
VT-CRA	**LJ45**	**019**
VT-CSP	**C56X**	**5368**
VT-DBA	**GLEX**	**9289**
VT-DBC	**LJ60**	**384**
VT-DBG	**CL64**	**5342**
VT-DHA	**GLEX**	**9111**
VT-DLF	GLF4	1231
VT-DOV	**C52A**	**0222**
VT-EAU	HS25	258120
VT-EHS	LJ28	29-003
VT-EHT	GALX	149
VT-EIH	LJ28	29-004
VT-ENR	GLF3	420
VT-EQZ	HS25	25133
VT-ERO	WW24	33
VT-ETG	**CS55**	**0089**
VT-EUN	C550	393
VT-EUX	**C560**	**0299**
VT-FAF	**HS25**	**258745**
VT-FTL	**HS25**	**258980**
VT-GKB	**G150**	**280**
VT-GRG	BE40	RK-566
VT-HBC	HS25	258531
VT-HCB	HS25	258476
VT-HDL	**F2TH**	**70**
VT-HGL	**F2TH**	**231**
VT-HJA	**HA4T**	**RC-26**
VT-HMA	**GLEX**	**9317**
VT-IAG	**E50P**	**50000203**
VT-IAJ	E50P	50000192
VT-IAM	**C510**	**0438**
VT-IBG	**GLEX**	**9658**
VT-IBR	**CL64**	**5425**
VT-IBS	**C550**	**550-1076**
VT-ICA	**HS25**	**HA-0061**
VT-IPA	**C650**	**0203**
VT-ISH	**F9EX**	**166**
VT-JHP	**HS25**	**258794**
VT-JSB	GLEX	9114
VT-JSE	**CL30**	**20196**
(VT-JSI)	GLEX	9410
VT-JSK	**GLEX**	**9214**
VT-JSP	C52A	0207
VT-JSS	**C56X**	**5594**
VT-JSY	**GLEX**	**9527**
VT-JUA	CL30	20273
VT-JUI	**CL30**	**20591**
VT-JUM	GALX	213
VT-KAV	CL64	5370
VT-KBN	**PRM1**	**RB-239**
VT-KJB	**GLEX**	**9446**
VT-KMB	**CS55**	**0135**
VT-KNB	**HS25**	**258815**
VT-LTA	**HS25**	**HA-0165**
VT-LTC	**HS25**	**HA-0185**
VT-MAM	**LJ60**	**394**
VT-MGF	CL64	5401
VT-MKJ	**CL65**	**5848**
VT-MON	**C52A**	**0126**
VT-MPA	HS25	257172
VT-MST	GLF4	1379
VT-NAB	**C525**	**0619**
VT-NGS	**CL64**	**5314**
VT-NJB	**C52A**	**0163**
(VT-NKL)	CL65	5813
VT-NKR	GLF6	6115
VT-OAM	BE40	RJ-38
VT-OBE	HS25	257215
VT-OBR	**HS25**	**258838**
VT-ONE	**GLF4**	**1231**
VT-OPJ	**C525**	**0112**
VT-PIL	**CL30**	**20006**
VT-PLA	**GALX**	**077**
VT-PLL	GLF4	1254
VT-PLP	GLF4	1254
VT-PSB	**C52A**	**0402**
VT-RAK	**CL30**	**20174**
VT-RAL	PRM1	RB-23
VT-RAN	HS25	258521
VT-RAY	HS25	258165
VT-RBK	HS25	258716
VT-RGX	**FA7X**	**49**
VT-RHM	CS55	0089
VT-RKA	**C52A**	**0520**
VT-RPG	**BE40**	**RK-190**
VT-RPL	**HS25**	**258465**
VT-RSP	**CL30**	**20356**
VT-RSR	**HS25**	**HB-7**
VT-RTR	PRM1	RB-192
VT-RVL	**F2TH**	**101**
VT-SBK	**F9EX**	**89**
VT-SDK	**GLEX**	**9228**
VT-SFM	**E50P**	**50000210**
VT-SGT	C550	709
VT-SMI	**GLF5**	**525**
VT-SNG	**GLEX**	**9493**
VT-SNP	**GALX**	**244**
VT-SRA	**HS25**	**258422**
VT-SRR	HS25	257191
VT-SSF	**PRM1**	**RB-243**
VT-SSN	HS25	258805
VT-STV	CL65	5750
VT-STV	GLEX	9262
VT-SWC	C56X	5168
VT-SWP	LJ25	367
VT-TAT	**F2TH**	**65**
VT-TAX	**C52A**	**0047**
VT-TAY	C52A	0176
VT-TBT	**F2TH**	**49**
VT-TDT	**F2EX**	**159**
VT-TEL	BE40	RJ-46
VT-TMS	GLF5	5294
VT-TRI	**LJ45**	**290**
VT-TSK	**E50P**	**50000238**
VT-TTA	FA20	511
VT-TVM	**C52A**	**0470**
VT-TVR	**BE40**	**RK-511**
VT-UBG	HS25	25254
VT-UDR	**HS25**	**HA-0187**
VT-UNO	**LJ60**	**412**
VT-UPM	**HS25**	**HA-0100**
VT-UPN	**PRM1**	**RB-236**
VT-VAP	**HS25**	**258384**
VT-VDD	**C56X**	**5783**
VT-VDM	**HA4T**	**RC-41**
VT-VED	C680	0056
VT-VID	**C52A**	**0378**
(VT-VIP)	HA4T	RC-25
VT-VKR	**F2TH**	**604**
VT-VLM	**F2TH**	**8**
VT-VLN	**F2EX**	**117**
VT-VPA	**HS25**	**258415**
VT-VPS	C550	269
VT-VRL	**PRM1**	**RB-219**
VT-VSA	LJ40	2101
(VT-XLS)	C56X	5594
VT-ZAP	**E50P**	**50000338**
VT-ZST	**CL64**	**5629**

Antigua

V2-LSF	HS25	256065

Namibia

V5-ACE	**C500**	**347**
V5-CAL	**C500**	**071**
V5-CDM	C560	0151
V5-GON	**FA7X**	**127**
V5-KJY	LJ24	165
V5-LOW	C500	071
V5-LRJ	**LJ45**	**228**
V5-NAG	**LJ31**	**091**
V5-NAM	**F900**	**103**
V5-NDB	**C56X**	**5267**
V5-NPC	**LJ31**	**138**
V5-OGL	**C500**	**080**
V5-PJM	**GLF3**	**341**
V5-RON	**LJ45**	**476**
V5-TTO	**LJ45**	**181**
V5-TUC	**LJ31**	**101**
V5-WAW	**BE40**	**RK-499**

Brunei

V8-001	GLF5	509
V8-001	GLF5	515
V8-007	GLF3	436
V8-007	GLF4	1059
V8-007	GLF4	1109
V8-007	GLF5	515
V8-008	GLF4	1176
V8-009	GLF3	436
V8-009	GLF4	1150
V8-009	GLF4	1202
V8-009	GLF5	509
V8-A11	GLF3	436
V8-ALI	GLF4	1059
V8-ALI	GLF4	1109
V8-ALI	GLF4	1150
V8-HB3	GLF3	436
V8-MSB	GLF4	1202
V8-RB1	GLF4	1059
V8-SR1	GLF4	1059
V8-SR1	GLF4	1109
V8-SR1	GLF4	1150

Mexico

XA-	LJ24	197
XA-...	**C500**	**475**
XA-...	**C550**	**240**
XA-...	**C550**	**247**
XA-...	**C550**	**716**
XA-...	**C650**	**0239**
XA-...	**CL60**	**1055**
XA-...	**CL64**	**5578**
XA-...	**E50P**	**50000313**
XA-...	**EA50**	**000108**
XA-...	**F900**	**170**
XA-...	**FA20**	**489**
XA-...	**GLF2**	**169**
XA-...	**HS25**	**25216**
XA-...	**HS25**	**257010**
XA-...	**HS25**	**257066**
XA-...	**HS25**	**258543**
XA-...	**HS25**	**258691**
XA-...	LJ24	039
XA-...	LJ24	093
XA-...	LJ24	213
XA-...	**LJ24**	**216**
XA-...	LJ24	237
XA-...	LJ24	252
XA-...	**LJ25**	**102**
XA-...	**LJ25**	**190**
XA-...	**LJ25**	**216**
XA-...	**LJ25**	**264**
XA-...	LJ25	268
XA-...	**LJ25**	**273**
XA-...	**LJ25**	**277**
XA-...	LJ25	280
XA-...	**LJ25**	**360**
XA-...	**LJ35**	**221**
XA-...	**LJ35**	**326**
XA-...	**LJ35**	**329**
XA-...	**LJ35**	**620**
XA-...	**LJ40**	**2026**
XA-...	**LJ45**	**252**
XA-...	**LJ60**	**347**
XA-...	**MU30**	**A081SA**
XA-...	**SBRL**	**276-25**
XA-...	**SBRL**	**306-109**
XA-...	**SBRL**	**306-121**
XA-...	**SBRL**	**380-21**
XA-...	**SBRL**	**380-47**
XA-...	SBRL	380-54
XA-...	SBRL	465-23
XA-...	WW24	56
(XA-...)	C500	443
(XA-...)	C560	0268
(XA-...)	C650	0078
(XA-...)	CL61	5142
(XA-...)	FA10	56
(XA-...)	GLF3	318
(XA-...)	HS25	25018
(XA-...)	HS25	25066
(XA-...)	JSTR	5089
(XA-...)	LJ24	065
(XA-...)	LJ35	077
XA-AAA	LJ24	208
(XA-AAF)	SBRL	277-7
(XA-AAG)	SBRL	277-2
(XA-AAH)	SBRL	285-25

(XA-AAI)	SBRL	277-6
(XA-AAJ)	SBRL	285-1
XA-AAK	C550	486
XA-AAL	JSTR	5231
XA-AAP	LJ31	032
XA-AAS	FA50	31
XA-AAS	LJ25	305
XA-AAW	SBRL	282-85
XA-AAY	**FA10**	**27**
XA-ABA	GLF2	136
XA-ABA	**GLF3**	**426**
XA-ABA	GLF4	1425
XA-ABB	LJ24	299
XA-ABC	GLF2	161
XA-ABC	SBRL	306-63
XA-ABD	GLF3	393
XA-ABD	**LJ45**	**338**
XA-ABE	**C550**	**550-0887**
XA-ABF	**CL61**	**5163**
XA-ABF	FA20	327
XA-ABH	LJ25	298
XA-ABS	**BE40**	**RK-574**
XA-ACA	FA20	179
XA-ACC	JSTR	5212
XA-ACC	LJ24	297
XA-ACC	LJ35	176
XA-ACD	SBRL	380-50
XA-ACE	SBRL	306-12
XA-ACH	C650	0218
XA-ACI	FA20	7
XA-ACN	HS25	256038
XA-ACR	**C52B**	**0091**
XA-ACX	LJ25	373
XA-ADC	SBRL	306-6
XA-ADD	LJ24	298
XA-ADJ	**LJ24**	**060**
XA-ADR	**G150**	**257**
XA-ADR	HS25	25146
XA-AEA	**C56X**	**5503**
XA-AEB	**C650**	**0099**
XA-AED	LJ45	140
XA-AEI	**C500**	**213**
XA-AEM	HS25	HB-22
XA-AEN	HS25	258232
XA-AET	HS25	258502
XA-AET	**HS25**	**HA-0045**
XA-AEV	SBRL	306-125
XA-AEX	**GLF4**	**1064**
XA-AEZ	CS55	0090
XA-AFA	**BE40**	**RK-316**
XA-AFG	SBRL	306-130
(XA-AFG)	FA50	94
XA-AFH	**LJ25**	**332**
XA-AFP	GLF2	136
XA-AFS	**HS25**	**HB-16**
XA-AFS	BE40	RK-259
XA-AFU	C550	661
XA-AFW	SBRL	282-63
XA-AFX	**LJ31**	**159**
XA-AGA	**C500**	**469**
XA-AGL	**HS25**	**25236**
XA-AGL	HS25	256046
XA-AGN	C550	082
XA-AGT	SBRL	306-58
XA-AHC	**GLF2**	**161**
XA-AHM	GLF2	161
XA-AHM	**GLF5**	**548**
XA-AIG	**LJ60**	**403**
XA-AIM	LJ45	077
XA-AIS	GLF4	1098
XA-AJL	**LJ25**	**120**
XA-ALA	FA50	188
XA-ALA	LJ45	210
XA-ALC	**GLF5**	**5116**
XA-ALE	LJ35	047
XA-ALF	**LJ45**	**127**
XA-ALN	**LJ45**	**231**
XA-ALT	**C52B**	**0307**
XA-ALV	LJ25	124
XA-AMI	**HS25**	**257098**
XA-AMY	**BE40**	**RK-447**
XA-AOV	**SBRL**	**380-60**
XA-APC	**SBRL**	**465-16**
XA-APD	SBRL	282-123
XA-APD	SBRL	306-33
XA-APE	**F900**	**178**
XA-ARA	GLF2	79
XA-ARB	**LJ45**	**284**
XA-ARD	**LJ31**	**209**
XA-ARE	SBRL	306-146
XA-ARE	SBRL	465-27
XA-ARG	LJ24	068
XA-ARO	**CL30**	**20200**
XA-ARQ	**LJ31**	**141**
XA-ARS	C650	0156
XA-ASH	**HS25**	**258082**
XA-ASI	**GLF4**	**1180**
XA-ASP	**LJ25**	**315**
XA-ASR	C500	199
XA-ASS	**E50P**	**50000271**
XA-AST	CL64	5357
XA-ATA	C550	486
XA-ATA	LJ35	264
XA-ATC	**HS25**	**256026**
XA-ATC	SBRL	282-114
XA-ATE	**SBRL**	**306-123**
XA-ATI	**GLF4**	**4254**
XA-ATL	**GLF5**	**5052**
(XA-ATP)	G150	290
XA-ATT	**E50P**	**50000342**
XA-ATT	HA4T	RC-40
XA-ATZ	**G150**	**290**
XA-AVE	**F2TH**	**175**
XA-AVE	FA50	22
XA-AVE	WW24	160
XA-AVR	GLF2	200
XA-AVR	SBRL	465-27
XA-AVV	**LJ25**	**079**
XA-AVX	**C52B**	**0192**
XA-AVZ	**GLF4**	**1010**
XA-AYL	**GLEX**	**9119**
XA-AZT	**GLF5**	**554**
XA-BAE	**C750**	**0136**
XA-BAF	SBRL	282-39
XA-BAL	GLF2	237/43
XA-BAL	GLF4	1114
XA-BAL	GLF5	546
XA-BAL	**GLF6**	**6033**
XA-BAT	C510	0044
XA-BAY	**G280**	**2007**
XA-BBA	LJ25	223
XA-BBE	LJ24	255
XA-BBO	GLF2	164
XA-BCC	CRVT	36
XA-BCC	FA20	284
XA-BCE	JSTR	5053/2
XA-BEB	**JSTR**	**5132/57**
XA-BEG	**F9EX**	**242**
XA-BEG	F9EX	33
XA-BEG	FA50	224
XA-BEM	HS25	25068
XA-BET	**C500**	**296**
XA-BFX	LJ45	111
XA-BLE	PRM1	RB-193
XA-BLZ	**F2EX**	**251**
XA-BLZ	GLF4	1467
XA-BNG	**HS25**	**HA-0028**
XA-BNG	BE40	RJ-33
XA-BNM	F9EX	55
XA-BNO	LJ35	336
XA-BOA	C500	607
XA-BOJ	HS25	25060
XA-BOM	**CL30**	**20439**
XA-BQA	WW24	276
XA-BRE	GLF2	185
XA-BRE	LJ35	373
XA-BRE	LJ60	058
XA-BRG	LJ31	032
XA-BUA	GLEX	9322
XA-BUA	**GLF5**	**5464**
XA-BUD	**HA4T**	**RC-71**
XA-BUX	LJ35	020
XA-BUX	**LJ35**	**176**
XA-BUY	LJ24	270
XA-BVG	GLF4	1013
XA-BWB	**HS25**	**258581**
XA-BYP	HS25	257041
XA-BZA	**LJ55**	**090**
XA-CAB	**HS25**	**HA-0208**
XA-CAG	GLF4	1197
XA-CAH	C525	0210
XA-CAH	HS25	256044
XA-CAN	**E55P**	**50500064**
XA-CAO	**LJ25**	**282**
XA-CAP	**C550**	**550-1070**
XA-CAP	LJ24	349
XA-CAR	**C680**	**0050**
XA-CCB	SBRL	306-12
XA-CCC	LJ25	219
XA-CCC	**LJ31**	**082**
XA-CDF	C560	0433
XA-CDF	**C680**	**0206**
XA-CDT	**F2EX**	**20**
XA-CEG	FA10	146
XA-CEN	SBRL	306-26
XA-CFX	**LJ45**	**209**
XA-CGF	LJ40	2040
XA-CHA	HS25	258241
XA-CHA	SBRL	380-58
XA-CHC	**CL30**	**20024**
XA-CHD	**F2EX**	**308**
XA-CHE	**GLF4**	**4201**
XA-CHG	**GLF4**	**1524**
XA-CHG	HA4T	RC-48
XA-CHG	HS25	258731
XA-CHK	**HS25**	**258727**
XA-CHP	SBRL	306-22
XA-CHR	GLF2	98/38
XA-CHR	GLF4	1195
XA-CHR	GLF4	1250
XA-CHR	**GLF5**	**5182**
XA-CHY	**G150**	**265**
XA-CIA	**C680**	**0004**
XA-CIS	SBRL	306-63
XA-CLA	BE40	RK-3
XA-CMA	**LJ45**	**189**
XA-CMM	**F2EX**	**121**
XA-CMN	SBRL	306-56
XA-COC	LJ25	194
XA-COI	LJ35	620
XA-COI	LJ60	174
XA-COL	HS25	25086
XA-CON	**JSTR**	**5228**
XA-CPL	**G150**	**269**
XA-CPQ	**GLF5**	**533**
XA-CPQ	SBRL	282-48
XA-CRS	**C680**	**0061**
XA-CSM	**C550**	**726**
XA-CSS	**E55P**	**50500335**
XA-CST	**LJ25**	**213**
XA-CTK	C650	7069
XA-CTL	**LJ31**	**070**
XA-CUN	SBRL	306-128
XA-CUR	SBRL	306-127
XA-CUZ	HS25	25279
XA-CVD	LJ35	370
XA-CVE	JSTR	5214
XA-CVS	**GLF2**	**167**
XA-CXW	**FA7X**	**32**
XA-CYA	**LJ31**	**021**
XA-CYS	**SBRL**	**282-79**
XA-CZG	**LJ35**	**162**
XA-DAB	**GLF5**	**546**
XA-DAD	HS25	258799
XA-DAJ	C500	241
XA-DAK	**HS25**	**258702**
XA-DAK	LJ25	190
XA-DAN	**HS25**	**25158**
XA-DAN	SBRL	282-26
XA-DAR	**HS25**	**258753**
XA-DAS	HS25	258176
XA-DAT	LJ24	322
XA-DAZ	LJ25	309
XA-DAZ	**LJ35**	**340**
XA-DCO	SBRL	306-38
XA-DCS	**HS25**	**25078**
XA-DET	**LJ24**	**337**
XA-DFN	**F2EX**	**289**
XA-DGO	LJ60	172
XA-DGP	C525	0329
XA-DHM	**GLF3**	**455**
XA-DIJ	LJ24	269
XA-DIN	HS25	25273
XA-DIN	LJ31	026
XA-DIW	HS25	25226
XA-DLA	**CL30**	**20203**
(XA-DMS)	FA50	249
XA-DOS	BE40	RK-238
XA-DPA	**HS25**	**HB-10**
XA-DPS	GLF4	1227
XA-DRE	**GALX**	**062**
XA-DRM	C56X	5307
XA-DSC	SBRL	306-56
XA-DST	**C56X**	**5819**
XA-DUB	LJ25	306
XA-DUC	**FA20**	**269**
XA-DUQ	FA50	146
XA-DVH	**BE40**	**RK-603**
XA-EAJ	**GLF5**	**5267**
XA-EAJ	GLF5	604
XA-EAJ	GLF6	6182
XA-EAS	LJ25	355
XA-EBF	**HS25**	**258646**
XA-ECM	SBRL	306-89
XA-ECR	FA20	513
XA-EEA	LJ45	102
XA-EEU	SBRL	282-54
XA-EFL	**HS25**	**257123**
XA-EFM	**LJ45**	**089**
XA-EFX	LJ31	234
XA-EGC	SBRL	282-61
XA-EGE	**HS25**	**HB-25**
XA-EGL	**C510**	**0324**
XA-EGS	**BE40**	**RK-487**
XA-EGU	**LJ31**	**143**
XA-EHR	GLF2	30/4
XA-EKO	C500	140
XA-EKT	JSTR	5234
XA-ELK	**GLF4**	**4218**
XA-ELM	**HS25**	**258051**
XA-ELR	LJ25	290
XA-ELU	LJ35	261
XA-ELX	**HS25**	**258413**
XA-EMA	HS25	25282
XA-EMB	**LEG5**	**55000030**
XA-EMM	**LJ45**	**139**
XA-EMO	JSTR	5140
XA-EMY	**C650**	**7014**
XA-EOF	GLF4	1473
XA-EOF	GLF5	5008
XA-EPM	SBRL	380-19
XA-ERH	GLF3	323
XA-ERM	**HS25**	**257164**
XA-ESC	GLF2	164
XA-ESP	**HS25**	**HA-0068**
XA-ESQ	HS25	25028
XA-ESQ	LJ25	234
XA-ESR	SBRL	282-59
XA-ESR	**BE40**	**RK-331**
XA-ESS	LJ24	037
XA-ETP	**BE40**	**RK-494**
XA-EVG	**CL64**	**5357**
XA-EXC	**HS25**	**258170**
XA-EXE	LJ45	271
XA-EXL	HS25	256061
XA-EYA	GLF2	96
XA-EYA	GLF4	1388
XA-EZI	**CL30**	**20367**
XA-FAF	**BE40**	**RK-359**
XA-FAX	**G280**	**2053**
XA-FCP	C650	0165
XA-FCP	GLF2	136
XA-FCP	**GLF4**	**1404**
XA-FEM	**GLF5**	**5281**
XA-FES	JSTR	5155/32
XA-FEX	F9EX	46
XA-FFF	LJ35	042
XA-FGL	**C750**	**0287**
XA-FGP	**LJ60**	**221**
XA-FGS	**HS25**	**258047**
XA-FHR	GLF2	30/4
XA-FHR	JSTR	5158
XA-FHR	JSTR	5231
XA-FHS	JSTR	5215
XA-FIR	C550	718
XA-FIU	FA10	83
XA-FIU	JSTR	5100/41
XA-FIW	LJ24	296
XA-FJM	**C750**	**0221**
XA-FLC	**F2EX**	**242**
XA-FLG	**FA20**	**364**
XA-FLM	**C680**	**0137**
XA-FLM	FA20	364
XA-FLX	**BE40**	**RK-503**
XA-FLY	**LJ60**	**250**
XA-FMK	**HS25**	**257068**
XA-FMR	**LJ25**	**274**
XA-FMT	LJ35	672
XA-FMT	**LJ60**	**337**
XA-FMU	LJ25	249
XA-FMX	C750	0119
XA-FMX	G280	2053
XA-FNP	SBRL	306-63
XA-FNY	GLF2	175
XA-FNY	GLF2	211
XA-FOU	GLF2	152
XA-FOU	GLF3	449
XA-FRC	**HS25**	**259023**
XA-FRD	CL30	20078
XA-FRI	C650	7081
XA-FRO	**BE40**	**RK-110**
"XA-FRO"	CL30	20078
XA-FRP	HS25	25185
XA-FSA	**HS25**	**258664**
XA-FSB	**F900**	**114**
XA-FTC	FA50	80
XA-FTN	SBRL	282-80
XA-FUD	**C680**	**0053**
XA-FVK	FA50	35
XA-FVK	SBRL	465-27
XA-FXL	F900	174
XA-FYN	HS25	258386
XA-GAA	**C550**	**082**
XA-GAC	GLF2	155/14
XA-GAE	F900	137
XA-GAM	LJ24	033
XA-GAN	C650	0218
XA-GAN	**C680**	**0043**
XA-GAO	**BE40**	**RK-353**
XA-GAP	SBRL	465-8
XA-GAV	**C650**	**7019**
XA-GBA	LJ24	260
XA-GBM	**C650**	**0234**
XA-GBP	**HS25**	**258749**
XA-GCC	**HS25**	**258252**
XA-GCD	CL61	5121
XA-GCH	FA50	50
XA-GCH	SBRL	282-115
XA-GCM	LJ31	230
XA-GDO	LJ35	449
XA-GDW	SBRL	265-86
XA-GEG	GLF2	253
XA-GEN	**C550**	**550-0999**
XA-GEO	CL61	5059
XA-GEO	LJ24	337
XA-GFB	HS25	258075
XA-GFC	FA50	80
XA-GGG	**LJ25**	**147**
XA-GGP	**HS25**	**258476**
XA-GGR	SBRL	282-65
XA-GHR	SBRL	380-58
XA-GIC	HS25	257206
XA-GIC	HS25	258183
XA-GIE	HS25	258302
XA-GIH	SBRL	306-72
XA-GIM	**C680**	**0231**
XA-GIT	C650	7025
XA-GJC	**C650**	**0035**
XA-GLG	HS25	258583
XA-GLS	**HS25**	**25179**
XA-GMD	F9EX	99
XA-GMD	FA50	291
XA-GMD	LJ31	005
XA-GME	**C680**	**0522**
XA-GME	CL61	5128
XA-GMG	C650	0201
XA-GMG	**C750**	**0001**
XA-GMM	HS25	258314
XA-GMO	C680	0004
XA-GMO	**F2TS**	**719**
XA-GMP	**C550**	**254**
XA-GMX	**GLF4**	**4102**
XA-GNI	F2EX	20
XA-GNI	F2TH	60
XA-GNI	**FA7X**	**252**
XA-GNL	LJ25	329
XA-GOB	**BE40**	**RK-301**
XA-GOC	HS25	25107
XA-GOR	**FA7X**	**261**
XA-GPA	FA10	23
(XA-GPE)	LJ40	2040
XA-GPO	**C550**	**550-1012**
XA-GPR	**CL30**	**20084**
XA-GPS	**C650**	**0226**
XA-GRB	CL61	5149
XA-GRB	CL64	5375
XA-GRB	**CL65**	**5829**
XA-GRB	HS25	259021
XA-GRB	LJ25	309
XA-GRE	**CL65**	**6063**
XA-GRR	**LJ40**	**2013**
XA-GSL	**LJ60**	**183**
XA-GSS	**C560**	**0533**
XA-GTC	**HS25**	**25205**
XA-GTE	HS25	258554
XA-GTP	**LJ45**	**256**
XA-GTR	F900	107
XA-GUA	**CL61**	**5076**
XA-GUB	HS25	25185
XA-GUR	SBRL	306-122
XA-GUR	SBRL	306-131
XA-GUR	SBRL	306-98
XA-GXG	**CL30**	**20043**
XA-GYA	C550	287
XA-GYR	SBRL	282-6
XA-GZA	JSTR	5100/41
XA-GZZ	**C52C**	**0003**
XA-HEV	C500	382
XA-HEW	FA20	250
XA-HFM	HS25	25107
XA-HFM	LJ45	246
XA-HGF	FA50	236
XA-HGF	LJ31	026
XA-HHF	**F2TH**	**85**
XA-HHF	FA20	327
XA-HHF	FA50	236
XA-HHH	**HS25**	**258554**
XA-HHR	SBRL	306-6
XA-HIT	**C680**	**0014**
XA-HMX	**CL61**	**5131**
XA-HNY	**GLF4**	**1338**
XA-HNY	JSTR	5162
XA-HOF	**C52C**	**0038**
XA-HOK	SBRL	282-17
XA-HOM	HS25	257199
XA-HOM	**HS25**	**258171**
XA-HOO	C500	175
XA-HOS	LJ35	045
XA-HOS	LJ35	341
XA-HOU	HS25	25060
XA-HPR	**C525**	**0618**
XA-HRM	JSTR	5066/46
XA-HRM	LJ31	026
XA-HRM	LJ31	044
XA-HTL	**C56X**	**5248**
XA-HUR	**LJ45**	**385**
XA-HVP	C650	0032
XA-HXM	HS25	257084
XA-HYS	LJ35	243
XA-IAS	PRM1	RB-9
XA-IBC	**LJ60**	**124**
XA-ICA	LJ60	027
XA-ICF	HS25	258581
XA-ICG	FA20	159
XA-ICK	SBRL	306-86
XA-ICO	C560	0461
XA-ICO	C56X	5196
XA-ICO	**C680**	**0318**
XA-ICP	C550	631
XA-ICU	**LJ35**	**171**
XA-IEM	C500	384
XA-IGE	CL64	5580
XA-III	FA20	264
XA-IIT	HS25	25152
XA-IIX	C500	274
XA-IJC	**HS25**	**258904**
XA-IKE	**LJ45**	**176**
XA-ILV	GLF2	195
XA-IMY	CL61	5189
XA-INF	C650	0198
XA-INF	CS55	0010
XA-INK	CS55	0010
XA-INM	**SBRL**	**465-24**
XA-IRE	**LJ60**	**058**
XA-ISH	HS25	258036
XA-ISR	CL60	1057
XA-ISR	F900	147
XA-IZA	HS25	258129
XA-JAI	HS25	257171
XA-JAM	BE40	RK-56
XA-JAO	**LJ45**	**042**
XA-JAX	LJ25	104
XA-JBG	**HS25**	**258715**
XA-JBT	**F2EX**	**125**
XA-JBT	HS25	258715
XA-JCE	C500	544
XA-JCE	SBRL	306-93
XA-JCG	**CL64**	**5328**
XA-JCG	JSTR	5140
XA-JCP	CL30	20014
XA-JCT	HS25	258581
XA-JDN	**SBRL**	**282-24**
XA-JEF	GLF5	604
XA-JEL	C500	250
XA-JEP	**CL64**	**5653**

XA-JEQ	HS25	256047
XA-JET	**HS25**	**258628**
XA-JET	BE40	RK-163
(XA-JEW)	C500	533
XA-JEX	C500	530
XA-JEZ	C550	140
XA-JFE	C500	544
XA-JFE	CL61	5059
XA-JFE	**CL64**	**5525**
XA-JFE	JSTR	5145
XA-JGC	**LJ60**	**311**
XA-JGT	**CL30**	**20007**
XA-JHE	**GALX**	**086**
XA-JHR	JSTR	5066/46
XA-JHS	**FA7X**	**192**
XA-JIK	SBRL	306-130
XA-JIN	LJ25	210
XA-JIQ	**LJ24**	**317**
XA-JIX	HS25	257079
XA-JJA	BE40	RJ-33
XA-JJJ	LJ35	460
XA-JJS	CL61	5097
XA-JJS	**GLF4**	**1113**
XA-JJS	JSTR	5101/15
XA-JJS	LJ60	131
XA-JKM	**LJ60**	**175**
XA-JLV	C500	021
XA-JLV	LJ24	136
XA-JMB	**LJ31**	**230**
XA-JMC	HS25	258035
XA-JMD	SBRL	306-119
XA-JMF	**LJ45**	**178**
XA-JML	JSTR	5206
XA-JML	**SBRL**	**306-125**
XA-JMM	**BE40**	**RJ-33**
XA-JMN	JSTR	5134/50
XA-JMR	**HS25**	**258530**
XA-JMS	HS25	258582
XA-JOC	**LJ25**	**303**
XA-JOV	C500	035
XA-JPA	C550	689
XA-JPA	**BE40**	**RK-56**
XA-JPF	**HS25**	**258327**
XA-JPG	**LJ45**	**235**
XA-JPS	GLF4	1250
XA-JRF	C550	642
XA-JRF	HS25	25202
XA-JRF	HS25	256018
XA-JRF	HS25	257059
XA-JRF	**SBRL**	**380-32**
XA-JRH	LJ35	609
XA-JRM	ASTR	039
XA-JRS	**LJ45**	**281**
XA-JRT	**C510**	**0034**
XA-JRV	C500	136
XA-JSC	LJ24	123
XA-JSC	LJ25	152
XA-JSC	**LJ25**	**173**
XA-JSO	LJ24	123
XA-JUA	C500	247
XA-JUD	SBRL	282-43
XA-JUE	SBRL	282-48
XA-JUL	**HS25**	**258006**
XA-JUZ	HS25	25014
XA-JVG	**HS25**	**HB-73**
XA-JWM	LJ60	221
XA-JWM	**LJ60**	**430**
XA-JYC	LJ31	030
XA-JYL	**LJ25**	**336**
XA-JYO	C550	689
XA-JZL	**CL61**	**5158**
XA-KAC	HS25	257110
XA-KAH	C500	289
XA-KAJ	LJ28	28-004
XA-KAR	**F2TS**	**710**
XA-KBA	HS25	258984
XA-KBL	**HS25**	**HA-0052**
XA-KCM	LJ45	418
XA-KCM	**LJ60**	**291**
XA-KEW	HS25	257096
XA-KEY	LJ25	222
XA-KIM	CL61	3015
XA-KIM	**CL65**	**5838**
XA-KIQ	C550	181
XA-KIS	HS25	257102
XA-KJM	BE40	RK-56
XA-KKK	**LJ25**	**169**
XA-KLZ	**LJ60**	**297**
XA-KMX	C550	247
XA-KMX	C650	0039
XA-KMX	**FA50**	**292**
XA-KOF	**HS25**	**25065**
XA-KON	HS25	257108
XA-KTX	**GLF4**	**1250**
XA-KTY	**HS25**	**258004**
XA-KUG	WW24	224
XA-KUJ	C500	313
XA-KUO	**GLF5**	**604**
XA-KUT	HS25	256028
XA-KYE	**C750**	**0204**
XA-LAA	GLF4	4026
XA-LAN	LJ35	267
XA-LAP	**C56X**	**5618**
XA-LAP	LJ25	336
XA-LAR	LJ24	074
XA-LAS	**HS25**	**258626**
XA-LAU	**HS25**	**258295**
XA-LBS	**LJ35**	**332**
XA-LCA	GLF3	489
XA-LEG	HS25	257046
XA-LEG	SBRL	282-100
XA-LEG	SBRL	380-15
XA-LEG	BE40	RJ-60
XA-LEG	BE40	RK-171
(XA-LEI)	SBRL	306-115
XA-LEL	SBRL	282-68
XA-LEO	C500	273
XA-LET	LJ25	244
XA-LEX	**HS25**	**258187**
XA-LEY	C650	0073
XA-LEY	**HS25**	**258731**
XA-LFA	**F2EX**	**77**
XA-LFJ	**C550**	**264**
XA-LFU	HS25	25112
XA-LGM	LJ24	033
XA-LIJ	WW24	285
XA-LIM	C500	571
XA-LIO	FA10	40
XA-LIX	SBRL	282-128
XA-LLA	CL30	20191
XA-LLL	**LJ25**	**015**
XA-LMA	SBRL	282-137
XA-LMG	BE40	RK-416
XA-LML	HS25	257076
XA-LML	LJ35	296
XA-LML	**SBRL**	**282-115**
XA-LMS	**LJ31**	**012**
XA-LNK	**LJ24**	**174**
XA-LNP	**GLF3**	**323**
XA-LOA	BE40	RK-242
(XA-LOA)	LJ40	2117
XA-LOB	E55P	50500064
XA-LOB	**E55P**	**50500303**
XA-LOB	FA20	39
XA-LOF	**C550**	**550-0989**
XA-LOF	LJ25	338
XA-LOH	FA50	9
XA-LOK	FA10	175
XA-LOQ	SBRL	306-145
XA-LOR	WW24	319
XA-LOS	**C56X**	**6065**
XA-LOT	C550	244
XA-LOV	HS25	25283
XA-LPK	**C52C**	**0025**
XA-LPZ	**CL65**	**5810**
XA-LRA	FA50	238
XA-LRA	SBRL	306-63
XA-LRD	**LJ31**	**176**
XA-LRJ	LJ25	359
XA-LRL	C550	619
XA-LRX	LJ45	067
XA-LTH	C550	462
XA-LTH	C650	0101
XA-LUC	SBRL	465-55
XA-LUD	C500	587
XA-LUF	CL64	5321
XA-LUN	C500	353
XA-LUN	**HS25**	**257127**
XA-LUV	C500	598
XA-LUZ	LJ25	314
XA-LVS	**LJ45**	**191**
XA-LVV	**C550**	**550-0855**
XA-LYM	WW24	133
XA-LZZ	GLF2	18
XA-MAH	HS25	256065
XA-MAK	GALX	013
XA-MAK	WW24	342
XA-MAK	WW24	350
"XA-MAK"	GALX	013
XA-MAL	C500	373
XA-MAL	C550	274
XA-MAM	**FA20**	**506**
XA-MAR	**FA7X**	**10**
XA-MAR	WW24	264
XA-MAV	F2TH	149
XA-MAV	**GLF5**	**5393**
XA-MAZ	JSTR	5079/33
XA-MBC	**LJ45**	**521**
XA-MBD	**LJ45**	**482**
XA-MBM	HS25	25030
XA-MBM	**HS25**	**25101**
XA-MBO	**LJ45**	**524**
XA-MBS	**LJ45**	**522**
XA-MBT	**LJ45**	**492**
XA-MBU	**LJ45**	**457**
XA-MCA	**LJ31**	**071**
XA-MCB	SBRL	380-36
XA-MCC	**LJ25**	**219**
XA-MDC	**GLF3**	**427**
XA-MDK	**GALX**	**080**
XA-MDM	**LJ60**	**089**
XA-MEG	**ASTR**	**154**
XA-MEM	GLF2	69
XA-MER	**HS25**	**258027**
XA-MES	**LJ60**	**321**
XA-MET	**LJ25**	**305**
XA-MEX	BE40	RK-196
XA-MEX	BE40	RK-396
XA-MEY	GLF3	252
XA-MGM	FA10	100
XA-MGM	LJ31	101
XA-MGM	LJ60	052
XA-MGM	**LJ60**	**405**
XA-MGM	BE40	RK-16
XA-MHA	LJ25	222
XA-MHP	**LJ60**	**131**
XA-MHU	**HDJT**	**42000019**
XA-MIC	GLF3	323
XA-MII	BE40	RJ-58
XA-MII	BE40	RK-83
XA-MIK	JSTR	5066/46
XA-MIL	**C750**	**0124**
XA-MIR	HS25	25068
XA-MIX	GLF2	237/43
XA-MJE	**SBRL**	**282-65**
XA-MJG	LJ31	044
XA-MJI	HS25	257033
XA-MKA	**C52C**	**0002**
XA-MKI	CL61	5158
XA-MKI	**GLF5**	**664**
XA-MKY	CL61	5158
XA-MKY	HS25	256064
XA-MLA	**HS25**	**HB-1**
XA-MLG	SBRL	465-48
XA-MLP	HS25	258383
XA-MMA	**HA4T**	**RC-13**
XA-MMD	**LJ24**	**326**
XA-MMM	**FA10**	**36**
XA-MMO	LJ25	352
XA-MMX	C56X	5639
XA-MNA	SBRL	282-115
XA-MOV	LJ24	269
XA-MPS	**GLF5**	**654**
XA-MPS	LJ35	460
XA-MRS	LJ31	024
XA-MSA	FA20	327
XA-MSH	HS25	257128
XA-MSH	LJ35	380
XA-MSL	**BE40**	**RK-298**
XA-MSO	**E50P**	**50000347**
XA-MTZ	C650	0218
XA-MUI	WW24	160
XA-MUL	SBRL	306-50
XA-MUU	**LJ25**	**008**
XA-MVG	LJ45	251
XA-MVG	SBRL	282-134
XA-MVR	FA50	94
XA-MVT	SBRL	380-42
XA-MXN	**C550**	**550-1099**
XA-MYM	**GALX**	**099**
XA-MYN	**CL61**	**5142**
XA-NAY	FA20	269
XA-NCC	**FA20**	**264**
XA-NDY	**CL65**	**5944**
XA-NEM	HS25	257158
XA-NGS	GLEX	9014
XA-NGS	HS25	258232
XA-NIC	**HS25**	**258552**
XA-NJM	**LJ40**	**2067**
XA-NLA	**LJ24**	**180**
XA-NLK	LJ24	109
XA-NOG	LJ25	349
XA-NOI	**HA4T**	**RC-15**
XA-NSA	HS25	257126
XA-NTE	HS25	256020
XA-NTE	HS25	257098
XA-NTE	**HS25**	**258638**
XA-NTG	**CL30**	**20348**
XA-NTR	**LJ31**	**195**
XA-NXT	**HS25**	**HB-22**
XA-OAC	C500	514
XA-OAC	C550	297
XA-OAC	**HS25**	**HB-9**
XA-OAC	BE40	RJ-29
XA-OAC	BE40	RJ-36
XA-OAF	SBRL	380-55
XA-ODC	C500	217
XA-ODC	C550	553
XA-OEM	**GLF5**	**540**
XA-OFA	LJ35	370
XA-OFM	**CL61**	**5155**
XA-OHS	CL61	5087
XA-OLA	**HS25**	**258757**
XA-OLE	**LJ31**	**044**
XA-OLI	JSTR	5148
XA-ONE	**LJ60**	**127**
(XA-ONE)	LJ60	220
XA-ORA	LJ60	245
XA-ORI	**LJ60**	**334**
XA-ORO	**LJ35**	**290**
XA-OVA	**CL30**	**20232**
XA-OVA	F900	141
XA-OVG	GLEX	9119
XA-OVR	F900	141
XA-OVR	FA50	88
XA-OVR	GLEX	9119
XA-OVR	**GLEX**	**9564**
XA-OVR	SBRL	306-130
XA-OVR	SBRL	465-12
XA-PAG	**HS25**	**259032**
XA-PAR	**LJ40**	**2042**
XA-PAX	SBRL	306-123
XA-PAZ	C500	060
XA-PAZ	G150	255
XA-PAZ	**G280**	**2048**
XA-PAZ	LJ25	309
XA-PBT	**HS25**	**258601**
XA-PBX	**LJ45**	**171**
XA-PCC	**FA20**	**159**
XA-PCH	GLF3	397
XA-PCO	**GALX**	**056**
XA-PEI	SBRL	306-20
XA-PEK	SBRL	306-38
XA-PEN	LJ31	005
XA-PES	JSTR	5130
(XA-PEV)	C500	607
XA-PFA	LJ24	329
XA-PFM	FA20	515
XA-PGB	F9EX	129
XA-PGO	JSTR	5069/20
XA-PIC	C500	141
XA-PIC	LJ31	076
XA-PIC	SBRL	282-39
XA-PIH	SBRL	282-102
XA-PIJ	C550	082
XA-PIL	GLEX	9100
XA-PIL	LJ55	014
XA-PIM	LJ25	368
XA-PIN	LJ35	201
XA-PIP	C650	0146
XA-PIU	**LJ25**	**293**
XA-PLA	C56X	5077
XA-PMH	**C650**	**0188**
XA-POG	LJ25	080
XA-POI	LJ25	152
XA-POJ	WW24	161
XA-PON	SBRL	380-39
XA-POO	JSTR	5158
XA-POP	LJ25	324
XA-POQ	LJ25	351
XA-POR	C550	273
XA-POR	SBRL	306-49
XA-POS	**GALX**	**103**
XA-POS	LJ24	249
XA-POU	JSTR	5053/2
XA-PRA	**LJ45**	**067**
XA-PRO	**C650**	**0032**
XA-PRO	LJ25	216
XA-PRO	SBRL	306-72
XA-PRR	FA50	319
XA-PSD	GLF2	98/38
XA-PSD	JSTR	5132/57
XA-PTR	CL61	5165
XA-PTR	**GLF4**	**1467**
XA-PUE	FA20	393
XA-PUF	**WW24**	**153**
XA-PUI	LJ35	277
XA-PUL	JSTR	5151
XA-PUR	SBRL	306-2
XA-PUV	GLF4	1079
XA-PVM	FA20	179
XA-PVR	C650	0076
XA-PVR	SBRL	465-12
XA-PVR	WW24	174
XA-PWR	JSTR	5211
XA-PYC	**HS25**	**258644**
XA-PYC	LJ35	336
XA-PYN	C650	0099
XA-PYN	C650	7088
XA-PYN	BE40	RK-68
XA-QLO	**LJ45**	**271**
XA-QPL	**HS25**	**258161**
XA-QUE	LJ45	067
XA-RAA	**HS25**	**258220**
XA-RAB	**LJ40**	**2047**
XA-RAD	**HS25**	**258527**
XA-RAN	**LJ31**	**179**
(XA-RAN)	LJ45	509
XA-RAP	CL60	1057
XA-RAP	**SBRL**	**306-88**
XA-RAQ	LJ24	329
XA-RAR	**BE40**	**RJ-32**
XA-RAV	LJ35	290
XA-RAV	**LJ60**	**400**
XA-RAX	LJ25	218
XA-RBP	**GLF2**	**14**
XA-RBS	GLF2	14
XA-RBS	GLF4	1102
XA-RBV	**HS25**	**258275**
XA-RCF	**LJ31**	**061**
XA-RCG	LJ25	330
XA-RCH	HS25	25101
XA-RCH	**LJ25**	**373**
XA-RCL	**HS25**	**258150**
XA-RCM	GLF3	312
XA-RCM	**GLF4**	**1081**
XA-RCR	JSTR	5214
XA-RDD	HS25	25030
XA-RDL	**LJ31**	**078**
XA-RDM	C560	0342
XA-RDY	SBRL	380-60
XA-REA	LJ24	331
XA-REC	SBRL	306-1
XA-RED	**HS25**	**258690**
XA-RED	SBRL	282-26
XA-REE	LJ25	314
XA-REG	SBRL	282-130
XA-REI	SBRL	306-20
XA-REK	LJ24	285
XA-REN	C550	273
XA-REO	WW24	124
XA-RET	F2TH	184
XA-RET	F9EX	203
XA-RET	**GLF5**	**5282**
XA-RET	HS25	258004
XA-RET	WW24	409
XA-REY	FA20	127
XA-REY	FA20	393
XA-RFB	SBRL	306-87
XA-RFC	**BE40**	**RK-416**
XA-RFS	LJ31	005
XA-RGB	F900	15
XA-RGB	F9EX	129
XA-RGB	GLF5	5282
XA-RGB	JSTR	5079/33
XA-RGC	SBRL	282-39
XA-RGC	SBRL	282-48
XA-RGC	SBRL	282-61
XA-RGC	SBRL	306-125
XA-RGG	HS25	259037
XA-RGH	**LJ35**	**412**
XA-RGO	**HS25**	**HA-0036**
XA-RGS	**C650**	**0189**
XA-RHA	**F2TH**	**107**
XA-RHA	FA20	379
XA-RIA	LJ36	050
XA-RIB	**C650**	**0150**
XA-RIC	LJ24	251
XA-RIE	C650	0170
XA-RIH	SBRL	380-46
XA-RIL	HS25	25237
XA-RIN	**GLF4**	**1509**
XA-RIN	LJ25	104
XA-RIN	LJ35	152
XA-RIN	LJ60	172
XA-RIR	SBRL	306-36
XA-RIU	**LJ45**	**038**
XA-RIV	**C550**	**381**
XA-RIW	WW24	86
XA-RIZ	**WW24**	**160**
XA-RJT	LJ35	011
XA-RKE	FA20	508
XA-RKG	SBRL	282-106
XA-RKH	C560	0156
XA-RKP	LJ25	353
XA-RKX	C560	0147
XA-RKY	LJ35	370
XA-RLE	C500	544
XA-RLH	SBRL	282-129
XA-RLI	LJ25	353
XA-RLL	SBRL	306-83
XA-RLP	SBRL	380-4
XA-RLR	SBRL	306-100
XA-RLR	SBRL	380-50
XA-RLS	SBRL	306-57
XA-RLV	**HS25**	**258035**
XA-RLX	FA10	226
XA-RMA	FA20	39
XA-RMD	JSTR	5228
XA-RMF	LJ24	290
XA-RMF	LJ25	308
XA-RMN	HS25	25185
XA-RMT	**LJ45**	**046**
XA-RMY	C650	0179
XA-RNB	FA20	142
XA-RNE	BE40	RJ-61
XA-RNG	BE40	RJ-58
XA-RNK	LJ31	021
XA-RNR	SBRL	306-49
XA-ROC	LJ25	357
XA-ROD	SBRL	380-50
XA-ROF	JSTR	5133
XA-ROF	JSTR	5148
XA-ROI	GLF2	10
XA-ROJ	HS25	25206
XA-ROK	JSTR	5133
XA-ROK	JSTR	5148
XA-ROO	LJ25	227
XA-ROX	LJ24	260
XA-ROZ	LJ25	286
XA-RPS	SBRL	282-56
XA-RPT	**HS25**	**25161**
XA-RPV	LJ25	210
XA-RQB	LJ24	150
XA-RQI	LJ25	032
XA-RQP	LJ24	179
XA-RQT	WW24	124
XA-RRC	LJ24	259
XA-RRG	PRM1	RB-154
XA-RRK	LJ24	307
XA-RRQ	C650	7025
XA-RSP	HS25	25091
XA-RSR	HS25	25017
XA-RSU	LJ25	363
XA-RTH	SBRL	306-39
XA-RTM	SBRL	282-39
XA-RTP	SBRL	306-110
XA-RTS	C650	7025
XA-RTS	**C680**	**0016**
XA-RTT	C560	0092
XA-RTV	LJ24	124
XA-RUA	**CL30**	**20404**
XA-RUD	C550	631
XA-RUI	GLF4	1250
XA-RUJ	LJ24	289
XA-RUQ	SBRL	306-15
XA-RUR	C500	273
XA-RUS	GLF2	161
XA-RUU	LJ31	012
XA-RUX	HS25	25101
XA-RUY	FA50	252
XA-RUY	HS25	258302
XA-RUY	LJ35	373
XA-RVB	LJ24	066
XA-RVB	LJ35	321

XA-RVG	JSTR	5139/54
XA-RVI	LJ25	286
XA-RVT	**SBRL**	**306-138**
XA-RVV	FA50	213
XA-RWN	HS25	25226
XA-RWY	SBRL	306-97
XA-RXA	LJ24	197
XA-RXB	LJ25	325
XA-RXO	C560	0118
XA-RXP	SBRL	306-56
XA-RXQ	LJ25	342
XA-RXZ	FA50	168
XA-RYB	HS25	259043
XA-RYD	SBRL	306-72
XA-RYE	C500	068
XA-RYE	C510	0039
XA-RYH	LJ25	334
XA-RYJ	**SBRL**	**370-5**
XA-RYK	**CL61**	**5122**
XA-RYK	HS25	256047
XA-RYM	**HS25**	**258075**
XA-RYN	LJ24	164
XA-RYO	SBRL	465-55
XA-RYR	C550	664
XA-RYR	**GLF4**	**1417**
XA-RYW	HS25	25064
XA-RZB	C550	654
XA-RZC	LJ24	071
XA-RZD	CL61	5087
XA-RZE	LJ25	274
XA-RZG	BE40	RK-36
XA-RZK	C650	0204
XA-RZM	LJ24	070
XA-RZQ	C650	0126
XA-RZT	LJ25	330
XA-RZW	SBRL	370-9
XA-RZY	LJ25	133
XA-RZZ	LJ35	485
XA-SAA	LJ24	306
XA-SAA	**LJ45**	**236**
XA-SAD	CL64	5630
XA-SAE	JSTR	5066/46
XA-SAE	LJ25	341
XA-SAG	FA20	287
XA-SAG	SBRL	282-111
XA-SAH	**SBRL**	**306-137**
XA-SAI	HS25	256016
XA-SAM	C500	255
XA-SAP	**LJ45**	**246**
XA-SAR	C750	0119
XA-SAR	FA10	125
XA-SAR	FA10	96
(XA-SAR)	FA10	54
XA-SAU	**HS25**	**257027**
XA-SAV	LJ24	306
XA-SBA	LJ35	380
XA-SBF	LJ35	376
XA-SBQ	JSTR	5124
XA-SBR	LJ24	180
XA-SBS	SBRL	282-6
XA-SBV	SBRL	306-109
XA-SBX	SBRL	306-40
XA-SBZ	LJ24	251
XA-SCA	LJ35	418
XA-SCE	**LJ24**	**271**
XA-SCL	FA20	130
XA-SCN	SBRL	282-105
(XA-SCO)	F9EX	186
XA-SCR	SBRL	465-65
(XA-SCV)	WW24	122
XA-SCY	LJ24	324
XA-SDE	GLF2	18
XA-SDI	C500	395
XA-SDI	**C550**	**550-0983**
XA-SDK	FA50	224
XA-SDM	GLF2	237/43
XA-SDN	C550	247
XA-SDP	LJ24	066
XA-SDQ	LJ25	005
XA-SDS	C500	313
XA-SDT	C560	0162
XA-SDU	**C650**	**0052**
XA-SDV	C550	037
XA-SDW	WW24	162
XA-SEB	C560	0375
XA-SEB	SBRL	380-58
XA-SEC	GLF4	1172
XA-SEG	**LJ45**	**165**
XA-SEH	HS25	258004
XA-SEJ	C560	0196
XA-SEN	C500	060
XA-SEN	HS25	257077
XA-SEN	SBRL	282-7
XA-SEP	C650	0076
XA-SET	C550	458
XA-SEU	SBRL	282-104
XA-SEX	C550	642
XA-SEY	C500	631
XA-SFB	GLF2	79
XA-SFE	C500	125
XA-SFP	FA50	22
XA-SFQ	**HS25**	**25273**
XA-SFS	WW24	13
XA-SGK	LJ35	380
XA-SGM	HS25	25283
XA-SGP	HS25	25114
XA-SGR	SBRL	370-6
XA-SGU	LJ24	101
XA-SGW	F900	122
XA-SHA	WW24	86
XA-SHN	LJ24	093
XA-SHO	C500	111
XA-SHZ	CL61	3012
XA-SID	**C56X**	**5083**
XA-SIF	FA50	231
XA-SIG	C500	175
XA-SIM	F900	114
XA-SIM	FA50	215
XA-SIM	SBRL	306-143
XA-SIN	JSTR	5005
XA-SIO	LJ25	121
XA-SIT	C560	0218
XA-SIV	HS25	258185
XA-SJC	C560	0197
XA-SJM	HS25	258713
XA-SJM	SBRL	306-128
XA-SJN	LJ25	365
XA-SJO	LJ25	370
XA-SJS	LJ25	076
XA-SJV	C500	189
XA-SJW	C500	169
XA-SJX	F900	97
XA-SJZ	C550	041
XA-SKA	LJ25	282
XA-SKA	**LJ45**	**493**
XA-SKB	SBRL	306-111
XA-SKE	HS25	25253
XA-SKH	HS25	256067
XA-SKI	JSTR	5124
XA-SKI	**LJ35**	**488**
XA-SKO	FA20	505
XA-SKW	C525	0044
XA-SKX	C560	0118
XA-SKY	GLF4	1487
XA-SKY	**GLF5**	**5293**
(XA-SKY)	LJ45	170
XA-SKZ	HS25	25121
XA-SLA	C560	0228
XA-SLB	**C650**	**0228**
XA-SLD	C550	014
XA-SLH	SBRL	306-39
XA-SLJ	SBRL	306-125
XA-SLP	**HS25**	**256002**
XA-SLQ	C500	111
XA-SLR	**HS25**	**25112**
XA-SMF	SBRL	306-6
XA-SMH	C500	084
XA-SML	C525	0636
XA-SMP	SBRL	282-13
XA-SMQ	SBRL	282-50
XA-SMR	SBRL	282-71
XA-SMS	CL61	3019
XA-SMT	C550	722
XA-SMU	LJ24	255
XA-SMV	C550	720
XA-SND	SBRL	306-7
XA-SNG	GLF3	434
XA-SNH	HS25	256021
XA-SNI	**LJ40**	**2030**
XA-SNI	SBRL	282-126
XA-SNM	LJ31	078
XA-SNN	HS25	257009
XA-SNO	LJ25	355
XA-SNP	BE40	RK-83
XA-SNX	C560	0229
XA-SNZ	LJ24	157
XA-SOA	CL60	1063
XA-SOC	JSTR	5152
XA-SOD	MU30	A049SA
XA-SOH	**LJ25**	**366**
XA-SOK	C650	7029
XA-SOL	**CL64**	**5501**
XA-SOL	FA50	116
XA-SON	HS25	257079
XA-SOR	**CL61**	**5147**
XA-SOU	C525	0060
XA-SOX	C500	217
XA-SOY	JSTR	5142
XA-SPL	LJ25	268
XA-SPM	FA50	242
XA-SPM	**SBRL**	**465-14**
XA-SPQ	C650	7028
XA-SPR	LJ31	076
XA-SQA	**SBRL**	**282-125**
XA-SQQ	C550	280
XA-SQR	C550	464
XA-SQS	FA20	198/466
XA-SQU	GLF2	173
XA-SQV	**C550**	**221**
XA-SQW	C550	226
XA-SQX	C500	428
XA-SQY	C500	243
XA-SQZ	C500	193
XA-SRB	C500	197
XA-SSS	FA50	119
XA-SSU	**LJ24**	**230**
XA-SSV	HS25	25187
XA-SSV	**SBRL**	**306-140**
XA-SSY	HS25	257199
XA-STG	JSTR	5206
XA-STI	SBRL	306-89
XA-STK	**HS25**	**258383**
XA-STO	GLF2	79
XA-STS	**GLF4**	**1308**
XA-STT	C500	310
XA-STT	GLF2	30/4
XA-STT	GLF3	406
XA-STU	SBRL	282-7
XA-STX	HS25	257186
XA-SUK	LJ45	057
XA-SUN	SBRL	306-143
XA-SUP	LJ24	319
(XA-SUY)	LJ24	324
XA-SVG	LJ25	079
XA-SVG	**SBRL**	**306-97**
XA-SVH	SBRL	306-97
XA-SVX	**LJ35**	**012**
XA-SWC	FA20	21
XA-SWD	JSTR	5108
XA-SWF	LJ35	391
XA-SWK	HS25	256026
XA-SWM	C650	7034
XA-SWP	GLF2	166/15
XA-SWX	LJ25	366
XA-SXD	LJ25	105
XA-SXG	LJ25	194
XA-SXK	SBRL	380-39
XA-SXY	LJ25	308
XA-SYS	SBRL	306-121
XA-SYY	FA10	4
XA-TAB	FA10	204
XA-TAB	FA50	177
XA-TAK	LJ25	305
XA-TAL	HS25	25064
XA-TAM	LJ25	341
XA-TAN	FA20	272
XA-TAQ	LJ25	286
XA-TAQ	LJ25	305
XA-TAV	JSTR	5103
XA-TAZ	JSTR	5103
XA-TBA	C650	0019
XA-TBL	FA10	203
XA-TBV	LJ25	325
XA-TCA	LJ24	224
XA-TCB	HS25	257082
XA-TCI	LJ35	349
XA-TCM	C550	717
XA-TCN	JSTR	5229
XA-TCO	GLF3	403
XA-TCO	LJ60	376
XA-TCR	HS25	257102
XA-TCY	LJ25	048
XA-TCZ	C650	7019
XA-TDD	FA50	252
XA-TDG	**JSTR**	**5158**
XA-TDK	GLF2	114
XA-TDP	LJ24	128
XA-TDQ	SBRL	380-50
XA-TDQ	BE40	RK-281
XA-TDU	F2TH	29
XA-TDX	SBRL	276-27
XA-TEI	**F9EX**	**186**
XA-TEL	C550	275
XA-TEL	**F900**	**168**
XA-TEM	**HS25**	**258431**
XA-TEN	**BE40**	**RK-459**
XA-TFC	SBRL	265-12
XA-TFD	SBRL	265-10
XA-TFL	SBRL	265-48
XA-TGA	C650	0036
XA-TGA	SBRL	306-126
XA-TGK	HS25	259037
XA-TGM	**LJ31**	**052**
XA-TGO	SBRL	276-6
XA-THD	LJ35	243
XA-THF	WW24	109
XA-THO	C555	0035
XA-TIE	LJ25	364
XA-TII	LJ24	070
XA-TIP	LJ24	227
XA-TIP	LJ24	293
XA-TIV	CL60	1057
XA-TIW	SBRL	276-44
XA-TIX	SBRL	276-21
XA-TIY	SBRL	265-14
XA-TJF	ASTR	050
XA-TJG	F900	131
XA-TJU	SBRL	276-8
XA-TJV	JSTR	5130
XA-TJW	JSTR	5129
XA-TJY	SBRL	276-39
XA-TJZ	SBRL	265-76
XA-TKC	LJ24	164
XA-TKQ	HS25	258111
XA-TKW	**SBRL**	**282-13**
XA-TKY	C500	411
XA-TKZ	C560	0474
XA-TKZ	**C56X**	**5208**
XA-TLL	SBRL	306-20
XA-TLM	CL61	5097
XA-TMF	**SBRL**	**306-100**
XA-TMH	F9EX	33
XA-TMI	C555	0080
XA-TMX	C650	7069
XA-TMZ	**C650**	**0068**
XA-TNP	SBRL	265-62
XA-TNW	SBRL	306-73
XA-TNX	HS25	256018
XA-TNY	**HS25**	**25196**
XA-TOF	C500	345
XA-TOM	SBRL	465-55
XA-TOO	GLF4	1114
(XA-TOT)	GLF3	302
XA-TPA	**E50P**	**50000272**
XA-TPB	HS25	258176
XA-TPB	**HS25**	**258409**
XA-TPD	JSTR	5134/50
XA-TPJ	JSTR	5231
XA-TPU	SBRL	306-143
XA-TQA	**C550**	**504**
XA-TQL	C550	268
XA-TQR	SBRL	276-4
XA-TRE	C650	7019
XA-TRG	GLF2	30/4
XA-TRI	C525	0060
XA-TRQ	**LJ24**	**112**
XA-TSA	LJ60	202
XA-TSL	LJ25	315
XA-TSN	PRM1	RB-12
XA-TSS	SBRL	306-63
XA-TSZ	**SBRL**	**380-71**
XA-TTC	**C52B**	**0308**
(XA-TTC)	C52A	0482
XA-TTD	CL61	5059
XA-TTE	JSTR	5058/4
XA-TTG	C525	0475
XA-TTH	**HS25**	**25148**
XA-TTQ	**C52A**	**0491**
XA-TTS	**BE40**	**RK-302**
XA-TTT	**LJ24**	**199**
XA-TUB	**LEG5**	**55000018**
XA-TUD	SBRL	380-5
XA-TUH	FA50	22
XA-TUL	LJ31	012
XA-TVG	**C56X**	**6167**
XA-TVG	CL64	5520
XA-TVH	C550	668
XA-TVI	HS25	258004
XA-TVK	**JSTR**	**5098/28**
XA-TVQ	FA50	94
XA-TVZ	SBRL	306-113
XA-TWH	**LJ25**	**289**
XA-TWW	**BE40**	**RK-332**
XA-TXB	FA50	210
XA-TYD	**BE40**	**RK-321**
XA-TYG	**HS25**	**257171**
XA-TYH	HS25	258491
XA-TYK	**HS25**	**258597**
XA-TYP	**BE40**	**RK-152**
XA-TYT	F2TH	60
XA-TYW	**LJ25**	**361**
XA-TYZ	SBRL	282-124
XA-TZF	**CL64**	**5527**
XA-TZF	LJ60	088
XA-TZI	**LJ60**	**088**
XA-TZV	JSTR	5130
XA-TZW	JSTR	5129
XA-UAF	**C56X**	**5356**
XA-UAG	LJ45	139
XA-UAM	C650	7073
XA-UAW	BE40	RK-359
XA-UBG	SBRL	282-112
XA-UBH	SBRL	380-40
XA-UBI	**LJ31**	**235**
XA-UBK	**HS25**	**25107**
XA-UCI	**LJ55**	**032**
XA-UCN	FA50	177
XA-UCS	SBRL	282-6
XA-UCU	HS25	257056
XA-UCV	**BE40**	**RK-375**
XA-UDP	FA10	204
XA-UDW	FA50	291
XA-UEA	HS25	257061
XA-UEC	GLF2	167
XA-UEF	C560	0687
XA-UEH	HS25	258044
XA-UEK	SBRL	380-40
XA-UEQ	SBRL	380-58
XA-UEV	BE40	RK-434
XA-UEW	CL61	5063
XA-UEX	**HS25**	**25066**
XA-UEY	**SBRL**	**282-112**
XA-UFB	**LJ45**	**295**
XA-UFK	**HS25**	**258287**
XA-UFQ	SBRL	306-130
XA-UFR	**BE40**	**RK-452**
XA-UFS	**BE40**	**RK-415**
XA-UGB	**SBRL**	**282-102**
XA-UGG	C550	590
XA-UGK	LJ35	488
XA-UGO	HS25	258731
XA-UGQ	C56X	5667
XA-UGX	C650	7088
XA-UHI	HS25	258055
XA-UHJ	WW24	174
XA-UHO	C650	7025
XA-UHQ	**C56X**	**5709**
XA-UHT	**LJ24**	**283**
XA-UIC	MU30	A055SA
XA-UIS	**C650**	**0186**
XA-UJG	FA10	146
XA-UJP	C56X	5771
XA-UJP	**C680**	**0186**
XA-UJQ	**LJ31**	**020**
XA-UJR	**LJ45**	**135**
XA-UJW	**SBRL**	**306-20**
XA-UJY	**C52A**	**0395**
XA-UJZ	**LJ45**	**188**
XA-UKD	FA10	100
XA-UKF	**LJ35**	**316**
XA-UKH	**LJ25**	**221**
XA-UKK	**LJ25**	**337**
XA-UKQ	**C56X**	**5813**
XA-UKR	HS25	257191
XA-UKU	BE40	RK-259
XA-ULG	**LJ25**	**334**
XA-ULO	**C510**	**0174**
XA-ULQ	CL61	5087
XA-ULS	**LJ25**	**210**
XA-ULT	**HS25**	**257003**
XA-UMA	LJ35	646
XA-UME	**C550**	**662**
XA-UML	FA10	100
XA-UMS	**C510**	**0166**
XA-UMV	**LJ31**	**234**
XA-UNC	LJ25	222
XA-UND	C650	0007
XA-UNV	**SBRL**	**282-114**
XA-UOB	E50P	50000172
"XA-UOC"	LJ60	406
XA-UOO	**SBRL**	**306-7**
XA-UOW	**HS25**	**257036**
XA-UPE	**HS25**	**257019**
XA-UPO	**FA20**	**327**
XA-UPR	**LJ35**	**308**
XA-UPX	**C550**	**730**
XA-UPZ	**C52A**	**0482**
XA-UQG	**C52C**	**0054**
XA-UQJ	**BE40**	**RK-474**
XA-UQN	HS25	257059
XA-UQO	**C550**	**550-0947**
XA-UQP	**LJ60**	**202**
XA-UQZ	**HA4T**	**RC-36**
XA-URG	LJ60	172
XA-URI	**SBRL**	**306-143**
XA-URK	F2TH	149
XA-URN	HS25	258327
XA-URQ	**C56X**	**6080**
XA-USA	C750	0001
XA-USD	LJ35	255
XA-USF	**LJ31**	**164**
XA-USI	**LJ35**	**401**
XA-USP	**LJ40**	**2054**
XA-USS	**C550**	**550-0965**
XA-USZ	**LJ60**	**429**
XA-UTB	**HS25**	**259009**
XA-UTD	**C56X**	**5148**
XA-UTG	**C52C**	**0026**
XA-UTI	**C550**	**550-1041**
XA-UTL	**CL61**	**5175**
XA-UTP	**GLF2**	**211**
XA-UUB	**LJ45**	**102**
XA-UUG	HA4T	RC-48
XA-UUP	**LJ60**	**132**
XA-UUQ	**LJ31**	**056**
XA-UUS	**SBRL**	**465-22**
XA-UUU	LJ25	276
XA-UUV	**HS25**	**258029**
XA-UUX	**G150**	**255**
XA-UVA	C550	550-0999
XA-UVA	C56X	5033
XA-UVA	LJ45	016
XA-UVH	**HS25**	**258152**
XA-UVS	**FA50**	**319**
XA-UVV	**C650**	**0177**
XA-UVW	**LJ45**	**057**
XA-UVY	**HS25**	**259011**
XA-UWJ	FA50	32
XA-UWR	**CL64**	**5321**
XA-UXC	**LJ45**	**526**
XA-UXD	**LJ45**	**527**
XA-UXK	**CL61**	**3015**
(XA-VAD)	GLF4	1227
XA-VAL	**F900**	**127**
XA-VDG	**CL61**	**5004**
XA-VEL	SBRL	306-42
XA-VER	C750	0072
XA-VFV	**CL30**	**20427**
XA-VFV	LJ40	2077
XA-VGF	C555	0080
XA-VGR	C56X	5776
XA-VGR	**C56X**	**6169**
XA-VIG	**LJ60**	**116**
XA-VIO	SBRL	306-34
XA-VIT	C650	0020
XA-VIT	SBRL	306-50
XA-VLA	**LJ60**	**217**
XA-VMC	**LJ25**	**114**
XA-VMX	**C510**	**0059**
(XA-VMX)	LJ31	224
XA-VRM	**LJ45**	**509**
XA-VRO	BE40	RK-238
XA-VTO	**F900**	**129**
XA-VTR	LJ31	231
XA-VVI	LJ24	230
XA-VWA	**PRM1**	**RB-293**
XA-VYA	LJ25	336
XA-VYC	**LJ45**	**034**
XA-VYF	C500	265
XA-VYM	**C650**	**0071**
XA-WIN	**LJ35**	**152**
XA-WNG	**HS25**	**258397**
XA-WNG	LJ45	016
XA-WOW	**GLF5**	**5368**
XA-WWG	C550	730

XA-WWW	**LJ25**	**193**
XA-XDC	**C680**	**0165**
XA-XEL	**HS25**	**HA-0149**
XA-XET	HS25	256022
XA-XGX	**C650**	**0198**
XA-XIS	C650	7032
(XA-XOX)	LJ60	196
XA-XPA	**SBRL**	**465-18**
XA-XTR	**GLF4**	**4008**
XA-YCC	**BE40**	**RK-571**
XA-YSM	HS25	25208
XA-YUR	**FA20**	**475**
XA-YYY	**LJ25**	**263**
XA-ZAP	**LJ35**	**129**
XA-ZOM	SBRL	306-47
XA-ZTA	CL61	5158
XA-ZTA	**LJ60**	**134**
XA-ZTH	LJ31	004
XA-ZTK	**GLF5**	**5054**
XA-ZUL	PRM1	RB-9
XA-ZUM	SBRL	306-47
XA-ZUM	SBRL	465-15
XA-ZYZ	LJ25	032
XA-ZYZ	LJ25	287
XA-ZYZ	**LJ31**	**073**
XA-ZZZ	LJ25	287
XA-ZZZ	LJ25	346
XA-ZZZ	**LJ45**	**243**
XB-ACD	**SBRL**	**380-50**
XB-ACS	C500	062
XB-ACS	**C550**	**674**
XB-ADR	**LJ24**	**103**
XB-ADZ	**HS25**	**256018**
XB-AER	WW24	172
XB-AFA	**LJ24**	**290**
XB-AGV	**C550**	**429**
XB-AKW	HS25	25102
XB-ALO	FA20	287
XB-AMO	**C500**	**152**
XB-APD	SBRL	306-33
XB-AQU	FA20	248/483
(XB-ASO)	HS25	25202
XB-ATH	C525	0148
XB-AXP	HS25	25112
XB-AXP	HS25	25233
XB-AYJ	SBRL	282-41
XB-AZD	LJ25	224
XB-BAK	FA10	65
XB-BBL	SBRL	282-116
XB-BBO	**GLF2**	**164**
XB-BEA	HS25	25068
XB-BIP	SBRL	306-63
XB-BON	C550	654
XB-BRT	C550	650
XB-CAM	FA10	107
XB-CAR	**CL61**	**5052**
XB-CCM	HS25	25226
XB-CCO	C500	175
XB-CSI	**C500**	**345**
XB-CTC	**MU30**	**A024SA**
XB-CUX	HS25	25262
XB-CVS	**SBRL**	**306-47**
XB-CXF	C500	143
XB-CXK	HS25	257153
XB-CXO	JSTR	5141
XB-CXZ	HS25	25060
XB-CYA	CRVT	36
XB-CYA	**SBRL**	**380-53**
XB-CYI	CRVT	40
XB-DBA	C500	067
XB-DBJ	JSTR	5145
XB-DBS	JSTR	5159
XB-DBT	**C550**	**550-0986**
XB-DBT	JSTR	5156
XB-DDG	**LJ25**	**224**
XB-DGA	**C525**	**0329**
XB-DKS	LJ25	309
XB-DLV	JSTR	5005
XB-DNY	WW24	183
XB-DSQ	HS25	25185
XB-DUH	JSTR	5157
XB-DUS	SBRL	282-106
XB-DVF	**C500**	**587**
XB-DVP	SBRL	380-53
XB-DYF	C500	313
XB-DZD	LJ24	349
XB-DZN	HS25	257158
XB-DZQ	LJ25	332
XB-DZR	**LJ24**	**273**
XB-EAL	HS25	25060
XB-EBI	GLF2	96
XB-ECR	FA20	513
XB-EDU	FA20	39
XB-EEP	C555	0070
XB-EFR	C500	090
XB-EGO	**SBRL**	**282-124**
XB-EGP	LJ25	194
XB-ELJ	**C650**	**0211**
XB-ELU	C500	544
XB-EPB	FA20	127
XB-EPM	SBRL	380-19
XB-EPN	C500	241
XB-EQR	SBRL	282-82
XB-ERN	HS25	25148
XB-ERU	SBRL	370-7
XB-ERX	C500	460
XB-ESG	**C500**	**292**
XB-ESS	**SBRL**	**282-123**
XB-ESX	SBRL	306-47
XB-ETE	C500	274
XB-ETV	**SBRL**	**306-96**
XB-EWF	CRVT	36
XB-EWQ	C500	141
XB-EXC	**HS25**	**256061**
XB-EXJ	GLF4	1055
XB-EZV	SBRL	282-7
XB-FDH	BE40	RJ-54
XB-FDN	C500	068
XB-FFV	HS25	25112
XB-FIR	**C550**	**550-0854**
XB-FIS	HS25	25060
XB-FIS	JSTR	5033/56
XB-FJI	WW24	115
XB-FJO	MS76	005
XB-FJW	LJ24	141
XB-FKT	**LJ31**	**029**
XB-FKV	WW24	137
XB-FMB	**SBRL**	**306-90**
XB-FMF	HS25	256033
XB-FMK	HS25	257068
XB-FNF	LJ35	210
XB-FNW	LJ35	255
XB-FPK	C500	084
XB-FQO	C500	278
XB-FRP	HS25	25185
XB-FST	SBRL	306-63
XB-FSZ	SBRL	306-50
XB-FUZ	SBRL	306-63
XB-FVH	FA20	393
XB-FVL	GLF2	100
XB-FWX	FA10	107
XB-FXD	GLF3	434
XB-FXO	C500	550
XB-GAM	**HS25**	**25075**
XB-GBC	LJ24	285
XB-GBF	**C500**	**273**
XB-GBZ	WW24	133
XB-GCC	HS25	258252
XB-GCP	**LJ25**	**325**
XB-GCR	FA20	127
XB-GDJ	**C500**	**598**
XB-GDO	**LJ35**	**449**
XB-GDR	LJ25	308
XB-GDU	SBRL	265-12
XB-GDV	SBRL	276-27
XB-GDW	SBRL	265-86
XB-GGK	HS25	25064
XB-GHC	HS25	25121
XB-GHO	LJ24	141
XB-GJO	SBRL	370-9
XB-GJS	LJ24	299
XB-GLZ	**C550**	**281**
XB-GMD	SBRL	465-12
XB-GNF	HS25	25283
XB-GRE	C500	550
XB-GRN	C650	0069
XB-GRN	WW24	301
XB-GRQ	LJ24	074
XB-GRR	LJ24	068
XB-GSM	**LJ35**	**672**
XB-GSN	GLF2	161
XB-GSP	**SBRL**	**380-55**
XB-GTH	**LJ45**	**326**
XB-GTT	**C650**	**0219**
XB-GVY	C500	368
XB-GXV	C650	0101
XB-GYB	LJ31	166
XB-HDL	SBRL	306-7
XB-HGE	LJ25	325
XB-HHF	SBRL	282-6
XB-HIZ	GLF3	403
XB-HJS	**SBRL**	**306-110**
XB-HND	C500	255
XB-HRA	**FA20**	**127**
XB-HZF	C550	473
XB-IFW	LJ25	366
XB-IHB	**SBRL**	**282-63**
XB-IJW	C500	198
XB-IKS	C500	010
XB-IKY	C550	642
XB-ILD	HS25	25190
XB-IML	**C560**	**0084**
XB-INI	**BE40**	**RK-126**
XB-IPX	**HS25**	**25188**
XB-IRH	**LJ24**	**308**
XB-IRZ	HS25	257084
XB-IUW	C500	198
XB-IWL	LJ35	379
XB-IXE	**C500**	**328**
XB-IXJ	SBRL	306-93
XB-IXT	**C500**	**685**
XB-IYK	FA20	282
XB-IYS	**SBRL**	**306-6**
XB-IZK	C550	473
XB-IZR	**SBRL**	**306-42**
XB-JCG	LJ60	131
XB-JCM	**C650**	**7053**
XB-JDG	C500	110
XB-JFE	JSTR	5145
XB-JFV	**C500**	**530**
XB-JGI	SBRL	282-80
XB-JHD	C560	0127
XB-JHE	BE40	RJ-48
XB-JHV	**LJ28**	**29-002**
XB-JIZ	JSTR	5058/4
XB-JJS	**LJ25**	**369**
XB-JKG	HS25	25146
XB-JKK	LJ25	334
XB-JKV	SBRL	282-102
XB-JLJ	C550	310
XB-JLU	LJ25	328
XB-JLY	HS25	25139
XB-JMM	SBRL	306-130
XB-JMR	**SBRL**	**306-35**
XB-JND	HS25	257106
XB-JOA	**LJ35**	**370**
XB-JOY	LJ24	263
XB-JPL	GLF2	10
XB-JPR	**C510**	**0287**
XB-JPS	**SBRL**	**282-128**
XB-JPX	**LJ36**	**043**
XB-JRS	C510	0247
XB-JTG	**SBRL**	**306-127**
XB-JTN	**HS25**	**257185**
XB-JVK	C500	199
XB-JVL	HS25	25052
XB-JXG	**C500**	**378**
XB-JXZ	**LJ24**	**346**
XB-JYS	HS25	257033
XB-JYZ	**SBRL**	**380-48**
XB-KBE	GLF2	114
XB-KBO	GLF2	30/4
XB-KBW	FA20	364
XB-KCV	JSTR	5161/43
XB-KCW	GLF2	114
XB-KCX	GLF2	30/4
XB-KDK	**LJ31**	**032**
XB-KDQ	**LJ25**	**365**
XB-KFR	JSTR	5161/43
XB-KFU	**GLF2**	**24**
XB-KHL	**C500**	**542**
XB-KIV	GLF2	91
XB-KJW	**LJ24**	**349**
XB-KKS	HS25	25225
XB-KKU	GLF2	119/22
XB-KLQ	SBRL	306-132
XB-KLV	**JSTR**	**5162**
XB-KMY	**LJ24**	**070**
XB-KNH	**HS25**	**25225**
XB-KPB	LJ35	379
XB-KPC	SBRL	306-7
XB-KPR	**LJ25**	**096**
XB-KQB	HS25	25139
XB-KQN	**LJ25**	**006**
XB-KQY	**SBRL**	**306-83**
XB-KSL	SBRL	306-86
XB-KVX	LJ25	122
XB-KWN	**LJ25**	**309**
XB-KYK	LJ25	194
XB-KYZ	LJ60	175
XB-LAW	SBRL	306-100
XB-LBO	LJ60	175
XB-LCI	LJ25	122
XB-LEJ	LJ60	175
XB-LHS	LJ35	255
XB-LHS	LJ35	648
XB-LHW	GLF2	253
XB-LLT	LJ60	175
XB-LOA	**SBRL**	**306-18**
XB-LPD	LJ25	270
XB-LRD	SBRL	306-21
XB-LSA	**C500**	**110**
XB-LTD	LJ25	076
XB-LTH	C550	462
XB-LVL	**C500**	**643**
XB-LVV	C550	550-0855
XB-LVY	**C500**	**010**
XB-LWC	**HS25**	**25220**
XB-LWN	**C550**	**654**
XB-LWW	**LJ35**	**091**
XB-LXL	LJ25	122
XB-LXP	HS25	25233
XB-LYG	**LJ25**	**364**
XB-LYY	**C500**	**577**
XB-MAR	**HS25**	**25202**
XB-MBM	HS25	25030
XB-MBP	**LJ31**	**221**
XB-MBV	**SBRL**	**306-63**
XB-MBW	**LJ25**	**328**
XB-MCB	**HS25**	**258320**
XB-MCN	**C500**	**062**
XB-MCW	**LJ25**	**291**
XB-MDG	SBRL	282-114
XB-MDO	**SBRL**	**306-124**
XB-MEH	LJ25	122
XB-MGM	HS25	25175
XB-MGM	LJ25	224
XB-MGS	**C500**	**261**
XB-MKO	**LJ25**	**122**
XB-MLC	HS25	257171
XB-MMN	**SBRL**	**306-72**
XB-MMW	SBRL	306-132
XB-MNV	**C550**	**550-1071**
XB-MQN	**SBRL**	**306-126**
XB-MRQ	E50P	50000271
XB-MRU	**SBRL**	**306-86**
XB-MSV	HS25	25185
XB-MSW	**LJ25**	**194**
XB-MSZ	**BE40**	**RK-247**
XB-MTG	**HS25**	**258063**
XB-MTR	**C525**	**0653**
XB-MTS	C560	0030
XB-MUL	E50P	50000271
XB-MUX	**GLF2**	**180**
XB-MVG	SBRL	282-134
XB-MWQ	HS25	257084
XB-MXG	**SBRL**	**306-93**
XB-MXK	**C650**	**0225**
XB-MXU	**SBRL**	**306-98**
XB-MXZ	**LJ25**	**359**
XB-MYA	**HS25**	**25227**
XB-MYE	**LJ24**	**066**
XB-MYG	**LJ25**	**295**
XB-MYO	**C555**	**0095**
XB-MYP	**SBRL**	**465-50**
XB-MZK	GLF2	27
XB-MZX	**LJ24**	**269**
XB-NAG	LJ24	270
XB-NBJ	CL30	20367
XB-NCM	FA20	487
XB-NCR	**C550**	**287**
XB-NET	**FA20**	**248/483**
XB-NHM	LJ45	271
XB-NIB	SBRL	282-125
XB-NKR	LJ35	488
XB-NKS	GLF2	114
XB-NKT	**C500**	**214**
XB-NOA	**SBRL**	**306-128**
XB-NOR	**FA20**	**179**
XB-NRX	**GLF2**	**27**
XB-NUR	LJ24	275
XB-NVE	**HS25**	**257084**
XB-NVT	**FA20**	**487**
XB-NWD	**CL65**	**5808**
XB-NXC	GLF2	112
XB-NXX	**C500**	**210**
XB-NYM	**HS25**	**258054**
XB-NYV	**C500**	**295**
XB-NZJ	**JSTR**	**5234**
XB-NZS	**LJ31**	**208**
XB-OAC	**LJ25**	**317**
XB-OAE	**HS25**	**258537**
XB-OAP	**FA20**	**504**
XB-OBE	C500	273
XB-OBM	C650	0177
XB-OBS	**HS25**	**257106**
XB-OCC	**GLF2**	**112**
XB-ODN	**C550**	**650**
XB-ODO	**CL60**	**1006**
XB-ODY	**EA50**	**000010**
XB-OEM	FA20	248/483
XB-OEM	FA50	80
XB-OEM	GLF4	1055
XB-OFK	C550	590
XB-OIQ	**C500**	**338**
XB-OMG	G150	290
XB-OZA	LJ25	224
XB-PAM	**HS25**	**257033**
XB-PAX	**C555**	**0065**
XB-PBT	**C500**	**054**
XB-PCJ	**SBRL**	**306-87**
XB-PEM	**C560**	**0162**
XB-PGC	**C650**	**0038**
XB-PMH	CL61	5164
XB-PMR	**C500**	**588**
XB-PTC	**SBRL**	**465-72**
XB-PUE	HS25	25158
XB-PYC	C560	0261
XB-QND	SBRL	306-21
XB-RDB	SBRL	380-55
XB-RGB	**LJ60**	**380**
XB-RGO	SBRL	282-114
XB-RGO	**SBRL**	**306-34**
XB-RGS	SBRL	282-114
XB-RMT	LJ45	046
XB-RRC	GLF2	97
XB-RSC	**C650**	**7028**
XB-RSC	SBRL	465-55
XB-RSG	SBRL	380-60
XB-RSH	SBRL	465-22
XB-RTT	C560	0092
XB-RYE	C510	0039
XB-RYO	SBRL	465-55
XB-RYP	**HS25**	**256066**
XB-RYT	**LJ35**	**042**
XB-SBC	HS25	25068
XB-SGT	**C550**	**218**
XB-SHA	**C500**	**648**
XB-SHA	SBRL	380-60
XB-SII	FA10	4
XB-SJA	**FA20**	**507**
XB-SLL	LJ60	183
XB-SOL	FA50	116
XB-SOL	SBRL	306-128
XB-SUD	LJ24	197
XB-SVV	**HS25**	**257069**
XB-TMG	**C500**	**504**
XB-TNY	BE40	RK-152
XB-TRN	**C500**	**198**
XB-TRY	C500	210
XB-TTT	**C550**	**642**
XB-UAG	C500	278
XB-ULF	**SBRL**	**306-129**
XB-UNA	**SBRL**	**465-8**
XB-UOC	**LJ60**	**406**
XB-USD	LJ35	255
XB-UVA	C550	550-0999
XB-VGT	**C500**	**068**
XB-VIW	JSTR	5140
XB-VLM	HS25	258013
XB-VRM	FA20	248/483
XB-VUI	HS25	25068
XB-WID	**LJ35**	**011**
XB-YJA	**FA50**	**136**
XB-ZNP	SBRL	306-63
XB-ZRB	FA10	107
(XB-ZRB)	LJ31	029
XB-ZUM	SBRL	306-47
XB-ZZZ	C550	711
XC-AA24	LJ36	050
XC-AA26	SBRL	306-12
XC-AA28	LJ24	037
XC-AA51	**SBRL**	**282-130**
XC-AA60	LJ35	321
XC-AA63	LJ24	249
XC-AA70	**GLF2**	**18**
XC-AA73	SBRL	282-105
XC-AA83	LJ25	286
XC-AA84	LJ25	330
XC-AA89	**SBRL**	**380-46**
XC-AA104	LJ24	070
XC-AAC	**SBRL**	**306-21**
XC-AAJ	SBRL	306-20
XC-AGR	LJ25	295
XC-AGU	**LJ24**	**260**
XC-ASA	C500	061
XC-ASB	C500	251
XC-AZU	LJ24	285
XC-BCS	C550	268
(XC-BDA)	WW24	340
XC-BEN	C500	243
XC-BEZ	C500	072
XC-BIN	FA20	198/466
XC-BJG	**BE40**	**RK-434**
XC-BOC	C500	169
XC-BUR	C500	245
XC-CAM	**SBRL**	**306-145**
XC-CFE	**C650**	**0218**
XC-CFE	GLF2	161
XC-CFM	LJ25	284
XC-CIR	C500	466
XC-COL	WW24	135
XC-COL	WW24	279
XC-CON	C500	169
XC-CUZ	**LJ35**	**213**
XC-DAA	LJ25	283
XC-DAD	LJ25	223
XC-DDA	**SBRL**	**380-34**
XC-DFS	LJ28	29-002
XC-DGA	C500	010
XC-DGA	HFB3	1049
XC-DGO	**LJ35**	**336**
XC-DIP	FA20	282
XC-DOK	C550	221
XC-DOP	LJ24	273
XC-DUF	C550	226
(XC-DUF)	C550	206
XC-FEZ	**C500**	**596**
XC-FEZ	GLF2	161
XC-FIA	SBRL	380-53
XC-FIF	LJ25	332
XC-FIT	C500	010
XC-FIU	C500	012
XC-FIV	**C500**	**013**
XC-FOO	C550	249
XC-FVH	FA20	393
XC-GAD	C500	061
(XC-GAM)	FA20	198/466
XC-GAW	**C500**	**586**
XC-GDC	**C52B**	**0062**
XC-GDT	**C560**	**0689**
XC-GII	LJ24	179
XC-GNL	LJ25	329
XC-GOB	HS25	25216
XC-GOV	C500	189
XC-GOW	C500	193
XC-GOX	C500	197
XC-GOY	C500	243
XC-GTO	**C500**	**533**
XC-GUB	**LJ25**	**306**
XC-GUH	C500	221
XC-GUO	C500	201
XC-GUQ	C500	143
XC-HAD	WW24	85
XC-HCP	WW24	230
XC-HDA	WW24	230
(XC-HDA)	WW24	339
XC-HEP	C550	464
XC-HEQ	C550	280
XC-HEY	SBRL	282-130
XC-HFY	SBRL	380-46
XC-HGY	SBRL	306-38
XC-HGZ	**C550**	**659**
XC-HHA	C550	673
XC-HHJ	**LJ35**	**435**
XC-HHL	SBRL	306-12
XC-HID	**FA20**	**282**
XC-HIE	LJ28	29-002
XC-HIE	**LJ45**	**026**
XC-HIF	**LJ45**	**111**
XC-HIS	**LJ25**	**312**
XC-HIX	FA20	248/483
XC-HIX	**FA20**	**471**
(XC-HIX)	FA20	111
XC-HJC	**C550**	**677**

XC-HJE	**C550**	**680**
XC-HJF	**C550**	**652**
XC-IPP	C500	329
XC-IPP	LJ35	028
XC-IST	**LJ28**	**29-001**
XC-JAY	C550	505
XC-JAZ	C550	602
XC-JBQ	C550	497
XC-JBR	**C550**	**494**
XC-JBS	**C550**	**666**
XC-JBT	C550	593
XC-JCC	JSTR	5053/2
XC-JCK	SBRL	282-1
XC-JCN	LJ24	299
XC-JCV	**C550**	**595**
XC-JCW	C550	607
XC-JCX	**C550**	**663**
XC-JCY	C550	096
XC-JCZ	**C550**	**670**
XC-JDA	C550	185
XC-JDC	SBRL	306-145
XC-JDX	LJ24	070
XC-JOA	LJ24	081
XC-LGD	LJ24	037
XC-LHA	**C550**	**681**
XC-LHH	**C550**	**655**
XC-LIT	**JSTR**	**5063**
XC-LJE	LJ24	346
XC-LJS	**BE40**	**RJ-48**
XC-LKA	**GLF2**	**69**
XC-LKB	**SBRL**	**380-58**
XC-LKL	GLF2	114
XC-LKN	**GLF2**	**30/4**
XC-LKS	**GLF2**	**91**
XC-LLL	**C550**	**473**
XC-LLZ	BE40	RK-168
XC-LMC	BE40	RK-293
XC-LMF	**GLF4**	**4128**
XC-LMP	**SBRL**	**306-113**
XC-LNC	HS25	259032
XC-LND	HS25	258004
XC-LNE	LJ35	340
XC-LNF	LJ31	078
XC-LNG	HS25	258150
XC-LNH	LJ35	401
XC-LNI	SBRL	465-16
XC-LNJ	HS25	257199
XC-LNN	**C560**	**0687**
XC-LNS	CL65	5808
XC-LOH	**G150**	**313**
XC-LOI	**G150**	**314**
XC-LOJ	**GLF4**	**4333**
XC-LOK	**GLF5**	**5508**
XC-MEX	GLF2	96
XC-MIC	**FA20**	**169**
XC-MMM	**C500**	**035**
XC-NSP	LJ25	194
XC-OAH	LJ35	488
XC-OAH	SBRL	282-1
XC-OAH	SBRL	306-73
XC-ONA	SBRL	380-39
XC-PET	GLF2	173
XC-PFJ	FA20	287
XC-PFM	**GLF4**	**4016**
XC-PFN	SBRL	306-111
XC-PFP	LJ24	260
XC-PFT	**GLF2**	**175**
XC-PGE	SBRL	282-130
XC-PGM	**C550**	**644**
XC-PGN	**C650**	**0165**
XC-PGP	C550	648
XC-PGR	GLF2	81
XC-PGR	LJ35	460
XC-PMX	C500	428
XC-PPM	C500	329
XC-QEO	C500	251
XC-QER	**FA20**	**287**
XC-ROO	C550	249
XC-ROO	C550	598
XC-RPP	**LJ25**	**236**
XC-SAG	LJ24	255
XC-SCT	C500	010
XC-SCT	**C550**	**153**
XC-SEY	FA20	169
XC-SKI	**JSTR**	**5124**
XC-SON	**FA20**	**393**
XC-SRA	SBRL	282-130
XC-SRH	JSTR	5154
XC-SST	**C550**	**731**
XC-SUB	SBRL	282-114
XC-SUP	LJ24	319
XC-TIJ	HFB3	1049
XC-TJN	**LJ40**	**2046**
XC-UJC	SBRL	380-67
XC-UJD	SBRL	380-68
XC-UJE	SBRL	306-139
XC-UJF	SBRL	306-144
XC-UJG	**LJ35**	**321**
XC-UJG	SBRL	282-130
XC-UJH	HS25	25216
XC-UJH	SBRL	282-117
XC-UJI	SBRL	282-130
XC-UJK	GLF2	161
XC-UJN	GLF3	352
XC-UJO	GLF3	386
XC-UJP	LJ24	037
XC-UJP	**LJ36**	**050**
XC-UJS	**SBRL**	**306-139**
XC-UJU	SBRL	380-68
XC-VMC	LJ45	028
XC-VSA	**LJ28**	**28-002**
XC-ZRB	FA10	107

Burkino Faso

XT-AOK	C550	726
XT-COK	C550	550-0924
XT-EBO	FA7X	108

Cambodia/Kampuchea

XU-008	FA20	323/520

Iraq

YI-AHH	FA20	337/529
YI-AHI	FA20	342/532
YI-AHJ	FA20	343/533
YI-AKA	JSTR	5233
YI-AKB	JSTR	5235
YI-AKC	JSTR	5237
YI-AKD	JSTR	5238
YI-AKE	JSTR	5239
YI-AKF	JSTR	5240
YI-AKG	HS25	257184
YI-AKH	HS25	257187
YI-AKI	GLF3	408
YI-AKJ	GLF3	419
YI-ALB	FA50	71
YI-ALC	FA50	101
YI-ALD	FA50	120
YI-ALE	FA50	122
YI-ASB	**HS25**	**258504**
YI-ASC	**HS25**	**258520**

Syria

YK-ASA	FA20	328/522
YK-ASB	**FA20**	**331/524**
YK-ASC	**F900**	**100**

Latvia

YL-ABA	LJ60	300
YL-KSC	**PRM1**	**RB-20**
YL-KSD	**HS25**	**258845**
YL-KSG	PRM1	RB-46
YL-MAR	HS25	258389
YL-MLV	PRM1	RB-216
YL-NST	HS25	258424
YL-SKY	**CL64**	**5532**
YL-VIP	HS25	257103
YL-VIP	HS25	258078
YL-VIR	HS25	257103
YL-WBD	CL64	5442

Nicaragua

YN-BPR	HS25	256037
YN-BVO	LJ35	280
YN-BZH	FA20	128/436

Romania

YR-CJF	F900	26
YR-DAD	C510	0266
YR-DAE	C510	0281
YR-DDM	**E50P**	**50000293**
YR-DIP	CL64	5475
YR-DPH	C56X	5793
YR-DSA	FA20	236
YR-DSB	FA20	242
YR-DVA	HS25	256024
YR-ELV	C560	0652
YR-FNA	FA50	148
YR-GCI	C56X	6033
YR-MSS	HS25	HB-34
YR-NAY	**HS25**	**HA-0182**
YR-NVY	CL30	20402
YR-RPB	LJ60	030
YR-RPG	C560	0665
YR-RPR	C56X	5337
YR-RUS	C510	0045
YR-SMD	**C560**	**0200**
YR-TIC	C560	0200
YR-TIG	GALX	012
YR-TII	**GALX**	**089**
YR-TIK	**GLEX**	**9229**
YR-TOY	C52A	0455
YR-TRC	**CL30**	**20261**
YR-TRQ	**C510**	**0433**
YR-TYA	**C56X**	**6075**
YR-TYC	LJ31	205
YR-VPA	HS25	258389

Yugoslavia/Serbia

YU-BIA	C500	031
YU-BIH	LJ24	320
YU-BJG	LJ25	187
YU-BJH	LJ25	186
YU-BKJ	LJ25	205
YU-BKR	LJ25	221
YU-BKZ	C500	415
YU-BLY	SBRL	380-65
YU-BME	HS25	256048
YU-BML	C500	554
YU-BNA	**FA50**	**43**
YU-BOE	CS55	0045
YU-BOL	LJ35	618
YU-BPL	C550	480
YU-BPU	C550	144
YU-BPY	LJ35	173
YU-BPZ	FA50	25
YU-BRA	LJ25	202
YU-BRB	LJ25	203
YU-BRZ	**LJ31**	**045**
YU-BSG	C550	550-1049
YU-BSM	C550	550-0808
YU-BST	**C525**	**0022**
YU-BTB	**C550**	**550-1037**
YU-BTM	**C650**	**7080**
YU-BTN	**C52B**	**0193**
YU-BTT	**C550**	**246**
YU-BUU	**C52A**	**0411**
YU-BVA	BE40	RK-124
YU-BVV	C550	307
YU-BZM	**C56X**	**6037**
YU-BZZ	**C550**	**550-0924**
YU-FCS	C550	347
YU-MDV	C500	616
YU-MPC	**C525**	**0911**
YU-MTU	**C525**	**0295**
YU-RDA	**C56X**	**6199**
YU-SEG	C500	276
YU-SMK	**C56X**	**5641**
YU-SPA	C56X	5760
YU-SPB	**C56X**	**5807**
YU-SPC	**C56X**	**6136**
YU-SPM	C510	0049
YU-SVL	**C56X**	**5772**
YU-VER	C52A	0401

Venezuela

YV-....	**HS25**	**25244**
YV-01CP	CRVT	35
YV-01CP	LJ24	040
YV-01CP	LJ35	157
YV-03CP	JSTR	5106/9
(YV-04CP)	C550	455
YV-05C	C550	463
YV-05CP	C550	018
YV-06CP	C550	020
YV-07CP	FA10	47
YV-07P	C500	253
YV-12CP	LJ55	031
(YV-15CP)	LJ35	191
(YV-15CP)	LJ35	270
YV-15CP	C500	095
YV-15CP	LJ24	047
YV-15CP	LJ35	342
YV-17CP	FA10	100
YV-19CP	C550	003
YV-19P	C500	253
YV-21CP	C500	115
YV-26CP	LJ25	098
YV-29CP	MU30	A049SA
YV-36CP	C550	080
(YV-37CP)	WW24	193
YV-38CP	FA20	287
(YV-41CP)	LJ55	015
YV-41CP	LJ55	019
YV-43CP	C500	284
YV-50CP	C500	289
YV-52CP	C500	399
YV-55CP	C500	215
YV-58CP	WW24	172
(YV-60CP)	GLF2	163
YV-62CP	C500	297
(YV-64CP)	SBRL	282-134
YV-65CP	LJ35	161
YV-70CP	FA10	66
YV-78CP	FA20	28
YV-79CP	C550	397
YV-88CP	LJ25	033
YV-89CP	LJ36	002
YV-99CP	FA10	172
YV-100CP	LJ35	083
YV-101CP	FA10	47
YV-119P	WW24	184
YV-120CP	C500	368
YV-123CP	WW24	16
YV-125CP	LJ55	126
YV-126CP	FA20	30
YV-130P	LJ25	071
(YV-131CP)	LJ35	193
YV-132CP	LJ25	071
(YV-135CP)	C500	384
YV-137CP	C550	049
YV-140CP	C550	014
YV-141CP	HS25	25195
YV-147CP	C550	106
YV-151CP	C550	016
YV-159CP	C500	393
YV-160CP	WW24	211
YV-161P	LJ36	002
YV-162CP	C550	332
YV-163CP	MS76	103
YV-166CP	C500	384
YV-169CP	C550	018
YV-169CP	C560	0230
YV-173CP	LJ35	163
YV-178CP	LJ24	342
YV-187CP	C550	197
YV-187CP	JSTR	5107
YV-190CP	WW24	219
YV-200C	FA20	200
YV-203CP	LJ25	061
YV-205CP	C550	024
(YV-209CP)	C550	175
YV-210CP	WW24	308
YV-213CP	C550	076
YV-221CP	FA10	47
YV-232CP	C500	449
YV-253CP	C500	418
YV-253P	C500	418
YV-265CP	LJ35	247
(YV-269CP)	FA50	126
(YV-270CP)	LJ35	375
(YV-274CP)	MU30	A046SA
YV-276CP	C550	385
YV-278CP	LJ24	036
YV-286CP	LJ35	268
YV-292CP	LJ55	052
YV-297CP	WW24	202
YV-298CP	C550	175
YV-299CP	C550	133
YV-300CP	C550	172
YV-301CP	C550	174
YV-301P	C500	518
YV-309P	MU30	A049SA
(YV-325CP)	LJ55	112
YV-326CP	LJ35	352
YV-327CP	LJ35	344
(YV-328CP)	LJ35	309
YV-332CP	WW24	330
YV-370CP	C500	171
YV-374CP	LJ55	053
YV-376CP	C550	637
YV-387CP	WW24	306
YV-388CP	HFB3	1057
YV-388CP	WW24	307
YV-393CP	WW24	262
YV-432CP	LJ35	437
YV-433CP	LJ35	431
YV-434CP	LJ35	422
YV-450CP	FA50	219
YV-451CP	WW24	343
YV-452CP	FA50	4
YV-455CP	FA50	136
YV-462CP	FA50	4
(YV-553CP)	FA50	30
YV-572CP	CRVT	17
YV-589CP	CRVT	35
YV-601CP	FA10	73
YV-604P	C550	385
YV-606CP	C550	035
YV-625CP	C500	210
YV-646CP	C500	031
YV-662CP	C550	682
YV-666CP	WW24	347
YV-678CP	C550	106
YV-688CP	C500	524
YV-697CP	C500	446
YV-701CP	C550	683
YV-707CP	C500	070
YV-713CP	C550	463
YV-717CP	C500	135
YV-735CP	HS25	258203
YV-737CP	BE40	RJ-6
YV-738CP	BE40	RJ-6
YV-754CP	BE40	RK-152
YV-757CP	ASTR	060
YV-770CP	WW24	258
YV-771CP	ASTR	077
YV-772CP	GALX	041
YV-777CP	WW24	191
YV-778CP	C550	385
YV-785CP	ASTR	057
YV-800CP	HS25	258209
YV-810CP	C550	467
YV-811CP	C560	0134
YV-814CP	HS25	258234
YV-815CP	HS25	25098
YV-824CP	LJ24	173
YV-825CP	HS25	25175
YV-826CP	JSTR	5205
YV-838CP	BE40	RJ-6
YV-850CP	LJ35	596
YV-876C	FA20	200
YV-881CP	C500	052
YV-888CP	C550	235
YV-900CP	C550	214
YV-901CP	C500	058
YV-909CP	C550	317
YV-911CP	C550	698
YV-939CP	C500	031
YV-940CP	C500	299
YV-943CP	BE40	RK-142
YV-952CP	LJ31	168
YV-962CP	WW24	385
YV-968CP	BE40	RK-306
YV-997CP	LJ35	458
YV-999P	HFB3	1037
YV-1049CP	LJ25	253
YV-1055CP	C550	335
(YV-1071CP)	C500	200
(YV-1107)	C550	449
YV-1111CP	CL60	1028
YV-1111CP	HS25	25224
YV-1122CP	HS25	25248
YV-1133CP	C500	317
YV-1144CP	SBRL	282-106
YV-1145CP	HS25	25191
YV-1478P	C550	106
YV-2199P	ASTR	057
YV-2267P	C500	052
YV-2295P	C500	472
YV-2338P	**C550**	**449**
YV-2426P	C550	300
YV-2454P	WW24	96
YV-2477P	C500	052
YV-2479P	C500	035
YV-2482P	WW24	172
YV-2564P	ASTR	057
YV-2567P	C550	200
YV-2605P	C500	518
YV-2628P	C500	052
YV-2671P	C550	076
YV-2711P	C550	550-0943
YV-2821P	C500	167
YV-E-GPA	LJ24	047
YV-O-CVG-1	WW24	308
YV-O-CVG-2	C550	020
YV-O-CVG-3	WW24	343
YV-O-FMO-6	WW24	343
YV-O-MAC-1	C500	336
YV-O-MRI-1	LJ35	270
YV-O-MTC	C550	251
YV-O-MTC-2	C500	472
YV-O-MTC-20	C550	251
YV-O-SATA-12	FA50	4
YV-O-SID-3	C500	397
YV-T-000	C500	215
YV-T-AFA	C500	115
YV-T-ASG	LJ36	002
YV-T-AVA	FA20	287
YV-T-DTT	LJ25	071
YV-T-MMM	C500	253
YV....	**C500**	**088**
YV....	**C500**	**121**
YV....	**C500**	**187**
YV....	**C500**	**298**
YV....	**C550**	**064**
YV....	**C550**	**148**
YV....	**C550**	**157**
YV....	**C550**	**210**
YV....	**C550**	**248**
YV....	**C550**	**550-1035**
YV....	**C550**	**733**
YV....	**C560**	**0097**
YV....	**C560**	**0509**
YV....	**C650**	**0020**
YV....	**CS55**	**0012**
YV....	**CS55**	**0039**
YV....	**CS55**	**0071**
YV....	**CS55**	**0109**
YV....	**CS55**	**0130**
YV....	**FA20**	**492**
YV....	**GALX**	**039**
YV....	**GLF2**	**138**
YV....	**GLF3**	**422**
YV....	**LJ25**	**092**
YV....	**LJ25**	**346**
YV....	**LJ35**	**035**
YV....	**LJ35**	**327**
YV....	**LJ55**	**014**
YV....	**LJ55**	**025**
YV....	**LJ55**	**043**
YV....	**LJ55**	**101**
YV....	**WW24**	**235**
YV....	**WW24**	**236**
YV....	**WW24**	**320**
YV....	**WW24**	**356**
YV....	**WW24**	**401**
(YV....)	ASTR	012
(YV....)	ASTR	143
(YV....)	C550	550-0817
(YV....)	C550	560
(YV....)	C650	0170
(YV....)	GLF2	245/30
YV113T	**HS25**	**25231**
YV120T	SBRL	282-106
YV129T	LJ25	253
YV182T	**C550**	**182**
YV195T	MU30	A064SA
YV198T	BE40	RK-306
YV205T	C550	236
YV210T	C550	477
YV213T	BE40	RK-152
YV225T	**SBRL**	**282-120**
YV232T	C500	446
YV233T	C500	317
YV238T	**C500**	**072**
YV251T	**WW24**	**362**
YV252T	**C550**	**231**
YV255T	**C550**	**335**
YV265T	**SBRL**	**380-2**
YV266T	C550	550-0943
YV289T	C52A	0318
YV299T	**HS25**	**25176**
YV305T	C52A	0221
YV317T	C500	093
YV327T	CS55	0146
YV338T	**SBRL**	**380-44**
YV345T	HS25	256063
YV351T	LJ45	006
YV363T	**BE40**	**RK-38**
YV374T	**WW24**	**315**
YV415T	SBRL	465-37
YV416T	SBRL	282-98
YV436T	**LJ25**	**217**
YV448T	**LJ25**	**298**

YV453T	BE40	RK-299
YV457T	BE40	RK-557
YV463T	C560	0175
YV470T	C550	163
YV471T	BE40	RK-593
YV474T	C550	239
YV483T	C560	0204
YV484T	ASTR	057
YV487T	LJ55	003
YV499T	LJ35	117
YV501T	ASTR	024
YV504T	C560	0475
YV508T	C56X	5229
YV516T	C560	0339
YV521T	C550	550-0818
YV523T	LJ35	655
YV525T	LJ25	162
YV526T	LJ35	605
YV527T	C650	0182
YV533T	C525	0244
YV534T	C560	0526
YV540T	C56X	5282
YV543T	LJ35	246
YV544T	LJ25	356
YV546T	C560	0781
YV549T	C525	0084
YV552T	C650	7074
YV564T	BE40	RK-512
YV565T	C550	636
YV569T	GLF2	151/24
YV572T	HS25	258430
YV575T	HS25	257208
YV576T	CL61	5099
YV580T	BE40	RK-551
YV586T	HS25	25239
YV588T	WW24	379
YV589T	C550	369
YV592T	LJ25	302
YV593T	C500	397
YV598T	LJ55	013
YV600T	C550	171
YV602T	BE40	RK-177
YV603T	C550	647
YV606T	WW24	434
YV611T	C550	550-0813
YV616T	C560	0103
YV1018	C560	0408
YV1022	C560	0134
YV1079	LJ24	173
YV1083	FA50	22
YV1118	LJ45	396
YV1128	FA50	53
YV1129	FA50	63
YV1152	C500	043
YV1192	C550	683
YV1316	C500	052
YV1346	LJ25	253
YV1401	GALX	041
YV1432	C500	167
YV1475.	C500	125
YV1495	FA50	136
YV1496	FA50	219
YV1504	C550	719
YV1541	C500	399
YV1563	C550	463
YV1677	C500	109
YV1681	GLF2	25
YV1685	WW24	330
YV1686	C500	216
YV1687	HS25	25191
YV1713	C500	058
YV1738	LJ25	363
YV1771	ASTR	077
YV1776	C550	200
YV1794	LJ55	031
YV1813	C550	385
YV1820	C550	300
YV1828	LJ35	019
(YV1969)	C750	0134
YV2030	C500	215
YV2032	WW24	205
YV2039	F900	108
YV2040	F900	133
YV2044	LJ35	437
YV2053	F9EX	60
YV2073	C550	076
YV2103	C550	235
YV2110	C560	0511
YV2152	C52A	0121
YV2165	FA50	4
YV2166	C550	467
YV2245	C500	031
YV2246	C550	332
YV2254	C500	399
YV2286	C550	637
YV2315	HS25	25241
YV2317	C550	124
YV2331	C525	0631
YV2332	C550	309
YV2346	FA50	44
YV2347	MU30	A064SA
(YV2365)	LJ25	061
YV2389	C560	0757
YV2416	HS25	25098
YV2443	C550	236
YV2452	BE40	RK-68
YV2465	LJ25	126
YV2469	CS55	0099
YV2470	C750	0134
YV2474	FA10	67
YV2477	HS25	258149
YV2485	F9EX	196
YV2486	F9EX	197
YV2495	C500	147
YV2498	C500	139
YV2502	C500	352
YV2565	LJ45	389
YV2567	LJ45	390
YV2596	C550	262
YV2609	E50P	50000080
YV2611	LJ25	310
YV2619	C550	401
YV2620	C500	217
YV2655	C560	0050
YV2661	LJ35	360
YV2662	C550	076
YV2670	LJ45	407
YV2671	CS55	0146
YV2674	BE40	RK-298
YV2675	LJ25	235
YV2679	ASTR	061
YV2680	HS25	256063
YV2681	LJ25	234
YV2682	ASTR	050
YV2686	C560	0093
YV2692	CS55	0081
YV2696	C500	310
YV2698	BE40	RK-306
YV2699	LJ25	310
YV2716	LJ45	415
YV2723	FA20	322
YV2726	F900	136
YV2734	LJ45	407
YV2736	BE40	RK-299
YV2737	C500	194
YV2738	LJ45	424
YV2739	LJ45	425
YV2753	C500	317
YV2766	C550	719
YV2770	LJ55	131
YV2786	LJ25	148
YV2788	C550	317
YV2798	C560	0333
YV2800	C500	132
YV2806	FA10	109
(YV2818)	C750	0134
YV2831	C550	573
YV2837	HS25	258201
YV2839	BE40	RK-273
YV2844	C52A	0318
YV2853	CS55	0133
YV2855	C550	426
YV2864	C510	0112
YV2868	LJ55	004
YV2871	SBRL	282-98
YV2872	ASTR	036
YV2873	LJ25	372
YV2875	C550	610
YV2877	C550	550-1072
YV2896	GLF3	469
YV2904	LJ55	003
YV2908	WW24	307
YV2919	FA20	476
YV2932	C550	477
YV2940	C560	0391
YV2959	C550	397
YV2961	LJ55	058
YV2968	C550	213
YV2975	C56X	5287
YV2981	WW24	403
YV2982	C500	067
YV2988	CS55	0107
YV3009	C500	516
YV3019	CS55	0093
YV3023	C550	721
YV3025	C500	444
YV3027	LJ35	117
YV3029	C500	218
YV3030	C500	074
YV3040	CS55	0159
YV3046	ASTR	016
YV3049	ASTR	018
YV3057	BE40	RK-227
YV3065	LJ60	333
YV3086	C550	550-0943
YV3095.	C500	250
YV3098	CS55	0160
YV3102	LJ55	138
YV3103	C560	0516
YV3106	BE40	RK-87
YV3111	C550	186
YV3116	LJ25	302
YV3119	G150	312
YV3124	C550	087
YV3125	CS55	0085
YV3128	C560	0526
YV3130	GALX	033
YV3140	WW24	429
YV3146	LJ60	157
YV3147	C56X	5327
YV3148	C510	0266
YV3152	CS55	0125
YV3153	BE40	RJ-52
YV3164	LJ55	055
YV3167	LJ60	333
YV3170	C560	0479
YV3173	BE40	RK-141
YV3178	C560	0091
YV3179	LJ55	147
YV3182	C525	0244
YV3183	C550	550-1080
YV3184	C525	0084
YV3188	C550	365
YV3190	C560	0522
YV3191	LJ25	368
YV3193	LJ45	319
YV3194	ASTR	145
YV3198	LJ25	097
YV3213	C650	0159
YV3219	WW24	389
YV3221	CL61	3061
YV3225	C560	0282
YVO157	BE40	RK-103

Zimbabwe

Z-TBX	HS25	25067
Z-VEC	HS25	25215
Z-WKY	LJ25	160
Z-WSY	C500	387

Albania

ZA-AMA	C550	075
ZA-EVA	F2EX	182

Jersey

ZJ-THC	C52C	0200

New Zealand

(ZK-ABC)	HA4T	RC-21
ZK-AWK	C560	0396
ZK-EUI	HS25	258058
(ZK-EUR)	HS25	258058
ZK-JAK	C510	0347
ZK-JTH	C680	0058
ZK-KFB	GLF4	1362
ZK-KFB	GLF5	5260
ZK-KFB	GLF6	6043
ZK-LCA	C510	0011
ZK-LJL	C500	123
ZK-MAY	FA20	505
ZK-MAZ	FA10	213
ZK-MOT	C510	0054
ZK-MRM	HS25	258074
ZK-MUS	C510	0054
ZK-MUS	C510	0300
ZK-NBR	C500	602
ZK-NDT	C500	602
ZK-NLJ	BE40	0133
ZK-NXJ	BE40	RK-210
ZK-OCB	C52C	0112
ZK-PGA	C510	0033
ZK-PGA	C52C	0112
ZK-PJA	WW24	339
ZK-RGB	GALX	158
(ZK-RHP)	HS25	258088
ZK-RJI	HS25	258082
ZK-RJZ	C510	0398
ZK-RML	WW24	339
ZK-TBM	C525	0511
ZK-TBM	C52B	0027
ZK-TCB	HS25	258001
(ZK-VGL)	GALX	233
(ZK-WNL)	FA10	50
ZK-XVL	LJ35	649
ZK-YDZ	C510	0070

Paraguay

ZP-	WW24	41
ZP-...	C510	0139
ZP-...	C56X	5217
ZP-AGD	WW24	151
ZP-BJB	BE40	RK-19
ZP-BMG	C550	089
ZP-BTP	C560	0034
ZP-BZH	C560	0357
ZP-PNB	C500	335
ZP-PNB	C550	320
ZP-PUP	C500	335
ZP-TCA	C550	710
ZP-TDF	HS25	25173
ZP-TKO	HS25	25173
ZP-TNB	C550	320
ZP-TWN	C550	374
ZP-TYO	C500	008
ZP-TYO	C550	039
ZP-TYP	C500	008
ZP-TZH	C500	185
ZP-TZY	C500	275

South Africa

ZS-AAM	PRM1	RB-265
ZS-ABG	HS25	259024
ZS-ABG	PRM1	RB-70
ZS-ACE	C500	652
ZS-ACT	CL30	20034
ZS-ACT	HS25	259026
(ZS-ACT)	CL30	20038
ZS-AFD	C510	0134
ZS-AFG	HS25	258724
ZS-AGT	LJ31	146
ZS-AJD	LJ31	202
ZS-AJD	LJ45	369
(ZS-AJN)	LJ45	181
ZS-AJZ	GLF5	634
ZS-AKG	C680	0254
ZS-ALT	CL64	5552
ZS-AMB	C500	071
ZS-AML	C52C	0064
ZS-AMP	GLEX	9230
ZS-ANZ	CL61	5152
ZS-AOA	HS25	258160
ZS-AOL	GLF5	5343
ZS-AOL	GLF5	634
ZS-AOT	HS25	258670
ZS-AOT	BE40	RK-453
ZS-ARA	LJ35	349
ZS-ARG	C550	132
(ZS-ARK)	HS25	258658
ZS-AVL	CL64	5328
ZS-AVL	HS25	259017
ZS-AVM	PRM1	RB-31
ZS-BAR	LJ45	046
ZS-BAR	LJ45	219
(ZS-BAR)	LJ45	007
ZS-BCT	ASTR	075
ZS-BDC	FA10	148
ZS-BDG	PRM1	RB-68
ZS-BEN	CS55	0041
(ZS-BFB)	FA50	91
ZS-BFS	C500	262
ZS-BGA	CL60	1072
ZS-BLE	LJ35	304
ZS-BMB	FA50	91
ZS-BOT	HS25	HA-0032
ZS-BPG	HS25	258165
(ZS-BSS)	C525	0124
ZS-BTC	C500	161
ZS-BVO	C550	550-0942
ZS-BXR	LJ25	141
ZS-CAG	HS25	257172
ZS-CAL	HS25	25172
ZS-CAQ	FA50	133
ZS-CAR	CS55	0078
ZS-CAS	FA50	91
ZS-CAT	LJ25	366
ZS-CBI	PRM1	RB-214
ZS-CCT	CL61	5176
ZS-CCT	HS25	259026
ZS-CCW	C56X	5112
ZS-CDS	C560	0414
ZS-CEW	LJ35	341
ZS-CFA	HS25	259024
ZS-CJB	LJ45	037
ZS-CJT	C52A	0163
ZS-CJT	C52B	0116
ZS-CMB	CL64	5479
ZS-CNA	HS25	25159
ZS-CRH	LJ36	055
ZS-CSB	E55P	50500133
ZS-CTF	C510	0060
ZS-CTL	GLF2	218
ZS-CVU	LJ45	250
ZS-CWD	C500	420
ZS-CWG	CS55	0138
(ZS-DAJ)	GLEX	9094
ZS-DAV	F900	149
ZS-DBS	C500	061
ZS-DCA	LJ45	117
ZS-DCK	HS25	258403
ZS-DCT	LJ45	052
(ZS-DCT)	LJ31	146
ZS-DDA	HS25	258601
ZS-DDM	PRM1	RB-238
ZS-DDM	PRM1	RB-63
ZS-DDT	HA4T	RC-15
ZS-DDT	HA4T	RC-56
ZS-DDT	HS25	258465
ZS-DES	CS55	0087
ZS-DFI	C510	0093
(ZS-DFN)	GLEX	9099
ZS-DGB	CL64	5390
ZS-DGW	GLF2	166/15
(ZS-DHL)	LJ31	170
ZS-DIY	C510	0092
ZS-DJA	GLF2	156/31
ZS-DJB	LJ35	647
ZS-DKS	EA50	000142
ZS-DLJ	GLEX	9094
ZS-DPP	C52B	0211
ZS-DRS	C680	0209
ZS-DSA	C500	044
ZS-DTD	HA4T	RC-12
ZS-EAG	LJ31	142
ZS-EDA	CS55	0126
(ZS-EFD)	LJ35	594
ZS-EHL	C500	431
ZS-ELI	LJ55	084
ZS-ELJ	LJ55	109
ZS-ESA	GLEX	9061
ZS-ETN	PRM1	RB-295
ZS-EXG	HS25	258406
ZS-FCB	C56X	5018
(ZS-FCB)	C560	0503
ZS-FCI	F9EX	38
ZS-FCN	F9EX	91
ZS-FCW	C525	0834
ZS-FGS	FA10	150
ZS-FLJ	C560	0536
ZS-FOS	C56X	5352
ZS-FOX	FA10	72
ZS-FSI	HS25	258078
(ZS-FUL)	LJ45	181
(ZS-FUL)	LJ45	270
ZS-FUN	LJ24	354
ZS-GJB	GLEX	9122
ZS-GLD	LJ24	291
(ZS-GSB)	SBRL	282-53
ZS-GSG	LJ60	301
(ZS-HWK)	HS25	HA-0102
ZS-ICC	JSTR	5223
ZS-ICU	HS25	257113
ZS-IDC	C56X	5352
ZS-IDC	C680	0224
ZS-IDC	CS55	0148
ZS-IGP	LJ35	608
ZS-INS	LJ35	238
ZS-IPE	HS25	257202
(ZS-IPI)	HS25	257202
ZS-ISA	C500	224
ZS-ISA	CL60	1081
(ZS-ITT)	LJ45	007
ZS-IYY	C500	078
ZS-JBA	HS25	25259
(ZS-JBR)	LJ45	007
ZS-JCC	F900	181
ZS-JDL	C680	0033
ZS-JDL	C680	0193
ZS-JDL	CL30	20332
ZS-JDL	CL30	20556
ZS-JDM	C510	0079
ZS-JGC	GLF3	312
ZS-JHL	HS25	256049
ZS-JIH	HS25	25260
ZS-JIS	GLF2	136
ZS-JJO	LJ24	317
ZS-JKR	C500	268
ZS-JLK	FA10	207
ZS-JOK	C500	329
ZS-JOO	C500	291
ZS-JPO	CL30	20383
ZS-JPS	BE40	RK-453
(ZS-JRM)	LJ60	149
ZS-JRO	BE40	RK-101
ZS-JVS	FA20	493
ZS-JWC	LJ24	030
ZS-KAA	LJ45	305
ZS-KBS	HS25	HA-0017
ZS-KBS	PRM1	RB-147
ZS-KDR	GLEX	9023
ZS-KEN	CL64	5318
(ZS-KGF)	C500	538
ZS-KGS	FA20	385
ZS-KJY	LJ24	165
ZS-KOO	C550	154
ZS-KPA	C500	567
ZS-KPM	C510	0091
ZS-LAC	FA50	257
ZS-LAH	GLF3	328
ZS-LAL	FA20	228/473
ZS-LBB	FA50	42
ZS-LDK	C550	310
ZS-LDO	C500	652
ZS-LDV	C500	656
ZS-LEE	C550	380
ZS-LEO	CL64	5318
ZS-LHP	C500	667
ZS-LHT	C550	439
ZS-LHU	C550	179
ZS-LHW	C550	416
ZS-LIG	C550	474
ZS-LII	LJ35	062
ZS-LJC	LJ31	101
(ZS-LJM)	FA50	107
ZS-LKG	C510	0090
ZS-LLG	FA20	228/473
ZS-LLG	LJ24	210
ZS-LLO	C550	235
ZS-LME	HS25	25242
ZS-LMF	BE40	RK-146
ZS-LMH	C500	262
ZS-LNP	C550	560
ZS-LOG	GLF2	19
ZS-LOW	C500	514
ZS-LOW	LJ45	092
ZS-LOW	LJ45	228
ZS-LPE	HS25	25184
ZS-LPF	HS25	25269
ZS-LPH	C500	402
(ZS-LRI)	LJ25	366
ZS-LRJ	LJ45	223
ZS-LTK	LJ24	103
ZS-LUD	LJ25	295
ZS-LUX	GLF3	327
ZS-LWU	LJ24	209
ZS-LXH	LJ25	206
ZS-LXT	C500	622
ZS-LYB	C500	278
ZS-MAN	HS25	25067
ZS-MBR	LJ24	064
ZS-MBS	C500	340
ZS-MBX	C550	587
ZS-MCO	PRM1	RB-72
ZS-MCP	C500	130
ZS-MCU	C500	137
ZS-MDA	ASTR	055

ZS-MDN	LJ24	081
ZS-MEG	HS25	25233
ZS-MGD	F2EX	51
ZS-MGH	C500	299
ZS-MGJ	**LJ24**	**207**
ZS-MGK	LJ35	357
ZS-MGK	PRM1	RB-54
ZS-MGK	PRM1	RB-67
ZS-MGL	C500	384
ZS-MGS	**FA50**	**232**
ZS-MHN	**BE40**	**RJ-59**
ZS-MJD	**BE40**	**RK-18**
ZS-MLN	**C550**	**266**
ZS-MLS	C550	621
ZS-MMG	**GLF2**	**85**
ZS-MNU	**HS25**	**258435**
ZS-MPD	E55P	50500021
ZS-MPD	**E55P**	**50500127**
ZS-MPI	C500	334
ZS-MPN	C500	393
ZS-MPT	C560	0089
ZS-MRH	C750	0194
ZS-MTD	**LJ25**	**160**
ZS-MTG	C510	0405
ZS-MUS	**C510**	**0137**
ZS-MVV	C560	0062
ZS-MVX	C525	0010
ZS-MVZ	C560	0064
ZS-MWW	LJ35	157
(ZS-MYN)	C560	0064
ZS-MZM	WW24	390
ZS-MZO	C500	453
ZS-NAN	**F900**	**99**
ZS-NAT	C550	554
ZS-NDT	C560	0160
ZS-NDU	C560	0151
ZS-NDW	C560	0166
ZS-NDX	**C560**	**0152**
ZS-NER	CL60	1019
ZS-NEW	HS25	259017
(ZS-NEX)	LJ35	671
ZS-NFK	LJ35	671
ZS-NFL	C550	697
(ZS-NFS)	LJ35	671
ZS-NGG	LJ24	280
ZS-NGL	C560	0202
ZS-NGM	C560	0201
ZS-NGR	C500	080
ZS-NGS	**C560**	**0241**
ZS-NHC	C560	0203
ZS-NHD	C560	0255
ZS-NHE	C525	0033
ZS-NHF	C500	296
ZS-NHL	HS25	259032
ZS-NHO	C550	264
ZS-NID	LJ35	426
ZS-NII	**C550**	**184**
ZS-NJF	LJ25	311
ZS-NJH	HS25	258224
ZS-NKD	CL61	5060
ZS-NMO	GLF4	1129
ZS-NNF	F2TH	2
"ZS-NNV"	C560	0322
ZS-NOD	BE40	RJ-18
ZS-NPV	HS25	25215
ZS-NRZ	LJ35	077
ZS-NSB	LJ35	654
ZS-NTV	LJ60	052
ZS-NUW	C525	0150
ZS-NUZ	C560	0398
ZS-NVP	LJ60	210
ZS-NVV	C560	0322
ZS-NYG	**LJ25**	**098**
ZS-NYV	LJ31	115
ZS-NZO	BE40	RK-57
ZS-OAK	**GLEX**	**9631**
ZS-OAM	C500	077
ZS-OCG	BE40	RK-140
(ZS-ODP)	WW24	171
ZS-OEA	**LJ24**	**267**
ZS-OFM	C560	0467
ZS-OFW	LJ31	031
ZS-OGS	C500	260
ZS-OHZ	**C56X**	**5079**
ZS-OIE	**C550**	**480**
ZS-OIF	**HS25**	**25221**
ZS-OIZ	LJ45	006
"ZS-OJO"	LJ31	058
ZS-OLJ	LJ45	046
ZS-OML	**LJ31**	**170**
ZS-ONE	C500	002
ZS-ONG	**FA50**	**287**
ZS-ONL	CL61	3006
ZS-ONP	BE40	RK-157
ZS-OPD	LJ45	007
ZS-OPM	LJ45	308
ZS-OPN	LJ45	321
ZS-OPO	LJ45	342
ZS-OPR	**LJ45**	**219**
ZS-OPY	**LJ45**	**218**
ZS-ORW	**BE40**	**RJ-37**
ZS-OSG	CL64	5486
(ZS-OSP)	LJ45	130
ZS-OUU	BE40	RJ-25
ZS-OXB	LJ45	046
ZS-OXY	HS25	258095
(ZS-OZU)	HS25	25219

ZS-PAJ	C52A	0457
ZS-PAR	HS25	258050
(ZS-PBA)	LJ35	263
(ZS-PBI)	LJ24	145
ZS-PCY	HS25	258589
ZS-PDB	BE40	RK-162
ZS-PDG	LJ45	092
ZS-PDZ	**C52A**	**0422**
ZS-PFB	FA50	177
ZS-PFE	**PRM1**	**RB-94**
ZS-PFG	**C500**	**122**
ZS-PHP	**C500**	**490**
ZS-PJE	HS25	25023
ZS-PKD	GALX	098
ZS-PKR	**F2TH**	**114**
ZS-PKY	HS25	258429
ZS-PLC	HS25	25204
ZS-PMA	**C500**	**123**
ZS-PMC	C550	141
ZS-PNP	LJ31	202
ZS-PNP	**LJ45**	**059**
ZS-POT	BE40	RK-400
ZS-PPH	**HS25**	**258717**
(ZS-PPR)	HA4T	RC-13
(ZS-PPR)	LJ45	092
(ZS-PRF)	PRM1	RB-24
ZS-PRM	PRM1	RB-24
ZS-PSE	HS25	258231
ZS-PSG	**CS55**	**0112**
ZS-PTJ	SBRL	282-53
ZS-PTL	LJ45	046
ZS-PTL	LJ45	181
(ZS-PTL)	LJ35	594
ZS-PTP	HS25	258633
ZS-PTT	**C500**	**085**
ZS-PWT	**C500**	**076**
ZS-PWU	C525	0431
ZS-PXD	**C500**	**257**
ZS-PYY	**GLF2**	**26**
ZS-PZA	HS25	258632
ZS-PZX	HS25	258670
ZS-RCC	C500	106
ZS-RCS	C550	065
ZS-RKV	**C550**	**060**
ZS-SAB	C750	0080
ZS-SAB	**F2EX**	**212**
ZS-SAH	HS25	HA-0026
ZS-SAP	**C680**	**0190**
(ZS-SCT)	CL30	20038
(ZS-SCT)	LJ60	239
ZS-SCX	C550	569
ZS-SDU	**HS25**	**257053**
ZS-SDZ	CL65	5706
ZS-SEA	**FA10**	**156**
ZS-SEB	**FA10**	**127**
(ZS-SEB)	FA10	160
ZS-SES	LJ35	185
ZS-SFV	**LJ35**	**275**
ZS-SFY	ASTR	158
ZS-SGC	**CL61**	**5070**
ZS-SGH	LJ24	187
ZS-SGJ	HS25	HA-0032
ZS-SGS	PRM1	RB-72
ZS-SGT	**C500**	**224**
ZS-SGU	**LJ45**	**365**
ZS-SGV	HS25	HA-0067
ZS-SHC	**PRM1**	**RB-137**
ZS-SIO	C510	0156
ZS-SKC	**CL60**	**1030**
ZS-SMB	C560	0359
ZS-SME	**HS25**	**HA-0104**
ZS-SMT	HS25	25128
ZS-SOI	**HS25**	**257144**
ZS-SOM	C52A	0401
ZS-SOS	FA20	493
ZS-SRU	**PRM1**	**RB-63**
ZS-SSM	**LJ25**	**022**
ZS-STS	**E50P**	**50000069**
ZS-SUA	**C550**	**550-1059**
ZS-SUM	**C680**	**0047**
ZS-SUW	**PRM1**	**RB-66**
ZS-SYH	GLEX	9470
ZS-SYS	**HS25**	**257040**
ZS-SYU	**E55P**	**50500021**
ZS-TBN	**HS25**	**25023**
ZS-TBT	**HS25**	**257210**
ZS-TCW	**CL60**	**1066**
ZS-TDF	**GLEX**	**9603**
ZS-TEJ	**LJ60**	**173**
ZS-TEX	**GLF3**	**355**
ZS-TGG	GLF2	8
ZS-TJS	**LJ45**	**083**
ZS-TMG	C500	149
ZS-TNF	**HS25**	**258724**
ZS-TOW	**LJ35**	**475**
ZS-TOY	**LJ24**	**219**
ZS-TPG	GLF2	150
ZS-TSB	**C560**	**0398**
ZS-TSN	**CL60**	**1071**
ZS-UCH	C500	0607
ZS-ULT	**LJ45**	**194**
ZS-VIP	**GLF3**	**444**
ZS-WHG	GLF2	67
ZS-WJW	**HS25**	**257159**
ZS-XPH	**BE40**	**RK-402**
ZS-XRS	GLEX	9260
ZS-YAG	**CL60**	**1076**

ZS-YES	C510	0303
ZS-YES	CL30	20044
ZS-YES	LJ45	194
ZS-YTC	**EA50**	**000131**
ZS-ZBB	F900	143
ZS-ZBB	GLEX	9253
ZS-ZIM	**HS25**	**258499**
ZS-ZOT	HA4T	RC-23
(ZS-ZZZ)	LJ35	172

Macedonia

Z3-BAA	**LJ25**	**205**
Z3-MKD	**LJ60**	**279**

Guernsey

2-JFJC	**CL61**	**5023**
2-LIFE	**EA50**	**000023**
2-MATO	**CL61**	**5114**
2-SEXY	**CL61**	**5125**
2-TRAV	**GLF4**	**1224**

Monaco

3A-MDB	HS25	25131
3A-MDE	HS25	25131
3A-MGA	F2TH	167
3A-MGA	F9EX	195
3A-MGA	**FA7X**	**200**
3A-MGC	F9EX	195
3A-MGR	F2TH	167
3A-MGR	FA20	473
3A-MGT	FA10	19
3A-MJV	FA20	473
3A-MMA	F2TH	167
3A-MPP	MS76	098
3A-MRB	C550	421
3A-MRG	C52B	0096
3A-MTB	C500	482
3A-MWA	C550	063

Mauritius

3B-GFI	CL60	1019
3B-NGT	CL30	20133
3B-NSY	FA50	230
3B-PGF	**GLF4**	**1046**
3B-PGT	**GLEX**	**9676**
3B-RGT	CL65	5850
3B-SSD	CL30	20126
3B-XLA	F900	7

Equatorial Guinea

3C-LGE	**FA50**	**246**
3C-LLX	**GLF5**	**669**
3C-ONM	**F900**	**167**
3C-QQU	**JSTR**	**5082/36**
3C-QRK	JSTR	5202

Swaziland

3D-AAB	HS25	25080
3D-AAC	GLF2	136
3D-AAC	GLF3	354
3D-AAI	GLF3	354
3D-ABZ	HS25	25242
3D-ACB	FA10	21
3D-ACQ	C550	179
3D-ACR	C500	268
3D-ACT	C550	264
3D-ACZ	LJ35	238
3D-ADC	LJ35	475
3D-ADH	C500	667
3D-ADR	FA10	202
3D-AEZ	LJ25	160
3D-AFH	MU30	A062SA
3D-AFJ	LJ24	064
3D-ART	FA10	61
3D-AVH	C550	341
3D-AVL	HS25	25254
3D-AVL	HS25	258025
3D-BIS	LJ45	104
3D-BOS	HS25	256021
3D-IER	C500	489
3D-LLG	FA20	228/473
3D-TCB	GLF2	73/9

Guinea

(3X-GBD)	GLF2	74
3X-GCI	FA10	89

Azerbaijan

4K-AI06	**GLF5**	**5277**
4K-AI88	**GLF6**	**6107**
4K-AZ208	**G280**	**2016**
4K-AZ280	**G280**	**2008**
4K-AZ888	**GALX**	**189**
4K-AZ888	**GLF4**	**4045**
4K-MEK8	**GLF5**	**5204**

Georgia

4L-ALF	**E50P**	**50000250**
4L-GAF	**GLF4**	**4106**
4L-MPX	**C500**	**679**
4L-VIP	BE40	RK-394

Montenegro

4O-BBB	LJ45	372
4O-BVA	**BE40**	**RK-124**
4O-MNE	**LJ45**	**044**
4O-OOO	C500	489
4O-SEV	**LJ45**	**104**

Yemen

4W-ACA	HS25	25219
4W-ACE	HS25	257046
4W-ACM	HS25	257178
4W-ACN	HS25	258037

Israel

4X-...	**G280**	**2102**
4X-...	**G280**	**2103**
4X-...	G150	300
4X-AIP	WW24	243
4X-CJA	WW24	154
4X-CJB	WW24	153
4X-CJC	WW24	152
4X-CJD	WW24	151
4X-CJE	WW24	155
4X-CJF	WW24	156
4X-CJG	WW24	157
4X-CJH	WW24	158
4X-CJI	WW24	159
4X-CJJ	WW24	160
4X-CJK	WW24	161
4X-CJL	WW24	162
4X-CJM	WW24	163
4X-CJN	WW24	164
4X-CJO	WW24	165
4X-CJP	WW24	166
4X-CJP	WW24	376
4X-CJQ	WW24	167
4X-CJR	WW24	168
4X-CJR	WW24	404
4X-CJS	WW24	169
4X-CJS	WW24	413
4X-CJT	WW24	170
4X-CJU	WW24	171
4X-CJV	WW24	172
4X-CJW	WW24	173
4X-CJX	WW24	174
4X-CJY	WW24	175
4X-CJZ	WW24	176
4X-CKA	WW24	177
4X-CKB	WW24	178
4X-CKC	WW24	179
4X-CKD	WW24	180
4X-CKE	WW24	181
4X-CKF	WW24	182
4X-CKG	WW24	183
4X-CKH	WW24	184
4X-CKI	WW24	185
4X-CKJ	WW24	186
4X-CKK	WW24	187
4X-CKL	WW24	188
4X-CKM	WW24	189
4X-CKN	WW24	190
4X-CKO	WW24	191
4X-CKP	WW24	192
4X-CKQ	WW24	193
4X-CKR	WW24	194
4X-CKS	WW24	195
4X-CKT	WW24	196
4X-CKU	WW24	197
4X-CKV	WW24	198
4X-CKW	WW24	199
4X-CKX	WW24	200
4X-CKY	WW24	201
4X-CKZ	WW24	202
4X-CLA	WW24	203
4X-CLB	WW24	204
4X-CLC	WW24	205
4X-CLD	WW24	206
4X-CLE	WW24	207
4X-CLF	WW24	208
4X-CLG	WW24	209
4X-CLH	WW24	210
4X-CLI	WW24	211
4X-CLJ	WW24	212
4X-CLK	WW24	213
4X-CLL	**GALX**	**040**
4X-CLL	WW24	214
4X-CLM	WW24	215
4X-CLN	WW24	216
4X-CLO	WW24	217
4X-CLP	WW24	218
4X-CLQ	WW24	219
4X-CLR	WW24	220
4X-CLS	WW24	221
4X-CLT	WW24	222
4X-CLU	WW24	223
4X-CLV	WW24	224
4X-CLW	WW24	225
4X-CLX	WW24	226
4X-CLY	WW24	227
4X-CLZ	WW24	228
4X-CLZ	**HS25**	**258290**
4X-CMA	**C510**	**0299**
4X-CMA	WW24	229
4X-CMB	WW24	230
(4X-CMB)	GLEX	9349
4X-CMC	WW24	231
4X-CMD	WW24	232
4X-CME	WW24	233
4X-CMF	WW24	234
4X-CMF	CL64	5522
4X-CMG	WW24	235
4X-CMG	C500	535
4X-CMH	WW24	236
4X-CMH	CL61	5174
4X-CMI	WW24	237
4X-CMJ	WW24	238
4X-CMK	WW24	239
4X-CML	WW24	240
4X-CMM	WW24	241
(4X-CMM)	GLF3	369
4X-CMN	WW24	242
4X-CMN	**E50P**	**50000329**
4X-CMO	WW24	243
4X-CMP	WW24	244
4X-CMQ	WW24	245
4X-CMR	C650	0185
4X-CMR	WW24	246
4X-CMS	WW24	247
4X-CMT	WW24	248
4X-CMU	WW24	249
4X-CMV	WW24	250
4X-CMW	WW24	251
4X-CMX	WW24	252
4X-CMY	WW24	253
4X-CMY	CL64	5388
4X-CMZ	WW24	254
4X-CMZ	CL64	5450
4X-CNA	WW24	255
4X-CNB	WW24	256
4X-CNC	WW24	257
4X-CND	WW24	258
4X-CNE	WW24	259
4X-CNF	WW24	260
4X-CNG	WW24	261
4X-CNH	WW24	262
4X-CNI	WW24	263
4X-CNJ	WW24	264
4X-CNK	WW24	265
4X-CNL	WW24	266
4X-CNM	WW24	267
4X-CNN	WW24	268
4X-CNO	WW24	269
4X-CNP	WW24	270
4X-CNQ	WW24	271
4X-CNR	WW24	272
4X-CNS	WW24	273
4X-CNT	WW24	274
4X-CNU	WW24	275
4X-CNV	WW24	276
4X-CNW	WW24	277
4X-CNX	WW24	278
4X-CNY	WW24	279
4X-CNZ	WW24	280
4X-COA	WW24	71
4X-COB	WW24	138
4X-COC	WW24	422
4X-COE	CL64	5352
4X-COF	GLEX	9424
4X-COG	GALX	018
4X-COH	GLEX	9431
4X-COI	GLEX	9130
4X-COJ	WW24	29
(4X-COK)	WW24	107
4X-COL	WW24	107
4X-COM	WW24	126
4X-CON	WW24	55
4X-COO	CS55	0086
4X-COP	WW24	134
4X-COT	CL61	5032
4X-COV	HS25	258283
4X-COY	CL61	5154
4X-COZ	**CS55**	**0118**
(4X-COZ)	HS25	258114
4X-CPA	WW24	110
4X-CPB	WW24	113
4X-CPC	WW24	114
4X-CPD	WW24	130
4X-CPE	WW24	131
4X-CPF	WW24	139
4X-CPG	WW24	140
4X-CPH	WW24	141
4X-CPI	WW24	142
4X-CPJ	WW24	143
4X-CPK	WW24	144
4X-CPL	WW24	148
4X-CPM	WW24	149
4X-CPN	WW24	150
4X-CPO	WW24	414
4X-CPS	HS25	258391
4X-CPT	CS55	0145
4X-CPU	C56X	5074
4X-CPV	CL30	20065
4X-CPW	C550	550-0941
4X-CPX	**GLF4**	**1481**
4X-CPY	**BE40**	**RK-219**
4X-CQA	WW24	281
4X-CQB	WW24	282
4X-CQC	WW24	283
4X-CQD	WW24	284
4X-CQE	WW24	285
4X-CQF	WW24	286
4X-CQG	WW24	287
4X-CQH	WW24	288
4X-CQI	WW24	289
4X-CQJ	WW24	290
4X-CQK	WW24	291
4X-CQL	WW24	292
4X-CQM	WW24	293
4X-CQN	WW24	294

4X-CQO	WW24	295
4X-CQP	WW24	296
4X-CQQ	WW24	297
4X-CQR	WW24	298
4X-CQS	WW24	299
4X-CQT	WW24	300
4X-CQU	WW24	301
4X-CQV	WW24	302
4X-CQW	WW24	303
4X-CQX	WW24	304
4X-CQY	WW24	305
4X-CQZ	WW24	306
4X-CRA	WW24	307
4X-CRB	WW24	308
4X-CRC	WW24	309
4X-CRD	WW24	310
4X-CRE	WW24	311
4X-CRF	WW24	312
4X-CRG	WW24	313
4X-CRH	WW24	314
4X-CRI	WW24	315
4X-CRJ	WW24	316
4X-CRK	WW24	317
4X-CRL	WW24	318
4X-CRM	WW24	319
4X-CRN	WW24	320
4X-CRO	WW24	321
4X-CRP	WW24	322
4X-CRQ	WW24	323
4X-CRR	WW24	324
4X-CRS	WW24	325
4X-CRT	WW24	326
4X-CRU	HS25	258682
4X-CRU	WW24	327
4X-CRV	WW24	328
4X-CRW	WW24	329
4X-CRX	WW24	330
4X-CRY	HS25	258538
4X-CRY	WW24	331
4X-CRZ	WW24	332
4X-CTA	WW24	333
4X-CTB	WW24	334
4X-CTC	WW24	335
4X-CTD	WW24	336
4X-CTE	WW24	337
4X-CTF	WW24	338
4X-CTG	WW24	339
4X-CTH	WW24	340
4X-CTI	WW24	341
4X-CTJ	WW24	342
4X-CTK	WW24	343
4X-CTL	WW24	344
4X-CTM	WW24	345
4X-CTN	WW24	346
4X-CTO	WW24	347
4X-CTP	WW24	348
4X-CTQ	WW24	349
4X-CTR	WW24	350
4X-CTS	WW24	351
4X-CTT	WW24	352
4X-CTU	WW24	353
4X-CTV	WW24	354
4X-CUA	ASTR	004
4X-CUA	WW24	340
4X-CUA	WW24	392
4X-CUA	WW24	406
4X-CUB	WW24	341
4X-CUB	WW24	372
4X-CUB	WW24	384
4X-CUB	WW24	390
4X-CUB	WW24	408
4X-CUB	WW24	418
4X-CUC	WW24	385
4X-CUC	WW24	395
4X-CUC	WW24	411
4X-CUC	WW24	414
4X-CUC	WW24	423
4X-CUC	WW24	434
4X-CUD	ASTR	017
4X-CUD	WW24	367
4X-CUD	WW24	413
4X-CUD	WW24	416
4X-CUE	ASTR	019
4X-CUE	WW24	368
4X-CUE	WW24	386
4X-CUE	WW24	417
4X-CUE	WW24	436
4X-CUF	WW24	369
4X-CUF	WW24	375
4X-CUF	WW24	389
4X-CUF	WW24	399
4X-CUF	WW24	419
4X-CUF	WW24	426
4X-CUF	WW24	437
4X-CUG	ASTR	023
4X-CUG	ASTR	056
4X-CUG	ASTR	061
4X-CUG	ASTR	064
4X-CUG	WW24	370
4X-CUG	WW24	391
4X-CUG	WW24	404
4X-CUG	WW24	435
4X-CUG	WW24	439
4X-CUH	ASTR	025
4X-CUH	ASTR	057
4X-CUH	WW24	371
4X-CUH	WW24	376
4X-CUH	WW24	388
4X-CUH	WW24	403
4X-CUH	WW24	420
4X-CUH	WW24	432
4X-CUH	WW24	433
4X-CUI	ASTR	026
4X-CUI	ASTR	030
4X-CUI	ASTR	055
4X-CUI	ASTR	063
4X-CUI	WW24	355
4X-CUI	WW24	378
4X-CUI	WW24	422
4X-CUJ	ASTR	027
4X-CUJ	ASTR	034
4X-CUJ	ASTR	062
4X-CUJ	ASTR	065
4X-CUJ	WW24	356
4X-CUJ	WW24	377
4X-CUJ	WW24	379
4X-CUJ	WW24	387
4X-CUJ	WW24	405
4X-CUJ	WW24	421
4X-CUJ	WW24	424
4X-CUJ	WW24	438
4X-CUJ	WW24	440
4X-CUK	ASTR	011
4X-CUK	ASTR	016
4X-CUK	WW24	357
4X-CUK	WW24	373
4X-CUK	WW24	393
4X-CUK	WW24	407
4X-CUK	WW24	425
4X-CUK	WW24	429
4X-CUL	ASTR	012
4X-CUL	WW24	358
4X-CUL	WW24	374
4X-CUM	ASTR	013
4X-CUM	WW24	359
4X-CUM	WW24	380
4X-CUM	WW24	394
4X-CUM	WW24	409
4X-CUM	WW24	430
4X-CUM?	WW24	409
4X-CUN	ASTR	014
4X-CUN	ASTR	032
4X-CUN	WW24	360
4X-CUN	WW24	397
4X-CUN	WW24	427
4X-CUN	WW24	431
4X-CUO	WW24	361
4X-CUO	WW24	381
4X-CUO	WW24	398
4X-CUO	WW24	409
4X-CUO	WW24	410
4X-CUO	WW24	428
4X-CUO	WW24	442
4X-CUP	ASTR	015
4X-CUP	ASTR	033
4X-CUP	WW24	362
4X-CUP	WW24	382
4X-CUP	WW24	400
4X-CUP	WW24	412
4X-CUP	WW24	441
4X-CUQ	WW24	363
4X-CUQ	WW24	383
4X-CUQ	WW24	401
4X-CUR	ASTR	018
4X-CUR	ASTR	021
4X-CUR	WW24	364
4X-CUR	WW24	396
4X-CUR	**CL64**	**5645**
4X-CUS	ASTR	020
4X-CUS	WW24	365
4X-CUS	WW24	402
4X-CUS	WW24	415
4X-CUT	ASTR	022
4X-CUT	ASTR	024
4X-CUT	WW24	366
4X-CUU	ASTR	087
4X-CUV	ASTR	076
4X-CUW	ASTR	071
4X-CUW	ASTR	075
4X-CUX	ASTR	079
4X-CUY	ASTR	080
4X-CUZ	ASTR	119
4X-CVC	G280	2043
4X-CVC	G280	2050
4X-CVC	G280	2058
4X-CVC	G280	2066
4X-CVC	G280	2074
4X-CVC	G280	2082
4X-CVC	G280	2090
4X-CVC	G280	2097
4X-CVD	G280	2044
4X-CVD	G280	2051
4X-CVD	G280	2059
4X-CVD	G280	2067
4X-CVD	G280	2075
4X-CVD	G280	2083
4X-CVD	G280	2091
4X-CVD	G280	2098
4X-CVE	GALX	012
4X-CVE	GALX	022
4X-CVE	GALX	026
4X-CVE	GALX	032
4X-CVE	GALX	035
4X-CVE	GALX	038
4X-CVE	GALX	039
4X-CVE	GALX	041
4X-CVE	GALX	044
4X-CVE	GALX	047
4X-CVE	GALX	050
4X-CVE	GALX	053
4X-CVE	GALX	056
4X-CVE	GALX	059
4X-CVE	GALX	063
4X-CVE	GALX	068
4X-CVE	GALX	079
4X-CVE	GALX	083
4X-CVE	GALX	087
4X-CVE	GALX	109
4X-CVE	GALX	114
4X-CVE	GALX	120
4X-CVE	ASTR	124
4X-CVE	GALX	128
4X-CVE	GALX	133
4X-CVE	GALX	140
4X-CVE	GALX	146
4X-CVE	ASTR	152
4X-CVE	GALX	152
4X-CVE	GALX	158
4X-CVE	GALX	165
4X-CVE	GALX	171
4X-CVE	GALX	177
4X-CVE	GALX	182
4X-CVE	GALX	192
4X-CVE	GALX	198
4X-CVE	G280	2007
4X-CVE	G280	2013
4X-CVE	G280	2019
4X-CVE	G280	2025
4X-CVE	GALX	203
4X-CVE	G280	2031
4X-CVE	G280	2037
4X-CVE	G280	2045
4X-CVE	G280	2052
4X-CVE	G280	2060
4X-CVE	G280	2068
4X-CVE	GALX	207
4X-CVE	G280	2076
4X-CVE	G280	2084
4X-CVE	G280	2092
4X-CVE	G280	2099
4X-CVE	GALX	213
4X-CVE	GALX	219
4X-CVE	GALX	225
4X-CVE	GALX	232
4X-CVE	GALX	236
4X-CVE	GALX	240
4X-CVE	GALX	242
4X-CVE	GALX	244
4X-CVE	GALX	247
4X-CVF	GALX	004
4X-CVF	GALX	017
4X-CVF	GALX	021
4X-CVF	GALX	027
4X-CVF	GALX	030
4X-CVF	GALX	034
4X-CVF	GALX	042
4X-CVF	GALX	045
4X-CVF	GALX	048
4X-CVF	GALX	051
4X-CVF	GALX	055
4X-CVF	GALX	060
4X-CVF	GALX	064
4X-CVF	GALX	069
4X-CVF	GALX	073
4X-CVF	GALX	095
4X-CVF	GALX	099
4X-CVF	GALX	107
4X-CVF	GALX	115
4X-CVF	GALX	116
4X-CVF	GALX	124
4X-CVF	ASTR	128
4X-CVF	GALX	129
4X-CVF	GALX	136
4X-CVF	GALX	142
4X-CVF	ASTR	147
4X-CVF	GALX	147
4X-CVF	GALX	153
4X-CVF	GALX	159
4X-CVF	GALX	164
4X-CVF	GALX	169
4X-CVF	GALX	175
4X-CVF	GALX	180
4X-CVF	GALX	184
4X-CVF	GALX	189
4X-CVF	GALX	195
4X-CVF	G280	2008
4X-CVF	GALX	201
4X-CVF	G280	2014
4X-CVF	G280	2020
4X-CVF	G280	2026
4X-CVF	G280	2032
4X-CVF	G280	2038
4X-CVF	G280	2046
4X-CVF	G280	2053
4X-CVF	G280	2061
4X-CVF	G280	2069
4X-CVF	G280	2077
4X-CVF	GALX	208
4X-CVF	G280	2085
4X-CVF	G280	2093
4X-CVF	G280	2100
4X-CVF	GALX	214
4X-CVF	GALX	220
4X-CVF	GALX	226
4X-CVF	GALX	233
4X-CVF	GALX	237
4X-CVF	GALX	241
4X-CVF	GALX	245
4X-CVF	GALX	248
4X-CVG	GALX	013
4X-CVG	GALX	052
4X-CVG	GALX	057
4X-CVG	GALX	061
4X-CVG	GALX	065
4X-CVG	GALX	070
4X-CVG	GALX	075
4X-CVG	GALX	081
4X-CVG	GALX	096
4X-CVG	GALX	106
4X-CVG	GALX	110
4X-CVG	GALX	117
4X-CVG	GALX	122
4X-CVG	ASTR	125
4X-CVG	GALX	126
4X-CVG	ASTR	127
4X-CVG	ASTR	129
4X-CVG	GALX	130
4X-CVG	ASTR	131
4X-CVG	ASTR	133
4X-CVG	ASTR	134
4X-CVG	GALX	135
4X-CVG	ASTR	136
4X-CVG	ASTR	138
4X-CVG	GALX	141
4X-CVG	GALX	148
4X-CVG	ASTR	151
4X-CVG	GALX	154
4X-CVG	GALX	160
4X-CVG	GALX	166
4X-CVG	GALX	172
4X-CVG	GALX	178
4X-CVG	GALX	183
4X-CVG	GALX	188
4X-CVG	GALX	193
4X-CVG	GALX	199
4X-CVG	G280	2002
4X-CVG	G280	2009
4X-CVG	G280	2015
4X-CVG	G280	2021
4X-CVG	G280	2027
4X-CVG	G280	2033
4X-CVG	G280	2039
4X-CVG	GALX	204
4X-CVG	G280	2047
4X-CVG	G280	2054
4X-CVG	G280	2062
4X-CVG	G280	2070
4X-CVG	G280	2078
4X-CVG	G280	2086
4X-CVG	GALX	210
4X-CVG	**G280**	**2101**
4X-CVG	GALX	216
4X-CVG	GALX	222
4X-CVG	GALX	227
4X-CVG	GALX	231
4X-CVG	GALX	235
4X-CVG	GALX	238
4X-CVG	GALX	243
4X-CVG	GALX	249
4X-CVH	GALX	018
4X-CVH	GALX	023
4X-CVH	GALX	028
4X-CVH	GALX	031
4X-CVH	GALX	037
4X-CVH	GALX	040
4X-CVH	GALX	043
4X-CVH	GALX	046
4X-CVH	GALX	049
4X-CVH	GALX	062
4X-CVH	GALX	066
4X-CVH	GALX	071
4X-CVH	GALX	077
4X-CVH	GALX	086
4X-CVH	GALX	089
4X-CVH	GALX	092
4X-CVH	GALX	103
4X-CVH	GALX	111
4X-CVH	GALX	121
4X-CVH	GALX	127
4X-CVH	GALX	131
4X-CVH	GALX	137
4X-CVH	ASTR	143
4X-CVH	GALX	143
4X-CVH	GALX	149
4X-CVH	GALX	155
4X-CVH	GALX	161
4X-CVH	GALX	167
4X-CVH	GALX	174
4X-CVH	GALX	185
4X-CVH	GALX	190
4X-CVH	GALX	196
4X-CVH	G280	2010
4X-CVH	G280	2016
4X-CVH	GALX	202
4X-CVH	G280	2022
4X-CVH	G280	2028
4X-CVH	G280	2034
4X-CVH	G280	2040
4X-CVH	G280	2055
4X-CVH	G280	2063
4X-CVH	G280	2071
4X-CVH	G280	2079
4X-CVH	G280	2087
4X-CVH	GALX	209
4X-CVH	G280	2094
4X-CVH	GALX	215
4X-CVH	GALX	221
4X-CVH	GALX	228
4X-CVH	GALX	234
4X-CVH	GALX	239
4X-CVH	GALX	246
4X-CVH	GALX	250
4X-CVI	GALX	015
4X-CVI	GALX	020
4X-CVI	GALX	024
4X-CVI	GALX	054
4X-CVI	GALX	058
4X-CVI	GALX	094
4X-CVI	GALX	097
4X-CVI	GALX	100
4X-CVI	GALX	104
4X-CVI	GALX	108
4X-CVI	GALX	112
4X-CVI	GALX	119
4X-CVI	GALX	125
4X-CVI	ASTR	130
4X-CVI	ASTR	132
4X-CVI	GALX	132
4X-CVI	ASTR	135
4X-CVI	ASTR	137
4X-CVI	GALX	138
4X-CVI	ASTR	139
4X-CVI	ASTR	141
4X-CVI	GALX	144
4X-CVI	ASTR	146
4X-CVI	ASTR	148
4X-CVI	GALX	150
4X-CVI	GALX	156
4X-CVI	GALX	162
4X-CVI	GALX	168
4X-CVI	GALX	173
4X-CVI	GALX	194
4X-CVI	GALX	200
4X-CVI	G280	2005
4X-CVI	G280	2011
4X-CVI	G280	2017
4X-CVI	G280	2023
4X-CVI	G280	2029
4X-CVI	G280	2035
4X-CVI	G280	2041
4X-CVI	G280	2048
4X-CVI	G280	2056
4X-CVI	GALX	206
4X-CVI	G280	2064
4X-CVI	G280	2072
4X-CVI	G280	2080
4X-CVI	G280	2088
4X-CVI	G280	2095
4X-CVI	GALX	211
4X-CVI	GALX	217
4X-CVI	GALX	224
4X-CVI	GALX	229
4X-CVJ	GALX	074
4X-CVJ	GALX	078
4X-CVJ	GALX	082
4X-CVJ	GALX	085
4X-CVJ	GALX	088
4X-CVJ	GALX	091
4X-CVJ	GALX	101
4X-CVJ	GALX	105
4X-CVJ	GALX	118
4X-CVJ	ASTR	123
4X-CVJ	GALX	123
4X-CVJ	ASTR	126
4X-CVJ	GALX	134
4X-CVJ	GALX	139
4X-CVJ	GALX	145
4X-CVJ	GALX	151
4X-CVJ	ASTR	153
4X-CVJ	ASTR	155
4X-CVJ	GALX	157
4X-CVJ	ASTR	158
4X-CVJ	GALX	163
4X-CVJ	GALX	170
4X-CVJ	GALX	176
4X-CVJ	GALX	181
4X-CVJ	GALX	186
4X-CVJ	GALX	191
4X-CVJ	GALX	197
4X-CVJ	G280	2006
4X-CVJ	G280	2012
4X-CVJ	G280	2018
4X-CVJ	G280	2024
4X-CVJ	G280	2030
4X-CVJ	G280	2036
4X-CVJ	G280	2042
4X-CVJ	G280	2049
4X-CVJ	GALX	205
4X-CVJ	G280	2057
4X-CVJ	G280	2065
4X-CVJ	G280	2073
4X-CVJ	G280	2081
4X-CVJ	G280	2089
4X-CVJ	G280	2096
4X-CVJ	GALX	212

4X-CVJ	GALX	218
4X-CVJ	GALX	223
4X-CVJ	GALX	230
4X-CVK	GALX	016
4X-CVK	GALX	019
4X-CVK	GALX	025
4X-CVK	GALX	029
4X-CVK	GALX	033
4X-CVK	GALX	036
4X-CVK	GALX	067
4X-CVK	GALX	072
4X-CVK	GALX	076
4X-CVK	GALX	080
4X-CVK	GALX	084
4X-CVK	GALX	090
4X-CVK	GALX	093
4X-CVK	GALX	098
4X-CVK	GALX	102
4X-CVK	GALX	113
4X-CVK	ASTR	140
4X-CVK	ASTR	142
4X-CVK	ASTR	144
4X-CVK	ASTR	145
4X-CVK	ASTR	150
4X-CVK	ASTR	157
4X-CVK	G150	203
4X-CVK	G150	205
4X-CVK	G150	207
4X-CVK	G150	209
4X-CVK	G150	211
4X-CVK	G150	213
4X-CVK	G150	215
4X-CVK	G150	217
4X-CVK	G150	223
4X-CVK	G150	227
4X-CVK	G150	230
4X-CVK	G150	234
4X-CVK	G150	239
4X-CVK	G150	244
4X-CVK	G150	249
4X-CVK	G150	252
4X-CVK	G150	258
4X-CVK	G150	263
4X-CVK	G150	268
4X-CVK	G150	273
4X-CVK	G150	277
4X-CVK	G150	281
4X-CVK	G150	286
4X-CVK	G150	291
4X-CVK	G150	296
4X-CVK	G150	301
4X-CVK	G150	304
4X-CVK	G150	307
4X-CVK	G150	311
4X-CVK	G150	313
4X-CVK	G150	318
4X-CVK	G150	321
4X-CVL	G150	219
4X-CVL	G150	222
4X-CVL	G150	226
4X-CVL	G150	231
4X-CVL	G150	235
4X-CVL	G150	241
4X-CVL	G150	246
4X-CVL	G150	251
4X-CVL	G150	256
4X-CVL	G150	261
4X-CVL	G150	265
4X-CVL	G150	270
4X-CVL	G150	276
4X-CVL	G150	283
4X-CVL	G150	289
4X-CVL	G150	294
4X-CVL	G150	297
4X-CVL	G150	302
4X-CVL	G150	305
4X-CVL	G150	310
4X-CVL	G150	316
4X-CVL	G150	319
4X-CVM	GALX	179
4X-CVM	G150	220
4X-CVM	G150	224
4X-CVM	G150	228
4X-CVM	G150	232
4X-CVM	G150	237
4X-CVM	G150	242
4X-CVM	G150	247
4X-CVM	G150	254
4X-CVM	G150	259
4X-CVM	G150	264
4X-CVM	G150	269
4X-CVM	G150	274
4X-CVM	G150	279
4X-CVM	G150	285
4X-CVM	G150	290
4X-CVM	G150	295
4X-CVM	G150	298
4X-CVM	G150	303
4X-CVM	G150	306
4X-CVM	G150	317
4X-CVM	G150	320
4X-CVP	G280	2004
4X-CYH	LJ45	336
4X-CZA	**C650**	**0187**
4X-CZD	**C550**	**079**
4X-CZI	**CL60**	**1042**
4X-CZM	HS25	258279
4X-CZO	**HS25**	**258183**
4X-DFZ	C510	0090
4X-FVN	WW24	134
4X-IGA	GALX	003
4X-IGB	GALX	005
4X-IGO	GALX	004
4X-JYF	WW24	152
4X-JYG	WW24	107
4X-JYJ	WW24	185
4X-JYJ	**WW24**	**185**
4X-JYO	WW24	186
4X-JYO	**WW24**	**186**
4X-JYR	WW24	152
4X-JYR	**WW24**	**152**
(4X-NOY)	WW24	213
4X-TRA	G150	201
4X-TRA	G150	236
4X-TRA	G150	240
4X-TRA	G150	245
4X-TRA	G150	250
4X-TRA	G150	255
4X-TRA	G150	260
4X-TRA	G150	267
4X-TRA	G150	272
4X-TRA	G150	278
4X-TRA	G150	282
4X-TRA	G150	287
4X-TRA	G150	292
4X-TRA	G150	299
4X-TRA	G150	308
4X-TRA	G150	312
4X-TRA	G150	314
4X-WBJ	G280	2003
4X-WIA	**ASTR**	**002**
4X-WID	G150	202
4X-WID	G150	204
4X-WID	G150	206
4X-WID	G150	208
4X-WID	G150	210
4X-WID	G150	212
4X-WID	G150	214
4X-WID	G150	216
4X-WID	G150	218
4X-WID	G150	221
4X-WID	G150	225
4X-WID	G150	229
4X-WID	G150	233
4X-WID	G150	238
4X-WID	G150	243
4X-WID	G150	248
4X-WID	G150	253
4X-WID	G150	257
4X-WID	G150	262
4X-WID	G150	266
4X-WID	G150	271
4X-WID	G150	275
4X-WID	G150	280
4X-WID	G150	284
4X-WID	G150	288
4X-WID	G150	293
4X-WID	G150	309
4X-WID	G150	315
4X-WIN	ASTR	001
4X-WIX	ASTR	073
4X-WSJ	G280	2001
4X-WSM	G280	2002

Libya

5A-DAC	LJ24	074
5A-DAD	LJ24	075
5A-DAF	FA20	128/436
5A-DAG	**FA20**	**143/442**
5A-DAJ	JSTR	5136
5A-DAR	JSTR	5221
5A-DBZ	**JSTR**	**5114/18**
5A-DCK	**CRVT**	**38**
5A-DCM	**FA50**	**68**
5A-DCN	**F9EX**	**148**
5A-DCO	**FA20**	**190/465**
5A-DDR	GLF2	240
5A-DDS	**GLF2**	**242**
5A-DGI	FA50	17
5A-DKQ	FA20	175
5A-DRK	**C56X**	**5710**
5A-DRL	**C56X**	**5808**
5A-UAA	**CL30**	**20175**
5A-UAB	**GLEX**	**9285**
5A-UAC	**GLEX**	**9257**
5A-UAE	**LJ60**	**385**

Cyprus

5B-...	**HS25**	**25088**
5B-CGB	FA20	32
5B-CGP	JSTR	5128/16
5B-CHE	JSTR	5114/18
5B-CHX	CL60	1028
5B-CIQ	C550	660
5B-CIS	C550	200
5B-CJG	ASTR	099
(5B-CKG)	HS25	258554
5B-CKK	CL61	5094
5B-CKL	HS25	258495
5B-CKN	FA50	339
5B-CKO	**F2EX**	**96**
5B-CSM	C650	0094

Tanzania

5H-APH	JSTR	5219
5H-BLM	HS25	259027
5H-ETG	**C560**	**0070**
5H-LUX	**C510**	**0342**
5H-ONE	**GLF5**	**5030**
5H-SMZ	HS25	257172

Nigeria

5N-...	**GALX**	**180**
5N-...	**CL61**	**5157**
5N-...	**HS25**	**HA-0194**
(5N-...)	HS25	259016
(5N-...)	HS25	259025
5N-AAN	HS25	25125
5N-AER	HS25	25099
5N-AET	HS25	25117
5N-AGU	HS25	25085
5N-AGV	GLF2	177
5N-AGZ	HS25	258143
5N-AKT	HS25	25117
5N-ALH	**HS25**	**25089**
5N-ALX	HS25	256012
5N-ALY	HS25	25106
5N-AMF	HFB3	1028
5N-AMK	HS25	25010
5N-AML	GLF2	186
5N-AMM	SBRL	380-17
5N-AMN	GLF2	13
5N-AMR	C550	045
5N-AMX	HS25	257115
5N-AMY	HS25	25227
5N-ANG	HS25	256050
5N-AOC	LJ25	322
5N-AOG	HS25	25143
5N-AOL	HS25	256050
5N-APN	C500	286
5N-APZ	**CL61**	**5026**
5N-AQY	HS25	25231
5N-ARD	HS25	256030
5N-ARE	FA50	110
5N-ARN	HS25	256056
5N-ASQ	LJ25	344
5N-ASZ	HS25	25063
5N-AVJ	HS25	257118
5N-AVK	**HS25**	**257160**
5N-AVL	C500	651
5N-AVM	C500	653
5N-AVV	HS25	25138
5N-AVZ	HS25	25113
5N-AWB	HS25	25025
5N-AWD	HS25	25008
5N-AWJ	C550	252
5N-AWS	HS25	256042
5N-AXO	HS25	257196
5N-AXP	HS25	257203
5N-AYA	C550	632
5N-AYK	HS25	256060
5N-AYM	FA20	228/473
5N-AYN	FA20	427
5N-AYO	FA20	383/550
5N-AZK	**GLF4**	**4323**
5N-BCI	C500	085
5N-BEL	C555	0079
5N-BEX	**HS25**	**257197**
5N-BFC	**HS25**	**257150**
5N-BGR	LJ45	163
5N-BGV	GLF2	177
5N-BJS	**C56X**	**5703**
"5N-BLV"	GLF2	177
5N-BLW	**LJ45**	**350**
5N-BMM	C56X	5830
5N-BMR	**HS25**	**258264**
5N-BMT	**HS25**	**258231**
5N-BNE	**HS25**	**258265**
5N-BNM	**HS25**	**258429**
5N-BOD	**GLF4**	**1126**
5N-BOH	**F900**	**52**
5N-BOO	**HS25**	**258143**
5N-BOQ	C56X	5629
5N-BSP	**CL64**	**5356**
5N-BUA	HS25	25178
5N-DAL	**LJ45**	**358**
5N-DAO	**HS25**	**257182**
5N-DGN	**HS25**	**259018**
5N-DIA	**C52C**	**0092**
5N-DNL	HS25	256052
5N-DOT	HS25	256062
5N-DUK	C550	550-0925
5N-EAS	**HS25**	**25217**
5N-EMA	HS25	256069
5N-EMS	**C680**	**0342**
5N-EPN	FA20	273
5N-EXJ	**HS25**	**258312**
5N-EZE	WW24	141
5N-FGE	F900	96
5N-FGO	F900	52
5N-FGP	GLF4	1126
5N-FGR	HS25	259018
5N-FGS	**GLF5**	**643**
5N-FGU	**FA7X**	**90**
5N-FGV	**FA7X**	**126**
5N-FGW	**GLF5**	**5310**
5N-FGX	**HA4T**	**RC-66**
5N-HAR	**C56X**	**6067**
5N-IGY	CL61	5037
5N-IMR	C560	0087
5N-IMR	GLF3	344
5N-IZY	**HS25**	**258514**
5N-IZZ	C550	550-0872
5N-JMA	HS25	258658
5N-JMB	**HS25**	**258659**
5N-LDM	**LJ45**	**327**
5N-MAO	**HS25**	**257186**
5N-MAY	HS25	256062
5N-MAZ	HS25	257169
5N-NBC	HS25	256052
5N-NOC	**HA4T**	**RC-38**
5N-NPC	**HS25**	**258109**
5N-NPF	**C550**	**138**
5N-NPF	HS25	258143
5N-OIL	F900	96
5N-OPT	HS25	256063
5N-PAZ	**CL61**	**5180**
5N-PZE	**GLF4**	**1175**
5N-QTS	**HS25**	**258020**
5N-RNO	HS25	256054
5N-SPL	**HS25**	**258984**
5N-WMA	**HS25**	**25178**
5N-YET	**HS25**	**256013**
5N-YFS	HS25	256054
5N-YYY	**HS25**	**HA-0072**

Malagasy (Madagascar)

5R-...	**C500**	**308**
5R-AHF	**C56X**	**5131**
5R-HMR	**C56X**	**5209**
5R-MBR	CRVT	16
5R-MGX	**C550**	**550-1054**
5R-MHF	C550	141
5R-MHK	**CRVT**	**34**
5R-MVD	CRVT	35
5R-MVN	CRVT	16

Mauritania

5T-UPR	GLF2	175

Togo

5V-MBG	FA10	167
5V-TAA	GLF2	149
5V-TAC	GLF2	167
5V-TAE	FA10	167
5V-TTM	**HS25**	**258632**
5V-TTP	**HS25**	**256049**
5V-TTS	**F900**	**33**

Uganda

5X-AAB	WW24	134
5X-UEF	GLF4	1413
5X-UGF	**GLF5**	**5208**
5X-UOI	GLF3	345
5X-UPF	GLF2	133

Kenya

5Y-BYD	C550	550-0932
5Y-CAX	**FA10**	**140**
5Y-CCB	**C550**	**550-1088**
5Y-GEO	LJ24	273
5Y-HAB	C550	028
5Y-MNG	**C550**	**550-0876**
5Y-MSR	**C550**	**550-0975**
5Y-PAA	**C680**	**0094**
5Y-SIR	**C550**	**550-0995**
(5Y-TCI)	C525	0217
5Y-TWE	C550	569
(5Y-WEC)	C550	353
5Y-WHB	**C56X**	**5085**
5Y-YAH	**C650**	**0217**

Senegal

6V-AEA	CRVT	8
6V-AFL	GLF2	136
6V-AGQ	GLF2	136
6V-AIM	HS25	257062
6V-AIN	**HS25**	**25261**
6V-AIQ	C550	347

Yemen Republic

7O-ADC	HS25	258037

Lesotho

7P-TCB	GLF2	73/9

Malawi

7Q-ONE	F9EX	38
7Q-YJI	HS25	257076
7Q-YLF	C550	706
7Q-YTL	C500	605

Algeria

7T-VCW	**HS25**	**257163**
7T-VCX	**C56X**	**6023**
7T-VHB	GLF2	230
7T-VHP	JSTR	5233
7T-VNC	**C56X**	**6171**
7T-VNF	**C52A**	**0436**
7T-VPA	F900	81
7T-VPB	F900	82
7T-VPC	**GLF4**	**1418**
7T-VPG	**GLF5**	**617**
7T-VPM	**GLF4**	**1421**
7T-VPR	**GLF4**	**1288**
7T-VPS	**GLF4**	**1291**
7T-VRB	GLF3	368
7T-VRC	GLF3	396
7T-VRD	GLF3	399
7T-VRE	FA20	156/448
7T-VRP	FA20	271/493
7T-VVL	**HS25**	**25131**

Barbados

8P-BAB	C500	525
8P-BAR	C550	256
8P-BAR	WW24	396
8P-BAR	C500	525
8P-GAC	GLF3	355
8P-KAM	C650	0119
8P-LAD	GLF2	210
8P-MAK	GLF4	1186
8P-MAK	GLF5	537
8P-MSD	**GLF5**	**5137**

Croatia

9A-BLY	SBRL	380-65
9A-BPU	C550	144
9A-CAD	C525	0199
(9A-CAD)	C525	0151
9A-CGH	C525	0151
9A-CHC	C500	529
9A-CLN	C52A	0434
9A-CRL	FA10	173
9A-CRO	CL61	5067
9A-CRO	**CL64**	**5322**
9A-CRT	CL61	5067
9A-CSG	C510	0049
9A-DOF	**C550**	**496**
9A-DVR	C500	638
9A-DWA	**C52A**	**0412**
9A-DWD	C510	0289
9A-JSB	**C525**	**0143**
9A-JSC	**C52A**	**0049**

Ghana

9G-ABF	**JSTR**	**5217**
9G-CTH	**HS25**	**258460**
9G-EXE	**F9EX**	**241**
9G-UHI	**HS25**	**258548**

Malta

9H-ABO	SBRL	465-22
9H-ACR	C550	025
9H-AEE	LJ60	170
9H-AFB	LJ60	327
9H-AFC	**CL65**	**5713**
9H-AFG	CL65	5762
9H-AFJ	**LJ60**	**030**
9H-AFP	GLEX	9167
9H-AFQ	CL65	5709
9H-AFR	**GLEX**	**9249**
9H-AJJ	**C500**	**245**
9H-ALF	CL65	5759
9H-ALL	**C52A**	**0005**
9H-AMF	**GLEX**	**9437**
9H-AMZ	**GLEX**	**9656**
9H-AVE	**FA50**	**295**
9H-BCP	**LJ45**	**287**
9H-BEC	**F2EX**	**63**
9H-BGL	GLEX	9348
9H-BOA	HA4T	RC-69
9H-BOB	HS25	258115
9H-BOF	HS25	HA-0177
9H-BOM	**CL65**	**5785**
9H-BSA	**HS25**	**HB-24**
9H-CFL	**LJ40**	**2024**
9H-CIO	**GLEX**	**9535**
9H-CMA	**GLEX**	**9693**
9H-COL	GLEX	9234
9H-DDJ	**LJ45**	**494**
9H-ERO	GLEX	9409
9H-FAM	**E50P**	**50000100**
9H-FED	GLEX	9234
9H-FGV	**E50P**	**50000193**
9H-FLN	**GLEX**	**9353**
9H-FOM	**E50P**	**50000092**
9H-FWW	**PRM1**	**RB-131**
9H-GBT	GLEX	9020
9H-GCM	**GLEX**	**9076**
9H-GFI	**GLEX**	**9701**
9H-GMT	**F9EX**	**247**
9H-GVA	**GLEX**	**9458**
9H-GVG	**GLEX**	**9470**
9H-GVI	**GLF6**	**6006**
9H-GYB	**HS25**	**HA-0161**
9H-HAM	**F2EX**	**245**
9H-ICS	CL65	5847
9H-IGH	**GLEX**	**9570**
9H-III	**GLEX**	**9036**
9H-IKO	GLF6	6120
9H-INV	**CL64**	**5628**
9H-IPG	CL64	5589
9H-IRA	**GLEX**	**9319**
9H-IRI	**C56X**	**5723**
9H-JCD	**CL65**	**5958**
9H-JET	G150	283
9H-JGR	**CL64**	**5624**
9H-JRF	C52B	0016
9H-KAS	**CL65**	**5856**
9H-KAZ	**HS25**	**HA-0034**
9H-LDV	**CL65**	**5756**
9H-LEO	**C550**	**154**
9H-LJE	**LJ60**	**362**

Reg	Type	MSN
9H-LLC	GLEX	9098
9H-LXX	**GLEX**	**9429**
9H-MAK	FA7X	114
9H-MAL	CL64	5508
9H-MAT	F2TH	216
9H-MCM	CS55	0028
9H-MIR	CL64	5368
9H-MMM	GLEX	9430
9H-MRQ	LJ35	429
9H-MSL	FA50	215
9H-OKI	GLEX	9336
9H-OMK	GLEX	9578
9H-OPE	GLEX	9440
9H-OVB	GLEX	9373
9H-PAL	C550	550-0932
9H-PVL	GLEX	9334
9H-SFA	F2EX	39
9H-SMB	GLEX	9549
9H-SMI	CL30	20071
9H-SRT	GLEX	9274
9H-STM	GLEX	9086
9H-SVA	F900	54
9H-TOR	GLEX	9547
9H-TRT	C550	414
9H-VCA	CL30	20513
9H-VCB	CL30	20514
9H-VCC	CL30	20535
9H-VCD	CL30	20538
9H-VCE	CL30	20540
9H-VCF	CL30	20541
9H-VCG	CL30	20545
9H-VCH	CL30	20546
9H-VCI	CL30	20550
9H-VCJ	CL30	20560
9H-VCK	CL30	20592
9H-VCL	CL30	20606
9H-VFA	CL65	5970
9H-VFB	CL65	5971
9H-VFC	CL65	5972
9H-VFD	CL65	5973
9H-VFE	CL65	5974
9H-VFF	CL65	5977
9H-VFG	CL65	5978
9H-VFH	CL65	5979
9H-VFI	CL65	5984
9H-VFJ	CL65	5987
9H-VJA	**GLEX**	**9441**
9H-VJB	GLEX	9440

Reg	Type	MSN
9H-VJC	**GLEX**	**9448**
(9H-VJC)	GLEX	9472
9H-VJD	GLEX	9472
9H-VJE	GLEX	9502
9H-VJF	GLEX	9503
9H-VJG	GLEX	9580
9H-VJH	GLEX	9585
9H-VJI	GLEX	9593
9H-VJJ	GLEX	9604
9H-VJK	GLEX	9619
9H-VJL	GLEX	9626
9H-VJM	GLEX	9630
9H-VJN	GLEX	9662
9H-VJO	GLEX	9669
9H-VJP	GLEX	9677
9H-VJQ	GLEX	9691
9H-VJR	GLEX	9703
9H-VJS	GLEX	9711
9H-VJT	GLEX	9721
9H-VJU	GLEX	9724
9H-VJV	GLEX	9725
9H-VJW	GLEX	9728
9H-VJX	GLEX	9730
9H-VJY	**GLEX**	**9667**
9H-VLZ	C560	0446
9H-VMK	**C56X**	**5674**
9H-VSM	GLEX	9430
9H-VTA	GLEX	9565
9H-VTB	**GLEX**	**9566**
9H-VTC	**GLEX**	**9571**
9H-WII	**C650**	**7090**
9H-WLD	F900	62
9H-XRS	GLEX	9329
(9H-YES)	CL65	5966
9H-ZAT	HS25	HA-0143
9H-ZMB	GLF6	6116
9H-ZSN	**FA7X**	**228**

Zambia

Reg	Type	MSN
9J-ADF	LJ24	249
9J-ADU	C500	153
9J-AED	LJ25	225
9J-AEJ	C500	359
9J-EPK	HS25	25067
9J-ONE	**CL64**	**5486**
9J-RAN	HS25	25067
9J-RON	CL61	3057
9J-SAS	HS25	25067

Kuwait

Reg	Type	MSN
9K-ACO	JSTR	5156
9K-ACQ	FA20	13G/439
(9K-ACQ)	FA50	21
9K-ACR	HS25	25238
9K-ACT	LJ35	025
9K-ACX	GLF2	164
9K-ACY	GLF2	4/8
9K-ACZ	HS25	256015
9K-AEA	HS25	25219
9K-AEB	GLF2	244
9K-AEC	GLF2	248
9K-AED	HS25	256054
9K-AEE	FA50	21
9K-AEF	FA50	40
9K-AEG	GLF3	408
9K-AEH	GLF3	419
9K-AGA	HS25	257184
9K-AGB	HS25	257187
9K-AJA	GLF4	1157
9K-AJB	GLF4	1159
9K-AJC	GLF4	1161
9K-AJD	**GLF5**	**560**
9K-AJE	**GLF5**	**569**
9K-AJF	**GLF5**	**573**
9K-GFA	**GLF5**	**5248**
9K-GGA	**GLF6**	**6103**
9K-GGB	**GLF6**	**6155**
9K-GGC	GLF6	6183

Sierra Leone

Reg	Type	MSN
9L-LAW	SBRL	380-61

Malaysia

Reg	Type	MSN
(9M-...)	HS25	258226
(9M-...)	GLF3	305
9M-ABC	GLF4	1312
9M-ARR	GLF2	116
9M-ATM	C750	0242
9M-ATM	FA10	216
9M-ATM	**CL65**	**5844**
9M-ATM	BE40	RJ-22
9M-ATT	GLF2	131/23
(9M-AYI)	HS25	25015
9M-AZZ	HS25	258219
9M-BAB	F900	121
9M-BAN	F900	106

Reg	Type	MSN
9M-BCR	FA20	35
9M-BDK	FA20	304/511
9M-CAL	**LJ60**	**034**
9M-CJG	**GLEX**	**9003**
9M-DDW	HS25	258079
9M-DRL	HS25	258237
9M-FAZ	C500	245
9M-FCL	**LJ60**	**072**
9M-FRA	**FA20**	**224**
9M-HLG	HS25	25257
9M-ISJ	**GLF4**	**1106**
9M-JJS	F9EX	5
9M-JMF	C550	610
9M-LLJ	**FA20**	**292**
9M-NOR	LJ35	673
9M-NSA	C550	610
9M-NSK	CL61	5166
9M-SSB	HS25	25215
9M-SSL	HS25	257112
9M-STR	HS25	257094
9M-SWG	CL61	5104
9M-TAA	C550	671
9M-TAN	CL30	20135
9M-TAN	CL61	5154
9M-TAN	**GLEX**	**9350**
9M-TMJ	**GLF5**	**5493**
9M-TRI	GLF4	1230
9M-TST	**CL30**	**20135**
(9M-UEM)	C550	610
(9M-VAM)	C750	0242
(9M-VVV)	HS25	258337
9M-WAN	C550	307
(9M-WCM)	HS25	258219
9M-ZAB	C550	550-1121

Democratic Republic of Congo

Reg	Type	MSN
9Q-...	**HS25**	**257035**
9Q-...	**GLF2**	**73/9**
(9Q-...)	HS25	25032
9Q-CAI	**HS25**	**256047**
9Q-CBC	LJ24	248
9Q-CBC	HS25	25258
9Q-CBS	CL61	5018
9Q-CBS	CL61	5061
9Q-CCA	FA10	150
9Q-CCF	HS25	25247
9Q-CDR	CL60	1080
"9Q-CFG"	HS25	256031

Reg	Type	MSN
9Q-CFJ	**HS25**	**256051**
9Q-CFW	HS25	256031
9Q CGC	**GLF4**	**1063**
9Q-CGF	HS25	256031
9Q-CGK	FA50	177
9Q-CGM	LJ24	038
9Q-CGM	HS25	25217
9Q-CHB	LJ24	038
9Q-CHC	LJ25	009
9Q-CHD	HS25	25217
9Q-CJF	**HS25**	**256031**
9Q-CKZ	FA20	73/419
9Q-COH	HS25	25246
9Q-CPF	**HS25**	**25287**
9Q-CPK	FA50	177
9Q-CPR	**HS25**	**25247**
9Q-CRD	**CL60**	**1080**
9Q-CSN	HS25	25247
9Q-CTT	FA20	193
9Q-CVA	CL60	1072
9Q-CVF	**HS25**	**25118**
9Q-CYA	HS25	256047

Burundi

Reg	Type	MSN
9U-BKB	**GLF4**	**1151**
9U-BTB	FA50	66

Singapore

Reg	Type	MSN
9V-...	**FA10**	**157**
9V-...	**HS25**	**257101**
9V-ATA	LJ31	033
9V-ATB	LJ31	034
9V-ATC	LJ31	033A
9V-ATD	LJ31	033B
9V-ATE	LJ31	033C
9V-ATF	LJ31	033D
9V-ATG	LJ45	029
9V-ATH	LJ45	031
9V-ATI	LJ45	033
9V-ATJ	LJ45	035
9V-BEE	JSTR	5011/1
(9V-PUW)	C550	141

Rwanda

Reg	Type	MSN
9XR-NN	FA50	6

MILITARY INDEX

Current marks (as at publication date) are in **bold** typeface.

Preserved aircraft and others not in service are shown in normal typeface.

Argentina

0653	HS25	25251
5-T-30	HS25	25251
A-01	MS76	003
A-02	MS76	004
A-03	MS76	007
A-04	MS76	010
A-05	MS76	011
A-06	MS76	013
A-07	MS76	015
A-08	MS76	016
A-09	MS76	017
A-10	MS76	018
A-11	MS76	021
A-12	MS76	022
AE-129	C550	117
AE-175	**SBRL**	**380-13**
AE-185	C500	366
AE-186	**C550**	**550-1086**
E-201	MS76	003
E-202	MS76	004
E-203	MS76	007
E-204	MS76	010
E-205	MS76	011
E-206	MS76	013
E-207	MS76	015
E-208	MS76	016
E-209	MS76	017
E-210	MS76	018
E-211	MS76	021
E-212	MS76	022
E-213	MS76	A-1
E-214	MS76	A-2
E-215	MS76	A-3
E-216	MS76	A-4
E-217	MS76	A-5
E-218	MS76	A-6
E-219	MS76	A-7
E-220	MS76	A-8
E-221	MS76	A-9
E-222	MS76	A-10
E-223	MS76	A-11
E-224	MS76	A-12
E-225	MS76	A-13
E-226	MS76	A-14
E-227	MS76	A-15
E-228	MS76	A-16
E-229	MS76	A-17
E-230	MS76	A-18
E-231	MS76	A-19
E-232	MS76	A-20
E-233	MS76	A-21
E-234	MS76	A-22
E-235	MS76	A-23
E-236	MS76	A-24
E-237	MS76	A-25
E-238	MS76	A-26
E-239	MS76	A-27
E-240	MS76	A-28
E-241	MS76	A-29
E-242	MS76	A-30
E-243	MS76	A-31
E-244	MS76	A-32
E-245	MS76	A-33
E-246	MS76	A-34
E-247	MS76	A-35
E-248	MS76	A-36
T-03	LJ24	316
T-10	**LJ60**	**140**
T-10	SBRL	380-3
T-11	SBRL	380-3
T-21	LJ35	115
T-22	**LJ35**	**136**
T-23	**LJ35**	**319**
T-24	LJ35	333
T-24	LJ35	369
T-25	**LJ35**	**484**
T-26	**LJ35**	**369**
VR-17	LJ35	369
VR-18	LJ35	484
VR-24	**LJ35**	**395**

Australia

A11-078	FA20	78/412
A11-085	FA20	85/425
A11-090	FA20	90/426
A26-070	F900	70
A26-073	F900	73
A26-074	F900	74
A26-076	F900	76
A26-077	F900	77
A37-001	**CL64**	**5521**
A37-002	**CL64**	**5534**
A37-003	**CL64**	**5538**

Belgium

CD-01	**F900**	**109**
CM-01	**FA20**	**276/494**
CM-02	**FA20**	**278/495**
(OT-JFA)	FA20	104/454

Bolivia

FAB-001	**F9EX**	**209**
FAB-001	SBRL	306-115
FAB-002	**FA50**	**289**
FAB-002	SBRL	306-115
FAB-008	LJ25	192
FAB-009	LJ35	152
FAB-010	**LJ25**	**192**
FAB-010	**LJ25**	**211**

Botswana

OK-1	HS25	258112
OK1	**GLEX**	**9259**
OK1	GLF4	1173
OK1	HS25	258164
OK2	GLF4	1173
OK2	HS25	258164
Z-1	HS25	258112

Brazil

2710	LJ35	631
2711	LJ35	632
2712	LJ35	633
2713	**LJ35**	**636**
2714	**LJ35**	**638**
2715	**LJ35**	**639**
2716	**LJ35**	**640**
2717	**LJ35**	**641**
2718	**LJ35**	**642**
3601	**LEG5**	**55000015**
3602	**LEG5**	**55000023**
6000	**LJ35**	**613**
6001	**LJ35**	**615**
6002	**LJ35**	**617**
FAB6100	**LJ55**	**140**
C41-2910	MS76	053
C41-2911	MS76	052
C41-2912	MS76	051
C41-2913	MS76	054
C41-2914	MS76	055
C41-2915	MS76	056
C41-2916	MS76	059
C41-2917	MS76	060
C41-2918	MS76	057
C41-2919	MS76	061
C41-2920	MS76	058
C41-2921	MS76	062
C41-2922	MS76	064
C41-2923	MS76	063
C41-2924	MS76	065
C41-2925	MS76	066
C41-2926	MS76	067
C41-2927	MS76	068
C41-2928	MS76	070
C41-2929	MS76	071
C41-2930	MS76	074
C41-2931	MS76	075
C41-2932	MS76	076
C41-2933	MS76	077
C41-2934	MS76	078
C41-2935	MS76	079
C41-2936	MS76	080
C41-2937	MS76	081
C41-2938	MS76	082
C41-2939	MS76	083
EC93-2125	HS25	25164
EU93-2119	HS25	25274
EU93-2121	HS25	25165
EU93-2125	**HS25**	**25164**
EU93A-6050	**HS25**	**258401**
EU93A-6051	**HS25**	**258421**
EU93A-6052	**HS25**	**258434**
EU93A-6053	**HS25**	**258447**
VC93-2120	HS25	25162
VC93-2121	HS25	25165
VC93-2122	HS25	25166
VC93-2123	HS25	25167
VC93-2124	HS25	25168
VU93-2113	**HS25**	**25136**
VU93-2114	HS25	25212
VU93-2117	HS25	25210
VU93-2118	**HS25**	**25200**
VU93-2120	**HS25**	**25162**
VU93-2123	**HS25**	**25167**
VU93-2124	HS25	25168
VU93-2126	**HS25**	**25277**
VU93-2127	HS25	25288
VU93-2128	HS25	25289
VU93-2129	HS25	25290
XU93-2117	HS25	25210

Canada

20501	FA20	82/418
20502	FA20	87/424
20503	FA20	92/421
20504	FA20	97/422
20505	FA20	103/423
20506	FA20	109/427
20507	FA20	114/420
117501	FA20	82/418
117502	FA20	87/424
117503	FA20	92/421
117504	FA20	97/422
117505	FA20	103/423
117506	FA20	109/427
117507	FA20	114/420
117508	FA20	157
144601	CL60	1040
144602	CL60	1065
144603	CL60	1006
144604	CL60	1007
144605	CL60	1008
144606	CL60	1009
144607	CL60	1014
144608	CL60	1015
144609	CL60	1017
144610	CL60	1022
144611	CL60	1030
144612	CL60	1002
144613	CL61	3035
144614	**CL61**	**3036**
144615	**CL61**	**3037**
144616	**CL61**	**3038**
144617	**CL64**	**5533**
144618	**CL64**	**5535**

Chile

130	WW24	409
301	FA20	401
302	FA20	496
303	C650	0131
304	**C680**	**0045**
351	**LJ35**	**050**
352	**LJ35**	**066**
361	**C525**	**0463**
362	**C525**	**0464**
363	**C525**	**0465**
364	**C525**	**0507**
911	GLF3	465
911	**GLF4**	**1089**
912	**GLF4**	**1182**
C-53	**C550**	**550-0996**
E-301	C550	146
E-302	C650	0033
E-303	C650	0131

China

090	C550	359
091	C550	357
092	C550	362
HY984	LJ36	053
HY985	LJ36	034
HY986	**LJ35**	**601**
HY987	LJ35	602
HY988	LJ35	603

Ciskei

CA-01	WW24	107

Colombia

FAC1211	**C550**	**582**
FAC1214	**LJ60**	**066**
FAC1216	**LJ60**	**317**
FAC5760	**C560**	**0350**
FAC5761	**C560**	**0374**
FAC5763	**C560**	**0365**
FAC5762	**C560**	**0386**
FAC5764	**C560**	**0381**

Czech Republic

5105	**CL61**	**5105**

Denmark

C-066	CL64	5366
C-080	**CL64**	**5380**
C-168	**CL64**	**5468**
C-172	**CL64**	**5472**
C-215	**CL64**	**5515**
F-085	GLF2	85
F-249	GLF3	249
F-313	GLF3	313
F-330	GLF3	330
F-400	GLF3	401

Ecuador

043	**SBRL**	**282-43**
047	**SBRL**	**282-109**
049	**SBRL**	**306-68**
068	SBRL	282-68
AEE-402	SBRL	380-45
AEE-403	SBRL	380-34
ANE-201	C500	481
FAE-001A	SBRL	306-117
FAE-034	SBRL	380-34
FAE-045	SBRL	380-45
FAE-052	**FA7X**	**185**
FAE050	**HS25**	**25190**
IGM-401	LJ24	312
IGM-628	**C550**	**628**

Eritrea

901	ASTR	063

Finland

LJ-1	**LJ35**	**430**
LJ-2	**LJ35**	**451**
LJ-3	**LJ35**	**470**

France

1	CRVT	1
1	FA20	1/401
1	MS76	001
2	CRVT	2
2	FA50	2
2	**F900**	**2**
02	**FA10**	**02**
03	MS76	03
4	**F900**	**4**
5	**FA50**	**5**
10	**CRVT**	**10**
12	MS76	012
14	MS76	014
19	MS76	019
20	MS76	020
22	FA20	22/404
23	MS76	023
24	MS76	024
25	MS76	025
26	MS76	026
27	FA50	27
27	**FA50**	**27**
27	MS76	027
29	MS76	029
30	**FA50**	**30**
30	MS76	030
31	MS76	031
32	**FA10**	**32**
32	MS76	032
33	MS76	033
34	**FA50**	**34**
34	MS76	034
35	MS76	035
36	**FA50**	**36**
36	MS76	036
37	MS76	037
38	MS76	038
39	FA10	39
40	MS76	040
41	MS76	041
42	MS76	042
44	MS76	044
45	MS76	045
46	MS76	046
47	MS76	047
48	**FA20**	**448**
48	MS76	048
49	FA20	49/408
51	MS76	051
53	MS76	053
54	MS76	054
56	MS76	056
57	MS76	057
58	MS76	058
59	MS76	059
60	MS76	060
61	MS76	061
62	MS76	062
65	**FA20**	**465**
65	MS76	065
68	**FA7X**	**68**
68	MS76	068
70	MS76	070
71	MS76	071
72	**FA20**	**472**
73	**MS76**	**073**
74	MS76	074
75	MS76	075
76	FA20	476
77	**FA20**	**477**
77	MS76	077
78	**FA50**	**78**
78	MS76	078
79	**FA20**	**79/415**
79	MS76	079
80	**FA20**	**480**
80	MS76	080
81	MS76	081
82	MS76	082
83	MS76	083
84	MS76	084
85	**MS76**	**085**
86	**FA7X**	**86**
87	MS76	087
88	MS76	088
91	MS76	091
92	MS76	092
93	FA20	93/435
93	MS76	093
94	MS76	094
95	MS76	095
96	**FA20**	**96**
96	MS76	096
97	MS76	097
100	**MS76**	**100**
101	**FA10**	**101**
101	MS76	101
104	**FA20**	**104/454**
113	MS76	113
114	MS76	114
115	MS76	115
115	FA20	115/432
116	MS76	116
117	MS76	117
118	MS76	118
119	MS76	119
124	FA20	124/433
129	**FA10**	**129**
131	FA20	131/437
132	**FA50**	**132**
133	**FA10**	**133**
138	**FA20**	**138/440**
143	**FA10**	**143**
145	**FA20**	**145/443**
154	FA20	154/447
167	FA20	167/453
182	FA20	182/461
185	**FA10**	**185**
188	**FA20**	**188/464**
231	**F2EX**	**231**
237	**F2EX**	**237**
238	FA20	238/477
252	**FA20**	**252/485**
260	FA20	260/488
263	**FA20**	**263/489**
268	FA20	268/492
288	**FA20**	**288/499**
291	FA20	291/505
309	FA20	309/514
339	FA20	451
342	FA20	342/532
375	**FA20**	**375/547**
422	**FA20**	**422**
463	FA20	186/463
483	**FA20**	**483**
20-Q	MS76	020
34-Z	MS76	037
41-A	MS76	038
41-A.	MS76	054
41-A.	MS76	059
41-A.	MS76	081
41-AC	MS76	057
41-AR	MS76	019
41-AT	MS76	060
42-AP	MS76	025
43-B.	MS76	045
43-BB	MS76	034
43-BL	**MS76**	**035**
44-CC	MS76	036
4D-L	MS76	044
65-KW	MS76	024
65-L.	MS76	082
65-L.	MS76	094
65-LB	MS76	058
65-LC	MS76	029
65-LD	MS76	093
65-LE	MS76	071
65-LF	MS76	065
65-LF	MS76	070
65-LG	MS76	056
65-LH	MS76	097
65-LI	MS76	030
65-LP	MS76	077
65-LU	MS76	091
65-LU	MS76	096
65-LV	MS76	062
65-LY	MS76	078
65-LZ	MS76	075
80/DE	MS76	080
113-CG	MS76	034

115-ME	MS76	038
115-ME	MS76	078
116-CB	MS76	025
118-DA	MS76	092
133-CF	MS76	059
133-CM	MS76	056
312-DF	MS76	014
312-DG	MS76	058
314-D	MS76	080
314-DO	MS76	062
316-DH	MS76	036
316-DI	MS76	045
316-DL	MS76	092
330-DB	MS76	001
330-DC	MS76	051
330-DO	MS76	023
330-DP	**MS76**	**065**
ELA61	MS76	081
GE-316	MS76	080
NB	**MS76**	**068**
NC	MS76	083
OD	MS76	053
__-DE	MS76	027
__-LN	MS76	026
__-LY	MS76	061

Germany

1101	JSTR	5025
1102	JSTR	5121
1103	JSTR	5071
1201	CL61	3031
1202	CL61	3040
1203	CL61	3043
1204	CL61	3049
1205	CL61	3053
1206	CL61	3056
1207	CL61	3059
1401	**GLEX**	**9395**
1402	**GLEX**	**9404**
1403	**GLEX**	**9411**
1404	**GLEX**	**9417**
1601	HFB3	1041
1602	HFB3	1042
1603	HFB3	1043
1604	HFB3	1046
1605	HFB3	1047
1606	HFB3	1048
1607	HFB3	1024
1608	HFB3	1025
1621	HFB3	1058
1622	HFB3	1059
1623	HFB3	1060
1624	HFB3	1061
1625	HFB3	1062
1626	HFB3	1063
1627	HFB3	1064
1628	HFB3	1065
9825	HFB3	1059
9826	HFB3	1060
9848	GLEX	9395
CA101	JSTR	5025
CA102	JSTR	5035
CA103	JSTR	5071
(CA111)	HFB3	1024
(CA112)	HFB3	1025
D9536	HFB3	1024
D9537	HFB3	1025
(YA111)	HFB3	1024
(YA112)	HFB3	1025

Ghana

G.511	HS25	25028
G540	GLF3	493

Greece

678	**GLF5**	**678**

Honduras

318	WW24	183

India

K-2960	GLF3	420
K-2961	**GLF3**	**494**
K-2962	**GLF3**	**495**
K-2995	LJ28	29-003
K-2996	LJ28	29-004
L3458	**ASTR**	**126**
L3467	**ASTR**	**148**
GB8001	**GLEX**	**9424**
GB8002	**GLEX**	**9431**

Indonesia

A-1645	JSTR	5059
A-9208	**PRM1**	**RB-56**
A-9446	JSTR	5046
P-2034	BE40	RK-362
P-8001	**BE40**	**RK-362**
T-1645	JSTR	5059
T-9446	JSTR	5046
T17845	JSTR	5011/1

Iran

0110	**FA20**	**251/484**
803	**FA20**	**340/531**
1003	JSTR	5203
1004	JSTR	5137
5-2801	FA20	333/526
5-2802	FA20	336/528
5-2803	FA20	340/531
5-2804	FA20	346/535
5-3020	FA20	348/536
5-3021	**FA20**	**350/537**
5-4039	FA20	348/536
5-4040	FA20	350/537
5-9001	FA20	351/538
5-9001	**JSTR**	**5137**
5-9002	FA20	353/539
5-9003	FA20	354/540
5-9003	**JSTR**	**5237**
5-9011	FA50	120
5-9012	FA50	101
5-9013	**FA50**	**122**
5-9014	**FA20**	**337/529**
5-9015	**FA20**	**343/533**
5-9016	**FA20**	**354/540**
15-2233	FA20	333/526
15-2234	**FA20**	**286/498**
15-2235	**FA20**	**318/518**

Ireland

238	HS25	257082
239	HS25	256015
249	GLF3	413
251	GLF4	1160
258	**LJ45**	**234**
IAC236	HS25	25256

Israel

027	WW24	185
029	WW24	152
031	WW24	186
035	WW24	152
064	WW24	107
429	GLF5	5429
514	GLF5	5014
532	GLF5	5132
537	**GLF5**	**5037**
544	GLF5	5044
569	**GLF5**	**5069**
676	**GLF5**	**676**
679	**GLF5**	**679**
684	**GLF5**	**684**
927	**WW24**	**185**
929	**WW24**	**152**
931	**WW24**	**186**

Italy

CSX62026	FA50	193
(MM151)	FA50	151
MM577	P808	501
MM578	P808	502
MM61948	P808	506
MM61949	P808	507
MM61950	P808	508
MM61951	P808	509
MM61952	P808	510
MM61953	P808	511
MM61954	P808	512
MM61955	P808	513
MM61956	P808	514
MM61957	P808	515
MM61958	P808	505
MM61959	P808	516
MM61960	P808	517
MM61961	P808	518
MM61962	P808	519
MM61963	P808	520
MM62014	P808	521
MM62015	P808	522
MM62016	P808	523
MM62017	P808	524
MM62020	FA50	151
MM62021	FA50	155
MM62022	GLF3	451
MM62025	GLF3	479
MM62026	**FA50**	**193**
MM62029	**FA50**	**211**
MM62171	**F9EX**	**45**
MM62172	**F9EX**	**52**
MM62210	**F9EX**	**116**
MM62244	**F9EX**	**149**
MM62245	**F9EX**	**156**

Japan

9201	**LJ36**	**054**
9202	LJ36	056
9203	LJ36	058
9204	**LJ36**	**059**
9205	**LJ36**	**060**
9206	**LJ36**	**061**
01-5060	**BE40**	**TX-10**
02-3013	**HS25**	**258370**
02-3014	**HS25**	**258381**
02-3015	**HS25**	**258407**
02-3016	**HS25**	**258427**
02-3027	**HS25**	**258824**
05-3255	**GLF4**	**1359**
12-3017	**HS25**	**258445**
12-3018	**HS25**	**258469**
12-3028	**HS25**	**258843**
21-5061	**BE40**	**TX-11**
21-5062	**BE40**	**TX-12**
22-3019	**HS25**	**258493**
22-3020	**HS25**	**258513**
29-3041	**HS25**	**258215**
32-3021	**HS25**	**258533**
39-3042	**HS25**	**258227**
41-5051	**BE40**	**TX-1**
41-5052	**BE40**	**TX-2**
41-5053	**BE40**	**TX-3**
41-5054	**BE40**	**TX-4**
41-5055	**BE40**	**TX-5**
41-5063	**BE40**	**TX-13**
42-3022	**HS25**	**258610**
49-3043	HS25	258242
51-5056	**BE40**	**TX-6**
51-5057	**BE40**	**TX-7**
51-5058	**BE40**	**TX-8**
52-3001	**HS25**	**258245**
52-3002	**HS25**	**258247**
52-3003	**HS25**	**258250**
52-3023	**HS25**	**258629**
62-3004	**HS25**	**258268**
62-3024	HS25	258685
71-5059	**BE40**	**TX-9**
72-3005	HS25	258288
72-3006	**HS25**	**258305**
72-3025	**HS25**	**258735**
75-3251	**GLF4**	**1270**
75-3252	**GLF4**	**1271**
82-3007	**HS25**	**258306**
82-3008	**HS25**	**258325**
82-3009	**HS25**	**258333**
82-3026	HS25	258797
85-3253	**GLF4**	**1303**
92-3010	**HS25**	**258341**
92-3011	**HS25**	**258348**
92-3012	**HS25**	**258360**
92-3026	**HS25**	**258797**
95-3254	**GLF4**	**1326**

Jordan

122	FA20	255/487

Libya

001	JSTR	5136
002	FA20	190/465

Malawi

MAAW-J1	HS25	257076
MAAW-J1	HS25	258064

Malaysia

FM1200	HS25	25189
FM1201	HS25	25209
FM1801	HS25	25189
FM1802	HS25	25209
M24-01	HS25	25189
M24-02	HS25	25209
M31-01	CL60	1062
M31-02	CL60	1064
M37-01	**F900**	**64**
M48-01	GLEX	9007
M48-02	**GLEX**	**9096**
M52-01	GLEX	9096
M102-01	**LJ35**	**673**

Mexico

3908	JSTR	5144
3909	**LJ35**	**321**
3910	**GLF5**	**5296**
3911	**CL65**	**5967**
3912	**LJ45**	**325**
3913	G150	313
3914	G150	314
3915	GLF4	4333
3916	GLF5	5508
3929	**C500**	**090**
3930	**C680**	**0284**
3931	C500	532
3933	**C500**	**351**
3934	**C500**	**525**
AMT-200	LJ60	152
AMT-201	**LJ31**	**174**
AMT-202	**LJ25**	**339**
AMT-203	SBRL	306-34
AMT-204	**SBRL**	**306-144**
AMT-205	GLF4	4128
AMT-206	LJ31	191
AMT-208	CL65	5969
ANX-1200	**LJ60**	**152**
ANX-1206	**LJ31**	**191**
ANX-1207	**GLF5**	**5305**
ANX-1208	**CL65**	**5969**
ANX-207	GLF5	5305
DN-01	JSTR	5144
ETE-1329	C500	090
JS10201	JSTR	5144
MTX-01	LJ24	313
MTX-01	LJ60	152
MTX-01	SBRL	306-34
MTX-02	LJ24	313
MTX-02	LJ31	174
MTX-02	SBRL	306-34
MTX-03	LJ25	339
MTX-04	SBRL	306-34
PF-201	LJ28	29-002
PF-239	FA20	287
TP-04	GLF2	161
TP-06	GLF3	352
TP-06	**GLF4**	**4333**
TP-07	GLF3	386
TP-07	**GLF5**	**5508**
TP-08	**G150**	**313**
TP-09	**G150**	**314**
TP-10	**LJ36**	**050**
T 101	SBRL	380-67
T 102	SBRL	380-68
T 103	SBRL	380-67
TP103	SBRL	306-139
T 104	SBRL	380-68
TP104	**LJ35**	**028**
TP104	SBRL	306-144
TP105	SBRL	306-139
TP105	SBRL	282-130
TP-106	LJ35	321
TP106	SBRL	306-144
TP107	SBRL	282-130
TP108	HS25	25216
TP108	SBRL	282-117
TP0206	HS25	25216

Mozambique

FAM-002	**HS25**	**258750**

Myanmar

4400	**C550**	**389**

Netherlands

V-11	**GLF4**	**1009**

Nigeria

NAF050	C550	632
NAF960	**C550**	**632**
NAF961	**F900**	**96**

Norway

041	**FA20**	**41/407**
053	**FA20**	**53/417**
0125	**FA20**	**125**

Oman

557	**GLF4**	**1168**
558	**GLF4**	**1196**
601	GLF2	214

Pakistan

0233	**C560**	**0233**
1003	**C550**	**550-1003**
101	**HS25**	**258982**
4270	**GLF4**	**4270**
EYE77	**CL65**	**5955**
EYE77	HA4T	RC-32
HBC21	HA4T	RC-21
J-468	**FA20**	**468**
J-469	**FA20**	**469**
J-753	**FA20**	**277/501**
J-754	**C56X**	**5004**
J-755	**GLF4**	**1325**
J-756	**GLF4**	**4090**
V-4101	**E50P**	**50000017**
V-4102	**E50P**	**50000014**
V-4103	**E50P**	**50000047**
V-4104	**E50P**	**50000113**

Panama

SAN-301	WW24	56

Peru

300	FA20	434
FAP_522	LJ25	159
FAP_523	LJ25	164
524	**LJ36**	**051**
525	**LJ36**	**052**
526	**LJ45**	**345**
721	C560	0365
EP-861	**C56X**	**5679**

Portugal

7401	FA50	195
7402	FA50	198
7403	FA50	221
8101	FA20	211
8102	FA20	215
8103	FA20	217
17101	FA20	211
17102	FA20	215
17103	FA20	217
17401	**FA50**	**195**
17402	**FA50**	**198**
17403	**FA50**	**221**

Russia

62	GLF2	62

(black or dark blue)

Saudi Arabia

101	JSTR	5129
102	JSTR	5130
103	GLF3	453
103	JSTR	5130
104	HS25	258115
105	HS25	258118
110	HS25	258148
130	HS25	258164

Seychelles

SY-001	C560	0003

Singapore

010	**GLF5**	**5014**
016	**GLF5**	**5044**
017	**GLF5**	**5132**
018	**GLF5**	**5143**

Slovenia

L1-01	**F2EX**	**15**

South Africa

01	HS25	25181
02	HS25	25177
03	HS25	25182
04	HS25	25184
05	HS25	25259
06	HS25	25260
07	HS25	25269
(431)	FA20	41/407

South Korea

701	**CL64**	**5429**
5327	C500	327
70327	C500	327
258-342	**HS25**	**258342**
258-343	**HS25**	**258343**
258-346	**HS25**	**258346**
258-350	**HS25**	**258350**
258-351	**HS25**	**258351**
258-352	**HS25**	**258352**
258-353	**HS25**	**258353**
258-357	**HS25**	**258357**

Spain

01-405	**C550**	**424**
01-406	**C550**	**446**
01-407	**C550**	**592**
45-01	FA20	332/525
45-02	FA20	253/486
45-03	FA20	222/471
45-04	FA20	219/470
45-05	FA20	475
45-20	FA50	84
45-40	**F900**	**38**
45-41	**F900**	**90**
45-42	**F900**	**77**
45-43	**F900**	**74**
45-44	**F900**	**73**
47-21	**FA20**	**253/486**
47-22	**FA20**	**222/471**
47-23	**FA20**	**219/470**
47-24	**FA20**	**332/525**
401-02	FA20	253/486
401-03	FA20	222/471
401-04	FA20	219/470
401-05	FA20	332/525
401-09	FA50	84
403-11	**C560**	**0161**
403-12	**C560**	**0193**
408-11	FA20	219/470
408-12	FA20	332/525
T.11-1	**FA20**	**253/486**
T.11-5	FA20	475
T.16-1	FA50	84
T.18-1	**F900**	**38**
T.18-2	**F900**	**90**
T.18-3	**F900**	**77**
T.18-4	**F900**	**74**
T.18-5	**F900**	**73**
TM.11-2	**FA20**	**222/471**
TM.11-3	**FA20**	**219/470**
TM.11-4	**FA20**	**332/525**
TR.20-01	**C560**	**0161**
TR.20-02	**C560**	**0193**
TR.20-03	**C560**	**0183**
U.20-1	**C550**	**424**
U.20-2	**C550**	**446**
U.20-3	**C550**	**592**
U.21-01	**C650**	**7079**

Sweden

86001	**SBRL**	**282-49**
86002	**SBRL**	**282-91**
102001	**GLF4**	**1014**
102002	**GLF4**	**1215**
102003	**GLF4**	**1216**
102004	**GLF4**	**1274**
102005	**GLF5**	**5200**
103001	C550	307
103002	C550	717

Switzerland

J-4117	MS76	069
T-781	LJ35	068
T-782	LJ35	145
T-783	FA50	67
T-784	**C56X**	**5269**
T-785	**F9EX**	**195**

Thailand

30 40207	**LJ35**	**623**
30 60504	LJ35	623
31 40208	LJ35	635
31 60505	LJ35	635
B.TL12-1	**LJ35**	**623**
B.TL12-2	LJ35	635

Turkey

001	GLF4	1027
007	**C550**	**502**
008	**C550**	**503**
09-001	**GLF5**	**5241**
10-002	GLF5	5254
12-001	C550	502
12-002	C550	503
12-003	GLF4	1163
84-007	C550	502
84-008	C550	503
91-003	**GLF4**	**1163**
93-004	**C650**	**7024**
93-005	**C650**	**7026**
93-7024	C650	7024
93-7026	C650	7026
ETI-024	C650	7024
ETI-026	C650	7026
EM-805	**C56X**	**6079**
TT2020	**C650**	**0229**
TT4010	**CL64**	**5459**

Uganda

UAF1	WW24	134

United Arab Emirates

800	LJ35	429
801	LJ35	265

United Kingdom

9246M	HS25	25054
9259M	HS25	25012
9260M	HS25	25061
9273M	HS25	25044
9274M	HS25	25077
9275M	HS25	25049
9276M	HS25	25059
XS709	HS25	25011
XS710	HS25	25012
XS711	HS25	25024
XS712	HS25	25040
XS713	HS25	25041
XS714	HS25	25054
XS726	HS25	25044
XS727	HS25	25045
XS728	HS25	25048
XS729	HS25	25049
XS730	HS25	25050
XS731	HS25	25055
XS732	HS25	25056
XS733	HS25	25059
XS734	HS25	25061
XS735	HS25	25071
XS736	HS25	25072
XS737	HS25	25076
XS738	HS25	25077
XS739	HS25	25081
XW788	HS25	25255
XW789	HS25	25264
XW790	HS25	25266
XW791	HS25	25268
XW930	HS25	25009
XX505	HS25	25252
XX506	HS25	25271
XX507	HS25	256006
XX508	HS25	256008
ZD620	HS25	257181
ZD621	HS25	257190
ZD703	HS25	257183
ZD704	HS25	257194
ZE395	HS25	257205
ZE396	HS25	257211
ZF130	HS25	256059
ZJ690	**GLEX**	**9107**
ZJ691	**GLEX**	**9123**
ZJ692	**GLEX**	**9131**
ZJ693	**GLEX**	**9132**
ZJ694	**GLEX**	**9135**

United States of America

59-2868	SBRL	265-1
59-2869	SBRL	265-2
59-2870	SBRL	265-3
59-2871	SBRL	265-4
59-2872	SBRL	265-5
59-2873	SBRL	270-1
59-2874	SBRL	270-2
59-5958	JSTR	5010
59-5959	JSTR	5026
59-5960	JSTR	5028
59-5961	JSTR	5030
59-5962	JSTR	5032
60-3474	SBRL	270-3
60-3475	SBRL	270-4
60-3476	SBRL	270-5
60-3477	SBRL	270-6
60-3478	SBRL	265-6
60-3479	SBRL	265-7
60-3480	SBRL	265-8
60-3481	SBRL	265-9
60-3482	SBRL	265-10
60-3483	SBRL	265-11
60-3484	SBRL	265-12
60-3485	SBRL	265-13
60-3486	SBRL	265-14
60-3487	SBRL	265-15
60-3488	SBRL	265-16
60-3489	SBRL	265-17
60-3490	SBRL	265-18
60-3491	SBRL	265-19
60-3492	SBRL	265-20
60-3493	SBRL	265-21
60-3494	SBRL	265-22
60-3495	SBRL	265-23
60-3496	SBRL	265-24
60-3497	SBRL	265-25
60-3498	SBRL	265-26
60-3499	SBRL	265-27
60-3500	SBRL	265-28
60-3501	SBRL	265-29
60-3502	SBRL	265-30
60-3503	SBRL	265-31
60-3504	SBRL	265-32
60-3505	SBRL	265-33
60-3506	SBRL	265-34
60-3507	SBRL	265-35
60-3508	SBRL	265-36
61-0634	SBRL	265-37
61-0635	SBRL	265-38
61-0636	SBRL	265-39
61-0637	SBRL	265-40
61-0638	SBRL	265-41
61-0639	SBRL	265-42
61-0640	SBRL	265-43
61-0641	SBRL	265-44
61-0642	SBRL	265-45
61-0643	SBRL	265-46
61-0644	SBRL	265-47
61-0645	SBRL	265-48
61-0646	SBRL	265-49
61-0647	SBRL	265-50
61-0648	SBRL	265-51
61-0649	SBRL	265-52
61-0650	SBRL	265-53
61-0651	SBRL	265-54
61-0652	SBRL	265-55
61-0653	SBRL	265-56
61-0654	SBRL	265-57
61-0655	SBRL	265-58
61-0656	SBRL	265-59
61-0657	SBRL	265-60
61-0658	SBRL	265-61
61-0659	SBRL	265-62
61-0660	SBRL	265-63
61-0661	SBRL	265-64
61-0662	SBRL	265-65
61-0663	SBRL	265-66
61-0664	SBRL	265-67
61-0665	SBRL	265-68
61-0666	SBRL	265-69
61-0667	SBRL	265-70
61-0668	SBRL	265-71
61-0669	SBRL	265-72
61-0670	SBRL	265-73
61-0671	SBRL	265-74
61-0672	SBRL	265-75
61-0673	SBRL	265-76
61-0674	SBRL	265-77
61-0675	SBRL	265-78
61-0676	SBRL	265-79
61-0677	SBRL	265-80
61-0678	SBRL	265-81
61-0679	SBRL	265-82
61-0680	SBRL	265-83
61-0681	SBRL	265-84
61-0682	SBRL	265-85
61-0683	SBRL	265-86
61-0684	SBRL	265-87
61-0685	SBRL	265-88
61-2488	JSTR	5017
61-2489	JSTR	5022
61-2490	JSTR	5024
61-2491	JSTR	5027
61-2492	JSTR	5031
61-2493	JSTR	5034
(62-12166)	JSTR	5025
(62-12167)	JSTR	5035
(62-12845)	JSTR	5071
62-4197	JSTR	5041
62-4198	JSTR	5042
62-4199	JSTR	5043
62-4200	JSTR	5044
62-4201	JSTR	5045
62-4448	SBRL	276-1
62-4449	SBRL	276-2
62-4450	SBRL	276-3
62-4451	SBRL	276-4
62-4452	SBRL	276-5
62-4453	SBRL	276-6
62-4454	SBRL	276-7
62-4455	SBRL	276-8
62-4456	SBRL	276-9
62-4457	SBRL	276-10
62-4458	SBRL	276-11
62-4459	SBRL	276-12
62-4460	SBRL	276-13
62-4461	SBRL	276-14
62-4462	SBRL	276-15
62-4463	SBRL	276-16
62-4464	SBRL	276-17
62-4465	SBRL	276-18
62-4466	SBRL	276-19
62-4467	SBRL	276-20
62-4468	SBRL	276-21
62-4469	SBRL	276-22
62-4470	SBRL	276-23
62-4471	SBRL	276-24
62-4472	SBRL	276-25
62-4473	SBRL	276-26
62-4474	SBRL	276-27
62-4475	SBRL	276-28
62-4476	SBRL	276-29
62-4477	SBRL	276-30
62-4478	SBRL	276-31
62-4479	SBRL	276-32
62-4480	SBRL	276-33
62-4481	SBRL	276-34
62-4482	SBRL	276-35
62-4483	SBRL	276-36
62-4484	SBRL	276-37
62-4485	SBRL	276-38
62-4486	SBRL	276-39
62-4487	SBRL	276-40
62-4488	SBRL	276-41
62-4489	SBRL	276-42
62-4490	SBRL	276-43
62-4491	SBRL	276-44
62-4492	SBRL	276-45
62-4493	SBRL	276-46
62-4494	SBRL	276-47
62-4495	SBRL	276-48
62-4496	SBRL	276-49
62-4497	SBRL	276-50
62-4498	SBRL	276-51
62-4499	SBRL	276-52
62-4500	SBRL	276-53
62-4501	SBRL	276-54
62-4502	SBRL	276-55
83-0500	GLF3	382
83-0501	GLF3	383
83-0502	**GLF3**	**389**
84-0063	LJ35	509
84-0064	LJ35	510
84-0065	**LJ35**	**511**
84-0066	LJ35	512
84-0067	LJ35	513
84-0068	LJ35	514
84-0069	LJ35	515
84-0070	**LJ35**	**516**
84-0071	**LJ35**	**517**
84-0072	**LJ35**	**518**
84-0073	LJ35	519
84-0074	LJ35	520
84-0075	LJ35	521
84-0076	LJ35	522
84-0077	**LJ35**	**523**
84-0078	LJ35	524
84-0079	**LJ35**	**525**
84-0080	LJ35	526
84-0081	LJ35	527
84-0082	LJ35	528
84-0083	**LJ35**	**529**
84-0084	LJ35	530
84-0085	**LJ35**	**531**
84-0086	LJ35	532
84-0087	**LJ35**	**533**
84-0088	LJ35	534
84-0089	LJ35	535
84-0090	LJ35	536
84-0091	LJ35	537
84-0092	LJ35	538
84-0093	LJ35	539
84-0094	**LJ35**	**540**
84-0095	**LJ35**	**541**
84-0096	**LJ35**	**542**
84-0097	LJ35	543
84-0098	LJ35	544
84-0099	**LJ35**	**545**
84-0100	LJ35	546
84-0101	LJ35	547
84-0102	LJ35	548
84-0103	**LJ35**	**549**
84-0104	LJ35	550
84-0105	LJ35	551
84-0106	**LJ35**	**552**
84-0107	LJ35	553
84-0108	LJ35	554
84-0109	**LJ35**	**555**
84-0110	**LJ35**	**556**
84-0111	LJ35	557
84-0112	LJ35	558
84-0113	LJ35	559
84-0114	LJ35	560
84-0115	LJ35	561
84-0116	LJ35	562
84-0117	LJ35	563
84-0118	LJ35	564
84-0119	LJ35	565
84-0120	**LJ35**	**566**
84-0121	LJ35	567
84-0122	LJ35	568
84-0123	LJ35	569
84-0124	**LJ35**	**570**
84-0125	**LJ35**	**571**
84-0126	**LJ35**	**572**
84-0127	LJ35	573
84-0128	LJ35	575
84-0129	**LJ35**	**576**
84-0130	LJ35	577
84-0131	LJ35	578
84-0132	LJ35	579
84-0133	LJ35	580
84-0134	LJ35	581
84-0135	**LJ35**	**582**
84-0136	LJ35	583
84-0137	**LJ35**	**585**
84-0138	LJ35	574
84-0139	**LJ35**	**587**
84-0140	LJ35	588
84-0141	LJ35	584
84-0142	**LJ35**	**586**
85-0049	GLF3	456
85-0050	GLF3	458
86-0200	GLF3	465
86-0201	**GLF3**	**470**
86-0202	GLF3	468
86-0203	**GLF3**	**475**
86-0204	**GLF3**	**476**
86-0205	GLF3	477
86-0206	**GLF3**	**478**
86-0374	**LJ35**	**624**
86-0375	LJ35	625
86-0376	LJ35	628
86-0377	**LJ35**	**629**
86-0403	GLF3	473
87-0026	LJ35	280
87-0139	GLF3	497
87-0140	GLF3	498
88-0269	HS25	258129
88-0270	HS25	258131
88-0271	HS25	258134
88-0272	HS25	258154
88-0273	HS25	258156
88-0274	HS25	258158
89-0266	GLF2	45
89-0284	**BE40**	**TT-5**
90-0300	**GLF4**	**1181**
90-0400	**BE40**	**TT-3**
90-0401	**BE40**	**TT-7**
90-0402	**BE40**	**TT-8**
90-0403	**BE40**	**TT-9**
90-0404	**BE40**	**TT-6**
90-0405	**BE40**	**TT-4**
90-0406	**BE40**	**TT-11**
90-0407	**BE40**	**TT-10**
90-0408	**BE40**	**TT-12**
90-0409	**BE40**	**TT-13**
90-0410	**BE40**	**TT-14**
90-0411	**BE40**	**TT-15**
90-0412	**BE40**	**TT-2**
90-0413	**BE40**	**TT-16**
91-0075	**BE40**	**TT-18**
91-0076	**BE40**	**TT-17**
91-0077	**BE40**	**TT-1**
91-0078	**BE40**	**TT-19**
91-0079	**BE40**	**TT-20**
91-0080	**BE40**	**TT-21**
91-0081	**BE40**	**TT-22**
91-0082	**BE40**	**TT-23**
91-0083	**BE40**	**TT-24**
91-0084	**BE40**	**TT-25**
91-0085	**BE40**	**TT-26**
91-0086	**BE40**	**TT-27**
91-0087	**BE40**	**TT-28**
91-0088	**BE40**	**TT-29**
91-0089	**BE40**	**TT-30**
91-0090	**BE40**	**TT-31**
91-0091	**BE40**	**TT-32**
91-0092	**BE40**	**TT-33**
91-0093	BE40	TT-34
91-0094	**BE40**	**TT-35**
91-0095	**BE40**	**TT-36**
91-0096	**BE40**	**TT-37**
91-0097	**BE40**	**TT-38**
91-0098	**BE40**	**TT-39**
91-0099	**BE40**	**TT-40**
91-0100	**BE40**	**TT-41**
91-0101	**BE40**	**TT-42**
91-0102	**BE40**	**TT-43**
91-0108	**GLF4**	**1162**
92-0330	**BE40**	**TT-44**
92-0331	**BE40**	**TT-45**
92-0332	**BE40**	**TT-46**
92-0333	**BE40**	**TT-47**
92-0334	**BE40**	**TT-48**
92-0335	**BE40**	**TT-49**
92-0336	**BE40**	**TT-50**
92-0337	**BE40**	**TT-51**
92-0338	**BE40**	**TT-52**
92-0339	**BE40**	**TT-53**
92-0340	**BE40**	**TT-54**
92-0341	**BE40**	**TT-55**
92-0342	**BE40**	**TT-56**
92-0343	**BE40**	**TT-57**
92-0344	**BE40**	**TT-58**
92-0345	**BE40**	**TT-59**
92-0346	**BE40**	**TT-60**
92-0347	**BE40**	**TT-61**
92-0348	**BE40**	**TT-62**
92-0349	**BE40**	**TT-63**
92-0350	**BE40**	**TT-64**
92-0351	**BE40**	**TT-65**
92-0352	**BE40**	**TT-66**
92-0353	**BE40**	**TT-67**
92-0354	**BE40**	**TT-68**
92-0355	**BE40**	**TT-69**
92-0356	**BE40**	**TT-70**
92-0357	**BE40**	**TT-71**
92-0358	**BE40**	**TT-72**
92-0359	**BE40**	**TT-73**
92-0360	**BE40**	**TT-74**
92-0361	**BE40**	**TT-75**
92-0362	**BE40**	**TT-76**
92-0363	**BE40**	**TT-77**
92-0375	**GLF4**	**1256**
93-0621	**BE40**	**TT-78**
93-0622	**BE40**	**TT-79**
93-0623	**BE40**	**TT-80**
93-0624	**BE40**	**TT-81**
93-0625	**BE40**	**TT-82**
93-0626	**BE40**	**TT-83**
93-0627	**BE40**	**TT-84**
93-0628	**BE40**	**TT-85**
93-0629	**BE40**	**TT-86**
93-0630	**BE40**	**TT-87**
93-0631	**BE40**	**TT-88**
93-0632	**BE40**	**TT-89**
93-0633	BE40	TT-90
93-0634	**BE40**	**TT-91**
93-0635	**BE40**	**TT-92**
93-0636	**BE40**	**TT-93**
93-0637	**BE40**	**TT-94**
93-0638	**BE40**	**TT-95**
93-0639	**BE40**	**TT-96**
93-0640	**BE40**	**TT-97**
93-0641	**BE40**	**TT-98**
93-0642	**BE40**	**TT-99**
93-0643	**BE40**	**TT-100**
93-0644	**BE40**	**TT-101**
93-0645	**BE40**	**TT-102**
93-0646	**BE40**	**TT-103**
93-0647	**BE40**	**TT-104**
93-0648	**BE40**	**TT-105**
93-0649	**BE40**	**TT-106**
93-0650	**BE40**	**TT-107**
93-0651	**BE40**	**TT-108**
93-0652	**BE40**	**TT-109**
93-0653	**BE40**	**TT-110**
93-0654	**BE40**	**TT-111**
93-0655	**BE40**	**TT-112**
93-0656	**BE40**	**TT-113**
94-0114	**BE40**	**TT-114**
94-0115	**BE40**	**TT-115**
94-0116	**BE40**	**TT-116**
94-0117	**BE40**	**TT-117**
94-0118	**BE40**	**TT-118**
94-0119	**BE40**	**TT-119**
94-0120	**BE40**	**TT-120**
94-0121	**BE40**	**TT-121**
94-0122	**BE40**	**TT-122**
94-0123	**BE40**	**TT-123**
94-0124	**BE40**	**TT-124**
94-0125	**BE40**	**TT-125**
94-0126	**BE40**	**TT-126**
94-0127	**BE40**	**TT-127**
94-0128	**BE40**	**TT-128**
94-0129	**BE40**	**TT-129**
94-0130	**BE40**	**TT-130**
94-0131	**BE40**	**TT-131**
94-0132	**BE40**	**TT-132**
94-0133	**BE40**	**TT-133**
94-0134	**BE40**	**TT-134**
94-0135	**BE40**	**TT-135**
94-0136	**BE40**	**TT-136**
94-0137	**BE40**	**TT-137**
94-0138	**BE40**	**TT-138**
94-0139	**BE40**	**TT-139**
94-0140	**BE40**	**TT-140**
94-0141	**BE40**	**TT-141**
94-0142	**BE40**	**TT-142**
94-0143	**BE40**	**TT-143**
94-0144	**BE40**	**TT-144**
94-0145	**BE40**	**TT-145**
94-0146	**BE40**	**TT-146**
94-0147	**BE40**	**TT-147**
94-0148	**BE40**	**TT-148**
94-1569	**ASTR**	**088**
94-1570	**ASTR**	**090**
95-0040	**BE40**	**TT-149**
95-0041	**BE40**	**TT-150**
95-0042	**BE40**	**TT-151**
95-0043	**BE40**	**TT-152**
95-0044	**BE40**	**TT-153**
95-0045	**BE40**	**TT-154**
95-0046	**BE40**	**TT-155**
95-0047	**BE40**	**TT-156**
95-0048	**BE40**	**TT-157**
95-0049	**BE40**	**TT-158**
95-0050	**BE40**	**TT-159**
95-0051	**BE40**	**TT-160**
95-0052	**BE40**	**TT-161**
95-0053	**BE40**	**TT-162**
95-0054	**BE40**	**TT-163**
95-0055	**BE40**	**TT-164**
95-0056	**BE40**	**TT-165**
95-0057	**BE40**	**TT-166**
95-0058	**BE40**	**TT-167**
95-0059	**BE40**	**TT-168**
95-0060	**BE40**	**TT-169**
95-0061	**BE40**	**TT-170**
95-0062	**BE40**	**TT-171**
95-0063	**BE40**	**TT-172**
95-0064	**BE40**	**TT-173**
95-0065	**BE40**	**TT-174**
95-0066	**BE40**	**TT-175**

95-0067	BE40	TT-176			
95-0068	BE40	TT-177			
95-0069	BE40	TT-178			
95-0070	BE40	TT-179			
95-0071	BE40	TT-180			
95-0123	C560	0387			
95-0124	C560	0392			
96-0107	C560	0404			
96-0108	C560	0410			
96-0109	C560	0415			
96-0110	C560	0420			
96-0111	C560	0426			
97-0049	GLF5	566			
97-0101	C560	0452			
97-0102	C560	0456			
97-0103	C560	0462			
97-0104	C560	0468			
97-0105	C560	0472			
97-0400	GLF5	521			
97-0401	GLF5	542			
98-0006	C560	0495			
98-0007	C560	0501			
98-0008	C560	0505			
98-0009	C560	0508			
98-0010	C560	0513			
99-0100	C560	0532			
99-0101	C560	0534			
99-0102	C560	0538			
99-0103	C560	0545			
99-0104	C560	0548			
99-0402	GLF5	571			
99-0404	GLF5	590			
(99-0405)	GLF5	596			
"97-0231"	C525	0231			
00-1051	C560	0565			
00-1052	C560	0574			
00-1053	C560	0577			
01-0028	GLF5	620			
01-0029	GLF5	624			
01-0030	GLF5	663			
01-0065	GLF5	652			
01-0076	GLF5	645			
01-0301	C560	0589			
02-1863	GLF5	670			
03-0016	C560	0649			
03-0726	C560	0667			
04-1778	GLF5	5034			
05-1944	GLF5	566			
06-0500	GLF5	5152			
09-0501	GLF5	5247			
09-0525	GLF5	5247			
11-0550	GLF5	5297			
11-9001	GLEX	9001			

11-9355	GLEX	9355
11-9358	GLEX	9358
12-9506	GLEX	9506

US Coast Guard

01	GLF3	477
01	GLF5	653
02	CL64	5427
02	GLF5	638
160	WW24	160
519	C500	019
2101	FA20	374
2102	FA20	386
2103	FA20	394
2104	FA20	390
2105	FA20	398
2106	FA20	402
2107	FA20	409
2108	FA20	405
2109	FA20	407
2110	FA20	411
2111	FA20	413
2112	FA20	415
2113	FA20	417
2114	FA20	418
2115	FA20	419
2116	FA20	420
2117	FA20	421
2118	FA20	423
2119	FA20	424
2120	FA20	425
2121	FA20	431
2122	FA20	433
2123	FA20	435
2124	FA20	437
2125	FA20	439
2126	FA20	441
2127	FA20	443
2128	FA20	445
2129	FA20	447
2130	FA20	450
2131	FA20	452
2132	FA20	454
2133	FA20	456
2134	FA20	458
2135	FA20	459
2136	FA20	460
2137	FA20	462
2138	FA20	464
2139	FA20	466
2140	FA20	467
2141	FA20	371

Navy/Marines

150542	SBRL	277-1
150543	SBRL	277-2
150544	SBRL	277-3
150545	SBRL	277-4
150546	SBRL	277-5
150547	SBRL	277-6
150548	SBRL	277-7
150549	SBRL	277-8
150550	SBRL	277-9
150551	SBRL	277-10
150969	SBRL	285-1
150970	SBRL	285-2
150971	SBRL	285-3
150972	SBRL	285-4
150973	SBRL	285-5
150974	SBRL	285-6
150975	SBRL	285-7
150976	SBRL	285-8
150977	SBRL	285-9
150978	SBRL	285-10
150979	SBRL	285-11
150980	SBRL	285-12
150981	SBRL	285-13
150982	SBRL	285-14
150983	SBRL	285-15
150984	SBRL	285-16
150985	SBRL	285-17
150986	SBRL	285-18
150987	SBRL	285-19
150988	SBRL	285-20
150989	SBRL	285-21
150990	SBRL	285-22
150991	SBRL	285-23
150992	SBRL	285-24
151336	SBRL	285-25
151337	SBRL	285-26
151338	SBRL	285-27
151339	SBRL	285-28
151340	SBRL	285-29
151341	SBRL	285-30
151342	SBRL	285-31
151343	SBRL	285-32
157352	SBRL	282-46
157353	SBRL	282-84
157354	SBRL	282-85
158380	SBRL	282-95
158381	SBRL	282-93
158382	SBRL	282-92
158383	SBRL	282-96
158843	SBRL	306-52
158844	SBRL	306-55
159361	SBRL	306-65

159362	SBRL	306-66
159363	SBRL	306-67
159364	SBRL	306-69
159365	SBRL	306-70
160053	SBRL	306-104
160054	SBRL	306-105
160055	SBRL	306-106
160056	SBRL	306-107
160057	SBRL	306-108
162755	C552	0001
162756	C552	0002
162757	C552	0003
162758	C552	0004
162759	C552	0005
162760	C552	0006
162761	C552	0007
162762	C552	0008
162763	C552	0009
162764	C552	0010
162765	C552	0011
162766	C552	0012
162767	C552	0013
162768	C552	0014
162769	C552	0015
163691	GLF3	480
163692	GLF3	481
165093	GLF4	1187
165094	GLF4	1189
165151	GLF4	1199
165152	GLF4	1201
165153	GLF4	1200
165509	SBRL	282-9
165510	SBRL	282-81
165511	SBRL	282-29
165512	SBRL	282-2
165513	SBRL	282-66
165514	SBRL	282-30
165515	SBRL	282-72
165516	SBRL	282-90
165517	SBRL	282-61
165518	SBRL	282-77
165519	SBRL	282-19
165520	SBRL	282-32
165521	SBRL	282-94
165522	SBRL	282-28
165523	SBRL	282-20
165524	SBRL	282-60
165525	SBRL	282-100
165740	C560	0524
165741	C560	0529
165938	C560	0567
165939	C560	0570
166374	C560	0592

166375	GLF5	657
166376	GLF5	5041
166377	GLF5	5087
166378	GLF5	5098
166474	C560	0630
166500	C560	0651
166712	C560	0672
166713	C560	0677
166714	C560	0679
166715	C560	0682
166766	C560	0693
166767	C560	0696
830500	GLF3	382

Uruguay

FAU_500	LJ35	378

Venda

VDF-030	C550	266

Venezuela

0002	C550	012
0004	GLF2	124
0005	GLF3	400
0006	LJ24	250
0010	GLF2	75/7
0018	FA50	22
0222	C500	092
0403	C550	371
0442	FA20	235
1060	C750	0134
1107	C550	449
1113	C550	309
1650	FA20	476
1967	C550	020
2222	C550	251
5761	FA20	23
5840	FA20	216
FAV0013	LJ35	270

Yugoslavia

10401	LJ25	202
10402	LJ25	203
70401	LJ25	202
70402	LJ25	203
72102	FA50	43

Odds and ends

"40420"	GLF3	420

AIRCRAFT WHOSE C/N IS NOT YET KNOWN

Reg'n	Type	Remarks
EC-207	HS25	reported at Koln/Bonn 13Nov88.
F-WWMF	F2EX	noted at Bordeaux Feb16 (possibly a F2TS)
F-WWMI	F2EX	noted at Bordeaux Feb16 (possibly a F2TS)
F-WWMJ	F2EX	noted at Bordeaux Feb16 (possibly a F2TS)
F-WWMK	F2EX	noted at Bordeaux Feb16 (possibly a F2TS)
F-WWMM	F2EX	noted at Bordeaux Feb16 (possibly a F2TS)
F-WWQI	FA8X	noted at Little Rock 03Mar16, c/n 408 or 409
F-WWQJ	FA8X	noted at Little Rock 06Apr16, c/n 409 or 410
F-WWQK	FA8X	noted at Bordeaux Apr16, c/n 410 or 411
F-WWQL	FA8X	noted at Bordeaux Apr16, c/n 411 or 412
F-WWUM	FA7X	noted at Little Rock 31Mar16
F-WWUN	FA7X	noted at Little Rock 18Feb16
F-WWUO	FA7X	noted at Little Rock 14Mar16
F-WWZU	FA7X	reported at Little Rock 02Dec15
HK-3452X	C550	registered to Aviaco Ltda – ntu?
LZ-OIF	HS25	reported at Cairo 29May03.
M-JEAI	GLEX	reported at Montreal/Dorval Oct15
N5AF	GLF5	reported at Long Beach 10Jan99 – possibly c/n 531 N531AF incorrectly painted.
N198GT	HS25	wfu at Inyoken, CA, fake marks.
N142HC	GLEX	reported at Montreal/Dorval 05Feb15
N175BA	LJ35	destroyed by Venezuelan military nr San Fernando de Apure 30Nov14, drug-running with fake marks
N780JR	ASTR	reported at Teterboro 30Jun93.
N1015G	C550	noted at Wichita 05Aug92.
N1123B	C650	noted at Wichita 21Jan97.
N2808B	BE40	noted at Beech Field, Wichita 28May91.
N2810B	BE40	noted at Beech Field, Wichita 01Apr93.
N2826B	BE40	flew St John's-Reykjavik-Shannon-Rome/Ciampino 15Feb94 and returned Ciampino-Shannon-Reykjavik 04Mar94.
N4074Z	C510	noted at Independence 23Jan08
N5000E	LJ31	noted at Wichita 10Mar92.
N5000E	LJ31	noted at Wichita 22Feb93.
N5010U	LJ31	noted at Wichita 21Apr92.
N5012G	LJ31	noted at Wichita 14Jan93.
N5012G	LJ60	noted at Tucson 10Sep00.
N5012H	LJ31	noted at Wichita 26Mar92.
N5012K	LJ31	noted at Wichita 05Aug92.
N5012K	LJ45	noted at Wichita 15Oct99.
N5012Z	LJ45	noted at Tucson 1999, German flag, possibly c/n 45-044.
N5013Y	LJ31	noted at Wichita 05May92.
N5014E	LJ31	noted at Wichita 03Feb92.
N5014E	LJ60	noted at Wichita 18Mar93.
N5014F	LJ35	noted at Wichita 09Jun92.
N5015U	LJ60	noted at Tucson 15Oct99.
N5016V	LJ31	noted at Wichita 26Mar92.
N5016V	LJ31	noted at Wichita 31Mar93.
N5017J	LJ31	noted at Wichita 13Apr93.
N5018G	LJ31	noted at Wichita 02Nov92.
N5076K	C560	noted at Wichita 22Apr99.
N5093D	C560	noted at Wichita 25Feb99.
N5093L	C550	noted at Wichita 15Oct99.
N5124F	C525	noted at Wichita 20Aug96.
N5126L	C525	noted at Wichita 17Sep99.
N5135A	C750	noted at Wichita 18Mar02.
N5148B	C550	noted at Wichita 18Nov98.
N5163K	C525	noted at Wichita 16Oct98.
N5197A	525A	noted at Wichita 19Jan03.
N5200Z	C560	noted at Wichita 10Jun94.
N5243K	C750	noted at Wichita 08Oct02.
N5244F	C525	noted at Wichita 16Sep99.
N5266F	C550	noted at Wichita 16Aug99.
N40078	LJ45	noted at Wichita 22Jun02.
N50111	LJ31	noted at Wichita 28Apr93.
N50126	LJ31	noted at Wichita 17Sep91.
N50126	LJ35	noted at Wichita 05Aug92.
N40335	BE40	noted Wichita/Beech Field 05Aug93.
N50154	LJ31	noted at Wichita 19Nov91.
N50157	LJ31	noted at Wichita 12Aug91.
N50163	LJ31	noted at Wichita 20Jly92.
N51613	C525	noted at Wichita 27Feb97.
N51983	C56X	noted at Wichita 01Oct99.
N52542	525A	noted at Wichita 30Jly02.
N82787	BE40	noted at Beech Field, Wichita 13Feb94.
OB-668	SBRL	registered in Peru, c/n quoted as '308-025'.
PT-MMY	C560	noted at Wichita 05May97.
P4-ALN	H25B	reported at Little Rock Apr2012.
UP-HA002	H25B	reported at Vilnius 09Mar13.
VP-CPR	GLF6	reported at Long Beach 13Feb16/
VQ-BLV	GLF6	reported at Teterboro 14Apr16 – possibly c/n 6176
VT-CLF	F2TH	noted at Dubai/World Central 26Oct15
XA-ABV	C550	noted at Fort Lauderdale Int'l 01Apr01
XA-AVJ	C52B	reported at Tucson 16Aug12.
XA-DCX	LJ35	noted at Toluca in Jan07.
XA-DIJ	LJ35	photographed at Las Vegas/McCarran Jan15
XA-HEI	SBRL	reported at Mexico City 23Sep90.
XA-JMB	LJ31	reported at Houston Intercontinental 28Mar15 – possibly c/n 31A-230 ex-N558HD.
XA-JMN	HS25	reported at Houston/Hobby 22Aug13.
XA-JPR	LJ25	noted at Toluca 26Dec08 and Miami 14Feb09.
XA-LDV	HS25	reported at Toluca in Sep05 – possibly XA-LOV misread?
XA-LED	SBRL	reported at Toluca Jan15
XA-MME	LJ25	operated by Air One Ambulance
XA-MMI	LJ25	photographed at San Jose, Costa Rica, 09Aug14
XA-NMT	HS25	noted at Miami 04Dec09.
XA-PPV	C500	photographed at Toluca 02Apr08
XA-RLF	SBRL	reported at Mexico City in Nov91.
XA-RPM	C56X	reported at Toluca in Mar06.
XA-TJX	SBRL	reported at Cancun 09Jun06.
XA-TOY	JSTR	reported at Teterboro 15Apr04 (marks on a Cessna 208 by Feb07).
XA-TRI	SBRL	reported at Toluca 22Mar00 (marks on an ATR-42 by Feb03).
XA-UJO	LJ35	noted at Toluca 28Jun08.
XA-ULN	HS25	noted at Ciudad Mante 27Jun09.
XA-UOF	HS25	photographed in Mexico Nov12, a 5-window model
XA-UTV	LJ25	reported at Hollywood-Burbank 20Jul14
XA-UWF	HS25	photographed at Orlando Executive 28Dec15, model 750 or 800
XA-VAL	LJ31	reported at San Antonio 03Dec08.
XA-VYA	LJ45	reported at Houston/Hobby 03Feb10.
XA-VYR	C500	reported at Dallas/Love Field.
XA-ZTJ	HS25	reported at Las Vegas 26Jul08.
XB-CMA	LJ25	photographed at Toluca Nov07.
XB-GCU	SBRL	reported at Las Vegas/McCarran 13Sep14
XB-JER	GLF1	reported at Acarigua, Venezuela, 04May06.
XB-JHU	SBRL	reported at Toluca 02Aug95.
XB-JTB	HS25	reported at Toluca Apr10.
XB-JTO	LJ25	noted at Toluca in Apr07.
XB-JVP	SBRL	photographed at Aguascalientes 20Mar09, a series 40.
XB-KMY	LJ24	photographed at Toluca in Nov07.
XB-LKH	C650	noted at Guadalajara 22Oct09.
XB-LTP	LJ25	photographed at Orlando Executive 21Jul10.
XB-LVG	LJ25	photographed at Houston/Hobby 09Jul10.
XB-LVL	C500	reported at Houston/Hobby 17Sep10.
XB-MLH	LJ24	photographed at Toluca 06Oct11.
XB-MTV	HS25	reported wfu at Caracas/La Carlota
XB-NNA	C500	reported at San Antonio 05Jan14.
XB-NNL	LJ25	photographed at Alajuela-San Jose, Costa Rica, 02Sep13
XB-NPQ	HS25	reported at Toluca 06Mar14
XB-NXR	C550	reported at Toluca 19Mar15 – possibly c/n 550-0216 ex-N550PG
XB-NYS	FA20	reported at White Plains 03Aug14
XB-NZF	C650	photographed in Mexico 2015
XB-NZW	LJ25	photographed at Las Vegas/McCarran 01May15
XB-OAF	HS25	photographed at Las Vegas/McCarran 17Dec14
XB-OBM	C650	noted at Toluca 18Mch15 – possibly c/n 650-0177
XB-ODW	LJ35	noted at Las Vegas/McCarran 26Oct15 – possibly c/n 35A-620
XB-OEC	LJ35	noted at San Antonio, TX, 18Oct15 – possibly c/n 35A-326
XB-OJA	C650	noted at Oakland, CA, 07Feb16
XB-RUA	C650	noted at Las Vegas/McCarran 14Sep15 – possibly c/n 650-7019
XB-TTT	C550	reported at Toluca May11.
XC-AGH	LJ25	reported at Houston/Hobby 09Oct07.
XC-ANL	HS25	instructional airframe at CONALEP Apodaca, Monterrey.
XC-ASG	LJ35	reported at Mexico City 27Jan94.
XC-GDH	FA20	noted at Toluca 18Mar15
XC-JEG	C550	reported at Davis-Monthan Nov02.
YA-GAB	HS25	reported at Termez, Uzbekistan, Apr04.
YV-94C	C500	reported at Fort Lauderdale Executive 12Sep93.
YV561T	C500	reported at Charallave 27Oct14
YV690T	C650	noted at Miami/Opa Locka 31Mar16, possibly c/n 650-0020
YV2461	C550	reported at Fort Lauderdale Executive 03Dec10.
YV2595	BE40	reported at Fort Lauderdale Executive 5Dec09
YV3051	C550	reported at St Maarten, Lesser Antilles, 11Dec14
YV3084	LJ25	photographed at Guyana, Venezuela Sep15
YV3087	LJ25	noted at Fort Lauderdale Executive 29Aug15
YV3120	WW24	photographed at Miami/Opa Locka 30Dec15, model 1124.
ZC-PMC	C550	noted at Wichita 2May90 and later at Mexico City – presumably should have been painted as XC-PMC …
ZS-KDR	GLEX	reported at Dallas/Love Field 21Mar15
4X-CVH	G280	reported at Tel Aviv 25Mar14
5A-DMH	HFB3	photographed at Mitiga, Libya, Oct09.
9M-CHX	HS25	reported at Kuala Lumpur 16Mar95.
A-9208	PRM1	reported at Bali 02Jan15, Indonesian Army
ES-7960	JSTR	displayed at petrol station San Luis Potosi, Mexico – fake marks.
GN-708	SBRL	photographed at Buenos Aires/Aeroparque in 1997, Gendarmerie Nacional Argentina, a series 75.
0313	C560	reported wfu at Caracas/La Carlota 27Oct14, Venezuelan Air Force
1113	C550	photographed at Caracas/Miranda 22Jun12, Venezuelan Air Force.
1603	C550	photographed at Guayana, Venezuela 12Nov15; Venezuelan Air Force
6005	LJ35	Brazilian Air Force R-35AM photographed at Anapolis Air Base 02Sep14 – either c/n 631, 632 or 633
15-2233	FA20	reported at Tehran Dec02, Iranian Air Force.
90-0400	BE40	noted in USAF colours at Wichita 20Mar90, probably painted as such for publicity purposes in connection with the T-1 Jayhawk programme. Possibly c/n RJ-45 – the marks are now genuinely worn by c/n TT-3.

GRUMMAN G159 GULFSTREAM 1

C/n	Series	Identities										
1		N701G	[ff14Aug58]	ZS-NVG	5Y-EMK	5Y-XXX	3X-GER	9Q-CTC				
2		N702G	N1	N3	N3003	N40CE	N42CE	N40CE	N116GA	N39PP	86-0402	[b/u 30Sep90]
3		N703G	CF-MAR	C-FMAR	[b/u for spares Montreal, Canada]							
4		N704G	N704HC	N717	N99DE	N89DE	N371BG	[wfu 1985; b/u for spares 1985]				
5		N705G	N601HK	N601HP	N700PR	N43AS	N9EB	N159AJ	N925WL	N159AJ	F-GFGT	ZS-OOE
6		N2425	(VR-B..)	S9-NAU	N221AP	[b/u Pawaukee apt, IL, on 15Feb96]						
7		CF-LOO	N5VX	N99EL	[cx 19May15; CofR expired]							
8		N708G	[wfu for spares in 1985, fuselage in yard by Cosgrove A/c Services, south of Houston Hobby apt, TX]									
9		N709G	N43M	N436M	N436	N436M	G-BNCE	[wfu Oct91 Aberdeen, UK due to corrosion; parted out; cx 04May93; fuselage to Dundee apt, UK fire/emergency training]				
10		N710G	N1623	N1623Z	XB-CIJ	[wfu 05Oct88 following landing accident]						
11		N711G	N650ST	N650BT	N100FL	N100EL	N7SL	[wfu Valencia, Venezuela]				
12		N712G	N400P	N4009	N166NK	N91JR	N8VB	XA-TBT	[parted out by Dodson Av'n, Rantoul, KS, circa Sep97]			
13		[airframe not built]										
14		N714G	N1607Z	N723RA	[cx Nov88; b/u for spares 1988 Shreveport, LA]							
15		N715G	N1501	N1501C	N72EZ	N26KW	XB-ESO	[wfu 11Oct90 following landing accident]				
16		N716G	N2998	N707WA	N8001J	N20H	N202HA	N615C	[cx 27Jun12; wfu]			
17		N717G	N199M	CF-TPC	N9971F	[wfu 1985; b/u for spares 1986]						
18		N718G	N300UP	N3UP	N48PA	YV-.....	[impounded in Venezuela Nov05 for drug-running, still marked N48PA]					
19		N719G	N80L	N80LR	N70LR	N12GW	PK-WWG	N12GW	[b/u for spares Oct87; cx Sep89]			
20		N720G	N266P	N227LS	N227LA	N250AL	N5PC	VR-CTN	N732US	F-GFMH	TJ-WIN	TU-TDM	N19FF	[wfu Madrid/Barajas, Spain, to be parted out]
21		N721G	N361G	N361Q	XC-BIO	N6653Z	[b/u for spares 01Aug91 Savannah, GA; cx Nov95]					
22		N722G	N860AC	N80G	N8BG	C-GKFG	[cx Feb97, wfu]					
23		N723G	N1929Y	N1929B	OE-BAZ	OE-HAZ	N193PA	N186PA	N810CB			
24		N724G	N1620	N1625	N1625B	YV-P-AEA	YV-09CP	N713US	HK-3315X	HK-3315	[w/o 06Feb90 El Salado Mt, nr Ibague, Colombia; cx 26Jun90]	
25		N725G	(OE-...)	N725G	(OK-NEA)	N725G	4X-ARH	3D-DLH	ZS-PHK	9Q-CKM		
26		N726G	N726S	N505S	N120S	N348DA	YV-82CP	N185PA				
27	1C	N727G	N100P	N1009	XB-FUB	XB-VIW	XB-VAD	N2150M	N80M	N114GA	N415CA	N198PA
28		N728G	N900JL	N9006L	N666ES	N11SX	N118X	N719RA	[parted out by Dodson Aviation, KS]			
29		N729G	N785GP	N1844S	N1845S	N1925P	N222SG	N222SE	N431G	C-....	[US marks cx Jun99; parted out Toronto/Lester B Pearson apt, Canada circa Nov00 still as N431G]	
30		N730G	N901G	N961G	[wfu 01Apr89 for spares; cx Nov91]							
31		N731G	CF-JFC	N715RA	[wfu; parted out by Int'l Turbine Services, TX]							
32		N732G	N734ET	N734EB	N733EB	N297X	N300MC	[cx Dec88; wfu]				
33		N126J	N88Y	N261L	N295SA	HR-IAJ	TG-TJB	(N23AH)	N21AH	9Q-CBY		
34		N734G	N620K	N48TE	HK-3634X	N34LE	5Y-BLR					
35		N735G	XC-IMS	XB-DVG	XA-PUA	N86MA	9Q-CBD					
36		N130A	N230E	[wfu 01Nov88 Detroit-Willow Run, MI; by Jan03 El Mirage CA; bare metal]								
37		N130G	N130B	N716RD	N716R	N20S	N91G	[w/o 24Sep78 Houston, TX]				
38		N738G	ZS-AAC	VQ-ZIP	3D-AAC	N7001N	N38JK	N333AH	N717RS	XA-...		
39		N40Y	N39TG	EC-376	EC-EVJ							
40		N6PG	N8ZA	N40AG	EC-493	EC-FIO	N19TZ	[wfu Madrid/Barajas, Spain; cx 26Nov13]				
41		N7PG	N9ZA	N41TG	EC-494	EC-EZO	[wfu Madrid-Barajas, Spain]					
42		N366P	N430H	N888PR	XA-MAS	XC-AA61	ZS-OCA	3D-TRE	3D-DOM	TL-ADN		
43		N344DJ	N140NT	C-GNOR	N39289	N716RA	[wfu for spares Jul88; cx Jan91]					
44		N285AA	N121NC	N717JF	N717RW	N717RD	F-GFGV	5Y-JET				
45		N745G	N7788	N329CT	N65CE	[cx 24Mar04; donated to Des Moines Central Campus Aviation laboratory, IA for use as instructional airframe]						
46		N746G	[wfu Oct86; used for spares]									
47		N747G	N20CC	N20CQ	N20HF	[b/u Oct86 Texas; cx Feb90]						
48		N748G	VR-BBY	N302K	G-AWYF	N213GA	[b/u Palwaukee, IL circa Apr97]					
49		N749G	N456	F-GFIC								
50		N80J	N8BJ	N6PA	N3100E	N8200E	N820CE	N28CG	[cx Jun90; to Schweizer Maintenance School, Elmira, NY by Aug91]			
51		N80K	N80KA	XC-HYC	N90PM	I-MGGG	[b/u 1994 Geneva, Switzerland]					
52		N752G	VH-ASJ	N3858H	N18TF	(N18TZ)	N612DT					
53		N753G	N700JW	(N701JW)	[wfu 21Apr89; b/u for spares by White Industries, Bates City, MO; cx Jun94]							
54		CF-MUR	C-FMUR	N26AJ	N164PA							
55		N755G	N255AA	N1234X	N429X	N429W	N9MH	N429W	N27L	N300PH	VR-CAE	N9446E	N118LT	[b/u for spares 1986 Lawton, TX; cx Jul91]
56		N756G	N220B	N510E	YV-46CP	N168PA	[b/u for spares; cx Mar05]					
57		N757G	I-CKET	N66JD	PK-TRM							
58		N758G	N358AA	5N-AAI	N16776	N46TE	N47TE	XB-FLL	XA-TTU	XC-VNC	[wfu Toluca, Mexico]	
59		N759G	N205AA	N23D	N11CZ	HK-3316X	HK-3316	[w/o 02May90 Los Garcones apt, Monteria, Colombia]				
60		CF-IOM	C-FIOM	PK-TRL								
61		N761G	N594AR	N734HR	N191SA	[b/u for spares Jun88 Wiley Post, OK; remains to Dodson Aviation, KS]						
62		N205M	[w/o 25Jul67 New Cumberland, PA]	N400NL	[cx 6Oct14, CofR expired]							
63		N763G	N144NK	N580BC	[to Aviation Warehouse Film Prop Yard, El Mirage, CA circa 2000]							
64		N764G	N466P	CF-COL	N49401	N64TG	EC-460	EC-EXS	[wfu Madrid, Spain]			
65		N765G	N345TW	N340WB	N641B	N721RA	[cx Nov89; b/u for spares 1988]					
66		N766G	N623W	N65H	N65HC	N111DR	XC-GEI	[wfu 04Sep86; b/u for spares]				
67		N767G	N376	N48	N806S	N5241Z	N806W	[cx 29Oct14; CofR expired]				
68		N768G	N768GP	N15GP	N4765P	N4765C	N7ZA	N68TG	[w/o 15Jul83 Tri-Cities apt, Bristol, TN]			
69		N769G	N377	N47	N47R	[wfu 1986; to Votec School, Rexburg, ID; then to Pratt Community College, KS circa 1998]						
70		N770G	N331H	[Parted out by Dodson Aviation, Ottawa, KS]								
71		N771G	N530AA	N60CR	VR-BTI	N222EF	(N15SQ)	N222EF	F-GFIB	XA-MYR	XB-MDM	XB-MVT	[wfu circa Mar06 Toluca, Mexico]
72		N772G	CF-NOC	N743G	(N93SA)	N743G	[wfu 01Apr89; b/u for spares]					
73		N773G	N773WJ	N207M	N720X	[cx Nov88; w/o pre Feb87 (buried by sand in Arizona Desert after drug-running flight)]						
74		N774G	N212H	N5619D	N701BN							
75		N775G	N304K	PT-KYF								
76		N776G	N305K	G-BRAL	P4-JML							
77		N777G	N706G	N73M	N748M	N748MN	N748M	9Q-CFK	G-BOBX	[wfu for spares 25Apr89]		
78		N778G	N1040	N778G	N1040	N7040	N431H	N33CP	(PT-...)	HK-3681		
79		N779G	N190DM	N79HS	(EC-491)	[parted out 1993 Fort Lauderdale Int'l, FL]						
80		N780G	N605AA	N605AB	N20GB	N200GJ	F-GGGY	D2-EXC				
81		N781G	N22G	N2PQ	C-GMJS	I-TASO	"5Y-BMT"	5Y-BMR				
82		N782G	N798S	N98R	N798R	N629JM	(N801CC)	SE-LFV	SE-LDV	N12RW	3C-...	
83	1C	N783G	N437A	N117GA	N245CA	[to White Inds, Bates City, MO for spares]						
84		N784G	N362G	N362GP	N184K	N183K	[destroyed by Colombian military 03Jun06 in anti-drug-running operation]					
85		N706G	N1150S	XC-BAU	(N66534)	[wfu 01Aug91; b/u for spares Savannah, GA; cx Nov95]						
86		N786G	N678RW	N231GR	N712MW	N712MR	N712MP	N106GH	N106GA	N86JK	N10TB	ZS-ALX	9Q-CTH
87		N787G	N10VM	N102PL	N711BT	N87CH	N87CE	(N87MK)	N845JB	[wfu and scrapped; cx Sep97]		
88	1C	N788G	N410AA	N1M	N357H	N857H	C-GPTN	N195PA	[wfu Cartersville, GA, Dec14]			

GRUMMAN G159 GULFSTREAM 1

C/n	Series	Identities									
89		N789G									
90		N790G	N4567	N18N	N80R	N41JK	HK-3330X	[remains with Dodson Av'n, Rantoul, KS Dec92]			
91		N791G	USCG 1380	USCG 02	USCG 03						
92		N710G	NASA3	N3NA	USCG 02	N3NA	YV....				
93		N740AA	N574DU	N574K	N674C	N137C	XA-ILV	N137C	N197PA	N820CB	[cx 20Feb13; wfu]	
94		N794G	N8E								
95		N795G	N50UC	N500RL	N500RN						
96		NASA1	N1NA	N2NA	N444BC	N361BL					
97		N797G	N5152	N671NC	N49DE	YV-85CP	N184PA	[cx 21Apr09, wfu]			
98		N798G	NASA2	N2NA	N29AY	N98MK	[wfu Apr91; b/u for spares by White Inds, Bates City, MO]				
99		N799G	N67B	N102M	N364G	N364L	N750BR	[w/o 13Nov88 nr Frankfurt, Germany; b/u; cx Dec89]			
100		N715G	N166KJ	N116K	VH-FLO	(ZK-...)	[cx May95; wfu]				
101		N716G	N222H	N300SB	F-GFGU	4X-ARV	F-GNGU				
102		N717G	N621A	N28CG	N48CG	N48CQ	(N73CG)	N48CQ	HA-ACV	C6-UNO	N11UN	[wfu 2004 Kendall-Tamiami Executive, FL]
103		N718G	N608RP	N608R	PT-	XC-AA57					
104		N719G	CF-HBO	C-FHBO							
105		N702G	[CofA expired 01Jun90; wfu Jul93 Milan-Linate, Italy; cx; in use as snack bar at Bacong Negros Oriental, Philippines 2004]								
106		N706G	N780AC	N72X	N72XL	N38CG	N64CG	C-FAWG	9XR-WR	YV1020	[destroyed by military action 26Sep05 while drug-running at secret airstrip nr San Andres, Colombia]
107		N722G	N34C	N73B	N7ZB	N71CR	N71CJ	[b/u Houston Hobby, TX circa Jan04]			
108		N723G	N1707Z	N23UG	[b/u for spares late 1986; cx Feb90]						
109		N724G	N1000	N823GA	N5000C	N2000C	N1000	N1091	N804CC	N307AT	N109P	[cx 02Oct99, b/u]
110		N727G	N533CS	C-GTDL	[cx May86; b/u for spares 1989]						
111		N728G	N363G	N3630	F-GJGC	[semi-derelict Oct91 Marseille, France]					
112		N729G	N942PM	N300PM	N300PE	(N300BP)	N803CC	[wfu Mar89; cx Sep89; noted derelict Sep91 Detroit-Willow Run, MI]			
113		[not built]									
114		N712G	N205M	N705M	N705RS	N9300P	VH-WPA	N724RA	[wfu 01Mar88; b/u for spares by Intl Turbine Services, TX; cx Jan89]		
115		CF-ASC	N61SB	[stored Dallas-Love Field, TX with engines removed]							
116	1C	N706G	N26L	N5400G	N5400C	N110GA	N159AN	N328CA	[parted out by White Inds, Bates City, MO; cx 12Sep12]		
117		N710G	N519M	N23AK	N41KD	YV-08CP	N167PA	[b/u for spares; cx Mar05]			
118		N715G	[b/u for spares 1983; cx 1984]								
119		N734G	YV-P-EPC	YV-28CP	N165PA	[wfu Cartersville, GA; cx]					
120		Greece P-9	[used callsign I-FRIS while in use by King Constantine in exile late 1960s/early 1970s]					Greece 120	[wfu 1995; preserved Tatoi-Dekelia, Greece, circa 1998]		
121		N732G	N234MM	[wfu 1992; displayed Disney-MGM Studio Theme Park, Orlando, FL]							
122		N738G	N153SR	N152SR	N707MP	F-GFEF	[cx 26Nov14; wfu]				
123	1C	N736G	N687RW	N714MW	N714MR	N2602M	N17CA	[to White Inds, Bates City, MO for spares]			
124		N737G	N504C	N725MK	N476S	ZS-NKT	D2-EXD				
125		N738G	N205G	N10NA	N5NA	N193PA					
126		N739G	N913BS	N913PS	N100TV	N63AU	N110RB				
127		N741GA	N500S	N50LS	N717JP	XA-TDJ	[wfu by 2004 Merida, Mexico]				
128		N122Y	N516DM	N910BS	F-GIIX	[dbf 28Jun94 Lyon-Satolas, France; cx 04Aug94]					
129		N743G	N770AC	N770A	N834H	N812CC	N113GA	N129AF	YV....		
130		N744G	N902JL	N3416	PK-TRO						
131		N750G	N730T	N1TX	N21TX	C-FRTT	5Y-BLF	[wfu Nairobi-Wilson apt, Kenya circa Oct00]			
132		N120HC	N1207C	N944H	N27G	N154SR	N154NS	N154RH	[b/u; cx Nov03]		
133		N752G	N2010	N7776	TU-VAC	N33TF	[wfu; b/u for spares by White Industries, Bates City, MO]				
134		N754G	N914BS	N920BS	G-BMPA	(F-....)	4X-ARF	3D-ARF	4X-ARF	3D-ARF	ZS-ONO	3D-DUE	ZS-PHJ	9Q-CTG
135		N755G	G-ASXT	[b/u Sep83 Denver, CO; cx 09Aug82]							
136		N756G	XB-GAW	XA-TBT	[wfu Urapan, Mexico]						
137		N757G	CF-DLO	N36DD	N42CA	(N811CC)	[noted 07Sep91 derelict Detroit-Willow Run, MI; cx Jun95]				
138		N758G	N126K	XA-ALK	XA-RLK						
139		N759G	N42G	N7972S	N8500N	N8500C	N157WC	N62J	C-FRTU	N196PA	
140		N760G	N40G	N140A	N300A	N92K	N92SA	F-GFCQ			
141		N762G	N228H	N800PA	ZS-NHW						
142		N764G	N10ZA	N142TG	EC-461	EC-EXQ	[wfu Madrid-Barajas, Spain]				
143		N720G	N914P	I-MDDD	[CofA expired 26Sep91; with Dodson Av'n, KS; cx]						
144		N766G	N860E	N70CR	N70QR	[wfu 1986; cx Mar91]					
145		N767G	N233U	N149X	N7FD	N155T	HK-3329X	HK-3580W			
146		N772G	N2011	N906F	OE-GSN	OE-HSN	Israel 001/4X-JUD	N906F	[b/u Opa-Locka, FL, late 2001]		
147		N774G	N861H	[w/o 11Jul67 Le Centre, MN]							
148		N775G	N804CC	N120S	(N9036P)	N107GH	N1701C	C-FWAM	XC-LIE	[wfu Toluca, Mexico]	
149		N776G	N636	N636G	N400HT	N684FM	N192PA				
150		N706G	N777G	YV-121CP	[wfu Jun88 following landing accident]						
151		N741G	NASA4	N4NA	[wfu circa Sep03 to display Pima Air & Space Museum, Tucson, AZ]						
152		N718G	N705G	HP-799	OB-M-1235	HP-799	N705G	[wfu 01May89; b/u for spares]			
153		N733G	N733NM	N80AC	N153TG	EC-433	EC-EXB	N19BX	[wfu Madrid/Barajas, Spain; cx 26Nov13]		
154		N736G	N267AA	N736G	N72B	N800PM	N800PD	N802CC	G-BNKO	C-GNAK	[w/o 19Jul00 nr Linneus, ME, USA]
155		N778G	N992CP	N22CP	N24CP	N900PM	N900PA	N805CC	G-BMOW	9Q-CJB	
156		N737G	N22AS	N41LH	(N159KK)	9Q-COE					
157		N741G	N94SA	[cx Aug91; sale in Panama possible, current status?]							
158		N779G	N697A	N1697A	N72CR	N2NR	N2NC	5Y-MIA	5Y-EMJ	[w/o 24Jan03 Busia, Kenya]	
159		N751G	N287AA	N940PM	N200PM	N200PF	N809CC	G-BNKN	XA-RJB	XB-JGU	
160		N752G	N3	"N965CJ"	N599TR	[wfu Lakeland, FL]					
161		N790G	N307EL	N925GC	[wfu Lawrenceville, GA by Oct03 but cx to Mexico 09Apr04]						
162		N724G	N547Q	N547QR	N547BN	N5470R	N31CN	N300GP	C-GPTA	[w/o 19Nov96 Lester B Pearson Airport, Toronto, Canada]	
163		N727G	N618M	N71CR	[w/o 11Jul75 Addison, TX]						
164		N738G	N8PG	N88PP	N590AS	N590AQ	N290AS	ZS-PHI	3X-GGI	9Q-CNP	
165		N739G	N75M	N75MT	N657PC	N657P	N500WN	N501WN			
166		N791G	N67CR	N20CR	N76DM	N725RA	F-GKES	(OO-IBG)	HB-IRQ	4X-ARG	D2-EXB
167		N794G	N908LN	C-GDWM	N717RA	[cx 01May06, wfu in Sao Tome]					
168		N754G	N209T	N722RA	[b/u for spares 1988; cx Nov88]						
169		N725HG	N725HC	N400WP	N400WF	N200AE					
170		N790G	N89K	N189K	YV-620CP	YV-627C					
171		VH-CRA	N171LS	(N1PC)	N728GM	YV-621CP	YV-628C	YV2054			
172		N700DB	N44MC	N11NY	N172RD	TC-SMA	[b/u Geneva, Switzerland, Jul08]				
173		N360WT	N944H	N944HL	N49CB	I-TASC	5Y-BMT	YV-988C	N173BT	YV-903CP	[disappeared, believed hijacked by drug traffickers 12Jun06]
174		N774G	N7004	N7004B	N718RA	[wfu; b/u for spares by Int'l Turbine Service, TX; cx Feb91]					
175		N795G	N10CR	N55AE	N578KB	YV-453CP	N173PA	[b/u for parts; cx Jan05]			
176	TC-4C	N798G	US Navy 155722	[preserved at Pensacola NAS, FL]							
177		N751G	N307K	N4PC	OY-BEG	N12GP	G-BRWN	PK-CTE	PK-CDM		
178	TC-4C	N778G	US Navy 155723	[w/o 16Oct75 Cherry Point, NC]							
179		N779G	N1916M	N61UT	N60AC	N60WK	HK-3622	XC-AA53			

GRUMMAN G159 GULFSTREAM 1

C/n	Series	Identities
180	TC-4C	N786G US Navy 155724 [stored by Oct94 Davis-Monthan AFB, AZ; park code 4G002]
181		N759G N966H N966HL N25W N25WL N181TG [w/o 01Jun85 Nashville, TN]
182	TC-4C	N762G US Navy 155725 [stored by Sep95 Davis-Monthan AFB, AZ; park code 4G007]
183	TC-4C	N766G US Navy 155726 [stored by Sep95 Davis-Monthan AFB, AZ; park code 4G006]
184	TC-4C	US Navy 155727 [stored by Oct94 Davis-Monthan AFB, AZ; park code 4G004]
185	TC-4C	US Navy 155728 [stored by Oct94 Davis-Monthan AFB, AZ; park code 4G003]
186	TC-4C	US Navy 155729 [stored by Oct94 Davis-Monthan AFB, AZ; park code 4G001]
187	TC-4C	US Navy 155730 [stored by Apr95 Davis-Monthan AFB, AZ; park code 4G005]
188		N17582 HB-LDT C-FAWE
189		N776G C-GPTG [cx Mar01 as wfu; b/u Nov02 Montreal-Dorval, Canada]
190		N1901W HK-3579X HK-4022X N190LE [w/o 02Aug96 in Sudan whilst on delivery to Kenya]
191		N200P N300P (N300XZ) G-BKJZ VH-JPJ PK-RJA [cx Mar06, b/u]
192		N712G N67H YV-76CP N171PA
193		N713G N754G PK-TRN 3D-TRN ZS-JIS 9Q-CIT [dbr Pweto, DR Congo, 20Jun12]
194		N718G N6702 N702E N702EA N81T I-MKKK 4X-CST I-MKKK 5Y-BMS YV-989C
195		N724G N1900W N190PA [cx 18Nov14; wfu]
196		N728G N752RB N752R N93AC (N811CC) N93AC I-EHAJ N134PA N659PC N100EG 9Q-CGI
197		N385M N777JS (N725RB) (N811CC) N977JS (N385M) N20H N20HE N197RM N520JG N748AA [stored Bristol/Filton, UK]
198		N740G N1902P N1902D N100C N80RD [w/o 23Aug90 Houston Intercontinental apt, TX; cx Oct91]
199		N745G XA-RIV N745G YV-83CP N183PA N167PA
200		N750G N255TK N159GS
322		N769G N90M N9QM N71RD [at Palwaukee, IL circa May00 – to be parted out?]
323		N900 N988AA N346DA S9-NAV N22320 "N900TT" N980TT HI-678CA HI-678CT

Production complete

Notes: c/n unknown aircraft
D2-FXG   reported at Rand, South Africa, 20Nov01
XB-JER   reported at Acarigua, Venezuela, 04May06
YV-78CP   reported as being carried by a Gulfstream 1 at Caracas 02Dec90; could this be connected with c/n 117,
YV-08CP   these marks have also been reported on a PA-31T?
ARC-701   (Colombian Navy) at Bogota wfu on 02Jul01.

G159 Gulfstream 1 Registration Cross-Reference

Note: Current Registrations are in **bold** type

Canada

C-....	G159	29
C-FAWE	**G159**	**188**
C-FAWG	G159	106
C-FHBO	**G159**	**104**
C-FIOM	G159	60
C-FMAR	G159	3
C-FMUR	G159	54
C-FRTT	G159	131
C-FRTU	G159	139
C-FWAM	G159	148
C-GDWM	G159	167
C-GKFG	G159	22
C-GMJS	G159	81
C-GNAK	G159	154
C-GNOR	G159	43
C-GPTA	G159	162
C-GPTG	G159	189
C-GPTN	G159	88
C-GTDL	G159	110
CF-ASC	G159	115
CF-COL	G159	64
CF-DLO	G159	137
CF-HBO	G159	104
CF-IOM	G159	60
CF-JFC	G159	31
CF-LOO	G159	7
CF-MAR	G159	3
CF-MUR	G159	54
CF-NOC	G159	72
CF-TPC	G159	17

Bahamas

C6-UNO	G159	102

Angola

D2-EXB	**G159**	**166**
D2-EXC	**G159**	**80**
D2-EXD	**G159**	**124**

Spain

EC-376	G159	39
EC-433	G159	153
EC-460	G159	64
EC-461	G159	142
(EC-491)	G159	79
EC-493	G159	40
EC-494	G159	41
EC-EVJ	**G159**	**39**
EC-EXB	G159	153
EC-EXQ	G159	142
EC-EXS	G159	64
EC-EZO	G159	41
EC-FIO	G159	40

France

(F-....)	G159	134
F-GFCQ	**G159**	**140**
F-GFEF	G159	122
F-GFGT	G159	5
F-GFGU	G159	101
F-GFGV	G159	44
F-GFIB	G159	71
F-GFIC	**G159**	**49**
F-GFMH	G159	20
F-GGGY	G159	80
F-GIIX	G159	128
F-GJGC	G159	111
F-GKES	G159	166
F-GNGU	**G159**	**101**

United Kingdom

G-ASXT	G159	135
G-AWYF	G159	48
G-BKJZ	G159	191
G-BMOW	G159	155
G-BMPA	G159	134
G-BMSR	G159	128
G-BNCE	G159	9
G-BNKN	G159	159
G-BNKO	G159	154
G-BOBX	G159	77
G-BRAL	G159	76
G-BRWN	G159	177

Hungary

HA-ACV	G159	102

Switzerland

HB-IRQ	G159	166
HB-LDT	G159	188

Dominican Republic

HI-678CA	G159	323
HI-678CT	**G159**	**323**

Colombia

HK-3315	G159	24
HK-3315X	G159	24
HK-3316	G159	59
HK-3316X	G159	59
HK-3329X	G159	145
HK-3330X	G159	90
HK-3579X	G159	190
HK-3580W	**G159**	**145**
HK-3622	G159	179
HK-3634X	G159	34
HK-3681	**G159**	**78**
HK-4022X	G159	190

Panama

HP-799	G159	152

Honduras

HR-IAJ	G159	33

Italy

I-CKET	G159	57
I-EHAJ	G159	196
I-MDDD	G159	143
I-MGGG	G159	51
I-MKKK	G159	194
I-TASB	G159	105
I-TASC	G159	173
I-TASO	G159	81

United States

N1	G159	2
N1M	G159	88
N1NA	G159	96
(N1PC)	G159	171
N1TX	G159	131
N2NA	G159	96
N2NA	G159	98
N2NC	G159	158
N2NR	G159	158
N2PQ	G159	81
N3	G159	160
N3	G159	2
N3NA	G159	92
N3UP	G159	18
N4NA	G159	151
N4PC	G159	177
N5NA	G159	125
N5PC	G159	20
N5VX	G159	7
N6PA	G159	50
N6PG	G159	40
N7FD	G159	145
N7PG	G159	41
N7SL	G159	11
N7ZA	G159	68
N7ZB	G159	107
N8BG	G159	22
N8BJ	G159	50
N8E	**G159**	**94**
N8PG	G159	164
N8VB	G159	12
N8ZA	G159	40
N9EB	G159	5
N9MH	G159	55
N9QM	G159	322
N9ZA	G159	41
N10CR	G159	175
N10NA	G159	125
N10TB	G159	86
N10VM	G159	87
N10ZA	G159	142
N11CZ	G159	59
N11NY	G159	172
N11SX	G159	28
N11UN	G159	102
N12GP	G159	177
N12GW	G159	19
N12RW	G159	82
N15GP	G159	68
(N15SQ)	G159	71
N17CA	G159	123
N18N	G159	90
N18TF	G159	52
(N18TZ)	G159	52
N19BX	G159	153
N19FF	G159	20
N19TZ	G159	40
N20CC	G159	47
N20CQ	G159	47
N20CR	G159	166
N20GB	G159	80
N20H	G159	16
N20H	G159	197
N20HE	G159	197
N20HF	G159	47
N20S	G159	37
N21AH	G159	33
N21TX	G159	131
N22AS	G159	156
N22CP	G159	155
N22G	G159	81
(N23AH)	G159	33
N23AK	G159	117
N23D	G159	59
N23UG	G159	108
N24CP	G159	155
N25W	G159	181
N25WL	G159	181
N26AJ	G159	54
N26KW	G159	15
N26L	G159	116
N27G	G159	132
N27L	G159	55
N28CG	G159	102
N28CG1	G159	50
N29AY	G159	98
N31CN	G159	162
N33CP	G159	78
N33TF	G159	133
N34C	G159	107
N34LE	G159	34
N36DD	G159	137
N38CG	G159	106
N38JK	G159	38
N39PP	G159	2
N39TG	G159	39
N40AG	G159	40
N40CE	G159	2
N40G	G159	140
N40Y	G159	39
N41JK	G159	90
N41KD	G159	117
N41LH	G159	156
N41TG	G159	41
N42CA	G159	137
N42CE	G159	2
N42G	G159	139
N43AS	G159	5
N43M	G159	9
N44MC	G159	172
N46TE	G159	58
N47	G159	69
N47R	G159	69
N47TE	G159	58
N48	G159	67
N48CG	G159	102
N48CQ	G159	102
N48PA	G159	18
N48TE	G159	34
N49CB	G159	173
N49DE	G159	97
N50LS	G159	127
N50UC	G159	95
N55AE	G159	175
N60AC	G159	179
N60CR	G159	71
N60WK	G159	179
N61SB	G159	115
N61UT	G159	179
N62J	G159	139
N63AU	G159	126
N64CG	G159	106
N64TG	G159	64
N65CE	G159	45
N65H	G159	66
N65HC	G159	66
N66JD	G159	57
N67B	G159	99
N67CR	G159	166
N67H	G159	192
N68TG	G159	68
N70CR	G159	144
N70LR	G159	19
N70QR	G159	144
N71CJ	G159	107
N71CR	G159	107
N71CR	G159	163
N71RD	G159	322
N72B	G159	154
N72CR	G159	158
N72EZ	G159	15
N72X	G159	106
N72XL	G159	106
N73B	G159	107
(N73CG)	G159	102
N73M	G159	77
N75M	G159	165
N75MT	G159	165
N76DM	G159	166
N79HS	G159	79
N80AC	G159	153
N80G	G159	22
N80J	G159	50
N80K	G159	51
N80KA	G159	51
N80L	G159	19
N80LR	G159	19
N80M	G159	27
N80R	G159	90
N80RD	G159	198
N81T	G159	194
N86JK	G159	86
N86MA	G159	35
N87CE	G159	87
N87CH	G159	87
(N87MK)	G159	87
N88PP	G159	164
N88Y	G159	33
N89DE	G159	4
N89K	G159	170
N90M	G159	322
N90PM	G159	51
N91G	G159	37
N91JR	G159	12
N92K	G159	140
N92SA	G159	140
N93AC	G159	196
(N93SA)	G159	72
N94SA	G159	157
N98MK	G159	98
N98R	G159	82
N99DE	G159	4
N99EL	G159	7
N100C	G159	198
N100EG	G159	196
N100EL	G159	11
N100FL	G159	11
N100P	G159	27
N100TV	G159	126
N102M	G159	99
N102PL	G159	87
N106GA	G159	86
N106GH	G159	86
N107GH	G159	148
N109P	G159	109
N110GA	G159	116
N110RB	**G159**	**126**
N111DR	G159	66
N113GA	G159	129
N114GA	G159	27
N116GA	G159	2
N116K	G159	100
N117GA	G159	83
N118LT	G159	55
N118X	G159	28
N120HC	G159	132
N120S	G159	148
N120S	G159	26
N121NC	G159	44
N122Y	G159	128
N126J	G159	33
N126K	G159	138
N129AF	G159	129
N130A	G159	36
N130B	G159	37
N130G	G159	37
N134PA	G159	196
N137C	G159	93
N140A	G159	140
N140NT	G159	43
N142TG	G159	142
N144NK	G159	63
N149X	G159	145
N152SR	G159	122
N153SR	G159	122
N153TG	G159	153
N154NS	G159	132
N154RH	G159	132
N154SR	G159	132
N155T	G159	145
N157WC	G159	139
N159AJ	G159	5
N159AN	G159	116
N159GS	**G159**	**200**
(N159KK)	G159	156
N164PA	**G159**	**54**
N165PA	G159	119
N166KJ	G159	100
N166NK	G159	12
N167PA	G159	117
N167PA	**G159**	**199**
N168PA	G159	56
N171LS	G159	171
N171PA	**G159**	**192**
N172RD	G159	172
N173BT	G159	173
N173PA	G159	175
N181TG	G159	181
N183K	G159	84
N183PA	G159	199
N184K	G159	84
N184PA	G159	97
N185PA	**G159**	**26**
N186PA	G159	23
N189K	G159	170
N190DM	G159	79
N190LE	G159	190
N190PA	G159	195
N191SA	G159	61
N192PA	**G159**	**149**
N193PA	G159	23
N193PA	**G159**	**125**
N195PA	G159	88
N196PA	**G159**	**139**
N197PA	G159	93
N197RM	G159	197
N198PA	**G159**	**27**
N199M	G159	17
N200AE	**G159**	**169**
N200GJ	G159	80
N200P	G159	191
N200PF	G159	159
N200PM	G159	159
N202HA	G159	16
N205AA	G159	59
N205G	G159	125
N205M	G159	114
N205M	G159	62
N207M	G159	73
N209T	G159	168
N212H	G159	74
N213GA1	G159	48
N220B	G159	56
N221AP	G159	6
N222EF	G159	71
N222H	G159	101
N222SE	G159	29
N222SG	G159	29
N227LA	G159	20
N227LS	G159	20
N228H	G159	141
N230E	G159	36
N231GR	G159	86
N233U	G159	145
N234MM	G159	121
N245CA	G159	83
N250AL	G159	20
N255AA	G159	55
N255TK	G159	200
N261L	G159	33
N266P	G159	20
N267AA	G159	154
N285AA	G159	44
N287AA	G159	159
N290AS	G159	164
N295SA	G159	33
N297X	G159	32
N300A	G159	140
(N300BP)	G159	112
N300GP	G159	162
N300MC	G159	32
N300P	G159	191
N300PE	G159	112
N300PH	G159	55
N300PM	G159	112
N300SB	G159	101
N300UP	G159	18
(N300XZ)	G159	191
N302K	G159	48
N304K	G159	75
N305K	G159	76
N307AT	G159	109
N307EL	G159	161
N307K	G159	177
N328CA	G159	116
N329CT	G159	45
N331H	G159	70
N333AH	G159	38
N340WB	G159	65
N344DJ	G159	43
N345TW	G159	65
N346DA	G159	323
N348DA	G159	26
N357H	G159	88
N358AA	G159	58
N360WT	G159	173
N361BL	**G159**	**96**
N361G	G159	21
N361Q	G159	21
N362G	G159	84
N362GP	G159	84
N363G	G159	111
N364G	G159	99
N364L	G159	99
N366P	G159	42
N371BG	G159	4
N376	G159	67
N377	G159	69
(N385M)	G159	197
N400HT	G159	149
N400NL	G159	62
N400P	G159	12
N400WF	G159	169
N400WP	G159	169
N410AA	G159	88
N415CA	G159	27
N429W	G159	55
N429X	G159	55

N430H G159 42
N431G G159 29
N431H G159 78
N436 G159 9
N436M G159 9
N437A G159 83
N444BC G159 96
N456 G159 49
N466P G159 64
N476S G159 124
N500RL G159 95
N500RN G159 95
N500S G159 127
N500WN G159 165
N501WN G159 165
N504C G159 124
N505S G159 26
N510E G159 56
N516DM G159 128
N519M G159 117
N520JG G159 197
N530AA G159 71
N533CS G159 110
N547BN G159 162
N547Q G159 162
N547QR G159 162
N574DU G159 93
N574K G159 93
N578KB G159 175
N580BC G159 63
N590AQ G159 164
N590AS G159 164
N594AR G159 61
N599TR G159 160
N601HK G159 5
N601HP G159 5
N605AA G159 80
N605AB G159 80
N608R G159 103
N608RP G159 103
N612DT G159 52
N615C G159 16
N618M G159 163
N620K G159 34
N621A G159 102
N623W G159 66
N629JM G159 82
N636 G159 149
N636G G159 149
N641B G159 65
N650BT G159 11
N650ST G159 11
N657P G159 165
N657PC G159 165
N659PC G159 196
N666ES G159 28
N671NC G159 97
N674C G159 93
N678RW G159 86
N684FM G159 149
N687RW G159 123
N697A G159 158
N700DB G159 172
N700JW G159 53
N700PR G159 5
N701BN G159 74
N701G G159 1
(N701JW) G159 53
N702E G159 194
N702EA G159 194
N702G G159 105
N702G G159 2
N703G G159 3
N704G G159 4
N704HC G159 4
N705G G159 152
N705G G159 5
N705M G159 114
N705RS G159 114
N706G G159 106
N706G G159 116
N706G G159 150
N706G G159 77
N706G G159 85
N707MP G159 122
N707WA G159 16
N708G G159 8
N709G G159 9
N710G G159 10
N710G G159 117
N710G G159 92
N711BT G159 87
N711G G159 11
N712G G159 114
N712G G159 12
N712G G159 192
N712MP G159 86
N712MR G159 86
N712MW G159 86
N713G G159 193
N713US G159 24
N714G G159 14
N714MR G159 123
N714MW G159 123
N715G G159 100
N715G G159 118
N715G G159 15
N715RA G159 31
N716G G159 101
N716G G159 16
N716R G159 37
N716RA G159 43
N716RD G159 37
N717 G159 4
N717G G159 102
N717G G159 17
N717JF G159 44
N717JP G159 127
N717RA G159 167
N717RD G159 44
N717RS G159 38
N717RW G159 44
N718G G159 103
N718G G159 152
N718G G159 18
N718G G159 194
N718RA G159 174
N719G G159 104
N719G G159 19
N719RA G159 28
N720G G159 143
N720G G159 20
N720X G159 73
N721G G159 21
N721RA G159 65
N722G G159 107
N722G G159 22
N722RA G159 168
N723G G159 108
N723G G159 23
N723RA G159 14
N724G G159 109
N724G G159 162
N724G G159 195
N724G G159 24
N724RA G159 114
N725G G159 25
N725HC G159 169
N725HG G159 169
N725MK G159 124
N725RA G159 166
(N725RB) G159 197
N726G G159 26
N726S G159 26
N727G G159 110
N727G G159 163
N727G G159 27
N728G G159 111
N728G G159 196
N728G G159 28
N728GM G159 171
N729G G159 112
N729G G159 29
N730G G159 30
N730T G159 131
N730TL G159 131
N731G G159 31
N732G G159 121
N732G G159 32
N732US G159 20
N733EB G159 32
N733G G159 153
N733NM G159 153
N734EB G159 32
N734ET G159 32
N734G G159 119
N734G G159 34
N734HR G159 61
N735G G159 35
N736G G159 123
N736G G159 154
N737G G159 124
N737G G159 156
N738G G159 122
N738G G159 125
N738G G159 164
N738G G159 38
N739G G159 126
N739G G159 165
N740AA G159 93
N740G G159 198
N741G G159 151
N741G G159 157
N741GA G159 127
N743G G159 129
N743G G159 72
N744G G159 130
N745G G159 199
N745G G159 45
N746G G159 46
N747G G159 47
N748AA G159 197
N748G G159 48
N748M G159 77
N748MN G159 77
N749G G159 49
N750BR G159 99
N750G G159 131
N750G G159 200
N751G G159 159
N751G G159 177
N752G G159 133
N752G G159 160
N752G G159 52
N752R G159 196
N752RB G159 196
N753G G159 53
N754G G159 134
N754G G159 168
N754G G159 193
N755G G159 135
N755G G159 55
N756G G159 136
N756G G159 56
N757G G159 137
N757G G159 57
N758G G159 138
N758G G159 58
N759G G159 139
N759G G159 181
N759G G159 59
N760G G159 140
N761G G159 61
N762G G159 141
N762G G159 182
N763G G159 63
N764G G159 142
N764G G159 64
N765G G159 65
N766G G159 144
N766G G159 183
N766G G159 66
N767G G159 145
N767G G159 67
N768G G159 68
N768GP G159 68
N769G G159 322
N769G G159 69
N770A G159 129
N770AC G159 129
N770G G159 70
N771G G159 71
N772G G159 146
N772G G159 72
N773G G159 73
N773WJ G159 73
N774G G159 147
N774G G159 174
N774G G159 74
N775G G159 148
N775G G159 75
N776G G159 149
N776G G159 189
N776G G159 76
N777G G159 150
N777G G159 77
N777JS G159 197
N778G G159 155
N778G G159 178
N778G G159 78
N779G G159 158
N779G G159 179
N779G G159 79
N780AC G159 106
N780G G159 80
N781G G159 81
N782G G159 82
N783G G159 83
N784G G159 84
N785GP G159 29
N786G G159 180
N786G G159 86
N787G G159 87
N788G G159 88
N789G G159 89
N790G G159 161
N790G G159 170
N790G G159 90
N791G G159 166
N791G G159 91
N794G G159 167
N794G G159 94
N795G G159 175
N795G G159 95
N797G G159 97
N798G G159 176
N798G G159 98
N798R G159 82
N798S G159 82
N799G G159 99
N800PA G159 141
N800PD G159 154
N800PM G159 154
(N801CC) G159 82
N802CC G159 154
N803CC G159 112
N804CC G159 109
N804CC G159 148
N805CC G159 155
N806S G159 67
N806W G159 67
N809CC G159 159
N810CB G159 23
(N811CC) G159 196
(N811CC) G159 197
(N811CC) G159 137
N812CC G159 129
N820CB G159 93
N820CE G159 50
N823GA G159 109
N834H G159 129
N845JB G159 87
N857H G159 88
N860AC G159 22
N860E G159 144
N861H G159 147
N888PR G159 42
N900 G159 323
N900JL G159 28
N900PA G159 155
N900PM G159 155
"N900TT" G159 323
N901G G159 30
N902JL G159 130
N906F G159 146
N908LN G159 167
N910BS G159 128
N913BS G159 126
N913PS G159 126
N914BS G159 134
N914P G159 143
N920BS G159 134
N925GC G159 161
N925WL G159 5
N940PM G159 159
N942PM G159 112
N944H G159 132
N944H G159 173
N944HL G159 173
N961G G159 30
"N965CJ" G159 160
N966H G159 181
N966HL G159 181
N977JS G159 197
N980TT G159 323
N988AA G159 323
N992CP G159 155
N1000 G159 109
N1009 G159 27
N1040 G159 78
N1091 G159 109
N1150S G159 85
N1207C G159 132
N1234X G159 55
N1501 G159 15
N1501C G159 15
N1607Z G159 14
N1620 G159 24
N1623 G159 10
N1623Z G159 10
N1625 G159 24
N1625B G159 24
N1697A G159 158
N1701L G159 148
N1707Z G159 108
N1844S G159 29
N1845S G159 29
N1900W G159 195
N1901W G159 190
N1902D G159 198
N1902P G159 198
N1916M G159 179
N1925P G159 29
N1929B G159 23
N1929Y G159 23
N2000C G159 109
N2010 G159 133
N2011 G159 146
N2150M G159 27
N2425 G159 6
N2602M G159 123
N2998 G159 16
N3003 G159 2
N3100E G159 50
N3416 G159 130
N3630 G159 111
N3858H G159 52
N4009 G159 12
N4567 G159 90
N4765C G159 68
N4765P G159 68
N5000C G159 109
N5152 G159 97
N5241Z G159 67
N5400C G159 116
N5400G G159 116
N5470R G159 162
N5619D G159 74
N6653Z G159 21
N6702 G159 194
N7001N G159 38
N7004 G159 174
N7004B G159 174
N7040 G159 78
N7776 G159 133
N7788 G159 45
N7972S G159 139
N8001J G159 16
N8200E G159 50
N8500C G159 139
N8500N G159 139
N9006L G159 28
(N9036P) G159 148
N9300P G159 114
N9446E G159 55
N9971F G159 17
N16776 G159 58
N17582 G159 188
N22320 G159 323
N39289 G159 43
N49401 G159 64
(N66534) G159 85

Peru
OB-M-1235 G159 152

Austria
(OE-...) G159 25
OE-BAZ G159 23
OE-GSN G159 146
OE-HAZ G159 23
OE-HSN G159 146

Czech Republic
(OK-NEA) G159 25

Belgium
(OO-IBG) G159 166

Denmark
OY-BEG G159 177

Indonesia
PK-CDM G159 177
PK-CTE G159 177
PK-RJA G159 191
PK-TRL G159 60
PK-TRM G159 57
PK-TRN G159 193
PK-TRO G159 130
PK-WWG G159 19

Brazil
PT- G159 103
(PT-...) G159 78
PT-KYF G159 75

Aruba
P4-JML G159 76

Sweden
SE-LDV G159 82
SE-LFV G159 82

Sao Tome
S9-NAU G159 6
S9-NAV G159 323

Turkey
TC-SMA G159 172

Guatemala
TG-TJB G159 33

Cameroon
TJ-WIN G159 20

Central African Republic
TL-ADN G159 42

Ivory Coast
TU-TDM G159 20
TU-VAC G159 133

Australia
VH-ASJ G159 52
VH-CRA G159 171
VH-FLO G159 100
VH-JPJ G159 191
VH-WPA G159 114

Swaziland
VQ-ZIP G159 38

Bermuda
VR-BBY G159 48
VR-BTI G159 71
(VR-B..) G159 6

Cayman Islands
VR-CAE G159 55
VR-CTN G159 20

Mexico
XA-... G159 38
XA-ALK G159 138
XA-ILV G159 93
XA-MAS G159 42
XA-MYR G159 71
XA-PUA G159 35
XA-RIV G159 199
XA-RJB G159 159
XA-RLK G159 138
XA-TBT G159 12
XA-TBT G159 136
XA-TDJ G159 127
XA-TTU G159 58
XB-CIJ G159 10
XB-DVG G159 35
XB-ESO G159 15
XB-FLL G159 58
XB-FUB G159 27
XB-GAW G159 136
XB-JGU G159 159
XB-MDM G159 71

XB-MVT	G159	71
XB-VAD	G159	27
XB-VIW	G159	27
XC-AA53	**G159**	**179**
XC-AA57	**G159**	**103**
XC-AA61	G159	42
XC-BAU	G159	85
XC-BIO	G159	21
XC-GEI	G159	66
XC-HYC	G159	51
XC-IMS	G159	35
XC-LIE	G159	148
XC-VNC	G159	58

Venezuela

YV-.....	G159	18
YV-08CP	G159	117
YV-09CP	G159	24
YV-46CP	G159	56
YV-121CP	G159	150
YV-28CP	G159	119
YV-76CP	G159	192
YV-82CP	G159	26
YV-83CP	G159	199
YV-85CP	G159	97
YV-453CP	G159	175
YV-620CP	G159	170
YV-621CP	G159	171

YV-627C	**G159**	**170**
YV-628C	G159	171
YV-903CP	G159	173
YV-988C	G159	173
YV-989C	**G159**	**194**
YV-P-AEA	G159	24
YV-P-EPC	G159	119
YV....	**G159**	**129**
YV....	**G159**	**92**
YV1020	G159	106
YV2054	**G159**	**171**

New Zealand

(ZK-...)	G159	100

South Africa

ZS-AAC	G159	38
ZS-ALX	G159	86
ZS-JIS	G159	193
ZS-NHW	**G159**	**141**
ZS-NKT	G159	124
ZS-NVG	G159	1
ZS-OCA	G159	42
ZS-ONO	G159	134
ZS-OOE	**G159**	**5**
ZS-PHI	G159	164
ZS-PHJ	G159	134
ZS-PHK	G159	25

Equatorial Guinea

3C-...	**G159**	**82**

Swaziland

3D-AAC	G159	38
3D-ARF	G159	134
3D-DLH	G159	25
3D-DOM	G159	42
3D-DUE	G159	134
3D-TRE	G159	42
3D-TRN	G159	193

Guinea

3X-GER	G159	1
3X-GGI	G159	164

Israel

4X-ARF	G159	134
4X-ARG	G159	166
4X-ARH	G159	25
4X-ARV	G159	101
4X-CST	G159	194

Nigeria

5N-AAI	G159	58

Kenya

5Y-BLF	G159	131

5Y-BLR	**G159**	**34**
5Y-BMR	**G159**	**81**
5Y-BMS	G159	194
5Y-BMT	G159	173
"5Y-BMT"	G159	81
5Y-EMJ	G159	158
5Y-EMK	G159	1
5Y-JET	**G159**	**44**
5Y-MIA	G159	158
5Y-XXX	G159	1

Democratic Republic of Congo

9Q-CBD	**G159**	**35**
9Q-CBY	**G159**	**33**
9Q-CFK	G159	77
9Q-CGI	**G159**	**196**
9Q-CIT	G159	193
9Q-CJB	**G159**	**155**
9Q-CKM	**G159**	**25**
9Q-CNP	**G159**	**164**
9Q-COE	**G159**	**156**
9Q-CTC	**G159**	**1**
9Q-CTG	**G159**	**134**
9Q-CTH	**G159**	**86**

Rwanda

9XR-WR	G159	106

MILITARY

Greece

120	G159	120
P-9	G159	120

Israel

001	G159	146

United States

NASA1	G159	96
NASA2	G159	98
NASA3	G159	92
NASA4	G159	151
86-0402	G159	2
USCG 02	G159	91
USCG 02	G159	92
USCG 03	**G159**	**91**
USCG 1380	G159	91
155722	G159	176
155723	G159	178
155724	G159	180
155725	G159	182
155726	G159	183
155727	G159	184
155728	G159	185
155729	G159	186
155730	G159	187

AIRBUS A319CJ/A318 Elite*/A320CJ%

C/n	Series	Identities							
0910	133X	D-AVYB	(OE-L..)	F-WWIC	D-AWFR	D-AWFR	A6-ESH		
0913	132	D-AVYL	G-OMAK	F-WWIF	G-OMAK	VP-CAJ	HZ-NAS	EK-RA01	Armenia 701 [not a 319CJ but a 319 built as a VIP aircraft]
1002	115X	D-AVYJ	D-AJWF	Italy MM62173		TC-TCB	TC-ANA		
1053	133X	D-AVYN	D-ADNA						
1157	115X	D-AVYO	D-AVWE	D-AACI	Italy MM62174		D-AACI	Italy MM62174	
1212	133X	D-AVYE	(D-AIKA)	VP-CVX					
1256	133X	D-AVYZ	F-WWIF	D-AVYZ	VP-BCS	D-AVYZ	(F-GVBG)	F-GSVU	CS-TLU
1335	133X	D-AVYK	A7-ABZ	A7-HHJ					
1468	133X	D-AVYQ	Venezuela 0001	[stored Toulouse]					
1485	115X	D-AVYV	F-GXFA	France 1485/F-RBFA	VQ-BKK				
1556	115X	D-AVYI	F-GXFB	France 1556/F-RBFB	6V-ONE				
1589	133X	D-AVYF	VP-CIE						
1599*	122	F-WWIA	D-AUAH	D-AIJA	A6-AAM	[built as standard A318 but used in the Elite development programme]			
1656	13LR	D-AVYT	A7-CJA	[A 319LR built as a VIP aircraft]					
1795	115X	D-AVYW	D-AWOR	Italy MM62209					
1908	115X	D-AVWP	D-AIJO	F-WWID	HS-TYR/60221		HS-TYR/60202		
1999	115X	D-AVYQ	F-GYAS	VH-VHD					
2111	133X	[not built]							
2192	133X	D-AVYB	"D-AVXB"	F-WWBN	D-AVYB	D-AIJO	P4-ARL	TU-VAS	
2263	133X	D-AVWJ	D-AICY	Brazil 2101	[VC-1A]				
2341	133LR	D-AVWK	A7-CJB	[A 319LR built as a VIP aircraft]					
2421	115X	D-AVYO	VP-CCJ						
2487	115X	D-AVWA	4K-AZ01	4K-AI02	4K-8888				
2507	115X	D-AVWN	D-AVIP	Italy MM62243					
2550	115X	D-AVYH	G-NMAK						
2592	115X	D-AVXK	D-AIMM	HB-IPO	UN-A1901	HB-IPO	9H-AFK	9H-MCE	LX-MCE
2650	132X	D-AVYA	D-AICY	VT-VJM					
2675	115X	D-AVYP	D-AIJO	VP-BEY	CS-TQJ				
2706	115X	D-AVYB	D-AVIP	VP-BEX					
2748	115X	D-AVWB	N3618F						
2801	115X	D-AVWU	D-AIFR	D-AVWU	Czech Republic 2801				
2837	115X	D-AVXS	D-AIMM	VT-IAH					
2910*	112	D-AUAA	F-WWIB	D-AUAA	D-AIJA	HB-IPP	9H-AFM	HZ-A5	
2921	115X	D-AVXQ	P4-VML	P4-VNL					
2949	115X	D-AVXC	D-AIDR	9M-NAA					
3046	115X	D-AVYF	OE-LGS	D-APGS					
3073	115X	D-AVXP	D-AIFR	VP-BED					
3085	115X	D-AVYU	D-AICY	Czech Republic 3085					
3100*	112X	D-AUAN	F-WWDJ	D-AUAN	D-AIEA	LX-GJC			
3133	115X	D-AVXC	P4-MIS						
3164%	214X	F-WWIJ	VP-BXT	HZ-AJ2	HZ-A2	HZ-SKY3			
3199%	3199	F-WWIY	UP-A2001						
3238*	112X	D-AUAJ	VP-CKS						
3243	115X	D-AVWD	F-WWDA	VP-CBN	F-WBGY	VP-CBN	D-ACBN		
3260	115X	D-AVXN	(UR-ABA)	OE-IAC	UR-ABA				
3333*	112X	D-AUAA	D-AIMM	B-6186					
3356	115X	D-AVYV	VP-BGF	F-WBGX	9H-SNA	VP-CSN			
3363*	112X	D-AUAB	D-AVIP	(HB-IPQ)	9H-AFL	B-77777			
3513	115X	D-AVYX	(D-ALHM)	D-ALEY	OE-LOV				
3530*	115X	D-AUAC	D-AIJA	VP-CKH					
3542	115X	D-AVWG	VP-BVA	9H-GVV	LX-GVV				
3617*	112	D-AUAH	D-AIJO	B-6188					
3632	115X	D-AVYO	D-AHAD	OE-LIP					
3723%	214X	F-WWDE	Oman 554						
3751*	112	D-AUAC	D-AYYC	VQ-BDD					
3826	115X	D-AVYJ	G-NOAH						
3856	115X	D-AVWB	M-RBUS						
3886*	112	D-AUAB	(OE-ICP)	D-AIMM	B-6411	2-CCLN	B-55411		
3897	115X	D-AWVM	98+46	15+01					
3957	115X	D-AVIP	9K-GEA						
3985*	112CJ	D-AUAE	VP-CAH	A6-AJC					
3994	115X	D-AVYR	F-WJKO	(9H-ERO)	A7-MHH				
4024	115X	D-AVYI	VP-CVW	F-WHUF	RA-73025				
4042	133X	D-AVYO	F-WWDA	D-AIDR	B-6418				
4060	155X	D-AGAF	15+02						
4114	133X	D-AVWA	A7-MED						
4117%	214X	F-WWID	Oman 555						
4151	133X	D-AVYB	M-KATE						
4169*	112	D-AIFR	9H-AFT	OE-LUX					
4170%	232	F-WWDF	A7-MBK						
4199%	214X	F-WWIV	N105AL	9H-AWK	9M-NAB				
4211*	112	D-AUAD	(A6-AJE)	VP-CCH	A6-CAS				
4228	115X	D-AVYL	VQ-BSF	VP-CIA	A6-AFH				
4319	133X	D AVXD	F WHUE	P4-RLA					
4353	115X	D-AVYN	VP-BJP	VP-CJG	OE-LJG				
4388%	232X	F-WWDG	(D-ARGL)	F-WHUH	N60FC	EI-FMX	B-8415		
4428	133X	D-AVXN	D-ALHT	B-6435					
4470	115X	D-AVYG	9H-ALX	D-ALXX					
4503*	112X	D-AUAF	F-WHUG	OE-ICE					
4583	133X	D-AVWE	VP-CAS	9H-AGC	B-6933				
4622	115X	D-AVWJ	9H-AVK						
4650*	112X	D-AUAG	F-WHUI	M-HHHH					
4679	115X	D-AVYN	F-WHUJ	(RA-32002)	RA-73026				
4732*	112X	D-AUAB	F-WHUK	B-6936					
4795%	214X	F-WWIE	Oman 556						
4822	119	D-AVWC	F-WHUL	A6-CJE					
4842	113	D-AVWI	VQ-BVQ						
4878*	112	D-AUAC	F-WHUM	VP-BKG					
4956	115	D-AVYD	VP-CGX	B-8319					
4992	115	D-AVYE	F-WXAH	A4O-AJ					
5040	115	D-AVXK	VP-CAD						
5182%	232	F-WWBG	(A7-AHV)	F-WHUG	VP-CHA				
5255%	232	F-WWDO	A7-HSJ						
5261	133	D-AVYC	9H-AGF						

AIRBUS A319CJ/A318 Elite*/A320CJ%

C/n	Series	Identities			
5277	115	D-AVYW	A6-RRJ		
5445	115	D-AVYJ	F-WBGU	P4-MGU	
5478*	112	D-AUAC	F-WXAE	N777UE	
5538	211	D-AVZA	9H-AGE	UP-A2010	[A321CJ]
5545*	118	D-AUAA	F-WXAH	VP-CYB	
5768	115X	D-AVXE	F-WTBJ	HL8080	
5792	115X	D-AVXJ	F-WTAD	B-54111	
5963	115X	D-AVWF	D-ALEX		
6069%	214X	F-WWDT	M-YBUS		
6112%	214X	F-WWBB	F-WHUE	60203	HS-TYT
6285%	214X	F-WWIQ	4K-A107		
6659%	232X	F-WWBS	A6-SHJ		
6727	115X	D-AVYJ	HZ-AC		

BOEING BBJ

Note: BBJ1s have series numbers starting with 7 while BBJ2s have numbers starting with 8

C/n	Line	Series	Identities						
28579	312	75V	N367G	N920DS	N737LE				
28581	126	75V	N1787B	N366G	N781TS	N43PR			
28976	158	75U	(VP-BOC)	N1786B	VP-BRM	5U-GRN			
29024	131	72T	N50TC						
29054	143	73T	N1787B	N1780B	N6067E	N500LS			
29102	101	73Q	N737BZ	VT-HSS	N772BC	N2TS	N834BA		
29135	206	74Q	N60436	N737CC					
29136	225	74Q	N1779B	N1787B	N737GG	TT-ABD			
29139	189	74T	N5573L	N73721	N21KR	VP-BEL			
29142	167	75T	N1787B	N1782B	N700WH	N737WH	N260DV		
29149	348	7H3	N5573L	TS-IOO					
29188	217	7P3	N1787B	N1779B	HZ-TAA	VQ-BTA			
29200	234	73U	N742PB						
29233	197	74U	N4AS	N66ZB	5R-MRP	N887LS			
29251	150	7EO	"AB-HRS"	A6-HRS					
29268	280	7Z5	N1786B	A6-AIN					
29269	432	7Z5	A6-SIR	A6-RJZ					
29272	323	74V	N737SP	N7378P	Colombia FAC0001				
29273	146	72U	N1787B	"N1001N"	N1011N	VP-BBJ			
29274	397	7H6	N1787B	N1785B	N6055X	9M-BBJ	Malaysia M53-01		
29317	265	79T	N1787B	VP-BWR					
29441	111	79U	N1787B	N1779B	"N1101N"	N1011N	VP-BPF	N88WZ	N88WR	N788DP
29749	456	7AH	N1787B	N73711	C6-TTB	N134AR	N888TY		
29791	336	7BH	N348BA	P4-TBN	P4-KSA	P4-ASL			
29857	445	7Z5	N1795B	A6-AUH	A6-LIW	A6-RJY			
29858	530	7Z5	A6-DAS						
29865	241	7AK	HB-IIO	A6-RJX					
29866	408	7AK	N1779B	HB-IIP	N720CH	B-5266			
29971	684	7DM	N731BJ	01-0040	[C-40B]				
29972	642	7AN	VP-BYA						
29979	496	7AF	N1003N	165829	[C-40A]				
29980	568	7AF	N1786B	N1003M	165830	[C-40A]			
30031	251	7AW	N1787B	N73715	(VP-CBB)	VP-CEC	VP-CPA	N737KY	VP-CPA	
30070	244	7AV	N1787B	N18NC	N889NC	P4-BBJ			
30076	179	7BJ	N1784B	N374MC	N737MC	D-AXXL	N737MC	VP-CZT	P4-CZT	N373BF	VP-BBW
30200	651	7AF	N1786B	165831	[C-40A]				
30327	356	7BC	N127QS	N796BA	N721UF				
30328	377	7DW	N1787B	N128QS	N164RJ	P4-PRM	TZ-PRM		
30329	384	7BC	N1787B	N129QS	N162WC				
30330	415	7BC	N130QS	VP-BJB	HB-JGV	N888NB	VP-BJJ		
30496	301	7BF	N1795B	N224TA	N180SM	N180AD	N737AG		
30547	423	7BQ	N79711	(HZ-DG5)					
30572	491	7BC	N1005S	N171QS	N254SJ	N339BA	N835BA		
30751	401	7CG	N1784B	N800GK	N888GW	P4-GJC	VP-BMC	N888NY	N737L	
30752	451	7CN	N1026G	HB-IIQ	(D-ABPA)	D-AWBB			
30753	481	7CP	N1787B	N329K	VP-BFE	N754BC	02-0202	[C-40C]		
30754	516	7CJ	N79715	N61MJ	N737ER				
30755	545	7CP	N330K	VP-BFO	N752BC	02-0201	[C-40C]		
30756	569	7BC	N1787B	N1003W	N156QS	N836BA			
30772	554	7CU	N1790B	N1784B	N315TS				
30781	742	7AF	N1787B	165832	[C-40A]				
30782	586	7BC	N1006F	(N182QS)	N515GM	N800KS			
30789	602	73Q	N349BA	N377CJ	N977CJ				
30790	613	7DF	N1787B	N10040	Australia A36-002				
30791	623	7BC	N191QS	LX-GVV	9H-BBJ				
30829	738	7DT	N1787B	N372BJ	Australia A36-001				
30884	747	7BC	N184QS	VP-BFA	VP-BFE	A6-DFR			
32438	779	8AN	"VP-BNH"	VP-BHN	HZ-HR5				
32450	787	8EC	N1787B	A6-MRM					
32451	836	8DP	N374BJ	HZ-101	HZ-102				
32575	861	7BC	N182QS	PR-BBS					
32597	1069	7AF	165833	[C-40A]					
32598	1174	7AF	165834	[C-40A]					
32627	826	7ED	N373BJ	ZS-RSA					
32628	953	7BC	N1787B	N102QS	N7600K				
32774	853	7EJ	N1784B	XA-AEX	N774EC	P4-KAZ			
32775	889	7EL	N376BJ	N90R					
32777	882	8DR	N1795B	N379BJ	N5537L	G-OBBJ	P4-BBJ	OE-ILX		
32805	940	7DP	N372BC	HZ-102	HZ-101				
32806	912	8AW	N73721	VP-CBB					
32807	926	7EG	N1787B	N375BJ	HL7770	N8767			
32825	1602	8AJ	A6-HEH						
32915	969	8DV	N99ZL	HB-ISG	N99ZL	D-ABZL	VP-BZL	D-ABZL	VP-BZL	
32916	979	7DM	N378BJ	01-0015	[C-40B]				
32970	988	7BC	N103QS	N707BZ	VP-BRT				
32971	996	8EF	N371BC						
33010	1037	7ET	(N104QS)	N313P	N4476S	N720MM			
33036	1060	7BC	N110QS	N888YF					
33079	1075	8EV	N375BC	EW-001PA					
33080	1089	7DM	N374BC	(01-0005)	01-0041	[C-40B]			
33102	1111	7BC	N105QS	N108MS					
33361	1124	8EQ	N737SP	N737M					
33367	1189	7FB	N377JC	3C-EGE					
33405	1204	7FG	N373JM	HZ-MF1					
33434	1211	7BC	N109QS	N703BC	02-0203	N236BA	02-0203	[C-40C]		
33473	1196	8EX	N379BC	A6-AUH					
33499	1217	7AJ	N365BJ	HZ-MF2					
33500	1223	7FD	N357BJ	N708BC	02-0042	N237BA	02-0042	[C-40C]		
33826	1548	7AF	N6065Y	165835	N543BA	165835	[C-40A]		
33836	1604	7AF	N1786B	165836	[C-40A]				
34260	1746	7NG	N1786B	N1781B	5N-FGT	Nigeria 001			
34303	1758	7AK	N1780B	VQ-BBS	HB-JJA				
34304	1849	7AF	166693	[C-40A]					

BOEING BBJ

C/n	Line	Series	Identities				
34477	1825	7AU	N5002K	N746BA	VP-BIZ		
34620	1803	8GG	N1784B	N852AK	VP-CSK		
34622	1785	7GC	N357BJ	P4-RUS	M-URUS		
34683	1859	7E1	N2121	B-LEX			
34807	1908	7DM	N1779B	N365BJ	05-0730	[C-40C]	
34808	2008	7DM	N366BJ	05-0932	[C-40C]		
34809	2141	7DM	N368BJ	05-4613	[C-40C]		
34865	1865	7EM	N786BA	VP-CLR			
35238	1966	8EO	N1786B	A6-MRS			
35792	2351	8GQ	N737GQ	VQ-BOS			
35959	2029	7HD	VP-BNZ				
35977	2047	7HF	VP-CLL	N888AQ	HL7227		
35990	2107	7EG	N737DB	HL7759			
36027	2068	7HE	N111NB	M-YBBJ			
36090	2196	7GV	N111VM				
36106	2118	7HI	N370BJ	India K5012			
36107	2325	7HI	N1786B	N719BA	India K5013		
36108	2425	7HI	N372BJ	Indian K5014			
36493	2211	7FY	N1786B	N493AG	P4-AFK		
36714	2340	7JB	N1787B	N1779B	VP-BFT		
36756	2405	7HJ	N529PP	N737AT	[BBJ C]		
36852	2475	75G	N1786B	N730MM	HL7787		
37111	2595	7JR	N721BA	N92SR			
37545	2696	8KB	A7-AAZ	CN-MVI			
37546	2725	9HWER	N375BJ	VP-CEC			
37560	2664	9JAER	N1768B	N6046P	N376BJ	HZ-103S	VP-CKK
37583	2869	7HZ	P4-NGK				
37592	2752	7JF	N54AG	P4-LIG			
37632	2965	9BQER	N373BJ	9K-GCC			
37660	2997	7B5	N719V	HL8222			
37663	3024	8JM	N379BJ	D-AACM			
37700	3128	7JZ	N380BJ				
38028	4072	76N	N668CP				
38408	4730	7JW	G-CICL	M-GEAA	VP-CZW		
38608	3208	7XK	N382BJ	VP-CAE	VP-CAM		
38633	3329	73W	N384BJ	B-5273			
38854	3727	7JV	N450BJ	N301SR			
38751	3796	7ZH	N930HB				
38854	3727	7JV	N450BJ	N301SR			
38855	3825	7JU	N1786B	N451BJ	OE-IRF		
38890	3033	9LBER	N374BJ	VP-BDB			
39095	4148	7LT	N709JM	N2708E	B-....		
39109	3461	7JY	N1TS				
39317	3219	9FGER	N383BJ	HZ-ATR			
39318	3399	9FGER	HZ-MF6				
39899	4035	8LX	VP-BBZ				
40116	4465	73W	N712JM				
40117	3701	73W	N449BJ	VP-BOP			
40118	3369	8KT	N447BJ	N737GG			
40119	4620	7ZX	9H-GGG				
40577	3676	7AF	166696	[C-90A]			
40586	4130	7EG	N705JM	HL8270	N688FD		
40706	3512	7DM	N736JS	09-0540	[C-40C]		
40761	3425	7HZ	P4-MAK				
41090	3636	79L	D-ACBJ	N448BJ	B-3999		
41375	4325	7GE	N710JM	HL8290			
41658	3866	7GJ	N453BJ	B-5286			
41706	3902	8U3	N454BJ	A-001 (Indonesia)			
42215	4952	8ZE	N502BJ				
42510	4499	8LZ	N713JM				
43826	4593	7ZW	N457BJ	B-5818			
60406	5028	7ZF	LY-TVG				
60686	5129	82Z	N504BJ				
61040	5279	79V	N506BJ	F-WTBR	B-09590		
62699	5749	7ZW	N839BA				

NOTE: Inverted commas around an identity indicate the marks concerned were incorrectly applied to the airframe

CANADAIR 100SE/CHALLENGER 800

C/n	Series	Identities						
7008	100SE	C-FMKV	N5100X	N501LS	N601LS	N764CC		
7075	100SE	C-FMLQ	N877SE	N135BC	N999YG			
7099	800	C-FMNW	N253SE	N305CC	N405CC	N168CK	[w/o 13Feb07 Moscow-Vnukovo, Russia]	
7136	100SE	C-FMNQ	N136SE	VR-CRJ	VP-CRJ	HB-IDJ	VQ-BNQ	C-GZCU	XY-AGW
7140	800	C-FMMB	C-FZKS	N260SE	Malaysia M47-01	N140WC	N711WM	
7152	100SE	C-FMLT	N150SE	N655CC	N529DB			
7176	100SE	C-FMMX	N176SE	HB-IVU	LX-GJC	P4-CRJ	VP-BHX	9H-AFU	VH-VMX	N678RS
7351	800	C-FMLS	N351EJ	(ZS-OGB)	ZS-OGH	N351BA	VP-BCI	(D-ADLY)	N387AA	VT-KML	M-ABGH	N1800C
7717	100SE	C-FMNX	C-GZSQ	VP-BCC	N481ES	N890RL	[stored as N481ES]	
7846	800	C-FMMB	C-GZLM	N846PR	N500PR			
8043	850	C-FFHA	OE-ISA					
8046	850	C-FFOY	OY-YVI	4L-GAF	4L-GAA			
8047	850	C-FMLF	C-FGKZ	C-GSUW				
8048	850	C-FMLI	C-FFVE	(N604XJ)	OE-ILI	9H-ILI		
8049	850	C-FMLQ	(N605XJ)	C-FHGK	UN-C8502	UP-C8502		
8051	850	C-FGQR	(A6-DSK)	VP-BSD	9H-BOO			
8052	850	C-FGQS	OY-NAD	OE-IZZ				
8053	800	C-FGAX	N854SA	P4-GJL	N296TX			
8054	850	C-FMNH	C-FHTO	UN-C8501	UP-C8501	P4-AST	UP-C8504	P4-AST	UP-C8505
8055	850	C-FGEL	N850RJ	G-GJMB	LY-LTY			
8056	850	C-	N850TS	OH-SPB	OE-ISF			
8057	850	C-FHCN	C-GWWW	EW-301PJ				
8060	850	C-FVAZ	C-FGTV	VH-LEF	C-GVFT	M-LILJ		
8063	850	C-FJBK	OE-IKG	9H-CLG				
8065	850	C-FMMB	C-FJRN	[stored by 06Mar07]	D-AAIJ			
8066	850	C-FMML	C-FLBV	D-AKSA	G-SHAL			
8067	850	C-FLKA	G-CMBL	C-GDTD				
8068	850	C-FMMQ	C-FLOA	M-FZMH				
8069	850	C-FMMW	C-FMGV	VP-BNH	A6-BNH	D-AJOY		
8070	850	C-FMMX	C-FMGW	(D-AAJA)	(D-ATOQ)	C-FMGW	VT-IBP	
8071	850	C-FMVS	VP-BVJ	9H-BVJ				
8072	850	C-FNII	UR-ICD					
8073	850	C-FMKV	C-FOFW	D-AANN	OY-NNA			
8074	850	C-FMKW	C-FOMN	RA-67218				
8075	850	C-FMKZ	C-FOXW	OY-VEG				
8076	850	C-FMLB	C-FOYA	OE-ILY				
8077	850	C-FOBI	OY-VGA					
8078	850	C-FPTI	G-IGWT	N546JB				
8079	850	C-FMLQ	C-FPSB	(VP-CDN)	M-TAKE			
8080	850	C-FMLS	C-FQPV	M-ISLA	M-DWWW	ZS-ZOR		
8081	850	C-FQPY	(D-ATRE)	D-ATRI	G-RADY			
8082	850	C-FRPF	OE-ILV	9H-ILV				
8083	850	C-FRPU	VP-CON					
8084	850	C-FMNH	C-FSLD	"SX-FAC"	UR-OAM	T7-OAM		
8085	850	C-FTKR	C-FSLE	EI-EEZ				
8086	850	C-FMNX	C-FTKR	(N.....)	(D-....)	OE-ILZ	9H-ILZ	
8087	850	C-FTKS	LZ-BVH	5A-UAD				
8088	850	C-FTKZ	RP-C6226	N288ZZ	N850JL			
8089	850	C-FMOW	C-FTSH	B-7697				
8090	850	C-FVAZ	C-FTSV	RA-67219				
8091	850	C-FMND	C-FTSF	RA-67220				
8092	850	C-FMNQ	C-FUKH	C-FWEZ	VQ-BOV			
8093	850	C-FMLU	C-FUQW	UP-C8503				
8094	850	C-FMOI	C-FUQX	M-ANTA				
8095	850	C-FMMB	C-FUQY	N895CL				
8096	850	C-FMML	C-FUQZ	B-7797				
8097	850	C-FMMN	C-FVPF	VP-BNY				
8098	850	C-FMMQ	C-FVPV	B-7795				
8099	850	C-FVQB	RA-67232					
8100	850	C-FVQE	B-3563					
8101	850	C-FXOY	OE-ILA	9H-ILA				
8102	850	C-FXOV	B-3570					
8103	850	C-FXOO	C-GSLL					
8104	850	C-FXOK	A6-JET	M-HLAN				
8105	850	C-FXOJ	RA-67233					
8106	850	C-GFUC	B-7767					
8107	850	C-GIAX	OE-ILB	C-FIPF	B-3376			
8108	850	C-GIVW	M-LILY					
8109	850	C-GLUH	B-3073					
8110	850	C-GMGQ	B-3078					
8111	850	C-GONH						
8112	850	C-GRUW	B-3373					
8113	850	C-GUDE						

DORNIER 328 ENVOY 3

C/n	Identities								
3118	D-BDXB	N873JC	UR-WOG						
3120	D-BDXC	D-BABA	5N-SPN	5N-BNH					
3141	D-BDXR	(D-BMAA)	5N-SPM						
3151	D-BDXT	(D-BMAB)	5N-SPE						
3183	D-BDX-	N328FD	N328GT						
3184	D-BDX-	(D-BMAF)	N328PM	N804CE	N304CE				
3199	D-BDXM	N328PT	"I-AIRH"	N328PT	D-B…	N328PT	OE-HCM	HB-AEU	OY-JJB
3216	D-BDXD	D-BIUU	N328NP	D-BADC					
3220	D-B	TF-NPA	N3220U	Mexico PF-801					
3221	D-BERG	VP-CJD	5N-BQT						
3224	D-BDXB	D-BADA							

EMBRAER EMB-135BJ LEGACY

C/n	Identities						
145363	PP-XJO	(PT-SAA)	PP-XJO				
145412	PT-XSW	PT-SAB	(N135JM)	N912CW	Brazil 2580	[VC-99B]	
145462	PT-SVH	PP-XGM	PT-SAC	(N254JM)	N962CW	Brazil 2581	[VC-99B]
145484	PT-SAD	Greece 135L-484					
145495	PT-STA	VP-CSL	PR-LEG	N995CW	N902LX	Brazil 2582	[VC-99B]
145505	PT-SAF	G-REUB	G-WCCI	N600TN			
145516	PT-SAG	PK-OME					
145528	PT-SAH	VP-CVD	N928CW	N908LX	Brazil 2583	[VC-99B]	
145540	PT-SAI	EC-IIR	XA-MAX	T7-JSJ			
145549	PT-SAJ	P4-VVP	RA-02857				
145555	PT-SAK	HB-JEA	VP-CUP	M-YCUP	(PP-JFP)	N419LP	
145586	PT-SAM	P4-SIS	RA-02858				
145591	(PT-SAN)	[not built]					
145600	N302GC	[then converted back to 135LR Jly04]		N846RP	Brazil 2560	[VC99C]	
145608	N303GC	[then converted back to 135LR Jly04]		N847RP	Brazil 2561	[VC99C]	
145625	PT-SDN	PR-ORE	PK-TFS				
145637	PT-SAP	VP-CFA	VP-CFB	N611BV			
145642	PT-SAQ	N642AG	N660JM				
145644	PT-SAR	HB-JED	(N168PY)	B-99999			
145648	PT-SEI	N89LD					
145678	PT-SAS	N494TG					
145686	PT-SAT	N686SG	P4-IVM	M-NJSS			
145699	PT-SIA	N691AN	OE-ISL+	N676TC	N188JT	[+ marks applied at EBACE04 at Geneva, display Switzerland for purposes only]	
145706	PT-SAX	N135SG					
145711	PT-SAY	N135SL					
145717	PT-SAZ	PR-RIO	N719DB	PR-IUH			
145730	PT-SHG	N730BH	N661JM				
145770	PP-XMB	PT-SIB	(N770SG)	N3005	N53NA		
145775	PT-SIC	(N105SG)	N905LX	N905FL			
145780	PT-SID	N780SG	N904LX	N904FL			
145789	PT-SIE	(HB-JEF)	(F-GRYS)	N456MT	N451DJ	N894JW	
145796	PT-SIF	OK-SLN					
14500802	PT-SIG	(N802SB)	HB-JEO	VP-CHP	M-ARSL		
14500809	PT-SII	N809SG	N809TD				
14500818	PT-SIM	N888ML					
14500825	PT-SIK	N825SG	N906LX	N925FL			
14500832	PT-SIL	(N832SG)	OE-IAS	G-SIRA	ZS-ECB		
14500841	PT-SIN	OE-IWP	HB-IWX	D-ARIF	LX-MOI	LX-GLS	
14500851	PT-SIO	OE-ISN	M-DSCL				
14500854	PT-SIP	N854SG	VP-CNG	HB-JGS	G-HUBY		
14500863	PT-SIQ	G-YIAN	EC-KHT	M-PMPM	N600LP		
14500867	PT-SIR	India K3601					
14500873	PT-SIS	OK-KKG	G-PEPI				
14500880	PT-SIT	India K3602					
14500884	PT-SIU	N617WA	N742SP				
14500891	PT-SIV	5N-RSG					
14500901	PT-SIX	VT-BSF					
14500903	PT-SIW	N900DP	N752SP				
14500910	PT-SIY	India K3603					
14500913	PT-SIZ	N551VB	(N590RB)	P4-MSG			
14500916	PT-SOM	OE-IRK					
14500919	PT-SON	India K3604					
14500925	PT-SOO	N702CM	N702DR	N189DR			
14500933	PT-SCB	HB-JEL	F-HFKD				
14500937	PT-SCI	G-SYLJ					
14500939	PT-SCK	N939AJ					
14500941	PT-SCM	D-ARTN	P4-RYY				
14500942	PT-SCN	N909LX	N908FL				
14500944	PT-SCP	A6-NKL					
14500946	PT-SCR	N470DC					
14500948	PT-SCT	N124LS					
14500950	PT-SCX	N515JT					
14500952	PT-SFB	N910LX	N910FL				
14500954	PT-SFC	G-RUBN	G-RRAZ	G-THFC			
14500955	PT-SFD	A6-DPW					
14500957	PT-SFF	N373RB					
14500960	PT-SFH	P4-NRA	OE-IBR	M-ABGF	A6-CPC		
14500961	PT-SFI	G-ONJC	M-YNJC	D-AFOR	VP-BGL	[stored?]	
14500963	PT-SFK	OK-SUN					
14500965	PT-SFN	N600XL	[mid-air collision 29Sep06 with GOL 737 PR-GTD but landed safely Novo Proresso-Cachimbo AFB]		N965LL	XA-MHA	
14500966	PT-SFP	(N911LX)	N907LX	N966JS			
14500967	PT-SFQ	G-RLGG	OE-IGR	LX-RLG			
14500969	PT-SFW	PK-RJG	N184SP	XA-RWS			
14500970	PT-SFX	VP-BBY	M-AKAK	N970EC	XA-LBO		
14500971	PT-SFY	N775SM	N827TV				
14500972	PT-SFZ	G-MGYB	A6-PJE	A6-GCC			
14500973	PT-SHA	N135SH	A6-KWT	9K-PAA	M-KPCO		
14500974	PT-SHD	N10SV	N974EC				
14500975	PT-SHH	A9C-MTC					
14500976	PT-SHI	N900EM					
14500977	PT-SHK	N983JC					
14500978	PT-SHM	A9C-MAN	A6-MAZ	P4-KUL			
14500979	PT-SHQ	VP-BVS	PH-ARO	N979PF			
14500980	PT-SHS	N605WG					
14500981	PT-SHT	Angola T-501					
14500982	PT-SHV	G-RBRO	P4-PAM	N84AW			
14500983	PT-SKA	N473MM	N6GD				
14500985	PT-SKB	N728PH					
14500986	PT-SKC	OK-GGG					
14500987	PT-SKF	(D-ATWO)	(5N-BJT)	HC-CGO			
14500988	PT-SKD	D-AONE	9H-WFC				
14500989	PT-SKJ	N556JT	N135SK				
14500990	PT-SKK	N580ML					
14500991	PT-SKL	D-AAAI	M-OLEG				

EMBRAER EMB-135BJ LEGACY

C/n	Identities					
14500993	PT-SKM	N912LX	A6-UGH	M-BIRD		
14500994	PT-SKN	P4-SAO	G-CJMD	N994PF		
14500995	PT-SKO	EC-KFQ	G-CGSE	LX-OLA		
14500997	PT-SKP	(D-ATWO)	Brazil 2584			
14500998	PT-SKQ	SX-CDK	G-XCJM	G-GLEG		
14500999	PT-SKR	OE-IDB				
14501001	PT-SKS	A6-SUN	TC-ICH	G-CHPJ	N661EC	
14501002	PT-SKT	P4-NVB	LX-NVB			
14501003	PT-SKU	HB-JGZ	VP-CLI	N703TS	TC-GVS	
14501004	PT-SKV	N615PG				
14501006	PT-SKW					
14501007	PT-SKX	N913LX	N914FL	N317LL		
14501008	PT-SKY	S5-ABL	OE-IFF			
14501010	PT-SKZ	D-ATWO	9H-JPC			
14501011	PT-SVE	G-CMAF	M-CMAF	N909MT		
14501012	PT-SVG	PR-NIO				
14501014	PT-SVH	N226HY				
14501015	PT-SVI	N912JC	N578HS	N597CJ		
14501016	PT-SVD	D-ACBG	M-ESGR			
14501017	PT-SVK	D-ATON	G-LALE			
14501018	PT-SVV	N227WE				
14501020	PT-SVW	G-FECR	PK-RJO	PK-RSS		
14501021	PT-SVX	N915LX	M-NATH	ZS-LRK	T7-LRK	
14501023	PT-SVY	SX-DGM				
14501025	PT-SVZ	VP-CNJ	EC-LGG	G-LEGC		
14501026	PT-SZA	VP-CDH	OE-IDH			
14501029	PT-SZB	S5-ALA	OE-IMW	9H-IMW	AP-SSH	
14501031	PT-SZC	P4-MIV	M-ABEC			
14501032	PT-SZD	N518JT	N918JT	N503JT	N325SH	
14501034	PT-SZE	N18BM	N924AK	N725BD		
14501035	PT-SZF	PR-BEB	N867VP	XA-KAD		
14501037	PT-SZG	PR-AVX				
14501038	PT-SZH	N916LX	D-AKAT			
14501039	PT-SZI	OK-ROM				
14501041	PT-SZL	A6-SSV	G-CHLR	N401EC	Honduras FAH-001	
14501042	PT-SZM	SE-DJG				
14501044	PT-SEB	N909TT				
14501045	PT-SEC	EC-KOK	G-CFJA	PK-RJE	PK-RNI	
14501046	PT-SED	PK-DHK				
14501048	PT-SEE	G-IRSH	M-INTS	OE-IIM		
14501049	PT-SEF	VQ-BFP				
14501051	PT-SFG	A6-FLL				
14501052	PT-SEH	VP-CLL	N652PF			
14501054	PT-SEO	PR-ODF				
14501055	PT-SEI	D-ADCN	JY-KME	HZ-IAM		
14501057	PT-SEJ	N702SV	VP-CMM	A6-VVV	HB-JFL	
14501058	PT-SEK	N89FE				
14501060	PT-SEM	(D-ADCO)	P4-SVM			
14501061	PT-SEN	N63AG				
14501062	PT-SEP	VQ-BFQ	VQ-BCS			
14501064	PT-SEQ	N678RC	N448RC	N127BG		
14501066	PT-SER	HP-1A				
14501067	PT-SES	D-ADCP				
14501069	PT-SET	N975GR	N600YC			
14501071	PT-SEU	VT-KLJ	PT-SEU	N898JS		
14501072	PT-SEV	G-RHMS				
14501074	PT-SEW	G-OGSK	P4-SUN			
14501075	PT-SEX	A6-NLA	VP-CAN			
14501078	PT-SEZ	(OE-ITO)	Brazil 2585			
14501079	PT-SKA	N357TE	T7-KAS			
14501080	PT-SKB	N865LS				
14501082	PT-SKC	Ecuador FAE051				
14501083	PT-SKD	VP-CMK				
14501084	PT-SKE	HS-AMP/1084 [dual marks]			Thailand 1084 only	
14501086	PT-SKJ	VQ-BLU	M-ANGA			
14501087	PT-SKL	OK-JNT				
14501089	PT-SMB	A6-AJA	A6-KAP	2-KAPP	9H-KAP	
14501090	PT-SKM	"SX-KDK"	PP-JLO			
14501091	PT-SKN	PR-LTC	N991EC	VP-CAA		
14501092	PT-SMC	D-AVAN				
14501094	PT-SMA	VP-CKP	VT-CKP			
14501095	PT-SME	N806D	Colombia FAC-1215			
14501096	PT-SMF	A6-FLO				
14501098	PT-SMG	A6-AJB	A6-ABC	N598SG	A6-AJB	C5-MAF
14501099	PT-SMI	PP-VVV				
14501100	PT-TKA	G-RUBE	SP-DLB			
14501102	PT-TKB	(OE-IMG)	G-PGRP	SP-FMG		
14501103	PT-TKC					
14501105	PT-TKD	N818HR				
14501106	PT-TKE	PK-RJW	N106EC			
14501107	PT-TKF	VH-VLT				
14501109	PT-TKG	D-AVIB				
14501110	PT-TKH	OE-IBK				
14501111	PT-TKJ	P4-AEG	OK-AEG	P4-AEG		
14501113	PT-TKS	M-RCCG				
14501114	PT-TKT	G-SHSI	CN-SSH			
14501115	PT-TKI					
14501117	PT-TKU	CN-MBP				
14501118	PT-TYE	PR-FPS				
14501119	PT-TKV	(VT-LKJ)	M-SAHA	M-ALEN		
14501120	PT-TKN	VP-CFA				
14501121	PT-TKO	G-RBNS	VQ-BFR			
14501122	PT-TKP	(CS-MPC)	ZS-UBS	T7-UBS		
14501123	PT-TKQ	P4-SMS				
14501126	PT-TKX	JY-CMC				

EMBRAER EMB-135BJ LEGACY

C/n	Identities				
14501127	PT-TKY	G-VILP	G-SYNA		
14501128	PT-TKZ	G-SUGA	N608EC		
14501131	PR-JDJ				
14501132	PT-XUS	N747AG	VQ-BFS		
14501133	PT-XUT	PT-TAQ	G-RBND	OE-ITA	
14501134	PT-TAR	D-ADCQ	PK-RJA		
14501135	PT-XUV	D-ADCR	India KW3556		
14501136	PT-TAS	G-PLVN	VP-CPL	M-RRBK	UP-EM011
14501137	(PT-XUW)	PT-TAT	PR-ITU		
14501138	(PT-XUX)	PT-TAU	PP-FJA		
14501139	(PT-XUY)	PT-TAV	N688JC		
14501140	PT-TAX	M-IMAK			
14501141	PT-TAY	A6-ADL			
14501142	PT-TAZ	G-CMAS			
14501143	PT-TID	OE-IML			
14501144	PT-TIE	VT-AML			
14501145	PT-TIF	B-3096			
14501146	PT-TIG	UP-EM007			
14501147	PT-TJC	P4-SLK			
14501148	PT-TRM	TC-DIA			
14501149	PT-TSC	PP-NLR			
14501150	PT-TSF	M-MHFZ			
14501151	PT-TSI	B-3097			
14501152	PT-TSJ	VP-CWJ			
14501153	PT-TSN	N286SJ			
14501154	PT-TSK	UP-EM010			
14501155	PT-TSL	B-3098			
14501156	PT-TCL	A6-VAS	A6-SSV		
14501157	PT-TCO	VT-AOK			
14501158	PT-TCQ	VT-AOL			
14501159	PT-TCR	N386AZ			
14501160	PT-TCT	G-PPBA	M-PPBA	G-PPBA	M-CPRS
14501161	PT-TCV	B-3799			
14501162	PT-TCW	G-OTGL			
14501163	PT-TCX	RA-02777			
14501164	PR-TLC				
14501165	PT-TFP	N912JC	N665PF	G-TCMZ	
14501166	PT-TFK	D-AJET			
14501167	PT-TFT	N333BH			
14501168	PT-TFV	N650EE	D-AFUN		
14501169	PR-CRG				
14501170	PP-LEG				
14501171	PT-TJX	N671EE	D-AHOI		
14501172	PT-TJV	PK-RJP			
14501173	PT-TJZ	B-3099			
14501174	PR-LBE	B-3296			
14501175	PR-LBJ	N8587H			
14501176	PR-LBN	M-IRON	UP-EM017		
14501179	PP-INC				
14501180	B-812L	B3293			
14501181	PR-LBU	N650JV			
14501182	PR-LBV	M-JCCA			
14501183	PR-LBX	M-AAKV			
14501184	PR-LBY	G-WIRG			
14501185	PR-LBH	N286CH			
14501186	PR-LBI	N286FM			
14501187	PR-CBY				
14501188	PR-LBZ	PT-FKK			
14501189	PR-LBW	OK-SYN			
14501190	PR-LBO	A6-YMA	A6-LGI		
14501191	PR-LBE	ER-KKL			
14501192	PR-LEJ	OE-LPV	OE-IIG	M-ILAN	
14501193	PR-LEZ	VP-CTB			
14501194	PR-LEK	N810TD			
14501195	PR-LFD	N598DB			
14501196	PR-LFY	VP-CRA			
14501197	PT-TJE	N697EE	PT-LEG	[N697EE reg as a 145 145-1197 & current]	
14501198	PT-TJD	N698EE	N1977H		
14501199	PR-LBQ	G-SUGR			
14501200	PT-TJF	OK-OWN			
14501201	PR-LFE	OE-IZA			
14501202	PR-LCY	VT-KJG			
14501203	B-3295				
14501204	PR-LFU*				
14501205	PR-LFZ*				
14501206	PR-LDI	B-3290	N798MS		
14501207	PR-LDU	B-3291	N799MS		
14501208	PR-LEQ	N798MS			
14501209	PR-LEU	N866MS			
14501210	B-3280				
14501211	PR-LHZ	M-YKBO			
14501212	PR-PID	N650AP			
14501213	PR-PIG	D-AHOX			
14501214	PR-LHV	OO-ARO			
14501215	PR-LHI	N912JC			
14501216	PR-LHD	D-AERO			
14501217	PR-LIH	VP-CLL			
14501218	PR-LHR	VT-OMM			
14501219	PR-LKC	D-AZUR			
14501220	PR-LKD*				
14501221	PR-LJQ	M-SEXY			
14501222	B-116L	B-3281			
14501223	PR-LKS*				

EMBRAER 190-100 LINEAGE

C/n	Identities			
19000109	PT-SQD	PT-XOL	A6-ARK	
19000140	PT-XTE	"A6-DWA"	A6-AJH	N588AH
19000159	PP-XTF	(A6-DWB)	N227GV	
19000177	PT-SDD	Brazil 2952	PR-LET	YV3016
19000203	PT-SGL	G-RBNB	VT-AOP	
19000225	PT-SHK	M-SBAH		
19000236	PT-SII	A6-KAH		
19000243	PT-SIO	XA-AYJ		
19000261	PT-TLC	A6-AJI		
19000278	PT-TLS	JY-AAG	VP-CCC	
19000296	PT-TZK	A6-HHS		
19000307	PT-XUZ	CN-SHS		
19000317	PT-TXF	PT-TOE	N666GL	
19000362	PT-TPB	A6-IGT		
19000438	PT-TPE	N889ML		
19000453	PT-TSO	B-3203		
19000534	PT-TDI	B-3219		
19000559	PT-TCK	N981EE		
19000568	PP-ADV			
19000571	PT-TDZ	N28888	OE-LUV	
19000611	PT-TIG	OO-NGI		
19000632	PR-LCW	N730MM		
19000641	PR-LBS	B-3220		
19000683	PR-LEV	N966MS		
19000691	PR-LHH	N527AH		
19000695	PR-LJT*			

NOTES

NOTES

NOTES

NOTES

NOTES

NOTES

NOTES

NOTES

NOTES

NOTES

NOTES

Would you like to know more about Air-Britain?

Check out our website at www.air-britain.co.uk

If you are not currently a member of Air-Britain, the publishers of this book, you may be interested in what we have on offer to provide for your interest in aviation.

Air-Britain membership offers many advantages, not least reduced prices on all our publications as shown below. All members receive the quarterly A4 magazine *Aviation World* which contains 52-pages of news, features and photographs, many in colour. In addition there is a further choice of three other magazines. The 160-page monthly A5 *Air-Britain News* contains data on Aircraft Registrations worldwide,and news of Airlines and Airliners, Business Jets, Local Airfield News, Civil and Military Air Show Reports and International Military Aviation. Then there are two other 48-page A4 quarterlies – *Archive* and *Aeromilitaria* – for the civil and military enthusiast respectively.

Air-Britain News is also available in an electronic format, offering full colour throughout and extra photo pages. In this format it is published a week before the printed version pops through UK letterboxes and there is a great saving in time and postal charges for overseas members.

Members also have exclusive access to the Air-Britain e-mail Information Exchange Service (ab-ix) where they can exchange information and solve each other's queries, and to an on-line UK airfield residents database. Other benefits include numerous Branches, use of the Specialists' Information Service; Air-Britain trips and access to black and white and colour photograph libraries. During the summer we also host our own popular FLY-IN.

Membership in 2016, including Aviation World and Air-Britain News, costs £48 (UK), £67 (Europe) and £72 (Rest of the World). There are several possible combinations of the four magazines available.

Full details may be found on www.air-britain.co.uk or, write to 'Air-Britain' at 1 Rose Cottages, 179 Penn Road, Hazlemere, High Wycombe, Bucks HP15 7NE, UK. for a free information pack.

Other annual Air-Britain titles available in 2016

AIRLINE FLEETS 2016 Listing over 2,500 operators' fleets by country worldwide with registrations, c/ns, line numbers, fleet numbers and names, plus numerous appendices including airliners in non-airline service, IATA and ICAO airline and base codes, operator index, airline alliances, etc. New data spot-marked for easy reference. A5 size hardback, 784 pages.

CIVIL AIRCRAFT REGISTERS OF THE BRITISH ISLES 2016 £22.95 (Members) £28.95 (Non-members) Acknowledged as the most comprehensive register published in the UK. Lists all current G-, EI-, M-, 2-, and ZJ-, allocations plus overseas registered aircraft based in the UK & Ireland. Full C of A details, alphabetical index by type, military serials decode, British Gliding Association registers, museums and private collections. A5 Hardback. 640 pages.

BRITISH ISLES CIVIL AIRCRAFT REGISTERS QUICK REFERENCE 2016 (UKQR) £8.95 (Members) £10.95 (Non-members) Basic easy-to-carry current registration and type listing for G-, EI-, M-, ZT- and 2- registers, including foreign aircraft based in UK, current military serials, aircraft museums and expanded base index. A5 size softback, 160 pages.

BUSINESS JETS & TURBOPROPS QUICK REFERENCE 2016 (BizQR) £8.95 (Members) £10.95 (Non-members) Includes all purpose-built business jets and business turboprops in both civil and military use, in registration or serial order by country. Easy-to-carry A5 size softback, 160 pages.

AIRLINE FLEETS QUICK REFERENCE 2016 (AFQR) £8.95 (Members) £10.95 (Non-members) Pocket guide to airliners of over 19 seats of 1700 major operators likely to be seen worldwide; regn, type, c/n, fleet numbers. Now includes corporate and VIP airliners. Listed by country and airline. A5 size softback, 288 pages.

EUROPEAN REGISTERS HANDBOOK 2016 is a mixed-media publication with current civil registers of 46 countries (not UK) in QR registration/type format in an A4 softback book or as a fully searchable CD giving full c/ns, identities and additional information, plus photographs from 2015 events. CD available May, Book available June 2016.

Full details of prices and availabilty of these and of our non-annual publications may be found on our web based shop at www.air-britain.co.uk